**GABRIEL MANTZ**

# YEARBOOK OF EUROPEAN FOOTBALL

# 2023-2024

British Library Cataloguing in Publication Data
A catalogue record for this book is available from the British Library

ISBN 978-1-86223-509-0

Copyright © 2023   SOCCER BOOKS LIMITED  (01472 696226)
72 St. Peter's Avenue, Cleethorpes, N.E. Lincolnshire, DN35 8HU, United Kingdom

Web site   www.soccer-books.co.uk

e-mail   info@soccer-books.co.uk

**Printed in the UK by 4edge Ltd**

Dear Readers

The 2022-2023 season was the "World Cup in the middle of the season" for Europe. After dominating every edition of the World Cup since 2002, for this tournament, Europe lost out to South America or to be more precise, Lionel Messi's Argentina. Europe still leads the score of victories with their teams winning 12 of the 22 tournaments played to date, but it remains to be seen how this balance will change in 2026, when the Finals tournament of the World Cup will be played in North America.

In the Final, a dramatic match won on penalties after the score was tied 3-3 following extra-time, Argentina faced a strong and talented young French team coached by Didier Deschamps and *Les Bleus* undoubtedly remain the strongest national team of the old Continent. England were also among the pre-tournament favourites but were narrowly defeated 2-1 by France in their quarter-final after the normally unflappable Harry Kane missed a late chance to equalise, smashing his penalty over the crossbar. The Netherlands had a resolute team and were undefeated for well over a year by the time they reached the quarter-final stage, but Argentina eventually prevailed on penalties in a lively game nicknamed the "Battle of Lusail" by some as the referee brandished a record 18 yellow cards and 1 red card. Croatia, runners-up in 2018, had another excellent tournament, eliminating Brazil in the quarter-finals on penalties, although somewhat fortunately in a match clearly dominated by the Brazilians. Argentina defeated the Croats comfortably in the semi-final, but the performances of this small country with a population of less than 4 million are still remarkable, even though the former Yugoslavia (of which Croatia was a part for many decades) has always been known for producing many talented players.

For the rest of the European teams, the World Cup was rather less successful. Portugal and Spain stumbled against the "revelation" of the tournament, Morocco, who eliminated both teams without conceding a single goal. It was perhaps a tournament too far for the ageing Cristiano Ronaldo who disappointed, but the rest of his team did not stand out for most of the competition either. Poland played some quite poor football and required a fair amount of good fortune to reach the Round of 16 where France proved much too strong. Switzerland had performed well in the group stage to reach the final 16 teams but were then surprisingly crushed 6-1 by Portugal.

Serbia still remains a country whose team promises much with their talented players, but achieves little and they finished bottom of their group. Denmark, semi-finalists at Euro 2020, similarly could not progress past the group stage, although they faced a relatively easy series of matches and they were ultimately eliminated following a defeat by Australia. For Wales, this tournament proved to be a step too far, with Gareth Bale unable to lift his team enough to win a single game.

Finally, there remain two teams that pose many questions: Belgium and Germany. The Belgians, once again considered among the favourites for the trophy, showed that they had probably reached the limit for this particular talented generation. The overall performance of the team did not impress and, even in their must-win decisive group match against Croatia, the "Red Devils" failed to impose themselves, indicating a new generation of players may be required. In the case of Germany, the problems run much deeper. For the second time in a row, the 2014 World Champions failed to progress past the group stage and the team had put in some similarly unimpressive performances during Euro 2020. Since Qatar 2022, Hansi Flick's team has continued their run of poor results with just 2 wins in 7 matches and the question now arises about the quality of the selected players, not just the team's lack of form.

In September 2022, the final matches of the UEFA Nations League groups were played, to determine the four teams that would play in the final tournament during June 2023 in League A. Similarly, decisive matches in the other Leagues were played to decide promotion or relegation. In League A, England's terrible form in the competition continued and they were deservedly relegated to League B. Italy were able to take advantage of the weaknesses of England and Germany and then defeated the up-and-coming Hungary team in Budapest to top the group, offering fans some small consolation for missing out on the World Cup. Despite home advantage, Portugal lost their decisive match against Spain in Group 2, thus missing out on the semi-finals. France, the title-holders following their victory in 2021, played poorly in the group matches, but did at least avoid the ignominy of relegation.

In League B, Israel took advantage of Russia's disqualification from the competition for well-known reasons and finished top of a relatively easy group – Iceland is a notably weaker team at present, although it is only a few years ago they were the revelation of the continent. Bosnia and Herzegovina outperformed Finland, while Scotland proved better than Ukraine. Serbia achieved promotion to League A for the next competition 2024/2025, at the expense of Norway, despite young striker Erling Haaland scoring no fewer than six goals in his four appearances in the competition! Turkey, Greece, Kazakhstan and Georgia were all promoted to League B, and Kazakhstan in particular has achieved some excellent results over the previous 12 months.

The final tournament of the UEFA Nations League was held in June 2023 in the Netherlands, where Croatia once again played very well, but also lost somewhat unluckily to Spain, who won a penalty shoot-out to obtain their first Nations League title.

During March 2023, the preliminaries for Euro 2024 began, the final tournament of which will be held in Germany. The 53 teams (Germany qualify automatically as hosts and Russia are disqualified from entering) were drawn into 10 preliminary groups, the top two teams of each group will qualify. The remaining 4 slots will then be allocated to the next best team in the Nations League overall ranking (Play-offs will be held during March 2024). Scotland, England and France all started confidently, each winning their first four matches, but impressive performances from Czech Republic and Moldova saw them both beat Poland whose chances of qualification must now be quite remote. Austria are well ahead of Sweden in their group, though this is not perhaps too surprising as the Scandinavian team has not been very strong for several years. Slovenia is also on the way back and top their group, while Kazakhstan achieved a surprising and resounding victory against Denmark (3-2 in Astana, after the Danes led 2-0 at half-time!). The decisive matches will be played in the Autumn of 2023 and only then will we find out the 20 teams that will travel to Germany next summer.

At club level, the season started as usual with the UEFA Super Cup Final which was played in Helsinki. Real Madrid CF won the trophy for the fifth time, comfortably beating Eintracht Frankfurt 2-0.

The 2022/2023 Champions League was won by Manchester City FC, marking their first European trophy for over half a century, the club's previous success coming in the 1972 Cup Winners' Cup, at the end of a particularly fruitful season which also saw Guardiola's team win the Premier League and the FA Cup! In a game which the English club were expected to dominate, the well-organised FC Internazionale Milano team played extremely well and were somewhat unlucky to lose. Inter had already surprised most observers by qualifying from the group stage ahead of FC Barcelona but perhaps the best Italian team of the season, SSC Napoli, were eliminated by AC Milan who were in turn beaten by FC Internazionale in the semi-finals...

After three years of waiting, Sevilla FC once again won the Europa League, a remarkable seventh victory (including UEFA Cup wins) in European club football's second competition. The Final in Budapest against an AS Roma team led by José Mourinho, was a bad-tempered affair with no fewer than 40 fouls committed, but the Spanish team were probably worthy winners finally overcoming their opponents in a penalty shoot-out.

The Europa Conference League 2022/2023 was the second edition of this competition and the venue for the Final was the Fortuna Stadium in Prague. Unfortunately, as with the first edition of the competition, this was a stadium with a relatively low spectator capacity and this is perhaps something which needs to be reconsidered in the future. West Ham United FC London finished off a very good season by lifting their first European trophy since an Intertoto Cup victory in 1999, winning 2-1 against ACF Fiorentina. A little over 17,300 fans watched a game which many more would have been happy be able to pay to attend!

This sixth edition of the Yearbook of European Football contains complete statistics for the national championships of all European countries with league results and tables. Player appearances and goals scored are presented for all top division clubs from Europe. You will also find national cup competition details including final match statistics and there are also complete statistics for national teams and the international players for each country and their clubs. Also contained, of course, is detailed information about the Final Tournament of the 2022 World Cup in Qatar, including the squads for all the European teams.

Many thanks go to Mr. Dirk Karsdorp who has once again made a great contribution to this book by providing full line-ups and complete statistics for both of the major European Club competitions during the 2022/2023 season.


Please enjoy the read!


The Author

# FIFA COUNTRY CODES

## EUROPE

| | | | | | | | |
|---|---|---|---|---|---|---|---|
| **ALB** | Albania | **GER** | Germany | **NIR** | Northern Ireland |
| **AND** | Andorra | **GIB** | Gibraltar | **NOR** | Norway |
| **ARM** | Armenia | **GRE** | Greece | **POL** | Poland |
| **AUT** | Austria | **HUN** | Hungary | **POR** | Portugal |
| **AZE** | Azerbaijan | **ISL** | Iceland | **IRL** | Republic of Ireland |
| **BLR** | Belarus | **ISR** | Israel | **ROU** | Romania |
| **BEL** | Belgium | **ITA** | Italy | **RUS** | Russia |
| **BIH** | Bosnia-Herzegovina | **KAZ** | Kazakhstan | **SMR** | San Marino |
| **BUL** | Bulgaria | **KOS** | Kosovo | **SCO** | Scotland |
| **CRO** | Croatia | **LVA** | Latvia | **SRB** | Serbia |
| **CYP** | Cyprus | **LIE** | Liechtenstein | **SVK** | Slovakia |
| **CZE** | Czech Republic | **LTU** | Lithuania | **SVN** | Slovenia |
| **DEN** | Denmark | **LUX** | Luxembourg | **ESP** | Spain |
| **ENG** | England | **MLT** | Malta | **SWE** | Sweden |
| **EST** | Estonia | **MDA** | Moldova | **SUI** | Switzerland |
| **FRO** | Faroe Islands | **MNE** | Montenegro | **TUR** | Turkey |
| **FIN** | Finland | **NED** | Netherlands | **UKR** | Ukraine |
| **FRA** | France | **MKD** | North Macedonia | **WAL** | Wales |
| **GEO** | Georgia | | | | |

## ASIA

| | |
|---|---|
| **AUS** | Australia |
| **CHN** | China P.R. |
| **IDN** | Indonesia |
| **IRN** | Iran |
| **IRQ** | Iraq |
| **JPN** | Japan |
| **JOR** | Jordan |
| **KOR** | Korea Republic |
| **KGZ** | Kyrgyzstan |
| **MAS** | Malaysia |
| **PLE** | Palestine |
| **PHI** | Philippines |
| **QAT** | Qatar |
| **KSA** | Saudi Arabia |
| **SYR** | Syria |
| **TJK** | Tajikistan |
| **THA** | Thailand |
| **TLS** | Timor-Leste |
| **UAE** | United Arab Emirates |
| **UZB** | Uzbekistan |

## AFRICA

| | |
|---|---|
| **ALG** | Algeria |
| **ANG** | Angola |
| **BEN** | Benin |
| **BFA** | Burkina Faso |
| **BDI** | Burundi |
| **CMR** | Cameroon |
| **CPV** | Cape Verde Islands |
| **CTA** | Central African Republic |
| **CHA** | Chad |
| **COM** | Comoros Islands |
| **CGO** | Congo |
| **COD** | D.R. Congo |
| **EGY** | Egypt |
| **EQG** | Equatorial Guinea |
| **ERI** | Eritrea |
| **GAB** | Gabon |
| **GAM** | Gambia |
| **GHA** | Ghana |
| **GUI** | Guinea |
| **GNB** | Guinea-Bissau |
| **CIV** | Ivory Coast |
| **KEN** | Kenya |
| **LBR** | Liberia |
| **LBY** | Libya |
| **MAD** | Madagascar |
| **MWI** | Malawi |
| **MLI** | Mali |
| **MTN** | Mauritania |
| **MRI** | Mauritius |
| **MAR** | Morocco |
| **MOZ** | Mozambique |
| **NAM** | Namibia |
| **NIG** | Niger |
| **NGA** | Nigeria |
| **RWA** | Rwanda |
| **SEN** | Senegal |
| **SLE** | Sierra Leone |
| **SOM** | Somalia |
| **RSA** | South Africa |
| **SSD** | South Sudan |
| **TAN** | Tanzania |
| **TOG** | Togo |
| **TUN** | Tunisia |
| **UGA** | Uganda |
| **ZAM** | Zambia |
| **ZIM** | Zimbabwe |

## NORTH AND CENTRAL AMERICA

| | |
|---|---|
| **BRB** | Barbados |
| **BER** | Bermuda |
| **VGB** | British Virgin Islands |
| **CAN** | Canada |
| **CRC** | Costa Rica |
| **CUB** | Cuba |
| **CUW** | Curaçao |
| **DMA** | Dominica |
| **DOM** | Dominican Republic |
| **SLV** | El Salvador |
| **GUF** | French Guiana |
| **GRN** | Grenada |
| **GLP** | Guadeloupe |
| **GUA** | Guatemala |
| **HAI** | Haiti |
| **HON** | Honduras |
| **JAM** | Jamaica |
| **MTQ** | Martinique |
| **MEX** | Mexico |
| **NCA** | Nicaragua |
| **PAN** | Panama |
| **LCA** | Saint Lucia |
| **SUR** | Suriname |
| **TRI** | Trinidad and Tobago |
| **USA** | United States |
| **VIR** | U.S. Virgin Islands |

## SOUTH AMERICA

| | |
|---|---|
| **ARG** | Argentina |
| **BOL** | Bolivia |
| **BRA** | Brazil |
| **CHI** | Chile |
| **COL** | Colombia |
| **ECU** | Ecuador |
| **PAR** | Paraguay |
| **PER** | Peru |
| **URU** | Uruguay |
| **VEN** | Venezuela |

## OCEANIA

| | |
|---|---|
| **NZL** | New Zealand |
| **PNG** | Papua New Guinea |
| **SOL** | Solomon Islands |

## OTHER ABBREVIATIONS

**DOB** Date of birth

**M** Matches played
**G** Goals
**(s)** Matches played as a substitute

**(F)** International friendly matches
**(WC)** 2022 FIFA World Cup Finals
**(UNL)** 2022-2023 UEFA Nations League
**(ECQ)** 2024 Euro Championship Qualifiers
**(BC)** 2022 Baltic Cup

# SUMMARY

## COMPETITIONS FOR NATIONAL TEAMS

## EUROPEAN CLUB COMPETITIONS

## NATIONAL ASSOCIATIONS

# COMPETITIONS FOR NATIONAL TEAMS

## 2022 FIFA WORLD CUP
## FINAL TOURNAMENT

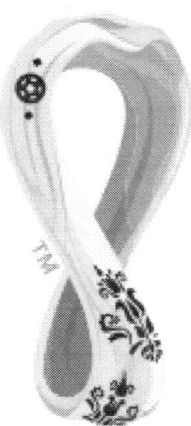

The 22$^{nd}$ FIFA World Cup Final Tournament took place in Qatar from 20 November to 18 December 2022. Thirteen teams represented the European Football Confederation (UEFA). As best European team, France – the defending World Champions from 2018 - reached the Final game, being defeated by Argentina after extra-time and penalties shoot-outs.

## GROUP STAGE
(teams in bold were qualified for the 2$^{th}$ Roundof 16)

### GROUP A

| Results | | | |
|---|---|---|---|
| 20.11.2022 | Al Khor | Qatar - Ecuador | 0-2(0-2) |
| 21.11.2022 | Doha | Senegal - Netherlands | 0-2(0-0) |
| 25.11.2022 | Doha | Qatar - Senegal | 1-3(0-1) |
| 25.11.2022 | Al Rayyan | Netherlands - Ecuador | 1-1(1-0) |
| 29.11.2022 | Al Khor | Netherlands - Qatar | 2-0(1-0) |
| 29.11.2022 | Al Rayyan | Ecuador - Senegal | 1-2(0-1) |

| | Final Standings | | | | | | | | |
|---|---|---|---|---|---|---|---|---|---|
| 1. | **Netherlands** | 3 | 2 | 1 | 0 | 5 | - | 1 | 7 |
| 2. | **Senegal** | 3 | 2 | 0 | 1 | 5 | - | 4 | 6 |
| 3. | Ecuador | 3 | 1 | 1 | 1 | 4 | - | 3 | 4 |
| 4. | Qatar | 3 | 0 | 0 | 3 | 1 | - | 7 | 0 |

### GROUP B

| Results | | | |
|---|---|---|---|
| 21.11.2022 | Al Rayyan | England - Iran | 6-2(3-0) |
| 21.11.2022 | Al Rayyan | United States - Wales | 1-1(1-0) |
| 25.11.2022 | Al Rayyan | Wales - Iran | 0-2(0-0) |
| 25.11.2022 | Al Khor | England - United States | 0-0 |
| 29.11.2022 | Al Rayyan | Wales - England | 0-3(0-0) |
| 29.11.2022 | Doha | Iran - United States | 0-1(0-1) |

| | Final Standings | | | | | | | | |
|---|---|---|---|---|---|---|---|---|---|
| 1. | **England** | 3 | 2 | 1 | 0 | 9 | - | 2 | 7 |
| 2. | **United States** | 3 | 1 | 2 | 0 | 2 | - | 1 | 5 |
| 3. | Iran | 3 | 1 | 0 | 2 | 4 | - | 7 | 3 |
| 4. | Wales | 3 | 0 | 1 | 2 | 1 | - | 6 | 1 |

### GROUP C

| Results | | | |
|---|---|---|---|
| 22.11.2022 | Lusail | Argentina - Saudi Arabia | 1-2(1-0) |
| 22.11.2022 | Doha | Mexico - Poland | 0-0 |
| 26.11.2022 | Al Rayyan | Poland - Saudi Arabia | 2-0(1-0) |
| 26.11.2022 | Lusail | Argentina - Mexico | 2-0(0-0) |
| 30.11.2022 | Doha | Poland - Argentina | 0-2(0-0) |
| 30.11.2022 | Lusail | Saudi Arabia - Mexico | 1-2(0-0) |

| | Final Standings | | | | | | | | |
|---|---|---|---|---|---|---|---|---|---|
| 1. | **Argentina** | 3 | 2 | 0 | 1 | 5 | - | 2 | 6 |
| 2. | **Poland** | 3 | 1 | 1 | 1 | 2 | - | 2 | 4 |
| 3. | Mexico | 3 | 1 | 1 | 1 | 2 | - | 3 | 4 |
| 4. | Saudi Arabia | 3 | 1 | 0 | 2 | 3 | - | 5 | 3 |

## GROUP D

### Results

| | | | | |
|---|---|---|---|---|
| 22.11.2022 | Al Rayyan | Denmark - Tunisia | 0-0 |
| 22.11.2022 | Al Wakrah | France - Australia | 4-1(2-1) |
| 26.11.2022 | Al Wakrah | Tunisia - Australia | 0-1(0-1) |
| 26.11.2022 | Doha | France - Denmark | 2-1(0-0) |
| 30.11.2022 | Al Wakrah | Australia - Denmark | 1-0(0-0) |
| 30.11.2022 | Al Rayyan | Tunisia - France | 1-0(0-0) |

### Final Standings

| | | | | | | | | | |
|---|---|---|---|---|---|---|---|---|---|
| 1. | **France** | 3 | 2 | 0 | 1 | 6 | - | 3 | 6 |
| 2. | **Australia** | 3 | 2 | 0 | 1 | 3 | - | 4 | 6 |
| 3. | Tunisia | 3 | 1 | 1 | 1 | 1 | - | 1 | 4 |
| 4. | Denmark | 3 | 0 | 1 | 2 | 1 | - | 3 | 1 |

## GROUP E

### Results

| | | | | |
|---|---|---|---|---|
| 23.11.2022 | Al Rayyan | Germany - Japan | 1-2(1-0) |
| 23.11.2022 | Doha | Spain - Costa Rica | 7-0(3-0) |
| 27.11.2022 | Al Rayyan | Japan - Costa Rica | 0-1(0-0) |
| 27.11.2022 | Al Khor | Spain - Germany | 1-1(0-0) |
| 01.12.2022 | Al Rayyan | Japan - Spain | 2-1(0-1) |
| 01.12.2022 | Al Khor | Costa Rica - Germany | 2-4(0-1) |

### Final Standings

| | | | | | | | | | |
|---|---|---|---|---|---|---|---|---|---|
| 1. | **Japan** | 3 | 2 | 0 | 1 | 4 | - | 3 | 6 |
| 2. | **Spain** | 3 | 1 | 1 | 1 | 9 | - | 3 | 4 |
| 3. | Germany | 3 | 1 | 1 | 1 | 6 | - | 5 | 4 |
| 4. | Costa Rica | 3 | 1 | 0 | 2 | 3 | - | 11 | 3 |

## GROUP F

### Results

| | | | | |
|---|---|---|---|---|
| 23.11.2022 | Al Khor | Morocco - Croatia | 0-0 |
| 23.11.2022 | Al Rayyan | Belgium - Canada | 1-0(1-0) |
| 27.11.2022 | Doha | Belgium - Morocco | 0-2(0-0) |
| 27.11.2022 | Al Rayyan | Croatia - Canada | 4-1(2-1) |
| 01.12.2022 | Al Rayyan | Croatia - Belgium | 0-0 |
| 01.12.2022 | Doha | Canada - Morocco | 1-2(1-2) |

### Final Standings

| | | | | | | | | | |
|---|---|---|---|---|---|---|---|---|---|
| 1. | **Morocco** | 3 | 2 | 1 | 0 | 4 | - | 1 | 7 |
| 2. | **Croatia** | 3 | 1 | 2 | 0 | 4 | - | 1 | 5 |
| 3. | Belgium | 3 | 1 | 1 | 1 | 1 | - | 2 | 4 |
| 4. | Canada | 3 | 0 | 0 | 3 | 2 | - | 7 | 0 |

## GROUP G

### Results

| | | | | |
|---|---|---|---|---|
| 24.11.2022 | Al Wakrah | Switzerland - Cameroon | 1-0(0-0) |
| 24.11.2022 | Lusail | Brazil - Serbia | 2-0(0-0) |
| 28.11.2022 | Al Wakrah | Cameroon - Serbia | 3-3(1-2) |
| 28.11.2022 | Doha | Brazil - Switzerland | 1-0(0-0) |
| 02.12.2022 | Doha | Serbia - Switzerland | 2-3(2-2) |
| 02.12.2022 | Lusail | Cameroon - Brazil | 1-0(0-0) |

### Final Standings

| | | | | | | | | | |
|---|---|---|---|---|---|---|---|---|---|
| 1. | **Brazil** | 3 | 2 | 0 | 1 | 3 | - | 1 | 6 |
| 2. | **Switzerland** | 3 | 2 | 0 | 1 | 4 | - | 3 | 6 |
| 3. | Cameroon | 3 | 1 | 1 | 1 | 4 | - | 4 | 4 |
| 4. | Serbia | 3 | 0 | 1 | 2 | 5 | - | 8 | 1 |

## GROUP H

### Results

| | | | | |
|---|---|---|---|---|
| 24.11.2022 | Al Rayyan | Uruguay - Korea Republic | 0-0 |
| 24.11.2022 | Doha | Portugal - Ghana | 3-2(0-0) |
| 28.11.2022 | Al Rayyan | Korea Republic - Ghana | 2-3(0-2) |
| 28.11.2022 | Lusail | Portugal - Uruguay | 2-0(0-0) |
| 02.12.2022 | Al Wakrah | Ghana - Uruguay | 0-2(0-2) |
| 02.12.2022 | Al Rayyan | Korea Republic - Portugal | 2-1(1-1) |

### Final Standings

| | | | | | | | | | |
|---|---|---|---|---|---|---|---|---|---|
| 1. | **Portugal** | 3 | 2 | 0 | 1 | 6 | - | 4 | 6 |
| 2. | **Korea Rep.** | 3 | 1 | 1 | 1 | 4 | - | 4 | 4 |
| 3. | Uruguay | 3 | 1 | 1 | 1 | 2 | - | 2 | 4 |
| 4. | Ghana | 3 | 1 | 0 | 2 | 5 | - | 7 | 3 |

| | | SECOND ROUND OF 16 | |
|---|---|---|---|
| 03.12.2022 | Al Rayyan | Netherlands - United States | 3-1(2-0) |
| 03.12.2022 | Al Rayyan | Argentina - Australia | 2-1(1-0) |
| 04.12.2022 | Doha | France - Poland | 3-1(1-0) |
| 04.12.2022 | Al Khor | England - Senegal | 3-0(2-0) |
| 05.12.2022 | Al Wakrah | Japan - Croatia | 1-1(1-0,1-1,1-1); 1-3 pen |
| 05.12.2022 | Doha | Brazil - Korea Republic | 4-1(4-0) |
| 06.12.2022 | Al Rayyan | Morocco - Spain | 0-0; 3-0 pen |
| 06.12.2022 | Lusail | Portugal - Switzerland | 6-1(2-0) |

| | | QUARTER-FINALS | |
|---|---|---|---|
| 09.12.2022 | Al Rayyan | Croatia - Brazil | 1-1(0-0,0-0,1-1); 4-2 pen |
| 09.12.2022 | Lusail | Netherlands - Argentina | 2-2(0-1,2-2,2-2); 3-4 pen |
| 10.12.2022 | Doha | Morocco - Portugal | 1-0(1-0) |
| 10.12.2022 | Al Khor | England - France | 1-2(0-1) |

| | | SEMI-FINALS | |
|---|---|---|---|
| 13.12.2022 | Lusail | Argentina - Croatia | 3-0(2-0) |
| 14.12.2022 | Al Khor | France - Morocco | 2-0(1-0) |

| | | THIRD PLACE PLAY-OFF | |
|---|---|---|---|
| 17.12.2022 | Al Rayyan | Croatia - Morocco | 2-1(2-1) |

| | | FINAL | |
|---|---|---|---|
| 18.12.2022 | Lusail | Argentina - France | 3-3(2-0,2-2,3-3); 4-2 pen |

# FINAL TOURNAMENT – SQUADS OF EUROPEAN TEAMS

| FRANCE | | |
|---|---|---|
| **Trainer**: Didier Claude Deschamps | | |

| **Goalkeepers:** | | |
|---|---|---|
| 1 | Hugo Hadrien Dominique Lloris | 26.12.1986 |
| 16 | Steve Mandanda Mpidi | 28.03.1985 |
| 23 | Alphonse Francis Aréola | 27.02.1993 |
| **Defenders:** | | |
| 2 | Benjamin Jacques Marcel Pavard | 28.03.1996 |
| 3 | Axel Wilson Arthur Disasi Mhakinis Belho | 11.03.1998 |
| 4 | Raphaël Xavier Varane | 25.04.1993 |
| 5 | Jules Olivier Koundé | 12.11.1998 |
| 17 | William Alain André Gabriel Saliba | 24.03.2001 |
| 18 | Dayotchanculle Oswald Upamecano | 27.10.1998 |
| 21 | Lucas François Bernard Hernández | 14.02.1996 |
| 22 | Théo Bernard François Hernández | 06.10.1997 |
| 24 | Ibrahima Konaté | 25.05.1999 |
| **Midfielders:** | | |
| 6 | Mattéo Elias Kenzo Guendouzi Olié | 14.04.1999 |
| 8 | Aurélien Djani Tchouaméni | 27.01.2000 |
| 13 | Youssuf Fofana | 10.01.1999 |
| 14 | Adrien Thibaut Marie Rabiot | 03.04.1995 |
| 15 | Jordan Marcel Gilbert Veretout | 01.03.1993 |
| 25 | Eduardo Celmi Camavinga | 10.11.2002 |
| **Forwards:** | | |
| 7 | Antoine Griezmann | 21.03.1991 |
| 9 | Olivier Jonathan Giroud | 30.09.1986 |
| 10 | Kylian Sanmi Mbappé Lottin | 20.12.1998 |
| 11 | Masour Ousmane Dembélé | 15.05.1997 |
| 12 | Randal Kolo Muani | 05.12.1998 |
| 19 | Karim Mostafa Benzema | 19.12.1987 |
| 20 | Kingsley Junior Coman | 13.06.1996 |
| 26 | Marcus Lilian Thuram-Ulien | 06.08.1997 |

## BELGIUM

**Trainer**: Roberto Martínez Montoliu (Spain)

### Goalkeepers:

| | | |
|---|---|---|
| 1 | Thibaut Nicolas Marc Courtois | 11.05.1992 |
| 12 | Simon Luc Hildebert Mignolet | 06.03.1988 |
| 13 | Koen Casteels | 25.06.1992 |

### Defenders:

| | | |
|---|---|---|
| 2 | Toby Albertine Maurits Alderweireld | 02.03.1989 |
| 3 | Arthur Nicolas Theate | 25.05.2000 |
| 4 | Wout Felix Lina Faes | 03.04.1998 |
| 5 | Jan Bert Lieve Vertonghen | 24.04.1987 |
| 15 | Thomas Meunier | 12.09.1991 |
| 19 | Leander Dendoncker | 15.04.1995 |
| 21 | Timothy Castagne | 05.12.1995 |
| 26 | Zeno Koen Debast | 24.10.2003 |

### Midfielders:

| | | |
|---|---|---|
| 6 | Axel Tomas Laurent Angel Lambert Witsel | 12.01.1989 |
| 7 | Kevin De Bruyne | 28.06.1991 |
| 8 | Youri Marion Tielemans | 07.05.1997 |
| 16 | Thorgan Ganael Francis Hazard | 29.03.1993 |
| 18 | Amadou Zeund Georges Ba Mvom Onana | 16.08.2001 |
| 20 | Hans Vanaken | 24.08.1992 |

### Forwards:

| | | |
|---|---|---|
| 9 | Romelu Menama Lukaku Bolingoli | 13.05.1993 |
| 10 | Eden Michael Hazard | 07.01.1991 |
| 11 | Yannick Ferreira Carrasco | 04.09.1993 |
| 14 | Dries Mertens | 06.05.1987 |
| 17 | Leandro Trossard | 04.12.1994 |
| 22 | Charles Marc De Ketelaere | 10.03.2001 |
| 23 | Michy Batshuayi-Atunga | 02.10.1993 |
| 24 | Ikoma Loïs Openda | 16.02.2000 |
| 25 | Jérémy Baffour Doku | 27.05.2002 |

## CROATIA

**Trainer**: Zlatko Dalić

### Goalkeepers:

| | | |
|---|---|---|
| 1 | Dominik Livaković | 09.01.1995 |
| 12 | Ivo Grbić | 18.01.1996 |
| 23 | Ivica Ivušić | 01.02.1995 |

### Defenders:

| | | |
|---|---|---|
| 2 | Josip Stanišić | 02.04.2000 |
| 3 | Borna Barišić | 10.11.1992 |
| 5 | Martin Erlić | 24.01.1998 |
| 6 | Dejan Lovren | 05.07.1989 |
| 19 | Borna Sosa | 21.01.1998 |
| 20 | Joško Gvardiol | 23.01.2002 |
| 21 | Domagoj Vida | 29.04.1989 |
| 22 | Josip Juranović | 16.08.1995 |
| 24 | Josip Šutalo | 28.02.2000 |

### Midfielders:

| | | |
|---|---|---|
| 7 | Lovro Majer | 17.01.1998 |
| 8 | Mateo Kovačić | 06.05.1994 |
| 10 | Luka Modrić | 09.09.1985 |
| 11 | Marcelo Brozović | 16.11.1992 |
| 13 | Nikola Vlašić | 04.10.1997 |
| 15 | Mario Pašalić | 09.02.1995 |
| 25 | Luka Sučić | 08.09.2002 |
| 26 | Kristijan Jakić | 14.05.1997 |

### Forwards:

| | | |
|---|---|---|
| 4 | Ivan Perišić | 02.02.1989 |
| 9 | Andrej Kramarić | 19.06.1991 |
| 14 | Marko Livaja | 26.08.1993 |
| 16 | Bruno Petković | 16.09.1994 |
| 17 | Ante Budimir | 22.07.1991 |
| 18 | Mislav Oršić | 29.12.1992 |

## DENMARK

**Trainer**: Kasper Hjulmand

### Goalkeepers:

| | | |
|---|---|---|
| 1 | Kasper Peter Schmeichel | 05.11.1986 |
| 16 | Oliver Christensen | 22.03.1999 |
| 22 | Frederik Riis Rønnow | 04.08.1992 |

### Defenders:

| | | |
|---|---|---|
| 2 | Joachim Christian Andersen | 31.05.1996 |
| 3 | Victor Enok Nelsson | 14.10.1998 |
| 4 | Simon Thorup Kjær | 26.03.1989 |
| 5 | Joakim Mæhle Pedersen | 20.05.1997 |
| 6 | Andreas Bødtker Christensen | 10.04.1996 |
| 13 | Rasmus Nissen Kristensen | 11.07.1997 |
| 17 | Jens Stryger Larsen | 21.02.1991 |
| 26 | Alexander Hartmann Bah | 09.12.1997 |

### Midfielders:

| | | |
|---|---|---|
| 7 | Mathias Jensen | 01.01.1996 |
| 8 | Thomas Joseph Delaney | 03.09.1991 |
| 10 | Christian Dannemann Eriksen | 14.02.1992 |
| 14 | Mikkel Krogh Damsgaard | 03.07.2000 |
| 15 | Christian Thers Nørgaard | 10.03.1994 |
| 18 | Daniel Wass | 31.05.1989 |
| 23 | Pierre-Emile Kordt Højbjerg | 05.08.1995 |
| 24 | Robert Skov | 20.05.1996 |
| 25 | Jesper Grænge Lindstrøm | 29.02.2000 |

### Forwards:

| | | |
|---|---|---|
| 9 | Martin Braithwaite Christensen | 05.06.1991 |
| 11 | Andreas Skov Olsen | 02.12.1999 |
| 12 | Kasper Dolberg Rasmussen | 06.10.1997 |
| 19 | Jonas Older Wind | 07.02.1999 |
| 20 | Yussuf Yurary Poulsen | 15.06.1994 |
| 21 | Andreas Evald Cornelius | 16.03.1993 |

## ENGLAND

**Trainer**: Gareth Southgate

### Goalkeepers:

| | | |
|---|---|---|
| 1 | Jordan Lee Pickford | 07.03.1994 |
| 13 | Nicholas David Pope | 19.04.1992 |
| 23 | Aaron Christopher Ramsdale | 14.05.1998 |

### Defenders:

| | | |
|---|---|---|
| 2 | Kyle Andrew Walker | 28.05.1990 |
| 3 | Luke Paul Hoare Shaw | 12.07.1995 |
| 5 | John Stones | 28.05.1994 |
| 6 | Jacob Harry Maguire | 05.03.1993 |
| 12 | Kieran John Trippier | 19.09.1990 |
| 16 | Conor David Coady | 25.02.1993 |
| 18 | Trent John Alexander-Arnold | 07.10.1998 |
| 21 | Benjamin William White | 08.10.1997 |

### Midfielders:

| | | |
|---|---|---|
| 4 | Declan Rice | 14.01.1999 |
| 8 | Jordan Brian Henderson | 17.06.1990 |
| 14 | Kalvin Mark Phillips | 02.12.1995 |
| 15 | Eric Jeremy Edgar Dier | 15.01.1994 |
| 19 | Mason Tony Mount | 10.01.1999 |
| 20 | Philip Walter Foden | 28.05.2000 |
| 22 | Jude Victor William Bellingham | 29.06.2003 |
| 25 | James Daniel Maddison | 23.11.1996 |
| 26 | Conor John Gallagher | 06.02.2000 |

### Forwards:

| | | |
|---|---|---|
| 7 | Jack Peter Grealish | 10.09.1995 |
| 9 | Harry Edward Kane | 28.07.1993 |
| 10 | Raheem Shaquille Sterling | 08.12.1994 |
| 11 | Marcus Rashford | 31.10.1997 |
| 17 | Bukayo Ayoyinka Saka | 05.09.2001 |
| 24 | Callum Eddie Graham Wilson | 27.02.1992 |

## GERMANY

**Trainer**: Hans-Dieter Flick

### Goalkeepers:
| | | |
|---|---|---|
| 1 | Manuel Peter Neuer | 27.03.1986 |
| 12 | Kevin Trapp | 08.07.1990 |
| 22 | Marc-André ter Stegen | 30.04.1992 |

### Defenders:
| | | |
|---|---|---|
| 2 | Antonio Rüdiger | 03.03.1993 |
| 3 | David Raum | 22.04.1998 |
| 4 | Matthias Lukas Ginter | 19.01.1994 |
| 5 | Jan Thilo Kehrer | 21.09.1996 |
| 15 | Niklas Süle | 03.09.1995 |
| 16 | Lukas Manuel Klostermann | 03.06.1996 |
| 20 | Christian Günter | 28.02.1993 |
| 23 | Nico Schlotterbeck | 01.12.1999 |
| 25 | Armel Bella-Kotchap | 11.12.2001 |

### Midfielders:
| | | |
|---|---|---|
| 6 | Joshua Walter Kimmich | 08.02.1995 |
| 8 | Leon Christoph Goretzka | 06.02.1995 |
| 11 | Mario Götze | 03.06.1992 |
| 13 | Thomas Müller | 13.09.1989 |
| 14 | Jamal Musiala | 26.02.2003 |
| 17 | Julian Brandt | 02.05.1996 |
| 18 | Jonas Hofmann | 14.07.1992 |
| 19 | Leroy Aziz Sané | 11.01.1996 |
| 21 | İlkay Gündoğan | 24.10.1990 |

### Forwards:
| | | |
|---|---|---|
| 7 | Kai Lukas Havertz | 11.06.1999 |
| 9 | Niclas Füllkrug | 09.02.1993 |
| 10 | Serge David Gnabry | 14.07.1995 |
| 24 | Karim-David Adeyemi | 18.01.2002 |
| 26 | Youssoufa Moukoko | 20.11.2004 |

## NETHERLANDS

**Trainer**: Aloysius Paulus Maria "Louis" van Gaal

### Goalkeepers:
| | | |
|---|---|---|
| 1 | Remko Jurian Pasveer | 08.11.1983 |
| 13 | Justin Bijlow | 22.01.1998 |
| 23 | Andries Noppert | 07.04.1994 |

### Defenders:
| | | |
|---|---|---|
| 2 | Jurriën David Norman Timber | 17.06.2001 |
| 3 | Matthijs de Ligt | 12.08.1999 |
| 4 | Virgil van Dijk | 08.07.1991 |
| 5 | Nathan Benjamin Aké | 18.02.1995 |
| 6 | Stefan de Vrij | 05.02.1992 |
| 16 | Tyrell Malacia | 17.08.1999 |
| 17 | Daley Blind | 09.03.1990 |
| 22 | Denzel Justus Morris Dumfries | 18.04.1996 |
| 26 | Jeremie Agyekum Frimpong | 10.12.2000 |

### Midfielders:
| | | |
|---|---|---|
| 11 | Steven Berghuis | 19.12.1991 |
| 14 | Davy Klaassen | 21.02.1993 |
| 15 | Marten Elco de Roon | 29.03.1991 |
| 20 | Teun Koopmeiners | 28.02.1998 |
| 21 | Frenkie de Jong | 12.05.1997 |
| 24 | Kenneth Ina Dorothea Taylor | 16.05.2002 |
| 25 | Xavi Quentin Shay Simons | 21.04.2003 |

### Forwards:
| | | |
|---|---|---|
| 7 | Steven Charles Bergwijn | 08.10.1997 |
| 8 | Cody Mathès Gakpo | 07.05.1999 |
| 9 | Luuk de Jong | 27.08.1990 |
| 10 | Memphis Depay | 13.02.1994 |
| 12 | Noa Noëll Lang | 17.06.1999 |
| 18 | Vincent Petrus Anna Sebastiaan Janssen | 15.06.1994 |
| 19 | Wout François Maria Weghorst | 07.08.1992 |

## POLAND

**Trainer**: Czesław Michniewicz

### Goalkeepers:
| | | |
|---|---|---|
| 1 | Wojciech Tomasz Szczęsny | 18.04.1990 |
| 12 | Łukasz Skorupski | 05.05.1991 |
| 22 | Kamil Mieczysław Grabara | 08.01.1999 |

### Defenders:
| | | |
|---|---|---|
| 2 | Matthew Stuart Cash | 07.08.1997 |
| 3 | Artur Jędrzejczyk | 04.11.1987 |
| 4 | Mateusz Wieteska | 11.02.1997 |
| 5 | Jan Kacper Bednarek | 12.04.1996 |
| 14 | Jakub Piotr Kiwior | 15.02.2000 |
| 15 | Kamil Jacek Glik | 03.02.1988 |
| 18 | Bartosz Bereszyński | 12.07.1992 |
| 25 | Robert Gumny | 04.06.1998 |

### Midfielders:
| | | |
|---|---|---|
| 6 | Krystian Bielik | 04.01.1998 |
| 8 | Damian Szymański | 16.06.1995 |
| 10 | Grzegorz Krychowiak | 29.01.1990 |
| 11 | Kamil Piotr Grosicki | 08.06.1988 |
| 13 | Jakub Kamiński | 05.06.2002 |
| 17 | Szymon Piotr Żurkowski | 25.09.1997 |
| 19 | Sebastian Szymański | 10.05.1999 |
| 20 | Piotr Sebastian Zieliński | 20.05.1994 |
| 21 | Nicola Zalewski | 23.01.2002 |
| 24 | Przemysław Frankowski | 12.04.1995 |
| 26 | Michał Skóraś | 15.02.2000 |

### Forwards:
| | | |
|---|---|---|
| 7 | Arkadiusz Krystian Milik | 28.02.1994 |
| 9 | Robert Lewandowski | 21.08.1988 |
| 16 | Karol Świderski | 23.01.1997 |
| 23 | Krzysztof Piątek | 01.07.1995 |

## PORTUGAL

**Trainer**: Fernando Manuel Fernandes da Costa Santos

### Goalkeepers:
| | | |
|---|---|---|
| 1 | *Rui* Pedro dos Santos *Patrício* | 15.02.1988 |
| 12 | *José* Pedro Malheiro de *Sá* | 17.01.1993 |
| 22 | *Diogo* Meireles da *Costa* | 19.09.1999 |

### Defenders:
| | | |
|---|---|---|
| 2 | José *Diogo Dalot* Teixeira | 18.03.1999 |
| 3 | Képler Laveran Lima Ferreira *"Pepe"* | 26.02.1983 |
| 4 | *Rúben* Santos Gato Alves *Dias* | 14.05.1997 |
| 5 | Raphaël Adelino José *Guerreiro* | 22.12.1993 |
| 13 | *Danilo* Luís Hélio *Pereira* | 09.09.1991 |
| 19 | *Nuno* Alexandre Tavares *Mendes* | 19.06.2002 |
| 20 | *João* Pedro Cavaco *Cancelo* | 27.05.1994 |
| 24 | *António* João Pereira de Albuquerque Tavares da *Silva* | 30.10.2003 |

### Midfielders:
| | | |
|---|---|---|
| 6 | *João* Maria Lobo Alves *Palhinha* Gonçalves | 09.07.1995 |
| 8 | *Bruno* Miguel Borges *Fernandes* | 08.09.1994 |
| 14 | *William* Silva de *Carvalho* | 07.04.1992 |
| 16 | *Vítor* Machado Ferreira *"Vitinha"* | 13.02.2000 |
| 17 | *João Mário* Naval da Costa Eduardo | 19.01.1993 |
| 18 | *Rúben* Diogo da Silva *Neves* | 13.03.1997 |
| 23 | *Matheus* Luiz *Nunes* | 27.08.1998 |
| 25 | *Otávio* Edmilson da Silva Monteiro | 09.02.1995 |

### Forwards:
| | | |
|---|---|---|
| 7 | *Cristiano Ronaldo* dos Santos Aveiro | 05.02.1985 |
| 9 | *André* Miguel Valente *Silva* | 06.11.1995 |
| 10 | *Bernardo* Mota Veiga de Carvalho e *Silva* | 10.08.1994 |
| 11 | *João Félix* Sequeira | 10.11.1999 |
| 15 | *Rafael* Alexandre da Conceição *Leão* | 10.06.1999 |
| 21 | *Ricardo* Jorge Luz *Horta* | 15.09.1994 |
| 26 | *Gonçalo* Matías *Ramos* | 20.06.2001 |

## SERBIA
**Trainer**: Dragan Stojković

### Goalkeepers:
| 1 | Marko Dmitrović | 24.01.1992 |
|---|---|---|
| 12 | Predrag Rajković | 31.10.1995 |
| 23 | Vanja Milinković-Savić | 20.02.1997 |

### Defenders:
| 2 | Strahinja Pavlović | 24.05.2001 |
|---|---|---|
| 3 | Strahinja Eraković | 22.01.2001 |
| 4 | Nikola Milenković | 12.10.1997 |
| 5 | Miloš Veljković | 26.09.1995 |
| 13 | Stefan Mitrović | 22.05.1990 |
| 15 | Srđan Babić | 22.04.1996 |
| 25 | Filip Mladenović | 15.08.1991 |

### Midfielders:
| 6 | Nemanja Maksimović | 26.01.1995 |
|---|---|---|
| 8 | Nemanja Gudelj | 16.11.1991 |
| 14 | Andrija Živković | 11.07.1996 |
| 16 | Saša Lukić | 13.08.1996 |
| 17 | Filip Kostić | 01.11.1992 |
| 19 | Uroš Račić | 17.03.1998 |
| 20 | Sergej Milinković-Savić | 27.02.1995 |
| 21 | Filip Đuričić | 30.01.1992 |
| 22 | Darko Lazović | 15.09.1990 |
| 24 | Ivan Ilić | 17.03.2001 |
| 26 | Marko Grujić | 13.04.1996 |

### Forwards:
| 7 | Nemanja Radonjić | 15.02.1996 |
|---|---|---|
| 9 | Aleksandar Mitrović | 16.09.1994 |
| 10 | Dušan Tadić | 20.11.1988 |
| 11 | Luka Jović | 23.12.1997 |
| 18 | Dušan Vlahović | 28.01.2000 |

## SPAIN
**Trainer**: Luis Enrique Martínez García

### Goalkeepers:
| 1 | *Robert* Lynch *Sánchez* | 18.11.1997 |
|---|---|---|
| 13 | *David Raya* Martín | 15.09.1995 |
| 23 | *Unai Simón* Mendibil | 11.06.1997 |

### Defenders:
| 2 | *César Azpilicueta* Tanco | 28.08.1989 |
|---|---|---|
| 3 | *Eric García* Martret | 09.01.2001 |
| 4 | *Pau* Francisco *Torres* | 16.01.1997 |
| 14 | *Alejandro Balde* Martínez | 18.10.2003 |
| 15 | *Hugo Guillamón* Sanmartín | 31.01.2000 |
| 18 | *Jordi Alba* Ramos | 21.03.1989 |
| 20 | Daniel "*Dani*" *Carvajal* Ramos | 11.01.1992 |
| 24 | *Aymeric* Jean Louis Gérard Alphonse *Laporte* | 27.05.1994 |

### Midfielders:
| 5 | *Sergio Busquets* i Burgos | 16.07.1988 |
|---|---|---|
| 6 | *Marcos Llorente* Moreno | 30.01.1995 |
| 8 | Joge Resurrección Merodio "*Koke*" | 08.01.1992 |
| 9 | Pablo Martín Páez Gavira "*Gavi*" | 05.08.2004 |
| 10 | *Marco Asensio* Willemsen | 21.01.1996 |
| 16 | Rodrigo Hernández Cascante "*Rodri*" | 22.06.1996 |
| 19 | *Carlos Soler* Barragán | 02.01.1997 |
| 22 | *Pablo Sarabia* García | 11.05.1992 |
| 26 | Pedro González López "*Pedri*" | 25.11.2002 |

### Forwards:
| 7 | *Álvaro* Borja *Morata* Martín | 23.10.1992 |
|---|---|---|
| 11 | *Ferran Torres* García | 29.02.2000 |
| 12 | Nicholas "*Nico*" *Williams* Arthuer | 12.07.2002 |
| 17 | *Yeremi* Jesús *Pino* Santos | 20.10.2002 |
| 21 | Daniel "*Dani*" *Olmo* Carvajal | 07.05.1998 |
| 25 | Anssumane "*Ansu*" *Fati* Vieira | 31.10.2002 |

## SWITZERLAND
**Trainer**: Murat Yakin

### Goalkeepers:
| 1 | Yann Sommer | 17.12.1988 |
|---|---|---|
| 12 | Jonas Omlin | 10.01.1994 |
| 21 | Gregor Kobel | 06.12.1997 |
| 24 | Philipp François Köhn | 02.04.1998 |

### Defenders:
| 2 | Edimilson Fernandes Ribeiro | 15.04.1996 |
|---|---|---|
| 3 | Silvan Dominic Widmer | 05.03.1993 |
| 4 | Nico Elvedi | 30.09.1996 |
| 5 | Manuel Obafemi Akanji | 19.07.1995 |
| 11 | Renato Steffen | 03.11.1991 |
| 13 | Ricardo Iván Rodríguez Araya | 25.08.1992 |
| 18 | Eray Ervin Cömert | 04.02.1998 |
| 22 | Fabian Lukas Schär | 20.12.1991 |

### Midfielders:
| 6 | Denis Lemi Zakaria Lako Lado | 20.11.1996 |
|---|---|---|
| 8 | Remo Marco Freuler | 15.04.1992 |
| 10 | Granit Xhaka | 27.09.1992 |
| 14 | Michel Aebischer | 06.01.1997 |
| 15 | Mohameth Djibril Ibrahima Sow | 06.02.1997 |
| 16 | Christian Fassnacht | 11.11.1993 |
| 20 | Fabian Frei | 08.01.1989 |
| 23 | Xherdan Shaqiri | 10.10.1991 |
| 25 | Fabian Rieder | 16.02.2002 |
| 26 | Ardon Jashari | 30.07.2002 |

### Forwards:
| 7 | Breel Donald Embolo | 14.02.1997 |
|---|---|---|
| 9 | Haris Seferović | 22.02.1992 |
| 17 | Rubén Estephan Vargas Martínez | 05.08.1998 |
| 19 | Noah Okafor | 24.05.2000 |

## WALES
**Trainer**: Robert John Page

### Goalkeepers:
| 1 | Wayne Robert Hennessey | 24.01.1987 |
|---|---|---|
| 12 | Daniel Ward | 22.06.1993 |
| 21 | Adam Rhys Davies | 17.07.1992 |

### Defenders:
| 2 | Christopher Ross Gunter | 21.07.1989 |
|---|---|---|
| 3 | Neco Shay Williams | 13.04.2001 |
| 4 | Benjamin Thomas Davies | 24.04.1993 |
| 5 | Christopher James Mepham | 05.10.1997 |
| 6 | Joseph Peter Rodon | 22.10.1997 |
| 14 | Connor Richard John Roberts | 23.09.1995 |
| 17 | Thomas Alun Lockyer | 03.12.1994 |
| 24 | Benjamin George Cabango | 30.05.2000 |

### Midfielders:
| 7 | Joseph Michael Allen | 14.03.1990 |
|---|---|---|
| 8 | Harry Wilson | 22.03.1997 |
| 10 | Aaron James Ramsey | 26.12.1990 |
| 15 | Ethan Kwame Colm Raymond Ampadu | 14.09.2000 |
| 16 | Joseff John Morrell | 03.01.1997 |
| 18 | Jonathan Peter Williams | 09.10.1993 |
| 22 | Benjamin Sorba William Thomas | 25.01.1999 |
| 23 | Dylan James Christopher Levitt | 17.11.2000 |
| 25 | Rubin James Colwill | 27.04.2002 |
| 26 | Matthew Robert Smith | 22.11.1999 |

### Forwards:
| 9 | Brennan Price Johnson | 23.05.2001 |
|---|---|---|
| 11 | Gareth Frank Bale | 16.07.1989 |
| 13 | Kieffer Roberto Francisco Moore | 08.08.1992 |
| 19 | Mark Thomas Harris | 29.12.1998 |
| 20 | Daniel Owen James | 10.11.1997 |

# 2022/2023 UEFA NATIONS LEAGUE

The 2022/2023 UEFA Nations League is the third season of the UEFA Nations League, a competition involving the men's national teams of the 55 member associations of UEFA. The competition continued in September 2022 with the remaining matches from the League Phase. In June 2023, the Nations League Finals (between League A Group winners) were played, while the relegation play-outs (League C) are scheduled for March 2024.

## LEAGUE A

### GROUP A1

| Results | | |
|---|---|---|
| 03.06.2022 | Croatia - Austria | 0-3(0-1) |
| 03.06.2022 | France - Denmark | 1-2(0-0) |
| 06.06.2022 | Croatia - France | 1-1(0-0) |
| 06.06.2022 | Austria - Denmark | 1-2(0-1) |
| 10.06.2022 | Austria - France | 1-1(1-0) |
| 10.06.2022 | Denmark - Croatia | 0-1(0-0) |
| 13.06.2022 | Denmark - Austria | 2-0(2-0) |
| 13.06.2022 | France - Croatia | 0-1(0-1) |
| 22.09.2022 | Croatia - Denmark | 2-1(0-0) |
| 22.09.2022 | France - Austria | 2-0(0-0) |
| 25.09.2022 | Austria - Croatia | 1-3(1-1) |
| 25.09.2022 | Denmark - France | 2-0(2-0) |

| Final Standings | | | | | | | | |
|---|---|---|---|---|---|---|---|---|
| 1. | **Croatia** | 6 | 4 | 1 | 1 | 8 - 6 | 13 |
| 2. | Denmark | 6 | 4 | 0 | 2 | 9 - 5 | 12 |
| 3. | France | 6 | 1 | 2 | 3 | 5 - 7 | 5 |
| 4. | *Austria* | 6 | 1 | 1 | 4 | 6 - 10 | 4 |

Croatia - Qualification for Nations League Finals
Austria - Relegation to League B

### GROUP A2

| Results | | |
|---|---|---|
| 02.06.2022 | Czech Republic - Switzerland | 2-1(1-1) |
| 02.06.2022 | Spain - Portugal | 1-1(1-0) |
| 05.06.2022 | Czech Republic - Spain | 2-2(1-1) |
| 05.06.2022 | Portugal - Switzerland | 4-0(3-0) |
| 09.06.2022 | Portugal - Czech Republic | 2-0(2-0) |
| 09.06.2022 | Switzerland - Spain | 0-1(0-1) |
| 12.06.2022 | Spain - Czech Republic | 2-0(1-0) |
| 12.06.2022 | Switzerland - Portugal | 1-0(1-0) |
| 24.09.2022 | Czech Republic - Portugal | 0-4(0-2) |
| 24.09.2022 | Spain - Switzerland | 1-2(0-1) |
| 27.09.2022 | Portugal - Spain | 0-1(0-0) |
| 27.09.2022 | Switzerland - Czech Republic | 2-1(2-1) |

| Final Standings | | | | | | | | |
|---|---|---|---|---|---|---|---|---|
| 1. | **Spain** | 6 | 3 | 2 | 1 | 8 - 5 | 11 |
| 2. | Portugal | 6 | 3 | 1 | 2 | 11 - 3 | 10 |
| 3. | Switzerland | 6 | 3 | 0 | 3 | 6 - 9 | 9 |
| 4. | *Czech Republic* | 6 | 1 | 1 | 4 | 5 - 13 | 4 |

Spain - Qualification for Nations League Finals
Czech Republic - Relegation to League B

### GROUP A3

| Results | | |
|---|---|---|
| 04.06.2022 | Hungary - England | 1-0(0-0) |
| 04.06.2022 | Italy - Germany | 1-1(0-0) |
| 07.06.2022 | Germany - England | 1-1(0-0) |
| 07.06.2022 | Italy - Hungary | 2-1(2-0) |
| 11.06.2022 | England - Italy | 0-0 |
| 11.06.2022 | Hungary - Germany | 1-1(1-1) |
| 14.06.2022 | England - Hungary | 0-4(0-1) |
| 14.06.2022 | Germany - Italy | 5-2(2-0) |
| 23.09.2022 | Germany - Hungary | 0-1(0-1) |
| 23.09.2022 | Italy - England | 1-0(0-0) |
| 26.09.2022 | England - Germany | 3-3(0-0) |
| 26.09.2022 | Hungary - Italy | 0-2(0-1) |

| Final Standings | | | | | | | | |
|---|---|---|---|---|---|---|---|---|
| 1. | **Italy** | 6 | 3 | 2 | 1 | 8 - 7 | 11 |
| 2. | Hungary | 6 | 3 | 1 | 2 | 8 - 5 | 10 |
| 3. | Germany | 6 | 1 | 4 | 1 | 11 - 9 | 7 |
| 4. | *England* | 6 | 0 | 3 | 3 | 4 - 10 | 3 |

Italy - Qualification for Nations League Finals
England - Relegation to League B

### GROUP A4

| Results | | |
|---|---|---|
| 01.06.2022 | Poland - Wales | 2-1(0-0) |
| 03.06.2022 | Belgium - Netherlands | 1-4(0-1) |
| 08.06.2022 | Belgium - Poland | 6-1(1-1) |
| 08.06.2022 | Wales - Netherlands | 1-2(0-0) |
| 11.06.2022 | Netherlands - Poland | 2-2(0-1) |
| 11.06.2022 | Wales - Belgium | 1-1(0-0) |
| 14.06.2022 | Netherlands - Wales | 3-2(2-1) |
| 14.06.2022 | Poland - Belgium | 0-1(0-1) |
| 22.09.2022 | Belgium - Wales | 2-1(2-0) |
| 22.09.2022 | Poland - Netherlands | 0-2(0-1) |
| 25.09.2022 | Netherlands - Belgium | 1-0(0-0) |
| 25.09.2022 | Wales - Poland | 0-1(0-0) |

| Final Standings | | | | | | | | |
|---|---|---|---|---|---|---|---|---|
| 1. | **Netherlands** | 6 | 5 | 1 | 0 | 14 - 6 | 16 |
| 2. | Belgium | 6 | 3 | 1 | 2 | 11 - 8 | 10 |
| 3. | Poland | 6 | 2 | 1 | 3 | 6 - 12 | 7 |
| 4. | *Wales* | 6 | 0 | 1 | 5 | 6 - 11 | 1 |

Netherlands - Qualification for Nations League Finals
Wales - Relegation to League B

# FINAL TOURNAMENT

## SEMI-FINALS

| 14.06.2023 | Rotterdam | Netherlands - Croatia | 2-4(1-0,2-2) |
| 15.06.2023 | Enschede | Spain - Italy | 2-1(1-1) |

## THIRD PLACE PLAY-OFF

| 18.06.2023 | Enschede | Netherlands - Italy | 2-3(0-2) |

## FINAL

| 18.06.2023 | Rotterdam | Croatia - **Spain** | 0-0 aet; 4-5 pen |

## UEFA NATIONS LEAGUE (2018-2023) TABLE OF HONOURS

| 2018/2019 | Portugal |
|---|---|
| 2020/2021 | France |
| 2022/2023 | Spain |

# LEAGUE B

## GROUP B1

### Results

| 04.06.2022 | Armenia - Republic of Ireland | 1-0(0-0) |
| 08.06.2022 | Scotland - Armenia | 2-0(2-0) |
| 08.06.2022 | Republic of Ireland - Ukraine | 0-1(0-0) |
| 11.06.2022 | Ukraine - Armenia | 3-0(0-0) |
| 11.06.2022 | Republic of Ireland - Scotland | 3-0(2-0) |
| 14.06.2022 | Armenia - Scotland | 1-4(1-2) |
| 14.06.2022 | Ukraine - Republic of Ireland | 1-1(0-1) |
| 21.09.2022 | Scotland - Ukraine | 3-0(0-0) |
| 24.09.2022 | Armenia - Ukraine | 0-5(0-1) |
| 24.09.2022 | Scotland - Republic of Ireland | 2-1(0-1) |
| 27.09.2022 | Republic of Ireland - Armenia | 3-2(1-0) |
| 27.09.2022 | Ukraine - Scotland | 0-0 |

### Final Standings

| 1. | **Scotland** | 6 | 4 | 1 | 1 | 11 | - | 5 | 13 |
|---|---|---|---|---|---|---|---|---|---|
| 2. | Ukraine | 6 | 3 | 2 | 1 | 10 | - | 4 | 11 |
| 3. | Republic of Ireland | 6 | 2 | 1 | 3 | 8 | - | 7 | 7 |
| 4. | *Armenia* | 6 | 1 | 0 | 5 | 4 | - | 17 | 3 |

Scotland - Promotion to League A
Armenia - Relegation to League C

## GROUP B2

### Results

| 02.06.2022 | Albania - Russia | * |
| 02.06.2022 | Israel - Iceland | 2-2(1-1) |
| 06.06.2022 | Israel - Russia | * |
| 06.06.2022 | Iceland - Albania | 1-1(0-1) |
| 10.06.2022 | Russia - Iceland | * |
| 10.06.2022 | Albania - Israel | 1-2(1-0) |
| 13.06.2022 | Russia - Albania | * |
| 13.06.2022 | Iceland - Israel | 2-2(1-1) |
| 24.09.2022 | Iceland - Russia | * |
| 24.09.2022 | Israel - Albania | 2-1(0-0) |
| 27.09.2022 | Russia - Israel | * |
| 27.09.2022 | Albania - Iceland | 1-1(1-0) |

### Final Standings

| 1. | **Israel** | 4 | 2 | 2 | 0 | 8 | - | 6 | 8 |
|---|---|---|---|---|---|---|---|---|---|
| 2. | Iceland | 4 | 0 | 4 | 0 | 6 | - | 6 | 4 |
| 3. | Albania | 4 | 0 | 2 | 2 | 4 | - | 6 | 2 |
| 4. | *Russia* (suspended) | | | | | | - | | |

Israel - Promotion to League A
Russia - Relegation to League C

*matches cancelled due to suspension of Russia*

## GROUP B3

### Results

| 04.06.2022 | Finland - Bosnia and Herzegovina | 1-1(1-0) |
| 04.06.2022 | Montenegro - Romania | 2-0(0-0) |
| 07.06.2022 | Finland - Montenegro | 2-0(2-0) |
| 07.06.2022 | Bosnia and Herzegovina - Romania | 1-0(0-0) |
| 11.06.2022 | Montenegro - Bosnia and Herzegovina | 1-1(0-0) |
| 11.06.2022 | Romania - Finland | 1-0(1-0) |
| 14.06.2022 | Bosnia and Herzegovina - Finland | 3-2(2-2) |
| 14.06.2022 | Romania - Montenegro | 0-3(0-1) |
| 23.09.2022 | Bosnia and Herzegovina - Montenegro | 1-0(1-0) |
| 23.09.2022 | Finland - Romania | 1-1(1-0) |
| 26.09.2022 | Montenegro - Finland | 0-2(0-0) |
| 26.09.2022 | Romania - Bosnia and Herzegovina | 4-1(1-0) |

### Final Standings

| 1. | **Bosnia and Herzegovina** | 6 | 3 | 2 | 1 | 8 | - | 8 | 11 |
|---|---|---|---|---|---|---|---|---|---|
| 2. | Finland | 6 | 2 | 2 | 2 | 8 | - | 6 | 8 |
| 3. | Montenegro | 6 | 2 | 1 | 3 | 6 | - | 6 | 7 |
| 4. | *Romania* | 6 | 2 | 1 | 3 | 6 | - | 8 | 7 |

Bosnia and Herzegovina - Promotion to League A
Romania - Relegation to League C

## Results

| | | |
|---|---|---|
| 02.06.2022 | Serbia - Norway | 0-1(0-1) |
| 02.06.2022 | Slovenia - Sweden | 0-2(0-1) |
| 05.06.2022 | Serbia - Slovenia | 4-1(1-1) |
| 05.06.2022 | Sweden - Norway | 1-2(0-1) |
| 09.06.2022 | Norway - Slovenia | 0-0 |
| 09.06.2022 | Sweden - Serbia | 0-1(0-1) |
| 12.06.2022 | Norway - Sweden | 3-2(1-0) |
| 12.06.2022 | Slovenia - Serbia | 2-2(0-2) |
| 24.09.2022 | Slovenia - Norway | 2-1(0-0) |
| 24.09.2022 | Serbia - Sweden | 4-1(2-1) |
| 27.09.2022 | Norway - Serbia | 0-2(0-1) |
| 27.09.2022 | Sweden - Slovenia | 1-1(1-1) |

## Final Standings

| | | | | | | | | | |
|---|---|---|---|---|---|---|---|---|---|
| 1. | Serbia | 6 | 4 | 1 | 1 | 13 | - | 5 | 13 |
| 2. | Norway | 6 | 3 | 1 | 2 | 7 | - | 7 | 10 |
| 3. | Slovenia | 6 | 1 | 3 | 2 | 6 | - | 10 | 6 |
| 4. | *Sweden* | 6 | 1 | 1 | 4 | 7 | - | 11 | 4 |

Serbia - Promotion to League A
Sweden - Relegation to League C

# LEAGUE C

## GROUP C1

## Results

| | | |
|---|---|---|
| 04.06.2022 | Lithuania - Luxembourg | 0-2(0-1) |
| 04.06.2022 | Turkey - Faroe Islands | 4-0(1-0) |
| 07.06.2022 | Faroe Islands - Luxembourg | 0-1(0-0) |
| 07.06.2022 | Lithuania - Turkey | 0-6(0-2) |
| 11.06.2022 | Faroe Islands - Lithuania | 2-1(2-1) |
| 11.06.2022 | Luxembourg - Turkey | 0-2(0-1) |
| 14.06.2022 | Luxembourg - Faroe Islands | 2-2(1-0) |
| 14.06.2022 | Turkey - Lithuania | 2-0(1-0) |
| 22.09.2022 | Lithuania - Faroe Islands | 1-1(1-1) |
| 22.09.2022 | Turkey - Luxembourg | 3-3(2-2) |
| 25.09.2022 | Luxembourg - Lithuania | 1-0(0-0) |
| 25.09.2022 | Faroe Islands - Turkey | 2-1(0-0) |

## Final Standings

| | | | | | | | | | |
|---|---|---|---|---|---|---|---|---|---|
| 1. | Turkey | 6 | 4 | 1 | 1 | 18 | - | 5 | 13 |
| 2. | Luxembourg | 6 | 3 | 2 | 1 | 9 | - | 7 | 11 |
| 3. | Faroe Islands | 6 | 2 | 2 | 2 | 7 | - | 10 | 8 |
| 4. | *Lithuania* | 6 | 0 | 1 | 5 | 2 | - | 14 | 1 |

Turkey - Promotion to League B
Lithuania - Qualification for relegation play-outs

## GROUP C2

## Results

| | | |
|---|---|---|
| 02.06.2022 | Cyprus - Kosovo | 0-2(0-0) |
| 02.06.2022 | Northern Ireland - Greece | 0-1(0-1) |
| 05.06.2022 | Cyprus - Northern Ireland | 0-0 |
| 05.06.2022 | Kosovo - Greece | 0-1(0-1) |
| 09.06.2022 | Kosovo - Northern Ireland | 3-2(2-1) |
| 09.06.2022 | Greece - Cyprus | 3-0(2-0) |
| 12.06.2022 | Northern Ireland - Cyprus | 2-2(0-1) |
| 12.06.2022 | Greece - Kosovo | 2-0(0-0) |
| 24.09.2022 | Northern Ireland - Kosovo | 2-1(0-0) |
| 24.09.2022 | Cyprus - Greece | 1-0(1-0) |
| 27.09.2022 | Kosovo - Cyprus | 5-1(2-0) |
| 27.09.2022 | Greece - Northern Ireland | 3-1(1-1) |

## Final Standings

| | | | | | | | | | |
|---|---|---|---|---|---|---|---|---|---|
| 1. | Greece | 6 | 5 | 0 | 1 | 10 | - | 2 | 15 |
| 2. | Kosovo | 6 | 3 | 0 | 3 | 11 | - | 8 | 9 |
| 3. | Northern Ireland | 6 | 1 | 2 | 3 | 7 | - | 10 | 5 |
| 4. | *Cyprus* | 6 | 1 | 2 | 3 | 4 | - | 12 | 5 |

Greece - Promotion to League B
Cyprus - Qualification for relegation play-outs

## GROUP C3

## Results

| | | |
|---|---|---|
| 03.06.2022 | Kazakhstan - Azerbaijan | 2-0(0-0) |
| 03.06.2022 | Belarus - Slovakia | 0-1(0-0) |
| 06.06.2022 | Belarus - Azerbaijan | 0-0 |
| 06.06.2022 | Slovakia - Kazakhstan | 0-1(0-1) |
| 10.06.2022 | Azerbaijan - Slovakia | 0-1(0-0) |
| 10.06.2022 | Belarus - Kazakhstan | 1-1(0-1) |
| 13.06.2022 | Kazakhstan - Slovakia | 2-1(2-0) |
| 13.06.2022 | Azerbaijan - Belarus | 2-0(0-0) |
| 22.09.2022 | Kazakhstan - Belarus | 2-1(1-1) |
| 22.09.2022 | Slovakia - Azerbaijan | 1-2(0-1) |
| 25.09.2022 | Slovakia - Belarus | 1-1(0-1) |
| 25.09.2022 | Azerbaijan - Kazakhstan | 3-0(0-0) |

## Final Standings

| | | | | | | | | | |
|---|---|---|---|---|---|---|---|---|---|
| 1. | Kazakhstan | 6 | 4 | 1 | 1 | 8 | - | 6 | 13 |
| 2. | Azerbaijan | 6 | 3 | 1 | 2 | 7 | - | 4 | 10 |
| 3. | Slovakia | 6 | 2 | 1 | 3 | 5 | - | 6 | 7 |
| 4. | *Belarus* | 6 | 0 | 3 | 3 | 3 | - | 7 | 3 |

Kazakhstan - Promotion to League B
Belarus - Qualification for relegation play-outs

## GROUP C4

| Results | | |
|---|---|---|
| 02.06.2022 | Georgia - Gibraltar | 4-0(2-0) |
| 02.06.2022 | Bulgaria - North Macedonia | 1-1(1-0) |
| 05.06.2022 | Gibraltar - North Macedonia | 0-2(0-1) |
| 05.06.2022 | Bulgaria - Georgia | 2-5(0-2) |
| 09.06.2022 | Gibraltar - Bulgaria | 1-1(0-1) |
| 09.06.2022 | North Macedonia - Georgia | 0-3(0-0) |
| 12.06.2022 | Georgia - Bulgaria | 0-0 |
| 12.06.2022 | North Macedonia - Gibraltar | 4-0(4-0) |
| 23.09.2022 | Georgia - North Macedonia | 2-0(1-0) |
| 23.09.2022 | Bulgaria - Gibraltar | 5-1(2-1) |
| 26.09.2022 | Gibraltar - Georgia | 1-2(0-1) |
| 26.09.2022 | North Macedonia - Bulgaria | 0-1(0-0) |

| | Final Standings | | | | | | | | |
|---|---|---|---|---|---|---|---|---|---|
| 1. | **Georgia** | 6 | 5 | 1 | 0 | 16 | - | 3 | 16 |
| 2. | Bulgaria | 6 | 2 | 3 | 1 | 10 | - | 8 | 9 |
| 3. | North Macedonia | 6 | 2 | 1 | 3 | 7 | - | 7 | 7 |
| 4. | *Gibraltar* | 6 | 0 | 1 | 5 | 3 | - | 18 | 1 |

Georgia - Promotion to League B
Gibraltar - Qualification for relegation play-outs

## RELEGATION PLAY-OUTS

Gibraltar - Cyprus
Lithuania - Belarus

Matches are scheduled for
21-23.03.2024 (1$^{st}$ leg) / 24-26.03.2024 (2$^{nd}$ leg)

# LEAGUE D

## GROUP D1

| Results | | |
|---|---|---|
| 03.06.2022 | Latvia - Andorra | 3-0(1-0) |
| 03.06.2022 | Liechtenstein - Moldova | 0-2(0-1) |
| 06.06.2022 | Latvia - Liechtenstein | 1-0(0-0) |
| 06.06.2022 | Andorra - Moldova | 0-0 |
| 10.06.2022 | Moldova - Latvia | 2-4(1-2) |
| 10.06.2022 | Andorra - Liechtenstein | 2-1(0-0) |
| 14.06.2022 | Moldova - Andorra | 2-1(1-1) |
| 14.06.2022 | Liechtenstein - Latvia | 0-2(0-2) |
| 22.09.2022 | Latvia - Moldova | 1-2(0-2) |
| 22.09.2022 | Liechtenstein - Andorra | 0-2(0-1) |
| 25.09.2022 | Andorra - Latvia | 1-1(0-0) |
| 25.09.2022 | Moldova - Liechtenstein | 2-0(0-0) |

| | Final Standings | | | | | | | | |
|---|---|---|---|---|---|---|---|---|---|
| 1. | **Latvia** | 6 | 4 | 1 | 1 | 12 | - | 5 | 13 |
| 2. | Moldova | 6 | 4 | 1 | 1 | 10 | - | 6 | 13 |
| 3. | Andorra | 6 | 2 | 2 | 2 | 6 | - | 7 | 8 |
| 4. | Liechtenstein | 6 | 0 | 0 | 6 | 1 | - | 11 | 0 |

Latvia - Promotion to League C

## GROUP D2

| Results | | |
|---|---|---|
| 02.06.2022 | Estonia - San Marino | 2-0(2-0) |
| 05.06.2022 | San Marino - Malta | 0-2(0-0) |
| 09.06.2022 | Malta - Estonia | 1-2(0-1) |
| 12.06.2022 | Malta - San Marino | 1-0(0-0) |
| 23.09.2022 | Estonia - Malta | 2-1(1-0) |
| 26.09.2022 | San Marino - Estonia | 0-4(0-1) |

| | Final Standings | | | | | | | | |
|---|---|---|---|---|---|---|---|---|---|
| 1. | **Estonia** | 4 | 4 | 0 | 0 | 10 | - | 2 | 12 |
| 2. | Malta | 4 | 2 | 0 | 2 | 5 | - | 4 | 6 |
| 3. | San Marino | 4 | 0 | 0 | 4 | 0 | - | 9 | 0 |

Estonia - Promotion to League C

# 2024 EUROPEAN CHAMPIONSHIP QUALIFIERS

The 2024 UEFA European Football Championship will be the 17th edition of the UEFA European Championship, the quadrennial international football championship organised by UEFA for the men's national teams of its member associations. Germany will host final the tournament, which is scheduled to take place from 14 June to 14 July 2024. The competition began with the qualifying tournament, which is being played from March 2023 to March 2024 to determine the 23 UEFA member men's national teams that will join the automatically qualified host team Germany in the 2024 final tournament. As four years ago, the competition is linked with the 2022/2023 UEFA Nations League, which gives countries a secondary route to qualify for the final tournament.

53 UEFA member associations were divided into ten groups, with seven groups containing five teams and three containing six teams. From each group, winners and runners-up were directly qualified for the final tournament. The four UEFA Nations League Finals participants were drawn into groups of five teams, so they were able to compete in the Nations League Finals in June 2023. Following the qualifying group stage, the remaining three teams will be decided through the play-offs, to be held in March 2024. Twelve teams will be selected based on their performance in the 2022/2023 UEFA Nations League. These teams will be divided into three paths, each containing four teams, with one team from each path qualifying for the final tournament. The group winners of Nations Leagues A, B, and C will automatically qualify for the play-off path of their league unless they have qualified for the final tournament via the qualifying group stage. If a group winner has already qualified through the qualifying group stage, they will be replaced by the next best-ranked team in the same league.

The teams were seeded based on the September 2022 UEFA Nations League overall rankings.

| UNL Pot | Pot 2 | Pot 3 | Pot 4 | Pot 5 | Pot 6 |
|---|---|---|---|---|---|
| Netherlands | France | Ukraine | Georgia | Slovakia | Andorra |
| Croatia | Austria | Iceland | Greece | Northern Ireland | San Marino |
| Spain | Czech Republic | Norway | Turkey | Cyprus | Liechtenstein |
| Italy (title holders) | England | Slovenia | Kazakhstan | Belarus | |
| **Pot 1** | Wales | Republic of Ireland | Luxembourg | Lithuania | |
| Denmark | Israel | Albania | Azerbaijan | Gibraltar | |
| Portugal | Bosnia and Herzegovina | Montenegro | Kosovo | Estonia | |
| Belgium | Serbia | Romania | Bulgaria | Latvia | |
| Hungary | Scotland | Sweden | Faroe Islands | Moldova | |
| Switzerland | Finland | Armenia | North Macedonia | Malta | |
| Poland | | | | | |

The draw for the qualifying group stage took place on 09.10.2022. Russia remains suspended from FIFA and UEFA competitions following their country's invasion of Ukraine.

## Qualifiers - Results from March to June 2023

### GROUP A

| Results | | |
|---|---|---|
| 25.03.2023 | Scotland - Cyprus | 3-0(1-0) |
| 25.03.2023 | Spain - Norway | 3-0(1-0) |
| 28.03.2023 | Georgia - Norway | 1-1(0-1) |
| 28.03.2023 | Scotland - Spain | 2-0(1-0) |
| 17.06.2023 | Norway - Scotland | 1-2(0-0) |
| 17.06.2023 | Cyprus - Georgia | 1-2(1-1) |
| 20.06.2023 | Scotland - Georgia | 2-0(1-0) |
| 20.06.2023 | Norway - Cyprus | 3-1(1-0) |

| | Standings | | | | | | | | |
|---|---|---|---|---|---|---|---|---|---|
| 1. | Scotland | 4 | 4 | 0 | 0 | 9 | - | 1 | 12 |
| 2. | Georgia | 3 | 1 | 1 | 1 | 3 | - | 4 | 4 |
| 3. | Norway | 4 | 1 | 1 | 2 | 5 | - | 7 | 4 |
| 4. | Spain | 2 | 1 | 0 | 1 | 3 | - | 2 | 3 |
| 5. | Cyprus | 3 | 0 | 0 | 3 | 2 | - | 8 | 0 |

**Next matches:**

| | |
|---|---|
| 08.09.2023 | Georgia - Spain, Cyprus - Scotland |
| 12.09.2023 | Norway - Georgia, Spain - Cyprus |
| 12.10.2023 | Cyprus - Norway, Spain - Scotland |
| 15.10.2023 | Georgia - Cyprus, Norway - Spain |
| 16.11.2023 | Georgia - Scotland, Cyprus - Spain |
| 19.11.2023 | Spain - Georgia, Scotland - Norway |

## GROUP B

| Results | | |
|---|---|---|
| 24.03.2023 | France - Netherlands | 4-0(3-0) |
| 24.03.2023 | Gibraltar - Greece | 0-3(0-2) |
| 27.03.2023 | Ireland - France | 0-1(0-0) |
| 27.03.2023 | Netherlands - Gibraltar | 3-0(1-0) |
| 16.06.2023 | Gibraltar - France | 0-3(0-2) |
| 16.06.2023 | Greece - Ireland | 2-1(1-1) |
| 19.06.2023 | France - Greece | 1-0(0-0) |
| 19.06.2023 | Ireland - Gibraltar | 3-0(0-0) |

| Standings | | | | | | | | |
|---|---|---|---|---|---|---|---|---|
| 1. | France | 4 | 4 | 0 | 0 | 9 | - 0 | 12 |
| 2. | Greece | 3 | 2 | 0 | 1 | 5 | - 2 | 6 |
| 3. | Republic of Ireland | 3 | 1 | 0 | 2 | 4 | - 3 | 3 |
| 4. | Netherlands | 2 | 1 | 0 | 1 | 3 | - 4 | 3 |
| 5. | Gibraltar | 4 | 0 | 0 | 4 | 0 | - 12 | 0 |

**Next matches:**

| | |
|---|---|
| 07.09.2023 | France - Ireland, Netherlands - Greece |
| 10.09.2023 | Greece - Gibraltar, Ireland - Netherlands |
| 13.10.2023 | Netherlands - France, Ireland - Greece |
| 16.10.2023 | Gibraltar - Ireland, Greece - Netherlands |
| 18.11.2023 | France - Gibraltar, Netherlands - Ireland |
| 21.11.2023 | Greece - France, Gibraltar - Netherlands |

## GROUP C

| Results | | |
|---|---|---|
| 23.03.2023 | Italy - England | 1-2(0-2) |
| 23.03.2023 | North Macedonia - Malta | 2-1(0-0) |
| 26.03.2023 | England - Ukraine | 2-0(2-0) |
| 26.03.2023 | Malta - Italy | 0-2(0-2) |
| 16.06.2023 | Malta - England | 0-4(0-3) |
| 16.06.2023 | North Macedonia - Ukraine | 2-3(2-0) |
| 19.06.2023 | Ukraine - Malta | 1-0(0-0) |
| 19.06.2023 | England - North Macedonia | 7-0(3-0) |

| Standings | | | | | | | | |
|---|---|---|---|---|---|---|---|---|
| 1. | England | 4 | 4 | 0 | 0 | 15 | - 1 | 12 |
| 2. | Ukraine | 3 | 2 | 0 | 1 | 4 | - 4 | 6 |
| 3. | Italy | 2 | 1 | 0 | 1 | 3 | - 2 | 3 |
| 4. | North Macedonia | 3 | 1 | 0 | 2 | 4 | - 11 | 3 |
| 5. | Malta | 4 | 0 | 0 | 4 | 1 | - 9 | 0 |

**Next matches:**

| | |
|---|---|
| 09.09.2023 | Ukraine - England, North Macedonia - Italy |
| 12.09.2023 | Italy - Ukraine, Malta - North Macedonia |
| 14.10.2023 | Ukraine - North Macedonia, Italy - Malta |
| 17.10.2023 | England - Italy, Malta - Ukraine |
| 17.11.2023 | England - Malta, Italy - North Macedonia |
| 20.11.2023 | North Macedonia - England, Ukraine - Italy |

## GROUP D

| Results | | |
|---|---|---|
| 25.03.2023 | Armenia - Turkey | 1-2(1-1) |
| 25.03.2023 | Croatia - Wales | 1-1(1-0) |
| 28.03.2023 | Turkey - Croatia | 0-2(0-2) |
| 28.03.2023 | Wales - Latvia | 1-0(1-0) |
| 16.06.2023 | Wales - Armenia | 2-4(1-2) |
| 16.06.2023 | Latvia - Turkey | 2-3(0-1) |
| 19.06.2023 | Armenia - Latvia | 2-1(1-0) |
| 19.06.2023 | Turkey - Wales | 2-0(0-0) |

| Standings | | | | | | | | |
|---|---|---|---|---|---|---|---|---|
| 1. | Turkey | 4 | 3 | 0 | 1 | 7 | - 5 | 9 |
| 2. | Armenia | 3 | 2 | 0 | 1 | 7 | - 5 | 6 |
| 3. | Croatia | 2 | 1 | 1 | 0 | 3 | - 1 | 4 |
| 4. | Wales | 4 | 1 | 1 | 2 | 4 | - 7 | 4 |
| 5. | Latvia | 3 | 0 | 0 | 3 | 3 | - 6 | 0 |

**Next matches:**

| | |
|---|---|
| 08.09.2023 | Turkey - Armenia, Croatia - Latvia |
| 11.09.2023 | Armenia - Croatia, Latvia - Wales |
| 12.10.2023 | Latvia - Armenia, Croatia - Turkey |
| 15.10.2023 | Wales - Croatia, Turkey - Latvia |
| 18.11.2023 | Armenia - Wales, Latvia - Croatia |
| 21.11.2023 | Croatia - Armenia, Wales - Turkey |

## GROUP E

### Results

| | | | |
|---|---|---|---|
| 24.03.2023 | Moldova - Faroe Islands | 1-1(0-1) |
| 24.03.2023 | Czech Republic - Poland | 3-1(2-0) |
| 27.03.2023 | Poland - Albania | 1-0(1-0) |
| 27.03.2023 | Moldova - Czech Republic | 0-0 |
| 17.06.2023 | Albania - Moldova | 2-0(0-0) |
| 17.06.2023 | Faroe Islands - Czech Republic | 0-3(0-2) |
| 20.06.2023 | Faroe Islands - Albania | 1-3(1-1) |
| 20.06.2023 | Moldova - Poland | 3-2(0-2) |

### Standings

| | | | | | | | | |
|---|---|---|---|---|---|---|---|---|
| 1. | Czech Republic | 3 | 2 | 1 | 0 | 6 | - 1 | 7 |
| 2. | Albania | 3 | 2 | 0 | 1 | 5 | - 2 | 6 |
| 3. | Moldova | 4 | 1 | 2 | 1 | 4 | - 5 | 5 |
| 4. | Poland | 3 | 1 | 0 | 2 | 4 | - 6 | 3 |
| 5. | Faroe Islands | 3 | 0 | 1 | 2 | 2 | - 7 | 1 |

### Next matches:

| | |
|---|---|
| 07.09.2023 | Czech Republic - Albania, Poland - Faroe Islands |
| 10.09.2023 | Faroe Islands - Moldova, Albania - Poland |
| 12.10.2023 | Albania - Czech Republic, Faroe Islands - Poland |
| 15.10.2023 | Czech Republic - Faroe Islands, Poland - Moldova |
| 17.11.2023 | Moldova - Albania, Poland - Czech Republic |
| 20.11.2023 | Albania - Faroe Islands, Czech Republic - Moldova |

## GROUP F

### Results

| | | | |
|---|---|---|---|
| 24.03.2023 | Austria - Azerbaijan | 4-1(2-0) |
| 24.03.2023 | Sweden - Belgium | 0-3(0-1) |
| 27.03.2023 | Sweden - Azerbaijan | 5-0(1-0) |
| 27.03.2023 | Austria - Estonia | 2-1(0-1) |
| 17.06.2023 | Azerbaijan - Estonia | 1-1(0-1) |
| 17.06.2023 | Belgium - Austria | 1-1(0-1) |
| 20.06.2023 | Estonia - Belgium | 0-3(0-2) |
| 20.06.2023 | Austria - Sweden | 2-0(0-0) |

### Standings

| | | | | | | | | |
|---|---|---|---|---|---|---|---|---|
| 1. | Austria | 4 | 3 | 1 | 0 | 9 | - 3 | 10 |
| 2. | Belgium | 3 | 2 | 1 | 0 | 7 | - 1 | 7 |
| 3. | Sweden | 3 | 1 | 0 | 2 | 5 | - 5 | 3 |
| 4. | Estonia | 3 | 0 | 1 | 2 | 2 | - 6 | 1 |
| 5. | Azerbaijan | 3 | 0 | 1 | 2 | 2 | - 10 | 1 |

### Next matches:

| | |
|---|---|
| 09.09.2023 | Azerbaijan - Belgium, Estonia - Sweden |
| 12.09.2023 | Belgium - Estonia, Sweden - Austria |
| 13.10.2023 | Estonia - Azerbaijan, Austria - Belgium |
| 16.10.2023 | Azerbaijan - Austria, Belgium - Sweden |
| 16.11.2023 | Azerbaijan - Sweden, Estonia - Austria |
| 19.11.2023 | Belgium - Azerbaijan, Sweden - Estonia |

## GROUP G

### Results

| | | | |
|---|---|---|---|
| 24.03.2023 | Bulgaria - Montenegro | 0-1(0-0) |
| 24.03.2023 | Serbia - Lithuania | 2-0(1-0) |
| 27.03.2023 | Hungary - Bulgaria | 3-0(3-0) |
| 27.03.2023 | Montenegro - Serbia | 0-2(0-0) |
| 17.06.2023 | Lithuania - Bulgaria | 1-1(1-1) |
| 17.06.2023 | Montenegro - Hungary | 0-0 |
| 20.06.2023 | Bulgaria - Serbia | 1-1(0-0) |
| 20.06.2023 | Hungary - Lithuania | 2-0(1-0) |

### Standings

| | | | | | | | | |
|---|---|---|---|---|---|---|---|---|
| 1. | Hungary | 3 | 2 | 1 | 0 | 5 | - 0 | 7 |
| 2. | Serbia | 3 | 2 | 1 | 0 | 5 | - 1 | 7 |
| 3. | Montenegro | 3 | 1 | 1 | 1 | 1 | - 2 | 4 |
| 4. | Bulgaria | 4 | 0 | 2 | 2 | 2 | - 6 | 2 |
| 5. | Lithuania | 3 | 0 | 1 | 2 | 1 | - 5 | 1 |

### Next matches:

| | |
|---|---|
| 07.09.2023 | Lithuania - Montenegro, Serbia - Hungary |
| 10.09.2023 | Montenegro - Bulgaria, Lithuania - Serbia |
| 14.10.2023 | Bulgaria - Lithuania, Hungary - Serbia |
| 17.10.2023 | Lithuania - Hungary, Serbia - Montenegro |
| 16.11.2023 | Bulgaria - Hungary, Montenegro - Lithuania |
| 19.11.2023 | Serbia - Bulgaria, Hungary - Montenegro |

## GROUP H

### Results

| | | |
|---|---|---|
| 23.03.2023 | Kazakhstan - Slovenia | 1-2(1-0) |
| 23.03.2023 | Denmark - Finland | 3-1(1-0) |
| 23.03.2023 | San Marino - Northern Ireland | 0-2(0-1) |
| 26.03.2023 | Kazakhstan - Denmark | 3-2(0-2) |
| 26.03.2023 | Slovenia - San Marino | 2-0(0-0) |
| 26.03.2023 | Northern Ireland - Finland | 0-1(0-1) |
| 16.06.2023 | Finland - Slovenia | 2-0(1-0) |
| 16.06.2023 | Denmark - Northern Ireland | 1-0(0-0) |
| 16.06.2023 | San Marino - Kazakhstan | 0-3(0-1) |
| 19.06.2023 | Finland - San Marino | 6-0(2-0) |
| 19.06.2023 | Slovenia - Denmark | 1-1(1-1) |
| 19.06.2023 | Northern Ireland - Kazakhstan | 0-1(0-0) |

### Standings

| | | | | | | | | | |
|---|---|---|---|---|---|---|---|---|---|
| 1. | Finland | 4 | 3 | 0 | 1 | 10 | - | 3 | 9 |
| 2. | Kazakhstan | 4 | 3 | 0 | 1 | 8 | - | 4 | 9 |
| 3. | Denmark | 4 | 2 | 1 | 1 | 7 | - | 5 | 7 |
| 4. | Slovenia | 4 | 2 | 1 | 1 | 5 | - | 4 | 7 |
| 5. | Northern Ireland | 4 | 1 | 0 | 3 | 2 | - | 3 | 3 |
| 6. | SanMarino | 4 | 0 | 0 | 4 | 0 | - | 13 | 0 |

### Next matches:

| | |
|---|---|
| 07.09.2023 | Kazakhstan - Finland, Denmark - San Marino, Slovenia - Northern Ireland |
| 10.09.2023 | Kazakhstan - Northern Ireland, Finland - Denmark, San Marino - Slovenia |
| 14.10.2023 | Northern Ireland - San Marino, Slovenia - Finland, Denmark - Kazakhstan |
| 17.10.2023 | Finland - Kazakhstan, San Marino - Denmark, Northern Ireland - Slovenia |
| 17.11.2023 | Kazakhstan - San Marino, Finland - Northern Ireland, Denmark - Slovenia |
| 20.11.2023 | Northern Ireland - Denmark, San Marino - Finland, Slovenia - Kazakhstan |

## GROUP I

### Results

| | | |
|---|---|---|
| 25.03.2023 | Belarus - Switzerland | 0-5(0-3) |
| 25.03.2023 | Israel - Kosovo | 1-1(0-1) |
| 25.03.2023 | Andorra - Romania | 0-2(0-1) |
| 28.03.2023 | Kosovo - Andorra | 1-1(0-0) |
| 28.03.2023 | Romania - Belarus | 2-1(2-0) |
| 28.03.2023 | Switzerland - Israel | 3-0(1-0) |
| 16.06.2023 | Andorra - Switzerland | 1-2(0-2) |
| 16.06.2023 | Belarus - Israel | 1-2(1-0) |
| 16.06.2023 | Kosovo - Romania | 0-0 |
| 19.06.2023 | Israel - Andorra | 2-1(1-0) |
| 19.06.2023 | Belarus - Kosovo | 2-1(0-0) |
| 19.06.2023 | Switzerland - Romania | 2-2(2-0) |

### Standings

| | | | | | | | | | |
|---|---|---|---|---|---|---|---|---|---|
| 1. | Switzerland | 4 | 3 | 1 | 0 | 12 | - | 3 | 10 |
| 2. | Romania | 4 | 2 | 2 | 0 | 6 | - | 3 | 8 |
| 3. | Israel | 4 | 2 | 1 | 1 | 5 | - | 6 | 7 |
| 4. | Belarus | 4 | 1 | 0 | 3 | 4 | - | 10 | 3 |
| 5. | Kosovo | 4 | 0 | 3 | 1 | 3 | - | 4 | 3 |
| 6. | Andorra | 4 | 0 | 1 | 3 | 3 | - | 7 | 1 |

### Next matches:

| | |
|---|---|
| 09.09.2023 | Andorra - Belarus, Romania - Israel, Kosovo - Switzerland |
| 12.09.2023 | Switzerland - Andorra, Israel - Belarus, Romania - Kosovo |
| 12.10.2023 | Andorra - Kosovo, Belarus - Romania, Israel - Switzerland |
| 15.10.2023 | Switzerland - Belarus, Romania - Andorra, Kosovo - Israel |
| 18.11.2023 | Belarus - Andorra, Israel - Romania, Switzerland - Kosovo |
| 21.11.2023 | Andorra - Israel, Kosovo - Belarus, Romania - Switzerland |

## GROUP J

### Results

| | | |
|---|---|---|
| 23.03.2023 | Bosnia-Herzegovina - Iceland | 3-0(2-0) |
| 23.03.2023 | Portugal - Liechtenstein | 4-0(1-0) |
| 23.03.2023 | Slovakia - Luxembourg | 0-0 |
| 26.03.2023 | Liechtenstein - Iceland | 0-7(0-2) |
| 26.03.2023 | Slovakia - Bosnia-Herzegovina | 2-0(2-0) |
| 26.03.2023 | Luxembourg - Portugal | 0-6(0-4) |
| 17.06.2023 | Luxembourg - Liechtenstein | 2-0(0-0) |
| 17.06.2023 | Portugal - Bosnia-Herzegovina | 3-0(1-0) |
| 17.06.2023 | Iceland - Slovakia | 1-2(1-1) |
| 20.06.2023 | Bosnia-Herzegovina - Luxembourg | 0-2(0-1) |
| 20.06.2023 | Iceland - Portugal | 0-1(0-0) |
| 20.06.2023 | Liechtenstein - Slovakia | 0-1(0-1) |

### Standings

| | | | | | | | | | |
|---|---|---|---|---|---|---|---|---|---|
| 1. | Portugal | 4 | 4 | 0 | 0 | 14 | - | 0 | 12 |
| 2. | Slovakia | 4 | 3 | 1 | 0 | 5 | - | 1 | 10 |
| 3. | Luxembourg | 4 | 2 | 1 | 1 | 4 | - | 6 | 7 |
| 4. | Bosnia and Herzegovina | 4 | 1 | 0 | 3 | 3 | - | 7 | 3 |
| 5. | Iceland | 4 | 1 | 0 | 3 | 8 | - | 6 | 3 |
| 6. | Liechtenstein | 4 | 0 | 0 | 4 | 0 | - | 14 | 0 |

### Next matches:

| | |
|---|---|
| 08.09.2023 | Bosnia-Herzegovina - Liechtenstein, Luxembourg - Iceland, Slovakia - Portugal |
| 11.09.2023 | Iceland - Bosnia-Herzegovina , Slovakia - Liechtenstein, Portugal - Luxembourg |
| 13.10.2023 | Liechtenstein - Bosnia-Herzegovina, Iceland - Luxembourg, Portugal - Slovakia |
| 16.10.2023 | Bosnia-Herzegovina - Portugal, Iceland - Liechtenstein, Luxembourg - Slovakia |
| 16.11.2023 | Luxembourg - Bosnia-Herzegovina, Slovakia - Iceland, Liechtenstein - Portugal |
| 19.11.2023 | Bosnia-Herzegovina - Slovakia, Portugal - Iceland, Liechtenstein - Luxembourg |

# EUROPEAN CLUB COMPETITIONS 2022/2023

## UEFA SUPERCUP 2022

The 2022 UEFA Super Cup was the 47th edition of the UEFA Super Cup, an annual football match organised by UEFA and contested by the winners of the two main European club competitions, the UEFA Champions League and the UEFA Europa League. The 2022 final match featured Real Madrid CF (winners of the 2021/2022 UEFA Champions League) and Eintracht Frankfurt (winners of the 2021/2022 UEFA Europa League).

11.08.2022; Olympic Stadium, Helsinki (Finland); Referee: Michael Oliver (England); Attendance: 31,042
### Real Madrid CF – Eintracht Frankfurt  2-0(1-0)
**Real Madrid**: Thibaut Nicolas Marc Courtois, Daniel „Dani" Carvajal Ramos (85.Antonio Rüdiger), Eder Gabriel Militão, David Olatukunbo Alaba, Ferland Mendy, Luka Modrić (67.Rodrygo Silva de Goes), Carlos Henrique Casimiro „Casemiro", Toni Kroos (85.Aurélien Djani Tchouaméni), Federico Santiago Valverde Dipetta (76.Eduardo Celmi Camavinga), Karim Mostafa Benzema (Cap), Vinícius José Paixão de Oliveira Júnior (85.Daniel „Dani" Ceballos Fernández). Trainer: Carlo Ancelotti (Italy).
**Eintracht Frankfurt**: Kevin Trapp, Almamy Touré (70.Lucas Nicolás Alario), Lucas Silva Melo „Tuta", Evan N'Dicka, Mohameth Djibril Ibrahima Sow, Sebastian Rode (Cap) (58.Mario Götze), Christopher Lenz, Daichi Kamada, Jesper Lindstrøm (58.Randal Kolo Muani), Ansgar Knauff, Rafael Santos Borré Maury. Trainer: Oliver Glasner (Austria).
**Goals**: 1-0 David Olatukunbo Alaba (37), 2-0 Karim Mostafa Benzema (65).

UEFA Supercup Winner 2022: **Real Madrid CF** (Spain)

## UEFA SUPER CUP (SINCE 1972)
### TABLE OF HONOURS

|  |  |  |
|---|---|---|
| 1972 | AFC Ajax Amsterdam (not official) | *Netherlands* |
| 1973 | AFC Ajax Amsterdam | *Netherlands* |
| 1974 | *Not played* | |
| 1975 | FK Dinamo Kyiv | *Soviet Union* |
| 1976 | RSC Anderlecht Bruxelles | *Belgium* |
| 1977 | Liverpool FC | *England* |
| 1978 | RSC Anderlecht Bruxelles | *Belgium* |
| 1979 | Nottingham Forest FC | *England* |
| 1980 | CF Valencia | *Spain* |
| 1981 | *Not played* | |
| 1982 | Aston Villa FC Birmingham | *England* |
| 1983 | Aberdeen FC | *Scotland* |
| 1984 | Juventus FC Torino | *Italy* |
| 1985 | *Not played* | |
| 1986 | FC Steaua Bucureşti | *Romania* |
| 1987 | FC do Porto | *Portugal* |
| 1988 | KV Mechelen | *Belgium* |
| 1989 | AC Milan | *Italy* |
| 1990 | AC Milan | *Italy* |
| 1991 | Manchester United FC | *England* |
| 1992 | FC Barcelona | *Spain* |
| 1993 | Parma AC | *Italy* |
| 1994 | AC Milan | *Italy* |
| 1995 | AFC Ajax Amsterdam | *Netherlands* |
| 1996 | Juventus FC Torino | *Italy* |
| 1997 | FC Barcelona | *Spain* |
| 1998 | Chelsea FC London | *England* |
| 1999 | SS Lazio Roma | *Italy* |
| 2000 | Galatasaray SK Istanbul | *Turkey* |
| 2001 | Liverpool FC | *England* |
| 2002 | Real Madrid CF | *Spain* |
| 2003 | AC Milan | *Italy* |
| 2004 | Valencia CF | *Spain* |
| 2005 | Liverpool FC | *England* |
| 2006 | Sevilla FC | *Spain* |
| 2007 | AC Milan | *Italy* |
| 2008 | FK Zenit Saint Petersburg | *Russia* |
| 2009 | FC Barcelona | *Spain* |
| 2010 | Club Atlético de Madrid | *Spain* |
| 2011 | FC Barcelona | *Spain* |
| 2012 | Club Atlético de Madrid | *Spain* |
| 2013 | FC Bayern München | *Germany* |
| 2014 | Real Madrid CF | *Spain* |
| 2015 | FC Barcelona | *Spain* |
| 2016 | Real Madrid CF | *Spain* |
| 2017 | Real Madrid CF | *Spain* |
| 2018 | Club Atlético de Madrid | *Spain* |
| 2019 | Liverpool FC | *England* |
| 2020 | FC Bayern München | *Germany* |
| 2021 | Chelsea FC London | *England* |
| 2022 | Real Madrid CF | *Spain* |

## PRELIMINARY ROUND – SEMI-FINALS

21.06.2022; Vikingsvöllur, Reykjavík (Iceland); Attendance: 39
Referee: Rohit Saggi (Norway)
**SP La Fiorita Montegiardino – Inter Club d'Escaldes 1-2(1-0)**
SP La Fiorita: Gianluca Vivan, Andrea Grandoni, Manuel Miori, Moises Sanchez (71.Mattia Anastasi), Lorenzo Fatica, Danilo Rinaldi, Armando Amati (90+2.Davide Vaierani), Nicola Palazzi (71.David Tomassini), Andrea Grassi, Martin Lago (63.Sami Abouzziane), Francesco Cinotti. Trainer: Oscar Lasagni.
Inter Club d'Escaldes: Jesús Coca, Adrià Gallego, Chus Rubio (88.Jordi Rubio), Iván de Nova, Raul Feher, Jordi Roca, Viti Martínez (69.Sergi Moreno), Víctor Casadesús (69.Ángel Pérez), Aridai Cabrera (60.Ahmed Belhadji), Genís Soldevila (88.Ildefons Lima), Sascha. Trainer: Raul Obiols Rodriguez.
Goals: 45+2' Danilo Rinaldi 1-0, 55', 66' Genís Soldevila 1-1, 1-2.

21.06.2022; Vikingsvöllur, Reykjavík; Attendance: 725
Referee: Tomasz Musial (Poland)
**FCI Levadia Tallinn – Víkingur Reykjavík 1-6(1-3)**
FCI Levadia: Karl Vallner, Maximiliano Uggè, Milan Mitrovic, Artur Pikk (54.Liliu), Rasmus Peetson, Marko Putincanin (74.Ilja Antonov), Zakaria Beglarishvili (74.Karl Oigus), Brent Lepistu, Mark Roosnupp, Ernest Agyiri (81.Murad Velijev), Robert Kirss. Trainer: Vladimir Vassiljev.
Víkingur Reykjavík: Thórdur Ingason, Halldór Sigurdsson, Davíd Atlason (74.Karl Gunnarsson), Oliver Ekroth, Kyle McLagan, Pablo Punyed (74.Logi Tómasson), Júlíus Magnússon, Viktor Örlygur Andrason, Nikolaj Hansen (68.Ari Sigurpálsson), Erlingur Agnarsson (68.Helgi Gudjónsson), Kristall Máni Ingason (78.Birnir Snær Ingason). Trainer: Arnar Gunnlaugsson.
Goals: 5' Zakaria Beglarishvili 1-0 (penalty), 10' Kyle McLagan 1-1, 27' Kristall Máni Ingason 1-2, 45+1' Halldór Sigurdsson 1-3, 49' Nikolaj Hansen 1-4, 71' Helgi Gudjónsson 1-5, 77' Júlíus Magnússon 1-6.

## PRELIMINARY ROUND – FINALS

24.06.2022; Vikingsvöllur, Reykjavík; Attendance: 925
Referee: Urs Schnyder (Switzerland)
**Inter Club d'Escaldes – Víkingur Reykjavík 0-1(0-0)**
Inter Club d'Escaldes: Jesús Coca, Adrià Gallego, Chus Rubio (86.Ildefons Lima), Iván de Nova, Raul Feher, Jordi Rubio (65.Genís Soldevila), Jordi Roca, Ahmed Belhadji (75.Jordi Betriu), Viti Martínez (86.Víctor Casadesús), Aridai Cabrera (75.Ángel Pérez), Sascha. Trainer: Raul Obiols Rodriguez.
Víkingur Reykjavík: Thórdur Ingason, Halldór Sigurdsson (55.Logi Tómasson), Davíd Atlason (55.Karl Gunnarsson), Oliver Ekroth, Kyle McLagan, Pablo Punyed (67.Birnir Snær Ingason), Júlíus Magnússon, Viktor Örlygur Andrason (80.Helgi Gudjónsson), Nikolaj Hansen, Erlingur Agnarsson (67.Ari Sigurpálsson), Kristall Máni Ingason. Trainer: Arnar Gunnlaugsson.
Goal: Vikingur Reykjavík: 68' Kristall Máni Ingason 0-1.

## FIRST QUALIFYING ROUND

05.07.2022; „Vazgen Sargsyan" Hanrapetakan Stadium, Yerevan; Attendance: 8,000; Referee: Bastian Dankert (Germany)
**FC Pyunik Yerevan – FC CFR 1907 Cluj-Napoca 0-0**
Pyunik Erevan: David Yurchenko, Alexander González (90+3.Gevorg Najaryan), Anton Bratkov, Sergiy Vakulenko, Mikhail Kovalenko, Juninho, Artak Dashyan, Renzo Zambrano (90+3.Yuri Gareginyan), Eugeniu Cociuc (77.Hovhannes Harutyunyan), David Davidyan (46.Uros Nenadovic), Yusuf Otubanjo (77.Nemanja Mladenovic). Trainer: Eghishe Melikyan.
CFR Cluj: Cristian Balgradean, Camora, Denis Kolinger, Andrei Burca, Cristian Manea, Ciprian Deac (90+1.Adrian Paun), Vito Hammershøy-Mistrati (64.Jefté Betancor), Nana Adjei-Boateng (82.Mihai Bordeianu), Lovro Cvek, Roger Junio (82.Claudiu Petrila), Gabriel Debeljuh (90+1.Marko Dugandzic). Trainer: Dan Petrescu.

13.07.2022; Stadionul "Dr. Constantin Rădulescu", Cluj-Napoca; Attendance: 7,017; Referee: Michael Fabbri (Italy)
**FC CFR 1907 Cluj-Napoca – FC PYUNIK YEREVAN 2-2(1-0,1-1,1-1) 3-4 on penalties;**
CFR Cluj: Cristian Balgradean, Camora, Daniel Graovac, Andrei Burca, Cristian Manea, Ciprian Deac (114.Karlo Muhar), Adrian Paun (71.Claudiu Petrila), Nana Adjei-Boateng (114.Yuri Matias), Lovro Cvek (87.Mihai Bordeianu), Roger Junio (96.Emmanuel Damoah Yeboah), Gabriel Debeljuh (87.Marko Dugandzic). Trainer: Dan Petrescu.
Pyunik Erevan: David Yurchenko, Zoran Gajic, Alexander González (64.Nemanja Mladenovic), Sergiy Vakulenko (90+2.Gevorg Najaryan), Mikhail Kovalenko, Juninho (103.Artur Avagyan), Artak Dashyan, Renzo Zambrano (64.Hovhannes Harutyunyan), Eugeniu Cociuc, Yusuf Otubanjo (85.David Davidyan), Uros Nenadovic (46.Luka Juricic). Trainer: Eghishe Melikyan.
Goals: 6' Nana Adjei-Boateng 1-0, 89' Zoran Gajic 1-1, 94' Claudiu Petrila 2-1, 119' Zoran Gajic 2-2.
Penalties: Marko Dugandzic 1-0; Eugeniu Cociuc 1-1; Claudiu Petrila (missed); Artak Dashyan 1-2; Andrei Burca 2-2; Hovhannes Harutyunyan 2-3; Karlo Muhar 3-3; Artur Avagyan 3-4; Camora (missed).

05.07.2022; Eleda Stadion, Malmö; Attendance: 11,830
Referee: Dumitri Muntean (Moldova)
**Malmö FF – Víkingur Reykjavík 3-2(2-1)**
Malmö FF: Johan Dahlin, Martin Olsson (71.Jonas Knudsen), Niklas Moisander (56.Felix Beijmo), Lasse Nielsen, Dennis Hadzikadunic, Anders Christiansen (71.Sebastian Nanasi), Jo Inge Berget, Sergio Peña, Erdal Rakip (80.Hugo Larsson), Veljko Birmancevic, Ola Toivonen (71.Patriot Sejdiu). Trainer: Miloš Milojević (Serbia).
Víkingur Reykjavík: Thórdur Ingason, Halldór Sigurdsson, Oliver Ekroth, Logi Tómasson (57.Davíd Atlason), Karl Gunnarsson, Pablo Punyed, Júlíus Magnússon, Viktor Örlygur Andrason, Nikolaj Hansen (80.Helgi Gudjónsson), Erlingur Agnarsson (78.Ari Sigurpálsson), Kristall Máni Ingason [sent off 39]. Trainer: Arnar Gunnlaugsson.
Goals: 16' Martin Olsson 1-0, 38' Kristall Máni Ingason 1-1, 42' Ola Toivonen 2-1, 84' Veljko Birmancevic 3-1, 90+3' Helgi Gudjónsson 3-2.

05.07.2022; Huvepharma Arena, Razgrad; Attendance: 3,963
Referee: Vitor Jorge Fernandes Ferreira (Portugal)
**PFC Ludogorets Razgrad – FK Sutjeska Nikšić 2-0(0-0)**
Ludogorets Razgrad: Sergio Padt, Cicinho, Igor Plastun, Anton Nedyalkov, Olivier Verdon, Claude Gonçalves, Alex Santana, Dominik Yankov (79.Spas Delev), Pieros Sotiriou (84.Matías Tissera), Bernard Tekpetey (67.Cauly), Rick (84.Kiril Despodov). Trainer: Ante Šimundža (Slovenia).
Sutjeska Nikšić: Vladan Giljen, Nikola Stijepovic, Ilija Tucevic, Dragan Grivic, Adrijan Rudovic, Milos Drincic, Srdjan Krstovic, Novica Erakovic, Marko Matanovic (90+3.Milos Kalezic), Yulian Nenov (85.Igor Pajovic), Zakaria Al Harish (75.Tyrone Conraad). Trainer: Milija Savovic.
Goals: 74' Alex Santana 1-0, 90+1' Matías Tissera 2-0.

05.07.2022; Stadiumi „Fadil Vokrri", Prishtina; Attendance: 4,000
Referee: Robert Harwey (Republic of Ireland)
**KF Ballkani Suva Reka – FK Žalgiris Vilnius 1-1(1-1)**
Ballkani: Stivi Frashëri, Bajram Jashanica (79.Leonit Abazi), Astrit Thaqi, Armend Thaçi, Lumbardh Dellova, Edvin Kuc, Meriton Korenica (85.Dilivio Hoffman), Lindon Emërllahu, Nazmi Gripshi (72.Albion Rrahmani), Albin Berisha (72.Qendrim Zyba), Ermal Krasniqi. Trainer: Ilir Daja.
Žalgiris: Edvinas Gertmonas, Saulius Mikoliūnas, Mario Pavelic, Petar Mamic, Nemanja Ljubisavljevic, Nicolás Gorobsov, Oliver Buff (65.Marko Milickovic), Fabien Ourega, Francis Kyeremeh (86.Gustas Jarusevicius), Josip Tadic (65.Mathias Oyewusi), Renan Oliveira (81.Donatas Kazlauskas). Trainer: Vladimir Cherubin (Kazakhstan).
Goals: 15' Nazmi Gripshi 1-0, 25' Oliver Buff 1-1.

05.07.2022; Park Hall Stadium, Oswestry; Attendance: 1,034
Referee: Andrei Florin Chivulete (Romania)
**The New Saints FC – Linfield FC Belfast 1-0(0-0)**
The New Saints: Connor Roberts, Chris Marriott, Keston Davies, Daniel Davies, Ryan Astles, Jon Routledge, Daniel Redmond (90+1.Ben Clack), Ryan Brobbel, Leo Smith, Declan McManus, Jordan Williams (76.Adrian Cieslewicz). Trainer: Anthony Limbrick.
Linfield FC: Chris Johns, Matthew Clarke, Ben Hall, Sam Roscoe-Byrne, Danny Finlayson, Jamie Mulgrew (67.Kyle McClean), Chris Shields, Kirk Millar (73.Jordan Stewart), Stephen Fallon, Joel Cooper, Robbie McDaid (79.Chris McKee). Trainer: David Healy.
Goal: 57' Ryan Brobbel 1-0.

05.07.2022; Stadion Miejski, Poznań; Attendance: 25,118
Referee: José Luis Munuera Montero (Spain)
**KKS Lech Poznań – Qarabağ FK Baki 1-0(1-0)**
Lech Poznań: Artur Rudko, Antonio Milic, Lubomir Satka, Pedro Rebocho, Joel Pereira, Jesper Karlström, Radoslaw Murawski (83.Alan Czerwinski), João Amaral (62.Filip Szymczak), Michal Skóras, Kristoffer Velde (62.Adriel Ba Loua), Mikael Ishak (80.Nika Kvekveskiri). Trainer: John van den Brom (Netherlands).
Qarabağ FK: Sahrudin Mahammadaliyev, Marko Vesovic, Maksim Medvedev, Qara Qarayev, Kevin Medina, Richard Almeyda (62.Marko Jankovic), Abdellah Zoubir, Kady (82.Owusu Kwabena), Elvin Cafarquliyev (82.Tural Bayramov), Leandro Andrade (62.Filip Ozobic), Ibrahima Wadji (62.Ramil Sheydaev). Trainer: Qurban Qurbanov.
Goal: 41' Mikael Ishak 1-0.

12.07.2022; Víkingsvöllur, Reykjavík; Attendance: 1,080
Referee: John Beaton (Scotland)
**Víkingur Reykjavík – MALMÖ FF 3-3(1-2)**
Víkingur Reykjavík: Ingvar Jónsson, Halldór Sigurdsson (44.Davíd Atlason), Oliver Ekroth, Logi Tómasson (46.Ari Sigurpálsson), Karl Gunnarsson, Pablo Punyed, Júlíus Magnússon, Viktor Örlygur Andrason, Nikolaj Hansen, Erlingur Agnarsson, Helgi Gudjónsson (64.Birnir Snær Ingason). Trainer: Arnar Gunnlaugsson.
Malmö FF: Johan Dahlin, Martin Olsson, Niklas Moisander, Lasse Nielsen (79.Dennis Hadzikadunic), Felix Beijmo, Anders Christiansen (62.Ola Toivonen), Jo Inge Berget, Sergio Peña, Veljko Birmancevic (87.Eric Larsson), Hugo Larsson, Isaac Kiese Thelin (62.Erdal Rakip). Trainer: Miloš Milojević (Serbia).
Goals: 15' Karl Gunnarsson 1-0, 34' Veljko Birmancevic 1-1, 44' Felix Beijmo 1-2, 47' Anders Christiansen 1-3, 56' Nikolaj Hansen 2-3, 74' Karl Gunnarsson 3-3.

12.07.2022; DG Arena, Podgorica; Attendance: 1,000
Referee: Gergő Bogár (Hungary)
**FK Sutjeska Nikšić – PFC LUDOGORETS RAZGRAD 0-1(0-0)**
Sutjeska Nikšić: Vladan Giljen, Nikola Stijepovic, Dragan Grivic, Adrijan Rudovic, Milos Drincic, Srdjan Krstovic (74.Ilija Tucevic), Novica Erakovic, Marko Matanovic (80.Nikola Djurkovic), Yulian Nenov (79.Fahd Saad Mohamed), Zakaria Al Harish (80.Dusan Vukovic), Vuk Strikovic (65.Tyrone Conraad). Trainer: Milija Savovic.
Ludogorets Razgrad: Sergio Padt, Igor Plastun, Anton Nedyalkov (90.Danny Gruper), Olivier Verdon, Zan Karnicnik, Cauly, Alex Santana, Show (74.Dominik Yankov), Spas Delev (65.Rick), Pieros Sotiriou (74.Igor Thiago), Kiril Despodov (66.Bernard Tekpetey). Trainer: Ante Šimundža (Slovenia).
Goal: 53' Pieros Sotiriou 0-1.

12.07.2022; LFF stadionas, Vilnius; Attendance: 3,542
Referee: Kristoffer Hagenes (Norway)
**FK ŽALGIRIS VILNIUS – KF Ballkani Suva Reka 1-0(0-0,0-0)**
Žalgiris: Edvinas Gertmonas, Saulius Mikoliūnas (90+4.Joël Fey d'Or Bopesu), Mario Pavelic, Petar Mamic, Nemanja Ljubisavljevic, Nicolás Gorobsov (90+4.Mantas Kuklys), Oliver Buff (62.Mathias Oyewusi), Fabien Ourega (105.Josip Tadic), Francis Kyeremeh (62.Gustas Jarusevicius), Marko Milickovic, Renan Oliveira (90.Donatas Kazlauskas). Trainer: Vladimir Cherubin (Kazakhstan).
Ballkani: Stivi Frashëri, Bajram Jashanica (107.Leonit Abazi), Astrit Thaqi, Armend Thaçi, Lumbardh Dellova, Edvin Kuc (107.Lucas), Meriton Korenica, Lindon Emërllahu (94.Qendrim Zyba), Nazmi Gripshi, Albin Berisha (56.Dilivio Hoffman, 119.Theophilus Solomon), Ermal Krasniqi (94.Albion Rrahmani). Trainer: Ilir Daja.
Goal: 97' Mathias Oyewusi 1-0.

13.07.2022; Windsor Park, Belfast; Attendance: 2,971
Referee: Duje Strukan (Croatia)
**LINFIELD FC BELFAST – The New Saints FC 2-0(0-0,1-0)**
Linfield FC: Chris Johns, Matthew Clarke, Ben Hall (78.Jamie Mulgrew), Sam Roscoe-Byrne, Danny Finlayson (67.Chris McKee), Chris Shields, Kirk Millar (100.Conor Pepper), Stephen Fallon (100.Cammy Palmer), Joel Cooper, Kyle McClean (67.Jordan Stewart), Robbie McDaid (78.Ethan Devine). Trainer: David Healy.
The New Saints: Connor Roberts, Chris Marriott, Keston Davies (111.Blaine Hudson), Daniel Davies (83.Josh Pask), Ryan Astles, Jon Routledge, Daniel Redmond (68.Ben Clack), Ryan Brobbel, Leo Smith (105.Joshua Daniels), Declan McManus, Jordan Williams (78.Adrian Cieslewicz). Trainer: Anthony Limbrick.
Goals: 90+4' Jamie Mulgrew 1-0, 95' Ethan Devine 2-0.

12.07.2022; „Tofiq Bəhramov" Stadionu; Attendance: 27,652
Referee: Andrew Madley (England)
**QARABAĞ FK BAKI – KKS Lech Poznań 5-1(2-1)**
Qarabağ FK: Sahrudin Mahammadaliyev, Marko Vesovic (76.Abbas Hüseynov), Maksim Medvedev, Kevin Medina, Richard Almeyda, Filip Ozobic (77.Owusu Kwabena), Abdellah Zoubir, Kady, Elvin Cafarquliyev (76.Tural Bayramov), Marko Jankovic (83.Ismayil Ibrahimli), Ibrahima Wadji (66.Ramil Sheydaev). Trainer: Qurban Qurbanov.
Lech Poznań: Artur Rudko, Antonio Milic, Lubomír Satka, Pedro Rebocho (85.Barry Douglas), Joel Pereira, Jesper Karlström (85.Nika Kvekveskiri), Radoslaw Murawski (85.Filip Marchwinski), João Amaral (72.Georgiy Tsitaishvili), Michal Skóras (72.Filip Szymczak), Kristoffer Velde, Mikael Ishak. Trainer: John van den Brom (Netherlands).
Goals: 1' Kristoffer Velde 0-1, 14' Kady 1-1, 42' Filip Ozobic 2-1, 56' Kevin Medina 3-1, 74' Kady 4-1, 77' Abbas Hüseynov 5-1.

05.07.2022; Tallaght Stadium, Dublin; Attendance: 7,019
Referee: Morten Krogh (Denmark)
**Shamrock Rovers FC Dublin – Hibernians FC Paola 3-0(2-0)**
Shamrock Rovers: Alan Mannus, Roberto Lopes, Sean Hoare, Lee Grace, Andy Lyons, Ronan Finn (81.Sean Gannon), Chris McCann, Gary O'Neill, Dylan Watts (81.Richie Towell), Rory Gaffney (85.Justin Ferizaj), Aaron Greene (67.Aidomo Emakhu). Trainer: Stephen Bradley.
Hibernians FC: Ibrahim Koné, Joseph Zerafa (90.Lorenzo Fonseca), Rodolfo Soares, Gonzalo Llerena, Zachary Grech (90.Lucas Caruana), Gabriel Izquier, Dunstan Vella, Ali Diakité, Jurgen Degabriele, Thaylor Lubanzadio (81.Ayrton Attard), Gabriel Mensah (46.Terence Groothusen). Trainer: Stefano Sanderra.
Goals: 25' Ronan Finn 1-0, 40' Dylan Watts 2-0, 78' Rory Gaffney 3-0.

05.07.2022; Nacionalna Arena "Toše Proeski", Skopje; Attendance: 2,500; Referee: Sebastian Gishamer (Austria)
**KF Shkupi Čair – Lincoln Red Imps FC 3-0(2-0)**
KF Shkupi: Kristijan Naumovski, Vladica Brdarovski, Gagi Margvelashvili [sent off 54], Faustin Senghor, Blerton Sheji, Freddy Álvarez, Queven, Mamadou Danfa (76.Aleks Zlatkov), Walid Hamidi (89.Pepi Georgiev), Sunday Adetunji, Renaldo Cephas (59.Melos Bajrami). Trainer: Goce Sedloski.
Lincoln Red Imps: Dayle Coleing, Scott Wiseman, Nano, Bernardo Lopes, Roy Chipolina (76.Kian Ronan), Ethan Britto, Juampe Rico (46.Graeme Torrilla), Liam Walker, Mustapha Yahaya, Marco Rosa (65.Kike Gómez), Juanfri (78.Lee Casciaro). Trainer: Raúl Castillo.
Goals: 11' Mamadou Danfa 1-0, 28' Sunday Adetunji 2-0, 62' Scott Wiseman 3-0 (own goal).

06.07.2022; Ortaliq Stadion, Kostanay; Attendance: 8,420
Referee: Dario Bel (Croatia)
**FC Tobol Kostanay – Ferencvárosi TC 0-0**
Tobol Kostanay: Aleksandr Mokin, Zarko Tomasevic, Sergiy Maliy, Aleksa Amanovic, Bagdat Kairov, Zoran Tosic, Rúben Brígido (64.Igor Sergeev), Askhat Tagybergen, Dusan Jovancic, Samat Zharynbetov (69.Serikzhan Muzhikov), Aybar Zhaksylykov (76.Miljan Vukadinovic). Trainer: Milan Milanović (Serbia).
Ferencvárosi TC: Dénes Dibusz, Endre Botka (77.Henry Wingo), Adnan Kovacevic, Eldar Civic, Samy Mmaee, Bálint Vécsei (51.Anderson Esiti), Kristoffer Zachariassen (62.Marquinhos), Aïssa Laïdouni, Tokmac Nguen, Franck Boli (62.Fortune Bassey), Adama Traoré (I). Trainer: Stanislav Cherchesov (Russia).

06.07.2022; Bolt Arena, Helsinki; Attendance: 3,874
Referee: Juxhin Xhaja (Albania)
**HJK Helsinki – FK Rīgas Futbola Skola 1-0(1-0)**
HJK Helsinki: Conor Hazard, Jukka Raitala, Miro Tenho, Murilo, Arttu Hoskonen, Matti Peltola, Pyry Soiri (84.Casper Terho), Manuel Martic (75.Përparim Hetemaj), Santeri Väänänen, Anthony Olusanya, Bojan Radulovic. Trainer: Toni Koskela.
Rīgas Futbola skola: Vytautas Cerniauskas, Vitalijs Jagodinskis, Vladislavs Sorokins, Ziga Lipuscek, Artūrs Zjuzins (79.Ismael Diomandé), Tomislav Saric, Petr Mares, Stefan Panic, Kevin Friesenbichler (90+2.Renārs Varslavāns), Emerson Deocleciano, Andrej Ilic. Trainer: Viktors Morozs.
Goal: 11' Manuel Martic 1-0.

06.07.2022; Aspmyra Stadion, Bodø; Attendance: 4,227
Referee: Mohammed Al-Hakim (Sweden)
**FK Bodø/Glimt – KÍ Klaksvík 3-0(2-0)**
FK Bodø/Glimt: Nikita Haikin, Marius Høibråten, Brede Moe (63.Japhet Sery), Brice Wembangomo, Alfons Sampsted, Ulrik Saltnes, Amahl Pellegrino (46.Sondre Sørli), Hugo Vetlesen (85.Anders Konradsen), Elias Hagen, Ola Solbakken (46.Joel Mvuka), Victor Boniface (76.Runar Espejord). Trainer: Kjetil Knutsen.
KÍ Klaksvík: Mathias Rosenørn, Heini Vatnsdal, Jesper Brinck, Patrick da Silva, Claes Kronberg (73.Anders Holvad), René Joensen, Deni Pavlovic, Jákup Andreasen, Jóannes Bjartalíd (90+2.Jóannes Danielsen), Mads Mikkelsen, Páll Klettskard (85.Árni Frederiksberg). Trainer: Mikkjal Thomassen.
Goals: 11', 31', 58' Victor Boniface 1-0, 2-0, 3-0 (penalty).

12.07.2022; MFA Centenary Stadium, Ta'Qali; Attendance: 979
Referee: Manfredas Lukjančukas (Lithuania)
**Hibernians FC Paola – SHAMROCK ROVERS FC DUBLIN 0-0**
Hibernians FC: Ibrahim Koné, Rodolfo Soares (84.Lorenzo Fonseca), Gonzalo Llerena (84.Andreas Bækskov Laursen), Zachary Grech (76.Gabriel Mensah), Gabriel Izquier (68.Joseph Zerafa), Dunstan Vella, Jake Grech, Ali Diakité, Jurgen Degabriele, Terence Groothusen, Ayrton Attard (68.Thaylor Lubanzadio). Trainer: Andrea Pisanu (Italy).
Shamrock Rovers: Alan Mannus, Roberto Lopes, Sean Hoare, Lee Grace, Andy Lyons, Ronan Finn (77.Sean Gannon), Chris McCann (77.Sean Kavanagh), Gary O'Neill, Dylan Watts (77.Jack Byrne), Rory Gaffney (81.Aidomo Emakhu), Aaron Greene (59.Richie Towell). Trainer: Stephen Bradley.

12.07.2022; Victoria Stadium, Gibraltar; Attendance: 896
Referee: Filip Glova (Slovakia)
**Lincoln Red Imps FC – KF SHKUPI ČAIR 2-0(1-0)**
Lincoln Red Imps: Dayle Coleing, Scott Wiseman, Nano, Bernardo Lopes, Jesús Toscano (68.Ethan Britto), Jack Sergeant, Liam Walker, Marco Rosa (46.Kian Ronan), Graeme Torrilla, Juanfri (78.Juampe Rico), Kike Gómez (61.Lee Casciaro). Trainer: Raúl Castillo.
KF Shkupi: Kristijan Naumovski, Vladica Brdarovski, Dzhelil Abdula, Faustin Senghor, Blerton Sheji, Freddy Álvarez, Queven, Aleks Zlatkov (46.Kristijan Trapanovski), Mamadou Danfa (90+1.Melos Bajrami), Sunday Adetunji, Renaldo Cephas (65.Antonio Kalanoski). Trainer: Goce Sedloski.
Goals: 32' Juanfri 1-0, 69' Lee Casciaro 2-0.

13.07.2022; Groupama Aréna, Budapest; Attendance: 17,347
Referee: Krzysztof Jakubik (Poland)
**FERENCVÁROSI TC – FC Tobol Kostanay 5-1(3-1)**
Ferencvárosi TC: Dénes Dibusz, Adnan Kovacevic (83.Mats Knoester), Eldar Civic, Henry Wingo, Samy Mmaee, Anderson Esiti (75.Stjepan Loncar), Kristoffer Zachariassen (83.Xavier Mercier), Aïssa Laïdouni, Tokmac Nguen (68.Carlos Auzqui), Franck Boli (69.Fortune Bassey), Adama Traoré (I). Trainer: Stanislav Cherchesov (Russia).
Tobol Kostanay: Aleksandr Mokin, Zarko Tomasevic, Sergiy Maliy, Aleksa Amanovic, Bagdat Kairov, Zoran Tosic (78.Aybar Zhaksylykov), Rúben Brígido (75.Miljan Vukadinovic), Askhat Tagybergen, Dusan Jovancic, Samat Zharynbetov (68.Serikzhan Muzhikov [sent off 81]), Igor Sergeev (75.Serge Deblé). Trainer: Milan Milanović (Serbia).
Goals: 4', 17' Adama Traoré 1-0, 2-0, 21' Aïssa Laïdouni 3-0, 23' Igor Sergeev 3-1, 74', 90+1' Fortune Bassey 4-1, 5-1.

12.07.2022; Slokas stadions, Jūrmala; Attendance: 1,631
Referee: David Fuxman (Israel)
**FK Rīgas Futbola Skola – HJK HELSINKI 2-1(0-0,2-1, 2-1); 4-5 on penalties**
Rīgas Futbola skola: Pāvels Steinbors, Vitalijs Jagodinskis, Ziga Lipuscek, Jovan Vlalukin, Artūrs Zjuzins (56.Kevin Friesenbichler), Tomislav Saric, Petr Mares, Stefan Panic, Alfusainey Jatta, Emerson Deocleciano, Andrej Ilic (105.Elvis Stuglis). Trainer: Viktors Morozs.
HJK Helsinki: Conor Hazard, Jukka Raitala, Miro Tenho, Murilo, Arttu Hoskonen, Matti Peltola (54.Santeri Hostikka), Përparim Hetemaj, Pyry Soiri (19.Anthony Olusanya, 76.Fabian Serrarens), Santeri Väänänen, David Browne (100.Casper Terho), Bojan Radulovic. Trainer: Toni Koskela.
Goals: 48' Artūrs Zjuzins 1-0, 56' Stefan Panic 2-0, 75' Murilo 2-1.
Penalties: Vitalijs Jagodinskis 1-0; Santeri Väänänen 1-1; Tomislav Saric 2-1; Murilo 2-2; Stefan Panic (missed); Bojan Radulovic 2-3; Ziga Lipuscek 3-3; Fabian Serrarens 3-4; Petr Mares 4-4; Casper Terho 4-5.

13.07.2022; Vid Djúpumýrar, Klaksvík; Attendance: 883
Referee: Horațiu Feșnic (Romania)
**KÍ Klaksvík – FK BODØ/GLIMT 3-1(2-0)**
KÍ Klaksvík: Mathias Rosenørn, Heini Vatnsdal, Jesper Brinck, Patrick da Silva, Claes Kronberg (76.Anders Holvad), René Joensen, Deni Pavlovic, Jákup Andreasen, Jóannes Bjartalíd, Mads Mikkelsen, Páll Klettskard. Trainer: Mikkjal Thomassen.
FK Bodø/Glimt: Nikita Haikin, Marius Høibråten, Brice Wembangomo, Alfons Sampsted, Isak Amundsen, Ulrik Saltnes, Hugo Vetlesen, Elias Hagen, Joel Mvuka, Gilbert Koomson, Victor Boniface. Trainer: Kjetil Knutsen.
Goals: 12' Mads Mikkelsen 1-0, 20' Jákup Andreasen 2-0, 55' Victor Boniface 2-1 (penalty), 85' Jákup Andreasen 3-1.

06.07.2022; Stade „Jos Nosbaum", Dudelange; Attendance: 1,555
Referee: Rohit Saggi (Norway)
**F91 Dudelange – KF Tiranë 1-0(0-0)**
F91 Dudelange: Lucas Fox, Manuel da Costa, Jules Diouf, Mehdi Kirch [*sent off 54*], Dejvid Sinani (82.Hugo Antunes), Eliot Gashi (60.Sylvio Ouassiero), Filip Bojic (76.Vova), Aldin Skenderovic, Charles Morren, Samir Hadji (60.Chris Stumpf), Mohcine Hassan Nader (82.Ninte Junior). Trainer: Carlos Manuel Fangueiro Soares (Portugal).
KF Tiranë: Visar Bekaj, Kristijan Tosevski, Marsel Ismajlgeci, Jocelin Behiratche, Filip Najdovski, Albano Aleksi, Ennur Totre (85.Klevi Qefalija), Vesel Limaj [*sent off 68*], Taulant Seferi, Devid (77.Florent Hasani), Redon Xhixha. Trainer: Orges Shehi.
Goal: 71' Mohcine Hassan Nader 1-0.

06.07.2022; Stadion pod Bijelim Brijegom, Mostar; Attendance: 5,400
Referee: Fabio Maresca (Italy)
**HŠK Zrinjski Mostar – FC Sheriff Tiraspol 0-0**
Zrinjski Mostar: Josip Condric, Mario Ticinovic (90+1.Matija Malekinusic), Almir Bekic (72.Kerim Memija), Hrvoje Barisic, Marin Magdic, Josip Corluka, Ivan Jukic (71.Nikola Mandic), Mario Cuze, Igor Savic (72.Damir Zlomislic), Nemanja Bilbija, Petar Sucic (46.Karlo Kamenar). Trainer: Sergej Jakirovic.
Sheriff Tiraspol: Razak Abalora, Patrick Kpozo, Stjepan Radeljic, Gaby Kiki, Renan Guedes, Regi Lushkja, Abou Ouattara (78.Iyayi Atiemwen, 86.Keston Julien), Cédric Badolo, Moussa Kyabou, Momo Yansané, Ibrahim Rasheed (74.Pernambuco). Trainer: Stjepan Tomas (Croatia).

06.07.2022; Ljudski vrt, Maribor; Attendance: 6,450
Referee: Anastasios Papapetrou (Greece)
**NK Maribor – FC Shakhtyor Solihorsk 0-0**
NK Maribor: Menno Bergsen, Martin Milec, Nemanja Mitrovic, Gregor Sikosek, Max Watson, Jan Repas, Antoine Makoumbou, Nino Zugelj (67.Rok Kronaveter), Marko Bozic, Roko Baturina (74.Rok Sirk), Ivan Brnic (74.Ignacio Guerrico). Trainer: Radovan Karanovic.
Shakhtyor Solihorsk: Maksim Plotnikov, Sergey Politevich, Nikola Antic, Milos Satara, Roman Yuzepchuk (46.Igor Ivanovic), Gleb Shevchenko, Valon Ahmedi, Ardit Krymi, Zaim Divanovic (90+2.Nikita Korzun), Vitor Feijão, Dembo Darboe (85.Euloge Placca Fessou). Trainer: Sergey Tashuev.

06.07.2022; Štadión Tehelné pole, Bratislava; Attendance: 10,589
Referee: David Coote (England)
**ŠK Slovan Bratislava – FC Dinamo Batumi 0-0**
Slovan Bratislava: Adrián Chovan, Guram Kashia, Vernon De Marco (58.Giorgi Chakvetadze), Jurij Medvedev, Myenty Abena, Juraj Kucka (86.Dávid Holman), Jaba Kankava, Vladimír Weiss (78.Aleksandar Cavric), Jaromír Zmrhal, Tigran Barseghyan (58.Andre Green), Eric Ramírez (58.Iván Saponjic). Trainer: Vladimír Weiss.
Dinamo Batumi: Lazare Kupatadze, Mamuka Kobakhidze [*sent off 42*], Oleksandr Azatskyi, Grigol Chabradze, Irakli Azarov, Benjamin Teidi, Vladimer Manuchashvili, Irakli Bidzinashvili (44.Giorgi Rekhviashvili), Sandro Altunashvili (86.Giorgi Navalovski), Zuriko Davitashvili (72.Mate Vatsadze), Flamarion (72.Milán Rádin). Trainer: George Geguchadze.

12.07.2022; Air Albania Stadium, Tiranë; Attendance: 6,000
Referee: César Soto Grado (Spain)
**KF Tiranë – F91 DUDELANGE 1-2(0-0)**
KF Tiranë: Visar Bekaj, Kristijan Tosevski (59.Florjan Pergjoni), Marsel Ismajlgeci, Jocelin Behiratche, Filip Najdovski, Ardit Hila (58.Klevi Qefalija), Albano Aleksi, Ennur Totre (63.Florent Hasani), Taulant Seferi, Devid, Redon Xhixha. Trainer: Orges Shehi.
F91 Dudelange: Lucas Fox, Manuel da Costa, Jules Diouf, Chris Stumpf (85.Edis Agovic), Dejvid Sinani, Eliot Gashi (49.Sylvio Ouassiero), Filip Bojic (73.Vova), Aldin Skenderovic (73.Vincent Decker), Charles Morren, Samir Hadji, Mohcine Hassan Nader (85.Ninte Junior). Trainer: Carlos Manuel Fangueiro Soares (Portugal).
Goals: 49' Filip Bojic 0-1, 61' Dejvid Sinani 0-2, 78' Redon Xhixha 1-2.

12.07.2022; Stadionul Zimbru, Chişinău; Attendance: 4,242
Referee: Radu Marian Petrescu (Romania)
**FC SHERIFF TIRASPOL – HŠK Zrinjski Mostar 1-0(1-0)**
Sheriff Tiraspol: Razak Abalora, Patrick Kpozo, Stjepan Radeljic, Gaby Kiki, Renan Guedes, Regi Lushkja (90+3.Serafim Cojocari), Abou Ouattara (85.Stefanos Evangelou), Cédric Badolo, Moussa Kyabou, Momo Yansané, Ibrahim Rasheed (76.Pernambuco). Trainer: Stjepan Tomas (Croatia).
Zrinjski Mostar: Josip Condric, Mario Ticinovic (73.Ivan Jukic), Almir Bekic (46.Kerim Memija), Hrvoje Barisic, Marin Magdic, Damir Zlomislic (46.Karlo Kamenar), Josip Corluka, Mario Cuze (46.Nikola Mandic), Igor Savic, Niko Jankovic (85.Franko Sabljic), Nemanja Bilbija. Trainer: Sergej Jakirovic.
Goal: 22' Igor Savic 1-0 (own goal).

13.07.2022; Yeni Sakarya Atatürk Stadyumu, Adapazari (Turkey); Attendance: 0; Referee: Enea Jorgji (Albania)
**FC Shakhtyor Solihorsk – NK MARIBOR 0-2(0-1)**
Shakhtyor Solihorsk: Maksim Plotnikov, Nikola Antic, Milos Satara, Roman Yuzepchuk, Gleb Shevchenko (46.Euloge Placca Fessou), Valon Ahmedi (59.Nikita Korzun), Igor Ivanovic, Ardit Krymi, Zaim Divanovic, Vitor Feijão (61.Maksim Skavysh), Dembo Darboe. Trainer: Sergey Tashuev.
NK Maribor: Menno Bergsen, Martin Milec, Nemanja Mitrovic, Gregor Sikosek, Max Watson, Jan Repas, Antoine Makoumbou (86.Aljaz Antolin), Nino Zugelj (63.Ignacio Guerrico), Marko Bozic (86.Aleks Pihler), Roko Baturina (71.Rok Sirk), Ivan Brnic (63.Rok Kronaveter). Trainer: Radovan Karanovic.
Goals: 12', 56' Roko Baturina 0-1, 0-2.

13.07.2022; Batumi Arena, Batumi; Attendance: 20,022
Referee: António Emanuel Carvalho Nobre (Portugal)
**FC Dinamo Batumi – ŠK SLOVAN BRATISLAVA 1-2(0-0,0-0)**
Dinamo Batumi: Lazare Kupatadze, Giorgi Rekhviashvili, Oleksandr Azatskyi, Grigol Chabradze (85.Mate Vatsadze), Irakli Azarov (105.Giorgi Navalovski), Benjamin Teidi (85.Guga Palavandishvili), Vladimer Manuchashvili, Irakli Bidzinashvili (62.Jaba Jigauri), Sandro Altunashvili (113.Milán Rádin), Zuriko Davitashvili, Flamarion. Trainer: George Geguchadze.
Slovan Bratislava: Adrián Chovan, Guram Kashia, Lukás Pauschek (105.Eric Ramírez), Jurij Medvedev (114.Andre Green), Myenty Abena, Juraj Kucka (114.Alen Mustafic), Jaba Kankava, Vladimír Weiss, Dávid Holman (46.Iván Saponjic), Giorgi Chakvetadze (62.Tigran Barseghyan), Aleksandar Cavric (67.Jaromír Zmrhal). Trainer: Vladimír Weiss.
Goals: 104' Zuriko Davitashvili 1-0, 115' Tigran Barseghyan 1-1, 120+3' Vladimír Weiss 1-2.

19.07.2022; „Tofiq Bəhramov" Stadionu; Attendance: 30,782
Referee: Irfan Peljto (Bosnia and Herzegovina)
**Qarabağ FK Bakı – FC Zürich 3-2(2-0)**
Qarabağ FK: Sahrudin Mahammadaliyev, Marko Vesovic (78.Abbas Hüseynov), Maksim Medvedev, Kevin Medina, Richard Almeyda, Filip Ozobic (59.Ramil Sheydaev), Abdellah Zoubir, Kady, Elvin Cafarquliyev (71.Tural Bayramov), Marko Jankovic (71.Ismayil Ibrahimli), Ibrahima Wadji (78.Owusu Kwabena). Trainer: Qurban Qurbanov.
FC Zürich: Yanick Brecher, Marc Hornschuh (46.Cheick Conde), Nikola Boranijasevic, Fidan Aliti, Mirlind Kryeziu, Adrián Guerrero, Lindrit Kamberi, Blerim Dzemaili (75.Ole Selnæs), Antonio Marchesano (76.Bledian Krasniqi), Fabian Rohner (76.Aiyegun Tosin), Wilfried Gnonto (90.Jonathan Okita). Trainer: Franco Foda (Germany).
Goals: 17' Kady 1-0, 36' Ibrahima Wadji 2-0, 65' Lindrit Kamberi 2-1, 66' Ibrahima Wadji 3-1, 85' Mirlind Kryeziu 3-2 (penalty).

19.07.2022; LFF stadionas, Vilnius; Attendance: 4,918
Referee: Georgi Kabakov (Bulgaria)
**FK Žalgiris Vilnius – Malmö FF 1-0(0-0)**
Žalgiris: Edvinas Gertmonas, Mario Pavelic, Petar Mamic, Joël Fey d'Or Bopesu, Nemanja Ljubisavljevic, Nicolás Gorobsov, Oliver Buff (82.Mantas Kuklys), Fabien Ourega (73.Gustas Jarusevicius), Marko Milickovic (90+5.Josip Tadic), Renan Oliveira (82.Donatas Kazlauskas), Mathias Oyewusi (73.Francis Kyeremeh). Trainer: Vladimir Cherubin (Kazakhstan).
Malmö FF: Johan Dahlin, Martin Olsson (74.Niklas Moisander), Lasse Nielsen, Dennis Hadzikadunic, Felix Beijmo (70.Eric Larsson), Anders Christiansen (70.Ola Toivonen), Jo Inge Berget, Sergio Peña (70.Hugo Larsson), Veljko Birmancevic (46.Moustafa Zeidan), Mahamé Siby, Isaac Kiese Thelin. Trainer: Miloš Milojević (Serbia).
Goal: 49' Fabien Ourega 1-0.

19.07.2022; „Vazgen Sargsyan" Hanrapetakan Stadium, Yerevan; Attendance: 9,000; Referee: Craig Pawson (England)
**FC Pyunik Yerevan – F91 Dudelange 0-1(0-0)**
Pyunik Erevan: David Yurchenko, Zoran Gajic, Alexander González (84.Gevorg Najaryan), Mikhail Kovalenko, Juninho, Artak Dashyan, Eugeniu Cociuc (84.André Mensalão), Hovhannes Harutyunyan (64.Renzo Zambrano), David Davidyan (74.Nemanja Mladenovic), Yusuf Otubanjo, Luka Juricic (64.Uros Nenadovic). Trainer: Eghishe Melikyan.
F91 Dudelange: Lucas Fox, Manuel da Costa, Jules Diouf, Mehdi Kirch, Sylvio Ouassiero (79.Chris Stumpf), Dejvid Sinani (85.Bruno Frere), Filip Bojic (79.Edis Agovic), Aldin Skenderovic, Charles Morren, Samir Hadji, Mohcine Hassan Nader (90+1.Ninte Junior). Trainer: Carlos Manuel Fangueiro Soares (Portugal).
Goal: 72' Samir Hadji 0-1 (penalty).

19.07.2022; Huvepharma Arena, Razgrad; Attendance: 4,983
Referee: João Pedro Silva Pinheiro (Portugal)
**PFC Ludogorets Razgrad – Shamrock Rovers FC Dublin 3-0(2-0)**
Ludogorets Razgrad: Sergio Padt, Cicinho, Igor Plastun, Anton Nedyalkov, Olivier Verdon, Cauly (89.Igor Thiago), Alex Santana, Show, Pieros Sotiriou (89.Matías Tissera), Bernard Tekpetey (71.Kiril Despodov), Rick (78.Spas Delev). Trainer: Ante Šimundža (Slovenia).
Shamrock Rovers: Alan Mannus, Roberto Lopes, Sean Hoare, Lee Grace, Andy Lyons, Ronan Finn (76.Sean Gannon), Chris McCann, Richie Towell (78.Sean Kavanagh), Gary O'Neill, Dylan Watts (61.Graham Burke), Rory Gaffney. Trainer: Stephen Bradley.
Goals: 26', 35' Pieros Sotiriou 1-0, 2-0, 90+4' Igor Thiago 3-0.

27.07.2022; Stadion Letzigrund, Zürich; Attendance: 10,237
Referee: Allard Lindhout (Netherlands)
**FC Zürich – QARABAĞ FK BAKI 2-2(1-0,2-1)**
FC Zürich: Yanick Brecher, Nikola Boranijasevic, Fidan Aliti, Mirlind Kryeziu, Adrián Guerrero (70.Jonathan Okita), Lindrit Kamberi, Antonio Marchesano (79.Ivan Santini), Ole Selnæs (71.Marc Hornschuh), Fabian Rohner (70.Aiyegun Tosin), Cheick Conde (119.Becir Omeragic), Wilfried Gnonto (105+1.Bledian Krasniqi). Trainer: Franco Foda (Germany).
Qarabağ FK: Sahrudin Mahammadaliyev, Marko Vesovic (117.Abbas Hüseynov), Maksim Medvedev (90+1.Bahlul Mustafazade), Kevin Medina (45.Badavi Hüseynov), Richard Almeyda (66.Qara Qarayev), Abdellah Zoubir, Kady, Elvin Cafarquliyev (46.Tural Bayramov), Marko Jankovic, Ramil Sheydaev, Ibrahima Wadji (67.Owusu Kwabena). Trainer: Qurban Qurbanov.
Goals: 4' Maksim Medvedev 1-0 (own goal), 55' Kady 1-1, 90+5' Ivan Santini 2-1, 98' Owusu Kwabena 2-2.

27.07.2022; Eleda Stadion, Malmö; Attendance: 17,234
Referee: Kristo Tohver (Estonia)
**Malmö FF – FK ŽALGIRIS VILNIUS 0-2(0-1)**
Malmö FF: Johan Dahlin, Niklas Moisander, Lasse Nielsen, Jonas Knudsen (57.Søren Rieks), Felix Beijmo (71.Eric Larsson), Anders Christiansen [sent off 77], Jo Inge Berget (57.Patriot Sejdiu), Sergio Peña (76.Hugo Larsson), Moustafa Zeidan, Veljko Birmancevic (46.Isaac Kiese Thelin), Ola Toivonen. Trainer: Miloš Milojević (Serbia).
Žalgiris: Edvinas Gertmonas, Mario Pavelic, Petar Mamic, Joël Fey d'Or Bopesu, Nemanja Ljubisavljevic, Nicolás Gorobsov, Oliver Buff (81.Saulius Mikoliūnas), Fabien Ourega (71.Gustas Jarusevicius), Marko Milickovic, Renan Oliveira (71.Donatas Kazlauskas), Mathias Oyewusi (57.Francis Kyeremeh). Trainer: Vladimir Cherubin (Kazakhstan).
Goals: 34' Mathias Oyewusi 0-1, 52' Renan Oliveira 0-2.

26.07.2022; Stade „Jos Nosbaum", Dudelange; Attendance: 1,495
Referee: José Luis Munuera Montero (Spain)
**F91 Dudelange – FC PYUNIK YEREVAN 1-4(1-1)**
F91 Dudelange: Lucas Fox, Manuel da Costa, Jules Diouf, Mehdi Kirch (82.Chris Stumpf), Sylvio Ouassiero (90.Ninte Junior), Dejvid Sinani, Filip Bojic (60.Vova), Aldin Skenderovic (81.Edis Agovic), Charles Morren (90.Bruno Frere), Samir Hadji, Mohcine Hassan Nader. Trainer: Carlos Manuel Fangueiro Soares (Portugal).
Pyunik Erevan: David Yurchenko, Zoran Gajic, Mikhail Kovalenko, Juninho, Artak Dashyan, André Mensalão (46.Eugeniu Cociuc), Renzo Zambrano (77.Yuri Gareginyan), Hovhannes Harutyunyan, David Davidyan (67.Alexander González), Yusuf Otubanjo (87.Gevorg Najaryan), Uros Nenadovic (46.Luka Juricic). Trainer: Eghishe Melikyan.
Goals: 21' Mohcine Hassan Nader 1-0, 24' Juninho 1-1, 53' Luka Juricic 1-2, 76' Yusuf Otubanjo 1-3, 85' Luka Juricic 1-4.

26.07.2022; Tallaght Stadium, Dublin; Attendance: 6,322
Referee: Fabio Maresca (Italy)
**Shamrock Rovers FC Dublin – PFC LUDOGORETS RAZGRAD 2-1(1-0)**
Shamrock Rovers: Alan Mannus, Sean Gannon, Sean Hoare, Lee Grace, Andy Lyons, Ronan Finn (71.Neil Farrugia), Chris McCann (83.Justin Ferizaj), Richie Towell (78.Aidomo Emakhu), Gary O'Neill (71.Rory Gaffney), Aaron Greene, Graham Burke (71.Dylan Watts). Trainer: Stephen Bradley.
Ludogorets Razgrad: Sergio Padt, Igor Plastun, Anton Nedyalkov, Olivier Verdon, Zan Karnicnik, Cauly (90+2.Georgi Terziev), Alex Santana, Show [sent off 51], Pieros Sotiriou (86.Igor Thiago), Kiril Despodov (46.Rick), Bernard Tekpetey (46.Spas Delev). Trainer: Ante Šimundža (Slovenia).
Goals: 21' Aaron Greene 1-0, 88' Aidomo Emakhu 2-0, 90+1' Cauly 2-1.

19.07.2022; Windsor Park, Belfast; Attendance: 3,168
Referee: Andris Treimanis (Latvia)
**Linfield FC Belfast – FK Bodø/Glimt 1-0(0-0)**
Linfield FC: Chris Johns, Matthew Clarke, Ben Hall, Sam Roscoe-Byrne, Danny Finlayson, Jamie Mulgrew (64.Kyle McClean), Chris Shields, Kirk Millar, Stephen Fallon, Robbie McDaid (64.Eetu Vertainen), Jordan Stewart (89.Niall Quinn). Trainer: David Healy.
FK Bodø/Glimt: Nikita Haikin, Marius Høibråten, Brice Wembangomo, Alfons Sampsted, Isak Amundsen, Ulrik Saltnes, Hugo Vetlesen, Elias Hagen (86.Anders Konradsen), Joel Mvuka (86.Gilbert Koomson), Runar Espejord (66.Victor Boniface), Sondre Sørli (66.Amahl Pellegrino). Trainer: Kjetil Knutsen.
Goal: 83' Kirk Millar 1-0.

19.07.2022; Stadion Maksimir, Zagreb; Attendance: 7,912
Referee: Radu Marian Petrescu (Romania)
**GNK Dinamo Zagreb – KF Shkupi Čair 2-2(1-1)**
Dinamo Zagreb: Dominik Livakovic, Dino Peric, Sadegh Moharrami (77.Stefan Ristovski), Josip Sutalo (17.Kévin Théophile-Catherine), Arijan Ademi, Josip Misic (64.Martin Baturina), Luka Ivanusec, Robert Ljubicic, Josip Drmic (64.Mislav Orsic), Bruno Petkovic, Dario Spikic (46.Luka Menalo). Trainer: Ante Cacic.
KF Shkupi: Kristijan Naumovski, Vladica Brdarovski, Dzhelil Abdula, Gagi Margvelashvili, Faustin Senghor, Blerton Sheji (69.Angelce Timovski), Freddy Álvarez (87.Renaldo Cephas), Queven, Mamadou Danfa (78.Kristijan Trapanovski), Walid Hamidi (69.Pepi Georgiev), Sunday Adetunji (87.Ali Adem). Trainer: Goce Sedloski.
Goals: 25' Queven 0-1, 44' Arijan Ademi 1-1, 86' Bruno Petkovic 2-1, 89' Renaldo Cephas 2-2.

20.07.2022; Bolt Arena, Helsinki; Attendance: 5,236
Referee: Nikola Dabanović (Montenegro)
**HJK Helsinki – FC Viktoria Plzeň 1-2(0-1)**
HJK Helsinki: Conor Hazard, Jukka Raitala, Miro Tenho (72.Matti Peltola), Murilo (79.Pyry Soiri), Arttu Hoskonen, Përparim Hetemaj (79.Johannes Yli-Kokko), Santeri Väänänen, David Browne, Santeri Hostikka (71.Nassim Boujellab), Bojan Radulovic, Malik Abubakari. Trainer: Toni Koskela.
Viktoria Plzeň: Jindrich Stanek, Radim Rezník, Lukás Hejda, Ludek Pernica, Milan Havel, Jan Kopic (85.Libor Holík), Jan Sýkora (85.Kristi Qose), Jhon Mosquera, Lukás Kalvach, Pavel Bucha, Tomás Chorý (81.René Dedic). Trainer: Michal Bílek.
Goals: 6' Tomás Chorý 0-1 (penalty), 50' Bojan Radulovic 1-1, 57' Jan Kopic 1-2.

20.07.2022; „Sammy Ofer" Stadium, Haifa; Attendance: 29,654
Referee: Sascha Stegemann (Germany)
**Maccabi Haifa FC – Olympiacos SFP Peiraiás 1-1(0-1)**
Maccabi Haifa: Josh Cohen, Daniel Sundgren, Bogdan Planic, Shon Goldberg, Pierre Cornud (79.Sun Menachem), Tjaronn Chery, Ali Muhammad, Neta Lavi (61.Mohammad Abu Fani), Dolev Haziza, Omer Atzili (50.Nikita Rukavytsya), Din David (60.Frantzdy Pierrot). Trainer: Barak Bakhar.
Olympiacos: Tomás Vaclík, Kostas Manolas, Sime Vrsaljko (81.Sokratis Papastathopoulos), Pape Cissé, Oleg Reabciuk, Yann M'Vila (72.Andreas Bouchalakis), Georgios Masouras (81.Pipa Ávila), Mamadou Kané, Aguibou Camara (46.Mady Camara), Tiquinho Soares, Philip Zinckernagel (46.Aboubakar Kamara). Trainer: Pedro Rui da Mota Vieira Martins (Portugal).
Goals: 7' Philip Zinckernagel 0-1, 90+2' Dolev Haziza 1-1.

20.07.2022; Groupama Aréna, Budapest; Attendance: 20,459
Referee: Ricardo de Burgos Bengoetxea (Spain)
**Ferencvárosi TC – ŠK Slovan Bratislava 1-2(0-0)**
Ferencvárosi TC: Dénes Dibusz, Adnan Kovacevic, Eldar Civic, Henry Wingo, Samy Mmaee, Anderson Esiti, Kristoffer Zachariassen, Aïssa Laïdouni (72.Xavier Mercier), Tokmac Nguen (80.Carlos Auzqui), Franck Boli (72.Fortune Bassey), Adama Traoré (I) (57.Stjepan Loncar). Trainer: Stanislav Cherchesov (Russia).
Slovan Bratislava: Adrián Chovan, Guram Kashia, Lukás Pauschek (73.Aleksandar Cavric), Vernon De Marco, Jurij Medvedev, Myenty Abena, Juraj Kucka (90+3.Dávid Holman), Jaba Kankava, Vladimír Weiss (73.Giorgi Chakvetadze), Tigran Barseghyan (90+3.Uche Agbo), Iván Saponjic (69.Eric Ramírez). Trainer: Vladimír Weiss.
Goals: 70' Kristoffer Zachariassen 1-0, 81' Guram Kashia 1-1, 86' Tigran Barseghyan 1-2.

27.07.2022; Aspmyra Stadion, Bodø; Attendance: 5,110
Referee: Roi Reinshreiber (Israel)
**FK BODØ/GLIMT – Linfield FC Belfast 8-0(4-0)**
FK Bodø/Glimt: Nikita Haikin, Marius Høibråten, Brice Wembangomo (46.Ask Tjærandsen-Skau), Alfons Sampsted, Isak Amundsen, Ulrik Saltnes (46.Anders Konradsen), Amahl Pellegrino (69.Sondre Sørli), Hugo Vetlesen, Elias Hagen, Joel Mvuka (64.Gilbert Koomson), Victor Boniface (46.Runar Espejord). Trainer: Kjetil Knutsen.
Linfield FC: Chris Johns, Matthew Clarke (75.Joshua Archer), Ben Hall, Sam Roscoe-Byrne, Danny Finlayson, Jamie Mulgrew (56.Kyle McClean), Chris Shields, Kirk Millar [sent off 20], Stephen Fallon (56.Andrew Clarke), Robbie McDaid (61.Niall Quinn), Jordan Stewart (56.Cammy Palmer). Trainer: David Healy.
Goals: 7' Hugo Vetlesen 1-0, 21' Victor Boniface 2-0 (penalty), 24' Amahl Pellegrino 3-0, 28' Ulrik Saltnes 4-0, 52' Runar Espejord 5-0, 54' Amahl Pellegrino 6-0 (penalty), 73' Alfons Sampsted 7-0, 88' Runar Espejord 8-0.

26.07.2022; Nacionalna Arena "Toše Proeski", Skopje; Attendance: 12,500; Referee: Jakob Kehlet (Denmark)
**KF Shkupi Čair – GNK DINAMO ZAGREB 0-1(0-0)**
KF Shkupi: Kristijan Naumovski, Vladica Brdarovski (83.Kristijan Trapanovski), Dzhelil Abdula (60.Ali Adem), Gagi Margvelashvili, Faustin Senghor, Blerton Sheji, Freddy Álvarez, Queven, Walid Hamidi (38.Pepi Georgiev), Sunday Adetunji, Renaldo Cephas. Trainer: Goce Sedloski.
Dinamo Zagreb: Dominik Livakovic, Stefan Ristovski (90+3.Sadegh Moharrami), Dino Peric, Rasmus Lauritsen, Arijan Ademi (80.Martin Baturina), Josip Misic, Luka Ivanusec, Robert Ljubicic, Mislav Orsic (90+6.Amer Gojak), Bruno Petkovic, Dario Spikic (46.Luka Menalo). Trainer: Ante Cacic.
Goal: 47' Arijan Ademi 0-1.

26.07.2022; Doosan Arena, Plzeň; Attendance: 10,810
Referee: Aleksandar Stavrev (North Macedonia)
**FC VIKTORIA PLZEŇ – HJK Helsinki 5-0(3-0)**
Viktoria Plzeň: Jindrich Stanek, Radim Rezník (46.Libor Holík), Lukás Hejda (63.Filip Kasa), Ludek Pernica, Milan Havel, Jan Kopic (77.Matej Trusa), Jan Sýkora, Jhon Mosquera (70.Václav Pilar), Lukás Kalvach, Pavel Bucha, Tomás Chorý (63.Jan Kliment). Trainer: Michal Bílek.
HJK Helsinki: Conor Hazard, Jukka Raitala, Miro Tenho, Murilo (58.Pyry Soiri), Arttu Hoskonen, Matti Peltola (72.Johannes Yli-Kokko), Përparim Hetemaj, David Browne, Santeri Hostikka (81.Casper Terho), Bojan Radulovic (46.Paulus Arajuuri), Malik Abubakari (58.Fabian Serrarens). Trainer: Toni Koskela.
Goals: 11' Ludek Pernica 1-0, 21' Jan Sýkora 2-0, 31' Lukás Hejda 3-0, 73' Jan Sýkora 4-0, 84' Jan Kliment 5-0.

27.07.2022; Stádio „Giórgos Karaïskáki", Peiraiás; Attendance: 21,705
Referee: Daniel Stefanski (Poland)
**Olympiacos SFP Peiraiás – MACCABI HAIFA FC 0-4(0-1)**
Olympiacos: Tomás Vaclík, Kostas Manolas, Sime Vrsaljko, Pape Cissé, Oleg Reabciuk, Andreas Bouchalakis (46.João Carvalho), Georgios Masouras (68.Mathieu Valbuena), Mady Camara (77.Yann M'Vila), Mamadou Kané (62.Youssef El-Arabi), Tiquinho Soares, Philip Zinckernagel (63.Pierre Kunde Malong). Trainer: Pedro Rui da Mota Vieira Martins (Portugal).
Maccabi Haifa: Josh Cohen, Daniel Sundgren, Bogdan Planic, Shon Goldberg, Pierre Cornud (72.Sun Menachem), Tjaronn Chery (78.Omer Atzili), Ali Muhammad, Neta Lavi, Dolev Haziza (72.Ofri Arad), Din David (78.Mohammad Abu Fani), Frantzdy Pierrot (86.Nikita Rukavytsya). Trainer: Barak Bakhar.
Goals: 5' Tjaronn Chery 0-1, 61', 65' Frantzdy Pierrot 0-2, 0-3, 86' Mohammad Abu Fani 0-4.

27.07.2022; Štadión Tehelné pole, Bratislava; Attendance: 21,500
Referee: Marco Di Bello (Italy)
**ŠK Slovan Bratislava – FERENCVÁROSI TC 1-4(0-2)**
Slovan Bratislava: Adrián Chovan, Guram Kashia, Lukás Pauschek (87.Vladimír Weiss, 90+3.Dávid Holman), Vernon De Marco, Jurij Medvedev (11.Andre Green), Myenty Abena, Juraj Kucka, Jaba Kankava (90+2.Uche Agbo), Giorgi Chakvetadze, Tigran Barseghyan, Iván Saponjic (87.Aleksandar Cavric). Trainer: Vladimír Weiss.
Ferencvárosi TC: Dénes Dibusz, Endre Botka, Eldar Civic, Samy Mmaee, Mats Knoester, Anderson Esiti, Kristoffer Zachariassen, Aïssa Laïdouni, Tokmac Nguen (90+3.Rasmus Thelander), Franck Boli (63.Bálint Vécsei), Adama Traoré (I). Trainer: Stanislav Cherchesov (Russia).
Goals: 20' Franck Boli 0-1, 30' Kristoffer Zachariassen 0-2, 70' Vernon De Marco 1-2, 89' Adama Traoré (I) 1-3, 90+5' Aïssa Laïdouni 1-4.

20.07.2022; Ljudski vrt, Maribor; Attendance: 7,150
Referee: Harald Lechner (Austria)
**NK Maribor – FC Sheriff Tiraspol 0-0**
NK Maribor: Menno Bergsen, Martin Milec, Nemanja Mitrovic, Gregor Sikosek, Max Watson, Aleks Pihler (67.Aljaz Antolin), Jan Repas, Nino Zugelj (82.Rok Kronaveter), Danijel Sturm (82.Ignacio Guerrico), Roko Baturina, Ivan Brnic. Trainer: Radovan Karanovic.
Sheriff Tiraspol: Razak Abalora, Patrick Kpozo, Stjepan Radeljic, Gaby Kiki, Renan Guedes, Regi Lushkja, Cédric Badolo, Moussa Kyabou, Momo Yansané (65.Kay Tejan), Pernambuco, Ibrahim Rasheed (77.Abou Ouattara). Trainer: Stjepan Tomas (Croatia).

26.07.2022; Stadionul Zimbru, Chişinău; Attendance: 6,738
Referee: Tamás Bognár (Hungary)
**FC SHERIFF TIRASPOL – NK Maribor 1-0(0-0)**
Sheriff Tiraspol: Razak Abalora, Patrick Kpozo, Stjepan Radeljic, Gaby Kiki, Renan Guedes, Regi Lushkja (90+3.Stefanos Evangelou), Cédric Badolo, Moussa Kyabou, Kay Tejan (85.Momo Yansané), Pernambuco (69.Abou Ouattara), Ibrahim Rasheed. Trainer: Stjepan Tomas (Croatia).
NK Maribor: Menno Bergsen, Nemanja Mitrovic, Gregor Sikosek, Max Watson (90+2.Danijel Sturm), Sven Karic, Jan Repas, Nino Zugelj (45.Ignacio Guerrico, 90+2.Zan Vipotnik), Aljaz Antolin (73.Luka Uskokovic), Rok Sirk (73.Rok Kronaveter), Roko Baturina, Ivan Brnic. Trainer: Radovan Karanovic.
Goal: 88' Momo Yansané 1-0.

19.07.2022; MCH Arena, Herning; Attendance: 7,008
Referee: Novak Simović (Serbia)
**FC Midtjylland Herning – AEK Larnaca FC 1-1(0-0)**
FC Midtjylland: Elías Ólafsson, Erik Sviatchenko, Henrik Dalsgaard, Joel Andersson (60.Mads Thychosen), Paulinho (60.Nikolas Dyhr), Juninho, Anders Dreyer, Evander (44.Charles), Gustav Isaksen (75.Sory Kaba), Edward Chilufya (59.Victor Lind), Raphael Onyedika. Trainer: Bo Henriksen.
AEK Larnaca: Kenan Piric, Nenad Tomovic, Oier, Ángel García, Kypros Christoforou (72.Roberto Rosales), Gus Ledes, Hrvoje Milicevic, Ádám Gyurcsó (90.Mikel González), Ivan Trickovski (82.Omri Altman), Imad Faraj (83.Rafail Mamas), Victor Olatunji (72.Rafael Lopes). Trainer: José Luis Oltra Castaner (Spain).
Goals: 81' Ádám Gyurcsó 0-1, 84' Erik Sviatchenko 1-1.

26.07.2022; AEK Arena "Georgios Karapatakis", Larnaca; Attendance: 6,163; Referee: István Vad (II) (Hungary)
**AEK Larnaca FC – FC Midtjylland Herning 1-1(1-1,1-1); 3-4 on penalties**
AEK Larnaca: Kenan Piric, Roberto Rosales (88.Kypros Christoforou), Nenad Tomovic, Oier, Ángel García, Gus Ledes, Hrvoje Milicevic, Ádám Gyurcsó (83.Bruno Gama), Ivan Trickovski (90.José Romo), Imad Faraj (65.Omri Altman), Victor Olatunji (65.Rafael Lopes, 118.Rafail Mamas). Trainer: José Luis Oltra Castaner (Spain).
FC Midtjylland: Elías Ólafsson, Erik Sviatchenko, Henrik Dalsgaard, Joel Andersson, Paulinho (46.Nikolas Dyhr), Juninho (72.Mads Thychosen), Anders Dreyer, Charles (84.Oliver Sørensen), Gustav Isaksen (83.Sory Kaba), Edward Chilufya (46. Pione Sisto), Raphael Onyedika (114.Chris Kouakou). Trainer: Bo Henriksen.
Goals: 9' Victor Olatunji 1-0, 12' Henrik Dalsgaard 1-1.
Penalties: Anders Dreyer 0-1, Omri Altman (missed), Pione Sisto 0-2, Hrvoje Milicevic 1-2, Oliver Sørensen 1-3, José Romo 2-3, Nikolas Dyhr 2-4, Bruno Gama 3-4, Sory Kaba (missed), Gus Ledes (missed).

20.07.2022; Stadion Miejski, Lódz (Poland); Attendance: 11,603
Referee: Glenn Nyberg (Sweden)
**FK Dinamo Kyiv – Fenerbahçe JK Istanbul 0-0**
Dinamo Kyiv: Georgiy Bushchan, Tomasz Kedziora, Vladyslav Dubinchak, Denys Popov (83.Oleksandr Syrota), Ilya Zabarnyi, Sergiy Sydorchuk, Vitaliy Buyalskyi (77.Denys Garmash), Benjamin Verbic (83.Vladyslav Vanat), Viktor Tsygankov (88.Oleksandr Karavayev), Mykola Shaparenko, Artem Besedin. Trainer: Mircea Lucescu (Romania).
Fenerbahçe: Altay Bayindir, Serdar Aziz (46.Marcel Tisserand), Attila Szalai, Willian Arão, Irfan Kahveci (63.Bruma), Bright Osayi-Samuel, Ferdi Kadioglu, Ismail Yüksek, Joshua King (63.Lincoln), Enner Valencia (72.Serdar Dursun), Diego Rossi (72.Arda Güler). Trainer: Jorge Fernando Pinheiro de Jesus (Portugal).

27.07.2022; „Şükrü Saracoğlu" Stadyumu, Istanbul; Attendance: 40,000
Referee: Massimiliano Irrati (Italy)
**Fenerbahçe JK Istanbul – FK DINAMO KYIV 1-2(0-0,1-1)**
Fenerbahçe: Altay Bayindir, Marcel Tisserand (85.Lincoln), Attila Szalai, Willian Arão (95.Filip Novák), Irfan Kahveci (46.Emre Mor, 77.Bruma), Bright Osayi-Samuel, Ferdi Kadioglu, Ismail Yüksek [sent off 53], Joshua King (63.Miguel Crespo), Enner Valencia (77.Serdar Dursun), Diego Rossi. Trainer: Jorge Fernando Pinheiro de Jesus (Portugal).
Dinamo Kyiv: Georgiy Bushchan, Tomasz Kedziora (90.Oleksandr Karavayev), Vladyslav Dubinchak (105.Kostiantyn Vivcharenko), Denys Popov, Ilya Zabarnyi, Sergiy Sydorchuk (105.Oleksnadr Andriyevskyi), Vitaliy Buyalskyi (67.Denys Garmash), Benjamin Verbic (37.Vladyslav Vanat), Viktor Tsygankov, Mykola Shaparenko, Artem Besedin (67.Volodymyr Shepelyev). Trainer: Mircea Lucescu (Romania).
Goals: 57' Vitaliy Buyalskyi 0-1, 88' Attila Szalai 1-1, 114' Oleksandr Karavayev 1-2.

02.08.2022; Stadionul Zimbru, Chişinău; Attendance: 8,153
Referee: Danny Desmond Makkelie (Netherlands)
**FC Sheriff Tiraspol – FC Viktoria Plzeň 1-2(1-1)**
Sheriff Tiraspol: Razak Abalora, Patrick Kpozo, Stjepan Radeljic, Gaby Kiki, Renan Guedes, Regi Lushkja (72.Giannis Botos), Cédric Badolo, Moussa Kyabou, Kay Tejan, Pernambuco, Ibrahim Rasheed (89.Abou Ouattara). Trainer: Stjepan Tomas (Croatia).
Viktoria Plzeň: Jindrich Stanek, Lukás Hejda, Ludek Pernica, Milan Havel, Jan Kopic, Jan Sýkora, Jhon Mosquera (75.Libor Holík), Lukás Kalvach, Pavel Bucha (90+2.Kristi Qose), Tomás Chorý (66.René Dedic), Jan Kliment (75.Matej Trusa). Trainer: Michal Bílek.
Goals: 36' Ibrahim Rasheed 1-0 (penalty), 41' Tomás Chorý 1-1 (penalty), 55' Pavel Bucha 1-2.

02.08.2022; Huvepharma Arena, Razgrad; Attendance: 7,505
Referee: Cüneyt Çakir (Turkey)
**PFC Ludogorets Razgrad – GNK Dinamo Zagreb 1-2(1-2)**
Ludogorets Razgrad: Sergio Padt (46.Simon Sluga), Cicinho, Igor Plastun, Anton Nedyalkov, Olivier Verdon, Cauly (46.Dominik Yankov), Jakub Piotrowski, Ivan Yordanov, Pieros Sotiriou (79.Igor Thiago), Bernard Tekpetey (73.Kiril Despodov), Rick (79.Spas Delev). Trainer: Ante Šimundža (Slovenia).
Dinamo Zagreb: Dominik Livakovic, Stefan Ristovski, Dino Peric, Rasmus Lauritsen, Arijan Ademi, Josip Misic, Luka Ivanusec (46.Dario Spikic), Robert Ljubicic, Martin Baturina (86.Bosko Sutalo), Mislav Orsic (71.Luka Menalo), Josip Drmic (60.Bruno Petkovic). Trainer: Ante Cacic.
Goals: 6' Dino Peric 0-1, 9' Sergio Padt 0-2 (own goal), 22' Bernard Tekpetey 1-2.

03.08.2022; „Tofiq Bəhramov" Stadionu; Attendance: 31,200
Referee: Andreas Ekberg (Sweden)
**Qarabağ FK Bakı – Ferencvárosi TC 1-1(1-1)**
Qarabağ FK: Sahrudin Mahammadaliyev, Marko Vesovic, Qara Qarayev, Badavi Hüseynov, Bahlul Mustafazade, Filip Ozobic (79.Ramil Sheydaev), Abdellah Zoubir, Tural Bayramov, Marko Jankovic (83.Júlio Romão), Ibrahima Wadji (90+3.Leandro Andrade), Owusu Kwabena. Trainer: Qurban Qurbanov.
Ferencvárosi TC: Dénes Dibusz, Endre Botka, Eldar Civic, Samy Mmaee (57.Rasmus Thelander), Mats Knoester (68.Adnan Kovacevic), Anderson Esiti, Kristoffer Zachariassen, Aïssa Laïdouni (88.Muhamed Besic), Tokmac Nguen, Franck Boli (68.Bálint Vécsei), Adama Traoré (I). Trainer: Stanislav Cherchesov (Russia).
Goals: 17' Franck Boli 0-1, 34' Owusu Kwabena 1-1.

03.08.2022; Aspmyra Stadion, Bodø; Attendance: 6,117
Referee: István Vad (II) (Hungary)
**FK Bodø/Glimt – FK Žalgiris Vilnius 5-0(2-0)**
FK Bodø/Glimt: Nikita Haikin, Marius Høibråten, Brede Moe (19.Isak Amundsen), Brice Wembangomo, Alfons Sampsted, Ulrik Saltnes, Amahl Pellegrino (80.Sondre Sørli), Hugo Vetlesen, Elias Hagen, Joel Mvuka (88.Gilbert Koomson), Lars-Jørgen Salvesen (80.Runar Espejord). Trainer: Kjetil Knutsen.
Žalgiris: Edvinas Gertmonas, Mario Pavelic, Petar Mamic, Joël Fey d'Or Bopesu (68.Donatas Kazlauskas), Nemanja Ljubisavljevic, Nicolás Gorobsov, Oliver Buff (88.Mantas Kuklys), Fabien Ourega (68.Gustas Jarusevicius), Marko Milickovic, Renan Oliveira (88.Francis Kyeremeh), Mathias Oyewusi (68.Saulius Mikoliūnas). Trainer: Vladimir Cherubin (Kazakhstan).
Goals: 33' Hugo Vetlesen 1-0 (penalty), 36' Amahl Pellegrino 2-0, 58' Lars-Jørgen Salvesen 3-0, 61' Marius Høibråten 4-0, 90+3' Runar Espejord 5-0.

09.08.2022; Doosan Aréna, Plzeň; Attendance: 10,770
Referee: Orel Grinfeld (Israel)
**FC VIKTORIA PLZEŇ – FC Sheriff Tiraspol 2-1(1-0)**
Viktoria Plzeň: Jindrich Stanek, Lukás Hejda, Ludek Pernica, Milan Havel, Jan Kopic, Jan Sýkora (90.Matej Trusa), Jhon Mosquera (90.Václav Pilar), Lukás Kalvach, Pavel Bucha, Tomás Chorý (73.René Dedic), Jan Kliment (59.Libor Holík). Trainer: Michal Bílek.
Sheriff Tiraspol: Razak Abalora, Stefanos Evangelou [sent off 85], Patrick Kpozo, Gaby Kiki, Renan Guedes, Abou Ouattara (80.Keston Julien), Cédric Badolo (70.Giannis Botos), Salifu Mudasiru, Moussa Kyabou, Pernambuco (46.Kay Tejan), Ibrahim Rasheed. Trainer: Stjepan Tomas (Croatia).
Goals: 10' Jan Kliment 1-0, 47' Ibrahim Rasheed 1-1 (penalty), 62' Jhon Mosquera 2-1.

09.08.2022; Stadion Maksimir, Zagreb; Attendance: 13,658
Referee: Benoît Bastien (France)
**GNK DINAMO ZAGREB – PFC Ludogorets Razgrad 4-2(3-1)**
Dinamo Zagreb: Dominik Livakovic, Stefan Ristovski (46.Sadegh Moharrami), Dino Peric, Bosko Sutalo, Arijan Ademi, Josip Misic (46.Amer Gojak), Robert Ljubicic, Martin Baturina (46.Luka Ivanusec), Mislav Orsic, Josip Drmic (71.Bruno Petkovic), Dario Spikic (90+1.Luka Menalo). Trainer: Ante Cacic.
Ludogorets Razgrad: Simon Sluga, Cicinho (46.Zan Karnicnik [sent off 87]), Igor Plastun (46.Spas Delev), Anton Nedyalkov, Olivier Verdon, Show (46.Ivan Yordanov), Dominik Yankov [sent off 17], Kiril Despodov (85.Jorghinho), Rick [sent off 73], Igor Thiago (66.Matías Tissera). Trainer: Ante Šimundža (Slovenia).
Goals: 13' Josip Drmic 1-0, 27', 44' Mislav Orsic 2-0 (penalty), 3-0, 45+4', 49' Kiril Despodov 3-1, 3-2 (penalty), 87' Bruno Petkovic 4-2 (penalty).

09.08.2022; Groupama Aréna, Budapest; Attendance: 18,875
Referee: Carlos del Cerro Grande (Spain)
**Ferencvárosi TC – QARABAĞ FK BAKI 1-3(0-1)**
Ferencvárosi TC: Dénes Dibusz, Rasmus Thelander, Endre Botka, Adnan Kovacevic (51.Mats Knoester), Eldar Civic (84.Lóránd Pászka), Anderson Esiti (51.Bálint Vécsei), Kristoffer Zachariassen, Aïssa Laïdouni, Tokmac Nguen (84.Marquinhos), Franck Boli (61.Ryan Mmaee), Adama Traoré (I). Trainer: Stanislav Cherchesov (Russia).
Qarabağ FK: Sahrudin Mahammadaliyev, Marko Vesovic, Qara Qarayev (86.Júlio Romão), Badavi Hüseynov, Bahlul Mustafazade, Abdellah Zoubir (86.Leandro Andrade), Kady, Tural Bayramov, Marko Jankovic (58.Richard Almeida), Ramil Sheydaev, Ibrahima Wadji (82.Owusu Kwabena). Trainer: Qurban Qurbanov.
Goals: 7' Abdellah Zoubir 0-1, 54', 78' Ibrahima Wadji 0-2, 0-3, 86' Adama Traoré (I) 1-3.

09.08.2022; LFF stadionas, Vilnius; Attendance: 4,629
Referee: Sandro Schärer (Switzerland)
**FK Žalgiris Vilnius – FK BODØ/GLIMT 1-1(1-0)**
Žalgiris: Edvinas Gertmonas, Saulius Mikoliūnas, Mario Pavelic, Petar Mamic [sent off 57], Nemanja Ljubisavljevic (82.Kipras Kazukolovas), Nicolás Gorobsov, Oliver Buff, Fabien Ourega (64.Joël Fey d'Or Bopesu), Francis Kyeremeh (64.Mathias Oyewusi), Marko Milickovic, Renan Oliveira (76.Donatas Kazlauskas). Trainer: Vladimir Cherubin (Kazakhstan).
FK Bodø/Glimt: Nikita Haikin (15.Julian Lund), Marius Høibråten, Alfons Sampsted, Isak Amundsen, Ulrik Saltnes, Amahl Pellegrino (63.Sondre Sørli), Hugo Vetlesen (81.Anders Konradsen), Elias Hagen, Ask Tjærandsen-Skau, Joel Mvuka (63.Gilbert Koomson), Lars-Jørgen Salvesen (63.Runar Espejord). Trainer: Kjetil Knutsen.
Goals: 39' Francis Kyeremeh 1-0, 51' Joel Mvuka 1-1.

03.08.2022; „Sammy Ofer" Stadium, Haifa; Attendance: 29,876
Referee: Maurizio Mariani (Italy)
**Maccabi Haifa FC – Apollon Limassol FC 4-0(1-0)**
Maccabi Haifa: Josh Cohen, Daniel Sundgren, Bogdan Planic, Shon Goldberg, Pierre Cornud (74.Sun Menachem), Tjaronn Chery, Ali Muhammad (74.Mohammad Abu Fani), Neta Lavi, Dolev Haziza (80.Mavis Tchibota), Din David (65.Omer Atzili), Frantzdy Pierrot (80.Nikita Rukavytsya). Trainer: Barak Bakhar.
Apollon Limassol: Aleksandar Jovanovic, Valentin Roberge, Mathieu Peybernes, Vukasin Jovanovic [sent off 61], Amine Khammas (90+3.Ido Shahar), Nicolas Diguiny (64.Euclides Cabral), Israel Coll, Danilo Spoljaric (45.Chambos Kyriakou), Hervin Ongenda (45.Vá), Andreas Panayiotou (64.Rangelo Janga), Ioannis Pittas. Trainer: Alexander Zorniger (Germany).
Goals: 38' Mathieu Peybernes 1-0 (own goal), 54', 62' Ali Muhammad 2-0, 3-0, 79' Frantzdy Pierrot 4-0.

03.08.2022; Stadion „Rajko Mitić", Beograd; Attendance: 40,456
Referee: Artur Manuel Ribeiro Soares Dias (Portugal)
**FK Crvena Zvezda Beograd – FC Pyunik Yerevan 5-0(3-0)**
Crvena Zvezda Beograd: Milan Borjan, Aleksandar Dragovic, Nemanja Milunovic, Milan Rodic [sent off 89], Strahinja Erakovic, Aleksandar Katai (67.Slavoljub Srnic), Guélor Kanga (76.Sékou Sanogo), Mirko Ivanic (76.Stefan Mitrovic), Kings Kangwa, Aleksandar Pesic (69.Milan Pavkov), Osman Bukari (76.Ibrahim Mustapha). Trainer: Dejan Stankovic.
Pyunik Erevan: David Yurchenko, Zoran Gajic, Mikhail Kovalenko, Juninho, Artak Dashyan, Renzo Zambrano, Eugeniu Cociuc (88.Gevorg Najaryan), Hovhannes Harutyunyan (66.Uros Nenadovic), David Davidyan (46.Alexander González), Yusuf Otubanjo (56.Marjan Radeski), Luka Juricic (88.Nemanja Mladenovic). Trainer: Eghishe Melikyan.
Goals: 29' Osman Bukari 1-0, 33' Kings Kangwa 2-0, 44', 70' Osman Bukari 3-0, 4-0, 77' Stefan Mitrovic 5-0.

09.08.2022; Stádio Neo GSP, Nicosia; Attendance: 3,936
Referee: Felix Zwayer (Germany)
**Apollon Limassol FC – MACCABI HAIFA FC 2-0(2-0)**
Apollon Limassol: Aleksandar Jovanovic, Valentin Roberge (73.Panagiotis Artymatas), Mathieu Peybernes, Chambos Kyriakou (73.Vá), Amine Khammas, Euclides Cabral, Nicolas Diguiny, Israel Coll, Rangelo Janga (57.Bagaliy Dabo), Hervin Ongenda (73.Ido Shahar), Ioannis Pittas. Trainer: Alexander Zorniger (Germany).
Maccabi Haifa: Josh Cohen, Daniel Sundgren, Bogdan Planic, Shon Goldberg, Sun Menachem (60.Pierre Cornud), Ofri Arad (46.Ali Muhammad), Neta Lavi, Mohammad Abu Fani, Omer Atzili (60.Dolev Haziza), Din David (76.Maor Levi), Frantzdy Pierrot (90+3.Nikita Rukavytsya). Trainer: Barak Bakhar.
Goals: 19' Hervin Ongenda 1-0, 26' Israel Coll 2-0.

09.08.2022; „Vazgen Sargsyan" Hanrapetakan Stadium, Yerevan; Attendance: 6,000; Referee: William Sean Collum (Scotland)
**FC Pyunik Yerevan – FK CRVENA ZVEZDA BEOGRAD 0-2(0-1)**
Pyunik Erevan: Stanislav Buchnev, Artur Avagyan (78.Gevorg Najaryan), Alexander González, Anton Bratkov (78.Yuri Gareginyan), Mikhail Kovalenko, Juninho, Artak Dashyan, Eugeniu Cociuc, Hovhannes Harutyunyan (79.Alan Aussi), Yusuf Otubanjo (62.Marjan Radeski), Luka Juricic (83.Nemanja Mladenovic). Trainer: Eghishe Melikyan.
Crvena Zvezda Beograd: Milan Borjan, Aleksandar Dragovic, Nemanja Milunovic, Marko Gobeljic, Strahinja Erakovic (64.Nikola Stankovic), Aleksandar Katai (64.El Fardou Ben Mohamed), Sékou Sanogo (46.Stefan Mitrovic), Guélor Kanga (77.Slavoljub Srnic), Kings Kangwa, Milan Pavkov, Osman Bukari (69.Ibrahim Mustapha). Trainer: Dejan Stankovic.
Goals: 44' Guélor Kanga 0-1 (penalty), 60' Milan Pavkov 0-2.

LEAGUE PATH

02.08.2022; Stade „Louis II", Monaco; Attendance: 10,802
Referee: Davide Massa (Italy)
**AS Monaco FC – PSV Eindhoven 1-1(0-1)**
AS Monaco: Alexander Nübel, Guillermo Maripán, Axel Disasi, Vanderson, Aleksandr Golovin (76.Breel Embolo), Youssouf Fofana, Eliot Matazo, Kevin Volland (76.Gelson Martins), Wissam Ben Yedder (84.Sofiane Diop), Takumi Minamino (67.Krépin Diatta), Ismail Jakobs. Trainer: Philippe Clement (Belgium).
PSV Eindhoven: Walter Benítez, Phillipp Mwene (76.Fredrik Oppegård), Philipp Max (61.André Ramalho), Armando Obispo, Jordan Teze, Ibrahim Sangaré (78.Marco van Ginkel), Guus Til (62.Érick Gutiérrez), Joey Veerman, Ismael Saibari (76.Xavi Simons), Luuk de Jong, Cody Gakpo. Trainer: Ruud van Nistelrooij.
Goals: 38' Joey Veerman 0-1, 80' Axel Disasi 1-1.

02.08.2022; King Power at Den Dreef, Heverlee; Attendance: 1,100
Referee: Irfan Peljto (Bosnia and Herzegovina)
**Royale Union Saint-Gilloise – Rangers FC Glasgow 2-0(1-0)**
Union Saint-Gilloise: Anthony Moris, Bart Nieuwkoop, Christian Burgess, Siebe Van Der Heyden, Ross Sykes, Teddy Teuma (90+2.Cameron Puertas), Senne Lynen, Jean Amani, Dante Vanzeir (90+2.Guillaume François), Loïc Lapoussin, Simon Adingra (85.Ilyes Ziani). Trainer: Karel Geraerts.
Rangers FC: Jon McLaughlin, James Tavernier, Connor Goldson, Borna Barisic (67.Ridvan Yilmaz), Ryan Jack (67.Ben Davies), John Lundstram, Glen Kamara, James Sands, Antonio Colak, Rabbi Matondo (77.Tom Lawrence), Malik Tillman (77.Scott Wright). Trainer: Giovanni van Bronckhorst (Netherlands).
Goals: 27' Teddy Teuma 1-0, 76' Dante Vanzeir 2-0 (penalty).

09.08.2022; Philips Stadion, Eindhoven; Attendance: 33,000
Referee: Jesús Gil Manzano (Spain)
**PSV EINDHOVEN – AS Monaco FC 3-2(1-0,2-2)**
PSV Eindhoven: Walter Benítez, Phillipp Mwene (77.Johan Bakayoko), Philipp Max (77.Fredrik Oppegård), Armando Obispo (88.Marco van Ginkel), Jordan Teze, Ibrahim Sangaré, Guus Til (65.Érick Gutiérrez), Joey Veerman (107.Jarrad Branthwaite), Ismael Saibari (65.André Ramalho), Luuk de Jong, Cody Gakpo. Trainer: Ruud van Nistelrooij.
AS Monaco: Alexander Nübel, Guillermo Maripán, Axel Disasi, Vanderson, Aleksandr Golovin (53.Krépin Diatta), Youssouf Fofana, Eliot Matazo (105.Jean Lucas), Kevin Volland (46.Breel Embolo), Wissam Ben Yedder (82.Sofiane Diop), Takumi Minamino (68.Gelson Martins), Ismail Jakobs (53.Caio Henrique). Trainer: Philippe Clement (Belgium).
Goals: 21' Joey Veerman 1-0, 58' Guillermo Maripán 1-1, 70' Wissam Ben Yedder 1-2, 89' Érick Gutiérrez 2-2, 109' Luuk de Jong 3-2.

09.08.2022; Ibrox Stadium, Glasgow; Attendance: 48,454
Referee: Anastasios Sidiropoulos (Greece)
**Rangers FC Glasgow – Royale Union Saint-Gilloise 3-0(1-0)**
Rangers FC: Jon McLaughlin, James Tavernier, Connor Goldson, Borna Barisic, Scott Arfield (64.Rabbi Matondo), Tom Lawrence (87.Glen Kamara), John Lundstram, James Sands (79.Ben Davies), Antonio Colak (79.Alfredo Morelos), Ryan Kent, Malik Tillman. Trainer: Giovanni van Bronckhorst (Netherlands).
Union Saint-Gilloise: Anthony Moris, Bart Nieuwkoop (77.Guillaume François), Christian Burgess, Siebe Van Der Heyden, Ross Sykes (83.Dennis Eckert-Ayensa), Teddy Teuma (87.Cameron Puertas), Jean Amani [sent off 90+4], Dante Vanzeir, Loïc Lapoussin, Simon Adingra. Trainer: Karel Geraerts.
Goals: 45' James Tavernier 1-0 (penalty), 58' Antonio Colak 2-0, 78' Malik Tillman 3-0.

02.08.2022; Estádio do Sport Lisboa e Benfica, Lisboa; Attendance: 53,346; Referee: Alejandro José Hernández Hernández (Spain)

**Sport Lisboa e Benfica – FC Midtjylland Herning 4-1(3-0)**

Benfica: Odisseas Vlachodimos, Nicolás Otamendi, Gilberto, Álex Grimaldo, Morato, João Mário, Rafa Silva (78.Henrique Araújo), Florentino Luís, Enzo Fernández, David Neres (87.Chiquinho), Gonçalo Ramos (79.Roman Yaremchuk). Trainer: Roger Schmidt (Germany).

FC Midtjylland: Elías Ólafsson, Erik Sviatchenko, Henrik Dalsgaard, Joel Andersson (67.Mads Thychosen), Juninho, Nikolas Dyhr (62.Paulinho), Pione Sisto, Anders Dreyer (46.Edward Chilufya), Charles (79.Chris Kouakou), Oliver Sørensen, Sory Kaba (67.Gustav Isaksen). Trainer: Henrik Jensen.

Goals: 17', 33' Gonçalo Ramos 1-0, 2-0, 40' Enzo Fernández 3-0, 61' Gonçalo Ramos 4-0, 78' Pione Sisto 4-1 (penalty).

03.08.2022; Stadion Miejski, Lódz (Poland); Attendance: 6,092
Referee: François Letexier (France)

**FK Dinamo Kyiv – SK Sturm Graz 1-0(1-0)**

Dinamo Kyiv: Georgiy Bushchan, Tomasz Kedziora, Oleksandr Karavayev, Vladyslav Dubinchak (71.Kostiantyn Vivcharenko), Denys Popov, Ilya Zabarnyi, Sergiy Sydorchuk, Vitaliy Buyalskyi, Mykola Shaparenko, Volodymyr Shepelyev (71.Denys Garmash), Artem Besedin (83.Vladyslav Vanat). Trainer: Mircea Lucescu (Romania).

Sturm Graz: Jörg Siebenhandl, Jon Gorenc-Stankovic, Gregory Wüthrich, Jusuf Gazibegovic, David Affengruber, Amadou Dante (68.David Schnegg), Stefan Hierländer (67.Ivan Ljubic), Tomi Horvat, Alexander Prass (78.Vesel Demaku), Manprit Sarkaria, Rasmus Højlund (89.Christoph Lang). Trainer: Christian Ilzer.

Goal: 28' Oleksandr Karavayev 1-0.

09.08.2022; Cepheus Park, Randers; Attendance: 5,111
Referee: Srđan Jovanović (Serbia)

**FC Midtjylland Herning – SPORT LISBOA E BENFICA 1-3(0-1)**

FC Midtjylland: Elías Ólafsson, Henrik Dalsgaard, Joel Andersson, Mads Thychosen, Paulinho (87.Nikolas Dyhr), Juninho, Pione Sisto (77.Edward Chilufya), Anders Dreyer (70.Gustav Isaksen), Evander (46.Oliver Sørensen), Raphael Onyedika, Sory Kaba (70.Júnior Brumado). Trainer: Henrik Jensen.

Benfica: Odisseas Vlachodimos, Nicolás Otamendi, Gilberto (76.Alexander Bah), Álex Grimaldo, Morato, João Mário (89.Diego Moreira), Rafa Silva (46.Henrique Araújo), Chiquinho (79.Diogo Gonçalves), Florentino Luís, Enzo Fernández, Gonçalo Ramos (46.Roman Yaremchuk). Trainer: Roger Schmidt (Germany).

Goals: 23' Enzo Fernández 0-1, 56' Henrique Araújo 0-2, 63' Pione Sisto 1-2, 88' Diogo Gonçalves 1-3.

09.08.2022; Merkur Arena, Graz; Attendance: 14,007
Referee: Ivan Kružliak (Slovakia)

**SK Sturm Graz – FK Dinamo Kyiv 1-2(1-0,1-0)**

Sturm Graz: Jörg Siebenhandl, Jon Gorenc-Stankovic (102.Mohammed Fuseini), Gregory Wüthrich, Jusuf Gazibegovic, David Affengruber, Amadou Dante (102.David Schnegg), Stefan Hierländer (103.Vesel Demaku), Tomi Horvat (84.Christoph Lang), Alexander Prass (115.Moritz Wels), Manprit Sarkaria [sent off 105], Rasmus Højlund (75.Ivan Ljubic). Trainer: Christian Ilzer.

Dinamo Kyiv: Georgiy Bushchan, Tomasz Kedziora (71.Oleksandr Karavayev), Vladyslav Dubinchak (71.Kostiantyn Vivcharenko), Oleksandr Syrota, Ilya Zabarnyi, Sergiy Sydorchuk, Vitaliy Buyalskyi, Viktor Tsygankov, Mykola Shaparenko, Volodymyr Shepelyev (82.Denys Garmash, 99.Oleksandr Andriyevskyi), Artem Besedin (76.Vladyslav Vanat). Trainer: Mircea Lucescu (Romania).

Goals: 27' Rasmus Højlund 1-0, 97' Kostiantyn Vivcharenko 1-1, 112' Viktor Tsyhankov 1-2.

---

**PLAY-OFFS**

Please note: the winners of the ties advanced to the Group Stage, while the losers were transferred to the UEFA Europa League Group Stage.

**CHAMPIONS PATH**

16.08.2022; Aspmyra Stadion, Bodø; Attendance: 7,762
Referee: Danny Desmond Makkelie (Netherlands)

**FK Bodø/Glimt – GNK Dinamo Zagreb 1-0(1-0)**

FK Bodø/Glimt: Nikita Haikin, Marius Høibråten, Brice Wembangomo, Alfons Sampsted, Isak Amundsen, Ulrik Saltnes, Hugo Vetlesen, Elias Hagen (82.Albert Grønbæk Erlykke), Amahl Pellegrino, Lars-Jørgen Salvesen (68.Runar Espejord), Joel Mvuka (81.Gilbert Koomson). Trainer: Kjetil Knutsen.

Dinamo Zagreb: Dominik Livakovic, Stefan Ristovski, Rasmus Lauritsen, Bosko Sutalo, Arijan Ademi, Josip Misic, Robert Ljubicic, Martin Baturina (77.Amer Gojak), Mislav Orsic (69.Mahir Emreli), Josip Drmic (46.Bruno Petkovic), Dario Spikic (46.Luka Ivanusec). Trainer: Ante Cacic.

Goal: 37' Amahl Pellegrino 1-0.

16.08.2022; Telia Parken, København; Attendance: 27,520
Referee: Michael Oliver (England)

**FC København – Trabzonspor Kulübü 2-1(1-0)**

FC København: Mathew Ryan, Davit Khocholava, Denis Vavro, Kevin Diks (81.Peter Ankersen), Victor Kristiansen, Rasmus Falk (89.Marko Stamenic), Zeca, Victor Claesson, Lukas Lerager, Pep Biel (81.Ísak Bergmann Jóhannesson), Hákon Haraldsson (67.William Bøving). Trainer: Jess Thorup.

Trapzonspor: Ugurcan Çakir, Jens Stryger Larsen, Vitor Hugo, Stefano Denswil (58.Marc Bartra), Eren Elmali, Anastasios Bakasetas, Manolis Siopis (58.Enis Bardhi), Trézéguet, Abdülkadir Ömür (89.Dorukhan Toköz), Jean Kouassi (46.Djaniny), Andreas Cornelius. Trainer: Abdullah Avci.

Goals: 9' Victor Claesson 1-0, 48' Lukas Lerager 2-0, 79' Anastasios Bakasetas 2-1.

24.08.2022; Stadion Maksimir, Zagreb; Attendance: 18,349
Referee: Antonio Miguel Mateu Lahoz (Spain)

**GNK DINAMO ZAGREB – FK Bodø/Glimt 4-1(2-0,2-1)**

Dinamo Zagreb: Dominik Livakovic, Stefan Ristovski (91.Sadegh Moharrami), Dino Peric (71.Emir Dilaver), Bosko Sutalo, Arijan Ademi (91.Petar Bockaj), Luka Ivanusec, Robert Ljubicic, Martin Baturina (60.Amer Gojak), Mislav Orsic (82.Josip Drmic), Bruno Petkovic, Dario Spikic (60.Mahir Emreli). Trainer: Ante Cacic.

FK Bodø/Glimt: Nikita Haikin, Marius Høibråten, Brice Wembangomo (111.Ask Tjærandsen-Skau), Alfons Sampsted, Isak Amundsen (106.Gaute Vetti), Ulrik Saltnes, Hugo Vetlesen (106.Anders Konradsen), Elias Hagen (63.Albert Grønbæk Erlykke), Amahl Pellegrino, Lars-Jørgen Salvesen (63.Runar Espejord), Joel Mvuka (104.Gilbert Koomson). Trainer: Kjetil Knutsen.

Goals: 4' Mislav Orsic 1-0, 35' Bruno Petkovic 2-0, 70' Albert Grønbæk Erlykke 2-1, 116' Josip Drmic 3-1, 120' Petar Bockaj 4-1.

24.08.2022; „Şenol Güneş" Stadyumu, Trabzon; Attendance: 36,128
Referee: Danny Desmond Makkelie (Netherlands)

**Trabzonspor Kulübü – FC KØBENHAVN 0-0**

Trapzonspor: Ugurcan Çakir, Jens Stryger Larsen, Marc Bartra, Stefano Denswil, Eren Elmali, Manolis Siopis, Enis Bardhi, Dorukhan Toköz (73.Jean Kouassi), Abdülkadir Ömür (66.Trézéguet), Djaniny (78.Anastasios Bakasetas), Andreas Cornelius. Trainer: Abdullah Avci.

FC København: Mathew Ryan, Davit Khocholava, Denis Vavro, Kevin Diks, Victor Kristiansen, Rasmus Falk, Zeca, Victor Claesson (78.Hákon Haraldsson), Lukas Lerager (85.Valdemar Lund Jensen), Pep Biel (79.Mamoudou Karamoko), Mohamed Daramy (63.Paul Mukairu). Trainer: Jess Thorup.

17.08.2022; „Tofiq Bəhramov" Stadionu; Attendance: 31,150
Referee: Slavko Vinčić (Slovenia)
**Qarabağ FK Bakı – FC Viktoria Plzeň 0-0**
Qarabağ FK: Sahrudin Mahammadaliyev, Marko Vesovic, Qara Qarayev, Badavi Hüseynov, Bahlul Mustafazade, Abdellah Zoubir, Kady, Tural Bayramov, Marko Jankovic (73.Richard Almeida), Ramil Sheydaev (62.Filip Ozobic), Ibrahima Wadji (73.Owusu Kwabena). Trainer: Qurban Qurbanov.
Viktoria Plzeň: Jindrich Stanek, Lukás Hejda, Ludek Pernica, Milan Havel, Václav Jemelka, Jan Kopic (90+1.Libor Holík), Jan Sýkora (71.Erik Jirka), Jhon Mosquera (59.Václav Pilar), Lukás Kalvach, Pavel Bucha, Tomás Chorý (71.Jan Kliment). Trainer: Michal Bílek.

17.08.2022; „Sammy Ofer" Stadium, Haifa; Attendance: 29,132
Referee: Carlos del Cerro Grande (Spain)
**Maccabi Haifa FC – FK Crvena Zvezda Beograd 3-2(1-2)**
Maccabi Haifa: Josh Cohen, Daniel Sundgren, Bogdan Planic, Shon Goldberg, Pierre Cornud (62.Sun Menachem), Tjaronn Chery, Ali Muhammad, Neta Lavi, Dolev Haziza (76.Mohammad Abu Fani), Din David (62.Omer Atzili), Frantzdy Pierrot (70.Nikita Rukavytsya). Trainer: Barak Bakhar.
Crvena Zvezda Beograd: Milan Borjan, Aleksandar Dragovic, Nemanja Milunovic, Milan Rodic, Strahinja Erakovic, Aleksandar Katai (56.Slavoljub Srnic), Guélor Kanga, Mirko Ivanic (72.Sékou Sanogo), Kings Kangwa, Aleksandar Pesic (72.El Fardou Ben Mohamed), Osman Bukari (60.Stefan Mitrovic). Trainer: Dejan Stankovic.
Goals: 18' Frantzdy Pierrot 1-0, 27' Aleksandar Pesic 1-1, 39' Guélor Kanga 1-2, 51' Frantzdy Pierrot 2-2, 61' Tjaronn Chery 3-2.

23.08.2022; Doosan Aréna, Plzeň; Attendance: 10,963
Referee: Artur Manuel Ribeiro Soares Dias (Portugal)
**FC VIKTORIA PLZEŇ – Qarabağ FK Bakı 2-1(0-1)**
Viktoria Plzeň: Jindrich Stanek, Ludek Pernica, Milan Havel, Libor Holík, Václav Jemelka, Jan Kopic (90+4.Filip Cihák), Jan Sýkora (46.Jan Kliment, 74.Erik Jirka), Jhon Mosquera, Lukás Kalvach, Pavel Bucha, Tomás Chorý (86.René Dedic). Trainer: Michal Bílek.
Qarabağ FK: Sahrudin Mahammadaliyev, Marko Vesovic, Qara Qarayev, Badavi Hüseynov, Bahlul Mustafazade, Richard Almeida (54.Marko Jankovic), Filip Ozobic (70.Ramil Sheydaev), Abdellah Zoubir, Kady, Tural Bayramov, Ibrahima Wadji (81.Owusu Kwabena). Trainer: Qurban Qurbanov.
Goals: 38' Filip Ozobic 0-1, 58' Jan Kopic 1-1, 73' Jan Kliment 2-1.

23.08.2022; Stadion „Rajko Mitić", Beograd; Attendance: 47,731
Referee: Anthony Taylor (England)
**FK Crvena Zvezda Beograd – MACCABI HAIFA FC 2-2(2-1)**
Crvena Zvezda Beograd: Milan Borjan, Aleksandar Dragovic, Nemanja Milunovic, Milan Rodic (84.Sékou Sanogo), Strahinja Erakovic, Aleksandar Katai, Slavoljub Srnic, Guélor Kanga (53.Kings Kangwa), Mirko Ivanic, Aleksandar Pesic (78.Milan Pavkov), Osman Bukari (84.Ibrahim Mustapha). Trainer: Dejan Stankovic.
Maccabi Haifa: Josh Cohen, Daniel Sundgren, Bogdan Planic, Shon Goldberg, Pierre Cornud, Tjaronn Chery (90+3.Rami Gershon), Ali Muhammad, Neta Lavi, Dolev Haziza, Din David (72.Omer Atzili), Frantzdy Pierrot. Trainer: Barak Bakhar.
Goals: 27' Aleksandar Pesic 1-0, 43' Mirko Ivanic 2-0, 45+5' Daniel Sundgren 2-1, 90' Milan Pavkov 2-2 (own goal).

---

## LEAGUE PATH

16.08.2022; Ibrox Stadium, Glasgow; Attendance: 49,097
Referee: Daniele Orsato (Italy)
**Rangers FC Glasgow – PSV Eindhoven 2-2(1-1)**
Rangers FC: Jon McLaughlin, James Tavernier, Connor Goldson, Borna Barisic, Steven Davis (71.Glen Kamara), John Lundstram, James Sands, Tom Lawrence, Antonio Colak, Ryan Kent, Malik Tillman (71.Scott Wright). Trainer: Giovanni van Bronckhorst (Netherlands).
PSV Eindhoven: Walter Benítez, André Ramalho, Philipp Max, Armando Obispo (79.Jarrad Branthwaite), Jordan Teze, Érick Gutiérrez, Ibrahim Sangaré, Joey Veerman, Luuk de Jong, Cody Gakpo, Ismael Saibari. Trainer: Ruud van Nistelrooij.
Goals: 37' Ibrahim Sangaré 0-1, 40' Antonio Colak 1-1, 70' Tom Lawrence 2-1, 78' Armando Obispo 2-2.

17.08.2022; Stadion Miejski, Lódz (Poland); Attendance: 16,450
Referee: Felix Zwayer (Germany)
**FK Dinamo Kyiv – Sport Lisboa e Benfica 0-2(0-2)**
Dinamo Kyiv: Georgiy Bushchan, Tomasz Kedziora, Vladyslav Dubinchak (63.Kostiantyn Vivcharenko), Denys Popov (80.Oleksandr Syrota), Ilya Zabarnyi, Vitaliy Buyalskyi, Oleksandr Andriyevskyi, Viktor Tsygankov (64.Oleksandr Karavayev), Mykola Shaparenko, Volodymyr Shepelyev (73.Anton Tsarenko), Artem Besedin (74.Vladyslav Vanat). Trainer: Mircea Lucescu (Romania).
Benfica: Odisseas Vlachodimos, Nicolás Otamendi, Gilberto (69.Alexander Bah), Álex Grimaldo, Morato, João Mário, Rafa Silva (84.Chiquinho), Florentino Luís, Enzo Fernández, David Neres (63.Henrique Araújo), Gonçalo Ramos (63.Roman Yaremchuk). Trainer: Roger Schmidt (Germany).
Goals: 9' Gilberto 0-1, 37' Gonçalo Ramos 0-2.

24.08.2022; Philips Stadion, Eindhoven; Attendance: 34,893
Referee: Szymon Marciniak (Poland)
**PSV Eindhoven – RANGERS FC GLASGOW 0-1(0-0)**
PSV Eindhoven: Walter Benítez, André Ramalho (62.Phillipp Mwene), Philipp Max (85.Marco van Ginkel), Armando Obispo, Jordan Teze, Érick Gutiérrez (62.Guus Til), Ibrahim Sangaré, Joey Veerman, Luuk de Jong (46.Xavi Simons), Cody Gakpo, Ismael Saibari (76.Carlos Vinícius). Trainer: Ruud van Nistelrooij.
Rangers FC: Jon McLaughlin, James Tavernier, Connor Goldson, Borna Barisic, John Lundstram, Glen Kamara (73.Scott Arfield), James Sands, Tom Lawrence (73.Scott Wright), Antonio Colak (90+2.Fashion Sakala), Ryan Kent, Malik Tillman. Trainer: Giovanni van Bronckhorst (Netherlands).
Goal: 60' Antonio Colak 0-1.

23.08.2022; Estádio do Sport Lisboa e Benfica, Lisboa; Attendance: 58,705; Referee: Clément Turpin (France)
**SPORT LISBOA E BENFICA – FK Dinamo Kyiv 3-0(3-0)**
Benfica: Odisseas Vlachodimos, Nicolás Otamendi, Gilberto, Álex Grimaldo, Morato, João Mário, Rafa Silva (70.Henrique Araújo), Florentino Luís (70.Julian Weigl), Enzo Fernández (90.Paulo Bernardo), David Neres (70.Diogo Gonçalves), Gonçalo Ramos (52.Petar Musa). Trainer: Roger Schmidt (Germany).
Dinamo Kyiv: Georgiy Bushchan, Tomasz Kedziora, Oleksandr Karavayev (87.Oleksandr Tymchyk), Oleksandr Syrota, Kostiantyn Vivcharenko (63.Vladyslav Dubinchak), Ilya Zabarnyi, Sergiy Sydorchuk, Vitaliy Buyalskyi (90+3.Oleksandr Yatsyk), Mykola Shaparenko, Volodymyr Shepelyev (87.Anton Tsarenko), Artem Besedin (63.Vladyslav Vanat). Trainer: Mircea Lucescu (Romania).
Goals: 27' Nicolás Otamendi 1-0, 40' Rafa Silva 2-0, 42' David Neres 3-0.

Please note: Winners and runners-up of each group were qualified for the Round of 16. Teams ranked third were transferred to the UEFA Europa League Knockout Round Play-offs.

| GROUP A | | | | | | | | |
|---|---|---|---|---|---|---|---|---|
| 1. **SSC Napoli** | 6 | 5 | 0 | 1 | 20 | - | 6 | 15 |
| 2. **Liverpool FC** | 6 | 5 | 0 | 1 | 17 | - | 6 | 15 |
| 3. *AFC Ajax Amsterdam* | 6 | 2 | 0 | 4 | 11 | - | 15 | 6 |
| 4. Rangers FC Glasgow | 6 | 0 | 0 | 6 | 2 | - | 22 | 0 |

07.09.2022; „Johan Cruijff" ArenA, Amsterdam; Attendance: 52,862
Referee: Tobias Stieler (Germany)
**AFC Ajax Amsterdam – Rangers FC Glasgow 4-0(3-0)**
AFC Ajax: Remko Pasveer, Daley Blind (81.Youri Baas), Calvin Bassey, Jurriën Timber, Devyne Rensch, Edson Álvarez (88.Jorge Sánchez), Kenneth Taylor, Mohammed Kudus (89.Brian Brobbey), Dusan Tadic, Steven Berghuis (81.Davy Klaassen), Steven Bergwijn (81.Lucas Ocampos). Trainer: Alfred Schreuder.
Rangers FC: Jon McLaughlin, James Tavernier (46.Leon King), Connor Goldson, Borna Barisic, John Lundstram, Glen Kamara (78.Steven Davis), Scott Wright (46.Rabbi Matondo), James Sands, Antonio Colak, Ryan Kent, Malik Tillman (46.Ryan Jack). Trainer: Giovanni van Bronckhorst (Netherlands).
Goals: 17' Edson Álvarez 1-0, 32' Steven Berghuis 2-0, 33' Mohammed Kudus 3-0, 80' Steven Bergwijn 4-0.

13.09.2022; Anfield Road, Liverpool; Attendance: 52,387
Referee: Artur Manuel Ribeiro Soares Dias (Portugal)
**Liverpool FC – AFC Ajax Amsterdam 2-1(1-1)**
Liverpool FC: Alisson, Joel Matip, Virgil van Dijk, Kostas Tsimikas, Trent Alexander-Arnold, Thiago Alcântara (90+4.Stefan Bajcatic), Fabinho, Harvey Elliott (66.Roberto Firmino), Mohamed Salah, Diogo Jota (66.Darwin Núñez), Luis Díaz (90+2.James Milner). Trainer: Jürgen Klopp (Germany).
AFC Ajax: Remko Pasveer, Daley Blind, Calvin Bassey, Jurriën Timber, Devyne Rensch (68.Jorge Sánchez), Edson Álvarez, Kenneth Taylor (80.Florian Grillitsch), Mohammed Kudus (86.Brian Brobbey), Dusan Tadic, Steven Berghuis, Steven Bergwijn. Trainer: Alfred Schreuder.
Goals: 17' Mohamed Salah 1-0, 27' Mohammed Kudus 1-1, 89' Joel Matip 2-1.

04.10.2022; Anfield Road, Liverpool; Attendance: 49,512
Referee: Clément Turpin (France)
**Liverpool FC – Rangers FC Glasgow 2-0(1-0)**
Liverpool FC: Alisson, Joel Matip, Virgil van Dijk, Kostas Tsimikas, Trent Alexander-Arnold (90+3.Joe Gomez), Jordan Henderson (70.Fabinho), Thiago Alcântara (81.James Milner), Mohamed Salah, Diogo Jota (69.Roberto Firmino), Luis Díaz, Darwin Núñez (80.Harvey Elliott). Trainer: Jürgen Klopp (Germany).
Rangers FC: Allan McGregor, James Tavernier, Connor Goldson, Ben Davies (81.Glen Kamara), Borna Barisic, Leon King, Steven Davis (66.Ryan Jack), John Lundstram, Alfredo Morelos (73.Antonio Colak), Ryan Kent (81.Rabbi Matondo), Malik Tillman (66.Fashion Sakala). Trainer: Giovanni van Bronckhorst (Netherlands).
Goals: 7' Trent Alexander-Arnold 1-0, 53' Mohamed Salah 2-0 (penalty).

12.10.2022; Stadio „Diego Armando Maradona", Napoli; Attendance: 52,229; Referee: Felix Zwayer (Germany)
**SSC Napoli – AFC Ajax Amsterdam 4-2(2-0)**
SSC Napoli: Alex Meret, Juan Jesus, Giovanni Di Lorenzo, Mathías Olivera, Kim Min-Jae, Piotr Zielinski (89.Gianluca Gaetano), Stanislav Lobotka, Frank Zambo Anguissa (49.Tanguy Ndombèlé), Hirving Lozano (77.Matteo Politano), Khvicha Kvaratskhelia (77.Eljif Elmas), Giacomo Raspadori (50.Victor Osimhen). Trainer: Luciano Spalletti.
AFC Ajax: Remko Pasveer, Daley Blind, Jorge Sánchez (65.Youri Baas), Calvin Bassey, Jurriën Timber, Davy Klaassen, Edson Álvarez, Kenneth Taylor (64.Florian Grillitsch), Mohammed Kudus (65.Brian Brobbey), Steven Berghuis (84.Francisco Conceição), Steven Bergwijn (84.Lucas Ocampos). Trainer: Alfred Schreuder.
Goals: 4' Hirving Lozano 1-0, 16' Giacomo Raspadori 2-0, 49' Dany Klaassen 2-1, 62' Khvicha Kvaratskhelia 3-1 (penalty), 83' Steven Bergwijn 3-2 (penalty), 89' Victor Osimhen 4-2.

07.09.2022; Stadio „Diego Armando Maradona", Napoli; Attendance: 51,793; Referee: Carlos del Cerro Grande (Spain)
**SSC Napoli – Liverpool FC 4-1(3-0)**
SSC Napoli: Alex Meret, Giovanni Di Lorenzo, Amir Rrahmani, Mathías Olivera (74.Mário Rui), Kim Min-Jae, Piotr Zielinski (74.Eljif Elmas), Stanislav Lobotka, Frank Zambo Anguissa, Matteo Politano (58.Hirving Lozano), Victor Osimhen (41.Giovanni Simeone), Khvicha Kvaratskhelia (57.Alessio Zerbin). Trainer: Luciano Spalletti.
Liverpool FC: Alisson, Virgil van Dijk, Andy Robertson, Joe Gomez (46.Joe Matip), Trent Alexander-Arnold, James Milner (62.Thiago Alcântara), Fabinho, Harvey Elliott (77.Arthur), Roberto Firmino (62.Darwin Núñez), Mohamed Salah (62.Diogo Jota), Luis Díaz. Trainer: Jürgen Klopp (Germany).
Goals: 5' Piotr Zielinski 1-0 (penalty), 31' Frank Zambo Anguissa 2-0, 44' Giovanni Simeone 3-0, 47' Piotr Zielinski 4-0, 49' Luis Díaz 4-1.

14.09.2022; Ibrox Stadium, Glasgow; Attendance: 50,121
Referee: Antonio Miguel Mateu Lahoz (Spain)
**Rangers FC Glasgow – SSC Napoli 0-3(0-0)**
Rangers FC: Allan McGregor, James Tavernier (82.Glen Kamara), Connor Goldson, Borna Barisic, Steven Davis (82.Malik Tillman), Scott Arfield (72.Rabbi Matondo), Ryan Jack (63.Leon King), John Lundstram, James Sands [*sent off 55*], Alfredo Morelos (72.Antonio Colak), Ryan Kent. Trainer: Giovanni van Bronckhorst (Netherlands).
SSC Napoli: Alex Meret, Mário Rui (77.Mathías Olivera), Giovanni Di Lorenzo, Amir Rrahmani, Kim Min-Jae, Piotr Zielinski (83.Tanguy Ndombèlé), Stanislav Lobotka, Frank Zambo Anguissa, Matteo Politano (77.Alessio Zerbin), Giovanni Simeone (77.Giacomo Raspadori), Khvicha Kvaratskhelia (90.Eljif Elmas). Trainer: Luciano Spalletti.
Goals: 68' Matteo Politano 0-1 (penalty), 85' Giacomo Raspadori 0-2, 90+1' Tanguy Ndombèlé 0-3.

04.10.2022; „Johan Cruijff" ArenA, Amsterdam; Attendance: 52,896
Referee: François Letexier (France)
**AFC Ajax Amsterdam – SSC Napoli 1-6(1-3)**
AFC Ajax: Remko Pasveer, Daley Blind, Calvin Bassey, Jurriën Timber (80.Florian Grillitsch), Devyne Rensch (84.Youri Baas), Edson Álvarez, Kenneth Taylor (72.Davy Klaassen), Mohammed Kudus, Dusan Tadic [*sent off 73*], Steven Berghuis (72.Brian Brobbey), Steven Bergwijn. Trainer: Alfred Schreuder.
SSC Napoli: Alex Meret, Giovanni Di Lorenzo (84.Alessandro Zanoli), Amir Rrahmani, Mathías Olivera, Kim Min-Jae, Piotr Zielinski (46.Tanguy Ndombèlé), Stanislav Lobotka (80.Gianluca Gaetano), Frank Zambo Anguissa, Hirving Lozano, Khvicha Kvaratskhelia (64.Eljif Elmas), Giacomo Raspadori (64.Giovanni Simeone). Trainer: Luciano Spalletti.
Goals: 9' Mohammed Kudus 1-0, 18' Giacomo Raspadori 1-1, 33' Giovanni Di Lorenzo 1-2, 45' Piotr Zielinski 1-3, 47' Giacomo Raspadori 1-4, 63' Khvicha Kvaratskhelia 1-5, 81' Giovanni Simeone 1-6.

12.10.2022; Ibrox Stadium, Glasgow; Attendance: 48,820
Referee: Slavko Vinčić (Slovenia)
**Rangers FC Glasgow – Liverpool FC 1-7(1-1)**
Rangers FC: Allan McGregor, James Tavernier, Connor Goldson (45.Leon King), Ben Davies, Borna Barisic, Scott Arfield, Ryan Jack (60.Steven Davis), John Lundstram, Antonio Colak (76.Alfredo Morelos), Ryan Kent (76.Scott Wright), Fashion Sakala (76.Rabbi Matondo). Trainer: Giovanni van Bronckhorst (Netherlands).
Liverpool FC: Alisson, Virgil van Dijk, Joe Gomez, Kostas Tsimikas (67.Andy Robertson), Ibrahima Konaté (79.James Milner), Jordan Henderson (67.Thiago Alcântara), Fabinho, Fábio Carvalho, Harvey Elliott, Roberto Firmino (73.Diogo Jota), Darwin Núñez (68.Mohamed Salah). Trainer: Jürgen Klopp (Germany).
Goals: 17' Scott Arfield 1-0, 24', 55' Roberto Firmino 1-1, 1-2, 66' Darwin Núñez 1-3, 76', 80', 81' Mohamed Salah 1-4, 1-5, 1-6, 87' Harvey Elliott 1-7.

26.10.2022; Stadio „Diego Armando Maradona", Napoli; Attendance: 39,835; Referee: Halil Umut Meler (Turkey)
**SSC Napoli – Rangers FC Glasgow 3-0(2-0)**
SSC Napoli: Alex Meret, Mário Rui, Giovanni Di Lorenzo (86.Alessandro Zanoli), Leo Østigård, Kim Min-Jae, Stanislav Lobotka (83.Piotr Zielinski), Tanguy Ndombèlé, Eljif Elmas (73.Gianluca Gaetano), Matteo Politano (73.Hirving Lozano), Giovanni Simeone, Giacomo Raspadori (83.Alessio Zerbin). Trainer: Luciano Spalletti.
Rangers FC: Allan McGregor, James Tavernier, Ben Davies, Ridvan Yilmaz, Leon King (76.Borna Barisic), John Lundstram, Scott Wright (46.Fashion Sakala), James Sands, Alfredo Morelos (68.Antonio Colak), Ryan Kent, Malik Tillman (67.Scott Arfield). Trainer: Giovanni van Bronckhorst (Netherlands).
Goals: 11', 16' Giovanni Simeone 1-0, 2-0, 80' Leo Østigård 3-0.

01.11.2022; Anfield Road, Liverpool; Attendance: 52,077
Referee: Tobias Stieler (Germany)
**Liverpool FC – SSC Napoli 2-0(0-0)**
Liverpool FC: Alisson, Virgil van Dijk, Kostas Tsimikas, Trent Alexander-Arnold (87.Calvin Ramsay), Ibrahima Konaté, James Milner (48.Harvey Elliott), Thiago Alcântara (87.Stefan Bajcetic), Fabinho, Curtis Jones (73.Darwin Núñez), Roberto Firmino (87.Fábio Carvalho), Mohamed Salah. Trainer: Jürgen Klopp (Germany).
SSC Napoli: Alex Meret, Giovanni Di Lorenzo, Mathías Olivera, Leo Østigård, Kim Min-Jae, Stanislav Lobotka (83.Piotr Zielinski), Tanguy Ndombèlé (87.Giacomo Raspadori), Frank Zambo Anguissa, Matteo Politano (70.Hirving Lozano), Victor Osimhen (87.Giovanni Simeone), Khvicha Kvaratskhelia (83.Eljif Elmas). Trainer: Luciano Spalletti.
Goals: 85' Mohamed Salah 1-0, 90+8' Darwin Núñez 2-0.

26.10.2022; „Johan Cruijff" ArenA, Amsterdam; Attendance: 53,327
Referee: José María Sánchez Martínez (Spain)
**AFC Ajax Amsterdam – Liverpool FC 0-3(0-1)**
AFC Ajax: Remko Pasveer, Daley Blind (58.Owen Wijndal), Jorge Sánchez, Calvin Bassey, Jurriën Timber, Davy Klaassen (58.Mohammed Kudus), Edson Álvarez (85.Florian Grillitsch), Dusan Tadic, Steven Berghuis (85.Francisco Conceição), Steven Bergwijn, Brian Brobbey (63.Kenneth Taylor). Trainer: Alfred Schreuder.
Liverpool FC: Alisson, Virgil van Dijk, Andy Robertson (87.Kostas Tsimikas), Joe Gomez, Trent Alexander-Arnold, Jordan Henderson (70.James Milner), Fabinho (71.Stefan Bajcetic), Harvey Elliott (71.Fábio Carvalho), Roberto Firmino, Mohamed Salah, Darwin Núñez (63.Curtis Jones). Trainer: Jürgen Klopp (Germany).
Goals: 42' Mohamed Salah 0-1, 49' Darwin Núñez 0-2, 52' Harvey Elliott 0-3.

01.11.2022; Ibrox Stadium, Glasgow; Attendance: 48,817
Referee: Glenn Nyberg (Sweden)
**Rangers FC Glasgow – AFC Ajax Amsterdam 1-3(0-2)**
Rangers FC: Allan McGregor, James Tavernier, Borna Barisic, Leon King, Steven Davis (60.Glen Kamara), Scott Arfield (83.Alex Lowry), James Sands, Antonio Colak (60.Alfredo Morelos), Ryan Kent (83.Rabbi Matondo), Fashion Sakala, Malik Tillman (60.Scott Wright). Trainer: Giovanni van Bronckhorst (Netherlands).
AFC Ajax: Remko Pasveer, Jorge Sánchez, Owen Wijndal (44.Devyne Rensch), Calvin Bassey, Jurriën Timber, Edson Álvarez, Kenneth Taylor (87.Florian Grillitsch), Mohammed Kudus, Dusan Tadic, Steven Berghuis (55.Davy Klaassen), Steven Bergwijn (88.Francisco Conceição). Trainer: Alfred Schreuder.
Goals: 4' Steven Berghuis 0-1, 29' Mohammed Kudus 0-2, 87' James Tavernier 1-2 (penalty), 89' Francisco Conceição 1-3.

| | | | | | | | |
|---|---|---|---|---|---|---|---|
| 1. **FC Porto** | 6 | 4 | 0 | 2 | 12 - 7 | 12 |
| 2. **Club Brugge KV** | 6 | 3 | 2 | 1 | 7 - 4 | 11 |
| 3. *Bayer 04 Leverkusen* | 6 | 1 | 2 | 3 | 4 - 8 | 5 |
| 4. Club Atlético de Madrid | 6 | 1 | 2 | 3 | 5 - 9 | 5 |

**GROUP B**

07.09.2022; Estádio Cívitas Metropolitano, Madrid; Attendance: 51,777
Referee: Szymon Marciniak (Poland)
**Club Atlético de Madrid – FC Porto 2-1(0-0)**
Atlético Madrid: Jan Oblak, José Giménez, Reinildo, Nahuel Molina (46.Rodrigo de Paul), Axel Witsel, Saúl (61.Antoine Griezmann), Koke, Yannick Carrasco (46.Thomas Lemar), Marcos Llorente, Álvaro Morata (68.Mario Hermoso), João Félix (71.Ángel Correa). Trainer: Diego Pablo Simeone (Argentina).
FC Porto: Diogo Costa, Pepe, Zaidu Sanusi, David Carmo, Mateus Uribe, Otávio (77.Bruno Costa), Stephen Eustáquio, Mehdi Taremi [*sent off 81*], Galeno (88.Gabriel Veron), Pepê Aquino (62.João Mário), Evanilson (78.Toni Martínez). Trainer: Sérgio Paulo Marceneiro da Conceição.
Goals: 90+2' Mario Hermoso 1-0, 90+6' Mateus Uribe 1-1 (penalty), 90+11' Antoine Griezmann 2-1.

13.09.2022; Estádio do Dragão, Porto; Attendance: 39,225
Referee: Anastasios Sidiropoulos (Greece)
**FC Porto – Club Brugge KV 0-4(0-1)**
FC Porto: Diogo Costa, Pepe, Zaidu Sanusi (76.Wendell), João Mário (46.Daniel Namaso Loader), David Carmo, Mateus Uribe, Otávio (61.Gonçalo Borges), Stephen Eustáquio, Galeno (61.Gabriel Veron), Pepê Aquino, Evanilson (46.Toni Martínez). Trainer: Sérgio Paulo Marceneiro da Conceição.
Club Brugge: Simon Mignolet, Denis Odoi, Brandon Mechele, Bjorn Meijer (75.Eduard Sobol), Abakar Sylla (65.Dedryck Boyata), Hans Vanaken, Casper Nielsen, Raphael Onyedika, Andreas Skov Olsen (71.Roman Yaremchuk), Kamal Sowah, Ferrán Jutglà (75.Antonio Nusa). Trainer: Carl Hoefkens.
Goals: 15' Ferrán Jutglà 0-1 (penalty), 47' Kamal Sowah 0-2, 52' Andreas Skov Olsen 0-3, 89' Antonio Nusa 0-4.

07.09.2022; Jan Breydelstadion, Brugge; Attendance: 21,235
Referee: Irfan Peljto (Bosnia and Herzegovina)
**Club Brugge KV – Bayer 04 Leverkusen 1-0(1-0)**
Club Brugge: Simon Mignolet, Denis Odoi, Brandon Mechele, Bjorn Meijer, Abakar Sylla, Hans Vanaken, Casper Nielsen, Raphael Onyedika (83.Éder Balanta), Andreas Skov Olsen (83.Cisse Sandra), Kamal Sowah (89.Eduard Sobol), Ferrán Jutglà (64.Roman Yaremchuk). Trainer: Carl Hoefkens.
Bayer Leverkusen: Lukás Hrádecký, Jonathan Tah, Jeremie Frimpong (86.Sardar Azmoun), Mitchel Bakker (67.Adam Hlozek), Odilon Kossounou, Piero Hincapié, Charles Aránguiz (46.Exequiel Palacios), Robert Andrich (67.Kerem Demirbay), Callum Hudson-Odoi (86.Nadiem Amiri), Patrik Schick, Moussa Diaby. Trainer: Gerardo Seoane Castro (Switzerland).
Goal: 42' Abakar Sylla 1-0.

13.09.2022; BayArena, Leverkusen; Attendance: 25,825
Referee: Michael Oliver (England)
**Bayer 04 Leverkusen – Club Atlético de Madrid 2-0(0-0)**
Bayer Leverkusen: Lukás Hrádecký, Jonathan Tah, Edmond Tapsoba (89.Mitchel Bakker), Odilon Kossounou, Piero Hincapié, Kerem Demirbay, Robert Andrich, Callum Hudson-Odoi (90+1.Nadiem Amiri), Patrik Schick (89.Charles Aránguiz), Moussa Diaby (89.Sardar Azmoun), Adam Hlozek (69.Jeremie Frimpong). Trainer: Gerardo Seoane Castro (Switzerland).
Atlético Madrid: Ivo Grbic, Felipe Monteiro, Reinildo (62.Yannick Carrasco), Mario Hermoso, Nahuel Molina (63.Antoine Griezmann), Axel Witsel, Saúl (46.Rodrigo de Paul), Koke, Marcos Llorente, Álvaro Morata (73.Matheus Cunha), João Félix (73.Ángel Correa). Trainer: Diego Pablo Simeone (Argentina).
Goals: 84' Robert Andrich 1-0, 87' Moussa Diaby 2-0.

04.10.2022; Estádio do Dragão, Porto; Attendance: 42,399
Referee: Anthony Taylor (England)
**FC Porto – Bayer 04 Leverkusen 2-0(0-0)**
FC Porto: Diogo Costa, Pepe, Wendell (63.Zaidu Sanusi), João Mário (63.Galeno), David Carmo, Mateus Uribe (83.Marko Grujic), Bruno Costa (46.Otávio), Stephen Eustáquio, Mehdi Taremi, Pepê Aquino, Evanilson (71.Toni Martínez). Trainer: Sérgio Paulo Marceneiro da Conceição.
Bayer Leverkusen: Lukás Hrádecký, Jonathan Tah, Jeremie Frimpong [*sent off 88*], Edmond Tapsoba, Piero Hincapié, Charles Aránguiz (79.Nadiem Amiri), Robert Andrich (72.Kerem Demirbay), Callum Hudson-Odoi (86.Timothy Fosu-Mensah), Patrik Schick, Moussa Diaby, Adam Hlozek (72.Amine Adli). Trainer: Gerardo Seoane Castro (Switzerland).
Goals: 69' Zaidu Sanusi 1-0, 87' Galeno 2-0.

12.10.2022; Estádio Cívitas Metropolitano, Madrid; Attendance: 60,810
Referee: Danny Desmond Makkelie (Netherlands)
**Club Atlético de Madrid – Club Brugge KV 0-0**
Atlético Madrid: Jan Oblak, Stefan Savic, José Giménez, Reinildo, Nahuel Molina, Saúl (73.Matheus Cunha), Geoffrey Kondogbia, Koke (60.Rodrigo de Paul), Thomas Lemar (60.Álvaro Morata), Antoine Griezmann (79.Axel Witsel), Ángel Correa (60.Yannick Carrasco). Trainer: Diego Pablo Simeone (Argentina).
Club Brugge: Simon Mignolet, Denis Odoi, Brandon Mechele, Abakar Sylla, Hans Vanaken, Casper Nielsen, Raphael Onyedika, Andreas Skov Olsen (50.Bjorn Meijer), Tajon Buchanan (83.Clinton Mata), Kamal Sowah [*sent off 82*], Ferrán Jutglà (73.Éder Balanta). Trainer: Carl Hoefkens.

26.10.2022; Jan Breydelstadion, Brugge; Attendance: 26,144
Referee: Michael Oliver (England)
**Club Brugge KV – FC Porto 0-4(0-1)**
Club Brugge: Simon Mignolet, Denis Odoi (71.Bjorn Meijer), Brandon Mechele, Abakar Sylla (71.Dedryck Boyata), Hans Vanaken, Casper Nielsen (80.Lynnt Audoor), Noa Lang, Raphael Onyedika (81.Éder Balanta), Andreas Skov Olsen (71.Antonio Nusa), Tajon Buchanan, Ferrán Jutglà. Trainer: Carl Hoefkens.
FC Porto: Diogo Costa, Fábio Cardoso, Zaidu Sanusi (76.Wendell), David Carmo, Mateus Uribe, Otávio, Stephen Eustáquio (77.Bruno Costa), Mehdi Taremi, Galeno (77.Gabriel Veron), Pepê Aquino (88.Toni Martínez), Evanilson (88.Rodrigo Conceição). Trainer: Sérgio Paulo Marceneiro da Conceição.
Goals: 33' Mehdi Taremi 0-1, 57' Evanilson 0-2, 60' Stephen Eustáquio 0-3, 70' Mehdi Taremi 0-4.

01.11.2022; Estádio do Dragão, Porto; Attendance: 47,546
Referee: Daniele Orsato (Italy)
**FC Porto – Club Atlético de Madrid 2-1(2-0)**
FC Porto: Diogo Costa, Iván Marcano, Fábio Cardoso, Zaidu Sanusi (53.Wendell), Otávio (89.Gonçalo Borges), Marko Grujic, Stephen Eustáquio, Mehdi Taremi, Galeno (89.Bernardo Folha), Pepê Aquino (89.Rodrigo Conceição), Evanilson (81.Toni Martínez). Trainer: Sérgio Paulo Marceneiro da Conceição.
Atlético Madrid: Jan Oblak, Stefan Savic, José Giménez, Reinildo, Nahuel Molina, Axel Witsel, Saúl (60.Yannick Carrasco), Rodrigo de Paul, Antoine Griezmann, Ángel Correa (85.Pablo Barrios), João Félix (61.Matheus Cunha). Trainer: Diego Pablo Simeone (Argentina).
Goals: 5' Mehdi Taremi 1-0, 24' Stephen Eustáquio 2-0, 90+5' Iván Marcano 2-1 (own goal).

04.10.2022; Jan Breydelstadion, Brugge; Attendance: 25,667
Referee: István Kovács (Romania)
**Club Brugge KV – Club Atlético de Madrid 2-0(1-0)**
Club Brugge: Simon Mignolet, Denis Odoi, Brandon Mechele, Bjorn Meijer (78.Eduard Sobol), Abakar Sylla (89.Jorne Spileers), Hans Vanaken, Casper Nielsen, Raphael Onyedika, Tajon Buchanan (79.Éder Balanta), Kamal Sowah, Ferrán Jutglà (86.Antonio Nusa). Trainer: Carl Hoefkens.
Atlético Madrid: Jan Oblak, Stefan Savic, José Giménez (46.Geoffrey Kondogbia), Reinildo, Nahuel Molina, Koke, Yannick Carrasco (80.João Félix), Marcos Llorente (33.Ángel Correa), Antoine Griezmann, Álvaro Morata (65.Matheus Cunha). Trainer: Diego Pablo Simeone (Argentina).
Goals: 36' Kamal Sowah 1-0, 62' Ferrán Jutglà 2-0.

12.10.2022; BayArena, Leverkusen; Attendance: 30,210
Referee: István Kovács (Romania)
**Bayer 04 Leverkusen – FC Porto 0-3(0-1)**
Bayer Leverkusen: Lukás Hrádecký, Jonathan Tah, Mitchel Bakker, Odilon Kossounou (69.Edmond Tapsoba), Piero Hincapié, Charles Aránguiz, Kerem Demirbay, Callum Hudson-Odoi (69.Adam Hlozek), Patrik Schick, Moussa Diaby (88.Timothy Fosu-Mensah), Amine Adli (57.Paulinho). Trainer: Xabier „Xabi" Alonso Olano (Spain).
FC Porto: Diogo Costa, Fábio Cardoso, Zaidu Sanusi, João Mário (46.Evanilson), David Carmo, Mateus Uribe (85.Bernardo Folha), Otávio, Stephen Eustáquio (90+2.Toni Martínez), Mehdi Taremi (90+2.Daniel Namaso Loader), Galeno (85.Gonçalo Borges), Pepê Aquino. Trainer: Sérgio Paulo Marceneiro da Conceição.
Goals: 6' Galeno 0-1, 53', 64' Mehdi Taremi 0-2 (penalty), 0-3 (penalty).

26.10.2022; Estádio Cívitas Metropolitano, Madrid; Attendance: 63,803
Referee: Clément Turpin (France)
**Club Atlético de Madrid – Bayer 04 Leverkusen 2-2(1-2)**
Atlético Madrid: Jan Oblak, José Giménez (87.João Félix), Reinildo, Mario Hermoso (46.Saúl), Nahuel Molina, Axel Witsel, Geoffrey Kondogbia, Yannick Carrasco, Antoine Griezmann, Álvaro Morata (61.Matheus Cunha), Ángel Correa (46.Rodrigo de Paul). Trainer: Diego Pablo Simeone (Argentina).
Bayer Leverkusen: Lukás Hrádecký, Jeremie Frimpong, Mitchel Bakker, Edmond Tapsoba (61.Jonathan Tah), Odilon Kossounou, Piero Hincapié, Robert Andrich, Nadiem Amiri, Callum Hudson-Odoi (60.Amine Adli), Moussa Diaby (76.Paulinho), Adam Hlozek (89.Timothy Fosu-Mensah). Trainer: Xabier „Xabi" Alonso Olano (Spain).
Goals: 9' Moussa Diaby 0-1, 22' Yannick Carrasco 1-1, 29' Callum Hudson-Odoi 1-2, 50 Rodrigo de Paul 2-2.

01.11.2022; BayArena, Leverkusen; Attendance: 30,210
Referee: Maurizio Mariani (Italy)
**Bayer 04 Leverkusen – Club Brugge KV 0-0**
Bayer Leverkusen: Lukás Hrádecký, Jonathan Tah, Jeremie Frimpong, Mitchel Bakker, Edmond Tapsoba, Odilon Kossounou, Robert Andrich, Exequiel Palacios (46.Kerem Demirbay), Callum Hudson-Odoi (76.Nadiem Amiri), Patrik Schick (89.Adam Hlozek), Moussa Diaby (76.Amine Adli). Trainer: Xabier „Xabi" Alonso Olano (Spain).
Club Brugge: Simon Mignolet, Dedryck Boyata, Eduard Sobol (79.Cyle Larin), Brandon Mechele, Bjorn Meijer, Hans Vanaken, Casper Nielsen, Noa Lang (67.Andreas Skov Olsen), Tajon Buchanan, Kamal Sowah, Ferrán Jutglà (87.Roman Yaremchuk). Trainer: Carl Hoefkens.

| | | | | | | | |
|---|---|---|---|---|---|---|---|
| **GROUP C** | 1. **FC Bayern München** | 6 | 6 | 0 | 0 | 18 - 2 | 18 |
| | 2. **FC Internazionale Milano** | 6 | 3 | 1 | 2 | 10 - 7 | 10 |
| | 3. *FC Barcelona* | 6 | 2 | 1 | 3 | 12 - 12 | 7 |
| | 4. FC Viktoria Plzeň | 6 | 0 | 0 | 6 | 5 - 24 | 0 |

07.09.2022; Estadio Camp Nou, Barcelona; Attendance: 77,411
Referee: Lawrence Visser (Belgium)
**FC Barcelona – FC Viktoria Plzeň 5-1(3-1)**
FC Barcelona: Marc-André ter Stegen, Jordi Alba, Sergi Roberto (46.Piqué), Andreas Christensen, Jules Koundé, Franck Kessié (81.Pablo Torre), Frenkie de Jong, Pedri (75.Gavi), Robert Lewandowski, Ousmane Dembélé (75.Memphis Depay), Ansu Fati (66.Ferrán Torres). Trainer: Xavier Hernández i Creus „Xavi".
Viktoria Plzeň: Jindrich Stanek, Lukás Hejda, Ludek Pernica, Milan Havel, Václav Jemelka (86.Libor Holík), Jan Sýkora (79.Václav Pilar), Jhon Mosquera (79.Erik Jirka), Adam Vlkanova (78.Ales Cermák), Lukás Kalvach, Pavel Bucha, Tomás Chorý (66.Fortune Bassey). Trainer: Michal Bílek.
Goals: 13' Franck Kessié 1-0, 34' Robert Lewandowski 2-0, 44' Jan Sýkora 2-1, 45+3', 67' Robert Lewandowski 3-1, 4-1, 71' Ferrán Torres 5-1).

13.09.2022; Doosan Aréna, Plzeň; Attendance: 11,252
Referee: Sandro Schärer (Switzerland)
**FC Viktoria Plzeň – FC Internazionale Milano 0-2(0-1)**
Viktoria Plzeň: Jindrich Stanek, Lukás Hejda, Ludek Pernica, Milan Havel (76.Libor Holík), Václav Jemelka, Jan Sýkora (71.Erik Jirka), Jhon Mosquera, Adam Vlkanova (84.Ales Cermák), Lukás Kalvach (76.Modou N'Diaye), Pavel Bucha [*sent off 61*], Tomás Chorý (71.Fortune Bassey). Trainer: Michal Bílek.
Internazionale Milano: André Onana, Francesco Acerbi, Milan Skriniar, Robin Gosens, Denzel Dumfries, Alessandro Bastoni (64.Danilo D'Ambrosio), Henrikh Mkhitaryan (72.Hakan Çalhanoglu), Marcelo Brozovic (84.Kristjan Asllani), Nicolò Barella (72.Roberto Gagliardini), Edin Dzeko, Joaquín Correa (72.Lautaro Martínez). Trainer: Simone Inzaghi.
Goals: 20' Edin Dzeko 0-1, 71' Denzel Dumfries 0-2.

04.10.2022; Allianz Arena, München; Attendance: 75,000
Referee: Nikola Dabanović (Montenegro)
**FC Bayern München – FC Viktoria Plzeň 5-0(3-0)**
Bayern München: Manuel Neuer, Noussair Mazraoui, Dayot Upamecano (72.Benjamin Pavard), Matthijs de Ligt, Alphonso Davies (46.Josip Stanisic), Leon Goretzka (73.Marcel Sabitzer), Ryan Gravenberch, Sadio Mané, Serge Gnabry, Leroy Sané (58.Mathys Tel), Jamal Musiala (46.Eric Maxim Choupo-Moting). Trainer: Julian Nagelsmann.
Viktoria Plzeň: Marián Tvrdon, Lukás Hejda (63.Mohamed Tijani), Ludek Pernica, Milan Havel, Libor Holík, Jan Kopic (58.Erik Jirka), Jhon Mosquera (86.Václav Pilar), Adam Vlkanova (46.Václav Jemelka), Lukás Kalvach, Modou N'Diaye, Tomás Chorý (58.Fortune Bassey). Trainer: Michal Bílek
Goals: 7' Leroy Sané 1-0, 13' Serge Gnabry 2-0, 21' Sadio Mané 3-0, 50' Leroy Sané 4-0, 59' Eric Maxim Choupo-Moting 5-0.

12.10.2022; Estadio Camp Nou, Barcelona; Attendance: 92,302
Referee: Szymon Marciniak (Poland)
**FC Barcelona – FC Internazionale Milano 3-3(1-0)**
FC Barcelona: Marc-André ter Stegen, Piqué, Sergi Roberto (72.Franck Kessié), Marcos Alonso (72.Álex Baldé), Eric García, Sergio Busquets (63.Frenkie de Jong), Pedri, Gavi (82.Ferrán Torres), Robert Lewandowski, Ousmane Dembélé, Raphinha (64.Ansu Fati). Trainer: Xavier Hernández i Creus „Xavi".
Internazionale Milano: André Onana, Stefan de Vrij, Milan Skriniar, Federico Dimarco (67.Matteo Darmian), Denzel Dumfries, Alessandro Bastoni (85.Francesco Acerbi), Henrikh Mkhitaryan, Hakan Çalhanoglu (76.Robin Gosens), Nicolò Barella (85.Kristjan Asllani), Edin Dzeko (76.Raoul Bellanova), Lautaro Martínez. Trainer: Simone Inzaghi.
Goals: 40' Ousmane Dembélé 1-0, 50' Nicolò Barella 1-1, 63' Lautaro Martínez 1-2, 82' Robert Lewandowski 2-2, 89' Robin Gosens 2-3, 90+2' Robert Lewandowski 3-3.

07.09.2022; Stadio „Giuseppe Meazza", Milano; Attendance: 58,951
Referee: Clément Turpin (France)
**FC Internazionale Milano – FC Bayern München 0-2(0-1)**
Internazionale Milano: André Onana, Danilo D'Ambrosio, Milan Skriniar (72.Stefan de Vrij), Robin Gosens, Denzel Dumfries (71.Matteo Darmian), Alessandro Bastoni (72.Federico Dimarco), Henrikh Mkhitaryan, Marcelo Brozovic, Hakan Çalhanoglu (81.Roberto Gagliardini), Edin Dzeko (71.Joaquín Correa), Lautaro Martínez. Trainer: Simone Inzaghi.
Bayern München: Manuel Neuer, Lucas Hernández (84.Josip Stanisic), Benjamin Pavard, Matthijs de Ligt (75.Dayot Upamecano), Alphonso Davies, Marcel Sabitzer (61.Leon Goretzka), Joshua Kimmich, Thomas Müller, Sadio Mané, Kingsley Coman (75.Serge Gnabry), Leroy Sané (84.Jamal Musiala). Trainer: Julian Nagelsmann.
Goals: 25' Leroy Sané 0-1, 66' Danilo D'Ambrosio 0-2 (own goal).

13.09.2022; Allianz Arena, München; Attendance: 75,000
Referee: Danny Desmond Makkelie (Netherlands)
**FC Bayern München – FC Barcelona 2-0(0-0)**
Bayern München: Manuel Neuer, Lucas Hernández, Benjamin Pavard (21.Noussair Mazraoui), Dayot Upamecano, Alphonso Davies, Marcel Sabitzer (46.Leon Goretzka), Joshua Kimmich, Thomas Müller, Sadio Mané (70.Serge Gnabry), Leroy Sané (79.Mathys Tel), Jamal Musiala (80.Ryan Gravenberch). Trainer: Julian Nagelsmann.
FC Barcelona: Marc-André ter Stegen, Marcos Alonso, Andreas Christensen (70.Eric García), Jules Koundé, Ronald Araújo, Sergio Busquets (80.Franck Kessié), Pedri, Gavi (61.Frenkie de Jong), Robert Lewandowski, Ousmane Dembélé (80.Ansu Fati), Raphinha (61.Ferrán Torres). Trainer: Xavier Hernández i Creus „Xavi".
Goals: 51' Lucas Hernández 1-0, 54' Leroy Sané 2-0.

04.10.2022; Stadio „Giuseppe Meazza", Milano; Attendance: 71,368
Referee: Slavko Vinčić (Slovenia)
**FC Internazionale Milano – FC Barcelona 1-0(1-0)**
Internazionale Milano: André Onana, Matteo Darmian (77.Robin Gosens), Stefan de Vrij (77.Francesco Acerbi), Milan Skriniar, Federico Dimarco (76.Denzel Dumfries), Alessandro Bastoni, Henrikh Mkhitaryan, Hakan Çalhanoglu (85.Kristjan Asllani), Nicolò Barella, Joaquín Correa (56.Edin Dzeko), Lautaro Martínez. Trainer: Simone Inzaghi.
FC Barcelona: Marc-André ter Stegen, Sergi Roberto, Marcos Alonso (64.Álex Baldé), Andreas Christensen (58.Piqué), Eric García, Sergio Busquets, Pedri, Gavi (83.Franck Kessié), Robert Lewandowski, Ousmane Dembélé, Raphinha (63.Ansu Fati). Trainer: Xavier Hernández i Creus „Xavi".
Goal: 45+2' Hakan Çalhanoglu 1-0.

12.10.2022; Doosan Aréna, Plzeň; Attendance: 11,326
Referee: Bartosz Frankowski (Poland)
**FC Viktoria Plzeň – FC Bayern München 2-4(0-4)**
Viktoria Plzeň: Jindrich Stanek, Lukás Hejda, Milan Havel (46.Libor Holík), Václav Jemelka (46.Ludek Pernica), Mohamed Tijani, Jan Kopic (25.Erik Jirka), Jhon Mosquera, Adam Vlkanova (81.Václav Pilar), Lukás Kalvach, Pavel Bucha, Tomás Chorý (46.Jan Kliment). Trainer: Michal Bílek.
Bayern München: Sven Ulreich, Benjamin Pavard, Noussair Mazraoui, Dayot Upamecano (70.Paul Wanner), Josip Stanisic, Leon Goretzka (56.Ryan Gravenberch), Joshua Kimmich, Thomas Müller (28.Mathys Tel), Sadio Mané, Kingsley Coman (46.Eric Maxim Choupo-Moting), Leroy Sané (70.Marcel Sabitzer). Trainer: Julian Nagelsmann.
Goals: 10' Sadio Mané 0-1, 14' Thomas Müller 0-2, 25', 35' Leon Goretzka 0-3, 0-4, 62' Adam Vlkanova 1-4, 75' Jan Kliment 2-4.

26.10.2022; Stadio „Giuseppe Meazza", Milano; Attendance: 71,849
Referee: Andreas Ekberg (Sweden)
**FC Internazionale Milano – FC Viktoria Plzeň 4-0(2-0)**
Internazionale Milano: André Onana, Francesco Acerbi, Milan Skriniar, Federico Dimarco (77.Robin Gosens), Denzel Dumfries, Alessandro Bastoni, Henrikh Mkhitaryan (83.Roberto Gagliardini), Hakan Çalhanoglu (71.Kristjan Asllani), Nicolò Barella, Edin Dzeko (71.Joaquín Correa), Lautaro Martínez (83.Romelu Lukaku). Trainer: Simone Inzaghi.
Viktoria Plzeň: Jindrich Stanek, Lukás Hejda, Ludek Pernica, Milan Havel, Mohamed Tijani (51.Václav Jemelka), Jhon Mosquera, Adam Vlkanova (84.Václav Pilar), Lukás Kalvach (70.Modou N'Diaye), Erik Jirka (46.Libor Holík), Pavel Bucha, Fortune Bassey (46.Tomás Chorý). Trainer: Michal Bílek.
Goals: 35' Henrikh Mkhitaryan 1-0, 42', 66' Edin Dzeko 2-0, 3-0, 87' Romelu Lukaku 4-0.

01.11.2022; Allianz Arena, München; Attendance: 75,000
Referee: Ivan Kružliak (Slovakia)
**FC Bayern München – FC Internazionale Milano 2-0(1-0)**
Bayern München: Sven Ulreich, Benjamin Pavard, Noussair Mazraoui (65.Jamal Musiala), Dayot Upamecano (46.Alphonso Davies), Josip Stanisic, Marcel Sabitzer, Joshua Kimmich, Ryan Gravenberch, Eric Maxim Choupo-Moting (73.Mathys Tel), Sadio Mané (66.Serge Gnabry), Kingsley Coman (76.Paul Wanner). Trainer: Julian Nagelsmann.
Internazionale Milano: André Onana, Matteo Darmian, Stefan de Vrij (76.Milan Skriniar), Francesco Acerbi, Robin Gosens, Raoul Bellanova, Roberto Gagliardini (60.Hakan Çalhanoglu), Nicolò Barella (60.Henrikh Mkhitaryan), Kristjan Asllani, Joaquín Correa (76.Valentin Carboni), Lautaro Martínez (60.Edin Dzeko). Trainer: Simone Inzaghi.
Goals: 32' Benjamin Pavard 1-0, 72' Eric Maxim Choupo-Moting 2-0.

26.10.2022; Estadio Camp Nou, Barcelona; Attendance: 84,016
Referee: Anthony Taylor (England)
**FC Barcelona – FC Bayern München 0-3(0-2)**
FC Barcelona: Marc-André ter Stegen, Marcos Alonso, Héctor Bellerín, Jules Koundé (67.Eric García), Álex Baldé, Sergio Busquets (58.Ferrán Torres), Franck Kessié, Frenkie de Jong, Pedri (58.Raphinha), Robert Lewandowski (82.Pablo Torre), Ousmane Dembélé (68.Ansu Fati). Trainer: Xavier Hernández i Creus „Xavi".
Bayern München: Sven Ulreich, Noussair Mazraoui (79.Josip Stanisic), Dayot Upamecano (63.Benjamin Pavard), Matthijs de Ligt, Alphonso Davies (46.Marcel Sabitzer), Leon Goretzka, Joshua Kimmich, Eric Maxim Choupo-Moting (63.Thomas Müller), Sadio Mané, Serge Gnabry, Jamal Musiala (67.Ryan Gravenberch). Trainer: Julian Nagelsmann.
Goals: 10' Sadio Mané 0-1, 31' Eric Maxim Choupo-Moting 0-2, 90+5' Benjamin Pavard 0-3.

01.11.2022; Doosan Aréna, Plzeň; Attendance: 11,258
Referee: Radu Marian Petrescu (Romania)
**FC Viktoria Plzeň – FC Barcelona 2-4(0-2)**
Viktoria Plzeň: Jindrich Stanek, Lukás Hejda, Ludek Pernica, Libor Holík, Václav Jemelka (57.Milan Havel), Václav Pilar (88.Adam Kronus), Adam Vlkanova, Lukás Kalvach (78.Ales Cermák), Erik Jirka, Modou N'Diaye (57.Pavel Bucha), Tomás Chorý (79.Fortune Bassey). Trainer: Michal Bílek.
FC Barcelona: Iñaki Peña, Piqué, Jordi Alba (57.Álex Baldé), Marcos Alonso, Héctor Bellerín, Franck Kessié (67.Marc Casadó), Gavi, Pablo Torre (77.Álvaro Sanz), Ferrán Torres, Raphinha (78.Ousmane Dembélé), Ansu Fati. Trainer: Xavier Hernández i Creus „Xavi".
Goals: 6' Marcos Alonso 0-1, 44' Ferrán Torres 0-2, 51' Tomás Chorý 1-2 (penalty), 54' Ferrán Torres 1-3, 63' Tomás Chorý 2-3, 75' Pablo Torre 2-4.

| | GROUP D | | | | | | | | | |
|---|---|---|---|---|---|---|---|---|---|---|
| 1. | **Tottenham Hotspur FC London** | 6 | 3 | 2 | 1 | 8 | - | 6 | | 11 |
| 2. | **Eintracht Frankfurt** | 6 | 3 | 1 | 2 | 7 | - | 8 | | 10 |
| 3. | *Sporting Clube de Portugal Lisboa* | 6 | 2 | 1 | 3 | 8 | - | 9 | | 7 |
| 4. | Olympique de Marseille | 6 | 2 | 0 | 4 | 8 | - | 8 | | 6 |

07.09.2022; Deutsche Bank Park, Frankfurt am Main; Attendance: 50,500; Referee: Orel Grinfeld (Israel)
**Eintracht Frankfurt – Sporting Clube de Portugal Lisboa 0-3(0-0)**
Eintracht Frankfurt: Kevin Trapp, Christopher Lenz (46.Luca Pellegrini), Evan Ndicka, Tuta, Mario Götze, Djibril Sow, Daichi Kamada (84.Makoto Hasebe), Kristijan Jakic (83.Ansgar Knauff), Éric Dina-Ebimbe (66.Rafael Borré), Jesper Lindstrøm (74.Lucas Alario), Randal Kolo Muani. Trainer: Oliver Glasner (Austria).
Sporting: Antonio Adán, Sebastián Coates, Matheus Reis, Jerry St. Juste (52.Luís Carlos Neto), Pedro Porro, Gonçalo Inácio, Manuel Ugarte, Pedro Gonçalves "Pote" (79.Nuno Santos), Hidemasa Morita, Marcus Edwards (73.Rochinha), Trincão (79.Paulinho). Trainer: Rúben Filipe Marques Amorim.
Goals: 65' Marcus Edwards 0-1, 67' Trincão 0-2, 82' Nuno Santos 0-3.

13.09.2022; Estádio „José Alvalade", Lisboa; Attendance: 39,899
Referee: Srđan Jovanović (Serbia)
**Sporting Clube de Portugal Lisboa – Tottenham Hotspur FC London 2-0(0-0)**
Sporting: Antonio Adán, Sebastián Coates, Matheus Reis, Pedro Porro, Gonçalo Inácio, Nuno Santos (90+2.Ricardo Esgaio), Manuel Ugarte, Pedro Gonçalves "Pote", Hidemasa Morita (71.Sotirios Alexandropoulos), Marcus Edwards (90+2.Arthur Gomes), Trincão (76.Paulinho). Trainer: Rúben Filipe Marques Amorim.
Tottenham Hotspur: Hugo Lloris, Ben Davies, Eric Dier, Cristian Romero, Emerson Royal, Ivan Perisic, Pierre-Emile Højbjerg, Rodrigo Bentancur, Heung-Min Son (72.Dejan Kulusevski), Harry Kane, Richarlison. Trainer: Antonio Conte (Italy).
Goals: 90' Paulinho 1-0, 90+3' Arthur Gomes 2-0.

07.09.2022; Tottenham Hotspur Stadium, London; Attendance: 57,367
Referee: Slavko Vinčić (Slovenia)
**Tottenham Hotspur FC London – Olympique de Marseille 2-0(0-0)**
Tottenham Hotspur: Hugo Lloris, Clément Lenglet (73.Ben Davies), Eric Dier, Cristian Romero (73.Japhet Tanganga), Emerson Royal (61.Dejan Kulusevski), Ivan Perisic, Pierre-Emile Højbjerg, Rodrigo Bentancur (85.Yves Bissouma), Heung-Min Son (86.Matt Doherty), Harry Kane, Richarlison. Trainer: Antonio Conte (Italy).
Olympique Marseille: Pau López, Jonathan Clauss (70.Sead Kolasinac), Chancel Mbemba [*sent off 47*], Samuel Gigot (87.Cengiz Ünder), Eric Bailly, Nuno Tavares, Jordan Veretout (87.Pape Gueye), Valentin Rongier, Gerson (50.Leonardo Balerdi), Mattéo Guendouzi, Luis Suárez (71.Amine Harit). Trainer: Igor Tudor (Croatia).
Goals: 76', 81' Richarlison 1-0, 2-0.

13.09.2022; Stade Orange Vélodrome, Marseille; Attendance: 62,500
Referee: José María Sánchez Martínez (Spain)
**Olympique de Marseille – Eintracht Frankfurt 0-1(0-1)**
Olympique Marseille: Pau López, Jonathan Clauss, Sead Kolasinac (82.Issa Kaboré), Eric Bailly (65.Mattéo Guendouzi), Nuno Tavares, Leonardo Balerdi, Dimitri Payet (60.Cengiz Ünder), Jordan Veretout, Valentin Rongier, Gerson (59.Amine Harit), Alexis Sánchez (59.Luis Suárez). Trainer: Igor Tudor (Croatia).
Eintracht Frankfurt: Kevin Trapp, Makoto Hasebe, Evan Ndicka, Tuta, Mario Götze (71.Sebastian Rode), Djibril Sow, Daichi Kamada (88.Éric Dina-Ebimbe), Kristijan Jakic (79.Timothy Chandler), Jesper Lindstrøm (79.Rafael Borré), Randal Kolo Muani (88.Lucas Alario), Ansgar Knauff. Trainer: Oliver Glasner (Austria).
Goal: 43' Jesper Lindstrøm 0-1.

04.10.2022; Stade Orange Vélodrome, Marseille; Attendance: 618
Referee: Davide Massa (Italy)

**Olympique de Marseille–Sporting Clube de Portugal Lisboa 4-1(3-1)**
Olympique Marseille: Pau López, Jonathan Clauss (32.Issa Kaboré), Chancel Mbemba, Eric Bailly (77.Samuel Gigot), Nuno Tavares, Leonardo Balerdi, Jordan Veretout (62.Valentin Rongier), Amine Harit (77.Gerson), Mattéo Guendouzi, Alexis Sánchez, Cengiz Ünder (62.Pape Gueye). Trainer: Igor Tudor (Croatia).
Sporting: Antonio Adán [*sent off 23*], Ricardo Esgaio, Matheus Reis, Jerry St. Juste (46.José Martínez Marsà), Gonçalo Inácio, Nuno Santos (46.Paulinho), Manuel Ugarte (46.Flávio Nazinho), Pedro Gonçalves "Pote" (46.Sotirios Alexandropoulos), Hidemasa Morita, Marcus Edwards (26.Franco Israel *goalkeeper*), Trincão. Trainer: Rúben Filipe Marques Amorim.
Goals: 1' Trincão 0-1, 13' Alexis Sánchez 1-1, 16' Amine Harit 2-1, 28' Leonardo Balerdi 3-1, 84' Chancel Mbemba 4-1.

12.10.2022; Tottenham Hotspur Stadium, London; Attendance: 55,180
Referee: Carlos del Cerro Grande (Spain)

**Tottenham Hotspur FC London – Eintracht Frankfurt 3-2(3-1)**
Tottenham Hotspur: Hugo Lloris, Clément Lenglet, Eric Dier (78.Davinson Sánchez), Cristian Romero, Emerson Royal, Pierre-Emile Højbjerg (85.Bryan Gil), Rodrigo Bentancur (67.Yves Bissouma), Ryan Sessegnon, Heung-Min Son (86.Lucas Moura), Harry Kane, Richarlison (67.Oliver Skipp). Trainer: Antonio Conte (Italy).
Eintracht Frankfurt: Kevin Trapp, Makoto Hasebe (69.Éric Dina-Ebimbe), Christopher Lenz (70.Faride Alidou), Evan Ndicka, Tuta [*sent off 59*], Sebastian Rode (69.Hrvoje Smolcic), Djibril Sow, Daichi Kamada (78.Mario Götze), Kristijan Jakic, Jesper Lindstrøm, Randal Kolo Muani (69.Rafael Borré). Trainer: Oliver Glasner (Austria).
Goals: 14' Daichi Kamada 0-1, 19' Heung-Min Son 1-1, 28' Harry Kane 2-1 (penalty), 36' Heung-Min Son 3-1, 87' Faride Alidou 3-2.

26.10.2022; Tottenham Hotspur Stadium, London; Attendance: 59,588
Referee: Danny Desmond Makkelie (Netherlands)

**Tottenham Hotspur FC London – Sporting Clube de Portugal Lisboa 1-1(0-1)**
Tottenham Hotspur: Hugo Lloris, Matt Doherty (71.Bryan Gil), Ben Davies (81.Clément Lenglet), Eric Dier, Cristian Romero, Ivan Perisic, Pierre-Emile Højbjerg, Rodrigo Bentancur, Heung-Min Son, Lucas Moura (81.Emerson Royal), Harry Kane. Trainer: Antonio Conte (Italy).
Sporting: Antonio Adán, Sebastián Coates, Matheus Reis, Pedro Porro, Gonçalo Inácio, Nuno Santos (61.Flávio Nazinho), Manuel Ugarte, Hidemasa Morita (61.Mateus Fernandes), Paulinho (75.Jerry St. Juste), Marcus Edwards (71.Abdul Fatawu Issahaku), Trincão (71.Arthur Gomes). Trainer: Rúben Filipe Marques Amorim.
Goals: 22' Marcus Edwards 0-1, 80' Rodrigo Bentancur 1-1.

01.11.2022; Estádio „José Alvalade", Lisboa; Attendance: 41,744
Referee: Slavko Vinčić (Slovenia)

**Sporting Clube de Portugal Lisboa – Eintracht Frankfurt 1-2(1-0)**
Sporting: Antonio Adán, Sebastián Coates, Jerry St. Juste (78.Jovane Cabral), Pedro Porro, Gonçalo Inácio, Nuno Santos (32.Matheus Reis), Arthur Gomes, Manuel Ugarte (63.Dário Essugo), Pedro Gonçalves "Pote", Paulinho, Marcus Edwards (63.Trincão). Trainer: Rúben Filipe Marques Amorim.
Eintracht Frankfurt: Kevin Trapp, Luca Pellegrini, Evan Ndicka, Tuta, Mario Götze (90.Faride Alidou), Djibril Sow, Daichi Kamada, Kristijan Jakic (81.Hrvoje Smolcic), Éric Dina-Ebimbe (69.Ansgar Knauff), Jesper Lindstrøm (46.Sebastian Rode), Randal Kolo Muani (80.Rafael Borré). Trainer: Oliver Glasner (Austria).
Goals: 39' Arthur Gomes 1-0, 62' Daichi Kamada 1-1 (penalty), 72' Randal Kolo Muani 1-2.

04.10.2022; Deutsche Bank Park, Frankfurt am Main; Attendance: 50,500; Referee: Daniele Orsato (Italy)

**Eintracht Frankfurt – Tottenham Hotspur FC London 0-0**
Eintracht Frankfurt: Kevin Trapp, Makoto Hasebe, Evan Ndicka, Tuta, Sebastian Rode (71.Luca Pellegrini), Djibril Sow, Daichi Kamada, Kristijan Jakic, Jesper Lindstrøm (87.Éric Dina-Ebimbe), Randal Kolo Muani (57.Rafael Borré), Ansgar Knauff. Trainer: Oliver Glasner (Austria).
Tottenham Hotspur: Hugo Lloris, Clément Lenglet (78.Ben Davies), Eric Dier, Cristian Romero, Emerson Royal, Ivan Perisic (71.Ryan Sessegnon), Pierre-Emile Højbjerg, Rodrigo Bentancur, Heung-Min Son, Harry Kane, Richarlison (79.Bryan Gil). Trainer: Antonio Conte (Italy).

12.10.2022; Estádio „José Alvalade", Lisboa; Attendance: 38,126
Referee: Alejandro José Hernández Hernández (Spain)

**Sporting Clube de Portugal Lisboa – Olympique de Marseille 0-2(0-2)**
Sporting: Franco Israel, Sebastián Coates (35.José Martínez Marsà), Ricardo Esgaio [*sent off 19*], Matheus Reis, Gonçalo Inácio, Nuno Santos (59.Pedro Porro), Manuel Ugarte, Pedro Gonçalves "Pote" [*sent off 61*], Hidemasa Morita (22.Abdul Fatawu Issahaku), Marcus Edwards (35.Sotirios Alexandropoulos), Trincão (46.Flávio Nazinho). Trainer: Rúben Filipe Marques Amorim.
Olympique Marseille: Pau López, Jonathan Clauss (64.Issa Kaboré), Chancel Mbemba, Eric Bailly (64.Samuel Gigot), Nuno Tavares, Leonardo Balerdi, Jordan Veretout (87.Pape Gueye), Valentin Rongier, Amine Harit (72.Dimitri Payet), Mattéo Guendouzi (64.Cengiz Ünder), Alexis Sánchez. Trainer: Igor Tudor (Croatia).
Goals: 20' Mattéo Guendouzi 0-1 (penalty), 30' Alexis Sánchez 0-2.

26.10.2022; Deutsche Bank Park, Frankfurt am Main; Attendance: 48,700; Referee: Jesús Gil Manzano (Spain)

**Eintracht Frankfurt – Olympique de Marseille 2-1(2-1)**
Eintracht Frankfurt: Kevin Trapp, Christopher Lenz (45.Luca Pellegrini), Evan Ndicka, Hrvoje Smolcic, Mario Götze, Djibril Sow, Daichi Kamada, Kristijan Jakic, Éric Dina-Ebimbe (79.Faride Alidou), Jesper Lindstrøm (69.Sebastian Rode), Randal Kolo Muani (79.Rafael Borré). Trainer: Oliver Glasner (Austria).
Olympique Marseille: Pau López, Jonathan Clauss (86.Luis Suárez), Chancel Mbemba, Samuel Gigot (60.Sead Kolasinac), Nuno Tavares, Leonardo Balerdi, Jordan Veretout, Valentin Rongier, Amine Harit, Mattéo Guendouzi (60.Cengiz Ünder), Alexis Sánchez. Trainer: Igor Tudor (Croatia).
Goals: 3' Daichi Kamada 1-0, 22' Mattéo Guendouzi 1-1, 27' Randal Kolo Muani 2-1.

01.11.2022; Stade Orange Vélodrome, Marseille; Attendance: 50,768
Referee: Szymon Marciniak (Poland)

**Olympique de Marseille – Tottenham Hotspur FC London 1-2(1-0)**
Olympique Marseille: Pau López, Jonathan Clauss (74.Issa Kaboré), Chancel Mbemba, Eric Bailly (9.Samuel Gigot, 73.Sead Kolasinac), Nuno Tavares, Leonardo Balerdi, Jordan Veretout (74.Cengiz Ünder), Valentin Rongier (83.Luis Suárez), Amine Harit, Mattéo Guendouzi, Alexis Sánchez. Trainer: Igor Tudor (Croatia).
Tottenham Hotspur: Hugo Lloris, Ben Davies, Clément Lenglet, Eric Dier, Ivan Perisic, Pierre-Emile Højbjerg, Rodrigo Bentancur (84.Oliver Skipp), Ryan Sessegnon (46.Emerson Royal), Heung-Min Son (29.Yves Bissouma), Lucas Moura (90+3.Bryan Gil), Harry Kane. Trainer: Antonio Conte (Italy).
Goals: 45+2' Chancel Mbemba 1-0, 54' Clément Lenglet 1-1, 90+5' Pierre-Emile Højbjerg 1-2.

| | | | | | | | | |
|---|---|---|---|---|---|---|---|---|
| **GROUP E** | 1. **Chelsea FC London** | 6 | 4 | 1 | 1 | 10 - 4 | 13 |
| | 2. **AC Milan** | 6 | 3 | 1 | 2 | 12 - 7 | 10 |
| | 3. *FC Red Bull Salzburg* | 6 | 1 | 3 | 2 | 5 - 9 | 6 |
| | 4. GNK Dinamo Zagreb | 6 | 1 | 1 | 4 | 4 - 11 | 4 |

06.09.2022; Stadion Maksimir, Zagreb; Attendance: 20,607
Referee: István Kovács (Romania)
**GNK Dinamo Zagreb – Chelsea FC London 1-0(1-0)**
Dinamo Zagreb: Dominik Livakovic, Stefan Ristovski, Dino Peric, Sadegh Moharrami (76.Rasmus Lauritsen), Josip Sutalo, Arijan Ademi (88.Martin Baturina), Josip Misic, Luka Ivanusec, Robert Ljubicic, Mislav Orsic (76.Dario Spikic), Bruno Petkovic (90+8.Josip Drmic). Trainer: Ante Cacic.
Chelsea FC: Kepa, César Azpilicueta (46.Hakim Ziyech), Kalidou Koulibaly, Ben Chilwell (71.Marc Cucurella), Reece James, Wesley Fofana, Mateo Kovacic (59.Jorginho), Mason Mount, Kai Havertz, Pierre-Emerick Aubameyang (59.Armando Broja), Raheem Sterling (75.Christian Pulisic). Trainer: Thomas Tuchel (Germany).
Goal: 13' Mislav Orsic 1-0.

14.09.2022; Stadio „Giuseppe Meazza", Milano; Attendance: 61,341
Referee: Jesús Gil Manzano (Spain)
**AC Milan – GNK Dinamo Zagreb 3-1(1-0)**
AC Milan: Mike Maignan, Davide Calabria, Fikayo Tomori, Theo Hernández, Pierre Kalulu, Ismaël Bennacer (78.Rade Krunic), Brahim Díaz (78.Sergiño Dest), Alexis Saelemaekers (78.Junior Messias), Sandro Tonali (78.Tommaso Pobega), Olivier Giroud (68.Charles De Ketelaere), Rafael Leão. Trainer: Stefano Pioli.
Dinamo Zagreb: Dominik Livakovic, Stefan Ristovski (78.Josip Drmic), Dino Peric, Sadegh Moharrami (63.Dario Spikic), Josip Sutalo, Arijan Ademi, Josip Misic, Luka Ivanusec, Robert Ljubicic, Mislav Orsic (84.Antonio Marin), Bruno Petkovic (84.Martin Baturina). Trainer: Ante Cacic.
Goals: 45' Olivier Giroud 1-0 (penalty), 47' Alexis Saelemaekers 2-0, 56' Mislav Orsic 2-1, 77' Tommaso Pobega 3-1.

05.10.2022; Red Bull Arena, Wals-Siezenheim; Attendance: 28,864
Referee: Andris Treimanis (Latvia)
**FC Red Bull Salzburg – GNK Dinamo Zagreb 1-0(0-0)**
Red Bull Salzburg: Philipp Köhn, Andreas Ulmer (79.Max Wöber), Oumar Solet, Strahinja Pavlovic, Amar Dedic, Nicolas Seiwald, Luka Sucic (90+2.Lucas Gourna-Douath), Nicolás Capaldo, Maurits Kjærgaard, Noah Okafor (79.Junior Chikwubuike Adamu), Benjamin Sesko. Trainer: Matthias Jaissle (Germany).
Dinamo Zagreb: Dominik Livakovic, Kévin Théophile-Catherine (76.Josip Drmic), Dino Peric, Sadegh Moharrami (80.Petar Bockaj), Josip Sutalo, Arijan Ademi, Josip Misic, Luka Ivanusec (87.Martin Baturina), Robert Ljubicic, Mislav Orsic (80.Dario Spikic), Bruno Petkovic. Trainer: Ante Cacic.
Goal: 71' Noah Okafor 1-0 (penalty).

11.10.2022; Stadion Maksimir, Zagreb; Attendance: 20,779
Referee: Tobias Stieler (Germany)
**GNK Dinamo Zagreb – FC Red Bull Salzburg 1-1(1-1)**
Dinamo Zagreb: Dominik Livakovic, Stefan Ristovski (79.Sadegh Moharrami), Dino Peric, Josip Sutalo, Arijan Ademi (67.Josip Drmic), Josip Misic (86.Marko Bulat), Luka Ivanusec (80.Martin Baturina), Robert Ljubicic, Mislav Orsic, Bruno Petkovic, Dario Spikic (80.Petar Bockaj). Trainer: Ante Cacic.
Red Bull Salzburg: Philipp Köhn, Andreas Ulmer, Oumar Solet, Strahinja Pavlovic, Amar Dedic, Nicolas Seiwald, Luka Sucic, Maurits Kjærgaard, Lucas Gourna-Douath, Noah Okafor (62.Junior Chikwubuike Adamu), Benjamin Sesko (86.Roko Simic). Trainer: Matthias Jaissle (Germany).
Goals: 12' Nicolas Seiwald 0-1, 40' Robert Ljubicic 1-1.

06.09.2022; Red Bull Arena, Wals-Siezenheim; Attendance: 29,520
Referee: Srđan Jovanović (Serbia)
**FC Red Bull Salzburg – AC Milan 1-1(1-1)**
Red Bull Salzburg: Philipp Köhn, Andreas Ulmer, Oumar Solet (42.Bernardo), Strahinja Pavlovic, Amar Dedic, Nicolas Seiwald, Nicolás Capaldo, Maurits Kjærgaard, Dijon Kameri (65.Lucas Gourna-Douath), Noah Okafor (90+3.Junior Chikwubuike Adamu), Fernando (65.Benjamin Sesko). Trainer: Matthias Jaissle (Germany).
AC Milan: Mike Maignan, Davide Calabria (57.Sergiño Dest), Fikayo Tomori, Theo Hernández, Pierre Kalulu, Ismaël Bennacer (57.Tommaso Pobega), Alexis Saelemaekers (80.Junior Messias), Sandro Tonali, Charles De Ketelaere (70.Brahim Díaz), Olivier Giroud (57.Divock Origi), Rafael Leão. Trainer: Stefano Pioli.
Goals: 28' Noah Okafor 1-0, 40' Alexis Saelemaekers 1-1.

14.09.2022; Stamford Bridge, London; Attendance: 38,818
Referee: Ivan Kružliak (Slovakia)
**Chelsea FC London – FC Red Bull Salzburg 1-1(0-0)**
Chelsea FC: Kepa, Thiago Silva, César Azpilicueta (81.Hakim Ziyech), Marc Cucurella, Reece James, Mateo Kovacic (81.Conor Gallagher), Jorginho, Mason Mount, Kai Havertz (66.Ruben Loftus-Cheek), Pierre-Emerick Aubameyang (66.Armando Broja), Raheem Sterling (84.Christian Pulisic). Trainer: Graham Potter.
Red Bull Salzburg: Philipp Köhn, Andreas Ulmer, Bernardo, Strahinja Pavlovic, Amar Dedic, Nicolas Seiwald, Luka Sucic (70.Dijon Kameri), Nicolás Capaldo, Maurits Kjærgaard (46.Lucas Gourna-Douath), Noah Okafor (85.Sékou Koïta), Benjamin Sesko (70.Junior Chikwubuike Adamu). Trainer: Matthias Jaissle (Germany).
Goals: 48' Raheem Sterling 1-0, 75' Noah Okafor 1-1.

05.10.2022; Stamford Bridge, London; Attendance: 39,537
Referee: Danny Desmond Makkelie (Netherlands)
**Chelsea FC London – AC Milan 3-0(1-0)**
Chelsea FC: Kepa, Thiago Silva, Kalidou Koulibaly, Ben Chilwell, Reece James, Wesley Fofana (38.Trevoh Chalobah), Mateo Kovacic (66.Jorginho), Ruben Loftus-Cheek, Mason Mount (74.Kai Havertz), Pierre-Emerick Aubameyang (65.Conor Gallagher), Raheem Sterling (75.Armando Broja). Trainer: Graham Potter.
AC Milan: Ciprian Tatarusanu, Fodé Ballo-Touré, Fikayo Tomori, Sergiño Dest, Pierre Kalulu, Rade Krunic (65.Matteo Gabbia), Ismaël Bennacer (73.Tommaso Pobega), Sandro Tonali, Charles De Ketelaere (64.Ante Rebic), Olivier Giroud (73.Divock Origi), Rafael Leão (72.Brahim Díaz). Trainer: Stefano Pioli.
Goals: 24' Wesley Fofana 1-0, 56' Pierre-Emerick Aubameyang 2-0, 62' Reece James 3-0.

11.10.2022; Stadio „Giuseppe Meazza", Milano; Attendance: 75,051
Referee: Daniel Siebert (Germany)
**AC Milan – Chelsea FC London 0-2(0-2)**
AC Milan: Ciprian Tatarusanu, Fikayo Tomori [*sent off 18*], Theo Hernández (80.Fodé Ballo-Touré), Matteo Gabbia, Pierre Kalulu, Rade Krunic, Ismaël Bennacer (62.Tommaso Pobega), Brahim Díaz (37.Sergiño Dest), Sandro Tonali, Olivier Giroud (62.Ante Rebic), Rafael Leão (80.Divock Origi). Trainer: Stefano Pioli.
Chelsea FC: Kepa, Thiago Silva, Kalidou Koulibaly, Trevoh Chalobah, Ben Chilwell (89.Marc Cucurella), Reece James (62.César Azpilicueta), Mateo Kovacic, Jorginho, Mason Mount (46.Conor Gallagher), Pierre-Emerick Aubameyang (79.Kai Havertz), Raheem Sterling (62.Ruben Loftus-Cheek). Trainer: Graham Potter.
Goals: 21' Jorginho 0-1 (penalty), 34' Pierre-Emerick Aubameyang 0-2.

25.10.2022; Red Bull Arena, Wals-Siezenheim; Attendance: 29,520
Referee: Sandro Schärer (Switzerland)
**FC Red Bull Salzburg – Chelsea FC London 1-2(0-1)**
Red Bull Salzburg: Philipp Köhn, Bernardo, Max Wöber (78.Andreas Ulmer), Strahinja Pavlovic, Amar Dedic, Nicolas Seiwald, Luka Sucic (61.Benjamin Sesko), Maurits Kjærgaard, Lucas Gourna-Douath, Noah Okafor (78.Roko Simic), Junior Chikwubuike Adamu (82.Dijon Kameri). Trainer: Matthias Jaissle (Germany).
Chelsea FC: Kepa, Thiago Silva, Marc Cucurella, Trevoh Chalobah, Mateo Kovacic (68.Ruben Loftus-Cheek), Jorginho, Christian Pulisic (75.César Azpilicueta), Kai Havertz, Conor Gallagher (88.Hakim Ziyech), Pierre-Emerick Aubameyang (75.Armando Broja), Raheem Sterling (88.Mason Mount). Trainer: Graham Potter.
Goals: 23' Mateo Kovacic 0-1, 49' Junior Chikwubuike Adamu 1-1, 64' Kai Havertz 1-2.

02.11.2022; Stamford Bridge, London; Attendance: 39,392
Referee: François Letexier (France)
**Chelsea FC London – GNK Dinamo Zagreb 2-1(2-1)**
Chelsea FC: Édouard Mendy, César Azpilicueta, Kalidou Koulibaly (65.Thiago Silva), Trevoh Chalobah, Ben Chilwell, Jorginho, Mason Mount, Denis Zakaria (71.Ruben Loftus-Cheek), Kai Havertz (64.Conor Gallagher), Pierre-Emerick Aubameyang (65.Armando Broja), Raheem Sterling (83.Christian Pulisic). Trainer: Graham Potter.
Dinamo Zagreb: Dominik Livakovic, Stefan Ristovski (69.Mahir Emreli), Dino Peric, Sadegh Moharrami, Josip Sutalo, Arijan Ademi (83.Marko Bulat), Josip Misic, Luka Ivanusic, Robert Ljubicic, Mislav Orsic (89.Dario Spikic), Bruno Petkovic (83.Josip Drmic). Trainer: Ante Cacic.
Goals: 7' Bruno Petkovic 0-1, 18' Raheem Sterling 1-1, 30' Denis Zakaria 2-1.

25.10.2022; Stadion Maksimir, Zagreb; Attendance: 20,572
Referee: Szymon Marciniak (Poland)
**GNK Dinamo Zagreb – AC Milan 0-4(0-1)**
Dinamo Zagreb: Dominik Livakovic, Stefan Ristovski (58.Dario Spikic), Dino Peric, Sadegh Moharrami, Josip Sutalo, Arijan Ademi (57.Martin Baturina), Josip Misic (75.Marko Bulat), Luka Ivanusec, Robert Ljubicic, Mislav Orsic (75.Petar Bockaj), Bruno Petkovic (58.Josip Drmic). Trainer: Ante Cacic.
AC Milan: Ciprian Tatarusanu, Simon Kjær, Theo Hernández (70.Fodé Ballo-Touré), Matteo Gabbia, Pierre Kalulu, Ismaël Bennacer (70.Tommaso Pobega), Sandro Tonali, Charles De Ketelaere (52.Rade Krunic), Olivier Giroud (81.Divock Origi), Ante Rebic, Rafael Leão (70.Junior Messias). Trainer: Stefano Pioli.
Goals: 39' Matteo Gabbia 0-1, 49' Rafael Leão 0-2, 59' Olivier Giroud 0-3 (penalty), 69' Robert Ljubicic 0-4 (own goal).

02.11.2022; Stadio „Giuseppe Meazza", Milano; Attendance: 74,292
Referee: Antonio Miguel Mateu Lahoz (Spain)
**AC Milan – FC Red Bull Salzburg 4-0(1-0)**
AC Milan: Ciprian Tatarusanu, Simon Kjær, Fikayo Tomori, Theo Hernández (78.Fodé Ballo-Touré), Pierre Kalulu (86.Matteo Gabbia), Rade Krunic (78.Charles De Ketelaere), Ismaël Bennacer (69.Tommaso Pobega), Sandro Tonali, Olivier Giroud, Ante Rebic, Rafael Leão (69.Junior Messias). Trainer: Stefano Pioli.
Red Bull Salzburg: Philipp Köhn, Max Wöber (77.Andreas Ulmer), Oumar Solet (46.Bernardo), Strahinja Pavlovic, Amar Dedic, Nicolas Seiwald, Luka Sucic, Maurits Kjærgaard, Lucas Gourna-Douath (64.Dijon Kameri), Noah Okafor (77.Sékou Koïta), Junior Chikwubuike Adamu (62.Benjamin Sesko). Trainer: Matthias Jaissle (Germany).
Goals: 14' Olivier Giroud 1-0, 46' Rade Krunic 2-0, 57' Olivier Giroud 3-0, 90+1' Junior Messias 4-0.

| | | | | | | | | | |
|---|---|---|---|---|---|---|---|---|---|
| **GROUP F** | 1. | **Real Madrid CF** | 6 | 4 | 1 | 1 | 15 - 6 | 13 |
| | 2. | **RasenBallsport Leipzig** | 6 | 4 | 0 | 2 | 13 - 9 | 12 |
| | 3. | *FK Shakhtar Donetsk* | 6 | 1 | 3 | 2 | 8 - 10 | 6 |
| | 4. | Celtic FC Glasgow | 6 | 0 | 2 | 6 | 6 - 15 | 2 |

06.09.2022; Celtic Park, Glasgow; Attendance: 57,057
Referee: Sandro Schärer (Switzerland)
**Celtic FC Glasgow – Real Madrid CF 0-3(0-0)**
Celtic FC: Joe Hart, Cameron Carter-Vickers, Josip Juranovic, Greg Taylor, Moritz Jenz, Callum McGregor, Matt O'Riley (72.Aaron Mooy), Reo Hatate (72.David Turnbull), Georgios Giakoumakis (72.Kyogo Furuhashi), Jota (82.Sead Haksabanovic), Liel Abada (46.Daizen Maeda). Trainer: Angelos Postecoglou (Australia).
Real Madrid: Thibaut Courtois, David Alaba, Dani Carvajal, Ferland Mendy, Éder Militão (46.Antonio Rüdiger), Luka Modric (81.Marco Asensio), Toni Kroos, Federico Valverde, Aurélien Tchouaméni (71.Eduardo Camavinga), Karim Benzema (30.Eden Hazard), Vinícius Júnior (80.Rodrygo). Trainer: Carlo Ancelotti.
Goals: 56' Vinícius Júnior 0-1, 60' Luka Modric 0-2, 77' Eden Hazard 0-3.

14.09.2022; Stadion Wojska Polskiego, Warszawa (Poland); Attendance: 20,697; Referee: Glenn Nyberg (Sweden)
**FK Shakhtar Donetsk – Celtic FC Glasgow 1-1(1-1)**
Shakhtar Donetsk: Anatoliy Trubin, Mykola Matvienko, Lucas Taylor, Valeriy Bondar, Yukhym Konoplya, Taras Stepanenko, Artem Bondarenko (74.Neven Djurasek), Mykhaylo Mudryk, Georgiy Sudakov (78.Oleh Ocheretko), Oleksandr Zubkov (61.Lassina Traoré), Marian Shved (60.Ivan Petryak). Trainer: Igor Jovićević (Croatia).
Celtic FC: Joe Hart, Cameron Carter-Vickers, Josip Juranovic, Greg Taylor, Moritz Jenz, Callum McGregor, Sead Haksabanovic (46.Daizen Maeda), Matt O'Riley (68.Aaron Mooy), Reo Hatate (68.David Turnbull), Jota (86.Liel Abada), Kyogo Furuhashi (68.Georgios Giakoumakis). Trainer: Angelos Postecoglou (Australia).
Goals: 10' Artem Bondarenko 0-1 (own goal), 29' Mykhaylo Mudryk 1-1.

06.09.2022; Red Bull Arena, Leipzig; Attendance: 41,591
Referee: João Pedro Silva Pinheiro (Portugal)
**RasenBallsport Leipzig – FK Shakhtar Donetsk 1-4(0-1)**
RB Leipzig: Péter Gulácsi, Marcel Halstenberg (46.David Raum), Willi Orbán, Abdou Diallo, Mohamed Simakan, Konrad Laimer (82.Amadou Haïdara), Xaver Schlager (70.Benjamin Henrichs), Dominik Szoboszlai, André Silva, Timo Werner (70.Emil Forsberg), Christopher Nkunku. Trainer: Domenico Tedesco (Italy).
Shakhtar Donetsk: Anatoliy Trubin, Mykola Matvienko, Lucas Taylor, Valeriy Bondar, Yukhym Konoplya, Taras Stepanenko (86.Sergiy Kryvtsov), Artem Bondarenko (62.Neven Djurasek), Mykhaylo Mudryk, Georgiy Sudakov, Oleksandr Zubkov (70.Lassina Traoré), Marian Shved (61.Ivan Petryak). Trainer: Igor Jovićević (Croatia).
Goals: 16' Marian Shved 0-1, 57' Mohamed Simakan 1-1, 58' Marian Shved 1-2, 76' Mykhaylo Mudryk 1-3, 85' LassinaTraoré 1-4.

14.09.2022; Estadio „Santiago Bernabéu", Madrid; Attendance: 54,289
Referee: Maurizio Mariani (Italy)
**Real Madrid CF – RasenBallsport Leipzig 2-0(0-0)**
Real Madrid: Thibaut Courtois, David Alaba (81.Ferland Mendy), Nacho, Dani Carvajal, Antonio Rüdiger, Luka Modric (81.Toni Kroos), Federico Valverde, Aurélien Tchouaméni, Eduardo Camavinga (64.Marco Asensio), Vinícius Júnior (85.Dani Ceballos), Rodrygo (85.Mariano Díaz). Trainer: Carlo Ancelotti.
RB Leipzig: Péter Gulácsi, Willi Orbán, Abdou Diallo, David Raum, Mohamed Simakan (75.Benjamin Henrichs), Emil Forsberg (81.Yussuf Poulsen), Xaver Schlager, Amadou Haïdara (75.Kevin Kampl), Dominik Szoboszlai, Timo Werner (81.André Silva), Christopher Nkunku. Trainer: Marco Rose.
Goals: 80' Federico Valverde 1-0, 90+1' Marco Asensio 2-0.

05.10.2022; Red Bull Arena, Leipzig; Attendance: 45,228
Referee: Espen Eskås (Norway)
**RasenBallsport Leipzig – Celtic FC Glasgow 3-1(1-0)**
RB Leipzig: Péter Gulácsi (13.Janis Blaswich), Willi Orbán, David Raum (81.Marcel Halstenberg), Mohamed Simakan, Josko Gvardiol, Kevin Kampl (71.Amadou Haïdara), Xaver Schlager, Dominik Szoboszlai (82.Yussuf Poulsen), André Silva, Timo Werner (71.Emil Forsberg), Christopher Nkunku. Trainer: Marco Rose.
Celtic FC: Joe Hart, Josip Juranovic, Greg Taylor, Stephen Welsh, Moritz Jenz, Callum McGregor (37.Oliver Abildgaard), Matt O'Riley (75.Sead Haksabanovic), Reo Hatate (82.James McCarthy), Jota, Daizen Maeda (75.James Forrest), Kyogo Furuhashi (82.Georgios Giakoumakis). Trainer: Angelos Postecoglou (Australia).
Goals: 27' Christopher Nkunku 1-0, 47' Jota 1-1, 64', 77' André Silva 2-1, 3-1.

11.10.2022; Stadion Wojska Polskiego, Warszawa (Poland); Attendance: 29,030; Referee: Orel Grinfeld (Israel)
**FK Shakhtar Donetsk – Real Madrid CF 1-1(0-0)**
Shakhtar Donetsk: Anatoliy Trubin, Mykola Matvienko, Bogdan Mykhaylichenko, Valeriy Bondar, Yukhym Konoplya, Taras Stepanenko, Artem Bondarenko, Mykhaylo Mudryk (85.Ivan Petryak), Georgiy Sudakov (81.Neven Djurasek), Oleksandr Zubkov (82.Lucas Taylor), Lassina Traoré (77.Danylo Sikan). Trainer: Igor Jovićević (Croatia).
Real Madrid: Andriy Lunin, Nacho, Antonio Rüdiger, Ferland Mendy (68.David Alaba), Toni Kroos, Lucas Vázquez, Federico Valverde (68.Eduardo Camavinga), Aurélien Tchouaméni (57.Luka Modric), Karim Benzema, Eden Hazard (57.Vinícius Júnior), Rodrygo (68.Marco Asensio). Trainer: Carlo Ancelotti.
Goals: 46' Oleksandr Zubkov 1-0, 90+5' Antonio Rüdiger 1-1.

25.10.2022; Celtic Park, Glasgow; Attendance: 57,478
Referee: Serdar Gözübüyük (Netherlands)
**Celtic FC Glasgow – FK Shakhtar Donetsk 1-1(1-0)**
Celtic FC: Joe Hart, Cameron Carter-Vickers, Josip Juranovic, Greg Taylor, Moritz Jenz, Sead Haksabanovic (66.Daizen Maeda), Matt O'Riley, Reo Hatate (84.David Turnbull), Georgios Giakoumakis, Kyogo Furuhashi (65.Aaron Mooy), Liel Abada (65.James Forrest). Trainer: Angelos Postecoglou (Australia).
Shakhtar Donetsk: Anatoliy Trubin, Mykola Matvienko, Bogdan Mykhaylichenko, Lucas Taylor, Valeriy Bondar, Taras Stepanenko, Artem Bondarenko, Mykhaylo Mudryk (90.Ivan Petryak), Georgiy Sudakov (90.Sergiy Kryvtsov), Oleksandr Zubkov (57.Danylo Sikan). Trainer: Igor Jovićević (Croatia).
Goals: 34' Georgios Giakoumakis 1-0, 58' Mykhaylo Mudryk 1-1.

02.11.2022; Estadio „Santiago Bernabéu", Madrid; Attendance: 52,511
Referee: Stéphanie Frappart (France)
**Real Madrid CF – Celtic FC Glasgow 5-1(2-0)**
Real Madrid: Thibaut Courtois, David Alaba (66.Nacho), Dani Carvajal (64.Lucas Vázquez), Ferland Mendy, Éder Militão (73.Jesús Vallejo), Luka Modric (66.Dani Caballos), Toni Kroos, Federico Valverde, Marco Asensio, Vinícius Júnior (63.Karim Benzema), Rodrygo. Trainer: Carlo Ancelotti.
Celtic FC: Joe Hart, Carl Starfelt, Josip Juranovic, Greg Taylor, Moritz Jenz, Aaron Mooy (63.David Turnbull), Matt O'Riley, Reo Hatate (82.Oliver Abildgaard), Daizen Maeda (63.Sead Haksabanovic), Kyogo Furuhashi (62.Georgios Giakoumakis), Liel Abada (63.Jota). Trainer: Angelos Postecoglou (Australia).
Goals: 6' Luka Modric 1-0 (penalty), 21' Rodrygo 2-0 (penalty), 51' Marco Asensio 3-0, 61' Vinícius Júnior 4-0, 71' Federico Valverde 5-0, 84' Jota 5-1.

05.10.2022; Estadio „Santiago Bernabéu", Madrid; Attendance: 56,011
Referee: Ivan Kružliak (Slovakia)
**Real Madrid CF – FK Shakhtar Donetsk 2-1(2-1)**
Real Madrid: Andriy Lunin, David Alaba, Dani Carvajal, Ferland Mendy, Éder Militão, Toni Kroos, Federico Valverde, Aurélien Tchouaméni (75.Eduardo Camavinga), Karim Benzema, Vinícius Júnior, Rodrygo (80.Marco Asensio). Trainer: Carlo Ancelotti.
Shakhtar Donetsk: Anatoliy Trubin, Mykola Matvienko, Bogdan Mykhaylichenko, Valeriy Bondar, Yukhym Konoplya, Taras Stepanenko (88.Lassina Traoré), Artem Bondarenko, Mykhaylo Mudryk, Georgiy Sudakov (88.Neven Djurasek), Oleksandr Zubkov (67.Danylo Sikan), Marian Shved (67.Ivan Petryak). Trainer: Igor Jovićević (Croatia).
Goals: 13' Rodrygo 1-0, 28' Vinícius Júnior 2-0, 39' Oleksandr Zubkov 2-1.

11.10.2022; Celtic Park, Glasgow; Attendance: 57,565
Referee: Halil Umut Meler (Turkey)
**Celtic FC Glasgow – RasenBallsport Leipzig 0-2(0-0)**
Celtic FC: Joe Hart, Cameron Carter-Vickers, Josip Juranovic, Greg Taylor, Moritz Jenz, Sead Haksabanovic (66.David Turnbull), Matt O'Riley, Reo Hatate (66.Aaron Mooy), Daizen Maeda (80.Alexandro Bernabei), Kyogo Furuhashi (66.Georgios Giakoumakis), Liel Abada (42.James Forrest). Trainer: Angelos Postecoglou (Australia).
RB Leipzig: Janis Blaswich, Willi Orbán, David Raum, Mohamed Simakan (76.Benjamin Henrichs), Josko Gvardiol, Xaver Schlager, Amadou Haïdara (84.Abdou Diallo), Dominik Szoboszlai (76.Emil Forsberg), André Silva (77.Yussuf Poulsen), Timo Werner, Christopher Nkunku (88.Hugo Novoa). Trainer: Marco Rose.
Goals: 75' Timo Werner 0-1, 84' Emil Forsberg 0-2.

25.10.2022; Red Bull Arena, Leipzig; Attendance: 45,228
Referee: Daniele Orsato (Italy)
**RasenBallsport Leipzig – Real Madrid CF 3-2(2-1)**
RB Leipzig: Janis Blaswich, Willi Orbán, David Raum (69.Abdou Diallo), Mohamed Simakan (89.Benjamin Henrichs), Josko Gvardiol, Emil Forsberg (69.Dani Olmo), Xaver Schlager, Amadou Haïdara (84.Kevin Kampl), Dominik Szoboszlai, André Silva (69.Timo Werner), Christopher Nkunku. Trainer: Marco Rose.
Real Madrid: Thibaut Courtois, Nacho (68.David Alaba), Antonio Rüdiger, Éder Militão, Toni Kroos (76.Eden Hazard), Lucas Vázquez (68.Dani Carvajal), Aurélien Tchouaméni, Eduardo Camavinga, Marco Asensio, Vinícius Júnior, Rodrygo. Trainer: Carlo Ancelotti.
Goals: 13' Josko Gvardiol 1-0, 18' Christopher Nkunku 2-0, 44' Vinícius Júnior 2-1, 81' Timo Werner 3-1, 90+4' Rodrygo 3-2 (penalty).

02.11.2022; Stadion Wojska Polskiego, Warszawa (Poland); Attendance: 26,045; Referee: Michael Oliver (England)
**FK Shakhtar Donetsk – RasenBallsport Leipzig 0-4(0-1)**
Shakhtar Donetsk: Anatoliy Trubin, Mykola Matvienko, Bogdan Mykhaylichenko, Valeriy Bondar, Yukhym Konoplya (59.Lucas Taylor), Taras Stepanenko, Ivan Petryak, Artem Bondarenko (81.Dmytro Kryskiv), Mykhaylo Mudryk (74.Andriy Totovytskyi), Georgiy Sudakov (59.Neven Djurasek), Lassina Traoré (59.Danylo Sikan). Trainer: Igor Jovićević (Croatia).
RB Leipzig: Janis Blaswich, Willi Orbán, David Raum (67.Marcel Halstenberg), Mohamed Simakan (67.Benjamin Henrichs), Josko Gvardiol, Kevin Kampl, Xaver Schlager (74.Abdou Diallo), Dominik Szoboszlai (67.Dani Olmo), André Silva, Timo Werner (19.Emil Forsberg), Christopher Nkunku. Trainer: Marco Rose.
Goals: 10' Christopher Nkunku 0-1, 50' André Silva 0-2, 62' Dominik Szoboszlai 0-3, 68' Valeriy Bondar 0-4 (own goal).

| | | | | | | | | |
|---|---|---|---|---|---|---|---|---|
| **GROUP G** | 1. **Manchester City FC** | 6 | 4 | 2 | 0 | 14 - 2 | 14 |
| | 2. **BV 09 Borussia Dortmund** | 6 | 2 | 3 | 1 | 19 - 5 | 9 |
| | 3. *Sevilla FC* | 6 | 1 | 2 | 3 | 6 - 12 | 5 |
| | 4. FC København | 6 | 0 | 3 | 3 | 1 - 12 | 3 |

06.09.2022; Signal Iduna Park, Dortmund; Attendance: 81,365
Referee: François Letexier (France)
**BV 09 Borussia Dortmund – FC København 3-0(2-0)**
Borussia Dortmund: Alexander Meyer, Thomas Meunier, Raphaël Guerreiro (86.Tom Rothe), Niklas Süle, Nico Schlotterbeck, Marco Reus (86.Marius Wolf), Thorgan Hazard (23.Gio Reyna), Julian Brandt, Salih Özcan (66.Emre Can), Jude Bellingham, Anthony Modeste (67.Youssoufa Moukoko). Trainer: Edin Terzic.
FC København: Mathew Ryan, Davit Khocholava (81.Nicolai Boilesen), Denis Vavro, Kevin Diks (81.Elias Jelert), Victor Kristiansen, Rasmus Falk, Zeca Rodrigues (72.Christian Sørensen), Victor Claesson, Lukas Lerager, Andreas Cornelius, Mohamed Daramy (60.Hákon Haraldsson). Trainer: Jess Thorup.
Goals: 35' Marco Reus 1-0, 42' Raphaël Guerreiro 2-0, 83' Jude Bellingham 3-0.

14.09.2022; Etihad Stadium, Manchester; Attendance: 50,441
Referee: Daniele Orsato (Italy)
**Manchester City FC – BV 09 Borussia Dortmund 2-1(0-0)**
Manchester City: Ederson, João Cancelo, Nathan Aké, John Stones, Manuel Akanji, Ilkay Gündogan (58.Bernardo Silva), Kevin De Bruyne, Jack Grealish (58.Phil Foden), Rodri, Riyad Mahrez (58.Julián Álvarez), Erling Haaland (90+2.Kalvin Phillips). Trainer: Josep Guardiola (Spain).
Borussia Dortmund: Alexander Meyer, Mats Hummels, Thomas Meunier, Raphaël Guerreiro, Niklas Süle, Marco Reus (88.Youssoufa Moukoko), Emre Can, Salih Özcan (88.Karim Adeyemi), Gio Reyna (62.Donyell Malen), Jude Bellingham, Anthony Modeste (78.Nico Schlotterbeck). Trainer: Edin Terzic.
Goals: 56' Jude Bellingham 0-1, 80' John Stones 1-1, 84' Erling Haaland 2-1.

05.10.2022; Etihad Stadium, Manchester; Attendance: 51,765
Referee: Donatas Rumšas (Lithuania)
**Manchester City FC – FC København 5-0(3-0)**
Manchester City: Ederson, João Cancelo (57.Rico Lewis), Aymeric Laporte, Rúben Dias, Ilkay Gündogan, Jack Grealish, Bernardo Silva (66.Josh Wilson-Esbrand), Sergio Gómez, Riyad Mahrez, Erling Haaland (46.Cole Palmer), Julián Álvarez. Trainer: Josep Guardiola (Spain).
FC København: Kamil Grabara, Davit Khocholava, Denis Vavro, Kevin Diks (66.Peter Ankersen), Victor Kristiansen, Victor Claesson (66.Paul Mukairu), Lukas Lerager (79.Christian Sørensen), Ísak Bergmann Jóhannesson, Marko Stamenic, Mamoudou Karamoko (46.Valdemar Lund Jensen), Mohamed Daramy (56.Hákon Haraldsson). Trainer: Jacob Neestrup.
Goals: 7', 33' Erling Haaland 1-0, 2-0, 39' Davit Khocholava 3-0 (own goal), 55' Riyad Mahrez 4-0 (penalty), 76' Julián Álvarez 5-0.

11.10.2022; Telia Parken , København; Attendance: 35,447
Referee: Artur Manuel Ribeiro Soares Dias (Portugal)
**FC København – Manchester City FC 0-0**
FC København: Kamil Grabara, Nicolai Boilesen, Davit Khocholava (80.Kevin Diks), Victor Kristiansen, Valdemar Lund Jensen, Elias Jelert, Victor Claesson, Lukas Lerager, Hákon Haraldsson (59.Ísak Bergmann Jóhannesson), Marko Stamenic (90+3.Paul Mukairu), Mohamed Daramy. Trainer: Jacob Neestrup.
Manchester City: Ederson, João Cancelo, Aymeric Laporte (88.Nathan Aké), Manuel Akanji, Ilkay Gündogan, Kevin De Bruyne (77.Bernardo Silva), Jack Grealish (77.Phil Foden), Rodri, Sergio Gómez [*sent off 30*], Riyad Mahrez (32.Rúben Dias), Julián Álvarez. Trainer: Josep Guardiola (Spain).

06.09.2022; Estadio „Ramón Sánchez Pizjuán", Sevilla; Attendance: 38,764; Referee: Davide Massa (Italy)
**Sevilla FC – Manchester City FC 0-4(0-1)**
Sevilla FC: Yassine Bounou "Bono", Jesús Navas, Alex Telles (57.Kasper Dolberg), Marcos Acuña, Tanguy Nianzou, José Ángel Carmona, Ivan Rakitic (46.Rafa Mir), Papu Gómez (73.Suso), Thomas Delaney (46.Joan Jordán), Nemanja Gudelj, Isco (78.Adnan Januzaj). Trainer: Julen Lopetegui Agote.
Manchester City: Ederson, João Cancelo, Rúben Dias, Manuel Akanji, Kevin De Bruyne (78.Riyad Mahrez), Jack Grealish (62.Ilkay Gündogan), Bernado Silva, Rodri (78.Kalvin Phillips), Phil Foden (70.Cole Palmer), Sergio Gómez, Erling Haaland (70.Julián Álvarez). Trainer: Josep Guardiola (Spain).
Goals: 20' Erling Haaland 0-1, 58' Phil Foden 0-2, 67' Erling Haaland 0-3, 90+2' Rúben Dias 0-4.

14.09.2022; Telia Parken, København; Attendance: 34,910
Referee: Irfan Peljto (Bosnia and Herzegovina)
**FC København – Sevilla FC 0-0**
FC København: Mathew Ryan, Davit Khocholava, Denis Vavro, Kevin Diks, Victor Kristiansen, Rasmus Falk (79.Lukas Lerager), Zeca Rodrigues, Victor Claesson (79.Hákon Haraldsson), Ísak Bergmann Jóhannesson (87.Christian Sørensen), Marko Stamenic, Mohamed Daramy (73.Paul Mukairu). Trainer: Jess Thorup.
Sevilla FC: Marko Dmitrovic, Alex Telles, José Ángel Carmona, Kike Salas, Ivan Rakitic (67.Joan Jordán), Fernando, Érik Lamela (73.Suso), Thomas Delaney (67.Papu Gómez), Nemanja Gudelj, Isco (84.Adnan Januzaj), Youssef En-Nesyri (74.Kasper Dolberg). Trainer: Julen Lopetegui Agote.

05.10.2022; Estadio „Ramón Sánchez Pizjuán", Sevilla; Attendance: 34,596; Referee: Maurizio Mariani (Italy)
**Sevilla FC – BV 09 Borussia Dortmund 1-4(0-3)**
Sevilla FC: Yassine Bounou "Bono", Jesús Navas (46.Gonzalo Montiel), Alex Telles, José Ángel Carmona, Kike Salas, Ivan Rakitic (62.Thomas Delaney), Nemanja Gudelj, Isco (62.Papu Gómez), Suso (46.Érik Lamela), Joan Jordán (77.Kasper Dolberg), Youssef En-Nesyri. Trainer: Julen Lopetegui Agote.
Borussia Dortmund: Alexander Meyer, Thomas Meunier, Raphaël Guerreiro (80.Tom Rothe), Niklas Süle, Nico Schlotterbeck, Emre Can, Julian Brandt (85.Thorgan Hazard), Salih Özcan (85.Antonios Papadopoulos), Jude Bellingham, Karim Adeyemi (64.Donyell Malen), Youssoufa Moukoko (80.Anthony Modeste). Trainer: Edin Terzic.
Goals: 6' Raphaël Guerreiro 0-1, 41' Jude Bellingham 0-2, 43' Karim Adeyemi 0-3, 51' Youssef En-Nesyri 1-3, 75' Julian Brandt 1-4.

11.10.2022; Signal Iduna Park, Dortmund; Attendance: 81,000
Referee: Srđan Jovanović (Serbia)
**BV 09 Borussia Dortmund – Sevilla FC 1-1(1-1)**
Borussia Dortmund: Gregor Kobel, Mats Hummels, Thomas Meunier (83.Nico Schlotterbeck), Niklas Süle, Tom Rothe (46.Raphaël Guerreiro), Julian Brandt, Salih Özcan, Jude Bellingham, Anthony Modeste (64.Youssoufa Moukoko), Donyell Malen (71.Gio Reyna), Karim Adeyemi (71.Thorgan Hazard). Trainer: Edin Terzic.
Sevilla FC: Yassine Bounou "Bono", Jesús Navas (90+1.Gonzalo Montiel), Marcus Acuña (71.Alex Telles), Marcão (90+1.Joan Jordán), Tanguy Nianzou, José Ángel Carmona, Ivan Rakitic, Érik Lamela, Nemanja Gudelj, Suso (59.Adnan Januzaj), Youssef En-Nesyri (59.Isco). Trainer: Jorge Luis Sampaoli Moya (Argentina).
Goals: 18' Tanguy Nianzou 0-1, 35' Jude Bellingham 1-1.

25.10.2022; Estadio „Ramón Sánchez Pizjuán", Sevilla; Attendance: 29,884; Referee: Benoît Bastien (France)
**Sevilla FC – FC København 3-0(0-0)**
Sevilla FC: Marko Dmitrovic, Alex Telles, Marcão, Gonzalo Montiel, Ivan Rakitic, Papu Gómez (77.Marcus Acuña), Nemanja Gudelj, Isco, Suso (55.Érik Lamela), Joan Jordán, Kasper Dolberg (46.Youssef En-Nesyri, 70.Rafa Mir). Trainer: Jorge Luis Sampaoli Moya (Argentina).
FC København: Kamil Grabara, Davit Khocholava [*sent off 90+5*], Victor Kristiansen, Valdemar Lund Jensen (80.Kevin Diks), Elias Jelert (81.Christian Sørensen), Victor Claesson, Lukas Lerager, Ísak Bergmann Jóhannesson (63.Roony Bardghji), Hákon Haraldsson (72.Andreas Cornelius), William Clem (81.Orri Óskarsson), Mohamed Daramy. Trainer: Jacob Neestrup.
Goals: 61' Youssef En-Nesyri 1-0, 88' Isco 2-0, 90+2' Gonzalo Montiel 3-0.

02.11.2022; Etihad Stadium, Manchester; Attendance: 51,610
Referee: Orel Grinfeld (Israel)
**Manchester City FC – Sevilla FC 3-1(0-1)**
Manchester City: Stefan Ortega, Aymeric Laporte, Rúben Dias, Rico Lewis (85.João Cancelo), Ilkay Gündogan (57.Bernardo Silva), Jack Grealish (46.Rodri), Phil Foden, Sergio Gómez (70.Josh Wilson-Esbrand), Cole Palmer (70.Kevin De Bruyne), Riyad Mahrez, Julián Álvarez. Trainer: Josep Guardiola (Spain).
Sevilla FC: Yassine Bounou "Bono", Karim Rekik, Marcus Acuña (46.Alex Telles), Marcão (45+1.Nemanja Gudelj), Gonzalo Montiel, José Ángel Carmona, Ivan Rakitic (67.Joan Jordán), Papu Gómez (46.Suso), Thomas Delaney, Isco (57.Érik Lamela), Rafa Mir. Trainer: Jorge Luis Sampaoli Moya (Argentina).
Goals: 31' Rafa Mir 0-1, 52' Rico Lewis 1-1, 73' Julián Álvarez 2-1, 83' Riyad Mahrez 3-1.

25.10.2022; Signal Iduna Park, Dortmund; Attendance: 81,000
Referee: Davide Massa (Italy)
**BV 09 Borussia Dortmund – Manchester City FC 0-0**
Borussia Dortmund: Gregor Kobel, Mats Hummels, Niklas Süle, Nico Schlotterbeck, Thorgan Hazard (82.Marius Wolf), Emre Can, Julian Brandt, Gio Reyna (87.Antonios Papadopoulos), Jude Bellingham, Karim Adeyemi (73.Donyell Malen), Youssoufa Moukoko (82.Anthony Modeste). Trainer: Edin Terzic.
Manchester City: Stefan Ortega, João Cancelo (46.Manuel Akanji), Nathan Aké, John Stones, Rúben Dias, Ilkay Gündogan, Rodri, Phil Foden (81.Jack Grealish), Riyad Mahrez (88.Cole Palmer), Erling Haaland (46.Bernardo Silva), Julián Álvarez. Trainer: Josep Guardiola (Spain).

02.11.2022; Telia Parken , København; Attendance: 31,900
Referee: Əliyar Ağayev (Azerbaijan)
**FC København – BV 09 Borussia Dortmund 1-1(1-1)**
FC København: Kamil Grabara, Christian Sørensen (58.Victor Kristiansen), Denis Vavro, Kevin Diks (79.Elias Jelert), Valdemar Lund Jensen, Victor Claesson (70.Rasmus Falk), Lukas Lerager, Hákon Haraldsson, Roony Bardghji (70.Ísak Bergmann Jóhannesson), William Clem, Mohamed Daramy (79.Orri Óskarsson). Trainer: Jacob Neestrup.
Borussia Dortmund: Gregor Kobel (46.Alexander Meyer), Mats Hummels (46.Niklas Süle), Nico Schlotterbeck, Thorgan Hazard (72.Soumaïla Coulibaly), Emre Can, Felix Passlack, Salih Özcan (63.Youssoufa Moukoko), Gio Reyna (63.Julian Brandt), Anthony Modeste, Donyell Malen, Karim Adeyemi. Trainer: Edin Terzic.
Goals: 23' Thorgan Hazard 0-1, 41' Hákon Haraldsson 1-1.

| GROUP H | | | | | | | | |
|---|---|---|---|---|---|---|---|---|
| 1. **Sport Lisboa e Benfica** | 6 | 4 | 2 | 0 | 16 | - | 7 | 14 |
| 2. **Paris Saint-Germain FC** | 6 | 4 | 2 | 0 | 16 | - | 7 | 14 |
| 3. *Juventus FC Torino* | 6 | 1 | 0 | 5 | 6 | - | 13 | 3 |
| 4. Maccabi Haifa FC | 6 | 1 | 0 | 5 | 7 | - | 21 | 3 |

06.09.2022; Stade Parc des Princes, Paris; Attendance: 47,415
Referee: Anthony Taylor (England)
**Paris Saint-Germain FC – Juventus FC Torino 2-1(2-0)**
Paris Saint-Germain: Gianluigi Donnarumma, Sergio Ramos, Marquinhos, Presnel Kimpembe, Achraf Hakimi (78.Nordi Mukiele), Nuno Mendes, Marco Verratti (87.Renato Sanches), Vitinha (78.Danilo Pereira), Lionel Messi (84.Carlos Soler), Neymar, Kylian Mbappé. Trainer: Christophe Galtier.
Juventus: Mattia Perin, Leonardo Bonucci, Danilo, Bremer, Juan Cuadrado (74.Mattia De Sciglio), Filip Kostic, Leandro Paredes, Adrien Rabiot (87.Moise Kean), Fabio Miretti (46.Weston McKennie), Arkadiusz Milik (68.Manuel Locatelli), Dusan Vlahovic. Trainer: Massimiliano Allegri.
Goals: 5', 22' Kylian Mbappé 1-0, 2-0, 53' Weston McKennie 2-1.

14.09.2022; Allianz Stadium, Torino; Attendance: 34,015
Referee: Felix Zwayer (Germany)
**Juventus FC Torino – Sport Lisboa e Benfica 1-2(1-1)**
Juventus: Mattia Perin, Leonardo Bonucci, Danilo, Bremer, Juan Cuadrado (58.Mattia De Sciglio), Filip Kostic (70.Moise Kean), Leandro Paredes, Weston McKennie, Fabio Miretti (58.Ángel Di María), Arkadiusz Milik (70.Nicolò Fagioli), Dusan Vlahovic. Trainer: Massimiliano Allegri.
Benfica: Odisseas Vlachodimos, Nicolás Otamendi, Álex Grimaldo, Alexander Bah, António Silva, João Mário (86.Julian Draxler), Rafa Silva (86.Diogo Gonçalves), Florentino, Enzo Fernández (81.Fredrik Aursnes), David Neres (81.Chiquinho), Gonçalo Ramos (81.Petar Musa). Trainer: Roger Schmidt (Germany).
Goals: 4' Arkadiusz Milik 1-0, 43' João Mário 1-1 (penalty), 55' David Neres 1-2.

06.09.2022; Estádio do Sport Lisboa e Benfica, Lisboa; Attendance: 55,130; Referee: Andreas Ekberg (Sweden)
**Sport Lisboa e Benfica – Maccabi Haifa FC 2-0(0-0)**
Benfica: Odisseas Vlachodimos, Nicolás Otamendi, Ález Grimaldo, Alexander Bah, António Silva, João Mário (79.Chiquinho), Rafa Silva (79.Diogo Gonçalves), Florentino, Enzo Fernández, David Neres (65.Fredrik Aursnes), Gonçalo Ramos (46.Petar Musa). Trainer: Roger Schmidt (Germany).
Maccabi Haifa: Josh Cohen, Daniel Sundgren, Shon Goldberg, Dylan Batubinsika, Abdoulaye Seck (67.Suf Podgoreanu, 78.Sun Menachem), Tjaronn Chery, Ali Muhammad (31.Mohammad Abu Fani), Neta Lavi, Dolev Haziza, Din David (46.Omer Atzili), Frantzdy Pierrot (78.Nikita Rukavytsya). Trainer: Barak Bakhar.
Goals: 49' Rafa Silva 1-0, 54' Álex Grimaldo 2-0.

14.09.2022; „Sammy Ofer" Stadium, Haifa; Attendance: 30,421
Referee: Daniel Siebert (Germany)
**Maccabi Haifa FC – Paris Saint-Germain FC 1-3(1-1)**
Maccabi Haifa: Josh Cohen, Daniel Sundgren (55.Abdoulaye Seck), Shon Goldberg, Dylan Batubinsika, Pierre Cornud (90+1.Mavis Tchibota), Tjaronn Chery, Neta Lavi, Dolev Haziza, Mohammad Abu Fani, Omer Atzili (76.Din David), Frantzdy Pierrot (90+1.Nikita Rukavytsya). Trainer: Barak Bakhar.
Paris Saint-Germain: Gianluigi Donnarumma, Sergio Ramos, Marquinhos, Nordi Mukiele (83.Achraf Hakimi), Nuno Mendes, Marco Verratti, Danilo Pereira, Vitinha (74.Fabián Ruiz), Lionel Messi, Neymar (90+1.Carlos Soler), Kylian Mbappé. Trainer: Christophe Galtier.
Goals: 24' Tjaronn Chery 1-0, 37' Lionel Messi 1-1, 69' Kylian Mbappé 1-2, 88' Neymar 1-3.

05.10.2022; Allianz Stadium, Torino; Attendance: 28,498
Referee: Sandro Schärer (Switzerland)
**Juventus FC Torino – Maccabi Haifa FC 3-1(1-0)**
Juventus: Wojciech Szczesny, Danilo, Mattia De Sciglio (46.Alex Sandro), Bremer, Ángel Di María, Juan Cuadrado (67.Leonardo Bonucci), Filip Kostic (66.Manuel Locatelli), Leandro Paredes (85.Fabio Miretti), Adrien Rabiot, Weston McKennie, Dusan Vlahovic (73.Moise Kean). Trainer: Massimiliano Allegri.
Maccabi Haifa: Josh Cohen, Daniel Sundgren, Shon Goldberg, Dylan Batubinsika, Pierre Cornud (60.Dolev Haziza), Abdoulaye Seck, Tjaronn Chery, Ali Muhammad (84.Nikita Rukavytsya), Mohammad Abu Fani (72.Neta Lavi), Mavis Tchibota (59.Omer Atzili), Frantzdy Pierrot (72.Din David). Trainer: Barak Bakhar.
Goals: 35' Adrien Rabiot 1-0, 50' Dusan Vlahovic 2-0, 75' Din David 2-1, 83' Adrien Rabiot 3-1.

11.10.2022; „Sammy Ofer" Stadium, Haifa; Attendance: 30,074
Referee: Antonio Miguel Mateu Lahoz (Spain)
**Maccabi Haifa FC – Juventus FC Torino 2-0(2-0)**
Maccabi Haifa: Josh Cohen, Daniel Sundgren, Shon Goldberg, Dylan Batubinsika, Pierre Cornud (71.Sun Menachem), Tjaronn Chery, Ali Muhammad (86.Mavis Tchibota), Neta Lavi, Omer Atzili (66.Abdoulaye Seck), Din David (72.Mohammad Abu Fani), Frantzdy Pierrot (86.Nikita Rukavytsya). Trainer: Barak Bakhar.
Juventus: Wojciech Szczesny, Leonardo Bonucci, Danilo (68.Moise Kean), Alex Sandro (74.Matías Soulé), Daniele Rugani, Ángel Di María (24.Arkadiusz Milik), Juan Cuadrado, Leandro Paredes (46.Manuel Locatelli), Adrien Rabiot, Weston McKennie (46.Filip Kostic), Dusan Vlahovic. Trainer: Massimiliano Allegri.
Goals: 7', 42' Omer Atzili 1-0, 2-0.

25.10.2022; Stade Parc des Princes, Paris; Attendance: 46,435
Referee: Felix Zwayer (Germany)
**Paris Saint-Germain FC – Maccabi Haifa FC 7-2(4-1)**
Paris Saint-Germain: Gianluigi Donnarumma, Sergio Ramos, Marquinhos (79.Presnel Kimpembe), Juan Bernat, Achraf Hakimi, Renato Sanches (68.Carlos Soler), Fabián Ruiz (83.Pablo Sarabia), Vitinha (79.Warren Zaïre-Emery), Lionel Messi, Neymar, Kylian Mbappé (79.Hugo Ekitike). Trainer: Christophe Galtier.
Maccabi Haifa: Josh Cohen, Shon Goldberg, Dylan Batubinsika, Pierre Cornud (70.Sun Menachem), Abdoulaye Seck, Tjaronn Chery, Ali Muhammad (83.Ofri Arad), Neta Lavi, Mohammad Abu Fani (71.Raz Meir), Omer Atzili (65.Din David), Frantzdy Pierrot (83.Nikita Rukavytsya). Trainer: Barak Bakhar.
Goals: 19' Lionel Messi 1-0, 32' Kylian Mbappé 2-0, 35' Neymar 3-0, 38' Abdoulaye Seck 3-1, 44' Lionel Messi 4-1, 50' Abdoulaye Seck 4-2, 64' Kylian Mbappé 5-2, 67' Shon Goldberg 6-2 (own goal), 84' Carlos Soler 7-2.

02.11.2022; Allianz Stadium, Torino; Attendance: 41,089
Referee: Carlos del Cerro Grande (Spain)
**Juventus FC Torino – Paris Saint-Germain FC 1-2(1-1)**
Juventus: Wojciech Szczesny, Leonardo Bonucci, Alex Sandro, Federico Gatti, Juan Cuadrado (88.Enzo Barrenechea), Filip Kostic, Adrien Rabiot, Manuel Locatelli (85.Matías Soulé), Nicolò Fagioli (88.Tommaso Barbieri), Fabio Miretti (74.Federico Chiesa), Arkadiusz Milik. Trainer: Massimiliano Allegri.
Paris Saint-Germain: Gianluigi Donnarumma, Sergio Ramos, Marquinhos, Juan Bernat (68.Nuno Mendes), Achraf Hakimi, Marco Verratti (88.Danilo Pereira), Fabián Ruiz (21.Renato Sanches), Carlos Soler (68.Hugo Ekitike), Vitinha, Lionel Messi, Kylian Mbappé. Trainer: Christophe Galtier.
Goals: 13' Kylian Mbappé 0-1, 39' Leonardo Bonucci 1-1, 69' Nuno Mendes 1-2.

05.10.2022; Estádio do Sport Lisboa e Benfica, Lisboa; Attendance: 62,295; Referee: Jesús Gil Manzano (Spain)
**Sport Lisboa e Benfica – Paris Saint-Germain FC 1-1(1-1)**
Benfica: Odisseas Vlachodimos, Nicolás Otamendi, Álex Grimaldo, Alexander Bah, António Silva, João Mário, Rafa Silva, Florentino, Enzo Fernández (78.Fredrik Aursnes), David Neres (90+1.Rodrigo Pinho), Gonçalo Ramos (78.Julian Draxler). Trainer: Roger Schmidt (Germany).
Paris Saint-Germain: Gianluigi Donnarumma, Sergio Ramos, Marquinhos, Achraf Hakimi, Nuno Mendes (67.Juan Bernat), Marco Verratti, Danilo Pereira, Vitinha (87.Fabián Ruiz), Lionel Messi (81.Pablo Sarabia), Neymar, Kylian Mbappé. Trainer: Christophe Galtier.
Goals: 22' Lionel Messi 0-1, 42' Danilo Pereira 1-1 (own goal).

11.10.2022; Stade Parc des Princes, Paris; Attendance: 46,435
Referee: Michael Oliver (England)
**Paris Saint-Germain FC – Sport Lisboa e Benfica 1-1(1-0)**
Paris Saint-Germain: Gianluigi Donnarumma, Sergio Ramos, Marquinhos, Juan Bernat (85.Nordi Mukiele), Achraf Hakimi, Marco Verratti, Pablo Sarabia (74.Hugo Ekitike), Danilo Pereira, Vitinha (85.Fabián Ruiz), Neymar, Kylian Mbappé (90.Carlos Soler). Trainer: Christophe Galtier.
Benfica: Odisseas Vlachodimos, Nicolás Otamendi, Álex Grimaldo, Alexander Bah (63.Gilberto), António Silva, João Mário (90+3.Chiquinho), Fredrik Aursnes, Rafa Silva (78.Julian Draxler), Florentino (78.Diogo Gonçalves), Enzo Fernández, Gonçalo Ramos (77.Rodrigo Pinho). Trainer: Roger Schmidt (Germany).
Goals: 39' Kylian Mbappé 1-0 (penalty), 62' João Mário 1-1 (penalty).

25.10.2022; Estádio do Sport Lisboa e Benfica, Lisboa; Attendance: 60,131; Referee: Srđan Jovanović (Serbia)
**Sport Lisboa e Benfica – Juventus FC Torino 4-3(3-1)**
Benfica: Odisseas Vlachodimos, Nicolás Otamendi, Álex Grimaldo, Alexander Bah (81.Gilberto), António Silva, João Mário (90+4.Chiquinho), Fredrik Aursnes, Rafa Silva (87.Petar Musa), Florentino, Enzo Fernández, Gonçalo Ramos (87.David Neres). Trainer: Roger Schmidt (Germany).
Juventus: Wojciech Szczesny, Leonardo Bonucci (60.Alex Sandro), Danilo, Federico Gatti, Juan Cuadrado (60.Fabio Miretti), Filip Kostic (70.Samuel Iling-Junior), Adrien Rabiot, Manuel Locatelli, Weston McKennie, Moise Kean (46.Arkadiusz Milik), Dusan Vlahovic (70.Matías Soulé). Trainer: Massimiliano Allegri.
Goals: 17' António Silva 1-0, 21' Moise Kean 1-1, 28' João Mário 2-1 (penalty), 35', 50' Rafa Silva 3-1, 4-1, 77' Arkadiusz Milik 4-2, 79' Weston McKennie 4-3.

02.11.2022; „Sammy Ofer" Stadium, Haifa; Attendance: 30,464
Referee: Anthony Taylor (England)
**Maccabi Haifa FC – Sport Lisboa e Benfica 1-6(1-1)**
Maccabi Haifa: Josh Cohen, Shon Goldberg, Pierre Cornud (85.Sun Menachem), Abdoulaye Seck, Tjaronn Chery, Raz Meir (63.Omer Atzili), Ali Muhammad (77.Ofri Arad), Neta Lavi, Mohammad Abu Fani, Din David (63.Mavis Tchibota), Frantzdy Pierrot (77.Nikita Rukavytsya). Trainer: Barak Bakhar.
Benfica: Odisseas Vlachodimos, Nicolás Otamendi, Álex Grimaldo, Alexander Bah, António Silva (88.Lucas Veríssimo), João Mário, Fredrik Aursnes (32.Chiquinho), Rafa Silva (82.Henrique Araújo), Florentino, David Neres (82.Diogo Gonçalves), Gonçalo Ramos (32.Petar Musa). Trainer: Roger Schmidt (Germany).
Goals: 20' Gonçalo Ramos 0-1, 26' Tjaronn Chery 1-1 (penalty), 59' Petar Musa 1-2, 69' Álex Grimaldo 1-3, 73' Rafa Silva 1-4, 88' Henrique Araújo 1-5, 90+2' João Mário 1-6.

14.02.2023; Stadio „Giuseppe Meazza", Milano; Attendance: 74,320
Referee: Sandro Schärer (Switzerland)
**AC Milan – Tottenham Hotspur FC London 1-0(1-0)**
AC Milan: Ciprian Tatarusanu, Simon Kjær, Theo Hernández, Pierre Kalulu, Malick Thiaw, Rade Krunic, Brahim Díaz (77.Charles De Ketelaere), Alexis Saelemaekers (77.Junior Messias), Sandro Tonali (86.Tommaso Pobega), Olivier Giroud, Rafael Leão (90+1.Ante Rebic). Trainer: Stefano Pioli.
Tottenham Hotspur: Fraser Forster, Clément Lenglet (81.Ben Davies), Eric Dier, Cristian Romero, Emerson Royal, Ivan Perisic, Oliver Skipp, Dejan Kulusevski (70.Richarlison), Pape Sarr, Heung-Min Son (81.Arnaut Danjuma), Harry Kane. Trainer: Antonio Conte (Italy).
Goal: 7' Brahim Díaz 1-0.

14.02.2023; Stade Parc des Princes, Paris; Attendance: 46,435
Referee: Michael Oliver (England)
**Paris Saint-Germain FC – FC Bayern München 0-1(0-0)**
Paris Saint-Germain: Gianluigi Donnarumma, Sergio Ramos, Marquinhos, Achraf Hakimi (46.Presnel Kimpembe), Nuno Mendes, Marco Verratti, Danilo Pereira (75.Vitinha), Carlos Soler (57.Kylian Mbappé), Warren Zaïre-Emery (57.Fabián Ruiz), Lionel Messi, Neymar. Trainer: Christophe Galtier.
Bayern München: Yann Sommer, João Cancelo (46.Alphonso Davies), Benjamin Pavard [*sent off 90+2*.], Dayot Upamecano, Matthijs de Ligt, Leon Goretzka, Joshua Kimmich, Eric Maxim Choupo-Moting (76.Thomas Müller), Kingsley Coman (75.Serge Gnabry), Leroy Sané (90.Josip Stanisic), Jamal Musiala (87.Ryan Gravenberch). Trainer: Julian Nagelsmann.
Goal: 53' Kingsley Coman 0-1.

15.02.2023; Jan Breydelstadion, Brugge; Attendance: 24,136
Referee: Davide Massa (Italy)
**Club Brugge KV – Sport Lisboa e Benfica 0-2(0-0)**
Club Brugge: Simon Mignolet, Denis Odoi (65.Casper Nielsen), Clinton Mata, Brandon Mechele, Jack Hendry, Bjorn Meijer, Hans Vanaken, Noa Lang, Raphael Onyedika, Tajon Buchanan, Kamal Sowah (79.Ferrán Jutglà). Trainer: Scott Matthew Parker (England).
Benfica: Odisseas Vlachodimos, Nicolás Otamendi, Álex Grimaldo, Alexander Bah, António Silva, João Mário (90+4.João Neves), Fredrik Aursnes, Rafa Silva (65.David Neres), Chiquinho, Florentino, Gonçalo Ramos (65.Gonçalo Guedes). Trainer: Roger Schmidt (Germany).
Goals: 51' João Mário 0-1 (penalty), 88' David Neres 0-2.

15.02.2023; Signal Iduna Park, Dortmund; Attendance: 81,365
Referee: Jesús Gil Manzano (Spain)
**BV 09 Borussia Dortmund – Chelsea FC London 1-0(0-0)**
Borussia Dortmund: Gregor Kobel, Raphaël Guerreiro, Niklas Süle, Nico Schlotterbeck, Emre Can, Julian Brandt, Marius Wolf (73.Julian Ryerson), Salih Özcan, Jude Bellingham, Sébastien Haller (68.Anthony Modeste), Karim Adeyemi (79.Jamie Bynoe-Gittens). Trainer: Edin Terzic.
Chelsea FC: Kepa, Thiago Silva, Kalidou Koulibaly, Ben Chilwell (71.Marc Cucurella), Reece James, Hakim Ziyech, Ruben Loftus-Cheek, Kai Havertz, Mykhaylo Mudryk (71.Mason Mount), Enzo Fernández, João Félix. Trainer: Graham Potter.
Goal: 63' Karim Adeyemi 1-0.

21.02.2023; Anfield Road, Liverpool; Attendance: 52,337
Referee: István Kovács (Romania)
**Liverpool FC – Real Madrid CF 2-5(2-2)**
Liverpool FC: Alisson, Virgil van Dijk, Andy Robertson, Joe Gomez (73.Joel Matip), Trent Alexander-Arnold, Stefan Bajcetic (85.Harvey Elliott), Jordan Henderson (73.James Milner), Fabinho, Mohamed Salah, Cody Gakpo (64.Roberto Firmino), Darwin Núñez (64.Diogo Jota). Trainer: Jürgen Klopp (Germany).
Real Madrid: Thibaut Courtois, David Alaba (27.Nacho), Dani Carvajal, Antonio Rüdiger, Éder Militão, Luka Modric (87.Toni Kroos), Federico Valverde, Eduardo Camavinga, Karim Benzema (87.Marco Asensio), Vinícius Júnior, Rodrygo (81.Dani Caballos). Trainer: Carlo Ancelotti.
Goals: 4' Darwin Núñez 1-0 14' Mohamed Salah 2-0, 21', 36' Vinícius Júnior 1-2, 2-2, 47' Éder Militão 2-3, 55', 67' Karim Benzema 2-4, 2-5.

08.03.2023; Tottenham Hotspur Stadium, London; Attendance: 61,602
Referee: Clément Turpin (France)
**Tottenham Hotspur FC London – AC MILAN 0-0**
Tottenham Hotspur: Fraser Forster, Ben Davies, Clément Lenglet, Cristian Romero [*sent off 77*], Emerson Royal (70.Richarlison), Ivan Perisic (53.Pedro Porro), Pierre-Emile Højbjerg, Oliver Skipp, Dejan Kulusevski (83.Davinson Sánchez), Heung-Min Son, Harry Kane. Trainer: Antonio Conte (Italy).
AC Milan: Mike Maignan, Fikayo Tomori, Theo Hernández, Pierre Kalulu, Malick Thiaw, Rade Krunic, Brahim Díaz (81.Ismaël Bennacer), Sandro Tonali, Olivier Giroud (81.Divock Origi), Rafael Leão (89.Ante Rebic), Junior Messias (56.Alexis Saelemaekers). Trainer: Stefano Pioli.

08.03.2023; Allianz Arena, München; Attendance: 75,000
Referee: Daniele Orsato (Italy)
**FC BAYERN MÜNCHEN – Paris Saint-Germain FC 2-0(0-0)**
Bayern München: Yann Sommer, Dayot Upamecano, Matthijs de Ligt, Josip Stanisic, Leon Goretzka, Joshua Kimmich, Eric Maxim Choupo-Moting (68.Leroy Sané), Thomas Müller (86.João Cancelo), Kingsley Coman (86.Serge Gnabry), Alphonso Davies, Jamal Musiala (82.Sadio Mané). Trainer: Julian Nagelsmann.
Paris Saint-Germain: Gianluigi Donnarumma, Sergio Ramos, Marquinhos (36.Nordi Mukiele, 46.El Chadaïlle Bitshiabu), Achraf Hakimi, Nuno Mendes, Marco Verratti, Danilo Pereira, Fabián Ruiz (76.Warren Zaïre-Emery), Vitinha (81.Hugo Ekitike), Lionel Messi, Kylian Mbappé. Trainer: Christophe Galtier.
Goals: 61' Eric Maxim Choupo-Moting 1-0, 89' Serge Gnabry 2-0.

07.03.2023; Estádio do Sport Lisboa e Benfica, Lisboa; Attendance: 60,960; Referee: Halil Umut Meler (Turkey)
**SPORT LISBOA E BENFICA – Club Brugge KV 5-1(2-0)**
Benfica: Odisseas Vlachodimos, Nicolás Otamendi (74.Morato), Álex Grimaldo, Alexander Bah (63.Gilberto), António Silva (88.Lucas Veríssimo), João Mário (74.João Neves), Fredrik Aursnes, Rafa Silva, Chiquinho (63.David Neres), Florentino, Gonçalo Ramos. Trainer: Roger Schmidt (Germany).
Club Brugge: Simon Mignolet, Clinton Mata (62.Denis Odoi), Brandon Mechele, Bjorn Meijer, Abakar Sylla, Hans Vanaken (74.Mats Rits), Casper Nielsen, Noa Lang (46.Raphael Onyedika), Roman Yaremchuk (62.Ferrán Jutglà), Tajon Buchanan, Kamal Sowah (75.Antonio Nusa). Trainer: Scott Matthew Parker (England).
Goals: 38' Rafa Silva 1-0, 45+2', 57' Gonçalo Ramos 2-0, 3-0, 71' João Mário 4-0 (penalty), 78' David Neres 5-0, 87' Bjorn Meijer 5-1.

07.03.2023; Stamford Bridge, London; Attendance: 38,882
Referee: Danny Desmond Makkelie (Netherlands)
**CHELSEA FC LONDON – BV 09 Borussia Dortmund 2-0(1-0)**
Chelsea FC: Kepa, Kalidou Koulibaly, Marc Cucurella, Ben Chilwell, Reece James, Wesley Fofana, Mateo Kovacic (83.Christian Pulisic), Kai Havertz, Enzo Fernández (87.Denis Zakaria), Raheem Sterling (82.Ruben Loftus-Cheek), João Félix (67.Conor Gallagher). Trainer: Graham Potter.
Borussia Dortmund: Alexander Meyer, Raphaël Guerreiro, Niklas Süle, Nico Schlotterbeck, Marco Reus, Emre Can, Julian Brandt (5.Gio Reyna), Marius Wolf, Salih Özcan (64.Jamie Bynoe-Gittens), Jude Bellingham, Sébastien Haller (77.Donyell Malen). Trainer: Edin Terzic.
Goals: 43' Raheem Sterling 1-0, 53' Kai Havertz 2-0 (penalty).

15.03.2023; Estadio „Santiago Bernabéu", Madrid; Attendance: 63,127
Referee: Felix Zwayer (Germany)
**REAL MADRID CF – Liverpool FC 1-0(0-0)**
Real Madrid: Thibaut Courtois, Nacho, Dani Carvajal (86.Lucas Vázquez), Antonio Rüdiger, Éder Militão, Luka Modric (82.Dani Caballos), Toni Kroos (84.Aurélien Tchouaméni), Federico Valverde, Eduardo Camavinga, Karim Benzema (82.Rodrygo), Vinícius Júnior (84.Marco Asensio). Trainer: Carlo Ancelotti.
Liverpool FC: Alisson, Virgil van Dijk, Andy Robertson (90+1.Kostas Tsimikas), Trent Alexander-Arnold, Ibrahima Konaté, James Milner (73.Alex Oxlade-Chamberlain), Fabinho, Mohamed Salah, Diogo Jota (57.Harvey Elliott), Cody Gakpo (90+1.Fábio Carvalho), Darwin Núñez (57.Roberto Firmino). Trainer: Jürgen Klopp (Germany).
Goal: 78' Karim Benzema 1-0.

21.02.2023; Deutsche Bank Park, Frankfurt am Main; Attendance: 47,500; Referee: Artur Manuel Ribeiro Soares Dias (Portugal)
**Eintracht Frankfurt – SSC Napoli 0-2(0-1)**
Eintracht Frankfurt: Kevin Trapp, Philipp Max (90+2.Christopher Lenz), Aurélio Buta (69.Ansgar Knauff), Evan Ndicka, Tuta, Mario Götze (81.Faride Alidou), Djibril Sow, Daichi Kamada, Kristijan Jakic, Jesper Lindstrøm (69.Rafael Borré), Randal Kolo Muani [*sent off 58*]. Trainer: Oliver Glasner (Austria).
SSC Napoli: Alex Meret, Giovanni Di Lorenzo, Amir Rrahmani, Mathías Olivera, Kim Min-Jae, Piotr Zielinski, Stanislav Lobotka, Frank Zambo Anguissa (80.Tanguy Ndombèlé), Hirving Lozano (80.Eljif Elmas), Victor Osimhen (84.Giovanni Simeone), Khvicha Kvaratskhelia (84.Matteo Politano). Trainer: Luciano Spalletti.
Goals: 40' Victor Osimhen 0-1, 65' Giovanni Di Lorenzo 0-2.

22.02.2023; Red Bull Arena, Leipzig; Attendance: 45,228
Referee: Serdar Gözübüyük (Netherlands)
**RasenBallsport Leipzig – Manchester City FC 1-1(0-1)**
RB Leipzig: Janis Blaswich, Marcel Halstenberg (89.David Raum), Willi Orbán, Lukas Klostermann (46.Benjamin Henrichs), Josko Gvardiol, Emil Forsberg (66.Christopher Nkunku), Konrad Laimer, Xaver Schlager (82.Amadou Haïdara), Dominik Szoboszlai, André Silva (82.Yussuf Poulsen), Timo Werner. Trainer: Marco Rose.
Manchester City: Ederson, Kyle Walker, Nathan Aké, Rúben Dias, Manuel Akanji, Ilkay Gündogan, Jack Grealish, Bernardo Silva, Rodri, Riyad Mahrez, Erling Haaland. Trainer: Josep Guardiola (Spain).
Goals: 27' Riyad Mahrez 0-1, 70' Josko Gvardiol 1-1.

22.02.2023; Stadio „Giuseppe Meazza", Milano; Attendance: 75,374
Referee: Srđan Jovanović (Serbia)
**FC Internazionale Milano – FC Porto 1-0(0-0)**
Internazionale Milano: André Onana, Matteo Darmian, Francesco Acerbi, Milan Skriniar (81.Denzel Dumfries), Federico Dimarco (58.Robin Gosens), Alessandro Bastoni, Henrikh Mkhitaryan (72.Marcelo Brozović), Hakan Çalhanoglu, Nicolò Barella, Edin Dzeko (58.Romelu Lukaku), Lautaro Martínez. Trainer: Simone Inzaghi.
FC Porto: Diogo Costa, Pepe, Iván Marcano, Zaidu Sanusi, João Mário (90+2.Gonçalo Borges), Mateus Uribe, Otávio [*sent off 78*], Marko Grujic, Mehdi Taremi (83.Wendell), Galeno (51.Evanilson), Pepê Aquino. Trainer: Sérgio Paulo Marceneiro da Conceição.
Goal: 86' Romelu Lukaku 1-0.

15.03.2023; Stadio „Diego Armando Maradona", Napoli;
Attendance: 49,082; Referee: Anthony Taylor (England)
**SSC NAPOLI – Eintracht Frankfurt 3-0(1-0)**
SSC Napoli: Alex Meret, Mário Rui, Giovanni Di Lorenzo, Amir Rrahmani, Kim Min-Jae (66.Juan Jesus), Piotr Zielinski (74.Tanguy Ndombèlé), Stanislav Lobotka, Frank Zambo Anguissa, Matteo Politano (67.Hirving Lozano), Victor Osimhen (81.Giovanni Simeone), Khvicha Kvaratskhelia (74.Eljif Elmas). Trainer: Luciano Spalletti.
Eintracht Frankfurt: Kevin Trapp, Christopher Lenz (67.Philipp Max), Aurélio Buta, Evan Ndicka, Tuta, Sebastian Rode (74.Kristijan Jakic), Mario Götze, Djibril Sow, Daichi Kamada, Rafael Borré, Ansgar Knauff (62.Faride Alidou). Trainer: Oliver Glasner (Austria).
Goals: 45+2', 53' Victor Osimhen 1-0, 2-0, 64' Piotr Zielinski 3-0 (penalty).

14.03.2023; Etihad Stadium, Manchester; Attendance: 52,038
Referee: Slavko Vinčić (Slovenia)
**MANCHESTER CITY FC – RasenBallsport Leipzig 7-0(3-0)**
Manchester City: Ederson, Nathan Aké, John Stones (64.Sergio Gómez), Rúben Dias, Manuel Akanji, Ilkay Gündogan (55.Riyad Mahrez), Kevin De Bruyne, Jack Grealish (55.Phil Foden), Bernardo Silva, Rodri (64.Kalvin Phillips), Erling Haaland (63.Julián Álvarez). Trainer: Josep Guardiola (Spain).
RB Leipzig: Janis Blaswich, Willi Orbán, Benjamin Henrichs (80.Lukas Klostermann), David Raum, Josko Gvardiol, Emil Forsberg (62.André Silva), Kevin Kampl, Konrad Laimer, Amadou Haïdara (63.Mohamed Simakan), Dominik Szoboszlai (72.Dani Olmo), Timo Werner (62.Yussuf Poulsen). Trainer: Marco Rose.
Goals: 22', 24', 45+2' Erling Haaland 1-0 (penalty), 2-0, 3-0, 49' Ilkay Gündogan 4-0, 53', 57' Erling Haaland 5-0, 6-0, 90+2' Kevin De Bruyne 7-0.

14.03.2023; Estádio do Dragão, Porto; Attendance: 48,015
Referee: Szymon Marciniak (Poland)
**FC Porto – FC INTERNAZIONALE MILANO 0-0**
FC Porto: Diogo Costa, Iván Marcano, Fábio Cardoso, Zaidu Sanusi (85.Wendell), Mateus Uribe (85.Danny Namaso Loader), Marko Grujic, Stephen Eustáquio (70.André Franco), Mehdi Taremi, Galeno, Pepê Aquino [*sent off 90+7*], Evanilson (71.Toni Martínez). Trainer: Sérgio Paulo Marceneiro da Conceição.
Internazionale Milano: André Onana, Matteo Darmian (80.Milan Skriniar), Francesco Acerbi, Federico Dimarco (70.Danilo D'Ambrosio), Denzel Dumfries, Alessandro Bastoni (74.Stefan de Vrij), Henrikh Mkhitaryan, Hakan Çalhanoglu, Nicolò Barella (80.Marcelo Brozović), Edin Dzeko (70.Romelu Lukaku), Lautaro Martínez. Trainer: Simone Inzaghi.

11.04.2023; Estádio do Sport Lisboa e Benfica, Lisboa; Attendance: 62,594; Referee: Michael Oliver (England)
**Sport Lisboa e Benfica – FC Internazionale Milano 0-2(0-0)**
Benfica: Odisseas Vlachodimos, Gilberto, Álex Grimaldo, Morato, António Silva, João Mário, Fredrik Aursnes, Rafa Silva, Chiquinho, Florentino (64.David Neres), Gonçalo Ramos. Trainer: Roger Schmidt (Germany).
Internazionale Milano: André Onana, Matteo Darmian, Francesco Acerbi, Federico Dimarco (63.Robin Gosens), Denzel Dumfries (87.Danilo D'Ambrosio), Alessandro Bastoni (90+1.Stefan de Vrij), Henrikh Mkhitaryan, Marcelo Brozovic, Nicolò Barella, Edin Dzeko (63.Romelu Lukaku), Lautaro Martínez (63.Joaquín Correa). Trainer: Simone Inzaghi.
Goals: 51' Nicolò Barella 0-1, 82' Romelu Lukaku 0-2 (penalty).

11.04.2023; Etihad Stadium, Manchester; Attendance: 52,257
Referee: Jesús Gil Manzano (Spain)
**Manchester City FC – FC Bayern München 3-0(1-0)**
Manchester City: Ederson, Nathan Aké, John Stones, Rúben Dias, Manuel Akanji, Ilkay Gündogan, Kevin De Bruyne (68.Julián Álvarez), Jack Grealish, Bernardo Silva, Rodri, Erling Haaland. Trainer: Josep Guardiola (Spain).
Bayern München: Yann Sommer, Benjamin Pavard, Dayot Upamecano, Matthijs de Ligt, Leon Goretzka, Joshua Kimmich, Serge Gnabry (80.Thomas Müller), Kingsley Coman, Leroy Sané, Alphonso Davies (80.João Cancelo), Jamal Musiala (69.Sadio Mané). Trainer: Thomas Tuchel (Germany).
Goals: 27' Rodri 1-0, 70' Bernardo Silva 2-0, 76' Erling Haaland 3-0.

12.04.2023; Estadio „Santiago Bernabéu", Madrid; Attendance: 63,142
Referee: François Letexier (France)
**Real Madrid CF – Chelsea FC London 2-0(1-0)**
Real Madrid: Thibaut Courtois, David Alaba, Dani Carvajal, Éder Militão, Luka Modric (81.Dani Ceballos), Toni Kroos (84.Aurélien Tchouaméni), Federico Valverde, Eduardo Camavinga (71.Antonio Rüdiger), Karim Benzema, Vinícius Júnior, Rodrygo (71.Marco Asensio). Trainer: Carlo Ancelotti.
Chelsea FC: Kepa, Thiago Silva (76.Mason Mount), Kalidou Koulibaly (55.Marc Cucurella), Ben Chilwell [sent off 59], Reece James, Wesley Fofana, Mateo Kovacic, N'Golo Kanté (75.Conor Gallagher), Enzo Fernández, Raheem Sterling (65.Kai Havertz), João Félix (65.Trevoh Chalobah). Trainer: Frank Lampard.
Goals: 21' Karim Benzema 1-0, 74' Marco Asencio 2-0.

12.04.2023; Stadio „Giuseppe Meazza", Milano; Attendance: 74,742
Referee: István Kovács (Romania)
**AC Milan – SSC Napoli 1-0(1-0)**
AC Milan: Mike Maignan, Simon Kjær, Davide Calabria, Fikayo Tomori, Theo Hernández, Rade Krunic, Ismaël Bennacer (67.Alexis Saelemaekers), Brahim Díaz (80.Ante Rebic), Sandro Tonali, Olivier Giroud, Rafael Leão. Trainer: Stefano Pioli.
SSC Napoli: Alex Meret, Mário Rui (81.Mathías Olivera), Giovanni Di Lorenzo, Amir Rrahmani, Kim Min-Jae, Piotr Zielinski (80.Tanguy Ndombèlé), Stanislav Lobotka, Frank Zambo Anguissa [sent off 74], Eljif Elmas, Hirving Lozano (69.Giacomo Raspadori), Khvicha Kvaratskhelia (81.Matteo Politano). Trainer: Luciano Spalletti.
Goal: 40' Ismaël Bennacer 1-0.

19.04.2023; Stadio „Giuseppe Meazza", Milano; Attendance: 75,380
Referee: Carlos del Cerro Grande (Spain)
**FC INTERNAZIONALE MILANO – Sport Lisboa e Benfica 3-3(1-1)**
Internazionale Milano: André Onana, Matteo Darmian, Francesco Acerbi, Federico Dimarco (80.Robin Gosens), Denzel Dumfries, Alessandro Bastoni (80.Danilo D'Ambrosio), Henrikh Mkhitaryan, Marcelo Brozovic, Nicolò Barella (76.Hakan Çalhanoglu), Edin Dzeko (76.Romelu Lukaku), Lautaro Martínez (76.Joaquín Correa). Trainer: Simone Inzaghi.
Benfica: Odisseas Vlachodimos, Nicolás Otamendi, Gilberto (46.David Neres), Álex Grimaldo, António Silva, João Mário (89.Andreas Schjelderup), Fredrik Aursnes, Rafa Silva (80.João Neves), Chiquinho (80.Petar Musa), Florentino, Gonçalo Ramos (74.Gonçalo Guedes). Trainer: Roger Schmidt (Germany).
Goals: 14' Nicolò Barella 1-0, 38' Fredrik Aursnes 1-1, 65' Lautaro Martínez 2-1, 78' Joaquín Correa 3-1, 86' António Silva 3-2, 90+5' Petar Musa 3-3.

19.04.2023; Allianz Arena, München; Attendance: 75,000
Referee: Clément Turpin (France)
**FC Bayern München – MANCHESTER CITY FC 1-1(0-0)**
Bayern München: Yann Sommer, João Cancelo (63.Alphonso Davies), Benjamin Pavard (77.Josip Stanisic), Dayot Upamecano, Matthijs de Ligt, Leon Goretzka, Joshua Kimmich, Eric Maxim Choupo-Moting (71.Mathys Tel), Kingsley Coman, Leroy Sané (64.Sadio Mané), Jamal Musiala (72.Thomas Müller). Trainer: Thomas Tuchel (Germany).
Manchester City: Ederson, Nathan Aké (66.Aymeric Laporte), John Stones, Rúben Dias, Manuel Akanji, Ilkay Gündogan, Kevin De Bruyne (88.Kyle Walker), Jack Grealish, Bernardo Silva, Rodri, Erling Haaland (84.Julián Álvarez). Trainer: Josep Guardiola (Spain).
Goals: 57' Erling Haaland 0-1, 83' Joshua Kimmich 1-1 (penalty).

18.04.2023; Stamford Bridge, London; Attendance: 39,453
Referee: Daniele Orsato (Italy)
**Chelsea FC London – REAL MADRID CF 0-2(0-0)**
Chelsea FC: Kepa, Thiago Silva, Marc Cucurella (68.Mykhaylo Mudryk), Trevoh Chalobah, Reece James, Wesley Fofana, Mateo Kovacic, N'Golo Kanté, Kai Havertz (77.Mason Mount), Conor Gallagher (67.João Félix), Enzo Fernández (67.Raheem Sterling). Trainer: Frank Lampard.
Real Madrid: Thibaut Courtois, David Alaba (46.Antonio Rüdiger), Dani Carvajal (81.Nacho), Éder Militão, Luka Modric, Toni Kroos (76.Dani Ceballos), Federico Valverde, Eduardo Camavinga (71.Aurélien Tchouaméni), Karim Benzema, Vinícius Júnior, Rodrygo (81.Marco Asensio). Trainer: Carlo Ancelotti.
Goals: 58', 80' Rodrygo 0-1, 0-2.

18.04.2023; Stadio "Diego Armando Maradona", Napoli; Attendance: 52,728; Referee: Szymon Marciniak (Poland)
**SSC Napoli – AC MILAN 1-1(0-1)**
SSC Napoli: Alex Meret, Juan Jesus, Mário Rui (34.Mathías Olivera), Giovanni Di Lorenzo, Amir Rrahmani (74.Leo Østigård), Piotr Zielinski (74.Giacomo Raspadori), Stanislav Lobotka, Tanguy Ndombèlé (63.Eljif Elmas), Matteo Politano (34.Hirving Lozano), Victor Osimhen, Khvicha Kvaratskhelia. Trainer: Luciano Spalletti.
AC Milan: Mike Maignan, Simon Kjær, Davide Calabria, Fikayo Tomori, Theo Hernández, Rade Krunic, Ismaël Bennacer, Brahim Díaz (59.Junior Messias), Sandro Tonali, Olivier Giroud (68.Divock Origi), Rafael Leão (84.Alexis Saelemaekers). Trainer: Stefano Pioli.
Goals: 43' Olivier Giroud 0-1, 90+3' Victor Osimhen 1-1.

09.05.2023; Estadio „Santiago Bernabéu", Madrid; Attendance: 63,485
Referee: Artur Manuel Ribeiro Soares Dias (Portugal)
**Real Madrid CF – Manchester City FC 1-1(1-0)**
Real Madrid: Thibaut Courtois, David Alaba, Dani Carvajal, Antonio Rüdiger, Luka Modric (87.Nacho), Toni Kroos (84.Aurélien Tchouaméni), Federico Valverde, Eduardo Camavinga, Karim Benzema, Vinícius Júnior, Rodrygo (81.Marco Asensio). Trainer: Carlo Ancelotti.
Manchester City: Ederson, Kyle Walker, John Stones, Rúben Dias, Manuel Akanji, Ilkay Gündogan, Kevin De Bruyne, Jack Grealish, Bernardo Silva, Rodri, Erling Haaland. Trainer: Josep Guardiola (Spain).
Goals: 36' Vinícius Júnior 1-0, 67' Kevin De Bruyne 1-1.

10.05.2023; Stadio „Giuseppe Meazza", Milano; Attendance: 75,532
Referee: Jesús Gil Manzano (Spain)
**AC Milan – FC Internazionale Milano 0-2(0-2)**
AC Milan: Mike Maignan, Simon Kjær (59.Malick Thiaw), Davide Calabria (82.Pierre Kalulu), Fikayo Tomori, Theo Hernández, Rade Krunic, Ismaël Bennacer (17.Junior Messias), Brahim Díaz (82.Tommaso Pobega), Alexis Saelemaekers (59.Divock Origi), Sandro Tonali, Olivier Giroud. Trainer: Stefano Pioli.
Internazionale Milano: André Onana, Matteo Darmian, Francesco Acerbi, Federico Dimarco (70.Stefan de Vrij), Denzel Dumfries, Alessandro Bastoni, Henrikh Mkhitaryan (62.Marcelo Brozovic), Hakan Çalhanoglu (78.Roberto Gagliardini), Nicolò Barella, Edin Dzeko (70.Romelu Lukaku), Lautaro Martínez (78.Joaquín Correa). Trainer: Simone Inzaghi.
Goals: 8' Edin Dzeko 0-1, 11' Henrikh Mkhitaryan 0-2.

17.05.2023; Etihad Stadium, Manchester; Attendance: 52,313
Referee: Szymon Marciniak (Poland)
**MANCHESTER CITY FC – Real Madrid CF 4-0(2-0)**
Manchester City: Ederson, Kyle Walker, John Stones, Rúben Dias, Manuel Akanji, Ilkay Gündogan (79.Riyad Mahrez), Kevin De Bruyne (84.Phil Foden), Jack Grealish, Bernardo Silva, Rodri, Erling Haaland (89.Julián Álvarez). Trainer: Josep Guardiola (Spain).
Real Madrid: Thibaut Courtois, David Alaba, Dani Carvajal (80.Lucas Vázquez), Éder Militão, Luka Modric (63.Antonio Rüdiger), Toni Kroos (70.Marco Asensio), Federico Valverde, Eduardo Camavinga (79.Aurélien Tchouaméni), Karim Benzema, Vinícius Júnior, Rodrygo (79.Dani Ceballos). Trainer: Carlo Ancelotti.
Goals: 23', 37' Bernardo Silva 1-0, 2-0, 76' Manuel Akanji 3-0, 90+1' Julián Álvarez 4-0.

16.05.2023; Stadio „Giuseppe Meazza", Milano; Attendance: 75,567
Referee: Clément Turpin (France)
**FC INTERNAZIONALE MILANO – AC Milan 1-0(0-0)**
Internazionale Milano: André Onana, Matteo Darmian, Francesco Acerbi, Federico Dimarco (66.Robin Gosens), Denzel Dumfries, Alessandro Bastoni, Henrikh Mkhitaryan (44.Marcelo Brozovic), Hakan Çalhanoglu, Nicolò Barella (84.Roberto Gagliardini), Edin Dzeko (66.Romelu Lukaku), Lautaro Martínez (84.Joaquín Correa). Trainer: Simone Inzaghi.
AC Milan: Mike Maignan, Davide Calabria, Fikayo Tomori, Theo Hernández, Malick Thiaw (64.Pierre Kalulu), Rade Krunic, Brahim Díaz (76.Divock Origi), Sandro Tonali, Olivier Giroud, Rafael Leão, Junior Messias (76.Alexis Saelemaekers). Trainer: Stefano Pioli.
Goal: 74' Lautaro Martínez 1-0.

10.06.2023; Atatürk Olimpiyat Stadi, Istanbul (Turkey); Referee: Szymon Marciniak (Poland); Attendance: 71,412
**Manchester City FC – FC Internazionale Milano 1-0(0-0)**
Manchester City: Ederson, Nathan Aké, John Stones (82.Kyle Walker), Rúben Dias, Manuel Akanji, Ilkay Gündogan, Kevin De Bruyne (36.Phil Foden), Jack Grealish, Bernardo Silva, Rodri, Erling Haaland. Trainer: Josep Guardiola (Spain).
Internazionale Milano: André Onana, Matteo Darmian (84.Danilo D'Ambrosio), Francesco Acerbi, Federico Dimarco, Denzel Dumfries (76.Raoul Bellanova), Alessandro Bastoni (76.Robin Gosens), Marcelo Brozovic, Hakan Çalhanoglu (84.Henrikh Mkhitaryan), Nicolò Barella, Edin Dzeko (57.Romelu Lukaku), Lautaro Martínez. Trainer: Simone Inzaghi.
Goals: 68' Rodri 1-0.

UEFA Champions League Winner 2022/2023: **Manchester City FC** (England)

Best Goalscorer: Erling Braut Haaland (NOR, Manchester City FC) – 12 goals

# EUROPEAN CHAMPION CLUBS' CUP (1955 – 1992)
## UEFA CHAMPIONS LEAGUE (1992 – 2023)
### TABLE OF HONOURS

| | | |
|---|---|---|
| 1955/1956 | Real Madrid CF | Spain |
| 1956/1957 | Real Madrid CF | Spain |
| 1957/1958 | Real Madrid CF | Spain |
| 1958/1959 | Real Madrid CF | Spain |
| 1959/1960 | Real Madrid CF | Spain |
| 1960/1961 | Sport Lisboa e Benfica | Portugal |
| 1961/1962 | Sport Lisboa e Benfica | Portugal |
| 1962/1963 | AC Milan | Italy |
| 1963/1964 | FC Internazionale Milano | Italy |
| 1964/1965 | FC Internazionale Milano | Italy |
| 1965/1966 | Real Madrid CF | Spain |
| 1966/1967 | Celtic FC Glasgow | Scotland |
| 1967/1968 | Manchester United FC | England |
| 1968/1969 | AC Milan | Italy |
| 1969/1970 | SC Feijenoord Rotterdam | Netherlands |
| 1970/1971 | AFC Ajax Amsterdam | Netherlands |
| 1971/1972 | AFC Ajax Amsterdam | Netherlands |
| 1972/1973 | AFC Ajax Amsterdam | Netherlands |
| 1973/1974 | FC Bayern München | Germany |
| 1974/1975 | FC Bayern München | Germany |
| 1975/1976 | FC Bayern München | Germany |
| 1976/1977 | Liverpool FC | England |
| 1977/1978 | Liverpool FC | England |
| 1978/1979 | Nottingham Forest FC | England |
| 1979/1980 | Nottingham Forest FC | England |
| 1980/1981 | Liverpool FC | England |
| 1981/1982 | Aston Villa FC Birmingham | England |
| 1982/1983 | Hamburger SV | Germany |
| 1983/1984 | Liverpool FC | England |
| 1984/1985 | Juventus FC Torino | Italy |
| 1985/1986 | FC Steaua Bucureşti | Romania |
| 1986/1987 | FC do Porto | Portugal |
| 1987/1988 | PSV Eindhoven | Netherlands |
| 1988/1989 | AC Milan | Italy |
| 1989/1990 | AC Milan | Italy |
| 1990/1991 | FK Crvena Zvezda Beograd | Serbia |
| 1991/1992 | FC Barcelona | Spain |
| 1992/1993 | Olympique de Marseille | France |
| 1993/1994 | AC Milan | Italy |
| 1994/1995 | AFC Ajax Amsterdam | Netherlands |
| 1995/1996 | Juventus FC Torino | Italy |
| 1996/1997 | BV Borussia 09 Dortmund | Germany |
| 1997/1998 | Real Madrid CF | Spain |
| 1998/1999 | Manchester United FC | England |
| 1999/2000 | Real Madrid CF | Spain |
| 2000/2001 | FC Bayern München | Germany |
| 2001/2002 | Real Madrid CF | Spain |
| 2002/2003 | AC Milan | Italy |
| 2003/2004 | FC do Porto | Portugal |
| 2004/2005 | Liverpool FC | England |
| 2005/2006 | FC Barcelona | Spain |
| 2006/2007 | AC Milan | Italy |
| 2007/2008 | Manchester United FC | England |
| 2008/2009 | FC Barcelona | Spain |
| 2009/2010 | FC Internazionale Milano | Italy |
| 2010/2011 | FC Barcelona | Spain |
| 2011/2012 | Chelsea FC London | England |
| 2012/2013 | FC Bayern München | Germany |
| 2013/2014 | Real Madrid CF | Spain |
| 2014/2015 | FC Barcelona | Spain |
| 2015/2016 | Real Madrid CF | Spain |
| 2016/2017 | Real Madrid CF | Spain |
| 2017/2018 | Real Madrid CF | Spain |
| 2018/2019 | Liverpool FC | England |
| 2019/2020 | FC Bayern München | Germany |
| 2020/2021 | Chelsea FC London | England |
| 2021/2022 | Real Madrid CF | Spain |
| 2022/2023 | Manchester City FC | England |

## THIRD QUALIFYING ROUND

The winners of the ties advanced to the Play-off Round.
The losers were transferred to the UEFA Europa Conference League Play-off Round of their respective path.

### CHAMPIONS PATH

04.08.2022; Eleda Stadion, Malmö; Attendance: 11,172
Referee: Enea Jorgji (Albania)
**Malmö FF – F91 Dudelange 3-0(0-0)**
Malmö FF: Johan Dahlin, Martin Olsson (76.Eric Larsson), Niklas Moisander, Lasse Nielsen, Felix Beijmo, Jo Inge Berget (69.Veljko Birmancevic), Sergio Peña (76.Hugo Larsson), Erdal Rakip, Moustafa Zeidan, Joseph Ceesay (82.Mohamed Buya Turay), Isaac Kiese Thelin (76.Ola Toivonen). Trainer: Andreas Georgson.
F91 Dudelange: Lucas Fox, Manuel da Costa, Jules Diouf (64.Ninte Junior), Mehdi Kirch, Sylvio Ouassiero (42.Eliot Gashi), Dejvid Sinani (63.Vova), Aldin Skenderovic, Charles Morren [sent off 31], Bruno Frere (63.Chris Stumpf), Samir Hadji (38.Filip Bojic), João Magno. Trainer: Carlos Manuel Fangueiro Soares (Portugal).
Goals: 54' Isaac Kiese Thelin 1-0, 81' Ola Toivonen 2-0, 85' Veljko Birmancevic 3-0.

04.08.2022; Ljudski vrt, Maribor; Attendance: 6,000
Referee: Georgi Kabakov (Bulgaria)
**NK Maribor – HJK Helsinki 0-2(0-0)**
NK Maribor: Menno Bergsen, Nemanja Mitrovic, Gregor Sikosek, Max Watson, Andraz Zinic (76.Marin Lausic), Jan Repas, Vladan Vidakovic (76.Sven Karic), Aljaz Antolin (87.Luka Bozickovic), Roko Baturina, Zan Vipotnik (65.Rok Kronaveter), Ivan Brnic (65.Marko Bozic). Trainer: Radovan Karanovic.
HJK Helsinki: Conor Hazard, Jukka Raitala, Miro Tenho, Murilo, Matti Peltola, Lucas Lingman (73.Johannes Yli-Kokko), Santeri Väänänen (46.Atomu Tanaka), David Browne (53.Pyry Soiri), Santeri Hostikka, Anthony Olusanya (46.Bojan Radulovic), Malik Abubakari (87.Fabian Serrarens). Trainer: Toni Koskela.
Goals: 47' David Browne 0-1, 64' Bojan Radulovic 0-2.

04.08.2022; Windsor Park, Belfast; Attendance: 3,044
Referee: Marco Di Bello (Italy)
**Linfield FC Belfast – FC Zürich 0-2(0-1)**
Linfield FC: Chris Johns, Matthew Clarke (87.Ethan Devine), Ben Hall, Sam Roscoe-Byrne, Danny Finlayson, Jamie Mulgrew (68.Cammy Palmer), Chris Shields, Stephen Fallon, Kyle McClean (68.Jordan Stewart), Robbie McDaid (53.Joel Cooper), Eetu Vertainen (68.Chris McKee). Trainer: David Healy.
FC Zürich: Yanick Brecher, Nikola Boranijasevic, Fidan Aliti, Mirlind Kryeziu, Lindrit Kamberi, Antonio Marchesano (72.Donis Avdijaj), Ole Selnæs (62.Marc Hornschuh), Cheick Oumar Condé, Jonathan Okita (62.Karol Mets), Aiyegun Tosin (72.Fabian Rohner), Wilfried Gnonto (85.Bledian Krasniqi). Trainer: Franco Foda (Germany).
Goals: 8' Aiyegun Tosin 0-1, 64' Wilfried Gnonto 0-2.

04.08.2022; Tallaght Stadium, Dublin; Attendance: 6,455
Referee: Bartosz Frankowski (Poland)
**Shamrock Rovers FC Dublin – KF Shkupi Čair 3-1(2-0)**
Shamrock Rovers: Alan Mannus, Sean Gannon, Sean Hoare, Lee Grace, Andy Lyons, Ronan Finn (73.Neil Farrugia), Chris McCann (61.Richie Towell), Gary O'Neill, Dylan Watts (73.Sean Kavanagh), Rory Gaffney (73.Aidomo Emakhu), Graham Burke (54.Aaron Greene). Trainer: Stephen Bradley.
KF Shkupi: Kristijan Naumovski, Gagi Margvelashvili, Faustin Senghor, Angelce Timovski, Freddy Álvarez (64.Ali Adem), Besir Demiri (46.Vladica Brdarovski), Queven (90.Dzhelil Abdula), Walid Hamidi [sent off 84], Sunday Adetunji (64.Pepi Georgiev), Albert Diène, Renaldo Cephas (64.Kristijan Trapanovski). Trainer: Goce Sedloski.
Goals: 13' Graham Burke 1-0 (penalty), 29' Dylan Watts 2-0, 77' Queven 2-1, 90+7' Gary O'Neill 3-1.

11.08.2022; Stade de Luxembourg, Lëtzebuerg; Attendance: 898
Referee: Ricardo de Burgos Bengoetxea (Spain)
**F91 Dudelange – MALMÖ FF 2-2(0-0)**
F91 Dudelange: Lucas Fox, Mehdi Kirch, Vincent Decker (77.Chris Stumpf), Dejvid Sinani, Vova, Eliot Gashi (67.Evann Mendes), Filip Bojic (77.Jules Diouf), Aldin Skenderovic, Samir Hadji, Edis Agovic (60.Bruno Frere), João Magno. Trainer: Carlos Manuel Fangueiro Soares (Portugal).
Malmö FF: Johan Dahlin, Martin Olsson (78.Eric Larsson), Lasse Nielsen, Dennis Hadzikadunic, Felix Beijmo, Anders Christiansen (88.Moustafa Zeidan), Sergio Peña (67.Niklas Moisander), Joseph Ceesay, Hugo Larsson, Ola Toivonen (67.Isaac Kiese Thelin), Mohamed Buya Turay (68.Søren Rieks). Trainer: Andreas Georgson.
Goals: 50' Mohamed Buya Turay 0-1, 52' Ola Toivonen 0-2, 56' Samir Hadji 1-2, 60' Dejvid Sinani 2-2.

11.08.2022; Bolt Arena, Helsinki; Attendance: 6,487
Referee: Tobias Stieler (Germany)
**HJK HELSINKI – NK Maribor 1-0(0-0)**
HJK Helsinki: Conor Hazard, Jukka Raitala, Miro Tenho, Murilo (84.Casper Terho), Arttu Hoskonen, Lucas Lingman (70.Përparim Hetemaj), Santeri Väänänen (57.Atomu Tanaka), David Browne, Santeri Hostikka (84.Anthony Olusanya), Bojan Radulovic, Malik Abubakari (57.Pyry Soiri). Trainer: Toni Koskela.
NK Maribor: Menno Bergsen, Nemanja Mitrovic, Gregor Sikosek, Sven Karic, Andraz Zinic (72.Ignacio Guerrico), Rok Kronaveter (46.Zan Vipotnik), Jan Repas, Vladan Vidakovic (72.Aljaz Antolin), Marko Bozic (60.Rok Sirk), Roko Baturina, Ivan Brnic (46.Marin Lausic). Trainer: Radovan Karanovic.
Goal: 54' Santeri Hostikka 1-0.

11.08.2022; Stadion Letzigrund, Zürich; Attendance: 7,904
Referee: Harm Osmers (Germany)
**FC ZÜRICH – Linfield FC Belfast 3-0(2-0)**
FC Zürich: Yanick Brecher, Nikola Boranijasevic (66.Fabian Rohner), Fidan Aliti, Mirlind Kryeziu, Adrián Guerrero, Lindrit Kamberi, Antonio Marchesano (74.Ivan Santini), Ole Selnæs (74.Blerim Dzemaili), Cheick Oumar Condé (46.Marc Hornschuh), Donis Avdijaj (46.Bledian Krasniqi), Aiyegun Tosin. Trainer: Franco Foda (Germany).
Linfield FC: Chris Johns, Matthew Clarke, Conor Pepper (85.Kirk Millar), Michael Newberry, Sam Roscoe-Byrne, Danny Finlayson, Jamie Mulgrew (85.Joshua Archer), Joel Cooper (63.Ethan Devine), Kyle McClean, Cammy Palmer (78.Andrew Clarke), Chris McKee (63.Eetu Vertainen). Trainer: David Healy.
Goals: 11', 25' Donis Avdijaj 1-0, 2-0, 84' Ivan Santini 3-0.

09.08.2022; Nacionalna Arena "Toše Proeski", Skopje; Attendance: 4,870; Referee: Aleksei Kulbakov (Belarus)
**KF Shkupi Čair – SHAMROCK ROVERS FC DUBLIN 1-2(0-0)**
KF Shkupi: Kristijan Naumovski, Gagi Margvelashvili, Faustin Senghor, Blerton Sheji (46.Vladica Brdarovski), Angelce Timovski (79.Besir Demiri), Freddy Álvarez, Queven, Ali Adem (46.Kristijan Trapanovski), Pepi Georgiev (79.Antonio Kalanoski), Sunday Adetunji, Albert Diène (46.Dzhelil Abdula). Trainer: Goce Sedloski.
Shamrock Rovers: Alan Mannus, Sean Hoare, Dan Cleary, Lee Grace, Andy Lyons (81.Neil Farrugia), Ronan Finn (68.Sean Gannon), Richie Towell (62.Graham Burke), Gary O'Neill, Dylan Watts, Rory Gaffney (69.Sean Kavanagh), Aaron Greene (81.Aidomo Emakhu). Trainer: Stephen Bradley.
Goals: 65' Rory Gaffney 0-1, 85' Aidomo Emakhu 0-2, 90+4' Sunday Adetunji 1-2.

04.08.2022; Stádio „Giórgos Karaïskáki", Peiraiás; Attendance: 15,585
Referee: Lawrence Visser (Belgium)
**Olympiacos SFP Peiraiás – ŠK Slovan Bratislava 1-1(0-0)**
Olympiacos: Tomás Vaclík, Sokratis Papastathopoulos, Pape Cissé, Pipa Ávila, Oleg Reabciuk, Yann M'Vila, Pierre Kunde Malong, Georgios Masouras (78.Garry Rodrigues), Mady Camara (68.Mathieu Valbuena), Tiquinho Soares (68.Youssef El-Arabi), Philip Zinckernagel (55.Lazar Randjelovic). Trainer: Carlos Corberán Vallet (Spain).
Slovan Bratislava: Adrián Chovan, Guram Kashia, Lukás Pauschek, Vernon De Marco, Myenty Abena, Juraj Kucka (90+1.Uche Agbo), Jaba Kankava, Jaromír Zmrhal (85.Jurij Medvedev), Giorgi Chakvetadze (90+1.Aleksandar Cavric), Tigran Barseghyan (82.Eric Ramírez), Andre Green. Trainer: Vladimir Weiss.
Goals: 63' Andre Green 0-1, 86' Youssef El-Arabi 1-1.

11.08.2022; Štadion Tehelné pole, Bratislava; Attendance: 18,133
Referee: Glenn Nyberg (Sweden)
**ŠK Slovan Bratislava – OLYMPIACOS SFP PEIRAIÁS 2-2(0-0,1-1,2-2); 3-4 on penalties**
Slovan Bratislava: Adrián Chovan, Guram Kashia, Lukás Pauschek (90+1.Jurij Medvedev), Vernon De Marco (69.Uche Agbo), Myenty Abena [*sent off 90+7*], Juraj Kucka, Jaba Kankava (90+1.Aleksandar Cavric), Jaromír Zmrhal (85.Eric Ramírez), Giorgi Chakvetadze, Tigran Barseghyan (69.Iván Saponjic), Andre Green. Trainer: Vladimir Weiss.
Olympiacos: Tomás Vaclík, Pape Cissé, Pipa Ávila, Oleg Reabciuk, Ousseynou Ba (85.Andreas Bouchalakis), Yann M'Vila, Pierre Kunde Malong, Georgios Masouras, Lazar Randjelovic (80.Kostas Manolas), Youssef El-Arabi (68.Tiquinho Soares, 91.Mamadou Kané, 110.Mathieu Valbuena), Philip Zinckernagel (69.Aguibou Camara). Trainer: Carlos Corberán Vallet (Spain).
Goals: 54' Philip Zinckernagel 0-1, 90+4' Iván Saponjic 1-1, 101' Aguibou Camara 1-2, 108' Andre Green 2-2.
Penalties: Eric Ramírez 1-0; Pierre Kunde Malong (missed); Iván Saponjic 2-0; Andreas Bouchalakis 2-1; Juraj Kucka (missed); Georgios Masouras 2-2; Andre Green 3-2; Pipa Ávila 3-3; Giorgi Chakvetadze (missed); Mathieu Valbuena 3-4.

---

## MAIN PATH

---

04.08.2022; AEK Arena "Georgios Karapatakis", Larnaca; Attendance: 4,250; Referee: Andris Treimanis (Latvia)
**AEK Larnaca FC – FK Partizan Beograd 2-1(1-1)**
AEK Larnaca: Kenan Piric, Roberto Rosales, Nenad Tomovic, Oier, Ángel García (81.Kypros Christoforou), Gus Ledes, Hrvoje Milicevic, Ádám Gyurcsó (61.Bruno Gama), Ivan Trickovski (62.Omri Altman), Imad Faraj (89.Rafail Mamas), Victor Olatunji (61.Rafael Lopes). Trainer: José Luis Oltra (Spain).
Partizan Beograd: Nemanja Stevanovic, Aleksander Filipovic (63.Marko Zivkovic), Igor Vujacic, Slobodan Urosevic, Sinisa Sanicanin, Ljubomir Fejsa, Bibras Natcho (74.Samed Bazdar), Patrick Andrade (81.Kristijan Belic), Ricardo Gomes, Queensy Menig (81.Aleksandar Lutovac), Fousséni Diabaté (81.Nikola Terzic). Coaches: Aleksandar Stanojevic & Ilija Stolica.
Goals: 18' Queensy Menig 0-1, 34' Ángel García 1-1, 70' Hrvoje Milicevic 2-1.

04.08.2022; „Şükrü Saracoğlu" Stadyumu, Istanbul; Attendance: 35,536
Referee: João Pedro Silva Pinheiro (Portugal)
**Fenerbahçe SK Istanbul – 1. FC Slovácko Uherské Hradiště 3-0(2-0)**
Fenerbahçe: Ertugrul Çetin, Gustavo Henrique, Attila Szalai, Miha Zajc (60.Miguel Crespo), Willian Arão, Emre Mor (60.Bruma), Lincoln, Bright Osayi-Samuel, Ferdi Kadioglu (77.Filip Novák), Enner Valencia (77.Arda Güler), Diego Rossi (60.Serdar Dursun). Trainer: Jorge Fernando Pinheiro de Jesus (Portugal).
1. FC Slovácko: Filip Nguyen, Michal Kadlec, Petr Reinberk (69.Filip Vecheta), Stanislav Hofmann [*sent off 48*], Jan Kalabiska, Milan Petrzela (63.Michal Tomic), Vlastimil Daníček, Marek Havlík (46.Vladislav Levin), Michal Trávník (86.Michal Kohút), Daniel Holzer (63.Vlasiy Sinyavskiy), Merchas Doski. Trainer: Martin Svedík.
Goals: 17' Emre Mor 1-0, 45+2', 81' Lincoln 2-0, 3-0.

11.08.2022; Stadion Partizana, Beograd; Attendance: 10,802
Referee: José María Sánchez Martínez (Spain)
**FK Partizan Beograd – AEK LARNACA FC 2-2(1-0)**
Partizan Beograd: Aleksandar Popovic, Aleksander Filipovic, Igor Vujacic, Slobodan Urosevic, Svetozar Markovic, Ljubomir Fejsa, Bibras Natcho (64.Nemanja Jovic), Patrick Andrade, Ricardo Gomes (84.Samed Bazdar), Queensy Menig (80.Aleksandar Lutovac), Fousséni Diabaté. Coaches: Aleksandar Stanojevic & Ilija Stolica.
AEK Larnaca: Kenan Piric, Roberto Rosales, Nenad Tomovic, Oier, Gus Ledes, Hrvoje Milicevic, Ádám Gyurcsó (66.Bruno Gama), Omri Altman (79.Rafail Mamas), Nikos Englezou (66.Ismael Casas), Rafael Lopes (79.Victor Olatunji), Imad Faraj (89.Mikel González). Trainer: José Luis Oltra (Spain).
Goals: 24' Ricardo Gomes 1-0, 51' Ádám Gyurcsó 1-1, 54' Ricardo Gomes 2-1, 56' Imad Faraj 2-2.

11.08.2022; Městský fotbalový stadion "Miroslava Valenty", Uherské Hradiště; Attendance: 6,520; Referee: Nikola Dabanović (Montenegro)
**1. FC Slovácko Uherské Hradiště – FENERBAHÇE SK ISTANBUL 1-1(0-0)**
1. FC Slovácko: Filip Nguyen, Michal Kadlec, Patrik Simko (63.Petr Reinberk), Michal Tomic (84.Vlasiy Sinyavskiy), Milan Petrzela, Vlastimil Daníček, Michal Trávník, Daniel Holzer (64.Jan Kalabiska), Vladislav Levin (64.Michal Kohút), Merchas Doski, Ondrej Sasinka (72.Libor Kozák). Trainer: Martin Svedík.
Fenerbahçe: Altay Bayindir, Luan Peres (65.Filip Novák), Mauricio Lemos (74.Gustavo Henrique), Attila Szalai, Bright Osayi-Samuel, Miguel Crespo (65.Miha Zajc), Ismail Yüksek, Arda Güler (80.Lincoln), Serdar Dursun, Bruma (65.Emre Mor), Diego Rossi. Trainer: Jorge Fernando Pinheiro de Jesus (Portugal).
Goals: 56' Serdar Dursun 0-1, 58' Ondrej Sasinka 1-1.

The winners of the ties advanced to the Group Stage.
The losers were transferred to the UEFA Europa Conference League Group Stage.

18.08.2022; Bolt Arena, Helsinki; Attendance: 8,237
Referee: João Pedro Silva Pinheiro (Portugal)
**HJK Helsinki – Silkeborg IF 1-0(0-0)**
HJK Helsinki: Conor Hazard, Jukka Raitala, Miro Tenho, Murilo, Arttu Hoskonen, Lucas Lingman, Santeri Väänänen (73.Nassim Boujellab), Atomu Tanaka (62.Përparim Hetemaj), David Browne, Santeri Hostikka (73.Bojan Radulovic), Malik Abubakari (88.Anthony Olusanya). Trainer: Toni Koskela.
Silkeborg IF: Nicolai Larsen, André Calisir [sent off 68], Tobias Salquist, Lukas Engel, Oliver Sonne, Mark Brink (90+1.Pelle Mattsson), Stefán Teitur Thórdarson (71.Joel Felix), Nicolai Vallys, Sebastian Jørgensen (70.Søren Tengstedt), Anders Klynge (85.Mads Kaalund), Nicklas Helenius. Trainer: Kent Nielsen.
Goal: 80' David Browne 1-0.

18.08.2022; Groupama Aréna, Budapest; Attendance: 15,239
Referee: Glenn Nyberg (Sweden)
**Ferencvárosi TC – Shamrock Rovers FC Dublin 4-0(2-0)**
Ferencvárosi TC: Dénes Dibusz, Endre Botka, Henry Wingo, Lóránd Pászka (84.Eldar Civic), Mats Knoester, Muhamed Besic (70.Bálint Vécsei), Aïssa Laïdouni, Carlos Auzqui (63.Marquinhos), Tokmac Nguen, Adama Traoré (I) (84.Xavier Mercier), Ryan Mmaee (64.Franck Boli). Trainer: Stanislav Cherchesov (Russia).
Shamrock Rovers: Alan Mannus, Sean Kavanagh (60.Richie Towell), Sean Gannon (61.Neil Farrugia), Sean Hoare, Dan Cleary, Lee Grace, Andy Lyons, Gary O'Neill, Dylan Watts (70.Justin Ferizaj), Rory Gaffney (60.Jack Byrne), Aaron Greene (79.Gideon Tetteh). Trainer: Stephen Bradley.
Goals: 13' Carlos Auzqui 1-0, 34', 48' Adama Traoré 2-0, 3-0, 90+3' Eldar Civic 4-0.

18.08.2022; Kybunpark, St. Gallen; Attendance: 7,958
Referee: Bartosz Frankowski (Poland)
**FC Zürich – Heart of Midlothian FC Edinburgh 2-1(2-1)**
FC Zürich: Yanick Brecher, Karol Mets (83.Fidan Aliti), Nikola Boranijasevic, Mirlind Kryeziu, Becir Omeragic, Blerim Dzemaili (74.Cheick Oumar Condé), Antonio Marchesano, Ole Selnæs, Adrián Guerrero, Donis Avdijaj (71.Wilfried Gnonto), Bogdan Vyunnyk (71.Fabian Rohner). Trainer: Franco Foda (Germany).
Heart of Midlothian: Craig Gordon, Stephen Kingsley, Criag Halkett (7.Toby Sibbick), Kye Rowles, Alex Cochrane, Nathaniel Atkinson (46.Michael Smith), Peter Haring (70.Liam Boyce), Jorge Grant (70.Alan Forrest), Cameron Devlin, Lawrence Shankland (90+3.Josh Ginnelly), Barrie McKay. Trainer: Robbie Neilson.
Goals: 22' Lawrence Shankland 0-1 (penalty), 32' Adrián Guerrero 1-1, 34' Blerim Dzemaili 2-1.

18.08.2022; Eleda Stadion, Malmö; Attendance: 12,167
Referee: William Sean Collum (Scotland)
**Malmö FF – Sivasspor Kulübü 3-1(2-1)**
Malmö FF: Johan Dahlin, Niklas Moisander, Lasse Nielsen, Dennis Hadzikadunic, Felix Beijmo, Anders Christiansen (84.Hugo Larsson), Erdal Rakip (71.Sergio Peña), Moustafa Zeidan (71.Emmanuel Lomotey), Veljko Birmancevic, Joseph Ceesay, Isaac Kiese Thelin (88.Jo Inge Berget). Trainer: Andreas Georgson.
Sivasspor: Muammer Yildirim, Caner Osmanpasa, Ugur Çiftçi, Dimitrios Goutas, Max Gradel, Hakan Arslan (84.Kader Keita), Fredrik Ulvestad (74.Clinton N'Jie), Robin Yalçin (74.Mustapha Yatabaré), Erdogan Yesilyurt, Kerem Kesgin (61.Charilaos Charisis), Leke James. Trainer: Riza Çalimbay.
Goals: 18' Moustafa Zeidan 1-0, 30' Leke James 1-1, 37' Anders Christiansen 2-1, 68' Niklas Moisander 3-1.

25.08.2022; JYSK Park, Silkeborg; Attendance: 6,334
Referee: Maurizio Mariani (Italy)
**Silkeborg IF – HJK HELSINKI 1-1(0-1)**
Silkeborg IF: Nicolai Larsen, Tobias Salquist, Joel Felix, Lukas Engel, Oliver Sonne, Mark Brink, Stefán Teitur Thórdarson (46.Mads Kaalund), Nicolai Vallys, Sebastian Jørgensen (60.Tonni Adamsen), Anders Klynge (85.Søren Tengstedt), Nicklas Helenius. Trainer: Kent Nielsen.
HJK Helsinki: Conor Hazard, Jukka Raitala, Aapo Halme (66.Matti Peltola), Murilo, Arttu Hoskonen, Lucas Lingman, Santeri Väänänen, Atomu Tanaka (46.Përparim Hetemaj), David Browne (78.Pyry Soiri), Santeri Hostikka (78.Nassim Boujellab), Malik Abubakari (86.Anthony Olusanya). Trainer: Toni Koskela.
Goals: 40' Malik Abubakari 0-1, 74' Joel Felix 1-1.

25.08.2022; Tallaght Stadium, Dublin; Attendance: 7,163
Referee: François Letexier (France)
**Shamrock Rovers FC Dublin – FERENCVÁROSI TC 1-0(0-0)**
Shamrock Rovers: Alan Mannus, Sean Kavanagh (73.Dylan Watts), Sean Gannon, Sean Hoare, Lee Grace, Ronan Finn (64.Andy Lyons), Richie Towell (73.Jack Byrne), Gary O'Neill, Neil Farrugia, Justin Ferizaj (72.Gideon Tetteh), Aidomo Emakhu (64.Aaron Greene). Trainer: Stephen Bradley.
Ferencvárosi TC: Ádám Bogdán, Adnan Kovacevic, Eldar Civic, Henry Wingo, Mats Knoester, Anderson Esiti (57.Bálint Vécsei), Aïssa Laïdouni, Carlos Auzqui (57.Marquinhos), Tokmac Nguen (71.Xavier Mercier), Adama Traoré (I) (79.Krisztián Lisztes), Ryan Mmaee (71.Franck Boli). Trainer: Stanislav Cherchesov (Russia).
Goal: 89' Andy Lyons 1-0.

25.08.2022; Tynecastle Park, Edinburgh; Attendance: 17,225
Referee: Lawrence Visser (Belgium)
**Heart of Midlothian FC Edinburgh – FC ZÜRICH 0-1(0-0)**
Heart of Midlothian: Craig Gordon, Michael Smith, Stephen Kingsley (78.Toby Sibbick), Kye Rowles, Alex Cochrane, Jorge Grant [sent off 54], Cameron Devlin (84.Connor Smith), Liam Boyce (64.Peter Haring), Lawrence Shankland, Barrie McKay, Alan Forrest (64.Josh Ginnelly). Trainer: Robbie Neilson.
FC Zürich: Yanick Brecher, Karol Mets, Nikola Boranijasevic, Mirlind Kryeziu, Becir Omeragic, Antonio Marchesano (79.Fabian Rohner), Ole Selnæs, Adrián Guerrero (90+1.Fidan Aliti), Cheick Oumar Condé (46.Marc Hornschuh), Donis Avdijaj (46.Wilfried Gnonto), Bogdan Vyunnyk (63.Aiyegun Tosin). Trainer: Franco Foda (Germany).
Goal: 80' Fabian Rohner 0-1.

25.08.2022; 4 Eylül Stadyumu, Sivas; Attendance: 16,873
Referee: Srđan Jovanović (Serbia)
**Sivasspor Kulübü – MALMÖ FF 0-2(0-0)**
Sivasspor: Ali Vural, Ugur Çiftçi, Dimitrios Goutas, Aaron Appindangoyé, Max Gradel, Fredrik Ulvestad, Erdogan Yesilyurt, Charilaos Charisis (69.Hakan Arslan), Kader Keita, Mustapha Yatabaré (80.Clinton N'Jie), Leke James (80.Karol Angielski). Trainer: Riza Çalimbay.
Malmö FF: Ismael Diawara, Niklas Moisander, Lasse Nielsen, Dennis Hadzikadunic, Felix Beijmo, Anders Christiansen, Jo Inge Berget, Erdal Rakip, Moustafa Zeidan (82.Hugo Larsson), Veljko Birmancevic (89.Joseph Ceesay), Isaac Kiese Thelin. Trainer: Andreas Georgson.
Goals: 76' Veljko Birmancevic 0-1, 89' Isaac Kiese Thelin 0-2.

18.08.2022; Stádio Neo GSP, Nicosia; Attendance: 10,479
Referee: José María Sánchez Martínez (Spain)
**Apollon Limassol FC – Olympiacos SFP Peiraiás 1-1(1-1)**
Apollon Limassol: Aleksandar Jovanovic, Valentin Roberge, Mathieu Peybernes, Chambos Kyriakou (60.El-Hadji Ba), Amine Khammas, Euclides Cabral, Nicolas Diguiny (74.Ezekiel Henty), Israel Coll, Rangelo Janga (60.Ido Shahar), Ioannis Pittas, Vá (46.Hervin Ongenda). Trainer: David Catalá Jiménez (Spain).
Olympiacos: Tomás Vaclík, Pape Cissé, Pipa Ávila, Oleg Reabciuk, Ousseynou Ba, Yann M'Vila, Pierre Kunde Malong (90+2.Andreas Bouchalakis), Hwang In-beom (66.Aguibou Camara), Lazar Randjelovic (79.Marios Vrousai), Youssef El-Arabi (66.Ahmed Hassan "Koka"), Philip Zinckernagel (79.Konrad de la Fuente). Trainer: Carlos Corberán Vallet (Spain).
Goals: 18' Rangelo Janga 1-0, 28' Hwang In-beom 1-1.

18.08.2022; „Vazgen Sargsyan" Hanrapetakan Stadium, Yerevan; Attendance: 9,000; Referee: Alejandro José Hernández Hernández (Spain)
**FC Pyunik Yerevan – FC Sheriff Tiraspol 0-0**
Pyunik Yerevan: David Yurchenko, Zoran Gajic (44.Mikhail Kovalenko), Alexander González, Anton Bratkov, Sergiy Vakulenko, Juninho, Artak Dashyan, Eugeniu Cociuc, Hovhannes Harutyunyan (61.Renzo Zambrano), Yusuf Otubanjo (61.Marjan Radeski), Luka Juricic (73.Uros Nenadovic). Trainer: Eghishe Melikyan.
Sheriff Tiraspol: Dumitru Celeadnic, Patrick Kpozo, Gaby Kiki, Renan Guedes, Heron, Abou Ouattara (72.Iyayi Atiemwen), Cédric Badolo, Moussa Kyabou, Mouhamed Diop (83.Salifu Mudasiru), Kay Tejan, Ibrahim Rasheed. Trainer: Stjepan Tomas (Croatia).

18.08.2022; Huvepharma Arena, Razgrad Attendancce: 4,951
Referee: Ivan Kružliak (Slovakia)
**PFC Ludogorets Razgrad – FK Žalgiris Vilnius 1-0(1-0)**
Ludogorets Razgrad: Simon Sluga, Cicinho, Anton Nedyalkov, Olivier Verdon, Jakub Piotrowski, Ivan Yordanov (90.Petar Georgiev), Danny Gruper, Spas Delev (66.Matías Tissera), Kiril Despodov, Bernard Tekpetey (79.Jorghinho), Thiago (79.Show). Trainer: Ante Šimundža (Slovenia).
Žalgiris: Edvinas Gertmonas, Saulius Mikoliūnas, Ivan Tatomirovic, Mario Pavelic, Kipras Kazukolovas (72.Marko Milickovic), Nemanja Ljubisavljevic, Nicolás Gorobsov, Oliver Buff (83.Gustas Jarusevicius), Fabien Ourega (90+3.Mantas Kuklys), Renan Oliveira (72.Josip Tadic), Mathias Oyewusi (72.Donatas Kazlauskas [sent off 90+4]). Trainer: Vladimir Cheburin (Kazakhstan).
Goal: 2' Ivan Tatomirovic 1-0 (own goal).

18.08.2022; Kosická futbalová aréna, Košice (Slovakia); Attendance: 3,450; Referee: Tobias Stieler (Germany)
**SC Dnipro-1 – AEK Larnaca FC 1-2(0-2)**
SC Dnipro-1: Max Walef, Volodymyr Tanchyk, Volodymyr Adamyuk, Oleksandr Svatok, Emiliano Purita (61.Oleksandr Nazarenko), Busanello, Domingo Blanco, Oleksandr Pikhalyonok, Igor Kogut (46.Artem Gromov), Eduard Sarapyi [sent off 90+5], Artem Dovbyk. Trainer: Oleksandr Kucher.
AEK Larnaca: Ioakim Toumpas, Mikel González, Roberto Rosales, Oier, Gus Ledes (86.Rafail Mamas), Hrvoje Milicevic, Ádám Gyurcsó (86.Ivan Trickovski), Omri Altman, Nikos Englezou (59.Ismael Casas), Rafael Lopes (59.José Romo), Imad Faraj (66.Bruno Gama). Trainer: José Luis Oltra (Spain).
Goals: 16' Omri Altman 0-1, 29' Oleksandr Svatok 0-2 (own goal), 90' Oleksandr Svatok 1-2.

25.08.2022; Stádio „Giórgos Karaïskáki", Peiraiás; Attendance: 20,054
Referee: Sandro Schärer (Switzerland)
**OLYMPIACOS SFP PEIRAIÁS – Apollon Limassol FC 1-1(1-0,1-1,1-1); 3-1 on penalties**
Olympiacos: Tomás Vaclík, Pape Cissé, Pipa Ávila, Oleg Reabciuk, Ousseynou Ba [sent off 100], Yann M'Vila, Pierre Kunde Malong (84.Aguibou Camara), Georgios Masouras (84.Konrad de la Fuente), Hwang In-beom (79.Mathieu Valbuena), Youssef El-Arabi (103.Kostas Manolas), Philip Zinckernagel (55.Lazar Randjelovic). Trainer: Carlos Corberán Vallet (Spain).
Apollon Limassol: Aleksandar Jovanovic, Valentin Roberge, Mathieu Peybernes, Amine Khammas, Nicolas Diguiny (81.Rangelo Janga), Charis Mavrias, Israel Coll (81.Chambos Kyriakou), Ido Shahar (67.El-Hadji Ba), Ezekiel Henty (57.Bassel Jradi, 97.Euclides Cabral), Ioannis Pittas, Vá (67.Hervin Ongenda). Trainer: David Catalá Jiménez (Spain).
Goals: 2' Giannis Masouras 1-0, 90' Ioannis Pittas 1-1.
Penalties: Yann M'Vila 1-0; Chambos Kyriakou (missed); Konrad de la Fuente 2-0; Ioannis Pittas 2-1; Pipa Ávila 3-1; Hervin Ongenda (missed); Lazar Randjelovic (missed); El-Hadji Ba (missed).

25.08.2022; Stadionul Zimbru, Chişinău; Attendance: 6,154
Referee: Andreas Ekberg (Sweden)
**FC SHERIFF TIRASPOL – FC Pyunik Yerevan 0-0 aet; 3-2 on penalties**
Sheriff Tiraspol: Dumitru Celeadnic, Patrick Kpozo, Stjepan Radeljic, Gaby Kiki, Renan Guedes, Iyayi Atiemwen (72.Kay Tejan), Abou Ouattara (81.Steve Ambri), Cédric Badolo (102.Salifu Mudasiru), Moussa Kyabou, Mouhamed Diop, Ibrahim Rasheed (90+4.Giannis Botos). Trainer: Stjepan Tomas (Croatia).
Pyunik Yerevan: David Yurchenko, Alexander González (80.Renzo Zambrano), Anton Bratkov, Sergiy Vakulenko, Mikhail Kovalenko, Juninho (90.Yuri Gareginyan), Artak Dashyan, Eugeniu Cociuc (80.Aleksandar Miljkovic), Hovhannes Harutyunyan, Yusuf Otubanjo (70.Uros Nenadovic; 105.Boris Varga), Marjan Radeski (46.Luka Juricic). Trainer: Eghishe Melikyan.
Penalties: Hovhannes Harutyunyan (missed); Kay Tejan 1-0; Artak Dashyan (missed); Steve Ambri (missed); Renzo Zambrano (missed); Mouhamed Diop (missed); Yuri Gareginyan 1-1; Patrick Kpozo 2-1; Sergiy Vakulenko 2-2; Gaby Kiki (missed); Mikhail Kovalenko (missed); Stjepan Radeljic 3-2.

25.08.2022; LFF stadionas, Vilnius; Attendance: 4,601
Referee: Harm Osmers (Germany)
**FK Žalgiris Vilnius – PFC LUDOGORETS RAZGRAD 3-3(2-1,3-2)**
Žalgiris: Edvinas Gertmonas, Mario Pavelic, Joël Bopesu, Kipras Kazukolovas, Nemanja Ljubisavljevic, Nicolás Gorobsov, Oliver Buff (100.Mantas Kuklys), Fabien Ourega (101.Petar Mamic), Marko Milickovic (109.Motiejus Burba), Renan Oliveira (71.Francis Kyeremeh), Mathias Oyewusi (71.Josip Tadic). Trainer: Vladimir Cheburin (Kazakhstan).
Ludogorets Razgrad: Simon Sluga, Cicinho, Anton Nedyalkov, Olivier Verdon, Jakub Piotrowski, Ivan Yordanov (80.Show), Danny Gruper (71.Zan Karnicnik), Bernard Tekpetey (64.Spas Delev), Matías Tissera (64.Cauly), Rick (100.Jorghinho), Thiago. Trainer: Ante Šimundža (Slovenia).
Goals: 1' Fabien Ourega 1-0, 8' Matías Tissera 1-1, 15' Oliver Buff 2-1, 57' Matías Tissera 2-2, 63' Renan Oliveira 3-2, 120' Olivier Verdon 3-3 (penalty).

25.08.2022; AEK Arena "Georgios Karapatakis", Larnaca; Attendance: 4,893; Referee: Davide Massa (Italy)
**AEK LARNACA FC – SC Dnipro-1 3-0(2-0)**
AEK Larnaca: Kenan Piric, Mikel González, Roberto Rosales, Oier, Gus Ledes, Hrvoje Milicevic, Ádám Gyurcsó (83.Giorgos Naoum), Omri Altman (74.Ángel García), Nikos Englezou (87.Bruno Gama), Rafael Lopes (74.Victor Olatunji), Imad Faraj (74.Rafail Mamas). Trainer: José Luis Oltra (Spain).
SC Dnipro-1: Max Walef, Volodymyr Tanchyk, Sergiy Loginov (73.Valentyn Rubchynskyi), Oleksandr Svatok, Busanello, Ruslan Babenko, Domingo Blanco, Oleksandr Pikhalyonok, Oleksiy Hutsulyak (58.Oleksandr Nazarenko), Artem Gromov (69.Igor Kogut), Artem Dovbyk. Trainer: Oleksandr Kucher.
Goals: 21' Ádám Gyurcsó 1-0, 45' Rafael Lopes 2-0, 78' Nikos Englezou 3-0.

18.08.2022; Ghelamco Arena, Gent; Attendance: 10,496
Referee: Irfan Peljto (Bosnia and Herzegovina)
**KAA Gent – AC Omonia Nicosia 0-2(0-1)**
KAA Gent: Dany Roef, Michael Ngadeu-Ngadjui, Núrio Fortuna (46.Vadis Odjidja-Ofoe), Jordan Torunarigha (81.Bruno Godeau), Andreas Hanche-Olsen (80.Joseph Okumu), Sven Kums, Andrew Hjulsager, Alessio Castro-Montes (81.Matisse Samoise), Hong Hyun-seok, Hugo Cuypers, Jens Hauge (62.Laurent Depoitre). Trainer: Hein Vanhaezebrouck.
Omonia Nicosia: Fabiano, Jan Lecjaks, Adam Matthews, Nemanja Miletic, Héctor Yuste, Mix Diskerud (70.Roman Bezus), Fouad Bachirou, Bruno Souza (74.Fotis Papoulis), Nikos Panagiotou, Charalampos Charalampous (74.Brandon Barker), Andronikos Kakoullis (86.Tim Matavz). Trainer: Neil Lennon (Northern Ireland).
Goals: 19' Charalampos Charalampous 0-1, 76' Brandon Barker 0-2.


18.08.2022; Generali Arena, Wien; Attendance: 14,000
Referee: Daniel Siebert (Germany)
**FK Austria Wien – Fenerbahçe SK Istanbul 0-2(0-1)**
Austria Wien: Christian Früchtl, Lucas Galvão [*sent off 83*], Marvin Martins, Lukas Mühl, Billy Koumetio, Reinhold Ranftl, Manfred Fischer, Matthias Braunöder, Florian Wustinger (22.Haris Tabakovic, 86.Johannes Handl), Dominik Fitz (75.Can Keles), Muharem Huskovic (46.Aleksandar Jukic). Trainer: Manfred Schmid.
Fenerbahçe: Altay Bayindir, Ezgjan Alioski (79.Filip Novák), Luan Peres, Mauricio Lemos (75.Gustavo Henrique), Attila Szalai, Miguel Crespo (60.Miha Zajc), Ferdi Kadioglu, Ismail Yüksek (79.Willian Arão), Joshua King (59.Lincoln), Serdar Dursun, Diego Rossi. Trainer: Jorge Fernando Pinheiro de Jesus (Portugal).
Goals: 8' Joshua King 0-1, 89' Serdar Dursun 0-2.


25.08.2022; Stádio Neo GSP, Nicosia; Attendance: 17,002
Referee: Georgi Kabakov (Bulgaria)
**AC OMONIA NICOSIA – KAA Gent 2-0(2-0)**
Omonia Nicosia: Fabiano, Jan Lecjaks, Adam Matthews, Nemanja Miletic, Héctor Yuste, Mix Diskerud (79.Fotis Papoulis), Fouad Bachirou, Bruno Souza (67.Brandon Barker), Nikos Panagiotou, Charalampos Charalampous (67.Roman Bezus), Andronikos Kakoullis (79.Pangiotis Zachariou). Trainer: Neil Lennon (Northern Ireland).
KAA Gent: Dany Roef, Michael Ngadeu-Ngadjui, Jordan Torunarigha, Joseph Okumu (84.Andreas Hanche-Olsen), Vadis Odjidja-Ofoe (63.Andrew Hjulsager), Sven Kums (72.Jens Hauge), Alessio Castro-Montes, Hong Hyun-seok (72.Sulayman Marreh), Matisse Samoise, Laurent Depoitre (63.Darko Lemajic), Hugo Cuypers. Trainer: Hein Vanhaezebrouck.
Goals: 18' Andronikos Kakoullis 1-0, 36' Charalampos Charalampous 2-0.


25.08.2022; „Şükrü Saracoğlu" Stadyumu, Istanbul; Attendance: 35,350
Referee: Jesús Gil Manzano (Spain)
**FENERBAHÇE SK ISTANBUL – FK Austria Wien 4-1(2-1)**
Fenerbahçe: Altay Bayindir, Ezgjan Alioski, Gustavo Henrique, Luan Peres (80.Attila Szalai), Mauricio Lemos, Írfan Kahveci (77.Arda Güler), Bright Osayi-Samuel, Miguel Crespo (77.Mert Hakan Yandas), Ísmail Yüksek, Serdar Dursun (80.Enner Valencia), Diego Rossi (85.Emre Mor). Trainer: Jorge Fernando Pinheiro de Jesus (Portugal).
Austria Wien: Christian Früchtl, Marvin Martins (46.Can Keles), Johannes Handl (81.Dario Kreiker), Lukas Mühl, Billy Koumetio, Reinhold Ranftl, Manfred Fischer, Matthias Braunöder (46.James Holland), Andreas Gruber (66.Marco Djuricin), Haris Tabakovic, Dominik Fitz (65.Romeo Vucic). Trainer: Manfred Schmid.
Goals: 12' Ísmail Yüksek 1-0, 44' Írfan Kahveci 2-0, 45+1' Marvin Martins 2-1, 70' Írfan Kahveci 3-1, 79' Mert Hakan Yandas 4-1.

Group Winners advanced to Round of 16.
Runners-up advanced to Knockout Round Play-offs (with 8 transferred teams from the UEFA Champions League).
Third ranked teams were transferred to Europa Conference League.

| GROUP A | | | | | | | | |
|---|---|---|---|---|---|---|---|---|
| 1. **Arsenal FC London** | 6 | 5 | 0 | 1 | 8 | - | 3 | 15 |
| 2. **PSV Eindhoven** | 6 | 4 | 1 | 1 | 15 | - | 4 | 13 |
| 3. *FK Bodø/Glimt* | 6 | 1 | 1 | 4 | 5 | - | 10 | 4 |
| 4. FC Zürich | 6 | 1 | 0 | 5 | 5 | - | 16 | 3 |

08.09.2022; Kybunpark, St. Gallen; Attendance: 17,070
Referee: Mohammed Al-Hakim (Sweden)
**FC Zürich – Arsenal FC London 1-2(1-1)**
FC Zürich: Yanick Brecher, Nikola Boranijasevic, Fidan Aliti, Mirlind Kryeziu, Lindrit Kamberi, Blerim Dzemaili (67.Cheick Condé), Ole Selnæs, Adrián Guerrero (67.Fabian Rohner), Bledian Krasniqi (67.Antonio Marchesano), Jonathan Okita (80.Donis Avdijaj), Aiyegun Tosin (80.Ivan Santini). Trainer: Franco Foda (Germany).
Arsenal: Matt Turner, Kieran Tierney (69.Oleksandr Zinchenko), Rob Holding, Takehiro Tomiyasu, Gabriel Magalhães, Granit Xhaka, Albert Lokonga, Fábio Vieira (69.Martin Ødegaard), Eddie Nketiah (78.Gabriel Jesus), Gabriel Martinelli, Marquinhos (69.Bukayo Saka). Trainer: Mikel Arteta Amatriain (Spain).
Goals: 17' Marquinhos 0-1, 44' Mirlind Kryeziu 1-1 (penalty), 62' Eddie Nketiah 1-2.

15.09.2022; Aspmyra Stadion, Bodø; Attendance: 8,000
Referee: Stéphanie Frappart (France)
**FK Bodø/Glimt – FC Zürich 2-1(0-0)**
FK Bodø/Glimt: Nikita Haikin, Marius Høibråten, Marius Lode (77.Isak Amundsen), Brice Wembangomo, Alfons Sampsted, Ulrik Saltnes, Patrick Berg, Hugo Vetlesen, Lars-Jørgen Salvesen (46.Runar Espejord), Ola Solbakken (77.Albert Grønbæk Erlykke), Joel Mvuka (67.Amahl Pellegrino). Trainer: Kjetil Knutsen.
FC Zürich: Yanick Brecher, Nikola Boranijasevic, Mirlind Kryeziu, Lindrit Kamberi, Blerim Dzemaili (71.Cheick Condé), Ole Selnæs, Adrián Guerrero, Fabian Rohner (61.Donis Avdijaj), Bledian Krasniqi (61.Antonio Marchesano), Jonathan Okita (71.Bogdan Viunnyk), Aiyegun Tosin (82.Ivan Santini). Trainer: Franco Foda (Germany).
Goals: 54' Ole Selnæs 1-0 (own goal), 58' Hugo Vetlesen 2-0, 81' Donis Avdijaj 2-1.

06.10.2022; Emirates Stadium, London; Attendance: 59,724
Referee: Harm Osmers (Germany)
**Arsenal FC London – FK Bodø/Glimt 3-0(2-0)**
Arsenal: Matt Turner, Kieran Tierney (70.Ben White), Rob Holding, Takehiro Tomiyasu, Gabriel Magalhães, Granit Xhaka (58.Martin Ødegaard), Albert Lokonga, Fábio Vieira, Eddie Nketiah (82.Reiss Nelson), Gabriel Martinelli (59.Gabriel Jesus), Marquinhos (59.Bukayo Saka). Trainer: Mikel Arteta Amatriain (Spain).
FK Bodø/Glimt: Nikita Haikin, Brede Moe, Marius Lode (88.Marius Høibråten), Brice Wembangomo, Alfons Sampsted (88.Morten Konradsen), Ulrik Saltnes, Patrick Berg, Hugo Vetlesen (73.Albert Grønbæk Erlykke), Amahl Pellegrino, Runar Espejord (88.Lars-Jørgen Salvesen), Joel Mvuka (73.Ola Solbakken). Trainer: Kjetil Knutsen.
Goals: 23' Eddie Nketiah 1-0, 27' Rob Holding 2-0, 84' Fábio Vieira 3-0.

13.10.2022; Philips Stadion, Eindhoven; Attendance: 30,000
Referee: Ali Palabıyık (Turkey)
**PSV Eindhoven – FC Zürich 5-0(3-0)**
PSV Eindhoven: Walter Benítez, Phillipp Mwene, André Ramalho, Philipp Max, Armando Obispo (74.Jordan Teze), Érick Gutiérrez, Ibrahim Sangaré (63.Sávio), Guus Til, Joey Veerman (56.Johan Bakayoko), Xavi Simons (46.Richy Ledezma), Cody Gakpo (46.Anwar El Ghazi). Trainer: Ruud van Nistelrooij.
FC Zürich: Yanick Brecher, Marc Hornschuh (82.Fabian Rohner), Karol Mets, Nikola Boranijasevic, Nikola Katic, Lindrit Kamberi, Antonio Marchesano (70.Bledian Krasniqi), Adrián Guerrero, Cheick Condé (59.Ole Selnæs), Aiyegun Tosin (70.Donis Avdijaj), Bogdan Viunnyk (59.Jonathan Okita). Trainer: Bo Henriksen (Denmark).
Goals: 9' Érick Gutiérrez 1-0, 15' Joey Veerman 2-0, 34' Ibrahim Sangaré 3-0, 55' Joey Veerman 4-0, 84' Anwar El Ghazi 5-0.

08.09.2022; Philips Stadion, Eindhoven; Attendance: 28,627
Referee: Georgi Kabakov (Bulgaria)
**PSV Eindhoven – FK Bodø/Glimt 1-1(0-1)**
PSV Eindhoven: Walter Benítez, Phillipp Mwene, Philipp Max, Armando Obispo, Jordan Teze, Ibrahim Sangaré, Joey Veerman, Xavi Simons, Cody Gakpo, Yorbe Vertessen (62.Anwar El Ghazi), Ismael Saibari (62.Sávio). Trainer: Ruud van Nistelrooij.
FK Bodø/Glimt: Nikita Haikin, Marius Høibråten, Marius Lode (70.Isak Amundsen), Brice Wembangomo, Alfons Sampsted, Ulrik Saltnes, Patrick Berg, Hugo Vetlesen, Albert Grønbæk Erlykke, Runar Espejord (58.Lars-Jørgen Salvesen), Joel Mvuka. Trainer: Kjetil Knutsen.
Goals: 44' Albert Grønbæk Erlykke 0-1, 62' Cody Gakpo 1-1.

06.10.2022; Stadion Letzigrund, Zürich; Attendance: 10,626
Referee: William Sean Collum (Scotland)
**FC Zürich – PSV Eindhoven 1-5(0-4)**
FC Zürich: Yanick Brecher, Nikola Boranijasevic (56.Jonathan Okita), Fidan Aliti (56.Karol Mets), Mirlind Kryeziu (71.Nikola Katic), Lindrit Kamberi, Blerim Dzemaili (56.Marc Hornschuh), Antonio Marchesano (71.Donis Avdijaj), Ole Selnæs, Adrián Guerrero, Fabian Rohner, Aiyegun Tosin. Trainer: Genesio Colatrella.
PSV Eindhoven: Walter Benítez, Phillipp Mwene, André Ramalho, Philipp Max (66.Ki-Jana Hoever), Armando Obispo (46.Jordan Teze), Ibrahim Sangaré, Joey Veerman, Xavi Simons (61.Guus Til), Cody Gakpo (62.Johan Bakayoko), Yorbe Vertessen (61.Anwar El Ghazi), Ismael Saibari. Trainer: Ruud van Nistelrooij.
Goals: 10', 16' Yorbe Vertessen 0-1, 0-2, 21' Cody Gakpo 0-3, 35' Xavi Simons 0-4, 55' Cody Gakpo 0-5, 87' Jonathan Okita 1-5.

13.10.2022; Aspmyra Stadion, Bodø; Attendance: 7,922
Referee: Irfan Peljto (Bosnia and Herzegovina)
**FK Bodø/Glimt – Arsenal FC London 0-1(0-1)**
FK Bodø/Glimt: Nikita Haikin, Marius Høibråten (89.Brede Moe), Marius Lode, Brice Wembangomo, Alfons Sampsted, Ulrik Saltnes (12.Albert Grønbæk Erlykke), Patrick Berg, Hugo Vetlesen, Amahl Pellegrino (89.Joel Mvuka), Runar Espejord (76.Lars-Jørgen Salvesen), Ola Solbakken. Trainer: Kjetil Knutsen.
Arsenal: Matt Turner, Kieran Tierney, Rob Holding, Ben White (70.Takehiro Tomiyasu), William Saliba, Martin Ødegaard (70.Marquinhos), Albert Lokonga (84.Thomas Partey), Bukayo Saka (59.Granit Xhaka), Fábio Vieira, Eddie Nketiah, Reiss Nelson (59.Gabriel Martinelli). Trainer: Mikel Arteta Amatriain (Spain).
Goal: 24' Bukayo Saka 0-1.

20.10.2022; Emirates Stadium, London; Attendance: 52,200
Referee: Alejandro José Hernández Hernández (Spain)
**Arsenal FC London – PSV Eindhoven 1-0(0-0)**
Arsenal: Matt Turner, Kieran Tierney, Rob Holding, Takehiro Tomiyasu (76.Ben White), Gabriel Magalhães, Granit Xhaka, Albert Lokonga (67.Thomas Partey), Bukayo Saka (85.Reiss Nelson), Fábio Vieira (67.Martin Ødegaard), Gabriel Jesus (76.Gabriel Martinelli), Eddie Nketiah. Trainer: Mikel Arteta Amatriain (Spain).
PSV Eindhoven: Walter Benítez, Phillipp Mwene, André Ramalho, Philipp Max (66.Jordan Teze), Armando Obispo, Érick Gutiérrez, Ibrahim Sangaré, Guus Til (65.Noni Madueke), Joey Veerman (77.Luuk de Jong), Xavi Simons (90+1.Richy Ledezma), Cody Gakpo. Trainer: Ruud van Nistelrooij.
Goal: 71' Granit Xhaka 1-0.

27.10.2022; Stadion Letzigrund, Zürich; Attendance: 10,168
Referee: Yevhen Aranovskiy (Ukraine)
**FC Zürich – FK Bodø/Glimt 2-1(0-1)**
FC Zürich: Yanick Brecher, Nikola Boranijasevic, Fidan Aliti (84.Karol Mets), Nikola Katic, Lindrit Kamberi, Blerim Dzemaili (71.Antonio Marchesano), Ole Selnæs, Adrián Guerrero (60.Fabian Rohner), Cheick Condé, Jonathan Okita (84.Bogdan Viunnyk), Aiyegun Tosin (84.Selmin Hodza). Trainer: Bo Henriksen (Denmark).
FK Bodø/Glimt: Nikita Haikin, Marius Høibråten, Brede Moe (82.Marius Lode), Brice Wembangomo, Alfons Sampsted, Ulrik Saltnes, Hugo Vetlesen, Albert Grønbæk Erlykke (87.Elias Hagen), Amahl Pellegrino (78.Joel Mvuka), Runar Espejord (78.Lars-Jørgen Salvesen), Ola Solbakken. Trainer: Kjetil Knutsen.
Goals: 45+1' Amahl Pellegrino 0-1, 67' Nikola Boranijasevic 1-1, 90+4' Antonio Marchesano 2-1.

03.11.2022; Emirates Stadium, London; Attendance: 48,500
Referee: Erik Lambechts (Belgium)
**Arsenal FC London – FC Zürich 1-0(1-0)**
Arsenal: Aaron Ramsdale, Kieran Tierney, Rob Holding, Gabriel Magalhães, Ben White (73.Takehiro Tomiyasu, 88.Cédric Soares), Mohamed Elneny (63.Thomas Partey), Albert Lokonga, Fábio Vieira (73.Martin Ødegaard), Gabriel Jesus (63.Bukayo Saka), Eddie Nketiah, Reiss Nelson. Trainer: Mikel Arteta Amatriain (Spain).
FC Zürich: Yanick Brecher, Nikola Boranijasevic, Fidan Aliti (89.Ivan Santini), Nikola Katic, Lindrit Kamberi, Ole Selnæs (77.Marc Hornschuh), Adrián Guerrero, Fabian Rohner (46.Antonio Marchesano), Cheick Condé (82.Bledian Krasniqi), Jonathan Okita, Aiyegun Tosin (78.Bogdan Viunnyk). Trainer: Bo Henriksen (Denmark).
Goal: 17' Kieran Tierney 1-0

27.10.2022; Philips Stadion, Eindhoven; Attendance: 35,000
Referee: Marco Di Bello (Italy)
**PSV Eindhoven – Arsenal FC London 2-0(0-0)**
PSV Eindhoven: Walter Benítez, Phillipp Mwene, André Ramalho, Philipp Max, Jarrad Branthwaite (81.Jordan Teze), Érick Gutiérrez, Ibrahim Sangaré, Joey Veerman (81.Guus Til), Xavi Simons (80.Noni Madueke), Anwar El Ghazi (46.Luuk de Jong), Cody Gakpo (84.Mauro Júnior). Trainer: Ruud van Nistelrooij.
Arsenal: Aaron Ramsdale, Kieran Tierney (74.Gabriel Magalhães), Rob Holding (64.Gabriel Jesus), Takehiro Tomiyasu (74.Ben White), William Saliba, Granit Xhaka, Martin Ødegaard (57.Bukayo Saka), Albert Lokonga (56.Thomas Partey), Fábio Vieira, Eddie Nketiah, Gabriel Martinelli. Trainer: Mikel Arteta Amatriain (Spain).
Goals: 55' Joey Veerman 1-0, 63' Luuk de Jong 2-0.

03.11.2022; Aspmyra Stadion, Bodø; Attendance: 7,985
Referee: Donatas Rumšas (Lithuania)
**FK Bodø/Glimt – PSV Eindhoven 1-2(0-1)**
FK Bodø/Glimt: Nikita Haikin, Marius Høibråten, Marius Lode, Alfons Sampsted, Japhet Sery Larsen (75.Morten Konradsen), Patrick Berg, Hugo Vetlesen (75.Ulrik Saltnes), Albert Grønbæk Erlykke, Runar Espejord (83.Lars-Jørgen Salvesen), Ola Solbakken (75.Nino Zugelj), Joel Mvuka (75.Amahl Pellegrino). Trainer: Kjetil Knutsen.
PSV Eindhoven: Joël Drommel, Armando Obispo (46.André Ramalho), Jordan Teze, Ki-Jana Hoever (90+1.Emmanuel van de Blaak), Fredrik Oppegård, Guus Til, Joey Veerman (46.Érick Gutiérrez), Richy Ledezma, Luuk de Jong (46.Anwar El Ghazi), Noni Madueke (70.Yorbe Vertessen), Johan Bakayoko. Trainer: Ruud van Nistelrooij.
Goals: 36' Alfons Sampsted 0-1 (own goal), 52' Johan Bakayoko 0-2, 90+3' Nino Zugelj 1-2.

| | GROUP B | | | | | | | | |
|---|---|---|---|---|---|---|---|---|---|
| 1. | **Fenerbahçe SK Istanbul** | 6 | 4 | 2 | 0 | 13 | - | 7 | 14 |
| 2. | **Stade Rennais FC** | 6 | 3 | 3 | 0 | 11 | - | 8 | 12 |
| 3. | *AEK Larnaca FC* | 6 | 1 | 2 | 3 | 7 | - | 10 | 5 |
| 4. | FK Dinamo Kyiv | 6 | 0 | 1 | 5 | 5 | - | 11 | 1 |

08.09.2022; AEK Arena "Georgios Karapatakis", Larnaca; Attendance: 4,103; Referee: Giorgi Kruashvili (Georgia)
**AEK Larnaca FC – Stade Rennais FC 1-2(1-1)**
AEK Larnaca: Kenan Piric, Roberto Rosales (46.Kypros Christoforou), Nenad Tomovic, Oier, Ángel García, Gus Ledes, Hrvoje Milicevic, Omri Altman (63.Ádám Gyurcsó), Ivan Trickovski (79.Pere Pons), Imad Faraj (90+3.Giorgos Naoum), Victor Olatunji (80.Rafael Lopes). Trainer: José Luis Oltra (Spain).
Stade Rennais: Steve Mandanda, Hamari Traoré, Birger Meling (57.Martin Terrier), Joe Rodon, Arthur Theate, Adrien Truffert, Flavien Tait, Baptiste Santamaría, Lovro Majer (83.Lorenz Assignon), Kamaldeen Sulemana, Matthis Abline (58.Benjamin Bourigeaud). Trainer: Bruno Génésio.
Goals: 29' Arthur Theate 0-1, 33' Oier 1-1, 90+4' Lorenz Assignon 1-2.

15.09.2022; Stadion Cracovii im. Józefa Piłsudskiego, Kraków (Poland); Attendance: 3,362; Referee: Jakob Kehlet (Denmark)
**FK Dinamo Kyiv – AEK Larnaca FC 0-1(0-1)**
Dinamo Kyiv: Denis Boyko, Tomasz Kedziora (67.Oleksandr Karavaev), Vladyslav Dubinchak, Oleksandr Syrota, Ilya Zabarnyi, Sergiy Sydorchuk, Denys Garmash (46.Artem Besedin), Vitaliy Buyalskyi, Oleksandr Andriyevskyi (67.Volodymyr Shepelyev), Viktor Tsygankov, Vladyslav Kabaev (84.Vladyslav Vanat). Trainer: Mircea Lucescu (Romania).
AEK Larnaca: Kenan Piric, Nenad Tomovic, Ángel García, Kypros Christoforou, Hrvoje Milicevic, Ádám Gyurcsó (77.Nikos Englezou), Omri Altman, Pere Pons (74.Giorgos Naoum), Rafail Mamas (64.Oier), Ivan Trickovski (64.Gus Ledes), Victor Olatunji (73.Rafael Lopes). Trainer: José Luis Oltra (Spain).
Goal: 8' Ádám Gyurcsó 0-1.

08.09.2022; „Şükrü Saracoğlu" Stadyumu, Istanbul; Attendance: 41,895
Referee: Tamás Bognár (Hungary)
**Fenerbahçe SK Istanbul – FK Dinamo Kyiv 2-1(1-0)**
Fenerbahçe: Altay Bayindir, Ezgjan Alioski (83.Lincoln), Gustavo Henrique, Luan Peres, Attila Szalai, Willian Arão, Miguel Crespo (83.Mert Hakan Yandas), Ferdi Kadioglu, Joshua King (69.Enner Valencia), João Pedro (69.Michy Batshuayi), Diego Rossi (69.Irfan Kahveci). Trainer: Jorge Fernando Pinheiro de Jesus (Portugal).
Dinamo Kyiv: Georgiy Bushchan, Tomasz Kedziora, Mykyta Burda, Vladyslav Dubinchak (59.Kostiantyn Vivcharenko), Oleksandr Syrota, Sergiy Sydorchuk, Denys Garmash (88.Mykyta Kravchenko), Vitaliy Buyalskyi, Viktor Tsygankov, Mykola Shaparenko (68.Volodymyr Shepelyev), Vladyslav Kabaev. Trainer: Mircea Lucescu (Romania).
Goals: 35' Gustavo Henrique 1-0, 63' Viktor Tsygankov 1-1, 90+3' Michy Batshuayi 2-1.

15.09.2022; Roazhon Park, Rennes; Attendance: 20,993
Referee: Aleksei Kulbakov (Belarus)
**Stade Rennais FC – Fenerbahçe SK Istanbul 2-2(0-0)**
Stade Rennais: Steve Mandanda, Hamari Traoré [sent off 83], Birger Meling, Joe Rodon, Arthur Theate, Benjamin Bourigeaud, Lovro Majer (78.Flavien Tait), Lesley Chimuanya Ugochukwu (78.Jérémy Doku), Kamaldeen Sulemana (65.Désiré Doué), Martin Terrier (74.Matthis Abline), Amine Gouiri (64.Adrien Truffert). Trainer: Bruno Génésio.
Fenerbahçe: Altay Bayindir, Gustavo Henrique, Luan Peres (57.Ezgjan Alioski), Attila Szalai, Irfan Kahveci, Mert Hakan Yandas (86.Diego Rossi), Lincoln (67.Emre Mor), Bright Osayi-Samuel, Ismail Yüksek, Joshua King (67.João Pedro), Michy Batshuayi (66.Enner Valencia). Trainer: Jorge Fernando Pinheiro de Jesus (Portugal).
Goals: 52' Martin Terrier 1-0, 54' Lovro Majer 2-0, 60' Irfan Kahveci 2-1, 90+3' Enner Valencia 2-2 (penalty).

06.10.2022; Roazhon Park, Rennes; Attendance: 24,671
Referee: José María Sánchez Martínez (Spain)
**Stade Rennais FC – FK Dinamo Kyiv 2-1(1-1)**
Stade Rennais: Steve Mandanda, Birger Meling, Joe Rodon, Arthur Theate, Lorenz Assignon, Flavien Tait, Benjamin Bourigeaud (85.Adrien Truffert), Lovro Majer (65.Arnaud Kalimuendo), Lesley Chimuanya Ugochukwu, Martin Terrier (79.Matthis Abline), Amine Gouiri (64.Désiré Doué). Trainer: Bruno Génésio.
Dinamo Kyiv: Denis Boyko, Tomasz Kedziora, Vladyslav Dubinchak, Denys Popov (90+2.Kostiantyn Vivcharenko), Ilya Zabarnyi, Sergiy Sydorchuk, Vitaliy Buyalskyi, Viktor Tsygankov (86.Oleksandr Karavaev), Volodymyr Shepelyev, Vladyslav Kabaev (79.Vladyslav Vanat), Artem Besedin. Trainer: Mircea Lucescu (Romania).
Goals: 23' Martin Terrier 1-0, 33' Viktor Tsygankov 1-1, 89' Désiré Doué 2-1.

13.10.2022; Stadion Cracovii im. Józefa Pilsudskiego, Kraków (Poland); Attendance: 5,398; Referee: Serdar Gözübüyük (Netherlands)
**FK Dinamo Kyiv – Stade Rennais FC 0-1(0-0)**
Dinamo Kyiv: Ruslan Neshcheret, Oleksandr Tymchk (77.Oleksandr Karavaev), Vladyslav Dubinchak (67.Kostiantyn Vivcharenko), Oleksandr Syrota, Ilya Zabarnyi, Sergiy Sydorchuk, Denys Garmash (66.Vladyslav Kabaev), Vitaliy Buyalskyi, Viktor Tsygankov, Volodymyr Shepelyev (70.Oleksandr Andriyevskyi), Artem Besedin (66.Vladyslav Vanat). Trainer: Mircea Lucescu (Romania).
Stade Rennais: Steve Mandanda, Birger Meling, Christopher Wooh, Arthur Theate, Lorenz Assignon, Benjamin Bourigeaud (84.Adrien Truffert), Lovro Majer, Lesley Chimuanya Ugochukwu, Désiré Doué (73.Flavien Tait), Martin Terrier (66.Kamaldeen Sulemana), Arnaud Kalimuendo (73.Amine Gouiri). Trainer: Bruno Génésio.
Goal: 48' Christopher Wooh 0-1.

27.10.2022; „Şükrü Saracoğlu" Stadyumu, Istanbul; Attendance: 34,840
Referee: Novak Simović (Serbia)
**Fenerbahçe SK Istanbul – Stade Rennais FC 3-3(1-3)**
Fenerbahçe: Altay Bayindir, Serdar Aziz, Gustavo Henrique (60.Ezgjan Alioski), Attila Szalai, Willian Arão (61.Miha Zajc), Irfan Kahveci (60.Emre Mor), Lincoln (78.Arda Güler), Bright Osayi-Samuel, Miguel Crespo, Enner Valencia, João Pedro (61.Michy Batshuayi). Trainer: Jorge Fernando Pinheiro de Jesus (Portugal).
Stade Rennais: Steve Mandanda (52.Dogan Alemdar), Hamari Traoré, Joe Rodon, Arthur Theate, Adrien Truffert, Flavien Tait, Benjamin Bourigeaud (70.Lorenz Assignon), Lovro Majer (70.Désiré Doué), Lesley Chimuanya Ugochukwu, Martin Terrier (83.Kamaldeen Sulemana), Amine Gouiri (84.Arnaud Kalimuendo). Trainer: Bruno Génésio.
Goals: 5' Amine Gouiri 0-1,16' Martin Terrier 0-2, 30' Amine Gouiri 0-3, 42' Enner Valencia 1-3, 82' Miha Zajc 2-3, 88' Emre Mor 3-3.

03.11.2022; Stadion Cracovii im. Józefa Pilsudskiego, Kraków (Poland); Attendance: 6,304; Referee: Duje Strukan (Croatia)
**FK Dinamo Kyiv – Fenerbahçe SK Istanbul 0-2(0-2)**
Dinamo Kyiv: Georgiy Bushchan, Oleksandr Tymchk, Denys Popov, Kostiantyn Vivcharenko (70.Oleksandr Syrota), Ilya Zabarnyi [sent off 68], Sergiy Sydorchuk, Vitaliy Buyalskyi (70.Oleksandr Karavaev), Viktor Tsygankov (86.Samba Diallo), Volodymyr Shepelyev (46.Denys Garmash), Artem Besedin (46.Vladyslav Kabaev), Vladyslav Vanat. Trainer: Mircea Lucescu (Romania).
Fenerbahçe: Altay Bayindir, Serdar Aziz, Attila Szalai, Willian Arão (73.Miha Zajc), Lincoln (79.Ezgjan Alioski), Bright Osayi-Samuel, Miguel Crespo, Ferdi Kadioglu, Arda Güler (64.Emre Mor), Enner Valencia (64.Irfan Kahveci), Michy Batshuayi (64.João Pedro). Trainer: Jorge Fernando Pinheiro de Jesus (Portugal).
Goals: 23' Arda Güler 0-1, 45+2' Willian Arão 0-2.

06.10.2022; „Şükrü Saracoğlu" Stadyumu, Istanbul; Attendance: 38,860
Referee: Chris Kavanagh (England)
**Fenerbahçe SK Istanbul – AEK Larnaca FC 2-0(1-0)**
Fenerbahçe: Altay Bayindir, Ezgjan Alioski, Gustavo Henrique, Attila Szalai, Emre Mor (72.Irfan Kahveci), Lincoln (72.Enner Valencia), Bright Osayi-Samuel (72.Ferdi Kadioglu), Miguel Crespo, Ismail Yüksek, Michy Batshuayi (88.Arda Güler), Diego Rossi (87.Serdar Aziz). Trainer: Jorge Fernando Pinheiro de Jesus (Portugal).
AEK Larnaca: Kenan Piric, Roberto Rosales, Nenad Tomovic, Oier (70.Giorgos Naoum), Ángel García, Gus Ledes (80.Pere Pons), Hrvoje Milicevic, Omri Altman (69.Victor Olatunji), Rafail Mamas, Rafael Lopes (81.Ivan Trickovski), Imad Faraj. Trainer: José Luis Oltra (Spain).
Goals: 26' Michy Batshuayi 1-0, 79' Rafail Mamas 2-0 (own goal).

13.10.2022; AEK Arena "Georgios Karapatakis", Larnaca; Attendance: 6,947; Referee: Pawel Raczkowski (Poland)
**AEK Larnaca FC – Fenerbahçe SK Istanbul 1-2(0-1)**
AEK Larnaca: Kenan Piric, Roberto Rosales, Nenad Tomovic, Oier (82.Mikel González), Ángel García [sent off 84], Gus Ledes (75.Pere Pons), Hrvoje Milicevic, Omri Altman (75.Victor Olatunji), Rafail Mamas (64.Giorgos Naoum), Ivan Trickovski (75.Rafael Lopes), Imad Faraj. Trainer: José Luis Oltra (Spain).
Fenerbahçe: Altay Bayindir, Serdar Aziz, Ezgjan Alioski (68.Bright Osayi-Samuel), Gustavo Henrique, Attila Szalai, Lincoln (76.Miguel Crespo), Ferdi Kadioglu, Ismail Yüksek, Arda Güler (69.Michy Batshuayi), João Pedro (69.Enner Valencia), Diego Rossi (90+2.Irfan Kahveci). Trainer: Jorge Fernando Pinheiro de Jesus (Portugal).
Goals: 16' João Pedro 0-1, 52' Ivan Trickovski 1-1 (penalty), 80' Michy Batshuayi 1-2 (penalty).

27.10.2022; AEK Arena "Georgios Karapatakis", Larnaca; Attendance: 4,321; Referee: John Beaton (Scotland)
**AEK Larnaca FC – FK Dinamo Kyiv 3-3(1-1)**
AEK Larnaca: Kenan Piric, Roberto Rosales (88.Mikel González), Nenad Tomovic, Gus Ledes, Hrvoje Milicevic, Ádám Gyurcsó (89.Giorgos Naoum), Omri Altman (83.Victor Olatunji), Pere Pons, Nikos Englezou, Rafael Lopes (66.Rafail Mamas), Imad Faraj (84.Kypros Christoforou). Trainer: José Luis Oltra (Spain).
Dinamo Kyiv: Ruslan Neshcheret, Oleksandr Tymchk, Oleksandr Syrota, Kostiantyn Vivcharenko, Ilya Zabarnyi, Sergiy Sydorchuk, Vitaliy Buyalskyi (75.Kaheem Parris), Viktor Tsygankov, Volodymyr Shepelyev (83.Samba Diallo), Vladyslav Kabaev (65.Denys Garmash), Vladyslav Vanat (83.Artem Besedin). Trainer: Mircea Lucescu (Romania).
Goals: 26' Omri Altman 1-0, 45' Vladyslav Vanat 1-1, 53' Rafael Lopes 2-1, 72' Omri Altman 3-1, 82', 90+2' Denys Garmash 3-2, 3-3.

03.11.2022; Roazhon Park, Rennes; Attendance: 27,210
Referee: Mohammed Al-Hakim (Sweden)
**Stade Rennais FC – AEK Larnaca FC 1-1(1-0)**
Stade Rennais: Dogan Alemdar, Birger Meling, Joe Rodon, Lorenz Assignon, Jeanuël Belocian, Flavien Tait, Benjamin Bourigeaud (63.Désiré Doué), Lovro Majer (63.Lesley Chimuanya Ugochukwu), Martin Terrier (56.Jérémy Doku), Arnaud Kalimuendo (71.Adrien Truffert), Matthis Abline (56.Amine Gouiri). Trainer: Bruno Génésio.
AEK Larnaca: Kenan Piric, Roberto Rosales, Nenad Tomovic, Ángel García, Kypros Christoforou, Gus Ledes (88.Mikel González), Hrvoje Milicevic, Ádám Gyurcsó (88.Nikos Englezou), Pere Pons, Rafail Mamas (74.Rafael Lopes), Victor Olatunji (90+2.Henry Andreou). Trainer: José Luis Oltra (Spain).
Goals: 17' Matthis Abline 1-0, 76' Rafael Lopes 1-1.

| | | | | | | | | |
|---|---|---|---|---|---|---|---|---|
| **GROUP C** | 1. **Real Betis Balompié Sevilla FC** | 6 | 5 | 1 | 0 | 12 - 4 | 16 |
| | 2. **AS Roma** | 6 | 3 | 1 | 2 | 11 - 7 | 10 |
| | 3. *PFC Ludogorets Razgrad* | 6 | 2 | 1 | 3 | 8 - 9 | 7 |
| | 4. HJK Helsinki | 6 | 0 | 1 | 5 | 2 - 13 | 1 |

08.09.2022; Huvepharma Arena, Razgrad; Attendance: 10,011
Referee: Craig Pawson (England)
**PFC Ludogorets Razgrad – AS Roma 2-1(0-0)**
Ludogorets Razgrad: Sergio Padt, Cicinho, Anton Nedyalkov, Aslak Witry (87.Georgi Terziev), Olivier Verdon, Cauly (86.Spas Delev), Jakub Piotrowski, Show (77.Nonato), Kiril Despodov (71.Rick), Bernard Tekpetey, Thiago. Trainer: Ante Šimundža (Slovenia).
AS Roma: Mile Svilar, Chris Smalling, Zeki Çelik (67.Leonardo Spinazzola), Gianluca Mancini (75.Cristian Volpato), Ibañez, Nemanja Matic (76.Mady Camara), Bryan Cristante (76.Edoardo Bove), Lorenzo Pellegrini, Paulo Dybala, Andrea Belotti (67.Eldor Shomurodov), Nicola Zalewski. Trainer: José Mário dos Santos Félix Mourinho (Portugal).
Goals: 72' Cauly 1-0, 86' Eldor Shomurodov 1-1, 88' Nonato 2-1.

15.09.2022; Estadio „Benito Villamarín", Sevilla; Attendance: 43,113
Referee: Andris Treimanis (Latvia)
**Real Betis Balompié Sevilla FC – PFC Ludogorets Razgrad 3-2(2-1)**
Real Betis: Claudio Bravo, Édgar González, Luiz Felipe (73.Germán Pezzella), Juan Miranda, Joaquín (72.Rodri), Andrés Guardado, Sergio Canales (85.Álex Moreno), Paul Akouokou (56.Guido Rodríguez), Willian José, Aitor Ruibal, Luiz Henrique (84.William Carvalho). Trainer: Manuel Luis Pellegrini Ripamonti (Chile).
Ludogorets Razgrad: Sergio Padt, Cicinho, Anton Nedyalkov, Aslak Witry (62.Danny Gruper), Olivier Verdon, Cauly, Jakub Piotrowski, Show (62.Nonato), Kiril Despodov (69.Spas Delev), Bernard Tekpetey (70.Rick), Thiago (80.Matías Tissera). Trainer: Ante Šimundža (Slovenia).
Goals: 25' Luiz Henrique 1-0, 39' Joaquín 2-0, 45+2' Kiril Despodov 2-1, 59' Sergio Canales 3-1, 74' Rick 3-2.

06.10.2022; Bolt Arena, Helsinki; Attendance: 9,751
Referee: Yevhen Aranovskiy (Ukraine)
**HJK Helsinki – PFC Ludogorets Razgrad 1-1(0-1)**
HJK Helsinki: Conor Hazard, Jukka Raitala, Arttu Hoskonen, Matti Peltola, Përparim Hetemaj (74.Bojan Radulovic), Pyry Soiri, Lucas Lingman, Santeri Väänänen, David Browne, Santeri Hostikka (74.Nassim Boujellab), Malik Abubakari (64.Anthony Olusanya). Trainer: Toni Koskela.
Ludogorets Razgrad: Sergio Padt, Igor Plastun, Anton Nedyalkov, Aslak Witry, Olivier Verdon, Cauly, Jakub Piotrowski, Show (69.Nonato), Kiril Despodov (87.Pedro Naressi), Bernard Tekpetey (61.Rick), Matías Tissera (70.Thiago). Trainer: Ante Šimundža (Slovenia).
Goals: 10' Matías Tissera 0-1, 55' Përparim Hetemaj 1-1.

13.10.2022; Estadio „Benito Villamarín", Sevilla; Attendance: 52,472
Referee: Anastasios Sidiropoulos (Greece)
**Real Betis Balompié Sevilla FC – AS Roma 1-1(1-0)**
Real Betis: Claudio Bravo, Germán Pezzella, Luiz Felipe, Juan Miranda (86.Álex Moreno), Joaquín (69.Luiz Henrique), Andrés Guardado (80.William Carvalho), Sergio Canales (81.Guido Rodríguez), Paul Akouokou, Rodri, Willian José (69.Borja Iglesias), Aitor Ruibal. Trainer: Manuel Luis Pellegrini Ripamonti (Chile).
AS Roma: Rui Patrício, Chris Smalling, Leonardo Spinazzola (71.Matías Viña), Gianluca Mancini, Ibañez, Nemanja Matic (46.Mady Camara), Bryan Cristante, Lorenzo Pellegrini (88.Stephan El Shaarawy), Andrea Belotti (76.Edoardo Bove), Tammy Abraham, Nicola Zalewski. Trainer: José Mário dos Santos Félix Mourinho (Portugal).
Goals: 34' Sergio Canales 1-0, 53' Andrea Belotti 1-1.

08.09.2022; Bolt Arena, Helsinki; Attendance: 10,164
Referee: Roi Reinshreiber (Israel)
**HJK Helsinki – Real Betis Balompié Sevilla FC 0-2(0-1)**
HJK Helsinki: Conor Hazard, Jukka Raitala, Miro Tenho, Arttu Hoskonen (87.Matti Peltola), Pyry Soiri (74.Casper Terho), Lucas Lingman (88.Përparim Hetemaj), Nassim Boujellab (74.Murilo), Santeri Väänänen, David Browne, Santeri Hostikka, Malik Abubakari (74.Anthony Olusanya). Trainer: Toni Koskela.
Real Betis: Claudio Bravo, Víctor Ruíz (46.Luiz Felipe), Germán Pezzella, Juan Miranda, Joaquín (60.Sergio Canales), William Carvalho (75.Guido Rodríguez), Paul Akouokou, Willian José, Juanmi (6.Rodri), Aitor Ruibal, Luiz Henrique (74.Andrés Guardado). Trainer: Manuel Luis Pellegrini Ripamonti (Chile).
Goals: 45+3', 64' Willian José 0-1 (penalty), 0-2.

15.09.2022; Stadio Olimpico, Roma; Attendance: 60,193
Referee: Radu Marian Petrescu (Romania)
**AS Roma – HJK Helsinki 3-0(0-0)**
AS Roma: Rui Patrício, Leonardo Spinazzola, Rick Karsdorp, Gianluca Mancini, Matías Viña (46.Paulo Dybala), Ibañez (46.Chris Smalling), Nemanja Matic, Bryan Cristante (64.Mady Camara), Lorenzo Pellegrini (69.Edoardo Bove), Nicolò Zaniolo (76.Tammy Abraham), Andrea Belotti. Trainer: José Mário dos Santos Félix Mourinho (Portugal).
HJK Helsinki: Conor Hazard, Jukka Raitala, Miro Tenho [sent off 14], Arttu Hoskonen (46.Paulus Arajuuri), Përparim Hetemaj (46.Aapo Halme), Pyry Soiri (66.Anthony Olusanya), Lucas Lingman (69.Nassim Boujellab), Santeri Väänänen, David Browne, Santeri Hostikka (23.Matti Peltola), Malik Abubakari. Trainer: Toni Koskela.
Goals: 47' Paulo Dybala 1-0, 49' Lorenzo Pellegrini 2-0, 68' Andrea Belotti 3-0.

06.10.2022; Stadio Olimpico, Roma; Attendance: 62,294
Referee: Matej Jug (Slovenia)
**AS Roma – Real Betis Balompié Sevilla FC 1-2(1-1)**
AS Roma: Rui Patrício, Chris Smalling, Zeki Çelik (5.Leonardo Spinazzola), Gianluca Mancini, Ibañez, Nemanja Matic, Bryan Cristante (80.Mady Camara), Nicolò Zaniolo [sent off 90+3], Paulo Dybala (80.Stephan El Shaarawy), Tammy Abraham (72.Andrea Belotti), Nicola Zalewski. Trainer: José Mário dos Santos Félix Mourinho (Portugal).
Real Betis: Claudio Bravo, Germán Pezzella, Luiz Felipe, Juan Miranda (76.Álex Moreno), Joaquín (61.Rodri), Andrés Guardado (75.William Carvalho), Sergio Canales, Guido Rodríguez, Willian José (76.Borja Iglesias), Nabil Fekir (22.Luiz Henrique), Aitor Ruibal. Trainer: Manuel Luis Pellegrini Ripamonti (Chile).
Goals: 34' Paulo Dybala 1-0 (penalty), 40' Guido Rodríguez 1-1, 88' Luiz Henrique 1-2.

13.10.2022; Huvepharma Arena, Razgrad; Attendance: 4,623
Referee: Kristo Tohver (Estonia)
**PFC Ludogorets Razgrad – HJK Helsinki 2-0(1-0)**
Ludogorets Razgrad: Sergio Padt, Cicinho, Anton Nedyalkov, Olivier Verdon, Cauly, Jakub Piotrowski (86.Nonato), Show (77.Pedro Naressi), Danny Gruper, Bernard Tekpetey (86.Spas Delev), Matías Tissera (67.Thiago), Rick. Trainer: Ante Šimundža (Slovenia).
HJK Helsinki: Conor Hazard, Jukka Raitala [sent off 90+3], Miro Tenho, Arttu Hoskonen, Përparim Hetemaj, Pyry Soiri (58.Casper Terho), Lucas Lingman (70.Atomu Tanaka), Santeri Väänänen (59.Nassim Boujellab), David Browne (46.Matti Peltola), Santeri Hostikka (70.Anthony Olusanya), Malik Abubakari. Trainer: Toni Koskela.
Goals: 39' Danny Gruper 1-0, 64' Rick 2-0.

27.10.2022; Huvepharma Arena, Razgrad; Attendance: 9,487
Referee: Harald Lechner (Austria)
**PFC Ludogorets Razgrad – Real Betis Balompié Sevilla FC 0-1(0-0)**
Ludogorets Razgrad: Sergio Padt, Cicinho, Anton Nedyalkov, Aslak Witry (83.Danny Gruper), Olivier Verdon, Cauly, Jakub Piotrowski (74.Nonato), Pedro Naressi (84.Claude Gonçalves), Bernard Tekpetey, Rick (74.Spas Delev), Thiago (65.Matías Tissera). Trainer: Ante Šimundža (Slovenia).
Real Betis: Claudio Bravo, Víctor Ruíz, Édgar González, Juan Miranda (46.Álex Moreno), Joaquín (28.Luiz Henrique), Sergio Canales, Guido Rodríguez (73.Enrique "Quique" Fernández), Paul Akouokou (46.Nabil Fekir), Rodri, Willian José (83.Borja Iglesias), Aitor Ruibal. Trainer: Manuel Luis Pellegrini Ripamonti (Chile).
Goal: 56' Nabil Fekir 0-1.

03.11.2022; Stadio Olimpico, Roma; Attendance: 60,807
Referee: Nikola Dabanović (Montenegro)
**AS Roma – PFC Ludogorets Razgrad 3-1(0-1)**
AS Roma: Rui Patrício, Chris Smalling, Rick Karsdorp (46.Bryan Cristante), Matías Viña, Ibañez, Nemanja Matic (61.Nicola Zalewski), Lorenzo Pellegrini, Mady Camara (46.Cristian Volpato, 80.Edoardo Bove), Stephan El Shaarawy, Andrea Belotti (46.Nicolò Zaniolo), Tammy Abraham. Trainer: José Mário dos Santos Félix Mourinho (Portugal).
Ludogorets Razgrad: Sergio Padt, Cicinho (87.Danny Gruper), Anton Nedyalkov, Aslak Witry (87.Spas Delev), Olivier Verdon [sent off 90], Cauly, Jakub Piotrowski (71.Nonato), Pedro Naressi, Bernard Tekpetey (71.Kiril Despodov), Rick, Thiago (71.Matías Tissera). Trainer: Ante Šimundža (Slovenia).
Goals: 41' Rick 0-1, 56', 65' Lorenzo Pellegrini 1-1 (penalty), 2-1 (penalty), 85' Nicolò Zaniolo 3-1.

27.10.2022; Bolt Arena, Helsinki; Attendance: 9,751
Referee: Tiago Bruno Lopes Martins (Portugal)
**HJK Helsinki – AS Roma 1-2(0-1)**
HJK Helsinki: Conor Hazard, Aapo Halme, Arttu Hoskonen, Matti Peltola, Përparim Hetemaj (69.Nassim Boujellab), Pyry Soiri, Lucas Lingman, Santeri Väänänen, David Browne, Santeri Hostikka, Anthony Olusanya (46.Malik Abubakari). Trainer: Toni Koskela.
AS Roma: Rui Patrício, Chris Smalling, Gianluca Mancini, Matías Viña, Bryan Cristante (84.Marash Kumbulla), Lorenzo Pellegrini (78.Eldor Shomurodov), Mady Camara (78.Edoardo Bove), Cristian Volpato (77.Giacomo Faticanti), Stephan El Shaarawy (89.Leonardo Spinazzola), Tammy Abraham, Nicola Zalewski. Trainer: José Mário dos Santos Félix Mourinho (Portugal).
Goals: 41' Tammy Abraham 0-1, 54' Përparim Hetemaj 1-1, 62' Arttu Hoskonen 1-2 (own goal).

03.11.2022; Estadio „Benito Villamarín", Sevilla; Attendance: 35,384
Referee: William Sean Collum (Scotland)
**Real Betis Balompié Sevilla FC – HJK Helsinki 3-0(2-0)**
Real Betis: Rui Silva, Víctor Ruíz, Youssouf Sabaly (46.Sergio Canales), Édgar González, Juan Miranda, William Carvalho (46.Borja Iglesias), Paul Akouokou (77.Andrés Guardado), Rodri, Willian José (67.Dani Pérez), Aitor Ruibal, Luiz Henrique (67.Nabil Fekir). Trainer: Manuel Luis Pellegrini Ripamonti (Chile).
HJK Helsinki: Conor Hazard, Jukka Raitala (54.Joona Toivio), Arttu Hoskonen, Matti Peltola, Pyry Soiri, Lucas Lingman, Nassim Boujellab (80.Johannes Yli-Kokko), Santeri Väänänen (80.Atomu Tanaka), David Browne, Santeri Hostikka (68.Anthony Olusanya), Malik Abubakari (80.Bojan Radulovic). Trainer: Toni Koskela.
Goals: 20', 40' Aitor Ruibal 1-0, 2-0, 90+3' Nabil Fekir 3-0.

| | | | | | | | |
|---|---|---|---|---|---|---|---|
| **GROUP D** | 1. **Royale Union Saint-Gilloise** | 6 | 4 | 1 | 1 | 11 - 7 | 13 |
| | 2. **1. FC Union Berlin** | 6 | 4 | 0 | 2 | 4 - 2 | 12 |
| | 3. *Sporting Clube de Braga* | 6 | 3 | 1 | 2 | 9 - 7 | 10 |
| | 4. Malmö FF | 6 | 0 | 0 | 6 | 3 - 11 | 0 |

08.09.2022; Eleda Stadion, Malmö; Attendance: 13,721
Referee: Duje Strukan (Croatia)
**Malmö FF – Sporting Clube de Braga 0-2(0-1)**
Malmö FF: Ismael Diawara, Martin Olsson (88.Jonas Knudsen), Niklas Moisander, Lasse Nielsen, Dennis Hadzikadunic, Felix Beijmo (56.Joseph Ceesay), Anders Christiansen, Jo Inge Berget, Oscar Lewicki (46.Sergio Peña), Erdal Rakip (25.Mohamed Buya Turay), Isaac Kiese Thelin (46.Ola Toivonen). Trainer: Åge Hareide (Norway).
Sporting Braga: Matheus Magalhães, Paulo Oliveira, Nuno Sequeira (85.Cristian Borja), Fabiano Silva, Bruno Rodrigues, Ali Al Musrati, André Horta (73.Uros Racic), Diego Lainez (74.Rodrigo Gomes), Ricardo Horta (85.Andre Castro), Abel Ruiz, Vítinha (61.Álvaro Djaló). Trainer: Artur Jorge Braga Melo Teixeira (Portugal).
Goals: 30' Bruno Rodrigues 0-1, 70' Ricardo Horta 0-2 (penalty).

15.09.2022; King Power at Den Dreef Stadion, Heverlee; Attendance: 4,373
Referee: Bartosz Frankowski (Poland)
**Royale Union Saint-Gilloise – Malmö FF 3-2(1-1)**
Union Saint-Gilloise: Anthony Moris, Guillaume François (66.Gustaf Nilsson), Christian Burgess, Siebe Van Der Heyden, Ismaël Kandouss, Teddy Teuma, Senne Lynen, Jean Lazare Amani, Dennis Eckert-Ayensa (53.Simon Adingra), Loïc Lapoussin, Victor Boniface (80.José Rodríguez). Trainer: Karel Geraerts.
Malmö FF: Johan Dahlin, Martin Olsson, Lasse Nielsen, Jonas Knudsen (46.Søren Rieks), Dennis Hadzikadunic, Felix Beijmo, Jo Inge Berget, Oscar Lewicki, Moustafa Zeidan (61.Hugo Larsson), Joseph Ceesay (74.Ola Toivonen), Isaac Kiese Thelin. Trainer: Åge Hareide (Norway).
Goals: 6' Joseph Ceesay 0-1, 17' Christian Burgess 1-1, 57' Isaac Kiese Thelin 1-2, 69' Teddy Teuma 2-2, 71' Victor Boniface 3-2.

08.09.2022; Stadion An der Alten Försterei, Berlin; Attendance: 21,512
Referee: Serhiy Boyko (Ukraine)
**1. FC Union Berlin – Royale Union Saint-Gilloise 0-1(0-1)**
Union Berlin: Frederik Rønnow, Christopher Trimmel (70.Julian Ryerson), Niko Gießelmann, Robin Knoche, Paul Jaeckel, Danilho Doekhi (82.Jamie Leweling), Genki Haraguchi (60.András Schäfer), Rani Khedira, Janik Haberer (69.Tim Skarke), Kevin Behrens (60.Sven Michel [sent off 90+6]), Sheraldo Becker. Trainer: Urs Fischer (Switzerland).
Union Saint-Gilloise: Anthony Moris, Bart Nieuwkoop, Christian Burgess, Siebe Van Der Heyden, Ismaël Kandouss, José Rodríguez (69.Cameron Puertas), Teddy Teuma, Senne Lynen, Dante Vanzeir (75.Simon Adingra), Loïc Lapoussin, Victor Boniface (83.Dennis Eckert-Ayensa). Trainer: Karel Geraerts.
Goal: 39' Senne Lynen 0-1.

15.09.2022; Estádio Municipal de Braga, Braga; Attendance: 17,782
Referee: Filip Glova (Slovakia)
**Sporting Clube de Braga – 1. FC Union Berlin 1-0(0-0)**
Sporting Braga: Matheus Magalhães, Paulo Oliveira, Nuno Sequeira, Vítor Tormena, Fabiano Silva, Ali Al Musrati, Uros Racic (61.André Horta), Ricardo Horta, Simon Banza (70.Abel Ruiz), Álvaro Djaló (61.Iuri Medeiros), Vítinha (86.Andre Castro). Trainer: Artur Jorge Braga Melo Teixeira (Portugal).
Union Berlin: Frederik Rønnow, Robin Knoche (82.Jamie Leweling), Julian Ryerson, Paul Jaeckel, Diogo Leite, Tymoteusz Puchacz (64.Christopher Trimmel), Rani Khedira, Janik Haberer (82.Tim Skarke), András Schäfer (68.Genki Haraguchi), Sheraldo Becker (82.Kevin Behrens), Jordan Siebatcheu. Trainer: Urs Fischer (Switzerland).
Goal: 77' Vítinha 1-0.

06.10.2022; Eleda Stadion, Malmö; Attendance: 16,057
Referee: Halil Umut Meler (Turkey)
**Malmö FF – 1. FC Union Berlin 0-1(0-0)**
Malmö FF: Ismael Diawara, Martin Olsson, Dennis Hadzikadunic, Felix Beijmo, Anders Christiansen, Jo Inge Berget (64.Ola Toivonen), Oscar Lewicki, Erdal Rakip, Joseph Ceesay (80.Patriot Sejdiu), Hugo Larsson (80.Moustafa Zeidan), Isaac Kiese Thelin. Trainer: Åge Hareide (Norway).
Union Berlin: Frederik Rønnow, Christopher Trimmel, Robin Knoche, Julian Ryerson (74.Niko Gießelmann), Diogo Leite, Danilho Doekhi, Rani Khedira, Janik Haberer (84.Genki Haraguchi), András Schäfer [*sent off 45*], Sheraldo Becker (90+1.Morten Thorsby), Jordan Siebatcheu (74.Kevin Behrens). Trainer: Urs Fischer (Switzerland).
Goal: 68' Sheraldo Becker 0-1.

13.10.2022; King Power at Den Dreef Stadion, Heverlee; Attendance: 7,851; Referee: Əliyar Ağayev (Azerbaijan)
**Royale Union Saint-Gilloise – Sporting Clube de Braga 3-3(1-3)**
Union Saint-Gilloise: Anthony Moris, Bart Nieuwkoop (90+4.Ross Sykes), Christian Burgess (46.Loïc Lapoussin), Siebe Van Der Heyden, Ismaël Kandouss, Teddy Teuma, Senne Lynen, Jean Lazare Amani (63.Cameron Puertas), Dante Vanzeir (82.Gustaf Nilsson), Victor Boniface (90+5.Oussama El Azzouzi), Simon Adingra. Trainer: Karel Geraerts.
Sporting Braga: Matheus Magalhães, Nuno Sequeira, Vítor Tormena, Sikou Niakaté (76.Paulo Oliveira), Fabiano Silva (46.Víctor Gómez), Ali Al Musrati, André Horta (69.Uros Racic), Ricardo Horta, Abel Ruiz (90+1.Simon Banza), Rodrigo Gomes (69.Iuri Medeiros), Vítinha. Trainer: Artur Jorge Braga Melo Teixeira (Portugal).
Goals: 15' Vítinha 0-1, 20' Victor Boniface 1-1, 36', 41' Vítinha 1-2, 1-3, 49' Dante Vanzeir 2-3, 62' Victor Boniface 3-3.

27.10.2022; Eleda Stadion, Malmö; Attendance: 10,912
Referee: Roi Reinshreiber (Israel)
**Malmö FF – Royale Union Saint-Gilloise 0-2(0-2)**
Malmö FF: Ismael Diawara, Dennis Hadzikadunic, Matej Chalus, Felix Beijmo, Søren Rieks (72.Jonas Knudsen), Anders Christiansen, Oscar Lewicki (46.Erdal Rakip), Patriot Sejdiu, Hugo Larsson (72.Sergio Peña), Isaac Kiese Thelin, Mohamed Buya Turay. Trainer: Åge Hareide (Norway).
Union Saint-Gilloise: Anthony Moris, Bart Nieuwkoop, Christian Burgess, Siebe Van Der Heyden, Ismaël Kandouss, Teddy Teuma (82.Oussama El Azzouzi), Senne Lynen, Jean Lazare Amani (46.Cameron Puertas), Dante Vanzeir (88.Guillaume François), Loïc Lapoussin (70.Simon Adingra), Victor Boniface (46.Gustaf Nilsson). Trainer: Karel Geraerts.
Goals: 10' Teddy Teuma 0-1, 41' Jean Lazare Amani 0-2.

03.11.2022; King Power at Den Dreef Stadion, Heverlee; Attendance: 5,597; Referee: Andris Treimanis (Latvia)
**Royale Union Saint-Gilloise – 1. FC Union Berlin 0-1(0-1)**
Union Saint-Gilloise: Anthony Moris, Bart Nieuwkoop, Christian Burgess, Ross Sykes, Ismaël Kandouss (72.Loïc Lapoussin), Teddy Teuma (72.José Rodríguez), Senne Lynen, Jean Lazare Amani (64.Oussama El Azzouzi), Gustaf Nilsson (46.Victor Boniface), Dante Vanzeir (64.Dennis Eckert-Ayensa), Simon Adingra. Trainer: Karel Geraerts.
Union Berlin: Frederik Rønnow (46.Lennart Grill), Christopher Trimmel, Robin Knoche, Julian Ryerson, Diogo Leite, Danilho Doekhi, Genki Haraguchi (62.András Schäfer), Rani Khedira, Janik Haberer (62.Morten Thorsby), Sheraldo Becker (89.Jamie Leweling), Sven Michel (62.Kevin Behrens). Trainer: Urs Fischer (Switzerland).
Goal: 6' Sven Michel 0-1.

06.10.2022; Estádio Municipal de Braga, Braga; Attendance: 14,044
Referee: Stéphanie Frappart (France)
**Sporting Clube de Braga – Royale Union Saint-Gilloise 1-2(0-0)**
Sporting Braga: Matheus Magalhães, Paulo Oliveira, Nuno Sequeira, Vítor Tormena, Fabiano Silva, Andre Castro (90+1.Jean-Baptiste Gorby), André Horta (65.Rodrigo Gomes), Uros Racic, Ricardo Horta (79.Diego Lainez), Abel Ruiz (89.Álvaro Djaló), Vítinha (79.Simon Banza). Trainer: Artur Jorge Braga Melo Teixeira (Portugal).
Union Saint-Gilloise: Anthony Moris, Bart Nieuwkoop (83.Guillaume François), Christian Burgess, Siebe Van Der Heyden, Ismaël Kandouss (83.Gustaf Nilsson), Teddy Teuma, Senne Lynen, Jean Lazare Amani (89.Cameron Puertas), Dante Vanzeir (90+1.Ross Sykes), Loïc Lapoussin (67.Simon Adingra), Victor Boniface. Trainer: Karel Geraerts.
Goals: 49' Abel Ruiz 1-0, 86', 90+4' Gustaf Nilsson 1-1, 1-2.

13.10.2022; Stadion An der Alten Försterei, Berlin; Attendance: 21,800
Referee: Aleksandar Stavrev (North Macedonia)
**1. FC Union Berlin – Malmö FF 1-0(0-0)**
Union Berlin: Frederik Rønnow, Christopher Trimmel, Robin Knoche, Julian Ryerson, Paul Jaeckel, Diogo Leite, Genki Haraguchi (67.Morten Thorsby), Rani Khedira, Janik Haberer (85.Kevin Behrens), Sheraldo Becker (90+6.Niko Gießelmann), Jordan Siebatcheu (67.Sven Michel). Trainer: Urs Fischer (Switzerland).
Malmö FF: Ismael Diawara, Martin Olsson (84.Jonas Knudsen), Dennis Hadzikadunic, Felix Beijmo, Anders Christiansen, Jo Inge Berget (37.Erdal Rakip), Oscar Lewicki (81.Emmanuel Lomotey [*sent off 90+2*]), Sergio Peña, Joseph Ceesay, Hugo Larsson, Isaac Kiese Thelin. Trainer: Åge Hareide (Norway).
Goal: 89' Robin Knoche 1-0 (penalty).

27.10.2022; Stadion An der Alten Försterei, Berlin; Attendance: 21,082
Referee: Craig Pawson (England)
**1. FC Union Berlin – Sporting Clube de Braga 1-0(0-0)**
Union Berlin: Frederik Rønnow, Christopher Trimmel, Robin Knoche, Julian Ryerson, Diogo Leite, Danilho Doekhi, Rani Khedira, Janik Haberer (90+4.Genki Haraguchi), Morten Thorsby (46.András Schäfer), Sheraldo Becker (90+1.Jamie Leweling), Jordan Siebatcheu (63.Kevin Behrens). Trainer: Urs Fischer (Switzerland).
Sporting Braga: Matheus Magalhães, Paulo Oliveira, Nuno Sequeira (90+1.Álvaro Djaló), Vítor Tormena, Fabiano Silva (80.Simon Banza), Andre Castro (75.André Horta), Ali Al Musrati, Iuri Medeiros (75.Rodrigo Gomes), Ricardo Horta, Abel Ruiz, Vítinha. Trainer: Artur Jorge Braga Melo Teixeira (Portugal).
Goal: 68' Robin Knoche 1-0 (penalty).

03.11.2022; Estádio Municipal de Braga, Braga; Attendance: 11,805
Referee: Ruddy Buquet (France)
**Sporting Clube de Braga – Malmö FF 2-1(1-0)**
Sporting Braga: Matheus Magalhães, Paulo Oliveira, Nuno Sequeira (79.Cristian Borja), Vítor Tormena, Víctor Gómez, Andre Castro, Ali Al Musrati (60.Uros Racic), Ricardo Horta (74.Diego Lainez), Simon Banza, Abel Ruiz (46.Álvaro Djaló), Rodrigo Gomes (59.Hernâni Infande). Trainer: Artur Jorge Braga Melo Teixeira (Portugal).
Malmö FF: Johan Dahlin, Dennis Hadzikadunic, Matej Chalus, Felix Beijmo, Søren Rieks, Anders Christiansen, Erdal Rakip (74.Sergio Peña), Romain Gall, Hugo Larsson, Ola Toivonen (61.Isaac Kiese Thelin), Mohamed Buya Turay (62.Patriot Sejdiu). Trainer: Åge Hareide (Norway).
Goals: 36' Ricardo Horta 1-0, 55' Álvaro Djaló 2-0, 77' Patriot Sejdiu 2-1.

| | | | | | | | |
|---|---|---|---|---|---|---|---|
| **GROUP E** | 1. **Real Sociedad de Fútbol San Sebastián** | 6 | 5 | 0 | 1 | 10 - 2 | 15 |
| | 2. **Manchester United FC** | 6 | 5 | 0 | 1 | 10 - 3 | 15 |
| | 3. *FC Sheriff Tiraspol* | 6 | 2 | 0 | 4 | 4 - 10 | 6 |
| | 4. AC Omonia Nicosia | 6 | 0 | 0 | 6 | 3 - 12 | 0 |

08.09.2022; Old Trafford, Manchester; Attendance: 74,310
Referee: Marco Di Bello (Italy)
### Manchester United FC – Real Sociedad de Fútbol San Sebastián 0-1(0-0)
Manchester United: David de Gea, Victor Lindelöf, Harry Maguire, Diogo Dalot (46.Lisandro Martínez), Tyrell Malacia (83.Charlie McNeill), Christian Eriksen (46.Bruno Fernandes), Casemiro, Fred, Cristiano Ronaldo, Antony (71.Jadon Sancho), Anthony Elanga (71.Alejandro Garnacho). Trainer: Erik ten Hag (Netherlands).
Real Sociedad: Álex Remiro, Aritz Elustondo, Andoni Gorosabel (84.Álex Sola), Aihen Muñoz, Jon Pacheco, David Silva (65.Mohamed Cho), Brais Méndez (84.Beñat Turrientes), Mikel Merino, Martín Zubimendi, Takefusa Kubo (78.Ander Barrenetxea), Umar Sadiq (46.Alexander Sørloth). Trainer: Imanol Alguacil.
Goal: 59' Brais Méndez 0-1 (penalty).

15.09.2022; Stadionul Zimbru, Chişinău; Attendance: 8,734
Referee: Pawel Raczkowski (Poland)
### FC Sheriff Tiraspol – Manchester United FC 0-2(0-2)
Sheriff Tiraspol: Maksim Koval, Patrick Kpozo, Stjepan Radeljic, Gaby Kiki, Armel Zohouri, Iyayi Atiemwen (81.Mudasiru Salifu), Abou Ouattara (73.Pernambuco), Cédric Badolo, Moussa Kyabou, Mouhamed Diop, Ibrahim Rasheed (73.Felipe Vizeu). Trainer: Stjepan Tomas (Croatia).
Manchester United: David de Gea, Raphaël Varane, Diogo Dalot (70' Luke Shaw), Tyrell Malacia, Lisandro Martínez (90' Harry Maguire), Christian Eriksen, Bruno Fernandes, Scott McTominay (46' Casemiro), Cristiano Ronaldo (81' Anthony Elanga), Jadon Sancho, Antony (90' Alejandro Garnacho). Trainer: Erik ten Hag (Netherlands).
Goals: 17' Jadon Sancho 0-1, 39' Cristiano Ronaldo 0-2 (penalty).

06.10.2022; Stadionul Zimbru, Chişinău; Attendance: 5,427
Referee: Harald Lechner (Austria)
### FC Sheriff Tiraspol – Real Sociedad de Fútbol San Sebastián 0-2(0-0)
Sheriff Tiraspol: Maksim Koval, Stjepan Radeljic, Gaby Kiki, Armel Zohouri, Iyayi Atiemwen (66.Mudasiru Salifu), Cédric Badolo, Moussa Kyabou [*sent off 61*], Mouhamed Diop, Felipe Vizeu (77.Patrick Kpozo), Pernambuco (67.Abou Ouattara), Ibrahim Rasheed. Trainer: Stjepan Tomas (Croatia).
Real Sociedad: Álex Remiro, Diego Rico, Aritz Elustondo, Álex Sola (69.Aritz Arambarri), Jon Pacheco, David Silva (69.Carlos Fernández), Brais Méndez (77.Beñat Turrientes), Mikel Merino (77.Illarramendi), Guevara, Takefusa Kubo, Alexander Sørloth (81.Jon Karrikaburu). Trainer: Imanol Alguacil.
Goals: 53' David Silva 0-1, 62' Aritz Elustondo 0-2.

13.10.2022; Old Trafford, Manchester; Attendance: 74,310
Referee: Jérôme Brisard (France)
### Manchester United FC – AC Omonia Nicosia 1-0(0-0)
Manchester United: David de Gea, Victor Lindelöf, Diogo Dalot, Tyrell Malacia (60.Luke Shaw), Lisandro Martínez, Casemiro (81.Scott McTominay), Fred (70.Christian Eriksen), Bruno Fernandes, Cristiano Ronaldo, Marcus Rashford, Antony (60.Jadon Sancho). Trainer: Erik ten Hag (Netherlands).
Omonia Nicosia: Francis Uzoho, Adam Matthews (65.Paris Psaltis), Ádám Lang, Nemanja Miletic, Héctor Yuste, Moreto Cassamá (86.Mix Diskerud), Bruno Felipe (74.Loizos Loizou), Nikos Panagiotou, Charalampos Charalampous (74.Fotis Papoulis), Fotios Kitsos, Andronikos Kakoullis (64.Karim Ansarifard). Trainer: Neil Lennon (Northern Ireland).
Goal: 90+3' Scott McTominay 1-0.

08.09.2022; Stádio Neo GSP, Nicosia; Attendance: 11,271
Referee: Rade Obrenović (Slovenia)
### AC Omonia Nicosia – FC Sheriff Tiraspol 0-3(0-1)
Omonia Nicosia: Fabiano (46.Francis Uzoho), Jan Lecjaks, Adam Matthews, Ádám Lang, Nemanja Miletic, Mix Diskerud, Moreto Cassamá (73.Fotis Papoulis), Bruno Felipe (81.Roman Bezus), Nikos Panagiotou, Charalampos Charalampous (82.Ioannis Kousoulos), Brandon Barker (73.Karim Ansarifard). Trainer: Neil Lennon (Northern Ireland).
Sheriff Tiraspol: Maksim Koval, Patrick Kpozo (90+10.Heron), Stjepan Radeljic, Gaby Kiki, Armel Zohouri (90+10.Renan Guedes), Iyayi Atiemwen (74.Mudasiru Salifu), Abou Ouattara (90+4.Pernambuco), Cédric Badolo, Moussa Kyabou, Mouhamed Diop, Ibrahim Rasheed (90+5.Felipe Vizeu). Trainer: Stjepan Tomas (Croatia).
Goals: 2' Ibrahim Rasheed 0-1, 55' Iyayi Atiemwen 0-2 (penalty), 76' Mouhamed Diop 0-3.

15.09.2022; Reale Arena, San Sebastián; Attendance: 28,587
Referee: Kristo Tohver (Estonia)
### Real Sociedad de Fútbol San Sebastián – AC Omonia Nicosia 2-1(1-0)
Real Sociedad: Álex Remiro, Diego Rico, Aritz Elustondo, Álex Sola (75.Andoni Gorosabel), Illarramendi (75.Beñat Turrientes), Brais Méndez, Mikel Merino (61.Robert Navarro), Zubeldía, Guevara, Jon Karrikaburu (61.Alexander Sørloth), Mohamed Cho (61.Takefusa Kubo). Trainer: Imanol Alguacil.
Omonia Nicosia: Fabiano, Nemanja Miletic, Paris Psaltis (65.Adam Matthews), Héctor Yuste (51.Ádám Lang), Mix Diskerud (65.Fotis Papoulis), Fouad Bachirou, Moreto Cassamá (13.Charalampos Charalampous), Nikos Panagiotou, Fotios Kitsos, Karim Ansarifard (66.Bruno Felipe), Loizos Loizou. Trainer: Neil Lennon (Northern Ireland).
Goals: 30' Guevara 1-0, 72' Bruno Felipe 1-1, 80' Alexander Sørloth 2-1.

06.10.2022; Stádio Neo GSP, Nicosia; Attendance: 20,011
Referee: João Pedro Silva Pinheiro (Portugal)
### AC Omonia Nicosia – Manchester United FC 2-3(1-0)
Omonia Nicosia: Fabiano, Jan Lecjaks, Adam Matthews, Ádám Lang, Nemanja Miletic (82.Roman Bezus), Héctor Yuste, Mix Diskerud (72.Nikos Panagiotou), Bruno Felipe (71.Loizos Loizou), Charalampos Charalampous, Karim Ansarifard (61.Andronikos Kakoullis), Brandon Barker (61.Fotis Papoulis). Trainer: Neil Lennon (Northern Ireland).
Manchester United: David de Gea, Victor Lindelöf, Diogo Dalot, Tyrell Malacia (46.Luke Shaw), Lisandro Martínez, Christian Eriksen, Casemiro (82.Scott McTominay), Bruno Fernandes (61.Anthony Martial), Cristiano Ronaldo, Jadon Sancho (46.Marcus Rashford), Antony (74.Fred). Trainer: Erik ten Hag (Netherlands).
Goals: 34' Karim Ansarifard 1-0, 53' Marcus Rashford 1-1, 63' Anthony Martial 1-2, 84' Marcus Rashford 1-3, 85' Nikos Panagiotou 2-3.

13.10.2022; Reale Arena, San Sebastián; Attendance: 25,806
Referee: Enea Jorgji (Albania)
### Real Sociedad de Fútbol San Sebastián – FC Sheriff Tiraspol 3-0(1-0)
Real Sociedad: Álex Remiro, Diego Rico, Aritz Elustondo (74.Aritz Arambarri), Robin Le Normand, Jon Pacheco, David Silva (46.Robert Navarro), Brais Méndez (62.Urko González), Guevara, Beñat Turrientes, Alexander Sørloth (62.Takefusa Kubo), Carlos Fernández (46.Jon Karrikaburu). Trainer: Imanol Alguacil.
Sheriff Tiraspol: Dumitru Celeadnic, Patrick Kpozo, Stjepan Radeljic, Gaby Kiki (85.Danila Ignatov), Renan Guedes, Armel Zohouri [*sent off 33*], Cédric Badolo, Mudasiru Salifu, Mouhamed Diop, Pernambuco (75.Heron), Ibrahim Rasheed (80.Felipe Vizeu). Trainer: Stjepan Tomas (Croatia).
Goals: 45+1' Alexander Sørloth 1-0, 66' Diego Rico 2-0, 81' Robert Navarro 3-0.

27.10.2022; Old Trafford, Manchester; Attendance: 73,764
Referee: Anastasios Sidiropoulos (Greece)
**Manchester United FC – FC Sheriff Tiraspol 3-0(1-0)**
Manchester United: David de Gea, Victor Lindelöf, Diogo Dalot (63.Luke Shaw), Tyrell Malacia, Lisandro Martínez (46.Harry Maguire), Christian Eriksen, Casemiro (63.Scott McTominay), Bruno Fernandes, Cristiano Ronaldo, Antony (46.Marcus Rashford), Alejandro Garnacho (79.Donny van de Beek). Trainer: Erik ten Hag (Netherlands).
Sheriff Tiraspol: Maksim Koval, Patrick Kpozo, Stjepan Radeljic, Gaby Kiki, Renan Guedes, Iyayi Atiemwen (89.Nichita Covali), Cédric Badolo (90+4.Eugeniu Gliga), Mudasiru Salifu, Moussa Kyabou, Mouhamed Diop (79.Adrian Hatman), Ibrahim Rasheed (79.Pernambuco). Trainer: Victor Mihailov.
Goals: 44' Diogo Dalot 1-0, 65' Marcus Rashford 2-0, 81' Cristiano Ronaldo 3-0.

03.11.2022; Reale Arena, San Sebastián; Attendance: 36,744
Referee: Georgi Kabakov (Bulgaria)
**Real Sociedad de Fútbol San Sebastián – Manchester United FC 0-1(0-1)**
Real Sociedad: Álex Remiro, Diego Rico, Andoni Gorosabel (58.Aritz Elustondo), Robin Le Normand, Jon Pacheco, Brais Méndez (83.Zubeldía), Mikel Merino, Martín Zubimendi, Pablo Marín (58.Robert Navarro), Alexander Sørloth (83.Jon Magunazelaia), Carlos Fernández (73.Guevara). Trainer: Imanol Alguacil.
Manchester United: David de Gea, Victor Lindelöf (58.Scott McTominay), Luke Shaw, Diogo Dalot, Lisandro Martínez, Christian Eriksen (82.Fred), Casemiro, Bruno Fernandes, Donny van de Beek (58.Marcus Rashford), Cristiano Ronaldo, Alejandro Garnacho (82.Harry Maguire). Trainer: Erik ten Hag (Netherlands).
Goal: 17' Alejandro Garnacho 0-1.

27.10.2022; Stádio Neo GSP, Nicosia; Attendance: 11,780
Referee: Tamás Bognár (Hungary)
**AC Omonia Nicosia – Real Sociedad de Fútbol San Sebastián 0-2(0-1)**
Omonia Nicosia: Francis Uzoho, Jan Lecjaks, Adam Matthews (80.Nikos Panagiotou), Ádám Lang, Nemanja Miletic (64.Héctor Yuste), Roman Bezus, Moreto Cassamá, Bruno Felipe (64.Karim Ansarifard), Charalampos Charalampous (72.Ioannis Kousoulos), Brandon Barker (46.Fotis Papoulis), Andronikos Kakoullis. Trainer: Yannick Ferrera y Caro (Belgium).
Real Sociedad: Álex Remiro, Diego Rico (69.Aritz Arambarri), Aritz Elustondo, Jon Pacheco, Illarramendi (80.Beñat Turrientes), Mikel Merino (46.Brais Méndez), Zubeldía, Guevara, Takefusa Kubo (46.Pablo Marín), Robert Navarro, Jon Karrikaburu (70.Jon Magunazelaia). Trainer: Imanol Alguacil.
Goals: 45+2' Robert Navarro 0-1, 60' Brais Méndez 0-2.

03.11.2022; Stadionul Zimbru, Chişinău; Attendance: 2,295
Referee: Fran Jović (Croatia)
**FC Sheriff Tiraspol – AC Omonia Nicosia 1-0(0-0)**
Sheriff Tiraspol: Maksim Koval, Patrick Kpozo, Stjepan Radeljic, Gaby Kiki, Armel Zohouri, Cédric Badolo, Mudasiru Salifu (69.Iyayi Atiemwen), Moussa Kyabou (90+2.Heron), Mouhamed Diop, Pernambuco (86.Renan Guedes), Ibrahim Rasheed. Trainer: Victor Mihailov.
Omonia Nicosia: Francis Uzoho, Jan Lecjaks (63.Paris Psaltis), Nemanja Miletic, Héctor Yuste, Roman Bezus, Moreto Cassamá (76.Mix Diskerud), Bruno Felipe (81.Brandon Barker), Charalampos Charalampous (63.Fotis Papoulis), Fotios Kitsos, Andronikos Kakoullis, Loizos Loizou (63.Pangiotis Zachariou). Trainer: Yannick Ferrera y Caro (Belgium).
Goal: 87' Ibrahim Rasheed 1-0.

| | | | | | | | | |
|---|---|---|---|---|---|---|---|---|
| **GROUP F** | 1. **Feyenoord Rotterdam** | 6 | 2 | 2 | 2 | 13 - 9 | 8 |
| | 2. **FC Midtjylland Herning** | 6 | 2 | 2 | 2 | 12 - 8 | 8 |
| | 3. *SS Lazio Roma* | 6 | 2 | 2 | 2 | 9 - 11 | 8 |
| | 4. SK Sturm Graz | 6 | 2 | 2 | 2 | 4 - 10 | 8 |

08.09.2022; Stadio Olimpico, Roma; Attendance: 22,763
Referee: Ricardo de Burgos Bengoetxea (Spain)
**SS Lazio Roma – Feyenoord Rotterdam 4-2(3-0)**
Lazio Roma: Ivan Provedel, Elseid Hysaj, Alessio Romagnoli (73.Patric), Adam Marusic (76.Stefan Radu), Mario Gila, Matías Vecino (70.Sergej Milinkovic-Savic), Luis Alberto (69.Toma Basic), Felipe Anderson, Mattia Zaccagni, Danilo Cataldi, Ciro Immobile (70.Matteo Cancellieri). Trainer: Maurizio Sarri.
Feyenoord Rotterdam: Justin Bijlow, Gernot Trauner, Dávid Hancko, Marcus Pedersen, Quilindschy Hartman, Sebastian Szymanski (46.Alireza Jahanbakhsh), Quinten Timber (86.Igor Paixão), Orkun Kökçü, Javairô Dilrosun (64.Mats Wieffer), Danilo (64.Santiago Giménez), Patrik Wålemark (69.Oussama Idrissi). Trainer: Arne Slot.
Goals: 4' Luis Alberto 1-0, 15' Felipe Anderson 2-0, 28', 63' Matías Vecino 3-0, 4-0, 69', 88' Santiago Giménez 4-1 (penalty), 4-2.

15.09.2022; MCH Arena, Herning; Attendance: 9,052
Referee: Nikola Dabanović (Montenegro)
**FC Midtjylland Herning – SS Lazio Roma 5-1(2-0)**
FC Midtjylland: Jonas Lössl, Erik Sviatchenko, Henrik Dalsgaard, Mads Thychosen, Paulinho, Kristoffer Olsson, Evander, Emiliano Martínez (62.Charles), Anders Dreyer (62.Pione Sisto), Gustav Isaksen (77.Edward Chilufya), Sory Kaba (87.Valdemar Andreasen). Trainer: Albert Capellas Herms (Spain).
Lazio Roma: Ivan Provedel, Stefan Radu (53.Adam Marusic), Elseid Hysaj, Alessio Romagnoli, Mario Gila, Matías Vecino (52.Sergej Milinkovic-Savic), Luis Alberto, Felipe Anderson, Danilo Cataldi (69.Marcos Antônio), Pedro (53.Matteo Cancellieri), Ciro Immobile (76.Luka Romero). Trainer: Maurizio Sarri.
Goals: 26' Paulinho 1-0, 30' Sory Kaba 2-0, 52' Evander 3-0 (penalty), 57' Sergej Milinkovic-Savic 3-1, 67' Gustav Isaksen 4-1, 72' Erik Sviatchenko 5-1.

08.09.2022; Merkur Arena, Graz; Attendance: 10,521
Referee: Əliyar Ağayev (Azerbaijan)
**SK Sturm Graz – FC Midtjylland Herning 1-0(1-0)**
Sturm Graz: Jörg Siebenhandl, Jon Gorenc Stankovic (79.Dominik Oroz), Gregory Wüthrich, Jusuf Gazibegovic, David Affengruber, Amadou Danté, Stefan Hierländer [sent off 73], Tomi Horvat (78.Ivan Ljubic), Alexander Prass, William Bøving (62.Mohammed Fuseini), Emanuel Emegha (69.Albian Ajeti). Trainer: Christian Ilzer.
FC Midtjylland: Jonas Lössl, Erik Sviatchenko, Henrik Dalsgaard (81.Edward Chilufya), Paulinho (81.Mads Thychosen), Juninho, Evander, Oliver Sørensen (57.Kristoffer Olsson), Pione Sisto (70.Emiliano Martínez), Anders Dreyer, Gustav Isaksen, Sory Kaba. Trainer: Albert Capellas Herms (Spain).
Goal: 8' Emanuel Emegha 1-0.

15.09.2022; Stadion Feijenoord, Rotterdam; Attendance: 34,332
Referee: Jérôme Brisard (France)
**Feyenoord Rotterdam – SK Sturm Graz 6-0(4-0)**
Feyenoord Rotterdam: Justin Bijlow, Gernot Trauner, Dávid Hancko, Marcos López (55.Quilindschy Hartman), Marcus Pedersen, Alireza Jahanbakhsh (64.Patrik Wålemark), Quinten Timber (75.Mats Wieffer), Orkun Kökçü (75.Ezequiel Bullaude), Oussama Idrissi, Javairô Dilrosun, Danilo (64.Santiago Giménez). Trainer: Arne Slot.
Sturm Graz: Jörg Siebenhandl, Jon Gorenc Stankovic (46.Dominik Oroz), Gregory Wüthrich (46.David Affengruber), Aleksandar Borkovic, Jusuf Gazibegovic, Amadou Danté, Tomi Horvat (72.Otar Kiteishvili), Alexander Prass, William Bøving (63.Christoph Lang), Manprit Sarkaria, Emanuel Emegha (19.Ivan Ljubic). Trainer: Christian Ilzer.
Goals: 9' Alireza Jahanbakhsh 1-0, 31' Dávid Hancko 2-0, 34' Danilo 3-0, 41' Alireza Jahanbakhsh 4-0, 66' Santiago Giménez 5-0, 78' Oussama Idrissi 6-0.

06.10.2022; Merkur Arena, Graz; Attendance: 14,171
Referee: Benoît Bastien (France)
### SK Sturm Graz – SS Lazio Roma 0-0
Sturm Graz: Jörg Siebenhandl, Jon Gorenc Stankovic, Gregory Wüthrich, Jusuf Gazibegovic [*sent off 82*], David Affengruber, Amadou Danté, Stefan Hierländer (75.Ivan Ljubic), Tomi Horvat (69.Otar Kiteishvili), Alexander Prass (84.Sandro Ingolitsch), William Bøving (70.Mohammed Fuseini), Albian Ajeti (76.Manprit Sarkaria). Trainer: Christian Ilzer.
Lazio Roma: Ivan Provedel, Elseid Hysaj, Alessio Romagnoli, Adam Marusic (46.Manuel Lazzari), Mario Gila (74.Patric), Luis Alberto, Felipe Anderson (46.Mattia Zaccagni), Danilo Cataldi, Sergej Milinkovic-Savic (63.Matías Vecino), Pedro (72.Matteo Cancellieri), Ciro Immobile. Trainer: Maurizio Sarri.


13.10.2022; Stadion Feijenoord, Rotterdam; Attendance: 43,086
Referee: Rade Obrenović (Slovenia)
### Feyenoord Rotterdam – FC Midtjylland Herning 2-2(1-1)
Feyenoord Rotterdam: Justin Bijlow, Gernot Trauner, Dávid Hancko, Marcos López, Lutsharel Geertruida, Marcus Pedersen, Alireza Jahanbakhsh (71.Patrik Wålemark), Sebastian Szymanski, Quinten Timber (71.Javairô Dilrosun), Orkun Kökçü, Santiago Giménez (77.Danilo). Trainer: Arne Slot.
FC Midtjylland: Jonas Lössl, Erik Sviatchenko, Henrik Dalsgaard (42.Juninho), Mads Thychosen, Paulinho, Kristoffer Olsson, Evander (88.Oliver Sørensen), Emiliano Martínez (88.Charles), Pione Sisto (66.Sory Kaba), Anders Dreyer (88.Edward Chilufya), Gustav Isaksen. Trainer: Albert Capellas Herms (Spain).
Goals: 16' Emiliano Martínez 0-1, 32' Quinten Timber 1-1, 48' Dávid Hancko 2-1, 58' Erik Sviatchenko 2-2.


27.10.2022; Stadio Olimpico, Roma; Attendance: 17,756
Referee: Daniel Stefanski (Poland)
### SS Lazio Roma – FC Midtjylland Herning 2-1(1-1)
Lazio Roma: Ivan Provedel, Elseid Hysaj, Alessio Romagnoli, Adam Marusic, Mario Gila (82.Nicolò Casale), Felipe Anderson, Mattia Zaccagni (73.Luka Romero), Sergej Milinkovic-Savic, Toma Basis (55.Matías Vecino), Marcos Antônio (55.Danilo Cataldi), Matteo Cancellieri (55.Pedro). Trainer: Maurizio Sarri.
FC Midtjylland: Jonas Lössl, Erik Sviatchenko, Henrik Dalsgaard, Joel Andersson (53.Mads Thychosen), Paulinho (82.Nikolas Dyhr), Evander, Charles (61.Sory Kaba), Emiliano Martínez (82.Juninho), Anders Dreyer, Gustav Isaksen, Edward Chilufya (53.Pione Sisto). Trainer: Albert Capellas Herms (Spain).
Goals: 8' Gustav Isaksen 0-1, 36' Sergej Milinkovic-Savic 1-1, 58' Pedro 2-1.


03.11.2022; MCH Arena, Herning; Attendance: 9,134
Referee: Matej Jug (Slovenia)
### FC Midtjylland Herning – SK Sturm Graz 2-0(1-0)
FC Midtjylland: Jonas Lössl, Erik Sviatchenko (89.Juninho), Joel Andersson, Stefan Gartenmann, Paulinho (67.Nikolas Dyhr), Kristoffer Olsson, Evander (66.Oliver Sørensen), Emiliano Martínez, Anders Dreyer (90+1.Gustav Christensen), Gustav Isaksen, Edward Chilufya (66.Valdemar Andreasen). Trainer: Albert Capellas Herms (Spain).
Sturm Graz: Jörg Siebenhandl, Jon Gorenc Stankovic, Gregory Wüthrich, Jusuf Gazibegovic, David Affengruber (80.Aleksandar Borkovic), Amadou Danté (46.David Schnegg), Otar Kiteishvili (80.Manprit Sarkaria), Tomi Horvat, Alexander Prass, William Bøving (46.Emanuel Emegha), Albian Ajeti (74.Jakob Jantscher). Trainer: Christian Ilzer.
Goals: 15', 72' Anders Dreyer 1-0, 2-0.


06.10.2022; MCH Arena, Herning; Attendance: 9,044
Referee: Mohammed Al-Hakim (Sweden)
### FC Midtjylland Herning – Feyenoord Rotterdam 2-2(0-2)
FC Midtjylland: Jonas Lössl, Erik Sviatchenko (46.Juninho), Henrik Dalsgaard, Joel Andersson (73.Mads Thychosen), Paulinho (84.Nikolas Dyhr), Kristoffer Olsson, Evander, Emiliano Martínez, Pione Sisto (73.Edward Chilufya), Gustav Isaksen, Sory Kaba (46.Anders Dreyer). Trainer: Albert Capellas Herms (Spain).
Feyenoord Rotterdam: Justin Bijlow, Gernot Trauner, Dávid Hancko, Marcos López, Lutsharel Geertruida, Sebastian Szymanski (79.Santiago Giménez), Quinten Timber, Orkun Kökçü (66.Marcus Pedersen), Oussama Idrissi (32.Alireza Jahanbakhsh), Javairô Dilrosun (66.Patrik Wålemark), Danilo (80.Mats Wieffer). Trainer: Arne Slot.
Goals: 21' Sebastian Szymanski 0-1, 45' Orkun Kökçü 0-2 (penalty), 54' Gustav Isaksen 1-2, 85' Juninho 2-2.


13.10.2022; Stadio Olimpico, Roma; Attendance: 21,059
Referee: Sascha Stegemann (Germany)
### SS Lazio Roma – SK Sturm Graz 2-2(1-0)
Lazio Roma: Ivan Provedel, Elseid Hysaj, Patric, Mario Gila, Luis Alberto (58.Felipe Anderson), Manuel Lazzari [*sent off 45+2*], Mattia Zaccagni (46.Adam Marusic), Danilo Cataldi (57.Matías Vecino), Toma Basis (57.Sergej Milinkovic-Savic), Pedro, Ciro Immobile (79.Matteo Cancellieri). Trainer: Maurizio Sarri.
Sturm Graz: Jörg Siebenhandl, Jon Gorenc Stankovic (79.Ivan Ljubic), Gregory Wüthrich, Sandro Ingolitsch, David Affengruber, Amadou Danté, Stefan Hierländer (79.Manprit Sarkaria), Otar Kiteishvili (57.Tomi Horvat), Alexander Prass, Albian Ajeti (79.Jakob Jantscher), Emanuel Emegha (46.William Bøving). Trainer: Christian Ilzer.
Goals: 45' Ciro Immobile 1-0 (penalty), 56' William Bøving 1-1, 71' Pedro 2-1, 83' William Bøving 2-2.


27.10.2022; Merkur Arena, Graz; Attendance: 13,987
Referee: Espen Eskås (Norway)
### SK Sturm Graz – Feyenoord Rotterdam 1-0(0-0)
Sturm Graz: Jörg Siebenhandl, Gregory Wüthrich, Jusuf Gazibegovic, David Affengruber, Amadou Danté (90+1.David Schnegg), Stefan Hierländer (56.Otar Kiteishvili), Ivan Ljubic, Tomi Horvat, Alexander Prass, William Bøving (83.Jakob Jantscher), Albian Ajeti (56.Emanuel Emegha). Trainer: Christian Ilzer.
Feyenoord Rotterdam: Justin Bijlow, Gernot Trauner, Dávid Hancko, Marcos López, Lutsharel Geertruida, Alireza Jahanbakhsh (60.Patrik Wålemark), Sebastian Szymanski (68.Marcus Pedersen), Quinten Timber, Orkun Kökçü, Javairô Dilrosun, Danilo (85.Santiago Giménez). Trainer: Arne Slot.
Goal: 90+3' Otar Kiteishvili 1-0.


03.11.2022; Stadion Feijenoord, Rotterdam; Attendance: 43,268
Referee: Irfan Peljto (Bosnia and Herzegovina)
### Feyenoord Rotterdam – SS Lazio Roma 1-0(0-0)
Feyenoord Rotterdam: Justin Bijlow, Gernot Trauner, Dávid Hancko, Marcos López (46.Quilindschy Hartman), Lutsharel Geertruida, Sebastian Szymanski, Quinten Timber (90+2.Mats Wieffer), Orkun Kökçü, Javairô Dilrosun, Danilo (63.Santiago Giménez), Igor Paixão (73.Patrik Wålemark). Trainer: Arne Slot.
Lazio Roma: Ivan Provedel, Elseid Hysaj, Patric, Nicolò Casale, Felipe Anderson, Manuel Lazzari (46.Adam Marusic), Mattia Zaccagni (63.Pedro), Sergej Milinkovic-Savic, Toma Basis (67.Matías Vecino), Marcos Antônio (67.Danilo Cataldi), Matteo Cancellieri (81.Luka Romero [*sent off 90+6*]). Trainer: Maurizio Sarri.
Goal: 64' Santiago Giménez 1-0.

| | | | | | | | |
|---|---|---|---|---|---|---|---|
| 1. **SC Freiburg** | 6 | 4 | 2 | 0 | 13 - 3 | 14 |
| 2. **FC Nantes** | 6 | 3 | 0 | 3 | 6 - 11 | 9 |
| 3. *Qarabağ FK Bakı* | 6 | 2 | 2 | 2 | 9 - 5 | 8 |
| 4. Olympiacos SFP Peiraiás | 6 | 0 | 2 | 4 | 2 - 11 | 2 |

**GROUP G**

08.09.2022; Stade de la Beaujoire „Louis Fonteneau", Nantes; Attendance: 31,276; Referee: Harald Lechner (Austria)

**FC Nantes – Olympiacos SFP Peiraiás 2-1(1-0)**

FC Nantes: Alban Lafont, Nicolas Pallois, Dennis Appiah, Andrei Girotto, Pedro Chirivella, Samuel Moutoussamy (69.Moussa Sissoko), Ludovic Blas, Quentin Merlin, Mostafa Mohamed, Ignatius Ganago (69.Moses Simon), Evann Guessand. Trainer: Antoine Kombouaré.

Olympiacos: Tomás Vaclík, Kostas Manolas, Panagiotis Retsos, Pape Cissé, Pipa, Oleg Reabciuk, Andreas Bouchalakis, Pep Biel (86.Youssef El-Arabi), Pierre Kunde, Georgios Masouras (59.Josh Bowler), Ui-Jo Hwang (77.Aboubakar Kamara). Trainer: Carlos Corberán Vallet (Spain).

Goals: 32' Mostafa Mohamed 1-0, 50' Samuel Moutoussamy 1-1 (own goal), 90+3' Evann Guessand 2-1.

15.09.2022; Stádio „Giórgos Karaïskáki", Peiraiás; Attendance: 23,104 Referee: Matej Jug (Slovenia)

**Olympiacos SFP Peiraiás – SC Freiburg 0-3(0-2)**

Olympiacos: Tomás Vaclík, Sime Vrsaljko (71.Pipa), Panagiotis Retsos (46.Pierre Kunde), Pape Cissé, Ousseynou Ba, Yann M'Vila, Andreas Bouchalakis (46.Oleg Reabciuk), Pep Biel, Georgios Masouras (63.Garry Rodrigues), Josh Bowler (63.Youssef El-Arabi), Ui-Jo Hwang. Trainer: Carlos Corberán Vallet (Spain).

SC Freiburg: Mark Flekken, Matthias Ginter, Christian Günter, Philipp Lienhart, Kiliann Sildillia (78.Lukas Kübler), Nicolas Höfler, Vincenzo Grifo (78.Yannik Keitel), Maximilian Eggestein, Daniel Kyereh (62.Jeong Woo-yeong), Michael Gregoritsch (62.Kevin Schade), Ritsu Dōan (69.Nils Petersen). Trainer: Christian Streich.

Goals: 5' Nicolas Höfler 0-1, 25', 52' Michael Gregoritsch 0-2, 0-3.

06.10.2022; Stádio „Giórgos Karaïskáki", Peiraiás; Attendance: 21,677 Referee: Irfan Peljto (Bosnia and Herzegovina)

**Olympiacos SFP Peiraiás – Qarabağ FK Bakı 0-3(0-0)**

Olympiacos: Konstantinos Tzolakis, Sime Vrsaljko, Pape Cissé (83.Mathieu Valbuena), Pipa, Oleg Reabciuk, Yann M'Vila, Andreas Bouchalakis (60.Marcelo), Pep Biel, Pierre Kunde (74.In-Beom Hwang), Garry Rodrigues (60.Georgios Masouras), Ui-Jo Hwang (74.Aboubakar Kamara). Trainer: José Miguel González Martín „Míchel" (Spain).

Qarabağ FK: Sahrudin Mahammadaliyev, Marko Vesovic (90+1.Abbas Hüseynov), Qara Qarayev, Badavi Hüseynov, Bahlul Mustafazada, Richard Almeyda (65.Júlio Romão), Abdellah Zoubir, Kady, Elvin Cafarquliyev (46.Toral Bayramov), Leandro Andrade (65.Ramil Sheydayev), Owusu Kwabena (90+1.Filip Ozobic). Trainer: Qurban Qurbanov.

Goals: 68' Owusu Kwabena 0-1, 82' Marko Vesovic 0-2, 86' Ramil Sheydayev 0-3.

13.10.2022; Stade de la Beaujoire „Louis Fonteneau", Nantes; Attendance: 31,845; Referee: Horaţiu Mircea Feşnic (Romania)

**FC Nantes – SC Freiburg 0-4(0-1)**

FC Nantes: Alban Lafont, Sébastien Corchia, Nicolas Pallois (80.Jean-Charles Castelletto), Andrei Girotto (88.Dennis Appiah), Moussa Sissoko (73.Marcus Coco), Pedro Chirivella (80.Samuel Moutoussamy), Ludovic Blas, Quentin Merlin, Moses Simon (73.Abdoul Kader Bamba), Mostafa Mohamed, Evann Guessand. Trainer: Antoine Kombouaré.

SC Freiburg: Mark Flekken, Lukas Kübler, Matthias Ginter, Christian Günter, Philipp Lienhart, Nicolas Höfler (87.Keven Schlotterbeck), Vincenzo Grifo (65.Kevin Schade), Yannik Keitel (75.Maximilian Eggestein), Jeong Woo-yeong, Nils Petersen (65.Michael Gregoritsch), Ritsu Dōan (75.Noah Weißhaupt). Trainer: Christian Streich.

Goals: 26' Lukas Kübler 0-1, 71' Michael Gregoritsch 0-2, 82' Kevin Schade 0-3, 87' Jeong Woo-yeong 0-4.

08.09.2022; Europa-Park Stadion, Freiburg im Breisgau; Attendance: 31,500; Referee: Erik Lambrechts (Belgium)

**SC Freiburg – Qarabağ FK Bakı 2-1(2-1)**

SC Freiburg: Mark Flekken, Matthias Ginter, Christian Günter, Philipp Lienhart, Kiliann Sildillia, Nicolas Höfler, Vincenzo Grifo (71.Daniel Kyereh), Maximilian Eggestein, Jeong Woo-yeong (88.Noah Weißhaupt), Nils Petersen (71.Michael Gregoritsch), Ritsu Dōan (90+3.Yannik Keitel). Trainer: Christian Streich.

Qarabağ FK: Sahrudin Mahammadaliyev, Marko Vesovic, Qara Qarayev (77.Richard Almeyda), Badavi Hüseynov, Bahlul Mustafazada, Abdellah Zoubir, Kady, Toral Bayramov (90+2.Elvin Cafarquliyev), Marko Jankovic (84.Leandro Andrade), Ramil Sheydayev (76.Júlio Romão), Owusu Kwabena. Trainer: Qurban Qurbanov.

Goals: 7' Vincenzo Grifo 1-0 (penalty), 15' Ritsu Dōan 2-0, 39' Marko Vesovic 2-1.

15.09.2022; „Tofiq Bahramov", Bakı; Attendance: 26,495 Referee: Enea Jorgji (Albania)

**Qarabağ FK Bakı – FC Nantes 3-0(0-0)**

Qarabağ FK: Sahrudin Mahammadaliyev, Marko Vesovic, Qara Qarayev (89.Júlio Romão), Badavi Hüseynov, Bahlul Mustafazada, Filip Ozobic (62.Ramil Sheydayev), Abdellah Zoubir (90+1.Musa Qurbanli), Kady, Elvin Cafarquliyev, Marko Jankovic (88.Richard Almeyda), Owusu Kwabena (88.Leandro Andrade). Trainer: Qurban Qurbanov.

FC Nantes: Alban Lafont, Fábio, Sébastien Corchia, Nicolas Pallois, Jean-Charles Castelletto, Moussa Sissoko (65.Pedro Chirivella), Samuel Moutoussamy (76.Andrei Girotto), Ludovic Blas, Moses Simon (76.Marcus Coco), Mostafa Mohamed (84.Dennis Appiah), Ignatius Ganago (64.Evann Guessand). Trainer: Antoine Kombouaré.

Goals: 60' Owusu Kwabena 1-0, 65' Abdellah Zoubir 2-0, 72' Marko Jankovic 3-0.

06.10.2022; Europa-Park Stadion, Freiburg im Breisgau; Attendance: 33,200; Referee: Glenn Nyberg (Sweden)

**SC Freiburg – FC Nantes 2-0(0-0)**

SC Freiburg: Mark Flekken, Matthias Ginter, Christian Günter, Philipp Lienhart, Kiliann Sildillia, Nicolas Höfler, Vincenzo Grifo (82.Noah Weißhaupt), Maximilian Eggestein (71.Yannik Keitel), Daniel Kyereh (82.Kevin Schade), Michael Gregoritsch (20.Nils Petersen), Ritsu Dōan (83.Lukas Kübler). Trainer: Christian Streich.

FC Nantes: Alban Lafont, Nicolas Pallois, Dennis Appiah (78.Sébastien Corchia), Andrei Girotto (78.Evann Guessand), Jean-Charles Castelletto, Pedro Chirivella (69.Moussa Sissoko), Samuel Moutoussamy, Ludovic Blas, Quentin Merlin, Moses Simon (69.Ignatius Ganago), Mostafa Mohamed (84.Abdoul Kader Bamba). Trainer: Antoine Kombouaré.

Goals: 48' Daniel Kyereh 1-0, 72' Vincenzo Grifo 2-0.

13.10.2022; „Tofiq Bahramov", Bakı; Attendance: 31,200 Referee: Craig Pawson (England)

**Qarabağ FK Bakı – Olympiacos SFP Peiraiás 0-0**

Qarabağ FK: Sahrudin Mahammadaliyev, Marko Vesovic, Qara Qarayev (68.Júlio Romão), Badavi Hüseynov, Bahlul Mustafazada, Richard Almeyda (68.Marko Jankovic), Abdellah Zoubir, Kady (62.Filip Ozobic), Elvin Cafarquliyev (85.Toral Bayramov), Ramil Sheydayev, Owusu Kwabena (85.Abbas Hüseynov). Trainer: Qurban Qurbanov.

Olympiacos: Alexandros Paschalakis, Sokratis Papastathopoulos, Sime Vrsaljko, Oleg Reabciuk, Andreas Bouchalakis (86.In-Beom Hwang), Pep Biel (60.Mathieu Valbuena), Pierre Kunde (69.Yann M'Vila), Andreas Ntoj, Ui-Jo Hwang (60.Marcelo), Aboubakar Kamara, Marios Vrousai (86.Garry Rodrigues). Trainer: José Miguel González Martín „Míchel" (Spain).

27.10.2022; Europa-Park Stadion, Freiburg im Breisgau; Attendance: 33,000; Referee: Kristo Tohver (Estonia)
**SC Freiburg – Olympiacos SFP Peiraiás 1-1(0-1)**
SC Freiburg: Mark Flekken, Lukas Kübler, Matthias Ginter, Christian Günter, Philipp Lienhart (78.Kiliann Sildillia), Nicolas Höfler, Vincenzo Grifo, Daniel Kyereh (64.Jeong Woo-yeong), Yannik Keitel (63.Maximilian Eggestein), Michael Gregoritsch (72.Nils Petersen), Ritsu Dōan (64.Noah Weißhaupt). Trainer: Christian Streich.
Olympiacos: Alexandros Paschalakis, Pipa, Ousseynou Ba [*sent off 90+6*], Yann M'Vila, Pep Biel (69.Pierre Kunde, 82.Mathieu Valbuena), In-Beom Hwang, Andreas Ntoj, Youssef El-Arabi (83.Ui-Jo Hwang), Garry Rodrigues (39.Oleg Reabciuk), Marios Vrousai (82.Panagiotis Retsos). Trainer: José Miguel González Martín „Míchel" (Spain).
Goals: 17' Youssef El-Arabi 0-1, 90+3' Lukas Kübler 1-1.


03.11.2022; „Tofiq Bahramov", Bakı; Attendance: 30,430
Referee: Aleksei Kulbakov (Belarus)
**Qarabağ FK Bakı – SC Freiburg 1-1(0-1)**
Qarabağ FK: Sahrudin Mahammadaliyev, Marko Vesovic (88.Abbas Hüseynov), Bahlul Mustafazada, Kevin Medina [*sent off 62*], Richard Almeyda (87.Musa Qurbanli), Abdellah Zoubir, Kady, Elvin Cafarquliyev (88.Toral Bayramov), Marko Jankovic (88.Júlio Romão), Ramil Sheydayev (63.Maksim Medvedev), Owusu Kwabena. Trainer: Qurban Qurbanov.
SC Freiburg: Noah Atubolu, Christian Günter (46.Lukas Kübler), Keven Schlotterbeck, Hugo Siquet (73.Matthias Ginter), Kiliann Sildillia, Yannik Keitel, Robert Wagner, Nils Petersen, Lucas Höler (84.Vincenzo Grifo), Noah Weißhaupt (72.Jeong Woo-yeong), Kevin Schade (62.Roland Sallai). Trainer: Christian Streich.
Goals: 25' Nils Petersen 0-1 (penalty), 90+2' Owusu Kwabena 1-1.


27.10.2022; Stade de la Beaujoire „Louis Fonteneau", Nantes; Attendance: 30,927; Referee: Jakob Kehlet (Denmark)
**FC Nantes – Qarabağ FK Bakı 2-1(1-0)**
FC Nantes: Alban Lafont, Sébastien Corchia (68.Moussa Sissoko), Andrei Girotto, Jean-Charles Castelletto, Pedro Chirivella (88.Marcus Coco), Samuel Moutoussamy (78.Ignatius Ganago), Ludovic Blas, Quentin Merlin, Abdoul Kader Bamba (68.Dennis Appiah), Mostafa Mohamed, Evann Guessand (67.Moses Simon). Trainer: Antoine Kombouaré.
Qarabağ FK: Sahrudin Mahammadaliyev, Marko Vesovic (88.Abbas Hüseynov), Qara Qarayev (79.Júlio Romão), Bahlul Mustafazada, Kevin Medina, Richard Almeyda (69.Marko Jankovic), Filip Ozobic (69.Ramil Sheydayev), Abdellah Zoubir, Kady, Toral Bayramov (88.Elvin Cafarquliyev), Owusu Kwabena. Trainer: Qurban Qurbanov.
Goals: 16' Ludovic Blas 1-0, 56' Filip Ozobic 1-1 (penalty), 90+5' Ignatius Ganago 2-1.


03.11.2022; Stádio „Giórgos Karaïskáki", Peiraiás; Attendance: 16,254
Referee: Serhiy Boyko (Ukraine)
**Olympiacos SFP Peiraiás – FC Nantes 0-2(0-0)**
Olympiacos: Konstantinos Tzolakis, Panagiotis Retsos, Alexios Kalogeropoulos (60.Pape Cissé), Andreas Bouchalakis, Pierre Kunde, Athanasios Androutsos, Josh Bowler (85.Pipa), Youssef El-Arabi (46.Anastasios Sapountzis), Ui-Jo Hwang, Aboubakar Kamara (69.Marcelo), Marios Vrousai (46.Sime Vrsaljko). Trainer: José Miguel González Martín „Míchel" (Spain).
FC Nantes: Alban Lafont, Fábio (5.Dennis Appiah), Nicolas Pallois, Jean-Charles Castelletto, Moussa Sissoko, Samuel Moutoussamy (73.Pedro Chirivella), Moses Simon (46.Ludovic Blas), Mostafa Mohamed, Ignatius Ganago (73.Abdoul Kader Bamba), Evann Guessand (80.Marcus Coco). Trainer: Antoine Kombouaré.
Goals: 79' Mostafa Mohamed 0-1, 90' Ludovic Blas 0-2.


| | **GROUP H** | | | | | | | |
|---|---|---|---|---|---|---|---|---|
| 1. | **Ferencvárosi TC** | 6 | 3 | 1 | 2 | 8 - 9 | 10 |
| 2. | **AS Monaco** | 6 | 3 | 1 | 2 | 9 - 8 | 10 |
| 3. | *Trabzonspor Kulübü* | 6 | 3 | 0 | 3 | 11 - 9 | 9 |
| 4. | FK Crvena Zvezda Beograd | 6 | 2 | 0 | 4 | 9 - 11 | 6 |

08.09.2022; Stadion "Rajko Mitić", Beograd; Attendance: 40,226
Referee: Harm Osmers (Germany)
**FK Crvena Zvezda Beograd – AS Monaco 0-1(0-0)**
Crvena Zvezda: Milan Borjan, Aleksandar Dragovic, Nemanja Milunovic, Milan Rodic, Strahinja Erakovic, Aleksandar Katai (87.Kalifa Coulibaly), Slavoljub Srnic (76.Veljko Nikolic), Sékou Sanogo (88.Stefan Mitrovic), Guélor Kanga, Aleksandar Pesic (54.El Fardou Ben Mohamed), Osman Bukari. Trainer: Milos Milojevic.
AS Monaco: Alexander Nübel, Guillermo Maripán, Axel Disasi, Caio Henrique, Benoît Badiashile, Vanderson, Takumi Minamino (57.Krépin Diatta), Aleksandr Golovin (83.Ismail Jakobs), Youssouf Fofana (57.Jean Lucas), Mohamed Camara, Wissam Ben Yedder (66.Breel Embolo). Trainer: Philippe Clement (Belgium).
Goal: 74' Breel Embolo 0-1 (penalty).


15.09.2022; „Şenol Güneş" Stadyumu, Trabzon; Attendance: 24,884
Referee: Sascha Stegemann (Germany)
**Trabzonspor Kulübü – FK Crvena Zvezda Beograd 2-1(1-0)**
Trabzonspor: Ugurcan Çakir, Jens Stryger Larsen (69.Vitor Hugo), Marc Bartra, Stefano Denswil, Eren Elmali, Marek Hamsík (61.Enis Bardhi), Anastasios Bakasetas, Emmanouil "Manolis" Siopis, Trézéguet, Djaniny (79.Umut Bozok), Maximiliano Gómez (61.Abdülkadir Ömür, 79.Montassir Lahtimi). Trainer: Abdullah Avci.
Crvena Zvezda: Milan Borjan, Aleksandar Dragovic, Nemanja Milunovic, Milan Rodic, Strahinja Erakovic, Slavoljub Srnic (46.Aleksandar Katai), Sékou Sanogo (59.Ibrahim Mustapha), Guélor Kanga (84.Radovan Pankov), Kings Kangwa [*sent off 63*], Aleksandar Pesic (59.Kalifa Coulibaly), Osman Bukari (70.Veljko Nikolic). Trainer: Milos Milojevic.
Goals: 16' Marek Hamsík 1-0, 68' Trézéguet 2-0, 89' Veljko Nikolic 2-1.


08.09.2022; Groupama Aréna, Budapest Attendancce: 17,987
Referee: Fabio Maresca (Italy)
**Ferencvárosi TC – Trabzonspor Kulübü 3-2(3-1)**
Ferencvárosi TC: Dénes Dibusz, Eldar Civic [*sent off 16*], Henry Wingo, Samy Mmaee, Mats Knoester, Muhamed Besic (90.Adnan Kovacevic), Bálint Vécsei (76.Aïssa Laïdouni), Kristoffer Zachariassen, Tokmac Nguen (76.Amer Gojak), Franck Boli (20.Endre Botka), Adama Traoré (I). Trainer: Stanislav Cherchesov (Russia).
Trabzonspor: Muhammet Taha Tepe, Jens Stryger Larsen, Vitor Hugo (46.Eren Elmali), Marc Bartra, Stefano Denswil (72.Djaniny), Anastasios Bakasetas, Trézéguet, Jean-Philippe Gbamin (46.Marek Hamsík), Enis Bardhi (46.Yusuf Yazici), Abdülkadir Ömür (60.Umut Bozok), Maximiliano Gómez. Trainer: Abdullah Avci.
Goals: 5' Tokmac Nguen 1-0, 29' Adama Traoré 2-0, 39' Maximiliano Gómez 2-1, 44' Tokmac Nguen 3-1 (penalty), 71' Umut Bozok 3-2.


15.09.2022; Stade „Louis II", Monaco; Attendance: 3,931
Referee: Espen Eskås (Norway)
**AS Monaco – Ferencvárosi TC 0-1(0-0)**
AS Monaco: Alexander Nübel, Axel Disasi, Malang Sarr (81.Myron Boadu), Caio Henrique, Benoît Badiashile, Vanderson (46.Ruben Aguilar), Aleksandr Golovin (73.Ismail Jakobs), Youssouf Fofana, Mohamed Camara, Wissam Ben Yedder (66.Breel Embolo), Krépin Diatta (46.Maghnes Akliouche). Trainer: Philippe Clement (Belgium).
Ferencvárosi TC: Dénes Dibusz, Endre Botka, Henry Wingo, Samy Mmaee, Mats Knoester, Muhamed Besic (70.Bálint Vécsei), Kristoffer Zachariassen (90.Anderson Esiti), Aïssa Laïdouni, Tokmac Nguen (63.Amer Gojak), Adama Traoré (I), Ryan Mmaee (64.Franck Boli). Trainer: Stanislav Cherchesov (Russia).
Goal: 79' Bálint Vécsei 0-1.

06.10.2022; Stadion "Rajko Mitić", Beograd; Attendance: 26,244
Referee: Lawrence Visser (Belgium)
**FK Crvena Zvezda Beograd – Ferencvárosi TC 4-1(2-0)**
Crvena Zvezda: Milan Borjan, Aleksandar Dragovic (72.Veljko Nikolic), Milan Rodic, Marko Gobeljic, Strahinja Erakovic, Aleksandar Katai (72.Nemanja Motika), Sékou Sanogo (62.Slavoljub Srnic), Guélor Kanga (80.Ibrahim Mustapha), Mirko Ivanic, Aleksandar Pesic, Stefan Mitrovic (62.Radovan Pankov). Trainer: Milos Milojevic.
Ferencvárosi TC: Dénes Dibusz, Endre Botka (77.Lóránd Pászka), Henry Wingo, Samy Mmaee, Mats Knoester, Muhamed Besic (57.Bálint Vécsei), Kristoffer Zachariassen, Aïssa Laïdouni (67.Amer Gojak), Tokmac Nguen (66.Marquinhos), Franck Boli (57.Ryan Mmaee), Adama Traoré (I). Trainer: Stanislav Cherchesov (Russia).
Goals: 27' Guélor Kanga 1-0 (penalty), 35' Stefan Mitrovic 2-0, 50' Aleksandar Katai 3-0, 60' Guélor Kanga 4-0, 71' Kristoffer Zachariassen 4-1.

13.10.2022; "Şenol Güneş" Stadyumu, Trabzon; Attendance: 24,343
Referee: Jakob Kehlet (Denmark)
**Trabzonspor Kulübü – AS Monaco 4-0(1-0)**
Trabzonspor: Ugurcan Çakir, Marc Bartra, Stefano Denswil, Hüseyin Türkmen (46.Vitor Hugo), Eren Elmali (77.Yusuf Erdogan), Marek Hamsík (58.Emmanouil "Manolis" Siopis), Anastasios Bakasetas, Jean-Philippe Gbamin, Enis Bardhi (64.Trézéguet), Djaniny (58.Abdülkadir Ömür), Umut Bozok. Trainer: Abdullah Avci.
AS Monaco: Alexander Nübel, Axel Disasi, Malang Sarr, Caio Henrique (83.Ismail Jakobs), Vanderson, Aleksandr Golovin (60.Takumi Minamino), Youssouf Fofana, Mohamed Camara, Wissam Ben Yedder (68.Kevin Volland), Breel Embolo (60.Myron Boadu), Krépin Diatta (60.Gelson Martins). Trainer: Philippe Clement (Belgium).
Goals: 44' Malang Sarr 1-0 (own goal), 48' Vitor Hugo 2-0, 57' Enis Bardhi 3-0, 69' Trézéguet 4-0.

27.10.2022; Stadion "Rajko Mitić", Beograd; Attendance: 30,431
Referee: João Pedro Silva Pinheiro (Portugal)
**FK Crvena Zvezda Beograd – Trabzonspor Kulübü 2-1(1-1)**
Crvena Zvezda: Milan Borjan, Aleksandar Dragovic, Nemanja Milunovic, Milan Rodic, Strahinja Erakovic, Aleksandar Katai (75.Kings Kangwa), Slavoljub Srnic (60.Mirko Ivanic), Guélor Kanga, Aleksandar Pesic (83.Jovan Mijatovic), Osman Bukari, Stefan Mitrovic (83.Ibrahim Mustapha). Trainer: Milos Milojevic.
Trabzonspor: Ugurcan Çakir, Jens Stryger Larsen, Vitor Hugo, Marc Bartra, Eren Elmali, Marek Hamsík (82.Yusuf Yazici), Anastasios Bakasetas, Trézéguet, Jean-Philippe Gbamin (68.Abdülkadir Ömür), Enis Bardhi (83.Montassir Lahtimi), Umut Bozok (69.Djaniny). Trainer: Abdullah Avci.
Goals: 37' Aleksandar Katai 1-0, 39' Anastasios Bakasetas 1-1, 64' Aleksandar Pesic 2-1.

03.11.2022; "Şenol Güneş" Stadyumu, Trabzon; Attendance: 22,840
Referee: Harm Osmers (Germany)
**Trabzonspor Kulübü – Ferencvárosi TC 1-0(1-0)**
Trabzonspor: Ugurcan Çakir, Jens Stryger Larsen, Vitor Hugo, Marc Bartra, Eren Elmali, Marek Hamsík (62.Jean-Philippe Gbamin), Anastasios Bakasetas (70.Naci Ünüvar), Emmanouil "Manolis" Siopis, Trézéguet (85.Dogucan Haspolat), Abdülkadir Ömür (69.Enis Bardhi), Yusuf Yazici (62.Djaniny). Trainer: Abdullah Avci.
Ferencvárosi TC: Dénes Dibusz, Henry Wingo, Lóránd Pászka (90+1.Damir Redzic), Samy Mmaee, Mats Knoester, Bálint Vécsei, Anderson Esiti (61.Xavier Mercier), Kristoffer Zachariassen, Aïssa Laïdouni, Tokmac Nguen (82.Adnan Kovacevic), Ryan Mmaee. Trainer: Stanislav Cherchesov (Russia).
Goal: 7' Anastasios Bakasetas 1-0.

06.10.2022; Stade „Louis II", Monaco; Attendance: 5,050
Referee: Giorgi Kruashvili (Georgia)
**AS Monaco – Trabzonspor Kulübü 3-1(2-0)**
AS Monaco: Alexander Nübel, Axel Disasi, Caio Henrique, Benoît Badiashile, Vanderson (65.Guillermo Maripán), Aleksandr Golovin (73.Takumi Minamino), Youssouf Fofana, Mohamed Camara (65.Jean Lucas), Wissam Ben Yedder (57.Myron Boadu), Breel Embolo (57.Kevin Volland), Krépin Diatta. Trainer: Philippe Clement (Belgium).
Trabzonspor: Ugurcan Çakir, Jens Stryger Larsen, Marc Bartra, Stefano Denswil, Eren Elmali, Marek Hamsík (56.Anastasios Bakasetas), Emmanouil "Manolis" Siopis (72.Abdülkadir Ömür), Trézéguet (72.Djaniny), Enis Bardhi (82.Naci Ünüvar), Yusuf Yazici (56.Umut Bozok), Maximiliano Gómez [sent off 11]. Trainer: Abdullah Avci.
Goals: 14', 45+2' Wissam Ben Yedder 1-0, 2-0 (penalty), 55' Axel Disasi 3-0, 72' Anastasios Bakasetas 3-1.

13.10.2022; Groupama Aréna, Budapest; Attendance: 20,675
Referee: Daniel Stefanski (Poland)
**Ferencvárosi TC – FK Crvena Zvezda Beograd 2-1(1-0)**
Ferencvárosi TC: Dénes Dibusz, Endre Botka, Lóránd Pászka, Samy Mmaee, Mats Knoester, Muhamed Besic (81.Anderson Esiti), Bálint Vécsei, Amer Gojak (66.Tokmac Nguen), Kristoffer Zachariassen, Adama Traoré (I), Ryan Mmaee (90+4.Franck Boli). Trainer: Stanislav Cherchesov (Russia).
Crvena Zvezda: Milan Borjan, Aleksandar Dragovic (81.Nemanja Milunovic), Milan Rodic, Marko Gobeljic, Strahinja Erakovic, Aleksandar Katai (61.Osman Bukari), Sékou Sanogo (27.Kings Kangwa), Guélor Kanga (82.Jovan Mijatovic), Mirko Ivanic, Aleksandar Pesic, Stefan Mitrovic. Trainer: Milos Milojevic.
Goals: 23' Kristoffer Zachariassen 1-0, 55' Stefan Mitrovic 1-1, 61' Samy Mmaee 2-1.

27.10.2022; Groupama Aréna, Budapest; Attendance: 20,517
Referee: Enea Jorgji (Albania)
**Ferencvárosi TC – AS Monaco 1-1(0-1)**
Ferencvárosi TC: Dénes Dibusz, Endre Botka, Henry Wingo, Lóránd Pászka (65.Tokmac Nguen), Samy Mmaee, Bálint Vécsei (56.Muhamed Besic), Amer Gojak (46.Marquinhos, 90+1.Anderson Esiti), Kristoffer Zachariassen, Aïssa Laïdouni, Adama Traoré (I), Ryan Mmaee. Trainer: Stanislav Cherchesov (Russia).
AS Monaco: Alexander Nübel, Guillermo Maripán, Axel Disasi, Caio Henrique, Benoît Badiashile, Vanderson (41.Krépin Diatta), Aleksandr Golovin, Youssouf Fofana (83.Jean Lucas), Mohamed Camara, Kevin Volland (83.Breel Embolo), Wissam Ben Yedder. Trainer: Philippe Clement (Belgium).
Goals: 31' Wissam Ben Yedder 0-1, 81' Kristoffer Zachariassen 1-1.

03.11.2022; Stade „Louis II", Monaco; Attendance: 6,341
Referee: Serdar Gözübüyük (Netherlands)
**AS Monaco – FK Crvena Zvezda Beograd 4-1(2-0)**
AS Monaco: Alexander Nübel, Guillermo Maripán, Axel Disasi, Caio Henrique, Benoît Badiashile, Aleksandr Golovin (85.Ismail Jakobs), Youssouf Fofana, Mohamed Camara (85.Eliot Matazo), Kevin Volland (90.Eliesse Ben Seghir), Wissam Ben Yedder (76.Breel Embolo), Krépin Diatta (75.Vanderson). Trainer: Philippe Clement (Belgium).
Crvena Zvezda: Milan Borjan, Nemanja Milunovic, Milan Rodic (84.Irakli Azarov), Marko Gobeljic, Strahinja Erakovic, Aleksandar Katai (60.Kings Kangwa), Guélor Kanga (71.Ibrahim Mustapha), Mirko Ivanic, Aleksandar Pesic, Osman Bukari (71.El Fardou Ben Mohamed), Stefan Mitrovic (46.Slavoljub Srnic). Trainer: Milos Milojevic.
Goals: 5', 27' Kevin Volland 1-0, 2-0, 50' Milan Rodic 3-0 (own goal), 54' Guélor Kanga 3-1 (penalty), 87' Kevin Volland 4-1.

Please note: AFC Ajax Amsterdam, Bayer 04 Leverkusen, FC Barcelona, Sporting Clube de Portugal Lisboa, FC Red Bull Salzburg, FK Shakhtar Donetsk, Sevilla FC and Juventus FC Torino entered the UEFA Europa League as the group stage third-placed teams from the UEFA Champions League.

16.02.2023; Estadio Camp Nou, Barcelona; Attendance: 90,225
Referee: Maurizio Mariani (Italy)
**FC Barcelona – Manchester United FC 2-2(0-0)**
FC Barcelona: Marc-André ter Stegen, Jordi Alba (67.Alejandro (Álex) Baldé), Marcos Alonso (67.Andreas Christensen), Jules Koundé, Ronald Araújo, Franck Kessié (67.Ansu Fati), Frenkie de Jong, Pedri (41.Sergi Roberto), Gavi, Robert Lewandowski, Raphinha (83.Ferrán Torres). Trainer: Xavier Hernández i Creus "Xavi".
Manchester United: David de Gea, Raphaël Varane, Luke Shaw, Tyrell Malacia, Aaron Wan-Bissaka, Casemiro, Fred, Bruno Fernandes, Wout Weghorst, Marcus Rashford, Jadon Sancho (81.Alejandro Garnacho). Trainer: Erik ten Hag (Netherlands).
Goals: 50' Marcos Alonso 1-0, 53' Marcus Rashford 1-1, 59' Jules Koundé 1-2 (own goal), 76' Raphinha 2-2.

16.02.2023; Stadion Wojska Polskiego, Warszawa (Poland); Attendance: 13,415; Referee: Irfan Peljto (Bosnia and Herzegovina)
**FK Shakhtar Donetsk – Stade Rennais FC 2-1(2-0)**
Shakhtar Donetsk: Anatoliy Trubin, Mykola Matviyenko, Bogdan Mykhailichenko, Valeriy Bondar, Yukhym Konoplya, Taras Stepanenko, Dmytro Kryskiv (76.Ivan Petryak), Artem Bondarenko, Georgiy Sudakov, Oleksandr Zubkov, Lassina Traoré (77.Danylo Sikan). Trainer: Igor Jovićević (Croatia).
Stade Rennais: Steve Mandanda, Djed Spence, Warmed Omari, Adrien Truffert, Jeanuël Belocian, Benjamin Bourigeaud, Lesley Chimuanya Ugochukwu (77.Baptiste Santamaría), Karl Toko Ekambi (77.Lovro Majer), Amine Gouiri (71.Désiré Doué), Jérémy Doku (71.Ibrahim Salah), Arnaud Kalimuendo (86.Birger Meling). Trainer: Bruno Génésio.
Goals: 11' Dmytro Kryskiv 1-0, 45' Artem Bondarenko 2-0 (penalty), 59' Karl Toko Ekambi 2-1.

16.02.2023; „Johan Cruyff" ArenA, Amsterdam; Attendance: 54,322
Referee: Halil Umut Meler (Turkey)
**AFC Ajax Amsterdam – 1. FC Union Berlin  0-0**
AFC Ajax: Gerónimo Rulli, Owen Wijndal (46.Brian Brobbey), Calvin Bassey, Jurriën Timber, Devyne Rensch, Edson Álvarez, Kenneth Taylor, Mohammed Kudus, Dusan Tadic, Steven Berghuis, Steven Bergwijn (75.Davy Klaassen). Trainer: John Heitinga.
Union Berlin: Frederik Rønnow, Robin Knoche, Jérôme Roussillon (90.Niko Gießelmann), Diogo Leite, Danilho Doekhi, Rani Khedira, Morten Thorsby, Aïssa Laïdouni, Kevin Behrens (70.Jordan Siebatcheu), Sheraldo Becker (82.Sven Michel). Trainer: Urs Fischer (Switzerland).

16.02.2023; Red Bull Arena, Wals-Siezenheim; Attendance: 29,520
Referee: Dennis Higler (Netherlands)
**FC Red Bull Salzburg – AS Roma 1-0(0-0)**
Red Bull Salzburg: Philipp Köhn, Andreas Ulmer, Oumar Solet, Strahinja Pavlovic, Amar Dedic, Nicolas Seiwald, Luka Sucic (82.Oscar Gloukh), Nicolás Capaldo, Lucas Gourna-Douath, Noah Okafor (82.Sékou Koïta), Fernando (60.Junior Chikwubuike Adamu). Trainer: Matthias Jaissle (Germany).
AS Roma: Rui Patrício, Chris Smalling, Gianluca Mancini, Ibañez, Nemanja Matic, Bryan Cristante, Lorenzo Pellegrini (74.Georginio Wijnaldum), Stephan El Shaarawy, Paulo Dybala (46.Zeki Çelik), Tammy Abraham (74.Andrea Belotti), Nicola Zalewski. Trainer: José Mário dos Santos Félix Mourinho (Portugal).
Goal: 88' Nicolás Capaldo 1-0.

23.02.2023; Old Trafford, Manchester; Attendance: 73,021
Referee: Clément Turpin (France)
**MANCHESTER UNITED FC – FC Barcelona 2-1(0-1)**
Manchester United: David de Gea, Raphaël Varane, Luke Shaw, Aaron Wan-Bissaka (67.Diogo Dalot), Lisandro Martínez, Casemiro, Fred, Bruno Fernandes, Wout Weghorst (46.Antony), Marcus Rashford, Jadon Sancho (67.Alejandro Garnacho). Trainer: Erik ten Hag (Netherlands).
FC Barcelona: Marc-André ter Stegen, Sergi Roberto (70.Ferrán Torres), Andreas Christensen, Jules Koundé, Ronald Araújo (82.Marcos Alonso), Alejandro (Álex) Baldé, Sergio Busquets, Franck Kessié, Frenkie de Jong, Robert Lewandowski, Raphinha (75.Ansu Fati). Trainer: Xavier Hernández i Creus "Xavi".
Goals: 18' Robert Lewandowski 0-1 (penalty), 47' Fred 1-1, 73' Antony 2-1.

23.02.2023; Roazhon Park, Rennes; Attendance: 27,781
Referee: Tobias Stieler (Germany)
**Stade Rennais FC – FK SHAKHTAR DONETSK 2-1(0-0,1-0,1-0); 4-5 on penalties**
Stade Rennais: Steve Mandanda, Djed Spence, Warmed Omari, Adrien Truffert (97.Birger Meling), Jeanuël Belocian, Baptiste Santamaría (96.Désiré Doué), Lovro Majer (71.Lesley Chimuanya Ugochukwu), Karl Toko Ekambi (96.Ibrahim Salah), Amine Gouiri, Jérémy Doku, Arnaud Kalimuendo (84.Flavien Tait). Trainer: Bruno Génésio.
Shakhtar Donetsk: Anatoliy Trubin, Mykola Matviyenko, Bogdan Mykhailichenko, Valeriy Bondar, Yukhym Konoplya, Taras Stepanenko (100.Yegor Nazaryna), Artem Bondarenko, Georgiy Sudakov, Oleksandr Zubkov (112.Kevin Kelsy), Dmytro Topalov (80.Neven Djurasek), Lassina Traoré (79.Danylo Sikan). Trainer: Igor Jovićević (Croatia).
Goals: 52' Karl Toko Ekambi 1-0, 106' Ibrahim Salah 2-0, 119' Jeanuël Belocian 2-1 (own goal).
Penalties: Désiré Doué 1-0; Yegor Nazaryna 1-1; Jérémy Doku (missed); Georgiy Sudakov 1-2; Birger Meling (missed); Artem Bondarenko 1-3; Amine Gouiri 2-3; Valeriy Bondar (missed); Flavien Tait 3-3; Danylo Sikan (missed); Warmed Omari 4-3; Yukhym Konoplya 4-4; Lesley Chimuanya Ugochukwu (missed); Kevin Kelsy 4-5.

23.02.2023; Stadion An der Alten Försterei, Berlin; Attendance: 21,800
Referee: Ricardo de Burgos Bengoetxea (Spain)
**1. FC UNION BERLIN – AFC Ajax Amsterdam 3-1(2-0)**
Union Berlin: Frederik Rønnow, Robin Knoche, Jérôme Roussillon (90+4.Niko Gießelmann), Josip Juranovic (90+4.Christopher Trimmel), Diogo Leite, Danilho Doekhi, Rani Khedira, Janik Haberer, Aïssa Laïdouni (65.Morten Thorsby), Kevin Behrens (65.Jordan Siebatcheu), Sheraldo Becker (85.Jamie Leweling). Trainer: Urs Fischer (Switzerland).
AFC Ajax: Gerónimo Rulli, Calvin Bassey, Jurriën Timber, Devyne Rensch (84.Francisco Conceição), Davy Klaassen (64.Brian Brobbey), Edson Álvarez [sent off 90+7], Kenneth Taylor, Mohammed Kudus, Dusan Tadic, Steven Berghuis, Steven Bergwijn (80.Lorenzo Lucca). Trainer: John Heitinga.
Goals: 20' Robin Knoche 1-0 (penalty), 44' Josip Juranovic 2-0, 47' Mohammed Kudus 2-1, 50' Danilho Doekhi 3-1.

23.02.2023; Stadio Olimpico, Roma; Attendance: 62,593
Referee: Slavko Vinčić (Slovenia)
**AS ROMA – FC Red Bull Salzburg 2-0(2-0)**
AS Roma: Rui Patrício, Chris Smalling, Leonardo Spinazzola, Gianluca Mancini, Ibañez, Nemanja Matic, Bryan Cristante, Lorenzo Pellegrini (81.Georginio Wijnaldum), Paulo Dybala (90+3.Stephan El Shaarawy), Andrea Belotti (87.Tammy Abraham), Nicola Zalewski (81.Rick Karsdorp). Trainer: José Mário dos Santos Félix Mourinho (Portugal).
Red Bull Salzburg: Philipp Köhn, Andreas Ulmer, Bernardo, Oumar Solet, Amar Dedic (74.Ignace Van Der Brempt), Nicolas Seiwald (75.Oscar Gloukh), Nicolás Capaldo (84.Sékou Koïta), Maurits Kjærgaard (46.Luka Sucic), Lucas Gourna-Douath, Noah Okafor, Junior Chikwubuike Adamu (74.Benjamin Sesko). Trainer: Matthias Jaissle (Germany).
Goals: 33' Andrea Belotti 1-0, 40' Paulo Dybala 2-0.

16.02.2023; Allianz Stadium, Torino; Attendance: 41,019
Referee: João Pedro Silva Pinheiro (Portugal)
**Juventus FC Torino – FC Nantes 1-1(1-0)**
Juventus: Wojciech Szczesny, Danilo, Alex Sandro, Mattia De Sciglio (73.Juan Cuadrado), Bremer, Ángel Di María (73.Matías Soulé), Leandro Paredes (63.Manuel Locatelli), Adrien Rabiot, Nicolò Fagioli (63.Filip Kostic), Dusan Vlahovic (86.Moise Kean), Federico Chiesa. Trainer: Massimiliano Allegri.
FC Nantes: Alban Lafont, Nicolas Pallois (83.Sébastien Corchia), Andrei Girotto, Jean-Charles Castelletto (88.Evann Guessand), Fabien Centonze, Moussa Sissoko, Pedro Chirivella (77.Florent Mollet), Samuel Moutoussamy, Ludovic Blas, Marcus Coco (77.Charles Traoré), Mostafa Mohamed (77.Moses Simon). Trainer: Antoine Kombouaré.
Goals: 13' Dusan Vlahovic 1-0, 60' Ludovic Blas 1-1.

16.02.2023; Estádio „José Alvalade", Lisboa; Attendance: 23,279
Referee: François Letexier (France)
**Sporting Clube de Portugal Lisboa – FC Midtjylland Herning 1-1(0-0)**
Sporting: Antonio Adán, Sebastián Coates, Ricardo Esgaio (65.Héctor Bellerín), Matheus Reis (78.Gonçalo Inácio), Jerry St.Juste, Nuno Santos, Arthur Gomes (65.Trincão), Manuel Ugarte (86.Mateo Tanlongo), Pedro Gonçalves "Pote", Paulinho (77.Youssef Chermiti), Marcus Edwards. Trainer: Rúben Amorim.
FC Midtjylland: Jonas Lössl, Henrik Dalsgaard, Joel Andersson, Stefan Gartenmann, Paulinho (67.Victor Bak), Kristoffer Olsson, Emiliano Martínez (67.Emam Ashour), Armin Gigovic, Valdemar Andreasen (46.Edward Chilufya), Gustav Isaksen (86.Aral Simsir), Frederik Heiselberg (59.Oliver Sørensen). Trainer: Albert Capellas Herms (Spain).
Goals: 77' Emam Ashour 0-1, 90+4' Sebastián Coates 1-1.

16.02.2023; BayArena, Leverkusen; Attendance: 27,864
Referee: Orel Grinfeld (Israel)
**Bayer 04 Leverkusen – AS Monaco 2-3(0-1)**
Bayer Leverkusen: Lukás Hrádecký, Jonathan Tah, Jeremie Frimpong (88.Callum Hudson-Odoi), Edmond Tapsoba, Piero Hincapié, Robert Andrich, Nadiem Amiri (68.Odilon Kossounou), Exequiel Palacios, Florian Wirtz, Moussa Diaby (56.Amine Adli), Adam Hlozek (88.Patrik Schick). Trainer: Xabier „Xabi" Alonso Olano (Spain).
AS Monaco: Alexander Nübel, Ruben Aguilar (80.Chrislain Matsima), Guillermo Maripán, Axel Disasi, Caio Henrique, Takumi Minamino (46.Eliesse Ben Seghir), Aleksandr Golovin (71.Ismail Jakobs), Youssouf Fofana, Mohamed Camara (71.Eliot Matazo), Breel Embolo (62.Wissam Ben Yedder), Krépin Diatta. Trainer: Philippe Clement (Belgium).
Goals: 9' Lukás Hrádecký 0-1 (own goal), 48' Moussa Diaby 1-1, 59' Florian Wirtz 2-1, 74' Krépin Diatta 2-2, 90+2' Axel Disasi 2-3.

16.02.2023; Estadio „Ramón Sánchez Pizjuán", Sevilla; Attendance: 29,593; Referee: Radu Marian Petrescu (Romania)
**Sevilla FC – PSV Eindhoven 3-0(1-0)**
Sevilla FC: Yassine Bounou "Bono", Jesús Navas, Marcos Acuña (70.Gonzalo Montiel), Loïc Badé (16.Fernando), Tanguy Nianzou, Ivan Rakitic, Nemanja Gudelj, Óliver Torres (70.Érik Lamela), Joan Jordán, Youssef En-Nesyri (63.Suso), Bryan Gil (46.Lucas Ocampos). Trainer: Jorge Luis Sampaoli Moya (Argentina).
PSV Eindhoven: Walter Benítez, Patrick van Aanholt (75.Mauro Júnior), André Ramalho (90+1.Armando Obispo), Jordan Teze, Jarrad Branthwaite, Ibrahim Sangaré, Guus Til (62.Thorgan Hazard), Joey Veerman, Xavi Simons, Luuk de Jong (62.Fábio Silva), Ismael Saibari (90+1.Philipp Mwene). Trainer: Ruud van Nistelrooij.
Goals: 45+2' Youssef En-Nesyri 1-0, 50' Lucas Ocampos 2-0, 55' Nemanja Gudelj 3-0).

23.02.2023; Stade de la Beaujoire „Louis Fonteneau", Nantes; Attendance: 34,420; Referee: José María Sánchez Martínez (Spain)
**FC Nantes – JUVENTUS FC TORINO 0-3(0-2)**
FC Nantes: Alban Lafont, Nicolas Pallois [sent off 17], Andrei Girotto, Jean-Charles Castelletto, Fabien Centonze, Moussa Sissoko (46.Samuel Moutoussamy), Florent Mollet (73.Evann Guessand), Pedro Chirivella (24.Charles Traoré), Ludovic Blas, Andy Delort (46.Ignatius Ganago), Moses Simon (73.Mostafa Mohamed). Trainer: Antoine Kombouaré.
Juventus: Wojciech Szczesny, Danilo (82.Leonardo Bonucci), Alex Sandro, Mattia De Sciglio (65.Juan Cuadrado), Bremer, Ángel Di María (82.Leandro Paredes), Filip Kostic (82.Samuel Iling-Junior), Adrien Rabiot, Manuel Locatelli, Nicolò Fagioli, Moise Kean (64.Dusan Vlahovic). Trainer: Massimiliano Allegri.
Goals: 5', 20', 78' Ángel Di María 0-1, 0-2 (penalty), 0-3.

23.02.2023; MCH Arena, Herning; Attendance: 9,576
Referee: Ivan Kružliak (Slovakia)
**FC Midtjylland Herning – SPORTING CLUBE DE PORTUGAL LISBOA 0-4(0-1)**
FC Midtjylland: Jonas Lössl, Henrik Dalsgaard, Joel Andersson (72.Mads Thychosen), Stefan Gartenmann, Paulinho, Kristoffer Olsson, Oliver Sørensen (46.Victor Bak), Armin Gigovic, Valdemar Andreasen (46.Emam Ashour), Astrit Selmani (46.Edward Chilufya), Gustav Isaksen (79.Frederik Heiselberg). Trainer: Albert Capellas Herms (Spain).
Sporting: Antonio Adán, Sebastián Coates, Ricardo Esgaio (46.Héctor Bellerín), Jerry St.Juste, Gonçalo Inácio, Arthur Gomes (65.Nuno Santos), Manuel Ugarte (78.Mateo Tanlongo), Pedro Gonçalves "Pote", Hidemasa Morita (53.Mateus Fernandes), Paulinho [sent off 38], Marcus Edwards (65.Trincão). Trainer: Rúben Amorim.
Goals: 21' Sebastián Coates 0-1, 50', 77' Pedro Gonçalves "Pote" 0-2, 0-3, 85' Stefan Gartenmann 0-4 (own goal).

23.02.2023; Stade „Louis II", Monaco; Attendance: 8,504
Referee: Alejandro José Hernández Hernández (Spain)
**AS Monaco – BAYER 04 LEVERKUSEN 2-3(1-2,2-3,2-3)**
AS Monaco: Alexander Nübel, Axel Disasi, Malang Sarr, Caio Henrique, Chrislain Matsima (61.Edan Diop), Aleksandr Golovin (78.Myron Boadu), Youssouf Fofana, Mohamed Camara (70.Eliot Matazo), Eliesse Ben Seghir (78.Ismail Jakobs), Wissam Ben Yedder (78.Breel Embolo), Krépin Diatta (110.Kevin Volland). Trainer: Philippe Clement (Belgium).
Bayer Leverkusen: Lukás Hrádecký, Jonathan Tah, Jeremie Frimpong (103.Moussa Diaby), Mitchel Bakker, Edmond Tapsoba, Piero Hincapié, Robert Andrich, Exequiel Palacios, Florian Wirtz (115.Sardar Azmoun), Adam Hlozek (70.Patrik Schick), Amine Adli (74.Nadiem Amiri). Trainer: Xabier „Xabi" Alonso Olano (Spain).
Goals: 13' Florian Wirtz 0-1, 19' Wissam Ben Yedder 1-1 (penalty), 21' Exequiel Palacios 1-2, 58' Amine Adli 1-3, 84' Breel Embolo 2-3.
Penalties: Sardar Azmoun 0-1; Axel Disasi 1-1; Nadiem Amiri 1-2; Eliot Matazo (missed); Edmond Tapsoba 1-3; Breel Embolo 2-3; Patrik Schick 2-4; Kevin Volland 3-4; Moussa Diaby 3-5.

23.02.2023; Philips Stadion, Eindhoven; Attendance: 34,000
Referee: Daniele Orsato (Italy)
**PSV Eindhoven – SEVILLA FC 2-0(0-0)**
PSV Eindhoven: Walter Benítez, Patrick van Aanholt (62.Mauro Júnior [sent off 90+7]), Philipp Mwene, André Ramalho, Jarrad Branthwaite, Érick Gutiérrez (62.Fábio Silva), Guus Til, Joey Veerman, Xavi Simons, Luuk de Jong, Johan Bakayoko. Trainer: Ruud van Nistelrooij.
Sevilla FC: Marko Dmitrovic, Jesús Navas (80.Gonzalo Montiel), Alex Telles, Marcos Acuña, Tanguy Nianzou, Ivan Rakitic, Fernando, Óliver Torres (68.Suso), Joan Jordán, Youssef En-Nesyri (69.Lucas Ocampos), Bryan Gil (86.Rafa Mir). Trainer: Jorge Luis Sampaoli Moya (Argentina).
Goals: 77' Luuk de Jong 1-0, 90+5' Fábio Silva 2-0.

09.03.2023; Stadion An der Alten Försterei, Berlin; Attendance: 21,605
Referee: Orel Grindfeld (Israel)
**1. FC Union Berlin – Royale Union Saint-Gilloise 3-3(1-1)**
Union Berlin: Frederik Rønnow, Christopher Trimmel (77.Niko Gießelmann), Robin Knoche, Josip Juranovic, Diogo Leite, Danilho Doekhi, Rani Khedira, Janik Haberer (63.Aïssa Laïdouni), Morten Thorsby (77.Jamie Leweling), Kevin Behrens (64.Jordan Siebatcheu), Sheraldo Becker (77.Sven Michel). Trainer: Urs Fischer (Switzerland).
Union Saint-Gilloise: Anthony Moris, Bart Nieuwkoop, Christian Burgess, Siebe Van Der Heyden, Ismaël Kandouss, Senne Lynen, Jean Lazare Amani (86.Cameron Puertas), Oussama El Azzouzi, Loïc Lapoussin, Yorbe Vertessen (80.Simon Adingra), Victor Boniface (86.Gustaf Nilsson). Trainer: Karel Geraerts.
Goals: 28' Victor Boniface 0-1, 42' Josip Juranovic 1-1, 58' Yorbe Vertessen 1-2, 69' Robin Knoche 2-2, 72' Victor Boniface 2-3, 89' Sven Michel 3-3.

09.03.2023; BayArena, Leverkusen; Attendance: 25,001
Referee: Davide Massa (Italy)
**Bayer 04 Leverkusen – Ferencvárosi TC 2-0(1-0)**
Bayer Leverkusen: Lukás Hrádecký, Jonathan Tah, Jeremie Frimpong, Edmond Tapsoba, Odilon Kossounou, Piero Hincapié, Kerem Demirbay, Nadiem Amiri, Florian Wirtz (89.Patrik Schick), Sardar Azmoun (60.Amine Adli), Moussa Diaby (71.Adam Hlozek). Trainer: Xabier „Xabi" Alonso Olano (Spain).
Ferencvárosi TC: Dénes Dibusz, Endre Botka (87.Henry Wingo), Eldar Civic, Myenty Abena, Mats Knoester, Bálint Vécsei, Anderson Esiti, Kristoffer Zachariassen, Adama Traoré (I) (87.Nikolai Baden Frederiksen), Ryan Mmaee, Marquinhos (78.Amer Gojak). Trainer: Stanislav Cherchesov (Russia).
Goals: 10' Kerem Demirbay 1-0, 86' Edmond Tapsoba 2-0.

09.03.2023; Estádio „José Alvalade", Lisboa; Attendance: 36,006
Referee: Tobias Stieler (Germany)
**Sporting Clube de Portugal Lisboa – Arsenal FC London 2-2(1-1)**
Sporting: Antonio Adán, Sebastián Coates, Ricardo Esgaio (76.Ousmane Diomande), Matheus Reis, Jerry St.Juste, Gonçalo Inácio, Pedro Gonçalves "Pote", Hidemasa Morita, Paulinho (76.Youssef Chermiti), Marcus Edwards (89.Abdul Issahaku Fatawu), Trincão (71.Nuno Santos). Trainer: Rúben Amorim.
Arsenal: Matt Turner, Ben White, Jakub Kiwior (71.Gabriel Magalhães), William Saliba, Granit Xhaka, Jorginho (71.Thomas Partey), Oleksandr Zinchenko (63.Takehiro Tomiyasu), Bukayo Saka, Fábio Vieira, Reiss Nelson (71.Emile Smith Rowe), Gabriel Martinelli. Trainer: Mikel Arteta Amatriain (Spain).
Goals: 22' William Saliba 0-1, 34' Gonçalo Inácio 1-1, 55' Paulinho 2-1, 62' Hidemasa Morita 2-2 (own goal).

09.03.2023; Stadio Olimpico, Roma; Attendance: 61,608
Referee: Sandro Schärer (Switzerland)
**AS Roma – Real Sociedad de Fútbol San Sebastián 2-0(1-0)**
AS Roma: Rui Patrício, Chris Smalling, Diego Llorente (46.Marash Kumbulla), Rick Karsdorp, Gianluca Mancini, Nemanja Matic, Bryan Cristante, Lorenzo Pellegrini (60.Georginio Wijnaldum), Stephan El Shaarawy (60.Leonardo Spinazzola), Paulo Dybala (88.Edoardo Bove), Tammy Abraham (61.Andrea Belotti). Trainer: José Mário dos Santos Félix Mourinho (Portugal).
Real Sociedad: Álex Remiro, Diego Rico, Andoni Gorosabel (83.Álex Sola), Robin Le Normand, David Silva (83.Beñat Turrientes), Illarramendi (75.Brais Méndez), Mikel Merino, Zubeldía, Martín Zubimendi, Takefusa Kubo (75.Mohamed Cho), Alexander Sørloth (67.Mikel Oyarzabal). Trainer: Imanol Alguacil.
Goals: 13' Stephan El Shaarawy 1-0, 87' Marash Kumbulla 2-0.

16.03.2023; Lotto Park, Bruxelles; Attendance: 15,681
Referee: José María Sánchez Martínez (Spain)
**ROYALE UNION SAINT-GILLOISE – 1. FC Union Berlin 3-0(1-0)**
Union Saint-Gilloise: Anthony Moris, Bart Nieuwkoop, Christian Burgess, Siebe Van Der Heyden, Ismaël Kandouss, Teddy Teuma (85.Oussama El Azzouzi), Senne Lynen, Jean Lazare Amani, Loïc Lapoussin, Victor Boniface (90+2.Casper Terho), Simon Adingra (67.Gustaf Nilsson). Trainer: Karel Geraerts.
Union Berlin: Frederik Rønnow, Robin Knoche, Jérôme Roussillon (74.Christopher Trimmel), Josip Juranovic (74.Niko Gießelmann), Diogo Leite, Danilho Doekhi, Rani Khedira, Morten Thorsby (67.Jamie Leweling), Aïssa Laïdouni (56.Janik Haberer [sent off 80]), Sheraldo Becker, Sven Michel (56.Jordan Siebatcheu). Trainer: Urs Fischer (Switzerland).
Goals: 18' Teddy Teuma 1-0, 63' Jean Lazare Amani 2-0, 90+4' Loïc Lapoussin 3-0.

16.03.2023; 16.03.2023; Puskás Aréna, Budapest; Attendance: 50,675
Referee: Artur Manuel Ribeiro Soares Dias (Portugal)
**Ferencvárosi TC – BAYER 04 LEVERKUSEN 0-2(0-1)**
Ferencvárosi TC: Dénes Dibusz, Eldar Civic, Henry Wingo (14.Marquinhos, 90+1.Krisztián Lisztes), Myenty Abena, Mats Knoester, Bálint Vécsei, Anderson Esiti, Amer Gojak (78.Balász Manner), Kristoffer Zachariassen, Adama Traoré (I), Ryan Mmaee (90+1.Nikolai Baden Frederiksen). Trainer: Stanislav Cherchesov (Russia).
Bayer Leverkusen: Lukás Hrádecký, Jonathan Tah, Jeremie Frimpong (82.Timothy Fosu-Mensah), Mitchel Bakker, Edmond Tapsoba, Piero Hincapié (82.Odilon Kossounou), Robert Andrich (86.Kerem Demirbay), Exequiel Palacios, Florian Wirtz (71.Amine Adli), Sardar Azmoun (71.Adam Hlozek), Moussa Diaby. Trainer: Xabier „Xabi" Alonso Olano (Spain).
Goals: 3' Moussa Diaby 0-1, 81' Amine Adli 0-2.

16.03.2023; Emirates Stadium, London; Attendance: 59,929
Referee: Antonio Mateu Lahoz (Spain)
**Arsenal FC London – SPORTING CLUBE DE PORTUGAL LISBOA 1-1(1-0,1-1,1-1); 3-5 on penalties**
Arsenal: Aaron Ramsdale, Takehiro Tomiyasu (9.Ben White), Gabriel Magalhães, William Saliba (21.Rob Holding), Granit Xhaka, Jorginho (65.Thomas Partey), Oleksandr Zinchenko, Fábio Vieira (101.Martin Ødegaard), Gabriel Jesus (46.Leandro Trossard), Reiss Nelson (66.Bukayo Saka), Gabriel Martinelli. Trainer: Mikel Arteta Amatriain (Spain).
Sporting: Antonio Adán, Ricardo Esgaio, Matheus Reis (94.Nuno Santos), Jerry St.Juste, Gonçalo Inácio, Ousmane Diomande, Manuel Ugarte [sent off 118], Pedro Gonçalves "Pote" (94.Dário Essugo), Paulinho (89.Youssef Chermiti), Marcus Edwards (119.Mateo Tanlongo), Trincão (105.Arthur Gomes). Trainer: Rúben Amorim.
Goals: 19' Granit Xhaka 1-0, 62' Pedro Gonçalves "Pote" 1-1.
Penalties: Jerry St. Juste 0-1; Martin Ødegaard 1-1; Ricardo Esgaio 1-2; Bukayo Saka 2-2; Gonçalo Inácio 2-3; Leandro Trossard 3-3; Arthur Gomes 3-4; Gabriel Martinelli (missed); Nuno Santos 3-5.

16.03.2023; Reale Arena, San Sebastián; Attendance: 35,054
Referee: István Kovács (Romania)
**Real Sociedad de Fútbol San Sebastián – AS ROMA 0-0**
Real Sociedad: Álex Remiro, Diego Rico, Andoni Gorosabel (72.Álex Sola), Robin Le Normand, David Silva, Brais Méndez (79.Mohamed Cho), Mikel Merino, Zubeldía, Martín Zubimendi, Alexander Sørloth (62.Carlos Fernández [sent off 90+9]), Mikel Oyarzabal (71.Takefusa Kubo). Trainer: Imanol Alguacil.
AS Roma: Rui Patrício, Chris Smalling, Leonardo Spinazzola, Rick Karsdorp (41.Nicola Zalewski), Gianluca Mancini, Ibañez, Georginio Wijnaldum, Bryan Cristante, Lorenzo Pellegrini (87.Edoardo Bove), Paulo Dybala (75.Stephan El Shaarawy), Andrea Belotti (76.Tammy Abraham). Trainer: José Mário dos Santos Félix Mourinho (Portugal).

09.03.2023; Estadio „Ramón Sánchez Pizjuán", Sevilla; Attendance: 24,480; Referee: François Letexier (France)

**Sevilla FC – Fenerbahçe SK Istanbul 2-0(0-0)**

Sevilla FC: Marko Dmitrovic, Jesús Navas, Alex Telles (46.Joan Jordán), Marcos Acuña (87.Suso), Tanguy Nianzou, Ivan Rakitic, Fernando, Nemanja Gudelj, Óliver Torres (70.Lucas Ocampos), Youssef En-Nesyri (87.Rafa Mir), Bryan Gil (70.Érik Lamela). Trainer: Jorge Luis Sampaoli Moya (Argentina).

Fenerbahçe: Altay Bayindir, Serdar Aziz, Samet Akaydin, Attila Szalai, Willian Arão, Irfan Kahveci (87.Arda Güler), Lincoln (82.Bright Osayi-Samuel), Miguel Crespo (67.Diego Rossi), Ferdi Kadioglu, Joshua King (67.Michy Batshuayi), Enner Valencia (82.João Pedro). Trainer: Jorge Fernando Pinheiro de Jesus (Portugal).

Goals: 56' Joan Jordán 1-0, 85' Érik Lamela 2-0.


09.03.2023; Allianz Stadium, Torino; Attendance: 37,474
Referee: Anastasios Sidiropoulos (Greece)

**Juventus FC Torino – SC Freiburg 1-0(0-0)**

Juventus: Wojciech Szczesny, Danilo, Alex Sandro (23.Leonardo Bonucci), Bremer, Ángel Di María, Juan Cuadrado, Filip Kostic (78.Moise Kean), Adrien Rabiot, Manuel Locatelli, Fabio Miretti (46.Nicolò Fagioli), Dusan Vlahovic (67.Federico Chiesa). Trainer: Massimiliano Allegri.

SC Freiburg: Mark Flekken, Lukas Kübler, Matthias Ginter, Christian Günter, Philipp Lienhart (68.Manuel Gulde), Kiliann Sildillia, Nicolas Höfler, Vincenzo Grifo, Maximilian Eggestein (59.Yannik Keitel), Roland Sallai (59.Ritsu Dōan), Lucas Höler (88.Michael Gregoritsch). Trainer: Christian Streich.

Goal: 53' Ángel Di María 1-0.


09.03.2023; Old Trafford, Manchester; Attendance: 72,998
Referee: Daniel Siebert (Germany)

**Manchester United FC – Real Betis Balompié Sevilla FC 4-1(1-1)**

Manchester United: David de Gea, Raphaël Varane, Luke Shaw (65.Tyrell Malacia), Diogo Dalot (46.Aaron Wan-Bissaka), Lisandro Martínez, Casemiro, Fred (81.Scott McTominay), Bruno Fernandes, Wout Weghorst, Marcus Rashford (65.Jadon Sancho), Antony (82.Facundo Pellistri). Trainer: Erik ten Hag (Netherlands).

Real Betis: Claudio Bravo, Germán Pezzella, Youssouf Sabaly, Luiz Felipe, Abner Vinicius, Joaquín (59.Sergio Canales), William Carvalho, Guido Rodríguez (65.Andrés Guardado), Juanmi (80.Willian José), Ayoze Pérez (65.Borja Iglesias), Luiz Henrique (59.Aitor Ruibal). Trainer: Manuel Luis Pellegrini Ripamonti (Chile).

Goals: 6' Marcus Rashford 1-0, 32' Ayoze Pérez 1-1, 52' Antony 2-1, 58' Bruno Fernandes 3-1, 82' Wout Weghorst 4-1.


09.03.2023; Stadion Wojska Polskiego, Warszawa (Poland); Attendance: 17,423; Referee: Ivan Kružliak (Slovakia)

**FK Shakhtar Donetsk – Feyenoord Rotterdam 1-1(0-0)**

Shakhtar Donetsk: Anatoliy Trubin, Yaroslav Rakitskyi, Mykola Matviyenko, Lucas Taylor, Taras Stepanenko, Dmytro Kryskiv (62.Neven Djurasek), Artem Bondarenko (90.Yegor Nazaryna), Georgiy Sudakov (90.Ivan Petryak), Oleksandr Zubkov (77.Marian Shved), Dmytro Topalov, Lassina Traoré (62.Kevin Kelsy). Trainer: Igor Jovićević (Croatia).

Feyenoord Rotterdam: Timon Wellenreuther, Dávid Hancko, Lutsharel Geertruida, Marcus Pedersen (57.Gernot Trauner), Quilindschy Hartman, Sebastian Szymanski (72.Javairô Dilrosun), Orkun Kökçü, Mats Wieffer, Alireza Jahanbakhsh (86.Ezequiel Bullaude), Oussama Idrissi (72.Igor Paixão), Danilo. Trainer: Arne Slot.

Goals: 79' Yaroslav Rakitskyi 1-0, 88' Ezequiel Bullaude 1-1).


16.03.2023; „Şükrü Saracoğlu" Stadyumu, Istanbul; Attendance: 44,775
Referee: Michael Oliver (England)

**Fenerbahçe SK Istanbul – SEVILLA FC 1-0(1-0)**

Fenerbahçe: Altay Bayindir, Serdar Aziz (84.Diego Rossi), Samet Akaydin, Attila Szalai, Jayden Oosterwolde, Miha Zajc (75.Mert Hakan Yandas), Ferdi Kadioglu, Ismail Yüksel, Arda Güler (84.Emre Mor), Enner Valencia (84.João Pedro), Michy Batshuayi (19.Joshua King). Trainer: Jorge Fernando Pinheiro de Jesus (Portugal).

Sevilla FC: Marko Dmitrovic, Alex Telles, Marcos Acuña, Gonzalo Montiel (83.Jesús Navas), Loïc Badé, Ivan Rakitic (83.Joan Jordán), Fernando, Nemanja Gudelj, Óliver Torres (73.Suso), Rafa Mir (73.Lucas Ocampos), Youssef En-Nesyri (59.Érik Lamela). Trainer: Jorge Luis Sampaoli Moya (Argentina).

Goal: 41' Enner Valencia 1-0 (penalty).


16.03.2023; Europa-Park Stadion, Freiburg im Breisgau; Attendance: 33,420; Referee: Serdar Gözübüyük (Netherlands)

**SC Freiburg – JUVENTUS FC TORINO 0-2(0-1)**

SC Freiburg: Mark Flekken, Manuel Gulde [sent off 44], Lukas Kübler, Matthias Ginter, Christian Günter (74.Npah Weißhaupt), Kiliann Sildillia, Nicolas Höfler, Maximilian Eggestein (46.Kenneth Schmidt), Michael Gregoritsch (74.Nils Petersen), Lucas Höler (62.Vincenzo Grifo), Ritsu Dōan (62.Roland Sallai). Trainer: Christian Streich.

Juventus: Wojciech Szczesny, Danilo, Bremer, Federico Gatti, Juan Cuadrado (85.Mattia De Sciglio), Filip Kostic (70.Samuel Iling-Junior), Adrien Rabiot, Manuel Locatelli (84.Enzo Barrenechea), Nicolò Fagioli, Moise Kean (90+1.Matías Soulé), Dusan Vlahovic (70.Federico Chiesa). Trainer: Massimiliano Allegri.

Goals: 45' Dusan Vlahovic 0-1 (penalty), 90+5' Federico Chiesa 0-2.


16.03.2023; Estadio „Benito Villamarín", Sevilla; Attendance: 54,643
Referee: Srđan Jovanović (Serbia)

**Real Betis Balompié Sevilla FC – MANCHESTER UNITED FC 0-1(0-0)**

Real Betis: Rui Silva, Germán Pezzella, Youssouf Sabaly, Aitor Ruibal (59.Borja Iglesias), Édgar González, Abner Vinicius (26.Juan Miranda), Joaquín (59.Sergio Canales), William Carvalho, Guido Rodríguez (66.Andrés Guardado), Juanmi, Ayoze Pérez (59.Willian José). Trainer: Manuel Luis Pellegrini Ripamonti (Chile).

Manchester United: David de Gea, Harry Maguire, Tyrell Malacia, Aaron Wan-Bissaka (75.Diogo Dalot), Lisandro Martínez (75.Victor Lindelöf), Casemiro, Fred (60.Marcel Sabitzer), Bruno Fernandes (68.Anthony Elanga), Facundo Pellistri, Wout Weghorst, Marcus Rashford (60.Jadon Sancho). Trainer: Erik ten Hag (Netherlands).

Goal: 56' Marcus Rashford 0-1.


16.03.2023; Stadion Feijenoord, Rotterdam; Attendance: 37,500
Referee: Jesús Gil Manzano (Spain)

**FEYENOORD ROTTERDAM – FK Shakhtar Donetsk 7-1(3-0)**

Feyenoord Rotterdam: Timon Wellenreuther, Gernot Trauner, Dávid Hancko, Marcos López (57.Jacob Rasmussen), Lutsharel Geertruida, Sebastian Szymanski (58.Ezequiel Bullaude), Orkun Kökçü (68.Mo Taabouni), Mats Wieffer, Alireza Jahanbakhsh, Oussama Idrissi (62.Igor Paixão), Santiago Giménez (57.Danilo). Trainer: Arne Slot.

Shakhtar Donetsk: Anatoliy Trubin, Mykola Matviyenko, Bogdan Mykhailichenko, Valeriy Bondar, Yukhym Konoplya, Taras Stepanenko (54.Yegor Nazaryna), Dmytro Kryskiv (46.Neven Djurasek), Artem Bondarenko (54.Danylo Sikan), Georgiy Sudakov, Oleksandr Zubkov (63.Ivan Petryak), Lassina Traoré (54.Kevin Kelsy). Trainer: Igor Jovićević (Croatia).

Goals: 9' Santiago Giménez 1-0, 24', 38' Orkun Kökçü 2-0, 3-0 (penalty), 49', 60' Oussama Idrissi 4-0, 5-0, 64' Alireza Jahanbakhsh 6-0, 66' Danilo 7-0, 87' Kevin Kelsy 7-1.

13.04.2023; Stadion Feijenoord, Rotterdam; Attendance: 42,960
Referee: José María Sánchez Martínez (Spain)
**Feyenoord Rotterdam – AS Roma 1-0(0-0)**
Feyenoord Rotterdam: Justin Bijlow, Gernot Trauner, Dávid Hancko, Lutsharel Geertruida, Quilindschy Hartman, Sebastian Szymanski, Orkun Kökçü, Mats Wieffer, Alireza Jahanbakhsh (72.Danilo), Oussama Idrissi (64.Igor Paixão), Santiago Giménez (83.Marcos López). Trainer: Arne Slot.
AS Roma: Rui Patrício, Chris Smalling, Leonardo Spinazzola (84.Zeki Çelik), Gianluca Mancini, Ibañez, Nemanja Matic, Bryan Cristante, Lorenzo Pellegrini (46.Georginio Wijnaldum), Nicola Zalewski, Paulo Dybala (26.Stephan El Shaarawy), Tammy Abraham (58.Andrea Belotti). Trainer: José Mário dos Santos Félix Mourinho (Portugal).
Goal: 53' Mats Wieffer 1-0.

13.04.2023; Old Trafford, Manchester; Attendance: 72,825
Referee: Felix Zwayer (Germany)
**Manchester United FC – Sevilla FC 2-2(2-0)**
Manchester United: David de Gea, Raphaël Varane (46.Harry Maguire), Tyrell Malacia, Aaron Wan-Bissaka, Lisandro Martínez, Casemiro, Marcel Sabitzer, Bruno Fernandes (62.Christian Eriksen), Anthony Martial (62.Wout Weghorst), Jadon Sancho (62.Anthony Elanga), Antony (81.Facundo Pellistri). Trainer: Erik ten Hag (Netherlands).
Sevilla FC: Yassine Bounou "Bono", Marcos Acuña, Marcão, Gonzalo Montiel (90.Papu Gómez), Tanguy Nianzou (73.Suso), Ivan Rakitic, Fernando, Érik Lamela (66.Youssef En-Nesyri), Nemanja Gudelj, Lucas Ocampos, Óliver Torres (46.Jesús Navas). Trainer: José Luis Mendilíbar.
Goals: 14', 21' Marcel Sabitzer 1-0, 2-0, 84' Tyrell Malacia 2-1 (own goal), 90+2' Harry Maguire 2-2 (own goal).

13.04.2023; Allianz Stadium, Torino; Attendance: 38,490
Referee: Halil Umut Meler (Turkey)
**Juventus FC Torino – Sporting Clube de Portugal Lisboa 1-0(0-0)**
Juventus: Wojciech Szczesny (44.Mattia Perin), Danilo, Bremer, Federico Gatti, Ángel Di María (85.Paul Pogba), Juan Cuadrado, Filip Kostic (62.Nicolò Fagioli), Adrien Rabiot, Manuel Locatelli (85.Leandro Paredes), Arkadiusz Milik (62.Dusan Vlahovic), Federico Chiesa. Trainer: Massimiliano Allegri.
Sporting: Antonio Adán, Sebastián Coates, Ricardo Esgaio (77.Héctor Bellerín), Jerry St.Juste (45+4.Ousmane Diomande), Gonçalo Inácio, Nuno Santos (62.Matheus Reis), Pedro Gonçalves "Pote", Hidemasa Morita, Marcus Edwards (77.Dário Essugo), Trincão, Youssef Chermiti (62.Arthur Gomes). Trainer: Rúben Amorim.
Goal: 73' Federico Gatti 1-0.

13.04.2023; BayArena, Leverkusen; Attendance: 30,210
Referee: Ivan Kružliak (Slovakia)
**Bayer 04 Leverkusen – Royale Union Saint-Gilloise 1-1(0-0)**
Bayer Leverkusen: Lukás Hrádecký, Jonathan Tah, Jeremie Frimpong, Mitchel Bakker, Edmond Tapsoba, Piero Hincapié, Robert Andrich, Exequiel Palacios (46.Kerem Demirbay), Florian Wirtz, Moussa Diaby (87.Adam Hlozek), Amine Adli (67.Sardar Azmoun). Trainer: Xabier „Xabi" Alonso Olano (Spain).
Union Saint-Gilloise: Anthony Moris, Bart Nieuwkoop, Christian Burgess, Siebe Van Der Heyden, Ismaël Kandouss, Teddy Teuma, Senne Lynen (80.Oussama El Azzouzi), Jean Lazare Amani, Loïc Lapoussin, Yorbe Vertessen (75.Cameron Puertas), Victor Boniface (89.Gustaf Nilsson). Trainer: Karel Geraerts.
Goals: 51' Victor Boniface 0-1, 82' Florian Wirtz 1-1.

20.04.2023; Stadio Olimpico, Roma; Attendance: 66,742
Referee: Anthony Taylor (England)
**AS ROMA – Feyenoord Rotterdam 4-1(0-0,2-1)**
AS Roma: Rui Patrício, Chris Smalling (78.Zeki Çelik), Leonardo Spinazzola, Diego Llorente (72.Ibañez), Gianluca Mancini, Georginio Wijnaldum (21.Stephan El Shaarawy, 105.Marash Kumbulla), Nemanja Matic, Bryan Cristante, Lorenzo Pellegrini, Nicola Zalewski (73.Paulo Dybala), Andrea Belotti (73.Tammy Abraham). Trainer: José Mário dos Santos Félix Mourinho (Portugal).
Feyenoord Rotterdam: Justin Bijlow, Gernot Trauner (105.Ezequiel Bullaude), Dávid Hancko, Lutsharel Geertruida, Quilindschy Hartman (105.Marcos López), Sebastian Szymanski (90.Marcus Pedersen), Orkun Kökçü, Mats Wieffer (105.Javairô Dilrosun), Alireza Jahanbakhsh (74.Danilo), Oussama Idrissi (64.Igor Paixão), Santiago Giménez [sent off 120]. Trainer: Arne Slot.
Goals: 60' Leonardo Spinazzola 1-0, 80' Igor Paixão 1-1, 89' Paulo Dybala 2-1, 101' Stephan El Shaarawy 3-1, 109' Lorenzo Pellegrini 4-1.

20.04.2023; Estadio „Ramón Sánchez Pizjuán", Sevilla; Attendance: 41,974; Referee: Artur Manuel Ribeiro Soares Dias (Portugal)
**SEVILLA FC – Manchester United FC 3-0(1-0)**
Sevilla FC: Yassine Bounou "Bono", Jesús Navas, Marcos Acuña (85.Alex Telles), Marcão (29.Suso), Loïc Badé, Ivan Rakitic, Fernando, Érik Lamela (80.Bryan Gil), Nemanja Gudelj, Lucas Ocampos, Youssef En-Nesyri. Trainer: José Luis Mendilíbar.
Manchester United: David de Gea, Victor Lindelöf, Harry Maguire, Diogo Dalot, Aaron Wan-Bissaka (46.Luke Shaw), Christian Eriksen (86.Anthony Elanga), Casemiro, Marcel Sabitzer (68.Fred), Anthony Martial (54.Wout Weghorst), Jadon Sancho (46.Marcus Rashford), Antony. Trainer: Erik ten Hag (Netherlands).
Goals: Sevilla FC: 8' Youssef En-Nesyri 1-0, 47' Loïc Badé 2-0, 81' Youssef En-Nesyri 3-0.

20.04.2023; Estádio „José Alvalade", Lisboa; Attendance: 45,903
Referee: François Letexier (France)
**Sporting Clube de Portugal Lisboa – JUVENTUS FC TORINO 1-1(1-1)**
Sporting: Antonio Adán, Sebastián Coates, Ricardo Esgaio, Gonçalo Inácio (81.Matheus Reis), Ousmane Diomande, Nuno Santos (87.Arthur Gomes), Manuel Ugarte, Pedro Gonçalves "Pote", Hidemasa Morita, Marcus Edwards, Trincão (81.Youssef Chermiti). Trainer: Rúben Amorim.
Juventus: Wojciech Szczesny, Danilo, Alex Sandro, Bremer (73.Federico Gatti), Ángel Di María, Juan Cuadrado, Adrien Rabiot, Manuel Locatelli, Fabio Miretti (72.Paul Pogba), Dusan Vlahovic (71.Arkadiusz Milik), Federico Chiesa (78.Filip Kostic). Trainer: Massimiliano Allegri.
Goals: 9' Adrien Rabiot 0-1, 20' Marcus Edwards 1-1 (penalty).

20.04.2023; Lotto Park, Bruxelles; Attendance: 17,069
Referee: Antonio Miguel Mateu Lahoz (Spain)
**Royale Union Saint-Gilloise – BAYER 04 LEVERKUSEN 1-4(0-2)**
Union Saint-Gilloise: Anthony Moris, Bart Nieuwkoop, Christian Burgess, Koki Machida, Ismaël Kandouss (46.Casper Terho), Teddy Teuma (87.Oussama El Azzouzi), Senne Lynen, Jean Lazare Amani (81.Cameron Puertas), Loïc Lapoussin, Yorbe Vertessen (32 Simon Adingra), Victor Boniface (81.Gustaf Nilsson). Trainer: Karel Geraerts.
Bayer Leverkusen: Lukás Hrádecký, Jonathan Tah, Jeremie Frimpong (71.Amine Adli), Mitchel Bakker, Edmond Tapsoba (59.Odilon Kossounou), Piero Hincapié, Robert Andrich, Nadiem Amiri (59.Kerem Demirbay), Florian Wirtz, Moussa Diaby (86.Karim Bellarabi), Adam Hlozek (86.Sardar Azmoun). Trainer: Xabier „Xabi" Alonso Olano (Spain).
Goals: 2' Moussa Diaby 0-1, 37' Mitchel Bakker 0-2, 60' Jeremie Frimpong 0-3, 64' Casper Terho 1-3, 79' Adam Hlozek 1-4.

11.05.2023; Allianz Stadium, Torino; Attendance: 34,816
Referee: Daniel Siebert (Germany)
**Juventus FC Torino – Sevilla FC 1-1(0-1)**
Juventus: Wojciech Szczesny, Leonardo Bonucci (61.Federico Gatti), Danilo, Alex Sandro, Ángel Di María (70.Paul Pogba), Juan Cuadrado, Filip Kostic (46.Samuel Iling-Junior), Adrien Rabiot, Manuel Locatelli, Fabio Miretti (46.Federico Chiesa), Dusan Vlahovic (61.Arkadiusz Milik). Trainer: Massimiliano Allegri.
Sevilla FC: Yassine Bounou "Bono", Jesús Navas, Marcos Acuña, Loïc Badé, Ivan Rakitic, Fernando, Nemanja Gudelj, Lucas Ocampos (34.Gonzalo Montiel), Óliver Torres (74.Papu Gómez), Youssef En-Nesyri, Bryan Gil (82.Érik Lamela). Trainer: José Luis Mendilíbar.
Goals: 26' Youssef En-Nesyri 0-1, 90+7' Federico Gatti 1-1.

11.05.2023; Stadio Olimpico, Roma; Attendance: 63,123
Referee: Michael Oliver (England)
**AS Roma – Bayer 04 Leverkusen 1-0(0-0)**
AS Roma: Rui Patrício, Leonardo Spinazzola, Zeki Çelik, Gianluca Mancini, Ibañez, Nemanja Matic, Bryan Cristante, Lorenzo Pellegrini, Edoardo Bove (76.Georginio Wijnaldum), Andrea Belotti (77.Paulo Dybala), Tammy Abraham. Trainer: José Mário dos Santos Félix Mourinho (Portugal).
Bayer Leverkusen: Lukás Hrádecký, Jonathan Tah, Jeremie Frimpong, Edmond Tapsoba, Odilon Kossounou (36.Mitchel Bakker), Piero Hincapié, Robert Andrich (90+2.Nadiem Amiri), Exequiel Palacios, Florian Wirtz, Moussa Diaby (72.Amine Adli), Adam Hlozek (72.Sardar Azmoun). Trainer: Xabier „Xabi" Alonso Olano (Spain).
Goal: 63' Edoardo Bove 1-0.

18.05.2023; Estadio "Ramón Sánchez Pizjuán", Sevilla; Attendance: 42,186; Referee: Danny Desmond Makkelie (Netherlands)
**SEVILLA FC – Juventus FC Torino 2-1(0-0,0-0)**
Sevilla FC: Yassine Bounou "Bono", Jesús Navas (107.Papu Gómez), Marcos Acuña [sent off 115], Loïc Badé, Ivan Rakitic, Fernando, Nemanja Gudelj, Lucas Ocampos (70.Érik Lamela), Óliver Torres (62.Suso, 118.Karim Rekik), Youssef En-Nesyri, Bryan Gil (100.Gonzalo Montiel). Trainer: José Luis Mendilíbar.
Juventus: Wojciech Szczesny, Danilo, Bremer, Federico Gatti, Ángel Di María (64.Federico Chiesa), Juan Cuadrado (106.Arkadiusz Milik), Adrien Rabiot, Manuel Locatelli (86.Fabio Miretti), Nicolò Fagioli (41.Leandro Paredes), Moise Kean (63.Dusan Vlahovic), Samuel Iling-Junior (86.Filip Kostic). Trainer: Massimiliano Allegri.
Goals: 65' Dusan Vlahovic 0-1, 71' Suso 1-1, 95' Érik Lamela 2-1.

18.05.2023; BayArena, Leverkusen; Attendance: 30,210
Referee: Slavko Vinčić (Slovenia)
**Bayer 04 Leverkusen – AS ROMA 0-0**
Bayer Leverkusen: Lukás Hrádecký, Jonathan Tah (86.Nadiem Amiri), Jeremie Frimpong, Mitchel Bakker (73.Amine Adli), Edmond Tapsoba, Piero Hincapié, Kerem Demirbay, Exequiel Palacios (80.Adam Hlozek), Florian Wirtz, Sardar Azmoun, Moussa Diaby. Trainer: Xabier „Xabi" Alonso Olano (Spain).
AS Roma: Rui Patrício, Leonardo Spinazzola (34.Nicola Zalewski), Zeki Çelik (78.Chris Smalling), Gianluca Mancini, Ibañez, Nemanja Matic, Bryan Cristante, Lorenzo Pellegrini, Edoardo Bove, Andrea Belotti (46.Georginio Wijnaldum), Tammy Abraham. Trainer: José Mário dos Santos Félix Mourinho (Portugal).

31.05.2023; Puskas Aréna, Budapest (Hungary); Referee: Anthony Taylor (England), Attendance: 61,476
**Sevilla FC – AS Roma 1-1(0-1,1-1,1-1); 4-1 on penalties**
Sevilla FC: Yassine Bounou "Bono", Alex Telles (95.Karim Rekik), Nemanja Gudelj (120+8.Marcão), Loïc Badé, Jesús Navas (95.Gonzalo Montiel), Ivan Rakitic, Fernando (120+9.Joan Jordán), Bryan Gil (46.Érik Lamela), Óliver Torres (46.Suso), Lucas Ocampos, Youssef En-Nesyri. Trainer: José Luis Mendilíbar.
AS Roma: Rui Patrício, Gianluca Mancini, Chris Smalling, Ibañez, Zeki Çelik (90.Nicola Zalewski). Bryan Cristante, Nemanja Matic (120.Edoardo Bove), Leonardo Spinazzola (105.Diego Llorente), Paolo Dybala (68.Georginio Wijnaldum), Lorenzo Pellegrini (105.Stephan El Shaarawy),Tammy Abraham (75.Andrea Belotti). Trainer: José Mário dos Santos Félix Mourinho (Portugal).
Goals: 34' Paolo Dybala 0-1, 55' Gianluca Mancini 1-1 (own goal).
Penalties: Lucas Ocampos 1-0; Bryan Cristante 1-1; Érik Lamela 2-1; Gianluca Mancini (saved); Ivan Rakitic 3-1; Ibañez (saved); Gonzalo Montiel 4-1.

UEFA Europa League Winner 2022/2023: **Sevilla FC** (Spain)

Best Goalscorer: Victor Okoh Boniface (NGA, Royale Union Saint-Gilloise) & Marcus Rashford (Manchester United FC) – 6 goals each

**FAIRS CUP (1958-1971)**
**UEFA CUP (1972-2009)**
**UEFA EUROPA LEAGUE (2010-2023)**
**TABLE OF HONOURS**

| | | |
|---|---|---|
| 1955/1958 | FC Barcelona | *Spain* |
| 1958/1960 | FC Barcelona | *Spain* |
| 1960/1961 | AS Roma | *Italy* |
| 1961/1962 | Valencia CF | *Spain* |
| 1962/1963 | Valencia CF | *Spain* |
| 1963/1964 | Real Zaragoza | *Spain* |
| 1964/1965 | Ferencvárosi TC | *Hungary* |
| 1965/1966 | FC Barcelona | *Spain* |
| 1966/1967 | GNK Dinamo Zagreb | *Croatia* |
| 1967/1968 | Leeds United FC | *England* |
| 1968/1969 | Newcastle United FC | *England* |
| 1969/1970 | Arsenal FC London | *England* |
| 1970/1971 | Leeds United FC | *England* |
| 1971/1972 | Tottenham Hotspur FC London | *England* |
| 1972/1973 | Liverpool FC | *England* |
| 1973/1974 | Feyenoord Rotterdam | *Netherlands* |
| 1974/1975 | Borussia VfL Mönchengladbach | *Germany* |
| 1975/1976 | Liverpool FC | *England* |
| 1976/1977 | Juventus FC Torino | *Italy* |
| 1977/1978 | PSV Eindhoven | *Netherlands* |
| 1978/1979 | Borussia VfL Mönchengladbach | *Germany* |
| 1979/1980 | Eintracht Frankfurt | *Germany* |
| 1980/1981 | Ipswich Town FC | *England* |
| 1981/1982 | IFK Göteborg | *Sweden* |
| 1982/1983 | RSC Anderlecht Bruxelles | *Belgium* |
| 1983/1984 | Tottenham Hotspur FC London | *England* |
| 1984/1985 | Real Madrid CF | *Spain* |
| 1985/1986 | Real Madrid CF | *Spain* |
| 1986/1987 | IFK Göteborg | *Sweden* |
| 1987/1988 | TSV Bayer 04 Leverkusen | *Germany* |
| 1988/1989 | SSC Napoli | *Italy* |
| 1989/1990 | Juventus FC Torino | *Italy* |
| 1990/1991 | FC Internazionale Milano | *Italy* |
| 1991/1992 | AFC Ajax Amsterdam | *Netherlands* |
| 1992/1993 | Juventus FC Torino | *Italy* |
| 1993/1994 | FC Internazionale Milano | *Italy* |
| 1994/1995 | Parma AC | *Italy* |
| 1995/1996 | FC Bayern München | *Germany* |
| 1996/1997 | FC Schalke 04 Gelsenkirchen | *Germany* |
| 1997/1998 | FC Internazionale Milano | *Italy* |
| 1998/1999 | Parma AC | *Italy* |
| 1999/2000 | Galatasaray SK Istanbul | *Turkey* |
| 2000/2001 | Liverpool FC | *England* |
| 2001/2002 | Feyenoord Rotterdam | *Netherlands* |
| 2002/2003 | FC do Porto | *Portugal* |
| 2003/2004 | Valencia CF | *Spain* |
| 2004/2005 | FK CSKA Moskva | *Russia* |
| 2005/2006 | Sevilla FC | *Spain* |
| 2006/2007 | Sevilla FC | *Spain* |
| 2007/2008 | FK Zenit Saint Petersburg | *Russia* |
| 2008/2009 | FK Shakhtar Donetsk | *Ukraine* |
| 2009/2010 | Club Atlético de Madrid | *Spain* |
| 2010/2011 | FC do Porto | *Portugal* |
| 2011/2012 | Club Atlético de Madrid | *Spain* |
| 2012/2013 | Chelsea FC London | *England* |
| 2013/2014 | Sevilla FC | *Spain* |
| 2014/2015 | Sevilla FC | *Spain* |
| 2015/2016 | Sevilla FC | *Spain* |
| 2016/2017 | Manchester United FC | *England* |
| 2017/2018 | Club Atlético de Madrid | *Spain* |
| 2018/2019 | Chelsea FC London | *England* |
| 2019/2020 | Sevilla FC | *Spain* |
| 2020/2021 | Villarreal CF | *Spain* |
| 2021/2022 | Eintracht Frankfurt | *Germany* |
| 2022/2023 | Sevilla FC | *Spain* |

# UEFA EUROPA CONFERENCE LEAGUE
## 2022/2023

| | | |
|---|---|---|
| FC Alashkert Yerevan - **Hamrun Spartans FC** | 1-0(1-0) | 1-4(0-0) |
| **KS Lechia Gdańsk** - Fudbalska Akademija Pandev Strumica | 4-1(3-0) | 2-1(1-0) |
| FC Inter Turku - **KF Drita Gjilan** | 1-0(0-0) | 0-3(0-1) |
| FC Dinamo Tbilisi - **Paide Linnameeskond** | 2-3(1-0) | 2-1(0-0,1-0,2-1); 5-6 pen |
| FK Panevėžys - **FC Milsami Orhei** | 0-0 | 0-2(0-1) |
| **KF Laçi** - FK Iskra Danilovgrad | 0-0 | 1-0(1-0) |
| SC Gjilani - **FK Liepāja** | 1-0(1-0) | 1-3(0-0) |
| FC Sfîntul Gheorghe - **NŠ Mura Murska Sobota** | 1-2(0-0) | 1-2(0-0) |
| **Kuopion Palloseura** - FC Dila Gori | 2-0(1-0) | 0-0 |
| **MFK Ružomberok** - FK Kauno Žalgiris Kaunas | 2-0(1-0) | 0-0 |
| **FK Budućnost Podgorica** - KF Llapi Podujevë | 2-0(2-0) | 2-2(1-1) |
| **Gżira United FC** - Atlètic Club d'Escaldes | 1-1(0-0) | 1-0(0-0,0-0) |
| FK Borac Banja Luka - **B36 Tórshavn** | 2-0(1-0) | 1-3(0-1,1-3,1-3); 3-4 pen |
| **NK Olimpija Ljubljana** - FC Differdange 03 | 1-1(0-1) | 2-1(0-1,1-1) |
| **St Joseph's Gibraltar** - Larne FC | 0-0 | 1-0(0-0) |
| UE Santa Coloma - **Breiðablik Kópavogur** | 0-1(0-1) | 1-4(1-1) |
| **FK DAC 1904 Dunajská Streda** - Cliftonville FAC | 2-1(1-1) | 3-0(1-0) |
| **Víkingur Gøta** - Europa FC Gibraltar | 1-0(0-0) | 2-1(2-0) |
| Bala Town FC - **Sligo Rovers FC** | 1-2(1-1) | 1-0(1-0,1-0,1-0); 3-4 pen |
| CS Fola Esch - **SP Tre Fiori Fiorentino** | 0-1(0-0) | 1-3(1-2) |
| FC Dinamo Minsk - **FK Dečić Tuzi** | 1-1(1-1) | 2-1(1-0) |
| SP Tre Penne Città di San Marino - **FK Tuzla City** | 0-2(0-0) | 0-6(0-1) |
| **FC Saburtalo Tbilisi** - FK Partizani Tiranë | 0-1(0-0) | 1-0(0-0,1-0,1-0); 5-4 pen |
| **KF Shkëndija Tetovo** - FC Ararat Yerevan | 2-0(2-0) | 2-2(2-0) |
| Floriana FC - **CS Petrocub Hîncești** | 0-0 | 0-1(0-1) |
| **MKS Pogoń Szczecin** - KR Reykjavík | 4-1(3-0) | 0-1(0-1) |
| HB Tórshavn - **Newtown AFC** | 1-0(0-0) | 1-2(0-2,1-2,1-2); 2-4 pen |
| FC Bruno's Magpies Gibraltar - **Crusaders FC Belfast** | 2-1(1-0) | 1-3(1-1) |
| FC Flora Tallinn - **SJK Seinäjoki** | 1-0(1-0) | 2-4(1-0,2-3) |
| Derry City FC - **Rīga FC** | 0-2(0-1) | 0-2(0-1) |

**Champions Path:**

| | | |
|---|---|---|
| **FC Shakhtyor Solihorsk** (bye) | | |
| **FK Rīgas Futbola Skola** (bye) | | |
| SP La Fiorita Montegiardino - **KF Ballkani Suva Reka** | 0-4(0-2) | 0-6(0-2) |
| **Víkingur Reykjavík** - The New Saints FC | 2-0(1-0) | 0-0 |
| FK Sutjeska Nikšić - **KÍ Klaksvík** | 0-0 | 0-1(0-0) |
| **Hibernians FC Paola** - FCI Levadia Tallinn | 3-2(2-0) | 1-1(0-0) |
| KF Tiranë - **HŠK Zrinjski Mostar** | 0-1(0-1) | 2-3(0-2) |
| **KKS Lech Poznań** - FC Dinamo Batumi | 5-0(3-0) | 1-1(0-0) |
| **FC CFR 1907 Cluj-Napoca** - Inter Club d'Escaldes | 3-0(2-0) | 1-1(0-1) |
| **FC Tobol Kostanay** - Lincoln Red Imps FC | 2-0(0-0) | 1-0(1-0) |

**League Path:**

| | | |
|---|---|---|
| **Gżira United FC** - Serbia Radnički Niš | 2-2(0-1) | 3-3(1-1,2-2,3-3); 3-1 pen |
| **Aris Thessaloníki** - FC Gomel | 5-1(3-1) | 2-1(1-0) |
| PFC Botev Plovdiv - **APOEL Nicosia** | 0-0 | 0-2(0-1) |
| **Fehérvár FC Székesfehérvár** - Qəbələ FK | 4-1(1-1) | 1-2(1-1) |
| **Istanbul Başakşehir FK** - Maccabi Netanya FC | 1-1(0-1) | 1-0(1-0) |
| Aris Limassol FC - **Neftçi PFK Bakı** | 2-0(0-0) | 0-3(0-1) |
| FK Velež Mostar - **Hamrun Spartans FC** | 0-1(0-1) | 0-1(0-1) |
| FC Saburtalo Tbilisi - **SC FCSB București** | 1-0(1-0) | 2-4(0-1) |
| FK Makedonija Gjorče Petrov Skopje - **PFC CSKA Sofia** | 0-0 | 0-4(0-1) |
| **Hapoel Be'er Sheva FC** - FC Dinamo Minsk | 2-1(1-0) | 1-0(0-0) |
| Zirə FK Bakı - **Maccabi Tel Aviv FC** | 0-3(0-2) | 0-0 |
| KF Vllaznia Shkodër - **CS Universitatea Craiova** | 1-1(0-1) | 0-3(0-0) |
| FC Ararat-Armenia Yerevan - **Paide Linnameeskond** | 0-0 | 0-0; 3-5 pen |
| FC Kairat Almaty - **Kisvárda FC** | 0-1(0-0) | 0-1(0-1) |
| FC BATE Borisov - **Konyaspor Kulübü** | 0-3(0-1) | 0-2(0-2) |
| **ACS Sepsi OSK Sfântu Gheorghe** - NK Olimpija Ljubljana | 3-1(1-1) | 0-2(0-0,0-2,0-2); 4-2 pen |
| **FC Kyzylzhar SK Petropavl** - NK Osijek | 1-2(0-0) | 2-0(0-0) |
| FK Liepāja - **BSC Young Boys Bern** | 0-1(0-0) | 0-3(0-2) |
| **SK Rapid Wien** - KS Lechia Gdańsk | 0-0 | 2-1(2-0) |
| SJK Seinäjoki - **Lillestrøm SK** | 0-1(0-0) | 2-5(1-2) |
| **Breiðablik Kópavogur** - FK Budućnost Podgorica | 2-0(0-0) | 1-2(0-1) |
| **St. Patrick's Athletic FC Dublin** - NŠ Mura Murska Sobota | 1-1(0-1) | 0-0; 6-5 pen |
| St Joseph's Gibraltar - **SK Slavia Praha** | 0-4(0-3) | 0-7(0-4) |
| **FC Spartak Trnava** - Newtown AFC | 4-1(3-1) | 2-1(1-0) |
| FK Sūduva Marijampolė - **Viborg FF** | 0-1(0-0) | 0-1(0-1) |
| Víkingur Gøta - **FK DAC 1904 Dunajská Streda** | 0-2(0-1) | 0-2(0-2) |

| | | |
|---|---|---|
| MKS Pogoń Szczecin - **Brøndby IF** | 1-1(0-1) | 0-4(0-2) |
| **AZ Alkmaar** - FK Tuzla City | 1-0(1-0) | 4-0(1-0) |
| Motherwell FC - **Sligo Rovers FC** | 0-1(0-1) | 0-2(0-1) |
| **Molde FK** - IF Elfsborg Borås | 4-1(0-1) | 2-1(0-1) |
| FC Koper - **FC Vaduz** | 0-1(0-0) | 1-1(0-0,1-0) |
| **B36 Tórshavn** - SP Tre Fiori Fiorentino | 1-0(0-0) | 0-0 |
| MFK Ružomberok - **Rīga FC** | 0-3(0-2) | 1-2(0-1) |
| **FC Basel** - Crusaders FC Belfast | 2-0(1-0) | 1-1(1-0) |
| **Royal Antwerp FC** - KF Drita Gjilan | 0-0 | 2-0(0-0) |
| **CS Petrocub Hînceşti** - KF Laçi | 0-0 | 4-1(0-1) |
| Racing FC Union Lëtzebuerg - **FK Čukarički** | 1-4(1-2) | 0-4(0-2) |
| **PFC Levski Sofia** - PAOK Thessaloníki | 2-0(2-0) | 1-1(1-0) |
| **Vitória SC Guimarães** - Puskás Ferenc Labdarugó Akadémia Felcsút | 3-0(2-0) | 0-0 |
| HNK Rijeka - **Djurgårdens IF Stockholm** | 1-2(1-1) | 0-2(0-0) |
| Vorskla Poltava Ukraine - **AIK Stockholm** | 3-2(2-2) | 0-2(0-1,0-1) |
| Valmiera Latvia - **KF Shkëndija Tetovo** | 1-2(1-1) | 1-3(1-2) |
| **RKS Raków Częstochowa** - Astana FC | 5-0(2-0) | 1-0(1-0) |
| **Kuopion Palloseura** - FC Milsami Orhei | 2-2(1-0) | 4-1(1-1) |
| AC Sparta Praha - **Viking FK Stavanger** | 0-0 | 1-2(1-1) |

## THIRD QUALIFYING ROUND [03/04.08 - (0910/11.08.2022]

**Champions Path:**

| | | |
|---|---|---|
| Víkingur Reykjavík - **KKS Lech Poznań** | 1-0(1-0) | 1-4(0-2,1-2) |
| **FK Rīgas Futbola Skola** - Hibernians FC Paola | 1-1(0-1) | 3-1(1-0) |
| **KF Ballkani Suva Reka** - KÍ Klaksvík | 3-2(2-0) | 1-2(0-0,1-2,1-2); 4-3 pen |
| **HŠK Zrinjski Mostar** - FC Tobol Kostanay | 1-0(0-0) | 1-1(1-0) |
| FC Shakhtyor Solihorsk - **FC CFR 1907 Cluj-Napoca** | 0-0 | 0-1(0-1) |

**League Path:**

| | | |
|---|---|---|
| FC Spartak Trnava - **RKS Raków Częstochowa** | 0-2(0-2) | 0-1(0-0) |
| **AIK Stockholm** - KF Shkëndija Tetovo | 1-1(1-1) | 1-1(0-1,1-1,1-1); 3-2 pen |
| **Viking FK Stavanger** - Sligo Rovers FC | 5-1(2-0) | 0-1(0-1) |
| Breiðablik Kópavogur - **Istanbul Başakşehir FK** | 1-3(0-1) | 0-3(0-1) |
| Kuopion Palloseura - **BSC Young Boys Bern** | 0-2(0-2) | 0-3(0-2) |
| Paide Linnameeskond - **RSC Anderlecht Bruxelles** | 0-2(0-2) | 0-3(0-0) |
| Viborg FF - **B36 Tórshavn** | 3-0(1-0) | 2-1(0-0) |
| **HNK Hajduk Split** - Vitória SC Guimarães | 3-1(0-0) | 0-1(0-1) |
| Brøndby IF - **FC Basel** | 1-0(0-0) | 1-2(1-2,1-2,1-2); 1-3 pen |
| Lillestrøm SK - **Royal Antwerp FC** | 1-3(1-1) | 0-2(0-1) |
| **PFC CSKA Sofia** - St. Patrick's Athletic FC Dublin | 0-1(0-0) | 2-0(1-0) |
| Dundee United Scotland - **AZ Alkmaar** | 1-0(0-0) | 0-7(0-5) |
| **APOEL Nicosia** - FC Kyzylzhar SK Petropavl | 1-0(1-0) | 0-0 |
| FK DAC 1904 Dunajská Streda - **SC FCSB Bucureşti** | 0-1(0-0) | 0-1(0-1) |
| **Rīga FC** - Gil Vicente FC Barcelos | 1-1(1-0) | 0-4(0-3) |
| **Wolfsberger AC** - Gżira United FC | 0-0 | 4-0(2-0) |
| **Maccabi Tel Aviv FC** - Aris Thessaloníki | 2-0(1-0) | 1-2(0-0) |
| **Molde FK** - Kisvárda FC | 3-0(0-0) | 1-2(0-2) |
| Neftçi PFK Bakı - **SK Rapid Wien** | 2-1(1-0) | 0-2(0-0,0-1) |
| Lugano Switzerland - **Hapoel Be'er Sheva FC** | 0-2(0-1) | 1-3(0-0) |
| **Hamrun Spartans FC** - PFC Levski Sofia | 0-1(0-0) | 2-1(0-0,2-1,2-1); 4-1 pen |
| FK Čukarički - **FC Twente Enschede** | 1-3(0-3) | 1-4(1-2) |
| Zorya Luhansk Ukraine - **CS Universitatea Craiova** | 1-0(0-0) | 0-3(0-1) |
| **FC Vaduz** - Konyaspor Kulübü | 1-1(0-0) | 4-2(2-1) |
| ACS Sepsi OSK Sfântu Gheorghe - **Djurgårdens IF Stockholm** | 1-3(0-2) | 1-3(1-2) |
| **Fehérvár FC Székesfehérvár** - CS Petrocub Hînceşti | 5-0(3-0) | 2-1(2-1) |
| **SK Slavia Praha** - Greece Panathinaikos | 2-0(1-0) | 1-1(0-0) |

## PLAY-OFF ROUND [17/18.08. - 23/25.08.2022]

**Champions Path:**

| | | |
|---|---|---|
| NK Maribor - **FC CFR 1907 Cluj-Napoca** | 0-0 | 0-1(0-0) |
| **FK Rīgas Futbola Skola** - Linfield FC Belfast | 2-2(0-1) | 1-1(0-0,0-1,1-1); 4-2 pen |
| **KKS Lech Poznań** - F91 Dudelange | 2-0(1-0) | 1-1(0-1) |
| KF Shkupi Čair - **KF Ballkani Suva Reka** | 1-2(1-1) | 0-1(0-0) |
| HŠK Zrinjski Mostar - **ŠK Slovan Bratislava** | 1-0(0-0) | 1-2(0-0,0-1,1-2); 5-6 pen |

**League Path:**

| | | |
|---|---|---|
| PFC CSKA Sofia - **FC Basel** | 1-0(0-0) | 0-2(0-0) |
| **FC Vaduz** - SK Rapid Wien | 1-1(1-0) | 1-0(1-0) |
| RKS Raków Częstochowa - **SK Slavia Praha** | 2-1(1-0) | 0-2(0-0,0-1) |
| **Djurgårdens IF Stockholm** - APOEL Nicosia | 3-0(1-0) | 2-3(0-2) |
| Maccabi Tel Aviv FC - **OGC Nice** | 1-0(0-0) | 0-2(0-1,0-1) |
| CS Universitatea Craiova - **Hapoel Be'er Sheva FC** | 1-1(0-0) | 1-1(0-0,0-1,1-1); 3-4 pen |
| **Istanbul Başakşehir FK** - Royal Antwerp FC | 1-0(1-0) | 3-1(1-0) |
| **SC FCSB Bucureşti** - Viking FK Stavanger | 1-2(1-2) | 3-1(1-1) |
| **FK Partizan Beograd** - Hamrun Spartans FC | 4-1(3-0) | 3-3(1-1) |
| **ACF Fiorentina** - FC Twente Enschede | 2-1(2-0) | 0-0 |
| **Villarreal CF** - HNK Hajduk Split | 4-2(4-1) | 2-0(1-0) |

| | | | |
|---|---|---|---|
| **1. FC Köln** - Fehérvár FC Székesfehérvár | 1-2(1-2) | 3-0(1-0) | |
| **West Ham United FC London** - Viborg FF | 3-1(1-0) | 3-0(1-0) | |
| BSC Young Boys Bern - **RSC Anderlecht Bruxelles** | 0-1(0-0) | 1-0(1-0,1-0,1-0); 1-3 pen | |
| **1. FC Slovácko Uherské Hradiště** - AIK Stockholm | 3-0(1-0) | 1-0(0-0) | |
| **Molde FK** - Wolfsberger AC | 0-1(0-1) | 4-0(2-0) | |
| **AZ Alkmaar** - Gil Vicente FC Barcelos | 4-0(1-0) | 2-1(0-0) | |

---

## GROUP STAGE [08.09. - 03.11.2022]

Please note: group winners were qualified for the Round of 16, while runners-up will advance to the Knock-Out Round Play-offs.

---

### GROUP A

| | | | |
|---|---|---|---|
| Heart of Midlothian FC Edinburgh - Istanbul Başakşehir FK | 0-4(0-1) | ACF Fiorentina - eart of Midlothian FC Edinburgh | 5-1(4-0) |
| ACF Fiorentina - FK Rīgas Futbola Skola | 1-1(0-0) | Istanbul Başakşehir FK - FK Rīgas Futbola Skola | 3-0(2-0) |
| Istanbul Başakşehir FK - ACF Fiorentina | 3-0(0-0) | ACF Fiorentina - Istanbul Başakşehir FK | 2-1(1-1) |
| FK Rīgas Futbola Skola - eart of Midlothian FC Edinburgh | 0-2(0-1) | eart of Midlothian FC Edinburgh- FK Rīgas Futbola Skola | 2-1(2-1) |
| eart of Midlothian FC Edinburgh- ACF Fiorentina | 0-3(0-2) | Istanbul Başakşehir FK - eart of Midlothian FC Edinburgh | 3-1(2-0) |
| FK Rīgas Futbola Skola - Istanbul Başakşehir FK | 0-0 | FK Rīgas Futbola Skola - ACF Fiorentina | 0-3(0-3) |

| | | | | | | | | | |
|---|---|---|---|---|---|---|---|---|---|
| 1. | **Istanbul Başakşehir FK** | 6 | 4 | 1 | 1 | 14 | - | 3 | 13 |
| 2. | *ACF Fiorentina* | 6 | 4 | 1 | 1 | 14 | - | 6 | 13 |
| 3. | Heart of Midlothian FC | 6 | 2 | 0 | 4 | 6 | - | 16 | 6 |
| 4. | FK Rīgas Futbola Skola | 6 | 0 | 2 | 4 | 2 | - | 11 | 2 |

---

### GROUP B

| | | | |
|---|---|---|---|
| RSC Anderlecht Bruxelles - Silkeborg IF | 1-0(0-0) | West Ham United FC London - RSC Anderlecht Bruxelles | 2-1(2-0) |
| West Ham United FC London - SC FCSB Bucureşti | 3-1(0-1) | SC FCSB Bucureşti - Silkeborg IF | 0-5(0-2) |
| SC FCSB Bucureşti - RSC Anderlecht Bruxelles | 0-0 | RSC Anderlecht Bruxelles - SC FCSB Bucureşti | 2-2(1-0) |
| Silkeborg IF - West Ham United FC London | 2-3(1-3) | West Ham United FC London - Silkeborg IF | 1-0(1-0) |
| RSC Anderlecht Bruxelles - West Ham United FC London | 0-1(0-0) | SC FCSB Bucureşti - West Ham United FC London | 0-3(0-1) |
| Silkeborg IF - SC FCSB Bucureşti | 5-0(3-0) | Silkeborg IF - RSC Anderlecht Bruxelles | 0-2(0-1) |

| | | | | | | | | | |
|---|---|---|---|---|---|---|---|---|---|
| 1. | **West Ham United FC** | 6 | 6 | 0 | 0 | 13 | - | 4 | 18 |
| 2. | *RSC Anderlecht Bruxelles* | 6 | 2 | 2 | 2 | 6 | - | 5 | 8 |
| 3. | Silkeborg IF | 6 | 2 | 0 | 4 | 12 | - | 7 | 6 |
| 4. | SC FCSB Bucureşti | 6 | 0 | 2 | 4 | 3 | - | 18 | 2 |

---

### GROUP C

| | | | |
|---|---|---|---|
| FK Austria Wien - Hapoel Be'er Sheva FC | 0-0 | FK Austria Wien - Villarreal CF | 0-1(0-0) |
| Villarreal CF - KKS Lech Poznań | 4-3(3-1) | Hapoel Be'er Sheva FC - KKS Lech Poznań | 1-1(1-1) |
| Hapoel Be'er Sheva FC - Villarreal CF | 1-2(0-1) | Villarreal CF - Hapoel Be'er Sheva FC | 2-2(0-0) |
| KKS Lech Poznań - FK Austria Wien | 4-1(1-1) | FK Austria Wien - KKS Lech Poznań | 1-1(0-0) |
| KKS Lech Poznań - Hapoel Be'er Sheva FC | 0-0 | Hapoel Be'er Sheva FC - FK Austria Wien | 4-0(2-0) |
| Villarreal CF - FK Austria Wien | 5-0(2-0) | KKS Lech Poznań - Villarreal CF | 3-0(1-0) |

| | | | | | | | | | |
|---|---|---|---|---|---|---|---|---|---|
| 1. | **Villarreal CF** | 6 | 4 | 1 | 1 | 14 | - | 9 | 13 |
| 2. | *KKS Lech Poznań* | 6 | 2 | 3 | 1 | 12 | - | 7 | 9 |
| 3. | Hapoel Be'er Sheva FC | 6 | 1 | 4 | 1 | 8 | - | 5 | 7 |
| 4. | FK Austria Wien | 6 | 0 | 2 | 4 | 2 | - | 15 | 2 |

---

### GROUP D

| | | | |
|---|---|---|---|
| 1. FC Slovácko Uherské Hradiště - FK Partizan Beograd | 3-3(2-0) | FK Partizan Beograd - 1. FC Köln | 2-0(1-0) |
| OGC Nice - 1. FC Köln | 1-1(0-1) | OGC Nice - 1. FC Slovácko Uherské Hradiště | 1-2(1-0) |
| FK Partizan Beograd - OGC Nice | 1-1(0-1) | OGC Nice - FK Partizan Beograd | 2-1(1-0) |
| 1. FC Köln - 1. FC Slovácko Uherské Hradiště | 4-2(2-0) | 1. FC Slovácko Uherské Hradiště - 1. FC Köln | 0-1(0-0) |
| 1. FC Slovácko Uherské Hradiště - OGC Nice | 0-1(0-0) | 1. FC Köln - OGC Nice | 2-2(0-2) |
| 1. FC Köln - FK Partizan Beograd | 0-1(0-1) | FK Partizan Beograd - 1. FC Slovácko Uherské Hradiště | 1-1(1-0) |

| | | | | | | | | | |
|---|---|---|---|---|---|---|---|---|---|
| 1. | **OGC Nice** | 6 | 2 | 3 | 1 | 8 | - | 7 | 9 |
| 2. | *FK Partizan Beograd* | 6 | 2 | 3 | 1 | 9 | - | 7 | 9 |
| 3. | 1. FC Köln | 6 | 2 | 2 | 2 | 8 | - | 8 | 8 |
| 4. | 1. FC Slovácko Uherské Hradiště | 6 | 1 | 2 | 3 | 8 | - | 11 | 5 |

## GROUP E

| | |
|---|---|
| FC Vaduz - Apollon Limassol FC | 0-0 |
| SK Dnipro-1 - AZ Alkmaar | 0-1(0-0) |
| AZ Alkmaar - FC Vaduz | 4-1(1-1) |
| Apollon Limassol FC - SK Dnipro-1 | 1-3(0-3) |
| SK Dnipro-1 - FC Vaduz | 2-2(1-1) |
| AZ Alkmaar - Apollon Limassol FC | 3-2(1-1) |

| | |
|---|---|
| Apollon Limassol FC - AZ Alkmaar | 1-0(1-0) |
| FC Vaduz - SK Dnipro-1 | 1-2(1-1) |
| FC Vaduz - AZ Alkmaar | 1-2(0-0) |
| SK Dnipro-1 - Apollon Limassol FC | 1-0(1-0) |
| Apollon Limassol FC - FC Vaduz | 1-0(1-0) |
| AZ Alkmaar - SK Dnipro-1 | 2-1(1-1) |

| | | | | | | | | |
|---|---|---|---|---|---|---|---|---|
| 1. | **AZ Alkmaar** | 6 | 5 | 0 | 1 | 12 | - | 6 | 15 |
| 2. | *SC Dnipro-1* | 6 | 3 | 1 | 2 | 9 | - | 7 | 10 |
| 3. | Apollon Limassol FC | 6 | 2 | 1 | 3 | 5 | - | 7 | 7 |
| 4. | FC Vaduz | 6 | 0 | 2 | 4 | 5 | - | 11 | 2 |

## GROUP F

| | |
|---|---|
| Molde FK - KAA Gent | 0-0 |
| Shamrock Rovers FC Dublin - Djurgårdens IF Stockholm | 0-0 |
| KAA Gent - Shamrock Rovers FC Dublin | 3-0(2-0) |
| Djurgårdens IF Stockholm - Molde FK | 3-2(0-1) |
| Molde FK - Shamrock Rovers FC Dublin | 3-0(1-0) |
| KAA Gent - Djurgårdens IF Stockholm | 0-1(0-1) |

| | |
|---|---|
| Djurgårdens IF Stockholm - KAA Gent | 4-2(3-0) |
| Shamrock Rovers FC Dublin - Molde FK | 0-2(0-1) |
| Shamrock Rovers FC Dublin - KAA Gent | 1-1(1-0) |
| Molde FK - Djurgårdens IF Stockholm | 2-3(2-1) |
| KAA Gent - Molde FK | 4-0(0-0) |
| Djurgårdens IF Stockholm - Shamrock Rovers FC Dublin | 1-0(1-0) |

| | | | | | | | | |
|---|---|---|---|---|---|---|---|---|
| 1. | **Djurgårdens IF Stockholm** | 6 | 5 | 1 | 0 | 12 | - | 6 | 16 |
| 2. | *KAA Gent* | 6 | 2 | 2 | 2 | 10 | - | 6 | 8 |
| 3. | Molde FK | 6 | 2 | 1 | 3 | 9 | - | 10 | 7 |
| 4. | Shamrock Rovers FC Dublin | 6 | 0 | 2 | 4 | 1 | - | 10 | 2 |

## GROUP G

| | |
|---|---|
| KF Ballkani Suva Reka - FC CFR 1907 Cluj-Napoca | 1-1(0-0) |
| Sivasspor Kulübü - SK Slavia Praha | 1-1(1-1) |
| FC CFR 1907 Cluj-Napoca - Sivasspor Kulübü | 0-1(0-1) |
| SK Slavia Praha - KF Ballkani Suva Reka | 3-2(3-2) |
| Sivasspor Kulübü - KF Ballkani Suva Reka | 3-4(1-2) |
| SK Slavia Praha - FC CFR 1907 Cluj-Napoca | 0-1(0-1) |

| | |
|---|---|
| FC CFR 1907 Cluj-Napoca - SK Slavia Praha | 2-0(1-0) |
| KF Ballkani Suva Reka - Sivasspor Kulübü | 1-2(1-0) |
| Sivasspor Kulübü - FC CFR 1907 Cluj-Napoca | 3-0(1-0) |
| KF Ballkani Suva Reka - SK Slavia Praha | 0-1(0-0) |
| SK Slavia Praha - Sivasspor Kulübü | 1-1(0-1) |
| FC CFR 1907 Cluj-Napoca - KF Ballkani Suva Reka | 1-0(1-0) |

| | | | | | | | | |
|---|---|---|---|---|---|---|---|---|
| 1. | **Sivasspor Kulübü** | 6 | 3 | 2 | 1 | 11 | - | 7 | 11 |
| 2. | *FC CFR 1907 Cluj-Napoca* | 6 | 3 | 1 | 2 | 5 | - | 5 | 10 |
| 3. | SK Slavia Praha | 6 | 2 | 2 | 2 | 6 | - | 7 | 8 |
| 4. | KF Ballkani Suva Reka | 6 | 1 | 1 | 4 | 8 | - | 11 | 4 |

## GROUP H

| | |
|---|---|
| ŠK Slovan Bratislava - FK Žalgiris Vilnius | 0-0 |
| FC Basel - FC Pyunik Yerevan | 3-1(1-1) |
| FK Žalgiris Vilnius - FC Basel | 0-1(0-0) |
| FC Pyunik Yerevan - ŠK Slovan Bratislava | 2-0(2-0) |
| FC Pyunik Yerevan - FK Žalgiris Vilnius | 2-0(1-0) |
| FC Basel - ŠK Slovan Bratislava | 0-2(0-2) |

| | |
|---|---|
| ŠK Slovan Bratislava - FC Basel | 3-3(1-1) |
| FK Žalgiris Vilnius - FC Pyunik Yerevan | 2-1(2-0) |
| FC Basel - FK Žalgiris Vilnius | 2-2(2-1) |
| ŠK Slovan Bratislava - FC Pyunik Yerevan | 2-1(0-0) |
| FK Žalgiris Vilnius - ŠK Slovan Bratislava | 1-2(0-2) |
| FC Pyunik Yerevan - FC Basel | 1-2(0-2) |

| | | | | | | | | |
|---|---|---|---|---|---|---|---|---|
| 1. | **ŠK Slovan Bratislava** | 6 | 3 | 2 | 1 | 9 | - | 7 | 11 |
| 2. | *FC Basel* | 6 | 3 | 2 | 1 | 11 | - | 9 | 11 |
| 3. | FC Pyunik Yerevan | 6 | 2 | 0 | 4 | 8 | - | 9 | 6 |
| 4. | FK Žalgiris Vilnius | 6 | 1 | 2 | 3 | 5 | - | 8 | 5 |

## KNOCK-OUT ROUND PLAY-OFFS [16.02. - 23.02.2023]

Please note: FK Bodø/Glimt, AEK Larnaca FC, PFC Ludogorets Razgrad, Sporting Clube de Braga, FC Sheriff Tiraspol, SS Lazio Roma, Qarabağ FK Bakı and Trabzonspor Kulübü entered the UEFA Europa Conference League as the group stage third-placed teams from the UEFA Europa League.

| | | |
|---|---|---|
| Qarabağ FK - **KAA Gent** | 1-0(0-0) | 0-1(0-0,0-1,0-1); 3-5 pen |
| Trabzonspor Kulübü - **FC Basel** | 1-0(0-0) | 0-2(0-1) |
| FK Bodø/Glimt - **KKS Lech Poznań** | 0-0 | 0-1(0-0) |
| Sporting Clube de Braga - **ACF Fiorentina** | 0-4(0-1) | 2-3(2-1) |
| **SS Lazio Roma** - FC CFR 1907 Cluj-Napoca | 1-0(1-0) | 0-0 |
| **AEK Larnaca FC** - SC Dnipro-1 | 1-0(0-0) | 0-0 |
| **FC Sheriff Tiraspol** - FK Partizan Beograd | 0-1(0-1) | 3-1(2-1) |
| PFC Ludogorets Razgrad - **RSC Anderlecht Bruxelles** | 1-0(1-0) | 1-2(0-1,1-2,1-2); 0-3 pen |

## ROUND OF 16 [07/09.03. - 15/16.03.2023]

| | | |
|---|---|---|
| SS Lazio Roma - **AZ Alkmaar** | 1-2(1-1) | 1-2(1-1) |
| AEK Larnaca FC - **West Ham United FC London** | 0-2(0-2) | 0-4(0-1) |
| FC Sheriff Tiraspol - **OGC Nice** | 0-1(0-1) | 1-3(0-1) |
| **RSC Anderlecht Bruxelles** - Villarreal CF | 1-1(0-1) | 1-0(0-0) |
| **ACF Fiorentina** - Sivasspor Kulübü | 1-0(0-0) | 4-1(1-1) |
| **KKS Lech Poznań** - Djurgårdens IF Stockholm | 2-0(1-0) | 3-0(0-0) |
| **FC Basel** - ŠK Slovan Bratislava | 2-2(2-1) | 2-2(0-2,2-2,2-2); 4-1 pen |
| **KAA Gent** - Istanbul Başakşehir FK | 1-1(1-1) | 4-1(4-0) |

## QUARTER-FINALS [13.04. - 20.04.2023]

| | | |
|---|---|---|
| KAA Gent - **West Ham United FC London** | 1-1(0-1) | 1-4(1-1) |
| KKS Lech Poznań - **ACF Fiorentina** | 1-4(1-2) | 3-2(1-0) |
| RSC Anderlecht Bruxelles - **AZ Alkmaar** | 2-0(1-0) | 0-2(0-2,0-2,0-2); 1-4 pen |
| **FC Basel** - OGC Nice | 2-2(1-2) | 2-1(0-1,1-1) |

## SEMI-FINALS [11.05. - 18.05.2023]

| | | |
|---|---|---|
| **ACF Fiorentina** - FC Basel | 1-2(1-0) | 3-1(1-0,2-1) |
| **West Ham United FC London** - AZ Alkmaar | 2-1(0-1) | 1-0(0-0) |

## FINAL

07.06.2023; Fortuna Arena, Praha (Czech Republic); Referee: Carlos del Cerro Grande (Spain); Attendance: 17,363

**ACF Fiorentina - West Ham United FC London**      **1-2(0-0)**

ACF Fiorentina: Pietro Terracciano, Domilson Cordeiro dos Santos „Dodô", Nikola Milenković, Luca Ranieri (84.Igor Julio dos Santos de Paulo), Cristiano Biraghi (Cap), Sofyan Amrabat, Rolando Mandragora (90+3.Antonín Barák), Giacomo Bonaventura, Nicolás Iván González, Christian Michael Kouamé Kouakou (61.Riccardo Saponara), Luka Jović (46.Arthur Mendonça Cabral). Trainer: Vincenzo Italiano.

West Ham United FC: Alphonse Francis Aréola, Vladimír Coufal, Kurt Happy Zouma (61.Jan Thilo Kehrer), Nayef Aguerd, Emerson Palmieri dos Santos, Tomáš Souček, Declan Rice (Cap), Lucas Tolentino Coelho de Lima „Lucas Paquetá", Jarrod Bowen, Saïd Benrahma (76.Pablo Fornals Malla), Michail Gregory Antonio (90+4.Obinze Angelo Ogbonna). Trainer: David William Moyes (Scotland)

Goals: 62' Saïd Benrahma (penalty) 0-1, 67' Giacomo Bonaventura 1-1, 90' Jarrod Bowen 1-2.

UEFA Europa Conference League Winner 2022/2023: **West Ham United FC London** (England)

Best Goalscorer: Mohamed Zeki Amdouni (MAR, FC Basel) & Arthur Mendonça Cabral (BRA, ACF Fiorentina) - 7 goals each

## EUROPA CONFERENCE LEAGUE (2021-2023)
## TABLE OF HONOURS

| 2021/2022 | AS Roma | *Italy* |
|---|---|---|
| 2022/2023 | West Ham United FC London | *England* |

# ALBANIA

### The Country:
Republic of Albania (Republika e Shqipërisë)
Capital: Tiranë
Surface: 28,748 km²
Inhabitants: 2,793,592 [2022]
Time: UTC+1

### The FA:
Federata Shqiptare e Futbollit
Rr. Liman Kaba Nd5, Hyrja 1, Njësia Administrative 5, 1019 Tiranë
Tel: +35542 346 601
Foundation date: 06.06.1930
Member of FIFA since: 12.06.1932
Member of UEFA since: 1954
Website: www.fshf.org

## NATIONAL TEAM RECORDS

| RECORDS | |
|---|---|
| **First international match:** | 07.10.1946, Tiranë: Albania – Yugoslavia 2-3 |
| **Most international caps:** | Lorik Cana - 93 caps (2003-2016) |
| **Most international goals:** | Erjon Bogdani - 18 goal / 74 caps (1996-2013) |

### UEFA EUROPEAN CHAMPIONSHIP
| | |
|---|---|
| 1960 | Qualifiers |
| 1964 | Qualifiers |
| 1968 | Qualifiers |
| 1972 | Qualifiers |
| 1976 | Did not enter |
| 1980 | Did not enter |
| 1984 | Qualifiers |
| 1988 | Qualifiers |
| 1992 | Qualifiers |
| 1996 | Qualifiers |
| 2000 | Qualifiers |
| 2004 | Qualifiers |
| 2008 | Qualifiers |
| 2012 | Qualifiers |
| 2016 | Final Tournament (Group Stage) |
| 2020 | Qualifiers |

### FIFA WORLD CUP
| | |
|---|---|
| 1930 | Did not enter |
| 1934 | Did not enter |
| 1938 | Did not enter |
| 1950 | Did not enter |
| 1954 | Did not enter |
| 1958 | Did not enter |
| 1962 | Did not enter |
| 1966 | Qualifiers |
| 1970 | *Entry not accepted by FIFA* |
| 1974 | Qualifiers |
| 1978 | Did not enter |
| 1982 | Qualifiers |
| 1986 | Qualifiers |
| 1990 | Qualifiers |
| 1994 | Qualifiers |
| 1998 | Qualifiers |
| 2002 | Qualifiers |
| 2006 | Qualifiers |
| 2010 | Qualifiers |
| 2014 | Qualifiers |
| 2018 | Qualifiers |
| 2022 | Qualifiers |

### OLYMPIC TOURNAMENTS
| | |
|---|---|
| 1908 | - |
| 1912 | - |
| 1920 | - |
| 1924 | - |
| 1928 | - |
| 1936 | - |
| 1948 | - |
| 1952 | - |
| 1956 | - |
| 1960 | - |
| 1964 | - |
| 1968 | - |
| 1972 | - |
| 1976 | - |
| 1980 | - |
| 1984 | *Withdrew* |
| 1988 | - |
| 1992 | *Withdrew* |
| 1996 | - |
| 2000 | Qualifiers |
| 2004 | Qualifiers |
| 2008 | Qualifiers |
| 2012 | Qualifiers |
| 2016 | Qualifiers |
| 2020 | Qualifiers |

### UEFA NATIONS LEAGUE
| | |
|---|---|
| 2018/2019 | League C (Group Stage) |
| 2020/2021 | League C (Group Stage -> promoted to League B) |
| 2022/2023 | League B (Group Stage) |

## ALBANIAN CLUB HONOURS IN EUROPEAN CLUB COMPETITIONS:

| European Champion Clubs' Cup (1956-1992) / UEFA Champions League (1993-2023) |
|---|
| None |

| Fairs Cup (1858-1971) / UEFA Cup (1972-2009) / UEFA Europa League (2010-2023) |
|---|
| None |

| UEFA Europa Conference League (2021-2023) |
|---|
| None |

| UEFA Super Cup (1972-2022) |
|---|
| None |

| *European Cup Winners' Cup 1961-1999** |
|---|
| None |

*defunct competition

## NATIONAL COMPETITIONS
## TABLE OF HONOURS

| | CHAMPIONS | CUP WINNERS | BEST GOALSCORERS | |
|---|---|---|---|---|
| 1930 | SK Tiranë | - | - | |
| 1931 | SK Tiranë | - | Teli Samsuri (Skënderbeu Korçë) | 9 |
| 1932 | SK Tiranë | - | - | |
| 1933 | Skënderbeu Korçë | - | Servet Tefik Agai (Skënderbeu Korçë) | 7 |
| 1934 | SK Tiranë | - | Mark Gurashi (SK Tiranë) | 12 |
| 1935 | *No competition* | - | *No competition* | |
| 1936 | SK Tiranë | - | Riza Lushta (SK Tiranë) | 11 |
| 1937 | SK Tiranë | - | Riza Lushta (SK Tiranë) | 25 |
| 1938 | *No competition* | - | *No competition* | |
| 1939 | SK Tiranë (*unofficial*) | SK Tiranë | - | |
| 1940 | Vllaznia Shkodër (*unofficial*) | *No competition* | - | |
| 1941 | *No competition* | *No competition* | *No competition* | |
| 1942 | SK Tiranë (*unofficial*) | *No competition* | - | |
| 1943 | *No competition* | *No competition* | *No competition* | |
| 1944 | *No competition* | *No competition* | *No competition* | |
| 1945 | Vllaznia Shkodër | *No competition* | Loro Boriçi (Vllaznia Shkodër) | 11 |
| 1946 | Vllaznia Shkodër | *No competition* | Xhevdet Shaqiri (Vllaznia Shkodër) | 11 |
| 1947 | Partizani Tiranë | *No competition* | Hamdi Bakalli (Partizani Tiranë) | 7 |
| 1948 | Partizani Tiranë | Partizani Tiranë | Tish Daija (Flamurtari Vlorë) Zihni Gjinali (Partizani Tiranë) | 11 |
| 1949 | Partizani Tiranë | Partizani Tiranë | Zihni Gjinali (Partizani Tiranë) | 14 |
| 1950 | Dinamo Tiranë | Dinamo Tiranë | Refik Resmja (Partizani Tiranë) | ? |
| 1951 | Dinamo Tiranë | Dinamo Tiranë | Refik Resmja (Partizani Tiranë) | 59 |
| 1952 | Dinamo Tiranë | Dinamo Tiranë | Refik Resmja (Partizani Tiranë) | 17 |
| 1953 | Dinamo Tiranë | Dinamo Tiranë | Refik Resmja (Partizani Tiranë) | 9 |
| 1954 | Partizani Tiranë | Dinamo Tiranë | Refik Resmja (Partizani Tiranë) | 13 |
| 1955 | Dinamo Tiranë | *No competition* | Refik Resmja (Partizani Tiranë) Skënder Jareci (Dinamo Tiranë) | 23 |
| 1956 | Dinamo Tiranë | *No competition* | Refik Resmja (Partizani Tiranë) | 17 |
| 1957 | Partizani Tiranë | Partizani Tiranë | Niko Bespalla (Teuta) | 15 |
| 1958 | Partizani Tiranë | Partizani Tiranë | Skënder Jareci (Dinamo Tiranë) | 14 |
| 1959 | Partizani Tiranë | *No competition* | Stavri Lubonja (Dinamo Tiranë) | 11 |
| 1960 | Dinamo Tiranë | Dinamo Tiranë | Skënder Jareci (Dinamo Tiranë) | 16 |
| 1961 | Partizani Tiranë | Partizani Tiranë | Panajot Pano (Partizani Tiranë) | 17 |
| 1962/1963 | Partizani Tiranë | *No competition* | Robert Jashari (Partizani Tiranë) | 18 |
| 1963/1964 | Partizani Tiranë | 17 Nëntori Tiranë | Robert Jashari (Partizani Tiranë) | 9 |
| 1964/1965 | 17 Nëntori Tiranë | Partizani Tiranë | Robert Jashari (Partizani Tiranë) | 14 |
| 1965/1966 | 17 Nëntori Tiranë | Vllaznia Shkodër | Sajmir Dauti (Dinamo Tiranë) | 13 |
| 1966/1967 | Dinamo Tiranë | Partizani Tiranë | Medin Zhega (Dinamo Tiranë) | 19 |
| 1968 | 17 Nëntori Tiranë | Partizani Tiranë | Skënder Hyka (17 Nëntori Tiranë) | 19 |
| 1969/1970 | 17 Nëntori Tiranë | Partizani Tiranë | Panajot Pano (Partizani Tiranë) | 17 |
| 1970/1971 | Partizani Tiranë | Dinamo Tiranë | Ilir Përnaska (Dinamo Tiranë) | 19 |
| 1971/1972 | Vllaznia Shkodër | Vllaznia Shkodër | Ilir Përnaska (Dinamo Tiranë) | 17 |
| 1972/1973 | Dinamo Tiranë | Partizani Tiranë | Ilir Përnaska (Dinamo Tiranë) | 12 |
| 1973/1974 | Vllaznia Shkodër | Dinamo Tiranë | Ilir Përnaska (Dinamo Tiranë) | 19 |
| 1974/1975 | Dinamo Tiranë | Elbasani | Ilir Përnaska (Dinamo Tiranë) | 17 |
| 1975/1976 | Dinamo Tiranë | 17 Nëntori Tiranë | Ilir Përnaska (Dinamo Tiranë) | 18 |
| 1976/1977 | Dinamo Tiranë | 17 Nëntori Tiranë | Agim Murati (Partizani Tiranë) | 12 |
| 1977/1978 | Vllaznia Shkodër | Dinamo Tiranë | Agim Murati (Partizani Tiranë) | 14 |
| 1978/1979 | Partizani Tiranë | Vllaznia Shkodër | Agim Murati (Partizani Tiranë) Petrit Dibra (17 Nëntori Tiranë) | 14 |
| 1979/1980 | Dinamo Tiranë | Partizani Tiranë | Përparim Kovaçi (Tomori Berat) | 18 |
| 1980/1981 | Partizani Tiranë | Vllaznia Shkodër | Dashnor Bajaziti (Besa Kavajë) | 12 |
| 1981/1982 | KF Tiranë | Dinamo Tiranë | Vasil Ruci (Flamurtari Vlorë) | 12 |
| 1982/1983 | Vllaznia Shkodër | 17 Nëntori Tiranë | Dashnor Bajaziti (Besa Kavajë) | 16 |
| 1983/1984 | Elbasani | 17 Nëntori Tiranë | Vasil Ruci (Flamurtari Vlorë) | 12 |
| 1984/1985 | 17 Nëntori Tiranë | Flamurtari Vlorë | Faslli Fakja (Vllaznia Shkodër) Arben Minga (17 Nëntori Tiranë) | 13 |
| 1985/1986 | Dinamo Tiranë | 17 Nëntori Tiranë | Kujtim Majaci (Apolonia Fier) | 20 |
| 1986/1987 | Partizani Tiranë | Vllaznia Shkodër | Arben Arbëri (Tomori Berat) | 14 |
| 1987/1988 | 17 Nëntori Tiranë | Flamurtari Vlorë | Agustin Kola (17 Nëntori Tiranë) | 18 |
| 1988/1989 | 17 Nëntori Tiranë | Dinamo Tiranë | Agustin Kola (17 Nëntori Tiranë) | 19 |
| 1989/1990 | Dinamo Tiranë | Dinamo Tiranë | Kujtim Majaci (Apolonia Fier) | 19 |
| 1990/1991 | KS Flamurtari Vlorë | FK Partizani Tiranë | Kliton Bozgo (FK Tomori Berat) | 29 |
| 1991/1992 | KF Vllaznia Shkodër | KF Elbasani | Edmir Bilali (KF Vllaznia Shkodër) | 21 |
| 1992/1993 | FK Partizani Tiranë | Partizani Tiranë | Edmond Dosti (FK Partizani Tiranë) | 20 |
| 1993/1994 | KF Teuta Durrës | KF Tiranë | Edi Martini (KF Vllaznia Shkodër) | 14 |
| 1994/1995 | KF Tiranë | KF Teuta Durrës | Arben Shehu (Luftëtari Gjirokastër FC) | 21 |
| 1995/1996 | KF Tiranë | KF Tiranë | Altin Çuko (FK Tomori Berat & KF Laçi) | 21 |
| 1996/1997 | KF Tiranë | FK Partizani Tiranë | Viktor Paço (KS Flamurtari Vlorë) | 14 |
| 1997/1998 | KF Vllaznia Shkodër | KF Apolonia Fier | Dorian Bubeqi (KS Shkumbini Peqin) | 26 |

| 1998/1999 | KF Tiranë | KF Tiranë | Artan Bano (KS Lushnja) | 22 |
|---|---|---|---|---|
| 1999/2000 | KF Tiranë | KF Teuta Durrës | Klodian Arbëri (FK Tomori Berat) | 18 |
| 2000/2001 | KF Vllaznia Shkodër | KF Tiranë | Indrit Fortuzi (KF Tiranë) | 31 |
| 2001/2002 | FK Dinamo Tiranë | KF Tiranë | Indrit Fortuzi (KF Tiranë) | 24 |
| 2002/2003 | KF Tiranë | FK Dinamo Tiranë | Mahir Halili (KF Tiranë) | 20 |
| 2003/2004 | KF Tiranë | FK Partizani Tiranë | Vioresin Sinani (KF Vllaznia Shkodër) | 36 |
| 2004/2005 | KF Tiranë | KF Teuta Durrës | Dorian Bylykbashi (FK Partizani Tiranë) | 24 |
| 2005/2006 | KF Elbasani | KF Tiranë | Hamdi Salihi (KF Tiranë) | 29 |
| 2006/2007 | KF Tiranë | KS Besa Kavajë | Vioresin Sinani (KF Tiranë) | 23 |
| 2007/2008 | FK Dinamo Tiranë | KF Vllaznia Shkodër | Vioresin Sinani (KF Vllaznia Shkodër) | 20 |
| 2008/2009 | KF Tiranë | KS Flamurtari Vlorë | Migen Memelli (KF Tiranë) | 23 |
| 2009/2010 | FK Dinamo Tiranë | KS Besa Kavajë | Daniel Xhafa (KS Besa Kavajë) | 18 |
| 2010/2011 | KF Skënderbeu Korçë | KF Tiranë | Daniel Xhafa (KS Flamurtari Vlorë) | 19 |
| 2011/2012 | KF Skënderbeu Korçë | KF Tiranë | Roland Dervishi (KS Shkumbini Peqin) | 20 |
| 2012/2013 | KF Skënderbeu Korçë | KF Laçi | Migen Memelli (KS Flamurtari Vlorë) | 19 |
| 2013/2014 | KF Skënderbeu Korçë | KS Flamurtari Vlorë | Pero Pejić (CRO, KF Skënderbeu Korçë) | 20 |
| 2014/2015 | KF Skënderbeu Korçë | KF Laçi | Pero Pejić (CRO, FK Kukësi) | 31 |
| 2015/2016 | KF Skënderbeu Korçë | FK Kukësi | Hamdi Salihi (KF Skënderbeu Korçë) | 27 |
| 2016/2017 | FK Kukësi | KF Tiranë | Pero Pejić (CRO, FK Kukësi) | 28 |
| 2017/2018 | KF Skënderbeu Korçë | KF Skënderbeu Korçë | Ali Sowe (GAM, KF Skënderbeu Korçë) | 21 |
| 2018/2019 | FK Partizani Tiranë | FK Kukësi | Reginaldo Artur Faife (MOZ, FK Kukësi) | 13 |
| 2019/2020 | KF Tiranë | KF Teuta Durrës | Kyrian Chinazorm Nwabueze (NGA, KF Laçi) | 24 |
| 2020/2021 | KF Teuta Durrës | KF Vllaznia Shkodër | Dejvi Bregu (KF Teuta Durrës) | 16 |
| 2021/2022 | KF Tiranë | KF Vllaznia Shkodër | Saliou Guindo (MLI, KF Laçi) Taulant Fatmir Seferi (KF Tiranë) | 19 |
| 2022/2023 | FK Partizani Tiranë | KF Egnatia Rrogozhinë | Florent Hasani (KOS, KF Tiranë) | 16 |

# NATIONAL CHAMPIONSHIP
## Albanian Superliga / Kategoria Superiore 2022/2023
### (19.08.2022 – 29.05.2023)

### Results

**Round 1 [19-21.08.2022]**
FK Kukësi - KF Tiranë 1-1(1-0)
KF Erzeni - FK Vllaznia 1-0(1-0)
FK Partizani - Egnatia Rrogozhinë 2-1(0-1)
KF Laçi - Teuta Durrës 3-1(1-0)
KF Bylis - KS Kastrioti 2-0(0-0)

**Round 2 [27-29.08.2022]**
KS Kastrioti - KF Erzeni 0-0
Teuta Durrës - KF Bylis 1-1(0-1)
Egnatia Rrogozhinë - KF Tiranë 0-2(0-1)
FK Vllaznia - FK Kukësi 2-1(1-0)
FK Partizani - KF Laçi 1-0(1-0)

**Round 3 [02-04.09.2022]**
KF Tiranë - FK Vllaznia 1-2(0-2)
KF Erzeni - Teuta Durrës 0-0
FK Kukësi - KS Kastrioti 1-2(0-0)
KF Laçi - Egnatia Rrogozhinë 0-1(0-0)
KF Bylis - FK Partizani 0-1(0-1)

**Round 4 [09-11.09.2022]**
Teuta Durrës - FK Kukësi 0-0
Egnatia Rrogozhinë - FK Vllaznia 3-0(2-0)
KS Kastrioti - KF Tiranë 0-0
KF Laçi - KF Bylis 0-1(0-0)
FK Partizani - KF Erzeni 0-1(0-1)

**Round 5 [16-19.09.2022]**
KF Tiranë - Teuta Durrës 4-0(1-0)
KF Bylis - Egnatia Rrogozhinë 0-0
KF Erzeni - KF Laçi 1-0(0-0)
FK Vllaznia - KS Kastrioti 1-0(1-0)
FK Kukësi - FK Partizani 1-2(0-1)

**Round 6 [30.09.-02.10.2022]**
KF Bylis - KF Erzeni 4-1(2-0)
Teuta Durrës - FK Vllaznia 0-0
Egnatia Rrogozhinë - KS Kastrioti 0-0
KF Laçi - FK Kukësi 0-1(0-1)
FK Partizani - KF Tiranë 0-2(0-1)

**Round 7 [07-08.10.2022]**
KF Erzeni - Egnatia Rrogozhinë 0-0
KF Tiranë - KF Laçi 3-3(2-1)
FK Vllaznia - FK Partizani 1-2(1-0)
FK Kukësi - KF Bylis 2-0(1-0)
KS Kastrioti - Teuta Durrës 2-1(2-1)

**Round 8 [15-17.10.2022]**
Egnatia Rrogozhinë - Teuta Durrës 1-2(0-0)
KF Laçi - FK Vllaznia 1-1(0-0)
KF Bylis - KF Tiranë 0-1(0-0)
FK Partizani - KS Kastrioti 0-0
KF Erzeni - FK Kukësi 0-2(0-1)

**Round 9 [21-22.10.2022]**
Teuta Durrës - FK Partizani 1-4(1-3)
FK Vllaznia - KF Bylis 2-1(1-0)
FK Kukësi - Egnatia Rrogozhinë 0-1(0-0)
KS Kastrioti - KF Laçi 0-1(0-1)
KF Tiranë - KF Erzeni 0-1(0-1)

**Round 10 [29-30.10.2022]**
KS Kastrioti - KF Bylis 3-0(1-0)
Teuta Durrës - KF Laçi 0-1(0-0)
FK Vllaznia - KF Erzeni 2-2(0-0)
Egnatia Rrogozhinë - FK Partizani 3-0(2-0)
KF Tiranë - FK Kukësi 4-1(1-1)

**Round 11 [02-03.11.2022]**
KF Erzeni - KS Kastrioti 1-1(0-1)
KF Bylis - Teuta Durrës 0-0
FK Kukësi - FK Vllaznia 0-1(0-1)
KF Laçi - FK Partizani 1-0(1-0)
KF Tiranë - Egnatia Rrogozhinë 1-0(0-0)

**Round 12 [13-14.11.2022]**
Egnatia Rrogozhinë - KF Laçi 2-0(0-0)
KS Kastrioti - FK Kukësi 1-1(0-0)
FK Vllaznia - KF Tiranë 0-0
Teuta Durrës - KF Erzeni 1-2(0-0)
FK Partizani - KF Bylis 2-1(1-0)

**Round 13 [11-12.12.2022]**
FK Kukësi - Teuta Durrës 0-1(0-0)
KF Bylis - KF Laçi 0-1(0-1)
KF Erzeni - FK Partizani 3-3(1-1)
FK Vllaznia - Egnatia Rrogozhinë 0-1(0-1)
KF Tiranë - KS Kastrioti 4-0(3-0)

**Round 14 [15-16.12.2022]**
KF Laçi - KF Erzeni 1-0(1-0)
FK Partizani - FK Kukësi 2-1(2-0)
Egnatia Rrogozhinë - KF Bylis 0-1(0-0)
KS Kastrioti - FK Vllaznia 1-0(0-0)
Teuta Durrës - KF Tiranë 1-0(0-0)

**Round 15 [21-22.12.2022]**
FK Kukësi - KF Laçi 1-0(1-0)
KF Tiranë - FK Partizani 0-1(0-1)
KF Erzeni - KF Bylis 1-1(0-1)
KS Kastrioti - Egnatia Rrogozhinë 2-3(1-1)
FK Vllaznia - Teuta Durrës 4-0(2-0)

**Round 16 [13-14.01.2023]**
KF Laçi - KF Tiranë 1-2(1-1)
KF Bylis - FK Kukësi 0-0
FK Partizani - FK Vllaznia 1-2(0-0)
Egnatia Rrogozhinë - KF Erzeni 1-1(0-0)
Teuta Durrës - KS Kastrioti 2-0(1-0)

**Round 17 [21-22.01.2023]**
KS Kastrioti - FK Partizani 1-1(0-0)
KF Tiranë - KF Bylis 4-1(3-0)
FK Vllaznia - KF Laçi 4-1(2-0)
FK Kukësi - KF Erzeni 0-2(0-1)
Teuta Durrës - Egnatia Rrogozhinë 1-1(0-0)

**Round 18 [25-26.01.2023]**
KF Laçi - KS Kastrioti 4-1(2-0)
KF Bylis - FK Vllaznia 1-0(0-0)
Egnatia Rrogozhinë - FK Kukësi 1-2(1-0)
FK Partizani - Teuta Durrës 0-2(0-1)
KF Erzeni - KF Tiranë 0-2(0-0)

**Round 19 [29-30.01.2023]**
FK Kukësi - KF Tiranë 2-0(1-0)
KF Bylis - KS Kastrioti 1-0(0-0)
KF Laçi - Teuta Durrës 4-3(2-2)
KF Erzeni - FK Vllaznia 3-2(2-0)
FK Partizani - Egnatia Rrogozhinë 1-1(0-0)

**Round 20 [06-07.02.2023]**
Egnatia Rrogozhinë - KF Tiranë 1-2(1-1)
FK Partizani - KF Laçi 1-2(1-1)
KS Kastrioti - KF Erzeni 2-2(0-2)
Teuta Durrës - KF Bylis 1-0(0-0)
FK Vllaznia - FK Kukësi 2-0(2-0)

**Round 21 [11-13.02.2023]**
FK Kukësi - KS Kastrioti 1-0(0-0)
KF Laçi - Egnatia Rrogozhinë 0-1(0-1)
KF Erzeni - Teuta Durrës 1-1(0-1)
KF Tiranë - FK Vllaznia 0-1(0-0)
KF Bylis - FK Partizani 0-1(0-0)

**Round 22 [18-19.02.2023]**
KF Laçi - KF Bylis 0-1(0-0)
Teuta Durrës - FK Kukësi 1-0(1-0)
FK Partizani - KF Erzeni 3-0(1-0)
Egnatia Rrogozhinë - FK Vllaznia 0-0
KS Kastrioti - KF Tiranë 0-1(0-0)

**Round 23 [24-25.02.2023]**
FK Kukësi - FK Partizani 1-0(1-0)
KF Bylis - Egnatia Rrogozhinë 2-3(0-0)
KF Erzeni - KF Laçi 1-0(0-0)
KF Tiranë - Teuta Durrës 0-2(0-1)
FK Vllaznia - KS Kastrioti 0-1(0-1)

**Round 24 [05-06.03.2023]**
Egnatia Rrogozhinë - KS Kastrioti 4-1(2-1)
KF Bylis - KF Erzeni 1-1(0-0)
KF Laçi - FK Kukësi 1-2(1-1)
Teuta Durrës - FK Vllaznia 1-1(1-1)
FK Partizani - KF Tiranë 2-0(1-0)

**Round 25 [10-11.03.2023]**
FK Kukësi - KF Bylis 2-0(0-0)
KS Kastrioti - Teuta Durrës 0-0
KF Erzeni - Egnatia Rrogozhinë 2-1(2-1)
KF Tiranë - KF Laçi 3-2(3-0)
FK Vllaznia - FK Partizani 1-1(1-1)

**Round 26 [18-19.03.2023]**
KF Bylis - KF Tiranë 1-1(0-0)
KF Erzeni - FK Kukësi 1-1(1-0)
Egnatia Rrogozhinë - Teuta Durrës 1-1(1-1)
KF Laçi - FK Vllaznia 2-0(2-0)
FK Partizani - KS Kastrioti 4-1(3-1)

**Round 27 [01-02.04.2023]**
FK Kukësi - Egnatia Rrogozhinë 0-3(0-1)
FK Vllaznia - KF Bylis 0-0
Teuta Durrës - FK Partizani 0-2(0-1)
KS Kastrioti - KF Laçi 2-1(0-0)
KF Tiranë - KF Erzeni 3-1(0-0)

**Round 28 [09-10.04.2023]**
Teuta Durrës - KF Laçi 1-2(0-0)
FK Vllaznia - KF Erzeni 3-1(1-0)
Egnatia Rrogozhinë - FK Partizani 1-1(0-1)
KF Tiranë - FK Kukësi 2-1(1-0)
KS Kastrioti - KF Bylis 0-2(0-2) [19.04.2023]

**Round 29 [15-16.04.2023]**
KF Bylis - Teuta Durrës 2-2(1-1)
KF Erzeni - KS Kastrioti 0-0
FK Kukësi - FK Vllaznia 0-0
KF Laçi - FK Partizani 3-2(1-1)
KF Tiranë - Egnatia Rrogozhinë 2-1(1-1)

**Round 30 [22-23.04.2023]**
Egnatia Rrogozhinë - KF Laçi 1-1(0-0)
Teuta Durrës - KF Erzeni 2-0(0-0)
FK Vllaznia - KF Tiranë 0-1(0-1)
KS Kastrioti - FK Kukësi 1-0(1-0)
FK Partizani - KF Bylis 2-1(1-1)

**Round 31 [29-30.04.2023]**
KF Bylis - KF Laçi 0-2(0-1)
KF Erzeni - FK Partizani 1-2(0-0)
FK Kukësi - Teuta Durrës 0-0
KF Tiranë - KS Kastrioti 1-0(0-0)
FK Vllaznia - Egnatia Rrogozhinë 0-4(0-1)

**Round 32 [06-07.05.2023]**
Egnatia Rrogozhinë - KF Bylis 2-0(0-0)
KS Kastrioti - FK Vllaznia 2-2(1-1)
FK Partizani - FK Kukësi 3-1(2-1)
Teuta Durrës - KF Tiranë 2-1(0-0)
KF Laçi - KF Erzeni 1-1(1-0)

**Round 33 [17.05.2023]**
KF Erzeni - KF Bylis 1-2(0-0)
FK Kukësi - KF Laçi 3-0(0-0)
KS Kastrioti - Egnatia Rrogozhinë 1-0(0-0)
FK Vllaznia - Teuta Durrës 1-0(1-0)
KF Tiranë - FK Partizani 1-1(0-0)

**Round 34 [21.05.2023]**
Egnatia Rrogozhinë - KF Erzeni 3-2(2-0)
KF Laçi - KF Tiranë 1-3(0-1)
KF Bylis - FK Kukësi 1-1(0-0)
FK Partizani - FK Vllaznia 2-1(2-0)
Teuta Durrës - KS Kastrioti 1-0(1-0)

**Round 35 [25.05.2023]**
FK Kukësi - KF Erzeni 0-0
KS Kastrioti - FK Partizani 1-4(1-2)
KF Tiranë - KF Bylis 2-2(1-1)
Teuta Durrës - Egnatia Rrogozhinë 1-0(1-0)
FK Vllaznia - KF Laçi 1-1(0-0)

**Round 36 [29.05.2023]**
Egnatia Rrogozhinë - FK Kukësi 0-1(0-0)
KF Erzeni - KF Tiranë 1-2(1-1)
KF Laçi - KS Kastrioti 3-0(1-0)
KF Bylis - FK Vllaznia 1-2(1-1)
FK Partizani - Teuta Durrës 2-0(1-0)

## Final Standings

| | | | | | | | Total | | | Home | | | | | Away | | | |
|---|---|---|---|---|---|---|---|---|---|---|---|---|---|---|---|---|---|---|
| 1. | **FK Partizani Tiranë** | 36 | 20 | 7 | 9 | 56 - 37 | 67 | 11 | 2 | 5 | 28 - 17 | 9 | 5 | 4 | 28 - 20 |
| 2. | KF Tiranë | 36 | 20 | 7 | 9 | 56 - 33 | 67 | 10 | 3 | 5 | 35 - 20 | 10 | 4 | 4 | 21 - 13 |
| 3. | KF Egnatia Rrogozhinë | 36 | 14 | 10 | 12 | 46 - 32 | 52 | 6 | 6 | 6 | 24 - 17 | 8 | 4 | 6 | 22 - 15 |
| 4. | KF Vllaznia Shkodër | 36 | 13 | 11 | 12 | 39 - 37 | 50 | 8 | 5 | 5 | 24 - 17 | 5 | 6 | 7 | 15 - 20 |
| 5. | KF Laçi | 36 | 14 | 6 | 16 | 45 - 46 | 48 | 8 | 2 | 8 | 26 - 21 | 6 | 4 | 8 | 19 - 25 |
| 6. | KF Teuta Durrës | 36 | 12 | 12 | 12 | 33 - 40 | 48 | 8 | 5 | 5 | 17 - 15 | 4 | 7 | 7 | 16 - 25 |
| 7. | FK Kukësi | 36 | 12 | 9 | 15 | 31 - 35 | 45 | 7 | 4 | 7 | 15 - 13 | 5 | 5 | 8 | 16 - 22 |
| 8. | KF Erzeni Shijak (*Relegation Play-off*) | 36 | 8 | 16 | 12 | 36 - 48 | 40 | 4 | 9 | 5 | 18 - 21 | 4 | 7 | 7 | 18 - 27 |
| 9. | KF Bylis Ballsh (*Relegated*) | 36 | 9 | 11 | 16 | 31 - 42 | 38 | 4 | 7 | 7 | 16 - 17 | 5 | 4 | 9 | 15 - 25 |
| 10. | KS Kastrioti Krujë (*Relegated*) | 36 | 8 | 11 | 17 | 26 - 49 | 35 | 6 | 7 | 5 | 19 - 19 | 2 | 4 | 12 | 7 - 30 |

## Top goalscorers:

| | | |
|---|---|---|
| 16 | **Florent Hasani (KOS)** | *KF Tiranë* |
| 13 | Vitor Matheus Da Silva Matos (BRA) | *FK Partizani Tiranë* |
| 12 | Patrick Carvalho Nonato (BRA) | *KF Erzeni Shijak* |

## Relegation Play-off [04.06.2023]

KF Erzeni Shijak - KS Korabi Peshkopi     2-1(1-1,1-1)

KF Erzeni Shijak remains at First Level for 2023/2024.

### 1/8-Finals [17-18.01./02-03.02.2023]

| First Leg | | Second Leg | |
|---|---|---|---|
| KF Lushnja - KF Tiranë | 0-3(0-3) | KF Tiranë - KF Lushnja | 1-0(0-0) |
| KS Korabi Peshkopi - FK Partizani Tiranë | 1-3(0-1) | FK Partizani Tiranë - KS Korabi Peshkopi | 3-0(2-0) |
| KF Bylis Ballsh - KF Vllaznia Shkodër | 0-2(0-1) | KF Vllaznia Shkodër - KF Bylis Ballsh | 1-1(0-0) |
| FK Dinamo Tiranë - KS Kastrioti Krujë | 1-3(1-1) | KS Kastrioti Krujë - FK Dinamo Tiranë | 0-0 |
| KF Tomori Berat - KF Laçi | 1-3(0-1) | KF Laçi - KF Tomori Berat | 2-1(0-0) |
| KF Apolonia Fier - FK Kukësi | 0-0 | FK Kukësi - KF Apolonia Fier | 5-0(1-0) |
| KF Skënderbeu Korçë - KF Egnatia Rrogozhinë | 0-1(0-0) | KF Egnatia Rrogozhinë - KF Skënderbeu Korçë | 1-1(0-1) |
| KF Erzeni Shijak - KF Teuta Durrës | 1-1(0-0) | KF Teuta Durrës - KF Erzeni Shijak | 1-0(0-0) |

### Quarter-Finals [28.02.-01.03./14-15.03.2023]

| First Leg | | Second Leg | |
|---|---|---|---|
| KS Kastrioti Krujë - KF Tiranë | 1-4(0-0) | KF Tiranë - KS Kastrioti Krujë | 2-2(2-0) |
| KF Egnatia Rrogozhinë - KF Laçi | 0-0 | KF Laçi - KF Egnatia Rrogozhinë | 0-3(0-1) |
| KF Vllaznia Shkodër - FK Partizani Tiranë | 3-1(2-1) | FK Partizani Tiranë - KF Vllaznia Shkodër | 1-0(1-0) |
| KF Teuta Durrës - FK Kukësi | 2-0(0-0) | FK Kukësi - KF Teuta Durrës | 2-1(0-1) |

### Semi-Finals [26.04./10.05.2023]

| First Leg | | Second Leg | |
|---|---|---|---|
| KF Tiranë - KF Teuta Durrës | 3-0(1-0) | KF Teuta Durrës - KF Tiranë | 0-0 |
| KF Vllaznia Shkodër - KF Egnatia Rrogozhinë | 1-1(0-0) | KF Egnatia Rrogozhinë - KF Vllaznia Shkodër | 1-0(0-0) |

### Final

01.06.2023; Elbasan Arena, Elbasan; Referee: Enea Jorgji; Attendance: n/a
**KF Tiranë - KF Egnatia Rrogozhinë**          **0-1(0-0,0-0)**

**KF Tiranë**: Ilion Lika, Kristijan Toševski (108.Ermal Meta), Florjan Pergjoni, Jocelin Behiratche, Filip Najdovski, Ardit Hila, Ardit Deliu (119.Serxhio Tafa), Elvi Berisha [*sent off 25*], Rimal Haxhiu, Klevi Qefalija (95.Hajrulla Tola), Kristal Abazaj. Trainer: Orges Shehi.

**KF Egnatia**: Alen Sherri, Renato Malota (72.Sodiq Ololade Atanda), Emiljano Musta, Hysen Memolla, Abdurraman Fangaj (111.Bledar Lila), Donald Mëllugja (88.Gytis Paulauskas), Fernando Medeiros Da Silva, Arbin Zejnullai (63.Michael Agbekpornu), Jackson Kenio Santos Laurentino [*sent off 120+3*], Raphael Dwamena, Redi Kasa. Trainer: Edlir Tetova.

**Goal**: 0-1 Jackson Kenio Santos Laurentino (114).

## THE CLUBS 2022/2023

### Klubi i Futbollit Bylis Ballsh

| | | |
|---|---|---|
| **Founded**: | 1972 | |
| **Stadium**: | Stadiumi „Adush Muça", Ballsh (5,200) | |
| **Trainer**: | Arjan Bellaj | 01.02.1971 |
| [23.01.2023] | Naci Şensoy (KOS) | 20.02.1958 |

| Goalkeepers: | DOB | M | (s) | G |
|---|---|---|---|---|
| Renato Beqaj | 22.06.2004 | | (1) | |
| Oltjan Haremi | 02.09.1992 | 3 | | |
| Aldo Teqja | 04.05.1995 | 33 | (1) | |
| **Defenders:** | **DOB** | **M** | **(s)** | **G** |
| Mevlan Adili (MKD) | 30.03.1994 | 15 | (1) | 1 |
| Aleksandar Damčevski (MKD) | 21.11.1992 | 29 | (2) | 1 |
| Stivian Janku | 23.06.1997 | 18 | (2) | |
| Bleart Kastrati (KOS) | 17.02.2003 | | (2) | |
| Ariel Muçollari | 19.04.2001 | 4 | (6) | 1 |
| Xhejson Ndreu | 18.08.2003 | 1 | (4) | |
| Marcelino Preka | 02.08.2003 | 2 | | |
| Krenar Skenderaj | 29.12.2004 | 1 | (1) | |
| Aleksandër Trumci | 31.12.2000 | 34 | | 2 |
| Vangjel Zguro | 04.03.1993 | 17 | | 1 |
| Vasilis Zogos (GRE) | 29.07.1999 | 9 | (2) | |
| **Midfielders:** | **DOB** | **M** | **(s)** | **G** |
| Marin Abazaj | 31.03.2001 | 6 | (12) | |
| Sanaido Pereira Da Silva „Esquerdinha"(BRA) | 21.05.1991 | 22 | (6) | 3 |

| | DOB | M | (s) | G |
|---|---|---|---|---|
| Kristi Kote | 26.09.1998 | 1 | (1) | |
| Xhonatan Lajthia | 01.02.1999 | 21 | (8) | 3 |
| *Lorran* de Oliveira Quintanilha (BRA) | 28.01.1996 | 32 | (2) | |
| Xhoeli Maçolli | 23.09.2001 | 30 | (1) | |
| Eridon Qardaku | 10.08.2000 | 9 | (17) | |
| Aldo Qoshku (GRE) | 20.10.2000 | 13 | (10) | |
| Flamur Ruçi | 19.01.2002 | 20 | (13) | 2 |
| **Forwards:** | **DOB** | **M** | **(s)** | **G** |
| *Aires* Rodrigo Encarnação *Sousa* (POR) | 17.09.1998 | 3 | (5) | 1 |
| Amos Beji Anthony (NGA) | 04.01.1999 | 9 | (3) | 3 |
| Charles Atshimene (NGA) | 05.02.2001 | 1 | (12) | |
| Aboubacar Camara (CIV) | 04.01.2002 | | (2) | |
| Abu Danladi (GHA) | 18.10.1995 | 6 | (4) | 1 |
| Tomoyuki Doi (JPN) | 24.09.1997 | 2 | (5) | 1 |
| Babacar Fall (SEN) | 23.06.1905 | | (1) | |
| *Felipe Souza* Barros Ferreira (BRA) | 21.05.1998 | 11 | (5) | 3 |
| Joálisson Santos Oliveira „Jô Santos" (BRA) | 31.03.1991 | 12 | (1) | 3 |
| Luis Kaçorri | 24.02.1995 | 32 | (2) | 5 |
| Brice Tutu (FRA) | 11.01.1998 | | (5) | |

## Klubi i Futbollit Egnatia Rrogozhinë

| | | | |
|---|---|---|---|
| **Founded**: | 1934 | | |
| **Stadium**: | Arena Egnatia, Rrogozhinë (4,000) | | |
| **Trainer**: | Edlir Tetova | | 14.04.1983 |
| [16.10.2022] | Shpëtim Duro | | 24.12.1959 |
| [27.01.2023] | Edlir Tetova | | 14.04.1983 |

| Goalkeepers: | DOB | M | (s) | G |
|---|---|---|---|---|
| Bruno Puja | 20.01.2000 | 1 | | |
| Alen Sherri | 15.12.1997 | 35 | | |
| **Defenders:** | **DOB** | **M** | **(s)** | **G** |
| Sodiq Ololade Atanda (NGA) | 26.08.1993 | 31 | (4) | 1 |
| Abdurraman Fangaj | 12.10.1997 | 33 | | |
| Jurgen Goxha | 29.12.1992 | 1 | (1) | |
| Alessandro Kacbufi (ITA) | 13.05.2001 | 11 | (10) | |
| Bledar Lila | 19.10.2000 | 8 | (16) | |
| Renato Malota | 24.06.1989 | 30 | (1) | 1 |
| Hysen Memolla | 03.07.1992 | 10 | (3) | |
| Emiljano Musta | 31.01.1992 | 31 | (2) | 2 |
| Geri Selita | 08.03.2001 | 1 | (4) | |
| **Midfielders:** | **DOB** | **M** | **(s)** | **G** |
| Michael Agbekpornu (GHA) | 31.08.1998 | 20 | (6) | 1 |
| Eduards Emsis (LVA) | 23.02.1996 | 2 | (12) | |
| *Fernando Medeiros* Da Silva (BRA) | 10.02.1996 | 35 | (1) | 7 |
| Erald Hyseni | 12.11.1999 | | (1) | |
| Skerdilajd Levendi | 01.10.2001 | | (2) | |
| Donald Mëllugja | 31.05.1995 | 17 | (13) | 1 |
| Hamzat Basit Ojediran (NGA) | 14.11.2003 | 10 | (1) | |
| Arbin Zejnullai | 15.02.1999 | 26 | (7) | 3 |
| **Forwards:** | **DOB** | **M** | **(s)** | **G** |
| James Gbenga Ayinde (NGA) | 17.09.2001 | | (10) | |
| Claudivan dos Santos Bezerra "Bambam" (BRA) | 06.02.1994 | 2 | (6) | |
| Ilir Camaj (MNE) | 24.06.1996 | 10 | (2) | 2 |
| Dzon Delarge (CGO) | 24.06.1990 | 9 | (3) | 4 |
| Lorougnon Doukouo (CIV) | 16.11.2002 | | (6) | |
| Raphael Dwamena (GHA) | 12.09.1995 | 18 | | 11 |
| *Jackson* Kenio Santos Laurentino (BRA) | 24.04.1999 | 24 | (7) | 7 |
| Redi Kasa (ITA) | 01.09.2001 | 13 | (4) | 4 |
| Flavio Mecja | 15.04.2001 | 2 | (15) | |
| Redon Mihana | 28.06.1999 | 4 | (6) | |
| Gytis Paulauskas (LTU) | 27.09.1999 | 12 | (7) | 1 |

## Klubi Futbollit Erzeni Shijak

| | | | |
|---|---|---|---|
| **Founded**: | 1931 | | |
| **Stadium**: | Stadiumi „Niko Dovana", Durrës (12,040) | | |
| **Trainer**: | Xhevahir Kapllani | | 21.06.1974 |
| [20.05.2023] | Alfred Deliallisi | | 28.03.1993 |

| Goalkeepers: | DOB | M | (s) | G |
|---|---|---|---|---|
| Klevis Hasanbelli | 30.06.1997 | 3 | | |
| Dashamir Xhika | 23.05.1989 | 33 | | |
| **Defenders:** | **DOB** | **M** | **(s)** | **G** |
| Xhelil Asani | 12.09.1995 | 11 | (11) | 1 |
| *Enck* Pablo Oliveira de Souza (BRA) | 13.01.2000 | 20 | (5) | 2 |
| Ergi Goga | 25.10.2002 | | (1) | |
| Ardit Iljazi (MKD) | 16.06.2000 | 27 | (4) | 1 |
| Gëzim Krasniqi | 05.01.1990 | 19 | (3) | |
| Anteo Osmanllari | 11.10.1998 | 11 | (10) | |
| Ardit Peposhi | 14.03.1993 | 29 | | |
| Nehar Sadiki (MKD) | 16.03.1998 | 20 | (2) | 2 |
| *Vitor Leão* Damasceno (BRA) | 11.09.1998 | 5 | (7) | 1 |
| **Midfielders:** | **DOB** | **M** | **(s)** | **G** |
| *Alan Calbergue* Leite Rodrigues (BRA) | 11.07.1998 | 27 | (7) | 3 |
| Amir Kahrimanović (CRO) | 28.04.1999 | 31 | (4) | 8 |
| Elvis Kovaçi | 03.10.1998 | | (9) | |
| Marko Krivičič (SVN) | 01.02.1996 | 27 | (6) | |
| Adnard Mehmeti (KOS) | 23.01.2001 | 34 | | |
| Rejnaldo Troplini | 09.11.1994 | | (7) | |
| **Forwards:** | **DOB** | **M** | **(s)** | **G** |
| Ilirid Ademi (MKD) | 04.03.1995 | 28 | (3) | 3 |
| Shefki Aliti (SRB) | 27.07.2003 | | (2) | |
| Argel Avdiu | 29.05.2002 | 1 | (9) | |
| Florijan Kadriu (MKD) | 29.08.1996 | 30 | (2) | 1 |
| Dejvid Kapllani | 03.06.2001 | 5 | (12) | 1 |
| Sokol Kiqina (KOS) | 23.03.2002 | | (7) | |
| Progon Maloku | 27.01.2000 | 2 | (6) | |
| *Patrick* Carvalho Nonato (BRA) | 27.06.1997 | 33 | (1) | 12 |
| Thierno Thioub (SEN) | 01.06.1998 | | (10) | |

## Klubi Sportiv Kastrioti Krujë

| | | | |
|---|---|---|---|
| **Founded**: | 1926 | | |
| **Stadium**: | Stadiumi Kamëz, Kamëz (5,500) | | |
| **Trainer**: | Emiliano Çela | | 21.07.1985 |
| [14.12.2022] | Ardian Mema | | 16.11.1971 |
| [13.02.2023] | Emiliano Çela | | 21.07.1985 |

| Goalkeepers: | DOB | M | (s) | G |
|---|---|---|---|---|
| Livio Malaj | 25.05.2001 | 1 | (2) | |
| Edmir Sali | 07.08.1997 | 35 | | |
| **Defenders:** | **DOB** | **M** | **(s)** | **G** |
| Bekim Dida | 27.08.1997 | 2 | (3) | |
| Eneid Kodra | 04.11.1999 | 28 | (1) | |
| Martin Prenkočević (MNE) | 17.02.1999 | 9 | (8) | 1 |
| Armando Rami | 24.09.1997 | 23 | (1) | |
| Adolf Selmani | 26.06.2000 | 30 | | |
| Miloš Stojanović (SRB) | 18.01.1997 | 33 | (1) | 1 |
| Mikael Sulka | 10.01.2001 | 2 | (4) | |
| **Midfielders:** | **DOB** | **M** | **(s)** | **G** |
| Abjel Bejzade | 30.10.2001 | 4 | (6) | |
| Fjorest Grimci | 19.12.2002 | | (2) | |
| Edon Hasani | 09.01.1992 | 32 | (1) | 1 |
| Aaron Kacinari (SVN) | 18.08.2001 | 1 | (3) | |
| Abaz Karakaçi | 25.08.1992 | 32 | (1) | 1 |
| Xhuljo Mehmeti | 29.12.1993 | 20 | (5) | 1 |
| Olawale Onanuga (NGA) | 27.12.1997 | 23 | (5) | |
| **Forwards:** | **DOB** | **M** | **(s)** | **G** |
| Spartak Ajazi | 03.07.1994 | 5 | (17) | 1 |
| Zajsar Arapi | 20.10.2003 | 3 | (18) | |
| Moustapha Camara (SEN) | 05.06.2003 | 4 | (6) | |
| Joan Çela | 06.01.2000 | 8 | (10) | 1 |
| *Gabriel* Argolo *Morbeck* (BRA) | 20.08.1997 | 8 | (5) | 3 |
| Bedri Greca | 23.10.1990 | 32 | (2) | 5 |
| Franc Marinaj | 20.12.2001 | | (6) | |
| Redon Mihana | 28.06.1999 | 5 | (7) | 4 |
| *Reginaldo* Artur Faife (MOZ) | 14.06.1990 | 10 | (6) | 1 |
| Santiago Selmani | 22.01.2002 | 15 | (12) | 3 |
| Yousuf Salwan Zetuna (IRQ) | 10.03.1999 | 1 | (1) | |
| Silvio Zogaj | 25.07.1997 | 30 | (3) | 2 |

## Futboll Klub Kukësi

**Founded**: 04.03.1930
**Stadium**: Kukës Arena, Kukës (6,322)
**Trainer**: Skënder Gega — 14.11.1963
[11.09.2022] Enkeleid Dobi — 23.05.1975
[12.12.2022] Rrahman Hallaçi — 12.11.1983

| Goalkeepers: | DOB | M | (s) | G |
|---|---|---|---|---|
| Marvin Brozi | 07.07.2001 | 2 | | |
| Betim Halimi (KOS) | 28.02.1996 | 9 | | |
| Angelo Tafas | 05.07.2000 | 25 | | |
| **Defenders:** | **DOB** | **M** | **(s)** | **G** |
| Altin Bytyçi (KOS) | 14.01.2001 | 27 | (5) | 1 |
| Redon Dragoshi | 18.03.2000 | 12 | (4) | |
| Ebert Cardoso da Silva (BRA) | 25.05.1993 | 28 | (1) | 1 |
| Antonio Ilieski (MKD) | 23.07.1996 | 13 | (3) | |
| Franko Lamçe | 30.07.1998 | 12 | (2) | |
| Jorgo Meksi | 21.03.1995 | 4 | (3) | |
| Endri Murati | 15.11.2001 | 1 | (2) | |
| Edison Ndreca | 05.07.1994 | 34 | | 2 |
| Tiago Emanuel Canelas Almeida Ferreira (POR) | 10.07.1993 | 13 | | 1 |
| **Midfielders:** | **DOB** | **M** | **(s)** | **G** |
| Agnaldo Pinto de Moraes Júnior (BRA) | 11.03.1994 | 5 | (2) | |
| Olalekan Ibrahim Alliu (NGA) | | | (1) | |
| Mirza Delimeđac (SRB) | 24.10.1999 | 7 | (8) | 1 |
| Abdou M'Bark El Id (MTN) | 16.06.1999 | 19 | (4) | |
| Françesko Hasaj | 22.07.2001 | 4 | (9) | |
| Rimal Haxhiu | 04.03.1999 | 17 | | |
| Kristi Kote | 26.09.1998 | 2 | (4) | |
| Daniel Momoh (NGA) | 15.03.2002 | 9 | (3) | |
| Layton Julius Ndukwu (ENG) | 07.09.1998 | 1 | (4) | |
| Darling Peposhi | 28.11.2005 | | (1) | |
| Eogen Sula | 23.06.2003 | 1 | (10) | |
| Gjelbrim Taipi (KOS) | 13.12.1992 | 36 | | 5 |
| Šçiprim Taipi | 19.02.1997 | 28 | (5) | 2 |
| **Forwards:** | **DOB** | **M** | **(s)** | **G** |
| Edwin Oppong Anane-Gyasi (GHA) | 01.07.1991 | 7 | (3) | |
| Gabriel Barbosa Avelino (BRA) | 17.03.1999 | 18 | (11) | 5 |
| Edi Baša (CRO) | 29.06.1993 | 26 | (5) | 4 |
| Jakup Berisha (MKD) | 20.02.2000 | 4 | (12) | |
| Klejdi Daci | 22.04.1999 | 4 | (7) | 2 |
| Fluturim Domi | 14.10.2000 | 2 | (9) | |
| Marjus Kola | 18.05.2001 | | (1) | |
| Juan David Martínez Sánchez (COL) | 03.05.2001 | | (3) | |
| Johnson Owusu (GHA) | 05.02.1998 | 8 | (5) | 1 |
| Ergys Peposhi | 26.08.2000 | 4 | (19) | |
| Atdhe Rashiti | 02.05.1999 | 11 | (2) | 3 |
| Ante Živković (CRO) | 21.05.1993 | 3 | (5) | 2 |

## Klubi i Futbollit Laçi

**Founded**: 1960
**Stadium**: Stadiumi Laçi, Laçi (2,300)
**Trainer**: Dejan Vukićević (MNE) — 27.04.1968
[20.11.2022] Gentian Mezani — 13.10.1979
[05.04.2023] Stavri Nica — 08.07.1954

| Goalkeepers: | DOB | M | (s) | G |
|---|---|---|---|---|
| Mario Dajsinani | 23.12.1998 | 19 | (1) | |
| Gentian Selmani | 09.03.1998 | 17 | | |
| **Defenders:** | **DOB** | **M** | **(s)** | **G** |
| Albi Alla (GRE) | 01.02.1993 | 11 | (4) | |
| Luka Cucin (SRB) | 24.11.1998 | 9 | (4) | |
| Nikolin Duka | 01.05.2000 | 7 | (7) | |
| Arlind Kurti | 24.01.2005 | 2 | (4) | |
| Endrit Marku | 22.02.2001 | 1 | (3) | |
| Marko Roganović (MNE) | 21.06.1996 | 33 | | |
| Rudolf Turkaj | 03.02.1995 | 26 | (3) | 1 |
| Viktor Velkoski (MKD) | 14.11.1995 | 32 | (1) | 1 |
| Renato Ziko | 16.11.1997 | 33 | | |
| **Midfielders:** | **DOB** | **M** | **(s)** | **G** |
| Michel Babatunde (NGA) | 24.12.1992 | 10 | (14) | 2 |
| Mario Barjamaj | 27.06.1998 | 5 | (12) | |
| Stiven Bibo | 26.09.2003 | 6 | (1) | 2 |
| Ariel Borysiuk (POL) | 29.07.1991 | 12 | (2) | 1 |
| Isi Manellari | 31.01.1998 | 27 | (4) | |
| Olsi Myrta | 20.01.2006 | 1 | | |
| Mykyta Peterman (UKR) | 12.06.1999 | 4 | (2) | |
| Klinti Qato | 23.12.1997 | 3 | (6) | |
| Sebastjan Spahiu (BEL) | 30.10.1999 | 27 | (6) | 2 |
| Serxho Ujka | 27.08.1998 | 30 | (1) | 7 |
| **Forwards:** | **DOB** | **M** | **(s)** | **G** |
| Adeleke Akinola Akinyemi (NGA) | 11.08.1998 | 19 | | 6 |
| Segerso Geci | 16.08.2001 | 1 | (7) | 1 |
| Saliou Guindo (MLI) | 12.09.1996 | 15 | (3) | 11 |
| Đorđe Ivković (SRB) | 06.03.1996 | 1 | (3) | |
| Mentor Mazrekaj | 08.02.1989 | 29 | (5) | 3 |
| Fatmir Prengaj | 01.05.2001 | 1 | (5) | |
| Vasil Shkurtaj | 27.02.1992 | 15 | (11) | 6 |

## Futboll Klub Partizani Tiranë

**Founded**: 04.02.1946
**Stadium**: Kompleksi Sportiv Partizani, Tiranë (4,500)
**Trainer**: Giovanni Colella (ITA) — 10.08.1966

| Goalkeepers: | DOB | M | (s) | G |
|---|---|---|---|---|
| Alban Hoxha | 23.11.1987 | 4 | | |
| Bekim Redjepi (MKD) | 27.10.1996 | 32 | | |
| **Defenders:** | **DOB** | **M** | **(s)** | **G** |
| David Atanaskoski (MKD) | 21.10.1996 | 20 | (11) | 1 |
| Eneo Bitri | 26.08.1996 | 17 | | 2 |
| Paulo Buxhelaj | 01.05.2003 | 16 | (10) | |
| Andi Hadroj | 22.02.1999 | 34 | | |
| Jozef Menich (SVK) | 15.09.1994 | 9 | (14) | |
| Marcelino Preka | 02.08.2003 | 9 | (2) | |
| Saliou Sembene (SEN) | 26.10.2001 | | (2) | |
| Elion Sota | 24.05.1998 | 30 | (1) | 1 |
| Henri Zuna | 24.05.2003 | 1 | (3) | |
| **Midfielders:** | **DOB** | **M** | **(s)** | **G** |
| Galip Arapi | 20.01.2001 | | (2) | |
| Sabit Bilali (MKD) | 15.08.1997 | 3 | (8) | |
| Maguette Gueye (SEN) | 30.12.2002 | 7 | (9) | 1 |
| Xhafer Hodo | 03.05.2003 | 4 | (3) | |
| Engjell Hoti (KOS) | 26.02.1997 | 16 | (13) | 7 |
| Mal Januzi (MKD) | 05.05.2004 | | (1) | |
| Chandrel Géraud Massanga Matondo (CGO) | 17.08.1999 | 27 | (3) | 1 |
| Valentino Murataj | 15.08.1996 | 31 | (3) | 1 |
| Hermes Aristóteles Romero Espinoza (VEN) | 18.10.1995 | 1 | (1) | |
| Arinaldo Rrapaj | 09.08.2001 | 33 | (1) | 6 |
| Bruno Telushi | 14.11.1990 | 20 | (6) | |
| Vitor Matheus Da Silva Matos (BRA) | 04.01.1995 | 23 | (3) | 13 |
| Leart Zekolli (KOS) | 24.10.2001 | | (11) | |
| **Forwards:** | **DOB** | **M** | **(s)** | **G** |
| Tedi Cara | 15.04.2000 | 20 | (15) | 6 |
| Matej Cvetanoski (MKD) | 18.08.1997 | | (8) | |
| Klevis Dragaj | 22.03.2003 | | (4) | |
| Christian Mba (NGA) | 12.10.1999 | 16 | (2) | 5 |
| Alfred Mensah (GHA) | 08.08.1999 | 4 | (23) | 1 |
| Orjel Murati | 10.01.2002 | | (1) | |
| Remzi Selmani (MKD) | 05.05.1997 | 3 | (2) | 1 |
| Fabian Shahaj | 16.06.2002 | | (2) | |
| Xhuliano Skuka | 02.08.1998 | 16 | (1) | 10 |

## Klubi Futbollit Teuta Durrës

| Founded: | 1920 | |
|---|---|---|
| Stadium: | Stadiumi „Niko Dovana", Durrës (12,040) | |
| Trainer: | Renato Arapi | 28.08.1986 |
| [06.09.2022] | Bledi Shkëmbi | 13.08.1979 |
| [23.11.2022] | Eduard Martini | 02.01.1975 |

| Goalkeepers: | DOB | M | (s) | G |
|---|---|---|---|---|
| Endri Dema | 17.04.2004 | 2 | (1) | |
| Panajot Qirko | 26.06.1999 | 34 | | |
| **Defenders:** | **DOB** | **M** | **(s)** | **G** |
| David Gjinollari | 17.04.1999 | 12 | (12) | |
| Jurgen Goxha | 29.12.1992 | 6 | (5) | 1 |
| Klaid Hoxha | 14.08.2001 | | (1) | |
| Hektor Idrizaj | 15.04.1989 | 7 | (2) | |
| Artan Jazxhi | 06.07.2001 | 26 | (1) | 2 |
| Blerim Kotobelli | 10.08.1992 | 32 | (1) | 1 |
| Alexandros Kouros (GRE) | 21.08.1993 | 33 | | |
| Reild Kurti | 17.10.2002 | 1 | (3) | |
| Albion Marku | 14.10.2000 | 34 | | 2 |
| Harallamb Qaqi | 17.09.1993 | 15 | (3) | |
| **Midfielders:** | **DOB** | **M** | **(s)** | **G** |
| Ledjo Beqja | 18.06.2001 | 34 | | 1 |
| Muço Boçi | 09.06.2003 | 4 | (9) | |
| Alban Çejku | 23.07.2001 | 2 | (5) | |
| Arbër Çyrbja | 18.09.1993 | 4 | (22) | |
| Devid Fejzulla | 13.02.2003 | | (3) | |
| Danilo Gecaj | 21.07.2000 | | (1) | |
| Arseld Halilaj | 11.01.2004 | | (3) | |
| Uheid Hoxha | 01.08.2000 | | (2) | |
| Sherif Kallaku | 01.03.1998 | 20 | | 6 |
| Erando Karabeci | 06.09.1988 | 23 | (1) | 1 |
| Jurgen Muka | 19.07.2002 | 2 | | |
| Emiljano Vila | 12.03.1988 | 29 | (3) | 3 |
| **Forwards:** | **DOB** | **M** | **(s)** | **G** |
| Klejdi Daci | 22.04.1999 | 6 | (9) | 1 |
| Ildi Gruda | 13.02.1999 | 17 | (9) | 4 |
| Rubin Hebaj | 30.07.1998 | 13 | (2) | 1 |
| Dejvid Kapllani | 03.06.2001 | | (2) | |
| Aldrit Oshafi | 26.03.2000 | 5 | (16) | 1 |
| Lorenco Vila | 14.12.1998 | 35 | | 9 |

## Klubi i Futbollit Tirana

| Founded: | 15.08.1920 (*as Shoqata Sportive Agimi*) | |
|---|---|---|
| Stadium: | Stadiumi"Selman Stërmasi", Tiranë (9,500) | |
| Trainer: | Orges Shehi | 25.09.1977 |

| Goalkeepers: | DOB | M | (s) | G |
|---|---|---|---|---|
| Visar Bekaj (KOS) | 24.05.1997 | 34 | | |
| Ilion Lika | 17.05.1980 | 2 | | |
| **Defenders:** | **DOB** | **M** | **(s)** | **G** |
| Jocelin Behiratche (CIV) | 08.05.2000 | 22 | (6) | 1 |
| Arbër Bytyqi | 16.10.2003 | | (1) | |
| Lukman Hussein (NGA) | 28.08.1996 | 3 | (2) | |
| Besir Iseni (MKD) | 02.05.2000 | 2 | (5) | |
| Marsel Ismajlgeci | 14.03.2000 | 16 | (2) | |
| Bruno Lulaj | 02.04.1995 | 18 | (6) | 2 |
| Florjan Pergjoni | 22.06.1997 | 28 | (4) | 1 |
| Kristijan Toševski (MKD) | 06.05.1994 | 22 | (2) | |
| Realf Zhivanaj | 15.03.1998 | 2 | (1) | |
| **Midfielders:** | **DOB** | **M** | **(s)** | **G** |
| Albano Aleksi | 10.10.1992 | 33 | | |
| Danilo Bajraktari | 08.07.2004 | | (1) | |
| Ardit Deliu | 26.10.1997 | 27 | (4) | 1 |
| Rimal Haxhiu | 04.03.1999 | 16 | (1) | 2 |
| Ardit Hila | 06.01.1993 | 16 | (13) | 6 |
| Sherif Kallaku | 01.03.1998 | 14 | (1) | 2 |
| Vesel Limaj (GER) | 01.12.1996 | 6 | (8) | 1 |
| Regi Lushkja | 17.05.1996 | 13 | (3) | |
| Filip Najdovski (MKD) | 13.09.1992 | 30 | | |
| Klevi Qefalija | 12.12.2003 | 3 | (9) | |
| Hajrulla Tola | 01.07.2004 | | (1) | |
| **Forwards:** | **DOB** | **M** | **(s)** | **G** |
| Kristal Abazaj | 06.07.1996 | 9 | (5) | 4 |
| Elvi Berisha | 02.03.1999 | 2 | (14) | |
| Aldi Gjumsi | 15.03.2002 | 3 | (14) | |
| Florent Hasani (KOS) | 30.03.1997 | 34 | | 16 |
| Dijar Nikqi | 20.10.2004 | 5 | (16) | 2 |
| *Patrick* Robson de Souza Monteiro (BRA) | 11.05.1998 | 18 | (4) | 6 |
| Taulant Fatmir Seferi (MKD) | 15.11.1996 | 1 | | |
| Redon Xhixha | 14.07.1998 | 17 | | 11 |

## Klubi I Futbollit Vllaznia Shkodër

| Founded: | 16.02.1919 (*as Shoqëria Sportive Vllaznia*) | |
|---|---|---|
| Stadium: | Stadiumi „Loro Boriçi", Shkodër (16,000) | |
| Trainer: | Mirel Josa | 01.06.1963 |
| [20.03.2023] | Auron Selaudin Miloti | 04.08.1974 |
| [03.04.2023] | Goce Sedloski (MKD) | 10.04.1974 |

| Goalkeepers: | DOB | M | (s) | G |
|---|---|---|---|---|
| Bojan Zogović (MNE) | 16.02.1989 | 36 | | |
| **Defenders:** | **DOB** | **M** | **(s)** | **G** |
| Darko Bulatović (MNE) | 05.09.1989 | 22 | (1) | |
| Erdenis Gurishta | 24.04.1995 | 30 | | |
| Ersin Hakaj | 06.12.1996 | 28 | (1) | 2 |
| Marko Jurić (CRO) | 07.10.1994 | 23 | (1) | 1 |
| Dajan Shehi | 19.03.1997 | 17 | (5) | |
| Geralb Smajli | 16.05.2002 | 15 | (3) | |
| **Midfielders:** | **DOB** | **M** | **(s)** | **G** |
| Rejan Alivoda | 05.06.2003 | 20 | (10) | |
| Lorik Boshnjaku (KOS) | 07.07.1995 | 23 | (3) | |
| Antonio Delaj | 06.09.2003 | | (5) | |
| Elvedin Herić (BIH) | 09.02.1997 | 6 | (15) | 1 |
| Fjoart Jonuzi | 09.07.1996 | 34 | (1) | 7 |
| Arsid Kruja | 08.06.1993 | 11 | (15) | |
| Esat Mala | 18.10.1998 | 23 | (1) | 3 |
| Herald Marku | 18.05.1996 | 29 | (6) | 7 |
| Kristijan Vulaj (MNE) | 25.06.1998 | | (7) | |
| **Forwards:** | **DOB** | **M** | **(s)** | **G** |
| Ante Aralica (CRO) | 23.07.1996 | 5 | (4) | 1 |
| Bekim Balaj | 11.01.1991 | 18 | (2) | 3 |
| Mehdi Çoba | 09.03.2000 | 12 | (13) | 3 |
| Ardit Hoxhaj | 20.07.1994 | 22 | (14) | 5 |
| *Kainã* Nunes da Silva Amarante (BRA) | 31.05.1997 | 9 | (24) | 4 |
| Liridon Latifi | 06.02.1994 | 13 | (4) | 2 |

# SECOND LEVEL
## Albanian First Division / Kategoria e Parë 2022/2023

| | | | | | | | | | | |
|---|---|---|---|---|---|---|---|---|---|---|
| 1. | KF Skënderbeu Korçë (*Promoted*) | 26 | 13 | 10 | 3 | 37 | - | 13 | 49 |
| 2. | FK Dinamo Tiranë (*Promoted*) | 26 | 14 | 5 | 7 | 48 | - | 23 | 47 |
| 3. | Flamurtari FC Vlorë | 26 | 13 | 7 | 6 | 40 | - | 16 | 46 |
| 4. | KF Tomori Berat | 26 | 13 | 4 | 9 | 29 | - | 27 | 43 |
| 5. | KS Korabi Peshkopi | 26 | 10 | 9 | 7 | 32 | - | 24 | 39 |
| 6. | KF Apolonia Fier | 26 | 10 | 8 | 8 | 31 | - | 30 | 38 |
| 7. | KF Luzi I Vogël 2008 | 26 | 10 | 8 | 8 | 31 | - | 26 | 38 |
| 8. | KF Besa Kavajë | 26 | 10 | 7 | 9 | 32 | - | 26 | 37 |
| 9. | KF Lushnja | 26 | 8 | 8 | 10 | 30 | - | 42 | 32 |
| 10. | KF Burreli | 26 | 7 | 10 | 9 | 22 | - | 29 | 31 |
| 11. | KF Oriku (*Relegated*) | 26 | 9 | 3 | 14 | 27 | - | 33 | 30 |
| 12. | KF Turbina Cërrik (*Relegated*) | 26 | 7 | 5 | 14 | 24 | - | 45 | 26 |
| 13. | KF Tërbuni Pukë* (*Relegated*) | 26 | 6 | 6 | 14 | 16 | - | 41 | 24 |
| 14. | KF Besëlidhja Lezhë** (*Relegated*) | 26 | 3 | 8 | 15 | 17 | - | 41 | 14 |

Teams ranked 3-6 were qualified for the Promotion Play-offs, while teams ranked 9-10 were qualified for the Relegation Play-out.

\* KF Tërbuni Pukë was excluded and relegated after violent incidents during a league match (Round 21, against KF Turbina Cërrik).
\*\*3 points deducted for no showing in one league match (against KS Korabi Peshkopi).

## Promotion Play-offs

| Semi-Finals [23.05.2023] | Flamurtari FC Vlorë* - KF Apolonia Fier | 1-1(1-0) |
|---|---|---|
| | KF Tomori Berat - KS Korabi Peshkopi | 0-1(0-0) |

*qualified as having higher ranking.*

| Final [28.05.2023] | Flamurtari FC Vlorë - KS Korabi Peshkopi | 1-2(0-1) |
|---|---|---|

KS Korabi Peshkopi were qualified for the Promotion Play-off against the 8th ranked team of Kategoria Superiore.

## Relegation Play-out (2nd / 3rd Level) [23-26.05.2023]

| KF Lushnja - KF Valbona | 1-0(1-0) |
|---|---|
| KF Burreli - KS Pogradeci | 2-1(0-1) |

KF Lushnja and KF Burreli will play at second level in 2023/2024.

# NATIONAL TEAM

## INTERNATIONAL MATCHES
### (16.07.2022 – 15.07.2023)

| 24.09.2022 | Tel Aviv | *Israel - Albania* | *2-1(0-0)* | (UNL) |
|---|---|---|---|---|
| 27.09.2022 | Tiranë | *Albania - Iceland* | *1-1(1-0)* | (UNL) |
| 26.10.2022 | Abu Dhabi | *Saudi Arabia - Albania* | *1-1(1-0)* | (F) |
| 09.11.2022 | Marbella | *Qatar - Albania* | *1-0(1-0)* | (F) |
| 16.11.2022 | Tiranë | *Albania - Italy* | *1-3(1-2)* | (F) |
| 19.11.2022 | Tiranë | *Albania - Armenia* | *2-0(1-0)* | (F) |
| 27.03.2023 | Warszawa | *Poland - Albania* | *1-0(1-0)* | (ECQ) |
| 17.06.2023 | Tiranë | *Albania - Moldova* | *2-0(0-0)* | (ECQ) |
| 20.06.2023 | Tórshavn | *Faroe Islands - Albania* | *1-3(1-1)* | (ECQ) |

**24.09.2022    ISRAEL - ALBANIA**              **2-1(0-0)**              3rd UEFA Nations League B, Group 2
Bloomfield Stadium, Tel Aviv; Referee: Donatas Rumšas (Lithuania); Attendance: 29,200
**ALB:** Thomas Fotaq Strakosha, Iván Salvador Balliu Campeny (46.Frédéric Shtjefan Veseli), Ardian Ilmi Ismajli, Arlind Afrim Ajeti (78.Enea Mihaj), Elseid Gëzim Hysaj (Cap), Qazim Laçi, Klaus Fatmir Gjasula, Amir Malush Abrashi (67.Ylber Latif Ramadani), Kristjan Asllani (67.Nedim Bajrami), Armando Broja, Sokol Cikalleshi (78.Myrto Artan Uzuni). Trainer: Edoardo Reja (Italy).
**Goal:** Myrto Artan Uzuni (88).

**27.09.2022    ALBANIA - ICELAND**              **1-1(1-0)**              3rd UEFA Nations League B, Group 2
Arena Kombëtare, Tiranë; Referee: Ricardo de Burgos Bengoetxea (Spain); Attendance: 8,800
**ALB:** Thomas Fotaq Strakosha, Iván Salvador Balliu Campeny, Ardian Ilmi Ismajli, Frédéric Shtjefan Veseli, Klaus Fatmir Gjasula (83.Enea Mihaj), Ermir Limon Lenjani (77.Elseid Gëzim Hysaj), Amir Malush Abrashi (69.Qazim Laçi), Ylber Latif Ramadani, Nedim Bajrami (83.Enis Çokaj), Myrto Artan Uzuni, Sokol Cikalleshi (Cap) (69.Armando Broja). Trainer: Edoardo Reja (Italy).
**Goal:** Ermir Limon Lenjani (38).

**26.10.2022    SAUDI ARABIA - ALBANIA**              **1-1(1-0)**              Friendly International
Al Nahyan Stadium, Abu Dhabi (United Arab Emirates); Referee: Adel Ali Ahmed Khamis Al Naqbi (United Arab Emirates); Attendance: 0
**ALB:** Elhan Kastrati (46.Gentian Selmani), Albion Marku (46.Odise Roshi), Eneo Bitri (61.Stivian Janku), Rudolf Turkaj (61.Esin Hakaj), Erdenis Gurishta, Andi Hadroj (46.Mario Mitaj), Ardit Deliu (61.Ardit Toli), Esat Mala (46.Arinaldo Rrapaj), Arbnor Muçolli (46.Sherif Kallaku), Redon Xhixha (47.Xhuliano Skuka), Sokol Cikalleshi (Cap) (46.Bekim Abdyl Balaj; 78.Lorenco Vila). Trainer: Edoardo Reja (Italy).
**Goal:** Bekim Abdyl Balaj (47).

**09.11.2022    QATAR - ALBANIA**                    **1-0(1-0)**                    Friendly International
Estadio Municipal "Antonio Lorenzo Cuevas", Marbella (Spain); Referee: Jason Lee Barcelo (Gibraltar); Attendance: 0
**ALB:** Mario Dajsinani (46.Alen Sherri), Andi Hadroj, Stivian Janku (46.Eneo Bitri), Rudolf Turkaj, Erdenis Gurishta, Esin Hakaj (64.Marsel Ismailgeci), Arinaldo Rrapaj, Serxho Ujka, Sherif Kallaku (Cap) (46.Herald Marku), Kristal Abazaj (81.Redon Xhixha), Tedi Cara (65.Xhuliano Skuka). Trainer: Edoardo Reja (Italy).

**16.11.2022    ALBANIA - ITALY**                    **1-3(1-2)**                    Friendly International
Arena Kombëtare, Tiranë; Referee: Genc Nuza (Kosovo); Attendance: 22,000
**ALB:** Etrit Fadil Berisha (Cap), Elseid Gëzim Hysaj, Ardian Ilmi Ismajli (71.Adrian Bajrami), Marash Kumbulla, Enea Mihaj, Ermir Limon Lenjani, Amir Malush Abrashi (77.Ylber Latif Ramadani), Keidi Bare (87.Qazim Laçi), Nedim Bajrami (71.Kristjan Asllani), Myrto Artan Uzuni (77.Xhuliano Skuka), Armando Broja (51.Odise Roshi). Trainer: Edoardo Reja (Italy).
**Goal:** Ardian Ilmi Ismajli (16).

**19.11.2022    ALBANIA - ARMENIA**                    **2-0(1-0)**                    Friendly International
Arena Kombëtare, Tiranë; Referee: Aleksandar Stavrev (North Macedonia); Attendance: n/a
**ALB:** Etrit Fadil Berisha (Cap), Andi Hadroj (65.Elseid Gëzim Hysaj), Adrian Bajrami, Marash Kumbulla (67.Eneo Bitri), Enea Mihaj, Ermir Limon Lenjani, Kristjan Asllani, Enis Çokaj (46.Keidi Bare), Qazim Laçi (46.Ylber Latif Ramadani), Ernest Muçi (46.Tedi Cara), Xhuliano Skuka (71.Arbnor Muçolli). Trainer: Edoardo Reja (Italy).
**Goals:** Xhuliano Skuka (28), Kristjan Asllani (64 penalty).

**27.03.2023    POLAND - ALBANIA**                    **1-0(1-0)**                    17th EC. Qualifiers
Stadion Narodowy, Warszawa; Referee: Slavko Vinčić (Slovenia); Attendance: 56,227
**ALB:** Thomas Fotaq Strakosha, Iván Salvador Balliu Campeny, Enea Mihaj, Marash Kumbulla, Elseid Gëzim Hysaj (Cap), Ylber Latif Ramadani, Jasir Fadil Asani (70.Anis Mehmeti), Klaus Fatmir Gjasula (88.Qazim Laçi), Kristjan Asllani (76.Nedim Bajrami), Myrto Artan Uzuni, Sokol Cikalleshi (76.Taulant Fatmir Seferi). Trainer: Sylvio Mendes Campos Junior "Sylvinho" (Brazil).

**17.06.2023    ALBANIA - MOLDOVA**                    **2-0(0-0)**                    17th EC. Qualifiers
Arena Kombëtare, Tiranë; Referee: Dennis Higler (Netherlands); Attendance: 20,944
**ALB:** Etrit Fadil Berisha, Elseid Gëzim Hysaj (Cap), Ardian Ilmi Ismajli, Berat Ridvan Gjimshiti, Mario Mitaj, Ylber Latif Ramadani, Keidi Bare (67.Kristjan Asllani), Nedim Bajrami (88.Ernest Muçi), Jasir Fadil Asani (67.Anis Mehmeti), Myrto Artan Uzuni (87.Taulant Fatmir Seferi), Sokol Cikalleshi. Trainer: Sylvio Mendes Campos Junior "Sylvinho" (Brazil).
**Goals:** Jasir Fadil Asani (52), Adrian Bajrami (76).

**20.06.2023    FAROE ISLANDS - ALBANIA**                    **1-3(1-1)**                    17th EC. Qualifiers
Tórsvøllur, Tórshavn; Referee: Chrysovalantis Theouli (Cyprus); Attendance: 2,507
**ALB:** Etrit Fadil Berisha, Elseid Gëzim Hysaj (Cap), Ardian Ilmi Ismajli, Berat Ridvan Gjimshiti, Mario Mitaj, Kristjan Asllani (88.Keidi Bare), Ylber Latif Ramadani, Jasir Fadil Asani (75.Anis Mehmeti), Nedim Bajrami (75.Ernest Muçi), Taulant Fatmir Seferi (89.Armando Durim Sadiku), Sokol Cikalleshi (67.Myrto Artan Uzuni). Trainer: Sylvio Mendes Campos Junior "Sylvinho" (Brazil).
**Goals:** Adrian Bajrami (20), Kristjan Asllani (51), Ernest Muçi (90+1).

| NATIONAL TEAM PLAYERS (16.07.2022 – 15.07.2023) | | | | |
|---|---|---|---|---|
| **Name** | **DOB** | **Caps** | **Goals** | **Club** |
| Goalkeepers | | | | |
| Etrit Fadil BERISHA | 10.03.1989 | 77 | 0 | 2022/2023: *Torino FC (ITA)* |
| Mario DAJSINANI | 23.12.1998 | 1 | 0 | 2022: *KF Laçi* |
| Elhan KASTRATI | 02.02.1997 | 2 | 0 | 2022: *AS Cittadella (ITA)* |
| Gentian SELMANI | 09.03.1998 | 4 | 0 | 2022: *Boluspor Kulübü (TUR)* |
| Alen SHERRI | 15.12.1997 | 1 | 0 | 2022: *KF Egnatia Rrogozhinë* |
| Thomas Fotaq STRAKOSHA | 19.03.1995 | 19 | 0 | 2022/2023: *Brentford FC London (ENG)* |
| Defenders | | | | |
| Arlind Afrim AJETI | 25.09.1993 | 22 | 1 | 2022: *Pordedone Calcio (ITA)* |
| Adrian BAJRAMI | 05.04.2002 | 3 | 0 | 2022: *Sport Lisboa e Benfica (POR)* |
| Iván Salvador BALLIU Campeny | 01.01.1992 | 9 | 0 | 2022/2023: *Rayo Vallecano de Madrid (ESP)* |
| Eneo BITRI | 26.08.1996 | 3 | 0 | 2022: *FK Partizani Tiranë* |
| Berat Ridvan GJIMSHITI | 19.02.1993 | 50 | 1 | 2023: *Atalanta Bergamasca Calcio (ITA)* |
| Erdenis GURISHTA | 24.04.1995 | 2 | 0 | 2022: *KF Vllaznia Shkodër* |
| Andi HADROJ | 22.02.1999 | 3 | 0 | 2022: *FK Partizani Tiranë* |
| Esin HAKAJ | 06.12.1996 | 2 | 0 | 2022: *KF Vllaznia Shkodër* |
| Elseid Gëzim HYSAJ | 02.02.1994 | 77 | 2 | 2022/2023: *SS Lazio Roma (ITA)* |
| Marsel ISMAILGECI | 14.03.2000 | 2 | 0 | 2022: *KF Tiranë* |
| Ardian Ilmi ISMAJLI | 30.09.1996 | 32 | 2 | 2022/2023: *Empoli FC (ITA)* |
| Stivian JANKU | 23.06.1997 | 2 | 0 | 2022: *KF Bylis Ballsh* |
| Marash KUMBULLA | 08.02.2000 | 18 | 0 | 2022/2023: *AS Roma (ITA)* |
| Ermir Limon LENJANI | 05.08.1989 | 45 | 5 | 2022: *Ümraniyespor Kulübü (TUR)* |
| Albion MARKU | 14.10.2000 | 1 | 0 | 2022: *KF Teuta Durrës* |
| Enea MIHAJ | 05.07.1998 | 14 | 0 | 2022/2023: *FC Famalicão (POR)* |
| Mario MITAJ | 06.08.2003 | 4 | 0 | 2022/2023: *FK Lokomotiv Moskva (RUS)* |

| Ardit TOLI | 12.07.1997 | 1 | 0 | 2022: | FK Vorskla Poltava (UKR) |
| Rudolf TURKAJ | 03.02.1995 | 2 | 0 | 2022: | KF Laçi |
| Frédéric Shtjefan VESELI | 20.11.1992 | 44 | 0 | 2022: | Benevento Calcio (ITA) |

### Midfielders

| | | | | | |
|---|---|---|---|---|---|
| Kristal ABAZAJ | 06.07.1996 | 2 | 0 | 2022: | Istanbulspor Kulübü (TUR) |
| Amir Malush ABRASHI | 27.03.1990 | 50 | 1 | 2022: | Grasshopper Club Zürich (SUI) |
| Kristjan ASLLANI | 09.03.2002 | 10 | 2 | 2022/2023: | FC Internazionale Milano (ITA) |
| Nedim BAJRAMI | 28.02.1999 | 8 | 0 | 2022: 31.01.2023-> | Empoli FC (ITA); US Sassuolo Calcio (ITA) |
| Keidi BARE | 28.08.1997 | 25 | 2 | 2022/2023: | RCD Espanyol Barcelona (ESP) |
| Enis ÇOKAJ | 23.02.1999 | 5 | 0 | 2022: | PAE Panathinaïkos Athína (GRE) |
| Ardit DELIU | 26.10.1997 | 1 | 0 | 2022: | KF Tiranë |
| Klaus Fatmir GJASULA | 14.12.1989 | 22 | 0 | 2022/2023: | SV Darmstadt 98 (GER) |
| Sherif KALLAKU | 01.03.1998 | 7 | 0 | 2022: | KF Tiranë |
| Qazim LAÇI | 19.01.1996 | 21 | 1 | 2022: 01.01.2023-> | AC Ajaccio (FRA); AC Sparta Praha (CZE) |
| Esat MALA | 18.10.1998 | 1 | 0 | 2022: | KF Vllaznia Shkodër |
| Herald MARKU | 18.05.1996 | 1 | 0 | 2022: | KF Vllaznia Shkodër |
| Anis MEHMETI | 09.01.2001 | 3 | 0 | 2023: | Bristol City FC (ENG) |
| Arbnor MUÇOLLI | 15.09.1999 | 3 | 0 | 2022: | Vejle Boldklub (DEN) |
| Ylber Latif RAMADANI | 12.04.1996 | 27 | 1 | 2022/2023: | Aberdeen FC (SCO) |
| Odise ROSHI | 22.05.1991 | 71 | 5 | 2022: | Sakaryaspor Kulübü (TUR) |
| Arinaldo RRAPAJ | 09.08.2001 | 2 | 0 | 2022: | FK Partizani Tiranë |
| Serxho UJKA | 27.08.1998 | 1 | 0 | 2022: | KF Laçi |

### Forwards

| | | | | | |
|---|---|---|---|---|---|
| Jasir Fadil ASANI | 19.05.1995 | 3 | 1 | 2023: | Gwangju FC (KOR) |
| Bekim Abdyl BALAJ | 11.01.1991 | 48 | 9 | 2022: | Ankara Keçiörengücü SK (TUR) |
| Armando BROJA | 10.09.2001 | 17 | 4 | 2022: | Chelsea FC London (ENG) |
| Tedi CARA | 15.04.2000 | 2 | 0 | 2022: | FK Partizani Tiranë |
| Sokol CIKALLESHI | 27.07.1990 | 54 | 12 | 2022/2023: | Khaleej FC Saihat (KSA) |
| Ernest MUÇI | 19.03.2001 | 4 | 1 | 2022/2023: | Legia Warszawa (POL) |
| Armando Durim SADIKU | 27.05.1991 | 39 | 12 | 2023: | FC Cartagena (ESP) |
| Taulant Fatmir SEFERI | 15.11.1996 | 13 | 1 | 2023: | KF Tiranë |
| Xhuliano SKUKA | 02.08.1998 | 4 | 1 | 2022: | FK Partizani Tiranë |
| Myrto Artan UZUNI | 31.05.1995 | 31 | 5 | 2022/2023: | Granada CF (ESP) |
| Lorenco VILA | 14.12.1998 | 1 | 0 | 2022: | KF Teuta Durrës |
| Redon XHIXHA | 14.07.1998 | 2 | 0 | 2022: | KF Tiranë |

### Trainer

| | | |
|---|---|---|
| Edoardo REJA (Italy) [17.04.2019 – 31.12.2022] | 10.10.1945 | 38 M; 15 W; 9 D; 15 L; 45-45 |
| Sylvio Mendes Campos Junior "SYLVINHO" (Brazil) [from 02.01.2023] | 12.04.1974 | 3 M; 2 W; 0 D; 1 L; 5-2 |

# ANDORRA

**The Country:**
Principality of Andorra (Principat d'Andorra)
Capital: Andorra la Vella
Surface: 467,63 km²
Inhabitants: 79,535 [2021]
Time: UTC+1

**The FA:**
Federació Andorrana de Futbol
c/ Batlle Tomàs, 4 Baixos, AD700 Escaldes-Engordany
Tel: +376 805 830
Foundation date: 1994
Member of FIFA since: 1996
Member of UEFA since: 1996
Website: www.faf.ad

## NATIONAL TEAM RECORDS

| RECORDS | | |
|---|---|---|
| **First international match:** | 13.11.1996, Andorra la Vella: | Andorra – Estonia 1-6 |
| **Most international caps:** | Ildefons Lima Solà | - 135 caps (since 1997) |
| **Most international goals:** | Ildefons Lima Solà | - 11 goal / 135 caps (since 1997) |

| UEFA EUROPEAN CHAMPIONSHIP | |
|---|---|
| 1960 | - |
| 1964 | - |
| 1968 | - |
| 1972 | - |
| 1976 | - |
| 1980 | - |
| 1984 | - |
| 1988 | - |
| 1992 | - |
| 1996 | Did not enter |
| 2000 | Qualifiers |
| 2004 | Qualifiers |
| 2008 | Qualifiers |
| 2012 | Qualifiers |
| 2016 | Qualifiers |
| 2020 | Qualifiers |

| FIFA WORLD CUP | |
|---|---|
| 1930 | - |
| 1934 | - |
| 1938 | - |
| 1950 | - |
| 1954 | - |
| 1958 | - |
| 1962 | - |
| 1966 | - |
| 1970 | - |
| 1974 | - |
| 1978 | - |
| 1982 | - |
| 1986 | - |
| 1990 | - |
| 1994 | Did not enter |
| 1998 | Did not enter |
| 2002 | Qualifiers |
| 2006 | Qualifiers |
| 2010 | Qualifiers |
| 2014 | Qualifiers |
| 2018 | Qualifiers |
| 2022 | Qualifiers |

| OLYMPIC TOURNAMENTS | |
|---|---|
| 1908 | - |
| 1912 | - |
| 1920 | - |
| 1924 | - |
| 1928 | - |
| 1936 | - |
| 1948 | - |
| 1952 | - |
| 1956 | - |
| 1960 | - |
| 1964 | - |
| 1968 | - |
| 1972 | - |
| 1976 | - |
| 1980 | - |
| 1984 | *Withdrew* |
| 1988 | - |
| 1992 | *Withdrew* |
| 1996 | - |
| 2000 | Qualifiers |
| 2004 | Qualifiers |
| 2008 | Did not enter |
| 2012 | Qualifiers |
| 2016 | Qualifiers |
| 2020 | Qualifiers |

| UEFA NATIONS LEAGUE | |
|---|---|
| 2018/2019 | League D (Group Stage) |
| 2020/2021 | League D (Group Stage) |
| 2022/2023 | League D (Group Stage) |

## ANDORRAN CLUB HONOURS IN EUROPEAN CLUB COMPETITIONS:

| European Champion Clubs.Cup (1956-1992) / UEFA Champions League (1993-2023) |
|---|
| None |

| Fairs Cup (1858-1971) / UEFA Cup (1972-2009) / UEFA Europa League (2010-2023) |
|---|
| None |

| UEFA Europa Conference League (2021-2023) |
|---|
| None |

| UEFA Super Cup (1972-2022) |
|---|
| None |

| *European Cup Winners' Cup 1961-1999* |
|---|
| None |

*defunct competition

## NATIONAL COMPETITIONS
## TABLE OF HONOURS

| | CHAMPIONS | CUP WINNERS | BEST GOALSCORERS | |
|---|---|---|---|---|
| 1990/1991 | - | FC Santa Coloma | - | |
| 1991/1992 | - | *No competition* | - | |
| 1992/1993 | - | *No competition* | - | |
| 1993/1994 | - | CE Principat Andorra La Vella | - | |
| 1994/1995 | FC Santa Colomaa | CE Principat Andorra La Vella | - | |
| 1995/1996 | FC Encamp | CE Principat Andorra La Vella | - | |
| 1996/1997 | CE Principat Andorra La Vella | CE Principat Andorra La Vella | Patricio González Fernández (CE Principat Andorra La Vella) | 25 |
| 1997/1998 | CE Principat Andorra La Vella | CE Principat Andorra La Vella | Rafael Sánchez Pedrosa (ESP, FC Santa Coloma) | 36 |
| 1998/1999 | CE Principat Andorra La Vella | CE Principat Andorra La Vella | - | |
| 1999/2000 | Constel·lació Esportiva Andorra La Vella | Constel·lació Esportiva Andorra La Vella | - | |
| 2000/2001 | FC Santa Coloma | FC Santa Coloma | - | |
| 2001/2002 | FC Encamp | FC Lusitanos Andorra La Vella | - | |
| 2002/2003 | FC Santa Coloma | FC Santa Coloma | - | |
| 2003/2004 | FC Santa Coloma | FC Santa Coloma | Jorge Filipe Sa Silva Carneiro (POR, UE Sant Julià) | 16 |
| 2004/2005 | UE Sant Julià | FC Santa Coloma | - | |
| 2005/2006 | FC Rànger's Andorra La Vella | FC Santa Coloma | - | |
| 2006/2007 | FC Rànger's Andorra La Vella | FC Santa Coloma | Norberto Urbani (ARG, FC Rànger's Andorra La Vella) Joan Carles Toscano Beltrán (FC Santa Coloma) | 14 |
| 2007/2008 | FC Santa Coloma | UE Sant Julià | - | - |
| 2008/2009 | UE Sant Julià | FC Santa Coloma | Norberto Urbani (ARG, FC Rànger's Andorra La Vella) | 22 |
| 2009/2010 | FC Santa Coloma | UE Sant Julià | Gabriel Riera Lancha (UE Sant Julià) | 19 |
| 2010/2011 | FC Santa Coloma | UE Sant Julià | Victor Bernat Cuadros (ESP, UE Santa Coloma) | 16 |
| 2011/2012 | FC Lusitanos Andorra La Vella | FC Santa Coloma | Victor Bernat Cuadros (ESP, UE Santa Coloma) | 14 |
| 2012/2013 | FC Lusitanos Andorra La Vella | UE Santa Coloma | Bruno Filipe Raposo Fernandes "Bruninho" (POR, FC Lusitanos Andorra La Vella) | 17 |
| 2013/2014 | FC Santa Coloma | UE Sant Julià | Luis Miguel dos Reis (POR, FC Lusitanos Andorra La Vella) | 13 |
| 2014/2015 | FC Santa Coloma | UE Sant Julià | Cristian Martínez Alejo (FC Santa Coloma) | 22 |
| 2015/2016 | FC Santa Coloma | UE Santa Coloma | Victor Bernat Cuadros (ESP, UE Santa Coloma) | 12 |
| 2016/2017 | FC Santa Coloma | UE Santa Coloma | Victor Bernat Cuadros (ESP, UE Santa Coloma) | 18 |
| 2017/2018 | FC Santa Coloma | FC Santa Coloma | Jesús David Sosa Sebastiá "Chus Sosa" (ESP, FC Santa Coloma) | 14 |
| 2018/2019 | FC Santa Coloma | UE Engordany | Nicolás Esteban Medina Ríos (CHI, FC Lusitanos Andorra La Vella) Joel Méndez del Río (ESP, UE Sant Julià) Enric Pi Solá (ESP, UE Sant Julià) Genís Soldevila Solduga (ESP, Inter Club d'Escaldes) | 10 |
| 2019/2020 | Inter Club d'Escaldes | Inter Club d'Escaldes | Genís Soldevila Solduga (ESP, Inter Club d'Escaldes) | 15 |
| 2020/2021 | Inter Club d'Escaldes | UE Sant Julià | Guillaume Silvain López (FRA, UE Engordany) | 16 |
| 2021/2022 | Inter Club d'Escaldes | Atlètic Club d'Escaldes | Guillaume Silvain López (FRA, FC Santa Coloma) | 21 |
| 2022/2023 | Atlètic Club d'Escaldes | Inter Club d'Escaldes | Guillaume Silvain López (FRA, Atlètic Club d'Escaldes) | 15 |

## NATIONAL CHAMPIONSHIP
### Primera Divisió 2022/2023
(11.09.2022 – 21.05.2023)

## Results

**Round 1** [11.09.2022]
UE Engordany - FC Santa Coloma 0-1
UE Santa Coloma - AC d'Escaldes 2-3
UE Sant Julià - FC Penya 0-0
Inter Club d'Escaldes - FC Ordino 2-1

**Round 2** [18.09.2022]
FC Penya - UE Santa Coloma 1-1
FC Santa Coloma - Inter Club d'Escaldes 2-2
AC d'Escaldes - UE Engordany 1-0
FC Ordino - UE Sant Julià 0-1

**Round 3** [02.10.2022]
Inter Club d'Escaldes - UE Sant Julià 1-1
UE Engordany - FC Penya 1-0
UE Santa Coloma - FC Ordino 0-0
FC Santa Coloma - AC d'Escaldes 1-1

**Round 4** [09.10.2022]
AC d'Escaldes - Inter Club d'Escaldes 2-1
FC Ordino - UE Engordany 5-3
FC Penya - FC Santa Coloma 0-2
UE Sant Julià - UE Santa Coloma 0-3

**Round 5** [16.10.2022]
FC Santa Coloma - FC Ordino 1-1
UE Engordany - UE Sant Julià 2-1
Inter Club d'Escaldes - UE Santa Coloma 1-3
AC d'Escaldes - FC Penya 3-0

**Round 6** [23.10.2022]
FC Ordino - AC d'Escaldes 0-3
Inter Club d'Escaldes - FC Penya 2-0
UE Sant Julià - FC Santa Coloma 1-2
UE Santa Coloma - UE Engordany 1-1

**Round 7** [30.10.2022]
FC Penya - FC Ordino 1-0
AC d'Escaldes - UE Sant Julià 5-1
UE Engordany - Inter Club d'Escaldes 0-3
FC Santa Coloma - UE Santa Coloma 0-1

**Round 8** [06.11.2022]
UE Engordany - UE Sant Julià 4-0
FC Penya - UE Santa Coloma 0-2
FC Ordino - Inter Club d'Escaldes 0-3
AC d'Escaldes - FC Santa Coloma 0-0

**Round 9** [13.11.2022]
UE Sant Julià - AC d'Escaldes 0-3 *awarded*
UE Santa Coloma - UE Engordany 2-1
FC Santa Coloma - FC Ordino 1-0
Inter Club d'Escaldes - FC Penya 8-0
*not played, UE Sant Julià forfeited.*

**Round 10** [20-24.11.2022]
AC d'Escaldes - FC Ordino 1-1
FC Penya - FC Santa Coloma 0-3
UE Sant Julià - UE Santa Coloma 1-3
UE Engordany - Inter Club d'Escaldes 0-4

**Round 11** [27.11.2022]
FC Santa Coloma - UE Engordany 6-0
Inter Club d'Escaldes - UE Sant Julià 12-0
UE Santa Coloma - AC d'Escaldes 0-0
FC Ordino - FC Penya 1-1

**Round 12** [04.12.2022]
UE Sant Julià - FC Santa Coloma 0-3 *awarded*
AC d'Escaldes - FC Penya 4-0
UE Santa Coloma - Inter Club d'Escaldes 2-2
UE Engordany - FC Ordino 0-3 *awarded*

**Round 13** [11.12.2022]
AC d'Escaldes - Inter Club d'Escaldes 2-2
FC Santa Coloma - UE Santa Coloma 3-0
FC Ordino - UE Sant Julià 2-3
FC Penya - UE Engordany 1-1

**Round 14** [17-18.12.2022]
UE Engordany - AC d'Escaldes 0-3 *awarded*
Inter Club d'Escaldes - FC Santa Coloma 2-1
UE Sant Julià - FC Penya 2-3
UE Santa Coloma - FC Ordino 1-1

**Round 15** [29.01.2023]
FC Penya - UE Santa Coloma 1-1
FC Ordino - FC Santa Coloma 1-4
AC d'Escaldes - UE Engordany 2-0
UE Sant Julià - Inter Club d'Escaldes 0-6

**Round 16** [05.02.2023]
Inter Club d'Escaldes - FC Ordino 0-1
UE Santa Coloma - AC d'Escaldes 2-0
FC Santa Coloma - FC Penya 3-2
UE Engordany - UE Sant Julià 2-0

**Round 17** [12.02.2023]
AC d'Escaldes - UE Sant Julià 6-1
FC Ordino - UE Engordany 1-2
UE Santa Coloma - FC Santa Coloma 0-0
FC Penya - Inter Club d'Escaldes 2-2

**Round 18** [19.02.2023]
UE Engordany - FC Penya 1-0
UE Sant Julià - FC Ordino 3-2
Inter Club d'Escaldes - UE Santa Coloma 1-0
FC Santa Coloma - AC d'Escaldes 0-3

**Round 19** [26.02.2023]
AC d'Escaldes - FC Ordino 6-1
FC Santa Coloma - Inter Club d'Escaldes 1-1
FC Penya - UE Sant Julià 1-1
UE Santa Coloma - UE Engordany 1-1

**Round 20** [04-05.03.2023]
UE Engordany - FC Santa Coloma 0-3
UE Sant Julià - UE Santa Coloma 1-3
AC d'Escaldes - Inter Club d'Escaldes 1-2
FC Ordino - FC Penya 0-3

**Round 21** [12.03.2023]
FC Santa Coloma - UE Sant Julià 4-0
FC Penya - AC d'Escaldes 0-1
Inter Club d'Escaldes - UE Engordany 2-0
UE Santa Coloma - FC Ordino 3-1

**Round 22** [02.04.2023]
Engordany - Inter Club d'Esc. 0-3 *awarded*
FC Ordino - FC Penya 1-1
UE Santa Coloma - UE Sant Julià 1-1
FC Santa Coloma - AC d'Escaldes 0-1

**Round 23** [16.04.2023]
UE Sant Julià - UE Engordany 3-0 *awarded*
Inter Club d'Escaldes - FC Santa Coloma 0-0
FC Penya - UE Santa Coloma 4-1
AC d'Escaldes - FC Ordino 1-1

**Round 24** [23.04.2023]
UE Santa Coloma - AC d'Escaldes 1-3
UE Engordany - FC Santa Coloma 0-7
FC Ordino - Inter Club d'Escaldes 3-5
UE Sant Julià - FC Penya 1-2

**Round 25** [30.04.2023]
FC Penya - UE Engordany 0-0
Inter Club d'Escaldes - UE Santa Coloma 1-0
AC d'Escaldes - UE Sant Julià 2-0
FC Santa Coloma - FC Ordino 3-1

**Round 26** [07.05.2023]
UE Sant Julià - Inter Club d'Escaldes 0-5
FC Penya - AC d'Escaldes 0-3
UE Santa Coloma - FC Santa Coloma 0-0
UE Engordany - FC Ordino 1-2

**Round 27** [14.05.2023]
Inter Club d'Escaldes - FC Penya 1-0
UE Engordany - AC d'Escaldes 1-7
FC Ordino - UE Santa Coloma 1-1
FC Santa Coloma - UE Sant Julià 4-0

**Round 28** [19-21.05.2023]
FC Penya - FC Santa Coloma 2-0
AC d'Escaldes - Inter Club d'Escaldes 1-2
UE Sant Julià - FC Ordino 1-2
UE Santa Coloma - UE Engordany 5-0

Please note: both UE Sant Julià (Rounds 9 & 12) and UE Engordany (Round 22 & 23) forfeited 2 matches, all this matches were awarded 0-3 losses against them.

### Final Standings

| | | | | | | | | Home | | | | Away | | | | |
|---|---|---|---|---|---|---|---|---|---|---|---|---|---|---|---|---|---|
| 1. | **Atlètic Club d'Escaldes** | 28 | 19 | 6 | 3 | 68 - 19 | 63 | 9 | 4 | 2 | 37 - 12 | 10 | 2 | 1 | 31 - 7 |
| 2. | Inter Club d'Escaldes | 28 | 18 | 7 | 3 | 76 - 23 | 61 | 9 | 2 | 2 | 33 - 7 | 9 | 5 | 1 | 43 - 16 |
| 3. | FC Santa Coloma | 28 | 15 | 8 | 5 | 55 - 19 | 53 | 7 | 4 | 3 | 29 - 13 | 8 | 4 | 2 | 26 - 6 |
| 4. | UE Santa Coloma | 28 | 10 | 12 | 6 | 40 - 29 | 42 | 4 | 9 | 2 | 21 - 14 | 6 | 3 | 4 | 19 - 15 |
| 5. | FC Penya d'Andorra | 28 | 6 | 9 | 13 | 25 - 46 | 27 | 3 | 6 | 5 | 13 - 18 | 3 | 3 | 8 | 12 - 28 |
| 6. | FC Ordino | 28 | 5 | 8 | 15 | 33 - 55 | 23 | 1 | 3 | 8 | 15 - 30 | 4 | 5 | 7 | 18 - 25 |
| 7. | UE Engordany (*Relegation Play-offs*) | 28 | 6 | 4 | 18 | 21 - 67 | 22 | 5 | 0 | 10 | 12 - 37 | 1 | 4 | 8 | 9 - 30 |
| 8. | UE Sant Julià (*Relegated*) | 28 | 4 | 4 | 20 | 23 - 83 | 16 | 2 | 1 | 11 | 13 - 37 | 2 | 3 | 9 | 10 - 46 |

### Top goalscorers:

| | | |
|---|---|---|
| 15 | **Guillaume Silvain Lopez (FRA)** | *Atlètic Club d'Escaldes* |
| 14 | Sascha Fernando Andreu Lahrach (ESP) | *Inter Club d'Escaldes* |
| 13 | Faysal Chouaib Hassany (ESP) | *UE Santa Coloma* |

### Relegation Play-offs [27-31.05.2023]

CE Carroi - UE Engordany      2-0 (1-0)      2-0 (0-0)
CE Carroi promoted for the first level 2023/2024.

## NATIONAL CUP
### Copa Constitució Final 2022/2023

| First Round [15.01.2023] | | | | |
|---|---|---|---|---|
| CF Atlètic Amèrica - UE Engordany | 3-0 | | UE Santa Coloma - Inter Club d'Escaldes | 0-2 |
| FC Santa Coloma - CE Carroi | 3-2 | | Atlètic Club d'Escaldes - FC Pas de la Casa | 0-3 |
| UE Sant Julià - FC Encamp | 4-2 | | FS La Massana - FC Penya d'Andorra | 0-4 |

| Quarter-Finals [22.01.2023] | | | | |
|---|---|---|---|---|
| UE Sant Julià - Inter Club d'Escaldes | 0-3 | | FC Ordino - FC Penya d'Andorra | 2-0 |
| CF Atlètic Amèrica - FC Santa Coloma | 0-3 | | FC Rànger's Andorra la Vella - FC Pas de la Casa | 0-3 |

| Semi-Finals [05-06.04.2023] | | | | |
|---|---|---|---|---|
| FC Pas de la Casa - FC Santa Coloma | 0-4 | | Inter Club d'Escaldes - FC Ordino | 1-1 aet; 4-3 pen |

### Final

28.05.2023; Estadi Nacional, Andorra la Vella; Referee: Manuel Antonio Nogueira Fernandes; Attendance: n/a

**FC Santa Coloma - Inter Club d'Escaldes**                                                     **1-2(1-0)**

**FC Santa Coloma**: Josep Antoni Gomes Moreira, Gerard Gómez Gómez (71.David Crespo Zurita), Marc Rebés Ruiz (90.Cristian Novoa Sandin), Daniel Toribio Gutiérrez, Maksim Valadzko, David Virgili Fernández (71.Eric Ruiz Naranjo), Jordi Aláez Peña, Andriy Markovych (81.Kilian Grant Carvalheira), Sergio Rodríguez Cidoncha, Miguel López Míguez, Eloy Gila Marín. Trainer: Dmitriy Cheryshev (Russia).

**Inter Club d'Escaldes**: Adrià Muñoz Fernández, Adrià Gallego Arias, Jesús Rubio Gómez (56.Jean Luc Gbayara Assoubre), Iván De Nova Ruiz, Pau Bosch Hueso, Domingo Berlanga Ouggouti (90+1.Sergio Moreno Marín), Raúl Mihai Fehér, Marc Caballé Naranjo, Jordi Roca Grau (56.Ángel de la Torre Pérez), Cristian González López „Chete", Sascha Fernando Andreu Lahrach. Trainer: Otger Canals Xifró (Spain).

**Goals:** 1-0 Eloy Gila Marín (34), 1-1 Domingo Berlanga Ouggouti (70), 1-2 Sascha Fernando Andreu Lahrach (89).

## THE CLUBS 2022/2023

### Atlètic Club d'Escaldes Escaldes-Engordany

**Founded**: 2002
**Stadium**: Camp de Fútbol d'Aixovall (1,000)
**Trainer**: Federico Bessone Luna (ARG)            23.01.1984

| Goalkeepers: | DOB | M | (s) | G |
|---|---|---|---|---|
| Julián Ezequiel Pedernera Escurti | 01.07.2002 | | (1) | |
| Saúl Gracia Campillos (ESP) | 11.04.2000 | 15 | | |
| Víctor López Medel (ESP) | 28.11.2001 | 12 | | |
| **Defenders:** | **DOB** | **M** | **(s)** | **G** |
| Sébastien Jacques Manuel Agüero (FRA) | 17.08.1993 | 13 | (5) | 1 |
| Álex Sánchez Rodríguez (ESP) | 19.01.1992 | 17 | (3) | |
| Aleix Císteró Serna (ESP) | 25.06.1994 | 7 | | 3 |
| Javier „Javi" Morales Aguilera (ESP) | 03.02.1993 | 19 | | 1 |
| Víctor Alfonso Maffeo Becerra (ESP) | 18.09.2000 | 14 | (7) | |
| Marcel Sgrò i Cabré | 27.05.1997 | 13 | (3) | |
| Moisés San Nicolás Schellens | 17.09.1993 | 1 | (2) | |
| Jilmar Steed Torres Martínez (COL) | 18.05.1994 | 8 | (2) | |

| Midfielders: | DOB | M | (s) | G |
|---|---|---|---|---|
| Julen Bernaola Cuezva (ESP) | 29.04.1999 | 7 | (2) | 2 |
| Gemelson Nayry Fay Bill Vieira (GNB) | 04.08.1992 | 4 | (15) | |
| Hamza Ryahi Bouharma (ESP) | 11.03.1994 | 11 | (11) | |
| Martí Riverola Bataller (ESP) | 26.01.1991 | 22 | (3) | 6 |
| Víctor Alonso Madueño (ESP) | 23.12.1994 | 15 | (4) | 2 |
| Víctor Pérez Alonso | 12.01.1988 | 22 | | 3 |
| Xavier "Xavi" Puerto Bellart (ESP) | 12.09.1991 | 10 | (10) | 4 |
| **Forwards:** | **DOB** | **M** | **(s)** | **G** |
| Alexandre "Álex" Martínez Palau | 10.10.1998 | 12 | (5) | 4 |
| David Rodríguez López „David Rodri" (ESP) | 02.07.1999 | 18 | (8) | 2 |
| Jorge Bolívar Cano (ESP) | 18.07.1997 | 12 | (14) | 7 |
| Guillaume Silvain López (FRA) | 30.01.1999 | 23 | (3) | 15 |
| Víctor Manuel Casadesús Castaño (ESP) | 28.02.1985 | 19 | (7) | 5 |
| Carlos Sagüés Curini (ESP) | 10.11.1997 | 3 | (7) | 4 |

### Unió Esportiva Engordany

**Founded**: 1980
**Stadium**: Estadi Comunal d'Andorra la Vella (1,300)
**Trainer**: Jesús Barón Téllez (ESP)            09.09.1982
[19.02.2023] Óscar Antonio Ochoa Hernández (MEX)            07.01.1992

| Goalkeepers: | DOB | M | (s) | G |
|---|---|---|---|---|
| Jesús Coca Noguerol (ESP) | 22.05.1989 | 23 | | |
| José Carlos Cortaberría Gasso (URU) | 30.08.1990 | 1 | | |
| Jordi Rodríguez Bertrán „Tete" | 01.12.1993 | 2 | (1) | |
| **Defenders:** | **DOB** | **M** | **(s)** | **G** |
| Xavier Carmona Velasco (ESP) | 21.01.1993 | 16 | | |
| Eric del Pozo Sanjaume | 02.05.2003 | | (1) | |
| Julián Fernández (ARG) | 18.07.1989 | 22 | | 4 |
| Jhon Wilmar Herrera López (COL) | 12.08.1991 | | (2) | |
| Jaime Ruiz Sánchez | 15.09.1998 | 8 | (4) | |
| Cristian Martínez Alejo „Kiki" | 16.10.1989 | 2 | (1) | |
| Steven Leblanc (GUF) | 24.09.2001 | 4 | (2) | |
| Marc García Renom | 21.03.1988 | 22 | (1) | |
| Juan Carlos Machuca de Lira (MEX) | 21.11.1993 | | (2) | |
| Mario Valentín Spano Páez (URU) | 07.02.1986 | 12 | | |
| **Midfielders:** | **DOB** | **M** | **(s)** | **G** |
| Adrià Torres Castañé (ESP) | 21.03.1999 | | (2) | |
| Daniel Miguel Cerqueira Carvalho (POR) | 05.01.2003 | 2 | (3) | |
| Diogo Filipe Leite Silva | 08.11.2005 | | (1) | |

| | DOB | M | (s) | G |
|---|---|---|---|---|
| Jordi Pérez Burgos (ESP) | 1999 | 3 | (3) | |
| Jordi Rubio Gómez | 01.11.1987 | 24 | | |
| Luis Emilio Blanco Coto „Lluís" (ESP) | 15.01.1990 | 20 | (3) | 1 |
| Marc Pujol Pons | 21.08.1992 | 16 | (1) | 2 |
| Marcelo Alejandro Tabárez Rodríguez (URU) | 10.02.1993 | 4 | (1) | 3 |
| Xavier „Xavi" Vieira de Vasconcelos | 14.01.1992 | 18 | (2) | |
| **Forwards:** | **DOB** | **M** | **(s)** | **G** |
| Eric Balastegui Martínez | 29.06.2003 | 7 | (11) | 2 |
| Cristian Manuel Millán Pichel | 02.06.2003 | 1 | (3) | |
| José Antonio Aguilar Gómez "Josele" (ESP) | 11.10.1989 | 4 | | |
| Gabriel Marcel Leighton Mateos (FRA) | 16.10.2000 | 6 | (11) | |
| Marcel Oliva Ruiz (ESP) | 16.12.2002 | 5 | (6) | |
| Diego Alejandro Nájera Quintero (MEX) | 11.12.1994 | 13 | (12) | 3 |
| Joan Palomino Abril (ESP) | 2001 | | (4) | |
| Roberto López López „Rober" (ESP) | 19.09.1992 | 8 | (3) | |
| Sebastián Gómez Pérez „Sebas" (ESP) | 01.11.1983 | 22 | (3) | 2 |
| Víctor Bernat Cuadros (ESP) | 17.05.1987 | 18 | (2) | 3 |
| Bruno Volpi (ARG) | 23.06.1993 | 3 | (1) | |

## Inter Club d'Escaldes

| Founded: | 1991 | | |
|---|---|---|---|
| Stadium: | Estadi Comunal d'Andorra la Vella (1,300) | | |
| Trainer: | Juan Velasco Damas (ESP) | | 17.05.1977 |
| [20.10.2022] | Otger Canals Xifró (ESP) | | 20.05.1986 |

| Goalkeepers: | DOB | M | (s) | G |
|---|---|---|---|---|
| Adrià „Adri" Muñoz Fernández | 13.05.1994 | 26 | | |
| Alejandro „Álex" Iglesias Rodríguez (ESP) | 07.04.1997 | 1 | | |
| **Defenders:** | **DOB** | **M** | **(s)** | **G** |
| Adrià Gallego Arias (ESP) | 09.04.1990 | 16 | (6) | 6 |
| Josep María Cabanes Foix | 02.04.1996 | | (1) | |
| Cristian González López „Chete" (ESP) | 12.05.1995 | 18 | (4) | 3 |
| Jesús „Chus" Rubio Gómez | 09.09.1994 | 18 | (7) | 1 |
| Iván De Nova Ruiz (ESP) | 22.09.1996 | 18 | (2) | 1 |
| Raúl Mihai Fehér (ROU) | 12.03.1997 | 20 | (5) | 2 |
| Roger Marcè Torres (ESP) | 02.05.1997 | 23 | (2) | 1 |
| **Midfielders:** | **DOB** | **M** | **(s)** | **G** |
| Alain Petxarromán Eizaguirre (ESP) | 08.09.1992 | | (7) | |

| | DOB | M | (s) | G |
|---|---|---|---|---|
| Marc Caballé Naranjo (ESP) | 22.06.1991 | 13 | | 3 |
| Pau Bosch Hueso (ESP) | 30.03.1988 | 23 | (2) | 1 |
| Jordi Roca Grau (ESP) | 23.08.1989 | 17 | (7) | 2 |
| Sergio "Sergi" Moreno Marín | 25.11.1987 | | (7) | |
| Víctor Martínez Manrique „Viti" (ESP) | 25.05.1997 | 17 | (1) | |
| **Forwards:** | **DOB** | **M** | **(s)** | **G** |
| Ángel de la Torre Pérez (ESP) | 04.11.1994 | 20 | (7) | 7 |
| Aridai Cabrera Suárez (ESP) | 26.09.1988 | 11 | (1) | 6 |
| Gerard Artigas Fonullet (ESP) | 10.01.1995 | 8 | (3) | 12 |
| Jean Luc Gbayara Assoubre (CIV) | 08.08.1992 | 7 | (2) | |
| Íñigo Sánchez Etxegarai (ESP) | 22.09.1999 | 6 | (19) | 3 |
| Domingo Berlanga Ouggouti (MAR) | 06.05.1995 | 16 | (7) | 8 |
| Sascha Fernando Andreu Lahrach (ESP) | 12.08.1986 | 19 | (7) | 14 |

## Fútbol Club Ordino

| Founded: | 2010 | |
|---|---|---|
| Stadium: | Centre d'Entrenament de la FAF, Andorra la Vella (300) | |
| Trainer: | Mario Sebastián Galles Fernández (ARG) | 20.04.1987 |

| Goalkeepers: | DOB | M | (s) | G |
|---|---|---|---|---|
| Luis Ángel Ferreiro (ARG) | 28.10.1988 | 9 | | |
| Luis Miguel Ibáñez Lera „Luismi" (ESP) | 11.08.1996 | 19 | (2) | |
| **Defenders:** | **DOB** | **M** | **(s)** | **G** |
| Juan Esteban Gómez Michellod (ESP) | 01.10.1997 | 14 | (2) | |
| Jorge David Guerrero Guio (COL) | | 9 | (3) | |
| Francisco Javier "Javi" López Martín (ESP) | 21.04.1990 | 14 | (3) | |
| Germán Mendoza Ogazón (ESP) | 2003 | 25 | | |
| Pedro Maria Henriques Lobo (POR) | 17.05.1999 | 18 | (7) | |
| Sergi Caballero Mateo (ESP) | 08.07.1998 | 9 | (3) | 1 |
| Ezequiel Ricardo Vargas (ARG) | 13.03.1996 | 24 | (1) | |
| Víctor Rodríguez Cámara (ESP) | 08.03.2001 | 10 | (1) | 1 |
| **Midfielders:** | **DOB** | **M** | **(s)** | **G** |
| David Corominas Saura "Coro" (ESP) | 29.08.1985 | 17 | (4) | 4 |
| Johnatan Estrada Campillo (COL) | 27.01.1983 | 21 | (3) | 1 |

| | DOB | M | (s) | G |
|---|---|---|---|---|
| Lucas Emanuel Gálvez (ARG) | 05.04.1992 | 1 | (3) | |
| Joao Pedro da Silva Teixeira (POR) | 17.07.1996 | 25 | (1) | 4 |
| Jorge Vicente Camargo „Junior" (ESP) | 17.10.2002 | 21 | (4) | 3 |
| Lucas Blas Regueira (ARG) | 04.06.1997 | 1 | (5) | |
| **Forwards:** | **DOB** | **M** | **(s)** | **G** |
| Agustín Filosa | | 9 | (3) | 2 |
| Aleix Tuset Badia | 01.09.1987 | 2 | (3) | |
| Roberto Andoni Gómez Michellod (ESP) | 21.02.2001 | | (9) | 1 |
| Brian Pubill dos Santos | 26.07.2000 | 11 | (11) | 2 |
| Josep María Tizón Fernández „Josete" | 03.10.1997 | 8 | (8) | |
| Cristian Martínez Alejo „Kiki" | 16.10.1999 | 6 | (3) | |
| Óscar Julián Martínez Peñaloza (COL) | 09.06.1994 | 9 | (3) | 1 |
| Izan Maldonado Moya (ESP) | 27.03.2003 | 9 | (3) | 6 |
| Alberto Rabassó Osuna (ESP) | 05.08.1998 | 17 | (2) | 3 |
| Samuel Sánchez Fajardo (COL) | | | (2) | |

## Fútbol Club Penya d'Andorra

| Founded: | 2009 | |
|---|---|---|
| Stadium: | Centre d'Entrenament de la FAF, Andorra la Vella (300) | |
| Trainer: | Richard Imbernón Ríos | 21.12.1975 |
| [29.12.2022] | Alejandro Esteve Power (ESP) | 28.03.1980 |

| Goalkeepers: | DOB | M | (s) | G |
|---|---|---|---|---|
| Matías Basterrechea (ARG) | 02.01.1994 | 18 | (2) | |
| Mauro Rabelo Pascual | 01.07.2002 | 3 | | |
| Víctor Silverio Pinto | 15.04.1997 | 7 | | |
| **Defenders:** | **DOB** | **M** | **(s)** | **G** |
| Aleix Viladot Caramés | 26.06.1997 | 9 | (1) | |
| Alexandre Correia Alfaiate "Alex" (POR) | 17.08.1995 | 13 | | |
| Patricio Basterrechea (ARG) | 02.02.1995 | 6 | (5) | |
| Eneko Agegnehu Clemente Galíndez | 24.09.2003 | | (2) | |
| Francisco Javier Denches Galán | 03.06.2000 | 9 | (3) | |
| Federico "Fede" Ondo Obama Ondo (EQG) | 04.02.2000 | 6 | (3) | |
| Junah Cyrille Fekoua-Youta (FRA) | | 2 | (2) | |
| Quentin Pierrick Laffont (FRA) | 17.01.1996 | 6 | (2) | |
| Lilian de Palmas (ESP) | 02.02.2002 | 7 | (4) | |
| David Maneiro Ton | 16.02.1989 | 4 | (1) | |
| Miguel Ruiz Enamorado (ESP) | 16.07.1982 | 14 | (1) | |
| Ignacio "Nacho" García Antuña | 14.04.2001 | 4 | | |
| Pedro Muñoz Fontalba "Peter" (ESP) | 09.01.1988 | 9 | (1) | |
| Sofiane Seffoud (FRA) | 13.02.1999 | | (1) | |
| Yanis Mohammed Miloud Teurki (FRA) | 29.05.2001 | 2 | (1) | |
| **Midfielders:** | **DOB** | **M** | **(s)** | **G** |
| Jamal Zarioh Taouil "Ángel" | 09.01.1988 | 6 | (4) | |
| Kemal Cecen (FRA) | 2003 | 1 | (2) | |

| | DOB | M | (s) | G |
|---|---|---|---|---|
| César Escribá Recuero (ESP) | 26.03.2001 | 19 | (6) | |
| Fabio Alexandre Cruz Martins (POR) | 10.02.1996 | 13 | | 5 |
| João Paulo da Silva Tomaz (POR) | 13.08.1999 | 13 | | 2 |
| Joel "Jou" Marques da Rocha (POR) | 19.11.1984 | 1 | (3) | |
| Yann Marie Bernard Kouakou | 17.08.1999 | 1 | | |
| Marc Ferré Nazzaro | 11.01.1994 | 8 | | |
| Eric Massinissa Oufella (ALG) | 19.08.2001 | 9 | (1) | |
| Japhet Mbati Ingatsio (FRA) | 25.03.2002 | | (1) | |
| Birahim Sarr (FRA) | 27.07.1991 | 8 | | |
| Shems-Dean Nedjoum (FRA) | | 2 | (8) | |
| Matías Nicolás Vaamonde (ARG) | 30.11.1989 | 20 | (3) | 1 |
| **Forwards:** | **DOB** | **M** | **(s)** | **G** |
| Adrián "Adri" Ferrer Pérez (ESP) | 12.02.2001 | 12 | (1) | |
| Brayan Glenn Andrew Aleme Ondoua (FRA) | 08.02.2001 | 4 | (1) | |
| Alejandro „Álex" Briega de la Cruz (ESP) | 19.12.2001 | 12 | | 2 |
| Alejandro "Álex" Poves Ruiz (ESP) | 09.03.1992 | 10 | (3) | 1 |
| Brayan Caicedo Mosquera (COL) | 27.04.1996 | 6 | (2) | |
| José Pastor Alemañ "Coke" (ESP) | 23.02.2002 | 1 | (6) | 1 |
| Eloy Ordóñez Muñiz (ESP) | 26.05.1999 | 13 | (1) | |
| Rodrigo Piloto de Oliveira (POR) | 09.06.2001 | 18 | (2) | 11 |
| Daniel Alberto Rojas Gómez (COL) | 09.07.1996 | 9 | (4) | |
| Héctor Jesús Alonso Urrunaga Orellana (PER) | 14.07.1995 | 1 | (7) | |
| Yves Roland Zama (CIV) | 26.12.1993 | 2 | (1) | 1 |

## Unió Esportiva Sant Julià de Lòria

| Founded: | 1982 | | |
|---|---|---|---|
| Stadium: | Estadi Comunal d'Andorra la Vella (1,300) | | |
| Trainer: | Albert Gómez Genies (ESP) | | 03.08.1966 |
| [22.11.2022] | Pablo Huerga Lorenzana (ESP) | | 02.06.1988 |

| Goalkeepers: | DOB | M | (s) | G |
|---|---|---|---|---|
| Alejandro „Álex" *Iglesias* Rodríguez (ESP) | 07.04.1997 | 7 | | |
| Alejandro „Álex" *Ruiz* Campagne (FRA) | 03.09.1991 | 10 | | |
| Billal Amar Djattit (FRA) | 16.11.1999 | 2 | | |
| Roberto Veiga Gomes „Robi" | 18.08.1987 | 3 | | |
| Alberto Buenestado Sánchez „Tito" (ESP) | 2001 | 2 | | |
| **Defenders:** | **DOB** | **M** | **(s)** | **G** |
| José *Adonay* Sierra Alvarado (ESP) | 20.10.2001 | 21 | (1) | |
| *César* Rodríguez Martínez (ESP) | 01.03.1994 | 22 | (1) | 2 |
| Jesús María Meneses Sabater "Chechu" (ESP) | 04.01.1995 | 16 | (1) | |
| Luis *Felipe* Alarcón Guzmán | 02.02.2002 | 2 | (2) | |
| Alfonso Alejandro Huerta Martínez (MEX)* | 19.11.1990 | 16 | (3) | 1 |
| *Jagoba* Gil Roz (ESP) | 09.04.1998 | 11 | | |
| *Joel* Rodríguez Giadas (ESP) | 11.06.2005 | | (3) | |
| Juan Manuel „Juanma" *Miranda* Rodríguez | 01.04.1994 | 4 | | |
| Sekouba Kaba (FRA) | 12.02.1992 | 7 | | |
| Quentin Pierrick Laffont (FRA) | 17.01.1996 | 2 | (2) | |
| **Midfielders:** | **DOB** | **M** | **(s)** | **G** |
| *Álvaro* Luis Correa Gómez (ESP) | 08.11.1996 | 9 | (2) | |
| Juan Diego Gutiérrez de las Casas (PER) | 28.04.1992 | 9 | (1) | |
| Ramiro Osvaldo Maldonado (ARG) | 20.07.1991 | 4 | | |

| | DOB | M | (s) | G |
|---|---|---|---|---|
| *Marc* Ferré Nazzaro | 11.01.1994 | 4 | | |
| Zoltán Mari (HUN) | 19.10.2003 | 10 | (7) | |
| Noah Arthurahmed Morillon Schieber-Herrbach (FRA) | 26.12.2004 | 11 | (2) | |
| Mike *Nosso* | 03.07.1996 | | (3) | |
| *Pedro* Santos Escolano (ESP) | 01.06.1993 | 5 | (1) | 1 |
| Jonathan Tassin (COD) | 31.01.1998 | 10 | | |
| **Forwards:** | **DOB** | **M** | **(s)** | **G** |
| Christian Bekamenga Bekamenga Aymard (CMR) | 09.05.1986 | 2 | (1) | |
| Celyan Belaid Djattit (FRA) | 05.01.2003 | 9 | (3) | 3 |
| Chang Seung-cheol (KOR) | 20.12.1998 | 11 | (9) | 2 |
| *Cristian* Torres Hernández (ESP) | 28.08.1998 | 2 | (2) | |
| *David* Pérez Doval (ESP) | 12.02.2002 | 6 | (8) | |
| José *Ginés* Hernández Martínez (ESP) | 28.02.1996 | 1 | (3) | |
| *Giovanni* Goran Rodríguez Rivero (ESP) | 25.08.1998 | 2 | | |
| *Iván* Rodríguez *Tato* (ESP) | 28.01.1998 | 11 | (2) | |
| *Marc* Pérez Morcillo (ESP) | 03.06.2003 | 16 | (3) | 2 |
| José Antonio Almeida Exposito „Nene" (ESP) | 17.02.2000 | 5 | (3) | 2 |
| Adoum Oueddo (FRA) | 22.09.1996 | 4 | (8) | |
| Ryan Alexis Ndri (FRA) | 30.11.2001 | 1 | (4) | |
| Zsolt Tibor Szilvási (HUN) | 02.11.2002 | 18 | (7) | 2 |

*Please note: Alfonso Alejandro Huerta Martínez played as goalkeeper in Round 14.*

---

## Fútbol Club Santa Coloma

| Founded: | 1986 | | |
|---|---|---|---|
| Stadium: | Estadi Comunal d'Andorra la Vella (1,300) | | |
| Trainer: | Dmitriy Cheryshev (RUS) | | 11.05.1969 |

| Goalkeepers: | DOB | M | (s) | G |
|---|---|---|---|---|
| José *Bejarano* Leandro (ESP) | 10.02.2002 | 8 | | |
| Adrià *Collet* Sallarés (ESP) | 21.10.1999 | 10 | (3) | |
| Josep Antoni *Gomes* Moreira | 03.12.1985 | 9 | | |
| **Defenders:** | **DOB** | **M** | **(s)** | **G** |
| *Andreu* Ramos Isus (ESP) | 19.01.1989 | 16 | (6) | |
| *Cristian* Orosa Lodeiro (ESP) | 12.12.1990 | 1 | (3) | |
| *David* Crespo Zurita (ESP) | 26.08.1995 | 8 | (4) | |
| *Eric* Ruiz Naranjo (ESP) | 23.04.1999 | 21 | (1) | |
| Santiago Antonio Fernández Alves (VEN) | 19.06.2000 | | (5) | |
| *Gerard* Gómez Gómez (ESP) | 02.08.2002 | 9 | (13) | 1 |
| Andriy Markovych (UKR) | 25.06.1995 | 3 | (4) | |
| *Robert* Ramos Isus (ESP) | 11.12.1992 | 8 | (6) | |
| *Sergio* Rodríguez Cidoncha (ESP) | 05.10.1989 | 10 | (2) | |
| Maksim Valadzko (BLR) | 10.11.1992 | 22 | (1) | 1 |

| **Midfielders:** | **DOB** | **M** | **(s)** | **G** |
|---|---|---|---|---|
| Daniel „Dani" *Toribio* Gutiérrez | 05.10.1988 | 23 | (1) | 2 |
| *Marc* Cintas Sánchez (ESP) | 07.04.2002 | | (5) | |
| *Marc* Rebés Ruiz | 03.07.1994 | 9 | (10) | 1 |
| *Miguel Ángel* Gómez Morera | 23.02.1993 | 15 | (8) | 1 |
| *Miguel* Ángel *Laborda* Gil (ESP) | 18.02.1995 | | (1) | |
| *Miguel* López Míguez (ESP) | 18.01.1998 | 26 | (1) | 3 |
| Octavio Andrés Páez Gil (VEN) | 28.02.2000 | 14 | (5) | 2 |
| **Forwards:** | **DOB** | **M** | **(s)** | **G** |
| Jordi *Aláez* Peña | 23.01.1998 | 2 | (2) | |
| Carles *Coto* Pagés (ESP) | 11.02.1988 | 17 | (4) | 6 |
| *Eloy Gila* Marín (ESP) | 21.06.1988 | 22 | (2) | 12 |
| *Kilian* Grant Carvalheira (ESP) | 05.05.1994 | 19 | (1) | 3 |
| Mario *Mourelo* del Huerto (ESP) | 03.01.1997 | 11 | (8) | 4 |
| Cristian Novoa Sandin (VEN) | 09.07.1991 | 2 | (19) | 10 |
| David *Virgili* Fernández (ESP) | 30.09.1998 | 12 | (4) | 4 |

---

## Unió Esportiva Santa Coloma

| Founded: | 1986 | | |
|---|---|---|---|
| Stadium: | Estadi Comunal d'Andorra la Vella (1,300) | | |
| Trainer: | Boris Antón Codina | | 27.02.1987 |

| Goalkeepers: | DOB | M | (s) | G |
|---|---|---|---|---|
| Alejandro „Alejo" *Agüera* Lasala (ESP) | 07.01.1999 | 3 | (1) | |
| *Jacobo* Martínez García (ESP) | 02.07.2002 | 18 | | |
| Idris Carlos Kameni (CMR) | 18.02.2004 | 7 | | |
| **Defenders:** | **DOB** | **M** | **(s)** | **G** |
| José Carlos Caballero Vargas „Checa" (ESP) | 09.05.1998 | 11 | | |
| *Christian García* González | 04.02.1999 | 17 | (2) | 3 |
| Adrián da Cunha Costa Gomes "Dacu" | 16.05.2001 | 9 | (9) | |
| Eric *de Pablos* Solà | 08.03.1999 | 22 | | |
| *Emili* Josep García Miramontes | 11.01.1989 | 6 | (7) | |
| Juan Manuel Miranda Rodríguez „Juanma" (ESP) | 01.03.1994 | 9 | (3) | |
| Gerard Aloy Soler „Kongo" | 17.04.1989 | | (3) | |
| Tiago Venancio Alves Pires „Tiago Portuga" (POR) | 20.10.1991 | 19 | (4) | 3 |
| Juan Camilo Puentes Londoño (COL) | 15.04.1998 | 22 | (2) | |
| **Midfielders:** | **DOB** | **M** | **(s)** | **G** |
| *Albert* Reyes Roig | 24.03.1996 | 14 | (2) | |
| Toussaint Bérenger Assamoa (CMR) | 2001 | 2 | (2) | |
| Alexandre *Cardoso* García (BRA) | 30.04.1992 | 6 | | |
| *Douglas* Abner Almeida dos Santos (BRA) | 30.01.1996 | 1 | (9) | 1 |
| *Iván* Aldair *Quintero* Ortiz | 21.03.2000 | | (8) | 1 |
| José Miguel Alias Trigos "Largo" (ESP) | 07.03.1993 | 2 | (5) | |

| | DOB | M | (s) | G |
|---|---|---|---|---|
| *Ludovic* Clemente Garcés | 09.06.1987 | 3 | (11) | |
| Sergio Clen Mendoza Espíndola (ARG) | 25.03.1994 | 23 | | 1 |
| Gonçalo José Gonçalves *Paulino* (POR) | 31.12.1998 | 21 | (5) | 5 |
| *Salomão* Ludy Luvunga Coxi (ANG) | 24.07.2002 | 1 | (2) | |
| *Youssef* El Ghzaoui Darir (ESP) | 25.10.2000 | 12 | | 1 |
| **Forwards:** | **DOB** | **M** | **(s)** | **G** |
| *Aarón* Sánchez Alburquerque | 05.06.1996 | 1 | (2) | |
| *Cristian* del Pozo Morenilla (ESP) | 12.08.1999 | 6 | (10) | 1 |
| Imad El Kabbou Elazz (MAR) | 02.04.2000 | 6 | (3) | 1 |
| Monsif Khttar El Yousfi (MAR) | 09.07.1999 | 17 | (7) | 3 |
| *Faysal* Chouaib Hassany (ESP) | 07.01.2000 | 23 | (2) | 13 |
| João Gabriel Carvalho Castro „Gabi" | 19.11.2001 | 7 | (3) | 2 |
| *Jordan* Gutiérrez Nsang (ESP) | 08.07.1998 | 14 | | 2 |
| Oscar Vicente *Mendes* (POR) | 08.10.1996 | | (2) | |
| Bruno Marcelo Gavim „Moicano" (BRA) | 09.04.1999 | 4 | (5) | 1 |
| *Pablo* Gil González (ESP) | 22.01.2003 | 1 | (5) | |
| *Roberto* Carlos *Gomes* Rebelo | 21.10.1999 | 1 | (3) | |
| Rui *Társio* Alves da Silva (ANG) | 07.04.1997 | | (3) | |
| Evangelos Skraparas (GER) | 05.03.1991 | | (2) | |
| Wilson Filipe de Menezes Viana da Conceição (POR) | 09.07.1994 | | (6) | |

**Regular Season - League table**

| | | | | | | | | | |
|---|---|---|---|---|---|---|---|---|---|
| 1. | FC Pas de la Casa | 18 | 15 | 3 | 0 | 99 | - | 7 | 48 |
| 2. | CF Atlètic Amèrica | 18 | 14 | 2 | 2 | 57 | - | 21 | 44 |
| 3. | CF Esperança d'Andorra | 18 | 12 | 4 | 2 | 49 | - | 17 | 40 |
| 4. | CE Carroi | 18 | 10 | 3 | 5 | 50 | - | 30 | 33 |
| 5. | FS La Massana | 18 | 8 | 4 | 6 | 48 | - | 28 | 28 |
| 6. | FC Encamp | 18 | 9 | 1 | 8 | 42 | - | 41 | 28 |
| 7. | FC Rànger's Andorra la Vella | 18 | 7 | 1 | 10 | 35 | - | 54 | 22 |
| 8. | FC Santa Coloma "B" | 18 | 2 | 0 | 16 | 17 | - | 87 | 6 |
| 9. | UE Endorgany "B" | 18 | 2 | 0 | 16 | 12 | - | 70 | 6 |
| 10. | UE Santa Coloma "B" | 18 | 2 | 0 | 16 | 18 | - | 72 | 6 |
| 11. | FC Ordino "B"* | 8 | 1 | 1 | 6 | 4 | - | 19 | 4 |

Top-7 teams were qualified for the Play-off Round. Reserve teams are not eligible to promote.
* FC Ordino "B" withdrew after Round 8, all their results were annulled.

**Play-off Round**

| | | | | | | | | | |
|---|---|---|---|---|---|---|---|---|---|
| 1. | FC Pas de la Casa (*Promoted*) | 24 | 20 | 4 | 0 | 119 | - | 10 | 64 |
| 2. | CF Atlètic Amèrica (*Promoted*) | 24 | 17 | 4 | 3 | 71 | - | 27 | 55 |
| 3. | CF Esperança d'Andorra (*Promoted*) | 24 | 15 | 5 | 4 | 58 | - | 25 | 50 |
| 4. | CE Carroi (*Promotion Play-offs*) | 24 | 15 | 3 | 6 | 65 | - | 34 | 48 |
| 5. | FS La Massana | 24 | 10 | 4 | 10 | 56 | - | 40 | 34 |
| 6. | FC Rànger's Andorra la Vella | 24 | 8 | 1 | 15 | 39 | - | 73 | 25 |
| 7. | FC Encamp** | 24 | 9 | 1 | 14 | 42 | - | 59 | 28 |

** FC Encamp withdrew, all their results were awarded 0-3 losses against them.

## INTERNATIONAL MATCHES
### (16.07.2022 – 15.07.2023)

| 22.09.2022 | Vaduz | *Liechtenstein - Andorra* | *0-2(0-1)* | (UNL) |
|---|---|---|---|---|
| 25.09.2022 | Andorra la Vella | *Andorra - Latvia* | *1-1(0-0)* | (UNL) |
| 16.11.2022 | Málaga | *Andorra - Austria* | *0-1(0-0)* | (F) |
| 19.11.2022 | Gibraltar | *Gibraltar - Andorra* | *1-0(1-0)* | (F) |
| 25.03.2023 | Andorra la Vella | *Andorra - Romania* | *0-2(0-1)* | (ECQ) |
| 28.03.2023 | Prishtina | *Kosovo - Andorra* | *1-1(0-0)* | (ECQ) |
| 16.06.2023 | Andorra la Vella | *Andorra - Switzerland* | *1-2(0-2)* | (ECQ) |
| 19.06.2023 | Jerusalem | *Israel - Andorra* | *2-1(1-0)* | (ECQ) |

**22.09.2022  LIECHTENSTEIN - ANDORRA**　　　　**0-2(0-1)**　　　　3<sup>rd</sup> UEFA Nations League D, Group 1

Rheinpark Stadion, Vaduz; Referee: Juxhin Xhaja (Albania); Attendance: 914
**AND:** Iker Álvarez de Eulate Molné, Jesús Rubio Gómez, Max Llovera González-Adrio, Albert Alavedra Jiménez, Joan Cervós Moro, Marc Vales González (84.Márcio Vieira de Vasconcelos), Xavier Vieira de Vasconcelos (77.Marc Rebés Ruiz), Ricard Fernández Betriu (77.Victor Bernat Cuadros), Àlexandre Martínez Palau, Marc Pujol Pons (Cap) (66.Francisco Pomares Ortega), Albert Rosas Ubach (84.Jordi Rubio Gómez). Trainer: Jesús Luis Álvarez de Eulate Güergue "Koldo".
**Goals:** Albert Rosas Ubach (4), Joan Cervós Moro Moro (80).

**25.09.2022  ANDORRA - LATVIA**　　　　**1-1(0-0)**　　　　3<sup>rd</sup> UEFA Nations League D, Group 1

Estadi Nacional, Andorra la Vella; Referee: Anastasios Papapetrou (Greece); Attendance: 1,102
**AND:** Iker Álvarez de Eulate Molné, Eric de Pablos Solà, Max Llovera González-Adrio, Albert Alavedra Jiménez (74.Victor Bernat Cuadros), Francisco Pomares Ortega, Jordi Rubio Gómez (54.Àlexandre Martínez Palau), Márcio Vieira de Vasconcelos (Cap) (74.Luis Emilio Blanco Coto), Marc Vales González, Marc Rebés Ruiz (87.Marc Pujol Pons), Joan Cervós Moro, Ricard Fernández Betriu (54.Albert Rosas Ubach). Trainer: Jesús Luis Álvarez de Eulate Güergue "Koldo".
**Goal:** Albert Rosas Ubach (88).

**16.11.2022  ANDORRA - AUSTRIA**　　　　**0-1(0-0)**　　　　Friendly International

Estadio La Rosaleda, Málaga (Spain); Referee: José Luis Munuera Montero (Spain); Attendance: 150
**AND:** Iker Álvarez de Eulate Molné, Jesús Rubio Gómez (88.Aleix Viladot Caramés), Joel Guillén García, Max Llovera González-Adrio, Albert Alavedra Jiménez, Marc García Renom, Marc Rebés Ruiz (67.Éric Vales Ramos), Joan Cervós Moro (87.Jordi Rubio Gómez), Márcio Vieira de Vasconcelos (Cap) (88.Albert Reyes Roig), Àlexandre Martínez Palau (76.Izan Fernández Vieitez), Ricard Fernández Betriu (62.Albert Rosas Ubach). Trainer: Jesús Luis Álvarez de Eulate Güergue "Koldo".

**19.11.2022  GIBRALTAR - ANDORRA**　　　　**1-0(1-0)**　　　　Friendly International

Victoria Stadium, Gibraltar; Referee: Abdullah Al Kandari (Kuwait); Attendance: 2,206
**AND:** Iker Álvarez de Eulate Molné, Max Llovera González-Adrio, Albert Alavedra Jiménez, Joan Cervós Moro, Francisco Pomares Ortega (59.Victor Bernat Cuadros), Jesús Rubio Gómez (90.Izan Fernández Vieitez), Albert Rosas Ubach, Àlexandre Martínez Palau (76.Marc Rebés Ruiz), Marc Vales González (Cap) (90.Joel Guillén García), Xavier Vieira de Vasconcelos (59.Luis Emilio Blanco Coto), Ricard Fernández Betriu (59.Márcio Vieira de Vasconcelos). Trainer: Jesús Luis Álvarez de Eulate Güergue "Koldo".

**25.03.2023  ANDORRA - ROMANIA**　　　　**0-2(0-1)**　　　　17<sup>th</sup> EC. Qualifiers

Estadi Nacional, Andorra la Vella; Referee: Dario Bel (Croatia); Attendance: 2,927
**AND:** Iker Álvarez de Eulate Molné, Jesús Rubio Gómez, Albert Alavedra Jiménez, Max Llovera González-Adrio, Moisés San Nicolás Schellens (86.Marc García Renom), Joan Cervós Moro (86.Marc Pujol Pons), Marc Vales González (60.Joel Guillén García), Marc Rebés Ruiz [*sent off 61*], Márcio Vieira de Vasconcelos (Cap), Àlexandre Martínez Palau (72.Éric Vales Ramos), Albert Rosas Ubach (72.Ricard Fernández Betriu). Trainer: Jesús Luis Álvarez de Eulate Güergue "Koldo".

**28.03.2023  KOSOVO - ANDORRA**　　　　**1-1(0-0)**　　　　17<sup>th</sup> EC. Qualifiers

Stadiumi "Fadil Vokrri", Prishtina; Referee: Sebastian Gishamer (Austria); Attendance: 12,600
**AND:** Iker Álvarez de Eulate Molné, Jesús Rubio Gómez, Max Llovera González-Adrio, Albert Alavedra Jiménez, Joel Guillén García, Marc Vales González (Cap), Éric Vales Ramos, Marc García Renom (78.Moisés San Nicolás Schellens), Joan Cervós Moro (90+1.Victor Bernat Cuadros), Jordi Rubio Gómez (68.Àlexandre Martínez Palau), Albert Rosas Ubach (90+1.Marc Pujol Pons). Trainer: Jesús Luis Álvarez de Eulate Güergue "Koldo".
**Goal:** Albert Rosas Ubach (61).

**16.06.2023  ANDORRA - SWITZERLAND**　　　　**1-2(0-2)**　　　　17<sup>th</sup> EC. Qualifiers

Estadi Nacional, Andorra la Vella; Referee: Balázs Berke (Hungary); Attendance: 2,490
**AND:** Iker Álvarez de Eulate Molné, Jesús Rubio Gómez (23.Marc García Renom), Albert Alavedra Jiménez, Joel Guillén García (86.Ildefons Lima Solà), Max Llovera González-Adrio, Moisés San Nicolás Schellens (Cap), Marc Rebés Ruiz (64.Márcio Vieira de Vasconcelos), Éric Vales Ramos, Joan Cervós Moro, Jordi Aláez Peña (64.Àlexandre Martínez Palau), Albert Rosas Ubach (64.Ricard Fernández Betriu). Trainer: Jesús Luis Álvarez de Eulate Güergue "Koldo".
**Goal:** Márcio Vieira de Vasconcelos (67).

**19.06.2023  ISRAEL - ANDORRA**　　　　**2-1(1-0)**　　　　17<sup>th</sup> EC. Qualifiers

Teddy Stadium, Jerusalem; Referee: Dragomir Draganov (Bulgaria); Attendance: 13,300
**AND:** Iker Álvarez de Eulate Molné, Moisés San Nicolás Schellens, Albert Alavedra Jiménez, Joel Guillén García, Max Llovera González-Adrio, Joan Cervós Moro, Márcio Vieira de Vasconcelos (Cap) (81.Marc Rebés Ruiz), Éric Vales Ramos (89.Marc Pujol Pons), Marc García Renom (89.Àlexandre Martínez Palau), Jordi Aláez Peña (81.Izan Fernández Vieitez), Albert Rosas Ubach (67.Ricard Fernández Betriu). Trainer: Jesús Luis Álvarez de Eulate Güergue "Koldo".
**Goal:** Albert Rosas Ubach (52).

## NATIONAL TEAM PLAYERS
### (16.07.2022 – 15.07.2023)

| Name | DOB | Caps | Goals | Club | |
|------|-----|------|-------|------|---|
| **Goalkeepers** | | | | | |
| Iker ÁLVAREZ de Eulate Molné | 25.07.2001 | 15 | 0 | 2022/2023: | *Villarreal CF "B" (ESP)* |
| **Defenders** | | | | | |
| Albert ALAVEDRA Jiménez | 26.02.1999 | 26 | 0 | 2022:<br>30.01.2023-> | *CF Badalona (ESP)*<br>*ND Primorje Ajdovščina (SVN)* |
| Joan CERVÓS Moro | 24.02.1998 | 47 | 1 | 2022/2023: | *FK Rudar Prijedor (BIH)* |
| Eric DE PABLOS Solà | 08.03.1999 | 7 | 0 | 2022: | *UE Santa Coloma* |
| Joel GUILLÉN García | 28.08.2001 | 6 | 0 | 2022/2023: | *CF Atlético de Monzón (ESP)* |
| Ildefons LIMA Solà | 10.12.1979 | 135 | 11 | 2023: | *FC Andorra* |
| Max LLOVERA González-Adrio | 08.01.1997 | 62 | 1 | 2022/2023: | *CP San Cristóbal Tarrasa (ESP)* |
| Francisco "KIKO" POMARES Ortega | 21.09.1998 | 5 | 0 | 2022: | *FC Jove Español San Vicente del Raspeig (ESP)* |
| Marc PUJOL Pons | 21.08.1982 | 108 | 4 | 2022/2023: | *UE Engordany* |
| Marc REBÉS Ruiz | 03.07.1994 | 57 | 3 | 2022/2023: | *FC Santa Coloma* |
| Jesús "TXUS" RUBIO Gómez | 09.09.1994 | 41 | 1 | 2022/2023: | *Inter Club d'Escaldes* |
| Jordi RUBIO Gómez | 01.11.1987 | 64 | 0 | 2022/2023: | *UE Engordany* |
| Marc VALES González | 04.04.1990 | 86 | 5 | 2022:<br>13.02.2023-> | *Kelab Bola Sepak Kedah Darul Aman (MAS)*<br>*Real Unión Club Irún (ESP)* |
| Aleix VILADOT Caramés | | 1 | 0 | 2022: | *CD Arnedo (ESP)* |
| **Midfielders** | | | | | |
| Jordi ALÁEZ Peña | 23.01.1998 | 53 | 3 | 2023: | *FC Santa Coloma* |
| Luis Emilio BLANCO Coto | 15.01.1990 | 5 | 0 | 2022: | *UE Engordany* |
| Marc GARCÍA Renom „Chiqui" | 21.03.1988 | 62 | 0 | 2022/2023: | *UE Engordany* |
| Albert REYES Roig | 24.03.1996 | 4 | 0 | 2022: | *UE Santa Coloma* |
| Moisés SAN NICOLÁS Schellens | 17.09.1993 | 72 | 0 | 2023: | *Atlètic Club d'Escaldes Escaldes-Engordany* |
| Éric VALES Ramos | 18.08.2000 | 5 | 0 | 2022/2023: | *CDJ Tamarite (ESP)* |
| Márcio VIEIRA de Vasconcelos | 10.10.1984 | 121 | 2 | 2022/2023: | *CF Atlético de Monzón (ESP)* |
| Xavier VIEIRA de Vasconcelos | 14.01.1992 | 12 | 0 | 2022: | *UE Engordany* |
| **Forwards** | | | | | |
| Victor BERNAT Cuadros | 17.05.1987 | 18 | 1 | 2022/2023: | *UE Engordany* |
| Izan FERNÁNDEZ Vieitez | 03.10.2001 | 3 | 0 | 2022/2023: | *CF Atlético de Monzón (ESP)* |
| Ricard FERNÁNDEZ Betriu | 19.03.1999 | 33 | 1 | 2022/2023: | *CP San Cristóbal Tarrasa (ESP)* |
| Àlexandre "ÁLEX" MARTÍNEZ Palau | 10.10.1998 | 48 | 1 | 2022/2023: | *Atlètic Club d'Escaldes Escaldes-Engordany* |
| Albert ROSAS Ubach | 19.08.2002 | 14 | 4 | 2022:<br>31.01.2023-> | *Utebo FC (ESP)*<br>*Real Betis Balompié Sevilla "B" (ESP)* |
| **Trainer** | | | | | |
| Jesús Luis Álvarez de Eulate „KOLDO" [from 02.02.2010] | 04.09.1970 | | | 111 M; 10 W; 17 D; 84 L; 39-233 | |

# ARMENIA

## The Country:
Republic of Armenia (Hayastani Hanrapetut'yun)
Capital: Yerevan
Surface: 29,743 km²
Inhabitants: 3,000,756 [2022]
Time: UTC+4

## The FA:
Football Federation of Armenia
Khanjyan Street 27, 0010 Yerevan
Tel: +374 11 888 808
Foundation date: 18.01.1992
Member of FIFA since: 1992
Member of UEFA since: 1993
Website: www.ffa.am

## NATIONAL TEAM RECORDS

| RECORDS | | |
|---|---|---|
| **First international match:** | 14.10.1992, Yerevan | Armenia – Moldova 0-0 |
| **Most international caps:** | Sargis Hovsepyan | - 132 caps (1992-2012) |
| **Most international goals:** | Henrikh Mkhitaryan | - 32 goals / 95 caps (2007-2021) |

| UEFA EUROPEAN CHAMPIONSHIP | |
|---|---|
| 1960 | - |
| 1964 | - |
| 1968 | - |
| 1972 | - |
| 1976 | - |
| 1980 | - |
| 1984 | - |
| 1988 | - |
| 1992 | Did not enter |
| 1996 | Qualifiers |
| 2000 | Qualifiers |
| 2004 | Qualifiers |
| 2008 | Qualifiers |
| 2012 | Qualifiers |
| 2016 | Qualifiers |
| 2020 | Qualifiers |

| FIFA WORLD CUP | |
|---|---|
| 1930 | - |
| 1934 | - |
| 1938 | - |
| 1950 | - |
| 1954 | - |
| 1958 | - |
| 1962 | - |
| 1966 | - |
| 1970 | - |
| 1974 | - |
| 1978 | - |
| 1982 | - |
| 1986 | - |
| 1990 | - |
| 1994 | Did not enter |
| 1998 | Qualifiers |
| 2002 | Qualifiers |
| 2006 | Qualifiers |
| 2010 | Qualifiers |
| 2014 | Qualifiers |
| 2018 | Qualifiers |
| 2022 | Qualifiers |

| OLYMPIC TOURNAMENTS | |
|---|---|
| 1908 | - |
| 1912 | - |
| 1920 | - |
| 1924 | - |
| 1928 | - |
| 1936 | - |
| 1948 | - |
| 1952 | - |
| 1956 | - |
| 1960 | - |
| 1964 | - |
| 1968 | - |
| 1972 | - |
| 1976 | - |
| 1980 | - |
| 1984 | - |
| 1988 | - |
| 1992 | Did not enter |
| 1996 | Did not enter |
| 2000 | Qualifiers |
| 2004 | Qualifiers |
| 2008 | Qualifiers |
| 2012 | Qualifiers |
| 2016 | Qualifiers |
| 2020 | Qualifiers |

Please note: *was part of Soviet Union from 1920 to 1991.*

| UEFA NATIONS LEAGUE | |
|---|---|
| 2018/2019 | League D (Group Stage) |
| 2020/2021 | League C (Group Stage -> promoted to League B) |
| 2022/2023 | League B (Group Stage- > relegated to League C) |

## ARMENIAN CLUB HONOURS IN EUROPEAN CLUB COMPETITIONS:

| European Champion Clubs.Cup (1956-1992) / UEFA Champions League (1993-2023) |
|---|
| None |

| Fairs Cup (1858-1971) / UEFA Cup (1972-2009) / UEFA Europa League (2010-2023) |
|---|
| None |

| UEFA Europa Conference League (2021-2023) |
|---|
| None |

| UEFA Super Cup (1972-2022) |
|---|
| None |

| *European Cup Winners' Cup 1961-1999* |
|---|
| None |

*defunct competition*

# NATIONAL COMPETITIONS
## TABLE OF HONOURS

### ARMENIAN SSR (SOVIET ERA) CHAMPIONS

| Year | Champion | Year | Champion | Year | Champion |
|------|----------|------|----------|------|----------|
| 1936 | Dinamo Yerevan | 1955 | Khimik Kirovakan | 1971 | FIMA Yerevan |
| 1937 | Dinamo Yerevan | 1956 | FIMA Yerevan | 1972 | Zvezda Yerevan |
| 1938 | Spartak Yerevan | 1957 | Karmir Drosh Leninakan | 1973 | Kotayk Abovyan |
| 1939 | Spartak Yerevan | 1958 | FIMA Yerevan | 1974 | FIMA Yerevan |
| 1940 | Spartak Yerevan | 1959 | FIMA Yerevan | 1975 | Kotayk Abovyan |
| 1941-44 | *No competition* | 1960 | Tekstilshchik Leninakan | 1976 | Kotayk Abovyan |
| 1945 | Spartak Yerevan | 1961 | Tekstilshchik Leninakan | 1977 | Araks Yerevan |
| 1946 | Dinamo Yerevan | 1962 | Tekstilshchik Leninakan | 1978 | Kanaz Yerevan |
| 1947 | Dinamo Yerevan | 1963 | Lokomotiv Yerevan | 1979 | Aragats Leninakan |
| 1948 | Dinamo Yerevan | 1964 | Khimik Kirovakan | 1980 | Aragats Leninakan |
| 1949 | Dinamo Yerevan | 1965 | Araks Yerevan | 1981-86 | *No competition* |
| 1950 | Urozhai Yerevan | 1966 | Elektrotekhnik Yerevan | 1987 | Aragats Leninakan |
| 1951 | Shinarar Yerevan | 1967 | Kotayk Abovyan | 1988 | Elektrotekhnik Yerevan |
| 1952 | Spartak Yerevan | 1968 | Araks Yerevan | 1989 | FC Kapan |
| 1953 | Karmir Drosh Leninakan | 1969 | Araks Yerevan | 1990 | Ararat-2 Yerevan |
| 1954 | Spartak Yerevan | 1970 | Motor Yerevan | 1991 | Syunik Kapan |

| | CHAMPIONS | CUP WINNERS | BEST GOALSCORERS | |
|------|-----------|-------------|------------------|---|
| 1992 | Shirak SC Gyumri<br>Homenetmen Yerevan (shared) | FC Banants Yerevan | Vahe Yaghmuryan (FC Ararat Yerevan) | 38 |
| 1993 | FC Ararat Yerevan | FC Ararat Yerevan | Andranik Hovsepyan (Banants)<br>Gegham Hovhannisyan (Homenetmen Yerevan) | 26 |
| 1994 | Shirak SC Gyumri | FC Ararat Yerevan | Arsen Avetisyan (Homenetmen Yerevan) | 39 |
| 1995 | *Transitional Season (No Winner)* | FC Ararat Yerevan | - | |
| 1995/1996 | FC Pyunik Yerevan | FC Pyunik Yerevan | Arayik Adamyan (Shirak SC Gyumri) | 28 |
| 1996/1997 | FC Pyunik Yerevan | FC Ararat Yerevan | Arsen Avetisyan (FC Pyunik Yerevan) | 24 |
| 1997 | FC Yerevan | - | Artur Petrosyan (Shirak SC Gyumri) | 18 |
| 1998 | FC Tsement Ararat | FC Tsement Ararat | Ara Hakobyan (Dvin Artashat) | 20 |
| 1999 | Shirak SC Gyumri | FC Tsement Ararat | Shirak SC Gyumri Sarikyan (FC Tsement Ararat) | 21 |
| 2000 | Araks Ararat FC | FC Mika Yerevan | Ara Hakobyan (Araks Ararat FC) | 21 |
| 2001 | FC Pyunik Yerevan | FC Mika Yerevan | Arman Karamyan (FC Pyunik Yerevan) | 21 |
| 2002 | FC Pyunik Yerevan | FC Pyunik Yerevan | Arman Karamyan (FC Pyunik Yerevan) | 36 |
| 2003 | FC Pyunik Yerevan | FC Mika Yerevan | Ara Hakobyan (FC Banants Yerevan) | 45 |
| 2004 | FC Pyunik Yerevan | FC Pyunik Yerevan | Edgar Manucharyan (FC Pyunik Yerevan)<br>Galust Petrosyan (FC Pyunik Yerevan) | 21 |
| 2005 | FC Pyunik Yerevan | FC Mika Yerevan | Nshan Erzrumyan (Kilikia FC Yerevan) | 18 |
| 2006 | FC Pyunik Yerevan | FC Mika Yerevan | Aram Hakobyan (FC Banants Yerevan) | 25 |
| 2007 | FC Pyunik Yerevan | FC Banants Yerevan | Marcos Pinheiro Pizzelli (Ararat Yerevan) | 22 |
| 2008 | FC Pyunik Yerevan | FC Ararat Yerevan | Marcos Pinheiro Pizzelli (Ararat Yerevan) | 17 |
| 2009 | FC Pyunik Yerevan | FC Pyunik Yerevan | Artur Kocharyan (Ulisses FC Yerevan) | 15 |
| 2010 | FC Pyunik Yerevan | FC Pyunik Yerevan | Marcos Pinheiro Pizzelli (FC Pyunik Yerevan)<br>Gevorg Ghazaryan (FC Pyunik Yerevan) | 16 |
| 2011 | Ulisses FC Yerevan | FC Mika Yerevan | Bruno César Correa (BRA, FC Banants Yerevan) | 16 |
| 2011/2012 | *Transitional Season (No winner)* | Shirak SC Gyumri | - | |
| 2012/2013 | Shirak SC Gyumri | FC Pyunik Yerevan | Norayr Gyozalyan (Impuls FC Dilijan) | 21 |
| 2013/2014 | FC Banants Yerevan | FC Pyunik Yerevan | Mihran Manasyan (FC Alashkert Yerevan) | 17 |
| 2014/2015 | FC Pyunik Yerevan | FC Pyunik Yerevan | César Romero Zamora (USA, FC Pyunik Yerevan)<br>Jean-Jacques Bougouhi (CIV, Shirak SC Gyumri) | 21 |
| 2015/2016 | FC Alashkert Yerevan | FC Banants Yerevan | Héber Araujo dos Santos (BRA, FC Alashkert Yerevan);<br>Mihran Manasyan (FC Alashkert Yerevan) | 16 |
| 2016/2017 | FC Alashkert Yerevan | Shirak SC Gyumri | Artak Yedigaryan (FC Alashkert Yerevan)<br>Mihran Manasyan (FC Alashkert Yerevan) | 13 |
| 2017/2018 | FC Alashkert Yerevan | FC Gandzasar Kapan | Artak Yedigaryan (FC Alashkert Yerevan)<br>Gegham Harutyunyan (FC Gandzasar Kapan) | 12 |
| 2018/2019 | FC Ararat-Armenia Yerevan | FC Alashkert Yerevan | Jonel Désiré (HAI, Lori FC Vanadzor) | 17 |
| 2019/2020 | FC Ararat-Armenia Yerevan | FC Noah Yerevan | Mory Koné (CIV, Shirak SC Gyumri) | 23 |
| 2020/2021 | FC Alashkert Yerevan | FC Ararat Yerevan | Yusuf Olaitan Otubanjo (NGA, FC Ararat-Armenia Yerevan) | 10 |
| 2021/2022 | FC Pyunik Yerevan | Noravank SC Vayk | Serges Deblé (CIV, FC Ararat Yerevan / FC Pyunik Yerevan) | 22 |
| 2022/2023 | FC Urartu Yerevan | FC Urartu Yerevan | Luka Juričić (BIH) & Yusuf Olaitan Otubanjo (NGA)<br>(both FC Pyunik Yerevan) | 17 |

Please note: Homenetmen Yerevan became FC Pyunik Yerevan (1995); Tsement Ararat changed its name to Araks Ararat FC (2000).

# NATIONAL CHAMPIONSHIP
## Armenian Premier League / Bardsragujn chumb 2022/2023
### (29.07.2022 – 06.06.2023)

## Results

### Round 1 [29-31.07.2022]
Lernayin Artsakh - FC Van 0-1
FC Noah - FC Alashkert 3-4
FC Pyunik - FC Ararat 0-1
BKMA Yerevan - FC Shirak 0-1
FC Urartu - FC Ararat-Armenia 1-0

### Round 2 [06-08.08.2022]
FC Noah - Lernayin Artsakh 0-1
FC Alashkert - FC Ararat 2-0
FC Van - BKMA Yerevan 2-2
FC Shirak - FC Urartu 0-2
FC Ararat-Armenia - FC Pyunik 0-0 [10.11.22]

### Round 3 [11-13.08.2022]
FC Ararat - FC Ararat-Armenia 0-2
Lernayin Artsakh - FC Alashkert 0-1
BKMA Yerevan - FC Noah 2-2
FC Pyunik - FC Shirak 1-0
FC Urartu - FC Van 0-1

### Round 4 [19-21.08.2022]
FC Alashkert - FC Ararat-Armenia 1-1
Lernayin Artsakh - BKMA Yerevan 1-1
FC Shirak - FC Ararat 0-0
FC Noah - FC Urartu 0-6
FC Pyunik - FC Van 0-1

### Round 5 [26-29.08.2022]
BKMA Yerevan - FC Alashkert 2-4
FC Ararat - FC Van 1-0
FC Ararat-Armenia - FC Shirak 3-0
FC Urartu - Lernayin Artsakh 2-3
FC Pyunik - FC Noah 3-0

### Round 6 [02-04.09.2022]
FC Alashkert - FC Shirak 3-0
FC Van - FC Ararat-Armenia 0-4
FC Noah - FC Ararat 0-0
FC Pyunik - Lernayin Artsakh 1-0
BKMA Yerevan - FC Urartu 1-4

### Round 7 [08-12.09.2022]
FC Shirak - FC Van 1-1
Lernayin Artsakh - FC Ararat 2-1
FC Ararat-Armenia - FC Noah 3-0
FC Urartu - FC Alashkert 1-1
FC Pyunik - BKMA Yerevan 3-1

### Round 8 [16-19.09.2022]
FC Alashkert - FC Van 0-0
FC Noah - FC Shirak 1-3
BKMA Yerevan - FC Ararat 2-1
Lernayin Artsakh - FC Ararat-Armenia 0-1
FC Urartu - FC Pyunik 2-1

### Round 9 [30.09.-02.10.2022]
FC Ararat-Armenia - BKMA Yerevan 1-0
FC Ararat - FC Urartu 0-2
FC Shirak - Lernayin Artsakh 1-2
FC Pyunik - FC Alashkert 5-1
FC Van - FC Noah 2-2

### Round 10 [09-11.10.2022]
FC Ararat-Armenia - FC Urartu 0-1
FC Ararat - FC Pyunik 1-0
FC Alashkert - FC Noah 5-0
FC Van - Lernayin Artsakh 1-1
FC Shirak - BKMA Yerevan 1-0

### Round 11 [14-17.10.2022]
FC Ararat - FC Alashkert 0-1
Lernayin Artsakh - FC Noah 0-0
BKMA Yerevan - FC Van 0-3
FC Urartu - FC Shirak 1-0
FC Pyunik - FC Ararat-Armenia 2-1

### Round 12 [19-21.10.2022]
FC Noah - BKMA Yerevan 0-0
FC Van - FC Urartu 0-1
FC Alashkert - Lernayin Artsakh 2-1
FC Ararat-Armenia - FC Ararat 2-1
FC Shirak - FC Pyunik 0-1

### Round 13 [23-26.10.2022]
FC Urartu - FC Noah 3-1
BKMA Yerevan - Lernayin Artsakh 0-1
FC Ararat - FC Shirak 0-1
FC Ararat-Armenia - FC Alashkert 4-1
FC Van - FC Pyunik 0-3 [24.02.2023]

### Round 14 [29-31.10.2022]
Lernayin Artsakh - FC Urartu 1-2
FC Van - FC Ararat 0-2
FC Alashkert - BKMA Yerevan 1-0
FC Shirak - FC Ararat-Armenia 0-5
FC Noah - FC Pyunik 0-1

### Round 15 [03-06.11.2022]
FC Ararat-Armenia - FC Van 4-0
FC Shirak - FC Alashkert 0-2
FC Urartu - BKMA Yerevan 1-0
FC Ararat - FC Noah 2-1
Lernayin Artsakh - FC Pyunik 1-1

### Round 16 [09-13.11.2022]
FC Van - FC Shirak 2-1
FC Alashkert - FC Urartu 0-0
FC Ararat - Lernayin Artsakh 0-0
FC Noah - FC Ararat-Armenia 1-2
BKMA Yerevan - FC Pyunik 1-1

### Round 17 [08-09.12.2022]
FC Van - FC Alashkert 1-0 [13.11.2022]
FC Shirak - FC Noah 2-0
FC Ararat - BKMA Yerevan 0-0
FC Ararat-Armenia - Lernayin Artsakh 1-0
FC Pyunik - FC Urartu 0-3

### Round 18 [20-22.11.2022]
Lernayin Artsakh - FC Shirak 0-0
FC Noah - FC Van 2-2
FC Alashkert - FC Pyunik 1-2
BKMA Yerevan - FC Ararat-Armenia 2-2
FC Urartu - FC Ararat 2-1

### Round 19 [28-30.11.2022]
Lernayin Artsakh - FC Van 0-2
FC Noah - FC Alashkert 3-2
BKMA Yerevan - FC Shirak 0-1
FC Pyunik - FC Ararat 2-0
FC Urartu - FC Ararat-Armenia 0-3

### Round 20 [03-05.12.2022]
FC Van - BKMA Yerevan 0-1
FC Noah - Lernayin Artsakh 2-0
FC Alashkert - FC Ararat 0-1
FC Shirak - FC Urartu 2-3
FC Ararat-Armenia - FC Pyunik 1-1

### Round 21 [27.02.-01.03.2023]
BKMA Yerevan - FC Noah 0-1
FC Ararat - FC Ararat-Armenia 1-3
Lernayin Artsakh - FC Alashkert 1-3
FC Urartu - FC Van 2-0
FC Pyunik - FC Shirak 4-1

### Round 22 [04-06.03.2023]
Lernayin Artsakh - BKMA Yerevan 0-3
FC Van - FC Pyunik 1-3
FC Alashkert - FC Ararat-Armenia 0-0
FC Ararat - FC Shirak 1-2
FC Noah - FC Urartu 0-2

### Round 23 [10-12.03.2023]
BKMA Yerevan - FC Alashkert 1-1
FC Ararat - FC Van 1-3
FC Urartu - Lernayin Artsakh 3-0
FC Pyunik - FC Noah 2-0
FC Ararat-Armenia - FC Shirak 1-0

### Round 24 [16-18.03.2023]
Lernayin Artsakh - FC Pyunik 0-6
BKMA Yerevan - FC Urartu 0-2
FC Alashkert - FC Shirak 3-0
FC Van - FC Ararat-Armenia 1-2
FC Noah - FC Ararat 2-1

### Round 25 [31.03.-02.04.2023]
FC Ararat - Lernayin Artsakh 2-0
FC Pyunik - BKMA Yerevan 3-0
FC Shirak - FC Van 1-0
FC Ararat-Armenia - FC Noah 3-0
FC Urartu - FC Alashkert 1-0

### Round 26 [09-11.04.2023]
FC Alashkert - FC Van 3-1
BKMA Yerevan - FC Ararat 0-1
Lernayin Artsakh - FC Ararat-Armenia 0-2
FC Noah - FC Shirak 3-3
FC Urartu - FC Pyunik 1-3

### Round 27 [15-17.04.2023]
FC Ararat-Armenia - BKMA Yerevan 2-1
FC Ararat - FC Urartu 0-0
FC Shirak - Lernayin Artsakh 1-0
FC Van - FC Noah 1-1
FC Pyunik - FC Alashkert 1-0

### Round 28 [20-22.04.2023]
FC Shirak - BKMA Yerevan 1-1
FC Van - Lernayin Artsakh 4-0
FC Alashkert - FC Noah 3-0
FC Ararat - FC Pyunik 0-2
FC Ararat-Armenia - FC Urartu 2-2

### Round 29 [25-27.04.2023]
Lernayin Artsakh - FC Noah 0-2
BKMA Yerevan - FC Van 5-1
FC Ararat - FC Alashkert 2-4
FC Urartu - FC Shirak 3-1
FC Pyunik - FC Ararat-Armenia 4-1

### Round 30 [01-03.05.2023]
FC Alashkert - Lernayin Artsakh 1-0
FC Noah - BKMA Yerevan 1-2
FC Van - FC Urartu 0-5
FC Shirak - FC Pyunik 0-4
FC Ararat-Armenia - FC Ararat 2-1

| Round 31 [07-10.05.2023] | Round 32 [15-17.05.2023] | Round 33 [20-22.05.2023] |
|---|---|---|
| FC Pyunik - FC Van 4-0 | FC Van - FC Ararat 3-1 | FC Ararat - FC Noah 1-0 |
| FC Urartu - FC Noah 1-0 | FC Noah - FC Pyunik 1-3 | FC Pyunik - Lernayin Artsakh 2-0 |
| FC Shirak - FC Ararat 0-0 | FC Alashkert - BKMA Yerevan 1-2 | FC Shirak - FC Alashkert 0-1 |
| BKMA Yerevan - Lernayin Artsakh 2-1 | Lernayin Artsakh - FC Urartu 0-4 | FC Ararat-Armenia - FC Van 4-1 |
| FC Ararat-Armenia - FC Alashkert 0-1 | FC Shirak - FC Ararat-Armenia 0-2 | FC Urartu - BKMA Yerevan 1-0 |

| Round 34 [25-27.05.2023] | Round 35 [30.05.-02.06.2023] | Round 36 [04-06.06.2023] |
|---|---|---|
| Lernayin Artsakh - FC Ararat 0-3 | FC Ararat - BKMA Yerevan 1-1 | FC Noah - FC Van 1-0 |
| FC Van - FC Shirak 3-0 | FC Van - FC Alashkert 0-1 | Lernayin Artsakh - FC Shirak 0-1 |
| BKMA Yerevan - FC Pyunik 1-1 | FC Shirak - FC Noah 0-2 | BKMA Yerevan - FC Ararat-Armenia 2-5 |
| FC Alashkert - FC Urartu 3-2 | FC Ararat-Armenia - Lernayin Artsakh 0-0 | FC Alashkert - FC Pyunik 1-2 |
| FC Noah - FC Ararat-Armenia 2-1 | FC Pyunik - FC Urartu 0-1 | FC Urartu - FC Ararat 1-1 |

## Final Standings

| | | Total | | | | | | Home | | | | | Away | | | |
|---|---|---|---|---|---|---|---|---|---|---|---|---|---|---|---|---|---|
| 1. | **FC Urartu Yerevan** | 36 | 26 | 5 | 5 | 68 - 25 | **83** | 12 | 2 | 4 | 26 - 16 | 14 | 3 | 1 | 42 - 9 |
| 2. | FC Pyunik Yerevan | 36 | 25 | 5 | 6 | 72 - 23 | **80** | 14 | 0 | 4 | 37 - 11 | 11 | 5 | 2 | 35 - 12 |
| 3. | FC Ararat-Armenia Yerevan | 36 | 23 | 7 | 6 | 70 - 27 | **76** | 12 | 4 | 2 | 33 - 10 | 11 | 3 | 4 | 37 - 17 |
| 4. | FC Alashkert Yerevan | 36 | 20 | 6 | 10 | 58 - 37 | **66** | 10 | 4 | 4 | 30 - 12 | 10 | 2 | 6 | 28 - 25 |
| 5. | FC Van Charentsavan | 36 | 11 | 7 | 18 | 38 - 59 | **40** | 5 | 4 | 9 | 21 - 30 | 6 | 3 | 9 | 17 - 29 |
| 6. | FC Ararat Yerevan | 36 | 10 | 8 | 18 | 29 - 42 | **38** | 5 | 4 | 9 | 13 - 22 | 5 | 4 | 9 | 16 - 20 |
| 7. | FC Shirak Gyumri | 36 | 10 | 6 | 20 | 25 - 55 | **36** | 4 | 4 | 10 | 10 - 26 | 6 | 2 | 10 | 15 - 29 |
| 8. | FC Noah Armavir | 36 | 8 | 8 | 20 | 34 - 66 | **32** | 5 | 4 | 9 | 22 - 33 | 3 | 4 | 11 | 12 - 33 |
| 9. | BKMA Yerevan | 36 | 7 | 11 | 18 | 36 - 53 | **32** | 3 | 5 | 10 | 21 - 33 | 4 | 6 | 8 | 15 - 20 |
| 10. | Lernayin Artsakh FC Stepanakert (Relegated) | 36 | 5 | 7 | 24 | 16 - 59 | **22** | 1 | 4 | 13 | 6 - 34 | 4 | 3 | 11 | 10 - 25 |

| Top goalscorers: | |
|---|---|
| 17  Luka Juričić (BIH) | *FC Pyunik Yerevan* |
| 17  Yusuf Olaitan Otubanjo (NGA) | *FC Pyunik Yerevan* |
| 13  Wilfried Kwassi Ezza (CIV) | *FC Ararat-Armenia Yerevan* |

## NATIONAL CUP
### Armenian Cup / Arrajin chumb 2022/2023

| First Round [04-06.10.2022] | | | |
|---|---|---|---|
| FC Ararat Yerevan - FC Ararat-Armenia Yerevan | 0-4(0-1) | FC Syunik Kapan - FC Shirak Gyumri | 1-5(0-2) |
| FC Mika Yerevan - FC Gandzasar Kapan | 1-2(0-0) | Lernayin Artsakh FC - FC Van Charentsavan | 1-3(0-2) |
| FC West Armenia - FC Alashkert Yerevan | 1-4(1-2) | BKMA Yerevan - FC Noah Armavir | 0-1(0-1) |

| Quarter-Finals [24-26.11.2022] | | | |
|---|---|---|---|
| FC Shirak Gyumri - FC Van Charentsavan | 2-0(1-0) | FC Ararat-Armenia Yerevan - FC Urartu Yerevan | 0-4(0-1) |
| FC Gandzasar Kapan - FC Alashkert Yerevan | 0-0 aet; 5-4 pen | FC Pyunik Yerevan - FC Noah Armavir | 3-0(1-0) |

| Semi-Finals [05-06.04.2023] | | | |
|---|---|---|---|
| FC Shirak Gyumri - FC Pyunik Yerevan | 1-1 aet; 5-3 pen | FC Urartu Yerevan - FC Gandzasar Kapan | 4-0(0-0) |

## Final

13.05.2023; „Vazgen Sargsyan" Hanrapetakan Stadium, Yerevan; Referee: Andris Treimanis (Latvia); Attendance: n/a
**FC Shirak Gyumri - FC Urartu Yerevan**      **1-2(1-1)**

**FC Shirak**: Egor Achinov, Arsen Sadoyan, Aleksa Vidić, Marko Prljević, Robert Darbinyan, Rafik Misakyan (74.Levon Darbinyan), Junior Magico Traoré, Donald Alvine Kodia, Moussa Bakayoko [*sent off 72*], Lyova Mryan (64.Allasana Doumbia), Vally Cissé (79.Robert Hakobyan). Trainer: Edgar Torosyan.

**FC Urartu**: Aleksandr Melikhov, Nana Antwi (80.Karen Melkonyan), Yevhen Tsymbalyuk, Erik Piloyan, Zhirayr Margaryan, Ugochukwu Christus Iwu, Aras Özbiliz (90+1.Maksim Mayrovich), David Khurtsidze, Marcos Antônio Candido Ferreira Junior (90+1.Dramane Salou), Oleg Polyakov (46.Narek Grigoryan), Dmytro Khlyobas (66.Leon Sabua). Trainer: Dmitriy Gunko (Russia).

**Goals:** 0-1 David Khurtsidze (1), 1-1 Moussa Bakayoko (6), 1-2 Karen Melkonyan (85).

## Football Club Alashkert Yerevan

| | | | |
|---|---|---|---|
| **Founded**: | 1990 | | |
| **Stadium**: | Alashkert Stadium, Yerevan (6,850) | | |
| **Trainer**: | Karen Barseghyan | | 15.03.1975 |
| [24.12.2022] | Vahe Gevorgyan | | 21.09.1987 |

| Goalkeepers: | DOB | M | (s) | G |
|---|---|---|---|---|
| Ognjen Čančarević (SRB) | 25.09.1989 | 33 | | |
| Roman Mysak (UKR) | 09.09.1991 | 3 | | |
| **Defenders:** | **DOB** | **M** | **(s)** | **G** |
| Vahagn Ayvazyan | 16.04.1992 | 2 | (4) | |
| Daniel José Carrillo Montilla (VEN) | 02.12.1995 | 15 | | |
| Deou Dosa Olatunji (NGA) | 29.07.1998 | 2 | (3) | |
| Serob Grigoryan | 04.02.1995 | 1 | (5) | |
| James Santos das Neves (BRA) | 15.07.1995 | 18 | | 1 |
| Didier Kadio (CIV) | 05.04.1990 | 12 | (4) | |
| Arman Khachatryan | 09.06.1997 | 1 | | |
| Annan Mensah (GHA) | 06.07.1996 | 28 | (2) | 3 |
| Mateo Mužek (CRO) | 29.04.1995 | 15 | (1) | 2 |
| Timur Rudoselskiy (KAZ) | 21.12.1994 | 4 | (5) | |
| Tiago Coelho Andrade "Tiago Cametá" (BRA) | 05.05.1992 | 12 | | |
| Vitaliy Ustinov (RUS) | 03.05.1991 | 15 | | 2 |
| Taron Voskanyan | 22.02.1993 | 23 | (1) | 1 |
| Andranik Voskanyan | 11.04.1990 | 3 | (1) | |
| Artak Yedigaryan | 18.03.1990 | 31 | (2) | 10 |
| **Midfielders:** | **DOB** | **M** | **(s)** | **G** |
| Wbeymar Angulo Mosquera | 06.03.1992 | 8 | (3) | |
| Wangu Batista Gome (NAM) | 13.02.1993 | 7 | (8) | |
| Artak Grigoryan | 19.10.1987 | 28 | (5) | |
| Benik Hovhannisyan | 01.05.1993 | 5 | (5) | |
| Rumyan Hovsepyan | 13.11.1991 | 4 | (7) | |
| Sergey Ivanov (RUS) | 07.01.1997 | 7 | (6) | 3 |
| David Khurtsidze (RUS) | 04.07.1993 | 1 | | |
| Aram Kocharyan | 05.03.1996 | 7 | (5) | |
| Karen Nalbandyan | 14.04.2002 | 4 | (7) | |
| Yeison Bossa Racines (ECU) | 07.10.1998 | 9 | (3) | 2 |
| Sargis Shahinyan | 10.09.1995 | 21 | (10) | |
| Tiago Galvão da Silva (BRA) | 24.08.1989 | 25 | (8) | 9 |
| **Forwards:** | **DOB** | **M** | **(s)** | **G** |
| Agdon Santos Menezes (BRA) | 26.01.1993 | 6 | (6) | 2 |
| Fáider Fabio Burbano Castillo (COL) | 19.06.1992 | 1 | (5) | |
| Ronald Cuéllar Ortíz (BOL) | 09.06.1997 | | (13) | 2 |
| Bladimir Yovany Díaz Saavedra (COL) | 10.07.1992 | 12 | (6) | 11 |
| Ismaël Fofana (CIV) | 08.09.1988 | 2 | (3) | |
| Aleksandr Karapetyan | 23.12.1987 | 2 | (1) | |
| Lucas Ventura Lopes (BRA) | 23.05.1997 | 4 | (3) | |
| Karapet Manukyan | 25.07.1992 | 3 | (3) | |
| Narek Manukyan | 19.12.2003 | | (1) | |
| Sargis Metoyan | 06.09.1997 | 2 | (11) | 1 |
| Artur Miranyan | 27.12.1995 | 10 | (6) | 3 |
| Uros Nenadović (SRB) | 28.01.1994 | 4 | (8) | 1 |
| Grigor Nikoghosyan | 28.04.2006 | | (1) | |
| Ivan Pešić (CRO) | 06.04.1992 | 2 | (9) | 1 |
| Kevin Stivens Reyes Ortíz (SLV) | 28.08.1997 | 4 | (5) | 3 |
| Aleksandr Ter-Tovmasyan | 01.06.2003 | | (1) | |

## Football Club Ararat Yerevan

| | | | |
|---|---|---|---|
| **Founded**: | 10.05.1935 | | |
| **Stadium**: | „Vazgen Sargsyan" Hanrapetakan Stadium, Yerevan (14,403) | | |
| **Trainer**: | Aram Voskanyan | | 26.08.1975 |
| [04.10.2022] | Rafael Safaryan | | 30.01.1986 |
| [16.10.2022] | Gagik Simonyan | | 21.08.1971 |
| [29.10.2022] | Aleksandr Petrosyan | | 28.05.1986 |
| [31.03.2023] | Gagik Simonyan | | 21.08.1971 |

| Goalkeepers: | DOB | M | (s) | G |
|---|---|---|---|---|
| Nemanja Lemajić (MNE) | 14.05.1998 | 3 | | |
| Gor Manukyan | 27.09.1993 | 6 | | |
| Artem Potapov (RUS) | 28.06.1994 | 18 | | |
| Sergey Revyakin (RUS) | 02.04.1995 | 9 | | |
| **Defenders:** | **DOB** | **M** | **(s)** | **G** |
| Vardan Arzoyan | 30.04.1995 | 5 | (4) | |
| Aymen Ben Mahmoud (TUN) | 24.04.1996 | 9 | | 1 |
| Juan David Bravo Padilla (COL) | 01.04.1990 | 14 | (3) | |
| Robert Darbinyan | 04.10.1995 | 11 | (3) | |
| Arman Hovhannisyan | 07.07.1993 | 6 | | |
| Hayk Ishkhanyan | 24.06.1989 | 25 | (1) | |
| Christian Dimitri Legbo Oueghi (CIV) | 30.08.2001 | 14 | (1) | |
| Yuri Maghakyan | 22.06.2000 | | (1) | |
| Teddy Mézague (FRA) | 27.05.1990 | 8 | (1) | 1 |
| Dušan Mijić (SRB) | 22.06.1993 | 15 | | 2 |
| Hrayr Mkoyan | 02.09.1986 | 29 | | |
| Arman Mkrtchyan | 09.07.1999 | 9 | (5) | |
| Hovhannes Nazaryan | 11.03.1998 | 2 | (3) | |
| **Midfielders:** | **DOB** | **M** | **(s)** | **G** |
| Petros Afajanyan | 31.10.1998 | 1 | (6) | |
| Isah Aliyu (NGA) | 08.08.1999 | 14 | (4) | |
| Alik Arakelyan | 21.05.1996 | 8 | (8) | 1 |
| Erik Azizyan | 04.03.2000 | | (3) | |
| Georgi Babaliev (BUL) | 14.05.2001 | 4 | (4) | |
| Babou Cham (GAM) | 03.03.1999 | | (8) | |
| Alasan Faye (SEN) | 28.09.2003 | 6 | (3) | |
| Eduard Galstyan | 01.05.2004 | | (2) | |
| Serob Galstyan | 23.09.2002 | 12 | (20) | 1 |
| Kassim Hadji (COM) | 23.03.2000 | 13 | (1) | 2 |
| Gor Malakyan | 12.06.1994 | 26 | (3) | |
| David Manoyan | 05.07.1990 | 9 | (10) | |
| Rudik Mkrtchyan | 26.10.1998 | 32 | (1) | 3 |
| Hadji Issa Moustapha (CMR) | 04.12.2003 | 7 | (5) | |
| Timur Pukhov (RUS) | 17.06.1998 | 3 | (4) | |
| Sosthène Tiehide (CIV) | 10.01.2002 | 2 | (4) | |
| **Forwards:** | **DOB** | **M** | **(s)** | **G** |
| Armand Dagrou (CIV) | 30.06.2000 | 14 | (6) | 1 |
| Aleksandar Glišić (BIH) | 03.09.1992 | 12 | (5) | 3 |
| Razmik Hakobyan | 09.02.1996 | 14 | (15) | 7 |
| Mohamed Koné (CIV) | 07.08.2003 | 4 | (6) | |
| Edgar Malakyan | 22.09.1990 | 12 | (4) | 1 |
| Ibeh Ransom Jidechukwu (NGA) | 29.06.2003 | 9 | (5) | 3 |
| Amara Traoré (CIV) | 02.01.2001 | 11 | (8) | 3 |

## Football Club Ararat-Armenia Yerevan

| | | | |
|---|---|---|---|
| **Founded**: | 2017 | | |
| **Stadium**: | Yerevan Football Academy Stadium, Yerevan (1,428) | | |
| **Trainer**: | Vardan Bichakhchyan | | 09.10.1977 |

| Goalkeepers: | DOB | M | (s) | G |
|---|---|---|---|---|
| Vsevolod Ermakov (RUS) | 06.01.1996 | 36 | | |
| **Defenders:** | **DOB** | **M** | **(s)** | **G** |
| Guilherme António de Souza "Alemão" (BRA) | 07.12.1992 | 24 | | 5 |
| Edgar Grigoryan | 25.08.1998 | 9 | | |
| Hakob Hakobyan | 29.03.1997 | 20 | (4) | 2 |
| Arman Hovhannisyan | 07.07.1993 | 3 | (3) | |
| José Junior Julio Bueno (COL) | 03.09.1996 | 23 | | 1 |
| Dragan Lovrić (CRO) | 03.01.1996 | 8 | (1) | |
| Styopa Mkrtchyan | 17.02.2003 | 8 | | |
| Carlos Anderson Pérez Ochoa (COL) | 15.06.1995 | 8 | | 1 |
| Romércio Pereira da Conceição (BRA) | 25.02.1997 | 14 | | 2 |
| Erik Smbatyan | 10.02.2003 | | (1) | |
| Milos Stamenković (SRB) | 01.06.1990 | 4 | | |
| Davit Terteryan | 17.12.1997 | 15 | (4) | |
| **Midfielders:** | **DOB** | **M** | **(s)** | **G** |
| Armen Ambartsumyan | 11.04.1994 | 18 | (12) | 3 |
| Wbeymar Angulo Mosquera | 06.03.1992 | 1 | (5) | |
| Artem Avanesyan | 17.07.1999 | 16 | (14) | 1 |
| Michel Ayvazyan | 21.06.2005 | | (1) | |
| Karen Muradyan | 01.11.1992 | 27 | (7) | |
| Amos Nondi Obiero (KEN) | 10.02.1999 | 14 | | 1 |
| Alwyn Luheni Tera (KEN) | 18.01.1997 | 22 | (7) | 1 |
| Solomon Ime Udo | 15.07.1995 | 11 | (11) | |
| **Forwards:** | **DOB** | **M** | **(s)** | **G** |
| Agdon Santos Menezes (BRA) | 26.01.1993 | 6 | (5) | 3 |
| Jesse Akila (NGA) | 27.12.2001 | | (16) | 1 |
| Jonathan Alexander Duarte Durán (COL) | 25.05.1997 | 10 | (10) | 3 |
| Wilfried Eza (CIV) | 28.12.1996 | 25 | (9) | 13 |
| Hugo Filipe Pinto Servulo Firmino (POR) | 22.12.1988 | 16 | (7) | 9 |
| Gevorg Ghazaryan | 05.04.1988 | 1 | (20) | 2 |
| Hilary Chukwah Gong (NGA) | 10.10.1998 | | (10) | |
| Taofiq Jibril (NGA) | 23.04.1998 | 1 | (14) | 4 |
| Mailson Lima Duarte Lopes (CPV) | 29.05.1994 | 9 | (10) | 2 |
| Artur Serobyan | 02.07.2003 | 15 | | 5 |
| Tenton Yenne (NGA) | 07.07.2000 | 32 | (2) | 10 |

## Banaki Kentronakan Marzakan Akumb Yerevan (Central Sport Club of the Army)

**Founded**: 1947
**Stadium**: Yerevan Football Academy Stadium, Yerevan (1,428)
**Trainer**: Rafael Nazaryan     26.03.1975

| Goalkeepers: | DOB | M | (s) | G |
|---|---|---|---|---|
| Henri Avagyan | 16.01.1996 | 16 | | |
| Gor Matinyan | 23.06.2004 | 5 | (1) | |
| Arman Nersesyan | 19.10.2001 | 15 | | |
| **Defenders:** | **DOB** | **M** | **(s)** | **G** |
| Ruben Abrahamyan | 07.08.2003 | 8 | (5) | 1 |
| Arsen Galstyan | 01.05.2002 | 5 | (1) | |
| Erjanik Ghubasaryan | 21.02.2001 | 2 | | |
| Serob Grigoryan | 04.02.1995 | 14 | (2) | 1 |
| Mher Kankanyan | 19.03.2004 | | (1) | |
| Albert Khachumyan | 23.06.1999 | 27 | (4) | 1 |
| Styopa Mkrtchyan | 17.02.2003 | 8 | (1) | 2 |
| Norayr Nikoghosyan | 09.03.2002 | 8 | (6) | |
| Argishti Petrosyan | 16.10.1992 | 35 | | 1 |
| Volodya Samsonyan | 24.02.2001 | 15 | (5) | |
| Erik Simonyan | 12.06.2003 | 25 | (3) | |
| **Midfielders:** | **DOB** | **M** | **(s)** | **G** |
| Daniel Aghbalyan | 12.03.1999 | 29 | (2) | 3 |
| Narek Alaverdyan | 19.02.2002 | 17 | (13) | |
| Eduard Avagyan | 21.03.1996 | | (2) | |
| Erik Azizyan | 04.03.2000 | 1 | (8) | |
| Artur Grigoryan | 10.07.1993 | 30 | (4) | |
| Aram Khamoyan | 10.01.2000 | 14 | (4) | |
| Gor Lulukyan | 02.01.2003 | 16 | (12) | 4 |
| Mikayel Mirzoyan | 06.02.2001 | 28 | (8) | 4 |
| Hamlet Sargsyan | 20.05.2004 | 1 | (3) | |
| **Forwards:** | **DOB** | **M** | **(s)** | **G** |
| David Arshakyan | 16.08.1994 | 1 | (3) | |
| Arayik Eloyan | 16.03.2004 | 1 | (6) | 2 |
| Davit Hakobyan | 09.08.2005 | | (3) | |
| Misak Hakobyan | 11.06.2004 | 17 | (12) | 1 |
| Akhmed Jindoyan | 02.10.1997 | 2 | (4) | |
| Hamlet Minasyan | 15.01.2003 | | (1) | |
| Grenik Petrosyan | 05.12.2001 | 14 | (3) | 4 |
| Artur Serobyan | 02.07.2003 | 14 | (4) | 2 |
| Zhirayr Shaghoyan | 10.04.2001 | 6 | | 5 |
| Gevorg Tarakhchyan | 15.03.2002 | 22 | (13) | 4 |

## Lernayin Artsakh Football Club Vayk

**Founded**: 1927
**Stadium**: Arevik Stadium, Vayk (1,000)
**Trainer**: Artashes Adamyan     12.11.1970
[14.04.2023]    Armen Adamyan     14.10.1967

| Goalkeepers: | DOB | M | (s) | G |
|---|---|---|---|---|
| Poghos Ayvazyan | 09.06.1995 | 3 | | |
| Vyacheslav Grigoryan (RUS) | 23.04.1999 | 25 | (1) | |
| Arman Harutyunyan | 05.03.2002 | 8 | | |
| **Defenders:** | **DOB** | **M** | **(s)** | **G** |
| Deou Dosa Olatunji (NGA) | 29.07.1998 | 9 | | |
| Tobi Jnohope (DMA) | 04.10.1997 | 27 | (2) | |
| Shogo Kagawa (JPN) | 04.10.1998 | 2 | (1) | |
| Ruben Karagulyan | 15.05.2003 | 2 | | |
| Artur Khachatryan | 09.04.1999 | 29 | (3) | |
| Vladimir Kharatyan (RUS) | 14.07.1996 | 25 | (4) | |
| Aram Kostandyan | 20.06.1989 | 27 | (2) | 1 |
| Simon Obonde (GHA) | 10.05.2001 | 28 | (7) | |
| Daniel Palomera Landero (MEX) | 29.06.2000 | 1 | | |
| Gor Poghosyan | 11.06.1988 | 15 | (3) | |
| Akito Saito (JPN) | 15.08.1999 | 1 | | |
| **Midfielders:** | **DOB** | **M** | **(s)** | **G** |
| Ashot Adamyan | 15.06.1997 | 12 | (8) | 1 |
| Alik Arakelyan | 21.05.1996 | 8 | (2) | |
| Ararat Chilingaryan | 08.08.2000 | 11 | (15) | |
| Sebastián Díaz Bedoya (COL) | 30.04.2001 | 2 | (3) | |
| Arsen Hovhannisyan | 01.03.1996 | | (6) | |
| Marat Karapetyan | 17.05.1991 | 5 | (8) | |
| Aramayis Mardiyan | 17.09.2002 | | (8) | |
| Davit Nalbandyan | 09.08.1999 | 1 | (3) | |
| Valdo Junior Ntone Bilunga (CMR) | 28.05.1995 | 29 | (4) | 1 |
| Juan David Barrenechi Palacios (COL) | 12.08.2000 | 14 | (17) | 2 |
| Tigran Simonyan | 09.06.1998 | 9 | (11) | 1 |
| Khalifa Ababacar Sow (SEN) | 15.12.1999 | 28 | (3) | |
| Jun Toba (JPN) | 12.08.1999 | 11 | (7) | |
| **Forwards:** | **DOB** | **M** | **(s)** | **G** |
| Marvin Santiago Angulo Perea (COL) | 02.03.2000 | 3 | (13) | 2 |
| *Emmanuel Vieira* De Souza Altenburg (BRA) | 24.03.2000 | 3 | (4) | |
| Norik Mkrtchyan | 09.03.1997 | 3 | (12) | |
| Olaoluwa Ayanwale Ojetunde (NGA) | 06.11.2002 | 28 | (7) | 2 |
| Michael Peprah (GHA) | 02.09.1995 | | (2) | |
| Yeison Bossa Racines (ECU) | 07.10.1998 | 18 | | 4 |
| Ipehe Williams (CIV) | 07.08.2001 | 9 | (5) | |

## Football Club Noah Armavir

**Founded**: 2017
**Stadium**: Armavir City Stadium, Armavir (3,100)
**Trainer**: Igor Picusceac (MDA)     27.03.1983
[23.08.2022]    Robert Arzumanyan     24.07.1985

| Goalkeepers: | DOB | M | (s) | G |
|---|---|---|---|---|
| Anatoliy Ayvazov | 08.06.1996 | 8 | | |
| Raul Andrei Bălbărău (ROU) | 07.04.2001 | 10 | | |
| Harutyun Melkonyan | 28.06.2001 | 6 | | |
| Vardan Shahatuni | 13.03.1998 | 12 | | |
| Arman Simonyan | 28.07.1997 | | (1) | |
| **Defenders:** | **DOB** | **M** | **(s)** | **G** |
| Artur Danielyan | 09.02.1998 | 18 | (2) | |
| Okezie Prince Ebenezer (NGA) | 28.02.2001 | 26 | (3) | |
| Arsen Galstyan | 01.05.2002 | 4 | (3) | |
| Erjanik Ghubasaryan | 21.02.2001 | 3 | (3) | |
| Arman Khachatryan | 09.06.1997 | 9 | (3) | |
| Karen Muradyan | 01.04.2001 | 20 | (2) | |
| Haik Moussakhanian (FRA) | 20.03.1998 | 19 | (6) | |
| Sergey Muradyan | 27.08.2004 | 13 | (1) | |
| Aleksandr Nesterov (RUS) | 24.03.2000 | 9 | | |
| Norayr Nikoghosyan | 09.03.2002 | 7 | (5) | |
| **Midfielders:** | **DOB** | **M** | **(s)** | **G** |
| Gor Abrahamyan | 07.12.2005 | 1 | (3) | |
| Petros Afajanyan | 31.10.1998 | 4 | (6) | 1 |
| Patvakan Avetisyan | 24.08.2001 | 2 | (11) | |
| Robert Baghramyan | 29.06.2002 | 26 | (1) | |
| Adams Friday (NGA) | 23.11.2002 | 30 | (3) | 2 |
| Hayk Ghevondyan | 01.07.2001 | 14 | (8) | 2 |
| Arsen Hayrapetyan (RUS) | 16.02.1997 | 13 | (13) | |
| Vahagn Hayrapetyan | 14.06.1997 | 15 | (3) | |
| Haggai Katoh (NGA) | 30.12.1998 | 3 | (10) | |
| Armen Nahapetyan | 24.07.1999 | 2 | (6) | |
| Karen Nalbandyan | 14.04.2002 | 6 | (7) | |
| Dramane Salou (BFA) | 22.05.1998 | 18 | (2) | 3 |
| Kim Yeon-seung (KOR) | 15.07.1999 | 20 | (9) | 2 |
| Ruben Tigran Yesayan | 14.02.2002 | 13 | (20) | 3 |
| **Forwards:** | **DOB** | **M** | **(s)** | **G** |
| Samvel Hakobyan | 30.04.2003 | 1 | (10) | |
| Goodnews Igbokwe (NGA) | 26.02.2003 | 10 | (13) | 6 |
| Alexandre Llovet (FRA) | 26.11.1997 | 15 | (1) | 6 |
| Peter Ukeme Olawale (NGA) | 26.07.2002 | 7 | (4) | |
| Israel Nana Opoku (GHA) | 10.05.2004 | 2 | (5) | 1 |
| Levon Vardanyan | 02.11.2003 | 30 | (3) | 8 |

# Football Club Pyunik Yerevan

**Founded**: 1992 (*as Homenetmen Yerevan*)
**Stadium**: „Vazgen Sargsyan" Hanrapetakan Stadium, Yerevan (14,403)
**Trainer**: Eghishe Melikyan 13.08.1979

| Goalkeepers: | DOB | M | (s) | G |
|---|---|---|---|---|
| Henri Avagyan | 16.01.1996 | 2 | | |
| Stanislav Buchnev | 17.07.1990 | 28 | | |
| Sergey Mikaelyan | 21.07.2002 | | (1) | |
| David Yurchenko | 27.03.1986 | 6 | | |
| **Defenders:** | **DOB** | **M** | **(s)** | **G** |
| Alan Aussi (UKR) | 30.06.2001 | 3 | | |
| Arthur Avagyan | 04.07.1987 | 5 | (2) | |
| Nikita Baranov (EST) | 19.08.1992 | 13 | | |
| Anton Bratkov (UKR) | 14.05.1993 | 17 | (2) | |
| Juan David Bravo Padilla (COL) | 01.04.1990 | 2 | (5) | 1 |
| Zoran Gajić (SRB) | 18.05.1990 | 2 | (1) | |
| Alexander David González Sibulo (VEN) | 13.09.1992 | 4 | (1) | |
| *James* Santos das Neves (BRA) | 15.07.1995 | 10 | (3) | 2 |
| Carlos Jamisson Teles dos Santos Jr. „Juninho" (BRA) | 29.07.1995 | 21 | (1) | |
| Mikhail Kovalenko (RUS) | 25.01.1995 | 22 | (7) | 2 |
| Aleksandar Miljković (SRB) | 26.02.1990 | 25 | (1) | 2 |
| Kire Ristevski (MKD) | 22.10.1990 | 9 | (3) | |
| Sergiy Vakulenko (UKR) | 07.09.1993 | 5 | | |
| Boris Varga (SRB) | 14.08.1993 | 5 | (1) | |
| **Midfielders:** | **DOB** | **M** | **(s)** | **G** |
| Vyacheslav Afyan | 28.10.2005 | | (1) | |
| José Enrique Caraballo Rosal (VEN) | 21.02.1996 | 17 | (11) | 6 |
| Eugeniu Cociuc (MDA) | 11.05.1993 | 7 | (2) | |
| Artak Dashyan | 20.11.1989 | 24 | (7) | 4 |

| | DOB | M | (s) | G |
|---|---|---|---|---|
| David Davidyan | 14.12.1997 | 21 | (3) | 1 |
| Yuri Gareginyan | 03.02.1994 | 8 | (12) | |
| Hovhannes Harutyunyan | 25.05.1999 | 22 | (7) | 5 |
| Karlen Hovhannisyan | 26.04.2005 | | (2) | |
| Roman Karasyuk (UKR) | 27.03.1991 | 14 | (7) | |
| André Luiz Leão Lima „André Mensalão" (BRA) | 21.06.1990 | 6 | (7) | 1 |
| Gevorg Nadzharyan (KAZ) | 06.01.1998 | 3 | | |
| Stefan Spirovski (MKD) | 23.08.1990 | 8 | (8) | 1 |
| *Lucas Villela* Rezende (BRA) | 24.03.1994 | 4 | (12) | 1 |
| Renzo José Zambrano (VEN) | 26.08.1994 | 2 | (3) | 1 |
| **Forwards:** | **DOB** | **M** | **(s)** | **G** |
| Narek Baroyan | 05.05.2005 | | (1) | |
| Vrezh Chiloyan | 06.04.2002 | | (1) | |
| Jonel Désiré (HAI) | 12.02.1997 | 12 | (3) | 4 |
| Dame Diop (SEN) | 15.02.1993 | 4 | (9) | 1 |
| Robert Gegedosh (UKR) | 02.05.1993 | 3 | (3) | |
| Luka Juričić (BIH) | 25.11.1996 | 13 | (15) | 17 |
| Aleksandr Karapetyan | 23.12.1987 | 4 | (3) | |
| Edgar Malakyan | 22.09.1990 | 12 | (1) | 4 |
| Nemanja Mladenović (SRB) | 03.03.1993 | 3 | | |
| Uros Nenadović (SRB) | 28.01.1994 | 3 | (1) | |
| Yusuf Otubanjo (NGA) | 12.09.1992 | 20 | (10) | 17 |
| Aras Özbiliz | 09.03.1990 | 1 | (8) | 1 |
| Grenik Petrosyan | 05.12.2001 | 1 | (6) | |
| Marjan Radeski (MKD) | 10.02.1995 | 5 | (2) | |

# Football Club Shirak Gyumri

**Founded**: 1927
**Stadium**: Gyumri City Stadium, Gyumri (4,000)
**Trainer**: Tigran Davtyan 10.06.1978
[01.04.2023] Edgar Torosyan 02.07.1984

| Goalkeepers: | DOB | M | (s) | G |
|---|---|---|---|---|
| Egor Achinov (RUS) | 11.08.2004 | 12 | | |
| Poghos Ayvazyan | 09.06.1995 | 11 | | |
| Sokrat Hovhannisyan | 05.04.1996 | 2 | (1) | |
| Lyova Karapetyan | 01.03.2001 | 11 | | |
| **Defenders:** | **DOB** | **M** | **(s)** | **G** |
| Robert Darbinyan | 04.10.1995 | 11 | (1) | |
| Robert Hakobyan | 22.10.1996 | 5 | (6) | |
| Artyom Mikaelyan | 12.07.1991 | 25 | (2) | |
| Hamlet Mnatsakanyan | 21.08.2002 | 3 | (5) | |
| Marko Prljević (SRB) | 02.08.1988 | 25 | (3) | |
| Arsen Sadoyan | 16.03.1999 | 33 | (2) | |
| Seryozha Urushanyan | 01.08.1997 | 18 | (6) | |
| Aleksa Vidić (SRB) | 29.09.1994 | 29 | (2) | |
| **Midfielders:** | **DOB** | **M** | **(s)** | **G** |
| Levon Darbinyan | 24.01.2002 | 8 | (16) | |
| Levon Gevorgyan | 2003 | | (1) | |
| Samvel Ghukasyan | 19.05.2002 | 1 | (9) | |
| Narek Janoyan | 28.10.2005 | | (3) | |

| | DOB | M | (s) | G |
|---|---|---|---|---|
| Sergey Manukyan | 03.04.2004 | 1 | (7) | |
| Rafik Misakyan | 02.01.2000 | 22 | (7) | 3 |
| Mher Tarloyan | 07.03.2005 | 4 | (2) | |
| Junior Magico Traoré (CIV) | 30.03.2003 | 30 | (1) | |
| Suren Tsarukyan | 19.08.2005 | 4 | (8) | 1 |
| Erik Vardanyan | 08.03.1999 | 18 | (6) | |
| **Forwards:** | **DOB** | **M** | **(s)** | **G** |
| Moussa Bakayoko (CIV) | 27.12.1996 | 32 | (2) | 7 |
| Vally Cissé (CIV) | 15.05.1999 | 9 | (2) | 1 |
| Allasana Doumbia (CIV) | 28.12.2002 | 26 | (3) | 2 |
| Artem Gevorkyan (RUS) | 21.05.1993 | 13 | (7) | 3 |
| Narek Khachatryan | 28.01.2004 | 3 | (3) | |
| Donald Alvine Kodia (CIV) | 2003 | 27 | (4) | 3 |
| Abdul Samir Koné (CIV) | 15.05.2000 | 3 | | 1 |
| Lyova Mryan | 11.05.2000 | 10 | (18) | 2 |
| Grigor Muradyan | 06.08.2002 | | (1) | |
| Emil Papikyan | 21.01.2007 | | (3) | 1 |
| Vrezh Torosyan | 08.07.2002 | | (4) | |

# Football Club Urartu Yerevan

**Founded**: 20.01.1992 (*as FC Banants Yerevan*)
**Stadium**: Urartu Stadium, Yerevan (4,860)
**Trainer**: Dmitriy Gunko (RUS) 01.03.1976

| Goalkeepers: | DOB | M | (s) | G |
|---|---|---|---|---|
| Arsen Beglaryan | 18.02.1993 | 14 | | |
| Aleksandr Melikhov (RUS) | 23.03.1998 | 22 | | |
| **Defenders:** | **DOB** | **M** | **(s)** | **G** |
| Nana Antwi (GHA) | 10.08.2000 | 23 | (4) | |
| Khariton Ayvazyan | 08.11.2003 | 4 | (5) | |
| Isaac Barry (NGA) | 28.08.2001 | 1 | | |
| *Rafael* Bruno Cajueiro da Silva „Carioca" (BRA) | 18.07.1992 | 2 | (7) | |
| *Éverson Bispo* Pereira (BRA) | 24.07.1997 | 5 | | |
| Arman Ghazaryan | 24.07.2001 | 22 | (6) | 1 |
| Edgar Grigoryan | 25.08.1998 | 3 | (6) | |
| Zhirayr Margaryan | 13.09.1997 | 32 | (2) | 3 |
| Evgeniy Nazarov (RUS) | 07.04.1997 | | (2) | |
| Vadym Paramonov (UKR) | 18.03.1991 | 12 | (5) | |
| Erik Piloyan | 29.01.2001 | 11 | (2) | 1 |
| Yevhen Tsymbalyuk (UKR) | 19.06.1996 | 24 | (1) | 4 |
| Ivan Zotko (UKR) | 09.07.1996 | 5 | (3) | 1 |
| **Midfielders:** | **DOB** | **M** | **(s)** | **G** |
| Narek Aghasaryan | 15.07.2001 | 22 | (9) | |
| Tigran Ayunts | 15.03.2000 | | (1) | |
| Levon Bashoyan | 15.09.2005 | | (1) | |

| | DOB | M | (s) | G |
|---|---|---|---|---|
| David Ghiasyan | 21.04.2006 | | (1) | |
| Ugochukwu Christus Iwu | 28.10.1999 | 31 | (1) | 1 |
| *Marcos* Antônio Candido Ferreira *Junior* (BRA) | 13.05.1995 | 19 | (14) | 4 |
| David Khurtsidze (RUS) | 04.07.1993 | 18 | (10) | 2 |
| Garnik Minasyan | 12.07.2005 | 1 | | |
| Sergey Mkrtchyan | 26.06.2001 | 13 | (6) | 1 |
| Dramane Salou (BFA) | 22.05.1998 | 4 | (6) | |
| Hamlet Sargsyan | 20.05.2004 | | (1) | |
| **Forwards:** | **DOB** | **M** | **(s)** | **G** |
| Deividi Oliveira da Silva „Buiu" (BRA) | 24.06.2004 | | (1) | |
| Temur Dzhikiya (RUS) | 08.05.1998 | 4 | (1) | 3 |
| Narek Grigoryan | 17.06.2001 | 21 | (11) | 8 |
| Artur Israelyan | 16.01.2004 | | (1) | |
| Dmytro Khlyobas (UKR) | 09.05.1994 | 6 | (19) | 9 |
| Maksim Mayrovich (RUS) | 06.02.1996 | 19 | (7) | 8 |
| Karen Melkonyan | 25.03.1999 | 21 | (12) | 4 |
| Aras Özbiliz | 09.03.1990 | 3 | (4) | 2 |
| Oleg Polyakov (RUS) | 29.11.1990 | 23 | (8) | 4 |
| Leon Sabua (RUS) | 01.09.2000 | 11 | (11) | 7 |
| Yaya Sanogo (FRA) | 27.01.1993 | | (2) | 2 |
| Edik Vardanyan | 25.03.2005 | | (1) | |

## Football Club Van Charentsavan

| | | |
|---|---|---|
| **Founded**: | 2019 | |
| **Stadium**: | Charentsavan City Stadium, Charentsavan (5,000) | |
| **Trainer**: | Artur Asoyan | 03.12.1970 |
| [14.01.2023] | Humberto Viviani Ribera (BOL) | 10.12.1980 |
| [04.05.2023] | Hayk Hovhannisyan | 26.02.1990 |

| Goalkeepers: | DOB | M | (s) | G |
|---|---|---|---|---|
| Samur Agamagomedov (RUS) | 30.11.1998 | 22 | | |
| Yevgen Grytsenko (UKR) | 05.02.1995 | 2 | | |
| Artur Melkonyan | 13.06.2004 | | (1) | |
| Diego Zamora Roca (BOL) | 12.09.1993 | 12 | | |
| **Defenders:** | **DOB** | **M** | **(s)** | **G** |
| Hamlet Asoyan | 13.01.1995 | 28 | (5) | |
| Daur Chanba (RUS) | 07.07.2000 | 1 | (1) | |
| Juan Daniel Cifuentes Vergara (COL) | 21.04.1999 | 10 | | 1 |
| Josue Gaba (CIV) | 12.01.2002 | 14 | (12) | 1 |
| Silvio Patricio Gutiérrez Álvarez (ECU) | 28.02.1993 | 10 | (4) | |
| Alexander Hovhannisyan | 20.07.1996 | 1 | | |
| Artur Kartashyan | 08.01.1997 | 8 | (1) | |
| Milan Lalić (SRB) | 25.07.1995 | 7 | (1) | |
| Armen Manucharyan | 03.02.1995 | 12 | (1) | |
| Vaspurak Minasyan | 29.06.1994 | 33 | (2) | 1 |
| Arman Mkrtchyan | 09.07.1999 | 8 | (4) | |
| Manuel Morello (ARG) | 20.10.1994 | 14 | (2) | 1 |
| Bogdan Mytsyk (UKR) | 08.03.1998 | 10 | (1) | 2 |
| Alan Tataev (RUS) | 03.08.1995 | 13 | | |
| Ibrahim Yahaya (NGA) | 28.03.2000 | 1 | (4) | |

| Midfielders: | DOB | M | (s) | G |
|---|---|---|---|---|
| Edvard Avagyan | 21.03.1996 | 1 | (2) | |
| Artem Biliy (UKR) | 03.10.1999 | 14 | (2) | 2 |
| Christopher Boniface (NGA) | 01.01.2002 | 9 | (12) | 2 |
| Mohammed Fatau (GHA) | 24.12.1992 | | (1) | |
| Pavel Gorelov | 22.01.2003 | 21 | (13) | 3 |
| Shota Gvazava (GEO) | 26.10.1992 | 19 | | |
| Narek Hovhannisyan | 11.06.2002 | 6 | (23) | 1 |
| Rumyan Hovsepyan | 13.11.1991 | 10 | (2) | 3 |
| David Manoyan | 05.07.1990 | 9 | (1) | 1 |
| Gevorg Nadzharyan (KAZ) | 06.01.1998 | 15 | (6) | |
| Artur Stepanyan | 17.11.1999 | 1 | (5) | |
| **Forwards:** | **DOB** | **M** | **(s)** | **G** |
| Mubarak Mohammed Ahmed (NGA) | 25.03.2003 | 5 | (9) | 1 |
| Danil Ankudinov (KAZ) | 31.07.2003 | 12 | (5) | 4 |
| Wilson José Barrios Rondón (VEN) | 23.08.2000 | 5 | (3) | |
| Sani Buhari (NGA) | 10.01.2004 | 10 | (13) | 2 |
| Gegham Harutyunyan | 23.08.1990 | 10 | (6) | |
| Goodnews Igbokwe (NGA) | 26.02.2003 | | (1) | |
| Gegam Kadimyan | 19.10.1992 | 3 | (7) | 1 |
| Edgar Movsesyan | 09.09.1998 | 29 | (7) | 9 |
| Bismark Ubah (NGA) | 05.01.1994 | 1 | (1) | |
| Ipehe Williams (CIV) | 07.08.2001 | 10 | (6) | 1 |

| | | | | | | | | | |
|---|---|---|---|---|---|---|---|---|---|
| | **SECOND LEVEL** **Armenian First League 2022/2023** | | | | | | | | |
| 1. | FC West Armenia Yerevan (*Promoted*) | 33 | 23 | 6 | 4 | 85 | - | 34 | 75 |
| 2. | BKMA-2 Yerevan | 33 | 23 | 3 | 7 | 81 | - | 30 | 72 |
| 3. | FC Gandzasar Kapan | 33 | 22 | 4 | 7 | 85 | - | 33 | 70 |
| 4. | FC Ararat-2 Yerevan | 33 | 19 | 3 | 11 | 65 | - | 48 | 60 |
| 5. | FC Ararat-Armenia-2 Yerevan | 33 | 18 | 4 | 11 | 65 | - | 52 | 58 |
| 6. | FC Urartu-2 Yerevan | 33 | 13 | 7 | 13 | 61 | - | 57 | 46 |
| 7. | Pyunik Academy Yerevan | 33 | 14 | 3 | 16 | 57 | - | 55 | 45 |
| 8. | FC Shirak-2 Gyumri | 33 | 13 | 5 | 15 | 39 | - | 38 | 44 |
| 9. | FC Syunik Kapan | 33 | 12 | 2 | 19 | 49 | - | 52 | 38 |
| 10. | FC Mika Yerevan | 33 | 11 | 3 | 19 | 35 | - | 77 | 36 |
| 11. | FC Alashkert-2 Yerevan | 33 | 8 | 2 | 23 | 47 | - | 99 | 26 |
| 12. | Lernayin Artsakh-2 FC Stepanakert (*withdrew*)* | 33 | 0 | 2 | 31 | 18 | - | 112 | 2 |

*Please note: Lernayin Artsakh-2 FC Stepanakert withdrew after Round 18. All remaining matches were awarded as a 3-0 win for the opponents.

## INTERNATIONAL MATCHES
(16.07.2022 – 15.07.2023)

| | | | | |
|---|---|---|---|---|
| 24.09.2022 | Yerevan | *Armenia - Ukraine* | *0-5(0-1)* | (UNL) |
| 27.09.2022 | Dublin | *Republic of Ireland - Armenia* | *3-2(1-0)* | (UNL) |
| 16.11.2022 | Prishtina | *Kosovo - Armenia* | *2-2(0-1)* | (F) |
| 19.11.2022 | Tiranë | *Albania - Armenia* | *2-0(1-0)* | (F) |
| | | | | |
| 25.03.2023 | Yerevan | *Armenia - Turkey* | *1-2(1-1)* | (ECQ) |
| 28.03.2023 | Yerevan | *Armenia - Cyprus* | *2-2(0-1)* | (F) |
| 16.06.2023 | Cardiff | *Wales - Armenia* | *2-4(1-2)* | (ECQ) |
| 19.06.2023 | Yerevan | *Armenia - Latvia* | *2-1(1-0)* | (ECQ) |

**24.09.2022    ARMENIA - UKRAINE**              **0-5(0-1)**              3rd UEFA Nations League B, Group 1
„Vazgen Sargsyan" Hanrapetakan Stadium, Yerevan; Referee: João Pedro da Silva Pinheiro (Portugalia); Attendance: 7,200
**ARM:** David Yurchenko, Hovhannes Hambartsumyan, Hrayr Mkoyan (Cap) (75.Taron Voskanyan), André Jack Calisir, Zhirayr Margaryan (75.Jordy João Monroy Ararat), Artak Grigoryan, Artak Dashyan, Tigran Barseghyan (63.Zhirayr Shaghoyan), Khoren Bayramyan, Vahan Bichakhchyan (46.Hovhannes Harutyunyan), Lucas Manuel Zelarayán (82.Artur Serobyan). Trainer: Joaquín de Jesús Caparrós Camino (Spain).

**27.09.2022    REPUBLIC OF IRELAND - ARMENIA**              **3-2(1-0)**              3rd UEFA Nations League B, Group 1
Aviva Stadium, Dublin; Referee: Rade Obrenovič (Slovenia); Attendance: 41,719
**ARM:** David Yurchenko, Hovhannes Hambartsumyan [*sent off 89*], André Jack Calisir (82.Karen Muradyan), Varazdat Haroyan (Cap), Hrayr Mkoyan (60.Taron Voskanyan), Jordy João Monroy Ararat (60.Artak Dashyan [*sent off 90*]), Khoren Bayramyan, Artak Grigoryan, Eduard Spertsyan, Tigran Barseghyan (82.Zhirayr Shaghoyan), Lucas Manuel Zelarayán (69.Vahan Bichakhchyan). Trainer: Joaquín de Jesús Caparrós Camino (Spain).
**Goals:** Artak Dashyan (71), Eduard Spertsyan (73).

**16.11.2022    KOSOVO - ARMENIA**              **2-2(0-1)**              Friendly International
Stadiumi „Fadil Vokrri", Prishtina; Referee: Eldorjan Hamiti (Albania); Attendance: 2,000
**ARM:** Stanislav Buchnev, Kamo Hovhannisyan (85.Petros Avetisyan), Varazdat Haroyan (Cap), Styopa Mkrtchyan, Hakob Hakobyan (77.David Terteryan), Hovhannes Harutyunyan, Artak Grigoryan (63.Sergey Mkrtchyan), Artak Dashyan, Vahan Bichakhchyan (77.Artur Serobyan), Edgar Babayan (63.Narek Grigorian), Zhirayr Shaghoyan (85.Zhirayr Margaryan). Trainer: Roman Berezovskiy.
**Goals:** Zhirayr Shaghoyan (24), Kamo Hovhannisyan (82).

**19.11.2022    ALBANIA - ARMENIA**              **2-0(1-0)**              Friendly International
Arena Kombëtare, Tiranë; Referee: Aleksandar Stavrev (North Macedonia); Attendance: n/a
**ARM:** Stanislav Buchnev, Taron Voskanyan (46.Sergey Mkrtchyan), Styopa Mkrtchyan (76.Arman Ghazaryan), Varazdat Haroyan (Cap), Hovhannes Harutyunyan (89.Petros Avetisyan), Artak Grigoryan (46.Artur Galoyan), Artak Dashyan, Kamo Hovhannisyan, Vahan Bichakhchyan, Edgar Babayan (66.Narek Grigorian), Zhirayr Shaghoyan (66.Artur Serobyan). Trainer: Roman Berezovskiy.

**25.03.2023    ARMENIA - TURKEY**              **1-2(1-1)**              17th EC. Qualifiers
„Vazgen Sargsyan" Hanrapetakan Stadium, Yerevan; Referee: José María Sánchez Martínez (Spain); Attendance: 14,125
**ARM:** Arsen Beglaryan, Kamo Hovhannisyan, Varazdat Haroyan (Cap), Georgiy Harutyunyan, Taron Voskanyan (28.Styopa Mkrtchyan; 54.Khoren Bayramyan), Nair Tiknizyan, Ugochukwu Christus Iwu, Eduard Spertsyan, Tigran Barseghyan, Lucas Manuel Zelarayán (75.Sargis Adamyan), Norberto Alejandro Briasco Balekian (76.Vahan Bichakhchyan). Trainer: Oleksandr Petrakov (Ukraine).
**Goal:** Ozan Muhammed Kabak (10 own goal).

**28.03.2023    ARMENIA - CYPRUS**              **2-2(0-1)**              Friendly International
„Vazgen Sargsyan" Hanrapetakan Stadium, Yerevan; Referee: Dumitru Muntean (Moldova); Attendance: n/a
**ARM:** Stanislav Buchnev, David Davidyan (46.Kamo Hovhannisyan), Varazdat Haroyan (Cap), Erik Piloyan (46.Georgiy Harutyunyan), Erjanik Ghubasaryan, Nair Tiknizyan (78.Zhirayr Margaryan), Ugochukwu Christus Iwu, Eduard Spertsyan, Vahan Bichakhchyan (65.Tigran Barseghyan), Grant-Leon Ranos (65.Zhirayr Shaghoyan), Sargis Adamyan (65.Artur Serobyan). Trainer: Oleksandr Petrakov (Ukraine).
**Goals:** Grant-Leon Ranos (50, 59).

**16.06.2023    WALES - ARMENIA**              **2-4(1-2)**              17th EC. Qualifiers
Cardiff City Stadium, Cardiff; Referee: Georgi Kabakov (Bulgaria); Attendance: 32,774
**ARM:** Ognjen Čančarević, Artak Dashyan, André Jack Calisir (62.Varazdat Haroyan), Georgiy Harutyunyan, Styopa Mkrtchyan, Nair Tiknizyan, Ugochukwu Christus Iwu, Eduard Spertsyan (Cap), Tigran Barseghyan (62.Vahan Bichakhchyan), Lucas Manuel Zelarayán (75.Norberto Alejandro Briasco Balekian), Grant-Leon Ranos (88.Artur Serobyan). Trainer: Oleksandr Petrakov (Ukraine).
**Goals:** Lucas Manuel Zelarayán (19), Grant-Leon Ranos (30, 66), Lucas Manuel Zelarayán (75).

**19.06.2023    ARMENIA - LATVIA**              **2-1(1-0)**              17th EC. Qualifiers
„Vazgen Sargsyan" Hanrapetakan Stadium, Yerevan; Referee: Peter Kráľovič (Slovakia); Attendance: 13,450
**ARM:** Ognjen Čančarević, Artak Dashyan, Varazdat Haroyan (Cap), Georgiy Harutyunyan, Styopa Mkrtchyan, Nair Tiknizyan, Ugochukwu Christus Iwu (90+5.Hovhannes Harutyunyan), Eduard Spertsyan, Norberto Alejandro Briasco Balekian (33.Vahan Bichakhchyan), Lucas Manuel Zelarayán (77.Artur Serobyan), Grant-Leon Ranos (77.Tigran Barseghyan). Trainer: Oleksandr Petrakov (Ukraine).
**Goals:** Nair Tiknizyan (35), Tigran Barseghyan (90+1 penalty).

## NATIONAL TEAM PLAYERS
### (16.07.2022 – 15.07.2023)

| Name | DOB | Caps | Goals | Club |
|------|-----|------|-------|------|

### Goalkeepers

| Name | DOB | Caps | Goals | Club | |
|------|-----|------|-------|------|---|
| Arsen BEGLARYAN | 18.02.1993 | 15 | 0 | 2023: | *FC Urartu Yerevan* |
| Stanislav BUCHNEV | 17.07.1990 | 4 | 0 | 2022/2023: | *FC Pyunik Yerevan* |
| Ognjen ČANČAREVIĆ | 25.09.1989 | 2 | 0 | 2023: | *FC Alashkert Yerevan* |
| David YURCHENKO | 27.03.1986 | 25 | 0 | 2022: | *FC Pyunik Yerevan* |

### Defenders

| Name | DOB | Caps | Goals | Club | |
|------|-----|------|-------|------|---|
| Jordy João Monroy ARARAT | 03.01.1996 | 8 | 0 | 2022: | *Deportivo Independiente Medellín (COL)* |
| André Jack CALISIR | 13.06.1990 | 24 | 0 | 2022: | *Silkeborg IF (DEN)* |
| | | | | 21.02.2023-> | *IF Brommapojkarna (SWE)* |
| Arman GHAZARYAN | 24.07.2001 | 1 | 0 | 2022: | *FC Urartu Yerevan* |
| Erjanik GHUBASARYAN | 21.02.2001 | 1 | 0 | 2023: | *FC Noah Armavir* |
| Hakob HAKOBYAN | 29.03.1997 | 4 | 0 | 2022: | *FC Ararat-Armenia Yerevan* |
| Hovhannes HAMBARTSUMYAN | 04.10.1990 | 50 | 4 | 2022: | *Anorthosis Famagusta FC (CYP)* |
| Varazdat HAROYAN | 24.08.1992 | 75 | 3 | 2022: | *Anorthosis Famagusta FC (CYP)* |
| | | | | 21.03.2023-> | *Astana FC (KAZ)* |
| Georgiy HARUTYUNYAN | 09.08.2004 | 4 | 0 | 2023: | *FK Krasnodar (RUS)* |
| Kamo HOVHANNISYAN | 05.10.1990 | 75 | 3 | 2022/2023: | *Astana FC (KAZ)* |
| Zhirayr MARGARYAN | 13.09.1997 | 5 | 0 | 2022/2023: | *FC Urartu Yerevan* |
| Hrayr MKOYAN | 02.09.1986 | 52 | 1 | 2022/2023: | *FC Ararat Yerevan* |
| Styopa MKRTCHYAN | 17.02.2003 | 10 | 0 | 2022: | *FC Ararat-Armenia Yerevan* |
| | | | | 28.02.2023-> | *BKMA Yerevan* |
| Erik PILOYAN | 29.01.2001 | 1 | 0 | 2023: | *FC Urartu Yerevan* |
| David TERTERYAN | 17.12.1997 | 11 | 0 | 2022: | *FC Ararat -Armenia Yerevan* |
| Nair TIKNIZYAN | 12.05.1999 | 4 | 1 | 2023: | *FK Lokomotiv Moskva (RUS)* |
| Taron VOSKANYAN | 22.02.1993 | 45 | 0 | 2022/2023: | *FC Alashkert Yerevan* |

### Midfielders

| Name | DOB | Caps | Goals | Club | |
|------|-----|------|-------|------|---|
| Petros AVETISYAN | 07.01.1996 | 7 | 0 | 2022: | *FC Akzhayik Oral (KAZ)* |
| Edgar BABAYAN | 28.10.1995 | 16 | 1 | 2022: | *Randers FC (DEN)* |
| Khoren BAYRAMYAN | 07.01.1992 | 22 | 2 | 2022/2023: | *FK Rostov (RUS)* |
| Vahan BICHAKHCHYAN | 09.07.1999 | 25 | 3 | 2022/2023: | *MKS Pogoń Szczecin (POL)* |
| Artak DASHYAN | 20.11.1989 | 17 | 1 | 2022/2023: | *FC Pyunik Yerevan* |
| David DAVIDYAN | 14.12.1997 | 1 | 0 | 2023: | *FC Pyunik Yerevan* |
| Artur GALOYAN | 25.06.1999 | 1 | 0 | 2022: | *FK Alania Vladikavkaz (RUS)* |
| Narek GRIGORIAN | 17.06.2001 | 4 | 0 | 2022: | *FC Urartu Yerevan* |
| Artak GRIGORYAN | 19.10.1987 | 51 | 1 | 2022: | *FC Alashkert Yerevan* |
| Hovhannes HARUTYUNYAN | 25.05.1999 | 7 | 0 | 2022/2023: | *FC Pyunik Yerevan* |
| Ugochukwu Christus IWU | 28.11.1999 | 4 | 0 | 2023: | *FC Urartu Yerevan* |
| Sergey MKRTCHYAN | 26.06.2001 | 2 | 0 | 2022: | *FC Urartu Yerevan* |
| Karen MURADYAN | 01.11.1992 | 11 | 0 | 2022: | *FC Ararat-Armenia Yerevan* |
| Artur SEROBYAN | 02.07.2003 | 8 | 0 | 2022: | *BKMA Yerevan* |
| | | | | 26.02.2023-> | *FC Ararat-Armenia Yerevan* |
| Zhirayr SHAGHOYAN | 10.04.2001 | 11 | 1 | 2022/2023: | *FC CSKA 1948 Sofia (BUL)* |
| Eduard SPERTSYAN | 07.06.2000 | 17 | 3 | 2022/2023: | *FK Krasnodar (RUS)* |

### Forwards

| Name | DOB | Caps | Goals | Club | |
|------|-----|------|-------|------|---|
| Sargis ADAMYAN | 23.05.1993 | 35 | 2 | 2023: | *1. FC Köln (GER)* |
| Tigran BARSEGHYAN | 22.09.1993 | 56 | 9 | 2022/2023: | *ŠK Slovan Bratislava (SVK)* |
| Norberto Alejandro BRIASCO Balekian | 29.02.1996 | 13 | 0 | 2023: | *CA Boca Juniors Buenos Aires (ARG)* |
| Grant-Leon RANOS | 20.07.2003 | 3 | 4 | 2023: | *FC Bayern München II (GER)* |
| Lucas Manuel ZELARAYÁN | 20.06.1992 | 9 | 2 | 2022/2023: | *Columbus Crew SC (USA)* |

### Trainer

| Name | DOB | Record | |
|------|-----|--------|---|
| Joaquín de Jesús CAPARRÓS Camino (ESP) [10.03.2020 – 29.09.2022] | 15.10.1955 | 26 M; 8 W; 6 D; 12 L; 25-56 | |
| Roman BEREZOVSKIY [08.11.2022 - 13.01.2023] | 05.08.1974 | 2 M; 0 W; 1 D; 1 L; 2-4 | |
| Oleksandr PETRAKOV (Ukraine) [from 14.01.2023] | 06.08.1957 | 4 M; 2 W; 1 D; 1 L; 9-7 | |

# AUSTRIA

### The Country:
Republic of Austria (Republik Österreich)
Capital: Vienna
Surface: 83,879 km²
Inhabitants: 9,027,999 [2022]
Time: UTC+1

### The FA:
Österreichischer Fußball-Bund
Ernst-Happel-Stadion - Sektor A/F, Meiereistrasse 7, 1021 Wien
Tel: +43 1 727 180
Foundation date: 1904
Member of FIFA since: 1905
Member of UEFA since: 1954
Website: www.oefb.at

## NATIONAL TEAM RECORDS

| RECORDS | | |
|---|---|---|
| **First international match:** | 12.10.1902, Wien: | Austria – Hungary 5-0 |
| **Most international caps:** | Marko Arnautović | - 108 caps (since 2008) |
| **Most international goals:** | Anton Polster | - 44 goals / 95 caps (1982-2000) |

| UEFA EUROPEAN CHAMPIONSHIP | |
|---|---|
| 1960 | Qualifiers |
| 1964 | Qualifiers |
| 1968 | Qualifiers |
| 1972 | Qualifiers |
| 1976 | Qualifiers |
| 1980 | Qualifiers |
| 1984 | Qualifiers |
| 1988 | Qualifiers |
| 1992 | Qualifiers |
| 1996 | Qualifiers |
| 2000 | Qualifiers |
| 2004 | Qualifiers |
| 2008 | Final Tournament (Group Stage) |
| 2012 | Qualifiers |
| 2016 | Final Tournament (Group Stage) |
| 2020 | Final Tournament (2nd Round of 16) |

| FIFA WORLD CUP | |
|---|---|
| 1930 | Did not enter |
| 1934 | Final Tournament (4th Place) |
| 1938 | *Withdrew* |
| 1950 | *Withdrew* |
| 1954 | Final Tournament (3rd Place) |
| 1958 | Final Tournament (Group Stage) |
| 1962 | *Withdrew* |
| 1966 | Qualifiers |
| 1970 | Qualifiers |
| 1974 | Qualifiers |
| 1978 | Final Tournament (2nd Round) |
| 1982 | Final Tournament (2nd Round) |
| 1986 | Qualifiers |
| 1990 | Final Tournament (Group Stage) |
| 1994 | Qualifiers |
| 1998 | Final Tournament (Group Stage) |
| 2002 | Qualifiers |
| 2006 | Qualifiers |
| 2010 | Qualifiers |
| 2014 | Qualifiers |
| 2018 | Qualifiers |
| 2022 | Qualifiers |

| OLYMPIC TOURNAMENTS | |
|---|---|
| 1908 | - |
| 1912 | FT/ Quarter-Finals |
| 1920 | Did not enter |
| 1924 | Did not enter |
| 1928 | Did not enter |
| 1936 | FT/ Runners-up |
| 1948 | FT/ 1/8-Finals |
| 1952 | FT/ Quarter-Finals |
| 1956 | Did not enter |
| 1960 | Qualifiers |
| 1964 | Qualifiers |
| 1968 | Qualifiers |
| 1972 | Qualifiers |
| 1976 | Qualifiers |
| 1980 | Qualifiers |
| 1984 | Did not enter |
| 1988 | Qualifiers |
| 1992 | Qualifiers |
| 1996 | Qualifiers |
| 2000 | Qualifiers |
| 2004 | Qualifiers |
| 2008 | Qualifiers |
| 2012 | Qualifiers |
| 2016 | Qualifiers |
| 2020 | Qualifiers |

| UEFA NATIONS LEAGUE | |
|---|---|
| 2018/2019 | League B (Group Stage) |
| 2020/2021 | League B (Group Stage -> promoted to League A) |
| 2022/2023 | League A (Group Stage -> relegated to League B) |

## AUSTRIAN CLUB HONOURS IN EUROPEAN CLUB COMPETITIONS:

| European Champion Clubs.Cup (1956-1992) / UEFA Champions League (1993-2023) |
|---|
| None |

| Fairs Cup (1858-1971) / UEFA Cup (1972-2009) / UEFA Europa League (2010-2023) |
|---|
| None |

| UEFA Europa Conference League (2021-2023) |
|---|
| None |

| UEFA Super Cup (1972-2022) |
|---|
| None |

| *European Cup Winners' Cup 1961-1999** |
|---|
| None |

*defunct competition

## NATIONAL COMPETITIONS
## TABLE OF HONOURS

| | CHAMPIONS | CUP WINNERS | BEST GOALSCORERS | |
|---|---|---|---|---|
| 1911/1912 | SK Rapid Wien | - | Johann Schwarz II (First Vienna FC 1894 Wien) | 22 |
| 1912/1913 | SK Rapid Wien | - | Richard Kuthan (SK Rapid Wien) | 16 |
| 1913/1914 | Wiener AF | - | Johann Neumann (Wiener AC) | 25 |
| 1914/1915 | Wiener AC | - | Leopold Deutsch (Floridsdorfer AC & Wiener AC) | 12 |
| 1915/1916 | SK Rapid Wien | - | Richard Kuthan (SK Rapid Wien) | 24 |
| 1916/1917 | SK Rapid Wien | - | Eduard Bauer (SK Rapid Wien)<br>Leopold Neubauer (Wiener AF) | 21 |
| 1917/1918 | Floridsdorfer AC | - | Eduard Bauer (SK Rapid Wien) | 21 |
| 1918/1919 | SK Rapid Wien | SK Rapid Wien | Josef Uridil (SK Rapid Wien) | 16 |
| 1919/1920 | SK Rapid Wien | SK Rapid Wien | Josef Uridil (SK Rapid Wien)<br>Ernst Winkler (SpC Rudolfshügel) | 21 |
| 1920/1921 | SK Rapid Wien | Wiener SV Amateure | Josef Uridil (SK Rapid Wien) | 35 |
| 1921/1922 | Wiener Sport-Club | Wiener AF | Richard Kuthan (SK Rapid Wien) | 20 |
| 1922/1923 | SK Rapid Wien | Wiener Sport-Club | Ferdinand Swatosch (Wiener SV Amateure) | 22 |
| 1923/1924 | Wiener SV Amateure | Wiener SV Amateure | Gustav Wieser (Wiener SV Amateure) | 16 |
| 1924/1925 | SC Hakoah Wien | Wiener SV Amateure | Gustav Wieser (Wiener SV Amateure) | 19 |
| 1925/1926 | Wiener SV Amateure | Wiener SV Amateure | Gustav Wieser (Wiener SV Amateure) | 25 |
| 1926/1927 | SK Admira Wien | SK Rapid Wien | Anton Schall (SK Admira Wien) | 27 |
| 1927/1928 | SK Admira Wien | SK Admira Wien | Anton Schall (SK Admira Wien) | 36 |
| 1928/1929 | SK Rapid Wien | First Vienna FC 1894 Wien | Anton Schall (SK Admira Wien) | 21 |
| 1929/1930 | SK Rapid Wien | First Vienna FC 1894 Wien | Franz Weselik (SK Rapid Wien) | 24 |
| 1930/1931 | First Vienna FC 1894 Wien | Wiener AC | Anton Schall (SK Admira Wien) | 25 |
| 1931/1932 | SK Admira Wien | SK Admira Wien | Anton Schall (SK Admira Wien) | 22 |
| 1932/1933 | First Vienna FC 1894 Wien | FK Austria Wien | Franz Binder (SK Rapid Wien) | 25 |
| 1933/1934 | SK Admira Wien | SK Admira Wien | Josef Bican (SK Rapid Wien) | 29 |
| 1934/1935 | SK Rapid Wien | FK Austria Wien | Matthias Kaburek (SK Rapid Wien) | 29 |
| 1935/1936 | SK Admira Wien | FK Austria Wien | Wilhelm Hahnemann (SK Admira Wien) | 23 |
| 1936/1937 | SK Admira Wien | First Vienna FC 1894 Wien | Franz Binder (SK Rapid Wien) | 29 |
| 1937/1938 | SK Rapid Wien | Wiener AC – Schwarz-Rot Wien | Franz Binder (SK Rapid Wien) | 22 |
| 1938/1939 | SK Admira Wien | - | Franz Binder (SK Rapid Wien) | 27 |
| 1939/1940 | SK Rapid Wien | - | Franz Binder (SK Rapid Wien) | 18 |
| 1940/1941 | SK Rapid Wien | - | Franz Binder (SK Rapid Wien) | 27 |
| 1941/1942 | Vienna FC Wien | - | Ernst Reitermaier (SC Wacker Wien) | 20 |
| 1942/1943 | Vienna FC Wien | - | Karl Kerbach (Floridsdorfer AC) | 31 |
| 1943/1944 | Vienna FC Wien | - | Karl Decker (First Vienna FC 1894 Wien) | 32 |
| 1944/1945 | SK Rapid Wien | - | Richard Fischer (First Vienna FC 1894 Wien) | 15 |
| 1945/1946 | SK Rapid Wien | SK Rapid Wien | Ernst Stojaspal I (FK Austria Wien) | 34 |
| 1946/1947 | SC Wacker Wien | SC Wacker Wien | Ernst Stojaspal I (FK Austria Wien) | 18 |
| 1947/1948 | SK Rapid Wien | FK Austria Wien | Ernst Stojaspal I (FK Austria Wien) | 24 |
| 1948/1949 | FK Austria Wien | FK Austria Wien | Erich Habitzl (SK Admira Wien) | 23 |
| 1949/1950 | FK Austria Wien | - | Karl Decker (First Vienna FC 1894 Wien) | 23 |
| 1950/1951 | SK Rapid Wien | - | Robert Dienst (SK Rapid Wien) | 32 |
| 1951/1952 | SK Rapid Wien | - | Ernst Stojaspal I (FK Austria Wien) | 31 |
| 1952/1953 | FK Austria Wien | - | Ernst Stojaspal I (FK Austria Wien)<br>Robert Dienst (SK Rapid Wien) | 30 |
| 1953/1954 | SK Rapid Wien | - | Robert Dienst (SK Rapid Wien) | 25 |
| 1954/1955 | First Vienna FC 1894 Wien | - | Richard Brousek (SC Wacker Wien) | 31 |
| 1955/1956 | SK Rapid Wien | - | Johann Buzek (First Vienna FC 1894 Wien) | 33 |
| 1956/1957 | SK Rapid Wien | - | Robert Dienst (SK Rapid Wien) | 32 |
| 1957/1958 | Wiener Sport-Club | - | Walter Horak (Wiener Sport-Club) | 33 |
| 1958/1959 | Wiener Sport-Club | Wiener AC | Erich Hof (Wiener Sport-Club) | 32 |
| 1959/1960 | SK Rapid Wien | FK Austria Wien | Friedrich Cejka (Wiener Sport-Club) | 28 |
| 1960/1961 | FK Austria Wien | SK Rapid Wien | Horst Nemec (FK Austria Wien) | 31 |
| 1961/1962 | FK Austria Wien | FK Austria Wien | Horst Nemec (FK Austria Wien) | 24 |
| 1962/1963 | FK Austria Wien | FK Austria Wien | Erich Hof (Wiener Sport-Club) | 21 |
| 1963/1964 | SK Rapid Wien | ESV Admira Energie Wien | Horst Nemec (FK Austria Wien) | 21 |
| 1964/1965 | Linzer ASK | Linzer ASK | Wolfgang Gayer (Wiener Sport-Club) | 18 |
| 1965/1966 | ESV Admira Energie Wien | ESV Admira Energie Wien | Johann Buzek (FK Austria Wien) | 18 |
| 1966/1967 | SK Rapid Wien | FK Austria Wien | August Starek (SK Rapid Wien) | 21 |
| 1967/1968 | SK Rapid Wien | SK Rapid Wien | Jørn Bjerregaard (DEN, SK Rapid Wien) | 23 |
| 1968/1969 | FK Austria Wien | SK Rapid Wien | Helmut Köglberger (FK Austria Wien) | 31 |
| 1969/1970 | FK Austria Wien | FC Wacker Innsbruck | Günter Kaltenbrunner (Wiener Sport-Club) | 22 |
| 1970/1971 | FC Wacker Innsbruck | FK Austria Wien | Wilhelm Kreuz (ESV Admira Energie Wien) | 26 |
| 1971/1972 | SSW Innsbruck | Wiener Sport-Club | Alfred Riedl (FK Austria Wien) | 16 |
| 1972/1973 | SSW Innsbruck | SSW Innsbruck | Wolfgang Breuer (SSW Innsbruck) | 22 |
| 1973/1974 | SK VÖEST Linz | FK Austria Wien | Johann Krankl (SK Rapid Wien) | 36 |
| 1974/1975 | SSW Innsbruck | SSW Innsbruck | Helmut Köglberger (FK Austria/WAC Wien - Linzer ASK) | 22 |
| 1975/1976 | FK Austria/WAC Wien | SK Rapid Wien | Hans Pirkner (FK Austria/WAC Wien) | 21 |
| 1976/1977 | SSW Innsbruck | FK Austria Wien | Johann Krankl (SK Rapid Wien) | 32 |
| 1977/1978 | FK Austria Wien | SSW Innsbruck | Johann Krankl (SK Rapid Wien) | 32 |
| 1978/1979 | FK Austria Wien | SSW Innsbruck | Walter Schachner (FK Austria Wien) | 24 |
| 1979/1980 | FK Austria Wien | FK Austria Wien | Walter Schachner (FK Austria Wien) | 34 |

| | | | | |
|---|---|---|---|---|
| 1980/1981 | FK Austria Wien | Grazer AK | Gernot Jurtin (SK Sturm Graz) | 20 |
| 1981/1982 | SK Rapid Wien | FK Austria Wien | Božo Bakota (YUG, SK Sturm Graz) | 24 |
| 1982/1983 | SK Rapid Wien | SK Rapid Wien | Johann Krankl (SK Rapid Wien) | 23 |
| 1983/1984 | FK Austria Wien | SK Rapid Wien | Tibor Nyilasi (HUN, FK Austria Wien) | 26 |
| 1984/1985 | FK Austria Wien | SK Rapid Wien | Anton Polster (FK Austria Wien) | 24 |
| 1985/1986 | FK Austria Wien | FK Austria Wien | Anton Polster (FK Austria Wien) | 33 |
| 1986/1987 | SK Rapid Wien | SK Rapid Wien | Anton Polster (FK Austria Wien) | 39 |
| 1987/1988 | SK Rapid Wien | Kremser SC | Zoran Stojadinović (YUG, SK Rapid Wien) | 27 |
| 1988/1989 | FC Swarovski Tirol Innsbruck | FC Swarovski Tirol Innsbruck | Peter Pacult (FC Swarovski Tirol) | 26 |
| 1989/1990 | FC Swarovski Tirol Innsbruck | FK Austria Wien | Gerhard Rodax (FC Admira/Wacker Wien) | 35 |
| 1990/1991 | FK Austria Wien | SV Stockerau | Václav Daněk (TCH, FC Swarovski Tirol) | 29 |
| 1991/1992 | FK Austria Wien | FK Austria Wien | Christoph Westerthaler (FC Swarovski Tirol) | 17 |
| 1992/1993 | FK Austria Wien | FC Wacker Innsbruck | Václav Daněk (TCH, FC Wacker Tirol) | 24 |
| 1993/1994 | SV Austria Salzburg | FK Austria Wien | Nikola Jurčević (CRO, SV Austria Salzburg) Heimo Pfeifenberger (SV Austria Salzburg) | 14 |
| 1994/1995 | SV Austria Salzburg | SK Rapid Wien | Souleyman Sané (SEN, FC Tirol Innsbruck) | 20 |
| 1995/1996 | SK Rapid Wien | SK Sturm Graz | Ivica Vastic (SK Sturm Graz) | 20 |
| 1996/1997 | SV Austria Salzburg | SK Sturm Graz | René Wagner (CZE, SK Rapid Wien) | 28 |
| 1997/1998 | SK Sturm Graz | SV Ried im Innkreis | Geir Frigård (NOR, LASK Linz) | 23 |
| 1998/1999 | SK Sturm Graz | SK Sturm Graz | Eduard Glieder (SV Austria Salzburg) | 22 |
| 1999/2000 | FC Tirol Innsbruck | Grazer AK | Ivica Vastic (SK Sturm Graz) | 32 |
| 2000/2001 | FC Tirol Innsbruck | FC Kärnten | Radosław Gilewicz (POL, FC Tirol Innsbruck) | 22 |
| 2001/2002 | FC Tirol Innsbruck | Grazer AK | Ronald Brunmayr (Grazer AK) | 27 |
| 2002/2003 | FK Austria Wien | FK Austria Wien | Axel Lawarée (BEL, SC Schwarz-Weiß Bregenz) | 21 |
| 2003/2004 | Grazer AK | Grazer AK | Roland Kollmann (Grazer AK) | 24 |
| 2004/2005 | SK Rapid Wien | FK Austria Wien | Christian Mayrleb (Grazer AK) | 27 |
| 2005/2006 | FK Austria Wien | FK Austria Wien | Sanel Kuljic (SV Ried) Roland Linz (FK Austria Wien) | 15 |
| 2006/2007 | FC Red Bull Salzburg | FK Austria Wien | Alexander Zickler (GER, FC Red Bull Salzburg) | 22 |
| 2007/2008 | SK Rapid Wien | - | Alexander Zickler (GER, FC Red Bull Salzburg) | 16 |
| 2008/2009 | FC Red Bull Salzburg | FK Austria Wien | Marc Janko (FC Red Bull Salzburg) | 39 |
| 2009/2010 | FC Red Bull Salzburg | SK Sturm Graz | Steffen Hofmann (GER, SK Rapid Wien) | 20 |
| 2010/2011 | SK Sturm Graz | SV Ried im Innkreis | Roland Linz (FK Austria Wien) Roman Kienast (SK Sturm Graz) | 21 |
| 2011/2012 | FC Red Bull Salzburg | FC Red Bull Salzburg | Jakob Jantscher (FC Red Bull Salzburg) Stefan Maierhofer (FC Red Bull Salzburg) | 14 |
| 2012/2013 | FK Austria Wien | FC Pasching | Philipp Hosiner (FK Austria Wien) | 32 |
| 2013/2014 | FC Red Bull Salzburg | FC Red Bull Salzburg | Jonathan Soriano Casas (ESP, FC Red Bull Salzburg) | 31 |
| 2014/2015 | FC Red Bull Salzburg | FC Red Bull Salzburg | Jonathan Soriano Casas (ESP, FC Red Bull Salzburg) | 31 |
| 2015/2016 | FC Red Bull Salzburg | FC Red Bull Salzburg | Jonathan Soriano Casas (ESP, FC Red Bull Salzburg) | 21 |
| 2016/2017 | FC Red Bull Salzburg | FC Red Bull Salzburg | Olarenwaju Ayobami Kayode (NGA, FK Austria Wien) | 17 |
| 2017/2018 | FC Red Bull Salzburg | SK Sturm Graz | Moanes Dabour (ISR, FC Red Bull Salzburg) | 22 |
| 2018/2019 | FC Red Bull Salzburg | FC Red Bull Salzburg | Moanes Dabour (ISR, FC Red Bull Salzburg) | 20 |
| 2019/2020 | FC Red Bull Salzburg | FC Red Bull Salzburg | Shon Zalman Weissman (ISR, Wolfsberger AC) | 30 |
| 2020/2021 | FC Red Bull Salzburg | FC Red Bull Salzburg | Patson Daka (ZAM, FC Red Bull Salzburg) | 27 |
| 2021/2022 | FC Red Bull Salzburg | FC Red Bull Salzburg | Karim-David Adeyemi (GER, FC Red Bull Salzburg) | 17 |
| 2022/2023 | FC Red Bull Salzburg | SK Sturm Graz | Guido Burgstaller (SK Rapid Wien) | 21 |

## NATIONAL CHAMPIONSHIP
### Österreichische Fußballmeisterschaft – Bundesliga 2022/2023
(22.07.2022 – 03.06.2023)

### Regular Season - Results

**Round 1** [22-24.07.2022]
RB Salzburg - Austria Wien 3-0(1-0)
Linzer ASK - Austria Klagenfurt 3-1(2-0)
Wolfsberger AC - Sturm Graz 1-1(1-1)
Austria Lustenau - WSG Tirol 2-1(1-0)
TSV Hartberg - SCR Altach 2-1(1-0)
Rapid Wien - SV Ried 1-0(0-0)

**Round 2** [30-31.07.2022]
SV Ried - Austria Lustenau 1-0(1-0)
SCR Altach - Wolfsberger AC 2-2(1-0)
Sturm Graz - RB Salzburg 2-1(1-0)
WSG Tirol - TSV Hartberg 2-1(1-1)
Austria Klagenfurt - Rapid Wien 0-1(0-0)
Austria Wien - Linzer ASK 1-1(0-0)

**Round 3** [06-07.08.2022]
SV Ried - Sturm Graz 1-1(0-1)
Wolfsberger AC - Linzer ASK 1-5(0-4)
TSV Hartberg - RB Salzburg 0-2(0-0)
SCR Altach - Austria Wien 3-2(0-1)
WSG Tirol - Austria Klagenfurt 2-2(2-0)
Rapid Wien - Austria Lustenau 1-1(1-0)

**Round 4** [13-14.08.2022]
Austria Wien - WSG Tirol 2-1(1-0)
Austria Klagenfurt - SV Ried 1-0(0-0)
Sturm Graz - SCR Altach 4-0(1-0)
Austria Lustenau - TSV Hartberg 4-1(2-1)
RB Salzburg - Wolfsberger AC 2-1(2-0)
Linzer ASK - Rapid Wien 2-1(2-0)

**Round 5** [20-21.08.2022]
RB Salzburg - Austria Klagenfurt 2-0(0-0)
SCR Altach - Austria Lustenau 1-2(1-1)
Sturm Graz - Linzer ASK 0-1(0-0)
SV Ried - WSG Tirol 1-2(1-0)
Wolfsberger AC - Austria Wien 1-2(1-1)
Rapid Wien - Hartberg 5-1(1-1) [26.10.2022]

**Round 6** [27-28.08.2022]
Austria Lustenau - RB Salzburg 0-6(0-2)
TSV Hartberg - SV Ried 2-0(0-0)
Linzer ASK - SCR Altach 4-1(1-0)
WSG Tirol - Wolfsberger AC 1-3(1-1)
Austria Klagenfurt - Austria Wien 3-3(1-1)
Rapid Wien - Sturm Graz 1-2(1-1)

**Round 7 [03-04.09.2022]**
RB Salzburg - WSG Tirol 2-0(1-0)
Austria Wien - Austria Lustenau 2-2(1-2)
Sturm Graz - TSV Hartberg 0-0
SCR Altach - Rapid Wien 0-1(0-1)
Wolfsberger AC - Austria Klagenfurt 3-4(2-2)
Linzer ASK - SV Ried 1-1(1-0)

**Round 8 [10-11.09.2022]**
Rapid Wien - Wolfsberger AC 1-3(0-2)
SV Ried - RB Salzburg 0-3(0-2)
WSG Tirol - SCR Altach 0-0
Austria Lustenau - Linzer ASK 1-1(0-1)
TSV Hartberg - Austria Wien 0-3(0-1)
Austria Klagenfurt - Sturm Graz 0-2(0-0)

**Round 9 [17-18.09.2022]**
Linzer ASK - WSG Tirol 1-4(1-3)
Wolfsberger AC - TSV Hartberg 3-1(1-1)
SCR Altach - Austria Klagenfurt 1-4(1-1)
Austria Wien - SV Ried 3-0(1-0)
Sturm Graz - Austria Lustenau 2-0(1-0)
RB Salzburg - Rapid Wien 1-1(1-1)

**Round 10 [01-02.10.2022]**
RB Salzburg - Linzer ASK 1-1(0-0)
Austria Lustenau - Wolfsberger AC 1-3(1-1)
WSG Tirol - Rapid Wien 0-5(0-1)
SV Ried - SCR Altach 2-3(2-1)
TSV Hartberg - Austria Klagenfurt 2-3(1-2)
Austria Wien - Sturm Graz 0-3(0-1)

**Round 11 [08-09.10.2022]**
Linzer ASK - TSV Hartberg 0-3(0-0)
Austria Klagenfurt - Austria Lustenau 2-1(1-0)
SCR Altach - RB Salzburg 2-3(0-0)
Wolfsberger AC - SV Ried 1-2(0-2)
Sturm Graz - WSG Tirol 2-1(2-1)
Rapid Wien - Austria Wien 1-2(0-2)

**Round 12 [15-16.10.2022]**
Austria Klagenfurt - Linzer ASK 1-3(0-1)
WSG Tirol - Austria Lustenau 3-2(3-0)
SV Ried - Rapid Wien 1-0(0-0)
Sturm Graz - Wolfsberger AC 3-2(0-1)
SCR Altach - TSV Hartberg 1-0(0-0)
Austria Wien - RB Salzburg 1-3(1-1)

**Round 13 [22-23.10.2022]**
RB Salzburg - Sturm Graz 0-0
TSV Hartberg - WSG Tirol 1-5(1-2)
Rapid Wien - Austria Klagenfurt 0-1(0-1)
Austria Lustenau - SV Ried 0-0
Wolfsberger AC - SCR Altach 2-3(2-2)
Linzer ASK - Austria Wien 2-2(0-0)

**Round 14 [29-30.10.2022]**
RB Salzburg - TSV Hartberg 1-0(0-0)
Austria Klagenfurt - WSG Tirol 2-3(1-2)
Austria Lustenau - Rapid Wien 3-3(1-0)
Austria Wien - SCR Altach 2-1(0-0)
Linzer ASK - Wolfsberger AC 4-1(3-0)
Sturm Graz - SV Ried 2-1(1-0)

**Round 15 [05-06.11.2022]**
SV Ried - Austria Klagenfurt 2-2(1-0)
TSV Hartberg - Austria Lustenau 1-1(0-1)
Wolfsberger AC - RB Salzburg 1-2(0-2)
WSG Tirol - Austria Wien 0-0
SCR Altach - Sturm Graz 1-1(1-1)
Rapid Wien - Linzer ASK 1-0(1-0)

**Round 16 [12-13.11.2022]**
Austria Lustenau - SCR Altach 3-0(2-0)
TSV Hartberg - Rapid Wien 1-2(1-1)
WSG Tirol - SV Ried 2-0(2-0)
Austria Klagenfurt - RB Salzburg 0-1(0-0)
Austria Wien - Wolfsberger AC 0-1(0-0)
Linzer ASK - Sturm Graz 1-1(0-0)

**Round 17 [10-12.02.2023]**
Sturm Graz - Rapid Wien 1-0(0-0)
RB Salzburg - Austria Lustenau 4-0(0-0)
Wolfsberger AC - WSG Tirol 1-2(0-0)
SV Ried - TSV Hartberg 0-1(0-0)
SCR Altach - Linzer ASK 0-1(0-1)
Austria Wien - Austria Klagenfurt 3-1(1-0)

**Round 18 [18-19.02.2023]**
TSV Hartberg - Sturm Graz 1-2(0-2)
Austria Klagenfurt - Wolfsberger AC 0-3(0-3)
SV Ried - Linzer ASK 1-1(1-0)
WSG Tirol - RB Salzburg 1-3(0-1)
Austria Lustenau - Austria Wien 1-0(1-0)
Rapid Wien - SCR Altach 3-0(0-0)

**Round 19 [24-26.02.2023]**
Linzer ASK - Austria Lustenau 1-0(0-0)
Sturm Graz - Austria Klagenfurt 1-2(1-1)
Austria Wien - TSV Hartberg 3-0(1-0)
Wolfsberger AC - Rapid Wien 1-2(0-2)
SCR Altach - WSG Tirol 0-0
RB Salzburg - SV Ried 2-0(1-0)

**Round 20 [04-05.03.2023]**
TSV Hartberg - Wolfsberger AC 2-1(1-1)
SV Ried - Austria Wien 1-3(1-1)
Austria Lustenau - Sturm Graz 0-2(0-0)
WSG Tirol - Linzer ASK 2-3(1-2)
Austria Klagenfurt - SCR Altach 3-0(3-0)
Rapid Wien - RB Salzburg 2-4(1-1)

**Round 21 [12.03.2023]**
Linzer ASK - RB Salzburg 0-2(0-0)
Sturm Graz - Austria Wien 3-1(1-1)
SCR Altach - SV Ried 1-2(1-1)
Wolfsberger AC - Austria Lustenau 0-1(0-0)
Austria Klagenfurt - TSV Hartberg 1-0(1-0)
Rapid Wien - WSG Tirol 2-0(0-0)

**Round 22 [19.03.2023]**
TSV Hartberg - Linzer ASK 2-2(1-1)
SV Ried - Wolfsberger AC 0-0
WSG Tirol - Sturm Graz 0-2(0-0)
Austria Lustenau - Austria Klagenfurt 4-2(2-1)
Austria Wien - Rapid Wien 2-0(1-0)
RB Salzburg - SCR Altach 1-1(0-0)

**Final Standings**

| | | | | | | | | | |
|---|---|---|---|---|---|---|---|---|---|
| 1. | FC Red Bull Salzburg | 22 | 17 | 4 | 1 | 49 | - | 13 | 55 |
| 2. | SK Sturm Graz | 22 | 14 | 6 | 2 | 37 | - | 15 | 48 |
| 3. | Linzer ASK | 22 | 10 | 8 | 4 | 38 | - | 28 | 38 |
| 4. | SK Rapid Wien | 22 | 10 | 3 | 9 | 34 | - | 26 | 33 |
| 5. | FK Austria Wien* | 22 | 10 | 5 | 7 | 37 | - | 31 | 32 |
| 6. | SK Austria Klagenfurt | 22 | 9 | 3 | 10 | 35 | - | 40 | 30 |
| 7. | WSG Tirol Wattens | 22 | 8 | 4 | 10 | 32 | - | 37 | 28 |
| 8. | SC Austria Lustenau | 22 | 7 | 6 | 9 | 29 | - | 37 | 27 |
| 9. | Wolfsberger AC | 22 | 6 | 3 | 13 | 35 | - | 41 | 21 |
| 10. | TSV Hartberg | 22 | 5 | 3 | 14 | 22 | - | 42 | 18 |
| 11. | SV Ried im Innkreis | 22 | 4 | 6 | 12 | 16 | - | 32 | 18 |
| 12. | SC Rheindorf Altach | 22 | 4 | 5 | 13 | 22 | - | 44 | 17 |

*Please note: FK Austria Wien were deducted 3 points due to license violation.
Teams ranked 1-6 were qualified for the Championship Round, while teams ranked 7-12 were qualified for the Relegation Round.

The points obtained during the regular season were halved (and rounded down) before the start of the play-offs.
As a result, the teams started with the following points:
**Championship Round**: FC Red Bull Salzburg 27, SK Sturm Graz 24, Linzer ASK 19, SK Rapid Wien 16, FK Austria Wien 16, SK Austria Klagenfurt 15.
**Relegation Round**: WSG Tirol Wattens 14, SC Austria Lustenau 13, Wolfsberger AC 10, TSV Hartberg 9, SV Ried im Innkreis 9, SC Rheindorf Altach 8.

## Championship Round

### Results

**Round 23** [02.04.2023]
Austria Wien - Linzer ASK 2-2(0-0)
Austria Klagenfurt - RB Salzburg 0-3(0-1)
Sturm Graz - Rapid Wien 3-1(2-1)

**Round 24** [09.04.2023]
RB Salzburg - Austria Wien 3-3(2-0)
Rapid Wien - Austria Klagenfurt 3-1(1-0)
Linzer ASK - Sturm Graz 2-1(0-0)

**Round 25** [16.04.2023]
RB Salzburg - Linzer ASK 0-0
Austria Klagenfurt - Sturm Graz 0-2(0-0)
Rapid Wien - Austria Wien 3-3(2-2)

**Round 26** [23.04.2023]
Austria Wien - Austria Klagenfurt 1-2(0-0)
Linzer ASK - Rapid Wien 3-1(2-0)
Sturm Graz - RB Salzburg 0-2(0-0)

**Round 27** [26.04.2023]
Sturm Graz - Austria Wien 3-2(1-2)
Rapid Wien - RB Salzburg 1-1(1-1)
Linzer ASK - Klagenfurt 4-0(0-0)[30.04.2023]

**Round 28** [07.05.2023]
Austria Klagenfurt - Linzer ASK 1-1(1-0)
Austria Wien - Sturm Graz 1-2(0-2)
RB Salzburg - Rapid Wien 2-1(1-0)

**Round 29** [14.05.2023]
Linzer ASK - RB Salzburg 0-1(0-0)
Sturm Graz - Austria Klagenfurt 4-1(2-1)
Austria Wien - Rapid Wien 3-1(2-1)

**Round 30** [21.05.2023]
Austria Klagenfurt - Austria Wien 1-1(0-0)
Rapid Wien - Linzer ASK 1-1(1-0)
RB Salzburg - Sturm Graz 2-1(0-1)

**Round 31** [28.05.2023]
Linzer ASK - Austria Wien 3-1(1-0)
RB Salzburg - Austria Klagenfurt 3-2(0-2)
Rapid Wien - Sturm Graz 3-2(2-2)

**Round 32** [03.06.2023]
Austria Wien - RB Salzburg 1-1(0-1)
Austria Klagenfurt - Rapid Wien 2-1(0-0)
Sturm Graz - Linzer ASK 2-0(2-0)

### Final Standings

| | | | | | | Total | | | | | Home | | | | | Away | | |
|---|---|---|---|---|---|---|---|---|---|---|---|---|---|---|---|---|---|---|
| 1. | **FC Red Bull Salzburg** | 32 | 23 | 8 | 1 | 67 | - | 22 | **49** | 10 | 6 | 0 | 29 | - | 11 | 13 | 2 | 1 | 38 - 11 |
| 2. | SK Sturm Graz | 32 | 20 | 6 | 6 | 57 | - | 29 | **42** | 12 | 1 | 3 | 32 | - | 15 | 8 | 5 | 3 | 25 - 14 |
| 3. | Linzer ASK | 32 | 14 | 12 | 6 | 54 | - | 38 | **35** | 9 | 3 | 4 | 31 | - | 21 | 5 | 9 | 2 | 23 - 17 |
| 4. | SK Rapid Wien | 32 | 12 | 6 | 14 | 50 | - | 47 | **25** | 7 | 4 | 5 | 29 | - | 22 | 5 | 2 | 9 | 21 - 25 |
| 5. | FK Austria Wien | 32 | 11 | 10 | 11 | 55 | - | 52 | **24** | 7 | 4 | 5 | 27 | - | 21 | 4 | 6 | 6 | 28 - 31 |
| 6. | SK Austria Klagenfurt | 32 | 11 | 5 | 16 | 45 | - | 63 | **23** | 5 | 3 | 8 | 17 | - | 25 | 6 | 2 | 8 | 28 - 38 |

FK Austria Wien were qualified for the Europa Conference League Play-offs Final.

## Relegation Round

### Results

**Round 23** [31.03.-01.04.2023]
TSV Hartberg - Austria Lustenau 0-1(0-1)
Wolfsberger AC - SV Ried 1-0(0-0)
SCR Altach - WSG Tirol 1-0(0-0)

**Round 24** [07-08.04.2023]
WSG Tirol - Wolfsberger AC 4-0(3-0)
SV Ried - TSV Hartberg 1-3(0-1)
Austria Lustenau - SCR Altach 1-0(0-0)

**Round 25** [14-15.04.2023]
SV Ried - WSG Tirol 1-1(1-1)
TSV Hartberg - SCR Altach 2-2(0-2)
Austria Lustenau - Wolfsberger AC 1-3(1-0)

**Round 26** [21-22.04.2023]
Wolfsberger AC - TSV Hartberg 2-2(0-1)
SCR Altach - SV Ried 1-1(0-0)
WSG Tirol - Austria Lustenau 0-2(0-0)

**Round 27** [28-29.04.2023]
SCR Altach - Wolfsberger AC 0-2(0-1)
SV Ried - Austria Lustenau 4-4(1-3)
WSG Tirol - TSV Hartberg 1-1(1-0)

**Round 28** [05-06.05.2023]
Wolfsberger AC - SCR Altach 0-0
Austria Lustenau - SV Ried 2-2(1-0)
TSV Hartberg - WSG Tirol 5-0(4-0)

**Round 29** [12-13.05.2023]
WSG Tirol - SV Ried 1-1(1-1)
SCR Altach - TSV Hartberg 0-1(0-1)
Wolfsberger AC - Austria Lustenau 2-2(2-2)

**Round 30** [19-20.05.2023]
SV Ried - SCR Altach 0-1(0-0)
TSV Hartberg - Wolfsberger AC 0-2(0-1)
Austria Lustenau - WSG Tirol 2-4(0-2)

**Round 31** [27.05.2023]
Wolfsberger AC - WSG Tirol 2-0(2-0)
TSV Hartberg - SV Ried 2-0(0-0)
SCR Altach - Austria Lustenau 1-1(1-0)

**Round 32** [02.06.2023]
Austria Lustenau - TSV Hartberg 5-1(3-0)
SV Ried - Wolfsberger AC 1-2(1-0)
WSG Tirol - SCR Altach 1-1(1-0)

### Final Standings

| | | | | | | Total | | | | | Home | | | | | Away | | |
|---|---|---|---|---|---|---|---|---|---|---|---|---|---|---|---|---|---|---|
| 1. | Wolfsberger AC | 32 | 12 | 6 | 14 | 51 | - | 51 | **31** | 3 | 4 | 9 | 22 | - | 29 | 9 | 2 | 5 | 29 - 25 |
| 2. | SC Austria Lustenau | 32 | 11 | 10 | 11 | 50 | - | 54 | **29** | 7 | 4 | 5 | 30 | - | 29 | 4 | 6 | 6 | 20 - 25 |
| 3. | WSG Tirol Wattens | 32 | 10 | 8 | 14 | 44 | - | 53 | **24** | 4 | 6 | 6 | 20 | - | 26 | 6 | 2 | 8 | 24 - 27 |
| 4. | TSV Hartberg | 32 | 9 | 6 | 17 | 39 | - | 56 | **24** | 5 | 3 | 8 | 23 | - | 27 | 4 | 3 | 9 | 16 - 29 |
| 5. | SC Rheindorf Altach | 32 | 6 | 10 | 16 | 29 | - | 53 | **19** | 3 | 5 | 8 | 15 | - | 23 | 3 | 5 | 8 | 14 - 30 |
| 6. | SV Ried im Innkreis (*Relegated*) | 32 | 4 | 11 | 17 | 27 | - | 50 | **14** | 2 | 6 | 8 | 17 | - | 27 | 2 | 5 | 9 | 10 - 23 |

Wolfsberger AC and SC Austria Lustenau were qualified for the Europa Conference League Play-offs Semi-Final.

| Top goalscorers: | |
|---|---|
| **21  Guido Burgstaller** | *SK Rapid Wien* |
| 17  Haris Tabaković (SUI) | *FK Austria Wien* |
| 17  Tai Baribo (ISR) | *Wolfsberger AC* |
| 16  Benjamin Šeško (SVN) | *FC Red Bull Salzburg* |
| 16  Markus Pink | *SK Austria Klagenfurt* |

### Europa Conference League Play-offs – Semi-Finals [05.06.2023]

| Wolfsberger AC - SC Austria Lustenau | 1-2(0-0,1-1) | |
|---|---|---|

### Europa Conference League Play-offs – Final [08.-11.06.2023]

| SC Austria Lustenau - FK Austria Wien | 1-1(1-0) | 0-5(0-1) |
|---|---|---|

# NATIONAL CUP
## ÖFB Cup 2022/2023

### First Round [15-17/19.07.2022]

| | | | | |
|---|---|---|---|---|
| SV Opbacher Fügen - FC Red Bull Salzburg | 0-3(0-1) | SV Frauental - USV Allerheiligen | 0-5(0-3) |
| SR Donaufeld - SKU Amstetten | 0-4(0-1) | SC Schwarz-Weiß Bregenz - SV Seekirchen | 3-0(2-0) |
| SC Admira Dornbirn 1946 - SK Austria Klagenfurt | 1-8(1-4) | ASKÖ Köttmannsdorf - Grazer AK | 1-3(1-1) |
| SK Treibach - SK Rapid Wien | 0-1(0-0) | TWL Elektra - SC Rheindorf Altach | 1-3(1-2) |
| ASV Draßburg - SV Horn | 0-3(0-2) | SV Stripfing/Weiden - FCM Traiskirchen | 0-1(0-0) |
| DSV Leoben - TSV Hartberg | 1-2(1-2) | SC Schwaz - Linzer ASK | 1-9(1-3) |
| SC Neusiedl/See 1919 - WSG Tirol Wattens | 1-3(0-0,1-1) | SV Leobendorf - SKN St. Pölten | 1-2(0-0) |
| SAK Klagenfurt - Wiener Sport-Club | 0-3(0-1) | VfB Hohenems - FC Blau Weiß Linz | 1-10(0-4) |
| Deutschlandsberger SC - USV Scheiblingkirchen-Warth | 2-0(1-0) | ASV Siegendorf - First Vienna FC | 2-2 aet; 4-3 pen |
| Sportunion Vöcklamarkt - FC Dornbirn 1913 | 0-5(0-2) | SVg Purgstall - FC Admira Wacker Mödling | 2-4(0-2) |
| SC/ESV Parndorf 1919 - SV Lafnitz | 2-3(1-0) | SC Imst - TSV St. Johann | 2-0(1-0) |
| Union Gurten - Sportunion St. Martin | 3-2(1-1) | SV Telfs - SV Austria Salzburg | 2-4(0-0) |
| SC Röthis - SK Sturm Graz | 0-6(0-4) | SV Kuchl - Wolfsberger AC | 1-4(1-2) |
| FC Marchfeld Donauauen - SC Austria Lustenau | 2-3(1-0) | WSC Hertha - SK Vorwärts Steyr | 1-0(1-0) |
| FC Stadlau - SV Ried im Innkreis | 0-4(0-3) | TuS Bad Gleichenberg - Floridsdorfer AC Wien | 0-2(0-1) |
| FC Wels - FK Austria Wien | 0-7(0-3) | SV Dellach/Gail - Kapfenberger SV | 1-2(0-0) |

### Second Round [30.08.-01.09.2022]

| | | | | |
|---|---|---|---|---|
| FC Admira Wacker Mödling - SC Rheindorf Altach | 3-0(3-0) | Deutschlandsberger SC - Wolfsberger AC | 1-5(0-2) |
| Kapfenberger SV 1919 - Floridsdorfer AC Wien | 1-2(1-0,1-1) | SKU Amstetten - FC Blau Weiß Linz | 0-3(0-2) |
| SV Lafnitz - Grazer AK | 1-2(0-0) | FC Dornbirn 1913- TSV Hartberg | 3-2(2-1) |
| Wiener Sport-Club - SC Austria Lustenau | 2-0(2-0) | SC Schwarz-Weiß Bregenz - SK Austria Klagenfurt | 0-5(0-3) |
| SV Horn - SKN St. Pölten | 3-1(2-0) | FCM Traiskirchen - WSG Tirol Wattens | 0-5(0-3) |
| Union Gurten - FC Red Bull Salzburg | 0-3(0-1) | WSC Hertha - SV Ried im Innkreis | 2-4(2-1) |
| SC Imst - Linzer ASK | 1-4(0-0,1-1) | ASV Siegendorf - FK Austria Wien | 0-5(0-4) |
| SK Sturm Graz - SV Austria Salzburg | 3-1(2-0) | USV Allerheiligen - SK Rapid Wien | 0-2(0-0) |

### 1/8-Finals [18-20.10.2022]

| | | | | |
|---|---|---|---|---|
| WSG Tirol Wattens - SK Rapid Wien | 1-4(1-1) | Grazer AK - SK Sturm Graz | 0-1(0-0) |
| FC Dornbirn 1913- SK Austria Klagenfurt | 1-2(1-1) | FC Blau Weiß Linz - Wolfsberger AC | 1-3(0-1) |
| SV Horn - SV Ried im Innkreis | 2-3(2-3) | FC Admira Wacker Mödling - FC Red Bull Salzburg | 1-6(0-4) |
| Floridsdorfer AC Wien - Linzer ASK | 1-2(1-2) | Wiener Sport-Club - FK Austria Wien | 3-1(1-1) |

### Quarter-Finals [03-05.02.2023]

| | | | | |
|---|---|---|---|---|
| Wolfsberger AC - SK Rapid Wien | 1-3(0-0,1-1) | Wiener Sport-Club - SV Ried im Innkreis | 0-2(0-0) |
| FC Red Bull Salzburg - SK Sturm Graz | 1-1 aet; 4-5 pen | Linzer ASK - SK Austria Klagenfurt | 1-0(0-0) |

### Semi-Finals [05-06.04.2023]

| | | | | |
|---|---|---|---|---|
| SK Rapid Wien - SV Ried im Innkreis | 2-1(1-0) | SK Sturm Graz - Linzer ASK | 1-0(0-0) |

### Final

30.04.2023; Wörthersee Stadion, Klagenfurt; Referee: Christopher Jäger; Attendance: 30,000

**SK Rapid Wien - SK Sturm Graz**                                    **0-2(0-0)**

**Rapid Wien**: Niklas Hedl, Thorsten Schick, Martin Moormann, Kevin Wimmer, Jonas Auer, Roman Kerschbaum, Aleksa Pejić, Patrick Greil (81.Ferdy Druijf), Nicolas Kühn (73.Ante Bajić), Marco Grüll (81.Oliver Strunz), Guido Burgstaller (Cap). Trainer: Zoran Barišić.

**Sturm Graz**: Arthur Okonkwo, Jusuf Gazibegović, David Affengruber, Gregory Wüthrich, David Schnegg, Jon Gorenc Stanković, Stefan Hierländer (Cap), Alexander Prass (89.Niklas Geyrhofer), Otar Kiteishvili (75.Tomi Horvat), Manprit Sarkaria (90+5.Bryan Silva Teixeira), Emanuel Esseh Emegha. Trainer: Christian Ilzer.

**Goals:** 0-1 Manprit Sarkaria (66), 0-2 Manprit Sarkaria (85).

Please note: appearances and goals includes statistics of both regular season and play-offs (Championship Round & Relegation Round).

## Sportklub Austria Klagenfurt

| Founded: | 1920 | | |
|---|---|---|---|
| Stadium: | 28 Black Arena [Wörthersee Stadion], Klagenfurt (29,863) | | |
| Trainer: | Peter Pacult | | 28.10.1959 |

| Goalkeepers: | DOB | M | (s) | G |
|---|---|---|---|---|
| Marco Knaller | 26.03.1987 | 2 | | |
| Phillip Menzel (GER) | 18.08.1998 | 30 | | |
| Defenders: | DOB | M | (s) | G |
| Michael Blauensteiner | 11.02.1995 | 8 | (8) | 1 |
| Solomon Owusu Bonnah (NED) | 19.08.2003 | 3 | (9) | 1 |
| Nikola Đorić (SRB) | 03.03.2000 | | (12) | |
| Kosmas Gkezos (GRE) | 15.08.1992 | 25 | (3) | 4 |
| Thorsten Mahrer | 22.01.1990 | 31 | | 1 |
| Maximiliano Moreira Romero (URU) | 11.06.1994 | 20 | (6) | 1 |
| Till Schumacher (GER) | 10.12.1997 | 17 | (4) | |
| Nicolas Wimmer | 15.03.1995 | 28 | (1) | 3 |
| Midfielders: | DOB | M | (s) | G |
| Rico Benatelli (GER) | 17.03.1992 | 14 | (10) | |
| Christopher Cvetko | 02.04.1997 | 30 | | 1 |
| Vesel Demaku | 05.02.2000 | 8 | (5) | |
| Andrew Irving (SCO) | 13.05.2000 | 28 | (3) | 5 |
| Florian Jaritz | 18.10.1997 | 7 | (10) | 1 |
| Sinan Karweina (GER) | 29.03.1999 | 17 | (3) | 1 |
| Emilian Metu | 18.04.2003 | | (1) | |
| Fabian Miesenböck | 07.07.1993 | 1 | (9) | |
| Florian Rieder | 16.05.1996 | 19 | (4) | 4 |
| Simon Straudi (ITA) | 27.01.1999 | 8 | (4) | |
| Christopher Wernitznig | 24.02.1990 | 23 | (8) | |
| Forwards: | DOB | M | (s) | G |
| Jonas Arweiler (GER) | 10.04.1997 | | (20) | 3 |
| Nicolas Binder | 13.01.2002 | 5 | (4) | |
| Markus Pink | 24.02.1991 | 22 | | 16 |
| Sebastian Guerra Soto (USA) | 28.07.2000 | 6 | (5) | 1 |

## Sportclub Austria Lustenau

| Founded: | 1914 | | |
|---|---|---|---|
| Stadium: | Planet Pure Stadion [Reichshofstadion], Lustenau (8,800) | | |
| Trainer: | Markus Mader | | 19.05.1968 |

| Goalkeepers: | DOB | M | (s) | G |
|---|---|---|---|---|
| Ammar Helac | 13.06.1998 | 3 | | |
| Domenik Schierl | 20.07.1994 | 29 | | |
| Defenders: | DOB | M | (s) | G |
| Anderson dos Santos Gomes (BRA) | 03.01.1998 | 29 | | 5 |
| Tobias Berger | 02.11.2001 | 4 | (14) | 1 |
| Fabian Gmeiner | 27.01.1997 | 16 | (9) | |
| Darijo Grujcic | 19.05.1999 | 14 | (7) | 2 |
| Hakim Guenouche (FRA) | 30.05.2000 | 27 | (3) | 1 |
| Jean Hugonet (FRA) | 24.11.1999 | 29 | | 1 |
| Hannes Küng | 02.02.2003 | | (1) | |
| Matthias Maak | 12.05.1992 | 24 | (3) | 1 |
| Midfielders: | DOB | M | (s) | G |
| Adriel Tadeu Ferreira da Silva (BRA) | 22.05.1997 | 10 | (10) | 1 |
| Yuliwes Bellache (ALG) | 15.12.2002 | | (7) | |
| Yadaly Diaby (FRA) | 09.08.2000 | 12 | (10) | 4 |
| Pius Grabher | 11.08.1993 | 29 | (1) | 1 |
| Henri Koudossou (GER) | 03.09.1999 | 2 | (4) | |
| Torben Rhein (GER) | 12.01.2003 | 10 | (11) | |
| Daniel Tiefenbach (HUN) | 10.08.1999 | 8 | (4) | |
| Cem Türkmen (TUR) | 29.03.2002 | 18 | (11) | |
| Stefano Surdanović (SRB) | 23.11.1998 | 30 | (2) | 4 |
| Forwards: | DOB | M | (s) | G |
| Michael Cheukoua (CMR) | 13.01.1997 | 4 | (14) | 3 |
| Lukas Fridrikas | 30.12.1997 | 22 | (7) | 13 |
| Emrehan Gedikli (GER) | 25.04.2003 | 1 | (3) | 1 |
| Nemanja Motika (SRB) | 20.03.2003 | 8 | (7) | 1 |
| Anthony Schmid | 18.01.1999 | 8 | (17) | 4 |
| Jan Stefanon | 02.01.1999 | | (2) | |
| Bryan Silva Teixeira (FRA) | 01.09.2000 | 15 | (1) | 6 |

## Fußballklub Austria Wien

| Founded: | 15.03.1911 | | |
|---|---|---|---|
| Stadium: | Generali Arena, Wien (17,500) | | |
| Trainer: | Manfred Schmid | | 20.02.1971 |
| [05.12.2022] | Michael Wimmer | | 18.06.1980 |

| Goalkeepers: | DOB | M | (s) | G |
|---|---|---|---|---|
| Christian Früchtl (GER) | 28.01.2000 | 32 | | |
| Mirko Kos | 12.04.1997 | | (1) | |
| Defenders: | DOB | M | (s) | G |
| Matan Baltaxa (ISR) | 20.09.1995 | 4 | (1) | 1 |
| Ziad El Sheiwi | 11.03.2004 | 1 | | |
| Johannes Handl | 07.05.1998 | 16 | (2) | |
| Billy Dawson Koumetio (FRA) | 14.11.2002 | 3 | (2) | |
| Doron Leidner (ISR) | 26.04.2002 | 7 | (3) | 1 |
| Lucas Galvão da Costa Souza (BRA) | 22.06.1991 | 14 | | |
| Marvin Martins (LUX) | 17.02.1995 | 29 | (1) | 1 |
| Matteo Meisl | 27.12.2000 | 11 | (5) | |
| Lukas Mühl (GER) | 27.01.1997 | 22 | (2) | |
| Reinhold Ranftl | 24.01.1992 | 31 | | 4 |
| Georg Teigl | 09.02.1991 | 2 | (11) | |
| Midfielders: | DOB | M | (s) | G |
| Matthias Braunöder | 27.03.2002 | 27 | (4) | 2 |
| Manfred Fischer | 06.08.1995 | 32 | | 2 |
| Dominik Fitz | 16.06.1999 | 24 | (3) | 7 |
| James Holland (AUS) | 15.05.1989 | 10 | (7) | |
| Aleksandar Jukić | 26.07.2000 | 19 | (8) | 3 |
| Dario Kreiker | 07.01.2003 | 1 | (2) | |
| Florian Wustinger | 21.07.2003 | 1 | (3) | |
| Forwards: | DOB | M | (s) | G |
| Marco Djuričin | 12.12.1992 | | (3) | 1 |
| Nikola Dovedan | 06.07.1994 | 9 | (11) | 1 |
| Ibrahima Dramé (SEN) | 06.10.2001 | | (3) | |
| Andreas Gruber | 29.06.1995 | 18 | (6) | 8 |
| Muharem Husković | 05.03.2003 | 6 | (2) | 1 |
| Can Keles | 02.09.2001 | 3 | (15) | 3 |
| Manuel Polster | 23.12.2002 | 12 | (9) | 1 |
| Haris Tabaković (SUI) | 20.06.1994 | 17 | (11) | 17 |
| Romeo Vučić | 30.01.2003 | 1 | (8) | |

## Linzer Athletik-Sport-Klub

| | | |
|---|---|---|
| **Founded**: | 07.08.1908 [as Athletiksportklub Siegfried] | |
| **Stadium**: | Raiffeisen-Arena [Waldstadion], Pasching (19,080) | |
| **Trainer**: | Dominik Thalhammer | 02.10.1970 |
| [13.09.2021] | Andreas Wieland | 16.08.1983 |
| [03.05.2022] | Dietmar Kühbauer | 04.04.1971 |

| Goalkeepers: | DOB | M | (s) | G |
|---|---|---|---|---|
| Tobias Lawal | 07.06.2000 | 7 | | |
| Alexander Schlager | 01.02.1996 | 25 | | |
| **Defenders:** | DOB | M | (s) | G |
| Jan Boller (GER) | 14.03.2000 | 1 | | |
| Ákos Kecskés (HUN) | 04.01.1996 | 1 | (5) | |
| Felix Luckeneder | 21.03.1994 | 30 | | |
| Marvin Potzmann | 07.12.1993 | 6 | (9) | |
| René Renner | 29.11.1993 | 29 | | 1 |
| Filip Stojković (MNE) | 22.01.1993 | 28 | | 1 |
| Maksym Taloverov (UKR) | 28.06.2000 | 5 | (7) | |
| Philipp Wiesinger | 23.05.1994 | 1 | (1) | |
| Philipp Ziereis (GER) | 14.03.1993 | 29 | | 1 |
| **Midfielders:** | DOB | M | (s) | G |
| Nemanja Celić | 26.04.1999 | 1 | (6) | |
| Florian Flecker | 29.10.1995 | 4 | (22) | 2 |
| Hong Hyun-seok (KOR) | 16.06.1999 | 3 | | |
| Sascha Horvath | 22.08.1996 | 25 | (6) | 2 |

| | DOB | M | (s) | G |
|---|---|---|---|---|
| Branko Jović (SRB) | 18.03.1993 | 21 | (7) | 1 |
| Peter Michorl | 09.05.1995 | 25 | (3) | |
| Stefan Radulović | 01.01.2002 | | (2) | |
| Fredy Alexander Valencia Ramos (COL) | 16.08.2001 | | (1) | |
| Luca Wimhofer | 27.02.2004 | | (1) | |
| Gabriel Zirngast | 20.01.2002 | | (2) | |
| Robert Žulj | 05.02.1992 | 21 | (4) | 11 |
| **Forwards:** | DOB | M | (s) | G |
| Husein Balić (BIH) | 15.02.1996 | | (5) | |
| Thomas Goiginger | 15.03.1993 | 17 | (8) | 4 |
| Efthimios Koulouris (GRE) | 06.03.1996 | 2 | (12) | 1 |
| Marin Ljubičić (CRO) | 28.02.2002 | 21 | (7) | 12 |
| Ibrahim Mustapha (GHA) | 18.06.2000 | 9 | (6) | 3 |
| Keito Nakamura (JPN) | 28.07.2000 | 30 | (1) | 14 |
| Alexander Schmidt | 19.01.1998 | | (2) | |
| Adil Taoui (FRA) | 10.08.2001 | | (4) | |
| Moses Usor (NGA) | 05.02.2002 | 11 | (5) | 1 |

## Sportklub Rapid Wien

| | | |
|---|---|---|
| **Founded**: | 08.01.1899 | |
| **Stadium**: | Allianz Stadion, Wien (28,000) | |
| **Trainer**: | Ferdinand Feldhofer | 23.10.1979 |
| [16.10.2022] | Zoran Barišić | 22.05.1970 |

| Goalkeepers: | DOB | M | (s) | G |
|---|---|---|---|---|
| Paul Gartler | 10.03.1997 | 1 | | |
| Niklas Hedl | 17.03.2001 | 31 | | |
| **Defenders:** | DOB | M | (s) | G |
| Jonas Auer | 05.08.2000 | 25 | (3) | |
| Christopher Dibon | 02.11.1990 | 2 | | |
| Maximilian Hofmann | 07.08.1993 | 4 | (2) | |
| Denso Kasius (NED) | 06.10.2002 | 8 | (2) | |
| Martin Koscelník (SVK) | 02.03.1995 | 14 | (4) | |
| Martin Moormann | 30.04.2001 | 14 | (7) | |
| Leopold Querfeld | 20.12.2003 | 21 | (2) | 1 |
| Thorsten Schick | 19.05.1990 | 13 | (12) | |
| Michael Sollbauer | 15.05.1990 | 24 | | |
| Kevin Wimmer | 15.11.1992 | 8 | (2) | |
| **Midfielders:** | DOB | M | (s) | G |
| Patrick Greil | 08.09.1996 | 17 | (11) | 1 |
| Roman Kerschbaum | 19.01.1994 | 23 | (5) | 2 |

| | DOB | M | (s) | G |
|---|---|---|---|---|
| Christoph Knasmüllner | 30.04.1992 | 7 | (5) | |
| Moritz Oswald | 05.01.2002 | 7 | (5) | |
| Aleksa Pejić (SRB) | 09.07.1999 | 24 | (2) | |
| Dejan Petrovič (SVN) | 12.01.1998 | 2 | (2) | |
| Nikolas Sattlberger | 18.01.2004 | 2 | (1) | |
| **Forwards:** | DOB | M | (s) | G |
| Ante Bajić | 22.08.1995 | 11 | (13) | 1 |
| Guido Burgstaller | 29.04.1989 | 27 | (4) | 21 |
| Yusuf Demir | 02.06.2003 | 1 | | 1 |
| Ferdy Druijf (NED) | 12.02.1998 | 11 | (12) | 3 |
| Marco Grüll | 06.07.1998 | 25 | (5) | 6 |
| Rene Kriwak | 30.04.1999 | 2 | (1) | |
| Nicolas Kühn (GER) | 01.01.2000 | 12 | (8) | 3 |
| Dragoljub Savić (SRB) | 25.04.2001 | 1 | (1) | |
| Oliver Strunz | 14.06.2000 | 7 | (7) | 4 |
| Bernhard Zimmermann | 15.02.2002 | 8 | (17) | 7 |

## Football Club Red Bull Salzburg

| | | |
|---|---|---|
| **Founded**: | 13.09.1933 (as SV Austria Salzburg) | |
| **Stadium**: | Red Bull Arena, Wals-Siezenheim (30,188) | |
| **Trainer**: | Matthias Jaissle (GER) | 05.04.1988 |

| Goalkeepers: | DOB | M | (s) | G |
|---|---|---|---|---|
| Philipp Köhn (SUI) | 02.04.1998 | 31 | (1) | |
| Alexander Walke (GER) | 06.06.1983 | 1 | | |
| **Defenders:** | DOB | M | (s) | G |
| Samson Baidoo | 31.03.2004 | 2 | (2) | |
| Bernardo Fernandes da Silva Junior (BRA) | 14.05.1995 | 15 | (3) | |
| Amar Dedić (BIH) | 18.08.2002 | 26 | (1) | 1 |
| Bryan Ikemefuna Okoh (SUI) | 16.05.2003 | | (1) | |
| Strahinja Pavlović (SRB) | 24.05.2001 | 23 | (1) | 1 |
| Kamil Piątkowski (POL) | 21.06.2000 | 2 | (1) | |
| Oumar Solet (FRA) | 07.02.2000 | 25 | | 1 |
| Andreas Ulmer | 30.10.1985 | 15 | (6) | |
| Ignace Van Der Brempt (BEL) | 01.04.2002 | 6 | (9) | |
| Maximilian Wöber | 04.02.1998 | 14 | (1) | 1 |
| **Midfielders:** | DOB | M | (s) | G |
| Lawrence Agyekum (GHA) | 23.11.2003 | 2 | (1) | |
| Antoine Bernède (FRA) | 26.05.1999 | | (2) | |
| Nicolás Capaldo Toaboas (ARG) | 14.09.1998 | 21 | (2) | 5 |

| | DOB | M | (s) | G |
|---|---|---|---|---|
| Mamady Diambou (MLI) | 11.11.2002 | | (4) | |
| Hamaciré Youba Diarra (MLI) | 24.03.1998 | 2 | (5) | 1 |
| Amankwah Forson (GHA) | 31.12.2002 | 3 | (9) | |
| Oscar Gloukh (ISR) | 04.01.2004 | 8 | (7) | 2 |
| Lucas Gourna-Douath (FRA) | 05.08.2003 | 17 | (4) | |
| Dijon Kameri | 20.04.2004 | 7 | (5) | 1 |
| Maurits Kjærgaard (DEN) | 26.06.2003 | 17 | (9) | 2 |
| Nicolas Seiwald | 04.05.2001 | 29 | (2) | 3 |
| Luka Sučić (CRO) | 08.09.2002 | 13 | (2) | |
| **Forwards:** | DOB | M | (s) | G |
| Chukwubuike Junior Adamu | 06.06.2001 | 13 | (15) | 10 |
| Fernando Dos Santos Pedro (BRA) | 01.03.1999 | 8 | (1) | 6 |
| Sékou Koïta (MLI) | 28.11.1999 | 14 | (8) | 6 |
| Karim Konaté (CIV) | 21.03.2004 | 1 | (8) | 3 |
| Noah Okafor (SUI) | 24.05.2000 | 11 | (10) | 7 |
| Benjamin Šeško (SVN) | 31.05.2003 | 23 | (7) | 16 |
| Roko Šimić (CRO) | 10.09.2003 | 3 | (6) | |

## Sportclub Rheindorf Altach

Founded: 26.12.1929
Stadium: Stadion Schnabelholz, Altach (8,500)
Trainer: Miroslav Josef Klose (GER) 09.06.1978
[20.03.2023] Klaus Schmidt 21.10.1967

| Goalkeepers: | DOB | M | (s) | G |
|---|---|---|---|---|
| Tino Casali | 14.11.1995 | 23 | | |
| Andreas Kristoffer Jungdal (DEN) | 22.02.2002 | 6 | | |
| Jakob Odehnal | 10.08.2001 | 3 | | |
| **Defenders:** | DOB | M | (s) | G |
| Nosa Iyobosa Edokpolor (NGA) | 22.09.1996 | 25 | (1) | |
| Lukas Gugganig | 14.02.1995 | 17 | (4) | 1 |
| David Herold (GER) | 20.02.2003 | 13 | (2) | |
| Samuel Mischitz | 14.08.2003 | | (3) | |
| Pape-Alioune Ndiaye (FRA) | 04.02.1998 | 4 | (3) | |
| Simon Nelson | 03.02.2002 | 3 | (1) | |
| Felix Strauß | 26.03.2001 | 19 | (2) | |
| Manuel Thurnwald | 16.07.1998 | 15 | (6) | |
| Emre Yabantas | 26.01.2004 | | (1) | |
| Jan Zwischenbrugger | 16.06.1990 | 18 | (5) | |
| **Midfielders:** | DOB | M | (s) | G |
| Sebastian Aigner | 03.01.2001 | 4 | (13) | |
| Mike-Steven Bähre (GER) | 10.08.1995 | 5 | (2) | 1 |
| Amankwah Forson | 31.12.2002 | 10 | (6) | 1 |
| Stefan Haudum | 27.11.1994 | 22 | (5) | |
| Lukas Jäger | 12.02.1994 | 30 | | 1 |
| Jan Jurčec (CRO) | 27.11.2000 | 22 | (9) | 2 |
| Bakary Nimaga (MLI) | 06.12.1994 | 8 | (2) | |
| Emanuel Schreiner | 02.02.1989 | 8 | (5) | 1 |
| Johannes Tartarotti | 02.08.1999 | 4 | (14) | 1 |
| **Forwards:** | DOB | M | (s) | G |
| Amir Abdijanović | 03.03.2001 | 9 | (11) | 1 |
| Husein Balić (BIH) | 15.02.1996 | 11 | (1) | |
| Noah Bischof | 07.12.2002 | 18 | (5) | 3 |
| Csaba Bukta (HUN) | 25.07.2001 | 8 | (19) | |
| Jurica Jurčec (CRO) | 04.04.2002 | 2 | (2) | |
| Marko Lazetić (SRB) | 22.01.2004 | 1 | (9) | |
| Damian Maksimović | 18.11.2004 | | (1) | |
| Atdhe Nuhiu (KOS) | 29.07.1989 | 24 | (6) | 10 |
| Dominik Reiter | 04.01.1998 | 5 | (2) | |
| Alexis Ronaldo Tibidi (FRA) | 03.11.2003 | 15 | (1) | 5 |

## Sportklub Sturm Graz

Founded: 1909
Stadium: Merkur-Arena, Graz (16,364)
Trainer: Christian Ilzer 21.10.1977

| Goalkeepers: | DOB | M | (s) | G |
|---|---|---|---|---|
| Arthur Okonkwo (ENG) | 09.09.2001 | 15 | | |
| Tobias Schützenauer | 19.05.1997 | 1 | | |
| Jörg Siebenhandl | 18.01.1990 | 16 | | |
| **Defenders:** | DOB | M | (s) | G |
| David Affengruber | 19.03.2001 | 21 | (6) | 4 |
| Alexandar Borković | 11.06.1999 | 16 | (4) | 1 |
| Amadou Dante (MLI) | 07.10.2000 | 12 | (9) | |
| Jusuf Gazibegović (BIH) | 11.03.2000 | 28 | (1) | 2 |
| Niklas Geyrhofer | 11.02.2000 | 1 | (6) | |
| Alois Dominik Oroz | 29.10.2000 | | (2) | |
| Sandro Ingolitsch | 18.04.1997 | 4 | (1) | |
| David Schnegg | 29.09.1998 | 20 | (10) | 3 |
| Gregory Wüthrich (SUI) | 04.12.1994 | 26 | (2) | 1 |
| **Midfielders:** | DOB | M | (s) | G |
| Vesel Demaku | 05.02.2000 | 1 | (2) | |
| Stefan Hierländer | 03.02.1991 | 25 | (3) | |
| Tomi Horvat (SVN) | 24.03.1999 | 25 | (7) | 4 |
| Otar Kiteishvili (GEO) | 26.03.1996 | 13 | (7) | 6 |
| Ivan Ljubić | 07.07.1996 | 2 | (20) | 1 |
| Alexander Prass | 26.05.2001 | 29 | (3) | 3 |
| Jon Gorenc Stanković (SVN) | 14.01.1996 | 30 | (1) | 2 |
| Moritz Wels | 25.09.2004 | | (2) | 1 |
| **Forwards:** | DOB | M | (s) | G |
| Albian Ajeti (SUI) | 26.02.1997 | 8 | (7) | 3 |
| William Bøving (DEN) | 01.03.2003 | 7 | (10) | 1 |
| Emanuel Esseh Emegha (NED) | 03.02.2003 | 16 | (11) | 9 |
| Mohammed Fuseini (GHA) | 16.05.2002 | | (7) | 2 |
| Leon Grgić | 22.01.2006 | | (2) | |
| Rasmus Højlund (DEN) | 04.02.2003 | 4 | (1) | 3 |
| Jakob Jantscher | 08.01.1989 | 1 | (8) | 1 |
| Christoph Lang | 07.01.2002 | 2 | (1) | 1 |
| Manprit Sarkaria | 26.08.1996 | 23 | (5) | 9 |
| Bryan Silva Teixeira (FRA) | 01.09.2000 | 6 | (8) | |

## Sportvereinigung Ried von 1912

Founded: 1912
Stadium: Keine Sorgen Arena, Ried im Innkreis (7,680)
Trainer: Christian Heinle 30.03.1985
[01.03.2023] Maximilian Senft 04.08.1989

| Goalkeepers: | DOB | M | (s) | G |
|---|---|---|---|---|
| Samuel Şahin-Radlinger | 07.11.1992 | 26 | | |
| Jonas Wendlinger | 17.07.2000 | 6 | | |
| **Defenders:** | DOB | M | (s) | G |
| Matthias Gragger | 03.11.2001 | 11 | (7) | 2 |
| Roko Jurišić (CRO) | 28.09.2001 | 14 | | |
| Markus Lackner | 05.04.1991 | 19 | (2) | |
| Tin Plavotić | 30.06.1997 | 29 | | 4 |
| Felix Seiwald | 20.08.2000 | | (1) | |
| Julian Turi | 03.07.2001 | 13 | (6) | |
| David Ungar | 17.03.2000 | 27 | | |
| Josef Weberbauer | 13.03.1998 | 4 | (7) | |
| Nico Wiesinger | 20.02.2003 | | (2) | |
| **Midfielders:** | DOB | M | (s) | G |
| Denizcan Cosgun | 16.02.2002 | 3 | (8) | |
| Gontie Junior Diomande (CIV) | 20.05.2003 | 2 | (6) | 1 |
| Oliver Kragl (GER) | 12.05.1990 | 1 | (4) | |
| Aleksandar Lutovac (SRB) | 28.06.1997 | 12 | (1) | |
| Diego Madritsch | 02.08.2005 | 8 | (3) | 1 |
| Michael Martin (GER) | 10.07.2000 | 27 | (1) | |
| Jonas Mayer | 29.06.2004 | | (1) | |
| Kingsley Dogo Michael (NGA) | 26.08.1999 | 8 | (5) | |
| Stefan Nutz | 15.02.1992 | 21 | | 2 |
| Philipp Pomer | 12.08.1997 | 27 | (1) | 2 |
| Tizian-Valentino Scharmer | 13.02.2004 | | (1) | |
| Nikola Stošić (SRB) | 29.01.2000 | 1 | (3) | |
| Julian Wießmeier (GER) | 04.11.1992 | 13 | (8) | 1 |
| Ben Wörndl | 26.09.2002 | | (1) | |
| Marcel Ziegl | 20.12.1992 | 12 | (2) | |
| **Forwards:** | DOB | M | (s) | G |
| Belmin Beganović (BIH) | 09.09.2004 | 7 | (5) | 1 |
| Seifedin Chabbi | 04.07.1993 | 11 | (14) | 4 |
| Agyemang Diawusie (GER) | 12.02.1998 | | (1) | |
| Luca Kronberger | 15.02.2002 | 3 | (13) | |
| Christoph Lang | 07.01.2002 | 12 | (3) | 3 |
| Leo Mikić (CRO) | 06.05.1997 | 21 | (6) | 2 |
| Christoph Monschein | 22.10.1992 | 14 | (11) | 3 |

## Turn- und Sportverein Hartberg

| Founded: | 29.04.1946 | | |
| Stadium: | Profertil Arena, Hartberg (4,635) | | |
| Trainer: | Klaus Schmidt | | 21.10.1967 |
| [14.11.2022] | Markus Schopp | | 22.02.1974 |

| Goalkeepers: | DOB | M | (s) | G |
|---|---|---|---|---|
| Florian Faist | 10.04.1989 | | (1) | |
| Raphael Sallinger | 08.12.1995 | 20 | | |
| Rene Swete | 01.06.1990 | 12 | | |
| **Defenders:** | **DOB** | **M** | **(s)** | **G** |
| Patrick Farkas | 09.09.1992 | 10 | (7) | |
| Manfred Gollner | 22.12.1990 | 2 | (6) | |
| Marin Karamarko (CRO) | 14.04.1998 | 11 | (2) | |
| Christian Klem | 21.04.1991 | 3 | (4) | |
| Thomas Kofler | 07.07.1998 | 5 | (3) | |
| Manuel Pfeifer | 10.09.1999 | 16 | | |
| Thomas Rotter | 27.01.1992 | 14 | (3) | |
| Marcel Schantl | 17.08.2000 | 1 | | |
| Mario Sonnleitner | 08.10.1986 | 19 | (1) | |
| Michael Steinwender | 04.05.2000 | 18 | (4) | |
| **Midfielders:** | **DOB** | **M** | **(s)** | **G** |
| Okan Aydin (TUR) | 08.05.1994 | 12 | (2) | 3 |
| Ousmane Diakité (MLI) | 25.07.2000 | 7 | (8) | |
| Albert Ejupi (SWE) | 28.08.1992 | 5 | (5) | |
| Lukas Fadinger | 27.09.2000 | 19 | (11) | 2 |
| Jürgen Heil | 04.04.1997 | 29 | | 2 |
| Matija Horvat (CRO) | 07.05.1999 | 15 | (9) | 1 |
| Tobias Kainz | 31.10.1992 | 24 | (7) | |
| Mario Kröpfl | 21.12.1989 | 2 | (11) | |
| Dominik Prokop | 02.06.1997 | 8 | (3) | 4 |
| Mamadou Sangaré (MLI) | 26.06.2002 | 10 | (5) | 2 |
| Philipp Sturm | 23.02.1999 | 1 | (3) | |
| **Forwards:** | **DOB** | **M** | **(s)** | **G** |
| Eylon Haim Almog (ISR) | 08.01.1999 | 5 | (4) | 1 |
| Donis Avdijaj (KOS) | 25.08.1996 | 15 | (1) | 7 |
| Dominik Frieser | 09.09.1993 | 26 | (1) | 1 |
| Jakob Knollmüller | 26.07.2003 | | (3) | |
| Rene Kriwak | 30.04.1999 | 7 | (17) | 2 |
| Seth Paintsil (GHA) | 20.05.1996 | 7 | (4) | |
| Ruben Providence (FRA) | 07.07.2001 | 15 | (6) | 6 |
| Dario Tadić | 11.05.1990 | 14 | (12) | 7 |

## Wolfsberger Athletik Club

| Founded: | 1931 | | |
| Stadium: | Lavanttal-Arena, Wolfsberg (7,300) | | |
| Trainer: | Robin Dutt (GER) | | 24.01.1965 |
| [05.03.2023] | Manfred Schmid | | 20.02.1971 |

| Goalkeepers: | DOB | M | (s) | G |
|---|---|---|---|---|
| Hendrik Bonmann (GER) | 22.01.1994 | 31 | | |
| David Skubl | 18.09.2001 | 1 | | |
| **Defenders:** | **DOB** | **M** | **(s)** | **G** |
| Matteo Anzolin (ITA) | 11.11.2000 | 18 | (1) | |
| Dominik Baumgartner | 20.07.1996 | 18 | (1) | |
| Kevin Bukusu (GER) | 27.02.2001 | 7 | (1) | |
| David Gugganig | 10.02.1997 | 4 | (4) | |
| Adis Jasic | 12.02.2003 | 18 | (6) | 2 |
| Luka Lochoshvili (GEO) | 29.05.1998 | 1 | (1) | |
| Michael Novak | 30.12.1990 | 8 | (14) | 1 |
| Tim Oermann (GER) | 06.10.2003 | 14 | | |
| Simon Piesinger | 13.05.1992 | 24 | (1) | 1 |
| Jonathan Scherzer | 22.07.1995 | 11 | (2) | |
| Raphael Schifferl | 29.07.1999 | 16 | (4) | 1 |
| **Midfielders:** | **DOB** | **M** | **(s)** | **G** |
| Thierno Ballo | 02.01.2002 | 14 | (13) | 6 |
| Augustine Boakye (GHA) | 03.11.2000 | 4 | (10) | 3 |
| Konstantin Kerschbaumer | 01.07.1992 | 20 | (7) | 2 |
| Mario Leitgeb | 30.06.1988 | 19 | (3) | 1 |
| Pascal Müller | 15.02.2003 | 1 | (2) | |
| Ervin Omić | 20.01.2003 | 19 | (7) | |
| Matthäus Taferner | 30.01.2001 | 18 | (7) | |
| Nikolas Veratschnig | 24.01.2003 | 20 | (9) | 1 |
| **Forwards:** | **DOB** | **M** | **(s)** | **G** |
| Tai Baribo (ISR) | 15.01.1998 | 30 | (2) | 16 |
| Maurice Malone (GER) | 17.08.2000 | 25 | (1) | 8 |
| Thorsten Röcher | 11.06.1991 | 7 | (21) | 6 |
| Nikolaos Vergos (GRE) | 13.01.1996 | 2 | (9) | 1 |
| Dario Vizinger (CRO) | 06.06.1998 | 2 | (3) | 1 |

## Wattener Sportgemeinschaft Tirol Wattens

| Founded: | 1930 | |
| Stadium: | Tivoli Stadion Tirol, Innsbruck (16,008) | |
| Trainer: | Thomas Silberberger | 03.06.1973 |

| Goalkeepers: | DOB | M | (s) | G |
|---|---|---|---|---|
| Ferdinand Oswald (GER) | 05.10.1990 | 27 | | |
| Benjamin Ožegović | 09.08.1999 | 5 | | |
| **Defenders:** | **DOB** | **M** | **(s)** | **G** |
| Felix Bacher | 25.10.2000 | 29 | (1) | 1 |
| Raffael Behounek | 16.04.1997 | 29 | (2) | 1 |
| David Jaunegg | 28.02.2003 | 1 | (2) | |
| Osarenren Okungbowa | 13.05.1994 | 4 | (11) | |
| Alexander Ranacher | 20.11.1998 | 14 | (13) | 3 |
| Kofi Schulz (GER) | 21.07.1989 | 28 | | 2 |
| Dominik Stumberger | 17.04.1999 | 16 | (2) | 1 |
| **Midfielders:** | **DOB** | **M** | **(s)** | **G** |
| Kilian Bauernfeind | 23.04.2002 | | (2) | |
| Bror Blume (DEN) | 22.01.1992 | 23 | (2) | |
| Julius Ertlthaler | 25.04.1997 | 13 | (5) | 2 |
| Valentino Müller | 19.01.1999 | 30 | | 3 |
| Johannes Naschberger | 25.01.2000 | 9 | (17) | 1 |
| Sandi Ogrinec (SVN) | 05.06.1998 | 17 | (1) | 3 |
| Žan Rogelj (SVN) | 25.11.1999 | 17 | (12) | 3 |
| Stefan Skrbo | 23.01.2001 | 2 | (7) | |
| Lukas Sulzbacher | 06.04.2000 | 25 | (1) | 1 |
| Cem Üstündag | 20.01.2001 | 1 | (5) | |
| **Forwards:** | **DOB** | **M** | **(s)** | **G** |
| Justin Forst | 21.02.2003 | 7 | (19) | 1 |
| Thomas Geris | 16.10.2002 | | (1) | |
| Nik Prelec (SVN) | 10.06.2001 | 12 | (1) | 6 |
| Bo Tim Rade Tiger Prica (SWE) | 23.04.2002 | 17 | (12) | 8 |
| Lautaro Patricio Rinaldi (ARG) | 30.12.1993 | 4 | (8) | 1 |
| Thomas Sabitzer | 12.10.2000 | 20 | (2) | 4 |
| Denis Tomić | 17.01.1998 | 2 | (16) | 1 |

### SECOND LEVEL
### 2. Liga 2022/2023

| | | | | | | | | | |
|---|---|---|---|---|---|---|---|---|---|
| 1. | FC Blau-Weiß Linz (*Promoted*) | 30 | 19 | 4 | 7 | 63 | - | 27 | 61 |
| 2. | Grazer AK | 30 | 17 | 9 | 4 | 52 | - | 29 | 60 |
| 3. | SKN St. Pölten | 30 | 17 | 5 | 8 | 53 | - | 27 | 56 |
| 4. | SV Horn | 30 | 13 | 9 | 8 | 38 | - | 33 | 48 |
| 5. | SKU Amstetten | 30 | 12 | 9 | 9 | 49 | - | 49 | 45 |
| 6. | Floridsdorfer AC Wien | 30 | 12 | 9 | 9 | 41 | - | 30 | 45 |
| 7. | First Vienna FC | 30 | 12 | 7 | 11 | 34 | - | 33 | 43 |
| 8. | SV Lafnitz | 30 | 12 | 5 | 13 | 47 | - | 46 | 41 |
| 9. | FC Liefering | 30 | 10 | 4 | 15 | 52 | - | 54 | 34 |
| 10. | FC Admira Wacker Mödling | 30 | 10 | 6 | 14 | 39 | - | 42 | 36 |
| 11. | FC Dornbirn 1913 | 30 | 10 | 5 | 15 | 43 | - | 44 | 35 |
| 12. | Kapfenberger SV | 30 | 9 | 7 | 14 | 40 | - | 56 | 34 |
| 13. | SK Sturm Graz II | 30 | 10 | 4 | 16 | 41 | - | 56 | 34 |
| 14. | SK Vorwärts Steyr (*Relegated*) | 30 | 8 | 8 | 14 | 36 | - | 54 | 32 |
| 15. | SK Rapid Wien II (*Relegated*) | 30 | 7 | 9 | 14 | 33 | - | 55 | 30 |
| 16. | FK Austria Wien II (*Relegated*) | 30 | 7 | 8 | 15 | 34 | - | 61 | 29 |

## INTERNATIONAL MATCHES
### (16.07.2022 – 15.07.2023)

| 22.09.2022 | Paris | France - Austria | 2-0(0-0) | (UNL) |
|---|---|---|---|---|
| 25.09.2022 | Wien | Austria - Croatia | 1-3(1-1) | (UNL) |
| 16.11.2022 | Málaga | Andorra - Austria | 0-1(0-0) | (F) |
| 20.11.2022 | Wien | Austria - Italy | 2-0(2-0) | (F) |
| 24.03.2023 | Linz | Austria - Azerbaijan | 4-1(2-0) | (ECQ) |
| 27.03.2023 | Linz | Austria - Estonia | 2-1(0-1) | (ECQ) |
| 17.06.2023 | Bruxelles | Belgium - Austria | 1-1(0-1) | (ECQ) |
| 20.06.2023 | Wien | Austria - Sweden | 2-0(0-0) | (ECQ) |

**22.09.2022**  **FRANCE - AUSTRIA**  2-0(0-0)  3rd UEFA Nations League A, Group 1
Stade de France, Saint-Denis, Paris; Referee: Andreas Ekberg (Sweden); Attendance: 70,188
**AUT:** Patrick Pentz, Christopher Trimmel, Philipp Lienhart, David Olatukunbo Alaba (Cap) (70.Stefan Posch), Maximilian Wöber, Xaver Schlager, Nicolas Seiwald, Marcel Sabitzer (69.Romano Christian Schmid), Andreas Weimann (50.Dejan Ljubičić), Marko Arnautović (64.Michael Gregoritsch), Karim Onisiwo (64.Christoph Baumgartner). Trainer: Ralf Rangnick (Germany).

**25.09.2022**  **AUSTRIA - CROATIA**  1-3(1-1)  3rd UEFA Nations League A, Group 1
"Heinz Happel" Stadion, Wien; Referee: Artur Manuel Ribeiro Soares Dias (Portugal); Attendance: 45,700
**AUT:** Heinz Lindner, Stefan Posch (62.Maximilian Wöber), David Olatukunbo Alaba (Cap), Kevin Danso, Christopher Trimmel (62.Stefan Lainer), Xaver Schlager, Nicolas Seiwald, Christoph Baumgartner (82.Romano Christian Schmid), Marcel Sabitzer, Michael Gregoritsch (82.Karim Onisiwo), Marko Arnautović (62.Muhammed-Cham Saracevic). Trainer: Ralf Rangnick (Germany).
**Goal:** Christoph Baumgartner (9).

**16.11.2022**  **ANDORRA - AUSTRIA**  0-1(0-0)  Friendly International
Estadio La Rosaleda, Málaga (Spain); Referee: José Luis Munuera Montero (Spain); Attendance: 150
**AUT:** Alexander Schlager (46.Niklas Hedl), Stefan Posch, Maximilian Wöber (67.David Olatukunbo Alaba), Gernot Trauner, Xaver Schlager (46.Junior Chukwubuike Adamu), Florian Grillitsch, Phillipp Mwene (46.Andreas Weimann), Alexander Prass (46.Christoph Baumgartner), Florian Kainz, Marcel Sabitzer (Cap), Michael Gregoritsch (46.Marko Arnautović). Trainer: Ralf Rangnick (Germany).
**Goal:** Marko Arnautović (87).

**20.11.2022**  **AUSTRIA - ITALY**  2-0(2-0)  Friendly International
"Ernst Happel" Stadion, Wien; Referee: Christian Dingert (Germany); Attendance: 18,000
**AUT:** Heinz Lindner, Stefan Posch, Philipp Lienhart, David Olatukunbo Alaba (Cap), Maximilian Wöber (72.Phillipp Mwene), Xaver Schlager, Nicolas Seiwald, Christoph Baumgartner (81.Florian Grillitsch), Marcel Sabitzer, Marko Arnautović (72.Michael Gregoritsch), Junior Chukwubuike Adamu (81.Romano Christian Schmid). Trainer: Ralf Rangnick (Germany).
**Goals:** Xaver Schlager (6), David Olatukunbo Alaba (35).

**24.03.2023**  **AUSTRIA - AZERBAIJAN**  4-1(2-0)  17th EC. Qualifiers
Raiffeisen Arena, Linz; Referee: Bartosz Frankowski (Poland); Attendance: 16,500
**AUT:** Heinz Lindner, Phillipp Mwene, Gernot Trauner (74.Andreas Ulmer), Kevin Danso, Maximilian Wöber (34.Stefan Posch), Marcel Sabitzer (Cap) (74.Dejan Ljubičić), Nicolas Seiwald, Patrick Wimmer (68.Florian Kainz), Konrad Laimer, Christoph Baumgartner, Michael Gregoritsch (68.Junior Chukwubuike Adamu). Trainer: Ralf Rangnick (Germany).
**Goals:** Marcel Sabitzer (28), Michael Gregoritsch (29), Marcel Sabitzer (50), Christoph Baumgartner (69).

**27.03.2023**  **AUSTRIA - ESTONIA**  2-1(0-1)  17th EC. Qualifiers
Raiffeisen Arena, Linz; Referee: Enea Jorgji (Albania); Attendance: 16,500
**AUT:** Heinz Lindner, Stefan Posch (82.Karim Onisiwo), Flavius David Daniliuc (46.David Olatukunbo Alaba), Kevin Danso, Phillipp Mwene, Nicolas Seiwald, Dejan Ljubičić (46.Junior Chukwubuike Adamu), Konrad Laimer (Cap), Christoph Baumgartner (90+2.Romano Christian Schmid), Patrick Wimmer (61.Florian Kainz), Michael Gregoritsch. Trainer: Ralf Rangnick (Germany).
**Goals:** Florian Kainz (68), Michael Gregoritsch (88).

**17.06.2023**  **BELGIUM - AUSTRIA**  1-1(0-1)  17th EC. Qualifiers
Stade "Roi Baudouin", Bruxelles; Referee: Jérôme Brisard (France); Attendance: 39,237
**AUT:** Alexander Schlager, Stefan Posch, Philipp Lienhart, David Olatukunbo Alaba (Cap), Maximilian Wöber (46.Phillipp Mwene), Patrick Wimmer (60.Florian Kainz), Xaver Schlager (87.Dejan Ljubičić), Nicolas Seiwald, Christoph Baumgartner, Michael Gregoritsch (87.Karim Onisiwo), Marko Arnautović (60.Marcel Sabitzer). Trainer: Ralf Rangnick (Germany).
**Goal:** Michael Gregoritsch (21).

**20.06.2023**  **AUSTRIA - SWEDEN**  2-0(0-0)  17th EC. Qualifiers
"Ernst Happel" Stadion, Wien; Referee: Marco Guida (Italy); Attendance: 46,300
**AUT:** Alexander Schlager, Stefan Posch (46.Maximilian Wöber), Philipp Lienhart, David Olatukunbo Alaba (Cap), Phillipp Mwene, Patrick Wimmer (59.Marcel Sabitzer), Xaver Schlager (71.Florian Grillitsch), Nicolas Seiwald, Christoph Baumgartner (90+1.Dejan Ljubičić), Michael Gregoritsch, Junior Chukwubuike Adamu (46.Marko Arnautović). Trainer: Ralf Rangnick (Germany).
**Goals:** Christoph Baumgartner (81, 89).

## NATIONAL TEAM PLAYERS
### (16.07.2022 – 15.07.2023)

| Name | DOB | Caps | Goals | Club | |
|------|-----|------|-------|------|---|

#### Goalkeepers

| Name | DOB | Caps | Goals | Club | |
|------|-----|------|-------|------|---|
| Niklas HEDL | 17.03.2001 | 1 | 0 | 2022: | *SK Rapid Wien* |
| Heinz LINDNER | 17.07.1990 | 36 | 0 | 2022/2023: | *FC Sion (SUI)* |
| Patrick PENTZ | 02.01.1997 | 4 | 0 | 2022: | *Stade de Reims (FRA)* |
| Alexander SCHLAGER | 01.02.1996 | 9 | 0 | 2022/2023: | *Linzer ASK* |

#### Defenders

| Name | DOB | Caps | Goals | Club | |
|------|-----|------|-------|------|---|
| David Olatukunbo ALABA | 24.06.1992 | 101 | 15 | 2022/2023: | *Real Madrid CF (ESP)* |
| Flavius David DANILIUC | 27.04.2001 | 1 | 0 | 2023: | *US Salernitana 1919 (ITA)* |
| Stefan LAINER | 27.08.1992 | 38 | 2 | 2022: | *Borussia VfL Mönchengladbach (GER)* |
| Philipp LIENHART | 11.07.1996 | 13 | 0 | 2022/2023: | *SC Freiburg (GER)* |
| Phillipp MWENE | 29.01.1994 | 7 | 0 | 2022/2023: | *PSV Eindhoven (NED)* |
| Stefan POSCH | 14.05.1997 | 24 | 1 | 2022/2023: | *Bologna FC 1909 (ITA)* |
| Gernot TRAUNER | 25.03.1992 | 10 | 1 | 2022/2023: | *Feyenoord Rotterdam (NED)* |
| Christopher TRIMMEL | 24.02.1987 | 25 | 1 | 2022: | *1. FC Union Berlin (GER)* |
| Andreas ULMER | 30.10.1985 | 32 | 0 | 2023: | *FC Red Bull Salzburg* |
| Maximilian WÖBER | 04.02.1998 | 16 | 0 | 2022: 03.01.2023-> | *FC Red Bull Salzburg; Leeds United FC (ENG)* |

#### Midfielders

| Name | DOB | Caps | Goals | Club | |
|------|-----|------|-------|------|---|
| Christoph BAUMGARTNER | 01.08.1999 | 29 | 10 | 2022/2023: | *TSG 1899 Hoffenheim (GER)* |
| Kevin DANSO | 19.09.1998 | 13 | 0 | 2022/2023: | *Racing Club de Lens (FRA)* |
| Florian GRILLITSCH | 07.08.1995 | 36 | 1 | 2022/2023: | *AFC Ajax Amsterdam (NED)* |
| Florian KAINZ | 24.10.1992 | 24 | 1 | 2022/2023: | *1.FC Köln (GER)* |
| Konrad LAIMER | 27.05.1997 | 26 | 2 | 2023: | *RasenBallsport Leipzig (GER)* |
| Dejan LJUBIČIĆ | 08.10.1997 | 8 | 1 | 2022/2023: | *1.FC Köln (GER)* |
| Alexander PRASS | 26.05.2001 | 1 | 0 | 2022: | *SK Sturm Graz* |
| Marcel SABITZER | 17.03.1994 | 71 | 13 | 2022: 31.01.2023-> | *FC Bayern München (GER); 31.01.2023-> Manchester United FC (ENG)* |
| Muhammed-Cham SARACEVIC | 26.09.2000 | 1 | 0 | 2022: | *Clermont Foot 63 (FRA)* |
| Xaver SCHLAGER | 28.09.1997 | 35 | 3 | 2022/2023: | *RasenBallsport Leipzig (GER)* |
| Romano Christian SCHMID | 27.01.2000 | 4 | 0 | 2022/2023: | *SV Werder Bremen (GER)* |
| Nicolas SEIWALD | 04.05.2001 | 14 | 0 | 2022/2023: | *FC Red Bull Salzburg* |
| Patrick WIMMER | 30.05.2001 | 5 | 0 | 2023: | *VfL Wolfsburg (GER)* |

#### Forwards

| Name | DOB | Caps | Goals | Club | |
|------|-----|------|-------|------|---|
| Junior Chukwubuike ADAMU | 06.06.2001 | 6 | 0 | 2022/2023: | *FC Red Bull Salzburg* |
| Marko ARNAUTOVIĆ | 19.04.1989 | 108 | 34 | 2022/2023: | *Bologna FC 1909 (ITA)* |
| Michael GREGORITSCH | 18.04.1994 | 47 | 10 | 2022/2023: | *SC Freiburg (GER)* |
| Karim ONISIWO | 17.03.1992 | 22 | 1 | 2022/2023: | *1.FSV Mainz 05 (GER)* |
| Andreas WEIMANN | 05.08.1991 | 21 | 1 | 2022: | *Bristol City FC (ENG)* |

#### Trainer

| | | | |
|------|-----|------|------|
| Ralf RANGNICK (Germany) [from 01.06.2022] | 29.06.1958 | 12 M; 6 W; 2 D; 4 L; 18-13 | |

# AZERBAIJAN

**The Country:**
Republic of Azerbaijan (Azərbaycan Respublikası)
Capital: Bakı
Surface: 86,600 km²
Inhabitants: 10,353,296 [2022]
Time: UTC+4

**The FA:**
Azərbaycan Futbol Federasiyaları Assosiasiyası
8 November avenue 163, Bakı
Tel: +994 12 404 27 77
Foundation date: 1992
Member of FIFA since: 1994
Member of UEFA since: 1994
Website: www.affa.az

## NATIONAL TEAM RECORDS

| RECORDS | | |
|---|---|---|
| **First international match:** | 17.09.1992, Gurdzhaani: | Georgia – Azerbaijan 6-3 |
| **Most international caps:** | Rəşad Ferhad Sadıqov | - 111 caps (2001-2017) |
| **Most international goals:** | Qurban Osman Qurbanov | - 12 goals / 65 caps (1992-2005) |

| UEFA EUROPEAN CHAMPIONSHIP | |
|---|---|
| 1960 | - |
| 1964 | - |
| 1968 | - |
| 1972 | - |
| 1976 | - |
| 1980 | - |
| 1984 | - |
| 1988 | - |
| 1992 | - |
| 1996 | Qualifiers |
| 2000 | Qualifiers |
| 2004 | Qualifiers |
| 2008 | Qualifiers |
| 2012 | Qualifiers |
| 2016 | Qualifiers |
| 2020 | Qualifiers |

| FIFA WORLD CUP | |
|---|---|
| 1930 | - |
| 1934 | - |
| 1938 | - |
| 1950 | - |
| 1954 | - |
| 1958 | - |
| 1962 | - |
| 1966 | - |
| 1970 | - |
| 1974 | - |
| 1978 | - |
| 1982 | - |
| 1986 | - |
| 1990 | - |
| 1994 | *Did not enter* |
| 1998 | Qualifiers |
| 2002 | Qualifiers |
| 2006 | Qualifiers |
| 2010 | Qualifiers |
| 2014 | Qualifiers |
| 2018 | Qualifiers |
| 2022 | Qualifiers |

| OLYMPIC TOURNAMENTS | |
|---|---|
| 1908 | - |
| 1912 | - |
| 1920 | - |
| 1924 | - |
| 1928 | - |
| 1936 | - |
| 1948 | - |
| 1952 | - |
| 1956 | - |
| 1960 | - |
| 1964 | - |
| 1968 | - |
| 1972 | - |
| 1976 | - |
| 1980 | - |
| 1984 | - |
| 1988 | - |
| 1992 | - |
| 1996 | Qualifiers |
| 2000 | Qualifiers |
| 2004 | Qualifiers |
| 2008 | Qualifiers |
| 2012 | Qualifiers |
| 2016 | Qualifiers |
| 2020 | Qualifiers |

*Please note: was part of Soviet Union until 1920-1991.*

| UEFA NATIONS LEAGUE | |
|---|---|
| 2018/2019 | League D (Group Stage) |
| 2020/2021 | League C (Group Stage) |
| 2022/2023 | League C (Group Stage) |

## AZERBAIJAN CLUB HONOURS IN EUROPEAN CLUB COMPETITIONS:

| European Champion Clubs.Cup (1956-1992) / UEFA Champions League (1993-2023) |
|---|
| None |

| Fairs Cup (1858-1971) / UEFA Cup (1972-2009) / UEFA Europa League (2010-2023) |
|---|
| None |

| UEFA Europa Conference League (2021-2023) |
|---|
| None |

| UEFA Super Cup (1972-2022) |
|---|
| None |

| *European Cup Winners' Cup 1961-1999** |
|---|
| None |

*\*defunct competition*

# NATIONAL COMPETITIONS
## TABLE OF HONOURS

### AZERBAIJAN SSR (SOVIET ERA) CHAMPIONS

| Year | Champion | Year | Champion | Year | Champion |
|------|----------|------|----------|------|----------|
| 1928 | Progress-2 Baku | 1954 | Zavod S.M. Budennogo Baku | 1973 | Araz Baku |
| 1929–33 | *Not known* | 1955 | Ordjonikidzeneft Baku | 1974 | Araz Baku |
| 1934 | Profsoyuz Baku | 1956 | NPU Ordgonikidzeneft Baku | 1975 | Araz Baku |
| 1935 | Stroitel Yuga Baku | 1957 | NPU Ordjonikidzeneft Baku | 1976 | Araz Baku |
| 1936 | Stroitel Yuga Baku | 1958 | NPU Ordjonikidzeneft Baku | 1977 | Karabakh Khankendi |
| 1937 | Lokomotiv Baku | 1959 | Baku Teams (Spartakiada) | 1978 | SKIF Baku |
| 1938 | Lokomotiv Baku | 1960 | SKA Baku | 1979 | SKA Baku |
| 1939 | Lokomotiv Baku | 1961 | Spartak Guba | 1980 | Energetik Ali-Bayramly |
| 1940 | Lokomotiv Baku | 1962 | SKA Baku | 1981 | Gandjlik Baku |
| 1941–43 | *Not known* | 1963 | Araz Baku | 1982 | Tokhudju Baku |
| 1944 | Dinamo Baku | 1964 | Polad Sumgait | 1983 | Termist Baku |
| 1945 | *No competition* | 1965 | Vostok Baku | 1984 | Termist Baku |
| 1946 | Lokomotiv Baku | 1966 | Vostok Baku | 1985 | Khazar Sumgayit |
| 1947 | Trudovye Rezervy Baku | 1967 | Araz Baku | 1986 | Göyəzən |
| 1948 | KKF Baku | 1968 | SKA Baku | 1987 | Araz Naxçıvan |
| 1949 | KKF Baku | 1969 | Araz Baku | 1988 | Qarabağ Ağdam |
| 1950 | Iskra Baku | 1970 | SKA Baku | 1989 | Stroitel Sabirabad |
| 1951 | Ordjonikidzeneft Baku | 1971 | Khimik Salyany | 1990 | Qarabağ Ağdam |
| 1952 | Ordjonikidzeneft Baku | 1972 | Surahanets Baku | 1991 | Khazar Sumgayit |
| 1953 | Ordjonikidzeneft Baku | | | | |

| | CHAMPIONS | CUP WINNERS | BEST GOALSCORERS | |
|---|-----------|-------------|------------------|---|
| 1992 | Neftçi PFK Bakı | İnşaatçı Bakı FK | Nazim Aliyev (FK Xəzər Lənkəran Sumqayit) | 39 |
| 1993 | Qarabağ FK Ağdam | Qarabağ FK Ağdam | Samir Alakbarov (Neftçi PFK Bakı) | 16 |
| 1993/1994 | FK Turan Tovuz | Kəpəz FK Gəncə | Musa Gurbanov (FK Turan Tovuz) | 35 |
| 1994/1995 | Kəpəz FK Gəncə | Neftçi PFK Bakı | Nazim Aliyev (Neftçi PFK Bakı) | 26 |
| 1995/1996 | Neftçi PFK Bakı | Neftçi PFK Bakı | Fazil Parvarov (Kəpəz FK Gəncə) | |
| | | | Rovshan Ahmadov (Kəpəz FK Gəncə) | 23 |
| 1996/1997 | Neftçi PFK Bakı | Kəpəz FK Gəncə | Gurban Gurbanov (Neftçi PFK Bakı) | 34 |
| 1997/1998 | Kəpəz FK Gəncə | Kəpəz FK Gəncə | Nazim Aliyev (Bakı FK) | 23 |
| 1998/1999 | Kəpəz FK Gəncə | Neftçi PFK Bakı | Alay Bahramov (FK Viləş Masallı) | 24 |
| 1999/2000 | FK Şəmkir | Kəpəz FK Gəncə | Badri Kvaratskhelia (FK Şəmkir) | 16 |
| 2000/2001 | FK Şəmkir | Şəfa Bakı FK | Pasha Aliyev (Bakılı PFK Bakı) | 12 |
| 2001/2002 | *Championship abandoned* | Neftçi PFK Bakı | - | |
| 2002/2003 | *No competition* | *No competition* | - | |
| 2003/2004 | Neftçi PFK Bakı | Neftçi PFK Bakı | Samir Musayev (Qarabağ FK Ağdam) | 20 |
| 2004/2005 | Neftçi PFK Bakı | Bakı FK | Zaur Ramazanov (Karvan FK) | 21 |
| 2005/2006 | Bakı FK | Qarabağ FK Bakı | Yacouba Bamba (CIV, Karvan FK) | 16 |
| 2006/2007 | Xəzər Lənkəran FK | Xəzər Lənkəran FK | Zaur Ramazanov (Xəzər Lənkəran FK) | 20 |
| 2007/2008 | İnter PİK Bakı | Xəzər Lənkəran FK | Khagani Mammadov (İnter PİK Bakı) | 19 |
| 2008/2009 | Bakı FK | Qarabağ FK Bakı | Walter Guglielmone Gómez (URU, İnter PİK Bakı) | 17 |
| 2009/2010 | İnter PİK Bakı | Bakı FK | Farid Guliyev (Standard FK Sumqayit) | 16 |
| 2010/2011 | Neftçi PFK Bakı | Xəzər Lənkəran FK | Georgi Adamia (GEO, Qarabağ FK Bakı) | 18 |
| 2011/2012 | Neftçi PFK Bakı | Bakı FK | Bahodir Nasimov (UZB, Neftçi PFK Bakı) | 16 |
| 2012/2013 | Neftçi PFK Bakı | Neftçi PFK Bakı | Nicolás Sebastián Canales Calas (CHI, Neftçi PFK Bakı) | 26 |
| 2013/2014 | Qarabağ FK Bakı | Neftçi PFK Bakı | Reynaldo dos Santos Silva (Qarabağ FK Bakı) | 22 |
| 2014/2015 | Qarabağ FK Bakı | Qarabağ FK Bakı | Nurlan Novruzov (Bakı FK) | 15 |
| 2015/2016 | Qarabağ FK Bakı | Qarabağ FK Bakı | Daniel Quintana Sosa "Dani Quintana" (ESP, Qarabağ FK Bakı) | 15 |
| 2016/2017 | Qarabağ FK Bakı | Qarabağ FK Bakı | Filip Ozobić (CRO, Qəbələ FK) | 11 |
| | | | Rauf Aliyev (İnter PİK Bakı) | |
| 2017/2018 | Qarabağ FK Bakı | Keşlə FK Bakı | Bagaliy Dabo (FRA, Qəbələ FK) | 13 |
| 2018/2019 | Qarabağ FK Bakı | Qəbələ FK | Mahir Anar Mədətov (Qarabağ FK Bakı) | 16 |
| 2019/2020 | Qarabağ FK Bakı | *Competition cancelled* | Peyman Babaei (IRN, Sumqayıt FK) | |
| | | | Steeven Joseph-Monrose (FRA, Neftçi PFK Bakı) | |
| | | | Bagaliy Dabo (FRA, Neftçi PFK Bakı) | |
| | | | Mahir Anar Emreli (Qarabağ FK Bakı) | 7 |
| 2020/2021 | Neftçi PFK Bakı | Keşlə FK Bakı | Namiq Ələsgərov (Neftçi PFK Bakı) | 19 |
| 2021/2022 | Qarabağ FK Bakı | Qarabağ FK Bakı | Kady Iuri Borges Malinowski (BRA, Qarabağ FK Bakı) | 12 |
| 2022/2023 | Qarabağ FK Bakı | Qəbələ FK | Ramil Sheydaev (Qarabağ FK Bakı) | 22 |

Please note: Qarabağ FK moved 1993 from Ağdam to Bakı.

# NATIONAL CHAMPIONSHIP
## Azerbaijan Premier League – Azərbaycan Premyer Liqası 2022/2023
### (05.08.2022 – 28.05.2023)

## Results

**Round 1** [05-08.08.2022]
Kəpəz PFK - Zira FK 1-2(1-1)
Qarabağ FK - Səbail FK 3-1(2-0)
Şamaxı FK - Neftçi PFK Bakı 0-1(0-0)
Sabah FK - Sumqayıt FK 3-0(1-0)
Turan Tovuz - Qəbələ FK 0-2(0-0)

**Round 2** [12-14.08.2022]
Zira FK - Sabah FK 1-3(1-2)
Sumqayıt FK - Qarabağ FK 0-2(0-0)
Səbail FK - Turan Tovuz 0-1(0-0)
Qəbələ FK - Şamaxı FK 3-1(3-0)
Neftçi PFK Bakı - Kəpəz PFK 5-2(3-0)

**Round 3** [19-21.08.2022]
Şamaxı FK - Səbail FK 1-1(0-1)
Sabah FK - Neftçi PFK Bakı 2-1(0-1)
Kəpəz PFK - Qəbələ FK 0-3(0-2)
Zira FK - Sumqayıt FK 0-0
Turan Tovuz-Qarabağ FK 0-2(0-2) [09.11.22]

**Round 4** [26-28.08.2022]
Sumqayıt FK - Turan Tovuz 0-0
Neftçi PFK Bakı - Zira FK 2-1(1-0)
Səbail FK - Kəpəz PFK 4-1(0-1)
Qarabağ FK - Şamaxı FK 4-0(1-0)
Qəbələ FK - Sabah FK 0-2(0-0)

**Round 5** [01-04.09.2022]
Kəpəz PFK - Qarabağ FK 0-1(0-1)
Şamaxı FK - Turan Tovuz 0-1(0-0)
Neftçi PFK Bakı - Sumqayıt FK 3-0(1-0)
Sabah FK - Səbail FK 0-0
Zira FK - Qəbələ FK 2-1(1-1)

**Round 6** [09-11.09.2022]
Turan Tovuz - Kəpəz PFK 2-0(1-0)
Qəbələ FK - Neftçi PFK Bakı 1-2(1-0)
Səbail FK - Zira FK 1-2(1-2)
Sumqayıt FK - Şamaxı FK 1-1(1-1)
Qarabağ FK - Sabah FK 4-3(1-1)

**Round 7** [16-18.09.2022]
Sabah FK - Turan Tovuz 3-1(2-0)
Neftçi PFK Bakı - Səbail FK 2-0(0-0)
Qəbələ FK - Sumqayıt FK 1-0(1-0)
Kəpəz PFK - Şamaxı FK 2-1(0-1)
Zira FK - Qarabağ FK 1-7(1-1)

**Round 8** [30.09.-02.10.2022]
Səbail FK - Qəbələ FK 1-2(0-0)
Turan Tovuz - Zira FK 1-3(1-2)
Qarabağ FK - Neftçi PFK Bakı 3-1(0-1)
Şamaxı FK - Sabah FK 0-1(0-0)
Sumqayıt FK - Kəpəz PFK 0-0

**Round 9** [07-09.10.2022]
Zira FK - Şamaxı FK 1-0(0-0)
Səbail FK - Sumqayıt FK 1-0(1-0)
Neftçi PFK Bakı - Turan Tovuz 0-0
Qəbələ FK - Qarabağ FK 0-1(0-0)
Sabah FK - Kəpəz PFK 5-0(3-0)

**Round 10** [14-16.10.2022]
Şamaxı FK - Qəbələ FK 1-1(0-0)
Turan Tovuz - Səbail FK 2-2(2-1)
Sabah FK - Zira FK 1-0(0-0)
Kəpəz PFK - Neftçi PFK Bakı 0-2(0-1)
Qarabağ FK - Sumqayıt FK 3-1(0-0)

**Round 11** [20-23.10.2022]
Qarabağ FK - Turan Tovuz 3-0(2-0)
Qəbələ FK - Kəpəz PFK 1-1(1-0)
Sumqayıt FK - Zira FK 0-2(0-1)
Səbail FK - Şamaxı FK 0-0
Neftçi PFK Bakı - Sabah FK 2-3(0-2)

**Round 12** [28-30.10.2022]
Turan Tovuz - Sumqayıt FK 1-0(0-0)
Kəpəz PFK - Səbail FK 3-0(1-0)
Zira FK - Neftçi PFK Bakı 0-3(0-1)
Şamaxı FK - Qarabağ FK 0-4(0-0)
Sabah FK - Qəbələ FK 2-1(0-1)

**Round 13** [04-06.11.2022]
Turan Tovuz - Şamaxı FK 1-3(1-2)
Qəbələ FK - Zira FK 1-0(0-0)
Sumqayıt FK - Neftçi PFK Bakı 2-2(1-0)
Səbail FK - Sabah FK 0-2(0-1)
Qarabağ FK - Kəpəz PFK 3-1(1-0)

**Round 14** [11-13.11.2022]
Şamaxı FK - Sumqayıt FK 4-2(2-1)
Zira FK - Səbail FK 1-0(0-0)
Neftçi PFK Bakı - Qəbələ FK 2-0(1-0)
Kəpəz PFK - Turan Tovuz 0-0
Sabah FK - Qarabağ FK 0-0

**Round 15** [27-29.11.2022]
Səbail FK - Neftçi PFK Bakı 1-3(0-1)
Şamaxı FK - Kəpəz PFK 1-1(0-1)
Qarabağ FK - Zira FK 0-0
Turan Tovuz - Sabah FK 0-1(0-0)
Sumqayıt FK - Qəbələ FK 1-1(0-0)

**Round 16** [02-04.12.2022]
Neftçi PFK Bakı - Qarabağ FK 0-4(0-1)
Qəbələ FK - Səbail FK 2-1(1-1)
Sabah FK - Şamaxı FK 1-1(1-0)
Kəpəz PFK - Sumqayıt FK 0-1(0-0)
Zira FK - Turan Tovuz 2-1(0-0)

**Round 17** [13-15.12.2022]
Şamaxı FK - Zira FK 0-0
Qarabağ FK - Qəbələ FK 1-0(0-0)
Kəpəz PFK - Sabah FK 2-2(1-1)
Sumqayıt FK - Səbail FK 2-0(1-0)
Turan Tovuz - Neftçi PFK Bakı 0-1(0-0)

**Round 18** [23-25.12.2022]
Neftçi PFK Bakı - Şamaxı FK 3-0(1-0)
Sumqayıt FK - Sabah FK 0-6(0-4)
Qəbələ FK - Turan Tovuz 0-0
Səbail FK - Qarabağ FK 0-3(0-0)
Zira FK - Kəpəz PFK 2-2(1-2)

**Round 19** [24-26.01.2023]
Kəpəz PFK - Qəbələ FK 2-2(2-0)
Turan Tovuz - Qarabağ FK 2-3(1-2)
Zira FK - Sumqayıt FK 3-1(0-1)
Şamaxı FK - Səbail FK 2-1(0-1)
Sabah FK - Neftçi PFK Bakı 2-0(2-0)

**Round 20** [30.01.-01.02.2023]
Sumqayıt FK - Turan Tovuz 2-1(1-1)
Qarabağ FK - Şamaxı FK 3-1(1-0)
Səbail FK - Kəpəz PFK 1-0(0-0)
Qəbələ FK - Sabah FK 0-3(0-0)
Neftçi PFK Bakı - Zira FK 1-0(0-0)

**Round 21** [04-06.02.2023]
Kəpəz PFK - Qarabağ FK 1-1(0-1)
Zira FK - Qəbələ FK 2-2(1-1)
Neftçi PFK Bakı - Sumqayıt FK 2-0(0-0)
Şamaxı FK - Turan Tovuz 0-1(0-0)
Sabah FK - Səbail FK 4-0(3-0)

**Round 22** [10-12.02.2023]
Qəbələ FK - Neftçi PFK Bakı 0-0
Turan Tovuz - Kəpəz PFK 2-0(1-0)
Qarabağ FK - Sabah FK 1-1(1-0)
Səbail FK - Zira FK 2-0(0-0)
Sumqayıt FK - Şamaxı FK 1-0(1-0)

**Round 23** [17-19.02.2023]
Kəpəz PFK - Şamaxı FK 3-2(1-1)
Qəbələ FK - Sumqayıt FK 2-1(1-0)
Neftçi PFK Bakı - Səbail FK 3-0(1-0)
Sabah FK - Turan Tovuz 0-2(0-1)
Zira FK - Qarabağ FK 0-1(0-0)

**Round 24** [24-27.02.2023]
Turan Tovuz - Zira FK 0-2(0-2)
Səbail FK - Qəbələ FK 2-2(0-1)
Şamaxı FK - Sabah FK 2-1(0-0)
Sumqayıt FK - Kəpəz PFK 1-2(0-2)
Qarabağ FK - Neftçi PFK Bakı 1-1(0-1)

**Round 25** [03-05.03.2023]
Zira FK - Şamaxı FK 2-2(1-0)
Səbail FK - Sumqayıt FK 0-1(0-0)
Sabah FK - Kəpəz PFK 2-0(1-0)
Qəbələ FK - Qarabağ FK 1-3(1-1)
Neftçi PFK Bakı - Turan Tovuz 4-0(2-0)

**Round 26** [10-12.03.2023]
Kəpəz PFK - Zira FK 1-1(1-0)
Sabah FK - Sumqayıt FK 4-0(1-0)
Turan Tovuz - Qəbələ FK 1-1(1-1)
Qarabağ FK - Səbail FK 3-0(2-0)
Şamaxı FK - Neftçi PFK Bakı 0-1(0-0)

**Round 27** [15-17.03.2023]
Sumqayıt FK - Qarabağ FK 0-6(0-4)
Zira FK - Sabah FK 0-2(0-0)
Səbail FK - Turan Tovuz 1-1(1-1)
Neftçi PFK Bakı - Kəpəz PFK 2-2(0-0)
Qəbələ FK - Şamaxı FK 2-0(2-0)

**Round 28** [31.03.-02.04.2023]
Turan Tovuz - Sumqayıt FK 2-3(2-1)
Kəpəz PFK - Səbail FK 1-0(0-0)
Zira FK - Neftçi PFK Bakı 1-1(0-1)
Şamaxı FK - Qarabağ FK 0-1(0-1)
Sabah FK - Qəbələ FK 3-2(1-2)

**Round 29** [07-09.04.2023]
Qəbələ FK - Zira FK 2-1(0-0)
Səbail FK - Sabah FK 2-1(1-0)
Sumqayıt FK - Neftçi PFK Bakı 0-4(0-1)
Turan Tovuz - Şamaxı FK 1-1(1-1)
Qarabağ FK - Kəpəz PFK 3-1(1-1)

**Round 30** [14-16.04.2023]
Zira FK - Səbail FK 3-1(0-0)
Neftçi PFK Bakı - Qəbələ FK 1-2(0-2)
Kəpəz PFK - Turan Tovuz 1-0(1-0)
Şamaxı FK - Sumqayıt FK 0-0
Sabah FK - Qarabağ FK 2-1(0-0)

| Round 31 [21-23.04.2023] |
|---|
| Şamaxı FK - Kəpəz PFK 1-1(1-1) |
| Qarabağ FK - Zira FK 2-2(0-0) |
| Turan Tovuz - Sabah FK 0-2(0-1) |
| Səbail FK - Neftçi PFK Bakı 1-1(1-1) |
| Sumqayıt FK - Qəbələ FK 2-3(0-0) |

| Round 32 [29.04.-02.05.2023] |
|---|
| Kəpəz PFK - Sumqayıt FK 0-1(0-0) |
| Sabah FK - Şamaxı FK 1-0(1-0) |
| Qəbələ FK - Səbail FK 4-2(2-0) |
| Zira FK - Turan Tovuz 1-3(0-1) |
| Neftçi PFK Bakı - Qarabağ FK 2-4(1-2) |

| Round 33 [05-08.05.2023] |
|---|
| Kəpəz PFK - Sabah FK 0-3(0-2) |
| Şamaxı FK - Zira FK 0-3(0-1) |
| Turan Tovuz - Neftçi PFK Bakı 4-0(3-0) |
| Sumqayıt FK - Səbail FK 1-3(1-0) |
| Qarabağ FK - Qəbələ FK 3-0(1-0) |

| Round 34 [12-17.05.2023] |
|---|
| Zira FK - Kəpəz PFK 1-1(0-1) |
| Qəbələ FK - Turan Tovuz 1-2(0-0) |
| Səbail FK - Qarabağ FK 0-3(0-0) |
| Neftçi PFK Bakı - Şamaxı FK 1-1(1-0) |
| Sumqayıt FK - Sabah FK 0-4(0-3) |

| Round 35 [21-22.05.2023] |
|---|
| Kəpəz PFK - Neftçi PFK Bakı 1-3(1-0) |
| Turan Tovuz - Səbail FK 2-2(1-0) |
| Qarabağ FK - Sumqayıt FK 1-2(0-2) |
| Sabah FK - Zira FK 0-0 |
| Şamaxı FK - Qəbələ FK 0-0 |

| Round 36 [27-28.05.2023] |
|---|
| Qəbələ FK - Kəpəz PFK 1-1(1-0) |
| Sumqayıt FK - Zira FK 0-3(0-1) |
| Səbail FK - Şamaxı FK 1-0(1-0) |
| Neftçi PFK Bakı - Sabah FK 1-0(1-0) |
| Qarabağ FK - Turan Tovuz 3-1(1-0) |

## Final Standings

| | | | | | | | | Total | | Home | | | | | Away | | | |
|---|---|---|---|---|---|---|---|---|---|---|---|---|---|---|---|---|---|---|
| 1. | Qarabağ FK Bakı | 36 | 28 | 6 | 2 | 91 - 25 | 90 | | 13 | 4 | 1 | 44 - 16 | | 15 | 2 | 1 | 47 - 9 |
| 2. | Sabah FK Bakı | 36 | 25 | 6 | 5 | 75 - 24 | 81 | | 13 | 4 | 1 | 35 - 9 | | 12 | 2 | 4 | 40 - 15 |
| 3. | Neftçi PFK Bakı | 36 | 20 | 8 | 8 | 63 - 38 | 68 | | 11 | 3 | 4 | 37 - 20 | | 9 | 5 | 4 | 26 - 18 |
| 4. | Qəbələ FK | 36 | 13 | 11 | 12 | 47 - 47 | 50 | | 8 | 4 | 6 | 22 - 21 | | 5 | 7 | 6 | 25 - 26 |
| 5. | Zirə FK Bakı | 36 | 13 | 11 | 12 | 45 - 46 | 50 | | 6 | 6 | 6 | 23 - 31 | | 7 | 5 | 6 | 22 - 15 |
| 6. | Turan Tovuz | 36 | 10 | 9 | 17 | 36 - 49 | 39 | | 4 | 4 | 10 | 21 - 28 | | 6 | 5 | 7 | 15 - 21 |
| 7. | Sumqayıt FK | 36 | 8 | 7 | 21 | 26 - 70 | 31 | | 3 | 5 | 10 | 13 - 40 | | 5 | 2 | 11 | 13 - 30 |
| 8. | Kəpəz PFK Gəncə | 36 | 6 | 13 | 17 | 34 - 62 | 31 | | 5 | 5 | 8 | 18 - 25 | | 1 | 8 | 9 | 16 - 37 |
| 9. | Səbail FK Bakı | 36 | 7 | 8 | 21 | 32 - 62 | 29 | | 6 | 4 | 8 | 17 - 22 | | 1 | 4 | 13 | 15 - 40 |
| 10. | Şamaxı FK (Relegated) | 36 | 4 | 13 | 19 | 26 - 52 | 25 | | 3 | 7 | 8 | 12 - 21 | | 1 | 6 | 11 | 14 - 31 |

| Top goalscorers: | |
|---|---|
| 22 Ramil Sheydaev | Qarabağ FK Bakı |
| 21 Musa Qurbanly | Qarabağ FK Bakı |
| 17 Joy-Lance Mickels (GER) | Sabah FK Bakı |
| 17 Emin Makhmudov | Neftçi PFK Bakı |

## NATIONAL CUP
### Azərbaycan Kuboku 2022/2023

| First Round [22-23.11.2022] | | | |
|---|---|---|---|
| MOIK Bakı - Səbail FK Bakı | 0-4(0-2) | Kəpəz PFK Gəncə - Sumqayıt FK | 1-0(1-0) |
| Şamaxı FK - Turan Tovuz | 0-1(0-0) | Energetik FK Mingəçevir - Zirə FK Bakı | 0-2(0-1) |
| Qəbələ FK - Araz-Naxçıvan PFK | 5-0(1-0) | Sabah FK Bakı - Qaradağ Lökbatan FK | 5-0(2-0) |

| Quarter-Finals [08-09./19-20.12.2022] | | | |
|---|---|---|---|
| **First Leg** | | **Second Leg** | |
| Zirə FK Bakı - Neftçi PFK Bakı | 1-0(0-0) | Neftçi PFK Bakı - Zirə FK Bakı | 3-1(2-0,2-1) |
| Qarabağ FK Bakı - Qəbələ FK | 2-0(0-1) | Qəbələ FK - Qarabağ FK Bakı | 1-0(0-0) |
| Kəpəz PFK Gəncə - Turan Tovuz | 1-2(1-0) | Turan Tovuz - Kəpəz PFK Gəncə | 2-2(2-2) |
| Səbail FK Bakı - Sabah FK Bakı | 3-2(1-0) | Sabah FK Bakı - Səbail FK Bakı | 0-1(0-0) |

| Semi-Finals [18-19/26-27.04.2023] | | | |
|---|---|---|---|
| **First Leg** | | **Second Leg** | |
| Qəbələ FK - Səbail FK Bakı | 3-2(1-2) | Səbail FK Bakı - Qəbələ FK | 0-1(0-0) |
| Turan Tovuz - Neftçi PFK Bakı | 1-0(0-0) | Neftçi PFK Bakı - Turan Tovuz | 2-0(0-0) |

## Final

03.06.2023; Bakcell Arena, Bakı; Referee: Inqilab Mammadov; Attendance: 9,000

**Neftçi PFK Bakı - Qəbələ FK**                                                    0-1(0-0,0-0)

**Neftçi PFK:** Ivan Brkić, Ömər Buludov (106.Egor Bogomolskiy), Solomon Kvirkvelia, Vojislav Stanković (106.Höccət Haqverdi), Kenny Saief, Ataa Jabir (106.César Daniel Meza Colli), İsmayıl Zülfüqarlı (81.Azer Əliyev), Eddi Silvestr Paskual İsrafilov (90+2.Farid Yusifli), Emin Mahmudov (Cap), Keelan Lebon, Matheus Bonifacio Saldanha Marinho. Trainer: Laurenţiu Aurelian Reghecampf (Romania).

**Qəbələ FK:** Christophe Atangana Assimba, İlkin Qırtımov, Ruan Renato Bonifácio Augusto, Murad Musayev (Cap), Məqsəd İsayev (95.Ürfan Abbasov), Emil Səfərov, Isnik Alimi, Ayyoub Allach (80.Ülvi İsgəndərov), Raphael Schorr Utzig „Raphael Alemão" (96.Rövlan Muradov), Felipe Silva Correa dos Santos (96.Omar Hani Ismail Al Zebdieh), Ramon Machado de Macedo. Trainer: Elmar Baxşiyev.

**Goal:** 0-1 Isnik Alimi (102 penalty).

## Kəpəz Peşəkar Futbol Klubu Gəncə

| | | |
|---|---|---|
| **Founded**: | 1959 | |
| **Stadium**: | Gəncə şəhər stadionu, Gəncə (27,000) | |
| **Trainer**: | Yaşar Vahabzadə | 08.04.1960 |
| [29.08.2022] | Xaliq Mərdanov | 21.03.1971 |
| [04.09.2022] | Tərlan Əhmədov | 17.11.1971 |

| Goalkeepers: | DOB | M | (s) | G |
|---|---|---|---|---|
| Kamran İbrahimov | 07.06.1999 | 6 | | |
| Mario Mustapić (CRO) | 22.10.1999 | 8 | (1) | |
| Orkhan Sadıqlı | 19.03.1993 | 22 | | |
| **Defenders:** | **DOB** | **M** | **(s)** | **G** |
| Tural Axundov | 01.08.1988 | 12 | (4) | |
| Elchin Əlicanov | 15.07.1999 | 28 | (5) | |
| Arzu Atakişiyev | 05.09.2005 | | (1) | |
| Zamiq Əliyev | 05.05.2001 | 16 | (4) | |
| Peyman Keshavarzi Nazarloo (IRN) | 06.03.1996 | 5 | (1) | |
| Yegor Khvalko (BLR) | 18.02.1997 | 26 | (1) | 2 |
| Zahir Mərdanov | 09.08.2000 | | (1) | |
| Yusif Nəbiyev | 03.09.1997 | 34 | | 1 |
| Abdulla Rzayev | 12.03.2002 | 18 | | |
| Elvin Yunuszadə | 22.08.1992 | 4 | (1) | |
| **Midfielders:** | **DOB** | **M** | **(s)** | **G** |
| Nihat Fərəci | 30.03.2003 | | (1) | |
| Mahir Həsənov | 12.01.2002 | 4 | (3) | |
| İdris İnqilablı | 06.10.2001 | 5 | (7) | |

| | DOB | M | (s) | G |
|---|---|---|---|---|
| Əfran İsmayılov | 08.10.1988 | 1 | (2) | 1 |
| Giorgi Kantaria (GEO) | 27.04.1997 | 31 | | |
| Samir Məhərrəmli | 17.07.2002 | 2 | (7) | |
| Nicat Məmmədov | 24.01.2001 | | (1) | |
| Tural Rzayev | 26.08.1993 | 8 | (18) | |
| Əli Səmədov | 06.09.1997 | 7 | | |
| Nizami Səmədov | 26.08.2000 | | (1) | |
| Ümid Səmədov | 07.10.2003 | | (1) | |
| Nicat Süleymanov | 15.11.1998 | 11 | (17) | 1 |
| Ruslan Süleymanov | 31.12.1999 | 2 | (1) | |
| **Forwards:** | **DOB** | **M** | **(s)** | **G** |
| Salif Cissé (FRA) | 12.07.1992 | 2 | (11) | 1 |
| Ahmed Isaiah (NGA) | 10.10.1995 | 31 | (1) | 4 |
| Alessandro Pinheiro Martins Júnior „Juninho" (BRA) | 07.11.1999 | 17 | (1) | 2 |
| Mate Kvirkvia (GEO) | 14.06.1996 | 31 | (2) | 3 |
| Farid Nəbiyev | 22.07.1999 | 28 | (2) | 4 |
| Abdullahi Shuaibu (NGA) | 22.01.2002 | 28 | (6) | 11 |
| Mikheil Ergemlidze (GEO) | 28.09.1999 | 5 | (9) | 2 |
| Rauf Əliyev | 12.02.1989 | 4 | | |

## Neftçi Peşəkar Futbol Klubu Bakı

| | | |
|---|---|---|
| **Founded**: | 18.03.1937 | |
| **Stadium**: | Bakcell Arena, Bakı (10,200) | |
| **Trainer**: | Laurenţiu Aurelian Reghecampf (ROU) | 19.09.1975 |

| Goalkeepers: | DOB | M | (s) | G |
|---|---|---|---|---|
| Ivan Brkić (CRO) | 29.06.1995 | 26 | | |
| Rza Cəfərov | 03.07.2003 | 1 | | |
| Aqil Məmmədov | 01.05.1989 | 9 | | |
| Əlirza Müştəfazadə | 05.12.2001 | | (1) | |
| **Defenders:** | **DOB** | **M** | **(s)** | **G** |
| Rüfat Abbasov | 01.01.2005 | 1 | | |
| Ömər Buludov | 15.12.1998 | 19 | (11) | 2 |
| Mert Çelik | 10.06.2000 | 5 | (7) | |
| Azer Əliyev (RUS) | 12.05.1994 | 21 | | 1 |
| Höccət Haqverdi | 03.02.1993 | 15 | (1) | |
| Solomon Kvirkvelia (GEO) | 06.02.1992 | 29 | (4) | 2 |
| Pape Mamadou Mbodj (SEN) | 12.03.1993 | 7 | (3) | |
| Azər Salahlı | 11.04.1994 | 15 | (8) | |
| Vojislav Stanković (SRB) | 22.09.1987 | 29 | | 2 |
| İsmayıl Zülfüqarlı | 16.04.2001 | 11 | (14) | 2 |
| **Midfielders:** | **DOB** | **M** | **(s)** | **G** |
| Vusal Əsgərov | 23.08.2001 | 1 | (1) | |

| | DOB | M | (s) | G |
|---|---|---|---|---|
| Rəhman Hacıyev | 25.07.1993 | 4 | (11) | 2 |
| Eddi Silvestr Paskual İsrafilov | 02.08.1992 | 18 | (3) | 3 |
| Ataa Jabir (PLE) | 03.10.1994 | 26 | (2) | 5 |
| Emin Mahmudov | 27.04.1992 | 33 | (3) | 17 |
| César Daniel Meza Colli (PAR) | 05.10.1991 | 7 | (10) | 2 |
| Ramin Nəsirli | 24.09.2002 | | (1) | |
| Ömer Qurbanov | 06.04.2005 | | (1) | |
| Kenny Saief (USA) | 17.12.1993 | 31 | (1) | 4 |
| Farid Yusifli | 20.02.2002 | 10 | (9) | |
| **Forwards:** | **DOB** | **M** | **(s)** | **G** |
| Vato Arveladze (GEO) | 04.03.1998 | 2 | (16) | |
| Egor Bogomolskiy (BLR) | 03.06.2000 | 10 | (17) | 3 |
| Godsway Donyoh (GHA) | 14.10.1994 | 15 | | 4 |
| Guilherme „Pato" Nunes Rodrigues (BRA) | 17.02.2001 | 2 | (10) | 1 |
| Yusuf Lawal (NGA) | 23.03.1998 | 17 | (1) | 1 |
| Keelan Lebon (FRA) | 04.07.1997 | 17 | | 4 |
| Matheus Bonifacio Saldanha Marinho (BRA) | 18.08.1999 | 15 | (2) | 5 |
| Ağadadaş Salyanski | 19.06.2004 | | (4) | 1 |

## Qarabağ Futbol Klubu Bakı

| | | |
|---|---|---|
| **Founded**: | 1951 | |
| **Stadium**: | Azersun Arena, Bakı (5,200) | |
| **Trainer**: | Qurban Qurbanov | 13.04.1992 |

| Goalkeepers: | DOB | M | (s) | G |
|---|---|---|---|---|
| Luka Gugeshashvili (GEO) | 29.04.1999 | 20 | | |
| Şahrudin Məhəmmədəliyev | 12.06.1994 | 11 | | |
| Amin Ramazanov | 20.01.2003 | 5 | | |
| **Defenders:** | **DOB** | **M** | **(s)** | **G** |
| Toral Bayramov | 23.02.2001 | 10 | (8) | 1 |
| Elvin Cəfərquliyev | 26.10.2000 | 26 | (3) | 5 |
| Abbas Hüseynov | 13.06.1995 | 10 | (3) | |
| Bədavi Hüseynov | 11.07.1991 | 13 | (7) | |
| Rahil Məmmədov | 24.11.1995 | 11 | (2) | |
| Kevin David Medina Rentería (COL) | 09.03.1993 | 19 | (4) | |
| Maksim Medvedev | 29.09.1989 | 12 | (3) | |
| Bəhlul Mustafazadə | 27.02.1997 | 25 | | 2 |
| Marko Vešović (MNE) | 28.08.1991 | 17 | (6) | |
| **Midfielders:** | **DOB** | **M** | **(s)** | **G** |
| Richard Almeida de Oliveira | 20.03.1989 | 16 | (10) | 3 |

| | DOB | M | (s) | G |
|---|---|---|---|---|
| Yassine Benzia (ALG) | 08.09.1994 | 2 | (1) | |
| İsmayıl İbrahimli | 13.02.1998 | 8 | (9) | |
| Marko Janković (MNE) | 09.07.1995 | 15 | (8) | 1 |
| Júlio Rodrigues Romão (BRA) | 29.03.1998 | 24 | (6) | 1 |
| Leandro Livramento Andrade (CPV) | 24.09.1999 | 23 | (3) | 7 |
| Filip Ozobić | 08.04.1991 | 10 | (10) | 3 |
| Qara Qarayev | 12.10.1992 | 17 | (11) | 1 |
| Abdellah Zoubir (FRA) | 05.12.1991 | 21 | (11) | 8 |
| **Forwards:** | **DOB** | **M** | **(s)** | **G** |
| Nəriman Axundzadə | 23.04.2004 | 2 | (7) | |
| Adama Diakhaby (FRA) | 05.07.1996 | 4 | (4) | |
| Kady Iuri Borges Malinowski (BRA) | 02.05.1996 | 9 | (7) | 4 |
| Owusu Kwabena (GHA) | 18.06.1997 | 11 | (7) | 5 |
| Musa Qurbanlı | 13.04.2002 | 26 | (6) | 21 |
| Ramil Şeydayev | 15.03.1996 | 24 | (11) | 22 |
| Redon Xhixha (ALB) | 14.07.1998 | 5 | (8) | 1 |

## Qəbələ Futbol Klubu

| | | | | |
|---|---|---|---|---|
| **Founded**: | 01.09.1955 | | | |
| **Stadium**: | Qəbələ şəhər stadionu, Qəbələ (4,500) | | | |
| **Trainer**: | Elmar Baxşiyev | | | 03.08.1980 |

| Goalkeepers: | DOB | M | (s) | G |
|---|---|---|---|---|
| Sələhət Ağayev | 04.01.1991 | 30 | | |
| Christophe Atangana Assimba (CMR) | 02.03.2000 | 6 | | |
| **Defenders:** | **DOB** | **M** | **(s)** | **G** |
| Ürfan Abbasov | 14.10.1992 | 11 | (3) | |
| Məqsəd İsayev | 07.06.1994 | 34 | | 2 |
| Hüseyn Mürsəlov | 12.07.2002 | | (1) | |
| Murad Musayev | 13.06.1994 | 25 | (5) | 1 |
| İlkin Qırtımov | 04.11.1990 | 30 | | |
| Ruan Renato Bonifácio Augusto (BRA) | 14.01.1994 | 33 | | 2 |
| **Midfielders:** | **DOB** | **M** | **(s)** | **G** |
| Fares Abu Akel (ISR) | 08.02.1997 | 30 | (1) | 2 |
| Isnik Alimi (ALB) | 02.02.1994 | 34 | | 9 |
| Ayyoub Allach (BEL) | 28.01.1998 | 9 | (4) | 3 |

| | DOB | M | (s) | G |
|---|---|---|---|---|
| Asif Məmmədov | 05.08.1986 | 18 | (12) | |
| Rauf Rüstəmli | 11.01.2003 | | (1) | |
| Andriy Stryzhak (UKR) | 22.10.1999 | | (6) | |
| **Forwards:** | **DOB** | **M** | **(s)** | **G** |
| Yaovi Akakpo (TOG) | 11.03.1999 | | (4) | |
| Omar Hani Ismail Al Zebdieh (JOR) | 27.06.1999 | 10 | (23) | 1 |
| Mehrac Baxşalı | 11.06.2003 | | (1) | |
| *Felipe* Silva Correa dos *Santos* (BRA) | 03.01.1997 | 35 | | 3 |
| Ülvi İsgəndərov | 24.10.1997 | 9 | (24) | 6 |
| Rövlan Muradov | 28.03.1998 | 20 | (13) | 2 |
| *Ramon* Machado de Macedo (BRA) | 04.04.1991 | 26 | (6) | 8 |
| Raphael Schorr Utzig „Raphael Alemão" (BRA) | 08.08.1996 | 24 | (6) | 4 |
| Emil Səfərov | 30.10.2002 | 12 | (19) | 1 |

## Sabah Futbol Klubu Bakı

| | | | | |
|---|---|---|---|---|
| **Founded**: | 2016 | | | |
| **Stadium**: | Bank Respublika Arena, Masazır (13,000) | | | |
| **Trainer**: | Murad Musayev (RUS) | | | 10.11.1983 |

| Goalkeepers: | DOB | M | (s) | G |
|---|---|---|---|---|
| Yusif İmanov | 27.09.2002 | 33 | | |
| Nicat Mehbalıyev | 11.09.2000 | 1 | | |
| Rustam Samiqullin | 23.12.2002 | 2 | | |
| **Defenders:** | **DOB** | **M** | **(s)** | **G** |
| Abdoulaye Ba (SEN) | 01.01.1991 | 22 | | 2 |
| Bəxtiyar Həsənəlizadə | 29.12.1992 | 16 | (3) | 1 |
| Jon *Irazábal* Iraurgui (ESP) | 28.11.1996 | 29 | (1) | 2 |
| Bojan Letić (BIH) | 21.12.1992 | 33 | (1) | |
| Tellur Mütallimov | 08.04.1995 | 6 | (22) | |
| Zurab Ochihava (UKR) | 18.05.1995 | 5 | | |
| Amin Seydiyev | 15.11.1998 | 33 | (1) | |
| **Midfielders:** | **DOB** | **M** | **(s)** | **G** |
| *Christian* da Silva Fiel (BRA) | 14.06.1989 | 14 | (5) | 1 |
| *Cristian Ceballos* Prieto (ESP) | 03.12.1992 | 3 | (16) | 3 |

| | DOB | M | (s) | G |
|---|---|---|---|---|
| Elvin Camalov | 04.02.1995 | 31 | (2) | 2 |
| Namiq Ələsgərov | 03.02.1995 | 9 | (14) | 2 |
| Aleksey Isaev | 09.11.1995 | 34 | | 3 |
| Seymur Məmmədov | 29.05.2003 | | (2) | 1 |
| Anatoliy Nuriyev | 20.05.1996 | 21 | (11) | 4 |
| Ceyhun Nurıyev | 30.03.2001 | 3 | (20) | 2 |
| Abdulax Xaybulayev | 19.08.2001 | | (4) | |
| **Forwards:** | **DOB** | **M** | **(s)** | **G** |
| Emmanuel Apeh (NGA) | 25.10.1996 | 13 | (21) | 8 |
| Camal Cəfərov | 25.02.2002 | | (4) | |
| İldar Ələkbərov | 27.04.2001 | | (18) | |
| Oleksiy Kashchuk (UKR) | 29.06.2000 | 30 | (1) | 16 |
| Joy-Lance Mickels (GER) | 29.03.1994 | 35 | | 17 |
| Davit Volkovi (GEO) | 03.06.1995 | 23 | (12) | 10 |

## Səbail Futbol Klubu Bakı

| | | | | |
|---|---|---|---|---|
| **Founded**: | 2016 | | | |
| **Stadium**: | Bayil Arena, Bakı (5,000) | | | |
| **Trainer**: | Mahmud Qurbanov | | | 10.05.1973 |
| [28.12.2022] | Şahin Diniyev | | | 12.07.1966 |

| Goalkeepers: | DOB | M | (s) | G |
|---|---|---|---|---|
| Emil Balayev | 17.04.1994 | 32 | (1) | |
| Hüseynali Quliyev | 11.08.1999 | 4 | (1) | |
| **Defenders:** | **DOB** | **M** | **(s)** | **G** |
| Facundo Cardozo (ARG) | 06.04.1995 | 12 | (1) | |
| Cabir Əmirli | 06.01.1997 | 29 | (4) | |
| Gustavo Moreno de *França* (BRA) | 20.07.1996 | 23 | (3) | |
| Vüqar Həsənov | 05.12.1997 | 11 | (2) | |
| Turan Manafov | 19.08.1998 | 12 | (5) | 1 |
| Adil Nağıyev | 11.09.1995 | 17 | | |
| Nihad Qurbanlı | 10.04.2001 | 10 | (2) | |
| Petro Stasyuk (UKR) | 24.02.1995 | 27 | (3) | |
| **Midfielders:** | **DOB** | **M** | **(s)** | **G** |
| Samir Abdullayev | 24.04.2002 | 7 | (14) | |
| Tural Bayramlı | 07.01.1998 | 1 | (2) | |
| Maksym Chekh (UKR) | 03.01.1999 | 23 | (6) | 1 |
| Rahid Əmirquliyev | 01.09.1989 | 8 | (4) | |

| | DOB | M | (s) | G |
|---|---|---|---|---|
| Ruslan Hacıyev | 26.03.1998 | 7 | (15) | 2 |
| Matija Ljujić (SRB) | 28.10.1993 | 12 | (2) | 3 |
| Rafael Məhərrəmli | 01.10.1999 | 14 | (6) | 1 |
| Emil Martinov (BUL) | 18.03.1992 | 15 | (10) | |
| Franco Eduardo Mazurek (ARG) | 24.09.1993 | 28 | (4) | 6 |
| İlkin Muradov | 05.03.1996 | 11 | (2) | |
| Vüsal Qənbərov | 25.04.2003 | | (2) | |
| Ədilxan Qarahmədov | 05.06.2001 | 2 | (7) | |
| Elmir Tağıyev | 23.05.2000 | 19 | (12) | 1 |
| Emin Zamanov | 26.12.1997 | 1 | (3) | |
| **Forwards:** | **DOB** | **M** | **(s)** | **G** |
| Mirabdulla Abbasov | 27.04.1995 | 5 | (14) | 3 |
| David Cafimipon Gomis (GNB) | 21.12.1992 | 15 | (3) | 3 |
| Luwagga Kizito (UGA) | 20.12.1993 | 8 | (11) | 1 |
| Agabala Ramazanov | 20.01.1993 | 20 | (3) | 5 |
| Elysée Goba Zakpa (POR) | 17.08.1992 | 23 | (7) | 5 |

## Sumqayıt Futbol Klubu

| | | | | |
|---|---|---|---|---|
| **Founded**: | 1961 (*as Metallurg Sumqayit*) | | | |
| **Stadium**: | Kapital Bank Arena, Sumqayit (1,400) | | | |
| **Trainer**: | Alyaksey Baha (BLR) | | | 04.02.1981 |
| [26.09.2022] | Samir Abbasov | | | 01.02.1978 |

| Goalkeepers: | DOB | M | (s) | G |
|---|---|---|---|---|
| Aydin Bayramov | 18.02.1996 | 31 | | |
| Ilnur Valiev (RUS) | 25.06.2003 | 5 | | |
| **Defenders:** | **DOB** | **M** | **(s)** | **G** |
| Elvin Bədəlov | 14.06.1995 | 33 | (1) | |
| Damjan Daničić (SRB) | 24.01.2000 | 8 | (3) | |
| Süleyman Əhmədov | 25.11.1999 | 19 | (9) | |
| Vurğun Hüseynov | 25.04.1988 | 25 | | 1 |
| Hasrat Mürsalov | 31.03.2004 | | (1) | |
| Steven Fernandes Pereira (CPV) | 13.04.1994 | 22 | | 1 |
| Aykhan Süleymanlı | 16.01.2004 | 1 | (3) | |
| Todor Todoroski (MKD) | 26.02.1999 | 31 | | 3 |
| **Midfielders:** | **DOB** | **M** | **(s)** | **G** |
| Araz Abdullayev | 18.04.1992 | 3 | (8) | |
| Rüfət Abdullazadə | 17.01.2001 | 5 | (13) | 1 |
| Sabuhi Abdullazadə | 18.12.2001 | 32 | (3) | 1 |
| Vüqar Bəybalayev | 05.08.1993 | 4 | (2) | |
| Nihad Əhmədzadə | 23.07.2006 | 1 | (8) | |

| | DOB | M | (s) | G |
|---|---|---|---|---|
| Carlos *Filipe* Fonseca *Chaby* (POR) | 22.01.1994 | 8 | (7) | |
| Masaki Murata (JPN) | 29.08.1999 | 16 | | |
| Vüqar Mustafayev | 05.08.1994 | 31 | | |
| Murad Xaçayev | 14.04.1998 | 27 | (3) | 1 |
| **Forwards:** | **DOB** | **M** | **(s)** | **G** |
| Elşan Abdullayev | 05.02.1994 | | (6) | |
| Karim Aboubakar (GHA) | 30.07.1995 | 15 | (3) | 3 |
| Almir Aganspahić | 12.09.1996 | 8 | (5) | 2 |
| Kamran Aliev (RUS) | 15.10.1998 | 12 | (3) | 2 |
| İbrahim Əliyev | 17.07.1999 | | (3) | |
| *Diego* Santos *Carioca* (BRA) | 06.02.1998 | 8 | (2) | 1 |
| Richard Gadze (GHA) | 23.08.1994 | 6 | (1) | 1 |
| Vüsal İsgəndərli | 03.11.1995 | 30 | (4) | 6 |
| Xəzər Mahmudov | 23.11.2000 | | (1) | |
| Rifat Nurmugamet (KAZ) | 22.05.1996 | 2 | (7) | |
| Terrence Tisdell (LBR) | 16.03.1998 | 8 | (5) | 1 |
| Alya Touré (GUI) | 04.01.2002 | 3 | (9) | |
| Ouro-Nile Touré (TOG) | 31.12.1998 | 2 | (1) | |

## Şamaxı Futbol Klubu

**Founded**: 1997 (*as Khazar University*)
**Stadium**: Şamaxı şəhər stadionu, Şamaxı (2,200)
**Trainer**: Vüqar Əsgərli     26.06.1984

| Goalkeepers: | DOB | M | (s) | G |
|---|---|---|---|---|
| Rəşad Əzizli | 01.01.1994 | 33 | (1) | |
| Əkpar Vəliyev | 07.09.2001 | 3 | | |
| **Defenders:** | **DOB** | **M** | **(s)** | **G** |
| Arsen Ağcabayov | 11.09.2000 | 4 | (9) | |
| İbrahim Aslanlı | 01.12.1996 | 4 | (11) | |
| Fuad Bayramov | 20.05.1998 | 35 | | 4 |
| Rahman Daşdəmirov | 20.10.1999 | 36 | | 1 |
| Rauf Hüseynli | 25.01.2000 | 28 | (3) | 1 |
| Calal Hüseynov | 02.01.2003 | 32 | (1) | |
| Zahid Mərdanov | 09.08.2000 | 12 | | |
| Elçin Mustafayev | 05.07.2000 | 14 | (16) | |
| Adil Nağıyev | 11.09.1995 | 17 | | |
| Nihad Quliyev | 19.07.2001 | 27 | (4) | 2 |
| Bəhruz Teymurov | 01.01.1994 | | (4) | |
| **Midfielders:** | **DOB** | **M** | **(s)** | **G** |
| Ramin Əhmədov | 01.06.2001 | 5 | (9) | |

| | DOB | M | (s) | G |
|---|---|---|---|---|
| Asim Əlizadə | 05.02.2000 | 2 | (8) | |
| Bahadur Həziyev | 26.03.1999 | 31 | (4) | 3 |
| Elvin Məmmədov | 18.07.1988 | 22 | (7) | |
| Kamal Mirzəyev | 14.09.1994 | 8 | (8) | |
| Elçin Rəhimli | 17.06.1996 | | (11) | |
| Abdulla Rzayev | 12.03.2002 | | (4) | |
| Qurban Səfərov | 05.09.2004 | 9 | (12) | |
| Əli Səmədov | 06.09.1997 | 7 | (7) | |
| Emin Zamanov | 26.12.1997 | 12 | (6) | 1 |
| **Forwards:** | **DOB** | **M** | **(s)** | **G** |
| Uğur Cahangirov | 22.09.2001 | | (4) | |
| Tapdıq Əhmədov | 08.05.1997 | | (1) | |
| Emil Qasımov | 09.04.2000 | 3 | (7) | 1 |
| Kamran Quliyev | 11.03.2000 | 24 | (8) | 5 |
| Rövşən Şahmuradov | 11.05.1999 | 13 | (13) | 1 |
| Amil Yunanov | 06.01.1993 | 15 | (7) | 7 |

## Turan Tovuz

**Founded**: 23.02.1992
**Stadium**: Tovuz şəhər stadionu, Tovuz (6,800)
**Trainer**: Ayxan Abbasov     25.08.1981

| Goalkeepers: | DOB | M | (s) | G |
|---|---|---|---|---|
| Kamal Bayramov | 19.08.1985 | 9 | | |
| Tarlan Əhmədli | 21.11.1994 | 26 | | |
| Mehman Hacıyev | 28.01.1995 | 1 | (1) | |
| **Defenders:** | **DOB** | **M** | **(s)** | **G** |
| Ben Aziz Dao (BFA) | 08.07.1999 | 6 | (3) | |
| Şəhriyar Əliyev | 25.12.1992 | 32 | | 3 |
| Faiq Hacıyev | 22.05.1999 | 9 | (3) | |
| Hüseyn Hüseynov | 25.07.2006 | | (1) | |
| Denis Marandici (MDA) | 18.09.1996 | 16 | | |
| Vüsal Məsimov | 03.04.2000 | 3 | (6) | |
| Roderick Alonso Miller Molina (PAN) | 03.04.1992 | 6 | | 2 |
| Sadiq Quliyev | 09.03.1995 | 14 | (6) | 1 |
| Tarlan Quliyev | 19.04.1992 | 21 | (3) | 1 |
| Siyanda Xulu (RSA) | 30.12.1991 | 22 | (2) | 1 |
| **Midfielders:** | **DOB** | **M** | **(s)** | **G** |
| Abbas Ağazadə | 10.02.1999 | 1 | (10) | |
| Səbayıl Bağirov | 30.01.1995 | 3 | (9) | |
| Piruz Marakvelidze (GEO) | 21.01.1995 | 17 | (1) | |

| | DOB | M | (s) | G |
|---|---|---|---|---|
| Divine Naah (GHA) | 20.04.1996 | 1 | (5) | |
| Xəyal Nəcəfov | 19.12.1997 | 28 | (6) | 1 |
| Henry Chimuchem Okebugwu (NGA) | 19.06.1998 | 8 | (9) | 1 |
| Elçin Qasımov | 04.09.2002 | | (1) | |
| Veysal Rzayev | 24.10.2002 | 8 | (16) | |
| Şakir Seyidov | 31.12.2000 | 24 | (4) | |
| Eltun Turabov | 18.02.1997 | 19 | (4) | |
| Turan Vəlizadə | 01.01.2001 | 14 | (12) | 1 |
| **Forwards:** | **DOB** | **M** | **(s)** | **G** |
| Imeda Ashortia (GEO) | 30.10.1996 | 3 | (10) | |
| Famil Camalov | 08.04.1998 | | (2) | |
| Rooney Eva Wankewai (CMR) | 25.12.1996 | 31 | (1) | 16 |
| Aykhan Guseynov (RUS) | 03.09.1999 | 18 | (13) | 3 |
| Nathan Kolade Oduwa (ENG) | 05.03.1996 | 26 | (2) | 5 |
| Belajdi Pusi (ALB) | 23.01.1998 | 10 | (8) | |
| Sadig Şəfiyev | 13.10.2005 | | (2) | |
| Ehtiram Şahverdiyev | 01.10.1996 | 19 | (7) | 1 |
| Cavid Tağıyev | 22.07.1992 | 1 | (11) | |

## Zirə Futbol Klubu Bakı

**Founded**: 28.07.2014
**Stadium**: Zirə Olympic Spot Complex Stadium, Bakı (1,300)
**Trainer**: Rəşad Sadıqov     16.06.1982

| Goalkeepers: | DOB | M | (s) | G |
|---|---|---|---|---|
| Mehdi Cənnətov | 26.01.1992 | 23 | | |
| Anar Nəzirov | 08.09.1985 | 13 | (1) | |
| **Defenders:** | **DOB** | **M** | **(s)** | **G** |
| Ruslan Abışov | 10.10.1987 | | (1) | |
| Moïse Adiléhou (BEN) | 01.11.1995 | 22 | (3) | 1 |
| Slavik Alxasov | 06.02.1993 | 7 | (13) | |
| Nemanja Anđelković (SRB) | 26.04.1997 | 24 | (2) | |
| Dimitrios Chantakias (GRE) | 04.01.1995 | 31 | (3) | 4 |
| Wilde-Donald Guerrier (HAI) | 31.03.1989 | 7 | (3) | |
| Sertan Taşqın | 08.10.1997 | 12 | (17) | 5 |
| Təmkin Xəlilzadə | 06.08.1993 | 8 | (3) | |
| **Midfielders:** | **DOB** | **M** | **(s)** | **G** |
| Mirsahib Abbasov | 19.01.1993 | | (1) | |
| Samir Ağayev | 25.05.2002 | | (1) | |
| Qismat Alıyev | 24.10.1996 | 30 | (4) | |
| Pərviz Azadov | 19.10.2000 | | (1) | |
| Coşqun Diniyev | 13.09.1995 | 21 | (9) | 2 |

| | DOB | M | (s) | G |
|---|---|---|---|---|
| Ramin Əhmədov | 01.05.2001 | | (7) | |
| Hacıağa Hacılı | 30.01.1998 | 18 | (8) | |
| Abbas Ibrahim (NGA) | 02.01.1998 | 4 | (4) | |
| Eldar Kuliev (UKR) | 24.03.2002 | 11 | (3) | 2 |
| Andrija Luković (SRB) | 24.10.1994 | 17 | (11) | |
| İlkin Muradov | 05.03.1996 | 6 | (7) | |
| Ramiz Muradov | 06.07.2005 | | (1) | |
| **Forwards:** | **DOB** | **M** | **(s)** | **G** |
| Rustam Əhmədzadə | 25.12.2000 | 18 | (14) | 2 |
| Loris Brogno (BEL) | 18.09.1992 | 18 | (8) | 3 |
| Issa Djibrilla (NIG) | 01.01.1996 | 6 | (3) | |
| *Filipe* Pachtmann (BRA) | 11.04.2000 | 3 | (8) | 1 |
| Mohamed Hamdaoui (NED) | 10.06.1993 | 21 | (8) | 1 |
| Hamidou Keyta (FRA) | 17.12.1994 | 32 | | 8 |
| Vladyslav Kulach (UKR) | 07.05.1993 | 4 | (4) | 3 |
| Rahim Sadıxov | 18.07.1996 | 36 | | 7 |
| *Toni* Correia *Gomes* (GNB) | 16.11.1998 | 4 | (20) | 3 |

| | | | | | | | | | |
|---|---|---|---|---|---|---|---|---|---|
| 1. | Araz-Naxçıvan PFK (*Promoted*) | 28 | 22 | 3 | 3 | 69 | - | 22 | 69 |
| 2. | Neftçi PFK-2 Bakı | 28 | 18 | 5 | 5 | 67 | - | 32 | 59 |
| 3. | Turan-2 Tovuz | 28 | 15 | 3 | 10 | 49 | - | 37 | 48 |
| 4. | Səbail FK-2 Bakı | 28 | 13 | 5 | 10 | 46 | - | 44 | 44 |
| 5. | Qəbələ FK-2 | 28 | 12 | 8 | 8 | 45 | - | 28 | 44 |
| 6. | Zaqatala PFK | 28 | 13 | 5 | 10 | 49 | - | 48 | 44 |
| 7. | Kəpəz PFK-2 Gəncə | 28 | 13 | 4 | 11 | 41 | - | 36 | 43 |
| 8. | MOIK Bakı | 28 | 12 | 7 | 9 | 43 | - | 42 | 43 |
| 9. | Qaradağ Lökbatan FK | 28 | 12 | 5 | 11 | 30 | - | 23 | 41 |
| 10. | Şamaxı FK-2 | 28 | 11 | 4 | 13 | 40 | - | 56 | 37 |
| 11. | Qarabağ FK-2 Bakı | 28 | 9 | 4 | 15 | 32 | - | 39 | 31 |
| 12. | Zirə FK-2 Bakı | 28 | 6 | 10 | 12 | 28 | - | 41 | 28 |
| 13. | Sumqayıt FK-2 | 28 | 6 | 4 | 18 | 36 | - | 60 | 22 |
| 14. | Energetik FK Mingəçevir | 28 | 5 | 5 | 18 | 29 | - | 51 | 20 |
| 15. | Mil-Muğan FK İmişli | 28 | 6 | 2 | 20 | 21 | - | 66 | 20 |

# NATIONAL TEAM

## INTERNATIONAL MATCHES
(16.07.2022 – 15.07.2023)

| 22.09.2022 | Trnava | *Slovakia - Azerbaijan* | *1-2(0-1)* | (UNL) |
|---|---|---|---|---|
| 25.09.2022 | Bakı | *Azerbaijan - Kazakhstan* | *3-0(0-0)* | (UNL) |
| 16.11.2022 | Chişinău | *Moldova - Azerbaijan* | *1-2(0-2)* | (F) |
| 20.11.2022 | Skopje | *North Macedonia - Azerbaijan* | *1-3(1-1)* | (F) |
| 24.03.2023 | Linz | *Austria - Azerbaijan* | *4-1(2-0)* | (ECQ) |
| 27.03.2023 | Stockholm | *Sweden - Azerbaijan* | *5-0(1-0)* | (ECQ) |
| 17.06.2023 | Bakı | *Azerbaijan - Estonia* | *1-1(0-1)* | (ECQ) |

**22.09.2022   SLOVAKIA - AZERBAIJAN               1-2(0-1)**          3rd UEFA Nations League C, Group 3
Štadión "Antona Malatinského", Trnava; Referee: William Sean Collum (Scotland); Attendance: 2,875
**AZE:** Şahruddin Məhəmmədəliyev, Hoccət Haqqverdi, Bəhlul Mustafazadə, Badavi Hüseynov, Elvin Cəfərquliyev, Richard Almeyda de Oliveira (72.Aleksey Isaev), Eddi Silvestr Paskual İsrafilov, Emin Mahmudov (Cap) (83.Elvin Camalov), Ozan Kökçü (72.Amin Seydiyev), Ramil Şeydayev, Renat Dadaşov (77.Musa Qurbanlı). Trainer: Giovanni Girolamo De Biasi (Italy).
**Goals:** Renat Dadaşov (44), Hoccət Haqqverdi (90+5).

**25.09.2022   AZERBAIJAN - KAZAKHSTAN               3-0(0-0)**          3rd UEFA Nations League C, Group 3
Dalğa Arena, Bakı; Referee: Harm Osmers (Germany); Attendance: 2,950
**AZE:** Şahruddin Məhəmmədəliyev, Hoccət Haqqverdi, Bəhlul Mustafazadə, Badavi Hüseynov, Elvin Cəfərquliyev (57.Toral Bayramov), Eddi Silvestr Paskual İsrafilov (46.Aleksey Isaev), Emin Mahmudov (Cap), Filip Ozobić (88.Anatoli Nuriyev), Ozan Kökçü (46.Mahir Emreli), Ramil Şeydayev, Renat Dadaşov (46.Musa Qurbanlı). Trainer: Giovanni Girolamo De Biasi (Italy).
**Goals:** Aleksandr Marochkin (66 own goal), Filip Ozobić (74), Anatoli Nuriyev (90+1).

**16.11.2022   MOLDOVA - AZERBAIJAN               1-2(0-2)**          Friendly International
Stadionul Zimbru, Chişinău; Referee: Denys Shurman (Ukraine); Attendance: 3,742
**AZE:** Şahruddin Məhəmmədəliyev, Hoccət Haqqverdi, Bəxtiyar Həsənalızadə, Anton Krivotsyuk, Elvin Cəfərquliyev (84.Azər Salahlı), Richard Almeyda de Oliveira (66.Elvin Camalov), Emin Mahmudov (Cap) (84.Anatoli Nuriyev), Aleksey Isaev, Ozan Kökçü (46.Mahir Emreli), Ramil Şeydayev (84.Namiq Ələsgərov), Musa Qurbanlı (66.Renat Dadaşov). Trainer: Giovanni Girolamo De Biasi (Italy).
**Goals:** Emin Mahmudov (28), Aleksey Isaev (43).

**20.11.2022   NORTH MACEDONIA - AZERBAIJAN               1-3(1-1)**          Friendly International
Nacionalna Arena "Toše Proeski", Skopje; Referee: Enea Jorgji (Albania); Attendance: 1,000
**AZE:** Şahruddin Məhəmmədəliyev, Hoccət Haqqverdi [*sent off 75*], Bəhlul Mustafazadə (68.Anton Krivotsyuk), Bəxtiyar Həsənalızadə, Elvin Cəfərquliyev (79.Azər Salahlı), Richard Almeyda de Oliveira (79.Qismət Alıyev), Emin Mahmudov (Cap) (68.Ceyhun Nuriyev), Ramil Şeydayev, Aleksey Isaev (59.Elvin Camalov), Ozan Kökçü (59.Mahir Emreli), Musa Qurbanlı. Trainer: Giovanni Girolamo De Biasi (Italy).
**Goals:** Elvin Cəfərquliyev (35), Musa Qurbanlı (65), Ramil Şeydayev (88).

**24.03.2023   AUSTRIA - AZERBAIJAN               4-1(2-0)**          17th EC. Qualifiers
Raiffeisen Arena, Linz; Referee: Bartosz Frankowski (Poland); Attendance: 16,500
**AZE:** Yusif İmanov, Hoccət Haqqverdi, Bəxtiyar Həsənalızadə (46.Anton Krivotsyuk), Bəhlul Mustafazadə, Elvin Cəfərquliyev (46.Azər Əliyev), Richard Almeyda de Oliveira (77.Aleksey Isaev), Eddi Silvestr Paskual İsrafilov (60.Elvin Camalov), Emin Mahmudov (Cap), Ozan Kökçü (46.Namiq Ələsgərov), Ramil Şeydayev, Renat Dadaşov. Trainer: Giovanni Girolamo De Biasi (Italy).
**Goal:** Emin Mahmudov (64).

**27.03.2023   SWEDEN - AZERBAIJAN               5-0(1-0)**          17th EC. Qualifiers
Friends Arena, Stockholm; Referee: Stéphanie Frappart (France); Attendance: 23,674
**AZE:** Emil Balayev, Hoccət Haqqverdi (73.Cəlal Hüseynov), Bəhlul Mustafazadə, Anton Krivotsyuk, Elvin Cəfərquliyev (73.Namiq Ələsgərov), Richard Almeyda de Oliveira, Aleksey Isaev (82.Musa Qurbanlı), Emin Mahmudov (Cap), Ramil Şeydayev, Toral Bayramov, Renat Dadaşov. Trainer: Giovanni Girolamo De Biasi (Italy).

**17.06.2023**    **AZERBAIJAN - ESTONIA**                    **1-1(0-1)**                    17th EC. Qualifiers

Dalga Arena, Bakı; Referee: Ondřej Berka (Czech Republic); Attendance: 3,900

**AZE:** Şahruddin Məhəmmədəliyev, Hoccət Haqqverdi (46.Qismət Alıyev), Badavi Hüseynov, Bəhlul Mustafazadə, Elvin Cəfərquliyev (46.Toral Bayramov), Elvin Camalov (46.Anton Krivotsyuk), Emin Mahmudov (Cap), Aleksey Isaev (80.Filip Ozobić), Mahir Emreli, Ramil Şeydayev, Renat Dadaşov (80.Musa Qurbanlı). Trainer: Giovanni Girolamo De Biasi (Italy).

**Goal:** Anton Krivotsyuk (62).

| NATIONAL TEAM PLAYERS | | | | |
|---|---|---|---|---|
| (16.07.2022 – 15.07.2023) | | | | |

| Name | DOB | Caps | Goals | Club |
|---|---|---|---|---|
| **Goalkeepers** | | | | |
| Emil BALAYEV | 17.04.1994 | 14 | 0 | 2023: *Səbail FK Bakı* |
| Yusif İMANOV | 27.09.2002 | 1 | 0 | 2023: *Sabah FK Bakı* |
| Şahruddin MƏHƏMMƏDƏLIYEV | 12.06.1994 | 20 | 0 | 2022/2023: *Qarabağ FK Bakı* |
| **Defenders** | | | | |
| Elvin CƏFƏRQULIYEV | 26.10.2000 | 11 | 1 | 2022/2023: *Qarabağ FK Bakı* |
| Hoccət HAQQVERDI | 03.02.1993 | 20 | 1 | 2022: *Tractor CSEC Tabriz (IRN)* |
| | | | | 09.01.2023-> *Neftçi PFK Bakı* |
| Bədavi HÜSEYNOV | 11.07.1991 | 67 | 1 | 2022/2023: *Qarabağ FK Bakı* |
| Cəlal HÜSEYNOV | 02.01.2003 | 5 | 0 | 2023: *Şamaxı FK* |
| Bəxtiyar HƏSƏNALIZADƏ | 29.12.1992 | 3 | 0 | 2022/2023: *Sabah FK Bakı* |
| Anton KRIVOTSYUK | 20.08.1998 | 30 | 1 | 2022: *Wisła Płock (POL)* |
| | | | | 21.02.2023-> *Daejeon Hana Citizen FC (KOR)* |
| Bəhlul MUSTAFAZADƏ | 27.02.1997 | 24 | 0 | 2022/2023: *Qarabağ FK Bakı* |
| Azər SALAHLI | 11.04.1994 | 24 | 1 | 2022: *Neftçi PFK Bakı* |
| Amin SEYDIYEV | 15.11.1998 | 7 | 0 | 2022: *Sabah FK Bakı* |
| **Midfielders** | | | | |
| Richard (Riçard) ALMEYDA de Oliveira | 20.03.1989 | 31 | 3 | 2022/2023: *Qarabağ FK Bakı* |
| Qismət ALIYEV | 24.10.1996 | 3 | 0 | 2022/2023: *Zirə FK Bakı* |
| Toral BAYRAMOV | 23.02.2001 | 13 | 0 | 2022/2023: *Qarabağ FK Bakı* |
| Elvin CAMALOV | 04.02.1995 | 11 | 0 | 2022/2023: *Sabah FK Bakı* |
| Namiq ƏLƏSGƏROV | 03.02.1995 | 39 | 0 | 2022/2023: *Sabah FK Bakı* |
| Azər ƏLIYEV | 12.05.1994 | 1 | 0 | 2023: *Neftçi PFK Bakı* |
| Aleksey ISAYEV | 09.11.1995 | 14 | 1 | 2022/2023: *Sabah FK Bakı* |
| Eddi Silvestr Paskual İSRAFILOV | 02.08.1992 | 22 | 0 | 2022/2023: *Neftçi PFK Bakı* |
| Ozan KÖKÇÜ | 18.08.1998 | 5 | 0 | 2022/2023: *FC Eindhoven (NED)* |
| Emin MAHMUDOV | 27.04.1992 | 39 | 10 | 2022/2023: *Neftçi PFK Bakı* |
| Ceyhun NURIYEV | 30.03.2001 | 1 | 0 | 2022: *Sabah FK Bakı* |
| Filip OZOBIĆ | 08.04.1991 | 11 | 1 | 2022/2023: *Qarabağ FK Bakı* |
| **Forwards** | | | | |
| Renat DADAŞOV | 17.05.1999 | 22 | 1 | 2022/2023: *Grasshopper Club Zürich (SUI)* |
| Mahir EMRELI | 01.07.1997 | 40 | 5 | 2022: *GNK Dinamo Zagreb (CRO)* |
| | | | | 14.02.2023-> *Konyaspor Kulübü (TUR)* |
| Musa QURBANLI | 13.04.2002 | 7 | 1 | 2022/2023: *Qarabağ FK Bakı* |
| Anatoli NURIYEV | 20.05.1996 | 13 | 1 | 2022: *Sumqayıt FK* |
| Ramil ŞEYDAYEV | 15.03.1996 | 55 | 9 | 2022/2023: *Qarabağ FK Bakı* |
| **Trainer** | | | | |
| Giovanni Girolamo DE BIASI (ITA) [from 11.07.2020] | 16.06.1956 | 33 M; 7 W; 8 D; 18 L; 27-48 | | |

# BELARUS

## The Country:
Рэспубліка Беларусь (Republic of Belarus)
Capital: Minsk
Surface: 207,595 km$^2$
Inhabitants: 9,413,505 [2022]
Time: UTC+3

## The FA:
Belaruskaya Federatiya Futbola
Prospekt Pobeditelei, 20/3 220020, Minsk
Tel: +375 17 254 56 00
Foundation date: 1889
Member of FIFA since: 1992
Member of UEFA since: 1993
Website: www.bff.by

## NATIONAL TEAM RECORDS

### RECORDS
| | |
|---|---|
| **First international match:** | 28.10.1992, Minsk: Belarus – Ukraine 1-1 |
| **Most international caps:** | Alyaksandr Kulchy - 102 caps (1996-2012) |
| **Most international goals:** | Maxym Romashchenko - 20 goal / 64 caps (1998-2008) |

### UEFA EUROPEAN CHAMPIONSHIP
|  |  |
|---|---|
| 1960 | - |
| 1964 | - |
| 1968 | - |
| 1972 | - |
| 1976 | - |
| 1980 | - |
| 1984 | - |
| 1988 | - |
| 1992 | - |
| 1996 | Qualifiers |
| 2000 | Qualifiers |
| 2004 | Qualifiers |
| 2008 | Qualifiers |
| 2012 | Qualifiers |
| 2016 | Qualifiers |
| 2020 | Qualifiers |

### FIFA WORLD CUP
|  |  |
|---|---|
| 1930 | - |
| 1934 | - |
| 1938 | - |
| 1950 | - |
| 1954 | - |
| 1958 | - |
| 1962 | - |
| 1966 | - |
| 1970 | - |
| 1974 | - |
| 1978 | - |
| 1982 | - |
| 1986 | - |
| 1990 | - |
| 1994 | Did not enter |
| 1998 | Qualifiers |
| 2002 | Qualifiers |
| 2006 | Qualifiers |
| 2010 | Qualifiers |
| 2014 | Qualifiers |
| 2018 | Qualifiers |
| 2022 | Qualifiers |

### OLYMPIC TOURNAMENTS
|  |  |
|---|---|
| 1908 | - |
| 1912 | - |
| 1920 | - |
| 1924 | - |
| 1928 | - |
| 1936 | - |
| 1948 | - |
| 1952 | - |
| 1956 | - |
| 1960 | - |
| 1964 | - |
| 1968 | - |
| 1972 | - |
| 1976 | - |
| 1980 | - |
| 1984 | - |
| 1988 | - |
| 1992 | - |
| 1996 | Qualifiers |
| 2000 | Qualifiers |
| 2004 | Qualifiers |
| 2008 | Qualifiers |
| 2012 | Final Tournament (Group Stage) |
| 2016 | Qualifiers |
| 2020 | Qualifiers |

Please note: *was part of Soviet Union until 1990.*

## UEFA NATIONS LEAGUE
| | |
|---|---|
| 2018/2019 | League D (Group Stage -> promoted to League League C) |
| 2020/2021 | League C (Group Stage) |
| 2022/2023 | League C (Group Stage -> relegation Play-outs in March 2024) |

## BELARUSIAN CLUB HONOURS IN EUROPEAN CLUB COMPETITIONS:

### European Champion Clubs.Cup (1956-1992) / UEFA Champions League (1993-2023)
None

### Fairs Cup (1858-1971) / UEFA Cup (1972-2009) / UEFA Europa League (2010-2023)
None

### UEFA Europa Conference League (2021-2023)
None

### UEFA Super Cup (1972-2022)
None

### European Cup Winners' Cup 1961-1999*
None

*defunct competition*

# NATIONAL COMPETITIONS
## TABLE OF HONOURS

### BELARUS SSR (SOVIET ERA) CHAMPIONS

| | | | | | | |
|---|---|---|---|---|---|---|
| 1922 | Minsk (city team) | 1949 | Traktor MTZ Minsk | 1970 | Torpedo Zhodino |
| 1923 | *Not known* | 1950 | ODO Minsk | 1971 | Torpedo Zhodino |
| 1924 | Minsk (city team) | 1951 | Dinamo Minsk | 1972 | Stroitel.Bobruisk |
| 1925 | *Not known* | 1952 | ODO Minsk | 1973 | Stroitel.Bobruisk |
| 1926 | Bobruisk (city team) | 1953 | Spartak Minsk | 1974 | BATE Borisov |
| 1927 | Unknown | 1954 | ODO Minsk | 1975 | Dinamo Minsk |
| 1928 | Gomel (city team) | 1955 | FSM Minsk | 1976 | BATE Borisov |
| 1929–32 | *Not known* | 1956 | Spartak Minsk | 1977 | Sputnik Minsk |
| 1933 | Gomel (city team) | 1957 | Sputnik Minsk | 1978 | Shinnik Bobruisk |
| 1934 | BVO Minsk | 1958 | Spartak Bobruisk | 1979 | BATE Borisov |
| 1935 | BVO Minsk | 1959 | Minsk (city team) | 1980 | Torpedo Zhodino |
| 1936 | BVO Minsk | 1960 | Sputnik Minsk | 1981 | Torpedo Zhodino |
| 1937 | Dinamo Minsk | 1961 | Volna Pinsk | 1982 | Torpedo Mogilev |
| 1938 | Dinamo Minsk | 1962 | Torpedo Minsk | 1983 | Obuvschik Lida |
| 1939 | Dinamo Minsk | 1963 | Naroch.Molodechno | 1984 | Orbita Minsk |
| 1940 | DKA Minsk | 1964 | SKA Minsk | 1985 | Obuvschik Lida |
| 1941–44 | *Not known* | 1965 | SKA Minsk | 1986 | Obuvschik Lida |
| 1945 | Dinamo Minsk | 1966 | Torpedo Minsk | 1987 | Shinnik Bobruisk |
| 1946 | ODO Minsk | 1967 | Torpedo Minsk | 1988 | Sputnik Minsk |
| 1947 | Torpedo Minsk | 1968 | Sputnik Minsk | 1989 | Obuvschik Lida |
| 1948 | Traktor MTZ Minsk | 1969 | Torpedo Minsk | 1990 | Sputnik Minsk |
| | | | | 1991 | Metallurg Molodechno |

| | CHAMPIONS | CUP WINNERS | BEST GOALSCORERS | |
|---|---|---|---|---|
| 1992 | FC Dinamo Minsk | FC Dinamo Minsk | Andrey Skorobogatko (FC Dnepr Mogilev) | 11 |
| 1992/1993 | FC Dinamo Minsk | FC Neman Grodno | Syarhey Baranovsky (FC Dinamo Minsk) Miroslav Romaschenko (FC Vedrich Rechitsa / FC Dnepr Mogilev) | 19 |
| 1993/1994 | FC Dinamo Minsk | FC Dinamo Minsk | Pyotr Kachuro (FC Dinamo-93 Minsk / FC Dinamo Minsk) | 21 |
| 1994/1995 | FC Dinamo Minsk | - | Pavel Shavrov (FC Dinamo-93 Minsk) | 19 |
| 1995 | FC Dinamo Minsk | FC Dinamo-93 Minsk | Syarhey Yaromko (MPKC Mozyr) | 16 |
| 1996 | MPKC Mozyr | MPKC Mozyr | Andrey Khlebasolaw (FC Belshina Bobruisk) | 34 |
| 1997 | FC Dinamo Minsk | FC Belshina Bobruisk | Andrey Khlebasolaw (FC Belshina Bobruisk) | 19 |
| 1998 | FC Dnepr Mogilev | FC Lokomotiv-96 Vitebsk | Syarhey Yaromko (FC Torpedo Minsk) | 19 |
| 1999 | FC BATE Borisov | FC Belshina Bobruisk | Valery Strypeykis (FC Slavia Mozyr) | 21 |
| 2000 | FC Slavia Mozyr | FC Slavia Mozyr | Raman Vasilyuk (FC Slavia Mozyr) | 31 |
| 2001 | FC Belshina Bobruisk | FC Belshina Bobruisk | Sergei Davydov (RUS, FC Neman Grodno) | 25 |
| 2002 | FC BATE Borisov | FC Gomel | Valery Strypeykis (FC Belshina Bobruisk) | 18 |
| 2003 | FC Gomel | FC Dinamo Minsk | Gennadi Bliznyuk (FC Gomel) | 18 |
| 2004 | FC Dinamo Minsk | FC Shakhtyor Solihorsk | Valery Strypeykis (Naftan Novopolotsk) | 18 |
| 2005 | FC Shakhtyor Solihorsk | MTZ-RIPO Minsk | Valery Strypeykis (Naftan Novopolotsk) | 16 |
| 2006 | FC BATE Borisov | FC BATE Borisov | Alyaksandr Klimenka (FC Shakhtyor Solihorsk) | 17 |
| 2007 | FC BATE Borisov | FC Dynamo Brest | Raman Vasilyuk (FC Gomel) | 24 |
| 2008 | FC BATE Borisov | MTZ-RIPO Minsk | Gennadi Bliznyuk (FC BATE Borisov) Vitali Rodionov (FC BATE Borisov) | 16 |
| 2009 | FC BATE Borisov | FC Naftan Novopolotsk | Maycon Rogério Silva Calijuri (BRA, FC Gomel) | 15 |
| 2010 | FC BATE Borisov | FC BATE Borisov | Renan Bardini Bressan (BRA, FC BATE Borisov) | 15 |
| 2011 | FC BATE Borisov | FC Gomel | Renan Bardini Bressan (BRA, FC BATE Borisov) | 13 |
| 2012 | FC BATE Borisov | FC Naftan Novopolotsk | Dzmitry Asipenka (FC Shakhtyor Solihorsk) | 14 |
| 2013 | FC BATE Borisov | FC Minsk | Vitali Rodionov (FC BATE Borisov) | 14 |
| 2014 | FC BATE Borisov | FC Shakhtyor Solihorsk | Mikalay Yanush (FC Shakhtyor Solihorsk) | 15 |
| 2015 | FC BATE Borisov | FC BATE Borisov | Mikalay Yanush (FC Shakhtyor Solihorsk) | 15 |
| 2016 | FC BATE Borisov | FC Torpedo-BelAZ Zhodino | Vitali Rodionov (FC BATE Borisov) Mikhayl Gordeichuk (FC BATE Borisov) | 16 |
| 2017 | FC BATE Borisov | FC Dinamo Brest | Mikhayl Gordeichuk (FC BATE Borisov) | 18 |
| 2018 | FC BATE Borisov | FC Dinamo Brest | Pavel Savitski (FC Dinamo Brest) | 15 |
| 2019 | FC Dinamo Brest | FC Shakhtyor Solihorsk | Ilya Shkurin (FC Energetik-BGU Minsk) | 19 |
| 2020 | FC Shakhtyor Solihorsk | FC BATE Borisov | Maksim Skavysh (FC BATE Borisov) | 19 |
| 2021 | FC Shakhtyor Solihorsk | FC BATE Borisov | Dembo Darboe (GAM, FC Shakhtyor Solihorsk) | 19 |
| 2022 | FC Shakhtyor Solihorsk | FC Gomel | Bobir Abdukhalikov (UZB, FC Energetik-BGU Minsk) | 26 |

## NATIONAL CHAMPIONSHIP
### Belarusian Premier League 2022
(18.03.2022 – 12.11.2022)

Please note: FC Rukh Brest withdrew from the league on 28.02.2022 due to financial problems, being replaced by FC Dnepr Mogilev.

## Results

### Round 1 [18-20.03.2022]
FC Minsk - Dinamo Minsk 0-1(0-0)
Energetik-BGU - FC Vitebsk 3-1(0-0)
Neman Grodno - Torpedo-BelAZ 2-0(1-0)
Dinamo Brest - Shakhtyor Solihorsk 1-1(0-0)
Isloch Minsk - FC Slutsk 1-2(0-1)
Arsenal Dzerzhinsk - FC Gomel 1-2(0-1)
Belshina Bobruisk - Dnepr Mogilev 0-0
FC Slaviya Mozyr - BATE Borisov 0-3(0-1)

### Round 2 [02-03.04.2022]
FC Slutsk - Neman Grodno 0-0
Dinamo Minsk - Arsenal Dzerzhinsk 1-1(0-1)
Belshina Bobruisk - BATE Borisov 0-3(0-1)
Dinamo Brest - Isloch Minsk 2-2(0-2)
FC Vitebsk - FC Minsk 1-1(1-0)
Energetik-BGU - Torpedo-BelAZ 3-1(1-1)
FC Gomel - FC Slaviya Mozyr 0-2(0-2)
Shakhtyor Solihorsk - Dnepr Mogilev 4-0(1-0)

### Round 3 [09-11.04.2022]
Energetik-BGU - FC Slutsk 1-1(0-1)
FC Slaviya Mozyr - Dinamo Minsk 1-2(1-0)
FC Minsk - Torpedo-BelAZ 1-0(1-0)
Neman Grodno - Dinamo Brest 2-1(1-0)
Dnepr Mogilev - BATE Borisov 0-3(0-2)
Isloch Minsk - Shakhtyor Solihorsk 1-1(1-1)
Arsenal Dzerzhinsk - FC Vitebsk 0-0
Belshina Bobruisk - FC Gomel 2-3(2-1)

### Round 4 [15-17.04.2022]
FC Slutsk - FC Minsk 2-4(1-2)
Isloch Minsk - Neman Grodno 1-1(0-0)
Torpedo-BelAZ - Arsenal Dzerzhinsk 1-0(1-0)
Shakhtyor Solihorsk - BATE Borisov 0-1(0-1)
Dinamo Minsk - Belshina Bobruisk 0-0
FC Vitebsk - FC Slaviya Mozyr 0-3(0-0)
FC Gomel - Dnepr Mogilev 3-1(1-0)
Dinamo Brest - Energetik-BGU 1-2(0-0)

### Round 5 [21-23.04.2022]
Arsenal Dzerzhinsk - FC Slutsk 1-1(0-1)
Belshina Bobruisk - FC Vitebsk 2-2(0-1)
Neman Grodno - Shakhtyor Solihorsk 1-1(1-0)
BATE Borisov - FC Gomel 2-1(1-0)
Energetik-BGU - Isloch Minsk 1-2(1-1)
FC Slaviya Mozyr - Torpedo-BelAZ 2-2(1-2)
FC Minsk - Dinamo Brest 2-0(1-0)
Dnepr Mogilev - Dinamo Minsk 0-2(0-1)

### Round 6 [30.04.-02.05.2022]
Torpedo-BelAZ - Belshina Bobruisk 1-3(1-2)
FC Slutsk - FC Slaviya Mozyr 1-0(0-0)
Isloch Minsk - FC Minsk 2-0(2-0)
Dinamo Brest - Arsenal Dzerzhinsk 0-0
FC Vitebsk - Dnepr Mogilev 2-1(1-0)
Neman Grodno - Energetik-BGU 1-4(1-2)
Shakhtyor Solihorsk - FC Gomel 1-0(0-0)
Dinamo Minsk - BATE Borisov 2-2(0-0)

### Round 7 [07-08.05.2022]
Arsenal Dzerzhinsk - Isloch Minsk 1-3(0-2)
Dnepr Mogilev - Torpedo-BelAZ 0-1(0-1)
Belshina Bobruisk - FC Slutsk 0-2(0-2)
FC Slaviya Mozyr - Dinamo Brest 3-1(2-0)
FC Minsk - Neman Grodno 3-2(2-0)
BATE Borisov - FC Vitebsk 2-1(1-1)
Energetik-BGU-Shakhtyor Solihorsk 0-1(0-0)
FC Gomel - Dinamo Minsk 0-1(0-0)

### Round 8 [13-15.05.2022]
FC Vitebsk - FC Gomel 1-1(0-0)
Torpedo-BelAZ - BATE Borisov 0-0
Energetik-BGU - FC Minsk 2-0(0-0)
Dinamo Brest - Belshina Bobruisk 1-1(0-0)
Shakhtyor Solihorsk - Dinamo Minsk 1-0(0-0)
Isloch Minsk - FC Slaviya Mozyr 0-2(0-0)
FC Slutsk - Dnepr Mogilev 2-2(2-1)
Neman Grodno - Arsenal Dzerzhinsk 2-0(1-0)

### Round 9 [20-22.05.2022]
FC Minsk - Shakhtyor Solihorsk 1-0(0-0)
Arsenal Dzerzhinsk - Energetik-BGU 0-2(0-2)
Belshina Bobruisk - Isloch Minsk 3-1(0-0)
Dnepr Mogilev - Dinamo Brest 2-0(0-0)
FC Slaviya Mozyr - Neman Grodno 1-1(0-1)
Dinamo Minsk - FC Vitebsk 2-1(1-0)
BATE Borisov - FC Slutsk 4-0(2-0) [29.06.22]
Gomel - Torpedo-BelAZ 1-0(1-0) [29.06.22]

### Round 10 [26-29.05.2022]
FC Minsk - Arsenal Dzerzhinsk 2-0(1-0)
Isloch Minsk - Dnepr Mogilev 3-2(0-0)
FC Slutsk - FC Gomel 2-0(0-0)
Dinamo Brest - BATE Borisov 0-3(0-2)
Torpedo-BelAZ - Dinamo Minsk 3-4(2-2)
Shakhtyor Solihorsk - FC Vitebsk 2-0(1-0)
Energetik-BGU - FC Slaviya Mozyr 5-0(2-0)
Neman Grodno - Belshina Bobruisk 2-2(1-0)

### Round 11 [17-19.06.2022]
Belshina Bobruisk - Energetik-BGU 0-1(0-0)
FC Vitebsk - Torpedo-BelAZ 0-1(0-1)
Dnepr Mogilev - Neman Grodno 1-3(0-0)
BATE Borisov - Isloch Minsk 0-1(0-0)
Dinamo Minsk - FC Slutsk 1-1(1-1)
Arsenal Dz. - Shakhtyor Solihorsk 1-2(0-1)
FC Gomel - Dinamo Brest 1-0(0-0)
FC Slaviya Mozyr - FC Minsk 4-2(2-1)

### Round 12 [25-27.06.2022]
Isloch Minsk - FC Gomel 1-1(1-1)
FC Slutsk - FC Vitebsk 0-2(0-1)
Shakhtyor Solihorsk-Torpedo-BelAZ 0-1(0-1)
Neman Grodno - BATE Borisov 0-0
FC Minsk - Belshina Bobruisk 2-4(1-1)
Dinamo Brest - Dinamo Minsk 1-3(0-1)
Arsenal Dzerzh. - FC Slaviya Mozyr 3-2(2-1)
Energetik-BGU - Dnepr Mogilev 1-1(1-0)

### Round 13 [02-04.07.2022]
Belshina Bobruisk - Arsenal Dzerzh. 1-0(1-0)
Dinamo Minsk - Isloch Minsk 1-2(0-0)
FC Vitebsk - Dinamo Brest 0-1(0-0)
BATE Borisov - Energetik-BGU 1-1(1-0)
FC Gomel - Neman Grodno 3-0 *awarded*
Dnepr Mogilev - FC Minsk 2-4(0-1)
Torpedo-BelAZ - FC Slutsk 3-0(2-0)
Slaviya M. - Shakhtyor S. 1-3(1-1) [24.07.22]

### Round 14 [08-10.07.2022]
Isloch Minsk - FC Vitebsk 2-0(1-0)
Slaviya Mozyr - Belshina Bobruisk 2-0(1-0)
Energetik-BGU - FC Gomel 0-0
FC Minsk - BATE Borisov 2-2(2-0)
Arsenal Dzerzhinsk - Dnepr Mogilev 1-0(1-0)
Dinamo Brest - Torpedo-BelAZ 0-1(0-1)
Shakhtyor S. - FC Slutsk 2-1(2-0) [29.07.22]
Neman G.-Dinamo Minsk 2-3(1-2) [31.08.22]

### Round 15 [15-18.07.2022]
BATE Borisov - Arsenal Dzerzhinsk 1-2(1-2)
FC Gomel - FC Minsk 0-3(0-1)
FC Vitebsk - Neman Grodno 2-2(1-2)
Torpedo-BelAZ - Isloch Minsk 0-1(0-1)
Dnepr Mogilev - FC Slaviya Mozyr 1-3(0-2)
FC Slutsk - Dinamo Brest 2-0(1-0)
Belshina Bobruisk - Shakhtyor S. 1-2(0-0)
Dinamo Minsk - Energetik 1-4(1-1) [02.11.22]

### Round 16 [05-07.08.2022]
FC Vitebsk - Energetik-BGU 0-3(0-2)
FC Slutsk - Isloch Minsk 2-4(0-2)
Torpedo-BelAZ - Neman Grodno 2-2(1-1)
Dnepr Mogilev - Belshina Bobruisk 4-3(1-0)
FC Gomel - Arsenal Dzerzhinsk 4-1(1-0)
BATE Borisov - FC Slaviya Mozyr 4-0(2-0)
Dinamo Minsk - FC Minsk 3-1(0-1)
Shakhtyor - Dinamo Brest 2-0(2-0) [02.11.22]

### Round 17 [12-15.08.2022]
Torpedo-BelAZ - Energetik-BGU 4-0(1-0)
Neman Grodno - FC Slutsk 1-0(0-0)
Isloch Minsk - Dinamo Brest 1-2(0-0)
FC Minsk - FC Vitebsk 2-0(0-0)
FC Slaviya Mozyr - FC Gomel 0-1(0-1)
BATE Borisov - Belshina Bobruisk 2-2(1-0)
Arsenal Dzerzhinsk - Dinamo Minsk 0-1(0-0)
Dnepr Mogilev - Shakhtyor Solihorsk 0-7(0-3)

### Round 18 [19-22.08.2022]
Torpedo-BelAZ - FC Minsk 1-1(0-0)
FC Slutsk - Energetik-BGU 1-2(1-0)
FC Vitebsk - Arsenal Dzerzhinsk 3-0(3-0)
FC Gomel - Belshina Bobruisk 0-3(0-2)
BATE Borisov - Dnepr Mogilev 2-1(1-1)
Dinamo Minsk - FC Slaviya Mozyr 0-0
Shakhtyor Solihorsk - Isloch Minsk 1-0(1-0)
Dinamo Brest - Neman Grodno 0-0

### Round 19 [26-28.08.2022]
Arsenal Dzerzhinsk - Torpedo-BelAZ 1-2(0-1)
FC Minsk - FC Slutsk 1-0(1-0)
Energetik-BGU - Dinamo Brest 0-0
Belshina Bobruisk - Dinamo Minsk 0-0
Neman Grodno - Isloch Minsk 1-0(1-0)
FC Slaviya Mozyr - FC Vitebsk 0-2(0-1)
Dnepr Mogilev - FC Gomel 0-4(0-2)
BATE Borisov - Shakhtyor Solihorsk 0-2(0-0)

### Round 20 [02-04.09.2022]
FC Slutsk - Arsenal Dzerzhinsk 1-0(0-0)
Dinamo Brest - FC Minsk 3-1(2-1)
Isloch Minsk - Energetik-BGU 2-3(0-0)
FC Vitebsk - Belshina Bobruisk 2-2(2-1)
Torpedo-BelAZ - FC Slaviya Mozyr 1-1(1-1)
Dinamo Minsk - Dnepr Mogilev 4-0(3-0)
Shakhtyor Solihorsk - Neman Grodno 2-2(1-1)
FC Gomel - BATE Borisov 0-1(0-1)

### Round 21 [09-11.09.2022]
Arsenal Dzerzhinsk - Dinamo Brest 0-2(0-1)
FC Slaviya Mozyr - FC Slutsk 1-1(0-1)
FC Minsk - Isloch Minsk 1-5(1-2)
Dnepr Mogilev - FC Vitebsk 2-1(1-0)
BATE Borisov - Dinamo Minsk 0-0
Energetik-BGU - Neman Grodno 2-1(1-0)
Belshina Bobruisk - Torpedo-BelAZ 1-3(1-2)
FC Gomel - Shakhtyor Solihorsk 0-3(0-1)

## Round 22 [16-18.09.2022]
Dinamo Minsk - FC Gomel 3-0(2-0)
FC Vitebsk - BATE Borisov 1-1(0-0)
Shakhtyor Solihorsk-Energetik-BGU 0-1(0-1)
FC Slutsk - Belshina Bobruisk 0-0
Isloch Minsk - Arsenal Dzerzhinsk 2-1(1-0)
Dinamo Brest - FC Slaviya Mozyr 1-3(0-2)
Torpedo-BelAZ - Dnepr Mogilev 1-0(1-0)
Neman Grodno - FC Minsk 1-1(1-0)

## Round 23 [30.09.-02.10.2022]
Dnepr Mogilev - FC Slutsk 1-2(1-0)
FC Gomel - FC Vitebsk 1-0(1-0)
Belshina Bobruisk - Dinamo Brest 2-2(1-2)
Dinamo Minsk - Shakhtyor Solihorsk 1-0(0-0)
BATE Borisov - Torpedo-BelAZ 1-1(0-0)
Arsenal Dzerzhinsk - Neman Grodno 1-1(0-0)
FC Minsk - Energetik-BGU 0-0
FC Slaviya Mozyr - Isloch Minsk 0-1(0-0)

## Round 24 [07-09.10.2022]
Dinamo Brest - Dnepr Mogilev 4-0(1-0)
FC Slutsk - BATE Borisov 0-0
Torpedo-BelAZ - FC Gomel 1-1(1-1)
FC Vitebsk - Dinamo Minsk 0-0
Shakhtyor Solihorsk - FC Minsk 2-1(0-1)
Energetik-BGU - Arsenal Dzerzhinsk 0-1(0-0)
Isloch Minsk - Belshina Bobruisk 2-0(0-0)
Neman Grodno - FC Slaviya Mozyr 2-0(0-0)

## Round 25 [14-15.10.2022]
Arsenal Dzerzhinsk - FC Minsk 0-0
Dinamo Minsk - Torpedo-BelAZ 2-2(1-1)
FC Vitebsk - Shakhtyor Solihorsk 0-5(0-2)
FC Slaviya Mozyr - Energetik-BGU 0-1(0-1)
Belshina Bobruisk - Neman Grodno 1-0(1-0)
Dnepr Mogilev - Isloch Minsk 0-2(0-1)
FC Gomel - FC Slutsk 1-0(0-0)
BATE Borisov - Dinamo Brest 4-1(3-0)

## Round 26 [18-20.10.2022]
FC Minsk - FC Slaviya Mozyr 5-0(3-0)
Torpedo-BelAZ - FC Vitebsk 1-0(1-0)
Shakhtyor S. - Arsenal Dzerzhinsk 3-0(2-0)
Energetik-BGU - Belshina Bobruisk 3-1(1-1)
FC Slutsk - Dinamo Minsk 0-5(0-0)
Dinamo Brest - FC Gomel 1-1(0-0)
Isloch Minsk - BATE Borisov 0-0
Neman Grodno - Dnepr Mogilev 2-0(1-0)

## Round 27 [22-24.10.2022]
Slaviya Mozyr - Arsenal Dzerzhinsk 1-1(0-1)
Belshina Bobruisk - FC Minsk 2-2(2-0)
Dinamo Minsk - Dinamo Brest 0-0
FC Vitebsk - FC Slutsk 0-1(0-0)
Torpedo-BelAZ-Shakhtyor Solihorsk 0-1(0-1)
FC Gomel - Isloch Minsk 3-1(1-1)
Dnepr Mogilev - Energetik-BGU 0-2(0-0)
BATE Borisov - Neman Grodno 2-1(1-0)

## Round 28 [29-30.10.2022]
Energetik-BGU - BATE Borisov 0-2(0-1)
Isloch Minsk - Dinamo Minsk 2-2(2-2)
Dinamo Brest - FC Vitebsk 4-4(3-2)
Shakhtyor Solih. - FC Slaviya Mozyr 1-1(0-1)
FC Slutsk - Torpedo-BelAZ 1-1(0-0)
FC Minsk - Dnepr Mogilev 1-0(0-0)
Arsenal Dzerzhinsk - Belshina Bobruisk 0-0
Neman Grodno - FC Gomel 3-0(0-0)

## Round 29 [06.11.2022]
BATE Borisov - FC Minsk 3-2(1-0)
Dinamo Minsk - Neman Grodno 2-0(0-0)
Belshina Bobruisk-FC Slaviya Mozyr 1-4(0-2)
FC Slutsk - Shakhtyor Solihorsk 0-1(0-1)
FC Vitebsk - Isloch Minsk 1-3(0-1)
FC Gomel - Energetik-BGU 1-2(1-1)
Dnepr Mogilev - Arsenal Dzerzhinsk 0-1(0-1)
Torpedo-BelAZ - Dinamo Brest 0-0

## Round 30 [12.11.2022]
Arsenal Dzerzhinsk - BATE Borisov 0-2(0-1)
Dinamo Brest - FC Slutsk 0-0
Energetik-BGU - Dinamo Minsk 1-3(0-0)
FC Minsk - FC Gomel 1-1(0-1)
Isloch Minsk - Torpedo-BelAZ 3-0(1-0)
Neman Grodno - FC Vitebsk 1-1(1-0)
Shakhtyor Solih. - Belshina Bobruisk 4-1(0-0)
FC Slaviya Mozyr - Dnepr Mogilev 5-0(2-0)

## Final Standings

| | | | | | | | | Total | | Home | | | | | Away | | | | |
|---|---|---|---|---|---|---|---|---|---|---|---|---|---|---|---|---|---|---|---|
| 1. | FC Shakhtyor Solihorsk | 30 | 20 | 5 | 5 | 55 - 17 | 65 | 10 | 2 | 3 | 25 - 9 | 10 | 3 | 2 | 30 - 8 |
| 2. | FC Energetik-BGU Minsk | 30 | 18 | 6 | 6 | 50 - 27 | 60 | 6 | 4 | 5 | 22 - 15 | 12 | 2 | 1 | 28 - 12 |
| 3. | FC BATE Borisov | 30 | 16 | 11 | 3 | 51 - 21 | 59 | 8 | 4 | 3 | 28 - 16 | 8 | 7 | 0 | 23 - 5 |
| 4. | FC Dinamo Minsk | 30 | 16 | 11 | 3 | 50 - 25 | 59 | 6 | 7 | 2 | 23 - 14 | 10 | 4 | 1 | 27 - 11 |
| 5. | FC Isloch Minsk Raion | 30 | 16 | 6 | 8 | 51 - 33 | 54 | 6 | 5 | 4 | 23 - 17 | 10 | 1 | 4 | 28 - 16 |
| 6. | FC Minsk | 30 | 12 | 8 | 10 | 47 - 43 | 44 | 9 | 3 | 3 | 24 - 15 | 3 | 5 | 7 | 23 - 28 |
| 7. | FC Gomel | 30 | 12 | 7 | 11 | 36 - 37 | 43 | 8 | 0 | 7 | 18 - 18 | 4 | 7 | 4 | 18 - 19 |
| 8. | FC Torpedo-BelAZ Zhodino | 30 | 11 | 10 | 9 | 35 - 32 | 43 | 5 | 6 | 4 | 19 - 14 | 6 | 4 | 5 | 16 - 18 |
| 9. | FC Neman Grodno | 30 | 9 | 13 | 8 | 39 - 36 | 40 | 8 | 5 | 2 | 23 - 13 | 1 | 8 | 6 | 16 - 23 |
| 10. | FC Slavia Mozyr | 30 | 10 | 7 | 13 | 42 - 46 | 37 | 4 | 4 | 7 | 21 - 21 | 6 | 3 | 6 | 21 - 25 |
| 11. | FC Slutsk | 30 | 7 | 11 | 12 | 26 - 41 | 32 | 3 | 6 | 6 | 14 - 23 | 4 | 5 | 6 | 12 - 18 |
| 12. | FC Belshina Bobruisk | 30 | 6 | 12 | 12 | 37 - 50 | 30 | 3 | 5 | 7 | 15 - 25 | 3 | 7 | 5 | 22 - 25 |
| 13. | FC Dinamo Brest | 30 | 5 | 12 | 13 | 29 - 43 | 27 | 2 | 8 | 5 | 19 - 22 | 3 | 4 | 8 | 10 - 21 |
| 14. | FC Arsenal Dzerzhinsk (Relegation Play-offs) | 30 | 5 | 8 | 17 | 18 - 42 | 23 | 2 | 5 | 8 | 10 - 20 | 3 | 3 | 9 | 8 - 22 |
| 15. | FC Vitebsk (Relegated) | 30 | 4 | 10 | 16 | 28 - 49 | 22 | 2 | 6 | 7 | 13 - 25 | 2 | 4 | 9 | 15 - 24 |
| 16. | FC Dnepr Mogilev (Relegated) | 30 | 3 | 3 | 24 | 21 - 73 | 12 | 3 | 0 | 12 | 13 - 38 | 0 | 3 | 12 | 8 - 35 |

## Top goalscorers:
| | | |
|---|---|---|
| 26 | Bobir Abdukhalikov (UZB) | FC Energetik-BGU Minsk |
| 21 | Uladzimir Khvashchynski | FC Minsk |
| 11 | Ivan Bakhar | FC Dinamo Minsk |

## Relegation Play-offs [16-20.11.2022]

FC Arsenal Dzerzhinsk - FC Rogachev          3-2(2-0)          1-3(0-1)

FC Rogachev were promoted to Belarusian Premier League 2023.

## NATIONAL CUP
### Kubak Belarusi 2021/2022

### Third Round [22-23.06./10.07./19.07.2021]

| | | | |
|---|---|---|---|
| NFC Krumkachy Minsk - FC Neman Grodno | 1-1 aet; 4-5 pen | FC Belshina Bobruisk - FC Rukh Brest | 1-3(1-2) |
| FC Baranovichi - FC BATE Borisov | 1-6(1-0) | FC Lokomotiv Gomel - FC Isloch Minsk Raion | 3-3 aet; 4-2 pen |
| FC Volna Pinsk - FC Slavia Mozyr | 0-1(0-1) | FC Smolevichy-STI - FC Vitebsk | 1-3(1-0) |
| FC Orsha - FC Gomel | 2-6(1-1) | FC Lida - FC Dinamo Minsk | 0-3(0-0) |
| FC Molodechno - FC Energetik-BGU Minsk | 0-4(0-1) | FC Partizan Solihorsk - FC Sputnik Rechytsa | 2-2 aet; 1-3 pen |
| FC Arsenal Dzerzhinsk - FC Smorgon | 2-1(0-0) | FC Naftan Novopolotsk - FC Dinamo Brest | 2-2 aet; 4-5 pen |
| FC Dnepr Mogilev - FC Minsk | 2-1(1-0) | Dyush-3 Stenles Pinsk - FC Torpedo-BelAZ Zhodino | 0-2(0-2) |
| FC Malorita - FC Slutsk | 1-2(0-1) | FC Uzda - FC Shakhtyor Solihorsk | 0-3(0-2) |

### 1/8-Finals [07-09.08.2021]

| | | | |
|---|---|---|---|
| FC Energetik-BGU Minsk - FC Neman Grodno | 0-4(0-2) | FC Slaviya Mozyr - FC BATE Borisov | 1-2(0-1) |
| FC Sputnik Rechytsa - FC Dnepr Mogilev | 0-3 awarded | FC Torpedo-BelAZ Zhodino - FC Lokomotiv Gomel | 0-0 aet; 5-4 pen |
| FC Slutsk - FC Dinamo Minsk | 0-4(0-2) | FC Dinamo Brest - FC Rukh Brest | 2-0(1-0) |
| FC Vitebsk - FC Arsenal Dzerzhinsk | 0-0 aet; 5-4 pen | FC Shakhtyor Solihorsk - FC Gomel | 1-2(1-0,1-1) |

### Quarter-Finals [06-09./12-13.03.2022]

| First Leg | | Second Leg | |
|---|---|---|---|
| FC Dinamo Minsk - FC Gomel | 1-1(0-0) | FC Gomel - FC Dinamo Minsk | 3-1(2-1) |
| FC Vitebsk - FC Dinamo Brest | 2-0(1-0) | FC Dinamo Brest - FC Vitebsk | 1-0(0-0) |
| FC Neman Grodno - FC Dnepr Mogilev | 3-0(1-0) | FC Dnepr Mogilev - Neman Grodno | 0-0 |
| FC BATE Borisov - FC Torpedo-BelAZ Zhodino | 1-1(0-1) | FC Torpedo-BelAZ Zhodino - FC BATE Borisov | 0-1(0-0) |

### Semi-Finals [06-07./27.04.2022]

| First Leg | | Second Leg | |
|---|---|---|---|
| FC Neman Grodno - FC BATE Borisov | 2-1(0-1) | FC BATE Borisov - FC Neman Grodno | 2-0(1-0) |
| FC Gomel - FC Vitebsk | 2-0(1-0) | FC Vitebsk - FC Gomel | 1-0(0-0) |

### Final

21.05.2022; Dinamo National Olympic Stadium, Minsk; Referee: Vitaly Sevostyanik; Attendance: 10,587
**FC BATE Borisov - FC Gomel**                                                     **1-2(1-0)**

**BATE Borisov**: Andrey Kudravets, Danila Nechaev, Jakov Filipović, Maksim Bordachev, Aleksander Filipović, Alyaksey Nosko (73.Valeriy Hramyka), Willum Þór Willumsson, Stanislaw Drahun (Cap), Dzmitryi Bessmertny (63.Artsyom Shumanskiy), Vladislav Malkevich, Nemanja Milić. Trainer: Aleksandr Mikhailov.

**FC Gomel**: Denis Sadovskiy, Konstantin Kuchinskiy, Syarhey Matvejchik, Artsyom Sokol, Yann Emmanuel Affi, Igor Costrov (Cap), Andrey Potapenko (56.Vasili Sovpel), Ilya Aleksievich, Aleksandr Anufriev (88.Kiryl Yermakovich), Raymond Adeola (90+3.Ihar Kuzmenok), Giorgi Gogolashvili (82.Yuriy Pantya). Trainer: Uladzimir Nevinskiy.

**Goals:** 1-0 Jakov Filipović (21), 1-1 Maksim Bordachev (62 own goal), 1-2 Syarhey Matvejchik (67).

## THE CLUBS 2022

### Football Club Arsenal Dzerzhinsk

| | |
|---|---|
| **Founded**: | 2019 |
| **Stadium**: | Gorodeya Stadium, Gorodeya (1,625) |
| **Trainer**: | Pavel Kirilchik                   04.01.1981 |

| Goalkeepers: | DOB | M | (s) | G |
|---|---|---|---|---|
| Evgeni Abramovich | 17.09.1995 | 29 | | |
| Artsyom Soroko | 01.04.1992 | 1 | | |
| **Defenders:** | **DOB** | **M** | **(s)** | **G** |
| Evgeniy Guletskiy | 15.01.2001 | 17 | (4) | 2 |
| Dzmitry Kaplunov | 21.04.1994 | 11 | (7) | |
| Igor Khaymanov (RUS) | 26.03.1994 | 6 | (1) | |
| Yahor Khvalko | 18.02.1997 | 13 | | 1 |
| Syarhey Kontsevoy | 21.06.1986 | 17 | | |
| Uladislaw Liakh | 13.08.1999 | 7 | (1) | |
| Stanislav Sazonovich | 06.03.1992 | 23 | (4) | 2 |
| Mikita Supranovich | 27.02.2001 | 13 | (1) | |
| Raman Vegerya | 14.07.2000 | 26 | (3) | 1 |
| **Midfielders:** | **DOB** | **M** | **(s)** | **G** |
| Anton Abramovich | 27.04.1999 | 6 | (6) | |
| Stanislav Atrashkevich | 22.10.2002 | 9 | | |
| Fabrice Boudega (CMR) | 24.07.1998 | 5 | (3) | |
| Maksim Gaevoy | 27.05.2002 | | (6) | |

| | DOB | M | (s) | G |
|---|---|---|---|---|
| Fedor Lebedev (RUS) | 25.12.2002 | | (1) | |
| Ruslan Myalkovskiy | 07.05.2006 | 5 | (5) | 1 |
| Mikita Patsko | 23.02.1995 | 14 | (1) | 2 |
| Pavel Seleznev | 11.06.2000 | 1 | (9) | |
| Valery Senko | 07.04.1998 | 17 | (12) | 1 |
| Alyaksandr Skshinetskiy | 28.02.1990 | 27 | (1) | 1 |
| Anton Susha | 25.01.2000 | | (3) | |
| Artiom Vaskov | 21.10.1988 | 14 | | 1 |
| Mikita Yereminok | 25.01.2002 | | (4) | |
| **Forwards:** | **DOB** | **M** | **(s)** | **G** |
| Artsyom Kiyko | 13.01.1996 | 27 | (1) | 2 |
| Dzmitry Matyash | 03.06.2000 | 7 | (14) | 2 |
| Artsyom Miroevskiy | 31.05.1999 | 2 | (10) | |
| Idris Nuradin (NGA) | 15.01.2002 | 2 | (5) | |
| Dmitriy Osipenko | 12.12.1982 | 15 | (9) | 1 |
| Gleb Rassadkin | 05.04.1995 | 10 | (4) | 1 |
| Anton Saroka | 05.03.1992 | 6 | (4) | |

## Football Club BATE Borisov

| | | | |
|---|---|---|---|
| Founded: | 1996 | | |
| Stadium: | Borisov Arena, Borisov (12,896) | | |
| Trainer: | Aleksandr Mikhailov | 21.12.1984 | |
| [17.08.2022] | Siarhey Zenevich | 23.01.1976 | |
| [10.10.2022] | Kirill Alshevsky | 27.01.1982 | |

| Goalkeepers: | DOB | M | (s) | G |
|---|---|---|---|---|
| Vyacheslav Dergachev | 01.07.2001 | 3 | | |
| Andrey Kudravets | 02.09.2003 | 25 | | |
| Denis Scherbitskiy | 14.04.1996 | 2 | | |
| **Defenders:** | **DOB** | **M** | **(s)** | **G** |
| Sidi Bane (SEN) | 14.01.2004 | 4 | (4) | |
| Maksim Bordachev | 18.05.1986 | 24 | (1) | 1 |
| Aleksander Filipović (SRB) | 20.12.1994 | 8 | | 3 |
| Jakov Filipović (CRO) | 17.10.1992 | 28 | | |
| Alyaksandr Martynaw | 15.06.2004 | | (1) | |
| Uladislaw Melko | 19.07.2004 | | (2) | |
| Danila Nyachayew | 30.10.1999 | 28 | | 1 |
| Viktar Sotnikaw | 27.07.2001 | 9 | (1) | |
| Maksim Volodko | 10.11.1992 | 3 | (4) | |
| **Midfielders:** | **DOB** | **M** | **(s)** | **G** |
| Valeriy Bacharow | 10.08.2000 | 27 | | 1 |
| Yamoussa Camara (GUI) | 26.04.2000 | | (2) | |
| Stanislaw Drahun | 04.06.1988 | 27 | (3) | 10 |

| Valeriy Hramyka | 23.01.1997 | 26 | (3) | 5 |
|---|---|---|---|---|
| Wladzislaw Malkevich | 09.12.1999 | 27 | | 4 |
| Alyaksey Nosko | 15.08.1996 | 4 | (3) | |
| Yaroslav Oreshkevich | 08.09.2000 | 7 | (8) | 1 |
| Syarhey Sazonchik | 20.10.2000 | 3 | (11) | |
| Timofey Sharkovsky | 04.02.2004 | 1 | (12) | |
| Willum Þór Willumsson (ISL) | 23.10.1998 | 10 | | 4 |
| Danila Zhulpa | 16.07.2004 | | (1) | |
| **Forwards:** | **DOB** | **M** | **(s)** | **G** |
| Dzmitryi Bessmertny | 03.01.1997 | 25 | (3) | 5 |
| Damjan Dostanić (SRB) | 03.12.2001 | 1 | (9) | |
| Alyaksandr Frantsuzov | 19.05.2004 | | (4) | |
| Nemanja Milić (SRB) | 25.05.1990 | 27 | | 6 |
| Mikita Nyakrasaw | 13.10.2000 | | (7) | 1 |
| Idris Nuradin (NGA) | 15.01.2002 | | (1) | |
| Artsyom Shumanskiy | 25.11.2004 | 4 | (18) | 4 |
| Ilya Vasilevich | 14.04.2000 | 7 | (16) | 3 |

## Football Club Belshina Bobruisk

| | | | |
|---|---|---|---|
| Founded: | 1976 | | |
| Stadium: | Spartak Stadium, Bobruisk (1,625) | | |
| Trainer: | Albert Rybak | 16.05.1973 | |

| Goalkeepers: | DOB | M | (s) | G |
|---|---|---|---|---|
| Artsyom Denisenko | 12.04.1999 | 24 | | |
| Alyaksey Kharitonovich | 30.04.1995 | 1 | | |
| Maksim Vysotsky | 29.01.1995 | 5 | | |
| **Defenders:** | **DOB** | **M** | **(s)** | **G** |
| Alyaksey Matlakh | 31.05.2000 | 4 | (6) | |
| Kirill Rodionov | 09.05.2000 | 20 | (4) | |
| Artur Slabashevich | 09.02.1989 | 24 | (1) | 1 |
| Mikita Sokolovsky | 14.02.2002 | 4 | (12) | 1 |
| Uladislaw Solanovich | 26.05.1999 | 18 | (4) | |
| Ihar Troyakov | 24.02.1995 | 29 | | 5 |
| Dzmitry Zinovich | 29.03.1995 | 21 | | 2 |
| **Midfielders:** | **DOB** | **M** | **(s)** | **G** |
| Alyaksandr Aleksandrovich | 06.07.1997 | 4 | (8) | |
| Ivan Baklanov (RUS) | 16.03.1995 | 8 | | |
| Uladislaw Bolotnikov | 23.01.2004 | | (1) | |
| Dzmitry Denisenko | 23.02.2004 | 5 | (1) | |
| Musa Isah (NGA) | 04.01.2002 | 28 | | 2 |
| Mikhail Kolyadko | 21.11.1988 | 11 | (11) | 1 |

| Ilya Kukharchyk | 10.03.1997 | 23 | (6) | 2 |
|---|---|---|---|---|
| Ilya Vasilyev (RUS) | 24.04.1997 | 16 | (2) | 9 |
| Dzmitry Velisevich | 09.02.1995 | 12 | (14) | |
| Yuri Volovik | 19.06.1993 | | (1) | |
| **Forwards:** | **DOB** | **M** | **(s)** | **G** |
| Sagir Abdulmajeed (NGA) | 30.08.2002 | | (3) | |
| Ilya Belous (RUS) | 01.01.1995 | 2 | (1) | |
| Islam Chesnokov (KAZ) | 21.11.1999 | 24 | (3) | 4 |
| Dmitry Gomza | 03.05.1987 | 19 | (8) | 6 |
| Artsyom Gurenko | 18.06.1994 | 12 | (2) | |
| Ioann Guzov | 07.04.2004 | 1 | (3) | |
| Ramazan Isayev (RUS) | 17.01.1998 | 3 | (7) | |
| Stanislav Lomako | 17.03.2002 | | (2) | 1 |
| Marat Lukyanov | 01.07.2004 | | (2) | |
| Vladislav Nuriev (UZB) | 20.02.1996 | 1 | (5) | |
| Alyaksey Skvorchevskiy | 27.02.1998 | | (4) | |
| Mikita Solonovich | 27.01.2005 | | (2) | |
| Dzmitry Vashkevich | 07.01.2000 | 11 | (13) | 2 |

## Football Club Dinamo Brest

| | | | |
|---|---|---|---|
| Founded: | 1960 | | |
| Stadium: | Regional Sport Complex Brestsky (10,600) | | |
| Trainer: | Syarhey Kovalchuk | 16.12.1973 | |
| [26.05.2022] | Alyaksandr Khrapkovskiy | 12.03.1975 | |
| [13.06.2022] | Andrey Prokopyuk | 21.10.1978 | |

| Goalkeepers: | DOB | M | (s) | G |
|---|---|---|---|---|
| Mikhail Kozakevich | 19.05.2002 | 22 | (1) | |
| Rodion Syamuk | 11.03.1989 | 8 | | |
| **Defenders:** | **DOB** | **M** | **(s)** | **G** |
| Ilya Bogdanovich | 30.01.2004 | | (1) | |
| Munashe Garananga (ZIM) | 18.01.2001 | 24 | | 2 |
| Illya Kolpachuk | 09.10.1990 | 17 | (3) | 1 |
| Uladislaw Krivitsky | 03.07.1995 | 5 | (4) | |
| Vadim Milyutin (RUS) | 08.04.2002 | 6 | (1) | |
| Daniil Miroshnikov | 01.11.2000 | 11 | | |
| Uladzimir Shcherba | 01.04.1986 | 16 | (2) | |
| Andrey Shemruk | 27.04.1994 | 24 | (3) | 1 |
| Uladislaw Yasyukevich | 30.05.1994 | 21 | (2) | 1 |
| Evgeni Yudchits | 25.11.1996 | 22 | (4) | 1 |
| **Midfielders:** | **DOB** | **M** | **(s)** | **G** |
| Alyaksandr Bulychev | 19.11.1999 | 7 | (6) | |
| Dávid Ivan (SVK) | 26.02.1995 | 17 | (3) | |
| Maksim Kolmakov (RUS) | 05.01.2003 | 5 | | 1 |
| Maksim Kovalchuk | 05.03.2000 | 1 | (4) | |

| Kirill Kovalyuk | 19.09.2003 | | (3) | |
|---|---|---|---|---|
| Dzmitry Lesnyak | 06.03.2004 | 8 | (4) | |
| Edgar Olekhnovich | 17.05.1987 | 23 | | 2 |
| Gbenga Muhammed Opamoye (NGA) | 06.04.1998 | 2 | (3) | |
| Yaroslav Oreshkevich | 08.09.2000 | 8 | (1) | 3 |
| Uladislaw Sugak | 30.07.2002 | | (10) | 1 |
| **Forwards:** | **DOB** | **M** | **(s)** | **G** |
| Maksim Artemchuk (RUS) | 09.08.1999 | 9 | (6) | 2 |
| Mikhail Gordeychuk | 23.10.1989 | 15 | | 5 |
| Abdulfatohi Khudoidodzoda | 15.07.2004 | | (5) | |
| Cédric Khaleb Kouadio (CIV) | 25.07.1997 | 11 | (2) | 1 |
| Yevgeni Kozel | 22.02.2001 | 5 | (6) | |
| Syarhey Lynko | 16.10.1989 | 14 | (9) | 2 |
| Daniil Pavlov (RUS) | 05.06.2002 | 9 | (1) | |
| Mukhtar Abayomi Sanusi (NGA) | 28.04.2002 | 1 | (5) | |
| Pavel Satsuk | 14.07.2003 | | (8) | |
| Alyaksandr Shestyuk | 05.06.2002 | 3 | (9) | 4 |
| Kirill Tsepenkov | 08.07.2004 | 16 | (6) | 2 |

## Football Club Dinamo Minsk

**Founded**: 18.06.1927
**Stadium**: Dinamo National Olympic Stadium, Minsk (22,246)
**Trainer**: Vadim Skripchenko     26.11.1975

| Goalkeepers: | DOB | M | (s) | G |
|---|---|---|---|---|
| Yahor Hatkevich | 09.07.1988 | 27 | (1) | |
| Denis Shpakovski | 26.05.2001 | 3 | | |
| **Defenders:** | **DOB** | **M** | **(s)** | **G** |
| Raman Begunov | 22.03.1993 | 13 | (6) | 1 |
| Higor Gabriel Fernandes Alves (BRA) | 28.04.1999 | 12 | | |
| Uladislaw Kalinin | 14.01.2002 | 10 | (1) | |
| Mikita Naumov | 15.11.1989 | 11 | (4) | |
| Edilson Borba De Aquino „Orinho" (BRA) | 24.05.1995 | 12 | (11) | |
| Alyaksandr Sachivko | 05.01.1986 | 9 | (3) | 2 |
| Maksim Shvyatsow | 02.04.1998 | 25 | (2) | 1 |
| Alyaksey Vakulich | 24.06.1998 | 21 | (3) | |
| João William Alves de Jesus (BRA) | 11.06.1996 | 4 | | 1 |
| **Midfielders:** | **DOB** | **M** | **(s)** | **G** |
| Dzmitry Borodin | 19.07.1999 | 2 | (1) | |
| Alyaksey Butarevich | 12.01.1997 | 1 | (2) | |

| | DOB | M | (s) | G |
|---|---|---|---|---|
| Artsyom Bykaw | 19.10.1992 | 24 | (2) | 6 |
| Nikita Demchenko | 06.09.2002 | 8 | (12) | |
| Dzyanis Grachyha | 22.05.1999 | 26 | (1) | 4 |
| Syarhey Kislyak | 06.08.1987 | 15 | (7) | 2 |
| Ivan Khovalko | 09.06.2003 | | (2) | |
| Mikhail Kozlov | 19.02.1990 | 17 | (7) | |
| Anton Putsila | 10.06.1987 | 10 | (2) | 2 |
| Filip Valenčič (SVN) | 07.01.1992 | 4 | (3) | |
| **Forwards:** | **DOB** | **M** | **(s)** | **G** |
| Ivan Bakhar | 10.07.1998 | 24 | (6) | 11 |
| Dušan Bakić (MNE) | 23.02.1999 | 19 | (7) | 8 |
| Zoran Josipović (SUI) | 25.08.1995 | 2 | (9) | 2 |
| Artsyom Kontsevoy | 26.08.1999 | 17 | | 3 |
| Dmitry Latykhov | 25.03.2003 | 2 | (11) | |
| Uladislaw Lozhkin | 25.03.2002 | 10 | (15) | 6 |
| Ivan Pešić (CRO) | 06.04.1992 | 2 | (2) | |

## Football Club Dnepr Mogilev

**Founded**: 1960
**Stadium**: Spartak Stadium, Mogilev (7,350)
**Trainer**: Yevgeniy Molchan     07.07.1986
[13.07.2022] Yuriy Lukasov     29.12.1974
[08.09.2022] Yevgeniy Molchan     07.07.1986

| Goalkeepers: | DOB | M | (s) | G |
|---|---|---|---|---|
| Andrey Ignatovich | 02.05.2003 | 2 | (1) | |
| Vladimir Pyatigorets | 12.04.1990 | 7 | | |
| Nikita Sednev | 21.01.2003 | | (1) | |
| Uladzimir Zhuraw | 09.03.1991 | 21 | | |
| **Defenders:** | **DOB** | **M** | **(s)** | **G** |
| Alyaksey Dunaev | 11.09.2004 | 23 | (1) | |
| Alyaksey Firsov | 07.02.2002 | 15 | (6) | |
| Pavel Markaw | 04.12.1991 | 26 | (1) | 1 |
| Dmitriy Tereshchenko (UKR) | 04.04.1987 | 22 | (1) | |
| Fedor Yurkevich | 06.02.2003 | 10 | (6) | |
| **Midfielders:** | **DOB** | **M** | **(s)** | **G** |
| Pavel Bordukov | 10.04.1993 | 27 | (2) | 1 |
| Artsyom Fedyanin | 25.04.1994 | 11 | (12) | 2 |
| Yuri Klochkov (RUS) | 03.10.1998 | 21 | (7) | 2 |

| | DOB | M | (s) | G |
|---|---|---|---|---|
| Mikita Krasnov | 09.07.2004 | 16 | (6) | 1 |
| Raman Kuleshov | 14.06.2003 | | (5) | |
| Anton Lukashov | 16.09.2004 | 10 | (8) | |
| Alyaksandr Nemirko | 08.02.2000 | 25 | (1) | |
| Uladislaw Puninskiy | 01.07.2002 | 4 | (11) | |
| Pavel Tseslyukevich | 11.05.1995 | 24 | (5) | |
| Gleb Zheleznikov | 31.07.1997 | 14 | (11) | 1 |
| **Forwards:** | **DOB** | **M** | **(s)** | **G** |
| Kirill Gusev | 06.04.1999 | 14 | (12) | 4 |
| Krasimir Kapov | 14.07.1999 | 16 | (12) | 2 |
| Yahor Malatkov | 24.07.2003 | 3 | (7) | |
| Mark Mokin | 26.01.2006 | 3 | (14) | 1 |
| Gleb Vershinin | 11.01.2002 | | (1) | |
| Raman Volkov | 08.01.1987 | 16 | (1) | 4 |

## Football Club Energetik-BGU Minsk

**Founded**: 1996
**Stadium**: RCOR BGU Stadium, Minsk (1,500)
**Trainer**: Pavel Rodnenok     30.07.1964

| Goalkeepers: | DOB | M | (s) | G |
|---|---|---|---|---|
| Stanislau Kliashchuk | 11.04.2000 | 1 | | |
| Artsyom Makavchik | 04.07.2000 | 29 | | |
| **Defenders:** | **DOB** | **M** | **(s)** | **G** |
| Abdukodir Khusanov (UZB) | 29.02.2004 | 27 | | 3 |
| Zaurbek Kokaev (RUS) | 12.04.2000 | 2 | (1) | |
| Aleksei Lavrik | 07.08.2000 | 28 | | 2 |
| Illia Lukashevich | 01.08.1998 | 23 | (2) | |
| Yaroslav Makushinskiy | 05.03.1998 | 28 | | |
| **Midfielders:** | **DOB** | **M** | **(s)** | **G** |
| Shokhrubek Abdurakhmonov (UZB) | 08.03.1999 | 13 | | 1 |
| Ivan Aheyew | 21.04.2005 | | (2) | |
| Maksim Burko | 23.01.2004 | | (2) | |
| Beka Gvaradze (GEO) | 11.08.1997 | 2 | (6) | |
| Abbosbek Jumakulov (UZB) | 01.06.1999 | | (2) | |
| Miroslav Khlebosolov | 18.01.1999 | | (5) | |
| Konstantin Malitskiy (RUS) | 20.05.2000 | | (3) | |
| Albert Mikhailov | 15.10.2002 | | (1) | |

| | DOB | M | (s) | G |
|---|---|---|---|---|
| Maxim Omelyanchuk | 05.09.2003 | 1 | (12) | |
| Pavel Pashevich | 04.06.2001 | 21 | (6) | 1 |
| Oleg Pliev (RUS) | 16.02.1998 | 6 | (7) | |
| Andrey Rylach | 05.06.2002 | 24 | (5) | 1 |
| Maksim Samotoi | 11.10.2001 | | (8) | |
| Alyaksey Semenov | 17.12.2002 | | (4) | |
| Daniil Silinskiy | 06.01.2000 | 30 | | |
| Aliaksandr Svirepa | 24.08.1999 | 29 | | 7 |
| Artsyom Turich | 23.01.2005 | 2 | (13) | 1 |
| Artsyom Zhurko | 08.04.2003 | | (1) | |
| **Forwards:** | **DOB** | **M** | **(s)** | **G** |
| Bobir Abdukhalikov (UZB) | 23.04.1997 | 30 | | 26 |
| Amirbek Bakaev (UZB) | 23.07.2004 | | (4) | |
| Danila Chul | 14.02.2005 | | (12) | |
| Ilya Grishchenko (RUS) | 18.12.2000 | 6 | (23) | 5 |
| Maksim Kunskiy | 09.01.2003 | | (7) | |
| Roman Paparyga (UKR) | 09.07.1999 | 28 | (1) | 2 |

## Football Club Gomel

**Founded**: 1959
**Stadium**: Central Stadium, Gomel (14,307)
**Trainer**: Uladzimir Nevinskiy     14.09.1973

| Goalkeepers: | DOB | M | (s) | G |
|---|---|---|---|---|
| Aleh Kavalyow | 24.05.1987 | 9 | | |
| Denis Sadovskiy | 11.08.1997 | 21 | | |
| **Defenders:** | **DOB** | **M** | **(s)** | **G** |
| Yann Emmanuel Affi (CIV) | 11.11.1995 | 24 | (2) | 1 |
| Konstantin Kuchinskiy | 15.07.1998 | 19 | (6) | |
| Ihar Kuzmenok | 06.07.1990 | 3 | (2) | |
| Syarhey Matvejchik | 05.06.1988 | 21 | (1) | |
| Daniil Miroshnikov | 01.11.2000 | 2 | (1) | |
| Yuriy Pantya (UKR) | 05.04.1990 | 26 | (2) | 1 |
| Kiryl Shawchenka | 26.02.2002 | 2 | (8) | |
| Artsyom Sokol | 30.03.1994 | 25 | (1) | 1 |
| **Midfielders:** | **DOB** | **M** | **(s)** | **G** |
| Ilya Aleksievich | 10.02.1991 | 20 | (3) | 2 |
| Aleksandr Anufriev | 21.07.1995 | 20 | (3) | 5 |

| | DOB | M | (s) | G |
|---|---|---|---|---|
| Dzmitry Baga | 04.01.1990 | 13 | (3) | 1 |
| Igor Costrov (MDA) | 03.08.1987 | 27 | (2) | 1 |
| Uladislaw Drapeza | 31.08.2001 | | (3) | |
| Dzmitry Yemyalyanaw | 02.06.2004 | | (1) | |
| Andrey Potapenko | 09.02.2000 | 25 | | 1 |
| Pavel Sedko | 03.04.1998 | 13 | (4) | 4 |
| Vasili Sovpel | 23.03.1999 | 2 | (15) | |
| Mikita Tsarenko | 09.07.2002 | 1 | | |
| **Forwards:** | **DOB** | **M** | **(s)** | **G** |
| Raymond Adeola (NGA) | 12.05.2001 | 13 | (2) | 2 |
| Giorgi Gogolashvili (GEO) | 02.08.1997 | 4 | (15) | 2 |
| Denis Kozlovskiy | 15.05.1993 | 5 | (5) | 2 |
| Alyaksandr Makas | 08.10.1991 | 22 | (6) | 8 |
| Evgeni Malashevich | 10.12.2002 | 1 | (8) | |
| Kiryl Yermakovich | 11.01.1999 | 12 | (11) | 2 |

## Football Club Isloch Minsk Raion

**Founded**: 2007
**Stadium**: FC Minsk Stadium, Minsk (3,000)
**Trainer**: Artsyom Radzkow      26.08.1985

| Goalkeepers: | DOB | M | (s) | G |
|---|---|---|---|---|
| Syarhey Ignatovich | 29.06.1992 | 24 | | |
| Konstantin Rudenok | 15.12.1990 | 3 | | |
| Timofey Yurasov | 25.02.2003 | 3 | (1) | |
| **Defenders:** | DOB | M | (s) | G |
| Ilya Boltrushevich | 30.03.1999 | 5 | (3) | |
| Junior Yvan Nyabeye Dibango (CMR) | 10.03.2002 | 16 | | 2 |
| Kirill Glushchenkov (RUS) | 05.02.2000 | 13 | (3) | |
| Fard Ibrahim (GHA) | 07.01.2000 | 14 | | 1 |
| Ilya Kalachev (RUS) | 18.01.2000 | 10 | (3) | |
| Maxim Kovel | 12.01.1999 | 10 | (8) | 1 |
| Aleksandr Mikhalenko | 12.12.2001 | 4 | (2) | |
| Vadzim Pigas | 08.08.2001 | 25 | (3) | 1 |
| Mikita Stepanov | 06.04.1996 | 29 | | 2 |
| **Midfielders:** | DOB | M | (s) | G |
| Stanislav Atrashkevich | 22.10.2002 | | (2) | |
| Yamoussa Camara (GUI) | 26.04.2000 | 5 | (4) | |
| Abdoulaye Conde (GUI) | 01.02.2002 | | (1) | |

| | DOB | M | (s) | G |
|---|---|---|---|---|
| Kirill Gomanov | 17.02.2005 | | (2) | |
| Alyaksandr Guz | 22.05.2004 | 3 | (4) | 1 |
| Dzmitry Lisakovich | 10.10.1999 | 28 | | 2 |
| Ruslan Lisakovich | 22.03.2002 | 19 | (4) | 4 |
| Oleg Patotskiy | 24.06.1991 | 15 | | 1 |
| Artsyom Zimin | 24.03.2003 | | (1) | |
| **Forwards:** | DOB | M | (s) | G |
| Martin Artyukh | 06.05.1996 | 2 | (10) | 2 |
| German Barkovskiy | 25.06.2002 | 10 | (4) | 5 |
| Artyom Davidovich | 17.01.2005 | | (1) | |
| Yurii Kozyrenko (UKR) | 27.11.1999 | 13 | | 1 |
| Kirill Leonovich | 21.04.1998 | 5 | (7) | 2 |
| Uladzislaw Marozaw | 12.10.2000 | 16 | (13) | 7 |
| Oleg Nikiforenko | 17.03.2001 | 21 | (6) | 5 |
| Gleb Rovdo | 04.06.2002 | 8 | (12) | 1 |
| Shakhrom Samiev (TJK) | 08.02.2001 | | (8) | 1 |
| Daniel Sosah (NIG) | 21.09.1998 | 29 | | 10 |
| Uladislaw Zhuravlev | 02.07.2004 | | (2) | |

## Football Club Minsk

**Founded**: 2006
**Stadium**: FC Minsk Stadium, Minsk (3,000)
**Trainer**: Vadzim Skripchenko      26.11.1975

| Goalkeepers: | DOB | M | (s) | G |
|---|---|---|---|---|
| Yegor Generalov (RUS) | 24.01.1993 | 6 | | |
| Aleksey Kozlov (RUS) | 23.01.1999 | 13 | | |
| Pavel Prishivalko | 25.07.1999 | 11 | (1) | |
| **Defenders:** | DOB | M | (s) | G |
| Bourama Fomba (MLI) | 10.07.1999 | 12 | (1) | |
| Uladzislaw Grekovich | 01.06.2005 | | (2) | |
| Gleb Gurban | 15.05.2001 | 12 | (5) | |
| Mikita Khalimonchik | 03.01.2000 | 19 | (2) | |
| Andrey Lebedev | 01.02.1991 | 10 | (1) | |
| Alyaksandr Poznyak | 23.07.1994 | 12 | | |
| Gleb Yakushevich | 31.07.2002 | 9 | | |
| Eduard Zhevnerov | 01.11.1987 | 14 | (1) | |
| **Midfielders:** | DOB | M | (s) | G |
| Taysir Adamchik | 11.05.2002 | 1 | | |
| Kirill Chernook | 02.01.2003 | 5 | (20) | 3 |
| Daniil Dushevskiy | 01.03.2004 | 20 | (6) | 2 |
| Alyaksandr Dzhigero | 15.04.1996 | 20 | (9) | 2 |
| Oleg Evdokimov | 25.02.1994 | 15 | | |

| | DOB | M | (s) | G |
|---|---|---|---|---|
| Nikolai Ivanov | 02.01.2000 | | (15) | |
| Yuliy Kuznetsov | 02.08.2003 | | (3) | |
| Andrei Levkovets | 07.05.1996 | 14 | (1) | 1 |
| Aleksa Matić (SRB) | 20.09.2002 | 8 | (3) | |
| Rodion Pechura | 24.03.2004 | 8 | (10) | 2 |
| Syarhey Pushnyakov | 08.02.1993 | 15 | | 1 |
| Mikhail Shibun | 01.01.1996 | | (4) | |
| Maksim Shilo | 17.04.1993 | 8 | (9) | |
| Denis Yaskovich | 30.08.1995 | 26 | (1) | |
| **Forwards:** | DOB | M | (s) | G |
| Yahor Bogomolskiy | 03.06.2000 | 14 | (1) | 8 |
| Saagi Avah Mmbi Dzenyagha (CMR) | 12.12.2001 | 1 | (8) | |
| Uladzimir Khvashchynski | 10.05.1990 | 27 | | 20 |
| Pavel Klenye | 28.04.1999 | | (8) | |
| Evgeni Malashevich | 10.12.2002 | | (1) | |
| Timofey Martynov | 06.05.2005 | 1 | (13) | |
| Semen Penchuk | 17.01.2001 | | (5) | |
| Anton Shramchenko | 12.02.1993 | 29 | | 7 |

## Football Club Neman Grodno

**Founded**: 1964
**Stadium**: Neman Stadium, Grodno (8,479)
**Trainer**: Ihar Kovalevich      03.02.1968

| Goalkeepers: | DOB | M | (s) | G |
|---|---|---|---|---|
| Syarhey Kurganski | 15.05.1986 | 3 | | |
| Artur Maliyevski | 21.08.2001 | 10 | | |
| Konstantin Rudenok | 15.12.1990 | 2 | (1) | |
| Uladislaw Vasilyuchek | 28.03.1994 | 15 | | |
| **Defenders:** | DOB | M | (s) | G |
| Alyaksandr Anyukevich | 10.04.1992 | 5 | (13) | 1 |
| Sherif Olatunde Jimoh (CIV) | 04.05.1996 | 26 | | 1 |
| Syarhey Karpovich | 29.03.1994 | 12 | | |
| Alyaksey Legchilin | 11.04.1992 | 27 | | |
| Evgeni Leshko | 24.06.1996 | 4 | | |
| Ivan Sadownichy | 11.05.1987 | 23 | | 3 |
| Aleksei Shalashnikov | 22.03.2002 | 10 | | |
| Andrey Vasilyev (RUS) | 11.02.1992 | 8 | (1) | |
| **Midfielders:** | DOB | M | (s) | G |
| Nenad Adamović (SRB) | 12.01.1989 | 16 | (2) | 1 |
| Alfred Mazurich | 05.12.2003 | | (2) | |

| | DOB | M | (s) | G |
|---|---|---|---|---|
| Yuri Pavlyukovets | 24.06.1994 | 19 | (6) | |
| Evgeniy Sakuta | 03.02.2000 | | (12) | |
| Anton Suchkow | 29.05.2002 | 5 | (5) | |
| Alimardon Şukurov (KGZ) | 28.09.1999 | 25 | (3) | 1 |
| Maksim Yablonskiy | 15.08.1996 | 6 | (18) | 1 |
| Andrey Yakimov | 17.11.1989 | 25 | (3) | 4 |
| Valeriy Zhukovskiy | 21.05.1984 | 15 | (8) | 3 |
| **Forwards:** | DOB | M | (s) | G |
| Raman Gribovskiy | 17.07.1995 | 1 | (2) | 1 |
| Pa Omar Jobe (GAM) | 26.12.1998 | 1 | (1) | |
| Gegam Kadimyan (ARM) | 19.10.1992 | 1 | (10) | 2 |
| Cédric Khaleb Kouadio (CIV) | 25.07.1997 | 3 | (5) | 2 |
| Kirill Leonovich | 21.04.1998 | | (2) | |
| Raman Pasevich | 28.11.1999 | 22 | (8) | 1 |
| Pavel Savitski | 12.07.1994 | 22 | (1) | 9 |
| Uladislaw Varaksa | 26.01.2004 | 8 | (6) | |
| Yahor Zubovich | 01.06.1989 | 16 | (5) | 7 |

## Football Club Shakhtyor Solihorsk

**Founded**: 1961
**Stadium**: Stroitel Stadium, Solihorsk (4,200)
**Trainer**: Ivan Bionchik — 07.10.1985
[12.04.2022] Sergey Tashuev (RUS) — 01.01.1959
[22.09.2022] Milić Ćurčić (SRB) — 26.01.1981

| Goalkeepers: | DOB | M | (s) | G |
|---|---|---|---|---|
| Syarhey Chernik | 20.07.1988 | 18 | | |
| Maksim Plotnikaw | 29.01.1998 | 12 | | |
| Raman Stsyapanaw | 06.08.1991 | | (1) | |
| **Defenders:** | **DOB** | **M** | **(s)** | **G** |
| Nikola Antić (SRB) | 04.01.1994 | 21 | (4) | 3 |
| Yahor Filipenko | 10.04.1988 | 8 | (2) | 1 |
| Denis Gruzhevsky | 10.03.2000 | 3 | (1) | |
| Ruslan Hadarkevich | 18.06.1993 | 4 | (2) | |
| Syarhey Palitsevich | 09.04.1990 | 22 | | 4 |
| Miloš Šatara (BIH) | 28.10.1995 | 16 | | 1 |
| Hleb Shawchenka | 17.02.1999 | 25 | (3) | |
| Viktor Sotnikov | 27.07.2001 | | (6) | |
| Ilya Sviridenko | 02.10.2002 | | (1) | |
| Luka Šimunović (CRO) | 24.05.1997 | 2 | (4) | |
| Raman Yuzepchuk | 24.07.1997 | 19 | (5) | |
| **Midfielders:** | **DOB** | **M** | **(s)** | **G** |
| Valon Ahmedi (ALB) | 07.10.1994 | 16 | (9) | 2 |
| Zaim Divanović (MNE) | 09.12.2000 | 15 | (8) | 1 |
| Mikita Korzun | 06.03.1995 | 19 | (2) | |
| Ardit Krymi (ALB) | 02.05.1996 | 4 | (7) | |
| Aleksa Pejić (SRB) | 09.07.1999 | 3 | (2) | |
| Pavel Zabelin | 30.06.1995 | 12 | (6) | |
| **Forwards:** | **DOB** | **M** | **(s)** | **G** |
| Ilya Chernyak | 19.05.2002 | 22 | (4) | 7 |
| Dembo Darboe (GAM) | 17.08.1998 | 7 | (4) | 5 |
| Raman Davyskiba | 31.03.2001 | 2 | (6) | |
| Euloge Mêmê Placca Fessou (TOG) | 31.12.1994 | 8 | (8) | 4 |
| Igor Ivanović (SRB) | 28.07.1997 | 19 | (7) | 7 |
| Yahor Karpitsky | 27.11.2003 | 3 | (12) | 3 |
| Dario Kolobarić (SVN) | 06.02.2000 | 1 | (1) | |
| Denis Kozlovskiy | 15.05.1993 | | (2) | |
| Dzmitry Padstrelaw | 06.09.1998 | 18 | (10) | 5 |
| Maksim Skavysh | 13.11.1989 | 23 | (6) | 9 |
| Andrey Solovey | 13.12.1994 | 6 | (13) | 1 |
| Vitor Correia da Silva „Vitor Feijão" (BRA) | 01.08.1996 | 2 | (3) | |

## Football Club Slavia Mozyr

**Founded**: 1987
**Stadium**: Yunost [Junactva] Stadium, Mozyr (5,300)
**Trainer**: Mikhail Martinovich — 14.09.1979
[21.10.2022] Ivan Bionchik — 07.10.1985

| Goalkeepers: | DOB | M | (s) | G |
|---|---|---|---|---|
| Yevgeniy Ivanenko | 22.12.1995 | 3 | | |
| Danila Sokol | 27.02.2001 | 27 | | |
| **Defenders:** | **DOB** | **M** | **(s)** | **G** |
| Andrey Alshanik | 03.05.1999 | 20 | (4) | 2 |
| Georgiy Bugulov (RUS) | 17.03.1993 | 24 | (2) | 1 |
| Vladimir Esin (RUS) | 11.01.1995 | 7 | (9) | |
| Dmitriy Ignatenko | 01.02.1995 | 5 | (6) | 1 |
| Daniil Prudnik | 04.04.2004 | | (1) | |
| Ilya Rutskiy | 03.12.1999 | 20 | (8) | 1 |
| Semen Shestilovskiy | 30.05.1994 | 21 | | 4 |
| Ihar Tymonyuk | 31.03.1994 | 16 | (4) | |
| **Midfielders:** | **DOB** | **M** | **(s)** | **G** |
| Andrey Chukhley | 02.10.1987 | 15 | (2) | |
| Andrei Cobeț (MDA) | 03.01.1997 | 20 | (9) | 5 |
| Cristian Dros (MDA) | 15.04.1998 | 23 | (4) | 1 |
| Yuri Lovets | 11.07.1996 | 28 | | 4 |
| Gbenga Muhammed Opamoye (NGA) | 06.04.1998 | 1 | (1) | |
| Uladislaw Poloz | 06.06.2001 | 2 | (17) | |
| Valeri Potorocha | 16.04.1996 | 21 | (8) | 4 |
| Nikolai Ryabykh | 11.02.2001 | | (3) | 1 |
| Evgeny Zemko | 16.02.1996 | 7 | (3) | |
| Uladislaw Zhuk | 11.06.1994 | 7 | (9) | |
| **Forwards:** | **DOB** | **M** | **(s)** | **G** |
| Evgeni Barsukov | 05.07.1990 | 14 | (10) | 4 |
| Emmanuel Romess Ovono Essogo (GAB) | 26.03.2001 | 21 | (4) | 2 |
| Artsyom Pyatrenka | 01.03.2000 | 1 | (13) | 1 |
| Danila Slesarchuk | 20.09.2001 | | (2) | |
| Gleb Zherdev | 18.05.2000 | 27 | (2) | 10 |

## Football Club Slutsk

**Founded**: 1998
**Stadium**: City Stadium, Slutsk (1,896)
**Trainer**: Alyaksandr Brazevich — 01.06.1973
[31.08.2022] Alyaksandr Gurinovich — 12.05.1985

| Goalkeepers: | DOB | M | (s) | G |
|---|---|---|---|---|
| Ilya Branovets | 16.04.1990 | 30 | | |
| **Defenders:** | **DOB** | **M** | **(s)** | **G** |
| Mikita Bylinkin | 27.01.1999 | 25 | (1) | |
| Pavel Grechishko | 23.03.1989 | 18 | (4) | 1 |
| Denis Obrazov | 24.04.1988 | 20 | (2) | |
| Yuriy Ostroukh | 21.01.1988 | 24 | (2) | 1 |
| Andrei Rum | 19.01.2002 | 6 | (1) | |
| Evgeni Veljko | 23.02.1997 | 15 | (3) | 1 |
| Uladislaw Yatskevich | 29.09.1998 | 3 | (3) | |
| Ihar Zayats | 08.01.1999 | 12 | (1) | |
| Eduard Zhevnerov | 01.11.1987 | 9 | | |
| **Midfielders:** | **DOB** | **M** | **(s)** | **G** |
| Lukuman Aliu (NGA) | 25.03.2003 | 1 | (6) | |
| Dzmitry Girs | 11.06.1997 | 20 | (7) | 1 |
| Syarhey Glebko | 23.08.1992 | 13 | (11) | 3 |
| Arseny Kontsedaylov (RUS) | 15.07.1997 | 22 | (4) | 5 |
| Konstantin Kotov (RUS) | 25.06.1998 | 16 | (1) | 1 |
| Yao Assamoi Kouassi (CIV) | 12.08.2002 | 1 | (1) | |
| Andrey Kren | 11.11.2003 | | (6) | |
| Uladislaw Kulchintski | 25.01.2002 | | (1) | |
| Ivan Mikhnyuk | 01.06.2003 | 6 | (3) | |
| Syarhey Rusak | 03.09.1993 | 4 | (15) | 1 |
| Mikhail Sachkovsky | 21.11.2002 | 24 | (2) | |
| Anton Susha | 25.01.2000 | | (5) | |
| Andrii Vyskrebentsevys (UKR) | 27.10.2000 | 17 | (2) | |
| Yaroslav Yarotski | 28.03.1996 | 7 | (8) | |
| **Forwards:** | **DOB** | **M** | **(s)** | **G** |
| Evgeni Apanasovich | 19.07.2002 | | (2) | |
| Abdoul Gafar Kassoum Sina Sirima (BFA) | 30.12.1998 | 1 | | |
| Jeremie Moussango Obounet (GAB) | 17.08.2002 | 10 | (12) | 2 |
| Raman Piletskij | 14.06.2003 | 1 | (3) | |
| Maksim Sanets | 04.04.1997 | 3 | (9) | 2 |
| Kirill Vergeychik | 23.08.1991 | 22 | (5) | 7 |

## Football Club Torpedo-BelAZ Zhodino

**Founded**: 1961
**Stadium**: Torpedo Stadium, Zhodino (3,020)
**Trainer**: Dzmitry Molosh — 10.12.1981

| Goalkeepers: | DOB | M | (s) | G |
|---|---|---|---|---|
| Vladimir Bushma | 24.11.1983 | 4 | | |
| Dzmitry Dudar | 08.11.1991 | 26 | | |
| **Defenders:** | **DOB** | **M** | **(s)** | **G** |
| Ihar Burko | 08.09.1988 | 21 | (3) | 1 |
| Alyaksandr Chyzh | 10.02.1997 | 8 | (4) | 1 |
| Aleksey Ivanov | 19.02.1997 | 8 | (5) | |
| Grigori Martyanov | 22.08.2002 | 3 | (2) | |
| Vitali Ustinov (RUS) | 03.05.1991 | 27 | | |
| Dmitriy Yashin (RUS) | 25.04.1993 | 14 | (3) | |
| Alyaksey Zaleskiy | 07.10.1994 | 27 | | 1 |
| **Midfielders:** | **DOB** | **M** | **(s)** | **G** |
| Evgeniy Berezkin | 05.07.1996 | 26 | (2) | 3 |
| Andrey Khachaturyan | 02.09.1987 | 3 | (9) | |
| Luiz Felipe Veloso Santos „Lipe" (BRA) | 07.04.1997 | 14 | (2) | 1 |
| Anatoli Makarov | 10.04.1996 | 17 | (8) | |
| Maksim Myakish | 03.03.2000 | 23 | (2) | 1 |
| Yahor Mychelkin | 17.10.2002 | 1 | (6) | |
| Mikita Patsko | 23.02.1995 | 6 | (5) | 1 |
| Kirill Premudrov | 11.06.1992 | 11 | (6) | 1 |
| **Forwards:** | **DOB** | **M** | **(s)** | **G** |
| Alyaksey Antilevskiy | 02.02.2002 | 3 | (19) | 2 |
| Valery Gorbachik | 19.01.1995 | 23 | (5) | 8 |
| Kirill Kirilenko | 08.10.2000 | 1 | (10) | |
| Anton Kovalev | 19.04.2000 | 17 | (10) | 3 |
| Vadzim Pobudey | 17.12.1994 | 24 | (3) | 3 |
| Shakhrom Samiev (TJK) | 08.02.2001 | | (2) | |
| Yevgeniy Shevchenko | 06.06.1996 | 23 | (7) | 6 |

## Football Club Vitebsk

| | | | |
|---|---|---|---|
| **Founded**: | 1960 | | |
| **Stadium**: | Vitebsky Central Sport Complex, Vitebsk (8,100) | | |
| **Trainer**: | Yawhen Chernukhin | | 02.03.1984 |
| [16.08.2022] | Siarhey Yasinskiy | | 07.01.1965 |

| Goalkeepers: | DOB | M | (s) | G |
|---|---|---|---|---|
| Dzmitry Gushchenko | 12.05.1988 | 30 | | |
| **Defenders:** | **DOB** | **M** | **(s)** | **G** |
| Mikita Baranok | 31.03.2004 | 18 | (2) | 2 |
| Sergey Bugriev (RUS) | 16.03.1998 | 1 | (1) | |
| Vladislav Davydov (RUS) | 18.06.1999 | | (6) | |
| Júlio César Basílio da Silva (BRA) | 06.12.1996 | 29 | | 1 |
| Mikita Kostomarov | 29.06.1999 | 8 | (2) | |
| Andrey Lebedev | 01.02.1991 | 7 | (3) | |
| Aleksandr Sakovich (RUS) | 31.03.1998 | 10 | (9) | |
| Artsyom Skitov | 21.01.1991 | 27 | | |
| Oleg Veretilo | 10.07.1988 | 23 | | 1 |
| **Midfielders:** | **DOB** | **M** | **(s)** | **G** |
| Maksim Drobysh | 30.01.2001 | 1 | (6) | |
| Uladislaw Glinskiy | 29.05.2000 | 3 | (4) | |
| Aram Kocharyan (ARM) | 05.03.1996 | 13 | (2) | |
| Yevgeniy Krasnov | 09.02.1998 | 26 | (3) | 2 |

| | DOB | M | (s) | G |
|---|---|---|---|---|
| Alyaksandr Ksenofontov | 05.05.1999 | 12 | (2) | 3 |
| Raman Lisovskiy | 22.11.2001 | 14 | (9) | |
| Shada Ouedraogo (CIV) | 01.06.2003 | | (9) | |
| Yan Skibskiy | 25.12.2002 | 18 | (11) | 1 |
| Syarhey Volkov | 27.01.1999 | 27 | (1) | |
| Yaroslav Yarotskiy | 28.03.1996 | 2 | (4) | 1 |
| Maksim Zhumabekov (RUS) | 23.06.1999 | 13 | (2) | 5 |
| **Forwards:** | **DOB** | **M** | **(s)** | **G** |
| Vladlen Anikeev | 09.02.2004 | | (5) | |
| Aria Barzegar (IRN) | 10.10.2002 | | (5) | |
| Zakhar Chervyakov | 30.08.2002 | | (12) | |
| Anton Matveenko | 03.09.1986 | 10 | (16) | 2 |
| Fröl Panarin | 10.09.2002 | | (2) | |
| Gleb Rassadkin | 05.04.1995 | 9 | (4) | 1 |
| Ruslan Teverov | 01.05.1994 | 28 | (2) | 7 |
| Karen Vardanyan | 09.09.2003 | 1 | (14) | 1 |

## SECOND LEVEL
### First League 2022

| | | | | | | | | | |
|---|---|---|---|---|---|---|---|---|---|
| 1. | FC Naftan Novopolotsk (*Promoted*) | 24 | 16 | 5 | 3 | 55 | - | 19 | 53 |
| 2. | FC Smorgon (*Promoted*) | 24 | 16 | 4 | 4 | 46 | - | 27 | 52 |
| 3. | FC Shakhtyor Petrikov | 24 | 13 | 6 | 5 | 69 | - | 20 | 45 |
| 4. | FC Rogachev (*Promotion Play-offs*) | 24 | 12 | 5 | 7 | 45 | - | 34 | 41 |
| 5. | FC Ostrovets | 24 | 11 | 7 | 6 | 42 | - | 34 | 40 |
| 6. | FC Lokomotiv Gomel | 24 | 10 | 9 | 5 | 39 | - | 24 | 39 |
| 7. | FC Volna Pinsk | 24 | 10 | 6 | 8 | 44 | - | 35 | 36 |
| 8. | FC Molodechno | 24 | 7 | 8 | 9 | 30 | - | 45 | 29 |
| 9. | FC Orsha | 24 | 7 | 6 | 11 | 33 | - | 52 | 27 |
| 10. | FC Lida | 24 | 6 | 8 | 10 | 35 | - | 43 | 26 |
| 11. | FC Slonim-2017 | 24 | 5 | 3 | 16 | 24 | - | 53 | 18 |
| 12. | FC Osipovich | 24 | 3 | 4 | 17 | 21 | - | 53 | 13 |
| 13. | FC Baranovichi | 24 | 3 | 3 | 18 | 25 | - | 69 | 12 |

## INTERNATIONAL MATCHES
### (16.07.2022 – 15.07.2023)

| | | | | |
|---|---|---|---|---|
| 22.09.2022 | Nur-Sultan | *Kazakhstan - Belarus* | *2-1(1-1)* | (UNL) |
| 25.09.2022 | Bačka Topola | *Slovakia - Belarus* | *1-1(0-1)* | (UNL) |
| 17.11.2022 | Dubai | *Syria - Belarus* | *0-1(0-0)* | (F) |
| 20.11.2022 | Al Ain | *Oman - Belarus* | *2-0(0-0)* | (F) |
| | | | | |
| 25.03.2023 | Novi Sad | *Belarus - Switzerland* | *0-5(0-3)* | (ECQ) |
| 28.03.2023 | Bucureşti | *Romania - Belarus* | *2-1(2-0)* | (ECQ) |
| 16.06.2023 | Budapest | *Belarus - Israel* | *1-2(1-0)* | (ECQ) |
| 19.06.2023 | Budapest | *Belarus - Kosovo* | *2-1(0-0)* | (ECQ) |

**22.09.2022    KAZAKHSTAN - BELARUS                      2-1(1-1)**                    3<sup>rd</sup> UEFA Nations League C, Group 3

Astana Arena, Astana; Referee: Horaţiu Feşnic (Romania); Attendance: 29,637
**BLR:** Yahor Hatkevich, Ruslan Yudzyankow, Dzyanis Palyakow, Maksim Shvyatsow, Kiryl Pyachenin, Hleb Shawchenka (84.Wladzislaw Malkevich), Afrid Max Ebong Ngome, Uladislaw Klimovich (61.Ruslan Lisakovich), Yawhen Yablonski (Cap), Pavel Savitski (76.Valeriy Hramyka), Yahor Bahamolski (61.Ivan Bakhar). Trainer: Heorhiy Kandratsyew.
**Goal:** Pavel Savitski (45+3).

**25.09.2022    SLOVAKIA - BELARUS                         1-1(0-1)**                    3<sup>rd</sup> UEFA Nations League C, Group 3

TSC Arena, Bačka Topola (Serbia); Referee: Nikola Dabanović (Montenegro); Attendance: 524
**BLR:** Maksim Plotnikaw, Ruslan Yudzyankow, Ruslan Hadarkevich, Dzyanis Palyakow, Valeriy Bacharow, Yawhen Yablonski (Cap), Danila Nyachayew, Wladzislaw Malkevich, Valeriy Hramyka (39.Kiryl Pyachenin), Uladislaw Klimovich, Ivan Bakhar (68.Yahor Bahamolski; 89.Pavel Savitski). Trainer: Heorhiy Kandratsyew.
**Goal:** Ivan Bakhar (45).

**17.11.2022    SYRIA - BELARUS                             0-1(0-0)**                    Friendly International

Al Maktoum Stadium, Dubai (United Arab Emirates); Referee: Yahya Mohammed Ali Hassan Al Mulla (United Arab Emirates); Attendance: 710
**BLR:** Andrey Kudravets, Zahar Volkaw, Syarhey Palitsevich, Dzyanis Palyakow, Kiryl Kaplenka, Yawhen Yablonski (Cap) (77.Valeriy Bacharow), Danila Nyachayew (60.Afrid Max Ebong Ngome), Wladzislaw Malkevich (68.Kiryl Pyachenin), Dzyanis Grachyha (68.Valeriy Hramyka), Uladislaw Klimovich (60.Hleb Shawchenka), Uladzimir Khvashchynski (77.Yahor Bahamolski). Trainer: Heorhiy Kandratsyew.
**Goal:** Thaer Sami Krouma (81 own goal).

**20.11.2022    OMAN - BELARUS                              2-0(0-0)**                    Friendly International

"Hazza bin Zayed" Stadium, Al Ain (United Arab Emirates); Referee: Adel Al Naqbi (United Arab Emirates); Attendance: 150
**BLR:** Syarhey Ignatovich, Zahar Volkaw, Dzyanis Palyakow, Maksim Shvyatsow (81.Dzmitry Padstrelaw), Hleb Shawchenka (46.Danila Nyachayew), Kiryl Kaplenka, Yawhen Yablonski (Cap) (74.Wladzislaw Malkevich), Kiryl Pyachenin, Dzyanis Grachyha (74.Valeriy Bacharow), Uladislaw Klimovich (46.Valeriy Hramyka), Uladzimir Khvashchynski (81.Yahor Bahamolski).Trainer: Heorhiy Kandratsyew.

**25.03.2023    BELARUS - SWITZERLAND                     0-5(0-3)**                    17<sup>th</sup> EC. Qualifiers

Karađorđe Stadium, Novi Sad (Serbia); Referee: Alejandro José Hernández Hernández (Spain); Attendance: *played behind closed doors**
**BLR:** Andrey Kudravets, Raman Yuzapchuk (33.Artsyom Bykaw), Zahar Volkaw, Dzyanis Palyakow, Wladzislaw Malkevich, Yawhen Yablonski (Cap) (46.Uladislaw Klimovich), Dzyanis Grachyha, Afrid Max Ebong Ngome, Alyaksandr Syalyava (81.Valeriy Bacharow), Yury Kavalyow (46.Ivan Bakhar), Uladzimir Khvashchynski (61.Uladzislaw Marozaw). Trainer: Heorhiy Kandratsyew.
*Please note:* due to the Belarusian country's involvement in the Russian invasion of Ukraine, Belarus are required to play their home matches at neutral venues and behind closed doors until further notice.

**28.03.2023    ROMANIA - BELARUS                          2-1(2-0)**                    17<sup>th</sup> EC. Qualifiers

Arena Naţională, Bucureşti; Referee: Allard Lindhout (Netherlands); Attendance: 27,837
**BLR:** Maksim Plotnikaw, Zahar Volkaw, Ruslan Hadarkevich, Wladzislaw Malkevich, Artsyom Bykaw, Alyaksandr Syalyava, Yawhen Yablonski (Cap) (64.Uladislaw Klimovich), Yury Kavalyow (85.Dzyanis Grachyha), Afrid Max Ebong Ngome, Uladzimir Khvashchynski 46.46.Raman Yuzapchuk), Ivan Bakhar (77.Uladzislaw Marozaw). Trainer: Heorhiy Kandratsyew.
**Goal:** Uladzislaw Marozaw (86).

**16.06.2023    BELARUS - ISRAEL                            1-2(1-0)**                    17<sup>th</sup> EC. Qualifiers

"Szusza Ferenc" Stadion, Budapest (Hungary); Referee: Jarred Gavan Gillett (Australia); Attendance: *played behind closed doors*
**BLR:** Syarhey Ignatovich, Dzyanis Palyakow, Syarhey Palitsevich (Cap), Kiryl Pyachenin, Artsyom Bykaw, Kiryl Kaplenka (78.Uladislaw Klimovich), Alyaksandr Syalyava (57.Yawhen Yablonski), Yury Kavalyow (64.Valeriy Bacharow), Raman Yuzapchuk, Afrid Max Ebong Ngome (78.Pavel Savitski), Uladzislaw Marozaw (46.Ivan Bakhar). Trainer: Heorhiy Kandratsyew.
**Goal:** Afrid Max Ebong Ngome (16).

**19.06.2023    BELARUS - KOSOVO                            2-1(0-0)**                    17<sup>th</sup> EC. Qualifiers

"Szusza Ferenc" Stadion, Budapest (Hungary); Referee: Julian Weinberger (Austria); Attendance: *played behind closed doors*
**BLR:** Syarhey Ignatovich, Zahar Volkaw, Dzyanis Palyakow, Kiryl Pyachenin (88.Wladzislaw Malkevich), Artsyom Bykaw, Kiryl Kaplenka, Raman Yuzapchuk (63.Yury Kavalyow), Valeriy Bacharow (65.Alyaksandr Syalyava), Yawhen Yablonski (Cap) (88.Uladislaw Klimovich), Afrid Max Ebong Ngome, Pavel Savitski (63.Uladzislaw Marozaw). Trainer: Heorhiy Kandratsyew.
**Goals:** Uladzislaw Marozaw (73), Afrid Max Ebong Ngome (75).

## NATIONAL TEAM PLAYERS
### (16.07.2022 – 15.07.2023)

| Name | DOB | Caps | Goals | Club | |
|------|-----|------|-------|------|---|
| **Goalkeepers** | | | | | |
| Yahor HATKEVICH | 09.07.1988 | 7 | 0 | 2022: | *FC Dinamo Minsk* |
| Syarhey IGNATOVICH | 29.06.1992 | 4 | 0 | 2022: | *FC Isloch Minsk Raion* |
| | | | | 05.01.2023-> | *FC Shakhtyor Solihorsk* |
| Andrey KUDRAVETS | 02.09.2003 | 2 | 0 | 2022/2023: | *FC BATE Borisov* |
| Maksim PLOTNIKAW | 29.01.1998 | 4 | 0 | 2022: | *FC Shakhtyor Solihorsk;* |
| | | | | 02.02.2023-> | *FC Caspiy Aqtau (KAZ)* |
| **Defenders** | | | | | |
| Ruslan HADARKEVICH | 18.06.1993 | 9 | 0 | 2022: | *FC Shakhtyor Solihorsk* |
| | | | | 01.01.2023-> | *FC Dinamo Minsk* |
| Danila NYACHAYEW | 30.10.1999 | 7 | 0 | 2022: | *FC BATE Borisov* |
| Syarhey PALITSEVICH | 09.04.1990 | 38 | 1 | 2022: | *FC Shakhtyor Solihorsk;* |
| | | | | 05.01.2023-> | *FC Dinamo Minsk* |
| Dzyanis PALYAKOW | 17.04.1991 | 55 | 1 | 2022: | *Astana FC (KAZ)* |
| | | | | 01.01.2023-> | *Hapoel Haifa FC (ISR)* |
| Kiryl PYACHENIN | 18.03.1997 | 20 | 0 | 2022/2023: | *FK Orenburg (RUS)* |
| Hleb SHAWCHENKA | 17.02.1999 | 15 | 0 | 2022: | *FC Shakhtyor Solihorsk* |
| Maksim SHVYATSOW | 02.04.1998 | 12 | 0 | 2022: | *FC Dinamo Minsk* |
| Zahar VOLKAW | 12.08.1997 | 9 | 0 | 2022: | *FK Khimki (RUS)* |
| | | | | 01.02.2023-> | *FC BATE Borisov* |
| **Midfielders** | | | | | |
| Valeriy BACHAROW | 10.08.2000 | 9 | 0 | 2022/2023: | *FC BATE Borisov* |
| Ivan BAKHAR | 10.07.1998 | 25 | 2 | 2022: | *FC Dinamo Minsk* |
| | | | | 01.01.2023-> | *Hapoel Ironi Kiryat Shmona FC (ISR)* |
| Artsyom BYKAW | 19.10.1992 | 25 | 1 | 2023: | *FC Dinamo Minsk* |
| Afrid Max EBONG Ngome | 26.08.1999 | 30 | 4 | 2022/2023: | *Astana FC (KAZ)* |
| Dzyanis GRACHYHA | 22.05.1999 | 5 | 0 | 2022: | *FC Dinamo Minsk* |
| | | | | 01.01.2023-> | *FC BATE Borisov* |
| Valeriy HRAMYKA | 23.01.1997 | 11 | 1 | 2022: | *FC BATE Borisov* |
| Kiryl KAPLENKA | 15.06.1999 | 4 | 0 | 2022/2023: | *FK Orenburg (RUS)* |
| Yury KAVALYOW | 27.01.1993 | 20 | 1 | 2023: | *FK Orenburg (RUS)* |
| Uladislaw KLIMOVICH | 12.06.1996 | 33 | 1 | 2022/2023: | *Nea Salamis Famagusta FC (CYP)* |
| Ruslan LISAKOVICH | 22.03.2002 | 5 | 0 | 2022: | *FC Isloch Minsk Raion* |
| Wladzislaw MALKEVICH | 04.12.1999 | 11 | 1 | 2022/2023: | *FC BATE Borisov* |
| Alyaksandr SYALYAVA | 17.05.1992 | 9 | 0 | 2023: | *FK Rostov (RUS)* |
| Yawhen YABLONSKI | 10.05.1995 | 32 | 3 | 2022/2023: | *Aris Limassol FC (CYP)* |
| Ruslan YUDZYANKOW | 28.04.1987 | 10 | 0 | 2022: | *FC Maqtaaral Jetisay (KAZ)* |
| Raman YUZAPCHUK | 24.07.1997 | 20 | 1 | 2023: | *FK Torpedo Moskva (RUS)* |
| **Forwards** | | | | | |
| Yahor BAHAMOLSKI | 03.06.2000 | 6 | 0 | 2022: | *Neftçi PFK Bakı (AZE)* |
| Uladzimir KHVASHCHYNSKI | 10.05.1990 | 8 | 1 | 2022/2023: | *FC Minsk* |
| Uladzislaw MAROZAW | 12.10.2000 | 4 | 2 | 2023: | *FC Dinamo Minsk* |
| Dzmitry PADSTRELAW | 06.09.1998 | 14 | 1 | 2022: | *FC Shakhtyor Solihorsk* |
| Pavel SAVITSKI | 12.07.1994 | 26 | 7 | 2022/2023: | *FC Neman Grodno* |

### Trainer

| | | |
|---|---|---|
| Heorhiy KANDRATSYEW [from 06.04.2021] | 07.01.1960 | 22 M; 5 W; 3 D; 14 L; 17-35 |
| | | Complete record as trainer of Belarus: |
| | | 50 M; 14 W; 11 D; 25 L; 54-70 |
| | | (29.02.2012 – 12.10.2014) & (06.04.2021 – 19.06.2023) |

# BELGIUM

ROYAL BELGIAN FA·1895

## The Country:
Royaume de Belgique / Koninkrijk België (Kingdom of Belgium)
Capital: Bruxelles
Surface: 30,528 km²
Inhabitants: 11,697,557 [2023]
Time: UTC+1

## The FA:
Union royale belge des sociétés de football association / Koninklijke Belgische Voetbalbond
Brusselsestraat 480, 1480 Tubeke
Tel: +32 2 477 1211
Foundation date: 1895
Member of FIFA since: 1904
Member of UEFA since: 1954
Website: www.belgianfootball.be

## NATIONAL TEAM RECORDS

### RECORDS
| | |
|---|---|
| **First international match:** | 01.05.1994, Bruxelles: Belgium – France 3-3 |
| **Most international caps:** | Jan Bert Lieve Vertonghen - 148 caps (since 2007) |
| **Most international goals:** | Romelu Menama Lukaku Bolingoli - 75 goals / 108 caps (since 2010) |

### UEFA EUROPEAN CHAMPIONSHIP
| | |
|---|---|
| 1960 | Did not enter |
| 1964 | Qualifiers |
| 1968 | Qualifiers |
| 1972 | Final Tournament (3rd Place) |
| 1976 | Qualifiers |
| 1980 | Final Tournament (Runners-up) |
| 1984 | Final Tournament (Group Stage) |
| 1988 | Qualifiers |
| 1992 | Qualifiers |
| 1996 | Qualifiers |
| 2000 | Final Tournament (Group Stage) |
| 2004 | Qualifiers |
| 2008 | Qualifiers |
| 2012 | Qualifiers |
| 2016 | Final Tournament (Quarter-Finals) |
| 2020 | Final Tournament (Quarter-Finals) |

### FIFA WORLD CUP
| | |
|---|---|
| 1930 | Final Tournament (Group Stage) |
| 1934 | Final Tournament (1st Round) |
| 1938 | Final Tournament (1st Round) |
| 1950 | *Withdrew* |
| 1954 | Final Tournament (Group Stage) |
| 1958 | Qualifiers |
| 1962 | Qualifiers |
| 1966 | Qualifiers |
| 1970 | Final Tournament (Group Stage) |
| 1974 | Qualifiers |
| 1978 | Qualifiers |
| 1982 | Final Tournament (2nd Round) |
| 1986 | Final Tournament (4th Place) |
| 1990 | Final Tournament (2nd Round of 16) |
| 1994 | Final Tournament (2nd Round of 16) |
| 1998 | Final Tournament (Group Stage) |
| 2002 | Final Tournament (2nd Round of 16) |
| 2006 | Qualifiers |
| 2010 | Qualifiers |
| 2014 | Final Tournament (Quarter-Finals) |
| 2018 | Final Tournament (3rd Place) |
| 2022 | Final Tournament (Group Stage) |

### OLYMPIC TOURNAMENTS
| | |
|---|---|
| 1908 | - |
| 1912 | - |
| 1920 | **Winners** |
| 1924 | Final Tournament (1/8-Finals) |
| 1928 | Quarter-Finals |
| 1936 | Did not enter |
| 1948 | Did not enter |
| 1952 | Did not enter |
| 1956 | Did not enter |
| 1960 | Did not enter |
| 1964 | Did not enter |
| 1968 | Did not enter |
| 1972 | Did not enter |
| 1976 | Did not enter |
| 1980 | Qualifiers |
| 1984 | Qualifiers |
| 1988 | Qualifiers |
| 1992 | Qualifiers |
| 1996 | Qualifiers |
| 2000 | Qualifiers |
| 2004 | Qualifiers |
| 2008 | Final Tournament (4th Place) |
| 2012 | Qualifiers |
| 2016 | Qualifiers |
| 2020 | Qualifiers |

### UEFA NATIONS LEAGUE
| | |
|---|---|
| 2018/2019 | League A (Group Stage) |
| 2020/2021 | League A (Group Stage -> Final Tournament: 4th Place) |
| 2022/2023 | League A (Group Stage) |

## BELGIAN CLUB HONOURS IN EUROPEAN CLUB COMPETITIONS:

### European Champion Clubs' Cup (1956-1992) / UEFA Champions League (1993-2023)
| | | |
|---|---|---|
| None | | |

### Fairs Cup (1858-1971) / UEFA Cup (1972-2009) / UEFA Europa League (2010-2023)
| | | |
|---|---|---|
| RSC Anderlecht Bruxelles | 1 | 1982/1983 |

### UEFA Europa Conference League (2021-2023)
| | | |
|---|---|---|
| None | | |

### UEFA Super Cup (1972-2022)
| | | |
|---|---|---|
| RSC Anderlecht Bruxelles | 2 | 1976, 1978 |
| KV Mechelen | 1 | 1988 |

### European Cup Winners' Cup 1961-1999*
| | | |
|---|---|---|
| RSC Anderlecht Bruxelles | 2 | 1975/1976, 1977/1978 |
| KV Mechelen | 1 | 1987/1988 |

*defunct competition

## NATIONAL COMPETITIONS
## TABLE OF HONOURS

| | CHAMPIONS | CUP WINNERS | BEST GOALSCORERS | |
|---|---|---|---|---|
| 1895/1896 | FC Liégeois | - | Samuel Hickson (ENG, FC Liégeois) | ? |
| 1896/1897 | Racing Club de Bruxelles | - | Samuel Hickson (ENG, FC Liégeois) | ? |
| 1897/1898 | FC Liégeois | - | Franz König (SUI, Racing Club de Bruxelles) | ? |
| 1898/1899 | FC Liégeois | - | Franz König (SUI, Racing Club de Bruxelles) | ? |
| 1899/1900 | Racing Club de Bruxelles | - | Charles Richard Atkinson-Grimshaw (ENG, Racing Club de Bruxelles) | ? |
| 1900/1901 | Racing Club de Bruxelles | - | Herbert Alfred Potts (ENG, K Beerschot VAC) | 26 |
| 1901/1902 | Racing Club de Bruxelles | - | Herbert Alfred Potts (ENG, K Beerschot VAC) | 16 |
| 1902/1903 | Racing Club de Bruxelles | - | Gustave Vanderstappen (Royale Union Saint-Gilloise) | ? |
| 1903/1904 | Royale Union Saint-Gilloise | - | Gustave Vanderstappen (Royale Union Saint-Gilloise) | 30 |
| 1904/1905 | Royale Union Saint-Gilloise | - | Robert De Veen (FC Brugeois) | ? |
| 1905/1906 | Royale Union Saint-Gilloise | - | Robert De Veen (FC Brugeois) | 26 |
| 1906/1907 | Royale Union Saint-Gilloise | - | Maurice Vertongen (Racing Club de Bruxelles) | 29 |
| 1907/1908 | Racing Club de Bruxelles | - | Maurice Vertongen (Racing Club de Bruxelles) | 23 |
| 1908/1909 | Royale Union Saint-Gilloise | - | Vahram Kevorkian (RUS, Racing Club de Bruxelles) | 30 |
| 1909/1910 | Royale Union Saint-Gilloise | - | Maurice Vertongen (Royale Union Saint-Gilloise) | 36 |
| 1910/1911 | CS Brugeois | - | Alphonse Six (CS Brugeois) | 40 |
| 1911/1912 | Daring Club de Bruxelles | Racing Club de Bruxelles | Maurice Taylor Bunyan (ENG, Racing Club de Bruxelles) | 35 |
| 1912/1913 | Royale Union Saint-Gilloise | Royale Union Saint-Gilloise | Sylva Brébart (Daring Club de Bruxelles) | 31 |
| 1913/1914 | Daring Club de Bruxelles | Royale Union Saint-Gilloise | Maurice Bunyan (ENG, Racing Club de Bruxelles) | 28 |
| 1915-1919 | *No competition* | *No competition* | - | |
| 1919/1920 | FC Brugeois | *No competition* | Honoré Vlamynck (Daring Club de Bruxelles) | 26 |
| 1920/1921 | Daring Club de Bruxelles | *No competition* | Ivan Thys (K Beerschot VAC) | 23 |
| 1921/1922 | K Beerschot VAC | *No competition* | Ivan Thys (K Beerschot VAC) | 21 |
| 1922/1923 | Royale Union Saint-Gilloise | *No competition* | Achille Meyskens (Royale Union Saint-Gilloise) | 24 |
| 1923/1924 | K Beerschot VAC | *No competition* | Charles Jooris (Racing Club de Bruxelles) | 18 |
| 1924/1925 | K Beerschot VAC | *No competition* | Joseph Taeymans (K Berchem Sport) | 20 |
| 1925/1926 | K Beerschot VAC | *No competition* | Laurent Grimmonprez (RC Gent) | 28 |
| 1926/1927 | RCS Brugeois | RCS Brugeois | Lucien Fabry (R Standard Liège) | 28 |
| 1927/1928 | K Beerschot VAC | *No competition* | Raymond Braine (K Beerschot VAC) | 35 |
| 1928/1929 | R Antwerp FC | *No competition* | Raymond Braine (K Beerschot VAC) | 30 |
| 1929/1930 | RCS Brugeois | *No competition* | Pierre De Vidts (Daring Club de Bruxelles) | 26 |
| 1930/1931 | R Antwerp FC | *No competition* | Jacques Secretin (RCFC Montegnée) Joseph Van Beeck (R Antwerp FC | 21 |
| 1931/1932 | K Lierse SK | *No competition* | Bernard Delmez (K Lierse SK) | 26 |
| 1932/1933 | Royale Union Saint-Gilloise | *No competition* | Willy Ulens (R Antwerp FC) | 26 |
| 1933/1934 | Royale Union Saint-Gilloise | *No competition* | Vital Van Landeghem (Royale Union Saint-Gilloise) | 29 |
| 1934/1935 | Royale Union Saint-Gilloise | Daring Club de Bruxelles | Marius Mondelé (Daring Club de Bruxelles) | 28 |
| 1935/1936 | Daring Club de Bruxelles SR | *No competition* | Flor Lambrechts (R Antwerp FC) | 37 |
| 1936/1937 | Daring Club de Bruxelles SR | *No competition* | Jean Collet (White Star WAC Bruxelles) | 22 |
| 1937/1938 | R Beerschot AC Antwerp | *No competition* | Marius Mondelé (Daring Club de Bruxelles) | 32 |
| 1938/1939 | R Beerschot AC Antwerp | *No competition* | Jozef Wagner (R Antwerp FC) | 31 |
| 1939-1941 | *No competition* | *No competition* | - | |
| 1941/1942 | K Liersche SK | *No competition* | Bert De Cleyn (R Antwerp FC) | 34 |
| 1942/1943 | RFC Malinois | *No competition* | Arthur Ceuleers (K Beerschot VAC) Jules Van Craen (K Lierse SK) | 41 |
| 1943/1944 | R Antwerp FC | *No competition* | Jan Goossens (ROC Charleroi) | 34 |
| 1944/1945 | *No competition* | *No competition* | - | |
| 1945/1946 | RFC Malinois | *No competition* | - | |
| 1946/1947 | RSC Anderlecht Bruxelles | *No competition* | Jef Mermans (RSC Anderlecht Bruxelles) | 39 |
| 1947/1948 | RFC Malinois | *No competition* | Jef Mermans (RSC Anderlecht Bruxelles) | 23 |
| 1948/1949 | RSC Anderlecht Bruxelles | *No competition* | René Thirifays (R Charleroi SC) | 26 |
| 1949/1950 | RSC Anderlecht Bruxelles | *No competition* | Jef Mermans (RSC Anderlecht Bruxelles) | 37 |
| 1950/1951 | RSC Anderlecht Bruxelles | *No competition* | Albert Dehert (K Berchem Sport) | 27 |
| 1951/1952 | RFC Liégeois | *No competition* | Jozef Mannaerts (KRC Mechelen) | 25 |
| 1952/1953 | RFC Liégeois | *No competition* | Rik Coppens (K Beerschot VAC) | 35 |
| 1953/1954 | RSC Anderlecht Bruxelles | R Standard Liège | Hippolyte Van Den Bosch (RSC Anderlecht Bruxelles) | 29 |
| 1954/1955 | RSC Anderlecht Bruxelles | R Antwerp FC | Rik Coppens (K Beerschot VAC) | 35 |
| 1955/1956 | RSC Anderlecht Bruxelles | RRC Tournaisien | Jean Mathonet (R Standard Liège) | 26 |
| 1956/1957 | R Antwerp FC | *No competition* | Maurice Willems (KAA Gent) | 35 |
| 1957/1958 | R Standard Liège | *No competition* | Jef Vliers (K Beerschot VAC) | 25 |
| 1958/1959 | RSC Anderlecht Bruxelles | *No competition* | Victor Wegria (RFC Liégeois) | 26 |
| 1959/1960 | K Lierse SK | *No competition* | Victor Wegria (RFC Liégeois) | 21 |
| 1960/1961 | R Standard Liège | *No competition* | Victor Wegria (RFC Liégeois) | 23 |
| 1961/1962 | RSC Anderlecht Bruxelles | *No competition* | Jacky Stockman (RSC Anderlecht Bruxelles) | 29 |
| 1962/1963 | R Standard Liège | *No competition* | Victor Wegria (RFC Liégeois) | 29 |
| 1963/1964 | RSC Anderlecht Bruxelles | ARA La Gantoise | Paul Van Himst (RSC Anderlecht Bruxelles) | 26 |
| 1964/1965 | RSC Anderlecht Bruxelles | RSC Anderlecht Bruxelles | Jean-Paul Colonval (RFC Tilleur Saint-Nicolas) | 25 |
| 1965/1966 | RSC Anderlecht Bruxelles | R Standard Liège | Paul Van Himst (RSC Anderlecht Bruxelles) | 25 |

| | | | | |
|---|---|---|---|---|
| 1966/1967 | RSC Anderlecht Bruxelles | R Standard Liège | Johan Mulder (NED, RSC Anderlecht Bruxelles) | 20 |
| 1967/1968 | RSC Anderlecht Bruxelles | Club Brugge KV | Roger Claessen (R Standard Liège Liège) Paul Van Himst (RSC Anderlecht Bruxelles) | 20 |
| 1968/1969 | R Standard Liège | K Lierse SK | Antal Nagy (HUN, R Standard Liège Liège) | 20 |
| 1969/1970 | R Standard Liège | Club Brugge KV | Lothar Emmerich (GER, K Beerschot VAC) | 29 |
| 1970/1971 | R Standard Liège | K Beerschot VAV | Erwin Kostedde (GER, R Standard Liège Liège) | 26 |
| 1971/1972 | RSC Anderlecht Bruxelles | RSC Anderlecht Bruxelles | Raoul Lambert (Club Brugge KV) | 17 |
| 1972/1973 | Club Brugge KV | RSC Anderlecht Bruxelles | Pieter Robert Rensenbrink (NED, RSC Anderlecht Bruxelles) Alfred Riedl (AUT, K Sint-Truidense VV) | 16 |
| 1973/1974 | RSC Anderlecht Bruxelles | KSV Waregem | Attila Ladynski (HUN, RSC Anderlecht Bruxelles) | 22 |
| 1974/1975 | R White Daring Molenbeek | RSC Anderlecht Bruxelles | Alfred Riedl (AUT, R Antwerp FC) | 28 |
| 1975/1976 | Club Brugge KV | RSC Anderlecht Bruxelles | Hans Posthumus (K Lierse SK) | 26 |
| 1976/1977 | Club Brugge KV | Club Brugge KV | François Van Der Elst (RSC Anderlecht Bruxelles) | 21 |
| 1977/1978 | Club Brugge KV | KSK Beveren | Harald Nickel (R Standard Liège Liège) | 22 |
| 1978/1979 | KSK Beveren | K Beerschot VAV | Erwin Albert (KSK Beveren) | 28 |
| 1979/1980 | Club Brugge KV | K Waterschei SV Thor Genk | Erwin Vandenbergh (K Lierse SK) | 39 |
| 1980/1981 | RSC Anderlecht Bruxelles | R Standard Liège | Erwin Vandenbergh (K Lierse SK) | 24 |
| 1981/1982 | R Standard Liège | K Waterschei SV Thor Genk | Erwin Vandenbergh (K Lierse SK) | 25 |
| 1982/1983 | R Standard Liège | KSK Beveren | Erwin Vandenbergh (RSC Anderlecht Bruxelles) | 20 |
| 1983/1984 | KSK Beveren | KAA Gent | Nicolaas Pieter Claesen (RFC Seraing) | 27 |
| 1984/1985 | RSC Anderlecht Bruxelles | Cercle Brugge KSV | Ronny Martens (KAA Gent) | 23 |
| 1985/1986 | RSC Anderlecht Bruxelles | Club Brugge KV | Erwin Vandenbergh (RSC Anderlecht Bruxelles) | 27 |
| 1986/1987 | RSC Anderlecht Bruxelles | KV Mechelen | Arnór Guðjohnsen (ISL, RSC Anderlecht Bruxelles) | 19 |
| 1987/1988 | Club Brugge KV | RSC Anderlecht Bruxelles | Francis Severeyns (R Antwerp FC) | 24 |
| 1988/1989 | KV Mechelen | RSC Anderlecht Bruxelles | Edward Krncevic (AUS, RSC Anderlecht Bruxelles) | 23 |
| 1989/1990 | Club Brugge KV | RFC Liégeois | Frank Farina (AUS, Club Brugge KV) | 24 |
| 1990/1991 | RSC Anderlecht Bruxelles | Club Brugge KV | Erwin Vandenbergh (KAA Gent) | 23 |
| 1991/1992 | Club Brugge KV | Royal Antwerp F.C. | Josip Weber (CRO, Cercle Brugge KSV) | 26 |
| 1992/1993 | RSC Anderlecht Bruxelles | R Standard Liège | Josip Weber (CRO, Cercle Brugge KSV) | 31 |
| 1993/1994 | RSC Anderlecht Bruxelles | RSC Anderlecht Bruxelles | Josip Weber (Cercle Brugge KSV) | 31 |
| 1994/1995 | RSC Anderlecht Bruxelles | Club Brugge KV | Aurelio Vidmar (AUS, R Standard Liège Liège) | 22 |
| 1995/1996 | Club Brugge KV | Club Brugge KV | Mario Stanić (CRO, Club Brugge KV) | 20 |
| 1996/1997 | K Lierse SK | KFC Germinal Ekeren | Robert Špehar (CRO, Club Brugge KV) | 26 |
| 1997/1998 | Club Brugge KV | KRC Genk | Branko Strupar (KRC Genk) | 22 |
| 1998/1999 | KRC Genk | Lierse S.K. | Jan Koller (CZE, Lokeren) | 24 |
| 1999/2000 | RSC Anderlecht Bruxelles | KRC Genk | Ole Martin Årst (NOR, KAA Gent) Antonio Brogno (KVC Westerlo) | 30 |
| 2000/2001 | RSC Anderlecht Bruxelles | KVC Westerlo | Tomasz Radzinski (CAN, RSC Anderlecht Bruxelles) | 23 |
| 2001/2002 | KRC Genk | Club Brugge KV | Wesley Sonck (KRC Genk) | 30 |
| 2002/2003 | Club Brugge KV | RAA La Louvière | Cédric Roussel (RAEC Mons) Wesley Sonck (KRC Genk) | 22 |
| 2003/2004 | RSC Anderlecht Bruxelles | Club Brugge KV | Luigi Pieroni (Mouscron) | 28 |
| 2004/2005 | Club Brugge KV | KFC Germinal Beerschot | Nenad Jestrović (SRB, RSC Anderlecht Bruxelles) | 18 |
| 2005/2006 | RSC Anderlecht Bruxelles | SV Zulte-Waregem | Tosin Dosunmu (NGA, KFC Germinal Beerschot Antwerpen) | 18 |
| 2006/2007 | RSC Anderlecht Bruxelles | Club Brugge KV | François Sterchele (KFC Germinal Beerschot Antwerpen) | 21 |
| 2007/2008 | R Standard Liège | RSC Anderlecht Bruxelles | Joseph Eneojo Akpala (NGA, R Charleroi SC) | 18 |
| 2008/2009 | R Standard Liège | KRC Genk | Jaime Alfonso Ruiz (COL, KVC Westerlo) | 18 |
| 2009/2010 | RSC Anderlecht Bruxelles | KAA Gent | Romelu Menama Lukaku Bolingoli (RSC Anderlecht Bruxelles) | 15 |
| 2010/2011 | KRC Genk | R Standard Liège | Ivan Perišić (CRO, Club Brugge KV) | 22 |
| 2011/2012 | RSC Anderlecht Bruxelles | KSC Lokeren | Jérémy Perbet (FRA, RAEC Mons) | 25 |
| 2012/2013 | RSC Anderlecht Bruxelles | KRC Genk | Carlos Arturo Bacca Ahumada (COL, Club Brugge KV) | 25 |
| 2013/2014 | RSC Anderlecht Bruxelles | KSC Lokeren | Hamdi Harbaoui (TUN, KSC Lokeren Oost-Vlaanderen) | 22 |
| 2014/2015 | KAA Gent | Club Brugge KV | Aleksandar Mitrović (SRB, RSC Anderlecht Bruxelles) | 20 |
| 2015/2016 | Club Brugge KV | R Standard Liège | Jérémy Perbet (FRA, R Charleroi SC) | 22 |
| 2016/2017 | RSC Anderlecht Bruxelles | SV Zulte Waregem | Łukasz Teodorczyk (POL, RSC Anderlecht Bruxelles) | 22 |
| 2017/2018 | Club Brugge KV | R Standard Liège | Hamdi Harbaoui (TUN, SV Zulte Waregem) | 22 |
| 2018/2019 | KRC Genk | KV Mechelen | Hamdi Harbaoui (TUN, SV Zulte Waregem) | 25 |
| 2019/2020 | Club Brugge KV | Royal Antwerp FC | Dieudonné Mbokani Bezua (COD, R Antwerp FC) Jonathan Christian David (CAN, KAA Gent) | 18 |
| 2020/2021 | Club Brugge KV | KRC Genk | Ebere Paul Onuachu (NGA, KRC Genk) | 33 |
| 2021/2022 | Club Brugge KV | KAA Gent | Deniz Undav (GER, Royale Union Saint-Gilloise) | 25 |
| 2022/2023 | Royal Antwerp FC | Royal Antwerp FC | Hugo Cuypers (KAA Gent) | 27 |

# NATIONAL CHAMPIONSHIP
## Eerste Divisie / Jupiler Pro League - 2022/2023
### (22.07.2022 – 04.06.2023)

**Regular Season - Results**

**Round 1 [22-24.07.2022]**
Standard Liège - KAA Gent 2-2(1-0)
Charleroi - KAS Eupen 3-1(1-0)
KV Kortrijk - OH Leuven 0-2(0-0)
Zulte Waregem - RFC Seraing 2-0(0-0)
Sint-Truidense - Union Saint-Gilloise 1-1(1-0)
Club Brugge - KRC Genk 3-2(1-1)
KV Mechelen - Antwerp FC 0-2(0-2)
Anderlecht - KV Oostende 2-0(1-0)
Westerlo - Cercle Brugge 2-0(1-0)

**Round 2 [29-31.07.2022]**
Union Saint-Gilloise - Charleroi 1-0(0-0)
Cercle Brugge - Anderlecht 1-0(0-0)
KV Oostende - KV Mechelen 2-1(2-0)
OH Leuven - Westerlo 2-0(1-0)
KAA Gent - Sint-Truidense VV 1-1(1-0)
KRC Genk - Standard Liège 3-1(3-1)
KAS Eupen - Club Brugge 2-1(2-1)
RFC Seraing - KV Kortrijk 0-1(0-0)
Antwerp FC - Zulte Waregem 1-0(0-0)

**Round 3 [05-07.08.2022]**
Club Brugge - Zulte Waregem 1-1(0-0)
KRC Genk - KAS Eupen 4-3(3-1)
KV Kortrijk - Sint-Truidense VV 0-0
Charleroi - KV Oostende 1-3(0-1)
KV Mechelen - Union Saint-Gilloise 3-0(1-0)
Standard Liège - Cercle Brugge 2-0(2-0)
KAA Gent - Westerlo 2-1(2-1)
Anderlecht - RFC Seraing 3-1(3-0)
Antwerp FC - OH Leuven 4-2(2-1)

**Round 4 [12-14.08.2022]**
KV Oostende - KAA Gent 1-3(1-2)
Westerlo - Standard Liège 4-2(1-0)
Cercle Brugge - KV Mechelen 0-0
RFC Seraing - Charleroi 0-1(0-0)
Union Saint-Gilloise - KV Kortrijk 2-1(1-0)
Sint-Truidense VV - Anderlecht 0-3(0-2)
KAS Eupen - Antwerp FC 0-1(0-0)
OH Leuven - Club Brugge 0-3(0-2)
Zulte Waregem - KRC Genk 1-4(1-3)

**Round 5 [19-21.08.2022]**
KAS Eupen - RFC Seraing 1-3(0-3)
KV Oostende - Sint-Truidense VV 0-1(0-1)
KRC Genk - Cercle Brugge 2-1(1-0)
Club Brugge - KV Kortrijk 2-1(2-1)
Zulte Waregem - Charleroi 1-3(1-1)
Standard Liège - OH Leuven 1-3(0-2)
KV Mechelen - Westerlo 5-4(1-1)
Antwerp FC - Union SG 4-2(4-1) [31.08.2022]
Anderlecht - KAA Gent 0-1(0-0) [01.09.2022]

**Round 6 [26-28.08.2022]**
Charleroi - Club Brugge 1-3(1-2)
RFC Seraing - KRC Genk 0-4(0-1)
Cercle Brugge - Zulte Waregem 1-1(1-1)
OH Leuven - KV Oostende 2-1(0-1)
Sint-Truidense VV - KV Mechelen 3-1(0-0)
KAA Gent - Antwerp FC 1-2(1-2)
KV Kortrijk - Standard Liège 0-1(0-0)
Union Saint-Gilloise - Anderlecht 2-1(2-1)
Westerlo - KAS Eupen 0-1(0-0)

**Round 7 [02-04.09.2022]**
Club Brugge - Cercle Brugge 4-0(1-0)
KRC Genk - Sint-Truidense VV 0-0
KAS Eupen - KV Kortrijk 0-1(0-0)
KV Mechelen - RFC Seraing 2-3(2-1)
Standard Liège - KV Oostende 1-0(0-0)
Anderlecht - OH Leuven 2-2(0-1)
Antwerp FC - Westerlo 3-0(1-0)
Charleroi - KAA Gent 2-1(1-1)
Zulte Waregem-Union Saint-Gilloise 1-3(0-1)

**Round 8 [09-11.09.2022]**
Sint-Truidense VV - Standard Liège 1-2(0-2)
KV Kortrijk - KV Mechelen 1-4(0-2)
KV Oostende - KAS Eupen 1-0(0-0)
RFC Seraing - Club Brugge 0-2(0-0)
OH Leuven - Charleroi 3-2(1-1)
Westerlo - Anderlecht 2-1(1-0)
Cercle Brugge - Antwerp FC 0-2(0-1)
Union Saint-Gilloise - KRC Genk 1-2(0-1)
KAA Gent - Zulte Waregem 2-0(0-0)

**Round 9 [16-18.09.2022]**
Antwerp FC - RFC Seraing 2-1(2-1)
KV Mechelen - OH Leuven 0-0
Cercle Brugge - KV Oostende 2-2(2-0)
Zulte Waregem - Sint-Truidense VV 0-3(0-1)
Charleroi - Westerlo 2-3(1-2)
KRC Genk - KAA Gent 1-0(0-0)
KAS Eupen - Union Saint-Gilloise 1-2(1-1)
Standard Liège - Club Brugge 3-0(1-0)
Anderlecht - KV Kortrijk 4-1(1-0)

**Round 10 [30.09.-02.10.2022]**
Standard Liège - RFC Seraing 0-2(0-1)
OH Leuven - Union Saint-Gilloise 0-3(0-2)
KV Oostende - KRC Genk 1-2(1-1)
Westerlo - Zulte Waregem 2-0(1-0)
Club Brugge - KV Mechelen 3-0(1-0)
Anderlecht - Charleroi 0-1(0-0)
KAA Gent - Cercle Brugge 3-4(0-1)
KV Kortrijk - Antwerp FC 2-1(2-0)
Sint-Truidense VV - KAS Eupen 0-1(0-0)

**Round 11 [07-09.10.2022]**
Antwerp FC - Sint-Truidense VV 2-0(1-0)
KRC Genk - KV Kortrijk 2-1(1-0)
RFC Seraing - KV Oostende 1-1(0-0)
Zulte Waregem - OH Leuven 2-5(1-0)
Club Brugge - Westerlo 0-2(0-0)
KV Mechelen - Anderlecht 1-3(1-0)
KAS Eupen - KAA Gent 0-4(0-2)
Charleroi - Standard Liège 0-1(0-1)
Union Saint-Gilloise - Cercle Brugge 2-1(1-0)

**Round 12 [14-16.10.2022]**
Westerlo - RFC Seraing 2-2(2-1)
KV Kortrijk - Zulte Waregem 1-3(1-0)
Cercle Brugge - KAS Eupen 5-1(3-1)
Sint-Truidense VV - Charleroi 2-1(1-0)
OH Leuven - KRC Genk 0-1(0-1)
Standard Liège - Antwerp FC 3-0(3-0)
KAA Gent - KV Mechelen 3-0(1-0)
Anderlecht - Club Brugge 0-1(0-0)
KV Oostende - Union Saint-Gilloise 1-6(0-2)

**Round 13 [18-20.10.2022]**
KAS Eupen - OH Leuven 4-2(2-2)
Charleroi - KV Kortrijk 2-2(2-0)
KRC Genk - Westerlo 6-1(5-1)
RFC Seraing - Cercle Brugge 0-1(0-1)
Union Saint-Gilloise - KAA Gent 2-0(1-0)
Club Brugge - Sint-Truidense VV 3-0(1-0)
KV Mechelen - Standard Liège 2-0(0-0)
Antwerp FC - KV Oostende 3-0(1-0)
Zulte Waregem - Anderlecht 3-2(1-1)

**Round 14 [21-23.10.2022]**
Cercle Brugge - Charleroi 4-1(1-0)
KV Kortrijk - Westerlo 0-2(0-0)
KV Mechelen - KAS Eupen 2-1(1-1)
Sint-Truidense VV - OH Leuven 0-0
Union Saint-Gilloise - Club Brugge 2-2(1-2)
Antwerp FC - KRC Genk 1-3(1-2)
KAA Gent - RFC Seraing 2-1(1-1)
Standard Liège - Anderlecht 5-0 *awarded**
KV Oostende - Zulte Waregem 2-1(1-0)

*awarded 5-0; abandoned at 3-1 after 60 mins
due to crowd trouble*

**Round 15 [28-30.10.2022]**
KRC Genk - KV Mechelen 3-1(1-1)
Zulte Waregem - Standard Liège 0-3(0-0)
KV Kortrijk - Cercle Brugge 1-1(0-1)
Westerlo - Sint-Truidense VV 2-3(0-2)
Club Brugge - KV Oostende 4-2(2-0)
Anderlecht - KAS Eupen 4-2(2-1)
RFC Seraing - Union Saint-Gilloise 1-2(0-0)
OH Leuven - KAA Gent 1-1(0-1)
Charleroi - Antwerp FC 1-0(1-0)

**Round 16 [04-06.11.2022]**
KRC Genk - Charleroi 4-1(2-0)
KV Mechelen - Zulte Waregem 2-2(2-0)
Cercle Brugge - OH Leuven 2-1(1-1)
RFC Seraing - Sint-Truidense VV 1-2(1-0)
KAS Eupen - Standard Liège 2-0(0-0)
KAA Gent - Club Brugge 2-0(2-0)
Union Saint-Gilloise - Westerlo 1-1(0-1)
Antwerp FC - Anderlecht 0-0
KV Oostende - KV Kortrijk 3-1(1-1)

**Round 17 [11-13.11.2022]**
OH Leuven - RFC Seraing 5-0(4-0)
Charleroi - KV Mechelen 0-5 *awarded ***
Westerlo - KV Oostende 6-0(3-0)
Zulte Waregem - KAS Eupen 5-5(2-3)
Sint-Truidense VV - Cercle Brugge 0-1(0-0)
Club Brugge - Antwerp FC 2-2(1-0)
Standard Liège - Union Saint-Gilloise 2-3(0-1)
Anderlecht - KRC Genk 0-2(0-1)
KV Kortrijk - KAA Gent 0-4(0-2)

*awarded 0-5; abandoned at 1-0 after 68 mins
due to crowd trouble*

**Round 18 [23-27.12.2022]**
RFC Seraing - KAS Eupen 0-1(0-0)
KAA Gent - Standard Liège 0-0
KV Mechelen - Cercle Brugge 1-1(0-1)
Club Brugge - OH Leuven 1-1(1-0)
Union Saint-Gilloise - KV Oostende 3-0(0-0)
KV Kortrijk - KRC Genk 1-0(0-0)
Charleroi - Anderlecht 0-1(0-0)
Westerlo - Antwerp FC 3-3(1-0)
Sint-Truidense VV - Zulte Waregem 2-0(1-0)

**Round 19** [06-08.01.2023]
Standard Liège - Sint-Truidense VV 1-1(0-0)
KAS Eupen - Charleroi 1-2(1-0)
Cercle Brugge - Westerlo 0-1(0-1)
KV Oostende - RFC Seraing 1-2(1-1)
Antwerp FC - KAA Gent 2-0(1-0)
KRC Genk - Club Brugge 3-1(1-1)
Zulte Waregem - KV Mechelen 2-0(1-0)
Anderlecht - Union Saint-Gilloise 1-3(0-0)
OH Leuven - KV Kortrijk 2-3(1-1)

**Round 20** [13-15.01.2023]
Westerlo - OH Leuven 1-2(0-0)
RFC Seraing - Standard Liège 1-1(1-1)
KAS Eupen - Sint-Truidense VV 0-2(0-1)
KV Mechelen - KV Oostende 2-1(1-0)
KRC Genk - Zulte Waregem 1-0(1-0)
Club Brugge - Anderlecht 1-1(0-0)
KAA Gent - KV Kortrijk 2-1(1-0)
Union Saint-Gilloise - Antwerp FC 2-0(1-0)
Charleroi - Cercle Brugge 2-1(1-1)

**Round 21** [17-19.01.2023]
OH Leuven - KAS Eupen 1-1(1-0)
Westerlo - KRC Genk 2-3(0-2)
Standard Liège - KV Mechelen 2-0(1-0)
Cercle Brugge - Union Saint-Gilloise 1-1(0-0)
KV Oostende - Antwerp FC 0-3(0-2)
KV Kortrijk - RFC Seraing 3-2(2-1)
Anderlecht - Zulte Waregem 2-3(2-1)
KAA Gent - Charleroi 0-0
Sint-Truidense VV - Club Brugge 1-1(0-1)

**Round 22** [21-22.01.2023]
Zulte Waregem - Westerlo 1-1(0-1)
KV Mechelen - KV Kortrijk 3-2(2-1)
KV Oostende - Cercle Brugge 1-2(0-1)
Union Saint-Gilloise - OH Leuven 1-0(0-0)
Antwerp FC - Standard Liège 4-1(3-1)
RFC Seraing - Anderlecht 0-1(0-0)
Club Brugge - Charleroi 2-2(1-2)
Sint-Truidense VV - KAA Gent 0-3(0-2)
KAS Eupen - KRC Genk 1-1(1-1) [01.02.23]

**Round 23** [27-29.01.2023]
Standard Liège - KAS Eupen 3-1(2-1)
Westerlo - KV Mechelen 2-0(1-0)
KV Kortrijk - KV Oostende 2-2(1-1)
OH Leuven - Sint-Truidense VV 1-1(0-1)
Charleroi - Union Saint-Gilloise 0-1(0-1)
Anderlecht - Antwerp FC 0-0
Cercle Brugge - KAA Gent 3-2(0-0)
Zulte Waregem - Club Brugge 1-2(1-2)
KRC Genk - RFC Seraing 4-0(2-0)

**Round 24** [03-05.02.2023]
KV Oostende - Anderlecht 0-2(0-1)
Cercle Brugge - Standard Liège 1-1(0-0)
KAS Eupen - Westerlo 1-1(0-1)
RFC Seraing - OH Leuven 2-1(1-1)
Sint-Truidense VV - KV Kortrijk 1-0(1-0)
Antwerp FC - Club Brugge 0-0
KV Mechelen - Charleroi 2-2(2-0)
KAA Gent - KRC Genk 2-3(1-1)
Union Saint-Gilloise-Zulte Waregem 4-0(1-0)

**Round 25** [10-12.02.2023]
OH Leuven - Cercle Brugge 0-0
Club Brugge - Union Saint-Gilloise 1-1(1-1)
KAS Eupen - KV Mechelen 2-1(0-1)
Westerlo - KAA Gent 3-3(2-2)
Charleroi - RFC Seraing 3-0(1-0)
KRC Genk - Antwerp FC 0-1(0-0)
Anderlecht - Sint-Truidense VV 3-1(0-0)
Standard Liège - KV Kortrijk 0-2(0-0)
Zulte Waregem - KV Oostende 1-1(1-0)

**Round 26** [17-19.02.2023]
KV Mechelen - KRC Genk 2-2(1-1)
Antwerp FC - KAS Eupen 2-0(2-0)
KV Oostende - Charleroi 0-0
RFC Seraing - Zulte Waregem 1-1(0-1)
Union Saint-Gilloise - Standard Liège 2-4(1-2)
Cercle Brugge - Club Brugge 2-2(0-1)
KAA Gent - OH Leuven 2-0(0-0)
KV Kortrijk - Anderlecht 2-2(0-1)
Sint-Truidense VV - Westerlo 0-1(0-1)

**Round 27** [24-26.02.2023]
Zulte Waregem - KV Kortrijk 3-3(1-2)
RFC Seraing - KV Mechelen 0-2(0-1)
KAS Eupen - Cercle Brugge 2-2(2-2)
KRC Genk - KV Oostende 3-0(2-0)
Westerlo - Union Saint-Gilloise 4-2(2-1)
Club Brugge - KAA Gent 2-0(0-0)
OH Leuven - Antwerp FC 1-1(1-0)
Anderlecht - Standard Liège 2-2(2-1)
Charleroi - Sint-Truidense VV 1-0(0-0)

**Round 28** [03-05.03.2023]
KV Oostende - Club Brugge 3-0(1-0)
KV Kortrijk - Charleroi 0-1(0-0)
Cercle Brugge - RFC Seraing 3-1(2-1)
OH Leuven - Zulte Waregem 4-2(3-0)
Standard Liège - Westerlo 2-0(1-0)
Sint-Truidense VV - KRC Genk 2-2(1-1)
Antwerp FC - KV Mechelen 5-0(3-0)
KAA Gent - Anderlecht 1-0(0-0)
Union Saint-Gilloise - KAS Eupen 2-1(1-0)

**Round 29** [10-12.03.2023]
Charleroi - OH Leuven 0-1(0-1)
KV Mechelen - Sint-Truidense VV 1-0(0-0)
KAS Eupen - KV Oostende 4-4(1-1)
Westerlo - KV Kortrijk 3-1(1-0)
RFC Seraing - Antwerp FC 0-2(0-2)
Club Brugge - Standard Liège 2-0(0-0)
Zulte Waregem - KAA Gent 2-6(0-2)
KRC Genk - Union Saint-Gilloise 1-2(1-2)
Anderlecht - Cercle Brugge 2-0(1-0)

**Round 30** [17-19.03.2023]
Cercle Brugge - KRC Genk 1-1(1-0)
KV Kortrijk - Club Brugge 1-0(1-0)
KV Oostende - Westerlo 1-2(0-1)
Sint-Truidense VV - RFC Seraing 2-1(1-0)
Standard Liège - Zulte Waregem 2-2(2-0)
Antwerp FC - Charleroi 0-1(0-1)
OH Leuven - Anderlecht 0-2(0-1)
Union Saint-Gilloise - KV Mechelen 2-1(1-1)
KAA Gent - KAS Eupen 3-0(1-0)

**Round 31** [31.03.-02.04.2023]
Zulte Waregem - Antwerp FC 0-2(0-0)
Cercle Brugge - KV Kortrijk 2-0(2-0)
Westerlo - Charleroi 2-3(1-2)
RFC Seraing - KAA Gent 0-5(0-1)
KV Oostende - Standard Liège 1-3(1-3)
KRC Genk - OH Leuven 2-1(1-0)
KAS Eupen - Anderlecht 0-1(0-0)
KV Mechelen - Club Brugge 0-3(0-2)
Union SG - Sint-Truidense VV 2-1(0-0)

**Round 32** [07-09.04.2023]
Club Brugge - RFC Seraing 2-0(0-0)
KV Kortrijk - KAS Eupen 0-2(0-0)
OH Leuven - KV Mechelen 4-1(2-0)
Charleroi - Zulte Waregem 3-2(0-1)
KAA Gent - Union Saint-Gilloise 1-1(0-1)
Anderlecht - Westerlo 0-0
Antwerp FC - Cercle Brugge 2-1(0-1)
Standard Liège - KRC Genk 2-0(2-0)
Sint-Truidense VV - KV Oostende 5-0(2-0)

**Round 33** [14-16.04.2023]
Standard Liège - Charleroi 3-1(1-0)
KAS Eupen - Zulte Waregem 1-5(0-4)
Cercle Brugge - Sint-Truidense VV 3-1(2-0)
KV Oostende - OH Leuven 0-4(0-2)
Westerlo - Club Brugge 0-0
KRC Genk - Anderlecht 5-2(2-1)
KV Mechelen - KAA Gent 1-1(1-1)
Antwerp FC - KV Kortrijk 1-0(0-0)
Union Saint-Gilloise - RFC Seraing 2-1(2-0)

**Round 34** [22-23.04.2023]
RFC Seraing - Westerlo 1-1(1-1)
Sint-Truidense VV - Antwerp FC 0-1(0-0)
Club Brugge - KAS Eupen 7-0(4-0)
KAA Gent - KV Oostende 1-2(0-0)
KV Kortrijk - Union Saint-Gilloise 2-4(2-1)
OH Leuven - Standard Liège 3-2(1-0)
Anderlecht - KV Mechelen 2-3(1-2)
Charleroi - KRC Genk 2-2(1-2)
Zulte Waregem - Cercle Brugge 2-3(0-2)

## Final Standings

| # | Team | Total | | | | | | Home | | | | | Away | | | | |
|---|------|---|---|---|---|---|---|---|---|---|---|---|---|---|---|---|---|
| 1. | KRC Genk | 34 | 23 | 6 | 5 | 78 - 37 | 75 | 14 | 1 | 2 | 44 - 15 | | 9 | 5 | 3 | 34 - 22 |
| 2. | Royale Union Saint-Gilloise | 34 | 23 | 6 | 5 | 70 - 41 | 75 | 13 | 2 | 2 | 33 - 16 | | 10 | 4 | 3 | 37 - 25 |
| 3. | Royal Antwerp FC | 34 | 22 | 6 | 6 | 59 - 26 | 72 | 13 | 2 | 2 | 36 - 11 | | 9 | 4 | 4 | 23 - 15 |
| 4. | Club Brugge KV | 34 | 16 | 11 | 7 | 61 - 36 | 59 | 10 | 6 | 1 | 40 - 15 | | 6 | 5 | 6 | 21 - 21 |
| 5. | KAA Gent | 34 | 16 | 8 | 10 | 64 - 38 | 56 | 9 | 4 | 4 | 28 - 16 | | 7 | 4 | 6 | 36 - 22 |
| 6. | R Standard Liège | 34 | 16 | 7 | 11 | 58 - 45 | 55 | 10 | 3 | 4 | 34 - 17 | | 6 | 4 | 7 | 24 - 28 |
| 7. | KVC Westerlo | 34 | 14 | 9 | 11 | 61 - 53 | 51 | 8 | 4 | 5 | 40 - 26 | | 6 | 5 | 6 | 21 - 27 |
| 8. | Cercle Brugge KSV | 34 | 13 | 11 | 10 | 50 - 46 | 50 | 8 | 7 | 2 | 31 - 18 | | 5 | 4 | 8 | 19 - 28 |
| 9. | R Charleroi SC | 34 | 14 | 6 | 14 | 45 - 52 | 48 | 7 | 2 | 8 | 23 - 27 | | 7 | 4 | 6 | 22 - 25 |
| 10. | Oud-Heverle Leuven | 34 | 13 | 9 | 12 | 56 - 48 | 48 | 7 | 5 | 5 | 29 - 24 | | 6 | 4 | 7 | 27 - 24 |
| 11. | RSC Anderlecht Bruxelles | 34 | 13 | 7 | 14 | 49 - 46 | 46 | 6 | 4 | 7 | 27 - 23 | | 7 | 3 | 7 | 22 - 23 |
| 12. | Sint-Truidense VV | 34 | 11 | 9 | 14 | 37 - 40 | 42 | 6 | 4 | 7 | 20 - 19 | | 5 | 5 | 7 | 17 - 21 |
| 13. | KV Mechelen | 34 | 11 | 7 | 16 | 49 - 63 | 40 | 7 | 6 | 4 | 29 - 27 | | 4 | 1 | 12 | 20 - 36 |
| 14. | KV Kortrijk | 34 | 8 | 7 | 19 | 37 - 61 | 31 | 4 | 5 | 8 | 16 - 29 | | 4 | 2 | 11 | 21 - 32 |
| 15. | KAS Eupen | 34 | 7 | 7 | 20 | 40 - 75 | 28 | 4 | 4 | 9 | 22 - 33 | | 3 | 3 | 11 | 18 - 42 |
| 16. | KV Oostende (*Relegated*) | 34 | 7 | 6 | 21 | 37 - 76 | 27 | 5 | 1 | 11 | 18 - 33 | | 2 | 5 | 10 | 19 - 43 |
| 17. | SV Zulte Waregem (*Relegated*) | 34 | 6 | 9 | 19 | 50 - 78 | 27 | 3 | 4 | 10 | 27 - 46 | | 3 | 5 | 9 | 23 - 32 |
| 18. | RFC Seraing (*Relegated*) | 34 | 5 | 5 | 24 | 28 - 68 | 20 | 1 | 4 | 12 | 8 - 29 | | 4 | 1 | 12 | 20 - 39 |

Teams ranked 1-4 were qualified for the Play-Off I (Championship), while teams ranked 5-8 were qualified for the Play-Off II (Europe).
The next season will be played with 16 teams.

## Play-Off I

Please note: the points obtained during the regular season were halved (and rounded up) before the start of the playoff. As a result, the teams started with the following points before the play-off: KRC Genk & Royale Union Saint-Gilloise 38, Royal Antwerp FC 36 and Club Brugge KV 30.

**Round 1 [30.04.-03.05.2023]**
KRC Genk - Club Brugge 3-1(1-1)
Union Saint-Gilloise - Antwerp FC 0-2(0-2)

**Round 2 [06-07.05.2023]**
Club Brugge - Union Saint-Gilloise 1-2(0-1)
Antwerp FC - KRC Genk 2-1(1-1)

**Round 3 [14.05.2023]**
Antwerp FC - Club Brugge 3-2(1-2)
Union Saint-Gilloise - KRC Genk 3-0(1-0)

**Round 4 [21.05.2023]**
Club Brugge - Antwerp FC 2-0(0-0)
KRC Genk - Union Saint-Gilloise 1-1(1-1)

**Round 5 [28.05.2023]**
Antwerp FC - Union Saint-Gilloise 1-1(1-0)
Club Brugge - KRC Genk 1-3(0-1)

**Round 6 [04.06.2023]**
KRC Genk - Antwerp FC 2-2(1-0)
Union Saint-Gilloise - Club Brugge 1-3(0-0)

### Final Standings

| # | Team | Total | | | | | | Home | | | | | Away | | | | |
|---|------|---|---|---|---|---|---|---|---|---|---|---|---|---|---|---|---|
| 1. | **Royal Antwerp FC** | 6 | 3 | 2 | 1 | 10 - 8 | 47 | 2 | 1 | 0 | 6 - 4 | | 1 | 1 | 1 | 4 - 4 |
| 2. | KRC Genk | 6 | 2 | 2 | 2 | 10 - 10 | 46 | 1 | 2 | 0 | 6 - 4 | | 1 | 0 | 2 | 4 - 6 |
| 3. | Royale Union Saint-Gilloise | 6 | 2 | 2 | 2 | 8 - 8 | 46 | 1 | 0 | 2 | 4 - 5 | | 1 | 2 | 0 | 4 - 3 |
| 4. | Club Brugge KV | 6 | 2 | 0 | 4 | 10 - 12 | 36 | 1 | 0 | 2 | 4 - 5 | | 1 | 0 | 2 | 6 - 7 |

## Play-Off II

Please note: the points obtained during the regular season were halved (and rounded up) before the start of the playoff. As a result, the teams started with the following points before the play-off: KAA Gent & R Standard Liège 28, KVC Westerlo 26 and Cercle Brugge KSV 25.

**Round 1 [28-29.04.2023]**
KAA Gent - Westerlo 3-1(0-1)
Cercle Brugge - Standard Liège 0-0

**Round 2 [06-07.05.2023]**
Standard Liège - KAA Gent 1-2(0-1)
Westerlo - Cercle Brugge 3-5(1-4)

**Round 3 [13.05.2023]**
Cercle Brugge - KAA Gent 0-4(0-1)
Standard Liège - Westerlo 2-2(1-0)

**Round 4 [20.05.2023]**
Westerlo - Standard Liège 3-0(2-0)
KAA Gent - Cercle Brugge 2-2(0-1)

**Round 5 [27.05.2023]**
Westerlo - KAA Gent 1-3(1-1)
Standard Liège - Cercle Brugge 0-4(0-1)

**Round 6 [03.06.2023]**
Cercle Brugge - Westerlo 2-0(0-0)
KAA Gent - Standard Liège 3-1(2-1)

### Final Standings

| # | Team | Total | | | | | | Home | | | | | Away | | | | |
|---|------|---|---|---|---|---|---|---|---|---|---|---|---|---|---|---|---|
| 5. | KAA Gent | 6 | 5 | 1 | 0 | 17 - 6 | 44 | 2 | 1 | 0 | 8 - 4 | | 3 | 0 | 0 | 9 - 2 |
| 6. | Cercle Brugge KSV | 6 | 3 | 2 | 1 | 13 - 9 | 36 | 1 | 1 | 1 | 2 - 4 | | 2 | 1 | 0 | 11 - 5 |
| 7. | R Standard Liège | 6 | 0 | 2 | 4 | 4 - 14 | 30 | 0 | 1 | 2 | 3 - 8 | | 0 | 1 | 2 | 1 - 6 |
| 8. | KVC Westerlo | 6 | 1 | 1 | 4 | 10 - 15 | 30 | 1 | 0 | 2 | 7 - 8 | | 0 | 1 | 2 | 3 - 7 |

KAA Gent were qualified for the Europa Conference League (second qualifying Round) 2023/2024.

| Top goalscorers (only regular season): | | |
|---|---|---|
| 27 | **Hugo Cuypers** | *KAA Gent* |
| 22 | Ayase Ueda (JPN) | *Cercle Brugge KSV* |
| 18 | Gianni Bruno | *Sint-Truidense VV* |
| 18 | Vincent Petrus Anna Sebastiaan Janssen (NED) | *Royal Antwerp FC* |

## NATIONAL CUP
### Coupe de Belgique / Beker van België Final 2022/2023

#### Sixth Round [08-10.11.2022]

| | | | | |
|---|---|---|---|---|
| RFC Seraing - R Charleroi SC | 4-1(0-1,1-1) | KSC Lokeren-Temse - KV Mechelen | 0-5(0-2) |
| KMSK Deinze - KAS Eupen | 3-0(2-0) | KVC Westerlo - KRC Genk | 0-1(0-1) |
| FCV Dender EH Denderleeuw - R Standard Liège | 0-1(0-0) | Sint-Truidense VV - RFC Meux | 1-0(0-0) |
| Royal Francs Borains Boussu - Oud-Heverle Leuven | 0-5(0-2) | KFC Dessel Sport - KAA Gent | 0-5(0-4) |
| Lommel SK - SV Zulte Waregem | 0-1(0-0) | K Patro Eisden Maasmechelen - Club Brugge KV | 0-2(0-0,0-0) |
| Cercle Brugge KSV - K Beerschot VA | 3-1(1-1) | SK Beveren - Royal Antwerp FC | 2-2 aet; 2-4 pen |
| KVV THES Sport Tessenderlo - KV Oostende | 1-4(0-0) | RWD Molenbeek - KV Kortrijk | 1-3(0-0) |
| R Cappellen FC - Royale Union Saint-Gilloise | 1-7(1-1) | Lierse Kempenzonen - RSC Anderlecht Bruxelles | 2-2 aet; 8-9 pen |

#### 1/8-Finals [20-21.12.2022]

| | | | | |
|---|---|---|---|---|
| KV Mechelen - RFC Seraing | 1-0(0-0) | Royal Antwerp FC - R Standard Liège | 4-0(1-0) |
| Royale Union Saint-Gilloise - KV Oostende | 2-1(1-1) | Club Brugge KV - Sint-Truidense VV | 1-4(1-1) |
| Oud-Heverle Leuven - KV Kortrijk | 1-3(0-0) | KMSK Deinze - SV Zulte Waregem | 1-2(0-0) |
| KAA Gent - Cercle Brugge KSV | 2-0(0-0,0-0) | KRC Genk - RSC Anderlecht Bruxelles | 1-0(0-0,0-0) |

#### Quarter-Finals [11-12.01.2023]

| | | | | |
|---|---|---|---|---|
| KV Kortrijk - KV Mechelen | 0-1(0-0) | KRC Genk - Royal Antwerp FC | 0-3(0-2) |
| SV Zulte Waregem - Sint-Truidense VV | 2-0(1-0) | Royale Union Saint-Gilloise - KAA Gent | 4-0(3-0) |

#### Semi-Finals [01-02.02./28.02.-02.03.2023]

| First Leg | | Second Leg | |
|---|---|---|---|
| Royale Union Saint-Gilloise - Royal Antwerp FC | 1-0(0-0) | Royal Antwerp FC - Royale Union Saint-Gilloise | 1-0 aet; 4-3 pen |
| SV Zulte Waregem - KV Mechelen | 1-2(1-1) | KV Mechelen - SV Zulte Waregem | 1-0(0-0) |

#### Final

30.04.2023; Stade "Roi Baudouin", Bruxelles; Referee: Jonathan Lardot; Attendance: 41,500
**KV Mechelen - Royal Antwerp FC**                                         **0-2(0-1)**

**KV Mechelen**: Gaëtan Coucke, Sandy Walsh, David Robert Bates (84.Enock Agyei), Jordi Vanlerberghe, Alec Van Hoorenbeeck (63.Boli Bolingoli-Mbombo), Dries Wouters, Dimitri Lavalée (46.Alessio Sergio Fernando Da Cruz), Rob Schoofs (Cap), Geoffry Hairemans, Abdallah Kerim Mrabti (75.Julien N'Goy), Nikola Storm. Trainer: Steven Arnold Defour.

**Antwerp FC**: Jean Butez, Ritchie De Laet, Tobias Albertine Maurits Alderweireld (Cap), William Joel Pacho Tenorio (69.Zeno Van den Bosch), Jelle Bataille (69.Gastón Ávila), Arthur Vermeeren, Calvin Stengs, Jurgen Ekkelenkamp (69.Mandela Keita), Gyrano Emilio Kerk (85.Christopher Scott), Arbnor Muja, Vincent Petrus Anna Sebastiaan Janssen (73.Michel Balikwisha). Trainer: Mark Peter Gertruda Andreas van Bommel (Netherlands).

**Goals:** 0-1 Vincent Petrus Anna Sebastiaan Janssen (35 penalty), 0-2 Michel Balikwisha (81).

## THE CLUBS 2022/2023

### Royal Sporting Club Anderlecht Bruxelles

| | | |
|---|---|---|
| **Founded**: | 27.05.1908 | |
| **Stadium**: | Lotto Park [Stade "Constant Vanden Stock"], Bruxelles (21,500) | |
| **Trainer**: | Felice Mazzù | 12.03.1966 |
| [24.10.2022] | Robin Veldman (NED) | 24.12.1985 |
| [02.12.2022] | Brian Riemer (DEN) | 22.09.1978 |

| Goalkeepers: | DOB | M | (s) | G |
|---|---|---|---|---|
| Hendrik Van Crombrugge | 30.04.1993 | 17 | | |
| Bart Verbruggen (NED) | 18.08.2002 | 17 | | |
| **Defenders:** | **DOB** | **M** | **(s)** | **G** |
| Zeno Debast | 24.10.2003 | 34 | | |
| Hannes Delcroix | 28.02.1999 | 13 | (3) | |
| Wesley Theodorus Hoedt (NED) | 06.03.1994 | 15 | | |
| Lucas Lissens | 25.07.2001 | | (1) | |
| Michael Amir Murillo Bermúdez (PAN) | 11.02.1996 | 27 | (2) | 3 |
| Moussa N'Diaye (SEN) | 18.06.2002 | 10 | (5) | |
| Noah Sadiki | 17.12.2004 | 4 | (8) | |
| Killian Sardella | 02.05.2002 | 12 | (4) | |
| *Sergio Gómez* Martín (ESP) | 04.09.2000 | | (1) | |
| Jan Bert Lieve Vertonghen | 24.04.1987 | 23 | (1) | 1 |
| **Midfielders:** | **DOB** | **M** | **(s)** | **G** |
| Ishaq Abdulrazak (NGA) | 05.05.2002 | 2 | (1) | |
| Nilson David Angulo Ramírez (ECU) | 19.06.2003 | | (6) | |
| Kristian Arnstad (NOR) | 07.09.2003 | 12 | (15) | 1 |
| Majeed Ashimeru (GHA) | 10.10.1997 | 21 | (7) | 2 |
| Amadou Diawara (GUI) | 17.07.1997 | 19 | (3) | 1 |
| Anouar Ait El Hadj | 20.04.2002 | 1 | (2) | 1 |
| Marco Kana | 08.08.2002 | 4 | (5) | |
| Théo Leoni | 21.04.2000 | 1 | (5) | |
| Kristoffer Olsson (SWE) | 30.06.1995 | | (3) | |
| Lior Refaelov (ISR) | 26.04.1986 | 17 | (12) | 4 |
| Adrien Trébel (FRA) | 03.03.1991 | 6 | (5) | |
| Yari Verschaeren | 12.07.2001 | 26 | (2) | 2 |
| **Forwards:** | **DOB** | **M** | **(s)** | **G** |
| Francis Amuzu | 23.08.1999 | 27 | (6) | 3 |
| Anders Dreyer (DEN) | 02.05.1998 | 13 | (1) | 4 |
| Julien Duranville | 05.05.2006 | 2 | (4) | 1 |
| Sebastiano Esposito (ITA) | 02.07.2002 | 5 | (9) | 1 |
| *Fábio* Daniel Soares *Silva* (POR) | 19.07.2002 | 17 | (3) | 7 |
| Benito Raman | 07.11.1994 | 9 | (13) | 5 |
| Islam Slimani (ALG) | 18.06.1988 | 7 | (3) | 8 |
| Lucas Stassin | 29.11.2004 | 2 | (1) | |
| Mario Stroeykens | 29.09.2004 | 11 | (15) | 4 |

## Royal Antwerp Football Club

| | | | |
|---|---|---|---|
| **Founded:** | 1880 | | |
| **Stadium:** | Bosuilstadion, Antwerp (12,975) | | |
| **Trainer:** | Mark Peter Gertruda Andreas van Bommel (NED) | | 22.04.1977 |

| Goalkeepers: | DOB | M | (s) | G |
|---|---|---|---|---|
| Jean Butez (FRA) | 08.06.1995 | 40 | | |
| **Defenders:** | **DOB** | **M** | **(s)** | **G** |
| Tobias Albertine Maurits Alderweireld | 02.03.1989 | 36 | | 7 |
| Gastón Ávila (ARG) | 30.09.2001 | 15 | (7) | |
| Jelle Bataille | 20.05.1999 | 28 | (9) | |
| Kobe Corbanie | 10.05.2005 | | (6) | |
| *Dinis* Costa Lima *Almeida* (POR) | 28.06.1995 | 3 | (5) | |
| Ritchie De Laet | 28.11.1988 | 24 | (8) | 1 |
| William Joel Pacho Tenorio (ECU) | 16.10.2001 | 39 | | |
| Zeno Van den Bosch | 06.07.2003 | 3 | (4) | |
| Samuel Marqus Lloyd Vines (USA) | 31.05.1999 | 15 | | 1 |
| **Midfielders:** | **DOB** | **M** | **(s)** | **G** |
| Jurgen Ekkelenkamp (NED) | 05.04.2000 | 28 | (5) | 6 |
| Pieter Gerkens | 13.08.1995 | 16 | (3) | 1 |
| Faris Haroun | 22.09.1985 | | (2) | |
| Mandela Keita | 10.05.2002 | 15 | (2) | 1 |
| Koji Miyoshi (JPN) | 26.03.1997 | 9 | (1) | 1 |
| Radja Nainggolan | 04.05.1988 | 7 | (5) | 1 |
| Christopher Scott (GER) | 07.06.2002 | | (22) | 1 |
| Milan Smits | 13.11.2004 | | (1) | |
| Calvin Stengs (NED) | 18.12.1998 | 21 | (4) | 1 |
| Gerard Vandeplas | 25.02.2006 | | (1) | |
| Arthur Vermeeren | 07.02.2005 | 24 | (2) | 1 |
| Birger Verstraete | 16.04.1994 | | (4) | |
| Alhassan Yusuf Abdullahi (NGA) | 18.07.2000 | 17 | (10) | |
| **Forwards:** | **DOB** | **M** | **(s)** | **G** |
| Michel Balikwisha | 10.05.2001 | 28 | (5) | 7 |
| *Benson* Manuel Hedilazio (ANG) | 28.03.1997 | | (1) | |
| Viktor Gorridsen Fischer (DEN) | 09.06.1994 | | (7) | |
| Michael Frey (SUI) | 19.07.1994 | 7 | (7) | 7 |
| Vincent Petrus Anna Sebastiaan Janssen(NED) | 15.06.1994 | 32 | (4) | 18 |
| Gyrano Emilio Kerk (NED) | 02.12.1995 | 11 | (7) | 6 |
| Arbnor Muja (KOS) | 29.11.1998 | 21 | (6) | 3 |
| Bruny Nsimba | 05.04.2000 | | (10) | 1 |
| Anthony Lenín Valencia Bajaña (ECU) | 21.07.2003 | 1 | (9) | 1 |

## Cercle Brugge Koninklijke Sportvereniging

| | | | |
|---|---|---|---|
| **Founded:** | 1899 | | |
| **Stadium:** | "Jan Breydel" Stadium, Brugge (29,042) | | |
| **Trainer:** | Dominik Thalhammer (AUT) | | 02.10.1970 |
| [28.11.2022] | Miron Muslić (AUT) | | 14.09.1982 |

| Goalkeepers: | DOB | M | (s) | G |
|---|---|---|---|---|
| Radosław Majecki (POL) | 16.11.1999 | 34 | | |
| *Warleson* Stellion Lisboa Oliveira (BRA) | 31.08.1996 | 6 | (1) | |
| **Defenders:** | **DOB** | **M** | **(s)** | **G** |
| Jesper Daland (NOR) | 06.01.2000 | 34 | (3) | 1 |
| Robbe Decostere | 08.05.1998 | 10 | (7) | |
| *Heitor* Rodrigues da Fonseca (BRA) | 05.11.2000 | | (7) | |
| Jean Marcelin (FRA) | 12.02.2000 | 13 | (7) | 1 |
| Senna Miangué (CGO) | 05.02.1997 | 4 | (4) | |
| Boris Popović (SRB) | 26.02.2000 | 37 | (2) | 2 |
| Christiaan Ravych | 30.07.2002 | 23 | (8) | 1 |
| Hugo Siquet | 09.07.2002 | 18 | (2) | 2 |
| Louis Alex Torres (FRA) | 29.04.2001 | 9 | (1) | 1 |
| Edgaras Utkus (LTU) | 22.06.2000 | 1 | (2) | |
| Dimitar Velkovski (BUL) | 22.01.1995 | 1 | (4) | |
| Tarick Ximines (JAM) | 07.10.2004 | | (1) | |
| **Midfielders:** | **DOB** | **M** | **(s)** | **G** |
| Francis Abu (GHA) | 27.04.2001 | 19 | (12) | 2 |
| Olivier Deman | 06.04.2000 | 34 | (2) | 1 |
| Gnantin Yann Gboho (FRA) | 14.01.2001 | 11 | (18) | 3 |
| Dino Hotič (BIH) | 26.07.1995 | 22 | (18) | 5 |
| *Leonardo* Adelino da Silva *Lopes* (POR) | 30.11.1998 | 27 | (3) | 1 |
| Hannes Van der Bruggen | 01.04.1993 | 15 | (12) | |
| Charles Vanhoutte | 16.09.1998 | 21 | (11) | 1 |
| **Forwards:** | **DOB** | **M** | **(s)** | **G** |
| Kévin Denkey (TOG) | 30.11.2000 | 28 | (10) | 11 |
| Emilio Kehrer (GER) | 20.03.2002 | | (11) | 1 |
| Aske Sampers | 20.05.2001 | | (3) | |
| Thibo Somers | 16.03.1999 | 36 | (1) | 7 |
| Ayase Ueda (JPN) | 28.08.1998 | 37 | (3) | 22 |
| Teun Sebastián Ángel Wilke Braams (MEX) | 14.03.2002 | | (3) | |

## Royal Charleroi Sporting Club

| | | | |
|---|---|---|---|
| **Founded:** | 01.01.1904 | | |
| **Stadium:** | Stade du Pays de Charleroi, Charleroi (14,000) | | |
| **Trainer:** | Edward Still | | 30.12.1990 |
| [22.10.2022] | Frank Defays | | 23.02.1974 |
| [28.11.2022] | Felice Mazzù | | 12.03.1966 |

| Goalkeepers: | DOB | M | (s) | G |
|---|---|---|---|---|
| Hervé Koffi Kouakou (BFA) | 16.10.1996 | 28 | | |
| Pierre Georges Patron (FRA) | 20.08.1997 | 6 | | |
| **Defenders:** | **DOB** | **M** | **(s)** | **G** |
| Stelios Andreou (CYP) | 24.07.2002 | 20 | (3) | |
| Jonas Valentin Bager (DEN) | 18.07.1996 | 21 | (2) | 1 |
| Loïc Bessilé (TOG) | 19.02.1999 | 7 | (5) | 1 |
| Mehdi Boukamir | 26.01.2004 | 8 | (2) | |
| Joris Kayembe | 08.08.1994 | 26 | (4) | 1 |
| Stefan Knežević (SUI) | 30.10.1996 | 14 | (1) | |
| Valentine James Ozornwafor (NGA) | 01.06.1999 | 1 | (2) | |
| Jules Van Cleemput | 11.04.1997 | 5 | (3) | |
| Martin Wasinski | 07.04.2004 | 4 | (3) | |
| **Midfielders:** | **DOB** | **M** | **(s)** | **G** |
| Ali Gholizadeh (IRN) | 10.03.1996 | 10 | (10) | 1 |
| Daan Heymans | 15.06.1999 | 20 | (13) | 6 |
| Amir Hosseinzadeh (IRN) | 30.10.2000 | 12 | (11) | 2 |
| Marco Ilaimaharitra (MAD) | 26.07.1995 | 31 | (1) | 3 |
| Damien Marcq (FRA) | 08.12.1988 | 17 | (4) | 2 |
| Ryota Morioka (JPN) | 12.04.1991 | 11 | (11) | 3 |
| Adem Zorgane (ALG) | 06.01.2000 | 31 | (1) | 4 |
| **Forwards:** | **DOB** | **M** | **(s)** | **G** |
| Youssouph Badji (SEN) | 20.12.2001 | 12 | (14) | 5 |
| Vakoun Issouf Bayo (CIV) | 10.01.1997 | 10 | | 3 |
| Nadhir Benbouali (ALG) | 17.04.2000 | 8 | (7) | 2 |
| Adrien Bongiovanni | 20.09.1999 | | (1) | |
| Anthony Descotte | 03.08.2003 | | (9) | |
| Josué Doké (TOG) | 20.04.2004 | | (2) | |
| Isaac Mbenza | 08.03.1996 | 25 | (9) | 4 |
| Ken Nkuba | 21.01.2002 | 25 | (3) | 4 |
| Nikola Štulić (SRB) | 08.09.2001 | 3 | (5) | |
| Jackson Tchatchoua | 23.06.2001 | 16 | (13) | 1 |
| Anass Zaroury | 07.11.2000 | 3 | (2) | 2 |

## Club Brugge Koninklijke Voetbalvereniging

| | | | |
|---|---|---|---|
| **Founded**: | 13.11.1891 | | |
| **Stadium**: | "Jan Breydel" Stadium, Brugge (29,042) | | |
| **Trainer**: | Carl Hoefkens | 06.10.1978 | |
| [31.12.2022] | Scott Matthew Parker (ENG) | 13.10.1980 | |
| [08.03.2023] | Rik De Mil | 15.09.1981 | |

| Goalkeepers: | DOB | M | (s) | G |
|---|---|---|---|---|
| Simon Luc Hildebert Mignolet | 06.03.1988 | 40 | | |
| **Defenders:** | **DOB** | **M** | **(s)** | **G** |
| Anga Dedryck Boyata | 28.11.1990 | 6 | (5) | |
| *Clinton* Mata Pedro Lourenço (ANG) | 07.11.1992 | 23 | (2) | 1 |
| Jack William Hendry (SCO) | 07.05.1995 | 7 | (1) | |
| Brandon Mechele | 28.01.1993 | 34 | (2) | 2 |
| Bjorn Thomas Meijer (NED) | 18.03.2003 | 33 | (2) | 3 |
| Stanley Pierre N'Soki (FRA) | 09.04.1999 | 2 | | |
| Denis Odoi | 27.05.1988 | 23 | (6) | |
| Kyriani Sabbe | 26.01.2005 | 1 | (2) | |
| Eduard Sobol (UKR) | 20.04.1995 | 5 | (4) | 1 |
| Jorne Spileers | 21.01.2005 | 10 | (1) | |
| Abakar Sylla (CIV) | 25.12.2002 | 16 | (4) | |
| **Midfielders:** | **DOB** | **M** | **(s)** | **G** |
| Lynnt Audoor | 13.10.2003 | | (6) | |
| Éder Fabián Álvarez Balanta (COL) | 28.02.1993 | 3 | (6) | |
| Noah Mbamba-Muanda | 05.01.2005 | 1 | (1) | |
| Casper Mørup Nielsen (DEN) | 29.04.1994 | 31 | (5) | 9 |
| Raphael Onyedika Nwadike (NGA) | 19.04.2001 | 26 | (5) | |
| Owen Otasowie (USA) | 06.01.2001 | 1 | | |
| Mats Rits | 18.07.1993 | 14 | (6) | 2 |
| Cisse Sandra | 16.12.2003 | 1 | (10) | 1 |
| Chemsdine Talbi | 09.05.2005 | | (5) | |
| Hans Vanaken | 24.08.1992 | 40 | | 14 |
| Ruud Vormer (NED) | 11.05.1988 | 1 | (1) | |
| **Forwards:** | **DOB** | **M** | **(s)** | **G** |
| Tajon Trevor Buchanan (CAN) | 08.02.1999 | 19 | (5) | 1 |
| *Ferrán* Jutglà Blanch (ESP) | 01.02.1999 | 28 | (6) | 13 |
| Shion Homma (JPN) | 09.08.2000 | | (2) | 1 |
| Noa Noëll Lang (NED) | 17.06.1999 | 25 | (8) | 9 |
| Cyle Christopher Larin (BEL) | 17.04.1995 | 1 | (8) | 1 |
| Antonio Eremensele Nordby Nusa (NOR) | 17.04.2005 | 7 | (19) | 1 |
| Andreas Skov Olsen (DEN) | 29.12.1999 | 18 | (5) | 7 |
| Kamal Sowah (GHA) | 09.01.2000 | 14 | (13) | |
| Romeo Vermant | 24.01.2004 | 1 | (9) | |
| Roman Yaremchuk (UKR) | 27.11.1995 | 9 | (14) | 2 |

## Königliche Allgemeine Sportvereinigung Eupen

| | | | |
|---|---|---|---|
| **Founded**: | 1945 | | |
| **Stadium**: | Kehrwegstadion, Eupen (8,363) | | |
| **Trainer**: | Bernd Storck (GER) | 25.01.1963 | |
| [24.10.2022] | Kristoffer Andersen & | 09.12.1985 | |
| | Mario Kohnen | 07.10.1986 | |
| [24.11.2022] | Edward Still | 30.12.1990 | |

| Goalkeepers: | DOB | M | (s) | G |
|---|---|---|---|---|
| Lennart Moser (GER) | 06.12.1999 | 30 | (1) | |
| Abdul Nurudeen (GHA) | 08.02.1999 | 4 | | |
| **Defenders:** | **DOB** | **M** | **(s)** | **G** |
| Teddy Alloh (FRA) | 23.01.2002 | 5 | (5) | |
| Loïc Bessilé (TOG) | 19.02.1999 | 7 | (1) | |
| Jason Alan Davidson (AUS) | 29.06.1991 | 30 | (3) | |
| Ibrahim Diakité (GUI) | 31.10.2003 | 2 | (8) | |
| Oleksandr Filin (UKR) | 25.06.1996 | 8 | (1) | |
| Jan Gorenc (SVN) | 26.07.1999 | 2 | (1) | |
| Sibiry Keita (MLI) | 30.01.2001 | | (1) | |
| Jan Král (CZE) | 05.04.1999 | 5 | (2) | |
| Boris Lambert | 10.04.2000 | 28 | (4) | 4 |
| Gary Magnée | 12.10.1999 | 25 | (6) | 3 |
| Rune Paeshuyse | 28.03.2002 | 23 | (5) | |
| Yentl Van Genechten | 18.08.2000 | 30 | (3) | |
| **Midfielders:** | **DOB** | **M** | **(s)** | **G** |
| Brandon Baiye | 27.12.2000 | 7 | (1) | 1 |
| Nathan Bitumazala (FRA) | 10.12.2002 | 9 | (6) | |
| Isaac Christie-Davies (WAL) | 18.10.1997 | 15 | (9) | |
| Jérôme Déom | 19.04.1999 | 6 | (10) | |
| James Alexander Jeggo (AUS) | 12.02.1992 | 11 | (3) | |
| Tyreek Magee (JAM) | 27.10.1999 | | (5) | |
| Stef Peeters | 09.02.1992 | 30 | (1) | 7 |
| Mubarak Wakaso (GHA) | 25.07.1990 | 6 | (3) | |
| **Forwards:** | **DOB** | **M** | **(s)** | **G** |
| Regan Evans Charles-Cook (GRN) | 14.02.1997 | 26 | (5) | 6 |
| Antonio David Álvarez Rey „Davo" (ESP) | 18.12.1994 | 1 | (6) | |
| Djeidi Gassama (FRA) | 10.09.2003 | 6 | (13) | 2 |
| Konan N'Dri (CIV) | 27.10.2000 | 22 | (11) | 7 |
| Isaac Nuhu (GHA) | 30.09.2001 | 13 | (6) | 2 |
| Lorenzo Offermann | 10.01.2002 | | (2) | |
| Smail Prevljak (BIH) | 10.05.1995 | 22 | (8) | 6 |
| Sambou Soumano (SEN) | 13.01.2001 | 1 | (6) | 1 |

## Koninklijke Racing Club Genk

| | | | |
|---|---|---|---|
| **Founded**: | 1988 | | |
| **Stadium**: | Luminus Arena, Genk (24,956) | | |
| **Trainer**: | Wouter Vrancken | 03.02.1979 | |

| Goalkeepers: | DOB | M | (s) | G |
|---|---|---|---|---|
| Maarten Vandevoordt | 26.02.2002 | 40 | | |
| **Defenders:** | **DOB** | **M** | **(s)** | **G** |
| Gerardo Daniel Arteaga Zamora (MEX) | 07.09.1998 | 38 | | 2 |
| Rasmus Carstensen (DEN) | 10.11.2000 | | (4) | |
| Carlos Eccohomo Cuesta Figueroa (COL) | 09.03.1999 | 33 | | 1 |
| Jhon Janer Lucumi Bonilla (COL) | 26.06.1998 | 3 | | |
| Mark Alexander McKenzie (USA) | 25.02.1999 | 36 | | 4 |
| *Mujaid* Sadick Aliu (ESP) | 14.03.2000 | 7 | (2) | |
| Daniel Muñoz Mejia (COL) | 25.05.1996 | 36 | | 8 |
| Aziz Ouattara (CIV) | 04.01.2001 | 3 | (15) | 2 |
| Ángelo Smit Preciado Quiñónez (ECU) | 18.02.1998 | 10 | (14) | |
| **Midfielders:** | **DOB** | **M** | **(s)** | **G** |
| Anouar Ait El Hadj | 20.04.2002 | | (10) | |
| Nicolás Federico Castro (ARG) | 01.11.2000 | 3 | (20) | |
| Matisse Didden | 08.10.2001 | | (1) | |
| Bilal El Khannouss (MAR) | 10.05.2004 | 35 | (4) | 1 |
| Matías Alejandro Galarza (ARG) | 04.03.2002 | | (8) | |
| Jay-Dee Geusens | 05.03.2002 | | (1) | |
| Bryan Heynen | 06.02.1997 | 38 | (1) | 11 |
| Patrik Hrošovský (SVK) | 22.04.1992 | 40 | | 3 |
| Luca Oyen | 14.03.2003 | 2 | (4) | |
| Yira Collins Sor (NGA) | 24.07.2000 | 4 | (16) | 2 |
| Mike Trésor Ndayishimiye | 28.05.1999 | 38 | (1) | 8 |
| **Forwards:** | **DOB** | **M** | **(s)** | **G** |
| Toluwalase Emmanuel Arokodare (NGA) | 23.11.2000 | 5 | (6) | 2 |
| Cyriel Dessers (NGA) | 08.12.1994 | 3 | | 3 |
| Junya Ito (JPN) | 09.03.1993 | 1 | | |
| András Németh (HUN) | 09.11.2002 | 4 | (11) | 1 |
| Ebere Paul Onuachu (NGA) | 28.05.1994 | 14 | (5) | 16 |
| Joseph Paintsil (GHA) | 01.02.1998 | 34 | (2) | 17 |
| Mbwana Samatta (TAN) | 23.12.1992 | 13 | (20) | 6 |

## Koninklijke Atletiek Associatie Gent

| | | | | |
|---|---|---|---|---|
| Founded: | 1900 | | | |
| Stadium: | Ghelamco Arena, Gent (20,000) | | | |
| Trainer: | Hein Vanhaezebrouck | | | 16.02.1964 |

| Goalkeepers: | DOB | M | (s) | G |
|---|---|---|---|---|
| Paul Nardi (FRA) | 18.05.1994 | 30 | | |
| Davy Roef | 06.02.1994 | 10 | (1) | |
| **Defenders:** | **DOB** | **M** | **(s)** | **G** |
| Brian Emo Agbor (CMR) | 14.06.2001 | | (3) | |
| Alessio Castro-Montes | 17.05.1997 | 22 | (9) | 1 |
| Bruno Godeau | 10.05.1992 | 4 | (11) | |
| Andreas Hanche-Olsen (NOR) | 17.01.1997 | 4 | (4) | |
| Bram Lagae | 14.01.2004 | | (3) | |
| Michael Ngadeu-Ngadjui (CMR) | 23.11.1990 | 30 | | 1 |
| *Núrio* Domingos Matias *Fortuna* (ANG) | 24.03.1995 | 11 | (5) | 1 |
| Joseph Stanley Okumu (KEN) | 26.05.1997 | 29 | (1) | 1 |
| Kamil Piątkowski (POL) | 21.06.2000 | 16 | (1) | |
| Jordan Torunarigha (GER) | 07.08.1997 | 33 | (1) | 3 |
| Cederick Van Daele | 25.08.2000 | | (1) | |
| **Midfielders:** | **DOB** | **M** | **(s)** | **G** |
| Noah De Ridder | 08.10.2003 | | (1) | |
| Julien De Sart | 23.12.1994 | 22 | (5) | 2 |
| Andrew Hjulsager (DEN) | 15.01.1995 | 17 | (7) | 3 |
| Hong Hyun-seok (KOR) | 16.06.1999 | 34 | (3) | 6 |
| Sven Kums | 26.02.1988 | 37 | (1) | 3 |
| Sulayman Marreh (GAM) | 15.01.1996 | 5 | (6) | 1 |
| Vadis Odjidja-Ofoe | 21.02.1989 | 19 | (10) | 1 |
| Elisha Owusu (FRA) | 07.11.1997 | 6 | (3) | |
| Ibrahim Salah (MAR) | 30.08.2001 | 8 | (6) | 3 |
| Matisse Samoise | 21.11.2001 | 31 | (2) | 2 |
| Rune Van den Bergh | 27.01.2003 | | (3) | |
| **Forwards:** | **DOB** | **M** | **(s)** | **G** |
| Hugo Cuypers | 07.02.1997 | 37 | (2) | 27 |
| Laurent Depoitre | 07.12.1988 | 7 | (21) | 5 |
| Matias Fernandez-Pardo | 03.02.2005 | | (1) | |
| Malick Fofana | 31.03.2005 | 8 | (14) | |
| Jens Petter Hauge (NOR) | 12.10.1999 | 1 | (18) | |
| Darko Lemajić (SRB) | 20.08.1993 | 1 | (7) | 2 |
| Gift Emmanuel Orban (NGA) | 17.07.2002 | 14 | (2) | 15 |
| Tarik Tissoudali (MAR) | 02.04.1993 | 4 | (8) | 2 |

## Koninklijke Voetbalclub Kortrijk

| | | | | |
|---|---|---|---|---|
| Founded: | 1901 | | | |
| Stadium: | Guldensporen Stadion, Kortrijk (9,399) | | | |
| Trainer: | Karim Belhocine (FRA) | | | 02.04.1978 |
| [01.09.2022] | Adnan Čustović (BIH) | | | 16.04.1978 |
| [18.11.2022] | Bernd Storck (GER) | | | 25.01.1963 |

| Goalkeepers: | DOB | M | (s) | G |
|---|---|---|---|---|
| Marko Ilić (SRB) | 03.02.1998 | 17 | | |
| Tom Vandenberghe | 17.08.1992 | 17 | | |
| **Defenders:** | **DOB** | **M** | **(s)** | **G** |
| Christalino Atemona (GER) | 26.04.2002 | 6 | (4) | |
| Kristof D'Haene | 06.06.1990 | 27 | (2) | 1 |
| Dorian Dessoleil | 07.08.1992 | 13 | | |
| Nikolas Langberg Dyhr (DEN) | 18.06.2001 | | (1) | |
| *João* Pedro Eira Antunes *Silva* (POR) | 14.01.1999 | 18 | (4) | 2 |
| Nayel Mehssatou | 08.08.2002 | 22 | (5) | |
| Aleksandar Radovanović (SRB) | 11.11.1993 | 10 | (1) | |
| Martin Wasinski | 07.04.2004 | 11 | (4) | 1 |
| Tsuyoshi Watanabe (JPN) | 05.02.1997 | 34 | | 1 |
| **Midfielders:** | **DOB** | **M** | **(s)** | **G** |
| Amine Benchaib | 18.06.1998 | 1 | (2) | |
| Youssef Challouk | 28.08.1995 | | (2) | |
| Alexandre De Bruyn | 04.06.1994 | 2 | (2) | |
| Dion De Neve | 12.06.2001 | 4 | (10) | 1 |
| Abdelkahar Kadri (ALG) | 24.06.2000 | 13 | (3) | 4 |
| Habib Keïta (MLI) | 05.02.2002 | 14 | (4) | 1 |
| Stjepan Lončar (BIH) | 10.11.1996 | 13 | (9) | |
| Faïz Selemani (COM) | 14.11.1993 | 24 | (4) | 8 |
| Sambou Sissoko (MLI) | 29.06.2000 | 3 | (1) | |
| Oleksiy Sych (UKR) | 01.04.2001 | 14 | | 1 |
| Satoshi Tanaka (JPN) | 13.08.2002 | 10 | (5) | |
| Kévin Vandendriessche (FRA) | 07.08.1989 | 7 | (3) | |
| **Forwards:** | **DOB** | **M** | **(s)** | **G** |
| Felipe Nicolás Avenatti Dovillabichus (URU) | 26.04.1993 | 21 | (7) | 7 |
| Massimo Bruno | 17.09.1993 | 13 | (9) | 3 |
| Pape Guèye (SEN) | 20.09.1999 | 13 | (13) | 3 |
| David Henen | 19.04.1996 | 8 | (9) | |
| Didier Lamkel Zé (CMR) | 17.09.1996 | 10 | | 1 |
| Dylan Mbayo | 11.10.2001 | 6 | (13) | 1 |
| Billal Messaoudi (ALG) | 21.12.1997 | 18 | (13) | 2 |
| Martin Regáli (SVK) | 12.10.1993 | 5 | (8) | |
| Luqman Hakim Shamsudin (MAS) | 05.03.2002 | | (1) | |

## Koninklijke Voetbalclub Mechelen

| | | | | |
|---|---|---|---|---|
| Founded: | 1904 | | | |
| Stadium: | AFAS-stadion Achter de Kazerne, Mechelen (16,672) | | | |
| Trainer: | Danny Buijs (NED) | | | 21.06.1982 |
| [17.10.2022] | Steven Arnold Defour | | | 15.04.1988 |

| Goalkeepers: | DOB | M | (s) | G |
|---|---|---|---|---|
| Gaëtan Coucke | 03.11.1998 | 29 | | |
| Yannick Thoelen | 18.07.1990 | 5 | (1) | |
| **Defenders:** | **DOB** | **M** | **(s)** | **G** |
| David Robert Bates (SCO) | 05.10.1996 | 22 | (3) | 2 |
| Lucas Bijker (NED) | 04.03.1993 | 3 | (1) | |
| Boli Bolingoli-Mbombo | 01.07.1995 | 15 | (4) | |
| Dimitri Lavalée | 13.01.1997 | 20 | (1) | |
| Thibault Peyre (FRA) | 03.10.1992 | 13 | (3) | 2 |
| Toon Raemaekers | 09.09.2000 | | (3) | |
| Iebe Swers | 27.12.1996 | | (9) | |
| Alec Van Hoorenbeeck | 30.12.1998 | 22 | (4) | |
| Jordi Vanlerberghe | 27.06.1996 | 17 | (3) | 2 |
| Sandy Walsh (IDN) | 14.03.1995 | 25 | | 2 |
| **Midfielders:** | **DOB** | **M** | **(s)** | **G** |
| Bilal Bafdili | 03.08.2004 | | (2) | |
| Alessio Sergio Fernando Da Cruz (NED) | 18.01.1997 | 23 | (5) | 3 |
| Samuel Yves Oum Gouet (CMR) | 14.12.1997 | 3 | (6) | |
| Jorge Hernandez (USA) | 08.11.2000 | | (9) | |
| Abdallah Kerim Mrabti (SWE) | 20.05.1994 | 10 | (2) | 1 |
| Ngal'Ayel Mukau | 03.11.2004 | | (9) | |
| Rob Schoofs | 23.03.1994 | 26 | (1) | 7 |
| Jannes Van Hecke | 15.01.2002 | 17 | (11) | |
| Birger Verstraete | 16.04.1994 | 19 | (1) | 2 |
| Dries Wouters | 28.01.1997 | 11 | (3) | 1 |
| **Forwards:** | **DOB** | **M** | **(s)** | **G** |
| Enock Agyei | 13.01.2005 | 3 | (5) | |
| Gustav Engvall (SWE) | 29.04.1996 | | (5) | |
| Geoffry Hairemans | 21.10.1991 | 31 | (2) | 9 |
| Yonas Malede (ISR) | 14.11.1999 | 10 | (17) | |
| Julien N'Goy | 02.11.1997 | 17 | (9) | 5 |
| Milan Robberechts | 04.03.2004 | | (3) | 2 |
| Frederic Leroi Soelle Soelle | 24.12.2005 | 1 | (11) | |
| Nikola Storm | 30.09.1994 | 30 | (1) | 4 |
| Marian Shved (UKR) | 16.07.1997 | 2 | (1) | |

## Koninklijke Voetbalclub Oostende

| Founded: | 1904 | | | |
|---|---|---|---|---|
| Stadium: | Versluys Arena, Ostend (8,432) | | | |
| Trainer: | Yves Vanderhaeghe | | 30.01.1970 | |
| [24.10.2022] | Dominik Thalhammer (AUT) | | 02.10.1970 | |

| Goalkeepers: | DOB | M | (s) | G |
|---|---|---|---|---|
| Guillaume Hubert | 11.01.1994 | 22 | | |
| Dillon Phillips (ENG) | 11.06.1995 | 12 | | |
| **Defenders:** | **DOB** | **M** | **(s)** | **G** |
| Mateo Barać (CRO) | 20.07.1994 | 5 | (1) | |
| Brecht Capon | 24.04.1988 | 11 | (10) | |
| Robbie D'Haese | 25.02.1999 | 14 | (5) | 1 |
| Fanos Katelaris (CYP) | 26.08.1996 | 9 | (4) | |
| Zech Medley (ENG) | 09.07.2000 | 11 | (4) | 1 |
| Théo Ndicka Matam (FRA) | 20.04.2000 | 16 | (7) | 2 |
| Manuel Osifo | 31.07.2003 | 1 | (5) | |
| Matej Rodin (CRO) | 13.02.1996 | 16 | | 1 |
| Anton Tanghe | 28.01.1999 | 29 | (1) | |
| Osaze Urhoghide (ENG) | 04.07.2000 | 24 | (3) | |
| Siebe Wylin | 27.05.2003 | 3 | (7) | |
| **Midfielders:** | **DOB** | **M** | **(s)** | **G** |
| Alfons Amade (GER) | 12.11.1999 | 15 | (5) | |
| Nick Bätzner (GER) | 15.03.2000 | 23 | (7) | 6 |
| Indy Boonen | 04.01.1999 | 4 | (7) | 1 |
| Maxime D'Arpino (FRA) | 17.06.1996 | | (4) | |
| Sieben Dewaele | 02.02.1999 | 18 | (5) | |
| Pierre Dwomoh | 21.06.2004 | 2 | (6) | |
| Milan Govaers | 23.03.2004 | | (1) | |
| Cameron McGeehan (NIR) | 06.04.1995 | 17 | (4) | 4 |
| Kenny Rocha Santos (CPV) | 03.01.2000 | 16 | (3) | |
| Tatsuhiro Sakamoto (JPN) | 22.10.1996 | 29 | (1) | |
| **Forwards:** | **DOB** | **M** | **(s)** | **G** |
| Alessandro Albanese | 12.01.2000 | 6 | (5) | |
| Thierry Winston Ambrose (GLP) | 28.03.1997 | 26 | (2) | 7 |
| Kelvin Arase (AUT) | 15.01.1999 | 6 | (4) | 1 |
| David Afänga (GHA) | 25.12.1996 | 13 | (15) | 5 |
| Adedapo Awokoya-Mebude (SCO) | 29.07.2001 | 2 | (3) | |
| Mohamed Berte | 25.03.2002 | | (13) | |
| Ivan Durdov (CRO) | 17.07.2000 | 3 | (5) | |
| Makhtar Gueye (SEN) | 04.12.1997 | | (4) | |
| Fraser Hornby (SCO) | 13.09.1999 | 19 | (2) | 8 |
| Andy Musayev | 17.04.2003 | 2 | (5) | |

## Oud-Heverlee Leuven

| Founded: | 2002 | | |
|---|---|---|---|
| Stadium: | Stadion Den Dreef, Leuven (10,000) | | |
| Trainer: | Marc Brys | 10.05.1962 | |

| Goalkeepers: | DOB | M | (s) | G |
|---|---|---|---|---|
| Valentin Alexandru Cojocaru (ROU) | 01.10.1995 | 34 | | |
| **Defenders:** | **DOB** | **M** | **(s)** | **G** |
| Joren Dom | 29.11.1989 | 11 | (20) | |
| Hamza Mendyl (MAR) | 21.10.1997 | 25 | (3) | |
| Pierre-Yves Ngawa | 09.02.1992 | | (4) | |
| Dylan Ouédraogo (BFA) | 22.07.1998 | 12 | (9) | |
| Louis Patris | 07.06.2001 | 31 | (2) | 2 |
| Ewoud Pletinckx | 10.10.2000 | 32 | | |
| Federico Ricca Rostagnol (URU) | 01.12.1994 | 28 | | 1 |
| Richie Sagrado | 30.01.2004 | 1 | (2) | |
| Joël Schingtienne | 14.08.2002 | | (1) | |
| Thibault Vlietinck | 19.08.1997 | 1 | (16) | |
| **Midfielders:** | **DOB** | **M** | **(s)** | **G** |
| Casper De Norre | 07.02.1997 | 34 | | 4 |
| Jo Gilis | 05.02.2000 | | (1) | |
| Raphael Holzhauser (AUT) | 16.02.1993 | 6 | (8) | 1 |
| João Pedro da Costa *Gamboa* (POR) | 31.08.1996 | 1 | (3) | |
| Mandela Keita | 10.05.2002 | | (6) | |
| Sofian Kiyine (MAR) | 02.10.1997 | 12 | (8) | 2 |
| Mathieu Maertens | 27.03.1995 | 23 | (1) | 5 |
| Kristiyan Malinov (BUL) | 30.03.1994 | 16 | (5) | |
| Siebe Schrijvers | 18.07.1996 | 13 | (3) | 2 |
| Emmanuel Tokú (GHA) | 10.07.2000 | | (3) | |
| **Forwards:** | **DOB** | **M** | **(s)** | **G** |
| Musa Suleiman Al Tamari (JOR) | 10.06.1997 | 30 | (4) | 6 |
| Franck Idumbo-Muzambo | 23.06.2002 | | (1) | |
| Mykola Kukharevych (UKR) | 01.07.2001 | | (4) | |
| *Mario* González Gutiérrez (ESP) | 25.02.1996 | 18 | (4) | 13 |
| Nachon Nsingi | 24.04.2001 | 13 | (12) | 5 |
| Nathan Opoku (GHA) | 22.07.2001 | 4 | (3) | 3 |
| Mai Traoré (GUI) | 24.11.1999 | | (1) | |
| Jón Dagur Þorsteinsson (ISL) | 26.11.1998 | 27 | (4) | 12 |

## Royal Football Club Seraing

| Founded: | 1922 | | | |
|---|---|---|---|---|
| Stadium: | Stade du Pairay, Seraing (8,207) | | | |
| Trainer: | José Jeunechamps | | 02.05.1967 | |
| [20.05.2023] | Jean-Sébastien Legros | | 16.02.1981 | |

| Goalkeepers: | DOB | M | (s) | G |
|---|---|---|---|---|
| Guillaume Dietsch (FRA) | 17.04.2001 | 23 | | |
| Timothy Galje | 05.06.2001 | 7 | | |
| Timothy Martin (LUX) | 27.03.2001 | 4 | | |
| **Defenders:** | **DOB** | **M** | **(s)** | **G** |
| Leroy Abanda Mfomo (FRA) | 07.06.2000 | 6 | (11) | |
| Mahamadou Dembélé (FRA) | 10.04.1999 | | (2) | |
| Gérald Kilota (FRA) | 02.01.1994 | 3 | (5) | |
| Moustapha Mbow (SEN) | 08.03.2000 | 25 | | 1 |
| John Mayanga Nekadio (COD) | 06.01.2002 | 1 | | |
| Dan Opare (GHA) | 18.10.1990 | 21 | (2) | |
| Morgan Paul Poaty (CGO) | 15.07.1997 | 24 | (7) | 3 |
| Fabrice Sambu | 03.06.1996 | 22 | (10) | |
| *Sérgio* Manuel Fernandes da *Conceição* (POR) | 12.11.1996 | 7 | (13) | |
| Elias Spago | 09.08.2001 | | (1) | |
| Abdoulaye Sylla (GUI) | 10.04.2000 | 17 | (5) | |
| Sandro Dennis Trémoulet (FRA) | 18.11.1999 | 13 | (3) | |
| Marvin Silver Tshibuabua (FRA) | 08.01.2002 | 18 | | |
| **Midfielders:** | **DOB** | **M** | **(s)** | **G** |
| Abou-Malal Ba (FRA) | 29.07.1998 | 9 | | |
| Denys Bunchukov (UKR) | 20.06.2003 | 3 | (4) | |
| Mathieu Cachbach | 23.05.2001 | 21 | (4) | |
| Valentin Guillaume | 17.04.2001 | 4 | (15) | |
| Sami Lahssaini | 18.09.1998 | 17 | (5) | |
| Christophe Lepoint | 24.10.1984 | 21 | (4) | 2 |
| Steve Regis Mvoué (CMR) | 02.02.2002 | 14 | (8) | 1 |
| Sambou Sissoko (FRA) | 27.04.1999 | 26 | (6) | 1 |
| Noah Solheid | 08.07.2003 | 3 | | |
| **Forwards:** | **DOB** | **M** | **(s)** | **G** |
| Antoine Bernier | 10.09.1997 | 20 | (2) | 3 |
| Simon Tom Elisor (FRA) | 22.07.1999 | 4 | (9) | 1 |
| Ejaita Ifoni (NGA) | 13.02.2000 | 1 | (8) | |
| Marius Mouandilmadji (CHA) | 22.01.1998 | 24 | (2) | 11 |
| Noah Serwy | 21.02.2003 | | (2) | |
| *Vagner* José Dias Gonçalves (CPV) | 10.01.1996 | 16 | (7) | 4 |

## Koninklijke Sint-Truidense Voetbalvereniging

| Founded: | 1924 | |
|---|---|---|
| Stadium: | Stayen Stadium, Sint-Truiden (14,600) | |
| Trainer: | Bernd Hollerbach (GER) | 08.12.1969 |

| Goalkeepers: | DOB | M | (s) | G |
|---|---|---|---|---|
| Jo Coppens | 21.12.1990 | 3 | (1) | |
| Daniel Yuji Yakubi Schmidt (JPN) | 03.02.1992 | 31 | | |
| **Defenders:** | **DOB** | **M** | **(s)** | **G** |
| Ameen Al Dakhil | 06.03.2002 | 16 | | |
| Robert Bauer (GER) | 09.04.1995 | 22 | (2) | |
| Eric Bocat (FRA) | 16.07.1999 | 18 | (4) | |
| Daiki Hashioka (JPN) | 17.05.1999 | 31 | (1) | |
| Wolke Janssens | 11.01.1995 | 24 | (7) | |
| Avelino *Jorge* Filipe *Teixeira* (POR) | 27.08.1986 | 10 | (3) | 1 |
| Toni Leistner (GER) | 19.08.1990 | 24 | | 1 |
| Matte Smets | 04.01.2004 | 12 | (2) | |
| **Midfielders:** | **DOB** | **M** | **(s)** | **G** |
| Frank Thierry Boya (CMR) | 01.07.1996 | 27 | (4) | 1 |
| Christian Brüls | 30.09.1988 | 14 | (4) | |
| Olivier Dumont | 06.03.2002 | 3 | (5) | 1 |
| Shinji Kagawa (JPN) | 17.03.1989 | 9 | (3) | 2 |
| Mory Konaté (GUI) | 15.11.1993 | 22 | (2) | 1 |
| Andrea Librici | 09.12.2004 | | (1) | |
| Rocco Reitz (GER) | 29.05.2002 | 9 | (3) | 1 |
| Stan Van Dessel | 24.07.2001 | 3 | (17) | |
| **Forwards:** | **DOB** | **M** | **(s)** | **G** |
| Gianni Bruno | 19.08.1991 | 23 | (7) | 18 |
| Taichi Hara (JPN) | 05.05.1999 | 4 | (7) | |
| Daichi Hayashi (JPN) | 23.05.1997 | 27 | (4) | 7 |
| Fatih Kaya (GER) | 13.11.1999 | | (15) | |
| Aboubakary Koita | 20.09.1998 | 12 | (17) | |
| Shinji Okazaki (JPN) | 16.04.1986 | 30 | | 1 |

## Royal Standard de Liège

| Founded: | 1898 | | |
| Stadium: | Stade "Maurice Dufrasne", Liège (30,023) | | |
| Trainer: | Ronny Deila (NOR) | 21.09.1975 |
| [25.05.2023] | Geoffrey Valenne | 15.04.1977 |

| Goalkeepers: | DOB | M | (s) | G |
|---|---|---|---|---|
| Arnaud Bodart | 11.03.1998 | 40 | | |
| **Defenders:** | **DOB** | **M** | **(s)** | **G** |
| Merveille Bopé Bokadi (COD) | 21.05.1996 | 34 | (3) | 1 |
| Alexandro Calut | 22.04.2003 | 1 | (1) | |
| Gilles Dewaele | 13.02.1996 | 8 | (3) | |
| Noë Dussenne | 07.04.1992 | 33 | (1) | 5 |
| Marlon Joseph Fossey (USA) | 09.09.1998 | 22 | (4) | 4 |
| Ibe Hautekiet | 13.04.2002 | 4 | (3) | |
| Kostas Laifis (CYP) | 19.05.1993 | 30 | (1) | 1 |
| Jacob Barrett Laursen (DEN) | 17.11.1994 | 8 | (14) | |
| Noah Mawete Kinsiona | 17.10.2005 | | (1) | |
| Nathan Ngoy | 10.06.2003 | 4 | (3) | |
| Lucas Noubi | 15.01.2005 | 3 | (14) | |
| **Midfielders:** | **DOB** | **M** | **(s)** | **G** |
| Steven Alzate (COL) | 08.09.1998 | 26 | (1) | 3 |
| Selim Amallah (MAR) | 15.11.1996 | 9 | | 4 |
| William Balikwisha | 12.05.1999 | 32 | (4) | 6 |
| Sacha Jordan Bansé | 16.03.2001 | | (1) | |
| Cihan Çanak | 24.01.2005 | 10 | (25) | 1 |
| Gojko Cimirot (BIH) | 19.12.1992 | 29 | (7) | |
| Léandre Kuavita | 31.05.2004 | | (2) | |
| Filippo Melegoni (ITA) | 18.02.1999 | 14 | (13) | 1 |
| Damjan Pavlović | 09.07.2001 | | (1) | |
| Nicolas Raskin | 23.02.2001 | 15 | (2) | 1 |
| Eden Shamir (ISR) | 25.06.1995 | | (4) | |
| Philip Aksel Frigast Zinckernagel (DEN) | 16.12.1994 | 25 | (2) | 10 |
| **Forwards:** | **DOB** | **M** | **(s)** | **G** |
| Aleksandar Boljević (MNE) | 12.12.1995 | 2 | (5) | |
| Osher Davida (ISR) | 18.02.2001 | 4 | (19) | |
| Aron Leonard Dønnum (NOR) | 20.04.1998 | 38 | (1) | 3 |
| Denis Mihai Drăguş (ROU) | 06.07.1999 | 13 | (6) | 4 |
| Renaud Emond | 05.12.1991 | 10 | (6) | 3 |
| Noah Chidiebere Junior Anyanwu Ohio (NED) | 16.01.2003 | 16 | (11) | 5 |
| Stipe Perica (CRO) | 07.07.1995 | 10 | (17) | 4 |
| Abdoul Tapsoba (BFA) | 23.08.2001 | | (3) | 1 |

## Royale Union Saint-Gilloise Bruxelles

| Founded: | 01.11.1897 | |
| Stadium: | Stade „Joseph Marien", Bruxelles (8,000) | |
| Trainer: | Karel Geraerts | 05.01.1982 |

| Goalkeepers: | DOB | M | (s) | G |
|---|---|---|---|---|
| Anthony Moris (LUX) | 29.04.1990 | 40 | | |
| **Defenders:** | **DOB** | **M** | **(s)** | **G** |
| Viktor Boone | 25.01.1998 | 1 | | |
| Christian Albert Elliot Burgess (ENG) | 07.10.1991 | 37 | | 5 |
| Arnaud Dony | 08.05.2004 | | (6) | |
| Guillaume François | 03.06.1990 | 5 | (12) | |
| Ismaël Kandouss (MAR) | 12.11.1997 | 31 | (2) | 1 |
| Koki Machida (JPN) | 25.08.1997 | 7 | (1) | |
| Bart Nieuwkoop (NED) | 07.03.1996 | 32 | (3) | 3 |
| Ross James Sykes (ENG) | 26.03.1999 | 12 | (8) | 2 |
| Siebe Van Der Heyden | 30.05.1998 | 32 | | 1 |
| **Midfielders:** | **DOB** | **M** | **(s)** | **G** |
| Lazare Amani (CIV) | 07.03.1998 | 34 | (2) | 3 |
| Oussama El Azzouzi (MAR) | 29.05.2001 | 6 | (17) | |
| José Rodríguez Martínez (ESP) | 16.12.1994 | 3 | (6) | |
| Loïc Lapoussin (MAD) | 27.03.1996 | 28 | (10) | 3 |
| Senne Lynen | 19.02.1999 | 36 | (1) | 1 |
| Cameron Puertas (SUI) | 18.08.1998 | 5 | (29) | 5 |
| Teddy Teuma (MLT) | 30.09.1993 | 36 | | 10 |
| **Forwards:** | **DOB** | **M** | **(s)** | **G** |
| Simon Adingra (CIV) | 01.01.2002 | 26 | (10) | 11 |
| Victor Okoh Boniface (NGA) | 23.12.2000 | 32 | (5) | 9 |
| Mohamed Boukammiri | 27.05.2004 | | (2) | |
| Dennis Eckert-Ayensa (GER) | 09.01.1997 | 1 | (7) | 2 |
| Håkan Gustaf Nilsson (SWE) | 23.05.1997 | 8 | (22) | 5 |
| Casper Terho (FIN) | 24.06.2003 | 1 | (5) | 2 |
| Dante Vanzeir | 16.04.1998 | 20 | | 10 |
| Yorbe Vertessen | 08.01.2001 | 6 | (9) | 3 |
| Ilyes Ziani | 20.06.2003 | 1 | (1) | |

## Koninklijke Voetbal Club Westerlo

| Founded: | 05.09.1933 | |
| Stadium: | Het Kuipje, Westerlo (8,035) | |
| Trainer: | Jonas De Roeck | 20.12.1979 |

| Goalkeepers: | DOB | M | (s) | G |
|---|---|---|---|---|
| Sinan Bolat (TUR) | 03.09.1988 | 36 | | |
| Nick Gillekens | 05.07.1995 | 4 | | |
| **Defenders:** | **DOB** | **M** | **(s)** | **G** |
| Maxim De Cuyper | 22.12.2000 | 39 | | 9 |
| Edisson Jordanov (BUL) | 08.06.1993 | 17 | (9) | 1 |
| Kouya Mabea (CIV) | 23.10.1998 | | (1) | |
| Pietro Perdichizzi | 16.12.1992 | 19 | (5) | |
| Bryan Keith Reynolds Jr. (USA) | 28.06.2001 | 28 | (4) | 1 |
| Rubin Seigers | 11.01.1998 | 17 | (8) | |
| Ravil Tagir (TUR) | 06.05.2003 | 23 | (5) | |
| **Midfielders:** | **DOB** | **M** | **(s)** | **G** |
| Ján Bernát (SVK) | 10.01.2001 | 3 | (3) | |
| Mathias Fixelles | 11.08.1996 | 21 | (11) | 3 |
| Muhammed Gümüşkaya (TUR) | 01.01.2001 | 2 | (13) | |
| Lucas Da Silva Izidoro (BRA) | 24.02.1996 | 6 | (3) | |
| Nicolas Martin Hautorp Madsen (DEN) | 17.03.2000 | 31 | (5) | 2 |
| Yusuke Matsuo (JPN) | 23.07.1997 | 10 | (4) | |
| Roman Neustädter (RUS) | 18.02.1988 | 27 | (7) | 1 |
| Thomas Van Den Keybus | 25.04.2001 | 23 | (6) | 3 |
| Lukas Van Eenoo | 06.02.1991 | 24 | (4) | 2 |
| **Forwards:** | **DOB** | **M** | **(s)** | **G** |
| Halil Akbunar (TUR) | 09.11.1993 | 9 | (5) | 2 |
| Nacer Chadli | 02.08.1989 | 25 | (2) | 6 |
| Erdon Daci (MKD) | 04.07.1998 | 2 | | 1 |
| Tuur Dierckx | 09.05.1995 | 13 | (19) | 5 |
| Lyle Brent Foster (RSA) | 03.09.2000 | 17 | (4) | 8 |
| Fernand Gouré Bi Irié (CIV) | 12.04.2002 | | (1) | |
| Dorgeles Nene (MLI) | 23.12.2002 | 20 | (15) | 13 |
| Kyan Vaesen | 13.04.2001 | 16 | (16) | 6 |
| Igor Mavuba Vetokele (ANG) | 23.03.1992 | 8 | (19) | 5 |
| Griffin McDorman Yow (USA) | 25.09.2002 | | (5) | |

<table>
<tr><td colspan="2">Sportvereniging Zulte Waregem</td></tr>
</table>

<table>
<tr><td>Founded:</td><td>01.07.2001</td><td></td></tr>
<tr><td>Stadium:</td><td>Regenboogstadion, Waregem (12,500)</td><td></td></tr>
<tr><td>Trainer:</td><td>Mbaye Leye (SEN)</td><td>01.12.1981</td></tr>
<tr><td>[15.03.2023]</td><td>Frederik D'Hollander &</td><td>20.05.1976</td></tr>
<tr><td></td><td>Davy De fauw</td><td>08.07.1981</td></tr>
</table>

| Goalkeepers: | DOB | M | (s) | G |
|---|---|---|---|---|
| Sammy Bossut | 11.08.1985 | 22 | | |
| Louis Bostyn | 04.10.1993 | 12 | | |

| Defenders: | DOB | M | (s) | G |
|---|---|---|---|---|
| *Borja López* Menéndez (ESP) | 02.02.1994 | 16 | (3) | 1 |
| Alessandro Ciranni | 28.06.1996 | 25 | (2) | 1 |
| Laurens De Bock | 07.11.1992 | | (1) | |
| Wout De Buyser | 29.06.2001 | | (4) | |
| Timothy Derijck | 25.05.1987 | 19 | (3) | 1 |
| Novatus Dismas Miroshi (TAN) | 02.09.2002 | 25 | (6) | |
| Oleksandr Drambaev (UKR) | 21.04.2001 | 12 | (10) | 1 |
| Karol Fila (POL) | 13.06.1998 | 11 | | 1 |
| Bent Sørmo (NOR) | 22.09.1996 | 5 | (3) | |
| Moudou Tambedou (SEN) | 04.04.2003 | 17 | (1) | 1 |
| Cheikh Thiam | 27.09.2003 | | (2) | |
| Ravy Dieuleriche Tsouka Dozi (CGO) | 23.12.1994 | 6 | (6) | |
| Lukas Willen | 25.04.2003 | 15 | (4) | 1 |

| Midfielders: | DOB | M | (s) | G |
|---|---|---|---|---|
| Christian Brüls | 30.09.1988 | 12 | (3) | |
| Daniel „*Dani*" *Ramírez* Fernández (ESP) | 18.06.1992 | 5 | (8) | |
| Dylan Demuynck | 06.05.2004 | | (2) | |
| Pape Demba Diop (SEN) | 04.09.2003 | | (1) | |
| Arthur Harinck | 11.12.2004 | | (1) | |
| David Hubert | 12.02.1988 | | (1) | |
| Kevor Palumets (EST) | 21.11.2002 | | (3) | |
| Nicolas Rommens | 17.12.1994 | 28 | (3) | 2 |
| Mamadou Sangaré (MLI) | 26.06.2002 | 4 | (6) | 1 |
| Abdoulaye Sissako (FRA) | 26.05.1998 | 28 | (3) | 1 |
| Lasse Vigen (DEN) | 15.08.1994 | 7 | (4) | |
| Ruud Willem Vormer (NED) | 11.05.1988 | 9 | (1) | 1 |

| Forwards: | DOB | M | (s) | G |
|---|---|---|---|---|
| Stan Braem | 25.11.1998 | | (16) | 2 |
| Jean-Luc Dompé (FRA) | 12.08.1995 | 4 | | |
| Alieu Fadera (GAM) | 03.11.2001 | 31 | (2) | 6 |
| Zinho Gano | 13.10.1993 | 17 | (3) | 12 |
| Lennert Hallaert | 17.04.2003 | 1 | (4) | |
| Alioune Ndour (SEN) | 21.10.1997 | 12 | (12) | 6 |
| Nnamdi Chinonso Offor (NGA) | 27.05.2000 | 4 | (9) | 2 |
| Youssuf Sylla | 19.12.2002 | | (1) | |
| Jelle Vossen | 22.03.1989 | 27 | (4) | 9 |

<table>
<tr><td colspan="9">SECOND LEVEL<br>Challenger Pro League 2022/2023</td></tr>
</table>

**Regular Season**

| | | | | | | | | | |
|---|---|---|---|---|---|---|---|---|---|
| 1. | RWD Molenbeek | 22 | 14 | 4 | 4 | 41 | - | 21 | 46 |
| 2. | SK Beveren | 22 | 12 | 7 | 3 | 52 | - | 25 | 43 |
| 3. | K Beerschot VA | 22 | 12 | 2 | 8 | 33 | - | 28 | 38 |
| 4. | Lierse Kempenzonen | 22 | 11 | 3 | 8 | 42 | - | 42 | 36 |
| 5. | Club NXT Brugge* | 22 | 10 | 6 | 6 | 38 | - | 30 | 36 |
| 6. | RSC Anderlecht Futures Bruxelles* | 22 | 9 | 7 | 6 | 42 | - | 35 | 34 |
| 7. | Lommel SK | 22 | 10 | 2 | 10 | 33 | - | 36 | 32 |
| 8. | KMSK Deinze | 22 | 9 | 3 | 10 | 29 | - | 33 | 30 |
| 9. | Jong KRC Genk* | 22 | 5 | 5 | 12 | 28 | - | 40 | 20 |
| 10. | FCV Dender EH Denderleeuw | 22 | 5 | 4 | 13 | 27 | - | 40 | 19 |
| 11. | R Standard Liège 16 FC* | 22 | 4 | 7 | 11 | 25 | - | 43 | 19 |
| 12. | Royal Excelsior Virton | 22 | 2 | 8 | 12 | 21 | - | 38 | 14 |

Team ranked 1-6 were qualified for the Promotion Round, while teams ranked 7-12 were qualified for the Relegation Round.
*reserve teams are not eligible for promotion.

**Promotion Round**

| | | | | | | | | | |
|---|---|---|---|---|---|---|---|---|---|
| 1. | RWD Molenbeek (*Promoted*) | 32 | 21 | 6 | 5 | 65 | - | 29 | 69 |
| 2. | SK Beveren | 32 | 20 | 8 | 4 | 76 | - | 34 | 68 |
| 3. | K Beerschot VA | 32 | 15 | 4 | 13 | 43 | - | 41 | 49 |
| 4. | Club NXT Brugge | 32 | 14 | 7 | 11 | 51 | - | 48 | 49 |
| 5. | Lierse Kempenzonen | 32 | 14 | 4 | 14 | 53 | - | 59 | 46 |
| 6. | RSC Anderlecht Futures Bruxelles | 32 | 9 | 10 | 13 | 46 | - | 56 | 37 |

**Relegation Round**

| | | | | | | | | | |
|---|---|---|---|---|---|---|---|---|---|
| 7. | Lommel SK | 32 | 16 | 3 | 13 | 53 | - | 46 | 51 |
| 8. | KMSK Deinze | 32 | 15 | 4 | 13 | 49 | - | 47 | 49 |
| 9. | FCV Dender EH Denderleeuw | 32 | 11 | 6 | 15 | 41 | - | 47 | 39 |
| 10. | R Standard Liège 16 FC | 32 | 5 | 12 | 15 | 31 | - | 60 | 27 |
| 11. | Jong KRC Genk | 32 | 6 | 8 | 18 | 36 | - | 58 | 26 |
| 12. | Royal Excelsior Virton (*Relegation*) | 32 | 5 | 10 | 17 | 32 | - | 51 | 25 |

## INTERNATIONAL MATCHES
### (16.07.2022 – 15.07.2023)

| | | | | |
|---|---|---|---|---|
| 22.09.2022 | Bruxelles | *Belgium - Wales* | *2-1(2-0)* | (UNL) |
| 25.09.2022 | Amsterdam | *Netherlands - Belgium* | *1-0(0-0)* | (UNL) |
| 18.11.2022 | Kuwait City | *Egypt - Belgium* | *2-1(1-0)* | (F) |
| 23.11.2022 | Al Rayyan | *Belgium - Canada* | *1-0(1-0)* | (WC) |
| 27.11.2022 | Doha | *Belgium - Morocco* | *0-2(0-0)* | (WC) |
| 01.12.2022 | Al Rayyan | *Croatia - Belgium* | *0-0* | (WC) |
| 24.03.2023 | Stockholm | *Sweden - Belgium* | *0-3(0-1)* | (ECQ) |
| 28.03.2023 | Köln | *Germany - Belgium* | *2-3(1-2)* | (F) |
| 17.06.2023 | Bruxelles | *Belgium - Austria* | *1-1(0-1)* | (ECQ) |
| 20.06.2023 | Tallinn | *Estonia - Belgium* | *0-3(0-2)* | (ECQ) |

**22.09.2022  BELGIUM - WALES**   2-1(2-0)   3rd UEFA Nations League A, Group 4
Stade "Roi Baudouin", Bruxelles,; Referee: Ali Palabıyık (Turkey); Attendance: 28,463
**BEL:** Thibaut Nicolas Marc Courtois, Thomas Meunier, Jan Vertonghen, Toby Albertine Maurits Alderweireld, Zeno Koen Debast, Axel Tomas Laurent Angel Lambert Witsel, Youri Marion Tielemans (76.Hans Vanaken), Kevin De Bruyne (90+2.Charles De Ketelaere), Yannick Ferreira Carrasco (65.Dries Mertens), Eden Hazard (Cap) (65.Leandro Trossard), Michy Batshuayi-Atunga (65.Ikoma Loïs OpEnda). Trainer: Roberto Martínez Montoliu (Spain).
**Goals:** Kevin De Bruyne (10), Michy Batshuayi-Atunga (37).

**25.09.2022  NETHERLANDS - BELGIUM**   1-0(0-0)   3rd UEFA Nations League A, Group 4
"Johan Cruyff" Arena, Amsterdam; Referee: Anthony Taylor (England); Attendance: 52,314
**BEL:** Thibaut Nicolas Marc Courtois, Thomas Meunier (46.Yannick Ferreira Carrasco), Jan Vertonghen, Toby Albertine Maurits Alderweireld, Timothy Castagne (82.Dodi Lukébakio Ngandoli), Zeno Koen Debast, Axel Tomas Laurent Angel Lambert Witsel, Amadou Zeund Georges Ba Mvom Onana (74.Youri Marion Tielemans), Kevin De Bruyne, Eden Hazard (Cap) (64.Leandro Trossard), Michy Batshuayi-Atunga (46.Charles De Ketelaere). Trainer: Roberto Martínez Montoliu (Spain).

**18.11.2022  EGYPT - BELGIUM**   2-1(1-0)   Friendly International
„Jaber Al Ahmad" International Stadium, Kuwait City (Kuwait); Referee: Ali Mahmoud Shaban (Kuwait); Attendance: 57,400
**BEL:** Thibaut Nicolas Marc Courtois, Toby Albertine Maurits Alderweireld, Timothy Castagne (82.Jérémy Baffour Doku), Arthur Nicolas Theate (71.Jan Vertonghen), Zeno Koen Debast, Axel Tomas Laurent Angel Lambert Witsel, Hans Vanaken (46.Youri Marion Tielemans), Kevin De Bruyne (46.Dries Mertens), Yannick Ferreira Carrasco, Eden Hazard (Cap) (71.Thomas Meunier), Michy Batshuayi-Atunga (46.Ikoma Loïs Openda). Trainer: Roberto Martínez Montoliu (Spain).
**Goal:** Ikoma Loïs Openda (76).

**23.11.2022  BELGIUM - CANADA**   1-0(1-0)   22nd FIFA WC. Group Stage.
„Ahmad bin Ali" Stadium, Al Rayyan (Qatar); Referee: Janny Sikazwe (Zambia); Attendance: 40,432
**BEL:** Thibaut Nicolas Marc Courtois, Leander Dendoncker, Toby Albertine Maurits Alderweireld, Jan Bert Lieve Vertonghen, Timothy Castagne, Youri Marion Tielemans (46.Amadou Zeund Georges Ba Mvom Onana), Axel Tomas Laurent Angel Lambert Witsel, Yannick Ferreira Carrasco (46.Thomas Meunier), Kevin De Bruyne, Michy Batshuayi-Atunga (78.Ikoma Loïs Openda), Eden Michael Hazard (Cap) (62.Leandro Trossard). Trainer: Roberto Martínez Montoliu (Spain).
**Goal:** Michy Batshuayi-Atunga (44).

**27.11.2022  BELGIUM - MOROCCO**   0-2(0-0)   22nd FIFA WC. Group Stage.
Al Thumama Stadium, Doha (Qatar); Referee: César Arturo Ramos Palazuelos (Mexico); Attendance: 43,738
**BEL:** Thibaut Nicolas Marc Courtois, Thomas Meunier (81.Romelu Menama Lukaku Bolingoli), Toby Albertine Maurits Alderweireld, Jan Bert Lieve Vertonghen, Timothy Castagne, Amadou Zeund Georges Ba Mvom Onana (60.Youri Marion Tielemans), Axel Tomas Laurent Angel Lambert Witsel, Thorgan Ganael Francis Hazard (75.Leandro Trossard), Kevin De Bruyne, Michy Batshuayi-Atunga (75.Charles Marc De Ketelaere), Eden Michael Hazard (Cap) (60.Dries Mertens). Trainer: Roberto Martínez Montoliu (Spain).

**01.12.2022  CROATIA - BELGIUM**   0-0   22nd FIFA WC. Group Stage.
„Ahmad bin Ali" Stadium, Al Rayyan (Qatar); Referee: Anthony Taylor (England); Attendance: 43,984
**BEL:** Thibaut Nicolas Marc Courtois, Leander Dendoncker (72.Youri Marion Tielemans), Toby Albertine Maurits Alderweireld, Jan Bert Lieve Vertonghen, Thomas Meunier (87.Eden Michael Hazard), Kevin De Bruyne (Cap), Axel Tomas Laurent Angel Lambert Witsel, Timothy Castagne, Leandro Trossard (59.Thorgan Ganael Francis Hazard), Dries Mertens (46.Romelu Menama Lukaku Bolingoli), Yannick Ferreira Carrasco (72.Jérémy Baffour Doku). Trainer: Roberto Martínez Montoliu (Spain).

**24.03.2023  SWEDEN - BELGIUM**   0-3(0-1)   17th EC. Qualifiers
Friends Arena, Stockholm; Referee: Orel Grinfeld (Israel); Attendance: 49,296
**BEL:** Thibaut Nicolas Marc Courtois, Jan Vertonghen, Timothy Castagne, Wout Felix Lina Faes, Arthur Nicolas Theate (85.Alexis Jesse Saelemaekers), Kevin De Bruyne (Cap), Amadou Zeund Georges Ba Mvom Onana, Leandro Trossard (61.Orel Mangala), Yannick Ferreira Carrasco (90.Ikoma Loïs Openda), Dodi Lukébakio Ngandoli (61.Saint-Cyr Johan Bakayoko), Romelu Menama Lukaku Bolingoli (85.Sebastiaan Bornauw). Trainer: Domenico Tedesco (Italy).
**Goals:** Romelu Menama Lukaku Bolingoli (35, 49, 83).

**28.03.2023  GERMANY - BELGIUM**   2-3(1-2)   Friendly International
RheinEnergieStadion, Köln; Referee: Willy Delajod (France); Attendance: 42,910
**BEL:** Koen Casteels, Jan Vertonghen (46.Alexis Jesse Saelemaekers), Timothy Castagne, Wout Felix Lina Faes, Arthur Nicolas Theate, Amadou Zeund Georges Ba Mvom Onana, Orel Mangala (79.Roméo Lavia), Kevin De Bruyne (Cap) (79.Ikoma Loïs Openda), Yannick Ferreira Carrasco (58.Leandro Trossard), Dodi Lukébakio Ngandoli (58.Saint-Cyr Johan Bakayoko), Romelu Menama Lukaku Bolingoli (68.Charles De Ketelaere). Trainer: Domenico Tedesco (Italy).
**Goals:** Yannick Ferreira Carrasco (6), Romelu Menama Lukaku Bolingoli (9), Kevin De Bruyne (78).

**17.06.2023**   **BELGIUM - AUSTRIA**   **1-1(0-1)**   17th EC. Qualifiers

Stade "Roi Baudouin", Bruxelles; Referee: Jérôme Brisard (France); Attendance: 39,237
**BEL:** Thibaut Nicolas Marc Courtois, Timothy Castagne, Wout Felix Lina Faes, Arthur Nicolas Theate, Leander Dendoncker (84.Ameen Al Dakhil), Orel Mangala (75.Aster Jan Vranckx), Youri Marion Tielemans, Yannick Ferreira Carrasco (75.Ikoma Loïs Openda), Dodi Lukébakio Ngandoli (69.Saint-Cyr Johan Bakayoko), Romelu Menama Lukaku Bolingoli (Cap), Jérémy Baffour Doku (84.Mike Trésor Ndayishimiye). Trainer: Domenico Tedesco (Italy).
**Goal:** Romelu Menama Lukaku Bolingoli (61).

**20.06.2023**   **ESTONIA - BELGIUM**   **0-3(0-2)**   17th EC. Qualifiers

A. Le Coq Arena, Tallinn; Referee: John Beaton (Scotland); Attendance: 11,772
**BEL:** Matz Willy Els Sels, Jan Vertonghen (57.Ameen Al Dakhil), Timothy Castagne, Wout Felix Lina Faes, Arthur Nicolas Theate (88.Olivier Deman), Youri Marion Tielemans, Mike Trésor Ndayishimiye (57.Jérémy Baffour Doku), Aster Jan Vranckx (57.Orel Mangala), Yannick Ferreira Carrasco, Saint-Cyr Johan Bakayoko, Romelu Menama Lukaku Bolingoli (Cap) (69.Michy Batshuayi-Atunga). Trainer: Domenico Tedesco (Italy).
**Goals:** Romelu Menama Lukaku Bolingoli (37, 40), Saint-Cyr Johan Bakayoko (90).

| NATIONAL TEAM PLAYERS (16.07.2022 – 15.07.2023) | | | | |
|---|---|---|---|---|
| **Name** | **DOB** | **Caps** | **Goals** | **Club** |

| Goalkeepers | | | | |
|---|---|---|---|---|
| Koen CASTEELS | 25.06.1992 | 5 | 0 | 2023: | VfL Wolfsburg (GER) |
| Thibaut Nicolas Marc COURTOIS | 11.05.1992 | 102 | 0 | 2022/2023: | Real Madrid CF (ESP) |
| Matz Willy Els SELS | 26.02.1992 | 3 | 0 | 2023: | Racing Club de Strasbourg (FRA) |

| Defenders | | | | |
|---|---|---|---|---|
| Ameen AL DAKHIL | 06.03.2002 | 2 | 0 | 2023: | Burnley FC (ENG) |
| Toby Albertine Maurits ALDERWEIRELD | 02.03.1989 | 127 | 5 | 2022: | Royal Antwerp FC |
| Sebastiaan BORNAUW | 22.03.1999 | 4 | 0 | 2023: | VfL Wolfsburg (GER) |
| Timothy CASTAGNE | 05.12.1995 | 33 | 2 | 2022/2023: | Leicester City FC (ENG) |
| Zeno Koen DEBAST | 24.10.2003 | 3 | 0 | 2022: | RSC Anderlecht Bruxelles |
| Leander DENDONCKER | 15.04.1995 | 32 | 1 | 2022/2023: | Aston Villa FC Birmingham (ENG) |
| Wout Felix Lina FAES | 03.04.1998 | 5 | 0 | 2023: | Leicester City FC (ENG) |
| Thomas MEUNIER | 12.09.1991 | 62 | 8 | 2022: | BV Borussia 09 Dortmund (GER) |
| Arthur Nicolas THEATE | 25.05.2000 | 8 | 0 | 2022/2023: | Stade Rennais FC (FRA) |
| Jan Bert Lieve VERTONGHEN | 24.04.1987 | 148 | 9 | 2022/2023: | RSC Anderlecht Bruxelles |

| Midfielders | | | | |
|---|---|---|---|---|
| Yannick Ferreira CARRASCO | 04.09.1993 | 66 | 9 | 2022/2023: | Club Atlético de Madrid (ESP) |
| Kevin DE BRUYNE | 28.06.1991 | 99 | 26 | 2022/2023: | Manchester City FC (ENG) |
| Olivier DEMAN | 06.04.2000 | 1 | 0 | 2023: | Cercle Brugge KSV |
| Roméo LAVIA | 06.01.2004 | 1 | 0 | 2023: | Southampton FC (ENG) |
| Orel MANGALA | 18.03.2001 | 6 | 0 | 2023: | Nottingham Forest FC (ENG) |
| Amadou Zeund Georges Ba Mvom ONANA | 16.08.2001 | 6 | 0 | 2022/2023: | Everton FC Liverpool (ENG) |
| Alexis Jesse SAELEMAEKERS | 27.06.1999 | 11 | 1 | 2023: | AC Milan (ITA) |
| Youri Marion TIELEMANS | 07.05.1997 | 60 | 5 | 2022/2023: | Leicester City FC (ENG) |
| Mike TRÉSOR Ndayishimiye | 28.05.1999 | 2 | 0 | 2023: | KRC Genk |
| Leandro TROSSARD | 04.12.1994 | 26 | 5 | 2022: 20.01.2023-> | Brighton & Hove Albion FC (ENG) Arsenal FC London (BEL) |
| Hans VANAKEN | 24.08.1992 | 23 | 5 | 2022: | Club Brugge KV |
| Axel Tomas Laurent Angel Lambert WITSEL | 12.01.1989 | 130 | 12 | 2022: | Club Atlético de Madrid (ESP) |
| Aster Jan VRANCKX | 04.10.2002 | 2 | 0 | 2023: | AC Milan (ITA) |

| Forwards | | | | |
|---|---|---|---|---|
| Saint-Cyr Johan BAKAYOKO | 20.04.2003 | 4 | 1 | 2023: | PSV Eindhoven (NED) |
| Michy BATSHUAYI-ATUNGA | 02.10.1993 | 51 | 27 | 2022/2023: | Fenerbahçe SK İstanbul (TUR) |
| Charles DE KETELAERE | 10.03.2001 | 12 | 1 | 2022/2023: | AC Milan (ITA) |
| Jérémy Baffour DOKU | 27.05.2002 | 14 | 2 | 2022/2023: | Stade Rennais FC (FRA) |
| Eden Michael HAZARD | 07.01.1991 | 126 | 33 | 2022: | Real Madrid CF (ESP) |
| Thorgan Ganael Francis HAZARD | 29.03.1993 | 47 | 9 | 2022: | BV Borussia 09 Dortmund (GER) |
| Romelu Menama LUKAKU Bolingoli | 13.05.1993 | 108 | 75 | 2022/2023: | FC Internazionale Milano (ITA) |
| Dodi LUKÉBAKIO Ngandoli | 24.09.1997 | 8 | 0 | 2022/2023: | Hertha BSC Berlin (GER) |
| Dries MERTENS | 06.05.1987 | 109 | 21 | 2022: | Galatasaray SK İstanbul (TUR) |
| Ikoma Loïs OPENDA | 16.02.2000 | 9 | 2 | 2022/2023: | Racing Club de Lens (FRA) |

| Trainer | | | |
|---|---|---|---|
| Roberto MARTÍNEZ Montoliu (Spain) [03.06.2016 – 31.12.2022] | 13.07.1973 | 80 M; 56 W; 13 D; 11 L; 210-70 |
| Domenico TEDESCO (Italy) [from 08.02.2023] | 12.09.1985 | 4 M; 3 W; 1 D; 0 L; 10-3 |

# BOSNIA AND HERZEGOVINA

## The Country:
Bosnia and Herzegovina (Bosna i Hercegovina / Босна и Херцеговина)
Capital: Sarajevo
Surface: 51,197 km²
Inhabitants: 3,824,782 [2021]
Time: UTC+1

## The FA:
Nogometni/Fudbalski Savez Bosne i Hercegovine
Bulevar Meše Selimovića 95, 71000 Sarajevo
Tel: +387 33 276 676
Foundation date: 1920 / 1992
Member of FIFA since: 1996
Member of UEFA since: 1998
Website: www.nfsbih.ba

## NATIONAL TEAM RECORDS

| RECORDS | | |
|---|---|---|
| **First international match:** | 30.11.1995, Tiranë | Albania - Bosnia and Herzegovina 2-0 |
| **Most international caps:** | Edin Džeko | - 129 caps (since 2007) |
| **Most international goals:** | Edin Džeko | - 64 goals / 129 caps (since 2007) |

| UEFA EUROPEAN CHAMPIONSHIP | |
|---|---|
| 1960 | - |
| 1964 | - |
| 1968 | - |
| 1972 | - |
| 1976 | - |
| 1980 | - |
| 1984 | - |
| 1988 | - |
| 1992 | - |
| 1996 | Did not enter |
| 2000 | Qualifiers |
| 2004 | Qualifiers |
| 2008 | Qualifiers |
| 2012 | Qualifiers |
| 2016 | Qualifiers |
| 2020 | Qualifiers |

| FIFA WORLD CUP | |
|---|---|
| 1930 | - |
| 1934 | - |
| 1938 | - |
| 1950 | - |
| 1954 | - |
| 1958 | - |
| 1962 | - |
| 1966 | - |
| 1970 | - |
| 1974 | - |
| 1978 | - |
| 1982 | - |
| 1986 | - |
| 1990 | - |
| 1994 | - |
| 1998 | Qualifiers |
| 2002 | Qualifiers |
| 2006 | Qualifiers |
| 2010 | Qualifiers |
| 2014 | Final Tournament (Group Stage) |
| 2018 | Qualifiers |
| 2022 | Qualifiers |

| OLYMPIC TOURNAMENTS | |
|---|---|
| 1908 | - |
| 1912 | - |
| 1920 | - |
| 1924 | - |
| 1928 | - |
| 1936 | - |
| 1948 | - |
| 1952 | - |
| 1956 | - |
| 1960 | - |
| 1964 | - |
| 1968 | - |
| 1972 | - |
| 1976 | - |
| 1980 | - |
| 1984 | - |
| 1988 | - |
| 1992 | - |
| 1996 | - |
| 2000 | Qualifiers |
| 2004 | Qualifiers |
| 2008 | - |
| 2012 | Qualifiers |
| 2016 | Qualifiers |
| 2020 | Qualifiers |

*was part of Yugoslavia until 01.03.1992*

| UEFA NATIONS LEAGUE | |
|---|---|
| 2018/2019 | League B (Group Stage -> promoted to League A) |
| 2020/2021 | League A (Group Stage -> relegated to League B) |
| 2022/2023 | League B (Group Stage -> promoted to League A) |

## BOSNIAN CLUB HONOURS IN EUROPEAN CLUB COMPETITIONS:

| European Champion Clubs' Cup (1956-1992) / UEFA Champions League (1993-2023) |
|---|
| None |

| Fairs Cup (1858-1971) / UEFA Cup (1972-2009) / UEFA Europa League (2010-2023) |
|---|
| None |

| UEFA Europa Conference League (2021-2023) |
|---|
| None |

| UEFA Super Cup (1972-2022) |
|---|
| None |

| *European Cup Winners' Cup 1961-1999** |
|---|
| None |

*defunct competition*

# NATIONAL COMPETITIONS
## TABLE OF HONOURS

| FIRST LEAGUE OF BOSNIA AND HERZEGOVINA CHAMPIONS | |
|---|---|
| 1994/1995 | NK Čelik Zenica |
| 1995/1996 | NK Čelik Zenica |
| 1996/1997 | NK Čelik Zenica |
| 1997/1998 | NK Bosna Visoko |
| 1998/1999 | FK Sarajevo |
| 1999/2000 | NK Jedinstvo Bihać |

| FIRST LEAGUE OF HERZEG-BOSNIA CHAMPIONS | |
|---|---|
| 1993/1994 | NK Široki Brijeg |
| 1994/1995 | NK Široki Brijeg |
| 1995/1996 | NK Široki Brijeg |
| 1996/1997 | NK Široki Brijeg |
| 1997/1998 | NK Široki Brijeg |
| 1998/1999 | NK Posušje |
| 1999/2000 | NK Posušje |

| FIRST LEAGUE OF THE REPUBLIKA SRPSKA CHAMPIONS | |
|---|---|
| 1995/1996 | FK Boksit Milići |
| 1996/1997 | FK Rudar Ugljevik |
| 1997/1998 | FK Rudar Ugljevik |
| 1998/1999 | FK Radnik Bijeljina |
| 1999/2000 | FK Boksit Milići |
| 2000/2001 | FK Borac Banja Luka |
| 2001/2002 | FK Leotar Trebinje |

| BOSNIA AND HERZEGOVINA CUP WINNERS | |
|---|---|
| 1994/1995 | NK Čelik Zenica |
| 1995/1996 | NK Čelik Zenica |
| 1996/1997 | FK Sarajevo |
| 1997/1998 | FK Sarajevo |
| 1998/1999 | NK Bosna Visoko |

| HERZEG-BOSNIA CUP WINNERS | |
|---|---|
| 1994/1995 | NK Bigeste Ljubuški |
| 1995/1996 | NK Bigeste Ljubuški |
| 1996/1997 | NK Troglav 1918 Livno |
| 1997/1998 | HNK Orašje |
| 1998/1999 | NK Brotnjo |
| 1999/2000 | HNK Orašje |

| REPUBLIKA SRPSKA CUP WINNERS | |
|---|---|
| 1993/1994 | FK Kozara Gradiška |
| 1994/1995 | FK Borac Banja Luka |
| 1995/1996 | FK Borac Banja Luka |
| 1996/1997 | FK Sloga Trn |
| 1997/1998 | FK Rudar Ugljevik |
| 1998/1999 | FK Rudar Ugljevik |
| 1999/2000 | FK Kozara Gradiška |

| | PLAYOFF CHAMPIONS | CUP WINNERS | BEST GOALSCORERS | |
|---|---|---|---|---|
| 1997/1998 | FK Željezničar Sarajevo | FK Sarajevo | Stanko Bubalo (CRO, NK Široki Brijeg) Hadis Zubanović (FK Željezničar Sarajevo) | 3 |
| 1998/1999 | FK Sarajevo (Regional NK Posušje winners FK Radnik Bijeljina shared) | No competition | - | |
| 1999/2000 | NK Brotnjo | FK Željezničar Sarajevo | Zikret Kuljaninović (FK Budućnost Banovići) Alen Škoro (FK Sarajevo) Halim Stupac (NK Jedinstvo Bihać) | 5 |
| | PREMIER LEAGUE | | | |
| 2000/2001 | FK Željezničar Sarajevo | FK Željezničar Sarajevo | Dželaludin Muharemović (FK Željezničar Sarajevo) | 31 |
| 2001/2002 | FK Željezničar Sarajevo | FK Sarajevo | Ivica Huljev (FK Željezničar Sarajevo) | 15 |
| 2002/2003 | FK Leotar Trebinje | FK Željezničar Sarajevo | Emir Obuća (FK Sarajevo) | 24 |
| 2003/2004 | NK Široki Brijeg | FK Modriča | Alen Škoro (FK Sarajevo) | 20 |
| 2004/2005 | HŠK Zrinjski Mostar | FK Sarajevo | Zoran Rajović (SRB, HŠK Zrinjski Mostar) | 17 |
| 2005/2006 | NK Široki Brijeg | HNK Orašje | Petar Jelić (FK Modriča) | 19 |
| 2006/2007 | FK Sarajevo | NK Široki Brijeg | Stevo Nikolić (FK Modriča) Dragan Benić (FK Borac Banja Luka) | 19 |
| 2007/2008 | FK Modriča | HŠK Zrinjski Mostar | Darko Spalević (SRB, FK Slavija Sarajevo) | 18 |
| 2008/2009 | HŠK Zrinjski Mostar | FK Slavija Sarajevo | Darko Spalević (SRB, FK Slavija Sarajevo) | 17 |
| 2009/2010 | FK Željezničar Sarajevo | FK Borac Banja Luka | Feđa Dudić (NK Travnik) | 16 |
| 2010/2011 | FK Borac Banja Luka | FK Željezničar Sarajevo | Ivan Lendrić (CRO, HŠK Zrinjski Mostar) | 16 |
| 2011/2012 | FK Željezničar Sarajevo | FK Željezničar Sarajevo | Eldin Adilović (FK Željezničar Sarajevo) | 19 |
| 2012/2013 | FK Željezničar Sarajevo | NK Široki Brijeg | Emir Hadžić (FK Sarajevo) | 20 |
| 2013/2014 | HŠK Zrinjski Mostar | FK Sarajevo | Wagner Santos Lago (BRA, NK Široki Brijeg) | 18 |
| 2014/2015 | FK Sarajevo | FK Olimpik Sarajevo | Riad Bajić (FK Željezničar Sarajevo) | 15 |
| 2015/2016 | HŠK Zrinjski Mostar | FK Radnik Bijeljina | Leon Benko (CRO, FK Sarajevo) | 17 |
| 2016/2017 | HŠK Zrinjski Mostar | NK Široki Brijeg | Ivan Lendrić (CRO, FK Željezničar Sarajevo) | 19 |
| 2017/2018 | HŠK Zrinjski Mostar | FK Željezničar Sarajevo | Miloš Filipović (SRB, HŠK Zrinjski Mostar) | 16 |
| 2018/2019 | FK Sarajevo | FK Sarajevo | Sulejman Krpić (FK Sarajevo) | 16 |
| 2019/2020 | FK Sarajevo | Competition cancelled | Mersudin Ahmetović (FK Sarajevo) | 13 |
| 2020/2021 | FK Borac Banja Luka | FK Sarajevo | Nemanja Bilbija (HŠK Zrinjski Mostar) | 17 |
| 2021/2022 | HŠK Zrinjski Mostar | FK Velež Mostar | Nemanja Bilbija (HŠK Zrinjski Mostar) | 33 |
| 2022/2023 | HŠK Zrinjski Mostar | HŠK Zrinjski Mostar | Nemanja Bilbija (HŠK Zrinjski Mostar) | 24 |

**Results**

Please note: FK Krupa na Vrbasu, initially promoted, didn't get a license for the first level, being replaced by FK Sloga Meridian Doboj.

**Round 1 [15-18.07.2022]**
HŠK Posušje - Velež Mostar 1-1(1-0)
Igman Konjic - Široki Brijeg 0-1(0-0)
FK Željezničar - Leotar Trebinje 1-1(1-1)
Sloga Doboj - Borac Banja Luka 2-2(0-2)
FK Sarajevo-FK Tuzla City 1-5(0-2) [10.08.22]
Sloboda T.-Zrinjski Mostar 0-1(0-0) [07.09.22]

**Round 2 [23-24.07.2022]**
Sloga Doboj - Leotar Trebinje 4-0(2-0)
Borac Banja Luka - FK Sarajevo 1-3(0-0)
Široki Brijeg - Sloboda Tuzla 2-0(2-0)
Zrinjski Mostar - FK Željezničar 1-2(1-0)
Velež Mostar-Igman Konjic 1-1(1-1) [17.08.22]
FK Tuzla City-HŠK Posušje 3-0(1-0)[17.08.22]

**Round 3 [30-31.07.2022]**
HŠK Posušje - Borac Banja Luka 0-2(0-1)
FK Sarajevo - Sloga Doboj 4-2(0-1)
FK Željezničar - Široki Brijeg 1-1(1-0)
Zrinjski Mostar - Leotar Trebinje 4-1(2-1)
Sloboda Tuzla-Velež Mostar 1-1(0-0)[14.09.22]
Igman Konjic - Tuzla City 3-2(1-1) [14.09.22]

**Round 4 [05-08.08.2022]**
Velež Mostar - FK Željezničar 3-1(1-0)
Borac Banja Luka - Igman Konjic 1-0(0-0)
FK Sarajevo - HŠK Posušje 1-0(0-0)
FK Tuzla City - Sloboda Tuzla 0-0
Široki Brijeg - Leotar Trebinje 1-0(1-0)
Sloga Doboj - Zrinjski M. 1-0(1-0) [14.09.22]

**Round 5 [12-14.08.2022]**
Leotar Trebinje - Velež Mostar 1-0(1-0)
Sloboda Tuzla - Borac Banja Luka 2-0(1-0)
HŠK Posušje - Sloga Doboj 3-2(1-1)
FK Željezničar - FK Tuzla City 4-2(1-0)
Igman Konjic - FK Sarajevo 2-0(1-0)
Zrinjski Mostar - Široki B. 3-0(1-0) [05.10.22]

**Round 6 [19-21.08.2022]**
FK Sarajevo - Sloboda Tuzla 1-1(0-1)
Borac Banja Luka - FK Željezničar 2-1(2-0)
FK Tuzla City - Leotar Trebinje 4-1(4-0)
Sloga Doboj - Široki Brijeg 1-1(0-1)
HŠK Posušje - Igman Konjic 2-2(0-2)
Zrinjski M. - Velež Mostar 1-0(1-0) [12.10.22]

**Round 7 [26-27.08.2022]**
Borac Banja Luka - Leotar Trebinje 0-1(0-1)
FK Željezničar - FK Sarajevo 2-2(0-0)
Igman Konjic - Sloga Doboj 0-2(0-0)
Sloboda Tuzla - HŠK Posušje 0-1(0-1)
Široki Brijeg - Velež Mostar 0-0
Zrinjski Mostar - Tuzla City 0-0 [26.10.22]

**Round 8 [30-31.08.2022]**
Sloga Doboj - Velež Mostar 3-0(1-0)
FK Sarajevo - Leotar Trebinje 3-0(2-0)
Borac Banja Luka - Zrinjski Mostar 1-0(1-0)
FK Tuzla City - Široki Brijeg 4-1(3-1)
Igman Konjic - Sloboda Tuzla 0-0
HŠK Posušje - FK Željezničar 1-2(0-2)

**Round 9 [03-05.09.2022]**
Sloboda Tuzla - Sloga Doboj 4-2(2-2)
Leotar Trebinje - HŠK Posušje 0-1(0-1)
Zrinjski Mostar - FK Sarajevo 4-1(3-1)
Široki Brijeg - Borac Banja Luka 2-0(2-0)
Velež Mostar - FK Tuzla City 4-0(1-0)
FK Željezničar - Igman Konjic 1-0(0-0)

**Round 10 [10-11.09.2022]**
Borac Banja Luka - Velež Mostar 0-0
Sloboda Tuzla - FK Željezničar 1-1(0-0)
Sloga Doboj - FK Tuzla City 0-3(0-1)
HŠK Posušje - Zrinjski Mostar 0-1(0-1)
Igman Konjic - Leotar Trebinje 3-1(2-1)
FK Sarajevo - Široki Brijeg 0-0

**Round 11 [17-19.09.2022]**
FK Tuzla City - Borac Banja Luka 0-1(0-0)
Leotar Trebinje - Sloboda Tuzla 0-0
Zrinjski Mostar - Igman Konjic 4-0(1-0)
FK Željezničar - Sloga Doboj 1-0(1-0)
Široki Brijeg - HŠK Posušje 1-0(0-0)
Velež Mostar - FK Sarajevo 1-1(0-0)

**Round 12 [30.09.-01.10.2022]**
FK Tuzla City - FK Sarajevo 1-0(0-0)
Velež Mostar - HŠK Posušje 1-1(1-1)
Zrinjski Mostar - Sloboda Tuzla 1-0(1-0)
Borac Banja Luka - Sloga Doboj 2-1(1-0)
Leotar Trebinje - FK Željezničar 0-1(0-1)
Široki Brijeg - Igman Konjic 3-2(1-0)

**Round 13 [07-09.10.2022]**
Igman Konjic - Velež Mostar 0-1(0-0)
Sloboda Tuzla - Široki Brijeg 0-3(0-2)
Leotar Trebinje - Sloga Doboj 4-1(2-0)
FK Željezničar - Zrinjski Mostar 0-1(0-1)
FK Sarajevo - Borac Banja Luka 1-0(0-0)
HŠK Posušje - FK Tuzla City 3-0(2-0)

**Round 14 [14-16.10.2022]**
Borac Banja Luka - HŠK Posušje 2-1(0-0)
Sloga Doboj - FK Sarajevo 1-0(0-0)
FK Tuzla City - Igman Konjic 2-3(0-2)
Široki Brijeg - FK Željezničar 1-0(0-0)
Leotar Trebinje - Zrinjski Mostar 1-1(1-1)
Velež Mostar - Sloboda Tuzla 1-0(0-0)

**Round 15 [22-23.10.2022]**
Leotar Trebinje - Široki Brijeg 1-0(0-0)
Igman Konjic - Borac Banja Luka 0-0
FK Željezničar - Velež Mostar 2-0(0-0)
Zrinjski Mostar - Sloga Doboj 3-0(2-0)
Sloboda Tuzla - FK Tuzla City 0-0
HŠK Posušje - FK Sarajevo 0-1(0-0)

**Round 16 [29-31.10.2022]**
Velež Mostar - Leotar Trebinje 1-0(0-0)
Sloga Doboj - HŠK Posušje 0-1(0-0)
Borac Banja Luka - Sloboda Tuzla 3-1(2-0)
Široki Brijeg - Zrinjski Mostar 1-1(0-0)
FK Sarajevo - Igman Konjic 3-1(1-1)
FK Tuzla City - FK Željezničar 1-2(0-1)

**Round 17 [05-06.11.2022]**
Sloboda Tuzla - FK Sarajevo 2-0(1-0)
Igman Konjic - HŠK Posušje 0-0
Leotar Trebinje - FK Tuzla City 4-0(3-0)
Široki Brijeg - Sloga Doboj 3-0(0-0)
FK Željezničar - Borac Banja Luka 1-2(1-1)
Velež Mostar - Zrinjski M. 1-3(1-2) [08.03.23]

**Round 18 [12-14.11.2022]**
Velež Mostar - Široki Brijeg 4-4(3-0)
HŠK Posušje - Sloboda Tuzla 2-1(0-1)
FK Tuzla City - Zrinjski Mostar 2-0(0-0)
Sloga Doboj - Igman Konjic 3-2(2-2)
Leotar Trebinje - Borac Banja Luka 0-1(0-0)
FK Sarajevo - FK Željezničar 0-0 [08.03.23]

**Round 19 [19-20.11.2022]**
Velež Mostar - Sloga Doboj 2-2(1-1)
Široki Brijeg - FK Tuzla City 1-0(0-0)
FK Željezničar - HŠK Posušje 1-1(1-0)
Sloboda Tuzla - Igman Konjic 5-1(1-0)
Leotar Trebinje - FK Sarajevo 2-0(0-0)
Zrinjski Mostar - Borac Banja Luka 1-0(0-0)

**Round 20 [24-26.02.2023]**
Borac Banja Luka - Široki Brijeg 1-0(0-0)
Igman Konjic - FK Željezničar 3-1(1-0)
Sloga Doboj - Sloboda Tuzla 2-2(1-1)
HŠK Posušje - Leotar Trebinje 1-1(1-1)
FK Tuzla City - Velež Mostar 0-1(0-0)
FK Sarajevo - Zrinjski Mostar 0-2(0-1)

**Round 21 [04-05.03.2023]**
Leotar Trebinje - Igman Konjic 1-1(0-0)
FK Željezničar - Sloboda Tuzla 1-0(1-0)
Velež Mostar - Borac Banja Luka 1-0(0-0)
Zrinjski Mostar - HŠK Posušje 5-0(1-0)
FK Tuzla City - Sloga Doboj 0-0
Široki Brijeg - FK Sarajevo 1-3(0-2)

**Round 22 [11-12.03.2023]**
Sloboda Tuzla - Leotar Trebinje 2-1(1-0)
Igman Konjic - Zrinjski Mostar 0-3(0-1)
Borac Banja Luka - FK Tuzla City 3-0(2-0)
HŠK Posušje - Široki Brijeg 0-1(0-1)
FK Sarajevo - Velež Mostar 0-1(0-0)
Sloga Doboj - FK Željezničar 0-1(0-0)

**Round 23 [18-20.03.2023]**
Zrinjski Mostar - Igman Konjic 2-1(0-0)
Borac Banja Luka - Leotar Trebinje 2-0(1-0)
FK Željezničar - Sloga Doboj 4-1(1-1)
Široki Brijeg - FK Tuzla City 1-1(0-1)
Velež Mostar - Sloboda Tuzla 0-0
FK Sarajevo - HŠK Posušje 3-1(0-0)

**Round 24 [31.03.-02.04.2023]**
FK Tuzla City - Borac Banja Luka 2-2(0-1)
Zrinjski Mostar - Široki Brijeg 3-1(1-0)
Igman Konjic - HŠK Posušje 3-0(1-0)
Leotar Trebinje - FK Željezničar 1-0(1-0)
Sloga Doboj - Velež Mostar 0-2(0-1)
Sloboda Tuzla - FK Sarajevo 2-3(2-2)

**Round 25 [07-10.04.2023]**
FK Sarajevo - Sloga Doboj 1-1(1-0)
HŠK Posušje - Sloboda Tuzla 2-0(2-0)
Velež Mostar - Leotar Trebinje 2-0(1-0)
Borac Banja Luka - Zrinjski Mostar 0-3(0-1)
FK Željezničar - FK Tuzla City 0-1(0-1)
Široki Brijeg - Igman Konjic 0-0

**Round 26 [14-15.04.2023]**
Zrinjski Mostar - FK Željezničar 2-0(2-0)
FK Tuzla City - Velež Mostar 1-1(0-0)
Igman Konjic - Sloboda Tuzla 1-1(1-0)
Leotar Trebinje - FK Sarajevo 0-3(0-1)
Sloga Doboj - HŠK Posušje 2-0(0-0)
Široki Brijeg - Borac Banja Luka 2-3(1-1)

**Round 27 [22-24.04.2023]**
Sloboda Tuzla - Sloga Doboj 0-1(0-0)
FK Željezničar - Široki Brijeg 1-0(0-0)
HŠK Posušje - Leotar Trebinje 1-0(0-0)
FK Sarajevo - FK Tuzla City 1-0(1-0)
Velež Mostar - Zrinjski Mostar 0-1(0-1)
Borac Banja Luka - Igman Konjic 1-0(1-0)

| Round 28 [26-27.04.2023] |  |
|---|---|
| FK Tuzla City - HŠK Posušje | 3-1(0-1) |
| Leotar Trebinje - Sloboda Tuzla | 0-0 |
| Zrinjski Mostar - FK Sarajevo | 2-3(1-1) |
| Široki Brijeg - Velež Mostar | 1-0(0-0) |
| Igman Konjic - Sloga Doboj | 3-0(0-0) |
| Borac Banja Luka - FK Željezničar | 2-0(0-0) |

| Round 29 [29.04.-02.05.2023] |  |
|---|---|
| FK Sarajevo - Široki Brijeg | 2-1(1-1) |
| HŠK Posušje - Zrinjski Mostar | 0-2(0-0) |
| Sloga Doboj - Leotar Trebinje | 1-1(1-0) |
| Sloboda Tuzla - FK Tuzla City | 1-0(0-0) |
| Velež Mostar - Borac Banja Luka | 2-0(1-0) |
| FK Željezničar - Igman Konjic | 1-1(0-1) |

| Round 30 [06-07.05.2023] |  |
|---|---|
| Zrinjski Mostar - Sloboda Tuzla | 4-1(2-1) |
| FK Tuzla City - Sloga Doboj | 1-2(1-1) |
| Široki Brijeg - HŠK Posušje | 1-1(1-1) |
| Igman Konjic - Leotar Trebinje | 2-0(0-0) |
| Borac Banja Luka - FK Sarajevo | 1-0(0-0) |
| FK Željezničar - Velež Mostar | 2-1(1-0) |

| Round 31 [12-15.05.2023] |  |
|---|---|
| Sloga Doboj - Zrinjski Mostar | 1-3(1-2) |
| Velež Mostar - Igman Konjic | 3-3(3-1) |
| FK Sarajevo - FK Željezničar | 2-2(1-0) |
| Leotar Trebinje - FK Tuzla City | 3-2(2-2) |
| HŠK Posušje - Borac Banja Luka | 1-0(0-0) |
| Sloboda Tuzla - Široki Brijeg | 2-1(0-0) |

| Round 32 [21.05.2023] |  |
|---|---|
| Borac Banja Luka - Sloboda Tuzla | 3-2(1-1) |
| Igman Konjic - FK Tuzla City | 0-1(0-1) |
| Široki Brijeg - Sloga Doboj | 1-0(1-0) |
| Velež Mostar - FK Sarajevo | 3-5(1-2) |
| FK Željezničar - HŠK Posušje | 3-0(0-0) |
| Zrinjski Mostar - Leotar Trebinje | 2-1(1-0) |

| Round 33 [28.05.2023] |  |
|---|---|
| FK Sarajevo - Igman Konjic | 2-4(2-3) |
| FK Tuzla City - Zrinjski Mostar | 3-0(1-0) |
| Leotar Trebinje - Široki Brijeg | 2-1(0-1) |
| HŠK Posušje - Velež Mostar | 2-1(1-1) |
| Sloboda Tuzla - FK Željezničar | 1-2(0-1) |
| Sloga Doboj - Borac Banja Luka | 2-1(1-1) |

### Final Standings

| | | Total | | | | | | Home | | | | | Away | | | |
|---|---|---|---|---|---|---|---|---|---|---|---|---|---|---|---|---|---|
| 1. | HŠK Zrinjski Mostar | 33 | 25 | 3 | 5 | 66 - 21 | 78 | 14 | 1 | 2 | 42 - 11 | 11 | 2 | 3 | 24 - 10 |
| 2. | FK Borac Banja Luka | 33 | 18 | 4 | 11 | 39 - 32 | 58 | 13 | 1 | 3 | 25 - 13 | 5 | 3 | 8 | 14 - 19 |
| 3. | FK Željezničar Sarajevo | 33 | 15 | 8 | 10 | 42 - 35 | 53 | 9 | 5 | 3 | 26 - 14 | 6 | 3 | 7 | 16 - 21 |
| 4. | FK Sarajevo | 33 | 15 | 7 | 11 | 50 - 46 | 52 | 8 | 5 | 4 | 25 - 21 | 7 | 2 | 7 | 25 - 25 |
| 5. | NK Široki Brijeg | 33 | 13 | 9 | 11 | 38 - 36 | 48 | 10 | 5 | 2 | 22 - 11 | 3 | 4 | 9 | 16 - 25 |
| 6. | FK Velež Mostar | 33 | 11 | 12 | 10 | 40 - 37 | 45 | 7 | 7 | 3 | 30 - 22 | 4 | 5 | 7 | 10 - 15 |
| 7. | FK Tuzla City | 33 | 10 | 7 | 16 | 43 - 46 | 37 | 6 | 4 | 6 | 26 - 17 | 4 | 3 | 10 | 17 - 29 |
| 8. | FK Igman Konjic | 33 | 9 | 10 | 14 | 42 - 48 | 37 | 7 | 4 | 5 | 20 - 13 | 2 | 6 | 9 | 22 - 35 |
| 9. | FK Sloga Meridian Doboj | 33 | 10 | 7 | 16 | 40 - 55 | 37 | 7 | 4 | 5 | 23 - 19 | 3 | 3 | 11 | 17 - 36 |
| 10. | HŠK Posušje | 33 | 10 | 7 | 16 | 28 - 46 | 37 | 7 | 3 | 6 | 19 - 17 | 3 | 4 | 10 | 9 - 29 |
| 11. | FK Leotar Trebinje (Relegated) | 33 | 9 | 7 | 17 | 29 - 46 | 34 | 8 | 4 | 4 | 20 - 12 | 1 | 3 | 13 | 9 - 34 |
| 12. | FK Sloboda Tuzla (Relegated) | 33 | 7 | 11 | 15 | 32 - 41 | 32 | 7 | 3 | 6 | 23 - 18 | 0 | 8 | 9 | 9 - 23 |

### Top goalscorers:

| | | |
|---|---|---|
| 24 | Nemanja Bilbija | HŠK Zrinjski Mostar |
| 19 | Mirsad Ramić | FK Igman Konjic |
| 12 | Nermin Haskić | FK Velež Mostar |

## NATIONAL CUP
### Kup Bosne i Hercegovine u nogometu 2022/2023

#### First Round [18-19.10.2022]

| | | | | |
|---|---|---|---|---|
| FK Krupa na Vrbasu - FK Borac Banja Luka | 1-3 | | NK Kolina Ustikolina - HŠK Posušje | 1-5 |
| NK Jedinstvo Bihać - FK Sloga Meridian Doboj | 1-2 | | FK Radnik Bijeljina - FK Tekstilac Derventa | 2-0 |
| FK Laktaši - FK Igman Konjic | 3-1 | | NK Zvijezda Gradačac - OFK Gradina Srebrenik | 4-1 |
| FK Zvijezda 09 Ugljevik - HŠK Zrinjski Mostar | 0-4 | | FK Sloboda Novi Grad - FK Rudar Prijedor | 1-4 |
| FK Budućnost Banovići - FK Željezničar Sarajevo | 1-2 | | FK Rudar Han Bila - FK Rudar Kakanj | 0-2 |
| FK Famos Hrasnica - NK Široki Brijeg | 0-3 | | HNK Sloga Uskoplje - FK Leotar Trebinje | 1-3 |
| FK Baton Sarajevo - FK Sloboda Tuzla | 2-8 | | FK Alfa Modriča - FK Tuzla City | 2-5 |
| NK TOŠK Tešanj - FK Velež Mostar | 0-2 | | NK Čelik Zenica - FK Sarajevo | 1-1 aet; 4-3 pen |

#### 1/8-Finals [18-19.02.2023]

| | | | | |
|---|---|---|---|---|
| FK Rudar Prijedor - FK Borac Banja Luka | 1-1 aet; 6-5 pen | | HŠK Zrinjski Mostar - FK Laktaši | 4-0(2-0) |
| NK Zvijezda Gradačac - FK Rudar Kakanj | 3-1(2-0) | | FK Sloboda Tuzla - FK Sloga Meridian Doboj | 1-1 aet; 6-7 pen |
| FK Željezničar Sarajevo - FK Leotar Trebinje | 2-1(1-1) | | NK Čelik Zenica - FK Radnik Bijeljina | 0-0 aet; 3-4 pen |
| FK Velež Mostar - HŠK Posušje | 2-0(1-0) | | NK Široki Brijeg - FK Tuzla City | 2-2 aet; 6-7 pen |

#### Quarter-Finals [28.02.-01.03./14-16.03.2023]

| First Leg | | | Second Leg | |
|---|---|---|---|---|
| FK Željezničar Sarajevo - NK Zvijezda Gradačac | 2-1(0-0) | | NK Zvijezda Gradačac - FK Željezničar Sarajevo | 2-3(1-0) |
| FK Tuzla City - FK Rudar Prijedor | 5-0(3-0) | | FK Rudar Prijedor - FK Tuzla City | 0-2(0-1) |
| FK Radnik Bijeljina - HŠK Zrinjski Mostar | 1-3(0-1) | | HŠK Zrinjski Mostar - FK Radnik Bijeljina | 2-0(1-0) |
| FK Sloga Meridian Doboj - FK Velež Mostar | 0-3(0-0) | | FK Velež Mostar - FK Sloga Meridian Doboj | 4-0(2-0) |

#### Semi-Finals [05.04./19.04.2023]

| First Leg | | | Second Leg | |
|---|---|---|---|---|
| FK Tuzla City - HŠK Zrinjski Mostar | 0-3(0-3) | | HŠK Zrinjski Mostar - FK Tuzla City | 4-0(1-0) |
| FK Velež Mostar - FK Željezničar Sarajevo | 1-0(1-0) | | FK Željezničar Sarajevo - FK Velež Mostar | 1-2(1-1) |

17.05.2023; Stadion Bilino Polje, Zenica; Referee: Luka Bilbija; Attendance: 5,000
**FK Velež Mostar - HŠK Zrinjski Mostar**                                    **0-1(0-0)**

**Velež Mostar**: Osman Hadžikić, Samir Zeljković, Ante Hrkać, Mitar Ćuković, Omar Pršeš [*sent off 90+5*], Nemanja Andušić, Tino Lauš [*sent off 90+5*], Tarik Šikalo (53.Emir Halilović), Nermin Haskić, Edo Vehabović [*sent off 90+5 on the bench*] (74.Wallace Menezes dos Santos), Alen Dejanović (85.Marko Karamarko). Trainer: Nedim Jusufbegović.

**Goal**: 0-1 Mario Čuže (52).

**Zrinjski Mostar**: Marko Marić, Slobodan Jakovljević, Hrvoje Barišić, Josip Čorluka, Kerim Memija, Antonio Ivančić (60.Karlo Kamenar), Mario Tičinović (60.Matija Malekinušić), Silvio Ilinković (80.Damir Zlomislić), Petar Sučić, Mario Čuže, Nemanja Bilbija. Trainer: Krunoslav Rendulić.

[*Tomislav Kiš and Franko Sabljić (90+5) were sent off on the bench*].

## THE CLUBS 2022/2023

### Fudbalski klub Borac Banja Luka

| | |
|---|---|
| **Founded**: | 04.07.1926 |
| **Stadium**: | Gradski stadion Banja Luka, Banja Luka (10,030) |
| **Trainer**: | Nenad Lalatović (SRB) 22.12.1977 |
| [28.08.2022] | Vinko Marinović 03.03.1971 |

| Goalkeepers: | DOB | M | (s) | G |
|---|---|---|---|---|
| Nikola Ćetković | 06.02.2002 | 25 | (1) | |
| Bojan Pavlović (SRB) | 08.11.1986 | 8 | | |
| **Defenders:** | **DOB** | **M** | **(s)** | **G** |
| Nikola Andrić (SRB) | 23.05.1992 | 13 | (1) | 1 |
| Dino Ćorić | 30.06.1990 | 5 | (3) | |
| Sergej Dojčinović | 14.04.2000 | 3 | (5) | |
| Marko Gajić (SRB) | 10.03.1992 | 13 | | |
| Milijan Kovačević | 17.10.2005 | | (1) | |
| Marko Kujunđić | 14.10.2002 | | (1) | |
| Ivan Lagunđić (CRO) | 14.06.1999 | 11 | | |
| Darko Lazić (SRB) | 19.07.1994 | 19 | (2) | 1 |
| Đorđe Milojević | 10.05.2001 | 1 | | |
| Nikola Pejović (SRB) | 22.09.1998 | 2 | (1) | |
| Filip Račić | 15.02.2003 | 6 | (1) | |
| Aleksandar Subić | 27.09.1993 | 18 | (6) | |
| Milan Spremo | 27.04.1995 | 10 | (2) | 1 |
| Savo Šušić | 27.01.2005 | 3 | | |
| Aleksandar Vojnović | 03.10.1996 | 29 | (1) | 3 |

| Midfielders: | DOB | M | (s) | G |
|---|---|---|---|---|
| Amar Begić | 07.08.2000 | 4 | (8) | |
| Dejan Meleg | 01.10.1994 | 3 | (2) | 2 |
| Danilo Moconja | 05.01.2005 | | (1) | |
| Nikola Ninković (SRB) | 19.12.1994 | 17 | (3) | 3 |
| Nedeljko Piščević (SRB) | 20.04.1995 | 27 | | 3 |
| Janez Pišek (SVN) | 04.05.1998 | 5 | (5) | |
| Dejan Popara | 10.03.2003 | 12 | (12) | |
| Fedor Predragović | 08.04.1995 | 17 | (4) | 1 |
| **Forwards:** | **DOB** | **M** | **(s)** | **G** |
| Jakov Blagaić (CRO) | 08.02.2000 | 5 | (6) | 2 |
| Obren Cvijanović | 30.08.1994 | 1 | (16) | |
| Alen Jurilj | 07.03.1996 | 8 | (10) | 1 |
| Enver Kulašin | 11.09.2003 | 27 | (4) | 4 |
| Jovo Lukić | 28.11.1998 | 14 | (16) | 2 |
| Stefan Marčetić | 02.12.2006 | 1 | (1) | |
| Momčilo Mrkaić | 21.09.1990 | 19 | (11) | 10 |
| Benjamin Tatar | 18.05.1994 | 28 | (1) | 1 |
| Goran Zakarić | 07.11.1992 | 9 | (7) | 1 |

### Fudbalski klub Igman Konjic

| | |
|---|---|
| **Founded**: | 1920 |
| **Stadium**: | Stadion Igmana, Konjic (5,000) |
| **Trainer**: | Adnan Elezović 26.04.1983 |
| [22.12.2022] | Husref Musemić 04.07.1961 |

| Goalkeepers: | DOB | M | (s) | G |
|---|---|---|---|---|
| Aldin Ćeman | 05.01.1995 | 29 | | |
| Dino Hamzić | 22.01.1988 | 1 | | |
| Mehmed Pajaziti | 25.05.1996 | | (1) | |
| Mićo Vukanović | 24.08.2000 | 3 | | |
| **Defenders:** | **DOB** | **M** | **(s)** | **G** |
| Almir Ćubara | 21.11.1997 | 3 | (9) | 1 |
| Amer Dupovac | 29.05.1991 | 20 | (5) | |
| Elvir Duraković | 07.02.2000 | 31 | | 2 |
| Kenan Hebibovic | 14.06.2001 | | (2) | |
| Azur Mahmić | 06.05.2003 | 27 | | |
| Amir Velić | 28.03.1999 | 22 | (5) | |
| **Midfielders:** | **DOB** | **M** | **(s)** | **G** |
| Nermin Alagić | 03.05.2001 | 10 | (4) | 1 |
| Berin Alić | 07.01.2000 | 2 | (4) | |
| Armin Besagić | 01.10.1998 | 19 | (10) | 1 |
| Edin Biber | 06.01.1999 | 3 | (13) | |
| Elvis Bibić | 04.03.1992 | | (1) | |

| | DOB | M | (s) | G |
|---|---|---|---|---|
| Petar Bojo | 08.01.1998 | 2 | (8) | 1 |
| Amer Drljević | 18.05.1994 | 28 | (1) | |
| Senad Kašić | 04.04.1995 | 3 | (11) | |
| Mirko Oremuš (CRO) | 06.09.1988 | 10 | (1) | |
| Amar Sabljica | 10.03.2001 | 1 | | |
| Anes Vazda | 24.07.1997 | 2 | (6) | |
| **Forwards:** | **DOB** | **M** | **(s)** | **G** |
| Mersudin Ahmetović | 19.03.1985 | 1 | (11) | 1 |
| Vahidin Alešević | 02.07.1997 | | (9) | |
| Dario Blagojević | 09.11.1989 | 3 | (7) | 1 |
| Darko Bodul (CRO) | 11.01.1989 | 27 | (2) | 1 |
| Stefan Denković (SRB) | 16.06.1991 | 8 | (3) | 5 |
| Anel Hebibović | 07.07.1990 | 26 | (1) | 1 |
| Damir Hrelja | 13.10.2001 | 29 | (3) | 4 |
| Demir Jakupović | 16.02.1996 | 26 | (2) | 4 |
| Iris Mandzuka | 05.04.2000 | | (1) | |
| Mirsad Ramić | 06.12.1992 | 27 | | 19 |

## Fudbalski klub Leotar Trebinje

**Founded**: 19.08.1925
**Stadium**: Stadion Police, Trebinje (8,550)
**Trainer**: Marko Vidojević    31.07.1975
[16.09.2022] Marko Maksimović    20.08.1984

| Goalkeepers: | DOB | M | (s) | G |
|---|---|---|---|---|
| Risto Perišić | 19.01.1997 | 1 | (2) | |
| Dušan Puletić (SRB) | 05.01.1989 | 32 | | |
| **Defenders:** | **DOB** | **M** | **(s)** | **G** |
| Mihailo Cmiljanović (SRB) | 15.06.1994 | 28 | | |
| Nemanja Cvetković (SRB) | 03.01.1996 | 10 | | |
| Marko Čubrilo | 03.05.1998 | 26 | (4) | |
| Darko Đajić | 30.08.1992 | 29 | (1) | |
| Zoran Milić | 11.04.1998 | 13 | (14) | 1 |
| Đoko Milović | 16.09.1992 | 23 | (1) | 1 |
| Dejan Uzelac | 29.11.1993 | 13 | (2) | 2 |
| Srđan Vulić | 07.10.1998 | | (5) | |
| **Midfielders:** | **DOB** | **M** | **(s)** | **G** |
| Boban Georgiev (MKD) | 26.01.1997 | 11 | (12) | 1 |
| Matija Glogovac | 04.08.2006 | 1 | | |
| Mahir Karić | 05.03.1992 | 14 | (18) | 1 |
| Dragan Matković | 09.06.2001 | 13 | (2) | |
| Aleksandar Milaković | 26.11.1992 | 5 | (6) | |
| Stefan Paranos | 20.09.1998 | | (2) | |
| Marko Perišić | 25.01.1991 | 10 | (5) | |
| Marko Pervan (CRO) | 04.04.1996 | 6 | (9) | 3 |
| Božo Prusina | 08.01.2004 | 11 | | |
| Aleksa Spaić (MNE) | 25.01.1999 | | (13) | |
| Miloš Stanojević (SRB) | 20.11.1993 | 4 | (5) | |
| Dennis Stojković (SRB) | 03.08.2002 | 5 | (12) | 1 |
| Danilo Šipovac | 17.04.2000 | 10 | (2) | 1 |
| Marko Šušnjar | 20.08.2003 | 4 | (5) | |
| Amar Tahrić | 04.05.2002 | 3 | (6) | |
| Ognjen Todorović | 24.03.1989 | 13 | (5) | 3 |
| **Forwards:** | **DOB** | **M** | **(s)** | **G** |
| Milos Ačimovič | 06.07.1997 | 26 | (7) | 3 |
| Milorad Albijanić | 04.10.1998 | | (4) | |
| David Čavić | 21.11.2002 | 23 | (2) | 4 |
| Ammar Đuderija | 06.08.2002 | 11 | (6) | 1 |
| Haris Handžić | 20.06.1990 | 17 | (2) | 6 |
| Filip Kolak | 30.12.2004 | | (1) | |
| Šaleta Kordić (MNE) | 19.04.1993 | 1 | (3) | |

## Hrvatski športski klub Posušje

**Founded**: 01.07.1950
**Stadium**: Stadion Mokri Dolac, Posušje (8,000)
**Trainer**: Ferdo Milin    15.12.1977
[29.09.2022] Goran Granić (CRO)    09.07.1975
[23.03.2023] Branko Karačić (CRO)    24.09.1960

| Goalkeepers: | DOB | M | (s) | G |
|---|---|---|---|---|
| Marko Galić | 13.02.1999 | | (1) | |
| Luka Kukić | 16.05.1996 | 33 | | |
| **Defenders:** | **DOB** | **M** | **(s)** | **G** |
| Tomislav Dadić (CRO) | 15.12.1997 | 18 | (8) | 1 |
| Kenan Horić | 13.09.1990 | 22 | | 1 |
| Josip Katavić (CRO) | 20.01.2000 | 1 | | |
| Ivor Krešić | 14.03.2001 | 4 | (3) | |
| Darijo Krišto (CRO) | 05.03.1988 | 22 | | 1 |
| Luka Lučić (CRO) | 02.01.1995 | 23 | (2) | |
| Frane Maglica (CRO) | 02.07.1997 | 9 | (2) | |
| Jovan Pavlović | 11.02.2000 | 19 | (7) | |
| **Midfielders:** | **DOB** | **M** | **(s)** | **G** |
| Luka Begić | 05.02.1994 | 2 | (23) | 1 |
| Zvonimir Begić | 22.09.1990 | 20 | (4) | 1 |
| Josip Bešlić (CRO) | 13.09.1999 | | (1) | |
| Arijan Brković (CRO) | 03.02.2001 | 26 | (4) | 2 |
| Marko Hanuljak (CRO) | 31.01.2000 | 16 | (1) | 1 |
| Davor Landeka | 18.09.1984 | 11 | (11) | |
| Luka Marković (CRO) | 28.07.2001 | 5 | (4) | 1 |
| Ivan Roca (CRO) | 31.03.1996 | 19 | (6) | |
| Nikša Šilić | 08.06.2002 | 6 | (7) | |
| **Forwards:** | **DOB** | **M** | **(s)** | **G** |
| Dominik Begić | 03.08.1997 | 4 | (17) | |
| Ivan Bešlić | 03.06.2001 | 17 | (4) | |
| Gabrijel Boban (CRO) | 23.07.1989 | 23 | (5) | 8 |
| Dejan Georgijević (SRB) | 19.01.1994 | 1 | (5) | 1 |
| Toni Jović (CRO) | 02.09.1992 | 24 | (1) | 4 |
| Marko Kraljević | 28.12.2005 | 1 | | |
| Slobodan Milanović | 27.08.1992 | 17 | (11) | 2 |
| Dario Pavkovic (CRO) | 28.05.1994 | 7 | (5) | 2 |
| Vinko Rozić (CRO) | 01.08.2003 | 9 | (4) | 1 |
| Zvonimir Vukoja (CRO) | 29.07.1997 | 4 | (10) | 1 |

## Fudbalski klub Sarajevo

**Founded**: 24.10.1946
**Stadium**: Stadion "Asim Ferhatović Hase", Sarajevo (34,500)
**Trainer**: Fedja Dudić    01.02.1983
[20.10.2022] Emir Obuca    11.12.1978
[12.12.2022] Mirza Varesanović    31.05.1972

| Goalkeepers: | DOB | M | (s) | G |
|---|---|---|---|---|
| Belmin Dizdarević | 09.08.2001 | 15 | | |
| Muhamed Šahinović | 30.09.2003 | 18 | | |
| **Defenders:** | **DOB** | **M** | **(s)** | **G** |
| Marin Aničić | 17.08.1989 | 2 | | |
| Vlatko Drobarov (MKD) | 02.11.1992 | 12 | (2) | |
| Ilija Martinović (MNE) | 31.01.1994 | 12 | | 2 |
| Musa Muhammed (NGA) | 31.10.1996 | 14 | (1) | 1 |
| Nihad Mujakić | 15.04.1998 | 2 | | |
| Enedin Mulalić | 10.01.2004 | 13 | (1) | 1 |
| Slaviša Radović (SRB) | 08.10.1993 | 7 | (4) | |
| Besim Šerbečić | 01.05.1998 | 13 | (1) | |
| Muharem Trako | 27.09.2003 | 14 | (5) | |
| Avdija Vršajević | 06.03.1986 | 5 | | |
| **Midfielders:** | **DOB** | **M** | **(s)** | **G** |
| Abdul Rashid Abubakar (GHA) | 16.03.2000 | 1 | (4) | |
| Haris Ališah | 03.11.2004 | 1 | (1) | |
| Muhamed Buljubašić | 04.07.2004 | | (1) | |
| Hamza Ćataković | 15.01.1997 | 17 | (11) | 6 |
| Frane Čirjak (CRO) | 23.06.1995 | 18 | (3) | |
| Adnan Džafić | 10.05.1990 | 14 | (13) | 2 |
| Andrej Đokanović | 01.03.2001 | 17 | | |
| Ivan Ikić (CRO) | 13.09.1999 | 11 | (6) | 5 |
| Ivan Jelić Balta (CRO) | 17.09.1992 | 12 | (1) | |
| Rifet Kapič | 03.07.1995 | 3 | (3) | |
| Rijad Kobiljar | 08.04.1996 | 1 | (11) | 1 |
| Mirza Mustafić | 20.06.1998 | 7 | (13) | 1 |
| Bakir Nurković | 05.04.2005 | | (2) | |
| Tarik Ramić | 07.04.2003 | 5 | (8) | |
| Đani Salčin | 19.03.2000 | | (7) | |
| Asmir Suljić | 11.09.1991 | 13 | (1) | |
| Dal Varešanović | 23.05.2001 | 25 | (5) | 8 |
| Mario Vrančić | 23.05.1989 | 12 | (2) | 1 |
| **Forwards:** | **DOB** | **M** | **(s)** | **G** |
| Mersudin Ahmetović | 19.03.1985 | 3 | (13) | 2 |
| Daniel Avramovski (MKD) | 20.02.1995 | 9 | (10) | 2 |
| Giorgi Guliashvili (GEO) | 05.09.2001 | 5 | (5) | |
| Francis Kyeremeh (GHA) | 23.06.1997 | 10 | | 1 |
| Nardin Mulahusejnović | 09.02.1998 | 9 | (7) | 3 |
| Irfan Ramić | 05.03.2004 | | (5) | |
| *Renan* Abner do Carmo Oliveira (BRA) | 08.05.1997 | 9 | (5) | 9 |
| Nemanja Tomašević (SRB) | 09.08.1999 | 21 | (4) | |
| Almedin Ziljkić | 25.02.1996 | 13 | (1) | 5 |

## Fudbalski klub Sloga Meridian Doboj

| | | | | |
|---|---|---|---|---|
| Founded: | 19.07.1945 | | | |
| Stadium: | Stadion Luke, Doboj (3,000) | | | |
| Trainer: | Zoran Curguz | | | 20.05.1971 |
| [23.03.2023] | Vlado Jagodić | | | 22.03.1964 |

| Goalkeepers: | DOB | M | (s) | G |
|---|---|---|---|---|
| Bakir Brajlović | 02.09.2002 | 5 | | |
| Mihajlo Dabić | 24.03.2002 | 9 | | |
| Danilo Djulčić (SRB) | 02.10.1998 | 5 | | |
| Ilia Gučmazov (RUS) | 14.04.2001 | 1 | | |
| Elvir Trako | 29.10.1998 | 13 | (3) | |
| **Defenders:** | **DOB** | **M** | **(s)** | **G** |
| David Čolić | 12.04.2000 | 15 | (6) | |
| Franko Dadić | 02.12.2000 | 11 | (12) | 2 |
| Eldin Hasanbegović | 17.09.2000 | 8 | (4) | 1 |
| Milan Lalić (SRB) | 25.07.1995 | 10 | (2) | 2 |
| Milan Milanović (SRB) | 31.03.1991 | 30 | | |
| Miloš Nikolić (SRB) | 03.10.1994 | 13 | | 2 |
| Albin Omić | 17.01.2004 | 1 | (2) | |
| Dušan Ristić | 04.10.2000 | 22 | (3) | |
| Karlo Stapić | 17.05.2002 | 15 | (1) | |
| Obrad Starčević | 15.09.2002 | 11 | (5) | |
| Ostoja Šaula | 17.03.1999 | 17 | (7) | |

| Midfielders: | DOB | M | (s) | G |
|---|---|---|---|---|
| Pavel Baranov (RUS) | 16.05.1999 | 5 | | |
| Staša Baštić | 24.12.2001 | 16 | (8) | 1 |
| Adonis Bilal | 05.08.1999 | 2 | (10) | |
| Ivan Djorić (SRB) | 07.07.1995 | 20 | (9) | 1 |
| Tarik Jasarević | 25.12.2004 | | (3) | 1 |
| Marko Kujundić | 14.10.2002 | 11 | (2) | |
| Aleksandar Milaković | 26.11.1992 | 11 | (6) | 3 |
| Nikola Popara | 08.03.1992 | 27 | (3) | |
| Dimitrije Zajić | 23.03.1995 | 16 | (14) | 4 |
| **Forwards:** | **DOB** | **M** | **(s)** | **G** |
| Milan Basrak (SRB) | 24.12.1994 | 2 | (9) | 1 |
| Leo Janković | 04.09.2000 | 4 | (10) | 2 |
| Mario Krstovski (MKD) | 03.04.1998 | 19 | (5) | 9 |
| Luka Kulenović | 29.09.1999 | 13 | (4) | 6 |
| Nemanja Mihajlović (SRB) | 19.01.1996 | 10 | (4) | |
| Demir Peco | 31.07.1996 | 3 | (7) | |
| Vasilije Perković | 21.08.2002 | 2 | (1) | |
| Uglješa Stevanović (SRB) | 09.09.1998 | 16 | (12) | 5 |
| Sergej Vitonji | 09.10.2002 | | (3) | |

## Fudbalski Klub Sloboda Tuzla

| | | | | |
|---|---|---|---|---|
| Founded: | 10.10.1919 | | | |
| Stadium: | Stadion Tušanj, Tuzla (7,200) | | | |
| Trainer: | Adnan Jahić | | | 28.02.1985 |
| [22.03.2023] | Danijel Pranjić | | | 02.12.1981 |

| Goalkeepers: | DOB | M | (s) | G |
|---|---|---|---|---|
| Semir Bukvić | 21.05.1991 | 24 | | |
| Filip Erić (SRB) | 10.10.1994 | 9 | | |
| **Defenders:** | **DOB** | **M** | **(s)** | **G** |
| Harun Beganović | 05.01.2002 | 11 | (8) | |
| Muharem Čivić | 04.01.1993 | 11 | (10) | |
| Kenin Devedžić | 01.01.2000 | 10 | (3) | |
| Emir Jusić | 13.06.1986 | 19 | (4) | 2 |
| Kemal Osmanković | 04.03.1997 | 23 | (4) | 2 |
| Jasmin Osmić | 13.07.2001 | 24 | (1) | 1 |
| Ivan Šubert (SRB) | 14.10.1993 | 9 | (2) | 1 |
| **Midfielders:** | **DOB** | **M** | **(s)** | **G** |
| Kenan Delić | 02.05.1999 | 25 | (4) | 1 |
| Haris Hasanović | 20.03.2004 | | (1) | |
| Said Husejinović | 17.05.1988 | 7 | (17) | 1 |
| Tarik Kapetanović | 06.06.2003 | 26 | (4) | 1 |
| Alen Kurtalić | 28.10.1999 | 14 | (10) | 1 |

| | DOB | M | (s) | G |
|---|---|---|---|---|
| Saša Maksimović | 18.12.1999 | 21 | (10) | 1 |
| Eldar Mehmedović | 10.04.2003 | 21 | (7) | 5 |
| Kemal Mujarić | 12.09.1999 | | (6) | |
| Melvin Osmić | 16.02.1999 | 24 | (4) | 2 |
| Marko Pervan (CRO) | 04.04.1996 | 8 | (5) | |
| Tarik Saletović | 20.10.2002 | | (1) | |
| Mak Varešanović | 28.08.1998 | 2 | (3) | |
| Adam Vošnjak (SVN) | 26.07.2000 | 19 | (3) | |
| Stojan Vranješ | 11.10.1986 | 20 | (1) | 5 |
| **Forwards:** | **DOB** | **M** | **(s)** | **G** |
| Adi Alić | 05.03.2002 | 8 | (6) | 1 |
| Amer Bekić | 05.08.1992 | 9 | (7) | 2 |
| Senad Jarović (GER) | 20.01.1998 | 2 | (6) | |
| Nikola Komazec (SRB) | 15.11.1987 | 14 | (12) | 5 |
| Aldin Mešić | 04.02.2004 | 3 | (4) | |
| Irman Sejmenović | 04.02.2003 | | (1) | |

## Nogometni klub Široki Brijeg

| | | | |
|---|---|---|---|
| Founded: | 1948 | | |
| Stadium: | Stadion Pecara, Široki Brijeg (7,000) | | |
| Trainer: | Ivica Barbarić (CRO) | | 23.02.1962 |

| Goalkeepers: | DOB | M | (s) | G |
|---|---|---|---|---|
| Renato Josipović (CRO) | 12.06.2001 | 25 | | |
| Tomislav Adolf Tomić (CRO) | 07.03.1997 | 8 | | |
| **Defenders:** | **DOB** | **M** | **(s)** | **G** |
| Branimir Barišić (CRO) | 31.05.1998 | 13 | (9) | 1 |
| *Bruno* de *Oliveira* Souza (BRA) | 09.06.1996 | 19 | (4) | |
| Mihael Kuprešak (CRO) | 15.05.2001 | 26 | | 1 |
| Mate Lasić | 29.03.2002 | | (1) | |
| Kristian Luburić (SUI) | 20.02.2001 | | (1) | |
| Ilija Mašić | 08.04.1999 | 31 | | 3 |
| Božo Musa (CRO) | 15.09.1988 | 11 | (6) | |
| Ivan Pranjić (CRO) | 06.08.1999 | 6 | (12) | |
| Mate Šuto (CRO) | 02.10.1996 | 6 | (15) | |
| Petar Turković (CRO) | 05.06.1997 | 1 | (1) | |
| Moris Valinčić (CRO) | 17.11.2002 | 28 | | |
| **Midfielders:** | **DOB** | **M** | **(s)** | **G** |
| *Alisson* Fabricio dos Santos *Taddei* (BRA) | 10.07.1997 | 5 | (4) | |
| Marijan Ćavar | 02.02.1998 | 31 | | 5 |

| | DOB | M | (s) | G |
|---|---|---|---|---|
| Tomislav Knežević (CRO) | 07.01.1999 | 2 | (9) | |
| Juraj Ljubić (CRO) | 26.05.2000 | | (2) | |
| Di Mateo Lovrić (CRO) | 08.01.2000 | 19 | (5) | 1 |
| Kristijan Medić | 17.03.2000 | 7 | (12) | |
| Božo Prusina | 08.01.2004 | | (3) | |
| Tomislav Tomić | 16.11.1990 | 2 | (5) | |
| Fran Vukelić (CRO) | 09.10.2001 | | (3) | |
| Bože Vukoja | 03.04.1998 | 28 | (2) | 10 |
| **Forwards:** | **DOB** | **M** | **(s)** | **G** |
| Ilija Bagarić (CRO) | 02.07.1999 | 19 | (7) | 5 |
| Carlos Eduardo de Sousa Leopoldino „Kadu" (BRA) | 03.03.2002 | 1 | (3) | |
| Cyrille Kpan (BFA) | 30.05.1998 | 24 | (2) | 2 |
| Daniel Lukić | 11.03.2001 | 24 | (5) | 6 |
| Frano Medić (CRO) | 20.07.2002 | | (7) | |
| Ilan Pejić (CRO) | 27.03.2001 | 17 | (11) | 1 |
| Dominik Radić (CRO) | 26.07.1996 | 9 | (11) | 2 |
| Vinko Rozić (CRO) | 01.08.2003 | 1 | (13) | 1 |

## Fudbalski klub Tuzla City

| | | |
|---|---|---|
| **Founded**: | 1955 (*as FK Sloga Simin Han*) | |
| **Stadium**: | Stadion Tušanj, Tuzla (7,200) | |
| **Trainer**: | Dragan Jović | 19.07.1963 |
| [19.12.2022] | Milenko Bošnjaković | 04.03.1968 |

| Goalkeepers: | DOB | M | (s) | G |
|---|---|---|---|---|
| Malcolm Barcola (TOG) | 14.05.1999 | 8 | | |
| Bakir Brajlović | 02.09.2002 | 1 | (1) | |
| Nevres Fejzić | 04.11.1990 | 24 | | |
| **Defenders:** | **DOB** | **M** | **(s)** | **G** |
| Anis Ćosić | 27.05.2004 | | (1) | |
| Fernando Darío Ferreyra (ARG) | 19.01.1997 | 10 | (6) | |
| Eldin Hasanbegović | 17.09.2000 | 1 | (1) | |
| Ante Hrkać | 11.03.1992 | 7 | (4) | |
| Damir Mehidić | 07.01.1992 | 28 | | 2 |
| Aleksey Nikitin (RUS) | 27.01.1992 | 5 | (1) | 1 |
| Robert Radić (CRO) | 17.05.1999 | 2 | | |
| Hamza Redžić | 10.06.2004 | | (1) | |
| Mustafa Šukilović | 01.01.2003 | 27 | (1) | |
| **Midfielders:** | **DOB** | **M** | **(s)** | **G** |
| Jasmin Čeliković | 07.01.1999 | 28 | (1) | 3 |
| Dino Ćorić | 30.06.1990 | 9 | | |
| Alassane Diaby (MLI) | 06.01.1995 | 5 | (5) | |
| Nebojša Gavrić (SRB) | 27.08.1991 | 13 | (7) | |
| Harun Karić | 30.11.2002 | 17 | (5) | 1 |
| Huso Karjašević | 10.07.1997 | 24 | (3) | 1 |
| Adrian Mendeš (CRO) | 21.08.2001 | 1 | (7) | |
| Belmin Mešinović | 06.12.2001 | 11 | (12) | |
| Petar Mišić (CRO) | 24.07.1994 | 17 | (5) | 3 |
| Kemal Mujarić | 12.09.1999 | | (2) | |
| Ajdin Nukić | 26.11.1997 | 17 | (11) | 1 |
| Dušan Pantelić (SRB) | 15.04.1993 | 17 | (6) | 2 |
| Mladen Veselinović | 04.01.1993 | 3 | (10) | 1 |
| **Forwards:** | **DOB** | **M** | **(s)** | **G** |
| Samir Burić | 08.06.1998 | 2 | (6) | |
| Amadou Coulibaly (MLI) | 05.05.1997 | 8 | (3) | 3 |
| Allan Eleouet (SUI) | 29.07.1994 | 7 | (8) | |
| Irfan Hadžić | 15.06.1993 | 6 | (6) | 4 |
| Giorgi Ivaniadze (GEO) | 27.01.2000 | 6 | (4) | 1 |
| Mićo Kuzmanović | 18.03.1996 | 29 | (1) | 6 |
| Ali Mahmud | 03.09.2004 | | (2) | |
| Eldin Mehmedović | 23.06.2000 | 5 | (5) | 1 |
| Salko Nargalić | 16.07.2001 | 5 | (5) | 3 |
| Đorđe Pantelić (SRB) | 29.11.1999 | 7 | (5) | 2 |
| Mahir Rahimić | 20.06.2005 | | (1) | |
| Semir Smajlagić | 18.09.1998 | 5 | (6) | 5 |
| Sedad Subašić | 16.02.2001 | 8 | (4) | |

## Fudbalski klub Velež Mostar

| | | |
|---|---|---|
| **Founded**: | 26.06.1922 | |
| **Stadium**: | Stadion Rođeni, Mostar (7,000) | |
| **Trainer**: | Amar Osim | 18.07.1967 |
| [01.12.2022] | Nedim Jusufbegović | 30.09.1974 |

| Goalkeepers: | DOB | M | (s) | G |
|---|---|---|---|---|
| Slaviša Bogdanović | 11.10.1993 | 21 | | |
| Osman Hadžikić (AUT) | 12.03.1996 | 11 | | |
| Edis Nanić | 13.02.2004 | 1 | | |
| **Defenders:** | **DOB** | **M** | **(s)** | **G** |
| Adin Bajrić | 22.07.2003 | 9 | | |
| Mehmed Ćosić | 25.06.1997 | 3 | (9) | |
| Mitar Ćuković (MNE) | 06.04.1995 | 7 | (2) | |
| Saša Domić (SRB) | 18.02.1998 | 7 | (3) | |
| Đanis Gosto | 28.01.2005 | 3 | (1) | |
| Ante Hrkać | 11.03.1992 | 11 | | |
| Frane Ikić (CRO) | 19.06.1994 | 16 | | 1 |
| Amar Kvakić | 30.10.2002 | 12 | (1) | |
| Elvir Muminović | 02.03.2001 | 2 | (1) | |
| Antonio Pavić (CRO) | 18.11.1994 | 6 | (1) | |
| Samir Zeljković | 04.09.1997 | 25 | (2) | |
| Denis Zvonić | 08.02.1992 | 14 | (5) | |
| **Midfielders:** | **DOB** | **M** | **(s)** | **G** |
| Nemanja Anđušić | 17.10.1996 | 19 | (8) | 7 |
| Stephane Joel Barou (CIV) | 21.12.2003 | | (3) | |
| Jovan Blagojević (SRB) | 15.03.1988 | 8 | (8) | |
| Emir Halilović | 04.11.1989 | 15 | (7) | 2 |
| Dino Hasanović | 21.01.1996 | 19 | (3) | |
| Haris Jogunović | 12.09.2006 | | (1) | |
| Faris Kadrić | 13.03.2005 | | (1) | |
| Marko Karamarko (CRO) | 27.03.1993 | 2 | (1) | |
| Tino Lauš (CRO) | 17.03.2001 | 11 | (1) | 1 |
| Ardonis Mućaj | 10.10.2003 | 3 | (4) | |
| Omar Pršeš | 07.05.1995 | 19 | (6) | |
| Dženan Puce | 14.08.2005 | | (2) | |
| Samir Radovac | 25.01.1996 | 1 | | |
| Tarik Šikalo | 26.03.2004 | 13 | (2) | |
| Edo Vehabović | 01.05.1995 | 13 | (12) | 3 |
| *Wallace* Menezes dos Santos (BRA) | 23.06.1998 | 4 | (6) | |
| **Forwards:** | **DOB** | **M** | **(s)** | **G** |
| Alen Dejanović | 19.01.2000 | 24 | (6) | 3 |
| Kenan Djuliman | 04.06.2006 | 1 | | |
| Arman Džanković | 24.03.2002 | 9 | | |
| Nedim Hadžić | 19.03.1999 | | (5) | |
| Nermin Haskić | 27.06.1989 | 25 | (5) | 12 |
| Raphael Ohanua Lea'i (SOL) | 09.09.2003 | 3 | (7) | 1 |
| Amar Milak | 25.05.2006 | | (1) | |
| Haris Ovčina | 24.10.1996 | 9 | (3) | |
| Đorđe Pantelić (SRB) | 29.11.1999 | 3 | (15) | 2 |
| Dževad Sijamija | 18.02.2002 | 5 | (3) | 1 |
| Dženan Zajmović | 11.11.1994 | 9 | (7) | 5 |

## Hrvatski športski klub Zrinjski Mostar

| | | |
|---|---|---|
| **Founded**: | 1905 | |
| **Stadium**: | Stadion pod Bijelim Brijegom, Mostar (9,000) | |
| **Trainer**: | Sergej Jakirović | 23.12.1976 |
| [30.11.2022] | Krunoslav Rendulić | 26.09.1973 |

| Goalkeepers: | DOB | M | (s) | G |
|---|---|---|---|---|
| Josip Čondrić (CRO) | 27.08.1993 | 15 | | |
| Marko Marić (CRO) | 03.01.1996 | 13 | | |
| Antonio Soldo | 12.01.1988 | 4 | | |
| Marin Topić (CRO) | 07.02.2001 | 1 | | |
| **Defenders:** | **DOB** | **M** | **(s)** | **G** |
| Hrvoje Barišić (CRO) | 03.02.1991 | 30 | | 2 |
| Almir Bekić | 01.06.1989 | 16 | (4) | 1 |
| Josip Čorluka (CRO) | 03.03.1995 | 28 | | 1 |
| Marsel Ismajlgeci (ALB) | 14.03.2000 | 5 | (3) | |
| Slobodan Jakovljević (SRB) | 26.05.1989 | 26 | | 3 |
| Marin Magdić (CRO) | 13.04.1999 | 6 | (3) | |
| Frane Maglica (CRO) | 02.07.1997 | 1 | | |
| Denis Marandici (MDA) | 18.09.1996 | 2 | (1) | |
| Kerim Memija | 06.01.1996 | 14 | (8) | |
| Matej Senić (CRO) | 21.02.1995 | 4 | (2) | |
| **Midfielders:** | **DOB** | **M** | **(s)** | **G** |
| Karim Emilio Roberto Gazzetta (SUI) †21.11.2022 | 01.04.1995 | | (1) | |
| Silvio Ilinković | 05.10.2002 | 20 | (3) | 2 |
| Antonio Ivančić (CRO) | 25.05.1995 | 11 | (1) | 1 |
| Niko Janković (CRO) | 25.08.2001 | 17 | (1) | 1 |
| Ivan Jukić | 21.06.1996 | 9 | (14) | 3 |
| Dragan Juranović (CRO) | 10.02.1994 | | (3) | |
| Karlo Kamenar (CRO) | 15.03.1994 | 2 | (17) | |
| Igor Savić | 08.10.2000 | 4 | | 2 |
| Domagoj Stranput (CRO) | 02.05.2001 | 4 | (6) | |
| Petar Sučić | 25.10.2003 | 22 | (5) | |
| Mario Tičinović (CRO) | 20.08.1991 | 14 | (4) | 6 |
| Milan Vukotić (MNE) | 05.10.2002 | 2 | (2) | |
| Damir Zlomislić | 20.07.1991 | 9 | (9) | |
| Abdul Musa Zubairu (NGA) | 03.10.1998 | | (7) | |
| **Forwards:** | **DOB** | **M** | **(s)** | **G** |
| Adnan Berbić | 11.02.2004 | | (1) | |
| Nemanja Bilbija | 02.11.1990 | 29 | (1) | 24 |
| Mario Čuže (CRO) | 24.04.1999 | 23 | (9) | 7 |
| Andrija Drljo | 06.09.2002 | 5 | (1) | |
| Irfan Hadžić | 15.06.1993 | 1 | (3) | |
| Tomislav Kiš (CRO) | 04.04.1994 | 5 | (8) | 5 |
| Matija Malekinušić (CRO) | 27.01.1999 | 6 | (14) | 1 |
| Nikola Mandić (CRO) | 19.03.1991 | 1 | (10) | 2 |
| Antonio Prskalo | 10.05.2004 | 4 | (3) | |
| Franko Sabljić | 17.09.2003 | 6 | (10) | 2 |
| Kristijan Stanić | 20.04.2001 | 4 | (3) | 1 |
| Matej Šakota | 16.08.2004 | | (1) | |

## Fudbalski klub Željezničar Sarajevo

| Founded: | 19.09.1921 | | |
|---|---|---|---|
| Stadium: | Stadion Grbavica, Sarajevo (13,146) | | |
| Trainer: | Edis Mulalić | | 23.10.1975 |
| [12.04.2023] | Nermin Bašić | | 24.11.1983 |

| Goalkeepers: | DOB | M | (s) | G |
|---|---|---|---|---|
| Josip Bender (CRO) | 01.03.1995 | 18 | | |
| Vedad Muftić | 25.10.2001 | 15 | | |
| **Defenders:** | **DOB** | **M** | **(s)** | **G** |
| Omar Beća | 01.01.2002 | 12 | (6) | |
| Amar Drina | 30.05.2002 | 22 | (2) | |
| Marin Galić | 21.09.1995 | 27 | (2) | |
| Irfan Jašarević | 24.08.1995 | 11 | (1) | 1 |
| Aleksandar Kosorić | 30.01.1987 | 20 | (3) | |
| Luka Malić | 07.05.2000 | 12 | (2) | |
| **Midfielders:** | **DOB** | **M** | **(s)** | **G** |
| Joseph Amoah (GHA) | 01.01.2002 | 20 | (7) | 8 |
| Samir Bekrić | 20.10.1984 | 1 | (14) | 1 |
| Edin Cocalić | 05.12.1987 | 25 | | 1 |
| Hamza Gasal | 16.12.2002 | 5 | (3) | 3 |

| | DOB | M | (s) | G |
|---|---|---|---|---|
| Haris Hajdarević | 07.10.1998 | 9 | (16) | |
| Armin Hodžić II | 29.02.2000 | 28 | (1) | 5 |
| Nedim Mekić | 15.04.1995 | 17 | (10) | 3 |
| Sedad Subašić | 16.02.2001 | 3 | (7) | |
| Semir Štilić | 08.10.1987 | 25 | (5) | 6 |
| Stjepan Vego (CRO) | 09.07.1997 | 6 | (4) | |
| **Forwards:** | **DOB** | **M** | **(s)** | **G** |
| Dženis Beganović | 23.03.1996 | 16 | (14) | |
| *Clarismario* Santos Rodrigus (BRA) | 27.07.2001 | 29 | (1) | 8 |
| Andrija Drljo | 06.09.2002 | 11 | (2) | |
| Dženan Haračić (CRO) | 30.07.1994 | 8 | (15) | 4 |
| Armin Hodžić | 17.11.1994 | 4 | (8) | |
| Sulejman Krpić | 01.01.1991 | 11 | (4) | 2 |
| Benjamin Šehić | 11.10.1998 | 8 | (5) | |

## SECOND LEVEL
### First League – m:tel Prva liga 2022/2023

### First League of the Federation of Bosnia and Herzegovina

| | | | | | | | | |
|---|---|---|---|---|---|---|---|---|
| 1. | NK GOŠK Gabela (*Promoted*) | 30 | 19 | 7 | 4 | 59 - 24 | 64 |
| 2. | NK Stupčanica Olovo | 30 | 16 | 4 | 10 | 46 - 27 | 52 |
| 3. | FK Budućnost Banovići | 30 | 14 | 8 | 8 | 41 - 37 | 50 |
| 4. | FK Goražde | 30 | 14 | 7 | 9 | 41 - 31 | 49 |
| 5. | NK Zvijezda Gradačac | 30 | 14 | 5 | 11 | 59 - 52 | 47 |
| 6. | OFK Gradina Srebrenik | 30 | 14 | 5 | 11 | 40 - 39 | 47 |
| 7. | HNK Tomislav | 30 | 12 | 7 | 11 | 43 - 39 | 43 |
| 8. | FK Rudar Kakanj | 30 | 13 | 4 | 13 | 40 - 41 | 43 |
| 9. | NK TOŠK Tešanj | 30 | 10 | 10 | 10 | 29 - 26 | 40 |
| 10. | NK Vis Simm Bau | 30 | 9 | 12 | 9 | 42 - 46 | 39 |
| 11. | NK Jedinstvo Bihać | 30 | 11 | 4 | 15 | 40 - 47 | 37 |
| 12. | NK Bratstvo Gračanica | 30 | 10 | 6 | 14 | 42 - 43 | 36 |
| 13. | FK Mladost Doboj Kakanj | 30 | 10 | 6 | 14 | 32 - 45 | 36 |
| 14. | FK Radnik Hadžići | 30 | 10 | 4 | 16 | 26 - 37 | 34 |
| 15. | NK Travnik (*Relegated*) | 30 | 10 | 1 | 19 | 26 - 49 | 31 |
| 16. | FK Radnički Lukavac (*Relegated*) | 30 | 6 | 6 | 18 | 34 - 57 | 24 |

### First League of of the Republika Srpska

| | | | | | | | | |
|---|---|---|---|---|---|---|---|---|
| 1. | FK Krupa na Vrbasu (*Promoted*) | 34 | 27 | 4 | 3 | 98 - 24 | 85 |
| 2. | FK Zvijezda 09 Ugljevik | 34 | 20 | 9 | 5 | 77 - 26 | 69 |
| 3. | FK Laktaši | 34 | 22 | 3 | 9 | 76 - 34 | 69 |
| 4. | FK Slavija Istočno Sarajevo | 34 | 15 | 10 | 9 | 56 - 40 | 55 |
| 5. | FK Sloboda Novi Grad | 34 | 16 | 7 | 11 | 51 - 42 | 55 |
| 6. | FK Rudar Prijedor | 34 | 15 | 8 | 11 | 47 - 33 | 53 |
| 7. | FK Radnik Bijeljina | 34 | 14 | 11 | 9 | 48 - 34 | 53 |
| 8. | FK Sutjeska Foča | 34 | 14 | 4 | 16 | 48 - 60 | 46 |
| 9. | FK Kozara Gradiška | 34 | 12 | 7 | 15 | 48 - 56 | 43 |
| 10. | FK Željezničar Banja Luka | 34 | 12 | 7 | 15 | 41 - 57 | 43 |
| 11. | FK Ljubić Prnjavor | 34 | 13 | 2 | 19 | 41 - 66 | 41 |
| 12. | FK Famos Istočna Ilidža | 34 | 12 | 4 | 18 | 40 - 53 | 40 |
| 13. | FK Sloboda Mrkonjić Grad | 34 | 11 | 7 | 16 | 45 - 59 | 40 |
| 14. | FK Drina Zvornik | 34 | 12 | 2 | 20 | 44 - 53 | 38 |
| 15. | FK Omarska | 34 | 11 | 5 | 18 | 42 - 76 | 38 |
| 16. | FK Alfa Modriča | 34 | 10 | 3 | 21 | 32 - 73 | 33 |
| 17. | FK Podrinje Janja (*Relegated*) | 34 | 8 | 7 | 19 | 38 - 62 | 31 |
| 18. | FK Tekstilac Derventa (*Relegated*) | 34 | 7 | 10 | 17 | 28 - 52 | 31 |

## INTERNATIONAL MATCHES
### (16.07.2022 – 15.07.2023)

| | | | | |
|---|---|---|---|---|
| 23.09.2022 | Zenica | *Bosnia and Herzegovina - Montenegro* | *1-0(1-0)* | (UNL) |
| 26.09.2022 | Bucureşti | *Romania - Bosnia and Herzegovina* | *4-1(1-0)* | (UNL) |
| | | | | |
| 23.03.2023 | Zenica | *Bosnia and Herzegovina - Iceland* | *3-0(2-0)* | (ECQ) |
| 26.03.2023 | Bratislava | *Slovakia - Bosnia and Herzegovina* | *2-0(2-0)* | (ECQ) |
| 17.06.2023 | Lisboa | *Portugal - Bosnia and Herzegovina* | *3-0(1-0)* | (ECQ) |
| 20.06.2023 | Zenica | *Bosnia and Herzegovina - Luxembourg* | *0-2(0-1)* | (ECQ) |

**23.09.2022    BOSNIA AND HERZEGOVINA - MONTENEGRO    1-0(1-0)**    3rd UEFA Nations League B, Group 3

Stadion Bilino Polje, Zenica; Referee: Szymon Marciniak (Poland); Attendance: 12,050
**BIH:** Ibrahim Šehić, Amar Dedić (90.Mateo Sušić), Dennis Hadžikadunić, Siniša Saničanin, Sead Kolašinac, Miralem Pjanić (67.Gojko Cimirot), Muhamed Bešić (73.Amer Gojak ), Amir Hadžiahmetović, Miroslav Stevanović (73.Kenan Kodro-Maksumić), Ermedin Demirović, Edin Džeko (Cap). Trainer: Ivaylo Petev (Bulgaria).
**Goal:** Ermedin Demirović (45+1).

**26.09.2022    ROMANIA - BOSNIA AND HERZEGOVINA    4-1(1-0)**    3rd UEFA Nations League B, Group 3

Stadionul Rapid-Giuleşti, Bucureşti; Referee: Halil Umut Meler (Turkey); Attendance: 12,693
**BIH:** Nikola Vasilj, Adnan Kovačević (25.Siniša Saničanin), Hrvoje Miličević (46.Haris Duljević), Besim Šerbečić, Eldar Ćivić (61.Sead Kolašinac), Amar Dedić, Gojko Cimirot (46.Vladan Danilović), Dario Šarić (71.Edin Džeko), Amer Gojak, Ermedin Demirović, Smail Prevljak (Cap). Trainer: Ivaylo Petev (Bulgaria).
**Goal:** Edin Džeko (77).

**23.03.2023    BOSNIA AND HERZEGOVINA - ICELAND    3-0(2-0)**    17th EC. Qualifiers

Stadion Bilino Polje, Zenica; Referee: Donatas Rumšas (Lithuania); Attendance: 9,234
**BIH:** Ibrahim Šehić (Cap), Siniša Saničanin, Anel Ahmedhodžić, Hrvoje Miličević, Amar Dedić (71.Dennis Hadžikadunić), Rade Krunić, Benjamin Tahirović (82.Gojko Cimirot), Amir Hadžiahmetović (71.Sanjin Prcić), Jusuf Gazibegović, Ermedin Demirović (82.Nemanja Bilbija), Smail Prevljak (67.Kenan Kodro-Maksumić). Trainer: Faruk Hadžibegić.
**Goals:** Rade Krunić (14, 40), Amar Dedić (63).

**26.03.2023    SLOVAKIA - BOSNIA AND HERZEGOVINA    2-0(2-0)**    17th EC. Qualifiers

Štadion Tehelné pole, Bratislava; Referee: Marco Di Bello (Italy); Attendance: 6,052
**BIH:** Ibrahim Šehić (Cap), Siniša Saničanin, Anel Ahmedhodžić, Hrvoje Miličević (46.Gojko Cimirot), Amar Dedić, Rade Krunić, Benjamin Tahirović (74.Miroslav Stevanović), Amir Hadžiahmetović (63.Sanjin Prcić), Jusuf Gazibegović, Ermedin Demirović, Smail Prevljak (63.Edin Džeko). Trainer: Faruk Hadžibegić.

**17.06.2023    PORTUGAL - BOSNIA AND HERZEGOVINA    3-0(1-0)**    17th EC. Qualifiers

Estádio da Luz, Lisboa; Referee: Davide Massa (Italy); Attendance: 55,058
**BIH:** Ibrahim Šehić, Siniša Saničanin, Anel Ahmedhodžić, Adrian Leon Barišić (71.Said Hamulić), Sead Kolašinac (78.Jusuf Gazibegović), Amar Dedić, Gojko Cimirot, Amir Hadžiahmetović (71.Benjamin Tahirović), Miralem Pjanić (78.Sanjin Prcić), Miroslav Stevanović, Edin Džeko (Cap) (78.Dal Varešanović). Trainer: Faruk Hadžibegić.

**20.06.2023    BOSNIA AND HERZEGOVINA - LUXEMBOURG    0-2(0-1)**    17th EC. Qualifiers

Stadion Bilino Polje, Zenica; Referee: Gal Leibovitz (Israel); Attendance: 8,600
**BIH:** Ibrahim Šehić, Sead Kolašinac, Adrian Leon Barišić, Siniša Saničanin, Benjamin Tahirović (46.Amir Hadžiahmetović), Amar Dedić, Miralem Pjanić, Gojko Cimirot (72.Smail Prevljak), Kenan Kodro-Maksumić (46.Said Hamulić), Miroslav Stevanović (72.Luka Menalo), Edin Džeko (Cap). Trainer: Faruk Hadžibegić.

## NATIONAL TEAM PLAYERS
### (16.07.2022 – 15.07.2023)

| Name | DOB | Caps | Goals | Club |
|------|-----|------|-------|------|
| **Goalkeepers** | | | | |
| Ibrahim ŠEHIĆ | 02.09.1988 | 50 | 0 | 2022/2023: *Konyaspor Kulübü (TUR)* |
| Nikola VASILJ | 02.12.1995 | 6 | 0 | 2022: *FC St. Pauli Hamburg (GER)* |
| **Defenders** | | | | |
| Anel AHMEDHODŽIĆ | 26.03.1999 | 21 | 1 | 2023: *Sheffield United FC (ENG)* |
| Adrian Leon BARIŠIĆ | 19.07.2001 | 2 | 0 | 2023: *NK Osijek (CRO)* |
| Eldar ČIVIĆ | 28.05.1996 | 25 | 1 | 2022: *Ferencvárosi TC (HUN)* |
| Amar DEDIĆ | 18.08.2002 | 7 | 0 | 2022/2023: *FC Red Bull Salzburg (AUT)* |
| Jusuf GAZIBEGOVIC | 11.03.2000 | 8 | 0 | 2023: *SK Sturm Graz (AUT)* |
| Dennis HADŽIKADUNIĆ | 09.07.1998 | 20 | 0 | 2022: *Malmö FF (SWE)*<br>18.01.2023-> *RCD Mallorca (ESP)* |
| Sead KOLAŠINAC | 20.06.1993 | 53 | 0 | 2022/2023: *Olympique de Marseille (FRA)* |
| Adnan KOVAČEVIĆ | 09.09.1993 | 11 | 0 | 2022: *Ferencvárosi TC (HUN)* |
| Hrvoje MILIČEVIĆ | 20.04.1993 | 6 | 0 | 2022/2023: *AEK Larnaca FC (CYP)* |
| Siniša SANIČANIN | 24.04.1995 | 23 | 0 | 2022/2023: *FK Partizan Beograd (SRB)* |
| Mateo SUŠIĆ | 18.11.1990 | 11 | 0 | 2022: *APOEL Nicosia (CYP)* |
| Besim ŠERBEČIĆ | 01.05.1998 | 1 | 0 | 2022: *Aalesunds FK (NOR)* |
| **Midfielders** | | | | |
| Muhamed BEŠIĆ | 10.09.1992 | 47 | 0 | 2022: *Ferencvárosi TC (HUN)* |
| Gojko CIMIROT | 19.12.1992 | 43 | 0 | 2022/2023: *R Standard Liège (BEL)* |
| Vladan DANILOVIĆ | 27.07.1999 | 7 | 0 | 2022: *CD Nacional Funchal (POR)* |
| Haris DULJEVIĆ | 16.11.1993 | 28 | 1 | 2022: *FC Hansa Rostock (GER)* |
| Amer GOJAK | 13.02.1997 | 35 | 4 | 2022: *Ferencvárosi TC (HUN)* |
| Amir HADŽIAHMETOVIĆ | 08.03.1997 | 25 | 0 | 2022: *Konyaspor Kulübü (TUR)*<br>02.02.2023-> *Beşiktaş JK İstanbul (TUR)* |
| Rade KRUNIĆ | 07.10.1993 | 29 | 4 | 2023: *AC Milan (ITA)* |
| Luka MENALO | 22.07.1996 | 14 | 3 | 2023: *GNK Dinamo Zagreb (CRO)* |
| Miralem PJANIĆ | 02.04.1990 | 110 | 17 | 2022: *FC Barcelona (ESP)*<br>07.09.2022-> *Sharjah FC (UAE)* |
| Sanjin PRCIĆ | 20.11.1993 | 17 | 0 | 2023: *Racing Club de Strasbourg (FRA)* |
| Miroslav STEVANOVIĆ | 29.07.1990 | 30 | 2 | 2022/2023: *Servette FC Genève (SUI)* |
| Dario ŠARIĆ | 30.05.1997 | 1 | 0 | 2022: *Palermo FC (ITA)* |
| Benjamin TAHIROVIĆ | 03.03.2003 | 4 | 0 | 2023: *AS Roma (ITA)* |
| Dal VAREŠANOVIĆ | 23.05.2001 | 1 | 0 | 2023: *FK Sarajevo* |
| **Forwards** | | | | |
| Nemanja BILBIJA | 02.11.1990 | 2 | 0 | 2023: *HŠK Zrinjski Mostar* |
| Ermedin DEMIROVIĆ | 25.03.1998 | 17 | 1 | 2022/2023: *FC Augsburg (GER)* |
| Edin DŽEKO | 17.03.1986 | 129 | 64 | 2022/2023: *FC Internazionale Milano (ITA)* |
| Said HAMULIĆ | 12.11.2000 | 2 | 0 | 2023: *Toulouse FC (FRA)* |
| Kenan KODRO-MAKSUMIĆ | 19.08.1993 | 13 | 2 | 2022/2023: *Fehérvár FC Székesfehérvár (HUN)* |
| Smail PREVLJAK | 10.05.1995 | 25 | 6 | 2022/2023: *KAS Eupen (BEL)* |

### Trainer

| | | |
|---|---|---|
| Ivaylo PETEV (Bulgaria) [27.01.2021 – 31.12.2022] | 09.07.1975 | 21 M; 6 W; 8 D; 7 L; 19-24 |
| Faruk HADŽIBEGIĆ [04.01.2023 – 23.06.2023] | 07.10.1957 | 4 M; 1 W; 0 D; 3 L; 3-7<br>Complete record as trainer of Bosnia and Herzegovina:<br>11 M; 3 W; 2 D; 6 L; 13-17<br>(10.03.1999 – 09.10.1999) & (04.01.2023 – 20.06.2023) |

# BULGARIA

**The Country:**
Република България (Republic of Bulgaria)
Capital: Sofia
Surface: 110,994 km$^2$
Inhabitants: 6,447,710 [2022]
Time: UTC+2

**The FA:**
Български футболен съюз (Bulgarian Football Union)
18 Vitoshko lale Str. BG - 1616, Sofia
Tel: +359 2 9426 253
Foundation date: 1923
Member of FIFA since: 1924
Member of UEFA since: 1954
Website: www.bfunion.bg

## NATIONAL TEAM RECORDS

| RECORDS | |
|---|---|
| **First international match:** | 21.05.1924, Wien: Austria – Bulgaria 6-0 |
| **Most international caps:** | Stilian Petrov - 105 caps (1998-2013) |
| **Most international goals:** | Dimitar Berbatov - 48 goals / 78 caps (1999-2010) |
| | Hristo Bonev - 48 goals / 96 caps (1967-1979) |

### UEFA EUROPEAN CHAMPIONSHIP

|  |  |
|---|---|
| 1960 | Qualifiers |
| 1964 | Qualifiers |
| 1968 | Qualifiers |
| 1972 | Qualifiers |
| 1976 | Qualifiers |
| 1980 | Qualifiers |
| 1984 | Qualifiers |
| 1988 | Qualifiers |
| 1992 | Qualifiers |
| 1996 | Final Tournament (Group Stage) |
| 2000 | Qualifiers |
| 2004 | Final Tournament (Group Stage) |
| 2008 | Qualifiers |
| 2012 | Qualifiers |
| 2016 | Qualifiers |
| 2020 | Qualifiers |

### FIFA WORLD CUP

|  |  |
|---|---|
| 1930 | Did not enter |
| 1934 | Qualifiers |
| 1938 | Qualifiers |
| 1950 | Did not enter |
| 1954 | Qualifiers |
| 1958 | Qualifiers |
| 1962 | Final Tournament (Group Stage) |
| 1966 | Final Tournament (Group Stage) |
| 1970 | Final Tournament (Group Stage) |
| 1974 | Final Tournament (Group Stage) |
| 1978 | Qualifiers |
| 1982 | Qualifiers |
| 1986 | Final Tournament (2$^{nd}$ Round of 16) |
| 1990 | Qualifiers |
| 1994 | Final Tournament (4$^{th}$ Place) |
| 1998 | Final Tournament (Group Stage) |
| 2002 | Qualifiers |
| 2006 | Qualifiers |
| 2010 | Qualifiers |
| 2014 | Qualifiers |
| 2018 | Qualifiers |
| 2022 | Qualifiers |

### OLYMPIC TOURNAMENTS

|  |  |
|---|---|
| 1908 | Did not enter |
| 1912 | Did not enter |
| 1920 | Did not enter |
| 1924 | 1$^{st}$ Round |
| 1928 | Did not enter |
| 1936 | Did not enter |
| 1948 | Did not enter |
| 1952 | 1$^{st}$ Round |
| 1956 | Semi-Finals |
| 1960 | Group Stage |
| 1964 | Qualifiers |
| 1968 | Runners-up |
| 1972 | Qualifiers |
| 1976 | Qualifiers |
| 1980 | Qualifiers |
| 1984 | Qualifiers |
| 1988 | Qualifiers |
| 1992 | Qualifiers |
| 1996 | Qualifiers |
| 2000 | Qualifiers |
| 2004 | Qualifiers |
| 2008 | Qualifiers |
| 2012 | Qualifiers |
| 2016 | Qualifiers |
| 2020 | Qualifiers |

### UEFA NATIONS LEAGUE

| | |
|---|---|
| 2018/2019 | League C (Group Stage -> promoted to League B) |
| 2020/2021 | League B (Group Stage -> relegated to League C) |
| 2022/2023 | League C (Group Stage) |

### BULGARIAN CLUB HONOURS IN EUROPEAN CLUB COMPETITIONS:

| European Champion Clubs' Cup (1956-1992) / UEFA Champions League (1993-2023) |
|---|
| None |

| Fairs Cup (1858-1971) / UEFA Cup (1972-2009) / UEFA Europa League (2010-2023) |
|---|
| None |

| UEFA Europa Conference League (2021-2023) |
|---|
| None |

| UEFA Super Cup (1972-2022) |
|---|
| None |

| *European Cup Winners' Cup 1961-1999** |
|---|
| None |

*defunct competition

# NATIONAL COMPETITIONS
## TABLE OF HONOURS

| | STATE CHAMPIONSHIPS CHAMPIONS | CUP WINNERS* | BEST GOALSCORERS | |
|---|---|---|---|---|
| 1924 | *Not finished* | - | - | |
| 1925 | Vladislav Varna | - | - | |
| 1926 | Vladislav Varna | - | - | |
| 1927 | *No competition* | - | - | |
| 1928 | Slavia Sofia | - | - | |
| 1929 | Botev Plovdiv | - | - | |
| 1930 | SK Slavia Sofia | - | - | |
| 1931 | AS 23 Sofia | - | - | |
| 1932 | Spartak Varna | - | - | |
| 1933 | SK Levski Sofia | - | - | |
| 1934 | Vladislav Varna | - | - | |
| 1935 | Sportklub Sofia | - | - | |
| 1936 | SK Slavia Sofia | - | - | |
| 1937 | SK Levski Sofia | - | - | |
| 1937/1938 | Ticha Varna | FC 13 Sofia | Krum Milev (Slavia Sofia) | 12 |
| 1938/1939 | SK Slavia Sofia | Shipka Sofia | Georgi Pachedzhiev (AS 23 Sofia) | 14 |
| 1939/1940 | Lokomotiv Sofia | FC 13 Sofia | - | |
| 1941 | SK Slavia Sofia | AS 23 Sofia | - | |
| 1942 | SK Levski Sofia | Levski Sofia | - | |
| 1943 | Slavia Sofia | - | - | |
| 1944 | *Not finished* | - | - | |

*called between 1938-1942 Tsar's Cup.

| | REPUBLIC CHAMPIONSHIPS CHAMPIONS | CUP WINNERS** | BEST GOALSCORERS | |
|---|---|---|---|---|
| 1945 | Lokomotiv Sofia | - | - | |
| 1946 | SK Levski Sofia | SK Levski Sofia | - | |
| 1947 | SK Levski Sofia | SK Levski Sofia | - | |
| 1948 | CDNV Sofia | Lokomotiv Sofia | - | |

| | „A" GROUP CHAMPIONS | CUP WINNERS** | BEST GOALSCORERS | |
|---|---|---|---|---|
| 1948/1949 | SK Levski Sofia | SK Levski Sofia | Dimitar Milanov (CSKA Sofia) Nedko Nedev (Cherno More Varna) | 11 |
| 1950 | SK Levski Sofia | SK Levski Sofia | Lyubomir Hranov (SK Levski Sofia) | 13 |
| 1951 | CDNA Sofia | CDNA Sofia | Dimitar Milanov (CDNA Sofia) | 14 |
| 1952 | CDNA Sofia | GUTP-DSO Udarnik Sofia | Dimitar Isakov (GUTP-DSO Udarnik Sofia) Dobromir Tashkov (Spartak Sofia) | 10 |
| 1953 | SK Levski Sofia | Lokomotiv Sofia | Dimitar Minchev (Spartak Pleven / VVS Sofia) | 15 |
| 1954 | CDNA Sofia | CDNA Sofia | Dobromir Tashkov (GUTP-DSO Udarnik Sofia) | 25 |
| 1955 | CDNA Sofia | CDNA Sofia | Todor Diev (Spartak Plovdiv) | 13 |
| 1956 | CDNA Sofia | SK Levski Sofia | Pavel Vladimirov (Minyor Pernik) | 16 |
| 1957 | CDNA Sofia | SK Levski Sofia | Hristo Iliev (SK Levski Sofia) Dimitar Milanov (CDNA Sofia) | 14 |
| 1958 | CDNA Sofia | Spartak Plovdiv | Dobromir Tashkov (FD Slavia Sofia) Georgi Arnaudov (Spartak Varna) | 9 |
| 1958/1959 | CDNA Sofia | SK Levski Sofia | Aleksandar Vasilev (FD Slavia Sofia) | 13 |
| 1959/1960 | CDNA Sofia | Septemvri Sofia | Dimitar Yordanov (SK Levski Sofia) Lyuben Kostov (Spartak Varna) | 12 |
| 1960/1961 | CDNA Sofia | CDNA Sofia | Ivan Sotirov (Botev Plovdiv) | 20 |
| 1961/1962 | CDNA Sofia | Botev Plovdiv | Nikola Yordanov (Dunav Ruse) Todor Diev (Spartak Plovdiv) | 23 |
| 1962/1963 | Spartak Plovdiv | FD Slavia Sofia | Todor Diev (Spartak Plovdiv) | 26 |
| 1963/1964 | Lokomotiv Sofia | FD Slavia Sofia | Nikola Tsanev (CDNA Sofia) | 26 |
| 1964/1965 | SK Levski Sofia | CSKA Cerveno Zname Sofia | Georgi Asparuhov (SK Levski Sofia) | 27 |
| 1965/1966 | CSKA Cerveno Zname Sofia | FD Slavia Sofia | Traycho Spasov (Marek Dupnitsa) | 21 |
| 1966/1967 | Botev Plovdiv | SK Levski Sofia | Petar Zhekov (Beroe Stara Zagora) | 21 |
| 1967/1968 | SK Levski Sofia | Spartak Sofia | Petar Zhekov (Beroe Stara Zagora) | 31 |
| 1968/1969 | CSKA Septemvrijsko Zname Sofia | CSKA Septemvrijsko Zname Sofia | Petar Zhekov (CSKA Septemvrijsko Zname Sofia) | 36 |
| 1969/1970 | DFS Levski-Spartak Sofia | DFS Levski-Spartak Sofia | Petar Zhekov (CSKA Septemvrijsko Zname Sofia) | 31 |
| 1970/1971 | CSKA Septemvrijsko Zname Sofia | DFS Levski-Spartak Sofia | Dimitar Yakimov (CSKA Septemvrijsko Zname Sofia) | 26 |
| 1971/1972 | CSKA Septemvrijsko Zname Sofia | CSKA Septemvrijsko Zname Sofia | Petar Zhekov (CSKA Septemvrijsko Zname Sofia) | 27 |
| 1972/1973 | CSKA Septemvrijsko Zname Sofia | CSKA Septemvrijsko Zname Sofia | Petar Zhekov (CSKA Septemvrijsko Zname Sofia) | 29 |
| 1973/1974 | DFS Levski-Spartak Sofia | CSKA Septemvrijsko Zname Sofia | Petko Petkov (Beroe Stara Zagora) Kiril Milanov (DFS Levski-Spartak Sofia) | 19 |
| 1974/1975 | CSKA Septemvrijsko Zname Sofia | DFS Slavia Sofia | Ivan Pritargov (Botev Plovdiv) | 20 |
| 1975/1976 | CSKA Septemvrijsko Zname Sofia | DFS Levski-Spartak Sofia | Petko Petkov (Beroe Stara Zagora) Pavel Panov (DFS Levski-Spartak Sofia) | 18 |
| 1976/1977 | DFS Levski-Spartak Sofia | DFS Levski-Spartak Sofia | Pavel Panov (DFS Levski-Spartak Sofia) | 20 |
| 1977/1978 | Lokomotiv Sofia | Marek Dupnitsa | Stoycho Mladenov (Beroe Stara Zagora) | 21 |
| 1978/1979 | DFS Levski-Spartak Sofia | DFS Levski-Spartak Sofia | Rusi Gochev (Chernomorets Burgas / DFS Levski-Spartak Sofia) | 19 |

| | | | | |
|---|---|---|---|---|
| 1979/1980 | CSKA Septemvrijsko Zname Sofia | DFS Slavia Sofia | Spas Dzhevizov (CSKA Sofia) | 23 |
| 1980/1981 | CSKA Septemvrijsko Zname Sofia | Botev Plovdiv | Georgi Slavkov (Botev Plovdiv) | 31 |
| 1981/1982 | CSKA Septemvrijsko Zname Sofia | Lokomotiv Sofia | Mihail Valchev (DFS Levski-Spartak Sofia) | 24 |
| 1982/1983 | CSKA Septemvrijsko Zname Sofia | CSKA Septemvrijsko Zname Sofia | Antim Pehlivanov (Botev Plovdiv) | 20 |
| 1983/1984 | DFS Levski-Spartak Sofia | DFS Levski-Spartak Sofia | Eduard Eranosyan (Lokomotiv Plovdiv) Emil Spasov (DFS Levski-Spartak Sofia) | 19 |
| 1984/1985 | DFS Levski-Spartak Sofia | CSKA Septemvrijsko Zname Sofia | Plamen Getov (Spartak Pleven) | 26 |
| 1985/1986 | Beroe Stara Zagora | FK Vitosha Sofia | Atanas Pashev (Botev Plovdiv) | 30 |
| 1986/1987 | FK Sredets Sofia | FK Sredets Sofia | Nasko Sirakov (FK Vitosha Sofia) | 36 |
| 1987/1988 | FK Vitosha Sofia | FK Sredets Sofia | Nasko Sirakov (FK Vitosha Sofia) | 28 |
| 1988/1989 | CFKA Sredets Sofia | FK Sredets Sofia | Hristo Stoichkov (CFKA Sredets Sofia) | 23 |
| 1989/1990 | CFKA Sofia | FC Sliven | Hristo Stoichkov (CFKA Sofia) | 38 |
| 1990/1991 | FC Etar Veliko Tarnovo | PFC Levski Sofia | Ivaylo Yordanov (FC Lokomotiv Gorna Oryahovitsa) | 21 |
| 1991/1992 | PFC CSKA Sofia | PFC Levski Sofia | Nasko Sirakov (PFC Levski Sofia) | 26 |
| 1992/1993 | PFC Levski Sofia | PFC CSKA Sofia | Plamen Getov (PFC Levski Sofia) | 26 |
| 1993/1994 | PFC Levski Sofia | PFC Levski Sofia | Nasko Sirakov (PFC Levski Sofia) | 30 |
| 1994/1995 | PFC Levski Sofia | PFC Lokomotiv Sofia | Petar Mihtarski (PFC CSKA Sofia) | 24 |
| 1995/1996 | PFC Slavia Sofia | PFC Slavia Sofia | Ivo Georgiev (FC Spartak Varna) | 21 |
| 1996/1997 | PFC CSKA Sofia | PFC CSKA Sofia | Todor Pramatarov (PFC Slavia Sofia) | 26 |
| 1997/1998 | PFC Litex Lovech | PFC Levski Sofia | Anton Spasov (PFC Naftex Burgas) Bontcho Guentchev (PFC CSKA Sofia) | 17 |
| 1998/1999 | PFC Litex Lovech | PFC CSKA Sofia | Dimcho Belyakov (PFC Litex Lovech) | 21 |
| 1999/2000 | PFC Levski Sofia | PFC Levski Sofia | Mihail Mihaylov (FC Velbazhd Kyustendil) | 20 |
| 2000/2001 | PFC Levski Sofia | PFC Litex Lovech | Georgi Ivanov (PFC Levski Sofia) | 22 |
| 2001/2002 | PFC Levski Sofia | PFC Levski Sofia | Vladimir Manchev (PFC CSKA Sofia) | 21 |
| 2002/2003 | PFC CSKA Sofia | PFC Levski Sofia | Georgi Chilikov (PFC Levski Sofia) | 23 |
| 2003/2004 | PFC Lokomotiv Plovdiv | PFC Litex Lovech | Martin Kamburov (PFC Lokomotiv Plovdiv) | 25 |
| 2004/2005 | PFC CSKA Sofia | PFC Levski Sofia | Martin Kamburov (PFC Lokomotiv Plovdiv) | 27 |
| 2005/2006 | PFC Levski Sofia | PFC CSKA Sofia | Milivoje Novaković (SVN, Litex Lovech) José Emílio Robalo Furtado (CPV, OFC Vihren Sandanski / PFC CSKA Sofia) | 16 |
| 2006/2007 | PFC Levski Sofia | PFC Levski Sofia | Tsvetan Genkov (PFC Lokomotiv Sofia) | 27 |
| 2007/2008 | PFC CSKA Sofia | PFC Litex Lovech | Georgi Hristov (PFC Botev Plovdiv) | 19 |
| 2008/2009 | PFC Levski Sofia | PFC Litex Lovech | Martin Kamburov (PFC Lokomotiv Sofia) | 17 |
| 2009/2010 | PFC Litex Lovech | PFC Beroe Stara Zagora | Wilfried Niflore (FRA, PFC Litex Lovech) | 19 |
| 2010/2011 | PFC Litex Lovech | PFC CSKA Sofia | Garra Dembélé (MLI, PFC Levski Sofia) | 26 |
| 2011/2012 | PFC Ludogorets Razgrad | PFC Ludogorets Razgrad | Ivan Stoyanov (PFC Ludogorets Razgrad) Aluísio Chaves Ribeiro Moraes Júnior (BRA, PFC CSKA Sofia) | 16 |
| 2012/2013 | PFC Ludogorets Razgrad | PFC Beroe Stara Zagora | Basile Salomon Pereira de Carvalho (GNB, PFC Levski Sofia) | 19 |
| 2013/2014 | PFC Ludogorets Razgrad | PFC Ludogorets Razgrad | Wilmar Jordán Gil (COL, PFC Litex Lovech) Martin Kamburov (PFC Lokomotiv Plovdiv) | 20 |
| 2014/2015 | PFC Ludogorets Razgrad | PFC Cherno More Varna | Antonio Salas Quinta „Añete" (ESP, PFC Levski Sofia) | 14 |
| 2015/2016 | PFC Ludogorets Razgrad | PFC CSKA Sofia | Martin Kamburov (PFC Lokomotiv Plovdiv) | 18 |
| 2016/2017 | PFC Ludogorets Razgrad | PFC Botev Plovdiv | Claudiu Andrei Keşerü (ROU, PFC Ludogorets Razgrad) | 22 |
| 2017/2018 | PFC Ludogorets Razgrad | PFC Slavia Sofia | Claudiu Andrei Keşerü (ROU, PFC Ludogorets Razgrad) | 26 |
| 2018/2019 | PFC Ludogorets Razgrad | PFC Lokomotiv Plovdiv | Stanislav Kostov (PFC Levski Sofia) | 24 |
| 2019/2020 | PFC Ludogorets Razgrad | PFC Lokomotiv Plovdiv | Martin Kamburov (PFC Beroe Stara Zagora) | 18 |
| 2020/2021 | PFC Ludogorets Razgrad | PFC CSKA Sofia | Claudiu Andrei Keşerü (ROU, PFC Ludogorets Razgrad) | 18 |
| 2021/2022 | PFC Ludogorets Razgrad | PFC Levski Sofia | Pieros Sotiriou (CYP, PFC Ludogorets Razgrad) | 17 |
| 2022/2023 | PFC Ludogorets Razgrad | PFC Ludogorets Razgrad | Ivaylo Chochev (FC CSKA 1948 Sofia) | 21 |

**called "Cup of the Soviet Army" (between 1945 - 1982) and Bulgarian Cup (from 1982 until today).

**FC CSKA Sofia** changed several times its name as following: 1948 CDNV Sofia, 1949 NV Sofia, 1950 NA Sofia, 1951 CDNA Sofia, 1953 Sofijski Garnizon Sofia, 1953 CDNA Sofia, 1964 CSKA Cerveno Zname Sofia, 1968 CSKA Septemvrijsko Zname Sofia, 1985 FK Sredets Sofia, 1987 CFKA Sredets Sofia, November 1989 CFKA Sofia, 1st january 1990 PFC CSKA Sofia.
**FC Levski Sofia** changed several times its name as following: 1914 CS Levski Sofia, SK Levski Sofia, 1949 Dinamo Sofia, 1957 FD Levski Sofia, 1969 DFS Levski-Spartak Sofia, 1985 FK Vitosha Sofia, 1990 FK Levski-1914 Sofia, 1998 PFC Levski Sofia.
**FC Slavia Sofia** changed several times its name as following: 1913 Botev Sofia, 1915 SK Slavia Sofia, 1945 NFD Slavia Sofia, 1949 DSO Strojtel Sofia, 1951 USS-DSO Udarnik Sofia, 1952 GUTP-DSO Udarnik Sofia, 1957 FD Slavia Sofia, 1969 ZSK Slavia Sofia, 1971 DFS Slavia Sofia, 1986 FC Slavia Sofia; 1990 PFC Slavia Sofia.

# NATIONAL CHAMPIONSHIP
## First Professional Football League – efbet League 2022/2023
### (08.07.2022 – 07.06.2023)

## Regular Season - Results

### Round 1 [08-11.07.2022]
Botev Plovdiv - Hebar Pazardzhik 0-1(0-0)
Septemvri Sofia - PFC Ludogorets 0-3(0-1)
Lokomotiv Plovdiv - Pirin Blagoevgr. 2-1(1-1)
CSKA 1948 Sofia - Levski Sofia 1-0(0-0)
Lokomotiv Sofia-Cherno More Varna 0-1(0-0)
CSKA Sofia - Arda Kardzhali 3-0(1-0)
Spartak Varna - Slavia Sofia 0-1(0-0)
Beroe Stara Zagora - Botev Vratsa 2-1(1-1)

### Round 2 [15-18.07.2022]
Botev Vratsa - Botev Plovdiv 3-2(2-0)
PFC Ludogorets - Lokomotiv Plovdiv 2-0(0-0)
Lokomotiv Sofia - CSKA Sofia 1-1(1-0)
Levski Sofia - Spartak Varna 5-0(1-0)
Cherno More Varna - Slavia Sofia 1-0(0-0)
Pirin Blagoevgrad-CSKA 1948 Sofia 1-1(1-0)
Hebar Pazardzhik - Septemvri Sofia 1-3(0-1)
Arda Kardzhali - Beroe Stara Zagora 1-0(0-0)

### Round 3 [22-25.07.2022]
Spartak Varna - Pirin Blagoevgrad 1-1(0-1)
CSKA 1948 Sofia - PFC Ludogorets 2-2(0-1)
Beroe Stara Zagora-Lokomotiv Sofia 1-1(1-0)
Botev Plovdiv - Arda Kardzhali 0-2(0-1)
Lokomotiv Plovdiv - Hebar Pazardzh. 2-1(1-1)
Septemvri Sofia - Botev Vratsa 1-1(0-0)
CSKA Sofia - Cherno More Varna 1-0(0-0)
Slavia Sofia - Levski Sofia 2-1(1-0) [12.10.22]

### Round 4 [29.07.-01.08.2022]
Hebar Pazardzhik - CSKA 1948 Sofia 0-1(0-1)
PFC Ludogorets - Spartak Varna 5-0(3-0)
Botev Vratsa - Lokomotiv Plovdiv 0-1(0-0)
Pirin Blagoevgrad - Slavia Sofia 1-2(0-2)
Lokomotiv Sofia - Botev Plovdiv 2-0(0-0)
CSKA Sofia - Beroe Stara Zagora 5-1(2-0)
Arda Kardzhali - Septemvri Sofia 3-2(2-1)
Cherno M. V. - Levski Sofia 0-0 [02.11.2022]

### Round 5 [05-08.08.2022]
Spartak Varna - Hebar Pazardzhik 0-1(0-0)
Beroe Stara Zagora - Cherno M. V. 0-2(0-1)
CSKA 1948 Sofia - Botev Vratsa 5-2(2-0)
Levski Sofia - Pirin Blagoevgrad 1-0(0-0)
Septemvri Sofia - Lokomotiv Sofia 0-3(0-3)
Lokomotiv Plovdiv - Arda Kardzhali 1-0(0-0)
Botev Plov. - CSKA Sofia 0-1(0-0) [19.10.22]
Slavia Sofia - Ludogorets 1-2(0-1) [26.11.22]

### Round 6 [12-15.08.2022]
Cherno M. Varna - Pirin Blagoevgrad 1-0(1-0)
Hebar Pazardzhik - Slavia Sofia 0-3(0-1)
Arda Kardzhali - CSKA 1948 Sofia 0-1(0-1)
Beroe Stara Zagora - Botev Plovdiv 1-1(0-0)
CSKA Sofia - Septemvri Sofia 1-0(0-0)
Lokomotiv Sofia - Lokomotiv Plovdiv 0-0
Botev Vratsa - Spartak Varna 1-0(1-0)
Ludogorets - Levski Sofia 0-0 [01.12.2022]

### Round 7 [19-22.08.2022]
Botev Plovdiv - Cherno More Varna 3-4(2-1)
Spartak Varna - Arda Kardzhali 1-3(1-1)
Levski Sofia - Hebar Pazardzhik 4-0(3-0)
CSKA 1948 Sofia - Lokomotiv Sofia 2-0(0-0)
Septemvri Sofia - Beroe Stara Zagora 3-1(2-1)
Slavia Sofia - Botev Vratsa 2-1(1-1)
Pirin Blagoevgrad - PFC Ludogorets 0-4(0-0)
Lokomotiv Plov.-CSKA S. 0-1(0-1) [01.11.22]

### Round 8 [26-29.08.2022]
Botev Plovdiv - Septemvri Sofia 3-1(1-0)
Beroe St.Zagora - Lokomotiv Plovdiv 2-0(0-0)
Arda Kardzhali - Slavia Sofia 1-0(0-0)
Lokomotiv Sofia - Spartak Varna 3-2(2-1)
Hebar Pazardzhik - Pirin Blagoevgrad 0-0
Botev Vratsa - Levski Sofia 0-2(0-1)
Cherno More V. - PFC Ludogorets 2-3(1-1)
CSKA Sofia - CSKA 1948 Sofia 2-1(0-0)

### Round 9 [02-05.09.2022]
Pirin Blagoevgrad - Botev Vratsa 2-1(1-1)
Slavia Sofia - Lokomotiv Sofia 2-1(0-1)
Spartak Varna - CSKA Sofia 0-1(0-1)
Lokomotiv Plovdiv - Botev Plovdiv 1-0(0-0)
CSKA 1948 Sofia - Beroe St. Zagora 4-0(2-0)
PFC Ludogorets - Hebar Pazardzhik 6-0(4-0)
Septemvri Sofia - Cherno More Varna 0-0
Levski Sofia - Arda Kardzhali 2-0(1-0)

### Round 10 [09-12.09.2022]
Beroe Stara Zagora - Spartak Varna 3-1(2-1)
Botev Plovdiv - CSKA 1948 Sofia 2-0(1-0)
Lokomotiv Sofia - Levski Sofia 3-2(1-1)
Cherno More V. - Hebar Pazardzhik 1-0(0-0)
CSKA Sofia - Slavia Sofia 2-0(0-0)
Botev Vratsa - PFC Ludogorets 0-4(0-3)
Arda Kardzhali - Pirin Blagoevgrad 0-0
Septemvri Sofia - Lokomotiv Plovdiv 0-1(0-0)

### Round 11 [16-18.09.2022]
Spartak Varna - Botev Plovdiv 3-2(0-0)
Hebar Pazardzhik - Botev Vratsa 0-2(0-2)
CSKA 1948 Sofia - Septemvri Sofia 1-0(0-0)
Pirin Blagoevgrad - Lokomotiv Sofia 0-1(0-1)
Lokomotiv Plovdiv - Cherno More V. 3-0(1-0)
Slavia Sofia - Beroe Stara Zagora 2-0(1-0)
Levski Sofia - CSKA Sofia 2-0(0-0)
PFC Ludogorets - Arda Kardzhali 1-1(1-1)

### Round 12 [29.09.-03.10.2022]
Arda Kardzhali - Hebar Pazardzhik 1-0(1-0)
Septemvri Sofia - Spartak Varna 1-1(1-1)
Cherno More Varna - Botev Vratsa 2-1(0-1)
Botev Plovdiv - Slavia Sofia 1-0(1-0)
Lokomotiv Sofia - PFC Ludogorets 1-0(0-0)
Lokomotiv Plovdiv - CSKA 1948 S. 1-3(0-0)
CSKA Sofia - Pirin Blagoevgrad 2-1(2-1)
Beroe Stara Zagora - Levski Sofia 0-1(0-1)

### Round 13 [07-10.10.2022]
Hebar Pazardzhik - Lokomotiv Sofia 3-2(2-2)
Pirin Blagoevgrad - Beroe Stara Zagora 0-0
Slavia Sofia - Septemvri Sofia 1-0(1-0)
Levski Sofia - Botev Plovdiv 1-0(1-0)
Botev Vratsa - Arda Kardzhali 0-0
CSKA 1948 Sofia - Cherno More Varna 0-0
Spartak Varna - Lokomotiv Plovdiv 0-2(0-0)
PFC Ludogorets - CSKA Sofia 2-1(1-0)

### Round 14 [14-17.10.2022]
Lokomotiv Sofia - Botev Vratsa 1-0(0-0)
Cherno More Varna - Arda Kardzhali 1-1(1-0)
Botev Plovdiv - Pirin Blagoevgrad 3-1(2-0)
CSKA Sofia - Hebar Pazardzhik 4-0(1-0)
CSKA 1948 Sofia - Spartak Varna 2-0(2-0)
Septemvri Sofia - Levski Sofia 0-0
Lokomotiv Plovdiv - Slavia Sofia 3-0(1-0)
Beroe Stara Zagora - PFC Ludogorets 0-4(0-0)

### Round 15 [21-24.10.2022]
Arda Kardzhali - Lokomotiv Sofia 2-2(1-2)
Spartak Varna - Cherno More Varna 0-0
Slavia Sofia - CSKA 1948 Sofia 1-1(0-1)
Levski Sofia - Lokomotiv Plovdiv 1-1(1-0)
Botev Vratsa - CSKA Sofia 0-4(0-2)
PFC Ludogorets - Botev Plovdiv 1-0(0-0)
Pirin Blagoevgrad - Septemvri Sofia 1-4(0-1)
Hebar Pazardzhik-Beroe Stara Zagora 1-1(1-1)

### Round 16 [28-31.10.2022]
Pirin Blagoevgrad - Lokomotiv Plovdiv 0-0
Arda Kardzhali - CSKA Sofia 1-3(0-1)
Cherno More V. - Lokomotiv Sofia 2-1(1-0)
Levski Sofia - CSKA 1948 Sofia 0-0
Slavia Sofia - Spartak Varna 2-2(0-1)
Hebar Pazardzhik - Botev Plovdiv 1-2(0-1)
PFC Ludogorets - Septemvri Sofia 3-1(1-1)
Botev Vratsa - Beroe Stara Zagora 2-0(2-0)

### Round 17 [04-08.11.2022]
Septemvri Sofia - Hebar Pazardzhik 1-1(0-1)
Botev Plovdiv - Botev Vratsa 6-0(2-0)
CSKA 1948 S. - Pirin Blagoevgrad 2-1(0-1)
Beroe Stara Zagora - Arda Kardzhali 2-0(0-0)
Slavia Sofia - Cherno More Varna 1-0(1-0)
Spartak Varna - Levski Sofia 2-2(0-1)
CSKA Sofia - Lokomotiv Sofia 0-0
Lokomotiv Plovdiv - PFC Ludogorets 2-3(1-3)

### Round 18 [11-14.11.2022]
Pirin Blagoevgrad - Spartak Varna 3-1(2-1)
Arda Kardzhali - Botev Plovdiv 2-1(0-1)
Cherno More Varna - CSKA Sofia 0-2(0-0)
Levski Sofia - Slavia Sofia 1-2(1-0)
Hebar Pazardzhik - Lokomotiv Plov. 1-2(0-1)
Lokomotiv Sofia - Beroe St. Zagora 1-2(0-0)
PFC Ludogorets - CSKA 1948 Sofia 1-1(0-0)
Botev Vratsa - Septemvri Sofia 0-0

### Round 19 [10-13.02.2023]
Botev Plovdiv - Lokomotiv Sofia 0-0
CSKA 1948 Sofia - Hebar Pazardzhik 2-0(1-0)
Levski Sofia - Cherno More Varna 0-1(0-0)
Spartak Varna - PFC Ludogorets 1-2(0-2)
Septemvri Sofia - Arda Kardzhali 0-1(0-1)
Beroe Stara Zagora - CSKA Sofia 1-4(0-0)
Lokomotiv Plovdiv - Botev Vratsa 0-0
Slavia Sofia - Pirin Blagoevgrad 2-0(2-0)

### Round 20 [17-20.02.2023]
Arda Kardzhali - Lokomotiv Plovdiv 5-0(1-0)
Lokomotiv Sofia - Septemvri Sofia 1-1(1-1)
Cherno More V. - Beroe St. Zagora 1-1(1-0)
CSKA Sofia - Botev Plovdiv 3-1(2-1)
Botev Vratsa - CSKA 1948 Sofia 1-0(1-0)
Pirin Blagoevgrad - Levski Sofia 1-1(1-1)
PFC Ludogorets - Slavia Sofia 2-1(1-0)
Hebar Pazardzhik - Spartak Varna 0-0

### Round 21 [25-28.02.2023]
CSKA 1948 Sofia - Arda Kardzhali 1-0(0-0)
Spartak Varna - Botev Vratsa 2-1(1-0)
Lokomotiv Plovd. - Lokomotiv Sofia 1-0(0-0)
Slavia Sofia - Hebar Pazardzhik 0-1(0-0)
Botev Plovdiv - Beroe Stara Zagora 1-0(1-0)
Septemvri Sofia - CSKA Sofia 0-1(0-1)
Pirin Blagoevgrad - Cherno More V. 0-1(0-1)
Levski Sofia - PFC Ludogorets 0-0

| Round 22 [03-06.03.2023] |
|---|
| Lokomotiv Sofia - CSKA 1948 Sofia 0-6(0-2) |
| Beroe Stara Zagora - Septemvri Sofia 1-2(1-0) |
| Cherno More Varna - Botev Plovdiv 1-2(1-1) |
| CSKA Sofia - Lokomotiv Plovdiv 1-1(1-1) |
| Botev Vratsa - Slavia Sofia 1-0(0-0) |
| Hebar Pazardzhik - Levski Sofia 0-2(0-1) |
| PFC Ludogorets - Pirin Blagoevgrad 0-1(0-1) |
| Arda Kardzhali - Spartak Varna 2-0(0-0) |

| Round 23 [10-13.03.2023] |
|---|
| Septemvri Sofia - Botev Plovdiv 2-1(1-1) |
| Pirin Blagoevgrad-Hebar Pazardzhik 2-0(0-0) |
| Spartak Varna - Lokomotiv Sofia 1-2(1-1) |
| Levski Sofia - Botev Vratsa 2-0(2-0) |
| Slavia Sofia - Arda Kardzhali 1-0(0-0) |
| PFC Ludogorets-Cherno More Varna 3-2(1-2) |
| CSKA 1948 Sofia - CSKA Sofia 0-1(0-0) |
| Lokomotiv Plovdiv - Beroe Stara Zagora 0-0 |

| Round 24 [17-19.03.2023] |
|---|
| Cherno More Varna-Septemvri Sofia 3-0(2-0) |
| Lokomotiv Sofia - Slavia Sofia 1-0(0-0) |
| Beroe Stara Zagora - CSKA 1948 S. 1-3(1-2) |
| Hebar Pazardzhik - PFC Ludogorets 1-3(1-1) |
| CSKA Sofia - Spartak Varna 1-0(1-0) |
| Botev Vratsa - Pirin Blagoevgrad 0-0 |
| Arda Kardzhali - Levski Sofia 0-3(0-2) |
| Botev Plovdiv - Lokomotiv Plovdiv 1-1(0-0) |

| Round 25 [07-10.04.2023] |
|---|
| Lokomotiv Plovdiv - Septemvri Sofia 2-1(1-0) |
| PFC Ludogorets - Botev Vratsa 8-1(3-0) |
| Levski Sofia - Lokomotiv Sofia 1-0(1-0) |
| Hebar Pazardzhik - Cherno M. Varna 0-1(0-0) |
| Spartak Varna - Beroe Stara Zagora 0-4(0-1) |
| Slavia Sofia - CSKA Sofia 0-2(0-0) |
| Pirin Blagoevgrad - Arda Kardzhali 1-1(0-0) |
| CSKA 1948 Sofia - Botev Plovdiv 2-1(2-0) |

| Round 26 [13-17.04.2023] |
|---|
| Botev Vratsa - Hebar Pazardzhik 0-0 |
| Lokomotiv Sofia - Pirin Blagoevgrad 2-0(1-0) |
| Septemvri Sofia - CSKA 1948 Sofia 1-3(1-2) |
| Arda Kardzhali - PFC Ludogorets 1-2(1-0) |
| Beroe Stara Zagora - Slavia Sofia 0-1(0-1) |
| Botev Plovdiv - Spartak Varna 1-1(1-0) |
| CSKA Sofia - Levski Sofia 0-0 |
| Cherno More V. - Lokomotiv Plovdiv 2-1(1-1) |

| Round 27 [21-24.04.2023] |
|---|
| Botev Vratsa - Cherno More Varna 0-2(0-0) |
| PFC Ludogorets - Lokomotiv Sofia 1-0(0-0) |
| Hebar Pazardzhik - Arda Kardzhali 0-1(0-1) |
| CSKA 1948 S. - Lokomotiv Plovdiv 1-0(0-0) |
| Pirin Blagoevgrad - CSKA Sofia 0-1(0-1) |
| Levski Sofia - Beroe Stara Zagora 1-0(0-0) |
| Spartak Varna - Septemvri Sofia 2-0(1-0) |
| Slavia Sofia - Botev Plovdiv 0-0 |

| Round 28 [28-30.04.2023] |
|---|
| Septemvri Sofia - Slavia Sofia 1-2(0-1) |
| Lokomotiv Plovdiv - Spartak Varna 3-1(1-1) |
| Lokomotiv Sofia - Hebar Pazardzhik 1-4(1-1) |
| Arda Kardzhali - Botev Vratsa 1-1(0-0) |
| Botev Plovdiv - Levski Sofia 0-1(0-0) |
| Beroe St. Zagora - Pirin Blagoevgrad 1-0(1-0) |
| Cherno More Varna - CSKA 1948 Sofia 0-0 |
| CSKA Sofia - PFC Ludogorets 0-1(0-0) |

| Round 29 [02-04.05.2023] |
|---|
| Botev Vratsa - Lokomotiv Sofia 2-1(2-0) |
| Slavia Sofia - Lokomotiv Plovdiv 1-1(0-0) |
| Spartak Varna - CSKA 1948 Sofia 3-3(0-0) |
| Arda Kardzhali - Cherno More Varna 2-2(0-1) |
| PFC Ludogorets - Beroe Stara Zagora 2-1(1-1) |
| Pirin Blagoevgrad - Botev Plovdiv 2-4(2-2) |
| Hebar Pazardzhik - CSKA Sofia 0-4(0-3) |
| Levski Sofia - Septemvri Sofia 2-0(1-0) |

| Round 30 [06-08.05.2023] |
|---|
| Lokomotiv Sofia - Arda Kardzhali 1-1(0-1) |
| CSKA 1948 Sofia - Slavia Sofia 0-1(0-0) |
| Septemvri Sofia - Pirin Blagoevgrad 0-1(0-1) |
| Cherno More Varna - Spartak Varna 3-2(1-0) |
| Botev Plovdiv - PFC Ludogorets 0-2(0-2) |
| Beroe St. Zagora - Hebar Pazardzhik 0-2(0-1) |
| Lokomotiv Plovdiv - Levski Sofia 1-0(0-0) |
| CSKA Sofia - Botev Vratsa 5-1(2-0) |

## Final Standings

| | | | | | | | | | |
|---|---|---|---|---|---|---|---|---|---|
| 1. | PFC Ludogorets Razgrad | 30 | 23 | 5 | 2 | 72 | - | 21 | 74 |
| 2. | PFC CSKA Sofia | 30 | 23 | 4 | 3 | 57 | - | 14 | 73 |
| 3. | FC CSKA 1948 Sofia | 30 | 17 | 8 | 5 | 49 | - | 22 | 59 |
| 4. | PFC Levski Sofia | 30 | 15 | 9 | 6 | 38 | - | 14 | 54 |
| 5. | PFC Cherno More Varna | 30 | 15 | 8 | 7 | 36 | - | 27 | 53 |
| 6. | PFC Lokomotiv Plovdiv | 30 | 14 | 8 | 8 | 33 | - | 28 | 50 |
| 7. | PFC Slavia Sofia | 30 | 15 | 4 | 11 | 31 | - | 27 | 49 |
| 8. | FC Arda 1924 Kardzhali | 30 | 11 | 9 | 10 | 33 | - | 32 | 42 |
| 9. | FC Lokomotiv 1929 Sofia | 30 | 10 | 8 | 12 | 32 | - | 38 | 38 |
| 10. | PFC Botev Plovdiv | 30 | 9 | 5 | 16 | 38 | - | 40 | 32 |
| 11. | POFC Botev Vratsa | 30 | 7 | 7 | 16 | 23 | - | 55 | 28 |
| 12. | PFC Beroe Stara Zagora | 30 | 7 | 6 | 17 | 26 | - | 47 | 27 |
| 13. | OFC Pirin Blagoevgrad | 30 | 5 | 9 | 16 | 21 | - | 39 | 24 |
| 14. | FC Hebar Pazardzhik | 30 | 6 | 5 | 19 | 19 | - | 51 | 23 |
| 15. | PFC Septemvri Sofia | 30 | 5 | 7 | 18 | 25 | - | 45 | 22 |
| 16. | FK Spartak 1918 Varna | 30 | 3 | 8 | 19 | 27 | - | 60 | 17 |

Teams ranked 1-6 were qualified for the Championship Round, teams ranked 7-10 were qualified for the Europa Conference League Round, while teams ranked 11-16 were qualified for the Relegation Round.

## Relegation Round

## Results

| Round 31 [12-13.05.2023] |
|---|
| Pirin Blagoevgrad-Hebar Pazardzhik 2-1(0-0) |
| Beroe Stara Zagora - Septemvri Sofia 2-0(1-0) |
| Botev Vratsa - Spartak Varna 1-1(0-1) |

| Round 32 [21-22.05.2023] |
|---|
| Septemvri Sofia - Pirin Blagoevgrad 2-0(0-0) |
| Spartak Varna - Hebar Pazardzhik 2-1(0-0) |
| Botev Vratsa - Beroe Stara Zagora 2-0(0-0) |

| Round 33 [25-27.05.2023] |
|---|
| Beroe Stara Zagora - Spartak Varna 1-1(1-1) |
| Hebar Pazardzhik - Septemvri Sofia 3-1(1-0) |
| Pirin Blagoevgrad - Botev Vratsa 2-0(0-0) |

| Round 34 [31.05.2023] |
|---|
| Spartak Varna - Septemvri Sofia 1-0(0-0) |
| Botev Vratsa - Hebar Pazardzhik 2-3(0-0) |
| Beroe St. Zagora - Pirin Blagoevgrad 1-1(1-0) |

| Round 35 [05.06.2023] |
|---|
| Pirin Blagoevgrad - Spartak Varna 2-0(2-0) |
| Hebar Pazardzhik-Beroe Stara Zagora 3-1(1-0) |
| Septemvri Sofia - Botev Vratsa 3-1(1-0) |

## Final Standings

| | | | | | | | | | | Total | | | | Home | | | | | Away | | | | |
|---|---|---|---|---|---|---|---|---|---|---|---|---|---|---|---|---|---|---|---|---|---|---|---|---|
| 1. | OFC Pirin Blagoevgrad | 35 | 8 | 10 | 17 | 28 | - | 43 | 34 | | 6 | 5 | 7 | 20 | - | 23 | | 2 | 5 | 10 | 8 | - | 20 |
| 2. | FC Hebar Pazardzhik | 35 | 9 | 5 | 21 | 30 | - | 59 | 32 | | 3 | 3 | 11 | 14 | - | 29 | | 6 | 2 | 10 | 16 | - | 30 |
| 3. | POFC Botev Vratsa | 35 | 8 | 8 | 19 | 29 | - | 64 | 32 | | 7 | 5 | 6 | 15 | - | 20 | | 1 | 3 | 13 | 14 | - | 44 |
| 4. | PFC Beroe Stara Zagora (Relegation Play-offs) | 35 | 8 | 8 | 19 | 31 | - | 54 | 32 | | 6 | 4 | 8 | 19 | - | 25 | | 2 | 4 | 11 | 12 | - | 29 |
| 5. | PFC Septemvri Sofia (Relegated) | 35 | 7 | 7 | 21 | 31 | - | 52 | 28 | | 4 | 5 | 8 | 15 | - | 21 | | 3 | 2 | 13 | 16 | - | 31 |
| 6. | FK Spartak 1918 Varna (Relegated) | 35 | 5 | 10 | 20 | 32 | - | 65 | 25 | | 5 | 4 | 8 | 19 | - | 26 | | 0 | 6 | 12 | 13 | - | 39 |

## Relegation Play-offs [09.06.2023]

PFC Beroe Stara Zagora - FC Sportist Svoge      1-0(1-0)
PFC Beroe Stara Zagora remains at first level for 2023/2024.

## Europa Conference League Round

### Results

**Round 31 [13-14.05.2023]**
Slavia Sofia - Botev Plovdiv 1-0(0-0)
Arda Kardzhali - Lokomotiv Sofia 3-0(2-0)

**Round 32 [19.05.2023]**
Slavia Sofia - Arda Kardzhali 0-0
Botev Plovdiv - Lokomotiv Sofia 0-2(0-1)

**Round 33 [23.05.2023]**
Lokomotiv Sofia - Slavia Sofia 1-1(1-0)
Arda Kardzhali - Botev Plovdiv 2-1(0-1)

**Round 34 [29.05.2023]**
Lokomotiv Sofia - Arda Kardzhali 1-3(0-2)
Botev Plovdiv - Slavia Sofia 0-0

**Round 35 [01.06.2023]**
Lokomotiv Sofia - Botev Plovdiv 1-2(1-1)
Arda Kardzhali - Slavia Sofia 3-2(0-1)

**Round 36 [06.06.2023]**
Botev Plovdiv - Arda Kardzhali 0-3(0-1)
Slavia Sofia - Lokomotiv Sofia 2-0(0-0)

### Final Standings

| | | Total | | | | | | Home | | | | | Away | | |
|---|---|---|---|---|---|---|---|---|---|---|---|---|---|---|---|---|
| 1. | FC Arda 1924 Kardzhali | 36 | 16 | 10 | 10 | 47 - 36 | 58 | 10 | 4 | 4 | 30 - 20 | 6 | 6 | 6 | 17 - 16 |
| 2. | PFC Slavia Sofia | 36 | 17 | 7 | 12 | 37 - 31 | 58 | 10 | 5 | 3 | 21 - 12 | 7 | 2 | 9 | 16 - 19 |
| 3. | FC Lokomotiv 1929 Sofia | 36 | 11 | 9 | 16 | 37 - 49 | 42 | 7 | 5 | 6 | 21 - 26 | 4 | 4 | 10 | 16 - 23 |
| 4. | PFC Botev Plovdiv | 36 | 10 | 6 | 20 | 41 - 49 | 36 | 6 | 4 | 8 | 21 - 20 | 4 | 2 | 12 | 20 - 29 |

FC Arda 1924 Kardzhali were qualified for the Europa Conference League Play-off Final.

## Championship Round

### Results

**Round 31 [14-15.05.2023]**
CSKA 1948 Sofia - Levski Sofia 2-2(1-2)
CSKA Sofia - Cherno More Varna 2-0(0-0)
PFC Ludogorets - Lokomotiv Plovdiv 1-0(1-0)

**Round 32 [20-21.05.2023]**
Cherno More V.- CSKA 1948 Sofia 1-1(0-1)
PFC Ludogorets - CSKA Sofia 2-2(1-2)
Lokomotiv Plovdiv - Levski Sofia 0-3(0-2)

**Round 33 [26-28.05.2023]**
Levski Sofia - Cherno More Varna 2-1(1-1)
CSKA Sofia - Lokomotiv Plovdiv 1-0(1-0)
CSKA 1948 Sofia - PFC Ludogorets 2-2(0-0)

**Round 34 [02-03.06.2023]**
Lokomotiv Plovdiv - Cherno More V.2-1(0-0)
CSKA Sofia - CSKA 1948 Sofia 1-1(1-1)
PFC Ludogorets - Levski Sofia 3-2(1-1)

**Round 35 [07.06.2023]**
Levski Sofia - CSKA Sofia 0-2(0-1)
CSKA 1948 Sofia - Lokomotiv Plovdiv 0-0
Cherno More V.- PFC Ludogorets 0-1(0-0)

### Final Standings

| | | Total | | | | | | Home | | | | | Away | | |
|---|---|---|---|---|---|---|---|---|---|---|---|---|---|---|---|---|
| 1. | **PFC Ludogorets Razgrad** | 35 | 26 | 7 | 2 | 81 - 27 | 85 | 13 | 4 | 1 | 43 - 14 | 13 | 3 | 1 | 38 - 13 |
| 2. | PFC CSKA Sofia | 35 | 26 | 6 | 3 | 65 - 17 | 84 | 13 | 4 | 1 | 34 - 8 | 13 | 2 | 2 | 31 - 9 |
| 3. | FC CSKA 1948 Sofia | 35 | 17 | 13 | 5 | 55 - 28 | 64 | 11 | 5 | 2 | 29 - 12 | 6 | 8 | 3 | 26 - 16 |
| 4. | PFC Levski Sofia | 35 | 17 | 10 | 8 | 47 - 22 | 61 | 11 | 3 | 3 | 25 - 7 | 6 | 7 | 5 | 22 - 15 |
| 5. | PFC Lokomotiv Plovdiv | 35 | 15 | 9 | 11 | 35 - 34 | 54 | 11 | 2 | 4 | 24 - 15 | 4 | 7 | 7 | 11 - 19 |
| 6. | PFC Cherno More Varna | 35 | 15 | 9 | 11 | 39 - 35 | 54 | 8 | 5 | 4 | 21 - 16 | 7 | 4 | 7 | 18 - 19 |

PFC Levski Sofia were qualified for the Europa Conference League Play-off.

## Europa Conference League Play-off [11.06.2023]

PFC Levski Sofia - FC Arda 1924 Kardzhali      2-0(1-0)

### Top goalscorers:

| | | |
|---|---|---|
| 21 | **Ivaylo Chochev** | *FC CSKA 1948 Sofia* |
| 18 | Duckens Moses Nazon (HAI) | *PFC CSKA Sofia* |
| 15 | Igor Thiago Nascimento Rodrigues (BRA) | *PFC Ludogorets Razgrad* |

### First Round [16/18-19/23/25-27.11.2022]

| | | | | |
|---|---|---|---|---|
| FC Strumska Slava Radomir - FK Spartak 1918 Varna | 0-2(0-1) | FC Sportist Svoge - PFC Slavia Sofia | 1-2(0-1,1-1) |
| FK Rozova Dolina - PFC Ludogorets Razgrad | 0-2(0-0) | FC Krumovgrad - PFC Septemvri Sofia | 0-1(0-0) |
| FC Maritsa Plovdiv - FC Hebar Pazardzhik | 4-2(2-1) | FC Chernomorets Balchik - PFC Botev Plovdiv | 0-3(0-2) |
| OFC Vihren Sandanski - PFC Levski Sofia | 1-4(1-2) | OFC Gigant Saedinenie - PFC CSKA Sofia | 1-1 aet; 6-7 pen |
| FK Chavdar Etropole - OFC Pirin Blagoevgrad | 2-0(2-0) | FC Minyor Pernik - PFC Beroe Stara Zagora | 0-2(0-1) |
| FC Vitosha Bistritsa - POFC Botev Vratsa | 1-0(0-0) | FK Sevlievo - FC CSKA 1948 Sofia | 0-4(0-1) |
| FC Dunav Ruse - FC Arda 1924 Kardzhali | 1-2(0-1) | FC Marek Dupnitsa - PFC Lokomotiv Plovdiv | 0-1(0-1) |
| OFK Spartak Pleven - FC Lokomotiv 1929 Sofia | 1-4(0-2) | PFC Litex Lovech - PFC Cherno More Varna | 0-2(0-0) |

### 1/8-Finals [26-28.11./02-04.12.2022]

| | | | | |
|---|---|---|---|---|
| FC Maritsa Plovdiv - FC Arda 1924 Kardzhali | 1-1 aet; 2-3 pen | PFC Beroe Stara Zagora - FC CSKA 1948 Sofia | 0-2(0-0) |
| FK Spartak 1918 Varna - FK Chavdar Etropole | 1-0(0-0,0-0) | PFC Slavia Sofia - PFC Botev Plovdiv | 2-1(1-1) |
| FC Lokomotiv 1929 Sofia - FC Vitosha Bistritsa | 3-0(1-0) | PFC Cherno More Varna - PFC Lokomotiv Plovdiv | 3-1(1-1) |
| PFC Septemvri Sofia - PFC CSKA Sofia | 1-2(0-0) | PFC Ludogorets Razgrad - PFC Levski Sofia | 2-1(0-0) |

### Quarter-Finals [03-05.04.2023]

| | | | | |
|---|---|---|---|---|
| FC Lokomotiv 1929 Sofia - PFC Slavia Sofia | 2-1(1-0) | PFC CSKA Sofia - PFC Cherno More Varna | 1-2(0-0) |
| PFC Ludogorets Razgrad - FK Spartak 1918 Varna | 2-1(1-1) | FC Arda 1924 Kardzhali - FC CSKA 1948 Sofia | 0-1(0-0,0-0) |

### Semi-Finals [25-26.04./10-11.05.2023]

| First Leg | | Second Leg | |
|---|---|---|---|
| PFC Cherno More Varna - PFC Ludogorets Razgrad | 1-2(1-2) | PFC Ludogorets Razgrad - PFC Cherno More Varna | 1-2 aet; 4-1 pen |
| FC Lokomotiv 1929 Sofia - FC CSKA 1948 Sofia | 2-3(1-3) | FC CSKA 1948 Sofia - FC Lokomotiv 1929 Sofia | 2-2(1-2,1-2) |

### Final

24.05.2023; Nationalen Stadion "Vasil Levski", Sofia; Referee: Dragomir Draganov; Attendance: 1,400

**FC CSKA 1948 Sofia - PFC Ludogorets Razgrad**          **1-3(0-2)**

**CSKA 1948**: Daniel Naumov (Cap), Reyan Daskalov (46.Steeve Furtado Pereira), Simeon Petrov, Héliton Jorge Tito dos Santos, Sidcley Ferreira Pereira, Emil Tsenov (46.Mario Topuzov), Georgi Rusev, Parvizdzhon Umarbaev (82.Svetoslav Dikov), Ivaylo Chochev, Radoslav Kirilov (56.Pedro Henrique Oliveira dos Santos „Pedrinho"), Aleksandar Kolev. Trainer: Todor Yanchev.

**Ludogorets**: Simon Sluga, Aslak Fonn Witry (55.Gonzalo Ávila Gordón "Pipa"), Igor Plastun, Olivier Verdon, Bernard Tekpetey, Manuel Luis da Silva Cafumana „Show", Pedro Henrique Naressi Machado (61.Gustavo Nonato Santana), Kiril Despodov (Cap) (71.Matías Fabián Tissera), Spas Delev (61.Rai Nascimento De Oliveira), Caio Vidal Rocha (55.Jakub Piotrowski), Igor Thiago Nascimento Rodrigues. Trainer: Ivaylo Petev.

**Goals:** 0-1 Caio Vidal Rocha (8), 0-2 Caio Vidal Rocha (43), 1-2 Ivaylo Chochev (59), 1-3 Matías Fabián Tissera (81).

## THE CLUBS 2022/2023

Please note: appearances and goals are including statistics of regular season and play-offs (Championship, Europa Conference League and Relegation Round).

### Professional Football Club Arda 1924 Kardzhali

| | |
|---|---|
| **Founded:** | 10.08.1924 |
| **Stadium:** | Arena Arda, Arda (11,114) |
| **Trainer:** | Aleksandar Tunchev          10.07.1981 |

| Goalkeepers: | DOB | M | (s) | G |
|---|---|---|---|---|
| Anatoli Gospodinov | 21.03.1994 | 29 | | |
| Vasil Simeonov | 04.02.1998 | 7 | (1) | |
| **Defenders:** | **DOB** | **M** | **(s)** | **G** |
| Dzhuneyt Ali | 05.09.1994 | 15 | (7) | |
| Aleksandar Georgiev | 10.11.1997 | 17 | (6) | |
| Kerimdzhan Ignatov | 15.02.2005 | | (2) | |
| Plamen Krachunov | 11.01.1989 | 11 | (5) | |
| Alex Petkov | 25.07.1999 | 25 | (1) | 1 |
| Oumar Sako (CIV) | 04.05.1996 | 27 | | 1 |
| Milen Stoev | 29.09.1999 | 11 | (6) | |
| Atanas Zehirov | 13.02.1989 | | (1) | |
| Milen Zhelev | 17.07.1993 | 23 | (5) | |
| **Midfielders:** | **DOB** | **M** | **(s)** | **G** |
| Chano Boukholda (ALG) | 24.05.1996 | 1 | (5) | |
| Stanislav Dyulgerov | 23.08.2003 | | (3) | |
| Hristo Ivanov | 16.12.2000 | 10 | (6) | 1 |

| | DOB | M | (s) | G |
|---|---|---|---|---|
| Stanislav Ivanov | 16.04.1999 | 13 | (4) | 3 |
| José Ederaldo da Silva *Júnior Palmares* (BRA) | 14.04.1997 | 4 | (13) | |
| Lachezar Kotev | 05.01.1998 | 17 | | 3 |
| Deyan Lozev | 26.10.1993 | 20 | (4) | |
| Rumen Rumenov | 07.06.1993 | | (2) | |
| Aboubacar Toungara (MLI) | 15.11.1994 | 14 | (1) | 1 |
| Radoslav Tsonev | 29.04.1995 | 17 | | 4 |
| Iliya Yurukov | 22.09.1999 | 28 | (3) | 1 |
| **Forwards:** | **DOB** | **M** | **(s)** | **G** |
| Georgi Atanasov | 06.03.2004 | | (1) | |
| Preslav Borukov | 23.04.2000 | 12 | (5) | 5 |
| Ivan Kokonov | 17.08.1991 | 16 | (16) | 1 |
| Svetoslav Kovachev | 14.03.1998 | 28 | (6) | 8 |
| Lassana N'Diaye (MLI) | 03.10.2000 | 14 | (21) | 8 |
| El Mamy Tetah (MTN) | 12.11.2001 | 11 | (12) | 3 |
| Ivan Tilev | 05.01.1999 | 17 | (14) | 4 |
| Tonislav Yordanov | 27.11.1998 | 9 | (9) | 1 |

## Professional Football Club Beroe Stara Zagora

| | | |
|---|---|---|
| **Founded**: | 06.05.1916 | |
| **Stadium**: | Stadion Beroe, Stara Zagora (12,128) | |
| **Trainer**: | Petar Hubchev | 26.02.1964 |
| [14.09.2022] | Nikolay Kirov | 12.06.1975 |
| [06.06.2023] | Veselin Penev | 11.08.1982 |

| Goalkeepers: | DOB | M | (s) | G |
|---|---|---|---|---|
| Ivan Goshev | 17.06.2000 | 4 | | |
| Ivan Karadzhov | 12.07.1989 | 31 | | |
| **Defenders:** | **DOB** | **M** | **(s)** | **G** |
| Gustavo *Cascardo* de Assis (BRA) | 24.03.1997 | 13 | (1) | |
| Maks Čelić (CRO) | 08.03.1996 | 13 | (1) | |
| Georgi Dinkov | 20.05.1991 | 10 | (6) | |
| Thomas Fontaine (MAD) | 08.05.1991 | 7 | | |
| Simeon Germanov | 01.01.2005 | | (1) | |
| *Klaidher* Vittorio Bravin *Macedo* (BRA) | 18.01.1999 | 12 | | |
| Zarija Lambulić (SRB) | 25.05.1998 | 9 | (2) | |
| Nikolay Nikolaev | 19.03.1997 | 3 | (4) | |
| Stiliyan Nikolov | 16.07.1991 | 12 | (2) | |
| *Pedro Henrique* Alves Santana (BRA) | 31.01.2001 | 12 | (4) | |
| Dimitar Pirgov | 26.10.1989 | 16 | | |
| Rui Pedro Coimbra Chaves „Ruca" (POR) | 11.09.1990 | 15 | | |
| *Saná* Gomes (GNB) | 10.10.1999 | 11 | (3) | |
| **Midfielders:** | **DOB** | **M** | **(s)** | **G** |
| Anicet Andrianantenaina Abel (MAD) | 13.03.1990 | 11 | | |
| Yoan Baurenski | 21.10.2001 | 4 | (7) | |
| *Lucas Willian* Cruzeiro Martins (BRA) | 12.05.1995 | 7 | (5) | |

| | | | | |
|---|---|---|---|---|
| *Luizinho* Silva (GNB) | 08.07.1995 | 6 | (8) | |
| Uerdi Mara (ALB) | 30.01.1999 | 7 | (3) | 1 |
| Simeon Mechev | 16.03.1990 | 31 | | 3 |
| Mitko Mitkov | 28.08.2000 | | (4) | |
| Romario Florin Moise (ROU) | 21.09.1995 | 5 | (6) | 1 |
| Bozhidar Penchev | 17.03.2002 | 13 | (14) | |
| Valentino Pugliese (SUI) | 18.07.1997 | | (7) | |
| Dimitar Stoyanov | 14.04.2001 | 9 | (3) | |
| Aboubacar Toungara (MLI) | 15.11.1994 | 17 | | 9 |
| Damian Yordanov | 30.05.2005 | | (1) | |
| Serkan Yusein | 31.03.1996 | 32 | (2) | 2 |
| **Forwards:** | **DOB** | **M** | **(s)** | **G** |
| Spas Georgiev | 21.06.1992 | 21 | (10) | |
| Kaloyan Krastev | 24.01.1999 | 7 | (10) | 1 |
| Denislav Stanchev | 28.03.2000 | | (3) | |
| Boubacar Traorè (SEN) | 26.07.1997 | 4 | (3) | |
| Steve Waren Traoré (FRA) | 18.02.1998 | 12 | (4) | 3 |
| Vinni Dugary Triboulet (CMR) | 18.06.1999 | 12 | (2) | 3 |
| Vasil Vasilev | 20.09.2005 | 6 | (4) | 1 |
| Tonislav Yordanov | 27.11.1998 | 13 | (3) | 6 |

## Professional Football Club Botev Plovdiv

| | | |
|---|---|---|
| **Founded**: | 12.03.1912 | |
| **Stadium**: | Stadion "Hristo Botev", Plovdiv (18,777) | |
| **Trainer**: | Azrudin Valentić (BIH) | 21.07.1970 |
| [29.07.2022] | Artur Hovhannisyan (ARM) | 20.02.1985 |
| [03.08.2022] | Željko Kopić (CRO) | 10.09.1977 |
| [03.01.2023] | Bruno Miguel Nunes Baltazar (POR) | 06.07.1977 |
| [25.05.2023] | Stefan Stoyanov | 24.01.1979 |

| Goalkeepers: | DOB | M | (s) | G |
|---|---|---|---|---|
| Georgi Argilashki | 13.06.1991 | 8 | | |
| Hidajet Hankič (AUT) | 29.06.1994 | 27 | | |
| Stefan Smarkalev | 14.05.2007 | 1 | | |
| **Defenders:** | **DOB** | **M** | **(s)** | **G** |
| Hugo Azzi (FRA) | 23.12.2003 | | (1) | |
| Dimitar Balinov | 19.01.2001 | 1 | | |
| Atanas Chernev | 25.03.2002 | | (5) | |
| James Armel Eto'o Eyenga (CMR) | 19.11.2000 | 27 | (2) | |
| Viktor Genev | 27.10.1988 | 31 | | 3 |
| Miroslav Georgiev | 19.10.2005 | 1 | (1) | |
| Roy Herman (ISR) | 21.06.2000 | 13 | (7) | 1 |
| Martin Hristov | 02.10.2003 | 1 | (1) | |
| Pa Momodou Konaté (GUI) | 25.04.1994 | 20 | (4) | 2 |
| Dimitar Papazov | 15.07.2006 | 3 | | |
| Roberto Punčec (CRO) | 27.10.1991 | 27 | | |
| Stanislav Rabotov | 14.06.2002 | 3 | | |
| Bozhidar Siderov | 25.04.2005 | | (1) | |
| Samuel Souprayen (FRA) | 02.02.1989 | 24 | (4) | |
| Jasper van Heertum (NED) | 10.11.1997 | 18 | (8) | |
| **Midfielders:** | **DOB** | **M** | **(s)** | **G** |
| Monir Hakam Al Badarin | 08.07.2005 | | (1) | |
| *Antonio Perera* Calderón (ESP) | 08.06.1997 | 7 | (3) | |
| Lachezar Baltanov | 11.07.1988 | 3 | (3) | |

| | | | | |
|---|---|---|---|---|
| Biser Bonev | 04.06.2003 | | (3) | |
| Daniel Gichev | 21.11.2004 | | (1) | |
| Krasian Kolev | 18.01.2004 | 11 | (4) | 1 |
| Dylan Mertens (NED) | 20.07.1995 | 21 | (5) | 1 |
| Tochukwu Nadi (NGA) | 30.06.2003 | 9 | (10) | |
| Todor Nedelev | 07.02.1993 | 3 | | |
| Dobromir Pavlov | 09.01.2005 | | (2) | |
| Stanislav Petkov | 10.06.2004 | 1 | | |
| Réda Rabeï (ALG) | 12.07.1994 | 15 | | |
| Martin Sitev | 06.09.2006 | 1 | (2) | |
| Emmanuel Tokú (GHA) | 10.07.2000 | 16 | (1) | 1 |
| Dimitar Tonev | 15.10.2001 | 5 | (8) | |
| **Forwards:** | **DOB** | **M** | **(s)** | **G** |
| Samuel Akere (NGA) | 16.02.2004 | 4 | (8) | |
| Antoine Baroan (FRA) | 24.06.2000 | 28 | (3) | 14 |
| Mohamed Brahimi (FRA) | 17.09.1998 | 14 | (2) | |
| Amadou Doumbouya (GUI) | 12.10.2002 | 1 | (3) | |
| Umeh Emmanuel (NGA) | 31.08.2004 | 9 | (5) | 1 |
| Elvis Manu (NED) | 13.08.1993 | 14 | | 7 |
| Nikolay Minkov | 13.08.1997 | 19 | (12) | 3 |
| Emil Naydenov | 12.02.2007 | | (1) | |
| Konstantin Pavlov | 14.08.2005 | 1 | (1) | |
| Martin Sekulić (CRO) | 04.01.1999 | 4 | (21) | 3 |
| Abdoulaye Traoré (CIV) | 28.06.2003 | 5 | (11) | 2 |

## Professional Football Club Botev Vratsa

| | | |
|---|---|---|
| **Founded**: | 1921 | |
| **Stadium**: | Stadion "Hristo Botev", Vratsa (6,417) | |
| **Trainer**: | Rosen Kirilov | 04.01.1973 |
| [06.09.2022] | Vladislav Vutov | 26.08.1980 |
| [14.09.2022] | Daniel Alexandre Morales Batagello (BRA) | 06.12.1975 |

| Goalkeepers: | DOB | M | (s) | G |
|---|---|---|---|---|
| Federico Barrios Rubio (COL) | 05.10.1996 | 1 | | |
| Krasimir Kostov | 11.02.1995 | 34 | | |
| **Defenders:** | **DOB** | **M** | **(s)** | **G** |
| Messie Biatoumoussoka (FRA) | 05.06.1998 | 19 | (5) | 1 |
| *Diego* Gustavo *Ferraresso* Scheda (BRA) | 21.05.1992 | 34 | | |
| Petko Ganev | 17.09.1996 | 3 | (3) | |
| Martin Kavdanski | 13.02.1987 | 21 | (3) | 1 |
| Petar Kepov | 22.11.2002 | 2 | (6) | 1 |
| *Luiz Felipe* de Souza Soares (BRA) | 23.02.1999 | 19 | | |
| Bryan Mendoza (ARG) | 07.03.1993 | 32 | (2) | 1 |
| Plamen Petrov | 06.11.2006 | | (1) | |
| Tom Rapnouil-Zarandona (FRA) | 09.02.2001 | 11 | (4) | |
| Momchil Tsvetanov | 03.12.1990 | 13 | (1) | |
| **Midfielders:** | **DOB** | **M** | **(s)** | **G** |
| Yhojan Iván Arenas Valbuena (COL) | 13.07.1997 | 8 | (2) | |
| Martin Atanasov | 19.01.2002 | 6 | (5) | |
| *Diogo* Barbosa (POR) | 13.01.1996 | 7 | (6) | |

| | | | | |
|---|---|---|---|---|
| Stefan Gavrilov | 09.07.2000 | 14 | (8) | |
| Antonio Georgiev | 26.10.1997 | 17 | (6) | |
| Chavdar Ivaylov | 09.07.1996 | 24 | (1) | 3 |
| *Lukas* Pivetta *Brambilla* (BRA) | 04.01.1995 | 2 | (4) | |
| Ivan Neshkov | 18.01.2005 | 1 | (1) | |
| Mitko Panov | 19.01.2006 | | (3) | |
| Santiago Ramírez Montoya (COL) | 27.11.1998 | 6 | (7) | |
| Kléry Serber (FRA) | 03.07.1998 | 14 | (10) | 1 |
| Krasimir Todorov | 02.03.2004 | 2 | (8) | 1 |
| **Forwards:** | **DOB** | **M** | **(s)** | **G** |
| Jean-Pierre Da Sylva (FRA) | 03.01.1997 | 14 | (14) | 1 |
| Daniel Genov | 19.05.1989 | 24 | (8) | 3 |
| Ventsislav Hristov | 09.11.1988 | 7 | (6) | 1 |
| Marco Ludivin Majouga (FRA) | 09.05.2001 | 6 | (10) | 1 |
| Miroslav Marinov | 07.03.2004 | 17 | (13) | 3 |
| Brayan Andrés Perea Vargas (COL) | 25.02.1993 | 26 | | 9 |
| Viktor Vasilev | 27.01.1999 | 1 | | |
| Radoslav Zahariev | 25.07.2004 | | (2) | |

## Professional Football Club Cherno More Varna

**Founded**: 03.03.1913
**Stadium**: Stadion Ticha, Varna (6,250)
**Trainer**: Ilian Iliev     02.07.1968

| Goalkeepers: | DOB | M | (s) | G |
|---|---|---|---|---|
| Ivan Dyulgerov | 15.07.1999 | 26 | | |
| Georgi Georgiev | 12.10.1988 | 9 | (1) | |
| **Defenders:** | **DOB** | **M** | **(s)** | **G** |
| Zhivko Atanasov | 03.02.1991 | 31 | | 1 |
| Petar Bosančić (CRO) | 19.04.1996 | 22 | | |
| Martin Dichev | 22.08.2000 | 6 | (9) | |
| Daniel Dimov | 21.01.1989 | 6 | (7) | 1 |
| Vlatko Drobarov (MKD) | 02.11.1992 | 11 | (1) | 2 |
| Tsvetomir Panov | 17.04.1989 | 21 | (3) | |
| Viktor Popov | 05.03.2000 | 30 | | 1 |
| Rosen Stefanov | 27.11.2002 | 7 | (1) | |
| Aleksandar Vasilev | 27.04.1995 | 15 | | |
| **Midfielders:** | **DOB** | **M** | **(s)** | **G** |
| Arlind Dakaj (SUI) | 13.10.2001 | 3 | (4) | |
| Atanas Iliev | 09.10.1994 | 8 | (8) | 3 |
| *Matheus* dos Santos *Clemente* (POR) | 10.06.1998 | 15 | (1) | 1 |
| *Matheus Machado* Ferreira (BRA) | 13.03.2003 | 3 | (5) | 2 |

| | DOB | M | (s) | G |
|---|---|---|---|---|
| Atair Mimito Rocha Biai „Mimito" (GNB) | 12.12.1997 | 11 | (5) | |
| Vasil Panayotov | 16.07.1990 | 31 | (1) | 4 |
| Mazire Soula (FRA) | 06.06.1998 | 23 | (6) | 2 |
| Stefan Velev | 02.05.1989 | 15 | (12) | |
| **Forwards:** | **DOB** | **M** | **(s)** | **G** |
| *Alex* Nascimento *Fernandes* (BRA) | 03.06.2002 | 19 | (6) | 3 |
| Angel Angelov | 17.11.1999 | | (5) | |
| Zakaria Benchaâ (ALG) | 11.01.1997 | 10 | (3) | 3 |
| Berk Beyhan | 29.10.2004 | | (1) | |
| Mathias Coureur (MTQ) | 22.03.1988 | 11 | (7) | 3 |
| *Edgar* Patricio Franco *Pacheco* (POR) | 23.06.2000 | 7 | (4) | |
| Ismail Isa | 26.06.1989 | 10 | (14) | 3 |
| *Michael* Santos Silva Alves (BRA) | 16.02.1996 | 1 | (6) | 2 |
| Madi Queta (POR) | 21.10.1998 | 14 | (3) | 1 |
| Velislav Vasilev | 08.05.2001 | 10 | (15) | 1 |
| Yevheniy Serdiuk (UKR) | 24.04.1998 | 4 | (1) | 3 |
| Nikolay Zlatev | 12.12.2004 | 6 | (17) | 2 |

## Professional Football Club Centralen Sporten Klub na Armiyata (CSKA) Sofia

**Founded**: 05.05.1948
**Stadium**: Balgarska Armiya Stadion, Sofia (22,995)
**Trainer**: Saša Ilić (SRB)     30.12.1977

| Goalkeepers: | DOB | M | (s) | G |
|---|---|---|---|---|
| Gustavo *Busatto* (BRA) | 23.10.1990 | 32 | | |
| Dimitar Evtimov | 07.09.1993 | 3 | | |
| **Defenders:** | **DOB** | **M** | **(s)** | **G** |
| Bradley de Nooijer (NED) | 07.11.1997 | 19 | (2) | 2 |
| Asen Donchev | 22.10.2001 | 2 | (5) | 1 |
| *Geferson* Cerqueira Teles (BRA) | 13.05.1994 | 14 | (7) | 1 |
| Menno Koch (NED) | 02.07.1994 | 9 | (9) | 3 |
| Enes Mahmutović (LUX) | 22.05.1997 | 15 | (3) | 1 |
| Jurgen Mattheij (NED) | 01.04.1993 | 26 | | 1 |
| Galin Minkov | 02.11.1997 | 2 | (1) | |
| Hristiyan Petrov | 24.06.2002 | 26 | | |
| Ivan Turitsov | 18.07.1999 | 24 | (3) | 5 |
| Thibaut Vion (FRA) | 11.12.1993 | 28 | (6) | |
| Amos Youga (CTA) | 08.12.1992 | 28 | (1) | 1 |
| **Midfielders:** | **DOB** | **M** | **(s)** | **G** |
| Yoan Baurenski | 21.10.2001 | 1 | (2) | |

| | DOB | M | (s) | G |
|---|---|---|---|---|
| Marcelino Jr. Carreazo Betín (VEN) | 17.02.1999 | 14 | (9) | 3 |
| Tobias Heintz (NOR) | 13.07.1998 | 13 | (3) | 3 |
| Jonathan Lindseth (NOR) | 25.02.1996 | 24 | (5) | 2 |
| Stanislav Shopov | 23.02.2002 | 18 | (11) | 1 |
| Lazar Tufegdžić (SRB) | 22.02.1997 | 15 | (11) | 3 |
| **Forwards:** | **DOB** | **M** | **(s)** | **G** |
| Simeon Aleksandrov | 24.09.2003 | | (1) | |
| Daouda Bamba (CIV) | 05.03.1995 | 4 | (7) | 1 |
| Kaloyan Krastev | 24.01.1999 | 3 | (1) | |
| Bismark Charles Kwarema (GHA) | 26.05.2001 | 1 | (11) | |
| *Mauricio Garcez* de Jésus (BRA) | 16.03.1997 | 24 | (7) | 10 |
| Brayan Moreno Álvarez (COL) | 02.08.1999 | 8 | (17) | 9 |
| Duckens Moses Nazon (HAI) | 07.04.1994 | 22 | (10) | 18 |
| Mark-Emilio Papazov | 08.10.2003 | | (1) | |
| Zhirayr Shaghoyan (ARM) | 10.04.2001 | 8 | (7) | |
| Georgi Yomov | 06.07.1997 | 2 | (1) | |
| Radoslav Zhivkov | 27.03.1999 | | (2) | |

## Football Club Central Sports Club of the Army 1948 Sofia

**Founded**: 19.07.2016
**Stadium**: Stadion Bistritsa, Sofia (2,500)
**Trainer**: Lyuboslav Penev     31.08.1966
[13.12.2022]   Todor Yanchev     19.05.1976
[25.05.2023]   Atanas Ribarski     25.03.1985

| Goalkeepers: | DOB | M | (s) | G |
|---|---|---|---|---|
| Gennady Ganev (UKR) | 15.05.1990 | 2 | (1) | |
| Daniel Naumov | 29.03.1998 | 33 | | |
| **Defenders:** | **DOB** | **M** | **(s)** | **G** |
| Aleksandar Aleksandrov | 30.07.1986 | 5 | (2) | |
| Ryan Bidounga (CGO) | 29.04.1997 | 3 | (1) | |
| Steeve Furtado Pereira (CPV) | 22.11.1994 | 21 | (5) | |
| Angel Granchov | 16.10.1992 | 2 | (1) | |
| *Héliton* Jorge Tito dos Santos (BRA) | 13.11.1995 | 25 | (2) | 4 |
| *Johnathan* Carlos Pereira (BRA) | 04.04.1995 | 19 | (4) | 1 |
| Angel Lyaskov | 16.03.1998 | 13 | (10) | |
| Lazar Marin | 09.02.1994 | 10 | (2) | |
| Simeon Petrov | 12.01.2000 | 18 | (1) | |
| *Sidcley* Ferreira Pereira (BRA) | 13.05.1993 | 9 | | |
| *Tiago Barbosa* Figueiredo (BRA) | 12.02.2001 | 1 | | |
| Stefan Tsonkov | 24.01.1995 | 1 | (1) | |
| **Midfielders:** | **DOB** | **M** | **(s)** | **G** |
| Ivaylo Chochev | 18.02.1993 | 30 | (1) | 21 |
| Reyan Daskalov | 10.02.1995 | 21 | (6) | |

| | DOB | M | (s) | G |
|---|---|---|---|---|
| *Octávio* Merlo Manteca (BRA) | 29.12.1993 | 16 | (14) | |
| Carlos Ohene (GHA) | 21.07.1993 | 13 | (4) | |
| Emil Tsenov | 26.04.2002 | 3 | (4) | |
| Parvizdzhon Umarbaev (TJK) | 01.11.1994 | 23 | (3) | 4 |
| **Forwards:** | **DOB** | **M** | **(s)** | **G** |
| Denislav Aleksandrov | 19.07.1997 | 1 | (7) | |
| Preslav Antonov | 02.10.1996 | | (2) | |
| Angel Bastunov | 15.05.1999 | 11 | (12) | 3 |
| Svetoslav Dikov | 18.04.1992 | 5 | (8) | 1 |
| *Henrique* Roberto Rafael (BRA) | 23.08.1993 | 5 | (6) | 1 |
| Birsent Karagaren | 06.12.1992 | 6 | (5) | 2 |
| Radoslav Kirilov | 29.06.1992 | 15 | (10) | 2 |
| Aleksandar Kolev | 08.12.1992 | 17 | (7) | 2 |
| Pedro Henrique Oliveira dos Santos „Pedrinho" (BRA) | 19.12.1996 | 8 | (5) | 3 |
| Georgi Rusev | 02.07.1998 | 27 | (7) | 7 |
| Yevgeniy Serdyuk (UKR) | 24.04.1998 | 9 | (2) | 3 |
| Stoyan Stoichkov | 18.07.2003 | | (2) | |
| Mario Topuzov | 25.07.1999 | 13 | (14) | |
| Valentin Yoskov | 05.06.1998 | | (1) | |

## Football Club Hebar Pazardzhik

**Founded**: 31.05.1918
**Stadium**: Stadion „Georgi Benkovski", Pazardzhik (13,128)
**Trainer**: Fulvio Pea (ITA)    26.08.1967
[23.09.2022]   Vladimir Manchev    06.10.1977
[21.03.2023]   Lyuboslav Penev    31.08.1966

| Goalkeepers: | DOB | M | (s) | G |
|---|---|---|---|---|
| Petar Debarliev | 19.06.1991 | 30 | (1) | |
| Zvonimir Mikulić (CRO) | 05.02.1990 | 2 | | |
| Khadim Ndiaye (SEN) | 12.04.2000 | 3 | | |
| **Defenders:** | **DOB** | **M** | **(s)** | **G** |
| Claudio Bonanni (ITA) | 05.03.1997 | 9 | (3) | |
| Hlib Bukhal (UKR) | 12.11.1995 | 14 | | 1 |
| Kamen Hadzhiev | 22.09.1991 | 5 | | |
| Arhan Isuf | 25.01.1999 | 8 | (4) | |
| Milan Kremenović (GER) | 08.03.2002 | | (1) | |
| Plamen Krumov | 04.11.1985 | 12 | (2) | 1 |
| *Mauro* Rafael Geral *Cerqueira* (POR) | 20.08.1992 | 4 | (3) | |
| Róbert Mazáň (SVK) | 09.02.1994 | 19 | (2) | |
| Martin Mihaylov | 03.01.2000 | 25 | (4) | |
| Nikolay Nikolaev | 19.03.1997 | 8 | (3) | |
| Kornel Osyra (POL) | 07.02.1993 | 25 | (2) | |
| Moussa Sylla (FRA) | 15.03.1999 | 8 | (7) | |
| Georgi Tartov | 03.12.1998 | 29 | (3) | 6 |
| Tsvetelin Tonev | 03.01.1992 | 8 | (4) | 1 |
| Stefan Tsonkov | 24.01.1995 | 12 | (2) | 3 |

| Midfielders: | DOB | M | (s) | G |
|---|---|---|---|---|
| Alejandro „*Álex*" *Serrano* García (ESP) | 06.02.1995 | 22 | | 1 |
| Bogomil Bozhurkin | 02.09.2002 | 12 | (6) | |
| Bojan Knežević (CRO) | 28.01.1997 | 6 | (2) | |
| Oleksiy Lobov | 16.08.1997 | 6 | (4) | |
| Emanuil Manev | 19.04.1992 | 7 | (2) | |
| Vincent Jean-Pierre Marcel (FRA) | 09.04.1997 | 22 | (4) | 2 |
| Stiliyan Tisovski | 01.10.2003 | 1 | (9) | |
| Georgi Valchev | 07.03.1991 | 11 | (1) | 1 |
| **Forwards:** | **DOB** | **M** | **(s)** | **G** |
| Todor Chavorski | 30.03.1993 | 6 | (2) | 1 |
| Aderinsola Khabib Eseola (UKR) | 28.06.1991 | 4 | (11) | |
| Oktai Hamdiev | 24.07.2000 | 30 | (3) | 2 |
| Loren Maružin (CRO) | 04.12.1997 | 5 | (12) | 1 |
| Ivaylo Mihaylov | 28.07.2000 | 8 | (9) | 2 |
| Patrik Ngingi Mavlyutova (COD) | 19.06.2003 | | (1) | |
| Mark-Emilio Papazov | 08.10.2003 | 2 | (11) | 2 |
| Stoyan Stoichkov | 18.07.2003 | 6 | (5) | 1 |
| Arsenio Jermaine Cedric Valpoort (NED) | 05.08.1992 | 11 | (7) | 3 |
| Ante Živković (CRO) | 21.05.1993 | 5 | (9) | 1 |

## Professional Football Club Levski Sofia

**Founded**: 24.05.1914
**Stadium**: Stadion Vivacom Arena „Georgi Asparuhov", Sofia (25,000)
**Trainer**: Stanimir Stoilov    13.02.1967
[12.04.2023]   Elin Topuzakov    05.02.1977

| Goalkeepers: | DOB | M | (s) | G |
|---|---|---|---|---|
| Plamen Andreev | 15.12.2004 | 32 | | |
| Nikolay Mihaylov | 28.06.1988 | 3 | | |
| **Defenders:** | **DOB** | **M** | **(s)** | **G** |
| Ante Blažević (CRO) | 05.05.1996 | 1 | | |
| José Ángel Córdoba Chambers (PAN) | 03.06.2001 | 25 | | |
| Kristian Dimitrov | 27.02.1997 | 2 | (6) | |
| Jérémy Arnaud Pétris (FRA) | 28.01.1998 | 22 | (3) | 1 |
| Noah Sonko Sundberg (GAM) | 06.06.1996 | 32 | | |
| Kellian van der Kaap (NED) | 08.11.1998 | 17 | (10) | |
| Wenderson de Freitas Soares „Tsunami"(BRA) | 04.01.1996 | 30 | (1) | 1 |
| **Midfielders:** | **DOB** | **M** | **(s)** | **G** |
| Asen Chandarov | 13.11.1998 | 5 | (11) | 2 |
| Patrick-Gabriel Galchev | 14.04.2001 | 8 | (6) | 1 |
| Nathan Christopher Adam Holder (CUW) | 02.05.2002 | | (3) | |
| Adrian Kraev | 14.02.1999 | 27 | (3) | 2 |

| | DOB | M | (s) | G |
|---|---|---|---|---|
| Filip Krastev | 15.10.2001 | 32 | (1) | 8 |
| David Mihalev | 27.03.2006 | | (2) | |
| Asen Mitkov | 17.02.2005 | 1 | (14) | |
| Ivelin Popov | 26.10.1987 | 23 | (4) | 5 |
| Borislav Rupanov | 01.08.2004 | 1 | (5) | |
| Abdullahi Shehu (NGA) | 12.03.1993 | 3 | (5) | |
| Iliyan Stefanov | 20.09.1998 | 13 | (12) | 4 |
| Kristiyan Yovov | 13.02.2006 | | (1) | |
| **Forwards:** | **DOB** | **M** | **(s)** | **G** |
| Bilal Bari (MAR) | 19.01.1998 | 3 | (3) | 2 |
| Jawad El Jemili Setti (ESP) | 04.09.2002 | 1 | (9) | |
| Georgi Milanov | 19.02.1992 | 15 | (3) | 2 |
| Marin Petkov | 02.10.2003 | 8 | (25) | 4 |
| Ricardo Viana Filho „Ricardinho" (BRA) | 23.04.2001 | 16 | | 9 |
| *Ronaldo* Cezar Soares dos Santos (BRA) | 07.12.2000 | 32 | (2) | 3 |
| *Welton* Felipe Paraguá de Melo (BRA) | 06.08.1997 | 33 | (1) | 3 |

## Professional Football Club Lokomotiv Plovdiv

**Founded**: 25.07.1926
**Stadium**: Stadion Lokomotiv, Plovdiv (8,610)
**Trainer**: Aleksandar Tomash    02.09.1978

| Goalkeepers: | DOB | M | (s) | G |
|---|---|---|---|---|
| Dinko Horkaš (CRO) | 10.03.1999 | 27 | | |
| Ilko Pirgov | 23.05.1986 | 7 | (2) | |
| Kristian Tomov | 17.08.2002 | 1 | | |
| **Defenders:** | **DOB** | **M** | **(s)** | **G** |
| Ryan Bidounga (FRA) | 29.04.1997 | 13 | | |
| Hristo Y. Ivanov | 16.12.2000 | 7 | (8) | |
| *Luan Leite* Da Silva (BRA) | 31.05.1996 | 3 | (5) | |
| *Matheus* de Barros da *Silva* (BRA) | 03.10.1997 | 30 | | 1 |
| Martin Paskalev | 25.12.2001 | 31 | (2) | 3 |
| Todor Pavlov | 16.06.2004 | 9 | (4) | |
| Miloš Petrović (SRB) | 05.05.1990 | 12 | (13) | |
| Jorge Andrés Segura Portocarrero (COL) | 18.01.1997 | 7 | (1) | 1 |
| Josip Tomašević (CRO) | 04.03.1994 | 22 | (7) | |
| Giovanni Troupée (CUW) | 20.03.1998 | 7 | (2) | |
| Aleksandar Vasilev | 27.04.1995 | 8 | (8) | |
| **Midfielders:** | **DOB** | **M** | **(s)** | **G** |
| Petar Andreev | 02.07.2004 | 1 | (7) | |

| | DOB | M | (s) | G |
|---|---|---|---|---|
| Hristo B. Ivanov | 05.12.2000 | | (5) | |
| Georgi Karakashev | 08.02.1999 | 18 | (13) | |
| Cristhian Alexander Mendoza Pineda (VEN) | 07.05.2002 | 1 | (3) | |
| Ivan Mihaylov | 28.10.2003 | | (4) | |
| Petar Vitanov | 10.03.1995 | 17 | (3) | |
| Pierre Zebli (CIV) | 06.12.1997 | 30 | (1) | |
| **Forwards:** | **DOB** | **M** | **(s)** | **G** |
| Denislav Aleksandrov | 19.07.1997 | 3 | (8) | |
| Preslav Borukov | 23.04.2000 | 13 | (5) | 3 |
| Ivaylo Dimitrov | 26.03.1989 | 2 | (15) | 1 |
| Babacar Dione (BEL) | 22.03.1997 | 30 | (5) | 4 |
| *Ewandro* Felipe de Lima Costa (BRA) | 15.03.1996 | 4 | (7) | |
| *Giovanny* Bariani Marques (BRA) | 19.09.1997 | 19 | (7) | 8 |
| Dimitar Iliev | 25.09.1988 | 34 | (1) | 4 |
| Birsent Karagaren | 06.12.1992 | 17 | | 6 |
| Erik Sorga (EST) | 08.07.1999 | 12 | (2) | 2 |
| Alex Velev | 26.01.2007 | | (3) | |

## Football Club Lokomotiv 1929 Sofia

**Founded**: 02.09.1929
**Stadium**: Stadion Lokomotiv, Sofia (22,000)
**Trainer**: Stanislav Genchev      20.03.1981

| Goalkeepers: | DOB | M | (s) | G |
|---|---|---|---|---|
| Baboucarr Gaye (GAM) | 24.02.1998 | 12 | (1) | |
| Aleksandar Lyubenov | 11.02.1995 | 24 | | |
| **Defenders:** | **DOB** | **M** | **(s)** | **G** |
| *Alan* Carlos de Paula *Dias* Filho (BRA) | 05.09.1998 | 28 | (1) | 2 |
| *Bruno* Alexandre *Franco* (BRA) | 10.04.1998 | 11 | (5) | |
| *Celso* Daniel Caeiro *Raposo* (POR) | 03.04.1996 | 29 | (4) | 1 |
| Kamen Hadzhiev | 22.09.1991 | 10 | (1) | |
| Luka Ivanov | 31.12.2003 | 7 | (9) | |
| *Kadu* Ribeiro Durval (BRA) | 09.02.1997 | 1 | | |
| Bozhidar Katsarov | 30.12.1993 | 28 | (2) | 1 |
| David Zeferino Malembana (MOZ) | 11.10.1995 | 15 | (3) | 2 |
| *Matheus Duarte* Rocha (BRA) | 12.05.1995 | 23 | (5) | |
| Miki Orachev | 19.03.1996 | 9 | (3) | |
| Mario Petkov | 04.12.1996 | 6 | (8) | |

| Midfielders: | DOB | M | (s) | G |
|---|---|---|---|---|
| Hristian Chipev | 23.07.2001 | 1 | (7) | |
| Teodor Ivanov | 04.05.2004 | | (4) | |
| Krasimir Miloshev | 05.04.2000 | 33 | | 3 |
| Ivaylo Naydenov | 22.03.1998 | 18 | (7) | 1 |
| Martin Raynov | 25.04.1992 | 9 | (4) | |
| Simeon Slavchev | 25.09.1993 | 16 | | |
| Antonio Vutov | 06.06.1996 | 26 | (2) | 5 |
| **Forwards:** | **DOB** | **M** | **(s)** | **G** |
| Aleksandar Aleksandrov | 28.03.1994 | 2 | (8) | |
| Dimo Bakalov | 19.12.1988 | 16 | (15) | 3 |
| Iliya Dimitrov | 10.07.1996 | 5 | (13) | 3 |
| Carlos Henrique *França* Freires (BRA) | 09.02.1995 | 32 | (2) | 5 |
| Stanislav Kostov | 02.10.1991 | 9 | (9) | 1 |
| Dimitar Mitkov | 27.01.2000 | 14 | (3) | 7 |
| Yulian Nenov | 17.11.1994 | 12 | (9) | 2 |
| Valentin Nikolov | 15.10.2003 | | (8) | |

## Professional Football Club Ludogorets Razgrad

**Founded**: 1945
**Stadium**: Huvepharma Arena, Razgrad (10,442)
**Trainer**: Ante Šimundža (SVN)      28.09.1971
[07.03.2023]    Ivaylo Petev      09.07.1975

| Goalkeepers: | DOB | M | (s) | G |
|---|---|---|---|---|
| Sergio Padt (NED) | 06.06.1990 | 32 | | |
| Simon Sluga (CRO) | 17.03.1993 | 3 | | |
| **Defenders:** | **DOB** | **M** | **(s)** | **G** |
| Neuciano de Jesus Gusmão „Cicinho" | 26.12.1988 | 8 | (5) | 1 |
| Žan Karničnik (SVN) | 18.09.1994 | 5 | | |
| Anton Nedyalkov | 30.04.1993 | 14 | (2) | |
| Gonzalo Ávila Gordón "Pipa" (ESP) | 26.01.1998 | 11 | (2) | |
| Igor Plastun (UKR) | 20.08.1990 | 20 | (6) | |
| Franco Matías Russo Panos (ARG) | 25.10.1994 | 14 | | 1 |
| Georgi Terziev | 18.04.1992 | 7 | (3) | 1 |
| Olivier Verdon (BEN) | 05.10.1995 | 25 | | 1 |
| Aslak Fonn Witry (NOR) | 10.03.1996 | 22 | (2) | |
| **Midfielders:** | **DOB** | **M** | **(s)** | **G** |
| *Alex* Paulo Menezes *Santana* (BRA) | 13.05.1995 | 3 | | 1 |
| *Cauly* Oliveira-Souza (BRA) | 15.09.1995 | 11 | (5) | 5 |
| Joaquim *Claude* Gonçalves Araújo (POR) | 09.04.1994 | 10 | (9) | 1 |
| Danny Gruper (ISR) | 16.03.1999 | 13 | (2) | |
| Todor Nedelev | 07.02.1993 | 5 | | 1 |
| *Pedro* Henrique *Naressi* Machado (BRA) | 10.01.1998 | 13 | (9) | |
| Jakub Piotrowski (POL) | 04.10.1997 | 21 | (9) | 3 |
| Manuel Luis da Silva Cafumana „Show" (ANG) | 06.03.1999 | 12 | (14) | 1 |
| Dominik Yankov | 28.07.2000 | 4 | (7) | |
| Ivan Yordanov | 07.11.2000 | 6 | (1) | 1 |
| **Forwards:** | **DOB** | **M** | **(s)** | **G** |
| *Caio Vidal* Rocha (BRA) | 04.11.2000 | 6 | (5) | 2 |
| Spas Delev | 22.09.1989 | 13 | (17) | 7 |
| Kiril Despodov | 11.11.1996 | 25 | (5) | 14 |
| Jorge Fernando Barbosa Intima „Jorghinho"(GNB) | 21.09.1995 | 1 | (2) | 1 |
| Gustavo *Nonato* Santana (BRA) | 03.03.1998 | 12 | (10) | 1 |
| *Rai Nascimento* De Oliveira (BRA) | 18.05.1998 | 1 | (6) | |
| *Rick* Jhonatan Lima Morais (BRA) | 02.09.1999 | 15 | (2) | 2 |
| Pieros Sotiriou (CYP) | 13.01.1993 | | (2) | 1 |
| Bernard Tekpetey (GHA) | 03.09.1997 | 18 | (9) | 8 |
| Igor *Thiago* Nascimento Rodrigues (BRA) | 26.06.2001 | 22 | (10) | 15 |
| Matías Fabián Tissera (ARG) | 06.09.1996 | 13 | (14) | 12 |

## Obshtinski futbolen klub Pirin Blagoevgrad

**Founded**: 1922
**Stadium**: Stadion „Hristo Bonev", Blagoevgrad (7,500)
**Trainer**: Krasimir Petrov      08.07.1981
[18.10.2022]    Svetoslav Dyakov      31.05.1984
[25.10.2022]    Hristo Yanev      04.05.1979

| Goalkeepers: | DOB | M | (s) | G |
|---|---|---|---|---|
| Yanko Georgiev | 22.10.1988 | 26 | | |
| Maksym Kovalov (UKR) | 11.07.2000 | 9 | (2) | |
| **Defenders:** | **DOB** | **M** | **(s)** | **G** |
| Martin Bachev | 28.06.2004 | 4 | (7) | |
| Marsel Bibishkov | 11.04.2007 | | (2) | |
| Nikolay Bodurov | 30.05.1986 | 12 | | |
| Ilker Budinov | 11.08.2000 | 7 | (3) | 1 |
| Alexander Dyulgerov | 19.04.1990 | 29 | | |
| Hristofor Hubchev | 24.11.1995 | 17 | | |
| Ilijan Kostov | 27.02.2005 | 2 | | |
| Julian Popev | 07.07.1986 | 2 | (7) | |
| Rayan Senhadji (FRA) | 13.06.1997 | 15 | | |
| Vyacheslav Velev (UKR) | 21.05.2000 | 24 | (2) | 1 |
| Emil Yanchev | 08.02.1999 | 2 | (6) | |
| Aizu Yuki (JPN) | 01.08.1996 | | (4) | |
| Petar Zanev | 18.10.1985 | 13 | (1) | |
| **Midfielders:** | **DOB** | **M** | **(s)** | **G** |
| Ventsislav Bengyuzov | 22.01.1991 | 25 | (5) | 2 |
| Čebrails Makreckis (LVA) | 10.05.2000 | 22 | (1) | 1 |
| Vladimir Medved (BLR) | 04.11.1999 | 1 | (2) | |
| Alex Pedinsky | 29.04.2006 | | (1) | |
| Dmytro Semeniv (UKR) | 24.06.1998 | 12 | (5) | 1 |
| Slavcho Shokolarov | 20.08.1989 | 16 | (12) | |
| Martin Smolenski | 08.03.2003 | 17 | (13) | 2 |
| Krasimir Stanoev | 14.09.1994 | 11 | (2) | 1 |
| Kazuki Takahashi (JPN) | 06.10.1996 | 7 | (6) | |
| Dimitar Tonev | 15.10.2001 | 8 | (2) | |
| Radoslav Tsonev | 29.04.1995 | 12 | | 2 |
| Andrey Yordanov | 06.09.2001 | 26 | (1) | 1 |
| **Forwards:** | **DOB** | **M** | **(s)** | **G** |
| Daniel Ivanov | 22.02.2002 | | (3) | |
| Danylo Kondrakov (UKR) | 19.01.1998 | 17 | | 5 |
| Stanislav Kostov | 02.10.1991 | 10 | (5) | 2 |
| Ivan Tasev | 27.04.2002 | 21 | (9) | 2 |
| Lyubomir Todorov | 13.01.2005 | | (5) | |
| Boris Tyutyukov | 28.10.1997 | 2 | (14) | 1 |
| Kitan Vasilev | 19.02.1997 | 5 | (7) | 1 |
| Preslav Yordanov | 21.07.1989 | 11 | (13) | 4 |

## Professional Football Club Septemvri Sofia

**Founded**: 05.11.1944
**Stadium**: Nationalen Stadion "Vasil Levski", Sofia (43,230)
**Trainer**: Slavko Matić (SRB) — 02.07.1976
[09.10.2022] Svetoslav Petrov — 12.02.1978
[05.05.2023] Krasimir Balakov — 29.03.1966

| Goalkeepers: | DOB | M | (s) | G |
|---|---|---|---|---|
| Dimitar Sheytanov | 15.03.1999 | 34 | | |
| Ivan Vasilev | 07.01.2000 | 1 | | |
| **Defenders:** | **DOB** | **M** | **(s)** | **G** |
| Martin Achkov | 10.07.1999 | 15 | (9) | |
| Ivan Arsov | 29.09.2000 | 24 | (1) | |
| Konstantin Cheshmedijev (MKD) | 29.01.1996 | 10 | (1) | |
| Petar Čuić (CRO) | 02.06.1999 | 12 | (2) | |
| Asen Georgiev | 09.07.1993 | 26 | (1) | 1 |
| Kubrat Jonashču | 06.07.2006 | 1 | (1) | |
| Stefan Milić (MNE) | 06.07.2000 | 8 | | |
| Martin Nikolov | 10.10.1993 | 17 | (7) | |
| Mikhail Polendakov | 06.05.2007 | | (4) | |
| Martin Stoychev | 17.10.2003 | 14 | | |
| Aleksandar Todorov | 25.06.2001 | 14 | (6) | |
| **Midfielders:** | **DOB** | **M** | **(s)** | **G** |
| Zahari Atanasov | 31.01.2005 | 1 | (4) | |
| Asen Chandarov | 13.11.1998 | 10 | (3) | 1 |
| Mirza Delimeđac (SRB) | 24.10.1999 | 4 | (3) | |
| Yoan Gavrilov | 25.01.1999 | 9 | (8) | |
| Sebastian Jakubiak (GER) | 21.06.1993 | 6 | (4) | |
| Redi Kasa (ITA) | 01.09.2001 | 4 | (10) | 1 |
| Krasian Kolev | 18.01.2004 | 15 | (2) | 1 |
| Dimitar Kostadinov | 14.08.1999 | 17 | (11) | 3 |
| Iliya Milanov | 19.02.1992 | 5 | (1) | |
| Mitko Mitkov | 28.08.2000 | 4 | (6) | 1 |
| Aleksandar Petrov | 19.04.2005 | | (4) | |
| Aykut Ramadan | 10.07.1998 | 10 | (14) | |
| Valentin Spasov | 27.06.1905 | | (1) | |
| Krasimir Stanoev | 14.09.1994 | 14 | (1) | 1 |
| Viktor Zorov | 26.11.2001 | 1 | (1) | |
| **Forwards:** | **DOB** | **M** | **(s)** | **G** |
| Simeon Aleksandrov | 24.09.2003 | 19 | (4) | 5 |
| Atanas Kabov | 11.04.1999 | 20 | (10) | 6 |
| Borislav Marinov | 02.03.2005 | | (3) | |
| Kristiyan Peshov | 16.06.1997 | 17 | (1) | 2 |
| Martin Petkov | 15.08.2002 | 20 | (6) | 4 |
| Martin Stojanov (MKD) | 03.03.1999 | 24 | (5) | |
| Vlatko Stojanovski (MKD) | 23.04.1997 | 4 | (4) | |
| Valentin Yoskov | 05.06.1998 | 5 | (10) | 2 |
| Radoslav Zhivkov | 27.03.1999 | | (7) | |

## Professional Football Club Slavia Sofia

**Founded**: 10.04.1913
**Stadium**: Stadion „Aleksandar Shalamanov", Sofia (25,556)
**Trainer**: Zlatomir Zagorčić — 15.06.1971
[04.05.2023] Angel Slavkov — 17.11.1962

| Goalkeepers: | DOB | M | (s) | G |
|---|---|---|---|---|
| Nikolay Krastev | 06.12.1996 | 7 | | |
| Georgi Petkov | 14.03.1976 | 1 | | |
| Svetoslav Vutsov | 09.07.2002 | 28 | | |
| **Defenders:** | **DOB** | **M** | **(s)** | **G** |
| Konstantin Cheshmedijev (MKD) | 29.01.1996 | 4 | (8) | |
| Nathan Gassama (FRA) | 05.01.2001 | 13 | (5) | |
| Veljko Jelenković (SRB) | 05.06.2003 | 10 | (3) | |
| Ventsislav Kerchev | 02.06.1997 | 22 | (7) | |
| Hristo Popadiyn | 06.01.1994 | 10 | (9) | |
| Ludovic Soares (FRA) | 08.05.1994 | 32 | (2) | |
| Ertan Tombak | 30.05.1999 | 30 | | |
| Emil Viyachki | 18.05.1990 | 34 | | 2 |
| **Midfielders:** | **DOB** | **M** | **(s)** | **G** |
| Erol Dost | 30.05.1999 | 15 | (16) | 2 |
| Galin Ivanov | 15.04.1988 | 31 | (1) | 4 |
| *Jon Bakero* González (ESP) | 05.11.1996 | 5 | | 2 |
| Ivan Minchev | 28.05.1991 | 9 | (11) | 1 |
| Kemelho Nguena (FRA) | 10.07.2000 | 15 | (3) | 4 |
| Nguyen Do Chung Thang | 23.05.2005 | 6 | (10) | |
| Valentin Petrov | 14.02.2004 | | (2) | |
| Emil Stoev | 17.01.1996 | 17 | (13) | 2 |
| Darko Tasevski (MKD) | 20.05.1984 | 4 | (4) | |
| Georgi Valchev | 07.03.1991 | 8 | (3) | |
| **Forwards:** | **DOB** | **M** | **(s)** | **G** |
| Ahmed Ahmedov | 04.03.1995 | 17 | (15) | 4 |
| Kristian Dobrev | 27.04.2001 | 14 | (11) | 3 |
| Radoslav Kirilov | 29.06.1992 | 5 | | 1 |
| Vladimir Nikolov | 07.02.2001 | 7 | (9) | 2 |
| Roberto Raychev | 07.12.2005 | | (4) | 1 |
| Martin Sorakov | 23.10.2003 | | (5) | |
| Kristian Stoyanov | 29.03.2003 | 20 | (6) | |
| Toni Tasev | 25.03.1994 | 32 | (3) | 7 |

## Football Club Spartak 1918 Varna

**Founded**: 28.08.1918 (*as SC Balgarski Sokol*)
**Stadium**: Stadion Spartak, Varna (7,500)
**Trainer**: Vasil Petrov — 05.10.1986
[11.08.2022] Georgi Ivanov — 22.05.1967
[23.08.2022] Todor Kiselichkov — 04.09.1975
[28.11.2022] Dimitar Dimitrov — 09.06.1959

| Goalkeepers: | DOB | M | (s) | G |
|---|---|---|---|---|
| *Cristiano* Pereira Figueiredo (POR) | 29.11.1990 | 14 | | |
| Ivan Dichevski | 24.04.2001 | 20 | | |
| Hristiyan Hristov | 09.04.1995 | 1 | | |
| **Defenders:** | **DOB** | **M** | **(s)** | **G** |
| Velislav Boev | 19.12.2003 | 6 | (5) | |
| Nikola Borisov | 21.11.2000 | 16 | (2) | 1 |
| Ilker Budinov | 11.08.2000 | 8 | (1) | |
| Plamen Dimov | 29.10.1990 | 17 | (5) | 1 |
| Sami El Anabi (BEL) | 21.06.2000 | 4 | (2) | |
| *Emanuel* Leone Moura (BRA) | 01.11.1999 | 8 | | |
| Ibryam Ibryam | 12.01.2001 | 4 | (2) | |
| Ben Karamoko (CIV) | 17.05.1995 | 12 | (3) | |
| *Luan Leite* Da Silva (BRA) | 31.05.1996 | 8 | | 3 |
| Prosper Mendy (FRA) | 07.06.1996 | 7 | (5) | |
| **Midfielders:** | **DOB** | **M** | **(s)** | **G** |
| Yancho Andreev | 08.01.1990 | 7 | (7) | |
| Alexandr Belousov (MDA) | 14.05.1998 | 10 | (5) | |
| Ruslan Chernenko (UKR) | 29.09.1992 | 5 | (2) | |
| Georgi Chukalov | 25.02.1998 | | (3) | |
| Nathan Christopher Adam Holder (CUW) | 02.05.2002 | | (4) | |
| Tsvetan Iliev | 29.04.1990 | 7 | (4) | |
| Nikolay Ivanov | 28.04.1995 | | (4) | |
| Ivaylo Klimentov | 03.02.1998 | 13 | (9) | 1 |
| Genadi Lugo | 06.05.1989 | 2 | (4) | |
| Daniel Nachev | 20.09.2003 | | (8) | |
| Roberto Manuel Sierra Giménez „Rober"(ESP) | 21.05.1996 | 17 | | |
| Rumen Rumenov | 07.06.1993 | 17 | (5) | 4 |
| Aleksandar Tsvetkov | 31.08.1990 | 16 | | |
| Bozhidar Vasev | 14.03.1993 | 16 | (5) | 2 |
| Ivan Yordanov | 07.11.2000 | 15 | (1) | 1 |
| **Forwards:** | **DOB** | **M** | **(s)** | **G** |
| Rodney Antwi (NED) | 03.11.1995 | 8 | (8) | 1 |
| Georgi Babaliev | 14.05.2001 | 4 | (6) | 1 |
| Denis Balanyuk (UKR) | 16.01.1997 | 12 | (12) | 5 |
| Zdravko Dimitrov | 24.08.1998 | 10 | (1) | 1 |
| *Ewandro* Felipe de Lima Costa (BRA) | 15.03.1996 | 11 | (4) | 5 |
| Romeesh Nathaniel Ivey Belgrave (PAN) | 14.07.1994 | 21 | (2) | 1 |
| *João Mário* Nunes Fernandes (GNB) | 11.10.1993 | 7 | (4) | 2 |
| Liandro Felipe Martis (CUW) | 13.11.1995 | 3 | (5) | |
| Mehmed Mehmed | 12.09.1998 | 8 | (6) | |
| Leroy-Jacques Mickels (GER) | 25.06.1995 | 15 | (2) | 1 |
| Viktor Mitev | 15.02.1992 | 31 | (3) | 1 |
| Martin Toshev | 17.04.1990 | 5 | (2) | |

| | | | | | | | | | |
|---|---|---|---|---|---|---|---|---|---|
| 1. | FC CSKA 1948 Sofia II* | 34 | 22 | 8 | 4 | 60 | - | 17 | 74 |
| 2. | SFC Etar Veliko Tarnovo (*Promoted*) | 34 | 18 | 9 | 7 | 47 | - | 22 | 63 |
| 3. | FC Krumovgrad (*Promoted*) | 34 | 17 | 9 | 8 | 43 | - | 33 | 60 |
| 4. | PFC Ludogorets Razgrad II* | 34 | 17 | 6 | 11 | 42 | - | 35 | 57 |
| 5. | FC Sportist Svoge (*Promotion Play-offs*) | 34 | 14 | 10 | 10 | 41 | - | 40 | 52 |
| 6. | FC Dunav Ruse | 34 | 13 | 11 | 10 | 47 | - | 38 | 50 |
| 7. | FC Maritsa Plovdiv | 34 | 14 | 5 | 15 | 36 | - | 46 | 47 |
| 8. | FC Yantra Gabrovo | 34 | 11 | 11 | 12 | 31 | - | 34 | 44 |
| 9. | PFC Litex Lovech | 34 | 11 | 11 | 12 | 32 | - | 28 | 44 |
| 10. | FC Montana | 34 | 12 | 8 | 14 | 37 | - | 39 | 44 |
| 11. | OFK Spartak Pleven | 34 | 10 | 12 | 12 | 44 | - | 44 | 42 |
| 12. | OFC Belasitsa Petrich | 34 | 12 | 5 | 17 | 33 | - | 41 | 41 |
| 13. | FC Dobrudzha Dobrich | 34 | 10 | 9 | 15 | 38 | - | 40 | 39 |
| 14. | FC Strumska Slava Radomir | 34 | 9 | 12 | 13 | 35 | - | 44 | 39 |
| 15. | FC Minyor Pernik (*Relegated*) | 34 | 9 | 11 | 14 | 33 | - | 35 | 38 |
| 16. | FC Sozopol (*Relegated*) | 34 | 9 | 11 | 14 | 32 | - | 52 | 38 |
| 17. | FC Vitosha Bistritsa (*Relegated*) | 34 | 9 | 9 | 16 | 34 | - | 50 | 36 |
| 18. | PFC Botev Plovdiv II (*Relegated*) | 34 | 7 | 7 | 20 | 25 | - | 52 | 28 |

*Please note: reserve teams are not eligible for promotion.

## NATIONAL TEAM

### INTERNATIONAL MATCHES
#### (16.07.2022 – 15.07.2023)

| | | | | |
|---|---|---|---|---|
| 23.09.2022 | Razgrad | *Bulgaria - Gibraltar* | *5-1(2-1)* | (UNL) |
| 26.09.2022 | Skopje | *North Macedonia - Bulgaria* | *0-1(0-0)* | (UNL) |
| 16.11.2022 | Larnaca | *Cyprus - Bulgaria* | *0-2(0-1)* | (F) |
| 20.11.2022 | Lëtzebuerg | *Luxembourg - Bulgaria* | *0-0* | (F) |
| 24.03.2023 | Razgrad | *Bulgaria - Montenegro* | *0-1(0-0)* | (ECQ) |
| 27.03.2023 | Budapest | *Hungary - Bulgaria* | *3-0(3-0)* | (ECQ) |
| 17.06.2023 | Kaunas | *Lithuania - Bulgaria* | *1-1(1-1)* | (ECQ) |
| 20.06.2023 | Razgrad | *Bulgaria - Serbia* | *1-1(0-0)* | (ECQ) |

**23.09.2022    BULGARIA - GIBRALTAR      5-1(2-1)      3rd UEFA Nations League C, Group 4**
Huvepharma Arena, Razgrad; Referee: Pavel Orel (Czech Republic); Attendance: 1,540
**BUL:** Daniel Naumov, Anton Nedyalkov, Valentin Antov, Petko Hristov, Ilia Gruev (72.Yanis Karabelyov), Filip Krastev, Ivan Turitsov (60.Yoni Stoyanov), Marin Petkov, Iliyan Stefanov (72.Nikola Iliev), Radoslav Kirilov (83.Martin Minchev), Kiril Despodov (Cap) (60.Georgi Rusev). Trainer: Mladen Krstajić (Serbia).
**Goals:** Valentin Antov (23), Kiril Despodov (36), Radoslav Kirilov (52), Iliyan Stefanov (55), Marin Petkov (81).

**26.09.2022    NORTH MACEDONIA - BULGARIA      0-1(0-0)      3rd UEFA Nations League C, Group 4**
Nacionalna Arena "Toše Proeski", Skopje; Referee: Julian Weinberger (Austria); Attendance: 20,173
**BUL:** Daniel Naumov, Anton Nedyalkov, Valentin Antov, Plamen Galabov, Ilia Gruev, Yanis Karabelyov (46.Nikola Iliev), Viktor Popov (82.Yoni Stoyanov), Marin Petkov, Iliyan Stefanov (46.Filip Krastev), Radoslav Kirilov (89.Georgi Rusev), Kiril Despodov (Cap) (90+3.Ivan Yordanov). Trainer: Mladen Krstajić (Serbia).
**Goal:** Kiril Despodov (50).

**16.11.2022    CYPRUS - BULGARIA      0-2(0-1)      Friendly International**
AEK Arena "Georgios Karapatakis", Larnaca; Referee: Trustin Farrugia Cann (Malta); Attendance: 1,000
**BUL:** Daniel Naumov, Anton Nedyalkov (69.Valentin Antov), Petko Hristov, Dimo Krastev, Ilia Gruev (46.Yanis Karabelyov), Ilian Iliev (82.Georgi Rusev), Yoni Stoyanov (63.Ivan Turitsov), Nikola Iliev (46.Filip Krastev), Marin Petkov (62.Dimitar Velkovski), Spas Delev, Kiril Despodov (Cap). Trainer: Mladen Krstajić (Serbia).
**Goals:** Kiril Despodov (24), Spas Delev (71).

**20.11.2022    LUXEMBOURG - BULGARIA      0-0      Friendly International**
Stade de Luxembourg, Lëtzebuerg; Referee: Manfredas Lukjančukas (Lithuania); Attendance: 4,700
**BUL:** Svetoslav Vutsov, Yoni Stoyanov, Petko Hristov, Valentin Antov (74.Plamen Galabov), Anton Nedyalkov, Ilia Gruev, Filip Krastev (74.Yanis Karabelyov), Dimitar Velkovski (62.Marin Petkov), Radoslav Kirilov (62.Nikola Iliev), Spas Delev (46.Ilian Iliev), Kiril Despodov (Cap) (90.Georgi Rusev). Trainer: Mladen Krstajić (Serbia).

**24.03.2023    BULGARIA - MONTENEGRO      0-1(0-0)      17th EC. Qualifiers**
Huvepharma Arena, Razgrad; Referee: Əliyar Ağayev (Azerbaijan); Attendance: 21,125
**BUL:** Daniel Naumov, Hristiyan Petrov (60.Yanis Karabelyov), Valentin Antov, Petko Hristov, Ilia Gruev, Ilian Iliev (59.Nikola Iliev), Filip Krastev (77.Radoslav Kirilov), Yoni Stoyanov, Ivan Yordanov (85.Georgi Rusev), Spas Delev (85.Marin Petkov), Kiril Despodov (Cap). Trainer: Mladen Krstajić (Serbia).

**27.03.2023    HUNGARY - BULGARIA      3-0(3-0)      17th EC. Qualifiers**
Puskás Aréna, Budapest; Referee: Halil Umut Meler (Turkey); Attendance: 53,000
**BUL:** Daniel Naumov, Ivaylo Markov (46.Hristiyan Petrov), Valentin Antov, Plamen Galabov, Yoni Stoyanov, Ilia Gruev (85.Stanislav Shopov), Yanis Karabelyov (46.Filip Krastev), Nikola Iliev, Marin Petkov, Spas Delev (46.Georgi Rusev), Kiril Despodov (Cap) (57.Radoslav Kirilov). Trainer: Mladen Krstajić (Serbia).

**17.06.2023**  **LITHUANIA - BULGARIA**                    **1-1(1-1)**                              17th EC. Qualifiers
„Steponas Darius ir Stasys Girėnas" Stadionas, Kaunas; Referee: Jakob Alexander Sundberg (Denmark); Attendance: 14,230
**BUL:** Ivan Dyulgerov, Ilia Gruev, Valentin Antov, Aleks Petkov, Patrick-Gabriel Galchev (81.Yoni Stoyanov), Stanislav Shopov (46.Ivan Yordanov), Marin Petkov, Ivaylo Chochev, Martin Minchev (63.Iliyan Stefanov), Spas Delev (46.Nikola Iliev), Kiril Despodov (Cap) (74.Georgi Rusev). Trainer: Mladen Krstajić (Serbia).
**Goal:** Marin Petkov (27).

**20.06.2023**  **BULGARIA - SERBIA**                    **1-1(0-0)**                              17th EC. Qualifiers
Ludogorets Arena, Razgrad; Referee: Craig Pawson (England); Attendance: 6,700
**BUL:** Ivan Dyulgerov, Viktor Popov (86.Patrick-Gabriel Galchev), Petko Hristov, Valentin Antov, Ilia Gruev, Andrian Kraev, Ivaylo Chochev (66.Filip Krastev), Nikola Iliev (66.Iliyan Stefanov), Marin Petkov, Georgi Rusev (86.Simeon Petrov), Kiril Despodov (Cap) (78.Spas Delev). Trainer: Mladen Krstajić (Serbia).
**Goal:** Kiril Despodov (47).

| NATIONAL TEAM PLAYERS (16.07.2022 – 15.07.2023) | | | | |
|---|---|---|---|---|
| **Name** | **DOB** | **Caps** | **Goals** | *Club* |

| Goalkeepers | | | | |
|---|---|---|---|---|
| Ivan DYULGEROV | 15.07.1999 | 2 | 0 | 2023: | PFC Cherno More Varna |
| Daniel NAUMOV | 29.03.1998 | 8 | 0 | 2022/2023: | FC CSKA 1948 Sofia |
| Svetoslav VUTSOV | 09.07.2002 | 4 | 0 | 2022: | PFC Slavia Sofia |

| Defenders | | | | |
|---|---|---|---|---|
| Valentin ANTOV | 09.11.2000 | 19 | 1 | 2022/2023: | AC Monza (ITA) |
| Plamen GALABOV | 02.11.1995 | 5 | 0 | 2022/2023: | Maccabi Netanya FC (ISR) |
| Patrick-Gabriel GALCHEV | 14.04.2001 | 2 | 0 | 2023: | PFC Levski Sofia |
| Petko HRISTOV | 01.03.1999 | 19 | 0 | 2022: 26.01.2023-> | Speza Calcio La Spezia (ITA) Venezia FC (ITA) |
| Dimo KRASTEV | 10.02.2003 | 1 | 0 | 2022: | ACF Fiorentina (ITA) |
| Ivaylo MARKOV | 05.06.1997 | 1 | 0 | 2023: | TS Podbeskidzie Bielsko-Biała (POL) |
| Anton NEDYALKOV | 30.04.1993 | 28 | 0 | 2022: | PFC Ludogorets Razgrad |
| Aleks PETKOV | 25.07.1999 | 2 | 1 | 2023: | FC Arda Kardzhali |
| Hristiyan PETROV | 24.06.2002 | 2 | 0 | 2023: | PFC CSKA Sofia |
| Simeon PETROV | 12.01.2000 | 1 | 0 | 2023: | FC CSKA 1948 Sofia |
| Viktor POPOV | 05.03.2000 | 7 | 0 | 2022/2023: | PFC Cherno More Varna |
| Ivan TURITSOV | 18.07.1999 | 15 | 0 | 2022: | PFC CSKA Sofia |
| Dimitar VELKOVSKI | 22.01.1995 | 9 | 0 | 2022: | Cercle Brugge KSV (BEL) |

| Midfielders | | | | |
|---|---|---|---|---|
| Ivaylo CHOCHEV | 18.02.1993 | 37 | 4 | 2023: | FC CSKA 1948 Sofia |
| Ilia GRUEV | 06.05.2000 | 8 | 0 | 2022/2023: | SV Werder Bremen (GER) |
| Ilian ILIEV | 20.08.1999 | 10 | 0 | 2022/2023: | Apollon Limassol FC (CYP) |
| Nikola ILIEV | 06.06.2004 | 8 | 0 | 2022/2023: | FC Internazionale Milano (ITA) |
| Yanis KARABELYOV | 23.01.1996 | 12 | 0 | 2022/2023: | Kisvárda FC (HUN) |
| Andrian KRAEV | 14.02.1999 | 3 | 0 | 2023: | PFC Levski Sofia |
| Filip KRASTEV | 15.10.2001 | 11 | 0 | 2022/2023: | PFC Levski Sofia |
| Marin PETKOV | 02.10.2003 | 8 | 2 | 2022/2023: | PFC Levski Sofia |
| Stanislav SHOPOV | 23.02.2002 | 2 | 0 | 2023: | PFC CSKA Sofia |
| Iliyan STEFANOV | 20.09.1999 | 8 | 2 | 2022/2023: | PFC Levski Sofia |
| Yoni STOYANOV | 22.05.2001 | 7 | 0 | 2022/2023: | Hapoel Be'er Sheva FC (ISR) |
| Ivan YORDANOV | 07.11.2000 | 3 | 0 | 2022: 18.01.2023-> | PFC Ludogorets Razgrad FK Spartak 1918 Varna |

| Forwards | | | | |
|---|---|---|---|---|
| Spas DELEV | 22.09.1989 | 42 | 4 | 2022/2023: | PFC Ludogorets Razgrad |
| Kiril DESPODOV | 11.11.1996 | 39 | 10 | 2022/2023: | PFC Ludogorets Razgrad |
| Radoslav KIRILOV | 29.06.1992 | 12 | 2 | 2022/2023: | FC CSKA 1948 Sofia |
| Martin MINCHEV | 22.04.2001 | 12 | 0 | 2022/2023: | AC Sparta Praha (CZE) |
| Georgi RUSEV | 02.07.1998 | 8 | 0 | 2022/2023: | FC CSKA 1948 Sofia |

| Trainer | | | |
|---|---|---|---|
| Mladen KRSTAJIĆ (Serbia) [from 21.07.2022] | 04.03.1974 | 8 M; 3 W; 3 D; 2 L; 10-7 | |

# CROATIA

## The Country:
Republika Hrvatska (Republic of Croatia)
Capital: Zagreb
Surface: 56,594 km²
Inhabitants: 3,871,833 [2021]
Time: UTC+1

## The FA:
Hrvatski nogometni savez
Vukovarska 269A, 10000 Zagreb
Tel: +385 1 2361 555
Foundation date: 16.07.1941 (as Independent State of Croatia); 03.07.1992 (as Croatia)
Member of FIFA since: 1992
Member of UEFA since: 1993
Website: www.hns-cff.hr

## NATIONAL TEAM RECORDS

| RECORDS | | |
|---|---|---|
| **First international match:** | 02.04.1940, Zagreb: | Croatia – Switzerland 4-0 |
| **Most international caps:** | Luka Modrić | - 166 caps (since 2006) |
| **Most international goals:** | Davor Šuker | - 45 goals / 69 caps (1990-2002) |

| UEFA EUROPEAN CHAMPIONSHIP | |
|---|---|
| 1960 | - |
| 1964 | - |
| 1968 | - |
| 1972 | - |
| 1976 | - |
| 1980 | - |
| 1984 | - |
| 1988 | - |
| 1992 | - |
| 1996 | Final Tournament (Quarter-Finals) |
| 2000 | Qualifiers |
| 2004 | Final Tournament (Group Stage) |
| 2008 | Final Tournament (Quarter-Finals) |
| 2012 | Final Tournament (Group Stage) |
| 2016 | Final Tournament (Group Stage) |
| 2020 | Final Tournament (2nd Round of 16) |

| FIFA WORLD CUP | |
|---|---|
| 1930 | - |
| 1934 | - |
| 1938 | - |
| 1950 | - |
| 1954 | - |
| 1958 | - |
| 1962 | - |
| 1966 | - |
| 1970 | - |
| 1974 | - |
| 1978 | - |
| 1982 | - |
| 1986 | - |
| 1990 | - |
| 1994 | Did not enter |
| 1998 | Final Tournament (3rd Place) |
| 2002 | Final Tournament (Group Stage) |
| 2006 | Final Tournament (Group Stage) |
| 2010 | Qualifiers |
| 2014 | Final Tournament (Group Stage) |
| 2018 | Final Tournament (Runners-up) |
| 2022 | Final Tournament (3rd Place) |

| OLYMPIC TOURNAMENTS | |
|---|---|
| 1908 | - |
| 1912 | - |
| 1920 | - |
| 1924 | - |
| 1928 | - |
| 1936 | - |
| 1948 | - |
| 1952 | - |
| 1956 | - |
| 1960 | - |
| 1964 | - |
| 1968 | - |
| 1972 | - |
| 1976 | - |
| 1980 | - |
| 1984 | - |
| 1988 | - |
| 1992 | - |
| 1996 | Qualifiers |
| 2000 | Qualifiers |
| 2004 | Qualifiers |
| 2008 | Qualifiers |
| 2012 | Qualifiers |
| 2016 | Qualifiers |
| 2020 | Qualifiers |

*Please note: was part of Yugoslavia (1918-1941 and 1945-1991)*

| UEFA NATIONS LEAGUE | |
|---|---|
| 2018/2019 | League A (Group Stage) |
| 2020/2021 | League A (Group Stage) |
| 2022/2023 | League A (Group Stage -> Final Tournament: Runners-up) |

## CROATIAN CLUB HONOURS IN EUROPEAN CLUB COMPETITIONS:

| European Champion Clubs.Cup (1956-1992) / UEFA Champions League (1993-2023) | | |
|---|---|---|
| None | | |

| Fairs Cup (1858-1971) / UEFA Cup (1972-2009) / UEFA Europa League (2010-2023) | | |
|---|---|---|
| GNK Dinamo Zagreb* | 1 | 1966/1967 |

*represented Yugoslavia

| UEFA Europa Conference League (2021-2023) | | |
|---|---|---|
| None | | |

| UEFA Super Cup (1972-2022) | | |
|---|---|---|
| None | | |

| European Cup Winners' Cup 1961-1999* | | |
|---|---|---|
| None | | |

*defunct competition

| | CHAMPIONS | CUP WINNERS | BEST GOALSCORERS | |
|---|---|---|---|---|
| 1992 | HNK Hajduk Split | NK Inter Zaprešić | Ardian Kozniku (HNK Hajduk Split) | 12 |
| 1992/1993 | NK Croatia Zagreb | HNK Hajduk Split | Goran Vlaović (NK Croatia Zagreb) | 23 |
| 1993/1994 | HNK Hajduk Split | NK Croatia Zagreb | Goran Vlaović (NK Croatia Zagreb) | 29 |
| 1994/1995 | HNK Hajduk Split | HNK Hajduk Split | Robert Špehar (NK Osijek) | 23 |
| 1995/1996 | NK Croatia Zagreb | NK Croatia Zagreb | Igor Cvitanović (NK Croatia Zagreb) | 19 |
| 1996/1997 | NK Croatia Zagreb | NK Croatia Zagreb | Igor Cvitanović (NK Croatia Zagreb) | 20 |
| 1997/1998 | NK Croatia Zagreb | NK Croatia Zagreb | Mate Baturina (NK Zagreb) | 18 |
| 1998/1999 | NK Croatia Zagreb | NK Osijek | Joško Popović (HNK Šibenik) | 21 |
| 1999/2000 | GNK Dinamo Zagreb | HNK Hajduk Split | Tomo Šokota (GNK Dinamo Zagreb) | 21 |
| 2000/2001 | HNK Hajduk Split | GNK Dinamo Zagreb | Tomo Šokota (GNK Dinamo Zagreb) | 20 |
| 2001/2002 | NK Zagreb | GNK Dinamo Zagreb | Ivica Olić (NK Zagreb) | 21 |
| 2002/2003 | GNK Dinamo Zagreb | HNK Hajduk Split | Ivica Olić (GNK Dinamo Zagreb) | 16 |
| 2003/2004 | HNK Hajduk Split | GNK Dinamo Zagreb | Robert Špehar (NK Osijek) | 18 |
| 2004/2005 | HNK Hajduk Split | HNK Rijeka | Tomislav Erceg (HNK Rijeka) | 17 |
| 2005/2006 | GNK Dinamo Zagreb | HNK Rijeka | Ivan Bošnjak (GNK Dinamo Zagreb) | 22 |
| 2006/2007 | GNK Dinamo Zagreb | GNK Dinamo Zagreb | Eduardo (GNK Dinamo Zagreb) | 34 |
| 2007/2008 | GNK Dinamo Zagreb | GNK Dinamo Zagreb | Želimir Terkeš (BIH, NK Zadar) | 21 |
| 2008/2009 | GNK Dinamo Zagreb | GNK Dinamo Zagreb | Mario Mandžukić (GNK Dinamo Zagreb) | 16 |
| 2009/2010 | GNK Dinamo Zagreb | HNK Hajduk Split | Davor Vugrinec (NK Zagreb) | 18 |
| 2010/2011 | GNK Dinamo Zagreb | GNK Dinamo Zagreb | Ivan Krstanović (BIH, NK Zagreb) | 19 |
| 2011/2012 | GNK Dinamo Zagreb | GNK Dinamo Zagreb | Fatos Bećiraj (MNE, GNK Dinamo Zagreb) | 15 |
| 2012/2013 | GNK Dinamo Zagreb | HNK Hajduk Split | Leon Benko (HNK Rijeka) | 19 |
| 2013/2014 | GNK Dinamo Zagreb | HNK Rijeka | Duje Čop (GNK Dinamo Zagreb) | 22 |
| 2014/2015 | GNK Dinamo Zagreb | GNK Dinamo Zagreb | Andrej Kramarić (HNK Rijeka) | 21 |
| 2015/2016 | GNK Dinamo Zagreb | GNK Dinamo Zagreb | Ilija Nestorovski (MKD, NK Inter Zaprešić) | 25 |
| 2016/2017 | HNK Rijeka | HNK Rijeka | Márkó Futács (HUN, HNK Hajduk Split) | 18 |
| 2017/2018 | GNK Dinamo Zagreb | GNK Dinamo Zagreb | El Arabi Hillel Soudani (ALG, GNK Dinamo Zagreb) | 17 |
| 2018/2019 | GNK Dinamo Zagreb | HNK Rijeka | Mijo Caktaš (HNK Hajduk Split) | 19 |
| 2019/2020 | GNK Dinamo Zagreb | HNK Rijeka | Antonio Čolak (HNK Rijeka) Mijo Caktaš (HNK Hajduk Split) Mirko Marić (NK Osijek) | 20 |
| 2020/2021 | GNK Dinamo Zagreb | GNK Dinamo Zagreb | Ramón Nazareno Miérez (ARG, NK Osijek) | 22 |
| 2021/2022 | GNK Dinamo Zagreb | HNK Hajduk Split | Marko Livaja (HNK Hajduk Split) | 28 |
| 2022/2023 | GNK Dinamo Zagreb | HNK Hajduk Split | Marko Livaja (HNK Hajduk Split) | 19 |

Please note: GNK Dinamo Zagreb were called NK Croatia Zagreb between 1993 and 2000.

## NATIONAL CHAMPIONSHIP
### Hrvatski Telekom Prva liga 2022/2023
(15.07.2022 – 28.05.2023)

### Results

**Round 1** [15-17.07.2022]
Dinamo Zagreb - Lokomotiva Zagreb 3-2(2-2)
NK Osijek - HNK Gorica 2-1(0-0)
HNK Šibenik - HNK Rijeka 0-1(0-0)
NK Varaždin - Slaven Belupo 0-1(0-0)
NK Istra 1961 - Hajduk Split 0-2(0-1)

**Round 2** [22-24.07.2022]
NK Istra 1961 - NK Varaždin 1-2(0-0)
HNK Gorica - HNK Šibenik 0-0
Slaven Belupo - Dinamo Zagreb 1-5(1-3)
Lokomotiva Zagreb - NK Osijek 2-1(0-1)
Hajduk Split - Rijeka 2-0(0-0) [14.09.2022]

**Round 3** [29-31.07.2022]
HNK Šibenik - Lokomotiva Zagreb 2-1(1-0)
Dinamo Zagreb - NK Istra 1961 4-1(2-0)
NK Varaždin - Hajduk Split 0-2(0-2)
NK Osijek - Slaven Belupo 0-0
HNK Rijeka - HNK Gorica 1-1(1-0)

**Round 4** [05-07.08.2022]
NK Varaždin - Dinamo Zagreb 1-1(0-1)
Slaven Belupo - HNK Šibenik 0-0
NK Istra 1961 - NK Osijek 1-0(0-0)
Lokomotiva Zagreb - HNK Rijeka 3-1(2-1)
Hajduk Split - Gorica 3-1(1-1) [26.10.2022]

**Round 5** [12-14.08.2022]
HNK Šibenik - NK Istra 1961 0-0
HNK Gorica - Lokomotiva Zagreb 3-2(0-1)
Dinamo Zagreb - Hajduk Split 4-1(0-1)
NK Osijek - NK Varaždin 2-2(0-0)
HNK Rijeka - Slaven Belupo 0-1(0-0)

**Round 6** [19-21.08.2022]
Slaven Belupo - HNK Gorica 2-1(0-1)
NK Varaždin - HNK Šibenik 2-2(1-1)
Dinamo Zagreb - NK Osijek 5-2(1-1)
NK Istra 1961 - HNK Rijeka 1-1(1-1)
Hajduk Split - Lokomotiva Zagreb 2-1(2-0)

**Round 7** [26-28.08.2022]
HNK Gorica - NK Istra 1961 0-2(0-0)
Lokomotiva Zagreb - Slaven Belupo 0-1(0-0)
HNK Rijeka - NK Varaždin 1-2(0-0)
HNK Šibenik - Dinamo Zagreb 1-2(1-1)
NK Osijek - Hajduk Split 2-1(2-0)

**Round 8** [02-04.09.2022]
Dinamo Zagreb - HNK Rijeka 3-1(2-0)
NK Varaždin - HNK Gorica 2-1(2-0)
NK Osijek - HNK Šibenik 1-1(1-0)
NK Istra 1961 - Lokomotiva Zagreb 1-2(0-1)
Hajduk Split - Slaven Belupo 5-1(0-1)

**Round 9** [09-11.09.2022]
HNK Šibenik - Hajduk Split 1-1(0-0)
HNK Rijeka - NK Osijek 0-3(0-2)
HNK Gorica - Dinamo Zagreb 0-1(0-0)
Slaven Belupo - NK Istra 1961 0-3(0-2)
Lokomotiva Zagreb - NK Varaždin 1-2(0-0)

**Round 10** [16-18.09.2022]
Slaven Belupo - NK Varaždin 1-0(1-0)
HNK Gorica - NK Osijek 0-1(0-1)
Hajduk Split - NK Istra 1961 2-2(0-0)
HNK Rijeka - HNK Šibenik 0-0
Lokomotiva Zagreb - Dinamo Zagreb 1-2(1-1)

**Round 11** [30.09.-02.10.2022]
NK Varaždin - NK Istra 1961 1-1(1-0)
NK Osijek - Lokomotiva Zagreb 4-1(3-0)
Dinamo Zagreb - Slaven Belupo 4-1(1-0)
HNK Rijeka - Hajduk Split 0-1(0-0)
HNK Šibenik - HNK Gorica 1-1(0-1)

**Round 12** [07-09.10.2022]
Lokomotiva Zagreb - HNK Šibenik 1-1(0-0)
Hajduk Split - NK Varaždin 2-1(1-0)
Slaven Belupo - NK Osijek 0-4(0-3)
HNK Gorica - HNK Rijeka 0-2(0-0)
NK Istra - Dinamo Zagreb 1-0(0-0) [15.03.23]

**Round 13 [14-16.10.2022]**
HNK Šibenik - Slaven Belupo 0-2(0-0)
NK Osijek - NK Istra 1961 2-0(0-0)
HNK Gorica - Hajduk Split 0-1(0-0)
Dinamo Zagreb - NK Varaždin 3-1(0-1)
HNK Rijeka - Lokomotiva Zagreb 3-0(2-0)

**Round 14 [21-23.10.2022]**
Hajduk Split - Dinamo Zagreb 1-1(1-0)
Lokomotiva Zagreb - HNK Gorica 2-1(1-0)
NK Varaždin - NK Osijek 4-1(3-1)
NK Istra 1961 - HNK Šibenik 0-0
Slaven Belupo - HNK Rijeka 2-1(1-0)

**Round 15 [28-30.10.2022]**
HNK Šibenik - NK Varaždin 1-2(0-0)
HNK Rijeka - NK Istra 1961 0-1(0-0)
NK Osijek - Dinamo Zagreb 1-0(0-0)
HNK Gorica - Slaven Belupo 1-1(1-1)
Lokomotiva Zagreb - Hajduk Split 2-2(0-0)

**Round 16 [04-06.11.2022]**
NK Istra 1961 - HNK Gorica 1-0(0-0)
Slaven Belupo - Lokomotiva Zagreb 0-0
Hajduk Split - NK Osijek 3-1(1-1)
NK Varaždin - HNK Rijeka 0-3(0-0)
Dinamo Zagreb - HNK Šibenik 3-0(2-0)

**Round 17 [12-13.11.2022]**
Lokomotiva Zagreb - NK Istra 1961 2-0(1-0)
Slaven Belupo - Hajduk Split 2-2(0-2)
HNK Šibenik - NK Osijek 0-2(0-2)
HNK Rijeka - Dinamo Zagreb 2-7(0-4)
HNK Gorica - NK Varaždin 0-0 [18.01.2023]

**Round 18 [20-22.01.2023]**
NK Istra 1961 - Slaven Belupo 0-0
NK Osijek - HNK Rijeka 1-1(1-1)
Dinamo Zagreb - HNK Gorica 0-0
Hajduk Split - HNK Šibenik 2-1(1-1)
NK Varaždin - Lokomotiva Zagreb 0-0

**Round 19 [27-29.01.2023]**
NK Varaždin - Slaven Belupo 1-0(0-0)
HNK Šibenik - HNK Rijeka 1-2(1-1)
Dinamo Zagreb - Lokomotiva Zagreb 2-1(1-0)
NK Osijek - HNK Gorica 2-0(1-0)
NK Istra 1961 - Hajduk Split 3-0(1-0)

**Round 20 [03-05.02.2023]**
NK Istra 1961 - NK Varaždin 2-1(1-0)
Lokomotiva Zagreb - NK Osijek 1-0(1-0)
Slaven Belupo - Dinamo Zagreb 1-1(1-1)
HNK Gorica - HNK Šibenik 0-3(0-1)
Hajduk Split - HNK Rijeka 1-2(0-0)

**Round 21 [10-12.02.2023]**
Dinamo Zagreb - NK Istra 1961 1-0(1-0)
NK Varaždin - Hajduk Split 1-4(0-0)
NK Osijek - Slaven Belupo 0-0
HNK Šibenik - Lokomotiva Zagreb 0-4(0-2)
HNK Rijeka - HNK Gorica 2-0(0-0)

**Round 22 [17-19.02.2023]**
Slaven Belupo - HNK Šibenik 0-1(0-1)
NK Istra 1961 - NK Osijek 1-0(0-0)
Lokomotiva Zagreb - HNK Rijeka 1-2(0-1)
NK Varaždin - Dinamo Zagreb 1-3(0-0)
Hajduk Split - HNK Gorica 2-1(0-0)

**Round 23 [24-26.02.2023]**
HNK Šibenik - NK Istra 1961 0-0
HNK Gorica - Lokomotiva Zagreb 1-0(0-0)
HNK Rijeka - Slaven Belupo 0-1(0-0)
Dinamo Zagreb - Hajduk Split 4-0(3-0)
NK Osijek - NK Varaždin 0-1(0-1)

**Round 24 [03-05.03.2023]**
NK Istra 1961 - HNK Rijeka 0-2(0-1)
NK Varaždin - HNK Šibenik 2-0(1-0)
Slaven Belupo - HNK Gorica 1-1(0-0)
Hajduk Split - Lokomotiva Zagreb 3-4(1-2)
Dinamo Zagreb - NK Osijek 1-1(0-0)

**Round 25 [10-12.03.2023]**
HNK Gorica - NK Istra 1961 5-4(1-2)
Lokomotiva Zagreb - Slaven Belupo 1-0(0-0)
HNK Šibenik - Dinamo Zagreb 2-1(2-0)
HNK Rijeka - NK Varaždin 3-1(1-0)
NK Osijek - Hajduk Split 0-2(0-2)

**Round 26 [17-19.03.2023]**
NK Varaždin - HNK Gorica 2-1(0-0)
NK Osijek - HNK Šibenik 0-0
Hajduk Split - Slaven Belupo 1-0(0-0)
NK Istra 1961 - Lokomotiva Zagreb 0-0
Dinamo Zagreb - HNK Rijeka 1-0(0-0)

**Round 27 [31.03.-02.04.2023]**
Slaven Belupo - NK Istra 1961 2-0(1-0)
HNK Gorica - Dinamo Zagreb 1-1(0-0)
HNK Šibenik - Hajduk Split 2-3(0-1)
HNK Rijeka - NK Osijek 1-1(1-0)
Lokomotiva Zagreb - NK Varaždin 1-1(1-0)

**Round 28 [07-08.04.2023]**
Slaven Belupo - NK Varaždin 1-1(1-0)
Hajduk Split - NK Istra 1961 2-2(2-2)
HNK Gorica - NK Osijek 2-0(0-0)
Lokomotiva Zagreb - Dinamo Zagreb 1-2(1-0)
HNK Rijeka - HNK Šibenik 1-0(0-0)

**Round 29 [14-16.04.2023]**
HNK Šibenik - HNK Gorica 0-4(0-4)
NK Osijek - Lokomotiva Zagreb 2-2(1-1)
Dinamo Zagreb - Slaven Belupo 4-0(3-0)
NK Varaždin - NK Istra 1961 0-0
HNK Rijeka - Hajduk Split 2-0(1-0)

**Round 30 [21-23.04.2023]**
Lokomotiva Zagreb - HNK Šibenik 1-0(0-0)
Slaven Belupo - NK Osijek 2-1(0-0)
NK Istra 1961 - Dinamo Zagreb 0-0
Hajduk Split - NK Varaždin 2-0(1-0)
HNK Gorica - HNK Rijeka 1-0(0-0)

**Round 31 [25-27.04.2023]**
HNK Šibenik - Slaven Belupo 3-1(2-0)
NK Osijek - NK Istra 1961 1-0(0-0)
Dinamo Zagreb - NK Varaždin 2-0(1-0)
HNK Gorica - Hajduk Split 0-0
HNK Rijeka - Lokomotiva Zagreb 2-0(0-0)

**Round 32 [29.04.-01.05.2023]**
NK Istra 1961 - HNK Šibenik 3-0(1-0)
NK Varaždin - NK Osijek 1-3(0-2)
Hajduk Split - Dinamo Zagreb 0-0
Lokomotiva Zagreb - HNK Gorica 2-2(1-0)
Slaven Belupo - HNK Rijeka 1-3(0-2)

**Round 33 [05-07.05.2023]**
HNK Šibenik - NK Varaždin 0-2(0-0)
HNK Gorica - Slaven Belupo 0-0
HNK Rijeka - NK Istra 1961 2-2(0-1)
NK Osijek - Dinamo Zagreb 0-0
Lokomotiva Zagreb - Hajduk Split 0-3(0-0)

**Round 34 [12-14.05.2023]**
Slaven Belupo - Lokomotiva Zagreb 0-0
Hajduk Split - NK Osijek 3-0(1-0)
NK Istra 1961 - HNK Gorica 1-0(1-0)
NK Varaždin - HNK Rijeka 2-0(0-0)
Dinamo Zagreb - HNK Šibenik 4-0(1-0)

**Round 35 [19-21.05.2023]**
Slaven Belupo - Hajduk Split 0-1(0-1)
HNK Šibenik - NK Osijek 1-4(0-1)
HNK Gorica - NK Varaždin 5-2(2-1)
Lokomotiva Zagreb - NK Istra 1961 3-1(2-0)
HNK Rijeka - Dinamo Zagreb 1-2(0-1)

**Round 36 [26-28.05.2023]**
NK Varaždin - Lokomotiva Zagreb 0-0
NK Istra 1961 - Slaven Belupo 1-1(0-0)
NK Osijek - HNK Rijeka 1-1(0-1)
Hajduk Split - HNK Šibenik 3-0(0-0)
Dinamo Zagreb - HNK Gorica 4-1(2-1)

## Final Standings

| | | Total | | | | | Home | | | | | Away | | | | |
|---|---|---|---|---|---|---|---|---|---|---|---|---|---|---|---|---|---|
| 1. | **GNK Dinamo Zagreb** | 36 | 24 | 9 | 3 | 81 - 28 | **81** | 16 | 2 | 0 | 52 - 12 | 8 | 7 | 3 | 29 - 16 |
| 2. | HNK Hajduk Split | 36 | 21 | 8 | 7 | 65 - 41 | **71** | 12 | 4 | 2 | 39 - 18 | 9 | 4 | 5 | 26 - 23 |
| 3. | NK Osijek | 36 | 13 | 11 | 12 | 46 - 41 | **50** | 7 | 9 | 2 | 21 - 13 | 6 | 2 | 10 | 25 - 28 |
| 4. | HNK Rijeka | 36 | 14 | 7 | 15 | 44 - 44 | **49** | 6 | 4 | 8 | 21 - 23 | 8 | 3 | 7 | 23 - 21 |
| 5. | NK Istra 1961 Pula | 36 | 11 | 13 | 12 | 36 - 38 | **46** | 8 | 6 | 4 | 17 - 11 | 3 | 7 | 8 | 19 - 27 |
| 6. | NK Varaždin | 36 | 12 | 10 | 14 | 41 - 51 | **46** | 6 | 6 | 6 | 20 - 23 | 6 | 4 | 8 | 21 - 28 |
| 7. | NK Lokomotiva Zagreb | 36 | 11 | 10 | 15 | 45 - 50 | **43** | 8 | 4 | 6 | 25 - 22 | 3 | 6 | 9 | 20 - 28 |
| 8. | NK Slaven Belupo Koprivnica | 36 | 10 | 13 | 13 | 27 - 46 | **43** | 5 | 7 | 6 | 16 - 25 | 5 | 6 | 7 | 11 - 21 |
| 9. | HNK Gorica | 36 | 7 | 11 | 18 | 36 - 50 | **32** | 6 | 6 | 6 | 19 - 20 | 1 | 5 | 12 | 17 - 30 |
| 10. | HNK Šibenik (*Relegated*) | 36 | 5 | 12 | 19 | 24 - 56 | **27** | 3 | 4 | 11 | 15 - 33 | 2 | 8 | 8 | 9 - 23 |

### Top goalscorers:

| | | |
|---|---|---|
| 19 | **Marko Livaja** | *HNK Hajduk Split* |
| 14 | Matija Frigan | *HNK Rijeka* |
| 12 | Fran Brodić | *NK Varaždin* |
| 12 | Luka Ivanušec | *GNK Dinamo Zagreb* |
| 12 | Ramón Nazareno Miérez (ARG) | *NK Osijek* |

| First Round [27.09./12.10./18-19.10.2022] | | | | |
|---|---|---|---|---|
| NK Borinci Jarmina - GNK Dinamo Zagreb | 0-4(0-3) | HNŠK Moslavina Kutina - HNK Rijeka | 1-1 aet; 4-5 pen |
| NK Tehničar Cvetkovec - HNK Hajduk Split | 1-5(0-3) | NK Bistra - NK Lokomotiva Zagreb | 1-6(1-1) |
| NK Papuk Orahovica - NK Osijek | 0-2(0-1) | NK Grobničan Čavle - NK Istra 1961 Pula | 1-2(1-1) |
| NK Dubrava Zagreb - HNK Gorica | 2-3(1-2) | NK Bednja Beletinec - NK Rudeš | 0-3(0-2) |
| NK Solin - NK Slaven Belupo Koprivnica | 1-2(0-1,1-1) | HNK Primorac Biograd na Moru - NK Varaždin | 1-4(1-0,1-1) |
| Jadran Poreč - HNK Šibenik | 1-2(1-1) | NK Bjelovar - NK Vinogradar Lokošin Dol | 4-2(2-2,2-2) |
| NK Mladost Ždralovi - NK Oriolik Oriovac | 6-0(4-0) | RNK Split - HNK Cibalia Vinkovci | 2-0(2-0) |
| NK Nedelišće - NK Inter Zaprešić | 3-0 awarded | NK Belišće - NK BSK Bijelo Brdo | 1-5(1-2) |

| 1/8-Finals [02.11./08-09.11.2022 & 14.02.2023] | | | |
|---|---|---|---|
| NK Nedelišće - NK Slaven Belupo Koprivnica | 0-6(0-3) | NK Bjelovar - NK Lokomotiva Zagreb | 0-1(0-1) |
| NK Mladost Ždralovi - HNK Hajduk Split | 0-2(0-2) | NK Varaždin - NK Osijek | 1-2(0-1) |
| NK Rudeš - NK Istra 1961 Pula | 2-1(2-0) | HNK Šibenik - HNK Gorica | 2-0(0-0) |
| NK BSK Bijelo Brdo - HNK Rijeka | 2-1(1-1) | RNK Split - GNK Dinamo Zagreb | 1-3(1-2) |

| Quarter-Finals [28.02.-01.03.2023] | | | |
|---|---|---|---|
| NK Slaven Belupo Koprivnica - NK Rudeš | 2-0(0-0) | GNK Dinamo Zagreb - NK Lokomotiva Zagreb | 3-1(0-1,1-1) |
| NK BSK Bijelo Brdo - HNK Šibenik | 0-2(0-1) | NK Osijek - HNK Hajduk Split | 1-2(0-1) |

| Semi-Finals [05/12.04.2023] | | | |
|---|---|---|---|
| HNK Šibenik - GNK Dinamo Zagreb | 2-1(0-1) | NK Slaven Belupo Koprivnica - HNK Hajduk Split | 0-1(0-0) |

## Final

24.05.2023; Stadion Rujevica, Rijeka; Referee: Igor Pajač; Attendance: 7,041
**HNK Hajduk Split - HNK Šibenik**                                                                                    **2-0(0-0)**

**Hajduk Split**: Ivan Lučić, Niko Sigur, Chidozie Collins Awaziem, Francisco Reis Ferreira „Ferro" (90+2.Luka Vušković), Dario Melnjak, Filip Krovinović, Rokas Pukštas, Emir Sahiti (79.Agustin Anello), Yassine Benrahou (86.Marco Fossati), Jan Mlakar, Marko Livaja (Cap). Trainer: Ivan Leko.

**HNK Šibenik**: Antonio Đaković, Zoran Kvržić (Cap), Stefan Perić, Josip Kvesič (69.Juan Camilo Mesa Antúnez), Marcos David Mina Lucumí (69.Iker Pozo La Rosa), Haruki Arai, Nikola Đorić (86.Doni Grdić), Marko Soldo (79.Josip Knežević), Amer Hiroš, Karlo Špeljak (69.Dario Čanađija), Ivan Dolček. Trainer: Damir Čanadi (Austria).

**Goals:** 1-0 Dario Melnjak (64), 2-0 Marko Livaja (90+4 penalty).

## THE CLUBS 2022/2023

### Građanski nogometni klub Dinamo Zagreb

| | | |
|---|---|---|
| **Founded**: | 09.06.1945 | |
| **Stadium**: | Stadion Maksimir, Zagreb (24,581) | |
| **Trainer**: | Ante Čačić | 29.09.1953 |
| [06.04.2023] | Igor Bišćan | 04.05.1978 |

| Goalkeepers: | DOB | M | (s) | G |
|---|---|---|---|---|
| Dominik Livaković | 09.01.1995 | 35 | | |
| Ivan Nevistić | 31.07.1998 | 1 | | |
| Danijel Zagorac | 07.02.1987 | | (1) | |
| **Defenders:** | **DOB** | **M** | **(s)** | **G** |
| Petar Bočkaj | 23.07.1996 | 16 | (6) | 3 |
| Emir Dilaver (AUT) | 07.05.1991 | 1 | (1) | |
| Jakov Gurlica | 10.01.2004 | | (1) | |
| Rasmus Lauritsen (DEN) | 27.02.1996 | 7 | (2) | 1 |
| Robert Ljubičić (AUT) | 14.07.1999 | 29 | (4) | 2 |
| Sadegh Moharrami (IRN) | 01.03.1996 | 16 | (9) | 1 |
| Dino Perić | 12.07.1994 | 22 | (1) | 3 |
| Mauro Perković | 22.03.2003 | 6 | (2) | |
| Stefan Ristovski (MKD) | 12.02.1992 | 26 | (2) | 4 |
| Daniel Štefulj | 08.11.1999 | 2 | (1) | |
| Boško Šutalo | 01.01.2000 | 4 | | 1 |
| Josip Šutalo | 28.02.2000 | 26 | (1) | 2 |
| Kévin Théophile-Catherine (MTQ) | 28.10.1989 | 6 | (1) | |
| Moreno Živković | 22.05.2004 | | (2) | |

| Midfielders: | DOB | M | (s) | G |
|---|---|---|---|---|
| Arijan Ademi (MKD) | 29.05.1991 | 13 | (6) | 4 |
| Martin Baturina | 16.02.2003 | 29 | (5) | 6 |
| Marko Bulat | 26.09.2001 | 8 | (13) | |
| Amer Gojak (BIH) | 13.02.1997 | | (2) | 1 |
| Josip Mišić | 28.06.1994 | 32 | (2) | 2 |
| Marko Tolić | 05.07.1996 | 1 | (1) | |
| **Forwards:** | **DOB** | **M** | **(s)** | **G** |
| Josip Drmić (SUI) | 08.08.1992 | 20 | (15) | 6 |
| Mahir Emreli (AZE) | 01.07.1997 | | (10) | 3 |
| Luka Ivanušec | 26.11.1998 | 29 | (4) | 12 |
| Toni Majić | 03.05.2006 | | (1) | |
| Antonio Marin | 09.01.2001 | 1 | (4) | |
| Luka Menalo (BIH) | 22.07.1996 | 4 | (18) | 2 |
| Mislav Oršić | 29.12.1992 | 11 | (4) | 8 |
| Bruno Petković | 16.09.1994 | 17 | (11) | 10 |
| Gabriel Rukavina | 16.01.2004 | | (6) | |
| Dario Špikić | 22.03.1999 | 31 | (3) | 7 |
| Fran Topić | 20.03.2004 | 3 | (6) | |

## Hrvatski Nogometni Klub Gorica

**Founded:** 16.07.2009
*(as merger of NK Radnik Velika Gorica and NK Polet Buševec)*
**Stadium:** Stadion Gradski, Velika Gorica (4,536)
**Trainer:** Samir Toplak — 23.04.1970
[27.08.2022] Igor Angelovski (MKD) — 02.06.1976
[28.11.2022] Željko Sopić — 26.07.1974

| Goalkeepers: | DOB | M | (s) | G |
|---|---|---|---|---|
| Ivan Banić | 18.07.1994 | 26 | | |
| Božidar Radošević | 04.04.1989 | 10 | | |
| **Defenders:** | **DOB** | **M** | **(s)** | **G** |
| Slavko Bralić | 15.12.1992 | 18 | | 3 |
| Robert Ćosić | 08.07.1997 | 1 | (1) | |
| Aleksandar Jovičić (BIH) | 18.07.1995 | 12 | (2) | |
| Cheick Keita (MLI) | 16.04.1996 | 5 | (1) | |
| Amet Ylber Kőrça (ALB) | 16.09.2000 | 2 | | |
| Krešimir Krizmanić | 03.07.2000 | 29 | (4) | |
| Mario Matković | 02.04.2003 | | (1) | |
| Momčilo Raspopović (MNE) | 18.03.1994 | 18 | (5) | 1 |
| Matthew Steenvoorden (NED) | 09.01.1993 | 24 | (1) | 1 |
| Dino Štiglec | 03.10.1990 | 10 | (5) | |
| Ivan Tomečak | 07.12.1989 | 17 | | |
| Matúš Vojtko (SVK) | 05.10.2000 | 10 | (14) | 1 |
| Moussa Wagué (SEN) | 04.10.1998 | 6 | (7) | |
| **Midfielders:** | **DOB** | **M** | **(s)** | **G** |
| Tyrese Jay Francois (AUS) | 16.07.2000 | 9 | (1) | 1 |
| Toni Fruk | 09.03.2001 | 22 | (2) | 7 |
| Paulius Golubickas (LTU) | 19.08.1999 | 7 | (4) | |
| Edin Julardžija | 21.01.2001 | 2 | (11) | |
| Anthony Kalik (AUS) | 05.11.1997 | 4 | | 2 |
| Luka Kapulica | 18.01.2005 | 4 | (6) | 1 |
| Filip Mrzljak | 16.04.1993 | 12 | | |
| Dominik Prokop (AUT) | 02.06.1997 | 3 | (3) | |
| Jurica Pršir | 29.05.2000 | 32 | (2) | 1 |
| Vinko Skrbin | 24.04.2003 | | (3) | |
| Joey Suk (NED) | 08.07.1989 | 18 | (12) | 2 |
| Fran Tomek | 25.06.2002 | | (1) | |
| *Wallace* Menezes dos Santos (BRA) | 23.06.1998 | | (5) | |
| **Forwards:** | **DOB** | **M** | **(s)** | **G** |
| *Caio* Da *Cruz* Oliveira Queiroz (BRA) | 13.03.2002 | 3 | (8) | 1 |
| Kristian Fućak | 14.11.1998 | 13 | (4) | 5 |
| Deni Jurić (AUS) | 03.09.1997 | 9 | (3) | |
| Ante Matej Jurič | 26.11.2002 | 7 | (8) | |
| Valentino Majstorović | 11.11.1995 | 3 | (16) | |
| Tim Matavž (SVN) | 13.01.1989 | 5 | (10) | |
| Josip Mitrović | 11.06.2000 | 26 | (4) | 4 |
| Merveil Valthy Streeker Ndockyt (CGO) | 20.07.1998 | 20 | (9) | 3 |
| Vinko Petković | 01.10.1995 | 3 | (4) | |
| Nikola Vujnović (MNE) | 11.01.1997 | 6 | (13) | 1 |

## Hrvatski nogometni klub Hajduk Split

**Founded:** 13.02.1911
**Stadium:** Stadion Poljud, Split (33,987)
**Trainer:** Valdas Dambrauskas (LTU) — 07.01.1977
[12.09.2022] Mislav Karoglan (BIH) — 14.04.1982
[31.12.2022] Ivan Leko — 07.02.1978

| Goalkeepers: | DOB | M | (s) | G |
|---|---|---|---|---|
| Lovre Kalinić | 03.04.1990 | 9 | | |
| Ivan Lučić (AUT) | 23.03.1995 | 12 | (1) | |
| Karlo Sentić | 03.06.2001 | 14 | (2) | |
| Danijel Subašić | 27.10.1984 | 1 | | |
| **Defenders:** | **DOB** | **M** | **(s)** | **G** |
| Chidozie Collins Awaziem (NGA) | 01.01.1997 | 24 | (4) | 5 |
| Toni Borevković | 18.06.1997 | 13 | (2) | |
| David Čolina | 19.07.2000 | 5 | (9) | 1 |
| Niko Đolonga | 24.05.2004 | | (1) | |
| Josip Elez | 25.04.1994 | 9 | (2) | |
| Francisco Reis Ferreira „Ferro" (POR) | 26.03.1997 | 9 | | |
| Elvis Letaj | 26.09.2003 | 1 | (3) | |
| Gergő Lovrencsics (HUN) | 01.09.1988 | 11 | (7) | |
| Dario Melnjak | 31.10.1992 | 33 | (2) | 4 |
| Dino Mikanović | 07.05.1994 | 14 | (10) | 1 |
| Dominik Prpić | 19.05.2004 | 4 | (1) | |
| Stefan Simič (CZE) | 20.01.1995 | 11 | (4) | |
| Luka Vušković | 24.02.2007 | 7 | (1) | |
| **Midfielders:** | **DOB** | **M** | **(s)** | **G** |
| Jani Atanasov (MKD) | 31.10.1999 | 3 | (8) | 2 |
| Yassine Benrahou (FRA) | 24.01.1999 | 11 | (6) | 4 |
| Marko Capan | 24.02.2004 | 3 | (1) | |
| Ivan Ćubelić | 02.06.2003 | | (11) | 1 |
| Marco Fossati (ITA) | 05.10.1992 | 20 | (7) | |
| Lukas Grgić (AUT) | 17.08.1995 | 17 | (9) | 1 |
| Anthony Kalik (AUS) | 05.11.1997 | 5 | (3) | 1 |
| Ivan Krolo | 23.01.2003 | | (4) | |
| Filip Krovinović | 29.08.1995 | 33 | (2) | 1 |
| Rokas Pukštas (USA) | 25.08.2004 | 15 | (6) | 4 |
| Niko Sigur (CAN) | 09.09.2003 | 7 | | |
| Josip Vuković | 02.05.1992 | 6 | (5) | |
| **Forwards:** | **DOB** | **M** | **(s)** | **G** |
| Agustin Anello (USA) | 22.04.2002 | 4 | (7) | |
| Stipe Biuk | 26.12.2002 | 14 | (1) | 1 |
| Roko Brajković | 03.07.2005 | 1 | (4) | 1 |
| Nikola Kalinić | 05.01.1988 | 3 | (15) | 4 |
| Marko Livaja | 26.08.1993 | 33 | (1) | 19 |
| Jan Mlakar (SVN) | 23.10.1998 | 24 | (9) | 11 |
| Emir Sahiti (ALB) | 29.11.1998 | 20 | (7) | 4 |
| Ivan Šarić | 16.01.2001 | | (1) | |

## Nogometni Klub Istra 1961 Pula

**Founded:** 1948
**Stadium:** Stadion "Aldo Drosina", Pula (9,921)
**Trainer:** Gonzalo Manuel García García (ESP) — 13.10.1983

| Goalkeepers: | DOB | M | (s) | G |
|---|---|---|---|---|
| Ivan Lučić (AUT) | 23.03.1995 | 1 | | |
| Lovro Majkić | 08.10.1999 | 35 | | |
| **Defenders:** | **DOB** | **M** | **(s)** | **G** |
| Filip Antovski (MKD) | 24.11.2000 | 1 | (9) | |
| Luka Bradarić | 08.09.2003 | 3 | (3) | |
| *Einar Galilea* Azaceta (ESP) | 22.05.1994 | 30 | (1) | 2 |
| Luka Hujber | 16.06.1999 | 32 | (1) | 1 |
| Iurie Iovu (MDA) | 06.07.2002 | 3 | | |
| Advan Kadušić (BIH) | 14.10.1997 | 32 | | 1 |
| Ante Majstorović | 06.11.1993 | 2 | (1) | |
| Dario Maresić (AUT) | 29.09.1999 | 25 | (2) | 1 |
| Luka Marin | 16.03.1998 | 23 | (6) | 1 |
| Mauro Perković | 22.03.2003 | 17 | | |
| Rafael „*Rafa*" Jesús *Navarro* Mazuelos (ESP) | 24.02.1994 | | (1) | |
| Mihael Rovis | 18.01.2002 | 5 | (4) | |
| Fran Vujnović | 23.06.2003 | | (1) | |
| **Midfielders:** | **DOB** | **M** | **(s)** | **G** |
| Slavko Blagojević | 21.03.1987 | | (4) | |
| Reda Boultam (NED) | 03.03.1998 | 14 | (8) | 2 |
| Facundo Agustín Cáseres (ARG) | 28.05.2001 | 32 | (1) | 2 |
| Tomislav Duvnjak | 05.02.2003 | 3 | (9) | |
| Tino Blaž Lauš | 17.03.2001 | | (4) | |
| Abdallahi Mohamed Mahmoud (MTN) | 04.05.2000 | 5 | (13) | 1 |
| Antonio Maurić | 04.11.2003 | 3 | (1) | |
| Robert Mišković | 20.10.1999 | 2 | | |
| Frano Mlinar | 30.03.1992 | 29 | (3) | 2 |
| Prince Mumba (ZAM) | 24.03.2001 | 1 | (8) | |
| Oleksandr Petrusenko (UKR) | 26.03.1998 | 30 | (1) | |
| Marin Žgomba | 30.05.2005 | 1 | (4) | |
| **Forwards:** | **DOB** | **M** | **(s)** | **G** |
| Monsef Bakrar (ALG) | 13.01.2001 | 18 | (13) | 8 |
| Bartol Barišić | 01.01.2003 | 3 | | |
| Marko Cukon | 01.04.2005 | | (1) | |
| Ante Erceg | 12.12.1989 | 17 | (4) | 11 |
| Zoran Josipović (SUI) | 25.08.1995 | 1 | (4) | |
| Lovre Knežević | 22.07.1998 | | (2) | |
| Kristijan Kopljar | 07.07.2001 | | (6) | |
| Mateo Lisica | 09.07.2003 | 5 | (12) | |
| Darwin Daniel Matheus Tovar (VEN) | 09.04.2001 | 3 | (5) | 2 |
| Vinko Petković | 01.10.1995 | 10 | (3) | 2 |
| Lorenzo Travaglia | 12.01.2005 | | (2) | |
| Matej Vuk | 10.06.2000 | 10 | (5) | |

## Nogometni klub Lokomotiva Zagreb

**Founded**: 01.05.1914 (*as ŽŠK Victoria Zagreb*)
**Stadium**: Stadion Kranjčevićeva, Zagreb (3,690)
**Trainer**: Silvijo Čabraja — 04.06.1968

| Goalkeepers: | DOB | M | (s) | G |
|---|---|---|---|---|
| Nikola Čavlina | 02.06.2002 | 30 | | |
| Krševan Santini | 11.04.1987 | 4 | | |
| Zvonimir Šubarić | 25.05.1997 | 2 | | |
| **Defenders:** | **DOB** | **M** | **(s)** | **G** |
| Branimir Cipetić (BIH) | 24.05.1995 | 30 | (3) | |
| Justin de Haas (NED) | 01.02.2000 | 18 | (3) | |
| Branimir Kalaica | 01.06.1998 | 15 | (2) | |
| Matej Matic | 05.06.2004 | | (1) | |
| Jon Mersinaj (ALB) | 08.02.1999 | 27 | (2) | |
| Ivan Miličević (BIH) | 16.07.1998 | 25 | (5) | |
| Josip Pivarić | 30.01.1989 | 23 | (5) | 2 |
| Hajdin Salihu (KOS) | 18.01.2002 | 5 | (2) | |
| Nikola Soldo | 25.01.2001 | 6 | | |
| Ivan Tomečak | 07.12.1989 | 2 | (4) | |
| Marko Vranjković | 05.02.1999 | 7 | (14) | |
| Fran Žilinski | 04.04.2003 | 2 | (1) | |
| **Midfielders:** | **DOB** | **M** | **(s)** | **G** |
| Blaž Bošković (BIH) | 15.12.2001 | 1 | (6) | 2 |

| | DOB | M | (s) | G |
|---|---|---|---|---|
| Vladan Bubanja (MNE) | 21.02.1999 | 23 | (6) | 3 |
| Enis Çokaj (ALB) | 23.02.1999 | 8 | | 1 |
| Gabriel Groznica | 12.03.2002 | 1 | (4) | |
| Lukas Kačavenda | 02.03.2003 | 11 | (4) | |
| Fabijan Krivak | 24.02.2005 | 2 | (3) | |
| Mate Maleš | 11.03.1989 | 1 | | |
| Mateo Marić (BIH) | 18.03.1998 | 31 | | 2 |
| Art Smakaj (KOS) | 04.02.2003 | 8 | (5) | |
| Luka Stojković | 28.10.2003 | 25 | (5) | 4 |
| Jakov-Anton Vasilj | 02.06.2002 | 10 | (12) | 3 |
| **Forwards:** | **DOB** | **M** | **(s)** | **G** |
| Ibrahim Aliyu (NGA) | 16.01.2002 | 23 | (3) | 6 |
| Marko Batur | 26.06.2004 | | (1) | |
| Raul Alexander Florucz (AUT) | 10.06.2001 | | (1) | |
| Silvio Goričan | 27.02.2000 | 21 | (14) | 6 |
| Sandro Kulenović | 04.12.1999 | 25 | (9) | 9 |
| Marin Šotiček | 18.09.2004 | 1 | (10) | |
| Indrit Tuci (ALB) | 14.09.2000 | 9 | (21) | 6 |
| Mario Veljača | 02.05.2002 | | (1) | |

## Nogometni klub Osijek

**Founded**: 27.02.1947
**Stadium**: Stadion Gradski vrt, Osijek (18,856)
**Trainer**: Nenad Bjelica — 20.08.1971
[01.09.2022] Rene Poms (AUT) — 05.07.1975
[29.09.2022] Ivica Kuleševic — 31.10.1969
[02.03.2023] Borimir Perković — 25.09.1967
[24.03.2023] Stjepan Tomas — 03.06.1976

| Goalkeepers: | DOB | M | (s) | G |
|---|---|---|---|---|
| Ivica Ivušić | 01.02.1995 | 17 | | |
| Marko Malenica | 08.02.1994 | 19 | | |
| **Defenders:** | **DOB** | **M** | **(s)** | **G** |
| Adrian Barišić (BIH) | 19.07.2001 | 26 | (1) | 1 |
| Karlo Bartolec | 20.04.1995 | 5 | (2) | |
| Slavko Bralić | 15.12.1992 | 3 | (4) | |
| Yevgen Cheberko (UKR) | 23.01.1998 | 18 | (2) | |
| Ivan Cvijanović | 09.10.2003 | | (1) | |
| Šime Gržan | 06.04.1994 | 18 | (7) | 1 |
| Mario Jurčević (SVN) | 01.06.1995 | 18 | (7) | |
| Marin Leovac | 07.08.1988 | 19 | (2) | 2 |
| Danijel Lončar | 26.06.1997 | 9 | (1) | |
| Mato Miloš | 30.06.1993 | 3 | (3) | |
| Mile Škorić | 19.06.1991 | 10 | (1) | |
| **Midfielders:** | **DOB** | **M** | **(s)** | **G** |
| Ognjen Bakić (MNE) | 06.01.2003 | 1 | (12) | |
| Diego Hernández Barriuso „Barri" (ESP) | 19.09.1995 | 4 | (6) | |
| Petar Brlek | 29.01.1994 | 5 | (4) | |
| Mijo Caktaš | 08.05.1992 | 28 | (1) | 8 |

| | DOB | M | (s) | G |
|---|---|---|---|---|
| Ivan Fiolić | 29.04.1996 | 15 | (6) | |
| Vedran Jugović | 31.07.1989 | 30 | (2) | 1 |
| László Kleinheisler (HUN) | 08.04.1994 | 14 | (2) | 6 |
| Darko Nejašmić | 25.01.1999 | 23 | (4) | 1 |
| Mihael Žaper | 11.08.1998 | 26 | (2) | 1 |
| **Forwards:** | **DOB** | **M** | **(s)** | **G** |
| Dominik Babić | 05.09.2006 | | (1) | |
| Dion Drena Beljo | 01.03.2002 | 13 | (3) | 8 |
| Domagoj Bukvić | 22.02.2004 | 8 | (2) | 1 |
| Kristian Fućak | 14.11.1998 | 3 | (1) | |
| Amer Hiroš (BIH) | 10.06.1996 | | (5) | |
| Nikola Janjić (MNE) | 14.07.2002 | 1 | (3) | |
| Kristijan Lovrić | 01.12.1995 | 11 | (8) | |
| Antonio Mance | 07.08.1995 | | (8) | |
| Filip Mažar | 24.03.2005 | | (1) | |
| Ramón Nazareno Miérez (ARG) | 13.05.1997 | 27 | (6) | 12 |
| Nail Omerović (BIH) | 20.10.2002 | 13 | (4) | |
| Josip Špoljarić | 05.01.1997 | 5 | (12) | 2 |
| Mihret Topčagić (AUT) | 21.06.1988 | 2 | (6) | |
| Filip Živković | 01.08.2006 | 2 | (8) | |

## Hrvatski Nogometni Klub Rijeka

**Founded**: 29.07.1946 (*as Sportsko Društvo Kvarner*)
**Stadium**: Stadion Rujevica, Rijeka (8,191)
**Trainer**: Dragan Tadić — 12.02.1973
[16.08.2022] Fausto Budicin — 01.05.1981
[05.09.2022] Serse Cosmi (ITA) — 05.05.1958
[25.11.2022] Sergej Jakirović (BIH) — 23.12.1976

| Goalkeepers: | DOB | M | (s) | G |
|---|---|---|---|---|
| Nediljko Labrović | 10.10.1999 | 36 | | |
| **Defenders:** | **DOB** | **M** | **(s)** | **G** |
| *Danilo* Filipe Melo *Veiga* (POR) | 25.09.2002 | 14 | (3) | |
| Emir Dilaver (AUT) | 07.05.1991 | 14 | | |
| Duje Dujmović | 15.12.2003 | | (1) | |
| Niko Galešić | 26.03.2001 | 23 | (2) | |
| Bruno Goda | 17.04.1998 | 6 | (5) | |
| Alen Grgić | 10.08.1994 | 14 | (14) | 1 |
| Roko Jurišić | 28.09.2001 | 3 | (1) | |
| Anton Krešić | 29.01.1996 | 10 | (4) | |
| Matej Mitrović | 10.11.1993 | 4 | (1) | |
| Mateo Pavlović | 09.06.1990 | 13 | | |
| Ivan Smolčić | 17.08.2000 | 14 | (7) | |
| Andrés Felipe Solano Dávila (COL) | 24.02.1998 | 2 | | |
| Nikita Vlasenko (SUI) | 20.03.2001 | 2 | (2) | 1 |
| Andrija Vukčević (MNE) | 11.10.1996 | 25 | (1) | |
| **Midfielders:** | **DOB** | **M** | **(s)** | **G** |
| Andro Babić | 08.09.2004 | | (1) | |
| Emmanuel Banda (ZAM) | 29.09.1997 | 6 | (13) | 2 |
| Alen Halilović | 18.06.1996 | 5 | (3) | 1 |
| Veldin Hodža | 15.10.2002 | 30 | (3) | 1 |
| Niko Janković | 25.08.2001 | 16 | (3) | 2 |
| Ivan Lepinjica | 09.07.1999 | 1 | | |

| | DOB | M | (s) | G |
|---|---|---|---|---|
| Adrian Liber | 09.01.2001 | 3 | (17) | 2 |
| *Pablo Álvarez* García (ESP) | 23.04.1997 | 5 | (3) | |
| Gabriel Antonio Lunetta (ITA) | 10.08.1996 | 3 | (4) | 1 |
| Damjan Pavlović (BEL) | 09.07.2001 | 5 | (1) | |
| Lindon Selahi (ALB) | 26.02.1999 | 30 | (3) | 2 |
| Mato Stanić (BIH) | 11.01.1998 | | (3) | |
| Mario Vrančić (BIH) | 23.05.1989 | 6 | (7) | 1 |
| **Forwards:** | **DOB** | **M** | **(s)** | **G** |
| Prince Ampem (GHA) | 13.04.1998 | 34 | (1) | 5 |
| Admir Bristrić (BIH) | 28.04.2003 | | (1) | |
| Bruno Bogojević | 29.06.1998 | | (1) | |
| Denis Bušnja | 14.04.2000 | 3 | (7) | |
| Naïs Djouahra (FRA) | 23.11.1999 | 8 | (11) | 1 |
| Marco Djuricin (AUT) | 12.12.1992 | 3 | (2) | |
| Matija Frigan | 11.02.2003 | 25 | (2) | 14 |
| Niko Gajzler | 21.12.2004 | | (1) | |
| Deni Jurić (AUS) | 03.09.1997 | | (6) | |
| Bernard Karrica (ALB) | 07.01.2001 | 1 | (3) | 1 |
| Antonio Marin | 09.01.2001 | 17 | (1) | 3 |
| Jorge Leonardo Obregón Rojas (COL) | 29.03.1997 | 6 | (20) | 3 |
| Dominik Simčić | 07.03.2003 | | (3) | |
| Haris Vučkić (SVN) | 21.08.1992 | 9 | (1) | 3 |
| Matej Vuk | 10.06.2000 | | (1) | |

## Nogometni klub Slaven Belupo Koprivnica

| | | | |
|---|---|---|---|
| **Founded**: | 1907 | | |
| **Stadium**: | Gradski Stadion "Ivan Kušek Apaš", Koprivnica (3,054) | | |
| **Trainer**: | Zoran Zekić | | 29.04.1974 |

| Goalkeepers: | DOB | M | (s) | G |
|---|---|---|---|---|
| Ivan Čović | 17.09.1990 | 20 | | |
| Antun Marković | 04.07.1992 | 10 | | |
| Ivan Sušak | 06.10.1997 | 6 | | |
| **Defenders:** | **DOB** | **M** | **(s)** | **G** |
| Marco Boras (GER) | 28.09.2001 | | (5) | 1 |
| Antonio Bosec | 28.08.1997 | 25 | (3) | |
| Tomislav Božić | 01.11.1987 | 27 | (2) | |
| Giannis Christopoulos (GRE) | 22.06.2000 | 6 | (5) | |
| Filip Hlevnjak | 05.08.2000 | 9 | (6) | |
| Filip Krušelj | 30.03.2005 | 1 | (2) | |
| Marko Martinaga | 27.05.1998 | 12 | (6) | |
| Vinko Soldo | 15.02.1998 | 30 | | |
| *Talys* Alves Pereira Oliveira (BRA) | 10.02.1999 | 19 | (2) | |
| Novak Tepšić | 16.03.2002 | 18 | (1) | |
| Matko Zirdum | 21.07.1998 | 4 | (1) | 1 |
| **Midfielders:** | **DOB** | **M** | **(s)** | **G** |
| Jakov Bašić | 25.11.1996 | 5 | (16) | |
| Seid Behram (BIH) | 12.07.1998 | | (4) | |
| Leon Bosnjak | 23.01.2006 | | (1) | |
| Mihail Caimacov (MDA) | 22.07.1998 | 5 | | |
| Nikola Jambor | 25.09.1995 | 17 | (6) | 1 |
| Mateo Kocijan | 27.03.1995 | 14 | (13) | 2 |
| Mario Marina (BIH) | 03.08.1989 | 26 | (1) | 1 |
| Josip Mihalić | 04.04.2003 | 3 | (9) | |
| Benedik Mioč | 06.10.1994 | 14 | (9) | |
| Robert Mudražija | 05.05.1997 | 26 | (1) | 1 |
| Nikola Turanjanin (BIH) | 12.04.2001 | | (2) | |
| **Forwards:** | **DOB** | **M** | **(s)** | **G** |
| Luka Branšteter | 19.06.2002 | 4 | | |
| Ante Crnac | 17.12.2003 | 28 | (7) | 6 |
| Matthias Olubori Ayodluwa Fanimo (ENG) | 28.01.1994 | 1 | (8) | |
| Arbër Hoxha (KOS) | 06.10.1998 | 32 | (1) | 7 |
| Ivan Krstanović (BIH) | 05.01.1983 | 7 | (25) | 5 |
| Zoran Kvržić (BIH) | 07.08.1988 | 11 | (3) | |
| Arb Manaj (KOS) | 23.07.1998 | 11 | (9) | 1 |
| Antonio Perošević | 06.03.1992 | 3 | (10) | |
| Frano Vlašić | 08.02.2006 | | (1) | |
| Marko Žuljević | 16.09.1997 | 2 | (19) | 1 |

## Hrvatski nogometni klub Šibenik

| | | | |
|---|---|---|---|
| **Founded**: | 01.12.1932 | | |
| **Stadium**: | Stadion Šubićevac, Šibenik (3,701) | | |
| **Trainer**: | Damir Čanadi (AUT) | | 06.05.1970 |
| [25.09.2022] | Mario Cvitanović | | 06.05.1975 |
| [31.01.2023] | Damir Čanadi (AUT) | | 06.05.1970 |

| Goalkeepers: | DOB | M | (s) | G |
|---|---|---|---|---|
| Antonio Đaković | 12.06.2001 | 2 | (1) | |
| Lovre Rogić | 27.08.1995 | 34 | | |
| **Defenders:** | **DOB** | **M** | **(s)** | **G** |
| Josip Baturina | 12.01.2004 | | (3) | |
| Nikola Đorić (SRB) | 03.03.2000 | 10 | (4) | |
| Doni Grdić (AUS) | 22.01.2002 | 2 | (1) | |
| Josip Kvesić (BIH) | 21.09.1990 | 6 | (8) | |
| Zoran Kvržić (BIH) | 07.08.1988 | 17 | | 1 |
| Mislav Matić | 06.01.2000 | 29 | (4) | 1 |
| Juan Camilo Mesa Antúnez (COL) | 23.02.1998 | 28 | (5) | |
| Marcos David Mina Lucumí (COL) | 12.04.1999 | 27 | (3) | 1 |
| Martin Pajić | 11.11.1999 | | (1) | |
| Stefan Perić (AUT) | 13.02.1997 | 30 | | 1 |
| Matija Rom (SVN) | 01.11.1998 | 4 | | |
| **Midfielders:** | **DOB** | **M** | **(s)** | **G** |
| Haruki Arai (JPN) | 12.04.1998 | 35 | | 2 |
| Moses Zambrang Barnabas (NGA) | 06.05.2003 | | (3) | |
| Mario Ćurić | 28.09.1998 | 6 | | |
| Marcel Čanadi (AUT) | 27.10.1997 | 6 | (4) | |
| Dario Čanađija | 17.04.1994 | 17 | (1) | |
| Marko Đira | 05.05.1999 | 8 | (2) | |
| *Iker Pozo* La Rosa (ESP) | 06.08.2000 | 1 | (6) | |
| Josip Knežević | 03.10.1988 | 3 | (9) | |
| Ivan Krolo | 23.01.2003 | 1 | | |
| Sacha Boris Roger Marasović (FRA) | 06.01.1998 | | (8) | |
| Bernardo Matić | 27.07.1994 | 12 | (3) | 1 |
| Niko Rak | 26.07.2003 | 9 | (6) | |
| Patrick Salomon (AUT) | 10.06.1988 | 14 | | 1 |
| Dino Skorup | 04.10.1999 | 4 | (11) | |
| Marko Soldo (BIH) | 22.11.2003 | 7 | (8) | |
| Ivica Vidović | 15.02.2002 | 7 | (5) | |
| **Forwards:** | **DOB** | **M** | **(s)** | **G** |
| Jorge Franco Alviz „Burgui" (ESP) | 29.10.1993 | | (8) | 1 |
| Duje Čop | 01.02.1990 | 17 | (4) | 4 |
| Ivan Delić | 29.09.1998 | 12 | (4) | 3 |
| Ivan Dolček | 24.04.2000 | 19 | (10) | 5 |
| Amer Hiroš (BIH) | 10.06.1996 | 12 | (4) | 1 |
| Nace Koprivnik (SVN) | 27.06.1999 | | (2) | |
| Leon Kreković | 07.05.2000 | 3 | (14) | |
| Dejan Radonjić | 23.07.1990 | 2 | (11) | |
| Karlo Špeljak | 14.03.2003 | 12 | (12) | 2 |

## Nogometni klub Varaždin

| | | | |
|---|---|---|---|
| **Founded**: | 01.07.2012 (*as NK Varaždin Škola nogometa*) | | |
| **Stadium**: | Stadion Varteks, Varaždin (8,818) | | |
| **Trainer**: | Nikola Šafarić | | 11.03.1981 |
| [ 14.01.2023] | Mario Kovačević | | 17.05.1975 |

| Goalkeepers: | DOB | M | (s) | G |
|---|---|---|---|---|
| Božidar Radošević | 04.04.1989 | 2 | | |
| Oliver Zelenika | 14.05.1993 | 34 | | |
| **Defenders:** | **DOB** | **M** | **(s)** | **G** |
| Lamine Ba (FRA) | 24.08.1997 | 16 | (3) | |
| Filip Brekalo | 20.01.2003 | 2 | (4) | |
| Luka Jelenić | 24.05.2000 | 27 | (3) | 1 |
| Jakov Karabatić | 23.03.2000 | 1 | | |
| Matija Katanec | 04.05.1990 | 2 | | |
| Matija Kolarić | 14.04.1996 | 19 | (8) | 2 |
| Jorgo Pëllumbi (ALB) | 15.07.2000 | 25 | (6) | |
| Jozo Stanić | 06.04.1999 | 29 | (2) | |
| Marko Stolnik | 08.07.1996 | 12 | (5) | |
| Luka Škaričić | 28.01.2002 | 1 | (4) | |
| Vito Tezak | 31.03.2005 | | (3) | 1 |
| Itsuki Urata (JPN) | 29.01.1997 | 19 | (8) | |
| **Midfielders:** | **DOB** | **M** | **(s)** | **G** |
| Leon Belcar | 04.01.2002 | 5 | (11) | |
| Ivan Ćubelić | 02.06.2003 | | (3) | |
| Agon Elezi (MKD) | 01.03.2001 | 29 | (3) | 3 |
| Karlo Lusavec | 30.10.2003 | 2 | (2) | |
| Marin Pilj | 03.12.1996 | 15 | (12) | 1 |
| Ivan Posavec | 05.07.1998 | 4 | (6) | 1 |
| Igor Postonjski | 04.02.1995 | 5 | (3) | 1 |
| David Puclin | 17.06.1992 | 17 | (4) | 1 |
| Rafael „*Rafa*" Reis *Pereira* (POR) | 26.05.2001 | | (4) | |
| Mato Stanić (BIH) | 11.01.1998 | 5 | (4) | |
| Tonio Teklić | 09.09.1999 | 32 | (1) | 8 |
| **Forwards:** | **DOB** | **M** | **(s)** | **G** |
| Lovro Banovec | 28.10.2001 | 6 | (14) | |
| Fran Brodić | 08.01.1997 | 32 | (2) | 12 |
| Niko Domjanić | 19.02.2003 | 5 | (12) | 3 |
| Domagoj Drožđek | 20.03.1996 | 9 | | 1 |
| Andris Jesús Herrera Palomino (VEN) | 20.10.1996 | 9 | (11) | |
| Dimitar Mitrovski (MKD) | 28.01.1999 | 2 | (7) | 1 |
| Nick Ocvirek | 12.10.2004 | | (2) | |
| Demir Peco (BIH) | 31.07.1996 | 6 | (2) | |
| Karlo Perić | 14.02.2001 | 1 | (10) | 1 |
| Ivan Šaranić | 12.05.2003 | | (4) | |
| Michele Šego | 05.08.2000 | 22 | (5) | 3 |
| Noa Vugrinec | 13.08.2002 | 1 | (4) | |
| Leonard Vuk | 23.05.1995 | | (1) | |

## SECOND LEVEL
## Druga liga 2022/2023

|  |  |  |  |  |  |  |  |  |
|---|---|---|---|---|---|---|---|---|
| 1. | NK Rudeš (*Promoted*) | 33 | 19 | 7 | 7 | 56 - 26 | 64 |
| 2. | HNK Vukovar 1991 | 33 | 17 | 12 | 4 | 57 - 25 | 63 |
| 3. | HNK Cibalia Vinkovci | 33 | 13 | 15 | 5 | 37 - 26 | 54 |
| 4. | NK BSK Bijelo Brdo | 33 | 12 | 8 | 13 | 41 - 37 | 44 |
| 5. | NK Jarun Zagreb | 33 | 13 | 5 | 15 | 43 - 57 | 44 |
| 6. | HNK Orijent 1919 Sušak | 33 | 10 | 13 | 10 | 45 - 45 | 43 |
| 7. | NK Croatia Zmijavci | 33 | 12 | 7 | 14 | 37 - 44 | 43 |
| 8. | NK Solin | 33 | 12 | 7 | 14 | 47 - 55 | 43 |
| 9. | NK Dubrava Zagreb | 33 | 11 | 9 | 13 | 38 - 39 | 42 |
| 10. | NK Dugopolje | 33 | 9 | 14 | 10 | 30 - 35 | 41 |
| 11. | NK Kustošija (*Relegation Play-off*) | 33 | 9 | 7 | 17 | 35 - 50 | 34 |
| 12. | NK Hrvatski Dragovoljac Zagreb (*Relegated*) | 33 | 4 | 10 | 19 | 31 - 58 | 22 |

### Relegation Play-offs 2nd / 3rd Level [10-17.06.2023]

NK Kustošija - NK Zrinski Jurjevac Punitovački          2-1          0-1

NK Zrinski Jurjevac Punitovački promoted for the 2023/2024 Druga Liga.

# NATIONAL TEAM

## INTERNATIONAL MATCHES
(16.07.2022 – 15.07.2023)

| | | | | |
|---|---|---|---|---|
| 22.09.2022 | Zagreb | *Croatia - Denmark* | *2-1(0-0)* | (UNL) |
| 25.09.2022 | Wien | *Austria - Croatia* | *1-3(1-1)* | (UNL) |
| 16.11.2022 | Riyadh | *Saudi Arabia - Croatia* | *0-1(0-0)* | (F) |
| 23.11.2022 | Al Khor | *Morocco - Croatia* | *0-0* | (WC) |
| 27.11.2022 | Al Rayyan | *Croatia - Canada* | *4-1(2-1)* | (WC) |
| 01.12.2022 | Al Rayyan | *Croatia - Belgium* | *0-0* | (WC) |
| 05.12.2022 | Al Wakrah | *Japan - Croatia* | *1-1(1-0,1-1,1-1); 1-3 pen* | (WC) |
| 09.12.2022 | Al Rayyan | *Croatia - Brazil* | *1-1(0-0,0-0,1-1); 4-2 pen* | (WC) |
| 13.12.2022 | Lusail | *Argentina - Croatia* | *3-0(2-0)* | (WC) |
| 17.12.2022 | Al Rayyan | *Croatia - Morocco* | *2-1(2-1)* | (WC) |
| 25.03.2023 | Split | *Croatia - Wales* | *1-1(1-0)* | (ECQ) |
| 28.03.2023 | Bursa | *Turkey - Croatia* | *0-2(0-2)* | (ECQ) |
| 14.06.2023 | Rotterdam | *Netherlands - Croatia* | *2-4(1-0,2-2)* | (UNL) |
| 18.06.2023 | Rotterdam | *Croatia - Spain* | *0-0; 4-5 pen* | (UNL) |

**22.09.2022    CROATIA - DENMARK**          **2-1(0-0)**          3rd UEFA Nations League A, Group 1
Stadion Maksimir, Zagreb; Referee: Davide Massa (Italy); Attendance: 22,715
**CRO:** Dominik Livaković, Josip Juranović, Josip Šutalo, Joško Gvardiol, Borna Sosa, Mateo Kovačić (78.Lovro Majer), Marcelo Brozović, Luka Modrić (Cap) (90+3.Domagoj Vida), Ivan Perišić (71.Mislav Oršić), Mario Pašalić (71.Nikola Vlašić), Andrej Kramarić (71.Bruno Petković). Trainer: Zlatko Dalić.
**Goals:** Borna Sosa (49), Lovro Majer (79).

**25.09.2022    AUSTRIA - CROATIA**          **1-3(1-1)**          3rd UEFA Nations League A, Group 1
"Ernst Happel" Stadion, Wien; Referee: Artur Manuel Ribeiro Soares Dias (Portugal); Attendance: 45,700
**CRO:** Dominik Livaković, Josip Stanišić, Dejan Lovren, Joško Gvardiol, Borna Barišić (62.Borna Sosa), Mateo Kovačić (85.Mario Pašalić), Marcelo Brozović (18.Lovro Majer), Luka Modrić (Cap), Ivan Perišić, Ante Budimir (62.Marko Livaja), Nikola Vlašić (84.Andrej Kramarić). Trainer: Zlatko Dalić.
**Goals:** Luka Modrić (6), Marko Livaja (69), Dejan Lovren (72).

**16.11.2022    SAUDI ARABIA - CROATIA**          **0-1(0-0)**          Friendly International
„Prince Faisal bin Fahd" Stadium, Riyadh; Referee: Adham Mohammad Tumah Makhadmeh (Jordan); Attendance: 8,287
**CRO:** Dominik Livaković, Josip Stanišić, Dejan Lovren (Cap) (58.Domagoj Vida), Martin Erlić, Borna Barišić, Luka Sučić (46.Mateo Kovačić), Marcelo Brozović (65.Luka Modrić), Mario Pašalić (65.Ivan Perišić), Nikola Vlašić (46.Mislav Oršić), Lovro Majer, Bruno Petković (58.Andrej Kramarić). Trainer: Zlatko Dalić.
**Goal:** Andrej Kramarić (82).

**23.11.2022    MOROCCO - CROATIA**          **0-0**          22nd FIFA WC. Group Stage.
Al Bayt Stadium, Al Khor (Qatar); Referee: Fernando Andrés Rapallini (Argentina); Attendance: 59,407
**CRO:** Dominik Livaković, Josip Juranović, Dejan Lovren, Joško Gvardiol, Borna Sosa, Luka Modrić (Cap), Marcelo Brozović, Mateo Kovačić (79.Lovro Majer), Nikola Vlašić (46.Mario Pašalić), Andrej Kramarić (71.Marko Livaja), Ivan Perišić (90.Mislav Oršić). Trainer: Zlatko Dalić.

**27.11.2022    CROATIA - CANADA**          **4-1(2-1)**          22nd FIFA WC. Group Stage.
Khalifa International Stadium, Al Rayyan (Qatar); Referee: Andrés Matías Matonte Cabrera (Uruguay); Attendance: 44,374
**CRO:** Dominik Livaković, Josip Juranović, Dejan Lovren, Joško Gvardiol, Borna Sosa, Luka Modrić (Cap) (86.Mario Pašalić), Marcelo Brozović, Mateo Kovačić (86.Lovro Majer), Marko Livaja (60.Bruno Petković), Andrej Kramarić (72.Nikola Vlašić), Ivan Perišić (86.Mislav Oršić). Trainer: Zlatko Dalić.
**Goals:** Andrej Kramarić (36), Marko Livaja (44), Andrej Kramarić (70), Lovro Majer (90+4).

**01.12.2022**   **CROATIA - BELGIUM**      **0-0**      22nd FIFA WC. Group Stage.
„Ahmad bin Ali" Stadium, Al Rayyan (Qatar); Attendance: 43,984
Referee: Anthony Taylor (England);
**CRO:** Dominik Livaković, Josip Juranović, Dejan Lovren, Joško Gvardiol, Borna Sosa, Luka Modrić (Cap), Marcelo Brozović, Mateo Kovačić (90+2.Lovro Majer), Andrej Kramarić (64.Mario Pašalić), Marko Livaja (64.Bruno Petković), Ivan Perišić. Trainer: Zlatko Dalić.

**05.12.2022**   **JAPAN - CROATIA**      **1-1(1-0,1-1,1-1); 1-3 on penalties**      22nd FIFA WC. 2nd Round of 16.
Al Janoub Stadium, Al Wakrah (Qatar); Referee: Ismail Elfath (United States); Attendance: 42,523
**CRO:** Dominik Livaković, Josip Juranović, Dejan Lovren, Joško Gvardiol, Borna Barišić, Luka Modrić (Cap) (99.Lovro Majer), Marcelo Brozović, Mateo Kovačić (99.Nikola Vlašić), Andrej Kramarić (68.Mario Pašalić), Bruno Petković (62.Ante Budimir; 106.Marko Livaja), Ivan Perišić (106.Mislav Oršić). Trainer: Zlatko Dalić.
**Goal:** Ivan Perišić (55).
**Penalties:** Nikola Vlašić, Marcelo Brozović, Marko Livaja (missed), Mario Pašalić.

**09.12.2022**   **CROATIA - BRAZIL**      **1-1(0-0,0-0,1-1); 4-2 on penalties**      22nd FIFA WC. Quarter-Finals.
Education City Stadium, Al Rayyan (Qatar); Referee: Michael Oliver (England); Attendance: 43,893
**CRO:** Dominik Livaković, Josip Juranović, Dejan Lovren, Joško Gvardiol, Borna Sosa (110.Ante Budimir), Marcelo Brozović (114.Mislav Oršić), Luka Modrić (Cap), Mateo Kovačić (106.Lovro Majer), Mario Pašalić (72.Nikola Vlašić), Andrej Kramarić (72.Bruno Petković), Ivan Perišić. Trainer: Zlatko Dalić.
**Goal:** Bruno Petković (117).
**Penalties:** Nikola Vlašić, Lovro Majer, Luka Modrić, Mislav Oršić.

**13.12.2022**   **ARGENTINA - CROATIA**      **3-0(2-0)**      22nd FIFA WC. Semi-Finals.
Lusail Stadium, Lusail (Qatar); Referee: Daniele Orsato (Italy); Attendance: 88,966
**CRO:** Dominik Livaković, Josip Juranović, Dejan Lovren, Joško Gvardiol, Borna Sosa (46.Mislav Oršić), Marcelo Brozović (50.Bruno Petković), Luka Modrić (Cap) (81.Lovro Majer), Mateo Kovačić, Mario Pašalić (46.Nikola Vlašić), Andrej Kramarić (72.Marko Livaja), Ivan Perišić. Trainer: Zlatko Dalić.

**17.12.2022**   **CROATIA - MOROCCO**      **2-1(2-1)**      22nd FIFA WC. Third Place Play-off.
Khalifa International Stadium, Al Rayyan (Qatar); Referee: Abdulrahman Ibrahim Al Jassim (Qatar); Attendance: 44,137
**CRO:** Dominik Livaković, Josip Stanišić, Josip Šutalo, Joško Gvardiol, Luka Modrić (Cap), Lovro Majer (66.Mario Pašalić), Mateo Kovačić, Mislav Oršić (90+5.Kristijan Jakić), Ivan Perišić, Andrej Kramarić (61.Nikola Vlašić), Marko Livaja (66.Bruno Petković). Trainer: Zlatko Dalić.
**Goals:** Joško Gvardiol (7), Mislav Oršić (42).

**25.03.2023**   **CROATIA - WALES**      **1-1(1-0)**      17th EC. Qualifiers
Stadion Poljud, Split; Referee: João Pedro da Silva Pinheiro (Portugal); Attendance: 33,474
**CRO:** Dominik Livaković, Josip Juranović, Josip Šutalo, Joško Gvardiol, Borna Sosa, Mateo Kovačić (76.Mario Pašalić), Marcelo Brozović, Luka Modrić (Cap) (90+2.Lovro Majer), Ivan Perišić, Marko Livaja (53.Petar Musa), Andrej Kramarić (74.Nikola Vlašić). Trainer: Zlatko Dalić.
**Goal:** Andrej Kramarić (28).

**28.03.2023**   **TURKEY - CROATIA**      **0-2(0-2)**      17th EC. Qualifiers
Bursa Büyükşehir Belediye Stadyumu, Bursa; Referee: Andreas Ekberg (Sweden); Attendance: 37,750
**CRO:** Dominik Livaković, Josip Stanišić, Josip Šutalo, Joško Gvardiol, Borna Barišić, Mateo Kovačić, Marcelo Brozović, Luka Modrić (Cap) (84.Lovro Majer), Ivan Perišić (90+2.Luka Ivanušec), Mario Pašalić (65.Josip Juranović), Andrej Kramarić (84.Petar Musa). Trainer: Zlatko Dalić.
**Goals:** Mateo Kovačić (20, 45+4).

**14.06.2023**   **NETHERLANDS - CROATIA**      **2-4(1-0,2-2)**      3rd UEFA Nations League, Semi-Finals
Stadion Feijenoord, Rotterdam; Referee: István Kovács (Romania); Attendance: 39,359
**CRO:** Dominik Livaković, Josip Juranović (79.Josip Stanišić), Domagoj Vida, Josip Šutalo (90.Bruno Petković), Mateo Kovačić (85.Lovro Majer), Marcelo Brozović, Luka Modrić (Cap) (119.Borna Barišić), Mario Pašalić, Ivan Perišić, Luka Ivanušec (78.Nikola Vlašić), Andrej Kramarić (90.Martin Erlić). Trainer: Zlatko Dalić.
**Goals:** Andrej Kramarić (55 penalty), Mario Pašalić (72), Bruno Petković (98), Luka Modrić (116 penalty).

**18.06.2023**   **CROATIA - SPAIN**      **0-0 aet; 4-5 on penalties**      3rd UEFA Nations League, Final
Stadion Feijenoord, Rotterdam (Netherlands); Referee: Felix Zwayer (Germany); Attendance: 41,110
**CRO:** Dominik Livaković, Josip Juranović (112.Josip Stanišić), Josip Šutalo, Martin Erlić, Mateo Kovačić, Marcelo Brozović, Luka Modrić (Cap), Ivan Perišić, Mario Pašalić (61.Bruno Petković), Luka Ivanušec (78.Nikola Vlašić), Andrej Kramarić (90+1.Lovro Majer). Trainer: Zlatko Dalić.
**Penalties:** Nikola Vlašić, Marcelo Brozović, Luka Modrić, Lovro Majer (saved), Ivan Perišić, Bruno Petković (saved).

## NATIONAL TEAM PLAYERS
### (16.07.2022 – 15.07.2023)

| Name | DOB | Caps | Goals | Club | |
|---|---|---|---|---|---|

### Goalkeepers

| Name | DOB | Caps | Goals | Club | |
|---|---|---|---|---|---|
| Dominik LIVAKOVIĆ | 09.01.1995 | 45 | 0 | 2022/2023: | *GNK Dinamo Zagreb* |

### Defenders

| Name | DOB | Caps | Goals | Club | |
|---|---|---|---|---|---|
| Borna BARIŠIĆ | 10.11.1992 | 31 | 1 | 2022/2023: | *Rangers FC Glasgow (SCO)* |
| Martin ERLIĆ | 24.01.1998 | 6 | 0 | 2022/2023: | *US Sassuolo Calcio (ITA)* |
| Joško GVARDIOL | 23.01.2002 | 21 | 2 | 2022/2023: | *RasenBallsport Leipzig (GER)* |
| Josip JURANOVIĆ | 16.08.1995 | 31 | 0 | 2022: 22.01.2023-> | *Celtic FC Glasgow (SCO)* *1. FC Union Berlin (GER)* |
| Dejan LOVREN | 05.07.1989 | 78 | 5 | 2022: | *FK Zenit Saint Petersburg (RUS)* |
| Borna SOSA | 21.01.1998 | 14 | 1 | 2022/2023: | *VfB Stuttgart (GER)* |
| Josip STANIŠIĆ | 02.04.2000 | 11 | 0 | 2022/2023: | *FC Bayern München (GER)* |
| Josip ŠUTALO | 28.02.2000 | 8 | 0 | 2022/2023: | *GNK Dinamo Zagreb* |
| Domagoj VIDA | 29.04.1989 | 101 | 4 | 2022/2023: | *AEK Athína (GRE)* |

### Midfielders

| Name | DOB | Caps | Goals | Club | |
|---|---|---|---|---|---|
| Marcelo BROZOVIĆ | 16.11.1992 | 87 | 7 | 2022/2023: | *FC Internazionale Milano (ITA)* |
| Luka IVANUŠEC | 26.11.1998 | 14 | 1 | 2023: | *GNK Dinamo Zagreb* |
| Kristijan JAKIĆ | 14.05.1997 | 5 | 0 | 2022: | *Eintracht Frankfurt (GER)* |
| Mateo KOVAČIĆ | 06.05.1994 | 95 | 5 | 2022/2023: | *Chelsea FC London (ENG)* |
| Lovro MAJER | 17.01.1998 | 22 | 4 | 2022/2023: | *Stade Rennais FC (FRA)* |
| Luka MODRIĆ | 09.09.1985 | 166 | 24 | 2022/2023: | *Real Madrid CF (ESP)* |
| Mario PAŠALIĆ | 09.02.1995 | 54 | 8 | 2022/2023: | *Atalanta Bergamasca Calcio (ITA)* |
| Ivan PERIŠIĆ | 02.02.1989 | 127 | 33 | 2022/2023: | *Tottenham Hotspur FC London (ITA)* |
| Luka SUČIĆ | 08.09.2002 | 4 | 0 | 2022: | *FC Red Bull Salzburg (AUT)* |
| Nikola VLAŠIĆ | 04.10.1997 | 51 | 7 | 2022/2023: | *Torino FC (ITA)* |

### Forwards

| Name | DOB | Caps | Goals | Club | |
|---|---|---|---|---|---|
| Ante BUDIMIR | 22.07.1991 | 17 | 1 | 2022: | *CA Osasuna Pamplona (ESP)* |
| Andrej KRAMARIĆ | 19.06.1991 | 85 | 24 | 2022/2023: | *TSG 1899 Hoffenheim (GER)* |
| Marko LIVAJA | 26.08.1993 | 21 | 4 | 2022/2023: | *HNK Hajduk Split* |
| Petar MUSA | 04.03.1998 | 2 | 0 | 2023: | *Sport Lisboa e Benfica (POR)* |
| Mislav ORŠIĆ | 29.12.1992 | 27 | 2 | 2022: | *GNK Dinamo Zagreb* |
| Bruno PETKOVIĆ | 16.09.1994 | 31 | 8 | 2022/2023: | *GNK Dinamo Zagreb* |

### Trainer

| Name | DOB | | | |
|---|---|---|---|---|
| Zlatko DALIĆ [from 07.10.2017] | 26.10.1966 | 74 M; 36 W; 20 D; 18 L; 120-89 |

# CYPRUS

## The Country:
Κυπριακή Δημοκρατία (Republic of Cyprus)
Capital: Nicosia
Surface: 9,251 km²
Inhabitants: 1,244,188 [2021]
Time: UTC+2

## The FA:
Cyprus Football Association
10 Achaion Street 2413 Engomi, PO Box 25071, 1306 Nicosia
Tel: +357 22 352 341
Foundation date: 23.09.1934
Member of FIFA since: 1948
Member of UEFA since: 1962
Website: www.cfa.com.cy

## NATIONAL TEAM RECORDS

| RECORDS | | |
|---|---|---|
| **First international match:** | 13.11.1960, Nicosia: | Cyprus – Israel 1-1 |
| **Most international caps:** | Yiannakis Okkas | - 103 caps (1997-2011) |
| **Most international goals:** | Michalis Konstantinou | - 32 goals / 84 caps (1997-2012) |

| UEFA EUROPEAN CHAMPIONSHIP | | FIFA WORLD CUP | | OLYMPIC TOURNAMENTS | |
|---|---|---|---|---|---|
| 1960 | Did not enter | 1930 | Did not enter | 1908 | - |
| 1964 | Did not enter | 1934 | Did not enter | 1912 | - |
| 1968 | Qualifiers | 1938 | Did not enter | 1920 | - |
| 1972 | Qualifiers | 1950 | Did not enter | 1924 | - |
| 1976 | Qualifiers | 1954 | Did not enter | 1928 | - |
| 1980 | Qualifiers | 1958 | Did not enter | 1936 | - |
| 1984 | Qualifiers | 1962 | Qualifiers | 1948 | - |
| 1988 | Qualifiers | 1966 | Qualifiers | 1952 | - |
| 1992 | Qualifiers | 1970 | Qualifiers | 1956 | - |
| 1996 | Qualifiers | 1974 | Qualifiers | 1960 | - |
| 2000 | Qualifiers | 1978 | Qualifiers | 1964 | - |
| 2004 | Qualifiers | 1982 | Qualifiers | 1968 | - |
| 2008 | Qualifiers | 1986 | Qualifiers | 1972 | - |
| 2012 | Qualifiers | 1990 | Qualifiers | 1976 | - |
| 2016 | Qualifiers | 1994 | Qualifiers | 1980 | - |
| 2020 | Qualifiers | 1998 | Qualifiers | 1984 | - |
| | | 2002 | Qualifiers | 1988 | - |
| | | 2006 | Qualifiers | 1992 | Qualifiers |
| | | 2010 | Qualifiers | 1996 | Qualifiers |
| | | 2014 | Qualifiers | 2000 | Qualifiers |
| | | 2018 | Qualifiers | 2004 | Qualifiers |
| | | 2022 | Qualifiers | 2008 | Qualifiers |
| | | | | 2012 | Qualifiers |
| | | | | 2016 | Qualifiers |
| | | | | 2020 | Qualifiers |

| UEFA NATIONS LEAGUE | |
|---|---|
| 2018/2019 | League C (Group Stage) |
| 2020/2021 | League C (Group Stage -> relegation Play-outs) |
| 2022/2023 | League C (Group Stage -> relegation Play-outs in March 2024) |

## CYPRIOT CLUB HONOURS IN EUROPEAN CLUB COMPETITIONS:

| European Champion Clubs' Cup (1956-1992) / UEFA Champions League (1993-2023) |
|---|
| None |

| Fairs Cup (1858-1971) / UEFA Cup (1972-2009) / UEFA Europa League (2010-2023) |
|---|
| None |

| UEFA Europa Conference League (2021-2023) |
|---|
| None |

| UEFA Super Cup (1972-2022) |
|---|
| None |

| *European Cup Winners' Cup 1961-1999** |
|---|
| None |

*defunct competition

# NATIONAL COMPETITIONS
## TABLE OF HONOURS

| | CHAMPIONS | CUP WINNERS | BEST GOALSCORERS | |
|---|---|---|---|---|
| 1934/1935 | Enosis Neon Trust Nicosia | Enosis Neon Trust Nicosia | - | |
| 1935/1936 | APOEL Nicosia | Enosis Neon Trust Nicosia | - | |
| 1936/1937 | APOEL Nicosia | APOEL Nicosia | - | |
| 1937/1938 | APOEL Nicosia | Enosis Neon Trust Nicosia | - | |
| 1938/1939 | APOEL Nicosia | AEL Limassol | - | |
| 1939/1940 | APOEL Nicosia | AEL Limassol | - | |
| 1940/1941 | AEL Limassol | APOEL Nicosia | - | |
| 1941-1944 | *No competition* | *No competition* | - | |
| 1944/1945 | EPA Larnaca FC | EPA Larnaca FC | - | |
| 1945/1946 | EPA Larnaca FC | EPA Larnaca FC | - | |
| 1946/1947 | APOEL Nicosia | APOEL Nicosia | - | |
| 1947/1948 | APOEL Nicosia | AEL Limassol | - | |
| 1948/1949 | APOEL Nicosia | Anorthosis Famagusta FC | - | |
| 1949/1950 | Anorthosis Famagusta FC | EPA Larnaca FC | - | |
| 1950/1951 | Çetinkaya Türk Spor Kulübü | APOEL Nicosia | - | |
| 1951/1952 | APOEL Nicosia | Çetinkaya Türk Spor Kulübü | - | |
| 1952/1953 | AEL Limassol | EPA Larnaca FC | - | |
| 1953/1954 | Pezoporikos Larnaca FC | Çetinkaya Türk Spor Kulübü | - | |
| 1954/1955 | AEL Limassol | EPA Larnaca FC | - | |
| 1955/1956 | AEL Limassol | *No competition* | - | |
| 1956/1957 | Anorthosis Famagusta FC | *No competition* | - | |
| 1957/1958 | Anorthosis Famagusta FC | *No competition* | - | |
| 1958/1959 | *No competition* | Anorthosis Famagusta FC | - | |
| 1959/1960 | Anorthosis Famagusta FC | *No competition* | - | |
| 1960/1961 | AC Omonia Nicosia | *No competition* | Panikos Krystallis (Apollon Limassol FC) | 26 |
| 1961/1962 | Anorthosis Famagusta FC | Anorthosis Famagusta FC | Michalis Shialis (Anorthosis Famagusta FC) | 22 |
| 1962/1963 | Anorthosis Famagusta FC | APOEL Nicosia | Panikos Papadopoulos (AEL Limassol) | 24 |
| 1963/1964 | *Championship Abandoned* | Anorthosis Famagusta FC | *Championship abandoned* | |
| 1964/1965 | APOEL Nicosia | AC Omonia Nicosia | Kostakis Pieridis (Olympiakos Nicosia FC) | 21 |
| 1965/1966 | AC Omonia Nicosia | Apollon Limassol FC | Panikos Efthymiades (Olympiakos Nicosia FC) | 20 |
| 1966/1967 | Olympiakos Nicosia FC | Apollon Limassol FC | Andreas Stylianou (APOEL Nicosia) | 29 |
| 1967/1968 | AEL Limassol | APOEL Nicosia | Charalambos Papadopoulos (AEL Limassol) | 31 |
| 1968/1969 | Olympiakos Nicosia FC | APOEL Nicosia | Panikos Efthymiades (Olympiakos Nicosia FC) | 17 |
| 1969/1970 | EPA Larnaca FC | Pezoporikos Larnaca FC | Tasos Constantinou (EPA Larnaca FC) | 24 |
| 1970/1971 | Olympiakos Nicosia FC | Anorthosis Famagusta FC | Andreas Stylianou (APOEL Nicosia) Kostas Vasiliades (Apollon Limassol FC) Panikos Efthymiades (Olympiakos Nicosia FC) | 11 |
| 1971/1972 | AC Omonia Nicosia | AC Omonia Nicosia | Sotiris Kaiafas (AC Omonia Nicosia) | 24 |
| 1972/1973 | APOEL Nicosia | APOEL Nicosia | Lakis Theodorou (EPA Larnaca FC) | 17 |
| 1973/1974 | AC Omonia Nicosia | AC Omonia Nicosia | Sotiris Kaiafas (AC Omonia Nicosia) | 20 |
| 1974/1975 | AC Omonia Nicosia | Anorthosis Famagusta FC | Andros Savva (AC Omonia Nicosia) | 21 |
| 1975/1976 | AC Omonia Nicosia | APOEL Nicosia | Sotiris Kaiafas (AC Omonia Nicosia) | 39 |
| 1976/1977 | AC Omonia Nicosia | Olympiakos Nicosia FC | Sotiris Kaiafas (AC Omonia Nicosia) | 44 |
| 1977/1978 | AC Omonia Nicosia | APOEL Nicosia | Andreas Kanaris (AC Omonia Nicosia) | 20 |
| 1978/1979 | AC Omonia Nicosia | APOEL Nicosia | Sotiris Kaiafas (AC Omonia Nicosia) | 28 |
| 1979/1980 | APOEL Nicosia | AC Omonia Nicosia | Sotiris Kaiafas (AC Omonia Nicosia) | 23 |
| 1980/1981 | AC Omonia Nicosia | AC Omonia Nicosia | Sotiris Kaiafas (AC Omonia Nicosia) | 14 |
| 1981/1982 | AC Omonia Nicosia | AC Omonia Nicosia | Sotiris Kaiafas (AC Omonia Nicosia) | 19 |
| 1982/1983 | AC Omonia Nicosia | AC Omonia Nicosia | Panikos Hatziloizou (Aris Limassol FC) | 17 |
| 1983/1984 | AC Omonia Nicosia | APOEL Nicosia | Sylvester Vernon (Pezoporikos Larnaca FC) Lenos Kittos (Ermis Aradippou FC) | 14 |
| 1984/1985 | AC Omonia Nicosia | AEL Limassol | Giorgos Savvidis (AC Omonia Nicosia) | 24 |
| 1985/1986 | APOEL Nicosia | Apollon Limassol FC | Yiannos Ioannou (APOEL Nicosia) | 22 |
| 1986/1987 | AC Omonia Nicosia | AEL Limassol | Spas Dzhevizov (BUL, AC Omonia Nicosia) | 32 |
| 1987/1988 | Pezoporikos Larnaca FC | AC Omonia Nicosia | Tasos Zouvanis (Enosis Neon Paralimni FC) | 23 |
| 1988/1989 | AC Omonia Nicosia | AEL Limassol | Nigel McNeal (ENG, Nea Salamis Famagusta FC) | 19 |
| 1989/1990 | APOEL Nicosia | Nea Salamis Famagusta FC | Siniša Gogić (YUG, APOEL Nicosia) | 19 |
| 1990/1991 | Apollon Limassol FC | AC Omonia Nicosia | Suad Beširević (YUG, Apollon Limassol FC) Panikos Xiourouppas (AC Omonia Nicosia) | 19 |
| 1991/1992 | APOEL Nicosia | Apollon Limassol FC | József Dzurják (HUN, AC Omonia Nicosia) | 21 |
| 1992/1993 | AC Omonia Nicosia | APOEL Nicosia | Slađan Šćepović (YUG, Apollon Limassol FC) | 25 |
| 1993/1994 | Apollon Limassol FC | AC Omonia Nicosia | Siniša Gogić (YUG, Anorthosis Famagusta FC) | 26 |
| 1994/1995 | Anorthosis Famagusta FC | APOEL Nicosia | Pambis Andreou (Nea Salamis Famagusta FC) | 25 |
| 1995/1996 | APOEL Nicosia | APOEL Nicosia | József Kiprich (HUN, APOEL Nicosia) | 25 |
| 1996/1997 | Anorthosis Famagusta FC | APOEL Nicosia | Michalis Konstantinou (Enosis Neon Paralimni FC) | 17 |
| 1997/1998 | Anorthosis Famagusta FC | Anorthosis Famagusta FC | Rainer Rauffmann (GER, AC Omonia Nicosia) | 42 |
| 1998/1999 | Anorthosis Famagusta FC | APOEL Nicosia | Rainer Rauffmann (GER, AC Omonia Nicosia) | 35 |
| 1999/2000 | Anorthosis Famagusta FC | AC Omonia Nicosia | Rainer Rauffmann (GER, AC Omonia Nicosia) | 34 |
| 2000/2001 | AC Omonia Nicosia | Apollon Limassol FC | Rainer Rauffmann (GER, AC Omonia Nicosia) | 30 |
| 2001/2002 | APOEL Nicosia | Anorthosis Famagusta FC | Wojciech Kowalczyk (POL, Anorthosis Famagusta FC) | 22 |
| 2002/2003 | AC Omonia Nicosia | Anorthosis Famagusta FC | Marios Neophytou (Anorthosis Famagusta FC) | 33 |

| 2003/2004 | APOEL Nicosia | AEK Larnaca FC | Łukasz Sosin (POL, Apollon Limassol FC) | |
| | | | Jozef Kožlej (SVK, AC Omonia Nicosia) | 21 |
| 2004/2005 | Anorthosis Famagusta FC | AC Omonia Nicosia | Łukasz Sosin (POL, Apollon Limassol FC) | 21 |
| 2005/2006 | Apollon Limassol FC | APOEL Nicosia | Łukasz Sosin (POL, Apollon Limassol FC) | 28 |
| 2006/2007 | APOEL Nicosia | Anorthosis Famagusta FC | Esteban Andrés Solari Poggio (ARG, APOEL Nicosia) | 20 |
| 2007/2008 | Anorthosis Famagusta FC | APOEL Nicosia | David Pereira da Costa (BRA, Doxa Katokopias FC) | |
| | | | Łukasz Sosin (POL, Anorthosis Famagusta FC) | 16 |
| 2008/2009 | APOEL Nicosia | APOP Kinyras Peyias FC | Sérgio Luis Gardino da Silva "Serjão" | |
| | | | (BRA, Doxa Katokopias FC) | 24 |
| 2009/2010 | AC Omonia Nicosia | Apollon Limassol FC | Joeano Pinto Chaves (BRA, Ermis Aradippou FC) | |
| | | | José Filipe CorreiaSemedo (CPV, APOP Kinyras) | 22 |
| 2010/2011 | APOEL Nicosia | AC Omonia Nicosia | Miljan Mrdaković (SRB, Apollon Limassol FC) | 21 |
| 2011/2012 | AEL Limassol | AC Omonia Nicosia | Frederico Castro Roque dos Santos "Freddy" | |
| | | | (ANG, AC Omonia Nicosia) | 17 |
| 2012/2013 | APOEL Nicosia | Apollon Limassol FC | Bernardo Lino Castro Paes Vasconcelos | |
| | | | (POR, Alki Larnaca FC) | 18 |
| 2013/2014 | APOEL Nicosia | APOEL Nicosia | Gastón Maximiliano Sangoy (ARG, Apollon Limassol FC) | |
| | | | Marco Tagbajumi (NGA, Ermis Aradippou FC) | |
| | | | Jorge Filipe Monteiro dos Santos Lourenço | |
| | | | (POR, AEL Limassol) | 18 |
| 2014/2015 | APOEL Nicosia | APOEL Nicosia | Mickaël Poté (BEN, AC Omonia Nicosia) | 17 |
| 2015/2016 | APOEL Nicosia | Apollon Limassol FC | Fernando Ezequiel Cavenaghi (ARG, APOEL Nicosia) | |
| | | | André Alves dos Santos (BRA, AEK Larnaca FC) | |
| | | | Dimitar Makriev (BUL, Nea Salamis Famagusta FC) | 19 |
| 2016/2017 | APOEL Nicosia | Apollon Limassol FC | Matthew Anthony Derbyshire (ENG, AC Omonia Nicosia) | 24 |
| 2017/2018 | APOEL Nicosia | AEK Larnaca FC | Matthew Anthony Derbyshire (ENG, AC Omonia Nicosia) | 23 |
| 2018/2019 | APOEL Nicosia | AEL Limassol | Adam Nemec (SVK, Pafos FC Paphos) | 16 |
| 2019/2020 | *Championship abandoned* | *Competition abandoned* | - | |
| 2020/2021 | AC Omonia Nicosia | Anorthosis Famagusta FC | Berat Sadik (FIN, Doxa Katokopias FC) | 18 |
| 2021/2022 | Apollon Limassol FC | AC Omonia Nicosia | Ivan Tričkovski (MKD, AEK Larnaca FC) | 15 |
| 2022/2023 | Aris Limassol FC | AC Omonia Nicosia | Ioannis Pittas (Apollon Limassol FC) | |
| | | | Jairo de Macedo da Silva (BRA, Pafos FC Paphos) | 18 |

## NATIONAL CHAMPIONSHIP
### Cypriot First Division 2022/2023
(26.08.2022 – 29.05.2023)

### Regular Season - Results

**Round 1** [26-30.08.2022]
Karmiotissa - Nea Salamis 1-2(0-1)
Olympiakos - Anorthosis 1-2(1-0)
Aris Limassol - AEL Limassol 2-1(0-1)
APOEL Nicosia - Pafos FC 1-1(0-1)
Akritas Chlorakas - AC Omonia 1-0(1-0)
AEK Larnaca - Doxa Katokopias 0-0
Apollon Limassol - Neon Paralimni 1-0(1-0)

**Round 2** [02-05.09.2022]
Aris Limassol - Olympiakos 5-0(2-0)
Pafos FC - Karmiotissa 4-0(2-0)
Doxa Katokopias - Apollon Limassol 0-1(0-0)
AC Omonia - AEK Larnaca 3-2(1-0)
AEL Limassol - Neon Paralimni 0-1(0-0)
Anorthosis - APOEL Nicosia 0-2(0-1)
Nea Salamis - Akritas Chlorakas 2-1(1-0)

**Round 3** [09-12.09.2022]
Neon Paralimni - Doxa Katokopias 1-2(1-0)
Karmiotissa - Anorthosis 0-2(0-1)
Akritas Chlorakas - Pafos FC 0-4(0-1)
APOEL Nicosia - Aris Limassol 0-1(0-1)
Apollon Limassol - AC Omonia 2-1(0-1)
AEK Larnaca - Nea Salamis 1-0(1-0)
Olympiakos - AEL Limassol 0-0

**Round 4** [15-18.09.2022]
Aris Limassol - Karmiotissa 1-2(0-1)
AEL Limassol - Doxa Katokopias 1-2(0-1)
Anorthosis - Akritas Chlorakas 1-1(0-0)
Olympiakos - APOEL Nicosia 0-2(0-2)
Nea Salamis - Apollon Limassol 1-1(1-1)
Pafos FC - AEK Larnaca 1-0(0-0)
AC Omonia - Neon Paralimni 4-0(2-0)

**Round 5** [01-03.10.2022]
Apollon Limassol - Pafos FC 1-1(0-1)
Doxa Katokopias - AC Omonia 0-2(0-1)
AEK Larnaca - Anorthosis 4-0(2-0)
APOEL Nicosia - AEL Limassol 0-0
Akritas Chlorakas - Aris Limassol 0-3(0-2)
Karmiotissa - Olympiakos 1-0(1-0)
Neon Paralimni - Nea Salamis 2-0(0-0)

**Round 6** [07-10.10.2022]
APOEL Nicosia - Karmiotissa 0-0
Nea Salamis - Doxa Katokopias 1-0(0-0)
Pafos FC - Neon Paralimni 3-0(1-0)
Olympiakos - Akritas Chlorakas 1-0(0-0)
Aris Limassol - AEK Larnaca 1-2(1-1)
AEL Limassol - AC Omonia 1-0(1-0)
Anorthosis - Apollon Limassol 0-1(0-0)

**Round 7** [14-18.10.2022]
Doxa Katokopias - Pafos FC 0-3(0-1)
Neon Paralimni - Anorthosis 1-1(1-1)
Karmiotissa - AEL Limassol 1-2(0-2)
Akritas Chlorakas - APOEL Nicosia 1-2(0-1)
AEK Larnaca - Olympiakos 4-2(2-0)
Apollon Limassol - Aris Limassol 0-3(0-0)
AC Omonia - Nea Salamis 0-1(0-0)

**Round 8** [21-24.10.2022]
Anorthosis - Doxa Katokopias 3-0(1-0)
Olympiakos - Apollon Limassol 1-1(0-0)
Pafos FC - AC Omonia 3-0(1-0)
APOEL Nicosia - AEK Larnaca 1-0(1-0)
Karmiotissa - Akritas Chlorakas 1-0(1-0)
Aris Limassol - Neon Paralimni 2-1(2-1)
AEL Limassol - Nea Salamis 1-0(0-0)

**Round 9** [28-31.10.2022]
Akritas Chlorakas - AEL Limassol 0-3(0-1)
Nea Salamis - Pafos FC 0-2(0-1)
Neon Paralimni - Olympiakos 2-1(1-1)
AEK Larnaca - Karmiotissa 4-0(2-0)
Apollon Limassol - APOEL Nicosia 0-1(0-0)
Doxa Katokopias - Aris Limassol 1-2(1-1)
AC Omonia - Anorthosis 2-0(1-0)

**Round 10** [04-07.11.2022]
APOEL Nicosia - Neon Paralimni 2-0(1-0)
Anorthosis - Nea Salamis 2-1(2-1)
Olympiakos - Doxa Katokopias 2-2(1-2)
AEL Limassol - Pafos FC 1-3(0-2)
Aris Limassol - AC Omonia 1-1(1-0)
Akritas Chlorakas - AEK Larnaca 1-2(0-1)
Karmiotissa - Apollon Limassol 1-1(1-0)

**Round 11** [10-13.11.2022]
Pafos FC - Anorthosis 1-0(1-0)
Nea Salamis - Aris Limassol 1-3(0-2)
AC Omonia - Olympiakos 4-0(1-0)
Neon Paralimni - Karmiotissa 0-0
Apollon Limassol-Akritas Chlorakas 2-0(2-0)
AEK Larnaca - AEL Limassol 1-0(0-0)
Doxa Katokopias - APOEL Nicosia 0-1(0-1)

**Round 12** [25-28.11.2022]
Akritas Chlorakas - Neon Paralimni 2-1(2-1)
Karmiotissa - Doxa Katokopias 2-1(0-1)
AEK Larnaca - Apollon Limassol 1-0(0-0)
APOEL Nicosia - AC Omonia 4-0(1-0)
AEL Limassol - Anorthosis 0-1(0-1)
Aris Limassol - Pafos FC 2-2(0-0)
Olympiakos - Nea Salamis 0-2(0-1)

## Round 13 [02-05.12.2022]
Doxa Katokopias - Akritas Chlorakas 2-0(2-0)
Neon Paralimni - AEK Larnaca 0-2(0-1)
Nea Salamis - APOEL Nicosia 1-3(0-2)
Pafos FC - Olympiakos 1-1(0-0)
Apollon Limassol - AEL Limassol *not played*\*
Anorthosis - Aris Limassol 0-2(0-1)
AC Omonia - Karmiotissa 4-0(1-0)

*\*match not played, declared void*

## Round 14 [09-12.12.2022]
Doxa Katokopias - AEK Larnaca 0-1(0-0)
Pafos FC - APOEL Nicosia 1-2(0-2)
Anorthosis - Olympiakos 1-1(0-0)
Neon Paralimni - Apollon Limassol 0-1(0-0)
AC Omonia - Akritas Chlorakas 1-0(0-0)
AEL Limassol - Aris Limassol 0-0
Nea Salamis - Karmiotissa 2-1(0-1)

## Round 15 [15-19.12.2022]
Apollon Limassol - Doxa Katokopias 1-0(1-0)
Neon Paralimni - AEL Limassol 0-1(0-1)
AEK Larnaca - AC Omonia 2-1(1-1)
Olympiakos - Aris Limassol 0-0
APOEL Nicosia - Anorthosis 1-0(1-0)
Akritas Chlorakas - Nea Salamis 1-2(1-0)
Karmiotissa - Pafos FC 0-1(0-1)

## Round 16 [21-23.12.2022]
Doxa Katokopias - Neon Paralimni 0-3(0-1)
Nea Salamis - AEK Larnaca 0-2(0-2)
Aris Limassol - APOEL Nicosia 1-1(1-1)
AC Omonia - Apollon Limassol 2-0(1-0)
Pafos FC - Akritas Chlorakas 5-2(2-2)
AEL Limassol - Olympiakos 2-0(1-0)
Anorthosis - Karmiotissa 0-3 *awarded*\*\*

*\*\*abandoned at 0-2 after 76 mins (crowd trouble)*

## Round 17 [02-05.01.2023]
Apollon Limassol - Nea Salamis 2-0(1-0)
Neon Paralimni - AC Omonia 0-3(0-2)
APOEL Nicosia - Olympiakos 1-0(1-0)
Doxa Katokopias - AEL Limassol 0-0
AEK Larnaca - Pafos FC 1-0(1-0)
Akritas Chlorakas - Anorthosis 1-0(0-0)
Karmiotissa - Aris Limassol 0-0

## Round 18 [06-09.01.2023]
Nea Salamis - Neon Paralimni 2-0(0-0)
AC Omonia - Doxa Katokopias 2-0(2-0)
Anorthosis - AEK Larnaca 0-0
Pafos FC - Apollon Limassol 2-2(1-0)
AEL Limassol - APOEL Nicosia 1-0(0-0)
Aris Limassol - Akritas Chlorakas 0-0
Olympiakos - Karmiotissa 0-0

## Round 19 [13-17.01.2023]
Akritas Chlorakas - Olympiakos 0-1(0-0)
Neon Paralimni - Pafos FC 0-2(0-1)
Karmiotissa - APOEL Nicosia 1-2(0-0)
AEK Larnaca - Aris Limassol 4-3(2-2)
Apollon Limassol - Anorthosis 3-0(1-0)
AC Omonia - AEL Limassol 1-0(1-0)
Doxa Katokopias - Nea Salamis 0-1(0-0)

## Round 20 [20-23.01.2023]
Olympiakos - AEK Larnaca 0-2(0-1)
AEL Limassol - Karmiotissa 2-0(0-0)
Pafos FC - Doxa Katokopias 3-1(2-1)
APOEL Nicosia - Akritas Chlorakas 2-0(0-0)
Nea Salamis - AC Omonia 2-1(1-0)
Aris Limassol - Apollon Limassol 3-1(2-0)
Anorthosis - Neon Paralimni 1-0(1-0)

## Round 21 [27-30.01.2023]
Apollon Limassol - Olympiakos 2-1(0-0)
Akritas Chlorakas - Karmiotissa 0-2(0-2)
AEK Larnaca - APOEL Nicosia 2-1(1-0)
Doxa Katokopias - Anorthosis 0-0
AC Omonia - Pafos FC 0-0
Nea Salamis - AEL Limassol 2-0(2-0)
Neon Paralimni - Aris Limassol 0-1(0-0)

## Round 22 [02-06.02.2023]
AEL Limassol - Akritas Chlorakas 2-1(1-0)
Anorthosis - AC Omonia 4-1(1-1)
Pafos FC - Nea Salamis 1-2(1-1)
APOEL Nicosia - Apollon Limassol 3-1(0-1)
Karmiotissa - AEK Larnaca 1-3(1-1)
Olympiakos - Neon Paralimni 1-2(1-0)
Aris Limassol - Doxa Katokopias 2-1(0-1)

## Round 23 [08-11.02.2023]
Pafos FC - AEL Limassol 1-0(0-0)
Apollon Limassol - Karmiotissa 3-4(2-1)
Nea Salamis - Anorthosis 0-1(0-1)
AEK Larnaca - Akritas Chlorakas 1-1(0-1)
AC Omonia - Aris Limassol 1-2(0-2)
Doxa Katokopias - Olympiakos 0-0
Neon Paralimni - APOEL Nicosia 1-2(0-1)

## Round 24 [17-20.02.2023]
Karmiotissa - Neon Paralimni 1-1(0-1)
Aris Limassol - Nea Salamis 3-0(3-0)
Akritas Chlorakas-Apollon Limassol 1-3(1-0)
AEL Limassol - AEK Larnaca 2-1(2-1)
APOEL Nicosia - Doxa Katokopias 1-1(1-0)
Anorthosis - Pafos FC 2-1(2-1)
Olympiakos - AC Omonia 0-1(0-1)

## Round 25 [24-27.02.2023]
Doxa Katokopias - Karmiotissa 3-2(0-1)
Pafos FC - Aris Limassol 1-1(0-1)
Anorthosis - AEL Limassol 1-1(0-0)
AC Omonia - APOEL Nicosia 0-2(0-0)
Neon Paralimni - Akritas Chlorakas 5-0(0-0)
Nea Salamis - Olympiakos 2-2(1-1)
Apollon Limassol - AEK Larnaca 2-1(0-0)

## Round 26 [04-07.03.2023]
AEK Larnaca - Neon Paralimni 3-1(2-0)
Karmiotissa - AC Omonia 1-2(0-0)
Akritas Chlorakas - Doxa Katokopias 1-2(1-2)
AEL Limassol - Apollon Limassol 0-2(0-1)
APOEL Nicosia - Nea Salamis 3-0(1-0)
Aris Limassol - Anorthosis 2-0(1-0)
Olympiakos - Pafos FC 1-1(1-1)

## Final Standings

| | | | | | | | | | |
|---|---|---|---|---|---|---|---|---|---|
| 1. | APOEL Nicosia | 26 | 18 | 5 | 3 | 40 | - | 13 | 59 |
| 2. | AEK Larnaca FC | 26 | 18 | 3 | 5 | 46 | - | 21 | 57 |
| 3. | Aris Limassol FC | 26 | 15 | 8 | 3 | 46 | - | 20 | 53 |
| 4. | Pafos FC Paphos | 26 | 14 | 8 | 4 | 48 | - | 20 | 50 |
| 5. | Apollon Limassol FC | 25 | 13 | 5 | 7 | 34 | - | 27 | 44 |
| 6. | AC Omonia Nicosia | 26 | 13 | 2 | 11 | 37 | - | 28 | 41 |
| 7. | Nea Salamis Famagusta FC | 26 | 12 | 2 | 12 | 27 | - | 34 | 38 |
| 8. | AEL Limassol | 25 | 10 | 5 | 10 | 21 | - | 20 | 35 |
| 9. | Anorthosis Famagusta FC | 26 | 9 | 6 | 11 | 22 | - | 30 | 33 |
| 10. | Karmiotissa Polemidion FC | 26 | 7 | 6 | 13 | 25 | - | 40 | 27 |
| 11. | Enosis Neon Paralimni FC | 26 | 6 | 3 | 17 | 22 | - | 38 | 21 |
| 12. | Doxa Katokopias FC | 26 | 5 | 6 | 15 | 18 | - | 36 | 21 |
| 13. | Olympiakos Nicosia FC | 26 | 2 | 10 | 14 | 16 | - | 40 | 16 |
| 14. | Akritas Chlorakas FC | 26 | 3 | 3 | 20 | 15 | - | 50 | 12 |

Teams ranked 1-6 were qualified for the Championship Round, while teams ranked 7-12 were qualified for the Relegation Round.

## Relegation Round

### Results

**Round 27** [10-13.03.2023]
Karmiotissa - Neon Paralimni 2-1(1-0)
Anorthosis - Doxa Katokopias 3-1(0-1)
Nea Salamis - Akritas Chlorakas 4-1(1-1)
AEL Limassol - Olympiakos 0-1(0-0)

**Round 28** [16-19.03.2023]
Doxa Katokopias - Karmiotissa 2-0(2-0)
Akritas Chlorakas - Neon Paralimni 2-2(0-0)
Nea Salamis - AEL Limassol 2-3(1-2)
Olympiakos - Anorthosis 1-2(0-1)

**Round 29** [31.03.-03.04.2023]
Anorthosis - Nea Salamis 4-4(2-1)
Karmiotissa - Olympiakos 0-2(0-1)
AEL Limassol - Akritas Chlorakas 2-2(0-1)
Neon Paralimni - Doxa Katokopias 1-2(0-2)

**Round 30** [07-09.04.2023]
Nea Salamis - Karmiotissa 1-0(1-0)
Akritas Chlorakas - Doxa Katokopias 1-2(1-0)
Olympiakos - Neon Paralimni 0-0
AEL Limassol - Anorthosis 0-2(0-1)

**Round 31** [12-13.04.2023]
Karmiotissa - AEL Limassol 2-0(1-0)
Anorthosis - Akritas Chlorakas 2-3(1-0)
Neon Paralimni - Nea Salamis 0-0
Doxa Katokopias - Olympiakos 1-0(0-0)

**Round 32** [18-19.04.2023]
Nea Salamis - Doxa Katokopias 1-1(0-0)
Akritas Chlorakas - Olympiakos 2-1(1-0)
AEL Limassol - Neon Paralimni 1-0(0-0)
Anorthosis - Karmiotissa 0-0

**Round 33** [22-24.04.2023]
Olympiakos - Nea Salamis 1-0(0-0)
Doxa Katokopias - AEL Limassol 0-0
Neon Paralimni - Anorthosis 0-0
Karmiotissa - Akritas Chlorakas 1-0(1-0)

**Round 34** [28-30.04.2023]
Akritas Chlorakas - Nea Salamis 1-0(0-0)
Neon Paralimni - Karmiotissa 0-1(0-1)
Doxa Katokopias - Anorthosis 0-5(0-3)
Olympiakos - AEL Limassol 1-1(1-1)

**Round 35** [03-04.05.2023]
Karmiotissa - Doxa Katokopias 2-1(1-1)
Neon Paralimni - Akritas Chlorakas 5-1(4-0)
AEL Limassol - Nea Salamis 3-3(3-1)
Anorthosis - Olympiakos 4-1(2-0)

**Round 36** [07-09.05.2023]
Nea Salamis - Anorthosis 0-2(0-1)
Olympiakos - Karmiotissa 1-2(1-1)
Doxa Katokopias - Neon Paralimni 0-1(0-0)
Akritas Chlorakas - AEL Limassol 1-0(1-0)

**Round 37** [12-15.05.2023]
Neon Paralimni - Olympiakos 3-0(1-0)
Karmiotissa - Nea Salamis 1-1(1-1)
Anorthosis - AEL Limassol 2-0(0-0)
Doxa Katokopias - Akritas Chlorakas 1-3(1-1)

**Round 38** [17-19.05.2023]
Nea Salamis - Neon Paralimni 4-2(2-0)
AEL Limassol - Karmiotissa 3-0(2-0)
Olympiakos - Doxa Katokopias 1-2(0-0)
Akritas Chlorakas - Anorthosis 3-1(0-1)

**Round 39** [20-23.05.2023]
Neon Paralimni - AEL Limassol 3-0(0-0)
Olympiakos - Akritas Chlorakas 2-2(1-1)
Doxa Katokopias - Nea Salamis 0-1(0-0)
Karmiotissa - Anorthosis 1-2(0-1)

**Round 40** [26-29.05.2023]
Nea Salamis - Olympiakos 3-2(2-0)
Akritas Chlorakas - Karmiotissa 0-0
Anorthosis - Neon Paralimni 1-0(0-0)
AEL Limassol - Doxa Katokopias 1-1(1-0)

### Standings

| | | Total | | | | | Home | | | | | Away | | | | |
|---|---|---|---|---|---|---|---|---|---|---|---|---|---|---|---|---|---|
| 7. | Anorthosis Famagusta FC | 40 | 18 | 9 | 13 | 52 - 44 | 63 | 9 | 6 | 5 | 31 - 23 | 9 | 3 | 8 | 21 - 21 |
| 8. | Nea Salamis Famagusta FC | 40 | 17 | 7 | 16 | 51 - 55 | 58 | 10 | 3 | 7 | 31 - 28 | 7 | 4 | 9 | 20 - 27 |
| 9. | AEL Limassol | 39 | 13 | 10 | 16 | 35 - 40 | 49 | 9 | 4 | 7 | 23 - 20 | 4 | 6 | 9 | 12 - 20 |
| 10. | Karmiotissa Polemidion FC | 40 | 13 | 9 | 18 | 37 - 54 | 48 | 7 | 4 | 9 | 20 - 24 | 6 | 5 | 9 | 17 - 30 |
| 11. | Doxa Katokopias FC | 40 | 10 | 9 | 21 | 32 - 56 | 39 | 4 | 4 | 12 | 10 - 26 | 6 | 5 | 9 | 22 - 30 |
| 12. | Enosis Neon Paralimni FC *(Relegated)* | 40 | 10 | 7 | 23 | 40 - 52 | 37 | 6 | 4 | 10 | 24 - 20 | 4 | 3 | 13 | 16 - 32 |
| 13. | Akritas Chlorakas FC *(Relegated)* | 40 | 9 | 7 | 24 | 37 - 73 | 34 | 7 | 2 | 11 | 19 - 31 | 2 | 5 | 13 | 18 - 42 |
| 14. | Olympiakos Nicosia FC *(Relegated)* | 40 | 5 | 13 | 22 | 30 - 62 | 28 | 2 | 9 | 9 | 14 - 24 | 3 | 4 | 13 | 16 - 38 |

## Championship Round

### Results

**Round 27** [11-13.03.2023]
AC Omonia - APOEL Nicosia 1-1(0-1)
Pafos FC - Aris Limassol 2-2(1-2)
AEK Larnaca - Apollon Limassol 0-1(0-1)

**Round 28** [17-20.03.2023]
APOEL Nicosia - Pafos FC 0-0
Apollon Limassol - AC Omonia 3-1(2-1)
Aris Limassol - AEK Larnaca 4-0(1-0)

**Round 29** [02-03.04.2023]
AC Omonia - Pafos FC 2-0(0-0)
Apollon Limassol - Aris Limassol 0-1(0-0)
AEK Larnaca - APOEL Nicosia 2-2(1-2)

**Round 30** [10-11.04.2023]
APOEL Nicosia - Apollon Limassol 0-2(0-1)
AC Omonia - Aris Limassol 0-3(0-1)
Pafos FC - AEK Larnaca 4-0(2-0)

**Round 31** [21-23.04.2023]
AEK Larnaca - AC Omonia 2-0(2-0)
Apollon Limassol - Pafos FC 0-1(0-1)
Aris Limassol - APOEL Nicosia 0-0

**Round 32** [30.04.-01.05.2023]
Apollon Limassol - AEK Larnaca 1-0(0-0)
APOEL Nicosia - AC Omonia 0-0
Aris Limassol - Pafos FC 2-1(0-0)

**Round 33** [06-07.05.2023]
AEK Larnaca - Aris Limassol 1-1(0-1)
Pafos FC - APOEL Nicosia 1-1(1-1)
AC Omonia - Apollon Limassol 1-2(1-0)

**Round 34** [13-14.05.2023]
Pafos FC - AC Omonia 0-1(0-1)
Aris Limassol - Apollon Limassol 2-0(2-0)
APOEL Nicosia - AEK Larnaca 2-1(1-1)

**Round 35** [20-21.05.2023]
Aris Limassol - AC Omonia 1-0(1-0)
Apollon Limassol - APOEL Nicosia 3-2(1-1)
AEK Larnaca - Pafos FC 1-1(0-1)

**Round 36** [27-28.05.2023]
APOEL Nicosia - Aris Limassol 4-3(3-3)
Pafos FC - Apollon Limassol 2-1(0-1)
AC Omonia - AEK Larnaca 0-2(0-1)

## Standings

| | | Total | | | | | Home | | | | | Away | | | |
|---|---|---|---|---|---|---|---|---|---|---|---|---|---|---|---|
| 1. Aris Limassol FC | 36 | 21 | 11 | 4 | 65 - 28 | 74 | 11 | 5 | 2 | 34 - 13 | 10 | 6 | 2 | 31 - 15 |
| 2. APOEL Nicosia | 36 | 20 | 11 | 5 | 52 - 26 | 71 | 10 | 6 | 2 | 25 - 10 | 10 | 5 | 3 | 27 - 16 |
| 3. AEK Larnaca FC | 36 | 20 | 6 | 10 | 55 - 37 | 66 | 12 | 5 | 1 | 34 - 14 | 8 | 1 | 9 | 21 - 23 |
| 4. Pafos FC Paphos | 36 | 17 | 12 | 7 | 60 - 30 | 63 | 10 | 5 | 3 | 36 - 16 | 7 | 7 | 4 | 24 - 14 |
| 5. Apollon Limassol FC | 35 | 19 | 5 | 11 | 47 - 37 | 62 | 11 | 1 | 5 | 26 - 17 | 8 | 4 | 6 | 21 - 20 |
| 6. AC Omonia Nicosia | 36 | 15 | 4 | 17 | 43 - 42 | 49 | 10 | 2 | 6 | 28 - 15 | 5 | 2 | 11 | 15 - 27 |

### Top goalscorers:

| | | |
|---|---|---|
| 18 | Ioannis Pittas | *Apollon Limassol FC* |
| 18 | Jairo de Macedo da Silva (BRA) | *Pafos FC Paphos* |
| 16 | Diego Fernando Dorregaray (ARG) | *Nea Salamis Famagusta FC* |
| 13 | Aleksandr Kokorin (RUS) | *Aris Limassol FC* |

## NATIONAL CUP
### Kypello Kyprou 2022/2023

#### 1/8-Finals [02.11./01.12.2022 & 12.01./17-19.01.2023]

| | | | | |
|---|---|---|---|---|
| PO Xylotymbou 2006- Olympiakos Nicosia FC | 0-2(0-2) | Doxa Katokopias FC - Ethnikos Achna FC | 5-1(2-1) |
| AC Omonia Nicosia - Karmiotissa Polemidion FC | 2-1(2-1) | Pafos FC Paphos - Akritas Chlorakas FC | 3-1(1-0) |
| AEL Limassol - Apollon Limassol FC | 0-0 aet; 5-4 pen | APOEL Nicosia - Aris Limassol FC | 4-2(3-1) |
| Nea Salamis Famagusta FC - AEK Larnaca FC | 4-0(1-0) | Anorthosis Famagusta FC-Enosis Neon Paralimni FC | 0-0 aet; 4-3 pen |

#### Quarter-Finals [14-16.02./28.02.-02.03.2023]

| First Leg | | Second Leg | |
|---|---|---|---|
| AEL Limassol - Nea Salamis Famagusta FC | 1-0(0-0) | Nea Salamis Famagusta FC - AEL Limassol | 1-1(1-1) |
| Doxa Katokopias FC - Pafos FC Paphos | 1-4(1-2) | Pafos FC Paphos - Doxa Katokopias FC | 1-1(1-0) |
| AC Omonia Nicosia - APOEL Nicosia | 1-2(1-0) | APOEL Nicosia - AC Omonia Nicosia | 0-2(0-1) |
| Olympiakos Nicosia FC - Anorthosis Famagusta FC | 2-1(1-1) | Anorthosis Famagusta FC - Olympiakos Nicosia FC | 1-1(0-1) |

#### Semi-Finals [05-06.04./26.04.2023]

| First Leg | | Second Leg | |
|---|---|---|---|
| Olympiakos Nicosia FC - AEL Limassol | 0-0 | AEL Limassol - Olympiakos Nicosia FC | 1-0(0-0) |
| Pafos FC Paphos - AC Omonia Nicosia | 1-1(0-1) | AC Omonia Nicosia - Pafos FC Paphos | 3-1(1-1) |

#### Final

24.05.2023; Stádio GSP, Nicosia; Referee: Szymon Marciniak (Poland); Attendance: 19,076

**AEL Limassol - AC Omonia Nicosia**                                         **0-1(0-0)**

**AEL Limassol**: Muriel Gustavo Becker, Sébastien Tony Dewaest, André Ferreira Teixeira (Cap), Djalma Antônio da Silva Filho, Slobodan Medojević, Javier Osvaldo Mendoza (90+1.Aaron Tshibola), Davor Zdravkovski, Stylianos Panteli (65.Jared Khasa), Evangelos Andreou (90+1.Fiodor Černych), Nicolae Milinceanu (65.Kevin Antonio Joel Gislain Mirallas y Castillo), Andreas Makris. Trainer: Christos Charalampous.

**AC Omonia**: Fabiano Ribeiro de Freitas, Jan Lecjaks, Nikos Panagiotou, Héctor Yuste Canton, Adam James Matthews, Ioannis Kousoulos (Cap), Mikkel Morgenstar Pålssønn Diskerud (57.Fotis Papoulis), Karim Ansarifard (90+1.Charalampos Charalampous), Loizos Loizou (90+1.Nemanja Miletić), Panagiotis Zachariou (57.Fouad Bachirou), Andronikos Kakoullis (73.Roman Bezus). Trainer: Sofronios Avgousti.

**Goal:** 0-1 Karim Ansarifard (85).

## THE CLUBS 2022/2023

<u>Please note</u>: appearances and goals are including statistics of regular season and play-offs (Championship and Relegation Round).

### Athletiki Enosi Kition Larnakas (AEK Larnaca)

| | |
|---|---|
| **Founded**: | 18.07.1994 |
| **Stadium**: | AEK Arena "Georgios Karapatakis", Larnaca (7,400) |
| **Trainer**: | José Luis Oltra Castañer (ESP)   24.03.1969 |

| Goalkeepers: | DOB | M | (s) | G |
|---|---|---|---|---|
| Kenan Pirić (BIH) | 07.07.1994 | 35 | | |
| Ioakim Toumpas | 19.02.1999 | 1 | | |
| **Defenders:** | **DOB** | **M** | **(s)** | **G** |
| Henry Andreou | 02.04.2001 | 1 | (1) | |
| *Ángel García* Cabezali (ESP) | 03.02.1993 | 20 | (6) | 1 |
| Kypros Christoforou | 24.04.1993 | 2 | (5) | |
| Nikos Englezou | 11.07.1993 | 13 | (2) | 1 |
| *Ismael* Casas Casado (ESP) | 07.03.2001 | 14 | (12) | |
| *Mikel* González de Martín Martínez (ESP) | 24.09.1985 | 15 | (5) | 1 |
| Hrvoje Miličević (CRO) | 20.04.1993 | 32 | (3) | 2 |
| Roberto José Rosales Altuve (VEN) | 20.11.1988 | 23 | (5) | |
| Nenad Tomović (SRB) | 30.08.1987 | 25 | (2) | |
| **Midfielders:** | **DOB** | **M** | **(s)** | **G** |
| Artem Gromov (UKR) | 14.01.1990 | 2 | (11) | |
| Luís Gustavo „*Gus*" *Ledes* Evangelista dos Santos (POR) | 28.09.1992 | 28 | (3) | |
| Rafail Mamas | 04.03.2001 | 6 | (15) | |

| | | | | |
|---|---|---|---|---|
| Giorgos Naoum | 21.02.2001 | 6 | (14) | |
| *Oier* Sanjurjo Maté (ESP) | 25.05.1986 | 11 | (17) | 2 |
| *Pere Pons* Riera (ESP) | 20.02.1993 | 29 | (1) | 4 |
| **Forwards:** | **DOB** | **M** | **(s)** | **G** |
| Omri Altman (ISR) | 23.03.1994 | 20 | (3) | 8 |
| Ernest Kwabena Asante (GHA) | 06.11.1988 | 6 | (5) | |
| *Bruno* Alexandre Vilela *Gama* (POR) | 15.11.1987 | 1 | (1) | |
| Imad Faraj (FRA) | 11.02.1999 | 25 | (6) | 5 |
| *Ádám* Gyurcsó (HUN) | 06.03.1991 | 24 | (2) | 6 |
| Marin Jakoliš (CRO) | 26.12.1996 | 6 | (7) | |
| Nemanja Nikolić (HUN) | 31.12.1987 | 3 | (9) | 1 |
| Victor Oluyemi Olatunji (NGA) | 05.09.1999 | 4 | (4) | 1 |
| *Rafael* Guimarães *Lopes* (POR) | 28.07.1991 | 20 | (12) | 6 |
| José Rafael Romo Pérez (VEN) | 06.12.1993 | 3 | (15) | 2 |
| Ivan Tričkovski (MKD) | 18.04.1987 | 21 | (8) | 11 |
| Marios Tziortzis | 02.02.2004 | | (1) | |

## Athlitiki Enosi Lemesou (AEL Limassol)

| | | |
|---|---|---|
| **Founded**: | 04.10.1930 | |
| **Stadium**: | Stádio Alphamega [Limassol Arena], Limassol (10,700) | |
| **Trainer**: | Jorge Manuel Rebelo Fernandes "Silas" (POR) | 01.09.1976 |
| [17.09.2022] | Čedomir Janevski (MKD) | 03.07.1961 |
| [14.04.2023] | Christos Charalampous | 03.10.1981 |

| Goalkeepers: | DOB | M | (s) | G |
|---|---|---|---|---|
| Michalis Kyriakou | 30.12.2002 | 1 | | |
| *Miguel* Aires Fernandes de *Oliveira* (POR) | 25.05.1994 | 13 | (1) | |
| *Muriel* Gustavo *Becker* (BRA) | 14.02.1987 | 25 | | |
| **Defenders:** | **DOB** | **M** | **(s)** | **G** |
| André Ferreira Teixeira (POR) | 14.08.1993 | 28 | (2) | 2 |
| Kristian Bilovar (UKR) | 05.02.2001 | 23 | (5) | |
| *Bruno* Araújo Dos *Santos* (BRA) | 07.02.1993 | 11 | (3) | 1 |
| Sébastien Tony Dewaest (BEL) | 27.05.1991 | 9 | (3) | 1 |
| Petar Filipović (CRO) | 14.09.1990 | 5 | (3) | |
| Christoforos Frantzis | 25.02.2001 | 14 | (8) | 1 |
| *Hugo* Cerqueira Pinto *Basto* (POR) | 14.05.1993 | 10 | | |
| Andreas Ioannou | 23.03.2005 | 2 | (2) | |
| Michalis Kolias | 02.08.2004 | 3 | (10) | |
| Kypros Neofytou | 13.08.2002 | 2 | (3) | |
| Djalma Antônio da *Silva* Filho (BRA) | 19.09.1994 | 32 | (1) | 2 |
| Marko Veselinovic (RSA) | 23.04.2003 | 1 | | |
| **Midfielders:** | **DOB** | **M** | **(s)** | **G** |
| Savvas Christodoulou | 02.01.2005 | 1 | (2) | |
| Vittorio Continella (ITA) | 31.12.2002 | 15 | (11) | 2 |
| Alexander Kačaniklić (SWE) | 13.08.1991 | 6 | (5) | 4 |
| Namanja Kerkez | 22.09.2005 | | (1) | |
| Slobodan Medojević (SRB) | 20.11.1990 | 10 | (7) | |
| Javier Osvaldo Mendoza (ARG) | 02.09.1992 | 7 | (3) | |
| Stylianos Panteli | 07.08.1999 | 17 | (5) | |
| Vasilios Papafotis | 10.08.1995 | 20 | (11) | 2 |
| Christos Sergiou | 10.06.2005 | 1 | | |
| Evdoras Silvestros | 19.06.1998 | 4 | (5) | |
| Aaron Tshibola (COD) | 02.01.1995 | 19 | (2) | 2 |
| Leontios Zacharia | 19.09.2005 | 2 | (2) | |
| Davor Zdravkovski (MKD) | 20.03.1998 | 27 | (5) | |
| **Forwards:** | **DOB** | **M** | **(s)** | **G** |
| Evangelos Andreou | 24.09.2002 | 4 | (7) | 1 |
| Saido Berahino (BDI) | 04.08.1993 | 13 | (15) | 4 |
| Fiodor Černych (LTU) | 21.05.1991 | 13 | (3) | 1 |
| Amadou Ciss (SEN) | 10.04.1999 | 11 | (4) | |
| Jared Khasa (FRA) | 04.11.1997 | 21 | (8) | 1 |
| Andreas Makris | 27.11.1995 | 14 | (9) | 2 |
| Nicolae Milinceanu (MDA) | 01.08.1992 | 15 | (14) | 2 |
| Kevin Antonio Joel Gislain Mirallas y Castillo (BEL) | 05.10.1987 | 17 | (4) | 4 |
| Panagiotis Neofytou | 02.01.2004 | | (1) | |
| Michael Odysseos | 08.12.2005 | 1 | (2) | |
| José Rafael Romo Pérez (VEN) | 06.12.1993 | 5 | (7) | 1 |
| Stefan Šćepović (SRB) | 10.01.1990 | 7 | (2) | |

## Akritas Chlorakas Football Club

| | | |
|---|---|---|
| **Founded**: | 1971 | |
| **Stadium**: | Stádio „Stelios Kyriakides", Paphos (9,394) | |
| **Trainer**: | David Badía Cequier (ESP) | 04.09.1974 |
| [30.12.2022] | Bruno Akrapović (BIH) | 26.09.1967 |
| [28.02.2023] | Denis Laktionov (RUS) | 04.09.1977 |

| Goalkeepers: | DOB | M | (s) | G |
|---|---|---|---|---|
| *Guilherme* Vicentini Castellani (BRA) | 25.05.2000 | 5 | | |
| Kleton Perntreou (ALB) | 08.01.1995 | 35 | | |
| **Defenders:** | **DOB** | **M** | **(s)** | **G** |
| Yago Balthazar Bernardi Gutiérrez (ARG) | 10.08.2001 | 6 | | |
| Hamed Dramé (FRA) | 13.06.2001 | 20 | (8) | 1 |
| Lois Sylvain Fauriel (FRA) | 17.07.2002 | 8 | (11) | |
| Souleymane Fofana (CIV) | 20.01.2002 | 7 | | |
| Konstantinos Karagiannis | 02.04.2000 | 29 | (2) | |
| Seid Korač (LUX) | 20.10.2001 | 13 | (2) | |
| Vinko Medimorec (CRO) | 01.06.1996 | 18 | | |
| Wilguens Paugain (FRA) | 24.08.2001 | 9 | (12) | |
| Ivan Šaravanja (BIH) | 24.08.1996 | 23 | (4) | |
| Edin Šehić (BIH) | 03.02.1995 | 32 | (2) | 1 |
| **Midfielders:** | **DOB** | **M** | **(s)** | **G** |
| *Abraham* González Casanova (ESP) | 16.07.1985 | 33 | (5) | 2 |
| Ivan Alekseev (RUS) | 29.06.2001 | 2 | (1) | |
| Vasilis Dimosthenous | 27.03.2000 | 7 | (6) | 1 |
| Nikita Dubov (RUS) | 15.08.2000 | 3 | (2) | |
| Javier *Eraso* Goñi (ESP) | 22.03.1990 | 25 | (9) | 6 |
| Stavros Gavriel | 29.01.2002 | 32 | | 5 |
| Ibrahim Pekegnon Koné (CIV) | 01.01.2002 | 25 | (5) | 1 |
| Loukas Kyriakidis | 01.06.2004 | | (1) | |
| *Matheus* dos Santos *Clemente* (POR) | 10.06.1998 | 10 | (10) | 2 |
| Giorgos Vasou | 26.07.1993 | 1 | (2) | |
| **Forwards:** | **DOB** | **M** | **(s)** | **G** |
| Besart Abdurahimi (MKD) | 31.07.1990 | 3 | (1) | |
| Magomedkhabib Abdusalamov (RUS) | 01.05.2003 | 4 | (14) | |
| *Davi* Machado dos Santos *Araújo* (BRA) | 20.03.1999 | 21 | (11) | |
| Jawad El Jemili Setti (ESP) | 04.09.2002 | 10 | (9) | 2 |
| Jose Roberto da Silva Lima Junior „Juninho Carpina"(BRA) | 09.03.2000 | 3 | (11) | |
| Pedro Antonio Pimentel Ferreira „Pedrinho"(BRA) | 20.02.2002 | | (1) | |
| Iasonas Pikis | 11.11.2000 | 15 | (8) | 1 |
| Reginaldo *Ramires* de Oliveira Albertino (BRA) | 25.04.2001 | 7 | (8) | 3 |
| *Rodrigo* Santos *Varanda* (BRA) | 11.01.2003 | 7 | (3) | 1 |
| Marcelo Luis Torres (ARG) | 06.11.1997 | 16 | (4) | 7 |
| *Vasco* Rafael Fortes *Lopes* (CPV) | 02.09.1999 | 11 | (12) | 3 |

## Anorthosis Famagusta Football Club

| | | |
|---|---|---|
| **Founded**: | 30.01.1911 | |
| **Stadium**: | Stádio "Antonis Papadopoulos", Larnaca (10,230) | |
| **Trainer**: | Darko Milanić (SVN) | 18.12.1967 |
| [03.10.2022] | Francisco Javier "Xisco" Muñoz Llompart (ESP) | 05.09.1980 |
| [05.01.2023] | Vesko Mihajlović (SRB) | 17.03.1968 |

| Goalkeepers: | DOB | M | (s) | G |
|---|---|---|---|---|
| Andreas Keravnos | 05.05.1999 | 9 | (1) | |
| Giorgi Loria (GEO) | 27.01.1986 | 25 | | |
| Neofytos Michail | 16.12.1993 | 4 | (2) | |
| Georgios Papadopoulos | 24.04.1991 | 2 | | |
| **Defenders:** | **DOB** | **M** | **(s)** | **G** |
| *Anderson Correia* de Barros (BRA) | 06.05.1991 | 30 | (2) | |
| Marios Antoniades | 14.05.1990 | 14 | (2) | 2 |
| Pavlos Correa | 14.07.1998 | 19 | (7) | |
| Hovhannes Hambardzumyan (ARM) | 04.10.1990 | 14 | (4) | 1 |
| Varazdat Haroyan (ARM) | 24.08.1992 | 18 | (2) | 1 |
| Francisco Manuel Geraldo Rosa „Kiko" (POR) | 20.01.1993 | 14 | (3) | 1 |
| Konstantinos Konstantinou | 07.09.2005 | 2 | (1) | |
| *Marco* João Costa *Baixinho* (POR) | 11.07.1989 | 33 | (1) | 2 |
| **Midfielders:** | **DOB** | **M** | **(s)** | **G** |
| Minas Antoniou | 22.02.1994 | 23 | (8) | |
| Kostakis Artymatas | 15.04.1993 | 23 | (2) | |
| Andreas Chrysostomou | 14.01.2001 | | (11) | 1 |
| Lazaros Christodoulopoulos (GRE) | 19.12.1986 | 3 | (5) | |
| Michalis Ioannou | 30.06.2000 | 22 | (6) | |
| Jason David Ian Puncheon (ENG) | 26.06.1986 | 10 | (6) | |
| Erik Sabo (SVK) | 22.11.1991 | 30 | (5) | 2 |
| *Sergio Tejera* Rodríguez (ESP) | 28.05.1990 | 13 | (1) | 2 |
| **Forwards:** | **DOB** | **M** | **(s)** | **G** |
| Antonio Cortés Heredia „Antoñín" (ESP) | 16.04.2000 | 10 | (8) | 4 |
| Sotiris Argyrou | 08.01.2005 | 1 | (5) | |
| Dimitris Christofi | 28.09.1988 | 10 | (22) | 5 |
| Avtandil Ebralidze (GEO) | 03.10.1991 | 8 | (7) | 1 |
| Miguel Ángel *Guerrero* Martín (ESP) | 12.07.1990 | 19 | (1) | 10 |
| *Hélder* José Castro Ferreira (POR) | 05.04.1997 | 15 | (19) | 3 |
| Dimitrianos Juliou | 19.01.2006 | | (4) | |
| Samuel Mráz (SVK) | 13.05.1997 | 10 | (9) | 6 |
| Casimir Rodrigue Ninga (CHA) | 17.05.1993 | 21 | (6) | 5 |
| Daniel Paroutis | 02.01.2001 | 14 | (7) | 2 |
| Dejan Radonjić (CRO) | 23.07.1990 | 1 | (9) | |
| Amr Warda (EGY) | 17.09.1993 | 10 | (2) | 1 |
| Majeed Waris (GHA) | 19.09.1991 | 13 | (14) | 1 |

## Athletikos Podosferikos Omilos Ellinon Lefkosias (APOEL Nicosia)

| Founded: | 08.11.1926 | | | |
|---|---|---|---|---|
| Stadium: | Stádio GSP, Nicosia (22,859) | | | |
| Trainer: | Sofronis Avgousti | | | 09.03.1977 |
| [04.10.2022] | Makis Sergidis | | | 02.10.1980 |
| [05.10.2022] | Vladan Milojević (SRB) | | | 09.03.1970 |
| [08.06.2023] | Ricardo Manuel da Silva Sá Pinto (POR) | | | 10.10.1972 |

| Goalkeepers: | DOB | M | (s) | G |
|---|---|---|---|---|
| Vid Belec (SVN) | 06.06.1990 | 32 | | |
| Andreas Christodoulou | 26.03.1997 | 4 | (1) | |
| **Defenders:** | DOB | M | (s) | G |
| José *Ángel Crespo* Rincón (ESP) | 09.02.1987 | 33 | | 2 |
| Issam Chebake (MAR) | 12.10.1989 | 11 | (5) | |
| Lasha Dvali (GEO) | 14.05.1995 | 20 | (5) | 4 |
| Franco Ariel Ferrari (ARG) | 09.05.1992 | 23 | (2) | |
| Konstantinos Giannakou | 25.04.2005 | | (1) | |
| Andreas Karo | 09.09.1996 | 21 | (4) | |
| Konstantinos Koromias | 31.03.2004 | | (1) | |
| Mateo Sušić (BIH) | 18.11.1990 | 24 | (1) | 3 |
| Christos Wheeler | 29.06.1997 | 12 | (3) | |
| **Midfielders:** | DOB | M | (s) | G |
| Danny Blum (GER) | 07.01.1991 | 5 | (9) | 2 |
| Euciodálcio Gomes „Dálcio" (POR) | 22.05.1996 | 27 | (7) | 2 |
| Murtaz Daushvili (GEO) | 01.05.1989 | 7 | (7) | |
| Giorgos Efrem | 05.07.1989 | 7 | (16) | 3 |
| Georgi Kostadinov (BUL) | 07.09.1990 | 24 | (1) | 2 |
| Amel Mujanić (SWE) | 01.04.2001 | | (1) | |
| Kingsley Sarfo (GHA) | 13.02.1995 | 31 | | 4 |
| Giannis Satsias | 28.12.2002 | 8 | (11) | 2 |
| Lucas Martín Villafáñez (ARG) | 04.10.1991 | 14 | (4) | |
| **Forwards:** | DOB | M | (s) | G |
| El Fardou Ben Mohamed (COM) | 10.06.1989 | 7 | (5) | 2 |
| Anastasios Donis (GRE) | 29.08.1996 | 12 | (4) | 5 |
| Marios Elia | 19.05.1996 | 1 | (12) | 1 |
| Stavros Georgiou | 19.10.2004 | | (1) | |
| Giorgi Kvilitaia (GEO) | 01.10.1993 | 26 | (4) | 8 |
| Federico Macheda (ITA) | 22.08.1991 | 6 | (9) | 2 |
| Anton Maglica (CRO) | 11.11.1991 | 6 | (4) | |
| Marcos Vinicius Sousa Natividade „Marquinhos" (BRA) | 26.01.1997 | 22 | (9) | 8 |
| Dieumerci Ndongala (COD) | 14.06.1991 | 11 | (12) | 1 |
| *Rafael* Mascarenhas *Moreira* (POR) | 05.04.2002 | 1 | (5) | |
| Dimitris Theodorou | 10.09.1997 | 1 | (2) | |

## Apollon Lemesou (Apollon Limassol Football Club)

| Founded: | 14.04.1954 | | | |
|---|---|---|---|---|
| Stadium: | Stádio Alphamega [Limassol Arena], Limassol (10,700) | | | |
| Trainer: | Alexander Zorniger (GER) | | | 08.10.1967 |
| [12.08.2022] | David Catalá Jiménez (ESP) | | | 03.05.1980 |
| [09.11.2022] | Konstantinos Makridis | | | 13.01.1982 |
| [11.02.2023] | Bogdan Ioan And one (ROU) | | | 07.01.1975 |

| Goalkeepers: | DOB | M | (s) | G |
|---|---|---|---|---|
| Dimitris Dimitriou | 15.01.1999 | 4 | | |
| Aleksandar Jovanović (SRB) | 06.12.1992 | 31 | | |
| **Defenders:** | DOB | M | (s) | G |
| Haitam Aleesami (NOR) | 31.07.1991 | 8 | (7) | |
| Panagiotis Artymatas | 12.11.1998 | 4 | (4) | |
| Elohor Godswill Ekpolo (NGA) | 14.05.1995 | 11 | (2) | 1 |
| *Euclides* da Silva *Cabral* (POR) | 05.01.1999 | 2 | (4) | |
| Vukašin Jovanović (SRB) | 17.05.1996 | 16 | | |
| Amine Khammas (MAR) | 06.04.1999 | 23 | (2) | 1 |
| Charis Mavrias (GRE) | 21.02.1994 | 16 | (5) | |
| Andreas Panayiotou Filiotis | 31.05.1995 | 17 | (4) | |
| Mathieu Philippe Peybernes (FRA) | 21.10.1990 | 21 | | |
| Valentin Sébastien Roger Roberge | 09.06.1987 | 25 | | 1 |
| Nearchos Zinonos | 29.01.2004 | | (2) | |
| **Midfielders:** | DOB | M | (s) | G |
| Marios Avgousti | 28.01.2004 | | (1) | |
| El-Hadji Ba (FRA) | 05.03.1993 | 2 | (1) | |
| Israel Emanuel Coll (ARG) | 22.07.1993 | 23 | (3) | 1 |
| Etzaz Muzafar Hussain (NOR) | 27.01.1993 | | (5) | |
| Ilian Iliev (BUL) | 20.08.1999 | 9 | (15) | 1 |
| Bassel Jradi (LIB) | 06.07.1993 | 8 | (11) | 3 |
| Chambos Kyriakou | 09.02.1995 | 18 | (7) | 2 |
| Hervin Ongenda (FRA) | 24.06.1995 | 2 | (3) | |
| José Luis García del Pozo „Recio" (ESP) | 11.01.1991 | 6 | (5) | |
| Oliver Michael Robinson (ENG) | 08.04.2005 | | (1) | |
| Ido Shahar (ISR) | 20.08.2001 | 14 | (11) | 2 |
| Danilo Špoljarić | 14.07.1999 | 11 | (10) | 1 |
| **Forwards:** | DOB | M | (s) | G |
| Bagaliy Dabo (FRA) | 27.07.1988 | 4 | (7) | |
| Nicolas Diguiny (FRA) | 31.05.1988 | 8 | (19) | 2 |
| Godsway Donyoh (GHA) | 14.10.1994 | 10 | (3) | 3 |
| Ezekiel Isoken Henty (NGA) | 13.05.1993 | 12 | (12) | 2 |
| Patrick Joosten (NED) | 14.04.1996 | 7 | (5) | |
| Dimitrios Pinakas (GRE) | 01.09.2001 | 3 | (1) | 1 |
| Ioannis Pittas | 10.07.1996 | 34 | (1) | 18 |
| Giorgos Pontikou | 08.01.2003 | | (1) | |
| Vladimiro Etson António Félix „Vá" (ANG) | 24.08.1998 | 18 | (8) | 2 |
| Amr Warda (EGY) | 17.09.1993 | 18 | (1) | 4 |

## Aris Lemesou (Aris Limassol Football Club)

| Founded: | 1930 | | | |
|---|---|---|---|---|
| Stadium: | Stádio Alphamega [Limassol Arena], Limassol (10,700) | | | |
| Trainer: | Aleksey Shpilevski (BLR) | | | 17.02.1988 |

| Goalkeepers: | DOB | M | (s) | G |
|---|---|---|---|---|
| Ellinas Sofroniou | 29.01.1995 | 3 | | |
| Vanailson Luciano de Souza Alves „Vaná" (BRA) | 25.04.1991 | 33 | | |
| **Defenders:** | DOB | M | (s) | G |
| Eric Boakye (GHA) | 19.11.1999 | 28 | (1) | 1 |
| Franz Brorsson (SWE) | 30.01.1996 | 30 | (2) | 1 |
| Wanderson de Jesus Martins „Caju" (BRA) | 17.07.1995 | 16 | (10) | 2 |
| Delmiro Évora Nascimento (CPV) | 29.08.1988 | 3 | (11) | |
| Abdel Medioub (ALG) | 28.08.1997 | 3 | (2) | |
| Alex Moucketou-Moussounda (GAB) | 10.10.2000 | 25 | (1) | |
| Kostas Pileas | 11.12.1998 | 15 | (5) | |
| Steeve Yago (BFA) | 16.12.1992 | 25 | (3) | |
| Ismael Patrick Yandal (CMR) | 13.09.2002 | | (1) | |
| **Midfielders:** | DOB | M | (s) | G |
| Morgan Brown (ENG) | 29.11.1999 | 16 | (14) | 3 |
| Matija Špoljarić | 02.04.1997 | 4 | (14) | 2 |
| Karol Struski (POL) | 18.01.2001 | 23 | (6) | 4 |
| Július Szőke (SVK) | 01.08.1995 | 27 | (4) | 2 |
| Evgeniy Yablonskiy (BLR) | 10.05.1995 | 7 | (19) | |
| **Forwards:** | DOB | M | (s) | G |
| Shavy Warren Babicka (GAB) | 01.06.2000 | 29 | (6) | 8 |
| Leo Bengtsson (SWE) | 26.05.1998 | 32 | (1) | 8 |
| Yannick Gomis (SEN) | 03.02.1992 | 23 | (5) | 8 |
| Aleksandr Kokorin (RUS) | 19.03.1991 | 24 | (5) | 13 |
| Mihlali Samson Mayambela (RSA) | 25.08.1996 | 19 | (11) | 4 |
| Kévin Monnet-Paquet (FRA) | 19.08.1988 | 1 | (3) | |
| Floriss Ndjave (GAB) | 15.11.1997 | 1 | (11) | 1 |
| Artem Shumanskiy (BLR) | 25.11.2004 | | (1) | |
| Daniel Sikorski (AUT) | 02.11.1987 | 2 | (6) | 1 |
| Mariusz Stępiński (POL) | 12.05.1995 | 7 | (22) | 4 |
| Martin Šlogar (CRO) | 21.09.2000 | | (3) | |

## Doxa Katokopias Football Club

| Founded: | 1954 | | |
|---|---|---|---|
| Stadium: | Stádio Katokopia, Peristona (3,500) | | |
| Trainer: | Nikos Andronikou | | 19.11.1961 |
| [11.08.2022] | Ricardo José Moutinho Chéu (POR) | | 14.05.1981 |
| [28.12.2022] | Kypros Mouzouros | | 27.09.1994 |
| [13.01.2023] | Víctor Manuel Basadre Orozco (ESP) | | 16.02.1970 |
| [23.01.2023] | Kostas Sakkas | | 1973 |

| Goalkeepers: | DOB | M | (s) | G |
|---|---|---|---|---|
| Damjan Shishkovski (MKD) | 18.03.1995 | 40 | | |
| **Defenders:** | DOB | M | (s) | G |
| Khaled Adénon (BEN) | 29.07.1985 | 30 | (3) | 1 |
| Sebastián Herrera Cardona (COL) | 23.01.1995 | 2 | (6) | |
| Andreas Karamanolis | 02.09.2001 | 31 | | 2 |
| Semir Kerla (BIH) | 26.09.1987 | 18 | (1) | |
| Bojan Kovačević (SRB) | 28.04.1996 | 35 | | 1 |
| Diego Armando Mesén Calvo (CRC) | 28.03.1999 | 3 | (3) | |
| Mac Bean Naggar (USA) | 10.06.1999 | | (1) | |
| Juhani Ojala (FIN) | 19.06.1989 | 3 | (7) | |
| Marios Stylianou | 23.09.1993 | 33 | (1) | |
| **Midfielders:** | DOB | M | (s) | G |
| Olamide Fawaz Abdullahi (NGA) | 04.05.2003 | 9 | (13) | |
| Alexander „Álex" Vallejo Mínguez (ESP) | 16.01.1992 | 17 | (1) | |
| Tidjani Anaane (BEN) | 29.03.1997 | 10 | (28) | 4 |
| Benjamin Asamoah (GHA) | 04.01.1994 | 26 | (13) | 1 |
| Bernardo Oliveira Dias „Benny" (POR) | 04.01.1997 | 33 | (7) | 2 |
| Christian Ilić (CRO) | 22.07.1996 | 16 | (18) | |
| Giorgos Pavlidis | 08.01.2003 | 6 | (3) | |
| Theodosis Siathas | 16.12.1998 | | (1) | |
| Duško Trajčevski (MKD) | 01.11.1990 | 24 | (8) | |
| **Forwards:** | DOB | M | (s) | G |
| Ernest Kwabena Asante (GHA) | 06.11.1988 | 21 | (3) | 6 |
| Marios Fasouliotis | 26.05.2005 | 6 | (3) | |
| Theodoros Iosifidis | 17.01.1997 | 5 | (1) | |
| Ibrahim Kargbo Junior (BEL) | 03.01.2000 | 1 | (6) | |
| Buomesca Tue Na Bangna „Mesca" (GNB) | 06.05.1993 | 8 | (19) | |
| Johan Arles Rodallega Gómez (COL) | 13.01.2001 | | (4) | |
| Berat Sadik (FIN) | 14.09.1986 | 38 | | 8 |
| Alex Sobczyk | 20.05.1997 | 7 | (10) | 2 |
| Nikola Trujić (SRB) | 14.04.1992 | 18 | (1) | 3 |

## Enosi Neon Paralimniou Football Club

| Founded: | 1936 | | |
|---|---|---|---|
| Stadium: | Stádio „Tasos Markou", Paralimni (5,800) | | |
| Trainer: | Marinos Satsias | | 24.05.1978 |

| Goalkeepers: | DOB | M | (s) | G |
|---|---|---|---|---|
| Ivan Kostić (SRB) | 24.10.1995 | 33 | | |
| Panagiotis Panagiotou | 30.04.1997 | 7 | | |
| **Defenders:** | DOB | M | (s) | G |
| Andreas Christofi | 31.10.1998 | 14 | (1) | |
| Pavel Dreksa (CZE) | 17.09.1989 | 31 | (3) | 1 |
| Marco Ehmann (ROU) | 03.08.2000 | 19 | (6) | 1 |
| Dimitris Flouris | 23.07.2002 | | (1) | |
| Marko Jevremović (SRB) | 23.02.1996 | 27 | (9) | 1 |
| Omer Korsia (ISR) | 07.10.2002 | 11 | (9) | |
| Fotis Kotsonis | 10.02.2003 | 23 | (8) | |
| Luís Marques Almeida Vieira Silva (POR) | 18.02.1999 | 38 | (1) | 3 |
| **Midfielders:** | DOB | M | (s) | G |
| Fernán Ferreiroa López (ESP) | 10.02.1995 | 1 | (5) | |
| Antonis Katsiaris | 14.10.1996 | 19 | (13) | 3 |
| Konstantinos Kolonias (GRE) | 20.01.2004 | | (4) | |
| Óscar Adrián Lucero (ARG) | 16.08.1985 | 23 | (10) | |
| Marcio Andre Meira Fernandes (POR) | 09.01.1994 | 31 | (5) | 2 |
| Dimitris Mavroudis | 03.05.2002 | 7 | (14) | |
| Paris Polykarpou | 23.09.2000 | 14 | (6) | |
| Stefan Vukčević (MNE) | 11.04.1997 | 15 | (13) | 1 |
| **Forwards:** | DOB | M | (s) | G |
| Kandet Diawara (FRA) | 10.02.2000 | 28 | (9) | 5 |
| Floriss Djave (GAB) | 29.07.2003 | 2 | (5) | 1 |
| Pantelis Gavriel | 07.01.2004 | 1 | (10) | |
| Konstantinos Konstantinou | 08.10.1994 | 26 | (3) | 1 |
| Julien Elie Lamy (FRA) | 06.11.1999 | 17 | (13) | 5 |
| Yehonatan Binyamin Levy (ISR) | 25.08.1999 | | (1) | |
| Branko Mihajlović (SRB) | 20.02.1991 | | (3) | |
| Rafael Mascarenhas Moreira (POR) | 05.04.2002 | | (3) | |
| Onisiforos Roushias | 15.07.1992 | 21 | (12) | 4 |
| Dimitris Solomou | 16.10.2006 | | (4) | |
| Víctor Fernández Satué (ESP) | 02.05.1998 | 10 | (8) | 3 |
| Aleksandar Vučenović (AUT) | 10.10.1997 | 22 | (14) | 9 |

## Karmiotissa Polemidion Football Club

| Founded: | 1979 | | |
|---|---|---|---|
| Stadium: | Stádio Tsirio, Limassol (13,331) | | |
| Trainer: | Dusan Uhrin Jr. (CZE) | | 11.10.1967 |
| [04.09.2022] | Christos Charalampous | | 03.10.1981 |
| [18.09.2022] | Aleksandr Khatskevich (BLR) | | 19.10.1973 |
| [31.10.2022] | Christos Charalampous | | 03.10.1981 |
| [14.12.2022] | Sofronios Avgousti | | 09.03.1977 |
| [08.02.2023] | Aleksandr Kerzhakov (RUS) | | 27.11.1982 |
| [25.03.2023] | Florin Daniel Bratu (ROU) | | 02.01.1980 |

| Goalkeepers: | DOB | M | (s) | G |
|---|---|---|---|---|
| Milan Knobloch (CZE) | 23.08.1992 | 35 | | |
| Aleksander Špoljarić | 28.11.1995 | 5 | | |
| **Defenders:** | DOB | M | (s) | G |
| Angelis Angeli | 31.05.1989 | 14 | (7) | |
| Tomáš Čelůstka (CZE) | 19.07.1991 | 24 | (8) | |
| Tomáš Hubočan (SVK) | 17.09.1985 | 26 | (1) | |
| Dion Malone (SUR) | 13.02.1989 | 35 | | 2 |
| Vinko Međimorec (CRO) | 01.06.1996 | 13 | | 1 |
| Antonio Miço (GRE) | 27.01.2000 | 8 | (4) | |
| Simranjit Singh Thandi (ENG) | 11.10.1999 | 18 | (2) | |
| Manolis Tzanakakis (GRE) | 30.04.1992 | 14 | (3) | |
| **Midfielders:** | DOB | M | (s) | G |
| Theodoros Andronikou | 07.07.2001 | 2 | (14) | |
| Samir Ben Sallam (NED) | 03.06.2001 | 19 | (9) | |
| Andreas Christou | 12.03.1994 | | (1) | |
| Mounir El Allouchi (NED) | 27.09.1994 | 38 | (1) | 10 |
| Jon Gaztañaga Arrospide (ESP) | 28.06.1991 | 19 | (1) | |
| Răzvan Toni Augustin Grădinaru (ROU) | 23.08.1995 | 14 | (7) | |
| Josef Hušbauer (CZE) | 16.03.1990 | 4 | (4) | |
| Giorgos Ikonomidis | 10.04.1990 | 11 | (10) | |
| Andreas Neophytou | 07.07.1998 | 15 | (8) | |
| Dimitris Stavrou | 10.09.2005 | | (1) | |
| Tomás Martins Podstawski (POR) | 30.01.1995 | 1 | (5) | |
| **Forwards:** | DOB | M | (s) | G |
| Andreas Avraam | 06.06.1987 | 6 | (8) | |
| Ioannis Chatzivasilis | 26.04.1990 | 5 | (11) | |
| Souleymane Coulibaly (CIV) | 26.12.1994 | 14 | (15) | 3 |
| Aboubacar Doumbia (CIV) | 12.11.1999 | 29 | (8) | 2 |
| Michal Ďuriš (SVK) | 01.06.1988 | 22 | (13) | 6 |
| Danzell Gravenberch (SUR) | 13.02.1994 | 9 | (8) | 1 |
| Nikolaos Kaltsas (GRE) | 03.05.1990 | 19 | (11) | 6 |
| Karim Loukili (MAR) | 28.04.1997 | 11 | (3) | 1 |
| Rasheed Oreoluwa Yusuf (NGA) | 14.05.2004 | | (6) | |
| Emilio José Zelaya (ARG) | 30.07.1987 | 10 | (5) | 3 |

## Nea Salamis Famagusta Football Club

| | | |
|---|---|---|
| **Founded**: | 1971 | |
| **Stadium**: | Stádio Ammochostos, Larnaca (5,500) | |
| **Trainer**: | Savvas Poursaitidis | 23.06.1976 |
| [16.05.2023] | Christodoulos Christodoulou | 04.09.1985 |

| Goalkeepers: | DOB | M | (s) | G |
|---|---|---|---|---|
| Giannis Kalanides | 12.05.2006 | 1 | | |
| Tasos Kissas | 18.01.1988 | 10 | | |
| Nikolaos Melissas (GRE) | 24.02.1993 | 29 | | |
| **Defenders:** | **DOB** | **M** | **(s)** | **G** |
| Zacharias Adoni | 13.07.1999 | 27 | (4) | 2 |
| Niko Datković (CRO) | 21.04.1993 | 16 | (1) | 1 |
| Abdelaye Diakitè (MLI) | 08.01.1990 | 20 | (2) | 4 |
| Loukas Kalogirou | 21.02.2002 | 2 | | |
| Giorgios Katsikas (GRE) | 14.06.1990 | 15 | (4) | |
| Serge Sedoine Tchaha Leuko (CMR) | 04.08.1993 | 13 | (5) | 1 |
| Giorgos Malekkidis | 14.07.1997 | 10 | (2) | |
| Thomas Nikolaou | 22.10.2001 | 4 | (5) | |
| Richard Ofori (GHA) | 24.04.1993 | 29 | (2) | |
| Konstantinos Sergiou | 02.10.2000 | 28 | | 1 |
| Giorgios Viktoros | 01.09.2005 | 1 | (1) | |
| **Midfielders:** | **DOB** | **M** | **(s)** | **G** |
| Norberto Carlos Costa dos Santos „Carlitos" (ANG) | 16.05.1999 | 24 | (8) | 2 |

| | DOB | M | (s) | G |
|---|---|---|---|---|
| *Edson* Martinho *Silva* (POR) | 17.05.2001 | 1 | (2) | |
| Efthymios Efthymiou | 03.11.2006 | | (1) | |
| Sotiris Fiakas | 08.09.1998 | 1 | (1) | |
| Andreas Frangos | 19.01.1997 | 16 | (9) | |
| *Juan Felipe* Alves Ribeiro (BRA) | 05.12.1987 | 18 | (13) | 2 |
| Uladzislaŭ Klimovič (BLR) | 12.06.1996 | 14 | (13) | 3 |
| Georges Constant Mandjeck (CMR) | 09.12.1988 | 27 | (4) | |
| Renato Joao Inacio *Margaça* | 17.07.1985 | 8 | (18) | |
| Luís Miguel Teixeira Ribeiro „Miguelito" (POR) | 09.03.1990 | 17 | (14) | 5 |
| **Forwards:** | **DOB** | **M** | **(s)** | **G** |
| Éric Bauthéac (FRA) | 24.08.1987 | 11 | (15) | |
| Francisco Gonçalves Sacalumbo „Chico Banza"(ANG) | 17.12.1998 | 22 | (10) | 2 |
| Diego Fernando Dorregaray (ARG) | 09.05.1992 | 28 | (8) | 16 |
| Michalis Koumouris | 31.10.1994 | 12 | (12) | 3 |
| Stallone Limbombe Ekango (BEL) | 26.03.1991 | 5 | (2) | |
| Sintayehu Sallalich (ISR) | 20.06.1991 | 6 | (6) | 1 |
| Thierry Alain Florian Taulemesse (FRA) | 31.01.1986 | 10 | (20) | 3 |
| *Thiago* Ferreira Dos Santos (BRA) | 12.07.1987 | 15 | (14) | 5 |

## Olympiakos Nicosia Football Club

| | | |
|---|---|---|
| **Founded**: | 1931 | |
| **Stadium**: | Stádio Makário, Nicosia (16,000) | |
| **Trainer**: | Nedim Tutić (BIH) | 17.07.1964 |
| [06.08.2022] | Giannis Petrakis | 20.05.1959 |
| [14.11.2022] | Makis Sergidis | 02.10.1980 |
| [10.04.2023] | Nedim Tutić (BIH) | 17.07.1964 |

| Goalkeepers: | DOB | M | (s) | G |
|---|---|---|---|---|
| *Charles* Marcelo da Silva (BRA) | 04.02.1994 | 5 | | |
| Adam Kováč (SVK) | 08.06.2000 | 1 | | |
| Joël Mall | 05.04.1991 | 34 | | |
| **Defenders:** | **DOB** | **M** | **(s)** | **G** |
| Charalambos Antoniou | 01.07.2005 | | (1) | |
| Pierre Luc Bardy-Alenda (FRA) | 27.08.1992 | 27 | (4) | |
| Bert Esselink (NED) | 16.08.1999 | 28 | (1) | 4 |
| Toni Gorupec (CRO) | 04.07.1993 | 10 | (3) | |
| Wilde-Donald Guerrier (HAI) | 31.03.1989 | 14 | | 3 |
| Nikolas Hadjimitsis | 10.09.2003 | 1 | (3) | |
| Thomas Ioannou | 19.07.1995 | 21 | (2) | |
| Sotiris Kaiafas | 27.10.2004 | 1 | (3) | |
| Artur Kartashyan (ARM) | 08.01.1997 | 10 | | |
| Evangelos Kyriakou | 03.02.1994 | 20 | (4) | |
| Thanasis Liasidis | 14.07.1997 | 12 | (2) | |
| Stephanos Mouktaris | 10.07.1994 | 25 | (1) | 1 |
| **Midfielders:** | **DOB** | **M** | **(s)** | **G** |
| Bryan Alcéus (HAI) | 01.02.1996 | 17 | (1) | |
| Stefanos Charalampous | 03.09.1999 | 9 | (7) | 1 |
| Charalambos Demetriou | 04.01.2005 | | (1) | |
| Marinos Dimitriou | 20.11.2004 | 1 | (3) | |

| | DOB | M | (s) | G |
|---|---|---|---|---|
| Nikolaos Dosis (SWE) | 25.01.2001 | 13 | (6) | 1 |
| Filip Duranski (MKD) | 17.07.1991 | | (1) | |
| Filippos Eftychidis | 26.02.2002 | 10 | (6) | |
| Abdul Rahman Khalili (SWE) | 07.06.1992 | 10 | (1) | 1 |
| Alexandar Marković (SRB) | 13.03.1991 | 3 | (4) | |
| Nanísio Justino Mendes Soares (GNB) | 17.09.1991 | 29 | (3) | |
| **Forwards:** | **DOB** | **M** | **(s)** | **G** |
| Michalis Christodoulou | 06.03.2000 | 11 | (6) | 1 |
| Jonel Désirè (HAI) | 12.02.1997 | 4 | (5) | 1 |
| Fiorin Durmishaj (ALB) | 14.11.1996 | 5 | (4) | 4 |
| Lewis Mbah Enoh (CMR) | 23.10.1992 | 5 | (6) | 1 |
| Petros Giakoumakis (GRE) | 03.07.1992 | 12 | (2) | |
| Sam Hendriks (NED) | 25.01.1995 | 18 | (15) | 2 |
| Fabrice Kah Nkwoh (CMR) | 09.03.1996 | 9 | (11) | 2 |
| Chrysovalantis Kapartis | 26.10.1991 | | (3) | |
| Osman Koroma (SLE) | 18.07.2002 | 15 | (17) | 1 |
| Marios Pechlivanis | 23.05.1995 | 27 | (6) | 2 |
| Petros Psychas | 28.08.1998 | 12 | (12) | 3 |
| Edgar Nicaise Constant Salli (CMR) | 17.08.1992 | 11 | (12) | |
| Martin Šlogar (CRO) | 21.09.2000 | 6 | (14) | 1 |
| Angelos Zefki | 15.04.2003 | 4 | (5) | |

## Athlitikos Sillogos Omonia Lefkosias
## (Athletic Club Omonia Nicosia)

| | | |
|---|---|---|
| **Founded**: | 04.06.1948 | |
| **Stadium**: | Stádio GSP, Nicosia (22,859) | |
| **Trainer**: | Neil Francis Lennon (NIR) | 25.06.1971 |
| [21.10.2022] | Yannick Ferrera y Caro (BEL) | 24.09.1980 |
| [06.02.2023] | Sofronios Avgousti | 09.03.1977 |

| Goalkeepers: | DOB | M | (s) | G |
|---|---|---|---|---|
| *Fabiano* Ribeiro de Freitas (BRA) | 29.02.1988 | 15 | | |
| Konstantinos Panagi | 08.10.1994 | 2 | (1) | |
| Francis Odinaka Uzoho (NGA) | 28.10.1998 | 19 | | |
| **Defenders:** | **DOB** | **M** | **(s)** | **G** |
| *Héctor Yuste* Canton (ESP) | 12.01.1988 | 15 | (6) | 2 |
| Fotis Kitsos (GRE) | 31.03.2003 | 20 | (5) | |
| Nikolas Kyriakides | 20.09.2004 | | (1) | |
| Ádám Lang (HUN) | 17.01.1993 | 28 | (1) | 1 |
| Jan Lecjaks (CZE) | 09.08.1990 | 25 | (5) | 2 |
| Adam James Matthews (WAL) | 13.01.1992 | 20 | (3) | |
| Nemanja Miletić (SRB) | 16.01.1991 | 22 | (1) | 1 |
| Nikos Panagiotou | 12.05.2000 | 10 | (5) | 1 |
| Paris Psaltis | 12.11.1996 | 9 | (2) | |
| Konstantinos Venizelou | 05.07.2004 | 2 | | |
| **Midfielders:** | **DOB** | **M** | **(s)** | **G** |
| Panagiotis Andreou | 29.04.2006 | | (1) | |
| Fouad Bachirou (COM) | 15.04.1990 | 17 | (4) | |
| Charalampos Charalampous | 04.04.2002 | 17 | (10) | |

| | DOB | M | (s) | G |
|---|---|---|---|---|
| Mikkel Morgenstar Pålssønn Diskerud (USA) | 02.10.1990 | 9 | (11) | |
| Ioannis Kousoulos | 14.06.1996 | 19 | (7) | |
| *Moreto* Moro *Cassamá* (GNB) | 16.02.1998 | 15 | (9) | |
| Fotis Papoulis (GRE) | 22.01.1985 | 9 | (16) | 1 |
| Andreas Savva | 21.07.2004 | | (3) | |
| **Forwards:** | **DOB** | **M** | **(s)** | **G** |
| Karim Ansarifard (IRN) | 03.04.1990 | 24 | (7) | 4 |
| Brandon Barker (ENG) | 04.10.1996 | 7 | (10) | 1 |
| Artem Besedin (UKR) | 31.03.1996 | 8 | (4) | 1 |
| Roman Bezus (UKR) | 26.09.1990 | 13 | (13) | 3 |
| *Bruno* Felipe Souza da Silva (BRA) | 26.05.1994 | 20 | | 8 |
| Gary Hooper (ENG) | 26.01.1988 | 4 | (9) | 2 |
| Andronikos Kakoullis | 03.05.2001 | 11 | (15) | 8 |
| Loizos Loizou | 18.07.2003 | 22 | (11) | 4 |
| Tim Matavž (SVN) | 13.01.1989 | | (4) | 1 |
| Angelos Neophytou | 23.05.2005 | | (1) | |
| Ismael Tajouri-Shradi (LBY) | 28.03.1994 | 5 | (6) | 1 |
| Panagiotis Zachariou | 26.02.1996 | 9 | (7) | 1 |

## Pafos Football Club Paphos

| Founded: | 10.06.2014 (after the merger of AEK Kouklia and AEP Paphos) | |
|---|---|---|
| Stadium: | Stádio „Stelios Kyriakides", Paphos (9,394) | |
| Trainer: | Henning Stille Berg (SVN) | 01.09.1969 |
| [06.04.2023] | Miguel Ángel Salgado Fernández (ESP) | 22.10.1975 |

| Goalkeepers: | DOB | M | (s) | G |
|---|---|---|---|---|
| Daniel Antosch (AUT) | 07.03.2000 | 19 | | |
| Ivica Ivušić (CRO) | 01.02.1995 | 16 | | |
| Oier Olazábal Paredes (ESP) | 14.09.1989 | 1 | | |
| **Defenders:** | **DOB** | **M** | **(s)** | **G** |
| Kenan Bajrič (SVN) | 20.12.1994 | 35 | | |
| Marios Demetriou | 25.12.1992 | 5 | (3) | |
| Jordan Ikoko (COD) | 03.02.1994 | 31 | (1) | |
| Leovigildo Júnior Reis Rodrigues „Juninho" (BRA) | 26.12.1995 | 31 | | 1 |
| Levan Kharabadze (GEO) | 26.01.2000 | 1 | (2) | |
| Josef Kvida (CZE) | 23.01.1997 | 34 | | 2 |
| Alexandros Michail | 28.01.2000 | | (1) | |
| Jeisson Andrés Palacios Murillo (COL) | 20.03.1994 | 13 | (3) | 1 |
| **Midfielders:** | **DOB** | **M** | **(s)** | **G** |
| Vlad Mihai Dragomir (ROU) | 24.04.1999 | 21 | (7) | 1 |
| Eirik Hestad (NOR) | 26.06.1995 | 8 | (14) | |

| | DOB | M | (s) | G |
|---|---|---|---|---|
| Deni Hočko (MNE) | 22.04.1994 | 11 | (9) | |
| Mamadou Kané (GUI) | 22.01.1997 | 31 | (1) | 3 |
| Moustapha Namé (SEN) | 05.05.1995 | 13 | (9) | 4 |
| *Pedro* Henrique Rocha *Pelágio* (POR) | 21.04.2000 | 7 | (9) | |
| Onni Johannes Simonpoika Valakari (FIN) | 18.08.1999 | 23 | (10) | 7 |
| **Forwards:** | **DOB** | **M** | **(s)** | **G** |
| Besart Abdurahimi (MKD) | 31.07.1990 | 12 | (13) | 8 |
| Hamadi Al Ghaddioui (MAR) | 22.09.1990 | | (9) | 1 |
| *Bruno* Felipe Souza da Silva (BRA) | 26.05.1994 | 8 | (7) | 1 |
| *Bruno* Miguel Costa Monteiro *Tavares* (POR) | 16.04.2002 | 1 | (2) | |
| *Jairo* De Macedo Da Silva (BRA) | 06.05.1992 | 27 | (2) | 18 |
| *Jefté* Betancor Sánchez (ESP) | 06.07.1993 | 1 | (7) | |
| Lysandros Papastylianou | 29.11.2005 | | (1) | |
| Muamer Tanković (SWE) | 22.02.1995 | 30 | (2) | 8 |
| *Willy* Johnson *Semedo* Afonso (CPV) | 27.04.1994 | 17 | (1) | 4 |

## SECOND LEVEL
### Cypriot Second Division 2022/2023

Please note: EN Achyronas Liopetriou FC and Onisilos Sotira 2014 merged into PO Achyronas Onisilos.

### Regular Season

| | | | | | | | | | | |
|---|---|---|---|---|---|---|---|---|---|---|
| 1. | AEZ Zakakiou | 15 | 9 | 4 | 2 | 23 | - | 9 | 31 |
| 2. | AC Othellos Athienou | 15 | 10 | 0 | 5 | 23 | - | 15 | 30 |
| 3. | Ethnikos Achna FC | 15 | 9 | 2 | 4 | 24 | - | 19 | 29 |
| 4. | PO Achyronas Onisilos | 15 | 8 | 3 | 4 | 26 | - | 13 | 27 |
| 5. | Peyia 2014 FC | 15 | 7 | 5 | 3 | 18 | - | 12 | 26 |
| 6. | ALS Omonia 29is Maiou | 15 | 7 | 4 | 4 | 18 | - | 12 | 25 |
| 7. | Omonia Aradippou FC | 15 | 6 | 5 | 4 | 22 | - | 18 | 23 |
| 8. | MEAP Pera Choriou Nisou | 15 | 7 | 1 | 7 | 13 | - | 15 | 22 |
| 9. | PAEEK Kyrenia | 15 | 6 | 4 | 5 | 16 | - | 16 | 22 |
| 10. | Ermis Aradippou FC | 15 | 5 | 5 | 5 | 16 | - | 18 | 20 |
| 11. | FC Krasava ENY Digenis Akrytas Ypsonas | 15 | 5 | 4 | 6 | 26 | - | 24 | 19 |
| 12. | Podosfairikos Omilos Xylotymbou 2006 | 15 | 5 | 3 | 7 | 23 | - | 28 | 18 |
| 13. | Athlitikos Omilos Ayia Napa FC | 15 | 5 | 2 | 8 | 18 | - | 18 | 17 |
| 14. | Anagennisi Deryneia FC | 15 | 3 | 4 | 8 | 17 | - | 24 | 13 |
| 15. | Alki Oroklini FC | 15 | 2 | 3 | 10 | 10 | - | 33 | 9 |
| 16. | Olympias Lympion | 15 | 1 | 1 | 13 | 8 | - | 27 | 4 |

Team ranked 1-8 were qualified for the Promotion Round, while teams ranked 9-16 were qualified for the Relegation Round.

### Promotion Round

| | | | | | | | | | | |
|---|---|---|---|---|---|---|---|---|---|---|
| 1. | AC Othellos Athienou (*Promoted*) | 14 | 9 | 2 | 3 | 23 | - | 13 | 59 |
| 2. | AEZ Zakakiou (*Promoted*) | 14 | 7 | 4 | 3 | 23 | - | 12 | 56 |
| 3. | Ethnikos Achna FC (*Promoted*) | 14 | 7 | 5 | 2 | 22 | - | 8 | 55 |
| 4. | ALS Omonia 29is Maiou | 14 | 7 | 4 | 3 | 14 | - | 11 | 50 |
| 5. | PO Achyronas Onisilos | 14 | 2 | 7 | 5 | 16 | - | 21 | 40 |
| 6. | Peyia 2014 FC | 14 | 3 | 4 | 7 | 7 | - | 17 | 39 |
| 7. | MEAP Pera Choriou Nisou | 14 | 3 | 2 | 9 | 11 | - | 26 | 33 |
| 8. | Omonia Aradippou FC | 14 | 1 | 6 | 7 | 7 | - | 15 | 32 |

### Relegation Round

| | | | | | | | | | | |
|---|---|---|---|---|---|---|---|---|---|---|
| 9. | Podosfairikos Omilos Xylotymbou 2006 | 12 | 6 | 3 | 3 | 23 | - | 11 | 39 |
| 10. | PAEEK Kyrenia | 12 | 4 | 5 | 3 | 19 | - | 14 | 39 |
| 11. | Ermis Aradippou FC | 12 | 5 | 2 | 5 | 16 | - | 14 | 37 |
| 12. | FC Krasava ENY Digenis Akrytas Ypsonas | 12 | 4 | 4 | 4 | 25 | - | 19 | 35 |
| 13. | Athlitikos Omilos Ayia Napa FC | 12 | 5 | 2 | 5 | 12 | - | 15 | 34 |
| 14. | Anagennisi Deryneia FC (*Relegation*) | 12 | 6 | 2 | 4 | 19 | - | 22 | 33 |
| 15. | Olympias Lympion (*Relegation*) | 12 | 1 | 4 | 7 | 13 | - | 32 | 11 |
| 16. | Alki Oroklini FC (*Relegation*) | (*withdrew*) | | | | | | | |

## INTERNATIONAL MATCHES
(16.07.2022 – 15.07.2023)

| 24.09.2022 | Larnaca | Cyprus - Greece | 1-0(1-0) | (UNL) |
|---|---|---|---|---|
| 27.09.2022 | Prishtina | Kosovo - Cyprus | 5-1(2-0) | (UNL) |
| 16.11.2022 | Larnaca | Cyprus - Bulgaria | 0-2(0-1) | (F) |
| 20.11.2022 | Petah Tikva | Israel - Cyprus | 2-3(0-2) | (F) |
| 25.03.2023 | Glasgow | Scotland - Cyprus | 3-0(1-0) | (ECQ) |
| 28.03.2023 | Yerevan | Armenia - Cyprus | 2-2(0-1) | (F) |
| 17.06.2023 | Larnaca | Cyprus - Georgia | 1-2(1-1) | (ECQ) |
| 20.06.2023 | Oslo | Norway - Cyprus | 3-1(1-0) | (ECQ) |

**24.09.2022**    **CYPRUS - GREECE**      **1-0(1-0)**      3rd UEFA Nations League C, Group 2
AEK Arena "Georgios Karapatakis", Larnaca; Referee: Aleksei Kulbakov (Belarus); Attendance: 4,548
**CYP:** Konstantinos Panagi, Stelios Andreou, Fanos Katelaris, Valentin Sébastien Roger Roberge, Nicholas Ioannou (76.Marios Antoniadis), Charalambos Kyriakou, Kostakis Artymatas (Cap), Loizos Loizou (58.Charalampos Charalampous), Grigoris Kastanos (75.Alexandros Gogić), Marinos Tzionis (64.Andreas Karo), Pieros Sotiriou (76.Andronikos Kakoullis). Trainer: Temur Ketsbaia (Georgia).
**Goal:** Marinos Tzionis (18).

**27.09.2022**    **KOSOVO - CYPRUS**      **5-1(2-0)**      3rd UEFA Nations League C, Group 2
Stadiumi „Fadil Vokrri", Prishtina; Referee: Kristo Tohver (Estonia); Attendance: 10,400
**CYP:** Konstantinos Panagi, Stelios Andreou, Fanos Katelaris, Valentin Sébastien Roger Roberge, Nicholas Ioannou, Charalambos Kyriakou (46.Charalampos Charalampous), Kostakis Artymatas (Cap), Grigoris Kastanos (59.Alexandros Gogić), Loizos Loizou (46.Dimitris Christofi), Marinos Tzionis (59.Fotios Papoulis), Pieros Sotiriou (72.Andronikos Kakoullis). Trainer: Temur Ketsbaia (Georgia).
**Goal:** Valentin Sébastien Roger Roberge (81).

**16.11.2022**    **CYPRUS - BULGARIA**      **0-2(0-1)**      Friendly International
AEK Arena "Georgios Karapatakis", Larnaca; Referee: Trustin Farrugia Cann (Malta); Attendance: 1,000
**CYP:** Konstantinos Panagi, Stelios Andreou (46.Danilo Špoljarić), Christos Sielis, Konstantinos Laifis, Marios Antoniadis (46.Minas Antoniou), Alexandros Gogić, Grigoris Kastanos, Charalambos Kyriakou (Cap) (46.Michalis Ioannou), Loizos Loizou (46.Christos Wheeler), Ioannis Pittas (78.Giorgos Efraim), Andronikos Kakoullis (65.Dimitris Christofi). Trainer: Temur Ketsbaia (Georgia).

**20.11.2022**    **ISRAEL - CYPRUS**      **2-3(0-2)**      Friendly International
HaMoshava Stadium, Petah Tikva; Referee: Arda Kardeşler (Turkey); Attendance: 7,352
**CYP:** Dimitris Dimitriou, Alexandros Gogić, Stelios Andreou, Minas Antoniou, Marios Antoniadis, Grigoris Kastanos (76.Matija Špoljarić; 88.Nikolas Panayiotou), Charalambos Kyriakou (Cap) (72.Michalis Ioannou), Danilo Špoljarić (76.Rafail Mamas), Christos Wheeler (88.Giorgos Ekonomidis), Charalampos Charalampous, Ioannis Pittas (72.Dimitris Christofi). Trainer: Temur Ketsbaia (Georgia).
**Goals:** Charalampos Charalampous (2), Ioannis Pittas (24), Michalis Ioannou (82).

**25.03.2023**    **SCOTLAND - CYPRUS**      **3-0(1-0)**      17th EC. Qualifiers
Hampden Park, Glasgow; Referee: Duje Strukan (Croatia); Attendance: 48,195
**CYP:** Dimitris Dimitriou, Minas Antoniou, Valentin Sébastien Roger Roberge, Alexandros Gogić (79.Loizos Loizou), Ioannis Kousoulos (46.Danilo Špoljarić), Nicholas Ioannou [*sent off 90+5*], Konstantinos Laifis, Kostakis Artymatas (Cap), Charalambos Kyriakou (68.Charalampos Charalampous), Grigoris Kastanos (79.Marinos Tzionis), Ioannis Pittas (68.Andronikos Kakoullis). Trainer: Temur Ketsbaia (Georgia).

**28.03.2023**    **ARMENIA - CYPRUS**      **2-2(0-1)**      Friendly International
„Vazgen Sargsyan" Hanrapetakan Stadium, Yerevan; Referee: Dumitru Muntean (Moldova); Attendance: n/a
**CYP:** Konstantinos Panagi, Valentin Sébastien Roger Roberge (46.Kostakis Artymatas [*sent off 89*]), Andreas Karo, Konstantinos Laifis (Cap), Ioannis Kousoulos (46.Charalambos Kyriakou), Danilo Špoljarić, Michalis Ioannou (47.Marios Antoniadis), Charalampos Charalampous (76.Loizos Loizou), Andreas Panayiotou Filiotis, Marinos Tzionis (67.Giorgos Efraim), Andronikos Kakoullis (67.Dimitris Christofi). Trainer: Temur Ketsbaia (Georgia).
**Goals:** Andreas Karo (43), Dimitris Christofi (83).

**17.06.2023**    **CYPRUS - GEORGIA**      **1-2(1-1)**      17th EC. Qualifiers
AEK Arena "Georgios Karapatakis", Larnaca; Referee: Fábio José Costa Veríssimo (Portugal); Attendance: 3,763
**CYP:** Joël Mall, Alexandros Gogić, Andreas Karo (63.Marios Antoniadis), Konstantinos Laifis, Charalampos Charalampous (77.Giannis Satsias), Ioannis Kousoulos, Minas Antoniou, Anderson Correia de Barros, Grigoris Kastanos (Cap), Marinos Tzionis (60.Loizos Loizou), Ioannis Pittas (77.Dimitris Christofi). Trainer: Temur Ketsbaia (Georgia).
**Goal:** Ioannis Pittas (40 penalty).

**20.06.2023**    **NORWAY - CYPRUS**      **3-1(1-0)**      17th EC. Qualifiers
Ullevaal Stadion, Oslo; Referee: Aleksandar Stavrev (North Macedonia); Attendance: 23,643
**CYP:** Joël Mall, Alexandros Gogić, Konstantinos Laifis, Nicholas Ioannou, Minas Antoniou (61.Loizos Loizou), Grigoris Kastanos (Cap), Ioannis Kousoulos (90+2.Giannis Satsias), Anderson Correia de Barros, Charalampos Charalampous (61.Marinos Tzionis), Kostas Pileas (61.Stelios Andreou), Ioannis Pittas (70.Dimitris Christofi). Trainer: Temur Ketsbaia (Georgia).
**Goal:** Grigoris Kastanos (90+3).

## NATIONAL TEAM PLAYERS
### (16.07.2022 – 15.07.2023)

| Name | DOB | Caps | Goals | Club | |
|------|-----|------|-------|------|--|

### Goalkeepers

| Name | DOB | Caps | Goals | Club | |
|------|-----|------|-------|------|--|
| Dimitris DIMITRIOU | 15.01.1999 | 9 | 0 | 2022/2023: | *Apollon Limassol FC* |
| Joël MALL | 05.04.1991 | 2 | 0 | 2023: | *Olympiakos Nicosia FC* |
| Konstantinos PANAGI | 08.10.1994 | 27 | 0 | 2022/2023: | *AC Omonia Nicosia* |

### Defenders

| Name | DOB | Caps | Goals | Club | |
|------|-----|------|-------|------|--|
| Stelios ANDREOU | 24.07.2002 | 10 | 0 | 2022/2023: | *R Charleroi SC (BEL)* |
| Marios ANTONIADIS | 14.05.1990 | 25 | 0 | 2022/2023: | *Anorthosis Famagusta FC* |
| Anderson CORREIA de Barros | 06.05.1991 | 2 | 0 | 2023: | *Anorthosis Famagusta FC* |
| Nicholas IOANNOU | 10.11.1995 | 43 | 2 | 2022/2023: | *Como 1907 (ITA)* |
| Andreas KARO | 09.09.1996 | 15 | 1 | 2022/2023: | *APOEL Nicosia* |
| Konstantinos LAIFIS | 19.04.1993 | 52 | 3 | 2022/2023: | *R Standard Liège (BEL)* |
| Andreas PANAYIOTOU Filiotis | 31.05.1995 | 6 | 0 | 2023: | *Apollon Limassol FC* |
| Nikolas PANAYIOTOU | 12.05.2000 | 10 | 0 | 2022: | *AC Omonia Nicosia* |
| Kostas PILEAS | 11.12.1998 | 1 | 0 | 2023: | *Aris Limassol FC* |
| Valentin Sébastien Roger ROBERGE | 09.06.1987 | 4 | 1 | 2022/2023: | *Apollon Limassol FC* |
| Christos SIELIS | 02.02.2000 | 5 | 0 | 2022: | *Vólos NPS (GRE)* |
| Christos WHEELER | 29.06.1997 | 6 | 0 | 2022: | *APOEL Nicosia* |

### Midfielders

| Name | DOB | Caps | Goals | Club | |
|------|-----|------|-------|------|--|
| Minas ANTONIOU | 22.02.1994 | 18 | 0 | 2022/2023: | *Anorthosis Famagusta FC* |
| Kostakis ARTYMATAS | 15.04.1993 | 65 | 1 | 2022/2023: | *Anorthosis Famagusta FC* |
| Charalampos CHARALAMPOUS | 04.04.2002 | 7 | 1 | 2022/2023: | *AC Omonia Nicosia* |
| Giorgos EFRAIM | 05.07.1989 | 51 | 5 | 2022/2023: | *APOEL Nicosia* |
| Giorgos EKONOMIDIS | 10.04.1990 | 13 | 0 | 2022: | *Karmiotissa Polemidion FC* |
| Alexandros GOGIĆ | 13.04.1994 | 21 | 0 | 2022/2023: | *St. Mirren FC Paisley (SCO)* |
| Michalis IOANNOU | 30.06.2000 | 6 | 1 | 2022/2023: | *Anorthosis Famagusta FC* |
| Grigoris KASTANOS | 30.01.1998 | 54 | 4 | 2022/2023: | *US Salernitana 1919 (ITA)* |
| Fanos KATELARIS | 20.08.1996 | 19 | 1 | 2022: | *KV Oostende (BEL)* |
| Ioannis KOUSOULOS | 14.06.1996 | 33 | 4 | 2023: | *AC Omonia Nicosia* |
| Charalambos KYRIAKOU | 09.02.1995 | 55 | 0 | 2022/2023: | *Apollon Limassol FC* |
| Loizos LOIZOU | 18.07.2003 | 25 | 1 | 2022/2023: | *AC Omonia Nicosia* |
| Rafail MAMAS | 04.03.2001 | 2 | 0 | 2022: | *AEK Larnaca FC* |
| Fotios PAPOULIS | 22.01.1985 | 31 | 3 | 2022: | *AC Omonia Nicosia* |
| Ioannis PITTAS | 10.07.1996 | 33 | 3 | 2022/2023: | *Apollon Limassol FC* |
| Giannis SATSIAS | 28.12.2002 | 2 | 0 | 2023: | *APOEL Nicosia* |
| Danilo ŠPOLJARIĆ | 14.07.1999 | 6 | 0 | 2022/2023: | *Apollon Limassol FC* |
| Matija ŠPOLJARIĆ | 02.04.1997 | 15 | 0 | 2022: | *Aris Thessaloníki (GRE)* |
| Marinos TZIONIS | 17.07.2001 | 24 | 2 | 2022/2023: | *Sporting Kansas City (USA)* |

### Forwards

| Name | DOB | Caps | Goals | Club | |
|------|-----|------|-------|------|--|
| Dimitris CHRISTOFI | 28.09.1988 | 71 | 9 | 2022/2023: | *Anorthosis Famagusta FC* |
| Andronikos KAKOULLIS | 03.05.2001 | 15 | 3 | 2022/2023: | *AC Omonia Nicosia* |
| Pieros SOTIRIOU | 13.01.1993 | 58 | 12 | 2022: | *Sanfrecce Hiroshima (JPN)* |

### Trainer

| | | | |
|--|--|--|--|
| Temur KETSBAIA (Georgia) [from 29.06.2022] | 18.03.1968 | 8 M; 2 W; 1 D; 5 L; 9-19 | |

# CZECH REPUBLIC

## The Country:
Česká republika (Czech Republic)
Capital: Praha
Surface: 78,866 km$^2$
Inhabitants: 10,827,529 [2023]
Time: UTC+1

## The FA:
Fotbalová asociace České republiky
Atletická 2474/8, 169 00 Praha 6
Tel: +420 233 029 111
Foundation date: 1901 (as Bohemia)
Member of FIFA since: 1907 (as Bohemia)
Member of UEFA since: 1954 (as Czechoslovakia)
Website: www.fotbal.cz

## NATIONAL TEAM RECORDS

| RECORDS | |
|---|---|
| **First international match:** | 28.08.1920, Antwerpen: Czechoslovakia - Yugoslavia 7-0 |
| **Most international caps:** Petr Čech | - 124 caps (2002-2016) |
| **Most international goals:** Jan Koller | - 55 goals / 91 caps (1999-2009) |

| UEFA EUROPEAN CHAMPIONSHIP | |
|---|---|
| 1960 | Final Tournament (3$^{rd}$ Place) |
| 1964 | Qualifiers |
| 1968 | Qualifiers |
| 1972 | Qualifiers |
| 1976 | **Final Tournament (Winners)** |
| 1980 | Final Tournament (3$^{rd}$ Place) |
| 1984 | Qualifiers |
| 1988 | Qualifiers |
| 1992 | Qualifiers |
| 1996 | Final Tournament (Runners-up) |
| 2000 | Final Tournament (Group Stage) |
| 2004 | Final Tournament (Semi-Finals) |
| 2008 | Final Tournament (Group Stage) |
| 2012 | Final Tournament (Quarter-Finals) |
| 2016 | Final Tournament (Qualified) |
| 2020 | Final Tournament (Quarter-Finals) |

| FIFA WORLD CUP | |
|---|---|
| 1930 | Did not enter |
| 1934 | Final Tournament (Runners-up) |
| 1938 | Final Tournament (Quarter-Finals) |
| 1950 | Did not enter |
| 1954 | Final Tournament (Group Stage) |
| 1958 | Final Tournament (Group Stage) |
| 1962 | Final Tournament (Runners-up) |
| 1966 | Qualifiers |
| 1970 | Final Tournament (Group Stage) |
| 1974 | Qualifiers |
| 1978 | Qualifiers |
| 1982 | Final Tournament (Group Stage) |
| 1986 | Qualifiers |
| 1990 | Final Tournament (Quarter-Finals) |
| 1994 | Qualifiers |
| 1998 | Qualifiers |
| 2002 | Qualifiers |
| 2006 | Final Tournament (Group Stage) |
| 2010 | Qualifiers |
| 2014 | Qualifiers |
| 2018 | Qualifiers |
| 2022 | Qualifiers |

| OLYMPIC TOURNAMENTS | |
|---|---|
| 1908 | - |
| 1912 | - |
| 1920 | Runners-up |
| 1924 | 1/8 Finals |
| 1928 | Did not enter |
| 1936 | Did not enter |
| 1948 | Did not enter |
| 1952 | Did not enter |
| 1956 | Did not enter |
| 1960 | Qualifiers |
| 1964 | Runners-up |
| 1968 | Group Stage |
| 1972 | Did not enter |
| 1976 | Qualifiers |
| 1980 | **Winners** |
| 1984 | Did not enter |
| 1988 | Qualifiers |
| 1992 | Qualifiers |
| 1996 | Qualifiers |
| 2000 | Group Stage |
| 2004 | Qualifiers |
| 2008 | Qualifiers |
| 2012 | Qualifiers |
| 2016 | Qualifiers |
| 2020 | Qualifiers |

| UEFA NATIONS LEAGUE | |
|---|---|
| 2018/2019 | League B (Group Stage) |
| 2020/2021 | League B (Group Stage -> promoted to League A) |
| 2022/2023 | League A (Group Stage -> relegated to League B) |

## CZECH CLUB HONOURS IN EUROPEAN CLUB COMPETITIONS:

| European Champion Clubs' Cup (1956-1992) / UEFA Champions League (1993-2023) |
|---|
| None |

| Fairs Cup (1858-1971) / UEFA Cup (1972-2009) / UEFA Europa League (2010-2023) |
|---|
| None |

| UEFA Europa Conference League (2021-2023) |
|---|
| None |

| UEFA Super Cup (1972-2022) |
|---|
| None |

| *European Cup Winners' Cup 1961-1999** |
|---|
| None |

*defunct competition

# NATIONAL COMPETITIONS
# TABLE OF HONOURS

## CZECHOSLOVAKIA 1925-1938 / BOHEMIA-MORAVIA 1938-1944 / CZECHOSLOVAKIA 1945-1993

| | CHAMPIONS | CUP WINNERS | BEST GOALSCORERS | |
|---|---|---|---|---|
| 1925 | SK Slavia Praha | - | Jan Vaník (SK Slavia Praha) | 13 |
| 1925/1926 | AC Sparta Praha | - | Jan Dvořáček (AC Sparta Praha) | 32 |
| 1927 | AC Sparta Praha | - | Antonín Puč (SK Slavia Praha) | |
| | | | Josef Šíma (AC Sparta Praha) | 13 |
| 1927/1928 | SK Viktoria Žižkov | - | Karel Meduna (SK Viktoria Žižkov) | 12 |
| 1928/1929 | SK Slavia Praha | - | Antonín Puč (SK Slavia Praha) | 13 |
| 1929/1930 | SK Slavia Praha | - | František Kloz (SK Kladno) | 15 |
| 1930/1931 | SK Slavia Praha | - | Josef Silný (AC Sparta Praha) | 18 |
| 1931/1932 | AC Sparta Praha | - | Raymond Braine (AC Sparta Praha) | 16 |
| 1932/1933 | SK Slavia Praha | - | Gejza Kocsis | |
| | | | (Teplitzer FK / Bohemians AFK Vršovice) | 23 |
| 1933/1934 | SK Slavia Praha | - | Raymond Braine (AC Sparta Praha) | |
| | | | Jiří Sobotka (SK Slavia Praha) | 18 |
| 1934/1935 | SK Slavia Praha | - | František Svoboda (SK Slavia Praha) | 27 |
| 1935/1936 | AC Sparta Praha | - | Vojtěch Bradáč (SK Slavia Praha) | 42 |
| 1936/1937 | SK Slavia Praha | - | František Kloz (SK Kladno) | 28 |
| 1937/1938 | AC Sparta Praha | - | Josef Bican (SK Slavia Praha) | 22 |
| 1938/1939 | AC Sparta Praha | - | Josef Bican (SK Slavia Praha) | 29 |
| 1939/1940 | SK Slavia Praha | - | Josef Bican (SK Slavia Praha) | 50 |
| 1940/1941 | SK Slavia Praha | - | Josef Bican (SK Slavia Praha) | 38 |
| 1941/1942 | SK Slavia Praha | - | Josef Bican (SK Slavia Praha) | 45 |
| 1942/1943 | SK Slavia Praha | - | Josef Bican (SK Slavia Praha) | 39 |
| 1943/1944 | AC Sparta Praha | - | Josef Bican (SK Slavia Praha) | 57 |
| 1944/1945 | *No competition* | - | - | |
| 1945/1946 | AC Sparta Praha | - | Josef Bican (SK Slavia Praha) | 31 |
| 1946/1947 | SK Slavia Praha | - | Josef Bican (SK Slavia Praha) | 43 |
| 1947/1948 | AC Sparta Praha | - | Jaroslav Cejp (AC Sparta Praha) | 21 |
| 1948 | *Championship abandoned* | - | Josef Bican (Sokol Slavia Praha) | 21 |
| 1949 | ŠK NV Bratislava | - | Ladislav Hlaváček (ZSJ Dynamo Slavia Praha) | 28 |
| 1950 | ŠK NV Bratislava | - | Josef Bican (Sokol Vítkovice Železárny) | 22 |
| 1951 | ŠK NV Bratislava | - | Alois Jaroš (ZSJ Vodotechna Teplice) | 16 |
| 1952 | Sparta ČKD Sokolovo | - | Miroslav Wiecek (OKD Ostrava) | 20 |
| 1953 | ÚDA Praha | - | Josef Majer (DSO Baník Kladno) | 13 |
| 1954 | TJ Spartak Praha Sokolovo | - | Jiří Pešek (TJ Spartak Praha Sokolovo) | 13 |
| 1955 | ŠK Slovan Bratislava | - | Emil Pažický | |
| | | | (ÚNV Slovan Bratislava / Jiskra Slovena Žilina) | 9 |
| 1956 | AS Dukla Praha | - | Milan Dvořák (AS Dukla Praha) | |
| | | | Miroslav Wiecek (DSO Baník Ostrava) | 15 |
| 1957/1958 | AS Dukla Praha | - | Miroslav Wiecek (DSO Baník Ostrava) | 25 |
| 1958/1959 | ČH Bratislava | - | Miroslav Wiecek (DSO Baník Ostrava) | 20 |
| 1959/1960 | DSO Spartak Hradec Králové | - | Michal Pucher (TJ Slovan Nitra) | 18 |
| 1960/1961 | AS Dukla Praha | AS Dukla Praha | Rudolf Kučera (AS Dukla Praha) | |
| | | | Ladislav Pavlovič (TJ Tatran Prešov) | 17 |
| 1961/1962 | AS Dukla Praha | Slovan CHZJD Bratislava | Adolf Scherer (TJ Červená Hviezda Bratislava) | 24 |
| 1962/1963 | AS Dukla Praha | Slovan CHZJD Bratislava | Karel Petroš (TJ Tatran Prešov) | 19 |
| 1963/1964 | AS Dukla Praha | Spartak Praha Sokolovo | Ladislav Pavlovič (TJ Tatran Prešov) | 21 |
| 1964/1965 | TJ Spartak Praha Sokolovo | AS Dukla Praha | Pavol Bencz (Jednota Trenčín) | 21 |
| 1965/1966 | AS Dukla Praha | AS Dukla Praha | Ladislav Michalík (TJ Baník Ostrava) | 15 |
| 1966/1967 | TJ Sparta ČKD Praha | Spartak Trnava | Jozef Adamec (Spartak Trnava) | 21 |
| 1967/1968 | Spartak TAZ Trnava | Slovan CHZJD Bratislava | Jozef Adamec (Spartak TAZ Trnava) | 18 |
| 1968/1969 | Spartak TAZ Trnava | AS Dukla Praha | Ladislav Petráš (AS Dukla Banská Bystrica) | 20 |
| 1969/1970 | Slovan CHZJD Bratislava | TJ Gottwaldov | Jozef Adamec (Spartak TAZ Trnava) | 18 |
| 1970/1971 | Spartak TAZ Trnava | Spartak TAZ Trnava | Jozef Adamec (Spartak TAZ Trnava) | |
| | | | Zdeněk Nehoda (TJ Gottwaldov) | 16 |
| 1971/1972 | Spartak TAZ Trnava | TJ Sparta ČKD Praha | Ján Čapkovič (Slovan CHZJD Bratislava) | 19 |
| 1972/1973 | Spartak TAZ Trnava | TJ Baník Ostrava OKD | Ladislav Józsa (TJ Lokomotíva Košice) | 21 |
| 1973/1974 | Slovan CHZJD Bratislava | Slovan CHZJD Bratislava | Ladislav Józsa (TJ Lokomotíva Košice) | |
| | | | Přemysl Bičovský (TJ Sklo Union Teplice) | 17 |
| 1974/1975 | Slovan CHZJD Bratislava | Spartak TAZ Trnava | Ladislav Petráš (TJ Internacionál Slovnaft Bratislava) | 20 |
| 1975/1976 | TJ Baník Ostrava OKD | TJ Sparta ČKD Praha | Dušan Galis (TJ VSS Košice) | 21 |
| 1976/1977 | ASVS Dukla Praha | TJ Lokomotíva Košice | Ladislav Józsa (TJ Lokomotíva Košice) | 18 |
| 1977/1978 | Zbrojovka Brno | TJ Baník Ostrava OKD | Karel Kroupa (Zbrojovka Brno) | 20 |
| 1978/1979 | ASVS Dukla Praha | TJ Lokomotíva Košice | Karel Kroupa (Zbrojovka Brno) | |
| | | | Zdeněk Nehoda (ASVS Dukla Praha) | 17 |
| 1979/1980 | TJ Baník Ostrava OKD | TJ Sparta ČKD Praha | Werner Lička (TJ Baník Ostrava OKD) | 18 |
| 1980/1981 | TJ Baník Ostrava OKD | ASVS Dukla Praha | Marián Masný (Slovan CHZJD Bratislava) | 16 |
| 1981/1982 | ASVS Dukla Praha | Slovan CHZJD Bratislava | Peter Herda (SK Slavia IPS Praha) | |
| | | | Ladislav Vízek (ASVS Dukla Praha) | 15 |
| 1982/1983 | Bohemians ČKD Praha | ASVS Dukla Praha | Pavel Chaloupka (Bohemians ČKD Praha) | 17 |

| 1983/1984 | TJ Sparta ČKD Praha | AC Sparta Praha | Werner Lička (TJ Baník Ostrava OKD) | 20 |
|---|---|---|---|---|
| 1984/1985 | TJ Sparta ČKD Praha | ASVS Dukla Praha | Ivo Knoflíček (SK Slavia IPS Praha) | 21 |
| 1985/1986 | TJ Vítkovice | Spartak TAZ Trnava | Stanislav Griga (TJ Sparta ČKD Praha) | 19 |
| 1986/1987 | TJ Sparta ČKD Praha | DAC Dunajská Streda | Václav Daněk (TJ Baník Ostrava OKD) | 24 |
| 1987/1988 | TJ Sparta ČKD Praha | TJ Sparta ČKD Praha | Milan Luhový (ASVS Dukla Praha) | 24 |
| 1988/1989 | TJ Sparta ČKD Praha | TJ Sparta ČKD Praha | Milan Luhový (ASVS Dukla Praha) | 25 |
| 1989/1990 | TJ Sparta ČKD Praha | ASVS Dukla Praha | Ľubomír Luhový (TJ Internacionál Slovnaft ZŤS Bratislava) | 20 |
| 1990/1991 | TJ Sparta Praha | FC Baník Ostrava | Roman Kukleta (TJ Sparta Praha) | 17 |
| 1991/1992 | ŠK Slovan Bratislava | AC Sparta Praha | Peter Dubovský (ŠK Slovan Bratislava) | 27 |
| 1992/1993 | AC Sparta Praha | 1. FC Košice | Peter Dubovský (ŠK Slovan Bratislava) | 24 |

## CZECH REPUBLIC (Since 1993)

| 1993/1994 | AC Sparta Praha | FK Viktoria Žižkov | Horst Siegl (AC Sparta Praha) | 20 |
|---|---|---|---|---|
| 1994/1995 | AC Sparta Praha | SK Hradec Králové | Radek Drulák (FK Drnovice) | 15 |
| 1995/1996 | SK Slavia Praha | AC Sparta Praha | Radek Drulák (FK Drnovice) | 22 |
| 1996/1997 | AC Sparta Praha | SK Slavia Praha | Horst Siegl (AC Sparta Praha) | 19 |
| 1997/1998 | AC Sparta Praha | FK Jablonec 97 | Horst Siegl (AC Sparta Praha) | 13 |
| 1998/1999 | AC Sparta Praha | SK Slavia Praha | Horst Siegl (AC Sparta Praha) | 18 |
| 1999/2000 | AC Sparta Praha | FC Slovan Liberec | Vratislav Lokvenc (AC Sparta Praha) | 22 |
| 2000/2001 | AC Sparta Praha | FK Viktoria Žižkov | Vítězslav Tuma (FK Drnovice) | 15 |
| 2001/2002 | FC Slovan Liberec | SK Slavia Praha | Jiří Štajner (FC Slovan Liberec) | 15 |
| 2002/2003 | AC Sparta Praha | FK Teplice | Jiří Kowalík (1. FC Synot Uherské Hradiště) | 16 |
| 2003/2004 | FC Baník Ostrava | AC Sparta Praha | Marek Heinz (FC Baník Ostrava) | 19 |
| 2004/2005 | AC Sparta Praha | FC Baník Ostrava | Tomáš Jun (AC Sparta Praha) | 14 |
| 2005/2006 | FC Slovan Liberec | AC Sparta Praha | Milan Ivana (FC Slovácko Uherské Hradiště) | 11 |
| 2006/2007 | AC Sparta Praha | AC Sparta Praha | Luboš Pecka (FK Mladá Boleslav) | 16 |
| 2007/2008 | SK Slavia Praha | AC Sparta Praha | Václav Svěrkoš (FC Baník Ostrava) | 15 |
| 2008/2009 | SK Slavia Praha | FK Teplice | Andrej Kerić (FC Slovan Liberec) | 15 |
| 2009/2010 | AC Sparta Praha | FC Viktoria Plzeň | Michal Ordoš (Sigma Olomouc) | 12 |
| 2010/2011 | FC Viktoria Plzeň | FK Mladá Boleslav | David Lafata (FK Baumit Jablonec) | 19 |
| 2011/2012 | FC Slovan Liberec | SK Sigma Olomouc | David Lafata (FK Baumit Jablonec) | 25 |
| 2012/2013 | FC Viktoria Plzeň | FK Baumit Jablonec | David Lafata (FK Baumit Jablonec / AC Sparta Praha) | 20 |
| 2013/2014 | AC Sparta Praha | AC Sparta Praha | Josef Hušbauer (AC Sparta Praha) | 18 |
| 2014/2015 | FC Viktoria Plzeň | FC Slovan Liberec | David Lafata (AC Sparta Praha) | 20 |
| 2015/2016 | FC Viktoria Plzeň | FK Mladá Boleslav | David Lafata (AC Sparta Praha) | 20 |
| 2016/2017 | SK Slavia Praha | FC Fastav Zlín | Milan Škoda (SK Slavia Praha) David Lafata (AC Sparta Praha) | 15 |
| 2017/2018 | FC Viktoria Plzeň | SK Slavia Praha | Michael Krmenčík (FC Viktoria Plzeň) | 16 |
| 2018/2019 | SK Slavia Praha | SK Slavia Praha | Nikolay Komlichenko (RUS, FK Mladá Boleslav) | 29 |
| 2019/2020 | SK Slavia Praha | AC Sparta Praha | Petar Musa (CRO, FC Slovan Liberec / SK Slavia Praha) Libor Kozák (AC Sparta Praha) | 14 |
| 2020/2021 | SK Slavia Praha | SK Slavia Praha | Jan Kuchta (SK Slavia Praha) Adam Hložek (AC Sparta Praha) | 15 |
| 2021/2022 | FC Viktoria Plzeň | 1. FC Slovácko Uherské Hradiště | Jean-David Beauguel (FRA, FC Viktoria Plzeň) | 19 |
| 2022/2023 | AC Sparta Praha | SK Slavia Praha | Václav Jurečka (SK Slavia Praha) | 20 |

Please note: FC Fastav Zlín changed its name to FC Trinity Zlín.

## Regular Season - Results

### Round 1 [30-31.07.2022]
Zbrojovka Brno - 1. FC Slovácko 2-2(2-1)
Baník Ostrava - Sigma Olomouc 0-3(0-1)
FC Trinity Zlín - Mladá Boleslav 0-0
FK Teplice - Viktoria Plzeň 2-2(1-0)
FC Hradec Králové - Slavia Praha 1-0(0-0)
FK Jablonec - Bohemians 1905 0-3(0-1)
FK Pardubice - SK Dynamo 0-2(0-1)
Sparta Praha - Slovan Liberec 1-2(0-2)

### Round 2 [06-07.08.2022]
Sigma Olomouc - Zbrojovka Brno 0-2(0-1)
Slovan Liberec - FK Teplice 5-1(3-1)
Viktoria Plzeň - FK Pardubice 2-1(1-0)
Bohemians 1905 - Baník Ostrava 3-3(3-1)
1. FC Slovácko - FC Hradec Králové 1-0(0-0)
SK Dynamo - Sparta Praha 0-2(0-2)
Mladá Boleslav - FK Jablonec 2-2(1-2)
Slavia Praha - FC Trinity Zlín 4-1(2-0)

### Round 3 [13-14.08.2022]
Zbrojovka Brno - Mladá Boleslav 3-1(0-1)
Baník Ostrava - FC Trinity Zlín 3-1(3-0)
FK Teplice - Bohemians 1905 0-1(0-0)
FC Hradec Králové - Viktoria Plzeň 1-2(1-1)
SK Dynamo - 1. FC Slovácko 2-2(1-1)
FK Jablonec - Slavia Praha 2-3(0-1)
FK Pardubice - Slovan Liberec 2-1(2-0)
Sparta Praha - Sigma Olomouc 2-0(1-0)

### Round 4 [20-22.08.2022]
Baník Ostrava - FK Teplice 1-2(1-1)
Mladá Boleslav - Sparta Praha 1-3(1-0)
FC Trinity Zlín - FK Jablonec 2-2(1-1)
Sigma Olomouc - 1. FC Slovácko 1-2(1-0)
Slovan Liberec - SK Dynamo 1-1(1-0)
Slavia Praha - FK Pardubice 7-0(2-0)
Bohemians 1905-FC Hradec Králové 1-2(1-2)
Viktoria P. - Zbrojovka B. 4-0(1-0) [09.11.22]

### Round 5 [27-28.08.2022]
SK Dynamo - Viktoria Plzeň 0-1(0-0)
FK Jablonec - Baník Ostrava 1-1(0-0)
FK Pardubice - Mladá Boleslav 0-3(0-3)
FK Teplice - FC Trinity Zlín 0-0
Sparta Praha - Bohemians 1905 1-1(0-1)
1. FC Slovácko - Slovan Liberec 1-2(0-1)
FC Hradec Králové - Sigma Olomouc 1-0(0-0)
Zbrojovka Brno - Slavia Praha 0-4(0-3)

### Round 6 [30-31.08.2022]
Bohemians 1905 - SK Dynamo 1-2(0-1)
FC Trinity Zlín - FK Pardubice 2-1(1-0)
FK Jablonec - Sparta Praha 1-1(1-1)
Baník Ostrava - Zbrojovka Brno 1-2(0-0)
Mladá Boleslav - FC Hradec Králové 1-2(0-1)
Sigma Olomouc - Slovan Liberec 1-1(1-0)
Viktoria Plzeň - 1. FC Slovácko 3-0(2-0)
Slavia Praha - FK Teplice 6-0(2-0)

### Round 7 [03-04.09.2022]
SK Dynamo - Mladá Boleslav 0-2(0-0)
FK Teplice - FK Jablonec 3-2(1-2)
Slovan Liberec - Viktoria Plzeň 0-1(0-1)
Sparta Praha - FC Trinity Zlín 0-0
Zbrojovka Brno - Bohemians 1905 1-2(0-2)
FC Hradec Králové - Baník Ostrava 0-0
FK Pardubice - Sigma Olomouc 0-2(0-1)
1. FC Slovácko - Slavia Praha 1-1(1-0)

### Round 8 [10-11.09.2022]
FC Trinity Zlín - Zbrojovka Brno 2-3(0-1)
Sigma Olomouc - Viktoria Plzeň 2-3(1-2)
FK Teplice - Sparta Praha 2-2(1-2)
Baník Ostrava - FK Pardubice 3-0(1-0)
Bohemians 1905 - Slovan Liberec 0-2(0-1)
FK Jablonec - FC Hradec Králové 3-0(0-0)
Mladá Boleslav - 1. FC Slovácko 1-1(0-1)
Slavia Praha - SK Dynamo 6-1(3-0)

### Round 9 [17-18.09.2022]
Zbrojovka Brno - FK Teplice 2-2(2-2)
SK Dynamo - Sigma Olomouc 0-3(0-2)
Slovan Liberec - Mladá Boleslav 1-3(1-0)
Sparta Praha - Baník Ostrava 1-1(0-1)
1. FC Slovácko - FK Jablonec 0-2(0-0)
FC Hradec Králové - FC Trinity Zlín 0-0
FK Pardubice - Bohemians 1905 0-1(0-0)
Viktoria Plzeň - Slavia Praha 3-0(2-0)

### Round 10 [01-02.10.2022]
Baník Ostrava - SK Dynamo 1-2(0-1)
Bohemians 1905 - Viktoria Plzeň 1-1(0-1)
Mladá Boleslav - Sigma Olomouc 1-1(1-0)
Sparta Praha - FC Hradec Králové 2-1(0-1)
FC Trinity Zlín - 1. FC Slovácko 0-2(0-0)
FK Jablonec - Zbrojovka Brno 3-1(1-0)
FK Teplice - FK Pardubice 5-1(2-0)
Slavia Praha - Slovan Liberec 3-0(3-0)

### Round 11 [08-09.10.2022]
Zbrojovka Brno - Sparta Praha 0-4(0-2)
FC Hradec Králové - FK Teplice 4-1(1-1)
FK Pardubice - FK Jablonec 1-0(0-0)
Viktoria Plzeň - Mladá Boleslav 2-0(0-0)
1. FC Slovácko - Bohemians 1905 2-4(0-2)
SK Dynamo - FC Trinity Zlín 2-2(2-1)
Slovan Liberec - Baník Ostrava 0-0
Sigma Olomouc - Slavia Praha 2-0(1-0)

### Round 12 [15-16.10.2022]
Bohemians 1905 - Sigma Olomouc 1-1(0-1)
FC Hradec Králové - Zbrojovka Brno 2-1(1-1)
FK Teplice - SK Dynamo 0-2(0-0)
Sparta Praha - FK Pardubice 5-2(2-1)
Baník Ostrava - 1. FC Slovácko 3-1(2-0)
FC Trinity Zlín - Slovan Liberec 2-1(1-0)
FK Jablonec - Viktoria Plzeň 0-3(0-1)
Slavia Praha - Mladá Boleslav 2-1(2-1)

### Round 13 [22-23.10.2022]
FK Pardubice - Zbrojovka Brno 1-3(0-1)
Sigma Olomouc - FC Trinity Zlín 2-1(0-1)
Slovan Liberec - FK Jablonec 2-0(1-0)
Viktoria Plzeň - Baník Ostrava 3-1(2-0)
SK Dynamo - FC Hradec Králové 0-3(0-0)
1. FC Slovácko - FK Teplice 2-1(0-1)
Mladá Boleslav - Bohemians 1905 4-3(1-1)
Slavia Praha - Sparta Praha 4-0(4-0)

### Round 14 [29-30.10.2022]
Baník Ostrava - Mladá Boleslav 3-1(1-0)
FC Hradec Králové - FK Pardubice 1-3(0-0)
FK Jablonec - SK Dynamo 3-0(1-0)
FC Trinity Zlín - Viktoria Plzeň 0-3(0-1)
Zbrojovka Brno - Slovan Liberec 3-0(0-0)
Bohemians 1905 - Slavia Praha 1-4(1-2)
FK Teplice - Sigma Olomouc 2-1(1-1)
Sparta Pr.-1. FC Slovácko 4-0(2-0) [09.11.22]

### Round 15 [05-06.11.2022]
Bohemians 1905 - FC Trinity Zlín 3-2(0-2)
SK Dynamo - Zbrojovka Brno 3-0(2-0)
Sigma Olomouc - FK Jablonec 3-0(1-0)
Viktoria Plzeň - Sparta Praha 0-1(0-0)
1. FC Slovácko - FK Pardubice 1-0(0-0)
Mladá Boleslav - FK Teplice 3-0(1-0)
Slovan Liberec - FC Hradec Králové 2-0(1-0)
Slavia Praha - Baník Ostrava 3-1(0-0)

### Round 16 [12-13.11.2022]
Baník Ostrava - Bohemians 1905 4-1(2-0)
FK Jablonec - Mladá Boleslav 1-2(1-1)
FK Teplice - Slovan Liberec 2-1(1-1)
Sparta Praha - SK Dynamo 1-0(1-0)
Zbrojovka Brno - Sigma Olomouc 2-3(1-2)
FC Hradec Králové - 1. FC Slovácko 1-2(1-0)
FK Pardubice - Viktoria Plzeň 1-1(0-0)
FC Trinity Zlín - Slavia Praha 0-4(0-3)

### Round 17 [28-29.01.2023]
1. FC Slovácko - SK Dynamo 1-0(0-0)
Bohemians 1905 - FK Teplice 2-0(0-0)
Viktoria Plzeň - FC Hradec Králové 1-2(1-1)
Sigma Olomouc - Sparta Praha 1-1(1-1)
Mladá Boleslav - Zbrojovka Brno 0-0
Slavia Praha - FK Jablonec 5-1(1-1)
Slovan Liberec - FK Pardubice 1-1(1-0)
FC Trinity Zlín - Baník Ostrava 1-1(0-1)

### Round 18 [04-05.02.2023]
1. FC Slovácko - Sigma Olomouc 0-0
FK Jablonec - FC Trinity Zlín 2-2(0-1)
FK Teplice - Baník Ostrava 0-5(0-0)
FK Pardubice - Slavia Praha 0-2(0-1)
Zbrojovka Brno - Viktoria Plzeň 1-3(1-0)
SK Dynamo - Slovan Liberec 0-2(0-1)
FC Hradec Králové-Bohemians 1905 0-2(0-2)
Sparta Praha - Mladá Boleslav 4-1(2-1)

### Round 19 [11-12.02.2023]
Baník Ostrava - FK Jablonec 1-2(0-1)
FC Trinity Zlín - FK Teplice 2-1(2-0)
Slovan Liberec - 1. FC Slovácko 0-1(0-0)
Slavia Praha - Zbrojovka Brno 2-0(0-0)
Mladá Boleslav - FK Pardubice 0-1(0-1)
Sigma Olomouc - FC Hradec Králové 2-2(1-1)
Viktoria Plzeň - SK Dynamo 2-1(1-0)
Bohemians 1905 - Sparta Praha 2-6(0-1)

### Round 20 [18-19.02.2023]
Zbrojovka Brno - Baník Ostrava 2-1(1-0)
FC Hradec Králové - Mladá Boleslav 0-1(0-0)
Slovan Liberec - Sigma Olomouc 2-2(1-1)
FK Teplice - Slavia Praha 1-1(1-0)
1. FC Slovácko - Viktoria Plzeň 2-0(1-0)
SK Dynamo - Bohemians 1905 1-0(0-0)
FK Pardubice - FC Trinity Zlín 2-1(1-0)
Sparta Praha - FK Jablonec 3-0(1-0)

### Round 21 [25-26.02.2023]
Bohemians 1905 - Zbrojovka Brno 1-1(0-0)
FC Trinity Zlín - Sparta Praha 2-3(0-2)
Mladá Boleslav - SK Dynamo 2-2(1-1)
Viktoria Plzeň - Slovan Liberec 2-1(1-0)
FK Jablonec - FK Teplice 4-1(2-0)
Sigma Olomouc - FK Pardubice 2-2(0-0)
Slavia Praha - 1. FC Slovácko 2-0(1-0)
Baník Ostrava - FC Hradec Králové 0-2(0-1)

| Round 22 [04-05.03.2023] |
|---|
| Zbrojovka Brno - FC Trinity Zlín 1-1(0-1) |
| FC Hradec Králové - FK Jablonec 1-4(1-0) |
| FK Pardubice - Baník Ostrava 1-1(1-1) |
| Viktoria Plzeň - Sigma Olomouc 1-1(0-0) |
| Sparta Praha - FK Teplice 4-1(2-0) |
| Slovan Liberec - Bohemians 1905 1-3(0-2) |
| 1. FC Slovácko - Mladá Boleslav 2-1(1-1) |
| SK Dynamo - Slavia Praha 1-0(0-0) |

| Round 23 [11-12.03.2023] |
|---|
| Baník Ostrava - Sparta Praha 0-3(0-2) |
| FC Trinity Zlín - FC Hradec Králové 2-2(2-1) |
| Sigma Olomouc - SK Dynamo 3-0(0-0) |
| Slavia Praha - Viktoria Plzeň 2-1(0-1) |
| Mladá Boleslav - Slovan Liberec 4-0(3-0) |
| FK Teplice - Zbrojovka Brno 1-1(0-0) |
| Bohemians 1905 - FK Pardubice 2-0(1-0) |
| Jablonec - 1. FC Slovácko 1-1(0-1) [05.04.23] |

| Round 24 [18-19.03.2023] |
|---|
| SK Dynamo - Baník Ostrava 2-1(1-1) |
| FC Hradec Králové - Sparta Praha 0-2(0-1) |
| Sigma Olomouc - Mladá Boleslav 2-0(1-0) |
| Slovan Liberec - Slavia Praha 2-2(1-1) |
| Zbrojovka Brno - FK Jablonec 1-2(1-0) |
| 1. FC Slovácko - FC Trinity Zlín 3-0(1-0) |
| FK Pardubice - FK Teplice 3-1(2-1) |
| Viktoria Plzeň - Bohemians 1905 1-2(1-0) |

| Round 25 [01-02.04.2023] |
|---|
| Baník Ostrava - Slovan Liberec 0-0 |
| FC Trinity Zlín - SK Dynamo 5-1(2-0) |
| Mladá Boleslav - Viktoria Plzeň 0-0 |
| Slavia Praha - Sigma Olomouc 4-0(1-0) |
| FK Jablonec - FK Pardubice 1-0(0-0) |
| FK Teplice - FC Hradec Králové 1-0(1-0) |
| Sparta Praha - Zbrojovka Brno 3-1(2-1) |
| Bohemians 1905 - 1. FC Slovácko 1-0(0-0) |

| Round 26 [08-09.04.2023] |
|---|
| Zbrojovka Brno - FC Hradec Králové 1-2(1-1) |
| 1. FC Slovácko - Baník Ostrava 0-1(0-1) |
| Slovan Liberec - FC Trinity Zlín 2-1(0-0) |
| Viktoria Plzeň - FK Jablonec 3-2(1-0) |
| SK Dynamo - FK Teplice 0-3(0-1) |
| Mladá Boleslav - Slavia Praha 1-1(1-1) |
| Sigma Olomouc - Bohemians 1905 2-2(1-1) |
| FK Pardubice - Sparta Praha 0-2(0-2) |

| Round 27 [15-16.04.2023] |
|---|
| FC Trinity Zlín - Sigma Olomouc 0-1(0-1) |
| FK Jablonec - Slovan Liberec 1-1(0-0) |
| FK Teplice - 1. FC Slovácko 1-3(0-1) |
| Sparta Praha - Slavia Praha 3-3(0-1) |
| Zbrojovka Brno - FK Pardubice 2-1(0-0) |
| Bohemians 1905 - Mladá Boleslav 4-0(1-0) |
| FC Hradec Králové - SK Dynamo 2-1(2-0) |
| Baník Ostrava - Viktoria Plzeň 2-1(1-0) |

| Round 28 [22-23.04.2023] |
|---|
| 1. FC Slovácko - Sparta Praha 1-1(1-0) |
| Mladá Boleslav - Baník Ostrava 1-0(1-0) |
| FK Pardubice - FC Hradec Králové 1-0(0-0) |
| Sigma Olomouc - FK Teplice 1-2(0-1) |
| Slavia Praha - Bohemians 1905 3-0(3-0) |
| SK Dynamo - FK Jablonec 5-1(3-0) |
| Slovan Liberec - Zbrojovka Brno 3-1(3-0) |
| Viktoria Plzeň - FC Trinity Zlín 4-0(1-0) |

| Round 29 [25-26.04.2023] |
|---|
| FK Pardubice - 1. FC Slovácko 3-1(0-1) |
| FK Teplice - Mladá Boleslav 1-1(1-0) |
| Baník Ostrava - Slavia Praha 0-2(0-0) |
| Zbrojovka Brno - SK Dynamo 1-1(1-0) |
| FC Trinity Zlín - Bohemians 1905 4-1(1-0) |
| FC Hradec Králové - Slovan Liberec 1-2(0-0) |
| FK Jablonec - Sigma Olomouc 2-2(2-0) |
| Sparta Praha - Viktoria Plzeň 2-1(1-1) |

| Round 30 [30.04.2023] |
|---|
| 1. FC Slovácko - Zbrojovka Brno 1-0(1-0) |
| Bohemians 1905 - FK Jablonec 4-1(2-0) |
| SK Dynamo - FK Pardubice 3-1(1-0) |
| Mladá Boleslav - FC Trinity Zlín 1-1(1-0) |
| Sigma Olomouc - Baník Ostrava 1-4(1-2) |
| Slavia Praha - FC Hradec Králové 1-1(1-1) |
| Slovan Liberec - Sparta Praha 1-3(1-0) |
| Viktoria Plzeň - FK Teplice 1-1(0-0) |

## Final Standings

| | | | | | | | | | | | | | | | | | |
|---|---|---|---|---|---|---|---|---|---|---|---|---|---|---|---|---|---|
| 1. | AC Sparta Praha | 30 | 20 | 8 | 2 | 70 - 29 | 68 | 10 | 4 | 1 | 36 - 14 | 10 | 4 | 1 | 34 - 15 |
| 2. | SK Slavia Praha | 30 | 20 | 6 | 4 | 81 - 25 | 66 | 14 | 1 | 0 | 54 - 7 | 6 | 5 | 4 | 27 - 18 |
| 3. | FC Viktoria Plzeň | 30 | 17 | 6 | 7 | 55 - 29 | 57 | 10 | 2 | 3 | 32 - 13 | 7 | 4 | 4 | 23 - 16 |
| 4. | Bohemians Praha 1905 | 30 | 14 | 6 | 10 | 53 - 49 | 48 | 6 | 4 | 5 | 27 - 25 | 8 | 2 | 5 | 26 - 24 |
| 5. | 1. FC Slovácko Uherské Hradiště | 30 | 13 | 7 | 10 | 36 - 38 | 46 | 8 | 3 | 4 | 18 - 13 | 5 | 4 | 6 | 18 - 25 |
| 6. | SK Sigma Olomouc | 30 | 10 | 11 | 9 | 45 - 40 | 41 | 5 | 5 | 5 | 25 - 22 | 5 | 6 | 4 | 20 - 18 |
| 7. | FC Slovan Liberec | 30 | 10 | 8 | 12 | 39 - 43 | 38 | 5 | 5 | 5 | 23 - 20 | 5 | 3 | 7 | 16 - 23 |
| 8. | FC Hradec Králové | 30 | 11 | 5 | 14 | 34 - 40 | 38 | 5 | 2 | 8 | 15 - 21 | 6 | 3 | 6 | 19 - 19 |
| 9. | FK Mladá Boleslav | 30 | 9 | 10 | 11 | 39 - 42 | 37 | 4 | 8 | 3 | 22 - 17 | 5 | 2 | 8 | 17 - 25 |
| 10. | SK Dynamo České Budějovice | 30 | 10 | 5 | 15 | 35 - 54 | 35 | 6 | 2 | 7 | 19 - 25 | 4 | 3 | 8 | 16 - 29 |
| 11. | FK Jablonec | 30 | 9 | 8 | 13 | 46 - 57 | 35 | 5 | 6 | 4 | 25 - 21 | 4 | 2 | 9 | 21 - 36 |
| 12. | FC Baník Ostrava | 30 | 9 | 8 | 13 | 43 - 42 | 35 | 6 | 1 | 8 | 22 - 23 | 3 | 7 | 5 | 21 - 19 |
| 13. | FK Teplice | 30 | 8 | 8 | 14 | 38 - 63 | 32 | 5 | 6 | 4 | 21 - 23 | 3 | 2 | 10 | 17 - 40 |
| 14. | FC Zbrojovka Brno | 30 | 8 | 7 | 15 | 40 - 56 | 31 | 4 | 4 | 7 | 22 - 29 | 4 | 3 | 8 | 18 - 27 |
| 15. | FK Pardubice | 30 | 8 | 4 | 18 | 29 - 58 | 28 | 6 | 2 | 7 | 15 - 21 | 2 | 2 | 11 | 14 - 37 |
| 16. | FC Trinity Zlín | 30 | 5 | 11 | 14 | 37 - 55 | 26 | 5 | 4 | 6 | 24 - 26 | 0 | 7 | 8 | 13 - 29 |

Teams ranked 1-6 were qualified for the Championship Round, teams ranked 7-10 were qualified for the Play-offs Round, while teams ranked 11-16 were qualified for the Relegation Round.

**Results**

**Round 31** [06.05.2023]
FC Trinity Zlín - FK Jablonec 1-1(0-0)
Baník Ostrava - Zbrojovka Brno 4-0(3-0)
FK Teplice - FK Pardubice 1-0(1-0)

**Round 32** [14.05.2023]
FK Jablonec - Baník Ostrava 1-1(1-0)
FK Teplice - FC Trinity Zlín 2-1(1-0)
Zbrojovka Brno - FK Pardubice 0-2(0-1)

**Round 33** [21.05.2023]
FK Jablonec - Zbrojovka Brno 1-0(1-0)
Baník Ostrava - FK Teplice 2-1(0-0)
FK Pardubice - FC Trinity Zlín 1-2(1-1)

**Round 34** [24.05.2023]
FK Pardubice - FK Jablonec 2-0(2-0)
FC Trinity Zlín - Baník Ostrava 2-1(0-0)
FK Teplice - Zbrojovka Brno 1-1(0-1)

**Round 35** [28.05.2023]
FK Jablonec - FK Teplice 0-2(0-1)
Baník Ostrava - FK Pardubice 2-4(1-1)
Zbrojovka Brno - FC Trinity Zlín 0-0

**Final Standings**

| | | Total | | | | | Home | | | | | Away | | | |
|---|---|---|---|---|---|---|---|---|---|---|---|---|---|---|---|
| 11. FC Baník Ostrava | 35 | 11 | 9 | 15 | 53 - 50 | 42 | 8 | 1 | 9 | 30 - 28 | 3 | 8 | 6 | 23 - 22 |
| 12. FK Teplice | 35 | 11 | 9 | 15 | 45 - 67 | 42 | 7 | 7 | 4 | 25 - 25 | 4 | 2 | 11 | 20 - 42 |
| 13. FK Jablonec | 35 | 10 | 10 | 15 | 49 - 63 | 40 | 6 | 7 | 5 | 27 - 24 | 4 | 3 | 10 | 22 - 39 |
| 14. FK Pardubice (*Relegation Play-offs*) | 35 | 11 | 4 | 20 | 38 - 63 | 37 | 7 | 2 | 8 | 18 - 23 | 4 | 2 | 12 | 20 - 40 |
| 15. FC Trinity Zlín (*Relegation Play-offs*) | 35 | 7 | 13 | 15 | 43 - 60 | 34 | 6 | 5 | 6 | 27 - 28 | 1 | 8 | 9 | 16 - 32 |
| 16. FC Zbrojovka Brno (*Relegated*) | 35 | 8 | 9 | 18 | 41 - 64 | 33 | 4 | 5 | 8 | 22 - 31 | 4 | 4 | 10 | 19 - 33 |

**Play-offs Round / Skupina o Evropu**

| | | | |
|---|---|---|---|
| **Semi-Finals** [07-13.05.2023] | SK Dynamo České Budějovice - FC Slovan Liberec | 3-2(2-2) | 0-4(0-1) |
| | FK Mladá Boleslav - FC Hradec Králové | 0-0 | 0-2(0-2) |
| **Final** [21-26.05.2023] | FC Hradec Králové - FC Slovan Liberec | 0-4(0-3) | 3-2(0-1) |

**Championship Round / Skupina o Titul**

**Results**

**Round 31** [06-07.05.2023]
Viktoria Plzeň - 1. FC Slovácko 2-2(0-0)
Sigma Olomouc - Sparta Praha 0-1(0-1)
Slavia Praha - Bohemians 1905 6-0(1-0)

**Round 32** [13-14.05.2023]
Viktoria Plzeň - Sigma Olomouc 1-3(1-1)
Sparta Praha - Slavia Praha 3-2(1-1)
Bohemians 1905 - 1. FC Slovácko 0-0

**Round 33** [20.05.2023]
1. FC Slovácko - Sigma Olomouc 2-2(1-0)
Sparta Praha - Bohemians 1905 2-1(0-0)
Slavia Praha - Viktoria Plzeň 2-1(1-0)

**Round 34** [23.05.2023]
1. FC Slovácko - Sparta Praha 0-0
Sigma Olomouc - Slavia Praha 2-3(2-2)
Viktoria Plzeň - Bohemians 1905 0-2(0-2)

**Round 35** [27.05.2023]
Sparta Praha - Viktoria Plzeň 0-1(0-0)
Slavia Praha - 1. FC Slovácko 4-0(2-0)
Bohemians 1905 - Sigma Olomouc 0-1(0-0)

**Final Standings**

| | | Total | | | | | Home | | | | | Away | | | |
|---|---|---|---|---|---|---|---|---|---|---|---|---|---|---|---|
| 1. **AC Sparta Praha** | 35 | 23 | 9 | 3 | 76 - 33 | 78 | 12 | 4 | 2 | 41 - 18 | 11 | 5 | 1 | 35 - 15 |
| 2. SK Slavia Praha | 35 | 24 | 6 | 5 | 98 - 31 | 78 | 17 | 1 | 0 | 66 - 8 | 7 | 5 | 5 | 32 - 23 |
| 3. FC Viktoria Plzeň | 35 | 18 | 7 | 10 | 60 - 38 | 61 | 10 | 3 | 5 | 35 - 20 | 8 | 4 | 5 | 25 - 18 |
| 4. Bohemians Praha 1905 | 35 | 15 | 7 | 13 | 56 - 58 | 52 | 6 | 5 | 6 | 27 - 26 | 9 | 2 | 7 | 29 - 32 |
| 5. 1. FC Slovácko Uherské Hradiště | 35 | 13 | 11 | 11 | 40 - 46 | 50 | 8 | 5 | 4 | 20 - 15 | 5 | 6 | 7 | 20 - 31 |
| 6. SK Sigma Olomouc | 35 | 12 | 12 | 11 | 53 - 47 | 48 | 5 | 5 | 7 | 27 - 26 | 7 | 7 | 4 | 26 - 21 |

**Relegation Play-offs** [01-04.06.2023]

| | | |
|---|---|---|
| FK Příbram - FK Pardubice | 0-2(0-0) | 0-0 |
| FC Trinity Zlín - MFK Vyškov | 1-0(0-0) | 0-0 |

Both FK Pardubice and FC Trinity Zlín remain at first level for 2023/2024.

**Top goalscorers:**

| | | |
|---|---|---|
| 20 | **Václav Jurečka** | *SK Slavia Praha* |
| 19 | Jakub Řezníček | *FC Zbrojovka Brno* |
| 15 | Jan Chramosta | *FK Jablonec* |

# NATIONAL CUP
## Pohár Českomoravského fotbalového svazu / MOL Cup 2022/2023

| Second Round [13-14/20-21.09.2022] | | | |
|---|---|---|---|
| SK Uničov - SK Sigma Olomouc | 2-4(1-0,2-2) | FC Hlučín - SK Líšeň | 2-0(1-0) |
| SK Kvítkovice - FK Třinec | 1-5(0-2) | Tatran Všechovice - MFK Vyškov | 2-9(0-5) |
| FK Viktoria Žižkov - FK Teplice | 1-2(0-1,1-1) | FK Frýdek-Místek - SFC Opava | 2-0(0-0) |
| FK Přepeře - FK Silon Táborsko | 0-1(0-0,0-0) | TJ Start Brno - FC Trinity Zlín | 0-3(0-3) |
| FC Rokycany - FC Slovan Liberec | 1-5(1-3) | FC Slovan Rosice - FC Zbrojovka Brno | 0-4(0-2) |
| FK Motorlet Praha - FK Jablonec | 0-4(0-2) | FC Viktoria Mariánské Lázně - FK Viagem Příbram | 2-3(1-1) |
| Slovan Velvary - FK Pardubice | 1-0(1-0) | SK Benátky nad Jizerou - FK Varnsdorf | 1-2(0-1) |
| SK Libčany - FK Dukla Praha | 1-3(0-1) | FC Libišany - FC Vysočina Jihlava | 1-3(0-1,1-1) |
| SK Zápy - MFK Chrudim | 2-1(2-1) | SK Hanácká Slávia Kroměříž - FC Baník Ostrava | 3-3 aet; 1-4 pen |
| TJ Jiskra Ústí nad Orlicí - FK Chlumec nad Cidlinou | 0-1(0-1) | FK Čáslav - FC Hradec Králové | 0-11(0-3) |
| TJ Spartak Soběslav - FK Robstav | 3-1(1-1) | FK Baník Most-Souš - FC Sellier & Bellot Vlašim | 1-4(1-3) |
| TJ Jiskra Domažlice - SK Aritma Praha | 4-1(2-0) | TJ Slovan Bzenec - MFK Karviná | 1-2(1-1) |
| TJ Sokol Tasovice - 1. SK Prostějov | 2-2 aet; 2-3 pen | FK Ústí nad Labem - Bohemians Praha 1905 | 0-3(0-1) |
| | | FC Chomutov - SK Dynamo České Budějovice | 0-5(0-2) |

| Third Round [11/18-19/25.10.2022] | | | |
|---|---|---|---|
| FK Jablonec - MFK Vyškov | 0-1(0-0) | FC Hlučín - FC Viktoria Plzeň | 3-2(0-0) |
| TJ Spartak Soběslav - MFK Karviná | 0-2(0-0) | FK Mladá Boleslav - 1. SK Prostějov | 4-0(3-0) |
| FK Viagem Příbram - FK Teplice | 0-3(0-1) | 1. FC Slovácko Uherské Hradiště - FK Varnsdorf | 6-0(1-0) |
| Slovan Velvary - FC Baník Ostrava | 0-2(0-0) | SK Dynamo České Budějovice - FC Sellier & Bellot Vlašim | 3-1(2-0) |
| FK Chlumec nad Cidlinou - FC Hradec Králové | 0-4(0-1) | Bohemians Praha 1905- FK Třinec | 2-1(1-1) |
| SK Zápy - SK Sigma Olomouc | 1-3(1-1) | FK Dukla Praha - SK Slavia Praha | 0-4(0-0) |
| FK Silon Táborsko - FC Zbrojovka Brno | 1-2(0-0) | FK Frýdek-Místek - FC Slovan Liberec | 0-6(0-3) |
| TJ Jiskra Domažlice - AC Sparta Praha | 1-6(1-4) | FC Trinity Zlín - FC Vysočina Jihlava | 2-0(1-0) |

| 1/8-Finals [17-19.11./26.11.2022 & 01.02.2023] | | | |
|---|---|---|---|
| FC Trinity Zlín - MFK Vyškov | 0-1(0-0) | FC Baník Ostrava - AC Sparta Praha | 2-3(1-1) |
| FK Teplice - FC Zbrojovka Brno | 2-3(1-1,2-2) | Bohemians Praha 1905- FC Hlučín | 3-0(1-0) |
| 1. FC Slovácko Uherské Hradiště - FK Mladá Boleslav | 1-0(0-0) | FC Slovan Liberec - SK Sigma Olomouc | 4-1(2-1) |
| MFK Karviná - SK Slavia Praha | 0-2(0-2) | SK Dynamo České Budějovice - FC Hradec Králové | 2-0(2-0) |

| Quarter-Finals [01.03.2023] | | | |
|---|---|---|---|
| SK Dynamo České Budějovice - FC Zbrojovka Brno | 2-1(2-0) | FC Slovan Liberec - AC Sparta Praha | 2-2 aet; 3-5 pen |
| 1. FC Slovácko Uh. Hradiště - Bohemians Praha 1905 | 1-2(0-2) | Slavia Praha - MFK Vyškov | 4-0(3-0) |

| Semi-Finals [05.04.2023] | | | |
|---|---|---|---|
| AC Sparta Praha - SK Dynamo České Budějovice | 2-0(1-0) | Slavia Praha - Bohemians Praha 1905 | 3-2(1-1,2-2) |

| Final |
|---|

03.05.2023; epet ARENA, Praha; Referee: Dalibor Černý; Attendance: 17,037
**AC Sparta Praha - SK Slavia Praha**                    **0-2(0-0)**

**Sparta Praha**: Matěj Kovář, Tomáš Wiesner (80.Adam Goljan), Filip Panák, Martin Vitík (80.David Pavelka), Ladislav Krejčí II (Cap), Kaan Kairinen, Lukáš Sadílek (68.Qazim Laçi), Jaroslav Zelený (68.Casper Højer Nielsen), Adam Karabec, Lukáš Haraslín (60.Kryštof Daněk), Jan Kuchta. Trainer: Brian Priske Pedersen (Denmark).

**Slavia Praha**: Ondřej Kolář, David Jurásek (86.Jakub Hromáda), Igoh Ogbu, Tomáš Holeš (Cap), David Douděra, Oscar Dorley, Ibrahim Traoré (55.Christos Zafeiris), Ivan Schranz (86.Ondřej Lingr), Matěj Jurásek (55.Lukáš Provod), Václav Jurečka, Mick van Buren (80.Stanislav Tecl). Trainer: Jindřich Trpišovský.

**Goals:** 0-1 David Douděra (59), 0-2 Filip Panák (64 own goal).

Please note: appearances and goals are including statistics of regular season and play-offs (Championship, Play-offs and Relegation Round).

## Football Club Baník Ostrava

| | | |
|---|---|---|
| Founded: | 1922 (*as SK Slezská Ostrava*) | |
| Stadium: | Městský stadion, Ostrava (15,123) | |
| Trainer: | Pavel Vrba | 06.12.1963 |
| [12.10.2022] | Pavel Hapal | 27.07.1969 |

| Goalkeepers: | DOB | M | (s) | G |
|---|---|---|---|---|
| Martin Hrubý | 22.03.2004 | 2 | | |
| Jan Laštůvka | 07.07.1982 | 24 | | |
| Jiří Letáček | 09.01.1999 | 9 | | |
| **Defenders:** | **DOB** | **M** | **(s)** | **G** |
| Eneo Bitri (ALB) | 26.08.1996 | 13 | | 2 |
| Jiří Fleišman | 02.10.1984 | 25 | (6) | 3 |
| Michal Frydrych | 27.02.1990 | 14 | | 2 |
| Jan Juroška | 02.03.1993 | 16 | (3) | 1 |
| David Lischka | 15.08.1997 | 13 | (2) | 1 |
| Patrik Měkota | 21.03.2004 | 1 | | |
| Gigli Nsungani Ndefe (NED) | 02.03.1994 | 10 | (1) | |
| Karel Pojezný | 23.09.2001 | 25 | (3) | |
| Jakub Pokorný | 11.09.1996 | 4 | | |
| Zdeněk Říha | 04.04.2002 | 1 | | |
| Muhammed Sanneh (GAM) | 19.02.2000 | 9 | (3) | |
| Eldar Šehić (BIH) | 28.04.2000 | 14 | (11) | |
| Jaroslav Svozil | 09.09.1993 | 1 | (2) | |

| Midfielders: | DOB | M | (s) | G |
|---|---|---|---|---|
| Jiří Boula | 08.04.1999 | 9 | (8) | 1 |
| David Buchta | 27.06.1999 | 15 | (13) | 1 |
| Lukáš Budínský | 27.03.1992 | | (1) | |
| Carlos Eduardo Lopes Cruz „Cadu" (BRA) | 08.08.1997 | 25 | (1) | 5 |
| Dominik Holaň | 01.07.2002 | 1 | (1) | |
| Filip Kaloč | 27.02.2000 | 29 | | 2 |
| Nemanja Kuzmanović (SRB) | 27.05.1989 | 20 | (13) | 3 |
| Robert Mišković (CRO) | 20.10.1999 | 9 | (14) | |
| Matěj Šín | 02.06.2004 | 6 | (5) | 1 |
| Laco Takács | 15.07.1996 | 3 | (2) | |
| Daniel Tetour | 17.07.1994 | 9 | (1) | 2 |
| **Forwards:** | **DOB** | **M** | **(s)** | **G** |
| Ladislav Almási (SVK) | 06.03.1999 | 12 | (9) | 6 |
| Petr Jaroň | 30.08.2001 | 7 | (17) | 1 |
| Jiří Klíma | 05.01.1997 | 23 | (4) | 5 |
| Srđan Plavšić (SRB) | 03.12.1995 | 23 | (1) | 5 |
| Daniel Smékal | 08.12.2001 | | (10) | 1 |
| Muhamed Tijani (NGA) | 26.07.2000 | 13 | (19) | 11 |

## Bohemians Praha 1905

| | | |
|---|---|---|
| Founded: | 1905 | |
| Stadium: | Stadion Ďolíček, Praha (6,300) | |
| Trainer: | Jaroslav Veselý | 08.08.1977 |

| Goalkeepers: | DOB | M | (s) | G |
|---|---|---|---|---|
| Hugo Bačkovský | 10.10.1999 | 3 | | |
| Martin Jedlička | 24.01.1998 | 15 | | |
| Lukáš Soukup | 06.01.1995 | 1 | | |
| Roman Valeš | 06.03.1990 | 16 | (1) | |
| **Defenders:** | **DOB** | **M** | **(s)** | **G** |
| Martin Dostál | 23.09.1989 | 23 | (9) | 1 |
| Lukáš Hůlka | 31.03.1995 | 34 | (1) | 3 |
| Adam Kadlec | 06.07.2003 | 6 | (2) | |
| Daniel Krch | 20.03.1992 | 1 | (7) | |
| Antonín Křapka | 22.01.1994 | 28 | (1) | 4 |
| Martin Nový | 23.06.1993 | | (15) | |
| Jan Vondra | 13.09.1995 | 15 | (2) | |
| **Midfielders:** | **DOB** | **M** | **(s)** | **G** |
| David Bartek | 13.02.1988 | 1 | (4) | |
| Michal Beran | 22.08.2000 | 8 | (16) | |
| Aleš Čermák | 01.10.1994 | 5 | | 2 |
| Martin Hála | 24.03.1992 | 13 | (12) | 2 |

| | DOB | M | (s) | G |
|---|---|---|---|---|
| Petr Hronek | 04.07.1993 | 13 | (1) | 2 |
| Adam Jánoš | 20.07.1992 | 23 | (8) | 3 |
| Josef Jindřišek | 14.02.1981 | 31 | (3) | 1 |
| Daniel Köstl | 23.05.1998 | 33 | | 2 |
| Jan Kovařík | 19.06.1988 | 27 | (7) | 2 |
| Roman Květ | 17.12.1997 | 13 | | 9 |
| Jan Morávek | 01.11.1989 | | (5) | |
| Vojtěch Novák | 20.01.2002 | | (5) | |
| Ondřej Petrák | 11.03.1992 | 10 | (2) | 1 |
| **Forwards:** | **DOB** | **M** | **(s)** | **G** |
| Václav Drchal | 25.07.1999 | 18 | (8) | 6 |
| Matěj Koubek | 10.01.2000 | | (4) | |
| Jan Matoušek | 09.05.1998 | 10 | (5) | 6 |
| Ladislav Mužík | 25.07.1998 | | (27) | |
| Tomáš Necid | 13.08.1989 | | (8) | |
| Erik Prekop (SVK) | 08.10.1997 | 21 | (3) | 5 |
| David Puškáč | 14.05.1993 | 17 | (8) | 6 |

## Sportovní klub Dynamo České Budějovice

| | | |
|---|---|---|
| Founded: | 1905 | |
| Stadium: | Stadion Střelecký ostrov, České Budějovice (6,681) | |
| Trainer: | Jozef Weber | 19.05.1977 |
| [31.10.2022] | Jiří Lerch | 17.10.1971 |
| [13.11.2022] | Marek Nikl | 20.02.1976 |

| Goalkeepers: | DOB | M | (s) | G |
|---|---|---|---|---|
| Martin Janáček | 22.09.2000 | 21 | | |
| Dávid Šipoš (SVK) | 14.08.1998 | 11 | | |
| **Defenders:** | **DOB** | **M** | **(s)** | **G** |
| David Broukal | 16.03.1996 | 10 | (12) | |
| Benjamin Čolić (BIH) | 23.07.1991 | 19 | (1) | 1 |
| Ondřej Čoudek | 25.10.2004 | 8 | | 1 |
| Lukáš Havel | 06.06.1996 | 31 | | 4 |
| Martin Králik (SVK) | 03.04.1995 | 30 | | 3 |
| Lukáš Skovajsa (SVK) | 27.03.1994 | 14 | (3) | |
| Martin Sladký | 01.03.1992 | 16 | (6) | |
| Branislav Sluka (SVK) | 23.01.1999 | 7 | (8) | 1 |
| **Midfielders:** | **DOB** | **M** | **(s)** | **G** |
| Patrik Čavoš | 07.01.1995 | 21 | (8) | 1 |
| Marcel Čermák | 25.11.1998 | 13 | (2) | 4 |
| Jakub Grič (SVK) | 05.07.1996 | 6 | (5) | |
| Patrik Hellebrand | 16.05.1999 | 27 | (5) | 3 |

| | DOB | M | (s) | G |
|---|---|---|---|---|
| Jakub Hora | 23.02.1991 | 25 | (2) | 2 |
| David Krch | 30.06.2003 | | (2) | |
| Matej Mršić (CRO) | 13.01.1994 | 4 | (4) | |
| Nicolas Penner | 19.06.2001 | 9 | (10) | |
| Jonáš Vais | 24.11.1999 | | (2) | |
| **Forwards:** | **DOB** | **M** | **(s)** | **G** |
| Quadri Adediran (NGA) | 10.10.2000 | 11 | (3) | 3 |
| Libor Bastl | 20.12.2003 | | (1) | |
| Lukáš Čmelík (SVK) | 13.04.1996 | 19 | (6) | 5 |
| Daniel Hais | 02.06.2003 | 5 | (12) | 2 |
| Vojtěch Hora | 05.05.2004 | | (1) | |
| Jakub Matoušek | 10.04.1998 | 2 | (15) | |
| Roman Potočný | 25.04.1991 | 21 | (9) | 2 |
| Michal Škoda | 01.03.1988 | 12 | (11) | 2 |
| Jakub Švec | 23.07.2000 | | (4) | |
| Tomáš Zajíc | 12.08.1996 | 10 | (11) | 1 |

## Football Club Hradec Králové

| Founded: | 1905 | | |
|---|---|---|---|
| Stadium: | Lokotrans Aréna, Mladá Boleslav (5,000) | | |
| Trainer: | Miroslav Koubek | | 01.09.1951 |
| [25.04.2023] | Stanislav Hejkal | | 03.01.1970 |

| Goalkeepers: | DOB | M | (s) | G |
|---|---|---|---|---|
| Pavol Bajza (SVK) | 04.09.1991 | 11 | (1) | |
| Michal Reichl | 14.09.1992 | 20 | (1) | |
| Patrik Vízek | 26.02.1993 | 3 | | |
| **Defenders:** | **DOB** | **M** | **(s)** | **G** |
| Vojtěch Baloun | 25.10.2002 | | (2) | |
| František Čech | 12.06.1998 | 25 | (2) | |
| Filip Čihák | 10.07.1999 | 11 | (2) | |
| Adam Gabriel | 28.05.2001 | 23 | (3) | 2 |
| Štěpán Harazim | 13.07.2000 | 14 | (5) | |
| Martin Hlaváč | 22.08.2002 | | (3) | |
| Jakub Klíma | 28.08.1998 | 30 | (1) | |
| Michal Leibl | 07.06.1992 | 14 | (2) | 2 |
| Ondřej Ševčík | 09.06.1995 | 4 | (5) | 1 |
| **Midfielders:** | **DOB** | **M** | **(s)** | **G** |
| Petr Kodeš | 31.01.1996 | 30 | (1) | 2 |

| | DOB | M | (s) | G |
|---|---|---|---|---|
| Jakub Kučera | 28.01.1997 | 24 | (4) | 2 |
| Filip Novotný | 17.08.1995 | 9 | (9) | 1 |
| Petr Pudhorocký | 13.06.2001 | 6 | (7) | 1 |
| Jakub Rada | 05.05.1987 | 19 | (10) | 2 |
| Vojtěch Smrž | 20.01.1997 | 29 | | 2 |
| Adam Vlkanova | 04.09.1994 | 5 | | 1 |
| **Forwards:** | **DOB** | **M** | **(s)** | **G** |
| Pavel Dvořák | 19.02.1989 | 2 | (16) | |
| Matěj Koubek | 10.01.2000 | 14 | (13) | 4 |
| Filip Kubala | 02.09.1999 | 24 | (3) | 7 |
| Erik Prekop (SVK) | 08.10.1997 | | (5) | |
| Petr Rybička | 14.01.1996 | 2 | (5) | |
| Matěj Ryneš | 30.05.2001 | 24 | (1) | 3 |
| Matej Trusa (SVK) | 29.11.2000 | 6 | (9) | 2 |
| Daniel Vasulin | 11.06.1998 | 25 | (2) | 7 |

## Fotbalový Klub Jablonec

| Founded: | 1945 | |
|---|---|---|
| Stadium: | Stadion Střelnice, Jablonec nad Nisou (6,108) | |
| Trainer: | David Horejš | 19.05.1977 |

| Goalkeepers: | DOB | M | (s) | G |
|---|---|---|---|---|
| Jan Hanuš | 28.04.1988 | 32 | | |
| Jakub Surovčík (SVK) | 28.06.2002 | 3 | | |
| **Defenders:** | **DOB** | **M** | **(s)** | **G** |
| Joshua Oghene Ochuko Akpudje (NGA) | 23.07.1998 | 13 | (1) | |
| Dion-Johan Chai Cools (MAS) | 04.06.1996 | 8 | | |
| David Heidenreich | 24.06.2000 | 18 | (2) | |
| Ishaku Konda (GHA) | 11.09.1999 | | (1) | |
| Jan Král | 05.04.1999 | 19 | | 1 |
| Jan Krob | 27.04.1987 | 8 | (1) | |
| Jakub Martinec | 13.03.1998 | 19 | (2) | 2 |
| Daniel Souček | 18.07.1998 | 19 | (5) | 1 |
| Michal Surzyn | 10.09.1997 | 9 | (14) | |
| David Štěpánek | 30.03.1997 | 6 | (8) | |
| **Midfielders:** | **DOB** | **M** | **(s)** | **G** |
| David Houska | 29.06.1993 | 14 | (1) | |
| Tomáš Hübschman | 04.09.1981 | 23 | (2) | 1 |

| | DOB | M | (s) | G |
|---|---|---|---|---|
| Miloš Kratochvíl | 26.04.1996 | 17 | (1) | 1 |
| Vojtěch Kubista | 19.03.1993 | 1 | (2) | |
| Tomáš Malínský | 25.08.1991 | | (8) | |
| Dominik Pleštil | 09.08.1999 | 1 | (3) | |
| Matěj Polidar | 20.12.1999 | 30 | | 7 |
| Jakub Považanec (SVK) | 31.01.1991 | 27 | (2) | 4 |
| Pavel Šulc | 29.12.2000 | 27 | (5) | 5 |
| **Forwards:** | **DOB** | **M** | **(s)** | **G** |
| Jan Chramosta | 12.10.1990 | 29 | (5) | 15 |
| Michal Černák | 01.09.2003 | 7 | (15) | 1 |
| Dāvis Ikaunieks (LVA) | 07.01.1994 | 3 | (17) | |
| Vladimir Jovović (MNE) | 26.10.1994 | 24 | (6) | 3 |
| Václav Kadlec | 20.05.1992 | | (2) | |
| Vojtěch Patrák | 18.03.2000 | 2 | (16) | |
| Václav Sejk | 18.05.2002 | 26 | (4) | 7 |
| Oliver Velich | 12.06.2001 | | (1) | |

## Fotbalový klub Mladá Boleslav

| Founded: | 1902 | |
|---|---|---|
| Stadium: | Lokotrans Aréna, Mladá Boleslav (5,000) | |
| Trainer: | Pavel Hoftych | 09.05.1967 |

| Goalkeepers: | DOB | M | (s) | G |
|---|---|---|---|---|
| Petr Mikulec | 05.04.1999 | 7 | | |
| Martin Polaček (SVK) | 02.04.1990 | 6 | | |
| Jan Šeda | 17.12.1985 | 19 | | |
| **Defenders:** | **DOB** | **M** | **(s)** | **G** |
| Denis Donát | 14.09.2001 | 10 | (10) | 1 |
| Ondřej Karafiát | 01.12.1994 | 30 | | |
| Radek Látal | 16.12.1997 | 1 | (1) | |
| David Šimek | 15.02.1998 | 26 | (2) | 2 |
| Martin Suchomel | 11.09.2002 | 10 | (3) | |
| Marek Suchý | 29.03.1988 | 31 | | |
| Michal Tomič (SVK) | 30.03.1999 | 4 | (5) | 1 |
| **Midfielders:** | **DOB** | **M** | **(s)** | **G** |
| Samuel Dancák (SVK) | 06.03.1998 | 12 | (10) | |
| Denis Darmovzal | 17.07.2000 | | (3) | |
| Denis Kaulfus | 03.06.2004 | 1 | (1) | |
| Vojtěch Kubista | 19.03.1993 | 21 | | 3 |

| | DOB | M | (s) | G |
|---|---|---|---|---|
| Daniel Mareček | 30.05.1998 | 27 | (3) | 5 |
| Marek Matějovský | 20.12.1981 | 20 | (8) | 2 |
| David Pech | 22.02.2002 | 16 | | 1 |
| Antonín Vaníček | 22.04.1998 | | (5) | |
| Patrik Žitný | 21.01.1999 | 3 | (12) | |
| **Forwards:** | **DOB** | **M** | **(s)** | **G** |
| Ubong Ekpai (NGA) | 17.10.1995 | 7 | (5) | |
| Jakub Fulnek | 26.04.1994 | 27 | (2) | 2 |
| Lamin Jawo (GAM) | 15.03.1995 | 7 | (4) | 3 |
| Ladislav Krobot | 01.04.2001 | 1 | (7) | 1 |
| Vasil Kušej | 24.05.2000 | 13 | (3) | 4 |
| Tomáš Ladra | 24.04.1997 | 28 | (4) | 7 |
| Lukáš Mašek | 08.05.2004 | 6 | (12) | 1 |
| Jiří Skalák | 12.03.1992 | 7 | (14) | 1 |
| Milan Škoda | 16.01.1986 | 10 | (8) | 4 |
| Vojtěch Stránský | 13.03.2003 | 2 | (13) | 1 |

## Fotbalový klub Pardubice

| Founded: | 2008 | |
| Stadium: | CFIG Aréna, Pardubice (4,600) | |
| Trainer: | Jiří Krejčí | 10.01.1965 |
| [29.08.2022] | Pavel Němeček | 12.01.1982 |
| [13.09.2022] | Radoslav Kováč | 27.11.1979 |

| Goalkeepers: | DOB | M | (s) | G |
|---|---|---|---|---|
| Viktor Budinský (SVK) | 09.05.1993 | 3 | | |
| Jakub Markovič | 13.07.2001 | 15 | (1) | |
| Florin Constantin Niţă (ROU) | 03.07.1987 | 17 | | |
| **Defenders:** | **DOB** | **M** | **(s)** | **G** |
| Martin Chlumecký | 11.01.1997 | 23 | (1) | 1 |
| Jan Halász | 28.02.2001 | | (1) | |
| Matěj Helešic | 12.11.1996 | 23 | (6) | |
| Robin Hranáč | 29.01.2000 | 29 | | 1 |
| Tomáš Koukola | 16.02.2002 | | (9) | |
| Petr Kůrka | 04.07.2002 | 1 | (2) | |
| Václav Svoboda | 16.09.1999 | 2 | | |
| Martin Toml | 25.03.1996 | 5 | | |
| Tomáš Vlček | 28.02.2001 | 32 | | 1 |
| **Midfielders:** | **DOB** | **M** | **(s)** | **G** |
| Bernardo Costa Da Rosa (BRA) | 20.09.2000 | 5 | (4) | |
| Denis Darmovzal | 17.07.2000 | 10 | (5) | 2 |
| Michal Hlavatý | 17.06.1998 | 32 | (1) | 5 |
| Marek Icha | 14.03.2002 | 23 | | |
| Dominik Janošek | 13.06.1998 | 33 | (1) | 8 |

| | | | | |
|---|---|---|---|---|
| Jan Jeřábek | 12.02.1984 | | (4) | |
| Dominik Kostka | 04.05.1996 | 22 | (4) | |
| Dominik Mareš | 03.02.2003 | 3 | (10) | 1 |
| Bartosz Pikul (POL) | 02.11.1997 | 10 | (7) | 1 |
| Tomáš Solil | 01.02.2000 | 7 | | 1 |
| Vojtěch Sychra | 30.11.2001 | 13 | (17) | 3 |
| Samuel Šimek | 12.04.2002 | | (7) | |
| Emil Tischler | 13.03.1998 | 13 | (8) | |
| Kamil Vacek | 18.05.1987 | 23 | (8) | 1 |
| Tomáš Zahradníček | 11.08.1993 | 4 | (2) | |
| **Forwards:** | **DOB** | **M** | **(s)** | **G** |
| Nana Akosah-Bempah (USA) | 29.08.1997 | | (4) | |
| Ondřej Chvěja | 17.07.1998 | 1 | (1) | |
| Pavel Černý | 28.01.1985 | 30 | (3) | 6 |
| Marek Červenka | 17.12.1992 | 1 | (7) | |
| David Huf | 23.01.1999 | | (9) | |
| Colet Kapanga (COD) | 15.04.2000 | | (2) | |
| Ladislav Krobot | 01.04.2001 | 3 | (12) | 4 |
| Leandro Matheus Rodrigues Lima (BRA) | 26.12.2001 | 2 | (16) | 1 |

## Sportovní Klub Sigma Olomouc

| Founded: | 1919 (as FK Hejčín Olomouc) | |
| Stadium: | Stadion Andrův, Olomouc (12,483) | |
| Trainer: | Václav Jílek | 16.05.1976 |

| Goalkeepers: | DOB | M | (s) | G |
|---|---|---|---|---|
| Matúš Macík (SVK) | 19.05.1993 | 13 | | |
| Tadeáš Stoppen | 30.12.2003 | 3 | | |
| Jakub Trefil | 09.02.2001 | 19 | | |
| **Defenders:** | **DOB** | **M** | **(s)** | **G** |
| Vít Beneš | 12.08.1988 | 27 | (3) | 4 |
| Juraj Chvátal (SVK) | 13.07.1996 | 24 | (2) | 3 |
| Václav Jemelka | 23.06.1995 | 2 | | |
| Jakub Pokorný | 11.09.1996 | 25 | (2) | 2 |
| Florent Poulolo (MTQ) | 02.01.1997 | 7 | (9) | 1 |
| Jiří Sláma | 08.01.1999 | 16 | (8) | 1 |
| Lukáš Vraštil | 10.03.1994 | 16 | (5) | 1 |
| Ondřej Zmrzlý | 22.04.1999 | 25 | (9) | 2 |
| **Midfielders:** | **DOB** | **M** | **(s)** | **G** |
| Radim Breite | 10.08.1989 | 32 | (1) | 1 |
| Jan Fortelný | 19.01.1999 | 3 | (6) | |
| Lukáš Greššák (SVK) | 23.01.1989 | 4 | (15) | |
| Jakub Matoušek | 25.10.1999 | | (14) | |

| | | | | |
|---|---|---|---|---|
| Jan Navrátil | 13.04.1990 | 33 | (2) | 5 |
| Martin Pospíšil | 26.06.1991 | 11 | (3) | |
| Jan Sedlák | 25.10.1994 | 1 | (4) | 1 |
| Jiří Spáčil | 11.02.1999 | 9 | (4) | 1 |
| Denis Ventúra (SVK) | 01.08.1995 | 21 | (2) | 3 |
| Jan Vodháněl | 25.04.1997 | 10 | (13) | 4 |
| Tomáš Zlatohlávek | 22.05.2000 | | (5) | |
| Filip Zorvan | 07.04.1996 | 15 | (12) | 1 |
| **Forwards:** | **DOB** | **M** | **(s)** | **G** |
| Mojmír Chytil | 29.04.1999 | 34 | | 12 |
| Israel Ola Dele (NGA) | 27.10.2001 | 2 | (3) | 1 |
| Martin Košťál (SVK) | 23.02.1996 | | (2) | |
| Denis Kramář | 08.08.2003 | | (7) | |
| Jakub Přichystal | 25.10.1995 | | (2) | |
| Antonín Růsek | 22.03.1999 | 22 | (2) | 3 |
| Jáchym Šíp | 22.01.2003 | | (7) | |
| David Vaněček | 09.03.1991 | | (8) | |
| Pavel Zifčak | 02.03.1999 | 11 | (17) | 4 |

## Sportovní klub Slavia Praha

| Founded: | 02.11.1902 (as Akademický cyklistický odbor Slavia) | |
| Stadium: | Fortuna Arena, Praha (19,370) | |
| Trainer: | Jindřich Trpišovský | 27.02.1976 |

| Goalkeepers: | DOB | M | (s) | G |
|---|---|---|---|---|
| Ondřej Kolář | 17.10.1994 | 25 | | |
| Aleš Mandous | 21.04.1992 | 10 | | |
| **Defenders:** | **DOB** | **M** | **(s)** | **G** |
| Jan Bořil | 11.01.1991 | | (2) | |
| Oscar Dorley (LBR) | 19.07.1998 | 20 | (5) | |
| David Douděra | 31.05.1998 | 28 | (1) | 5 |
| Eduardo Gonzaga Mendes Santos (BRA) | 28.11.1997 | 12 | | |
| David Jurásek | 07.08.2000 | 28 | (3) | 2 |
| Taras Kacharaba (UKR) | 07.01.1995 | 16 | (3) | 1 |
| Ondřej Kričfaluši | 29.03.2004 | | (6) | |
| Igoh Ogbu (NGA) | 08.02.2000 | 16 | | 1 |
| Aiham Ousou (SWE) | 09.01.2000 | 17 | (2) | 1 |
| **Midfielders:** | **DOB** | **M** | **(s)** | **G** |
| Daniel Fila | 21.08.2002 | | (2) | |
| Tomáš Holeš | 31.03.1993 | 17 | (4) | |
| Jakub Hromada (SVK) | 25.05.1996 | 14 | (5) | 1 |
| Petr Hronek | 04.07.1993 | 1 | (5) | |
| Marek Icha | 14.03.2002 | 1 | (2) | 1 |
| Ondřej Lingr | 07.10.1998 | 15 | (12) | 11 |

| | | | | |
|---|---|---|---|---|
| Lukáš Masopust | 12.02.1993 | 15 | (4) | 2 |
| Matouš Nikl | 02.02.2002 | | (1) | |
| David Pech | 22.02.2002 | 2 | (5) | |
| Dominik Pech | 04.09.2006 | | (1) | |
| Lukáš Provod | 23.10.1996 | 9 | (13) | 2 |
| Petr Ševčík | 04.05.1994 | 15 | (3) | |
| Christ Joël Tiehi (CIV) | 16.06.1998 | 6 | (7) | 1 |
| Ibrahim Traoré (CIV) | 16.09.1988 | 7 | (5) | 1 |
| Christos Zafeiris (NOR) | 23.02.2003 | 9 | (6) | 1 |
| **Forwards:** | **DOB** | **M** | **(s)** | **G** |
| Ewerton Paixao da Silva (BRA) | 28.12.1996 | 6 | (8) | 2 |
| Matěj Jurásek | 30.08.2003 | 7 | (14) | 7 |
| Václav Jurečka | 26.06.1994 | 22 | (5) | 20 |
| Peter Oladeji Olayinka (NGA) | 16.11.1995 | 21 | (2) | 11 |
| Ivan Schranz (SVK) | 13.09.1993 | 17 | (5) | 5 |
| Yira Sor (NGA) | 24.07.2000 | | (3) | |
| Daniel Šmiga | 02.01.2004 | | (2) | |
| Stanislav Tecl | 01.09.1990 | 16 | (14) | 11 |
| Moses Usor (NGA) | 05.02.2002 | 4 | (11) | 4 |
| Mick van Buren (NED) | 24.08.1992 | 9 | (10) | 5 |

## 1. Fudbalový Klub Slovácko Uherské Hradiště

| Founded: | 1927 (*as SK Staré Město*) |
| Stadium: | Městský fotbalový stadion "Miroslava Valenty", Uherské Hradiště (8,000) |
| Trainer: | Martin Svědík      27.06.1974 |

| Goalkeepers: | DOB | M | (s) | G |
|---|---|---|---|---|
| Jiří Borek | 23.09.2002 | 1 | | |
| Tomáš Fryšták | 18.08.1987 | 1 | | |
| Filip Nguyen | 14.09.1992 | 33 | (1) | |
| **Defenders:** | **DOB** | **M** | **(s)** | **G** |
| Tomáš Břečka | 12.05.1994 | 3 | (3) | |
| Merchas Ghazi Salih Doski (IRQ) | 07.12.1999 | 16 | (10) | 3 |
| Stanislav Hofmann | 17.06.1990 | 30 | (1) | 3 |
| Michal Kadlec | 13.12.1984 | 30 | (3) | 1 |
| Jan Kalabiška | 22.12.1986 | 21 | (9) | 4 |
| Petr Reinberk | 23.05.1989 | 24 | (3) | 3 |
| Patrik Šimko (SVK) | 08.07.1991 | 8 | (6) | |
| Michal Tomič (SVK) | 30.03.1999 | 9 | (3) | 1 |
| **Midfielders:** | **DOB** | **M** | **(s)** | **G** |
| Vlastimil Daníček | 15.07.1991 | 28 | (2) | 3 |
| Marek Havlík | 08.07.1995 | 31 | (2) | 1 |
| Daniel Holzer | 18.08.1995 | 15 | (10) | 2 |
| Pavel Juroška | 07.07.2001 | 4 | (9) | |
| Kim Seung-bin (KOR) | 28.12.2000 | 6 | (6) | 2 |
| Michal Kohút | 04.06.2000 | 11 | (6) | |
| Martin Kudela | 29.01.2003 | | (3) | |
| Vladislav Levin (RUS) | 28.03.1995 | 6 | (3) | |
| Milan Petržela | 19.06.1983 | 25 | (5) | 3 |
| Michal Trávník | 17.05.1994 | 16 | (11) | 2 |
| **Forwards:** | **DOB** | **M** | **(s)** | **G** |
| Patrik Brandner | 04.01.1994 | 8 | (10) | 1 |
| Libor Kozák | 30.05.1989 | 10 | (1) | 1 |
| Ondřej Mihálik | 02.04.1997 | 20 | (10) | 4 |
| Vlasiy Sinyavskiy (EST) | 27.11.1996 | 13 | (13) | 2 |
| Ondřej Šašinka | 21.03.1998 | 6 | (13) | |
| Filip Vecheta | 15.02.2003 | 10 | (17) | 3 |

## Football Club Slovan Liberec

| Founded: | 1958 |
| Stadium: | Stadion u Nisy, Liberec (9,900) |
| Trainer: | Luboš Kozel      16.03.1971 |

| Goalkeepers: | DOB | M | (s) | G |
|---|---|---|---|---|
| Hugo Bačkovský | 10.10.1999 | 6 | | |
| Olivier Vliegen (BEL) | 07.02.1999 | 28 | | |
| **Defenders:** | **DOB** | **M** | **(s)** | **G** |
| Michal Fukala | 22.10.2000 | 12 | (7) | |
| Theodor Gebre Selassie | 24.12.1986 | 16 | | 1 |
| Ondřej Lehoczki | 10.02.1998 | | (2) | |
| Jan Mikula | 05.01.1992 | 18 | (1) | 1 |
| Gigli Nsungani Ndefe (NED) | 02.03.1994 | 10 | (1) | |
| Dominik Plechatý | 18.04.1999 | 31 | (1) | |
| Marios Pourzitidis (GRE) | 08.05.1999 | 17 | (11) | 1 |
| Filip Prebsl | 04.03.2003 | 20 | (6) | 1 |
| Dominik Preisler | 20.09.1995 | 19 | (7) | |
| Maksym Taloverov (UKR) | 28.06.2000 | 13 | | 1 |
| **Midfielders:** | **DOB** | **M** | **(s)** | **G** |
| Lukáš Červ | 10.04.2001 | 31 | (1) | 4 |
| Mohamed Doumbia (CIV) | 25.12.1998 | 12 | (8) | 3 |
| Christian Frýdek | 01.02.1999 | 24 | (7) | 5 |
| Milan Lexa | 21.08.2004 | | (3) | |
| Youssouf Kamso Mara (GUI) | 24.12.1994 | 1 | (4) | |
| Jan Matoušek | 09.05.1998 | 8 | (3) | |
| Tomas Polyak | 07.05.2001 | 1 | (6) | |
| Matej Valenta | 09.02.2000 | 19 | (3) | 2 |
| Ivan Varfolomeyev (UKR) | 24.03.2004 | 5 | (9) | |
| Denis Višinský | 21.03.2003 | 9 | (6) | 1 |
| **Forwards:** | **DOB** | **M** | **(s)** | **G** |
| Ahmad Abubakar Ghali (NGA) | 23.06.2000 | 11 | (5) | |
| Matyáš Kozák | 04.05.2001 | 3 | (20) | 2 |
| Karol Mészáros (SVK) | 25.07.1993 | 4 | (11) | |
| Victor Oluyemi Olatunji (NGA) | 05.09.1999 | 13 | (5) | 8 |
| Michael Rabušic | 17.09.1989 | 4 | (18) | 1 |
| Imad Rondić (BIH) | 16.02.1999 | 12 | (16) | 4 |
| Ľubomír Tupta (SVK) | 27.03.1998 | 13 | (4) | 6 |
| Mick van Buren (NED) | 24.08.1992 | 14 | (1) | 9 |

## Athletic Club Sparta Praha

| Founded: | 16.11.1893 |
| Stadium: | epet ARENA, Praha (18,944) |
| Trainer: | Brian Priske Pedersen (DEN)      14.05.1977 |

| Goalkeepers: | DOB | M | (s) | G |
|---|---|---|---|---|
| Dominik Holec (SVK) | 28.07.1994 | 7 | | |
| Matěj Kovář | 17.05.2000 | 28 | | |
| **Defenders:** | **DOB** | **M** | **(s)** | **G** |
| Ondřej Čelůstka | 18.06.1989 | | (1) | |
| Dávid Hancko (SVK) | 13.12.1997 | 3 | | |
| Casper Højer Nielsen (DEN) | 20.11.1994 | 14 | (7) | 1 |
| Dimitrije Kamenović (SRB) | 16.07.2000 | | (2) | |
| Jan Mejdr | 11.05.1995 | 17 | (9) | |
| Filip Panák | 02.11.1995 | 12 | (3) | |
| Asger Strømgaard Sørensen (DEN) | 05.06.1996 | 32 | | 5 |
| Martin Vitík | 21.01.2003 | 21 | (1) | |
| Patrik Vydra | 20.06.2003 | 4 | (1) | |
| Tomáš Wiesner | 17.07.1997 | 18 | (10) | 3 |
| Jaroslav Zelený | 20.08.1992 | 30 | (4) | 1 |
| **Midfielders:** | **DOB** | **M** | **(s)** | **G** |
| Kryštof Daněk | 05.01.2003 | 12 | (15) | 2 |
| Jan Fortelný | 19.01.1999 | 1 | (4) | |
| Jakub Jankto | 19.01.1996 | 8 | (7) | 1 |
| Kaan Kairinen (FIN) | 22.12.1998 | 14 | (1) | 1 |
| Adam Karabec | 02.07.2003 | 9 | (14) | 2 |
| Daniel Kaštánek | 12.03.2003 | | (2) | |
| Ladislav Krejčí II | 20.04.1999 | 19 | | 13 |
| Qazim Laçi (ALB) | 19.01.1996 | 7 | (10) | |
| David Pavelka | 18.05.1991 | 13 | (5) | 1 |
| Michal Sáček | 19.09.1996 | | (5) | |
| Lukáš Sadílek | 23.05.1996 | 31 | (3) | 3 |
| **Forwards:** | **DOB** | **M** | **(s)** | **G** |
| Tomáš Čvančara | 13.08.2000 | 20 | (4) | 12 |
| Václav Drchal | 25.07.1999 | | (4) | |
| Adam Goljan (SVK) | 15.04.2001 | | (2) | |
| Lukáš Haraslín (SVK) | 26.05.1996 | 21 | (1) | 7 |
| Lukáš Juliš | 02.12.1994 | 4 | (4) | 1 |
| Jan Kuchta | 08.01.1997 | 29 | | 14 |
| Awer Bul Mabil (AUS) | 15.09.1995 | 1 | (13) | 2 |
| Martin Minchev (BUL) | 22.04.2001 | 7 | (22) | 5 |
| Jakub Pešek | 24.06.1993 | 3 | | |
| Tomáš Schánělec | 20.06.2002 | | (2) | |

## Fotbalový klub Teplice

**Founded**: 1945
**Stadium**: Stadion Na Stínadlech, Teplice (18,221)
**Trainer**: Jiří Jarošík  27.10.1977
[06.03.2023]  Zdenko Frťala (SVK)  03.08.1970

| Goalkeepers: | DOB | M | (s) | G |
|---|---|---|---|---|
| Tomáš Grigar | 01.02.1983 | 19 | | |
| Filip Mucha | 04.06.1992 | 15 | | |
| Luděk Němeček | 04.01.1999 | 1 | | |
| **Defenders:** | **DOB** | **M** | **(s)** | **G** |
| Štěpán Chaloupek | 08.03.2003 | 17 | (3) | |
| Soufiane Dramé (FRA) | 27.02.1996 | 5 | (10) | |
| Jakub Hora II | 08.03.2001 | 7 | (5) | |
| Matěj Hybš | 03.01.1993 | 29 | (1) | 4 |
| Alois Hyčka | 22.07.1990 | 24 | (4) | 1 |
| Jan Knapík | 11.12.2000 | 17 | (3) | 1 |
| Nemanja Mićević (SRB) | 28.01.1999 | 17 | | |
| Ibrahima Sarr (SEN) | 25.11.2000 | | (1) | |
| Tomáš Vondrášek | 26.10.1987 | 19 | | 1 |
| **Midfielders:** | **DOB** | **M** | **(s)** | **G** |
| Marek Beránek | 16.05.2003 | | (1) | |
| Adam Čičovský | 08.12.2002 | 2 | (3) | |
| Jakub Emmer | 30.03.2001 | | (1) | |
| Jakub Hora I | 23.02.1991 | 1 | | |

| | DOB | M | (s) | G |
|---|---|---|---|---|
| Robert Jukl | 28.10.1998 | 27 | (2) | 1 |
| Ladislav Kodad | 23.04.1998 | 4 | (17) | |
| Jakub Křišťan | 05.07.2002 | 4 | (4) | |
| Tomáš Kučera | 20.07.1991 | 25 | (3) | 3 |
| Lukáš Mareček | 17.04.1990 | 20 | (7) | 1 |
| Dominik Pleštil | 09.08.1999 | 3 | (1) | 1 |
| Matěj Radosta | 10.05.2001 | 5 | (6) | 1 |
| Jan Shejbal | 20.04.1994 | 5 | (3) | |
| Daniel Trubač | 17.07.1997 | 30 | (2) | 2 |
| Jakub Urbanec | 27.04.1992 | 22 | (6) | 6 |
| **Forwards:** | **DOB** | **M** | **(s)** | **G** |
| Roman Čerepkai (SVK) | 06.04.2002 | 1 | (3) | |
| Daniel Fila | 21.08.2002 | 10 | (5) | 4 |
| Abdallah Gning (SEN) | 29.09.1998 | 31 | (1) | 9 |
| Dominik Procházka | 25.01.2002 | 1 | (3) | |
| Babacar Sy (SEN) | 02.10.2000 | 1 | (9) | 1 |
| Tadeáš Vachoušek | 11.01.2004 | 5 | (11) | 2 |
| Mohamed Yasser Nour (EGY) | 05.05.2001 | 2 | (7) | |
| Filip Žák | 01.09.1995 | 16 | (14) | 7 |

## Football Club Trinity Zlín

**Founded**: 1919
**Stadium**: Stadion Letná, Zlín (5,783)
**Trainer**: Jan Jelínek  22.03.1982
[14.11.2022]  Vit Vrtelka  21.10.1982
[28.11.2022]  Pavel Vrba  06.12.1963

| Goalkeepers: | DOB | M | (s) | G |
|---|---|---|---|---|
| Stanislav Dostál | 20.06.1991 | 11 | | |
| Matej Rakovan (SVK) | 14.03.1990 | 24 | | |
| **Defenders:** | **DOB** | **M** | **(s)** | **G** |
| Lukáš Bartošák | 03.07.1990 | 17 | (8) | 2 |
| Martin Cedidla | 22.11.2001 | 24 | | 1 |
| Adam Hloušek | 20.12.1988 | | (2) | |
| Jakub Kolář | 16.01.2000 | 26 | | 2 |
| Václav Procházka | 08.05.1984 | 27 | | 1 |
| Dominik Simerský | 29.09.1992 | 30 | (3) | 2 |
| **Midfielders:** | **DOB** | **M** | **(s)** | **G** |
| Vakhtang Chanturishvili (GEO) | 05.08.1993 | 27 | (2) | 3 |
| Joss Didiba Moudoumbou (CMR) | 07.11.1997 | 19 | (9) | 1 |
| Antonín Fantiš | 15.04.1992 | 12 | (8) | 2 |
| Martin Fillo | 07.02.1986 | 14 | (6) | 3 |
| Jan Hellebrand | 02.03.2002 | | (7) | |

| | DOB | M | (s) | G |
|---|---|---|---|---|
| Marek Hlinka (SVK) | 04.10.1990 | 21 | (1) | |
| Robert Hrubý | 27.04.1994 | 24 | (5) | 3 |
| Jakub Janetzký | 12.06.1997 | 20 | (6) | 2 |
| Rudolf Reiter | 28.09.1994 | 12 | (8) | |
| Tom Slončík | 21.12.2004 | 10 | (4) | 2 |
| David Tkáč | 06.07.2002 | | (4) | |
| **Forwards:** | **DOB** | **M** | **(s)** | **G** |
| Filip Balaj (SVK) | 02.08.1997 | 8 | (8) | 3 |
| Libor Bobčik | 08.08.2002 | | (1) | |
| Youba Dramé (FRA) | 16.01.1998 | 8 | (20) | 2 |
| Lukas Hrdlička | 03.04.2001 | | (2) | |
| Lamin Jawo (GAM) | 15.03.1995 | 14 | (2) | 3 |
| Neđeljko Kovinić (MNE) | 07.02.2002 | 2 | (17) | 3 |
| Libor Kozák | 30.05.1989 | 11 | (1) | 4 |
| Jan Silný | 15.02.1995 | 6 | (10) | 1 |
| Vukadin Vukadinovič (SRB) | 14.12.1990 | 18 | (13) | 2 |

## Football Club Viktoria Plzeň

**Founded**: 11.06.1911
**Stadium**: Doosan Arena, Plzeň (11,700)
**Trainer**: Michal Bílek  13.04.1965

| Goalkeepers: | DOB | M | (s) | G |
|---|---|---|---|---|
| Jindřich Staněk | 27.04.1996 | 32 | (1) | |
| Marián Tvrdoň (SVK) | 18.08.1994 | 3 | | |
| **Defenders:** | **DOB** | **M** | **(s)** | **G** |
| Filip Číhák | 10.07.1999 | 1 | | |
| Milan Havel | 07.08.1994 | 25 | (4) | 3 |
| Lukáš Hejda | 09.03.1990 | 28 | (1) | 3 |
| Libor Holík | 12.05.1998 | 20 | (6) | |
| Václav Jemelka | 23.06.1995 | 27 | (3) | 1 |
| Filip Kaša | 01.01.1994 | 10 | (3) | |
| Luděk Pernica | 16.06.1990 | 20 | (1) | 1 |
| Radim Řezník | 20.01.1989 | 3 | (2) | |
| Mohamed Tijani (BEN) | 10.07.1997 | 4 | | |
| **Midfielders:** | **DOB** | **M** | **(s)** | **G** |
| Pavel Bucha | 11.03.1998 | 31 | (2) | 3 |
| Carlos Eduardo Lopes Cruz „Cadu" (BRA) | 08.08.1997 | 1 | (1) | |
| Aleš Čermák | 01.10.1994 | 2 | (7) | |
| Erik Jirka (SVK) | 19.09.1997 | 7 | (21) | 2 |

| | DOB | M | (s) | G |
|---|---|---|---|---|
| Lukáš Kalvach | 19.07.1995 | 28 | | 2 |
| Jan Kopic | 04.06.1990 | 13 | (8) | 3 |
| Adam Kronus | 29.07.2002 | | (1) | |
| Roman Květ | 17.12.1997 | 10 | (7) | 2 |
| Jhon Édison Mosquera Rebolledo (COL) | 08.05.1990 | 23 | (9) | 7 |
| Modou Birame N'Diaye (SEN) | 29.10.1996 | 4 | (7) | 1 |
| Václav Pilař | 13.10.1988 | 5 | (11) | 1 |
| Kristi Qose (ALB) | 10.06.1995 | 1 | | |
| Jan Sýkora | 29.12.1993 | 18 | (3) | 2 |
| Adam Vlkanova | 04.09.1994 | 18 | (10) | 4 |
| **Forwards:** | **DOB** | **M** | **(s)** | **G** |
| Fortune Akpan Bassey (NGA) | 06.10.1998 | 3 | (9) | 1 |
| Tomáš Chorý | 26.01.1995 | 30 | (4) | 13 |
| René Dedič (SVK) | 07.08.1993 | | (3) | |
| Rafiu Adekunle Durosinmi (NGA) | 01.01.2003 | 7 | (8) | 4 |
| Jan Kliment | 01.09.1993 | 5 | (7) | 3 |
| Matěj Vydra | 01.05.1992 | 6 | (10) | 4 |

## Football Club Zbrojovka Brno

| Founded: | 1913 (*as SK Židenice*) | |
|---|---|---|
| Stadium: | Městský fotbalový stadion Srbská, Brno (12,550) | |
| Trainer: | Richard Dostálek | 26.04.1974 |
| [11.04.2023] | Martin Hašek | 11.10.1969 |

| Goalkeepers: | DOB | M | (s) | G |
|---|---|---|---|---|
| Martin Berkovec | 12.02.1989 | 32 | | |
| Vlastimil Hrubý | 21.02.1985 | 1 | | |
| Jakub Šiman | 07.01.1995 | 2 | | |

| Defenders: | DOB | M | (s) | G |
|---|---|---|---|---|
| Josef Divíšek | 24.09.1990 | 6 | (7) | |
| Lukáš Endl | 17.06.2003 | 20 | | |
| Denis Granečný | 07.09.1998 | 25 | (3) | |
| Jan Hlavica | 17.07.1994 | 16 | (8) | |
| Matěj Hrabina | 29.04.1993 | 27 | (3) | |
| Josef Koželuh | 15.02.2002 | 7 | (1) | |
| Róbert Matějov (SVK) | 05.07.1988 | 7 | (5) | 1 |
| Jan Štěrba | 08.07.1994 | 6 | (1) | |
| Jakub Šural | 01.07.1996 | 24 | | 1 |
| Mohamed Tijani (BEN) | 10.07.1997 | 12 | (1) | |

| Midfielders: | DOB | M | (s) | G |
|---|---|---|---|---|
| Filip Blecha | 16.07.1997 | 7 | (15) | |
| Šimon Falta | 23.04.1993 | 18 | (9) | |
| Adam Fousek | 08.03.1994 | 5 | (18) | 1 |
| David Jambor | 31.01.2003 | | (1) | |
| Ondřej Pachlopník | 14.02.2000 | 2 | (12) | 1 |
| Filip Souček | 18.09.2000 | 19 | (1) | 1 |
| Michal Ševčík | 13.08.2002 | 31 | (3) | 9 |
| Jiří Texl | 03.01.1993 | 31 | (3) | 2 |

| Forwards: | DOB | M | (s) | G |
|---|---|---|---|---|
| Wale Musa Alli (NGA) | 31.12.2000 | 27 | (8) | 3 |
| Jan Hladík | 21.09.1993 | 16 | (15) | |
| Jakub Nečas | 26.01.1995 | 6 | (10) | |
| Jakub Přichystal | 25.10.1995 | 5 | (4) | 1 |
| Lukáš Rogožan | 01.12.1999 | | (13) | |
| Jakub Řezníček | 26.05.1988 | 33 | (2) | 19 |

## SECOND LEVEL
### Czech National Football League 2022/2023

| | | | | | | | | | | |
|---|---|---|---|---|---|---|---|---|---|---|
| 1. | MFK Karviná (*Promoted*) | 30 | 17 | 5 | 8 | 58 | - | 37 | 56 |
| 2. | MFK Vyškov (*Promotion Play-offs*) | 30 | 14 | 10 | 6 | 45 | - | 29 | 52 |
| 3. | FK Příbram (*Promotion Play-offs*) | 30 | 14 | 9 | 7 | 48 | - | 32 | 51 |
| 4. | FK Dukla Praha | 30 | 14 | 5 | 11 | 51 | - | 45 | 47 |
| 5. | SK Líšeň Brno | 30 | 13 | 7 | 10 | 38 | - | 27 | 46 |
| 6. | FK Varnsdorf | 30 | 12 | 7 | 11 | 54 | - | 46 | 43 |
| 7. | FC Silon Táborsko | 30 | 11 | 9 | 10 | 39 | - | 43 | 42 |
| 8. | MFK Chrudim | 30 | 8 | 15 | 7 | 32 | - | 32 | 39 |
| 9. | SK Sigma Olomouc "B" | 30 | 10 | 9 | 11 | 41 | - | 46 | 39 |
| 10. | AC Sparta Praha "B" | 30 | 11 | 6 | 13 | 32 | - | 39 | 39 |
| 11. | FC Sellier & Bellot Vlašim | 30 | 11 | 5 | 14 | 54 | - | 49 | 38 |
| 12. | 1. SK Prostějov | 30 | 9 | 9 | 12 | 39 | - | 57 | 36 |
| 13. | Slezský FC Opava | 30 | 8 | 10 | 12 | 26 | - | 29 | 34 |
| 14. | FC Vysočina Jihlava | 30 | 9 | 7 | 14 | 37 | - | 51 | 34 |
| 15. | SK Slavia Praha "B" (*Relegated*) | 30 | 8 | 8 | 14 | 42 | - | 56 | 32 |
| 16. | FK Třinec (*Relegated*) | 30 | 6 | 9 | 15 | 30 | - | 48 | 27 |

## INTERNATIONAL MATCHES
(16.07.2022 – 15.07.2023)

| | | | | |
|---|---|---|---|---|
| 24.09.2022 | Praha | *Czech Republic - Portugal* | *0-4(0-2)* | (UNL) |
| 27.09.2022 | St. Gallen | *Switzerland - Czech Republic* | *2-1(2-1)* | (UNL) |
| 16.11.2022 | Olomouc | *Czech Republic - Faroe Islands* | *5-0(4-0)* | (F) |
| 19.11.2022 | Gaziantep | *Turkey - Czech Republic* | *2-1(1-0)* | (F) |
| 24.03.2023 | Praha | *Czech Republic - Poland* | *3-1(2-0)* | (ECQ) |
| 27.03.2023 | Chişinău | *Moldova - Czech Republic* | *0-0* | (ECQ) |
| 17.06.2023 | Tórshavn | *Faroe Islands - Czech Republic* | *0-3(0-2)* | (ECQ) |
| 20.06.2023 | Podgorica | *Montenegro - Czech Republic* | *1-4(0-1)* | (F) |

**24.09.2022**    **CZECH REPUBLIC - PORTUGAL**             **0-4(0-2)**          3rd UEFA Nations League A, Group 2
Fortuna Arena, Praha; Referee: Srđan Jovanović (Serbia); Attendance: 19,322
**CZE:** Tomáš Vaclík, David Zima, Jakub Brabec (22.Ondřej Kúdela), Václav Jemelka, Alex Král, Tomáš Souček (Cap) (77.Jan Kuchta), Vladimír Coufal, Jaroslav Zelený (63.Adam Vlkanova), Antonín Barák (63.Petr Ševčík), Adam Hložek (63.Václav Černý), Patrik Schick. Trainer: Jaroslav Šilhavý.

**27.09.2022**    **SWITZERLAND - CZECH REPUBLIC**          **2-1(2-1)**          3rd UEFA Nations League A, Group 2
Kybunpark, St. Gallen; Referee: Irfan Peljto (Bosnia and Herzegovina); Attendance: 13,353
**CZE:** Tomáš Vaclík (46.Jindřich Staněk), Vladimír Coufal, Ondřej Kúdela (46.Milan Havel), David Zima, Václav Jemelka, Tomáš Souček (Cap), Lukáš Kalvach (64.Jan Kuchta), Václav Černý (79.Petr Ševčík), Antonín Barák (64.Lukáš Provod), Adam Vlkanova, Patrik Schick. Trainer: Jaroslav Šilhavý.
**Goal:** Patrik Schick (45).

**16.11.2022**    **CZECH REPUBLIC - FAROE ISLANDS**        **5-0(4-0)**                      Friendly International
Andrův stadion, Olomouc; Referee: Martin Dohál (Slovakia); Attendance: 10,762
**CZE:** Jiří Pavlenka, Vladimír Coufal, David Zima (85.Matěj Chaluš), Jakub Brabec (46.Patrizio Stronati), Jaromír Zmrhal, Alex Král, Tomáš Souček (Cap), Václav Černý (46.Ondřej Zmrzlý), Antonín Barák (77.Antonín Růsek), Jan Navrátil (46.Petr Schwarz), Mojmír Chytil (64.Tomáš Pekhart). Trainer: Jaroslav Šilhavý.
**Goals:** Mojmír Chytil (13, 19, 23), Václav Černý (42), Patrizio Stronati (76).

**19.11.2022**    **TURKEY - CZECH REPUBLIC**               **2-1(1-0)**                      Friendly International
Kalyon Stadyumu, Gaziantep; Referee: William Sean Collum (Scotland); Attendance: 29,017
**CZE:** Jiří Pavlenka (46.Tomáš Koubek), Vladimír Coufal, David Zima, Jakub Brabec, Aleš Matějů (90+1.Patrizio Stronati), Alex Král, Tomáš Souček (Cap), Václav Černý (73.Petr Schwarz), Antonín Barák (85.Antonín Růsek), Jaromír Zmrhal (73.Jan Navrátil), Tomáš Pekhart (46.Mojmír Chytil). Trainer: Jaroslav Šilhavý.
**Goal:** Václav Černý (56).

**24.03.2023**    **CZECH REPUBLIC - POLAND**               **3-1(2-0)**                      17th EC. Qualifiers
Eden Arena, Praha; Referee: Anastasios Sidiropoulos (Greece); Attendance: 19,045
**CZE:** Jiří Pavlenka, Ladislav Krejčí, Jakub Brabec, Tomáš Holeš, Vladimír Coufal (70.David Douděra), Alex Král, Tomáš Souček (Cap), David Jurásek (89.Jaroslav Zelený), Adam Hložek (89.Václav Černý), Tomáš Čvančara (64.Mojmír Chytil), Jan Kuchta (70.Antonín Barák). Trainer: Jaroslav Šilhavý.
**Goals:** Ladislav Krejčí (1), Tomáš Čvančara (3), Jan Kuchta (64).

**27.03.2023**    **MOLDOVA - CZECH REPUBLIC**              **0-0**                           17th EC. Qualifiers
Stadionul Zimbru, Chişinău; Referee: Daniel Schlager (Germany); Attendance: 5,120
**CZE:** Jiří Pavlenka, Tomáš Holeš, Jakub Brabec, Václav Jemelka, Vladimír Coufal, Antonín Barák (73.Petr Ševčík), Tomáš Souček (Cap), David Jurásek, Adam Hložek (83.Ondřej Lingr), Tomáš Čvančara, Jan Kuchta (73.Mojmír Chytil). Trainer: Jaroslav Šilhavý.

**17.06.2023**    **FAROE ISLANDS - CZECH REPUBLIC**        **0-3(0-2)**                      17th EC. Qualifiers
Tórsvøllur, Tórshavn; Referee: Arda Kardeşler (Turkey); Attendance: 2,232
**CZE:** Jiří Pavlenka, Vladimír Coufal, Tomáš Holeš, Ladislav Krejčí, David Jurásek, Alex Král (89.Lukáš Sadílek), Tomáš Souček (Cap), Václav Černý (80.Michal Sadílek), Adam Hložek (69.Lukáš Provod), Václav Jurečka (80.Jan Matoušek), Jan Kuchta (69.Mojmír Chytil). Trainer: Jaroslav Šilhavý.
**Goals:** Ladislav Krejčí (15), Václav Černý (44, 75).

**20.06.2023**    **MONTENEGRO - CZECH REPUBLIC**           **1-4(0-1)**                      Friendly International
Stadion pod Goricom, Podgorica; Referee: Matthew De Gabriele (Malta); Attendance: 1,792
**CZE:** Tomáš Vaclík, David Zima, Jakub Brabec, Patrizio Stronati, David Douděra, Michal Sadílek (76.Lukáš Sadílek), Tomáš Souček (Cap), Jaroslav Zelený (46.Jakub Jugas), Václav Černý (74.Adam Hložek), Jaromír Zmrhal (46.Lukáš Provod), Mojmír Chytil (85.Jan Matoušek). Trainer: Jaroslav Šilhavý.
**Goals:** Mojmír Chytil (28), Michal Sadílek (57), Lukáš Provod (75), Adam Hložek (85).

| Name | DOB | Caps | Goals | Club | |
|------|-----|------|-------|------|--|
| **Goalkeepers** | | | | | |
| Tomáš KOUBEK | 26.08.1992 | 12 | 0 | 2022: | FC Augsburg (GER) |
| Jiří PAVLENKA | 14.04.1992 | 19 | 0 | 2022/2023: | SV Werder Bremen (GER) |
| Jindřich STANĚK | 27.04.1996 | 5 | 0 | 2022: | FC Viktoria Plzeň |
| Tomáš VACLÍK | 29.03.1989 | 54 | 0 | 2022: | Olympiacos SFP Peiraiás (GRE) |
| | | | | 31.01.2023-> | Huddersfield Town AFC (ENG) |
| **Defenders** | | | | | |
| Jakub BRABEC | 06.08.1992 | 36 | 2 | 2022/2023: | Aris Thessaloníki (GRE) |
| Matěj CHALUŠ | 02.02.1998 | 1 | 0 | 2022: | Malmö FF (SWE) |
| Vladimír COUFAL | 22.08.1992 | 37 | 1 | 2022/2023: | West Ham United FC London (ENG) |
| Milan HAVEL | 07.08.1994 | 5 | 0 | 2022: | FC Viktoria Plzeň |
| Tomáš HOLEŠ | 31.03.1993 | 20 | 2 | 2023: | SK Slavia Praha |
| Václav JEMELKA | 23.06.1996 | 8 | 0 | 2022/2023: | FC Viktoria Plzeň |
| Jakub JUGAS | 05.05.1992 | 3 | 0 | 2023: | KS Cracovia Kraków (POL) |
| David JURÁSEK | 07.08.2000 | 3 | 0 | 2023: | SK Slavia Praha |
| Ondřej KÚDELA | 26.03.1987 | 10 | 0 | 2022: | Persatuan Sepakbola Indonesia Jakrata (IDN) |
| Aleš MATĚJŮ | 03.06.1996 | 15 | 0 | 2022: | US Città di Palermo (ITA) |
| Patrizio STRONATI | 17.11.1994 | 3 | 1 | 2022/2023: | Puskás Ferenc Labdarugó Akadémia Felcsút (HUN) |
| Jaroslav ZELENÝ | 20.08.1992 | 8 | 0 | 2022/2023: | AC Sparta Praha |
| David ZIMA | 08.11.2000 | 16 | 0 | 2022/2023: | Torino FC (ITA) |
| Ondřej ZMRZLÝ | 22.04.1999 | 1 | 0 | 2022: | SK Sigma Olomouc |
| **Midfielders** | | | | | |
| Antonín BARÁK | 03.12.1994 | 37 | 8 | 2022/2023: | ACF Fiorentina (ITA) |
| David DOUDĚRA | 31.05.1998 | 2 | 0 | 2023: | SK Slavia Praha |
| Lukáš KALVACH | 19.07.1995 | 4 | 0 | 2022: | FC Viktoria Plzeň |
| Alex KRÁL | 19.05.1998 | 36 | 2 | 2022/2023: | FC Schalke 04 Gelsenkirchen (GER) |
| Ladislav KREJČÍ | 20.04.1999 | 4 | 2 | 2023: | AC Sparta Praha |
| Ondřej LINGR | 07.10.1998 | 6 | 0 | 2023: | SK Slavia Praha |
| Jan NAVRÁTIL | 13.04.1990 | 2 | 0 | 2022: | SK Sigma Olomouc |
| Lukáš PROVOD | 23.10.1996 | 10 | 2 | 2022/2023: | SK Slavia Praha |
| Lukáš SADÍLEK | 23.05.1996 | 2 | 0 | 2023: | AC Sparta Praha |
| Michal SADÍLEK | 31.05.1999 | 16 | 1 | 2023: | FC Twente Enschede (NED) |
| Petr SCHWARZ | 12.11.1991 | 2 | 0 | 2022: | WKS Śląsk Wrocław (POL) |
| Tomáš SOUČEK | 27.02.1995 | 60 | 9 | 2022/2023: | West Ham United FC London (ENG) |
| Petr ŠEVČÍK | 04.05.1994 | 15 | 0 | 2022/2023: | SK Slavia Praha |
| Adam VLKANOVA | 04.09.1994 | 3 | 0 | 2022: | FC Viktoria Plzeň |
| Jaromír ZMRHAL | 02.08.1993 | 23 | 1 | 2022/2023: | ŠK Slovan Bratislava (SVK) |
| **Forwards** | | | | | |
| Mojmír CHYTIL | 29.04.1999 | 6 | 4 | 2022/2023: | SK Sigma Olomouc |
| Václav ČERNÝ | 17.10.1997 | 11 | 4 | 2022/2023: | FC Twente Enschede (NED) |
| Tomáš ČVANČARA | 13.08.2000 | 2 | 1 | 2023: | AC Sparta Praha |
| Adam HLOŽEK | 25.07.2002 | 23 | 2 | 2022/2023: | Bayer 04 Leverkusen (GER) |
| Václav JUREČKA | 26.06.2001 | 6 | 0 | 2023: | SK Slavia Praha |
| Jan KUCHTA | 08.01.1997 | 15 | 3 | 2022/2023: | AC Sparta Praha |
| Jan MATOUŠEK | 09.05.1998 | 2 | 0 | 2023: | Bohemians Praha 1905 |
| Tomáš PEKHART | 26.05.1989 | 26 | 2 | 2022: | Gaziantep FK (TUR) |
| Antonín RŮSEK | 22.03.1999 | 3 | 0 | 2022: | SK Sigma Olomouc |
| Patrik SCHICK | 24.01.1996 | 35 | 18 | 2022: | Bayer 04 Leverkusen (GER) |
| **Trainer** | | | | | |
| Jaroslav ŠILHAVÝ [from 18.09.2019] | 03.11.1961 | | | 53 M; 26 W; 7 D; 20 L; 84-64 | |

# DENMARK

### The Country:
Kongeriget Danmark (Kingdom of Denmark)
Capital: København
Surface: 42,925 km$^2$
Inhabitants: 5,935,619 [2023]
Time: UTC+1

### The FA:
Dansk Boldspil-Union
House of Football, DBU Allé 1, 2605 Brøndby
Tel: +45 43 262 222
Foundation date: 18.05.1889
Member of FIFA since: 1904
Member of UEFA since: 1954
Website: www.dbu.dk

## NATIONAL TEAM RECORDS

### RECORDS

| | | |
|---|---|---|
| **First international match:** | 19.10.1908, London: | France – Denmark 0-9 (5th OG. 1st Round) |
| **Most international caps:** | Peter Schmeichel | - 129 caps (1987-2001) |
| **Most international goals:** | Jon Dahl Tomasson | - 52 goals / 112 caps (1997-2008) |
| | Poul "Tist" Nielsen | - 52 goals / 38 caps (1910-1925) |

### UEFA EUROPEAN CHAMPIONSHIP

| | |
|---|---|
| 1960 | Qualifiers |
| 1964 | Final Tournament (4th Place) |
| 1968 | Qualifiers |
| 1972 | Qualifiers |
| 1976 | Qualifiers |
| 1980 | Qualifiers |
| 1984 | Final Tournament (Semi-Finals) |
| 1988 | Final Tournament (Group Stage) |
| 1992 | **Final Tournament (Winners)** |
| 1996 | Final Tournament (Group Stage) |
| 2000 | Final Tournament (Group Stage) |
| 2004 | Final Tournament (Quarter-Finals) |
| 2008 | Qualifiers |
| 2012 | Final Tournament (Group Stage) |
| 2016 | Qualifiers |
| 2020 | Final Tournament (Semi-Finals) |

### FIFA WORLD CUP

| | |
|---|---|
| 1930 | Did not enter |
| 1934 | Did not enter |
| 1938 | Did not enter |
| 1950 | Did not enter |
| 1954 | Did not enter |
| 1958 | Qualifiers |
| 1962 | Did not enter |
| 1966 | Qualifiers |
| 1970 | Qualifiers |
| 1974 | Qualifiers |
| 1978 | Qualifiers |
| 1982 | Qualifiers |
| 1986 | Final Tournament (2nd Round of 16) |
| 1990 | Qualifiers |
| 1994 | Qualifiers |
| 1998 | Final Tournament (Quarter-Finals) |
| 2002 | Final Tournament (2nd Round of 16) |
| 2006 | Qualifiers |
| 2010 | Final Tournament (Group Stage) |
| 2014 | Qualifiers |
| 2018 | Final Tournament (2nd Round of 16) |
| 2022 | Final Tournament (Group Stage) |

### OLYMPIC TOURNAMENTS

| | |
|---|---|
| 1908 | Runners-up |
| 1912 | Runners-up |
| 1920 | First Round |
| 1924 | Did not enter |
| 1928 | Did not enter |
| 1936 | Did not enter |
| 1948 | 3rd Place |
| 1952 | Quarter-Finals |
| 1956 | Did not enter |
| 1960 | Runners-up |
| 1964 | Qualifiers |
| 1968 | Did not enter |
| 1972 | Second Round |
| 1976 | Qualifiers |
| 1980 | Qualifiers |
| 1984 | Qualifiers |
| 1988 | Qualifiers |
| 1992 | Group Stage |
| 1996 | Qualifiers |
| 2000 | Qualifiers |
| 2004 | Qualifiers |
| 2008 | Qualifiers |
| 2012 | Qualifiers |
| 2016 | Quarter-Finals |
| 2020 | Qualifiers |

### UEFA NATIONS LEAGUE

| | |
|---|---|
| 2018/2019 | League B (Group Stage -> promoted to League A) |
| 2020/2021 | League A (Group Stage) |
| 2022/2023 | League A (Group Stage) |

### FIFA CONFEDERATIONS CUP 1992-2017

1995 (Winners)

### DANISH CLUB HONOURS IN EUROPEAN CLUB COMPETITIONS:

| European Champion Clubs' Cup (1956-1992) / UEFA Champions League (1993-2023) |
|---|
| None |

| Fairs Cup (1858-1971) / UEFA Cup (1972-2009) / UEFA Europa League (2010-2023) |
|---|
| None |

| UEFA Europa Conference League (2021-2023) |
|---|
| None |

| UEFA Super Cup (1972-2022) |
|---|
| None |

| *European Cup Winners' Cup 1961-1999** |
|---|
| None |

*defunct competition

## NATIONAL COMPETITIONS
## TABLE OF HONOURS

| | CHAMPIONS | CUP WINNERS* | BEST GOALSCORERS | |
|---|---|---|---|---|
| 1912/1913 | Kjøbenhavns Boldklub | - | - | |
| 1913/1914 | Kjøbenhavns Boldklub | - | - | |
| 1914/1915 | *No competition* | - | - | |
| 1915/1916 | B 93 København | - | - | |
| 1916/1917 | Kjøbenhavns Boldklub | - | - | |
| 1917/1918 | Kjøbenhavns Boldklub | - | - | |
| 1918/1919 | Akademisk BK København | - | - | |
| 1919/1920 | B 1903 København | - | - | |
| 1920/1921 | Akademisk BK København | - | - | |
| 1921/1922 | Kjøbenhavns Boldklub | - | - | |
| 1922/1923 | BK Frem København | - | - | |
| 1923/1924 | B 1903 København | - | - | |
| 1924/1925 | Kjøbenhavns Boldklub | - | - | |
| 1925/1926 | B 1903 København | - | - | |
| 1926/1927 | B 93 København | - | - | |
| 1927/1928 | *No competition* | - | | |
| 1928/1929 | B 93 København | - | *Not available* | |
| 1929/1930 | B 93 København | - | *Not available* | |
| 1930/1931 | BK Frem København | - | *Not available* | |
| 1931/1932 | Kjøbenhavns Boldklub | - | *Not available* | |
| 1932/1933 | BK Frem København | - | *Not available* | |
| 1933/1934 | B 93 København | - | *Not available* | |
| 1934/1935 | B 93 København | - | *Not available* | |
| 1935/1936 | BK Frem København | - | *Not available* | |
| 1936/1937 | Akademisk BK København | - | Pauli Jørgensen (BK Frem København) | 19 |
| 1937/1938 | B 1903 København | - | Knud Andersen (B 1903 København) | 23 |
| 1938/1939 | B 93 København | - | Erik Petersen (B 93 København) | 27 |
| 1939/1940 | Kjøbenhavns Boldklub | - | Frede Jensen (Køge BK)<br>Kaj Hansen (B 93 København) | 12 |
| 1940/1941 | BK Frem København | - | - | |
| 1941/1942 | B 93 København | - | - | |
| 1942/1943 | Akademisk BK København | - | - | |
| 1943/1944 | BK Frem København | - | - | |
| 1944/1945 | Akademisk BK København | - | - | |
| 1945/1946 | B 93 København | - | Jørgen Leschly Sørensen (B 93 København) | 16 |
| 1946/1947 | Akademisk BK København | - | Helge Broneé (Østerbros Boldklub) | 21 |
| 1947/1948 | Kjøbenhavns Boldklub | - | John Hansen (BK Frem København) | 20 |
| 1948/1949 | Kjøbenhavns Boldklub | - | Jørgen Leschly Sørensen (Odense Boldklub) | 16 |
| 1949/1950 | Kjøbenhavns Boldklub | - | James Rønvang (Akademisk BK København) | 15 |
| 1950/1951 | Akademisk BK København | - | James Rønvang (Akademisk BK København)<br>Henning Bjerregaard (B 93 København)<br>Jens Peter Hansen (Esbjerg fB) | 11 |
| 1951/1952 | Akademisk BK København | - | Valdemar Kendzior (Skovshoved IF)<br>Poul Erik Petersen (Køge BK) | 13 |
| 1952/1953 | Kjøbenhavns Boldklub | - | Valdemar Kendzior (Skovshoved IF) | 17 |
| 1953/1954 | Køge BK | - | Jens-Carl Kristensen (Akademisk BK København) | 12 |
| 1954/1955 | Aarhus GF | Aarhus GF | Henning Jensen (BK Frem København) | 17 |
| 1955/1956 | Aarhus GF | BK Frem København | Gunnar Kjeldberg (Aarhus GF) | 18 |
| 1956/1957 | Aarhus GF | Aarhus GF | Søren Andersen (BK Frem København) | 27 |
| 1958 | Vejle Boldklub | Vejle Boldklub | Henning Enoksen (Vejle Boldklub) | 27 |
| 1959 | B 1909 Odense | Vejle Boldklub | Per Jensen (Kjøbenhavns Boldklub) | 20 |
| 1960 | Aarhus GF | Aarhus GF | Harald Nielsen (Frederikshavn fI) | 19 |
| 1961 | Esbjerg fB | Aarhus GF | Jørgen Ravn (Kjøbenhavns Boldklub) | 26 |
| 1962 | Esbjerg fB | B 1909 Odense | Henning Enoksen (Aarhus GF)<br>Carl Emil Christiansen (Esbjerg fB) | 24 |
| 1963 | Esbjerg fB | B 1913 Odense | Mogens Haastrup (B 1909 Odense) | 21 |
| 1964 | B 1909 Odense | Esbjerg fB | Jørgen Ravn (Kjøbenhavns Boldklub) | 21 |
| 1965 | Esbjerg fB | Aarhus GF | Per Petersen (B 1903 København) | 18 |
| 1966 | Hvidovre IF | Aalborg BK | Henning Enoksen (Aarhus GF) | 16 |
| 1967 | Akademisk BK København | Randers Freja | Leif Nielsen (BK Frem København) | 15 |
| 1968 | Kjøbenhavns Boldklub | Randers Freja | Niels-Christian Holmstrøm (Kjøbenhavns Boldklub) | 23 |
| 1969 | B 1903 København | Kjøbenhavns Boldklub | Steen Rømer Larsen (B 1903 København) | 15 |
| 1970 | B 1903 København | Aalborg BK | Ole Forsing (B 1903 København) | 18 |
| 1971 | Vejle Boldklub | B 1909 Odense | Uffe Brage (Kjøbenhavns Boldklub)<br>John Nielsen (B 1901 Nykøbing) | 19 |
| 1972 | Vejle Boldklub | Vejle Boldklub | Karsten Lund (Vejle Boldklub)<br>John Nielsen (B 1901 Nykøbing) | 16 |
| 1973 | Hvidovre IF | Randers Freja | Hans Aabech (Hvidovre IF) | 28 |
| 1974 | Kjøbenhavns Boldklub | Vanløse IF | Niels-Christian Holmstrøm (Kjøbenhavns Boldklub) | 24 |
| 1975 | Køge BK | Vejle Boldklub | Bjarne Petersen (Kjøbenhavns Boldklub) | 25 |
| 1976 | B 1903 København | Esbjerg fB | Mogens Jespersen (Aalborg BK) | 22 |
| 1977 | Odense Boldklub | Vejle Boldklub | Allan Hansen (Odense Boldklub) | 23 |

| Year | Champions | Runners-up/Cup* | Top scorer | Goals |
|------|-----------|-----------------|------------|-------|
| 1978 | Vejle Boldklub | BK Frem København | John Eriksen (Odense Boldklub) | 22 |
| 1979 | Esbjerg fB | B 1903 København | John Eriksen (Odense Boldklub) | 20 |
| 1980 | Kjøbenhavns Boldklub | Hvidovre IF | Hans Aabech (Kjøbenhavns Boldklub) | 19 |
| 1981 | Hvidovre IF | Vejle Boldklub | Allan Hansen (Odense Boldklub) | 28 |
| 1982 | Odense Boldklub | B 93 København | Ib Jacquet (Vejle Boldklub) | 20 |
| 1983 | Lyngby Boldklub | Odense Boldklub | Vilhelm Munk Nielsen (Odense Boldklub) | 20 |
| 1984 | Vejle Boldklub | Lyngby Boldklub | Steen Thychosen (Vejle Boldklub) | 24 |
| 1985 | Brøndby IF | Lyngby Boldklub | Lars Bastrup (Ikast FS) | 20 |
| 1986 | Aarhus GF | B 1903 København | Claus Nielsen (Brøndby IF) | 16 |
| 1987 | Brøndby IF | Aarhus GF | Claus Nielsen (Brøndby IF) | 20 |
| 1988 | Brøndby IF | Aarhus GF | Bent Christensen (Brøndby IF) | 21 |
| 1989 | Odense Boldklub | Brøndby IF | Miklos Molnar (BK Frem København) Flemming Christensen (Lyngby Boldklub) Lars Jakobsen (Odense Boldklub) | 14 |
| 1990 | Brøndby IF | Lyngby Boldklub | Bent Christensen (Brøndby IF) | 17 |
| 1991 | Brøndby IF | Odense Boldklub | Bent Christensen (Brøndby IF) | 11 |
| 1991/1992 | Lyngby Boldklub | Aarhus GF | Peter Møller (Aalborg BK) | 17 |
| 1992/1993 | FC København | Odense Boldklub | Peter Møller (Aalborg BK) | 22 |
| 1993/1994 | Silkeborg IF | Brøndby IF | Søren Frederiksen (Silkeborg IF) | 18 |
| 1994/1995 | Aalborg BK | FC København | Erik Bo Andersen (Aalborg BK) | 24 |
| 1995/1996 | Brøndby IF | Aarhus GF | Thomas Thorninger (Aarhus GF) | 20 |
| 1996/1997 | Brøndby IF | FC København | Miklos Molnar (Lyngby Boldklub) | 26 |
| 1997/1998 | Brøndby IF | Brøndby IF | Ebbe Sand (Brøndby IF) | 28 |
| 1998/1999 | Aalborg BK | Akademisk BK København | Heine Fernandez (Viborg FF) | 23 |
| 1999/2000 | Herfølge BK | Viborg FF | Peter Lassen (Silkeborg IF) | 16 |
| 2000/2001 | FC København | Silkeborg IF | Peter Graulund (Brøndby IF) | 21 |
| 2001/2002 | Brøndby IF | Odense Boldklub | Peter Madsen (Brøndby IF) Kaspar Dalgas (Odense Boldklub) | 22 |
| 2002/2003 | FC København | Brøndby IF | Søren Frederiksen (Viborg FF) Jan Kristiansen (Esbjerg fB) | 18 |
| 2003/2004 | FC København | FC København | Steffen Højer (Odense Boldklub) Mohamed Zidan (EGY, FC Midtjylland Herning) Tommy Bechmann (Esbjerg fB) Mwape Miti (ZAM, Odense Boldklub) | 19 |
| 2004/2005 | Brøndby IF | Brøndby IF | Steffen Højer (Odense Boldklub) | 20 |
| 2005/2006 | FC København | Randers FC | Steffen Højer (Viborg FF) | 16 |
| 2006/2007 | FC København | Odense Boldklub | Rade Prica (SWE, Aalborg BK) | 19 |
| 2007/2008 | Aalborg BK | Brøndby IF | Jeppe Lund Curth (Aalborg BK) | 17 |
| 2008/2009 | FC København | FC København | Morten Nordstrand (FC København) Marc Nygaard (Randers FC) | 16 |
| 2009/2010 | FC København | FC Nordsjælland Farum | Peter Maduabuchi Utaka (NGA, Odense Boldklub) | 18 |
| 2010/2011 | FC København | FC Nordsjælland Farum | Dame N'Doye (SEN, FC København) | 25 |
| 2011/2012 | FC Nordsjælland Farum | FC København | Dame N'Doye (SEN, FC København) | 18 |
| 2012/2013 | FC København | Esbjerg fB | Andreas Evald Cornelius (FC København) | 18 |
| 2013/2014 | Aalborg BK | Aalborg BK | Thomas Dalgaard (Viborg FF) | 18 |
| 2014/2015 | FC Midtjylland Herning | FC København | Martin Pušić (AUT, Esbjerg fB / FC Midtjylland Herning) | 17 |
| 2015/2016 | FC København | FC København | Lukas Spalvis (LTU, Aalborg BK) | 18 |
| 2016/2017 | FC København | FC København | Marcus Ingvartsen (FC Nordsjælland Farum) | 23 |
| 2017/2018 | FC Midtjylland Herning | Brøndby IF | Pål Alexander Kirkevold (NOR, Hobro IK) | 22 |
| 2018/2019 | FC København | FC Midtjylland Herning | Robert Skov (FC København) | 29 |
| 2019/2020 | FC Midtjylland Herning | Sønderjysk Elitesport | Ronnie Schwartz (Silkeborg IF / FC Midtjylland Herning) | 18 |
| 2020/2021 | Brøndby IF | Randers FC | Mikael Uhre (Brøndby IF) | 19 |
| 2021/2022 | FC København | FC Midtjylland Herning | Nicklas Helenius Jensen (Silkeborg IF) | 17 |
| 2022/2023 | FC København | FC København | Gustav Tang Isaksen (FC Midtjylland Herning) | 18 |

*Cup competition called Landspokalturneringen (1954-1989), Giro Cup (1898-1996), Compaq Cup (1996-1999), DONG Cup (1999-2004), Landspokalturneringen (2004-2008), Ekstra Bladet Cup (2008-2011) and DBU Pokalen (since 2011).

# NATIONAL CHAMPIONSHIP
## 3F Superliga 2022/2023
### (15.07.2022 – 04.06.2023)

## Regular Season - Results

### Round 1 [15-18.07.2022]
FC Midtjylland - Randers FC 1-1(0-0)
Viborg FF - Aalborg BK 2-1(1-0)
Lyngby BK - Silkeborg IF 2-2(1-0)
FC København - AC Horsens 0-1(0-0)
Brøndby IF - Aarhus GF 1-0(0-0)
Odense BK - FC Nordsjælland 0-2(0-1)

### Round 2 [22-25.07.2022]
FC Midtjylland - Silkeborg IF 1-3(0-1)
Aarhus GF - Viborg FF 3-1(1-0)
Randers FC - Odense BK 2-2(0-2)
Brøndby IF - FC Nordsjælland 1-3(0-1)
Aalborg BK - FC København 1-3(0-1)
AC Horsens - Lyngby BK 1-0(1-0)

### Round 3 [29.07.-01.08.2022]
Odense BK - FC Midtjylland 1-5(1-1)
Aalborg BK - AC Horsens 0-0
Aarhus GF - Randers FC 0-0
Viborg FF - FC København 4-2(2-1)
Silkeborg IF - Brøndby IF 2-0(1-0)
FC Nordsjælland - Lyngby BK 2-1(1-0)

### Round 4 [05-08.08.2022]
Randers FC - AC Horsens 1-0(1-0)
Lyngby BK - FC Midtjylland 3-3(1-3)
FC Nordsjælland - Viborg FF 1-0(1-0)
FC København - Brøndby IF 4-1(3-1)
Odense BK - Aarhus GF 1-2(1-1)
Silkeborg IF - Aalborg BK 3-1(1-0)

### Round 5 [12-15.08.2022]
AC Horsens - FC Midtjylland 3-3(0-3)
FC København - Randers FC 1-3(0-0)
Viborg FF - Silkeborg IF 2-0(2-0)
Aalborg BK - FC Nordsjælland 0-0
Brøndby IF - Odense BK 2-0(2-0)
Aarhus GF - Lyngby BK 1-0(1-0)

### Round 6 [19-22.08.2022]
Lyngby BK - FC København 0-3(0-1)
FC Midtjylland - Aarhus GF 0-2(0-0)
FC Nordsjælland - Silkeborg IF 0-2(0-2)
Randers FC - Viborg FF 1-0(0-0)
Aalborg BK - Brøndby IF 2-1(1-0)
Odense BK - AC Horsens 1-0(0-0)

### Round 7 [26-29.08.2022]
AC Horsens - Aarhus GF 2-1(0-1)
Randers FC - Aalborg BK 1-1(1-0)
Viborg FF - Lyngby BK 2-1(0-0)
FC Nordsjælland - FC København 3-1(2-0)
Silkeborg IF - Odense BK 1-2(1-1)
Brøndby IF - FC Midtjylland 0-2(0-2)

### Round 8 [02-05.09.2022]
FC København - Silkeborg IF 1-0(1-0)
Lyngby BK - Randers FC 0-2(0-0)
Odense BK - Viborg FF 1-2(1-0)
AC Horsens - Brøndby IF 0-2(0-0)
FC Midtjylland - Aalborg BK 0-2(0-1)
Aarhus GF - FC Nordsjælland 2-3(1-2)

### Round 9 [10-12.09.2022]
Odense BK - FC København 2-1(1-1)
Aalborg BK - Lyngby BK 1-1(0-1)
FC Nordsjælland - FC Midtjylland 1-1(1-0)
Brøndby IF - Randers FC 2-2(1-1)
Silkeborg IF - Aarhus GF 1-0(1-0)
Viborg FF - AC Horsens 2-1(2-0)

### Round 10 [16-18.09.2022]
AC Horsens - FC Nordsjælland 1-0(1-0)
Aarhus GF - Aalborg BK 3-1(0-0)
Lyngby BK - Odense BK 0-2(0-1)
Randers FC - Silkeborg IF 3-2(1-1)
Viborg FF - Brøndby IF 0-0
FC Midtjylland - FC København 2-1(2-1)

### Round 11 [30.09.-03.10.2022]
Aalborg BK - Odense BK 1-1(1-0)
FC Midtjylland - Viborg FF 1-1(1-1)
Silkeborg IF - AC Horsens 2-1(1-0)
Brøndby IF - Lyngby BK 3-3(2-1)
FC København - Aarhus GF 1-0(0-0)
FC Nordsjælland - Randers FC 3-1(2-0)

### Round 12 [07-10.10.2022]
Lyngby BK - Viborg FF 1-1(1-1)
FC København - FC Nordsjælland 1-1(0-0)
Aarhus GF - FC Midtjylland 0-1(0-0)
Odense BK - Silkeborg IF 1-1(0-0)
Randers FC - Brøndby IF 2-3(1-1)
AC Horsens - Aalborg BK 0-0

### Round 13 [14-17.10.2022]
Lyngby BK - Aalborg BK 0-2(0-1)
Brøndby IF - FC København 1-1(1-0)
Viborg FF - Odense BK 0-0
FC Nordsjælland - Aarhus GF 1-1(1-0)
FC Midtjylland - AC Horsens 2-1(1-1)
Silkeborg IF - Randers FC 3-3(3-1)

### Round 14 [21-24.10.2022]
Odense BK - Lyngby BK 3-1(3-0)
FC København - FC Midtjylland 1-1(1-0)
Randers FC - FC Nordsjælland 0-2(0-1)
AC Horsens - Silkeborg IF 3-2(1-1)
Aarhus GF - Brøndby IF 2-2(1-0)
Aalborg BK - Viborg FF 1-3(1-1)

### Round 15 [28-31.10.2022]
FC Nordsjælland - AC Horsens 2-0(1-0)
Randers FC - FC København 0-2(0-0)
Lyngby BK - Aarhus GF 0-1(0-0)
Silkeborg IF - Viborg FF 1-3(1-0)
Brøndby IF - Aalborg BK 3-2(2-1)
FC Midtjylland - Odense BK 1-2(0-1)

### Round 16 [04-07.11.2022]
AC Horsens - Randers FC 5-1(2-1)
Aalborg BK - Silkeborg IF 1-2(1-0)
Viborg FF - Aarhus GF 1-1(0-1)
FC København - Lyngby BK 3-0(1-0)
Odense BK - Brøndby IF 1-1(0-1)
FC Midtjylland - FC Nordsjælland 0-0

### Round 17 [12-13.11.2022]
Silkeborg IF - Lyngby BK 0-2(0-0)
Aarhus GF - FC København 0-2(0-0)
AC Horsens - Odense BK 3-3(2-2)
Brøndby IF - Viborg FF 0-2(0-1)
FC Nordsjælland - Aalborg BK 5-1(1-0)
Randers FC - FC Midtjylland 0-0

### Round 18 [17-20.02.2023]
Aalborg BK - Aarhus GF 0-1(0-0)
Lyngby BK - FC Nordsjælland 1-1(0-0)
Odense BK - Randers FC 0-0
Silkeborg IF - FC København 0-3(0-1)
Brøndby IF - AC Horsens 5-2(1-2)
Viborg FF - FC Midtjylland 0-4(0-1)

### Round 19 [24-27.02.2023]
FC Nordsjælland - Odense BK 4-2(1-1)
AC Horsens - Viborg FF 0-3(0-3)
Randers FC - Lyngby BK 1-0(0-0)
FC København - Aalborg BK 1-0(0-0)
Aarhus GF - Silkeborg IF 1-1(1-0)
FC Midtjylland - Brøndby IF 0-1(0-0)

### Round 20 [03-06.03.2023]
Aarhus GF - AC Horsens 2-0(1-0)
Silkeborg IF - FC Nordsjælland 2-1(0-1)
Viborg FF - Randers FC 2-2(2-0)
Lyngby BK - Brøndby IF 1-0(0-0)
FC København - Odense BK 7-0(2-0)
Aalborg BK - FC Midtjylland 0-0

### Round 21 [10-13.03.2023]
Odense BK - Aalborg BK 2-1(1-0)
FC Midtjylland - Lyngby BK 1-3(0-1)
Viborg FF - FC Nordsjælland 1-1(0-1)
AC Horsens - FC København 1-4(1-0)
Brøndby IF - Silkeborg IF 2-1(1-0)
Randers FC - Aarhus GF 1-2(0-1)

### Round 22 [19.03.2023]
Aalborg BK - Randers FC 0-1(0-0)
Aarhus GF - Odense BK 1-0(1-0)
FC København - Viborg FF 2-1(1-0)
FC Nordsjælland - Brøndby IF 2-1(0-1)
Lyngby BK - AC Horsens 1-1(1-0)
Silkeborg IF - FC Midtjylland 3-3(1-2)

|  | | | | | | | | | |
|---|---|---|---|---|---|---|---|---|---|
| 1. | FC Nordsjælland Farum | 22 | 12 | 7 | 3 | 38 | - | 20 | 43 |
| 2. | FC København | 22 | 13 | 3 | 6 | 45 | - | 22 | 42 |
| 3. | Viborg FF | 22 | 10 | 7 | 5 | 32 | - | 25 | 37 |
| 4. | Aarhus GF | 22 | 10 | 5 | 7 | 26 | - | 20 | 35 |
| 5. | Randers FC | 22 | 8 | 8 | 6 | 28 | - | 30 | 32 |
| 6. | Brøndby IF | 22 | 8 | 6 | 8 | 32 | - | 34 | 30 |
| 7. | Silkeborg IF | 22 | 8 | 5 | 9 | 34 | - | 35 | 29 |
| 8. | FC Midtjylland Herning | 22 | 6 | 10 | 6 | 32 | - | 29 | 28 |
| 9. | Odense Boldklub | 22 | 7 | 7 | 8 | 27 | - | 38 | 28 |
| 10. | AC Horsens | 22 | 6 | 5 | 11 | 26 | - | 37 | 23 |
| 11. | Lyngby Boldklub | 22 | 3 | 7 | 12 | 21 | - | 36 | 16 |
| 12. | Aalborg BK | 22 | 3 | 6 | 13 | 18 | - | 33 | 15 |

Teams ranked 1-6 were qualified for the Championship Round, while teams ranked 7-12 were qualified for the Relegation Round.

## Relegation Round

### Results

**Round 23 [31.03.-02.04.2023]**
Odense BK - FC Midtjylland 1-3(1-2)
Lyngby BK - Silkeborg IF 1-1(1-1)
AC Horsens - Aalborg BK 0-4(0-2)

**Round 24 [10-11.04.2023]**
Aalborg BK - Odense BK 2-3(0-2)
FC Midtjylland - Lyngby BK 1-0(0-0)
Silkeborg IF - AC Horsens 1-2(0-1)

**Round 25 [14-16.04.2023]**
FC Midtjylland - Aalborg BK 1-1(0-1)
Lyngby BK - AC Horsens 2-1(1-1)
Odense BK - Silkeborg IF 2-0(0-0)

**Round 26 [21-24.04.2023]**
Silkeborg IF - Aalborg BK 2-2(2-1)
AC Horsens - FC Midtjylland 0-2(0-1)
Odense BK - Lyngby BK 2-2(0-1)

**Round 27 [28.04.-01.05.2023]**
AC Horsens - Odense BK 2-2(1-1)
Aalborg BK - Lyngby BK 1-0(0-0)
FC Midtjylland - Silkeborg IF 3-0(3-0)

**Round 28 [07.05.2023]**
Aalborg BK - AC Horsens 4-0(1-0)
Silkeborg IF - Odense BK 0-1(0-1)
Lyngby BK - FC Midtjylland 2-1(2-1)

**Round 29 [12-14.05.2023]**
Odense BK - Aalborg BK 1-1(1-0)
Silkeborg IF - Lyngby BK 1-0(0-0)
FC Midtjylland - AC Horsens 3-1(1-1)

**Round 30 [19-21.05.2023]**
AC Horsens - Silkeborg IF 0-1(0-0)
Aalborg BK - FC Midtjylland 0-2(0-1)
Lyngby BK - Odense BK 0-4(0-2)

**Round 31 [26-29.05.2023]**
Odense BK - AC Horsens 2-1(0-0)
Silkeborg IF - FC Midtjylland 3-3(1-1)
Lyngby BK - Aalborg BK 2-1(1-1)

**Round 32 [03.06.2023]**
FC Midtjylland - Odense BK 4-2(2-1)
Aalborg BK - Silkeborg IF 0-1(0-0)
AC Horsens - Lyngby BK 0-0

### Final Standings

|  | | Total | | | | | | | | Home | | | | | | Away | | | | |
|---|---|---|---|---|---|---|---|---|---|---|---|---|---|---|---|---|---|---|---|---|
| 1. | FC Midtjylland Herning | 32 | 13 | 12 | 7 | 55 | - | 39 | **51** | 6 | 4 | 6 | 21 | - | 21 | 7 | 8 | 1 | 34 | - | 18 |
| 2. | Odense Boldklub | 32 | 12 | 10 | 10 | 47 | - | 53 | **46** | 6 | 5 | 5 | 21 | - | 23 | 6 | 5 | 5 | 26 | - | 30 |
| 3. | Silkeborg IF | 32 | 11 | 8 | 13 | 44 | - | 49 | **41** | 6 | 4 | 6 | 25 | - | 26 | 5 | 4 | 7 | 19 | - | 23 |
| 4. | Lyngby Boldklub | 32 | 6 | 10 | 16 | 30 | - | 49 | **28** | 4 | 6 | 6 | 16 | - | 26 | 2 | 4 | 10 | 14 | - | 23 |
| 5. | AC Horsens (*Relegated*) | 32 | 7 | 7 | 18 | 33 | - | 58 | **28** | 5 | 5 | 6 | 21 | - | 28 | 2 | 2 | 12 | 12 | - | 30 |
| 6. | Aalborg BK (*Relegated*) | 32 | 6 | 9 | 17 | 34 | - | 45 | **27** | 3 | 5 | 8 | 14 | - | 19 | 3 | 4 | 9 | 20 | - | 26 |

Please note: FC Midtjylland Herning were qualified for the Europa Conference League Play-offs.

## Championship Round

### Results

**Round 23 [02-03.04.2023]**
Brøndby IF - Viborg FF 0-3(0-1)
FC København - FC Nordsjælland 2-1(0-1)
Aarhus GF - Randers FC 1-1(1-1)

**Round 24 [09-10.04.2023]**
Viborg FF - Aarhus GF 0-1(0-0)
Randers FC - FC København 1-0(0-0)
FC Nordsjælland - Brøndby IF 2-1(2-0)

**Round 25 [16-17.04.2023]**
FC København - Viborg FF 2-1(1-1)
Brøndby IF - Aarhus GF 1-0(1-0)
Randers FC - FC Nordsjælland 1-1(0-0)

**Round 26 [23.04.2023]**
Viborg FF - FC Nordsjælland 1-0(0-0)
Brøndby IF - Randers FC 0-4(0-2)
Aarhus GF - FC København 0-0

**Round 27 [30.04.2023]**
Viborg FF - Randers FC 3-1(1-0)
FC København - Brøndby IF 0-1(0-0)
FC Nordsjælland - Aarhus GF 0-1(0-1)

**Round 28 [07-08.05.2023]**
Randers FC - Brøndby IF 1-3(0-3)
Aarhus GF - Viborg FF 3-0(1-0)
FC Nordsjælland - FC København 3-2(1-0)

**Round 29 [14-15.05.2023]**
Brøndby IF - FC København 1-3(0-1)
Aarhus GF - FC Nordsjælland 1-1(0-0)
Randers FC - Viborg FF 0-2(0-0)

**Round 30 [21-22.05.2023]**
Viborg FF - Brøndby IF 1-1(0-1)
FC København - Aarhus GF 4-3(2-2)
FC Nordsjælland - Randers FC 3-1(1-1)

**Round 31 [29-30.05.2023]**
Viborg FF - FC København 1-2(0-2)
Brøndby IF - FC Nordsjælland 5-1(2-0)
Randers FC - Aarhus GF 1-3(1-1)

**Round 32** [04.06.2023]
FC Nordsjælland - Viborg FF 0-0
FC København - Randers FC 1-1(0-1)
Aarhus GF - Brøndby IF 3-3(0-2)

## Final Standings

| | | Total | | | | | | Home | | | | | Away | | | |
|---|---|---|---|---|---|---|---|---|---|---|---|---|---|---|---|---|---|
| 1. **FC København** | 32 | 18 | 5 | 9 | 61 - 35 | **59** | 10 | 3 | 3 | 31 - 15 | 8 | 2 | 6 | 30 - 20 |
| 2. FC Nordsjælland Farum | 32 | 15 | 10 | 7 | 50 - 35 | **55** | 11 | 3 | 2 | 32 - 16 | 4 | 7 | 5 | 18 - 19 |
| 3. Aarhus GF | 32 | 14 | 9 | 9 | 42 - 31 | **51** | 6 | 7 | 3 | 23 - 16 | 8 | 2 | 6 | 19 - 15 |
| 4. Viborg FF | 32 | 14 | 9 | 9 | 44 - 35 | **51** | 7 | 6 | 3 | 22 - 18 | 7 | 3 | 6 | 22 - 17 |
| 5. Brøndby IF | 32 | 12 | 8 | 12 | 48 - 52 | **44** | 7 | 3 | 6 | 27 - 29 | 5 | 5 | 6 | 21 - 23 |
| 6. Randers FC | 32 | 10 | 11 | 11 | 40 - 47 | **41** | 6 | 3 | 7 | 16 - 22 | 4 | 8 | 4 | 24 - 25 |

Please note: Viborg FF were qualified for the Europa Conference League Play-offs.

## Top goalscorers:

| | | |
|---|---|---|
| 18 | **Gustav Tang Isaksen** | *FC Midtjylland Herning* |
| 16 | Patrick Mortensen | *Aarhus GF* |
| 13 | Anthony Ohikhuaeme Omoijuanfo (NOR) | *Brøndby IF* |
| 13 | Viktor Johan Anton Claesson (SWE) | *FC København* |
| 12 | Ernest Nuamah (GHA) | *FC Nordsjælland Farum* |

## Europa Conference League Play-off [09.06.2023]

Viborg FF - FC Midtjylland Herning                                0-1(0-0)

# NATIONAL CUP
## DBU Pokalen / Sydbank Pokalen 2022/2023

### Third Round [28.09./05.10./12.10./18-20.10.2022]

| | | | | |
|---|---|---|---|---|
| Næstved BK - Silkeborg IF | 0-3(0-2) | HB Køge - Sønderjysk Elitesport | 1-4(0-2) |
| Sædding-Guldager IF - Middelfart Boldklub | 0-6(0-3) | FC Roskilde - BK Fremad Amager | 1-2(0-2) |
| Ballerup-Skovlunde Fodbold - FC Nordsjælland Farum | 0-5(0-1) | Aarhus Fremad - Brøndby IF | 4-0(3-0) |
| AB Gladsaxe - Aarhus GF | 0-3(0-2) | Ishøj IF - Viborg FF | 2-3(1-0,1-1) |
| Brabrand IF - Vejle Boldklub | 0-3(0-2) | FA 2000 Frederiksberg - FC Midtjylland Herning | 0-6(0-4) |
| Næsby BK - Nykøbing FC | 1-2(0-1) | Hobro IK - FC København | 1-1 aet; 3-5 pen |
| Vanløse IF - Aalborg BK | 1-3(1-0,1-1) | Hørsholm-Usserød IK - AC Horsens | 1-2(0-0) |
| Thisted FC - FC Helsingør | 2-1(1-0) | Vendsyssel FF - Randers FC | 0-2(0-2) |

### 1/8-Finals [08-10.11.2022]

| | | | |
|---|---|---|---|
| Nykøbing FC - Sønderjysk Elitesport | 1-2(1-1,1-1) | Thisted FC - FC København | 1-3(1-1,1-1) |
| Aarhus Fremad - BK Fremad Amager | 3-1(3-1) | Randers FC - Silkeborg IF | 1-3(1-0) |
| Middelfart Boldklub - Aalborg BK | 1-2(0-0) | Viborg FF - FC Midtjylland Herning | 3-1(3-0) |
| Vejle Boldklub - AC Horsens | 1-0(0-0) | Aarhus GF - FC Nordsjælland Farum | 0-2(0-1) |

### Quarter-Finals [28.02.-02.03./08.03.2023 & 05-06.04.2023]

| First Leg | | Second Leg | |
|---|---|---|---|
| Aarhus Fremad - FC Nordsjælland Farum | 0-3(0-3) | FC Nordsjælland Farum - Aarhus Fremad | 4-1(2-0) |
| FC København - Vejle Boldklub | 2-0(0-0) | Vejle Boldklub - FC København | 0-0 |
| Aalborg BK - Viborg FF | 2-0(0-0) | Viborg FF - Aalborg BK | 1-0(1-0) |
| Sønderjysk Elitesport - Silkeborg IF | 0-2(0-1) | Silkeborg IF - Sønderjysk Elitesport | 3-2(0-2) |

### Semi-Finals [25-26.04./04.05.2023]

| First Leg | | Second Leg | |
|---|---|---|---|
| Silkeborg IF - Aalborg BK | 1-1(0-0) | Aalborg BK - Silkeborg IF | 4-1(2-1) |
| FC Nordsjælland Farum - FC København | 3-2(1-0) | FC København - FC Nordsjælland Farum | 5-3(3-1) |

### Final

18.05.2023; Parken Stadium, København; Referee: Jakob Sundberg; Attendance: 34,937
**Aalborg BK - FC København**                                **0-1(0-0)**

**Aalborg BK**: Nico Mantl, Kasper Jørgensen (85.Kilian Ludewig), Rasmus Thelander, Lars Kramer, Daniel Granli (75.Jakob Ahlmann), Pedro Miguel Dinis Ferreira (75.Louka Prip), Iver Fossum, Malthe Højholt, Younes Bakiz (85.Oliver Ross), Lucas Andersen (Cap), Nicklas Helenius (75.Anosike Ementa). Trainer: Oscar Karl Niclas Hiljemark (Sweden).

**Goal:** 0-1 Diogo António Cupido Gonçalves (48).

**FC København**: Kamil Grabara, Elias Jelert, Denis Vavro, Valdemar Lund Jensen, Christian Sørensen, William Clem, Rasmus Falk (38.Roony Bardghji; 89.Kevin Diks), Victor Johan Anton Claesson (Cap), Jordan Larsson, Diogo António Cupido Gonçalves (70.Marko Seufatu Nikola Stamenić), Hákon Haraldsson (89.Ísak Bergmann Jóhannesson). Trainer: Jacob Neestrup.

Please note: appearances and goals are including statistics of both regular season and play-offs (Championship Round & Relegation Round).

## Aalborg Boldspilklub

| Founded: | 13.05.1985 | |
|---|---|---|
| Stadium: | Aalborg Portland Park (13,797) | |
| Trainer: | Lars Friis | 07.05.1966 |
| [15.09.2022] | Erik Hamrén (SWE) | 27.06.1957 |
| [20.03.2023] | Oscar Karl Niclas Hiljemark (SWE) | 28.06.1992 |

| Goalkeepers: | DOB | M | (s) | G |
|---|---|---|---|---|
| Nico Mantl (GER) | 06.02.2000 | 8 | | |
| Josip Posavec (CRO) | 10.03.1996 | 10 | | |
| Theo Sander | 08.01.2005 | 14 | | |
| **Defenders:** | **DOB** | **M** | **(s)** | **G** |
| Jakob Ahlmann | 18.01.1991 | 12 | (11) | |
| Daniel Granli (NOR) | 01.05.1994 | 17 | (5) | 2 |
| Anders Hagelskjær | 16.02.1997 | | (3) | 1 |
| Kasper Jørgensen | 07.11.1999 | 6 | (2) | |
| Lars Kramer (NED) | 11.07.1999 | 31 | | 2 |
| Kilian Ludewig (GER) | 05.03.2000 | 15 | (4) | |
| Yahya Nadrani (MAR) | 14.01.1997 | 3 | | |
| Sebastian Otoa | 13.05.2004 | 2 | (4) | |
| Kristoffer Pallesen | 30.04.1990 | 17 | (3) | |
| Andreas Poulsen | 13.10.1999 | 10 | (6) | 1 |
| Mathias Ross Jensen | 15.01.2001 | 8 | | 1 |
| Rasmus Thelander | 09.07.1991 | 11 | | |

| Midfielders: | DOB | M | (s) | G |
|---|---|---|---|---|
| Iver Fossum (NOR) | 15.07.1996 | 30 | | 3 |
| Malthe Højholt | 16.04.2001 | 20 | (6) | |
| Kasper Kusk | 10.11.1991 | 1 | (5) | 1 |
| Jeppe Pedersen | 03.03.2001 | | (6) | 1 |
| *Pedro* Miguel Dinis *Ferreira* (POR) | 05.01.1998 | 20 | (7) | 2 |
| **Forwards:** | **DOB** | **M** | **(s)** | **G** |
| *Allan* Gonçalves *Sousa* (BRA) | 27.01.1997 | 24 | (3) | 8 |
| Lucas Andersen | 13.09.1994 | 20 | (11) | 1 |
| Younes Bakiz | 05.02.1999 | 16 | (5) | 6 |
| Anosike Ementa | 03.05.2002 | 6 | (14) | |
| Nicklas Helenius | 08.05.1991 | 13 | (2) | 1 |
| Kasper Høgh | 06.12.2000 | | (4) | |
| Milan Makarić (SRB) | 04.10.1995 | 4 | (3) | |
| Louka Prip | 29.06.1997 | 26 | (6) | 1 |
| Marco Ramkilde | 09.05.1998 | 5 | (15) | 2 |
| Oliver Ross | 10.10.2004 | 3 | (19) | 1 |

## Aarhus Gymnastikforening

| Founded: | 1880 | |
|---|---|---|
| Stadium: | Ceres Park, Aarhus (20,032) | |
| Trainer: | Uwe Rösler (GER) | 15.11.1968 |

| Goalkeepers: | DOB | M | (s) | G |
|---|---|---|---|---|
| Jesper Hansen | 31.03.1985 | 32 | | |
| **Defenders:** | **DOB** | **M** | **(s)** | **G** |
| Felix Beijmo (SWE) | 31.01.1998 | 14 | | |
| Yann Aurel Bisseck (GER) | 29.11.2000 | 32 | | 4 |
| Peter Nicolai Kruse Bjur | 02.02.2000 | 4 | (7) | 1 |
| Anthony D'Alberto (BEL) | 13.10.1994 | 1 | (11) | |
| Sebastian Hausner | 11.04.2000 | 3 | (2) | |
| Eric Kahl (SWE) | 27.09.2001 | 15 | (16) | |
| Thomas Kristensen | 17.01.2002 | 19 | (1) | 1 |
| Oliver Lund | 21.08.1990 | | (2) | |
| Tobias Mølgaard | 22.07.1996 | 28 | (4) | |
| Alexander Munksgaard | 13.12.1997 | | (1) | |
| Frederik Tingager | 22.02.1993 | 30 | | 1 |
| **Midfielders:** | **DOB** | **M** | **(s)** | **G** |
| Frederik Brandhof | 05.07.1996 | 3 | (21) | |

| | DOB | M | (s) | G |
|---|---|---|---|---|
| Albert Grønbæk Erlykke | 23.05.2001 | 1 | (3) | |
| Benjamin Hvidt | 12.03.2000 | | (3) | |
| Mads Madsen | 14.01.1998 | 25 | (2) | 3 |
| Nikolai Poulsen | 15.08.1993 | 26 | (2) | |
| Mathias Sauer | 02.04.2004 | | (1) | |
| Kevin Yakob (SWE) | 10.10.2000 | 19 | (5) | 3 |
| **Forwards:** | **DOB** | **M** | **(s)** | **G** |
| Mikael Anderson (ISL) | 01.07.1998 | 24 | (2) | 5 |
| Adam Daghim | 28.09.2005 | | (3) | |
| Mikkel Duelund | 29.06.1997 | 8 | (4) | 2 |
| Jelle Duin (NED) | 27.01.1999 | 3 | (12) | 3 |
| Sebastian Grønning Andersen | 03.02.1997 | | (6) | 1 |
| Sigurd Haugen (NOR) | 17.07.1997 | 15 | (16) | 2 |
| Dawid Kurminowski (POL) | 24.02.1999 | | (4) | |
| Neo Gift Links (RSA) | 02.10.1998 | 18 | (10) | |
| Patrick Mortensen | 13.07.1989 | 32 | | 16 |

## Brøndbyernes Idrætsforening

| Founded: | 03.12.1964 | |
|---|---|---|
| Stadium: | Brøndby Stadion, Brøndby (29,000) | |
| Trainer: | Niels Frederiksen | 11.09.1968 |
| [02.01.2023] | Jesper Ingemann Sørensen | 10.06.1973 |

| Goalkeepers: | DOB | M | (s) | G |
|---|---|---|---|---|
| Mads Hermansen | 11.07.2000 | 27 | | |
| Thomas Mikkelsen | 27.08.1983 | 5 | | |
| **Defenders:** | **DOB** | **M** | **(s)** | **G** |
| Peter Nicolai Kruse Bjur | 02.02.2000 | 1 | (3) | |
| Jens Martin Gammelby | 05.02.1995 | 6 | (4) | 1 |
| Henrik Heggheim (NOR) | 22.04.2001 | 2 | | |
| Frederik Alves Ibsen | 08.11.1999 | 8 | (9) | |
| Rasmus Lauritsen | 27.02.1996 | 8 | (1) | |
| Andreas Maxsø | 18.03.1994 | 11 | | 1 |
| Kevin Mensah | 15.05.1991 | 8 | (1) | |
| Blas Miguel Riveros Galeano (PAR) | 03.02.1998 | 21 | (4) | |
| Sigurd Rosted (NOR) | 22.07.1994 | 6 | (4) | |
| Sebastian Sebulonsen (NOR) | 27.01.2000 | 11 | (8) | 1 |
| Kevin Tshiembe | 31.03.1997 | 23 | (5) | |
| Daniel Wass | 31.05.1989 | 23 | (1) | 1 |
| Frederik Winther | 04.01.2001 | 12 | (3) | |

| Midfielders: | DOB | M | (s) | G |
|---|---|---|---|---|
| Joe Zen Robert Bell (NZL) | 27.04.1999 | 13 | (5) | |
| Anis Ben Slimane (TUN) | 16.03.2001 | 13 | (17) | 3 |
| Christian Jaeger Cappis (USA) | 13.08.1999 | 8 | (11) | 2 |
| Håkon Evjen (NOR) | 14.02.2000 | 11 | (4) | 3 |
| Mathias Greve | 11.02.1995 | 21 | (4) | |
| Bertram Kvist | 19.03.2005 | | (1) | |
| Josip Radošević (CRO) | 03.04.1994 | 20 | (7) | 3 |
| Nicolai Vallys | 04.09.1996 | 24 | | 6 |
| **Forwards:** | **DOB** | **M** | **(s)** | **G** |
| Carl Björk (SWE) | 19.01.2000 | | (3) | |
| Marko Divković (CRO) | 11.06.1999 | 6 | (5) | |
| Simon Hedlund (SWE) | 11.03.1993 | 19 | (6) | 2 |
| Mathias Kvistgaarden | 15.04.2002 | 15 | (15) | 7 |
| Anthony Ohikhuaeme Omoijuanfo (NOR) | 10.01.1994 | 24 | | 13 |
| Yousef Salech | 17.01.2002 | | (4) | |
| Oscar Schwartau | 17.05.2006 | 6 | (12) | 4 |

## Football Club København

**Founded**: 01.07.1992
**Stadium**: Parken Stadion, København (38,065)
**Trainer**: Jess Thorup 21.02.1970
[20.09.2022] Jacob Neestrup 08.03.1988

| Goalkeepers: | DOB | M | (s) | G |
|---|---|---|---|---|
| Kamil Grabara (POL) | 08.01.1999 | 23 | | |
| Kalle Johnsson (SWE) | 28.01.1990 | 3 | (1) | |
| Mathew David Ryan (AUS) | 08.04.1992 | 6 | | |
| **Defenders:** | **DOB** | **M** | **(s)** | **G** |
| Peter Ankersen | 22.09.1990 | 9 | (3) | |
| Nicolai Boilesen | 16.02.1992 | 5 | (3) | |
| Kevin Diks (NED) | 06.10.1996 | 14 | (10) | 1 |
| Elias Jelert | 12.06.2003 | 21 | (5) | 1 |
| Davit Khocholava (GEO) | 08.02.1993 | 17 | | 1 |
| Victor Bernth Kristiansen | 16.12.2002 | 13 | (2) | 1 |
| Valdemar Lund Jensen | 28.05.2003 | 14 | (5) | 1 |
| Christian Sørensen | 06.08.1992 | 10 | (7) | 2 |
| Denis Vavro (SVK) | 10.04.1996 | 27 | (2) | 1 |
| **Midfielders:** | **DOB** | **M** | **(s)** | **G** |
| Victor Johan Anton Claesson (SWE) | 02.01.1992 | 30 | | 13 |
| Ísak Bergmann Jóhannesson (ISL) | 23.03.2003 | 8 | (14) | 1 |
| William Clem | 20.06.2004 | 11 | (6) | |
| Hákon Haraldsson (ISL) | 10.04.2003 | 26 | (3) | 4 |
| Lukas Lerager | 12.07.1993 | 24 | (6) | 6 |
| Paul Mukairu (NGA) | 18.01.2000 | | (5) | |
| *Pep Biel* Mas Jaume (ESP) | 05.09.1996 | 7 | | 6 |
| Marko Seufatu Nikola Stamenić (NZL) | 19.02.2002 | 8 | (7) | |
| José Carlos Gonçalves Rodrigues Zeca"(GRE) | 31.08.1988 | 4 | (3) | |
| **Forwards:** | **DOB** | **M** | **(s)** | **G** |
| Akinkunmi Ayobami Amoo (NGA) | 07.06.2002 | | (2) | |
| Khouma Babacar (SEN) | 17.03.1993 | | (3) | |
| Roony Bardghji (SWE) | 15.11.2005 | 4 | (15) | 3 |
| William Bøving | 01.03.2003 | 1 | (2) | |
| Andreas Evald Cornelius | 16.03.1993 | 4 | (7) | |
| Mohamed Daramy | 07.01.2002 | 26 | (2) | 8 |
| *Diogo* António Cupido *Gonçalves* (POR) | 06.02.1997 | 11 | (3) | 5 |
| Rasmus Falk | 15.01.1992 | 19 | (8) | 1 |
| Mamoudou Karamoko (FRA) | 08.09.1999 | 2 | (3) | |
| Jordan Larsson (SWE) | 20.06.1997 | 5 | (7) | 4 |
| Orri Steinn Óskarsson (ISL) | 29.08.2004 | | (4) | |

## Alliance Club Horsens

**Founded**: 1994
**Stadium**: CASA Arena, Horsens (10,400)
**Trainer**: Jens Berthel Askou 19.08.1982

| Goalkeepers: | DOB | M | (s) | G |
|---|---|---|---|---|
| Markus Bobjerg | 26.01.1998 | 2 | (1) | |
| Samuel Brolin (SWE) | 29.09.2000 | 3 | | |
| Matej Delač (CRO) | 20.08.1992 | 27 | | |
| **Defenders:** | **DOB** | **M** | **(s)** | **G** |
| Jacob Buus Jacobsen | 07.03.1997 | 7 | (4) | |
| James Gomez (GAM) | 14.11.2001 | 26 | (2) | 1 |
| Magnus Jensen | 27.10.1996 | 24 | (1) | 4 |
| Malte Kiilerich | 16.10.1995 | 30 | | |
| Mikkel Lassen | 19.06.2001 | 13 | (9) | 1 |
| Alexander Ludwig | 30.06.1993 | 11 | (2) | |
| **Midfielders:** | **DOB** | **M** | **(s)** | **G** |
| Janus Drachmann | 11.05.1988 | 14 | (12) | |
| Jonas Gemmer | 31.01.1996 | 11 | (18) | 1 |
| Marcus Hannesbo | 11.05.2002 | 1 | (9) | |
| David Kruse | 15.05.2002 | 25 | (6) | |
| Lubambo Musonda (ZAM) | 01.03.1995 | 27 | (3) | 3 |
| Moses Opondo (UGA) | 28.10.1997 | 30 | (1) | 2 |
| Thomas Santos | 10.10.1998 | 28 | (2) | 4 |
| Hjalte Toftegaard | 25.06.2006 | | (1) | |
| **Forwards:** | **DOB** | **M** | **(s)** | **G** |
| Jashar Beluli (ALB) | 07.06.2004 | | (2) | |
| Samson Iyede (NGA) | 28.01.1998 | 4 | (14) | |
| Anders Jacobsen | 27.10.1989 | 30 | (1) | 7 |
| Elijah Henry Just (NZL) | 01.05.2000 | 8 | (19) | |
| Simon Makienok | 21.11.1990 | 4 | (11) | 1 |
| Lirim Qamili (ALB) | 04.06.1998 | | (7) | |
| Aron Sigurðarson (ISL) | 08.10.1993 | 24 | (7) | 7 |
| Casper Tengstedt | 01.06.2000 | 3 | | |

## Lyngby Boldklub

**Founded**: 1921
**Stadium**: Lyngby Stadion, Lyngby (8,000)
**Trainer**: Freyr Alexandersson (ISL) 18.11.1982

| Goalkeepers: | DOB | M | (s) | G |
|---|---|---|---|---|
| Frederik Ibsen | 28.03.1997 | 6 | | |
| Mads Kikkenborg | 07.10.1999 | 26 | | |
| **Defenders:** | **DOB** | **M** | **(s)** | **G** |
| Andreas Bjelland | 11.07.1988 | 17 | (1) | |
| Kolbeinn Finnsson (ISL) | 25.08.1999 | 13 | (2) | 1 |
| Pascal Gregor | 18.02.1994 | 27 | (2) | |
| Brian Hämäläinen | 29.05.1989 | 13 | (13) | |
| Lucas Hey | 13.04.2003 | 21 | (3) | |
| Kasper Poul Mølgaard Jørgensen | 07.11.1999 | 17 | | 4 |
| Mikkel Juhl | 20.01.2000 | | (1) | |
| Willy Kumado (GHA) | 02.12.2002 | 6 | (3) | |
| Timo Letschert (NED) | 25.05.1993 | 4 | (1) | |
| Gustav Mortensen | 19.03.2004 | | (3) | |
| Kristian Riis | 17.02.1997 | 5 | (4) | 1 |
| Adam Sørensen | 11.11.2000 | 16 | | |
| **Midfielders:** | **DOB** | **M** | **(s)** | **G** |
| Parfait Bizoza (BDI) | 03.03.1999 | 1 | (7) | |
| Tochi Chukwuani | 24.03.2003 | 19 | (4) | 1 |
| Rezan Çorlu | 07.08.1997 | 13 | (13) | 2 |
| Magnus Kaastrup Refstrup Lauritsen | 28.12.2000 | 10 | (9) | |
| Sanders Ngabo | 04.07.2004 | | (8) | |
| Marcel Rømer | 08.08.1991 | 26 | (5) | 1 |
| Tobias Storm | 04.07.2004 | 8 | (7) | |
| Magnus Hee Westergaard | 27.05.1998 | 13 | (2) | |
| Casper Winther | 11.02.2003 | 14 | (13) | |
| **Forwards:** | **DOB** | **M** | **(s)** | **G** |
| Alfreð Finnbogason (ISL) | 01.02.1989 | 10 | (3) | 3 |
| Frederik Gytkjær | 16.03.1993 | 20 | (3) | 5 |
| Petur Knudsen (FRO) | 21.04.1998 | 5 | (3) | 2 |
| Sebastian Koch | 11.10.1996 | | (5) | |
| Mathias Kristensen | 24.06.1993 | 10 | (15) | 2 |
| Sævar Atli Magnússon (ISL) | 16.06.2000 | 20 | (8) | 6 |
| Lasse Emil Nielsen | 08.11.1993 | 7 | (2) | 2 |
| Rasmus Thellufsen Pedersen | 09.01.1997 | 5 | (4) | |

## Football Club Midtjylland Herning

| | | | |
|---|---|---|---|
| **Founded**: | 02.02.1999 | | |
| **Stadium**: | MCH Arena, Herning (11,800) | | |
| **Trainer**: | Bo Henriksen | | 07.02.1975 |
| [28.07.2022] | Henrik Jensen | | 11.01.1985 |
| [24.08.2022] | Albert Capellas Herms (ESP) | | 01.10.1967 |
| [23.03.2023] | Thomas Thomasberg | | 15.10.1974 |

| Goalkeepers: | DOB | M | (s) | G |
|---|---|---|---|---|
| Jonas Lössl | 01.02.1989 | 24 | | |
| Elías Ólafsson (ISL) | 11.03.2000 | 8 | | |
| **Defenders:** | **DOB** | **M** | **(s)** | **G** |
| Joel Andersson (SWE) | 11.11.1996 | 15 | (1) | |
| Victor Bak | 03.10.2003 | 4 | (7) | |
| Henrik Dalsgaard | 27.07.1989 | 22 | (2) | 1 |
| Nikolas Dyhr | 18.06.2001 | 8 | (5) | 1 |
| Stefan Gartenmann | 02.02.1997 | 17 | (8) | 3 |
| José Carlos Ferreira Júnior „Juninho" (BRA) | 01.02.1995 | 19 | (6) | 1 |
| Paulo Victor da Silva „Paulinho" (BRA) | 03.01.1995 | 18 | (10) | 1 |
| Erik Sviatchenko | 04.10.1991 | 15 | (1) | |
| Pontus Texel | 27.02.2004 | | (1) | |
| Mads Thychosen | 27.06.1997 | 15 | (9) | |
| **Midfielders:** | **DOB** | **M** | **(s)** | **G** |
| Valdemar Byskov | 25.01.2005 | | (5) | |
| *Charles* Rigon Matos (BRA) | 19.06.1996 | 3 | (16) | |
| *Evander* Da Silva Ferreira (BRA) | 09.06.1998 | 10 | | 4 |
| Armin Gigović (SWE) | 06.04.2002 | 12 | (3) | |
| Banhourin Chris Emmanuel Kouakou (CIV) | 15.12.1999 | | (1) | |
| Emiliano Martínez Toranza (URU) | 17.08.1999 | 23 | (1) | |
| Jamiu Musbaudeen (NGA) | 09.07.2004 | | (1) | |
| Kristoffer Olsson (SWE) | 30.06.1995 | 23 | | 5 |
| Raphael Onyedika Nwadike (NGA) | 19.04.2001 | 6 | | |
| Oliver Sørensen | 10.03.2002 | 20 | (6) | 1 |
| **Forwards:** | **DOB** | **M** | **(s)** | **G** |
| Emam Ashour Metwally Abdelghany (EGY) | 20.02.1998 | 4 | (1) | 1 |
| Edward Chilufya (ZAM) | 17.09.1999 | 4 | (22) | 1 |
| Anders Dreyer | 02.05.1998 | 15 | (1) | 8 |
| Frederik Heiselberg | 11.02.2003 | 3 | (7) | 1 |
| Gustav Isaksen | 19.04.2001 | 29 | (2) | 18 |
| José Francisco dos Santos *Júnior „Brumado"* (BRA) | 15.05.1999 | 4 | (7) | |
| Sory Kaba (GUI) | 28.07.1995 | 12 | (4) | 2 |
| Victor Lind | 12.07.2003 | 1 | (2) | |
| Astrit Selmani (KOS) | 13.05.1997 | 1 | (2) | |
| Aral Şimşir | 19.06.2002 | 8 | (7) | 2 |
| Pione Sisto Ifolo Emirmija | 04.02.1995 | 9 | (3) | 3 |

## Football Club Nordsjælland Farum

| | | | |
|---|---|---|---|
| **Founded**: | 01.07.2003 | | |
| **Stadium**: | Right to Dream Park, Farum (9,900) | | |
| **Trainer**: | Flemming Pedersen | | 30.06.1963 |
| [07.01.2023] | Johannes Hoff Thorup | | 19.02.1989 |

| Goalkeepers: | DOB | M | (s) | G |
|---|---|---|---|---|
| Andreas Hansen | 11.08.1995 | 32 | | |
| **Defenders:** | **DOB** | **M** | **(s)** | **G** |
| Kaare Barslund | 23.03.2004 | | (1) | |
| Martin Frese | 04.01.1998 | 24 | (2) | 2 |
| Kian Hansen | 03.03.1989 | 31 | | |
| Lucas Høgsberg | 23.06.2006 | | (1) | |
| Jonas Jensen-Abbew | 20.04.2002 | | (3) | |
| Ulrik Yttergård Jenssen (NOR) | 17.07.1996 | 1 | (1) | |
| Erik Marxen | 02.12.1990 | 3 | (16) | |
| Adamo Nagalo (BFA) | 22.09.2002 | 28 | | 1 |
| Daniel Svensson (SWE) | 12.02.2002 | 17 | (12) | 2 |
| Oliver Villadsen | 16.11.2001 | 31 | | |
| Leo Walta (FIN) | 24.06.2003 | | (5) | |
| **Midfielders:** | **DOB** | **M** | **(s)** | **G** |
| Rocco Ascone (FRA) | 12.09.2003 | 5 | (7) | 2 |
| Mads Bidstrup | 25.02.2001 | 30 | | |
| Jacob Christensen | 25.06.2001 | 30 | | |
| Lasso Coulibaly (CIV) | 19.10.2002 | 4 | (16) | 2 |
| Mohammed Diomandé (CIV) | 30.10.2001 | 30 | (2) | 5 |
| Mario Dorgeles (CIV) | 07.08.2004 | 4 | (11) | |
| Emiliano Marcondes | 09.03.1995 | 5 | (3) | 3 |
| Magnus Munck | 05.01.2005 | | (1) | |
| **Forwards:** | **DOB** | **M** | **(s)** | **G** |
| Oliver Antman (FIN) | 15.08.2001 | 4 | (12) | 2 |
| Wahid Faghir | 29.07.2003 | 6 | (10) | 4 |
| Mads Hansen | 28.07.2002 | 14 | (12) | 2 |
| Conrad Harder | 07.04.2005 | | (1) | |
| Ernest Nuamah (GHA) | 01.11.2003 | 30 | | 12 |
| Benjamin Nygren (SWE) | 08.07.2001 | 5 | (20) | 3 |
| Ibrahim Osman (GHA) | 14.12.2004 | 2 | (4) | |
| Andreas Schjelderup (NOR) | 01.06.2004 | 16 | (1) | 10 |

## Odense Boldklub

| | | | |
|---|---|---|---|
| **Founded**: | 12.07.1887 | | |
| **Stadium**: | Nature Energy Park, Odense (15,633) | | |
| **Trainer**: | Gert Andreas Alm (SWE) | | 19.06.1973 |

| Goalkeepers: | DOB | M | (s) | G |
|---|---|---|---|---|
| Hans Christian Bernat | 13.11.2000 | 7 | | |
| Martin Hansen | 15.06.1990 | 25 | | |
| **Defenders:** | **DOB** | **M** | **(s)** | **G** |
| Aske Adelgaard | 10.11.2003 | 16 | (6) | |
| Gustav Grubbe | 27.01.2003 | 19 | (8) | |
| Mihajlo Ivančević (SRB) | 07.04.1999 | 15 | | |
| Omar Jebali (TUN) | 19.02.2000 | | (1) | |
| Joel Bruce King (AUS) | 30.10.2000 | 3 | (3) | |
| Kasper Larsen | 25.01.1993 | 3 | (1) | |
| Look Saa Nicholas Kengkhetkid Mickelson (THA) | 24.07.1999 | 13 | (4) | |
| Bjørn Paulsen | 02.07.1991 | 25 | (1) | 1 |
| Jørgen Skjelvik (NOR) | 05.07.1991 | 23 | (4) | |
| Tobias Slotsager | 01.01.2006 | 10 | (2) | |
| Jeppe Tverskov | 12.03.1993 | 30 | | 2 |
| Robin Østrøm (NOR) | 09.08.2002 | 1 | | 1 |
| **Midfielders:** | **DOB** | **M** | **(s)** | **G** |
| Max Ejdum | 15.10.2004 | | (2) | |
| Mads Frøkjær-Jensen | 29.07.1999 | 26 | (2) | 8 |
| Armin Gigović (SWE) | 06.04.2002 | 9 | | 1 |
| Markus Jensen | 15.07.2005 | | (1) | |
| Noah Lassen | 13.01.2007 | | (1) | |
| Alasana Manneh (GAM) | 08.04.1998 | 15 | (3) | 1 |
| Alen Mustafić (BIH) | 05.07.1999 | 3 | (3) | 1 |
| Ayo Simon Okosun | 21.07.1993 | 3 | (2) | |
| Naatan Skyttä (FIN) | 07.05.2002 | 4 | (4) | 2 |
| Aron Þrándarson (ISL) | 10.11.1994 | 6 | (20) | 1 |
| **Forwards:** | **DOB** | **M** | **(s)** | **G** |
| Jakob Breum | 17.11.2003 | 8 | (13) | |
| Max Fenger | 07.08.2001 | 1 | (4) | |
| Issam Jebali (TUN) | 25.12.1991 | 13 | | 4 |
| Bashkim Kadrii | 09.07.1991 | 18 | (7) | 8 |
| Luca Kjerrumgaard | 09.02.2003 | | (4) | |
| Yankuba Minteh (GAM) | 22.07.2004 | 15 | (2) | 4 |
| Agon Muçolli (ALB) | 26.09.1998 | | (10) | |
| Charly Ngos Nouck Horneman | 21.03.2004 | 5 | (12) | 2 |
| Emmanuel Sabbi (USA) | 24.12.1997 | 15 | (4) | 8 |
| Sander Svendsen (NOR) | 06.08.1997 | 7 | | |
| Franco Tongya (ITA) | 13.03.2002 | 14 | (7) | 2 |
| Kenneth Zohoré | 31.01.1994 | | (4) | |

## Randers Football Club

| Founded: | 01.01.2003 | |
|---|---|---|
| Stadium: | Cepheus Park, Randers (12,000) | |
| Trainer: | Thomas Thomasberg | 15.10.1974 |
| [23.03.2023] | Rasmus Bertelsen | 21.12.1983 |

| Goalkeepers: | DOB | M | (s) | G |
|---|---|---|---|---|
| Patrik Carlgren (SWE) | 08.01.1992 | 31 | | |
| Alexander Nybo | 12.04.1995 | 1 | | |
| Aleksander Stanković | 25.05.1995 | | (1) | |
| **Defenders:** | **DOB** | **M** | **(s)** | **G** |
| Adam Andersson (SWE) | 11.11.1996 | 19 | (7) | 1 |
| Hugo Andersson (SWE) | 01.01.1999 | 22 | (4) | 3 |
| Oliver Bundgaard | 15.06.2001 | 2 | (1) | |
| Simon Graves | 22.05.1999 | 14 | (2) | 1 |
| Sabil Hansen | 14.11.2005 | | (1) | |
| Daniel Høegh | 06.01.1991 | 14 | (4) | 2 |
| Carl Johansson (SWE) | 23.05.1994 | 13 | | 1 |
| William Kaastrup | 21.03.2004 | 3 | (1) | |
| Mikkel Kallesøe | 20.04.1997 | 13 | (1) | |
| Björn Kopplin (GER) | 07.01.1991 | 27 | (3) | 2 |
| Jeppe Kudsk | 25.02.2003 | 2 | | |
| Jesper Lauridsen | 27.03.1991 | | (1) | |

| Midfielders: | DOB | M | (s) | G |
|---|---|---|---|---|
| Jakob Ankersen | 22.09.1990 | 17 | (12) | 3 |
| Lasse Berg Johnsen (NOR) | 18.08.1999 | 32 | | 1 |
| Mads Enggård | 20.01.2004 | 14 | (2) | 2 |
| Tosin Kehinde (NGA) | 18.06.1998 | 16 | (7) | 1 |
| Frederik Lauenborg | 18.05.1997 | 16 | | 1 |
| Mikkel Pedersen | 07.01.1996 | 6 | (18) | |
| **Forwards:** | **DOB** | **M** | **(s)** | **G** |
| Edgar Babayan (ARM) | 28.10.1995 | 7 | (16) | 2 |
| Nicolai Brock-Madsen | 09.01.1993 | 2 | (2) | |
| Filip Bundgaard | 03.07.2004 | 20 | (11) | 4 |
| Marvin Egho (AUT) | 09.05.1994 | 20 | (8) | 6 |
| Oliver Bjerrum Jensen | 30.04.2002 | | (1) | |
| Alhaji Kamara (SLE) | 16.04.1994 | 2 | (18) | 2 |
| Tobias Klysner | 03.07.2001 | 12 | (16) | 1 |
| Simen Nordli (NOR) | 25.12.1999 | 10 | (4) | 2 |
| Stephen Pius Odey (NGA) | 15.01.1998 | 17 | (12) | 4 |
| Mustapha Ubandoma (NGA) | 23.07.2004 | | (2) | |

## Silkeborg Idrætsforening

| Founded: | 26.04.1917 | |
|---|---|---|
| Stadium: | JYSK Park, Silkeborg (10,000) | |
| Trainer: | Kent Nielsen | 28.12.1961 |

| Goalkeepers: | DOB | M | (s) | G |
|---|---|---|---|---|
| Aske Andrésen | 12.07.2005 | | (1) | |
| Nicolai Larsen | 09.03.1991 | 32 | | |
| **Defenders:** | **DOB** | **M** | **(s)** | **G** |
| Alexander Busch | 25.07.2003 | 11 | | 1 |
| André Jack Calisir (ARM) | 13.06.1990 | 4 | | |
| Rasmus Carstensen | 10.11.2000 | 3 | | |
| Lukas Engel | 14.12.1998 | 25 | | 1 |
| Joel Felix | 13.01.1998 | 19 | (1) | |
| Lukas Klitten | 01.05.2000 | 4 | (5) | |
| Tobias Salquist | 18.05.1995 | 30 | | 2 |
| Oliver Sonne | 10.11.2000 | 27 | (2) | 4 |
| Robin Østrøm (NOR) | 09.08.2002 | 6 | (5) | |
| **Midfielders:** | **DOB** | **M** | **(s)** | **G** |
| Mark Brink | 15.03.1998 | 28 | (1) | |
| Anders Dahl | 01.05.2002 | | (3) | |
| Robert Gojani (SWE) | 19.10.1992 | 3 | (6) | |

| | DOB | M | (s) | G |
|---|---|---|---|---|
| Mads Kaalund | 16.08.1996 | 5 | (12) | |
| Anders Klynge | 14.10.2000 | 28 | (1) | 1 |
| Pelle Mattsson | 04.08.2001 | 9 | (15) | 1 |
| Andreas Oggesen | 18.03.1994 | 1 | (15) | 1 |
| Oskar Adam Rudkjøbing Boesen (ESP) | 05.05.2005 | | (3) | |
| Nicolai Vallys | 04.09.1996 | 6 | | 2 |
| Lasse Vigen | 15.08.1994 | 6 | (8) | |
| Stefán Teitur Þórðarson (ISL) | 16.10.1998 | 21 | (6) | 1 |
| **Forwards:** | **DOB** | **M** | **(s)** | **G** |
| Tonni Adamsen | 15.11.1994 | 19 | (9) | 10 |
| Asbjørn Bøndergaard | 05.05.2004 | | (2) | |
| Frederik Carstensen | 09.04.2002 | | (2) | |
| Nicklas Helenius Jensen | 08.05.1991 | 13 | (4) | 5 |
| Sebastian Jørgensen | 08.06.2000 | 25 | (3) | 6 |
| Kasper Kusk | 10.11.1991 | 15 | (9) | 2 |
| Alexander Lind Rasmussen | 26.06.2002 | | (11) | 2 |
| Søren Tengstedt | 30.06.2000 | 12 | (16) | 3 |

## Viborg Fodsports Forening

| Founded: | 01.04.1896 | |
|---|---|---|
| Stadium: | Energi Viborg Arena, Viborg (9,566) | |
| Trainer: | Jacob Friis | 11.12.1976 |

| Goalkeepers: | DOB | M | (s) | G |
|---|---|---|---|---|
| Lucas Lund Pedersen | 19.03.2000 | 32 | | |
| **Defenders:** | **DOB** | **M** | **(s)** | **G** |
| Martin Agnarsson (FRO) | 07.12.2003 | | (1) | |
| Daniel Anyembe | 22.07.1998 | 20 | (2) | |
| Oliver Bundgaard | 15.06.2001 | 16 | (5) | 1 |
| Nicolas Bürgy (SUI) | 07.08.1995 | 28 | | 1 |
| Anton Gaaei | 19.11.2002 | 26 | (1) | |
| Viktor Hjorth | 24.02.2005 | | (1) | |
| Mads Lauritsen | 14.04.1993 | 3 | (2) | 1 |
| Christian Sørensen | 06.08.1992 | 7 | | 2 |
| Jonas Søndberg Thorsen | 19.04.1990 | | (3) | |
| Žan Zaletel (SVN) | 16.09.1999 | 25 | (1) | |
| **Midfielders:** | **DOB** | **M** | **(s)** | **G** |
| Sofus Berger | 02.06.2003 | | (12) | |
| Jakob Bonde | 29.12.1993 | 29 | (2) | 3 |
| Jay-Roy Grot (NED) | 13.03.1998 | 17 | | 9 |

| | DOB | M | (s) | G |
|---|---|---|---|---|
| Jeppe Grønning | 24.05.1991 | 30 | | 1 |
| Clint Leemans (NED) | 15.09.1995 | 30 | (2) | 6 |
| Justin Lonwijk (NED) | 21.12.1999 | 8 | (1) | 2 |
| Mads Søndergaard | 26.12.2002 | 6 | (20) | |
| Jakob Vester | 01.12.2004 | 1 | (4) | |
| Magnus Westergaard | 27.05.1998 | 4 | (11) | 1 |
| Jan Žambůrek (CZE) | 13.02.2001 | 4 | (15) | 1 |
| **Forwards:** | **DOB** | **M** | **(s)** | **G** |
| Elias Achouri (TUN) | 10.02.1999 | 15 | (9) | 6 |
| Tobias Bech | 19.02.2002 | | (3) | 2 |
| Alassana Jatta (GAM) | 12.01.1999 | 7 | (13) | 2 |
| Marokhy Ndione (SEN) | 04.11.1999 | 2 | (3) | |
| *Nils Mortimer* Moreno (ESP) | 11.06.2001 | 5 | (16) | 1 |
| Paulo Rafael Pereira Araújo „Paulinho" (POR) | 21.09.1999 | 1 | (9) | 1 |
| *Renato* Barbosa dos Santos *Júnior* (BRA) | 05.06.2002 | 8 | (5) | |
| Ibrahim Muhammad Said (NGA) | 15.06.2002 | 28 | (3) | 4 |

## SECOND LEVEL
### 1. division - NordicBet Liga 2022/2023

### Regular Season

| | | | | | | | | | |
|---|---|---|---|---|---|---|---|---|---|
| 1. | Vejle Boldklub | 22 | 16 | 2 | 4 | 47 | - | 20 | 50 |
| 2. | Hvidovre IF | 22 | 13 | 5 | 4 | 50 | - | 28 | 44 |
| 3. | FC Helsingør | 22 | 12 | 1 | 9 | 32 | - | 35 | 37 |
| 4. | Sønderjysk Elitesport | 22 | 10 | 5 | 7 | 41 | - | 29 | 35 |
| 5. | Vendsyssel FF Hjørring | 22 | 10 | 3 | 9 | 35 | - | 31 | 33 |
| 6. | Næstved BK | 22 | 8 | 8 | 6 | 32 | - | 26 | 32 |
| 7. | Hillerød Fodbold | 22 | 9 | 4 | 9 | 29 | - | 35 | 31 |
| 8. | HB Køge | 22 | 7 | 4 | 11 | 29 | - | 33 | 25 |
| 9. | Hobro IK | 22 | 5 | 8 | 9 | 19 | - | 30 | 23 |
| 10. | BK Fremad Amager | 22 | 7 | 2 | 13 | 25 | - | 42 | 23 |
| 11. | FC Fredericia | 22 | 6 | 3 | 13 | 29 | - | 40 | 21 |
| 12. | Nykøbing FC | 22 | 4 | 5 | 13 | 26 | - | 44 | 17 |

Team ranked 1-6 were qualified for the Promotion Group, while teams ranked 7-12 were qualified for the Relegation Group.

### Promotion Group

| | | | | | | | | | |
|---|---|---|---|---|---|---|---|---|---|
| 1. | Vejle Boldklub (*Promoted*) | 32 | 20 | 7 | 5 | 61 | - | 30 | 67 |
| 2. | Hvidovre IF (*Promoted*) | 32 | 17 | 7 | 8 | 65 | - | 41 | 58 |
| 3. | Sønderjysk Elitesport | 32 | 16 | 8 | 8 | 60 | - | 45 | 56 |
| 4. | Vendsyssel FF Hjørring | 32 | 13 | 7 | 12 | 48 | - | 43 | 46 |
| 5. | Næstved BK | 32 | 11 | 10 | 11 | 50 | - | 48 | 43 |
| 6. | FC Helsingør | 32 | 13 | 3 | 16 | 47 | - | 54 | 42 |

### Relegation Group

| | | | | | | | | | |
|---|---|---|---|---|---|---|---|---|---|
| 7. | FC Fredericia | 32 | 13 | 6 | 13 | 56 | - | 48 | 45 |
| 8. | HB Køge | 32 | 13 | 5 | 14 | 50 | - | 51 | 44 |
| 9. | Hillerød Fodbold | 32 | 12 | 5 | 15 | 37 | - | 51 | 41 |
| 10. | Hobro IK | 32 | 9 | 11 | 12 | 33 | - | 42 | 38 |
| 11. | BK Fremad Amager (*Relegated*) | 32 | 10 | 4 | 18 | 38 | - | 60 | 34 |
| 12. | Nykøbing FC (*Relegated*) | 32 | 6 | 5 | 21 | 43 | - | 73 | 23 |

## INTERNATIONAL MATCHES
### (16.07.2022 – 15.07.2023)

| 22.09.2022 | Zagreb | *Croatia - Denmark* | *2-1(0-0)* | (UNL) |
|---|---|---|---|---|
| 25.09.2022 | København | *Denmark - France* | *2-0(2-0)* | (UNL) |
| 22.11.2022 | Al rayyan | *Denmark - Tunisia* | *0-0* | (WC) |
| 26.11.2022 | Doha | *France - Denmark* | *2-1(0-0)* | (WC) |
| 30.11.2022 | Al Wakrah | *Australia - Denmark* | *1-0(0-0)* | (WC) |
| | | | | |
| 23.03.2023 | København | *Denmark - Finland* | *3-1(1-0)* | (ECQ) |
| 26.03.2023 | Astana | *Kazakhstan - Denmark* | *3-2(0-2)* | (ECQ) |
| 16.06.2023 | København | *Denmark - Northern Ireland* | *1-0(0-0)* | (ECQ) |
| 19.06.2023 | Ljubljana | *Slovenia - Denmark* | *1-1(1-1)* | (ECQ) |

**22.09.2022  CROATIA - DENMARK**  **2-1(0-0)**  3rd UEFA Nations League A, Group 1
Stadion Maksimir, Zagreb; Referee: Davide Massa (Italy); Attendance: 22,715
**DEN:** Kasper Peter Schmeichel, Joachim Christian Andersen, Andreas Bødtker Christensen, Simon Thorup Kjær (Cap) (72.Mathias Jensen), Daniel Wass (60.Rasmus Nissen Kristensen), Thomas Joseph Delaney (60.Rasmus Winther Højlund), Pierre-Emile Kordt Højbjerg, Joakim Mæhle Pedersen, Christian Dannemann Eriksen, Andreas Skov Olsen (89.Kasper Dolberg Rasmussen), Martin Braithwaite Christensen (59.Mikkel Krogh Damsgaard). Trainer: Kasper Hjulmand.
**Goal:** Christian Dannemann Eriksen (77).

**25.09.2022  DENMARK - FRANCE**  **2-0(2-0)**  3rd UEFA Nations League A, Group 1
Parken Stadium, København; Referee: István Kovács (Romania); Attendance: 36,064
**DEN:** Kasper Peter Schmeichel (Cap), Rasmus Nissen Kristensen (90+1.Alexander Hartmann Bah), Andreas Bødtker Christensen, Joachim Christian Andersen, Joakim Mæhle Pedersen, Pierre-Emile Kordt Højbjerg, Thomas Joseph Delaney (71.Simon Thorup Kjær), Christian Dannemann Eriksen, Andreas Skov Olsen (71.Martin Braithwaite Christensen), Mikkel Krogh Damsgaard (59.Jesper Grænge Lindstrøm), Kasper Dolberg Rasmussen (59.Rasmus Winther Højlund). Trainer: Kasper Hjulmand.
**Goals:** Kasper Dolberg Rasmussen (34), Andreas Skov Olsen (39).

**22.11.2022  DENMARK - TUNISIA**  **0-0**  22nd FIFA WC. Group Stage.
Education City Stadium, Al Rayyan (Qatar); Referee: César Arturo Ramos Palazuelos (Mexico); Attendance: 42,925
**DEN:** Kasper Peter Schmeichel, Joachim Christian Andersen, Simon Thorup Kjær (Cap) (65.Mathias Jensen), Andreas Bødtker Christensen, Rasmus Nissen Kristensen, Pierre-Emile Kordt Højbjerg, Thomas Joseph Delaney (45+1.Mikkel Krogh Damsgaard), Christian Dannemann Eriksen, Joakim Mæhle Pedersen, Andreas Skov Olsen (65.Jesper Grænge Lindstrøm), Kasper Dolberg Rasmussen (65.Andreas Evald Cornelius). Trainer: Kasper Hjulmand.

**26.11.2022  FRANCE - DENMARK**  **2-1(0-0)**  22nd FIFA WC. Group Stage.
Stadium 974, Doha (Qatar); Referee: Szymon Marciniak (Poland); Attendance: 42,860
**DEN:** Kasper Peter Schmeichel (Cap), Joachim Christian Andersen, Andreas Bødtker Christensen, Victor Enok Nelsson, Rasmus Nissen Kristensen (90+2.Alexander Hartmann Bah), Pierre-Emile Kordt Højbjerg, Christian Dannemann Eriksen, Joakim Mæhle Pedersen, Jesper Grænge Lindstrøm (85.Christian Thers Nørgaard), Andreas Evald Cornelius (46. Martin Braithwaite Christensen), Mikkel Krogh Damsgaard (73.Kasper Dolberg Rasmussen). Trainer: Kasper Hjulmand.
**Goal:** Andreas Bødtker Christensen (68).

**30.11.2022  AUSTRALIA - DENMARK**  **1-0(0-0)**  22nd FIFA WC. Group Stage.
Al Janoub Stadium, Al Wakrah (Qatar); Referee: Mustapha Ghorbal (Algeria); Attendance: 41,232
**DEN:** Kasper Peter Schmeichel, Rasmus Nissen Kristensen (46.Alexander Hartmann Bah), Joachim Christian Andersen, Andreas Bødtker Christensen, Joakim Mæhle Pedersen (69.Andreas Evald Cornelius), Pierre-Emile Kordt Højbjerg, Mathias Jensen (59. Mikkel Krogh Damsgaard), Andreas Skov Olsen (69.Robert Skov), Christian Dannemann Eriksen (Cap), Jesper Grænge Lindstrøm, Martin Braithwaite Christensen (59.Kasper Dolberg Rasmussen). Trainer: Kasper Hjulmand.

**23.03.2023  DENMARK - FINLAND**  **3-1(1-0)**  17th EC. Qualifiers
Parken Stadium, København; Referee: Daniel Siebert (Germany); Attendance: 35,851
**DEN:** Kasper Peter Schmeichel, Alexander Hartmann Bah, Simon Thorup Kjær (Cap), Andreas Bødtker Christensen (18.Victor Enok Nelsson), Joakim Mæhle Pedersen (65.Jens Stryger Larsen), Christian Thers Nørgaard, Pierre-Emile Kordt Højbjerg, Mathias Jensen (77.Philip Anyanwu Billing), Mikkel Krogh Damsgaard (65.Mohammed Daramy), Martin Braithwaite Christensen (77.Jonas Wind), Rasmus Winther Højlund. Trainer: Kasper Hjulmand.
**Goals:** Rasmus Winther Højlund (21, 82, 90+3).

**26.03.2023  KAZAKHSTAN - DENMARK**  **3-2(0-2)**  17th EC. Qualifiers
Astana Arena, Astana; Referee: Novak Simović (Serbia); Attendance: 28,697
**DEN:** Kasper Peter Schmeichel, Alexander Hartmann Bah (65.Jens Stryger Larsen), Simon Thorup Kjær (Cap), Victor Enok Nelsson, Joakim Mæhle Pedersen (83.Rasmus Nissen Kristensen), Christian Thers Nørgaard, Mathias Jensen (65.Philip Anyanwu Billing), Pierre-Emile Kordt Højbjerg, Jonas Wind (87.Martin Braithwaite Christensen), Mikkel Krogh Damsgaard (65.Mohammed Daramy), Rasmus Winther Højlund. Trainer: Kasper Hjulmand.
**Goals:** Rasmus Winther Højlund (21, 36).

**16.06.2023  DENMARK - NORTHERN IRELAND**  **1-0(0-0)**  17th EC. Qualifiers
Parken Stadium, København; Referee: Daniel Stefański (Poland); Attendance: 35,701
**DEN:** Kasper Peter Schmeichel, Joachim Christian Andersen, Simon Thorup Kjær (Cap), Andreas Bødtker Christensen, Joakim Mæhle Pedersen (73.Jens Stryger Larsen), Pierre-Emile Kordt Højbjerg, Christian Dannemann Eriksen, Andreas Skov Olsen (80.Jesper Grænge Lindstrøm), Jonas Wind (80.Rasmus Nissen Kristensen), Martin Braithwaite Christensen (73.Mikkel Krogh Damsgaard), Rasmus Winther Højlund (90+2.Mohammed Daramy). Trainer: Kasper Hjulmand.
**Goal:** Jonas Wind (47).

**19.06.2023 SLOVENIA - DENMARK 1-1(1-1)** 17th EC. Qualifiers

Stadion Stožice, Ljubljana; Referee: François Letexier (France); Attendance: 14,382

**DEN:** Kasper Peter Schmeichel, Alexander Hartmann Bah, Andreas Bødtker Christensen, Simon Thorup Kjær (Cap), Mathias Jattah-Njie Jørgensen, Christian Dannemann Eriksen, Pierre-Emile Kordt Højbjerg, Jens Stryger Larsen (84.Victor Bernth Kristiansen), Andreas Skov Olsen (71.Yussuf Yurary Poulsen), Jonas Wind (59.Mikkel Krogh Damsgaard), Rasmus Winther Højlund (71.Martin Braithwaite Christensen). Trainer: Kasper Hjulmand.

**Goal:** Rasmus Winther Højlund (42).

## NATIONAL TEAM PLAYERS
(16.07.2022 – 15.07.2023)

| Name | DOB | Caps | Goals | *Club* | |
|---|---|---|---|---|---|
| | | | **Goalkeepers** | | |
| Kasper Peter SCHMEICHEL | 05.11.1986 | **93** | **0** | 2022/2023: | *OGC Nice (FRA)* |
| | | | **Defenders** | | |
| Joachim Christian ANDERSEN | 31.05.1996 | **23** | **0** | 2022/2023: | *Crystal Palace FC London (ENG)* |
| Alexander Hartmann BAH | 09.12.1997 | **9** | **1** | 2022/2023: | *Sport Lisboa e Benfica (POR)* |
| Andreas Bødtker CHRISTENSEN | 10.04.1996 | **64** | **3** | 2022/2023: | *FC Barcelona (ESP)* |
| Mathias Jattah-Njie JØRGENSEN | 23.04.1990 | **36** | **2** | 2023: | *Brentford FC London (ENG)* |
| Simon Thorup KJÆR | 26.03.1989 | **126** | **5** | 2022/2023: | *AC Milan (ITA)* |
| Rasmus Nissen KRISTENSEN | 11.07.1997 | **15** | **0** | 2022/2023: | *Leeds United FC (ENG)* |
| Victor Bernth KRISTIANSEN | 16.12.2002 | **1** | **0** | 2023: | *Leicester City FC (ENG)* |
| Joakim MÆHLE Pedersen | 20.05.1997 | **37** | **9** | 2022/2023: | *Atalanta Bergamasca Calcio (ITA)* |
| Victor Enok NELSSON | 14.10.1998 | **10** | **0** | 2022/2023: | *Galatasaray SK Istanbul (TUR)* |
| Jens STRYGER Larsen | 21.02.1991 | **53** | **3** | 2022/2023: | *Trabzonspor Kulübü (TUR)* |
| | | | **Midfielders** | | |
| Philip Anyanwu BILLING | 11.06.1996 | **5** | **0** | 2022/2023: | *AFC Bournemouth (ENG)* |
| Thomas Joseph DELANEY | 03.09.1991 | **72** | **7** | 2022: | *Sevilla FC (ESP)* |
| Christian Dannemann ERIKSEN | 14.02.1992 | **122** | **39** | 2022/2023: | *Manchester United FC (ENG)* |
| Pierre-Emile Kordt HØJBJERG | 05.08.1995 | **67** | **5** | 2022/2023: | *Tottenham Hotspur FC London (ENG)* |
| Mathias JENSEN | 01.01.1996 | **24** | **1** | 2022/2023: | *Brentford FC London (ENG)* |
| Jesper Grænge LINDSTRØM | 29.02.2000 | **10** | **1** | 2022/2023: | *Eintracht Frankfurt (GER)* |
| Christian Thers NØRGAARD | 10.03.1994 | **20** | **1** | 2022/2023: | *Brentford FC London (ENG)* |
| Daniel WASS | 31.05.1989 | **44** | **1** | 2022: | *Brøndby IF* |
| | | | **Forwards** | | |
| Martin BRAITHWAITE Christensen | 05.06.1991 | **68** | **10** | 2022/2023: | *RCD Espanyol Barcelona (ESP)* |
| Andreas Evald CORNELIUS | 16.03.1993 | **44** | **9** | 2022: | *FC København* |
| Mikkel Krogh DAMSGAARD | 03.07.2000 | **25** | **4** | 2022/2023: | *Brentford FC London (ENG)* |
| Mohammed DARAMY | 07.01.2002 | **7** | **0** | 2023: | *FC København* |
| Kasper DOLBERG Rasmussen | 06.10.1997 | **40** | **11** | 2022: | *Sevilla FC (ESP)* |
| Rasmus Winther HØJLUND | 04.02.2003 | **6** | **6** | 2022/2023: | *Atalanta Bergamasca Calcio (ITA)* |
| Andreas Skov OLSEN | 02.12.1999 | **27** | **8** | 2022/2023: | *Club Brugge KV (BEL)* |
| Yussuf Yurary POULSEN | 15.06.1994 | **69** | **11** | 2023: | *RasenBallsport Leipzig (GER)* |
| Robert SKOV | 20.05.1996 | **12** | **5** | 2022: | *TSG 1899 Hoffenheim (GER)* |
| Jonas Older WIND | 07.02.1999 | **19** | **6** | 2023: | *VfL Wolfsburg (GER)* |
| | | | **Trainer** | | |
| Kasper HJULMAND [from 01.08.2020] | 09.04.1972 | 41 M; 25 W; 4 D; 12 L; 81-35 | | | |

# ENGLAND

| The Country: |
| --- |
| England |
| Capital: London |
| Surface: 130,279 km² |
| Inhabitants: 56,489,800 [2021] |
| Time: UTC |

| The FA: |
| --- |
| The Football Association |
| Wembley Stadium, P.O. Box 1966, SWIP 9EQ, London |
| Tel: +44 844 980 8200 |
| Foundation date: 1863 |
| Member of FIFA: 1905-1918, 1924-1928, since 1946 |
| Member of UEFA since: 1954 |
| Website: www.thefa.com |

## NATIONAL TEAM RECORDS

| RECORDS | | |
| --- | --- | --- |
| **First international match:** | 30.11.1872, Glasgow: | Scotland – England 0-0 |
| **Most international caps:** | Peter Leslie Shilton | - 125 caps (1970-1990) |
| **Most international goals:** | Harry Edward Kane | - 58 goals / 84 caps (since 2015) |

| UEFA EUROPEAN CHAMPIONSHIP | |
| --- | --- |
| 1960 | Did not enter |
| 1964 | Qualifiers |
| 1968 | Final Tournament (3rd Place) |
| 1972 | Qualifiers |
| 1976 | Qualifiers |
| 1980 | Final Tournament (Group Stage) |
| 1984 | Qualifiers |
| 1988 | Final Tournament (Group Stage) |
| 1992 | Final Tournament (Group Stage) |
| 1996 | Final Tournament (Semi-Finals) |
| 2000 | Final Tournament (Group Stage) |
| 2004 | Final Tournament (Quarter-Finals) |
| 2008 | Qualifiers |
| 2012 | Final Tournament (Quarter-Finals) |
| 2016 | Final Tournament (2nd Round of 16) |
| 2020 | Final Tournament (Runners-up) |

| FIFA WORLD CUP | |
| --- | --- |
| 1930 | Did not enter |
| 1934 | Did not enter |
| 1938 | Did not enter |
| 1950 | Final Tournament (Group Stage) |
| 1954 | Final Tournament (Quarter-Finals) |
| 1958 | Final Tournament (Group Stage) |
| 1962 | Final Tournament (Quarter-Finals) |
| 1966 | **Final Tournament (Winners)** |
| 1970 | Final Tournament (Quarter-Finals) |
| 1974 | Qualifiers |
| 1978 | Qualifiers |
| 1982 | Final Tournament (2nd Round) |
| 1986 | Final Tournament (Quarter-Finals) |
| 1990 | Final Tournament (4th Place) |
| 1994 | Qualifiers |
| 1998 | Final Tournament (2nd Round of 16) |
| 2002 | Final Tournament (Quarter-Finals) |
| 2006 | Final Tournament (Quarter-Finals) |
| 2010 | Final Tournament (2nd Round of 16) |
| 2014 | Final Tournament (Group Stage) |
| 2018 | Final Tournament (4th Place) |
| 2022 | Final Tournament (Quarter-Finals) |

| OLYMPIC TOURNAMENTS | |
| --- | --- |
| 1908 | - |
| 1912 | - |
| 1920 | - |
| 1924 | - |
| 1928 | - |
| 1936 | - |
| 1948 | - |
| 1952 | - |
| 1956 | - |
| 1960 | - |
| 1964 | - |
| 1968 | - |
| 1972 | - |
| 1976 | - |
| 1980 | - |
| 1984 | - |
| 1988 | - |
| 1992 | - |
| 1996 | - |
| 2000 | - |
| 2004 | - |
| 2008 | - |
| 2012 | - |
| 2016 | - |
| 2020 | - |

| UEFA NATIONS LEAGUE | |
| --- | --- |
| 2018/2019 | League A (Group Stage -> Final Tournament – 3rd Place) |
| 2020/2021 | League A (Group Stage) |
| 2022/2023 | League A (Group Stage -> relegated to League B) |

## ENGLISH CLUB HONOURS IN EUROPEAN CLUB COMPETITIONS:

| European Champion Clubs' Cup (1956-1992) / UEFA Champions League (1993-2023) | | |
| --- | --- | --- |
| Liverpool FC | 6 | 1976/1977, 1977/1978, 1980/1981, 1983/1984, 2004/2005, 2018/2019 |
| Manchester United FC | 3 | 1967/1968, 1998/1999, 2007/2008 |
| Notthingam Forest FC | 2 | 1978/1979, 1979/1980 |
| Chelsea FC London | 2 | 2011/2012, 2020/2021 |
| Aston Villa FC Birmingham | 1 | 1981/1982 |
| Manchester City FC | 1 | 2022/2023 |
| Fairs Cup (1858-1971) / UEFA Cup (1972-2009) / UEFA Europa League (2010-2023) | | |
| Liverpool FC | 3 | 1972/1973, 1975/1976, 2000/2001 |
| Leeds United FC | 2 | 1967/1968, 1970/1971 |
| Tottenham Hotspur FC London | 2 | 1971/1972, 1983/1984 |
| Chelsea FC London | 2 | 2012/2013, 2018/2019 |
| Newcastle United FC | 1 | 1968/1969 |

| | | | |
|---|---|---|---|
| Arsenal FC London | 1 | 1969/1970 | |
| Ipswich Town FC | 1 | 1980/1981 | |
| Manchester United FC | 1 | 2016/2017 | |

| UEFA Europa Conference League (2021-2023) | | |
|---|---|---|
| West Ham United FC London | 1 | 2022/2023 |

| UEFA Super Cup (1972-2022) | | |
|---|---|---|
| Liverpool FC | 4 | 1977, 2001, 2005, 2019 |
| Chelsea FC London | 2 | 1998, 2021 |
| Notthingam Forest FC | 1 | 1979 |
| Aston Villa FC Birmingham | 1 | 1982 |
| Manchester United FC | 1 | 1991 |

| European Cup Winners' Cup 1961-1999* | | |
|---|---|---|
| Chelsea FC London | 2 | 1970/1971, 1997/1998 |
| Tottenham Hotspur FC London | 1 | 1962/1963 |
| West Ham United FC London | 1 | 1964/1965 |
| Manchester City FC | 1 | 1969/1970 |
| Everton FC Liverpool | 1 | 1984/1985 |
| Manchester United FC | 1 | 1990/1991 |
| Arsenal FC London | 1 | 1993/1994 |

*defunct competition

## NATIONAL COMPETITIONS
## TABLE OF HONOURS

| | CHAMPIONS | CUP WINNERS | BEST GOALSCORERS | |
|---|---|---|---|---|
| 1871/1872 | - | Wanderers FC London | - | |
| 1872/1873 | - | Wanderers FC London | - | |
| 1873/1874 | - | Oxford University AFC | - | |
| 1874/1875 | - | Royal Engineers AFC | - | |
| 1875/1876 | - | Wanderers FC London | - | |
| 1876/1877 | - | Wanderers FC London | - | |
| 1877/1878 | - | Wanderers FC London | - | |
| 1878/1879 | - | Old Etonians AFC | - | |
| 1879/1880 | - | Clapham Rovers FC | - | |
| 1880/1881 | - | Old Carthusians FC | - | |
| 1881/1882 | - | Old Etonians AFC | - | |
| 1882/1883 | - | Blackburn Olympic FC | - | |
| 1883/1884 | - | Blackburn Rovers FC | - | |
| 1884/1885 | - | Blackburn Rovers FC | - | |
| 1885/1886 | - | Blackburn Rovers FC | - | |
| 1886/1887 | - | Aston Villa FC Birmingham | - | |
| 1887/1888 | - | West Bromwich Albion FC | - | |
| 1888/1889 | Preston North End FC | Preston North End FC | John Goodall (Preston North End FC) | 21 |
| 1889/1890 | Preston North End FC | Blackburn Rovers FC | Jimmy Ross (SCO, Preston North End FC) | 24 |
| 1890/1891 | Everton FC Liverpool | Blackburn Rovers FC | Jack Southworth (Blackburn Rovers FC) | 26 |
| 1891/1892 | Sunderland AFC | West Bromwich Albion FC | John Campbell (SCO, Sunderland AFC) | 32 |
| 1892/1893 | Sunderland AFC | Wolverhampton Wanderers FC | John Campbell (SCO, Sunderland AFC) | 31 |
| 1893/1894 | Aston Villa FC Birmingham | Notts County FC | Jack Southworth (Everton FC Liverpool) | 27 |
| 1894/1895 | Sunderland AFC | Aston Villa FC Birmingham | John Campbell (SCO, Sunderland AFC) | 22 |
| 1895/1896 | Aston Villa FC Birmingham | The Wednesday Sheffield FC | John James Campbell (SCO, Aston Villa FC Birmingham) Stephen Bloomer (Derby County FC) | 20 |
| 1896/1897 | Aston Villa FC Birmingham | Aston Villa FC Birmingham | Stephen Bloomer (Derby County FC) | 22 |
| 1897/1898 | Sheffield United FC | Nottingham Forest FC | Fred Wheldon (Aston Villa FC Birmingham) | 21 |
| 1898/1899 | Aston Villa FC Birmingham | Sheffield United FC | Stephen Bloomer (Derby County FC) | 23 |
| 1899/1900 | Aston Villa FC Birmingham | Bury FC | Billy Garraty (Aston Villa FC Birmingham) | 27 |
| 1900/1901 | Liverpool FC | Tottenham Hotspur FC London | Stephen Bloomer (Derby County FC) | 23 |
| 1901/1902 | Sunderland AFC | Sheffield United FC | Jimmy Settle (Everton FC Liverpool) | 18 |
| 1902/1903 | The Wednesday Sheffield FC | Bury FC | Sam Raybould (Liverpool FC) | 31 |
| 1903/1904 | The Wednesday Sheffield FC | Manchester City FC | Stephen Bloomer (Derby County FC) | 20 |
| 1904/1905 | Newcastle United FC | Aston Villa FC Birmingham | Arthur Brown (Sheffield United FC) | 22 |
| 1905/1906 | Liverpool FC | Everton FC Liverpool | Albert Shepherd (Bolton Wanderers FC) | 26 |
| 1906/1907 | Newcastle United FC | The Wednesday Sheffield FC | Alex Young (SCO, Everton FC Liverpool) | 30 |
| 1907/1908 | Manchester United FC | Wolverhampton Wanderers FC | Enoch West (Nottingham Forest FC) | 27 |
| 1908/1909 | Newcastle United FC | Manchester United FC | Bert Freeman (Everton FC Liverpool) | 38 |
| 1909/1910 | Aston Villa FC Birmingham | Newcastle United FC | Jack Parkinson (Liverpool FC) | 30 |
| 1910/1911 | Manchester United FC | Bradford City AFC | Albert Shepherd (Newcastle United FC) | 25 |
| 1911/1912 | Blackburn Rovers FC | Barnsley FC | Harry Hampton (Aston Villa FC Birmingham) George Holley (Sunderland AFC) David McLean (The Wednesday Sheffield FC) | 25 |
| 1912/1913 | Sunderland AFC | Aston Villa FC Birmingham | David McLean (SCO, The Wednesday Sheffield FC) | 30 |
| 1913/1914 | Blackburn Rovers FC | Burnley FC | George Elliot (Middlesbrough FC) | 32 |
| 1914/1915 | Everton FC Liverpool | Sheffield United FC | Bobby Parker (SCO, Everton FC Liverpool) | 35 |
| 1915-1919 | *No competition* | *No competition* | - | |
| 1919/1920 | West Bromwich Albion FC | Aston Villa FC Birmingham | Fred Morris (West Bromwich Albion FC) | 37 |

| | | | |
|---|---|---|---|
| 1920/1921 | Burnley FC | Tottenham Hotspur FC London | Joe Smith (Bolton Wanderers FC) | 38 |
| 1921/1922 | Liverpool FC | Huddersfield Town AFC | Andy Wilson (SCO, Middlesbrough FC) | 31 |
| 1922/1923 | Liverpool FC | Bolton Wanderers FC | Charles Murray Buchan (SCO, Sunderland AFC) | 30 |
| 1923/1924 | Huddersfield Town AFC | Newcastle United FC | Wilf Chadwick (Everton FC Liverpool) | 28 |
| 1924/1925 | Huddersfield Town AFC | Sheffield United FC | Frank Roberts (Manchester City FC) | 31 |
| 1925/1926 | Huddersfield Town AFC | Bolton Wanderers FC | Ted Harper (Blackburn Rovers FC) | 43 |
| 1926/1927 | Newcastle United FC | Cardiff City FC (WAL) | Jimmy Trotter (The Wednesday Sheffield FC) | 37 |
| 1927/1928 | Everton FC Liverpool | Blackburn Rovers FC | William Ralph Dean (Everton FC Liverpool) | 60 |
| 1928/1929 | The Wednesday Sheffield FC | Bolton Wanderers FC | Dave Halliday (SCO, Sunderland AFC) | 43 |
| 1929/1930 | Sheffield Wednesday FC | Arsenal FC London | Victor Martin Watson (West Ham United FC) | 41 |
| 1930/1931 | Arsenal FC London | West Bromwich Albion FC | Thomas Waring (Aston Villa FC Birmingham) | 49 |
| 1931/1932 | Everton FC Liverpool | Newcastle United FC | William Ralph Dean (Everton FC Liverpool) | 44 |
| 1932/1933 | Arsenal FC London | Everton FC Liverpool | John William Anslow Bowers (Derby County FC) | 35 |
| 1933/1934 | Arsenal FC London | Manchester City FC | John William Anslow Bowers (Derby County FC) | 34 |
| 1934/1935 | Arsenal FC London | Sheffield Wednesday FC | Edward Joseph Drake (Arsenal FC London) | 42 |
| 1935/1936 | Sunderland AFC | Arsenal FC London | William "Ginger" Richardson (West Bromwich Albion FC) | 39 |
| 1936/1937 | Manchester City FC | Sunderland AFC | Frederick Charles Steele (Stoke City FC) | 33 |
| 1937/1938 | Arsenal FC London | Preston North End FC | Thomas Lawton (Everton FC Liverpool) | 28 |
| 1938/1939 | Everton FC Liverpool | Portsmouth FC | Thomas Lawton (Everton FC Liverpool) | 35 |
| 1939-1945 | *No competition* | *No competition* | - | |
| 1945/1946 | *No competition* | Derby County FC | - | |
| 1946/1947 | Liverpool FC | Charlton Athletic FC | Dennis Westcott (Wolverhampton Wanderers FC) | 37 |
| 1947/1948 | Arsenal FC London | Manchester United FC | Ronald Leslie Rooke (Arsenal FC London) | 33 |
| 1948/1949 | Portsmouth FC | Wolverhampton Wanderers FC | William Moir (SCO, Bolton Wanderers FC) | 25 |
| 1949/1950 | Portsmouth FC | Arsenal FC London | Richard Daniel Davis (Sunderland AFC) | 25 |
| 1950/1951 | Tottenham Hotspur FC London | Newcastle United FC | Stanley Harding Mortensen (Blackpool FC) | 30 |
| 1951/1952 | Manchester United FC | Newcastle United FC | Jorge Robledo Oliver (CHI, Newcastle United FC) | 33 |
| 1952/1953 | Arsenal FC London | Blackpool FC | Charles Wayman (Preston North End FC) | 24 |
| 1953/1954 | Wolverhampton Wanderers FC | West Bromwich Albion FC | Jimmy Glazzard (Huddersfield Town AFC) | 29 |
| 1954/1955 | Chelsea FC London | Newcastle United FC | Ronald Allen (West Bromwich Albion FC) | 27 |
| 1955/1956 | Manchester United FC | Manchester City FC | Nathaniel Lofthouse (Bolton Wanderers FC) | 33 |
| 1956/1957 | Manchester United FC | Aston Villa FC Birmingham | William John Charles (WAL, Leeds United FC) | 38 |
| 1957/1958 | Wolverhampton Wanderers FC | Bolton Wanderers FC | Robert Alfred Smith (Tottenham Hotspur FC) | 36 |
| 1958/1959 | Wolverhampton Wanderers FC | Nottingham Forest FC | James Peter Greaves (Chelsea FC London) | 33 |
| 1959/1960 | Burnley FC | Wolverhampton Wanderers FC | Dennis Sydney Viollet (Manchester United FC) | 32 |
| 1960/1961 | Tottenham Hotspur FC London | Tottenham Hotspur FC London | James Peter Greaves (Chelsea FC London) | 41 |
| 1961/1962 | Ipswich Town FC | Tottenham Hotspur FC London | Raymond Crawford (Ipswich Town FC) Derek Tennyson Kevan (West Bromwich Albion FC) | 33 |
| 1962/1963 | Everton FC Liverpool | Manchester United FC | James Peter Greaves (Tottenham Hotspur FC) | 37 |
| 1963/1964 | Liverpool FC | West Ham United FC London | James Peter Greaves (Tottenham Hotspur FC) | 35 |
| 1964/1965 | Manchester United FC | Liverpool FC | Andrew McEvoy (IRL, Blackburn Rovers FC) James Peter Greaves (Tottenham Hotspur FC) | 29 |
| 1965/1966 | Liverpool FC | Everton FC Liverpool | William John Irvine (NIR, Burnley FC) | 29 |
| 1966/1967 | Manchester United FC | Tottenham Hotspur FC London | Ron Davies (WAL, Southampton FC) | 37 |
| 1967/1968 | Manchester City FC | West Bromwich Albion FC | George Best (NIR, Manchester United FC) Ronald Tudor Davies (WAL, Southampton FC) | 28 |
| 1968/1969 | Leeds United FC | Manchester City FC | James Peter Greaves (Tottenham Hotspur FC) | 27 |
| 1969/1970 | Everton FC Liverpool | Chelsea FC London | Jeffrey Astle (West Bromwich Albion FC) | 25 |
| 1970/1971 | Arsenal FC London | Arsenal FC London | Anthony Brown (West Bromwich Albion FC) | 28 |
| 1971/1972 | Derby County FC | Leeds United FC | Francis Henry Lee (Manchester City FC) | 33 |
| 1972/1973 | Liverpool FC | Sunderland AFC | Bryan Stanley Robson (West Ham United FC) | 28 |
| 1973/1974 | Leeds United FC | Liverpool FC | Michael Roger Channon (Southampton FC) | 21 |
| 1974/1975 | Derby County FC | West Ham United FC London | Malcolm Ian Macdonald (Newcastle United FC) | 21 |
| 1975/1976 | Liverpool FC | Southampton FC | Edward John MacDougall (SCO, Norwich City FC) | 23 |
| 1976/1977 | Liverpool FC | Manchester United FC | Malcolm Ian Macdonald (Arsenal FC London) Andrew Mullen Gray (SCO, Aston Villa FC) | 25 |
| 1977/1978 | Nottingham Forest FC | Ipswich Town FC | Robert Dennis Latchford (Everton FC Liverpool) | 30 |
| 1978/1979 | Liverpool FC | Arsenal FC London | Frank Stewart Worthington (Bolton Wanderers FC) | 24 |
| 1979/1980 | Liverpool FC | West Ham United FC London | Philip John Boyer (Southampton FC) | 23 |
| 1980/1981 | Aston Villa FC Birmingham | Tottenham Hotspur FC London | Peter Withe (Aston Villa FC Birmingham) Steven Archibald (SCO, Tottenham Hotspur FC) | 20 |
| 1981/1982 | Liverpool FC | Tottenham Hotspur FC London | Joseph Kevin Keegan (Southampton FC) | 26 |
| 1982/1983 | Liverpool FC | Manchester United FC | Luther Loide Blissett (Watford FC) | 27 |
| 1983/1984 | Liverpool FC | Everton FC Liverpool | Ian James Rush (WAL, Liverpool FC) | 32 |
| 1984/1985 | Everton FC Liverpool | Manchester United FC | Kerry Michael Dixon (Chelsea FC London) Gary Winston Lineker (Leicester City FC) | 24 |
| 1985/1986 | Liverpool FC | Liverpool FC | Gary Winston Lineker (Everton FC Liverpool) | 30 |
| 1986/1987 | Everton FC Liverpool | Coventry City FC | Clive Darren Allen (Tottenham Hotspur FC London) | 33 |
| 1987/1988 | Liverpool FC | Wimbledon | John William Aldridge (IRL, Liverpool FC) | 26 |
| 1988/1989 | Arsenal FC London | Liverpool FC | Alan Martin Smith (Arsenal FC London) | 23 |
| 1989/1990 | Liverpool FC | Manchester United FC | Gary Winston Lineker (Tottenham Hotspur FC) | 24 |
| 1990/1991 | Arsenal FC London | Tottenham Hotspur FC London | Alan Martin Smith (Arsenal FC London) | 22 |
| 1991/1992 | Leeds United FC | Liverpool FC | Ian Edward Wright (Crystal Palace FC London/Arsenal FC London) | 29 |
| 1992/1993 | Manchester United FC | Arsenal FC London | Edward Paul Sheringham (Nottingham Forest FC/Tottenham Hotspur FC London) | 22 |
| 1993/1994 | Manchester United FC | Manchester United FC | Andrew Alexander Cole (Newcastle United FC) | 34 |

| Season | Champion | | Top scorer | |
|---|---|---|---|---|
| 1994/1995 | Blackburn Rovers FC | Everton FC Liverpool | Alan Shearer (Blackburn Rovers FC) | 34 |
| 1995/1996 | Manchester United FC | Manchester United FC | Alan Shearer (Blackburn Rovers FC) | 31 |
| 1996/1997 | Manchester United FC | Chelsea FC London | Alan Shearer (Newcastle United FC) | 25 |
| 1997/1998 | Arsenal FC London | Arsenal FC London | Christopher Roy Sutton (Blackburn Rovers FC) Dion Dublin (Coventry City FC) Michael James Owen (Liverpool FC) | 18 |
| 1998/1999 | Manchester United FC | Manchester United FC | Jimmy Floyd Hasselbaink (NED, Leeds United FC) Michael James Owen (Liverpool FC) Dwight Eversley Yorke (TRI, Manchester United) | 18 |
| 1999/2000 | Manchester United FC | Chelsea FC London | Kevin Mark Phillips (Sunderland AFC) | 30 |
| 2000/2001 | Manchester United FC | Liverpool FC | Jimmy Floyd Hasselbaink (NED, Chelsea FC London) | 23 |
| 2001/2002 | Arsenal FC London | Arsenal FC London | Thierry Daniel Henry (FRA, Arsenal FC London) | 24 |
| 2002/2003 | Manchester United FC | Arsenal FC London | Rutgerus Johannes Martinus "Ruud" van Nistelrooy (NED, Manchester United FC) | 25 |
| 2003/2004 | Arsenal FC London | Manchester United FC | Thierry Daniel Henry (FRA, Arsenal FC London) | 30 |
| 2004/2005 | Chelsea FC London | Arsenal FC London | Thierry Daniel Henry (FRA, Arsenal FC London) | 25 |
| 2005/2006 | Chelsea FC London | Liverpool FC | Thierry Daniel Henry (FRA, Arsenal FC London) | 27 |
| 2006/2007 | Manchester United FC | Chelsea FC London | Didier Yves Drogba Tébily (CIV, Chelsea FC London) | 20 |
| 2007/2008 | Manchester United FC | Portsmouth FC | Cristiano Ronaldo dos Santos Aveiro (POR, Manchester United FC) | 31 |
| 2008/2009 | Manchester United FC | Chelsea FC London | Nicolas Sébastien Anelka (FRA, Chelsea FC London) | 19 |
| 2009/2010 | Chelsea FC London | Chelsea FC London | Didier Yves Drogba Tébily (CIV, Chelsea FC London) | 29 |
| 2010/2011 | Manchester United FC | Manchester City FC | Dimitar Berbatov (BUL, Manchester United FC) Carlos Alberto Martínez Tevez (ARG, Manchester City FC) | 20 |
| 2011/2012 | Manchester City FC | Chelsea FC London | Robin van Persie (NED, Arsenal FC London) | 30 |
| 2012/2013 | Manchester United FC | Wigan Athletic FC | Robin van Persie (NED, Manchester United FC) | 26 |
| 2013/2014 | Manchester City FC | Arsenal FC London | Luis Alberto Suárez Díaz (URU, Liverpool FC) | 31 |
| 2014/2015 | Chelsea FC London | Arsenal FC London | Sergio Leonel Agüero del Castillo (ARG, Manchester City FC) | 26 |
| 2015/2016 | Leicester City FC | Manchester United FC | Harry Edward Kane (Tottenham Hotspur FC) | 25 |
| 2016/2017 | Chelsea FC London | Arsenal FC London | Harry Edward Kane (Tottenham Hotspur FC) | 29 |
| 2017/2018 | Manchester City FC | Chelsea FC London | Mohamed Salah Ghaly (EGY, Liverpool FC) | 32 |
| 2018/2019 | Manchester City FC | Manchester City FC | Pierre-Emerick Emiliano François Aubameyang (GAB, Arsenal FC London) Sadio Mané (SEN, Liverpool FC) Mohamed Salah Ghaly (EGY, Liverpool FC) | 22 |
| 2019/2020 | Liverpool FC | Arsenal FC London | Jamie Richard Vardy (Leicester City FC) | 23 |
| 2020/2021 | Manchester City FC | Leicester City FC | Harry Edward Kane (Tottenham Hotspur FC) | 23 |
| 2021/2022 | Manchester City FC | Liverpool FC | Mohamed Salah Ghaly (EGY, Liverpool FC) Son Heung-min (KOR, Tottenham Hotspur FC London) | 23 |
| 2022/2023 | Manchester City FC | Manchester City FC | Erling Braut Haaland (NOR, Manchester City FC) | 36 |

Please note: the championship was called Football League (1888–1892), Football League First Division (1892–1992) and Premier League (1992–present).

## EFL (LEAGUE) CUP WINNERS

| Season | Winner | Season | Winner | Season | Winner |
|---|---|---|---|---|---|
| 1960/1961 | Aston Villa FC Birmingham | 1981/1982 | Liverpool FC | 2002/2003 | Liverpool FC |
| 1961/1962 | Norwich City FC | 1982/1983 | Liverpool FC | 2003/2004 | Middlesbrough FC |
| 1962/1963 | Birmingham City FC | 1983/1984 | Liverpool FC | 2004/2005 | Chelsea FC London |
| 1963/1964 | Leicester City FC | 1984/1985 | Norwich City FC | 2005/2006 | Manchester United FC |
| 1964/1965 | Chelsea FC London | 1985/1986 | Oxford United FC | 2006/2007 | Chelsea FC London |
| 1965/1966 | West Bromwich Albion FC | 1986/1987 | Arsenal FC London | 2007/2008 | Tottenham Hotspur FC London |
| 1966/1967 | Queens Park Rangers FC | 1987/1988 | Luton Town FC | 2008/2009 | Manchester United FC |
| 1967/1968 | Leeds United FC | 1988/1989 | Nottingham Forest FC | 2009/2010 | Manchester United FC |
| 1968/1969 | Swindon Town FC | 1989/1990 | Nottingham Forest FC | 2010/2011 | Birmingham City FC |
| 1969/1970 | Manchester City FC | 1990/1991 | Sheffield Wednesday FC | 2011/2012 | Liverpool FC |
| 1970/1971 | Tottenham Hotspur FC London | 1991/1992 | Manchester United FC | 2012/2013 | Swansea City AFC |
| 1971/1972 | Stoke City FC | 1992/1993 | Arsenal FC London | 2013/2014 | Manchester City FC |
| 1972/1973 | Tottenham Hotspur FC London | 1993/1994 | Aston Villa FC Birmingham | 2014/2015 | Chelsea FC London |
| 1973/1974 | Wolverhampton Wanderers FC | 1994/1995 | Liverpool FC | 2015/2016 | Manchester City FC |
| 1974/1975 | Aston Villa FC Birmingham | 1995/1996 | Aston Villa FC Birmingham | 2016/2017 | Manchester United FC |
| 1975/1976 | Manchester City FC | 1996/1997 | Leicester City FC | 2017/2018 | Manchester City FC |
| 1976/1977 | Aston Villa FC Birmingham | 1997/1998 | Chelsea FC London | 2018/2019 | Manchester City FC |
| 1977/1978 | Nottingham Forest FC | 1998/1999 | Tottenham Hotspur FC London | 2019/2020 | Manchester City FC |
| 1978/1979 | Nottingham Forest FC | 1999/2000 | Leicester City FC | 2020/2021 | Manchester City FC |
| 1979/1980 | Wolverhampton Wanderers FC | 2000/2001 | Liverpool FC | 2021/2022 | Liverpool FC |
| 1980/1981 | Liverpool FC | 2001/2002 | Blackburn Rovers FC | 2022/2023 | Manchester United FC |

## Results

### Round 1 [05-07.08.2022]
Crystal Palace - Arsenal 0-2(0-1)
Fulham - Liverpool 2-2(1-0)
Bournemouth - Aston Villa 2-0(1-0)
Leeds United - Wolverhampton 2-1(1-1)
Newcastle United-Nottingham Forest 2-0(0-0)
Tottenham Hotspur - Southampton 4-1(2-1)
Everton - Chelsea 0-1(0-1)
Leicester City - Brentford 2-2(1-0)
Manchester United-Brighton & Hove 1-2(0-2)
West Ham United - Manchester City 0-2(0-1)

### Round 2 [13-15.08.2022]
Aston Villa - Everton 2-1(1-0)
Brighton & Hove - Newcastle United 0-0
Arsenal - Leicester City 4-2(2-0)
Southampton - Leeds United 2-2(0-0)
Manchester City - Bournemouth 4-0(3-0)
Wolverhampton - Fulham 0-0
Brentford - Manchester United 4-0(4-0)
Nottingham Forest-West Ham United 1-0(1-0)
Chelsea - Tottenham Hotspur 2-2(1-0)
Liverpool - Crystal Palace 1-1(0-1)

### Round 3 [20-22.08.2022]
Tottenham Hotspur - Wolverhampton 1-0(0-0)
Crystal Palace - Aston Villa 3-1(1-1)
Everton - Nottingham Forest 1-1(0-0)
Fulham - Brentford 3-2(2-1)
Leicester City - Southampton 1-2(0-0)
Bournemouth - Arsenal 0-3(0-2)
Leeds United - Chelsea 3-0(2-0)
West Ham United - Brighton & Hove 0-2(0-1)
Newcastle United - Manchester City 3-3(2-1)
Manchester United - Liverpool 2-1(1-0)

### Round 4 [27-28.08.2022]
Southampton - Manchester United 0-1(0-0)
Brighton & Hove - Leeds United 1-0(0-0)
Brentford - Everton 1-1(0-1)
Chelsea - Leicester City 2-1(0-0)
Liverpool - Bournemouth 9-0(5-0)
Manchester City - Crystal Palace 4-2(0-2)
Arsenal - Fulham 2-1(0-0)
Aston Villa - West Ham United 0-1(0-0)
Wolverhampton - Newcastle United 1-1(1-0)
Nottingham F. - Tottenham Hotspur 0-2(0-1)

### Round 5 [30.08.-01.09.2022]
Fulham - Brighton & Hove 2-1(0-0)
Crystal Palace - Brentford 1-1(0-0)
Southampton - Chelsea 2-1(2-1)
Leeds United - Everton 1-1(0-1)
Bournemouth - Wolverhampton 0-0
Arsenal - Aston Villa 2-1(1-0)
Manchester City - Nottingham Forest 6-0(3-0)
West Ham United - Tottenham Hots. 1-1(0-1)
Liverpool - Newcastle United 2-1(0-1)
Leicester City - Manchester United 0-1(0-1)

### Round 6 [03-04.09.2022]
Everton - Liverpool 0-0
Brentford - Leeds United 5-2(2-1)
Chelsea - West Ham United 2-1(0-0)
Newcastle United - Crystal Palace 0-0
Nottingham Forest - Bournemouth 2-3(2-0)
Tottenham Hotspur - Fulham 2-1(1-0)
Wolverhampton - Southampton 1-0(1-0)
Aston Villa - Manchester City 1-1(0-0)
Brighton & Hove - Leicester City 5-2(2-2)
Manchester United - Arsenal 3-1(1-0)

### Round 7
Fulham - Chelsea 2-1(1-0) [12.01.2023]
C. Palace - Manchester U. 1-1(0-1) [18.01.23]
Manchester C.-Tottenham 4-2(0-2) [19.01.23]
Arsenal - Everton 4-0(2-0) [01.03.2023]
Liverpool-Wolverhampton 2-0(0-0) [01.03.23]
Southampton - Brentford 0-2(0-1) [15.03.23]
Bournemouth-Brighton&H 0-2(0-1)[04.04.23]
Leeds - Nottingham Forest 2-1(2-1) [04.04.23]
Leicester - Aston Villa 1-2(1-1) [04.04.23]
West Ham - Newcastle 1-5(1-2) [05.04.23]

### Round 8 [16-18.09.2022]
Aston Villa - Southampton 1-0(1-0)
Nottingham Forest - Fulham 2-3(1-0)
Wolverhampton - Manchester City 0-3(0-2)
Newcastle United - Bournemouth 1-1(0-0)
Tottenham Hotspur - Leicester City 6-2(2-2)
Brentford - Arsenal 0-3(0-2)
Everton - West Ham United 1-0(0-0)
Manchester U. - Leeds U 2-2(0-1) [08.02.23]
Brighton&Hove-C. Palace 1-0(1-0) [15.03.23]
Chelsea - Liverpool 0-0 [04.04.2023]

### Round 9 [01-03.10.2022]
Arsenal - Tottenham Hotspur 3-1(1-1)
Bournemouth - Brentford 0-0
Crystal Palace - Chelsea 1-2(1-1)
Fulham - Newcastle United 1-4(0-3)
Liverpool - Brighton & Hove 3-3(1-2)
Southampton - Everton 1-2(0-0)
West Ham United - Wolverhampton 2-0(1-0)
Manchester City - Manchester United 6-3(4-0)
Leeds United - Aston Villa 0-0
Leicester City - Nottingham Forest 4-0(3-0)

### Round 10 [08-10.10.2022]
Bournemouth - Leicester City 2-1(0-1)
Chelsea - Wolverhampton 3-0(1-0)
Manchester City - Southampton 4-0(2-0)
Newcastle United - Brentford 5-1(2-0)
Brighton & Hove-Tottenham Hotspur 0-1(0-1)
Crystal Palace - Leeds United 2-1(1-1)
West Ham United - Fulham 3-1(1-1)
Arsenal - Liverpool 3-2(2-1)
Everton - Manchester United 1-2(1-2)
Nottingham Forest - Aston Villa 1-1(1-1)

### Round 11 [14-16.10.2022]
Brentford - Brighton & Hove 2-0(1-0)
Leicester City - Crystal Palace 0-0
Fulham - Bournemouth 2-2(1-2)
Wolverhampton - Nottingham Forest 1-0(0-0)
Tottenham Hotspur - Everton 2-0(0-0)
Aston Villa - Chelsea 0-2(0-1)
Southampton - West Ham United 1-1(1-0)
Leeds United - Arsenal 0-1(0-1)
Manchester United - Newcastle United 0-0
Liverpool - Manchester City 1-0(0-0)

### Round 12 [18-20.10.2022]
Brighton & Hove - Nottingham Forest 0-0
Crystal Palace - Wolverhampton 2-1(0-1)
Bournemouth - Southampton 0-1(0-1)
Brentford - Chelsea 0-0
Newcastle United - Everton 1-0(1-0)
Liverpool - West Ham United 1-0(1-0)
Manchester United - Tottenham 2-0(0-0)
Fulham - Aston Villa 3-0(1-0)
Leicester City - Leeds United 2-0(2-0)
Arsenal - Manchester City 1-3(1-1) [15.02.23]

### Round 13 [22-24.10.2022]
Nottingham Forest - Liverpool 1-0(0-0)
Everton - Crystal Palace 3-0(1-0)
Manchester City - Brighton & Hove 3-1(2-0)
Chelsea - Manchester United 1-1(0-0)
Aston Villa - Brentford 4-0(3-0)
Southampton - Arsenal 1-1(0-1)
Leeds United - Fulham 2-3(1-1)
Wolverhampton - Leicester City 0-4(0-2)
Tottenham - Newcastle United 1-2(0-2)
West Ham United - Bournemouth 2-0(1-0)

### Round 14 [29-30.10.2022]
Leicester City - Manchester City 0-1(0-0)
Bournemouth - Tottenham Hotspur 2-3(1-0)
Brighton & Hove - Chelsea 4-1(3-0)
Crystal Palace - Southampton 1-0(1-0)
Brentford - Wolverhampton 1-1(0-0)
Newcastle United - Aston Villa 4-0(1-0)
Fulham - Everton 0-0
Liverpool - Leeds United 1-2(1-1)
Arsenal - Nottingham Forest 5-0(1-0)
Manchester United-West Ham United 1-0(1-0)

### Round 15 [05-06.11.2022]
Leeds United - Bournemouth 4-3(1-2)
Manchester City - Fulham 2-1(1-1)
Nottingham Forest - Brentford 2-2(1-1)
Wolverhampton - Brighton & Hove 2-3(2-2)
Everton - Leicester City 0-2(0-1)
Chelsea - Arsenal 0-1(0-0)
Aston Villa - Manchester United 3-1(2-1)
Southampton - Newcastle United 1-4(0-1)
West Ham United - Crystal Palace 1-2(1-1)
Tottenham Hotspur - Liverpool 1-2(0-2)

### Round 16 [12-13.11.2022]
Manchester City - Brentford 1-2(1-1)
Bournemouth - Everton 3-0(2-0)
Liverpool - Southampton 3-1(3-1)
Nottingham Forest - Crystal Palace 1-0(0-0)
Tottenham Hotspur - Leeds United 4-3(1-2)
West Ham United - Leicester City 0-2(0-1)
Newcastle United - Chelsea 1-0(0-0)
Wolverhampton - Arsenal 0-2(0-0)
Brighton & Hove - Aston Villa 1-2(1-1)
Fulham - Manchester United 1-2(0-1)

### Round 17 [26-28.12.2022]
Brentford - Tottenham Hotspur 2-2(1-0)
Crystal Palace - Fulham 0-3(0-1)
Everton - Wolverhampton 1-2(1-1)
Southampton - Brighton & Hove 1-3(0-2)
Leicester City - Newcastle United 0-3(0-3)
Aston Villa - Liverpool 1-3(0-2)
Arsenal - West Ham United 3-1(0-1)
Chelsea - Bournemouth 2-0(2-0)
Manchester United - Nottingham 3-0(2-0)
Leeds United - Manchester City 1-3(0-1)

### Round 18 [30.12.2022-01.01.2023]
West Ham United - Brentford 0-2(0-2)
Liverpool - Leicester City 2-1(2-1)
Wolverhampton - Manchester United 0-1(0-0)
Bournemouth - Crystal Palace 0-2(0-2)
Fulham - Southampton 2-1(1-0)
Manchester City - Everton 1-1(1-0)
Newcastle United - Leeds United 0-0
Brighton & Hove - Arsenal 2-4(0-2)
Tottenham Hotspur - Aston Villa 0-2(0-0)
Nottingham Forest - Chelsea 1-1(0-1)

### Round 19 [02-05.01.2023]
Brentford - Liverpool 3-1(2-0)
Arsenal - Newcastle United 0-0
Everton - Brighton & Hove 1-4(0-1)
Leicester City - Fulham 0-1(0-1)
Manchester United - Bournemouth 3-0(1-0)
Southampton - Nottingham Forest 0-1(0-1)
Leeds United - West Ham United 2-2(1-1)
Aston Villa - Wolverhampton 1-1(0-1)
Crystal Palace - Tottenham Hotspur 0-4(0-0)
Chelsea - Manchester City 0-1(0-0)

### Round 20 [13-15.01.2023]
Aston Villa - Leeds United 2-1(1-0)
Manchester United - Manchester City 2-1(0-0)
Brighton & Hove - Liverpool 3-0(0-0)
Everton - Southampton 1-2(1-0)
Nottingham Forest - Leicester City 2-0(0-0)
Wolverhampton - West Ham United 1-0(0-0)
Brentford - Bournemouth 2-0(1-0)
Chelsea - Crystal Palace 1-0(0-0)
Newcastle United - Fulham 1-0(0-0)
Tottenham Hotspur - Arsenal 0-2(0-2)

### Round 21 [21-23.01.2023]
Liverpool - Chelsea 0-0
Bournemouth - Nottingham Forest 1-1(1-0)
Southampton - Aston Villa 0-1(0-0)
Leicester City - Brighton & Hove 2-2(1-1)
West Ham United - Everton 2-0(2-0)
Crystal Palace - Newcastle United 0-0
Leeds United - Brentford 0-0
Manchester City - Wolverhampton 3-0(1-0)
Arsenal - Manchester United 3-2(1-1)
Fulham - Tottenham Hotspur 0-1(0-1)

### Round 22 [03-05.02.2023]
Chelsea - Fulham 0-0
Everton - Arsenal 1-0(0-0)
Aston Villa - Leicester City 2-4(2-3)
Brighton & Hove - Bournemouth 1-0(0-0)
Brentford - Southampton 3-0(2-0)
Manchester United - Crystal Palace 2-1(1-0)
Wolverhampton - Liverpool 3-0(2-0)
Newcastle United - West Ham United 1-1(1-1)
Nottingham Forest - Leeds United 1-0(1-0)
Tottenham Hotspur-Manchester City 1-0(1-0)

### Round 23 [11-13.02.2023]
West Ham United - Chelsea 1-1(1-1)
Crystal Palace - Brighton & Hove 1-1(0-0)
Arsenal - Brentford 1-1(0-0)
Fulham - Nottingham Forest 2-0(1-0)
Southampton - Wolverhampton 1-2(1-0)
Leicester City - Tottenham Hotspur 4-1(3-1)
Bournemouth - Newcastle United 1-1(1-1)
Leeds United - Manchester United 0-2(0-0)
Manchester City - Aston Villa 3-1(3-0)
Liverpool - Everton 2-0(1-0)

### Round 24 [18-19.02.2023]
Aston Villa - Arsenal 2-4(2-1)
Brighton & Hove - Fulham 0-1(0-0)
Brentford - Crystal Palace 1-1(0-0)
Chelsea - Southampton 0-1(0-1)
Everton - Leeds United 1-0(0-0)
Nottingham Forest - Manchester City 1-1(0-1)
Wolverhampton - Bournemouth 0-1(0-0)
Newcastle United - Liverpool 0-2(0-2)
Manchester United - Leicester City 3-0(1-0)
Tottenham Hotspur - West Ham U. 2-0(0-0)

### Round 25 [24-26.02.2023]
Fulham - Wolverhampton 1-1(0-1)
Everton - Aston Villa 0-2(0-0)
Leeds United - Southampton 1-0(0-0)
Leicester City - Arsenal 0-1(0-0)
West Ham - Nottingham Forest 4-0(0-0)
Bournemouth - Manchester City 1-4(0-3)
Crystal Palace - Liverpool 0-0
Tottenham Hotspur - Chelsea 2-0(0-0)
Manchester U. - Brentford 1-0(1-0) [05.04.23]
Newcastle - Brighton & H. 4-1(2-0) [18.05.23]

### Round 26 [04-06.03.2023]
Manchester City - Newcastle United 2-0(1-0)
Aston Villa - Crystal Palace 1-0(1-0)
Brighton & Hove - West Ham United 4-0(1-0)
Arsenal - Bournemouth 3-2(0-1)
Chelsea - Leeds United 1-0(0-0)
Wolverhampton - Tottenham Hotspur 1-0(0-0)
Southampton - Leicester City 1-0(1-0)
Nottingham Forest - Everton 2-2(1-2)
Liverpool - Manchester United 7-0(1-0)
Brentford - Fulham 3-2(1-1)

### Round 27 [11-12.03.2023]
Bournemouth - Liverpool 1-0(1-0)
Everton - Brentford 1-0(1-0)
Leeds United - Brighton & Hove 2-2(1-1)
Leicester City - Chelsea 1-3(1-2)
Tottenham Hotspur - Nottingham 3-1(2-0)
Crystal Palace - Manchester City 0-1(0-0)
Fulham - Arsenal 0-3(0-3)
Manchester United - Southampton 0-0
West Ham United - Aston Villa 1-1(1-1)
Newcastle United - Wolverhampton 2-1(1-0)

### Round 28 [17-19.03.2023]
Nottingham - Newcastle United 1-2(1-1)
Aston Villa - Bournemouth 3-0(1-0)
Brentford - Leicester City 1-1(1-0)
Southampton - Tottenham Hotspur 3-3(0-1)
Wolverhampton - Leeds United 2-4(0-1)
Chelsea - Everton 2-2(0-0)
Arsenal - Crystal Palace 4-1(2-0)
Liverpool - Fulham 1-0(1-0) [03.05.2023]
Manchester C.-West Ham 3-0(0-0) [03.05.23]
Brighton - Manchester U. 1-0(0-0) [04.05.23]

### Round 29 [01-03.04.2023]
Manchester City - Liverpool 4-1(1-1)
Bournemouth - Fulham 2-1(0-1)
Brighton & Hove - Brentford 3-3(2-2)
Crystal Palace - Leicester City 2-1(0-0)
Arsenal - Leeds United 4-1(1-0)
Nottingham Forest - Wolverhampton 1-1(1-0)
Chelsea - Aston Villa 0-2(0-1)
West Ham United - Southampton 1-0(1-0)
Newcastle United-Manchester United 2-0(0-0)
Everton - Tottenham Hotspur 1-1(0-0)

### Round 30 [08-09.04.2023]
Manchester United - Everton 2-0(1-0)
Aston Villa - Nottingham Forest 2-0(0-0)
Brentford - Newcastle United 1-2(1-0)
Fulham - West Ham United 0-1(0-1)
Leicester City - Bournemouth 0-1(0-1)
Tottenham - Brighton & Hove 2-1(1-1)
Wolverhampton - Chelsea 1-0(1-0)
Southampton - Manchester City 1-4(0-1)
Leeds United - Crystal Palace 1-5(1-1)
Liverpool - Arsenal 2-2(1-2)

### Round 31 [15-17.04.2023]
Aston Villa - Newcastle United 3-0(1-0)
Chelsea - Brighton & Hove 1-2(1-1)
Everton - Fulham 1-3(1-1)
Southampton - Crystal Palace 0-2(0-0)
Wolverhampton - Brentford 2-0(1-0)
Tottenham Hotspur - Bournemouth 2-3(1-1)
Manchester City - Leicester City 3-1(3-0)
West Ham United - Arsenal 2-2(1-2)
Nottingham - Manchester United 0-2(0-1)
Leeds United - Liverpool 1-6(0-2)

### Round 32 [21-23.04.2023]
Arsenal - Southampton 3-3(1-2)
Fulham - Leeds United 2-1(0-0)
Crystal Palace - Everton 0-0
Brentford - Aston Villa 1-1(0-0)
Liverpool - Nottingham Forest 3-2(0-0)
Leicester City - Wolverhampton 2-1(1-1)
Bournemouth - West Ham United 0-4(0-3)
Newcastle - Tottenham Hotspur 6-1(5-0)
Brighton-Manchester City 1-1(1-1) [24.05.23]
Manchester Unit.-Chelsea 4-1(2-0) [25.05.23]

### Round 33 [25-27.04.2023]
Wolverhampton - Crystal Palace 2-0(1-0)
Aston Villa - Fulham 1-0(1-0)
Leeds United - Leicester City 1-1(1-0)
Nottingham - Brighton & Hove 3-1(1-1)
West Ham United - Liverpool 1-2(1-1)
Chelsea - Brentford 0-2(0-1)
Manchester City - Arsenal 4-1(2-0)
Everton - Newcastle United 1-4(0-1)
Southampton - Bournemouth 0-1(0-0)
Tottenham - Manchester United 2-2(0-2)

### Round 34 [29.04.-02.05.2023]
Crystal Palace - West Ham United 4-3(3-2)
Brighton & Hove - Wolverhampton 6-0(4-0)
Brentford - Nottingham Forest 2-1(0-1)
Bournemouth - Leeds United 4-1(2-1)
Fulham - Manchester City 1-2(1-2)
Manchester United - Aston Villa 1-0(1-0)
Newcastle United - Southampton 3-1(0-1)
Liverpool - Tottenham Hotspur 4-3(3-1)
Leicester City - Everton 2-2(2-1)
Arsenal - Chelsea 3-1(3-0)

### Round 35 [06-08.05.2023]
Bournemouth - Chelsea 1-3(1-1)
Manchester City - Leeds United 2-1(2-0)
Tottenham Hotspur - Crystal Palace 1-0(1-0)
Wolverhampton - Aston Villa 1-0(1-0)
Liverpool - Brentford 1-0(1-0)
Newcastle United - Arsenal 0-2(0-1)
West Ham United-Manchester United 1-0(1-0)
Fulham - Leicester City 5-3(3-0)
Brighton & Hove - Everton 1-5(0-3)
Nottingham Forest - Southampton 4-3(3-1)

### Round 36 [13-15.05.2023]
Leeds United - Newcastle United 2-2(1-1)
Aston Villa - Tottenham Hotspur 2-1(1-0)
Crystal Palace - Bournemouth 2-0(1-0)
Chelsea - Nottingham Forest 2-2(0-1)
Southampton - Fulham 0-2(0-0)
Manchester United - Wolverhampton 2-0(1-0)
Brentford - West Ham United 2-0(2-0)
Everton - Manchester City 0-3(0-2)
Arsenal - Brighton & Hove 0-3(0-0)
Leicester City - Liverpool 0-3(0-2)

| Round 37 [20-22.05.2023] |
| --- |
| Tottenham Hotspur - Brentford 1-3(1-0) |
| Bournemouth - Manchester United 0-1(0-1) |
| Fulham - Crystal Palace 2-2(1-1) |
| Liverpool - Aston Villa 1-1(0-1) |
| Wolverhampton - Everton 1-1(1-0) |
| Nottingham Forest - Arsenal 1-0(1-0) |
| West Ham United - Leeds United 3-1(1-1) |
| Brighton & Hove - Southampton 3-1(2-0) |
| Manchester City - Chelsea 1-0(1-0) |
| Newcastle United - Leicester City 0-0 |

| Round 38 [28.05.2023] |
| --- |
| Aston Villa - Brighton & Hove 2-1(2-1) |
| Crystal Palace - Nottingham Forest 1-1(0-1) |
| Arsenal - Wolverhampton 5-0(3-0) |
| Brentford - Manchester City 1-0(0-0) |
| Chelsea - Newcastle United 1-1(1-1) |
| Everton - Bournemouth 1-0(0-0) |
| Southampton - Liverpool 4-4(2-2) |
| Leeds United - Tottenham Hotspur 1-4(0-1) |
| Leicester City - West Ham United 2-1(1-0) |
| Manchester United - Fulham 2-1(1-1) |

## Final Standings

| | | | | | | | | | | Total | | | Home | | | | | Away | | | | |
| --- | --- | --- | --- | --- | --- | --- | --- | --- | --- | --- | --- | --- | --- | --- | --- | --- | --- | --- | --- | --- | --- | --- |
| 1. | **Manchester City FC** | 38 | 28 | 5 | 5 | 94 | - | 33 | **89** | 17 | 1 | 1 | 60 | - | 17 | 11 | 4 | 4 | 34 | - | 16 |
| 2. | Arsenal FC London | 38 | 26 | 6 | 6 | 88 | - | 43 | **84** | 14 | 3 | 2 | 53 | - | 25 | 12 | 3 | 4 | 35 | - | 18 |
| 3. | Manchester United FC | 38 | 23 | 6 | 9 | 58 | - | 43 | **75** | 15 | 3 | 1 | 36 | - | 10 | 8 | 3 | 8 | 22 | - | 33 |
| 4. | Newcastle United FC | 38 | 19 | 14 | 5 | 68 | - | 33 | **71** | 11 | 6 | 2 | 36 | - | 14 | 8 | 8 | 3 | 32 | - | 19 |
| 5. | Liverpool FC | 38 | 19 | 10 | 9 | 75 | - | 47 | **67** | 13 | 5 | 1 | 46 | - | 17 | 6 | 5 | 8 | 29 | - | 30 |
| 6. | Brighton & Hove Albion FC | 38 | 18 | 8 | 12 | 72 | - | 53 | **62** | 10 | 4 | 5 | 37 | - | 21 | 8 | 4 | 7 | 35 | - | 32 |
| 7. | Aston Villa FC Birmingham | 38 | 18 | 7 | 13 | 51 | - | 46 | **61** | 12 | 2 | 5 | 33 | - | 21 | 6 | 5 | 8 | 18 | - | 25 |
| 8. | Tottenham Hotspur FC London | 38 | 18 | 6 | 14 | 70 | - | 63 | **60** | 12 | 1 | 6 | 37 | - | 25 | 6 | 5 | 8 | 33 | - | 38 |
| 9. | Brentford FC London | 38 | 15 | 14 | 9 | 58 | - | 46 | **59** | 10 | 7 | 2 | 35 | - | 18 | 5 | 7 | 7 | 23 | - | 28 |
| 10. | Fulham FC London | 38 | 15 | 7 | 16 | 55 | - | 53 | **52** | 8 | 5 | 6 | 31 | - | 29 | 7 | 2 | 10 | 24 | - | 24 |
| 11. | Crystal Palace FC London | 38 | 11 | 12 | 15 | 40 | - | 49 | **45** | 7 | 7 | 5 | 21 | - | 23 | 4 | 5 | 10 | 19 | - | 26 |
| 12. | Chelsea FC London | 38 | 11 | 11 | 16 | 38 | - | 47 | **44** | 6 | 7 | 6 | 20 | - | 19 | 5 | 4 | 10 | 18 | - | 28 |
| 13. | Wolverhampton Wanderers FC | 38 | 11 | 8 | 19 | 31 | - | 58 | **41** | 9 | 3 | 7 | 19 | - | 20 | 2 | 5 | 12 | 12 | - | 38 |
| 14. | West Ham United FC London | 38 | 11 | 7 | 20 | 42 | - | 55 | **40** | 8 | 4 | 7 | 26 | - | 24 | 3 | 3 | 13 | 16 | - | 31 |
| 15. | AFC Bournemouth | 38 | 11 | 6 | 21 | 37 | - | 71 | **39** | 6 | 4 | 9 | 20 | - | 28 | 5 | 2 | 12 | 17 | - | 43 |
| 16. | Nottingham Forest FC | 38 | 9 | 11 | 18 | 38 | - | 68 | **38** | 8 | 6 | 5 | 27 | - | 24 | 1 | 5 | 13 | 11 | - | 44 |
| 17. | Everton FC Liverpool | 38 | 8 | 12 | 18 | 34 | - | 57 | **36** | 6 | 3 | 10 | 16 | - | 27 | 2 | 9 | 8 | 18 | - | 30 |
| 18. | Leicester City FC (Relegated) | 38 | 9 | 7 | 22 | 51 | - | 68 | **34** | 5 | 4 | 10 | 23 | - | 27 | 4 | 3 | 12 | 28 | - | 41 |
| 19. | Leeds United FC (Relegated) | 38 | 7 | 10 | 21 | 48 | - | 78 | **31** | 5 | 7 | 7 | 26 | - | 37 | 2 | 3 | 14 | 22 | - | 41 |
| 20. | Southampton FC (Relegated) | 38 | 6 | 7 | 25 | 36 | - | 73 | **25** | 2 | 5 | 12 | 19 | - | 37 | 4 | 2 | 13 | 17 | - | 36 |

## Top goalscorers:

| | | |
| --- | --- | --- |
| 36 | **Erling Braut Haaland (NOR)** | *Manchester City FC* |
| 30 | Harry Edward Kane | *Tottenham Hotspur FC London* |
| 20 | Ivan Benjamin Elijah Toney | *Brentford FC London* |
| 19 | Mohamed Salah Ghaly (EGY) | *Liverpool FC* |
| 18 | Callum Eddie Graham Wilson | *Newcastle United FC* |

## EFL (League) Cup Final 2022/2023

26.02.2023; Wembley Stadium, London; Referee: David Coote; Attendance: 0,000

**Manchester United FC - Newcastle United FC**                                             **2-0(2-0)**

**Manchester United**: David de Gea Quintana, José Diogo Dalot Teixeira (46.Aaron Wan-Bissaka), Raphaël Xavier Varane, Lisandro Martínez, Luke Paul Hoare Shaw, Frederico Rodrigues de Paula Santos "Fred" (70.Marcel Sabitzer), Carlos Henrique José Francisco Venancio Casimiro „Casemiro", Bruno Miguel Borges Fernandes (Cap), Antony Matheus dos Santos (83.Jadon Malik Sancho), Marcus Rashford (88.Jacob Harry Maguire), Wout Weghorst. Trainer: Erik ten Hag (Netherlands).

**Newcastle United**: Loris Karius, Kieran John Trippier (Cap), Fabian Schär, Sven Adriaan Botman, Daniel Johnson Burn, Bruno Guimarães Rodriguez Moura (79.Joseph George Willock), Sean David Longstaff (46.lexander Isak), Joelinton Cássio Apolinário de Lira, Miguel Ángel Almirón Rejala (90+1.Elliot Anderson), Callum Eddie Graham Wilson (90+1.Matthew Thomas Ritchie), Allan Irénée Saint-Maximin (78.Jacob Kai Murphy). Trainer: Edward John Frank Howe.

**Goals:** 1-0 Carlos Henrique José Francisco Venancio Casimiro „Casemiro" (33), 2-0 Marcus Rashford (39).

# NATIONAL CUP
## FA Cup 2022/2023

### Third Round [06-09.01./17-18.01./24.01.2023]

| | | | | | |
|---|---|---|---|---|---|
| Manchester United FC - Everton FC Liverpool | 3-1(1-1) | | Sheffield Wednesday FC - Newcastle United FC | 2-1(0-0) |
| Preston North End FC - Huddersfield Town AFC | 3-1(0-0) | | Liverpool FC - Wolverhampton | 2-2(1-1) |
| Tottenham Hotspur FC London - Portsmouth FC | 1-0(0-0) | | Derby County FC - Barnsley FC | 3-0(1-0) |
| Gillingham FC - Leicester City FC | 0-1(0-0) | | Bristol City FC - Swansea City AFC | 1-1(0-1) |
| Crystal Palace FC London - Southampton FC | 1-2(1-1) | | Stockport County FC - Walsall FC | 1-2(0-0) |
| Reading FC - Watford FC | 2-0(1-0) | | Cardiff City FC - Leeds United FC | 2-2(2-0) |
| Middlesbrough FC - Brighton & Hove Albion FC | 1-5(1-2) | | Norwich City FC - Blackburn Rovers FC | 0-1(0-1) |
| Chesterfield FC - West Bromwich Albion FC | 3-3(3-2) | | Hartlepool United FC - Stoke City FC | 0-3(0-2) |
| Boreham Wood FC - Accrington Stanley FC | 1-1(0-1) | | Manchester City FC - Chelsea FC London | 4-0(3-0) |
| AFC Bournemouth - Burnley FC | 2-4(1-3) | | Aston Villa FC Birmingham - Stevenage FC | 1-2(1-0) |
| Fleetwood Town FC - Queens Park Rangers FC London | 2-1(1-1) | | Oxford United FC - Arsenal FC London | 0-3(0-0) |
| Blackpool FC - Nottingham Forest FC | 4-1(1-0) | | Forest Green Rovers FC - Birmingham City FC | 1-2(1-0) |
| Hull City AFC - Fulham FC London | 0-2(0-1) | | *Replays:* | |
| Millwall FC London - Sheffield United FC | 0-2(0-2) | | Wigan Athletic FC - Luton Town FC | 1-2(0-0) |
| Shrewsbury Town FC - Sunderland AFC | 1-2(0-0) | | Wolverhampton - Liverpool FC | 0-1(0-1) |
| Ipswich Town FC - Rotherham United FC | 4-1(1-0) | | Swansea City AFC - Bristol City FC | 1-2(0-0,1-1) |
| Brentford FC London - West Ham United FC London | 0-1(0-0) | | West Bromwich Albion FC - Chesterfield FC | 4-0(1-0) |
| Coventry City FC - Wrexham AFC | 3-4(1-3) | | Leeds United FC - Cardiff City FC | 5-2(3-0) |
| Luton Town FC - Wigan Athletic FC | 1-1(1-1) | | Accrington Stanley FC - Boreham Wood FC | 1-0(0-0,0-0) |
| Grimsby Town FC - Burton Albion FC | 1-0(0-0) | | | |

### Fourth Round [27-31.01./07-08.02.2023]

| | | | | | |
|---|---|---|---|---|---|
| Manchester City FC - Arsenal FC London | 1-0(0-0) | | Brighton & Hove Albion FC - Liverpool FC | 2-1(1-1) |
| Walsall FC - Leicester City FC | 0-1(0-0) | | Stoke City FC - Stevenage FC | 3-1(1-0) |
| Accrington Stanley FC - Leeds United FC | 1-3(0-1) | | Wrexham AFC - Sheffield United FC | 3-3(0-1) |
| Southampton FC - Blackpool FC | 2-1(1-0) | | Derby County FC - West Ham United FC London | 0-2(0-1) |
| Ipswich Town FC - Burnley FC | 0-0 | | *Replays:* | |
| Luton Town FC - Grimsby Town FC | 2-2(0-1) | | Birmingham City FC - Blackburn Rovers FC | 0-1(0-0,0-0) |
| Sheffield Wednesday FC - Fleetwood Town FC | 1-1(0-0) | | Burnley FC - Ipswich Town FC | 2-1(1-1) |
| Fulham FC London - Sunderland AFC | 1-1(0-1) | | Grimsby Town FC - Luton Town FC | 3-0(3-0) |
| Bristol City FC - West Bromwich Albion FC | 3-0(2-0) | | Fleetwood Town FC - Sheffield Wednesday FC | 1-0(0-0) |
| Blackburn Rovers FC - Birmingham City FC | 2-2(1-1) | | Sheffield United FC - Wrexham AFC | 3-1(0-0) |
| Preston North End FC - Tottenham Hotspur FC London | 0-3(0-0) | | Sunderland AFC - Fulham FC London | 2-3(0-1) |
| Manchester United FC - Reading FC | 3-1(0-0) | | | |

### 1/8-Finals [28.02.-01.03.2023]

| | | | | | |
|---|---|---|---|---|---|
| Stoke City FC - Brighton & Hove Albion FC | 0-1(0-1) | | Southampton FC - Grimsby Town FC | 1-2(0-1) |
| Leicester City FC - Blackburn Rovers FC | 1-2(0-1) | | Burnley FC - Fleetwood Town FC | 1-0(0-0) |
| Fulham FC London - Leeds United FC | 2-0(1-0) | | Manchester United FC - West Ham United FC London | 3-1(0-0) |
| Bristol City FC - Manchester City FC | 0-3(0-1) | | Sheffield United FC - Tottenham Hotspur FC London | 1-0(0-0) |

### Quarter-Finals [18-19.03.2023]

| | | | | | |
|---|---|---|---|---|---|
| Manchester City FC - Burnley FC | 6-0(2-0) | | Brighton & Hove Albion FC - Grimsby Town FC | 5-0(1-0) |
| Sheffield United FC - Blackburn Rovers FC | 3-2(1-1) | | Manchester United FC - Fulham FC London | 3-1(0-0) |

### Semi-Finals [22-23.04.2023]

| | | | | | |
|---|---|---|---|---|---|
| Manchester City FC - Sheffield United FC | 3-0(1-0) | | Brighton & Hove Albion FC - Manchester United FC | 0-0 aet; 6-7pen |

### Final

03.06.2023; Wembley Stadium, London; Referee: Paul Tierney; Attendance: 83,179
**Manchester City FC - Manchester United FC**                                    **2-1(1-1)**

**Manchester City**: Stefan Ortega Moreno, Kyle Andrew Walker (90+5.Aymeric Jean Louis Gerard Alphonse Laporte), Manuel Obafemi Akanji, Rúben Santos Gato Alves Dias, John Stones, Rodrigo Hernández Cascante „Rodri", İlkay Gündoğan (Cap), Kevin De Bruyne (76.Philip Walter Foden), Jack Peter Grealish (89.Nathan Benjamin Aké), Bernardo Mota Veiga de Carvalho e Silva, Erling Braut Haaland. Trainer: Josep Guardiola Sala (Spain).

**Manchester United**: David de Gea Quintana, Aaron Wan-Bissaka, Raphaël Xavier Varane, Victor Jörgen Nilsson Lindelöf (83.Scott Francis McTominay), Luke Paul Hoare Shaw, Frederico Rodrigues de Paula Santos "Fred",Carlos Henrique José Francisco Venancio Casimiro „Casemiro", Christian Dannemann Eriksen (62.Alejandro Garnacho Ferreira), Bruno Miguel Borges Fernandes (Cap), Jadon Malik Sancho (78.Wout Weghorst), Marcus Rashford. Trainer: Erik ten Hag (Netherlands).

**Goals:** 1-0 İlkay Gündoğan (1), 1-1 Bruno Miguel Borges Fernandes (33 penalty), 2-1 İlkay Gündoğan (51).

## Arsenal Football Club London

| | Founded: | 1886 | |
|---|---|---|---|
| | Stadium: | Emirates Stadium, London (60,704) | |
| | Trainer: | Mikel Amatriain Arteta (ESP) | 26.03.1982 |

| Goalkeepers: | DOB | M | (s) | G |
|---|---|---|---|---|
| Aaron Christopher Ramsdale | 14.05.1998 | 38 | | |
| **Defenders:** | **DOB** | **M** | **(s)** | **G** |
| *Cédric* Ricardo Alves Soares (POR) | 31.08.1991 | | (2) | |
| *Gabriel* dos Santos Magalhaes (BRA) | 19.12.1997 | 38 | | 3 |
| Robert Samuel Holding | 20.09.1995 | 6 | (8) | 1 |
| Jakub Piotr Kiwior (POL) | 15.02.2000 | 5 | (2) | 1 |
| William Alain André Gabriel Saliba (FRA) | 24.03.2001 | 27 | | 2 |
| Kieran Tierney (SCO) | 05.06.1997 | 6 | (21) | |
| Takehiro Tomiyasu (JPN) | 05.11.1998 | 6 | (15) | |
| Benjamin William White | 08.10.1997 | 36 | (2) | 2 |
| Oleksandr Zinchenko (UKR) | 15.12.1996 | 26 | (1) | 1 |
| **Midfielders:** | **DOB** | **M** | **(s)** | **G** |
| Mohamed Naser Elsayed Elneny (EGY) | 11.07.1992 | 1 | (4) | |
| *Fábio* Daniel Ferreira *Vieira* (POR) | 30.05.2000 | 3 | (19) | 1 |
| Filho Jorge Luiz Frello „Jorginho" (ITA) | 20.12.1991 | 9 | (5) | |
| Albert Sambi Lokonga (BEL) | 22.10.1999 | 2 | (4) | |
| Ethan Chidiebere Nwaneri | 21.03.2007 | | (1) | |
| Martin Ødegaard (NOR) | 17.12.1998 | 37 | | 15 |
| Thomas Partey (GHA) | 13.06.1993 | 28 | (5) | 3 |
| Emile Smith Rowe | 28.07.2000 | | (12) | |
| Granit Xhaka (SUI) | 27.09.1992 | 36 | (1) | 7 |
| **Forwards:** | **DOB** | **M** | **(s)** | **G** |
| *Gabriel* Fernando de *Jesus* (BRA) | 03.04.1997 | 24 | (2) | 11 |
| *Gabriel* Teodoro *Martinelli* Silva (BRA) | 18.06.2001 | 34 | (2) | 15 |
| Marcus Vinícius Oliveira Alencar „Marquinhos"(BRA) | 07.04.2003 | | (1) | |
| Reiss Nelson | 10.12.1999 | | (11) | 3 |
| Edward Keddar Nketiah | 30.05.1999 | 9 | (21) | 4 |
| Bukayo Ayoyinka Saka | 05.09.2001 | 37 | (1) | 14 |
| Leandro Trossard (BEL) | 04.12.1994 | 10 | (10) | 1 |

## Aston Villa Football Club Birmingham

| | Founded: | 21.11.1874 | |
|---|---|---|---|
| | Stadium: | Villa Park, Birmingham (42,682) | |
| | Trainer: | Steven George Gerrard | 30.05.1980 |
| [21.10.2022] | | Aaron Danks | 15.06.1983 |
| [01.11.2022] | | Unai Emery Etxegoien (ESP) | 03.11.1971 |

| Goalkeepers: | DOB | M | (s) | G |
|---|---|---|---|---|
| Damián Emiliano Martínez Romero (ARG) | 02.09.1992 | 36 | | |
| Robin Patrick Olsen (SWE) | 08.01.1990 | 2 | (2) | |
| **Defenders:** | **DOB** | **M** | **(s)** | **G** |
| Alexandre Moreno Lopera „Álex Moreno" (ESP) | 08.06.1993 | 14 | (5) | |
| Hans Carl Ludwig Augustinsson (SWE) | 21.04.1994 | 1 | (2) | |
| Jan Kacper Bednarek (POL) | 12.04.1996 | 1 | (2) | |
| Matthew Stuart Cash (POL) | 07.08.1997 | 20 | (6) | |
| Calum Chambers | 20.01.1995 | 2 | (12) | |
| *Diego Carlos* Santos Silva (BRA) | 15.03.1993 | 2 | (1) | |
| Lucas Digne (FRA) | 20.07.1993 | 18 | (10) | 1 |
| Ezri Konsa Ngoyo | 23.10.1997 | 37 | (1) | |
| Tyrone Deon Mings | 13.03.1993 | 35 | | 1 |
| Ashley Simon Young | 09.07.1985 | 23 | (6) | 1 |
| **Midfielders:** | **DOB** | **M** | **(s)** | **G** |
| Leander Dendoncker (BEL) | 15.04.1995 | 7 | (13) | |
| *Douglas Luiz* Soares de Paulo (BRA) | 09.05.1998 | 33 | (4) | 6 |
| Boubacar Bernard Kamara (FRA) | 23.11.1999 | 21 | (3) | |
| John McGinn (SCO) | 18.10.1994 | 30 | (4) | 1 |
| *Philippe Coutinho* Correia (BRA) | 12.06.1992 | 7 | (13) | 1 |
| Jacob Ramsey | 28.05.2001 | 31 | (4) | 6 |
| Morgan Sanson (FRA) | 18.08.1994 | | (2) | |
| **Forwards:** | **DOB** | **M** | **(s)** | **G** |
| Cameron Desmond Archer | 09.12.2001 | | (6) | |
| Leon Patrick Bailey Butler (JAM) | 09.08.1997 | 26 | (7) | 4 |
| Emiliano Buendia Sutil (ARG) | 25.12.1996 | 27 | (11) | 5 |
| Jhon Jader Durán Palacio (COL) | 13.12.2003 | | (12) | |
| Daniel William John Ings | 23.07.1992 | 8 | (10) | 6 |
| Bertrand Traoré (BFA) | 06.09.1995 | 1 | (7) | 2 |
| Oliver George Arthur Watkins | 30.12.1995 | 36 | (1) | 15 |

## Association Football Club Bournemouth

| | Founded: | 1889 | |
|---|---|---|---|
| | Stadium: | Vitality Stadium [Dean Court], Bournemouth (11,307) | |
| | Trainer: | Scott Matthew Parker | 13.10.1980 |
| [30.08.2022] | | Gary Paul O'Neil | 18.05.1983 |

| Goalkeepers: | DOB | M | (s) | G |
|---|---|---|---|---|
| Norberto Murara *Neto* (BRA) | 19.07.1989 | 27 | | |
| Mark Travers (IRL) | 18.05.1999 | 11 | (1) | |
| **Defenders:** | **DOB** | **M** | **(s)** | **G** |
| Owen Bevan (WAL) | 26.10.2003 | | (1) | |
| Ryan Marlowe Fredericks | 10.10.1992 | 5 | (7) | |
| Lloyd Casius Kelly | 06.10.1998 | 23 | | |
| Christopher James Mepham (WAL) | 05.11.1997 | 24 | (2) | |
| Marcos Nicolás Senesi Barón (ARG) | 10.05.1997 | 29 | (2) | 2 |
| Adam James Smith | 29.04.1991 | 34 | (3) | |
| Jack William Stacey | 06.04.1996 | 3 | (7) | |
| Jack Stephens | 27.01.1994 | 13 | (2) | |
| Matías Nicolás Viña Susperreguy (URU) | 09.11.1997 | 5 | (7) | 2 |
| Ilya Zabarnyi (UKR) | 01.09.2002 | 3 | (2) | |
| Jordan Zemura (ZIM) | 14.11.1999 | 17 | (2) | |
| **Midfielders:** | **DOB** | **M** | **(s)** | **G** |
| Philip Anyabwu Billing (DEN) | 11.06.1996 | 34 | (2) | 7 |
| Emiliano Marcondes Camargo Hansen (DEN) | 09.03.1995 | | (1) | |
| Ryan Christie (SCO) | 22.02.1995 | 22 | (10) | 1 |
| Lewis John Cook | 03.02.1997 | 18 | (10) | |
| Jefferson Andrés Lerma Solís (COL) | 25.10.1994 | 37 | | 5 |
| Joseph Matthew Rothwell | 11.01.1995 | 12 | (8) | |
| Benjamin David Pearson | 04.01.1995 | 3 | (4) | |
| Marcus Joseph Tavernier | 22.03.1999 | 19 | (4) | 5 |
| Hamed Junior Traorè (CIV) | 16.02.2000 | 5 | (2) | |
| **Forwards:** | **DOB** | **M** | **(s)** | **G** |
| Jaidon Kya Denley Anthony | 01.12.1999 | 11 | (19) | 3 |
| David Robert Brooks (WAL) | 08.07.1997 | 2 | (4) | |
| Ben Siriki Dembélé (SCO) | 07.09.1996 | | (6) | |
| Jamal Akua Lowe (JAM) | 21.07.1994 | | (2) | |
| Kieffer Roberto Francisco Moore (WAL) | 08.08.1992 | 12 | (15) | 4 |
| Dango Ouattara (BFA) | 11.02.2002 | 15 | (4) | 1 |
| Antoine Semenyo (GHA) | 07.01.2000 | 2 | (9) | 1 |
| Dominic Ayodele Solanke-Mitchell | 14.09.1997 | 32 | (1) | 6 |
| Felix Junior Stanislas | 26.11.1989 | | (4) | |

## Brentford Football Club London

| | Founded: | 10.10.1889 | |
|---|---|---|---|
| | Stadium: | Brentford Community Stadium, Brentford, West London (17,250) | |
| | Trainer: | Thomas Frank (DEN) | 09.10.1973 |

| Goalkeepers: | DOB | M | (s) | G |
|---|---|---|---|---|
| *David Raya* Martín (ESP) | 15.09.1995 | 38 | | |
| **Defenders:** | **DOB** | **M** | **(s)** | **G** |
| Kristoffer Vassbakk Ajer (NOR) | 17.04.1998 | 9 | | |
| Mads Bech Sørensen (DEN) | 07.01.1999 | | (4) | |
| Rico Antonio Henry | 08.07.1997 | 37 | | |
| Aaron Buchanan Hickey (SCO) | 10.06.2002 | 23 | (3) | |
| Pontus Sven Gustav Jansson (SWE) | 13.02.1991 | 9 | (3) | 1 |
| Mathias Jattah-Njie Jørgensen (DEN) | 23.04.1990 | 11 | (7) | |
| Benjamin Thomas Mee | 21.09.1989 | 37 | | 3 |
| Ethan Rupert Pinnock (JAM) | 29.05.1993 | 30 | | 3 |
| Mads Roerslev Rasmussen (DEN) | 24.06.1999 | 12 | (8) | |
| **Midfielders:** | **DOB** | **M** | **(s)** | **G** |
| Shandon Harkeem Baptiste (GRN) | 08.04.1998 | 4 | (19) | |
| Pelenda Joshua Tunga Da Silva | 23.10.1998 | 14 | (22) | 4 |
| Saman Ghoddos (IRN) | 06.09.1993 | | (15) | |
| Vitaly Janelt (GER) | 10.05.1998 | 24 | (11) | 3 |
| Mathias Jensen (DEN) | 01.01.1996 | 37 | | 5 |
| Christian Thers Nørgaard (DEN) | 10.03.1994 | 21 | (1) | 1 |
| Frank Ogochukwu Onyeka (NGA) | 01.01.1998 | 8 | (13) | |
| **Forwards:** | **DOB** | **M** | **(s)** | **G** |
| Mikkel Krogh Damsgaard (DEN) | 03.07.2000 | 9 | (17) | |
| Halil İbrahim Dervişoğlu (TUR) | 08.12.1999 | | (1) | |
| Keane William Lewis-Potter | 22.02.2001 | 3 | (7) | |
| Bryan Tetsadong Marceau Mbeumo (CMR) | 07.08.1999 | 36 | (2) | 9 |
| Kevin Schade (GER) | 27.11.2001 | 7 | (11) | |
| *Sergi Canós* Tenés (ESP) | 02.02.1997 | | (5) | |
| Ivan Benjamin Elijah Toney | 16.03.1996 | 33 | | 20 |
| Yoane Wissa (COD) | 03.09.1996 | 16 | (22) | 7 |

## Brighton & Hove Albion Football Club

| | | | |
|---|---|---|---|
| **Founded:** | 24.06.1901 | | |
| **Stadium:** | Falmer Stadium, Brighton and Hove (31,800) | | |
| **Trainer:** | Graham Stephen Potter | 20.05.1975 | |
| [08.09.2022] | Andrew Lawrence Crofts (WAL) | 29.05.1984 | |
| [18.09.2022] | Roberto De Zerbi (ITA) | 06.06.1979 | |

| Goalkeepers: | DOB | M | (s) | G |
|---|---|---|---|---|
| Robert Lynch Sánchez (ESP) | 18.11.1997 | 23 | | |
| Jason Steele | 18.08.1990 | 15 | | |
| **Defenders:** | **DOB** | **M** | **(s)** | **G** |
| Levi Lemar Samuels Colwill | 26.02.2003 | 13 | (4) | |
| Lewis Carl Dunk | 21.11.1991 | 36 | | 1 |
| Pervis Josué Estupiñán Tenorio (ECU) | 21.01.1998 | 31 | (4) | 1 |
| Tariq Kwame Nii-Lante Lamptey (GHA) | 30.09.2000 | 3 | (17) | |
| Odeluga Joshua Offiah | 26.10.2002 | | (2) | |
| Jan Paul van Hecke (NED) | 08.06.2000 | 3 | (5) | |
| Joël Ivo Veltman (NED) | 15.01.1992 | 25 | (6) | 1 |
| Adam Harry Webster | 04.01.1995 | 23 | (4) | |
| **Midfielders:** | **DOB** | **M** | **(s)** | **G** |
| Yasin Abbas Ayari (SWE) | 06.10.2003 | 1 | (1) | |
| Facundo Buonanotte (ARG) | 23.12.2004 | 6 | (7) | 1 |
| Moisés Isaac Caicedo Corozo (ECU) | 02.11.2001 | 34 | (3) | 1 |
| Billy Clifford Gilmour (SCO) | 11.06.2001 | 7 | (7) | |

| | DOB | M | (s) | G |
|---|---|---|---|---|
| Pascal Groß (GER) | 15.06.1991 | 37 | | 9 |
| Jack Hinshelwood | 11.04.2005 | | (1) | |
| Adam David Lallana | 10.05.1988 | 12 | (4) | 2 |
| Alexis Mac Allister (ARG) | 24.12.1998 | 31 | (4) | 10 |
| Andrew Moran (IRL) | 15.10.2003 | | (1) | |
| Enock Mwepu (ZAM) | 01.01.1998 | 2 | (4) | |
| Cameron Paul Jacques Peupion (AUS) | 23.09.2002 | | (1) | |
| Jeremy Leonel Sarmiento Morante (ECU) | 16.06.2002 | 1 | (8) | |
| **Forwards:** | **DOB** | **M** | **(s)** | **G** |
| Julio César Enciso Espínola (PAR) | 23.01.2004 | 7 | (13) | 4 |
| Evan Ferguson (IRL) | 19.10.2004 | 10 | (9) | 6 |
| Solomon Benjamin March | 20.07.1994 | 31 | (2) | 6 |
| Kaoru Mitoma (JPN) | 20.05.1997 | 24 | (9) | 7 |
| Leandro Trossard (BEL) | 04.12.1994 | 16 | | 7 |
| Deniz Undav (GER) | 19.07.1996 | 6 | (16) | 5 |
| Daniel Nii Tackie Mensah Welbeck | 26.11.1990 | 21 | (10) | 6 |

## Chelsea Football Club London

| | | | |
|---|---|---|---|
| **Founded:** | 10.03.1905 | | |
| **Stadium:** | Stamford Bridge, London (40,343) | | |
| **Trainer:** | Thomas Tuchel (GER) | 29.08.1973 | |
| [08.09.2022] | Graham Stephen Potter | 20.05.1975 | |
| [02.04.2023] | Bruno Saltor Grau (ESP) | 01.10.1980 | |
| [06.04.2023] | Frank James Lampard | 20.06.1978 | |

| Goalkeepers: | DOB | M | (s) | G |
|---|---|---|---|---|
| Kepa Arrizabalaga Revuelta (ESP) | 03.10.1994 | 29 | | |
| Edouard Mendy (SEN) | 01.03.1992 | 9 | (1) | |
| **Defenders:** | **DOB** | **M** | **(s)** | **G** |
| César *Azpilicueta* Tanco (ESP) | 28.08.1989 | 16 | (9) | |
| Benoît Badiashile Mukinayi (FRA) | 26.03.2001 | 10 | (1) | 1 |
| Trevoh Thomas Chalobah | 05.07.1999 | 18 | (7) | |
| Benjamin James Chilwell | 21.12.1996 | 15 | (8) | 2 |
| Marc *Cucurella* Saseta (ESP) | 22.07.1998 | 21 | (3) | |
| Wesley Fofana (FRA) | 17.12.2000 | 12 | (3) | 1 |
| Lewis Hall | 08.09.2004 | 8 | (1) | |
| Reece James | 08.12.1999 | 14 | (2) | 1 |
| Kalidou Koulibaly (SEN) | 20.06.1991 | 20 | (3) | 2 |
| *Thiago* Emiliano *Silva* (BRA) | 22.09.1984 | 26 | (1) | |
| **Midfielders:** | **DOB** | **M** | **(s)** | **G** |
| Carney Chibueze Chukwuemeka | 20.10.2003 | 2 | (12) | |
| Enzo Jeremías Fernández (ARG) | 17.01.2001 | 18 | | |
| Conor John Gallagher | 06.02.2000 | 18 | (17) | 3 |

| | DOB | M | (s) | G |
|---|---|---|---|---|
| Omari Elijah Giraud-Hutchinson | 29.10.2003 | | (1) | |
| Filho Jorge Luiz Frello „Jorginho" (ITA) | 20.12.1991 | 15 | (3) | 2 |
| N'Golo Kanté (FRA) | 29.03.1991 | 6 | (1) | |
| Mateo Kovačić (CRO) | 06.05.1994 | 17 | (10) | 1 |
| Ruben Ira Loftus-Cheek | 23.01.1996 | 19 | (6) | |
| Mason Tony Mount | 10.01.1999 | 20 | (4) | 3 |
| Mykhaylo Mudryk (UKR) | 05.01.2001 | 7 | (8) | |
| Denis Lemi Zakaria Lako Lado (SUI) | 20.11.1996 | 5 | (2) | |
| **Forwards:** | **DOB** | **M** | **(s)** | **G** |
| Pierre-Emerick Emiliano François Aubameyang(GAB) | 18.06.1989 | 5 | (10) | 1 |
| Armando Broja (ALB) | 10.09.2001 | 2 | (10) | 1 |
| David Fofana (CIV) | 22.12.2002 | 1 | (2) | |
| Kai Lukas Havertz (GER) | 11.06.1999 | 30 | (5) | 7 |
| *João Félix* Sequeira (POR) | 10.11.1999 | 11 | (5) | 4 |
| Chukwunonso Tristan Madueke | 10.03.2002 | 7 | (5) | 1 |
| Christian Mate Pulišić (USA) | 18.09.1998 | 8 | (16) | 1 |
| Raheem Shaquille Sterling | 08.12.1994 | 23 | (5) | 6 |
| Hakim Ziyech (MAR) | 19.03.1993 | 6 | (12) | |

## Crystal Palace Football Club London

| | | | |
|---|---|---|---|
| **Founded:** | 10.09.1905 | | |
| **Stadium:** | Selhurst Park, London (25,486) | | |
| **Trainer:** | Patrick Donalé Vieira (FRA) | 23.06.1976 | |
| [17.03.2023] | Patrick Richard McCarthy (IRL) | 31.05.1983 | |
| [21.03.2023] | Roy Hodgson | 09.08.1947 | |

| Goalkeepers: | DOB | M | (s) | G |
|---|---|---|---|---|
| Vicente *Guaita* Panadero (ESP) | 10.01.1987 | 27 | | |
| Samuel Luke Johnstone | 25.03.1993 | 9 | | |
| Joseph Charles Whitworth | 29.02.2004 | 2 | | |
| **Defenders:** | **DOB** | **M** | **(s)** | **G** |
| Joachim Christian Andersen (DEN) | 31.05.1996 | 32 | | 1 |
| Nathaniel Edwin Clyne | 05.04.1991 | 19 | (3) | |
| Addji Keaninkin Marc-Israel Guéhi | 13.07.2000 | 37 | | 1 |
| Tyrick Kwon Mitchell | 01.09.1999 | 34 | (2) | |
| Christopher Jeffrey Richards (USA) | 28.03.2000 | 4 | (5) | |
| James Oliver Charles Tomkins | 29.03.1989 | 3 | (3) | 1 |
| Joel Edward Philip Ward | 29.10.1989 | 24 | (4) | 1 |
| **Midfielders:** | **DOB** | **M** | **(s)** | **G** |
| Naouirou Mohamed Ahamada (FRA) | 29.03.2002 | | (8) | |
| Cheick Doucouré (MLI) | 08.01.2000 | 34 | | |

| | DOB | M | (s) | G |
|---|---|---|---|---|
| Eberechi Oluchi Eze | 29.06.1998 | 30 | (8) | 10 |
| William James Hughes | 17.04.1995 | 7 | (20) | 1 |
| Albert Mboyo Sambi Lokonga (BEL) | 22.10.1999 | 6 | (3) | |
| James McFarlane McArthur (SCO) | 07.10.1987 | | (4) | |
| Luka Milivojević (SRB) | 07.04.1991 | 5 | (13) | |
| David Ozoh | 06.05.2005 | | (1) | |
| Jaïro Jocquim Riedewald (NED) | 09.09.1996 | | (6) | |
| Jeffrey Schlupp (GHA) | 23.12.1992 | 30 | (4) | 3 |
| **Forwards:** | **DOB** | **M** | **(s)** | **G** |
| Jordan Pierre Ayew (GHA) | 11.09.1991 | 31 | (7) | 4 |
| Malcolm Perewari Ebiowei | 04.09.2003 | | (3) | |
| Odsonne Édouard (FRA) | 16.01.1998 | 20 | (15) | 5 |
| Jean-Philippe Mateta (FRA) | 28.06.1997 | 6 | (23) | 2 |
| Michael Olise (FRA) | 12.12.2001 | 31 | (6) | 2 |
| Dazet Wilfried Armel Zaha (CIV) | 10.11.1992 | 27 | | 7 |

## Everton Football Club Liverpool

| | | |
|---|---|---|
| **Founded**: | 1878 | |
| **Stadium**: | Goodison Park, Liverpool (39,414) | |
| **Trainer**: | Frank James Lampard | 20.06.1978 |
| [24.01.2023] | Paul Tait & | 24.10.1974 |
| | Leighton John Baines | 11.12.1984 |
| [30.01.2023] | Sean Mark Dyche | 28.06.1971 |

| Goalkeepers: | DOB | M | (s) | G |
|---|---|---|---|---|
| Asmir Begović (BIH) | 20.06.1987 | 1 | | |
| Jordan Lee Pickford | 07.03.1994 | 37 | | |
| **Defenders:** | **DOB** | **M** | **(s)** | **G** |
| Conor David Coady | 25.02.1993 | 23 | (1) | 1 |
| Séamus Coleman (IRL) | 11.10.1988 | 20 | (3) | 1 |
| Benjamin Matthew Godfrey | 15.01.1998 | 10 | (3) | |
| Mason Anthony Holgate | 22.10.1996 | 5 | (3) | |
| Michael Vincent Keane | 11.01.1993 | 10 | (2) | 1 |
| Yerry Fernando Mina González (COL) | 23.09.1994 | 7 | | 2 |
| Vitaliy Mykolenko (UKR) | 29.05.1999 | 30 | (4) | |
| Nathan Kenneth Patterson (SCO) | 16.10.2001 | 14 | (5) | |
| *Rúben* Gonçalo Silva Nascimento *Vinagre* (POR) | 09.04.1999 | | (2) | |
| James Alan Tarkowski | 19.11.1992 | 38 | | 1 |
| **Midfielders:** | **DOB** | **M** | **(s)** | **G** |
| Bamidele Jermaine Alli | 11.04.1996 | | (2) | |

| | DOB | M | (s) | G |
|---|---|---|---|---|
| Thomas Davies | 30.06.1998 | 4 | (15) | |
| Abdoulaye Doucouré (MLI) | 01.01.1993 | 17 | (8) | 5 |
| James David Garner | 13.03.2001 | 7 | (9) | |
| Idrissa Gueye (SEN) | 26.09.1989 | 32 | (1) | |
| Alexander Chuka Iwobi (NGA) | 03.05.1996 | 38 | | 2 |
| Amadou Zeund Georges Ba Mvom Onana (BEL) | 16.08.2001 | 29 | (4) | 1 |
| Isaac Jude Price (NIR) | 26.09.2003 | | (1) | |
| **Forwards:** | **DOB** | **M** | **(s)** | **G** |
| Dominic Nathaniel Calvert-Lewin | 16.03.1997 | 15 | (2) | 2 |
| Thomas Christopher Cannon | 28.12.2002 | | (2) | |
| Anthony Michael Gordon | 24.02.2001 | 12 | (4) | 3 |
| Demarai Ramelle Gray (JAM) | 28.06.1996 | 27 | (6) | 4 |
| Neal Maupay (FRA) | 14.08.1996 | 11 | (16) | 1 |
| Dwight James Matthew McNeil | 22.11.1999 | 28 | (8) | 7 |
| José Salomón Rondón Giménez (VEN) | 16.09.1989 | 1 | (6) | |
| Ellis Rico Simms | 05.01.2001 | 2 | (9) | 1 |

## Fulham Football Club London

| | | |
|---|---|---|
| **Founded**: | 1879 (*as St. Andrews Cricket & Football Club*) | |
| **Stadium**: | Craven Cottage, London (22,384) | |
| **Trainer**: | Marco Alexandre Saraiva da Silva (POR) | 12.07.1977 |

| Goalkeepers: | DOB | M | (s) | G |
|---|---|---|---|---|
| Bernd Leno (GER) | 04.03.1992 | 36 | | |
| Marek Rodák (SVK) | 13.12.1996 | 2 | | |
| **Defenders:** | **DOB** | **M** | **(s)** | **G** |
| Abdul-Nasir Oluwatosin Oluwadoyinsolami Adarabioyo | 24.09.1997 | 23 | (2) | 1 |
| *Cédric* Ricardo Alves Soares (POR) | 31.08.1991 | 2 | (4) | |
| Issa Diop (FRA) | 09.01.1997 | 21 | (4) | 1 |
| Shane Patrick Michael Duffy (IRL) | 01.01.1992 | | (5) | |
| Layvin Marc Kurzawa (FRA) | 04.09.1992 | 2 | (1) | |
| Melingo Kevin Mbabu (SUI) | 19.04.1995 | 1 | (5) | |
| Timothy Michael Ream (USA) | 05.10.1987 | 33 | | 1 |
| Antonee Robinson (USA) | 08.08.1997 | 35 | | |
| Kenny Joelle Tete (NED) | 09.10.1995 | 29 | (2) | 1 |
| **Midfielders:** | **DOB** | **M** | **(s)** | **G** |
| *Andreas* Hugo Hoelgebaum *Pereira* (BRA) | 01.01.1996 | 33 | | 4 |
| Thomas Cairney | 20.01.1991 | 6 | (27) | 2 |
| Nathaniel Nyakie Chalobah | 12.12.1994 | 1 | (3) | |

| | DOB | M | (s) | G |
|---|---|---|---|---|
| Bobby Armani De Cordova-Reid (JAM) | 02.02.1993 | 29 | (7) | 4 |
| Tyrese Jay Francois (AUS) | 16.07.2000 | | (1) | |
| Luke Bernard Harris (WAL) | 03.04.2005 | | (3) | |
| *João* Maria Lobo Alves *Palhinha* Gonçalves (POR) | 09.07.1995 | 35 | | 3 |
| Saša Lukić (SRB) | 13.08.1996 | 4 | (8) | |
| Joshua Oghenetega Peter Onomah | 27.04.1997 | | (2) | |
| Harrison James Reed | 27.01.1995 | 35 | (2) | 3 |
| **Forwards:** | **DOB** | **M** | **(s)** | **G** |
| *Carlos Vinícius* Alves Morais (BRA) | 25.03.1995 | 11 | (17) | 5 |
| Daniel Owen James (WAL) | 10.11.1997 | 5 | (15) | 2 |
| Neeskens Kebano (COD) | 10.03.1992 | 9 | (8) | |
| Aleksandar Mitrović (SRB) | 16.09.1994 | 23 | (1) | 14 |
| Manor Solomon (ISR) | 24.07.1999 | 4 | (15) | 4 |
| Jay Stansfield | 24.11.2002 | 1 | (2) | |
| *Willian* Borges da Silva (BRA) | 09.08.1988 | 25 | (2) | 5 |
| Harry Wilson (WAL) | 22.03.1997 | 13 | (16) | 2 |

## Leeds United Football Club

| | | |
|---|---|---|
| **Founded**: | 17.10.1919 | |
| **Stadium**: | Elland Road, Leeds (37,608) | |
| **Trainer**: | Jesse Alan Marsch (USA) | 08.11.1973 |
| [06.02.2023] | Michael Skubala | 31.10.1982 |
| [21.02.2023] | Javier "Javi" Gracia Carlos (ESP) | 01.05.1970 |
| [03.05.2023] | Samuel Allardyce | 19.10.1954 |

| Goalkeepers: | DOB | M | (s) | G |
|---|---|---|---|---|
| *Joel* Robles Blázquez (ESP) | 17.06.1990 | 4 | | |
| Illan Stéphane Meslier (FRA) | 02.03.2000 | 34 | | |
| **Defenders:** | **DOB** | **M** | **(s)** | **G** |
| Luke Ayling | 25.08.1991 | 22 | (7) | 2 |
| Liam David Ian Cooper (SCO) | 30.08.1991 | 16 | (2) | 1 |
| Cody Callum Pierre Drameh | 08.12.2001 | 1 | | |
| Héctor *Junior Firpo* Adamés (ESP) | 22.08.1996 | 14 | (5) | 1 |
| Robin Koch (GER) | 17.07.1996 | 36 | | |
| Rasmus Nissen Kristensen (DEN) | 11.07.1997 | 21 | (5) | 3 |
| Diego Javier *Llorente* Ríos (ESP) | 16.08.1993 | 7 | (1) | |
| Pascal Struijk (NED) | 11.08.1999 | 26 | (3) | 2 |
| Maximilian Wöber (AUT) | 04.02.1998 | 14 | (2) | |
| **Midfielders:** | **DOB** | **M** | **(s)** | **G** |
| Brenden Russell Aaronson (USA) | 22.10.2000 | 28 | (8) | 1 |
| Tyler Shaan Adams (USA) | 14.02.1999 | 24 | | |
| Adam John Forshaw | 08.10.1991 | 5 | (7) | |

| | DOB | M | (s) | G |
|---|---|---|---|---|
| Sam Greenwood | 26.01.2002 | 3 | (15) | 1 |
| Darko Boateng Gyabi | 18.02.2004 | | (1) | |
| Mateusz Klich (POL) | 13.06.1990 | | (14) | |
| *Marc Roca* Junqué (ESP) | 26.11.1996 | 29 | (3) | 1 |
| Weston James Earl McKennie (USA) | 28.08.1998 | 16 | (3) | |
| **Forwards:** | **DOB** | **M** | **(s)** | **G** |
| Patrick James Bamford | 05.09.1993 | 18 | (10) | 4 |
| Joseph Paul Gelhardt | 04.05.2002 | 1 | (14) | |
| Degnand Wilfried Gnonto (ITA) | 05.11.2003 | 14 | (10) | 2 |
| Jack David Harrison | 20.11.1996 | 34 | (2) | 5 |
| Daniel Owen James (WAL) | 10.11.1997 | 2 | (2) | |
| *Mateo* Joseph *Fernández* Regatillo (ESP) | 19.10.2003 | | (3) | |
| *Rodrigo* Moreno Machado (ESP) | 06.03.1991 | 23 | (8) | 13 |
| Georginio Rutter (FRA) | 20.04.2002 | 1 | (10) | |
| Luis Fernando Sinisterra Lucumí (COL) | 17.06.1999 | 13 | (6) | 5 |
| Crysencio Jilbert Sylverio Summerville (NED) | 30.10.2001 | 12 | (16) | 4 |

## Leicester City Football Club

| Founded: | 1884 | |
|---|---|---|
| Stadium: | King Power Stadium, Leicester (32,262) | |
| Trainer: | Brendan Rodgers (NIR) | 26.01.1973 |
| [04.04.2023] | Adam Sadler | 09.01.1980 |
| [10.04.2023] | Dean Smith | 19.03.1971 |

| Goalkeepers: | DOB | M | (s) | G |
|---|---|---|---|---|
| Daniel Lønne Iversen (DEN) | 19.07.1997 | 12 | | |
| Daniel Ward (WAL) | 22.06.1993 | 26 | | |
| **Defenders:** | **DOB** | **M** | **(s)** | **G** |
| Daniel Amartey (GHA) | 21.12.1994 | 18 | (2) | |
| Timothy Castagne (BEL) | 05.12.1995 | 36 | (1) | 2 |
| Jonathan Grant Evans (NIR) | 03.01.1988 | 12 | (1) | |
| Wout Felix Lina Faes (BEL) | 03.04.1998 | 31 | | 1 |
| Wesley Fofana (FRA) | 17.12.2000 | 2 | | |
| James Michael Justin | 23.02.1998 | 14 | | |
| Victor Bernth Kristiansen (DEN) | 16.12.2002 | 11 | (1) | |
| *Ricardo* Domingos Barbosa *Pereira* (POR) | 06.10.1993 | 5 | (5) | 1 |
| Harry James Souttar (AUS) | 22.10.1998 | 11 | (1) | |
| Çağlar Söyüncü (TUR) | 23.05.1996 | 6 | (1) | 1 |
| Luke Jonathan Thomas | 10.06.2001 | 11 | (6) | |

| Midfielders: | DOB | M | (s) | G |
|---|---|---|---|---|
| Marc Kevin Albrighton | 18.11.1989 | 1 | (5) | 1 |
| Lewis Brunt | 06.11.2000 | | (1) | |
| Kiernan Frank Dewsbury-Hall | 06.09.1998 | 28 | (3) | 2 |
| James Daniel Maddison | 23.11.1996 | 28 | (3) | 10 |
| Nampalys Mendy (SEN) | 23.06.1992 | 7 | (12) | 1 |
| Onyinye Wilfred Ndidi (NGA) | 16.12.1996 | 19 | (8) | |
| Dennis Praet (BEL) | 14.05.1994 | 6 | (16) | 1 |
| Boubakary Soumaré (FRA) | 27.02.1999 | 20 | (6) | |
| Youri Marion Tielemans (BEL) | 07.05.1997 | 27 | (4) | 3 |
| **Forwards:** | **DOB** | **M** | **(s)** | **G** |
| Harvey Lewis Barnes | 09.12.1997 | 32 | (2) | 13 |
| *Ayoze Pérez* Gutiérrez (ESP) | 29.07.1993 | 3 | (5) | |
| Patson Daka (ZAM) | 09.10.1998 | 13 | (17) | 4 |
| Kelechi Promise Iheanacho (NGA) | 03.10.1996 | 11 | (17) | 5 |
| Mateus Cardoso Lemos Martins „Tetê" (BRA) | 15.02.2000 | 9 | (4) | 1 |
| Jamie Richard Vardy | 11.01.1987 | 19 | (18) | 3 |

## Liverpool Football Club

| Founded: | 03.06.1892 | |
|---|---|---|
| Stadium: | Anfield Road, Liverpool (53,394) | |
| Trainer: | Jürgen Norbert Klopp (GER) | 16.06.1967 |

| Goalkeepers: | DOB | M | (s) | G |
|---|---|---|---|---|
| Alisson Ramses Becker (BRA) | 02.10.1992 | 37 | | |
| Caoimhin Odhran Kelleher (IRL) | 23.11.1998 | 1 | | |
| **Defenders:** | **DOB** | **M** | **(s)** | **G** |
| Trent John Alexander-Arnold | 07.10.1998 | 34 | (3) | 2 |
| Joseph Dave Gomez | 23.05.1997 | 15 | (6) | |
| Ibrahima Konaté (FRA) | 25.05.1999 | 17 | (1) | |
| Job Joël André Matip (CMR) | 08.08.1991 | 12 | (2) | 1 |
| Nathaniel Harry Phillips | 21.03.1997 | 1 | (1) | |
| Andrew Robertson (SCO) | 11.03.1994 | 29 | (5) | |
| Konstantinos Tsimikas (GRE) | 12.05.1996 | 9 | (11) | |
| Virgil van Dijk (NED) | 08.07.1991 | 32 | | 3 |
| **Midfielders:** | **DOB** | **M** | **(s)** | **G** |
| Stefan Bajčetić Maqueira (ESP) | 22.10.2004 | 6 | (5) | 1 |
| Bobby Clark | 07.02.2005 | | (1) | |
| Harvey Scott Elliott | 04.04.2003 | 18 | (14) | 1 |

| | DOB | M | (s) | G |
|---|---|---|---|---|
| Fabio Henrique Tavares "Fabinho" (BRA) | 23.10.1993 | 31 | (5) | |
| *Fábio* Leandro Freitas Gouveia *Carvalho* (POR) | 30.08.2002 | 4 | (9) | 2 |
| Jordan Brian Henderson | 17.06.1990 | 23 | (12) | |
| Curtis Julian Jones | 30.01.2001 | 12 | (6) | 3 |
| Naby Keïta (GUI) | 10.02.1995 | 3 | (5) | |
| James Philip Milner | 04.01.1986 | 7 | (24) | |
| Alexander Mark David Oxlade-Chamberlain | 15.08.1993 | 4 | (5) | 1 |
| Thiago Alcântara do Nascimento (ESP) | 11.04.1991 | 14 | (4) | |
| **Forwards:** | **DOB** | **M** | **(s)** | **G** |
| Luis Fernando Díaz Marulanda (COL) | 13.01.1997 | 11 | (6) | 4 |
| Diogo José Teixeira da Silva „Diogo Jota" (POR) | 04.12.1996 | 12 | (10) | 7 |
| Ben Gannon Doak (SCO) | 11.11.2005 | | (2) | |
| Cody Mathès Gakpo (NED) | 07.05.1999 | 17 | (4) | 7 |
| Darwin Gabriel Núñez Ribeiro (URU) | 24.06.1999 | 19 | (10) | 9 |
| *Roberto Firmino* Barbosa de Oliveira (BRA) | 02.10.1991 | 13 | (12) | 11 |
| Mohamed Salah Ghaly (EGY) | 15.06.1992 | 37 | (1) | 19 |

## Manchester City Football Club

| Founded: | 1880 | |
|---|---|---|
| Stadium: | City of Manchester Stadium, Manchester (53,400) | |
| Trainer: | Josep "Pep" Guardiola Sala (ESP) | 18.01.1971 |

| Goalkeepers: | DOB | M | (s) | G |
|---|---|---|---|---|
| Ederson Santana de Moraes (BRA) | 17.08.1993 | 35 | | |
| Stefan Ortega Moreno (GER) | 06.11.1992 | 3 | | |
| **Defenders:** | **DOB** | **M** | **(s)** | **G** |
| Manuel Obafemi Akanji (SUI) | 19.07.1995 | 24 | (5) | |
| Nathan Benjamin Aké (NED) | 18.02.1995 | 22 | (4) | 1 |
| *João* Pedro Cavaco *Cancelo* (POR) | 27.05.1994 | 16 | (1) | 2 |
| Aymeric Jean Louis Gerard Alphonse Laporte (FRA) | 27.05.1994 | 11 | (1) | |
| Rico Mark Lewis | 21.11.2004 | 10 | (4) | |
| *Rúben* Santos Gato Alves *Dias* (POR) | 14.05.1997 | 22 | (4) | |
| *Sergio Gómez* Martín (ESP) | 04.09.2000 | 2 | (10) | |
| John Stones | 28.05.1994 | 21 | (2) | 2 |
| Kyle Andrew Walker | 28.05.1990 | 22 | (5) | |

| Midfielders: | DOB | M | (s) | G |
|---|---|---|---|---|
| *Bernardo* Mota Veiga de Carvalho e *Silva* (POR) | 10.08.1994 | 24 | (10) | 4 |
| Shea Emmanuel Charles (NIR) | 05.11.2003 | | (1) | |
| Kevin De Bruyne (BEL) | 28.06.1991 | 28 | (4) | 7 |
| İlkay Gündoğan (GER) | 24.10.1990 | 27 | (4) | 8 |
| Cole Jermaine Palmer | 06.05.2002 | 2 | (12) | |
| Máximo Perrone (ARG) | 07.01.2003 | | (1) | |
| Kalvin Mark Phillips | 02.12.1995 | 2 | (10) | |
| Rodrigo Hernández Cascante „Rodri" (ESP) | 22.06.1996 | 34 | (2) | 2 |
| **Forwards:** | **DOB** | **M** | **(s)** | **G** |
| Julián Álvarez (ARG) | 31.01.2000 | 13 | (18) | 9 |
| Philip Walter Foden | 28.05.2000 | 22 | (10) | 11 |
| Jack Peter Grealish | 10.09.1995 | 23 | (5) | 5 |
| Erling Braut Haaland (NOR) | 21.07.2000 | 33 | (2) | 36 |
| Riyad Karim Mahrez (ALG) | 21.02.1991 | 22 | (8) | 5 |

## Manchester United Football Club

| Founded: | 1878 | |
|---|---|---|
| Stadium: | Old Trafford, Manchester (74,310) | |
| Trainer: | Erik ten Hag (NED) | 02.02.1970 |

| Goalkeepers: | DOB | M | (s) | G |
|---|---|---|---|---|
| David de Gea Quintana (ESP) | 07.11.1990 | 38 | | |
| **Defenders:** | **DOB** | **M** | **(s)** | **G** |
| José *Diogo Dalot* Teixeira (POR) | 18.03.1999 | 24 | (2) | 1 |
| Victor Jörgen Nilsson Lindelöf (SWE) | 17.07.1994 | 14 | (6) | |
| Jacob Harry Maguire | 05.03.1993 | 8 | (8) | |
| Tyrell Johannes Chicco Malacia (NED) | 17.08.1999 | 14 | (8) | |
| Lisandro Martínez (ARG) | 18.01.1998 | 24 | (3) | 1 |
| Luke Paul Hoare Shaw | 12.07.1995 | 30 | (1) | 1 |
| Raphaël Xavier Varane (FRA) | 25.04.1993 | 22 | (2) | |
| Aaron Wan-Bissaka | 26.11.1997 | 16 | (3) | |
| **Midfielders:** | **DOB** | **M** | **(s)** | **G** |
| *Bruno* Miguel Borges *Fernandes* (POR) | 08.09.1994 | 37 | | 8 |
| Carlos Henrique José Francisco Venancio Casimiro (BRA) | 23.02.1992 | 24 | (4) | 4 |
| Christian Dannemann Eriksen (DEN) | 14.02.1992 | 25 | (3) | 1 |

| | DOB | M | (s) | G |
|---|---|---|---|---|
| *Antony* Matheus dos Santos (BRA) | 24.02.2000 | 23 | (2) | 4 |
| *Cristiano Ronaldo* dos Santos Aveiro (POR) | 05.02.1985 | 4 | (6) | 1 |
| Anthony David Junior Elanga (SWE) | 27.04.2002 | 5 | (11) | |
| Alejandro *Garnacho* Ferreira (ESP) | 01.07.2004 | 5 | (14) | 3 |
| Anthony Joran Martial (FRA) | 05.12.1995 | 11 | (10) | 6 |
| Facundo Pellistri Rebollo (URU) | 20.12.2001 | | (4) | |
| Marcus Rashford | 31.10.1997 | 32 | (3) | 17 |
| Jadon Malik Sancho | 25.03.2000 | 21 | (5) | 6 |
| Wout Weghorst (NED) | 07.08.1992 | 10 | (7) | |

The rows above that appear under the Manchester United second block also include the header row "Forwards:" before *Antony* Matheus dos Santos, and before it: Frederico Rodrigues de Paula Santos "Fred"(BRA) 05.03.1993 12 (23) 2; Kobbie Mainoo 19.04.2005 (1); Scott Francis McTominay (SCO) 08.12.1996 10 (14) 1; Marcel Sabitzer (AUT) 17.03.1994 7 (4); Donny van de Beek (NED) 18.04.1997 2 (5).

## Newcastle United Football Club

| Founded: | 09.12.1892 | | | |
|---|---|---|---|---|
| Stadium: | St James' Park, Newcastle upon Tyne (52,305) | | | |
| Trainer: | Edward John Frank Howe | | 29.11.1977 | |

| Goalkeepers: | DOB | M | (s) | G |
|---|---|---|---|---|
| Martin Dúbravka (SVK) | 15.01.1989 | 1 | (1) | |
| Nicholas David Pope | 19.04.1992 | 37 | | |
| Defenders: | DOB | M | (s) | G |
| Sven Adriaan Botman (NED) | 12.01.2000 | 35 | (1) | |
| Daniel Johnson Burn | 09.05.1992 | 35 | (3) | 1 |
| Emil Henry -Kristoffer Krafth (SWE) | 02.08.1994 | | (1) | |
| Jamaal Lascelles | 11.11.1993 | 2 | (5) | |
| Jamal Piaras Lewis (NIR) | 25.01.1998 | | (2) | |
| Javier *Manquillo* Gaitán (ESP) | 05.05.1994 | | (4) | |
| Fabian Schär (SUI) | 20.12.1991 | 36 | | 1 |
| Matthew Robert Targett | 18.09.1995 | 6 | (11) | |
| Kieran John Trippier | 19.09.1990 | 38 | | 1 |
| Midfielders: | DOB | M | (s) | G |
| Elliot Anderson (SCO) | 06.11.2002 | 3 | (19) | |
| *Bruno Guimarães* Rodriguez Moura (BRA) | 16.11.1997 | 32 | | 4 |
| *Joelinton* Cássio Apolinário de Lira (BRA) | 14.08.1996 | 30 | (2) | 6 |
| Sean David Longstaff | 30.10.1997 | 28 | (5) | 1 |
| Lewis Miley | 01.05.2006 | | (1) | |
| Matthew Thomas Ritchie (SCO) | 10.09.1989 | | (7) | |
| Jonjo Shelvey | 27.02.1992 | | (3) | |
| Joseph George Willock | 20.08.1999 | 31 | (4) | 3 |
| Forwards: | DOB | M | (s) | G |
| Miguel Ángel Almirón Rejala (PAR) | 10.02.1994 | 29 | (5) | 11 |
| Ryan Fraser (SCO) | 24.02.1994 | 3 | (5) | |
| Anthony Michael Gordon | 24.02.2001 | 4 | (12) | 1 |
| Alexander Isak (SWE) | 21.09.1999 | 17 | (5) | 10 |
| Jacob Kai Murphy | 24.02.1995 | 14 | (22) | 4 |
| Allan Irénée Saint-Maximin (FRA) | 12.03.1997 | 12 | (13) | 1 |
| Callum Eddie Graham Wilson | 27.02.1992 | 21 | (10) | 18 |
| Christopher Grant Wood (NZL) | 07.12.1991 | 4 | (14) | 2 |

## Nottingham Forest Football Club

| Founded: | 1865 | | | |
|---|---|---|---|---|
| Stadium: | City Ground, West Bridgford (30,332) | | | |
| Trainer: | Steve Cooper | | 10.12.1979 | |

| Goalkeepers: | DOB | M | (s) | G |
|---|---|---|---|---|
| Dean Bradley Henderson | 12.03.1997 | 18 | | |
| Wayne Robert Hennessey (WAL) | 24.01.1987 | 3 | (1) | |
| Keilor Antonio Navas Gamboa (CRC) | 15.12.1986 | 17 | | |
| Defenders: | DOB | M | (s) | G |
| Sèrge Alain Stephane Aurier (CIV) | 24.12.1992 | 22 | (2) | 1 |
| Giulian Biancone (FRA) | 31.03.2000 | | (2) | |
| Willy Arnaud Zobo Boly (CIV) | 03.02.1991 | 9 | (2) | |
| Steve Anthony Cook | 19.04.1991 | 11 | (1) | |
| *Felipe* Augusto de Almeida *Monteiro* (BRA) | 16.05.1989 | 15 | (1) | |
| Scott Fraser McKenna (SCO) | 12.11.1996 | 19 | (1) | |
| Moussa Niakhaté (FRA) | 08.03.1996 | 14 | | |
| *Renan* Augusto *Lodi* dos Santos (BRA) | 08.04.1998 | 26 | (2) | |
| Harry Stefano Toffolo | 19.08.1995 | 9 | (10) | |
| Neco Shay Williams (WAL) | 13.04.2001 | 20 | (11) | 1 |
| Joseph Adrian Worrall | 10.01.1997 | 21 | (9) | 1 |
| Midfielders: | DOB | M | (s) | G |
| Carlos Miguel Ribeiro Dias „Cafú" (POR) | 26.02.1993 | | (1) | |
| Jack Raymond Colback | 24.10.1989 | 4 | (7) | |
| *Danilo* dos Santos de Oliveira (BRA) | 29.04.2001 | 12 | (1) | 3 |
| Remo Freuler (SUI) | 15.04.1992 | 24 | (4) | |
| Morgan Anthony Gibbs-White | 27.01.2000 | 34 | (1) | 5 |
| *Gustavo* Henrique Furtado *Scarpa* (BRA) | 05.01.1994 | 2 | (4) | |
| Brennan Price Johnson (WAL) | 23.05.2001 | 33 | (5) | 8 |
| Cheikhou Kouyaté (SEN) | 21.12.1989 | 10 | (11) | 1 |
| Jesse Ellis Lingard | 15.12.1992 | 12 | (5) | |
| Orel Johnson Mangala (BEL) | 18.03.1998 | 20 | (7) | 1 |
| Lewis John O'Brien | 14.10.1998 | 6 | (7) | 1 |
| Jonjo Shelvey | 27.02.1992 | 6 | (2) | |
| Ryan James Yates | 21.11.1997 | 21 | (5) | |
| Forwards: | DOB | M | (s) | G |
| Taiwo Michael Awoniyi (NGA) | 12.08.1997 | 17 | (10) | 10 |
| André Morgan Rami Ayew (GHA) | 17.12.1989 | 1 | (12) | |
| Emmanuel Bonaventure Dennis (NGA) | 15.11.1997 | 6 | (13) | 2 |
| Alexander Cole Mighten | 11.04.2002 | | (1) | |
| Samuel William Surridge | 28.07.1998 | 1 | (19) | 1 |
| Christopher Grant Wood (NZL) | 07.12.1991 | 5 | (2) | 1 |

## Southampton Football Club

| Founded: | 21.11.1885 | | | |
|---|---|---|---|---|
| Stadium: | St. Mary's Stadium, Southampton (32,384) | | | |
| Trainer: | Ralph Hasenhüttl (AUT) | | 09.08.1967 | |
| [08.11.2023] | Rubén Sellés Salvador (ESP) | | 15.06.1983 | |
| [10.11.2022] | Nathan Jason Jones (WAL) | | 28.05.1973 | |
| [12.02.2023] | Rubén Sellés Salvador (ESP) | | 15.06.1983 | |

| Goalkeepers: | DOB | M | (s) | G |
|---|---|---|---|---|
| Gavin Okeroghene Bazunu (IRL) | 20.02.2002 | 32 | | |
| Alex Simon McCarthy | 03.12.1989 | 6 | | |
| Defenders: | DOB | M | (s) | G |
| Jan Bednarek (POL) | 12.04.1996 | 20 | | |
| Armel Bella-Kotchap (GER) | 11.12.2001 | 24 | | |
| James Patrick Bree | 11.12.1997 | 4 | (1) | |
| Duje Ćaleta-Car (CRO) | 17.09.1996 | 9 | (4) | 1 |
| *Juan Larios* López (ESP) | 12.01.2004 | 2 | (3) | |
| Valentino Francisco Livramento | 12.11.2002 | | (2) | |
| *Lyanco* Evangelista Silveira Neves Vojnović (SRB) | 01.02.1997 | 11 | (10) | 1 |
| Romain Perraud (FRA) | 22.09.1997 | 22 | (7) | 2 |
| Mohammed Salisu Abdul Karim (GHA) | 17.04.1999 | 21 | (1) | |
| Jack Stephens | 27.01.1994 | | (2) | |
| Yan Valery (FRA) | 22.02.1999 | 1 | | |
| Kyle Leonardus Walker-Peters | 13.04.1997 | 30 | (1) | 1 |
| Midfielders: | DOB | M | (s) | G |
| Carlos Jonas Alcaraz (ARG) | 30.11.2002 | 13 | (5) | 4 |
| Samuel Amo-Ameyaw | 18.07.2006 | | (1) | |
| Joseph Oluwaseyi Temitope Ayodele-Aribo(NGA) | 21.07.1996 | 13 | (8) | 2 |
| Stuart Armstrong (SCO) | 30.03.1992 | 14 | (18) | 2 |
| Ibrahima Diallo (FRA) | 08.03.1999 | 11 | (7) | |
| Kamari Doyle | 01.08.2005 | | (1) | |
| Roméo Lavia (BEL) | 06.01.2004 | 26 | (3) | 1 |
| Ainsley Cory Maitland-Niles | 29.08.1997 | 13 | (9) | |
| *Oriol Romeu* Vidal (ESP) | 24.09.1991 | 1 | | |
| James Michael Edward Ward-Prowse | 01.11.1994 | 38 | | 9 |
| Forwards: | DOB | M | (s) | G |
| Ché Zach Everton Fred Adams (SCO) | 13.07.1996 | 23 | (5) | 5 |
| Adam James Armstrong | 10.02.1997 | 14 | (16) | 2 |
| Dominic Ballard | 01.04.2005 | | (2) | |
| Moussa Djénépo (MLI) | 15.06.1998 | 7 | (9) | |
| Samuel Ikechukwu Edozie | 28.01.2003 | 5 | (12) | |
| Mohamed Elyounoussi (NOR) | 04.08.1994 | 27 | (6) | 1 |
| Sékou Mara (FRA) | 30.07.2002 | 4 | (18) | 1 |
| Paul Ebere Onuachu (NGA) | 28.05.1994 | 4 | (7) | |
| Mislav Oršić (CRO) | 29.12.1992 | | (1) | |
| Nathan Daniel Jerome Redmond | 06.03.1994 | | (1) | |
| Kamaldeen Sulemana (GHA) | 15.02.2002 | 10 | (8) | 2 |
| Theodore James Walcott | 16.03.1989 | 13 | (7) | 2 |

## Tottenham Hotspur Football Club London

| Founded: | 05.09.1882 | |
|---|---|---|
| Stadium: | Tottenham Hotspur Stadium, London (62,850) | |
| Trainer: | Antonio Conte (ITA) | 31.07.1969 |
| [26.03.2023] | Cristian Stellini | 27.04.1974 |
| [24.03.2023] | Ryan Glen Mason | 13.06.1991 |

| Goalkeepers: | DOB | M | (s) | G |
|---|---|---|---|---|
| Fraser Gerard Forster | 17.03.1988 | 13 | (1) | |
| Hugo Hadrien Dominique Lloris (FRA) | 26.12.1986 | 25 | | |
| **Defenders:** | **DOB** | **M** | **(s)** | **G** |
| Benjamin Thomas Davies (WAL) | 24.04.1993 | 26 | (5) | 2 |
| Eric Jeremy Edgar Dier | 15.01.1994 | 31 | (2) | 2 |
| Matthew James Doherty (IRL) | 16.01.1992 | 7 | (5) | 1 |
| *Emerson* Aparecido Leite de Souza Junior (BRA) | 14.01.1999 | 20 | (6) | 2 |
| Clément Nicolas Laurent Lenglet (FRA) | 17.06.1995 | 24 | (2) | |
| *Pedro* Antonio *Porro* Sauceda (ESP) | 13.09.1999 | 13 | (2) | 3 |
| Cristian Gabriel Romero (ARG) | 27.04.1998 | 26 | (1) | |
| Dávinson Sánchez Mina (COL) | 12.06.1996 | 8 | (10) | |
| Djed Tehuti Djed-Hotep Spence | 09.08.2000 | | (4) | |
| Japhet Manzambi Tanganga | 31.03.1999 | 2 | (2) | |
| **Midfielders:** | **DOB** | **M** | **(s)** | **G** |
| George Abbott | 17.08.2005 | | (1) | |
| Rodrigo Bentancur Colmán (URU) | 25.06.1997 | 17 | (1) | 5 |

| Yves Bissouma (MLI) | 30.08.1996 | 10 | (13) | |
|---|---|---|---|---|
| Matthew George Craig (SCO) | 16.04.2003 | | (1) | |
| Pierre-Emile Kordt Højbjerg (DEN) | 05.08.1995 | 35 | | 4 |
| Ivan Perišić (CRO) | 02.02.1989 | 23 | (11) | 1 |
| Pape Matar Sarr (SEN) | 14.09.2002 | 2 | (9) | |
| Kouassi Ryan Sessegnon | 18.05.2000 | 9 | (8) | 2 |
| Oliver William Skipp | 16.09.2000 | 18 | (5) | 1 |
| Harvey David White | 19.09.2001 | | (1) | |
| **Forwards:** | **DOB** | **M** | **(s)** | **G** |
| Arnaut Danjuma Adam Groeneveld (NED) | 31.01.1997 | 1 | (8) | 1 |
| *Bryan Gil* Salvatierra (ESP) | 11.02.2001 | 2 | (2) | |
| Harry Edward Kane | 28.07.1993 | 38 | | 30 |
| Dejan Kulusevski (SWE) | 25.04.2000 | 23 | (7) | 2 |
| *Lucas* Rodrigues *Moura* da Silva (BRA) | 13.08.1992 | | (15) | 1 |
| *Richarlison* de Andrade (BRA) | 10.05.1997 | 12 | (15) | 1 |
| Son Heung-min (KOR) | 08.07.1992 | 33 | (3) | 10 |

## West Ham United Football Club London

| Founded: | 29.06.1895 | |
|---|---|---|
| Stadium: | London Stadium, London (62,500) | |
| Trainer: | David William Moyes (SCO) | 25.04.1963 |

| Goalkeepers: | DOB | M | (s) | G |
|---|---|---|---|---|
| Alphonse Francis Aréola (FRA) | 27.02.1993 | 2 | (3) | |
| Łukasz Fabiański (POL) | 18.04.1985 | 36 | | |
| **Defenders:** | **DOB** | **M** | **(s)** | **G** |
| Nayef Aguerd (MAR) | 30.03.1996 | 17 | (1) | 2 |
| Vladimír Coufal (CZE) | 22.08.1992 | 24 | (3) | |
| Aaron William Cresswell | 15.12.1989 | 24 | (4) | |
| Craig Dawson | 06.05.1990 | 8 | | |
| *Emerson* Palmieri dos Santos (ITA) | 03.08.1994 | 16 | (6) | 1 |
| Benjamin Anthony Johnson | 24.01.2000 | 9 | (8) | |
| Jan Thilo Kehrer (GER) | 21.09.1996 | 25 | (2) | |
| Obinze Angelo Ogbonna (ITA) | 23.05.1988 | 13 | (3) | |
| Kurt Happy Zouma (FRA) | 27.10.1994 | 24 | (1) | 2 |
| **Midfielders:** | **DOB** | **M** | **(s)** | **G** |
| Conor James Coventry (IRL) | 25.03.2000 | | (1) | |

| Flynn Downes | 20.01.1999 | 7 | (14) | |
|---|---|---|---|---|
| Manuel Lanzini (ARG) | 15.02.1993 | 2 | (8) | 1 |
| Lucas Tolentino Coelho de Lima „Lucas Paquetá" (BRA) | 27.08.1997 | 27 | (1) | 4 |
| *Pablo Fornals* Malla (ESP) | 22.02.1996 | 17 | (15) | 3 |
| Declan Rice | 14.01.1999 | 36 | (1) | 4 |
| Tomáš Souček (CZE) | 27.02.1995 | 32 | (4) | 2 |
| **Forwards:** | **DOB** | **M** | **(s)** | **G** |
| Michail Gregory Antonio (JAM) | 28.03.1990 | 21 | (12) | 5 |
| Saïd Benrahma (ALG) | 10.08.1995 | 22 | (13) | 6 |
| Jarrod Bowen | 20.12.1996 | 36 | (2) | 6 |
| Maxwel Cornet (CIV) | 27.09.1996 | 2 | (12) | |
| Daniel William John Ings | 23.07.1992 | 7 | (10) | 2 |
| Divin Mubama | 25.10.2004 | | (3) | |
| Gianluca Scamacca (ITA) | 01.01.1999 | 11 | (5) | 3 |

## Wolverhampton Wanderers Football Club

| Founded: | 1877 (*as St. Luke's FC*) | |
|---|---|---|
| Stadium: | Molineux Stadium, Wolverhampton (31,750) | |
| Trainer: | Bruno Miguel Silva do Nascimento (POR) | 12.05.1976 |
| [02.10.2022] | Steve Peter Davis | 26.07.1965 |
| [14.11.2022] | Julen Lopetegui Agote (ESP) | 28.08.1966 |

| Goalkeepers: | DOB | M | (s) | G |
|---|---|---|---|---|
| Daniel Ian Bentley | 13.07.1993 | 2 | | |
| José Pedro Malheiro de Sá (POR) | 17.01.1993 | 36 | | |
| **Defenders:** | **DOB** | **M** | **(s)** | **G** |
| Rayan Aït Nouri (FRA) | 06.06.2001 | 9 | (12) | 1 |
| Nathan Michael Collins (IRL) | 30.04.2001 | 19 | (7) | |
| Craig Dawson | 06.05.1990 | 17 | | 1 |
| *Hugo Bueno* López (ESP) | 18.09.2002 | 16 | (5) | |
| Jonathan Castro Otto "Jonny" (ESP) | 03.03.1994 | 14 | (4) | 1 |
| Maximilian William Kilman | 23.05.1997 | 37 | | |
| Dexter Joeng Woo Lembikisa (JAM) | 04.11.2003 | | (1) | |
| *Nélson Cabral* Semedo (POR) | 16.11.1993 | 31 | (5) | |
| Tote António Gomes „Toti" (POR) | 16.01.1999 | 10 | (7) | 1 |
| **Midfielders:** | **DOB** | **M** | **(s)** | **G** |
| Chem Campbell (WAL) | 30.12.2002 | | (5) | |
| Leander Dendoncker (BEL) | 15.04.1995 | 2 | (2) | |
| Morgan Anthony Gibbs-White | 27.01.2000 | 2 | | |
| Joseph Shaun Hodge (IRL) | 14.09.2002 | 1 | (5) | |

| *João* Victor *Gomes* da Silva (BRA) | 12.02.2001 | 7 | (4) | 1 |
|---|---|---|---|---|
| *João* Filipe Iria Santos *Moutinho* (POR) | 08.09.1986 | 20 | (11) | |
| Mario René Junior Lemina (GAB) | 01.09.1993 | 17 | (2) | |
| *Matheus* Luiz Nunes (POR) | 27.08.1998 | 30 | (4) | 1 |
| Connor Patrick Ronan (IRL) | 06.03.1998 | | (1) | |
| *Rúben* Diogo da Silva *Neves* (POR) | 13.03.1997 | 33 | (2) | 6 |
| Boubacar Traoré (MLI) | 20.08.2001 | 4 | (6) | |
| **Forwards:** | **DOB** | **M** | **(s)** | **G** |
| *Daniel Castelo* Podence (POR) | 21.10.1995 | 20 | (12) | 6 |
| *Diego* da Silva *Costa* (ESP) | 07.10.1988 | 16 | (7) | 1 |
| *Gonçalo* Manuel Ganchinho *Guedes* (POR) | 29.11.1996 | 8 | (5) | 1 |
| Hwang Hee-chan (KOR) | 26.01.1996 | 12 | (15) | 3 |
| Raúl Alonso Jiménez Rodríguez (MEX) | 05.05.1991 | 8 | (7) | |
| Saša Kalajdžić (AUT) | 07.07.1997 | 1 | | |
| *Matheus* Santos Carneiro da *Cunha* (BRA) | 27.05.1999 | 12 | (5) | 2 |
| *Pablo Sarabia* García (ESP) | 11.05.1992 | 9 | (4) | 1 |
| *Pedro* Lomba *Neto* (POR) | 09.03.2000 | 13 | (5) | |
| Adama Traoré Diarra (ESP) | 25.01.1996 | 12 | (22) | 2 |

| | | | | | | | | | |
|---|---|---|---|---|---|---|---|---|---|
| 1. | Burnley FC (*Promoted*) | 46 | 29 | 14 | 3 | 87 | - | 35 | 101 |
| 2. | Sheffield United FC (*Promoted*) | 46 | 28 | 7 | 11 | 73 | - | 39 | 91 |
| 3. | Luton Town FC | 46 | 21 | 17 | 8 | 57 | - | 39 | 80 |
| 4. | Middlesbrough FC | 46 | 22 | 9 | 15 | 84 | - | 56 | 75 |
| 5. | Coventry City FC | 46 | 18 | 16 | 12 | 58 | - | 46 | 70 |
| 6. | Sunderland AFC | 46 | 18 | 15 | 13 | 68 | - | 55 | 69 |
| 7. | Blackburn Rovers FC | 46 | 20 | 9 | 17 | 52 | - | 54 | 69 |
| 8. | Millwall FC London | 46 | 19 | 11 | 16 | 57 | - | 50 | 68 |
| 9. | West Bromwich Albion FC | 46 | 18 | 12 | 16 | 59 | - | 53 | 66 |
| 10. | Swansea City AFC | 46 | 18 | 12 | 16 | 68 | - | 64 | 66 |
| 11. | Watford FC | 46 | 16 | 15 | 15 | 56 | - | 53 | 63 |
| 12. | Preston North End FC | 46 | 17 | 12 | 17 | 45 | - | 59 | 63 |
| 13. | Norwich City FC | 46 | 17 | 11 | 18 | 57 | - | 54 | 62 |
| 14. | Bristol City FC | 46 | 15 | 14 | 17 | 55 | - | 56 | 59 |
| 15. | Hull City AFC | 46 | 14 | 16 | 16 | 51 | - | 61 | 58 |
| 16. | Stoke City FC | 46 | 14 | 11 | 21 | 55 | - | 54 | 53 |
| 17. | Birmingham City FC | 46 | 14 | 11 | 21 | 47 | - | 58 | 53 |
| 18. | Huddersfield Town AFC | 46 | 14 | 11 | 21 | 47 | - | 62 | 53 |
| 19. | Rotherham United FC | 46 | 11 | 17 | 18 | 49 | - | 60 | 50 |
| 20. | Queens Park Rangers FC London | 46 | 13 | 11 | 22 | 44 | - | 71 | 50 |
| 21. | Cardiff City FC | 46 | 13 | 10 | 23 | 41 | - | 58 | 49 |
| 22. | Reading FC (*Relegated*) | 46 | 13 | 11 | 22 | 46 | - | 68 | 44 |
| 23. | Blackpool FC (*Relegated*) | 46 | 11 | 11 | 24 | 48 | - | 72 | 44 |
| 24. | Wigan Athletic FC (*Relegated*) | 46 | 10 | 15 | 21 | 38 | - | 65 | 42 |

Clubs ranked 3-6 were qualified for the Promotion Play-offs.

## Promotion Play-offs [13-27.05.2023]

| Play-off Semi-Finals | | | |
|---|---|---|---|
| | Sunderland AFC - Luton Town FC | 2-1(1-1) | 0-2(0-2) |
| | Coventry City FC - Middlesbrough FC | 0-0 | 1-0(0-0) |

| Play-off Finals | | |
|---|---|---|
| | Coventry City FC - Luton Town FC | 1-1(0-1,1-1,1-1); 5-6 pen |

Luton Town FC promoted to the 2022/2023 Premier League.

### INTERNATIONAL MATCHES
### (16.07.2022 – 15.07.2023)

| | | | | |
|---|---|---|---|---|
| 23.09.2022 | Milano | *Italy - England* | *1-0(0-0)* | (UNL) |
| 26.09.2022 | London | *England - Germany* | *3-3(0-0)* | (UNL) |
| 21.11.2022 | Al Rayyan | *England - Iran* | *6-2(3-0)* | (WC) |
| 25.11.2022 | Al Khor | *England - United States* | *0-0* | (WC) |
| 29.11.2022 | Al Rayyan | *Wales - England* | *0-3(0-0)* | (WC) |
| 04.12.2022 | Al Khor | *England - Senegal* | *3-0(2-0)* | (WC) |
| 10.12.2022 | Al Khor | *England - France* | *1-2(0-1)* | (WC) |
| | | | | |
| 23.03.2023 | Napoli | *Italy - England* | *1-2(0-2)* | (ECQ) |
| 26.03.2023 | London | *England - Ukraine* | *2-0(2-0)* | (ECQ) |
| 16.06.2023 | Attard | *Malta - England* | *0-4(0-3)* | (ECQ) |
| 19.06.2023 | Manchester | *England - North Macedonia* | *7-0(3-0)* | (ECQ) |

**23.09.2022**    **ITALY - ENGLAND**      **1-0(0-0)**      3<sup>rd</sup> UEFA Nations League A, Group 3

3<sup>rd</sup> UEFA Nations League A, Group 3

Stadio "Giuseppe Meazza", Milano; Referee: Jesús Gil Manzano (Spain); Attendance: 50,640
**ENG:** Nicholas David Pope, Kyle Andrew Walker (72.Luke Paul Hoare Shaw), Jacob Harry Maguire, Eric Jeremy Edgar Dier, Reece James, Jude Bellingham, Declan Rice, Philip Walter Foden, Bukayo Ayoyinka Saka (72.Jack Peter Grealish), Raheem Shaquille Sterling, Harry Edward Kane (Cap). Trainer: Gareth Southgate.

**26.09.2022**    **ENGLAND - GERMANY**      **3-3(0-0)**      3<sup>rd</sup> UEFA Nations League A, Group 3
Wembley Stadium, London; Referee: Danny Desmond Makkelie (Netherlands); Attendance: 78,949
**ENG:** Nicholas David Pope, Luke Paul Hoare Shaw, Jacob Harry Maguire, John Stones (37.Kyle Andrew Walker), Reece James, Eric Jeremy Edgar Dier, Jude Bellingham (90+1.Jordan Brian Henderson), Declan Rice, Philip Walter Foden (66.Bukayo Ayoyinka Saka), Raheem Shaquille Sterling (66.Mason Tony Mount), Harry Edward Kane (Cap). Trainer: Gareth Southgate.
**Goals:** Luke Paul Hoare Shaw (71), Mason Tony Mount (75), Harry Edward Kane (83 penalty).

**21.11.2022**    **ENGLAND - IRAN**      **6-2(3-0)**      22<sup>nd</sup> FIFA WC. Group Stage.
Khalifa International Stadium, Al Rayyan (Qatar); Referee: Raphael Claus (Brazil); Attendance: 45,334
**ENG:** Jordan Lee Pickford, Kieran John Trippier, John Stones, Jacob Harry Maguire (70.Eric Jeremy Edgar Dier), Luke Paul Hoare Shaw, Jude Victor William Bellingham, Declan Rice, Bukayo Ayoyinka Saka (70.Marcus Rashford), Mason Tony Mount (70.Philip Walter Foden), Raheem Shaquille Sterling (70.Jack Peter Grealish), Harry Edward Kane (Cap) (75.Callum Eddie Graham Wilson). Trainer: Gareth Southgate.
**Goals:** Jude Victor William Bellingham (35), Bukayo Ayoyinka Saka (43), Raheem Shaquille Sterling (45+1), Bukayo Ayoyinka Saka (62), Marcus Rashford (71), Jack Peter Grealish (90).

**25.11.2022**    **ENGLAND - UNITED STATES**      **0-0**      22<sup>nd</sup> FIFA WC. Group Stage.
Al Bayt Stadium, Al Khor (Qatar); Referee: Jesús Noel Valenzuela Sáez (Venezuela); Attendance: 68,463
**ENG:** Jordan Lee Pickford, Kieran John Trippier, John Stones, Jacob Harry Maguire, Luke Paul Hoare Shaw, Jude Victor William Bellingham (68.Jordan Brian Henderson), Declan Rice, Mason Tony Mount, Bukayo Ayoyinka Saka (77.Marcus Rashford), Harry Edward Kane (Cap), Raheem Shaquille Sterling (68.Jack Peter Grealish). Trainer: Gareth Southgate.

**29.11.2022**    **WALES - ENGLAND**      **0-3(0-0)**      22<sup>nd</sup> FIFA WC. Group Stage.
„Ahmad bin Ali" Stadium, Al Rayyan (Qatar); Referee: Slavko Vinčić (Slovenia); Attendance: 44,297
**ENG:** Jordan Lee Pickford, Kyle Andrew Walker (57.Trent John Alexander-Arnold), John Stones, Jacob Harry Maguire, Luke Paul Hoare Shaw (65.Kieran John Trippier), Jordan Brian Henderson, Declan Rice (57.Kalvin Mark Phillips), Jude Victor William Bellingham, Philip Walter Foden, Harry Edward Kane (Cap) (57.Callum Eddie Graham Wilson), Marcus Rashford (75.Jack Peter Grealish). Trainer: Gareth Southgate.
**Goals:** Marcus Rashford (50), Philip Walter Foden (51), Marcus Rashford (68).

**04.12.2022**    **ENGLAND - SENEGAL**      **3-0(2-0)**      22<sup>nd</sup> FIFA WC. 2<sup>nd</sup> Round of 16.
Al Bayt Stadium, Al Khor (Qatar); Referee: Iván Arcides Barton Cisneros (El Salvador); Attendance: 65,985
**ENG:** Jordan Lee Pickford, Kyle Andrew Walker, John Stones (76.Eric Jeremy Edgar Dier), Jacob Harry Maguire, Luke Paul Hoare Shaw, Jordan Brian Henderson (82.Kalvin Mark Phillips), Declan Rice, Jude Victor William Bellingham (76.Mason Tony Mount), Bukayo Ayoyinka Saka (65.Marcus Rashford), Harry Edward Kane (Cap), Philip Walter Foden (65.Jack Peter Grealish). Trainer: Gareth Southgate.
**Goals:** Jordan Brian Henderson (39), Harry Edward Kane (45+3), Bukayo Ayoyinka Saka (57).

**10.12.2022**    **ENGLAND - FRANCE**      **1-2(0-1)**      22<sup>nd</sup> FIFA WC. Quarter-Finals.
Al Bayt Stadium, Al Khor (Qatar); Referee: Wilton Pereira Sampaio (Brazil); Attendance: 68,895
**ENG:** Jordan Lee Pickford, Kyle Andrew Walker, John Stones (90+8.Jack Peter Grealish), Jacob Harry Maguire, Luke Paul Hoare Shaw, Jordan Brian Henderson (79.Mason Tony Mount), Declan Rice, Jude Victor William Bellingham, Bukayo Ayoyinka Saka (79.Raheem Shaquille Sterling), Harry Edward Kane (Cap), Philip Walter Foden (85.Marcus Rashford). Trainer: Gareth Southgate.
**Goal:** Harry Edward Kane (54 penalty).

**23.03.2023**    **ITALY - ENGLAND**      **1-2(0-2)**      17<sup>th</sup> EC. Qualifiers
Stadio "Diego Armando Maradona", Napoli; Referee: Srdan Jovanović (Serbia); Attendance: 44,536
**ENG:** Jordan Lee Pickford, Kyle Andrew Walker, Jacob Harry Maguire, John Stones, Luke Paul Hoare Shaw [*sent off 80*], Jude Bellingham (85.Conor John Gallagher), Declan Rice, Kalvin Mark Phillips, Bukayo Ayoyinka Saka (85.Reece James), Jack Peter Grealish (69.Philip Walter Foden; 81.Kieran John Trippier), Harry Edward Kane (Cap). Trainer: Gareth Southgate.
**Goals:** Declan Rice (13), Harry Edward Kane (44 penalty).

**26.03.2023**    **ENGLAND - UKRAINE**      **2-0(2-0)**      17<sup>th</sup> EC. Qualifiers
Wembley Stadium, London; Referee: Serdar Gözübüyük (Netherlands); Attendance: 83,947
**ENG:** Jordan Lee Pickford, Kyle Andrew Walker, Jacob Harry Maguire, John Stones, Benjamin James Chilwell, Jude Bellingham (85.Conor John Gallagher), James Daniel Maddison (85.Jack Peter Grealish), Declan Rice, Jordan Brian Henderson, Bukayo Ayoyinka Saka, Harry Edward Kane (Cap) (81.Ivan Benjamin Elijah Toney). Trainer: Gareth Southgate.
**Goals:** Harry Edward Kane (37), Bukayo Ayoyinka Saka (40).

**16.06.2023    MALTA - ENGLAND**                    **0-4(0-3)**                    17th EC. Qualifiers
Ta'Qali National Stadium, Attard; Referee: Igor Pajac (Croatia); Attendance: 16,277
**ENG:** Jordan Lee Pickford, Kieran John Trippier, Jacob Harry Maguire, Addji Keaninkin Marc-Israel Guéhi, Luke Paul Hoare Shaw (60.Tyrone Deon Mings), Trent John Alexander-Arnold, Jordan Brian Henderson (60.Marcus Rashford), James Daniel Maddison (69.Eberechi Oluchi Eze), Declan Rice, Bukayo Ayoyinka Saka (46.Philip Walter Foden), Harry Edward Kane (Cap) (60.Callum Eddie Graham Wilson). Trainer: Gareth Southgate.
**Goals:** Ferdinando Apap (8 own goal), Trent John Alexander-Arnold (28), Harry Edward Kane (31 penalty), Callum Eddie Graham Wilson (83 penalty).

**19.06.2023    ENGLAND - NORTH MACEDONIA**          **7-0(3-0)**                    17th EC. Qualifiers
Old Trafford, Manchester; Referee: István Kovács (Romania); Attendance: 70,708
**ENG:** Jordan Lee Pickford, Kyle Andrew Walker, Jacob Harry Maguire, John Stones, Luke Paul Hoare Shaw, Trent John Alexander-Arnold, Declan Rice (58.Kalvin Mark Phillips), Bukayo Ayoyinka Saka (58.Philip Walter Foden), Marcus Rashford (58.Jack Peter Grealish), Jordan Brian Henderson (58.Conor John Gallagher), Harry Edward Kane (Cap) (74.Callum Eddie Graham Wilson). Trainer: Gareth Southgate.
**Goals:** Harry Edward Kane (29), Bukayo Ayoyinka Saka (38), Marcus Rashford (45), Bukayo Ayoyinka Saka (47, 51), Kalvin Mark Phillips (64), Harry Edward Kane (73 penalty).

| NATIONAL TEAM PLAYERS | | | | |
|---|---|---|---|---|
| (16.07.2022 – 15.07.2023) | | | | |
| **Name** | **DOB** | **Caps** | **Goals** | *Club* |
| **Goalkeepers** | | | | |
| Jordan Lee PICKFORD | 07.03.1994 | 54 | 0 | 2022/2023: *Everton FC Liverpool* |
| Nicholas David POPE | 19.04.1992 | 10 | 0 | 2022: *Newcastle United FC* |
| **Defenders** | | | | |
| Trent John ALEXANDER-ARNOLD | 07.10.1998 | 20 | 2 | 2022/2023: *Liverpool FC* |
| Benjamin James CHILWELL | 21.12.1996 | 18 | 1 | 2023: *Chelsea FC London* |
| Eric Jeremy Edgar DIER | 15.01.1994 | 49 | 3 | 2022: *Tottenham Hotspur FC London* |
| Addji Keaninkin Marc-Israel GUÉHI | 13.07.2000 | 4 | 0 | 2023: *Crystal Palace FC London* |
| Reece JAMES | 08.12.1999 | 16 | 0 | 2022/2023: *Chelsea FC London* |
| Jacob Harry MAGUIRE | 05.03.1993 | 57 | 7 | 2022/2023: *Manchester United FC* |
| Tyrone Deon MINGS | 13.03.1993 | 18 | 2 | 2023: *Aston Villa FC Birmingham* |
| Luke Paul Hoare SHAW | 12.07.1995 | 31 | 3 | 2022/2023: *Manchester United FC* |
| John STONES | 28.05.1994 | 67 | 3 | 2022/2023: *Manchester City FC* |
| Kieran John TRIPPIER | 19.09.1990 | 42 | 1 | 2022/2023: *Newcastle United FC* |
| Kyle Andrew WALKER | 28.05.1990 | 76 | 0 | 2022/2023: *Manchester City FC* |
| **Midfielders** | | | | |
| Jude Victor William BELLINGHAM | 29.06.2003 | 24 | 1 | 2022/2023: *BV Borussia Dortmund (GER)* |
| Eberechi Oluchi EZE | 29.06.1998 | 1 | 0 | 2023: *Crystal Palace FC London* |
| Philip Walter FODEN | 28.05.2000 | 25 | 3 | 2022/2023: *Manchester City FC* |
| Conor John GALLAGHER | 06.02.2000 | 7 | 0 | 2023: *Chelsea FC London* |
| Jordan Brian HENDERSON | 17.06.1990 | 77 | 3 | 2022/2023: *Liverpool FC* |
| Mason Tony MOUNT | 10.01.1999 | 36 | 5 | 2022: *Chelsea FC London* |
| Kalvin Mark PHILLIPS | 02.12.1995 | 27 | 1 | 2022/2023: *Manchester City FC* |
| Declan RICE | 14.01.1999 | 43 | 3 | 2022/2023: *West Ham United FC London* |
| **Forwards** | | | | |
| Jack Peter GREALISH | 10.09.1995 | 32 | 2 | 2022/2023: *Manchester City FC* |
| Harry Edward KANE | 28.07.1993 | 84 | 59 | 2022/2023: *Tottenham Hotspur FC London* |
| James Daniel MADDISON | 23.11.1996 | 3 | 0 | 2023: *Leicester City FC* |
| Marcus RASHFORD | 31.10.1997 | 53 | 16 | 2022/2023: *Manchester United FC* |
| Bukayo Ayoyinka SAKA | 05.09.2001 | 28 | 11 | 2022/2023: *Arsenal FC London* |
| Raheem Shaquille STERLING | 08.12.1994 | 82 | 20 | 2022: *Chelsea FC London* |
| Ivan Benjamin Elijah TONEY | 16.03.1996 | 1 | 0 | 2023: *Brentford FC London* |
| Callum Eddie Graham WILSON | 27.02.1992 | 8 | 2 | 2022/2023: *Newcastle United FC* |
| **Trainer** | | | | |
| Gareth SOUTHGATE [from 30.11.2016] | 03.09.1970 | 85 M; 53 W; 18 D; 14 L; 189-58 | | |

# ESTONIA

## The Country:
Eesti Vabariik (Republic of Estonia)
Capital: Tallinn
Surface: 45,339 km²
Inhabitants: 1,331,796 [2022]
Time: UTC+2

## The FA:
Eesti Jalgpalli Liit
A. Le Coq Arena, Asula 4c, 11312 Tallinn
Tel: +372 627 9960
Foundation date: 14.12.1921
Member of FIFA since: 1923
Member of UEFA since: 1992
Website: www.jalgpall.ee

## NATIONAL TEAM RECORDS

| | | |
|---|---|---|
| **First international match:** | 20.10.1920, Helsinki: | Finland – Estonia 6-0 |
| **Most international caps:** | Martin Reim | - 157 caps (1991-2009) |
| **Most international goals:** | Andres Oper | - 38 goals / 134 caps (1995-2014) |

### UEFA EUROPEAN CHAMPIONSHIP

| | |
|---|---|
| 1960 | - |
| 1964 | - |
| 1968 | - |
| 1972 | - |
| 1976 | - |
| 1980 | - |
| 1984 | - |
| 1988 | - |
| 1992 | - |
| 1996 | Qualifiers |
| 2000 | Qualifiers |
| 2004 | Qualifiers |
| 2008 | Qualifiers |
| 2012 | Qualifiers |
| 2016 | Qualifiers |
| 2020 | Qualifiers |

### FIFA WORLD CUP

| | |
|---|---|
| 1930 | Did not enter |
| 1934 | Qualifiers |
| 1938 | Qualifiers |
| 1950 | - |
| 1954 | - |
| 1958 | - |
| 1962 | - |
| 1966 | - |
| 1970 | - |
| 1974 | - |
| 1978 | - |
| 1982 | - |
| 1986 | - |
| 1990 | - |
| 1994 | Qualifiers |
| 1998 | Qualifiers |
| 2002 | Qualifiers |
| 2006 | Qualifiers |
| 2010 | Qualifiers |
| 2014 | Qualifiers |
| 2018 | Qualifiers |
| 2022 | Qualifiers |

### OLYMPIC TOURNAMENTS

| | |
|---|---|
| 1908 | - |
| 1912 | - |
| 1920 | - |
| 1924 | - |
| 1928 | - |
| 1936 | - |
| 1948 | - |
| 1952 | - |
| 1956 | - |
| 1960 | - |
| 1964 | - |
| 1968 | - |
| 1972 | - |
| 1976 | - |
| 1980 | - |
| 1984 | - |
| 1988 | - |
| 1992 | - |
| 1996 | Qualifiers |
| 2000 | Qualifiers |
| 2004 | Qualifiers |
| 2008 | Qualifiers |
| 2012 | Qualifiers |
| 2016 | Qualifiers |
| 2020 | Qualifiers |

Please note: *was part of Soviet Union from 1945 to 1991.*

### UEFA NATIONS LEAGUE

| | |
|---|---|
| 2018/2019 | League C (Group Stage) |
| 2020/2021 | League C (Group Stage) |
| 2022/2023 | League D (Group Stage -> promoted to League C) |

### ESTONIAN CLUB HONOURS IN EUROPEAN CLUB COMPETITIONS:

| **European Champion Clubs' Cup (1956-1992) / UEFA Champions League (1993-2023)** |
|---|
| None |

| **Fairs Cup (1858-1971) / UEFA Cup (1972-2009) / UEFA Europa League (2010-2023)** |
|---|
| None |

| **UEFA Europa Conference League (2021-2023)** |
|---|
| None |

| **UEFA Super Cup (1972-2022)** |
|---|
| None |

| ***European Cup Winners' Cup 1961-1999**** |
|---|
| None |

*defunct competition*

# NATIONAL COMPETITIONS
## TABLE OF HONOURS

| | | | | | | | |
|---|---|---|---|---|---|---|---|
| 1945 | Dünamo Tallinn | 1961 | Kalev Kopli | 1977 | Baltika Narva | | |
| 1946 | BL Tallinn | 1962 | Kalev Ülemiste | 1978 | Dünamo Tallinn | | |
| 1947 | Dünamo Tallinn | 1963 | Tempo Tallinn | 1979 | Norma Tallinn | | |
| 1948 | Balti Laevastik Tallinn | 1964 | Norma Tallinn | 1980 | Dünamo Tallinn | | |
| 1949 | Dünamo Tallinn | 1965 | Balti Laevastik Tallinn | 1981 | Dünamo Tallinn | | |
| 1950 | Dünamo Tallinn | 1966 | Balti Laevastik Tallinn | 1982 | Tempo Tallinn | | |
| 1951 | Balti Laevastik Tallinn | 1967 | Norma Tallinn | 1983 | Dünamo Tallinn | | |
| 1952 | Balti Laevastik Tallinn | 1968 | Balti Laevastik Tallinn | 1984 | Estonia Jõhvi | | |
| 1953 | Dünamo Tallinn | 1969 | Dvigatel Tallinn | 1985 | Kalakombinaat/MEK Pärnu | | |
| 1954 | Dünamo Tallinn | 1970 | Norma Tallinn | 1986 | Zvezda Tallinn | | |
| 1955 | Kalev Tallinn | 1971 | Tempo Tallinn | 1987 | Tempo Tallinn | | |
| 1956 | Balti Laevastik Tallinn | 1972 | Balti Laevastik Tallinn | 1988 | Norma Tallinn | | |
| 1957 | Kalev Ülemiste | 1973 | Kreenholm Narva | 1989 | Zvezda Tallinn | | |
| 1958 | Kalev Ülemiste | 1974 | Baltika Narva | 1990 | Tallinna VMK | | |
| 1959 | Kalev Ülemiste | 1975 | Baltika Narva | 1991 | Tallinna VMK | | |
| 1960 | Balti Laevastik Tallinn | 1976 | Dvigatel Tallinn | | | | |

| | CHAMPIONS | CUP WINNERS | BEST GOALSCORERS | |
|---|---|---|---|---|
| 1921 | Sport Tallinn | - | - | |
| 1922 | Sport Tallinn | - | - | |
| 1923 | Kalev Tallinn | - | - | |
| 1924 | Sport Tallinn | - | - | |
| 1925 | Sport Tallinn | - | - | |
| 1926 | Jalgpalliklubi Tallinn | - | - | |
| 1927 | Sport Tallinn | - | - | |
| 1928 | Jalgpalliklubi Tallinn | - | - | |
| 1929 | Sport Tallinn | - | - | |
| 1930 | Kalev Tallinn | - | - | |
| 1931 | Sport Tallinn | - | - | |
| 1932 | Sport Tallinn | - | - | |
| 1933 | Sport Tallinn | - | - | |
| 1934 | Tallinn | - | - | |
| 1935 | Tallinn | - | - | |
| 1936 | Tallinn | - | - | |
| 1937/1938 | Tallinn | SK Tallinna Sport | - | |
| 1938/1939 | Tallinn | Jalgpalliklubi Tallinn | - | |
| 1939/1940 | Olümpia Tartu | - | - | |
| 1941 | *Championship not finished* | - | - | |
| 1942 | PSR Tartu (*unofficial*) | - | - | |
| 1943 | Tallinn (*unofficial*) | - | - | |
| 1944 | *Championship not finished* | - | - | |

----------------------------------------------------------------------------------------------------

| | CHAMPIONS | CUP WINNERS | BEST GOALSCORERS | |
|---|---|---|---|---|
| 1992 | FC Norma Tallinn | - | Sergei Bragin (FC Norma Tallinn) | 18 |
| 1992/1993 | FC Norma Tallinn | FC Nikol Tallinn | Sergei Bragin (FC Norma Tallinn) | 27 |
| 1993/1994 | FC Flora Tallinn | FC Norma Tallinn | Maksim Gruznov (JK Narva Trans/Tevalte Tallinn) | 21 |
| 1994/1995 | FC Flora Tallinn | FC Flora Tallinn | Serhiy Morozov (UKR, FC Lantana Tallinn) | 25 |
| 1995/1996 | FC Lantana Tallinn | JK Tallinna Sadam | Lembit Rajala (FC Flora Tallinn) | 16 |
| 1996/1997 | FC Lantana Tallinn | JK Tallinna Sadam | Sergei Bragin (FC Lantana Tallinn) | 18 |
| 1997/1998 | FC Flora Tallinn | - | Konstantin Kolbassenko (JK Tallinna Sadam) | 18 |
| 1998 | FC Flora Tallinn | FC Flora Tallinn | Konstantin Kolbassenko (JK Tallinna Sadam) | 13 |
| 1999 | FC Levadia Maardu | FC Levadia Maardu | Toomas Krõm (FC Levadia Maardu) | 19 |
| 2000 | FC Levadia Maardu | FC Levadia Maardu | Egidijus Juška (LTU, FC Tallinna VMK)<br>Toomas Krõm (FC Levadia Maardu) | 24 |
| 2001 | FC Flora Tallinn | JK Narva Trans | Maksim Gruznov (JK Narva Trans) | 37 |
| 2002 | FC Flora Tallinn | FC Levadia Maardu | Andrei Krõlov (FC Tallinna VMK) | 37 |
| 2003 | FC Flora Tallinn | FC Tallinna VMK | Tor Henning Hamre (NOR, FC Flora Tallinn) | 39 |
| 2004 | FC Levadia Maardu | FC Levadia Maardu | Vjatšeslav Zahovaiko (FC Flora Tallinn) | 28 |
| 2005 | FC Tallinna VMK | FC Levadia Tallinn | Tarmo Neemelo (FC Tallinna VMK) | 41 |
| 2006 | FC Levadia Tallinn | FC Tallinna VMK | Maksim Gruznov (JK Narva Trans) | 31 |
| 2007 | FC Levadia Tallinn | FC Levadia Tallinn | Russia Dmitri Lipartov (JK Narva Trans) | 30 |
| 2008 | FC Levadia Tallinn | FC Flora Tallinn | Ingemar Teever (Nõmme Kalju FC Tallinn) | 23 |
| 2009 | FC Levadia Tallinn | FC Flora Tallinn | Vitali Gussev (FC Levadia Tallinn) | 26 |
| 2010 | FC Flora Tallinn | FC Levadia Tallinn | Sander Post (FC Flora Tallinn) | 24 |
| 2011 | FC Flora Tallinn | FC Flora Tallinn | Latvia Aleksandrs Čekulajevs (JK Narva Trans) | 46 |
| 2012 | Nõmme Kalju FC Tallinn | FC Levadia Tallinn | Vladislav Ivanov (RUS, JK Sillamäe Kalev/JK Narva Trans) | 23 |
| 2013 | FC Levadia Tallinn | FC Flora Tallinn | Vladimir Voskoboinikov (Nõmme Kalju FC Tallinn) | 23 |
| 2014 | FC Levadia Tallinn | FC Levadia Tallinn | Russia Yevgeni Kabaev (JK Sillamäe Kalev) | 36 |
| 2015 | FC Flora Tallinn | Nõmme Kalju FC Tallinn | Ingemar Teever (FC Levadia Tallinn) | 24 |
| 2016 | FC Infonet Tallinn | FC Flora Tallinn | Russia Yevgeni Kabaev (JK Sillamäe Kalev) | 25 |
| 2017 | FC Flora Tallinn | FC Infonet Tallinn | Albert Prosa (FC Infonet Tallinn)<br>Rauno Sappinen (FC Flora Tallinn) | 27 |

| 2018 | Nõmme Kalju FC Tallinn | FCI Levadia Tallinn | Ellinton Antonio Costa Morais "Liliu" (BRA, Nõmme Kalju FC Tallinn) | 31 |
|------|------------------------|---------------------|-----------------------------------|----|
| 2019 | FC Flora Tallinn | JK Narva Trans | Erik Sorga (FC Flora Tallinn) | 31 |
| 2020 | FC Flora Tallinn | FC Flora Tallinn | Rauno Sappinen (FC Flora Tallinn) | 26 |
| 2021 | FCI Levadia Tallinn | FCI Levadia Tallinn | Henri Anier (Paide Linnameeskond) | 26 |
| 2022 | FC Flora Tallinn | Paide Linnameeskond | Zakaria Beglarishvili (GEO, FCI Levadia Tallinn) | 21 |

## NATIONAL CHAMPIONSHIP
### Meistriliiga / A.Le Coq Premium Liiga 2022
### (01.03.2022 – 12.11.2022)

### Results

**Round 1 [01-02.03.2022]**
FCI Levadia - Tallinna Kalev 5-1(2-0)
Pärnu Vaprus - Linnameeskond 1-3(1-3)
Nõmme Kalju - FC Kuressaare 2-0(0-0)
JK Tammeka - FC Flora 0-4(0-2)
Tallinna Legion - Narva Trans 0-2(0-1)

**Round 2 [05-06.03.2022]**
FC Kuressaare - Narva Trans 1-2(0-0)
Pärnu Vaprus - FCI Levadia 0-8(0-2)
Tallinna Legion - JK Tammeka 1-1(1-0)
FC Flora - Tallinna Kalev 7-1(3-1)
Linnameeskond - Nõmme Kalju 2-3(1-2)

**Round 3 [12-13.03.2022]**
Tallinna Kalev - FC Kuressaare 0-3(0-0)
Narva Trans - JK Tammeka 0-2(0-1)
FCI Levadia - Tallinna Legion 2-0(1-0)
Nõmme Kalju - Pärnu Vaprus 2-0(1-0)
Linnameeskond - FC Flora 1-2(0-1)

**Round 4 [19-20.03.2022]**
Nõmme Kalju - FC Flora 1-2(1-0)
Tallinna Legion - FC Kuressaare 2-2(1-0)
Pärnu Vaprus - Tallinna Kalev 3-1(0-0)
JK Tammeka - Linnameeskond 1-3(1-1)
Narva Trans - FCI Levadia 0-1(0-0) [20.04.22]

**Round 5 [01-03.04.2022]**
Tallinna Kalev - Linnameeskond 0-3(0-0)
Tallinna Legion - Nõmme Kalju 2-4(1-3)
FCI Levadia - JK Tammeka 4-0(2-0)
FC Flora - Narva Trans 1-0(1-0)
FC Kuressaare - Pärnu Vaprus 3-2(3-0)

**Round 6 [09-10.04.2022]**
FC Flora - Tallinna Legion 2-0(1-0)
Narva Trans - Pärnu Vaprus 3-1(1-0)
JK Tammeka - FC Kuressaare 1-0(1-0)
Nõmme Kalju - Tallinna Kalev 2-1(2-1)
Linnameeskond - FCI Levadia 0-1(0-0)

**Round 7 [12-13.04.2022]**
FC Kuressaare - FC Flora 0-3(0-1)
Pärnu Vaprus - JK Tammeka 1-2(0-1)
Linnameeskond - Tallinna Legion 5-0(2-0)
Narva Trans - Tallinna Kalev 5-0(2-0)
FCI Levadia - Nõmme Kalju 1-1(0-1)

**Round 8 [16-17.04.2022]**
Pärnu Vaprus - FC Flora 0-2(0-1)
Tallinna Legion - Tallinna Kalev 1-1(1-1)
Narva Trans - Linnameeskond 1-2(0-1)
JK Tammeka - Nõmme Kalju 1-1(0-1)
FCI Levadia - FC Kuressaare 1-0(0-0)

**Round 9 [22-24.04.2022]**
Tallinna Kalev - JK Tammeka 1-0(0-0)
Tallinna Legion - Pärnu Vaprus 3-0(1-0)
FC Kuressaare - Linnameeskond 2-1(2-1)
Nõmme Kalju - Narva Trans 3-0(1-0)
FC Flora - FCI Levadia 2-0(2-0)

**Round 10 [26-27.04.2022]**
Narva Trans - FC Kuressaare 0-1(0-1)
Nõmme Kalju - Tallinna Legion 3-0(1-0)
JK Tammeka - FCI Levadia 0-1(0-0)
Tallinna Kalev - FC Flora 2-4(2-3)
Linnameeskond - Pärnu Vaprus 6-2(3-1)

**Round 11 [29.04.-01.05.2022]**
FC Kuressaare - Tallinna Legion 1-0(0-0)
Pärnu Vaprus - Nõmme Kalju 0-1(0-0)
FCI Levadia - Narva Trans 6-0(3-0)
Linnameeskond - Tallinna Kalev 7-0(3-0)
FC Flora - JK Tammeka 3-2(2-1)

**Round 12 [06-08.05.2022]**
Pärnu Vaprus - FC Kuressaare 3-1(2-1)
Tallinna Kalev - FCI Levadia 0-1(0-0)
Tallinna Legion - Narva Trans 1-0(0-0)
Nõmme Kalju - JK Tammeka 3-1(0-1)
FC Flora - Linnameeskond 0-0

**Round 13 [13-15.05.2022]**
JK Tammeka - Pärnu Vaprus 3-1(1-0)
FC Kuressaare - Tallinna Kalev 1-0(1-0)
FCI Levadia - Linnameeskond 4-0(1-0)
Tallinna Legion - FC Flora 0-7(0-4) [22.07.22]
Narva Trans - Nõmme Kal.2-1(0-0) [23.07.22]

**Round 14 [17-18.05.2022]**
JK Tammeka - Tallinna Kalev 1-3(0-0)
FC Flora - FC Kuressaare 4-0(4-0)
Linnameeskond - Narva Trans 4-2(2-1)
Pärnu Vaprus - Tallinna Legion 1-1(0-1)
Nõmme Kalju - FCI Levadia 0-1(0-0)

**Round 15 [24-25.05.2022]**
FC Kuressaare - Nõmme Kalju 1-1(0-0)
Tallinna Legion - FCI Levadia 1-3(0-2)
Linnameeskond - JK Tammeka 3-0(1-0)
Tallinna Kalev - Pärnu Vaprus 1-0(0-0)
Narva Trans - FC Flora 0-3(0-1)

**Round 16 [28-29.05.2022]**
Tallinna Kalev - Tallinna Legion 2-2(0-0)
Nõmme Kalju - Linnameeskond 1-0(1-0)
FCI Levadia - FC Flora 1-1(0-1)
FC Kuressaare - JK Tammeka 3-0(0-0)
Pärnu Vaprus-Narva Trans 3-5(2-1) [09.07.22]

**Round 17 [16-19.06.2022]**
FCI Levadia - Pärnu Vaprus 4-1(2-1)
Narva Trans - Tallinna Kalev 1-1(1-0)
Linnameeskond - FC Kuressaare 1-1(0-1)
JK Tammeka - Tallinna Legion 1-4(0-2)
FC Flora - Nõmme Kalju 2-0(1-0)

**Round 18 [28-29.06.2022]**
FC Kuressaare - FCI Levadia 1-1(1-1)
Tallinna Kalev - Nõmme Kalju 0-3(0-2)
JK Tammeka - Narva Trans 1-0(0-0)
FC Flora - Pärnu Vaprus 6-1(2-1)
Tallinna Legion - Linnameeskond 1-2(1-0)

**Round 19 [01-03.07.2022]**
FCI Levadia - Tallinna Kalev 3-1(2-0)
Narva Trans - Linnameeskond 1-1(0-0)
Tallinna Legion - FC Flora 0-1(0-0)
Pärnu Vaprus - JK Tammeka 1-1(0-1)
Nõmme Kalju - FC Kuressaare 3-1(0-1)

**Round 20 [15-17.07.2022]**
JK Tammeka - FCI Levadia 0-3(0-2)
Nõmme Kalju - Narva Trans 1-1(0-1)
FC Kuressaare - Tallinna Legion 1-0(0-0)
FC Flora - Tallinna Kalev 2-0(1-0)
Linnameeskond - Pärnu V. 4-2(2-1) [17.08.22]

**Round 21 [29-31.07.2022]**
Pärnu Vaprus - Nõmme Kalju 0-3(0-3)
Tallinna Kalev - Narva Trans 5-2(2-2)
Linnameeskond - JK Tammeka 3-0(2-0)
FCI Levadia - Tallinna Legion 3-0(0-0)
FC Kuressaare - FC Flora 2-3(0-1)

**Round 22 [05-07.08.2022]**
JK Tammeka - FC Flora 0-1(0-1)
Pärnu Vaprus - FC Kuressaare 0-1(0-0)
Nõmme Kalju - Tallinna Kalev 6-0(5-0)
Narva Trans - FCI Levadia 0-1(0-0)
T.Legion-Linnameeskond 1-1(1-1) [14.09.22]

**Round 23 [12-14.08.2022]**
FCI Levadia - Pärnu Vaprus 3-0(2-0)
Tallinna Legion - Nõmme Kalju 1-2(0-2)
FC Flora - Narva Trans 1-1(1-1)
Tallinna Kalev - JK Tammeka 2-5(0-1)
Linnameeskond - FC Kuressaare 0-0

**Round 24 [20-21.08.2022]**
Tallinna Kalev - Linnameeskond 2-7(0-5)
Narva Trans - JK Tammeka 1-2(1-1)
FC Flora - Pärnu Vaprus 3-1(1-1)
Nõmme Kalju - JK Tammeka 1-1(0-1)
FC Kuressaare - FCI Levadia 2-3(2-0)

**Round 25 [26-28.08.2022]**
Pärnu Vaprus - Tallinna Kalev 2-3(1-0)
FC Kuressaare - Narva Trans 3-1(2-1)
JK Tammeka - Tallinna Legion 2-0(1-0)
Linnameeskond - FC Flora 1-2(0-1)
FCI Levadia - Nõmme Kalju 1-1(0-0)

**Round 26 [30-31.08.2022]**
Tallinna Legion - Tallinna Kalev 2-3(0-2)
Narva Trans - Pärnu Vaprus 1-0(0-0)
JK Tammeka - FC Kuressaare 1-1(1-1)
Linnameeskond - FCI Levadia 0-0
FC Flora - Nõmme Kalju 2-0(0-0)

**Round 27 [03-04.09.2022]**
Narva Trans - JK Tammeka 0-0
Nõmme Kalju - Linnameeskond 1-2(1-0)
Tallinna Kalev - FC Kuressaare 1-2(1-1)
FCI Levadia - FC Flora 1-2(0-1)
Pärnu Vaprus - Tallinna Legion 0-1(0-0)

| Round 28 [09-11.09.2022] |
|---|
| FC Flora - JK Tammeka 1-0(0-0) |
| FC Kuressaare - Nõmme Kalju 0-0 |
| Pärnu Vaprus - Linnameeskond 1-2(0-2) |
| Tallinna Kalev - FCI Levadia 0-3(0-2) |
| Tallinna Legion - Narva Trans 1-6(1-2) |

| Round 29 [16-18.09.2022] |
|---|
| Nõmme Kalju - Pärnu Vaprus 4-0(2-0) |
| Narva Trans - FC Flora 0-4(0-1) |
| JK Tammeka - Tallinna Kalev 1-3(0-2) |
| FCI Levadia - FC Kuressaare 2-3(0-2) |
| Linnameeskond - Tallinna Legion 10-0(6-0) |

| Round 30 [01-02.10.2022] |
|---|
| Tallinna Kalev - Pärnu Vaprus 1-0(1-0) |
| FC Kuressaare - JK Tammeka 2-2(1-1) |
| FC Flora - Tallinna Legion 4-1(2-0) |
| Linnameeskond - Narva Trans 2-0(0-0) |
| Nõmme Kalju - FCI Levadia 0-1(0-0) |

| Round 31 [08-09.10.2022] |
|---|
| Tallinna Legion - FCI Levadia 1-1(1-1) |
| Tallinna Kalev - Narva Trans 0-2(0-2) |
| JK Tammeka - Nõmme Kalju 3-0(2-0) |
| FC Kuressaare - Linnameeskond 3-3(3-1) |
| Pärnu Vaprus - FC Flora 1-7(0-3) |

| Round 32 [14-16.10.2022] |
|---|
| Tallinna Legion - FC Kuressaare 3-2(1-0) |
| Linnameeskond - Tallinna Kalev 1-2(1-0) |
| FCI Levadia - JK Tammeka 1-0(1-0) |
| Pärnu Vaprus - Narva Trans 1-0(1-0) |
| Nõmme Kalju - FC Flora 1-0(1-0) |

| Round 33 [22-23.10.2022] |
|---|
| Tallinna Kalev - Tallinna Legion 2-0(0-0) |
| FC Flora - FC Kuressaare 2-1(2-0) |
| JK Tammeka - Pärnu Vaprus 1-0(0-0) |
| Narva Trans - Nõmme Kalju 0-0 |
| FCI Levadia - Linnameeskond 1-2(0-0) |

| Round 34 [29-30.10.2022] |
|---|
| FC Kuressaare - Tallinna Kalev 1-1(1-0) |
| Pärnu Vaprus - FCI Levadia 2-3(1-0) |
| Nõmme Kalju - Tallinna Legion 1-0(0-0) |
| JK Tammeka - Narva Trans 2-0(2-0) |
| FC Flora - Linnameeskond 1-0(0-0) |

| Round 35 [05-06.11.2022] |
|---|
| Tallinna Kalev - FC Flora 1-1(0-0) |
| Tallinna Legion - JK Tammeka 1-1(0-1) |
| FCI Levadia - Narva Trans 1-1(0-0) |
| FC Kuressaare - Pärnu Vaprus 1-0(0-0) |
| Linnameeskond - Nõmme Kalju 1-0(0-0) |

| Round 36 [11-12.11.2022] |
|---|
| Tallinna Legion - Pärnu Vaprus 2-1(1-1) |
| Narva Trans - FC Kuressaare 2-2(1-0) |
| Tallinna Kalev - Nõmme Kalju 0-3(0-2) |
| FC Flora - FCI Levadia 2-1(1-1) |
| JK Tammeka - Linnameeskond 1-1(0-1) |

## Final Standings

| | | | Total | | | | | | | Home | | | | | | Away | | |
|---|---|---|---|---|---|---|---|---|---|---|---|---|---|---|---|---|---|---|
| 1. | **FC Flora Tallinn** | 36 | 31 | 4 | 1 | 94 - 21 | **97** | 16 | 2 | 0 | 45 - 9 | | 15 | 2 | 1 | 49 - 12 |
| 2. | FCI Levadia Tallinn | 36 | 24 | 7 | 5 | 74 - 25 | **79** | 11 | 4 | 3 | 41 - 14 | | 13 | 3 | 2 | 33 - 11 |
| 3. | Paide Linnameeskond | 36 | 19 | 8 | 9 | 84 - 37 | **65** | 10 | 3 | 5 | 51 - 17 | | 9 | 5 | 4 | 33 - 20 |
| 4. | Nõmme Kalju FC Tallinn | 36 | 19 | 8 | 9 | 59 - 30 | **65** | 12 | 2 | 4 | 35 - 11 | | 7 | 6 | 5 | 24 - 19 |
| 5. | FC Kuressaare | 36 | 13 | 11 | 12 | 49 - 51 | **50** | 8 | 6 | 4 | 28 - 23 | | 5 | 5 | 8 | 21 - 28 |
| 6. | Tartu JK Tammeka | 36 | 10 | 9 | 17 | 38 - 57 | **39** | 7 | 3 | 8 | 20 - 26 | | 3 | 6 | 9 | 18 - 31 |
| 7. | JK Narva Trans | 36 | 10 | 8 | 18 | 43 - 58 | **38** | 6 | 5 | 7 | 24 - 22 | | 4 | 3 | 11 | 19 - 36 |
| 8. | JK Tallinna Kalev | 36 | 10 | 5 | 21 | 42 - 92 | **35** | 5 | 2 | 11 | 20 - 41 | | 5 | 3 | 10 | 22 - 51 |
| 9. | Tallinna JK Legion* (Relegation Play-offs) | 36 | 6 | 8 | 22 | 34 - 82 | **22** | 4 | 6 | 8 | 23 - 34 | | 2 | 2 | 14 | 11 - 48 |
| 10. | Pärnu JK Vaprus (Relegated)** | 36 | 3 | 2 | 31 | 32 - 96 | **11** | 3 | 2 | 13 | 20 - 45 | | 0 | 0 | 18 | 12 - 51 |

*Please note: Tallinna JK Legion were deducted 4 points for failing to comply with club licensing procedures.

Viljandi JK Tulevik announced on 22.12.2021 voluntary relegation due to financial difficulties.

| Top goalscorers: | |
|---|---|
| 21  Zakaria Beglarishvili (GEO) | *FCI Levadia Tallinn* |
| 16  Robi Saarma | *Paide Linnameeskond* |
| 15  Sten Reinkort | *FC Kuressaare* |
| 14  Konstantin Vassiljev | *FC Flora Tallinn* |

## Relegation Play-offs [23-27.11.2022]

FC Elva - Tallinna JK Legion                    0-3(0-3)          1-0(0-0)

**Please note: despite winning the relegation play-offs, Tallinna JK Legion gave up its place in the Meistriliiga and were voluntary relegated into the 2023 Esiliiga. As a result of Tallinna JK Legion's withdrawal, Pärnu JK Vaprus will remain at firs tlevel for 2023.

## NATIONAL CUP
### Eesti Karikas 2021/2022

| Third Round [04/09/16-18/23/25.08. & 01-02/21-22.09 & 06.10. & 12.12.2021] | | | |
|---|---|---|---|
| Viljandi JK Tulevik - Viljandi JK Tulevik II | 10-0 | Tallinna FC Ararat - FC Vastseliina | 2-3 |
| Paide Linnameeskond III - Kristiine JK | 5-0 | Tartu FC Helios - Tartu JK Welco | 0-3 |
| JK Narva Trans - Tallinna FC Eston Villa | 3-0 *awarded* | JK Tallinna Kalev - JK Tabasalu II | 3-0 |
| FC Elva - Viimsi JK | 2-0 | FA Tartu Kalev - FC Nõmme United | 4-2 |
| Läänemaa JK - Tallinna JK Legion | 2-8 | FCI Tallinn - FC Flora U-21 Tallinn | 2-3 |
| Nõmme Kalju FC Tallinn - Tallinna FC Zapoos | 9-1 | FC Tallinn - Paide Linnameeskond | 1-4 |
| Tartu JK Tammeka - FC Kuressaare | 3-1 | Pärnu JK - JK Tabasalu | 0-1 |
| Raplamaa JK - FCI Levadia Tallinn | 0-5 | FC Flora U-19 Tallinn - FC Flora Tallinn | 0-14 |

| 1/8-Finals [23-24.10./16.12.2021 & 05.02.2022] | | | |
|---|---|---|---|
| Tallinna JK Legion - FC Elva | *not played* | FCI Levadia Tallinn - JK Tallinna Kalev | 3-0 |
| Paide Linnameeskond - FC Flora U-21 Tallinn | 14-0 | Tartu JK Tammeka - FA Tartu Kalev | 3-0 |
| Viljandi JK Tulevik - Nõmme Kalju FC Tallinn | 1-3 | FC Flora Tallinn - Paide Linnameeskond III | *not played* |
| JK Narva Trans - Tartu JK Welco | 3-0 | FC Vastseliina - Tabasalu JK | *not played* |

| Quarter-Finals [08-10.03.2022] | | | | |
|---|---|---|---|---|
| JK Narva Trans - Tartu JK Tammeka | 2-0 | FC Flora Tallinn - FCI Levadia Tallinn | 2-0 |
| Tallinna JK Legion - Paide Linnameeskond | 0-2 | Nõmme Kalju FC Tallinn - Tabasalu JK | 7-0 |

| Semi-Finals [05/15.05.2022] | | | |
|---|---|---|---|
| FC Flora Tallinn - Paide Linnameeskond | 0-0 aet; 4-5 pen | JK Narva Trans - Nõmme Kalju FC Tallinn | 0-1 |

## Final

21.05.2022; A. Le Coq Arena, Tallinn; Referee: Martti Pukk; Attendance: 1,358
**Nõmme Kalju FC Tallinn - Paide Linnameeskond**

**0-1(0-0,0-0)**

**Nõmme Kalju**: Marko Meerits, Andriy Markovych, Giannis Tsivelekidis (Cap), Yohann Mannone, Henri Järvelaid (98.Trevor Elhi), Mikhail Babichev, Nikita Komissarov, Igor Subbotin, Kaspar Paur (98.Welves Santos Damacena), Pavel Marin (80.Maksim Gussev), Aleksandr Volkov (105+2.Stanislav Tsõmbaljuk). Trainer: Eddie Walter Alves Cardoso (Portugal).

**Paide Linnameeskond**: Mihkel Aksalu, Abdul Yusif (98.Kristjan Pelt), Ragnar Klavan, Joseph Saliste, Andre Frolov (Cap), Edgar Tur (69.Sergei Mošnikov), Kevor Palumets (88.Dominique Simon), Karl Mööl, Siim Luts, Deabeas Owusu-Sekyere, Kaimar Saag (62.Ebrima Singhateh). Trainer: Karel Voolaid.

**Goal:** 0-1 Siim Luts (109).

## THE CLUBS 2022

### Football Club Flora Tallinn

| | |
|---|---|
| **Founded**: | 10.03.1990 |
| **Stadium**: | A. Le Coq Arena, Tallinn (14,336) |
| **Trainer**: | Jürgen Henn                02.06.1987 |

| Goalkeepers: | DOB | M | (s) | G |
|---|---|---|---|---|
| Evert Grünvald | 06.04.2001 | 5 | | |
| Kristen Lapa | 11.02.2000 | 2 | | |
| Karl-Romet Nõmm | 04.01.1998 | 29 | | |
| **Defenders:** | **DOB** | **M** | **(s)** | **G** |
| Kristo Hussar | 28.06.2002 | 10 | (7) | |
| Ken Kallaste | 31.08.1988 | 21 | (4) | 5 |
| Mihhail Kolobov | 02.03.2005 | 2 | | |
| Michael Lilander | 10.06.1997 | 35 | (1) | 1 |
| Marko Lipp | 19.03.1999 | 6 | (3) | |
| Marco Lukka | 04.12.1996 | 16 | | |
| Henrik Pürg | 03.06.1996 | 29 | | 5 |
| Markkus Seppik | 16.04.2001 | 11 | (1) | |
| Joonas Tamm | 02.02.1992 | 12 | (1) | 1 |

| Midfielders: | DOB | M | (s) | G |
|---|---|---|---|---|
| Mikhel Järviste | 28.05.2000 | 6 | (5) | |
| Vladislavs Kreida | 25.09.1999 | 7 | (2) | 1 |
| Martin Miller | 25.09.1997 | 29 | (4) | 11 |
| Markus Poom | 27.02.1999 | 16 | (7) | 4 |
| Markus Soomets | 02.03.2000 | 30 | (5) | 1 |
| Konstantin Vassiljev | 16.08.1984 | 22 | (9) | 13 |
| **Forwards:** | **DOB** | **M** | **(s)** | **G** |
| Rauno Alliku | 02.03.1990 | 23 | (7) | 12 |
| Tristan Koskor | 28.11.1995 | 3 | (6) | 2 |
| Danil Kuraksin | 04.04.2003 | 16 | (16) | 10 |
| Mark Anders Lepik | 10.09.2000 | 8 | (14) | 6 |
| Henrik Ojamaa | 20.05.1991 | 25 | (4) | 6 |
| Aleksandr Šapovalov | 28.02.2003 | 4 | (16) | 5 |
| Tony Varjund | 21.06.2007 | | (2) | |
| Sergei Zenjov | 20.04.1989 | 29 | (1) | 10 |

### Football Club Kuressaare

| | |
|---|---|
| **Founded**: | 14.03.1997 |
| **Stadium**: | Kuressaare linnastaadion, Kuressaare (1,000) |
| **Trainer**: | Roman Kozhukhovskyi (UKR)         24.01.1979 |

| Goalkeepers: | DOB | M | (s) | G |
|---|---|---|---|---|
| Magnus Karofeld | 20.08.1996 | 9 | (2) | |
| Kristen Lapa | 11.02.2000 | 15 | | |
| Ingmar Paplavskis | 17.05.1999 | 12 | | |
| **Defenders:** | **DOB** | **M** | **(s)** | **G** |
| Markus Allast | 05.09.2000 | 16 | (1) | |
| Sander Alex Liit | 11.04.2003 | 28 | (1) | |
| Mairo Miil | 15.02.2000 | 6 | (2) | |
| Märten Pajunurm | 29.04.1993 | 27 | | 4 |
| Rasmus Saar | 02.03.2000 | 4 | (5) | |
| Michael Schjønning-Larsen | 02.02.2001 | 18 | (5) | 3 |
| Ralf-Sander Suvinomm | 29.10.2001 | 5 | | |
| Moorits Veering | 26.12.1999 | 21 | (2) | |
| **Midfielders:** | **DOB** | **M** | **(s)** | **G** |
| Aleksander Iljin | 05.09.2002 | 4 | (5) | |

| | DOB | M | (s) | G |
|---|---|---|---|---|
| Silver Alex Kelder | 22.10.1995 | 30 | (2) | |
| Sten-Egert Paap | 12.01.2003 | | (3) | |
| Marcus Puust | 19.09.2003 | | (1) | |
| Oliver Rass | 25.05.2000 | 26 | (2) | |
| Sander Seeman | 12.09.1992 | 29 | (3) | |
| Tristan Teeväli | 19.05.2003 | 3 | (7) | |
| Daniel Tuhkanen | 26.02.2001 | 1 | (1) | |
| Rauno Tutk | 10.04.1988 | 23 | (7) | 1 |
| **Forwards:** | **DOB** | **M** | **(s)** | **G** |
| Andero Kivi | 07.11.2003 | | (4) | |
| Sander Laht | 26.09.1991 | 28 | (4) | 7 |
| Otto-Robert Lipp | 02.12.2000 | 12 | (20) | 7 |
| Mattias Männilaan | 08.09.2001 | 28 | | 9 |
| Sten Reinkort | 29.04.1998 | 36 | | 15 |
| Joonas Soomre | 17.05.2000 | 15 | (8) | 1 |

## Tallinna Jalgpalli Klubi Legion

**Founded**: 04.01.2007
**Stadium**: Kadriord staadion, Tallinn (5,000)
**Trainer**: Denis Belov    01.04.1977

| Goalkeepers: | DOB | M | (s) | G |
|---|---|---|---|---|
| Ivans Baturins (LVA) | 25.06.1997 | 34 | | |
| Pavel Londak | 14.05.1980 | 1 | | |
| Martin Žukov | 21.11.2003 | 1 | | |
| **Defenders:** | **DOB** | **M** | **(s)** | **G** |
| Mark Antonio Havier | 23.08.2004 | 3 | (7) | |
| Vladimir Ištšenko | 23.04.2001 | 5 | (11) | |
| Vladislav Jegorov | 27.09.2004 | 4 | (2) | |
| Mihhail Kolobov | 02.03.2005 | 13 | (3) | |
| Anton Mazur | 04.02.2003 | | (2) | |
| Aleksandr Nikolajev | 23.06.2003 | 26 | (3) | |
| Mathias Palts | 21.03.2001 | 10 | (8) | |
| Danil Pankov | 04.11.2002 | 24 | (1) | |
| Ivan Timofejev | 16.06.2002 | 25 | (3) | 1 |
| Nikita Salamatov (RUS) | 23.02.1994 | 11 | (2) | |
| Mihhail Tõsjatov | 05.06.2003 | | (2) | |
| Erko Jonne Tõugjas | 05.07.2003 | 14 | | 1 |
| Aleksandr Volodin | 29.03.1988 | 31 | | 2 |

| Midfielders: | DOB | M | (s) | G |
|---|---|---|---|---|
| Andrei Bespomoštšnov | 06.05.2001 | | (2) | |
| Pavel Dõmov | 31.12.1993 | 28 | (1) | 6 |
| Nikita Grankin | 29.08.2000 | 13 | (13) | 2 |
| Nikita Ivanov | 16.08.2003 | 31 | (2) | 11 |
| Stefan Tšendei | 13.05.1994 | 31 | (1) | 1 |
| **Forwards:** | **DOB** | **M** | **(s)** | **G** |
| Leonid Arhipov | 12.03.2002 | 9 | (3) | |
| Deniss Drabinko | 07.05.2002 | 1 | (3) | |
| Filipp Drabinko | 07.05.2002 | 2 | (2) | |
| Daniel Fedotov | 16.08.2001 | 12 | (15) | 2 |
| Nikita Kondratski | 07.05.2004 | 13 | (20) | |
| Vsevolod Pochekutov | 13.05.2005 | | (2) | |
| Denis Ruus | 11.10.2001 | | (1) | |
| Aleksander Švedovski | 26.11.2004 | 22 | (9) | 1 |
| Daniil Tarassenkov | 25.02.2003 | 14 | (3) | 1 |
| Markus Vaherna | 27.01.1999 | 18 | (11) | 5 |

## FCI Levadia Tallinn

**Founded**: 22.10.1998
**Stadium**: A. Le Coq Arena, Tallinn (14,336)
**Trainer**: Vladimir Vassiljev    13.02.1988
[03.07.2022] Ivan Stojković (SRB)    24.09.1989
[12.09.2022] Maksym Kalinichenko (UKR)    26.01.1979
[22.09.2022] Nikita Andreev (RUS)    22.09.1988

| Goalkeepers: | DOB | M | (s) | G |
|---|---|---|---|---|
| Artur Kotenko | 20.08.1981 | 4 | (1) | |
| Karl Vallner | 28.02.1998 | 32 | (1) | |
| **Defenders:** | **DOB** | **M** | **(s)** | **G** |
| Bourama Fomba (MLI) | 10.07.1999 | 5 | (6) | 1 |
| Andres Järve | 21.05.2002 | 1 | | |
| Markus Jürgenson | 09.09.1987 | 1 | (11) | |
| Milan Mitrović (SRB) | 02.07.1988 | 30 | | |
| Rasmus Peetson | 03.05.1995 | 25 | (2) | 3 |
| Artur Pikk | 05.03.1993 | 30 | (3) | 1 |
| Maksim Podholjuzin | 13.11.1992 | 10 | (7) | |
| Maximiliano Uggè (ITA) | 24.09.1991 | 30 | | 3 |
| **Midfielders:** | **DOB** | **M** | **(s)** | **G** |
| Mihkel Ainsalu | 08.03.1996 | 2 | (3) | |
| Ilja Antonov | 05.12.1992 | 16 | (11) | |
| Zakaria Beglarishvili (GEO) | 30.04.1990 | 32 | (4) | 21 |
| Artjom Komlov | 09.09.2002 | | (3) | 1 |
| Patrik Kristal | 12.11.2007 | 1 | (1) | |
| Brent Lepistu | 26.03.1993 | 30 | (2) | 2 |

| | DOB | M | (s) | G |
|---|---|---|---|---|
| Daniel Luts | 25.01.2004 | 2 | (5) | |
| Til Mavretič (SVN) | 19.11.1997 | 9 | | 1 |
| Marko Putinčanin (SRB) | 16.12.1987 | 16 | (1) | 4 |
| Artem Shchedry (UKR) | 09.11.1992 | 2 | (1) | 1 |
| Nikita Vassiljev | 07.10.2003 | 3 | (5) | |
| Bogdan Vaštšuk | 04.10.1995 | 12 | | 2 |
| **Forwards:** | **DOB** | **M** | **(s)** | **G** |
| Ernest Agyiri (GHA) | 06.03.1998 | 20 | (2) | 3 |
| Nikita Dronov | 25.04.2002 | | (2) | |
| Oleksiy Khoblenko (UKR) | 04.04.1994 | 2 | (4) | 1 |
| Robert Kirss | 03.09.1994 | 16 | (14) | 6 |
| Frank Liivak | 07.07.1996 | 3 | (14) | 3 |
| Ellinton Antonio Costa Morais „Liliu" (BRA) | 01.03.1990 | 20 | (3) | 9 |
| Karl Õigus | 05.11.1998 | 8 | (18) | 1 |
| Mark Oliver Roosnupp | 12.05.1997 | 24 | (9) | 8 |
| Rustam Soirov (TJK) | 12.09.2002 | | (5) | |
| Daniil Timofeev (RUS) | 17.03.2003 | | (1) | |
| Murad Velijev (AZE) | 27.03.2002 | 10 | (10) | 2 |

## Jalgpalliklubi Narva Trans

**Founded**: 1979 (*as Avtomobilist Narva*)
**Stadium**: Narva Kreenholm staadion, Narva (1,065)
**Trainer**: Aleksei Yeryomenko (RUS)    17.01.1964
[12.11.2022] Aleksey Yagudin (UZB)    14.01.1973

| Goalkeepers: | DOB | M | (s) | G |
|---|---|---|---|---|
| Aleksei Matrossov | 06.04.1991 | 31 | | |
| Maksim Pavlov | 17.07.2003 | 5 | | |
| **Defenders:** | **DOB** | **M** | **(s)** | **G** |
| Kevin Aloe | 07.05.1995 | 30 | | |
| Denis Dedechko (UKR) | 02.07.1987 | 31 | | 12 |
| Oleg Gonsevich | 13.05.2005 | 4 | (2) | |
| Martin Käos | 18.06.1998 | 16 | (8) | |
| Sergei Kondrattsev | 23.09.2001 | 12 | (3) | |
| Aleksandr Kulinitš | 24.05.1992 | 14 | (2) | |
| Ryan Lindsay (CAN) | 04.12.2001 | 9 | (2) | |
| Roman Nesterovski | 09.06.1989 | 15 | (11) | |
| Aleksei Stepanov | 13.02.2002 | | (2) | |
| Artjom Škinjov | 30.01.1996 | 7 | (4) | |
| Denis Taraduda (UKR) | 17.08.2000 | 18 | | |

| Midfielders: | DOB | M | (s) | G |
|---|---|---|---|---|
| Irié Bi Séhi Elysée (CIV) | 13.09.1989 | 32 | | |
| Cem Fələk (GER) | 12.05.1996 | 1 | (5) | |
| Arseni Kovaltšuk | 07.01.2001 | 28 | (1) | 3 |
| Viktor Kudriashov | 29.10.2005 | | (1) | |
| Nikita Mihhailov | 20.06.2002 | 28 | (1) | 3 |
| Denis Polyakov (RUS) | 21.02.1992 | 20 | (2) | |
| Aleksandr Zakarlyuka (RUS) | 24.06.1995 | 18 | (5) | 5 |
| Egor Zhuravlev | 11.07.2005 | 3 | (6) | |
| **Forwards:** | **DOB** | **M** | **(s)** | **G** |
| Jevgeni Demidov | 11.02.2000 | 9 | (14) | 4 |
| Eduard Golovljov | 25.01.1997 | 1 | (11) | 2 |
| Oleksandr Kozhevnikov (UKR) | 17.04.2000 | 20 | (8) | 6 |
| Gleb Pevtsov | 23.10.2000 | 15 | (14) | 2 |
| Volodimir Priyomov (UKR) | 02.01.1986 | 26 | (5) | 6 |
| Raivo Saar | 11.07.2000 | 3 | (14) | |

## Nõmme Kalju Football Club Tallinn

**Founded**: 1923 (Re-established in 1997)
**Stadium**: Hiiu staadion, Tallinn (300)
**Trainer**: Eddie Walter Alves Cardoso (POR) — 20.09.1978
[16.10.2022] Kaido Koppel — 09.05.1988

| Goalkeepers: | DOB | M | (s) | G |
|---|---|---|---|---|
| Sergei Lepmets | 05.04.1987 | 3 | | |
| Marko Meerits | 26.04.1992 | 25 | | |
| Henri Perk | 14.10.1999 | 8 | | |
| **Defenders:** | **DOB** | **M** | **(s)** | **G** |
| Vladimir Avilov | 10.03.1995 | 9 | | 4 |
| Trevor Elhi | 11.04.1993 | 25 | (7) | 2 |
| Henri Järvelaid | 11.12.1998 | 26 | (6) | |
| Kaur Georg Maksimovski | 03.01.2005 | | (1) | |
| Yohann Mannone (FRA) | 19.07.1995 | 20 | (2) | 2 |
| Andriy Markovych (UKR) | 25.06.1995 | 9 | (3) | |
| Artur Šarnin | 19.07.2000 | 3 | (8) | – |
| Giannis Tsivelekidis (GRE) | 04.06.1999 | 30 | (2) | 3 |
| **Midfielders:** | **DOB** | **M** | **(s)** | **G** |
| Mikhail Babichev (BLR) | 02.02.1995 | 29 | (2) | 1 |
| Andre Fortune II (TRI) | 03.07.1996 | 11 | (3) | 1 |
| Nikita Komissarov | 25.04.2000 | 21 | (10) | 1 |
| Rommi Siht | 30.06.2006 | | (4) | |
| Igor Subbotin | 26.06.1990 | 21 | (5) | 5 |
| Daniel Sudar (AUT) | 28.01.1998 | 2 | (3) | |
| German Šlein | 28.03.1996 | 32 | (2) | 1 |
| Stanislav Tsõmbaljuk | 25.11.2002 | | (7) | |
| **Forwards:** | **DOB** | **M** | **(s)** | **G** |
| Maksim Gussev | 20.07.1994 | 19 | (13) | 6 |
| William Jebor (LBR) | 10.11.1991 | 2 | (8) | 1 |
| Pavel Marin | 14.06.1995 | 22 | (4) | 1 |
| Kaspar Paur | 16.02.1995 | 30 | (5) | 9 |
| Alex Tamm | 24.07.2001 | 26 | (1) | 12 |
| Aleksandr Volkov | 11.10.1994 | 18 | (15) | 9 |
| Welves Santos Damacena (BRA) | 24.11.2000 | 5 | (3) | |

## Paide Linnameeskond

**Founded**: 2004
**Stadium**: Paide linnastaadion, Paide (500)
**Trainer**: Karel Voolaid — 04.07.1977

| Goalkeepers: | DOB | M | (s) | G |
|---|---|---|---|---|
| Mihkel Aksalu | 07.11.1984 | 17 | | |
| Ebrima Jarju (GAM) | 16.03.1998 | 18 | | |
| Mattias Sapp | 08.01.2001 | 1 | | |
| **Defenders:** | **DOB** | **M** | **(s)** | **G** |
| Siim Aer | 22.07.2001 | | (2) | |
| Rasmus Kallas | 18.11.2003 | 1 | (3) | |
| Ragnar Klavan | 30.10.1985 | 11 | | 1 |
| Hindrek Ojamaa | 12.06.1995 | 17 | (7) | 1 |
| Kristjan Pelt | 12.07.2001 | 28 | (2) | 3 |
| Joseph Saliste | 10.04.1995 | 35 | | |
| Abdul Yusif (GHA) | 09.08.2001 | 26 | (1) | 3 |
| **Midfielders:** | **DOB** | **M** | **(s)** | **G** |
| Foday Darboe (GAM) | 09.03.2003 | 3 | (5) | |
| Andre Frolov | 18.04.1988 | 25 | (8) | 2 |
| Marten Kelement | 24.10.2003 | | (2) | |
| Sergei Mošnikov | 07.01.1988 | 8 | (18) | 4 |
| Karl Mööl | 04.03.1992 | 34 | (2) | |
| Kevor Palumets | 21.11.2002 | 14 | (9) | 1 |
| Herol Riiberg | 14.04.1997 | 7 | (12) | |
| Dominique Simon (FRA) | 29.07.2000 | 21 | (6) | 2 |
| **Forwards:** | **DOB** | **M** | **(s)** | **G** |
| Raimond Eino | 15.02.2000 | | (1) | |
| Mechini Gomis (SEN) | 14.12.2001 | 5 | (3) | 4 |
| Siim Luts | 12.03.1989 | 16 | (7) | 3 |
| Deabeas Owusu-Sekyere (NED) | 04.11.1999 | 17 | (1) | 9 |
| Kristofer Piht | 24.04.2001 | 16 | (12) | 8 |
| Kaimar Saag | 05.08.1988 | 26 | (3) | 9 |
| Robi Saarma | 20.05.2001 | 22 | (12) | 16 |
| Ebrima Singhateh (GAM) | 06.05.2003 | 9 | (12) | 9 |
| Bubacarr Tambedou (GAM) | 05.04.2002 | 8 | (10) | 7 |
| Edgar Tur | 28.12.1996 | 11 | (8) | |
| Sten Jakob Viidas | 24.02.2003 | | (8) | |

## Jalgpalliklubi Tallinna Kalev

**Founded**: 1909 (as Meteor Tallinn); Re-established on 01.09.2002
**Stadium**: Kadriorg staadion, Tallinn (1,300)
**Trainer**: Daniel Meijel — 26.12.1974

| Goalkeepers: | DOB | M | (s) | G |
|---|---|---|---|---|
| Stiven Raider | 04.12.2001 | 24 | | |
| Maico Rimmel | 23.09.2003 | 12 | (1) | |
| **Defenders:** | **DOB** | **M** | **(s)** | **G** |
| Alexander Bergmann | 08.12.2004 | 1 | (6) | |
| Aron Kirt | 26.02.2006 | | (1) | |
| Kaspar Laur | 08.04.2000 | 23 | (5) | 3 |
| Hugo Palutaja | 02.03.2004 | 24 | (5) | |
| Georg Pank | 01.03.2004 | 2 | | |
| Daniil Shevyakov (RUS) | 29.07.1999 | 1 | (5) | |
| Mikk Siitam | 25.12.2003 | 5 | (9) | |
| Valerii Stepanenko (UKR) | 19.10.1998 | 21 | (9) | |
| Daniil Sõtšugov | 15.01.2003 | 24 | (2) | |
| Tanel Tamberg | 06.06.1992 | 26 | (1) | |
| **Midfielders:** | **DOB** | **M** | **(s)** | **G** |
| Marek Kaljumäe | 18.02.1991 | 20 | (7) | 1 |
| Mikk Kruusalu | 06.12.2000 | 2 | (1) | |
| Kenlou Laasner | 25.12.1999 | | (2) | |
| Markus Leivategija | 24.04.2006 | | (2) | |
| Sten Luht | 02.03.2005 | | (1) | |
| Daniil Petrunin | 22.03.2001 | 23 | | 2 |
| Reinhard Reimaa | 12.11.1998 | 29 | (5) | 1 |
| Markus Riisenberg | 15.07.2004 | | (5) | |
| Ramon Smirnov | 25.08.2004 | 7 | (5) | |
| Tristan Toomas Teeväli | 19.05.2003 | 15 | | 3 |
| Martin Tomberg | 05.03.2006 | | (1) | |
| Foday Trawally (GAM) | 28.03.2001 | 19 | (5) | 8 |
| **Forwards:** | **DOB** | **M** | **(s)** | **G** |
| Hannes Anier | 16.01.1993 | 21 | (5) | 3 |
| Taavi Jürisoo | 23.05.2005 | 2 | (9) | 1 |
| Karl Stefan Lill | 07.07.2002 | | (2) | |
| Pavel Marasov | 26.02.2003 | | (1) | |
| Mark Mälksoo | 07.04.2004 | | (3) | 1 |
| Vadim Mihailov | 06.06.1998 | 24 | (8) | 1 |
| Ats Purje | 03.08.1985 | 27 | (5) | 10 |
| Hannes Planken | 24.02.2006 | | (1) | |
| Ramol Sillamaa | 17.10.2004 | 10 | (15) | 2 |
| Evert Talviste | 19.11.2006 | 1 | (1) | |
| Daniil Timofeev | 17.03.2003 | | (3) | |
| Ioan Yakovlev (RUS) | 19.01.1998 | 33 | | 6 |

## Jalgpallikool Tammeka Tartu

**Founded**: 13.06.1989
**Stadium**: Tartu Tamme staadion, Tartu (1,500)
**Trainer**: Carlos Miguel Sousa Santos (POR) — 15.05.1984
[09.07.2021] Marti Pähn — 21.01.1989

| Goalkeepers: | DOB | M | (s) | G |
|---|---|---|---|---|
| Richard Aland | 15.03.1994 | 15 | | |
| Marcus Agarmaa | 19.09.2003 | 1 | | |
| Carl Kiidjärv | 05.12.2001 | 15 | (1) | |
| Karl Pechter | 02.03.1996 | 5 | (1) | |
| **Defenders:** | **DOB** | **M** | **(s)** | **G** |
| David Addy (GHA) | 21.02.1990 | 25 | | 1 |
| Kevin Anderson | 10.11.1993 | 9 | (2) | |
| Gerdo Juhkam | 19.06.1994 | 32 | | 2 |
| Karl Läänelaid | 07.07.2003 | 1 | (8) | |
| Carl Roberts Mägimets | 10.02.2002 | 4 | (11) | |
| Tanel Tammik | 14.06.2002 | 26 | (5) | 3 |
| Taijo Teniste | 31.01.1988 | 26 | (1) | 2 |
| Ats Toomsalu | 17.08.2002 | 6 | (4) | |
| **Midfielders:** | **DOB** | **M** | **(s)** | **G** |
| Reio Laabus | 14.03.1990 | 26 | (6) | 3 |
| Dominic Laaneots | 16.06.2001 | 16 | (14) | 1 |
| Tanel Lang | 15.08.1995 | 29 | | 1 |
| Herman Pedmanson | 12.08.2005 | 1 | (2) | |
| Sander Puri | 07.05.1988 | 29 | (1) | 1 |
| Giacomo Uggeri (ITA) | 04.04.2001 | 1 | (20) | |
| Henri Välja | 04.11.2001 | 25 | (1) | 2 |
| **Forwards:** | **DOB** | **M** | **(s)** | **G** |
| Kevin Burov | 27.04.2004 | 2 | (4) | |
| Martin Jõgi | 05.01.1995 | | (10) | 1 |
| Sander Kapper | 08.12.1994 | 26 | (5) | 1 |
| Henri Käblik | 19.04.2005 | 4 | (10) | 4 |
| Aleksandr Kukharev | 02.05.2002 | 11 | (13) | 3 |
| Kevin Mätas | 26.10.1999 | 27 | (6) | 10 |
| Egert Naruson | 26.04.2001 | | (4) | |
| Artur Uljanov | 25.03.1999 | 7 | (2) | 1 |
| Patrik Veelma | 15.04.2002 | 27 | (7) | 1 |

## Pärnu Jalgpalliklubi Vaprus

| | | |
|---|---|---|
| **Founded**: | 1922 | |
| **Stadium**: | Pärnu Rannastaadion, Pärnu (1,501) | |
| **Trainer**: | Dmitrijs Kalašņikovs (LVA) | 11.12.1983 |

| Goalkeepers: | DOB | M | (s) | G |
|---|---|---|---|---|
| Ott Nõmm | 23.10.2004 | 18 | | |
| Hendrik Vainu | 03.04.1996 | 18 | (1) | |
| **Defenders:** | **DOB** | **M** | **(s)** | **G** |
| Siim Aer | 22.07.2001 | 11 | (5) | |
| Martin Kase | 02.09.1993 | 30 | (3) | 2 |
| Kairo Kiltmaa | 22.02.2003 | 7 | (1) | |
| Uku Kõrre | 19.04.2000 | 32 | | |
| Luka Luković (SRB) | 16.07.2001 | 1 | | |
| Reno Mark | 16.11.2000 | 31 | | |
| Kevin Metso | 18.12.2002 | 11 | (7) | |
| Ranet Ristikivi | 19.11.2000 | 6 | (2) | |
| Magnus Villota | 11.02.1998 | 30 | (1) | 2 |
| **Midfielders:** | **DOB** | **M** | **(s)** | **G** |
| Kristjan Kask | 05.07.1999 | 31 | | 3 |

| | DOB | M | (s) | G |
|---|---|---|---|---|
| Anton Krutogolov | 05.04.2001 | 10 | (1) | |
| Robin Limberg | 10.10.2001 | | (2) | |
| Sander Sinilaid | 07.10.1990 | 34 | | 3 |
| Enrico Veensalu | 19.08.1999 | 11 | (13) | 1 |
| Mathias Villota | 28.06.2005 | 1 | (2) | |
| **Forwards:** | **DOB** | **M** | **(s)** | **G** |
| Aamir Yunis Abdallah (AUS) | 08.05.1999 | 12 | (3) | 1 |
| Kevin Kauber | 23.03.1995 | 30 | (1) | 6 |
| Andreas Kiivit | 05.07.2003 | 3 | (13) | |
| Markus Miiter | 02.09.2005 | | (1) | |
| Raul Tääker | 27.03.2002 | | (2) | |
| Ronaldo Tiismaa | 02.05.2001 | 22 | (7) | 7 |
| Taaniel Usta | 17.02.2003 | 19 | (2) | 4 |
| Igor Ustritski | 27.08.2001 | 2 | (12) | |
| Virgo Vallik | 03.02.2003 | 26 | (8) | 3 |

## SECOND LEVEL
### Esiliiga 2022

| | | | | | | | | | |
|---|---|---|---|---|---|---|---|---|---|
| 1. | Harju JK Laagri (*Promoted*) | 36 | 24 | 4 | 8 | 97 | - | 46 | 76 |
| 2. | FCI Levadia U-21 Tallinn | 36 | 21 | 5 | 10 | 85 | - | 45 | 68 |
| 3. | FC Elva (*Promotion Play-offs*) | 36 | 20 | 6 | 10 | 76 | - | 52 | 66 |
| 4. | Viimsi JK | 36 | 20 | 3 | 13 | 76 | - | 40 | 63 |
| 5. | FC Flora U-21 Tallinn | 36 | 19 | 5 | 12 | 88 | - | 52 | 62 |
| 6. | JK FC Nõmme United | 36 | 18 | 6 | 12 | 79 | - | 56 | 60 |
| 7. | Paide Linnameeskond U-21 | 36 | 17 | 1 | 18 | 75 | - | 88 | 52 |
| 8. | Ida-Virumaa FC Alliance (*Relegation Play-offs*) | 36 | 8 | 3 | 25 | 29 | - | 105 | 27 |
| 9. | Viljandi JK Tulevik (*Relegated*) | 36 | 6 | 5 | 25 | 28 | - | 102 | 23 |
| 10. | Pärnu JK (*Relegated*) | 36 | 4 | 8 | 24 | 30 | - | 77 | 20 |

Please note: reserve teams are not eligible to be promoted to the Meistriliiga.

## Relegation Play-offs (2nd/3rd Level) [16-20.11.2022]

| | | |
|---|---|---|
| Ida-Virumaa FC Alliance - JK Tallinna Kalev U-21 | 3-3(2-1) | 1-0(0-0) |

Ida-Virumaa FC Alliance remains at second level for 2023.

## NATIONAL TEAM

### INTERNATIONAL MATCHES
#### (16.07.2022 – 15.07.2023)

| | | | | |
|---|---|---|---|---|
| 23.09.2022 | Tallinn | *Estonia - Malta* | *2-1(1-0)* | (UNL) |
| 26.09.2022 | Serravalle | *San Marino - Estonia* | *0-4(0-1)* | (UNL) |
| 16.11.2022 | Rīga | *Latvia - Estonia* | *1-1(1-1,1-1,1-1); 5-3 on penalties* | (BC) |
| 19.11.2022 | Tallinn | *Estonia - Lithuania* | *2-0(0-0)* | (BC) |
| 08.01.2023 | Albufeira | *Iceland - Estonia* | *1-1(0-1)* | (F) |
| 12.01.2023 | Albufeira | *Finland - Estonia* | *0-1(0-0)* | (F) |
| 23.03.2023 | Budapest | *Hungary - Estonia* | *1-0(1-0)* | (F) |
| 27.03.2023 | Linz | *Austria - Estonia* | *2-1(0-1)* | (ECQ) |
| 17.06.2023 | Bakı | *Azerbaijan - Estonia* | *1-1(0-1)* | (ECQ) |
| 20.06.2023 | Tallinn | *Estonia - Belgium* | *0-3(0-2)* | (ECQ) |

**23.09.2022    ESTONIA - MALTA    2-1(1-0)    3rd UEFA Nations League D, Group 2**
A. Le Coq Arena, Tallinn; Referee: Daniel Siebert (Germany); Attendance: 5,539
**EST:** Karl Jakob Hein, Henrik Pürg, Joonas Tamm, Karol Mets, Ken Kallaste (46.Taijo Teniste), Henrik Ojamaa (77.Vlasiy Sinyavskiy), Markus Soomets, Bogdan Vaštšuk (68.Martin Miller), Konstantin Vassiljev (Cap), Sergei Zenjov (90+3.Robert Kirss), Rauno Sappinen (68.Henri Anier). Trainer: Thomas Häberli (Switzerland).
**Goals:** Rauno Sappinen (45+6 penalty), Henri Anier (86).

**26.09.2022    SAN MARINO - ESTONIA    0-4(0-1)    3rd UEFA Nations League D, Group 2**
San Marino Stadium, Serravalle; Referee: Kateryna Monzul (Ukraine); Attendance: 608
**EST:** Karl Jakob Hein, Joonas Tamm, Karol Mets, Henrik Pürg (61.Nikita Baranov), Markus Soomets, Taijo Teniste (61.Martin Miller), Bogdan Vaštšuk (68.Rocco Robert Shein), Konstantin Vassiljev (Cap) (83.Georgi Tunjov), Henrik Ojamaa, Henri Anier, Rauno Sappinen (83.Erik Sorga). Trainer: Thomas Häberli (Switzerland).
**Goals:** Henri Anier (38), Taijo Teniste (56), Rauno Sappinen (66), Henri Anier (78).

**16.11.2022    LATVIA - ESTONIA**                1-1(1-1,1-1,1-1); 5-3 on penalties        29th Baltic Cup, Semi-Finals
Daugava stadions, Rīga; Referee: Robertas Valikonis (Lithuania); Attendance: 1,657
**EST:** Karl Jakob Hein, Taijo Teniste (82.Vlasiy Sinyavskiy), Märten Kuusk, Karol Mets, Nikita Baranov, Ken Kallaste (90+1.Frank Liivak), Mattias Käit, Bogdan Vaštšuk (66.Martin Miller), Konstantin Vassiljev (Cap), Sergei Zenjov, Rauno Sappinen (67.Erik Sorga). Trainer: Thomas Häberli (Switzerland).
**Goal:** Sergei Zenjov (2).
**Penalties:** Karol Mets, Konstantin Vassiljev, Sergei Zenjov (missed), Erik Sorga.

**19.11.2022    ESTONIA - LITHUANIA**                2-0(0-0)        29th Baltic Cup, Third Place Play-off
A. Le Coq Arena, Tallinn; Referee: Vitalijs Spasjonņikovs (Latvia); Attendance: 1,563
**EST:** Karl Jakob Hein, Taijo Teniste (84.Taijo Teniste), Märten Kuusk, Karol Mets, Rasmus Peetson, Ken Kallaste (30.Vlasiy Sinyavskiy), Rocco Robert Shein (64.Mattias Käit), Markus Soomets, Konstantin Vassiljev (Cap) (64.Georgi Tunjov), Erik Sorga (64.Sergei Zenjov), Rauno Sappinen (84.Bogdan Vaštšuk). Trainer: Thomas Häberli (Switzerland).
**Goals:** Sergei Zenjov (65), Rasmus Peetson (89).

**08.01.2023    ICELAND - ESTONIA**                1-1(0-1)        Friendly International
Estadio da Nora, Albufeira (Portugal); Referee: Miguel Bertolo Nogueira (Portugal); Attendance: n/a
**EST:** Karl Andre Vallner, Taijo Teniste, Erko Jonne Tõugjas, Rasmus Peetson, Markus Soomets, Martin Miller, Markus Poom (63.Nikita Vassiljev), Konstantin Vassiljev (Cap) (85.Karl Mööl), Ken Kallaste (75.Marko Lipp), Henrik Ojamaa (63.Ioan Yakovlev), Sergei Zenjov (75.Alex Matthias Tamm). Trainer: Thomas Häberli (Switzerland).
**Goal:** Sergei Zenjov (45).

**12.01.2023    FINLAND - ESTONIA**                0-1(0-0)        Friendly International
Estadio da Nora, Albufeira (Portugal); Referee: Gustavo Fernandes Correia (Portugal); Attendance: n/a
**EST:** Marko Meerits (46.Karl-Romet Nõmm), Taijo Teniste (51.Hindrek Ojamaa), Marko Lipp, Rasmus Peetson, Erko Jonne Tõugjas, Ken Kallaste (81.Danil Kuraksin), Nikita Vassiljev, Martin Miller, Konstantin Vassiljev (Cap) (66.Markus Poom), Henrik Ojamaa (51.Sten Reinkort), Sergei Zenjov (66.Robi Saarma). Trainer: Thomas Häberli (Switzerland).
**Goal:** Martin Miller (84).

**23.03.2023    HUNGARY - ESTONIA**                1-0(1-0)        Friendly International
Puskás Aréna, Budapest; Referee: Walter Altmann (Austria); Attendance: 37,804
**EST:** Karl Jakob Hein, Maksim Paskotši, Märten Kuusk, Nikita Baranov (82.Erko Jonne Tõugjas), Artur Pikk (84.Sten Reinkort), Rocco Robert Shein (46.Martin Miller), Mattias Käit, Henrik Ojamaa (46.Erik Sorga), Konstantin Vassiljev (Cap) (64.Georgi Tunjov), Vlasiy Sinyavskiy, Rauno Sappinen (46.Sergei Zenjov). Trainer: Thomas Häberli (Switzerland).

**27.03.2023    AUSTRIA - ESTONIA**                2-1(0-1)        17th EC. Qualifiers
Raiffeisen Arena, LInz; Referee: Enea Jorgji (Albania); Attendance: 16,500
**EST:** Karl Jakob Hein, Maksim Paskotši, Karol Mets, Joonas Tamm, Martin Miller (78.Rocco Robert Shein), Vlasiy Sinyavskiy, Mattias Käit, Konstantin Vassiljev (Cap), Artur Pikk (90+1.Georgi Tunjov), Sergei Zenjov (90+2.Sten Reinkort), Rauno Sappinen (85.Henrik Ojamaa). Trainer: Thomas Häberli (Switzerland).
**Goal:** Rauno Sappinen (25).

**17.06.2023    AZERBAIJAN - ESTONIA**                1-1(0-1)        17th EC. Qualifiers
Dalga Arena, Bakı; Referee: Ondřej Berka (Czech Republic); Attendance: 3,900
**EST:** Karl Jakob Hein, Märten Kuusk, Karol Mets, Rasmus Peetson, Marco Lukka (83.Taijo Teniste), Konstantin Vassiljev (Cap), Mattias Käit, Martin Miller, Vlasiy Sinyavskiy, Henri Anier (56.Henrik Ojamaa), Rauno Sappinen (83.Sten Reinkort). Trainer: Thomas Häberli (Switzerland).
**Goal:** Rauno Sappinen (27).

**20.06.2023    ESTONIA - BELGIUM**                0-3(0-2)        17th EC. Qualifiers
A. Le Coq Arena, Tallinn; Referee: John Beaton (Scotland); Attendance: 11,772
**EST:** Karl Jakob Hein, Rasmus Peetson, Karol Mets (Cap), Märten Kuusk, Markus Poom (61.Henri Anier), Martin Miller (74.Rocco Robert Shein), Taijo Teniste (79.Sten Reinkort), Mattias Käit, Vlasiy Sinyavskiy, Henrik Ojamaa (46.Georgi Tunjov), Rauno Sappinen (74.Erik Sorga). Trainer: Thomas Häberli (Switzerland).

## NATIONAL TEAM PLAYERS
### (16.07.2022 – 15.07.2023)

| Name | DOB | Caps | Goals | Club | |
|---|---|---|---|---|---|

**Goalkeepers**

| Name | DOB | Caps | Goals | Club | |
|---|---|---|---|---|---|
| Karl Jakob HEIN | 13.04.2002 | 22 | 0 | 2022/2023: | *Arsenal FC London (ENG)* |
| Marko MEERITS | 26.04.1992 | 14 | 0 | 2023: | *Nõmme Kalju FC Tallinn* |
| Karl-Romet NÕMM | 04.01.1998 | 1 | 0 | 2023: | *FC Flora Tallinn* |
| Karl Andre VALLNER | 28.02.1998 | 1 | 0 | 2023: | *FCI Levadia Tallinn* |

**Defenders**

| Name | DOB | Caps | Goals | Club | |
|---|---|---|---|---|---|
| Nikita BARANOV | 19.08.1992 | 46 | 0 | 2022/2023: | *FC Pyunik Yerevan (ARM)* |
| Ken KALLASTE | 31.08.1988 | 57 | 0 | 2022/2023: | *FC Flora Tallinn* |
| Märten KUUSK | 05.04.1996 | 25 | 0 | 2022: | *Újpest FC (HUN)* |
| | | | | 09.02.2023-> | *FC Flora Tallinn* |
| Michael LILANDER | 20.06.1997 | 15 | 0 | 2022: | *FC Flora Tallinn* |
| Marko LIPP | 19.03.1999 | 2 | 0 | 2023: | *FC Flora Tallinn* |
| Marco LUKKA | 04.12.1996 | 5 | 0 | 2023: | *FC Flora Tallinn* |
| Karol METS | 16.05.1993 | 87 | 0 | 2022: | *FC Zürich (SUI)* |
| | | | | 05.01.2023-> | *FC St. Pauli Hamburg (GER)* |
| Hindrek OJAMAA | 12.06.1995 | 6 | 0 | 2022/2023: | *Paide Linnameeskond* |
| Maksim PASKOTŠI | 19.01.2003 | 18 | 0 | 2023: | *Tottenham Hotspur FC London (ENG)* |
| Rasmus PEETSON | 03.05.1995 | 8 | 1 | 2022/2023: | *FCI Levadia Tallinn* |
| Artur PIKK | 05.03.1993 | 50 | 1 | 2023: | *OKS Odra Opole (POL)* |
| Henrik PÜRG | 03.06.1996 | 11 | 0 | 2022: | *FC Flora Tallinn* |
| Joonas TAMM | 02.02.1992 | 50 | 4 | 2022/2023: | *SC FCSB Bucureşti (ROU)* |
| Taijo TENISTE | 31.01.1988 | 99 | 1 | 2022/2023: | *Tartu JK Tammeka* |
| Erko Jonne TÕUGJAS | 05.07.2003 | 3 | 0 | 2022: | *Tallinna JK Legion* |
| | | | | 15.01.2023-> | *FC Flora Tallinn* |
| Bogdan VAŠTŠUK | 04.10.1995 | 11 | 0 | 2022: | *FKS Stal Mielec (POL)* |

**Midfielders**

| Name | DOB | Caps | Goals | Club | |
|---|---|---|---|---|---|
| Danil KURAKSIN | 04.04.2003 | 1 | 0 | 2023: | *FC Flora Tallinn* |
| Mattias KÄIT | 29.06.1998 | 49 | 8 | 2022/2023: | *FC Rapid 1923 Bucureşti (ROU)* |
| Martin MILLER | 25.09.1997 | 26 | 2 | 2022/2023: | *FC Flora Tallinn* |
| Karl MÖÖL | 04.03.1992 | 10 | 0 | 2023: | *Paide Linnameeskond* |
| Markus POOM | 27.02.1999 | 16 | 0 | 2022: | *FC Flora Tallinn* |
| | | | | 16.01.2023-> | *Shamrock Rovers FC Dublin (IRL)* |
| Rocco Robert SHEIN | 14.07.2003 | 6 | 0 | 2022/2023: | *FC Utrecht (NED)* |
| Markus SOOMETS | 02.03.2000 | 12 | 0 | 2022/2023: | *FC Flora Tallinn* |
| Georgi TUNJOV | 17.04.2001 | 11 | 0 | 2022/2023: | *SPAL Ferrara (ITA)* |
| Konstantin VASSILJEV | 16.08.1984 | 151 | 26 | 2022/2023: | *FC Flora Tallinn* |
| Nikita VASSILJEV | 07.10.2003 | 2 | 0 | 2023: | *FCI Levadia Tallinn* |
| Ioan YAKOVLEV | 19.01.1998 | 1 | 0 | 2023: | *FCI Levadia Tallinn* |

**Forwards**

| Name | DOB | Caps | Goals | Club | |
|---|---|---|---|---|---|
| Henri ANIER | 17.12.1990 | 86 | 21 | 2022/2023: | *Muang Thong United FC (THA)* |
| Robert KIRSS | 03.09.1994 | 14 | 1 | 2022: | *FCI Levadia Tallinn* |
| Frank LIIVAK | 07.07.1996 | 25 | 3 | 2022: | *Sligo Rovers FC (IRL)* |
| Henrik OJAMAA | 20.05.1991 | 60 | 1 | 2022/2023: | *FC Flora Tallinn* |
| Sten REINKORT | 29.04.1998 | 5 | 0 | 2023: | *FC Flora Tallinn* |
| Robi SAARMA | 20.05.2001 | 1 | 0 | 2023: | *Paide Linnameeskond* |
| Rauno SAPPINEN | 23.01.1996 | 53 | 12 | 2022: | *GKS Piast Gliwice (POL)* |
| | | | | 24.01.2023-> | *FKS Stal Mielec (POL)* |
| Vlasiy SINYAVSKIY | 27.11.1996 | 26 | 0 | 2022/2023: | *1. FC Slovácko Uherské Hradiště (CZE)* |
| Erik SORGA | 08.07.1999 | 26 | 4 | 2022: | *IFK Göteborg (SWE)* |
| | | | | 01.01.2023-> | *PFC Lokomotiv Plovdiv (BUL)* |
| Alex Matthias TAMM | 24.07.2001 | 1 | 0 | 2023: | *Nõmme Kalju FC Tallinn* |
| Sergei ZENJOV | 20.04.1989 | 106 | 17 | 2022/2023: | *FC Flora Tallinn* |

**Trainer**

| | | | |
|---|---|---|---|
| Thomas HÄBERLI (Switzerland) [from 05.01.2021] | 11.04.1974 | 29 M; 10 W; 6 D; 13 L; 30-42 | |

# FAROE ISLANDS

## The Country:
Faroe Islands (Føroyar)
Capital: Tórshavn
Surface: 1,399 km²
Inhabitants: 54,000 [2022]
Time: UTC

## The FA:
Fótbóltssamband Føroya
Gundadalur P.O. Box 3028, 110 Tórshavn
Tel: +298 351 979
Foundation date: 1979
Member of FIFA since: 1988
Member of UEFA since: 1990
Website: www.football.fo

## NATIONAL TEAM RECORDS

| RECORDS | | |
|---|---|---|
| **First international match:** | 24.08.1988, Akranes: | Iceland – Faroe Islands 1-0 |
| **Most international caps:** | Fróði Benjaminsen | - 95 caps (1999-2017) |
| **Most international goals:** | Rógvi Jacobsen | - 10 goals / 53 caps (1999-2009) |
| | Klæmint Andrasson Olsen | - 10 goals / 56 caps (since 2012) |

| UEFA EUROPEAN CHAMPIONSHIP | |
|---|---|
| 1960 | - |
| 1964 | - |
| 1968 | - |
| 1972 | - |
| 1976 | - |
| 1980 | - |
| 1984 | - |
| 1988 | - |
| 1992 | Qualifiers |
| 1996 | Qualifiers |
| 2000 | Qualifiers |
| 2004 | Qualifiers |
| 2008 | Qualifiers |
| 2012 | Qualifiers |
| 2016 | Qualifiers |
| 2020 | Qualifiers |

| FIFA WORLD CUP | |
|---|---|
| 1930 | - |
| 1934 | - |
| 1938 | - |
| 1950 | - |
| 1954 | - |
| 1958 | - |
| 1962 | - |
| 1966 | - |
| 1970 | - |
| 1974 | - |
| 1978 | - |
| 1982 | Did not enter |
| 1986 | Did not enter |
| 1990 | Did not enter |
| 1994 | Qualifiers |
| 1998 | Qualifiers |
| 2002 | Qualifiers |
| 2006 | Qualifiers |
| 2010 | Qualifiers |
| 2014 | Qualifiers |
| 2018 | Qualifiers |
| 2022 | Qualifiers |

| OLYMPIC TOURNAMENTS | |
|---|---|
| 1908 | - |
| 1912 | - |
| 1920 | - |
| 1924 | - |
| 1928 | - |
| 1936 | - |
| 1948 | - |
| 1952 | - |
| 1956 | - |
| 1960 | - |
| 1964 | - |
| 1968 | - |
| 1972 | - |
| 1976 | - |
| 1980 | - |
| 1984 | Did not enter |
| 1988 | Did not enter |
| 1992 | Did not enter |
| 1996 | Did not enter |
| 2000 | Did not enter |
| 2004 | Did not enter |
| 2008 | Did not enter |
| 2012 | Qualifiers |
| 2016 | Qualifiers |
| 2020 | Qualifiers |

## UEFA NATIONS LEAGUE

| 2018/2019 | League D (Group Stage) |
|---|---|
| 2020/2021 | League D (Group Stage -> promotion to League C) |
| 2022/2023 | League C (Group Stage) |

## FAROE ISLANDS CLUB HONOURS IN EUROPEAN CLUB COMPETITIONS:

| European Champion Clubs' Cup (1956-1992) / UEFA Champions League (1993-2023) |
|---|
| None |

| Fairs Cup (1858-1971) / UEFA Cup (1972-2009) / UEFA Europa League (2010-2023) |
|---|
| None |

| UEFA Europa Conference League (2021-2023) |
|---|
| None |

| UEFA Super Cup (1972-2022) |
|---|
| None |

| *European Cup Winners' Cup 1961-1999** |
|---|
| None |

*defunct competition

# NATIONAL COMPETITIONS
# TABLE OF HONOURS

| | CHAMPIONS | CUP WINNERS | BEST GOALSCORERS | |
|---|---|---|---|---|
| 1942 | KÍ Klaksvík | - | - | |
| 1943 | TB Tvøroyri | - | - | |
| 1944 | No competition | - | - | |
| 1945 | KÍ Klaksvík | - | - | |
| 1946 | B36 Tórshavn | - | - | |
| 1947 | SÍ Sørvágur | - | - | |
| 1948 | B36 Tórshavn | - | - | |
| 1949 | TB Tvøroyri | - | - | |
| 1950 | B36 Tórshavn | - | - | |
| 1951 | TB Tvøroyri | - | - | |
| 1952 | KÍ Klaksvík | - | - | |
| 1953 | KÍ Klaksvík | - | - | |
| 1954 | KÍ Klaksvík | - | - | |
| 1955 | HB Tórshavn | HB Tórshavn | - | |
| 1956 | KÍ Klaksvík | TB Tvøroyri | - | |
| 1957 | KÍ Klaksvík | HB Tórshavn | - | |
| 1958 | KÍ Klaksvík | TB Tvøroyri | - | |
| 1959 | B36 Tórshavn | HB Tórshavn | - | |
| 1960 | HB Tórshavn | TB Tvøroyri | - | |
| 1961 | KÍ Klaksvík | TB Tvøroyri | - | |
| 1962 | B36 Tórshavn | HB Tórshavn | - | |
| 1963 | HB Tórshavn | HB Tórshavn | - | |
| 1964 | HB Tórshavn | HB Tórshavn | - | |
| 1965 | HB Tórshavn | B36 Tórshavn | - | |
| 1966 | KÍ Klaksvík | KÍ Klaksvík | - | |
| 1967 | KÍ Klaksvík | KÍ Klaksvík | - | |
| 1968 | KÍ Klaksvík | HB Tórshavn | - | |
| 1969 | KÍ Klaksvík | HB Tórshavn | - | |
| 1970 | KÍ Klaksvík | Cup Final not played | - | |
| 1971 | HB Tórshavn | HB Tórshavn | - | |
| 1972 | KÍ Klaksvík | HB Tórshavn | - | |
| 1973 | HB Tórshavn | HB Tórshavn | - | |
| 1974 | HB Tórshavn | VB Vágur | - | |
| 1975 | HB Tórshavn | HB Tórshavn | - | |
| 1976 | TB Tvøroyri | HB Tórshavn | - | |
| 1977 | TB Tvøroyri | TB Tvøroyri | - | |
| 1978 | HB Tórshavn | HB Tórshavn | - | |
| 1979 | ÍF Fuglafjørður | HB Tórshavn | - | |
| 1980 | TB Tvøroyri | HB Tórshavn | Jóan Petur Olgarsson (TB Tvøroyri) | 18 |
| 1981 | HB Tórshavn | HB Tórshavn | Jóannes Jakobsen (HB Tórshavn) | 14 |
| 1982 | HB Tórshavn | HB Tórshavn | Jóannes Jakobsen (HB Tórshavn) | 9 |
| 1983 | Gøtu Ítróttarfelag | Gøtu Ítróttarfelag | Petur Hans Hansen (B68 Toftir) Hans Leo í Bartalsstovu (Gøtu Ítróttarfelag) | 10 |
| 1984 | B68 Toftir | HB Tórshavn | Aksel Højgaard (B68 Toftir) Erling Jacobsen (HB Tórshavn) | 10 |
| 1985 | B68 Toftir | Gøtu Ítróttarfelag | Símun Petur Justinussen (Gøtu Ítróttarfelag) | 10 |
| 1986 | Gøtu Ítróttarfelag | NSÍ Runavík | Jesper Wiemer (DEN, B68 Toftir) Símun Petur Justinussen (Gøtu Ítróttarfelag) | 13 |
| 1987 | TB Tvøroyri | HB Tórshavn | Símun Petur Justinussen (Gøtu Ítróttarfelag) | 10 |
| 1988 | HB Tórshavn | HB Tórshavn | Jógvan Petersen (B68 Toftir) | 9 |
| 1989 | B71 Sandoy | HB Tórshavn | Egill Steinþórsson (ISL, VB Vágur) | 16 |
| 1990 | HB Tórshavn | KÍ Klaksvík | Gunnar Mohr (HB Tórshavn) Jens Erik Rasmussen (MB Miðvágur) | 10 |
| 1991 | Klaksvíkar Ítróttarfelag | B36 Tórshavn | Símun Petur Justinussen (Gøtu Ítróttarfelag) | 15 |
| 1992 | B68 Toftir | HB Tórshavn | Símun Petur Justinussen (Gøtu Ítróttarfelag) | 14 |
| 1993 | Gøtu Ítróttarfelag | B71 Sandur | Uni Arge (HB Tórshavn) | 11 |
| 1994 | Gøtu Ítróttarfelag | KÍ Klaksvík | John Petersen (Gøtu Ítróttarfelag) | 21 |
| 1995 | Gøtu Ítróttarfelag | HB Tórshavn | Súni Fríði Johannesen (B68 Toftir) | 24 |
| 1996 | Gøtu Ítróttarfelag | Gøtu Ítróttarfelag | Kurt Mørkøre (KÍ Klaksvík) | 20 |
| 1997 | B36 Tórshavn | Gøtu Ítróttarfelag | Uni Arge (HB Tórshavn) | 24 |
| 1998 | HB Tórshavn | HB Tórshavn | Jákup á Borg (B36 Tórshavn) | 20 |
| 1999 | Klaksvíkar Ítróttarfelag | KÍ Klaksvík | Jákup á Borg (B36 Tórshavn) | 17 |
| 2000 | VB Vágur | Gøtu Ítróttarfelag | Súni Fríði Johannesen (B36 Tórshavn) | 16 |
| 2001 | B36 Tórshavn | B36 Tórshavn | Helgi L. Petersen (Gøtu Ítróttarfelag) | 19 |
| 2002 | HB Tórshavn | NSÍ Runavík | Andrew av Fløtum (HB Tórshavn) | 18 |
| 2003 | HB Tórshavn | B36 Tórshavn | Hjalgrím Elttør (KÍ Klaksvík) | 13 |
| 2004 | HB Tórshavn | HB Tórshavn | Sonni L. Petersen (EB/Streymur) | 13 |
| 2005 | B36 Tórshavn | Gøtu Ítróttarfelag | Christian Høgni Jacobsen (NSÍ Runavík) | 18 |
| 2006 | HB Tórshavn | B36 Tórshavn | Christian Høgni Jacobsen (NSÍ Runavík) | 18 |
| 2007 | NSÍ Runavík | EB/Streymur | Amed Davy Sylla (FRA, B36 Tórshavn) | 18 |
| 2008 | EB/Streymur | EB/Streymur | Arnbjørn Hansen (EB/Streymur) | 20 |
| 2009 | HB Tórshavn | Víkingur Gøta | Finnur Justinussen (Víkingur Gøta) | 19 |

| 2010 | HB Tórshavn | EB/Streymur | Arnbjørn Hansen (EB/Streymur) | |
| | | | Christian Høgni Jacobsen (NSÍ Runavík) | 22 |
| 2011 | B36 Tórshavn | EB/Streymur | Finnur Justinussen (Víkingur Gøta) | 21 |
| 2012 | EB/Streymur | Víkingur Gøta | Clayton Soares do Nascimento | |
| | | | (BRA, ÍF Fuglafjørður) | 22 |
| | | | Páll Andrasson Klettskarð (KÍ Klaksvík) | |
| 2013 | HB Tórshavn | Víkingur Gøta | Klæmint Andrasson Olsen (NSÍ Runavík) | 21 |
| 2014 | B36 Tórshavn | Víkingur Gøta | Klæmint Andrasson Olsen (NSÍ Runavík) | 22 |
| 2015 | B36 Tórshavn | Víkingur Gøta | Klæmint Andrasson Olsen (NSÍ Runavík) | 21 |
| 2016 | Víkingur Gøta | KÍ Klaksvík | Klæmint Andrasson Olsen (NSÍ Runavík) | 23 |
| 2017 | Víkingur Gøta | NSÍ Runavík | Adeshina Abayomi Lawal (NGA, (Víkingur Gøta) | 17 |
| 2018 | HB Tórshavn | B36 Tórshavn | Adrian Justinussen (HB Tórshavn) | 20 |
| 2019 | KÍ Klaksvík | HB Tórshavn | Klæmint Andrasson Olsen (NSÍ Runavík) | 26 |
| 2020 | HB Tórshavn | HB Tórshavn | Klæmint Andrasson Olsen (NSÍ Runavík) | |
| | | | Uroš Stojanov (SRB, ÍF Fuglafjarðar) | 17 |
| 2021 | KÍ Klaksvík | B36 Tórshavn | Mikkel Dahl (DEN, HB Tórshavn) | 27 |
| 2022 | KÍ Klaksvík | Víkingur Gøta | Sølvi Vatnhamar (Víkingur Gøta) | 20 |

## NATIONAL CHAMPIONSHIP
### Faroe Islands Premier League - Betri deildin 2022
(05.03.2022 – 22.10.2022)

### Results

**Round 1 [05-06.03.2022]**
07 Vestur - Víkingur Gøta 2-3(2-1)
AB Argir - HB Tórshavn 1-3(1-1)
Skála ÍF - KÍ Klaksvík 0-3(0-2)
B36 Tórshavn - B68 Toftir 4-1(2-0)
EB/Streymur - NSÍ Runavík 3-4(3-3)

**Round 2 [12-13.03.2022]**
Víkingur Gøta - EB/Streymur 1-2(1-1)
KÍ Klaksvík - B36 Tórshavn 1-0(1-0)
AB Argir - 07 Vestur 3-3(2-1)
HB Tórshavn - NSÍ Runavík 5-1(4-1)
B68 Toftir - Skála ÍF 2-2(2-1)

**Round 3 [19-20.03.2022]**
NSÍ Runavík - B68 Toftir 0-2(0-2)
HB Tórshavn - B36 Tórshavn 1-0(0-0)
EB/Streymur - KÍ Klaksvík 0-2(0-2)
Skála ÍF - 07 Vestur 0-0
Víkingur Gøta - AB Argir 4-1(1-0) [03.05.22]

**Round 4 [02-03.04.2022]**
B68 Toftir - HB Tórshavn 1-1(0-0)
AB Argir - Skála ÍF 2-1(1-1)
B36 Tórshavn - Víkingur Gøta 0-3(0-2)
EB/Streymur - 07 Vestur 3-0(1-0)
NSÍ Runavík - KÍ Klaksvík 0-4(0-2)

**Round 5 [09-10.04.2022]**
Víkingur Gøta - Skála ÍF 4-2(3-1)
07 Vestur - B68 Toftir 1-0(0-0)
HB Tórshavn - EB/Streymur 2-2(0-1)
KÍ Klaksvík - AB Argir 6-1(4-1)
NSÍ Runavík - B36 Tórshavn 0-2(0-2)

**Round 6 [18.04.2022]**
KÍ Klaksvík - 07 Vestur 3-0(2-0)
Skála ÍF - HB Tórshavn 2-3(2-2)
B36 Tórshavn - EB/Streymur 5-0(3-0)
AB Argir - NSÍ Runavík 2-3(0-2)
B68 Toftir - Víkingur Gøta 0-4(0-3)

**Round 7 [24.04.2022]**
07 Vestur - NSÍ Runavík 3-2(1-0)
Skála ÍF - B36 Tórshavn 1-1(0-0)
Víkingur Gøta - HB Tórshavn 4-2(1-0)
B68 Toftir - KÍ Klaksvík 0-5(0-3)
EB/Streymur - AB Argir 1-0(0-0)

**Round 8 [30.04.-01.05.2022]**
EB/Streymur - B68 Toftir 2-1(1-1)
AB Argir - B36 Tórshavn 0-3(0-2)
KÍ Klaksvík - Víkingur Gøta 1-0(0-0)
HB Tórshavn - 07 Vestur 2-2(2-0)
NSÍ Runavík - Skála ÍF 2-1(2-0)

**Round 9 [07-08.05.2022]**
Skála ÍF - EB/Streymur 0-0
KÍ Klaksvík - HB Tórshavn 2-0(0-0)
Víkingur Gøta - NSÍ Runavík 3-0(1-0)
B36 Tórshavn - 07 Vestur 3-0(1-0)
AB Argir - B68 Toftir 4-1(3-0)

**Round 10 [14-15.05.2022]**
B68 Toftir - Víkingur Gøta 0-6(0-4)
EB/Streymur - B36 Tórshavn 1-5(1-4)
07 Vestur - KÍ Klaksvík 0-6(0-3)
Skála ÍF - HB Tórshavn 1-1(0-0)
NSÍ Runavík - AB Argir 1-4(0-0)

**Round 11 [21-22.05.2022]**
Skála ÍF - NSÍ Runavík 1-4(0-2)
HB Tórshavn - 07 Vestur 3-0(0-0)
Víkingur Gøta - KÍ Klaksvík 0-0
B68 Toftir - EB/Streymur 0-1(0-1)
B36 Tórshavn - AB Argir 1-2(0-0)

**Round 12 [26-28.05.2022]**
Víkingur Gøta - AB Argir 7-0(5-0)
B68 Toftir - NSÍ Runavík 0-1(0-0)
B36 Tórshavn - HB Tórshavn 0-1(0-1)
KÍ Klaksvík - EB/Streymur 3-0(1-0)
07 Vestur - Skála ÍF 2-0(1-0)

**Round 13 [19.06.2022]**
07 Vestur - AB Argir 1-3(0-1)
B36 Tórshavn - KÍ Klaksvík 0-1(0-1)
Skála ÍF - B68 Toftir 1-2(1-1)
NSÍ Runavík - HB Tórshavn 0-2(0-1)
EB/Streymur - Víkingur Gøta 1-2(1-1)

**Round 14 [24-26.06.2022]**
AB Argir - B68 Toftir 0-3(0-0)
EB/Streymur - Skála ÍF 0-1(0-0)
HB Tórshavn - KÍ Klaksvík 1-2(0-1)
NSÍ Runavík - Víkingur Gøta 1-3(1-2)
07 Vestur - B36 Tórshavn 0-1(0-0)

**Round 15 [29.06.-02.07.2022]**
KÍ Klaksvík - NSÍ Runavík 4-2(1-1)
Skála ÍF - AB Argir 5-0(2-0)
Víkingur Gøta - B36 Tórshavn 2-1(0-0)
B68 Toftir - HB Tórshavn 0-1(0-0)
07 Vestur - EB/Streymur 5-4(4-1)

**Round 16 [27-31.07.2022]**
AB Argir - EB/Streymur 1-1(0-0)
NSÍ Runavík - 07 Vestur 0-1(0-0)
KÍ Klaksvík - B68 Toftir 2-0(1-0)
HB Tórshavn-Víkingur G. 2-1(0-1) [02.08.22]
B36 Tórshavn-Skála ÍF 5-1(4-0) [12.08.2022]

**Round 17 [06-07.08.2022]**
Víkingur Gøta - 07 Vestur 6-1(3-0)
HB Tórshavn - AB Argir 3-0(1-0)
NSÍ Runavík - EB/Streymur 0-1(0-0)
KÍ Klaksvík - Skála ÍF 8-0(4-0) [22.10.22]
B68 Toftir - B36 Tórshavn 1-0(1-0) [22.10.22]

**Round 18 [14-17.08.2022]**
EB/Streymur - HB Tórshavn 1-4(0-2)
07 Vestur - B68 Toftir 2-6(2-1)
AB Argir - KÍ Klaksvík 0-2(0-1)
B36 Tórshavn - NSÍ Runavík 1-1(1-1)
Skála ÍF - Víkingur Gøta 1-3(0-3)

**Round 19 [21.08.2022]**
AB Argir - NSÍ Runavík 1-2(0-1)
EB/Streymur - B36 Tórshavn 3-2(1-1)
HB Tórshavn - Skála ÍF 3-0(3-0)
KÍ Klaksvík - 07 Vestur 2-0(1-0)
Víkingur Gøta - B68 Toftir 2-1(1-1)

**Round 20 [28.08.2022]**
HB Tórshavn - EB/Streymur 2-0(1-0)
KÍ Klaksvík - AB Argir 4-1(2-0)
NSÍ Runavík - B36 Tórshavn 1-2(1-0)
Víkingur Gøta - Skála ÍF 2-0(1-0)
B68 Toftir - 07 Vestur 0-1(0-1)

**Round 21 [04.09.2022]**
07 Vestur - Víkingur Gøta 1-1(1-0)
AB Argir - HB Tórshavn 2-1(1-1)
B36 Tórshavn - B68 Toftir 0-3 *awarded**
EB/Streymur - NSÍ Runavík 1-0(0-0)
Skála ÍF - KÍ Klaksvík 0-1(0-1)

*originally 3-1; awarded 0-3 as B36 Tórshavn
fielded ineligible player.*

| Round 22 [10-11.09.2022] |  |
|---|---|
| B68 Toftir - EB/Streymur | 1-1(1-0) |
| 07 Vestur - HB Tórshavn | 0-4(0-1) |
| AB Argir - B36 Tórshavn | 0-5(0-3) |
| Víkingur Gøta - KÍ Klaksvík | 1-2(0-0) |
| Skála ÍF - NSÍ Runavík | 1-1(1-0) |

| Round 23 [16-17.09.2022] |  |
|---|---|
| B36 Tórshavn - Skála ÍF | 5-0(3-0) |
| KÍ Klaksvík - B68 Toftir | 3-0(1-0) |
| EB/Streymur - AB Argir | 1-1(0-0) |
| NSÍ Runavík - 07 Vestur | 1-1(0-0) |
| HB Tórshavn - Víkingur Gøta | 2-1(1-0) |

| Round 24 [02-03.10.2022] |  |
|---|---|
| NSÍ Runavík - KÍ Klaksvík | 0-3(0-0) |
| B36 Tórshavn - Víkingur Gøta | 0-0 |
| HB Tórshavn - B68 Toftir | 1-2(1-1) |
| AB Argir - Skála ÍF | 2-0(1-0) |
| EB/Streymur-07 Vestur | 0-3(0-0) [12.10.2022] |

| Round 25 [08-09.10.2022] |  |
|---|---|
| B68 Toftir - AB Argir | 0-1(0-1) |
| Skála ÍF - EB/Streymur | 0-1(0-0) |
| 07 Vestur - B36 Tórshavn | 1-1(1-0) |
| KÍ Klaksvík - HB Tórshavn | 1-0(0-0) |
| Víkingur Gøta - NSÍ Runavík | 2-1(0-0) |

| Round 26 [16.10.2022] |  |
|---|---|
| AB Argir - Víkingur Gøta | 0-0 |
| B36 Tórshavn - HB Tórshavn | 0-3(0-1) |
| EB/Streymur - KÍ Klaksvík | 0-6(0-4) |
| NSÍ Runavík - B68 Toftir | 2-3(1-2) |
| Skála ÍF - 07 Vestur | 3-3(1-2) |

| Round 27 [22.10.2022] |  |
|---|---|
| B68 Toftir - Skála ÍF | 7-2(3-2) [07.08.22] |
| Klaksvík-B36 Tórshavn | 1-1(0-0) [01.09.22] |
| 07 Vestur - AB Argir | 1-1(0-1) |
| HB Tórshavn - NSÍ Runavík | 3-1(1-1) |
| Víkingur Gøta - EB/Streymur | 4-0(1-0) |

## Final Standings

|  |  | Total |  |  |  |  |  | Home |  |  |  |  | Away |  |  |  |
|---|---|---|---|---|---|---|---|---|---|---|---|---|---|---|---|---|
| 1. | KÍ Klaksvík | 27 | 25 | 2 | 0 | 78 - 7 | 77 | 13 | 1 | 0 | 41 - 5 | 12 | 1 | 0 | 37 - 2 |
| 2. | Víkingur Gøta | 27 | 18 | 4 | 5 | 69 - 24 | 58 | 11 | 1 | 2 | 42 - 13 | 7 | 3 | 3 | 27 - 11 |
| 3. | HB Tórshavn | 27 | 17 | 4 | 6 | 56 - 27 | 55 | 9 | 2 | 2 | 30 - 12 | 8 | 2 | 4 | 26 - 15 |
| 4. | B36 Tórshavn | 27 | 11 | 5 | 11 | 48 - 29 | 38 | 5 | 2 | 6 | 24 - 16 | 6 | 3 | 5 | 24 - 13 |
| 5. | EB/Streymur | 27 | 10 | 5 | 12 | 31 - 54 | 35 | 6 | 1 | 7 | 18 - 30 | 4 | 4 | 5 | 13 - 24 |
| 6. | B68 Toftir | 27 | 9 | 3 | 15 | 37 - 50 | 30 | 2 | 3 | 8 | 12 - 26 | 7 | 0 | 7 | 25 - 24 |
| 7. | 07 Vestur Sørvágur | 27 | 7 | 8 | 12 | 34 - 61 | 29 | 4 | 3 | 6 | 19 - 32 | 3 | 5 | 6 | 15 - 29 |
| 8. | AB Argir | 27 | 8 | 5 | 14 | 33 - 63 | 29 | 4 | 3 | 7 | 18 - 28 | 4 | 2 | 7 | 15 - 35 |
| 9. | NSÍ Runavík (*Relegated*) | 27 | 6 | 3 | 18 | 31 - 59 | 21 | 1 | 1 | 11 | 8 - 29 | 5 | 2 | 7 | 23 - 30 |
| 10. | Skála ÍF (*Relegated*) | 27 | 1 | 7 | 19 | 25 - 68 | 10 | 1 | 6 | 7 | 16 - 23 | 0 | 1 | 12 | 9 - 45 |

| Top goalscorers: |  |  |
|---|---|---|
| 20 | Sølvi Vatnhamar | *Víkingur Gøta* |
| 18 | Páll Andrasson Klettskarð | *KÍ Klaksvík* |
| 17 | Jóannes Bjartalíð | *KÍ Klaksvík* |
| 13 | Stefan Radosavljević | *HB Tórshavn* |

## NATIONAL CUP
### Løgmanssteypid 2022

| First Round [02-03.04.2022] |  |  |  |
|---|---|---|---|
| FC Hoyvík - MB Miðvágur | 8-0(7-0) | FC Suðuroy - Royn Hvalba | 5-0(2-0) |

| 1/8-Finals [14.04.2022] |  |  |  |
|---|---|---|---|
| ÍF Fuglafjarðar - B71 Sandoy | 4-0(4-0) | HB Tórshavn - FC Suðuroy | 9-1(6-0) |
| EB/Streymur - 07 Vestur Sørvágur | 2-4(2-1,2-2) | AB Argir - B68 Toftir | 4-2(1-1,2-2) |
| Víkingur Gøta - Undrið FF | 4-0(2-0) | Skála ÍF - KÍ Klaksvík | 0-3(0-3) |
| TB Tvøroyri - FC Hoyvík | 4-0(1-0) | NSÍ Runavík - B36 Tórshavn | 1-4(1-2) |

| Quarter-Finals [18.05.2022] |  |  |  |
|---|---|---|---|
| HB Tórshavn - AB Argir | 2-1(0-1) | TB Tvøroyri - 07 Vestur Sørvágur | 1-4(1-2) |
| KÍ Klaksvík - ÍF Fuglafjarðar | 3-0(0-0) | B36 Tórshavn - Víkingur Gøta | 0-2(0-2) |

| Semi-Finals [07.09./05.10.2022] |  |  |  |
|---|---|---|---|
| **First Leg** |  | **Second Leg** |  |
| Víkingur Gøta - HB Tórshavn | 2-2(2-1) | HB Tórshavn - Víkingur Gøta | 0-1(0-1) |
| 07 Vestur Sørvágur - KÍ Klaksvík | 2-2(1-0) | KÍ Klaksvík - 07 Vestur Sørvágur | 4-0(2-0) |

### Final

29.10.2022; Tórsvøllur, Tórshavn; Referee: Dagfinn Forná; Attendance: 4,175

**KÍ Klaksvík - Víkingur Gøta**                                                       **0-1(0-0)**

**KÍ Klaksvík**: Mathias Rosenørn, Jóannes Danielsen, Heini Vatnsdal, Odmar Færø (89.Jesper Brinck), René Shaki Joensen (60.Patrick da Silva), Dávid Andreasen (Cap), Jóannes Bjartalíð, Mads Boe Mikkelsen (89.Jonn Johannesen), Árni Frederiksberg, Claes Kronberg (77.Deni Pavlović; 89.Valērijs Šabala), Páll Andrasson Klettskarð. Trainer: Mikkjal Kjartansson Thomassen.

**Víkingur Gøta**: Bárður á Reynatrøð, Bárður Hansen (67.Ari Olsen), Arnbjørn Svensson, Gunnar Vatnhamar, Bergur Gregersen, Géza David Túri, Noah Mneney, Olaf Bárðarson (71.Ingi Jonhardsson), Jákup Johansen, Sølvi Vatnhamar (Cap), Andreas Lava Olsen (84.Martin Klein Joensen). Trainer: Jóhan Petur Poulsen.

**Goal:** 0-1 Sølvi Vatnhamar (87 penalty).

## 07 Vestur Sørvágur

| | | |
|---|---|---|
| **Founded**: | 06.11.2007 | |
| **Stadium**: | á Dungasandi, Sørvagur (2,000) | |
| **Trainer**: | Michael Schjønberg Christensen (DEN) | 19.01.1967 |

| Goalkeepers: | DOB | M | (s) | G |
|---|---|---|---|---|
| Silas Eyðsteinsson | 13.02.1998 | 11 | | |
| Ari Petersen | 07.12.2002 | 16 | | |
| **Defenders:** | **DOB** | **M** | **(s)** | **G** |
| Jóannis á Steig | 21.03.1997 | 15 | (8) | |
| Ári Arge | 02.05.2002 | 8 | (6) | |
| Hákun Edmundsson | 21.03.1996 | 6 | (2) | |
| Eiler Fróðason | 24.04.2003 | 9 | (10) | 1 |
| Asbjørn Heðinsson | 19.12.2000 | 5 | (9) | |
| Heri Ólason Klakkstein | 02.01.2005 | | (1) | |
| Rasmus Juel Knudsen (DEN) | 02.10.2002 | 14 | | |
| Dánial Pauli Lervig | 26.04.1991 | 15 | (5) | |
| Høgni Nielsen | 29.04.1997 | 22 | | 3 |
| Daniel Obbekjær (DEN) | 16.07.2002 | 15 | | 2 |
| Mathias Voss (DEN) | 26.01.2002 | 24 | | |
| Mads Winther (DEN) | 20.10.2001 | 8 | | |
| **Midfielders:** | **DOB** | **M** | **(s)** | **G** |
| Sølvi Egilson | 24.01.1995 | 10 | (10) | |
| Hjalmar Gudmundsen | 15.06.2006 | | (1) | |
| Marius Hagen (NOR) | 23.07.1992 | 2 | | |
| Julian Mouritsen | 10.10.2005 | 1 | (5) | |
| Jón í Horni Nielsen | 22.04.2005 | | (4) | |
| Teitur Olsen | 11.07.1998 | 7 | (11) | 1 |
| Janus Samuelsen | 27.09.1998 | 23 | | 3 |
| Martin Tausen | 04.05.1990 | 9 | (1) | |
| **Forwards:** | **DOB** | **M** | **(s)** | **G** |
| Mads Borchers (DEN) | 18.06.2002 | 25 | | 12 |
| Ronny Møller-Iversen (DEN) | 17.07.1994 | 24 | | 4 |
| Albert Theis Nielsen | 18.09.1999 | 2 | (4) | |
| Jasper Van der Heyden (BEL) | 03.07.1995 | 26 | | 8 |

## Bóltfelagið 1936 Tórshavn

| | | |
|---|---|---|
| **Founded**: | 28.03.1936 | |
| **Stadium**: | Gundadalur, Tórshavn (5,000) | |
| **Trainer**: | Dan Brimsvík | 30.06.1987 |

| Goalkeepers: | DOB | M | (s) | G |
|---|---|---|---|---|
| Mattias Lamhauge | 02.08.1999 | 27 | | |
| **Defenders:** | **DOB** | **M** | **(s)** | **G** |
| Martin Agnarsson | 07.12.2003 | 13 | (5) | 3 |
| Magnus Egilsson | 19.03.1994 | 23 | (2) | |
| Lukas Enevoldsen (DEN) | 24.05.1993 | 10 | (8) | |
| Andrias Eriksen | 22.02.1994 | 6 | (2) | |
| Thor Høholt (DEN) | 19.03.2001 | 17 | | |
| Mattias Joensen | 15.02.2003 | | (3) | |
| Alex Mellemgaard | 27.11.1991 | | (2) | |
| Sonni Nattestad | 05.08.1994 | 20 | (2) | 1 |
| Bjarni Petersen | 12.08.1998 | | (3) | |
| Andreas Thomsen | 04.10.2001 | 1 | (7) | |
| **Midfielders:** | **DOB** | **M** | **(s)** | **G** |
| Hannes Agnarsson | 26.02.1999 | 11 | (2) | 2 |
| Marius Árting Allansson | 27.02.2005 | | (1) | |
| Jógvan Gullfoss | 25.05.2004 | | (5) | |
| Benjamin Heinesen | 26.03.1996 | 11 | (8) | 1 |
| Mattias Johnnyson Hellisdal | 21.01.2006 | 1 | (4) | 1 |
| Magnus Holm Jacobsen | 23.05.2000 | 17 | (7) | 5 |
| Brian Jakobsen | 04.11.1991 | 13 | (10) | 8 |
| Carl Mikkelsen | 18.10.2005 | | (1) | |
| Eli Nielsen | 23.09.1992 | 22 | (2) | |
| Ragnar Samuelsen | 23.08.1999 | 9 | (15) | |
| Símun Sólheim | 25.02.2001 | 22 | (5) | 1 |
| Rani í Soylu | 29.08.2002 | | (3) | 1 |
| **Forwards:** | **DOB** | **M** | **(s)** | **G** |
| Tobias Hansen | 28.06.2005 | | (1) | |
| Andrass Johansen | 16.11.2001 | 20 | (1) | 4 |
| Bjarki Nielsen | 02.11.1998 | 18 | (8) | 3 |
| Rasmus Reihdar Nissen (DEN) | 25.06.2001 | 8 | (4) | 4 |
| Michał Przybylski (POL) | 29.12.1997 | 24 | (2) | 10 |
| Uroš Stojanov (SRB) | 05.01.1989 | 4 | (8) | 4 |

## Tofta Ítróttarfelag B68

| | | |
|---|---|---|
| **Founded**: | 21.12.1962 | |
| **Stadium**: | Svangaskarð, Toftir (6,000) | |
| **Trainer**: | Øssur Hansen | 07.01.1971 |
| [10.05.2022] | André Olsen | 23.10.1990 |
| [18.05.2022] | Jákup á Borg | 26.10.1979 |

| Goalkeepers: | DOB | M | (s) | G |
|---|---|---|---|---|
| Terji Þór Brynjarsson | 11.12.1991 | 3 | | |
| Jóannes Eyðfinnsson Davidsen | 19.09.2002 | 1 | | |
| Rói Hentze | 22.09.1999 | 10 | | |
| Meinhardt Pállsson Joensen | 27.11.1979 | 3 | | |
| Ragnar Lindholm | 17.08.1993 | 4 | (1) | |
| Benjamin Schubert (DEN) | 22.09.1996 | 6 | | |
| **Defenders:** | **DOB** | **M** | **(s)** | **G** |
| Hilmar Højgaard | 23.08.2003 | 1 | (7) | |
| Aleksandur Jensen | 07.05.2001 | 23 | | |
| Aidan Bardina Liu (USA) | 01.07.2000 | 25 | | 3 |
| Friði Petersen | 18.08.2003 | 9 | (10) | |
| Hjalti Strømsten | 21.01.1997 | 15 | (4) | 1 |
| Pedro Tarancón Antón (ESP) | 18.12.1985 | | (2) | |
| **Midfielders:** | **DOB** | **M** | **(s)** | **G** |
| Andri Benjaminsen | 12.01.1999 | 8 | (3) | |
| Łukasz Cieślewicz (POL) | 15.11.1987 | 4 | (3) | 1 |
| Esmar Clementsen | 29.09.1996 | 10 | (9) | 1 |
| Karstin Clementsen | 12.09.2001 | 4 | (9) | |
| Hanus Højgaard | 03.12.2005 | 1 | (2) | |
| Bárður Jensen | 07.05.2001 | 27 | | 1 |
| Áki Johannesen | 11.11.2002 | 16 | (2) | |
| Sebastian Nielsen (DEN) | 02.07.1996 | 23 | (1) | 8 |
| Jann Ingi Petersen | 07.01.1984 | 1 | (1) | |
| Hugin Samuelsen | 12.02.1999 | 9 | | 2 |
| Tonni Thomsen | 05.02.1999 | 17 | (6) | |
| **Forwards:** | **DOB** | **M** | **(s)** | **G** |
| Boubacar Dabo (SEN) | 10.10.1997 | 24 | (1) | 7 |
| Niels Jensen (DEN) | 20.10.1994 | 4 | (11) | |
| Steffan Løkin | 13.11.2000 | 14 | (9) | 3 |
| Óli Højgaard Olsen | 24.11.1985 | | (1) | |
| Muhammed Samba (GAM) | 09.11.1998 | 17 | (2) | 7 |
| Gilli Samuelsen | 12.02.1999 | 18 | (2) | |

## Eiðis Bóltfelag / Streymur

| | | | |
|---|---|---|---|
| **Founded**: | 1993 | | |
| **Stadium**: | Við Margáir, Streymnes (2,000) | | |
| **Trainer**: | Jákup Martin Joensen | | 07.05.1976 |

| Goalkeepers: | DOB | M | (s) | G |
|---|---|---|---|---|
| Kristian Pállsson Joensen | 21.12.1992 | 27 | | |
| **Defenders:** | **DOB** | **M** | **(s)** | **G** |
| Ragnar Danielsen | 24.02.1992 | 4 | (4) | |
| Rógvi Egilstoft | 07.12.1992 | 4 | | |
| Dánjal Godtfred | 07.03.1996 | 24 | (1) | 1 |
| Mikkjal Hellisá | 18.02.2002 | 10 | (5) | 1 |
| Sámal Jónsson | 10.05.2003 | | (1) | |
| Andras Olsen | 24.10.1995 | 20 | (1) | 1 |
| Rói Olsen | 03.03.1997 | 13 | (12) | 3 |
| Sørin Wardum | 13.05.1999 | | (5) | |
| **Midfielders:** | **DOB** | **M** | **(s)** | **G** |
| Hans Pauli á Bø | 29.10.2005 | 1 | (4) | |
| Gutti Dahl-Olsen | 19.01.2002 | 24 | (2) | 7 |
| Elias El Moustage Gilstón | 30.05.2001 | 12 | (12) | 2 |
| Jákup Hummeland | 10.12.2003 | 3 | (17) | 1 |
| Jóhann Joensen | 17.08.2001 | 27 | | 3 |
| Tóki Johannesen | 17.03.1997 | 17 | (7) | |
| Mattias Weihe Joensen | 15.02.2003 | 12 | | |
| Filip Johansen | 21.07.2003 | | (10) | |
| Virgar Jónsson | 13.06.2006 | | (1) | |
| Sverri Mariusarson | 02.08.2004 | | (3) | |
| Árni Grunnveit Olsen | 13.09.1993 | 18 | (2) | |
| Bogi Reinert-Petersen | 20.02.1993 | 20 | (1) | 1 |
| Jóhan J. Samuelsen | 16.06.2003 | | (1) | |
| Gutti við Streym Jóhansson | 18.08.2004 | | (2) | |
| **Forwards:** | **DOB** | **M** | **(s)** | **G** |
| Jacob Andersen (DEN) | 15.09.1993 | 10 | (1) | 3 |
| Niels Pauli Danielsen | 18.01.1989 | 14 | (4) | |
| Filip Đorđević (SRB) | 07.03.1994 | 25 | | 3 |
| Hannus Eiðisgarð | 18.09.2005 | | (1) | |
| Høgni Hummeland | 14.07.1996 | | (3) | |
| Niklas Kruse | 11.05.1999 | 12 | (2) | 3 |

## Argja Bóltfelag

| | | | |
|---|---|---|---|
| **Founded**: | 15.08.1973 | | |
| **Stadium**: | Skansi Arena (Inni í Vika), Argir (2,000) | | |
| **Trainer**: | Sámal Erik Hentze | | 27.01.1972 |
| [18.05.2022] | Jonas Dal Andersen (DEN) | | 07.07.1976 |
| [30.06.2022] | Henrik Larsen (DEN) | | 13.10.1965 |

| Goalkeepers: | DOB | M | (s) | G |
|---|---|---|---|---|
| Antonio Joseph Chavez Borelli (USA) | 23.11.1998 | 7 | | |
| Rasmus Jepsen-Jacob (DEN) | 27.05.2000 | 9 | | |
| Rói Zachariasen | 12.10.1998 | 11 | | |
| **Defenders:** | **DOB** | **M** | **(s)** | **G** |
| Tróndur á Høvdanum | 19.08.1995 | 11 | (3) | |
| Jákup Pauli Breckmann | 16.04.1998 | 16 | | |
| Dánjal Danielsen | 05.07.2004 | 1 | (1) | |
| Jake Lewis Gross (USA) | 30.03.2001 | 3 | (1) | |
| Ramzi Touré Idrissou (TOG) | 31.07.1996 | 11 | (1) | 1 |
| Erik McCue (USA) | 18.01.2001 | 22 | (1) | 1 |
| Jonas Alfio Sapienza (FIN) | 15.11.1998 | 8 | (1) | |
| Michael Alexander Smith (USA) | 13.01.1999 | 13 | (1) | |
| **Midfielders:** | **DOB** | **M** | **(s)** | **G** |
| Coby Atkinseon (JAM) | 21.05.2000 | 2 | (6) | |
| Jobin Drangastein | 01.11.1990 | 2 | (3) | 1 |
| Mikkjal Hentze | 08.12.1986 | 9 | | |
| Brandur Jákupsson | 27.11.1999 | 1 | (3) | |
| Santiago Nicolás Lebus (ARG) | 18.07.1996 | 12 | | |
| Marius Kryger Lindh (DEN) | 22.06.1999 | 19 | (1) | 6 |
| Fahad Fussad Mohammed (FIN) | 21.03.2000 | 2 | | |
| Teitur Olsen | 27.01.1998 | 26 | | 6 |
| Bartal Petersen | 22.11.2000 | 6 | (15) | 3 |
| Rógvi Poulsen | 31.10.1989 | 3 | (2) | |
| Matthias Præst Nielsen (DEN) | 21.06.2000 | 14 | (1) | |
| Gunnar Reynslág | 10.11.2004 | 4 | (3) | 2 |
| Bjarni Skála | 14.11.1997 | | (5) | |
| Ragnar Skála | 05.09.2000 | 23 | (1) | 1 |
| Rógvi Skála | 05.09.2000 | 2 | (4) | |
| Oleksandr Snyzhko (UKR) | 20.08.1996 | 2 | | |
| Emil Seedorff Sørensen (DEN) | 21.02.2003 | 6 | (3) | |
| Onni Tiihonen (FIN) | 06.06.2000 | 14 | | |
| **Forwards:** | **DOB** | **M** | **(s)** | **G** |
| Robbie Azodo (FIN) | 23.04.2001 | 6 | (7) | 1 |
| Thomas Kirkeby Junge (DEN) | 20.12.2002 | 6 | (5) | 1 |
| Yevgen Kholmetskiy (UKR) | 07.04.2004 | 1 | (3) | |
| Karl Dreier Leth (DEN) | 22.08.2002 | 12 | (3) | |
| Agustín Marsico (ARG) | 21.03.1997 | 8 | (6) | 5 |
| Rói Nielsen | 10.06.2005 | | (1) | |
| Ragnar Rasmussen | 13.07.2000 | | (2) | |
| Danis Zvirkić | 22.06.2002 | 5 | (5) | 1 |

## Havnar Bóltfelag Tórshavn

| | | | |
|---|---|---|---|
| **Founded**: | 04.10.1904 | | |
| **Stadium**: | Gundadalur, Tórshavn (5,000) | | |
| **Trainer**: | Kim Winkel Engstrøm (DEN) | | 29.10.1979 |
| [16.05.2022] | Dalibor Savić (SWE) | | 19.05.1979 |

| Goalkeepers: | DOB | M | (s) | G |
|---|---|---|---|---|
| Teitur Matras Gestsson | 19.08.1992 | 24 | | |
| Bjarti Mørk | 07.06.2001 | 3 | (2) | |
| **Defenders:** | **DOB** | **M** | **(s)** | **G** |
| Samuel Chukwudi | 25.06.2003 | | (2) | |
| Daniel Johansen | 09.07.1998 | 23 | (2) | 7 |
| Ári Jónsson | 22.06.1994 | 16 | (6) | |
| Gustav Kjeldsen (DEN) | 03.07.1999 | 9 | | |
| Hanus Sørensen | 19.02.2001 | 14 | (5) | |
| Bartal Wardum | 03.05.1997 | 15 | (3) | |
| **Midfielders:** | **DOB** | **M** | **(s)** | **G** |
| Hørður Askham | 22.09.1994 | 25 | (1) | 1 |
| Ási Dam | 18.12.2002 | 1 | (3) | |
| Leivur Guttesen | 17.01.2002 | 1 | (4) | |
| Heðin Hansen | 30.07.1993 | 23 | (2) | 2 |
| Tróndur Jensen | 06.02.1993 | 1 | | |
| Heri Mohr | 13.05.1997 | 12 | (4) | |
| Pætur Joensson Petersen | 29.03.1998 | 18 | (7) | 10 |
| Dan í Soylu | 09.07.1996 | 19 | (6) | 1 |
| **Forwards:** | **DOB** | **M** | **(s)** | **G** |
| Øssur Dalbúð | 28.03.1989 | 5 | (16) | 3 |
| Hilmar Leon Jakobsen | 02.08.1997 | 3 | (4) | 1 |
| Adrian Justinussen | 21.07.1998 | 25 | (4) | 6 |
| Thomas Bjørn Miezan | 15.04.2006 | | (1) | |
| Ejvind Restorff Mouritsen | 14.02.2004 | | (11) | 1 |
| Stefan Radosavljević | 08.09.2000 | 25 | (1) | 13 |
| Áki Samuelsen | 17.04.2004 | 24 | (2) | 5 |
| Rani Sørensen | 22.04.2004 | 1 | (5) | 1 |
| Jákup Thomsen | 23.11.1997 | 10 | (4) | 2 |

## Klaksvíkar Ítróttarfelag

**Founded:** 24.08.1904
**Stadium:** Við Djúpumýrar, Klaksvík (4,000)
**Trainer:** Mikkjal Kjartansson Thomassen    12.01.1976

| Goalkeepers: | DOB | M | (s) | G |
|---|---|---|---|---|
| Meinhardt Joensen | 27.11.1979 | | (1) | |
| Mathias Rosenørn (DEN) | 11.05.1993 | 27 | | |
| **Defenders:** | **DOB** | **M** | **(s)** | **G** |
| Jesper Brinck (DEN) | 22.03.1989 | 14 | (6) | |
| Patrick da Silva (DEN) | 23.10.1994 | 21 | (4) | |
| Jóannes Danielsen | 10.09.1997 | 12 | | 1 |
| Odmar Færø | 01.11.1989 | 16 | (2) | |
| Olaf Hansen | 20.02.2002 | | (2) | |
| Claes Kronberg (DEN) | 19.04.1987 | 11 | (7) | 1 |
| Dmytro Lytvyn (UKR) | 21.11.1996 | 3 | (3) | 1 |
| Deni Pavlović (SRB) | 01.09.1993 | 11 | (8) | 3 |
| Børge Petersen | 24.04.2002 | 4 | (5) | |
| Heini Vatnsdal | 18.10.1991 | 22 | (2) | 1 |

| Midfielders: | DOB | M | (s) | G |
|---|---|---|---|---|
| Dávid Andreasen | 27.06.2004 | | (12) | 1 |
| Jákup Biskopstø Andreasen | 31.05.1998 | 27 | | 2 |
| Árni Frederiksberg | 13.06.1992 | 26 | | 11 |
| Silas Gaard | 23.05.2004 | 1 | (1) | |
| René Shaki Joensen | 08.02.1993 | 20 | (4) | 1 |
| Jonn Johannesen | 30.12.2001 | 3 | (14) | 4 |
| Mads Mikkelsen | 11.12.1999 | 24 | | 6 |
| Óli Poulsen | 30.05.2001 | | (1) | |
| **Forwards:** | **DOB** | **M** | **(s)** | **G** |
| Jóannes Bjartalíð | 10.07.1996 | 26 | | 17 |
| Anders Holvad (DEN) | 24.06.1990 | 5 | (8) | 1 |
| Páll Andrasson Klettskarð | 17.05.1990 | 20 | (6) | 18 |
| Valērijs Šabala (LVA) | 12.10.1994 | 4 | (14) | 7 |

## Nes Sóknar Ítróttarfelag Runavík

**Founded:** 1957
**Stadium:** Við Løkin, Runavík (2,000)
**Trainer:** Todi Adam Jónsson    02.02.1972
[01.03.2022] Poul Helgi Jacobsen    13.10.1975
[01.07.2022] Sámal Erik Hentze    27.01.1972

| Goalkeepers: | DOB | M | (s) | G |
|---|---|---|---|---|
| Karstin Hansen | 05.10.1997 | 11 | | |
| Tórður Thomsen | 11.06.1986 | 16 | | |
| **Defenders:** | **DOB** | **M** | **(s)** | **G** |
| Meinhard Geyti | 03.05.2001 | 16 | (3) | |
| Lukas Grenaa Giessing | 09.05.2000 | 11 | (1) | 1 |
| Súni Hansen | 21.01.2003 | | (1) | |
| Pætur Hentze | 06.11.1999 | 25 | | 3 |
| Áron Høj | 13.01.2002 | 1 | (2) | |
| Oddur Højgaard | 12.09.1989 | 20 | (1) | |
| Bergur Johannesen | 03.05.1999 | 1 | (2) | |
| Mathias Aaris Kragh Nielsen (DEN) | 02.03.1991 | 10 | (1) | |
| Beinir Nolsøe | 07.07.2003 | 9 | (15) | 2 |
| Atli Petersen | 01.12.2000 | 16 | | |
| Miska Rautiola (FIN) | 20.06.1998 | 8 | | |
| Einar Tróndargjógv | 02.04.1988 | 11 | | |

| Midfielders: | DOB | M | (s) | G |
|---|---|---|---|---|
| Kristian Mamush Andersen (DEN) | 01.09.1994 | 6 | (2) | |
| Betuel Hansen | 14.03.1997 | 21 | | 1 |
| Jógvan Højgaard | 14.12.2000 | 6 | (5) | |
| Jóel Jacobsen | 04.11.2002 | | (1) | |
| Albert Róin Johannesen | 29.03.1995 | 9 | (6) | |
| Aron Knudsen | 05.11.1999 | 2 | (1) | |
| Mórits Heini Mortensen | 25.03.1999 | 18 | (4) | |
| Sølvi Sigvardsen | 18.10.2000 | 4 | (6) | 1 |
| Pætur Skipanes | 20.10.2000 | 13 | | |
| **Forwards:** | **DOB** | **M** | **(s)** | **G** |
| Hans Marius Davidsen | 12.05.1998 | 11 | (12) | 4 |
| Búi Egilsson | 04.01.1996 | 12 | (10) | |
| Meinhard Janusarson | 30.08.2002 | | (1) | |
| Yegor Korytskiy (UKR) | 09.01.2001 | 1 | (8) | |
| Jørgen Nielsen | 30.11.2003 | 14 | (1) | 6 |
| Marjus Nón | 11.04.2004 | | (1) | |
| Klæmint Andrasson Olsen | 17.07.1990 | 25 | | 9 |

## Skála Ítróttarfelag

**Founded:** 1965
**Stadium:** Undir Mýruhjalla, Skála (2,000)
**Trainer:** Michael Bjørn Nielsen (DEN)    31.08.1973

| Goalkeepers: | DOB | M | (s) | G |
|---|---|---|---|---|
| Joakim Jürs (DEN) | 15.12.1996 | 1 | (1) | |
| Jákup Olsen | 03.01.1999 | 26 | | |
| **Defenders:** | **DOB** | **M** | **(s)** | **G** |
| Mikal á Reynatrøð | 15.05.1999 | 4 | (5) | |
| Jákup Jakobsen | 22.11.1992 | 25 | | |
| Kristian Martin Jakobsen | 10.11.1996 | 11 | (8) | 1 |
| Karl Martin Johansen | 17.08.1999 | 14 | (6) | 1 |
| Julian Mikkelsen | 28.07.2000 | | (1) | |
| Djóni Petersen | 09.10.1999 | 21 | (2) | |
| Andreas Thomsen | 04.10.2001 | 10 | (1) | |
| Vukašin Tomić (SRB) | 08.04.1987 | 25 | | |
| **Midfielders:** | **DOB** | **M** | **(s)** | **G** |
| Ari Ellingsgaard | 03.02.1993 | 22 | | 1 |
| Jan Hansen | 08.10.1997 | 21 | (3) | 3 |

| | DOB | M | (s) | G |
|---|---|---|---|---|
| Pætur Jacobsen | 05.12.1982 | 19 | (4) | 1 |
| Emil Joensen | 19.11.2003 | 22 | (2) | |
| Jákup Joensen | 27.02.2000 | 3 | (3) | |
| Teitur Joensen | 10.11.1986 | 8 | | |
| Dávid Johansen | 08.02.1997 | 2 | (12) | 1 |
| Poul Kallsberg | 04.02.2003 | 23 | (2) | 6 |
| Steinbjørn Olsen | 11.09.1996 | 15 | (3) | 1 |
| **Forwards:** | **DOB** | **M** | **(s)** | **G** |
| Jamiu Ola Ajibade (NGA) | 02.01.2003 | | (2) | |
| Christian Høgh Sørensen (DEN) | 05.01.1995 | 2 | (1) | |
| Andreas Jacobsen | 25.11.1999 | 7 | | 1 |
| Martin Johansen | 08.12.2003 | 3 | (11) | |
| Uroš Stojanov (SRB) | 05.01.1989 | 13 | | 7 |
| Bjarti Thorleifsson | 28.01.2004 | | (2) | |

## Víkingur Gøta Norðragøta

**Founded:** 14.01.2008 (*after the merger of GÍ Gøta and Leirvík ÍF*)
**Stadium:** Sarpugerði, Norðragøta (3,000)
**Trainer:** Jóhan Petur Poulsen    08.05.1986

| Goalkeepers: | DOB | M | (s) | G |
|---|---|---|---|---|
| Bárður á Reynatrøð | 08.01.2000 | 27 | | |
| **Defenders:** | **DOB** | **M** | **(s)** | **G** |
| Signar á Brúnni | 19.11.2002 | | (5) | |
| Olaf Bárðarson | 20.10.2003 | 17 | (2) | 8 |
| Atli Gregersen | 15.06.1982 | 26 | | |
| Bergur Gregersen | 11.09.1994 | 20 | (3) | 1 |
| Noah Mneney | 06.12.2002 | 24 | (1) | 1 |
| Gunnar Vatnhamar | 29.03.1995 | 27 | | 5 |
| **Midfielders:** | **DOB** | **M** | **(s)** | **G** |
| Árni Nóa Atlason | 15.01.2006 | | (1) | |
| Aron Ellingsgaard | 16.09.2002 | | (7) | 1 |
| Bárður Hansen | 13.03.1992 | 21 | (1) | |

| | DOB | M | (s) | G |
|---|---|---|---|---|
| Rani Hansen | 27.11.2000 | | (1) | |
| Martin Klein Joensen | 26.12.1999 | 14 | (12) | 10 |
| Ari Olsen | 09.09.1998 | 5 | (6) | 1 |
| Arnbjørn Svensson | 01.07.1979 | 25 | (1) | 4 |
| Jákup Andrias Thomsen | 01.06.2004 | | (1) | |
| Géza David Túri (HUN) | 06.10.2001 | 25 | | |
| Sølvi Vatnhamar | 05.05.1986 | 26 | | 20 |
| **Forwards:** | **DOB** | **M** | **(s)** | **G** |
| Jákup Johansen | 27.04.1993 | 15 | (3) | 7 |
| Ingi Jonhardsson | 11.09.2001 | 12 | (12) | 1 |
| Finnur Justinussen | 30.03.1989 | 1 | (14) | 3 |
| Andreas Lava Olsen | 09.10.1987 | 12 | (6) | 7 |

| | | | | | | | | |
|---|---|---|---|---|---|---|---|---|
| 1. | ÍF Fuglafjarðar (*Promoted*) | 27 | 17 | 5 | 5 | 57 - 33 | 56 |
| 2. | Víkingur Gøta II | 27 | 17 | 4 | 6 | 81 - 40 | 55 |
| 3. | TB Tvøroyri (*Promoted*) | 27 | 16 | 4 | 7 | 69 - 39 | 52 |
| 4. | B71 Sandoy | 27 | 16 | 4 | 7 | 54 - 30 | 52 |
| 5. | KÍ Klaksvík II | 27 | 15 | 1 | 11 | 65 - 41 | 46 |
| 6. | Undrið FF Tórshavn | 27 | 13 | 3 | 11 | 46 - 42 | 42 |
| 7. | HB Tórshavn II | 27 | 10 | 3 | 14 | 45 - 59 | 33 |
| 8. | B36 Tórshavn II | 27 | 7 | 6 | 14 | 44 - 62 | 27 |
| 9. | NSÍ Runavík II (*Relegated*) | 27 | 3 | 6 | 18 | 31 - 92 | 15 |
| 10. | 07 Vestur Sørvágur II (*Relegated*) | 27 | 2 | 2 | 23 | 25 - 79 | 8 |

## NATIONAL TEAM

### INTERNATIONAL MATCHES
#### (16.07.2022 – 15.07.2023)

| | | | | |
|---|---|---|---|---|
| 22.09.2022 | Vilnius | *Lithuania - Faroe Islands* | *1-1(1-1)* | (UNL) |
| 25.09.2022 | Tórshavn | *Faroe Islands - Turkey* | *2-1(0-0)* | (UNL) |
| 16.11.2022 | Olomouc | *Czech Republic - Faroe Islands* | *5-0(4-0)* | (F) |
| 19.11.2022 | Prishtina | *Kosovo - Faroe Islands* | *1-1(0-0)* | (F) |
| 24.03.2023 | Chişinău | *Moldova - Faroe Islands* | *1-1(0-1)* | (ECQ) |
| 27.03.2023 | Skopje | *North Macedonia - Faroe Islands* | *1-0(0-0)* | (F) |
| 17.06.2023 | Tórshavn | *Faroe Islands - Czech Republic* | *0-3(0-2)* | (ECQ) |
| 20.06.2023 | Tórshavn | *Faroe Islands - Albania* | *1-3(1-1)* | (ECQ) |

**22.09.2022    LITHUANIA - FAROE ISLANDS    1-1(1-1)    3rd UEFA Nations League C, Group 1**
LFF stadionas, Vilnius; Referee: Vilhjálmur Alvar Þórarinsson (Iceland); Attendance: 2,376
**FRO:** Gunnar Nielsen, Gilli Rólantsson Sørensen, Gunnar Vatnhamar, Hørður Heðinsson Askham, Viljormur í Heiðunum Davidsen (Cap), Jákup Biskopstø Andreasen, René Shaki Joensen (90+2.Heðin Hansen), Jóannes Bjartalíð, Meinhard Egilsson Olsen (83.Mads Boe Mikkelsen), Jóan Símun Edmundsson (77.Patrik Johannesen), Klæmint Andrasson Olsen (90+1.Sonni Ragnar Nattestad). Trainer: Håkan Georg Ericson (Sweden).
**Goal:** Jákup Biskopstø Andreasen (22).

**25.09.2022    FAROE ISLANDS - TURKEY    2-1(0-0)    3rd UEFA Nations League C, Group 1**
Tórsvøllur, Tórshavn; Referee: Serhiy Boiko (Ukraine); Attendance: 2,056
**FRO:** Teitur Matras Gestsson, Gilli Rólantsson Sørensen, Gunnar Vatnhamar, Heini Vatnsdal, Viljormur í Heiðunum Davidsen (Cap), Jákup Biskopstø Andreasen, René Shaki Joensen (57.Mads Boe Mikkelsen), Meinhard Egilsson Olsen (90+4.Patrik Johannesen), Sølvi Vatnhamar, Jóan Símun Edmundsson (72.Klæmint Andrasson Olsen), Jóannes Bjartalíð. Trainer: Håkan Georg Ericson (Sweden).
**Goals:** Viljormur í Heiðunum Davidsen (51), Jóan Símun Edmundsson (59).

**16.11.2022    CZECH REPUBLIC - FAROE ISLANDS    5-0(4-0)    Friendly International**
Andrův stadion, Olomouc; Referee: Martin Dohál (Slovakia); Attendance: 10,762
**FRO:** Gunnar Nielsen, Hanus Sørensen (71.Samuel Johansen Chukwudi), Sølvi Vatnhamar (77.Stefan Radosavljević), Sonni Ragnar Nattestad, Viljormur í Heiðunum Davidsen (Cap), Mads Boe Mikkelsen (56.Gilli Rólantsson Sørensen), René Shaki Joensen, Gunnar Vatnhamar, Heðin Hansen (71.Kaj Leo í Bartalsstovu), Meinhard Egilsson Olsen (77.Pætur Joensson Petersen), Klæmint Andrasson Olsen (56.Patrik Johannesen). Trainer: Håkan Georg Ericson (Sweden).

**19.11.2022    KOSOVO - FAROE ISLANDS    1-1(0-0)    Friendly International**
Stadiumi „Fadil Vokrri", Prishtina; Referee: Juxhin Xhaja (Albania); Attendance: 2,000
**FRO:** Mattias Heðinsson Lamhauge, Gilli Rólantsson Sørensen, Gunnar Vatnhamar, Andrias Edmundsson (58.Samuel Johansen Chukwudi), Viljormur í Heiðunum Davidsen (Cap) (70.Martin Agnarsson), René Shaki Joensen (58.Kaj Leo í Bartalsstovu), Noah Hans Mneney, Sølvi Vatnhamar (70.Stefan Radosavljević), Meinhard Egilsson Olsen, Patrik Johannesen (79.Jann Julian Benjaminsen), Pætur Joensson Petersen (70.Klæmint Andrasson Olsen). Trainer: Håkan Georg Ericson (Sweden).
**Goal:** Stefan Radosavljević (77).

**24.03.2023    MOLDOVA - FAROE ISLANDS    1-1(0-1)    17th EC. Qualifiers**
Stadionul Zimbru, Chişinău; Referee: Nicolas Walsh (Scotland); Attendance: 4,732
**FRO:** Mattias Heðinsson Lamhauge, René Shaki Joensen, Sølvi Vatnhamar, Odmar Færø (79.Heini Vatnsdal), Viljormur í Heiðunum Davidsen (Cap), Meinhard Egilsson Olsen (79.Ári Mohr Jónsson), Jákup Biskopstø Andreasen, Gunnar Vatnhamar, Mads Boe Mikkelsen (71.Gilli Rólantsson Sørensen), Patrik Johannesen (63.Noah Hans Mneney), Klæmint Andrasson Olsen (79.Páll Andrasson Klettskarð). Trainer: Håkan Georg Ericson (Sweden).
**Goal:** Mads Boe Mikkelsen (27).

**27.03.2023    NORTH MACEDONIA - FAROE ISLANDS    1-0(0-0)    Friendly International**
Nacionalna Arena "Toše Proeski", Skopje; Referee: Miloš Savović (Montenegro); Attendance: 500
**FRO:** Bárður á Reynatrøð, Hanus Sørensen, Rógvi Asmundur Baldvinsson (72.Odmar Færø), Heini Vatnsdal (46.Andrias Edmundsson), Viljormur í Heiðunum Davidsen (Cap), Jákup Biskopstø Andreasen (72.Noah Hans Mneney), Sølvi Vatnhamar, René Shaki Joensen (84.Klæmint Andrasson Olsen), Stefan Radosavljević (63.Gilli Rólantsson Sørensen), Ári Mohr Jónsson (62.Daniel Johansen), Pætur Joensson Petersen. Trainer: Håkan Georg Ericson (Sweden).
**Goal:** Mads Boe Mikkelsen (27).

**17.06.2023    FAROE ISLANDS - CZECH REPUBLIC    0-3(0-2)    17th EC. Qualifiers**
Tórsvøllur, Tórshavn; Referee: Arda Kardeşler (Turkey); Attendance: 2,232
**FRO:** Teitur Matras Gestsson, Gilli Rólantsson Sørensen (83.Hannes Agnarsson), Odmar Færø, Gunnar Vatnhamar, Heini Vatnsdal, Viljormur í Heiðunum Davidsen (Cap), Jákup Biskopstø Andreasen (83.Rógvi Asmundur Baldvinsson), René Shaki Joensen, Sølvi Vatnhamar (84.Stefan Radosavljević), Jóannes Bjartalíð (58.Hanus Sørensen), Petur Knudsen (58.Jóan Símun Edmundsson). Trainer: Håkan Georg Ericson (Sweden).

**20.06.2023**    **FAROE ISLANDS - ALBANIA**     **1-3(1-1)**     17th EC. Qualifiers

Tórsvøllur, Tórshavn; Referee: Chrysovalantis Theouli (Cyprus); Attendance: 2,507
**FRO:** Teitur Matras Gestsson, Gilli Rólantsson Sørensen, Odmar Færø, Heini Vatnsdal, Viljormur í Heiðunum Davidsen (Cap), Sølvi Vatnhamar (80.Stefan Radosavljević), Jákup Biskopstø Andreasen (46.Jóannes Bjartalíð), Gunnar Vatnhamar (80.Brandur Hendriksson Olsen), René Shaki Joensen (64.Petur Knudsen), Jóan Símun Edmundsson (65.Andrass Johansen), Klæmint Andrasson Olsen. Trainer: Håkan Georg Ericson (Sweden).
**Goal:** Odmar Færø (45+1).

<table>
<tr><td colspan="5" align="center">NATIONAL TEAM PLAYERS<br>(16.07.2022 – 15.07.2023)</td></tr>
<tr><th>Name</th><th>DOB</th><th>Caps</th><th>Goals</th><th>Club</th></tr>
<tr><td colspan="5" align="center">Goalkeepers</td></tr>
<tr><td>Teitur Matras GESTSSON</td><td>19.08.1992</td><td>22</td><td>0</td><td>2022/2023:    HB Tórshavn</td></tr>
<tr><td>Mattias Heðinsson LAMHAUGE</td><td>02.08.1999</td><td>3</td><td>0</td><td>2022/2023:    B36 Tórshavn</td></tr>
<tr><td>Gunnar NIELSEN</td><td>07.10.1986</td><td>71</td><td>0</td><td>2022:    FH Hafnarfjarðar (ISL)</td></tr>
<tr><td>Bárður á REYNATRØÐ</td><td>08.01.2000</td><td>1</td><td>0</td><td>2023:    Víkingur Gøta</td></tr>
<tr><td colspan="5" align="center">Defenders</td></tr>
<tr><td>Martin AGNARSSON</td><td>07.12.2003</td><td>1</td><td>0</td><td>2022:    Viborg FF (DEN)</td></tr>
<tr><td>Hørður Heðinsson ASKHAM</td><td>22.09.1994</td><td>11</td><td>0</td><td>2022:    HB Tórshavn</td></tr>
<tr><td>Rógvi Asmundur BALDVINSSON</td><td>06.12.1989</td><td>53</td><td>4</td><td>2023:    Bryne FK (NOR)</td></tr>
<tr><td>Jann Julian BENJAMINSEN</td><td>03.04.1997</td><td>1</td><td>0</td><td>2022:    IL Hødd Ulsteinvik (NOR)</td></tr>
<tr><td>Samuel Johansen CHUKWUDI</td><td>25.06.2003</td><td>2</td><td>0</td><td>2022:    Royale Union Saint-Gilloise (BEL)</td></tr>
<tr><td>Viljormur í Heiðunum DAVIDSEN</td><td>19.07.1991</td><td>69</td><td>4</td><td>2022:    Helsingborgs IF (SWE)<br>09.01.2023->    HB Tórshavn</td></tr>
<tr><td>Andrias EDMUNDSSON</td><td>18.12.2000</td><td>2</td><td>0</td><td>2022/2023:    Águilas FC (ESP)</td></tr>
<tr><td>Odmar FÆRØ</td><td>01.11.1989</td><td>53</td><td>2</td><td>2023:    KÍ Klaksvík</td></tr>
<tr><td>Daniel JOHANSEN</td><td>09.07.1998</td><td>5</td><td>0</td><td>2023:    FC Fredericia (DEN)</td></tr>
<tr><td>Sonni Ragnar NATTESTAD</td><td>05.08.1994</td><td>46</td><td>3</td><td>2022:    B36 Tórshavn</td></tr>
<tr><td>Gilli RÓLANTSSON Sørensen</td><td>11.08.1992</td><td>65</td><td>1</td><td>2022/2023:    Odds BK Skien (NOR)</td></tr>
<tr><td>Hanus SØRENSEN</td><td>19.02.2001</td><td>3</td><td>0</td><td>2022/2023:    HB Tórshavn</td></tr>
<tr><td>Gunnar VATNHAMAR</td><td>29.03.1995</td><td>31</td><td>2</td><td>2022/2023:    Víkingur Gøta</td></tr>
<tr><td>Heini VATNSDAL</td><td>18.10.1991</td><td>37</td><td>1</td><td>2022/2023:    KÍ Klaksvík</td></tr>
<tr><td colspan="5" align="center">Midfielders</td></tr>
<tr><td>Jákup Biskopstø ANDREASEN</td><td>31.05.1998</td><td>18</td><td>2</td><td>2022/2023:    KÍ Klaksvík</td></tr>
<tr><td>Jóannes BJARTALÍÐ</td><td>10.07.1996</td><td>25</td><td>2</td><td>2022:    KÍ Klaksvík<br>26.01.2023->    Fredrikstad FK (NOR)</td></tr>
<tr><td>Heðin HANSEN</td><td>30.07.1993</td><td>9</td><td>0</td><td>2022:    HB Tórshavn</td></tr>
<tr><td>Brandur HENDRIKSSON Olsen</td><td>19.12.1995</td><td>51</td><td>6</td><td>2023:    Fredrikstad FK (NOR)</td></tr>
<tr><td>René Shaki JOENSEN</td><td>08.02.1993</td><td>44</td><td>3</td><td>2022/2023:    KÍ Klaksvík</td></tr>
<tr><td>Patrik JOHANNESEN</td><td>07.09.1995</td><td>21</td><td>1</td><td>2022:    Keflavík (ISL)<br>02.02.2023->    Breiðablik Kópavogur (ISL)</td></tr>
<tr><td>Andrass JOHANSEN</td><td>16.11.20001</td><td>1</td><td>0</td><td>2023:    B36 Tórshavn</td></tr>
<tr><td>Ári Mohr JÓNSSON</td><td>22.07.1994</td><td>17</td><td>1</td><td>2023:    HB Tórshavn</td></tr>
<tr><td>Noah Hans MNENEY</td><td>06.12.2002</td><td>3</td><td>0</td><td>2022:    Víkingur Gøta<br>21.02.2023->    Byrne FK (NOR)</td></tr>
<tr><td>Stefan RADOSAVLJEVIĆ</td><td>08.09.2000</td><td>5</td><td>1</td><td>2022:    HB Tórshavn<br>10.02.2023->    Sligo Rovers FC (IRL)</td></tr>
<tr><td>Sølvi VATNHAMAR</td><td>05.05.1986</td><td>66</td><td>2</td><td>2022/2023:    Víkingur Gøta</td></tr>
<tr><td colspan="5" align="center">Forwards</td></tr>
<tr><td>Hannes AGNARSSON</td><td>26.02.1999</td><td>4</td><td>0</td><td>2022:    B36 Tórshavn</td></tr>
<tr><td>Kaj Leo í BARTALSSTOVU</td><td>23.06.1991</td><td>30</td><td>1</td><td>2022:    ÍA Akranes (ISL)</td></tr>
<tr><td>Jóan Símun EDMUNDSSON</td><td>26.07.1991</td><td>80</td><td>8</td><td>2022/2023:    KVRS Waasland-Beveren (BEL)</td></tr>
<tr><td>Páll Andrasson KLETTSKARÐ</td><td>17.05.1990</td><td>15</td><td>0</td><td>2023:    KÍ Klaksvík</td></tr>
<tr><td>Petur KNUDSEN</td><td>21.04.1998</td><td>11</td><td>0</td><td>2023:    Lyngby BK (DEN)</td></tr>
<tr><td>Mads Boe MIKKELSEN</td><td>11.12.1999</td><td>7</td><td>1</td><td>2022/2023:    KÍ Klaksvík</td></tr>
<tr><td>Klæmint Andrasson OLSEN</td><td>17.07.1990</td><td>57</td><td>10</td><td>2022:    NSÍ Runavík<br>04.02.2023->    Breiðablik Kópavogur (ISL)</td></tr>
<tr><td>Meinhard Egilsson OLSEN</td><td>10.04.1997</td><td>26</td><td>1</td><td>2022/2023:    Mjøndalen IF (NOR)</td></tr>
<tr><td>Pætur Joensson PETERSEN</td><td>09.03.1998</td><td>3</td><td>0</td><td>2022:    HB Tórshavn;<br>04.02.2023->    KA Akureyri (ISL)</td></tr>
<tr><td colspan="5" align="center">Trainer</td></tr>
<tr><td>Håkan Georg ERICSON (Sweden) [since 16.12.2019]</td><td>29.05.1960</td><td colspan="3">34 M; 8 W; 9 D; 17 L; 33-60</td></tr>
</table>

# FINLAND

## The Country:
Suomen tasavalta (Republic of Finland)
Capital: Helsinki
Surface: 338,424 km²
Inhabitants: 5,553,000 [2022]
Time: UTC+2

## The FA:
Suomen Palloliitto
Urheilukatu 5, 00250 Helsinki
Tel: +358 9 742 151
Foundation date: 1907
Member of FIFA since: 1908
Member of UEFA since: 1954
Website:

## NATIONAL TEAM RECORDS

### RECORDS
| | | |
|---|---|---|
| **First international match:** | 22.10.1911, Helsinki: | Finland – Sweden 2-5 |
| **Most international caps:** | Jari Olavi Litmanen | - 137 caps (1989-2010) |
| **Most international goals:** | Teemu Eino Antero Pukki | - 38 goals / 112 caps (since 2011) |

### UEFA EUROPEAN CHAMPIONSHIP
| | |
|---|---|
| 1960 | Did not enter |
| 1964 | Did not enter |
| 1968 | Qualifiers |
| 1972 | Qualifiers |
| 1976 | Qualifiers |
| 1980 | Qualifiers |
| 1984 | Qualifiers |
| 1988 | Qualifiers |
| 1992 | Qualifiers |
| 1996 | Qualifiers |
| 2000 | Qualifiers |
| 2004 | Qualifiers |
| 2008 | Qualifiers |
| 2012 | Qualifiers |
| 2016 | Qualifiers |
| 2020 | Final Tournament (Group Stage) |

### FIFA WORLD CUP
| | |
|---|---|
| 1930 | Did not enter |
| 1934 | Did not enter |
| 1938 | Qualifiers |
| 1950 | *Withdrew* |
| 1954 | Qualifiers |
| 1958 | Qualifiers |
| 1962 | Qualifiers |
| 1966 | Qualifiers |
| 1970 | Qualifiers |
| 1974 | Qualifiers |
| 1978 | Qualifiers |
| 1982 | Qualifiers |
| 1986 | Qualifiers |
| 1990 | Qualifiers |
| 1994 | Qualifiers |
| 1998 | Qualifiers |
| 2002 | Qualifiers |
| 2006 | Qualifiers |
| 2010 | Qualifiers |
| 2014 | Qualifiers |
| 2018 | Qualifiers |
| 2022 | Qualifiers |

### OLYMPIC TOURNAMENTS
| | |
|---|---|
| 1908 | - |
| 1912 | - |
| 1920 | - |
| 1924 | - |
| 1928 | - |
| 1936 | Qualifiers |
| 1948 | - |
| 1952 | Round 1 |
| 1956 | - |
| 1960 | Qualifiers |
| 1964 | Qualifiers |
| 1968 | Qualifiers |
| 1972 | *Withdrew* |
| 1976 | Qualifiers |
| 1980 | Group Stage |
| 1984 | Qualifiers |
| 1988 | Qualifiers |
| 1992 | Qualifiers |
| 1996 | Qualifiers |
| 2000 | Qualifiers |
| 2004 | Qualifiers |
| 2008 | Qualifiers |
| 2012 | Qualifiers |
| 2016 | Qualifiers |
| 2020 | Qualifiers |

### UEFA NATIONS LEAGUE
| | |
|---|---|
| 2018/2019 | League C (Group Stage -> promotion to League B) |
| 2020/2021 | League B (Group Stage) |
| 2022/2023 | League B (Group Stage) |

### FINNISH CLUB HONOURS IN EUROPEAN CLUB COMPETITIONS:

| European Champion Clubs.Cup (1956-1992) / UEFA Champions League (1993-2023) |
|---|
| None |

| Fairs Cup (1858-1971) / UEFA Cup (1972-2009) / UEFA Europa League (2010-2023) |
|---|
| None |

| UEFA Europa Conference League (2021-2023) |
|---|
| None |

| UEFA Super Cup (1972-2022) |
|---|
| None |

| *European Cup Winners' Cup 1961-1999** |
|---|
| None |

*defunct competition

# NATIONAL COMPETITIONS
## TABLE OF HONOURS

| | CHAMPIONS | CUP WINNERS | BEST GOALSCORERS | |
|---|---|---|---|---|
| 1908 | Unitas Helsinki | - | - | |
| 1909 | PUS Helsinki | - | - | |
| 1910 | Åbo IFK Turku | - | - | |
| 1911 | HJK Helsinki | - | - | |
| 1912 | HJK Helsinki | - | - | |
| 1913 | KIF Helsinki | - | - | |
| 1914 | *No competition* | - | - | |
| 1915 | KIF Helsinki | - | - | |
| 1916 | KIF Helsinki | - | - | |
| 1917 | HJK Helsinki | - | - | |
| 1918 | HJK Helsinki | - | - | |
| 1919 | HJK Helsinki | - | - | |
| 1920 | Åbo IFK Turku | - | - | |
| 1921 | Helsingin Palloseura | - | - | |
| 1922 | Helsingin Palloseura | - | - | |
| 1923 | HJK Helsinki | - | - | |
| 1924 | Åbo IFK Turku | - | - | |
| 1925 | HJK Helsinki | - | - | |
| 1926 | Helsingin Palloseura | - | - | |
| 1927 | Helsingin Palloseura | - | - | |
| 1928 | TPS Turku | - | - | |
| 1929 | Helsingin Palloseura | - | - | |
| 1930 | IFK Helsingfors | - | Holger Salin (IFK Helsingfors) Olof Strömsten (KIF Helsinki) | 9 |
| 1931 | IFK Helsingfors | - | Holger Salin (IFK Helsingfors) | 11 |
| 1932 | Helsingin Palloseura | - | Lauri Lehtinen (TPS Turku) | 13 |
| 1933 | IFK Helsingfors | - | Olof Strömsten (IFK Helsingfors) | 18 |
| 1934 | Helsingin Palloseura | - | Olof Strömsten (IFK Helsingfors) | 15 |
| 1935 | Helsingin Palloseura | - | Aatos Lehtonen (HJK Helsinki) Nuutti Lintamo (VPS Vaasa) | 13 |
| 1936 | HJK Helsinki | - | Aatos Lehtonen (HJK Helsinki) | 14 |
| 1937 | IFK Helsingfors | - | Aatos Lehtonen (HJK Helsinki) | 25 |
| 1938 | HJK Helsinki | - | Aatos Lehtonen (HJK Helsinki) | 14 |
| 1939 | TPS Turku | - | Aatos Lehtonen (HJK Helsinki) | 15 |
| 1940 | Sudet Viipuri | - | *Not known* | |
| 1941 | TPS Turku | - | Jussi Valtonen (TPS Turku) | 14 |
| 1942 | HT Helsinki | - | *Not known* | |
| 1943 | *No competition* | - | - | |
| 1944 | VIFK Vaasa | - | Urho Teräs (TPS Turku) Leo Turunen (Sudet Viipuri) | 9 |
| 1945 | VPS Vaasa | - | *Not known* | |
| 1946 | VIFK Vaasa | - | *Not known* | |
| 1947 | IFK Helsingfors | - | *Not known* | |
| 1948 | VPS Vaasa | - | Stig-Göran Myntti (VIFK Vaasa) | 15 |
| 1949 | TPS Turku | - | Yrjö Asikainen (Ilves-Kissat Tampere) Kaimo Lintamo (VPS Vaasa) | 20 |
| 1950 | Ilves-Kissat Tampere | - | Yrjö Asikainen (Ilves-Kissat Tampere) Jorma Saarinen (VPS Vaasa) | 15 |
| 1951 | KTP Kotka | - | Åke Forsberg (KIF Helsinki) | 16 |
| 1952 | KTP Kotka | - | Mauri Vanhanen (KTP Kotka) | 16 |
| 1953 | VIFK Vaasa | - | Rainer Forss (Pyrkivä Turku) | 15 |
| 1954 | Pyrkivä Turku | - | Eino Koskinen (TuTo Turku) | 16 |
| 1955 | KIF Helsinki | FC Haka Valkeakoski | Yrjö Asikainen (KIF Helsinki) | 12 |
| 1956 | KuPS Kuopio | PPojat Helsinki | Pentti Styck (HJK Helsinki) | 20 |
| 1957 | Helsingin Palloseura | Drott Pietarsaari | Matti Sundelin (TPS Turku) | 21 |
| 1958 | KuPS Kuopio | KTP Kotka | Kalevi Lehtovirta (TPS Turku) Kai Pahlman (Helsingin Palloseura) | 17 |
| 1959 | IFK Helsingfors | FC Haka Valkeakoski | Matti Sundelin (TPS Turku) | 21 |
| 1960 | FC Haka Valkeakoski | FC Haka Valkeakoski | Matti Sundelin (TPS Turku) | 30 |
| 1961 | IFK Helsingfors | KTP Kotka | Kai Pahlman (Helsingin Palloseura) | 20 |
| 1962 | FC Haka Valkeakoski | Helsingin Palloseura | Tor Österlund (HIK Hanko) | 22 |
| 1963 | Reipas Lahti | FC Haka Valkeakoski | Juha Lyytikäinen (IFK Helsingfors) | 16 |
| 1964 | HJK Helsinki | Reipas Lahti | Arto Tolsa (KTP Kotka) | 26 |
| 1965 | FC Haka Valkeakoski | Åbo IFK Turku | Kai Pahlman (HJK Helsinki) | 22 |
| 1966 | KuPS Kuopio | HJK Helsinki | Markku Hyvärinen (KuPS Kuopio) | 16 |
| 1967 | Reipas Lahti | KTP Kotka | Tommy Lindholm (TPS Turku) | 22 |
| 1968 | TPS Turku | KuPS Kuopio | Tommy Lindholm (TPS Turku) | 23 |
| 1969 | KPV Kokkola | FC Haka Valkeakoski | Hannu Lamberg (KPV Kokkola) Pekka Talaslahti (HJK Helsinki) | 18 |
| 1970 | Reipas Lahti | MP Mikkeli | Matti Paatelainen (IFK Helsingfors) | 20 |
| 1971 | TPS Turku | MP Mikkeli | Pentti Toivola (MP Mikkeli) | 17 |

| Year | Champion | Runner-up / Cup | Top scorer | Goals |
|------|----------|-----------------|------------|-------|
| 1972 | TPS Turku | Reipas Lahti | Matti Paatelainen (IFK Helsingfors) Heikki Suhonen (TPS Turku) | 16 |
| 1973 | HJK Helsinki | Reipas Lahti | Hannu Lamberg (KPV Kokkola) | 13 |
| 1974 | KuPS Kuopio | Reipas Lahti | Erkki Salo (TPS Turku) | 17 |
| 1975 | TPS Turku | Reipas Lahti | Reijo Rantanen (MiPK Mikkeli) | 16 |
| 1976 | KuPS Kuopio | Reipas Lahti | Matti Paatelainen (FC Haka Valkeakoski) | 17 |
| 1977 | FC Haka Valkeakoski | FC Haka Valkeakoski | Matti Paatelainen (FC Haka Valkeakoski) | 20 |
| 1978 | HJK Helsinki | Reipas Lahti | Atik Ismail (HJK Helsinki) | 20 |
| 1979 | OPS Oulu | FC Ilves Tampere | Atik Ismail (HJK Helsinki) Heikki Suhonen (TPS Turku) | 15 |
| 1980 | OPS Oulu | KTP Kotka | Hannu Rajaniemi (Sepsi-78 Seinäjoki) | 19 |
| 1981 | HJK Helsinki | HJK Helsinki | Juhani Himanka (OPS Oulu) | 22 |
| 1982 | FC Kuusysi Lahti | FC Haka Valkeakoski | Atik Ismail (HJK Helsinki) | 19 |
| 1983 | FC Ilves Tampere | FC Kuusysi Lahti | Mika Lipponen (TPS Turku) | 22 |
| 1984 | FC Kuusysi Lahti | HJK Helsinki | Mika Lipponen (TPS Turku) | 25 |
| 1985 | HJK Helsinki | FC Haka Valkeakoski | Ismo Lius (FC Kuusysi Lahti) | 19 |
| 1986 | FC Kuusysi Lahti | RoPS Rovaniemi | Ismo Lius (FC Kuusysi Lahti) Jari Niinimäki (FC Ilves Tampere) | 13 |
| 1987 | HJK Helsinki | FC Kuusysi Lahti | Ari Hjelm (FC Ilves Tampere) | 20 |
| 1988 | HJK Helsinki | FC Haka Valkeakoski | Ismo Lius (FC Kuusysi Lahti) | 22 |
| 1989 | FC Kuusysi Lahti | KuPS Kuopio | Ismo Lius (FC Kuusysi Lahti) | 15 |
| 1990 | HJK Helsinki | FC Ilves Tampere | Marek Czakon (POL, FC Ilves Tampere) Kimmo Tarkkio (HJK Helsinki) | 16 |
| 1991 | FC Kuusysi Lahti | TPS Turku | Kimmo Tarkkio (FC Haka Valkeakoski) | 23 |
| 1992 | HJK Helsinki | MyPa Myllykoski | Luiz Antônio Moraes (BRA, FC Jazz Pori) | 21 |
| 1993 | FC Jazz Pori | HJK Helsinki | Antti Sumiala (FC Jazz Pori) | 20 |
| 1994 | TPV Tampere | TPS Turku | Dionísio Domingos Rangel (BRA, TPV Tampere) | 17 |
| 1995 | FC Haka Valkeakoski | MyPa Myllykoski | Valeri Popovitch (RUS, FC Haka Valkeakoski) | 21 |
| 1996 | FC Jazz Pori | HJK Helsinki | Luiz Antônio Moraes (BRA, FC Jazz Pori) | 17 |
| 1997 | HJK Helsinki | FC Haka Valkeakoski | Rafael Pires Vieira (BRA, HJK Helsinki) | 11 |
| 1998 | FC Haka Valkeakoski | HJK Helsinki | Matti Hiukka (RoPS Rovaniemi) | 11 |
| 1999 | FC Haka Valkeakoski | Jokerit Helsinki | Valeri Popovitch (FC Haka Valkeakoski) | 23 |
| 2000 | FC Haka Valkeakoski | HJK Helsinki | Shefki Kuqi (Jokerit Helsinki) | 19 |
| 2001 | TamU Tampere | Atlantis Helsinki | Paulus Roiha (HJK Helsinki) | 22 |
| 2002 | HJK Helsinki | FC Haka Valkeakoski | Mika Kottila (HJK Helsinki) | 18 |
| 2003 | HJK Helsinki | HJK Helsinki | Saku Puhakainen (MyPa Myllykoski) | 14 |
| 2004 | FC Haka Valkeakoski | MyPa Myllykoski | Antti Pohja (TamU Tampere) | 16 |
| 2005 | MyPa Myllykoski | FC Haka Valkeakoski | Juho Mäkelä (HJK Helsinki) | 16 |
| 2006 | TamU Tampere | HJK Helsinki | Hermanni Vuorinen (FC Honka Espoo) | 16 |
| 2007 | TamU Tampere | TamU Tampere | Rafael Pires Vieira (BRA, FC Lahti) | 14 |
| 2008 | FC Inter Turku | HJK Helsinki | Aleksandr Kokko (FC Honka Espoo) Henri Myntti (TamU Tampere) | 13 |
| 2009 | HJK Helsinki | FC Inter Turku | Hermanni Vuorinen (FC Honka Espoo) | 16 |
| 2010 | HJK Helsinki | TPS Turku | Juho Mäkelä (HJK Helsinki) | 16 |
| 2011 | HJK Helsinki | HJK Helsinki | Timo Furuholm (FC Inter Turku) | 22 |
| 2012 | HJK Helsinki | FC Honka Espoo | Irakli Sirbiladze (GEO, FC Inter Turku) | 17 |
| 2013 | HJK Helsinki | RoPS Rovaniemi | Tim Väyrynen (FC Honka Espoo) | 17 |
| 2014 | HJK Helsinki | HJK Helsinki | Jonas Emet (FF Jaro Pietarsaari) Luis Emilio Solignac (ARG, IFK Mariehamn) | 14 |
| 2015 | SJK Seinäjoki | IFK Mariehamn | Aleksandr Kokko (RoPS Rovaniemi) | 17 |
| 2016 | IFK Mariehamn | SJK Seinäjoki | Roope Vilhelmi Riski (SJK Seinäjoki) | 17 |
| 2017 | HJK Helsinki | HJK Helsinki | Aleksei Kangaskolkka (IFK Mariehamn) | 16 |
| 2018 | HJK Helsinki | FC Inter Turku | João Klauss De Mello (BRA, HJK Helsinki) | 21 |
| 2019 | Kuopion Palloseura | FC Ilves Tampere | Filip Valenčić (SVN, FC Inter Turku) | 17 |
| 2020 | HJK Helsinki | HJK Helsinki | Roope Vilhelmi Riski (HJK Helsinki) | 16 |
| 2021 | HJK Helsinki | Kuopion Palloseura | Benjamin Källman (FC Inter Turku) Ariel Thierry Ngueukam (CMR, SJK Seinäjoki) | 14 |
| 2022 | HJK Helsinki | Kuopion Palloseura | Lee Harry Erwin (SCO, FC Haka Valkeakoski) | 17 |

**Regular Season - Results**

**Round 1 [02.04.2022]**
HJK Helsinki - FC Honka 1-0(0-0)
Haka Valkeakoski - Ilves Tampere 2-1(2-1)
Kuopion PS - FC Inter Turku 2-1(2-1)
SJK Seinäjoki - Helsingfors IFK 2-1(0-0)
Vaasan PS - AC Oulu 2-2(1-0)
IFK Mariehamn - FC Lahti 0-0

**Round 2 [07-09.04.2022]**
FC Honka - Haka Valkeakoski 3-2(3-0)
FC Lahti - Vaasan PS 0-5(0-3)
SJK Seinäjoki - HJK Helsinki 0-1(0-0)
FC Inter Turku - AC Oulu 2-1(1-1)
Helsingfors IFK - IFK Mariehamn 1-1(1-0)
Ilves Tampere - Kuopion PS 1-2(1-1)

**Round 3 [15-18.04.2022]**
Kuopion PS - SJK Seinäjoki 2-0(1-0)
FC Inter Turku - Haka Valkeakoski 0-2(0-1)
AC Oulu - Ilves Tampere 2-2(2-0)
Helsingfors IFK - FC Lahti 0-3(0-0)
IFK Mariehamn - FC Honka 1-1(1-1)
Vaasan PS - HJK Helsinki 0-1(0-0)

**Round 4 [22-25.04.2022]**
Haka Valkeakoski - Helsingfors IFK 2-1(1-1)
FC Lahti - Kuopion PS 0-1(0-1)
HJK Helsinki - FC Inter Turku 1-4(1-1)
Ilves Tampere - Vaasan PS 3-2(2-1)
IFK Mariehamn - AC Oulu 2-1(1-1)
FC Honka - SJK Seinäjoki 5-1(2-0)

**Round 5 [28-29.04.2022]**
Helsingfors IFK - HJK Helsinki 0-2(0-1)
AC Oulu - Haka Valkeakoski 3-0(2-0)
FC Inter Turku - IFK Mariehamn 4-0(4-0)
FC Lahti - FC Honka 0-2(0-0)
Ilves Tampere - SJK Seinäjoki 3-1(1-1)
Kuopion PS - Vaasan PS 3-1(2-0)

**Round 6 [07-08.05.2022]**
SJK Seinäjoki - FC Lahti 1-2(0-1)
AC Oulu - Helsingfors IFK 1-1(1-0)
Haka Valkeakoski - Vaasan PS 0-2(0-0)
FC Honka - FC Inter Turku 2-1(0-0)
HJK Helsinki - Ilves Tampere 2-1(0-1)
IFK Mariehamn - Kuopion PS 1-1(0-0)

**Round 7 [12-15.05.2022]**
FC Lahti - HJK Helsinki 1-1(1-1)
Kuopion PS - Haka Valkeakoski 2-1(2-0)
AC Oulu - FC Honka 2-1(0-0)
Vaasan PS - SJK Seinäjoki 0-1(0-0)
FC Inter Turku - Helsingfors IFK 2-2(1-1)
Ilves Tampere - IFK Mariehamn 1-0(0-0)

**Round 8 [19-23.05.2022]**
Vaasan PS - FC Inter Turku 1-2(0-1)
FC Honka - Ilves Tampere 0-0
SJK Seinäjoki - IFK Mariehamn 1-0(0-0)
FC Lahti - AC Oulu 0-2(0-1)
HJK Helsinki - Haka Valkeakoski 4-1(1-1)
Helsingfors IFK - Kuopion PS 0-1(0-1)

**Round 9 [28-29.05.2022]**
AC Oulu - SJK Seinäjoki 1-0(0-0)
Haka Valkeakoski - FC Lahti 1-1(0-0)
FC Inter Turku - Ilves Tampere 2-2(0-0)
Helsingfors IFK - FC Honka 1-2(0-0)
Kuopion PS - HJK Helsinki 0-0
IFK Mariehamn - Vaasan PS 1-3(0-2)

**Round 10 [18.06.2022]**
Haka Valkeakoski - IFK Mariehamn 3-2(2-1)
FC Honka - Kuopion PS 2-0(2-0)
HJK Helsinki - AC Oulu 0-1(0-0)
Ilves Tampere - FC Lahti 3-2(1-1)
SJK Seinäjoki - FC Inter Turku 1-1(1-1)
Helsingfors IFK - Vaasan PS 1-5(0-2)

**Round 11 22.06.2022 [ ]**
FC Inter Turku - FC Lahti 5-1(1-0)
Ilves Tampere - Helsingfors IFK 0-1(0-0)
Kuopion PS - AC Oulu 2-1(0-1)
SJK Seinäjoki - Haka Valkeakoski 2-2(1-0)
Vaasan PS - FC Honka 0-1(0-1)
IFK Mariehamn - HJK Helsinki 2-1(1-1)

**Round 12 [02-04.07.2022]**
H. Valkeakoski - Seinäjoki 1-1(0-0) [17.05.22]
FC Honka - IFK Mariehamn 1-1(1-0)
AC Oulu - Vaasan PS 0-6(0-2)
HJK Helsinki - Kuopion PS 1-1(0-1)
FC Lahti - FC Inter Turku 2-1(1-1)
Helsingfors IFK - Ilves Tampere 0-1(0-1)

**Round 13 [09-11.07.2022]**
Inter Turku-HJK Helsinki 0-1(0-1) [03.05.22]
Helsingfors IFK - Haka Valkeakoski 0-2(0-1)
Vaasan PS - IFK Mariehamn 1-3(0-1)
Kuopion PS - FC Lahti 4-0(1-0)
SJK Seinäjoki - FC Honka 3-2(0-1)
Ilves Tampere - AC Oulu 0-2(0-1)

**Round 14 [15-18.07.2022]**
AC Oulu - Kuopion PS 0-3(0-1) [17.05.2022]
FC Honka - FC Lahti 5-0(3-0)
HJK Helsinki - Vaasan PS 3-1(1-1)
IFK Mariehamn - Helsingfors IFK 1-1(1-1)
SJK Seinäjoki - Ilves Tampere 3-3(1-1)
Haka Valkeakoski - FC Inter Turku 3-2(1-1)

**Round 15 [23-25.07.2022]**
Ilves Tampere - HJK Helsinki 1-2(1-0)
AC Oulu - IFK Mariehamn 3-1(2-1)
Vaasan PS - Haka Valkeakoski 3-3(2-2)
Kuopion PS - Helsingfors IFK 5-1(1-0)
FC Lahti - SJK Seinäjoki 1-3(0-2)
FC Inter Turku - FC Honka 0-1(0-0)

**Round 16 [29.07.-01.08.2022]**
FC Lahti - Ilves Tampere 1-1(0-1)
FC Honka - Vaasan PS 4-0(0-0)
HJK Helsinki - IFK Mariehamn 1-0(1-0)
Haka Valkeakoski - Kuopion PS 2-1(0-0)
SJK Seinäjoki - AC Oulu 3-2(1-0)
Helsingfors IFK - FC Inter Turku 0-3(0-2)

**Round 17 [06-08.08.2022]**
Vaasan PS - Ilves Tampere 3-0(3-0)
FC Inter Turku - SJK Seinäjoki 1-0(1-0)
IFK Mariehamn - Haka Valkeakoski 2-0(1-0)
Kuopion PS - FC Honka 1-1(1-0)
AC Oulu - HJK Helsinki 1-1(0-1)
FC Lahti - Helsingfors IFK 0-0

**Round 18 [12-15.08.2022]**
HJK Helsinki - FC Lahti 3-2(0-1) [17.05.22]
Haka Valkeakoski - AC Oulu 3-2(1-1)
FC Inter Turku - Vaasan PS 1-1(1-1)
Ilves Tampere - FC Honka 0-4(0-1)
Kuopion PS - IFK Mariehamn 1-0(0-0)
Helsingfors IFK - SJK Seinäjoki 0-2(0-1)

**Round 19 [20-22.08.2022]**
SJK Seinäjoki - Kuopion PS 2-1(1-1)
Vaasan PS - FC Lahti 2-3(1-1)
AC Oulu - FC Inter Turku 0-3 *awarded*
Haka Valkeakoski - HJK Helsinki 0-3(0-3)
IFK Mariehamn - Ilves Tampere 1-5(1-4)
FC Honka - Helsingfors IFK 4-1(1-0)

**Round 20 [26-28.08.2022]**
FC Lahti - IFK Mariehamn 0-2(0-0)
FC Honka - AC Oulu 2-2(0-1)
Ilves Tampere - Haka Valkeakoski 2-3(1-1)
FC Inter Turku - Kuopion PS 1-2(1-0)
Vaasan PS - Helsingfors IFK 1-1(0-1)
HJK Helsinki - SJK Seinäjoki 1-0(1-0)

**Round 21 [01-05.09.2022]**
Haka Valkeakoski - FC Honka 2-1(0-1)
Kuopion PS - Ilves Tampere 0-0
SJK Seinäjoki - Vaasan PS 2-0(1-0)
AC Oulu - FC Lahti 0-0
IFK Mariehamn - FC Inter Turku 2-3(0-1)
HJK Helsinki - Helsingfors IFK 2-1(1-1)

**Round 22 [11.09.2022]**
FC Honka - HJK Helsinki 1-2(0-1)
FC Lahti - Haka Valkeakoski 0-1(0-0)
Helsingfors IFK - AC Oulu 1-6(1-2)
IFK Mariehamn - SJK Seinäjoki 2-0(2-0)
Ilves Tampere - FC Inter Turku 1-1(0-1)
Vaasan PS - Kuopion PS 0-1(0-0)

| | | | | | | | | | | |
|---|---|---|---|---|---|---|---|---|---|---|
| 1. | HJK Helsinki | 22 | 15 | 4 | 3 | 34 | - | 18 | 49 |
| 2. | Kuopion Palloseura | 22 | 14 | 5 | 3 | 36 | - | 16 | 47 |
| 3. | FC Honka Espoo | 22 | 12 | 5 | 5 | 45 | - | 21 | 41 |
| 4. | FC Haka Valkeakoski | 22 | 11 | 4 | 7 | 36 | - | 38 | 37 |
| 5. | FC Inter Turku | 22 | 9 | 5 | 8 | 40 | - | 28 | 32 |
| 6. | SJK Seinäjoki | 22 | 9 | 4 | 9 | 29 | - | 32 | 31 |
| 7. | AC Oulu | 22 | 8 | 6 | 8 | 35 | - | 35 | 30 |
| 8. | FC Ilves Tampere | 22 | 6 | 7 | 9 | 31 | - | 36 | 25 |
| 9. | IFK Mariehamn | 22 | 6 | 6 | 10 | 25 | - | 33 | 24 |
| 10. | Vaasan Palloseura | 22 | 6 | 4 | 12 | 39 | - | 36 | 22 |
| 11. | FC Lahti | 22 | 4 | 6 | 12 | 19 | - | 43 | 18 |
| 12. | IFK Helsingfors | 22 | 1 | 6 | 15 | 15 | - | 48 | 9 |

Teams ranked 1-6 were qualified for the Championship Round, while teams ranked 7-12 were qualified for the Relegation Round.

## Relegation Round

### Results

**Round 23** [18.09.2022]
Ilves Tampere - Vaasan PS 2-3(0-0)
AC Oulu - Helsingfors IFK 4-1(1-0)
IFK Mariehamn - FC Lahti 6-0(1-0)

**Round 24** [28.09.2022]
Helsingfors IFK - Ilves Tampere 1-5(1-3)
FC Lahti - Vaasan PS 0-2(0-2)
IFK Mariehamn - AC Oulu 2-4(0-1)

**Round 25** [02.10.2022]
Ilves Tampere - IFK Mariehamn 2-3(1-1)
Vaasan PS - Helsingfors IFK 4-0(1-0)
AC Oulu - FC Lahti 2-1(2-0)

**Round 26** [08-09.10.2022]
Helsingfors IFK - IFK Mariehamn 2-3(1-3)
Vaasan PS - AC Oulu 2-1(1-1)
Ilves Tampere - FC Lahti 1-0(1-0)

**Round 27** [16.10.2022]
AC Oulu - Ilves Tampere 0-2(0-1)
IFK Mariehamn - Vaasan PS 2-2(0-1)
FC Lahti - Helsingfors IFK 6-1(3-1)

### Final Standings

| | | | | | | | | | | Total | | | | | | Home | | | | | | Away | | |
|---|---|---|---|---|---|---|---|---|---|---|---|---|---|---|---|---|---|---|---|---|---|---|---|---|
| 1. | AC Oulu | 27 | 11 | 6 | 10 | 46 | - | 43 | **39** | | 6 | 4 | 4 | 19 | - | 22 | | 5 | 2 | 6 | 27 | - | 21 |
| 2. | Vaasan Palloseura | 27 | 10 | 5 | 12 | 52 | - | 41 | **35** | | 3 | 3 | 7 | 19 | - | 19 | | 7 | 2 | 5 | 33 | - | 22 |
| 3. | FC Ilves Tampere | 27 | 9 | 7 | 11 | 43 | - | 43 | **34** | | 5 | 1 | 8 | 20 | - | 26 | | 4 | 6 | 3 | 23 | - | 17 |
| 4. | IFK Mariehamn | 27 | 9 | 7 | 11 | 41 | - | 43 | **34** | | 5 | 5 | 4 | 25 | - | 22 | | 4 | 2 | 7 | 16 | - | 21 |
| 5. | FC Lahti (*Relegation Play-offs*) | 27 | 5 | 6 | 16 | 26 | - | 55 | **21** | | 2 | 3 | 8 | 11 | - | 22 | | 3 | 3 | 8 | 15 | - | 33 |
| 6. | IFK Helsingfors (*Relegated*) | 27 | 1 | 6 | 20 | 20 | - | 70 | **9** | | 0 | 1 | 12 | 7 | - | 36 | | 1 | 5 | 8 | 13 | - | 34 |

## Championship Round

### Results

**Round 23** [28-29.09.2022]
SJK Seinäjoki - Kuopion PS 3-1(2-0)
FC Inter Turku - Haka Valkeakoski 0-1(0-0)
FC Honka - HJK Helsinki 3-1(0-1)

**Round 24** [02.10.2022]
Kuopion PS - FC Honka 3-2(2-1)
Haka Valkeakoski - SJK Seinäjoki 2-0(0-0)
HJK Helsinki - FC Inter Turku 3-0(0-0)

**Round 25** [05-06.10.2022]
HJK Helsinki - Seinäjoki 2-1(1-1) [18.09.22]
Kuopion PS - Haka Valkeakoski 0-0
FC Honka - FC Inter Turku 2-1(1-0)

**Round 26** [09-10.10.2022]
Kuopion PS - FC Inter Turku 2-0(1-0)
Haka Valkeakoski - HJK Helsinki 0-1(0-1)
SJK Seinäjoki - FC Honka 0-0

**Round 27** [16.10.2022]
HJK Helsinki - Kuopion PS 0-1(0-1)
FC Honka - Haka Valkeakoski 1-1(1-0)
FC Inter Turku - SJK Seinäjoki 1-0(0-0)

### Final Standings

| | | | | | | | | | | Total | | | | | | Home | | | | | | Away | | |
|---|---|---|---|---|---|---|---|---|---|---|---|---|---|---|---|---|---|---|---|---|---|---|---|---|
| 1. | **HJK Helsinki** | 27 | 18 | 4 | 5 | 41 | - | 23 | **58** | | 10 | 1 | 3 | 24 | - | 14 | | 8 | 3 | 2 | 17 | - | 9 |
| 2. | Kuopion Palloseura | 27 | 17 | 6 | 4 | 43 | - | 21 | **57** | | 10 | 4 | 0 | 27 | - | 8 | | 7 | 2 | 4 | 16 | - | 13 |
| 3. | FC Honka Espoo | 27 | 14 | 7 | 6 | 53 | - | 27 | **49** | | 9 | 4 | 1 | 35 | - | 13 | | 5 | 3 | 5 | 18 | - | 14 |
| 4. | FC Haka Valkeakoski | 27 | 13 | 6 | 8 | 40 | - | 40 | **45** | | 8 | 2 | 3 | 21 | - | 18 | | 5 | 4 | 5 | 19 | - | 22 |
| 5. | FC Inter Turku | 27 | 10 | 5 | 12 | 42 | - | 36 | **35** | | 5 | 3 | 5 | 19 | - | 14 | | 5 | 2 | 7 | 23 | - | 22 |
| 6. | SJK Seinäjoki | 27 | 10 | 5 | 12 | 33 | - | 38 | **35** | | 7 | 4 | 2 | 23 | - | 16 | | 3 | 1 | 10 | 10 | - | 22 |

| Top goalscorers: | |
|---|---|
| **20  Lee Harry Erwin (SCO)** | *FC Haka Valkeakoski* |
| 15  Agon Sadiku | *FC Honka Espoo* |
| 14  Kalle Multanen | *Vaasan Palloseura* |

| Europa Conference League Play-offs | | | |
|---|---|---|---|
| **Quarter-Finals [19.10.2022]** | FC Inter Turku - Vaasan Palloseura | 1-5(0-1) | |
| | SJK Seinäjoki - AC Oulu | 0-1(0-0) | |
| **Semi-Finals [22.10.2022]** | AC Oulu - Vaasan Palloseura | 0-1(0-0,0-0) | |
| **Final [26-30.10.2022]** | Vaasan Palloseura - **FC Haka Valkeakoski** | 0-3(0-3) | 2-1(1-1) |

| Relegation Play-offs [20-23.10.2022] | | | |
|---|---|---|---|
| Turun Palloseura Turku - FC Lahti | | 1-1(0-1) | 1-2(0-1) |

FC Lahti remains at first level for 2023.

# NATIONAL CUP
## Suomen cup 2022

| Fifth Round [24-26.05.2022] | | | | |
|---|---|---|---|---|
| Klubi 04 Helsinki - HJK Helsinki | 0-4(0-2) | Hämeenlinnan JS - FC Kiffen 08 Helsinki | 2-0(2-0) |
| FC Inter Turku - FC Inter Turku II | 10-0(5-0) | TV Ilves-Kissat Tampere - PK-35 Vantaa | 2-7(1-5) |
| HaPK Edustus - FC Lahti | 2-6(1-4) | JäPS Järvenpää - FC Komeetat Jyväskylä | 3-1(1-1) |
| AC Oulu - Ilves Tampere II | 4-0(2-0) | Mikkelin Palloilijat - FF Jaro Jakobstad | 0-0 aet; 4-3 pen |
| SJK Akatemia Seinäjoki - SJK Seinäjoki | 2-3(0-2) | Kotkan Työväen Palloilijat - FC Haka Valkeakoski | 2-4(2-1) |
| Espoon PS - IFK Mariehamn | 0-3(0-1) | SexyPöxyt Laaksolahti - IFK Helsingfors | 0-7(0-3) |
| Jippo Joensuu - Atlantis FC Helsinki | 1-3(0-1) | Kuopion Palloseura - Ekenäs IF | 5-1(1-0) |
| Vaasan Palloseura -Vantaan JS | 2-0(1-0) | Kuovolan JP - Salon Palloilijat | 3-6(3-1) |

| 1/8-Round [13-15.06.2022] | | | | |
|---|---|---|---|---|
| SJK Seinäjoki - FC Inter Turku | 1-1 aet; 3-5 pen | Hämeenlinnan JS - FC Haka Valkeakoski | 0-1(0-0) |
| Vaasan Palloseura - HJK Helsinki | 0-0 aet; 1-2 pen | JäPS Järvenpää - AC Oulu | 2-1(0-0) |
| Mikkelin Palloilijat - Kuopion Palloseura | 0-1(0-0) | FC Lahti - Atlantis FC Helsinki | 4-2(0-1) |
| IFK Mariehamn - IFK Helsingfors | 1-1 aet; 2-4 pen | PK-35 Vantaa - Salon Palloilijat | 1-0(0-0) |

| Quarter-Finals [28-29.06.2022] | | | | |
|---|---|---|---|---|
| FC Lahti - JäPS Järvenpää | 2-1(1-1) | FC Haka Valkeakoski - Kuopion Palloseura | 2-2 aet; 2-4 pen |
| FC Inter Turku - HJK Helsinki | 0-0 aet; 5-4 pen | PK-35 Vantaa - IFK Helsingfors | 2-2 aet; 4-5 pen |

| Semi-Finals [31.08.2022] | | | | |
|---|---|---|---|---|
| IFK Helsingfors - FC Inter Turku | 2-3(1-1) | FC Lahti - Kuopion Palloseura | 0-1(0-1) |

| Final |
|---|

17.09.2022; Olympiastadion, Helsinki; Referee: Mohammad Al Emara; Attendance: 3,372
**Kuopion Palloseura - FC Inter Turku**                                                    **1-0(0-0)**

**Kuopion Palloseura**: Johannes Kreidl, Diogo Alberto Soares Tomas, Paulo Ricardo Ferreira, Henri Toivomäki (Cap), Henry Uzochukwu Unuorah (77.Saku Savolainen), Sebastian Dahlström, Anton Popovitch, Daniel José Carrillo Montilla, Jaakko Tapio Oksanen, Joona Veteli (84.Gabriel Bispo dos Santos), Tim Väyrynen. Trainer: Simo Valakari.

**FC Inter Turku**: Matias Riikonen, Rodrigo Sebastián Arciero (90.Luka Kuittinen), Noah Nurmi, Juuso Hämäläinen (Cap), Roger Bonet Badía „Ruxi" (67.Juho Hyvärinen), Aleksi Paananen (84.Matias Ojala), Roberto Manuel Sierra Giménez „Rober",Tommi Jyry, Petteri Forsell, David Accam (89.Miguel Ángel Nazarit Mina), Matias Tamminen. Trainer: Miguel Grau Piles (Spain).

**Goal:** 1-0 Gabriel Bispo dos Santos (88).

# THE CLUBS 2022

| AC Oulu | | | | |
|---|---|---|---|---|

| **Founded**: | 2002 | | |
|---|---|---|---|
| **Stadium**: | Raatti Sradion, Oulu (4,392) | | |
| **Trainer**: | Ricardo Duarte (POR) | | 12.02.1980 |

| Goalkeepers: | DOB | M | (s) | G |
|---|---|---|---|---|
| Nuutti Kaikkonen | 10.04.2003 | 1 | | |
| Juhani Pennanen | 19.02.1993 | 1 | | |
| Calum Brian Joseph Ward (ENG) | 17.10.2000 | 25 | | |
| **Defenders:** | **DOB** | **M** | **(s)** | **G** |
| Sandro Sene Sakho Aníbal Embaló (POR) | 01.05.1996 | 8 | (2) | 1 |
| Mehdi Hetemaj (AUT) | 07.05.1997 | 11 | (4) | |
| Miika Koskela | 12.07.2003 | 14 | (4) | 1 |
| Noah Pallas | 09.02.2001 | 14 | (7) | 1 |
| Rafael da Silva Floro (POR) | 19.01.1994 | 19 | (4) | 5 |
| Rafael Scapini de Almeida „Rafinha" (BRA) | 29.06.1982 | 21 | (2) | |
| Riku Selander | 22.11.1994 | 21 | (3) | 1 |
| **Midfielders:** | **DOB** | **M** | **(s)** | **G** |
| Magnus Breitenmoser (SUI) | 06.08.1998 | 16 | (6) | 3 |
| Niklas Jokelainen | 30.03.2000 | 15 | (5) | 4 |
| Armend Kabashi | 04.12.1995 | 15 | (5) | 1 |

| Jere Kallinen | 10.01.2002 | 13 | (2) | |
|---|---|---|---|---|
| Marius Könkkölä | 31.10.2003 | 5 | (10) | |
| Otso Liimatta | 10.07.2004 | 23 | (3) | 5 |
| Raymond Roan Nogha Nogha (CMR) | 12.03.2004 | 2 | (10) | |
| Moshtagh Yaghoubi | 08.11.1994 | 6 | | |
| **Forwards:** | **DOB** | **M** | **(s)** | **G** |
| Samu Alanko | 16.05.1998 | 1 | (1) | |
| Samuel Anini Jr. | 07.09.2002 | 5 | (10) | 2 |
| Enoch Banza | 04.02.2000 | 5 | (4) | 1 |
| Aapo Heikkilä | 13.04.1994 | 7 | (4) | |
| Rasmus Joonatan Karjalainen | 04.04.1996 | 11 | (1) | 6 |
| Michael Steven López (ARG) | 19.08.1997 | 20 | (5) | 10 |
| Claudio Lucas Morais Ferreira dos Santos (BRA) | 22.04.1997 | 8 | (3) | 2 |
| Dennis Salanović (LIE) | 26.02.1996 | 3 | (1) | 1 |
| Onni Suutari | 29.04.2003 | 5 | (9) | 1 |
| Ibrahim Sekajja (ENG) | 31.10.1992 | 2 | (4) | 2 |

## Football Club Valkeakosken Haka

**Founded**: 1934
**Stadium**: Tehtaan kenttä, Valkeakoski (3,516)
**Trainer**: Teemu Tainio    27.11.1979

| Goalkeepers: | DOB | M | (s) | G |
|---|---|---|---|---|
| Aatu Hakala | 28.07.2000 | 24 | | |
| Mika Hilander | 17.08.1983 | 3 | | |

| Defenders: | DOB | M | (s) | G |
|---|---|---|---|---|
| Eero-Matti Auvinen | 05.03.1996 | 21 | (2) | |
| Elias Collin | 12.09.2003 | 7 | (6) | |
| Luiyi Ramón de Lucas Pérez (DOM) | 31.08.1994 | 23 | | 1 |
| Niklas Friberg | 14.03.1996 | 25 | | |
| Vigori Jean-Jaurès Gbe (CIV) | 10.02.2002 | 1 | | |
| Anthony Herbert (TRI) | 18.04.1998 | 3 | (7) | 1 |
| Henri Malundama | 08.06.1995 | 16 | (8) | |
| Konsta Mervelä | 24.03.2004 | | (1) | |
| Seth Saarinen | 05.05.2001 | 21 | (5) | 1 |
| Thomas Saarinen | 20.01.2004 | | (1) | |

| Midfielders: | DOB | M | (s) | G |
|---|---|---|---|---|
| Donaldo Açka (ALB) | 17.09.1997 | 8 | (14) | 1 |
| Jude Ekow Arthur (GHA) | 08.06.1999 | 7 | (3) | 2 |
| Janne-Pekka Laine | 25.01.2001 | 24 | (1) | 1 |
| Elias Mastokangas | 01.02.2001 | 7 | (3) | 2 |
| Tino Purme | 14.03.1998 | 11 | (16) | |
| Atte Sihvonen | 18.02.1996 | 18 | | |
| Oliver Whyte (NZL) | 20.01.2000 | 12 | (9) | 2 |

| Forwards: | DOB | M | (s) | G |
|---|---|---|---|---|
| Lee Harry Erwin (SCO) | 19.03.1994 | 26 | | 17 |
| Oiva Laaksonen | 19.09.2003 | | (6) | |
| Salomo Ojala | 17.04.1997 | 5 | (9) | 1 |
| Logan Rogerson (NZL) | 28.05.1998 | 23 | (4) | 4 |
| Stavros Zarokostas (USA) | 05.11.1997 | 12 | (12) | 7 |

## Football Club Honka Espoo

**Founded**: 1957
**Stadium**: Tapiolan Urheilupuisto, Espoo (6,000)
**Trainer**: Vesa-Pekka Vasara    16.08.1976

| Goalkeepers: | DOB | M | (s) | G |
|---|---|---|---|---|
| Roope Paunio | 14.12.2002 | 1 | | |
| Maksim Rudakov (RUS) | 22.01.1996 | 26 | | |

| Defenders: | DOB | M | (s) | G |
|---|---|---|---|---|
| Henri Aalto | 20.04.1989 | 19 | (2) | |
| Mohammed Adams (GHA) | 11.11.2000 | 3 | (2) | |
| Elias Äijälä | 24.03.2003 | 10 | (8) | |
| Florian Baak (GER) | 18.03.1999 | 2 | (2) | |
| Aldayr Hernández Basanta (COL) | 04.08.1995 | 25 | (2) | 3 |
| Ville Koski | 27.01.2002 | 23 | (1) | 2 |
| Jonas Levänen | 12.01.1994 | 2 | (1) | |
| Dario Naamo | 14.05.2005 | | (1) | |
| Matias Rale | 04.03.2001 | 21 | | 2 |
| Konsta Rasimus | 15.12.1990 | 1 | (9) | |

| Midfielders: | DOB | M | (s) | G |
|---|---|---|---|---|
| Daniel Heikkinen | 16.12.2002 | | (1) | |
| Saku Heiskanen | 29.09.2001 | 1 | (9) | |
| Kevin Jansen (NED) | 08.04.1992 | 24 | (1) | 4 |
| Otso Koskinen | 01.01.2003 | 3 | (12) | 2 |
| Florian Krebs (GER) | 04.02.1999 | 19 | (5) | 4 |
| Lucas Paz Kaufmann (BRA) | 26.03.1991 | 8 | (13) | 1 |
| Duarte Tammilehto | 15.02.1990 | 11 | (11) | |
| Jerry Voutilainen | 29.03.1995 | 25 | (1) | 6 |

| Forwards: | DOB | M | (s) | G |
|---|---|---|---|---|
| Edmund Arko-Mensah (GHA) | 09.09.2001 | 20 | (5) | 3 |
| Dražen Bagarić (CRO) | 12.11.1992 | 1 | (12) | 3 |
| Pauli Katajamäki | 04.01.2002 | | (1) | |
| Aleksandar Katanić (SRB) | 15.08.1995 | 1 | (7) | |
| Lauri Laine | 30.05.2005 | | (1) | |
| Rui Manuel Muati Modesto (POR) | 07.10.1999 | 25 | (1) | 7 |
| Niilo Saarikivi | 06.06.2003 | 2 | (6) | |
| Agon Sadiku | 10.03.2003 | 24 | (2) | 15 |

## Tampereen Ilves

**Founded**: 1931
**Stadium**: Tampere Stadion, Tampere (16,800)
**Trainer**: Toni Kari Mikael Kallio    09.08.1978

| Goalkeepers: | DOB | M | (s) | G |
|---|---|---|---|---|
| Eetu Huuhtanen | 31.01.2003 | 6 | | |
| Rasmus Leislahti | 16.06.2000 | 21 | (1) | |

| Defenders: | DOB | M | (s) | G |
|---|---|---|---|---|
| Mikael Almén | 08.03.2000 | 17 | (2) | 1 |
| Kalle Katz | 04.01.2000 | 15 | (2) | |
| Leo Kyllönen | 22.01.2004 | | (3) | |
| Aapo Mäenpää | 14.01.1998 | 21 | (1) | |
| Luc Landry Tabi Manga (CMR) | 17.11.1994 | 13 | (2) | |
| Tatu Miettunen | 24.04.1995 | 12 | (9) | 1 |
| Tuomas Ollila | 25.04.2000 | 23 | (3) | 6 |
| Jere Riissanen | 18.06.2005 | | (1) | |
| Najeeb Yakubu (GHA) | 01.05.2000 | 8 | | |

| Midfielders: | DOB | M | (s) | G |
|---|---|---|---|---|
| Doni Arifi | 11.04.2002 | 19 | (7) | |
| Noel Hasa | 06.02.2003 | 2 | (3) | |
| Teemu Jäntti | 02.03.2000 | 2 | (4) | |
| Patrick Steve Loa Loa (CMR) | 03.06.1999 | 3 | (11) | |
| Yussif Moussa (NIG) | 04.09.1998 | 6 | (2) | |
| Emmanuel Maker Lam Patut | 19.06.2003 | 2 | (4) | |
| Petteri Pennanen | 19.09.1990 | 26 | | 9 |
| Tuure Siira | 25.10.1994 | 15 | (7) | |
| Axel Vidjeskog | 14.04.2001 | 10 | | 1 |

| Forwards: | DOB | M | (s) | G |
|---|---|---|---|---|
| Badreddine Bushara | 04.01.2004 | | (11) | |
| Oiva Jukkola | 21.05.2002 | 4 | (3) | 2 |
| Adam Mikael Larsson (SWE) | 05.09.1999 | 12 | (1) | 3 |
| Kai Meriluoto | 02.01.2003 | 20 | (5) | 10 |
| Ariel Thierry Ngueukam (CMR) | 15.11.1988 | 23 | (2) | 6 |
| Eric Oteng (GHA) | 20.10.2001 | 11 | (10) | 3 |
| Momodou Sarr | 31.03.2000 | 3 | (8) | |
| Jorn Vancamp (BEL) | 28.10.1998 | | (3) | |
| Djair Terraii Carl Parfitt-Williams (BER) | 01.10.1996 | 3 | (3) | 1 |

## Football Club International Turku

**Founded**: 1990
**Stadium**: Veritas Stadion, Turku (9,372)
**Trainer**: Miguel Grau Piles (ESP)    22.04.1984
[20.09.2022] Ramiro Muñoz Calvo (ESP)    10.02.1994

| Goalkeepers: | DOB | M | (s) | G |
|---|---|---|---|---|
| Matias Riikonen | 24.02.2002 | 9 | | |
| Walter Viitala | 09.01.1992 | 18 | (1) | |

| Defenders: | DOB | M | (s) | G |
|---|---|---|---|---|
| Rodrigo Sebastián Arciero (ARG) | 12.03.1993 | 17 | (1) | |
| Juuso Hämäläinen | 30.11.1992 | 7 | | 1 |
| Juho Hyvärinen | 27.03.2000 | 14 | (4) | 1 |
| Rick Ketting (NED) | 15.01.1996 | 13 | | 3 |
| Luka Kuittinen | 29.03.2003 | 9 | (8) | |
| Ryan Mahuta | 07.07.2002 | 3 | (5) | |
| Miguel Ángel Nazarit Mina (COL) | 20.05.1997 | 2 | (2) | |
| Jussi Niska | 15.08.2002 | 18 | (2) | |
| Roger Bonet Badía „Ruxi" (ESP) | 11.04.1995 | 26 | | 3 |

| Midfielders: | DOB | M | (s) | G |
|---|---|---|---|---|
| Markus Arsalo | 21.10.2002 | 9 | (6) | |
| Petteri Forsell | 16.10.1990 | 26 | | 6 |
| Tommi Jyry | 16.08.1999 | 26 | (1) | 5 |
| Roope Kantola | 01.04.2002 | | (2) | |
| Elias Mastokangas | 01.02.2001 | 1 | (4) | |
| Noah Nurmi | 06.02.2001 | 14 | (4) | |
| Matias Ojala | 28.02.1995 | 6 | (5) | |
| Aleksi Paananen | 25.01.1993 | 12 | (7) | 3 |
| Roberto Manuel Sierra Giménez „Rober"(ESP) | 21.05.1996 | 12 | (1) | |

| Forwards: | DOB | M | (s) | G |
|---|---|---|---|---|
| David Accam (GHA) | 28.09.1990 | 4 | (6) | |
| David Haro Iniesta (ESP) | 17.07.1990 | 11 | (1) | 4 |
| Tobias Allan Diego Fagerström | 12.07.2000 | | (2) | |
| Benjamin Källman | 17.06.1998 | 12 | | 7 |
| Joel Rodríguez Satorres (ESP) | 25.09.1998 | 5 | (5) | |
| Otto Lehtisalo | 30.07.2004 | | (5) | |
| Joonas Lepistö | 22.06.1998 | 3 | (12) | |
| Matias Tamminen | 21.11.2001 | 20 | (6) | 5 |

## Helsingin Jalkapalloklubi

| Goalkeepers: | DOB | M | (s) | G |
|---|---|---|---|---|
| Conor William Hazard (NIR) | 05.03.1998 | 24 | | |
| Jakob Tånnander (SWE) | 10.08.2000 | 3 | | |
| **Defenders:** | **DOB** | **M** | **(s)** | **G** |
| Paulus Verneri Arajuuri | 15.06.1988 | 2 | | |
| Aapo Ilmari Halme | 22.05.1998 | 2 | | 1 |
| Arttu Hoskonen | 16.04.1997 | 16 | (5) | 3 |
| Valtteri Moren | 15.06.1991 | 4 | | |
| Murilo Henrique de Araujo Santos (BRA) | 02.12.1995 | 13 | (6) | |
| Matti Peltola | 03.07.2002 | 12 | (3) | |
| Jukka Raitala | 15.09.1988 | 21 | (2) | |
| Janne Saksela | 14.03.1993 | 1 | (1) | |
| Miro Tenho | 02.04.1995 | 20 | (1) | 2 |
| Joona Toivio | 10.03.1988 | 8 | (3) | |
| Miska Ylitolva | 23.05.2004 | 1 | (3) | |
| **Midfielders:** | **DOB** | **M** | **(s)** | **G** |
| Nassim Boujellab (MAR) | 20.06.1999 | 16 | (4) | 1 |
| Përparim Hetemaj | 12.12.1986 | 9 | (7) | 2 |

| Founded: | 19.06.1907 | | | |
|---|---|---|---|---|
| Stadium: | Bolt Arena, Helsinki (10,770) | | | |
| Trainer: | Toni Koskela | | 16.02.1983 | |

| | DOB | M | (s) | G |
|---|---|---|---|---|
| Jair Tavares Silva (BRA) | 03.08.1994 | 10 | (1) | 2 |
| Lucas Lingman | 25.01.1998 | 5 | (2) | |
| Manuel Martić (AUT) | 15.08.1995 | 5 | (5) | 1 |
| Atomu Tanaka (JPN) | 04.10.1987 | 12 | (7) | 1 |
| Aaro Toivonen | 19.04.2005 | | (1) | |
| Santeri Väänänen | 01.01.2002 | 8 | (5) | 1 |
| Johannes Yli-Kokko | 24.08.2001 | 10 | (7) | 1 |
| **Forwards:** | **DOB** | **M** | **(s)** | **G** |
| Abdul Malik Abubakari (GHA) | 10.05.2000 | 5 | (6) | 1 |
| David Eric Browne (PNG) | 27.12.1995 | 15 | (7) | 2 |
| Santeri Hostikka | 30.09.1997 | 11 | (9) | 2 |
| Anthony Olusanya | 01.02.2000 | 10 | (11) | 7 |
| Bojan Radulović (SRB) | 29.12.1999 | 14 | (9) | 8 |
| Riku Riski | 16.08.1989 | 1 | | |
| Roope Riski | 16.08.1991 | 1 | (1) | |
| Fabian Serrarens (NED) | 09.02.1991 | 11 | (5) | |
| Pyry Henri Hidipo Soiri | 22.09.1994 | 7 | (8) | 1 |
| Casper Terho | 24.06.2003 | 20 | (6) | 4 |

## Idrottsföreningen Kamraterna Helsingfors

| Goalkeepers: | DOB | M | (s) | G |
|---|---|---|---|---|
| António Alberto Bastos Pimparel „Beto"(POR) | 01.05.1982 | 12 | | |
| Felix Ferahyan | 29.11.1998 | 1 | | |
| Ramilson Almeida da Silva (BRA) | 21.08.1999 | 14 | | |
| **Defenders:** | **DOB** | **M** | **(s)** | **G** |
| Macario Hing-Glover (USA) | 04.04.1995 | 21 | | 1 |
| Oliver Kangaslahti | 01.05.2000 | 5 | (1) | |
| Serge Wilfried Kanon (CIV) | 06.07.1993 | 7 | (1) | |
| Daan Klinkenberg (NED) | 12.01.1996 | 19 | | |
| Jesse Nikki | 28.06.2003 | 17 | | |
| Felipe Sáez Carrillo „Pipe Sáez" (ESP) | 19.08.1995 | 12 | | 1 |
| Ståle Stehen Sæthre (NOR) | 02.04.1993 | 9 | | |
| Guillermo Sotelo (ARG) | 01.01.1991 | 10 | | |
| **Midfielders:** | **DOB** | **M** | **(s)** | **G** |
| Ifeanyi Emmanuel Ani (NGA) | 29.08.2002 | 5 | (4) | |
| Jani Bäckman | 20.03.1988 | 6 | (8) | |
| Roman Eremenko | 19.03.1987 | 11 | | 2 |
| Sergey Eremenko (RUS) | 06.01.1999 | 14 | (3) | 1 |

| Founded: | 1897 | | |
|---|---|---|---|
| Stadium: | Bolt Arena, Helsinki (10,770) | | |
| Trainer: | Fernando José Bernardo Tavares (POR) | 02.05.1980 | |
| [06.04.2022] | Pedro Miguel Dias Pires Henriques | 29.10.1985 | |
| [19.04.2022] | Mika-Matti Petteri Paatelainen | 03.02.1967 | |
| [06.10.2022] | Teemu Kankkunen | 13.01.1980 | |

| | DOB | M | (s) | G |
|---|---|---|---|---|
| Jukka Halme | 30.11.1984 | 7 | (4) | |
| Keaton Isaksson | 21.04.1994 | 4 | (3) | |
| Wilson Masakuba Kamavuaka (COD) | 29.03.1990 | 4 | (1) | 1 |
| Aatu Kujanpää | 27.07.1998 | 9 | (8) | 1 |
| Sakari Mattila | 14.07.1989 | 21 | | 1 |
| Obed Malolo | 18.04.1997 | 20 | (2) | |
| Fortuna Namputu (CGO) | 11.12.1996 | 2 | (5) | |
| Eetu Puro | 03.07.1997 | 6 | (5) | 1 |
| Sávio Roberto Juliao Figueiredo (BRA) | 30.04.1996 | 8 | (3) | 1 |
| Maximus Tainio | 24.05.2001 | 7 | (8) | 1 |
| **Forwards:** | **DOB** | **M** | **(s)** | **G** |
| Mosawer Ahadi | 08.03.2000 | 3 | (5) | |
| Jusif Ali | 04.05.2000 | 15 | (10) | 1 |
| Michael Bakare (ENG) | 01.12.1986 | 7 | (4) | 2 |
| Didis Lutumba-Pitah | 13.11.1998 | 7 | (12) | 1 |
| Eero Markkanen | 03.07.1991 | 11 | (12) | 3 |
| Ifeanyi David Onyeanula (NGA) | 13.07.2000 | 3 | (3) | 2 |

## Football Club Lahti

| Goalkeepers: | DOB | M | (s) | G |
|---|---|---|---|---|
| Antonio Reguero Chapinal (ESP) | 04.07.1982 | 19 | | |
| Joona Tiainen | 07.05.2000 | 8 | (1) | |
| **Defenders:** | **DOB** | **M** | **(s)** | **G** |
| Alan Henrique Ferreira Bastos Soares (BRA) | 19.06.1991 | 2 | (4) | |
| Martinos Christofi (CYP) | 26.07.1993 | 11 | (4) | |
| Lassi Järvenpää | 28.10.1996 | 8 | (1) | |
| Arian Kabashi (KOS) | 26.09.1996 | 8 | (1) | |
| Daniel Koskipalo | 03.05.2003 | 2 | (1) | |
| Kevin Kouassivi-Benissan | 25.01.1999 | 19 | (2) | 1 |
| Hysen Memolla (ALB) | 03.07.1992 | 22 | (4) | |
| Teemu Penninkangas | 24.07.1992 | 20 | (2) | 3 |
| Juho Pirttijoki | 30.07.1996 | 16 | (1) | 1 |
| Akseli Puukko | 24.08.2006 | 1 | | |
| **Midfielders:** | **DOB** | **M** | **(s)** | **G** |
| Nemanja Bosančić (SRB) | 01.03.1995 | 1 | (3) | |
| Eduards Emsis (LVA) | 23.02.1996 | 18 | | |

| Founded: | 1996 | | |
|---|---|---|---|
| Stadium: | Lahden Stadion, Lahti (7,465) | | |
| Trainer: | Ilir Zeneli | 15.01.1984 | |
| [26.06.2022] | Mikko Mannila | 02.03.1975 | |

| | DOB | M | (s) | G |
|---|---|---|---|---|
| Arttu Heinonen | 22.04.1999 | 11 | (8) | 1 |
| Loorents Hertsi | 13.11.1992 | 15 | (5) | 1 |
| Viljami Jokiranta | 23.07.2006 | | (1) | |
| Matti Klinga | 10.12.1994 | 15 | (5) | 2 |
| Berat Köse | 26.10.1999 | | (3) | 1 |
| Samuel Pasanen | 02.01.2006 | 1 | (2) | 2 |
| Eemeli Virta | 28.09.2000 | 19 | (3) | |
| **Forwards:** | **DOB** | **M** | **(s)** | **G** |
| Albion Ademi (ALB) | 19.02.1999 | 9 | (5) | |
| Chinedu Charles Geoffrey (NGA) | 01.10.1997 | 18 | (7) | 4 |
| Onni Hänninen | 29.04.2005 | 2 | (3) | |
| Macoumba Kandji (SEN) | 02.08.1985 | 12 | (12) | 3 |
| Pyry Lampinen | 07.03.2002 | 7 | (8) | 2 |
| Dennis Salanović (LIE) | 26.02.1996 | 3 | (3) | |
| Arlind Sejdiu | 11.08.2001 | 10 | (11) | 1 |
| Altin Zeqiri (KOS) | 01.03.2000 | 20 | (5) | 3 |

## Idrottsföreningen Kamraterna Mariehamn

Founded: 1919
Stadium: Wiklöf Holding Arena, Mariehamn (4,000)
Trainer: Daniel Norrmén (SWE)    11.02.1975

| Goalkeepers: | DOB | M | (s) | G |
|---|---|---|---|---|
| Yann-Alexandre Fillion (CAN) | 14.02.1996 | 9 | | |
| Elmo Henriksson | 10.03.2003 | 18 | | |
| **Defenders:** | **DOB** | **M** | **(s)** | **G** |
| Jean-Christophe Coubronne (FRA) | 30.07.1989 | 22 | (1) | |
| Eddie Albin Alexander Granlund | 01.09.1989 | 5 | (1) | 1 |
| Melvin Kahnberg | 26.11.2003 | 2 | (4) | |
| Timi Lahti | 28.06.1990 | 20 | | 1 |
| Baba Mensah (GHA) | 20.08.1994 | 9 | (8) | 1 |
| Jiri Nissinen | 30.05.1997 | 19 | (5) | |
| Patrik Raitanen | 13.06.2001 | 11 | (2) | |
| Mikko Sumusalo | 12.03.1990 | 16 | (1) | 1 |
| **Midfielders:** | **DOB** | **M** | **(s)** | **G** |
| Mohammed Abubakari (GHA) | 15.02.1986 | 17 | (1) | 2 |
| Leo Andersson | 11.06.2004 | | (1) | |
| Yanga Baliso (RSA) | 27.03.1997 | 20 | (4) | 1 |
| Jamie Ryan Hopcutt (ENG) | 23.06.1992 | 7 | (1) | 2 |
| Joakim Latonen | 24.02.1998 | 12 | (8) | 2 |
| Thadée Alvaro Ngamba (CMR) | 15.12.1998 | 18 | (5) | 1 |
| Robin Sid | 21.09.1994 | 17 | (7) | 2 |
| Oscar Wiklöf | 29.01.2003 | 1 | (5) | |
| **Forwards:** | **DOB** | **M** | **(s)** | **G** |
| Cledson Carvalho da Silva „Dé" (BRA) | 06.02.1998 | 21 | (4) | 9 |
| Luis Felipe Queiroz dos Santos (BRA) | 15.09.2000 | 1 | (6) | |
| Vahid Hambo | 03.02.1995 | 5 | (16) | 2 |
| Muhamed Tehe Olawale (CIV) | 20.02.1999 | 6 | (6) | 2 |
| John Owoeri (NGA) | 13.01.1987 | 19 | (3) | 11 |
| Riku Sjöroos | 10.03.1995 | 14 | (6) | 2 |
| Eero Tamminen | 19.05.1995 | 8 | (5) | 1 |

## Kuopion Palloseura

Founded: 1923
Stadium: Savon Sanomat Areena, Kuopio (5,000)
Trainer: Simo Valakari    28.04.1973

| Goalkeepers: | DOB | M | (s) | G |
|---|---|---|---|---|
| Johannes Kreidl (AUT) | 07.03.1996 | 23 | | |
| Otso Virtanen | 03.04.1994 | 4 | (1) | |
| **Defenders:** | **DOB** | **M** | **(s)** | **G** |
| Felipe Aspegren Berhönnr | 12.02.1994 | | (2) | |
| Daniel José Carrillo Montilla (VEN) | 02.12.1995 | 19 | (1) | 2 |
| Taneli Hämäläinen | 16.04.2001 | 15 | (1) | |
| Samuli Miettinen | 16.06.2004 | | (2) | |
| Tony Miettinen | 23.09.2002 | 2 | (2) | |
| Musah Nuhu (GHA) | 17.01.1997 | 3 | | |
| Paulo Ricardo Ferreira (BRA) | 13.07.1994 | 24 | | |
| Saku Savolainen | 13.08.1996 | 6 | (6) | 1 |
| Henri Toivomäki | 21.02.1991 | 16 | (3) | 1 |
| Diogo Alberto Soares Tomas | 31.07.1997 | 24 | (2) | 1 |
| Henry Uzochukwu Unuorah (NGA) | 22.01.1999 | 8 | (5) | |
| **Midfielders:** | **DOB** | **M** | **(s)** | **G** |
| Clinton Antwi (GHA) | 06.11.1999 | 14 | (4) | 3 |
| Sebastian Dahlström | 05.11.1996 | 14 | (5) | 1 |
| Gabriel Bispo dos Santos (BRA) | 05.03.1997 | 17 | (6) | 6 |
| Jānis Ikaunieks (LVA) | 16.02.1995 | 21 | (2) | 8 |
| Christian Tue Jensen (DEN) | 09.03.2000 | | (4) | |
| Jaakko Tapio Oksanen | 07.11.2000 | 12 | | 2 |
| Anton Popovitch | 11.07.1996 | 23 | (1) | 2 |
| Talles Brener de Paula (BRA) | 12.05.1998 | 5 | (3) | 2 |
| Filip Valenčič (SVN) | 07.01.1992 | 5 | (4) | |
| Joona Veteli | 21.04.1995 | 11 | (4) | 2 |
| Axel Vidjeskog | 14.04.2001 | 4 | (5) | 1 |
| **Forwards:** | **DOB** | **M** | **(s)** | **G** |
| Santeri Haarala | 17.12.1999 | 3 | (11) | |
| Iiro Järvinen | 03.11.1996 | 5 | (4) | |
| Okko Nenonen | 14.02.2004 | | (1) | |
| Nika Sitchinava (GEO) | 17.07.1994 | | (4) | |
| Tim Väyrynen | 30.03.1993 | 19 | (5) | 11 |

## Seinäjoen Jalkapallokerho

Founded: 05.11.2007
Stadium: OmaSP Stadion, Seinäjoki (6,000)
Trainer: Joaquín Gómez Blasco (ESP)    25.07.1986

| Goalkeepers: | DOB | M | (s) | G |
|---|---|---|---|---|
| Jesse Öst | 20.10.1990 | 16 | | |
| Markus Uusitalo | 15.05.1997 | 11 | (1) | |
| **Defenders:** | **DOB** | **M** | **(s)** | **G** |
| Felipe Aspegren Berhönnr | 12.02.1994 | 9 | (1) | |
| Bradley Diallo (FRA) | 20.07.1990 | 2 | (2) | |
| Babacar Fati (POR) | 01.02.2000 | 1 | (7) | |
| Martti Haukioja | 06.10.1994 | 11 | (1) | |
| Matej Hradecký | 17.04.1995 | 23 | (1) | 1 |
| Niko Markkula | 27.06.1990 | 10 | (2) | |
| Pablo Andrade Plaza da Silva (BRA) | 15.02.1994 | 14 | (3) | |
| Ville Tikkanen | 08.08.1999 | 16 | (3) | 1 |
| Matias Vainionpää | 02.10.2001 | 11 | (1) | 1 |
| Cristian Camilo Valencia Cifuentes (COL) | 04.12.1991 | 4 | | 1 |
| **Midfielders:** | **DOB** | **M** | **(s)** | **G** |
| Alfie Bates (ENG) | 03.05.2001 | 12 | (1) | |
| Jake Dunwoody (NIR) | 28.09.1998 | 17 | (7) | |
| Valentin Román Gasc (ARG) | 09.10.2000 | | (6) | |
| Vertti Hänninen | 01.06.2002 | | (5) | |
| Pyry Hannola | 21.10.2001 | 19 | (3) | |
| Mehmet Hetemaj | 08.12.1987 | 8 | (6) | |
| Nooa Laine | 22.11.2002 | 16 | (5) | 1 |
| Diego Nicolás Rojas Orellana (CHI) | 15.02.1995 | 17 | (5) | 3 |
| Moshtagh Hossain Yaghoubi | 08.11.1994 | 6 | (2) | |
| **Forwards:** | **DOB** | **M** | **(s)** | **G** |
| Serge Atakayi | 30.01.1999 | 4 | (5) | |
| Daniel Noel Mikael Håkans | 26.10.2000 | 12 | (3) | 1 |
| Eemeli Honkola | 28.01.2005 | | (1) | |
| Jake Mario Jervis (ENG) | 17.09.1991 | 12 | (5) | 6 |
| Tuomas Kaukua | 13.10.2000 | 13 | (8) | 5 |
| José Pablo Monreal Villablanca (CHI) | 01.04.1996 | 9 | (8) | 3 |
| Jonathan Muzinga | 10.11.2002 | 1 | | |
| Samson Ebuka Obioha (NGA) | 29.11.1999 | 5 | (9) | 1 |
| Kingsley Ofori (GHA) | 01.03.2002 | 10 | (7) | |
| Denys Oliynyk (UKR) | 16.06.1987 | 7 | (3) | 3 |
| Rafał Wolsztyński (POL) | 08.12.1994 | 1 | (4) | 1 |

## Vaasan Palloseura

Founded: 1924
Stadium: Hietalahden jalkapallostadion, Vaasa (6,005)
Trainer: Jussi Nuorela    11.08.1974

| Goalkeepers: | DOB | M | (s) | G |
|---|---|---|---|---|
| Oskari Forsman | 28.01.1988 | 18 | (1) | |
| Teppo Marttinen | 06.05.1997 | 9 | | |
| **Defenders:** | **DOB** | **M** | **(s)** | **G** |
| Jesper Engström | 24.04.1992 | 18 | (2) | 2 |
| Kareem Moses (TRI) | 11.02.1990 | 8 | (7) | |
| Luis Carlos Murillo (COL) | 16.10.1990 | 4 | | |
| Miika Niemi | 04.03.1994 | 10 | (14) | |
| Josep Nuorela | 19.06.2003 | 2 | (6) | |
| Juhani Pikkarainen | 30.07.1998 | 22 | | 2 |
| Mikko Pitkänen | 02.01.1997 | 24 | (1) | 2 |
| Tyler Reid (ENG) | 02.09.1997 | 22 | | 2 |
| Gabriel Sillanpää | 08.09.2005 | | (2) | |
| **Midfielders:** | **DOB** | **M** | **(s)** | **G** |
| Prosper Ahiabu (GHA) | 10.05.1999 | 26 | | |
| Gustaf Backaliden (SWE) | 15.09.1997 | 4 | (7) | |
| Samuel Lindeman | 29.12.1997 | 22 | | |
| Arttu Nuutinen | 29.07.1996 | | (1) | |
| Aleksi Pahkasalo | 18.07.1992 | 10 | (9) | 6 |
| Antti-Ville Räisänen | 04.04.1998 | 6 | (10) | 1 |
| Samba Sillah | 10.01.1999 | 14 | | 1 |
| Sebastian Strandvall | 16.09.1986 | 7 | (2) | 2 |
| Joonas Vahtera | 06.01.1996 | 12 | (7) | 5 |
| **Forwards:** | **DOB** | **M** | **(s)** | **G** |
| Samu Alanko | 16.05.1998 | 6 | (6) | 1 |
| Roni Hudd | 20.01.2005 | 1 | (14) | 1 |
| Riku Jääskä | 04.02.1998 | 2 | (7) | 1 |
| Steven Morrissey (JAM) | 25.07.1986 | 3 | (14) | 5 |
| Kalle Multanen | 07.04.1989 | 23 | (3) | 14 |
| Tete Yengi (AUS) | 28.11.2000 | 24 | | 7 |

## SECOND LEVEL
### Ykkönen 2022

#### Regular Season

| | | | | | | | | | |
|---|---|---|---|---|---|---|---|---|---|
| 1. | Kotkan Työväen Palloilijat | 22 | 14 | 4 | 4 | 44 | - | 20 | 46 |
| 2. | Turun Palloseura Turku | 22 | 13 | 6 | 3 | 39 | - | 16 | 45 |
| 3. | FF Jaro Jakobstad | 22 | 10 | 5 | 7 | 43 | - | 25 | 35 |
| 4. | Ekenäs IF | 22 | 8 | 8 | 6 | 39 | - | 34 | 32 |
| 5. | Kokkolan Palloveikot | 22 | 8 | 8 | 6 | 24 | - | 32 | 32 |
| 6. | JäPS Järvenpää | 22 | 9 | 4 | 9 | 31 | - | 39 | 31 |
| 7. | IF Gnistan Helsinki | 22 | 8 | 6 | 8 | 35 | - | 31 | 30 |
| 8. | Mikkelin Palloilijat | 22 | 7 | 6 | 9 | 35 | - | 33 | 27 |
| 9. | SJK Akatemia Seinäjoki | 22 | 6 | 7 | 9 | 31 | - | 32 | 25 |
| 10. | PePo Lappeenranta | 22 | 6 | 6 | 10 | 25 | - | 38 | 24 |
| 11. | PK-35 Helsinki | 22 | 5 | 7 | 10 | 28 | - | 44 | 22 |
| 12. | PIF Parainen | 22 | 4 | 1 | 17 | 21 | - | 51 | 13 |

Team ranked 1-6 were qualified for the Promotion Group, while teams ranked 7-12 were qualified for the Relegation Group.

#### Promotion Group

| | | | | | | | | | |
|---|---|---|---|---|---|---|---|---|---|
| 1. | Kotkan Työväen Palloilijat (*Promoted*) | 27 | 17 | 4 | 6 | 60 | - | 28 | 55 |
| 2. | Turun Palloseura Turku (*Promotion Play-offs*) | 27 | 15 | 7 | 5 | 47 | - | 23 | 52 |
| 3. | FF Jaro Jakobstad (*Promotion Play-offs*) | 27 | 15 | 5 | 7 | 55 | - | 29 | 50 |
| 4. | Ekenäs IF (*Promotion Play-offs*) | 27 | 10 | 8 | 9 | 46 | - | 41 | 38 |
| 5. | Kokkolan Palloveikot | 27 | 9 | 9 | 9 | 32 | - | 45 | 36 |
| 6. | JäPS Järvenpää | 27 | 10 | 4 | 13 | 37 | - | 57 | 34 |

#### Relegation Group

| | | | | | | | | | |
|---|---|---|---|---|---|---|---|---|---|
| 7. | IF Gnistan Helsinki | 27 | 11 | 7 | 9 | 45 | - | 38 | 40 |
| 8. | Mikkelin Palloilijat | 27 | 10 | 6 | 11 | 48 | - | 42 | 36 |
| 9. | SJK Akatemia Seinäjoki | 27 | 9 | 8 | 10 | 43 | - | 40 | 35 |
| 10. | PK-35 Helsinki (*Relegated*) | 27 | 8 | 7 | 12 | 36 | - | 52 | 31 |
| 11. | PePo Lappeenranta (*Relegated*) | 27 | 7 | 6 | 14 | 34 | - | 56 | 27 |
| 12. | PIF Parainen (*Relegated*) | 27 | 5 | 1 | 21 | 29 | - | 61 | 16 |

#### Promotion Play-offs

| | | |
|---|---|---|
| **Semi-Finals [12.10.2022]** | FF Jaro Jakobstad - Ekenäs IF | 2-1(2-1) |
| **Final [17.10.2022]** | Turun Palloseura Turku - FF Jaro Jakobstad | 4-0(2-0) |

## NATIONAL TEAM

### INTERNATIONAL MATCHES
#### (16.07.2022 – 15.07.2023)

| | | | | |
|---|---|---|---|---|
| 23.09.2022 | Helsinki | *Finland - Romania* | *1-1(1-0)* | (UNL) |
| 26.09.2022 | Podgorica | *Montenegro - Finland* | *0-2(0-0)* | (UNL) |
| 17.11.2022 | Skopje | *North Macedonia - Finland* | *1-1(0-1)* | (F) |
| 20.11.2022 | Oslo | *Norway - Finland* | *1-1(0-1)* | (F) |
| 09.01.2023 | Faro/Loulé | *Sweden - Finland* | *2-0(1-0)* | (F) |
| 12.01.2023 | Albufeira | *Finland - Estonia* | *0-1(0-0)* | (F) |
| 23.03.2023 | København | *Denmark - Finland* | *3-1(1-0)* | (ECQ) |
| 26.03.2023 | Belfast | *Northern Ireland - Finland* | *0-1(0-1)* | (ECQ) |
| 16.06.2023 | Helsinki | *Finland - Slovenia* | *2-0(1-0)* | (ECQ) |
| 19.06.2023 | Helsinki | *Finland - San Marino* | *6-0(2-0)* | (ECQ) |

**23.09.2022     FINLAND - ROMANIA**                **1-1(1-0)**                3rd UEFA Nations League B, Group 3

Olympiastadion, Helsinki; Referee: Carlos del Cerro Grande (Spain); Attendance: 20,130
**FIN:** Lukáš Hrádecký (Cap), Nikolai Aleksanteri Alho, Robert Ivanov, Richard Olav Jensen, Leo Onni Artturi Väisänen, Jere Juhani Uronen (87.Ilmari Niskanen), Rasmus Schüller (88.Kasper Kaan Kairinen), Glen Adjei Kamara , Onni Valakari (58.Lucas Lingman), Hans Fredrik Jensen (57.Benjamin Källman), Teemu Eino Antero Pukki (75.Joel Julius Ilmari Pohjanpalo). Trainer: Markku Tapio Kanerva.
**Goal:** Teemu Eino Antero Pukki (12).

**26.09.2022     MONTENEGRO - FINLAND**                **0-2(0-0)**                3rd UEFA Nations League B, Group 3

Stadion pod Goricom, Podgorica; Referee: François Letexier (France); Attendance: 2,522
**FIN:** Lukáš Hrádecký (Cap), Nikolai Aleksanteri Alho, Leo Onni Artturi Väisänen, Robert Ivanov, Richard Olav Jensen, Kasper Kaan Kairinen, Lucas Lingman (46.Joel Julius Ilmari Pohjanpalo), Glen Adjei Kamara , Benjamin Källman (74.Santeri Hostikka), Teemu Eino Antero Pukki (74.Marcus Forss), Oliver Antman (88.Pyry Henri Hidipo Soiri). Trainer: Markku Tapio Kanerva.
**Goals:** Oliver Antman (47), Benjamin Källman (53).

**17.11.2022**    **NORTH MACEDONIA - FINLAND**        **1-1(0-1)**        Friendly International
Nacionalna Arena "Toše Proeski", Skopje; Referee: Novak Simović (Serbia); Attendance: 2,000
**FIN:** Jesse Pekka Joronen, Nikolai Aleksanteri Alho (72.Diogo Alberto Soares Tomas), Robert Ivanov, Arttu Hoskonen, Tuomas Ollila (90+1.Ilmari Niskanen), Lucas Lingman (58.Niilo Mäenpää), Anssi Tapio Suhonen, Robert Thomas Taylor (72.Santeri Hostikka), Robin Lod (61.Mikael Antero Soisalo), Joel Julius Ilmari Pohjanpalo (Cap), Oliver Antman (83.Marcus Forss). Trainer: Markku Tapio Kanerva.
**Goal:** Oliver Antman (37).

**20.11.2022**    **NORWAY - FINLAND**        **1-1(0-1)**        Friendly International
Ullevaal Stadion, Oslo; Referee: Morten Krogh (Denmark); Attendance: 13,347
**FIN:** Lukáš Hrádecký (Cap), Leo Onni Artturi Väisänen (84.Diogo Alberto Soares Tomas), Robert Ivanov (76.Arttu Hoskonen), Daniel Michael O'Shaughnessy (61.Sauli Aapo Kasperi Väisänen), Pyry Henri Hidipo Soiri (90+1.Nikolai Aleksanteri Alho), Anssi Tapio Suhonen, Robin Lod (61.Lucas Lingman), Niilo Mäenpää, Ilmari Niskanen, Marcus Forss (83.Oliver Antman), Benjamin Källman. Trainer: Markku Tapio Kanerva.
**Goal:** Benjamin Källman (32).

**09.01.2023**    **SWEDEN - FINLAND**        **2-0(1-0)**        Friendly International
Estádio Algarve, Faro/Loulé (Portugal); Referee: Vitor Jorge Fernandes Ferreira (Portugal); Attendance: n/a
**FIN:** Lucas Carl Edvard Bergström, Richard Olav Jensen (Cap), Arttu Hoskonen, Robert Ivanov, Pyry Henri Hidipo Soiri (65.Felipe Aspegren Berhönnr), Niilo Mäenpää (65.Rasmus Schüller), Lucas Lingman (65.Santeri Hostikka), Santeri Väänänen, Tomas Galvez, Kai Meriluoto (77.Anthony Olusanya), Agon Sadiku. Trainer: Markku Tapio Kanerva.

**12.01.2023**    **FINLAND - ESTONIA**        **0-1(0-0)**        Friendly International
Estadio da Nora, Albufeira (Portugal); Referee: Gustavo Fernandes Correia (Portugal); Attendance: n/a
**FIN:** Viljami Kari Veikko Sinisalo, Robin Amin Tihi, Ville Koski, Diogo Alberto Soares Tomas, Noah Pallas, Rasmus Schüller (Cap) (72.Santeri Väänänen), Matti Peltola (72.Lucas Lingman), Jaakko Tapio Oksanen (90.Pyry Henri Hidipo Soiri), Santeri Hostikka (46.Kai Meriluoto), Saku Ylätupa (72.Agon Sadiku), Anthony Olusanya. Trainer: Markku Tapio Kanerva.

**23.03.2023**    **DENMARK - FINLAND**        **3-1(1-0)**        17th EC. Qualifiers
Parken Stadium, København; Referee: Daniel Siebert (Germany); Attendance: 35,851
**FIN:** Lukáš Hrádecký (Cap), Nikolai Aleksanteri Alho, Leo Onni Artturi Väisänen, Robert Ivanov, Richard Olav Jensen (73.Tuomas Ollila), Kasper Kaan Kairinen, Glen Adjei Kamara , Robin Lod (73.Marcus Forss), Oliver Antman (72.Anssi Tapio Suhonen), Joel Julius Ilmari Pohjanpalo, Teemu Eino Antero Pukki. Trainer: Markku Tapio Kanerva.
**Goal:** Oliver Antman (53).

**26.03.2023**    **NORTHERN IRELAND - FINLAND**        **0-1(0-1)**        17th EC. Qualifiers
Windsor Park, Belfast; Referee: Ivan Kružliak (Slovakia); Attendance: 17,936
**FIN:** Lukáš Hrádecký (Cap), Nikolai Aleksanteri Alho (86.Robert Thomas Taylor), Leo Onni Artturi Väisänen, Robert Ivanov, Richard Olav Jensen (52.Matti Peltola), Rasmus Schüller, Glen Adjei Kamara , Robin Lod, Anssi Tapio Suhonen (70.Pyry Henri Hidipo Soiri), Benjamin Källman (86.Joel Julius Ilmari Pohjanpalo), Teemu Eino Antero Pukki (70.Marcus Forss). Trainer: Markku Tapio Kanerva.
**Goal:** Benjamin Källman (28).

**16.06.2023**    **FINLAND - SLOVENIA**        **2-0(1-0)**        17th EC. Qualifiers
Olympiastadion, Helsinki; Referee: Guillermo Cuadra Fernández (Spain); Attendance: 32,560
**FIN:** Lukáš Hrádecký (Cap), Richard Olav Jensen (65.Matti Peltola), Arttu Hoskonen, Robert Ivanov, Nikolai Aleksanteri Alho (71.Jere Juhani Uronen), Rasmus Schüller (79.Glen Adjei Kamara ), Kasper Kaan Kairinen, Ilmari Niskanen, Oliver Antman (79.Anssi Tapio Suhonen), Joel Julius Ilmari Pohjanpalo, Teemu Eino Antero Pukki (65.Daniel Noel Mikael Håkans). Trainer: Markku Tapio Kanerva.
**Goals:** Joel Julius Ilmari Pohjanpalo (13), Oliver Antman (64).

**19.06.2023**    **FINLAND - SAN MARINO**        **6-0(2-0)**        17th EC. Qualifiers
Olympiastadion, Helsinki; Referee: Genc Nuza (Kosovo); Attendance: 32,812
**FIN:** Lukáš Hrádecký (Cap), Nikolai Aleksanteri Alho (81.Pyry Henri Hidipo Soiri), Robert Ivanov, Diogo Alberto Soares Tomas, Jere Juhani Uronen (46.Noah Pallas), Rasmus Schüller (60.Robert Thomas Taylor), Anssi Tapio Suhonen, Glen Adjei Kamara , Oliver Antman (60.Daniel Noel Mikael Håkans), Benjamin Källman, Joel Julius Ilmari Pohjanpalo (60.Teemu Eino Antero Pukki). Trainer: Markku Tapio Kanerva.
**Goals:** Glen Adjei Kamara (16), Benjamin Källman (39), Daniel Noel Mikael Håkans (65, 72, 74), Teemu Eino Antero Pukki (76).

| NATIONAL TEAM PLAYERS (16.07.2022 – 15.07.2023) | | | | |
|---|---|---|---|---|
| **Name** | **DOB** | **Caps** | **Goals** | **Club** |
| Goalkeepers | | | | |
| Lucas Carl Edvard BERGSTRÖM | 05.09.2002 | 1 | 0 | 2023: *Peterborough United FC (ENG)* |
| Lukáš HRÁDECKÝ | 24.11.1989 | 85 | 0 | 2022/2023: *Bayer 04 Leverkusen (GER)* |
| Jesse Pekka JORONEN | 21.03.1993 | 17 | 0 | 2022: *Venezia FC (ITA)* |
| Viljami Kari Veikko SINISALO | 11.10.2001 | 1 | 0 | 2023: *Burton Albion FC (ENG)* |
| Defenders | | | | |
| Nikolai Aleksanteri ALHO | 12.03.1993 | 29 | 0 | 2022/2023: *Vólos NPS (GRE)* |
| Felipe ASPEGREN Berhönnr | 12.02.1994 | 1 | 0 | 2023: *SJK Seinäjoki* |
| Tomas GALVEZ | 28.01.2005 | 1 | 0 | 2023: *Manchester City FC (ENG)* |
| Arttu HOSKONEN | 16.04.1997 | 4 | 0 | 2022: *HJK Helsinki* 23.01.2023-> *KS Cracovia Kraków (POL)* |
| Robert IVANOV | 19.09.1994 | 22 | 0 | 2022/2023: *KS Warta Poznań (POL)* |
| Richard Olav JENSEN | 17.03.1996 | 9 | 0 | 2022/2023: *KS Górnik Zabrze (POL)* |

| | | | | | |
|---|---|---|---|---|---|
| Ville KOSKI | 27.01.2002 | 1 | 0 | 2023: | FC Honka Espoo |
| Daniel Michael O'SHAUGHNESSY | 14.09.1994 | 22 | 1 | 2022: | Karlsruher SC (GER) |
| Tuomas OLLILA | 25.04.2000 | 2 | 0 | 2022: | FC Ilves Tampere |
| | | | | 01.01.2023-> | HJK Helsinki |
| Noah PALLAS | 09.02.2001 | 2 | 0 | 2023: | AC Oulu |
| Pyry Henri Hidipo SOIRI | 22.09.1994 | 40 | 5 | 2022/2023: | HJK Helsinki |
| Robin Amin TIHI | 16.03.2002 | 1 | 0 | 2023: | AIK Stockholm (SWE) |
| Diogo Alberto Soares TOMAS | 31.07.1997 | 4 | 0 | 2022: | Kuopion Palloseura |
| | | | | 04.03.2023-> | Odds BK Skien (NOR) |
| Jere Juhani URONEN | 13.07.1994 | 63 | 1 | 2022: | Stade Brestois 29 (FRA) |
| | | | | 07.01.2023-> | FC Schalke 04 Gelsenkirchen (GER) |
| Leo Onni Artturi VÄISÄNEN | 23.07.1997 | 25 | 0 | 2022: | IF Elfsborg Borås (SWE) |
| | | | | 31.01.2023-> | Austin FC (USA) |
| Sauli Aapo Kasperi VÄISÄNEN | 05.06.1994 | 23 | 0 | 2022: | Cosenza Calcio (ITA) |

| | | | | | |
|---|---|---|---|---|---|
| **Midfielders** | | | | | |
| Oliver ANTMAN | 15.08.2001 | 6 | 4 | 2022: | FC Nordsjælland Farum (DEN) |
| | | | | 31.01.2023-> | FC Groningen (NED) |
| Daniel Noel Mikael HÅKANS | 26.10.2000 | 2 | 3 | 2023: | Vålerenga Fotball Oslo (NOR) |
| Hans Fredrik JENSEN | 09.09.1997 | 26 | 7 | 2022: | FC Augsburg (GER) |
| Kasper Kaan KAIRINEN | 22.12.1998 | 9 | 0 | 2022: | Lillestrøm SK (NOR) |
| | | | | 01.01.2023-> | AC Sparta Praha (CZE) |
| Glen Adjei KAMARA | 28.10.1995 | 52 | 2 | 2022/2023: | Rangers FC Glasgow (SCO) |
| Benjamin KÄLLMAN | 17.06.1998 | 12 | 6 | 2022/2023: | KS Cracovia Kraków (POL) |
| Lucas LINGMAN | 25.01.1998 | 9 | 0 | 2022/2023: | HJK Helsinki |
| Robin LOD | 17.04.1993 | 62 | 5 | 2022/2023: | Minnesota United FC (USA) |
| Niilo MÄENPÄÄ | 14.01.1998 | 3 | 0 | 2022/2023: | KS Warta Poznań (POL) |
| Ilmari NISKANEN | 27.10.1997 | 14 | 1 | 2022/2023: | Dundee United FC (SCO) |
| Jaakko Tapio OKSANEN | 07.11.2000 | 1 | 0 | 2023: | Kuopion Palloseura |
| Matti PELTOLA | 03.07.2002 | 3 | 0 | 2023: | HJK Helsinki |
| Rasmus SCHÜLLER | 18.06.1991 | 69 | 0 | 2022/2023: | Djurgårdens IF Stockholm (SWE) |
| Mikael Antero SOISALO | 24.04.1998 | 4 | 0 | 2022: | Rīga FC (LVA) |
| Anssi Tapio SUHONEN | 14.01.2001 | 6 | 0 | 2022/2023: | Hamburger SV (GER) |
| Onni VALAKARI | 18.08.1999 | 11 | 1 | 2022: | Pafos FC Paphos (CYP) |
| Santeri VÄÄNÄNEN | 01.01.2002 | 2 | 0 | 2023: | Rosenborg BK Trondheim (NOR) |

| | | | | | |
|---|---|---|---|---|---|
| **Forwards** | | | | | |
| Marcus FORSS | 18.06.1999 | 19 | 2 | 2022/2023: | Middlesbrough FC (ENG) |
| Santeri HOSTIKKA | 30.09.1997 | 6 | 0 | 2022/2023: | HJK Helsinki |
| Kai MERILUOTO | 02.01.2003 | 2 | 0 | 2023: | HJK Helsinki |
| Anthony OLUSANYA | 01.02.2000 | 2 | 0 | 2023: | HJK Helsinki |
| Joel Julius Ilmari POHJANPALO | 13.09.1994 | 63 | 14 | 2022/2023: | Venezia FC (ITA) |
| Teemu Eino Antero PUKKI | 29.03.1990 | 112 | 38 | 2022/2023: | Norwich City FC (ENG) |
| Agon SADIKU | 10.03.2003 | 2 | 0 | 2023: | FC Honka Espoo |
| Robert Thomas TAYLOR | 21.10.1994 | 29 | 1 | 2022/2023: | CIF Miami (USA) |
| Saku YLÄTUPA | 04.08.1999 | 3 | 0 | 2023: | GIF Sundsvall (SWE) |

| | | | | | |
|---|---|---|---|---|---|
| **Trainer** | | | | | |
| Markku Tapio KANERVA [from 12.12.2016] | | 24.05.1964 | 73 M; 32 W; 13 D; 28 L; 88-75 | | |

Complete record as trainer of Finland:
79 M; 34 W; 16 D; 29 L; 93-80
(09.02.2011 – 29.03.2011) & (04.09.2015 – 11.10.2015) &
(09.01.2017 – 19.06.2023)

# FRANCE

**F F F**

| | |
|---|---|
| **The Country:** | |

French Republic (République française)
Capital: Paris
Surface: 643,801 km²
Inhabitants: 68,042,591 [2023]
Time: UTC+1

**The FA:**
Fédération Française de Football
87, Boulevard de Grenelle, 75738 Paris Cedex 15
Tel: +33 1 4431 3173 00
Foundation date: 07.04.1919
Member of FIFA since: 1907
Member of UEFA since: 1954
Website: www.fff.fr

## NATIONAL TEAM RECORDS

### RECORDS
| | | |
|---|---|---|
| **First international match:** | 01.05.1994, Bruxelles: | Belgium – France 3-3 |
| **Most international caps:** | Hugo Hadrien Dominique Lloris | - 145 caps (2008-2022) |
| **Most international goals:** | Olivier Jonathan Giroud | - 54 goals / 124 caps (since 2011) |

### UEFA EUROPEAN CHAMPIONSHIP
| | |
|---|---|
| 1960 | Final Tournament (4th Place) |
| 1964 | Qualifiers |
| 1968 | Qualifiers |
| 1972 | Qualifiers |
| 1976 | Qualifiers |
| 1980 | Qualifiers |
| 1984 | **Final Tournament (Winners)** |
| 1988 | Qualifiers |
| 1992 | Final Tournament (Group Stage) |
| 1996 | Final Tournament (Semi-Finals) |
| 2000 | **Final Tournament (Winners)** |
| 2004 | Final Tournament (Quarter-Finals) |
| 2008 | Final Tournament (Group Stage) |
| 2012 | Final Tournament (Quarter-Finals) |
| 2016 | Final Tournament (Runners-up) |
| 2020 | Final Tournament (2nd Round of 16) |

### FIFA WORLD CUP
| | |
|---|---|
| 1930 | Final Tournament (Group Stage) |
| 1934 | Final Tournament (1st Round) |
| 1938 | Final Tournament (Quarter-Finals) |
| 1950 | *Withdrew* |
| 1954 | Final Tournament (Group Stage) |
| 1958 | Final Tournament (3rd Place) |
| 1962 | Qualifiers |
| 1966 | Final Tournament (Group Stage) |
| 1970 | Qualifiers |
| 1974 | Qualifiers |
| 1978 | Final Tournament (Group Stage) |
| 1982 | Final Tournament (4th Place) |
| 1986 | Final Tournament (3rd Place) |
| 1990 | Qualifiers |
| 1994 | Qualifiers |
| 1998 | **Final Tournament (Winners)** |
| 2002 | Final Tournament (Group Stage) |
| 2006 | Final Tournament (Runners-up) |
| 2010 | Final Tournament (Group Stage) |
| 2014 | Final Tournament (Quarter-Finals) |
| 2018 | **Final Tournament (Winners)** |
| 2022 | Final Tournament (Runners-up) |

### OLYMPIC TOURNAMENTS
| | |
|---|---|
| 1908 | Final Tournament |
| 1912 | - |
| 1920 | Final Tournament (Semi-Finals) |
| 1924 | Final Tournament (Quarter-Finals) |
| 1928 | 1/8-Finals |
| 1936 | - |
| 1948 | Final Tournament (Quarter-Finals) |
| 1952 | Qualifiers |
| 1956 | - |
| 1960 | Final Tournament (Group Stage) |
| 1964 | Qualifiers |
| 1968 | Final Tournament (Quarter-Finals) |
| 1972 | Qualifiers |
| 1976 | Final Tournament (Quarter-Finals) |
| 1980 | Qualifiers |
| 1984 | **Winners** |
| 1988 | Qualifiers |
| 1992 | Qualifiers |
| 1996 | Final Tournament (Quarter-Finals) |
| 2000 | Qualifiers |
| 2004 | Qualifiers |
| 2008 | Qualifiers |
| 2012 | Qualifiers |
| 2016 | Qualifiers |
| 2020 | Final Tournament (Group Stage) |

### UEFA NATIONS LEAGUE
| | |
|---|---|
| 2018/2019 | League A (Group Stage) |
| 2020/2021 | League A (Group Stage -> Final Tournament – **Winners)** |
| 2022/2023 | League A (Group Stage) |

### FIFA CONFEDERATIONS CUP 1992-2017
**2001 (Winners), 2003 (Winners)**

### FRENCH CLUB HONOURS IN EUROPEAN CLUB COMPETITIONS:

| European Champion Clubs' Cup (1956-1992) / UEFA Champions League (1993-2023) | | |
|---|---|---|
| Olympique de Marseille | 1 | 1992/1993 |

| Fairs Cup (1858-1971) / UEFA Cup (1972-2009) / UEFA Europa League (2010-2023) | | |
|---|---|---|
| None | | |

| UEFA Europa Conference League (2021-2023) | | |
|---|---|---|
| None | | |

| UEFA Super Cup (1972-2022) | | |
|---|---|---|
| None | | |

| *European Cup Winners' Cup 1961-1999\** | | |
|---|---|---|
| Paris Saint-Germain FC | 1 | 1995/1996 |

*\*defunct competition*

## NATIONAL COMPETITIONS
## TABLE OF HONOURS

| | CHAMPIONS | CUP WINNERS | BEST GOALSCORERS | |
|---|---|---|---|---|
| 1893/1894 | Standard Athletic Club Paris | - | - | |
| 1894/1895 | Standard Athletic Club Paris | - | - | |
| 1895/1896 | Club Français Paris | - | - | |
| 1896/1897 | Standard Athletic Club Paris | - | - | |
| 1897/1898 | Standard Athletic Club Paris | - | - | |
| 1898/1899 | Le Havre AC | - | - | |
| 1899/1900 | Le Havre AC | - | - | |
| 1900/1901 | Standard Athletic Club Paris | - | - | |
| 1901/1902 | Racing Club de Roubaix | - | - | |
| 1902/1903 | Racing Club de Roubaix | - | - | |
| 1903/1904 | Racing Club de Roubaix | - | - | |
| 1904/1905 | Gallia Club Paris | - | - | |
| 1905/1906 | Racing Club de Roubaix | - | - | |
| 1906/1907 | Racing Club de France Paris | - | - | |
| 1907/1908 | Racing Club de Roubaix | - | - | |
| 1908/1909 | Stade Helvétique de Marseille | - | - | |
| 1909/1910 | US Tourcoing | - | - | |
| 1910/1911 | Stade Helvétique de Marseille | - | - | |
| 1911/1912 | Stade Saint-Raphaëlois | - | - | |
| 1912/1913 | Stade Helvétique de Marseille | - | - | |
| 1913/1914 | Olympique Lillois | - | - | |
| 1914/1915 | *No competition* | - | - | |
| 1915/1916 | *No competition* | - | - | |
| 1916/1917 | *No competition* | - | - | |
| 1917/1918 | *No competition* | Olympique de Pantin | - | |
| 1918/1919 | Le Havre AC | CASG Paris | - | |
| 1919/1920 | *No competition* | Cercle Athlétique de Paris | - | |
| 1920/1921 | *No competition* | Red Star FC Paris | - | |
| 1921/1922 | *No competition* | Red Star FC Paris | - | |
| 1922/1923 | *No competition* | Red Star FC Paris | - | |
| 1923/1924 | *No competition* | Olympique de Marseille | - | |
| 1924/1925 | *No competition* | CASG Paris | - | |
| 1925/1926 | *No competition* | Olympique de Marseille | - | |
| 1926/1927 | Cercle Athlétique de Paris | Olympique de Marseille | - | |
| 1927/1928 | Stade Français Paris | Red Star FC Paris | - | |
| 1928/1929 | Olympique de Marseille | Montpellier Hérault Sport Club | - | |
| 1929/1930 | *No competition* | FC Sète | - | |
| 1930/1931 | *No competition* | Club Français Paris | - | |
| 1931/1932 | *No competition* | AS Cannes | - | |
| 1932/1933 | Olympique Lillois | Excelsior Athlétic Club de Roubaix | Walter Kaiser (GER, Stade Rennais FC) Robert Mercier (Club Français Paris) | 15 |
| 1933/1934 | FC Sète | FC Sète | István Lukács (HUN, FC Sète) | 28 |
| 1934/1935 | Sochaux | Olympique de Marseille | André Abegglen (SUI, FC Sochaux-Montbéliard) | 30 |
| 1935/1936 | Racing Club de France Paris | RC Paris | Roger Courtois (FC Sochaux-Montbéliard) | 34 |
| 1936/1937 | Olympique de Marseille | FC FC Sochaux-Montbéliard | Oskar Rohr (GER, Racing Club de Strasbourg) | 30 |
| 1937/1938 | FC Sochaux-Montbéliard | Olympique de Marseille | Jean Nicolas (FC Rouen) | 26 |
| 1938/1939 | FC Sète | Racing Club de France Paris | Roger Courtois (FC Sochaux-Montbéliard) Désiré Koranyi (FC Sète) | 27 |
| 1939/1940 | *No competition* | Racing Club de France Paris | - | |
| 1940/1941 | *No competition* | FC Girondins de Bordeaux | - | |
| 1941/1942 | *No competition* | Red Star FC Paris | - | |
| 1942/1943 | *No competition* | Olympique de Marseille | - | |
| 1943/1944 | *No competition* | Équipe fédérale Nancy-Lorraine | - | |
| 1944/1945 | *No competition* | Racing Club de France Paris | - | |
| 1945/1946 | Lille OSC | Lille OSC | René Bihel (Lille OSC) | 28 |
| 1946/1947 | Racing Club de Roubaix–Tourcoing | Lille OSC | Pierre Sinibaldi (Stade de Reims) | 33 |
| 1947/1948 | Olympique de Marseille | Lille OSC | Jean Baratte (Lille OSC) | 31 |
| 1948/1949 | Stade de Reims | Racing Club de France Paris | Jean Baratte (Lille OSC) Josef Humpál (CZE, FC Sochaux-Montbéliard) | 26 |
| 1949/1950 | FC Girondins de Bordeaux | Stade de Reims | Jean Grumellon (Stade Rennais FC) | 25 |
| 1950/1951 | OGC Nice | Racing Club de Strasbourg | Roger Piantoni (AS Nancy-Lorraine) Jean Courteaux (OGC Nice) | 27 |
| 1951/1952 | OGC Nice | OGC Nice | Gunnar Andersson (SWE, Olympique de Marseille) | 31 |
| 1952/1953 | Stade de Reims | Lille OSC | Gunnar Andersson (SWE, Olympique de Marseille) | 35 |
| 1953/1954 | Lille OSC | OGC Nice | Édouard Kargu (FC Girondins de Bordeaux) | 27 |
| 1954/1955 | Stade de Reims | Lille OSC | René Bliard (Stade de Reims) | 30 |
| 1955/1956 | OGC Nice | CS Sedan | Thadée Cisowski (Racing Club de France Paris) | 31 |
| 1956/1957 | AS Saint-Étienne | Toulouse FC | Thadée Cisowski (Racing Club de France Paris) | 33 |
| 1957/1958 | Stade de Reims | Stade de Reims | Just Fontaine (Stade de Reims) | 34 |
| 1958/1959 | OGC Nice | Le Havre AC | Thadée Cisowski (Racing Club de France Paris) | 30 |
| 1959/1960 | Stade de Reims | AS Monaco FC | Just Fontaine (Stade de Reims) | 28 |

| | | | | |
|---|---|---|---|---|
| 1960/1961 | AS Monaco FC | CS Sedan | Roger Piantoni (Stade de Reims) | 28 |
| 1961/1962 | Stade de Reims | AS Saint-Étienne | Sékou Touré (CIV, Montpellier Hérault Sport Club) | 25 |
| 1962/1963 | AS Monaco FC | AS Monaco FC | Serge Masnaghetti (USVA Valenciennes) | 35 |
| 1963/1964 | AS Saint-Étienne | Olympique Lyonnais | Ahmed Oudjani (ALG, Racing Club de Lens) | 30 |
| 1964/1965 | FC Nantes | Stade Rennais FC | Jacques Simon (FC Nantes) | 24 |
| 1965/1966 | FC Nantes | Racing Club de Strasbourg | Philippe Gondet (FC Nantes) | 36 |
| 1966/1967 | AS Saint-Étienne | Olympique Lyonnais | Hervé Revelli (AS Saint-Étienne) | 31 |
| 1967/1968 | AS Saint-Étienne | AS Saint-Étienne | Étienne Sansonetti (AC Ajaccio) | 26 |
| 1968/1969 | AS Saint-Étienne | Olympique de Marseille | André Guy (Olympique Lyonnais) | 25 |
| 1969/1970 | AS Saint-Étienne | AS Saint-Étienne | Hervé Revelli (AS Saint-Étienne) | 28 |
| 1970/1971 | Olympique de Marseille | Stade Rennais FC | Josip Skoblar (YUG, Olympique de Marseille) | 44 |
| 1971/1972 | Olympique de Marseille | Olympique de Marseille | Josip Skoblar (YUG, Olympique de Marseille) | 30 |
| 1972/1973 | FC Nantes | Olympique Lyonnais | Josip Skoblar (YUG, Olympique de Marseille) | 26 |
| 1973/1974 | AS Saint-Étienne | AS Saint-Étienne | Carlos Arcecio Bianchi (ARG, Stade de Reims) | 30 |
| 1974/1975 | AS Saint-Étienne | AS Saint-Étienne | Delio Onnis (ARG, AS Monaco FC) | 30 |
| 1975/1976 | AS Saint-Étienne | Olympique de Marseille | Carlos Arcecio Bianchi (ARG, Stade de Reims) | 34 |
| 1976/1977 | FC Nantes | AS Saint-Étienne | Carlos Arcecio Bianchi (ARG, Stade de Reims) | 28 |
| 1977/1978 | AS Monaco FC | AS Nancy-Lorraine | Carlos Arcecio Bianchi (ARG, Paris Saint-Germain FC) | 37 |
| 1978/1979 | Racing Club de Strasbourg | FC Nantes | Carlos Arcecio Bianchi (ARG, Paris Saint-Germain FC) | 27 |
| 1979/1980 | FC Nantes | AS Monaco FC | Erwin Kostedde (GER, Stade Lavallois) Delio Onnis (ARG, AS Monaco FC) | 21 |
| 1980/1981 | AS Saint-Étienne | SC Bastia | Delio Onnis (ARG, Tours FC) | 24 |
| 1981/1982 | AS Monaco FC | Paris Saint-Germain FC | Delio Onnis (ARG, Tours FC) | 29 |
| 1982/1983 | FC Nantes | Paris Saint-Germain FC | Vahid Halilhodžić (YUG, FC Nantes) | 27 |
| 1983/1984 | FC Girondins de Bordeaux | FC Metz | Patrice Garande (AJ Auxerre) Delio Onnis (ARG, Sporting Club Toulon) | 21 |
| 1984/1985 | FC Girondins de Bordeaux | AS Monaco FC | Vahid Halilhodžić (YUG, FC Nantes) | 28 |
| 1985/1986 | Paris Saint-Germain FC | FC Girondins de Bordeaux | Jules François Bocandé (SEN, FC Metz) | 23 |
| 1986/1987 | FC Girondins de Bordeaux | FC Girondins de Bordeaux | Bernard Zénier (FC Metz) | 18 |
| 1987/1988 | AS Monaco FC | FC Metz | Jean-Pierre Papin (Olympique de Marseille) | 19 |
| 1988/1989 | Olympique de Marseille | Olympique de Marseille | Jean-Pierre Papin (Olympique de Marseille) | 22 |
| 1989/1990 | Olympique de Marseille | Montpellier Hérault Sport Club | Jean-Pierre Papin (Olympique de Marseille) | 30 |
| 1990/1991 | Olympique de Marseille | AS Monaco FC | Jean-Pierre Papin (Olympique de Marseille) | 23 |
| 1991/1992 | Olympique de Marseille | *Not played to end* | Jean-Pierre Papin (Olympique de Marseille) | 27 |
| 1992/1993 | *No winner was declared by FFF* | Paris Saint-Germain FC | Alen Bokšić (CRO, Olympique de Marseille) | 22 |
| 1993/1994 | Paris Saint-Germain FC | AJ Auxerre | Roger Zokou Boli (Racing Club de Lens) Youri Djorkaeff (AS Monaco FC) Nicolas Pierre Ouédec (FC Nantes) | 20 |
| 1994/1995 | FC Nantes | Paris Saint-Germain FC | Patrice Loko (FC Nantes) | 22 |
| 1995/1996 | AJ Auxerre | AJ Auxerre | Anderson da Silva (BRA, AS Monaco FC) | 21 |
| 1996/1997 | AS Monaco FC | OGC Nice | Stéphane Pierre Yves Guivarc'h (Stade Rennais FC) | 21 |
| 1997/1998 | Racing Club de Lens | Paris Saint-Germain FC | Stéphane Pierre Yves Guivarc'h (AJ Auxerre) | 21 |
| 1998/1999 | FC Girondins de Bordeaux | FC Nantes | Sylvain Wiltord (FC Girondins de Bordeaux) | 22 |
| 1999/2000 | AS Monaco FC | FC Nantes | Anderson da Silva (BRA, Olympique Lyonnais) | 23 |
| 2000/2001 | FC Nantes | Racing Club de Strasbourg | Anderson da Silva (BRA, Olympique Lyonnais) | 22 |
| 2001/2002 | Olympique Lyonnais | FC Lorient | Djibril Cissé (AJ Auxerre) Pedro Miguel Carreiro Resendes "Pauleta" (POR, FC Girondins de Bordeaux) | 22 |
| 2002/2003 | Olympique Lyonnais | AJ Auxerre | Shabani Christophe Nonda (COD, AS Monaco FC) | 26 |
| 2003/2004 | Olympique Lyonnais | Paris Saint-Germain FC | Djibril Cissé (AJ Auxerre) | 26 |
| 2004/2005 | Olympique Lyonnais | AJ Auxerre | Alexander Frei (SUI, Stade Rennais FC) | 20 |
| 2005/2006 | Olympique Lyonnais | Paris Saint-Germain FC | Pedro Miguel Carreiro Resendes "Pauleta" (POR, Paris Saint-Germain FC) | 21 |
| 2006/2007 | Olympique Lyonnais | FC Sochaux-Montbéliard | Pedro Miguel Carreiro Resendes "Pauleta" (POR, Paris Saint-Germain FC) | 15 |
| 2007/2008 | Olympique Lyonnais | Olympique Lyonnais | Karim Mostafa Benzema (Olympique Lyonnais) | 20 |
| 2008/2009 | FC Girondins de Bordeaux | En Avant de Guingamp | André-Pierre Christian Gignac (Toulouse FC) | 24 |
| 2009/2010 | Olympique de Marseille | Paris Saint-Germain FC | Mamadou Hamidou Niang (SEN, Olympique de Marseille) | 18 |
| 2010/2011 | Lille OSC | Lille OSC | Moussa Sow (SEN, Lille OSC) | 25 |
| 2011/2012 | Montpellier Hérault Sport Club | Olympique Lyonnais | Olivier Jonathan Giroud (Montpellier Hérault SC) Anderson Luiz de Carvalho "Nenê" (BRA, Paris Saint-Germain FC) | 21 |
| 2012/2013 | Paris Saint-Germain FC | FC Girondins de Bordeaux | Zlatan Ibrahimović (SWE, Paris Saint-Germain FC) | 30 |
| 2013/2014 | Paris Saint-Germain FC | En Avant de Guingamp | Zlatan Ibrahimović (SWE, Paris Saint-Germain FC) | 26 |
| 2014/2015 | Paris Saint-Germain FC | Paris Saint-Germain FC | Alexandre Lacazette (Olympique Lyonnais) | 27 |
| 2015/2016 | Paris Saint-Germain FC | Paris Saint-Germain FC | Zlatan Ibrahimović (SWE, Paris Saint-Germain FC) | 38 |
| 2016/2017 | AS Monaco FC | Paris Saint-Germain FC | Edinson Roberto Cavani Gómez (URU, Paris Saint-Germain FC) | 35 |
| 2017/2018 | Paris Saint-Germain FC | Paris Saint-Germain FC | Edinson Roberto Cavani Gómez (URU, Paris Saint-Germain FC) | 28 |
| 2018/2019 | Paris Saint-Germain FC | Stade Rennais FC | Kylian Sanmi Mbappé Lottin (Paris Saint-Germain FC) | 33 |
| 2019/2020 | Paris Saint-Germain FC | Paris Saint-Germain FC | Wissam Ben Yedder (AS Monaco FC) Kylian Sanmi Mbappé Lottin (Paris Saint-Germain FC) | 18 |
| 2020/2021 | Lille OSC | Paris Saint-Germain FC | Kylian Sanmi Mbappé Lottin (Paris Saint-Germain FC) | 27 |
| 2021/2022 | Paris Saint-Germain FC | FC Nantes | Kylian Sanmi Mbappé Lottin (Paris Saint-Germain FC) | 28 |
| 2022/2023 | Paris Saint-Germain FC | Toulouse FC | Kylian Sanmi Mbappé Lottin (Paris Saint-Germain FC) | 29 |

| 1963/1964 | Racing Club de Strasbourg |
|---|---|
| 1964/1965 | FC Nantes |
| 1981/1982 | Stade Lavallois |
| 1983/1984 | Stade Lavallois |
| 1985/1986 | FC Metz |
| 1990/1991 | Stade de Reims |
| 1991/1992 | Montpellier Hérault Sport Club |
| 1993/1994 | Racing Club de Lens |
| 1994/1995 | Paris Saint-Germain FC |
| 1995/1996 | FC Metz |
| 1996/1997 | Racing Club de Strasbourg |
| 1997/1998 | Paris Saint-Germain FC |

| 1998/1999 | Racing Club de Lens |
|---|---|
| 1999/2000 | FC Gueugnon |
| 2000/2001 | Olympique Lyonnais |
| 2001/2002 | FC Girondins de Bordeaux |
| 2002/2003 | AS Monaco FC |
| 2003/2004 | FC Sochaux-Montbéliard |
| 2004/2005 | Racing Club de Strasbourg |
| 2005/2006 | AS Nancy-Lorraine |
| 2006/2007 | FC Girondins de Bordeaux |
| 2007/2008 | Paris Saint-Germain FC |
| 2008/2009 | FC Girondins de Bordeaux |

| 2009/2010 | Olympique de Marseille |
|---|---|
| 2010/2011 | Olympique de Marseille |
| 2011/2012 | Olympique de Marseille |
| 2012/2013 | AS Saint-Étienne |
| 2013/2014 | Paris Saint-Germain FC |
| 2014/2015 | Paris Saint-Germain FC |
| 2015/2016 | Paris Saint-Germain FC |
| 2016/2017 | Paris Saint-Germain FC |
| 2017/2018 | Paris Saint-Germain FC |
| 2018/2019 | Racing Club de Strasbourg |
| 2019/2020 | Paris Saint-Germain FC |

*Competition called: Coupe de la Ligue (1963–1965), Coupe d'Été/Coupe de la Ligue (1982–1994) and Coupe de la Ligue (1994-2020).

## NATIONAL CHAMPIONSHIP
### Ligue 1 2022/2023
(05.08.2022 – 03.06.2023)

### Results

**Round 1 [05-07.08.2022]**
Olympique Lyon - AC Ajaccio 2-1(2-1)
Strasbourg - AS Monaco 1-2(0-1)
Clermont Foot - Paris Saint-Germain 0-5(0-3)
Toulouse FC - OGC Nice 1-1(1-0)
Montpellier - Troyes 3-2(2-2)
Lille OSC - Auxerre 4-1(3-0)
RC Lens - Stade Brestois 3-2(1-0)
Angers - FC Nantes 0-0
Stade Rennais - FC Lorient 0-1(0-0)
Marseille - Stade Reims 4-1(2-0)

**Round 2 [12-14.08.2022]**
FC Nantes - Lille OSC 1-1(1-0)
AS Monaco - Stade Rennais 1-1(0-0)
Paris Saint-Germain - Montpellier 5-2(2-0)
AC Ajaccio - RC Lens 0-0
Auxerre - Angers 2-2(2-1)
Troyes - Toulouse FC 0-3(0-1)
Stade Reims - Clermont Foot 2-4(2-0)
OGC Nice - Strasbourg 1-1(1-0)
Stade Brestois - Marseille 1-1(0-1)
FC Lorient - Ol. Lyon 3-1(2-1) [07.09.2022]

**Round 3 [19-21.08.2022]**
Olympique Lyon - Troyes 4-1(1-1)
AS Monaco - RC Lens 1-4(1-2)
Marseille - FC Nantes 2-1(0-0)
Strasbourg - Stade Reims 1-1(1-0)
Clermont Foot - OGC Nice 1-0(1-0)
Toulouse FC - FC Lorient 2-2(1-1)
Montpellier - Auxerre 1-2(1-0)
Angers - Stade Brestois 1-3(0-2)
Stade Rennais - AC Ajaccio 2-1(1-0)
Lille OSC - Paris Saint-Germain 1-7(0-4)

**Round 4 [26-28.08.2022]**
AC Ajaccio - Lille OSC 1-3(0-2)
Auxerre - Strasbourg 1-0(1-0)
RC Lens - Stade Rennais 2-1(0-0)
FC Nantes - Toulouse FC 3-1(0-1)
Troyes - Angers 3-1(1-0)
FC Lorient - Clermont Foot 2-1(2-0)
OGC Nice - Marseille 0-3(0-3)
Stade Brestois - Montpellier 0-7(0-5)
Stade Reims - Olympique Lyon 1-1(1-0)
Paris Saint-Germain - AS Monaco 1-1(0-1)

**Round 5 [31.08.2022]**
AS Monaco - Troyes 2-4(1-2)
Montpellier - AC Ajaccio 2-0(1-0)
Olympique Lyon - Auxerre 2-1(1-0)
Strasbourg - FC Nantes 1-1(1-0)
Angers - Stade Reims 2-4(0-2)
Toulouse FC - Paris Saint-Germain 0-3(0-1)
Marseille - Clermont Foot 1-0(0-0)
Lille OSC - OGC Nice 1-2(1-2)
RC Lens - FC Lorient 5-2(2-1)
Stade Rennais - Stade Brestois 3-1(0-0)

**Round 6 [03-04.09.2022]**
Auxerre - Marseille 0-2(0-1)
Olympique Lyon - Angers 5-0(2-0)
FC Nantes - Paris Saint-Germain 0-3(0-1)
Montpellier - Lille OSC 1-3(1-1)
AC Ajaccio - FC Lorient 0-1(0-0)
Clermont Foot - Toulouse FC 2-0(0-0)
Stade Brestois - Strasbourg 1-1(1-1)
Stade Reims - RC Lens 1-1(0-0)
Troyes - Stade Rennais 1-1(1-0)
OGC Nice - AS Monaco 0-1(0-0)

**Round 7 [09-11.09.2022]**
RC Lens - Troyes 1-0(1-0)
Paris Saint-Germain - Stade Brestois 1-0(1-0)
Marseille - Lille OSC 2-1(1-1)
Strasbourg - Clermont Foot 0-0
AC Ajaccio - OGC Nice 0-1(0-0)
FC Lorient - FC Nantes 3-2(1-1)
Toulouse FC - Stade Reims 1-0(1-0)
Angers - Montpellier 2-1(1-1)
Stade Rennais - Auxerre 5-0(1-0)
AS Monaco - Olympique Lyon 2-1(0-0)

**Round 8 [16-18.09.2022]**
Auxerre - FC Lorient 1-3(0-3)
Montpellier - Strasbourg 2-1(1-0)
Lille OSC - Toulouse FC 2-1(1-0)
Stade Reims - AS Monaco 0-3(0-0)
Clermont Foot - Troyes 1-3(1-1)
OGC Nice - Angers 0-1(0-1)
Marseille - Stade Rennais 1-1(0-1)
Stade Brestois - AC Ajaccio 0-1(0-0)
FC Nantes - RC Lens 0-0
Olymp. Lyon - Paris Saint-Germain 0-1(0-1)

**Round 9 [30.09.-02.10.2022]**
Angers - Marseille 0-3(0-1)
Strasbourg - Stade Rennais 1-3(0-1)
Paris Saint-Germain - OGC Nice 2-1(1-0)
FC Lorient - Lille OSC 2-1(1-0)
AC Ajaccio - Clermont Foot 1-3(0-1)
Auxerre - Stade Brestois 1-1(0-0)
Troyes - Stade Reims 2-2(0-1)
Toulouse FC - Montpellier 4-2(3-1)
AS Monaco - FC Nantes 4-1(3-0)
RC Lens - Olympique Lyon 1-0(0-0)

**Round 10 [07-09.10.2022]**
Olympique Lyon - Toulouse FC 1-1(1-0)
Marseille - AC Ajaccio 1-2(1-1)
Stade Reims - Paris Saint-Germain 0-0
Montpellier - AS Monaco 0-2(0-1)
Clermont Foot - Auxerre 2-1(0-0)
OGC Nice - Troyes 3-2(2-0)
Angers - Strasbourg 2-3(1-2)
Stade Brestois - FC Lorient 1-2(1-1)
Stade Rennais - FC Nantes 3-0(1-0)
Lille OSC - RC Lens 1-0(1-0)

**Round 11 [14-16.10.2022]**
Strasbourg - Lille OSC 0-3(0-1)
FC Lorient - Stade Reims 0-0
RC Lens - Montpellier 1-0(0-0)
Toulouse FC - Angers 3-2(2-1)
Auxerre - OGC Nice 1-1(1-1)
Troyes - AC Ajaccio 1-1(0-0)
FC Nantes - Stade Brestois 4-1(2-1)
Stade Rennais - Olympique Lyon 3-2(1-1)
AS Monaco - Clermont Foot 1-1(1-0)
Paris Saint-Germain - Marseille 1-0(1-0)

**Round 12 [21-23.10.2022]**
AC Ajaccio - Paris Saint-Germain 0-3(0-1)
Montpellier - Olympique Lyon 1-2(0-1)
Marseille - RC Lens 0-1(0-0)
Angers - Stade Rennais 1-2(0-1)
Clermont Foot - Stade Brestois 1-3(0-1)
Troyes - FC Lorient 2-2(1-0)
Toulouse FC - Strasbourg 2-2(1-0)
Stade Reims - Auxerre 2-1(1-1)
OGC Nice - FC Nantes 1-1(0-0)
Lille OSC - AS Monaco 4-3(2-2)

**Round 13** [28-30.10.2022]
RC Lens - Toulouse FC 3-0(0-0)
Paris Saint-Germain - Troyes 4-3(1-1)
Strasbourg - Marseille 2-2(0-2)
Auxerre - AC Ajaccio 1-0(1-0)
AS Monaco - Angers 2-0(0-0)
FC Nantes - Clermont Foot 1-1(0-0)
Stade Brestois - Stade Reims 0-0
Stade Rennais - Montpellier 3-0(2-0)
FC Lorient - OGC Nice 1-2(1-0)
Olympique Lyon - Lille OSC 1-0(0-0)

**Round 14** [04-06.11.2022]
Troyes - Auxerre 1-1(1-0)
AC Ajaccio - Strasbourg 4-2(4-2)
Angers - RC Lens 1-2(0-1)
FC Lorient - Paris Saint-Germain 1-2(0-1)
Clermont Foot - Montpellier 1-1(0-1)
Toulouse FC - AS Monaco 0-2(0-0)
OGC Nice - Stade Brestois 1-0(0-0)
Stade Reims - FC Nantes 1-0(0-0)
Lille OSC - Stade Rennais 1-1(1-0)
Marseille - Olympique Lyon 1-0(1-0)

**Round 15** [11-13.11.2022]
Olympique Lyon - OGC Nice 1-1(0-1)
RC Lens - Clermont Foot 2-1(0-1)
Stade Rennais - Toulouse FC 2-1(1-0)
Paris Saint-Germain - Auxerre 5-0(1-0)
FC Nantes - AC Ajaccio 2-2(0-0)
Montpellier - Stade Reims 1-1(0-0)
Lille OSC - Angers 1-0(1-0)
Stade Brestois - Troyes 2-1(0-0)
Strasbourg - FC Lorient 1-1(0-1)
AS Monaco - Marseille 2-3(1-1)

**Round 16** [28-29.12.2022]
AC Ajaccio - Angers 1-0(1-0)
Troyes - FC Nantes 0-0
Auxerre - AS Monaco 2-3(1-1)
Clermont Foot - Lille OSC 0-2(0-0)
Paris Saint-Germain - Strasbourg 2-1(1-0)
Stade Brestois - Olympique Lyon 2-4(1-3)
FC Lorient - Montpellier 0-2(0-2)
Stade Reims - Stade Rennais 3-1(2-1)
OGC Nice - RC Lens 0-0
Marseille - Toulouse FC 6-1(2-0)

**Round 17** [01-02.01.2023]
AS Monaco - Stade Brestois 1-0(0-0)
FC Nantes - Auxerre 1-0(0-0)
Toulouse FC - AC Ajaccio 2-0(0-0)
Angers - FC Lorient 1-2(1-0)
Olympique Lyon - Clermont Foot 0-1(0-0)
RC Lens - Paris Saint-Germain 3-1(2-1)
Strasbourg - Troyes 2-2(0-0)
Lille OSC - Stade Reims 1-1(1-0)
Montpellier - Marseille 1-2(0-0)
Stade Rennais - OGC Nice 2-1(1-1)

**Round 18** [11.01.2023]
AC Ajaccio - Stade Reims 0-1(0-1)
Auxerre - Toulouse FC 0-5(0-3)
Clermont Foot - Stade Rennais 2-1(1-0)
FC Nantes - Olympique Lyon 0-0
Stade Brestois - Lille OSC 0-0
Troyes - Marseille 0-2(0-1)
FC Lorient - AS Monaco 2-2(0-0)
OGC Nice - Montpellier 6-1(2-0)
Paris Saint-Germain - Angers 2-0(1-0)
Strasbourg - RC Lens 2-2(2-2)

**Round 19** [14-15.01.2023]
RC Lens - Auxerre 1-0(0-0)
Marseille - FC Lorient 3-1(1-1)
Olympique Lyon - Strasbourg 1-2(1-2)
Lille OSC - Troyes 5-1(2-0)
Toulouse FC - Stade Brestois 1-1(0-1)
Montpellier - FC Nantes 0-3(0-1)
Angers - Clermont Foot 1-2(0-1)
Stade Reims - OGC Nice 0-0
AS Monaco - AC Ajaccio 7-1(5-1)
Stade Rennais - Paris Saint-Germain 1-0(0-0)

**Round 20** [27-29.01.2023]
FC Lorient - Stade Rennais 2-1(2-0)
Troyes - RC Lens 1-1(0-0)
Marseille - AS Monaco 1-1(0-1)
OGC Nice - Lille OSC 1-0(1-0)
Auxerre - Montpellier 0-2(0-0)
Clermont Foot - FC Nantes 0-0
Strasbourg - Toulouse FC 1-2(1-1)
Stade Brestois - Angers 4-0(2-0)
AC Ajaccio - Olympique Lyon 0-2(0-1)
Paris Saint-Germain - Stade Reims 1-1(0-0)

**Round 21** [01.02.2023]
FC Nantes - Marseille 0-2(0-0)
Toulouse FC - Troyes 4-1(2-1)
Lille OSC - Clermont Foot 0-0
Angers - AC Ajaccio 1-2(1-0)
Stade Reims - FC Lorient 4-2(1-2)
AS Monaco - Auxerre 3-2(2-0)
Montpellier - Paris Saint-Germain 1-3(0-0)
Olympique Lyon - Stade Brestois 0-0
RC Lens - OGC Nice 0-1(0-0)
Stade Rennais - Strasbourg 3-0(2-0)

**Round 22** [04-05.02.2023]
Paris Saint-Germain - Toulouse FC 2-1(1-1)
Troyes - Olympique Lyon 1-3(0-1)
Stade Rennais - Lille OSC 1-3(1-0)
Clermont Foot - AS Monaco 0-2(0-2)
AC Ajaccio - FC Nantes 0-2(0-0)
Auxerre - Stade Reims 0-0
FC Lorient - Angers 0-0
Strasbourg - Montpellier 2-0(2-0)
Stade Brestois - RC Lens 1-1(0-0)
Marseille - OGC Nice 1-3(0-2)

**Round 23** [10-12.02.2023]
OGC Nice - AC Ajaccio 3-0(1-0)
AS Monaco - Paris Saint-Germain 3-1(3-1)
Clermont Foot - Marseille 0-2(0-1)
Toulouse FC - Stade Rennais 3-1(3-0)
Montpellier - Stade Brestois 3-0(2-0)
Lille OSC - Strasbourg 2-0(2-0)
Angers - Auxerre 1-1(1-1)
Stade Reims - Troyes 4-0(2-0)
FC Nantes - FC Lorient 1-0(0-0)
Olympique Lyon - RC Lens 2-1(1-1)

**Round 24** [17-19.02.2023]
Auxerre - Olympique Lyon 2-1(0-1)
OGC Nice - Stade Reims 0-0
Strasbourg - Angers 2-1(2-0)
Paris Saint-Germain - Lille OSC 4-3(2-1)
Troyes - Montpellier 0-1(0-0)
FC Lorient - AC Ajaccio 3-0(2-0)
Stade Brestois - AS Monaco 1-2(0-1)
Stade Rennais - Clermont Foot 2-0(1-0)
RC Lens - FC Nantes 3-1(2-1)
Toulouse FC - Marseille 2-3(1-0)

**Round 25** [24-26.02.2023]
Lille OSC - Stade Brestois 2-1(0-1)
Angers - Olympique Lyon 1-3(0-1)
Montpellier - RC Lens 1-1(0-1)
FC Lorient - Auxerre 0-1(0-0)
AC Ajaccio - Troyes 2-1(0-1)
Clermont Foot - Strasbourg 1-1(0-1)
FC Nantes - Stade Rennais 0-1(0-1)
Stade Reims - Toulouse FC 3-0(2-0)
AS Monaco - OGC Nice 0-3(0-3)
Marseille - Paris Saint-Germain 0-3(0-2)

**Round 26** [03-05.03.2023]
OGC Nice - Auxerre 1-1(1-1)
RC Lens - Lille OSC 1-1(1-0)
Paris Saint-Germain - FC Nantes 4-2(2-2)
Troyes - AS Monaco 2-2(1-0)
Toulouse FC - Clermont Foot 0-1(0-0)
Montpellier - Angers 5-0(3-0)
Strasbourg - Stade Brestois 0-1(0-1)
Stade Reims - AC Ajaccio 1-0(0-0)
Olympique Lyon - FC Lorient 0-0
Stade Rennais - Marseille 0-1(0-0)

**Round 27** [10-12.03.2023]
Lille OSC - Olympique Lyon 3-3(0-0)
Auxerre - Stade Rennais 0-0
Stade Brestois - Paris Saint-Germain 1-2(1-1)
Clermont Foot - RC Lens 0-4(0-3)
AC Ajaccio - Montpellier 0-1(0-0)
FC Lorient - Troyes 2-0(1-0)
FC Nantes - OGC Nice 2-2(1-1)
Angers - Toulouse FC 0-2(0-1)
AS Monaco - Stade Reims 0-1(0-0)
Marseille - Strasbourg 2-2(0-0)

**Round 28** [17-19.03.2023]
Olympique Lyon - FC Nantes 1-1(1-1)
Toulouse FC - Lille OSC 0-2(0-0)
RC Lens - Angers 3-0(2-0)
AC Ajaccio - AS Monaco 0-2(0-1)
Troyes - Stade Brestois 2-2(2-1)
Montpellier - Clermont Foot 2-1(0-1)
OGC Nice - FC Lorient 1-1(0-1)
Strasbourg - Auxerre 2-0(1-0)
Paris Saint-Germain - Stade Rennais 0-2(0-1)
Stade Reims - Marseille 1-2(1-2)

**Round 29** [31.03.-02.04.2023]
Marseille - Montpellier 1-1(1-1)
Auxerre - Troyes 1-0(0-0)
Stade Rennais - RC Lens 0-1(0-1)
Lille OSC - FC Lorient 3-1(1-0)
Clermont Foot - AC Ajaccio 2-1(0-1)
FC Nantes - Stade Reims 0-3(0-2)
Angers - OGC Nice 1-1(1-1)
Stade Brestois - Toulouse FC 3-1(1-1)
AS Monaco - Strasbourg 4-3(1-2)
Paris Saint-Germain - Olymp. Lyon 0-1(0-0)

**Round 30** [07-09.04.2023]
RC Lens - Strasbourg 2-1(1-0)
Angers - Lille OSC 1-0(0-0)
OGC Nice - Paris Saint-Germain 0-2(0-1)
Olympique Lyon - Stade Rennais 3-1(0-1)
AC Ajaccio - Auxerre 0-3(0-3)
Troyes - Clermont Foot 0-2(0-2)
Montpellier - Toulouse FC 1-2(0-1)
Stade Reims - Stade Brestois 1-1(0-1)
FC Nantes - AS Monaco 2-2(0-2)
FC Lorient - Marseille 0-0

| Round 31 [14-16.04.2023] |
|---|
| Toulouse FC - Olympique Lyon 1-2(1-1) |
| Stade Rennais - Stade Reims 3-0(2-0) |
| Paris Saint-Germain - RC Lens 3-1(3-0) |
| Lille OSC - Montpellier 2-1(0-1) |
| Auxerre - FC Nantes 2-1(2-0) |
| Clermont Foot - Angers 2-1(2-1) |
| Strasbourg - AC Ajaccio 3-1(1-0) |
| Stade Brestois - OGC Nice 1-0(1-0) |
| AS Monaco - FC Lorient 3-1(2-0) |
| Marseille - Troyes 3-1(2-0) |

| Round 32 [21-23.04.2023] |
|---|
| Angers - Paris Saint-Germain 1-2(0-2) |
| Auxerre - Lille OSC 1-1(0-1) |
| RC Lens - AS Monaco 3-0(2-0) |
| Stade Reims - Strasbourg 0-2(0-2) |
| AC Ajaccio - Stade Brestois 0-0 |
| FC Lorient - Toulouse FC 0-1(0-0) |
| FC Nantes - Troyes 2-2(1-0) |
| OGC Nice - Clermont Foot 1-2(1-1) |
| Montpellier - Stade Rennais 1-0(0-0) |
| Olympique Lyon - Marseille 1-2(0-1) |

| Round 33 [28.04.-03.05.2023] |
|---|
| Strasbourg - Olympique Lyon 1-2(1-2) |
| Lille OSC - AC Ajaccio 3-0(3-0) |
| AS Monaco - Montpellier 0-4(0-1) |
| Clermont Foot - Stade Reims 1-0(1-0) |
| Troyes - OGC Nice 0-1(0-1) |
| Stade Rennais - Angers 4-2(2-2) |
| Paris Saint-Germain - FC Lorient 1-3(1-2) |
| Marseille - Auxerre 2-1(0-1) |
| Toulouse FC - RC Lens 0-1(0-1) |
| Stade Brestois - FC Nantes 2-0(2-0) |

| Round 34 [06-07.05.2023] |
|---|
| OGC Nice - Stade Rennais 2-1(0-0) |
| Stade Reims - Lille OSC 1-0(1-0) |
| RC Lens - Marseille 2-1(1-0) |
| Angers - AS Monaco 1-2(0-1) |
| AC Ajaccio - Toulouse FC 0-0 |
| Auxerre - Clermont Foot 1-1(1-0) |
| FC Lorient - Stade Brestois 2-1(1-0) |
| FC Nantes - Strasbourg 0-2(0-1) |
| Olympique Lyon - Montpellier 5-4(1-2) |
| Troyes - Paris Saint-Germain 1-3(0-1) |

| Round 35 [12-14.05.2023] |
|---|
| RC Lens - Stade Reims 2-1(1-1) |
| Strasbourg - OGC Nice 2-0(1-0) |
| Paris Saint-Germain - AC Ajaccio 5-0(2-0) |
| Clermont Foot - Olympique Lyon 2-1(1-1) |
| Montpellier - FC Lorient 1-1(0-0) |
| Stade Brestois - Auxerre 1-0(0-0) |
| Stade Rennais - Troyes 4-0(1-0) |
| Toulouse FC - FC Nantes 0-0 |
| AS Monaco - Lille OSC 0-0 |
| Marseille - Angers 3-1(1-1) |

| Round 36 [19-21.05.2023] |
|---|
| Olympique Lyon - AS Monaco 3-1(1-1) |
| FC Nantes - Montpellier 0-3(0-1) |
| Lille OSC - Marseille 2-1(0-1) |
| AC Ajaccio - Stade Rennais 0-5(0-4) |
| Troyes - Strasbourg 1-1(0-1) |
| OGC Nice - Toulouse FC 0-0 |
| Stade Brestois - Clermont Foot 2-1(1-1) |
| Stade Reims - Angers 2-2(1-0) |
| FC Lorient - RC Lens 1-3(1-2) |
| Auxerre - Paris Saint-Germain 1-2(0-2) |

| Round 37 [27.05.2023] |
|---|
| Clermont Foot - FC Lorient 2-0(1-0) |
| Toulouse FC - Auxerre 1-1(1-1) |
| Montpellier - OGC Nice 2-3(2-0) |
| Marseille - Stade Brestois 1-2(0-0) |
| Olympique Lyon - Stade Reims 3-0(2-0) |
| Lille OSC - FC Nantes 2-1(0-1) |
| Strasbourg - Paris Saint-Germain 1-1(0-0) |
| RC Lens - AC Ajaccio 3-0(3-0) |
| Angers - Troyes 2-1(1-1) |
| Stade Rennais - AS Monaco 2-0(0-0) |

| Round 38 [03.06.2023] |
|---|
| AC Ajaccio - Marseille 1-0(0-0) |
| Auxerre - RC Lens 1-3(0-1) |
| AS Monaco - Toulouse FC 1-2(0-0) |
| Troyes - Lille OSC 1-1(0-0) |
| FC Lorient - Strasbourg 2-1(2-0) |
| FC Nantes - Angers 1-0(1-0) |
| OGC Nice - Olympique Lyon 3-1(3-1) |
| Paris Saint-Germain - Clermont Foot 2-3(2-2) |
| Stade Brestois - Stade Rennais 1-2(1-2) |
| Stade Reims - Montpellier 1-3(1-0) |

## Final Standings

| | | Total | | | | | | Home | | | | | Away | | | | |
|---|---|---|---|---|---|---|---|---|---|---|---|---|---|---|---|---|---|---|
| 1. | **Paris Saint-Germain FC** | 38 | 27 | 4 | 7 | 89 - 40 | **85** | 13 | 2 | 4 | 45 - 25 | | 14 | 2 | 3 | 44 - 15 |
| 2. | Racing Club de Lens | 38 | 25 | 9 | 4 | 68 - 29 | **84** | 17 | 1 | 1 | 41 - 13 | | 8 | 8 | 3 | 27 - 16 |
| 3. | Olympique de Marseille | 38 | 22 | 7 | 9 | 67 - 40 | **73** | 10 | 4 | 5 | 35 - 24 | | 12 | 3 | 4 | 32 - 16 |
| 4. | Stade Rennais FC | 38 | 21 | 5 | 12 | 69 - 39 | **68** | 15 | 0 | 4 | 43 - 14 | | 6 | 5 | 8 | 26 - 25 |
| 5. | Lille OSC | 38 | 19 | 10 | 9 | 65 - 44 | **67** | 13 | 4 | 2 | 40 - 25 | | 6 | 6 | 7 | 25 - 19 |
| 6. | AS Monaco FC | 38 | 19 | 8 | 11 | 70 - 58 | **65** | 9 | 3 | 7 | 37 - 33 | | 10 | 5 | 4 | 33 - 25 |
| 7. | Olympique Lyonnais | 38 | 18 | 8 | 12 | 65 - 47 | **62** | 10 | 5 | 4 | 35 - 19 | | 8 | 3 | 8 | 30 - 28 |
| 8. | Clermont Foot 63 | 38 | 17 | 8 | 13 | 45 - 49 | **59** | 9 | 3 | 7 | 20 - 28 | | 8 | 5 | 6 | 25 - 21 |
| 9. | OGC Nice | 38 | 15 | 13 | 10 | 48 - 37 | **58** | 7 | 7 | 5 | 24 - 18 | | 8 | 6 | 5 | 24 - 19 |
| 10. | FC Lorient-Bretagne Sud | 38 | 15 | 10 | 13 | 52 - 53 | **55** | 9 | 4 | 6 | 26 - 21 | | 6 | 6 | 7 | 26 - 32 |
| 11. | Stade de Reims | 38 | 12 | 15 | 11 | 45 - 45 | **51** | 8 | 6 | 5 | 28 - 23 | | 4 | 9 | 6 | 17 - 22 |
| 12. | Montpellier Hérault SC | 38 | 15 | 5 | 18 | 65 - 62 | **50** | 7 | 3 | 9 | 29 - 29 | | 8 | 2 | 9 | 36 - 33 |
| 13. | Toulouse FC | 38 | 13 | 9 | 16 | 51 - 57 | **48** | 6 | 6 | 7 | 27 - 27 | | 7 | 3 | 9 | 24 - 30 |
| 14. | Stade Brestois 29 | 38 | 11 | 11 | 16 | 44 - 54 | **44** | 7 | 5 | 7 | 24 - 26 | | 4 | 6 | 9 | 20 - 28 |
| 15. | Racing Club de Strasbourg | 38 | 9 | 13 | 16 | 51 - 59 | **40** | 5 | 7 | 7 | 25 - 26 | | 4 | 6 | 9 | 26 - 33 |
| 16. | FC Nantes | 38 | 7 | 15 | 16 | 37 - 55 | **36** | 5 | 8 | 6 | 20 - 26 | | 2 | 7 | 10 | 17 - 29 |
| 17. | AJ Auxerre (*Relegated*) | 38 | 8 | 11 | 19 | 35 - 63 | **35** | 5 | 7 | 7 | 18 - 28 | | 3 | 4 | 12 | 17 - 35 |
| 18. | AC Ajaccio (*Relegated*) | 38 | 7 | 5 | 26 | 23 - 74 | **26** | 4 | 3 | 12 | 10 - 30 | | 3 | 2 | 14 | 13 - 44 |
| 19. | ES Troyes Aube Champagne (*Relegated*) | 38 | 4 | 12 | 22 | 45 - 81 | **24** | 1 | 11 | 7 | 19 - 30 | | 3 | 1 | 15 | 26 - 51 |
| 20. | Angers SCO (*Relegated*) | 38 | 4 | 6 | 28 | 33 - 81 | **18** | 3 | 3 | 13 | 20 - 36 | | 1 | 3 | 15 | 13 - 45 |

Please note: four teams were relegated and only two teams promoted. Next season's Ligue 1 will be disputed with 18 teams.

| Top goalscorers: | |
|---|---|
| 29 **Kylian Sanmi Mbappé Lottin** | *Paris Saint-Germain FC* |
| 27 Alexandre Armand Lacazette | *Olympique Lyonnais* |
| 24 Jonathan Christian David (CAN) | *Lille OSC* |
| 21 Folarin Jerry Balogun (USA) | *Stade de Reims* |
| 21 Ikoma-Loïs Openda (BEL) | *Racing Club de Lens* |

# NATIONAL CUP
## Coupe de France 2022/2023

### Round of 64 [06-08/14.01.2023]

| | | | | |
|---|---|---|---|---|
| Racing Club de Strasbourg - Angers SCO | 0-0 aet; 4-5 pen | US Granvillaise - Chamois Niortais FC | 0-3(0-0) |
| Paris FC - Valenciennes FC | 3-1(1-1) | AS Monaco FC - Rodez Aveyron Football | 2-2 aet; 4-5 pen |
| Grenoble Foot 38 - Nîmes Olympique | 1-0(0-0) | Le Puy Foot 43 - OGC Nice | 1-0(1-0) |
| Pau FC - Montpellier Hérault SC | 2-1(1-0) | FC Girondins de Bordeaux - Stade Rennais FC | 1-2(1-1) |
| LB Châteauroux - Paris Saint-Germain FC | 1-3(1-1) | FC Chamalières - Bourges Foot 18 | 0-0 aet; 6-5 pen |
| Évreux FC 27 - Sporting Club Bastiais | 1-1 aet; 3-4 pen | ASM Belfort - Olympique Saint-Quentin | 3-1(2-1) |
| RC Grasse - La Tamponnaise | 1-0(1-0) | FC Loon-Plage - Stade de Reims | 0-7(0-1) |
| FCO Strasbourg Koenigshoffen - Clermont Foot 63 | 0-0 aet; 4-3 pen | AS La Châtaigneraie - FC Lorient-Bretagne Sud | 0-6(0-2) |
| Olympique Lyonnais - FC Metz | 2-1(0-0) | Jura Sud Foot - AC Ajaccio | 1-2(0-1) |
| ESA Linas-Montlhéry - Racing Club de Lens | 0-2(0-0) | Avoine OCC - Vierzon FC | 1-2(1-1) |
| US Avranches - Stade Brestois 29 | 0-2(0-0) | USL Dunkerque - AJ Auxerre | 2-2 aet; 4-5 pen |
| Olympique de Marseille - Hyères FC | 2-0(1-0) | Lannion FC - Toulouse FC | 1-7(1-3) |
| Villerupt Thil - FC d'Annecy | 1-6(1-4) | Stade Pontivyen - Les Herbiers Vendée Football | 1-4(0-2) |
| ES Thaon - Amiens SC | 0-0 aet; 4-2 pen | Aubagne FC - Chambéry SF | 1-3(0-0) |
| AF Virois - FC Nantes | 0-2(0-1) | Lille OSC - ES Troyes Aube Champagne | 2-0(1-0) |
| Stade Plabennécois - Vannes OC | 2-0(1-0) | US Pays de Cassel - Wasquehal Football | 1-1 aet; 5-4 pen |

### Round of 32 [20-23.01.2023]

| | | | | |
|---|---|---|---|---|
| Olympique de Marseille - Stade Rennais FC | 1-0(1-0) | FCO Strasbourg Koenigshoffen - Angers SCO | 0-1(0-1) |
| Chambéry SF - Olympique Lyonnais | 0-3(0-2) | Chamois Niortais FC - AJ Auxerre | 0-4(0-2) |
| Stade Plabennécois - Grenoble Foot 38 | 0-1(0-1) | Lille OSC - Pau FC | 2-0(1-0) |
| FC Chamalières - Paris FC | 0-4(0-2) | ES Thaon - FC Nantes | 0-0 aet; 2-4 pen |
| Sporting Club Bastiais - FC Lorient-Bretagne Sud | 1-1 aet; 1-4 pen | Le Puy Foot 43 - Vierzon FC | 0-0 aet; 3-5 pen |
| Les Herbiers Vendée Football - Stade de Reims | 0-3(0-1) | ASM Belfort - FC d'Annecy | 1-1 aet; 3-4 pen |
| Toulouse FC - AC Ajaccio | 2-0(0-0) | Stade Brestois 29- Racing Club de Lens | 1-3(1-3) |
| RC Grasse - Rodez Aveyron Football | 0-0 aet; 4-5 pen | US Pays de Cassel - Paris Saint-Germain FC | 0-7(0-4) |

### Round of 16 [08-09.02.2023]

| | | | | |
|---|---|---|---|---|
| Olympique Lyonnais - Lille OSC | 2-2 aet; 4-2 pen | Paris FC - FC d'Annecy | 1-1 aet; 5-6 pen |
| Toulouse FC - Stade de Reims | 3-1(2-0) | Angers SCO - FC Nantes | 1-1 aet; 2-4 pen |
| Vierzon FC - Grenoble Foot 38 | 0-1(0-0) | Olympique de Marseille - Paris Saint-Germain FC | 2-1(1-1) |
| AJ Auxerre - Rodez Aveyron Football | 2-3(1-1) | FC Lorient-Bretagne Sud - Racing Club de Lens | 1-1 aet; 2-4 pen |

### Quarter-Finals [28.02.-01.03.2023]

| | | | | |
|---|---|---|---|---|
| Olympique Lyonnais - Grenoble Foot 38 | 2-1(2-0) | Toulouse FC - Rodez Aveyron Football | 6-1(5-0) |
| FC Nantes - Racing Club de Lens | 2-1(1-1) | Olympique de Marseille - FC d'Annecy | 2-2 aet; 6-7 pen |

### Semi-Finals [05-06.04.2023]

| | | | | |
|---|---|---|---|---|
| FC Nantes - Olympique Lyonnais | 1-0(0-0) | FC d'Annecy - Toulouse FC | 1-2(1-1) |

### Final

29.04.2023; Stade de France, Saint-Denis, Paris; Referee: Benoît Millot; Attendance: 78,038
**FC Nantes - Toulouse FC**                                                    **1-5(0-4)**

**FC Nantes**: Alban Lafont, Fabien Centonze, Jean-Charles Castelletto, Nicolas Pallois (46.Andy Delort), João Victor Da Silva Marcelino (66.Quentin Merlin), Andrei Girotto, Moussa Sissoko, Florent Mollet (46.Samuel Moutoussamy), Ludovic Blas (Cap) (82.Marcus Coco), Moses Daddy-Ayala Simon (46.Ignatius Kpene Ganago), Mostafa Mohamed Ahmed Abdalla. Trainer: Antoine Krilone Kombouaré.

**Toulouse FC**: Christian Kjetil Haug, Mikkel Desler, Logan Costa (82.Anthony Rouault), Rasmus Schmidt Nicolaisen, Gabriel Alonso Suazo Urbina, Stijn Spierings (82.Moussa Diarra), Brecht Dejaegere (Cap) (69.Vincent Olivier Sierro), Branco van den Boomen, Zakaria Aboukhlal, Fares Chaïbi (76.Rafael Rogério da Silva „Rafael Ratão"), Thijs Dallinga (69.Ado Onaiwu). Trainer: Philippe Jacques William Montanier.

**Goals:** 0-1 Logan Costa (4), 0-2 Logan Costa (10), 0-3 Thijs Dallinga (23), 0-4 Thijs Dallinga (31), 1-4 Ludovic Blas (75), 1-5 Zakaria Aboukhlal (79).

## Athletic Club Ajaccio

| | | |
|---|---|---|
| **Founded**: | 1910 | |
| **Stadium**: | Stade "François Coty", Ajaccio (10,446) | |
| **Trainer**: | Olivier Pantaloni | 13.12.1966 |

| Goalkeepers: | DOB | M | (s) | G |
|---|---|---|---|---|
| Benjamin Leroy | 07.04.1989 | 32 | | |
| Ghjuvanni Quilichini | 01.09.2002 | | (1) | |
| François-Joseph Sollacaro | 21.03.1994 | 6 | | |
| **Defenders:** | **DOB** | **M** | **(s)** | **G** |
| Mickaël Alphonse (GLP) | 12.07.1989 | 14 | (12) | |
| Cédric Avinel | 11.09.1986 | 19 | (5) | 1 |
| Ismaël Diallo (CIV) | 29.01.1997 | 25 | (3) | |
| Oumar González | 25.02.1998 | 29 | (1) | |
| Anthony Khelifa | 20.09.2005 | | (2) | |
| Youssouf Koné (MLI) | 05.07.1995 | 12 | (1) | |
| Fernand Mayembo (CGO) | 09.01.1996 | 8 | (3) | |
| Tony Strata | 07.09.2004 | 1 | (2) | |
| Clément Vidal | 18.06.2000 | 21 | (5) | 1 |
| Mohamed Baki Youssouf (COM) | 26.03.1988 | 27 | (3) | |
| **Midfielders:** | **DOB** | **M** | **(s)** | **G** |
| Mickaël Barreto | 18.01.1991 | 15 | (5) | 1 |
| Florian Chabrolle | 07.04.1998 | 3 | (4) | |
| Yanis Cimignani | 22.01.2002 | 3 | (5) | |
| Mathieu Coutadeur | 20.03.1986 | 22 | (5) | |
| Qazim Laçi (ALB) | 19.01.1996 | 2 | (7) | |
| Thomas Mangani | 29.04.1987 | 14 | (12) | 1 |
| Vincent Marchetti | 04.07.1997 | 29 | (2) | |
| *Paolo Lebas* da Silva (POR) | 20.04.2003 | | (1) | |
| Mehdi Puch-Herrantz (ALG) | 20.01.2004 | | (4) | |
| **Forwards:** | **DOB** | **M** | **(s)** | **G** |
| Cyrille Barros Bayala (BFA) | 24.05.1996 | 25 | (8) | 1 |
| Youcef Belaïli (ALG) | 14.03.1992 | 15 | (2) | 6 |
| Kouame Jean Fiacre Botué (BFA) | 07.08.2002 | 2 | (6) | |
| Ivane Chegra (ALG) | 03.03.2004 | 1 | (5) | |
| Moussa Djitté (SEN) | 04.10.1999 | 1 | (5) | |
| Mounaïm El Idrissy | 10.02.1999 | 30 | (2) | 6 |
| Romain Hamouma | 29.03.1987 | 14 | (5) | 2 |
| Bevic Selad Moussiti-Oko (CGO) | 28.01.1995 | 7 | (10) | 1 |
| Riad Nouri | 07.06.1985 | 16 | (17) | 1 |
| *Ruan* Levine Camara Vitor (BRA) | 19.01.1999 | | (3) | |
| Moussa Soumano | 09.07.2005 | 5 | (9) | 1 |
| Kevin Spadanuda (SUI) | 16.01.1997 | 13 | (9) | |
| Ben Hamed Touré (CIV) | 21.08.2003 | 2 | (2) | |
| Yoann Touzghar (TUN) | 28.11.1986 | 5 | (6) | |

## Angers Sporting Club de l'Ouest

| | | |
|---|---|---|
| **Founded**: | 1919 | |
| **Stadium**: | Stade "Raymond Kopa", Angers (18,752) | |
| **Trainer**: | Gérald Baticle | 10.09.1969 |
| [28.11.2022] | Abdelaziz Bouhazama | 04.01.1969 |
| [07.03.2023] | Alexandre Dujeux | 08.01.1976 |

| Goalkeepers: | DOB | M | (s) | G |
|---|---|---|---|---|
| Paul Bernardoni | 18.04.1997 | 27 | | |
| Yahia Fofana | 21.08.2000 | 11 | | |
| **Defenders:** | **DOB** | **M** | **(s)** | **G** |
| Abdoulaye Bamba (CIV) | 25.04.1990 | 12 | (9) | |
| Miha Blažič (SVN) | 08.05.1993 | 22 | (2) | 2 |
| Ousmane Camara | 06.03.2003 | 6 | (3) | |
| Ilyes Chetti | 22.01.1995 | 2 | (4) | |
| Souleyman Doumbia (CIV) | 24.09.1996 | 21 | (3) | |
| Faouzi Ghoulam (ALG) | 01.02.1991 | 6 | (1) | |
| Cédric Hountondji (BEN) | 19.01.1994 | 35 | (1) | |
| Lillian Rao-Lisoa | 16.06.2000 | | (7) | 1 |
| Halid Šabanović (BIH) | 22.08.1999 | 8 | (7) | 2 |
| Yan Valery | 22.02.1999 | 30 | | |
| **Midfielders:** | **DOB** | **M** | **(s)** | **G** |
| Himad Abdelli | 17.11.1999 | 24 | (6) | 2 |
| Ibrahim Amadou | 06.04.1993 | 4 | (3) | |
| Jean-Mattéo Bahoya | 07.05.2005 | 2 | (8) | |
| Nabil Bentaleb (ALG) | 24.11.1994 | 29 | (1) | 4 |
| Antonin Bobichon | 14.09.1995 | | (3) | |
| Pierrick Capelle | 15.04.1987 | 15 | (11) | |
| Batista Mendy | 12.01.2000 | 35 | | |
| Zinédine Ould Khaled | 14.01.2000 | | (4) | |
| Azzedine Ounahi (MAR) | 19.04.2000 | 13 | (2) | |
| Waniss Taïbi | 07.03.2002 | 1 | (10) | |
| **Forwards:** | **DOB** | **M** | **(s)** | **G** |
| Sofiane Boufal (MAR) | 17.09.1993 | 9 | (4) | 4 |
| Loïs Diony | 20.12.1992 | 5 | (6) | 2 |
| Farid El Melali (ALG) | 05.05.1997 | 9 | (8) | |
| Adrien Hunou | 19.01.1994 | 28 | (6) | 4 |
| Marin Jakoliš (CRO) | 26.12.1996 | | (1) | |
| Justin-Noël Kalumba | 25.12.2004 | 7 | | |
| Jason Mbock | 01.11.1999 | | (2) | |
| Ibrahima Niane (SEN) | 11.03.1999 | 15 | (1) | 2 |
| Amine Salama | 18.07.2000 | 12 | (13) | 3 |
| Abdallah Sima (SEN) | 17.06.2001 | 19 | (15) | 5 |
| Sada Thioub | 01.06.1995 | 11 | (16) | 1 |

## Association de la Jeunesse Auxerroise

| | | |
|---|---|---|
| **Founded**: | 29.12.1905 | |
| **Stadium**: | Stade de l'Abbé-Deschamps, Auxerre (21,379) | |
| **Trainer**: | Jean-Marc Furlan | 20.11.1957 |
| [11.10.2022] | Michel Padovani | 21.01.1962 |
| [26.10.2022] | Christophe Pélissier | 05.10.1965 |

| Goalkeepers: | DOB | M | (s) | G |
|---|---|---|---|---|
| Benoît Costil | 03.07.1987 | 19 | | |
| Donovan René Léon (GUF) | 03.11.1992 | 2 | | |
| Ionuţ Andrei Radu (ROU) | 28.05.1997 | 17 | | |
| **Defenders:** | **DOB** | **M** | **(s)** | **G** |
| Denys Bain | 02.07.1993 | 1 | (1) | |
| Quentin Bernard | 07.07.1989 | 7 | | |
| Kenji-Van Boto | 07.03.1996 | 2 | | |
| Alexandre Serge Coeff | 20.02.1992 | 6 | (1) | |
| Julian Jeanvier | 31.03.1992 | 20 | (2) | 1 |
| Paul Joly | 07.06.2000 | 10 | | |
| *Jubal* Rocha Mendes *Júnior* (BRA) | 29.08.1993 | 35 | (2) | 3 |
| Gideon Mensah (GHA) | 18.07.1998 | 26 | | |
| Théo Pellenard | 04.03.1994 | 1 | (1) | |
| Brayann Pereira | 21.05.2003 | 2 | | |
| Isaak Touré | 28.03.2003 | 18 | (1) | 1 |
| Akim Zedadka (ALG) | 30.05.1995 | 19 | (1) | |
| **Midfielders:** | **DOB** | **M** | **(s)** | **G** |
| Mathias Autret | 01.03.1991 | 16 | (7) | 2 |
| Kévin Danois | 28.06.2004 | | (1) | |
| Youssouf Yacoub M'Changama (COM) | 29.08.1990 | 11 | (15) | |
| Han-Noah Massengo | 07.07.2001 | 13 | (1) | |
| Gaëtan Perrin | 07.06.1996 | 15 | (22) | 3 |
| Rayan Raveloson (MAD) | 16.01.1997 | 27 | (7) | 2 |
| Kays Ruiz-Atil | 26.08.2002 | 1 | | |
| Hamza Sakhi (MAR) | 07.06.1996 | 18 | (9) | 1 |
| Birama Touré (MLI) | 06.06.1992 | 38 | | 2 |
| **Forwards:** | **DOB** | **M** | **(s)** | **G** |
| Matthis Abline | 28.03.2003 | 8 | (11) | 2 |
| Ousmane Camara (GUI) | 03.11.2001 | | (3) | |
| Gaëtan Charbonnier | 27.12.1988 | 3 | (3) | 1 |
| Ben Siriki Dembélé (SCO) | 07.09.1996 | 4 | (8) | |
| Rémy Dugimont | 01.07.1986 | | (11) | |
| Gauthier Hein | 07.08.1996 | 23 | (12) | 2 |
| M'Baye Niang (SEN) | 19.12.1994 | 17 | (13) | 6 |
| *Nuno* Miguel *da Costa* Jóia (CPV) | 10.02.1991 | 23 | (10) | 5 |
| Lassine Sinayoko | 08.12.1999 | 16 | (17) | 1 |

## Stade Brestois 29

| Founded: | 1950 | | |
|---|---|---|---|
| Stadium: | Stade „Francis-Le Blé", Brest (15,931) | | |
| Trainer: | Michel Der Zakarian (ARM) | | 18.02.1963 |
| [11.10.2022] | Bruno Grougi | | 26.04.1983 |
| [03.01.2023] | Eric Serge Armand Roy | | 26.09.1967 |

| Goalkeepers: | DOB | M | (s) | G |
|---|---|---|---|---|
| Marco Bizot (NED) | 10.03.1991 | 37 | | |
| Joaquín Blázquez (ARG) | 28.01.2001 | 1 | | |
| **Defenders:** | **DOB** | **M** | **(s)** | **G** |
| Lilian Brassier | 02.11.1999 | 35 | (1) | |
| Brendan Chardonnet | 22.12.1994 | 27 | (3) | |
| Achraf Dari (MAR) | 06.05.1999 | 15 | (3) | 1 |
| Jean-Kévin Duverne | 12.07.1997 | 27 | (7) | |
| Noah Fadiga (SEN) | 03.12.1999 | 16 | (5) | 1 |
| Christophe Hérelle | 22.08.1992 | 12 | (4) | |
| Kenny Lala | 03.10.1991 | 16 | (1) | |
| Bradley Locko | 06.05.2002 | 2 | (5) | |
| Jere Uronen (FIN) | 13.07.1994 | 3 | (3) | |
| **Midfielders:** | **DOB** | **M** | **(s)** | **G** |
| Haris Belkebla (ALG) | 28.01.1994 | 30 | (8) | 2 |
| Mahdi Camara | 30.06.1998 | 20 | (11) | 2 |
| Axel Camblan | 18.06.2003 | | (7) | |

| Romain Del Castillo | 29.03.1996 | 16 | (11) | 6 |
|---|---|---|---|---|
| Pierre Lees-Melou | 25.05.1993 | 32 | | 5 |
| Félix Lemaréchal | 07.08.2003 | 2 | (11) | |
| Hugo Magnetti | 30.05.1998 | 19 | (13) | 1 |
| *Mathias* Pereira Lage (POR) | 30.11.1996 | 16 | (8) | 2 |
| Hiang'a Mbock | 28.12.1999 | | (2) | |
| **Forwards:** | **DOB** | **M** | **(s)** | **G** |
| Taïryk Arconte | 12.11.2003 | 1 | (3) | |
| Youcef Belaïli (ALG) | 14.03.1992 | 4 | (2) | |
| Irvin Cardona | 08.08.1997 | 1 | (9) | |
| Karamoko Kader Dembélé (ENG) | 22.02.2003 | | (15) | |
| Alberth Josué Elis Martínez (HON) | 12.02.1996 | 2 | (8) | |
| Franck Honorat | 11.08.1996 | 29 | (4) | 6 |
| Jérémy Le Douaron | 21.04.1998 | 24 | (8) | 10 |
| Steve Mounié (BEN) | 29.09.1994 | 20 | (3) | 6 |
| Islam Slimani (ALG) | 18.06.1988 | 11 | (5) | 1 |

## Clermont Foot 63

| Founded: | 1911 | |
|---|---|---|
| Stadium: | Stade „Gabriel Montpied", Clermont-Ferrand (11,980) | |
| Trainer: | Pascal Gastien | 02.12.1963 |

| Goalkeepers: | DOB | M | (s) | G |
|---|---|---|---|---|
| Mory Diaw | 22.06.1993 | 37 | | |
| Ouparine Djoco | 22.04.1998 | 1 | | |
| **Defenders:** | **DOB** | **M** | **(s)** | **G** |
| Jean-Claude Billong | 28.12.1993 | | (1) | |
| Maximiliano Caufriez (BEL) | 16.02.1997 | 25 | (1) | 1 |
| Souleymane Cissé | 08.08.2002 | | (2) | |
| Baïla Diallo (SEN) | 24.06.2001 | | (6) | |
| Cheick Oumar Konaté (MLI) | 02.04.2004 | 6 | (3) | |
| Arial Mendy (SEN) | 07.11.1994 | 1 | (4) | |
| Vivaldo Borges dos Santos Neto „Neto Borges" (BRA) | 13.09.1996 | 33 | | 3 |
| Florent Ogier | 21.03.1989 | 18 | (8) | |
| Alidu Seidu (GHA) | 04.06.2000 | 28 | | |
| Mateusz Wieteska (POL) | 11.02.1997 | 35 | | |
| Mehdi Zeffane | 19.05.1992 | 7 | (11) | 1 |

| Midfielders: | DOB | M | (s) | G |
|---|---|---|---|---|
| Jim Allevinah (GAB) | 27.02.1995 | 25 | (11) | 1 |
| Brandon Baiye (BEL) | 27.12.2000 | | (7) | |
| Jason Berthomier | 06.01.1990 | | (2) | |
| Muhammed Cham (AUT) | 26.09.2000 | 23 | (15) | 7 |
| Johan Gastien | 25.01.1988 | 29 | (2) | 4 |
| Maxime Gonalons | 10.03.1989 | 19 | (6) | 1 |
| Saîf-Eddine Khaoui (TUN) | 27.04.1995 | 23 | (11) | 7 |
| Yohann Magnin | 21.06.1997 | 25 | (13) | |
| Yanis Massolin | 20.09.2002 | | (6) | |
| Aïman Maurer (MAR) | 25.09.2004 | 6 | (4) | |
| **Forwards:** | **DOB** | **M** | **(s)** | **G** |
| Komnen Andrić (SRB) | 01.07.1995 | 16 | (18) | 4 |
| Jérémie Bela (ANG) | 08.04.1993 | 7 | (12) | 1 |
| Jodel Dossou (BEN) | 17.03.1992 | 2 | (7) | 1 |
| Grejohn Kyei | 12.08.1995 | 26 | (11) | 10 |
| Elbasan Rashani (KOS) | 09.05.1993 | 26 | (6) | 3 |

## Racing Club de Lens

| Founded: | 1906 | |
|---|---|---|
| Stadium: | Stade „Bollaert-Delelis", Lens (37,705) | |
| Trainer: | Franck Haise | 15.04.1971 |

| Goalkeepers: | DOB | M | (s) | G |
|---|---|---|---|---|
| Jean-Louis Leca | 21.09.1985 | 1 | | |
| Brice Lauriche Samba | 25.04.1994 | 37 | | |
| **Defenders:** | **DOB** | **M** | **(s)** | **G** |
| Ismaël Boura | 14.08.2000 | | (9) | |
| Kevin Danso (AUT) | 19.09.1998 | 37 | | 1 |
| Steven Fortès (CPV) | 17.04.1992 | | (1) | |
| Jonathan Gradit | 24.11.1992 | 33 | | 1 |
| Massadio Haïdara | 02.12.1992 | 17 | (19) | |
| Julien Le Cardinal | 03.08.1997 | 2 | (6) | |
| Deiver Andrés Machado Mena (COL) | 02.09.1993 | 26 | (7) | 4 |
| Facundo Axel Medina (ARG) | 28.05.1999 | 32 | | 2 |
| Christopher Wooh | 18.09.2001 | | (1) | |
| **Midfielders:** | **DOB** | **M** | **(s)** | **G** |
| Salis Abdul Samed (GHA) | 26.03.2000 | 33 | | 1 |
| Patrick Berg (NOR) | 24.11.1997 | | (3) | |
| Jimmy Cabot | 18.04.1994 | 5 | (6) | |

| Alexis Claude-Maurice | 06.06.1998 | 5 | (15) | 5 |
|---|---|---|---|---|
| *David* Pereira Da *Costa* (POR) | 05.01.2001 | 16 | (15) | 1 |
| Seko Fofana (CIV) | 07.05.1995 | 34 | (1) | 7 |
| Przemysław Frankowski (POL) | 12.04.1995 | 31 | (6) | 5 |
| Angelo Fulgini | 20.08.1996 | 12 | (5) | 1 |
| Gaël Romeo Kakuta Mabenga (COD) | 21.06.1991 | | (2) | |
| Jean Emile Junior Onana Onana (CMR) | 08.01.2000 | 9 | (12) | |
| Łukasz Poręba (POL) | 13.03.2000 | 3 | (7) | |
| Adrien Thomasson | 10.12.1993 | 16 | (4) | 5 |
| **Forwards:** | **DOB** | **M** | **(s)** | **G** |
| Adam Buksa (POL) | 12.07.1996 | | (8) | |
| Ignatius Kpene Ganago (CMR) | 16.02.1999 | | (4) | |
| Rémy Labeau Lascary (GLP) | 03.03.2003 | | (10) | |
| Ikoma Loïs Openda (BEL) | 16.02.2000 | 29 | (9) | 21 |
| Wesley Saïd | 19.04.1995 | 6 | (15) | 5 |
| Florian Sotoca | 25.10.1990 | 34 | (4) | 7 |

## Lille Olympique Sporting Club

| Founded: | 23.09.1944 | |
|---|---|---|
| Stadium: | Stade "Pierre Mauroy", Villeneuve-d'Ascq (50,186) | |
| Trainer: | Paulo Alexandre Rodrigues Fonseca (POR) | 05.03.1973 |

| Goalkeepers: | DOB | M | (s) | G |
|---|---|---|---|---|
| Lucas Chevalier | 06.11.2001 | 32 | | |
| Léonardo César Jardim „Léo Jardim" (BRA) | 20.03.1995 | 6 | | |
| **Defenders:** | **DOB** | **M** | **(s)** | **G** |
| *Alexsandro* Victor de Souza *Ribeiro* (BRA) | 09.08.1999 | 16 | (5) | 3 |
| Bafodé Diakité | 06.01.2001 | 29 | (4) | 3 |
| Gabriel Gudmundsson (SWE) | 29.04.1999 | 9 | (9) | |
| *Ismaily* Gonçalves dos Santos (BRA) | 11.01.1990 | 21 | (2) | 2 |
| *José* Miguel da Rocha *Fonte* (POR) | 22.12.1983 | 30 | (1) | 1 |
| Simon Ramet | 13.03.2003 | | (1) | |
| *Tiago* Emanuel Embaló *Djaló* (POR) | 09.04.2000 | 24 | (1) | 2 |
| Leny Yoro | 13.11.2005 | 8 | (5) | |
| Akim Zedadka (ALG) | 30.05.1995 | 4 | (4) | 1 |
| **Midfielders:** | **DOB** | **M** | **(s)** | **G** |
| Benjamin André | 03.08.1990 | 33 | (1) | 1 |

| *André* Filipe Tavares *Gomes* (POR) | 30.07.1993 | 18 | (8) | 3 |
|---|---|---|---|---|
| Carlos Noom Quomah Baleba (CMR) | 03.01.2004 | 5 | (14) | |
| Rémy Cabella | 08.03.1990 | 28 | (4) | 7 |
| Angel Almeida Gomes (ENG) | 31.08.2000 | 34 | (2) | 2 |
| Jonas Martin | 09.04.1990 | 2 | (10) | |
| Yusuf Yazıcı (TUR) | 29.01.1997 | 3 | (1) | 1 |
| **Forwards:** | **DOB** | **M** | **(s)** | **G** |
| Jonathan Bamba | 26.03.1996 | 32 | (2) | 6 |
| Mohamed Bayo (GUI) | 04.06.1998 | 6 | (21) | 4 |
| Jonathan Christian David (CAN) | 14.01.2000 | 36 | (1) | 24 |
| Amine Messoussa | 12.10.2004 | | (1) | |
| Adam Ounas (ALG) | 11.11.1996 | 12 | (9) | 1 |
| Alan Virginius | 03.01.2003 | 1 | (14) | 1 |
| Timothy Tarpeh Weah (USA) | 22.02.2000 | 18 | (11) | |
| Edon Zhegrova (KOS) | 31.03.1999 | 11 | (11) | 3 |

## Football Club Lorient-Bretagne Sud

**Founded:** 1926
**Stadium:** Stade du Moustoir, Lorient (18,890)
**Trainer:** Régis Le Bris          06.12.1975

| Goalkeepers: | DOB | M | (s) | G |
|---|---|---|---|---|
| Vito Mannone (ITA) | 02.03.1988 | 17 | (1) | |
| Yvon Landry Mvogo Nganoma (SUI) | 06.06.1994 | 21 | | |
| **Defenders:** | **DOB** | **M** | **(s)** | **G** |
| *Igor Silva* de Almeida (BRA) | 21.08.1996 | 5 | (2) | |
| Gédéon Kalulu Kyatengwa (COD) | 29.08.1997 | 28 | (1) | |
| Julien Laporte | 04.11.1993 | 19 | (1) | |
| Vincent Le Goff | 15.10.1989 | 37 | | |
| Chrislain Matsima | 15.05.2002 | 2 | (4) | |
| Abdoul Bamo Meité (CIV) | 03.12.2001 | 16 | (1) | 1 |
| Montassar Talbi (TUN) | 26.05.1998 | 38 | | 1 |
| Darlin Zidane Yongwa Ngameni (CMR) | 22.09.2000 | 8 | (6) | 1 |
| **Midfielders:** | **DOB** | **M** | **(s)** | **G** |
| Laurent Abergel | 01.02.1993 | 28 | (1) | |
| Adil Aouchiche | 15.07.2002 | 1 | (10) | |
| Quentin Boisgard | 17.03.1997 | 1 | (4) | 1 |
| Romain Faivre | 14.07.1998 | 14 | (2) | 5 |
| Bonke Innocent (NGA) | 20.01.1996 | 14 | (11) | |
| Ayman Kari | 19.11.2004 | | (5) | |
| Eli Kroupi | 23.06.2006 | | (1) | |
| Théo Le Bris | 01.10.2002 | 15 | (12) | 2 |
| Enzo Le Fée | 03.02.2000 | 35 | | 5 |
| Jean-Victor Makengo | 12.06.1998 | 12 | (3) | |
| Julien Ponceau | 28.11.2000 | 20 | (11) | 1 |
| **Forwards:** | **DOB** | **M** | **(s)** | **G** |
| Yoann Cathline | 22.07.2002 | 11 | (12) | 1 |
| Stéphane Diarra (CIV) | 09.12.1998 | 14 | (14) | 2 |
| Cheikh Bamba Dieng (SEN) | 23.03.2000 | 9 | (6) | 3 |
| Siriné Doucouré | 08.04.2002 | | (12) | |
| Adrian Grbić (AUT) | 04.08.1996 | | (2) | |
| Ibrahima Koné (MLI) | 16.06.1999 | 15 | (22) | 7 |
| Armand Laurienté | 04.12.1998 | 3 | | 1 |
| Terem Igobor Moffi (NGA) | 25.05.1999 | 17 | (1) | 12 |
| Dango Ouattara (BFA) | 11.02.2002 | 18 | | 6 |

## Olympique Lyonnais

**Founded:** 1950
**Stadium:** Groupama Stadium, Décines-Charpieu, Lyon (59,186)
**Trainer:** Peter Sylvester Bosz          21.11.1963
[09.10.2023] Laurent Robert Blanc          19.11.1965

| Goalkeepers: | DOB | M | (s) | G |
|---|---|---|---|---|
| Anthony Lopes (POR) | 01.10.1990 | 32 | | |
| Rémy Riou | 06.08.1987 | 6 | (1) | |
| **Defenders:** | **DOB** | **M** | **(s)** | **G** |
| Jérôme Agyenim Boateng (GER) | 03.09.1988 | 6 | (2) | |
| Damien Da Silva | 17.05.1988 | 3 | (4) | |
| Sinaly Diomandé (CIV) | 09.04.2001 | 22 | (2) | |
| Malo Gusto | 19.05.2003 | 19 | (2) | |
| *Henrique* Silva Milagres (BRA) | 25.04.1994 | 3 | (4) | |
| Saël Kumbedi | 26.03.2005 | 14 | (6) | |
| Dejan Lovren (CRO) | 05.07.1989 | 17 | | 1 |
| Castello Lukeba | 17.12.2002 | 33 | (1) | 2 |
| Mamadou Sarr | 29.08.2005 | | (1) | |
| Nicolás Alejandro Tagliafico (ARG) | 31.08.1992 | 34 | | 1 |
| **Midfielders:** | **DOB** | **M** | **(s)** | **G** |
| Houssem Aouar | 30.06.1998 | 6 | (10) | 1 |
| Maxence Caqueret | 15.02.2000 | 32 | (4) | 4 |
| Rayan Cherki | 17.08.2003 | 21 | (13) | 4 |
| Mohamed El Arouch | 06.04.2004 | | (1) | |
| Romain Faivre | 14.07.1998 | 3 | (7) | |
| Johann Lepenant | 22.10.2002 | 21 | (10) | 1 |
| *Lucas* Tolentino Coelho de Lima „Paquetá"(BRA) | 27.08.1997 | 2 | | |
| Jeff Reine-Adélaïde | 17.01.1998 | 1 | (13) | |
| *Thiago* Henrique *Mendes* Ribeiro (BRA) | 15.03.1992 | 22 | (9) | 1 |
| Corentin Tolisso | 03.08.1994 | 25 | (5) | 1 |
| **Forwards:** | **DOB** | **M** | **(s)** | **G** |
| Bradley Barcola | 02.09.2002 | 15 | (11) | 5 |
| Moussa Dembélé | 12.07.1996 | 8 | (15) | 3 |
| *Jefferson Ruan* Pereira dos Santos „Jeffinho" (BRA) | 30.12.1999 | 4 | (5) | 1 |
| Alexandre Armand Lacazette | 28.05.1991 | 34 | (1) | 27 |
| Amin Sarr (SWE) | 11.03.2001 | 6 | (7) | 1 |
| Mateus Cardoso Lemos Martins „Tetê" (BRA) | 15.02.2000 | 14 | (3) | 6 |
| Karl Brillant Toko Ekambi (CMR) | 14.09.1992 | 15 | (4) | 4 |

## Olympique de Marseille

**Founded:** 31.08.1899
**Stadium:** Stade Orange Vélodrome, Marseille (67,394)
**Trainer:** Igor Tudor (CRO)          16.04.1978

| Goalkeepers: | DOB | M | (s) | G |
|---|---|---|---|---|
| *Pau López* Sabata (ESP) | 13.12.1994 | 32 | (1) | |
| *Rubén Blanco* Veiga (ESP) | 25.07.1995 | 6 | | |
| **Defenders:** | **DOB** | **M** | **(s)** | **G** |
| Eric Bailly (CIV) | 12.04.1994 | 5 | (12) | |
| Leonardo Julián Balerdi Rosa (ARG) | 26.01.1999 | 30 | (5) | |
| Jonathan Clauss | 25.09.1992 | 32 | (2) | 2 |
| Duje Ćaleta-Car (CRO) | 17.09.1996 | | (1) | |
| Samuel Gigot | 12.10.1993 | 24 | (2) | 2 |
| Issa Kaboré (BFA) | 12.05.2001 | 9 | (13) | 1 |
| Sead Kolašinac (BIH) | 20.06.1993 | 26 | (7) | 4 |
| Chancel Mbemba Mangulu (COD) | 08.08.1994 | 32 | (4) | 5 |
| *Nuno* Albertino Varela *Tavares* (POR) | 26.01.2000 | 23 | (8) | 6 |
| Souleymane Isaak Touré | 28.03.2003 | | (5) | |
| **Midfielders:** | **DOB** | **M** | **(s)** | **G** |
| *Gerson* Santos da Silva (BRA) | 20.05.1997 | 6 | (4) | 2 |
| Matteo Elias Kenzo Guendouzi Olié | 14.04.1999 | 25 | (8) | 2 |
| Pape Alassane Gueye (SEN) | 24.01.1999 | 4 | (10) | 1 |
| Amine Harit (MAR) | 18.06.1997 | 6 | (4) | |
| Ruslan Malinovskiy (UKR) | 04.05.1993 | 13 | (7) | 1 |
| Azzedine Ounahi (MAR) | 19.04.2000 | 1 | (6) | 1 |
| Dimitri Payet | 29.03.1987 | 9 | (15) | 4 |
| Valentin Rongier | 07.12.1994 | 34 | (2) | 1 |
| Jordan Marcel Gilbert Veretout | 01.03.1993 | 31 | (7) | 4 |
| **Forwards:** | **DOB** | **M** | **(s)** | **G** |
| Cédric Bakambu (COD) | 11.04.1991 | | (3) | |
| Salim Ben Seghir | 24.02.2003 | | (1) | |
| Cheikh Bamba Dieng (SEN) | 23.03.2000 | 1 | (9) | 1 |
| Arkadiusz Milik (POL) | 28.02.1994 | 2 | | |
| François Régis Mughe (CMR) | 16.06.2004 | | (1) | |
| Alexis Alejandro Sánchez Sánchez (CHI) | 19.12.1988 | 32 | (3) | 14 |
| Luis Javier Suárez Charris (COL) | 02.12.1997 | 2 | (5) | 3 |
| Cengiz Ünder (TUR) | 14.07.1997 | 28 | (9) | 5 |
| *Vítor* Manuel Carvalho Oliveira „Vitinha" (POR) | 15.03.2000 | 5 | (9) | 2 |

## Association Sportive de Monaco Football Club

**Founded:** 23.08.1924
**Stadium:** Stade „Louis II", Monaco (18,523)
**Trainer:** Philippe Clement (BEL)          22.03.1974

| Goalkeepers: | DOB | M | (s) | G |
|---|---|---|---|---|
| Alexander Nübel (GER) | 30.09.1996 | 38 | | |
| **Defenders:** | **DOB** | **M** | **(s)** | **G** |
| Ruben Aguilar | 26.04.1993 | 14 | (6) | |
| Benoît Badiashile | 26.03.2001 | 9 | (2) | 2 |
| *Caio Henrique* Oliveira Silva (BRA) | 31.07.1997 | 32 | (3) | 1 |
| Axel Disasi | 11.03.1998 | 37 | (1) | 3 |
| Ismail Jakobs (SEN) | 17.08.1999 | 9 | (23) | |
| Guillermo Alfonso Maripán Loayza (CHI) | 06.05.1994 | 25 | (1) | 3 |
| Chrislain Matsima | 15.05.2002 | 5 | (3) | |
| Malang Sarr | 23.01.1999 | 8 | (5) | |
| *Vanderson* de Oliveira Campos (BRA) | 21.06.2001 | 24 | (7) | 1 |
| **Midfielders:** | **DOB** | **M** | **(s)** | **G** |
| Maghnes Akliouche (ALG) | 25.02.2002 | 5 | (6) | |
| Eliesse Ben Seghir | 16.02.2005 | 13 | (6) | 4 |
| Mohamed Camara (MLI) | 06.01.2000 | 25 | (4) | |
| Edan Diop | 28.08.2004 | 1 | (6) | 1 |
| Youssouf Fofana | 10.01.1999 | 35 | (1) | 2 |
| Aleksandr Golovin (RUS) | 30.05.1996 | 29 | (5) | 8 |
| *Jean Lucas* de Souza Oliveira (BRA) | 22.06.1998 | 3 | (3) | |
| Soungoutou Magassa | 08.10.2003 | | (2) | |
| Eliot Matazo (BEL) | 15.02.2002 | 13 | (10) | 1 |
| **Forwards:** | **DOB** | **M** | **(s)** | **G** |
| Wissam Ben Yedder | 12.08.1990 | 28 | (4) | 19 |
| Myron Boadu (NED) | 14.01.2001 | 3 | (9) | 3 |
| Krépin Diatta (SEN) | 25.02.1999 | 22 | (9) | 4 |
| Sofiane Diop | 09.06.2000 | 1 | | 1 |
| Breel-Donald Embolo (SUI) | 14.02.1997 | 19 | (13) | 12 |
| *Gelson* Dany Batalha *Martins* (POR) | 11.05.1995 | 3 | (8) | |
| Takumi Minamino (JPN) | 16.01.1995 | 10 | (8) | 1 |
| Kevin Volland (GER) | 30.07.1992 | 7 | (10) | 3 |

## Montpellier Hérault Sport Club

| | | | | |
|---|---|---|---|---|
| Founded: | 1919 | | | |
| Stadium: | Stade de la Mosson, Montpellier (32,939) | | | |
| Trainer: | Olivier Dall'Oglio | | 16.05.1964 | |
| [17.10.2022] | Romain Pitau | | 08.08.1977 | |
| [08.02.2023] | Michel Der Zakarian (ARM) | | 18.02.1963 | |

| Goalkeepers: | DOB | M | (s) | G |
|---|---|---|---|---|
| Matis Carvalho (POR) | 28.04.1999 | 1 | (1) | |
| Bingourou Kamara (SEN) | 21.10.1996 | 4 | (1) | |
| Benjamin Lecomte | 26.04.1991 | 19 | | |
| Jonas Omlin (SUI) | 10.01.1994 | 14 | | |
| **Defenders:** | **DOB** | **M** | **(s)** | **G** |
| Nicolas Cozza | 08.01.1999 | 14 | (3) | 2 |
| Maxime Estève | 26.05.2002 | 18 | (5) | |
| Christopher Jullien | 22.03.1993 | 30 | | |
| Boubacar Kouyaté (MLI) | 15.04.1997 | 15 | | |
| Faitout Maouassa | 06.07.1998 | 23 | (10) | 5 |
| *Pedro* Filipe Teodosio *Mendes* (POR) | 01.10.1990 | | (1) | |
| Falaye Sacko (MLI) | 01.05.1995 | 29 | (6) | 1 |
| Théo Sainte-Luce | 20.10.1998 | 7 | (2) | 1 |
| Mamadou Sakho | 13.02.1990 | 7 | (8) | 1 |
| Arnaud Souquet | 12.02.1992 | 3 | (9) | |
| Issiaga Sylla (GUI) | 01.01.1994 | 15 | | 1 |
| Thibault Tamas | 20.02.2001 | | (1) | |

| | DOB | M | (s) | G |
|---|---|---|---|---|
| Enzo Gianni Tchato Mbiayi (CMR) | 23.11.2002 | 11 | (10) | 1 |
| **Midfielders:** | **DOB** | **M** | **(s)** | **G** |
| Joris Chotard | 24.09.2001 | 26 | (9) | |
| Sacha Delaye | 23.04.2002 | | (3) | 1 |
| Khalil Fayad | 09.06.2004 | 7 | (17) | |
| Jordan Ferri | 12.03.1992 | 32 | (2) | 1 |
| Léo Leroy | 14.02.2000 | 14 | (13) | |
| Téji Savanier | 22.12.1991 | 30 | | 12 |
| **Forwards:** | **DOB** | **M** | **(s)** | **G** |
| Sérigné Faye (SEN) | 05.04.2004 | | (2) | |
| Valère Germain | 17.04.1990 | 5 | (26) | 2 |
| Axel Gueguin | 24.03.2005 | | (5) | |
| Wahbi Khazri (TUN) | 08.02.1991 | 20 | (7) | 4 |
| Béni Makouana (CGO) | 28.09.2002 | 1 | (7) | |
| Stephy Mavididi (ENG) | 31.05.1998 | 14 | (12) | 4 |
| Arnaud Nordin | 17.06.1998 | 30 | (6) | 9 |
| Elye Wahi | 02.01.2003 | 29 | (4) | 19 |

## Football Club de Nantes

| | | | | |
|---|---|---|---|---|
| Founded: | 1943 | | | |
| Stadium: | Stade de la Beaujoire, Nantes (35,322) | | | |
| Trainer: | Antoine Krilone Kombouaré | | 16.11.1963 | |
| [09.05.2023] | Pierre Aristouy | | 20.12.1979 | |

| Goalkeepers: | DOB | M | (s) | G |
|---|---|---|---|---|
| Rémy Descamps | 25.06.1996 | 1 | | |
| Alban Lafont | 23.01.1999 | 37 | | |
| **Defenders:** | **DOB** | **M** | **(s)** | **G** |
| *Andrei* Girotto (BRA) | 17.02.1992 | 36 | | 1 |
| Dennis Appiah | 09.06.1992 | 9 | (6) | |
| Jean-Charles Castelletto (CMR) | 26.01.1995 | 30 | (2) | |
| Fabien Centonze | 16.01.1996 | 19 | (4) | |
| Sébastien Corchia | 01.11.1990 | 6 | (16) | |
| *Fábio* Pereira Da Silva (BRA) | 09.07.1990 | 3 | (3) | |
| Jaouen Hadjam | 26.03.2003 | 8 | (5) | |
| *João Victor* Da Silva Marcelino (BRA) | 17.07.1998 | 9 | (4) | |
| Quentin Merlin | 16.05.2002 | 22 | (2) | 1 |
| Nicolas Pallois | 19.09.1987 | 26 | | 1 |
| Charles Traoré (MLI) | 01.01.1992 | 6 | (6) | |
| Nathan Zézé | 18.06.2005 | 1 | | |

| **Midfielders:** | **DOB** | **M** | **(s)** | **G** |
|---|---|---|---|---|
| Mohamed Achi | 16.01.2002 | | (2) | |
| Ludovic Blas | 31.12.1997 | 30 | (7) | 7 |
| Lohann Doucet | 14.09.2002 | | (9) | |
| Florent Mollet | 19.11.1991 | 11 | (8) | 1 |
| Samuel Moutoussamy (COD) | 12.08.1996 | 27 | (8) | |
| *Pedro Chirivella* Burgos (ESP) | 23.05.1997 | 25 | (1) | |
| Moussa Sissoko | 16.08.1989 | 22 | (8) | 2 |
| **Forwards:** | **DOB** | **M** | **(s)** | **G** |
| Stredair Appuah | 27.06.2004 | | (5) | |
| Abdoul Kader Bamba | 25.04.1994 | 1 | (3) | |
| Marcus Coco | 24.06.1996 | 6 | (20) | 1 |
| Andy Delort (ALG) | 09.10.1991 | 6 | (6) | |
| Ignatius Kpene Ganago (CMR) | 16.02.1999 | 16 | (12) | 5 |
| Evann Guessand | 01.07.2001 | 15 | (15) | 3 |
| Mostafa Mohamed Ahmed Abdalla (EGY) | 28.11.1997 | 18 | (18) | 8 |
| Moses Daddy-Ayala Simon (NGA) | 12.07.1995 | 28 | (6) | 5 |

## Olympique Gymnaste Club Nice Côte d'Azur

| | | | | |
|---|---|---|---|---|
| Founded: | 09.07.1904 (*as Le Gymnaste Club de Nice*) | | | |
| Stadium: | Allianz Riviera, Nice (35,624) | | | |
| Trainer: | Lucien Favre (SUI) | | 02.11.1957 | |
| [09.01.2023] | Didier Frédéric Thierry Digard | | 12.07.1986 | |

| Goalkeepers: | DOB | M | (s) | G |
|---|---|---|---|---|
| Marcin Bułka (POL) | 04.10.1999 | 2 | | |
| Kasper Peter Schmeichel (DEN) | 05.11.1986 | 36 | | |
| **Defenders:** | **DOB** | **M** | **(s)** | **G** |
| Ayoub Amraoui | 14.05.2004 | 3 | (4) | |
| Youcef Atal (ALG) | 17.05.1996 | 8 | (10) | 1 |
| Melvin Bard | 06.11.2000 | 28 | (5) | |
| Joseph Edward Bryan (ENG) | 17.09.1993 | 2 | (4) | |
| Flavius David Daniliuc (AUT) | 27.04.2001 | 1 | (1) | |
| Bonfim Costa Santos *Dante* (BRA) | 18.10.1983 | 37 | | 1 |
| Jordan Lotomba (SUI) | 29.09.1998 | 27 | (6) | |
| Antoine Mendy | 27.05.2004 | 7 | (4) | |
| Youssouf Ndayishimiye (BDI) | 27.10.1998 | 6 | (4) | 1 |
| Jean-Clair Todibo | 30.12.1999 | 33 | (1) | |
| Mattia Viti (ITA) | 24.01.2002 | 7 | (2) | 1 |
| **Midfielders:** | **DOB** | **M** | **(s)** | **G** |
| Ross Barkley (ENG) | 05.12.1993 | 9 | (18) | 4 |
| Alexis Beka Beka | 29.03.2001 | 7 | (7) | |
| Reda Belahyane | 01.06.2004 | 1 | (3) | |

| | DOB | M | (s) | G |
|---|---|---|---|---|
| Hichem Boudaoui (ALG) | 23.09.1999 | 22 | (5) | 1 |
| Alexis Claude-Maurice | 06.06.1998 | 1 | (1) | |
| Andréa Dacourt | 20.07.2005 | | (1) | |
| Mario René Junior Lemina (GAB) | 01.09.1993 | 11 | (3) | |
| Aaron James Ramsey (WAL) | 26.12.1990 | 18 | (9) | 1 |
| Pablo Paulino Rosario (NED) | 07.01.1997 | 17 | (14) | |
| Calvin Stengs (NED) | 18.12.1998 | 3 | (1) | |
| Khéphren Thuram-Ulien | 26.03.2001 | 30 | (5) | 2 |
| Théo Trinker | 20.06.2001 | | (1) | |
| **Forwards:** | **DOB** | **M** | **(s)** | **G** |
| Badredine Bouanani (ALG) | 08.12.2004 | 9 | (10) | |
| Bilal Brahimi (ALG) | 14.03.2000 | 5 | (21) | 3 |
| Andy Delort (ALG) | 09.10.1991 | 9 | (5) | 6 |
| Sofiane Diop | 09.06.2000 | 14 | (8) | 1 |
| Amine Gouiri | 16.02.2000 | 3 | | |
| Rareş Ilie (ROU) | 19.04.2003 | 2 | (2) | |
| Gaëtan Laborde | 03.05.1994 | 28 | (5) | 13 |
| Terem Igobor Moffi (NGA) | 25.05.1999 | 15 | (1) | 6 |
| Nicolas Pépé (CIV) | 29.05.1995 | 17 | (2) | 6 |

## Paris Saint-Germain Football Club

**Founded:** 12.08.1970
**Stadium:** Stade Parc des Princes, Paris (48,583)
**Trainer:** Christophe Galtier — 23.08.1966

| Goalkeepers: | DOB | M | (s) | G |
|---|---|---|---|---|
| Gianluigi Donnarumma (ITA) | 25.02.1999 | 38 | | |
| Alexandre Letellier | 11.12.1990 | | (1) | |
| **Defenders:** | **DOB** | **M** | **(s)** | **G** |
| El Chadaïlle Bitshiabu | 16.05.2005 | 6 | (7) | |
| Achraf Hakimi (MAR) | 04.11.1998 | 23 | (5) | 5 |
| Juan Bernat Velasco (ESP) | 01.03.1993 | 18 | (10) | 1 |
| Presnel Kimpembe | 13.08.1995 | 9 | (2) | |
| Marcos Aoás Corrêa „Marquinhos" (BRA) | 14.05.1994 | 30 | (3) | 2 |
| Nordi Mukiele Mulere | 01.11.1997 | 12 | (7) | |
| Nuno Alexandre Tavares Mendes (POR) | 19.06.2002 | 18 | (5) | 1 |
| Timothée Joseph Pembélé | 09.09.2002 | 4 | (1) | |
| Sergio Ramos García (ESP) | 30.03.1986 | 31 | (2) | 2 |
| **Midfielders:** | **DOB** | **M** | **(s)** | **G** |
| Carlos Soler Barragán (ESP) | 02.01.1997 | 14 | (12) | 3 |
| Danilo Luís Hélio Pereira (POR) | 09.09.1991 | 27 | (6) | 2 |
| Fabián Ruiz Peña (ESP) | 03.04.1996 | 21 | (6) | 3 |
| Ismaël Gharbi Álvarez (ESP) | 10.04.2004 | | (6) | |
| Leandro Daniel Paredes (ARG) | 29.06.1994 | | (3) | |
| Renato Júnior Luz Sanches (POR) | 18.08.1997 | 6 | (17) | 2 |
| Marco Verratti (ITA) | 05.11.1992 | 27 | (2) | |
| Vítor Machado Ferreira „Vitinha" (POR) | 13.02.2000 | 29 | (7) | 2 |
| Warren Zaire-Emery | 08.03.2006 | 8 | (18) | 2 |
| **Forwards:** | **DOB** | **M** | **(s)** | **G** |
| Hugo Ekitiké | 20.06.2002 | 12 | (13) | 3 |
| Ilyes Housni | 14.05.2005 | | (1) | |
| Kylian Sanmi Mbappé Lottin | 20.12.1998 | 32 | (2) | 29 |
| Lionel Andrés Messi Cuccitini (ARG) | 24.06.1987 | 32 | | 16 |
| Neymar da Silva Santos Júnior (BRA) | 05.02.1992 | 18 | (2) | 13 |
| Pablo Sarabia García (ESP) | 11.05.1992 | 3 | (11) | |

## Stade de Reims

**Founded:** 1931 (*as Société Sportive du Parc Pommery*)
**Stadium:** Stade „Auguste Delaune", Reims (21,684)
**Trainer:** Óscar García Junyent (ESP) — 26.04.1973
**[13.10.2022]** William Still (BEL) — 14.10.1992

| Goalkeepers: | DOB | M | (s) | G |
|---|---|---|---|---|
| Yehvann Diouf | 16.11.1999 | 31 | | |
| Patrick Pentz | 02.01.1997 | 7 | | |
| **Defenders:** | **DOB** | **M** | **(s)** | **G** |
| Yunis Abdelhamid (MAR) | 28.09.1987 | 37 | | 1 |
| Emmanuel Agbadou (CIV) | 17.06.1997 | 27 | (2) | |
| Maxime Busi (BEL) | 14.10.1999 | 11 | (10) | |
| Thibault De Smet (BEL) | 05.06.1998 | 20 | (2) | |
| Ibrahim Diakité | 31.10.2003 | 1 | (2) | |
| Wout Faes (BEL) | 03.04.1998 | 3 | | |
| Fallou Fall (SEN) | 15.04.2004 | | (1) | |
| Thomas Foket (BEL) | 25.09.1994 | 23 | (1) | |
| Andreaw Gravillon (GLP) | 08.02.1998 | 12 | (1) | |
| Cheick Keita | 02.04.2003 | 8 | (1) | |
| Bradley Locko | 06.05.2002 | 13 | (2) | |
| **Midfielders:** | **DOB** | **M** | **(s)** | **G** |
| Martin Adeline | 02.12.2003 | | (5) | |
| Valentin Atangana Edoa | 25.08.2005 | 2 | (5) | |
| Jens-Lys Cajuste (SWE) | 10.08.1999 | 14 | (17) | 3 |
| Kamory Doumbia (MLI) | 18.02.2003 | 13 | (13) | 2 |
| Rafik Guitane | 26.05.1999 | | (1) | |
| Samuel Koeberlé | 26.11.2004 | | (1) | |
| Dion Lopy (SEN) | 02.02.2002 | 16 | (13) | |
| Azor Matusiwa (NED) | 28.04.1998 | 29 | (1) | |
| Marshall Munetsi (ZIM) | 22.06.1996 | 31 | (3) | 7 |
| **Forwards:** | **DOB** | **M** | **(s)** | **G** |
| Folarin Jerry Balogun (USA) | 03.07.2001 | 34 | (3) | 21 |
| Mamadou Diakhon | 22.09.2005 | | (2) | |
| Alexis Flips | 18.01.2000 | 28 | (5) | 4 |
| Noah Emmanuel Jean Holm (NOR) | 23.05.2001 | 2 | (6) | |
| Junya Ito (JPN) | 09.03.1993 | 34 | (1) | 6 |
| Myziane Maolida | 14.02.1999 | 2 | (7) | 1 |
| Nathanaël Mbuku | 16.03.2002 | | (6) | |
| Kaj Sierhuis (NED) | 27.04.1998 | 1 | (13) | |
| El Bilal Touré (MLI) | 03.10.2001 | 1 | (2) | |
| Mohamed Touré (AUS) | 26.03.2004 | | (3) | |
| Mitchell van Bergen (NED) | 27.08.1999 | 6 | (22) | |
| Arbër Zeneli (KOS) | 25.02.1995 | 12 | (11) | |

## Stade Rennais Football Club

**Founded:** 10.03.1901
**Stadium:** Roazhon Park, Rennes (29,778)
**Trainer:** Bruno Génésio — 01.09.1966

| Goalkeepers: | DOB | M | (s) | G |
|---|---|---|---|---|
| Doğan Alemdar (TUR) | 29.10.2002 | 4 | (2) | |
| Steve Mandanda Mpidi | 28.03.1985 | 34 | | |
| **Defenders:** | **DOB** | **M** | **(s)** | **G** |
| Lorenz Assignon | 22.06.2000 | 2 | (10) | |
| Loïc Badé | 11.04.2000 | 1 | | |
| Jeanuël Belocian | 17.02.2005 | 6 | (2) | |
| Guela Doué | 17.10.2002 | | (2) | |
| Birger Meling (NOR) | 17.12.1994 | 10 | (17) | |
| Warmed Omari | 23.04.2000 | 15 | (1) | |
| Joseph Peter Rodon (WAL) | 22.10.1997 | 16 | | 1 |
| Djed Tehuti Djed-Hotep Spence (ENG) | 09.08.2000 | 7 | (1) | |
| Arthur Nicolas Theate (BEL) | 25.05.2000 | 35 | | 4 |
| Hamari Traoré (MLI) | 27.01.1992 | 28 | (3) | 1 |
| Adrien Truffert | 20.11.2001 | 24 | (4) | |
| Christopher Maurice Wooh (CMR) | 18.09.2001 | 12 | (1) | |
| **Midfielders:** | **DOB** | **M** | **(s)** | **G** |
| Benjamin Bourigeaud | 14.01.1994 | 37 | | 7 |
| Désiré Doué | 03.06.2005 | 11 | (15) | 3 |
| Lovro Majer (CRO) | 17.01.1998 | 18 | (14) | 2 |
| Baptiste Santamaría | 09.03.1995 | 20 | (5) | 2 |
| Flavien Tait | 02.02.1993 | 19 | (11) | 2 |
| Chimuanya Ugochukwu | 26.03.2004 | 14 | (12) | |
| Miguel Ângelo da Silva Rocha „Xeka" (POR) | 10.11.1994 | 6 | (2) | |
| **Forwards:** | **DOB** | **M** | **(s)** | **G** |
| Matthis Abline | 28.03.2003 | | (11) | 1 |
| Fabrice-Alan Do Marcolino (GAB) | 19.03.2002 | | (3) | |
| Jérémy Doku (BEL) | 27.05.2002 | 13 | (16) | 6 |
| Amine Gouiri | 16.02.2000 | 29 | (4) | 15 |
| Serhou Guirassy | 12.03.1996 | | (1) | |
| Arnaud Kalimuendo | 20.01.2002 | 24 | (6) | 7 |
| Gaëtan Laborde | 03.05.1994 | 3 | (1) | 2 |
| Ibrahim Salah (MAR) | 30.08.2001 | 1 | (12) | |
| Kamaldeen Sulemana (GHA) | 15.02.2002 | 2 | (12) | 1 |
| Martin Terrier | 04.03.1997 | 16 | | 9 |
| Karl Brillant Toko Ekambi (CMR) | 14.09.1992 | 11 | (6) | 3 |

## Racing Club de Strasbourg Alsace

| Founded: | 1906 | |
|---|---|---|
| Stadium: | Stade de la Meinau, Strasbourg (29,230) | |
| Trainer: | Julien Stéphan | 18.09.1980 |
| [09.01.2023] | Mathieu Le Scornet | 02.05.1983 |
| [13.02.2023] | Frédéric Antonetti | 19.08.1961 |

| Goalkeepers: | DOB | M | (s) | G |
|---|---|---|---|---|
| Matz Willy Els Sels (BEL) | 26.02.1992 | 38 | | |
| **Defenders:** | **DOB** | **M** | **(s)** | **G** |
| Franci Bouebari | 12.09.2003 | | (2) | |
| Colin Dagba | 09.09.1998 | 12 | (9) | |
| Thomas Delaine | 24.03.1992 | 13 | (4) | |
| Alexander Djiku (GHA) | 09.08.1994 | 31 | | 1 |
| Ismaël Doukouré | 24.07.2003 | 25 | (3) | 1 |
| Karol Fila (POL) | 13.06.1998 | | (2) | |
| Frédéric Guilbert | 24.12.1994 | 17 | (1) | |
| Maxime Le Marchand | 11.10.1989 | 23 | (3) | |
| Gerzino Nyamsi | 22.01.1997 | 19 | (1) | 1 |
| Lucas Perrin | 19.11.1998 | 18 | (8) | |
| Ronaël Julien Pierre-Gabriel | 13.06.1998 | 7 | (7) | |
| Marvin Senaya | 28.01.2001 | | (1) | |
| Eduard Sobol (UKR) | 20.04.1995 | 9 | (6) | |

| Midfielders: | DOB | M | (s) | G |
|---|---|---|---|---|
| Jean-Eudes Aholou (CIV) | 20.03.1994 | 16 | (14) | 3 |
| Jean-Ricner Bellegarde | 27.06.1998 | 29 | (1) | 2 |
| Mouhamadou Habib Diarra | 03.01.2004 | 18 | (11) | 3 |
| Dany Jean (HAI) | 28.11.2002 | | (2) | |
| Nordine Kandil | 31.10.2001 | | (7) | |
| Dimitri Liénard | 13.02.1988 | 18 | (10) | |
| Sanjin Prcić (BIH) | 20.11.1993 | 17 | (12) | 1 |
| Morgan Sanson | 18.08.1994 | 18 | | 1 |
| Ibrahima Sissoko | 27.10.1997 | 13 | (13) | |
| Yuito Suzuki (JPN) | 25.10.2001 | | (3) | 1 |
| Adrien Thomasson | 10.12.1993 | 10 | (5) | |
| **Forwards:** | **DOB** | **M** | **(s)** | **G** |
| Ludovic Ajorque | 25.02.1994 | 9 | (4) | 1 |
| Habib Diallo (SEN) | 18.06.1995 | 32 | (5) | 20 |
| Kevin Gameiro | 09.05.1987 | 23 | (11) | 10 |
| Lebogang Mothiba (RSA) | 28.01.1996 | 3 | (16) | 3 |

## Toulouse Football Club

| Founded: | 25.05.1970 | |
|---|---|---|
| Stadium: | Stade Municipal, Toulouse (33,150) | |
| Trainer: | Philippe Jacques William Montanier | 15.11.1964 |

| Goalkeepers: | DOB | M | (s) | G |
|---|---|---|---|---|
| Maxime Dupé | 04.03.1993 | 38 | | |
| **Defenders:** | **DOB** | **M** | **(s)** | **G** |
| Logan Costa (CPV) | 01.04.2001 | 4 | (2) | |
| Mikkel Desler (DEN) | 19.02.1995 | 26 | (1) | 1 |
| Moussa Diarra (MLI) | 10.11.2000 | 12 | (11) | |
| Warren Håkon Christofer Kamanzi (NOR) | 11.11.2000 | 7 | (4) | |
| Kévin Keben Biakolo (CMR) | 26.01.2004 | 4 | (7) | |
| Christian Mawissa Elebi | 18.04.2005 | 1 | (1) | |
| Rasmus Schmidt Nicolaisen (DEN) | 16.03.1997 | 34 | | |
| Anthony Rouault | 29.05.2001 | 37 | | 2 |
| Gabriel Alonso Suazo Urbina (CHI) | 09.08.1997 | 14 | (4) | |
| Issiaga Sylla (GUI) | 1994 | 16 | (1) | |
| Carl Oliver Zandén (SWE) | 14.08.2001 | 1 | (4) | |
| **Midfielders:** | **DOB** | **M** | **(s)** | **G** |
| Brecht Dejaegere (BEL) | 29.05.1991 | 25 | (5) | 4 |
| Denis Genreau (AUS) | 21.05.1999 | 7 | (13) | |
| Vincent Olivier Sierro (SUI) | 08.10.1995 | 7 | (8) | |
| Naatan Skyttä (FIN) | 07.05.2002 | | (2) | |
| Stijn Spierings (NED) | 12.03.1996 | 35 | (1) | 2 |
| Theocharis Tsingaras (GRE) | 20.08.2000 | | (1) | |
| Branco van den Boomen (NED) | 21.07.1995 | 32 | (3) | 5 |
| **Forwards:** | **DOB** | **M** | **(s)** | **G** |
| Zakaria Aboukhlal (MAR) | 18.02.2000 | 28 | (9) | 10 |
| Yanis Begraoui | 04.07.2001 | 1 | (2) | |
| Veljko Birmančević (SRB) | 05.03.1998 | 2 | (23) | |
| Fares Chaïbi | 28.11.2002 | 24 | (12) | 5 |
| Thijs Dallinga (NED) | 03.08.2000 | 28 | (8) | 12 |
| Rhys Evitt-Healey (ENG) | 06.12.1994 | | (4) | 2 |
| Saïd Hamulić (BIH) | 12.11.2000 | | (6) | |
| Nathan N'Goumou Minpole | 14.03.2000 | 1 | | |
| Ado Onaiwu (JPN) | 08.11.1995 | 9 | (25) | 2 |
| Rafael Rogério da Silva „Rafael Ratão" (BRA) | 30.11.1995 | 25 | (5) | 5 |

## Ésperance Sportive Troyes Aube Champagne

| Founded: | 1986 | |
|---|---|---|
| Stadium: | Stade de l'Aube, Troyes (21,684) | |
| Trainer: | Bruno Irles | 16.08.1975 |
| [08.11.2022] | Claude Robin | 10.12.1960 |
| [23.11.2022] | Patrick Fabio Maxime Kisnorbo (AUS) | 24.03.1981 |

| Goalkeepers: | DOB | M | (s) | G |
|---|---|---|---|---|
| Gauthier Gallon | 23.04.1993 | 30 | | |
| Mateusz Lis (POL) | 27.02.1997 | 8 | (1) | |
| **Defenders:** | **DOB** | **M** | **(s)** | **G** |
| *Abdu* Cadri *Conté* (POR) | 24.03.1998 | 15 | (4) | 1 |
| Thierno Baldé | 10.06.2002 | 25 | (6) | |
| Tanguy Banhie-Zoukrou | 07.05.2003 | 5 | (3) | |
| Andreas Bruus (DEN) | 16.01.1999 | 18 | (9) | |
| Mathis Hamdi | 18.10.2003 | | (2) | |
| Rudy Kohon | 23.05.2004 | | (1) | |
| Yasser Larouci | 01.01.2001 | 21 | (9) | 1 |
| Erik Palmer-Brown (USA) | 24.04.1997 | 36 | (2) | |
| Jackson Gabriel Porozo Vernaza (ECU) | 04.08.2000 | 17 | (5) | 2 |
| Adil Rami | 27.12.1985 | 18 | (2) | |
| Yoann Salmier (GUF) | 21.11.1992 | 31 | (1) | 1 |
| **Midfielders:** | **DOB** | **M** | **(s)** | **G** |
| Lucien Agoumé | 09.02.2002 | 14 | (1) | |
| Xavier Chavalerin | 07.03.1991 | 25 | (9) | 4 |
| Tristan Dingomé | 17.02.1991 | | (8) | |
| Danel Jordan Dongmo (CMR) | 31.01.2001 | | (2) | |
| Rominigue Kouamé (MLI) | 17.12.1996 | 31 | (1) | 1 |
| Derek Mazou-Sacko | 06.10.2004 | | (1) | |
| Ante Palaversa (CRO) | 06.04.2000 | | (2) | 1 |
| Jeff Reine-Adélaïde | 17.01.1998 | 3 | (3) | |
| Florian Tardieu | 22.04.1992 | 11 | (4) | 3 |
| **Forwards:** | **DOB** | **M** | **(s)** | **G** |
| Mama Samba Baldé (GNB) | 06.11.1995 | 30 | (4) | 12 |
| Kyliane Dong | 27.09.2004 | 2 | (4) | |
| Amar Abdirahman Ahmed Fatah (SWE) | 19.02.2004 | | (1) | |
| Wilson Odobert | 28.11.2004 | 19 | (13) | 4 |
| Renaud Ripart | 14.03.1993 | 15 | (11) | 4 |
| Marcos Paulo Mesquita Lopes „Rony Lopes" (POR) | 28.12.1995 | 29 | (3) | 7 |
| Alexis Tibidi | 03.11.2003 | | (3) | |
| Iké Dominique Ugbo (CAN) | 21.09.1998 | 9 | (16) | 2 |
| Pape Ndiaga Yade (SEN) | 05.01.2000 | 6 | (8) | |
| Marlos Moreno Durán (COL) | 20.09.1996 | | (2) | |

## SECOND LEVEL
### Ligue 2 2022/2023

| | | | | | | | | | |
|---|---|---|---|---|---|---|---|---|---|
| 1. | Le Havre AC (*Promoted*) | 38 | 20 | 15 | 3 | 46 | - | 19 | 75 |
| 2. | FC Metz (*Promoted*) | 38 | 20 | 12 | 6 | 61 | - | 33 | 72 |
| 3. | FC Girondins de Bordeaux | 38 | 20 | 9 | 9 | 51 | - | 28 | 69 |
| 4. | Sporting Club Bastiais | 38 | 17 | 9 | 12 | 52 | - | 45 | 60 |
| 5. | Stade Malherbe Caen | 38 | 16 | 11 | 11 | 52 | - | 43 | 59 |
| 6. | En Avant de Guingamp | 38 | 15 | 10 | 13 | 51 | - | 46 | 55 |
| 7. | Paris FC | 38 | 15 | 10 | 13 | 45 | - | 43 | 55 |
| 8. | AS Saint-Étienne* | 38 | 15 | 11 | 12 | 63 | - | 57 | 53 |
| 9. | FC Sochaux-Montbéliard (*Relegated*) | 38 | 15 | 7 | 16 | 54 | - | 41 | 52 |
| 10. | Grenoble Foot 38 | 38 | 14 | 9 | 15 | 33 | - | 36 | 51 |
| 11. | US Quevillaise-Rouen Métropole | 38 | 12 | 14 | 12 | 47 | - | 49 | 50 |
| 12. | Amiens SC | 38 | 13 | 8 | 17 | 40 | - | 52 | 47 |
| 13. | Pau FC | 38 | 12 | 11 | 15 | 40 | - | 52 | 47 |
| 14. | Rodez Aveyron Football | 38 | 11 | 13 | 14 | 39 | - | 44 | 46 |
| 15. | Stade Lavallois Mayenne FC | 38 | 14 | 4 | 20 | 44 | - | 56 | 46 |
| 16. | Valenciennes FC | 38 | 10 | 15 | 13 | 42 | - | 49 | 45 |
| 17. | FC d'Annecy | 38 | 11 | 12 | 15 | 39 | - | 51 | 45 |
| 18. | Dijon FCO (*Relegated*) | 38 | 10 | 12 | 16 | 38 | - | 43 | 42 |
| 19. | Nîmes Olympique (*Relegated*) | 38 | 10 | 6 | 22 | 44 | - | 62 | 36 |
| 20. | Chamois Niortais FC (*Relegated*) | 38 | 7 | 8 | 23 | 35 | - | 67 | 29 |

*3 points deducted for pitch invasion during the Relegation Play-off from last season.

<u>Please note</u>: FC Sochaux-Montbéliard was relegated to Championnat National (third level) due to financial problems.

## NATIONAL TEAM

### INTERNATIONAL MATCHES
#### (16.07.2022 – 15.07.2023)

| | | | | |
|---|---|---|---|---|
| 22.09.2022 | Paris | *France - Austria* | *2-0(0-0)* | (UNL) |
| 25.09.2022 | København | *Denmark - France* | *2-0(2-0)* | (UNL) |
| 22.11.2022 | Al Wakrah | *France - Australia* | *4-1(2-1)* | (WC) |
| 26.11.2022 | Doha | *France - Denmark* | *2-1(0-0)* | (WC) |
| 30.11.2022 | Al-Rayyan | *Tunisia - France* | *1-0(0-0)* | (WC) |
| 04.12.2022 | Doha | *France - Poland* | *3-1(1-0)* | (WC) |
| 10.12.2022 | Al Khor | *England - France* | *1-2(0-1)* | (WC) |
| 14.12.2022 | Al Khor | *France - Morocco* | *2-0(1-0)* | (WC) |
| 18.12.2022 | Lusail | *Argentina - France* | *3-3(1-0,2-2,2-2); 4-2 pen* | (WC) |
| | | | | |
| 24.03.2023 | Paris | *France - Netherlands* | *4-0(3-0)* | (ECQ) |
| 27.03.2023 | Dublin | *Republic of Ireland - France* | *0-1(0-0)* | (ECQ) |
| 16.06.2023 | Faro/Loulé | *Gibraltar - France* | *0-3(0-2)* | (ECQ) |
| 19.06.2023 | Paris | *France - Greece* | *1-0(0-0)* | (ECQ) |

**22.09.2022    FRANCE - AUSTRIA**          **2-0(0-0)**          3rd UEFA Nations League A, Group 1
Stade de France, Saint-Denis, Paris; Referee: Andreas Ekberg (Sweden); Attendance: 70,188
**FRA:** Mike Maignan (46.Alphonse Areola), Jonathan Clauss, Raphaël Varane (Cap), Ferland Sinna Mendy, Jules Olivier Koundé (23.William Alain André Gabriel Saliba), Benoît Ntambue Badiashile Mukinayi Baya, Aurélien Djani Tchouaméni, Youssouf Fofana, Antoine Griezmann (79.Masour Ousmane Dembélé), Olivier Jonathan Giroud (79.Christopher Alan Nkunku), Kylian Sanmi Mbappé Lottin (90+2.Randal Kolo Muani). Trainer: Didier Claude Deschamps.
**Goals:** Kylian Sanmi Mbappé Lottin (56), Olivier Jonathan Giroud (65).

**25.09.2022    DENMARK - FRANCE**          **2-0(2-0)**          3rd UEFA Nations League A, Group 1
Parken Stadium, København; Referee: István Kovács (Romania); Attendance: 36,064
**FRA:** Alphonse Areola, Benjamin Jacques Marcel Pavard, Ferland Sinna Mendy (65.Adrien Truffert), Dayotchanculle Oswald Upamecano, Benoît Ntambue Badiashile Mukinayi Baya, William Alain André Gabriel Saliba (46.Jonathan Clauss), Aurélien Djani Tchouaméni, Eduardo Celmi Camavinga (46.Youssouf Fofana), Antoine Griezmann (Cap) (81.Randal Kolo Muani), Olivier Jonathan Giroud (65.Christopher Alan Nkunku), Kylian Sanmi Mbappé Lottin. Trainer: Didier Claude Deschamps.

**22.11.2022    FRANCE - AUSTRALIA**          **4-1(2-1)**          22nd FIFA WC. Group Stage.
Al Janoub Stadium, Al Wakrah (Qatar); Referee: Victor Miguel de Freitas Gomes (South Africa); Attendance: 40,875
**FRA:** Hugo Hadrien Dominique Lloris (Cap), Benjamin Jacques Marcel Pavard (89.Jules Olivier Koundé), Ibrahima Konaté, Dayotchanculle Oswald Upamecano, Lucas François Bernard Hernández (13.Théo Bernard François Hernández), Aurélien Djani Tchouaméni (77.Youssouf Fofana), Adrien Thibaut Marie Rabiot-Provost, Masour Ousmane Dembélé (77.Kingsley Junior Coman), Antoine Griezmann, Kylian Sanmi Mbappé Lottin, Olivier Jonathan Giroud (89.Marcus Lilian Thuram-Ulien). Trainer: Didier Claude Deschamps.
**Goals:** Adrien Thibaut Marie Rabiot-Provost (27), Olivier Jonathan Giroud (32), Kylian Sanmi Mbappé Lottin (68), Olivier Jonathan Giroud (71).

**26.11.2022    FRANCE - DENMARK                2-1(0-0)                22nd FIFA WC. Group Stage.**
Stadium 974, Doha (Qatar); Referee: Szymon Marciniak (Poland); Attendance: 42,860
**FRA:** Hugo Hadrien Dominique Lloris (Cap), Jules Olivier Koundé, Raphaël Xavier Varane (75.Ibrahima Konaté), Dayotchanculle Oswald Upamecano, Théo Bernard François Hernández, Aurélien Djani Tchouaméni, Adrien Thibaut Marie Rabiot-Provost, Masour Ousmane Dembélé (75.Kingsley Junior Coman), Antoine Griezmann (90+3.Youssouf Fofana), Kylian Sanmi Mbappé Lottin, Olivier Jonathan Giroud (63.Marcus Lilian Thuram-Ulien). Trainer: Didier Claude Deschamps.
**Goals:** Kylian Sanmi Mbappé Lottin (61, 86).

**30.11.2022    TUNISIA - FRANCE                1-0(0-0)                22nd FIFA WC. Group Stage.**
Education City Stadium, Al Rayyan (Qatar); Referee: Matthew Conger (New Zealand); Attendance: 43,627
**FRA:** Steve Mandanda Mpidi, Axel Wilson Arthur Disasi Mhakinis Belho, Raphaël Xavier Varane (Cap) (63.William Alain André Gabriel Saliba), Ibrahima Konaté, Eduardo Celmi Camavinga, Aurélien Djani Tchouaméni, Youssouf Fofana (73.Antoine Griezmann), Mattéo Elias Kenzo Guendouzi Olié (79.Masour Ousmane Dembélé), Jordan Marcel Gilbert Veretout (63.Adrien Thibaut Marie Rabiot-Provost), Kingsley Junior Coman (63.Kylian Sanmi Mbappé Lottin), Randal Kolo Muani. Trainer: Didier Claude Deschamps.

**04.12.2022    FRANCE - POLAND                3-1(1-0)                22nd FIFA WC. 2nd Round of 16.**
Al Thumama Stadium, Doha (Qatar); Referee: Jesús Noel Valenzuela Sáez (Venezuela); Attendance: 40,989
**FRA:** Hugo Hadrien Dominique Lloris (Cap), Jules Olivier Koundé (90+2.Axel Wilson Arthur Disasi Mhakinis Belho), Raphaël Xavier Varane, Dayotchanculle Oswald Upamecano, Théo Bernard François Hernández, Aurélien Djani Tchouaméni (66.Youssouf Fofana), Adrien Thibaut Marie Rabiot-Provost, Masour Ousmane Dembélé (76.Kingsley Junior Coman), Antoine Griezmann, Kylian Sanmi Mbappé Lottin, Olivier Jonathan Giroud (76.Marcus Lilian Thuram-Ulien). Trainer: Didier Claude Deschamps.
**Goals:** Olivier Jonathan Giroud (44), Kylian Sanmi Mbappé Lottin (73, 90+1).

**10.12.2022    ENGLAND - FRANCE                1-2(0-1)                22nd FIFA WC. Quarter-Finals.**
Al Bayt Stadium, Al Khor (Qatar); Referee: Wilton Pereira Sampaio (Brazil); Attendance: 68,895
**FRA:** Hugo Hadrien Dominique Lloris (Cap), Jules Olivier Koundé, Raphaël Xavier Varane, Dayotchanculle Oswald Upamecano, Théo Bernard François Hernández, Aurélien Djani Tchouaméni, Adrien Thibaut Marie Rabiot-Provost, Masour Ousmane Dembélé (79.Kingsley Junior Coman), Antoine Griezmann, Kylian Sanmi Mbappé Lottin, Olivier Jonathan Giroud. Trainer: Didier Claude Deschamps.
**Goals:** Aurélien Djani Tchouaméni (17), Olivier Jonathan Giroud (78).

**14.12.2022    FRANCE - MOROCCO                2-0(1-0)                22nd FIFA WC. Semi-Finals.**
Al Bayt Stadium, Al Khor (Qatar); Referee: César Arturo Ramos Palazuelos (Mexico); Attendance: 68,294
**FRA:** Hugo Hadrien Dominique Lloris (Cap), Jules Olivier Koundé, Raphaël Xavier Varane, Ibrahima Konaté, Théo Bernard François Hernández, Aurélien Djani Tchouaméni, Youssouf Fofana, Masour Ousmane Dembélé (78.Randal Kolo Muani), Antoine Griezmann, Kylian Sanmi Mbappé Lottin, Olivier Jonathan Giroud (65.Marcus Lilian Thuram-Ulien). Trainer: Didier Claude Deschamps.
**Goals:** Théo Bernard François Hernández (5), Randal Kolo Muani (79).

**18.12.2022    ARGENTINA - FRANCE                3-3(1-0,2-2,2-2); 4-2 on penalties                22nd FIFA WC. Final.**
Lusail Stadium, Lusail (Qatar); Referee: Szymon Marciniak (Poland); Attendance: 88,966
**FRA:** Hugo Hadrien Dominique Lloris (Cap), Jules Olivier Koundé (120+1.Axel Wilson Arthur Disasi Mhakinis Belho), Raphaël Xavier Varane (112.Ibrahima Konaté), Dayotchanculle Oswald Upamecano, Théo Bernard François Hernández (71.Eduardo Celmi Camavinga), Aurélien Djani Tchouaméni, Adrien Thibaut Marie Rabiot-Provost (96.Youssouf Fofana), Masour Ousmane Dembélé (41.Randal Kolo Muani), Antoine Griezmann (71.Kingsley Junior Coman), Kylian Sanmi Mbappé Lottin, Olivier Jonathan Giroud (41.Marcus Lilian Thuram-Ulien). Trainer: Didier Claude Deschamps.
**Goals:** Kylian Sanmi Mbappé Lottin (80 penalty, 81, 118 penalty).
**Penalties:** Kylian Sanmi Mbappé Lottin, Kingsley Junior Coman (saved), Aurélien Djani Tchouaméni (missed), Randal Kolo Muani.

**24.03.2023    FRANCE - NETHERLANDS                4-0(3-0)                17th EC. Qualifiers**
Stade de France, Saint-Denis, Paris; Referee: Maurizio Mariani (Italy); Attendance: 77,328
**FRA:** Mike Maignan, Jules Olivier Koundé, Dayotchanculle Oswald Upamecano, Ibrahima Konaté, Theo Bernard François Hernández, Aurélien Djani Tchouaméni (76.Eduardo Celmi Camavinga), Adrien Thibaut Marie Rabiot-Provost (89.Khéphren Thuram-Ulien), Antoine Griezmann (76.Youssouf Fofana), Kingsley Junior Coman (67.Moussa Diaby), Randal Kolo Muani (76.Olivier Jonathan Giroud), Kylian Sanmi Mbappé Lottin (Cap). Trainer: Didier Claude Deschamps.
**Goals:** Antoine Griezmann (2), Dayotchanculle Oswald Upamecano (8), Kylian Sanmi Mbappé Lottin (21, 88).

**27.03.2023    REPUBLIC OF IRELAND - FRANCE                0-1(0-0)                17th EC. Qualifiers**
Aviva Stadium, Dublin; Referee: Artur Manuel Ribeiro Soares Dias (Portugal); Attendance: 50,219
**FRA:** Mike Maignan, Benjamin Jacques Marcel Pavard (81.Jules Olivier Koundé), Dayotchanculle Oswald Upamecano, Ibrahima Konaté, Theo Bernard François Hernández, Eduardo Celmi Camavinga, Adrien Thibaut Marie Rabiot-Provost (81.Aurélien Djani Tchouaméni), Antoine Griezmann, Randal Kolo Muani (90+2.Marcus Lilian Thuram-Ulien), Olivier Jonathan Giroud (65.Moussa Diaby), Kylian Sanmi Mbappé Lottin (Cap). Trainer: Didier Claude Deschamps.
**Goal:** Benjamin Jacques Marcel Pavard (50).

**16.06.2023    GIBRALTAR - FRANCE                0-3(0-2)                17th EC. Qualifiers**
Estádio Algarve, Faro/Loulé (Portugal); Referee: Yevhenii Aranovskiy (Ukraine); Attendance: 4,065
**FRA:** Brice Laurice Samba, Benjamin Jacques Marcel Pavard, Ibrahima Konaté (84.Axel Wilson Arthur Disasi Mhakinis Belho), Wesley Tidjan Fofana, Theo Bernard François Hernández, Aurélien Djani Tchouaméni, Eduardo Celmi Camavinga (79.Youssouf Fofana), Antoine Griezmann (65.Christopher Alan Nkunku), Kingsley Junior Coman (65.Masour Ousmane Dembélé), Olivier Jonathan Giroud (65.Randal Kolo Muani), Kylian Sanmi Mbappé Lottin (Cap). Trainer: Didier Claude Deschamps.
**Goals:** Olivier Jonathan Giroud (3), Kylian Sanmi Mbappé Lottin (45+3), Aymen Mouelhi (78 own goal).

**19.06.2023    FRANCE - GREECE                1-0(0-0)                17th EC. Qualifiers**
Stade de France, Saint-Denis, Paris; Referee: Antonio Mateu Lahoz (Spain); Attendance: 76,500
**FRA:** Mike Maignan, Jules Olivier Koundé, Dayotchanculle Oswald Upamecano, Ibrahima Konaté, Theo Bernard François Hernández, Aurélien Djani Tchouaméni, Eduardo Celmi Camavinga, Antoine Griezmann (85.Christopher Alan Nkunku), Kingsley Junior Coman (77.Masour Ousmane Dembélé), Randal Kolo Muani (85.Olivier Jonathan Giroud), Kylian Sanmi Mbappé Lottin (Cap). Trainer: Didier Claude Deschamps.
**Goal:** Kylian Sanmi Mbappé Lottin (55 penalty).

## NATIONAL TEAM PLAYERS
### (16.07.2022 – 15.07.2023)

| Name | DOB | Caps | Goals | Club | |
|---|---|---|---|---|---|
| **Goalkeepers** | | | | | |
| Alphonse AREOLA | 27.02.1993 | 5 | 0 | 2022: | *West Ham United FC London (ENG)* |
| Hugo Hadrien Dominique LLORIS | 26.12.1986 | 145 | 0 | 2022: | *Tottenham Hotspur FC London (ENG)* |
| Mike MAIGNAN | 03.07.1995 | 8 | 0 | 2022/2023: | *AC Milan (ITA)* |
| Steve MANDANDA Mpidi | 28.03.1985 | 35 | 0 | 2022: | *Stade Rennais FC* |
| Brice Laurice SAMBA | 25.04.1994 | 1 | 0 | 2023: | *Racing Club de Lens* |
| **Defenders** | | | | | |
| Benoît Ntambue BADIASHILE Mukinayi Baya | 26.03.2001 | 2 | 0 | 2022: | *AS Monaco FC* |
| Jonathan CLAUSS | 25.09.1992 | 6 | 0 | 2022: | *Olympique de Marseille* |
| Axel Wilson Arthur DISASI Mhakinis Belho | 11.03.1998 | 4 | 0 | 2022/2023: | *AS Monaco FC* |
| Wesley Tidjan FOFANA | 17.12.2000 | 1 | 0 | 2023: | *Chelsea FC London (ENG)* |
| Lucas François Bernard HERNÁNDEZ | 14.02.1996 | 33 | 0 | 2022: | *FC Bayern München (GER)* |
| Theo Bernard François HERNÁNDEZ | 06.10.1997 | 17 | 2 | 2022/2023: | *AC Milan (ITA)* |
| Ibrahima KONATÉ | 25.05.1999 | 11 | 0 | 2022/2023: | *Liverpool FC (ENG)* |
| Jules Olivier KOUNDÉ | 12.11.1998 | 21 | 0 | 2022/2023: | *FC Barcelona (ESP)* |
| Ferland Sinna MENDY | 08.06.1995 | 9 | 0 | 2022: | *Real Madrid CF (ESP)* |
| Benjamin Jacques Marcel PAVARD | 28.03.1996 | 49 | 3 | 2022/2023: | *FC Bayern München (GER)* |
| William Alain André Gabriel SALIBA | 24.03.2001 | 8 | 0 | 2022: | *Arsenal FC London (ENG)* |
| Adrien TRUFFERT | 20.11.2001 | 1 | 0 | 2022: | *Stade Rennais FC* |
| Dayotchanculle Oswald UPAMECANO | 27.10.1998 | 15 | 2 | 2022/2023: | *FC Bayern München (GER)* |
| Raphaël Xavier VARANE | 25.04.1993 | 93 | 5 | 2022: | *Manchester United FC (ENG)* |
| **Midfielders** | | | | | |
| Eduardo Celmi CAMAVINGA | 10.11.2002 | 10 | 1 | 2022/2023: | *Real Madrid CF (ESP)* |
| Youssouf FOFANA | 10.01.1999 | 10 | 0 | 2022/2023: | *AS Monaco FC* |
| Mattéo Elias Kenzo GUENDOUZI Olié | 14.04.1999 | 7 | 1 | 2022: | *Olympique de Marseille* |
| Adrien Thibaut Marie RABIOT-PROVOST | 03.04.1995 | 37 | 3 | 2022/2023: | *Juventus FC Torino (ITA)* |
| Aurélien Djani TCHOUAMÉNI | 27.01.2000 | 25 | 2 | 2022/2023: | *Real Madrid CF (ESP)* |
| Khéphren THURAM-ULIEN | 26.03.2001 | 1 | 0 | 2023: | *OGC Nice* |
| Jordan Marcel Gilbert VERETOUT | 01.03.1993 | 6 | 0 | 2022: | *Olympique de Marseille* |
| **Forwards** | | | | | |
| Kingsley Junior COMAN | 13.06.1996 | 49 | 5 | 2022/2023: | *FC Bayern München (GER)* |
| Masour Ousmane DEMBÉLÉ | 15.05.1997 | 37 | 4 | 2022/2023: | *FC Barcelona (ESP)* |
| Moussa DIABY | 07.07.1999 | 10 | 0 | 2023: | *Bayer 04 Leverkusen (GER)* |
| Olivier Jonathan GIROUD | 30.09.1986 | 124 | 54 | 2022/2023: | *AC Milan (ITA)* |
| Antoine GRIEZMANN | 21.03.1991 | 121 | 43 | 2022/2023: | *Club Atlético de Madrid (ESP)* |
| Randal KOLO MUANI | 05.12.1998 | 9 | 1 | 2022/2023: | *Eintracht Frankfurt (GER)* |
| Kylian Sanmi MBAPPÉ Lottin | 20.12.1998 | 70 | 40 | 2022/2023: | *Paris Saint-Germain FC* |
| Christopher Alan NKUNKU | 14.11.1997 | 10 | 0 | 2022/2023: | *RasenBallsport Leipzig (GER)* |
| Marcus Lilian THURAM-ULIEN | 06.08.1997 | 10 | 0 | 2022/2023: | *Borussia VfL Mönchengladbach (GER)* |
| **Trainer** | | | | | |
| Didier Claude DESCHAMPS [from 08.07.2012] | 15.10.1968 | | | 143 M; 93 W; 28 D; 22 L; 288-119 | |

# GEORGIA

## The Country:
Georgia (საქართველო)
Capital: Tbilisi
Surface: 69,700 km²
Inhabitants: 4,935,518 [2022]
Time: UTC+4

## The FA:
Georgian Football Federation
76a Chavchavadze Avenue, 0162 Tbilisi
Tel: +995 32 912 680
Founded: 1936/re-founded 1990
Member of FIFA since: 1992
Member of UEFA since: 1992
Website: www.gff.ge

## NATIONAL TEAM RECORDS

| RECORDS | | |
|---|---|---|
| **First international match:** | 27.05.1990, Tbilisi: | Georgia – Lithuania 2-2 |
| **Most international caps:** | Guram Kashia | - 104 caps (since 2009) |
| **Most international goals:** | Shota Arveladze | - 26 goals / 61 caps (1992-2007) |

| UEFA EUROPEAN CHAMPIONSHIP | |
|---|---|
| 1960 | - |
| 1964 | - |
| 1968 | - |
| 1972 | - |
| 1976 | - |
| 1980 | - |
| 1984 | - |
| 1988 | - |
| 1992 | - |
| 1996 | Qualifiers |
| 2000 | Qualifiers |
| 2004 | Qualifiers |
| 2008 | Qualifiers |
| 2012 | Qualifiers |
| 2016 | Qualifiers |
| 2020 | Qualifiers |

| FIFA WORLD CUP | |
|---|---|
| 1930 | - |
| 1934 | - |
| 1938 | - |
| 1950 | - |
| 1954 | - |
| 1958 | - |
| 1962 | - |
| 1966 | - |
| 1970 | - |
| 1974 | - |
| 1978 | - |
| 1982 | - |
| 1986 | - |
| 1990 | - |
| 1994 | Did not enter |
| 1998 | Qualifiers |
| 2002 | Qualifiers |
| 2006 | Qualifiers |
| 2010 | Qualifiers |
| 2014 | Qualifiers |
| 2018 | Qualifiers |
| 2022 | Qualifiers |

| OLYMPIC TOURNAMENTS | |
|---|---|
| 1908 | - |
| 1912 | - |
| 1920 | - |
| 1924 | - |
| 1928 | - |
| 1936 | - |
| 1948 | - |
| 1952 | - |
| 1956 | - |
| 1960 | - |
| 1964 | - |
| 1968 | - |
| 1972 | - |
| 1976 | - |
| 1980 | - |
| 1984 | - |
| 1988 | - |
| 1992 | - |
| 1996 | Qualifiers |
| 2000 | Qualifiers |
| 2004 | Qualifiers |
| 2008 | Qualifiers |
| 2012 | Qualifiers |
| 2016 | Qualifiers |
| 2020 | Qualifiers |

*was part of Soviet Union between 1930-1990*

| UEFA NATIONS LEAGUE | |
|---|---|
| 2018/2019 | League D (Group Stage -> promoted to League League C) |
| 2020/2021 | League C (Group Stage) |
| 2022/2023 | League C (Group Stage -> promoted to League League B) |

## GEORGIAN CLUB HONOURS IN EUROPEAN CLUB COMPETITIONS:

| European Champion Clubs.Cup (1956-1992) / UEFA Champions League (1993-2023) | | |
|---|---|---|
| None | | |

| Fairs Cup (1858-1971) / UEFA Cup (1972-2009) / UEFA Europa League (2010-2023) | | |
|---|---|---|
| None | | |

| UEFA Europa Conference League (2021-2023) | | |
|---|---|---|
| None | | |

| UEFA Super Cup (1972-2022) | | |
|---|---|---|
| None | | |

| European Cup Winners' Cup 1961-1999* | | |
|---|---|---|
| FC Dinamo Tbilisi* | 1 | 1980/1981 |
| *represented the Soviet Union | | |

*defunct competition*

# NATIONAL COMPETITIONS
## TABLE OF HONOURS

### GEORGIAN SSR (SOVIET ERA) CHAMPIONS

| Year | Champion | Year | Champion | Year | Champion |
|------|----------|------|----------|------|----------|
| 1927 | Batumi XI | 1953 | TTU Tbilisi | 1972 | Lokomotivi FC Samtredia |
| 1928 | Tbilisi XI | 1954 | TTU Tbilisi | 1973 | Dinamo Zugdidi |
| 1929-1935 | *No competition* | 1955 | Dinamo Kutaisi | 1974 | Metallurg Rustavi |
| 1936 | ZII Tbilisi | 1956 | FC FC Lokomotivi Tbilisi | 1975 | Magaroeli Chiatura |
| 1937 | FC FC Lokomotivi Tbilisi | 1957 | TTU Tbilisi | 1976 | SKIF Tbilisi |
| 1938 | FC FC Dinamo Batumi | 1958 | TTU Tbilisi | 1977 | Mziuri Gali |
| 1939 | Nauka Tbilisi | 1959 | Metallurg Rustavi | 1978 | Kolheti Poti |
| 1940 | FC FC Dinamo Batumi | 1960 | Imereti Kutaisi | 1979 | Metallurg Rustavi |
| 1941-1942 | *No competition* | 1961 | FC Guria Lanchkhuti | 1980 | Meshakhte Tkibuli |
| 1943 | ODKA Tbilisi | 1962 | Imereti Kutaisi | 1981 | Meshakhte Tkibuli |
| 1944 | *No competition* | 1963 | Imereti Kutaisi | 1982 | Mertskhali Makharadze |
| 1945 | FC FC Lokomotivi Tbilisi | 1964 | IngurGES Zugdidi | 1983 | Samgulari Tskhaltubo |
| 1946 | Dinamo Kutaisi | 1965 | Tolia Tbilisi | 1984 | Metallurg Rustavi |
| 1947 | FC Dinamo Sokhumi | 1966 | FC Guria Lanchkhuti | 1985 | Shadrevani-83 Tskhaltubo |
| 1948 | FC Dinamo Sokhumi | 1967 | Mertskhali Makharadze | 1986 | Shevardeni-1906 Tbilisi |
| 1949 | FC FC Torpedo Kutaisi | 1968 | SKA Tbilisi | 1987 | Mertskhali Makharadze |
| 1950 | TODO Tbilisi | 1969 | Sulori Vani | 1988 | Kolheti Poti |
| 1951 | TODO Tbilisi | 1970 | SKIF Tbilisi | 1989 | Shadrevani-83 Tskhaltubo |
| 1952 | TTU Tbilisi | 1971 | FC Guria Lanchkhuti | | |

| | CHAMPIONS | CUP WINNERS | BEST GOALSCORERS | |
|------|-----------|-------------|------------------|---|
| 1990 | FC Iberia Tbilisi | FC Guria Lanchkhuti | Gia Guruli (FC Iberia Tbilisi) Mamuka Pantsulaia (FC Gorda Rustavi) | 23 |
| 1991 | FC Iberia Tbilisi | FC Dinamo Tbilisi | Otar Korgalidze (FC Guria Lanchkhuti) | 14 |
| 1991/1992 | FC Dinamo Tbilisi | FC Dinamo Tbilisi | Otar Korgalidze (FC Guria Lanchkhuti) | 40 |
| 1992/1993 | FC Dinamo Tbilisi | FC Dinamo Tbilisi | Merab Megreladze (Samgurali Tskhaltubo) | 41 |
| 1993/1994 | FC Dinamo Tbilisi | FC Dinamo Tbilisi | Merab Megreladze (FC Margveti Zestafoni) | 31 |
| 1994/1995 | FC Dinamo Tbilisi | FC Dinamo Tbilisi | Giorgi Daraselia (FC Kolkheti-1913 Poti) | 26 |
| 1995/1996 | FC Dinamo Tbilisi | FC Dinamo Tbilisi | Zviad Endeladze (FC Margveti Zestafoni) | 40 |
| 1996/1997 | FC Dinamo Tbilisi | FC Dinamo Batumi | Giorgi Demetradze (FC Dinamo Tbilisi) David Ujmajuridze (FC Dinamo Batumi) | 26 |
| 1997/1998 | FC Dinamo Tbilisi | FC Torpedo Kutaisi | Levan Khomeriki (FC Dinamo Tbilisi) | 23 |
| 1998/1999 | FC Dinamo Tbilisi | FC Lokomotivi Tbilisi | Mikheil Ashvetia (FC Dinamo Tbilisi) | 26 |
| 1999/2000 | FC Torpedo Kutaisi | FC Torpedo Kutaisi | Zurab Ionanidze (FC Torpedo Kutaisi) | 24 |
| 2000/2001 | FC Torpedo Kutaisi | FC Lokomotivi Tbilisi | Zaza Zirakishvili (FC Dinamo Tbilisi) | 21 |
| 2001/2002 | FC Torpedo Kutaisi | FC Dinamo Tbilisi | Suliko Davitashvili (FC Lokomotivi Tbilisi / FC Merani Tbilisi) | 18 |
| 2002/2003 | FC Dinamo Tbilisi | FC Dinamo Tbilisi | Zurab Ionanidze (FC Torpedo Kutaisi) | 26 |
| 2003/2004 | FC WIT Georgia Tbilisi | FC Lokomotivi Tbilisi | Suliko Davitashvili (FC Torpedo Kutaisi) | 20 |
| 2004/2005 | FC Dinamo Tbilisi | FC Ameri Tbilisi | Levani Melkadze (FC Dinamo Tbilisi) | 27 |
| 2005/2006 | FC Sioni Bolnisi | FC Ameri Tbilisi | Jaba Dvali (FC Dinamo Tbilisi) | 21 |
| 2006/2007 | FC Olimpi Rustavi | FC Zestafoni | Sandro Iashvili (FC Dinamo Tbilisi) | 27 |
| 2007/2008 | FC Dinamo Tbilisi | FC Dinamo Tbilisi | Mikheil Khutsishvili (FC Dinamo Tbilisi) | 16 |
| 2008/2009 | FC WIT Georgia Tbilisi | FC WIT Georgia Tbilisi | Nikoloz Gelashvili (FC Zestafoni) | 20 |
| 2009/2010 | FC Olimpi Rustavi | FC Gagra | Brazil Anderson Aquino (FC Metalurgi Rustavi) | 26 |
| 2010/2011 | FC Zestafoni | FC Dila Gori | Nikoloz Gelashvili (FC Zestafoni) | 18 |
| 2011/2012 | FC Zestafoni | FC Dinamo Tbilisi | Jaba Dvali (FC Zestafoni) | 20 |
| 2012/2013 | FC Dinamo Tbilisi | FC Dinamo Tbilisi | Spain Xisco (FC Dinamo Tbilisi) | 24 |
| 2013/2014 | FC Dinamo Tbilisi | FC Dinamo Tbilisi | Spain Xisco (FC Dinamo Tbilisi) | 19 |
| 2014/2015 | FC Dila Gori | FC Dinamo Tbilisi | Irakli Modebadze (FC Dila Gori) | 16 |
| 2015/2016 | FC Dinamo Tbilisi | FC Torpedo Kutaisi | Giorgi Kvilitaia (FC Dinamo Tbilisi) | 24 |
| 2016 | FC Samtredia | FC Chikhura Sachkhere | Budu Zivzivadze (FC Samtredia) | 11 |
| 2017 | FC Torpedo Kutaisi | FC Guria Lanchkhuti | Irakli Sikharulidze (FC Lokomotivi Tbilisi) | 25 |
| 2018 | FC Saburtalo Tbilisi | FC Torpedo Kutaisi | Giorgi Gabedava (FC Chikhura Sachkhere) Budu Zivzivadze (FC Dinamo Tbilisi) | 22 |
| 2019 | FC Dinamo Tbilisi | FC Saburtalo Tbilisi | Levan Kutalia (FC Dinamo Tbilisi) | 20 |
| 2020 | FC Dinamo Tbilisi | FC Gagra | Mykola Kovtalyuk (UKR, FC Dila Gori) | 10 |
| 2021 | FC Dinamo Batumi | FC Saburtalo Tbilisi | Zoran Marušić (SRB, FC Dinamo Tbilisi) | 16 |
| 2022 | FC Dinamo Tbilisi | FC Torpedo Kutaisi | Flamarion Jovinho Filho (BRA, FC Dinamo Batumi) | 19 |

Please note: FC Dinamo Tbilisi changed its name to FC Iberia Tbilisi between 1990-1992; FC Olimpi Rustavi became FC Metalurgi Rustavi (2011-2015) and later FC Rustavi (since 2011).

## Results

### Round 1 [25-27.02.2022]
Dinamo Batumi - Sioni Bolnisi 4-0(1-0)
Dinamo Tbilisi - Torpedo Kutaisi 4-0(2-0)
Dila Gori - FC Gagra 2-1(2-0)
Lokomotivi Tbilisi - FC Telavi 0-1(0-0)
FC Saburtalo - FC Samgurali 2-1(1-1)

### Round 2 [04-05.03.2022]
FC Gagra - FC Saburtalo 1-0(1-0)
Torpedo Kutaisi - Dila Gori 1-0(1-0)
Dinamo Batumi - Dinamo Tbilisi 3-0(2-0)
Sioni Bolnisi - FC Telavi 0-2(0-0)
FC Samgurali - Lokomotivi Tbilisi 3-1(0-1)

### Round 3 [08-09.03.2022]
Dila Gori - Dinamo Batumi 2-1(0-0)
FC Saburtalo - Torpedo Kutaisi 2-0(2-0)
Dinamo Tbilisi - Sioni Bolnisi 1-0(0-0)
Lokomotivi Tbilisi - FC Gagra 0-2(0-2)
FC Telavi - FC Samgurali 0-0 [06.04.2022]

### Round 4 [13-15.03.2022]
Dinamo Batumi - FC Saburtalo 2-2(1-1)
Sioni Bolnisi - FC Samgurali 1-1(0-1)
FC Gagra - FC Telavi 2-2(1-2)
Dinamo Tbilisi - Dila Gori 2-1(2-0) [06.04.22]
Torpedo K.-Lokomotivi T. 4-2(2-0) [06.04.22]

### Round 5 [18-19.03.2022]
Lokomotivi Tbilisi - Dinamo Batumi 0-2(0-1)
Dila Gori - Sioni Bolnisi 2-1(0-0)
FC Samgurali-FC Gagra 1-1(1-0) [14.04.2022]
FC Telavi - Torpedo Kutaisi 0-0 [14.04.2022]
Saburtalo - Dinamo Tbilisi 1-1(1-0) [14.04.22]

### Round 6 [02-03.04.2022]
Torpedo Kutaisi - FC Samgurali 0-2(0-2)
Dinamo Batumi - FC Telavi 1-0(1-0)
Dila Gori - FC Saburtalo 1-0(0-0)
Dinamo Tbilisi - Lokomotivi Tbilisi 2-1(1-0)
Sioni Bolnisi - FC Gagra 2-1(1-1)

### Round 7 [10-11.04.2022]
FC Gagra - Torpedo Kutaisi 0-2(0-1)
FC Samgurali - Dinamo Batumi 0-3(0-1)
FC Saburtalo - Sioni Bolnisi 3-3(0-2)
FC Telavi - Dinamo Tbilisi 1-1(1-1)
Lokomotivi Tbilisi - Dila Gori 0-3(0-0)

### Round 8 [18.04.2022]
Sioni Bolnisi - Torpedo Kutaisi 1-1(1-1)
Dila Gori - FC Telavi 2-1(0-0)
Dinamo Tbilisi - FC Samgurali 0-0
Dinamo Batumi - FC Gagra 5-2(3-1)
FC Saburtalo - Lokomotivi Tbilisi 3-1(1-0)

### Round 9 [23.04.2022]
FC Samgurali - Dila Gori 0-0
FC Gagra - Dinamo Tbilisi 1-0(0-0)
Lokomotivi Tbilisi - Sioni Bolnisi 1-2(1-1)
FC Telavi - FC Saburtalo 0-2(0-1)
Torpedo Kutaisi - Dinamo Batumi 0-3(0-2)

### Round 10 [29.04.2022]
FC Gagra - Dila Gori 1-0(0-0)
FC Samgurali - FC Saburtalo 3-0(0-0)
Sioni Bolnisi - Dinamo Batumi 1-1(0-1)
FC Telavi - Lokomotivi Tbilisi 5-0(4-0)
Torpedo Kutaisi - Dinamo Tbilisi 0-*awarded*

### Round 11 [03-04.05.2022]
Dila Gori - Torpedo Kutaisi 2-0(1-0)
Dinamo Tbilisi - Dinamo Batumi 0-0
FC Saburtalo - FC Gagra 3-0(0-0)
FC Telavi - Sioni Bolnisi 2-0(2-0)
Lokomotivi Tbilisi - FC Samgurali 0-2(0-1)

### Round 12 [08-09.05.2022]
Sioni Bolnisi - Dinamo Tbilisi 3-7(2-4)
Torpedo Kutaisi - FC Saburtalo 0-1(0-0)
Dinamo Batumi - Dila Gori 3-0(1-0)
FC Samgurali - FC Telavi 2-1(2-0)
FC Gagra - Lokomotivi Tbilisi 5-3(1-1)

### Round 13 [12-13.05.2022]
FC Saburtalo - Dinamo Batumi 0-0
Dila Gori - Dinamo Tbilisi 0-1(0-1)
Sioni Bolnisi - FC Samgurali 0-2(0-1)
Lokomotivi Tbilisi - Torpedo Kutaisi 0-3(0-2)
FC Telavi - FC Gagra 1-0(0-0)

### Round 14 [16-17.05.2022]
Dinamo Tbilisi - FC Saburtalo 0-0
FC Gagra - FC Samgurali 0-2(0-2)
Sioni Bolnisi - Dila Gori 0-0
Torpedo Kutaisi - FC Telavi 1-1(0-0)
Dinamo Batumi - Lokomotivi Tbilisi 7-2(4-2)

### Round 15 [21-22.05.2022]
Lokomotivi Tbilisi - Dinamo Tbilisi 0-2(0-1)
FC Samgurali - Torpedo Kutaisi 3-0(0-0)
FC Telavi - Dinamo Batumi 0-2(0-2)
FC Gagra - Sioni Bolnisi 1-2(0-1)
FC Saburtalo - Dila Gori 0-2(0-0)

### Round 16 [25-27.05.2022]
Dinamo Tbilisi - FC Telavi 3-2(2-1)
Dinamo Batumi - FC Samgurali 4-4(3-2)
Torpedo Kutaisi - FC Gagra 1-0(0-0)
Sioni Bolnisi - FC Saburtalo 1-0(0-0)
Dila Gori - Lokomotivi Tbilisi 4-1(1-1)

### Round 17 [15-16.06.2022]
FC Telavi - Dila Gori 0-0
FC Gagra - Dinamo Batumi 0-3(0-1)
Lokomotivi Tbilisi - FC Saburtalo 2-1(1-0)
FC Samgurali - Dinamo Tbilisi 2-1(1-1)
Torpedo Kutaisi - Sioni Bolnisi 3-0(2-0)

### Round 18 [20-21.06.2022]
Sioni Bolnisi - Lokomotivi Tbilisi 5-1(2-1)
Dinamo Tbilisi - FC Gagra 5-0(1-0)
Dila Gori - FC Samgurali 0-0(0-0)
FC Saburtalo - FC Telavi 1-0(0-0)
Dinamo Batumi - Torpedo Kutaisi 4-0(1-0)

### Round 19 [24-26.06.2022]
Dila Gori - FC Gagra 1-1(0-0)
Dinamo Batumi - Sioni Bolnisi 3-0(0-0)
FC Saburtalo - FC Samgurali 3-1(1-1)
Dinamo Tbilisi - Torpedo Kutaisi 5-1(1-0)
Lokomotivi Tbilisi - FC Telavi 0-2(0-2)

### Round 20 [29.06.-02.07.2022]
Torpedo Kutaisi - Dila Gori 4-1(1-0)
FC Gagra - FC Saburtalo 3-3(1-1)
Dinamo Batumi - Dinamo Tbilisi 4-1(3-0)
FC Samgurali - Lokomotivi Tbilisi 4-1(1-1)
Sioni Bolnisi - FC Telavi 0-0

### Round 21 [13-15.08.2022]
FC Telavi - FC Samgurali 1-1(0-1)
Dinamo Tbilisi - Sioni Bolnisi 3-1(0-0)
Lokomotivi Tbilisi - FC Gagra 0-2(0-2)
Dila Gori - Dinamo Batumi 0-1(0-0)
FC Saburtalo - Torpedo Kutaisi 2-4(2-2)

### Round 22 [20-21.08.2022]
Sioni Bolnisi - FC Samgurali 0-0
Dinamo Tbilisi - Dila Gori 3-0(1-0)
FC Gagra - FC Telavi 1-1(1-0)
Torpedo Kutaisi - Lokomotivi Tbilisi 3-1(1-1)
Dinamo Batumi - FC Saburtalo 3-2(2-0)

### Round 23 [25-27.08.2022]
Dila Gori - Sioni Bolnisi 1-2(1-0)
FC Saburtalo - Dinamo Tbilisi 1-2(1-2)
FC Samgurali - FC Gagra 2-2(2-1)
Lokomotivi Tbilisi - Dinamo Batumi 1-1(0-0)
FC Telavi - Torpedo Kutaisi 1-1(0-1)

### Round 24 [30.08.-01.09.2022]
Dila Gori - FC Saburtalo 3-0(1-0)
Sioni Bolnisi - FC Gagra 0-0
Torpedo Kutaisi - FC Samgurali 3-2(1-1)
Dinamo Batumi - FC Telavi 4-0(1-0)
Dinamo Tbilisi - Lokomotivi Tbilisi 5-0(4-0)

### Round 25 [05-06.09.2022]
Lokomotivi Tbilisi - Dila Gori 2-2(0-2)
FC Saburtalo - Sioni Bolnisi 1-1(0-0)
FC Telavi - Dinamo Tbilisi 1-2(1-1)
FC Samgurali - Dinamo Batumi 3-0(2-0)
FC Gagra - Torpedo Kutaisi 0-2(0-1)

### Round 26 [09-10.09.2022]
Dila Gori - FC Telavi 0-0
Sioni Bolnisi - Torpedo Kutaisi 0-3(0-0)
Dinamo Tbilisi - FC Samgurali 3-0(2-0)
FC Saburtalo - Lokomotivi Tbilisi 5-1(3-1)
Dinamo Batumi - FC Gagra 2-0(2-0)

### Round 27 [17-18.09.2022]
FC Samgurali - Dila Gori 0-3(0-2)
Lokomotivi Tbilisi - Sioni Bolnisi 2-2(1-0)
Torpedo Kutaisi - Dinamo Batumi 1-0(1-0)
FC Gagra - Dinamo Tbilisi 0-1(0-0)
FC Telavi - FC Saburtalo 0-3(0-1)

### Round 28 [01-02.10.2022]
FC Gagra - Dila Gori 0-0
FC Samgurali - FC Saburtalo 0-3(0-2)
FC Telavi - Lokomotivi Tbilisi 0-0
Sioni Bolnisi - Dinamo Batumi 1-1(0-1)
Torpedo Kutaisi - Dinamo Tbilisi 0-0

### Round 29 [07-09.10.2022]
Dila Gori - Torpedo Kutaisi 2-1(2-1)
Dinamo Tbilisi - Dinamo Batumi 1-0(0-0)
FC Saburtalo - FC Gagra 2-1(1-0)
Lokomotivi Tbilisi - FC Samgurali 1-4(1-2)
FC Telavi - Sioni Bolnisi 0-0

### Round 30 [15-16.10.2022]
FC Gagra - Lokomotivi Tbilisi 2-0(2-0)
FC Samgurali - FC Telavi 2-0(0-0)
Sioni Bolnisi - Dinamo Tbilisi 0-2(0-0)
Torpedo Kutaisi - FC Saburtalo 1-1(1-1)
Dinamo Batumi - Dila Gori 3-2(3-0)

| Round 31 [21-23.10.2022] |
|---|
| FC Saburtalo - Dinamo Batumi 2-4(1-1) |
| Lokomotivi Tbilisi - Torpedo Kutaisi 0-0 |
| Dila Gori - Dinamo Tbilisi 2-3(1-1) |
| FC Samgurali - Sioni Bolnisi 2-1(0-1) |
| FC Telavi - FC Gagra 1-0(1-0) |

| Round 32 [29-30.10.2022] |
|---|
| Torpedo Kutaisi - FC Telavi 1-0(1-0) |
| Dinamo Tbilisi - FC Saburtalo 3-1(1-1) |
| Dinamo Batumi - Lokomotivi Tbilisi 4-2(2-0) |
| FC Gagra - FC Samgurali 1-1(0-0) |
| Sioni Bolnisi - Dila Gori 1-2(1-1) |

| Round 33 [04-06.11.2022] |
|---|
| FC Gagra - Sioni Bolnisi 2-1(1-0) |
| FC Telavi - Dinamo Batumi 0-2(0-0) |
| Lokomotivi Tbilisi - Dinamo Tbilisi 0-2(0-1) |
| FC Samgurali - Torpedo Kutaisi 2-2(1-1) |
| FC Saburtalo - Dila Gori 0-2(0-2) |

| Round 34 [10-12.11.2022] |
|---|
| Dinamo Tbilisi - FC Telavi 1-1(1-0) |
| Sioni Bolnisi - FC Saburtalo 1-0(0-0) |
| Torpedo Kutaisi - FC Gagra 0-1(0-0) |
| Dila Gori - Lokomotivi Tbilisi 1-0(1-0) |
| Dinamo Batumi - FC Samgurali 1-2(0-1) |

| Round 35 [26.11.2022] |
|---|
| FC Gagra - Dinamo Batumi 1-4(0-2) |
| Lokomotivi Tbilisi - FC Saburtalo 0-1(0-0) |
| FC Samgurali - Dinamo Tbilisi 1-1(1-0) |
| FC Telavi - Dila Gori 1-1(0-1) |
| Torpedo Kutaisi - Sioni Bolnisi 3-0(1-0) |

| Round 36 [03.12.2022] |
|---|
| Dinamo Batumi - Torpedo Kutaisi 2-2(1-1) |
| Dinamo Tbilisi - FC Gagra 2-1(1-0) |
| FC Saburtalo - FC Telavi 0-1(0-0) |
| Sioni Bolnisi - Lokomotivi Tbilisi 5-2(3-1) |
| Dila Gori - FC Samgurali 3-0(1-0) |

## Final Standings

| | | | | Total | | | | Home | | | | | Away | | | | |
|---|---|---|---|---|---|---|---|---|---|---|---|---|---|---|---|---|---|
| 1. | **FC Dinamo Tbilisi** | 36 | 24 | 8 | 4 | 73 - 29 | **80** | 14 | 4 | 0 | 43 - 9 | 10 | 4 | 4 | 30 - 20 |
| 2. | FC Dinamo Batumi | 36 | 23 | 8 | 5 | 87 - 34 | **77** | 14 | 3 | 1 | 59 - 21 | 9 | 5 | 4 | 28 - 13 |
| 3. | FC Dila Gori | 36 | 17 | 8 | 11 | 48 - 35 | **59** | 12 | 2 | 4 | 29 - 14 | 5 | 6 | 7 | 19 - 21 |
| 4. | FC Samgurali Tskhaltubo | 36 | 15 | 12 | 9 | 55 - 44 | **57** | 9 | 6 | 3 | 31 - 21 | 6 | 6 | 6 | 24 - 23 |
| 5. | FC Torpedo Kutaisi | 36 | 15 | 9 | 12 | 48 - 48 | **54** | 10 | 3 | 5 | 26 - 18 | 5 | 6 | 7 | 22 - 30 |
| 6. | FC Saburtalo Tbilisi | 36 | 13 | 8 | 15 | 51 - 49 | **47** | 8 | 4 | 6 | 31 - 25 | 5 | 4 | 9 | 20 - 24 |
| 7. | FC Telavi | 36 | 8 | 15 | 13 | 29 - 36 | **39** | 4 | 9 | 5 | 14 - 15 | 4 | 6 | 8 | 15 - 21 |
| 8. | FC Sioni Bolnisi (*Relegation Play-offs*) | 36 | 8 | 12 | 16 | 38 - 60 | **36** | 5 | 7 | 6 | 21 - 25 | 3 | 5 | 10 | 17 - 35 |
| 9. | FC Gagra (*Relegation Play-offs*) | 36 | 9 | 9 | 18 | 36 - 57 | **36** | 6 | 5 | 7 | 21 - 27 | 3 | 4 | 11 | 15 - 30 |
| 10. | FC Lokomotivi Tbilisi (*Relegated*) | 36 | 1 | 5 | 30 | 28 - 101 | **8** | 1 | 4 | 13 | 9 - 34 | 0 | 1 | 17 | 19 - 67 |

| Top goalscorers: | | |
|---|---|---|
| 19 | **Flamarion Jovinho Filho (BRA)** | *FC Dinamo Batumi* |
| 13 | Irakli Rukhadze | *FC Samgurali Tskhaltubo* |
| 12 | Irakli Sikharulidze | *FC Saburtalo Tbilisi* |

## Relegation Play-offs [07/08-11/12.12.2022]

| | | |
|---|---|---|
| FC Samtredia - FC Sioni Bolnisi | 1-0(0-0) | 2-0(1-0) |
| FC Gagra - FC Spaeri Tbilisi | 2-0(1-0) | 1-3 aet; 5-4 pen |

Both FC Samtredia and FC Gagra will play at first level in 2023.

## NATIONAL CUP
### "David Kipiani" Cup - Sakartvelos tasi 2022

| Fourth Round [06-08.08.2022] | | | | |
|---|---|---|---|---|
| FC WIT Georgia Tbilisi - FC Lokomotivi Tbilisi | 2-2 aet; 2-4 pen | | FC Gareji 1960 Sagarejo - FC Telavi | 0-1(0-0) |
| FC Dinamo-2 Tbilisi - FC Sioni Bolnisi | 3-2(2-0) | | FC Samegrelo Chkhorotsku - FC Merani Martvili | 0-3(0-0) |
| FC Shukura Kobuleti - FC Gagra | 2-0(1-0) | | FC Zana Abasha - FC Tskhumi Sukhumi | 1-0(1-0) |
| FC Varketili Tbilisi - FC Saburtalo-2 Tbilisi | 2-0(1-0) | | FC Lokomotivi-2 Tbilisi - FC Samgurali Tskhaltubo | 1-0(1-0) |
| FC Samtredia - FC Dinamo Tbilisi | 1-2(0-1) | | FC Merani Tbilisi - FC Spaeri Tbilisi | 2-2 aet; 3-4 pen |
| FC Guria Lanchkhuti - FC Kolkheti 1913 Poti | 1-0(1-0) | | FC WIT Georgia-2 Tbilisi - FC Torpedo Kutaisi | 1-2(0-2) |
| FC Gardabani - FC Rustavi | 1-8(0-3) | | FC Matchakhela Khelvachauri - FC Dila Gori | 1-6(0-1) |

| 1/8-Finals [13-14.09.2022] | | | | |
|---|---|---|---|---|
| FC Zana Abasha - FC Guria Lanchkhuti | 1-4(0-2) | | FC Spaeri Tbilisi - FC Torpedo Kutaisi | 0-1(0-1) |
| FC Varketili Tbilisi - FC Rustavi | 2-3(1-3) | | FC Merani Martvili - FC Saburtalo | 2-3(2-1,2-2) |
| FC Lokomotivi-2 Tbilisi - FC Telavi | 1-1 aet; 4-2 pen | | FC Shukura Kobuleti - FC Lokomotivi Tbilisi | 2-0(1-0) |
| FC Dinamo-2 Tbilisi - FC Dila Gori | 1-4(0-2) | | Dinamo Batumi - FC Dinamo Tbilisi | 0-0 aet; 0-3 pen |

| Quarter-Finals [12.10.2022] | | | | |
|---|---|---|---|---|
| FC Lokomotivi-2 Tbilisi - FC Guria Lanchkhuti | 1-0(0-0) | | FC Dinamo Tbilisi - FC Dila Gori | 2-1(1-1) |
| FC Shukura Kobuleti - FC Saburtalo | 0-2(0-1) | | FC Rustavi - FC Torpedo Kutaisi | 2-4(1-2) |

| Semi-Finals [02.11.2022] | | | | |
|---|---|---|---|---|
| FC Torpedo Kutaisi - FC Dinamo Tbilisi | 2-0(0-0) | | FC Lokomotivi-2 Tbilisi - FC Saburtalo | 0-0 aet; 7-6 pen |

07.12.2022; Adjarabet Arena, Batumi; Referee: Aleko Aptsiauri; Attendance: n/a
**FC Torpedo Kutaisi - FC Lokomotivi-2 Tbilisi**                    **2-0(0-0)**

**Torpedo Kutaisi**: Roin Kvaskhvadze (Cap), Levan Gegetchkori, Nika Sandokhadze, Pedro Filipe Tinoco Monteiro, Lasha Shergelashvili, Merab Gigauri, Giuli Mandzhgaladze (90+2.Vazha Tabatadze), Giorgi Kukhianidze (77.Mate Tsintsadze), Giorgi Arabidze (69.Akaki Shulaia), Mauro Andrés Caballero Aguilera (69.Tornike Akhvlediani), Giorgi Kimadze (69.Irakli Bugridze). Trainer: Kakhaber Chkhetiani.

**Lokomotivi-2 Tbilisi**: Soso Kopaliani, Giorgi Gabadze, Aleksandre Andronikashvili, Beka Kharaishvili, Giorgi Pirtakhia, Irakli Chiabrishvili (80.Givi Mukbaniani), Revaz Khinchiashvili (80.Ivane Okropiridze), Tornike Kurtanidze (72.Sandro Melikishvili), Lasha Menteshashvili (72.Lasha Ozbetelashvili), Vano Shermadini (66.Gabriel Khutsishvili), Saba Amiko Kiknadze (Cap). Trainer: Lasha Chaghiashvili.

**Goals:** 1-0 Mauro Andrés Caballero Aguilera (53), 2-0 Giorgi Kimadze (61).

# THE CLUBS 2022

## Football Club Dila Gori

| Founded: | 1949 |
|---|---|
| Stadium: | Stadioni „Tengiz Burjanadze", Gori (8,230) |
| Trainer: | Andriy Demchenko (UKR) 20.08.1976 |

| Goalkeepers: | DOB | M | (s) | G |
|---|---|---|---|---|
| Demetre Buliskeria | 09.01.2000 | 10 | (2) | |
| Danylo Kanevtsev (UKR) | 26.07.1996 | 26 | | |
| **Defenders:** | **DOB** | **M** | **(s)** | **G** |
| Anri Chitchinadze | 05.10.1997 | 30 | (1) | |
| Revaz Chiteishvili | 30.01.1994 | 31 | | 1 |
| Tornike Dzotsenidze | 07.11.1999 | 15 | (6) | 2 |
| Ramaric Presley Etou Thomaso (CGO) | 25.01.1995 | 1 | | |
| Aleksandre Gaprindashvili | 16.07.2004 | 6 | (15) | |
| Wanderson Henrique do Nascimento Silva (BRA) | 13.09.1991 | 36 | | |
| **Midfielders:** | **DOB** | **M** | **(s)** | **G** |
| Alef Santos de Araujo (BRA) | 06.11.1996 | 34 | | 3 |
| Alvaro Luis Tavares Vieira (BRA) | 10.03.1995 | 6 | (6) | |
| Yuriy Batyushyn (UKR) | 07.12.1992 | 10 | (3) | 1 |
| Nika Gagnidze | 20.03.2001 | 18 | | 3 |

| Giorgi Lomtadze | 30.10.2001 | 1 | (9) | |
|---|---|---|---|---|
| Francisco Madinga (MWI) | 11.02.2000 | 7 | (13) | 1 |
| Tsotne Mosiashvili | 14.02.1995 | 23 | (4) | 1 |
| Amos Nondi Obiero (KEN) | 10.02.1999 | 27 | (5) | |
| Jean Victor Gonçalves (BRA) | 21.03.1995 | 8 | (6) | 1 |
| **Forwards:** | **DOB** | **M** | **(s)** | **G** |
| Hadji Dramé (MLI) | 10.09.2000 | 2 | (23) | 3 |
| Thierry Gale (BRB) | 01.05.2002 | 16 | | 2 |
| Honoré Gomis (SEN) | 27.02.1996 | 20 | (6) | 4 |
| Paata Gudushauri | 07.06.1997 | 16 | (1) | 2 |
| Giorgi Ivaniadze | 27.01.2000 | 3 | (8) | |
| Tornike Kapanadze | 04.06.1992 | 26 | (2) | 9 |
| Tamaz Makatsaria | 03.10.1995 | 7 | (7) | 3 |
| Nugzar Spanderashvili | 16.01.1999 | 5 | (8) | 1 |
| Vagner Gonçalves Nogueira de Souza (BRA) | 27.04.1996 | 12 | (5) | 8 |

## Football Club Dinamo Batumi

| Founded: | 1923 |
|---|---|
| Stadium: | Batumi Stadium (Adjarabet Arena), Batumi (20,000) |
| Trainer: | Georgi Geguchadze 20.06.1965 |

| Goalkeepers: | DOB | M | (s) | G |
|---|---|---|---|---|
| Mikheil Alavidze | 05.11.1987 | 17 | | |
| Giorgi Begashvili | 12.02.1991 | 2 | | |
| Lazare Kupatadze | 08.02.1996 | 17 | | |
| **Defenders:** | **DOB** | **M** | **(s)** | **G** |
| Irakli Azarovi | 21.02.2002 | 18 | | |
| Oleksandr Azatsky (UKR) | 13.01.1994 | 26 | (3) | |
| Grigol Chabradze | 20.04.1996 | 28 | (4) | |
| Abraham Frimpong (GHA) | 06.04.1993 | | (1) | |
| Luka Kapianidze | 10.01.1999 | 1 | (3) | |
| Mamuka Kobakhidze | 23.08.1992 | 33 | (1) | 2 |
| Giorgi Navalovski | 28.06.1986 | 5 | (11) | |
| Giorgi Rekhviashvili | 01.02.1988 | 12 | (1) | |
| **Midfielders:** | **DOB** | **M** | **(s)** | **G** |
| Sandro Altunashvili | 19.05.1997 | 30 | (1) | 1 |
| Jano Ananidze | 10.10.1992 | 1 | (4) | |
| Irakli Bidzinashvili | 27.02.1997 | 10 | (17) | 7 |

| Jaba Jigauri | 08.07.1992 | 21 | (9) | 8 |
|---|---|---|---|---|
| Vladimer Mamuchashvili | 28.08.1997 | 32 | (2) | 7 |
| Guga Palavandishvili | 14.08.1993 | 12 | (17) | 1 |
| Milan Radin (SRB) | 25.06.1991 | 23 | (5) | 7 |
| Benjamin Teidi (NGA) | 07.05.1994 | 25 | (3) | 2 |
| Giorgi Zaria | 14.07.1997 | 2 | (26) | 1 |
| **Forwards:** | **DOB** | **M** | **(s)** | **G** |
| Zuriko Davitashvili | 15.02.2001 | 11 | (3) | 6 |
| Stefan Denković (MNE) | 16.06.1991 | | (4) | |
| Flamarion Jovinho Filho (BRA) | 30.07.1996 | 25 | (4) | 19 |
| Tornike Gaprindashvili | 20.07.1997 | 4 | (14) | 5 |
| Khvicha Kvaratskhelia | 12.02.2001 | 9 | (2) | 8 |
| Elguja Lobjanidze | 17.09.1992 | 3 | (8) | 1 |
| Giorgi Pantsulaia | 06.01.1994 | 16 | (13) | 6 |
| Paata Gudushauri | 07.06.1997 | 8 | (3) | 1 |
| Mate Vatsadze | 17.12.1988 | 5 | (10) | 4 |

## Football Club Dinamo Tbilisi

| Founded: | 1925 |
|---|---|
| Stadium: | „Boris Paichadze" Dinamo Arena, Tbilisi (54,139) |
| Trainer: | Kakhaber Tskhadadze 07.09.1968 |
| [19.06.2022] | Giorgi Chiabrishvili 07.10.1979 |

| Goalkeepers: | DOB | M | (s) | G |
|---|---|---|---|---|
| Davit Kereselidze | 19.08.1999 | 7 | | |
| Luka Kutaladze | 27.04.2001 | 11 | (1) | |
| Andrés Prieto (ESP) | 17.01.1993 | 18 | (1) | |
| **Defenders:** | **DOB** | **M** | **(s)** | **G** |
| Godfrey Bitok Stephen (NGA) | 22.08.2000 | 5 | (8) | |
| Giorgi Chkhetiani | 20.02.2003 | | (2) | |
| Simon Gbegnon Amoussou (TOG) | 27.10.1992 | 19 | (1) | 2 |
| Aleksandre Kalandadze | 09.05.2001 | 26 | (3) | |
| Levan Kharabadze | 26.01.2000 | 13 | (4) | |
| Saba Khvadagiani | 30.01.2003 | 18 | (6) | |
| Davit Kobouri | 24.01.1994 | 14 | (2) | |
| Giorgi Maisuradze | 31.01.2002 | 2 | (10) | |
| Nikoloz Mali | 27.01.1999 | 35 | | |
| Jemal Tabidze | 18.03.1996 | 12 | | |
| **Midfielders:** | **DOB** | **M** | **(s)** | **G** |
| Giorgi Kutsia | 27.10.1999 | 3 | (9) | |
| Nodar Lominadze | 04.04.2002 | 3 | (6) | |

| Anzor Mekvabishvili | 05.06.2001 | 29 | (1) | 5 |
|---|---|---|---|---|
| Giorgi Moistsrapishvili | 29.09.2001 | 22 | (8) | 7 |
| Levan Osikmashvili | 20.04.2002 | 10 | (10) | |
| Imran Oulad Omar (NED) | 11.12.1997 | 14 | (2) | 8 |
| Giorgi Papava | 16.02.1993 | 10 | (5) | 1 |
| Luka Parkadze | 06.04.2005 | | (3) | |
| Gabriel Sigua | 30.06.2005 | 2 | (7) | |
| **Forwards:** | **DOB** | **M** | **(s)** | **G** |
| Dmitriy Antilevskiy (BLR) | 12.06.1997 | 14 | (10) | 3 |
| Stanislav Bilenkiy (UKR) | 22.08.1998 | 17 | (11) | 10 |
| Ousmane Camara (GUI) | 28.12.1998 | 34 | (2) | 10 |
| Giorgi Gabedava | 03.10.1989 | 4 | (21) | 7 |
| Giorgi Gvishiani | 19.11.2003 | | (2) | |
| Tornike Kirkitadze | 23.07.1996 | 20 | (10) | 6 |
| Lasha Odisharia | 23.10.2002 | 1 | (6) | 1 |
| Barnes Osei (GHA) | 08.01.1995 | 21 | (7) | 4 |
| Davit Skhirtladze | 16.03.1993 | 12 | (10) | 7 |

## Football Club Gagra

| Founded: | 2004 | | | |
| Stadium: | „Boris Paichadze" Dinamo Arena, Tbilisi (54,139) | | | |
| Trainer: | Gaga Kirkitadze | | 18.10.1987 | |

| Goalkeepers: | DOB | M | (s) | G |
|---|---|---|---|---|
| Nika Kavtaradze | 17.06.1998 | 9 | | |
| Beka Kurdadze | 24.01.1997 | 19 | | |
| Oleksandr Vorobey (UKR) | 14.06.1995 | 8 | | |
| **Defenders:** | DOB | M | (s) | G |
| Nika Chanturia | 19.01.1995 | 21 | | |
| Koba Iadze | 27.01.2003 | | (2) | |
| Shota Kerdzevadze | 20.03.1993 | | (4) | |
| Vasil Khositashvili | 11.05.1996 | 32 | | 3 |
| Giorgi Kobuladze | 26.02.1997 | 36 | | 2 |
| Solomon Kvirkvelia | 06.02.1992 | 11 | (1) | |
| Luka Nozadze | 25.12.1996 | 29 | (1) | 2 |
| Valeri Olkhovi | 18.08.1998 | 1 | (10) | |
| Zurab Sekhniashvili | 24.06.1996 | 14 | (4) | |
| **Midfielders:** | DOB | M | (s) | G |
| Mario Charbel Bah (BEN) | 19.12.2001 | | (2) | |
| Nodar Lominadze | 04.04.2002 | 9 | (5) | 1 |
| Giorgi Lomtadze | 30.10.2001 | 3 | (10) | 1 |
| Tamimou Ouorou (BEN) | 03.05.2003 | | (8) | |
| Otar Parulava | 14.03.2001 | 15 | (21) | 2 |
| Yaroslav Ryazantsev (UKR) | 09.06.2005 | | (2) | |
| Sandro Shetsiruli | 07.04.1999 | 34 | (2) | |
| Teimuraz Shonia | 28.05.1990 | 30 | (4) | 6 |
| Erekle Sultanishvili | 11.07.1994 | 23 | (10) | |
| Giorgi Vekua | 24.08.1996 | 9 | (8) | |
| **Forwards:** | DOB | M | (s) | G |
| Giorgi Bukhaidze | 09.12.1991 | 8 | (23) | 4 |
| Temur Chogadze | 05.05.1998 | 14 | (5) | 1 |
| Arfang Daffé (SEN) | 24.06.1991 | 2 | (6) | |
| Giorgi Gvishiani | 19.11.2003 | 12 | (5) | 1 |
| Ivane Khabelashvili | 04.09.1993 | 10 | (19) | |
| Mate Kvirkvia | 14.06.1996 | 19 | (1) | 2 |
| Tamaz Makatsaria | 03.10.1995 | 11 | (4) | 3 |
| Mate Vatsadze | 17.12.1988 | 17 | (2) | |

## Football Club Lokomotivi Tbilisi

| Founded: | 1936 | | |
| Stadium: | Stadioni „Mikheil Meskhi", Tbilisi (27,223) | | |
| Trainer: | Lasha Chagiashvili | 17.02.1981 | |
| [14.04.2022] | Aleksandre Intskirveli | 24.08.1981 | |
| [25.06.2022] | Johannes Maria van Loen (NED) | 04.02.1965 | |
| [24.09.2022] | Giorgi Minashvili | | |

| Goalkeepers: | DOB | M | (s) | G |
|---|---|---|---|---|
| Oto Goshadze | 13.10.1997 | 15 | | |
| Soso Kopaliani | 07.07.2006 | 1 | | |
| Rezo Lomidze | 22.07.2001 | 9 | | |
| Ravaz Tevdoradze | 14.02.1988 | 11 | | |
| **Defenders:** | DOB | M | (s) | G |
| Bakar Abzhandadze | 13.02.2003 | 1 | | |
| Aleksandre Andronikashvili | 09.04.1999 | 23 | (5) | 1 |
| Lasha Atskureli | 11.04.2001 | 3 | (7) | 1 |
| Beka Buighlishvili | 27.09.2000 | 3 | (1) | 1 |
| Giorgi Gabadze | 02.03.1995 | 17 | (2) | |
| Andro Giorgadze | 03.05.1996 | 14 | (5) | 1 |
| Nikoloz Grigalashvili | 22.07.2004 | 1 | (1) | |
| Nodar Iashvili | 24.01.1993 | 16 | (1) | |
| Luka Japaridze | 22.12.2000 | 9 | (5) | |
| Beka Kharaishvili | 27.10.2001 | 19 | | |
| Luka Khorava | 12.02.2002 | 1 | | |
| Giorgi Kveladze | 14.12.2001 | 22 | (3) | 1 |
| Sandro Lominadze | 12.09.2005 | | (1) | |
| Rati Mchedlishvili | 17.06.2002 | 2 | (3) | |
| Giorgi Pirtakhia | 17.08.2004 | 2 | | |
| Dachi Popkhadze | 27.01.1984 | 5 | | |
| Davit Ubilava | 27.01.1994 | 11 | (2) | |
| Zura Zosiashvili | 25.08.2003 | 5 | (9) | |
| **Midfielders:** | DOB | M | (s) | G |
| Liban Abdulahi (SOM) | 02.11.1995 | 10 | (4) | |
| Dachi Aidarashvili | 05.11.2004 | | (1) | |
| Luka Babluani | 04.04.2003 | | (1) | |
| Revaz Bushelashvili | 20.01.2004 | 2 | (2) | 1 |
| Beka Dartsmelia | 21.03.2000 | 21 | | 2 |
| Giorgi Diasamidze | 08.05.1992 | 2 | (6) | 1 |
| Tornike Dzebniauri | 27.11.1999 | 32 | (1) | 2 |
| Luka Kekelidze | 07.01.2003 | 7 | (15) | |
| Revaz Khinchiashvili | 19.11.2000 | 1 | | |
| Gabriel Khutsishvili | 13.02.2002 | 1 | (11) | 1 |
| Bidzina Makharoblidze | 10.10.1992 | 4 | (5) | 4 |
| Lasha Menteshashvili | 15.12.2002 | 1 | | |
| Givi Mukbaniani | 20.12.2001 | 3 | (13) | |
| Ivane Okropiridze | 27.08.2000 | | (1) | |
| Davit Samurkasovi | 05.02.1998 | 12 | | |
| Sandro Shashiashvili | 01.09.2003 | 1 | | |
| Vano Shermadini | 20.04.2004 | 6 | (3) | |
| Levan Tavzarashvili | 06.10.2002 | 2 | (1) | 1 |
| Luka Ugrekhelidze | 27.04.2003 | 1 | | |
| **Forwards:** | DOB | M | (s) | G |
| Irakli Chiabrishvili | 02.09.2001 | 18 | (12) | 3 |
| Giorgi Iakobidze | 27.02.2001 | 13 | | 2 |
| Lasha Kalandadze | 08.05.2004 | 5 | (6) | |
| Kakha Kakhabrishvili | 08.07.1993 | 10 | (4) | 2 |
| Nika Khutsishvili | 13.02.2002 | 1 | (5) | |
| Saba-Amiko Kiknadze | 10.04.2001 | 3 | (2) | |
| Tornike Kurtanidze | 01.04.2001 | 1 | (2) | |
| Sandro Melikishvili | 16.05.2001 | | (1) | |
| Giorgi Omarashvili | 10.02.2002 | 20 | (12) | 2 |
| Lasha Ozbetelashvili | 20.01.1999 | 1 | (1) | |
| Shota Shekiladze | 15.02.2000 | 28 | (5) | 2 |

## Football Club Saburtalo Tbilisi

| Founded: | 20.08.1999 | | |
| Stadium: | Stadioni „Mikheil Meskhi", Tbilisi (27,223) | | |
| Trainer: | Levan Korgalidze | 21.02.1980 | |
| [13.06.2022] | Lasha Nozadze | 18.03.1980 | |
| [10.09.2022] | Temur Shalamberidze | 08.12.1969 | |

| Goalkeepers: | DOB | M | (s) | G |
|---|---|---|---|---|
| Oto Goshadze | 13.10.1997 | 10 | | |
| Beka Kurdadze | 24.01.1997 | 4 | | |
| Tornike Megrelishvili | 08.05.1999 | 22 | | |
| **Defenders:** | DOB | M | (s) | G |
| Giorgi Bartia | 03.03.2004 | | (1) | |
| Gia Chaduneli | 15.05.1994 | 16 | (4) | |
| Giorgi Gocholeishvili | 14.02.2001 | 29 | (1) | 4 |
| Nodar Iashvili | 24.01.1993 | 2 | (7) | |
| Giorgi Jgerenaia | 28.12.1993 | 29 | (1) | 1 |
| Jemali-Giorgi Jinjolava | 28.06.2000 | 11 | (2) | |
| Levan Kakubava | 15.10.1990 | 27 | | |
| Zurab Lataria | 18.05.2002 | | (1) | |
| Giorgi Latsabidze | 15.05.1995 | 7 | (1) | |
| Saba Mamatsashvili | 23.08.2002 | 9 | (6) | 1 |
| Davit Ubilava | 27.01.1994 | 7 | | |
| **Midfielders:** | DOB | M | (s) | G |
| Giorgi Ambrosidze | 23.11.2003 | 4 | (2) | |
| Gegi Geguchadze | 30.12.2003 | | (5) | |
| Bakar Kardava | 04.10.1994 | 36 | | 2 |
| Otar Mamageishvili | 15.01.2003 | 9 | (17) | 2 |
| Gizo Mamageishvili | 15.01.2001 | 1 | (19) | |
| Benedik Mioc (CRO) | 06.10.1994 | 9 | (7) | 2 |
| Levan Nonikashvili | 05.04.1995 | 28 | (5) | 2 |
| Shota Nonikashvili | 10.01.2001 | 21 | (5) | 5 |
| Lasha Parunashvili | 14.02.1993 | 4 | (4) | |
| Nikoloz Talakhadze | 23.08.2002 | | (2) | |
| Luka Tsulukidze | 08.02.2004 | | (1) | |
| **Forwards:** | DOB | M | (s) | G |
| Guram Goshteliani | 05.01.1997 | 14 | (1) | 3 |
| Giorgi Guliashvili | 05.09.2001 | 26 | (9) | 4 |
| Júlio Vinícius da Fonseca Souza (BRA) | 02.04.2002 | 1 | (6) | 1 |
| Nodar Kavtaradze | 02.01.1993 | 6 | (10) | 1 |
| Luka Kokosadze | 30.07.2001 | 1 | | |
| Lasha Shindagoridze | 30.01.1993 | 5 | (8) | 1 |
| Irakli Sikharulidze | 18.07.1990 | 28 | (5) | 12 |
| Iuri Tabatadze | 29.11.1999 | 30 | (4) | 8 |

## Football Club Samgurali Tskhaltubo

| Founded: | 1945 | | | |
|---|---|---|---|---|
| Stadium: | Stadioni 26 Mai, Tskhaltubo (12,000) | | | |
| Trainer: | Giorgi Mikadze | | 21.03.1980 | |

| Goalkeepers: | DOB | M | (s) | G |
|---|---|---|---|---|
| Maksime Kvilitaia | 17.09.1985 | 1 | (2) | |
| Levan Shovnadze | 19.11.1997 | 35 | | |
| **Defenders:** | **DOB** | **M** | **(s)** | **G** |
| Shalva Burjanadze | 29.10.1998 | 17 | (13) | 2 |
| Nika Kalandarishvili | 09.09.1998 | 29 | (4) | 4 |
| Tedo Kikabidze | 27.04.1996 | 34 | | 1 |
| Levan Kurdadze | 03.09.1990 | 23 | (9) | 1 |
| Davit Maisashvili | 18.02.1989 | 28 | (1) | 3 |
| Omar Patarkatsishvili | 05.02.1996 | 25 | (2) | 3 |
| Giorgi Tevzadze | 25.08.1996 | 5 | (6) | |
| **Midfielders:** | **DOB** | **M** | **(s)** | **G** |
| Mikheil Basheleishvili | 21.06.1997 | 28 | (3) | 3 |
| Georgi Chelidze (RUS) | 20.01.2000 | | (1) | |
| Demur Chikhladze | 23.09.1996 | 25 | (4) | 6 |
| Andria Devdariani | 09.09.2002 | | (16) | 1 |
| Luqman Gilmore (NGA) | 10.05.1996 | 27 | (1) | |
| Jeferson Geraldo de Almeida „Jefinho" (BRA) | 23.02.1989 | 34 | (2) | 7 |
| Elvis Sakyi (GHA) | 24.11.1996 | | (3) | |
| Mikhail Strelnik (RUS) | 27.05.2000 | 1 | (7) | |
| Yusuf Touré (CIV) | 01.01.2000 | 1 | (3) | |
| **Forwards:** | **DOB** | **M** | **(s)** | **G** |
| Ilia Akhvlediani | 05.10.1998 | 18 | (8) | 2 |
| Lado Chikhradze | 03.09.2001 | | (2) | |
| Grigol Dolidze | 25.10.1982 | 1 | (16) | 1 |
| Mamia Gavashelishvili | 08.01.1995 | 5 | (19) | 1 |
| Sergo Kukhianidze | 23.04.1999 | 6 | (16) | |
| Giorgi Nikabadze | 10.01.1991 | 12 | (6) | 5 |
| Irakli Rukhadze | 28.10.1996 | 26 | (4) | 13 |
| Nikita Simdyankin (RUS) | 03.01.2001 | 10 | (16) | 1 |
| Aleksandr Verulidze (RUS) | 25.09.1996 | 5 | (10) | |

## Football Club Sioni Bolnisi

| Founded: | 1936 | | |
|---|---|---|---|
| Stadium: | Stadioni „Tamaz Stepania", Bolnisi (3,000) | | |
| Trainer: | Giorgi Daraselia | | 16.09.1968 |
| [10.03.2022] | Ucha Sosiashvili | | 26.07.1989 |
| [09.11.2022] | Giorgi Chelidze | | 29.11.1984 |

| Goalkeepers: | DOB | M | (s) | G |
|---|---|---|---|---|
| Levan Isiani | 30.04.1998 | 34 | | |
| Giorgi Ugrekhelidze | 16.01.2002 | 1 | | |
| Konstantine Sepiashvili | 19.03.1986 | 1 | | |
| **Defenders:** | **DOB** | **M** | **(s)** | **G** |
| Luka Asatiani | 22.04.1999 | 4 | (2) | 2 |
| Temur Bekauri | 12.02.1994 | 11 | (2) | 1 |
| Ukwubile Raphael Chukwurah (NGA) | 17.05.1992 | 18 | | 1 |
| Giorgi Gadrani | 30.09.1994 | 8 | | |
| Iva Gelashvili | 08.04.2001 | 7 | (1) | |
| Zurab Japiashvili | 26.05.1996 | 13 | (4) | |
| Otar Javashvili | 17.08.1993 | 10 | (4) | |
| Davit Kikalishvili | 19.03.1999 | 13 | (1) | |
| Varlam Kilasonia | 09.01.1993 | 18 | | |
| Giorgi Koripadze | 03.10.1989 | 15 | (3) | 1 |
| Goderdzi Machaidze | 17.07.1992 | 6 | (8) | |
| Andro Nemsadze | 15.08.1997 | 29 | (2) | |
| Archil Tvildiani | 31.01.1993 | 4 | (9) | |
| Lasha Ugrekhelidze | 25.08.1999 | 8 | (2) | 1 |
| Vítor Francisco dos Santos de Carvalho (BRA) | 17.02.1993 | 14 | (1) | |
| **Midfielders:** | **DOB** | **M** | **(s)** | **G** |
| Luka Chaganava | 09.11.2004 | 8 | (16) | 1 |
| Abdoul Aziz Doumbia (CIV) | 17.12.2000 | 20 | (6) | 1 |
| Nika Ghambarashvili | 02.04.2003 | 1 | (7) | 1 |
| Levan Jordania | 01.01.1997 | 10 | (3) | |
| Luka Khorkheli | 31.01.2000 | 34 | | 6 |
| Luka Koberidze | 09.09.1994 | 3 | (6) | |
| Vladimir Medved (BLR) | 04.11.1999 | | (3) | |
| Anatoli Mesiachenko | 21.04.2001 | 2 | (7) | |
| Ivane Potskhveria | 24.07.2002 | 33 | | 5 |
| Giorgi Ugrekhelidze | 26.06.1997 | 1 | (3) | 1 |
| **Forwards:** | **DOB** | **M** | **(s)** | **G** |
| Raphael de la Sousa (ISR) | 16.11.1996 | | (3) | |
| Ramin Doobi (GHA) | 21.12.2001 | 3 | (2) | 1 |
| Guy Kassa Gnabouyou (FRA) | 01.12.1989 | 4 | (7) | 2 |
| Nika Khorkheli | 09.09.2001 | 32 | | 9 |
| Otar Kobakhidze | 29.02.1996 | 1 | (10) | |
| Mikheil Kochakidze | 15.10.2002 | 1 | (5) | 1 |
| Otar Kvernadze | 10.09.1993 | | (5) | |
| Toma Tabatadze | 17.12.1991 | 16 | (1) | 3 |
| Zaza Tsitskishvili | 04.07.1995 | 1 | | |
| Davit Zurabiani | 22.02.2002 | 12 | (12) | |

## Football Club Telavi

| Founded: | 2016 | | |
|---|---|---|---|
| Stadium: | Stadioni „Givi Chokheli", Telavi (12,000) | | |
| Trainer: | Giorgi Chelidze | | 29.11.1984 |
| [17.07.2022] | Giorgi Tsetsadze | | 03.09.1974 |

| Goalkeepers: | DOB | M | (s) | G |
|---|---|---|---|---|
| Bogdan Bezkrovnyi (UKR) | 21.11.1998 | 6 | | |
| Luka Sanikidze | 19.11.1998 | 21 | | |
| Levan Tandilashvili | 27.02.2003 | 9 | | |
| **Defenders:** | **DOB** | **M** | **(s)** | **G** |
| Vako Bachiashvili | 04.11.1992 | 2 | (7) | |
| Ilia Beriashvili | 09.07.1998 | 16 | | 1 |
| Ukwubile Raphael Chukwurah (NGA) | 17.05.1992 | 7 | (4) | |
| Tornike Dundua | 01.10.2003 | | (1) | |
| Konsantine Ghaghanidze | 03.02.1994 | | (2) | |
| Zurab Gigashvili | 20.11.2001 | 12 | (7) | |
| Tsotne Kapanadze | 30.08.2001 | 31 | (1) | |
| Vazha Patsatsia | 29.01.1998 | 27 | (3) | |
| Zurab Tevzadze | 28.08.1994 | 32 | (1) | 1 |
| Anton Tolordava | 02.08.1996 | 18 | | 2 |
| **Midfielders:** | **DOB** | **M** | **(s)** | **G** |
| Mirian Jikia | 14.10.1990 | 28 | (3) | |
| Giorgi Kantaria | 27.04.1997 | 11 | (2) | |
| Lasha Kochladze | 22.08.1995 | 22 | (13) | 2 |
| Bidzina Makharoblidze | 10.10.1992 | 8 | (7) | 1 |
| Piruz Marakvelidze | 21.01.1995 | 12 | (1) | 1 |
| Davit Mujiri | 02.01.1978 | 1 | | |
| Eldar Parkinashvili | 29.12.2002 | 4 | (22) | |
| Strahinja Pavišić (SRB) | 29.05.1996 | 22 | (6) | 1 |
| Saba Piranishvili | 19.10.1999 | 17 | (11) | |
| Dzmitriy Rekish (BLR) | 14.09.1988 | | (6) | |
| Victor Hugo Coelho Vieira „Vitinho" (BRA) | 08.09.1997 | 10 | (3) | |
| **Forwards:** | **DOB** | **M** | **(s)** | **G** |
| Imeda Ashortia | 30.10.1996 | 14 | (6) | 3 |
| Guram Goshteliani | 05.01.1997 | 14 | (3) | 2 |
| Levan Grdzelidze | 18.08.2000 | 1 | (5) | |
| Guram Kavelashvili | 18.08.2001 | 5 | (9) | 1 |
| Beka Kavtaradze | 15.06.1999 | 10 | (3) | 2 |
| Giorgi Khabuliani | 25.03.2004 | 4 | (11) | 2 |
| Lasha Kokhreidze | 18.11.1998 | 4 | (3) | 1 |
| Giorgi Kvernadze | 07.02.2003 | 13 | (8) | 3 |
| Davit Mujiri | 28.01.1999 | 15 | (13) | 1 |

## Football Club Torpedo Kutaisi

| Founded: | 1946 | |
|---|---|---|
| Stadium: | Stadioni „Ramaz Shengelia", Kutaisi (19,400) | |
| Trainer: | Giorgi Tsetsadze | 03.09.1974 |
| [03.05.2022] | Tornike Shekriladze | 14.02.1991 |
| [17.05.2022] | Shota Babunashvili | 17.11.1980 |
| [26.06.2022] | Kakhaber Chkhetiani | 24.02.1978 |

| Goalkeepers: | DOB | M | (s) | G |
|---|---|---|---|---|
| Dino Hamzić (BIH) | 22.01.1988 | 7 | | |
| Roin Kvaskhvadze | 31.05.1989 | 27 | | |
| Avtandil Labadze | 09.05.1998 | 2 | | |
| **Defenders:** | **DOB** | **M** | **(s)** | **G** |
| Mate Abuladze | 30.06.2000 | 12 | (5) | |
| Vakhtang Botchorishvili | 21.08.2001 | 1 | (2) | |
| Levan Gegetchkori | 05.06.1994 | 11 | (3) | |
| Saba Goglichidze | 25.06.2004 | 13 | (2) | |
| Giorgi Kimadze | 11.02.1992 | 23 | (6) | 3 |
| Giorgi Mchedlishvili | 18.01.1992 | 7 | (6) | |
| Bakar Mirtskhulava | 24.05.1992 | 13 | | |
| Tsotne Nadaraia | 21.02.1997 | 22 | (3) | 1 |
| Pedro Filipe Tinoco Monteiro (POR) | 30.01.1994 | 14 | (1) | |
| Nika Sandokhadze | 20.02.1994 | 23 | (4) | 1 |
| Lasha Shergelashvili | 17.01.1992 | 15 | (1) | 2 |
| **Midfielders:** | **DOB** | **M** | **(s)** | **G** |
| Levan Arveladze (UKR) | 06.04.1993 | 1 | (9) | |
| Vano Chargeishvili | 15.05.2001 | | (2) | |

| | DOB | M | (s) | G |
|---|---|---|---|---|
| Irakli Dzaria | 01.12.1988 | 1 | (7) | |
| Merab Gigauri | 05.06.1993 | 14 | | 1 |
| Vasilios Karagounis (GRE) | 18.01.1994 | 6 | (6) | |
| Giorgi Kukhianidze | 01.07.1992 | 26 | (3) | 9 |
| Giuli Mandzhgaladze | 09.09.1992 | 22 | (4) | 2 |
| Vazha Tabatadze | 01.02.1991 | 7 | (9) | 1 |
| Anzor Tevzadze | 25.06.2004 | | (3) | |
| Mate Tsintsadze | 07.01.1995 | 19 | (12) | 2 |
| Beka Vachiberadze | 05.03.1996 | 9 | (8) | |
| **Forwards:** | **DOB** | **M** | **(s)** | **G** |
| Tornike Akhvlediani | 24.07.1999 | 9 | (16) | 7 |
| Giorgi Arabidze | 04.03.1998 | 21 | (8) | 5 |
| Irakli Bugridze | 03.01.1998 | 11 | (17) | 4 |
| Mauro Andrés Caballero Aguilera (PAR) | 08.10.1994 | 9 | (3) | 1 |
| Nodar Kavtaradze | 02.01.1993 | 3 | (7) | |
| Levan Mchedlidze | 24.03.1990 | 11 | (8) | 3 |
| Giorgi Papunashvili | 02.09.1995 | 11 | (4) | |
| Akaki Shulaia | 06.09.1996 | 26 | (6) | 2 |

## SECOND LEVEL
### Erovnuli Liga 2 2022

| | | | | | | | | | | |
|---|---|---|---|---|---|---|---|---|---|---|
| 1. | FC Shukura Kobuleti (*Promoted*) | 28 | 19 | 3 | 6 | 52 | - | 23 | 60 |
| 2. | FC Spaeri Tbilisi (*Promotion Play-offs*) | 28 | 15 | 6 | 7 | 57 | - | 35 | 51 |
| 3. | FC Samtredia (*Promotion Play-offs*) | 28 | 14 | 6 | 8 | 43 | - | 28 | 48 |
| 4. | FC Merani Martvili | 28 | 12 | 6 | 10 | 55 | - | 53 | 42 |
| 5. | FC Gareji Sagarejo | 28 | 10 | 6 | 12 | 38 | - | 36 | 36 |
| 6. | FC Merani Tbilisi | 28 | 10 | 4 | 14 | 34 | - | 56 | 34 |
| 7. | FC Rustavi (*Relegation Play-offs*) | 28 | 6 | 5 | 17 | 34 | - | 54 | 23 |
| 8. | FC WIT Georgia Tbilisi (*Relegation Play-offs*) | 28 | 5 | 6 | 17 | 30 | - | 58 | 21 |
| 9. | FC Dinamo Zugdidi (*Relegated*) | 0 | 0 | 0 | 0 | 0 | | 0 | 0 |
| 10. | FC Shevardeni-1906 Tbilisi (*Relegated*) | 0 | 0 | 0 | 0 | 0 | | 0 | 0 |

Please note: FC Dinamo Zugdidi and FC Shevardeni-1906 Tbilisi were accused of match-fixing and expelled from the league with immediate effect on 22.05.2022 (after Round 13), based on decision made by GFF Disciplinary Committee. All their results and individual records have been annulled.

## Relegation Play-offs (2nd / 3rd Level) [06-10.12.2022]

| | | |
|---|---|---|
| FC WIT Georgia Tbilisi - FC Aragvi Dusheti | 0-0 | 1-0(1-0) |
| FC Kolkheti Khobi - FC Rustavi | 1-0(1-0) | 1-0(0-0) |

Both FC WIT Georgia Tbilisi and FC Kolkheti Khobi will play in next season's Erovnuli Liga 2.

## INTERNATIONAL MATCHES
(16.07.2022 – 15.07.2023)

| | | | | |
|---|---|---|---|---|
| 23.09.2022 | Tbilisi | *Georgia - North Macedonia* | *2-0(1-0)* | (UNL) |
| 26.09.2022 | Gibraltar | *Gibraltar - Georgia* | *1-2(0-1)* | (UNL) |
| 17.11.2022 | Sharjah | *Morocco - Georgia* | *3-0(2-0)* | (F) |
| 25.03.2023 | Batumi | *Georgia - Mongolia* | *6-1(1-1)* | (F) |
| 28.03.2023 | Batumi | *Georgia - Norway* | *1-1(0-1)* | (ECQ) |
| 17.06.2023 | Larnaca | *Cyprus - Georgia* | *1-2(1-1)* | (ECQ) |
| 20.06.2023 | Glasgow | *Scotland - Georgia* | *2-0(1-0)* | (ECQ) |

**23.09.2022   GEORGIA - NORTH MACEDONIA**      **2-0(1-0)**      3rd UEFA Nations League C, Group 4
"Boris Paichadze" Dinamo Arena, Tbilisi; Referee: Ivan Kružliak (Slovakia); Attendance: 54,200
**GEO:** Giorgi Mamardashvili, Solomon Kverkvelia, Guram Kashia (Cap), Davit Khocholava (72.Luka Lochoshvili), Giorgi Aburjania (87.Vladimer Mamuchashvili), Otar Kakabadze, Nika Kvekveskiri, Giorgi Tsitaishvili (72.Irakli Azarovi), Zuriko Davitashvili (78.Anzor Mekvabishvili), Budu Zivzivadze (78.Georges Mikautadze), Khvicha Kvaratskhelia. Trainer: William David Frédéric Sagnol (France).
**Goals:** Bojan Miovski (35 own goal), Khvicha Kvaratskhelia (64).

**26.09.2022   GIBRALTAR - GEORGIA**      **1-2(0-1)**      3rd UEFA Nations League C, Group 4
Victoria Stadium, Gibraltar; Referee: Robert Harvey (Republic of Ireland); Attendance: 1,199
**GEO:** Giorgi Loria (46.Giorgi Mamardashvili), Otar Kakabadze, Guram Kashia (Cap), Davit Khocholava, Nika Kvekveskiri, Anzor Mekvabishvili, Saba Lobjanidze (89.Luka Lochoshvili), Irakli Azarovi (60.Zuriko Davitashvili), Giorgi Tsitaishvili, Khvicha Kvaratskhelia (72.Valeri Qazaishvili), Budu Zivzivadze (60.Georges Mikautadze). Trainer: William David Frédéric Sagnol (France).
**Goals:** Khvicha Kvaratskhelia (19), Giorgi Tsitaishvili (48).

**17.11.2022   MOROCCO - GEORGIA**      **3-0(2-0)**      Friendly International
Sharjah Stadium, Sharjah (United Arab Emirates); Referee: Adel Ali Ahmed Khamis Al Naqbi (United Arab Emirates); Attendance: n/a
**GEO:** Giorgi Mamardashvili, Luka Lochoshvili, Guram Kashia (Cap), Solomon Kverkvelia (78.Saba Sazonov), Giorgi Gocholeishvili, Giorgi Aburjania (78.Anzor Mekvabishvili), Nika Kvekveskiri (78.Giorgi Beridze), Otar Kiteishvili, Zuriko Davitashvili (62.Saba Lobjanidze), Giorgi Tsitaishvili (35.Levan Shengelia), Davit Volkovi (62.Giorgi Kvilitaia). Trainer: William David Frédéric Sagnol (France).

**25.03.2023   GEORGIA - MONGOLIA**      **6-1(1-1)**      Friendly International
Adjarabet Arena, Batumi; Referee: Zaven Hovhannisyan (Armenia); Attendance: 12,685
**GEO:** Giorgi Loria (Cap) (46.Luka Gugeshashvili), Saba Sazonov, Lasha Dvali, Mamuka Kobakhidze, Saba Lobjanidze, Giorgi Aburjania (46.Nika Kvekveskiri), Luka Gagnidze (64.Zuriko Davitashvili), Giorgi Gocholeishvili, Giorgi Tsitaishvili (64.Gabriel Sigua), Giorgi Chakvetadze (64.Budu Zivzivadze), Davit Volkovi (71.Giorgi Beridze). Trainer: William David Frédéric Sagnol (France).
**Goals:** Davit Volkovi (15), Giorgi Chakvetadze (56, 58), Saba Lobjanidze (70), Giorgi Beridze (88), Budu Zivzivadze (90+1).

**28.03.2023   GEORGIA - NORWAY**      **1-1(0-1)**      17th EC. Qualifiers
Adjarabet Arena, Batumi; Referee: Andris Treimanis (Latvia); Attendance: 20,300
**GEO:** Giorgi Mamardashvili, Jemal Tabidze (59.Budu Zivzivadze), Guram Kashia (Cap), Solomon Kverkvelia, Giorgi Aburjania (90.Luka Gagnidze), Nika Kvekveskiri, Otar Kakabadze, Zuriko Davitashvili (59.Saba Lobjanidze), Irakli Azarovi (70.Giorgi Gocholeishvili), Khvicha Kvaratskhelia, Georges Mikautadze (90.Giorgi Beridze). Trainer: William David Frédéric Sagnol (France).
**Goal:** Georges Mikautadze (60).

**17.06.2023   CYPRUS - GEORGIA**      **1-2(1-1)**      17th EC. Qualifiers
AEK Arena "Georgios Karapatakis", Larnaca; Referee: Fábio José Costa Veríssimo (Portugal); Attendance: 3,763
**GEO:** Giorgi Mamardashvili, Otar Kakabadze, Guram Kashia (Cap), Luka Lochoshvili (87.Lasha Dvali), Giorgi Gocholeishvili (75.Saba Lobjanidze), Otar Kiteishvili, Nika Kvekveskiri (74.Luka Gagnidze), Irakli Azarovi, Giorgi Chakvetadze (74.Zuriko Davitashvili), Khvicha Kvaratskhelia, Georges Mikautadze (87.Budu Zivzivadze). Trainer: William David Frédéric Sagnol (France).
**Goals:** Georges Mikautadze (31), Zuriko Davitashvili (84).

**20.06.2023   SCOTLAND - GEORGIA**      **2-0(1-0)**      17th EC. Qualifiers
Hampden Park, Glasgow; Referee: István Vad (Hungary); Attendance: 50,062
**GEO:** Giorgi Mamardashvili, Otar Kakabadze, Solomon Kverkvelia, Guram Kashia (Cap), Lasha Dvali (56.Budu Zivzivadze), Luka Gagnidze, Nika Kvekveskiri (56.Giorgi Gocholeishvili), Saba Lobjanidze (64.Zuriko Davitashvili), Otar Kiteishvili, Khvicha Kvaratskhelia, Georges Mikautadze. Trainer: William David Frédéric Sagnol (France).

## NATIONAL TEAM PLAYERS
### (16.07.2022 – 15.07.2023)

| Name | DOB | Caps | Goals | Club | |
|------|-----|------|-------|------|---|
| **Goalkeepers** | | | | | |
| Luka GUGESHASHVILI | 29.04.1999 | 1 | 0 | 2023: | *Qarabağ FK Bakı (AZE)* |
| Giorgi LORIA | 27.01.1986 | 77 | 0 | 2022/2023: | *Anorthosis Famagusta FC (CYP)* |
| Giorgi MAMARDASHVILI | 29.09.2000 | 9 | 0 | 2022/2023: | *Valencia CF (ESP)* |
| **Defenders** | | | | | |
| Irakli AZAROVI | 21.01.2002 | 12 | 0 | 2022/2023: | *FC Dinamo Batumi* |
| Lasha DVALI | 14.05.1995 | 28 | 1 | 2023: | *APOEL Nicosia (CYP)* |
| Giorgi GOCHOLEISHVILI | 14.02.2001 | 5 | 0 | 2022: | *FC Saburtalo Tbilisi* |
| | | | | 01.01.2023-> | *FK Shakhtar Donetsk (UKR)* |
| Otar KAKABADZE | 27.06.1995 | 56 | 0 | 2022/2023: | *KS Cracovia Kraków (POL)* |
| Guram KASHIA | 04.07.1987 | 104 | 2 | 2022/2023: | *ŠK Slovan Bratislava (SVK)* |
| Davit KHOCHOLAVA | 08.02.1993 | 39 | 0 | 2022: | *FC København (DEN)* |
| Mamuka KOBAKHIDZE | 23.08.1992 | 5 | 0 | 2023: | *FC Dinamo Batumi* |
| Solomon KVIRKVELIA | 06.02.1992 | 50 | 0 | 2022/2023: | *Neftçi PFK Bakı (AZE)* |
| Luka LOCHOSHVILI | 29.05.1998 | 6 | 0 | 2022/2023: | *US Cremonese (ITA)* |
| Saba SAZONOV | 01.02.2002 | 2 | 0 | 2022/2023: | *FK Dinamo Moskva (RUS)* |
| Jemal TABIDZE | 18.03.1996 | 15 | 1 | 2023: | *FC Dinamo Tbilisi* |
| **Midfielders** | | | | | |
| Giorgi ABURJANIA | 02.01.1995 | 38 | 1 | 2022/2023: | *Gil Vicente FC Barcelos (POR)* |
| Giorgi CHAKVETADZE | 29.08.1999 | 16 | 7 | 2023: | *ŠK Slovan Bratislava (SVK)* |
| Zuriko DAVITASHVILI | 15.02.2001 | 26 | 4 | 2022/2023: | *FC Girondins de Bordeaux (FRA)* |
| Luka GAGNIDZE | 28.02.2003 | 4 | 0 | 2023: | *FK Dinamo Moskva (RUS)* |
| Otar KITEISHVILI | 26.03.1996 | 31 | 1 | 2022/2023: | *SK Sturm Graz (AUT)* |
| Khvicha KVARATSKHELIA | 12.02.2001 | 22 | 10 | 2022/2023: | *SSC Napoli (ITA)* |
| Nika KVEKVESKIRI | 29.05.1992 | 54 | 0 | 2022/2023: | *KKS Lech Poznań (POL)* |
| Saba LOBJANIDZE | 18.12.1994 | 33 | 3 | 2022: | *Hatayspor Antakya (TUR)* |
| | | | | 18.02.2023-> | *Fatih Karagümrük SK (TUR)* |
| Vladimer MAMUCHASHVILI | 29.08.1997 | 7 | 0 | 2022: | *FC Dinamo Batumi* |
| Anzor MEKVABISHVILI | 05.06.2001 | 7 | 0 | 2022: | *FC Dinamo Tbilisi* |
| Valeri QAZAISHVILI | 29.01.1993 | 63 | 13 | 2022: | *Ulsan Hyundai FC (KOR)* |
| Levan SHENGELIA | 27.10.1995 | 11 | 0 | 2022: | *Panetolikos GPS Agrinio (GRE)* |
| Gabriel SIGUA | 30.06.2005 | 1 | 0 | 2023: | *FC Dinamo Tbilisi* |
| **Forwards** | | | | | |
| Giorgi BERIDZE | 12.05.1997 | 8 | 1 | 2022/2023: | *MKE Ankaragücü (TUR)* |
| Giorgi KVILITAIA | 01.10.1993 | 35 | 6 | 2022: | *APOEL Nicosia (CYP)* |
| Georges MIKAUTADZE | 31.10.2000 | 16 | 4 | 2022/2023: | *RFC Seraing (BEL)* |
| Giorgi TSITAISHVILI | 18.11.2000 | 14 | 1 | 2022/2023: | *KKS Lech Poznań (POL)* |
| Davit VOLKOVI | 03.06.1995 | 5 | 2 | 2022/2023: | *Sabah FC Bakı (AZE)* |
| Budu ZIVZIVADZE | 10.03.1994 | 19 | 4 | 2022: | *Fehérvár FC Székesfehérvár (HUN)* |
| | | | | 31.01.2023-> | *Karlsruher SC (GER)* |
| **Trainer** | | | | | |
| William David Frédéric SAGNOL (France) [from 15.02.2021] | 18.03.1977 | | | 25 M; 12 W; 4 D; 9 L; 36-31 | |

# GERMANY

| The Country: |
|---|
| Bundesrepublik Deutschland (Federal Republic of Germany) |
| Capital: Berlin |
| Surface: 357,168 km² |
| Inhabitants: 84,270,625 [2022] |
| Time: UTC+1 |

| The FA: |
|---|
| Deutscher Fußball-Bund |
| Otto-Fleck-Schneise 6, Postfach 710265, 60492 Frankfurt am Main |
| Tel: +49 69 678 80 |
| Foundation date: 28.01.1900 |
| Member of FIFA since: 1904 |
| Member of UEFA since: 1954 |
| Website: www.dfb.de |

## NATIONAL TEAM RECORDS

### RECORDS

| | | |
|---|---|---|
| **First international match:** | 05.04.1908, Basel: Switzerland – Germany 5-3 | |
| **Most international caps:** | Lothar Herbert Matthäus | - 150 caps (1980-2000) |
| **Most international goals:** | Miroslav Klose | - 71 goals / 137 caps (2001-2014) |

| UEFA EUROPEAN CHAMPIONSHIP | |
|---|---|
| 1960 | Did not enter |
| 1964 | Did not enter |
| 1968 | Qualifiers |
| **1972** | **Final Tournament (Winners)** |
| 1976 | Final Tournament (Runners-up) |
| **1980** | **Final Tournament (Winners)** |
| 1984 | Final Tournament (Group Stage) |
| 1988 | Final Tournament (Semi-Finals) |
| 1992 | Final Tournament (Runners-up) |
| **1996** | **Final Tournament (Winners)** |
| 2000 | Final Tournament (Group Stage) |
| 2004 | Final Tournament (Group Stage) |
| 2008 | Final Tournament (Runners-up) |
| 2012 | Final Tournament (Semi-Finals) |
| 2016 | Final Tournament (Semi-Finals) |
| 2020 | Final Tournament (2nd Round of 16) |

| FIFA WORLD CUP | |
|---|---|
| 1930 | Did not enter |
| 1934 | Final Tournament (3rd Place) |
| 1938 | Final Tournament (1st Round) |
| 1950 | *Banned* |
| **1954** | **Final Tournament (Winners)** |
| 1958 | Final Tournament (3rd Place) |
| 1962 | Final Tournament (Quarter-Finals) |
| 1966 | Final Tournament (Runners-up) |
| 1970 | Final Tournament (3rd Place) |
| **1974** | **Final Tournament (Winners)** |
| 1978 | Final Tournament (Second Round) |
| 1982 | Final Tournament (Runners-up) |
| 1986 | Final Tournament (Runners-up) |
| **1990** | **Final Tournament (Winners)** |
| 1994 | Final Tournament (Quarter-Finals) |
| 1998 | Final Tournament (Quarter-Finals) |
| 2002 | Final Tournament (Runners-up) |
| 2006 | Final Tournament (3rd Place) |
| 2010 | Final Tournament (3rd Place) |
| **2014** | **Final Tournament (Winners)** |
| 2018 | Final Tournament (Group Stage) |
| 2022 | Final Tournament (Group Stage) |

| OLYMPIC TOURNAMENTS | |
|---|---|
| 1908 | - |
| 1912 | 1st Round |
| 1920 | - |
| 1924 | - |
| 1928 | Quarter-Finals |
| 1936 | Quarter-Finals |
| 1948 | - |
| 1952 | 4th Place |
| 1956 | 1st Round |
| 1960 | Qualifiers |
| 1964 | Qualifiers |
| 1968 | - |
| 1972 | Second Round |
| 1976 | Qualifiers |
| 1980 | Qualifiers |
| 1984 | Quarter-Finals |
| 1988 | 3rd Place |
| 1992 | Qualifiers |
| 1996 | Qualifiers |
| 2000 | Qualifiers |
| 2004 | Qualifiers |
| 2008 | Qualifiers |
| 2012 | Qualifiers |
| 2016 | Runners-up |
| 2020 | Final Tournament (Group Stage) |

## UEFA NATIONS LEAGUE

| 2018/2019 | League A (Group Stage) |
|---|---|
| 2020/2021 | League A (Group Stage) |
| 2022/2023 | League A (Group Stage) |

## FIFA CONFEDERATIONS CUP 1992-2017

1999 (Group Stage), 2005 (3rd Place), **2017 (Winners)**

## GERMAN CLUB HONOURS IN EUROPEAN CLUB COMPETITIONS:

| European Champion Clubs' Cup (1956-1992) / UEFA Champions League (1993-2023) | | |
|---|---|---|
| FC Bayern München | 6 | 1973/1974, 1974/1975, 1975/1976, 2000/2001, 2012/2013, 2019/2020 |
| Hamburger SV | 1 | 1982/1983 |
| BV Borussia Dortmund | 1 | 1996/1997 |
| **Fairs Cup (1858-1971) / UEFA Cup (1972-2009) / UEFA Europa League (2010-2023)** | | |
| Borussia VfL Mönchengladbach | 2 | 1974/1975, 1978/1979 |
| Eintracht Frankfurt | 2 | 1979/1980, 2021/2022 |
| TSV Bayer 04 Leverkusen | 1 | 1987/1988 |
| FC Bayern München | 1 | 1995/1996 |
| FC Schalke 04 Gelsenkirchen | 1 | 1996/1997 |

| UEFA Europa Conference League (2021-2023) | | |
|---|---|---|
| None | | |
| **UEFA Super Cup (1972-2022)** | | |
| FC Bayern München | 2 | 2013, 2020 |
| **European Cup Winners' Cup 1961-1999*** | | |
| BV Borussia Dortmund | 1 | 1965/1966 |
| Hamburger SV | 1 | 1976/1977 |
| FC Bayern München | 1 | 1966/1967 |
| SV Werder Bremen | 1 | 1991/1992 |

*defunct competition*

# NATIONAL COMPETITIONS
# TABLE OF HONOURS

| | CHAMPIONS | CUP WINNERS | BEST GOALSCORERS | |
|---|---|---|---|---|
| 1902/1903 | VfB Leipzig | - | - | |
| 1903/1904 | *No champions (final not played)* | - | - | |
| 1904/1905 | Berliner TuFC Union 1892 | - | - | |
| 1905/1906 | VfB Leipzig | - | - | |
| 1906/1907 | Freiburger FC | - | - | |
| 1907/1908 | Berliner TuFC Viktoria 1889 | - | - | |
| 1908/1909 | FC Phönix Karlsruhe | - | - | |
| 1909/1910 | Karlsruher FV | - | - | |
| 1910/1911 | Berliner TuFC Viktoria 1889 | - | - | |
| 1911/1912 | Holstein Kiel | - | - | |
| 1912/1913 | VfB Leipzig | - | - | |
| 1913/1914 | SpVgg Fürth | - | - | |
| 1914-1919 | *No competition* | - | - | |
| 1919/1920 | 1. FC Nürnberg | - | - | |
| 1920/1921 | 1. FC Nürnberg | - | - | |
| 1921/1922 | *No champions (title declined by DFB)* | - | - | |
| 1922/1923 | Hamburger SV | - | - | |
| 1923/1924 | 1. FC Nürnberg | - | - | |
| 1924/1925 | 1. FC Nürnberg | - | - | |
| 1925/1926 | SpVgg Fürth | - | - | |
| 1926/1927 | 1. FC Nürnberg | - | - | |
| 1927/1928 | Hamburger SV | - | - | |
| 1928/1929 | SpVgg Fürth | - | - | |
| 1929/1930 | Hertha BSC Berlin | - | - | |
| 1930/1931 | Hertha BSC Berlin | - | - | |
| 1931/1932 | FC Bayern München | - | - | |
| 1932/1933 | TSV Fortuna Düsseldorf | - | - | |
| 1933/1934 | FC Schalke 04 Gelsenkirchen | - | - | |
| 1934/1935 | FC Schalke 04 Gelsenkirchen | 1. FC Nürnberg | - | |
| 1935/1936 | 1. FC Nürnberg | VfB Leipzig | - | |
| 1936/1937 | FC Schalke 04 Gelsenkirchen | FC Schalke 04 Gelsenkirchen | - | |
| 1937/1938 | SV Hannover 96 | SK Rapid Wien | - | |
| 1938/1939 | FC Schalke 04 Gelsenkirchen | 1. FC Nürnberg | - | |
| 1939/1940 | FC Schalke 04 Gelsenkirchen | Dresdner SC | - | |
| 1940/1941 | SK Rapid Wien | Dresdner SC | - | |
| 1941/1942 | FC Schalke 04 Gelsenkirchen | TSV 1860 München | - | |
| 1942/1943 | Dresdner SC | 1894 First Vienna FC | - | |
| 1943/1944 | Dresdner SC | *No competition* | - | |
| 1944/1945 | *No competition* | *No competition* | - | |
| 1945/1946 | VfB Stuttgart | *No competition* | - | |
| 1946/1947 | 1. FC Nürnberg | *No competition* | - | |
| 1947/1948 | 1. FC Nürnberg | *No competition* | - | |
| 1948/1949 | VfR Mannheim | *No competition* | - | |
| 1949/1950 | VfB Stuttgart | *No competition* | - | |
| 1950/1951 | 1. FC Kaiserslautern | *No competition* | - | |
| 1951/1952 | VfB Stuttgart | *No competition* | - | |
| 1952/1953 | 1. FC Kaiserslautern | Rot-Weiss Essen | - | |
| 1953/1954 | SV Hannover 96 | VfB Stuttgart | - | |
| 1954/1955 | Rot-Weiss Essen | Karlsruher SC | - | |
| 1955/1956 | BV Borussia 09 Dortmund | Karlsruher SC | - | |
| 1956/1957 | BV Borussia 09 Dortmund | FC Bayern München | - | |
| 1957/1958 | FC Schalke 04 Gelsenkirchen | VfB Stuttgart | - | |
| 1958/1959 | Eintracht Frankfurt | TB Schwarz-Weiß Essen | - | |
| 1959/1960 | Hamburger SV | Borussia VfL Mönchengladbach | - | |
| 1960/1961 | 1. FC Nürnberg | SV Werder Bremen | - | |
| 1961/1962 | 1. FC Köln | 1. FC Nürnberg | - | |
| 1962/1963 | BV Borussia 09 Dortmund | Hamburger SV | - | |
| 1963/1964 | 1. FC Köln | TSV 1860 München | Uwe Seeler (Hamburger SV) | 30 |
| 1964/1965 | SV Werder Bremen | BV Borussia 09 Dortmund | Rudolf Brunnenmeier (TSV 1860 München) | 24 |
| 1965/1966 | TSV 1860 München | FC Bayern München | Lothar Emmerich (BV Borussia 09 Dortmund) | 31 |

| | | | |
|---|---|---|---|
| 1966/1967 | TSV Eintracht Braunschweig | FC Bayern München | Lothar Emmerich (BV Borussia 09 Dortmund) |
| | | | Gerhard Müller (FC Bayern München) 28 |
| 1967/1968 | 1. FC Nürnberg | 1. FC Köln 1. FC Köln | Johannes Löhr (1. FC Köln) 27 |
| 1968/1969 | FC Bayern München | FC Bayern München | Gerhard Müller (FC Bayern München) 30 |
| 1969/1970 | Borussia VfL Mönchengladbach | Kickers Offenbach FC | Gerhard Müller (FC Bayern München) 38 |
| 1970/1971 | Borussia VfL Mönchengladbach | FC Bayern München | Lothar Kobluhn (SC Rot-Weiß Oberhausen) 24 |
| 1971/1972 | FC Bayern München | FC Schalke 04 Gelsenkirchen | Gerhard Müller (FC Bayern München) 40 |
| 1972/1973 | FC Bayern München | Borussia VfL Mönchengladbach | Gerhard Müller (FC Bayern München) 36 |
| 1973/1974 | FC Bayern München | Eintracht Frankfurt | Gerhard Müller (FC Bayern München) |
| | | | Josef Heynckes (Borussia VfL Mönchengladbach) 30 |
| 1974/1975 | Borussia VfL Mönchengladbach | Eintracht Frankfurt | Josef Heynckes (Borussia VfL Mönchengladbach) 27 |
| 1975/1976 | Borussia VfL Mönchengladbach | Hamburger SV | Klaus Fischer (FC Schalke 04 Gelsenkirchen) 29 |
| 1976/1977 | Borussia VfL Mönchengladbach | 1. FC Köln | Dieter Müller (1. FC Köln) 34 |
| 1977/1978 | 1. FC Köln | 1. FC Köln | Dieter Müller (1. FC Köln) |
| | | | Gerhard Müller (FC Bayern München) 24 |
| 1978/1979 | Hamburger SV | TSV Fortuna Düsseldorf | Klaus Allofs (TSV TSV Fortuna Düsseldorf) 22 |
| 1979/1980 | FC Bayern München | TSV Fortuna Düsseldorf | Karl-Heinz Rummenigge (FC Bayern München) 26 |
| 1980/1981 | FC Bayern München | Eintracht Frankfurt | Karl-Heinz Rummenigge (FC Bayern München) 29 |
| 1981/1982 | Hamburger SV | FC Bayern München | Horst Hrubesch (Hamburger SV) 27 |
| 1982/1983 | Hamburger SV | 1. FC Köln | Rudolf Völler (SV Werder Bremen) 23 |
| 1983/1984 | VfB Stuttgart | FC Bayern München | Karl-Heinz Rummenigge (FC Bayern München) 26 |
| 1984/1985 | FC Bayern München | FC Bayer 05 Uerdingen | Klaus Allofs (1. FC Köln) 26 |
| 1985/1986 | FC Bayern München | FC Bayern München | Stefan Kuntz (VfL Bochum) 22 |
| 1986/1987 | FC Bayern München | Hamburger SV | Uwe Rahn (Borussia VfL Mönchengladbach) 24 |
| 1987/1988 | SV Werder Bremen | Eintracht Frankfurt | Jürgen Klinsmann (VfB Stuttgart) 19 |
| 1988/1989 | FC Bayern München | BV Borussia 09 Dortmund | Thomas Allofs (1. FC Köln) 17 |
| | | | Roland Wohlfarth (FC Bayern München) |
| 1989/1990 | FC Bayern München | 1. FC Kaiserslautern | Jørn Andersen (NOR, Eintracht Frankfurt) 18 |
| 1990/1991 | 1. FC Kaiserslautern | SV Werder Bremen | Roland Wohlfarth (FC Bayern München) 21 |
| 1991/1992 | VfB Stuttgart | SV Hannover 96 | Fritz Walter (VfB Stuttgart) 22 |
| 1992/1993 | SV Werder Bremen | TSV Bayer 04 Leverkusen | Ulf Kirsten (TSV Bayer 04 Leverkusen) |
| | | | Anthony Yeboah (GHA, Eintracht Frankfurt) 20 |
| 1993/1994 | FC Bayern München | SV Werder Bremen | Stefan Kuntz (1. FC Kaiserslautern) |
| | | | Anthony Yeboah (GHA, Eintracht Frankfurt) 18 |
| 1994/1995 | BV Borussia 09 Dortmund | Borussia VfL Mönchengladbach | Mario Basler (SV Werder Bremen) |
| | | | Heiko Herrlich (Borussia VfL Mönchengladbach) 20 |
| 1995/1996 | BV Borussia 09 Dortmund | 1. FC Kaiserslautern | Fredi Bobič (VfB Stuttgart) 17 |
| 1996/1997 | FC Bayern München | VfB Stuttgart | Ulf Kirsten (TSV Bayer 04 Leverkusen) 22 |
| 1997/1998 | 1. FC Kaiserslautern | FC Bayern München | Ulf Kirsten (TSV Bayer 04 Leverkusen) 22 |
| 1998/1999 | FC Bayern München | SV Werder Bremen | Michael Preetz (Hertha BSC Berlin) 23 |
| 1999/2000 | FC Bayern München | FC Bayern München | Martin Max (TSV 1860 München) 19 |
| 2000/2001 | FC Bayern München | FC Schalke 04 Gelsenkirchen | Sergej Barbarez (BIH, Hamburger SV) |
| | | | Ebbe Sand (DEN, FC Schalke 04 Gelsenkirchen) 22 |
| 2001/2002 | BV Borussia 09 Dortmund | FC Schalke 04 Gelsenkirchen | Márcio Amoroso dos Santos |
| | | | (BRA, BV Borussia 09 Dortmund) |
| | | | Martin Max (TSV 1860 München) 18 |
| 2002/2003 | FC Bayern München | FC Bayern München | Thomas Christiansen Tarín (DEN, VfL Bochum) |
| | | | Giovane Élber de Souza |
| | | | (BRA, FC Bayern München) 21 |
| 2003/2004 | SV Werder Bremen | SV Werder Bremen | Aílton Gonçalves da Silva |
| | | | (BRA, SV Werder Bremen) 28 |
| 2004/2005 | FC Bayern München | FC Bayern München | Marek Mintál (SVK, 1. FC Nürnberg) 24 |
| 2005/2006 | FC Bayern München | FC Bayern München | Miroslav Klose (SV Werder Bremen) 25 |
| 2006/2007 | VfB Stuttgart | 1. FC Nürnberg | Theofanis Gekas (GRE, VfL Bochum) 20 |
| 2007/2008 | FC Bayern München | FC Bayern München | Luca Toni Varchetta (ITA, FC Bayern München) 24 |
| 2008/2009 | VfL Wolfsburg | SV Werder Bremen | Edinaldo Batista Libânio "Grafite" |
| | | | (BRA, VfL Wolfsburg) 28 |
| 2009/2010 | FC Bayern München | FC Bayern München | Edin Džeko (BIH, VfL Wolfsburg) 22 |
| 2010/2011 | BV Borussia 09 Dortmund | FC Schalke 04 Gelsenkirchen | Mario Gómez García (FC Bayern München) 28 |
| 2011/2012 | BV Borussia 09 Dortmund | BV Borussia 09 Dortmund | Dirk Jan Klaas Huntelaar |
| | | | (NED, FC Schalke 04 Gelsenkirchen) 29 |
| 2012/2013 | FC Bayern München | FC Bayern München | Stefan Kießling (TSV Bayer 04 Leverkusen) 25 |
| 2013/2014 | FC Bayern München | FC Bayern München | Robert Lewandowski |
| | | | (POL, BV Borussia 09 Dortmund) 20 |
| 2014/2015 | FC Bayern München | VfL Wolfsburg | Alexander Meier (Eintracht Frankfurt) 19 |
| 2015/2016 | FC Bayern München | FC Bayern München | Robert Lewandowski (POL, FC Bayern München) 30 |
| 2016/2017 | FC Bayern München | BV Borussia 09 Dortmund | Pierre-Emerick Emiliano François Aubameyang |
| | | | (GAB, BV Borussia 09 Dortmund) 31 |
| 2017/2018 | FC Bayern München | Eintracht Frankfurt | Robert Lewandowski (POL, FC Bayern München) 29 |
| 2018/2019 | FC Bayern München | FC Bayern München | Robert Lewandowski (POL, FC Bayern München) 22 |
| 2019/2020 | FC Bayern München | FC Bayern München | Robert Lewandowski (POL, FC Bayern München) 34 |
| 2020/2021 | FC Bayern München | BV Borussia 09 Dortmund | Robert Lewandowski (POL, FC Bayern München) 41 |
| 2021/2022 | FC Bayern München | RasenBallsport Leipzig | Robert Lewandowski (POL, FC Bayern München) 35 |
| 2022/2023 | FC Bayern München | RasenBallsport Leipzig | Niclas Füllkrug (SV Werder Bremen) |
| | | | Christopher Alan Nkunku (FRA, RB Leipzig) 16 |

Please note: the Bundesliga was introduced at the start of the 1963/1964 season.

# NATIONAL CHAMPIONSHIP
## Bundesliga 2022/2023
### (05.08.2022 – 27.05.2023)

**Results**

### Round 1 [05-07.08.2022]
Eintracht Frankfurt-Bayern München 1-6(0-5)
Union Berlin - Hertha BSC 3-1(1-0)
Mönchengladbach - Hoffenheim 3-1(1-1)
VfL Wolfsburg - Werder Bremen 2-2(1-2)
VfL Bochum - FSV Mainz 05 1-2(1-1)
FC Augsburg - SC Freiburg 0-4(0-0)
Bor. Dortmund - Bayer Leverkusen 1-0(1-0)
VfB Stuttgart - RB Leipzig 1-1(1-1)
FC Köln - FC Schalke 04 3-1(0-0)

### Round 2 [12-14.08.2022]
SC Freiburg - Borussia Dortmund 1-3(1-0)
Bayer Leverkusen - FC Augsburg 1-2(1-1)
RB Leipzig - FC Köln 2-2(1-1)
Hoffenheim - VfL Bochum 3-2(2-2)
Hertha BSC - Eintracht Frankfurt 1-1(1-0)
Werder Bremen - VfB Stuttgart 2-2(1-1)
FC Schalke 04 - Mönchengladbach 2-2(1-0)
FSV Mainz 05 - Union Berlin 0-0
Bayern München - VfL Wolfsburg 2-0(2-0)

### Round 3 [19-21.08.2022]
Mönchengladbach - Hertha BSC 1-0(1-0)
Borussia Dortmund - Werder Bremen 2-3(1-0)
Bayer Leverkusen - Hoffenheim 0-3(0-2)
VfL Wolfsburg - FC Schalke 04 0-0
FC Augsburg - FSV Mainz 05 1-2(1-1)
VfB Stuttgart - SC Freiburg 0-1(0-1)
Union Berlin - RB Leipzig 2-1(2-0)
Eintracht Frankfurt - FC Köln 1-1(0-0)
VfL Bochum - Bayern München 0-7(0-4)

### Round 4 [26-28.08.2022]
SC Freiburg - VfL Bochum 1-0(0-0)
RB Leipzig - VfL Wolfsburg 2-0(1-0)
FSV Mainz 05 - Bayer Leverkusen 0-3(0-3)
Hoffenheim - FC Augsburg 1-0(1-0)
Hertha BSC - Borussia Dortmund 0-1(0-1)
FC Schalke 04 - Union Berlin 1-6(1-3)
Bayern München - Mönchengladbach 1-1(0-1)
FC Köln - VfB Stuttgart 0-0
Werder Bremen - Eintracht Frankfurt 3-4(2-3)

### Round 5 [02-04.09.2022]
Borussia Dortmund - Hoffenheim 1-0(1-0)
Bayer Leverkusen - SC Freiburg 2-3(1-0)
Union Berlin - Bayern München 1-1(1-1)
VfL Wolfsburg - FC Köln 2-4(1-3)
VfL Bochum - Werder Bremen 0-2(0-0)
VfB Stuttgart - FC Schalke 04 1-1(1-1)
Eintracht Frankfurt - RB Leipzig 4-0(2-0)
FC Augsburg - Hertha BSC 0-2(0-0)
Mönchengladbach - FSV Mainz 05 0-1(0-0)

### Round 6 [09-11.09.2022]
Werder Bremen - FC Augsburg 0-1(0-0)
Bayern München - VfB Stuttgart 2-2(1-0)
RB Leipzig - Borussia Dortmund 3-0(2-0)
Hoffenheim - FSV Mainz 05 4-1(0-0)
Eintracht Frankfurt - VfL Wolfsburg 0-1(0-0)
Hertha BSC - Bayer Leverkusen 2-2(0-0)
FC Schalke 04 - VfL Bochum 3-1(1-0)
FC Köln - Union Berlin 0-1(0-1)
SC Freiburg - Mönchengladbach 0-0

### Round 7 [16-18.09.2022]
FSV Mainz 05 - Hertha BSC 1-1(0-1)
Borussia Dortmund - FC Schalke 04 1-0(0-0)
Bayer Leverkusen - Werder Bremen 1-1(0-0)
FC Augsburg - Bayern München 1-0(0-0)
VfB Stuttgart - Eintracht Frankfurt 1-3(0-1)
Mönchengladbach - RB Leipzig 3-0(2-0)
Union Berlin - VfL Wolfsburg 2-0(0-0)
VfL Bochum - FC Köln 1-1(1-0)
Hoffenheim - SC Freiburg 0-0

### Round 8 [30.09.-02.10.2022]
Bayern München - Bayer Leverkusen 4-0(3-0)
RB Leipzig - VfL Bochum 4-0(2-0)
SC Freiburg - FSV Mainz 05 2-1(2-0)
FC Köln - Borussia Dortmund 3-2(0-1)
Eintracht Frankfurt - Union Berlin 2-0(2-0)
VfL Wolfsburg - VfB Stuttgart 3-2(2-2)
Werder Bremen - Mönchengladbach 5-1(4-0)
Hertha BSC - Hoffenheim 1-1(1-1)
FC Schalke 04 - FC Augsburg 2-3(1-2)

### Round 9 [07-09.10.2022]
Hoffenheim - Werder Bremen 1-2(1-1)
Bayer Leverkusen - FC Schalke 04 4-0(2-0)
FSV Mainz 05 - RB Leipzig 1-1(1-0)
VfL Bochum - Eintracht Frankfurt 3-0(0-0)
FC Augsburg - VfL Wolfsburg 1-1(0-1)
Borussia Dortmund-Bayern München 2-2(0-1)
Mönchengladbach - FC Köln 5-2(2-1)
Hertha BSC - SC Freiburg 2-2(1-1)
VfB Stuttgart - Union Berlin 0-1(0-0)

### Round 10 [14-16.10.2022]
FC Schalke 04 - Hoffenheim 0-3(0-2)
Eintracht Frankf. - Bayer Leverkusen 5-1(1-0)
VfL Wolfsburg - Mönchengladbach 2-2(1-1)
VfB Stuttgart - VfL Bochum 4-1(2-1)
Werder Bremen - FSV Mainz 05 0-2(0-1)
RB Leipzig - Hertha BSC 3-2(3-0)
FC Köln - FC Augsburg 3-2(0-1)
Union Berlin - Borussia Dortmund 2-0(2-0)
Bayern München - SC Freiburg 5-0(2-0)

### Round 11 [21-23.10.2022]
FSV Mainz 05 - FC Köln 5-0(3-0)
Borussia Dortmund - VfB Stuttgart 5-0(3-0)
Bayer Leverkusen - VfL Wolfsburg 2-2(1-1)
SC Freiburg - Werder Bremen 2-0(0-0)
Hoffenheim - Bayern München 0-2(0-2)
FC Augsburg - RB Leipzig 3-3(1-0)
Mönchengladbach - Eintracht Frankf. 1-3(0-3)
VfL Bochum - Union Berlin 2-1(1-0)
Hertha BSC - FC Schalke 04 2-1(0-0)

### Round 12 [28-30.10.2022]
Werder Bremen - Hertha BSC 1-0(0-0)
Bayern München - FSV Mainz 05 6-2(3-1)
RB Leipzig - Bayer Leverkusen 2-0(1-0)
VfL Wolfsburg - VfL Bochum 4-0(2-0)
VfB Stuttgart - FC Augsburg 2-1(1-1)
Eintracht Frankfurt - Bor. Dortmund 1-2(1-1)
Union Berlin - Mönchengladbach 2-1(0-1)
FC Schalke 04 - SC Freiburg 0-2(0-1)
FC Köln - Hoffenheim 1-1(1-1)

### Round 13 [04-06.11.2022]
Mönchengladbach - VfB Stuttgart 3-1(2-1)
Borussia Dortmund - VfL Bochum 3-0(3-0)
FSV Mainz 05 - VfL Wolfsburg 0-3(0-1)
Hoffenheim - RB Leipzig 1-3(0-1)
FC Augsburg - Eintracht Frankfurt 1-2(1-1)
Hertha BSC - Bayern München 2-3(2-3)
Werder Bremen - FC Schalke 04 2-1(1-0)
Bayer Leverkusen - Union Berlin 5-0(0-0)
SC Freiburg - FC Köln 2-0(0-0)

### Round 14 [08-09.11.2022]
VfL Wolfsburg - Borussia Dortmund 2-0(1-0)
Bayern München - Werder Bremen 6-1(4-1)
VfL Bochum - Mönchengladbach 2-1(2-0)
VfB Stuttgart - Hertha BSC 2-1(1-1)
FC Köln - Bayer Leverkusen 1-2(1-0)
RB Leipzig - SC Freiburg 3-1(0-0)
Union Berlin - FC Augsburg 2-2(2-2)
Eintracht Frankfurt - Hoffenheim 4-2(3-1)
FC Schalke 04 - FSV Mainz 05 1-0(1-0)

### Round 15 [11-13.11.2022]
Mönchengladbach - Bor. Dortmund 4-2(3-2)
Bayer Leverkusen - VfB Stuttgart 2-0(1-0)
Hoffenheim - VfL Wolfsburg 1-2(1-1)
FC Augsburg - VfL Bochum 0-1(0-0)
Hertha BSC - FC Köln 2-0(1-0)
Werder Bremen - RB Leipzig 1-2(0-1)
FC Schalke 04 - Bayern München 0-2(0-1)
FSV Mainz 05 - Eintracht Frankfurt 1-1(1-0)
SC Freiburg - Union Berlin 4-1(4-0)

### Round 16 [20-22.01.2023]
RB Leipzig - Bayern München 1-1(0-1)
Union Berlin - Hoffenheim 3-1(0-1)
Eintracht Frankfurt - FC Schalke 04 3-0(1-0)
VfL Wolfsburg - SC Freiburg 6-0(3-0)
VfL Bochum - Hertha BSC 3-1(2-0)
VfB Stuttgart - FSV Mainz 05 1-1(1-1)
FC Köln - Werder Bremen 7-1(5-1)
Borussia Dortmund - FC Augsburg 4-3(2-2)
Mönchengladbach-Bayer Leverkusen 2-3(0-2)

### Round 17 [24-25.01.2023]
FC Schalke 04 - RB Leipzig 1-6(0-4)
Bayern München - FC Köln 1-1(0-1)
Hoffenheim - VfB Stuttgart 2-2(1-1)
Hertha BSC - VfL Wolfsburg 0-5(0-3)
FSV Mainz 05 - Borussia Dortmund 1-2(1-1)
Bayer Leverkusen - VfL Bochum 2-0(1-0)
SC Freiburg - Eintracht Frankfurt 1-1(0-1)
FC Augsburg - Mönchengladbach 1-0(0-0)
Werder Bremen - Union Berlin 1-2(1-1)

### Round 18 [27-29.01.2023]
RB Leipzig - VfB Stuttgart 2-1(1-0)
Hertha BSC - Union Berlin 0-2(0-1)
Hoffenheim - Mönchengladbach 1-4(0-2)
Werder Bremen - VfL Wolfsburg 2-1(1-0)
FSV Mainz 05 - VfL Bochum 5-2(3-0)
SC Freiburg - FC Augsburg 3-1(2-1)
Bayern München-Eintracht Frankfurt 1-1(1-0)
FC Schalke 04 - FC Köln 0-0
Bayer Leverkusen - Bor. Dortmund 0-2(0-1)

**Round 19 [03-05.02.2023]**
FC Augsburg - Bayer Leverkusen 1-0(0-0)
FC Köln - RB Leipzig 0-0
Borussia Dortmund - SC Freiburg 5-1(1-1)
Union Berlin - FSV Mainz 05 2-1(1-0)
VfL Bochum - Hoffenheim 5-2(3-0)
Eintracht Frankfurt - Hertha BSC 3-0(2-0)
Mönchengladbach - FC Schalke 04 0-0
VfB Stuttgart - Werder Bremen 0-2(0-0)
VfL Wolfsburg - Bayern München 2-4(1-3)

**Round 20 [10-12.02.2023]**
FC Schalke 04 - VfL Wolfsburg 0-0
Werder Bremen - Borussia Dortmund 0-2(0-0)
Hoffenheim - Bayer Leverkusen 1-3(0-1)
Bayern München - VfL Bochum 3-0(1-0)
FSV Mainz 05 - FC Augsburg 3-1(2-1)
SC Freiburg - VfB Stuttgart 2-1(0-1)
RB Leipzig - Union Berlin 1-2(1-0)
Hertha BSC - Mönchengladbach 4-1(1-1)
FC Köln - Eintracht Frankfurt 3-0(0-0)

**Round 21 [17-19.02.2023]**
FC Augsburg - Hoffenheim 1-0(0-0)
Mönchengladbach - Bayern München 3-2(1-1)
VfL Wolfsburg - RB Leipzig 0-3(0-1)
VfL Bochum - SC Freiburg 0-2(0-1)
VfB Stuttgart - FC Köln 3-0(1-0)
Eintracht Frankfurt - Werder Bremen 2-0(1-0)
Union Berlin - FC Schalke 04 0-0
Borussia Dortmund - Hertha BSC 4-1(2-0)
Bayer Leverkusen - FSV Mainz 05 2-3(1-2)

**Round 22 [24-26.02.2023]**
FSV Mainz 05 - Mönchengladbach 4-0(1-0)
Hoffenheim - Borussia Dortmund 0-1(0-1)
RB Leipzig - Eintracht Frankfurt 2-1(2-0)
FC Köln - VfL Wolfsburg 0-2(0-1)
Werder Bremen - VfL Bochum 3-0(2-0)
Hertha BSC - FC Augsburg 2-0(0-0)
FC Schalke 04 - VfB Stuttgart 2-1(2-0)
SC Freiburg - Bayer Leverkusen 1-1(1-0)
Bayern München - Union Berlin 3-0(3-0)

**Round 23 [03-05.03.2023]**
Borussia Dortmund - RB Leipzig 2-1(2-0)
Mönchengladbach - SC Freiburg 0-0
Union Berlin - FC Köln 0-0
FSV Mainz 05 - Hoffenheim 1-0(1-0)
VfL Bochum - FC Schalke 04 0-2(0-1)
FC Augsburg - Werder Bremen 2-1(1-1)
VfB Stuttgart - Bayern München 1-2(0-1)
Bayer Leverkusen - Hertha BSC 4-1(2-0)
VfL Wolfsburg - Eintracht Frankfurt 2-2(2-2)

**Round 24 [10-12.03.2023]**
FC Köln - VfL Bochum 0-2(0-1)
Hertha BSC - FSV Mainz 05 1-1(1-0)
RB Leipzig - Mönchengladbach 3-0(0-0)
Bayern München - FC Augsburg 5-3(4-1)
Eintracht Frankfurt - VfB Stuttgart 1-1(0-0)
FC Schalke 04 - Borussia Dortmund 2-2(0-1)
SC Freiburg - Hoffenheim 2-1(1-0)
Werder Bremen - Bayer Leverkusen 2-3(1-1)
VfL Wolfsburg - Union Berlin 1-1(0-0)

**Round 25 [17-19.03.2023]**
Mönchengladbach - Werder Bremen 2-2(0-0)
VfL Bochum - RB Leipzig 1-0(0-0)
VfB Stuttgart - VfL Wolfsburg 0-1(0-0)
Hoffenheim - Hertha BSC 3-1(2-0)
FC Augsburg - FC Schalke 04 1-1(0-0)
Borussia Dortmund - FC Köln 6-1(4-1)
Union Berlin - Eintracht Frankfurt 2-0(0-0)
Bayer Leverkusen - Bayern München 2-1(0-1)
FSV Mainz 05 - SC Freiburg 1-1(0-0)

**Round 26 [31.03.-02.04.2023]**
Eintracht Frankfurt - VfL Bochum 1-1(1-1)
FC Schalke 04 - Bayer Leverkusen 0-3(0-0)
RB Leipzig - FSV Mainz 05 0-3(0-1)
VfL Wolfsburg - FC Augsburg 2-2(0-2)
Union Berlin - VfB Stuttgart 3-0(0-0)
SC Freiburg - Hertha BSC 1-0(1-0)
Bayern München-Borussia Dortmund 4-2(3-0)
FC Köln - Mönchengladbach 0-0
Werder Bremen - Hoffenheim 1-2(0-0)

**Round 27 [08-09.04.2023]**
SC Freiburg - Bayern München 0-1(0-0)
Borussia Dortmund - Union Berlin 2-1(1-0)
FC Augsburg - FC Köln 1-3(1-2)
Bayer Leverkusen - Eintracht Frankf. 3-1(2-0)
FSV Mainz 05 - Werder Bremen 2-2(0-0)
Hertha BSC - RB Leipzig 0-1(0-1)
Mönchengladbach - VfL Wolfsburg 2-0(1-0)
VfL Bochum - VfB Stuttgart 2-3(0-1)
Hoffenheim - FC Schalke 04 2-0(1-0)

**Round 28 [14-16.04.2023]**
FC Schalke 04 - Hertha BSC 5-2(2-1)
VfB Stuttgart - Borussia Dortmund 3-3(0-2)
FC Köln - FSV Mainz 05 1-1(0-1)
Bayern München - Hoffenheim 1-1(1-0)
RB Leipzig - FC Augsburg 3-2(3-1)
Eintracht Frankf. - Mönchengladbach 1-1(0-1)
Werder Bremen - SC Freiburg 1-2(0-0)
Union Berlin - VfL Bochum 1-1(1-0)
VfL Wolfsburg - Bayer Leverkusen 0-0

**Round 29 [21-23.04.2023]**
FC Augsburg - VfB Stuttgart 1-1(1-0)
FSV Mainz 05 - Bayern München 3-1(0-1)
Hoffenheim - FC Köln 1-3(0-2)
VfL Bochum - VfL Wolfsburg 1-5(0-3)
Hertha BSC - Werder Bremen 2-4(0-2)
Bor. Dortmund - Eintracht Frankfurt 4-0(3-0)
SC Freiburg - FC Schalke 04 4-0(2-0)
Bayer Leverkusen - RB Leipzig 2-0(1-0)
Mönchengladbach - Union Berlin 0-1(0-0)

**Round 30 [28-30.04.2023]**
VfL Bochum - Borussia Dortmund 1-1(1-1)
Union Berlin - Bayer Leverkusen 0-0
FC Köln - SC Freiburg 0-1(0-0)
RB Leipzig - Hoffenheim 1-0(1-0)
VfB Stuttgart - Mönchengladbach 2-1(1-0)
Eintracht Frankfurt - FC Augsburg 1-1(1-0)
FC Schalke 04 - Werder Bremen 2-1(0-1)
Bayern München - Hertha BSC 2-0(0-0)
VfL Wolfsburg - FSV Mainz 05 3-0(3-0)

**Round 31 [05-07.05.2023]**
Bayer Leverkusen - FC Köln 1-2(1-2)
FSV Mainz 05 - FC Schalke 04 2-3(0-1)
SC Freiburg - RB Leipzig 0-1(0-0)
FC Augsburg - Union Berlin 1-0(0-0)
Hoffenheim - Eintracht Frankfurt 3-1(3-0)
Mönchengladbach - VfL Bochum 2-0(1-0)
Hertha BSC - VfB Stuttgart 2-1(2-1)
Werder Bremen - Bayern München 1-2(0-0)
Borussia Dortmund - VfL Wolfsburg 6-0(3-0)

**Round 32 [12-14.05.2023]**
FC Köln - Hertha BSC 5-2(3-2)
Union Berlin - SC Freiburg 4-2(3-0)
Eintracht Frankfurt - FSV Mainz 05 3-0(2-0)
VfL Wolfsburg - Hoffenheim 2-1(1-0)
VfL Bochum - FC Augsburg 3-2(1-1)
Bayern München - FC Schalke 04 6-0(2-0)
Bor. Dortmund - Mönchengladbach 5-2(4-0)
VfB Stuttgart - Bayer Leverkusen 1-1(0-0)
RB Leipzig - Werder Bremen 2-1(0-0)

**Round 33 [19-21.05.2023]**
SC Freiburg - VfL Wolfsburg 2-0(0-0)
Hoffenheim - Union Berlin 4-2(2-1)
Werder Bremen - FC Köln 1-1(0-1)
FC Schalke 04 - Eintracht Frankfurt 2-2(1-1)
Hertha BSC - VfL Bochum 1-1(0-0)
Bayern München - RB Leipzig 1-3(1-0)
FSV Mainz 05 - VfB Stuttgart 1-4(1-1)
FC Augsburg - Borussia Dortmund 0-3(0-0)
Bayer Leverkusen-Mönchengladbach 2-2(2-0)

**Round 34 [27.05.2023]**
FC Köln - Bayern München 1-2(0-1)
VfL Bochum - Bayer Leverkusen 3-0(2-0)
Eintracht Frankfurt - SC Freiburg 2-1(0-1)
Borussia Dortmund - FSV Mainz 05 2-2(0-2)
VfB Stuttgart - Hoffenheim 1-1(0-0)
Mönchengladbach - FC Augsburg 2-0(2-0)
VfL Wolfsburg - Hertha BSC 1-2(1-0)
RB Leipzig - FC Schalke 04 4-2(2-1)
Union Berlin - Werder Bremen 1-0(0-0)

| | | | Total | | | | | | | Home | | | | | | | Away | | | | |
|---|---|---|---|---|---|---|---|---|---|---|---|---|---|---|---|---|---|---|---|---|---|
| 1. | FC Bayern München | 34 | 21 | 8 | 5 | 92 | - | 38 | 71 | 11 | 5 | 1 | 53 | - | 17 | 10 | 3 | 4 | 39 | - | 21 |
| 2. | BV Borussia 09 Dortmund | 34 | 22 | 5 | 7 | 83 | - | 44 | 71 | 14 | 2 | 1 | 55 | - | 17 | 8 | 3 | 6 | 28 | - | 27 |
| 3. | RasenBallsport Leipzig | 34 | 20 | 6 | 8 | 64 | - | 41 | 66 | 13 | 2 | 2 | 38 | - | 18 | 7 | 4 | 6 | 26 | - | 23 |
| 4. | 1. FC Union Berlin | 34 | 18 | 8 | 8 | 51 | - | 38 | 62 | 11 | 6 | 0 | 30 | - | 11 | 7 | 2 | 8 | 21 | - | 27 |
| 5. | SC Freiburg | 34 | 17 | 8 | 9 | 51 | - | 44 | 59 | 10 | 4 | 3 | 28 | - | 13 | 7 | 4 | 6 | 23 | - | 31 |
| 6. | Bayer 04 Leverkusen | 34 | 14 | 8 | 12 | 57 | - | 49 | 50 | 8 | 3 | 6 | 35 | - | 23 | 6 | 5 | 6 | 22 | - | 26 |
| 7. | Eintracht Frankfurt | 34 | 13 | 11 | 10 | 58 | - | 52 | 50 | 9 | 5 | 3 | 35 | - | 18 | 4 | 6 | 7 | 23 | - | 34 |
| 8. | VfL Wolfsburg | 34 | 13 | 10 | 11 | 57 | - | 48 | 49 | 6 | 7 | 4 | 34 | - | 25 | 7 | 3 | 7 | 23 | - | 23 |
| 9. | 1. FSV Mainz 05 | 34 | 12 | 10 | 12 | 54 | - | 55 | 46 | 6 | 6 | 5 | 31 | - | 25 | 6 | 4 | 7 | 23 | - | 30 |
| 10. | Borussia VfL Mönchengladbach | 34 | 11 | 10 | 13 | 52 | - | 55 | 43 | 10 | 3 | 4 | 33 | - | 18 | 1 | 7 | 9 | 19 | - | 37 |
| 11. | 1. FC Köln | 34 | 10 | 12 | 12 | 49 | - | 54 | 42 | 6 | 5 | 6 | 28 | - | 20 | 4 | 7 | 6 | 21 | - | 34 |
| 12. | TSG 1899 Hoffenheim | 34 | 10 | 6 | 18 | 48 | - | 57 | 36 | 7 | 2 | 8 | 28 | - | 29 | 3 | 4 | 10 | 20 | - | 28 |
| 13. | SV Werder Bremen | 34 | 10 | 6 | 18 | 51 | - | 64 | 36 | 5 | 2 | 10 | 26 | - | 28 | 5 | 4 | 8 | 25 | - | 36 |
| 14. | VfL Bochum | 34 | 10 | 5 | 19 | 40 | - | 72 | 35 | 8 | 2 | 7 | 28 | - | 32 | 2 | 3 | 12 | 12 | - | 40 |
| 15. | FC Augsburg | 34 | 9 | 7 | 18 | 42 | - | 63 | 34 | 6 | 4 | 7 | 16 | - | 24 | 3 | 3 | 11 | 26 | - | 39 |
| 16. | VfB Stuttgart (*Relegation Play-offs*) | 34 | 7 | 12 | 15 | 45 | - | 57 | 33 | 5 | 6 | 6 | 23 | - | 22 | 2 | 6 | 9 | 22 | - | 35 |
| 17. | FC Schalke 04 Gelsenkirchen (*Relegated*) | 34 | 7 | 10 | 17 | 35 | - | 71 | 31 | 5 | 5 | 7 | 23 | - | 36 | 2 | 5 | 10 | 12 | - | 35 |
| 18. | Hertha BSC Berlin (*Relegated*) | 34 | 7 | 8 | 19 | 42 | - | 69 | 29 | 5 | 6 | 6 | 24 | - | 27 | 2 | 2 | 13 | 18 | - | 42 |

| Top goalscorers: | |
|---|---|
| 16 Niclas Füllkrug | *SV Werder Bremen* |
| 16 Christopher Alan Nkunku (FRA) | *RasenBallsport Leipzig* |
| 15 Vincenzo Grifo | *SC Freiburg* |
| 15 Randal Kolo Muani (FRA) | *Eintracht Frankfurt* |
| 14 Serge David Gnabry | *FC Bayern München* |

## Relegation Play-offs (01-05.06.2023)

| | | |
|---|---|---|
| VfB Stuttgart - Hamburger SV | 3-0(1-0) | 3-1(0-1) |

VfB Stuttgart remains at first level for 2023/2024.

# NATIONAL CUP
## DFB Pokal 2022/2023

### First Round [29.07.-01.08./30-31.08.2022]

| | | | | |
|---|---|---|---|---|
| 1. FC Kaan-Marienborn Siegen - 1. FC Nürnberg | 0-2(0-1) | Bremer SV - FC Schalke 04 Gelsenkirchen | 0-5(0-4) |
| TSG Neustrelitz - Karlsruher SC | 0-8(0-3) | FV Engers 07 - DSC Arminia Bielefeld | 1-7(0-2) |
| SG Dynamo Dresden - VfB Stuttgart | 0-1(0-1) | TSV Schott Mainz - SV Hannover 96 | 0-3(0-2) |
| TSV 1860 München - BV Borussia 09 Dortmund | 0-3(0-3) | SV Rödinghausen - TSG 1899 Hoffenheim | 0-2(0-0,0-0) |
| FC Viktoria 1889 Berlin - VfL Bochum | 0-3(0-2) | 1. FC Kaiserslautern - SC Freiburg | 1-2(1-0,1-1) |
| SV 19 Straelen - FC St. Pauli Hamburg | 3-4(2-2) | SV Oberachern - Borussia VfL Mönchengladbach | 1-9(0-6) |
| SSV Jahn Regensburg - 1.FC Köln | 2-2 aet; 4-3 pen | Blau-Weiß Lohne - FC Augsburg | 0-4(0-0) |
| VfB Lübeck - FC Hansa Rostock | 1-0(0-0) | TSV Eintracht Braunschweig - Hertha BSC Berlin | 4-4 aet; 6-5 pen |
| SV 07 Elversberg - Bayer Leverkusen | 4-3(3-2) | SV Waldhof Mannheim - SV Holstein Kiel | 0-0 aet; 5-3 pen |
| FC Einheit Wernigerode - SC Paderborn 07 | 0-10(0-3) | FC Erzgebirge Aue - 1. FSV Mainz 05 | 0-3(0-1) |
| FV Illertissen - 1. FC Heidenheim 1846 | 0-2(0-0) | Chemnitzer FC - 1. FC Union Berlin | 1-2(0-0,1-1) |
| SpVgg Bayreuth - Hamburger SV | 1-3(1-0,1-1) | FC Ingolstadt 04 - SV Darmstadt 98 | 0-3(0-2) |
| Kickers Offenbach - TSV Fortuna Düsseldorf | 1-4(0-1) | FC Energie Cottbus - SV Werder Bremen | 1-2(0-1) |
| FC Carl Zeiss Jena - VfL Wolfsburg | 0-1(0-0) | 1. FC Magdeburg - Eintracht Frankfurt | 0-4(0-2) |
| Stuttgarter Kickers - SpVgg Greuther Fürth | 2-0(1-0) | FC Teutonia Ottensen - RasenBallsport Leipzig | 0-8(0-4) |
| BSV Schwarz-Weiß Rehden - SV Sandhausen | 0-4(0-3) | FC Viktoria Köln - FC Bayern München | 0-5(0-2) |

### Second Round [18-19.10.2022]

| | | | | |
|---|---|---|---|---|
| VfB Lübeck - 1. FSV Mainz 05 | 0-3(0-2) | SV Hannover 96- BV Borussia 09 Dortmund | 0-2(0-1) |
| Stuttgarter Kickers - Eintracht Frankfurt | 0-2(0-2) | SC Freiburg - FC St. Pauli Hamburg | 2-1(0-1,1-1) |
| SV Waldhof Mannheim - 1. FC Nürnberg | 0-1(0-0) | SV Sandhausen - Karlsruher SC | 2-2 aet; 8-7 pen |
| RasenBallsport Leipzig - Hamburger SV | 4-0(2-0) | SC Paderborn 07 - SV Werder Bremen | 2-2 aet; 5-4 pen |
| SV Darmstadt 98 - Borussia VfL Mönchengladbach | 2-1(1-0) | FC Augsburg - FC Bayern München | 2-5(1-1) |
| SV 07 Elversberg - VfL Bochum | 0-1(0-0) | VfB Stuttgart - DSC Arminia Bielefeld | 6-0(4-0) |
| TSV Eintracht Braunschweig - VfL Wolfsburg | 1-2(1-1) | 1. FC Union Berlin - 1. FC Heidenheim 1846 | 2-0(1-0) |
| TSG 1899 Hoffenheim - FC Schalke 04 Gelsenkirch. | 5-1(3-0) | SSV Jahn Regensburg - TSV Fortuna Düsseldorf | 0-3(0-3) |

### Third Round [31.01.-01.02./07-08.02.2023]

| | | | | |
|---|---|---|---|---|
| SC Paderborn 07 - VfB Stuttgart | 1-2(1-0) | SV Sandhausen - SC Freiburg | 0-2(0-0) |
| 1. FC Union Berlin - VfL Wolfsburg | 2-1(1-1) | Eintracht Frankfurt - SV Darmstadt 98 | 4-2(2-2) |
| RasenBallsport Leipzig - TSG 1899 Hoffenheim | 3-1(2-0) | 1. FC Nürnberg - TSV Fortuna Düsseldorf | 1-1 aet; 5-3 pen |
| 1. FSV Mainz 05 - FC Bayern München | 0-4(0-3) | VfL Bochum - BV Borussia 09 Dortmund | 1-2(0-1) |

| Quarter-Finals [04-05.04.2023] | | | |
|---|---|---|---|
| Eintracht Frankfurt - 1. FC Union Berlin | 2-0(2-0) | 1. FC Nürnberg - VfB Stuttgart | 0-1(0-0) |
| FC Bayern München - SC Freiburg | 1-2(1-1) | RasenBallsport Leipzig - BV Borussia 09 Dortmund | 2-0(1-0) |

| Semi-Finals [02-03.05.2023] | | | |
|---|---|---|---|
| SC Freiburg - RasenBallsport Leipzig | 1-5(0-4) | VfB Stuttgart - Eintracht Frankfurt | 2-3(1-0) |

## Final

03.06.2023; Olympiastadion, Berlin; Referee: Daniel Siebert; Attendance:
**RasenBallsport Leipzig - Eintracht Frankfurt**                                    **2-0(0-0)**

**RB Leipzig**: Janis Blaswich, Benjamin Paa Kwesi Henrichs, Lukas Manuel Klostermann, Vilmos Tamás Orbán (Cap), Marcel Halstenberg, Konrad Laimer, Amadou Haïdara (78.Xaver Schlager), Dominik Szoboszlai (90+1.Kevin Kampl), Daniel Olmo Carvajal „Dani Olmo",Christopher Alan Nkunku, Timo Werner (61.Yussuf Yurary Poulsen). Trainer: Marco Rose.

**Eintracht Frankfurt**: Kevin Trapp, Lucas Silva Melo „Tuta", Makoto Hasebe (78.Christopher Lenz), Evan N'Dicka, Aurélio Gabriel Ulineia Buta (87.Éric Junior Dina-Ebimbe), Sebastian Rode (Cap) (70.Jesper Lindstrøm), Philipp Max (78.Rafael Santos Borré Maury), Daichi Kamada, Mario Götze, Randal Kolo Muani. Trainer: Oliver Glasner (Austria).

**Goals:** 1-0 Christopher Alan Nkunku (71), 2-0 Dominik Szoboszlai (85).

## THE CLUBS 2022/2023

### Fußball-Club Augsburg 1907

| | | |
|---|---|---|
| **Founded**: | 08.08.1907 | |
| **Stadium**: | WWK Arena, Augsburg (30,660) | |
| **Trainer**: | Enrico Maaßen | 10.03.1984 |

| Goalkeepers: | DOB | M | (s) | G |
|---|---|---|---|---|
| Rafał Gikiewicz (POL) | 26.10.1987 | 23 | | |
| Tomáš Koubek (CZE) | 26.08.1992 | 11 | | |
| **Defenders:** | **DOB** | **M** | **(s)** | **G** |
| Maximilian Bauer | 09.02.2000 | 20 | (7) | |
| David Čolina (CRO) | 19.07.2000 | | (7) | 1 |
| Raphael Framberger | 06.09.1995 | 2 | (1) | |
| Jeffrey Gouweleeuw (NED) | 10.07.1991 | 32 | | |
| Robert Gumny (POL) | 04.06.1998 | 23 | (6) | 1 |
| Iago Amaral Borduchi (BRA) | 23.03.1997 | 19 | (3) | |
| Reece Joel Oxford (ENG) | 16.12.1998 | 1 | (2) | |
| Mads Giersing Valentin Pedersen (DEN) | 01.09.1996 | 20 | (8) | |
| Felix Uduokhai | 09.09.1997 | 16 | (3) | |
| Frederik Winther (DEN) | 04.01.2001 | 1 | | |
| Aaron Zehnter | 31.10.2004 | | (1) | |
| **Midfielders:** | **DOB** | **M** | **(s)** | **G** |
| Julian Baumgartlinger (AUT) | 02.01.1988 | 3 | (13) | |
| Niklas Dorsch | 15.01.1998 | 5 | (6) | |
| Arne Engels (BEL) | 08.09.2003 | 18 | | |

| | DOB | M | (s) | G |
|---|---|---|---|---|
| Carlos Armando Gruezo Arboleda (ECU) | 19.04.1995 | 12 | (1) | |
| Hans Fredrik Jensen (FIN) | 09.09.1997 | 8 | (12) | 2 |
| Arne Maier | 08.01.1999 | 24 | (6) | 5 |
| *Renato Palma Veiga* (POR) | 29.07.2003 | 7 | (6) | |
| Elvis Rexhbeçaj | 01.11.1997 | 30 | (1) | |
| **Forwards:** | **DOB** | **M** | **(s)** | **G** |
| Dion Beljo (CRO) | 01.03.2002 | 16 | (2) | 3 |
| Mërgim Berisha | 11.05.1998 | 20 | (3) | 9 |
| Daniel Caligiuri | 15.01.1988 | 2 | (11) | 1 |
| Irvin Charly José Cardona (FRA) | 08.08.1997 | | (10) | 1 |
| Ermedin Demirović (BIH) | 25.03.1998 | 30 | | 8 |
| André Hahn | 13.08.1990 | 4 | (3) | 2 |
| Nathanaël Mbuku (FRA) | 16.03.2002 | | (2) | |
| Florian Niederlechner | 24.10.1990 | 10 | (4) | 4 |
| Ricardo Daniel Pepi (USA) | 09.01.2003 | 1 | (3) | |
| Lukas Emanuel Petkov | 01.11.2000 | | (7) | |
| Noah Sarenren Bazee (NGA) | 21.08.1996 | | (2) | |
| Rubén Estephan Vargas Martínez (SUI) | 05.08.1998 | 13 | (10) | 3 |
| Kelvin Kwarteng Yeboah (GHA) | 06.05.2000 | 3 | (10) | 1 |

### Bayer 04 Leverkusen Fußball GmbH

| | | |
|---|---|---|
| **Founded**: | 01.07.1904 | |
| **Stadium**: | BayArena, Leverkusen (30,210) | |
| **Trainer**: | Gerardo Seoane (SUI) | 30.10.1978 |
| [05.10.2022] | Xabier "Xabi" Alonso Olano (ESP) | 25.11.1981 |

| Goalkeepers: | DOB | M | (s) | G |
|---|---|---|---|---|
| Lukáš Hrádecký (FIN) | 24.11.1989 | 33 | | |
| Andrey Lunev (RUS) | 13.11.1991 | 1 | | |
| **Defenders:** | **DOB** | **M** | **(s)** | **G** |
| Mitchel Bakker (NED) | 20.06.2000 | 19 | (9) | 3 |
| Timothy Fosu-Mensah (NED) | 02.01.1998 | 1 | (10) | |
| Jeremie Agyekum Frimpong (NED) | 10.12.2000 | 32 | (2) | 8 |
| Piero Martín Hincapié Reyna (ECU) | 09.01.2002 | 27 | (3) | 1 |
| Odilon Kossounou (CIV) | 04.01.2001 | 17 | (7) | |
| Daley Sinkgraven (NED) | 04.07.1995 | 4 | (8) | |
| Jonathan Glao Tah | 11.02.1996 | 28 | (5) | 1 |
| Edmond Tapsoba (BFA) | 02.02.1999 | 32 | (1) | 1 |
| **Midfielders:** | **DOB** | **M** | **(s)** | **G** |
| Nadiem Amiri | 27.10.1996 | 9 | (16) | 4 |
| Robert Andrich | 22.09.1994 | 28 | (1) | 2 |
| Charles Mariano Aránguiz Sandoval (CHI) | 17.04.1989 | 4 | (6) | 1 |

| | DOB | M | (s) | G |
|---|---|---|---|---|
| Ayman Azhil (MAR) | 10.04.2001 | | (1) | |
| Kerem Demirbay | 03.07.1993 | 17 | (8) | 4 |
| Noah Mbamba-Muanda (BEL) | 05.01.2005 | | (1) | |
| Exequiel Alejandro Palacios (ARG) | 05.10.1998 | 19 | (6) | 4 |
| Florian Richard Wirtz | 03.05.2003 | 11 | (6) | 1 |
| **Forwards:** | **DOB** | **M** | **(s)** | **G** |
| Amine Adli (FRA) | 10.05.2000 | 16 | (10) | 5 |
| Sardar Azmoun (IRN) | 01.01.1995 | 8 | (15) | 4 |
| Karim Bellarabi | 08.04.1990 | 1 | (7) | |
| Moussa Diaby (FRA) | 07.07.1999 | 33 | | 9 |
| Adam Hložek (CZE) | 25.07.2002 | 16 | (13) | 5 |
| Callum James Hudson-Odoi (ENG) | 07.11.2000 | 7 | (7) | |
| Paulo Henrique Sampaio Filho „Paulinho" (BRA) | 15.07.2000 | 1 | (3) | 1 |
| Joel Pohjanpalo (FIN) | 13.09.1994 | | (1) | |
| Patrik Schick (CZE) | 24.01.1996 | 10 | (4) | 3 |

## Fußball-Club Bayern München

| Founded: | 27.02.1900 | | |
| Stadium: | Allianz Arena, München (75,000) | | |
| Trainer: | Julian Nagelsmann | | 23.07.1987 |
| [24.03.2023] | Thomas Tuchel | | 29.08.1973 |

| Goalkeepers: | DOB | M | (s) | G |
|---|---|---|---|---|
| Manuel Peter Neuer | 27.03.1986 | 12 | | |
| Yann Sommer (SUI) | 17.12.1988 | 19 | | |
| Sven Ulreich | 03.08.1988 | 3 | | |
| **Defenders:** | **DOB** | **M** | **(s)** | **G** |
| Daley Blind (NED) | 09.03.1990 | 1 | (3) | |
| Alphonso Boyle Davies (CAN) | 02.11.2000 | 24 | (2) | 1 |
| Matthijs de Ligt (NED) | 12.08.1999 | 27 | (4) | 3 |
| Lucas François Bernard Hernández (FRA) | 14.02.1996 | 6 | (1) | |
| *João* Pedro Cavaco *Cancelo* (POR) | 27.05.1994 | 11 | (4) | 1 |
| Noussair Mazraoui (MAR) | 14.11.1997 | 11 | (8) | 1 |
| Benjamin Jacques Marcel Pavard (FRA) | 28.03.1996 | 27 | (3) | 4 |
| Bouna Sarr (SEN) | 31.01.1992 | | (1) | |
| Josip Stanišić (CRO) | 02.04.2000 | 4 | (10) | |
| Dayotchanculle Oswald Upamecano (FRA) | 27.10.1998 | 27 | (2) | |

| Midfielders: | DOB | M | (s) | G |
|---|---|---|---|---|
| Leon Christoph Goretzka | 06.02.1995 | 22 | (5) | 3 |
| Ryan Jiro Gravenberch (NED) | 15.06.2002 | 3 | (21) | |
| Arijon Ibrahimović | 11.12.2005 | | (1) | |
| Joshua Walter Kimmich | 08.02.1995 | 32 | (1) | 5 |
| Jamal Musiala | 26.02.2003 | 26 | (7) | 12 |
| Marcel Sabitzer (AUT) | 17.03.1994 | 7 | (8) | 1 |
| Leroy Aziz Sané | 11.01.1996 | 20 | (12) | 8 |
| Gabriel Vidović | 01.12.2003 | | (1) | |
| Paul Wanner | 23.12.2005 | | (2) | |
| **Forwards:** | **DOB** | **M** | **(s)** | **G** |
| Jean-Eric Maxim Choupo-Moting (CMR) | 23.03.1989 | 14 | (5) | 10 |
| Kingsley Junior Coman (FRA) | 13.06.1996 | 16 | (8) | 8 |
| Serge David Gnabry | 14.07.1995 | 22 | (12) | 14 |
| Sadio Mané (SEN) | 10.04.1992 | 18 | (7) | 7 |
| Thomas Müller | 13.09.1989 | 21 | (6) | 7 |
| Mathys Tel (FRA) | 27.04.2005 | 1 | (21) | 5 |

## Verein für Leibesübungen Bochum 1848 Fußballgemeinschaft

| Founded: | 26.07.1848 | | |
| Stadium: | Vonovia Ruhrstadion, Bochum (27,599) | | |
| Trainer: | Thomas Reis | | 04.10.1973 |
| [12.09.2022] | Heiko Butscher | | 28.07.1980 |
| [22.09.2022] | Thomas Letsch | | 26.08.1968 |

| Goalkeepers: | DOB | M | (s) | G |
|---|---|---|---|---|
| Manuel Riemann | 09.09.1988 | 34 | | |
| **Defenders:** | **DOB** | **M** | **(s)** | **G** |
| *Danilo* Teodoro *Soares* (BRA) | 29.10.1991 | 23 | | |
| Cristian Esteban Gamboa Luna (CRC) | 24.10.1989 | 17 | (2) | |
| Dominique Heintz | 15.08.1993 | 8 | (3) | |
| Jannes-Kilian Horn | 06.02.1997 | 1 | (1) | |
| Saidy Janko (SUI) | 22.10.1995 | 12 | (8) | |
| Vassilios Lampropoulos (GRE) | 31.03.1990 | 7 | (8) | |
| Erhan Mašović (SRB) | 22.11.1998 | 23 | (6) | 4 |
| Tim Oermann | 06.10.2003 | 2 | (2) | |
| Ivan Ordets (UKR) | 08.07.1992 | 28 | (2) | |
| Jordi Osei-Tutu (ENG) | 02.10.1998 | 8 | (12) | |
| Keven Schlotterbeck | 28.04.1997 | 8 | (5) | 2 |
| Kostas Stafylidis (GRE) | 02.12.1993 | 11 | (8) | |

| Midfielders: | DOB | M | (s) | G |
|---|---|---|---|---|
| Philipp Förster | 04.02.1995 | 15 | (10) | 3 |
| Jacek Góralski (POL) | 21.09.1992 | 2 | (2) | |
| Pierre Kunde Malong (CMR) | 26.07.1995 | 3 | (9) | 1 |
| Anthony Losilla (FRA) | 10.03.1986 | 31 | | 2 |
| Patrick Osterhage | 01.02.2000 | 11 | (12) | |
| Kevin Stöger (AUT) | 27.08.1993 | 29 | (3) | 5 |
| **Forwards:** | **DOB** | **M** | **(s)** | **G** |
| Christopher Antwi-Adjei (GHA) | 07.02.1994 | 22 | (7) | 3 |
| Takuma Asano (JPN) | 10.11.1994 | 21 | (4) | 3 |
| Moritz Broschinski | 23.09.2000 | | (11) | 2 |
| Silvère Ganvoula M'Boussy (CGO) | 29.06.1996 | | (16) | |
| Philipp Hofmann | 30.03.1993 | 31 | (3) | 8 |
| Gerrit Holtmann | 25.03.1995 | 8 | (15) | 1 |
| Simon Zoller | 26.06.1991 | 19 | (8) | 3 |

## Ballspielverein Borussia 09 Dortmund

| Founded: | 19.12.1909 | | |
| Stadium: | Signal Iduna Park, Dortmund (81,365) | | |
| Trainer: | Edin Terzić | | 30.10.1982 |

| Goalkeepers: | DOB | M | (s) | G |
|---|---|---|---|---|
| Gregor Kobel (SUI) | 06.12.1997 | 27 | | |
| Alexander Meyer | 13.04.1991 | 7 | | |
| **Defenders:** | **DOB** | **M** | **(s)** | **G** |
| Soumaïla Coulibaly (FRA) | 14.10.2003 | | (1) | |
| Raphaël Adelino José Guerreiro (POR) | 22.12.1993 | 26 | (1) | 4 |
| Mats Julian Hummels | 16.12.1988 | 24 | (6) | 1 |
| Thomas Meunier (BEL) | 12.09.1991 | 7 | (3) | |
| Felix Passlack | 29.05.1998 | | (3) | |
| Tom Rothe | 29.10.2004 | | (2) | |
| Julian Ryerson (NOR) | 17.11.1997 | 17 | | 1 |
| Nico Cedric Schlotterbeck | 01.12.1999 | 27 | (1) | 4 |
| Niklas Süle | 03.09.1995 | 23 | (6) | 2 |
| Marius Wolf | 27.05.1995 | 17 | (8) | 1 |
| **Midfielders:** | **DOB** | **M** | **(s)** | **G** |
| Jude Victor William Bellingham (ENG) | 29.06.2003 | 30 | (1) | 8 |
| Julian Brandt | 02.05.1996 | 29 | (3) | 9 |

| | DOB | M | (s) | G |
|---|---|---|---|---|
| Emre Can | 12.01.1994 | 20 | (7) | 2 |
| Mahmoud Dahoud | 01.01.1996 | 4 | (5) | |
| Thorgan Hazard (BEL) | 29.03.1993 | 2 | (12) | |
| Salih Özcan (TUR) | 11.01.1998 | 17 | (9) | |
| Antonios Papadopoulos | 10.09.1999 | | (1) | |
| Marco Pašalić (CRO) | 14.09.2000 | | (1) | |
| Marco Reus | 31.05.1989 | 14 | (11) | 6 |
| Giovanni Alejandro Reyna (USA) | 13.11.2002 | 4 | (18) | 7 |
| **Forwards:** | **DOB** | **M** | **(s)** | **G** |
| Karim-David Adeyemi | 18.01.2002 | 20 | (4) | 6 |
| Jamie Bynoe-Gittens (ENG) | 08.08.2004 | 4 | (11) | 3 |
| Julien Duranville (BEL) | 05.05.2006 | | (1) | |
| Sébastien Romain Teddy Haller (CIV) | 22.06.1994 | 15 | (4) | 9 |
| Donyell Malen (NED) | 19.01.1999 | 22 | (4) | 9 |
| Anthony Mbu Agogo Modeste (FRA) | 14.04.1988 | 7 | (12) | 2 |
| Youssoufa Moukoko | 20.11.2004 | 11 | (15) | 7 |
| Justin Gideon Njinmah | 15.11.2000 | | (1) | |

## Borussia Verein für Leibesübungen 1900 Mönchengladbach

| Founded: | 01.08.1900 | | |
| Stadium: | Borussia-Park, Mönchengladbach (54,057) | | |
| Trainer: | Daniel Farke | | 30.10.1976 |

| Goalkeepers: | DOB | M | (s) | G |
|---|---|---|---|---|
| Jan Olschowsky | 18.11.2001 | 4 | | |
| Jonas Omlin (SUI) | 10.01.1994 | 15 | | |
| Tobias Sippel | 22.03.1988 | 5 | (1) | |
| Yann Sommer (SUI) | 17.12.1988 | 10 | | |
| **Defenders:** | **DOB** | **M** | **(s)** | **G** |
| Ramy Bensebaini (ALG) | 16.04.1995 | 28 | | 6 |
| Nico Elvedi (SUI) | 30.09.1996 | 32 | | 3 |
| Marvin Friedrich | 13.12.1995 | 13 | (10) | 1 |
| Ko Itakura (JPN) | 27.01.1997 | 22 | (2) | |
| Tony Jantschke | 07.04.1990 | 1 | (7) | |
| Stefan Lainer (AUT) | 27.08.1992 | 9 | (8) | |
| Luca Netz | 15.05.2003 | 7 | (13) | 1 |
| Joseph Scally (USA) | 31.12.2002 | 25 | (3) | |
| **Midfielders:** | **DOB** | **M** | **(s)** | **G** |
| Oscar Luigi Fraulo (DEN) | 06.12.2003 | | (2) | |

| | DOB | M | (s) | G |
|---|---|---|---|---|
| Jonas Hofmann | 14.07.1992 | 30 | (1) | 12 |
| Kouadio Koné (FRA) | 17.05.2001 | 30 | | 1 |
| Christoph Kramer | 19.02.1991 | 27 | (2) | |
| Florian Christian Neuhaus | 16.03.1997 | 16 | (7) | 1 |
| Rocco Reitz | 29.05.2002 | | (1) | |
| Julian Weigl | 08.09.1995 | 21 | (2) | 1 |
| **Forwards:** | **DOB** | **M** | **(s)** | **G** |
| Yvandro Borges Sanches (LUX) | 24.05.2004 | | (3) | |
| Patrick Herrmann | 12.02.1991 | | (21) | 1 |
| Nathan N'Goumou (FRA) | 14.03.2000 | 7 | (13) | 1 |
| Alassane Pléa (FRA) | 10.03.1993 | 20 | (9) | 2 |
| Lars Stindl | 26.08.1988 | 20 | (9) | 8 |
| Semir Telalovic | 23.12.1999 | | (3) | |
| Marcus Lilian Thuram-Ulien (FRA) | 06.08.1997 | 28 | (2) | 13 |
| Hannes Wolf (AUT) | 16.04.1999 | 4 | (14) | 1 |

## Eintracht Frankfurt

**Founded**: 08.03.1899
**Stadium**: Deutsche Bank-Park (Waldstadion), Frankfurt (51,500)
**Trainer**: Oliver Glasner (AUT)  28.08.1974

| Goalkeepers: | DOB | M | (s) | G |
|---|---|---|---|---|
| Diant Ramaj | 19.09.2001 | 1 | | |
| Kevin Trapp | 08.07.1990 | 33 | | |
| **Defenders:** | **DOB** | **M** | **(s)** | **G** |
| Aurélio Gabriel Ulineia *Buta* (POR) | 10.02.1997 | 15 | (3) | 3 |
| Timothy Chandler (USA) | 29.03.1990 | | (6) | |
| Dario Gebuhr | 06.05.2003 | | (1) | |
| Makoto Hasebe (JPN) | 18.01.1984 | 15 | (3) | |
| Christopher Lenz | 22.09.1994 | 13 | (11) | |
| Philipp Max | 30.09.1993 | 8 | (2) | |
| Evan N'Dicka (FRA) | 20.08.1999 | 30 | | 1 |
| Luca Pellegrini (ITA) | 07.03.1999 | 7 | (2) | |
| Hrvoje Smolčić (CRO) | 17.08.2000 | 4 | (5) | |
| Almamy Touré (FRA) | 28.04.1996 | 5 | (2) | |
| Lucas Silva Melo „*Tuta*" (BRA) | 04.07.1999 | 30 | (1) | 2 |

| Midfielders: | DOB | M | (s) | G |
|---|---|---|---|---|
| Paxten Reid Aaronson (USA) | 26.08.2003 | | (7) | |
| Éric Junior Dina-Ebimbe (FRA) | 21.11.2000 | 10 | (9) | 3 |
| Mario Götze | 03.06.1992 | 32 | | 3 |
| Kristijan Jakić (CRO) | 14.05.1997 | 17 | (7) | 1 |
| Daichi Kamada (JPN) | 05.08.1996 | 25 | (7) | 9 |
| Filip Kostić (SRB) | 01.11.1992 | 1 | | |
| Jesper Lindstrøm (DEN) | 29.02.2000 | 22 | (5) | 7 |
| Sebastian Rode | 11.10.1990 | 19 | (8) | 4 |
| Mohameth Djibril Ibrahima Sow (SUI) | 06.02.1997 | 30 | (2) | 4 |
| Marcel Wenig | 04.05.2004 | | (1) | |
| **Forwards:** | **DOB** | **M** | **(s)** | **G** |
| Lucas Nicolás Alario (ARG) | 08.10.1992 | 2 | (18) | 1 |
| Faride Alidou | 18.07.2001 | | (15) | |
| Rafael Santos Borré Maury (COL) | 15.09.1995 | 10 | (22) | 2 |
| Ansgar Knauff | 10.01.2002 | 14 | (10) | 1 |
| Randal Kolo Muani (FRA) | 05.12.1998 | 31 | (1) | 15 |

## Sport-Club Freiburg

**Founded**: 1904
**Stadium**: Europa-Park Stadion, Freiburg (34,700)
**Trainer**: Christian Streich  11.06.1965

| Goalkeepers: | DOB | M | (s) | G |
|---|---|---|---|---|
| Mark Flekken (NED) | 13.06.1993 | 34 | | |
| **Defenders:** | **DOB** | **M** | **(s)** | **G** |
| Kimberly Ezekwem | 19.06.2001 | | (1) | |
| Matthias Lukas Ginter | 19.01.1994 | 34 | | 4 |
| Manuel Gulde | 12.02.1991 | 8 | (7) | 1 |
| Christian Günter | 28.02.1993 | 31 | (2) | 1 |
| Lukas Kübler | 30.08.1992 | 19 | (3) | 2 |
| Philipp Lienhart (AUT) | 11.07.1996 | 27 | (2) | 1 |
| Keven Schlotterbeck | 28.04.1997 | | (2) | |
| Jonathan Schmid (FRA) | 22.06.1990 | | (3) | |
| Kenneth Schmidt | 03.06.2002 | 3 | (2) | |
| Kiliann Sildillia (FRA) | 16.05.2002 | 23 | (4) | |
| Hugo Siquet (BEL) | 09.07.2002 | | (2) | |
| **Midfielders:** | **DOB** | **M** | **(s)** | **G** |
| Maximilian Eggestein | 08.12.1996 | 27 | (4) | 1 |

| | DOB | M | (s) | G |
|---|---|---|---|---|
| Nicolas Höfler | 09.03.1990 | 32 | | |
| Yannik Keitel | 15.02.2000 | 8 | (14) | |
| Daniel Kyereh (GHA) | 08.03.1996 | 7 | (5) | 2 |
| Merlin Röhl | 05.07.2002 | | (3) | |
| Robert Wagner | 14.07.2003 | | (4) | |
| **Forwards:** | **DOB** | **M** | **(s)** | **G** |
| Ritsu Dōan (JPN) | 16.06.1998 | 30 | (3) | 5 |
| Michael Gregoritsch (AUT) | 18.04.1994 | 27 | (3) | 10 |
| Vincenzo Grifo (ITA) | 07.04.1993 | 30 | (3) | 15 |
| Lucas Höler | 10.07.1994 | 16 | (10) | 5 |
| Jeong Woo-yeong (KOR) | 20.09.1999 | 4 | (22) | 1 |
| Nils Petersen | 06.12.1988 | | (27) | 1 |
| Roland Sallai (HUN) | 22.05.1997 | 10 | (9) | 1 |
| Kevin Schade | 27.11.2001 | 1 | (7) | 1 |
| Noah Weißhaupt | 20.09.2001 | 3 | (15) | |

## Hertha Berliner Sport-Club

**Founded**: 25.07.1892
**Stadium**: Olympiastadion, Berlin (74,649)
**Trainer**: Sandro Schwarz  17.10.1968
[16.04.2023]  Pál Dárdai (HUN)  16.03.1976

| Goalkeepers: | DOB | M | (s) | G |
|---|---|---|---|---|
| Oliver Christensen (DEN) | 22.03.1999 | 33 | | |
| Tjark Ernst | 15.03.2003 | 1 | | |
| **Defenders:** | **DOB** | **M** | **(s)** | **G** |
| Márton Dárdai | 12.02.2002 | 11 | (6) | 1 |
| Julian Eitschberger | 05.03.2004 | | (1) | |
| Marc Oliver Kempf | 28.01.1995 | 31 | | 1 |
| Jonjoe Kenny (ENG) | 15.03.1997 | 25 | (4) | |
| Pascal Klemens | 23.02.2005 | 1 | | |
| Maximilian Mittelstädt | 18.03.1997 | 7 | (10) | |
| Peter Pekarík (SVK) | 30.10.1986 | 2 | (3) | |
| Marvin Plattenhardt | 26.01.1992 | 29 | (2) | |
| Agustín Maximiliano Rogel Paita (URU) | 17.10.1997 | 14 | (6) | |
| Veit Stange | 08.02.2004 | | (1) | |
| Filip Uremović (CRO) | 11.02.1997 | 21 | (1) | |
| **Midfielders:** | **DOB** | **M** | **(s)** | **G** |
| Kevin-Prince Boateng (GHA) | 06.03.1987 | 5 | (11) | |
| Jean-Paul Boëtius (NED) | 22.03.1994 | 10 | (11) | |

| | DOB | M | (s) | G |
|---|---|---|---|---|
| Tolga Ciğerci (TUR) | 23.03.1992 | 10 | (1) | |
| Vladimír Darida (CZE) | 08.08.1990 | | (3) | |
| Suat Serdar | 11.04.1997 | 24 | (8) | 4 |
| Ivan Šunjić (CRO) | 09.10.1996 | 12 | (6) | |
| Lucas Tousart (FRA) | 29.04.1997 | 33 | | 5 |
| **Forwards:** | **DOB** | **M** | **(s)** | **G** |
| Chidera Ejuke (NGA) | 02.01.1998 | 9 | (11) | |
| Stevan Jovetić (MNE) | 02.11.1989 | 8 | (9) | 4 |
| Wilfried Kanga (FRA) | 21.02.1998 | 15 | (8) | 2 |
| Dodi Lukébakio (BEL) | 24.09.1997 | 27 | (5) | 11 |
| Myziane Maolida (FRA) | 14.02.1999 | 1 | (2) | |
| Ibrahim Maza | 24.11.2005 | | (2) | 1 |
| Jessic Ngankam | 20.07.2000 | 8 | (10) | 4 |
| Florian Niederlechner | 24.10.1990 | 11 | (5) | 1 |
| Marco Richter | 24.11.1997 | 21 | (8) | 6 |
| Tony Rölke | 22.01.2003 | | (1) | |
| Derry Scherhant | 10.11.2002 | 2 | (8) | 1 |
| Davie Selke | 20.01.1995 | 3 | (10) | 1 |

## Turn- und Sportgemeinschaft 1899 Hoffenheim

| Founded: | 01.07.1899 | |
|---|---|---|
| Stadium: | PreZero Arena, Sinsheim (30,150) | |
| Trainer: | André Breitenreiter | 02.10.1973 |
| [08.02.2023] | Pellegrino Matarazzo (USA) | 28.11.1977 |

| Goalkeepers: | DOB | M | (s) | G |
|---|---|---|---|---|
| Oliver Baumann | 02.06.1990 | 34 | | |
| **Defenders:** | **DOB** | **M** | **(s)** | **G** |
| Kevin Akpoguma (NGA) | 19.04.1995 | 21 | (7) | |
| José Ángel Esmorís Tasende „Angeliño" (ESP) | 04.01.1997 | 30 | (3) | |
| Ermin Bičakčić (BIH) | 24.01.1990 | | (9) | |
| John Anthony Brooks (USA) | 28.01.1993 | 15 | | |
| Eduardo Filipe Quaresma Vieira Coimbra Simões (POR) | 02.03.2002 | 1 | (3) | |
| Ozan Kabak (TUR) | 25.03.2000 | 28 | (2) | 2 |
| Pavel Kadeřábek (CZE) | 25.04.1992 | 17 | (9) | 1 |
| Stanley N'Soki (FRA) | 09.04.1999 | 14 | (5) | 1 |
| Stefan Posch (AUT) | 14.05.1997 | 1 | | |
| Joshua Quarshie | 26.07.2004 | | (1) | |
| Kevin Vogt | 23.09.1991 | 22 | | |
| **Midfielders:** | **DOB** | **M** | **(s)** | **G** |
| Christoph Baumgartner (AUT) | 01.08.1999 | 33 | | 7 |
| Finn Becker | 08.06.2000 | 6 | (7) | |
| Tom Bischof | 28.06.2005 | 3 | (8) | |

| | DOB | M | (s) | G |
|---|---|---|---|---|
| Muhammed Damar | 09.04.2004 | 1 | (5) | |
| Thomas Joseph Delaney (DEN) | 03.09.1991 | 4 | (2) | |
| Dennis Geiger | 10.06.1998 | 27 | | 1 |
| Grischa Prömel | 09.01.1995 | 17 | (1) | 1 |
| Sebastian Rudy | 28.02.1990 | 6 | (16) | |
| Diadié Samassékou (MLI) | 11.01.1996 | 1 | (1) | |
| Robert Faxe Skov (DEN) | 20.05.1996 | 16 | (7) | 3 |
| Angelo Stiller | 04.04.2001 | 6 | (14) | 1 |
| Umut Tohumcu | 11.08.2004 | 2 | (6) | |
| **Forwards:** | **DOB** | **M** | **(s)** | **G** |
| Fisnik Asllani | 08.08.2002 | | (8) | |
| Ihlas Bebou (TOG) | 23.04.1994 | 17 | (2) | 7 |
| Jacob Bruun Larsen (DEN) | 19.09.1998 | 3 | (9) | 1 |
| Munas Dabbur (ISR) | 14.05.1992 | 8 | (13) | 6 |
| Kasper Dolberg Rasmussen (DEN) | 06.10.1997 | 4 | (9) | 1 |
| Andrej Kramarić (CRO) | 19.06.1991 | 26 | (6) | 12 |
| Georginio Rutter (FRA) | 20.04.2002 | 11 | (4) | 2 |

## 1. Fußball-Club Köln 01/07

| Founded: | 13.02.1948 | |
|---|---|---|
| Stadium: | RheinEnergieStadion, Köln (49,698) | |
| Trainer: | Steffen Baumgart | 05.01.1972 |

| Goalkeepers: | DOB | M | (s) | G |
|---|---|---|---|---|
| Marvin Schwäbe | 25.04.1995 | 34 | | |
| **Defenders:** | **DOB** | **M** | **(s)** | **G** |
| Julian Chabot | 12.02.1998 | 21 | | |
| Kingsley Ehizibue (NGA) | 25.05.1995 | 1 | | |
| Jonas Armin Hector | 27.05.1990 | 32 | | |
| Timo Hübers | 20.07.1996 | 28 | (1) | 3 |
| Luca Kilian | 01.09.1999 | 13 | (3) | 1 |
| Kristian Pedersen (DEN) | 04.08.1994 | 3 | (3) | |
| Kingsley Schindler | 12.07.1993 | 8 | (21) | |
| Benno Schmitz | 17.11.1994 | 30 | (1) | 1 |
| Nikola Soldo (CRO) | 25.01.2001 | 6 | (1) | |
| **Midfielders:** | **DOB** | **M** | **(s)** | **G** |
| Ondrej Duda (SVK) | 05.12.1994 | 9 | (4) | |
| Denis Huseinbašić | 03.07.2001 | 7 | (17) | 4 |
| Dejan Ljubicic (AUT) | 08.10.1997 | 20 | (7) | 5 |

| | DOB | M | (s) | G |
|---|---|---|---|---|
| Eric Martel | 29.04.2002 | 23 | (6) | 1 |
| Mathias Olesen (LUX) | 21.03.2001 | 6 | (8) | |
| Ellyes Skhiri (TUN) | 10.05.1995 | 32 | | 7 |
| **Forwards:** | **DOB** | **M** | **(s)** | **G** |
| Sargis Adamyan (ARM) | 23.05.1993 | 4 | (20) | 1 |
| Justin Diehl | 27.11.2004 | | (2) | |
| Florian Dietz | 03.08.1998 | 4 | (7) | 1 |
| Florian Kainz (AUT) | 24.10.1992 | 31 | (1) | 6 |
| Tim Lemperle | 05.02.2002 | | (12) | |
| Dimitris Limnios (GRE) | 27.05.1998 | | (2) | |
| Linton Maina | 23.06.1999 | 27 | (6) | 3 |
| Davie Selke | 20.01.1995 | 12 | (5) | 5 |
| Jan Thielmann | 26.05.2002 | 6 | (17) | 2 |
| Steffen Tigges | 31.07.1998 | 17 | (13) | 6 |
| Mark Uth | 24.08.1991 | | (3) | |

## RasenBallsport Leipzig

| Founded: | 19.05.2009 | |
|---|---|---|
| Stadium: | Red Bull Arena, Leipzig (47,069) | |
| Trainer: | Domenico Tedesco (ITA) | 12.09.1985 |
| [08.09.2022] | Marco Rose | 11.09.1976 |

| Goalkeepers: | DOB | M | (s) | G |
|---|---|---|---|---|
| Janis Blaswich | 02.05.1991 | 26 | | |
| Péter Gulácsi (HUN) | 06.05.1990 | 6 | | |
| Ørjan Nyland (NOR) | 10.09.1990 | 2 | | |
| **Defenders:** | **DOB** | **M** | **(s)** | **G** |
| Sanoussy Ba | 05.01.2004 | | (1) | |
| Abdou Diallo (SEN) | 04.05.1996 | 5 | (3) | 1 |
| Joško Gvardiol (CRO) | 23.01.2002 | 24 | (6) | 1 |
| Marcel Halstenberg | 27.09.1991 | 17 | (14) | 1 |
| Benjamin Paa Kwesi Henrichs | 23.02.1997 | 23 | (7) | 2 |
| Lukas Manuel Klostermann | 03.06.1996 | 10 | (5) | |
| Vilmos Tamás „Willi" Orbán (HUN) | 03.11.1992 | 33 | | 4 |
| David Raum | 22.04.1998 | 19 | (9) | |
| Mohamed Simakan (FRA) | 03.05.2000 | 18 | (6) | 1 |

| Midfielders: | DOB | M | (s) | G |
|---|---|---|---|---|
| Daniel Olmo Carvajal „Dani Olmo" (ESP) | 07.05.1998 | 15 | (8) | 2 |
| Emil Forsberg (SWE) | 23.10.1991 | 16 | (14) | 6 |
| Amadou Haïdara (MLI) | 31.01.1998 | 15 | (16) | 2 |
| Kevin Kampl (SVN) | 09.10.1990 | 16 | (14) | 2 |
| Konrad Laimer (AUT) | 27.05.1997 | 17 | (4) | 3 |
| Xaver Schlager (AUT) | 28.09.1997 | 16 | (6) | 1 |
| Dominik Szoboszlai (HUN) | 25.10.2000 | 28 | (3) | 6 |
| **Forwards:** | **DOB** | **M** | **(s)** | **G** |
| André Miguel Valente da Silva (POR) | 06.11.1995 | 20 | (11) | 4 |
| Hugo Novoa Ramos (ESP) | 24.01.2003 | 2 | (5) | 1 |
| Christopher Alan Nkunku (FRA) | 14.11.1997 | 20 | (5) | 16 |
| Yussuf Yurary Poulsen (DEN) | 15.06.1994 | 3 | (16) | 2 |
| Alexander Sørloth (NOR) | 05.12.1995 | | (1) | |
| Timo Werner | 06.03.1996 | 23 | (4) | 9 |

## 1. Fußball- und Sportverein Mainz 05

| Founded: | 16.03.1905 | |
|---|---|---|
| Stadium: | Mewa Arena, Mainz (34,000) | |
| Trainer: | Bo Svensson (DEN) | 04.08.1979 |

| Goalkeepers: | DOB | M | (s) | G |
|---|---|---|---|---|
| Finn Dahmen | 27.03.1998 | 8 | | |
| Robin Zentner | 28.10.1994 | 26 | | |
| **Defenders:** | **DOB** | **M** | **(s)** | **G** |
| Aarón Martín Caricol (ESP) | 22.04.1997 | 20 | (8) | 5 |
| Stefan Bell | 24.08.1991 | 26 | (4) | |
| Anthony Caci (FRA) | 01.07.1997 | 23 | (8) | 2 |
| Danny da Costa | 13.07.1993 | 14 | (9) | |
| Alexander Hack | 08.09.1993 | 14 | (5) | |
| Andreas Hanche-Olsen (NOR) | 17.01.1997 | 17 | | 1 |
| Maxim Leitsch | 18.05.1998 | 7 | (2) | |
| Silvan Widmer (SUI) | 05.03.1993 | 19 | (7) | 2 |
| **Midfielders:** | **DOB** | **M** | **(s)** | **G** |
| Aymane Barkok (MAR) | 21.05.1998 | 3 | (20) | |
| Leandro Barreiro (LUX) | 03.01.2000 | 25 | (6) | 4 |
| Edimilson Fernandes Ribeiro (SUI) | 15.04.1996 | 28 | (4) | |

| | DOB | M | (s) | G |
|---|---|---|---|---|
| Angelo Fulgini (FRA) | 20.08.1996 | 5 | (11) | |
| Dominik Kohr | 31.01.1994 | 27 | (3) | 3 |
| Lee Jae-sung (KOR) | 10.08.1992 | 24 | (10) | 7 |
| Eniss Shabani | 29.05.2003 | | (1) | |
| Anton Stach | 15.11.1998 | 22 | (8) | 1 |
| Niklas Tauer | 17.02.2001 | | (3) | |
| **Forwards:** | **DOB** | **M** | **(s)** | **G** |
| Ludovic Ajorque (FRA) | 25.02.1994 | 15 | (2) | 6 |
| Delano Burgzorg (NED) | 07.11.1998 | | (13) | |
| Jonathan Burkardt | 11.07.2000 | 7 | (4) | 1 |
| Brajan Gruda | 31.05.2004 | | (2) | |
| Marcus Ingvartsen (DEN) | 04.01.1996 | 16 | (12) | 10 |
| Marlon Mustapha (AUT) | 24.05.2001 | | (6) | |
| Karim Onisiwo (AUT) | 17.03.1992 | 28 | (3) | 10 |
| Nelson Weiper | 17.03.2005 | | (9) | 2 |

## Fußballclub Gelsenkirchen-Schalke 04

| | | |
|---|---|---|
| Founded: | 04.05.1904 | |
| Stadium: | Veltins-Arena, Gelsenkirchen (62,271) | |
| Trainer: | Frank Kramer | 03.05.1972 |
| [20.10.2022] | Matthias Kreutzer | 23.12.1982 |
| [27.10.2022] | Thomas Reis | 04.10.1973 |

| Goalkeepers: | DOB | M | (s) | G |
|---|---|---|---|---|
| Ralf Fährmann | 27.09.1988 | 12 | | |
| Alexander Schwolow | 02.06.1992 | 22 | (1) | |
| **Defenders:** | **DOB** | **M** | **(s)** | **G** |
| Mehmet-Can Aydın | 09.02.2002 | 3 | (13) | |
| Cédric Brunner (SUI) | 17.02.1994 | 28 | | |
| Kerim Çalhanoğlu | 26.08.2002 | | (3) | |
| Leo Greiml (AUT) | 03.07.2001 | 3 | (4) | |
| Moritz Jenz | 30.04.1999 | 11 | | |
| Marcin Kamiński (POL) | 15.01.1992 | 7 | (1) | 2 |
| Timothée Kolodziejczak (FRA) | 01.10.1991 | | (1) | |
| Henning Matriciani | 14.03.2000 | 22 | | |
| Thomas Ouwejan (NED) | 30.09.1996 | 10 | (7) | |
| Malick Laye Thiaw | 08.08.2001 | 3 | | |
| Jere Juhani Uronen (FIN) | 13.07.1994 | 9 | (2) | |
| Sepp van den Berg (NED) | 20.12.2001 | 8 | (1) | 1 |
| Maya Yoshida (JPN) | 24.08.1988 | 28 | (1) | |
| **Midfielders:** | **DOB** | **M** | **(s)** | **G** |
| Éder Fabián Álvarez Balanta (COL) | 28.02.1993 | 3 | (3) | |
| Dominick Drexler | 26.05.1990 | 16 | (11) | 4 |

| | DOB | M | (s) | G |
|---|---|---|---|---|
| Florian Flick | 01.05.2000 | 5 | (3) | |
| Andreas Ionuţ Ivan (ROU) | 10.01.1995 | | (1) | |
| Soichiro Kozuki (JPN) | 22.12.2000 | 5 | | 1 |
| Alex Král (CZE) | 19.05.1998 | 26 | (3) | |
| Tom Krauß | 22.06.2001 | 31 | (1) | 2 |
| Danny Latza | 07.12.1989 | 8 | (12) | |
| Tobias Mohr | 24.08.1995 | 8 | (10) | |
| Florent Mollet (FRA) | 19.11.1991 | 4 | (5) | 1 |
| Rodrigo Zalazar Martínez (URU) | 12.08.1999 | 15 | (7) | 1 |
| **Forwards:** | **DOB** | **M** | **(s)** | **G** |
| Marius Bülter | 29.03.1993 | 30 | (3) | 11 |
| Michael Frey (SUI) | 19.07.1994 | 10 | (5) | |
| Kenan Karaman (TUR) | 05.03.1994 | 10 | (11) | 1 |
| Carl Henrik Jordan Larsson (SWE) | 20.06.1997 | 5 | (6) | |
| Sebastian Polter | 01.04.1991 | 5 | (14) | 2 |
| Sidi Sané | 21.04.2003 | | (1) | |
| Tim Skarke | 07.09.1996 | 6 | (3) | 1 |
| Simon Terodde | 02.03.1988 | 21 | (11) | 5 |
| Keke Topp | 25.03.2004 | | (1) | |

## Verein für Bewegungsspiele Stuttgart 1893

| | | |
|---|---|---|
| Founded: | 09.09.1893 | |
| Stadium: | Mercedes-Benz Arena, Stuttgart (60,449) | |
| Trainer: | Pellegrino Matarazzo (USA) | 28.11.1977 |
| [11.10.2022] | Michael Wimmer | 18.06.1980 |
| [05.12.2022] | Bruno Labbadia | 08.02.1966 |
| [03.04.2023] | Sebastian Hoeneß | 12.05.1982 |

| Goalkeepers: | DOB | M | (s) | G |
|---|---|---|---|---|
| Fabian Bredlow | 02.03.1995 | 15 | | |
| Florian Müller | 13.11.1997 | 19 | | |
| **Defenders:** | **DOB** | **M** | **(s)** | **G** |
| Waldemar Anton | 20.07.1996 | 34 | | 1 |
| Hiroki Ito (JPN) | 12.05.1999 | 29 | (1) | 1 |
| Konstantinos Mavropanos (GRE) | 11.12.1997 | 26 | (2) | 2 |
| Borna Sosa (CRO) | 21.01.1998 | 22 | (3) | 2 |
| Pascal Stenzel | 20.03.1996 | 3 | (9) | |
| Josha Vagnoman | 11.12.2000 | 16 | (7) | 2 |
| Dan-Axel Zagadou (FRA) | 03.06.1999 | 14 | (3) | |
| **Midfielders:** | **DOB** | **M** | **(s)** | **G** |
| Naouirou Ahamada (FRA) | 29.03.2002 | 17 | | 2 |
| Darko Churlinov (MKD) | 11.07.2000 | | (1) | |
| Lilian Egloff | 20.08.2002 | 2 | (8) | |
| Wataru Endo (JPN) | 09.02.1993 | 33 | | 5 |
| Genki Haraguchi (JPN) | 09.05.1991 | 9 | (2) | |

| | DOB | M | (s) | G |
|---|---|---|---|---|
| Atakan Karazor | 13.10.1996 | 22 | (7) | |
| Enzo Millot (FRA) | 17.07.2002 | 9 | (14) | |
| Clinton Mola (ENG) | 15.03.2001 | | (1) | |
| Nikolas Nartey (DEN) | 22.02.2000 | 5 | (4) | |
| Laurin Ulrich | 31.01.2005 | | (1) | |
| **Forwards:** | **DOB** | **M** | **(s)** | **G** |
| Tanguy Coulibaly (FRA) | 18.02.2001 | | (14) | 4 |
| Chris Führich | 09.01.1998 | 21 | (12) | 5 |
| *Gil* Bastião *Dias* (POR) | 28.09.1996 | 6 | (1) | 1 |
| Serhou Yadaly Guirassy (FRA) | 12.03.1996 | 20 | (2) | 11 |
| Saša Kalajdžić (AUT) | 07.07.1997 | 3 | | |
| Thomas Kastanaras | 09.01.2003 | 1 | (3) | |
| Silas Katompa Mvumpa (COD) | 06.10.1998 | 23 | (7) | 5 |
| Alou Kuol (AUS) | 05.07.2001 | | (1) | |
| Juan José Perea Mendoza (COL) | 23.02.2000 | 3 | (13) | 1 |
| Luca Pfeiffer | 20.08.1996 | 6 | (13) | |
| *Tiago* Barreiros de Melo *Tomás* (POR) | 16.06.2002 | 16 | (11) | 3 |

## 1. Fußballclub Union Berlin

| | | |
|---|---|---|
| Founded: | 20.01.1966 | |
| Stadium: | Stadion An der Alten Försterei, Berlin (22,012) | |
| Trainer: | Urs Fischer (SUI) | 20.02.1966 |

| Goalkeepers: | DOB | M | (s) | G |
|---|---|---|---|---|
| Lennart Grill | 25.01.1999 | 5 | | |
| Frederik Riis Rønnow (DEN) | 04.08.1992 | 29 | | |
| **Defenders:** | **DOB** | **M** | **(s)** | **G** |
| Timo Baumgartl | 04.03.1996 | 6 | (2) | |
| *Diogo* Filipe Monteiro Pinto *Leite* (POR) | 23.01.1999 | 26 | (2) | |
| Danilho Raimundo Doekhi (NED) | 30.06.1998 | 25 | | 5 |
| Niko Gießelmann | 26.09.1991 | 14 | (12) | |
| Paul Jaeckel | 22.07.1998 | 13 | (3) | 1 |
| Josip Juranović (CRO) | 16.08.1995 | 10 | (2) | 2 |
| Robin Knoche | 22.05.1992 | 32 | | 2 |
| Tymoteusz Puchacz (POL) | 23.01.1999 | 1 | | |
| Jérôme Roussillon (FRA) | 06.01.1993 | 11 | (5) | |
| Julian Ryerson (NOR) | 17.11.1997 | 12 | (1) | |
| Christopher Trimmel (AUT) | 24.02.1987 | 20 | (5) | |

| Midfielders: | DOB | M | (s) | G |
|---|---|---|---|---|
| Janik Haberer | 02.04.1994 | 30 | (2) | 5 |
| Genki Haraguchi (JPN) | 09.05.1991 | 6 | (5) | |
| Rani Khedira | 27.01.1994 | 33 | | 2 |
| Aïssa Laïdouni (TUN) | 13.12.1996 | 11 | (3) | 2 |
| Levin Öztunali | 15.03.1996 | | (2) | |
| Miloš Pantović (SRB) | 07.07.1996 | | (13) | 1 |
| András Schäfer (HUN) | 13.04.1999 | 10 | (6) | |
| Paul Seguin | 29.03.1995 | 4 | (16) | 1 |
| Morten Thorsby (NOR) | 05.05.1996 | 8 | (16) | 1 |
| **Forwards:** | **DOB** | **M** | **(s)** | **G** |
| Sheraldo Becker (SUR) | 09.02.1995 | 33 | (1) | 11 |
| Kevin Behrens | 03.02.1991 | 17 | (16) | 8 |
| Jamie Leweling | 26.02.2001 | | (16) | 1 |
| Sven Michel | 15.07.1990 | 2 | (19) | 3 |
| Theoson-Jordan Siebatcheu Pefok (USA) | 26.04.1996 | 16 | (15) | 4 |
| Tim Skarke | 07.09.1996 | | (3) | |

## Sportverein Werder Bremen von 1899

| Founded: | 04.02.1899 |
| Stadium: | Wohninvest Weserstadion, Bremen (42,100) |
| Trainer: | Ole Werner | 04.05.1988 |

| Goalkeepers: | DOB | M | (s) | G |
|---|---|---|---|---|
| Jiří Pavlenka (CZE) | 14.04.1992 | 33 | | |
| Michael Zetterer | 12.07.1995 | 1 | (1) | |
| **Defenders:** | **DOB** | **M** | **(s)** | **G** |
| Felix Agu | 27.09.1999 | | (3) | |
| Lee David Buchanan (ENG) | 07.03.2001 | 2 | (19) | 1 |
| Fabio Chiarodia (ITA) | 05.06.2005 | 1 | (2) | |
| Marco Friedl (AUT) | 16.03.1998 | 30 | | |
| Anthony Jung | 03.11.1991 | 32 | (2) | 2 |
| Amos Pieper | 17.01.1998 | 22 | (7) | 2 |
| Niklas Stark | 14.04.1995 | 23 | (4) | |
| Miloš Veljković (SRB) | 26.09.1995 | 25 | (4) | 1 |
| Mitchell-Elijah Weiser | 21.04.1994 | 29 | (1) | 2 |
| **Midfielders:** | **DOB** | **M** | **(s)** | **G** |
| Leonardo Jesus Loureiro Bittencourt | 19.12.1993 | 22 | (3) | 3 |

| | DOB | M | (s) | G |
|---|---|---|---|---|
| Christian Groß | 08.02.1989 | 23 | (3) | 1 |
| Ilia Gruev (BUL) | 06.05.2000 | 18 | (13) | |
| Jean-Manuel Mbom | 24.02.2000 | | (2) | |
| Nicolai Rapp | 13.12.1996 | | (7) | |
| Dikeni Salifou (TOG) | 08.06.2003 | | (1) | |
| Romano Christian Schmid (AUT) | 27.01.2000 | 15 | (12) | 1 |
| Niklas Schmidt | 01.03.1998 | 11 | (13) | 3 |
| Jens Dalsgaard Stage (DEN) | 08.11.1996 | 21 | (11) | 3 |
| **Forwards:** | **DOB** | **M** | **(s)** | **G** |
| Oliver Jasen Burke (SCO) | 07.04.1997 | 1 | (14) | 2 |
| Eren Dinkçi | 13.12.2001 | | (17) | |
| Marvin Ducksch | 07.03.1994 | 34 | | 12 |
| Niclas Füllkrug | 09.02.1993 | 28 | | 16 |
| Maximilian Philipp | 01.03.1994 | 3 | (12) | 1 |

## Verein für Leibesübungen Wolfsburg

| Founded: | 12.09.1945 |
| Stadium: | Volkswagen Arena, Wolfsburg (30,000) |
| Trainer: | Niko Kovač (CRO) | 15.10.1971 |

| Goalkeepers: | DOB | M | (s) | G |
|---|---|---|---|---|
| Koen Casteels (BEL) | 25.06.1992 | 34 | | |
| **Defenders:** | **DOB** | **M** | **(s)** | **G** |
| Bote Ridle Nzuzi Baku | 08.04.1998 | 29 | (4) | 5 |
| Sebastiaan Bornauw (BEL) | 22.03.1999 | 23 | (3) | 1 |
| Nicolas Cozza (FRA) | 08.01.1999 | | (5) | |
| Kilian Fischer | 12.10.2000 | 5 | (5) | |
| Maxence Lacroix (FRA) | 06.04.2000 | 18 | (6) | 1 |
| *Paulo Otávio* Rosa da Silva (BRA) | 23.11.1994 | 25 | | |
| Jérôme Roussillon (FRA) | 06.01.1993 | | (4) | |
| Micky van de Ven (NED) | 19.04.2001 | 33 | | 1 |
| **Midfielders:** | **DOB** | **M** | **(s)** | **G** |
| Lukáš Ambros (CZE) | 05.06.2004 | | (1) | |
| Maximilian Arnold | 27.05.1994 | 32 | | 5 |
| Bartol Franjić (CRO) | 14.01.2000 | 3 | (2) | |
| Yannick Gerhardt | 13.03.1994 | 22 | (7) | 6 |

| | DOB | M | (s) | G |
|---|---|---|---|---|
| Josuha Guilavogui (FRA) | 19.09.1990 | 11 | (12) | 1 |
| Max Kruse | 19.03.1988 | 2 | (3) | |
| Felix Kalu Nmecha | 10.10.2000 | 19 | (11) | 3 |
| Kevin Alexander Paredes (USA) | 07.05.2003 | 1 | (21) | 1 |
| Maximilian Philipp | 01.03.1994 | 1 | (2) | |
| Mattias Svanberg (SWE) | 05.01.1999 | 21 | (11) | 4 |
| Aster Vranckx (BEL) | 04.10.2002 | | (1) | |
| **Forwards:** | **DOB** | **M** | **(s)** | **G** |
| Josip Brekalo (CRO) | 23.06.1998 | 3 | (3) | |
| Jakub Kamiński (POL) | 05.06.2002 | 25 | (6) | 4 |
| Omar Marmoush (EGY) | 07.02.1999 | 15 | (18) | 5 |
| Lukas Okechukwu Nmecha | 14.12.1998 | 10 | (6) | 4 |
| Dženan Pejčinović | 15.02.2005 | | (1) | |
| Luca Waldschmidt | 19.05.1996 | 4 | (14) | 4 |
| Patrick Wimmer (AUT) | 30.05.2001 | 23 | (3) | 4 |
| Jonas Older Wind (DEN) | 07.02.1999 | 15 | (9) | 6 |

## SECOND LEVEL
### 2. Bundesliga 2022/2023

| | | | | | | | | | |
|---|---|---|---|---|---|---|---|---|---|
| 1. | 1. FC Heidenheim 1846 (*Promoted*) | 34 | 19 | 10 | 5 | 67 | - | 36 | 67 |
| 2. | SV Darmstadt 98 (*Promoted*) | 34 | 20 | 7 | 7 | 50 | - | 33 | 67 |
| 3. | Hamburger SV (*Promotion Play-offs*) | 34 | 20 | 6 | 8 | 70 | - | 45 | 66 |
| 4. | TSV Fortuna Düsseldorf | 34 | 17 | 7 | 10 | 60 | - | 43 | 58 |
| 5. | FC St. Pauli Hamburg | 34 | 16 | 10 | 8 | 55 | - | 39 | 58 |
| 6. | SC Paderborn 07 | 34 | 16 | 7 | 11 | 68 | - | 44 | 55 |
| 7. | Karlsruher SC | 34 | 13 | 7 | 14 | 56 | - | 53 | 46 |
| 8. | SV Holstein Kiel | 34 | 12 | 10 | 12 | 58 | - | 61 | 46 |
| 9. | 1.FC Kaiserslautern | 34 | 11 | 12 | 11 | 47 | - | 48 | 45 |
| 10. | SV Hannover 96 | 34 | 12 | 8 | 14 | 50 | - | 55 | 44 |
| 11. | 1.FC Magdeburg | 34 | 12 | 7 | 15 | 48 | - | 55 | 43 |
| 12. | SpVgg Greuther Fürth | 34 | 10 | 11 | 13 | 47 | - | 50 | 41 |
| 13. | FC Hansa Rostock | 34 | 12 | 5 | 17 | 32 | - | 48 | 41 |
| 14. | 1. FC Nürnberg | 34 | 10 | 9 | 15 | 32 | - | 49 | 39 |
| 15. | TSV Eintracht Braunschweig | 34 | 9 | 9 | 16 | 42 | - | 59 | 36 |
| 16. | DSC Arminia Bielefeld (*Relegation Play-offs*) | 34 | 9 | 7 | 18 | 50 | - | 62 | 34 |
| 17. | SSV Jahn Regensburg (*Relegated*) | 34 | 8 | 7 | 19 | 34 | - | 58 | 31 |
| 18. | SV Sandhausen (*Relegated*) | 34 | 7 | 7 | 20 | 35 | - | 63 | 28 |

### Relegation Play-offs [02-06.06.2023]

SV Wehen Wiesbaden - DSC Arminia Bielefeld                4-0(1-0)          2-1(2-1)

SV Wehen Wiesbaden promoted for the second level for 2023/2024.

### INTERNATIONAL MATCHES
(16.07.2022 – 15.07.2023)

| Date | City | Match | Score | Type |
|---|---|---|---|---|
| 23.09.2022 | Leipzig | *Germany - Hungary* | *0-1(0-1)* | (UNL) |
| 26.09.2022 | London | *England - Germany* | *3-3(0-0)* | (UNL) |
| 16.11.2022 | Muscat | *Oman - Germany* | *0-1(0-0)* | (F) |
| 23.11.2022 | Al Rayyan | *Germany - Japan* | *1-2(1-0)* | (WC) |
| 27.11.2022 | Al Khor | *Spain - Germany* | *1-1(0-0)* | (WC) |
| 01.12.2022 | Al Khor | *Costa Rica - Germany* | *2-4(0-1)* | (WC) |
| 25.03.2023 | Mainz | *Germany - Peru* | *2-0(2-0)* | (F) |
| 28.03.2023 | Köln | *Germany - Belgium* | *2-3(1-2)* | (F) |
| 12.06.2023 | Bremen | *Germany - Ukraine* | *3-3(1-2)* | (F) |
| 16.06.2023 | Warszawa | *Poland - Germany* | *1-0(1-0)* | (F) |
| 20.06.2023 | Gelsenkirchen | *Germany - Colombia* | *0-2(0-0)* | (F) |

**23.09.2022  GERMANY - HUNGARY    0-1(0-1)    3rd UEFA Nations League A, Group 3**
Red Bull Arena, Leipzig; Referee: Slavko Vinčić (Slovenia); Attendance: 39,513
**GER:** Marc-André ter Stegen, Niklas Süle, Antonio Rüdiger, David Raum, Jonas Hofmann, İlkay Gündoğan (69.Jamal Musiala), Joshua Walter Kimmich, Thomas Müller (Cap) (85.Lukas Nmecha), Leroy Aziz Sané, Serge David Gnabry (46.Jan Thilo Kehrer), Timo Werner (70.Kai Lukas Havertz). Trainer: Hans-Dieter Flick.

**26.09.2022  ENGLAND - GERMANY    3-3(0-0)    3rd UEFA Nations League A, Group 3**
Wembley Stadium, London; Referee: Danny Desmond Makkelie (Netherlands); Attendance: 78,949
**GER:** Marc-André ter Stegen, Jan Thilo Kehrer, Niklas Süle, Nico Cedric Schlotterbeck, David Raum (68.Robin Everardus Gosens), Jonas Hofmann (46.Timo Werner), İlkay Gündoğan, Joshua Walter Kimmich (Cap), Leroy Aziz Sané (68.Serge David Gnabry), Kai Lukas Havertz (90+1.Armel Bella-Kotchap), Jamal Musiala (79.Thomas Müller). Trainer: Hans-Dieter Flick.
**Goals:** İlkay Gündoğan (52 penalty), Kai Lukas Havertz (67, 87).

**16.11.2022  OMAN - GERMANY    0-1(0-0)    Friendly International**
"Sultan Qaboos" Sports Complex, Muscat; Referee: Mohammed Khaled Al Hoaish (Saudi Arabia); Attendance: 25,654
**GER:** Manuel Peter Neuer (Cap), Jan Thilo Kehrer, Matthias Lukas Ginter (46.Nico Cedric Schlotterbeck), Lukas Manuel Klostermann (34.Armel Bella-Kotchap), David Raum (46.Christian Günter), Jonas Hofmann, İlkay Gündoğan (65.Julian Brandt), Leon Christoph Goretzka (46.Joshua Walter Kimmich), Leroy Aziz Sané, Kai Lukas Havertz, Youssoufa Moukoko (46.Niclas Füllkrug). Trainer: Hans-Dieter Flick.
**Goal:** Niclas Füllkrug (80).

**23.11.2022  GERMANY - JAPAN    1-2(1-0)    22nd FIFA WC. Group Stage.**
Khalifa International Stadium, Al Rayyan (Qatar); Referee: Iván Arcides Barton Cisneros (El Salvador); Attendance: 42,608
**GER:** Manuel Peter Neuer (Cap), Niklas Süle, Antonio Rüdiger, Nico Cedric Schlotterbeck, David Raum, Joshua Walter Kimmich, İlkay Gündoğan (67.Leon Christoph Goretzka), Serge David Gnabry (90.Youssoufa Moukoko), Thomas Müller (67.Jonas Hofmann), Jamal Musiala (79.Mario Götze), Kai Lukas Havertz (79.Niclas Füllkrug). Trainer: Hans-Dieter Flick.
**Goal:** İlkay Gündoğan (33 penalty).

**27.11.2022  SPAIN - GERMANY    1-1(0-0)    22nd FIFA WC. Group Stage.**
Al Bayt Stadium, Al Khor (Qatar); Referee: Danny Desmond Makkelie (Netherlands); Attendance: 68,895
**GER:** Manuel Peter Neuer (Cap), Jan Thilo Kehrer (70.Lukas Manuel Klostermann), Niklas Süle, Antonio Rüdiger, David Raum (87.Nico Cedric Schlotterbeck), Joshua Walter Kimmich, Leon Christoph Goretzka, Serge David Gnabry (85.Jonas Hofmann), İlkay Gündoğan (70.Leroy Aziz Sané), Jamal Musiala, Thomas Müller (70.Niclas Füllkrug). Trainer: Hans-Dieter Flick.
**Goal:** Niclas Füllkrug (83).

**01.12.2022  COSTA RICA - GERMANY    2-4(0-1)    22nd FIFA WC. Group Stage.**
Al Bayt Stadium, Al Khor (Qatar); Referee: Stéphanie Frappart (France); Attendance: 67,054
**GER:** Manuel Peter Neuer (Cap), Joshua Walter Kimmich, Niklas Süle (90+3.Matthias Lukas Ginter), Antonio Rüdiger, David Raum (66.Mario Götze), Leon Christoph Goretzka (46.Lukas Manuel Klostermann), İlkay Gündoğan (55.Niclas Füllkrug), Leroy Aziz Sané, Jamal Musiala, Serge David Gnabry, Thomas Müller (66.Kai Lukas Havertz). Trainer: Hans-Dieter Flick.
**Goals:** Serge David Gnabry (10), Kai Lukas Havertz (73, 85), Niclas Füllkrug (89).

**25.03.2023  GERMANY - PERU    2-0(2-0)    Friendly International**
Mewa Arena, Mainz; Referee: Maria Sole Ferrieri Caputi (Italy); Attendance: 25,384
**GER:** Marc-André ter Stegen, Marius Wolf, Matthias Lukas Ginter, Nico Cedric Schlotterbeck (86.Jan Thilo Kehrer), David Raum, Emre Can (46.Leon Christoph Goretzka), Joshua Walter Kimmich (Cap), Kai Lukas Havertz (75.Kevin Schade), Florian Richard Wirtz (46.Mario Götze), Niclas Füllkrug (75.Mërgim Berisha), Timo Werner (46.Serge David Gnabry). Trainer: Hans-Dieter Flick.
**Goals:** Niclas Füllkrug (12, 33).

**28.03.2023  GERMANY - BELGIUM    2-3(1-2)    Friendly International**
RheinEnergieStadion, Köln; Referee: Willy Delajod (France); Attendance: 42,910
**GER:** Marc-André ter Stegen, Marius Wolf (80.Josha Mamadou Karaboue Vagnoman), Jan Thilo Kehrer, Matthias Lukas Ginter, David Raum (68.Christian Günter), Joshua Walter Kimmich (Cap), Leon Christoph Goretzka (32.Felix Kalu Nmecha), Florian Richard Wirtz (32.Emre Can), Serge David Gnabry, Niclas Füllkrug (80.Mërgim Berisha), Timo Werner (80.Kevin Schade). Trainer: Hans-Dieter Flick.
**Goals:** Niclas Füllkrug (44 penalty), Serge David Gnabry (87).

**12.06.2023  GERMANY - UKRAINE    3-3(1-2)    Friendly International**
Weserstadion, Bremen; Referee: Anastasios Sidiropoulos (Greece); Attendance: 35,795
**GER:** Kevin Christian Trapp, Matthias Lukas Ginter, Nico Cedric Schlotterbeck (46.Lukas Manuel Klostermann), Antonio Rüdiger, David Raum (71.Benjamin Paa Kwesi Henrichs), Marius Wolf (62.Jonas Hofmann), Joshua Walter Kimmich (Cap), Leon Christoph Goretzka (62.Jamal Musiala), Julian Brandt (71.Florian Richard Wirtz), Leroy Aziz Sané, Niclas Füllkrug (46.Kai Lukas Havertz). Trainer: Hans-Dieter Flick.
**Goals:** Niclas Füllkrug (6), Kai Lukas Havertz (83), Joshua Walter Kimmich (90+1 penalty).

**16.06.2023**    **POLAND - GERMANY**                                      **1-0(1-0)**                                    Friendly International
Stadion Narodowy, Warszawa; Referee: Orel Grinfeld (Israel); Attendance: 57,098
**GER:** Marc-André ter Stegen, Jan Thilo Kehrer, Antonio Rüdiger, Malick Laye Thiaw (87.Marius Wolf), Benjamin Paa Kwesi Henrichs (68.Leroy Aziz Sané), Jonas Hofmann (46.Robin Everardus Gosens), Emre Can, Joshua Walter Kimmich (Cap) (80.Leon Christoph Goretzka), Florian Richard Wirtz (80.Julian Brandt), Jamal Musiala (68.Niclas Füllkrug), Kai Lukas Havertz. Trainer: Hans-Dieter Flick.

**20.06.2023**    **GERMANY - COLOMBIA**                                   **0-2(0-0)**                                    Friendly International
Arena AufSchalke, Gelsenkirchen; Referee: Halil Umut Meler (Turkey); Attendance: 50,421
**GER:** Marc-André ter Stegen, Antonio Rüdiger, Malick Laye Thiaw, Robin Everardus Gosens, Marius Wolf (46.Benjamin Paa Kwesi Henrichs), İlkay Gündoğan (Cap) (79.Joshua Walter Kimmich), Emre Can (66.Niclas Füllkrug), Leon Christoph Goretzka, Jamal Musiala, Leroy Aziz Sané, Kai Lukas Havertz (79.Julian Brandt). Trainer: Hans-Dieter Flick.

| NATIONAL TEAM PLAYERS (16.07.2022 – 15.07.2023) | | | | |
|---|---|---|---|---|
| **Name** | **DOB** | **Caps** | **Goals** | **Club** |
| **Goalkeepers** | | | | |
| Manuel Peter NEUER | 27.03.1986 | 117 | 0 | 2022: | FC Bayern München |
| Marc-André TER STEGEN | 30.04.1992 | 34 | 0 | 2022/2023: | FC Barcelona (ESP) |
| Kevin Christian TRAPP | 08.07.1990 | 7 | 0 | 2023: | Eintracht Frankfurt |
| **Defenders** | | | | |
| Armel BELLA-KOTCHAP | 11.12.2001 | 2 | 0 | 2022: | Southampton FC (ENG) |
| Matthias Lukas GINTER | 19.01.1994 | 51 | 2 | 2022/2023: | SC Freiburg |
| Robin Everardus GOSENS | 05.07.1994 | 16 | 2 | 2022/2023: | FC Internazionale Milano (ITA) |
| Christian GÜNTER | 28.02.1993 | 8 | 0 | 2022/2023: | SC Freiburg |
| Benjamin Paa Kwesi HENRICHS | 23.02.1997 | 10 | 0 | 2023: | RasenBallsport Leipzig |
| Jan Thilo KEHRER | 21.09.1996 | 27 | 0 | 2022/2023: | West Ham United FC London (ENG) |
| Lukas Manuel KLOSTERMANN | 03.06.1996 | 22 | 0 | 2022/2023: | RasenBallsport Leipzig |
| David RAUM | 22.04.1998 | 18 | 0 | 2022/2023: | RasenBallsport Leipzig |
| Antonio RÜDIGER | 03.03.1993 | 60 | 2 | 2022/2023: | Real Madrid CF (ESP) |
| Nico Cedric SCHLOTTERBECK | 01.12.1999 | 10 | 0 | 2022/2023: | BV Borussia 09 Dortmund |
| Niklas SÜLE | 03.09.1995 | 45 | 1 | 2022: | BV Borussia 09 Dortmund |
| Malick Laye THIAW | 08.08.2001 | 2 | 0 | 2023: | AC Milan (ITA) |
| Josha Mamadou Karaboue VAGNOMAN | 11.12.2000 | 1 | 0 | 2023: | VfB Stuttgart |
| Marius WOLF | 27.05.1995 | 5 | 0 | 2023: | BV Borussia 09 Dortmund |
| **Midfielders** | | | | |
| Julian BRANDT | 02.05.1996 | 42 | 3 | 2022/2023: | BV Borussia 09 Dortmund |
| Emre CAN | 12.01.1994 | 41 | 1 | 2023: | BV Borussia 09 Dortmund |
| Leon Christoph GORETZKA | 06.02.1995 | 53 | 14 | 2022/2023: | FC Bayern München |
| Mario GÖTZE | 03.06.1992 | 66 | 17 | 2022/2023: | Eintracht Frankfurt |
| İlkay GÜNDOĞAN | 24.10.1990 | 67 | 17 | 2022/2023: | Manchester City FC (ENG) |
| Kai Lukas HAVERTZ | 11.06.1999 | 37 | 13 | 2022/2023: | Chelsea FC London (ENG) |
| Jonas HOFMANN | 14.07.1992 | 21 | 4 | 2022/2023: | Borussia VfL Mönchengladbach |
| Joshua Walter KIMMICH | 08.02.1995 | 79 | 6 | 2022/2023: | FC Bayern München |
| Jamal MUSIALA | 26.02.2003 | 23 | 1 | 2022/2023: | FC Bayern München |
| Thomas MÜLLER | 13.09.1989 | 121 | 44 | 2022: | FC Bayern München |
| Felix Kalu NMECHA | 10.10.2000 | 1 | 0 | 2023: | VfL Wolfsburg |
| Florian Richard WIRTZ | 03.05.2003 | 8 | 0 | 2023: | Bayer 04 Leverkusen |
| **Forwards** | | | | |
| Mërgim BERISHA | 11.05.1998 | 2 | 0 | 2023: | FC Augsburg |
| Niclas FÜLLKRUG | 09.02.1993 | 9 | 7 | 2022/2023: | SV Werder Bremen |
| Serge David GNABRY | 14.07.1995 | 41 | 22 | 2022/2023: | FC Bayern München |
| Youssoufa MOUKOKO | 20.11.2004 | 2 | 0 | 2022: | BV Borussia 09 Dortmund |
| Lukas NMECHA | 14.12.1998 | 7 | 0 | 2022: | VfL Wolfsburg |
| Leroy Aziz SANÉ | 11.01.1996 | 53 | 11 | 2022/2023: | FC Bayern München |
| Kevin SCHADE | 27.11.2001 | 2 | 0 | 2023: | Brentford FC London (ENG) |
| Timo WERNER | 06.03.1996 | 57 | 24 | 2022/2023: | RasenBallsport Leipzig |
| **Trainer** | | | | |
| Hans-Dieter FLICK [from 01.08.2021] | 24.02.1965 | 24 M; 12 W; 7 D; 5 L; 59-26 | | |

# GIBRALTAR

**The Country:**
Gibraltar [*British Overseas Territory*]
Capital: Gibraltar
Surface: 6,8 km²
Inhabitants: 34,003 [2020]
Time: UTC+1

**The FA:**
Gibraltar Football Association
7.01b World Trade Center 11, 1AA Gibraltar
Tel: +350 200 42 941
Foundation date: 1895
Member of FIFA since: 13.05.2016
Member of UEFA since: 24.05.2013
Website: www.gibraltarfa.com

## NATIONAL TEAM RECORDS

| RECORDS | | |
|---|---|---|
| **First international match:** | 19.11.2013, Faro/Loulé (POR): | Gibraltar – Slovakia 0-0 |
| **Most international caps:** | Liam Walker | - 69 caps (since 2013) |
| **Most international goals:** | Liam Walker | - 5 goals / 69 caps (since 2013) |
| | Roy Alan Chipolina | - 5 goals / 68 caps (since 2013) |

| UEFA EUROPEAN CHAMPIONSHIP | |
|---|---|
| 1960 | Not member of UEFA |
| 1964 | Not member of UEFA |
| 1968 | Not member of UEFA |
| 1972 | Not member of UEFA |
| 1976 | Not member of UEFA |
| 1980 | Not member of UEFA |
| 1984 | Not member of UEFA |
| 1988 | Not member of UEFA |
| 1992 | Not member of UEFA |
| 1996 | Not member of UEFA |
| 2000 | Not member of UEFA |
| 2004 | Not member of UEFA |
| 2008 | Not member of UEFA |
| 2012 | Not member of UEFA |
| 2016 | Qualifiers |
| 2020 | Qualifiers |

| FIFA WORLD CUP | |
|---|---|
| 1930 | Not member of FIFA |
| 1934 | Not member of FIFA |
| 1938 | Not member of FIFA |
| 1950 | Not member of FIFA |
| 1954 | Not member of FIFA |
| 1958 | Not member of FIFA |
| 1962 | Not member of FIFA |
| 1966 | Not member of FIFA |
| 1970 | Not member of FIFA |
| 1974 | Not member of FIFA |
| 1978 | Not member of FIFA |
| 1982 | Not member of FIFA |
| 1986 | Not member of FIFA |
| 1990 | Not member of FIFA |
| 1994 | Not member of FIFA |
| 1998 | Not member of FIFA |
| 2002 | Not member of FIFA |
| 2006 | Not member of FIFA |
| 2010 | Not member of FIFA |
| 2014 | Not member of FIFA |
| 2018 | Qualifiers |
| 2022 | Qualifiers |

| OLYMPIC TOURNAMENTS | |
|---|---|
| 1908 | Not member of FIFA |
| 1912 | Not member of FIFA |
| 1920 | Not member of FIFA |
| 1924 | Not member of FIFA |
| 1928 | Not member of FIFA |
| 1936 | Not member of FIFA |
| 1948 | Not member of FIFA |
| 1952 | Not member of FIFA |
| 1956 | Not member of FIFA |
| 1960 | Not member of FIFA |
| 1964 | Not member of FIFA |
| 1968 | Not member of FIFA |
| 1972 | Not member of FIFA |
| 1976 | Not member of FIFA |
| 1980 | Not member of FIFA |
| 1984 | Not member of FIFA |
| 1988 | Not member of FIFA |
| 1992 | Not member of FIFA |
| 1996 | Not member of FIFA |
| 2000 | Not member of FIFA |
| 2004 | Not member of FIFA |
| 2008 | Not member of FIFA |
| 2012 | Not member of FIFA |
| 2016 | Not member of FIFA |
| 2020 | Qualifiers |

| UEFA NATIONS LEAGUE | |
|---|---|
| 2018/2019 | League D (Group Stage) |
| 2020/2021 | League D (Group Stage -> promoted to League C) |
| 2022/2023 | League C (Group Stage -> relegation Play-outs in March 2024) |

## GIBRALTARIAN CLUB HONOURS IN EUROPEAN CLUB COMPETITIONS:

| European Champion Clubs' Cup (1956-1992) / UEFA Champions League (1993-2023) |
|---|
| None |

| Fairs Cup (1858-1971) / UEFA Cup (1972-2009) / UEFA Europa League (2010-2023) |
|---|
| None |

| UEFA Europa Conference League (2021-2023) |
|---|
| None |

| UEFA Super Cup (1972-2022) |
|---|
| None |

| *European Cup Winners' Cup 1961-1999** |
|---|
| None |

*defunct competition

## NATIONAL COMPETITIONS
## TABLE OF HONOURS

| | CHAMPIONS | CUP WINNERS |
|---|---|---|
| 1894/1895 | - | Gibraltar FC |
| 1895/1896 | Gibraltar FC | Not known |
| 1896/1897 | Jubilee FC | Not known |
| 1897/1898 | Jubilee FC | Not known |
| 1898/1899 | Albion FC | Not known |
| 1899/1900 | Exiles FC | Not known |
| 1900/1901 | Prince of Wales FC | Not known |
| 1901/1902 | Exiles FC | Not known |
| 1902/1903 | Prince of Wales FC | Not known |
| 1903/1904 | Prince of Wales FC | Not known |
| 1904/1905 | Athletic FC | Not known |
| 1905/1906 | Prince of Wales FC | Not known |
| 1906/1907 | No competition | Not known |
| 1907/1908 | FC Britannia XI | Not known |
| 1908/1909 | Prince of Wales FC | Not known |
| 1909/1910 | South United FC | Not known |
| 1910/1911 | South United FC | Not known |
| 1911/1912 | FC Britannia XI | Not known |
| 1912/1913 | FC Britannia XI | Not known |
| 1913/1914 | Prince of Wales FC | Not known |
| 1914/1915 | Royal Sovereign | Not known |
| 1915/1916 | No competition | Not known |
| 1916/1917 | Prince of Wales FC | Not known |
| 1917/1918 | FC Britannia XI | Not known |
| 1918/1919 | Prince of Wales FC | Not known |
| 1919/1920 | FC Britannia XI | Not known |
| 1920/1921 | Prince of Wales FC | Not known |
| 1921/1922 | Prince of Wales FC | Not known |
| 1922/1923 | Prince of Wales FC | Not known |
| 1923/1924 | Gibraltar FC | Not known |
| 1924/1925 | Prince of Wales FC | Not known |
| 1925/1926 | Prince of Wales FC | Not known |
| 1926/1927 | Prince of Wales FC | Not known |
| 1927/1928 | Prince of Wales FC | Not known |
| 1928/1929 | Europa FC | Not known |
| 1929/1930 | Europa FC | Not known |
| 1930/1931 | Prince of Wales FC | Not known |
| 1931/1932 | Europa FC | Not known |
| 1932/1933 | Europa FC | Not known |
| 1933/1934 | Commander of the Yard FC | Not known |
| 1934/1935 | Chief Construction FC | Not known |
| 1935/1936 | Chief Constructor FC | HMS Hood |
| 1936/1937 | FC Britannia XI | FC Britannia XI |
| 1937/1938 | Europa FC | Europa FC |
| 1938/1939 | Prince of Wales FC | 2nd Battalion The King's Regiment |
| 1939/1940 | Prince of Wales FC | FC Britannia XI |
| 1940/1941 | FC Britannia XI | No competition |
| 1941/1942 | No competition | A.A.R.A. |
| 1942/1943 | No competition | Royal Air Force New Camp |
| 1943/1944 | No competition | 4th Btallion Royal Scott |
| 1944/1945 | No competition | No competition |
| 1945/1946 | No competition | Europa FC |
| 1946/1947 | Gibraltar United FC | Gibraltar United FC |
| 1947/1948 | Gibraltar United FC | FC Britannia XI |
| 1948/1949 | Gibraltar United FC | Prince of Wales FC |
| 1949/1950 | Gibraltar United FC | Europa FC |
| 1950/1951 | Gibraltar United FC | Europa FC |
| 1951/1952 | Europa FC | Europa FC |
| 1952/1953 | Prince of Wales FC | Not known |
| 1953/1954 | Gibraltar United FC | Not known |
| 1954/1955 | FC Britannia XI | Not known |
| 1955/1956 | FC Britannia XI | Not known |
| 1956/1957 | FC Britannia XI | Not known |
| 1957/1958 | FC Britannia XI | Not known |
| 1958/1959 | FC Britannia XI | Not known |
| 1959/1960 | Gibraltar United FC | Not known |
| 1960/1961 | FC Britannia XI | Not known |
| 1961/1962 | Gibraltar United FC | Not known |
| 1962/1963 | FC Britannia XI | Not known |
| 1963/1964 | Gibraltar United FC | Not known |
| 1964/1965 | Gibraltar United FC | Not known |

| | | |
|---|---|---|
| 1965/1966 | Glacis United FC | *Not known* |
| 1966/1967 | Glacis United FC | *Not known* |
| 1967/1968 | Glacis United FC | *Not known* |
| 1968/1969 | Glacis United FC | *Not known* |
| 1969/1970 | Glacis United FC | *Not known* |
| 1970/1971 | Glacis United FC | *Not known* |
| 1971/1972 | Glacis United FC | *Not known* |
| 1972/1973 | Glacis United FC | *Not known* |
| 1973/1974 | Glacis United FC | Manchester United FC |
| 1974/1975 | Manchester United FC | Glacis United FC |
| 1975/1976 | Glacis United FC | 2nd Battalion Royal Green Jackets |
| 1976/1977 | Manchester United FC | Manchester United FC |
| 1977/1978 | *No competition* | *Not known* |
| 1978/1979 | Manchester United FC | St Joseph's FC |
| 1979/1980 | Manchester United FC | Manchester United FC |
| 1980/1981 | Glacis United FC | Glacis United FC |
| 1981/1982 | Glacis United FC | Glacis United FC |
| 1982/1983 | Glacis United FC | St Joseph's FC |
| 1983/1984 | Manchester United FC | St Joseph's FC |
| 1984/1985 | Glacis United FC & Lincoln Red Imps FC | St Joseph's FC |
| 1985/1986 | Lincoln Red Imps FC | Lincoln Red Imps FC |
| 1986/1987 | St Theresa's FC | St Joseph's FC |
| 1987/1988 | St Theresa's FC | Royal Air Force Gibraltar |
| 1988/1989 | Glacis United FC | Lincoln Red Imps FC |
| 1989/1990 | Lincoln Red Imps FC | Lincoln Red Imps FC |
| 1990/1991 | Lincoln Red Imps FC | *Not known* |
| 1991/1992 | Lincoln Red Imps FC | St Joseph's FC |
| 1992/1993 | Lincoln Red Imps FC | Lincoln Red Imps FC |
| 1993/1994 | Lincoln Red Imps FC | Lincoln Red Imps FC |
| 1994/1995 | Manchester United FC | St Theresa's FC |
| 1995/1996 | St Joseph's FC | St Joseph's FC |
| 1996/1997 | Glacis United FC | Manchester United FC |
| 1997/1998 | St Theresa's FC | Glacis United FC |
| 1998/1999 | Manchester United FC | Gibraltar United FC |
| 1999/2000 | Glacis United FC | Gibraltar United FC |
| 2000/2001 | Lincoln Red Imps FC | Gibraltar United FC |
| 2001/2002 | Gibraltar United FC | Lincoln Red Imps FC |
| 2002/2003 | Lincoln Red Imps FC | Manchester United FC |
| 2003/2004 | Lincoln Red Imps FC | Newcastle FC |
| 2004/2005 | Lincoln Red Imps FC | Newcastle FC |
| 2005/2006 | Lincoln Red Imps FC | Newcastle FC |
| 2006/2007 | Lincoln Red Imps FC | Newcastle FC |
| 2007/2008 | Lincoln Red Imps FC | Lincoln Red Imps FC |
| 2008/2009 | Lincoln Red Imps FC | Lincoln Red Imps FC |
| 2009/2010 | Lincoln Red Imps FC | Lincoln Red Imps FC |
| 2010/2011 | Lincoln Red Imps FC | Lincoln Red Imps FC |
| 2011/2012 | Lincoln Red Imps FC | St Joseph's FC |
| 2012/2013 | Lincoln Red Imps FC | St Joseph's FC |
| 2013/2014 | Lincoln Red Imps FC | Lincoln Red Imps FC |
| 2014/2015 | Lincoln Red Imps FC | Lincoln Red Imps FC |
| 2015/2016 | Lincoln Red Imps FC | Lincoln Red Imps FC |
| 2016/2017 | Europa FC | Europa FC |
| 2017/2018 | Lincoln Red Imps FC | Europa FC |
| 2018/2019 | Lincoln Red Imps FC | Europa FC |
| 2019/2020 | *Championship cancelled* | *Competition cancelled* |
| 2020/2021 | Lincoln Red Imps FC | Lincoln Red Imps FC |
| 2021/2022 | Lincoln Red Imps FC | Lincoln Red Imps FC |
| 2022/2023 | Lincoln Red Imps FC | FC Bruno's Magpies |

Please note: Manchester United FC changed its name to Manchester 62 FC (2013); Newcastle FC was a temporary name for Lincoln Red Imps FC.

# NATIONAL CHAMPIONSHIP
## Gibraltar National League 2022/2023
### (30.09.2022 – 23.04.2023)

## Regular Stage - Results

### Round 1 [30.09.-02.10.2022]
Europa FC - FCB Magpies 1-1
Mons Calpe SC - Lynx FC 1-2
Lincoln Red Imps - Manchester 62 FC 3-0
College 1975 FC - Europa Point FC 0-4
Lions Gibraltar - St. Joseph's FC 1-4

### Round 2 [07-09.10.2022]
Glacis United FC - Mons Calpe SC 1-0
Manchester 62 FC - Europa FC 1-4
Lynx FC - College 1975 FC 1-0
St. Joseph's FC - Lincoln Red Imps 2-2
Europa Point FC - Lions Gibraltar 0-1

### Round 3 [14-16.10.2022]
FCB Magpies - Manchester 62 FC 1-0
College 1975 FC - Glacis United FC 1-0
Europa FC - St. Joseph's FC 1-0
Lions Gibraltar - Lynx FC 0-0
Lincoln Red Imps - Europa Point FC 10-0

### Round 4 [21-23.10.2022]
Mons Calpe SC - College 1975 FC 2-1
St. Joseph's FC - FCB Magpies 1-2
Glacis United FC - Lions Gibraltar 1-0
Europa Point FC - Europa FC 0-9
Lynx FC - Lincoln Red Imps 1-2

### Round 5 [28-30.10.2022]
Manchester 62 FC - St. Joseph's FC 0-3
Lions Gibraltar - Mons Calpe SC 1-1
FCB Magpies - Europa Point FC 7-0
Lincoln Red Imps - Glacis United FC 4-1
Europa FC - Lynx FC 2-1

### Round 6 [04-06.11.2022]
Lions Gibraltar - College 1975 FC 5-1
Manchester 62 FC - Europa Point FC 2-2
Lincoln Red Imps - Mons Calpe SC 2-1
FCB Magpies - Lynx FC 0-1
Europa FC - Glacis United FC 7-0

### Round 7 [25-27.11.2022]
Europa Point FC - St. Joseph's FC 0-6
College 1975 FC - Lincoln Red Imps 0-5
Lynx FC - Manchester 62 FC 4-2
Mons Calpe SC - Europa FC 0-2
Glacis United FC - FCB Magpies 1-2

### Round 8 [02-04.12.2022]
Lincoln Red Imps - Lions Gibraltar 6-0
St. Joseph's FC - Lynx FC 2-1
Europa FC - College 1975 FC 5-0
Manchester 62 FC - Glacis United FC 3-2
FCB Magpies - Mons Calpe SC 2-0

### Round 9 [09-11.12.2022]
Lynx FC - Europa Point FC 5-1
Lions Gibraltar - Europa FC 0-3
Glacis United FC - St. Joseph's FC 2-1
College 1975 FC - FCB Magpies 0-4
Mons Calpe SC - Manchester 62 FC 1-0

### Round 10 [13-17.12.2022]
Europa FC - Lincoln Red Imps 0-1
Europa Point FC - Glacis United FC 0-4
FCB Magpies - Lions Gibraltar 2-0
St. Joseph's FC-Mons Calpe SC 3-0 *awarded**
Manchester 62 FC - College 1975 FC 2-0

### Round 11 [18-21.12.2022]
Lincoln Red Imps - FCB Magpies 1-3
Mons Calpe SC - Europa Point FC 1-0
Glacis United FC - Lynx FC 0-2
Lions Gibraltar - Manchester 62 FC 3-2
College 1975 FC - St. Joseph's FC 1-4

*originally 2-2.*

## Final Standings

| | | | | | | | | | |
|---|---|---|---|---|---|---|---|---|---|
| 1. | Europa FC | 10 | 8 | 1 | 1 | 34 | - | 4 | 25 |
| 2. | Lincoln Red Imps FC | 10 | 8 | 1 | 1 | 36 | - | 8 | 25 |
| 3. | FC Bruno's Magpies | 10 | 8 | 1 | 1 | 24 | - | 5 | 25 |
| 4. | St. Joseph's FC | 10 | 6 | 1 | 3 | 26 | - | 10 | 19 |
| 5. | Lynx FC | 10 | 6 | 1 | 3 | 19 | - | 9 | 19 |
| 6. | Glacis United FC | 10 | 4 | 0 | 6 | 14 | - | 20 | 12 |
| 7. | Lions Gibraltar FC | 10 | 3 | 2 | 5 | 11 | - | 20 | 11 |
| 8. | Mons Calpe SC | 10 | 3 | 1 | 6 | 7 | - | 14 | 10 |
| 9. | Manchester 62 FC | 10 | 2 | 1 | 7 | 12 | - | 23 | 7 |
| 10. | Europa Point FC | 10 | 1 | 1 | 8 | 7 | - | 45 | 4 |
| 11. | College 1975 FC | 10 | 1 | 0 | 9 | 4 | - | 32 | 3 |

Teams ranked 1-6 were qualified for the Championship Round, while teams ranked 7-11 were qualified for the Challenge (Relegation) Round.

## Challenge Round

### Results

### Round 1 [07-08.01.2023]
Europa Point FC - Lions Gibraltar 0-5
Manchester 62 FC - Mons Calpe SC 0-2

### Round 2 [21-22.01.2023]
College 1975 FC - Manchester 62 FC 2-4
Mons Calpe SC - Europa Point FC 2-1

### Round 3 [28-29.01.2023]
Lions Gibraltar - Mons Calpe SC 2-5
Europa Point FC - College 1975 FC 1-1

### Round 4 [04-05.02.2023]
Manchester 62 FC - Europa Point FC 2-0
College 1975 FC - Lions Gibraltar 4-1

### Round 5 [11-12.02.2023]
Mons Calpe SC - College 1975 FC 2-1
Lions Gibraltar - Manchester 62 FC 0-4

### Round 6 [25-26.02.2023]
Lions Gibraltar - Europa Point FC 0-0
Mons Calpe SC - Manchester 62 FC 1-2

### Round 7 [04-05.03.2023]
Manchester 62 FC - College 1975 FC 4-1
Europa Point FC - Mons Calpe SC 1-4

### Round 8 [09-11.04.2023]
College 1975 FC - Europa Point FC 2-2
Mons Calpe SC - Lions Gibraltar 0-3

### Round 9 [15-16.04.2023]
Europa Point FC - Manchester 62 FC 0-4
Lions Gibraltar - College 1975 FC 2-2

### Round 10 [22-23.04.2023]
College 1975 FC - Mons Calpe SC 2-3
Manchester 62 FC - Lions Gibraltar 2-1

| | | Total | | | | | | Home | | | | | Away | | | |
|---|---|---|---|---|---|---|---|---|---|---|---|---|---|---|---|---|---|
| 7. Mons Calpe SC | 18 | 9 | 1 | 8 | 34 - 30 | 28 | 5 | 1 | 3 | 16 - 15 | 4 | 0 | 5 | 18 - 15 |
| 8. Manchester 62 FC | 18 | 9 | 1 | 8 | 26 - 26 | 28 | 5 | 0 | 4 | 10 - 12 | 4 | 1 | 4 | 16 - 14 |
| 9. Lions Gibraltar FC | 18 | 5 | 4 | 9 | 25 - 37 | 19 | 2 | 4 | 4 | 14 - 22 | 3 | 0 | 5 | 11 - 15 |
| 10. College 1975 FC | 18 | 2 | 3 | 13 | 19 - 51 | 9 | 2 | 1 | 6 | 12 - 27 | 0 | 2 | 7 | 7 - 24 |
| 11. Europa Point FC | 18 | 1 | 4 | 13 | 12 - 65 | 7 | 0 | 1 | 7 | 2 - 34 | 1 | 3 | 6 | 10 - 31 |

## Championship Round

### Results

**Round 1** [06-08.01.2023]
Europa FC - Lynx FC 2-1
Glacis United FC - St. Joseph's FC 0-2
FCB Magpies - Lincoln Red Imps 1-5

**Round 2** [20-22.01.2023]
Europa FC - Glacis United FC 4-2
St. Joseph's FC - FCB Magpies 1-3
Lynx FC - Lincoln Red Imps 1-4

**Round 3** [27-29.01.2023]
Lincoln Red Imps - Glacis United FC 4-1
St. Joseph's FC - Europa FC 2-0
FCB Magpies - Lynx FC 1-1

**Round 4** [03-05.02.2023]
Europa FC - FCB Magpies 0-0
Glacis United FC - Lynx FC 0-2
Lincoln Red Imps - St. Joseph's FC 1-0

**Round 5** [11-15.02.2023]
Europa FC - Lincoln Red Imps 0-2
FCB Magpies - Glacis United FC 3-0
Lynx FC - St. Joseph's FC 1-1

**Round 6** [24-26.02.2023]
Lynx FC - Europa FC 2-0
Lincoln Red Imps - FCB Magpies 3-1
St. Joseph's FC - Glacis United FC 3-2

**Round 7** [03-05.03.2023]
Lincoln Red Imps - Lynx FC 4-0
FCB Magpies - St. Joseph's FC 0-1
Glacis United FC - Europa FC 0-1

**Round 8** [08-09.04.2023]
Lynx FC - FCB Magpies 0-5
Glacis United FC - Lincoln Red Imps 0-5
Europa FC - St. Joseph's FC 3-0

**Round 9** [14-16.04.2023]
St. Joseph's FC - Lincoln Red Imps 0-3
Lynx FC - Glacis United FC 5-2
FCB Magpies - Europa FC 1-2

**Round 10** [21-23.04.2023]
St. Joseph's FC - Lynx FC 0-2
Lincoln Red Imps - Europa FC 1-2
Glacis United FC - FCB Magpies 0-0

### Final Standings

| | | Total | | | | | | Home | | | | | Away | | | |
|---|---|---|---|---|---|---|---|---|---|---|---|---|---|---|---|---|---|
| 1. **Lincoln Red Imps FC** | 20 | 17 | 1 | 2 | 68 - 14 | 52 | 9 | 0 | 2 | 39 - 9 | 8 | 1 | 0 | 29 - 5 |
| 2. Europa FC | 20 | 14 | 2 | 4 | 48 - 15 | 44 | 7 | 2 | 2 | 25 - 8 | 7 | 0 | 2 | 23 - 7 |
| 3. FC Bruno's Magpies | 20 | 11 | 4 | 5 | 39 - 18 | 37 | 5 | 1 | 4 | 18 - 10 | 6 | 3 | 1 | 21 - 8 |
| 4. Lynx FC | 20 | 10 | 3 | 7 | 33 - 29 | 33 | 5 | 1 | 3 | 20 - 17 | 5 | 2 | 4 | 13 - 12 |
| 5. St. Joseph's FC | 20 | 10 | 2 | 8 | 36 - 25 | 32 | 4 | 1 | 4 | 14 - 15 | 6 | 1 | 4 | 22 - 10 |
| 6. Glacis United FC | 20 | 4 | 1 | 15 | 19 - 49 | 13 | 3 | 1 | 6 | 5 - 15 | 1 | 0 | 9 | 14 - 34 |

### Top goalscorers:

| | | |
|---|---|---|
| **21** | **Juan Francisco García Peña "Juanfri" (ESP)** | *Lincoln Red Imps FC* |
| 17 | Enrique "Kike" Gómez Bernal (PHI) | *Lincoln Red Imps FC* |
| 12 | Aldair Issac Ruiz Ruiz (CUB) | *Lynx FC* |
| 12 | Aodhán O'Hara (IRL) | *Manchester 62 FC* |

## NATIONAL CUP
### Rock Cup 2022/2023

#### First Round [19.01.2023]

| | | | |
|---|---|---|---|
| Lincoln Red Imps FC - Europa FC | 3-2(2-2) | Europa Point FC - FC Bruno's Magpies | 0-1(0-1) |
| FC Hound Dogs - Lions Gibraltar FC | 1-7(0-4) | College 1975 FC - Mons Calpe SC | 0-3(0-1) |

#### Quarter-Finals [18-19.02.2023]

| | | | |
|---|---|---|---|
| Lions Gibraltar FC - FC Bruno's Magpies | 1-2(0-0) | Manchester 62 FC - St. Joseph's FC | 0-2(0-1) |
| Lincoln Red Imps FC - Lynx FC | 5-0(2-0) | Glacis United FC - Mons Calpe SC | 0-1(0-1) |

#### Semi-Finals [04-05.04.2023]

| | | | |
|---|---|---|---|
| Mons Calpe SC - FC Bruno's Magpies | 0-1(0-1) | Lincoln Red Imps FC - St. Joseph's FC | 2-1(1-1,1-1) |

27.04.2023; Victoria Stadium, Gibraltar; Referee: Timothy Reoch; Attendance: n/a
**FC Bruno's Magpies - Lincoln Red Imps FC**

**1-1(0-1,1-1,1-1); 4-2 on penalties**

**FC Bruno's Magpies**: Jaylan Ernest Hankins, José Manuel Martínez Oliver „Joe", Francisco Javier Gil Zúñiga (Cap), Rubén Díaz Menacho (112.Julian Del Rio), Olmo González Casado (118.Alan Parker), Luke Bautista, Daniel Bent, Scott Glenn Ballantine, James Timothy Barry Coombes (87.José Antonio Pedrosa Galán), Jack Frederick Wendell Storer, Kyle Casciaro. Trainer: Nathan Rooney (England).

**Lincoln Red Imps FC**: Dayle Edward Coleing, Scott Nigel Kenneth Wiseman, Graeme Lee Torrilla (102.Roy Alan Chipolina), Bernardo Morgado Gaspar Lopes (Cap), John Iain Stephen Sergeant (106.Kyle Clinton), Mustapha Yahaya, Marco Rosa Blanco (78.Julian John Valarino), Mariano González Maroto „Nano", Juan Pedro Rico Domínguez „Juampe" (90.Jesús Toscano Serrano), Juan Francisco García Peña „Juanfri" (61.Ethan Britto), Enrique "Kike" Gómez Bernal. Trainer: Javier Muñoz Arévalo (Spain).

**Goals:** 0-1 Mustapha Yahaya (30), 1-1 Daniel Bent (60).

**Penalties:** Kyle Casciaro 1-0; Ethan Britto 1-1; Jack Frederick Wendell Storer (saved); Bernardo Morgado Gaspar Lopes (saved); Daniel Bent 2-1; Julian John Valarino (missed); Francisco Javier Gil Zúñiga 3-1; Enrique "Kike" Gómez Bernal 3-2; José Antonio Pedrosa Galán 4-2.

## THE CLUBS 2022/2023

### Football Club Bruno's Magpies

| Founded: | 2013 | | | |
|---|---|---|---|---|
| Stadium: | Victoria Stadium, Gibraltar (2,800) | | | |
| Trainer: | Nathan Rooney (ENG) | | 10.09.1989 | |

| Goalkeepers: | DOB | M | (s) | G |
|---|---|---|---|---|
| Jaylan Ernest Hankins | 17.11.2000 | 15 | | |
| Manuel „Lolo" Soler Ortuño (ESP) | 17.09.1986 | 2 | | |
| Matthew Manuel Silva (CAN) | 28.03.1991 | 3 | | |
| **Defenders:** | **DOB** | **M** | **(s)** | **G** |
| Ibrahim Ayew (GHA) | 16.04.1988 | 16 | (1) | |
| Luke Bautista | 09.11.2001 | 6 | (1) | |
| Lee Coombes | 20.06.1998 | 8 | | |
| Francisco Javier Gil Zúñiga (MEX) | 22.12.1990 | 14 | (1) | 2 |
| Olmo González Casado (ESP) | 15.06.1987 | 18 | (1) | 2 |
| Kevagn Ronco | 20.04.1998 | 9 | (2) | |
| Rubén Díaz Menacho (ESP) | 10.06.1989 | 13 | (5) | |
| **Midfielders:** | **DOB** | **M** | **(s)** | **G** |
| Scott Glenn Ballantine | 12.04.1996 | 3 | (3) | |
| Daniel Bent (ENG) | 10.01.1996 | 17 | (1) | 1 |
| James Timothy Barry Coombes | 27.05.1996 | 18 | (2) | 3 |
| Jack Horrocks (ENG) | 26.05.1993 | | (1) | |

| | DOB | M | (s) | G |
|---|---|---|---|---|
| José Manuel Martínez Oliver „Joe" (ESP) | 06.02.1991 | 14 | (2) | 4 |
| Shay Jones | 24.02.2002 | 1 | (10) | 2 |
| José Antonio Pedrosa Galán (ESP) | 02.02.1986 | 12 | (6) | 1 |
| Jeremy Joseph López | 09.07.1989 | 2 | (3) | |
| Alan Parker | 15.05.1996 | 2 | (5) | |
| Dylan Paul Peacock | 24.08.2001 | 5 | (5) | 2 |
| Frankie Samuel Perry (ENG) | 13.08.2004 | | (2) | |
| Luis Alberto Díez Ocerín „Tato" (ESP) | 09.07.1992 | 4 | (5) | |
| **Forwards:** | **DOB** | **M** | **(s)** | **G** |
| Olatunde Bayode (ENG) | 07.02.1999 | 4 | (6) | 1 |
| Kyle Casciaro | 02.12.1987 | 15 | (2) | 4 |
| Julian Del Rio | 15.02.2002 | 1 | (2) | 1 |
| Wesley George Martinez | 23.04.2002 | | (1) | |
| Emmanuel Ocran (GHA) | 19.02.1996 | 2 | (7) | |
| Juan Pablo "Pibe" Pereira Sastre (ESP) | 02.07.1987 | 13 | (1) | 11 |
| Jack Frederick Wendell Storer (ENG) | 02.01.1998 | 3 | (5) | 5 |

### College 1975 Football Club

| Founded: | 1975 | | | |
|---|---|---|---|---|
| Stadium: | Victoria Stadium, Gibraltar (2,800) | | | |
| Trainer: | Ángel Espinosa Domínguez (ESP) | | 16.12.1991 | |
| [16.01.2023] | Luis Manuel Blanco (ARG) | | 13.12.1958 | |

| Goalkeepers: | DOB | M | (s) | G |
|---|---|---|---|---|
| Leeor Brounchtine (USA) | 08.10.2001 | 8 | (2) | |
| Eduardo Oliva Ruiz "Edu Oliva" (ESP) | 29.03.1994 | 7 | (1) | |
| Dean John Penfold | 16.03.1996 | 3 | (1) | |
| **Defenders:** | **DOB** | **M** | **(s)** | **G** |
| Kivan Francharles Castle | 21.02.1990 | 2 | (3) | |
| Daniel "Dani" Guerrero Heredia (ESP) | 08.07.1983 | 8 | | |
| Angel Allen Field | 19.08.2002 | 4 | (7) | 1 |
| Nicholas Keith Fortuna | 22.06.2001 | | (1) | |
| Gerardo López Rico (ESP) | 18.10.1994 | 1 | (1) | |
| Julian Paul Laguea | 27.11.2003 | 8 | | |
| Jamie-Luke McCarthy | 21.07.1992 | 14 | (3) | 1 |
| Jordan McGrail | 21.09.2000 | 2 | (1) | |
| Kaylan Manuel Francis Muscat | 17.10.1989 | 1 | | |
| Liam Jay Preston (ENG) | 23.06.1999 | 1 | (3) | |
| Daniel Rodgers | 18.04.1991 | 2 | (2) | |
| **Midfielders:** | **DOB** | **M** | **(s)** | **G** |
| James Mark Caetano | 27.09.2004 | 6 | (2) | |
| Matthew Joseph Codali | 02.07.2005 | | (1) | |

| | DOB | M | (s) | G |
|---|---|---|---|---|
| José Domingo Utrera García (ESP) | 26.10.1988 | 2 | (2) | |
| Bilal Douah | 25.07.2003 | 6 | (1) | |
| Aidan Nicholas Enriles | 22.02.2001 | 1 | (2) | |
| Kaylan Edward Franco | 13.08.2001 | 14 | | |
| Ignacio Giampaoli (ARG) | 19.02.1992 | 3 | | 1 |
| José Gustavo Lima Velasco (ESP) | | 7 | | |
| Adam Maidany (USA) | 08.12.2001 | 9 | (4) | 1 |
| Jemar Maurice Matto | 19.01.2001 | 2 | | |
| Francisco Javier Moreno Jiménez (ESP) | 18.09.1990 | 17 | | |
| Christian Pacheco López (ESP) | 19.11.1998 | 7 | (8) | 1 |
| Nahuel Martín Sendín Saldaña (ARG) | 12.01.1993 | | (1) | |
| Jyron Joseph Zammitt Moreno | 04.11.2004 | 10 | (6) | 2 |
| **Forwards:** | **DOB** | **M** | **(s)** | **G** |
| Hugo Bartkowiak (POL) | 23.07.2000 | 7 | (1) | 3 |
| Germán Cortés Narváez (ESP) | 03.02.1994 | 13 | (1) | 4 |
| Adam Charles Gracia | 28.05.2001 | 15 | (1) | 3 |
| Javier "Javi" Anaya Rojas (ESP) | 12.07.1995 | 11 | (1) | |
| Charley John McMillan López (VGB) | 27.03.1997 | | (1) | |
| José Alberto Mateos Valdivia (ESP) | 18.01.1996 | 7 | (2) | 2 |

## Europa Football Club

| Founded: | 1925 | |
|---|---|---|
| Stadium: | Victoria Stadium, Gibraltar (2,800) | |
| Trainer: | Moisés García Fernández Arteaga (ESP) | 01.06.1969 |
| [02.09.2022] | Steven Cummings (ENG) | |
| [04.03.2023] | Miguel Ángel Berlanga Rodríguez (ESP) | 23.08.1982 |

| Goalkeepers: | DOB | M | (s) | G |
|---|---|---|---|---|
| Bradley James Banda | 20.01.1998 | 11 | | |
| Christian López | 10.02.2001 | 9 | | |
| **Defenders:** | **DOB** | **M** | **(s)** | **G** |
| Álvaro Benítez Huelva (ESP) | 20.04.1989 | 11 | (1) | 2 |
| Francisco Javier „Javi" Paul Curado (ESP) | 30.04.1999 | 19 | | |
| Ethan Terence Jolley | 29.03.1997 | 18 | (2) | |
| Jayce Lee Mascarenhas-Olivero | 02.07.1998 | 19 | | 1 |
| Samuel Yeo | 27.12.2002 | | (1) | |
| **Midfielders:** | **DOB** | **M** | **(s)** | **G** |
| Mohamed Badr Hassan | 18.11.1989 | 10 | (6) | |
| Sergio Rivera Barroso (ESP) | 08.04.2001 | 18 | (1) | 7 |
| Bobby Battisson (ENG) | 31.01.2004 | | (1) | |
| Mitchell Dean Gibson | 08.10.2001 | 3 | (8) | 3 |

| | DOB | M | (s) | G |
|---|---|---|---|---|
| Andrew Albert Hernandez | 10.01.1999 | 18 | | |
| Anthony Alland Hernandez | 03.02.1995 | 15 | (3) | 7 |
| Jocelyn Kola (CTA) | 10.03.1994 | 11 | (1) | |
| Cristian Orihuela Valle (ESP) | 08.01.1997 | 3 | (16) | 2 |
| Manuel Sánchez López (ESP) | 13.09.1988 | 18 | | 5 |
| Jaron Emmanuel Vinet | 16.12.1997 | 1 | (3) | |
| **Forwards:** | **DOB** | **M** | **(s)** | **G** |
| Dylan Borge | 15.10.2003 | 12 | (4) | 5 |
| José Antonio Ojeda Delgado "Cipri" (ESP) | 01.01.2000 | 1 | (6) | |
| Francisco Javier Jiménez Benítez „Fran Bolly" (ESP) | 28.05.2003 | | (2) | |
| Manuel „Manu" Heredia Montoya (ESP) | 12.01.1995 | 2 | (4) | 1 |
| Ibrahima Ndiaye (SEN) | 30.12.1992 | 4 | (5) | 8 |
| Antonio Manuel Sánchez Expósito (ESP) | 06.04.1991 | 7 | (6) | 4 |
| Juan Luis Becerra Gallego "Willy" (ESP) | 08.09.1989 | 10 | (6) | 1 |

## Europa Point Football Club

| Founded: | 2014 | |
|---|---|---|
| Stadium: | Victoria Stadium, Gibraltar (2,800) | |
| Trainer: | Garry Lowe | 13.07.1984 |

| Goalkeepers: | DOB | M | (s) | G |
|---|---|---|---|---|
| Jesse Gonzalez | 16.11.2005 | | (1) | |
| Daniel Tudela Barreira (ESP) | 09.03.1999 | 18 | | |
| **Defenders:** | **DOB** | **M** | **(s)** | **G** |
| Leon Gerald Avellano | 25.04.2004 | 6 | (1) | |
| Jesse Ballester | 30.06.1993 | 5 | | |
| Mark Anthony Ballester | 19.03.1995 | 2 | | |
| Kivan Francharles Castle | 21.02.1990 | 8 | | |
| Martin Filip Falkeborn (SWE) | 08.01.1993 | 7 | | |
| Dion William Hammond | 18.08.1994 | 7 | | 1 |
| Ryan Sean McCarthy (IRL) | 20.08.1995 | 2 | (1) | |
| Antony James Moulds | 04.02.1988 | 12 | | 1 |
| Daniel Rodgers | 18.04.1991 | 1 | (7) | |
| William James Sanders (ENG) | 25.11.2001 | 10 | | |
| Leon Danilo Thick | 30.10.2005 | | (1) | |
| Aiden John Victor | | 2 | (2) | |
| William Wallin (SWE) | 12.07.1994 | 5 | | |
| Jonathan Westerberg (SWE) | 05.01.2002 | 5 | | |
| Reed Wilson (ENG) | 30.07.1997 | 4 | (3) | |
| Michael Anthony Zapata | 29.01.2001 | 1 | (2) | |
| **Midfielders:** | **DOB** | **M** | **(s)** | **G** |
| Federico Nevel Canteros (ARG) | 1999 | | (2) | |
| Matthew Joseph Codali | 02.07.2005 | | (1) | |
| Andrew Viñas Cruz | 11.02.2005 | 1 | (3) | |

| | DOB | M | (s) | G |
|---|---|---|---|---|
| Ilyas El Ouahabi | 20.06.1999 | 2 | (1) | |
| Giles Fabre | | | (1) | |
| Germán García (ARG) | 18.02.1996 | | (1) | |
| Charlie Hardiman (ENG) | 24.07.2003 | 3 | | 1 |
| Zane Charles Holgado | 16.10.1995 | 2 | (1) | |
| Nazim Hughes | 08.10.1992 | 8 | (5) | |
| Oliver Stefan Johansson (SWE) | 13.07.2002 | 3 | (2) | 1 |
| Modoumatarr Mbye (SWE) | 23.08.2000 | 4 | | |
| Hampus Casper Orsing (SWE) | 12.01.2005 | | (2) | |
| Mathew Ian Plumb | 25.10.2004 | 12 | (4) | 1 |
| Oskar Skuza (POL) | 16.03.2002 | 7 | (3) | |
| Kai Alexander Soithongsuk | 23.08.1989 | 12 | (1) | |
| Austin Sparkes (ENG) | 11.11.2003 | 7 | (2) | |
| Christian John Witkowski Dickerson (BRA) | 01.10.1998 | 3 | (1) | |
| **Forwards:** | **DOB** | **M** | **(s)** | **G** |
| Álvaro Ruiz González (ESP) | 31.12.1998 | 1 | (3) | |
| Stephen Luke Black (ENG) | 19.02.2001 | 8 | (6) | 1 |
| Kegan Montgomery Caull (LCA) | 20.03.2004 | 6 | (3) | 4 |
| Louis Frye (GER) | 22.09.1997 | | (4) | |
| Kristoffer Krebs (SWE) | 06.04.2003 | 3 | (1) | |
| Charley John McMillan López (VGB) | 27.03.1997 | | (1) | |
| Lawrence Nzuruba (ENG) | 15.01.1990 | 9 | (1) | 2 |
| Tristan Francis Olivares | 25.03.2002 | 1 | (4) | |
| Ethan Perez | 14.10.1998 | 11 | (2) | |

## Glacis United Football Club

| Founded: | 1965 | |
|---|---|---|
| Stadium: | Victoria Stadium, Gibraltar (2,800) | |
| Trainer: | Michele Di Piedi (ITA) | 04.12.1980 |

| Goalkeepers: | DOB | M | (s) | G |
|---|---|---|---|---|
| Quinn Johnson (NED) | 09.07.2001 | 7 | (1) | |
| André Krul (NED) | 08.05.1987 | 3 | | |
| Domenico Pasqua (ITA) | 22.04.2003 | 9 | | |
| Jake Louis Victor | 28.06.1998 | 1 | (1) | |
| **Defenders:** | **DOB** | **M** | **(s)** | **G** |
| Luke Bautista | 09.11.2001 | 10 | (1) | |
| Julian Britto | 28.06.2004 | 14 | (2) | |
| James William Chiles-Cowell | 14.02.2003 | | (2) | |
| Joseph Louis Chipolina | 14.12.1987 | 15 | (1) | 1 |
| Daniel „Dani" Guerrero Heredia (ESP) | 08.07.1983 | 5 | (1) | |
| Fernando De La Flor Armario (ESP) | 24.04.1998 | 1 | (2) | |
| Ahmed Abdikarim Isse (ENG) | 03.02.2001 | 2 | (6) | |
| Ethan Jay Thorne-Llambias | 23.11.2000 | 16 | (1) | |
| **Midfielders:** | **DOB** | **M** | **(s)** | **G** |
| Soulemane Ba (ITA) | 19.08.2003 | | (1) | |
| Vincenzo Basile (ITA) | 04.11.2002 | 7 | (2) | |
| Julian Brinkman | 02.01.2003 | 1 | (7) | |
| Djumaney Burnet (NED) | 31.03.2001 | 14 | | |
| Leon Clinton | 19.07.1998 | 10 | (4) | 1 |
| Jayme Francis Colton | 29.08.2005 | | (3) | |

| | DOB | M | (s) | G |
|---|---|---|---|---|
| Naoufal El Andaloussi | 07.03.1991 | 5 | (7) | |
| Jeff Fati (ENG) | 13.04.1999 | | (1) | |
| Iván Ruiz Pecino (ESP) | 16.09.1990 | 10 | (2) | 2 |
| Shay Jones | 24.02.2002 | 5 | (1) | |
| Davan Victor Martin | 29.01.2003 | | (1) | |
| Luis McCoy | 02.09.1994 | 12 | (4) | 1 |
| Luis Ignacio "Nacho" Fernández Ríos (ESP) | 28.01.1988 | 11 | (8) | |
| Dylan Paul Peacock | 24.08.2001 | 6 | | 1 |
| Cecil Prescott | 10.05.1999 | 3 | (1) | 1 |
| Giammarco Schirru (ITA) | 04.11.2003 | 9 | (1) | |
| Hatim Anthony Smith | 25.12.2000 | | (2) | |
| Kaydrian Mark Verjaque | 25.09.2003 | 3 | (4) | |
| Oliver Hamilton Williams | 19.11.1991 | | (2) | |
| **Forwards:** | **DOB** | **M** | **(s)** | **G** |
| Francesco Di Piedi (ITA) | 17.06.2003 | 8 | (1) | 2 |
| Giuseppe Domanico (ITA) | 25.05.2002 | 8 | (1) | 1 |
| Arjun Bovind Sing Mann (CAN) | 06.02.2002 | 8 | (6) | |
| Xhelal Terziqi (ALB) | 26.10.2000 | 12 | (1) | 7 |
| Edvinas Valatka (LTU) | 09.01.1997 | | (1) | |
| Vittorio Vigolo (ITA) | 06.01.2000 | 5 | (4) | 2 |

## Lincoln Red Imps Football Club

Founded: 1976
Stadium: Victoria Stadium, Gibraltar (2,800)
Trainer: Raúl Castillo Pérez (ESP) 15.03.1981
[01.01.2023] Javier "Javi" Muñoz Arévalo (ESP) 27.01.1982

| Goalkeepers: | DOB | M | (s) | G |
|---|---|---|---|---|
| Dayle Edward Coleing | 23.10.1996 | 16 | | |
| Nauzet *García* Santana (ESP) | 08.04.1994 | 3 | | |
| Iván *Villanueva* Ramírez (ESP) | 28.02.1996 | 1 | | |
| **Defenders:** | **DOB** | **M** | **(s)** | **G** |
| Ethan Britto | 30.11.2000 | 18 | | 1 |
| Roy Alan Chipolina | 20.01.1983 | 7 | (3) | |
| Julian Paul Laguea | 27.11.2003 | | (1) | |
| Bernardo Morgado Gaspar Lopes | 30.07.1993 | 18 | | 1 |
| Javan Joseph Peacock | 31.07.2006 | | (2) | |
| Kian Joe Ronan | 09.03.2001 | 4 | (9) | 4 |
| John Iain Stephen Sergeant | 27.02.1995 | 18 | (1) | |
| Jesús *Toscano* Serrano (ESP) | 13.12.1990 | 7 | (4) | 2 |
| Scott Nigel Kenneth Wiseman | 09.10.1985 | 10 | (4) | 1 |
| **Midfielders:** | **DOB** | **M** | **(s)** | **G** |
| Shane Borda | 07.05.2005 | | (1) | |
| Lee Martin Chipolina | 27.02.2006 | | (2) | |
| Kyle Clinton | 18.03.2004 | | (6) | 1 |
| Javier Martinez | 30.11.2005 | | (1) | |
| Mariano González Maroto „Nano" (ESP) | 27.10.1984 | 17 | (2) | 2 |
| Marco *Rosa* Blanco (ESP) | 30.11.1995 | 13 | (4) | 1 |
| Graeme Lee Torrilla | 03.09.1997 | 11 | (2) | 2 |
| Julian John Valarino | 23.06.2000 | 5 | (8) | |
| Liam Walker | 13.04.1988 | 17 | | 7 |
| Mustapha Yahaya (GHA) | 09.01.1994 | 9 | (8) | 2 |
| **Forwards:** | **DOB** | **M** | **(s)** | **G** |
| Lee Henry Casciaro | 29.09.1981 | 4 | (10) | 2 |
| Juan Pedro Rico Domínguez „Juampe" (ESP) | 24.05.1984 | 14 | (6) | 5 |
| Juan Francisco García Peña „Juanfri" (ESP) | 01.10.1989 | 16 | (4) | 21 |
| Enrique "Kike" *Gómez* Bernal (PHI) | 04.05.1994 | 12 | (7) | 17 |
| Jonathan Sciortino | 29.12.2005 | | (2) | |

## Lions Gibraltar Football Club

Founded: 1966
Stadium: Victoria Stadium, Gibraltar (2,800)
Trainer: Adrian Parral 23.09.1970

| Goalkeepers: | DOB | M | (s) | G |
|---|---|---|---|---|
| *Borja* Valadés González (ESP) | 30.06.1988 | 17 | | |
| Juan Jesús *Muñoz* Sánchez (ESP) | 30.12.2000 | 1 | | |
| **Defenders:** | **DOB** | **M** | **(s)** | **G** |
| Shea Kevin Luke Breakspear | 22.11.1991 | 12 | | |
| *Joel David* Rodriguez Macias (ESP) | 10.06.1999 | 15 | (1) | |
| David Paul Gallardo | 04.05.1991 | 13 | | 2 |
| Jack Arthur William Lee (ENG) | 16.08.2004 | 5 | | |
| Francisco Luis *Morales* Sánchez (ESP) | 07.01.1994 | 7 | (7) | |
| Leon Mark Payas | 26.02.1998 | 8 | (7) | |
| Liam Jay Preston (ENG) | 23.06.1999 | 4 | (3) | 1 |
| Javan Keith Robertson | 19.06.2000 | | (7) | |
| Kaylan Alfred Rumbo | 12.12.1990 | 4 | (4) | |
| Adrián *Vera* Tovar (ESP) | 21.02.1990 | 12 | | |
| **Midfielders:** | **DOB** | **M** | **(s)** | **G** |
| Antonio *Cintas* Sánchez (ESP) | 11.05.1995 | 15 | | 2 |
| *Estiven* Morente Vélez (ESP) | 16.02.1991 | 3 | (4) | 1 |
| John Charles Gaivizo | 27.07.1993 | 1 | (1) | |
| Sykes Al Garro | 26.02.1993 | 11 | | 1 |
| Aaram William Marcial Hanglin | 18.08.2005 | | (1) | |
| Thomas Hastings | 23.09.1992 | 16 | | |
| Davan Victor Martin | 29.01.2003 | | (5) | |
| Kyron McGrail | 22.04.2003 | 1 | | |
| Harrison Wade Murray-Freeman | 16.10.2005 | 2 | | |
| Karl Poggio | 08.06.1998 | | (2) | |
| Cecil Prescott | 10.05.1999 | | (4) | |
| Antonio Jiménez Ramos "Ñito" (ESP) | 07.05.1996 | 7 | (7) | 2 |
| Aidan Charles Serra | 28.12.1994 | 6 | (1) | 1 |
| Etien Victory | 21.09.1999 | | (2) | |
| **Forwards:** | **DOB** | **M** | **(s)** | **G** |
| Byron Manuel Espinosa | 15.03.1999 | 3 | (1) | 1 |
| Evan James Greeen | 13.03.1993 | 12 | (1) | 2 |
| Juan Manuel Labrador Aguilar „Labra" (ESP) | 24.06.1995 | 17 | | 8 |
| Sergio Giovanni *Lengua* Esposito (ESP) | 04.11.2002 | | (1) | |
| José María *Marín* Criado (ESP) | 17.01.2001 | 4 | (7) | 4 |
| Ellis Lineker Wilson | 11.09.2003 | 2 | (2) | |

## Lynx Football Club

Founded: 2007
Stadium: Victoria Stadium, Gibraltar (2,800)
Trainer: Albert Parody 30.08.1968

| Goalkeepers: | DOB | M | (s) | G |
|---|---|---|---|---|
| Bradley Emile Avellano | 01.11.2002 | 13 | | |
| Jordan López Pérez | 13.11.1986 | 6 | (1) | |
| Robert Copello Rae | 30.05.1999 | 1 | | |
| **Defenders:** | **DOB** | **M** | **(s)** | **G** |
| David Alberto Bautista Martos „Bauti" (ESP) | 27.02.1992 | 16 | (1) | 2 |
| Daniel „*Dani*" Gallardo Aragón (ESP) | 26.07.1990 | 18 | | 1 |
| Jean-Carlos Garcia | 05.07.1992 | 19 | (1) | |
| Andrés Cristobal González Zapico (ARG) | 26.02.2001 | | (5) | |
| Serge Ilondelo (SWE) | 17.05.2003 | | (1) | |
| Santino Swanson Manuel (GER) | 29.12.2000 | | (2) | |
| Santino Encino Recine (CAN) | 13.01.1997 | 7 | (5) | 2 |
| Ethan James Santos | 22.12.1998 | 8 | | 1 |
| **Midfielders:** | **DOB** | **M** | **(s)** | **G** |
| Blas *Álvarez* Cortés (ESP) | 19.07.1995 | 7 | | |
| Bilal Douah | 25.07.2003 | 2 | (4) | |
| Ernesto *García* Gallego (ESP) | 23.01.1986 | 5 | | |
| *Antonio González* García (ESP) | 06.05.1996 | 2 | (8) | 2 |
| *José González* Morales (ESP) | 09.10.1994 | 1 | (6) | |
| Maximiliano Javier Mallemaci (ARG) | 29.04.1989 | 11 | (4) | |
| Michael Lee Negrette | 14.09.1998 | 8 | (7) | |
| Aiden Lee Olivares | 10.10.1999 | | (3) | |
| Jesse John Victory | 02.04.1996 | 13 | | |
| **Forwards:** | **DOB** | **M** | **(s)** | **G** |
| Hugo Bartkowiak (POL) | 23.07.2000 | | (5) | |
| Tejan Brima (SLE) | 28.08.1999 | 12 | (7) | 1 |
| George Cabrera | 14.12.1988 | 3 | (4) | 1 |
| Macauley Chrisantus (NGA) | 20.08.1990 | 7 | (2) | 6 |
| Gonzalo *Giménez* Munzón (ESP) | 24.12.2000 | 14 | (6) | 1 |
| José Antonio Almeida Exposito „Nene" (ESP) | 17.02.2000 | 1 | (5) | |
| Aldair Issac Ruiz Ruiz (CUB) | 13.11.1997 | 19 | (1) | 12 |
| Michael Francis Ruiz | 07.12.2000 | 9 | (9) | 2 |
| Omar Salah El-Din Farfan | 02.10.2003 | 18 | (2) | 1 |

## Manchester 62 Football Club

**Founded**: 1962
**Stadium**: Victoria Stadium, Gibraltar (2,800)
**Trainer**: David Wilson (SCO)    22.02.1974
[11.10.2022] James McDonough (ENG)    09.03.1989

| Goalkeepers: | DOB | M | (s) | G |
|---|---|---|---|---|
| Benjamin Maidens (ENG) | 14.07.1991 | 7 | (1) | |
| Fernando Ruiz Canto (ESP) | 01.06.1999 | 7 | | |
| Ayden Leigh Viñales | 13.02.1998 | 4 | (1) | |
| **Defenders:** | **DOB** | **M** | **(s)** | **G** |
| Jett Blaschka (VIR) | 16.09.1999 | 8 | (3) | |
| Jamie Ralph Bosio | 27.03.1991 | 17 | | |
| Kenneth George Chipolina | 08.04.1994 | 4 | (1) | |
| Matthew David Clenahan (ENG) | 11.02.1996 | 5 | (5) | |
| Ryan John Dean | 18.07.1998 | | (1) | |
| Mark Anthony Edzes (ENG) | 14.08.1991 | 18 | | |
| Tom Farmer (WAL) | 11.12.1996 | 4 | (1) | |
| Marquis McKinley Flowers-Gamboa (USA) | 27.12.1996 | 8 | (2) | |
| Daniel Edward Joseph Sánchez | 11.11.1997 | | (6) | |
| Ethan James Santos | 22.12.1998 | 8 | (1) | |
| Peter Sardeña | 03.03.1996 | 2 | (3) | |
| Jayden Louis Villa | 12.05.2005 | | (6) | |
| Reed Wilson (ENG) | 30.07.1997 | | (2) | |
| **Midfielders:** | **DOB** | **M** | **(s)** | **G** |
| Scott Glenn Ballantine | 12.04.1996 | 11 | | 1 |
| Michael Maximillian Philip Cottrell | 15.09.1999 | | (1) | |
| Carl de Torres | 26.02.2005 | 5 | (3) | |
| Kieron Joseph Garcia | 04.08.1998 | 10 | (6) | |
| Aodhán O'Hara (IRL) | 14.02.1999 | 18 | | 12 |
| Giles Paul Lopez | 29.06.1992 | | (1) | |
| Alberto Julmart Rafael Lubango (ENG) | 11.04.1999 | 18 | | 5 |
| Panashe Makwiramiti (ENG) | 01.07.2002 | 8 | (6) | |
| Jaydan Albert Parody | 08.05.1998 | 3 | (2) | |
| Frankie Samuel Perry (ENG) | 13.08.2004 | | (5) | |
| Lucas James Reed (SCO) | 06.01.2003 | 6 | | 2 |
| Stefan Glen Viagas | 13.07.2000 | | (1) | 1 |
| **Forwards:** | **DOB** | **M** | **(s)** | **G** |
| Jaiden Kamil Bartolo | 10.02.2006 | 2 | | |
| Samuel *Benítez* Fajardo (ESP) | 13.01.2000 | 4 | (2) | 4 |
| Fraser Carnegie | 14.11.2005 | | (2) | |
| Luke Coleman (ENG) | 02.01.2002 | | (1) | |
| Kevan Gonzalez | 19.10.2005 | 6 | (5) | 2 |
| Nicholas Keyamo (ENG) | 16.02.1996 | 2 | (4) | |
| Emmanuel Ocran (GHA) | 19.02.1996 | 7 | | 4 |
| Theo Charles Pizarro | 10.07.1998 | 6 | (5) | 2 |

## Mons Calpe Sports Club

**Founded**: 2013
**Stadium**: Victoria Stadium, Gibraltar (2,800)
**Trainer**: Allen Bula    04.01.1965
[12.10.2022] Andrés David Gutiérrez Cantero (ESP)    18.12.1972

| Goalkeepers: | DOB | M | (s) | G |
|---|---|---|---|---|
| Christian Hernán Fraiz García (ARG) | 22.02.1988 | 2 | | |
| Jordan López Pérez | 13.11.1986 | 9 | | |
| Jamie Payas-Carlin | 27.08.1992 | 1 | | |
| Charlie Preston (ENG) | 08.12.2003 | 3 | | |
| Adam Paul Stevens (ENG) | 20.05.1992 | 3 | | |
| **Defenders:** | **DOB** | **M** | **(s)** | **G** |
| Alejandro „*Álex*" Trujillo Torres (ESP) | 05.08.1997 | 11 | (3) | |
| *André* Luiz Dos Santos (BRA) | 19.02.1992 | 15 | | 2 |
| Kenneth George Chipolina | 08.04.1994 | 3 | (3) | 3 |
| Ryan John Dean | 18.07.1998 | 8 | | |
| Emanuel Alejandro Ojeda (ARG) | 25.11.1990 | 12 | (3) | |
| James Michael Parkinson | 21.05.2000 | 10 | (2) | |
| *Renan Bernardes* Alt (BRA) | 21.03.1992 | 17 | | |
| Mauricio Enrique Reygadas (MEX) | 19.10.2005 | 5 | (5) | |
| Jordan Wells (ENG) | 15.03.2000 | 2 | (2) | |
| **Midfielders:** | **DOB** | **M** | **(s)** | **G** |
| Alejandro Rodríguez Rivas „Álex Quillo" (ESP) | 07.10.1986 | 4 | (1) | |
| Julio Gil Bado | 03.06.1983 | 15 | (1) | |
| Dylan De Los Santos | 27.06.2002 | 1 | (4) | |
| Sykes Al Garro | 26.02.1993 | 4 | | |
| Guilherme "*Gee*" Fernandes Mateus *Baltazar* (POR) | 27.11.1999 | 4 | (2) | |
| Ignacio Giampaoli (ARG) | 19.02.1992 | 3 | (2) | |
| Moshe Shalom Hassan (CAN) | 2005 | | (1) | |
| Francisco Javier "*Javi*" Moreno Arjona (ESP) | 18.01.1999 | 11 | (5) | 4 |
| Ralph Max Alexander Kerrebijn (NED) | 16.05.1999 | | (1) | |
| Kody Maude (AUS) | 10.10.1996 | 2 | | |
| Kian Craig Tansley (ENG) | 12.01.2003 | 2 | (1) | |
| Etien Victory | 21.09.1999 | 5 | (3) | |
| **Forwards:** | **DOB** | **M** | **(s)** | **G** |
| George Cabrera | 14.12.1988 | 2 | (2) | 1 |
| Mark Joseph Chichon | 24.12.1994 | 13 | (1) | 3 |
| Fernando *Cosano* Diaz (ESP) | 20.07.1999 | 5 | (1) | 1 |
| John-Paul Duarte | 13.12.1986 | 4 | (1) | 1 |
| Luis Manuel *Gallardo* Monje (ESP) | 20.07.1992 | | (7) | 1 |
| Ashton Hancock | 05.10.2006 | 1 | (2) | 1 |
| *Jesús* María *Ayala* Sánchez (ESP) | 16.11.1993 | 5 | (1) | 5 |
| Robert Montovio | 03.08.1984 | 5 | (5) | 3 |
| Joseph Nahon | 2005 | | (2) | |
| Samir Omari | 28.08.1993 | 2 | (1) | 1 |
| Nathan Albert Santos | 11.10.1988 | 8 | (2) | |
| Cristian Alejandro Toncheff Ferberovich (ARG) | 25.03.1982 | 1 | (3) | 1 |

## St. Joseph's Football Club

**Founded**: 1912
**Stadium**: Victoria Stadium, Gibraltar (2,800)
**Trainer**: Abraham Paz Cruz (ESP)    29.06.1979

| Goalkeepers: | DOB | M | (s) | G |
|---|---|---|---|---|
| Alan Andrew Martin (SCO) | 01.01.1989 | 14 | (5) | |
| Jamie Kevagn Robba | 26.10.1991 | 6 | | |
| **Defenders:** | **DOB** | **M** | **(s)** | **G** |
| Erin Anthony Barnett | 02.09.1996 | 10 | (1) | 2 |
| Jules Cesar Boubane (NED) | 19.09.2003 | 6 | (2) | |
| Aymen Mouelhi | 14.09.1986 | 12 | (4) | |
| Alain Anthony Pons | 16.09.1995 | 19 | (1) | |
| Federico Martín Villar (ARG) | 24.11.1985 | 13 | | |
| **Midfielders:** | **DOB** | **M** | **(s)** | **G** |
| Christian *Aznar* Fernández (ESP) | 10.01.2003 | 14 | (6) | 3 |
| Dylan Duo | 17.01.2006 | | (1) | |
| Kaydan Glynn | 16.05.2005 | | (2) | |
| Juan Manuel Gonzáles Pérez "Juanma" (ESP) | 02.05.1991 | 16 | (1) | 1 |
| Manuel "*Manu*" Caballero González (ESP) | 10.04.1992 | 17 | (3) | 5 |
| Fernando „*Nando*" Cózar Torres (ESP) | 02.03.1991 | 4 | (4) | |
| Cristian *Pecci* Macías (ESP) | 10.05.1988 | 9 | (8) | |
| Kevagn Robba | 20.09.1994 | 16 | (4) | |
| Pablo *Rosa* Tristán (ESP) | 07.01.2003 | 3 | (9) | |
| **Forwards:** | **DOB** | **M** | **(s)** | **G** |
| Ishmael Kofi Antwi (GHA) | 04.09.1992 | 2 | (8) | 1 |
| Salvador Manuel Alegre Delgado "Boro"(ESP) | 04.05.1991 | 18 | (1) | 8 |
| Ayoub El Hmidi | 30.09.2000 | 10 | (9) | 2 |
| Kayden Gonzalez | 14.11.2006 | | (2) | |
| Kelvin Morgan | 14.11.1997 | 5 | (5) | 2 |
| *Pablo Rodríguez* Moreno (ESP) | 28.12.1997 | 8 | (1) | 4 |
| Michael Yome | 29.08.1994 | 14 | (6) | 6 |
| Maxim Zeulevoet (BEL) | 03.02.2000 | 4 | (7) | |

## INTERNATIONAL MATCHES
### (16.07.2022 – 15.07.2023)

| 23.09.2022 | Razgrad | Bulgaria - Gibraltar | 5-1(2-1) | (UNL) |
|---|---|---|---|---|
| 26.09.2022 | Gibraltar | Gibraltar - Georgia | 1-2(0-1) | (UNL) |
| 16.11.2022 | Gibraltar | Gibraltar - Liechtenstein | 2-0(2-0) | (F) |
| 19.11.2022 | Gibraltar | Gibraltar - Andorra | 1-0(1-0) | (F) |
| 24.03.2023 | Faro/Loulé | Gibraltar - Greece | 0-3(0-2) | (ECQ) |
| 27.03.2023 | Rotterdam | Netherlands - Gibraltar | 3-0(1-0) | (ECQ) |
| 16.06.2023 | Faro/Loulé | Gibraltar - France | 0-3(0-2) | (ECQ) |
| 19.06.2023 | Dublin | Republic of Ireland - Gibraltar | 3-0(0-0) | (ECQ) |

**23.09.2022  BULGARIA - GIBRALTAR  5-1(2-1)  3rd UEFA Nations League C, Group 4**
Huvepharma Arena, Razgrad; Referee: Pavel Orel (Czech Republic); Attendance: 1,540
**GIB:** Dayle Edward Coleing, Kian Joe Ronan, Bernardo Morgado Gaspar Lopes, Roy Alan Chipolina (Cap), Jayce Lee Mascarenhas-Olivero, Ethan Britto (83.Joseph Louis Chipolina), Louie Annesley (63.Ethan Terence Jolley), Graeme Lee Torrilla (63.John Iain Stephen Sergeant), Scott Nigel Kenneth Wiseman, Liam Walker (72.Nicholas Charles Pozo), Lee Henry Casciaro (63.Reece Styche). Trainer: Julio César Ribas Vlacovich (Uruguay).
**Goal:** Roy Alan Chipolina (26).

**26.09.2022  GIBRALTAR - GEORGIA  1-2(0-1)  3rd UEFA Nations League C, Group 4**
Victoria Stadium, Gibraltar; Referee: Robert Harvey (Republic of Ireland); Attendance: 1,199
**GIB:** Bradley James Banda, Scott Nigel Kenneth Wiseman (73.John Iain Stephen Sergeant), Bernardo Morgado Gaspar Lopes, Roy Alan Chipolina (Cap), Jayce Lee Mascarenhas-Olivero, Ethan Britto (84.Joseph Louis Chipolina), Louie Annesley, Liam Walker, Kian Joe Ronan (63.Reece Styche), Graeme Lee Torrilla (84.Kelvin John Morgan), Lee Henry Casciaro. Trainer: Julio César Ribas Vlacovich (Uruguay).
**Goal:** Louie Annesley (75).

**16.11.2022  GIBRALTAR - LIECHTENSTEIN  2-0(2-0)  Friendly International**
Victoria Stadium, Gibraltar; Referee: Ahmad Faisal Al Ali (Kuwait); Attendance: 558
**GIB:** Dayle Edward Coleing, John Iain Stephen Sergeant (46.Ethan Terence Jolley), Bernardo Morgado Gaspar Lopes, Roy Alan Chipolina (Cap), Jayce Lee Mascarenhas-Olivero, Louie Annesley (86.Nicholas Charles Pozo), Ethan Britto (86.James Timothy Barry Coombes), Graeme Lee Torrilla, Lee Henry Casciaro (75.Julian John Valarino), Liam Walker (86.Joseph Louis Chipolina), Andre Tjay De Barr (71.Reece Styche). Trainer: Julio César Ribas Vlacovich (Uruguay).
**Goals:** Roy Alan Chipolina (14), Liam Walker (21 penalty).

**19.11.2022  GIBRALTAR - ANDORRA  1-0(1-0)  Friendly International**
Victoria Stadium, Gibraltar; Referee: Abdullah Al Kandari (Kuwait); Attendance: 2,206
**GIB:** Dayle Edward Coleing, Ethan Terence Jolley (84.Joseph Louis Chipolina), Bernardo Morgado Gaspar Lopes, Roy Alan Chipolina (Cap), Jayce Lee Mascarenhas-Olivero, Louie Annesley, Ethan Britto, Graeme Lee Torrilla, Lee Henry Casciaro (65.Julian John Valarino), Liam Walker, Andre Tjay De Barr (87.Kelvin John Morgan). Trainer: Julio César Ribas Vlacovich (Uruguay).
**Goal:** Roy Alan Chipolina (34).

**24.03.2023  GIBRALTAR - GREECE  0-3(0-2)  17th EC. Qualifiers**
Estádio Algarve, Faro/Loulé (Portugal); Referee: Rohit Saggi (Norway); Attendance: 390
**GIB:** Dayle Edward Coleing, Jayce Lee Mascarenhas-Olivero, John Iain Stephen Sergeant, Roy Alan Chipolina (Cap), Julian John Valarino (62.James Timothy Barry Coombes), Bernardo Morgado Gaspar Lopes, Ethan Britto (85.Ethan Terence Jolley), Graeme Lee Torrilla (62.Aymen Mouelhi), Kian Joe Ronan (85.Joseph Louis Chipolina), Lee Henry Casciaro (85.Reece Styche), Liam Walker. Trainer: Julio César Ribas Vlacovich (Uruguay).

**27.03.2023  NETHERLANDS - GIBRALTAR  3-0(1-0)  17th EC. Qualifiers**
Stadion Feijenoord, Rotterdam; Referee: Morten Krogh (Denmark); Attendance: 36,327
**GIB:** Dayle Edward Coleing, John Iain Stephen Sergeant, Roy Alan Chipolina (Cap), Bernardo Morgado Gaspar Lopes, Jayce Lee Mascarenhas-Olivero, Ethan Britto, Kian Joe Ronan (76.Aymen Mouelhi), Graeme Lee Torrilla (86.Niels Mark Pieter Hartman), Liam Walker [*sent off 51*], Lee Henry Casciaro (86.Julian John Valarino), James Timothy Barry Coombes (65.Ethan Terence Jolley). Trainer: Julio César Ribas Vlacovich (Uruguay).

**16.06.2023  GIBRALTAR - FRANCE  0-3(0-2)  17th EC. Qualifiers**
Estádio Algarve, Faro/Loulé (Portugal); Referee: Yevhenii Aranovskiy (Ukraine); Attendance: 4,065
**GIB:** Dayle Edward Coleing, John Iain Stephen Sergeant, Roy Alan Chipolina (Cap), Bernardo Morgado Gaspar Lopes, Jayce Lee Mascarenhas-Olivero, Ethan Britto, Niels Mark Pieter Hartman (60.Louie Annesley), Nicholas Charles Pozo (84.Joseph Louis Chipolina), Lee Henry Casciaro (60.Andre Tjay De Barr), Kian Joe Ronan (72.Scott Nigel Kenneth Wiseman), Ayoub El Hmidi (60.Aymen Mouelhi). Trainer: Julio César Ribas Vlacovich (Uruguay).

**19.06.2023  REPUBLIC OF IRELAND - GIBRALTAR  3-0(0-0)  17th EC. Qualifiers**
Aviva Stadium, Dublin; Referee: Marian Alexandru Barbu (Romania); Attendance: 42,156
**GIB:** Dayle Edward Coleing, John Iain Stephen Sergeant (46.Scott Nigel Kenneth Wiseman), Roy Alan Chipolina (Cap) (43.Aymen Mouelhi), Bernardo Morgado Gaspar Lopes, Jayce Lee Mascarenhas-Olivero, Louie Annesley, Niels Mark Pieter Hartman, Nicholas Charles Pozo (68.Ethan Terence Jolley), Kian Joe Ronan, Ethan Britto (73.Scott Glenn Ballantine), Ayoub El Hmidi (46.Andre Tjay De Barr). Trainer: Julio César Ribas Vlacovich (Uruguay).

## NATIONAL TEAM PLAYERS
### (16.07.2022 – 15.07.2023)

| Name | DOB | Caps | Goals | Club | |
|------|-----|------|-------|------|---|

### Goalkeepers

| Name | DOB | Caps | Goals | Club | |
|------|-----|------|-------|------|---|
| Bradley James BANDA | 20.01.1998 | 5 | 0 | 2022: | *Europa FC* |
| Dayle Edward COLEING | 23.10.1996 | 25 | 0 | 2022/2023: | *Lincoln Red Imps FC* |

### Defenders

| Name | DOB | Caps | Goals | Club | |
|------|-----|------|-------|------|---|
| Ethan BRITTO | 30.11.2000 | 30 | 0 | 2022/2023: | *Lincoln Red Imps FC* |
| Joseph Louis CHIPOLINA | 14.12.1987 | 54 | 2 | 2022/2023: | *Glacis United FC* |
| Roy Alan CHIPOLINA | 20.01.1983 | 68 | 5 | 2022/2023: | *Lincoln Red Imps FC* |
| Ethan Terence JOLLEY | 29.03.1997 | 23 | 0 | 2022/2023: | *Europa FC* |
| Bernardo Morgado Gaspar LOPES | 30.07.1993 | 14 | 0 | 2022/2023: | *Lincoln Red Imps FC* |
| Jayce Lee MASCARENHAS-OLIVERO | 02.07.1998 | 50 | 0 | 2022/2023: | *Europa FC* |
| Aymen MOUELHI | 14.09.1986 | 30 | 0 | 2023: | *St. Joseph's FC* |
| John Iain Stephen SERGEANT | 27.02.1995 | 52 | 0 | 2022/2023: | *Lincoln Red Imps FC* |
| Scott Nigel Kenneth WISEMAN | 09.10.1985 | 38 | 0 | 2022/2023: | *Lincoln Red Imps FC* |

### Midfielders

| Name | DOB | Caps | Goals | Club | |
|------|-----|------|-------|------|---|
| Louie John ANNESLEY | 03.05.2000 | 37 | 1 | 2022: | *Blackburn Rovers FC (ENG)* |
| | | | | 10.01.2023-> | *Dundalk FC (IRL)* |
| Scott Glenn BALLANTINE | 12.04.1996 | 1 | 0 | 2023: | *FC Bruno's Magpies* |
| Niels Mark Pieter HARTMAN | 17.01.2001 | 3 | 0 | 2023: | *Loughborough University FC (ENG)* |
| Nicholas Charles POZO | 19.01.2003 | 5 | 0 | 2022/2023: | *Cádiz CF (ESP)* |
| Kian Joe RONAN | 09.03.2001 | 25 | 0 | 2022/2023: | *Lincoln Red Imps FC* |
| Graeme Lee TORRILLA | 03.09.1997 | 26 | 1 | 2022/2023: | *Lincoln Red Imps FC* |
| Julian John VALARINO | 23.06.2000 | 22 | 0 | 2022/2023: | *Lincoln Red Imps FC* |
| Liam WALKER | 13.04.1988 | 69 | 5 | 2022/2023: | *Lincoln Red Imps FC* |

### Forwards

| Name | DOB | Caps | Goals | Club | |
|------|-----|------|-------|------|---|
| Lee Henry CASCIARO | 29.09.1981 | 56 | 3 | 2022/2023: | *Lincoln Red Imps FC* |
| James Timothy Barry COOMBES | 27.05.1996 | 28 | 0 | 2022/2023: | *FC Bruno's Magpies* |
| Andre Tjay DE BARR | 13.03.2000 | 32 | 3 | 2022/2023: | *Wycombe Wanderers FC (ENG)* |
| Ayoub EL HMIDI | 30.09.2000 | 2 | 0 | 2023: | *St. Joseph's FC* |
| Kelvin John MORGAN | 14.11.1997 | 3 | 0 | 2022: | *St. Joseph's FC* |
| Reece STYCHE | 03.05.1989 | 31 | 3 | 2022: | *Stourbridge FC (ENG)* |
| | | | | 17.03.2023-> | *Matlock Town FC (ENG)* |

### Trainer

| | | | |
|------|-----|------|------|
| Julio César RIBAS Vlacovich (Uruguay) [from 01.07.2018] | 08.01.1957 | 48 M; 6 W; 6 D; 36 L; 21-133 | |

# GREECE

## The Country:
Ελληνική Δημοκρατία (Hellenic Republic)
Capital: Athína
Surface: 131,957 km²
Inhabitants: 10,482,487 [2021]
Time: UTC+2

## The FA:
Hellenic Football Federation
Goudi Park P.O. Box 14161, 11510 Athens
Tel: +30 210 930 6000
Foundation date: 1926
Member of FIFA since: 1927
Member of UEFA since: 1954
Website: www.epo.gr

## NATIONAL TEAM RECORDS

### RECORDS
| | | |
|---|---|---|
| **First international match:** | 07.04.1929, Athína: | Greece – Italy "B" 1-4 |
| **Most international caps:** | Georgios Karagoúnis | - 139 caps (1999-2014) |
| **Most international goals:** | Nikolaos Anastopoulos | - 29 goals / 74 caps (1977-1988) |

### UEFA EUROPEAN CHAMPIONSHIP
| | |
|---|---|
| 1960 | Qualifiers |
| 1964 | Did not enter |
| 1968 | Qualifiers |
| 1972 | Qualifiers |
| 1976 | Qualifiers |
| 1980 | Final Tournament (Group Stage) |
| 1984 | Qualifiers |
| 1988 | Qualifiers |
| 1992 | Qualifiers |
| 1996 | Qualifiers |
| 2000 | Qualifiers |
| 2004 | **Final Tournament (Winners)** |
| 2008 | Final Tournament (Group Stage) |
| 2012 | Final Tournament (Quarter-Finals) |
| 2016 | Qualifiers |
| 2020 | Qualifiers |

### FIFA WORLD CUP
| | |
|---|---|
| 1930 | Did not enter |
| 1934 | Qualifiers |
| 1938 | Qualifiers |
| 1950 | Did not enter |
| 1954 | Qualifiers |
| 1958 | Qualifiers |
| 1962 | Qualifiers |
| 1966 | Qualifiers |
| 1970 | Qualifiers |
| 1974 | Qualifiers |
| 1978 | Qualifiers |
| 1982 | Qualifiers |
| 1986 | Qualifiers |
| 1990 | Qualifiers |
| 1994 | Final Tournament (Group Stage) |
| 1998 | Qualifiers |
| 2002 | Qualifiers |
| 2006 | Qualifiers |
| 2010 | Final Tournament (Group Stage) |
| 2014 | Final Tournament (2nd Round of 16) |
| 2018 | Qualifiers |
| 2022 | Qualifiers |

### OLYMPIC TOURNAMENTS
| | |
|---|---|
| 1908 | - |
| 1912 | - |
| 1920 | Quarter-Finals |
| 1924 | - |
| 1928 | - |
| 1936 | - |
| 1948 | - |
| 1952 | Preliminary Round |
| 1956 | - |
| 1960 | Qualifiers |
| 1964 | Qualifiers |
| 1968 | Qualifiers |
| 1972 | Qualifiers |
| 1976 | Qualifiers |
| 1980 | Group Stage |
| 1984 | Qualifiers |
| 1988 | Qualifiers |
| 1992 | Qualifiers |
| 1996 | Qualifiers |
| 2000 | Qualifiers |
| 2004 | Group Stage |
| 2008 | Qualifiers |
| 2012 | Qualifiers |
| 2016 | Qualifiers |
| 2020 | Qualifiers |

### UEFA NATIONS LEAGUE
| | |
|---|---|
| 2018/2019 | League C (Group Stage) |
| 2020/2021 | League C (Group Stage) |
| 2022/2023 | League C (Group Stage -> promoted to League A) |

### FIFA CONFEDERATIONS CUP 1992-2017
2005 (Group Stage)

### GREEK CLUB HONOURS IN EUROPEAN CLUB COMPETITIONS:

| European Champion Clubs' Cup (1956-1992) / UEFA Champions League (1993-2023) |
|---|
| None |

| Fairs Cup (1858-1971) / UEFA Cup (1972-2009) / UEFA Europa League (2010-2023) |
|---|
| None |

| UEFA Europa Conference League (2021-2023) |
|---|
| None |

| UEFA Super Cup (1972-2022) |
|---|
| None |

| *European Cup Winners' Cup 1961-1999** |
|---|
| None |

*defunct competition

# NATIONAL COMPETITIONS
## TABLE OF HONOURS

| | CHAMPIONS | CUP WINNERS | BEST GOALSCORERS | |
|---|---|---|---|---|
| 1905/1906 | Ethnikos GS Athína | - | - | |
| 1906/1907 | Ethnikos GS Athína | - | - | |
| 1907/1908 | FC Goudi Athína | - | - | |
| 1908/1909 | Peiraikos Syndesmos | - | - | |
| 1909/1910 | FC Goudi Athína | - | - | |
| 1910/1911 | Podosferikos Omilos Athinon | - | - | |
| 1911/1912 | FC Goudi Athína | - | - | |
| 1912/1913 | *No competition* | - | - | |
| 1913/1914 | *No competition* | - | - | |
| 1914/1915 | *No competition* | - | - | |
| 1915/1916 | *No competition* | - | - | |
| 1916/1917 | *Championship not finished* | - | - | |
| 1917/1918 | *No competition* | - | - | |
| 1918/1919 | *No competition* | - | - | |
| 1919/1920 | *No competition* | - | - | |
| 1920/1921 | *No competition* | - | - | |
| 1921/1922 | Panellinios Podosferikos Omilos | - | - | |
| 1922/1923 | Peiraikos Syndesmos | - | - | |
| 1923/1924 | Apollonas Athína (Athína champions) APS Peiraiás (Athína/Peiraiás champions) Aris Thessaloníki (Thessaloníki champions) | - | - | |
| 1924/1925 | PAE Panathinaïkos Athína (Athína champions) Olympiacos SFP Peiraiás (Athína/Peiraiás champions) | - | - | |
| 1925/1926 | PAE Panathinaïkos Athína (Athína champions) Olympiacos SFP Peiraiás (Athína/Peiraiás champions) Aris Thessaloníki (Thessaloníki champions) | - | - | |
| 1926/1927 | PAE Panathinaïkos Athína (Athína champions) Olympiacos SFP Peiraiás (Athína/Peiraiás champions) Iraklis Thessaloníki (Thessaloníki champions) | - | - | |
| 1927/1928 | Aris Thessaloníki | - | - | |
| 1928/1929 | *No competition* | - | - | |
| 1929/1930 | PAE Panathinaïkos Athína | - | - | |
| 1930/1931 | Olympiacos SFP Peiraiás | - | - | |
| 1931/1932 | Aris Thessaloníki | AEK Athína | - | |
| 1932/1933 | Olympiacos SFP Peiraiás | Ethnikos Peiraiás | - | |
| 1933/1934 | Olympiacos SFP Peiraiás | *No competition* | - | |
| 1934/1935 | *Championship not finished* | *No competition* | - | |
| 1935/1936 | Olympiacos SFP Peiraiás | *No competition* | - | |
| 1936/1937 | Olympiacos SFP Peiraiás | *No competition* | - | |
| 1937/1938 | Olympiacos SFP Peiraiás | *No competition* | - | |
| 1938/1939 | AEK Athína | AEK Athína | - | |
| 1939/1940 | AEK Athína | PAE Panathinaïkos Athína | - | |
| 1940/1941 | *Championship not finished* | *No competition* | - | |
| 1941/1942 | *No competition* | *No competition* | - | |
| 1942/1943 | *Championship not finished* | *No competition* | - | |
| 1943/1944 | *No competition* | *No competition* | - | |
| 1944/1945 | *No competition* | *No competition* | - | |
| 1945/1946 | Aris Thessaloníki | *No competition* | - | |
| 1946/1947 | Olympiacos SFP Peiraiás | Olympiacos SFP Peiraiás | - | |
| 1947/1948 | Olympiacos SFP Peiraiás | PAE Panathinaïkos Athína | - | |
| 1948/1949 | PAE Panathinaïkos Athína | AEK Athína | - | |
| 1949/1950 | *No competition* | AEK Athína | - | |
| 1950/1951 | Olympiacos SFP Peiraiás | Olympiacos SFP Peiraiás | - | |
| 1951/1952 | *No competition* | Olympiacos SFP Peiraiás | - | |
| 1952/1953 | PAE Panathinaïkos Athína | Olympiacos SFP Peiraiás | - | |
| 1953/1954 | Olympiacos SFP Peiraiás | Olympiacos SFP Peiraiás | - | |
| 1954/1955 | Olympiacos SFP Peiraiás | PAE Panathinaïkos Athína | - | |
| 1955/1956 | Olympiacos SFP Peiraiás | AEK Athína | - | |
| 1956/1957 | Olympiacos SFP Peiraiás | Olympiacos SFP Peiraiás | - | |
| 1957/1958 | Olympiacos SFP Peiraiás | Olympiacos SFP Peiraiás | - | |
| 1958/1959 | Olympiacos SFP Peiraiás | Olympiacos SFP Peiraiás | - | |
| 1959/1960 | PAE Panathinaïkos Athína | Olympiacos SFP Peiraiás | Konstantinos Nestoridis (AEK Athína) | 30 |
| 1960/1961 | PAE Panathinaïkos Athína | Olympiacos SFP Peiraiás | Konstantinos Nestoridis (AEK Athína) | 27 |
| 1961/1962 | PAE Panathinaïkos Athína | *Final abandoned, no winner* | Konstantinos Nestoridis (AEK Athína) | 29 |
| 1962/1963 | AEK Athína | Olympiacos SFP Peiraiás | Konstantinos Nestoridis (AEK Athína) | 23 |
| 1963/1964 | PAE Panathinaïkos Athína | AEK Athína | Dimitrios Papaioannou (AEK Athína) | 29 |
| 1964/1965 | PAE Panathinaïkos Athína | Olympiacos SFP Peiraiás | Giorgos Sideris (Olympiacos SFP Peiraiás) | 29 |
| 1965/1966 | Olympiacos SFP Peiraiás | AEK Athína | Dimitrios Papaioannou (AEK Athína) | 23 |
| 1966/1967 | Olympiacos SFP Peiraiás | PAE Panathinaïkos Athína | Giorgos Sideris (Olympiacos SFP Peiraiás) | 24 |

| | | | |
|---|---|---|---|
| 1967/1968 | AEK Athína | Olympiacos SFP Peiraiás | Thanasis Intzoglou (Panionios GSS Athína) | 24 |
| 1968/1969 | PAE Panathinaïkos Athína | PAE Panathinaïkos Athína | Giorgos Sideris (Olympiacos SFP Peiraiás) | 35 |
| 1969/1970 | PAE Panathinaïkos Athína | Aris Thessaloníki | Antonis Antoniadis (PAE Panathinaïkos Athína) | 25 |
| 1970/1971 | AEK Athína | Olympiacos SFP Peiraiás | Giorgos Dedes (Panionios GSS Athína) | 28 |
| 1971/1972 | PAE Panathinaïkos Athína | PAOK Thessaloníki | Antonis Antoniadis (PAE Panathinaïkos Athína) | 39 |
| 1972/1973 | Olympiacos SFP Peiraiás | Olympiacos SFP Peiraiás | Antonis Antoniadis (PAE Panathinaïkos Athína) | 22 |
| 1973/1974 | Olympiacos SFP Peiraiás | PAOK Thessaloníki | Antonis Antoniadis (PAE Panathinaïkos Athína) | 26 |
| 1974/1975 | Olympiacos SFP Peiraiás | Olympiacos SFP Peiraiás | Antonis Antoniadis (PAE Panathinaïkos Athína) Roberto Calcadera (URU, Ethnikos Peiraiás) | 20 |
| 1975/1976 | PAOK Thessaloníki | Iraklis Thessaloníki | Giorgos Dedes (AEK Athína) | 15 |
| 1976/1977 | PAE Panathinaïkos Athína | PAE Panathinaïkos Athína | Thanasis Intzoglou (Ethnikos Peiraiás) Dimitrios Papadopoulos (OFI Heraklion) | 22 |
| 1977/1978 | AEK Athína | AEK Athína | Thomas Mavros (AEK Athína) | 22 |
| 1978/1979 | AEK Athína | Panionios GSS Athína | Thomas Mavros (AEK Athína) | 31 |
| 1979/1980 | Olympiacos SFP Peiraiás | AGSK Kastoria | Dušan Bajević (YUG, AEK Athína) | 25 |
| 1980/1981 | Olympiacos SFP Peiraiás | Olympiacos SFP Peiraiás | Dinos Kouis (Aris Thessaloníki) | 21 |
| 1981/1982 | Olympiacos SFP Peiraiás | PAE Panathinaïkos Athína | Grigoris Charalampidis (PAE Panathinaïkos Athína) | 21 |
| 1982/1983 | Olympiacos SFP Peiraiás | AEK Athína | Nikolaos Anastopoulos (Olympiacos SFP Peiraiás) | 29 |
| 1983/1984 | PAE Panathinaïkos Athína | PAE Panathinaïkos Athína | Nikolaos Anastopoulos (Olympiacos SFP Peiraiás) | 18 |
| 1984/1985 | PAOK Thessaloníki | AE Lárissa | Thomas Mavros (AEK Athína) | 27 |
| 1985/1986 | PAE Panathinaïkos Athína | PAE Panathinaïkos Athína | Nikolaos Anastopoulos (Olympiacos SFP Peiraiás) | 19 |
| 1986/1987 | Olympiacos SFP Peiraiás | OFI Heraklion | Nikolaos Anastopoulos (Olympiacos SFP Peiraiás) | 16 |
| 1987/1988 | AE Lárissa | PAE Panathinaïkos Athína | Henrik Nielsen (DEN, AEK Athína) | 20 |
| 1988/1989 | AEK Athína | PAE Panathinaïkos Athína | Imre Boda (HUN, Olympiakos Vólos) | 20 |
| 1989/1990 | PAE Panathinaïkos Athína | Olympiacos SFP Peiraiás | Thomas Mavros (Panionios GSS Athína) | 22 |
| 1990/1991 | PAE Panathinaïkos Athína | PAE Panathinaïkos Athína | Dimitrios Saravakos (PAE Panathinaïkos Athína) | 23 |
| 1991/1992 | AEK Athína | Olympiacos SFP Peiraiás | Vasilios Dimitriadis (AEK Athína) | 28 |
| 1992/1993 | AEK Athína | PAE Panathinaïkos Athína | Vasilios Dimitriadis (AEK Athína) | 33 |
| 1993/1994 | AEK Athína | PAE Panathinaïkos Athína | Alexandros Alexandris (AEK Athína) Krzysztof Warzycha (POL, PAE Panathinaïkos Athína) | 24 |
| 1994/1995 | PAE Panathinaïkos Athína | PAE Panathinaïkos Athína | Krzysztof Warzycha (POL, PAE Panathinaïkos Athína) | 29 |
| 1995/1996 | PAE Panathinaïkos Athína | AEK Athína | Vassilis Tsiartas (AEK Athína) | 26 |
| 1996/1997 | Olympiacos SFP Peiraiás | AEK Athína | Alexandros Alexandris (Olympiacos SFP Peiraiás) | 23 |
| 1997/1998 | Olympiacos SFP Peiraiás | Panionios GSS Athína | Krzysztof Warzycha (POL, PAE Panathinaïkos Athína) | 32 |
| 1998/1999 | Olympiacos SFP Peiraiás | Olympiacos SFP Peiraiás | Themistoklis Nikolaidis (AEK Athína) | 22 |
| 1999/2000 | Olympiacos SFP Peiraiás | AEK Athína | Dimitrios Nalitzis (Panionios, PAOK Thessaloníki) | 24 |
| 2000/2001 | Olympiacos SFP Peiraiás | PAOK Thessaloníki | Alexandros Alexandris (Olympiacos SFP Peiraiás) | 19 |
| 2001/2002 | Olympiacos SFP Peiraiás | AEK Athína | Alexandros Alexandris (Olympiacos SFP Peiraiás) | 19 |
| 2002/2003 | Olympiacos SFP Peiraiás | PAOK Thessaloníki | Nikolaos Liberopoulos (PAE Panathinaïkos Athína) | 16 |
| 2003/2004 | PAE Panathinaïkos Athína | PAE Panathinaïkos Athína | Giovanni Silva de Oliveira (BRA, Olympiacos SFP Peiraiás) | 21 |
| 2004/2005 | Olympiacos SFP Peiraiás | Olympiacos SFP Peiraiás | Theofanis Gekas (PAE Panathinaïkos Athína) | 18 |
| 2005/2006 | Olympiacos SFP Peiraiás | Olympiacos SFP Peiraiás | Dimitrios Salpingidis (PAOK Thessaloníki) | 17 |
| 2006/2007 | Olympiacos SFP Peiraiás | AE Lárissa | Nikolaos Liberopoulos (AEK Athína) | 18 |
| 2007/2008 | Olympiacos SFP Peiraiás | Olympiacos SFP Peiraiás | Ismael Alfonso Blanco (ARG, AEK Athína) | 19 |
| 2008/2009 | Olympiacos SFP Peiraiás | Olympiacos SFP Peiraiás | Ismael Alfonso Blanco (ARG, AEK Athína) Luciano Martín Galletti (ARG, Olympiacos SFP Peiraiás) | 14 |
| 2009/2010 | PAE Panathinaïkos Athína | PAE Panathinaïkos Athína | Djibril Cissé (FRA, PAE Panathinaïkos Athína) | 23 |
| 2010/2011 | Olympiacos SFP Peiraiás | AEK Athína | Djibril Cissé (FRA, PAE Panathinaïkos Athína) | 20 |
| 2011/2012 | Olympiacos SFP Peiraiás | Olympiacos SFP Peiraiás | Kevin Antonio Joel Gislain Mirallas y Castillo (BEL, Olympiacos SFP Peiraiás) | 22 |
| 2012/2013 | Olympiacos SFP Peiraiás | Olympiacos SFP Peiraiás | Rafik Djebbour (ALG, Olympiacos SFP Peiraiás) | 20 |
| 2013/2014 | Olympiacos SFP Peiraiás | PAE Panathinaïkos Athína | Esteban Andrés Solari Poggio (ARG, Skoda Xanthi AC) | 16 |
| 2014/2015 | Olympiacos SFP Peiraiás | Olympiacos SFP Peiraiás | Jerónimo Barrales (ARG, AGS Asteras Tripoli) | 17 |
| 2015/2016 | Olympiacos SFP Peiraiás | AEK Athína | Konstantinos Fortounis (Olympiacos SFP Peiraiás) | 18 |
| 2016/2017 | Olympiacos SFP Peiraiás | PAOK Thessaloníki | Bengt Erik Markus Berg (SWE, PAE Panathinaïkos Athína) | 22 |
| 2017/2018 | AEK Athína | PAOK Thessaloníki | Aleksandar Prijović (SRB, PAOK Thessaloníki) | 19 |
| 2018/2019 | PAOK Thessaloníki | PAOK Thessaloníki | Efthymis Koulouris (APS Atromitos Athína) | 19 |
| 2019/2020 | Olympiacos SFP Peiraiás | Olympiacos SFP Peiraiás | Youssef El-Arabi (MAR, Olympiacos SFP Peiraiás) | 20 |
| 2020/2021 | Olympiacos SFP Peiraiás | PAOK Thessaloníki | Youssef El-Arabi (MAR, Olympiacos SFP Peiraiás) | 22 |
| 2021/2022 | Olympiacos SFP Peiraiás | PAE Panathinaïkos Athína | Tom van Weert (NED, Vólos NPS) | 17 |
| 2022/2023 | AEK Athína | AEK Athína | Cédric Bakambu (COD, Olympiacos SFP Peiraiás) | 18 |

# NATIONAL CHAMPIONSHIP
## Super League 1 2022/2023
### (19.08.2022 – 14.05.2023)

**Regular Season - Results**

**Round 1 [19-21.08.2022]**
Vólos - Asteras Tripolis 3-3(1-1)
Atromitos - OFI Heraklion 3-1(2-1)
Lamia - AEK Athína 0-3(0-1)
PAOK Thessaloníki - Panetolikos 1-0(1-0)
Panathinaïkos - Ionikos Nikaia 1-0(1-0)
Aris Thessaloníki - Levadiakos 3-0(2-0)
Olympiacos - PAS Giannina 2-0(0-0)

**Round 2 [26-29.08.2022]**
Ionikos Nikaia - Levadiakos 0-0
PAS Giannina - Lamia 1-1(1-0)
AEK Athína - Vólos 0-1(0-1)
Panetolikos - Aris Thessaloníki 3-1(1-1)
OFI Heraklion - Panathinaïkos 0-2(0-2)
PAOK Thessaloníki - Atromitos 2-1(1-0)
Asteras Tripolis - Olympiacos 0-0

**Round 3 [03-04.09.2022]**
Lamia - Asteras Tripolis 0-0
Olympiacos - Ionikos Nikaia 3-1(2-0)
Panathinaïkos - Levadiakos 1-0(1-0)
Atromitos - Panetolikos 1-1(0-1)
Vólos - OFI Heraklion 0-1(0-1)
AEK Athína - PAS Giannina 2-0(1-0)
Aris Thessaloníki - PAOK Thessaloníki 0-0

**Round 4 [10-12.09.2022]**
OFI Heraklion - Panetolikos 1-2(1-1)
PAS Giannina - Levadiakos 2-1(1-1)
Ionikos Nikaia - Atromitos 1-4(1-0)
Olympiacos - Vólos 1-1(0-1)
Asteras Tripolis - Aris Thessaloníki 0-2(0-1)
Panathinaïkos - AEK Athína 2-1(2-1)
PAOK Thessaloníki - Lamia 1-0(1-0)

**Round 5 [17-18.09.2022]**
Atromitos - Lamia 0-0
Panetolikos - AEK Athína 0-2(0-0)
Panathinaïkos - PAS Giannina 3-0(1-0)
Levadiakos - Asteras Tripolis 1-1(0-0)
OFI Heraklion - PAOK Thessaloníki 1-1(0-1)
Aris Thessaloníki - Olympiacos 2-1(0-1)
Vólos - Ionikos Nikaia 2-0(1-0)

**Round 6 [01-03.10.2022]**
Lamia - Levadiakos 1-0(0-0)
Asteras Tripolis - OFI Heraklion 2-0(2-0)
Olympiacos - Atromitos 2-0(1-0)
Vólos - Aris Thessaloníki 2-0(2-0)
PAOK Thessaloníki - Panathinaïkos 1-2(1-0)
PAS Giannina - Panetolikos 1-4(1-2)
AEK Athína - Ionikos Nikaia 4-1(2-0)

**Round 7 [08-10.10.2022]**
Panetolikos - Vólos 2-3(2-2)
Ionikos Nikaia - Lamia 1-1(0-1)
OFI Heraklion - Olympiacos 1-2(1-0)
Levadiakos - PAOK Thessaloníki 1-1(0-0)
Panathinaïkos - Asteras Tripolis 1-0(0-0)
Aris Thessaloníki - AEK Athína 0-2(0-1)
Atromitos - PAS Giannina 2-1(0-0)

**Round 8 [15-17.10.2022]**
Vólos - Levadiakos 2-1(0-0)
Aris Thessaloníki - Ionikos Nikaia 2-1(0-1)
AEK Athína - Atromitos 1-0(0-0)
PAS Giannina - OFI Heraklion 2-2(1-0)
Lamia - Panathinaïkos 0-2(0-1)
Asteras Tripolis - Panetolikos 0-0
Olympiacos - PAOK Thessaloníki 1-2(1-1)

**Round 9 [22-24.10.2022]**
Atromitos - Vólos 0-2(0-1)
Panetolikos - Olympiacos 0-2(0-0)
Ionikos Nikaia - PAS Giannina 2-2(2-0)
Panathinaïkos - Aris Thessaloníki 1-0(0-0)
PAOK Thessaloníki-Asteras Tripolis 2-2(0-1)
Levadiakos - AEK Athína 0-2(0-0)
OFI Heraklion - Lamia 0-0

**Round 10 [29-31.10.2022]**
Ionikos Nikaia - Panetolikos 1-1(1-1)
Vólos - Panathinaïkos 1-5(0-2)
Olympiacos - Lamia 2-0(2-0)
Levadiakos - Atromitos 2-1(1-0)
AEK Athína - PAOK Thessaloníki 2-0(1-0)
Aris Thessaloníki - OFI Heraklion 1-1(0-0)
PAS Giannina - Asteras Tripolis 2-1(0-0)

**Round 11 [05-06.11.2022]**
Lamia - Vólos 2-2(2-1)
OFI Heraklion - Ionikos Nikaia 0-2(0-0)
Atromitos - Aris Thessaloníki 0-0
PAOK Thessaloníki - PAS Giannina 2-0(2-0)
Panetolikos - Levadiakos 0-0
Panathinaïkos - Olympiacos 1-1(0-0)
Asteras Tripolis - AEK Athína 1-1(0-0)

**Round 12 [08-10.11.2022]**
Aris Thessaloníki - Lamia 5-0(3-0)
Panetolikos - Panathinaïkos 0-1(0-0)
Atromitos - Asteras Tripolis 2-0(2-0)
AEK Athína - OFI Heraklion 3-0(2-0)
Levadiakos - Olympiacos 0-1(0-1)
Vólos - PAS Giannina 2-1(0-0)
Ionikos Nikaia - PAOK Thessaloníki 0-3(0-2)

**Round 13 [13-14.11.2022]**
PAS Giannina - Aris Thessaloníki 0-4(0-0)
Panathinaïkos - Atromitos 2-0(0-0)
Lamia - Panetolikos 1-3(1-2)
Olympiacos - AEK Athína 0-0
PAOK Thessaloníki - Vólos 3-0(2-0)
Asteras Tripolis - Ionikos Nikaia 1-0(1-0)
OFI Heraklion - Levadiakos 2-1(0-1)

**Round 14 [21-22.12.2022]**
Levadiakos - Aris Thessaloníki 1-1(1-0)
AEK Athína - Lamia 3-0(0-0)
Asteras Tripolis - Vólos 0-0
PAS Giannina - Olympiacos 2-2(0-2)
Ionikos Nikaia - Panathinaïkos 1-1(0-1)
OFI Heraklion - Atromitos 0-1(0-1)
Panetolikos - PAOK Thessaloníki 0-2(0-1)

**Round 15 [28-29.12.2022]**
Levadiakos - Ionikos Nikaia 1-0(1-0)
Olympiacos - Asteras Tripolis 5-0(2-0)
Vólos - AEK Athína 0-4(0-3)
Atromitos - PAOK Thessaloníki 1-1(0-1)
Panathinaïkos - OFI Heraklion 1-1(0-0)
Aris Thessaloníki - Panetolikos 1-0(0-0)
Lamia - PAS Giannina 1-1(0-0)

**Round 16 [03-04.01.2023]**
OFI Heraklion - Vólos 0-0
Levadiakos - Panathinaïkos 0-1(0-1)
PAS Giannina - AEK Athína 2-1(2-0)
Ionikos Nikaia - Olympiacos 0-2(0-2)
Asteras Tripolis - Lamia 3-0(3-0)
Panetolikos - Atromitos 2-0(0-0)
PAOK Thessaloníki - Aris Thessal. 1-0(1-0)

**Round 17 [07-09.01.2023]**
Levadiakos - PAS Giannina 1-3(0-1)
Lamia - PAOK Thessaloníki 0-3(0-2)
Vólos - Olympiacos 0-4(0-3)
Atromitos - Ionikos Nikaia 2-0(1-0)
Aris Thessaloníki - Asteras Tripolis 3-0(2-0)
AEK Athína - Panathinaïkos 1-0(0-0)
Panetolikos - OFI Heraklion 0-4(0-1)

**Round 18 [14-16.01.2023]**
Lamia - Atromitos 1-1(0-1)
PAOK Thessaloníki - OFI Heraklion 0-0
AEK Athína - Panetolikos 4-1(2-1)
Asteras Tripolis - Levadiakos 0-0
Olympiacos - Aris Thessaloníki 1-0(0-0)
PAS Giannina - Panathinaïkos 0-1(0-0)
Ionikos Nikaia - Vólos 0-1(0-0)

**Round 19 [20-22.01.2023]**
Panetolikos - PAS Giannina 1-1(0-0)
OFI Heraklion - Asteras Tripolis 1-0(0-0)
Aris Thessaloníki - Vólos 3-0(0-0)
Ionikos Nikaia - AEK Athína 1-2(1-0)
Levadiakos - Lamia 0-0
Panathinaïkos - PAOK Thessaloníki 0-3(0-1)
Atromitos - Olympiacos 1-1(0-0)

**Round 20 [28-30.01.2023]**
Vólos - Panetolikos 2-3(1-1)
PAS Giannina - Atromitos 1-1(1-0)
Olympiacos - OFI Heraklion 2-1(1-1)
AEK Athína - Aris Thessaloníki 3-0(1-0)
PAOK Thessaloníki - Levadiakos 3-2(2-1)
Lamia - Ionikos Nikaia 0-2(0-2)
Asteras Tripolis - Panathinaïkos 1-0(0-0)

**Round 21 [04-06.02.2023]**
OFI Heraklion - PAS Giannina 0-0
Ionikos Nikaia - Aris Thessaloníki 1-0(0-0)
Panathinaïkos - Lamia 2-0(1-0)
Panetolikos - Asteras Tripolis 0-0
PAOK Thessaloníki - Olympiacos 0-0
Levadiakos - Vólos 0-3(0-0)
Atromitos - AEK Athína 0-1(0-1)[08.03.2023]

**Round 22 [11-13.02.2023]**
PAS Giannina - Ionikos Nikaia 0-0
Vólos - Atromitos 2-1(0-0)
Aris Thessaloníki - Panathinaïkos 1-2(1-1)
Lamia - OFI Heraklion 1-4(0-2)
Asteras Tripolis-PAOK Thessaloníki 2-2(0-1)
AEK Athína - Levadiakos 3-0(2-0)
Olympiacos - Panetolikos 6-1(2-0)

**Round 23 [18-20.02.2023]**
Panathinaïkos - Vólos 2-0(0-0)
Asteras Tripolis - PAS Giannina 1-1(1-1)
Lamia - Olympiacos 0-3(0-1)
Panetolikos - Ionikos Nikaia 1-0(0-0)
PAOK Thessaloníki - AEK Athína 2-0(1-0)
Atromitos - Levadiakos 1-0(1-0)
OFI Heraklion - Aris Thessaloníki 0-3(0-2)

**Round 24 [24-26.02.2023]**
Vólos - Lamia 1-1(0-1)
AEK Athína - Asteras Tripolis 2-0(1-0)
PAS Giannina - PAOK Thessaloníki 0-0
Olympiacos - Panathinaïkos 0-0
Ionikos Nikaia - OFI Heraklion 0-2(0-0)
Levadiakos - Panetolikos 0-0
Aris Thessaloníki - Atromitos 2-1(2-0)

**Round 25 [04-06.03.2023]**
Asteras Tripolis - Atromitos 1-1(0-1)
Olympiacos - Levadiakos 6-0(2-0)
PAS Giannina - Vólos 0-1(0-0)
Lamia - Aris Thessaloníki 2-1(2-1)
OFI Heraklion - AEK Athína 0-3(0-1)
PAOK Thessaloníki - Ionikos Nikaia 6-0(4-0)
Panathinaïkos - Panetolikos 2-0(0-0)

**Round 26 [12.03.2023]**
AEK Athína - Olympiacos 1-3(0-0)
Aris Thessaloníki - PAS Giannina 3-1(2-1)
Atromitos - Panathinaïkos 0-2(0-0)
Ionikos Nikaia - Asteras Tripolis 1-0(1-0)
Levadiakos - OFI Heraklion 2-0(2-0)
Panetolikos - Lamia 1-1(0-0)
Vólos - PAOK Thessaloníki 0-1(0-1)

## Final Standings

| | | | | | | | | | | |
|---|---|---|---|---|---|---|---|---|---|---|
| 1. | PAE Panathinaïkos Athína | 26 | 19 | 4 | 3 | 38 | - | 12 | 61 |
| 2. | AEK Athína | 26 | 19 | 2 | 5 | 51 | - | 14 | 59 |
| 3. | Olympiacos SFP Peiraiás | 26 | 16 | 8 | 2 | 53 | - | 14 | 56 |
| 4. | PAOK Thessaloníki | 26 | 15 | 9 | 2 | 43 | - | 15 | 54 |
| 5. | Aris Thessaloníki | 26 | 12 | 4 | 10 | 38 | - | 24 | 40 |
| 6. | Vólos NPS | 26 | 11 | 6 | 9 | 31 | - | 38 | 39 |
| 7. | Panetolikos GPS Agrinio | 26 | 7 | 8 | 11 | 26 | - | 38 | 29 |
| 8. | APS Atromitos Athína | 26 | 7 | 8 | 11 | 25 | - | 29 | 29 |
| 9. | OFI Heraklion | 26 | 6 | 8 | 12 | 23 | - | 34 | 26 |
| 10. | AGS Asteras Tripolis | 26 | 4 | 13 | 9 | 19 | - | 30 | 25 |
| 11. | PAS Giannina | 26 | 4 | 11 | 11 | 24 | - | 41 | 23 |
| 12. | PAE Ionikos Nikaia | 26 | 4 | 6 | 16 | 16 | - | 42 | 18 |
| 13. | PAS Lamia | 26 | 2 | 11 | 13 | 13 | - | 45 | 17 |
| 14. | PAE Levadiakos Livadeia | 26 | 3 | 8 | 15 | 14 | - | 38 | 17 |

Teams ranked 1-6 were qualified for the Championship Round, while teams ranked 7-14 were qualified for the Relegation Round.

## Relegation Round

### Results

**Round 27 [18.03.2023]**
Asteras Tripolis - Panetolikos 2-1(1-0)
OFI Heraklion - Levadiakos 1-1(0-0)
Atromitos - Ionikos Nikaia 2-0(1-0)
Lamia - PAS Giannina 2-0(2-0)

**Round 28 [01.04.2023]**
Levadiakos - Atromitos 1-1(0-0)
Panetolikos - Lamia 1-3(0-0)
PAS Giannina - OFI Heraklion 0-1(0-1)
Ionikos Nikaia - Asteras Tripolis 1-0(1-0)

**Round 29 [08.04.2023]**
Atromitos - PAS Giannina 1-1(1-1)
OFI Heraklion - Lamia 4-1(2-1)
Asteras Tripolis - Levadiakos 0-1(0-1)
Panetolikos - Ionikos Nikaia 0-1(0-1)

**Round 30 [22.04.2023]**
Levadiakos - Ionikos Nikaia 2-2(0-1)
OFI Heraklion - Asteras Tripolis 1-1(1-1)
PAS Giannina - Panetolikos 3-2(1-1)
Lamia - Atromitos 1-0(0-0)

**Round 31 [29.04.2023]**
Asteras Tripolis - Lamia 0-0
Atromitos - OFI Heraklion 2-3(2-2)
Ionikos Nikaia - PAS Giannina 0-1(0-0)
Panetolikos - Levadiakos 2-2(0-2)

**Round 32 [06.05.2023]**
Atromitos - Panetolikos 2-0(1-0)
OFI Heraklion - Ionikos Nikaia 2-2(1-1)
PAS Giannina - Asteras Tripolis 1-0(0-0)
Lamia - Levadiakos 1-1(0-1)

**Round 33 [13.05.2023]**
Panetolikos - OFI Heraklion 0-2(0-0)
Asteras Tripolis - Atromitos 1-1(1-0)
Ionikos Nikaia - Lamia 2-2(2-0)
Levadiakos - PAS Giannina 3-3(2-2)

### Final Standings

| | | Total | | | | | | | | Home | | | | | | | Away | | | | | |
|---|---|---|---|---|---|---|---|---|---|---|---|---|---|---|---|---|---|---|---|---|---|---|---|
| 7. | OFI Heraklion | 33 | 10 | 11 | 12 | 37 | - | 41 | 41 | 3 | 7 | 7 | 14 | - | 22 | 7 | 4 | 5 | 23 | - | 19 |
| 8. | APS Atromitos Athína | 33 | 9 | 11 | 13 | 34 | - | 36 | 38 | 7 | 6 | 4 | 20 | - | 14 | 2 | 5 | 9 | 14 | - | 22 |
| 9. | PAS Giannina | 33 | 7 | 13 | 13 | 33 | - | 50 | 34 | 5 | 6 | 5 | 17 | - | 22 | 2 | 7 | 8 | 16 | - | 28 |
| 10. | AGS Asteras Tripolis | 33 | 5 | 16 | 12 | 23 | - | 36 | 31 | 5 | 10 | 2 | 15 | - | 10 | 0 | 6 | 10 | 8 | - | 26 |
| 11. | Panetolikos GPS Agrinio | 33 | 7 | 9 | 17 | 32 | - | 53 | 30 | 3 | 5 | 9 | 13 | - | 25 | 4 | 4 | 8 | 19 | - | 28 |
| 12. | PAS Lamia | 33 | 5 | 14 | 14 | 23 | - | 53 | 29 | 4 | 5 | 7 | 13 | - | 26 | 1 | 9 | 7 | 10 | - | 27 |
| 13. | PAE Ionikos Nikaia (Relegated) | 33 | 6 | 9 | 18 | 24 | - | 51 | 27 | 3 | 6 | 7 | 12 | - | 22 | 3 | 3 | 11 | 12 | - | 29 |
| 14. | PAE Levadiakos Livadeia (Relegated) | 33 | 4 | 14 | 15 | 25 | - | 48 | 26 | 3 | 8 | 5 | 15 | - | 20 | 1 | 6 | 10 | 10 | - | 28 |

## Championship Round

### Results

**Round 27 [19.03.2023]**
Vólos - Olympiacos 0-3(0-2)
Aris Thessal. - PAOK Thessaloníki 1-2(1-0)
AEK Athína - Panathinaïkos 0-0

**Round 28 [02.04.2023]**
Panathinaïkos - Vólos 0-0
PAOK Thessaloníki - AEK Athína 0-1(0-0)
Olympiacos - Aris Thessaloníki 2-2(1-0)

**Round 29 [05.04.2023]**
Vólos - AEK Athína 0-1(0-1)
Aris Thessaloníki - Panathinaïkos 0-1(0-0)
Olympiacos - PAOK Thessaloníki 3-1(0-1)

**Round 30 [09.04.2023]**
AEK Athína - Aris Thessaloníki 3-1(1-1)
PAOK Thessaloníki - Vólos 4-2(4-0)

**Round 31 [23.04.2023]**
Vólos - Aris Thessaloníki 0-3(0-1)
PAOK Thessaloníki - Panathinaïkos 1-2(0-1)

**Round 32 [26.04.2023]**
Vólos - Panathinaïkos 0-2(0-0)
Aris Thessaloníki - Olympiacos 2-1(1-0)

| Panathinaïkos - Olympiacos 2-0(2-0) | Olympiacos - AEK Athína 1-3(0-1) | AEK Athína - PAOK Thessaloníki 4-0(2-0) |
|---|---|---|

**Round 33** [30.04.2023]
Olympiacos - Vólos 5-0(3-0)
Panathinaïkos - AEK Athína 0-0
PAOK Thessaloníki - Aris Thessal. 3-2(0-1)

**Round 34** [03.05.2023]
AEK Athína - Olympiacos 0-0
Aris Thessaloníki - Vólos 4-2(2-0)
Panathinaïkos - PAOK Thessaloníki 1-1(1-0)

**Round 35** [08.05.2023]
Aris Thessaloníki - AEK Athína 1-2(1-2)
Vólos - PAOK Thessaloníki 0-2(0-1)
Olympiacos - Panathinaïkos 1-0(0-0)

**Round 36** [14.05.2023]
AEK Athína - Vólos 4-0(2-0)
Panathinaïkos - Aris Thessaloníki 1-1(1-1)
PAOK Thessaloníki - Olympiacos 0-1(0-1)

## Final Standings

| | | Total | | | | | | Home | | | | | Away | | | |
|---|---|---|---|---|---|---|---|---|---|---|---|---|---|---|---|---|---|
| 1. | **AEK Athína** | 36 | 26 | 5 | 5 | 69 - 17 | **83** | 14 | 2 | 2 | 40 - 7 | 12 | 3 | 3 | 29 - 10 |
| 2. | PAE Panathinaïkos Athína | 36 | 23 | 9 | 4 | 47 - 16 | **78** | 11 | 6 | 1 | 23 - 8 | 12 | 3 | 3 | 24 - 8 |
| 3. | Olympiacos SFP Peiraiás | 36 | 21 | 10 | 5 | 70 - 24 | **73** | 12 | 4 | 2 | 43 - 12 | 9 | 6 | 3 | 27 - 12 |
| 4. | PAOK Thessaloníki | 36 | 19 | 10 | 7 | 57 - 32 | **67** | 11 | 3 | 4 | 32 - 15 | 8 | 7 | 3 | 25 - 17 |
| 5. | Aris Thessaloníki | 36 | 15 | 6 | 15 | 55 - 41 | **51** | 11 | 2 | 5 | 34 - 17 | 4 | 4 | 10 | 21 - 24 |
| 6. | Vólos NPS | 36 | 11 | 7 | 18 | 35 - 66 | **40** | 5 | 2 | 11 | 17 - 36 | 6 | 5 | 7 | 18 - 30 |

**Top goalscorers:**

| | | |
|---|---|---|
| 18 | **Cédric Bakambu (COD)** | *Olympiacos SFP Peiraiás* |
| 14 | Levi Samuel García (TRI) | *AEK Athína* |
| 13 | Nikolaos Karelis | *Panetolikos GPS Agrinio* |

# NATIONAL CUP
## Greek Football Cup - Kypello Elladas 2022/2023

### Fifth Round [18-20.10.2022]

| | | | | |
|---|---|---|---|---|
| Vólos NPS - PAE Ionikos Nikaia | 4-0(2-0) | AGS Asteras Tripolis - APS Atromitos Athína | 1-3(0-0,0-0) |
| PS Kalamata - Panetolikos GPS Agrinio | 2-2 aet; 4-3 pen | AE Kifisia - OFI Heraklion | 1-0(0-0) |
| PAE Athens Kallithea - Veria FC | 1-0(1-0) | AO Agios Nikolaos - Almyros Gaziou | 2-0(1-0) |
| Panserraikós Serres - Panahaiki PAE Patras | 5-2(1-0,2-2) | Ionikos Ionias - PS Apollon Paralimnio | 0-4(0-2) |
| APO Almopos Arideas - PAS Lamia | 0-2(0-1) | Panelefsiniakos AO Elefsinas - PAE Apollon Póntou | 1-3(1-1) |
| AE Lárissa - PAE Levadiakos Livadeia | 1-2(1-2) | AEK Athína - PAS Giannina | 2-0(1-0) |

### 1/8-Finals [14-16.12.2022/10-12.01.2023]

| First Leg | | Second Leg | |
|---|---|---|---|
| PS Apollon Paralimnio - AO Agios Nikolaos | 2-2(1-1) | AO Agios Nikolaos - PS Apollon Paralimnio | 1-2(1-1,1-1) |
| PS Kalamata - PAOK Thessaloníki | 0-2(0-1) | PAOK Thessaloníki - PS Kalamata | 2-0(2-0) |
| PAS Lamia - PAE Athens Kallithea | 1-1(0-0) | PAE Athens Kallithea - PAS Lamia | 1-2(1-2) |
| PAE Panathinaïkos Athína - Vólos NPS | 3-0(1-0) | Vólos NPS - PAE Panathinaïkos Athína | 0-2(0-1) |
| Olympiacos SFP Peiraiás - APS Atromitos Athína | 4-1(1-1) | APS Atromitos Athína - Olympiacos SFP Peiraiás | 2-2(1-2) |
| AE Kifisia - AEK Athína | 0-2(0-2) | AEK Athína - AE Kifisia | 3-0(1-0) |
| Panserraikós Serres - PAE Apollon Póntou | 3-0(1-0) | PAE Apollon Póntou - Panserraikós Serres | 0-1(0-1) |
| PAE Levadiakos Livadeia - Aris Thessaloníki | 1-2(1-0) | Aris Thessaloníki - PAE Levadiakos Livadeia | 1-0(1-0) |

### Quarter-Finals [18.01./25-26.01.2023]

| First Leg | | Second Leg | |
|---|---|---|---|
| PS Apollon Paralimnio - PAS Lamia | 1-2(1-1) | PAS Lamia - PS Apollon Paralimnio | 4-2(3-1) |
| AEK Athína - Panserraikós Serres | 3-0(0-0) | Panserraikós Serres - AEK Athína | 1-3(0-1) |
| Olympiacos SFP Peiraiás - Aris Thessaloníki | 1-0(1-0) | Aris Thessaloníki - Olympiacos SFP Peiraiás | 0-1(0-0) |
| PAOK Thessaloníki - PAE Panathinaïkos Athína | 2-0(0-0) | PAE Panathinaïkos Athína - PAOK Thessaloníki | 1-1(1-0) |

### Semi-Finals [09.02.-08.03./12-13.04.2023]

| First Leg | | Second Leg | |
|---|---|---|---|
| AEK Athína - Olympiacos SFP Peiraiás | 3-0(2-0) | Olympiacos SFP Peiraiás - AEK Athína | 2-1(1-0) |
| PAS Lamia - PAOK Thessaloníki | 1-5(0-2) | PAOK Thessaloníki - PAS Lamia | 1-1(1-0) |

### Final

24.05.2023; Stádio Panthessaliko, Vólos; Referee: Dr. Felix Brych (Germany); Attendance: *played behind closed doors*
**AEK Athína - PAOK Thessaloníki**                                      **2-0(1-0)**

**AEK**: Cican Stanković, Lazaros Rota [*sent off 6*], Domagoj Vida, Harold-Desty Moukoudi, Ehsan Hajsafi, Damian Szymański (Cap) (61.Jens Jønsson), Niclas Eliasson Santana (82.Petros Mantalos), Mijat Gaćinović (86.Paolo Fernandes Cantin), Orbelín Pineda Alvarado (61.Djibril Sidibé), Levi Samuel García (61.Nordin Amrabat), Steven Zuber. Trainer: Matías Jesús Almeyda (Argentina).

**PAOK**: Dominik Kotarski, Joan Sastre Vanrell (62.Diego Marvin Biseswar), Sverrir Ingason (Cap), Luís Rafael Soares Alves (62.Adelino André Vieira de Freitas „Vieirinha"), Konstantinos Koulierakis (86.Tomasz Kędziora), Douglas Augusto Soares Gomes, Stefan Schwab (78.Omar El Kaddouri), Andrija Živković, Ioannis Konstantelias (86.Stefanos Tzimas), Taison Barcellos Freda, Brandon Thomas Llamas. Trainer: Răzvan Lucescu (Romania).

**Goals:** 1-0 Harold-Desty Moukoudi (26), 2-0 Paolo Fernandes Cantin (90+2).

# THE CLUBS 2022/2023

<u>Please note</u>: appearances and goals are including statistics of regular season and play-offs (Championship and Relegation Round).

## Athlitikí Énosis Konstantinoupóleos Athína

| | | |
|---|---|---|
| **Founded**: | 13.04.1924 | |
| **Stadium**: | Stádio „Agio Sophia" [OPAP Arena], Athína (31,100) | |
| **Trainer**: | Matías Jesús Almeyda (ARG) | 21.12.1973 |

| Goalkeepers: | DOB | M | (s) | G |
|---|---|---|---|---|
| Georgios Athanasiadis | 07.04.1993 | 30 | | |
| Cican Stanković (AUT) | 04.11.1992 | 6 | | |
| **Defenders:** | **DOB** | **M** | **(s)** | **G** |
| Ehsan Hajsafi (IRN) | 25.02.1990 | 28 | (1) | |
| Gerasimos Mitoglou | 20.10.1999 | 5 | (3) | 1 |
| Milad Mohammadi (IRN) | 29.09.1993 | 8 | (5) | |
| Harold-Desty Moukoudi (CMR) | 27.11.1997 | 26 | (1) | 2 |
| Lazaros Rota | 23.08.1997 | 28 | (3) | |
| Djibril Sidibé (FRA) | 29.07.1992 | 6 | (6) | |
| Giorgos Tzavellas | 26.11.1987 | 10 | (3) | |
| Domagoj Vida (CRO) | 29.04.1989 | 31 | | 1 |
| **Midfielders:** | **DOB** | **M** | **(s)** | **G** |
| Alexander Fransson (SWE) | 02.04.1994 | | (2) | |
| Mijat Gaćinović (SRB) | 08.02.1995 | 24 | (6) | 9 |
| Konstantinos Galanopoulos | 28.12.1997 | 1 | (11) | |
| Jens Jønsson (DEN) | 10.01.1993 | 27 | (7) | |
| Petros Mantalos | 31.08.1991 | 6 | (24) | 2 |
| *Paolo Fernandes* Cantin (ESP) | 09.08.1998 | 1 | (13) | 1 |
| Orbelin Pineda Alvarado (MEX) | 24.03.1996 | 31 | (5) | 9 |
| Damian Szymański (POL) | 16.06.1995 | 28 | (2) | 2 |
| **Forwards:** | **DOB** | **M** | **(s)** | **G** |
| Christos Albanis | 05.11.1994 | | (1) | |
| Nordin Amrabat (MAR) | 31.03.1987 | 19 | (12) | 7 |
| Sergio Ezequiel Araujo (ARG) | 28.01.1992 | 28 | (1) | 7 |
| Efthymios Christopoulos | 20.09.2000 | | (1) | |
| Niclas Eliasson Santana (SWE) | 07.12.1995 | 13 | (13) | |
| Levi Samuel García (TRI) | 20.11.1997 | 26 | (5) | 14 |
| Michalis Kosidis | 09.02.2002 | | (2) | |
| Theodosis Macheras | 09.05.2000 | | (1) | |
| Tom van Weert (NED) | 07.06.1990 | 3 | (10) | 5 |
| Ambrosini Antonio Cabaça Salvador „Zini"(ANG) | 03.07.2002 | | (2) | |
| Steven Zuber (SUI) | 17.08.1991 | 11 | (17) | 8 |

## Aris Thessaloníki

| | | |
|---|---|---|
| **Founded**: | 25.03.1914 | |
| **Stadium**: | Stádio " Kleanthis Vikelidis", Thessaloníki (22,800) | |
| **Trainer**: | Germán Adrián Ramón Burgos (ARG) | 16.04.1969 |
| [29.08.2022] | Apostolos Terzis | 13.03.1971 |
| [14.09.2022] | Alan Scott Pardew (ENG) | 18.07.1961 |
| [05.02.2023] | Apostolos Terzis | 13.03.1971 |

| Goalkeepers: | DOB | M | (s) | G |
|---|---|---|---|---|
| Julián *Cuesta* Díaz (ESP) | 28.03.1991 | 31 | | |
| Marios Siabanis | 28.09.1999 | 5 | | |
| **Defenders:** | **DOB** | **M** | **(s)** | **G** |
| Jakub Brabec (CZE) | 06.08.1992 | 23 | | 1 |
| *Fabiano* Leismann (BRA) | 18.11.1991 | 30 | (2) | 3 |
| Salem M'Bakata (FRA) | 19.04.1998 | 18 | (5) | 1 |
| Bradley Mazikou (CGO) | 02.06.1996 | 21 | (7) | |
| Nicolas Julio N'Koulou N'Doubena (CMR) | 27.03.1990 | 11 | (6) | 1 |
| Moses Adeshina Ayoola Junior Odubajo(ENG) | 28.07.1993 | 20 | (5) | 1 |
| Marvin Peersman (BEL) | 10.02.1991 | 24 | (5) | |
| **Midfielders:** | **DOB** | **M** | **(s)** | **G** |
| Lazaros Christodoulopoulos | 19.12.1986 | 3 | (10) | |
| Bryan Dabo (BFA) | 18.02.1992 | 16 | (11) | 1 |
| Vladimír Darida (CZE) | 08.08.1990 | 21 | | 5 |
| Pape Cheikh Diop Gueyé (SEN) | 08.08.1997 | 3 | (7) | |
| Cheick Doukouré (CIV) | 11.09.1992 | 11 | (5) | |
| Peter Etebo Oghenekaro (NGA) | 09.11.1995 | 23 | (2) | |
| Daniel Mancini (ARG) | 11.11.1996 | 16 | (1) | 3 |
| Manuel „Manu" García Alonso (ESP) | 02.01.1998 | 12 | (5) | 4 |
| Luis Enrique Palma Oseguera (HON) | 17.01.2000 | 20 | (9) | 11 |
| Lukas Rupp (GER) | 08.01.1991 | 3 | (5) | 1 |
| Rafail Sgouros | 28.05.2004 | 1 | (4) | |
| **Forwards:** | **DOB** | **M** | **(s)** | **G** |
| Christos Chatziioannou | 10.01.2004 | | (2) | |
| Mateo Ezequiel García (ARG) | 10.09.1996 | 27 | (6) | 3 |
| Gervais Lombe Yao Kouassi „Gervinho"(CIV) | 27.05.1987 | 5 | (6) | 1 |
| Andre Anthony Gray (JAM) | 26.06.1991 | 20 | (12) | 8 |
| Juan Manuel Iturbe Arévalos (PAR) | 04.06.1993 | 17 | (16) | 4 |
| Aboubakar Kamara (MTN) | 07.03.1995 | 10 | (4) | 4 |
| *Rafael* Euclides Soares *Camacho* (POR) | 22.05.2000 | 5 | (20) | 2 |
| Edwin Alexander Rodríguez Castillo (HON) | 25.09.1999 | | (1) | |

## Athletic Gymnastics Society Asteras Tripolis

| | | |
|---|---|---|
| **Founded**: | 26.03.1931 | |
| **Stadium**: | Stádio "Theodoros Kolokotronis", Tripolis (7,442) | |
| **Trainer**: | Iraklis Metaxas | 10.07.1967 |
| [23.12.2022] | Alexandros Maniatoglou | 14.10.1983 |
| [04.01.2023] | Apostolos Mantzios | 21.10.1969 |
| [10.04.2023] | Giannis Douvikas | 30.09.1965 |

| Goalkeepers: | DOB | M | (s) | G |
|---|---|---|---|---|
| Nikolaos Papadopoulos | 11.04.1990 | 26 | | |
| Antonis Tsiftsis | 21.07.1999 | 7 | | |
| **Defenders:** | **DOB** | **M** | **(s)** | **G** |
| Oluwatobiloba Adefunyibomi Alagbe (NGA) | 24.04.2000 | 7 | (3) | |
| Federico Hernán Álvarez (ARG) | 07.08.1994 | 25 | (4) | 1 |
| Georgios Antzoulas | 04.02.2000 | 1 | | |
| Francisco Javier *Atienza* Valverde (ESP) | 18.01.1990 | 22 | | 1 |
| Ilias Christopoulos | 02.02.2003 | | (1) | |
| *David Carmona* Sierra (ESP) | 11.01.1997 | 21 | (2) | |
| José Castaño Muñoz „Pepe Castaño" (ESP) | 10.12.1998 | 30 | | 1 |
| *Rubén García* Canales (ESP) | 23.10.1998 | 8 | (3) | |
| Christos Tasoulis | 03.05.1991 | 9 | (3) | |
| Ervin Zukanović (BIH) | 11.02.1987 | 14 | (4) | 1 |
| **Midfielders:** | **DOB** | **M** | **(s)** | **G** |
| Facundo Daniel Bertoglio (ARG) | 30.06.1990 | 10 | (12) | |
| *Daniel Santafé* Mena (ESP) | 03.07.1997 | 7 | (7) | |
| *Eneko Capilla* González (ESP) | 13.06.1995 | | (2) | |
| Michael Gardawski (GER) | 25.09.1990 | 13 | (8) | 1 |
| Walter Matías Iglesias (ARG) | 18.04.1985 | 16 | (5) | |
| *José Luis* Valiente Giménez (ESP) | 18.05.1991 | | (1) | |
| *Juan Domínguez* Lamas (ESP) | 08.01.1990 | 5 | (4) | |
| Juan Manuel Munafo Horta (ARG) | 20.03.1988 | 21 | (3) | 1 |
| Giorgos Prountzos | 19.08.2003 | 1 | (4) | |
| Caleb James Stanko (USA) | 26.07.1993 | 9 | (1) | 1 |
| **Forwards:** | **DOB** | **M** | **(s)** | **G** |
| *Adrián Riera* Torrecillas (ESP) | 19.04.1996 | 14 | (9) | 1 |
| *Asier Benito* Sasiain (ESP) | 11.02.1995 | 5 | (8) | 1 |
| Jerónimo Barrales (ARG) | 28.01.1986 | 22 | (6) | 2 |
| Julián Bartolo (ARG) | 15.04.1996 | 12 | (10) | 2 |
| Ivan Demydenko (UKR) | 11.06.2003 | | (2) | |
| Georgios Kosteas | 16.04.2003 | 1 | (10) | 1 |
| Leonardo Costa Silva „Léo Tilica" (BRA) | 20.04.1995 | 16 | (12) | 3 |
| Andrés Pascual Santoja „Sito" (ESP) | 18.11.1996 | 18 | (8) | 2 |
| Kévin Olivier Soni (CMR) | 17.04.1998 | | (2) | |
| Francesc *"Xesc"* Regis *Crespi* (ESP) | 30.09.1996 | 20 | (3) | 3 |
| Nikolaos Zouglis | 14.11.2003 | 3 | (3) | |

## PAE APS Atromitos Athinon Football Club

**Founded**: 30.04.1923
**Stadium**: Stádio Peristeri, Athína (10,050)
**Trainer**: Christopher Patrick Coleman (WAL)     10.06.1970

| Goalkeepers: | DOB | M | (s) | G |
|---|---|---|---|---|
| Laurenţiu Constantin Brănescu (ROU) | 30.03.1994 | 1 | | |
| Andreas Gianniotis | 18.12.1992 | 31 | | |
| Marko Marić (CRO) | 03.01.1996 | 1 | (1) | |
| **Defenders:** | **DOB** | **M** | **(s)** | **G** |
| Nikolaos Athanasiou | 16.03.2001 | 5 | | |
| Dimitrios Chatziisaias | 21.09.1992 | 31 | | 1 |
| Daniel *„Dani" Suárez* García-Osorio (ESP) | 05.07.1990 | 8 | (1) | |
| Laurens Henry Cristine De Bock (BEL) | 07.11.1992 | 29 | | |
| Wajdi Kechrida (TUN) | 05.11.1995 | 30 | | 1 |
| Kyriakos Kivrakidis | 21.07.1992 | 3 | | |
| Theofanis Mavrommatis | 16.01.1997 | 15 | (3) | |
| Stefanos Stroungis | 09.10.1997 | 11 | (1) | |
| **Midfielders:** | **DOB** | **M** | **(s)** | **G** |
| Aguibou Camara (GUI) | 20.05.2001 | 10 | (2) | 3 |
| *Eder González* Tortella (ESP) | 07.01.1997 | 30 | (2) | |
| August Erlingmark (SWE) | 22.04.1998 | 18 | (6) | 2 |
| Samúel Friðjónsson (ISL) | 22.02.1996 | 13 | (15) | 2 |
| Giannis Ikonomidis | 03.01.1998 | 3 | (15) | |
| *Juan Muñiz* Gallego (ESP) | 14.03.1992 | 7 | (4) | 1 |
| Andreas Kuen (AUT) | 24.03.1995 | 18 | (5) | 2 |
| Mattheos Mountes | 17.11.2003 | | (1) | |
| **Forwards:** | **DOB** | **M** | **(s)** | **G** |
| Viðar Kjartansson (ISL) | 11.03.1990 | 18 | (13) | 6 |
| Viktor Klonaridis (BEL) | 28.07.1992 | 16 | (9) | 1 |
| Konstantinos Kotsopoulos | 17.02.1997 | 4 | (5) | |
| Gaëtan Robail (FRA) | 09.01.1994 | 31 | (2) | 5 |
| Dorin Rotariu (ROU) | 29.07.1995 | 19 | (8) | 4 |
| Marios Tzavidas | 08.10.2003 | 10 | (21) | 2 |
| Giorgos Tzovaras | 03.11.1999 | 1 | (24) | 3 |

## Athlitikós Ómilos Ionikós Nikeas

**Founded**: 1965
**Stadium**: Stádio Neapoli, Nikeas (6,000)
**Trainer**: Dimitrios Spanos     13.07.1969
[26.01.2023]     Michalis Grigoriou     19.12.1973

| Goalkeepers: | DOB | M | (s) | G |
|---|---|---|---|---|
| Eleftherios Choutesiotis | 20.07.1994 | 33 | | |
| **Defenders:** | **DOB** | **M** | **(s)** | **G** |
| Rachid Bouhenna (ALG) | 29.06.1991 | 2 | (3) | |
| Dmitro Chigrinskiy (UKR) | 07.11.1986 | 26 | | 1 |
| *Hugo* Filipe Gonçalves Martins de *Sousa* (POR) | 04.06.1992 | 14 | (4) | |
| Federico Emanuel Milo (ARG) | 10.01.1992 | 2 | (5) | |
| Georgios Mygas | 07.04.1994 | 29 | | |
| Simon Rrumbullaku (ALB) | 30.12.1991 | 3 | (2) | |
| Emanuel Šakić (AUT) | 25.01.1991 | 24 | (2) | |
| Konstantinos Tsirigotis | 10.03.2001 | 2 | (1) | |
| Georgios Valerianos | 13.02.1992 | 24 | | 1 |
| **Midfielders:** | **DOB** | **M** | **(s)** | **G** |
| Fabien Antunes (FRA) | 19.11.1991 | 12 | (6) | |
| Aias Aosman (SYR) | 21.10.1994 | 13 | | 2 |
| José Alberto *Cañas* Ruiz Herrera (ESP) | 27.05.1987 | 21 | (6) | 1 |
| Raman Chibsah (GHA) | 10.03.1993 | 5 | (4) | |
| Bandiougou Fadiga (FRA) | 15.01.2001 | 25 | (3) | 1 |
| Christos Ioannidis | 28.07.2004 | | (1) | |
| Zinédine Machach (MAR) | 05.01.1996 | 11 | (12) | 2 |
| Javier Osvaldo Mendoza (ARG) | 02.09.1992 | 5 | (5) | 2 |
| Vasilios Poghosyan | 04.05.1998 | | (2) | |
| Jacques Alaixys Romao (TOG) | 18.01.1984 | 31 | | |
| **Forwards:** | **DOB** | **M** | **(s)** | **G** |
| Jerson Cabral (CPV) | 03.01.1991 | | (7) | |
| Christos Eleftheriadis | 30.09.1991 | 7 | (17) | 2 |
| Nikolaos Ioannidis | 26.04.1994 | 4 | (9) | |
| Sotirios Kokkinis | 11.07.2000 | | (1) | |
| Maximiliano Alberto Lovera (ARG) | 09.03.1999 | 19 | (5) | 2 |
| Dimitrios Manos | 16.09.1994 | | (10) | |
| Vasilios Mantzis | 04.12.1991 | 29 | (3) | 6 |
| Reagy Baah Ofosu (GER) | 20.09.1991 | 1 | (2) | |
| Sebastião de Freitas Couto Junior „Sebá" (BRA) | 08.06.1992 | 17 | (5) | 2 |
| Kaiyne River Woolery (ENG) | 11.01.1995 | 4 | (5) | |

## PAS Lamia 1964 Football Club

**Founded**: 01.06.1964
**Stadium**: Stádio Dimotiko, Lamia (5,500)
**Trainer**: Gianluca Festa (ITA)     16.03.1969
[16.11.2022]     Savvas Pantelidis     07.04.1965
[14.02.2023]     Leonidas Vokolos     31.08.1970

| Goalkeepers: | DOB | M | (s) | G |
|---|---|---|---|---|
| Athanasios Garavelis | 06.08.1992 | 10 | | |
| Alexei Koşelev (MDA) | 19.11.1993 | 4 | | |
| Bojan Šaranov (SRB) | 22.09.1987 | 19 | (1) | |
| **Defenders:** | **DOB** | **M** | **(s)** | **G** |
| Leroy Abanda (FRA) | 07.06.2000 | 15 | | |
| Daniel Adejo (NGA) | 07.08.1989 | 15 | (1) | |
| Oliver Paz Benítez (ARG) | 07.06.1991 | | (2) | |
| *David Simón* Rodríguez Santana (ESP) | 16.12.1988 | 29 | (2) | |
| Ivan Goranov (BUL) | 10.06.1992 | 16 | (1) | |
| Georgios Kornezos | 23.02.1998 | 22 | | 1 |
| Kyriakos Papadopoulos | 23.02.1992 | 9 | (1) | |
| Aleksandr Pavlovets (BLR) | 13.08.1996 | 3 | | |
| Konstantinos Provydakis | 21.05.1996 | 1 | (1) | |
| Giorgos Saramantas | 29.01.1992 | 1 | (8) | |
| Adam Tzanetopoulos | 10.02.1995 | 17 | (1) | |
| Stavros Vasilantonopoulos | 28.01.1992 | 6 | (6) | |
| **Midfielders:** | **DOB** | **M** | **(s)** | **G** |
| Paris Babis | 17.07.1999 | 1 | (4) | |
| Danny Bryan Bejarano Yañez (BOL) | 03.01.1994 | 15 | (8) | 1 |
| Tomás Sebastián De Vincenti (ARG) | 09.02.1989 | 17 | (7) | 4 |
| Savvas Gentsoglou | 19.09.1990 | 1 | | |
| Cristopher Antonio Núñez González (CRC) | 08.12.1997 | 24 | (5) | 3 |
| *Rubén Martínez* Granja (ESP) | 08.12.1989 | 14 | (3) | 3 |
| Vykintas Slivka (LTU) | 29.04.1995 | 21 | (8) | 1 |
| Caleb James Stanko (USA) | 26.07.1993 | 5 | (5) | |
| Theofanis Tzandaris | 13.06.1993 | 24 | (5) | |
| Theodoros Vasilakakis | 20.07.1988 | | (1) | |
| **Forwards:** | **DOB** | **M** | **(s)** | **G** |
| Stefan Aškovski (MKD) | 24.02.1992 | 8 | (8) | |
| Richmond Yiadom Boakye (GHA) | 28.01.1993 | 2 | (6) | 1 |
| Petros Giakoumakis | 03.07.1992 | 5 | (9) | |
| *Gustavo Marmentini* dos Santos (BRA) | 08.03.1994 | | (6) | |
| Anastasios Karamanos | 21.09.1990 | 1 | (8) | |
| Georgios Manousos | 03.12.1987 | 11 | (16) | |
| Jeison Medina Escobar (COL) | 27.02.1995 | 5 | (3) | 1 |
| Lazar Romanić (SRB) | 25.03.1998 | 7 | (5) | |
| Zoran Tošić (SRB) | 28.04.1987 | | (4) | 2 |
| Sotiris Tsiloulis | 14.02.1995 | 20 | (6) | 2 |
| Nikolaos Tsoukalos | 23.03.1992 | | (7) | |
| Nikolaos Vergos | 13.01.1996 | 15 | (1) | 4 |

## PAE Levadiakos Livadeia

| | | | |
|---|---|---|---|
| **Founded:** | 01.12.1961 | | |
| **Stadium:** | Stádio Dimotiko, Livadeia (5,915) | | |
| **Trainer:** | Giannis Taousianis | | 27.06.1972 |
| [21.09.2022] | Jasminko Velić (BIH) | | 01.09.1965 |
| [16.02.2023] | Giannis Petrakis | | 20.05.1959 |

| Goalkeepers: | DOB | M | (s) | G |
|---|---|---|---|---|
| Dávid Gróf (HUN) | 17.04.1989 | 11 | | |
| Matej Marković (CRO) | 22.07.1996 | 14 | | |
| Stefan Stojanović (SRB) | 09.02.1997 | 8 | | |
| **Defenders:** | **DOB** | **M** | **(s)** | **G** |
| Patrick Bahanack (CMR) | 03.08.1997 | 11 | (4) | |
| Antonis Dentakis | 13.03.1995 | 5 | (5) | |
| Dimitrios Konstantinidis | 02.06.1994 | 8 | (1) | |
| Panagiotis Liagas | 05.11.1999 | 17 | (3) | 1 |
| Stavros Panagiotou | 01.07.1993 | 16 | (3) | 1 |
| Gonzalo Ezequiel Paz (ARG) | 06.06.1993 | 12 | | |
| Triantafyllos Tsapras | 22.10.2001 | 26 | | 2 |
| Themistoklis Tzimopoulos (NZL) | 20.11.1985 | 8 | (8) | |
| Marios Vichos | 14.01.2000 | 15 | (3) | |
| Paulo Vinícius Souza Dos Santos (HUN) | 21.02.1990 | 22 | | 1 |
| **Midfielders:** | **DOB** | **M** | **(s)** | **G** |
| Anthony Belmonte (FRA) | 16.10.1995 | 6 | (9) | 1 |
| Abdoulaye Dabo (FRA) | 04.03.2001 | 4 | (5) | |
| Stephen Hammond (GHA) | 06.08.1996 | 23 | (3) | 1 |
| Alfredo Antonio Mejía Escobar (HON) | 03.04.1990 | 27 | (2) | 1 |
| Georgios Nikas | 17.09.1999 | 24 | (6) | 6 |
| *Régis Tosatti* Giacomin (BRA) | 16.01.1998 | | (2) | |
| Michal Škvarka (SVK) | 19.08.1992 | 6 | (9) | 1 |
| Georgios Vrakas | 28.04.2001 | 22 | (5) | 1 |
| Christos Voutsas | 31.07.2001 | | (2) | |
| **Forwards:** | **DOB** | **M** | **(s)** | **G** |
| *António* Manuel Pereira *Xavier* (POR) | 06.07.1992 | | (2) | |
| Konstantinos Doumtsios | 20.09.1997 | 16 | (5) | 1 |
| Giannis Gianniotas | 29.04.1993 | 12 | (4) | 2 |
| Alexander Thomas Jeremejeff (SWE) | 12.10.1993 | 6 | (4) | 1 |
| Kazenga LuaLua (ENG) | 10.12.1990 | 8 | (10) | |
| Thierry Rua *Moutinho* (POR) | 26.02.1991 | 16 | (1) | 3 |
| Adrian Tabarcea Petre (ROU) | 11.02.1998 | 3 | (2) | |
| Filip Filipos Lars Sachpekidis (SWE) | 03.07.1997 | 4 | (6) | |
| Bakary Sako (MLI) | 26.04.1988 | 2 | (8) | |
| Panagiotis Symelidis | 03.11.1992 | 6 | (5) | |
| Jonas Gabriel Da Silva Nunes „Toró" (BRA) | 30.05.1999 | 5 | (9) | |
| Theodoros Tsirigotis | 23.06.2000 | | (12) | |

## Ómilos Filáthlon Heraklíou

| | | | |
|---|---|---|---|
| **Founded:** | 1925 | | |
| **Stadium:** | Stádio „Theodoros Vardinogiannis", Heraklion (9,088) | | |
| **Trainer:** | Nikolaos Nioplias | | 17.01.1965 |
| [21.10.2022] | Pedro Caravela (POR) | | 21.12.1976 |
| [25.10.2022] | Valdas Dambrauskas (LTU) | | 07.01.1977 |

| Goalkeepers: | DOB | M | (s) | G |
|---|---|---|---|---|
| Nikolaos Christogeorgos | 03.01.2000 | 1 | | |
| Christos Mandas | 17.09.2001 | 26 | | |
| Sonny Stevens (NED) | 22.06.1992 | 6 | | |
| **Defenders:** | **DOB** | **M** | **(s)** | **G** |
| Konstantinos Balogiannis | 08.02.1999 | 20 | (3) | 1 |
| Apostolos Diamantis | 20.05.2000 | 28 | (2) | 2 |
| Konstantinos Giannoulis | 09.12.1987 | 6 | (4) | |
| Eric Larsson (SWE) | 15.07.1991 | 31 | | 2 |
| Nikolaos Marinakis | 12.09.1993 | 7 | (6) | |
| Triantafyllos Pasalidis | 19.07.1996 | 21 | (1) | |
| Praxitelis Vouros | 05.05.1995 | 28 | (1) | |
| Samuel Yohou (FRA) | 06.08.1991 | 4 | (3) | |
| Guðmundur Þórarinsson (ISL) | 15.04.1992 | 20 | (7) | |
| **Midfielders:** | **DOB** | **M** | **(s)** | **G** |
| Giannis Apostolakis | 24.09.2004 | | (3) | |
| Marko Bakić (MNE) | 01.11.1993 | 13 | (2) | 3 |
| Giannis Bouzoukis | 27.03.1998 | 4 | (3) | |
| Assane Dioussé (SEN) | 20.09.1997 | 28 | (5) | 3 |
| *Jon* Miquel *Toral* Harper (ESP) | 05.02.1995 | 21 | (3) | 8 |
| *Luis* Perea Hernández (ESP) | 25.08.1997 | 13 | (13) | 1 |
| Miguel Alberto Mellado (ARG) | 18.03.1993 | 27 | | 2 |
| Juan Ángel Neira (ARG) | 21.02.1989 | 6 | (9) | 2 |
| Paschalis Staikos | 08.02.1996 | 1 | (9) | |
| **Forwards:** | **DOB** | **M** | **(s)** | **G** |
| Thievy Bifouma (CGO) | 13.05.1992 | 2 | (9) | |
| Nouha Dicko (MLI) | 14.05.1992 | 27 | (3) | 6 |
| Fiorin Durmishaj (ALB) | 14.11.1996 | 3 | (9) | 1 |
| Sebastian Grønning (DEN) | 03.02.1997 | 1 | (7) | 1 |
| Miguel Ángel *Guerrero* Martín (ESP) | 12.07.1990 | 8 | (3) | |
| Bruce Kamau (AUS) | 28.03.1995 | | (3) | |
| *Luiz Phellype* Luciano Silva (BRA) | 27.09.1993 | 3 | (6) | 1 |
| *Mésaque* Geremias *Djú* (POR) | 18.03.1999 | 5 | (5) | |
| Hárold Santiago Mosquera Caicedo (COL) | 07.02.1995 | 1 | (11) | |
| Giannis Theodosoulakis | 11.09.2004 | | (6) | |
| Kosmas Tsilianidis | 09.05.1994 | 2 | (9) | 1 |

## Olympiakós Sýndesmos Filáthlon Peiraiós

| | | | |
|---|---|---|---|
| **Founded:** | 10.03.1925 | | |
| **Stadium:** | Stádio „Giórgos Karaïskáki", Peiraiás (32,115) | | |
| **Trainer:** | Pedro Rui da Mota Vieira Martins (POR) | | 17.07.1970 |
| [01.08.2022] | Carlos Corberán Vallet (ESP) | | 07.04.1983 |
| [20.09.2022] | José Miguel González Martín del Campo "Míchel"(ESP) | | 23.03.1963 |
| [04.04.2023] | José Anigo (FRA) | | 15.04.1961 |

| Goalkeepers: | DOB | M | (s) | G |
|---|---|---|---|---|
| Alexandros Paschalakis | 28.07.1989 | 24 | | |
| Konstantinos Tzolakis | 08.11.2002 | 7 | | |
| Tomáš Vaclík (CZE) | 29.03.1989 | 5 | | |
| **Defenders:** | **DOB** | **M** | **(s)** | **G** |
| Athanasios Androutsos | 06.05.1997 | 5 | (2) | 1 |
| Ousseynou Ba (SEN) | 11.11.1995 | 17 | (2) | |
| Pape Abou Cissé (SEN) | 14.09.1995 | 4 | (2) | |
| Konstantinos Manolas | 14.06.1991 | 3 | | |
| *Marcelo* Vieira da Silva Júnior (BRA) | 12.05.1988 | | (5) | |
| Andreas Ndoj (ALB) | 02.02.2003 | 18 | (3) | 1 |
| Sokratis Papastathopoulos | 09.06.1988 | 26 | (1) | 2 |
| Gonzalo Ávila Gordón „Pipa" (ESP) | 26.01.1998 | 7 | (4) | |
| *Ramon* Ramos Lima (BRA) | 13.03.2001 | 4 | (5) | |
| Oleg Reabciuk (MDA) | 16.01.1998 | 30 | | 1 |
| Panagiotis Retsos | 09.08.1998 | 4 | (3) | |
| *Rodinei* Marcelo de Almeida (BRA) | 29.01.1992 | 19 | | |
| Šime Vrsaljko (CRO) | 10.01.1992 | 3 | | |
| Philip Aksel Frigast Zinckernagel (DEN) | 16.12.1994 | 1 | | |
| **Midfielders:** | **DOB** | **M** | **(s)** | **G** |
| Andreas Bouchalakis | 05.04.1993 | 2 | (1) | 1 |
| Aguibou Camara (GUI) | 20.05.2001 | 3 | (3) | |
| Konstantinos Fortounis | 16.10.1992 | 21 | (4) | 4 |
| Hwang In-beom (KOR) | 20.09.1996 | 31 | (1) | 3 |
| Pajtim Kasami (SUI) | 02.06.1992 | 4 | (8) | 2 |
| Leonardo Pablo Koutris | 23.07.1995 | 1 | | |
| Pierre Kunde Malong (CMR) | 26.07.1995 | 1 | (1) | |
| Yann Gérard M'Vila (FRA) | 29.06.1990 | 28 | (3) | |
| *Pep Biel* Mas Jaume (ESP) | 05.09.1996 | 26 | (4) | 9 |
| Lazar Ranđelović (SRB) | 05.08.1997 | 2 | (1) | 1 |
| James David Rodríguez Rubio (COL) | 12.07.1991 | 18 | (2) | 5 |
| Diadié Samassékou (MLI) | 11.01.1996 | 8 | (12) | 2 |
| Mathieu Valbuena (FRA) | 28.09.1984 | 5 | (13) | 3 |
| **Forwards:** | **DOB** | **M** | **(s)** | **G** |
| Moustafa Hassan Mohamed Abdelmonem Mahgoub (EGY) | 05.03.1993 | 1 | | |
| Cédric Bakambu (COD) | 11.04.1991 | 27 | (5) | 18 |
| Joshua Luke Bowler (ENG) | 05.03.1999 | 1 | (3) | |
| Zymer Bytyqi (KOS) | 11.09.1996 | | (2) | |
| Konrad de la Fuente (USA) | 16.07.2001 | 2 | (1) | |
| Youssef El-Arabi (MAR) | 03.02.1987 | 7 | (27) | 6 |
| Hwang Ui-jo (KOR) | 28.08.1992 | 2 | (3) | |
| Aboubakar Kamara (MTN) | 07.03.1995 | | (1) | |
| Georgios Masouras | 01.01.1994 | 15 | (18) | 4 |
| Garry Mendes Rodrigues (CPV) | 27.11.1990 | 4 | (14) | 2 |
| *Sergi Canós* Tenés (ESP) | 02.02.1997 | 5 | (3) | 4 |
| Marios Vrousai | 02.07.1998 | 5 | (14) | |

## Panathinaïkós Athlitikós Ómilos Athína

**Founded**: 03.02.1908
**Stadium**: Stádio "Apostolos Nikolaidis", Athína (16,003)
**Trainer**: Ivan Jovanović (SRB)  08.07.1962

| Goalkeepers: | DOB | M | (s) | G |
|---|---|---|---|---|
| Alberto Brignoli (ITA) | 19.08.1991 | 34 | | |
| Yuriy Lodygin (RUS) | 26.05.1990 | 2 | | |
| **Defenders:** | **DOB** | **M** | **(s)** | **G** |
| Cristian George Ganea (ROU) | 24.05.1992 | 3 | (6) | |
| Juan Carlos Pérez López „Juankar" (ESP) | 30.03.1990 | 31 | (2) | |
| Giannis Kotsiras | 16.12.1992 | 19 | (6) | |
| Hörður Magnússon (ISL) | 11.02.1993 | 21 | (3) | 1 |
| Achilleas Poungouras | 13.12.1995 | 6 | (2) | |
| Tymoteusz Puchacz (POL) | 23.01.1999 | 2 | (11) | |
| Facundo Sánchez (ARG) | 07.03.1990 | 11 | (3) | 1 |
| Bart Schenkeveld (NED) | 28.08.1991 | 26 | (1) | |
| Zvonimir Šarlija (CRO) | 29.08.1996 | 19 | (2) | |
| Georgios Vagiannidis | 12.09.2001 | 7 | (12) | |
| **Midfielders:** | **DOB** | **M** | **(s)** | **G** |
| Sotirios Alexandropoulos | 26.11.2001 | | (1) | |
| Bernard Anício Caldeira Duarte (BRA) | 08.09.1992 | 26 | (5) | 2 |
| Enis Çokaj (ALB) | 23.02.1999 | 1 | (19) | |
| Leandro Frroku (ALB) | 03.09.2003 | | (1) | |
| Adam Gnezda Čerin (SVN) | 16.07.1999 | 29 | (5) | 1 |
| László Kleinheisler (HUN) | 08.04.1994 | 4 | (11) | 2 |
| Dimitrios Kourbelis | 02.11.1993 | 26 | (4) | 1 |
| Daniel Mancini (ARG) | 11.11.1996 | 11 | (6) | 3 |
| Rubén Salvador Pérez del Mármol (ESP) | 26.04.1989 | 33 | | |
| Alexis Trouillet (FRA) | 23.12.2000 | | (1) | |
| Benjamin Verbič (SVN) | 27.11.1993 | 11 | (15) | 2 |
| **Forwards:** | **DOB** | **M** | **(s)** | **G** |
| Aitor Cantalapiedra Fernández (ESP) | 10.02.1996 | 8 | (1) | 8 |
| Fotis Ioannidis | 10.01.2000 | 17 | (19) | 7 |
| Sebastián Alberto Palacios (ARG) | 20.01.1992 | 29 | (4) | 6 |
| Andraž Šporar (SVN) | 27.02.1994 | 20 | (12) | 11 |

## Panaetolikos Gymnastikos Philekpaideutikos Syllogos Agrinio

**Founded**: 09.03.1926
**Stadium**: Stádio Panetolikos, Agrinio (7,321)
**Trainer**: Giannis Anastasiou  05.03.1973

| Goalkeepers: | DOB | M | (s) | G |
|---|---|---|---|---|
| Giannis Anestis | 09.03.1991 | 21 | | |
| Joel David Graterol Nader (VEN) | 13.02.1997 | 5 | | |
| Vangelis Kontogiannis | 09.01.2002 | 2 | | |
| Antonis Stergiakis | 16.03.1999 | 5 | | |
| **Defenders:** | **DOB** | **M** | **(s)** | **G** |
| Panagiotis Anastasopoulos | 24.10.2003 | | (1) | |
| Konstantinos Apostolakis | 28.05.1999 | 17 | (4) | |
| Michalis Bakakis | 18.03.1991 | 5 | | |
| Ilias Chatzitheodoridis | 05.11.1997 | 12 | (6) | |
| Diamantis Chouchoumis | 17.07.1994 | 23 | (4) | 1 |
| Derek Austin Cornelius (CAN) | 25.11.1997 | 13 | | |
| Georgios Liavas | 12.02.2001 | 10 | (5) | 1 |
| Alexandros Malis | 19.03.1997 | 9 | (2) | 1 |
| Sebastian Mladen (ROU) | 11.12.1991 | 29 | (2) | |
| Nikola Stajić (SRB) | 08.09.2001 | 3 | (1) | |
| Jacob Une-Larsson (SWE) | 08.04.1994 | 31 | | |
| **Midfielders:** | **DOB** | **M** | **(s)** | **G** |
| Juan Pablo Añor Acosta (VEN) | 24.01.1994 | 7 | (2) | 1 |
| Giannis Bouzoukis | 27.03.1998 | 2 | (12) | |
| Deybi Aldair Flores Flores (HON) | 16.06.1996 | 10 | (6) | |
| Dimitrios Kolovos | 27.04.1993 | 19 | (10) | 3 |
| Johan Daniel Mårtensson (SWE) | 16.02.1989 | 17 | (10) | |
| Vangelis Nikolaou | 03.06.2004 | | (1) | |
| Afeez Nosiru (NGA) | 01.03.1998 | | (2) | |
| Angelos Tsingaras | 24.07.1999 | 1 | (2) | |
| Ivan Varone (ITA) | 11.10.1992 | | (1) | |
| Georgios Xenitidis | 04.09.1999 | 6 | (8) | |
| **Forwards:** | **DOB** | **M** | **(s)** | **G** |
| Nadrey Dago (CIV) | 07.05.1997 | 10 | (6) | 2 |
| Jorge Luis Díaz Gutiérrez (URU) | 28.06.1989 | 24 | (4) | |
| Frederico Fonseca Pires de Almeida Duarte (POR) | 30.03.1999 | 14 | (11) | 1 |
| João Pedro Sousa Silva (POR) | 13.11.1996 | 6 | (24) | 5 |
| Nikolaos Karelis | 24.02.1992 | 25 | (4) | 13 |
| Sahr Jonathan Morsay (SWE) | 05.10.1997 | 14 | (10) | 1 |
| Levan Shengelia (GEO) | 27.10.1995 | 22 | (9) | 3 |
| Alexandros Voilis | 26.05.2000 | 1 | (2) | |

## Panthessaloníkios Athlitikós Ómilos Konstantinoupolitón

**Founded**: 20.04.1926
**Stadium**: Stádio Toumba, Thessaloníki (28,703)
**Trainer**: Răzvan Lucescu (ROU)  17.02.1969

| Goalkeepers: | DOB | M | (s) | G |
|---|---|---|---|---|
| Dominik Kotarski (CRO) | 10.02.2000 | 34 | | |
| Živko Živković (SRB) | 14.04.1989 | 2 | | |
| **Defenders:** | **DOB** | **M** | **(s)** | **G** |
| Sverrir Ingason (ISL) | 05.08.1993 | 30 | | 3 |
| Joan Sastre Vanrell (ESP) | 30.04.1997 | 17 | (7) | |
| Giannis Kargas | 09.12.1994 | 7 | (1) | |
| Tomasz Kędziora (POL) | 11.06.1994 | 7 | (1) | 1 |
| Lefteris Lyratzis | 22.02.2000 | 12 | (2) | |
| Ivan Tarek Fjellstad Näsberg (NOR) | 22.04.1996 | 8 | (4) | 1 |
| Luís Rafael „Rafa" Soares Alves (POR) | 09.05.1995 | 26 | | |
| Marios Tsaousis | 11.05.2000 | 6 | (3) | |
| Adelino André Vieira de Freitas „Vieirinha"(POR) | 24.01.1986 | 7 | (8) | |
| **Midfielders:** | **DOB** | **M** | **(s)** | **G** |
| André Miguel Lapa Ricardo (POR) | 23.08.2000 | | (3) | |
| Diego Marvin Biseswar (SUR) | 08.03.1988 | 4 | (21) | |
| Douglas Augusto Soares Gomes (BRA) | 13.01.1997 | 29 | | 4 |
| Omar El Kaddouri (MAR) | 21.08.1990 | 9 | (14) | |
| Filipe Miguel Barros Soares (POR) | 20.05.1999 | 5 | (15) | 1 |
| Ioannis Konstantelias | 10.05.2003 | 26 | (4) | 2 |
| Jasmin Kurtić (SVN) | 10.01.1989 | 10 | | 3 |
| Stefan Schwab (AUT) | 27.09.1990 | 14 | (17) | 3 |
| Tiago Filipe Oliveira Dantas (POR) | 24.12.2000 | 24 | (8) | 4 |
| **Forwards:** | **DOB** | **M** | **(s)** | **G** |
| Brandon Thomas Llamas (ESP) | 04.02.1995 | 11 | (18) | 6 |
| Vasileios Gordeziani | 29.01.2002 | 1 | (1) | |
| Konstantinos Koulierakis | 28.11.2003 | 24 | (1) | 2 |
| Thomas Murg (AUT) | 14.11.1994 | 1 | (3) | |
| Khaled Narey (GER) | 23.07.1994 | 25 | (2) | 7 |
| Nélson Miguel Castro Oliveira (POR) | 08.08.1991 | 24 | (8) | 7 |
| Nicolás Quagliata Platero (URU) | 05.06.1999 | | (3) | |
| Taison Barcellos Freda (BRA) | 13.01.1988 | 5 | (9) | 1 |
| Stefanos Tzimas | 06.01.2006 | | (4) | 1 |
| Andrija Živković (SRB) | 11.07.1996 | 28 | (5) | 7 |

## Panepirotikos Athlitikos Syllogos Giannina

| | Founded: | 08.07.1966 | | |
|---|---|---|---|---|
| | Stadium: | Stádio Zosimades, , Giannina (7,652) | | |
| | Trainer: | Athanasios Staikos | | 29.11.1980 |

| Goalkeepers: | DOB | M | (s) | G |
|---|---|---|---|---|
| Vasilios Athanasiou | 24.07.1999 | 7 | (2) | |
| Jérôme Prior (FRA) | 08.08.1995 | 3 | | |
| Vasilios Soulis | 07.12.1994 | 8 | (1) | |
| Panagiotis Tsintotas | 04.07.1993 | 15 | | |
| Defenders: | DOB | M | (s) | G |
| Petros Bagalianis | 06.02.2001 | 5 | (3) | |
| Gerasimos Bakadimas | 06.06.2000 | 6 | (2) | |
| Gerónimo Bortagaray Derregibus (URU) | 05.08.2000 | 3 | (3) | |
| Carles Soria Grau (ESP) | 08.10.1996 | 31 | | |
| Rodrigo Nahuel Erramuspe (ARG) | 03.05.1990 | 31 | | 9 |
| Ioannis Kiakos | 14.02.1998 | 7 | (1) | |
| Epaminondas Pantelakis | 10.02.1995 | 23 | (2) | 1 |
| Stavros Pilios | 10.12.2000 | 23 | | |
| Louis Poznański (GER) | 24.05.2001 | 3 | | |
| Andrei Radu (ROU) | 21.06.1996 | 2 | | |
| Angelos Tsavos | 11.04.2002 | 2 | (1) | |
| Midfielders: | DOB | M | (s) | G |
| Federico Gino Acevedo Fagúndez (URU) | 26.02.1993 | 16 | | |

| Iker Bilbao Mendiguren (ESP) | 20.03.1996 | 14 | (2) | |
|---|---|---|---|---|
| Zisis Karachalios | 10.01.1996 | 21 | (2) | |
| Iason Kyrkos | 21.03.2003 | | (2) | |
| Angelos Liasos | 26.05.2000 | 14 | (9) | 2 |
| Nikolaos Lolis | 20.01.2005 | | (1) | |
| Sotiris Ninis | 03.04.1990 | 2 | (7) | |
| Daan Rienstra (NED) | 06.10.1994 | 18 | (3) | 1 |
| Angelos Tsiris | 18.08.2004 | | (2) | |
| Panagiotis Tzimas | 12.03.2001 | 14 | (14) | |
| Forwards: | DOB | M | (s) | G |
| Claudiu Cristian Bălan (ROU) | 22.06.1994 | 19 | (8) | 6 |
| Manssour Fofana (CIV) | 10.07.2002 | 1 | (4) | 1 |
| Jean-Baptiste Léo (FRA) | 03.05.1996 | | (4) | |
| Alexandros Lolis | 05.09.2002 | 4 | (7) | |
| Ahmad Mendes Moreira (GUI) | 27.06.1995 | 25 | (6) | 1 |
| Giorgos Pamlidis | 13.11.1993 | 24 | (4) | 6 |
| Pedro Pérez Conde (ESP) | 26.07.1988 | 3 | (2) | 1 |
| Kevin Duvan Ante Rosero (COL) | 03.12.1998 | 15 | (7) | 4 |
| Apostolos Stamatelopoulos (AUS) | 09.04.1999 | 4 | (13) | |

## Vólos Néos Podosfairikós Sýllogos

| | Founded: | 02.06.2017 | | |
|---|---|---|---|---|
| | Stadium: | Stádio Panthessaliko, Vólos (22,700) | | |
| | Trainer: | Oswald Tanchot (FRA) | | 07.08.1973 |
| [23.08.2022] | | Konstantinos Bratsos | | 26.04.1977 |

| Goalkeepers: | DOB | M | (s) | G |
|---|---|---|---|---|
| Panagiotis Avgerinos | 11.04.2003 | 2 | (1) | |
| Boris Klaiman (ISR) | 26.10.1990 | 29 | | |
| Matic Kotnik (SVN) | 23.07.1990 | 5 | | |
| Defenders: | DOB | M | (s) | G |
| Nikolai Alho (FIN) | 12.03.1993 | 32 | (2) | 1 |
| Antonio Manuel Luna Rodríguez (ESP) | 17.03.1991 | 30 | (3) | 2 |
| Kyriakos Aslanidis | 11.03.2002 | 3 | (2) | |
| Antonios Ikonomopoulos | 09.05.1998 | 1 | (4) | |
| João Rodrigo Pereira Escoval (POR) | 08.05.1997 | 29 | | |
| Odysseas Lyberakis | 05.06.1998 | | (1) | |
| Juha Pirinen (FIN) | 22.10.1991 | 15 | (9) | |
| Christos Shelis (CYP) | 02.02.2000 | 25 | (3) | |
| Harouna Sy (FRA) | 30.03.1996 | 10 | (5) | |
| Efstathios Tachatos | 12.08.2001 | 7 | (7) | 2 |
| Athanasios Triantafyllou | 22.07.2003 | | (2) | |
| Abdul Rahman Weiss (SYR) | 14.06.1998 | 5 | (6) | |
| Midfielders: | DOB | M | (s) | G |
| Jean Pierre Barrientos (URU) | 16.09.1990 | 20 | (3) | 2 |
| Cristian Damián Battocchio (ARG) | 10.02.1992 | | (4) | |

| Enzo Gaggi (ARG) | 14.01.1998 | 13 | (2) | 1 |
|---|---|---|---|---|
| Ergys Kaçe (ALB) | 08.07.1993 | 6 | (6) | |
| Javier Magro Matilla (ESP) | 16.08.1988 | 4 | (9) | |
| Alexandros Kartalis | 29.01.1995 | 2 | (14) | |
| Dimitrios Metaxas | 16.12.2003 | 14 | (7) | |
| Gabriel Nicolás Mezquida Sero (URU) | 21.01.1992 | 14 | (8) | 1 |
| Wandepanga Ismahila Ouédraogo (BFA) | 05.11.1999 | | (1) | |
| Paolo Fernandes Cantin (ESP) | 09.08.1998 | 13 | | 3 |
| Ilias Tselios | 06.10.1997 | | (2) | |
| Anastasios Tsokanis | 02.05.1991 | 24 | (3) | 4 |
| Forwards: | DOB | M | (s) | G |
| Michaell Anthony Chirinos Cortez (HON) | 17.06.1995 | 13 | (1) | 1 |
| Miloš Deletić (SRB) | 14.10.1993 | 32 | | 6 |
| Felipe Augusto Rodrigues Pires (BRA) | 18.04.1995 | 11 | (6) | 1 |
| Anthony Patrick Knockaert (FRA) | 20.11.1991 | 4 | (5) | |
| Georgios Koutsias | 08.02.2004 | 6 | (14) | 3 |
| Ognjen Ožegović (SRB) | 09.06.1994 | 22 | (3) | 6 |
| Sarantis Tselebakis | 02.11.2005 | | (2) | |
| Tom van Weert (NED) | 07.06.1990 | 3 | | 1 |
| Víctor Fernández Satué (ESP) | 02.05.1998 | 2 | (5) | |

---

## SECOND LEVEL
### Super League 2 2022/2023

| North Group | | | | | | | | | |
|---|---|---|---|---|---|---|---|---|---|
| 1. | Panserraikós Serres (Promoted) | 28 | 20 | 4 | 4 | 43 | - | 13 | 64 |
| 2. | AE Lárissa | 28 | 18 | 4 | 6 | 50 | - | 19 | 58 |
| 3. | PAE Níki Vólos | 28 | 15 | 7 | 6 | 41 | - | 20 | 52 |
| 4. | PAOK Thessaloníki „B" | 28 | 14 | 7 | 7 | 51 | - | 33 | 49 |
| 5. | GS Iraklís Thessaloníki[1] | 28 | 15 | 8 | 5 | 56 | - | 22 | 47 |
| 6. | PAE Anagennisi Karditsas[2] | 28 | 13 | 8 | 7 | 34 | - | 21 | 41 |
| 7. | APO Almopos Aridaias | 28 | 7 | 15 | 6 | 23 | - | 17 | 36 |
| 8. | AS Makedonikos Neapolis | 28 | 8 | 9 | 11 | 28 | - | 30 | 33 |
| 9. | PAE Panathinaïkós Athína "B" | 28 | 7 | 12 | 9 | 39 | - | 41 | 33 |
| 10. | PAE GS Diagoras 1905 Rhodos | 28 | 9 | 6 | 13 | 38 | - | 42 | 33 |
| 11. | PAE Apollon Póntou | 28 | 9 | 5 | 14 | 21 | - | 37 | 32 |
| 12. | NPS Véria (Relegated) | 28 | 8 | 7 | 13 | 28 | - | 32 | 31 |
| 13. | AE Iraklis Larissa (Relegated) | 28 | 7 | 5 | 16 | 17 | - | 42 | 26 |
| 14. | AS Thesprotos Igoumenitsa[1] (Relegated) | 28 | 4 | 8 | 16 | 26 | - | 49 | 17 |
| 15. | PAE Apollon Lárissa (Withdrew & Relegated) | 28 | 3 | 1 | 24 | 8 | - | 85 | 4 |

[1] 3 points deducted;
[2] 6 points deducted;

| | | | | | | | | | | |
|---|---|---|---|---|---|---|---|---|---|---|
| 1. | AE Kifisias (*Promoted*) | 28 | 20 | 6 | 2 | 62 | - | 16 | 66 |
| 2. | PAE Athens Kallithea | 28 | 20 | 5 | 3 | 54 | - | 22 | 65 |
| 3. | GS Apollon Smyrnis (*Relegated*) | 28 | 16 | 8 | 4 | 37 | - | 20 | 56 |
| 4. | PAE Chania Kissamikos | 28 | 14 | 9 | 5 | 38 | - | 18 | 51 |
| 5. | OF Ierapetra | 28 | 14 | 6 | 8 | 39 | - | 25 | 48 |
| 6. | PS Kalamata | 28 | 13 | 8 | 7 | 33 | - | 16 | 47 |
| 7. | GS Ilioupolis | 28 | 11 | 8 | 9 | 36 | - | 32 | 41 |
| 8. | Panahaiki PAE Patras[3] | 28 | 12 | 6 | 10 | 32 | - | 29 | 36 |
| 9. | Olympiacos SFP Peiraiás "B"[4] | 28 | 13 | 5 | 10 | 39 | - | 36 | 34 |
| 10. | AO Aigaleo Athína | 28 | 8 | 10 | 10 | 27 | - | 31 | 34 |
| 11. | AEK Athína "B" | 28 | 7 | 8 | 13 | 30 | - | 35 | 29 |
| 12. | AO Proodeftiki Neolea Peiraiás (*Relegated*) | 28 | 8 | 5 | 15 | 23 | - | 37 | 29 |
| 13. | AO Episkopis (*Relegated*) | 28 | 4 | 4 | 20 | 17 | - | 53 | 16 |
| 14. | PAO Rouf (*Relegated*) | 28 | 3 | 3 | 22 | 25 | - | 60 | 12 |
| 15. | PASA Irodotos[5] (*Expelled & Relegated*) | 28 | 1 | 1 | 26 | 6 | - | 68 | -11 |

[3] *3 points deducted;*
[4] *10 points deducted;*
[5] *15 points deducted;*

# NATIONAL TEAM

## INTERNATIONAL MATCHES
### (16.07.2022 – 15.07.2023)

| | | | | |
|---|---|---|---|---|
| 24.09.2022 | Larnaca | *Cyprus - Greece* | *1-0(1-0)* | (UNL) |
| 27.09.2022 | Athína | *Greece - Northern Ireland* | *3-1(1-1)* | (UNL) |
| 17.11.2022 | Attard | *Malta - Greece* | *2-2(0-1)* | (F) |
| 20.11.2022 | Budapest | *Hungary - Greece* | *2-1(1-0)* | (F) |
| 24.03.2023 | Faro/Loulé | *Gibraltar - Greece* | *0-3(0-2)* | (ECQ) |
| 27.03.2023 | Athína | *Greece - Lithuania* | *0-0* | (ECQ) |
| 16.06.2023 | Athína | *Greece - Republic of Ireland* | *2-1(1-1)* | (ECQ) |
| 19.06.2023 | Paris | *France - Greece* | *1-0(0-0)* | (ECQ) |

**24.09.2022   CYPRUS - GREECE**                    **1-0(1-0)**            3rd UEFA Nations League C, Group 2
AEK Arena "Georgios Karapatakis", Larnaca; Referee: Aleksei Kulbakov (Belarus); Attendance: 4,548
**GRE:** Odisseas Vlachodimos, George Henry Ivor Baldock, Konstantinos Mavropanos, Pantelis Hatzidiakos, Konstantinos Tsimikas, Emmanouil Siopis (46.Andreas Bouchalakis), Anastasios Bakasetas (Cap) (58.Fotis Ioannidis), Dimitrios Kourbelis (77.Anastasios Hatzigiovannis), Dimitrios Pelkas (78.Sotiris Polykarpos Alexandropoulos), Giorgos Masouras, Anastasios Douvikas (46.Taxiarchis Fountas). Trainer: Gustavo Augusto Poyet Domínguez (Uruguay).

**27.09.2022   GREECE - NORTHERN IRELAND**          **3-1(1-1)**            3rd UEFA Nations League C, Group 2
Stádio "Georgios Kamaras", Athína; Referee: Filip Glova (Slovakia); Attendance: 5,871
**GRE:** Odisseas Vlachodimos, George Henry Ivor Baldock, Konstantinos Mavropanos, Pantelis Hatzidiakos, Konstantinos Tsimikas, Dimitrios Kourbelis, Anastasios Bakasetas (Cap) (76.Andreas Bouchalakis), Petros Mantalos (90+2.Dimitrios Goutas), Giorgos Masouras (76.Anastasios Hatzigiovannis), Dimitrios Pelkas (67.Taxiarchis Fountas), Fotis Ioannidis (67.Anastasios Douvikas). Trainer: Gustavo Augusto Poyet Domínguez (Uruguay).
**Goals:** Dimitrios Pelkas (14), Giorgos Masouras (55), Petros Mantalos (80).

**17.11.2022   MALTA - GREECE**                     **2-2(0-1)**            Friendly International
Ta'Qali National Stadium, Attard; Referee: Alain Durieux (Luxembourg); Attendance: n/a
**GRE:** Alexandros Paschalakis, Lazaros Rota, Pantelis Hatzidiakos, Giorgos Tzavelas (46.Konstantinos Koulierakis), Dimitrios Hristos Giannoulis (80.Giorgos Kyriakopoulos), Emmanouil Siopis (80.Sotiris Polykarpos Alexandropoulos), Anastasios Bakasetas (Cap) (46.Andreas Bouchalakis), Petros Mantalos, Anastasios Hatzigiovannis, Dimitrios Pelkas [*sent off 79 on the bench*] (68.Taxiarchis Fountas), Fotis Ioannidis (68.Anastasios Douvikas). Trainer: Gustavo Augusto Poyet Domínguez (Uruguay).
**Goals:** Anastasios Bakasetas (39), Taxiarchis Fountas (86).

**20.11.2022   HUNGARY - GREECE**                   **2-1(1-0)**            Friendly International
Puskás Aréna, Budapest; Referee: Daniele Chiffi (Italy); Attendance: 50,893
**GRE:** Alexandros Paschalakis, Lazaros Rota, Panagiotis Retsos, Pantelis Hatzidiakos, Dimitrios Hristos Giannoulis (68.Giorgos Kyriakopoulos), Dimitrios Kourbelis (86.Giannis Papanikolaou), Andreas Bouchalakis (68.Anastasios Hatzigiovannis), Petros Mantalos, Anastasios Bakasetas (Cap), Giorgos Masouras (86.Anastasios Douvikas), Fotis Ioannidis (60.Taxiarchis Fountas). Trainer: Gustavo Augusto Poyet Domínguez (Uruguay).
**Goals:** Anastasios Bakasetas (81 penalty).

**24.03.2023   GIBRALTAR - GREECE**                 **0-3(0-2)**            17th EC. Qualifiers
Estádio Algarve, Faro/Loulé (Portugal); Referee: Rohit Saggi (Norway); Attendance: 390
**GRE:** Odisseas Vlachodimos, George Henry Ivor Baldock, Konstantinos Mavropanos, Pantelis Hatzidiakos, Konstantinos Tsimikas (85.Dimitrios Hristos Giannoulis), Emmanouil Siopis, Anastasios Bakasetas (Cap) (70.Konstantinos Fortounis), Petros Mantalos, Giorgos Masouras (85.Anastasios Hatzigiovannis), Dimitrios Pelkas (62.Giannis Konstantelias), Giorgos Giakoumakis (62.Vangelis Pavlidis). Trainer: Gustavo Augusto Poyet Domínguez (Uruguay).
**Goals:** Giorgos Masouras (11), Emmanouil Siopis (45), Anastasios Bakasetas (58).

**27.03.2023**  **GREECE - LITHUANIA**  **0-0**  Friendly International
OPAP Arena, Athína; Referee: Jonathan Lardot (Belgium); Attendance: 11,950
**GRE:** Odisseas Vlachodimos, Lazaros Rota, Konstantinos Mavropanos, Pantelis Hatzidiakos, Konstantinos Tsimikas (24.Dimitrios Hristos Giannoulis), Emmanouil Siopis, Anastasios Bakasetas (Cap) (69.Giannis Konstantelias), Petros Mantalos, Giorgos Masouras (80.Giannis Papanikolaou), Konstantinos Fortounis (80.Dimitrios Limnios), Vangelis Pavlidis (69.Giorgos Giakoumakis). Trainer: Gustavo Augusto Poyet Domínguez (Uruguay).

**16.06.2023**  **GREECE - REPUBLIC OF IRELAND**  **2-1(1-1)**  17<sup>th</sup> EC. Qualifiers
OPAP Arena, Athína; Referee: Harald Lechner (Austria); Attendance: 17,452
**GRE:** Odisseas Vlachodimos, George Henry Ivor Baldock, Konstantinos Mavropanos, Pantelis Hatzidiakos, Konstantinos Tsimikas, Dimitrios Kourbelis, Anastasios Bakasetas (Cap) (90+4.Giorgos Tzavelas), Petros Mantalos (90.Emmanouil Siopis), Giorgos Masouras, Dimitrios Pelkas (71.Taxiarchis Fountas), Vangelis Pavlidis (71.Giorgos Giakoumakis). Trainer: Gustavo Augusto Poyet Domínguez (Uruguay).
**Goals:** Anastasios Bakasetas (15 penalty), Giorgos Masouras (49).

**19.06.2023**  **FRANCE - GREECE**  **1-0(0-0)**  17<sup>th</sup> EC. Qualifiers
Stade de France, Saint-Denis, Paris; Referee: Antonio Mateu Lahoz (Spain); Attendance: 76,500
**GRE:** Odisseas Vlachodimos, George Henry Ivor Baldock, Konstantinos Mavropanos [*sent off 70*], Pantelis Hatzidiakos, Konstantinos Tsimikas, Dimitrios Kourbelis (86.Andreas Bouchalakis), Emmanouil Siopis (66.Taxiarchis Fountas), Anastasios Bakasetas (Cap) (71.Panagiotis Retsos), Giorgos Masouras (71.Konstantinos Koulierakis), Petros Mantalos, Giorgos Giakoumakis (66.Vangelis Pavlidis). Trainer: Gustavo Augusto Poyet Domínguez (Uruguay).

| NATIONAL TEAM PLAYERS (16.07.2022 – 15.07.2023) | | | | |
|---|---|---|---|---|
| **Name** | **DOB** | **Caps** | **Goals** | *Club* |
| **Goalkeepers** | | | | |
| Alexandros PASCHALAKIS | 28.07.1989 | 5 | 0 | 2022: *Olympiacos SFP Peiraiás* |
| Odisseas VLACHODIMOS | 26.04.1994 | 33 | 0 | 2022/2023: *Sport Lisboa e Benfica (POR)* |
| **Defenders** | | | | |
| George Henry Ivor BALDOCK | 09.03.1993 | 9 | 0 | 2022/2023: *Sheffield United FC (ENG)* |
| Dimitrios Hristos GIANNOULIS | 17.10.1995 | 23 | 0 | 2022/2023: *Norwich City FC (ENG)* |
| Dimitrios GOUTAS | 04.04.1994 | 3 | 0 | 2022: *Sivasspor Kulübü (TUR)* |
| Pantelis HATZIDIAKOS | 18.01.1997 | 27 | 0 | 2022/2023: *AZ Alkmaar (NED)* |
| Konstantinos KOULIERAKIS | 28.11.2003 | 2 | 0 | 2022/2023: *PAOK Thessaloníki* |
| Giorgos KYRIAKOPOULOS | 05.02.1996 | 7 | 0 | 2022: *US Sassuolo Calcio (ITA)* |
| Konstantinos MAVROPANOS | 11.12.1997 | 19 | 0 | 2022/2023: *VfB Stuttgart (GER)* |
| Panagiotis RETSOS | 09.08.1998 | 7 | 0 | 2022/2023: *Olympiacos SFP Peiraiás* |
| Lazaros ROTA | 23.08.1997 | 7 | 0 | 2022/2023: *AEK Athína* |
| Konstantinos TSIMIKAS | 12.05.1996 | 28 | 0 | 2022/2023: *Liverpool FC (ENG)* |
| Giorgos TZAVELAS | 26.11.1987 | 49 | 3 | 2022/2023: *AEK Athína* |
| **Midfielders** | | | | |
| Sotirios Polykarpos ALEXANDROPOULOS | 26.11.2001 | 7 | 0 | 2022: *Sporting Clube de Braga (POR)* |
| Anastasios BAKASETAS | 28.06.1993 | 57 | 12 | 2022/2023: *Trabzonspor Kulübü (TUR)* |
| Andreas BOUCHALAKIS | 05.04.1993 | 36 | 1 | 2022: *Olympiacos SFP Peiraiás* 02.02.2023-> *Konyaspor Kulübü (TUR)* |
| Konstantinos FORTOUNIS | 16.10.1992 | 56 | 9 | 2023: *Olympiacos SFP Peiraiás* |
| Giannis KONSTANTELIAS | 05.03.2003 | 2 | 0 | 2023: *PAOK Thessaloníki* |
| Dimitrios KOURBELIS | 02.11.1993 | 32 | 1 | 2022/2023: *PAE Panathinaïkos Athína* |
| Petros MANTALOS | 31.08.1991 | 54 | 6 | 2022/2023: *AEK Athína* |
| Giannis PAPANIKOLAOU | 18.11.1998 | 3 | 0 | 2022/2023: *RKS Raków Częstochowa (POL)* |
| Dimitrios PELKAS | 26.10.1993 | 31 | 2 | 2022/2023: *Hull City AFC (ENG)* |
| Emmanouil SIOPIS | 14.05.1994 | 25 | 1 | 2022/2023: *Trabzonspor Kulübü (TUR)* |
| **Forwards** | | | | |
| Anastasios DOUVIKAS | 02.08.1999 | 15 | 1 | 2022: *FC Utrecht (NED)* |
| Taxiarchis FOUNTAS | 04.09.1995 | 14 | 1 | 2022/2023: *Washington DC United (USA)* |
| Giorgos GIAKOUMAKIS | 09.12.1994 | 15 | 2 | 2023: *Atlanta United FC (USA)* |
| Anastasios HATZIGIOVANIS | 31.05.1997 | 11 | 0 | 2022/2023: *MKE Ankaragücü (TUR)* |
| Fotis IOANNIDIS | 10.01.2000 | 4 | 0 | 2022: *PAE Panathinaïkos Athína* |
| Dimitrios LIMNIOS | 27.05.1998 | 24 | 3 | 2023: *1.FC Köln (GER)* |
| Giorgos MASOURAS | 01.01.1994 | 33 | 3 | 2022/2023: *Olympiacos SFP Peiraiás* |
| Vangelis PAVLIDIS | 21.11.1998 | 31 | 6 | 2023: *AZ Alkmaar (NED)* |
| **Trainer** | | | | |
| Gustavo Augusto POYET Domínguez (Uruguay) [from 11.02.2022] | 15.11.1967 | | | 14 M; 8 W; 2 D; 4 L; 19-9 |

# HUNGARY

## The Country:
Magyarország (Hungary )
Capital: Budapest
Surface: 93,030 km²
Inhabitants: 9,678,000 [2023]
Time: UTC+1

## The FA:
Magyar Labdarúgó Szövetség
1112 Budapest, Kánai út 2.D
Tel: +36 1 577 9500
Foundation date: 00.00.1900
Member of FIFA since: 1901
Member of UEFA since: 1954
Website: www.mlsz.hu

## NATIONAL TEAM RECORDS

| RECORDS | | |
|---|---|---|
| First international match: | 12.10.1902, Wien: | Austria – Hungary 5-0 |
| Most international caps: | Balázs Dzsudzsák | - 109 caps (2007-2022) |
| Most international goals: | Ferenc Puskás | - 84 goals / 85 caps (1945-1956) |

### UEFA EUROPEAN CHAMPIONSHIP
| | |
|---|---|
| 1960 | Qualifiers |
| 1964 | Final Tournament (3rd Place) |
| 1968 | Qualifiers |
| 1972 | Final Tournament (4th Place) |
| 1976 | Qualifiers |
| 1980 | Qualifiers |
| 1984 | Qualifiers |
| 1988 | Qualifiers |
| 1992 | Qualifiers |
| 1996 | Qualifiers |
| 2000 | Qualifiers |
| 2004 | Qualifiers |
| 2008 | Qualifiers |
| 2012 | Qualifiers |
| 2016 | Final Tournament (2nd Round of 16) |
| 2020 | Final Tournament (Group Stage) |

### FIFA WORLD CUP
| | |
|---|---|
| 1930 | Did not enter |
| 1934 | Final Tournament (Quarter-Finals) |
| 1938 | Final Tournament (Runners-up) |
| 1950 | Did not enter |
| 1954 | Final Tournament (Runners-up) |
| 1958 | Final Tournament (Group Stage) |
| 1962 | Final Tournament (Quarter-Finals) |
| 1966 | Final Tournament (Quarter-Finals) |
| 1970 | Qualifiers |
| 1974 | Qualifiers |
| 1978 | Final Tournament (Group Stage) |
| 1982 | Final Tournament (Group Stage) |
| 1986 | Final Tournament (Group Stage) |
| 1990 | Qualifiers |
| 1994 | Qualifiers |
| 1998 | Qualifiers |
| 2002 | Qualifiers |
| 2006 | Qualifiers |
| 2010 | Qualifiers |
| 2014 | Qualifiers |
| 2018 | Qualifiers |
| 2022 | Qualifiers |

### OLYMPIC TOURNAMENTS
| | |
|---|---|
| 1908 | Did not enter |
| 1912 | Quarter-Finals |
| 1920 | Did not enter |
| 1924 | 1/8-Finals |
| 1928 | Did not enter |
| 1936 | 1/8-Finals |
| 1948 | Did not enter |
| 1952 | **Winners** |
| 1956 | Did not enter |
| 1960 | 3rd Place |
| 1964 | **Winners** |
| 1968 | **Winners** |
| 1972 | Runners-up |
| 1976 | Qualifiers |
| 1980 | Qualifiers |
| 1984 | Qualifiers |
| 1988 | Qualifiers |
| 1992 | Qualifiers |
| 1996 | Group Stage |
| 2000 | Qualifiers |
| 2004 | Qualifiers |
| 2008 | Qualifiers |
| 2012 | Qualifiers |
| 2016 | Qualifiers |
| 2020 | Qualifiers |

## UEFA NATIONS LEAGUE

| | |
|---|---|
| 2018/2019 | League C (Group Stage -> promoted to League B) |
| 2020/2021 | League B (Group Stage -> promoted to League A) |
| 2022/2023 | League A (Group Stage) |

## HUNGARIAN CLUB HONOURS IN EUROPEAN CLUB COMPETITIONS:

| European Champion Clubs' Cup (1956-1992) / UEFA Champions League (1993-2023) | | |
|---|---|---|
| None | | |

| Fairs Cup (1858-1971) / UEFA Cup (1972-2009) / UEFA Europa League (2010-2023) | | |
|---|---|---|
| Ferencvárosi FC | 1 | 1964/1965 |

| UEFA Europa Conference League (2021-2023) | | |
|---|---|---|
| None | | |

| UEFA Super Cup (1972-2022) | | |
|---|---|---|
| None | | |

| European Cup Winners' Cup 1961-1999* | | |
|---|---|---|
| None | | |

*defunct competition

## NATIONAL COMPETITIONS
## TABLE OF HONOURS

| | CHAMPIONS | CUP WINNERS | BEST GOALSCORERS | |
|---|---|---|---|---|
| 1901 | Budapesti Torna Club | - | Miltiades Manno (Budapesti Torna Club) | 17 |
| 1902 | Budapesti Torna Club | - | Miltiades Manno (Budapesti Torna Club) | 10 |
| 1903 | Ferencvárosi TC | - | Jenő Károly (MTK Budapest) | 15 |
| 1904 | MTK Budapest | - | József Pokorny (Ferencvárosi TC) | 12 |
| 1905 | Ferencvárosi TC | - | Jenő Károly (MTK Budapest) | 13 |
| 1906/1907 | Ferencvárosi TC | - | Béla Kelemen (Magyar Atlétikai Club) | 21 |
| 1907/1908 | MTK Budapest | - | Gyula Vangel (Magyar Atlétikai Club) | 21 |
| 1908/1909 | Ferencvárosi TC | - | Imre Schlosser (Ferencvárosi TC) | 30 |
| 1909/1910 | Ferencvárosi TC | MTK Budapest | Imre Schlosser (Ferencvárosi TC) | 18 |
| 1910/1911 | Ferencvárosi TC | MTK Budapest | Imre Schlosser (Ferencvárosi TC) | 38 |
| 1911/1912 | Ferencvárosi TC | MTK Budapest | Imre Schlosser (Ferencvárosi TC) | 34 |
| 1912/1913 | Ferencvárosi TC | Ferencvárosi TC | Imre Schlosser (Ferencvárosi TC) | 33 |
| 1913/1914 | MTK Budapest | MTK Budapest | Imre Schlosser (Ferencvárosi TC) | 21 |
| 1914/1915 | *No competition* | *No competition* | - | |
| 1915/1916 | *No competition* | *No competition* | | |
| 1916/1917 | MTK Budapest | *No competition* | Imre Schlosser (MTK Budapest) | 38 |
| 1917/1918 | MTK Budapest | *No competition* | Alfréd Schaffer (MTK Budapest) | 46 |
| 1918/1919 | MTK Budapest | *No competition* | Alfréd Schaffer (MTK Budapest) | 41 |
| 1919/1920 | MTK Budapest | *No competition* | György Orth (MTK Budapest) | 28 |
| 1920/1921 | MTK Budapest | *No competition* | György Orth (MTK Budapest) | 21 |
| 1921/1922 | MTK Budapest | Ferencvárosi TC | György Orth (MTK Budapest) | 26 |
| 1922/1923 | MTK Budapest | MTK Budapest | István Priboj (Újpesti TE) | 25 |
| 1923/1924 | MTK Budapest | *No competition* | József Jeszmás (Újpesti TE) | 15 |
| 1924/1925 | MTK Budapest | MTK Budapest | György Molnár (MTK Budapest) | 21 |
| 1925/1926 | Ferencvárosi TC | Kispest AC | József Takács (Vasas SC Budapest) | 29 |
| 1926/1927 | Ferencvárosi TC | Ferencvárosi TC | László Horváth (Ferencvárosi TC) | 14 |
| 1927/1928 | Ferencvárosi TC | Ferencvárosi TC | József Takács (Ferencvárosi TC) | 31 |
| 1928/1929 | Hungária MTK FC Budapest | *No competition* | József Takács (Ferencvárosi TC) | 41 |
| 1929/1930 | Újpesti TE | Debreceni Bocskai FC | József Takács (Ferencvárosi TC) | 40 |
| 1930/1931 | Újpesti TE | III. Kerületi TVE | Jenő Vincze (Debreceni Bocskai FC) | 20 |
| 1931/1932 | Ferencvárosi TC | Hungária MTK FC Budapest | József Takács (Ferencvárosi TC) | 42 |
| 1932/1933 | Újpesti TE | Ferencvárosi TC | Pál Jávor (Újpesti TE) | 31 |
| 1933/1934 | Ferencvárosi TC | Soroksár FC | Géza Toldi (Ferencvárosi TC) | 27 |
| 1934/1935 | Újpesti TE | Ferencvárosi TC | László Cseh II (MTK Budapest) | 23 |
| 1935/1936 | Hungária MTK FC Budapest | *No competition* | György Sárosi dr. (Ferencvárosi TC) | 36 |
| 1936/1937 | Hungária MTK FC Budapest | *No competition* | László Cseh II (MTK Budapest) | 36 |
| 1937/1938 | Ferencvárosi TC | *No competition* | Gyula Zsengellér (Újpesti TE) | 31 |
| 1938/1939 | Újpesti TE | *No competition* | Gyula Zsengellér (Újpesti TE) | 56 |
| 1939/1940 | Ferencvárosi TC | *No competition* | György Sárosi dr. (Ferencvárosi TC) | 23 |
| 1940/1941 | Ferencvárosi TC | Szolnoki MÁV SE | György Sárosi dr. (Ferencvárosi TC) | 29 |
| 1941/1942 | Csepel SC Budapest | Ferencvárosi TC | György Kalmár (Szegedi AK) | 35 |
| 1942/1943 | Csepel SC Budapest | Ferencvárosi TC | Gyula Zsengellér (Újpesti TE) Jenő Jenőfi (Vasas SC Budapest) | 26 |
| 1943/1944 | Nagyváradi AC | Ferencvárosi TC | Gyula Zsengellér (Újpesti TE) | 33 |
| 1945 | Újpesti TE | *No competition* | Gyula Zsengellér (Újpesti TE) | 36 |
| 1945/1946 | Újpesti TE | *No competition* | Ferenc Deák (Szentlőrinci AC) | 66 |
| 1946/1947 | Újpesti TE | *No competition* | Ferenc Deák (Szentlőrinci AC) | 48 |
| 1947/1948 | Csepel SC Budapest | *No competition* | Ferenc Puskás (Budapest Honvéd SE) | 50 |
| 1948/1949 | Ferencvárosi TC | *No competition* | Ferenc Deák (Ferencvárosi TC) | 59 |
| 1949/1950 | Budapest Honvéd SE | *No competition* | Ferenc Puskás (Budapest Honvéd SE) | 31 |
| 1950 | Budapest Honvéd SE | *No competition* | Ferenc Puskás (Budapest Honvéd SE) | 25 |
| 1951 | Budapesti Textiles SE | *No competition* | Sándor Kocsis (Budapest Honvéd SE) | 30 |
| 1952 | Budapest Honvéd SE | Budapesti Bástya SE | Sándor Kocsis (Budapest Honvéd SE) | 36 |
| 1953 | Budapesti Vörös Lobogó SE | *No competition* | Ferenc Puskás (Budapest Honvéd SE) | 27 |
| 1954 | Budapest Honvéd SE | *No competition* | Sándor Kocsis (Budapest Honvéd SE) | 33 |
| 1955 | Budapest Honvéd SE | Vasas SC Budapest | Zoltán Czibor (Budapest Honvéd SE) Ferenc Machos (Budapest Honvéd SE) | 20 |
| 1956 | *No competition* | *No competition* | - | |
| 1957 | Vasas SC Budapest | *No competition* | Gyula Szilágyi (Vasas SC Budapest) | 17 |
| 1957/1958 | MTK Budapest | Ferencvárosi TC | Zoltán Friedmanszky (Ferencvárosi TC) János Molnár (MTK Budapest) | 16 |
| 1958/1959 | Csepel SC Budapest | *No competition* | Róbert Kisuczky (Csepel) Tivadar Monostori (Dorog) Lajos Tichy (Honvéd) | 15 |
| 1959/1960 | Újpesti Dózsa SC | *No competition* | Flórián Albert (Ferencvárosi TC) | 27 |
| 1960/1961 | Vasas SC Budapest | *No competition* | Flórián Albert (Ferencvárosi TC) Lajos Tichy (Budapest Honvéd SE) | 21 |
| 1961/1962 | Vasas SC Budapest | *No competition* | Lajos Tichy (Budapest Honvéd SE) | 23 |
| 1962/1963 | Ferencvárosi TC | *No competition* | Ferenc Bene (Újpesti Dózsa SC) | 23 |
| 1963 | Győri Vasas ETO | *No competition* | Lajos Tichy (Budapest Honvéd SE) | 13 |
| 1964 | Ferencvárosi TC | Budapest Honvéd SE | Lajos Tichy (Budapest Honvéd SE) | 28 |

| | | | | |
|---|---|---|---|---|
| 1965 | Vasas SC Budapest | Rába Vasas ETO Győr | Flórián Albert (Ferencvárosi TC) | 27 |
| 1966 | Vasas SC Budapest | Rába Vasas ETO Győr | János Farkas (Vasas SC Budapest) | 25 |
| 1967 | Ferencvárosi TC | Rába Vasas ETO Győr | Antal Dunai II (Újpesti Dózsa SC) | 36 |
| 1968 | Ferencvárosi TC | MTK Budapest | Antal Dunai II (Újpesti Dózsa SC) | 31 |
| 1969 | Újpesti Dózsa SC | Újpesti Dózsa SC | Ferenc Bene (Újpesti Dózsa SC) | 27 |
| 1970 | Újpesti Dózsa SC | Újpesti Dózsa SC | Antal Dunai II (Újpesti Dózsa SC) | 14 |
| 1970/1971 | Újpesti Dózsa SC | *No competition* | Mihály Kozma (Budapest Honvéd SE) | 25 |
| 1971/1972 | Újpesti Dózsa SC | Ferencvárosi TC | Ferenc Bene (Újpesti Dózsa SC) | 29 |
| 1972/1973 | Újpesti Dózsa SC | Vasas Budapest SC | Ferenc Bene (Újpesti Dózsa SC) | 23 |
| 1973/1974 | Újpesti Dózsa SC | Ferencvárosi TC | Mihály Kozma (Budapest Honvéd SE) | 27 |
| 1974/1975 | Újpesti Dózsa SC | Újpesti Dózsa SC | Mihály Kozma (Budapest Honvéd SE) Ferenc Bene (Újpesti Dózsa SC) | 20 |
| 1975/1976 | Ferencvárosi TC | Ferencvárosi TC | László Fazekas (Újpesti Dózsa SC) | 19 |
| 1976/1977 | Vasas SC Budapest | Diósgyőri VTK | Béla Várady (Vasas SC Budapest) | 36 |
| 1977/1978 | Újpesti Dózsa SC | Ferencvárosi TC | László Fazekas (Újpesti Dózsa SC) | 24 |
| 1978/1979 | Újpesti Dózsa SC | Rába Vasas ETO Győr | László Fekete (Újpesti Dózsa SC) | 31 |
| 1979/1980 | Budapest Honvéd SE | Diósgyőri VTK | László Fekete (Újpesti Dózsa SC) | 36 |
| 1980/1981 | Ferencvárosi TC | Vasas Budapest SC | Tibor Nyilasi (Ferencvárosi TC) | 30 |
| 1981/1982 | Rába Vasas ETO Győr | Újpesti Dózsa SC | Péter Hannich (Rába Vasas ETO Győr) | 22 |
| 1982/1983 | Rába Vasas ETO Győr | Újpesti Dózsa SC | Lajos Dobány (Pécsi MSC / Szombathely) | 23 |
| 1983/1984 | Budapest Honvéd SE | Siófoki Bányász SK | József Szabó (Videoton SC Székesfehérvár) | 19 |
| 1984/1985 | Budapest Honvéd SE | Budapest Honvéd SE | Lajos Détári (Budapest Honvéd SE) József Kiprich (Tatabányai Bányász) | 18 |
| 1985/1986 | Budapest Honvéd SE | Vasas Budapest SC | Lajos Détári (Budapest Honvéd SE) | 27 |
| 1986/1987 | MTK-VM Budapest | Újpesti Dózsa SC | Lajos Détári (Budapest Honvéd SE) | 19 |
| 1987/1988 | Budapest Honvéd SE | Békéscsabai Előre SSC | Béla Melis (Debreceni VSC) | 19 |
| 1988/1989 | Budapest Honvéd SE | Budapest Honvéd SE | Tamás Petres (Videoton SC Székesfehérvár) | 19 |
| 1989/1990 | Újpesti TE | Pécsi MSC | József Dzurják (Ferencvárosi TC) | 18 |
| 1990/1991 | Budapest Honvéd SE | Ferencvárosi TC | József Gregor (Budapest Honvéd SE) | 19 |
| 1991/1992 | Ferencvárosi TC | Újpesti TE | Pál Fischer (Siófoki Bányász SK) Ferenc Orosz (Vác FC) | 16 |
| 1992/1993 | Kispest Honvéd FC | Ferencvárosi TC | László Répási (Vác FC) | 16 |
| 1993/1994 | Vác FC | Ferencvárosi TC | Béla Illés ( Kispest Honvéd FC) | 17 |
| 1994/1995 | Ferencvárosi TC | Ferencvárosi TC | Sándor Preisinger (Zalaegerszeg) | 21 |
| 1995/1996 | Ferencvárosi TC | Kispest Honvéd FC | Ihor Nichenko (UKR, Stadler FC / Ferencvárosi TC) | 18 |
| 1996/1997 | MTK Budapest FC | MTK Budapest FC | Béla Illés (MTK Budapest FC) | 23 |
| 1997/1998 | Újpesti TE | MTK Budapest FC | Krisztián Tiber (Gázszer FC Gárdony) | 20 |
| 1998/1999 | MTK Hungária FC Budapest | Debreceni VSC | Béla Illés (MTK Hungária FC Budapest) | 22 |
| 1999/2000 | Dunaferr SE Dunaújváros | MTK Hungária FC Budapest | Attila Tököli (Dunaferr SE Dunaújváros) | 22 |
| 2000/2001 | Ferencvárosi TC | Debreceni VSC | Péter Kabát (Vasas SC Budapest) | 24 |
| 2001/2002 | Zalaegerszegi TE FC | Újpesti TE | Attila Tököli (Dunaferr SE Dunaújváros) | 28 |
| 2002/2003 | MTK Hungária FC Budapest | Ferencvárosi TC | Krisztián Kenesei (Zalaegerszegi TE FC) | 23 |
| 2003/2004 | Ferencvárosi TC | Ferencvárosi TC | Mihály Tóth (Soproni VSE) | 17 |
| 2004/2005 | Debreceni VSC | Sopron FC | Tomáš Medveď (SVK, Pápai FC) | 18 |
| 2005/2006 | Debreceni VSC | FC Fehérvár Székesfehérvár | Péter Rajczi (Újpest FC) | 23 |
| 2006/2007 | Debreceni VSC | Budapest Honvéd FC | Ibrahim Sidibe (SEN, Debreceni VSC) Péter Bajzát (Győri ETO FC) | 18 |
| 2007/2008 | MTK Budapest FC | Debreceni VSC | Róbert Waltner (Zalaegerszegi TE FC) | 18 |
| 2008/2009 | Debreceni VSC | Budapest Honvéd FC | Péter Bajzát (Győri ETO FC) | 20 |
| 2009/2010 | Debreceni VSC | Debreceni VSC | Nemanja Nikolić (SRB, Videoton FC Székesfehérvár) | 18 |
| 2010/2011 | Videoton FC Székesfehérvár | Kecskeméti TE | André Alves dos Santos (BRA, Videoton FC Székesfehérvár) | 24 |
| 2011/2012 | Debreceni VSC | Debreceni VSC | Adamo Coulibaly (FRA, Debreceni VSC) | 20 |
| 2012/2013 | Győri ETO FC | Debreceni VSC | Adamo Coulibaly (FRA, Debreceni VSC) | 18 |
| 2013/2014 | Debreceni VSC | Újpest FC | Nemanja Nikolić (Videoton FC Székesfehérvár) Attila Simon (Paksi FC) | 21 |
| 2014/2015 | Videoton FC Székesfehérvár | Ferencvárosi TC | Nemanja Nikolić (Videoton FC Székesfehérvár) | 21 |
| 2015/2016 | Ferencvárosi TC | Ferencvárosi TC | Dániel Böde (Ferencvárosi TC) | 17 |
| 2016/2017 | Budapest Honvéd FC | Ferencvárosi TC | Márton Eppel (Budapest Honvéd FC) | 16 |
| 2017/2018 | Videoton FC Székesfehérvár | Újpest FC | Davide Lanzafame (ITA, Budapest Honvéd FC) | 18 |
| 2018/2019 | Ferencvárosi TC | MOL Vidi FC Székesfehérvár | Davide Lanzafame (ITA, Budapest Honvéd FC) Filip Holender (Budapest Honvéd FC) | 16 |
| 2019/2020 | Ferencvárosi TC | Budapest Honvéd FC | András Radó (Zalaegerszegi TE FC) | 13 |
| 2020/2021 | Ferencvárosi TC | Újpest FC | János Csaba Hahn (Paksi FC) | 22 |
| 2021/2022 | Ferencvárosi TC | Ferencvárosi TC | Ádám Martin (Paksi FC) | 31 |
| 2022/2023 | Ferencvárosi TC | Zalaegerszegi TE FC | Barnabás Varga (Paksi FC) | 26 |

# NATIONAL CHAMPIONSHIP
## Nemzeti Bajnokság I 2022/2023
### (29.07.2022 – 28.05.2023)

**Results**

**Round 1 [29-31.07.2022]**
Budapest Honvéd - Zalaegerszeg 0-1(0-0)
Kecskeméti TE - Vasas FC 0-0
Újpest FC - Mezőkövesd 1-1(1-0)
Kisvárda FC - Debreceni VSC 2-2(0-0)
Paksi FC - Fehérvár FC 2-0(1-0)
Ferencvárosi TC - Puskás Akadémia 1-0(0-0)

**Round 2 [05-07.08.2022]**
Vasas FC - Paksi FC 2-2(2-1)
Debreceni VSC - Kecskeméti TE 1-1(0-0)
Kisvárda FC - Mezőkövesd 4-2(2-1)
Puskás Akadémia - Újpest FC 2-0(1-0)
Fehérvár FC - Budapest Honvéd 4-0(2-0)
Zalaegerszeg - Ferencváros 1-2(1-1) [24.01.23]

**Round 3 [12-14.08.2022]**
Debreceni VSC - Vasas FC 1-1(0-1)
Kecskeméti TE - Mezőkövesd 1-0(1-0)
Újpest FC - Zalaegerszeg 1-1(0-1)
Kisvárda FC - Puskás Akadémia 1-1(0-1)
Ferencvárosi TC - Fehérvár FC 4-0(3-0)
Budapest Honvéd - Paksi FC 3-3(2-0)

**Round 4 [19-22.08.2022]**
Puskás Akadémia - Kecskeméti TE 1-1(0-1)
Zalaegerszeg - Kisvárda FC 1-3(1-1)
Vasas FC - Budapest Honvéd 1-2(1-1)
Mezőkövesd - Debreceni VSC 4-2(3-1)
Fehérvár - Újpest FC 0-1(0-0) [10.10.2022]
Paksi FC - Ferencváros 1-3(0-0) [01.02.2023]

**Round 5 [26-28.08.2022]**
Újpest FC - Paksi FC 2-3(0-1)
Mezőkövesd - Vasas FC 1-1(1-1)
Kecskeméti TE - Zalaegerszeg 3-1(1-1)
Debreceni VSC - Puskás Akadémia 1-1(1-0)
Kisvárda FC - Fehérvár FC 3-1(0-0)
Ferencvárosi TC - Budapest Honvéd 3-1(1-0)

**Round 6 [30.08.-01.09.2022]**
Puskás Akadémia - Mezőkövesd 1-0(0-0)
Zalaegerszeg - Debreceni VSC 4-2(1-0)
Paksi FC - Kisvárda FC 1-3(0-2)
Fehérvár FC - Kecskeméti TE 2-1(1-1)
Vasas FC - Ferencvárosi TC 0-1(0-1)
Budapest Honvéd - Újpest FC 0-0

**Round 7 [02-04.09.2022]**
Mezőkövesd - Zalaegerszeg 0-5(0-1)
Kecskeméti TE - Paksi FC 3-1(0-0)
Vasas FC - Puskás Akadémia 1-1(1-0)
Debreceni VSC - Fehérvár FC 1-0(1-0)
Kisvárda FC - Budapest Honvéd 0-1(0-1)
Újpest FC - Ferencvárosi TC 0-6(0-4)

**Round 8 [10-11.09.2022]**
Paksi FC - Debreceni VSC 1-0(1-0)
Budapest Honvéd - Kecskeméti TE 0-0
Fehérvár FC - Mezőkövesd 2-1(1-0)
Zalaegerszeg - Puskás Akadémia 1-2(1-0)
Ferencvárosi TC - Kisvárda FC 3-0(1-0)
Újpest FC - Vasas FC 2-1(1-1)

**Round 9 [30.09.-02.10.2022]**
Mezőkövesd - Paksi FC 1-2(1-0)
Újpest FC - Kisvárda FC 4-0(3-0)
Debreceni VSC - Budapest Honvéd 4-3(3-0)
Vasas FC - Zalaegerszeg 1-1(1-0)
Kecskeméti TE - Ferencvárosi TC 2-0(2-0)
Puskás Akadémia - Fehérvár FC 1-1(0-0)

**Round 10 [07-09.10.2022]**
Fehérvár FC - Zalaegerszeg 1-1(1-0)
Újpest FC - Kecskeméti TE 1-2(0-0)
Kisvárda FC - Vasas FC 2-0(2-0)
Budapest Honvéd - Mezőkövesd 2-2(2-2)
Paksi FC - Puskás Akadémia 1-3(1-1)
Ferencvárosi TC - Debreceni VSC 2-0(1-0)

**Round 11 [14-16.10.2022]**
Kecskeméti TE - Kisvárda FC 3-3(1-1)
Zalaegerszeg - Paksi FC 3-0(2-0)
Puskás Akadémia - Budapest Honvéd 1-0(1-0)
Vasas FC - Fehérvár FC 2-0(1-0)
Debreceni VSC - Újpest FC 4-1(1-1)
Mezőkövesd - Ferencvárosi TC 2-1(1-1)

**Round 12 [21-24.10.2022]**
Vasas FC - Kecskeméti TE 1-2(0-2)
Zalaegerszeg - Budapest Honvéd 0-2(0-1)
Fehérvár FC - Paksi FC 1-1(1-0)
Puskás Akadémia - Ferencvárosi TC 2-4(2-3)
Mezőkövesd - Újpest FC 1-0(0-0)
Debreceni VSC - Kisvárda FC 2-3(1-1)

**Round 13 [28-30.10.2022]**
Mezőkövesd - Kisvárda FC 1-1(0-0)
Budapest Honvéd - Fehérvár FC 0-1(0-1)
Kecskeméti TE - Debreceni VSC 2-2(1-0)
Paksi FC - Vasas FC 0-1(0-1)
Újpest FC - Puskás Akadémia 3-3(1-1)
Ferencvárosi TC - Zalaegerszeg 2-1(1-0)

**Round 14 [05-06.11.2022]**
Mezőkövesd - Kecskeméti TE 2-1(2-1)
Puskás Akadémia - Kisvárda FC 0-1(0-0)
Zalaegerszeg - Újpest FC 1-0(1-0)
Vasas FC - Debreceni VSC 0-3(0-3)
Paksi FC - Budapest Honvéd 5-0(2-0)
Fehérvár FC - Ferencvárosi TC 2-2(0-1)

**Round 15 [08-10.11.2022]**
Kisvárda FC - Zalaegerszeg 0-3(0-1)
Kecskeméti TE - Puskás Akadémia 1-1(0-1)
Debreceni VSC - Mezőkövesd 1-0(0-0)
Ferencvárosi TC - Paksi FC 3-2(2-2)
Újpest FC - Fehérvár FC 2-1(1-0)
Budapest Honvéd - Vasas FC 2-0(0-0)

**Round 16 [12-13.11.2022]**
Puskás Akadémia - Debreceni VSC 2-1(1-1)
Paksi FC - Újpest FC 3-1(1-0)
Zalaegerszeg - Kecskeméti TE 0-0
Fehérvár FC - Kisvárda FC 4-1(2-0)
Budapest Honvéd - Ferencvárosi TC 0-2(0-0)
Vasas FC - Mezőkövesd 1-0(1-0)

**Round 17 [28-29.01.2023]**
Kisvárda FC - Paksi FC 2-2(0-1)
Debreceni VSC - Zalaegerszeg 3-0(2-0)
Ferencvárosi TC - Vasas FC 0-0
Mezőkövesd - Puskás Akadémia 1-0(0-0)
Újpest FC - Budapest Honvéd 2-1(0-1)
Kecskeméti TE - Fehérvár FC 2-1(1-1)

**Round 18 [03-05.02.2023]**
Puskás Akadémia - Vasas FC 1-1(1-0)
Paksi FC - Kecskeméti TE 0-0
Budapest Honvéd - Kisvárda FC 1-1(0-0)
Fehérvár FC - Debreceni VSC 1-1(0-1)
Zalaegerszeg - Mezőkövesd 0-0
Ferencvárosi TC - Újpest FC 3-1(1-0)

**Round 19 [10-12.02.2023]**
Mezőkövesd - Fehérvár FC 2-1(1-1)
Kecskeméti TE - Budapest Honvéd 2-2(2-2)
Kisvárda FC - Ferencvárosi TC 0-0
Debreceni VSC - Paksi FC 2-1(0-0)
Puskás Akadémia - Zalaegerszeg 1-0(0-0)
Vasas FC - Újpest FC 0-1(0-0)

**Round 20 [17-19.02.2023]**
Kisvárda FC - Újpest FC 2-1(1-0)
Paksi FC - Mezőkövesd 0-2(0-0)
Ferencvárosi TC - Kecskeméti TE 1-1(1-0)
Fehérvár FC - Puskás Akadémia 1-1(0-0)
Zalaegerszeg - Vasas FC 0-0
Budapest Honvéd - Debreceni VSC 2-3(0-1)

**Round 21 [24-26.02.2023]**
Mezőkövesd - Budapest Honvéd 0-0
Zalaegerszeg - Fehérvár FC 2-1(1-1)
Puskás Akadémia - Paksi FC 1-4(1-2)
Vasas FC - Kisvárda FC 2-2(1-1)
Kecskeméti TE - Újpest FC 2-2(0-1)
Debreceni VSC - Ferencvárosi TC 0-2(0-1)

**Round 22 [03-05.03.2023]**
Ferencvárosi TC - Mezőkövesd 1-1(1-1)
Kisvárda FC - Kecskeméti TE 0-1(0-0)
Paksi FC - Zalaegerszeg 3-1(2-1)
Fehérvár FC - Vasas FC 2-1(1-1)
Budapest Honvéd - Puskás Akadémia 3-1(0-0)
Újpest FC - Debreceni VSC 1-1(1-1)

**Round 23 [11-12.03.2023]**
Kisvárda FC - Debreceni VSC 0-1(0-0)
Paksi FC - Fehérvár FC 2-1(1-1)
Budapest Honvéd - Zalaegerszeg 1-0(1-0)
Kecskeméti TE - Vasas FC 2-0(0-0)
Újpest FC - Mezőkövesd 1-0(1-0)
Ferencvárosi TC - Puskás Akadémia 1-2(0-2)

**Round 24 [18-19.03.2023]**
Mezőkövesd - Kisvárda FC 1-1(1-1)
Debreceni VSC - Kecskeméti TE 1-2(0-0)
Fehérvár FC - Budapest Honvéd 2-0(1-0)
Vasas FC - Paksi FC 2-3(0-1)
Puskás Akadémia - Újpest FC 5-1(1-0)
Zalaegerszeg - Ferencvárosi TC 1-0(1-0)

**Round 25 [01-02.04.2023]**
Kisvárda FC - Puskás Akadémia 2-2(1-0)
Újpest FC - Zalaegerszeg 3-2(1-0)
Budapest Honvéd - Paksi FC 1-2(0-1)
Kecskeméti TE - Mezőkövesd 0-1(0-0)
Ferencvárosi TC - Fehérvár FC 2-2(0-1)
Debreceni VSC - Vasas FC 3-1(2-0)

**Round 26 [07-09.04.2023]**
Mezőkövesd - Debreceni VSC 0-1(0-0)
Puskás Akadémia - Kecskeméti TE 0-3(0-1)
Fehérvár FC - Újpest FC 0-0
Paksi FC - Ferencvárosi TC 3-2(1-1)
Vasas FC - Budapest Honvéd 0-1(0-0)
Zalaegerszeg - Kisvárda FC 0-0

**Round 27 [14-16.04.2023]**
Debreceni VSC - Puskás Akadémia 0-1(0-0)
Kecskeméti TE - Zalaegerszeg 3-0(2-0)
Mezőkövesd - Vasas FC 1-4(1-2)
Ferencvárosi TC - Budapest Honvéd 3-0(1-0)
Kisvárda FC - Fehérvár FC 0-0
Újpest FC - Paksi FC 3-2(2-1)

| Round 28 [21-23.04.2023] | |
|---|---|
| Budapest Honvéd - Újpest FC | 0-1(0-0) |
| Fehérvár FC - Kecskeméti TE | 1-2(0-2) |
| Vasas FC - Ferencvárosi TC | 0-1(0-0) |
| Paksi FC - Kisvárda FC | 2-0(1-0) |
| Puskás Akadémia - Mezőkövesd | 2-1(2-0) |
| Zalaegerszeg - Debreceni VSC | 0-2(0-1) |

| Round 29 [28.04.-01.05.2023] | |
|---|---|
| Kecskeméti TE - Paksi FC | 2-3(2-0) |
| Mezőkövesd - Zalaegerszeg | 1-2(1-0) |
| Kisvárda FC - Budapest Honvéd | 2-2(1-1) |
| Vasas FC - Puskás Akadémia | 2-2(0-0) |
| Debreceni VSC - Fehérvár FC | 2-0(0-0) |
| Újpest FC - Ferencvárosi TC | 2-3(1-1) |

| Round 30 [05-07.05.2023] | |
|---|---|
| Budapest Honvéd - Kecskeméti TE | 1-0(0-0) |
| Újpest FC - Vasas FC | 1-1(1-1) |
| Paksi FC - Debreceni VSC | 0-0 |
| Ferencvárosi TC - Kisvárda FC | 3-0(0-0) |
| Zalaegerszeg - Puskás Akadémia | 2-1(2-1) |
| Fehérvár FC - Mezőkövesd | 1-1(1-0) |

| Round 31 [13-14.05.2023] | |
|---|---|
| Vasas FC - Zalaegerszeg | 1-1(0-1) |
| Debreceni VSC - Budapest Honvéd | 0-0 |
| Kecskeméti TE - Ferencvárosi TC | 2-0(1-0) |
| Mezőkövesd - Paksi FC | 6-1(2-0) |
| Kisvárda FC - Újpest FC | 2-0(0-0) |
| Puskás Akadémia - Fehérvár FC | 2-1(0-0) |

| Round 32 [19-21.05.2023] | |
|---|---|
| Paksi FC - Puskás Akadémia | 0-2(0-0) |
| Kisvárda FC - Vasas FC | 2-1(1-1) |
| Fehérvár FC - Zalaegerszeg | 3-0(2-0) |
| Ferencvárosi TC - Debreceni VSC | 1-3(1-0) |
| Budapest Honvéd - Mezőkövesd | 2-3(1-1) |
| Újpest FC - Kecskeméti TE | 3-0(2-0) |

| Round 33 [26-28.05.2023] | |
|---|---|
| Kecskeméti TE - Kisvárda FC | 1-0(0-0) |
| Zalaegerszeg - Paksi FC | 1-1(1-1) |
| Debreceni VSC - Újpest FC | 2-0(1-0) |
| Puskás Akadémia - Budapest Honvéd | 2-1(0-0) |
| Vasas FC - Fehérvár FC | 0-0 |
| Mezőkövesd - Ferencvárosi TC | 1-0(1-0) |

## Final Standings

| | | | | | | Total | | | | Home | | | | | Away | | | | |
|---|---|---|---|---|---|---|---|---|---|---|---|---|---|---|---|---|---|---|---|
| 1. | Ferencvárosi TC | 33 | 19 | 6 | 8 | 62 - 33 | 63 | 10 | 4 | 2 | 33 - 14 | | 9 | 2 | 6 | 29 - 19 |
| 2. | Kecskeméti TE | 33 | 15 | 12 | 6 | 48 - 32 | 57 | 9 | 6 | 2 | 31 - 17 | | 6 | 6 | 4 | 17 - 15 |
| 3. | Debreceni VSC | 33 | 15 | 9 | 9 | 52 - 39 | 54 | 9 | 4 | 4 | 28 - 17 | | 6 | 5 | 5 | 24 - 22 |
| 4. | Puskás Ferenc Labdarugó Akadémia Felcsút | 33 | 14 | 11 | 8 | 48 - 42 | 53 | 9 | 3 | 4 | 24 - 20 | | 5 | 8 | 4 | 24 - 22 |
| 5. | Paksi FC | 33 | 14 | 7 | 12 | 57 - 57 | 49 | 8 | 2 | 6 | 24 - 19 | | 6 | 5 | 6 | 33 - 38 |
| 6. | Kisvárda FC | 33 | 10 | 13 | 10 | 43 - 49 | 43 | 6 | 7 | 4 | 24 - 20 | | 4 | 6 | 6 | 19 - 29 |
| 7. | Mezőkövesdi SE | 33 | 11 | 9 | 13 | 40 - 43 | 42 | 8 | 4 | 5 | 25 - 23 | | 3 | 5 | 8 | 15 - 20 |
| 8. | Újpest FC | 33 | 11 | 8 | 14 | 42 - 55 | 41 | 8 | 5 | 4 | 32 - 28 | | 3 | 3 | 10 | 10 - 27 |
| 9. | Zalaegerszegi TE FC | 33 | 10 | 9 | 14 | 37 - 43 | 39 | 6 | 5 | 5 | 17 - 16 | | 4 | 4 | 9 | 20 - 27 |
| 10. | Fehérvár FC Székesfehérvár | 33 | 8 | 11 | 14 | 38 - 43 | 35 | 7 | 7 | 2 | 27 - 14 | | 1 | 4 | 12 | 11 - 29 |
| 11. | Budapest Honvéd FC (Relegated) | 33 | 8 | 9 | 16 | 34 - 51 | 33 | 4 | 5 | 7 | 18 - 20 | | 4 | 4 | 9 | 16 - 31 |
| 12. | Vasas FC Budapest (Relegated) | 33 | 4 | 14 | 15 | 29 - 43 | 26 | 2 | 7 | 8 | 16 - 23 | | 2 | 7 | 7 | 13 - 20 |

## Top goalscorers:

| | | |
|---|---|---|
| 26 | **Barnabás Varga** | *Paksi FC* |
| 14 | Stefan Dražić (SRB) | *Mezőkövesdi SE* |
| 13 | Dorian Babunski (MKD) | *Debreceni VSC* |
| 13 | Kenan Kodro-Maksumić (BIH) | *Fehérvár FC Székesfehérvár* |
| 13 | Nenad Lukić | *Budapest Honvéd FC* |

# NATIONAL CUP
## Magyar Kupa 2022/2023

### Eighth Round [18-19.10.2022]

| | | | | |
|---|---|---|---|---|
| Nyíregyháza Spartacus FC - Vasas FC Budapest | 1-2(0-1) | | Nagykanizsa FC - Békéscsaba 1912 Előre SE | 1-4(0-1) |
| Győri ETO FC - Kecskeméti TE | 1-0(1-0) | | ESMTK Budapest - BFC Siófok | 3-1(1-1,1-1) |
| Iváncsa KSE - Ferencvárosi TC | 3-2(1-2,2-2) | | Nagyatádi FC - Monori SE | 0-3(0-2) |
| Debreceni EAC - Debreceni VSC | 0-4(0-1) | | Nyergesújfalu SE - Mezőkövesdi SE | 1-4(0-3) |
| Balatonfüredi FC - Paksi FC | 0-3(0-1) | | Szombathelyi Haladás - Budapest Honvéd FC | 1-2(1-2) |
| Budafoki MTE - Szeged-Csanád Grosics Akadémia | 1-0(0-0,0-0) | | FC Ajka - Újpest FC | 1-3(1-1) |
| Mosónmagyaróvári TE - Kisvárda FC | 0-3(0-1) | | Kazincbarcikai SC - Zalaegerszegi TE FC | 0-2(0-1) |
| BTE Felsőzsolca - MTK Budapest FC | 0-6(0-1) | | Fehérvár FC - Puskás Ferenc Labdarugó Akadémia | 0-1(0-1) |

### 1/8-Finals [01.02.& 07-09.2023]

| | | | | |
|---|---|---|---|---|
| MTK Budapest FC - Mezőkövesdi SE | 0-2(0-1) | | Iváncsa KSE - Budafoki MTE | 1-2(1-0) |
| Vasas FC Budapest - Budapest Honvéd FC | 2-0(1-0) | | ESMTK Budapest - Kisvárda FC | 0-1(0-0,0-0) |
| Monori SE - Paksi FC | 1-5(1-2) | | Győri ETO FC - Debreceni VSC | 1-2(0-1,1-1) |
| Békéscsaba 1912 Előre SE - Zalaegerszegi TE FC | 0-2(0-0) | | Puskás Ferenc Labdarugó Akadémia - Újpest FC | 0-0 aet; 5-4 pen |

### Quarter-Finals [28.02.-02.03.2023]

| | | | | |
|---|---|---|---|---|
| Mezőkövesdi SE - Zalaegerszegi TE FC | 1-4(0-1) | | Paksi FC - Vasas FC Budapest | 2-3(1-2) |
| Budafoki MTE - Kisvárda FC | 2-0(2-0) | | Debreceni VSC-Puskás Ferenc Labdarugó Akadémia | 1-3(1-2) |

### Semi-Finals [04-05.04.2023]

| | | | | |
|---|---|---|---|---|
| Zalaegerszegi TE - Puskás Ferenc Labd. Akadémia | 1-0(0-0,0-0) | | Budafoki MTE - Vasas FC Budapest | 3-0(3-0) |

03.05.2023; Puskás Aréna, Budapest; Referee: István Vad; Attendance: 24,152
**Budafoki MTE - Zalaegerszegi TE FC**                    **0-2(0-0,0-0)**

**Budafok:** Bence Gundel-Takács, Botond Nándori (106.Andor Margitics), Márk Jagodics, Dominik Fótyik, Márk Bíró (89.Máté Fekete), András Csonka, Bálint Oláh, Olivér Kalmár (106.Gergő Vaszicsku), Dávid Kovács (Cap) (65.Márió Németh), Péter Beke (100.Balázs Bakti), Olivér Horváth (79.Zoltán Vasvári). Trainer: János Mátyus.

**Zalaegerszeg:** Patrik Demjén, Attila Mocsi, Dávid Kálnoki-Kis (Cap), Dániel Csóka, Gergő Mim (46.András Huszti), Bence Gergényi (98.Bence Bedi), Bojan Sanković (112.Barnabás Kovács), Norbert Szendrei, Meshack Izuchukwu Ubochioma (77.Szabolcs Szalay), Mátyás Tajti (120.Zoran Lesjak), Eduvie Marho Ikoba (46.Dániel Németh). Trainer: Gábor Boér.

**Goals:** 0-1 Dániel Németh (117), 0-2 Szabolcs Szalay (120+2).

## THE CLUBS 2022/2023

### Debreceni Vasutas Sport Club

| | | | |
|---|---|---|---|
| **Founded**: | 12.03.1902 | | |
| **Stadium**: | Nagyerdei Stadion, Debrecen (20,340) | | |
| **Trainer:** | João Pedro de Oliveira Janeiro (POR) | 29.06.1981 | |
| [31.08.2022] | Tibor Dombi | 11.11.1973 | |
| [21.09.2022] | Srđan Blagojević (SRB) | 06.06.1973 | |

| Goalkeepers: | DOB | M | (s) | G |
|---|---|---|---|---|
| Dávid Gróf | 17.04.1989 | 6 | | |
| Alex Hrabina | 05.04.1995 | 4 | | |
| Balázs Megyeri | 31.03.1990 | 19 | | |
| Marko Milošević (SRB) | 07.02.1991 | 4 | (1) | |
| **Defenders:** | **DOB** | **M** | **(s)** | **G** |
| Nimród Baranyai | 06.08.2003 | 2 | (2) | |
| *Charleston* Silva dos Santos (BRA) | 23.09.1996 | 3 | (2) | |
| *Christian* Manrique Díaz (ESP) | 02.10.1998 | 19 | (1) | 1 |
| Sylvain Boris Nabil Deslandes (FRA) | 25.04.1997 | 13 | (1) | 1 |
| Meldin Drešković (MNE) | 26.03.1998 | 20 | (4) | 2 |
| János Ferenczi | 03.04.1991 | 27 | (2) | |
| Erik Kusnyír | 07.02.2000 | 20 | (1) | |
| Dušan Lagator (MNE) | 29.03.1994 | 19 | (5) | 2 |
| Sámuel Major | 09.01.2002 | | (2) | |
| Oleksandr Romanchuk (UKR) | 16.12.1999 | 18 | (3) | |
| *Saná* Gomes (GNB) | 10.10.1999 | 2 | (2) | |
| **Midfielders:** | **DOB** | **M** | **(s)** | **G** |
| Okan Aydin (TUR) | 08.05.1994 | | (1) | |
| Péter Baráth | 21.02.2002 | 11 | (4) | 2 |

| | DOB | M | (s) | G |
|---|---|---|---|---|
| Zsombor Bévárdi | 30.01.1999 | 8 | (10) | 1 |
| Ádám Bódi | 18.10.1990 | 8 | (14) | 3 |
| Balázs Dzsudzsák | 23.12.1986 | 29 | (2) | 6 |
| Tamás Farkas | 14.07.2003 | | (1) | |
| Krisztofer György Horváth | 08.01.2002 | 4 | (3) | |
| Alexandros Kyziridis (GRE) | 16.09.2000 | 8 | (11) | |
| Stefan Lončar (MNE) | 19.02.1996 | 12 | (5) | 1 |
| Georgios Neofytidis (GRE) | 28.07.2000 | 5 | (5) | 1 |
| Hamzat Ojediran (NGA) | 14.11.2003 | 3 | (4) | |
| Bence Sós | 10.05.1994 | 11 | (13) | 2 |
| József Varga | 06.06.1988 | 16 | (6) | 2 |
| **Forwards:** | **DOB** | **M** | **(s)** | **G** |
| Dorian Babunski (MKD) | 29.08.1996 | 25 | (5) | 13 |
| Donát Bárány | 04.09.2000 | 5 | (12) | 4 |
| Matar Dièye (SEN) | 10.01.1998 | | (1) | |
| Norbert Kundrák | 18.05.1999 | 1 | (1) | |
| Antonio Mance (CRO) | 07.08.1995 | 3 | (12) | 2 |
| Peter Ukeme Olawale (NGA) | 26.07.2002 | | (4) | |
| Márk Szécsi | 22.05.1994 | 28 | (4) | 5 |
| Kevin Varga | 30.03.1996 | 10 | (2) | 2 |

### Fehérvár Football Club Székesfehérvár

| | | | |
|---|---|---|---|
| **Founded**: | 1941 | | |
| **Stadium**: | MOL Aréna Sóstó, Székesfehérvár (14,144) | | |
| **Trainer:** | Michael Boris (GER) | 03.06.1975 | |
| [17.10.2022] | Szabolcs Huszti | 18.04.1983 | |
| [15.03.2023] | Bartosz Grzelak (SWE) | 02.11.1978 | |

| Goalkeepers: | DOB | M | (s) | G |
|---|---|---|---|---|
| Dániel Kovács | 16.01.1994 | 32 | | |
| Emil Rockov (SRB) | 27.01.1995 | 1 | | |
| **Defenders:** | **DOB** | **M** | **(s)** | **G** |
| Barnabás Bese | 06.05.1994 | 11 | (5) | |
| Attila Csaba Fiola | 17.02.1990 | 19 | (2) | |
| Szilveszter Hangya | 02.01.1994 | 6 | (4) | |
| Marcel Heister (GER) | 29.07.1992 | 23 | (4) | |
| Kasper Larsen (DEN) | 25.01.1993 | 17 | (2) | 1 |
| Loïc Négo | 15.01.1991 | 22 | (4) | 1 |
| Nikola Serafimov (MKD) | 11.08.1999 | 11 | | 1 |
| Artem Shabanov (UKR) | 07.03.1992 | 4 | (1) | |
| Ianique dos Santos Tavares „Stopira" (CPV) | 20.05.1988 | 25 | | 2 |
| **Midfielders:** | **DOB** | **M** | **(s)** | **G** |
| *Alef* dos Santos Saldanha (BRA) | 28.01.1995 | 1 | (3) | |
| Claudiu Vasile Bumba (ROU) | 05.01.1994 | 5 | (6) | |
| Áron Csongvai | 31.10.2000 | 12 | | 1 |
| Deybi Aldair Flores Flores (HON) | 16.06.1996 | 14 | (1) | |
| Lyes Hafid Houri (FRA) | 19.01.1996 | 12 | (5) | |
| Mátyás Katona | 30.12.1999 | 7 | (6) | 2 |

| | DOB | M | (s) | G |
|---|---|---|---|---|
| Bence Kovács (SVK) | 14.01.2004 | | (1) | |
| Bogdan Lyednyev (UKR) | 07.04.1998 | 5 | (3) | |
| Evgeniy Makarenko (UKR) | 21.05.1991 | 9 | (8) | 1 |
| Milan Pető | 25.01.2005 | 1 | | |
| Peter Pokorný (SVK) | 08.08.2001 | 12 | (11) | |
| *Rúben* Rafael Melo Silva *Pinto* (POR) | 24.04.1992 | 9 | (1) | |
| **Forwards:** | **DOB** | **M** | **(s)** | **G** |
| Bence Babos | 12.02.2004 | | (1) | |
| Funsho Ibrahim Bamgboye (NGA) | 09.01.1999 | 3 | (8) | 2 |
| Tobias Christensen (NOR) | 11.05.2000 | 9 | (5) | |
| Palkó Dárdai | 24.04.1999 | 25 | (4) | 5 |
| Lirim Kastrati (KOS) | 16.01.1999 | 16 | (9) | 4 |
| Kenan Kodro-Maksumić (BIH) | 19.08.1993 | 30 | (3) | 13 |
| Zsombor Menyhárt | 24.06.2004 | 1 | (1) | |
| Ivan Petryak (UKR) | 13.03.1994 | 2 | (1) | |
| Szabolcs Schön | 27.09.2000 | 15 | (6) | 4 |
| Levente Szabó | 06.06.1999 | 1 | (5) | |
| Ákos Szendrei | 23.01.2003 | | (3) | |
| Budu Zivzivadze (GEO) | 10.03.1994 | 3 | (7) | 1 |

## Ferencvárosi Torna Club

| | | | | |
|---|---|---|---|---|
| **Founded**: | 03.05.1899 | | | |
| **Stadium**: | Groupama Aréna, Budapest (22,043) | | | |
| **Trainer**: | Stanislav Cherchesov (RUS) | | 02.09.1963 | |

| Goalkeepers: | DOB | M | (s) | G |
|---|---|---|---|---|
| Ádám Bogdán | 27.09.1987 | 3 | | |
| Dénes Dibusz | 16.11.1990 | 29 | | |
| Gergő Szécsi | 07.02.1989 | 1 | | |
| **Defenders:** | **DOB** | **M** | **(s)** | **G** |
| Myenty Abena (SUR) | 12.12.1994 | 7 | (3) | |
| Endre Botka | 25.08.1994 | 18 | (5) | 3 |
| Eldar Čivić (BIH) | 28.05.1996 | 15 | (2) | |
| Norbert Kaján | 11.09.2004 | 1 | (1) | |
| Mats Knoester (NED) | 19.11.1998 | 25 | (2) | |
| Adnan Kovačević (BIH) | 09.09.1993 | 18 | (2) | |
| Samy Mmaee A Nwambeben (MAR) | 08.09.1996 | 14 | (2) | 2 |
| Lóránd Pászka | 22.03.1996 | 18 | (1) | 2 |
| Rasmus Thelander (DEN) | 09.07.1991 | 3 | | |
| Henry Swensson Wingo (USA) | 04.10.1995 | 10 | (4) | |
| **Midfielders:** | **DOB** | **M** | **(s)** | **G** |
| Péter Baráth | 21.02.2002 | 4 | (4) | |
| Muhamed Bešić (BIH) | 10.09.1992 | 11 | (5) | |
| Mehdi Boudjemaa (FRA) | 07.04.1998 | 2 | (1) | |
| Anderson Esiti (NGA) | 24.05.1994 | 14 | (7) | 1 |
| Giorgi Kharaishvili (GEO) | 29.07.1996 | | (1) | |
| Aïssa Laïdouni (TUN) | 13.12.1996 | 7 | (3) | |
| Stjepan Lončar (BIH) | 10.11.1996 | 1 | | |
| Xavier Mercier (FRA) | 25.07.1989 | 11 | (5) | 1 |
| Dávid Sigér | 30.11.1990 | 8 | (4) | |
| Alex Tóth | 23.10.2005 | | (2) | |
| Bálint Máté Vécsei | 13.07.1993 | 12 | (7) | 1 |
| Kristoffer Zachariassen (NOR) | 27.01.1994 | 20 | (7) | 7 |
| **Forwards:** | **DOB** | **M** | **(s)** | **G** |
| Carlos Daniel Auzqui (ARG) | 16.03.1991 | 6 | (11) | 3 |
| Fortune Akpan Bassey (NGA) | 06.10.1998 | 1 | | |
| Bi Sylvestre Franck Fortune Boli (CIV) | 07.12.1993 | 5 | (4) | 3 |
| Nikolai Baden Frederiksen (DEN) | 18.05.2000 | 3 | (3) | |
| Amer Gojak (BIH) | 13.02.1997 | 13 | (6) | 2 |
| Owusu Kwabena (GHA) | 18.06.1997 | 5 | (5) | 2 |
| Krisztián Lisztes | 06.05.2005 | 2 | (7) | 5 |
| José Marcos Costa Martins „Marquinhos" (BRA) | 23.10.1999 | 17 | (12) | 6 |
| Ryan Mmaee Nwambeben Kabir (MAR) | 01.11.1997 | 18 | (6) | 12 |
| Tokmac Chol Nguen (NOR) | 20.10.1993 | 11 | (9) | 1 |
| Ángelo Nicolás Sagal Tapia (CHI) | 18.04.1993 | 4 | (3) | |
| Adama Traoré I (MLI) | 05.06.1995 | 26 | (4) | 11 |

## Budapest Honvéd Football Club

| | | | | |
|---|---|---|---|---|
| **Founded**: | 03.08.1909 | | | |
| **Stadium**: | Bozsik Aréna, Budapest (8,428) | | | |
| **Trainer**: | Thomas Courts (SCO) | | 10.08.1981 | |
| [24.10.2022] | Dean Klafurić (CRO) | | 26.07.1972 | |

| Goalkeepers: | DOB | M | (s) | G |
|---|---|---|---|---|
| Gellért Dúzs | 24.02.2002 | 7 | | |
| Péter Szappanos | 14.11.1990 | 23 | | |
| Tomáš Tujvel (SVK) | 19.09.1983 | 3 | (2) | |
| **Defenders:** | **DOB** | **M** | **(s)** | **G** |
| Barna Benczenleitner | 16.09.2003 | 3 | (1) | |
| Luka Capan (CRO) | 06.04.1995 | 17 | (1) | |
| Lazar Ćirković (SRB) | 22.08.1992 | 12 | (5) | |
| Albi Doka (ALB) | 26.06.1997 | 14 | (8) | |
| Christian Gomis (SEN) | 25.08.1998 | 22 | (4) | |
| Viðar Ari Jónsson (ISL) | 10.03.1994 | 6 | (16) | 1 |
| Łukasz Klemenz (POL) | 24.09.1995 | 9 | (1) | |
| Ivan Lovrić (CRO) | 11.07.1985 | 15 | (3) | |
| Herdi Prenga (ALB) | 31.08.1994 | 29 | (1) | 3 |
| Alex Szabó | 15.05.2002 | 14 | (2) | |
| Krisztián Tamás | 18.04.1995 | 27 | (2) | |
| **Midfielders:** | **DOB** | **M** | **(s)** | **G** |
| István Átrok | 06.12.2005 | 1 | (10) | |
| Bertalan Bocskay | 02.03.2002 | 14 | (5) | |
| Brandon Dominguès (FRA) | 06.06.2000 | 12 | (7) | 4 |
| *Jairo* Samperio Bustara (ESP) | 11.07.1993 | 14 | (3) | 4 |
| Noel Keresztes | 16.09.2004 | 1 | (8) | |
| Dominik Kocsis | 01.08.2002 | 21 | (10) | 2 |
| Nikola Mitrović (SRB) | 02.01.1987 | 23 | (6) | |
| Maxim Plakushchenko (ISR) | 04.01.1996 | 6 | (10) | |
| Donát Zsótér | 06.01.1996 | 16 | (5) | |
| **Forwards:** | **DOB** | **M** | **(s)** | **G** |
| Richlord Ennin (CAN) | 17.09.1998 | 13 | (8) | 2 |
| András Eördögh | 09.03.2002 | 7 | | |
| István Fábiánkovits | 30.04.2005 | | (1) | |
| Zalán Kerezsi | 17.02.2003 | 7 | (7) | 4 |
| Ábel Krajcsovics | 17.08.2004 | | (3) | |
| Nenad Lukić (SRB) | 02.09.1992 | 27 | (2) | 13 |
| Maksym Pukhtieiev (UKR) | 02.02.2004 | | (1) | |
| Boubacar Traoré (MLI) | 14.12.1999 | | (6) | |

## Kecskeméti Testedző Egyesület

| | | | | |
|---|---|---|---|---|
| **Founded**: | 11.06.1911 | | | |
| **Stadium**: | Széktói Stadion, Kecskemét (6,320) | | | |
| **Trainer**: | István Szabó | | 17.01.1967 | |

| Goalkeepers: | DOB | M | (s) | G |
|---|---|---|---|---|
| Ádám Varga | 12.02.1999 | 8 | (1) | |
| Bence Varga | 09.01.1996 | 25 | | |
| **Defenders:** | **DOB** | **M** | **(s)** | **G** |
| Csaba Belényesi | 03.03.1994 | 31 | | |
| Gábor Buna | 24.05.2002 | | (1) | |
| Attila Grünwald | 26.07.1991 | 3 | (5) | |
| Danilo Pejović | 21.06.1998 | 2 | (3) | |
| Imre Polyák | 05.07.2004 | | (2) | |
| Mykhaylo Ryashko (UKR) | 05.11.1996 | 9 | (10) | |
| Milán Sági | 19.07.1995 | 2 | (5) | |
| Alex Szabó | 26.08.1998 | 29 | (2) | 2 |
| Gábor Szalai | 09.06.2000 | 24 | (5) | 3 |
| Márió Zeke | 01.09.2000 | 25 | (3) | 1 |
| **Midfielders:** | **DOB** | **M** | **(s)** | **G** |
| Bence Banó-Szabó | 25.07.1999 | 27 | (4) | 5 |
| Zoltán Bodor | 04.03.2003 | | (1) | |
| Uroš Đuranović (MNE) | 01.02.1994 | 4 | (7) | 1 |
| Valentin Hadaró | 08.06.1995 | 5 | (3) | |
| Krisztofer Horváth | 08.01.2002 | 10 | (5) | 6 |
| Bálint Katona | 07.09.2002 | 19 | (14) | 8 |
| Máté Katona | 22.06.1997 | 4 | (13) | |
| Milán Májer | 28.06.1999 | 2 | (12) | |
| Mykhailo Meskhi (UKR) | 26.02.1997 | 3 | (17) | |
| Krisztián Nagy | 18.07.1995 | 30 | (3) | 6 |
| Tamás Nikitscher | 03.11.1999 | 10 | (4) | |
| Levente Vágó | 15.09.1992 | 30 | | 1 |
| **Forwards:** | **DOB** | **M** | **(s)** | **G** |
| Márton Gréczi | 10.07.2000 | | (3) | |
| Levente Szabó | 06.06.1999 | 3 | (13) | 4 |
| Soma Szuhodovszki | 30.12.1999 | 30 | (2) | 3 |
| Barna Tóth | 13.03.1995 | 28 | (3) | 6 |

## Kisvárda Futball Club

| Founded: | 1911 | | |
|---|---|---|---|
| Stadium: | Várkerti Stadion, Kisvárda (3,385) | | |
| Trainer: | László Török | | 25.12.1969 |
| [27.03.2023] | Miloš Kruščić (SRB) | | 03.10.1976 |

| Goalkeepers: | DOB | M | (s) | G |
|---|---|---|---|---|
| Otto Hindrich (ROU) | 05.08.2002 | 25 | | |
| Artem Odintsov (UKR) | 09.11.2000 | 3 | | |
| Danijel Petković (MNE) | 25.05.1993 | 5 | | |
| **Defenders:** | **DOB** | **M** | **(s)** | **G** |
| Enes Alić (BIH) | 03.09.1999 | 4 | (5) | |
| Viktor Hei (UKR) | 02.02.1996 | 30 | (1) | |
| Aleksandar Jovičić (BIH) | 18.07.1995 | 12 | | |
| Dominik Kovačić (CRO) | 05.01.1994 | 28 | (1) | 1 |
| Anton Kravchenko (UKR) | 23.03.1991 | 7 | (1) | 1 |
| *Matheus* Izidorio Leoni (BRA) | 20.09.1991 | 25 | (2) | 2 |
| Bogdan Melnyk (UKR) | 04.01.1997 | 23 | (9) | 3 |
| Ionuţ Andrei Peteleu (ROU) | 20.08.1992 | 6 | (3) | |
| Imre Széles | 30.11.1995 | 12 | (3) | |
| Miloš Vranjanin (SRB) | 11.06.1996 | 5 | (2) | |

| Midfielders: | DOB | M | (s) | G |
|---|---|---|---|---|
| Roland Biró | 30.05.2003 | | (2) | |
| Erik Czérna | 07.05.2003 | 1 | (4) | |
| Mario Ilievski (MKD) | 24.04.2002 | 8 | (24) | 5 |
| Yanis Karabelyov (BUL) | 23.01.1996 | 23 | (7) | 1 |
| *Lucas* Marcolini Dantas Bertucci (BRA) | 06.05.1989 | 8 | (10) | |
| Rafał Makowski (POL) | 05.08.1996 | 26 | (4) | 7 |
| Bence Ötvös | 13.03.1998 | 21 | (6) | 2 |
| Krisztófer Vida | 23.06.1995 | 1 | (18) | |
| **Forwards:** | **DOB** | **M** | **(s)** | **G** |
| Jasir Asani (ALB) | 19.05.1995 | 11 | (4) | |
| Driton Camaj (MNE) | 07.03.1997 | 27 | (6) | 6 |
| Yaroslav Gelesh (UKR) | 20.07.2004 | | (1) | |
| Jasmin Mešanović (BIH) | 06.01.1992 | 28 | (4) | 8 |
| Jaroslav Navrátil (CZE) | 30.12.1991 | 17 | (12) | 2 |
| Miloš Spasić (SRB) | 29.07.1997 | 7 | (9) | 2 |

## Mezőkövesdi Sport Egyesület

| Founded: | 31.01.1975 | | |
|---|---|---|---|
| Stadium: | Városi Stadion, Mezőkövesd (4,183) | | |
| Trainer: | Attile Supka | | 19.09.1962 |
| [06.09.2022] | Gábor Híres | | 26.02.1958 |
| [14.09.2022] | Attila Kuttor | | 29.05.1970 |

| Goalkeepers: | DOB | M | (s) | G |
|---|---|---|---|---|
| Riccardo Piscitelli (ITA) | 10.10.1993 | 31 | | |
| Árpád Tordai (ROU) | 11.03.1997 | 2 | (1) | |
| **Defenders:** | **DOB** | **M** | **(s)** | **G** |
| Nimrod Baranyai | 06.08.2003 | 1 | (2) | |
| Ilia Beriashvili (GEO) | 09.07.1998 | 11 | (2) | |
| Dávid Bobál | 31.08.1995 | 9 | | |
| Steliano Filip (ROU) | 15.05.1994 | 14 | (1) | |
| Milán Gábor Horváth | 30.01.2022 | | (1) | |
| Luka Lakvekheliani (GEO) | 20.10.1998 | | (3) | |
| Roland Lehoczky | 19.04.2002 | 4 | (4) | |
| Andrej Lukić (CRO) | 02.04.1994 | 28 | | 1 |
| Róbert Pillár (SVK) | 27.05.1991 | 19 | (1) | 1 |
| Philipp Schmiedl (AUT) | 23.07.1997 | 4 | (6) | |
| Dániel Vadnai | 19.02.1988 | 2 | (3) | |
| Younn Zahary (FRA) | 08.10.1998 | 4 | (3) | |
| **Midfielders:** | **DOB** | **M** | **(s)** | **G** |
| David Babunski (MKD) | 01.03.1994 | 15 | (9) | 3 |
| Dino Beširović (BIH) | 31.01.1994 | 28 | (3) | 8 |
| Marko Brtan (CRO) | 07.04.1991 | 8 | (11) | 1 |

| | DOB | M | (s) | G |
|---|---|---|---|---|
| Benjámin Cseke | 22.07.1994 | 3 | (1) | |
| Tamás Cseri | 15.01.1988 | 28 | | |
| Thomas Ephestion (MTQ) | 09.06.1995 | 1 | (6) | |
| Aleksandr Karnitskiy (BLR) | 14.02.1989 | 23 | (7) | 2 |
| Márk Madarász | 24.11.1995 | 2 | (4) | 1 |
| Attila Márkus | 29.12.1996 | | (5) | |
| Gergő Nagy | 07.01.1993 | 13 | (2) | |
| Kamer Qaka (ALB) | 11.04.1995 | 1 | (3) | |
| Sándor Vajda | 14.12.1991 | 21 | (10) | 3 |
| **Forwards:** | **DOB** | **M** | **(s)** | **G** |
| Gergely Bobál | 31.08.1995 | 4 | (10) | 1 |
| Stefan Dražić (SRB) | 14.08.1992 | 27 | (2) | 14 |
| Marin Jurina (BIH) | 26.11.1993 | 2 | (1) | 2 |
| Kevin Kállai | 14.01.2002 | 29 | (2) | |
| Zalán Kállai | 21.02.2004 | | (4) | |
| Tomislav Kiš (CRO) | 04.04.1994 | 1 | (4) | |
| Gábor Molnár | 16.05.1994 | 24 | (8) | 2 |
| Dominik Nagy | 08.05.1995 | 3 | (2) | |
| Nikolay Prudnikov (RUS) | 09.02.1998 | | (3) | |
| Remzifaik Selmani (MKD) | 05.05.1997 | 1 | (5) | |

## Paksi Futball Club

| Founded: | 28.11.1952 | | |
|---|---|---|---|
| Stadium: | Fehérvári úti Stadion, Paks (6,150) | | |
| Trainer: | Róbert Waltner | | 20.09.1977 |
| [14.02.2023] | György Bognár | | 05.11.1961 |

| Goalkeepers: | DOB | M | (s) | G |
|---|---|---|---|---|
| Gergely Nagy | 27.05.1994 | 23 | | |
| Gergő Rácz | 20.11.1995 | 5 | (1) | |
| Barnabás Simon | 13.02.2004 | 5 | (2) | |
| **Defenders:** | **DOB** | **M** | **(s)** | **G** |
| Tamás Kádár | 14.03.1990 | 28 | | |
| Ákos Kinyik | 12.05.1993 | 23 | | 1 |
| Bence Lenzsér | 09.04.1996 | 8 | | |
| Attila Osváth | 10.12.1995 | 24 | (4) | |
| János Szabó | 11.07.1989 | 25 | (1) | |
| Milán Szekszárdi | 08.02.2001 | | (1) | |
| Norbert Szélpál | 03.03.1996 | 17 | (5) | 2 |
| Olivér Tamás | 14.04.2001 | | (3) | |
| **Midfielders:** | **DOB** | **M** | **(s)** | **G** |
| Balász Balogh | 11.06.1990 | 23 | (5) | 1 |
| Lukács Bőle | 27.03.1990 | 18 | (9) | 3 |
| Zalán Debreceni | 06.07.2002 | | (6) | |
| Gergő Gyurkits | 05.06.2002 | 2 | (11) | |

| | DOB | M | (s) | G |
|---|---|---|---|---|
| Attila Haris | 23.01.1997 | 2 | (6) | |
| Nikolász Kovács | 27.02.1999 | 2 | (4) | |
| Richárd Nagy | 08.04.1994 | 1 | (5) | |
| Patrik Nyári | 09.04.2001 | | (1) | |
| Kristóf Papp | 14.05.1993 | 25 | (6) | 4 |
| Bálint Szabó | 18.01.2001 | 15 | (2) | 2 |
| Gábor Vas | 29.08.2003 | 14 | (8) | |
| József Windecker | 02.12.1992 | 21 | (2) | 6 |
| **Forwards:** | **DOB** | **M** | **(s)** | **G** |
| Dániel Böde | 24.10.1986 | 3 | (13) | 5 |
| János Csaba Hahn | 15.03.1995 | 17 | (11) | 3 |
| Zsolt Haraszti | 04.11.1991 | 14 | (4) | 1 |
| Kevin Horváth | 02.03.2005 | | (1) | |
| Zoltán Pesti | 24.04.2005 | | (1) | |
| Máté Sajbán | 19.12.1995 | 12 | (18) | 1 |
| Alen Skribek | 11.04.2001 | 5 | (7) | 1 |
| Barnabás Varga | 25.10.1994 | 31 | | 26 |
| Patrik Volter | 13.08.2002 | | (2) | |

## Puskás Ferenc Labdarugó Akadémia Felcsút

**Founded**: 2005
**Stadium**: Pancho Aréna, Felcsút (3,816)
**Trainer**: Zsolt Hornyák (SVK) 01.05.1973

| Goalkeepers: | DOB | M | (s) | G |
|---|---|---|---|---|
| Tamás Markek | 30.08.1991 | 13 | | |
| Balázs Tóth | 04.09.1997 | 20 | | |
| **Defenders:** | **DOB** | **M** | **(s)** | **G** |
| Karlo Bartolec (CRO) | 20.04.1995 | 7 | (6) | |
| Bence Batik | 08.11.1993 | 27 | | 3 |
| Wojciech Golla (POL) | 12.01.1992 | 11 | | |
| Zsolt Nagy | 25.05.1993 | 7 | (2) | 1 |
| Brandon Ormonde-Ottewill (ENG) | 21.12.1995 | 20 | (1) | |
| Patrik Posztobányi | 29.07.2002 | 2 | (2) | |
| Csaba Spandler | 07.03.1996 | 21 | | 1 |
| Patrizio Stronati (CZE) | 17.11.1994 | 24 | | |
| Roland Szolnoki | 21.01.1992 | 8 | (1) | |
| **Midfielders:** | **DOB** | **M** | **(s)** | **G** |
| Balázs Bakti | 31.12.2004 | | (4) | |
| Marius Corbu (ROU) | 07.05.2002 | 24 | (6) | 6 |
| Szabolcs Dusinszki | 06.08.2005 | | (2) | |
| Artem Favorov (UKR) | 19.03.1994 | 26 | (3) | 6 |
| Martin Kern | 23.03.2006 | 2 | | |
| Marcell Major | 17.03.2005 | | (2) | |
| Mohamed Mezghrani (BEL) | 02.06.1994 | 19 | (2) | |
| Jakub Plšek (CZE) | 13.12.1993 | 6 | (3) | 1 |
| Jozef Urblík (SVK) | 22.08.1996 | 2 | (6) | |
| Yoëll van Nieff (NED) | 17.06.1993 | 10 | (14) | 1 |
| **Forwards:** | **DOB** | **M** | **(s)** | **G** |
| Alexandru Mihail Băluţă (ROU) | 13.09.1993 | 17 | (5) | 2 |
| Lamin Colley (GAM) | 05.07.1993 | 9 | (10) | 3 |
| Zsombor Gruber | 07.09.2004 | 13 | (13) | 3 |
| Tamás Kiss | 24.11.2000 | 13 | (3) | |
| György Komáromi | 19.01.2002 | 16 | (9) | 3 |
| Jonathan Alberto Levi (SWE) | 23.01.1996 | 11 | (6) | 1 |
| Jakov Puljić (CRO) | 04.08.1993 | 13 | (6) | 4 |
| Alen Skribek | 11.04.2001 | 2 | (6) | |
| Luciano Slagveer (NED) | 05.10.1993 | 7 | (11) | 4 |
| Shahab Zahedi (IRN) | 18.08.1995 | 13 | (15) | 8 |

## Újpest Football Club

**Founded**: 16.06.1885
**Stadium**: "Szusza Ferenc" Stadion, Budapest (12,670)
**Trainer**: Miloš Kruščić (SRB) 03.10.1976
[23.03.2023] Nebojša Vignjević (SRB) 15.05.1968

| Goalkeepers: | DOB | M | (s) | G |
|---|---|---|---|---|
| Dávid Banai | 09.05.1994 | 8 | (1) | |
| Đorđe Nikolić (SRB) | 13.04.1997 | 24 | | |
| Filip Pajović (SRB) | 30.07.1993 | 1 | | |
| **Defenders:** | **DOB** | **M** | **(s)** | **G** |
| Nemanja Antonov (SRB) | 06.05.1995 | 25 | (3) | 3 |
| Georgios Antzoulas (GRE) | 04.02.2000 | 12 | (1) | 1 |
| Abdoulaye Diaby (MLI) | 04.07.2000 | 18 | (7) | 4 |
| Csanád Fehér | 13.06.2002 | 2 | | |
| Tim Hall (LUX) | 15.04.1997 | 14 | | |
| Lirim R. Kastrati (KOS) | 02.02.1999 | 14 | (4) | 1 |
| Dominik Kovács | 18.02.2001 | | (1) | |
| Märten Kuusk (EST) | 05.04.1996 | 5 | | |
| Luca Mack (GER) | 25.05.2000 | 16 | (7) | |
| Branko Pauljević (SRB) | 12.06.1989 | 25 | (7) | 1 |
| **Midfielders:** | **DOB** | **M** | **(s)** | **G** |
| Miroslav Bjeloš (SRB) | 29.10.1990 | 2 | (9) | |
| Petrus Boumal Mayega (CMR) | 20.04.1993 | 15 | (9) | |
| Áron Csongvai | 31.10.2000 | 18 | | 1 |
| Luis Jakobi (GER) | 15.12.2001 | 11 | (7) | |
| Stefan Jevtoski (MKD) | 02.09.1997 | 1 | (5) | |
| Mátyás Katona | 30.12.1999 | 16 | (2) | 2 |
| Matija Ljujić (SRB) | 28.10.1993 | 6 | (5) | |
| Heinz Mörschel (GER) | 24.08.1997 | 7 | (3) | 2 |
| Vincent Onovo (NGA) | 10.12.1995 | 26 | (3) | |
| Bálint Szabó | 18.02.2002 | 16 | (2) | 1 |
| **Forwards:** | **DOB** | **M** | **(s)** | **G** |
| Peter Ambrose (NGA) | 10.06.2002 | | (14) | 1 |
| Giuseppe Borello (ITA) | 28.04.1999 | 2 | (9) | |
| Yohan Croizet (FRA) | 15.02.1992 | 1 | (4) | |
| Kevin Csoboth | 20.06.2000 | 24 | (2) | 5 |
| Fernand Gouré (CIV) | 12.04.2002 | 18 | (6) | 8 |
| Mory Koné (CIV) | 13.07.1995 | | (1) | |
| Jack Daniel Kalichi Lahne (SWE) | 24.10.2001 | 1 | (5) | |
| Márk Mucsányi | 16.11.2001 | 1 | (2) | |
| Ognjen Mudrinski (SRB) | 15.11.1991 | 9 | | 3 |
| Krisztián Simon | 10.06.1991 | 10 | (10) | 5 |
| Gadji Celi Carmel Junior Tallo (CIV) | 21.12.1992 | 4 | (7) | 1 |
| György Varga | 23.10.2003 | 11 | (5) | 2 |

## Vasas Futball Club Budapest

**Founded**: 16.03.1911
**Stadium**: „Illovszky Rudolf" Stadion, Budapest (5,154)
**Trainer**: Attila Kuttor 29.05.1970
[06.09.2022] Elemér Kondás 11.09.1963
[06.04.2023] Szilárd Desits 28.07.1977

| Goalkeepers: | DOB | M | (s) | G |
|---|---|---|---|---|
| Dávid Dombó | 26.02.1993 | 4 | (1) | |
| Levente Jova | 30.01.1992 | 12 | | |
| János Uram | 09.02.2001 | 17 | | |
| **Defenders:** | **DOB** | **M** | **(s)** | **G** |
| Botond Baráth | 21.04.1992 | 15 | (5) | |
| László Deutsch | 09.03.1999 | 1 | (6) | |
| János Hegedűs | 04.10.1996 | 4 | (1) | |
| Patrick Iyinbor | 07.01.2002 | 25 | (2) | |
| Róbert Litauszki | 15.03.1990 | 7 | (2) | |
| Máté Ódor | 29.04.2001 | 11 | (6) | |
| Kenny Otigba | 29.08.1992 | 25 | (3) | 1 |
| Erik Silye | 12.06.1996 | 24 | (2) | |
| **Midfielders:** | **DOB** | **M** | **(s)** | **G** |
| Zsombor Berecz | 13.12.1995 | 31 | | 5 |
| Patrik Hidi | 27.11.1990 | 19 | (14) | 2 |
| Sándor Hidi | 20.02.2001 | 1 | (15) | |
| Kristóf Hinora | 05.02.1998 | 25 | (4) | 1 |
| Sebestyén Ihrig-Farkas | 28.01.1994 | 1 | (15) | 1 |
| Dávid Márkvárt | 20.09.1994 | 11 | (3) | |
| Máté Pátkai | 06.03.1988 | 5 | (1) | |
| Szabolcs Szilágyi | 23.09.2003 | 12 | (4) | |
| Donát Szivacski | 18.01.1997 | 25 | (1) | |
| Dominik Sztojka | 23.12.2003 | 1 | (4) | |
| Jozef Urblík (SVK) | 22.08.1996 | 10 | (1) | 3 |
| Máté Vida | 08.03.1996 | 4 | (1) | |
| **Forwards:** | **DOB** | **M** | **(s)** | **G** |
| Norbert Balogh | 21.02.1996 | 3 | (5) | |
| Gergely Bobál | 31.08.1995 | 1 | | |
| Dominik Cipf | 31.01.2001 | 3 | (16) | 1 |
| Róbert Feczesin | 22.02.1986 | | (8) | 1 |
| Krisztián Géresi | 14.06.1994 | 3 | (6) | |
| Filip Holender | 27.07.1994 | 26 | (4) | 8 |
| Soma Novothny | 16.06.1994 | 22 | (3) | 5 |
| András Radó | 09.09.1993 | 13 | (5) | 1 |
| József Szalai | 11.11.2002 | | (6) | |
| Dávid Zimonyi | 24.12.1997 | 2 | (9) | |

## Zalaegerszegi Torna Egylet Football Club

| Founded: | 1920 | |
|---|---|---|
| Stadium: | ZTE Aréna, Zalaegerszeg (11,200) | |
| Trainer: | Ricardo Moniz (NED) | 17.06.1964 |
| [24.04.2023] | Gábor Boér | 19.12.1982 |

| Goalkeepers: | DOB | M | (s) | G |
|---|---|---|---|---|
| Patrik Demjén | 22.03.1998 | 32 | | |
| Márton Gyurján | 01.12.1995 | 1 | | |
| **Defenders:** | **DOB** | **M** | **(s)** | **G** |
| Bence Bedi | 14.11.1996 | 15 | (5) | 1 |
| Bence Gergényi | 16.03.1998 | 29 | | 3 |
| András Huszti | 29.01.2001 | 17 | (7) | 1 |
| Dávid Kálnoki-Kis | 06.08.1991 | 22 | (1) | |
| Zoran Lesjak (CRO) | 01.02.1988 | 16 | (9) | 2 |
| Attila Mocsi | 29.05.2000 | 30 | | |
| Csongor Papp | 22.02.2005 | | (1) | |
| Oleksandr Safronov (UKR) | 11.06.1999 | 7 | (8) | |
| **Midfielders:** | **DOB** | **M** | **(s)** | **G** |
| Dániel Csóka | 04.04.2000 | 20 | (1) | 1 |
| Barnabás Kovács | 14.11.2002 | 7 | (9) | |

| | DOB | M | (s) | G |
|---|---|---|---|---|
| Gergő Mim | 07.06.1999 | 4 | (14) | 2 |
| Bojan Sanković (CRO) | 21.11.1993 | 23 | | |
| Norbert Szendrei | 27.03.2000 | 18 | (6) | |
| Mátyás Tajti | 02.06.1998 | 23 | (3) | 2 |
| **Forwards:** | **DOB** | **M** | **(s)** | **G** |
| Christopher Philip Baloteli (NGA) | 15.02.2004 | | (1) | |
| Diego Silva Nascimento Santos „Diego Carioca" (BRA) | 06.02.1998 | 1 | (3) | |
| Eros Grezda (ALB) | 15.04.1995 | 3 | (4) | 1 |
| Eduvie Marho Ikoba (USA) | 26.10.1997 | 22 | (6) | 11 |
| Milán Klausz | 24.02.2005 | 2 | (11) | 1 |
| Milán Májer | 28.06.1999 | 4 | (4) | |
| Christy Manzinga (FRA) | 31.01.1995 | 7 | (7) | 1 |
| Dániel Németh | 09.10.2003 | 19 | (8) | 3 |
| Szabolcs Szalay | 17.02.2002 | 20 | (11) | 3 |
| Meshack Izuchukwu Ubochioma (NGA) | 01.11.2001 | 21 | (11) | 4 |

## SECOND LEVEL
### Nemzeti Bajnokság II 2022/2023

| | | | | | | | | | |
|---|---|---|---|---|---|---|---|---|---|
| 1. | Diósgyőri VTK (*Promoted*) | 38 | 28 | 3 | 7 | 79 | - | 36 | 87 |
| 2. | MTK Budapest FC (*Promoted*) | 38 | 22 | 8 | 8 | 86 | - | 48 | 74 |
| 3. | FC Ajka | 38 | 20 | 8 | 10 | 54 | - | 37 | 68 |
| 4. | Szeged-Csanád Grosics Akadémia | 38 | 18 | 10 | 10 | 50 | - | 38 | 64 |
| 5. | Soroksár SC | 38 | 16 | 13 | 9 | 57 | - | 48 | 61 |
| 6. | Gyirmót FC Győr | 38 | 17 | 9 | 12 | 59 | - | 46 | 60 |
| 7. | Pécsi Mecsek FC | 38 | 14 | 16 | 8 | 38 | - | 31 | 58 |
| 8. | BFC Siófok | 38 | 15 | 11 | 12 | 45 | - | 51 | 56 |
| 9. | Szombathelyi Haladás | 38 | 14 | 9 | 15 | 54 | - | 56 | 51 |
| 10. | Budafoki MTE | 38 | 12 | 11 | 15 | 39 | - | 46 | 47 |
| 11. | Tiszakécske LC | 38 | 13 | 7 | 18 | 38 | - | 50 | 46 |
| 12. | Mosónmagyaróvári TE | 38 | 12 | 10 | 16 | 36 | - | 44 | 46 |
| 13. | Győri ETO FC | 38 | 11 | 13 | 14 | 37 | - | 42 | 46 |
| 14. | Kazincbarcikai SC | 38 | 12 | 9 | 17 | 41 | - | 56 | 45 |
| 15. | Aqvital FC Csákvár | 38 | 9 | 15 | 14 | 44 | - | 50 | 42 |
| 16. | Kozármisleny SE (*Relegation Play-offs*) | 38 | 11 | 8 | 19 | 46 | - | 63 | 41 |
| 17. | Szentlőrinc SE (*Relegation Play-offs*) | 38 | 9 | 12 | 17 | 44 | - | 58 | 39 |
| 18. | Nyíregyháza Spartacus FC (*Relegation Play-offs*) | 38 | 9 | 11 | 18 | 46 | - | 55 | 38 |
| 19. | Békéscsaba 1912 Előre SE (*Relegated*) | 38 | 8 | 13 | 17 | 47 | - | 56 | 37 |
| 20. | Dorogi FC (*Relegated*) | 38 | 7 | 10 | 21 | 32 | - | 61 | 31 |

## Relegation Play-offs [28.05.-04.06.2023]

| | | |
|---|---|---|
| **Kozármisleny SE** - Iváncsa KSE | 0-1(0-0) | 3-0(1-0) |
| Veszprém FC - **Nyíregyháza Spartacus FC** | 0-0 | 0-1(0-1) |
| **Budapesti VSC-Zugló KE** - Szentlőrinc SE | 0-0 | 2-1(0-0) |

Teams in bold were qualified for Nemzeti Bajnokság II 2023/2024.

## INTERNATIONAL MATCHES
(16.07.2022 – 15.07.2023)

| | | | | |
|---|---|---|---|---|
| 23.09.2022 | Leipzig | *Germany - Hungary* | *0-1(0-1)* | (UNL) |
| 26.09.2022 | Budapest | *Hungary - Italy* | *0-2(0-1)* | (UNL) |
| 17.11.2022 | Lëtzebuerg | *Luxembourg - Hungary* | *2-2(1-1)* | (F) |
| 20.11.2022 | Budapest | *Hungary - Greece* | *2-1(1-0)* | (F) |
| 23.03.2023 | Budapest | *Hungary - Estonia* | *1-0(1-0)* | (F) |
| 27.03.2023 | Budapest | *Hungary - Bulgaria* | *3-0(3-0)* | (ECQ) |
| 17.06.2023 | Podgorica | *Montenegro - Hungary* | *0-0* | (ECQ) |
| 20.06.2023 | Budapest | *Hungary - Lithuania* | *2-0(1-0)* | (ECQ) |

**23.09.2022 GERMANY - HUNGARY** 0-1(0-1) 3rd UEFA Nations League A, Group 3
Red Bull Arena, Leipzig; Referee: Slavko Vinčić (Slovenia); Attendance: 39,513
**HUN:** Péter Gulácsi, Ádám Lang, Vilmos Tamás Orbán, Attila Árpád Szalai, Attila Csaba Fiola, Ádám Nagy (78.Callum John Styles), Dániel Gazdag (67.László Kleinheisler), András Schäfer, Milos Kerkez, Dominik Szoboszlai (85.Loïc Négo), Ádám Csaba Szalai (Cap) (67.Martin Ádám). Trainer: Marco Rossi (Italy).
**Goal:** Ádám Csaba Szalai (17).

**26.09.2022 HUNGARY - ITALY** 0-2(0-1) 3rd UEFA Nations League A, Group 3
Puskás Aréna, Budapest; Referee: Benoît Bastien (France); Attendance: 57,300
**HUN:** Péter Gulácsi, Attila Csaba Fiola, Ádám Lang, Vilmos Tamás Orbán, Attila Árpád Szalai, Loïc Négo (75.Bendegúz Bolla), Ádám Nagy (46.Callum John Styles), András Schäfer, Milos Kerkez (57.Dániel Gazdag), Dominik Szoboszlai (85.László Kleinheisler), Ádám Csaba Szalai (Cap) (75.Martin Ádám). Trainer: Marco Rossi (Italy).

**17.11.2022 LUXEMBOURG - HUNGARY** 2-2(1-1) Friendly International
Stade de Luxembourg, Lëtzebuerg; Referee: Jonathan Lardot (Belgium); Attendance: 3,571
**HUN:** Dénes Dibusz, Ádám Lang, Vilmos Tamás Orbán, Attila Árpád Szalai, Attila Csaba Fiola (78.Endre Botka), Ádám Nagy (78.Péter Baráth), Dániel Gazdag (58.Roland Sallai), Callum John Styles, Zsolt Nagy (58.Milos Kerkez), Dominik Szoboszlai (Cap) (87.Zsolt Kalmár), Martin Ádám (58.András Németh). Trainer: Marco Rossi (Italy).
**Goals:** Attila Árpád Szalai (25), András Németh (67).

**20.11.2022 HUNGARY - GREECE** 2-1(1-0) Friendly International
Puskás Aréna, Budapest; Referee: Daniele Chiffi (Italy); Attendance: 50,893
**HUN:** Dénes Dibusz (90+2.Péter Szappanos), Attila Csaba Fiola, Endre Botka (71.Ádám Lang), Vilmos Tamás Orbán, Attila Árpád Szalai, Ádám Nagy, Callum John Styles, Milos Kerkez (53.Zsolt Nagy), Dominik Szoboszlai (90+2.Zsolt Kalmár), Balázs Dzsudzsák (Cap) (53.Martin Ádám), Roland Sallai (72.Palkó Dárdai). Trainer: Marco Rossi (Italy).
**Goals:** Roland Sallai (15), Zsolt Kalmár (90+4).

**23.03.2023 HUNGARY - ESTONIA** 1-0(1-0) Friendly International
Puskás Aréna, Budapest; Referee: Walter Altmann (Austria); Attendance: 37,804
**HUN:** Dénes Dibusz, Ádám Lang, Vilmos Tamás Orbán, Attila Árpád Szalai, Bendegúz Bolla (84.Endre Botka), Bálint Máté Vécsei (46.Ádám Nagy), Zsolt Kalmár (60.László Kleinheisler), Milos Kerkez, Dominik Szoboszlai (Cap) (76.Kevin Csoboth), Roland Sallai (76.András Németh), Martin Ádám (60.Dániel Gazdag). Trainer: Marco Rossi (Italy).
**Goal:** Martin Ádám (41).

**27.03.2023 HUNGARY - BULGARIA** 3-0(3-0) 17th EC. Qualifiers
Puskás Aréna, Budapest; Referee: Halil Umut Meler (Turkey); Attendance: 53,000
**HUN:** Dénes Dibusz, Ádám Lang, Vilmos Tamás Orbán, Attila Árpád Szalai, Bendegúz Bolla (86.Loïc Négo), Ádám Nagy (73.László Kleinheisler), Bálint Máté Vécsei (87.Zsolt Kalmár), Milos Kerkez, Dominik Szoboszlai (Cap), Roland Sallai (73.Kevin Csoboth), Martin Ádám (59.Barnabás Varga). Trainer: Marco Rossi (Italy).
**Goals:** Bálint Máté Vécsei (7), Dominik Szoboszlai (26), Martin Ádám (39).

**17.06.2023 MONTENEGRO - HUNGARY** 0-0 17th EC. Qualifiers
Stadion pod Goricom, Podgorica; Referee: Jesús Gil Manzano (Spain); Attendance: 6,761
**HUN:** Dénes Dibusz, Ádám Lang, Vilmos Tamás Orbán, Attila Árpád Szalai, Bendegúz Bolla (88.Endre Botka), Ádám Nagy, Callum John Styles (72.Zsolt Kalmár), Milos Kerkez, Dominik Szoboszlai (Cap), Roland Sallai (58.Kevin Csoboth), Martin Ádám (59.Barnabás Varga). Trainer: Marco Rossi (Italy).

**20.06.2023 HUNGARY - LITHUANIA** 2-0(1-0) 17th EC. Qualifiers
Puskás Aréna, Budapest; Referee: António Emanuel Carvalho Nobre (Portugal); Attendance: 58,274
**HUN:** Dénes Dibusz, Endre Botka, Vilmos Tamás Orbán, Attila Árpád Szalai, Ádám Nagy, Callum John Styles (60.László Kleinheisler), Milos Kerkez (79.János Ferenczi), Dániel Gazdag (79.Ádám Lang), Dominik Szoboszlai (Cap), Roland Sallai (88.Péter Baráth), Barnabás Varga (60.Martin Ádám). Trainer: Marco Rossi (Italy).
**Goals:** Barnabás Varga (32), Roland Sallai (83).

## NATIONAL TEAM PLAYERS
### (16.07.2022 – 15.07.2023)

| Name | DOB | Caps | Goals | Club | |
|---|---|---|---|---|---|

### Goalkeepers

| Name | DOB | Caps | Goals | Club | |
|---|---|---|---|---|---|
| Dénes DIBUSZ | 16.11.1990 | 28 | 0 | 2022/2023: | Ferencvárosi TC |
| Péter GULÁCSI | 06.05.1990 | 51 | 0 | 2022: | RasenBallsport Leipzig (GER) |
| Péter SZAPPANOS | 14.11.1990 | 1 | 0 | 2022: | Budapest Honvéd FC |

### Defenders

| Name | DOB | Caps | Goals | Club | |
|---|---|---|---|---|---|
| Bendegúz BOLLA | 22.11.1999 | 11 | 0 | 2022/2023: | Grasshopper Club Zürich (SUI) |
| Endre BOTKA | 25.08.1994 | 23 | 1 | 2022/2023: | Ferencvárosi TC |
| János FERENCZI | 03.04.1991 | 2 | 0 | 2023: | Debreceni VSC |
| Attila Csaba FIOLA | 17.02.1990 | 52 | 2 | 2022: | Fehérvár FC Székesfehérvár |
| Milos KERKEZ | 07.11.2003 | 8 | 0 | 2022/2023: | AZ Alkmaar (NED) |
| Ádám LANG | 17.01.1993 | 59 | 1 | 2022/2023: | AC Omonia Nicosia (CYP) |
| Zsolt NAGY | 25.05.1993 | 13 | 2 | 2022: | Puskás Ferenc Labdarugó Akadémia Felcsút |
| Loïc NÉGO | 15.01.1991 | 27 | 2 | 2022/2023: | Fehérvár FC Székesfehérvár |
| Vilmos Tamás „Willi" ORBÁN | 03.11.1992 | 41 | 5 | 2022/2023: | RasenBallsport Leipzig (GER) |
| Attila Árpád SZALAI | 20.01.1998 | 35 | 1 | 2022/2023: | Fenerbahçe SK İstanbul (TUR) |

### Midfielders

| Name | DOB | Caps | Goals | Club | |
|---|---|---|---|---|---|
| Péter BARÁTH | 21.02.2002 | 2 | 0 | 2022: | Debreceni VSC |
| | | | | 14.02.2023-> | Ferencvárosi TC |
| Dániel GAZDAG | 02.03.1996 | 20 | 4 | 2022/2023: | Philadelphia Union (USA) |
| Zsolt KALMÁR | 09.06.1995 | 32 | 3 | 2022/2023: | FC DAC 1904 Dunajská Streda (SVK) |
| László KLEINHEISLER | 08.04.1994 | 47 | 3 | 2022: | NK Osijek (CRO) |
| | | | | 12.01.2023-> | PAE Panathinaïkos Athína (GRE) |
| Ádám NAGY | 17.06.1995 | 71 | 1 | 2022/2023: | Pisa SC (ITA) |
| András SCHÄFER | 13.04.1999 | 22 | 3 | 2022: | 1. FC Union Berlin (GER) |
| Callum John STYLES | 28.03.2000 | 12 | 0 | 2022/2023: | Millwall FC London (ENG) |
| Dominik SZOBOSZLAI | 25.10.2000 | 32 | 7 | 2022/2023: | RasenBallsport Leipzig (GER) |
| Bálint Máté VÉCSEI | 13.07.1993 | 12 | 2 | 2023: | Ferencvárosi TC |

### Forwards

| Name | DOB | Caps | Goals | Club | |
|---|---|---|---|---|---|
| Martin ÁDÁM | 06.11.1994 | 14 | 2 | 2022/2023: | Ulsan Hyundai FC (KOR) |
| Kevin CSOBOTH | 20.06.2000 | 3 | 0 | 2023: | Újpest FC |
| Balázs DZSUDZSÁK | 23.12.1986 | 109 | 21 | 2022: | Debreceni VSC |
| Palkó DÁRDAI | 24.04.1999 | 1 | 0 | 2022: | Fehérvár FC Székesfehérvár |
| András NÉMETH | 09.11.2002 | 2 | 1 | 2022: | KRC Genk (BEL) |
| | | | | 27.01.2023-> | Hamburger SV (GER) |
| Roland SALLAI | 22.05.1997 | 42 | 10 | 2022/2023: | SC Freiburg (GER) |
| Ádám Csaba SZALAI | 09.12.1987 | 86 | 26 | 2022/2023: | FC Basel (SUI) |
| Barnabás VARGA | 25.10.1994 | 3 | 1 | 2023: | Paksi FC |

### Trainer

| Name | DOB | | | | |
|---|---|---|---|---|---|
| Marco ROSSI (Italy) [from 19.06.2019] | 09.09.1964 | 53 M; 26 W; 11 D; 16 L; 73-55 | | | |

# ICELAND

### The Country:
Ísland (Iceland)
Capital: Reykjavík
Surface: 102,775 km²
Inhabitants: 376,248 [2022]
Time: UTC

### The FA:
Knattspyrnusamband Íslands
Laugardal 104, Reykjavík
Tel: +354 510 2900
Foundation date: 1947
Member of FIFA since: 1947
Member of UEFA since: 1954
Website: www.ksi.is

## NATIONAL TEAM RECORDS

| RECORDS | | |
|---|---|---|
| **First international match:** | 17.07.1946, Reykjavík: | Iceland – Denmark 0-3 |
| **Most international caps:** | Birkir Bjarnason | - 113 caps (since 2010) |
| **Most international goals:** | Eiður Smári Guðjohnsen | - 26 goals / 88 caps (1996-2016) |
| | Kolbeinn Sigþórsson | - 26 goals / 64 caps (2010-2021) |

| UEFA EUROPEAN CHAMPIONSHIP | |
|---|---|
| 1960 | Did not enter |
| 1964 | Qualifiers |
| 1968 | Did not enter |
| 1972 | Did not enter |
| 1976 | Qualifiers |
| 1980 | Qualifiers |
| 1984 | Qualifiers |
| 1988 | Qualifiers |
| 1992 | Qualifiers |
| 1996 | Qualifiers |
| 2000 | Qualifiers |
| 2004 | Qualifiers |
| 2008 | Qualifiers |
| 2012 | Qualifiers |
| 2016 | Final Tournament (Quarter-Finals) |
| 2020 | Qualifiers |

| FIFA WORLD CUP | |
|---|---|
| 1930 | - |
| 1934 | - |
| 1938 | - |
| 1950 | - |
| 1954 | *Entry not accepted by FIFA* |
| 1958 | Qualifiers |
| 1962 | Did not enter |
| 1966 | Did not enter |
| 1970 | Did not enter |
| 1974 | Qualifiers |
| 1978 | Qualifiers |
| 1982 | Qualifiers |
| 1986 | Qualifiers |
| 1990 | Qualifiers |
| 1994 | Qualifiers |
| 1998 | Qualifiers |
| 2002 | Qualifiers |
| 2006 | Qualifiers |
| 2010 | Qualifiers |
| 2014 | Qualifiers |
| 2018 | Final Tournament (Group Stage) |
| 2022 | Qualifiers |

| OLYMPIC TOURNAMENTS | |
|---|---|
| 1908 | - |
| 1912 | - |
| 1920 | - |
| 1924 | - |
| 1928 | - |
| 1936 | - |
| 1948 | - |
| 1952 | - |
| 1956 | - |
| 1960 | Qualifiers |
| 1964 | Qualifiers |
| 1968 | Qualifiers |
| 1972 | Qualifiers |
| 1976 | Did not enter |
| 1980 | Did not enter |
| 1984 | Did not enter |
| 1988 | Qualifiers |
| 1992 | Qualifiers |
| 1996 | Qualifiers |
| 2000 | Qualifiers |
| 2004 | Qualifiers |
| 2008 | Qualifiers |
| 2012 | Qualifiers |
| 2016 | Qualifiers |
| 2020 | Qualifiers |

## UEFA NATIONS LEAGUE

| | |
|---|---|
| 2018/2019 | League A (Group Stage) |
| 2020/2021 | League A (Group Stage -> relegated to League B) |
| 2022/2023 | League B (Group Stage) |

## ICELANDIAN CLUB HONOURS IN EUROPEAN CLUB COMPETITIONS:

| European Champion Clubs' Cup (1956-1992) / UEFA Champions League (1993-2023) |
|---|
| None |

| Fairs Cup (1858-1971) / UEFA Cup (1972-2009) / UEFA Europa League (2010-2023) |
|---|
| None |

| UEFA Europa Conference League (2021-2023) |
|---|
| None |

| UEFA Super Cup (1972-2022) |
|---|
| None |

| *European Cup Winners' Cup 1961-1999*\* |
|---|
| None |

*\*defunct competition*

## NATIONAL COMPETITIONS
## TABLE OF HONOURS

| | CHAMPIONS | CUP WINNERS | BEST GOALSCORERS | |
|---|---|---|---|---|
| 1912 | KR Reykjavík | - | - | |
| 1913 | Fram Reykjavík | - | - | |
| 1914 | Fram Reykjavík | - | - | |
| 1915 | Fram Reykjavík | - | - | |
| 1916 | Fram Reykjavík | - | - | |
| 1917 | Fram Reykjavík | - | - | |
| 1918 | Fram Reykjavík | - | - | |
| 1919 | KR Reykjavík | - | - | |
| 1920 | Víkingur Reykjavík | - | - | |
| 1921 | Fram Reykjavík | - | - | |
| 1922 | Fram Reykjavík | - | - | |
| 1923 | Fram Reykjavík | - | - | |
| 1924 | Víkingur Reykjavík | - | - | |
| 1925 | Fram Reykjavík | - | - | |
| 1926 | KR Reykjavík | - | - | |
| 1927 | KR Reykjavík | - | - | |
| 1928 | KR Reykjavík | - | - | |
| 1929 | KR Reykjavík | - | - | |
| 1930 | Valur Reykjavík | - | - | |
| 1931 | KR Reykjavík | - | - | |
| 1932 | KR Reykjavík | - | - | |
| 1933 | Valur Reykjavík | - | - | |
| 1934 | KR Reykjavík | - | - | |
| 1935 | Valur Reykjavík | - | - | |
| 1936 | Valur Reykjavík | - | - | |
| 1937 | Valur Reykjavík | - | - | |
| 1938 | Valur Reykjavík | - | - | |
| 1939 | Fram Reykjavík | - | - | |
| 1940 | Valur Reykjavík | - | - | |
| 1941 | KR Reykjavík | - | - | |
| 1942 | Valur Reykjavík | - | - | |
| 1943 | Valur Reykjavík | - | - | |
| 1944 | Valur Reykjavík | - | - | |
| 1945 | Valur Reykjavík | - | - | |
| 1946 | Fram Reykjavík | - | - | |
| 1947 | Fram Reykjavík | - | - | |
| 1948 | KR Reykjavík | - | - | |
| 1949 | KR Reykjavík | - | - | |
| 1950 | KR Reykjavík | - | - | |
| 1951 | ÍA Akranes | - | - | |
| 1952 | KR Reykjavík | - | - | |
| 1953 | ÍA Akranes | - | - | |
| 1954 | ÍA Akranes | - | - | |
| 1955 | KR Reykjavík | - | - | |
| 1956 | Valur Reykjavík | - | - | |
| 1957 | ÍA Akranes | - | - | |
| 1958 | ÍA Akranes | - | - | |
| 1959 | KR Reykjavík | - | - | |
| 1960 | ÍA Akranes | KR Reykjavík | - | |
| 1961 | KR Reykjavík | KR Reykjavík | - | |
| 1962 | Fram Reykjavík | KR Reykjavík | - | |
| 1963 | KR Reykjavík | KR Reykjavík | - | |
| 1964 | Keflavík ÍF | KR Reykjavík | - | |
| 1965 | KR Reykjavík | Valur Reykjavík | - | |
| 1966 | Valur Reykjavík | KR Reykjavík | - | |
| 1967 | Valur Reykjavík | KR Reykjavík | - | |
| 1968 | KR Reykjavík | ÍBV Vestmannaeyjar | - | |
| 1969 | Keflavík ÍF | KA Akureyrar | - | |
| 1970 | ÍA Akranes | Fram Reykjavík | - | |
| 1971 | Keflavík ÍF | Víkingur Reykjavík | - | |
| 1972 | Fram Reykjavík | ÍBV Vestmannaeyjar | - | |
| 1973 | Keflavík ÍF | Fram Reykjavík | - | |
| 1974 | ÍA Akranes | Valur Reykjavík | - | |
| 1975 | ÍA Akranes | Keflavík ÍF | - | |
| 1976 | Valur Reykjavík | Valur Reykjavík | - | |
| 1977 | ÍA Akranes | Valur Reykjavík | - | |
| 1978 | Valur Reykjavík | ÍA Akranes | - | |
| 1979 | ÍBV Vestmannaeyjar | Fram Reykjavík | - | |
| 1980 | Valur Reykjavík | Fram Reykjavík | Matthias Hallgrimsson (Valur Reykjavík) | 15 |
| 1981 | Víkingur Reykjavík | ÍBV Vestmannaeyjar | Sigurlás Þorleifsson (ÍBV Vestmannaeyjar) | |
| | | | Larus Gudmundsson (Víkingur Reykjavík) | 12 |

| | | | | |
|---|---|---|---|---|
| 1982 | Víkingur Reykjavík | ÍA Akranes | Sigurlás Þorleifsson (ÍBV Vestmannaeyjar) | |
| | | | Heimir Karlsson (Víkingur Reykjavík) | 10 |
| 1983 | ÍA Akranes | ÍA Akranes | Ingi Björn Albertsson (Valur Reykjavík) | 14 |
| 1984 | ÍA Akranes | ÍA Akranes | Guðmundur Steinsson (Fram Reykjavík) | 10 |
| 1985 | Valur Reykjavík | Fram Reykjavík | Ómar Torfason (Fram Reykjavík) | 13 |
| 1986 | Fram Reykjavík | ÍA Akranes | Gudmundur Torfason (Fram Reykjavík) | 19 |
| 1987 | Valur Reykjavík | Fram Reykjavík | Petur Ormslev (Fram Reykjavík) | 12 |
| 1988 | Fram Reykjavík | Valur Reykjavík | Sigurjón Kristjánsson (Valur Reykjavík) | 13 |
| 1989 | KA Akureyri | Fram Reykjavík | Hörður Magnússon (FH Hafnarfjörður) | 12 |
| 1990 | Fram Reykjavík | Valur Reykjavík | Hörður Magnússon (FH Hafnarfjörður) | 13 |
| 1991 | Víkingur Reykjavík | Valur Reykjavík | Hörður Magnússon (FH Hafnarfjörður) | |
| | | | Guðmundur Steinsson (Víkingur Reykjavík) | 13 |
| 1992 | ÍA Akranes | Valur Reykjavík | Arnar Gunnlaugsson (ÍA Akranes) | 15 |
| 1993 | ÍA Akranes | ÍA Akranes | Þórður Guðjónsson (ÍA Akranes) | 19 |
| 1994 | ÍA Akranes | KR Reykjavík | Mihajlo Biberčić (SRB, ÍA Akranes) | 14 |
| 1995 | ÍA Akranes | KR Reykjavík | Arnar Gunnlaugsson (ÍA Akranes) | 15 |
| 1996 | ÍA Akranes | ÍA Akranes | Ríkharður Daðason (KR Reykjavík) | 14 |
| 1997 | ÍBV Vestmannaeyjar | Keflavík ÍF | Tryggvi Guðmundsson (ÍBV Vestmannaeyjar) | 19 |
| 1998 | ÍBV Vestmannaeyjar | ÍBV Vestmannaeyjar | Steingrímur Jóhannesson (ÍBV Vestmannaeyjar) | 16 |
| 1999 | KR Reykjavík | KR Reykjavík | Steingrímur Jóhannesson (ÍBV Vestmannaeyjar) | 12 |
| 2000 | KR Reykjavík | ÍA Akranes | Guðmundur Steinarsson (Keflavík ÍF) | |
| | | | Andri Sigþórsson (KR Reykjavík) | 14 |
| 2001 | ÍA Akranes | Fylkir Reykjavík | Hjörtur Hjartarson (ÍA Akranes) | 15 |
| 2002 | KR Reykjavík | Fylkir Reykjavík | Grétar Hjartarson (UMF Grindavík) | 13 |
| 2003 | KR Reykjavík | ÍA Akranes | Björgólfur Takefusa (Þróttur Reykjavík) | 10 |
| 2004 | FH Hafnarfjörður | Keflavík ÍF | Gunnar Heiðar Þorvaldsson (ÍBV Vestmannaeyjar) | 12 |
| 2005 | FH Hafnarfjörður | Valur Reykjavík | Tryggvi Guðmundsson (FH Hafnarfjörður) | 16 |
| 2006 | FH Hafnarfjörður | Keflavík ÍF | Marel Baldvinsson (Breiðablik Kópavogur) | 11 |
| 2007 | Valur Reykjavík | FH Hafnarfjörður | Jónas Grani Garðarsson (Fram Reykjavík) | 13 |
| 2008 | FH Hafnarfjörður | KR Reykjavík | Guðmundur Steinarsson (Keflavík ÍF) | 16 |
| 2009 | FH Hafnarfjörður | Breiðablik Kópavogur | Björgólfur Takefusa (KR Reykjavík) | 16 |
| 2010 | Breiðablik Kópavogur | FH Hafnarfjörður | Gilles Mbang Ondo (GAB, UMF Grindavík) | 14 |
| 2011 | KR Reykjavík | KR Reykjavík | Garðar Jóhannsson (Stjarnan Garðabær) | 15 |
| 2012 | FH Hafnarfjörður | KR Reykjavík | Atli Guðnason (FH Hafnarfjörður) | 12 |
| 2013 | KR Reykjavík | Fram Reykjavík | Atli Viðar Björnsson (FH Hafnarfjörður) | |
| | | | Viðar Örn Kjartansson (Fylkir Reykjavík) | |
| | | | Gary Martin (ENG, KR Reykjavík) | 13 |
| 2014 | Stjarnan Garðabær | KR Reykjavík | Gary Martin (ENG, KR Reykjavík) | 13 |
| 2015 | FH Hafnarfjörður | Valur Reykjavík | Patrick Pedersen (DEN, Valur Reykjavík) | 13 |
| 2016 | FH Hafnarfjörður | Valur Reykjavík | Garðar Gunnlaugsson (ÍA Akranes) | 14 |
| 2017 | Valur Reykjavík | ÍBV Vestmannaeyjar | Andri Rúnar Bjarnason (UMF Grindavík) | 19 |
| 2018 | Valur Reykjavík | Stjarnan Garðabær | Patrick Pedersen (DEN, Valur Reykjavík) | 17 |
| 2019 | KR Reykjavík | Víkingur Reykjavík | Gary John Martin | |
| | | | (ENG, Valur Reykjavík / ÍBV Vestmannaeyjar ) | 14 |
| 2020 | Valur Reykjavík | *Competition cancelled* | Steven Lennon (SCO, FH Hafnarfjörður) | 17 |
| 2021 | Víkingur Reykjavík | Víkingur Reykjavík | Nikolaj Hansen (DEN, Víkingur Reykjavík) | 16 |
| 2022 | Breiðablik Kópavogur | Víkingur Reykjavík | Nökkvi Þeyr Þórisson (KA Akureyri) | |
| | | | Guðmundur Magnússon (Fram Reykjavík) | 17 |

## NATIONAL CHAMPIONSHIP
### Úrvalsdeild karla 2022
(18.04.2022 – 29.10.2022)

### Regular Season - Results

**Round 1 [18-20.04.2022]**
Víkingur - FH Hafnarfjörður 2-1(1-1)
Valur Reykjavík - Vestmannaeyjar 2-1(1-1)
Stjarnan - ÍA Akranes 2-2(0-1)
Breiðablik - Keflavík 4-1(3-0)
KA Akureyri - Leiknir Reykjavík 1-0(0-0)
Fram Reykjavík - KR Reykjavík 1-4(0-3)

**Round 2 [24-25.04.2022]**
Vestmannaeyjar - KA Akureyri 0-3(0-1)
Leiknir Reykjavík - Stjarnan 0-3(0-2)
ÍA Akranes - Víkingur 3-0(2-0)
Keflavík - Valur Reykjavík 0-1(0-1)
FH Hafnarfjörður - Fram Reykjavík 4-2(1-2)
KR Reykjavík - Breiðablik 0-1(0-0)

**Round 3 [30.04.-02.05.2022]**
Valur Reykjavík - KR Reykjavík 2-1(1-1)
Vestmannaeyjar - Leiknir Reykjavík 1-1(1-1)
Breiðablik - FH Hafnarfjörður 3-0(1-0)
KA Akureyri - Keflavík 3-2(1-1)
Fram Reykjavík - ÍA Akranes 1-1(1-1)
Víkingur - Stjarnan 4-5(2-3)

**Round 4 [06-08.05.2022]**
FH Hafnarfjörður - Valur Reykjavík 2-2(1-0)
ÍA Akranes - Breiðablik 1-5(0-3)
Keflavík - Vestmannaeyjar 3-3(2-0)
KR Reykjavík - KA Akureyri 0-0
Stjarnan - Fram Reykjavík 1-1(0-1)
Leiknir Reykjavík - Víkingur 0-0

**Round 5 [11-12.05.2022]**
Vestmannaeyjar - KR Reykjavík 1-2(1-2)
KA Akureyri - FH Hafnarfjörður 1-0(0-0)
Breiðablik - Stjarnan 3-2(2-1)
Valur Reykjavík - ÍA Akranes 4-0(1-0)
Keflavík - Leiknir Reykjavík 3-0(1-0)
Víkingur - Fram Reykjavík 4-1(3-0)

**Round 6 [15-16.05.2022]**
FH Hafnarfjörður - Vestmannaeyjar 2-0(1-0)
ÍA Akranes - KA Akureyri 0-3(0-1)
Stjarnan - Valur Reykjavík 1-0(0-0)
KR Reykjavík - Keflavík 1-0(0-0)
Leiknir Reykjavík - Fram Reykjavík 1-2(0-1)
Víkingur - Breiðablik 0-3(0-0)

**Round 7 [21-22.05.2022]**
Vestmannaeyjar - ÍA Akranes 0-0
KA Akureyri - Stjarnan 0-2(0-1)
KR Reykjavík - Leiknir Reykjavík 1-1(1-0)
Keflavík - FH Hafnarfjörður 2-1(2-1)
Valur Reykjavík - Víkingur 1-3(0-0)
Breiðablik - Fram Reykjavík 4-3(2-1)

**Round 8 [29.05.2022]**
Fram Reykjavík - Valur Reykjavík 3-2(1-1)
Víkingur - KA Akureyri 2-1(0-0)
Stjarnan - Vestmannaeyjar 1-0(0-0)
ÍA Akranes - Keflavík 0-2(0-1)
FH Hafnarfjörður - KR Reykjavík 2-3(1-2)
Leiknir Reykjavík - Breiðablik 1-2(0-1)

**Round 9 [15-16.06.2022]**
Vestmannaeyjar - Víkingur 0-3(0-2)
KR Reykjavík - ÍA Akranes 3-3(1-1)
KA Akureyri - Fram Reykjavík 2-2(0-2)
FH Hafnarfjörður - Leiknir Reykjavík 2-2(2-1)
Keflavík - Stjarnan 2-2(1-2)
Valur Reykjavík - Breiðablik 3-2(2-0)

**Round 10 [20-21.06.2022]**
Víkingur - Keflavík 4-1(4-0) [28.04.2022]
Fram Reykjavík - Vestmannaeyjar 3-3(2-2)
Stjarnan - KR Reykjavík 1-1(1-0)
Breiðablik - KA Akureyri 4-1(1-0)
Valur Reykjavík - Leiknir Reykjavík 2-1(1-1)
ÍA Akranes - FH Hafnarfjörður 1-1(0-0)

**Round 11 [01-04.07.2022]**
KR Reykjavík - Víkingur 0-3(0-1)
Vestmannaeyjar - Breiðablik 0-0
Keflavík - Fram Reykjavík 3-1(2-0)
KA Akureyri - Valur Reykjavík 1-1(0-0)
FH Hafnarfjörður - Stjarnan 1-1(0-0)
Leiknir Reykjavík - ÍA Akranes 1-0(0-0)

**Round 12 [09-11.07.2022]**
Breiðablik - KR Reykjavík 4-0(2-0) [23.06.22]
KA Akureyri - Vestmannaeyjar 4-3(2-3)
Víkingur - ÍA Akranes 3-2(2-0)
Fram Reykjavík - FH Hafnarfjörður 1-0(0-0)
Stjarnan - Leiknir Reykjavík 0-3(0-3)
Valur Reykjavík - Keflavík 0-3(0-1)

**Round 13 [16-19.07.2022]**
FH Hafnarfjörður - Víkingur 0-3(0-0)
Vestmannaeyjar - Valur Reykjavík 3-2(1-0)
Leiknir Reykjavík - KA Akureyri 0-5(0-2)
ÍA Akranes - Stjarnan 0-3(0-2)
Keflavík - Breiðablik 2-3(1-1)
KR Reykjavík - Fram Reykjavík 1-1(0-1)

**Round 14 [24-25.07.2022]**
Leiknir Reykjavík - Vestmannaeyjar 1-4(0-2)
Keflavík - KA Akureyri 1-3(1-0)
FH Hafnarfjörður - Breiðablik 0-0
ÍA Akranes - Fram Reykjavík 0-4(0-2)
KR Reykjavík - Valur Reykjavík 3-3(1-1)
Stjarnan - Víkingur 2-2(0-0) [30.07.2022]

**Round 15 [30.07.-03.08.2022]**
Vestmannaeyjar - Keflavík 2-2(1-1)
Breiðablik - ÍA Akranes 3-1(0-0)
KA Akureyri - KR Reykjavík 0-1(0-1)
Fram Reykjavík - Stjarnan 2-2(2-1)
Valur Reykjavík - FH Hafnarfjörður 2-0(1-0)
Víkingur - Leiknir Reyk. 9-0(5-0) [07.09.22]

**Round 16 [07-08.08.2022]**
FH Hafnarfjörður - KA Akureyri 0-3(0-2)
KR Reykjavík - Vestmannaeyjar 4-0(2-0)
Stjarnan - Breiðablik 5-2(3-1)
Fram Reykjavík - Víkingur 3-3(1-0)
ÍA Akranes - Valur Reykjavík 1-2(0-0)
Leiknir Reykjavík - Keflavík 1-2(0-1)

**Round 17 [14-15.08.2022]**
Vestmannaeyjar - FH Hafnarfjörður 4-1(3-0)
KA Akureyri - ÍA Akranes 3-0(0-0)
Valur Reykjavík - Stjarnan 6-1(3-1)
Keflavík - KR Reykjavík 0-0
Breiðablik - Víkingur 1-1(1-0)
Fram Reykjavík - Leiknir Reykjavík 4-1(1-0)

**Round 18 [21-22.08.2022]**
ÍA Akranes - Vestmannaeyjar 2-1(1-0)
Stjarnan - KA Akureyri 2-4(2-3)
FH Hafnarfjörður - Keflavík 3-0(2-0)
Leiknir Reykjavík - KR Reykjavík 4-3(2-1)
Fram Reykjavík - Breiðablik 0-2(0-0)
Víkingur - Valur Reykjavík 2-2(2-1)

**Round 19 [28-29.08.2022]**
Vestmannaeyjar - Stjarnan 3-1(2-1)
KA Akureyri - Víkingur 2-3(1-1)
Keflavík - ÍA Akranes 0-1(0-0)
KR Reykjavík - FH Hafnarfjörður 0-0
Breiðablik - Leiknir Reykjavík 4-0(1-0)
Valur Reykjavík - Fram Reykjavík 1-1(1-0)

**Round 20 [04-05.09.2022]**
Leiknir Reykjavík - FH Hafnarfjörður 0-0
Víkingur - Vestmannaeyjar 2-2(1-2)
ÍA Akranes - KR Reykjavík 4-4(2-3)
Fram Reykjavík - KA Akureyri 2-2(0-0)
Stjarnan - Keflavík 0-2(0-0)
Breiðablik - Valur Reykjavík 1-0(0-0)

**Round 21 [11.09.2022]**
FH Hafnarfjörður - ÍA Akranes 6-1(3-1)
Vestmannaeyjar - Fram Reykjavík 2-2(1-1)
KA Akureyri - Breiðablik 2-1(1-0)
Keflavík - Víkingur 0-3(0-3)
KR Reykjavík - Stjarnan 3-1(2-0)
Leiknir Reykjavík - Valur Reykjavík 1-0(0-0)

**Round 22 [17.09.2022]**
Breiðablik - Vestmannaeyjar 3-0(0-0)
Fram Reykjavík - Keflavík 4-8(3-4)
ÍA Akranes - Leiknir Reykjavík 1-2(1-0)
Stjarnan - FH Hafnarfjörður 2-1(2-1)
Valur Reykjavík - KA Akureyri 0-1(0-0)
Víkingur - KR Reykjavík 2-2(1-0)

## Final Standings

| | | | | | | | | |
|---|---|---|---|---|---|---|---|---|
| 1. | Breiðablik Kópavogur | 22 | 16 | 3 | 3 | 55 - 23 | 51 |
| 2. | Víkingur Reykjavík | 22 | 12 | 7 | 3 | 58 - 32 | 43 |
| 3. | KA Akureyri | 22 | 13 | 4 | 5 | 45 - 26 | 43 |
| 4. | Valur Reykjavík | 22 | 9 | 5 | 8 | 38 - 32 | 32 |
| 5. | KR Reykjavík | 22 | 7 | 10 | 5 | 37 - 34 | 31 |
| 6. | Stjarnan Garðabær | 22 | 8 | 7 | 7 | 40 - 42 | 31 |
| 7. | Keflavík | 22 | 8 | 4 | 10 | 39 - 40 | 28 |
| 8. | Fram Reykjavík | 22 | 5 | 10 | 7 | 44 - 51 | 25 |
| 9. | ÍBV Vestmannaeyjar | 22 | 4 | 8 | 10 | 33 - 44 | 20 |
| 10. | Leiknir Reykjavík | 22 | 5 | 5 | 12 | 21 - 49 | 20 |
| 11. | FH Hafnarfjörður | 22 | 4 | 7 | 11 | 27 - 35 | 19 |
| 12. | ÍA Akranes | 22 | 3 | 6 | 13 | 24 - 53 | 15 |

Teams ranked 1-6 were qualified for the Championship Round, while teams ranked 7-12 were qualified for the Relegation Round.

## Relegation Round

### Results

**Round 23** [02-05.10.2022]
Keflavík - ÍA Akranes 3-2(2-1)
Fram Reykjavík - Leiknir Reykjavík 3-2(1-1)
Vestmannaeyjar - FH Hafnarfjörður 2-1(1-1)

**Round 24** [08-10.10.2022]
ÍA Akranes - Fram Reykjavík 3-2(1-2)
Vestmannaeyjar - Keflavík 2-1(2-0)
FH Hafnarfjörður - Leiknir Reykjavík 4-2(2-1)

**Round 25** [15-16.10.2022]
Leiknir Reykjavík - ÍA Akranes 2-2(2-2)
Keflavík - FH Hafnarfjörður 2-3(2-1)
Fram Reykjavík - Vestmannaeyjar 1-3(0-3)

**Round 26** [22-23.10.2022]
Leiknir Reykjavík - Keflavík 1-7(0-3)
ÍA Akranes - Vestmannaeyjar 3-2(0-1)
Fram Reykjavík - FH Hafnarfjörður 3-0(2-0)

**Round 27** [29.10.2022]
FH Hafnarfjörður - ÍA Akranes 1-2(1-1)
Keflavík - Fram Reykjavík 4-0(1-0)
Vestmannaeyjar - Leiknir Reykjavík 1-0(0-0)

### Final Standings

| | | | | | | | | Total | | Home | | | | | Away | | | | |
|---|---|---|---|---|---|---|---|---|---|---|---|---|---|---|---|---|---|---|---|
| 7. | Keflavík | 27 | 11 | 4 | 12 | 56 | - | 48 | 37 | 5 | 3 | 6 | 25 | - | 23 | 6 | 1 | 6 | 31 - 25 |
| 8. | ÍBV Vestmannaeyjar | 27 | 8 | 8 | 11 | 43 | - | 50 | 32 | 6 | 5 | 3 | 21 | - | 19 | 2 | 3 | 8 | 22 - 31 |
| 9. | Fram Reykjavík | 27 | 7 | 10 | 10 | 53 | - | 63 | 31 | 5 | 5 | 4 | 31 | - | 33 | 2 | 5 | 6 | 22 - 30 |
| 10. | FH Hafnarfjörður | 27 | 6 | 7 | 14 | 36 | - | 46 | 25 | 5 | 4 | 4 | 27 | - | 21 | 1 | 3 | 10 | 9 - 25 |
| 11. | ÍA Akranes (*Relegated*) | 27 | 6 | 7 | 14 | 36 | - | 63 | 25 | 4 | 2 | 7 | 19 | - | 31 | 2 | 5 | 7 | 17 - 32 |
| 12. | Leiknir Reykjavík (*Relegated*) | 27 | 5 | 6 | 16 | 28 | - | 66 | 21 | 3 | 3 | 7 | 13 | - | 30 | 2 | 3 | 9 | 15 - 36 |

## Championship Round

### Results

**Round 23** [02-05.10.2022]
KA Akureyri - KR Reykjavík 1-0(0-0)
Breiðablik - Stjarnan 3-0(1-0)
Víkingur - Valur Reykjavík 3-2(0-2)

**Round 24** [08-10.10.2022]
KA Akureyri - Breiðablik 1-2(0-1)
KR Reykjavík - Valur Reykjavík 2-1(0-0)
Stjarnan - Víkingur 2-1(0-0)

**Round 25** [15-16.10.2022]
Víkingur - KA Akureyri 2-2(1-1)
Breiðablik - KR Reykjavík 0-1(0-0)
Valur Reykjavík - Stjarnan 3-0(1-0)

**Round 26** [22-24.10.2022]
Valur Reykjavík - Breiðablik 2-5(2-2)
Stjarnan - KA Akureyri 0-3(0-1)
Víkingur - KR Reykjavík 2-2(0-1)

**Round 27** [29.10.2022]
KR Reykjavík - Stjarnan 0-2(0-0)
Breiðablik - Víkingur 1-0(1-0)
KA Akureyri - Valur Reykjavík 2-0(2-0)

### Final Standings

| | | | | | | | | Total | | Home | | | | | Away | | | | |
|---|---|---|---|---|---|---|---|---|---|---|---|---|---|---|---|---|---|---|---|
| 1. | **Breiðablik Kópavogur** | 27 | 20 | 3 | 4 | 66 | - | 27 | 63 | 12 | 1 | 1 | 38 | - | 10 | 8 | 2 | 3 | 28 - 17 |
| 2. | KA Akureyri | 27 | 16 | 5 | 6 | 54 | - | 30 | 53 | 8 | 2 | 4 | 23 | - | 17 | 8 | 3 | 2 | 31 - 13 |
| 3. | Víkingur Reykjavík | 27 | 13 | 9 | 5 | 66 | - | 41 | 48 | 7 | 5 | 2 | 41 | - | 26 | 6 | 4 | 3 | 25 - 15 |
| 4. | KR Reykjavík | 27 | 9 | 11 | 7 | 42 | - | 40 | 38 | 4 | 6 | 3 | 18 | - | 16 | 5 | 5 | 4 | 24 - 24 |
| 5. | Stjarnan Garðabær | 27 | 10 | 7 | 10 | 44 | - | 52 | 37 | 5 | 4 | 4 | 19 | - | 22 | 5 | 3 | 6 | 25 - 30 |
| 6. | Valur Reykjavík | 27 | 10 | 5 | 12 | 46 | - | 44 | 35 | 8 | 1 | 4 | 28 | - | 19 | 2 | 4 | 8 | 18 - 25 |

| Top goalscorers: | |
|---|---|
| 17 **Nökkvi Þeyr Þórisson** | *KA Akureyri* |
| 17 **Guðmundur Magnússon** | *Fram Reykjavík* |
| 14 Ísak Snær Þorvaldsson | *Breiðablik Kópavogur* |

# NATIONAL CUP
## Mjólkurbikarinn 2022

### Third Round [24-26.05.2022]

| | | | | |
|---|---|---|---|---|
| Huginn/Höttur - KF Ægir | 1-3(1-1) | | Fylkir Reykjavík - ÍBV Vestmannaeyjar | 2-1(1-0) |
| Sindri Höfn - ÍA Akranes | 3-5(1-1) | | FH Hafnarfjörður - Kári | 3-0(0-0) |
| UMF Selfoss - ÍF Magni | 1-1 aet; 5-3 pen | | Keflavík - UMF Njarðvík | 1-4(1-2) |
| IF Vestri Ísafjörður - UMF Afturelding Mosfellsbær | 2-3(0-0,1-1) | | Stjarnan Garðabær - KR Reykjavík | 0-3(0-2) |
| Hvíti riddarinn - Kórdrengir Reykjavík | 0-2(0-0) | | Fram Reykjavík - Leiknir Reykjavík | 3-2(1-1,2-2) |
| UMF Grindavík - ÍR Reykjavík | 1-2(0-1) | | KA Akureyri - Reynir Sandgerði | 4-1(1-1) |
| HK Kópavogur - IF Grótta Seltjarnarnes | 3-1(1-0) | | Haukar Hafnarfjörður - Víkingur Reykjavík | 0-7(0-3) |
| Dalvík/Reynir - Þór Akureyri | 2-0(1-0) | | Breiðablik Kópavogur - Valur Reykjavík | 6-2(2-2) |

### 1/8-Finals [26-28.06.2022]

| | | | | |
|---|---|---|---|---|
| HK Kópavogur - Dalvík/Reynir | 6-0(0-0) | | UMF Njarðvík - KR Reykjavík | 0-1(0-0) |
| KA Akureyri - Fram Reykjavík | 4-1(2-0) | | Kórdrengir Reykjavík - UMF Afturelding Mosfellsb. | 2-1(0-0,1-1) |
| FH Hafnarfjörður - ÍR Reykjavík | 6-1(2-0) | | ÍA Akranes - Breiðablik Kópavogur | 2-3(0-2) |
| KF Ægir - Fylkir Reykjavík | 1-0(0-0) | | UMF Selfoss - Víkingur Reykjavík | 0-6(0-2) |

### Quarter-Finals [10-11./18-19.08.2022]

| | | | | |
|---|---|---|---|---|
| KA Akureyri - KF Ægir | 3-0(0-0) | | Víkingur Reykjavík - KR Reykjavík | 5-3(2-1) |
| Kórdrengir Reykjavík - FH Hafnarfjörður | 2-4(2-3) | | HK Kópavogur - Breiðablik Kópavogur | 0-1(0-0) |

### Semi-Finals [31.08.-01.09.2022]

| | | | | |
|---|---|---|---|---|
| Breiðablik Kópavogur - Víkingur Reykjavík | 0-3(0-3) | | FH Hafnarfjörður - KA Akureyri | 2-1(0-1) |

### Final

01.10.2022; Laugardalsvöllur, Reykjavík; Referee: Ivar Orri Kristjansson; Attendance: 4,381
**Víkingur Reykjavík - FH Hafnarfjörður**                    **3-2(1-1,2-2)**

**Víkingur Reykjavík:** Ingvar Jónsson, Viktor Örlygur Andrason, Kyle McLagan, Oliver Ekroth, Logi Tómasson, Júlíus Magnússon (Cap), Pablo Oshan Battuto Punyed (106.Karl Fridleifur Gunnarsson), Danijel Dejan Djuric (75.Helgi Guðjónsson), Ari Sigurpálsson (75.Nikolaj Hansen), Birnir Snær Ingason (75.Arnór Borg Guðjohnsen), Erlingur Agnarsson (118.Gísli Þórðarson). Trainer: Arnar Gunnlaugsson.

**FH Hafnarfjörður:** Atli Gunnar Guðmundsson, Ástbjörn Þórðarson (106.Haraldur Einar Ásgrímsson), Eggert Gunnþór Jónsson (99.Jóhann Ægir Arnarsson), Guðmundur Kristjánsson, Ólafur Guðmundsson, Björn Daníel Sverrisson, Matthías Vilhjálmsson (Cap) (91.Máni Hilmarsson), Davíð Snær Jóhannsson, Oliver Heiðarsson (80.Baldur Logi Guðlaugsson), Vuk Oskar Dimitrijević (78.Kristinn Freyr Sigurðsson), Úlfur Ágúst Björnsson (78.Steven Lennon). Trainer: Eiður Smári Guðjohnsen.

**Goals:** 1-0 Pablo Oshan Battuto Punyed (26), 1-1 Oliver Heiðarsson (28), 2-1 Nikolaj Hansen (89), 2-2 Ingvar Jónsson (90 own goal), 3-2 Nikolaj Hansen (91).

# THE CLUBS 2022

## Breiðablik Kópavogur

| | |
|---|---|
| **Founded:** | 12.04.1950 |
| **Stadium:** | Kópavogsvöllur, Kópavogur (3,009) |
| **Trainer:** | Óskar Hrafn Þorvaldsson                25.10.1973 |

| Goalkeepers: | DOB | M | (s) | G |
|---|---|---|---|---|
| Brynjar Atli Bragason | 01.04.2000 | | (1) | |
| Anton Ari Einarsson | 25.08.1994 | 27 | | |
| **Defenders:** | **DOB** | **M** | **(s)** | **G** |
| Adam Örn Arnarson | 27.08.1995 | | (2) | |
| Höskuldur Gunnlaugsson | 26.09.1994 | 27 | | 6 |
| Elfar Freyr Helgason | 27.07.1989 | 1 | (4) | |
| Davíð Ingvarsson | 25.04.1999 | 20 | (3) | |
| Viktor Örn Margeirsson | 22.07.1994 | 25 | | 1 |
| Damir Muminović | 13.05.1990 | 24 | (1) | 1 |
| Mikkel Qvist (DEN) | 22.04.1993 | 4 | (5) | 1 |
| **Midfielders:** | **DOB** | **M** | **(s)** | **G** |
| William Cole Campbell | 20.02.2006 | | (1) | |
| Viktor Karl Einarsson | 30.01.1997 | 19 | (3) | 6 |
| Gísli Eyjólfsson | 31.05.1994 | 23 | (1) | 2 |

| | DOB | M | (s) | G |
|---|---|---|---|---|
| Viktor Elmar Gautason | 09.10.2003 | | (4) | |
| Sölvi Snær Guðbjargarson | 25.07.2001 | 2 | (7) | 3 |
| Anton Logi Lúðvíksson | 13.03.2003 | 4 | (11) | 2 |
| Gunnar Andri Pétursson | 21.11.1994 | | (1) | |
| Oliver Sigurjónsson | 03.03.1995 | 20 | (1) | |
| Kristinn Steindórsson | 29.04.1990 | 20 | (5) | 7 |
| Andri Rafn Yeoman | 18.04.1992 | 10 | (10) | |
| Dagur Dan Þórhallsson | 02.05.2000 | 21 | (4) | 9 |
| **Forwards:** | **DOB** | **M** | **(s)** | **G** |
| Pétur Theódór Árnason | 04.06.1995 | | (1) | |
| Galdur Guðmundsson | 14.04.2006 | | (4) | |
| Omar Sowe (USA) | 28.10.2000 | 2 | (15) | 2 |
| Jason Daði Svanþórsson | 31.12.1999 | 25 | (2) | 11 |
| Ísak Snær Þorvaldsson | 01.05.2001 | 23 | (1) | 14 |

## Fimleikafélag Hafnarfjarðar

| Founded: | 15.10.1929 | | |
| Stadium: | Kaplakriki, Hafnarfjörður (6,450) | | |
| Trainer: | Ólafur Davíð Jóhannesson | | 30.06.1957 |
| [19.06.2022] | Eiður Smári Guðjohnsen | | 15.09.1978 |
| [06.10.2022] | Sigurvin Ólafson | | 18.07.1976 |

| Goalkeepers: | DOB | M | (s) | G |
|---|---|---|---|---|
| Atli Gunnar Guðmundsson | 08.10.1993 | 12 | | |
| Heiðar Hermannsson | 12.10.2005 | | (1) | |
| Gunnar Nielsen (FRO) | 07.10.1986 | 15 | | |
| **Defenders:** | **DOB** | **M** | **(s)** | **G** |
| Jóhann Ægir Arnarsson | 09.12.2002 | 8 | (5) | 1 |
| Haraldur Einar Ásgrímsson | 16.06.2000 | 8 | (8) | |
| Arngrímur Bjartur Guðmundsson | 14.03.2005 | | (1) | |
| Ólafur Guðmundsson | 18.03.2002 | 21 | (1) | 4 |
| Guðmundur Kristjánsson | 01.03.1989 | 24 | (2) | 1 |
| Ástbjörn Þórðarson | 26.07.1999 | 20 | (1) | |
| **Midfielders:** | **DOB** | **M** | **(s)** | **G** |
| William Cole Campbell | 20.02.2006 | | (1) | |
| Baldur Logi Guðlaugsson | 21.01.2002 | 7 | (10) | 1 |
| Baldur Kári Helgason | 08.02.2005 | | (1) | |

| | DOB | M | (s) | G |
|---|---|---|---|---|
| Davíð Snær Jóhannsson | 15.06.2002 | 12 | (9) | 1 |
| Eggert Gunnþór Jónsson | 18.08.1988 | 20 | | |
| Finnur Orri Margeirsson | 08.03.1991 | 10 | (3) | |
| Lasse Petry (DEN) | 19.09.1992 | 6 | (3) | |
| Logi Hrafn Róbertsson | 22.07.2004 | 9 | (3) | 1 |
| Kristinn Freyr Sigurðsson | 25.12.1991 | 22 | (2) | 3 |
| Björn Daníel Sverrisson | 29.05.1990 | 23 | (4) | |
| **Forwards:** | **DOB** | **M** | **(s)** | **G** |
| Úlfur Ágúst Björnsson | 12.06.2003 | 8 | (6) | 4 |
| Vuk Oskar Dimitrijević | 28.02.2001 | 10 | (10) | 3 |
| Gils Gíslason | 15.12.2007 | | | |
| Máni Hilmarsson | 02.06.1998 | 5 | (11) | 2 |
| Oliver Heiðarsson | 23.02.2001 | 12 | (14) | 2 |
| Steven Lennon (SCO) | 20.01.1988 | 21 | (3) | 3 |
| Matthías Vilhjálmsson | 30.01.1987 | 24 | (2) | 9 |

## Íþróttabandalag Akraness

| Founded: | 1946 | | |
| Stadium: | Norðurálsvöllurinn, Akranes (3,054) | | |
| Trainer: | Jón Þór Haukson | | 02.05.1978 |

| Goalkeepers: | DOB | M | (s) | G |
|---|---|---|---|---|
| Árni Marinó Einarsson | 18.02.2002 | 10 | | |
| Árni Snær Ólafsson | 16.08.1991 | 17 | | |
| **Defenders:** | **DOB** | **M** | **(s)** | **G** |
| Alexander James Davey (SCO) | 24.11.1994 | 9 | | |
| Wout Droste (NED) | 20.05.1989 | 3 | (4) | |
| Hallur Flosason | 01.05.1993 | 1 | (5) | |
| Jón Gísli Eyland Gíslason | 25.02.2002 | 13 | (4) | |
| Hlynur Sævar Jónsson | 29.03.1999 | 15 | (6) | 1 |
| Aron Bjarki Jósepsson | 21.11.1989 | 18 | | 2 |
| Tobias Kirstrup Stagaard (DEN) | 29.01.2002 | 8 | (4) | |
| Oliver Stefánsson | 03.08.2002 | 19 | (4) | 1 |
| Johannes Vall (SWE) | 19.10.1992 | 23 | | 1 |
| **Midfielders:** | **DOB** | **M** | **(s)** | **G** |
| Ármann Ingi Finnbogason | 16.06.2004 | 1 | (4) | 1 |
| Sveinn Svavar Hallgrímsson | 2006 | | (1) | |
| Haukur Andri Haraldsson | 24.08.2005 | 8 | (7) | 1 |

| | DOB | M | (s) | G |
|---|---|---|---|---|
| Árni Salvar Heimisson | 10.03.2003 | 11 | (2) | |
| Breki Þór Hermannsson | 20.03.2003 | | (5) | |
| Daniel Ingi Jóhannesson | 03.04.2007 | | (1) | |
| Christian Køhler (DEN) | 10.04.1996 | 17 | (1) | |
| Brynjar Snær Pálsson | 11.11.2001 | 6 | (7) | |
| Ingi Þór Sigurðsson | 06.04.2004 | 3 | (9) | 3 |
| Gísli Luxdal Unnarsson | 28.02.2001 | 26 | (1) | 5 |
| Benedikt Warén | 03.10.2001 | 13 | (8) | 2 |
| Steinar Þorsteinsson | 06.12.1997 | 23 | (1) | 2 |
| **Forwards:** | **DOB** | **M** | **(s)** | **G** |
| Garðar Gunnlaugsson | 24.04.1983 | | (2) | |
| Kaj Leo í Bartalsstovu (FRO) | 23.06.1991 | 18 | (6) | 2 |
| Viktor Jónsson | 23.06.1994 | 4 | (2) | 2 |
| Kristian Ladewig Lindberg (DEN) | 14.02.1994 | 6 | (5) | 2 |
| Guðmundur Tyrfingsson | 01.02.2003 | 1 | (8) | |
| Eyþór Aron Wöhler | 28.01.2002 | 23 | (2) | 9 |
| Sigurður Hrannar Þorsteinsson | 19.04.2000 | 1 | (8) | |

## Knattspyrnufélag Akureyrar

| Founded: | 1928 | | |
| Stadium: | Akureyrarvöllur, Akureyri (1,645) | | |
| Trainer: | Arnar Grétarsson | | 20.02.1972 |
| [01.10.2022] | Hallgrímur Jónasson | | 04.05.1986 |

| Goalkeepers: | DOB | M | (s) | G |
|---|---|---|---|---|
| Steinþór Már Auðunsson | 23.02.1990 | 10 | (1) | |
| Kristijan Jajalo (BIH) | 04.03.1993 | 17 | | |
| **Defenders:** | **DOB** | **M** | **(s)** | **G** |
| Ívar Örn Árnason | 12.04.1996 | 26 | | 2 |
| Dušan Brković (SRB) | 20.01.1989 | 21 | (1) | |
| Oleksiy Bykov (UKR) | 29.03.1998 | 7 | (1) | |
| Gaber Dobrovoljc (SVN) | 27.01.1993 | 3 | (4) | 1 |
| Hallgrímur Jónasson | 04.05.1986 | | (2) | |
| Andri Fannar Stefánsson | 22.04.1991 | 9 | (9) | |
| Hrannar Björn Steingrímsson | 19.06.1992 | 13 | (3) | |
| Bryan Van Den Bogaert (BEL) | 14.12.1991 | 19 | (3) | 1 |
| Þorri Mar Þórisson | 13.08.1999 | 20 | (5) | 1 |

| **Midfielders:** | **DOB** | **M** | **(s)** | **G** |
|---|---|---|---|---|
| Bjarni Aðalsteinsson | 01.09.1999 | 5 | (16) | |
| Jakob Snær Árnason | 04.07.1997 | 5 | (18) | 4 |
| Sebastiaan Brebels (BEL) | 05.05.1995 | 3 | (4) | |
| Kári Gautason | 11.12.2003 | | (1) | |
| Daníel Hafsteinsson | 12.11.1999 | 25 | | 3 |
| Sveinn Margeir Hauksson | 02.11.2001 | 20 | (3) | 3 |
| Rodrigo Gómez Mateo „Rodri" (ESP) | 09.02.1989 | 22 | (1) | 2 |
| Mikael Breki Þórðarson | 2007 | | (2) | |
| **Forwards:** | **DOB** | **M** | **(s)** | **G** |
| Elfar Árni Aðalsteinsson | 12.08.1990 | 19 | (4) | 7 |
| Ásgeir Sigurgeirsson | 11.12.1996 | 13 | (6) | 2 |
| Hallgrímur Mar Steingrímsson | 02.10.1990 | 18 | (9) | 9 |
| Nökkvi Þeyr Þórisson | 13.08.1999 | 20 | | 17 |
| Steinþór Freyr Þorsteinsson | 29.07.1985 | 2 | (14) | |

## Knattspyrnufélagið Fram

| Founded: | 01.05.1908 | | |
| Stadium: | Laugardalsvöllur, Reykjavík (9,500) | | |
| Trainer: | Jón Þórir Sveinsson | | 05.08.1965 |

| Goalkeepers: | DOB | M | (s) | G |
|---|---|---|---|---|
| Stefán Þór Hannesson | 02.03.1996 | 1 | | |
| Ólafur Ólafsson | 08.05.1995 | 26 | | |
| **Defenders:** | **DOB** | **M** | **(s)** | **G** |
| Arnór Daði Aðalsteinsson | 06.03.1997 | | (1) | |
| Aron Kári Aðalsteinsson | 09.07.1999 | | (3) | |
| Hosine Bility (AUS) | 10.05.2001 | | (4) | |
| Alex Freyr Elísson | 09.10.1997 | 19 | (1) | 2 |
| Brynjar Gauti Guðjónsson | 27.02.1992 | 10 | | 2 |
| Þórir Guðjónsson | 07.04.1991 | 5 | (6) | 1 |
| Gunnar Gunnarsson | 22.09.1993 | 5 | (2) | |
| Orri Gunnarsson | 05.04.1992 | 2 | (13) | |
| Hlynur Atli Magnússon | 11.09.1990 | 21 | (3) | 1 |
| Delphin Tshiembe (COD) | 17.07.1991 | 22 | | 1 |
| Jesús Natividad Yendis Gómez (VEN) | 18.03.1998 | 7 | (7) | |

| **Midfielders:** | **DOB** | **M** | **(s)** | **G** |
|---|---|---|---|---|
| Már Ægisson | 11.01.2000 | 23 | | 2 |
| Breki Baldursson | 11.08.2006 | | (2) | |
| Tryggvi Snær Geirsson | 06.11.2000 | 8 | (15) | |
| Sigfús Árni Guðmundsson | 13.04.2004 | | (1) | |
| Albert Hafsteinsson | 05.06.1996 | 16 | (5) | 4 |
| Óskar Jónsson | 28.01.1997 | 4 | (4) | |
| Almarr Ormarsson | 25.02.1988 | 15 | (1) | |
| Tiago Manuel Da Silva Fernandes (POR) | 31.03.1995 | 21 | (2) | 5 |
| Magnús Þórðarson | 22.11.1999 | 9 | (13) | 4 |
| Indriði Áki Þorláksson | 02.08.1995 | 22 | (3) | |
| **Forwards:** | **DOB** | **M** | **(s)** | **G** |
| Jannik Holmsgaard (DEN) | 06.04.1996 | 14 | (5) | 8 |
| Aron Snær Ingason | 26.10.2001 | | (4) | |
| Guðmundur Magnússon | 10.06.1991 | 25 | (1) | 17 |
| Frederico „Fred" Bello Saraiva (BRA) | 15.08.1996 | 19 | (5) | 5 |
| Alexander Már Þorláksson | 02.08.1995 | 3 | (4) | 1 |

## Knattspyrnudeild Keflavík

| Goalkeepers: | DOB | M | (s) | G |
|---|---|---|---|---|
| Rúnar Gissurarson | 23.11.1986 | 2 | (2) | |
| Sindri Kristinn Ólafsson | 19.01.1997 | 25 | | |
| **Defenders:** | **DOB** | **M** | **(s)** | **G** |
| Stefán Jón Friðriksson | 12.02.2004 | | (1) | |
| Sindri Þór Guðmundsson | 11.08.1997 | 16 | (8) | |
| Dani Hatakka (FIN) | 12.03.1994 | 26 | | 4 |
| Axel Ingi Jóhannesson | 02.06.2004 | | (2) | |
| Ásgeir Páll Magnússon | 07.09.2000 | 4 | (11) | |
| Magnús Þór Magnússon | 20.02.1992 | 24 | | 1 |
| Ignacio Heras Anglada „Nacho Heras" (ESP) | 27.08.1991 | 21 | (1) | 3 |
| Rúnar Þór Sigurgeirsson | 28.12.1999 | 21 | (1) | 2 |
| **Midfielders:** | **DOB** | **M** | **(s)** | **G** |
| Ernir Bjarnason | 22.08.1997 | 10 | (8) | 1 |
| Frans Elvarsson | 14.08.1990 | 22 | | 3 |

| Founded: | 1929 | | | |
|---|---|---|---|---|
| Stadium: | Keflavíkurvöllur, Keflavík (5,200) | | | |
| Trainer: | Eysteinn Húni Hauksson & | | 12.08.1974 | |
| | Sigurdur Ragnar Eyjólfsson | | 01.12.1973 | |

| | DOB | M | (s) | G |
|---|---|---|---|---|
| Ingimundur Aron Guðnason | 29.03.1999 | 8 | (4) | 1 |
| Valur Þór Hákonarson | 20.01.2004 | | (2) | |
| Patrik Johannesen (FRO) | 07.09.1995 | 22 | | 12 |
| Ivan Kalyuzhniy (UKR) | 21.01.1998 | 6 | | |
| Sindri Snær Magnússon | 18.02.1992 | 11 | (2) | 1 |
| Edon Osmani | 25.03.2000 | 3 | (6) | |
| Adam Pálsson | 07.06.1998 | 24 | | 7 |
| Guðjón Pétur Stefánsson | 01.05.2003 | | (2) | |
| Dagur Ingi Valsson | 06.09.1999 | 5 | (12) | 5 |
| Kian Paul James Williams (ENG) | 01.07.2000 | 18 | (4) | 5 |
| **Forwards:** | **DOB** | **M** | **(s)** | **G** |
| Joseph Arthur Gibbs (AUS) | 13.06.1992 | 20 | (1) | 5 |
| Ari Steinn Guðmundsson | 31.12.1996 | | (2) | |
| Helgi Þór Jónsson | 01.03.1994 | | (13) | 1 |
| Adam Árni Róbertsson | 12.01.1999 | 9 | (11) | 5 |

## Knattspyrnufélag Reykjavíkur

| Goalkeepers: | DOB | M | (s) | G |
|---|---|---|---|---|
| Aron Snær Friðriksson | 29.01.1997 | 3 | | |
| Beitir Ólafsson | 02.07.1986 | 24 | | |
| **Defenders:** | **DOB** | **M** | **(s)** | **G** |
| Arnór Sveinn Aðalsteinsson | 26.01.1986 | 12 | (2) | 1 |
| Kennie Chopart (DEN) | 01.06.1990 | 25 | (1) | 1 |
| Grétar Snær Gunnarsson | 08.01.1997 | 15 | (1) | |
| Kristinn Jónsson | 04.08.1990 | 14 | (3) | 1 |
| Pontus Lindgren (SWE) | 13.12.2000 | 11 | (5) | |
| Finnur Tómas Pálmason | 12.02.2001 | 16 | | 1 |
| Jón Arnar Sigurðsson | 03.05.2007 | | (1) | |
| **Midfielders:** | **DOB** | **M** | **(s)** | **G** |
| Aron Þórður Albertsson | 27.06.1996 | 10 | (8) | 1 |
| Theodór Elmar Bjarnason | 04.03.1987 | 24 | (1) | 2 |

| Founded: | 16.02.1899 | | |
|---|---|---|---|
| Stadium: | Alvogenvöllurinn, Reykjavík (3,333) | | |
| Trainer: | Rúnar Kristinsson | | 05.09.1969 |

| | DOB | M | (s) | G |
|---|---|---|---|---|
| Gunnar Magnús Gunnarsson | 10.02.2006 | | (1) | |
| Hallur Hansson (FRO) | 08.07.1992 | 18 | (2) | 1 |
| Ægir Jarl Jónasson | 08.03.1998 | 20 | (5) | 6 |
| Aron Kristófer Lárusson | 17.09.1998 | 15 | (4) | 1 |
| Pálmi Rafn Pálmason | 09.11.1984 | 12 | (7) | |
| Þorsteinn Már Ragnarsson | 19.04.1990 | 7 | (10) | 1 |
| Atli Sigurjónsson | 01.07.1991 | 27 | | 8 |
| Jón Ívar Þórólfsson | 2006 | | (1) | |
| **Forwards:** | **DOB** | **M** | **(s)** | **G** |
| Kjartan Finnbogason | 09.07.1986 | 7 | (11) | 4 |
| Kristján Flóki Finnbogason | 12.01.1995 | 3 | (6) | 2 |
| Stefán Árni Geirsson | 06.11.2000 | 13 | (4) | 3 |
| Sigurður Bjartur Hallsson | 01.09.1999 | 15 | (9) | 4 |
| Stefan Ljubicic | 05.10.1999 | 6 | (12) | 2 |

## Íþróttafélagið Leiknir Reykjavík

| Goalkeepers: | DOB | M | (s) | G |
|---|---|---|---|---|
| Atli Jónasson | 12.03.1988 | 1 | | |
| Viktor Freyr Sigurðsson | 10.07.2000 | 26 | | |
| **Defenders:** | **DOB** | **M** | **(s)** | **G** |
| Bjarki Aðalsteinsson | 10.10.1991 | 24 | | 2 |
| Adam Örn Arnarson | 27.08.1995 | 7 | (3) | |
| Birgir Baldvinsson | 10.01.2001 | 19 | (1) | 2 |
| Loftur Páll Eiríksson | 11.12.1992 | 2 | (3) | |
| Gyrðir Hrafn Guðbrandsson | 30.03.1999 | 13 | (10) | |
| Óttar Bjarni Guðmundsson | 15.04.1990 | 4 | | |
| Dagur Austmann Hilmarsson | 02.06.1998 | 20 | (2) | |
| Arnór Ingi Kristinsson | 23.06.2001 | 8 | (6) | |
| Hjalti Sigurðsson | 19.09.2000 | 9 | (4) | |
| Ósvald Jarl Traustason | 22.10.1995 | 1 | (5) | |
| **Midfielders:** | **DOB** | **M** | **(s)** | **G** |
| Árni Elvar Árnason | 18.11.1996 | 9 | (4) | |

| Founded: | 17.05.1973 | | |
|---|---|---|---|
| Stadium: | Leiknisvöllur, Reykjavík (1,025) | | |
| Trainer: | Sigurður Heiðar Höskuldsson | | 15.05.1985 |

| | DOB | M | (s) | G |
|---|---|---|---|---|
| Jón Hrafn Barkarson | 14.09.2003 | 1 | (10) | |
| Emil Berger (SWE) | 23.05.1991 | 26 | | 6 |
| Sindri Björnsson | 29.03.1995 | 4 | (10) | |
| Daði Bærings Halldórsson | 08.04.1997 | 18 | (6) | 1 |
| Brynjar Hlöðversson | 03.04.1989 | 20 | | |
| Davíð Júlían Jónsson | 26.06.2004 | 4 | (4) | |
| Maciej Makuszewski (POL) | 29.09.1989 | 9 | (3) | 1 |
| Daníel Finns Matthíasson | 21.06.2000 | 2 | (1) | |
| Shkelzen Veseli | 02.06.2004 | | (3) | |
| **Forwards:** | **DOB** | **M** | **(s)** | **G** |
| Róbert Quental Árnason | 23.05.2005 | 1 | (4) | |
| Mikkel Dahl (DEN) | 22.06.1993 | 15 | (5) | 4 |
| Zean Peetz Dalügge (DEN) | 11.07.2003 | 12 | | 4 |
| Róbert Hauksson | 01.10.2001 | 15 | (10) | 3 |
| Mikkel Jakobsen (DEN) | 23.05.1999 | 18 | (8) | 2 |
| Kristófer Konráðsson | 31.03.1998 | 9 | (7) | |

## Ungmennafélagið Stjarnan Garðabær

| Goalkeepers: | DOB | M | (s) | G |
|---|---|---|---|---|
| Haraldur Björnsson | 11.01.1989 | 27 | | |
| Viktor Reynir Oddgeirsson | 24.02.2003 | | (1) | |
| **Defenders:** | **DOB** | **M** | **(s)** | **G** |
| Elís Rafn Björnsson | 13.10.1992 | 7 | (3) | 2 |
| Björn Berg Bryde | 08.07.1992 | 21 | (1) | |
| Brynjar Gauti Guðjónsson | 27.02.1992 | 1 | (3) | |
| Sindri Þór Ingimarsson | 24.11.1998 | 26 | | |
| Tristan Freyr Ingólfsson | 07.04.1999 | 2 | (1) | |
| Daníel Laxdal | 22.09.1986 | 23 | | 1 |
| Örvar Logi Örvarsson | 30.07.2003 | 1 | (7) | |
| Þórarinn Ingi Valdimarsson | 23.04.1990 | 23 | (1) | |
| **Midfielders:** | **DOB** | **M** | **(s)** | **G** |
| Hafþór Andri Benediktsson | 2006 | | (1) | |
| Ólafur Karl Finsen | 30.03.1992 | 4 | (13) | 1 |
| Eggert Aron Guðmundsson | 08.02.2004 | 20 | (5) | 4 |

| Founded: | 1960 | | |
|---|---|---|---|
| Stadium: | Samsung völlurinn, Garðabær (1,440) | | |
| Trainer: | Ágúst Þór Gylfason | | 01.08.1971 |

| | DOB | M | (s) | G |
|---|---|---|---|---|
| Jóhann Árni Gunnarsson | 06.04.2001 | 20 | (4) | 6 |
| Óskar Örn Hauksson | 22.08.1984 | 12 | (13) | 3 |
| Henrik Máni Hilmarsson | 16.02.2003 | 2 | (3) | |
| Helgi Fróði Ingason | 2005 | | (3) | |
| Einar Karl Ingvarsson | 08.10.1993 | 12 | (11) | 1 |
| Daníel Finns Matthíasson | 21.06.2000 | 8 | (12) | 1 |
| Gudmundur Baldvin Nökkvason | 27.04.2004 | 15 | (4) | 3 |
| Óli Valur Ómarsson | 09.01.2003 | 12 | | 1 |
| Þorsteinn Már Ragnarsson | 19.04.1990 | | (3) | |
| Róbert Frosti Þorkelsson | 18.08.2005 | 2 | (3) | |
| **Forwards:** | **DOB** | **M** | **(s)** | **G** |
| Emil Atlason | 22.07.1993 | 19 | | 11 |
| Adolf Daði Birgisson | 03.06.2004 | 12 | (4) | 3 |
| Oliver Haurits (DEN) | 12.12.2000 | | (8) | 1 |
| Kjartan Már Kjartansson | 14.07.2006 | 2 | (4) | |
| Ísak Andri Sigurgeirsson | 11.09.2003 | 26 | (1) | 5 |

## Knattspyrnufélagið Valur Reykjavík

**Founded**: 11.05.1911
**Stadium**: Valsvöllur, Reykjavík (2,465)
**Trainer**: Heimir Guðjónsson — 03.04.1969
[18.07.2022] Ólafur Davið Jóhannesson — 30.06.1957

| Goalkeepers: | DOB | M | (s) | G |
|---|---|---|---|---|
| Sveinn Sigurður Jóhannesson | 22.01.1995 | 1 | (1) | |
| Frederik August Albrecht Schram | 19.01.1995 | 16 | | |
| Guy Smit (NED) | 19.01.1996 | 10 | | |
| **Defenders:** | **DOB** | **M** | **(s)** | **G** |
| Heiðar Ægisson | 10.08.1995 | 4 | (9) | |
| Rasmus Christiansen (DEN) | 06.10.1989 | 3 | (8) | |
| Hólmar Örn Eyjólfsson | 06.08.1990 | 25 | | 2 |
| Sebastian Starke Hedlund (SWE) | 05.04.1995 | 19 | (2) | |
| Jesper Juelsgård (DEN) | 26.01.1989 | 24 | | 2 |
| Arnór Ingi Kristinsson | 23.06.2001 | | (3) | |
| Sverrir Þór Kristinsson | 06.11.2003 | | (1) | |
| Birkir Mar Sævarsson | 11.11.1984 | 25 | (1) | 2 |
| Ólafur Flóki Stephensen | 29.09.2004 | 1 | | |

| Midfielders: | DOB | M | (s) | G |
|---|---|---|---|---|
| Sigurður Dagsson | 07.08.2002 | | (1) | |
| Birkir Heimisson | 12.02.2000 | 18 | (5) | 1 |
| Ágúst Hlynsson | 28.03.2000 | 26 | | 2 |
| Orri Hrafn Kjartansson | 05.02.2002 | 10 | (10) | 1 |
| Almarr Ormarsson | 25.02.1988 | | (4) | |
| Lasse Petry Andersen (DEN) | 19.09.1992 | 4 | (7) | |
| Haukur Páll Sigurðsson | 05.08.1987 | 17 | (6) | 2 |
| Arnór Smárason | 07.09.1988 | 8 | (12) | 5 |
| **Forwards:** | **DOB** | **M** | **(s)** | **G** |
| Tryggvi Hrafn Haraldsson | 30.09.1996 | 17 | (4) | 7 |
| Frederik Dahl Ihler | 25.06.2003 | 1 | (2) | |
| Aron Jóhannsson (USA) | 10.11.1990 | 18 | (3) | 7 |
| Sigurður Egil Lárusson | 22.01.1992 | 17 | (6) | 2 |
| Patrick Pedersen (DEN) | 25.11.1991 | 18 | (3) | 8 |
| Guðmundur Andri Tryggvason | 04.11.1999 | 15 | (5) | 4 |

## Íþróttabandalag Vestmannaeyja

**Founded**: 1903
**Stadium**: Hásteinsvöllur, Vestmannaeyjar (2,300)
**Trainer**: Hermann Hreiðarsson — 11.07.1974

| Goalkeepers: | DOB | M | (s) | G |
|---|---|---|---|---|
| Jón Kristinn Elíasson | 20.03.2001 | 5 | | |
| Halldór Geirsson | 21.07.1994 | 5 | | |
| Guðjón Orri Sigurjónsson | 01.12.1992 | 17 | (1) | |
| **Defenders:** | **DOB** | **M** | **(s)** | **G** |
| Elvis Bwomono (ENG) | 29.11.1998 | 19 | | |
| Felix Örn Friðriksson | 16.03.1999 | 25 | (1) | 2 |
| Guðjón Ernir Hrafnkelsson | 19.08.2001 | 26 | | |
| Jón Ingason | 21.09.1995 | 8 | (6) | |
| Sigurður Arnar Magnússon | 30.06.1999 | 26 | | 3 |
| Nökkvi Már Nökkvason | 02.07.2000 | 1 | (3) | |
| Eiður Aron Sigurbjörnsson | 26.02.1990 | 26 | | 4 |
| **Midfielders:** | **DOB** | **M** | **(s)** | **G** |
| Atli Hrafn Andrason | 04.01.1999 | 12 | (9) | 1 |
| Kundai Benyu (ENG) | 12.12.1997 | 4 | (3) | |

| | DOB | M | (s) | G |
|---|---|---|---|---|
| Alex Freyr Hilmarsson | 26.07.1993 | 26 | | 4 |
| Óskar Dagur Jónasson | 22.09.2005 | | (1) | |
| Guðjón Lýðsson | 28.12.1987 | 6 | (4) | |
| Tómas Bent Magnússon | 14.08.2002 | 4 | (6) | 1 |
| Óskar Elías Zoega Óskarsson | 04.11.1995 | | (8) | |
| Telmo Ferreira Castanheira (POR) | 13.04.1992 | 26 | | 3 |
| **Forwards:** | **DOB** | **M** | **(s)** | **G** |
| Sigurður Grétar Benónýsson | 27.08.1996 | | (2) | |
| Andri Rúnar Bjarnason | 12.11.1990 | 17 | (8) | 10 |
| Arnar Breki Gunnarsson | 23.05.2002 | 16 | (7) | 4 |
| Hans Kamta Mpongo (NED) | 25.06.1905 | 1 | (3) | |
| Breki Ómarsson | 10.08.1998 | 2 | (12) | 1 |
| Sito Seoane (ESP) | 16.03.1989 | 5 | (11) | 2 |
| Halldór Jón Sigurdur Þórðarson | 12.07.1996 | 20 | (3) | 7 |

## Knattspyrnufélagið Víkingur Reykjavík

**Founded**: 21.04.1908
**Stadium**: Víkingsvöllur, Reykjavík (2,023)
**Trainer**: Arnar Gunnlaugsson — 06.03.1973

| Goalkeepers: | DOB | M | (s) | G |
|---|---|---|---|---|
| Þórður Ingason | 30.03.1988 | 5 | | |
| Ingvar Jónsson | 18.10.1989 | 22 | | |
| **Defenders:** | **DOB** | **M** | **(s)** | **G** |
| Davið Örn Atlason | 18.08.1994 | 8 | (5) | 1 |
| Oliver Ekroth (SWE) | 18.01.1992 | 24 | | 1 |
| Karl Fridleifur Gunnarsson | 06.07.2001 | 16 | (4) | 1 |
| Kyle McLagan (USA) | 14.10.1995 | 18 | (4) | 1 |
| Halldór Smári Sigurðsson | 04.10.1988 | 9 | (5) | 1 |
| Logi Tómasson | 13.09.2000 | 22 | (4) | 6 |
| Tómas Þórisson | 06.03.2003 | | (1) | |
| **Midfielders:** | **DOB** | **M** | **(s)** | **G** |
| Erlingur Agnarsson | 05.03.1998 | 22 | (3) | 8 |
| Viktor Örlygur Andrason | 05.02.2000 | 23 | (4) | 2 |

| | DOB | M | (s) | G |
|---|---|---|---|---|
| Danijel Dejan Djuric | 05.01.2003 | 11 | (3) | 5 |
| Axel Freyr Harðarson | 22.10.1999 | | (6) | |
| Júlíus Magnússon | 28.06.1998 | 24 | | 4 |
| Pablo Oshan Battuto Punyed (SLV) | 18.04.1990 | 17 | (2) | 1 |
| Gísli Þórðarson | 12.09.2004 | | (5) | |
| **Forwards:** | **DOB** | **M** | **(s)** | **G** |
| Sigurður Steinar Björnsson | 15.01.2004 | | (4) | |
| Arnór Borg Guðjohnsen | 16.09.2000 | 3 | (7) | |
| Helgi Guðjónsson | 04.08.1999 | 17 | (9) | 9 |
| Nikolaj Hansen (DEN) | 15.03.1993 | 12 | (9) | 6 |
| Birnir Snær Ingason | 04.12.1996 | 12 | (15) | 5 |
| Kristall Máni Ingason | 18.01.2002 | 12 | | 4 |
| Ari Sigurpálsson | 17.03.2003 | 20 | (7) | 8 |
| Stígur Diljan Þórðarson | 04.01.2006 | | (1) | |

## SECOND LEVEL
### 1. deild karla 2022

| | | | | | | | | |
|---|---|---|---|---|---|---|---|---|
| 1. | Fylkir Reykjavík (*Promoted*) | 22 | 16 | 3 | 3 | 63 - 23 | 51 |
| 2. | HK Kópavogur (*Promoted*) | 22 | 15 | 1 | 6 | 46 - 30 | 46 |
| 3. | IF Grótta Seltjarnarnes | 22 | 12 | 1 | 9 | 42 - 33 | 37 |
| 4. | Fjölnir Reykjavík | 22 | 11 | 3 | 8 | 51 - 37 | 36 |
| 5. | Kórdrengir Reykjavík | 22 | 9 | 6 | 7 | 36 - 30 | 33 |
| 6. | UMF Grindavík | 22 | 8 | 6 | 8 | 43 - 40 | 30 |
| 7. | Þór Akureyri | 22 | 9 | 3 | 10 | 31 - 35 | 30 |
| 8. | UMF Afturelding Mosfellsbær | 22 | 8 | 5 | 9 | 39 - 39 | 29 |
| 9. | UMF Selfoss | 22 | 8 | 5 | 9 | 36 - 39 | 29 |
| 10. | IF Vestri Ísafjörður | 22 | 7 | 7 | 8 | 36 - 44 | 28 |
| 11. | KV Vesturbæjar (*Relegated*) | 22 | 5 | 3 | 14 | 27 - 52 | 18 |
| 12. | Þróttur Vogar (*Relegated*) | 22 | 1 | 3 | 18 | 8 - 56 | 6 |

## INTERNATIONAL MATCHES
(16.07.2022 – 15.07.2023)

| | | | | |
|---|---|---|---|---|
| 22.09.2022 | Maria Enzersdorf | *Venezuela - Iceland* | *0-1(0-0)* | (F) |
| 27.09.2022 | Tiranë | *Albania - Iceland* | *1-1(1-0)* | (UNL) |
| 06.11.2022 | Abu Dhabi | *Saudi Arabia - Iceland* | *1-0(1-0)* | (F) |
| 11.11.2022 | Hwaseong | *Korea Republic - Iceland* | *1-0(1-0)* | (F) |
| 16.11.2022 | Vilnius | *Lithuania - Iceland* | *0-0; 5-6 pen* | (BC) |
| 19.11.2022 | Rīga | *Latvia - Iceland* | *1-1(0-0,1-1,1-1); 7-8 pen* | (BC) |
| | | | | |
| 08.01.2023 | Albufeira | *Iceland - Estonia* | *1-1(0-1)* | (F) |
| 12.01.2023 | Faro/Loulé | *Sweden - Iceland* | *2-1(0-1)⁻* | (F) |
| 23.03.2023 | Zenica | *Bosnia and Herzegovina - Iceland* | *3-0(2-0)* | (ECQ) |
| 26.03.2023 | Vaduz | *Liechtenstein - Iceland* | *0-7(0-2)* | (ECQ) |
| 17.06.2023 | Reykjavík | *Iceland - Slovakia* | *1-2(1-1)* | (ECQ) |
| 20.06.2023 | Reykjavík | *Iceland - Portugal* | *0-1(0-0)* | (ECQ) |

**22.09.2022　VENEZUELA - ICELAND　　0-1(0-0)　　Friendly International**
Motion invest Arena, Maria Enzersdorf (Austria); Referee: Sebastian Gishamer (Austria); Attendance: 50
**ISL:** Rúnar Alex Rúnarsson, Guðlaugur Victor Pálsson, Aron Einar Malmquist Gunnarsson (Cap), Hörður Björgvin Magnússon, Davíð Kristján Ólafsson, Birkir Bjarnason (58.Aron Elís Þrándarson), Stefán Teitur Þórðarson (58.Þórir Jóhann Helgason), Hákon Amar Haraldsson (58.Ísak Bergmann Jóhannesson), Arnór Sigurðsson (19.Mikael Egill Ellertsson), Jón Dagur Þorsteinsson (86.Mikael Neville Anderson), Alfreð Finnbogason (58.Andri Lucas Guðjohnsen). Trainer: Arnar Þór Viðarsson.
**Goal:** Ísak Bergmann Jóhannesson (87 penalty).

**27.09.2022　ALBANIA - ICELAND　　1-1(1-0)　　3ʳᵈ UEFA Nations League B, Group 2**
Arena Kombëtare, Tiranë; Referee: Ricardo de Burgos Bengoetxea (Spain); Attendance: 8,800
**ISL:** Rúnar Alex Rúnarsson, Guðlaugur Victor Pálsson, Aron Einar Malmquist Gunnarsson (Cap) [*sent off 11*], Hörður Björgvin Magnússon, Davíð Kristján Ólafsson, Birkir Bjarnason (81.Andri Lucas Guðjohnsen), Ísak Bergmann Jóhannesson (69.Hákon Amar Haraldsson), Þórir Jóhann Helgason, Jón Dagur Þorsteinsson (12.Daníel Leó Grétarsson Schmidt), Arnór Sigurðsson (70.Mikael Egill Ellertsson), Alfreð Finnbogason (70.Mikael Neville Anderson). Trainer: Arnar Þór Viðarsson.
**Goal:** Mikael Neville Anderson (90+7).

**06.11.2022　SAUDI ARABIA - ICELAND　　1-0(1-0)　　Friendly International**
"Mohammed bin Zayed" Stadium, Abu Dhabi (United Arab Emirates); Referee: Ahmed Eisa Mohamed Darwish (United Arab Emirates); Attendance: n/a
**ISL:** Hákon Rafn Valdimarsson, Höskuldur Gunnlaugsson, Damir Muminovic (70.Viktor Örn Margeirsson), Róbert Orri Þorkelsson, Rúnar Þór Sigurgeirsson (55.Logi Tómasson), Aron Einar Malmquist Gunnarsson (Cap) (84.Júlíus Magnússon), Dagur Dan Þórhallsson, Ísak Snær Þorvaldsson, Jónatan Ingi Jónsson (56.Jason Daði Svanþórsson), Valdimar Þór Ingimundarson (55.Viktor Karl Einarsson), Óttar Magnús Karlsson (55.Bjarki Steinn Bjarkason). Trainer: Arnar Þór Viðarsson.

**11.11.2022　KOREA REPUBLIC - ICELAND　　1-0(1-0)　　Friendly International**
Hwaseong Stadium, Hwaseong; Referee: Jumpei Iida (Japan); Attendance: 15,274
**ISL:** Frederik August Albrecht Schram, Höskuldur Gunnlaugsson (Cap), Damir Muminovic, Róbert Orri Þorkelsson, Hörður Ingi Gunnarsson 873.Logi Tómasson), Júlíus Magnússon, Viktor Örlygur Andrason (84.Daníel Hafsteinsson), Viktor Karl Einarsson (73.Dagur Dan Þórhallsson), Bjarki Steinn Bjarkason (62.Jónatan Ingi Jónsson), Danijel Dejan Djuric (73.Jason Daði Svanþórsson), Óttar Magnús Karlsson (62.Ísak Snær Þorvaldsson). Trainer: Arnar Þór Viðarsson.

**16.11.2022　LITHUANIA - ICELAND　　0-0; 5-6 on penalties　　29ᵗʰ Baltic Cup, Semi-Finals**
„Steponas Darius ir Stasys Girėnas" Stadionas, Kaunas; Referee: Andris Treimanis (Latvia); Attendance: 5,934
**ISL:** Rúnar Alex Rúnarsson, Valgeir Lunddal Friðriksson, Sverrir Ingi Ingason, Hörður Björgvin Magnússon [*sent off 84*], Davíð Kristján Ólafsson, Birkir Bjarnason (Cap) (82.Aron Elís Þrándarson), Ísak Bergmann Jóhannesson (62.Andri Lucas Guðjohnsen), Þórir Jóhann Helgason (62.Mikael Neville Anderson), Jóhann Berg Guðmundsson (62.Arnór Sigurðsson), Jón Dagur Þorsteinsson (75.Mikael Egill Ellertsson), Hákon Amar Haraldsson (75.Stefán Teitur Þórðarson). Trainer: Arnar Þór Viðarsson.
**Penalties:** Andri Lucas Guðjohnsen, Stefán Teitur Þórðarson, Arnór Sigurðsson, Mikael Neville Anderson, Sverrir Ingi Ingason, Aron Elís Þrándarson.

**19.11.2022　LATVIA - ICELAND　　1-1(0-0,1-1,1-1); 7-8 on penalties　　29ᵗʰ Baltic Cup, Final**
Daugava stadions, Rīga; Referee: Joonas Jaanovits (Estonia); Attendance: 997
**ISL:** Patrik Sigurður Gunnarsson, Alfons Sampsted, Aron Elís Þrándarson (Cap), Daníel Leó Grétarsson Schmidt, Davíð Kristján Ólafsson, Stefán Teitur Þórðarson, Ísak Bergmann Jóhannesson, Hákon Amar Haraldsson (76.Þórir Jóhann Helgason), Arnór Sigurðsson, Mikael Neville Anderson (76.Mikael Egill Ellertsson), Sveinn Aron Guðjohnsen. Trainer: Arnar Þór Viðarsson.
**Goal:** Ísak Bergmann Jóhannesson (62 penalty).
**Penalties:** Ísak Bergmann Jóhannesson, Sveinn Aron Guðjohnsen, Þórir Jóhann Helgason, Arnór Sigurðsson, Stefán Teitur Þórðarson, Aron Elís Þrándarson, Mikael Egill Ellertsson, Daníel Leó Grétarsson Schmidt.

**08.01.2023　ICELAND - ESTONIA　　1-1(0-1)　　Friendly International**
Estadio da Nora, Albufeira (Portugal); Referee: Miguel Bertolo Nogueira (Portugal); Attendance: n/a
**ISL:** Patrik Sigurður Gunnarsson, Guðlaugur Victor Pálsson (Cap) (37.Davíð Kristján Ólafsson), Damir Muminovic, Róbert Orri Þorkelsson, Valgeir Lunddal Friðriksson, Arnór Ingvi Traustason (46.Júlíus Magnússon), Aron Sigurðarson (75.Danijel Dejan Djuric), Dagur Dan Þórhallsson (75.Ísak Snær Þorvaldsson), Kristall Máni Ingason (63.Sævar Atli Magnússon), Nökkvi Þeyr Þórisson (63.Sveinn Aron Guðjohnsen), Andri Lucas Guðjohnsen. Trainer: Arnar Þór Viðarsson.
**Goal:** Andri Lucas Guðjohnsen (90+1 penalty).

**12.01.2023**     **SWEDEN - ICELAND**             **2-1(0-1)**                  Friendly International
Estádio Algarve, Faro/Loulé (Portugal); Referee: Luís Miguel Branco Godinho (Portugal); Attendance: 212
**ISL:** Frederik August Albrecht Schram (61.Hákon Rafn Valdimarsson), Höskuldur Gunnlaugsson (Cap), Damir Muminovic, Róbert Orri Þorkelsson (61.Bjarni Mark Antonsson Duffield), Davíð Kristján Ólafsson, Júlíus Magnússon, Dagur Dan Þórhallsson, Aron Sigurðarson (70.Danijel Dejan Djuric), Sævar Atli Magnússon (70.Kristall Máni Ingason), Aron Bjarnason (70.Viktor Örlygur Andrason), Sveinn Aron Guðjohnsen (81.Ísak Snær Þorvaldsson). Trainer: Arnar Þór Viðarsson.
**Goal:** Sveinn Aron Guðjohnsen (30).

**23.03.2023**     **BOSNIA AND HERZEGOVINA - ICELAND**         **3-0(2-0)**           17th EC. Qualifiers
Stadion Bilino Polje, Zenica; Referee: Donatas Rumšas (Lithuania); Attendance: 9,234
**ISL:** Rúnar Alex Rúnarsson, Guðlaugur Victor Pálsson, Hörður Björgvin Magnússon, Daníel Leó Grétarsson Schmidt, Davíð Kristján Ólafsson, Arnór Ingvi Traustason (82.Stefán Teitur Þórðarson), Jóhann Berg Guðmundsson (Cap), Arnór Sigurðsson (67.Mikael Neville Anderson), Hákon Arnar Haraldsson, Jón Dagur Þorsteinsson (67.Mikael Egill Ellertsson), Alfreð Finnbogason (82.Andri Lucas Guðjohnsen). Trainer: Arnar Þór Viðarsson.

**26.03.2023**     **LIECHTENSTEIN - ICELAND**             **0-7(0-2)**           17th EC. Qualifiers
Rheinpark Stadion, Vaduz; Referee: Jakob Kehlet (Denmark); Attendance: 1,692
**ISL:** Rúnar Alex Rúnarsson, Guðlaugur Victor Pálsson, Aron Einar Malmquist Gunnarsson (Cap) (74.Ísak Bergmann Jóhannesson), Hörður Björgvin Magnússon (65.Alfons Sampsted), Davíð Kristján Ólafsson, Stefán Teitur Þórðarson, Jóhann Berg Guðmundsson (46.Mikael Neville Anderson), Arnór Sigurðsson (65.Mikael Egill Ellertsson), Hákon Arnar Haraldsson, Jón Dagur Þorsteinsson, Alfreð Finnbogason (65.Andri Lucas Guðjohnsen). Trainer: Arnar Þór Viðarsson.
**Goals:** Davíð Kristján Ólafsson (3), Hákon Arnar Haraldsson (38), Aron Einar Malmquist Gunnarsson (48, 68, 73 penalty), Andri Lucas Guðjohnsen (85), Mikael Egill Ellertsson (87).

**17.06.2023**     **ICELAND - SLOVAKIA**                **1-2(1-1)**           17th EC. Qualifiers
Laugardalsvöllur, Reykjavík; Referee: Donald Robertson (Scotland); Attendance: 7,555
**ISL:** Rúnar Alex Rúnarsson, Alfons Sampsted (81.Sævar Atli Magnússon), Guðlaugur Victor Pálsson, Sverrir Ingi Ingason, Hörður Björgvin Magnússon, Valgeir Lunddal Friðriksson, Jóhann Berg Guðmundsson (Cap), Willum Þór Willumsson, Albert Guðmundsson, Jón Dagur Þorsteinsson (63.Mikael Egill Ellertsson), Alfreð Finnbogason (63.Hákon Arnar Haraldsson). Trainer: Åge Fridtjof Hareide (Norway).
**Goal:** Alfreð Finnbogason (41 penalty).

**20.06.2023**     **ICELAND - PORTUGAL**               **0-1(0-0)**           17th EC. Qualifiers
Laugardalsvöllur, Reykjavík; Referee: Daniel Siebert (Germany); Attendance: 9,517
**ISL:** Rúnar Alex Rúnarsson, Valgeir Lunddal Friðriksson (79.Alfons Sampsted), Guðlaugur Victor Pálsson, Sverrir Ingi Ingason, Hörður Björgvin Magnússon, Arnór Ingvi Traustason (75.Ísak Bergmann Jóhannesson), Jóhann Berg Guðmundsson (Cap), Willum Þór Willumsson [*sent off 81*], Albert Guðmundsson, Jón Dagur Þorsteinsson (79.Hákon Arnar Haraldsson), Alfreð Finnbogason (75.Sævar Atli Magnússon). Trainer: Åge Fridtjof Hareide (Norway).

| NATIONAL TEAM PLAYERS (16.07.2022 – 15.07.2023) | | | | |
|---|---|---|---|---|
| **Name** | **DOB** | **Caps** | **Goals** | ***Club*** |
| **Goalkeepers** | | | | |
| Patrik Sigurður GUNNARSSON | 15.11.2000 | 3 | 0 | 2022/2023: *Viking FK Stavanger (NOR)* |
| Rúnar Alex RÚNARSSON | 18.02.1995 | 24 | 0 | 2022/2023: *Alanyaspor Kulübü (TUR)* |
| Frederik August Albrecht SCHRAM | 19.01.1995 | 7 | 0 | 2022/2023: *Valur Reykjavík* |
| Hákon Rafn VALDIMARSSON | 13.10.2001 | 4 | 0 | 2022/2023: *IF Elfsborg Borås (SWE)* |
| **Defenders** | | | | |
| Valgeir Lunddal FRIÐRIKSSON | 24.09.2001 | 7 | 0 | 2022/2023: *BK Häcken Göteborg (SWE)* |
| Daníel Leó GRÉTARSSON Schmidt | 02.10.1995 | 13 | 0 | 2022/2023: *WKS Śląsk Wrocław (POL)* |
| Hörður Ingi GUNNARSSON | 14.08.1998 | 2 | 0 | 2022: *Sogndal Fotball (NOR)* |
| Höskuldur GUNNLAUGSSON | 26.09.1994 | 8 | 0 | 2022/2023: *Breiðablik Kópavogur* |
| Sverrir Ingi INGASON | 05.08.1993 | 42 | 3 | 2022/2023: *PAOK Thessaloníki (GRE)* |
| Hörður Björgvin MAGNÚSSON | 11.02.1993 | 48 | 2 | 2022/2023: *PAE Panathinaïkos Athína (GRE)* |
| Viktor Örn MARGEIRSSON | 22.07.1994 | 1 | 0 | 2022: *Breiðablik Kópavogur* |
| Damir MUMINOVIC | 13.05.1990 | 6 | 0 | 2022/2023: *Breiðablik Kópavogur* |
| Davíð Kristján ÓLAFSSON | 15.05.1995 | 15 | 1 | 2022/2023: *Kalmar FF (SWE)* |
| Alfons SAMPSTED | 06.04.1998 | 17 | 0 | 2022: *FK Bodø/Glimt (NOR)* <br> 01.01.2023-> *FC Twente Enschede (NED)* |
| Rúnar Þór SIGURGEIRSSON | 28.12.1999 | 2 | 0 | 2022: *Keflavík* |
| Logi TÓMASSON | 13.09.2000 | 2 | 0 | 2022: *Víkingur Reykjavík* |
| Róbert Orri ÞORKELSSON | 03.04.2002 | 4 | 0 | 2022/2023: *CF Montréal (CAN)* |

## Midfielders

| | | | | | |
|---|---|---|---|---|---|
| Mikael Neville ANDERSON | 01.07.1998 | 20 | 2 | 2022/2023: | *Aarhus GF (DEN)* |
| Viktor Örlygur ANDRASON | 05.02.2000 | 4 | 0 | 2022/2023: | *Víkingur Reykjavík* |
| Bjarni Mark ANTONSSON Duffield | 27.12.1995 | 3 | 0 | 2023: | *IK Start Kristiansand (NOR)* |
| Bjarki Steinn BJARKASON | 11.05.2000 | 2 | 0 | 2022: | *Venezia FC (ITA)* |
| Aron BJARNASON | 14.10.1995 | 1 | 0 | 2023: | *IK Sirius Uppsala (SWE)* |
| Birkir BJARNASON | 27.05.1988 | 113 | 15 | 2022: | *Adana Demirspor Kulübü (TUR)* |
| Viktor Karl EINARSSON | 30.01.1997 | 4 | 0 | 2022: | *Breiðablik Kópavogur* |
| Mikael Egill ELLERTSSON | 11.03.2002 | 13 | 1 | 2022: 26.01.2023-> | *Spezia Calcio La Spezia (ITA)* *Venezia FC (ITA)* |
| Aron Einar Malmquist GUNNARSSON | 22.04.1989 | 101 | 5 | 2022/2023: | *Al Arabi SC Doha (QAT)* |
| Jóhann Berg GUÐMUNDSSON | 27.10.1990 | 86 | 7 | 2022/2023: | *Burnley FC (ENG)* |
| Daníel HAFSTEINSSON | 12.11.1999 | 1 | 0 | 2022: | *KA Akureyri* |
| Hákon Amar HARALDSSON | 10.04.2003 | 11 | 1 | 2022/2023: | *FC København (DEN)* |
| Þórir Jóhann HELGASON | 28.09.2000 | 16 | 2 | 2022: | *US Lecce (ITA)* |
| Kristall Máni INGASON | 18.01.2002 | 4 | 0 | 2023: | *Rosenborg BK Trondheim (NOR)* |
| Valdimar Þór INGIMUNDARSON | 28.04.1999 | 2 | 0 | 2022: | *Strømsgodset IF Drammen (NOR)* |
| Ísak Bergmann JÓHANNESSON | 23.03.2003 | 19 | 3 | 2022/2023: | *FC København (DEN)* |
| Jónatan Ingi JÓNSSON | 15.03.1999 | 2 | 0 | 2022: | *Sogndal Fotball (NOR)* |
| Júlíus MAGNÚSSON | 28.06.1998 | 5 | 0 | 2022/2023: | *Víkingur Reykjavík* |
| Guðlaugur Victor PÁLSSON | 30.04.1991 | 36 | 1 | 2022/2023: | *Washington DC United (USA)* |
| Aron SIGURÐARSON | 08.10.1993 | 8 | 2 | 2023: | *AC Horsens (DEN)* |
| Arnór SIGURÐSSON | 15.05.1999 | 27 | 2 | 2022/2023: | *IFK Norrköping (SWE)* |
| Arnór Ingvi TRAUSTASON | 30.04.1993 | 47 | 5 | 2023: | *IFK Norrköping (SWE)* |
| Willum Þór WILLUMSSON | 23.10.1998 | 3 | 0 | 2023: | *Go Ahead Eagles Deventer (NED)* |
| Jón Dagur ÞORSTEINSSON | 26.11.1998 | 28 | 4 | 2022/2023: | *Oud-Heverle Leuven (BEL)* |
| Aron Elís ÞRÁNDARSON | 10.11.1994 | 17 | 1 | 2022: | *Odense BK (DEN)* |
| Dagur Dan ÞÓRHALLSSON | 02.05.2000 | 4 | 0 | 2022/2023: | *Breiðablik Kópavogur* |
| Nökkvi Þeýr ÞÓRISSON | 13.08.1999 | 1 | 0 | 2023: | *K Beerschot VA (BEL)* |
| Stefán Teitur ÞÓRÐARSON | 16.10.1998 | 17 | 1 | 2022/2023: | *Silkeborg IF (DEN)* |

## Forwards

| | | | | | |
|---|---|---|---|---|---|
| Danijel Dejan DJURIC | 05.01.2003 | 3 | 0 | 2022/2023: | *Víkingur Reykjavík* |
| Alfreð FINNBOGASON | 01.02.1989 | 67 | 16 | 2022/2023: | *Lyngby BK (DEN)* |
| Andri Lucas GUÐJOHNSEN | 29.01.2002 | 15 | 4 | 2022/2023: | *IFK Norrköping (SWE)* |
| Sveinn Aron GUÐJOHNSEN | 12.05.1998 | 19 | 2 | 2022/2023: | *IF Elfsborg Borås (SWE)* |
| Albert GUÐMUNDSSON | 15.06.1997 | 35 | 6 | 2023: | *Genoa C&FC (ITA)* |
| Óttar Magnús KARLSSON | 21.02.1997 | 11 | 0 | 2022: | *Oakland Roots SC (USA)* |
| Sævar Atli MAGNÚSSON | 16.06.2000 | 4 | 0 | 2023: | *Lyngby BK (DEN)* |
| Jason Daði SVANÞÓRSSON | 31.12.1999 | 3 | 0 | 2022: | *Breiðablik Kópavogur* |
| Ísak Snær ÞORVALDSSON | 01.05.2001 | 4 | 0 | 2022: 08.01.2023-> | *Breiðablik Kópavogur* *Rosenborg BK Trondheim (NOR)* |

## Trainer

| | | |
|---|---|---|
| Arnar Þór VIÐARSSON [22.12.2020 – 30.03.2023] | 15.03.1978 | 31 M; 6 W; 13 D; 12 L; 37-49 |
| Åge Fridtjof HAREIDE (Norway) [from 14.04.2023] | 23.09.1953 | 2 M; 0 W; 0 D; 2 L; 1-3 |

# ISRAEL

## The Country:
יִשְׂרָאֵל מְדִינַת (State of Israel)
Capital: Jerusalem
Surface: 20,770–22,072 km²
Inhabitants: 9,774,080 [2023]
Time: UTC+2

## The FA:
Israel Football Association
Ramat Gan Stadium, 299 Aba Hilell Street, P.O. Box 3591, 52134 Ramat Gan, Tel Aviv
Tel: +972 3 617 1500
Foundation date: 18.07.1928
Member of FIFA since: 1929
Member of UEFA since: 1994
Website: www.football.org.il

## NATIONAL TEAM RECORDS

| RECORDS | | |
|---|---|---|
| **First international match:** | 16.03.1934, Cairo: Egypt – Palestina 7-1 | |
| **Most international caps:** | Yosef Shay Benayoun | - 102 caps (1998-2017) |
| **Most international goals:** | Eran Zahavi | - 33 goals / 70 caps (2010-2021) |

### UEFA EUROPEAN CHAMPIONSHIP

| | |
|---|---|
| 1960 | - |
| 1964 | - |
| 1968 | - |
| 1972 | - |
| 1976 | - |
| 1980 | - |
| 1984 | - |
| 1988 | - |
| 1992 | - |
| 1996 | Qualifiers |
| 2000 | Qualifiers |
| 2004 | Qualifiers |
| 2008 | Qualifiers |
| 2012 | Qualifiers |
| 2016 | Qualifiers |
| 2020 | Qualifiers |

### FIFA WORLD CUP

| | |
|---|---|
| 1930 | Did not enter |
| 1934 | Qualifiers |
| 1938 | Qualifiers |
| 1950 | Qualifiers |
| 1954 | Qualifiers |
| 1958 | Qualifiers |
| 1962 | Qualifiers |
| 1966 | Qualifiers |
| 1970 | Final Tournament (Group Stage) |
| 1974 | Qualifiers |
| 1978 | Qualifiers |
| 1982 | Qualifiers |
| 1986 | Qualifiers |
| 1990 | Qualifiers |
| 1994 | Qualifiers |
| 1998 | Qualifiers |
| 2002 | Qualifiers |
| 2006 | Qualifiers |
| 2010 | Qualifiers |
| 2014 | Qualifiers |
| 2018 | Qualifiers |
| 2022 | Qualifiers |

### OLYMPIC TOURNAMENTS

| | |
|---|---|
| 1908 | - |
| 1912 | - |
| 1920 | - |
| 1924 | - |
| 1928 | - |
| 1936 | - |
| 1948 | - |
| 1952 | Qualifiers |
| 1956 | Qualifiers |
| 1960 | Qualifiers |
| 1964 | Qualifiers |
| 1968 | FT/Quarter-Finals |
| 1972 | Qualifiers |
| 1976 | FT/Quarter-Finals |
| 1980 | *Withdrew* |
| 1984 | Qualifiers |
| 1988 | Qualifiers |
| 1992 | Qualifiers |
| 1996 | Qualifiers |
| 2000 | Qualifiers |
| 2004 | Qualifiers |
| 2008 | Qualifiers |
| 2012 | Qualifiers |
| 2016 | Qualifiers |
| 2020 | Qualifiers |

## UEFA NATIONS LEAGUE

| 2018/2019 | League C (Group Stage -> promoted to League B) |
|---|---|
| 2020/2021 | League B (Group Stage) |
| 2022/2023 | League B (Group Stage -> promoted to League A) |

## ISRAELI CLUB HONOURS IN EUROPEAN CLUB COMPETITIONS:

| European Champion Clubs' Cup (1956-1992) / UEFA Champions League (1993-2023) |
|---|
| None |
| **Fairs Cup (1858-1971) / UEFA Cup (1972-2009) / UEFA Europa League (2010-2023)** |
| None |
| **UEFA Europa Conference League (2021-2023)** |
| None |
| **UEFA Super Cup (1972-2022)** |
| None |
| *European Cup Winners' Cup 1961-1999\** |
| None |

*\*defunct competition*

# NATIONAL COMPETITIONS
## TABLE OF HONOURS

| | CHAMPIONS | CUP WINNERS | BEST GOALSCORERS | |
|---|---|---|---|---|
| 1927/1928 | – | Hapoel Tel Aviv FC<br>Maccabi Hasmonean Jerusalem FC<br>(*shared*) | – | |
| 1928/1929 | – | Maccabi Tel Aviv FC | – | |
| 1929/1930 | – | Maccabi Tel Aviv FC | – | |
| 1930/1931 | – | *No competition* | – | |
| 1931/1932 | United Kingdom British Police | United Kingdom British Police | – | |
| 1932/1933 | *No Championship* | Maccabi Tel Aviv FC | – | |
| 1933/1934 | Hapoel Tel Aviv FC | Hapoel Tel Aviv FC | – | |
| 1934/1935 | Hapoel Tel Aviv FC | Maccabi Petah Tikva FC | – | |
| 1935/1936 | Maccabi Tel Aviv FC | *No competition* | – | |
| 1936/1937 | Maccabi Tel Aviv FC | Hapoel Tel Aviv FC | – | |
| 1937/1938 | Hapoel Tel Aviv FC | Hapoel Tel Aviv FC | – | |
| 1938/1939 | *No Championship* | Hapoel Tel Aviv FC | – | |
| 1939/1940 | Hapoel Tel Aviv FC | Beitar Tel Aviv FC | – | |
| 1940/1941 | *No Championship* | Maccabi Tel Aviv FC | – | |
| 1941/1942 | Maccabi Tel Aviv FC | Beitar Tel Aviv FC | – | |
| 1942/1943 | *Championship not finished* | *No competition* | – | |
| 1943/1944 | Hapoel Tel Aviv FC | *No competition* | – | |
| 1944/1945 | Hapoel Tel Aviv FC<br>Beitar Tel Aviv FC (*shared*) | *No competition* | – | |
| 1945/1946 | *No Championship* | Maccabi Tel Aviv FC | – | |
| 1946/1947 | Maccabi Tel Aviv FC | Maccabi Tel Aviv FC | – | |
| 1947/1948 | *Championship not finished* | *No competition* | – | |
| 1948 | *Championship not finished* | *No competition* | – | |
| 1949/1950 | Maccabi Tel Aviv FC | *No competition* | Yosef Merimovich (Maccabi Tel Aviv FC) | 25 |
| 1950/1951 | *No Championship* | *No competition* | – | – |
| 1951/1952 | Maccabi Tel Aviv FC | Maccabi Petah Tikva FC | Yehoshua Glazer (Maccabi Tel Aviv FC) | 24 |
| 1952/1953 | *No Championship* | *No competition* | – | – |
| 1953/1954 | Maccabi Tel Aviv FC | Maccabi Tel Aviv FC | Eliezer Spiegel (Maccabi Petah Tikva FC) | 16 |
| 1954/1955 | Hapoel Petah Tikva FC | Maccabi Tel Aviv FC | Nisim Elmaliah (Beitar Tel Aviv FC) | 30 |
| 1955/1956 | Maccabi Tel Aviv FC | *No competition* | Avraham Levi (Beitar Tel Aviv FC)<br>Michael Michaelov (Beitar Tel Aviv FC) | 16 |
| 1956/1957 | Hapoel Tel Aviv FC | Hapoel Petah Tikva FC | Avraham Ginzburg (Hapoel Haifa FC) | 16 |
| 1957/1958 | Maccabi Tel Aviv FC | Maccabi Tel Aviv FC | Rafi Levi (Maccabi Tel Aviv FC) | 14 |
| 1958/1959 | Hapoel Petah Tikva FC | Maccabi Tel Aviv FC | Aharon Amar (Maccabi Haifa FC) | 17 |
| 1959/1960 | Hapoel Petah Tikva FC | *No competition* | Rafi Levi (Maccabi Tel Aviv FC) | 19 |
| 1960/1961 | Hapoel Petah Tikva FC | Hapoel Tel Aviv FC | Shlomo Levi (Hapoel Haifa FC)<br>Zharia Ratzabi (Hapoel Petah Tikva FC) | 15 |
| 1961/1962 | Hapoel Petah Tikva FC | Maccabi Haifa FC | Shlomo Levi (Maccabi Haifa FC)<br>Itzhak Nizri (Hapoel Tiberias) | 16 |
| 1962/1963 | Hapoel Petah Tikva FC | Hapoel Haifa FC | Zharia Ratzabi (Hapoel Petah Tikva FC) | 12 |
| 1963/1964 | Hapoel Haifa FC | Maccabi Tel Aviv FC | Israel Ashkenazi (Maccabi Jaffa FC) | 21 |
| 1964/1965 | Hakoah Ramat Gan FC | Maccabi Tel Aviv FC | Israel Ashkenazi (Maccabi Jaffa FC)<br>Itzhak Mizrahi (Bnei Yehuda Tel Aviv FC) | 18 |
| 1965/1966 | Hapoel Tel Aviv FC | Hapoel Haifa FC | Moshe Romano (Shimshon Tel Aviv FC)<br>Mordechai Spiegler (Maccabi Netanya FC) | 17 |
| 1966/1967 | - | Maccabi Tel Aviv FC | | |
| 1967/1968 | Maccabi Tel Aviv FC [1966-1968] | Bnei Yehuda Tel Aviv FC | Mordechai Spiegler (Maccabi Netanya FC) | 38 |
| 1968/1969 | Hapoel Tel Aviv FC | Hakoah Ramat Gan FC | Mordechai Spiegler (Maccabi Netanya FC) | 25 |
| 1969/1970 | Maccabi Tel Aviv FC | Maccabi Tel Aviv FC | Moshe Romano (Shimshon Tel Aviv FC) | 15 |
| 1970/1971 | Maccabi Netanya FC | Hakoah Ramat Gan FC | Eli Ben Rimoz (Hapoel Jerusalem FC) | 20 |
| 1971/1972 | Maccabi Tel Aviv FC | Hapoel Tel Aviv FC | Yehouda Shaharabani (Hakoah Ramat Gan FC) | 21 |
| 1972/1973 | Hakoah Ramat Gan FC | Hapoel Jerusalem FC | Moshe Romano (Beitar Tel Aviv FC) | 18 |
| 1973/1974 | Maccabi Netanya FC | Hapoel Haifa FC | Benny Alon (Hapoel Haifa FC) | 15 |
| 1974/1975 | Hapoel Be'er Sheva FC | Hapoel Kfar Saba FC | Moshe Romano (Shimshon Tel Aviv FC) | 17 |
| 1975/1976 | Hapoel Be'er Sheva FC | Beitar Jerusalem FC | Oded Machnes (Maccabi Netanya FC) | 21 |
| 1976/1977 | Maccabi Tel Aviv FC | Maccabi Tel Aviv FC | Vicky Peretz (Maccabi Tel Aviv FC) | 17 |
| 1977/1978 | Maccabi Netanya FC | Maccabi Netanya FC | David Lavi (Maccabi Netanya FC) | 16 |
| 1978/1979 | Maccabi Tel Aviv FC | Beitar Jerusalem FC | Oded Machnes (Maccabi Netanya FC)<br>Eli Miali (Beitar Jerusalem FC) | 18 |
| 1979/1980 | Maccabi Netanya FC | Hapoel Kfar Saba FC | David Lavi (Maccabi Netanya FC) | 18 |
| 1980/1981 | Hapoel Tel Aviv FC | Bnei Yehuda Tel Aviv FC | Hertzel Fitusi (Hapoel Petah Tikva FC) | 22 |
| 1981/1982 | Hapoel Kfar Saba FC | Hapoel Yehud | Oded Machnes (Maccabi Netanya FC) | 26 |
| 1982/1983 | Maccabi Netanya FC | Hapoel Tel Aviv FC | Oded Machnes (Maccabi Netanya FC) | 22 |
| 1983/1984 | Maccabi Haifa FC | Hapoel Lod | David Lavi (Maccabi Netanya FC) | 16 |
| 1984/1985 | Maccabi Haifa FC | Beitar Jerusalem FC | David Lavi (Maccabi Netanya FC) | 18 |
| 1985/1986 | Hapoel Tel Aviv FC | Beitar Jerusalem FC | Uri Malmilian (Beitar Jerusalem FC)<br>Doron Rabinzon (Maccabi Petah Tikva FC) | 14 |
| 1986/1987 | Beitar Jerusalem FC | Maccabi Tel Aviv FC | Eli Yani (Hapoel Kfar Saba FC) | 16 |
| 1987/1988 | Hapoel Tel Aviv FC | Maccabi Tel Aviv FC | Zahi Armeli (Maccabi Haifa FC) | 25 |

| 1988/1989 | Maccabi Haifa FC | Beitar Jerusalem FC | Benny Tabak (Maccabi Tel Aviv FC) | 18 |
|---|---|---|---|---|
| 1989/1990 | Bnei Yehuda Tel Aviv FC | Hapoel Kfar Saba FC | Uri Malmilian (Maccabi Tel Aviv FC) | 16 |
| 1990/1991 | Maccabi Haifa FC | Maccabi Haifa FC | Nir Levine (Hapoel Petah Tikva FC) | 20 |
| 1991/1992 | Maccabi Tel Aviv FC | Hapoel Petah Tikva FC | Alon Mizrahi (Bnei Yehuda Tel Aviv FC) | 20 |
| 1992/1993 | Beitar Jerusalem FC | Maccabi Haifa FC | Alon Mizrahi (Bnei Yehuda Tel Aviv FC) | 26 |
| 1993/1994 | Maccabi Haifa FC | Maccabi Tel Aviv FC | Alon Mizrahi (Maccabi Haifa FC) | 28 |
| 1994/1995 | Maccabi Tel Aviv FC | Maccabi Haifa FC | Haim Revivo (Maccabi Haifa FC) <br> Amir Turgeman (Maccabi Ironi Ashdod FC FC) | 17 |
| 1995/1996 | Maccabi Tel Aviv FC | Maccabi Tel Aviv FC | Haim Revivo (Maccabi Haifa FC) | 26 |
| 1996/1997 | Beitar Jerusalem FC | Hapoel Be'er Sheva FC | Motti Kakoun (Hapoel Petah Tikva FC) | 21 |
| 1997/1998 | Beitar Jerusalem FC | Maccabi Haifa FC | Alon Mizrahi (Maccabi Haifa FC) | 18 |
| 1998/1999 | Hapoel Haifa FC | Hapoel Tel Aviv FC | Andrzej Kubica (Maccabi Tel Aviv FC) | 21 |
| 1999/2000 | Hapoel Tel Aviv FC | Hapoel Tel Aviv FC | Assi Tubi (Maccabi Petah Tikva FC) | 27 |
| 2000/2001 | Maccabi Haifa FC | Maccabi Tel Aviv FC | Avi Nimni (Maccabi Tel Aviv FC) | 25 |
| 2001/2002 | Maccabi Haifa FC | Maccabi Tel Aviv FC | Kobi Refua (Maccabi Petah Tikva FC) | 18 |
| 2002/2003 | Maccabi Tel Aviv FC | Hapoel Haifa FC | Yaniv Abargil (Hapoel Kfar Saba FC) <br> Shay Holtzman <br> (Ironi Rishon LeZion FC / FC Ashdod) | 18 |
| 2003/2004 | Maccabi Haifa FC | Bnei Sakhnin FC | Ofir Haim (Hapoel Be'er Sheva FC) <br> Shay Holtzman (FC Ashdod) | 16 |
| 2004/2005 | Maccabi Haifa FC | Maccabi Tel Aviv FC | Roberto Colautti (Maccabi Haifa FC) | 19 |
| 2005/2006 | Maccabi Haifa FC | Hapoel Tel Aviv FC | Shay Holtzman (FC Ashdod) | 18 |
| 2006/2007 | Beitar Jerusalem FC | Hapoel Tel Aviv FC | Yaniv Azran (FC Ashdod) | 15 |
| 2007/2008 | Beitar Jerusalem FC | Beitar Jerusalem FC | Samuel Yeboah (Hapoel Kfar Saba FC) | 15 |
| 2008/2009 | Maccabi Haifa FC | Beitar Jerusalem FC | Barak Yitzhaki (Beitar Jerusalem FC) <br> Shimon Abuhatzira (Hapoel Petah Tikva FC) <br> Eliran Atar (Bnei Yehuda Tel Aviv FC) | 14 |
| 2009/2010 | Hapoel Tel Aviv FC | Hapoel Tel Aviv FC | Shlomi Arbeitman (Maccabi Haifa FC) | 28 |
| 2010/2011 | Maccabi Haifa FC | Hapoel Tel Aviv FC | Toto Tamuz (Hapoel Tel Aviv FC) | 21 |
| 2011/2012 | Ironi Kiryat | Hapoel Tel Aviv FC | Achmad Saba'a (Maccabi Netanya FC) | 20 |
| 2012/2013 | Maccabi Tel Aviv FC | Hapoel Haifa FC | Eliran Atar (Maccabi Tel Aviv FC) | 22 |
| 2013/2014 | Maccabi Tel Aviv FC | Hapoel Ironi Kiryat Shmona FC | Eran Zahavi (Maccabi Tel Aviv FC) | 29 |
| 2014/2015 | Maccabi Tel Aviv FC | Maccabi Tel Aviv FC | Eran Zahavi (Maccabi Tel Aviv FC) | 27 |
| 2015/2016 | Hapoel Be'er Sheva FC | Maccabi Haifa FC | Eran Zahavi (Maccabi Tel Aviv FC) | 35 |
| 2016/2017 | Hapoel Be'er Sheva FC | Bnei Yehuda Tel Aviv FC | Viðar Örn Kjartansson (ISL, Maccabi Tel Aviv FC) | 19 |
| 2017/2018 | Hapoel Be'er Sheva FC | Hapoel Haifa FC | Dia Saba (Maccabi Netanya FC) | 24 |
| 2018/2019 | Maccabi Tel Aviv FC | Bnei Yehuda Tel Aviv FC | Ben Sahar (Hapoel Be'er Sheva FC) | 15 |
| 2019/2020 | Maccabi Tel Aviv FC | Hapoel Be'er Sheva FC | Nikita Rukavytsya (AUS, Maccabi Haifa FC) | 22 |
| 2020/2021 | Maccabi Haifa FC | Maccabi Tel Aviv FC | Nikita Rukavytsya (AUS, Maccabi Haifa FC) | 19 |
| 2021/2022 | Maccabi Haifa FC | Hapoel Be'er Sheva FC | Omer Atzili (Maccabi Haifa FC) | 20 |
| 2022/2023 | Maccabi Haifa FC | Beitar Jerusalem FC | Omer Atzili (Maccabi Haifa FC) | 21 |

## NATIONAL CHAMPIONSHIP
### Israeli Premier League (Ligat Winner) 2022/2023
(20.08.2022 – 20.05.2023)

### Regular Season - Results

**Round 1 [20-22.08.2022]**
Hapoel Haifa - Hapoel Tel Aviv 2-0(1-0)
Hapoel Jerusalem - Hapoel Hadera 1-1(1-0)
Maccabi Netanya - Beitar Jerusalem 4-1(3-1)
Maccabi Tel Aviv - Bnei Reineh 5-0(4-0)
Sektzia N. Tziona - Hapoel Ironi K.S. 0-2(0-1)
Bnei Sachnin – Macc. Haifa 0-1(0-0) [30.08.22]
Hapoel Be'er Sheva-Ashdod 1-2(1-1)[31.08.22]

**Round 2 [27-29.08.2022]**
Hapoel Ironi K.S. - Hapoel Jerusalem 1-1(1-0)
Hapoel Tel Aviv - Bnei Sachnin 0-2(0-2)
Maccabi Haifa - Maccabi Netanya 4-1(1-1)
FC Ashdod - Sektzia Ness Tziona 1-0(1-0)
Maccabi Bnei Reineh - Hapoel Haifa 1-1(0-0)
Beitar Jerusalem-Hapoel Be'er Sheva 0-5(0-1)
Hapoel Hadera - Maccabi Tel Aviv 0-6(0-4)

**Round 3 [03-05.09.2022]**
Maccabi Tel Aviv - Hapoel Ironi K.S. 3-1(1-0)
Hapoel Jerusalem - FC Ashdod 3-0(1-0)
Hapoel Haifa - Bnei Sachnin 1-2(0-0)
Hapoel Be'er Sheva - Maccabi Haifa 1-2(1-1)
Maccabi Bnei Reineh-Hapoel Hadera 1-2(1-1)
Sektzia Ness Tziona-Beitar Jerusalem 0-3(0-0)
Maccabi Netanya - Hapoel Tel Aviv 0-2(0-1)

**Round 4 [10-12.09.2022]**
Maccabi Haifa - Sektzia Ness Tziona 3-1(1-1)
Bnei Sachnin - Maccabi Netanya 0-0
Hapoel Hadera - Hapoel Haifa 1-1(0-0)
FC Ashdod - Maccabi Tel Aviv 0-0
Ironi K.S. - Maccabi Bnei Reineh 1-1(1-1)
Hapoel Tel Aviv-Hapoel Be'er Sheva 2-3(1-0)
Beitar Jerusalem - Hapoel Jerusalem 0-1(0-1)

**Round 5 [17-18.09.2022]**
Sektzia Ness Tziona-Hapoel Tel Aviv 4-3(2-3)
Maccabi Bnei Reineh - FC Ashdod 1-1(0-0)
Hapoel Haifa - Maccabi Netanya 0-0
Maccabi Tel Aviv - Beitar Jerusalem 4-0(2-0)
Hapoel Hadera - Hapoel Ironi K.S. 1-1(0-0)
Hapoel Be'er Sheva - Bnei Sachnin 1-0(0-0)
Hapoel Jerusalem - Maccabi Haifa 3-0(2-0)

**Round 6 [01-03.10.2022]**
Hapoel Ironi K.S. - Hapoel Haifa 1-1(0-1)
FC Ashdod - Hapoel Hadera 1-1(0-0)
Maccabi Netanya-Hapoel Be'er Sheva 1-2(0-0)
Maccabi Haifa - Maccabi Tel Aviv 2-0(0-0)
Bnei Sachnin - Sektzia Ness Tziona 2-0(1-0)
Hapoel Tel Aviv - Hapoel Jerusalem 1-3(1-2)
Beitar Jerus. - Maccabi Bnei Reineh 2-3(1-1)

**Round 7 [08-10.10.2022]**
Sektzia N. Tziona - Maccabi Netanya 1-1(1-1)
Hapoel Jerusalem - Bnei Sachnin 1-2(0-1)
Hapoel Hadera - Beitar Jerusalem 2-1(2-0)
Maccabi Bnei Reineh-Maccabi Haifa 1-0(1-0)
Hapoel Ironi K.S. - FC Ashdod 1-1(0-1)
Hapoel Be'er Sheva - Hapoel Haifa 2-2(1-1)
Maccabi Tel Aviv - Hapoel Tel Aviv 3-0(0-0)

**Round 8 [15-17.10.2022]**
Hapoel T. A. - Maccabi Bnei Reineh 2-0(0-0)
FC Ashdod - Hapoel Haifa 4-0(2-0)
Beitar Jerusalem - Hapoel Ironi K.S. 2-0(0-0)
Bnei Sachnin - Maccabi Tel Aviv 0-1(0-0)
Maccabi Netanya - Hapoel Jerusalem 0-2(0-0)
Hapoel Be'er Sheva - Sektzia N. Tzi. 1-1(0-1)
Maccabi Haifa - Hapoel Hadera 1-0(0-0)

**Round 9 [22-24.10.2022]**
Hapoel Jerusal. - Hapoel Be'er Sheva 1-4(1-3)
Hapoel Haifa - Sektzia Ness Tziona 0-1(0-0)
FC Ashdod - Beitar Jerusalem 0-2(0-1)
Hapoel Ironi K.S. - Maccabi Haifa 2-3(1-1)
Maccabi Bnei Reineh - Bnei Sachnin 2-0(1-0)
Hapoel Hadera - Hapoel Tel Aviv 0-0
Maccabi Tel Aviv - Maccabi Netanya 3-0(2-0)

| Round 10 [29-31.10.2022] |
|---|
| Maccabi Haifa - FC Ashdod 3-1(2-1) |
| Bnei Sachnin - Hapoel Hadera 1-4(1-3) |
| Sektzia N. Tziona - Hapoel Jerusalem 0-2(0-1) |
| Maccabi Netanya - Bnei Reineh 2-1(1-1) |
| Beitar Jerusalem - Hapoel Haifa 0-0 |
| Hapoel Tel Aviv - Hapoel Ironi K.S. 2-1(1-1) |
| Hapoel Be'er Sh. - Maccabi Tel Aviv 2-0(1-0) |

| Round 11 [05-06.11.2022] |
|---|
| Maccabi Tel Aviv - Sektzia N.Tziona 1-1(1-1) |
| Hapoel Hadera - Hapoel Jerusalem 3-1(3-1) |
| Hapoel Haifa - Hapoel Jerusalem 1-0(0-0) |
| Hapoel Ironi K.S. - Bnei Sachnin 1-1(0-1) |
| FC Ashdod - Hapoel Tel Aviv 1-0(0-0) |
| Bnei Reineh - Hapoel Be'er Sheva 0-3(0-1) |
| Beitar Jerusalem - Maccabi Haifa 1-4(1-1) |

| Round 12 [08-09.11.2022] |
|---|
| Bnei Sachnin - FC Ashdod 1-1(1-1) |
| Maccabi Netanya - Hapoel Ironi K.S. 1-0(1-0) |
| Hapoel Jerusalem - Maccabi Tel Aviv 0-3(0-1) |
| Sektzia Ness Tziona - Bnei Reineh 3-3(2-1) |
| Hapoel Be'er Sheva - Hapoel Hadera 3-0(1-0) |
| Hapoel Tel Aviv - Beitar Jerusalem 2-1(1-1) |
| Hapoel Haifa - Maccabi Haifa 0-1(0-0) |

| Round 13 [12-14.11.2022] |
|---|
| FC Ashdod - Maccabi Netanya 2-3(0-3) |
| Hapoel Hadera - Sektzia Ness Tziona 0-0 |
| Maccabi Tel Aviv - Hapoel Haifa 1-0(0-0) |
| Bnei Reineh - Hapoel Jerusalem 0-2(0-0) |
| Hapoel Ironi K.S. - Hapoel Be'er Sh. 0-2(0-1) |
| Maccabi Haifa - Hapoel Tel Aviv 5-2(4-1) |
| Beitar Jerusalem - Bnei Sachnin 2-1(0-1) |

| Round 14 [17-19.12.2022] |
|---|
| Hapoel Hadera - Hapoel Jerusalem 0-0 |
| Hapoel Tel Aviv - Hapoel Haifa 3-3(0-2) |
| Beitar Jerusalem - Maccabi Netanya 6-3(4-0) |
| FC Ashdod - Hapoel Be'er Sheva 0-1(0-0) |
| Hapoel Ironi K.S. - Sektzia N. Tziona 3-3(2-2) |
| Bnei Reineh - Maccabi Tel Aviv 0-2(0-1) |
| Maccabi Haifa - Bnei Sachnin 3-1(1-0) |

| Round 15 [24-26.12.2022] |
|---|
| Maccabi Tel Aviv - Hapoel Hadera 5-0(3-0) |
| Hapoel Jerusalem - Hapoel Ironi K.S. 1-1(1-0) |
| Hapoel Haifa - Maccabi Bnei Reineh 0-0 |
| Sektzia Ness Tziona - FC Ashdod 2-0(0-0) |
| Hapoel Be'er Sh. - Beitar Jerusalem 3-2(1-0) |
| Bnei Sachnin - Hapoel Tel Aviv 1-1(1-0) |
| Maccabi Netanya - Maccabi Haifa 0-2(0-0) |

| Round 16 [31.12.2022-01.01.2023] |
|---|
| Beitar Jerusalem-Sektzia Ness Tziona 3-2(3-1) |
| Hapoel Tel Aviv - Maccabi Bnei Reineh 1-1(1-0) |
| Bnei Sachnin - Hapoel Haifa 1-2(0-1) |
| FC Ashdod - Hapoel Jerusalem 1-1(0-0) |
| Hapoel Ironi K.S. - Maccabi Tel Aviv 1-1(1-0) |
| Hapoel Hadera-Maccabi Bnei Reineh 2-2(0-1) |
| Maccabi Haifa - Hapoel Be'er Sheva 2-0(1-0) |

| Round 17 [07-09.01.2023] |
|---|
| Maccabi Netanya - Bnei Sachnin 0-0 |
| Maccabi Tel Aviv - FC Ashdod 3-0(1-0) |
| Hapoel Haifa - Hapoel Hadera 3-0(1-0) |
| Hapoel Jerusalem - Beitar Jerusalem 1-1(0-0) |
| Bnei Reineh - Hapoel Ironi K.S. 0-1(0-0) |
| Sektzia Ness Tziona - Maccabi Haifa 0-2(0-1) |
| Hapoel Be'er Sheva-Hapoel Tel Aviv 6-0(3-0) |

| Round 18 [14-16.01.2023] |
|---|
| Hapoel Tel Aviv - Sektzia N. Tziona 1-1(0-0) |
| Hapoel Ironi K.S. - Hapoel Hadera 2-2(1-1) |
| FC Ashdod - Maccabi Bnei Reineh 3-0(2-0) |
| Maccabi Netanya - Hapoel Haifa 1-0(1-0) |
| Maccabi Haifa - Hapoel Jerusalem 2-1(2-1) |
| Beitar Jerusalem - Maccabi Tel Aviv 2-2(1-1) |
| Bnei Sachnin-Be'er Sheva 0-1(0-0)[08.02.2023] |

| Round 19 [21-23.01.2023] |
|---|
| Hapoel Jerusalem - Hapoel Tel Aviv 0-0 |
| Hapoel Haifa - Hapoel Ironi K.S. 1-0(0-0) |
| Hapoel Hadera - FC Ashdod 0-2(0-0) |
| Sektzia Ness Tziona - Bnei Sachnin 0-0 |
| Bnei Reineh - Beitar Jerusalem 0-2(0-2) |
| Be'er Sheva - Maccabi Netanya 2-2(2-2) |
| Maccabi Tel Aviv - Maccabi Haifa 3-0(1-0) |

| Round 20 [28-30.01.2023] |
|---|
| Maccabi Haifa - Maccabi Bnei Reineh 0-0 |
| FC Ashdod - Hapoel Ironi K.S. 1-1(0-0) |
| Maccabi Netanya - Sektzia N. Tziona 3-0(2-0) |
| Beitar Jerusalem - Hapoel Hadera 0-2(0-1) |
| Hapoel Tel Aviv - Maccabi Tel Aviv 0-0 |
| Hapoel Haifa - Hapoel Be'er Sheva 0-1(0-1) |
| Bnei Sachnin - Hapoel Jerusalem 2-1(1-1) |

| Round 21 [04-08.02.2023] |
|---|
| Sektzia N. Tziona - Hapoel Be'er Sh. 0-1(0-1) |
| Maccabi Tel Aviv - Bnei Reineh 1-1(0-1) |
| Hapoel Haifa - FC Ashdod 1-1(0-0) |
| Hapoel Jerusalem - Maccabi Netanya 0-2(0-0) |
| Hapoel Ironi K.S. - Beitar Jerusalem 0-3(0-0) |
| Bnei Reineh - Hapoel Tel Aviv 1-1(0-1) |
| Hapoel Hadera - Maccabi Haifa 1-1(0-0) |

| Round 22 [11-13.02.2023] |
|---|
| Beitar Jerusalem - FC Ashdod 2-1(2-0) |
| Hapoel Be'er Sheva - Hapoel Jerusalem 0-0 |
| Bnei Sachnin - Maccabi Bnei Reineh 1-1(0-0) |
| Sektzia Ness Tziona - Hapoel Haifa 0-2(0-1) |
| Maccabi Haifa - Hapoel Ironi K.S. 2-0(0-0) |
| Hapoel Tel Aviv - Hapoel Hadera 0-0 |
| Maccabi Netanya - Maccabi Tel Aviv 2-1(0-0) |

| Round 23 [18-20.02.2023] |
|---|
| Hapoel Ironi K.S. - Hapoel Tel Aviv 0-1(0-1) |
| Bnei Reineh - Maccabi Netanya 1-2(1-0) |
| Hapoel Hadera - Bnei Sachnin 1-3(1-1) |
| Hapoel Jerusalem - Sektzia N. Tziona 1-0(0-0) |
| FC Ashdod - Maccabi Haifa 3-1(2-0) |
| Hapoel Haifa - Beitar Jerusalem 0-0 |
| Maccabi Tel Aviv - Hapoel Be'er Sh. 1-0(1-0) |

| Round 24 [25-27.02.2023] |
|---|
| Hapoel Tel Aviv - FC Ashdod 1-2(1-0) |
| Sektzia N.Tziona - Maccabi Tel Aviv 0-2(0-2) |
| Bnei Sachnin - Hapoel Ironi K.S. 1-3(1-3) |
| Maccabi Netanya - Hapoel Hadera 1-0(0-0) |
| Maccabi Haifa - Beitar Jerusalem 2-1(1-1) |
| Hapoel Jerusalem - Hapoel Haifa 2-2(1-1) |
| Hapoel Be'er Sheva - Bnei Reineh 2-0(1-0) |

| Round 25 [04-06.03.2023] |
|---|
| Hapoel Ironi K.S. - Maccabi Netanya 2-2(1-2) |
| Hapoel Hadera - Hapoel Be'er Sheva 0-3(0-1) |
| FC Ashdod - Bnei Sachnin 1-1(0-1) |
| Bnei Reineh - Sektzia Ness Tziona 3-2(1-2) |
| Maccabi Tel Aviv - Hapoel Jerusalem 1-2(1-0) |
| Beitar Jerusalem - Hapoel Tel Aviv 1-3(1-1) |
| Maccabi Haifa - Hapoel Haifa 4-1(2-0) |

| Round 26 [11-13.03.2023] |
|---|
| Hapoel Haifa - Maccabi Tel Aviv 1-1(0-1) |
| Hapoel Jerusalem - Bnei Reineh 0-1(0-0) |
| Sektzia Ness Tziona - Hapoel Hadera 1-3(1-0) |
| Bnei Sachnin - Beitar Jerusalem 2-0(0-0) |
| Maccabi Netanya - FC Ashdod 0-2(0-0) |
| Hapoel Be'er Sh. - Hapoel Ironi K.S. 2-1(1-0) |
| Hapoel Tel Aviv - Maccabi Haifa 0-1(0-0) |

## Final Standings

| | | | | | | | | |
|---|---|---|---|---|---|---|---|---|
| 1. | Maccabi Haifa FC | 26 | 20 | 2 | 4 | 51 - 24 | 62 |
| 2. | Hapoel Be'er Sheva FC | 26 | 18 | 4 | 4 | 52 - 19 | 58 |
| 3. | Maccabi Tel Aviv FC | 26 | 15 | 7 | 4 | 53 - 15 | 52 |
| 4. | Maccabi Netanya FC | 26 | 10 | 7 | 9 | 33 - 38 | 37 |
| 5. | Hapoel Jerusalem FC | 26 | 9 | 9 | 8 | 30 - 26 | 36 |
| 6. | FC Ashdod | 26 | 9 | 9 | 8 | 32 - 30 | 36 |
| 7. | Beitar Jerusalem FC | 26 | 9 | 4 | 13 | 38 - 47 | 31 |
| 8. | Hapoel Haifa FC | 26 | 6 | 12 | 8 | 25 - 28 | 30 |
| 9. | Bnei Sakhnin FC | 26 | 7 | 9 | 10 | 26 - 30 | 30 |
| 10. | Hapoel Hadera–Giv'at Olga "Shulem Schwarz" | 26 | 6 | 11 | 9 | 26 - 41 | 29 |
| 11. | Hapoel Tel Aviv FC | 26 | 6 | 9 | 11 | 28 - 42 | 27 |
| 12. | Maccabi Bnei Reineh FC | 26 | 5 | 9 | 12 | 23 - 42 | 24 |
| 13. | Hapoel Ironi Kiryat Shmona FC | 26 | 3 | 12 | 11 | 27 - 39 | 21 |
| 14. | Sektzia Nes Tziona FC | 26 | 3 | 8 | 15 | 23 - 46 | 17 |

Teams ranked 1-6 were qualified for the Championship Round, while teams ranked 7-14 were qualified for the Relegation Round.

## Relegation Round

### Round 27 [18-19.03.2023]
Hapoel Hadera - Sektzia Ness Tziona 1-2(0-0)
Beitar Jerusalem - Hapoel Tel Aviv 2-1(0-0)
Bnei Sachnin - Maccabi Bnei Reineh 2-2(0-1)
Hapoel Haifa - Hapoel Ironi K.S. 1-1(0-0)

### Round 28 [01-03.04.2023]
Hapoel Tel Aviv-Sektzia Ness Tziona 2-1(0-0)
Maccabi Bnei Reineh-Hapoel Hadera 1-1(1-1)
Hapoel Ironi K.S. - Bnei Sachnin 2-2(0-1)
Beitar Jerusalem - Hapoel Haifa 2-0(1-0)

### Round 29 [15-16.04.2023]
Hapoel Haifa - Hapoel Tel Aviv 1-0(1-0)
Hapoel Hadera - Hapoel Ironi K.S. 1-1(1-0)
Sektzia N. Tz. - Maccabi Bnei Reineh 1-2(0-1)
Bnei Sachnin - Beitar Jerusalem 4-3(2-0)

### Round 30 [22-23.04.2023]
Hapoel T. A. - Maccabi Bnei Reineh 1-2(0-1)
Hapoel Ironi K.S. - Sektzia N. Tziona 1-1(1-0)
Hapoel Haifa - Bnei Sachnin 2-2(1-0)
Beitar Jerusalem - Hapoel Hadera 2-1(2-1)

### Round 31 [29-30.04.2023]
M. Bnei Reineh - Hapoel Ironi K.S. 1-3(0-0)
Sektzia Ness Tziona-Beitar Jerusalem 1-3(0-0)
Hapoel Hadera - Hapoel Haifa 1-2(1-1)
Bnei Sachnin - Hapoel Tel Aviv 0-1(0-1)

### Round 32 [06.05.2023]
Hapoel Haifa - Sektzia Ness Tziona 0-1(0-0)
Hapoel Tel Aviv - Hapoel Ironi K.S. 2-2(0-2)
Bnei Sachnin - Hapoel Hadera 2-3(1-1)
Beitar Jerusalem - Bnei Reineh 0-1(0-0)

### Round 33 [13.05.2023]
Sektzia Ness Tziona - Bnei Sachnin 1-1(1-1)
Hapoel Hadera - Hapoel Tel Aviv 1-2(0-2)
Maccabi Bnei Reineh - Hapoel Haifa 0-4(0-1)
Hapoel Ironi K.S. - Beitar Jerusalem 3-2(3-0)

## Final Standings

| | | | Total | | | | | | Home | | | | | Away | | |
|---|---|---|---|---|---|---|---|---|---|---|---|---|---|---|---|---|---|
| 7. | Hapoel Haifa FC | 33 | 9 | 14 | 10 | 35 - 35 | 41 | 5 | 7 | 5 | 14 - 11 | 4 | 7 | 5 | 21 - 24 |
| 8. | Beitar Jerusalem FC | 33 | 13 | 4 | 16 | 52 - 58 | 40 | 8 | 2 | 7 | 27 - 30 | 5 | 2 | 9 | 25 - 28 |
| 9. | Bnei Sakhnin FC | 33 | 8 | 13 | 12 | 39 - 44 | 37 | 4 | 5 | 8 | 20 - 25 | 4 | 8 | 4 | 19 - 19 |
| 10. | Hapoel Tel Aviv FC | 33 | 9 | 10 | 14 | 37 - 51 | 36 | 4 | 6 | 6 | 20 - 23 | 5 | 4 | 8 | 17 - 28 |
| 11. | Maccabi Bnei Reineh FC | 33 | 8 | 11 | 14 | 32 - 54 | 35 | 3 | 4 | 9 | 13 - 27 | 5 | 7 | 5 | 19 - 27 |
| 12. | Hapoel Hadera–Giv'at Olga "Shulem Schwarz" | 33 | 7 | 13 | 13 | 35 - 53 | 34 | 2 | 8 | 7 | 15 - 28 | 5 | 5 | 6 | 20 - 25 |
| 13. | Hapoel Ironi Kiryat Shmona FC (*Relegated*) | 33 | 5 | 17 | 11 | 40 - 49 | 32 | 1 | 11 | 4 | 21 - 27 | 4 | 6 | 7 | 19 - 22 |
| 14. | Sektzia Nes Tziona FC (*Relegated*) | 33 | 5 | 10 | 18 | 31 - 56 | 25 | 2 | 4 | 10 | 14 - 30 | 3 | 6 | 8 | 17 - 26 |

## Championship Round

### Results

### Round 27 [18.03.2023]
Hapoel Be'er Sh. - Hapoel Jerusalem 1-0(1-0)
Maccabi Tel Aviv - Maccabi Netanya 2-0(2-0)
Maccabi Haifa - FC Ashdod 2-1(2-1)

### Round 28 [01.04.2023]
Hapoel Jerusalem - Maccabi Tel Aviv 0-2(0-1)
FC Ashdod - Maccabi Netanya 3-2(2-1)
Maccabi Haifa - Hapoel Be'er Sheva 1-0(1-0)

### Round 29 [04.04.2023]
Maccabi Netanya - Hapoel Jerusalem 0-2(0-0)
Hapoel Be'er Sheva - FC Ashdod 3-1(1-0)
Maccabi Tel Aviv - Maccabi Haifa 1-1(1-0)

### Round 30 [08-10.04.2023]
FC Ashdod - Hapoel Jerusalem 0-1(0-1)
Maccabi Haifa - Maccabi Netanya 4-1(0-1)
Hapoel Be'er Sh. - Maccabi Tel Aviv 1-2(1-1)

### Round 31 [15-16.04.2023]
Hapoel Jerusalem - Maccabi Haifa 2-1(0-0)
Maccabi Tel Aviv - FC Ashdod 1-1(0-0)
Maccabi Netanya-Hapoel Be'er Sheva 1-1(1-1)

### Round 32 [22-23.04.2023]
Hapoel Jerusalem - Hapoel Be'er Sh. 1-2(0-1)
Maccabi Netanya - Maccabi Tel Aviv 0-0
FC Ashdod - Maccabi Haifa 1-2(0-0)

### Round 33 [29.04.-01.05.2023]
Maccabi Netanya - FC Ashdod 2-0(1-0)
Maccabi Tel Aviv - Hapoel Jerusalem 2-1(2-1)
Hapoel Be'er Sheva - Maccabi Haifa 2-1(1-1)

### Round 34 [07-08.05.2023]
Hapoel Jerusalem - Maccabi Netanya 1-4(1-2)
FC Ashdod - Hapoel Be'er Sheva 0-1(0-1)
Maccabi Haifa - Maccabi Tel Aviv 3-1(1-1)

### Round 35 [14-15.05.2023]
Hapoel Jerusalem - FC Ashdod 0-1(0-0)
Maccabi Netanya - Maccabi Haifa 1-5(1-1)
Maccabi Tel Aviv - Hapoel Be'er Sh. 3-0(2-0)

### Round 36 [20.05.2023]
FC Ashdod - Maccabi Tel Aviv 1-2(1-1)
Hapoel Be'er Sh. - Maccabi Netanya 2-0(1-0)
Maccabi Haifa - Hapoel Jerusalem 5-0(3-0)

## Final Standings

| | | | Total | | | | | | Home | | | | | Away | | |
|---|---|---|---|---|---|---|---|---|---|---|---|---|---|---|---|---|---|
| 1. | **Maccabi Haifa FC** | 36 | 27 | 3 | 6 | 76 - 34 | 81 | 17 | 1 | 0 | 48 - 12 | 10 | 2 | 6 | 28 - 22 |
| 2. | Hapoel Be'er Sheva FC | 36 | 24 | 5 | 7 | 65 - 29 | 74 | 11 | 4 | 3 | 35 - 16 | 13 | 1 | 4 | 30 - 13 |
| 3. | Maccabi Tel Aviv FC | 36 | 21 | 10 | 5 | 69 - 23 | 73 | 13 | 4 | 1 | 43 - 8 | 8 | 6 | 4 | 26 - 15 |
| 4. | Hapoel Jerusalem FC | 36 | 12 | 9 | 15 | 38 - 44 | 45 | 4 | 5 | 9 | 18 - 27 | 8 | 4 | 6 | 20 - 17 |
| 5. | Maccabi Netanya FC | 36 | 12 | 9 | 15 | 44 - 58 | 45 | 8 | 3 | 7 | 19 - 21 | 4 | 6 | 8 | 25 - 37 |
| 6. | FC Ashdod | 36 | 11 | 10 | 15 | 41 - 46 | 43 | 6 | 5 | 7 | 23 - 19 | 5 | 5 | 8 | 18 - 27 |

## Top goalscorers:

| | | |
|---|---|---|
| 21 | **Omer Atzili** | *Maccabi Haifa FC* |
| 20 | Eran Zahavi | *Maccabi Tel Aviv FC* |
| 17 | Danilo Moreno Asprilla (COL) | *Beitar Jerusalem FC* |

# NATIONAL CUP
## Israel State Cup (Gvia HaMedina) 2022/2023

### Eighth Round [11-12.12.2022]

| | | | | |
|---|---|---|---|---|
| Beitar Jerusalem FC - FC Kafr Qasim | 4-0 | Hapoel Rishon LeZion FC - Maccabi Bnei Reineh FC | 0-3 |
| Hapoel Ashdod FC - Ironi Tiberias FC | 1-2 | Hapoel Jerusalem FC - Maccabi Petah Tikva FC | 0-1 |
| Hapoel Hadera–Giv'at Olga - Hapoel Kfar Saba FC | 1-3 | Hapoel Acre FC - Sektzia Nes Tziona FC | 2-3 |
| Hapoel Ironi Kiryat Shmona - Maccabi Netanya FC | 1-1 aet; 3-4 pen | Maccabi Ahi Nazareth FC - FC Tzofi Haifa | 5-1 |
| Hapoel Umm al-Fahm FC - Maccabi Tel Aviv FC | 2-3 | FC Ashdod - Hapoel Be'er Sheva FC | 2-1 |
| Hapoel Qalansawe FC - Bnei Sakhnin FC | 0-3 | Hapoel Nir Ramat HaSharon FC - Holon Yermiyahu | 2-0 |
| Ihud Bnei Shefa-Amr - Hapoel Haifa FC | 4-4 aet; 2-4 pen | Hapoel Afula FC - Hapoel Tel Aviv FC | 1-0 |
| FC Tira - Hapoel Petah Tikva FC | 2-3 aet | Hapoel Nof HaGalil FC - Maccabi Haifa FC | 0-1 |

### 1/8-Finals [03-05.01.2023]

| | | | |
|---|---|---|---|
| Hapoel Nir Ramat HaSharon FC - FC Ashdod | 0-1 | Sektzia Nes Tziona FC - Maccabi Petah Tikva FC | 1-2 |
| Maccabi Ahi Nazareth FC - Maccabi Netanya FC | 0-1 | Maccabi Bnei Reineh FC - Hapoel Petah Tikva FC | 0-2 |
| Maccabi Tel Aviv FC - Bnei Sakhnin FC | 5-0 | Maccabi Haifa FC - Hapoel Haifa FC | 5-1 |
| Beitar Jerusalem FC - Ironi Tiberias FC | 1-1 aet; 7-6 pen | Hapoel Afula FC - Hapoel Kfar Saba FC | 3-0 |

### Quarter-Finals [31.01.-01.02./28.02.-01.03.2023]

| First Leg | | Second Leg | |
|---|---|---|---|
| Hapoel Petah Tikva FC - FC Ashdod | 1-1 | FC Ashdod - Hapoel Petah Tikva FC | 4-2 |
| Maccabi Netanya FC - Maccabi Haifa FC | 2-2 | Maccabi Haifa FC - Maccabi Netanya FC | 1-2 aet |
| Hapoel Afula FC - Beitar Jerusalem FC | 0-4 | Beitar Jerusalem FC - Hapoel Afula | 1-2 |
| Maccabi Tel Aviv FC - Maccabi Petah Tikva FC | 4-0 | Maccabi Petah Tikva FC - Maccabi Tel Aviv FC | 1-2 |

### Semi-Finals [02-03.05.2023]

| | | | |
|---|---|---|---|
| FC Ashdod - Maccabi Netanya FC | 1-3 | Beitar Jerusalem FC - Maccabi Tel Aviv FC | 3-1 |

### Final

23.05.2023; "Sammy Ofer" Stadium, Haifa; Referee: Gal Leibovitz; Attendance: n/a

**Maccabi Netanya FC - Beitar Jerusalem FC**  0-3(0-1)

**Maccabi Netanya**: Itamar Nitzan, Ido Vaier, Raz Shlomo, Plamen Galabov (63.Yuval Sade), Nassim Ouammou (76.Shay Konstantini), Aviv Avraham (Cap) (76.Liran Rotman), Boris Enow Takang, Ethane Azulay (63.Omri Gandelman), Oz Bilu (63.Igor Zlatanović), Patrick Twumasi, Stanislav Bilenkiy. Trainer: Ran Kojok.

**Beitar Jerusalem**: João Miguel Macedo Silva, Grigoriy Morozov, Ori Dahan, Orel Dgani, Avishay Cohen, Trazié Thomas (90+6.Lion Mizrahi), Ofir Kriaf (Cap), Dan Azaria (60.Adi Yona), Yarden Shua (90+6.Bar Cohen), Ion Nicolăescu (63.Imoh Fred Friday), Danilo Moreno Asprilla (90+6.Sergey Borodin). Trainer: Yossi Abukasis.

**Goals:** 0-1 Ion Nicolăescu (37), 0-2 Imoh Fred Friday (76), 0-3 Yarden Shua (90+5 penalty).

# THE CLUBS 2022/2023

Please note: appearances and goals are including statistics of both regular season and play-offs (Championship Round and Relegation Round).

## Beitar Jerusalem Football Club

| | |
|---|---|
| **Founded**: | 1936 |
| **Stadium**: | Teddy Stadium, Jerusalem (31,733) |
| **Trainer**: | Yossi Abukasis  10.09.1970 |

| Goalkeepers: | DOB | M | (s) | G |
|---|---|---|---|---|
| Netanel Daloya | 14.07.1998 | 3 | | |
| Itamar Israeli | 22.03.1992 | 18 | | |
| João *Miguel* Macedo *Silva* (POR) | 07.04.1995 | 12 | | |
| **Defenders:** | **DOB** | **M** | **(s)** | **G** |
| Shay Lee Ayzen | 27.08.2000 | 1 | (2) | |
| Sergey Borodin (RUS) | 30.01.1999 | 11 | (2) | |
| Amit Cohen | 21.11.1998 | 17 | (3) | 1 |
| Ori Dahan | 07.12.1999 | 18 | (3) | 1 |
| Orel Dgani | 08.01.1989 | 26 | | 1 |
| Hagai Goldenberg | 15.09.1990 | 2 | (1) | |
| Maksim Grechkin | 04.03.1996 | 13 | (1) | |
| David Houja | 27.04.2001 | 2 | (1) | |
| Josua Antonio Mejías García (VEN) | 01.08.1997 | 11 | | |
| Grigoriy Morozov (RUS) | 06.06.1994 | 11 | (2) | 1 |
| Adi Yona | 17.04.2004 | 6 | (18) | 1 |
| Or Zehavi | 23.04.1996 | 9 | (2) | |
| **Midfielders:** | **DOB** | **M** | **(s)** | **G** |
| Tamir Adi | 02.05.1993 | 9 | (2) | 2 |

| | DOB | M | (s) | G |
|---|---|---|---|---|
| Dan Azaria | 29.08.1995 | 4 | (2) | |
| Bar Cohen | 10.03.2001 | 13 | (20) | 1 |
| Ofir Kriaf | 17.03.1991 | 22 | (3) | 1 |
| Ilay Madmon | 23.02.2003 | 4 | (17) | 1 |
| Lion Mizrahi | 24.10.2002 | 6 | (10) | |
| Meron Tal | 01.01.2002 | 2 | (6) | |
| Trazié Thomas (CIV) | 01.07.1999 | 25 | (2) | 4 |
| Aviel Zargary | 11.12.2002 | 5 | (2) | |
| **Forwards:** | **DOB** | **M** | **(s)** | **G** |
| Avishay Cohen | 19.06.1995 | 20 | (6) | 1 |
| Nehoray Dabush | 18.10.2004 | | (3) | |
| Imoh Fred Friday (NGA) | 22.05.1995 | 4 | (5) | 1 |
| Eduardo Antonio Guerrero Locano (PAN) | 21.02.2000 | 5 | (8) | |
| Ronen Hanzis | 28.02.2002 | 1 | (8) | |
| Danilo Moreno Asprilla (COL) | 12.01.1989 | 28 | (3) | 17 |
| Stav Nachmani | 06.10.2002 | 4 | (5) | |
| Ion Nicolăescu (MDA) | 07.09.1998 | 26 | (1) | 15 |
| Yarden Shua | 16.06.1999 | 25 | (3) | 3 |
| Gleofilo Sabrino Rudewald Hasselbaink Vlijter (SUR) | 17.09.1999 | | (2) | |

## Bnei Sakhnin Football Club

| Founded: | 1991 | | |
|---|---|---|---|
| Stadium: | Doha Stadium, Sakhnin (8,500) | | |
| Trainer: | Haim Silvas | | 21.11.1975 |
| [29.11.2022] | Kobi Refua | | 03.09.1974 |

| Goalkeepers: | DOB | M | (s) | G |
|---|---|---|---|---|
| Gad Amos | 24.12.1988 | 29 | | |
| Mahmoud Kannadil | 11.08.1988 | 3 | (1) | |
| Abed Yassin | 01.05.2004 | 1 | (1) | |
| **Defenders:** | DOB | M | (s) | G |
| Ovadia Darwish | 24.09.1998 | 19 | (2) | 1 |
| Walid Darwish | 24.09.1998 | | (1) | |
| Abou Dosso (CIV) | 26.03.1996 | 15 | | |
| Maroun Gantus | 15.06.1996 | 26 | | |
| Hassan Hilo | 25.11.1999 | 22 | (7) | |
| Abdallah Jaber (PLE) | 17.02.1993 | 2 | (9) | |
| Ante Puljić (CRO) | 05.11.1987 | 28 | (2) | 2 |
| Fabian Sporkslede (SUR) | 03.08.1993 | 18 | (6) | 1 |
| Ahmad Taha | 09.01.2005 | 3 | | |
| Taleb Tawatha | 21.06.1992 | 12 | (7) | |
| **Midfielders:** | DOB | M | (s) | G |
| Yuval Ashkenazi | 13.02.1992 | 3 | (3) | 1 |
| Ibrahima Sory Conté I (GUI) | 03.04.1991 | 8 | (5) | |

| Ihab Ganayem | 11.06.1996 | 25 | (2) | |
|---|---|---|---|---|
| Gaby Joury | 16.10.2000 | 2 | (9) | |
| Marwan Kabha | 23.02.1991 | 15 | (3) | |
| Beram Kayal | 02.05.1988 | 28 | | 6 |
| Roei Shukrani | 26.06.1990 | 16 | (15) | |
| Saher Taji | 09.11.2000 | 6 | (8) | |
| **Forwards:** | DOB | M | (s) | G |
| Mohammad Awwad | 09.06.1997 | 1 | (9) | 1 |
| Mohamed Badarna | 15.11.1995 | 2 | (8) | |
| Nicolao Cardoso Dumitru (ITA) | 12.10.1991 | 18 | (10) | 3 |
| Dor Hugi | 10.07.1995 | 12 | (2) | 5 |
| Basil Khuri | 01.12.2003 | 2 | (2) | 3 |
| Jérémie Luvovadio-Lelo (BEL) | 20.03.2001 | | (9) | |
| Guy Melamed | 21.12.1992 | 28 | (1) | 12 |
| German Onugkha (RUS) | 06.07.1996 | 5 | (3) | |
| Ange-Freddy Plumain (GLP) | 02.03.1995 | 14 | (1) | 2 |
| Fadel Zbedat | 11.12.2002 | | (4) | |

## Football Club (Moadon Sport) Ashdod

| Founded: | 1999 | | |
|---|---|---|---|
| Stadium: | Yud-Alef Stadium, Ashdod (7,800) | | |
| Trainer: | Ran Ben Shimon | | 28.11.1970 |

| Goalkeepers: | DOB | M | (s) | G |
|---|---|---|---|---|
| Tomer Amar | 01.07.2002 | | (1) | |
| Yoav Gerafi | 29.08.1993 | 33 | | |
| Sahar Hasson | 24.04.1996 | 3 | | |
| **Defenders:** | DOB | M | (s) | G |
| Timothy Dennis Awany (UGA) | 06.08.1996 | 27 | (1) | |
| Tom Ben Zaken | 29.10.1994 | 24 | | |
| Gil Cohen | 08.11.2000 | 28 | (1) | |
| David Cuperman Coifman (COL) | 08.11.1996 | 19 | (5) | |
| Nenad Cvetković (SRB) | 06.01.1996 | 32 | | 3 |
| Shaked Hakmon | 15.06.2002 | 5 | (7) | |
| Montari Kamaheni (GHA) | 01.02.2000 | 6 | (3) | |
| Obeida Khattab | 14.07.1992 | | (3) | |
| Zohar Zasano | 21.11.2001 | 21 | (12) | |
| **Midfielders:** | DOB | M | (s) | G |
| Samuel Alabi Borquaye (GHA) | 06.05.2000 | 3 | (3) | 1 |
| Izhak Asefa | 19.11.1998 | 1 | (4) | |
| Martin Beautrel Atemengue Ndzie (CMR) | 16.01.2003 | | (3) | |
| Oz Bilu | 16.01.2001 | 5 | (6) | |
| Shalev Harush | 08.05.2002 | 13 | (14) | 3 |
| Nir Hasson | 19.12.2001 | | (3) | |

| Lucas Spinola Salinas (BRA) | 14.10.1995 | 6 | (1) | 1 |
|---|---|---|---|---|
| Noam Muche | 30.07.2003 | 1 | (2) | |
| Isaac Pappoe (GHA) | 20.12.2003 | | (1) | |
| Naor Sabag | 23.05.1993 | 32 | | 1 |
| Jordan Sebban (FRA) | 06.01.1997 | 24 | (8) | 1 |
| Elad Shahaf | 13.01.1998 | 17 | (1) | 2 |
| **Forwards:** | DOB | M | (s) | G |
| Ravid Abergel | 20.11.2003 | | (1) | |
| Elton Acolatse (NED) | 25.07.1995 | 6 | (9) | 3 |
| Roei Ben Shimon | 04.12.2000 | 3 | (1) | 1 |
| Ya'akov Berihon | 06.07.1993 | 11 | (18) | 5 |
| Dor Jan | 16.12.1994 | 1 | (4) | |
| Mohamad Knaan | 14.01.2000 | 26 | | 5 |
| Adir Levi | 06.01.2002 | 2 | (21) | 2 |
| Roy Levy | 13.01.2000 | 5 | (11) | 1 |
| Ebenezer Mamatah (GHA) | 07.11.2001 | 17 | (12) | 4 |
| Shavit Mazal | 29.11.2001 | 2 | (6) | |
| Yaniv Mizrahi | 30.08.1995 | 1 | (6) | |
| Zakaria Mugeese (GHA) | 27.12.2001 | 18 | (6) | 5 |
| Michael Ohana | 04.10.1995 | 4 | (1) | 1 |

## Hapoel Be'er Sheva Football Club

| Founded: | 01.05.1949 | | |
|---|---|---|---|
| Stadium: | "Yaakov Turner Toto" Stadium, Be'er Sheva (16,126) | | |
| Trainer: | Elyaniv Barda | | 15.12.1981 |

| Goalkeepers: | DOB | M | (s) | G |
|---|---|---|---|---|
| Omri Glazer | 11.03.1996 | 35 | | |
| Ariel Harush | 25.05.1988 | 1 | | |
| **Defenders:** | DOB | M | (s) | G |
| Iyad Abu Abaid | 31.12.1994 | 18 | (3) | |
| Amir Ariely | 03.03.2003 | 1 | (2) | |
| Itay Azut | | | (1) | |
| Or Blorian | 07.03.2000 | 2 | (4) | |
| Or Dadya | 12.07.1997 | 14 | (8) | |
| Hatem Abd Elhamed | 18.03.1991 | 3 | | |
| Hélder Filipe Oliveira Lopes (POR) | 04.01.1989 | 31 | | 4 |
| Miguel Ângelo Leonardo Vítor | 30.06.1989 | 30 | | 2 |
| Aviv Solomon | 10.01.1995 | 2 | (5) | |
| Eitan Tibi | 16.11.1987 | 18 | (7) | |
| **Midfielders:** | DOB | M | (s) | G |
| André Renato Soares Martins (POR) | 21.01.1990 | 4 | (3) | |
| Lucas Mariano Bareiro (ARG) | 08.03.1995 | 18 | (9) | 1 |
| Shay Elias | 25.02.1999 | 18 | (6) | 1 |
| Amir Ganach | 07.09.2004 | | (2) | |

| Roei Gordana | 06.07.1990 | 24 | (6) | 1 |
|---|---|---|---|---|
| David Keltjens | 11.06.1995 | | (1) | |
| Ilay Madmon | 23.02.2003 | 1 | (1) | |
| Roi Maman | 04.11.2003 | | (2) | |
| Dor Micha | 02.03.1992 | 22 | (14) | 1 |
| Constantin Adrian Alexandru Păun (ROU) | 01.04.1995 | 18 | (6) | 4 |
| Ramzi Safuri | 21.10.1995 | 15 | (9) | 8 |
| Eden Shamir | 25.06.1995 | 22 | (4) | 2 |
| Yoan Stoyanov (BUL) | 22.05.2001 | | (1) | |
| Sagiv Yehezkel | 21.03.1995 | 22 | (3) | 7 |
| Tomer Yosefi | 02.02.1999 | | (5) | |
| **Forwards:** | DOB | M | (s) | G |
| Eugène Ansah (GHA) | 16.12.1994 | 17 | (9) | 5 |
| Rotem Hatuel | 12.04.1998 | 10 | (19) | 11 |
| Tomer Hemed | 02.05.1987 | 10 | (14) | 6 |
| Patryk Klimala (POL) | 05.08.1998 | 9 | (6) | 3 |
| Itay Shechter | 22.02.1987 | 2 | (16) | 1 |
| Astrit Selmani (KOS) | 13.05.1997 | 7 | (3) | 2 |
| Shapi Suleymanov (RUS) | 16.12.1999 | 22 | (7) | 5 |

## Hapoel Hadera–Giv'at Olga "Shulem Schwarz" Football Club

| Founded: | 1936 | |
|---|---|---|
| Stadium: | Netanya Stadium, Netanya (13,610) | |
| Trainer: | Asaf Nimni | 07.03.1983 |
| [09.01.2023] | Menahem Koretski | 04.04.1974 |
| [01.05.2023] | Nisso Avitan | 29.09.1971 |

| Goalkeepers: | DOB | M | (s) | G |
|---|---|---|---|---|
| Shahar Golan | 01.07.2003 | | (1) | |
| Gai Herman | 19.06.2000 | 2 | (1) | |
| Rubi Levkovich | 31.08.1988 | 31 | | |
| **Defenders:** | DOB | M | (s) | G |
| Tarek Boshnak | 03.06.1999 | 13 | (3) | |
| Jonathan Cissé (CIV) | 18.05.1997 | 30 | | 3 |
| Philip Orite Ipole (NGA) | 06.06.2001 | 26 | (2) | |
| Rotem Keller | 09.11.2002 | 5 | (1) | |
| Diaa Lababidi | 26.07.1992 | 28 | (1) | |
| Ido Levy | 31.07.1990 | 31 | (1) | 2 |
| Tomer Machluf | 09.08.2000 | 6 | (8) | |
| Lidor Maimon | 02.03.2002 | 1 | | |
| Oren Sitbon | 19.03.2003 | | (12) | |
| Klemen Šturm (SVN) | 27.06.1994 | 18 | (4) | |
| Ron Unger | 05.09.2001 | 4 | (8) | |
| Amit Yeverbaum | 12.08.2001 | | (4) | |
| **Midfielders:** | DOB | M | (s) | G |
| Gilad Avramov | 30.03.2000 | 14 | (12) | 1 |
| Roslan Barsky | 03.01.1992 | 16 | | |

| Tom Berkovich | 07.01.2002 | | (1) | |
|---|---|---|---|---|
| Samy Bourard (BEL) | 10.07.1996 | 29 | (3) | 9 |
| Albert Ejupi (SWE) | 28.08.1992 | 4 | (6) | |
| Saar Fadida | 04.01.1997 | 24 | (6) | 5 |
| Niv Gotlieb | 29.10.2002 | 5 | (21) | 3 |
| Elad Madmon | 10.02.2004 | 3 | (4) | |
| Nicolás Olsak | 25.11.1991 | 3 | (1) | |
| Menashe Zalka | 01.07.1990 | 29 | (1) | |
| Ness Zamir | 31.10.1990 | | (2) | |
| **Forwards:** | DOB | M | (s) | G |
| Steven Alfred (NGA) | 11.10.1997 | 19 | (7) | 5 |
| Rom Alyagon | 24.12.2002 | | (2) | |
| Eyal Chen | 14.03.2000 | 1 | (12) | 1 |
| Nehorai Ifrah | 07.05.2003 | | (5) | |
| Afik Katan | 30.08.2000 | | (3) | |
| Mohamed Khatib | 24.11.1995 | 15 | (5) | 3 |
| Stav Nachmani | 06.10.2002 | 6 | (7) | 2 |
| Liav Prada | 18.07.2002 | | (2) | |
| Berthe Souleymane (CIV) | 08.01.2004 | | (1) | |

## Hapoel Haifa Football Club

| Founded: | 24.04.1924 | |
|---|---|---|
| Stadium: | „Sammy Ofer" Stadium, Haifa (30,780) | |
| Trainer: | Nir Klinger | 25.05.1966 |
| [23.10.2022] | Ronny Levy | 14.11.1966 |

| Goalkeepers: | DOB | M | (s) | G |
|---|---|---|---|---|
| Ran Kadosch | 04.10.1985 | 1 | | |
| Ohad Levita | 17.02.1986 | 32 | | |
| **Defenders:** | DOB | M | (s) | G |
| Hatem Abd Elhamed | 18.03.1991 | 17 | (5) | 1 |
| Noam Ben Harush | 13.05.2005 | | (2) | |
| Oren Biton | 16.06.1994 | 8 | (4) | |
| Nisso Kapiloto | 01.10.1989 | 3 | (2) | |
| Dor Malul | 30.04.1989 | 21 | (6) | 1 |
| George Andrei Miron (ROU) | 28.05.1994 | 5 | | |
| Guy Mizrahi | 30.03.2001 | 19 | (4) | 1 |
| Denis Polyakov (BLR) | 17.04.1991 | 9 | (3) | |
| Konstantinos Sotiriou (CYP) | 21.06.1996 | 24 | (5) | 2 |
| Dino Štiglec (CRO) | 03.10.1990 | 9 | | |
| Loai Taha | 26.11.1989 | 16 | | |
| Dudu Twito | 06.02.1990 | 20 | (4) | 1 |
| **Midfielders:** | DOB | M | (s) | G |
| Gal Arel | 09.07.1989 | 11 | (12) | 2 |
| Tamir Glazer | 30.05.2000 | 12 | (5) | |

| Gidi Kanyuk | 11.02.1993 | 9 | (11) | 1 |
|---|---|---|---|---|
| *Leandro* Miguel Pereira *Silva* (POR) | 04.05.1994 | 3 | | |
| Hanan Maman | 28.08.1989 | 23 | (6) | 2 |
| Amit Meir | 07.01.2001 | 1 | (5) | |
| Nichita Moţpan (MDA) | 17.07.2001 | | (4) | |
| Eliel Peretz | 18.11.1996 | 16 | (7) | 2 |
| Liran Sardal | 02.07.1994 | 21 | (4) | 4 |
| Yarin Sardal | 13.02.2001 | | (1) | |
| Aleksandar Šćekić (MNE) | 12.12.1991 | 10 | (2) | 1 |
| Tomer Yosefi | 02.02.1999 | 6 | (4) | 2 |
| **Forwards:** | DOB | M | (s) | G |
| Carnejy Antoine (FRA) | 27.07.1991 | 4 | (7) | |
| Itay Bogani | 29.05.2001 | 10 | (10) | |
| Jubayer Bushnaq | 21.05.2003 | 1 | (5) | |
| Shoval Gozlan | 25.04.1994 | 4 | (8) | 2 |
| Mohammed Kamara (LBR) | 31.10.1997 | 17 | (7) | 5 |
| Arvydas Novikovas (LTU) | 18.12.1990 | | (6) | |
| Kwame Quee (SLE) | 07.09.1996 | 7 | (11) | |
| Alon Turgeman | 09.06.1991 | 24 | (7) | 7 |

## Hapoel Jerusalem Football Club

| Founded: | 1926 | |
|---|---|---|
| Stadium: | Teddy Stadium, Jerusalem (31,733) | |
| Trainer: | Ziv Arie | 22.01.1971 |

| Goalkeepers: | DOB | M | (s) | G |
|---|---|---|---|---|
| Adebayo Adeleye (NGA) | 17.05.2000 | 29 | | |
| Omer Kabilo | 04.06.2003 | 1 | | |
| Yehonatan Shabi | 24.12.1996 | 6 | | |
| **Defenders:** | DOB | M | (s) | G |
| Ondřej Bačo (CZE) | 25.03.1996 | 34 | | 3 |
| Amit Glazer | 30.05.2000 | 11 | (6) | |
| Yorai Maliach | 26.03.1998 | 1 | (8) | |
| Noam Malmud | 02.08.2002 | 24 | (1) | |
| Roy Revivo | 22.05.2003 | 12 | (4) | |
| Harel Shalom | 12.12.1997 | 25 | (9) | |
| Eloge Yao (CIV) | 20.01.1996 | 35 | | 1 |
| **Midfielders:** | DOB | M | (s) | G |
| Omer Agvadish | 30.12.2000 | 6 | (11) | |
| Tomer Altman | 08.02.1998 | 13 | (13) | 1 |
| Guy Badash | 24.05.1994 | 31 | (2) | 11 |
| Noaf Bazea | 16.11.2000 | 1 | (6) | |

| Golan Beni | 31.10.2000 | 1 | (11) | |
|---|---|---|---|---|
| Ofek Biton | 27.09.1989 | 31 | (4) | 7 |
| Cédric Franck Don (CIV) | 03.05.2004 | 10 | (21) | 5 |
| Awaka Eshata | 05.09.1999 | 18 | (13) | |
| Ayano Farada | 29.04.2002 | 7 | (3) | |
| Lior Kasa | 01.05.2005 | | (2) | |
| Goni Naor | 23.04.1999 | 17 | | 1 |
| Nadav Nidam | 11.04.2001 | 24 | (8) | 1 |
| Itay Zada | 01.11.2002 | 1 | (19) | |
| **Forwards:** | DOB | M | (s) | G |
| Jordan Rolly Botaka (COD) | 24.06.1993 | 29 | (5) | 3 |
| Dor Jan | 16.12.1994 | 3 | (3) | |
| Ahmad Ebraheim Salman | 22.03.2004 | | (4) | |
| William Togui (CIV) | 07.08.1996 | 25 | (5) | 3 |
| Yoav Tomer | 17.01.1998 | 1 | (11) | |
| Karem Zoabi | 03.05.2006 | | (4) | |

## Hapoel Ironi Kiryat Shmona Football Club

| | | | |
|---|---|---|---|
| Founded: | 2000 | | |
| Stadium: | Kiryat Shmona Municipal Stadium, Kiryat Shmona (5,300) | | |
| Trainer: | Menahem Koretski | 04.04.1974 | |
| [22.12.2022] | Nir Berkovich | 23.01.1983 | |
| [14.02.2023] | Slobodan Drapić | 28.02.1965 | |

| Goalkeepers: | DOB | M | (s) | G |
|---|---|---|---|---|
| Džiugas Bartkus (LTU) | 07.11.1989 | 30 | | |
| Assaf Tzur | 28.08.1998 | 3 | | |
| **Defenders:** | **DOB** | **M** | **(s)** | **G** |
| Itay Ben Shabat | 09.07.2000 | 26 | (3) | |
| Ofir Benbenishti | 08.08.2000 | 15 | (5) | |
| Noam Cohen | 06.01.1999 | 27 | (2) | |
| Shalev Desta | 07.08.2001 | | (1) | |
| Nir Drori | 25.12.2001 | 8 | (8) | |
| Ayed Habashi | 10.05.1995 | 31 | | 4 |
| Ziv Morgan | 19.01.2000 | 25 | (2) | |
| **Midfielders:** | **DOB** | **M** | **(s)** | **G** |
| Mohamad Abu Rumi | 01.03.2004 | | (2) | |
| Tamir Adi | 02.05.1993 | 4 | (6) | |
| Samuel Bar On | 03.03.1998 | 17 | (11) | |
| *Gian* dos Santos *Martins* (BRA) | 01.04.1993 | 11 | (4) | 1 |

| Roy Harrell | 02.12.2003 | 2 | (5) | 1 |
|---|---|---|---|---|
| Yoav Hofmayster | 25.12.2000 | 22 | (5) | |
| Roi Kehat | 12.05.1992 | 24 | (4) | 4 |
| Yadin Lugasi | 04.04.1999 | 9 | (21) | 2 |
| Timothy Muzie | 24.08.2001 | 10 | (20) | |
| Ariel Sheratzky | 24.09.2001 | 12 | (5) | |
| **Forwards:** | **DOB** | **M** | **(s)** | **G** |
| Ivan Bakhar (BLR) | 10.07.1998 | 4 | (10) | 2 |
| *Marlon* dos Santos Prazeres (BRA) | 29.04.1995 | 2 | (10) | |
| Joseph Essien Mbong (MLT) | 15.07.1997 | 10 | (5) | |
| Yair Mordechai | 01.09.2003 | | (1) | |
| Senin Sebai (CIV) | 18.12.1993 | 15 | (13) | 5 |
| Bilal Shaheen | 27.03.2003 | | (1) | |
| Muhamad Shaker | 14.11.1996 | 25 | (6) | 6 |
| Itamar Shviro | 17.06.1998 | 31 | (2) | 12 |

## Hapoel Tel Aviv Football Club

| | | | |
|---|---|---|---|
| Founded: | 1923 | | |
| Stadium: | Bloomfield Stadium, Tel Aviv (29,150) | | |
| Trainer: | Kobi Refua | 03.09.1974 | |
| [19.09.2022] | Slobodan Drapić (SRB) | 28.02.1965 | |
| [09.01.2023] | Haim Silvas | 21.11.1975 | |

| Goalkeepers: | DOB | M | (s) | G |
|---|---|---|---|---|
| Stefan Tone Marinović (NZL) | 07.10.1991 | 18 | | |
| Ido Sharon | 06.06.2002 | 1 | | |
| Emilijus Zubas (LTU) | 10.07.1990 | 14 | | |
| **Defenders:** | **DOB** | **M** | **(s)** | **G** |
| Leo Benbenisti | 01.07.2004 | 1 | | |
| Ben Bitton | 03.01.1991 | 22 | | |
| Antoine Conté (FRA) | 29.01.1994 | 12 | (4) | |
| Abou Dosso (CIV) | 26.03.1996 | 9 | | |
| Dor Elo | 26.09.1993 | 7 | (5) | |
| Adi Gotlieb | 16.08.1992 | 28 | | |
| Yahav Gurfinkel | 27.06.1998 | 28 | (1) | |
| Or Israelov | 02.09.2004 | 14 | (2) | 1 |
| Stav Lemkin | 02.04.2003 | 15 | (7) | |
| **Midfielders:** | **DOB** | **M** | **(s)** | **G** |
| Roy Alkokin | 07.04.2004 | | (1) | |
| Tal Archel | 10.06.2003 | 1 | | |
| Shlomi Azulay II | 30.03.1990 | 5 | (10) | |
| Ran Binyamin | 06.02.2004 | 4 | (9) | |
| Ariel Cohen | 12.08.2003 | 3 | (7) | |
| Yuval Cohen | 01.02.2005 | | (1) | |
| Dan Einbinder | 16.02.1989 | 28 | (2) | 4 |

| Hrvoje Ilić (CRO) | 14.04.1999 | 6 | (4) | 2 |
|---|---|---|---|---|
| El Yam Kanzapolsky | 22.12.2003 | 13 | (9) | 1 |
| David Keltjens | 11.06.1995 | 23 | | |
| *Pablo González* Juárez (ESP) | 12.05.1993 | 4 | (2) | 2 |
| Godfried Roemeratoe (CUW) | 19.08.1999 | 16 | (8) | |
| **Forwards:** | **DOB** | **M** | **(s)** | **G** |
| Ravve Assayag | 05.01.2001 | | (2) | |
| Aleksandar Boljević (MNE) | 12.12.1995 | 8 | (6) | |
| Sagi Genis | 10.01.2004 | | (2) | |
| Qays Ghanem | 31.12.1997 | 19 | (3) | 3 |
| Sabastian Hernandez | 16.01.2003 | | (1) | |
| Hisham Layous | 13.11.2000 | 19 | (3) | 2 |
| Shavit Mazal | 29.11.2001 | 5 | (8) | |
| Alen Ožbolt (SVN) | 24.06.1996 | 29 | | 11 |
| Liad Ramot | 22.04.2004 | | (3) | 1 |
| Sintayehu Sallalich | 20.06.1991 | 2 | (6) | |
| Omer Senior | 23.02.2003 | 4 | (19) | 1 |
| Yoav Tomer | 17.01.1998 | | (1) | |
| Raz Twizer | 09.04.1999 | 2 | (3) | 3 |
| Idan Vered | 25.05.1989 | 2 | (6) | |
| Niv Zrihan | 24.05.1994 | 1 | (16) | 2 |

## Maccabi Bnei Reineh Football Club

| | | | |
|---|---|---|---|
| Founded: | 2005 (re-founded 2016) | | |
| Stadium: | Green Stadium, Nof HaGalil (5,200) | | |
| Trainer: | Adham Hadiya | 12.02.1985 | |
| [08.09.2022] | Sharon Mimer | 06.09.1973 | |

| Goalkeepers: | DOB | M | (s) | G |
|---|---|---|---|---|
| Muhamad Abu Nil | 03.05.2001 | 4 | | |
| Arik Yanko | 21.12.1991 | 29 | | |
| **Defenders:** | **DOB** | **M** | **(s)** | **G** |
| Ali Abbas | 31.05.2001 | | (3) | |
| Dolev Azrual | 20.02.1998 | 9 | (5) | |
| Nir Bardea | 25.01.1996 | 21 | (5) | |
| Eyad Hutava | 20.11.1987 | 18 | (9) | |
| Abdallah Jaber (PLE) | 17.02.1993 | 10 | (2) | |
| Ashraf Rabah | 10.02.1994 | 14 | (11) | |
| Mamadu Samba Candé „Sambinha" (POR) | 23.09.1992 | 18 | (2) | |
| Lukas Spendlhofer (AUT) | 02.06.1993 | 31 | (1) | 2 |
| **Midfielders:** | **DOB** | **M** | **(s)** | **G** |
| Namir Agha | 13.01.1995 | | (9) | |
| Basel Amer | 01.11.1998 | | (1) | |
| Anicet Andrianantenaina Abel (MAD) | 13.03.1990 | 9 | (2) | |
| Shlomi Azulay | 18.10.1989 | 23 | (5) | 7 |

| Roslan Barsky | 03.01.1992 | 7 | (2) | |
|---|---|---|---|---|
| Richard Boateng (GHA) | 10.07.1992 | 28 | (3) | 5 |
| Yaniv Brik | 28.05.1995 | 14 | (17) | |
| Guy Hadida | 23.07.1995 | 8 | (1) | 1 |
| Loai Halaf | 08.08.2000 | 9 | (18) | 3 |
| Amit Meir | 07.01.2001 | 11 | (4) | 1 |
| Isaac Nortey (GHA) | 13.04.2000 | 7 | (7) | |
| Oleksandr Noyok (UKR) | 15.05.1992 | 11 | (2) | |
| **Forwards:** | **DOB** | **M** | **(s)** | **G** |
| Ahmed Abed | 30.03.1990 | 15 | (9) | 2 |
| *Gustavo Marmentini* dos Santos (BRA) | 08.03.1994 | 8 | (4) | |
| Lazar Jovanović (SRB) | 13.07.1993 | 8 | (2) | |
| Osama Khalaila | 06.04.1998 | 12 | (12) | 1 |
| Márk Koszta (HUN) | 26.09.1996 | 12 | (1) | 8 |
| Mufalah Shalata | 03.07.2000 | 24 | (8) | |
| Amit Zenati | 02.04.1997 | 3 | (10) | 1 |

## Maccabi Haifa Football Club

| | Founded: | 1913 | | | |
|---|---|---|---|---|---|
| | Stadium: | "Sammy Ofer" Stadium, Haifa (30,780) | | | |
| | Trainer: | Barak Bakhar | | 21.09.1979 | |

| Goalkeepers: | DOB | M | (s) | G |
|---|---|---|---|---|
| Joshua Cohen (USA) | 18.08.1992 | 27 | | |
| Roei Mashpati | 23.11.1992 | 9 | | |
| **Defenders:** | **DOB** | **M** | **(s)** | **G** |
| Ofri Arad | 11.09.1998 | 3 | (1) | |
| Dylan Batubinsika (FRA) | 15.02.1996 | 20 | (5) | 2 |
| Pierre Cornud (FRA) | 12.12.1996 | 23 | (4) | |
| Yinon Eliyahu | 01.11.1993 | 3 | | |
| Rami Gershon | 12.08.1988 | 5 | (10) | 1 |
| Shon Goldberg | 13.06.1995 | 28 | | 1 |
| Raz Meir | 30.11.1996 | 9 | (6) | |
| Sun Menachem | 07.09.1993 | 7 | (7) | |
| Abdoulaye Seck (SEN) | 04.06.1992 | 26 | (2) | 3 |
| Daniel Andreas Sundgren (SWE) | 22.11.1990 | 20 | (4) | |
| **Midfielders:** | **DOB** | **M** | **(s)** | **G** |
| Mohammad Abu Fani | 27.04.1998 | 27 | (6) | 4 |

| | DOB | M | (s) | G |
|---|---|---|---|---|
| Omer Atzili | 27.07.1993 | 31 | (4) | 21 |
| Dolev Haziza | 05.07.1995 | 20 | (6) | 2 |
| Mahmoud Jaber | 05.10.1999 | 4 | (11) | |
| Neta Lavi | 25.08.1996 | 14 | (3) | |
| Maor Levi | 18.06.2000 | 3 | (3) | |
| Ali Mohamed Muhammad El Fazaz (NIG) | 07.10.1995 | 19 | (12) | |
| Goni Naor | 23.04.1999 | 1 | (8) | |
| Basam Zaarura | 13.11.2002 | | (1) | |
| **Forwards:** | **DOB** | **M** | **(s)** | **G** |
| Tjaronn Chery (SUR) | 04.06.1988 | 27 | (6) | 10 |
| Dean David | 14.03.1996 | 23 | (13) | 10 |
| Frantzdy Pierrot (HAI) | 29.03.1995 | 23 | (12) | 9 |
| Nikita Rukavytsya (AUS) | 22.06.1987 | 5 | (14) | 1 |
| Dia Saba | 18.11.1992 | 14 | (2) | 6 |
| Ben Sahar | 10.08.1989 | | (1) | |
| Mavis Tchibota Dufounou (CGO) | 07.05.1996 | 5 | (20) | |

## Maccabi Netanya Football Club

| | Founded: | 1934 | | |
|---|---|---|---|---|
| | Stadium: | Netanya Stadium, Netanya (13,610) | | |
| | Trainer: | Benyamin Lamm | 09.04.1959 | |
| | [07.11.2022] | Ran Kojok | 12.01.1981 | |

| Goalkeepers: | DOB | M | (s) | G |
|---|---|---|---|---|
| Raz Karmi | 27.01.1996 | 3 | (1) | |
| Itamar Nitzan | 23.06.1987 | 32 | | |
| Tomer Zarfati | 16.10.2003 | 1 | | |
| **Defenders:** | **DOB** | **M** | **(s)** | **G** |
| Plamen Galabov (BUL) | 02.11.1995 | 29 | (2) | |
| Florian Hartherz (GER) | 29.05.1993 | 8 | | |
| Karem Jaber | 31.10.2000 | 15 | (15) | |
| Rotem Keller | 09.11.2002 | 1 | (3) | |
| Denis Kolikov | 24.08.2004 | 2 | | |
| Shay Konstantini | 27.06.1996 | 17 | (5) | |
| Yuval Sade | 10.05.2000 | 10 | (7) | |
| Raz Shlomo | 13.08.1999 | 30 | | |
| Ido Vaier | 10.10.1996 | 11 | (7) | |
| **Midfielders:** | **DOB** | **M** | **(s)** | **G** |
| Yuval Ashkenazi | 13.02.1992 | 1 | (5) | |
| Aviv Avraham | 30.03.1996 | 18 | (10) | 1 |
| Ethane Azulay | 26.05.2002 | 16 | (11) | |
| Naftali Belay | 28.03.1997 | 6 | (11) | |

| | DOB | M | (s) | G |
|---|---|---|---|---|
| Oz Bilu | 16.01.2001 | 8 | (8) | |
| Boris Enow Takang (CMR) | 30.03.2000 | 27 | (4) | |
| Omri Gandelman | 16.05.2000 | 23 | (5) | 6 |
| Eden Karzev | 11.04.2000 | 17 | | 2 |
| Moshe Mula | 29.02.2000 | 1 | (1) | |
| Michael Ohana | 04.10.1995 | 2 | (8) | |
| Nassim Ouammou (FRA) | 27.04.1993 | 12 | (3) | |
| Liran Rotman | 07.06.1996 | 20 | (9) | 7 |
| **Forwards:** | **DOB** | **M** | **(s)** | **G** |
| Erich Berko (GER) | 06.09.1994 | 3 | (3) | |
| Amir Berkovits | 03.06.2000 | 7 | (12) | 1 |
| Stanislav Bilenkiy (UKR) | 22.08.1998 | 8 | (5) | 2 |
| Osher Eliyahu | 15.01.2003 | 2 | (4) | 1 |
| Gil Itzhak | 29.06.1993 | 5 | (9) | 1 |
| Roy Korine | 10.09.2002 | 4 | (8) | |
| Ahmad Salman | 22.03.2004 | 6 | (7) | |
| Patrick Twumasi (GHA) | 09.05.1994 | 21 | (4) | 7 |
| Igor Zlatanović (SRB) | 10.02.1998 | 30 | (4) | 15 |

## Maccabi Tel Aviv Football Club

| | Founded: | 1906 (*as HaRishon LeZion-Yaffo*) | | |
|---|---|---|---|---|
| | Stadium: | Bloomfield Stadium, Tel Aviv (29,150) | | |
| | Trainer: | Vladimir Ivić (SRB) | 07.05.1977 | |
| | [03.01.2023] | Aitor Karanka de la Hoz (ESP) | 18.09.1973 | |

| Goalkeepers: | DOB | M | (s) | G |
|---|---|---|---|---|
| Daniel Miller Tenenbaum | 19.04.1995 | 1 | | |
| Daniel Peretz | 10.07.2000 | 35 | | |
| **Defenders:** | **DOB** | **M** | **(s)** | **G** |
| Ofir Davidzada | 05.05.1991 | 28 | (2) | |
| André *Geraldes* de Barros (POR) | 02.05.1991 | 24 | (4) | 1 |
| Maor Kandil | 27.11.1993 | 13 | (5) | 1 |
| Derrick Luckassen (NED) | 03.07.1995 | 23 | (1) | |
| Idan Nachmias | 17.03.1997 | 1 | (1) | |
| Shahar Piven-Bachtiar | 21.09.1995 | 11 | (6) | |
| Enric *Saborit* Teixidor (ESP) | 27.04.1992 | 32 | | 3 |
| **Midfielders:** | **DOB** | **M** | **(s)** | **G** |
| Eylon Almog | 08.01.1999 | 1 | (4) | 2 |
| Dan Biton | 20.07.1995 | 8 | (7) | 1 |
| Nir Bitton | 30.10.1991 | 19 | (2) | 1 |
| Dan Glazer | 20.09.1996 | 23 | (3) | |
| Oscar Gloukh | 04.01.2004 | 14 | (3) | 4 |

| | DOB | M | (s) | G |
|---|---|---|---|---|
| Eyal Golasa | 07.10.1991 | 10 | (16) | 3 |
| Parfait Guiagon (CIV) | 22.02.2001 | 16 | (16) | 4 |
| Rareş Ilie (ROU) | 19.04.2003 | | (8) | |
| Gabriel Gilad Kanichowsky | 24.08.1997 | 25 | (9) | 5 |
| Anosh-Lin Nosh-Lin | 26.06.1905 | | (1) | |
| Dor Peretz | 17.05.1995 | 24 | (11) | 3 |
| Avi Rikan | 10.09.1988 | 6 | (15) | 1 |
| Joris van Overeem (NED) | 01.06.1994 | 1 | (8) | |
| Sheran Yeini | 08.12.1986 | 9 | (6) | 1 |
| **Forwards:** | **DOB** | **M** | **(s)** | **G** |
| Yonatan Cohen | 29.06.1996 | 5 | (9) | 1 |
| Matan Hozez | 12.08.1996 | 1 | (12) | |
| Đorđe Jovanović (SRB) | 15.02.1999 | 32 | (1) | 15 |
| Brandley Kuwas (CUW) | 19.09.1992 | | (1) | |
| Stipe Perica (CRO) | 07.07.1995 | 1 | | 2 |
| Dor Turgeman | 24.10.2003 | 1 | (10) | |
| Eran Zahavi | 25.07.1987 | 32 | | 20 |

<table>
<tr><td colspan="5">Sektzia Ness Ziona Football Club</td><td>Founded: 1955 (re-founded 2005)</td></tr>
</table>

## Sektzia Ness Ziona Football Club

| Founded: | 1955 (re-founded 2005) | |
|---|---|---|
| Stadium: | HaMoshava Stadium, Petah Tikva (11,500) | |
| Trainer: | Nir Berkovich | 23.01.1983 |
| [22.12.2022] | Ami Tayar | 20.03.1981 |
| [03.01.2023] | Shlomi Dora | 22.06.1973 |

| Goalkeepers: | DOB | M | (s) | G |
|---|---|---|---|---|
| Niv Antman | 02.08.1992 | 13 | | |
| Yossi Ginzburg | 11.10.1991 | 20 | | |
| **Defenders:** | **DOB** | **M** | **(s)** | **G** |
| Stephane Acka (CIV) | 11.10.1990 | 24 | (2) | 1 |
| Omri Ben Harush | 07.03.1990 | 15 | (1) | 1 |
| Stav Israeli | 11.12.1998 | 25 | (2) | |
| Nisso Kapiloto | 01.10.1989 | 12 | | |
| Or Rahih | 01.09.2003 | 1 | (1) | |
| Itay Rotman | 16.08.2002 | | (2) | |
| Michael Siroshtein | 25.04.1989 | 15 | (6) | |
| **Midfielders:** | **DOB** | **M** | **(s)** | **G** |
| Cristian Battocchio (ITA) | 10.02.1992 | 10 | (2) | |
| Or Inbrum | 12.01.1996 | | (5) | |
| Aboubakar Keita (CIV) | 05.11.1997 | 15 | (1) | |
| Dor Kochav | 06.05.1993 | 27 | (4) | |
| Ori Magbo | 12.09.1987 | 9 | (16) | |
| Ari Niejo | 01.12.2002 | | (1) | |
| Ben Binyamin Ozlavo | 01.03.2003 | | (2) | |

| | DOB | M | (s) | G |
|---|---|---|---|---|
| Yoan Stoyanov (BUL) | 22.05.2001 | 27 | | 5 |
| Amnon Tadela | 19.11.1997 | | (2) | |
| Sivan Talmi | 01.06.2003 | | (1) | |
| Ilay Trost | 31.03.1999 | 29 | (2) | 1 |
| Muhammed Usman Edu (NGA) | 02.03.1994 | 25 | (2) | 1 |
| Rotem Yatzkar | 14.08.2002 | | (1) | |
| Eylon Yerushalmi | 10.03.1997 | 6 | (3) | 1 |
| Kachal Yosef | 01.10.2002 | | (2) | |
| Ness Nissim Zamir | 31.10.1990 | 4 | (11) | |
| Liel Zana | 21.08.2000 | 2 | (14) | |
| **Forwards:** | **DOB** | **M** | **(s)** | **G** |
| *Ari Moura* Vieira Filho (BRA) | 31.07.1996 | 14 | (13) | 1 |
| Almog Buzaglo | 08.12.1992 | 27 | (3) | 8 |
| Bladimir Yovany Díaz Saavedra (COL) | 10.07.1992 | 2 | (2) | |
| Mor Fadida | 26.01.1997 | 5 | (7) | 1 |
| Levan Kutalia (GEO) | 19.07.1989 | 18 | (6) | 5 |
| Ange-Freddy Plumain (GLP) | 02.03.1995 | 12 | (4) | 1 |
| Or Roizman | 22.03.2002 | 6 | (22) | 4 |

## SECOND LEVEL
### Liga Leumit 2022/2023

### Regular Season

| | | | | | | | | | |
|---|---|---|---|---|---|---|---|---|---|
| 1. | Maccabi Petah Tikva FC | 30 | 19 | 4 | 7 | 57 | - | 30 | 61 |
| 2. | Hapoel Petah Tikva FC | 30 | 18 | 6 | 6 | 48 | - | 25 | 60 |
| 3. | Ironi Tiberias FC | 30 | 15 | 10 | 5 | 50 | - | 29 | 55 |
| 4. | Hapoel Umm al-Fahm FC | 30 | 14 | 9 | 7 | 37 | - | 21 | 51 |
| 5. | Hapoel Acre FC | 30 | 13 | 8 | 9 | 38 | - | 31 | 47 |
| 6. | Maccabi Jaffa FC | 30 | 13 | 5 | 12 | 42 | - | 42 | 44 |
| 7. | Hapoel Kfar Saba FC | 30 | 12 | 6 | 12 | 38 | - | 39 | 42 |
| 8. | Bnei Yehuda Tel Aviv FC | 30 | 11 | 8 | 11 | 43 | - | 39 | 41 |
| 9. | Hapoel Afula FC | 30 | 10 | 9 | 11 | 37 | - | 36 | 39 |
| 10. | Maccabi Ahi Nazareth FC | 30 | 10 | 6 | 14 | 30 | - | 42 | 36 |
| 11. | Hapoel Rishon LeZion FC | 30 | 9 | 8 | 13 | 33 | - | 38 | 35 |
| 12. | Hapoel Nir Ramat HaSharon FC | 30 | 9 | 8 | 13 | 29 | - | 35 | 35 |
| 13. | Hapoel Ramat Gan Givatayim FC | 30 | 8 | 10 | 12 | 30 | - | 40 | 34 |
| 14. | FC Kafr Qasim | 30 | 7 | 12 | 11 | 33 | - | 35 | 33 |
| 15. | Hapoel Nof HaGalil FC | 30 | 7 | 6 | 17 | 31 | - | 53 | 27 |
| 16. | Hapoel Ashdod FC* | 30 | 4 | 7 | 19 | 20 | - | 61 | 7 |

Teams ranked 1-8 were qualified for the Promotion Play-offs, while teams ranked 9-16 were qualified for the Relegation Play-offs.
*12 points deducted

### Promotion Play-offs

| | | | | | | | | | |
|---|---|---|---|---|---|---|---|---|---|
| 1. | Maccabi Petah Tikva FC (*Promoted*) | 37 | 23 | 6 | 8 | 73 | - | 34 | 75 |
| 2. | Hapoel Petah Tikva FC (*Promoted*) | 37 | 21 | 8 | 8 | 62 | - | 31 | 71 |
| 3. | Ironi Tiberias FC | 37 | 19 | 10 | 8 | 57 | - | 38 | 67 |
| 4. | Hapoel Umm al-Fahm FC | 37 | 17 | 9 | 11 | 44 | - | 32 | 60 |
| 5. | Hapoel Acre FC | 37 | 15 | 11 | 11 | 50 | - | 39 | 56 |
| 6. | Maccabi Jaffa FC | 37 | 15 | 7 | 15 | 47 | - | 50 | 52 |
| 7. | Hapoel Kfar Saba FC | 37 | 15 | 6 | 16 | 48 | - | 52 | 51 |
| 8. | Bnei Yehuda Tel Aviv FC | 37 | 13 | 9 | 15 | 51 | - | 59 | 48 |

### Relegation Play-offs

| | | | | | | | | | |
|---|---|---|---|---|---|---|---|---|---|
| 9. | Hapoel Ramat Gan Givatayim FC | 37 | 13 | 11 | 13 | 50 | - | 49 | 50 |
| 10. | Hapoel Afula FC | 37 | 12 | 10 | 15 | 49 | - | 51 | 46 |
| 11. | Hapoel Nir Ramat HaSharon FC | 37 | 12 | 10 | 15 | 45 | - | 47 | 46 |
| 12. | Hapoel Rishon LeZion FC | 37 | 11 | 11 | 15 | 45 | - | 48 | 44 |
| 13. | FC Kafr Qasim | 37 | 9 | 15 | 13 | 43 | - | 47 | 42 |
| 14. | Hapoel Nof HaGalil FC (*Relegation Play-off*) | 37 | 12 | 6 | 19 | 42 | - | 59 | 42 |
| 15. | Maccabi Ahi Nazareth FC (*Relegated*) | 37 | 11 | 9 | 17 | 37 | - | 55 | 42 |
| 16. | Hapoel Ashdod FC (*Relegated*) | 37 | 4 | 10 | 23 | 26 | - | 78 | 10 |

**Relegation Play-off**:  Hapoel Nof HaGalil FC – Hapoel Kfar Shalem FC        2-0(1-0)

Hapoel Nof HaGalil FC remains at Second Level for 2023/2024.

## INTERNATIONAL MATCHES
### (16.07.2022 – 15.07.2023)

| | | | | |
|---|---|---|---|---|
| 24.09.2022 | Tel Aviv | *Israel - Albania* | *2-1(0-0)* | (UNL) |
| 27.09.2022 | Attard | *Malta - Israel* | *2-1(0-1)* | (F) |
| 17.11.2022 | Petah Tikva | *Israel - Zambia* | *4-2(2-0)* | (F) |
| 20.11.2022 | Petah Tikva | *Israel - Cyprus* | *2-3(0-2)* | (F) |
| | | | | |
| 25.03.2023 | Tel Aviv | *Israel - Kosovo* | *1-1(0-1)* | (ECQ) |
| 28.03.2023 | Genève | *Switzerland - Israel* | *3-0(1-0)* | (ECQ) |
| 16.06.2023 | Budapest | *Belarus - Israel* | *1-2(1-0)* | (ECQ) |
| 19.06.2023 | Jerusalem | *Israel - Andorra* | *2-1(1-0)* | (ECQ) |

**24.09.2022    ISRAEL - ALBANIA**           **2-1(0-0)**           3rd UEFA Nations League B, Group 2
Bloomfield Stadium, Tel Aviv; Referee: Donatas Rumšas (Lithuania); Attendance: 29,200
**ISR:** Omri Glazer, Elazar Dasa (Cap), Miguel Ângelo Leonardo Vítor (87.Raz Shlomo), Sean Goldberg, Doron Leidner (73.Dan Leon Glazer), Eden Karzev (73.Denny Gropper), Neta Lavi, Gabriel Gilad Kanichowsky, Liel Abada (77.Omer Atzili), Dolev Haziza, Shon Zalman Weissman (86.Tai Baribo). Trainer: Alon Hazan.
**Goals:** Shon Zalman Weissman (46), Tai Baribo (90+1).

**27.09.2022    MALTA - ISRAEL**           **2-1(0-1)**           Friendly International
Ta' Qali National Stadium, Attard; Referee: Eldorjan Hamiti (Albania); Attendance: n/a
**ISR:** Ofir Meir Marciano (46.Yoav Pini Gerafi), Or Dadia (57.Elazar Dasa), Raz Shlomo, Maroun Gantous (74.Guy Badash), Denny Gropper, Bibras Natkho (Cap) (66.Shay Elias), Goni Naor, Omri Altman, Rotem Hatuel, Tai Baribo (57.Itamar Shviro), Shon Zalman Weissman (58.Guy Melamed). Trainer: Alon Hazan.
**Goal:** Bibras Natkho (32 penalty).

**17.11.2022    ISRAEL - ZAMBIA**           **4-2(2-0)**           Friendly International
HaMoshava Stadium, Petah Tikva; Referee: Arda Kardeşler (Turkey); Attendance: 5,243
**ISR:** Omri Glazer, Elazar Dasa (Cap), Miguel Ângelo Leonardo Vítor (59.Oscar Gloukh), Sean Goldberg (74.Dor Peretz), Doron Leidner (82.Itamar Shviro), Eden Karzev (74.Dan Leon Glazer), Neta Lavi (59.Raz Shlomo), Ramzi Safouri (74.Sagiv Yehezkel), Gabriel Gilad Kanichowsky, Dean David, Tai Baribo. Trainer: Alon Hazan.
**Goals:** Tai Baribo (21), Dean David (24), Rodrick Kabwe (89 own goal), Itamar Shviro (90+3).

**20.11.2022    ISRAEL - CYPRUS**           **2-3(0-2)**           Friendly International
HaMoshava Stadium, Petah Tikva; Referee: Arda Kardeşler (Turkey); Attendance: 7,352
**ISR:** Daniel Peretz, Elazar Dasa (46.Neta Lavi; 64.Ramzi Safouri), Raz Shlomo, Sean Goldberg (71.Liran Sardal), Doron Leidner (56.Maksim Grechkin), Dor Peretz, Bibras Natkho (Cap) (46.Tai Baribo), Oscar Gloukh, Sagiv Yehezkel, Omri Altman (46.Mohamad Kanaan), Itamar Shviro. Trainer: Alon Hazan.
**Goals:** Oscar Gloukh (66), Tai Baribo (67).

**25.03.2023    ISRAEL - KOSOVO**           **1-1(0-1)**           17th EC. Qualifiers
Bloomfield Stadium, Tel Aviv; Referee: William Sean Collum (Scotland); Attendance: 28,935
**ISR:** Omri Glazer, Elazar Dasa (Cap), Raz Shlomo, Miguel Ângelo Leonardo Vítor, Doron Leidner (88.Denny Gropper), Neta Lavi, Oscar Gloukh (79.Tai Baribo), Dor Peretz, Dolev Haziza (67.Mohamad Kanaan), Manor Solomon, Shon Zalman Weissman (88.Bibras Natkho). Trainer: Alon Hazan.
**Goal:** Dor Peretz (56).

**28.03.2023    SWITZERLAND - ISRAEL**           **3-0(1-0)**           17th EC. Qualifiers
Stade de Genève, Genève; Referee: Nikola Dabanović (Montenegro); Attendance: 14,819
**ISR:** Omri Glazer, Elazar Dasa (Cap), Raz Shlomo, Miguel Ângelo Leonardo Vítor, Doron Leidner, Neta Lavi, Dor Peretz (73.Gabriel Gilad Kanichowsky), Mahmoud Jaber (54.Oscar Gloukh), Dolev Haziza (53.Sagiv Yehezkel), Manor Solomon, Tai Baribo (63.Shon Zalman Weissman). Trainer: Alon Hazan.

**16.06.2023    BELARUS - ISRAEL**           **1-2(1-0)**           17th EC. Qualifiers
"Szusza Ferenc" Stadion, Budapest (Hungary); Referee: Jarred Gavan Gillett (Australia); Attendance: *played behind closed doors*
**ISR:** Omri Glazer, Elazar Dasa (Cap) (78.Sagiv Yehezkel), Raz Shlomo, Sean Goldberg, Ofir Davidzada, Dor Peretz (66.Gabriel Gilad Kanichowsky), Mohammad Abu Fani, Ramzi Safouri (57.Oscar Gloukh), Liel Abada (46.Dolev Haziza), Manor Solomon, Tai Baribo (46.Shon Zalman Weissman). Trainer: Alon Hazan.
**Goals:** Shon Zalman Weissman (85 penalty), Oscar Gloukh (90+2).

**19.06.2023    ISRAEL - ANDORRA**           **2-1(1-0)**           17th EC. Qualifiers
Teddy Stadium, Jerusalem; Referee: Dragomir Draganov (Bulgaria); Attendance: 13,300
**ISR:** Omri Glazer, Elazar Dasa (Cap), Raz Shlomo, Sean Goldberg, Roy Revivo, Neta Lavi, Gabriel Gilad Kanichowsky (75.Mohammad Abu Fani), Ramzi Safouri (57.Oscar Gloukh), Dolev Haziza (57.Sagiv Yehezkel), Manor Solomon, Shon Zalman Weissman (75.Tai Baribo). Trainer: Alon Hazan.
**Goals:** Raz Shlomo (42), Manor Solomon (61).

## NATIONAL TEAM PLAYERS
### (16.07.2022 – 15.07.2023)

| Name | DOB | Caps | Goals | Club |
|------|-----|------|-------|------|
| **Goalkeepers** | | | | |
| Yoav Pini GERAFI | 29.08.1993 | 1 | 0 | 2022: *FC Ashdod* |
| Omri GLAZER | 11.03.1996 | 7 | 0 | 2022/2023: *Hapoel Be'er Sheva FC* |
| Ofir Meir MARCIANO | 07.10.1989 | 40 | 0 | 2022/2023: *Feyenoord Rotterdam (NED)* |
| Daniel PERETZ | 10.07.2000 | 1 | 0 | 2022: *Maccabi Tel Aviv FC* |
| **Defenders** | | | | |
| Or DADIA | 12.07.1997 | 1 | 0 | 2022: *Hapoel Be'er Sheva FC* |
| Elazar DASA | 03.12.1992 | 56 | 0 | 2022/2023: *FK Dinamo Moskva (RUS)* |
| Ofir DAVIDZADA | 05.05.1991 | 17 | 0 | 2023: *Maccabi Tel Aviv FC* |
| Maroun GANTOUS | 15.06.1996 | 1 | 0 | 2022: *Bnei Sakhnin FC* |
| Sean GOLDBERG | 13.06.1995 | 10 | 0 | 2022/2023: *Maccabi Haifa FC* |
| Maksim GRECHKIN | 04.03.1996 | 1 | 0 | 2022: *Beitar Jerusalem FC* |
| Denny GROPPER | 16.03.1999 | 3 | 0 | 2022/2023: *PFC Ludogorets Razgrad (BUL)* |
| Eden KARZEV | 11.04.2000 | 5 | 0 | 2022: *Maccabi Netanya FC* |
| Doron LEIDNER | 26.04.2002 | 8 | 0 | 2022: *Olympiacos SFP Peiraiás (GRE)* |
| | | | | 19.01.2023-> *FK Austria Wien (AUT)* |
| MIGUEL Ângelo Leonardo VÍTOR | 30.06.1989 | 7 | 0 | 2022/2023: *Hapoel Be'er Sheva FC* |
| Roy REVIVO | 22.05.2003 | 1 | 0 | 2023: *Hapoel Jerusalem FC* |
| Raz SHLOMO | 13.08.1999 | 8 | 1 | 2022/2023: *Maccabi Netanya FC* |
| Sagiv YEHEZKEL | 21.03.1995 | 5 | 0 | 2022/2023: *Hapoel Be'er Sheva FC* |
| **Midfielders** | | | | |
| Mohammad ABU FANI | 27.04.1998 | 16 | 0 | 2023: *Maccabi Haifa FC* |
| Guy BADASH | 24.05.1994 | 1 | 0 | 2022: *Hapoel Jerusalem FC* |
| Shay ELIAS | 25.02.1999 | 1 | 0 | 2022: *Hapoel Be'er Sheva FC* |
| Dan Leon GLAZER | 20.09.1996 | 18 | 1 | 2022: *Maccabi Tel Aviv FC* |
| Oscar GLOUKH | 01.04.2004 | 6 | 2 | 2022: *Maccabi Tel Aviv FC* |
| | | | | 27.01.2023-> *FC Red Bull Salzburg (AUT)* |
| Rotem HATUEL | 12.04.1998 | 1 | 0 | 2022: *Hapoel Be'er Sheva FC* |
| Dolev HAZIZA | 05.07.1995 | 14 | 0 | 2022/2023: *Maccabi Haifa FC* |
| Mahmoud JABER | 05.10.1999 | 4 | 0 | 2023: *Maccabi Haifa FC* |
| Mohamad KANAAN | 14.01.2000 | 2 | 0 | 2022/2023: *FC Ashdod* |
| Gabriel Gilad KANICHOWSKY | 24.08.1997 | 7 | 0 | 2022/2023: *Maccabi Tel Aviv FC* |
| Neta LAVI | 26.08.1996 | 15 | 0 | 2022: *Maccabi Haifa FC* |
| | | | | 27.01.2023-> *Gamba Osaka (JPN)* |
| Goni NAOR | 23.04.1999 | 1 | 0 | 2022: *Hapoel Jerusalem FC* |
| Bibras NATKHO | 18.02.1988 | 88 | 4 | 2022/2023: *FK Partizan Beograd (SRB)* |
| Dor PERETZ | 17.05.1995 | 35 | 6 | 2022/2023: *Maccabi Tel Aviv FC* |
| Ramzi SAFOURI | 21.10.1995 | 8 | 0 | 2022/2023: *Hapoel Be'er Sheva FC* |
| Liran SARDAL | 02.07.1994 | 1 | 0 | 2022: *Hapoel Haifa FC* |
| **Forwards** | | | | |
| Liel ABADA | 03.10.2001 | 10 | 1 | 2022/2023: *Celtic FC Glasgow (SCO)* |
| Omri ALTMAN | 23.03.1994 | 2 | 0 | 2022: *AEK Larnaca FC (CYP)* |
| Omer ATZILI | 27.07.1993 | 6 | 0 | 2022: *Maccabi Haifa FC* |
| Tai BARIBO | 15.01.1998 | 11 | 3 | 2022/2023: *Wolfsberger AC (AUT)* |
| Dean DAVID | 14.03.1996 | 3 | 1 | 2022: *Maccabi Haifa FC* |
| Guy MELAMED | 21.12.1992 | 1 | 0 | 2022: *Bnei Sakhnin FC* |
| Itamar SHVIRO | 17.06.1998 | 3 | 1 | 2022: *Hapoel Ironi Kiryat Shmona FC* |
| Manor SOLOMON | 24.07.1999 | 35 | 7 | 2023: *Fulham FC London (ENG)* |
| Shon Zalman WEISSMAN | 14.02.1996 | 29 | 5 | 2022: *Real Valladolid CF (ESP)* |
| | | | | 31.01.2023-> *Granada CF (ESP)* |

| **Trainer** | | | |
|------|------|------|------|
| Alon HAZAN [from 08.07.2022] | 14.09.1967 | 12 M; 5 W; 3 D; 4 L; 21-21 | |
| | | Complete record as trainer of Israel: | |
| | | 13 M; 5 W; 3 D; 5 L; 21-23 (23.03.2016) & (from 08.07.2022) | |

# ITALY

## The Country:
Repubblica Italiana (Italian Republic)
Capital: Roma
Surface: 301,338 km²
Inhabitants: 60,317,116 [2020]
Time: UTC+1

## The FA:
Federazione Italiana Giuoco Calcio
Via Gregorio Allegri 14, CP 2450 00198, Roma
Tel: +39 06 84 912 553
Foundation date: 1898
Member of FIFA since: 1905
Member of UEFA since: 1954
Website: www.figc.it

## NATIONAL TEAM RECORDS

### RECORDS
| | | |
|---|---|---|
| **First international match:** | 15.05.1910, Milano: | Italy – France 6-2 |
| **Most international caps:** | Gianluigi Buffon | - 176 caps (1997-2018) |
| **Most international goals:** | Luigi Riva | - 35 goals / 42 caps (1965-1974) |

### UEFA EUROPEAN CHAMPIONSHIP
| | |
|---|---|
| 1960 | Did not enter |
| 1964 | Qualifiers |
| 1968 | **Final Tournament (Winners)** |
| 1972 | Qualifiers |
| 1976 | Qualifiers |
| 1980 | Final Tournament (4th Place) |
| 1984 | Qualifiers |
| 1988 | Final Tournament (Semi-Finals) |
| 1992 | Qualifiers |
| 1996 | Final Tournament (Group Stage) |
| 2000 | Final Tournament (Runners-up) |
| 2004 | Final Tournament (Group Stage) |
| 2008 | Final Tournament (Quarter-Finals) |
| 2012 | Final Tournament (Runners-up) |
| 2016 | Final Tournament (Quarter-Finals) |
| 2020 | **Final Tournament (Winners)** |

### FIFA WORLD CUP
| | |
|---|---|
| 1930 | Did not enter |
| 1934 | **Final Tournament (Winners)** |
| 1938 | **Final Tournament (Winners)** |
| 1950 | Final Tournament (Group Stage) |
| 1954 | Final Tournament (Group Stage) |
| 1958 | Qualifiers |
| 1962 | Final Tournament (Group Stage) |
| 1966 | Final Tournament (Group Stage) |
| 1970 | Final Tournament (Runners-up) |
| 1974 | Final Tournament (Group Stage) |
| 1978 | Final Tournament (4th Place) |
| 1982 | **Final Tournament (Winners)** |
| 1986 | Final Tournament (Second Round of 16) |
| 1990 | Final Tournament (3rd Place) |
| 1994 | Final Tournament (Runners-up) |
| 1998 | Final Tournament (Quarter-Finals) |
| 2002 | Final Tournament (Second Round of 16) |
| 2006 | **Final Tournament (Winners)** |
| 2010 | Final Tournament (Group Stage) |
| 2014 | Final Tournament (Group Stage) |
| 2018 | Qualifiers |
| 2022 | Qualifiers |

### OLYMPIC TOURNAMENTS
| | |
|---|---|
| 1908 | - |
| 1912 | Round 1 |
| 1920 | Quarter-Finals |
| 1924 | Quarter-Finals |
| 1928 | 3rd Place |
| 1936 | **Winners** |
| 1948 | Quarter-Finals |
| 1952 | Round 1 |
| 1956 | Did not enter |
| 1960 | 4th Place |
| 1964 | Qualifiers |
| 1968 | *Withdrew* |
| 1972 | Qualifiers |
| 1976 | Did not enter |
| 1980 | Group Stage |
| 1984 | 4th Place |
| 1988 | 4th Place |
| 1992 | Quarter-Finals |
| 1996 | Group Stage |
| 2000 | Quarter-Finals |
| 2004 | 3rd Place |
| 2008 | Quarter-Finals |
| 2012 | Qualifiers |
| 2016 | Qualifiers |
| 2020 | Qualifiers |

### UEFA NATIONS LEAGUE
| | |
|---|---|
| 2018/2019 | League A (Group Stage) |
| 2020/2021 | League A (Group Stage -> Final Tournament: 3rd Place) |
| 2022/2023 | League A (Group Stage -> Final Tournament: 3rd Place) |

### FIFA CONFEDERATIONS CUP 1992-2017
2009 (Group Stage), 2013 (3rd Place)

## ITALIAN CLUB HONOURS IN EUROPEAN CLUB COMPETITIONS:

| European Champion Clubs' Cup (1956-1992) / UEFA Champions League (1993-2023) | | |
|---|---|---|
| AC Milan | 7 | 1962/1963, 1968/1969, 1988/1989, 1989/1990, 1993/1994, 2002/2003, 2006/2007 |
| FC Internazionale Milano | 3 | 1963/1964, 1964/1965, 2009/2010 |
| Juventus FC Torino | 2 | 1984/1985, 1995/1996 |
| **Fairs Cup (1858-1971) / UEFA Cup (1972-2009) / UEFA Europa League (2010-2023)** | | |
| Juventus FC Torino | 3 | 1976/1977, 1989/1990, 1992/1993 |
| FC Internazionale Milano | 3 | 1990/1991, 1993/1994, 1997/1998 |
| AC Parma | 2 | 1994/1995, 1998/1999 |
| AS Roma | 1 | 1960/1961 |
| SSC Napoli | 1 | 1988/1989 |

| UEFA Europa Conference League (2021-2023) | | |
|---|---|---|
| AS Roma | 1 | 2021-2022 |

| UEFA Super Cup (1972-2022) | | |
|---|---|---|
| AC Milan | 5 | 1989, 1990, 1994, 2003, 2007 |
| Juventus FC Torino | 2 | 1984, 1996 |
| AC Parma | 1 | 1993 |
| SS Lazio Roma | 1 | 1999 |

| European Cup Winners' Cup 1961-1999* | | |
|---|---|---|
| AC Milan | 2 | 1967/1968, 1972/1973 |
| AC Fiorentina | 1 | 1960/1961 |
| Juventus FC Torino | 1 | 1983/1984 |
| UC Sampdoria Genova | 1 | 1989/1990 |
| AC Parma | 1 | 1992/1993 |

*defunct competition*

## NATIONAL COMPETITIONS
## TABLE OF HONOURS

| | CHAMPIONS | CUP WINNERS | BEST GOALSCORERS | |
|---|---|---|---|---|
| 1898 | Genoa CFC | - | - | |
| 1899 | Genoa CFC | - | - | |
| 1900 | Genoa CFC | - | - | |
| 1901 | AC Milan | - | - | |
| 1902 | Genoa CFC | - | - | |
| 1903 | Genoa CFC | - | - | |
| 1904 | Genoa CFC | - | - | |
| 1905 | Juventus FC Torino | - | - | |
| 1906 | AC Milan | - | - | |
| 1907 | AC Milan | - | - | |
| 1908 | FC Pro Vercelli | - | - | |
| 1909 | FC Pro Vercelli | - | - | |
| 1909/1910 | FC Internazionale Milano | - | - | |
| 1910/1911 | FC Pro Vercelli | - | - | |
| 1911/1912 | FC Pro Vercelli | - | - | |
| 1912/1913 | FC Pro Vercelli | - | - | |
| 1913/1914 | Casale FBC | - | - | |
| 1914/1915 | Genoa CFC | - | - | |
| 1915/1916 | *No competition* | - | - | |
| 1916/1917 | *No competition* | - | - | |
| 1917/1918 | *No competition* | - | - | |
| 1918/1919 | *No competition* | - | - | |
| 1919/1920 | FC Internazionale Milano | - | - | |
| 1920/1921 | FC Pro Vercelli | - | - | |
| 1921/1922 | USD Novese Novi Ligure (FIGC) FC Pro Vercelli (CCI) | FC Vado | - | |
| 1922/1923 | Genoa CFC | *No competition* | - | |
| 1923/1924 | Genoa CFC | *No competition* | Heinrich Schönfeld (AUT, FBC Torino) | 22 |
| 1924/1925 | Bologna SC | *No competition* | Mario Magnozzi (AS Livorno Calcio) | 19 |
| 1925/1926 | Juventus FC Torino | *No competition* | Ferenc Hirzer (HUN, Juventus FC Torino) | 35 |
| 1926/1927 | *Not awarded* | *No competition* | Anton Powolny (FC Internazionale Milano) | 22 |
| 1927/1928 | FBC Torino | *No competition* | Julio Libonatti (ARG, FBC Torino) | 35 |
| 1928/1929 | Bologna SC | *No competition* | Gino Rossetti (FBC Torino) | 36 |
| 1929/1930 | Ambrosiana-Inter Milano | *No competition* | Giuseppe Meazza (Ambrosiana-Inter Milano) | 31 |
| 1930/1931 | Juventus FC Torino | *No competition* | Rodolfo Volk (AS Roma) | 29 |
| 1931/1932 | Juventus FC Torino | *No competition* | Pedro Petrone Schiavione (URU, ACF Fiorentina) Angelo Schiavio (Bologna SC) | 25 |
| 1932/1933 | Juventus FC Torino | *No competition* | Felice Placido Borel (Juventus FC Torino) | 29 |
| 1933/1934 | Juventus FC Torino | *No competition* | Felice Placido Borel (Juventus FC Torino) | 31 |
| 1934/1935 | Juventus FC Torino | *No competition* | Enrico Guaita (ARG, AS Roma) | 31 |
| 1935/1936 | Bologna AGC | FBC Torino | Giuseppe Meazza (Ambrosiana-Inter Milano) | 25 |
| 1936/1937 | Bologna AGC | Genoa CFC | Silvio Piola (SS Lazio Roma) | 21 |
| 1937/1938 | Ambrosiana-Inter Milano | Juventus FC Torino | Giuseppe Meazza (Ambrosiana-Inter Milano) | 20 |
| 1938/1939 | Bologna AGC | FC Internazionale Milano | Aldo Boffi (AC Milan) Héctor Puricelli (URU, Bologna AGC) | 19 |
| 1939/1940 | Ambrosiana-Inter Milano | ACF Fiorentina | Aldo Boffi (AC Milan) | 24 |
| 1940/1941 | Bologna AGC | Venezia FBC | Héctor Puricelli (URU, Bologna AGC) | 22 |
| 1941/1942 | AS Roma | Juventus FC Torino | Aldo Boffi (AC Milan) | 22 |
| 1942/1943 | AC Torino | AC Torino | Silvio Piola (SS Lazio Roma) | 21 |
| 1944 | AC Spezia (*honorific title awarded in 2002*) | *No competition* | - | |
| 1944/1945 | *No competition* | *No competition* | - | |
| 1945/1946 | AC Torino | *No competition* | Guglielmo Gabetto (AC Torino) | 22 |
| 1946/1947 | AC Torino | *No competition* | Valentino Mazzola (AC Torino) | 29 |
| 1947/1948 | AC Torino | *No competition* | Giampiero Boniperti (Juventus FC Torino) | 27 |
| 1948/1949 | AC Torino | *No competition* | István Nyers (HUN, FC Internazionale Milano) | 26 |

| | | | | |
|---|---|---|---|---|
| 1949/1950 | Juventus FC Torino | *No competition* | Gunnar Nordahl (SWE, AC Milan) | 35 |
| 1950/1951 | AC Milan | *No competition* | Gunnar Nordahl (SWE, AC Milan) | 34 |
| 1951/1952 | Juventus FC Torino | *No competition* | John Hansen (DEN, Juventus FC Torino) | 30 |
| 1952/1953 | FC Internazionale Milano | *No competition* | Gunnar Nordahl (SWE, AC Milan) | 26 |
| 1953/1954 | FC Internazionale Milano | *No competition* | Gunnar Nordahl (SWE, AC Milan) | 23 |
| 1954/1955 | AC Milan | *No competition* | Gunnar Nordahl (SWE, AC Milan) | 26 |
| 1955/1956 | ACF Fiorentina | *No competition* | Gino Pivatelli (Bologna FC) | 29 |
| 1956/1957 | AC Milan | *No competition* | Dino da Costa (BRA, AS Roma) | 22 |
| 1957/1958 | Juventus FC Torino | SS Lazio Roma | William John Charles (WAL, Juventus FC Torino) | 28 |
| 1958/1959 | AC Milan | Juventus FC Torino | Antonio Valentin Angelillo (ARG, FC Internazionale Milano) | 33 |
| 1959/1960 | Juventus FC Torino | Juventus FC Torino | Enrique Omar Sivori (ARG, Juventus FC Torino) | 28 |
| 1960/1961 | Juventus FC Torino | ACF Fiorentina | Sergio Brighenti (UC Sampdoria Genova) | 27 |
| 1961/1962 | AC Milan | SSC Napoli | José João Altafini "Mazzola" (BRA, AC Milan) Aurelio Milani (ACF Fiorentina) | 22 |
| 1962/1963 | FC Internazionale Milano | Atalanta Bergamasca Calcio | Harald Nielsen (DEN, Bologna FC) Pedro Waldemar Manfredini (ARG, AS Roma) | 19 |
| 1963/1964 | Bologna FC | AS Roma | Harald Nielsen (DEN, Bologna FC) | 21 |
| 1964/1965 | FC Internazionale Milano | Juventus FC Torino | Alessandro Mazzola (FC Internazionale Milano) Alberto Orlando (ACF Fiorentina) | 17 |
| 1965/1966 | FC Internazionale Milano | ACF Fiorentina | Luis Vinicio (Lanerossi Vicenza) | 25 |
| 1966/1967 | Juventus FC Torino | AC Milan | Luigi Riva (US Cagliari) | 18 |
| 1967/1968 | AC Milan | AC Torino | Pierino Prati (AC Milan) | 15 |
| 1968/1969 | ACF Fiorentina | AS Roma | Luigi Riva (US Cagliari) | 21 |
| 1969/1970 | US Cagliari | Bologna FC | Luigi Riva (US Cagliari) | 21 |
| 1970/1971 | FC Internazionale Milano | AC Torino | Roberto Boninsegna (FC Internazionale Milano) | 24 |
| 1971/1972 | Juventus FC Torino | AC Milan | Roberto Boninsegna (FC Internazionale Milano) | 22 |
| 1972/1973 | Juventus FC Torino | AC Milan | Giuseppe Savoldi (Bologna FC) Paolino Pulici (AC Torino) Gianni Rivera (AC Milan) | 17 |
| 1973/1974 | SS Lazio Roma | Bologna FC | Giorgio Chinaglia (SS Lazio Roma) | 24 |
| 1974/1975 | Juventus FC Torino | ACF Fiorentina | Paolino Pulici (AC Torino) | 18 |
| 1975/1976 | AC Torino | SSC Napoli | Paolino Pulici (AC Torino) | 21 |
| 1976/1977 | Juventus FC Torino | AC Milan | Francesco Graziani (AC Torino) | 21 |
| 1977/1978 | Juventus FC Torino | FC Internazionale Milano | Paolo Rossi (Lanerossi Vicenza) | 24 |
| 1978/1979 | AC Milan | Juventus FC Torino | Bruno Giordano (SS Lazio Roma) | 19 |
| 1979/1980 | FC Internazionale Milano | AS Roma | Roberto Bettega (Juventus FC Torino) | 16 |
| 1980/1981 | Juventus FC Torino | AS Roma | Roberto Pruzzo (AS Roma) | 18 |
| 1981/1982 | Juventus FC Torino | FC Internazionale Milano | Roberto Pruzzo (AS Roma) | 15 |
| 1982/1983 | AS Roma | Juventus FC Torino | Michel Platini (FRA, Juventus FC Torino) | 16 |
| 1983/1984 | Juventus FC Torino | AS Roma | Michel Platini (FRA, Juventus FC Torino) | 20 |
| 1984/1985 | AC Hellas Verona | UC Sampdoria Genova | Michel Platini (FRA, Juventus FC Torino) | 18 |
| 1985/1986 | Juventus FC Torino | AS Roma | Roberto Pruzzo (AS Roma) | 19 |
| 1986/1987 | SSC Napoli | SSC Napoli | Pietro Paolo Virdis (AC Milan) | 17 |
| 1987/1988 | AC Milan | UC Sampdoria Genova | Diego Armando Maradona (ARG, SSC Napoli) | 15 |
| 1988/1989 | FC Internazionale Milano | UC Sampdoria Genova | Aldo Serena (FC Internazionale Milano) | 22 |
| 1989/1990 | SSC Napoli | Juventus FC Torino | Marcel van Basten (NED, AC Milan) | 19 |
| 1990/1991 | UC Sampdoria Genova | AS Roma | Gianluca Vialli (UC Sampdoria Genova) | 19 |
| 1991/1992 | AC Milan | AC Parma | Marcel van Basten (NED, AC Milan) | 25 |
| 1992/1993 | AC Milan | Torino Calcio | Giuseppe Signori (SS Lazio Roma) | 26 |
| 1993/1994 | AC Milan | UC Sampdoria Genova | Giuseppe Signori (SS Lazio Roma) | 23 |
| 1994/1995 | Juventus FC Torino | Juventus FC Torino | Gabriel Omar Batistuta (ARG, ACF Fiorentina) | 26 |
| 1995/1996 | AC Milan | ACF Fiorentina | Igor Protti (AS Bari) Giuseppe Signori (SS Lazio Roma) | 24 |
| 1996/1997 | Juventus FC Torino | Vicenza Calcio | Filippo Inzaghi (Atalanta Bergamasca Calcio) | 24 |
| 1997/1998 | Juventus FC Torino | SS Lazio Roma | Oliver Bierhoff (GER, Udinese Calcio) | 27 |
| 1998/1999 | AC Milan | AC Parma | Márcio Amoroso dos Santos (BRA, Udinese Calcio) | 22 |
| 1999/2000 | SS Lazio Roma | SS Lazio Roma | Andriy Shevchenko (UKR, AC Milan) | 24 |
| 2000/2001 | AS Roma | ACF Fiorentina | Hernán Jorge Crespo (ARG, SS Lazio Roma) | 26 |
| 2001/2002 | Juventus FC Torino | AC Parma | David Sergio Trezeguet (FRA, Juventus FC Torino) Dario Hübner (Piacenza Calcio) | 24 |
| 2002/2003 | Juventus FC Torino | AC Milan | Christian Vieri (FC Internazionale Milano) | 24 |
| 2003/2004 | AC Milan | SS Lazio Roma | Andriy Shevchenko (UKR, AC Milan) | 24 |
| 2004/2005 | *Not awarded* | FC Internazionale Milano | Cristiano Lucarelli (AS Livorno Calcio) | 24 |
| 2005/2006 | FC Internazionale Milano | FC Internazionale Milano | Luca Toni (ACF Fiorentina) | 31 |
| 2006/2007 | FC Internazionale Milano | AS Roma | Francesco Totti (AS Roma) | 26 |
| 2007/2008 | FC Internazionale Milano | AS Roma | Alessandro Del Piero (Juventus FC Torino) | 21 |
| 2008/2009 | FC Internazionale Milano | SS Lazio Roma | Zlatan Ibrahimović (SWE, FC Internazionale Milano) | 25 |
| 2009/2010 | FC Internazionale Milano | FC Internazionale Milano | Antonio Di Natale (Udinese Calcio) | 29 |
| 2010/2011 | AC Milan | FC Internazionale Milano | Antonio Di Natale (Udinese Calcio) | 28 |
| 2011/2012 | Juventus FC Torino | SSC Napoli | Zlatan Ibrahimović (SWE, AC Milan) | 28 |
| 2012/2013 | Juventus FC Torino | SS Lazio Roma | Edinson Roberto Cavani Gómez (URU, SSC Napoli) | 29 |
| 2013/2014 | Juventus FC Torino | SSC Napoli | Ciro Immobile (Torino FC) | 22 |
| 2014/2015 | Juventus FC Torino | Juventus FC Torino | Mauro Emanuel Icardi (ARG, FC Internazionale Milano) Luca Toni (Hellas Verona FC) | 22 |
| 2015/2016 | Juventus FC Torino | Juventus FC Torino | Gonzalo Gerardo Higuaín (ARG, SSC Napoli) | 36 |
| 2016/2017 | Juventus FC Torino | Juventus FC Torino | Edin Džeko (BIH, AS Roma) | 29 |

| 2017/2018 | Juventus FC Torino | Juventus FC Torino | Mauro Emanuel Icardi (ARG, FC Internazionale Milano) Ciro Immobile (SS Lazio Roma) | 29 |
| 2018/2019 | Juventus FC Torino | SS Lazio Roma | Fabio Quagliarella (UC Sampdoria Genova) | 26 |
| 2019/2020 | Juventus FC Torino | SSC Napoli | Ciro Immobile (SS Lazio Roma) | 36 |
| 2020/2021 | FC Internazionale Milano | Juventus FC Torino | Cristiano Ronaldo dos Santos Aveiro (POR, Juventus FC Torino) | 29 |
| 2021/2022 | AC Milan | FC Internazionale Milano | Ciro Immobile (SS Lazio Roma) | 27 |
| 2022/2023 | SSC Napoli | FC Internazionale Milano | Victor James Osimhen (NGA, SSC Napoli) | 26 |

## NATIONAL CHAMPIONSHIP
### Serie A 2022/2023
#### (13.08.2022 – 04.06.2023)

### Results

**Round 1** [13-15.08.2022]
AC Milan - Udinese 4-2(2-2)
Sampdoria - Atalanta 0-2(0-1)
AC Monza - Torino FC 1-2(0-1)
US Lecce - Internazionale 1-2(0-1)
Fiorentina - Cremonese 3-2(2-1)
Lazio Roma - Bologna 2-1(0-1)
Spezia - Empoli 1-0(1-0)
US Salernitana - AS Roma 0-1(0-1)
Hellas Verona - SSC Napoli 2-5(1-2)
Juventus - US Sassuolo 3-0(2-0)

**Round 2** [20-22.08.2022]
Torino FC - Lazio Roma 0-0
Udinese - US Salernitana 0-0
Internazionale - Spezia 3-0(1-0)
US Sassuolo - US Lecce 1-0(1-0)
Empoli - Fiorentina 0-0
SSC Napoli - AC Monza 4-0(2-0)
Atalanta - AC Milan 1-1(1-0)
Bologna - Hellas Verona 1-1(1-1)
AS Roma - Cremonese 1-0(0-0)
Sampdoria - Juventus 0-0

**Round 3** [26-28.08.2022]
AC Monza - Udinese 1-2(1-1)
Lazio Roma - Internazionale 3-1(1-0)
Juventus - AS Roma 1-1(1-0)
Cremonese - Torino FC 1-2(0-1)
AC Milan - Bologna 2-0(1-0)
Spezia - US Sassuolo 2-2(2-1)
Hellas Verona - Atalanta 0-1(0-0)
US Salernitana - Sampdoria 4-0(2-0)
Fiorentina - SSC Napoli 0-0
US Lecce - Empoli 1-1(1-1)

**Round 4** [30.08.-01.09.2022]
US Sassuolo - AC Milan 0-0
AS Roma - AC Monza 3-0(2-0)
Internazionale - Cremonese 3-1(2-0)
Empoli - Hellas Verona 1-1(1-0)
Sampdoria - Lazio Roma 1-1(0-1)
Udinese - Fiorentina 1-0(1-0)
Juventus - Spezia 2-0(1-0)
SSC Napoli - US Lecce 1-1(1-1)
Atalanta - Torino FC 3-1(1-0)
Bologna - US Salernitana 1-1(0-0)

**Round 5** [03-05.09.2022]
Fiorentina - Juventus 1-1(1-1)
AC Milan - Internazionale 3-2(1-1)
Lazio Roma - SSC Napoli 1-2(1-1)
Cremonese - US Sassuolo 0-0
Spezia - Bologna 2-2(1-1)
Hellas Verona - Sampdoria 2-1(2-1)
Udinese - AS Roma 4-0(1-0)
AC Monza - Atalanta 0-2(0-0)
US Salernitana - Empoli 2-2(1-1)
Torino FC - US Lecce 1-0(1-0)

**Round 6** [10-12.09.2022]
SSC Napoli - Spezia 1-0(0-0)
Internazionale - Torino FC 1-0(0-0)
Sampdoria - AC Milan 1-2(0-1)
Atalanta - Cremonese 1-1(0-0)
Bologna - Fiorentina 2-1(0-0)
US Sassuolo - Udinese 1-3(1-0)
US Lecce - AC Monza 1-0(1-0)
Lazio Roma - Hellas Verona 2-0(0-0)
Juventus - US Salernitana 2-2(0-2)
Empoli - AS Roma 1-2(1-1)

**Round 7** [16-18.09.2022]
US Salernitana - US Lecce 1-2(0-1)
Bologna - Empoli 0-1(0-0)
Spezia - Sampdoria 2-1(1-1)
Torino FC - US Sassuolo 1-0(0-0)
Udinese - Internazionale 3-1(1-1)
Fiorentina - Hellas Verona 2-0(1-0)
AC Monza - Juventus 1-0(0-0)
Cremonese - Lazio Roma 0-4(0-3)
AS Roma - Atalanta 0-1(0-1)
AC Milan - SSC Napoli 1-2(0-0)

**Round 8** [01-03.10.2022]
SSC Napoli - Torino FC 3-1(3-1)
Internazionale - AS Roma 1-2(1-1)
Empoli - AC Milan 1-3(0-0)
Lazio Roma - Spezia 4-0(2-0)
Sampdoria - AC Monza 0-3(0-1)
US Sassuolo - US Salernitana 5-0(2-0)
US Lecce - Cremonese 1-1(1-1)
Atalanta - Fiorentina 1-0(0-0)
Juventus - Bologna 3-0(1-0)
Hellas Verona - Udinese 1-2(1-0)

**Round 9** [08-10.10.2022]
US Sassuolo - Internazionale 1-2(0-1)
AC Milan - Juventus 2-0(1-0)
Bologna - Sampdoria 1-1(1-0)
Torino FC - Empoli 1-1(0-0)
AC Monza - Spezia 2-0(1-0)
Udinese - Atalanta 2-2(0-1)
US Salernitana - Hellas Verona 2-1(1-0)
Cremonese - SSC Napoli 1-4(0-1)
AS Roma - US Lecce 2-1(1-1)
Fiorentina - Lazio Roma 0-4(0-2)

**Round 10** [15-17.10.2022]
Empoli - AC Monza 1-0(1-0)
Torino FC - Juventus 0-1(0-0)
Atalanta - US Sassuolo 2-1(1-1)
Internazionale - US Salernitana 2-0(1-0)
Lazio Roma - Udinese 0-0
Spezia - Cremonese 2-2(2-1)
SSC Napoli - Bologna 3-2(1-1)
Hellas Verona - AC Milan 1-2(1-1)
Sampdoria - AS Roma 0-1(0-1)
US Lecce - Fiorentina 1-1(1-0)

**Round 11** [21-24.10.2022]
Juventus - Empoli 4-0(1-0)
US Salernitana - Spezia 1-0(0-0)
AC Milan - AC Monza 4-1(2-0)
Fiorentina - Internazionale 3-4(1-2)
Udinese - Torino FC 1-2(1-1)
Bologna - US Lecce 2-0(2-0)
Atalanta - Lazio Roma 0-2(0-1)
AS Roma - SSC Napoli 0-1(0-0)
Cremonese - Sampdoria 0-1(0-0)
US Sassuolo - Hellas Verona 2-1(1-1)

**Round 12** [29-31.10.2022]
SSC Napoli - US Sassuolo 4-0(3-0)
US Lecce - Juventus 0-1(0-0)
Internazionale - Sampdoria 3-0(2-0)
Empoli - Atalanta 0-2(0-1)
Spezia - Fiorentina 1-2(1-1)
Cremonese - Udinese 0-0
Lazio Roma - US Salernitana 1-3(1-0)
Torino FC - AC Milan 2-1(2-0)
Hellas Verona - AS Roma 1-3(1-1)
AC Monza - Bologna 1-2(0-0)

**Round 13** [04-06.11.2022]
Udinese - US Lecce 1-1(0-1)
Empoli - US Sassuolo 1-0(0-0)
US Salernitana - Cremonese 2-2(2-1)
Atalanta - SSC Napoli 1-2(1-2)
AC Milan - Spezia 2-1(1-0)
Bologna - Torino FC 2-1(0-1)
Sampdoria - Fiorentina 0-2(0-1)
AC Monza - Hellas Verona 2-0(0-0)
AS Roma - Lazio Roma 0-1(0-1)
Juventus - Internazionale 2-0(0-0)

**Round 14** [08-10.11.2022]
Spezia - Udinese 1-1(1-1)
SSC Napoli - Empoli 2-0(0-0)
Cremonese - AC Milan 0-0
US Sassuolo - AS Roma 1-1(0-0)
US Lecce - Atalanta 2-1(2-1)
Fiorentina - US Salernitana 2-1(1-0)
Torino FC - Sampdoria 2-0(1-0)
Internazionale - Bologna 6-1(3-1)
Hellas Verona - Juventus 0-1(0-0)
Lazio Roma - AC Monza 1-0(0-0)

**Round 15** [11-13.11.2022]
Empoli - Cremonese 2-0(0-0)
SSC Napoli - Udinese 3-2(2-0)
Sampdoria - US Lecce 0-2(0-1)
Bologna - US Sassuolo 3-0(1-0)
Atalanta - Internazionale 2-3(1-1)
AS Roma - Torino FC 1-0(0-0)
Hellas Verona - Spezia 1-2(1-0)
AC Monza - US Salernitana 3-0(2-0)
AC Milan - Fiorentina 2-1(1-1)
Juventus - Lazio Roma 3-0(1-0)

## Round 16 [04.01.2023]
US Sassuolo - Sampdoria 1-2(0-2)
US Salernitana - AC Milan 1-2(0-2)
Torino FC - Hellas Verona 1-1(0-1)
Spezia - Atalanta 2-2(2-0)
AS Roma - Bologna 1-0(1-0)
US Lecce - Lazio Roma 2-1(0-1)
Fiorentina - AC Monza 1-1(1-0)
Cremonese - Juventus 0-1(0-0)
Internazionale - SSC Napoli 1-0(0-0)
Udinese - Empoli 1-1(0-1)

## Round 17 [07-09.01.2023]
Fiorentina - US Sassuolo 2-1(0-0)
Juventus - Udinese 1-0(0-0)
AC Monza - Internazionale 2-2(1-2)
US Salernitana - Torino FC 1-1(0-1)
Lazio Roma - Empoli 2-2(1-0)
Spezia - US Lecce 0-0
Sampdoria - SSC Napoli 0-2(0-1)
AC Milan - AS Roma 2-2(1-0)
Hellas Verona - Cremonese 2-0(2-0)
Bologna - Atalanta 1-2(1-0)

## Round 18 [13-16.01.2023]
SSC Napoli - Juventus 5-1(2-1)
Cremonese - AC Monza 2-3(0-2)
US Lecce - AC Milan 2-2(2-0)
Internazionale - Hellas Verona 1-0(1-0)
US Sassuolo - Lazio Roma 0-2(0-1)
Torino FC - Spezia 0-1(0-1)
Udinese - Bologna 1-2(1-0)
Atalanta - US Salernitana 8-2(5-1)
AS Roma - Fiorentina 2-0(1-0)
Empoli - Sampdoria 1-0(0-0)

## Round 19 [21-24.01.2023]
Hellas Verona - US Lecce 2-0(1-0)
US Salernitana - SSC Napoli 0-2(0-1)
Fiorentina - Torino FC 0-1(0-1)
Sampdoria - Udinese 0-1(0-0)
AC Monza - US Sassuolo 1-1(0-1)
Spezia - AS Roma 0-2(0-1)
Juventus - Atalanta 3-3(2-1)
Bologna - Cremonese 1-1(0-0)
Internazionale - Empoli 0-1(0-0)
Lazio Roma - AC Milan 4-0(2-0)

## Round 20 [27-30.01.2023]
Bologna - Spezia 2-0(1-0)
US Lecce - US Salernitana 1-2(1-2)
Empoli - Torino FC 2-2(1-0)
Cremonese - Internazionale 1-2(1-1)
Atalanta - Sampdoria 2-0(1-0)
AC Milan - US Sassuolo 2-5(1-3)
Juventus - AC Monza 0-2(0-2)
Lazio Roma - Fiorentina 1-1(0-0)
SSC Napoli - AS Roma 2-1(1-0)
Udinese - Hellas Verona 1-1(1-1)

## Round 21 [04-07.02.2023]
Cremonese - US Lecce 0-2(0-0)
AS Roma - Empoli 2-0(2-0)
US Sassuolo - Atalanta 1-0(0-0)
Spezia - SSC Napoli 0-3(0-0)
Torino FC - Udinese 1-0(0-0)
Fiorentina - Bologna 1-2(1-1)
Internazionale - AC Milan 1-0(1-0)
Hellas Verona - Lazio Roma 1-1(0-1)
AC Monza - Sampdoria 2-2(1-1)
US Salernitana - Juventus 0-3(0-2)

## Round 22 [10-13.02.2023]
AC Milan - Torino FC 1-0(0-0)
Empoli - Spezia 2-2(0-2)
US Lecce - AS Roma 1-1(1-1)
Lazio Roma - Atalanta 0-2(0-1)
Udinese - US Sassuolo 2-2(2-2)
Bologna - AC Monza 0-1(0-1)
Juventus - Fiorentina 1-0(1-0)
SSC Napoli - Cremonese 3-0(1-0)
Hellas Verona - US Salernitana 1-0(1-0)
Sampdoria - Internazionale 0-0

## Round 23 [17-20.02.2023]
US Sassuolo - SSC Napoli 0-2(0-2)
Sampdoria - Bologna 1-2(0-1)
AC Monza - AC Milan 0-1(0-1)
Internazionale - Udinese 3-1(1-1)
Atalanta - US Lecce 1-2(0-1)
Fiorentina - Empoli 1-1(0-1)
US Salernitana - Lazio Roma 0-2(0-0)
Spezia - Juventus 0-2(0-1)
AS Roma - Hellas Verona 1-0(1-0)
Torino FC - Cremonese 2-2(1-0)

## Round 24 [25-28.02.2023]
Empoli - SSC Napoli 0-2(0-2)
US Lecce - US Sassuolo 0-1(0-0)
Bologna - Internazionale 1-0(0-0)
US Salernitana - AC Monza 3-0(0-0)
Udinese - Spezia 2-2(1-1)
AC Milan - Atalanta 2-0(1-0)
Hellas Verona - Fiorentina 0-3(0-2)
Lazio Roma - Sampdoria 1-0(0-0)
Cremonese - AS Roma 2-1(1-0)
Juventus - Torino FC 4-2(2-2)

## Round 25 [03-06.03.2023]
SSC Napoli - Lazio Roma 0-1(0-0)
AC Monza - Empoli 2-1(1-0)
Atalanta - Udinese 0-0
Fiorentina - AC Milan 2-1(0-0)
Spezia - Hellas Verona 0-0
Sampdoria - US Salernitana 0-0
Internazionale - US Lecce 2-0(1-0)
AS Roma - Juventus 1-0(0-0)
US Sassuolo - Cremonese 3-2(2-0)
Torino FC - Bologna 1-0(1-0)

## Round 26 [10-13.03.2023]
Spezia - Internazionale 2-1(0-0)
Empoli - Udinese 0-2(0-0)
SSC Napoli - Atalanta 2-0(0-0)
Bologna - Lazio Roma 0-0
US Lecce - Torino FC 0-2(0-2)
Hellas Verona - AC Monza 1-1(0-0)
Cremonese - Fiorentina 0-2(0-1)
AS Roma - US Sassuolo 3-4(1-3)
Juventus - Sampdoria 4-2(2-2)
AC Milan - US Salernitana 1-1(1-0)

## Round 27 [17-19.03.2023]
US Sassuolo - Spezia 1-0(0-0)
Atalanta - Empoli 2-1(0-1)
AC Monza - Cremonese 1-1(0-0)
US Salernitana - Bologna 2-2(1-1)
Udinese - AC Milan 3-1(2-1)
Sampdoria - Hellas Verona 3-1(2-0)
Fiorentina - US Lecce 1-0(1-0)
Torino FC - SSC Napoli 0-4(0-2)
Lazio Roma - AS Roma 1-0(0-0)
Internazionale - Juventus 0-1(0-1)

## Round 28 [01-03.04.2023]
Cremonese - Atalanta 1-3(0-1)
Internazionale - Fiorentina 0-1(0-0)
Juventus - Hellas Verona 1-0(0-0)
Bologna - Udinese 3-0(2-0)
Spezia - US Salernitana 1-1(0-1)
AC Monza - Lazio Roma 0-2(0-1)
AS Roma - Sampdoria 3-0(0-0)
SSC Napoli - AC Milan 0-4(0-2)
Empoli - US Lecce 1-0(0-0)
US Sassuolo - Torino FC 1-1(1-0)

## Round 29 [07-08.04.2023]
US Salernitana - Internazionale 1-1(0-1)
US Lecce - SSC Napoli 1-2(0-1)
AC Milan - Empoli 0-0
Udinese - AC Monza 2-2(1-0)
Fiorentina - Spezia 1-1(1-1)
Atalanta - Bologna 0-2(0-0)
Sampdoria - Cremonese 2-3(1-1)
Torino FC - AS Roma 0-1(0-1)
Hellas Verona - US Sassuolo 2-1(0-1)
Lazio Roma - Juventus 2-1(1-1)

## Round 30 [14-17.04.2023]
Cremonese - Empoli 1-0(1-0)
Spezia - Lazio Roma 0-3(0-1)
Bologna - AC Milan 1-1(1-1)
SSC Napoli - Hellas Verona 0-0
Internazionale - AC Monza 0-1(0-0)
US Lecce - Sampdoria 1-1(0-0)
Torino FC - US Salernitana 1-1(0-1)
US Sassuolo - Juventus 1-0(0-0)
AS Roma - Udinese 3-0(1-0)
Fiorentina - Atalanta 1-1(0-1)

## Round 31 [21-24.04.2023]
Hellas Verona - Bologna 2-1(1-0)
US Salernitana - US Sassuolo 3-0(2-0)
Lazio Roma - Torino FC 0-1(0-1)
Sampdoria - Spezia 1-1(1-0)
Empoli - Internazionale 0-3(0-0)
AC Monza - Fiorentina 3-2(2-2)
Udinese - Cremonese 3-0(3-0)
AC Milan - US Lecce 2-0(1-0)
Juventus - SSC Napoli 0-1(0-0)
Atalanta - AS Roma 3-1(1-0)

## Round 32 [28-30.04.2023]
US Lecce - Udinese 1-0(0-0)
Spezia - AC Monza 0-2(0-1)
AS Roma - AC Milan 1-1(0-0)
Torino FC - Atalanta 1-2(0-1)
Internazionale - Lazio Roma 3-1(0-1)
US Sassuolo - Empoli 2-1(0-1)
SSC Napoli - US Salernitana 1-1(0-0)
Cremonese - Hellas Verona 1-1(1-0)
Fiorentina - Sampdoria 5-0(1-0)
Bologna - Juventus 1-1(1-0)

## Round 33 [03-04.05.2023]
Atalanta - Spezia 3-2(1-1)
Juventus - US Lecce 2-1(2-1)
Sampdoria - Torino FC 0-2(0-1)
US Salernitana - Fiorentina 3-3(1-1)
AC Milan - Cremonese 1-1(0-0)
Hellas Verona - Internazionale 0-6(0-3)
Lazio Roma - US Sassuolo 2-0(1-0)
AC Monza - AS Roma 1-1(1-1)
Empoli - Bologna 3-1(2-0)
Udinese - SSC Napoli 1-1(1-0)

| Round 34 [06-08.05.2023] |
|---|
| AC Milan - Lazio Roma 2-0(2-0) |
| AS Roma - Internazionale 0-2(0-1) |
| Cremonese - Spezia 2-0(1-0) |
| Atalanta - Juventus 0-2(0-0) |
| Torino FC - AC Monza 1-1(0-0) |
| SSC Napoli - Fiorentina 1-0(0-0) |
| US Lecce - Hellas Verona 0-1(0-0) |
| Empoli - US Salernitana 2-1(1-0) |
| Udinese - Sampdoria 2-0(2-0) |
| US Sassuolo - Bologna 1-1(1-1) |

| Round 35 [12-15.05.2023] |
|---|
| Lazio Roma - US Lecce 2-2(1-1) |
| US Salernitana - Atalanta 1-0(0-0) |
| Spezia - AC Milan 2-0(0-0) |
| Internazionale - US Sassuolo 4-2(1-0) |
| Hellas Verona - Torino FC 0-1(0-1) |
| Fiorentina - Udinese 2-0(1-0) |
| AC Monza - SSC Napoli 2-0(1-0) |
| Bologna - AS Roma 0-0 |
| Juventus - Cremonese 2-0(0-0) |
| Sampdoria - Empoli 1-1(1-0) |

| Round 36 [19-22.05.2023] |
|---|
| US Sassuolo - AC Monza 1-2(1-0) |
| Cremonese - Bologna 1-5(0-3) |
| Atalanta - Hellas Verona 3-1(1-1) |
| AC Milan - Sampdoria 5-1(3-1) |
| US Lecce - Spezia 0-0 |
| Torino FC - Fiorentina 1-1(0-0) |
| SSC Napoli - Internazionale 3-1(0-0) |
| Udinese - Lazio Roma 0-1(0-0) |
| AS Roma - US Salernitana 2-2(0-1) |
| Empoli - Juventus 4-1(2-0) |

| Round 37 [26-28.05.2023] |
|---|
| Sampdoria - US Sassuolo 2-2(1-2) |
| Spezia - Torino FC 0-4(0-1) |
| US Salernitana - Udinese 3-2(1-2) |
| Fiorentina - AS Roma 2-1(0-1) |
| Internazionale - Atalanta 3-2(2-1) |
| Hellas Verona - Empoli 1-1(0-0) |
| Bologna - SSC Napoli 2-2(0-1) |
| AC Monza - US Lecce 0-1(0-0) |
| Lazio Roma - Cremonese 3-2(2-0) |
| Juventus - AC Milan 0-1(0-1) |

| Round 38 [02-04.06.2023] |
|---|
| US Sassuolo - Fiorentina 1-3(1-3) |
| Torino FC - Internazionale 0-1(0-1) |
| Empoli - Lazio Roma 0-2(0-0) |
| Cremonese - US Salernitana 2-0(1-0) |
| SSC Napoli - Sampdoria 2-0(0-0) |
| AC Milan - Hellas Verona 3-1(1-0) |
| AS Roma - Spezia 2-1(1-1) |
| Atalanta - AC Monza 5-2(2-0) |
| Udinese - Juventus 0-1(0-0) |
| US Lecce - Bologna 2-3(1-0) |

## Final Standings

| | | | | | | Total | | | | Home | | | | | | Away | | | | |
|---|---|---|---|---|---|---|---|---|---|---|---|---|---|---|---|---|---|---|---|---|
| 1. | **SSC Napoli** | 38 | 28 | 6 | 4 | 77 - 28 | **90** | 14 | 3 | 2 | 40 - 15 | | 14 | 3 | 2 | 37 - 13 |
| 2. | SS Lazio Roma | 38 | 22 | 8 | 8 | 60 - 30 | **74** | 11 | 4 | 4 | 32 - 18 | | 11 | 4 | 4 | 28 - 12 |
| 3. | FC Internazionale Milano | 38 | 23 | 3 | 12 | 71 - 42 | **72** | 14 | 0 | 5 | 37 - 14 | | 9 | 3 | 7 | 34 - 28 |
| 4. | AC Milan | 38 | 20 | 10 | 8 | 64 - 43 | **70** | 13 | 4 | 2 | 41 - 20 | | 7 | 6 | 6 | 23 - 23 |
| 5. | Atalanta Bergamasca Calcio | 38 | 19 | 7 | 12 | 66 - 48 | **64** | 10 | 3 | 6 | 38 - 26 | | 9 | 4 | 6 | 28 - 22 |
| 6. | AS Roma | 38 | 18 | 9 | 11 | 50 - 38 | **63** | 11 | 3 | 5 | 28 - 15 | | 7 | 6 | 6 | 22 - 23 |
| 7. | Juventus FC Torino* | 38 | 22 | 6 | 10 | 56 - 33 | **62** | 13 | 3 | 3 | 38 - 15 | | 9 | 3 | 7 | 18 - 18 |
| 8. | ACF Fiorentina | 38 | 15 | 11 | 12 | 53 - 43 | **56** | 9 | 6 | 4 | 30 - 22 | | 6 | 5 | 8 | 23 - 21 |
| 9. | Bologna FC 1909 | 38 | 14 | 12 | 12 | 53 - 49 | **54** | 7 | 9 | 3 | 24 - 14 | | 7 | 3 | 9 | 29 - 35 |
| 10. | Torino FC | 38 | 14 | 11 | 13 | 42 - 41 | **53** | 5 | 7 | 7 | 15 - 19 | | 9 | 4 | 6 | 27 - 22 |
| 11. | AC Monza | 38 | 14 | 10 | 14 | 48 - 52 | **52** | 7 | 5 | 7 | 25 - 22 | | 7 | 5 | 7 | 23 - 30 |
| 12. | Udinese Calcio | 38 | 11 | 13 | 14 | 47 - 48 | **46** | 6 | 9 | 4 | 30 - 20 | | 5 | 4 | 10 | 17 - 28 |
| 13. | US Sassuolo Calcio | 38 | 12 | 9 | 17 | 47 - 61 | **45** | 8 | 4 | 7 | 24 - 23 | | 4 | 5 | 10 | 23 - 38 |
| 14. | Empoli FC | 38 | 10 | 13 | 15 | 37 - 49 | **43** | 8 | 4 | 7 | 22 - 23 | | 2 | 9 | 8 | 15 - 26 |
| 15. | US Salernitana 1919 | 38 | 9 | 15 | 14 | 48 - 62 | **42** | 7 | 6 | 6 | 30 - 26 | | 2 | 9 | 8 | 18 - 36 |
| 16. | US Lecce | 38 | 8 | 12 | 18 | 33 - 46 | **36** | 3 | 8 | 8 | 18 - 24 | | 5 | 4 | 10 | 15 - 22 |
| 17. | Hellas Verona FC (*Relegation tie-breaker*) | 38 | 7 | 10 | 21 | 31 - 59 | **31** | 6 | 3 | 10 | 20 - 32 | | 1 | 7 | 11 | 11 - 27 |
| 18. | Spezia Calcio La Spezia (*Relegation tie-breaker*) | 38 | 6 | 13 | 19 | 31 - 62 | **31** | 4 | 8 | 7 | 18 - 30 | | 2 | 5 | 12 | 13 - 32 |
| 19. | US Cremonese (*Relegated*) | 38 | 5 | 12 | 21 | 36 - 69 | **27** | 4 | 4 | 11 | 15 - 31 | | 1 | 8 | 10 | 21 - 38 |
| 20. | UC Sampdoria Genova (*Relegated*) | 38 | 3 | 10 | 25 | 24 - 71 | **19** | 1 | 7 | 11 | 12 - 28 | | 2 | 3 | 14 | 12 - 43 |

*please note: Juventus FC Torino was deducted 10 points as a punishment for capital gain violation.

As both Hellas Verona FC and Spezia Calcio La Spezia finished with 31 points, a one-match relegation was held on neutral place (Reggio Emilia):

| Tie-breaker [11.06.2023] | Hellas Verona FC - Spezia Calcio La Spezia | 3-1(3-1) |
|---|---|---|

Hellas Verona FC remains at first level, while Spezia Calcio La Spezia were relegated to Serie B.

| Top goalscorers: | |
|---|---|
| 26 **Victor James Osimhen (NGA)** | *SSC Napoli* |
| 21 Lautaro Javier Martínez (ARG) | *FC Internazionale Milano* |
| 16 Boulaye Dia (SEN) | *US Salernitana 1919* |
| 15 Rafael Alexandre da Conceição Leão (POR) | *AC Milan* |

# NATIONAL CUP
## Coppa Italia 2022/2023

### First Round [05-08.08.2022]

| | | | | |
|---|---|---|---|---|
| Cagliari Calcio - AC Perugia Calcio | 3-2(1-1) | Venezia FC - Ascoli Calcio 1898 FC | 2-3(0-1) |
| Udinese - Feralpisalò | 2-1(1-0) | Hellas Verona FC - SSC Bari | 1-4(1-2) |
| US Lecce - AS Cittadella | 2-3(0-0,1-1) | US Salernitana 1919 - Parma Calcio 1913 | 0-2(0-0) |
| UC Sampdoria Genova - Reggina 1914 | 1-0(0-0) | AC Monza - Frosinone Calcio | 3-2(2-0) |
| Pisa Sporting Club - Brescia Calcio | 1-4(1-1) | Genoa C&FC - Benevento Calcio | 3-2(2-1) |
| Spezia Calcio La Spezia - Calcio Como | 5-1(1-0) | Modena FC - US Sassuolo Calcio | 3-2(2-1) |
| Empoli - SPAL Ferrara | 1-2(0-0,1-1) | US Cremonese - Ternana Calcio | 3-2(2-0) |
| Torino FC - Palermo FC | 3-0(0-0) | Bologna FC 1909- Cosenza Calcio | 1-0(0-0) |

### Second Round [18-20.10.2022]

| | | | |
|---|---|---|---|
| Genoa C&FC - SPAL Ferrara | 1-0(1-0) | Udinese Calcio - AC Monza | 2-3(0-1) |
| Torino FC - AS Cittadella | 4-0(1-0) | US Cremonese - Modena FC | 4-2(0-0,2-2) |
| Spezia Calcio La Spezia - Brescia Calcio | 3-1(1-0) | UC Sampdoria Genova - Ascoli Calcio 1898 FC | 2-2 aet; 9-8 pen |
| Parma Calcio 1913 - SSC Bari | 1-0(1-0) | Bologna FC 1909- Cagliari Calcio | 1-0(0-0) |

### 1/8-Finals [10-12/17/19.01.2023]

| | | | |
|---|---|---|---|
| FC Internazionale Milano - Parma Calcio 1913 | 2-1(0-1,1-1) | SSC Napoli - US Cremonese | 2-2 aet; 4-5 pen |
| AC Milan - Torino FC | 0-1(0-0,0-0) | Atalanta Bergamasca Calcio - Spezia Calcio La Spezia | 5-2(3-2) |
| ACF Fiorentina - UC Sampdoria Genova | 1-0(1-0) | SS Lazio Roma - Bologna FC 1909 | 1-0(1-0) |
| AS Roma - Genoa C&FC | 1-0(0-0) | Juventus FC Torino - AC Monza | 2-1(1-1) |

### Quarter-Finals [31.01.-02.02.2023]

| | | | |
|---|---|---|---|
| FC Internazionale Milano - Atalanta Bergamasca Calcio | 1-0(0-0) | AS Roma - US Cremonese | 1-2(0-1) |
| ACF Fiorentina - Torino FC | 2-1(0-0) | Juventus FC Torino - SS Lazio Roma | 1-0(1-0) |

### Semi-Finals [04-05.04./26-27.04.2023]

| First Leg | | Second Leg | |
|---|---|---|---|
| Juventus FC Torino - FC Internazionale Milano | 1-1(0-0) | FC Internazionale Milano - Juventus FC Torino | 1-0(1-0) |
| US Cremonese - ACF Fiorentina | 0-2(0-1) | ACF Fiorentina - US Cremonese | 0-0 |

### Final

24.05.2023; Stadio Olimpico, Roma; Referee: Massimiliano Irrati; Attendance: 68,500
**ACF Fiorentina - FC Internazionale Milano**                                        **1-2(1-2)**

**Fiorentina**: Pietro Terracciano, Domilson Cordeiro dos Santos „Dodô" (82.Aleksa Terzić), Nikola Milenković, Lucas Martínez Quarta (70.Luca Ranieri), Cristiano Biraghi (Cap), Giacomo Bonaventura, Sofyan Amrabat (70.Luka Jović), Nanitamo Jonathan Ikoné (60.Riccardo Sottil), Gaetano Castrovilli (60.Rolando Mandragora), Nicolás Iván González, Arthur Mendonça Cabral. Trainer: Vincenzo Italiano.

**Internazionale**: Samir Handanovič (Cap), Matteo Darmian, Francesco Acerbi, Alessandro Bastoni (58.Stefan de Vrij), Denzel Justus Morris Dumfries, Nicolò Barella, Hakan Çalhanoğlu (83.Roberto Gagliardini), Marcelo Brozović, Federico Dimarco (68.Robin Gosens), Edin Džeko (58.Romelu Menama Lukaku Bolingoli), Lautaro Javier Martínez (83.Carlos Joaquín Correa). Trainer: Simone Inzaghi.

**Goals:** 1-0 Nicolás Iván González (3), 1-1 Lautaro Javier Martínez (29), 1-2 Lautaro Javier Martínez (37).


# THE CLUBS 2022/2023

## Atalanta Bergamasca Calcio

| | |
|---|---|
| **Founded**: | 17.10.1907 |
| **Stadium**: | Gewiss Stadium [Stadio Atleti Azzurri d'Italia], Bergamo (21,000) |
| **Trainer**: | Gian Piero Gasperini          26.01.1958 |

| Goalkeepers: | DOB | M | (s) | G |
|---|---|---|---|---|
| Juan Agustín Musso (ARG) | 06.05.1994 | 24 | | |
| Francesco Rossi | 27.04.1991 | | (1) | |
| Marco Sportiello | 10.05.1992 | 14 | (1) | |
| **Defenders:** | **DOB** | **M** | **(s)** | **G** |
| Merih Demiral (TUR) | 05.03.1998 | 14 | (14) | 1 |
| Berat Djimsiti (ALB) | 19.02.1993 | 20 | (4) | |
| Hans Hateboer (NED) | 09.01.1994 | 17 | | 1 |
| Joakim Mæhle Pedersen (DEN) | 20.05.1997 | 25 | (9) | 3 |
| Caleb Okoli | 13.07.2001 | 9 | (8) | |
| José Luis Palomino (ARG) | 05.01.1990 | 8 | (7) | 1 |
| Matteo Ruggeri | 11.07.2002 | 8 | (7) | |
| Giorgio Scalvini | 11.12.2003 | 29 | (3) | 2 |
| Brandon Soppy (FRA) | 21.02.2002 | 8 | (7) | |
| Rafael Tolói | 10.10.1990 | 32 | | 2 |
| Davide Zappacosta | 11.06.1992 | 18 | (3) | 4 |

| | DOB | M | (s) | G |
|---|---|---|---|---|
| Nadir Zortea | 19.06.1999 | 1 | (8) | 1 |
| **Midfielders:** | **DOB** | **M** | **(s)** | **G** |
| Marten Elco de Roon (NED) | 29.03.1991 | 34 | (1) | 3 |
| *Éderson* José dos Santos Lourenço da Silva (BRA) | 07.07.1999 | 25 | (10) | 1 |
| Teun Koopmeiners (NED) | 28.02.1998 | 32 | (1) | 10 |
| Ruslan Malinovskiy (UKR) | 04.05.1993 | 5 | (10) | 1 |
| Mario Pašalić (CRO) | 09.02.1995 | 24 | (8) | 5 |
| **Forwards:** | **DOB** | **M** | **(s)** | **G** |
| Jérémie Boga (CIV) | 03.01.1997 | 5 | (18) | 2 |
| Tommaso De Nipoti | 23.07.2003 | | (1) | |
| Rasmus Winther Højlund (DEN) | 04.02.2003 | 20 | (12) | 9 |
| Ademola Lookman Olajide Alade Ayola Lookman (NGA) | 20.10.1997 | 20 | (11) | 13 |
| Luis Fernando Muriel Fruito (COL) | 16.04.1991 | 10 | (19) | 3 |
| Lukáš Vorlický (CZE) | 18.01.2002 | | (3) | |
| Duván Esteban Zapata Banguero (COL) | 01.04.1991 | 16 | (9) | 2 |

## Bologna Football Club 1909

| | | |
|---|---|---|
| **Founded**: | 03.10.1909 | |
| **Stadium**: | Stadio "Renato Dall'Ara", Bologna (36,462) | |
| **Trainer**: | Siniša Mihajlović (SRB) (†16.12.2022) | 20.02.1969 |
| [07.09.2022] | Luca Vigiani | 25.08.1976 |
| [12.09.2022] | Thiago Motta Santon Olivares | 28.08.1982 |

| Goalkeepers: | DOB | M | (s) | G |
|---|---|---|---|---|
| Francesco Bardi | 18.01.1992 | 1 | | |
| Łukasz Skorupski (POL) | 05.05.1991 | 37 | | |
| **Defenders:** | **DOB** | **M** | **(s)** | **G** |
| Kevin Bonifazi | 19.05.1996 | 9 | (4) | |
| Andrea Cambiaso | 20.02.2000 | 25 | (7) | |
| Lorenzo De Silvestri | 23.05.1988 | 6 | (9) | 1 |
| Denso Kasius (NED) | 06.10.2002 | 4 | (3) | |
| Giorgos Kyriakopoulos (GRE) | 05.02.1996 | 8 | (4) | |
| Jhon Janer Lucumi Bonilla (COL) | 26.06.1998 | 33 | | |
| Charalampos Lykogiannis (GRE) | 22.10.1993 | 11 | (10) | 2 |
| Gary Alexis Medel Soto (CHI) | 03.08.1987 | 17 | (12) | |
| Stefan Posch (AUT) | 14.05.1997 | 30 | | 6 |
| Enzo Joaquín Sosa Romanuk (URU) | 10.01.2002 | 7 | (3) | |
| Adama Soumaoro (FRA) | 18.06.1992 | 22 | (1) | |
| **Midfielders:** | **DOB** | **M** | **(s)** | **G** |
| Michel Aebischer (SUI) | 06.01.1997 | 18 | (14) | 1 |
| Nicolás Martín Domínguez (ARG) | 28.06.1998 | 26 | (5) | 3 |
| Lewis Ferguson (SCO) | 24.08.1999 | 27 | (5) | 7 |
| Nikola Moro (CRO) | 12.03.1998 | 12 | (14) | 1 |
| Niklas Pyyhtiä (FIN) | 25.09.2003 | | (6) | |
| Jerdy Schouten (NED) | 12.01.1997 | 29 | (4) | |
| Roberto Soriano | 08.02.1991 | 15 | (12) | 1 |
| **Forwards:** | **DOB** | **M** | **(s)** | **G** |
| Marko Arnautović (AUT) | 19.04.1989 | 18 | (3) | 10 |
| Musa Barrow (GAM) | 14.11.1998 | 26 | (6) | 3 |
| Riccardo Orsolini | 24.01.1997 | 22 | (10) | 11 |
| Antonio Raimondo | 18.03.2004 | | (2) | |
| Nicola Sansone | 10.09.1991 | 8 | (10) | 4 |
| Emanuel Vignato | 24.08.2000 | 2 | (6) | |
| Joshua Orobosa Zirkzee (NED) | 22.05.2001 | 5 | (14) | 2 |

## Unione Sportiva Cremonense

| | | |
|---|---|---|
| **Founded**: | 24.03.1903 | |
| **Stadium**: | Stadio „Giovanni Zini", Cremona (16,003) | |
| **Trainer**: | Massimiliano Alvini | 20.04.1970 |
| [15.01.2023] | Davide Ballardini | 06.01.1964 |

| Goalkeepers: | DOB | M | (s) | G |
|---|---|---|---|---|
| Marco Carnesecchi | 01.07.2000 | 27 | | |
| Ionuţ Andrei Radu (ROU) | 28.05.1997 | 9 | | |
| Mouhamadou Sarr (SEN) | 05.01.1997 | 2 | | |
| **Defenders:** | **DOB** | **M** | **(s)** | **G** |
| Emanuel Aiwu (AUT) | 25.12.2000 | 17 | (6) | |
| Matteo Bianchetti | 17.03.1993 | 22 | (3) | 1 |
| Vlad Iulian Chircheş (ROU) | 14.11.1989 | 14 | (2) | |
| Alex Ferrari | 01.07.1994 | 13 | (3) | |
| Paolo Ghiglione | 02.02.1997 | 8 | (7) | 1 |
| Jack William Hendry (SCO) | 07.05.1995 | 2 | (2) | |
| Luka Lochoshvili (GEO) | 29.05.1998 | 22 | (3) | 1 |
| Giacomo Quagliata | 19.02.2000 | 6 | (14) | |
| Leonardo Sernicola | 30.07.1997 | 27 | (5) | 2 |
| Emanuele Valeri | 07.12.1998 | 31 | (6) | 2 |
| Johan Felipe Vásquez Ibarra (MEX) | 22.10.1998 | 19 | (6) | 1 |
| **Midfielders:** | **DOB** | **M** | **(s)** | **G** |
| Christian Acella | 07.07.2002 | | (1) | |
| Santiago Lionel Ascacíbar (ARG) | 25.02.1997 | 7 | (6) | |
| Marco Benassi | 08.09.1994 | 11 | (4) | |
| Michele Castagnetti | 27.12.1989 | 14 | (13) | |
| Gonzalo Escalante (ARG) | 27.03.1993 | 7 | (2) | |
| Pablo Ignacio Galdames Millán (CHI) | 30.12.1996 | 10 | (3) | 1 |
| Soualiho Meïté (FRA) | 17.03.1994 | 28 | (3) | |
| Tommaso Pantaleo Milanese | 31.07.2002 | | (2) | |
| Charles Pickel (SUI) | 15.05.1997 | 30 | (3) | 1 |
| **Forwards:** | **DOB** | **M** | **(s)** | **G** |
| Felix Afena-Gyan (GHA) | 19.01.2003 | 7 | (16) | |
| Jaime Báez Stábile (URU) | 25.04.1995 | 1 | (1) | |
| Alberto Basso Ricci | 29.06.2004 | | (1) | |
| Cristian Buonaiuto | 29.12.1992 | 7 | (22) | 1 |
| Daniel Ciofani | 31.07.1985 | 10 | (22) | 8 |
| Cyriel Kolawole Dessers (NGA) | 08.12.1994 | 19 | (7) | 6 |
| Samuel Di Carmine | 29.09.1988 | | (2) | |
| David Chidozie Okereke (NGA) | 29.08.1997 | 25 | (8) | 7 |
| Frank Tsadjout | 28.07.1999 | 14 | (6) | 3 |
| Luca Zanimacchia | 19.07.1998 | 9 | (6) | |

## Empoli Football Club

| | | |
|---|---|---|
| **Founded**: | 1920 | |
| **Stadium**: | Stadio „Carlo Castellani", Empoli (16,284) | |
| **Trainer**: | Paolo Zanetti | 16.12.1982 |

| Goalkeepers: | DOB | M | (s) | G |
|---|---|---|---|---|
| Samuele Perisan | 21.08.1997 | 7 | | |
| Samir Ujkani (KOS) | 05.07.1988 | | (1) | |
| Guglielmo Vicario | 07.10.1996 | 31 | | |
| **Defenders:** | **DOB** | **M** | **(s)** | **G** |
| Liberato Gianpaolo Cacace (NZL) | 27.09.2000 | 5 | (7) | |
| Koni De Winter (BEL) | 12.06.2002 | 12 | (2) | |
| Tyronne Efe Ebuehi (NGA) | 16.12.1995 | 22 | (4) | 2 |
| Ardian Ismajli (ALB) | 30.09.1996 | 22 | (3) | |
| Sebastiano Luperto | 06.09.1996 | 36 | | 2 |
| Fabiano Parisi | 09.11.2000 | 33 | | 2 |
| Petar Stojanović (SVN) | 07.10.1995 | 16 | (11) | |
| Lorenzo Tonelli | 17.01.1990 | | (1) | |
| Sebastian Walukiewicz (POL) | 05.04.2000 | 6 | (5) | |
| **Midfielders:** | **DOB** | **M** | **(s)** | **G** |
| Jean-Daniel Akpa-Akpro (CIV) | 11.10.1992 | 16 | (8) | 1 |
| Nedim Bajrami (ALB) | 28.02.1999 | 8 | (11) | 1 |
| Tommaso Baldanzi | 23.03.2003 | 24 | (2) | 4 |
| Filippo Bandinelli | 29.03.1995 | 28 | (7) | 2 |
| Duccio Degli Innocenti | 28.04.2003 | | (1) | |
| Jacopo Fazzini | 16.03.2003 | 8 | (13) | |
| Alberto Grassi | 07.03.1995 | 14 | (11) | |
| Nicolas Haas (SUI) | 23.01.1996 | 12 | (12) | 1 |
| Liam Henderson (SCO) | 25.04.1996 | 11 | (14) | |
| Răzvan Gabriel Marin (ROU) | 23.05.1996 | 28 | (5) | 2 |
| **Forwards:** | **DOB** | **M** | **(s)** | **G** |
| Nicolò Cambiaghi | 28.12.2000 | 12 | (16) | 6 |
| Francesco Caputo | 06.08.1987 | 20 | (1) | 5 |
| Mattia Destro | 20.03.1991 | 6 | (11) | 1 |
| Emmanuel Ekong (SWE) | 25.06.2002 | | (2) | |
| *Herculano* Bucancil Nabian (POR) | 25.01.2004 | | (1) | |
| Sam Adrianus Martinus Lammers (NED) | 30.04.1997 | 10 | (4) | 1 |
| Roberto Piccoli | 27.01.2001 | 6 | (7) | 2 |
| Marko Pjaca (CRO) | 06.05.1995 | 5 | (12) | |
| Martín Adrián Satriano Costa (URU) | 20.02.2001 | 20 | (11) | 2 |
| Emanuel Vignato | 24.08.2000 | | (5) | 1 |

## Associazione Calcio Fiorentina Firenze

| | | |
|---|---|---|
| **Founded**: | 29.08.1926 (re-founded 01.08.2002) | |
| **Stadium**: | Stadio "Artemio Franchi", Firenze (43,147) | |
| **Trainer**: | Vincenzo Italiano | 10.12.1977 |

| Goalkeepers: | DOB | M | (s) | G |
|---|---|---|---|---|
| Michele Cerofolini | 04.01.1999 | 5 | | |
| Pierluigi Gollini | 18.03.1995 | 3 | | |
| Salvatore Sirigu | 12.01.1987 | 1 | | |
| Pietro Terracciano | 08.03.1990 | 29 | | |
| **Defenders:** | **DOB** | **M** | **(s)** | **G** |
| Cristiano Biraghi | 01.09.1992 | 30 | (3) | 2 |
| Domilson Cordeiro dos Santos „Dodô" (BRA) | 17.11.1998 | 28 | (5) | 1 |
| Igor Julio dos Santos de Paulo (BRA) | 07.02.1998 | 23 | (4) | |
| Lucas Martínez Quarta (ARG) | 10.05.1996 | 25 | (2) | 1 |
| Nikola Milenković (SRB) | 12.10.1997 | 23 | (4) | 2 |
| Luca Ranieri | 23.04.1999 | 5 | (4) | |
| Aleksa Terzić (SRB) | 17.08.1999 | 8 | (14) | 1 |
| Lorenzo Venuti | 12.04.1995 | 9 | (8) | |
| **Midfielders:** | **DOB** | **M** | **(s)** | **G** |
| Sofyan Amrabat (MAR) | 21.08.1996 | 24 | (5) | |
| Antonín Barák (CZE) | 03.12.1994 | 21 | (9) | 2 |

| | DOB | M | (s) | G |
|---|---|---|---|---|
| Marco Benassi | 08.09.1994 | 1 | (1) | |
| Alessandro Bianco | 01.10.2002 | 2 | (5) | |
| Giacomo Bonaventura | 22.08.1989 | 21 | (9) | 5 |
| Gaetano Castrovilli | 17.02.1997 | 7 | (8) | 2 |
| Alfred Duncan (GHA) | 10.03.1993 | 13 | (12) | 1 |
| Youssef Maleh (MAR) | 22.08.1998 | 4 | (3) | |
| Rolando Mandragora | 29.06.1997 | 22 | (7) | 2 |
| Riccardo Saponara | 21.12.1991 | 14 | (15) | 4 |
| Szymon Piotr Żurkowski (POL) | 25.09.1997 | | (2) | |
| **Forwards:** | **DOB** | **M** | **(s)** | **G** |
| Arthur Mendonça Cabral (BRA) | 25.04.1998 | 15 | (13) | 8 |
| Josip Brekalo (CRO) | 23.06.1998 | 1 | (5) | |
| Nicolás Iván González (ARG) | 06.04.1998 | 13 | (11) | 6 |
| Nanitamo Jonathan Ikoné (FRA) | 02.05.1998 | 24 | (9) | 4 |
| Luka Jović (SRB) | 23.12.1997 | 16 | (15) | 6 |
| Christian Michael Kouamé Kouakou (CIV) | 06.12.1997 | 22 | (6) | 4 |
| Riccardo Sottil | 03.06.1999 | 9 | (9) | |

## Hellas Verona Football Club

| | | |
|---|---|---|
| **Founded**: | 1903 (as AC Hellas Verona; re-founded 1995) | |
| **Stadium**: | Stadio „Marcantonio Bentegodi", Verona (31,045) | |
| **Trainer**: | Gabriele Cioffi | 07.09.1975 |
| [13.10.2022] | Salvatore Bocchetti | 30.11.1986 |
| [04.12.2022] | Marco Zaffaroni | 20.01.1969 |

| Goalkeepers: | DOB | M | (s) | G |
|---|---|---|---|---|
| Lorenzo Montipò | 20.02.1996 | 37 | | |
| Simone Perilli | 07.01.1995 | 1 | | |
| **Defenders:** | **DOB** | **M** | **(s)** | **G** |
| Bruno Agustín Amione (ARG) | 03.01.2002 | 1 | | |
| Juan David Cabal Murillo (COL) | 08.01.2001 | 3 | (8) | |
| Federico Ceccherini | 11.05.1992 | 18 | (4) | 2 |
| Diego Coppola | 28.12.2003 | 11 | (8) | |
| Paweł Dawidowicz (POL) | 20.05.1995 | 20 | (3) | 1 |
| Fabio Depaoli | 24.04.1997 | 24 | (7) | 2 |
| Josh Thomas Doig (SCO) | 18.05.2002 | 15 | (7) | 2 |
| Davide Faraoni | 25.10.1991 | 19 | (4) | 2 |
| Koray Günter (GER) | 16.08.1994 | 11 | (2) | 1 |
| Isak Hien (SWE) | 13.01.1999 | 28 | (4) | |
| Giangiacomo Magnani | 04.10.1995 | 19 | (5) | |
| Panagiotis Retsos (GRE) | 09.08.1998 | 1 | (1) | |
| Deyovaisio Evan Zeefuik (NED) | 11.03.1998 | | (1) | |
| **Midfielders:** | **DOB** | **M** | **(s)** | **G** |
| Oliver Abildgaard Nielsen (DEN) | 10.06.1996 | 6 | (7) | |
| Antonín Barák (CZE) | 03.12.1994 | | (1) | |

| | DOB | M | (s) | G |
|---|---|---|---|---|
| Alessandro Cortinovis | 25.01.2001 | | (1) | |
| Ondrej Duda (SVK) | 05.12.1994 | 11 | (4) | |
| Martin Hongla Yma (CMR) | 16.03.1998 | 6 | (3) | |
| Ajdin Hrustić (AUS) | 05.07.1996 | 3 | (3) | |
| Ivan Ilić (SRB) | 17.03.2001 | 10 | (1) | |
| Darko Lazović (SRB) | 15.09.1990 | 27 | (3) | 4 |
| Miguel Luís Pinto Veloso (POR) | 11.05.1986 | 14 | (8) | |
| Ibrahim Sulemana (GHA) | 22.05.2003 | 6 | (10) | |
| Adrien Tamèze (FRA) | 04.02.1994 | 35 | (2) | |
| Filippo Terracciano | 08.02.2003 | 7 | (13) | |
| Simone Verdi | 12.07.1992 | 12 | (12) | 5 |
| **Forwards:** | **DOB** | **M** | **(s)** | **G** |
| Jayden Jezairo Braaf (NED) | 31.08.2002 | 2 | (4) | |
| Milan Đurić (BIH) | 22.05.1990 | 14 | (14) | 1 |
| Adolfo Julián Gaich (ARG) | 26.02.1999 | 8 | (8) | 2 |
| Thomas Michel David Henry (FRA) | 20.09.1994 | 13 | (3) | 2 |
| Yayah Kallon (SLE) | 30.06.2001 | 8 | (14) | 1 |
| Kevin Lasagna | 10.08.1992 | 17 | (9) | 1 |
| Cyril Ngonge (BEL) | 26.05.2000 | 9 | (5) | 3 |
| Roberto Piccoli | 27.01.2001 | 2 | (5) | |

## Football Club Internazionale Milano

| | | |
|---|---|---|
| **Founded**: | 09.03.1908 | |
| **Stadium**: | Stadio "Giuseppe Meazza", Milano (75,923) | |
| **Trainer**: | Simone Inzaghi | 05.04.1976 |

| Goalkeepers: | DOB | M | (s) | G |
|---|---|---|---|---|
| Alex Cordaz | 01.01.1983 | | (1) | |
| Samir Handanović (SVN) | 14.07.1984 | 14 | | |
| André Onana Onana (CMR) | 02.04.1996 | 24 | | |
| **Defenders:** | **DOB** | **M** | **(s)** | **G** |
| Francesco Acerbi | 10.02.1988 | 25 | (6) | |
| Alessandro Bastoni | 13.04.1999 | 26 | (3) | |
| Raoul Bellanova | 17.05.2000 | 3 | (15) | |
| Danilo D'Ambrosio | 09.09.1988 | 8 | (7) | |
| Matteo Darmian | 02.12.1989 | 24 | (7) | 1 |
| Stefan de Vrij (NED) | 05.02.1992 | 22 | (5) | 1 |
| Federico Dimarco | 10.11.1997 | 26 | (7) | 4 |
| Milan Škriniar (SVK) | 11.02.1995 | 20 | (1) | |
| Mattia Zanotti | 11.01.2003 | | (2) | |

| Midfielders: | DOB | M | (s) | G |
|---|---|---|---|---|
| Kristjan Asllani (ALB) | 09.03.2002 | 5 | (15) | |
| Nicolò Barella | 07.02.1997 | 31 | (4) | 6 |
| Marcelo Brozović (CRO) | 16.11.1992 | 19 | (9) | 3 |
| Hakan Çalhanoğlu (TUR) | 08.02.1994 | 28 | (5) | 3 |
| Valentin Carboni | 05.03.2005 | | (5) | |
| Denzel Justus Morris Dumfries (NED) | 18.04.1996 | 25 | (9) | 1 |
| Roberto Gagliardini | 07.04.1994 | 7 | (12) | |
| Robin Gosens (GER) | 05.07.1994 | 11 | (21) | 3 |
| Henrikh Mkhitaryan (ARM) | 21.01.1989 | 24 | (7) | 3 |
| **Forwards:** | **DOB** | **M** | **(s)** | **G** |
| Carlos Joaquín Correa (ARG) | 13.08.1994 | 12 | (14) | 3 |
| Edin Džeko (BIH) | 17.03.1986 | 18 | (15) | 9 |
| Romelu Menama Lukaku Bolingoli (BEL) | 13.05.1993 | 19 | (6) | 10 |
| Lautaro Javier Martínez (ARG) | 22.08.1997 | 27 | (11) | 21 |

## Juventus Football Club Torino

**Founded**: 01.11.1897
**Stadium**: Allianz Stadium, Torino (41,507)
**Trainer**: Massimiliano Allegri     11.08.1967

| Goalkeepers: | DOB | M | (s) | G |
|---|---|---|---|---|
| Mattia Perin | 10.11.1992 | 10 | (1) | |
| Wojciech Szczęsny (POL) | 18.04.1990 | 28 | | |
| **Defenders:** | **DOB** | **M** | **(s)** | **G** |
| Alex Sandro Lobo Silva (BRA) | 26.01.1991 | 21 | (4) | |
| Tommaso Barbieri | 26.08.2002 | 2 | (1) | |
| Leonardo Bonucci | 01.05.1987 | 9 | (7) | 1 |
| Gleison Bremer Silva Nascimento (BRA) | 18.03.1997 | 30 | | 4 |
| Danilo Luiz da Silva (BRA) | 15.07.1991 | 35 | (2) | 3 |
| Mattia De Sciglio | 20.10.1992 | 11 | (6) | |
| Federico Gatti | 24.06.1998 | 16 | (2) | |
| Daniele Rugani | 29.07.1994 | 6 | (3) | |
| **Midfielders:** | **DOB** | **M** | **(s)** | **G** |
| Enzo Alan Tomás Barrenechea (ARG) | 22.05.2001 | 3 | | |
| Juan Guillermo Cuadrado Bello (COL) | 26.05.1988 | 24 | (7) | 1 |
| Nicolò Fagioli | 12.02.2001 | 17 | (9) | 3 |
| Filip Kostić (SRB) | 01.11.1992 | 33 | (4) | 3 |

| | DOB | M | (s) | G |
|---|---|---|---|---|
| Manuel Locatelli | 08.01.1998 | 29 | (3) | |
| Weston James Earl McKennie (USA) | 28.08.1998 | 13 | (2) | 1 |
| Fabio Miretti | 03.08.2003 | 14 | (13) | |
| Leandro Daniel Paredes (ARG) | 29.06.1994 | 8 | (17) | 1 |
| Paul Labile Pogba (FRA) | 15.03.1993 | 1 | (5) | |
| Adrien Thibaut Marie Rabiot-Provost (FRA) | 03.04.1995 | 31 | (1) | 8 |
| Nicolò Rovella | 04.12.2001 | | (3) | |
| Denis Lemi Zakaria Lako Lado (SUI) | 20.11.1996 | 1 | (1) | |
| **Forwards:** | **DOB** | **M** | **(s)** | **G** |
| Federico Chiesa | 25.10.1997 | 6 | (15) | 2 |
| Ángel Fabián Di María (ARG) | 14.02.1988 | 15 | (11) | 4 |
| Samuel Iling Junior (ENG) | 04.10.2003 | 1 | (11) | 1 |
| Moise Bioty Kean | 28.02.2000 | 11 | (17) | 6 |
| Arkadiusz Milik (POL) | 28.02.1994 | 17 | (10) | 7 |
| Matías Soulé Malvano (ARG) | 15.04.2003 | 4 | (9) | 1 |
| Dušan Vlahović (SRB) | 28.01.2000 | 22 | (5) | 10 |

## Società Sportiva Lazio Roma

**Founded**: 09.01.1900
**Stadium**: Stadio Olimpico, Roma (70,634)
**Trainer**: Maurizio Sarri     10.01.1959

| Goalkeepers: | DOB | M | (s) | G |
|---|---|---|---|---|
| Luís Manuel Arantes Maximiano (POR) | 05.01.1999 | 1 | | |
| Ivan Provedel | 17.03.1994 | 37 | (1) | |
| **Defenders:** | **DOB** | **M** | **(s)** | **G** |
| Nicolò Casale | 14.02.1998 | 27 | (2) | 1 |
| Mario Gila Fuentes (ESP) | 29.08.2000 | | (4) | |
| Elseid Hysaj (ALB) | 02.02.1994 | 22 | (12) | 1 |
| Manuel Lazzari | 29.11.1993 | 22 | (6) | |
| Adam Marušić (MNE) | 17.10.1992 | 31 | (2) | |
| Patricio Gabarrón Gil „Patric" (ESP) | 17.04.1993 | 16 | (2) | |
| Luca Pellegrini | 07.03.1999 | 1 | (6) | |
| Stefan Daniel Radu (ROU) | 22.10.1986 | | (1) | |
| Alessio Romagnoli | 12.01.1995 | 33 | (1) | 2 |

| Midfielders: | DOB | M | (s) | G |
|---|---|---|---|---|
| Toma Bašić (CRO) | 25.11.1996 | 4 | (21) | 1 |
| Marco Bertini | 07.08.2002 | | (1) | |
| Danilo Cataldi | 06.08.1994 | 26 | (3) | |
| Luis Alberto Romero Alconchel (ESP) | 28.09.1992 | 27 | (8) | 6 |
| Marcos Antônio Silva Santos (BRA) | 13.06.2000 | 6 | (10) | 1 |
| Sergej Milinković-Savić (SRB) | 27.02.1995 | 34 | (2) | 9 |
| Matías Vecino Falero (URU) | 24.08.1991 | 17 | (15) | 2 |
| **Forwards:** | **DOB** | **M** | **(s)** | **G** |
| Matteo Cancellieri | 12.02.2002 | 1 | (19) | |
| Felipe Anderson Pereira Gomes (BRA) | 15.04.1993 | 35 | (3) | 9 |
| Ciro Immobile | 20.02.1990 | 27 | (4) | 12 |
| Pedro Eliezer Rodríguez Ledesma (ESP) | 28.07.1987 | 17 | (19) | 4 |
| Luka Romero Bezzana (ARG) | 18.11.2004 | 1 | (5) | 1 |
| Mattia Zaccagni | 16.06.1995 | 33 | (2) | 10 |

## Unione Sportiva Lecce

**Founded**: 15.03.1908
**Stadium**: Stadio „Ettore Giardiniero" – Via del mare, Lecce (31,533)
**Trainer**: Marco Baroni     11.09.1963

| Goalkeepers: | DOB | M | (s) | G |
|---|---|---|---|---|
| Wladimiro Falcone | 12.04.1995 | 38 | | |
| **Defenders:** | **DOB** | **M** | **(s)** | **G** |
| Federico Baschirotto | 20.09.1996 | 37 | | 3 |
| Tommaso Cassandro | 09.01.2000 | | (1) | |
| Pietro Ceccaroni | 21.12.1995 | | (2) | |
| Yıldırım Mert Çetin (TUR) | 01.01.1997 | 1 | | |
| Kastriot Dermaku (KOS) | 15.01.1992 | | (1) | |
| Antonino Gallo | 05.01.2000 | 28 | (4) | |
| Valentin André Stanislas Gendrey (FRA) | 21.06.2000 | 35 | (2) | |
| Giuseppe Pezzella | 29.11.1997 | 10 | (6) | |
| Marin Pongračić (CRO) | 11.09.1997 | 9 | | |
| Simone Romagnoli | 09.02.1990 | 1 | (6) | |
| Alessandro Tuia | 08.06.1990 | 6 | (1) | |
| Samuel Yves Umtiti (FRA) | 14.11.1993 | 24 | (1) | |
| **Midfielders:** | **DOB** | **M** | **(s)** | **G** |
| Kristoffer Askildsen (NOR) | 09.01.2001 | 7 | (14) | |

| | DOB | M | (s) | G |
|---|---|---|---|---|
| Kristijan Bistrović (CRO) | 09.04.1998 | 5 | (6) | |
| Alexis Blin (FRA) | 16.09.1996 | 26 | (9) | 1 |
| Þórir Jóhann Helgason (ISL) | 28.09.2000 | 2 | (10) | |
| Morten Due Hjulmand (DEN) | 25.06.1999 | 34 | (1) | |
| Joan Gonzàlez Cañellas (ESP) | 01.02.2002 | 26 | (9) | 1 |
| Marcin Listkowski (POL) | 10.02.1998 | | (5) | |
| Youssef Maleh (MAR) | 22.08.1998 | 7 | (10) | |
| **Forwards:** | **DOB** | **M** | **(s)** | **G** |
| Lameck Banda (ZAM) | 29.01.2001 | 19 | (17) | 2 |
| Assan Ceesay (GAM) | 17.03.1994 | 20 | (14) | 6 |
| Lorenzo Colombo | 08.03.2002 | 18 | (15) | 5 |
| Federico Di Francesco | 14.06.1994 | 23 | (13) | 2 |
| Gabriel Tadeu Strefezza Rebelato (BRA) | 18.04.1997 | 30 | (5) | 8 |
| Rémi Oudin (FRA) | 18.11.1996 | 12 | (19) | 3 |
| Pablo Rodríguez Delgado (ESP) | 04.08.2001 | | (4) | |
| Joel Voelkerling Persson (SWE) | 15.01.2003 | | (9) | |

## Associazione Calcio Milan

**Founded**: 16.12.1899
**Stadium**: Stadio "Giuseppe Meazza", Milano (75,923)
**Trainer**: Stefano Pioli     20.10.1965

| Goalkeepers: | DOB | M | (s) | G |
|---|---|---|---|---|
| Mike Peterson Maignan (FRA) | 03.07.1995 | 22 | | |
| Antonio Mirante | 08.07.1983 | | (1) | |
| Ciprian Anton Tătăruşanu (ROU) | 09.02.1986 | 16 | | |
| **Defenders:** | **DOB** | **M** | **(s)** | **G** |
| Fodé Ballo-Touré (SEN) | 03.01.1997 | 5 | (5) | 1 |
| Davide Calabria | 06.12.1996 | 21 | (4) | 1 |
| Sergiño Gianni Dest (USA) | 03.11.2000 | 2 | (6) | |
| Alessandro Florenzi | 11.03.1991 | 2 | (4) | |
| Matteo Gabbia | 21.10.1999 | 6 | (6) | |
| Theo Bernard François Hernández (FRA) | 06.10.1997 | 32 | | 4 |
| Pierre Kalulu Kyatengwa (FRA) | 05.06.2000 | 26 | (8) | 1 |
| Simon Thorup Kjær (DEN) | 26.03.1989 | 12 | (5) | |
| Malick Laye Thiaw (GER) | 08.08.2001 | 15 | (5) | |
| Oluwafikayomi Oluwadamilola Tomori (ENG) | 19.12.1997 | 32 | (1) | 1 |
| **Midfielders:** | **DOB** | **M** | **(s)** | **G** |
| Yacine Adli (FRA) | 29.07.2000 | 1 | (5) | |

| | DOB | M | (s) | G |
|---|---|---|---|---|
| Tiemoué Bakayoko (FRA) | 17.08.1994 | | (3) | |
| Ismaël Bennacer (ALG) | 01.12.1997 | 24 | (4) | 2 |
| Brahim Abdelkader Díaz (ESP) | 03.08.1999 | 27 | (6) | 6 |
| Charles Marc De Ketelaere (BEL) | 10.03.2001 | 9 | (23) | |
| Rade Krunić (BIH) | 07.10.1993 | 18 | (5) | |
| Tommaso Pobega | 15.07.1999 | 9 | (10) | 2 |
| Sandro Tonali | 08.05.2000 | 30 | (4) | 2 |
| Aster Vranckx (BEL) | 04.10.2002 | 2 | (7) | |
| **Forwards:** | **DOB** | **M** | **(s)** | **G** |
| Olivier Jonathan Giroud (FRA) | 30.09.1986 | 25 | (8) | 13 |
| Zlatan Ibrahimović (SWE) | 03.10.1981 | 1 | (3) | 1 |
| Marko Lazetić (SRB) | 22.01.2004 | | (1) | |
| Walter Messias Junior (BRA) | 13.05.1991 | 19 | (6) | 5 |
| Divock Okoth Origi (BEL) | 18.04.1995 | 10 | (17) | 2 |
| Rafael Alexandre da Conceição Leão (POR) | 10.06.1999 | 28 | (7) | 15 |
| Ante Rebić (CRO) | 21.09.1993 | 10 | (13) | 3 |
| Alexis Saelemaekers (BEL) | 27.06.1999 | 14 | (16) | 2 |

## Associazione Calcio Monza

**Founded**: 01.09.1912
**Stadium**: Stadio Brianteo [U-Power Stadium], Monza (15,039)
**Trainer**: Giovanni Stroppa 24.01.1968
[13.09.2023] Raffaele Palladino 17.04.1984

| Goalkeepers: | DOB | M | (s) | G |
|---|---|---|---|---|
| Alessio Cragno | 28.06.1994 | 1 | | |
| Michele Di Gregorio | 27.07.1997 | 37 | | |
| **Defenders:** | **DOB** | **M** | **(s)** | **G** |
| Valentin Antov (BUL) | 09.11.2000 | 2 | (7) | |
| Samuele Birindelli | 19.07.1999 | 14 | (17) | |
| Luca Caldirola | 01.02.1991 | 27 | (4) | 2 |
| Andrea Carboni | 04.02.2001 | 1 | (3) | |
| Franco Ezequiel Carboni (ARG) | 04.04.2003 | | (3) | |
| *Carlos Augusto* Zopolato Neves (BRA) | 07.01.1999 | 35 | | 6 |
| Giulio Donati | 05.02.1990 | 4 | (4) | 1 |
| Armando Izzo | 02.03.1992 | 29 | (1) | 1 |
| *Marlon* Santos da Silva Barbosa (BRA) | 07.09.1995 | 18 | (10) | |
| Luca Marrone | 28.03.1990 | 2 | | |
| *Pablo Marí* Villar (ESP) | 31.08.1993 | 28 | (2) | 1 |
| Andrea Ranocchia | 16.02.1988 | 1 | | |
| **Midfielders:** | **DOB** | **M** | **(s)** | **G** |
| Andrea Barberis | 11.12.1993 | 3 | (6) | |
| Warren Pierre Bondo (FRA) | 15.09.2003 | | (4) | |
| Andrea Colpani | 11.05.1999 | 10 | (17) | 4 |
| Salvatore Andrea Molina | 01.01.1992 | 1 | (4) | |
| José Ndong Machín Dicombo „*Pepín*" (EQG) | 14.08.1996 | 11 | (14) | |
| Matteo Pessina | 21.04.1997 | 34 | (1) | 5 |
| Filippo Ranocchia | 14.05.2001 | 5 | (9) | 1 |
| Nicolò Rovella | 04.12.2001 | 21 | (4) | 1 |
| Stefano Sensi | 05.08.1995 | 21 | (7) | 3 |
| Mattia Valoti | 06.09.1993 | 4 | (12) | |
| Samuele Vignato | 24.02.2004 | | (5) | |
| **Forwards:** | **DOB** | **M** | **(s)** | **G** |
| Gianluca Caprari | 30.07.1993 | 32 | (5) | 5 |
| Patrick Ciurria | 09.02.1995 | 31 | (5) | 6 |
| Marco D'Alessandro | 17.02.1991 | 3 | (5) | |
| *Dany Mota* Carvalho (POR) | 02.05.1998 | 21 | (8) | 5 |
| Christian Lund Gytkjær (DEN) | 06.05.1990 | 3 | (19) | 1 |
| Andrea Petagna | 30.06.1995 | 19 | (12) | 4 |

## Società Sportiva Calcio Napoli

**Founded**: 01.08.1926 (*as Associazione Calcio Napoli*)
**Stadium**: Stadio "Diego Armando Maradona", Napoli (54,726)
**Trainer**: Luciano Spalletti 07.03.1959

| Goalkeepers: | DOB | M | (s) | G |
|---|---|---|---|---|
| Pierluigi Gollini | 18.03.1995 | 4 | | |
| Alex Meret | 22.03.1997 | 34 | | |
| **Defenders:** | **DOB** | **M** | **(s)** | **G** |
| Bartosz Bereszyński (POL) | 12.07.1992 | 2 | (1) | |
| Giovanni Di Lorenzo | 04.08.1993 | 36 | (1) | 3 |
| *Juan* Guilherme Nunes *Jesus* (BRA) | 10.06.1991 | 10 | (5) | 1 |
| Kim Min-jae (KOR) | 15.11.1996 | 35 | | 2 |
| *Mário Rui* Silva Duarte (POR) | 27.05.1991 | 21 | (1) | |
| Mathías Olivera Miramontes (URU) | 31.10.1997 | 17 | (13) | 2 |
| Leo Skiri Østigård (NOR) | 28.11.1999 | 4 | (3) | |
| Amir Rrahmani (KOS) | 24.02.1994 | 27 | (2) | 2 |
| Alessandro Zanoli | 03.10.2000 | | (1) | |
| **Midfielders:** | **DOB** | **M** | **(s)** | **G** |
| André-Frank Zambo Anguissa (CMR) | 16.11.1995 | 36 | | 3 |
| Diego Demme (GER) | 21.11.1991 | 2 | (5) | |
| Eljif Elmas (MKD) | 24.09.1999 | 14 | (22) | 6 |
| Gianluca Gaetano | 05.05.2000 | | (8) | 1 |
| Stanislav Lobotka (SVK) | 25.11.1994 | 34 | (4) | 1 |
| Tanguy Ndombèlé Alvaro (FRA) | 28.12.1996 | 8 | (22) | 1 |
| Karim Zedadka (FRA) | 09.06.2000 | | (3) | |
| Piotr Zieliński (POL) | 20.05.1994 | 27 | (10) | 3 |
| **Forwards:** | **DOB** | **M** | **(s)** | **G** |
| Khvicha Kvaratskhelia (GEO) | 12.02.2001 | 30 | (4) | 12 |
| Hirving Rodrigo Lozano Bahena (MEX) | 30.07.1995 | 20 | (12) | 3 |
| Victor James Osimhen (NGA) | 29.12.1998 | 30 | (2) | 26 |
| Adam Ounas (ALG) | 11.11.1996 | | (2) | |
| Matteo Politano | 03.08.1993 | 14 | (13) | 3 |
| Giacomo Raspadori | 18.02.2000 | 10 | (15) | 2 |
| Giovanni Pablo Simeone (ARG) | 05.07.1995 | 1 | (24) | 4 |
| Alessio Zerbin | 03.03.1999 | 2 | (8) | |

## Associazione Sportiva Roma

**Founded**: 07.06.1927
**Stadium**: Stadio Olimpico, Roma (70,634)
**Trainer**: José Mário dos Santos Mourinho Félix (POR) 26.01.1963

| Goalkeepers: | DOB | M | (s) | G |
|---|---|---|---|---|
| Rui Pedro dos Santos Patrício (POR) | 15.02.1988 | 35 | | |
| Mile Svilar (SRB) | 27.08.1999 | 3 | | |
| **Defenders:** | **DOB** | **M** | **(s)** | **G** |
| Zeki Çelik (TUR) | 17.02.1997 | 16 | (8) | |
| Roger Ibanez da Silva „*Ibañez*" (BRA) | 23.11.1998 | 32 | (1) | 3 |
| Rick Karsdorp (NED) | 11.02.1995 | 8 | (5) | |
| Marash Kumbulla (ALB) | 08.02.2000 | 5 | (2) | |
| Diego Javier *Llorente* Ríos (ESP) | 16.08.1993 | 5 | (4) | |
| Gianluca Mancini | 17.04.1996 | 33 | (2) | 1 |
| Filippo Missori | 24.03.2004 | 2 | (1) | |
| Christopher Lloyd Smalling (ENG) | 22.11.1989 | 31 | (1) | 3 |
| Leonardo Spinazzola | 25.03.1993 | 18 | (8) | 1 |
| Matías Nicolás Viña Susperreguy (URU) | 09.11.1997 | 1 | (2) | |
| **Midfielders:** | **DOB** | **M** | **(s)** | **G** |
| Edoardo Bove | 16.05.2002 | 10 | (12) | 1 |
| Mady Camara (GUI) | 28.02.1997 | 8 | (7) | |
| Bryan Cristante | 03.03.1995 | 34 | (2) | 1 |
| Nemanja Matić (SRB) | 01.08.1988 | 16 | (19) | 2 |
| Lorenzo Pellegrini | 19.06.1996 | 29 | (3) | 4 |
| Niccolò Pisilli | 23.09.2004 | | (1) | |
| Benjamin Tahirović (BIH) | 03.03.2003 | 4 | (7) | |
| Cristian Volpato (AUS) | 15.11.2003 | 2 | (5) | 1 |
| Georginio Gregion Emile Wijnaldum (NED) | 11.11.1990 | 10 | (4) | 2 |
| Nicola Zalewski (POL) | 23.01.2002 | 26 | (7) | 2 |
| Nicolò Zaniolo | 02.07.1999 | 12 | (1) | 1 |
| **Forwards:** | **DOB** | **M** | **(s)** | **G** |
| Kevin Oghenetega Tamaraebi Bakumo-Abraham (ENG) | 02.10.1997 | 24 | (14) | 8 |
| Andrea Belotti | 20.12.1993 | 11 | (20) | |
| Paulo Bruno Exequiel Dybala (ARG) | 15.11.1993 | 21 | (4) | 12 |
| Stephan Kareem El Shaarawy | 27.10.1992 | 14 | (15) | 7 |
| Jordan Majchrzak (POL) | 08.10.2004 | | (1) | |
| Eldor Shomurodov (UZB) | 29.06.1995 | 1 | (5) | |
| Ola Selvaag Solbakken (NOR) | 07.09.1998 | 7 | (7) | 1 |

## Unione Sportiva Salernitana 1919

**Founded**: 1919 (*refounded 2005 and 2011*)
**Stadium**: Stadio Arechi, Salerno (37,180)
**Trainer**: Davide Nicola 05.03.1973
[15.02.2023] Paulo Manuel Carvalho de Sousa (POR) 30.08.1970

| Goalkeepers: | DOB | M | (s) | G |
|---|---|---|---|---|
| Vincenzo Fiorillo | 13.01.1990 | 1 | | |
| Francisco Guillermo Ochoa Magaña (MEX) | 13.07.1985 | 20 | | |
| Luigi Sepe | 08.05.1991 | 17 | | |
| **Defenders:** | **DOB** | **M** | **(s)** | **G** |
| Domagoj Bradarić (CRO) | 10.12.1999 | 24 | (7) | |
| Dylan Bronn (TUN) | 19.06.1995 | 19 | (5) | |
| Flavius David Daniliuc (AUT) | 27.04.2001 | 23 | (4) | |
| Federico Julián Fazio (ARG) | 17.03.1987 | 12 | (2) | 1 |
| Norbert Gyömbér (SVK) | 03.07.1992 | 23 | (4) | |
| Matteo Lovato | 14.02.2000 | 8 | (9) | |
| Pasquale Mazzocchi | 27.07.1995 | 23 | (4) | 2 |
| Lorenzo Pirola | 20.02.2002 | 23 | (3) | 2 |
| Salomon Sambia (FRA) | 07.09.1996 | 7 | (15) | |
| William Paul Troost-Ekong (NGA) | 01.09.1993 | 4 | (5) | 1 |
| **Midfielders:** | **DOB** | **M** | **(s)** | **G** |
| Emil Bohinen (NOR) | 12.03.1999 | 9 | (15) | |
| Antonio Candreva | 28.02.1987 | 32 | (3) | 7 |
| Lassana Coulibaly (MLI) | 10.04.1996 | 34 | (1) | 3 |
| Domen Črnigoj (SVN) | 18.11.1995 | 4 | (3) | |
| Antonio Pio Iervolino | 23.05.2003 | | (1) | |
| Grigoris Kastanos (CYP) | 30.01.1998 | 13 | (15) | 2 |
| Giulio Maggiore | 12.03.1998 | 11 | (5) | |
| Hans Nicolussi Caviglia | 18.06.2000 | 6 | (6) | 1 |
| Ivan Radovanović (SRB) | 29.08.1988 | 7 | (3) | |
| Tonny Emilio Trindade de Vilhena (NED) | 03.01.1995 | 27 | (6) | 4 |
| **Forwards:** | **DOB** | **M** | **(s)** | **G** |
| Federico Bonazzoli | 21.05.1997 | 12 | (12) | 2 |
| Erik Botheim (NOR) | 10.01.2000 | 9 | (19) | 1 |
| Boulaye Dia (SEN) | 16.11.1996 | 27 | (6) | 16 |
| Julian Kristoffersen (NOR) | 10.05.1997 | | (1) | |
| Krzysztof Piątek (POL) | 01.07.1995 | 23 | (10) | 4 |
| Franck Bilal Ribéry (FRA) | 07.04.1983 | | (1) | |
| Diego Martín Valencia Morello (CHI) | 14.01.2000 | | (12) | |

## Unione Calcio Sampdoria Genova

**Founded**: 12.08.1946
**Stadium**: Stadio "Luigi Ferraris", Genova (36,599)
**Trainer**: Marco Giampaolo    02.08.1967
[06.10.2022] Dejan Stanković (SRB)    11.09.1978

| Goalkeepers: | DOB | M | (s) | G |
|---|---|---|---|---|
| Emil Audero | 18.01.1997 | 25 | | |
| Nicola Ravaglia | 12.12.1988 | 9 | | |
| Martin Turk (SVN) | 21.08.2003 | 4 | | |
| Defenders: | DOB | M | (s) | G |
| Bruno Agustín Amione (ARG) | 03.01.2002 | 25 | (1) | 1 |
| Tommaso Augello | 30.08.1994 | 35 | (2) | 2 |
| Bartosz Bereszyński (POL) | 12.07.1992 | 15 | | |
| Omar Colley (GAM) | 24.10.1992 | 15 | (1) | 1 |
| Andrea Conti | 02.03.1994 | | (1) | |
| Fabio Depaoli | 24.04.1997 | 1 | (2) | |
| Alex Ferrari | 01.07.1994 | 10 | (2) | |
| Koray Günter (GER) | 16.08.1994 | 8 | (2) | |
| Jeison Fabián Murillo Cerón (COL) | 27.05.1992 | 12 | (8) | |
| Nicola Murru | 16.12.1994 | 5 | (15) | |
| Bram Nuytinck (NED) | 04.05.1990 | 19 | | |
| Marios Oikonomou (GRE) | 06.10.1992 | 3 | (3) | |
| Alessandro Zanoli | 03.10.2000 | 16 | (6) | 2 |
| Midfielders: | DOB | M | (s) | G |
| Mickaël Bruno Dominique Cuisance (FRA) | 16.08.1999 | 9 | (3) | |
| Filip Đuričić (SRB) | 30.01.1992 | 27 | (5) | 3 |
| Gonzalo Villar del Fraile (ESP) | 23.03.1998 | 8 | (7) | |
| Emirhan İlkhan (TUR) | 01.06.2004 | | (8) | |
| Mehdi Léris (FRA) | 23.05.1998 | 29 | (3) | 1 |
| Lorenzo Malagrida | 24.10.2003 | | (6) | |
| Flavio Paoletti | 16.01.2003 | 1 | (11) | |
| Tomás Eduardo Rincón Hernández (VEN) | 13.01.1988 | 30 | (4) | |
| Abdelhamid Sabiri (MAR) | 28.11.1996 | 12 | (6) | 2 |
| Telasco José Segovia Pérez (VEN) | 02.04.2003 | | (1) | |
| Valerio Verre | 11.01.1994 | 6 | (12) | |
| Ronaldo Augusto Vieira Nan (ENG) | 19.07.1998 | 8 | (8) | |
| Harry Billy Winks (ENG) | 02.02.1996 | 19 | (1) | |
| Gerard Yepes Laut (ESP) | 25.08.2002 | 2 | (3) | |
| Forwards: | DOB | M | (s) | G |
| Francesco Caputo | 06.08.1987 | 13 | (2) | 1 |
| Manuel De Luca | 17.07.1998 | | (2) | |
| Manolo Gabbiadini | 26.11.1991 | 27 | (8) | 7 |
| Mihailo Ivanović (SRB) | 29.11.2004 | | (1) | |
| Jesé Rodríguez Ruíz (ESP) | 26.02.1993 | 1 | (10) | 1 |
| Sam Adrianus Martinus Lammers (NED) | 30.04.1997 | 13 | (6) | 1 |
| Samuel Ntanda Lukisa (BEL) | 30.06.2005 | | (1) | |
| Daniele Montevago | 18.03.2003 | 3 | (3) | |
| Ignacio Pussetto (ARG) | 21.12.1995 | 1 | (4) | |
| Fabio Quagliarella | 31.01.1983 | 7 | (16) | 1 |

## Unione Sportiva Sassuolo Calcio

**Founded**: 17.07.1920
**Stadium**: Mapei Stadium – Città del Tricolore, Reggio Emilia (21,525)
**Trainer**: Alessio Dionisi    01.04.1980

| Goalkeepers: | DOB | M | (s) | G |
|---|---|---|---|---|
| Andrea Consigli | 27.01.1987 | 35 | | |
| Gianluca Pegolo | 25.03.1981 | 2 | | |
| Alessandro Russo | 31.03.2001 | 1 | | |
| Defenders: | DOB | M | (s) | G |
| Kaan Ayhan (TUR) | 10.11.1994 | 5 | (5) | |
| Martin Erlić (CRO) | 24.01.1998 | 26 | (2) | |
| Gian Marco Ferrari | 15.05.1992 | 24 | (9) | 1 |
| Giorgos Kyriakopoulos (GRE) | 05.02.1996 | 9 | (3) | 1 |
| Riccardo Marchizza | 26.03.1998 | 3 | (7) | |
| Mert Müldür (TUR) | 03.04.1999 | 1 | (1) | |
| Rogério Oliveira da Silva (BRA) | 13.01.1998 | 34 | (2) | |
| Filippo Romagna | 26.05.1997 | | (2) | |
| Ruan Tressoldi Netto (BRA) | 07.06.1999 | 21 | (2) | |
| Jeremy Toljan (GER) | 08.08.1994 | 29 | (2) | |
| Nadir Zortea | 19.06.1999 | 7 | (3) | |
| Midfielders: | DOB | M | (s) | G |
| Nedim Bajrami (ALB) | 28.02.1999 | 7 | (11) | 1 |
| Davide Frattesi | 22.09.1999 | 35 | (1) | 7 |
| Abdou Harroui (MAR) | 13.01.1998 | 5 | (18) | 2 |
| Maxime López (FRA) | 04.12.1997 | 25 | (5) | |
| Matheus Henrique de Souza (BRA) | 19.12.1997 | 21 | (9) | 4 |
| Pedro Avomo Mba Obiang (EQG) | 27.03.1992 | 11 | (6) | |
| Kristian Thorstvedt (NOR) | 13.03.1999 | 13 | (18) | 2 |
| Hamed Junior Traorè (CIV) | 16.02.2000 | 6 | (5) | |
| Forwards: | | M | (s) | G |
| Agustín Álvarez Martínez (URU) | 19.05.2001 | 1 | (21) | 1 |
| Janis Antiste (FRA) | 18.08.2002 | | (2) | 1 |
| Domenico Berardi | 01.08.1994 | 22 | (4) | 12 |
| Emil Konradsen Ceide (NOR) | 03.09.2001 | 5 | (14) | |
| Luca D'Andrea | 06.09.2004 | 5 | | |
| Grégoire Defrel (MTQ) | 17.06.1991 | 13 | (14) | 2 |
| Armand Laurienté (FRA) | 04.12.1998 | 27 | (1) | 7 |
| Andrea Pinamonti | 19.05.1999 | 25 | (7) | 5 |
| Giacomo Raspadori | 18.02.2000 | | (1) | |

## Spezia Calcio La Spezia

**Founded**: 10.10.1906
**Stadium**: Stadio „Alberto Picco", La Spezia (11,512)
**Trainer**: Luca Gotti    13.09.1967
[15.02.2023] Fabrizio Lorieri    11.02.1964
[23.02.2023] Leonardo Semplici    18.07.1967

| Goalkeepers: | DOB | M | (s) | G |
|---|---|---|---|---|
| Bartłomiej Drągowski (POL) | 19.08.1997 | 34 | | |
| Federico Marchetti | 07.02.1983 | | (1) | |
| Jeroen Zoet (NED) | 06.01.1991 | 4 | (1) | |
| Petar Zovko (BIH) | 25.03.2002 | | (1) | |
| Defenders: | DOB | M | (s) | G |
| Kelvin Amian (FRA) | 08.02.1998 | 26 | (4) | |
| Ethan Kwame Colm Raymond Ampadu(WAL) | 14.09.2000 | 31 | | |
| Mattia Caldara | 05.05.1994 | 13 | (7) | |
| Petko Hristov (BUL) | 01.03.1999 | 4 | (5) | |
| Emil Alfons Holm (SWE) | 13.05.2000 | 17 | (3) | 1 |
| João Gervásio Bragança Moutinho (POR) | 12.01.1998 | | (4) | |
| Jakub Kiwior (POL) | 15.02.2000 | 17 | | |
| Dimitrios Nikolaou (GRE) | 13.08.1998 | 34 | (2) | 1 |
| Arkadiusz Reca (POL) | 17.06.1995 | 24 | (6) | 1 |
| Salvador „Salva" Ferrer Canals (ESP) | 21.01.1998 | | (5) | |
| Przemysław Wiśniewski (POL) | 27.07.1998 | 11 | (3) | 1 |
| Midfielders: | DOB | M | (s) | G |
| Kevin Andrés Agudelo Ardila (COL) | 14.11.1998 | 23 | (11) | |
| Simone Bastoni | 05.11.1996 | 15 | (4) | 2 |
| Julius Eskelund Beck (DEN) | 27.04.2005 | | (1) | |
| Mehdi Bourabia (FRA) | 07.08.1991 | 36 | (1) | 1 |
| Tio Cipot (SVN) | 20.04.2003 | | (8) | |
| Albin Ekdal (SWE) | 28.07.1989 | 18 | (13) | |
| Mikael Egill Ellertsson (ISL) | 11.03.2002 | 1 | (10) | |
| Salvatore Esposito | 07.10.2000 | 10 | (5) | 1 |
| Viktor Kovalenko (UKR) | 14.02.1996 | 7 | (11) | |
| Daniel Maldini | 11.10.2001 | 4 | (14) | 2 |
| Jacopo Sala | 05.12.1991 | 1 | (5) | |
| Szymon Żurkowski (POL) | 25.09.1997 | 3 | (7) | |
| Forwards: | DOB | M | (s) | G |
| Emmanuel Gyasi (GHA) | 11.01.1994 | 35 | | 2 |
| Raimonds Krollis (LVA) | 28.10.2001 | | (4) | |
| Leandro Mário Baldé Sanca (POR) | 04.01.2000 | | (4) | |
| M'Bala Nzola (ANG) | 18.08.1996 | 29 | (2) | 13 |
| Eldor Shomurodov (UZB) | 29.06.1995 | 9 | (6) | 1 |
| Dávid Strelec (SVK) | 04.04.2001 | 1 | (6) | |
| Daniele Verde | 20.06.1996 | 11 | (14) | 3 |

## Torino Football Club

| Founded: | 03.12.1906 |
| Stadium: | Stadio Olimpico Grande Torino, Torino (27,958) |
| Trainer: | Ivan Jurić (CRO) 25.08.1975 |

| Goalkeepers: | DOB | M | (s) | G |
|---|---|---|---|---|
| Vanja Milinković-Savić (SRB) | 20.02.1997 | 38 | | |
| **Defenders:** | **DOB** | **M** | **(s)** | **G** |
| Temitayo Olufisayo Olaoluwa Aina (NGA) | 08.10.1996 | 9 | (10) | |
| Alessandro Buongiorno | 06.06.1999 | 30 | (4) | 1 |
| Koffi Djidji (CIV) | 30.11.1992 | 26 | (8) | 1 |
| Andreaw Gravillon (GLP) | 08.02.1998 | 4 | (3) | |
| Valentino Lando Lazaro (AUT) | 24.03.1996 | 15 | (8) | |
| Ricardo Ivan Rodríguez Araya (SUI) | 25.08.1992 | 30 | (5) | |
| Perr Schuurs (NED) | 26.11.1999 | 28 | (2) | |
| Wilfried Stephane Singo (CIV) | 25.12.2000 | 24 | (7) | 2 |
| Mërgim Vojvoda (KOS) | 01.02.1995 | 18 | (11) | |
| David Zima (CZE) | 08.11.2000 | 4 | (5) | |
| **Midfielders:** | **DOB** | **M** | **(s)** | **G** |
| Michel Ndary Adopo (FRA) | 19.07.2000 | 3 | (6) | |
| Brian Jephte Bayeye (FRA) | 30.06.2000 | 1 | (1) | |
| Gvidas Gineitis (LTU) | 15.04.2004 | 2 | (1) | |
| Ivan Ilić (SRB) | 17.03.2001 | 13 | (1) | 2 |
| Emirhan İlkhan (TUR) | 01.06.2004 | 1 | (3) | |
| Karol Linetty (POL) | 02.02.1995 | 22 | (10) | 1 |
| Saša Lukić (SRB) | 13.08.1996 | 13 | (3) | 2 |
| Aleksey Miranchuk (RUS) | 17.10.1995 | 24 | (5) | 4 |
| Samuele Ricci | 21.08.2001 | 23 | (5) | 2 |
| Jacopo Segre | 17.02.1997 | | (1) | |
| Ronaldo Augusto Vieira Nan (ENG) | 19.07.1998 | | (2) | |
| Nikola Vlašić (CRO) | 04.10.1997 | 29 | (5) | 5 |
| **Forwards:** | **DOB** | **M** | **(s)** | **G** |
| Yann Karamoh (CIV) | 08.07.1998 | 7 | (14) | 4 |
| Pietro Pellegri | 17.03.2001 | 4 | (14) | |
| Nemanja Radonjić (SRB) | 15.02.1996 | 16 | (12) | 2 |
| Arnaldo Antonio Sanabria Ayala (PAR) | 04.03.1996 | 28 | (5) | 12 |
| Demba Seck (SEN) | 10.02.2001 | 6 | (13) | |

## Udinese Calcio

| Founded: | 30.11.1896 |
| Stadium: | Stadio Friuli, Udine (25,144) |
| Trainer: | Andrea Sottil 04.01.1974 |

| Goalkeepers: | DOB | M | (s) | G |
|---|---|---|---|---|
| Marco Silvestri | 02.03.1991 | 38 | | |
| **Defenders:** | **DOB** | **M** | **(s)** | **G** |
| James Abankwah (IRL) | 16.01.2004 | 1 | (1) | |
| Jaka Bijol (SVN) | 05.02.1999 | 32 | | 3 |
| Nicolò Cocetta | 19.12.2003 | | (1) | |
| Festy Oseiwe Ebosele (IRL) | 02.08.2002 | 4 | (13) | |
| Enzo Jacques Rodolphe Ebosse (CMR) | 11.03.1999 | 9 | (10) | |
| Kingsley Osezele Ehizibue (NGA) | 25.05.1995 | 16 | (11) | 2 |
| Axel Guessand (FRA) | 06.11.2004 | 1 | | |
| Leonardo Daniel Ulineia Buta (POR) | 05.06.2002 | | (2) | |
| Adam Masina (MAR) | 02.01.1994 | 8 | (6) | 2 |
| Bram Nuytinck (NED) | 04.05.1990 | 3 | (3) | |
| Patricio Nehuén Pérez (ARG) | 24.06.2000 | 33 | (1) | 2 |
| Rodrigo Nascimento Franca „Rodrigo Becão" (BRA) | 19.01.1996 | 28 | | 2 |
| Brandon Soppy (FRA) | 21.02.2002 | 1 | | |
| Destiny Udogie | 28.11.2002 | 31 | (2) | 3 |
| Marvin Zeegelaar (NED) | 12.08.1990 | 4 | (3) | 1 |
| **Midfielders:** | **DOB** | **M** | **(s)** | **G** |
| Tolgay Arslan (GER) | 16.08.1990 | 12 | (24) | 1 |
| Mato Jajalo (BIH) | 25.05.1988 | | (3) | |
| Sandi Lovrič (SVN) | 28.03.1998 | 28 | (9) | 5 |
| Jean-Victor Makengo (FRA) | 12.06.1998 | 11 | (5) | |
| Simone Pafundi | 14.03.2006 | | (8) | |
| Roberto Maximiliano Pereyra (ARG) | 07.01.1991 | 33 | (1) | 5 |
| Lazar Samardžić (SRB) | 24.02.2002 | 19 | (18) | 5 |
| Walace Souza Silva (BRA) | 04.04.1995 | 37 | | |
| **Forwards:** | **DOB** | **M** | **(s)** | **G** |
| Norberto Bercique Gomes Betuncal „Beto" (POR) | 31.01.1998 | 23 | (10) | 10 |
| Gerard Deulofeu Lázaro (ESP) | 13.03.1994 | 15 | (1) | 2 |
| Ilija Nestorovski (MKD) | 12.03.1990 | 5 | (16) | 2 |
| Isaac Success Ajayi (NGA) | 07.01.1996 | 21 | (9) | 1 |
| Vivaldo Leandro Semedo Moura Sousa (POR) | 28.01.2005 | | (5) | |
| Florian Tristan Mariano Thauvin (FRA) | 26.01.1993 | 5 | (11) | |

## SECOND LEVEL
### Serie B 2022/2023

| | | | | | | | | | |
|---|---|---|---|---|---|---|---|---|---|
| 1. | Frosinone Calcio (*Promoted*) | 38 | 24 | 8 | 6 | 63 | - | 26 | 80 |
| 2. | Genoa C&FC[1] (*Promoted*) | 38 | 21 | 11 | 6 | 53 | - | 28 | 73 |
| 3. | SSC Bari | 38 | 17 | 14 | 7 | 58 | - | 37 | 65 |
| 4. | Parma Calcio 1913[1] | 38 | 17 | 10 | 11 | 48 | - | 39 | 60 |
| 5. | Cagliari Calcio | 38 | 15 | 15 | 8 | 50 | - | 34 | 60 |
| 6. | FC Südtirol Bolzano | 38 | 14 | 16 | 8 | 38 | - | 34 | 58 |
| 7. | Reggina 1914[2] (*Relegated to Serie D*) | 38 | 17 | 4 | 17 | 49 | - | 45 | 50 |
| 8. | Venezia FC | 38 | 13 | 10 | 15 | 51 | - | 50 | 49 |
| 9. | Palermo FC | 38 | 11 | 16 | 11 | 48 | - | 49 | 49 |
| 10. | Modena FC 2018 | 38 | 13 | 9 | 16 | 47 | - | 53 | 48 |
| 11. | Pisa Sporting Club | 38 | 11 | 14 | 13 | 48 | - | 42 | 47 |
| 12. | Ascoli Calcio 1898 FC | 38 | 12 | 11 | 15 | 40 | - | 47 | 47 |
| 13. | Como 1907 | 38 | 10 | 17 | 11 | 47 | - | 48 | 47 |
| 14. | Ternana Calcio | 38 | 11 | 10 | 17 | 37 | - | 52 | 43 |
| 15. | AS Cittadella | 38 | 9 | 16 | 13 | 34 | - | 45 | 43 |
| 16. | Brescia Calcio (*Relegation Play-out*) | 38 | 9 | 13 | 16 | 36 | - | 57 | 40 |
| 17. | Cosenza Calcio (*Relegation Play-out*) | 38 | 9 | 13 | 16 | 30 | - | 53 | 40 |
| 18. | AC Perugia Calcio (*Relegated*) | 38 | 10 | 9 | 19 | 40 | - | 52 | 39 |
| 19. | SPAL Ferrara (*Relegated*) | 38 | 8 | 14 | 16 | 41 | - | 51 | 38 |
| 20. | Benevento Calcio (*Relegated*) | 38 | 7 | 14 | 17 | 33 | - | 49 | 35 |

Teams ranked 3-8 were qualified for the Promotion Play-offs.
[1] 1 point deducted due to tax payment irregularities;
[2] 5 points (initially 7 points) deducted for failing payments of tax and salaries; Reggina 1914 will start next season in Serie D (fourth level).

### Promotion Play-offs

**Preliminary Round [26-27.05.2023]**
| FC Südtirol Bolzano - Reggina 1914 | 1-0(0-0) | |
| Cagliari Calcio - Venezia FC | 2-1(2-0) | |

**Semi-Finals [29/30.05.-02/03.06.2023]**
| FC Südtirol Bolzano - SSC Bari* | 1-0(0-0) | 0-1(0-0) |
| Cagliari Calcio - Parma Calcio 1913 | 3-2(0-2) | 0-0 |

*qualified as higher-ranked teams.

**Finals [08-11.06.2023]**
| Cagliari Calcio - SSC Bari | 1-1(1-0) | 1-0(0-0) |

Cagliari Calcio promoted for the 2023/2024 Serie A.

Cosenza Calcio – Brescia Calcio       1-0(0-0)     1-1(0-0)*
*the second leg was awarded as a 3-0 win for Cosenza Calcio, they remains at second level.

## NATIONAL TEAM

### INTERNATIONAL MATCHES
#### (16.07.2022 – 15.07.2023)

| | | | | |
|---|---|---|---|---|
| 23.09.2022 | Milano | *Italy - England* | *1-0(0-0)* | (UNL) |
| 26.09.2022 | Budapest | *Hungary - Italy* | *0-2(0-1)* | (UNL) |
| 16.11.2022 | Tiranë | *Albania - Italy* | *1-3(1-2)* | (F) |
| 20.11.2022 | Wien | *Austria - Italy* | *2-0(2-0)* | (F) |
| 23.03.2023 | Napoli | *Italy - England* | *1-2(0-2)* | (ECQ) |
| 26.03.2023 | Attard | *Malta - Italy* | *0-2(0-2)* | (ECQ) |
| 15.06.2023 | Enschede | *Spain - Italy* | *2-1(1-1)* | (UNL) |
| 18.06.2023 | Enschede | *Netherlands - Italy* | *2-3(0-2)* | (UNL) |

**23.09.2022    ITALY - ENGLAND**      **1-0(0-0)**      3rd UEFA Nations League A, Group 3
Stadio "Giuseppe Meazza", Milano; Referee: Jesús Gil Manzano (Spain); Attendance: 50,640
**ITA:** Gianluigi Donnarumma, Francesco Acerbi, Leonardo Bonucci (Cap), Rafael Tolói, Giovanni Di Lorenzo, Bryan Cristante, Nicolò Barella (63.Tommaso Pobega), Jorge Luiz Frello Filho "Jorginho" (89.Emerson Palmieri dos Santos) Federico Dimarco (89.Davide Frattesi), Giacomo Raspadori (81.Manolo Gabbiadini), Gianluca Scamacca (63.Degnand Wilfried Gnonto). Trainer: Roberto Mancini.
**Goal:** Giacomo Raspadori (68).

**26.09.2022    HUNGARY - ITALY**      **0-2(0-1)**      3rd UEFA Nations League A, Group 3
Puskás Aréna, Budapest; Referee: Benoît Bastien (France); Attendance: 57,300
**ITA:** Gianluigi Donnarumma, Francesco Acerbi (46.Alessandro Bastoni), Leonardo Bonucci (Cap), Rafael Tolói, Giovanni Di Lorenzo (90.Pasquale Mazzocchi), Bryan Cristante, Nicolò Barella, Jorge Luiz Frello Filho "Jorginho" (72.Tommaso Pobega), Federico Dimarco, Giacomo Raspadori (72.Gianluca Scamacca), Degnand Wilfried Gnonto (65.Manolo Gabbiadini). Trainer: Roberto Mancini.
**Goals:** Giacomo Raspadori (27), Federico Dimarco (52).

**16.11.2022    ALBANIA - ITALY**      **1-3(1-2)**      Friendly International
Arena Kombëtare, Tiranë; Referee: Genc Nuza (Kosovo); Attendance: 22,000
**ITA:** Alex Meret, Giorgio Scalvini, Alessandro Bastoni, Leonardo Bonucci (Cap) (90+1.Andrea Pinamonti), Giovanni Di Lorenzo, Sandro Tonali (45+2.Samuele Ricci), Marco Verratti (90.Simone Pafundi), Federico Dimarco, Nicolò Zaniolo (77.Nicolò Fagioli), Vincenzo Grifo (77.Degnand Wilfried Gnonto), Giacomo Raspadori (90.Federico Chiesa). Trainer: Roberto Mancini.
**Goals:** Giovanni Di Lorenzo (20), Vincenzo Grifo (25, 64).

**20.11.2022    AUSTRIA - ITALY**      **2-0(2-0)**      Friendly International
"Ernst Happel" Stadion, Wien; Referee: Christian Dingert (Germany); Attendance: 18,000
**ITA:** Gianluigi Donnarumma, Federico Gatti (46.Matteo Pessina), Francesco Acerbi, Leonardo Bonucci (Cap), Giovanni Di Lorenzo (46.Giorgio Scalvini), Nicolò Barella (90.Fabio Miretti), Marco Verratti, Federico Dimarco, Matteo Politano (46.Federico Chiesa), Vincenzo Grifo (46.Nicolò Zaniolo), Giacomo Raspadori (71.Degnand Wilfried Gnonto). Trainer: Roberto Mancini.

**23.03.2023    ITALY - ENGLAND**      **1-2(0-2)**      17th EC. Qualifiers
Stadio "Diego Armando Maradona", Napoli; Referee: Srđan Jovanović (Serbia); Attendance: 44,536
**ITA:** Gianluigi Donnarumma, Giovanni Di Lorenzo, Rafael Tolói, Francesco Acerbi, Leonardo Spinazzola, Marco Verratti (Cap) (88.Gianluca Scamacca), Jorge Luiz Frello Filho "Jorginho" (69.Sandro Tonali), Nicolò Barella (62.Bryan Cristante), Domenico Berardi (62.Matteo Politano), Lorenzo Pellegrini (69.Degnand Wilfried Gnonto), Mateo Retegui. Trainer: Roberto Mancini.
**Goal:** Mateo Retegui (56).

**26.03.2023    MALTA - ITALY**      **0-2(0-2)**      17th EC. Qualifiers
Ta'Qali National Stadium, Attard; Referee: Georgi Kabakov (Bulgaria); Attendance: 16,015
**ITA:** Gianluigi Donnarumma (Cap), Giovanni Di Lorenzo (46.Matteo Darmian), Giorgio Scalvini (83.Rafael Tolói), Alessio Romagnoli, Emerson Palmieri dos Santos, Bryan Cristante, Matteo Pessina, Sandro Tonali (66.Marco Verratti), Matteo Politano, Mateo Retegui (66.Gianluca Scamacca), Degnand Wilfried Gnonto (22.Vincenzo Grifo). Trainer: Roberto Mancini.
**Goals:** Mateo Retegui (15), Matteo Pessina (27).

**15.06.2023    SPAIN - ITALY**      **2-1(1-1)**      3rd UEFA Nations League, Semi-Finals
De Grolsch Veste, Enschede (Netherlands); Referee: Slavko Vinčić (Slovenia); Attendance: 24,558
**ITA:** Gianluigi Donnarumma, Rafael Tolói, Francesco Acerbi, Leonardo Bonucci (Cap) (46.Matteo Darmian), Giovanni Di Lorenzo, Nicolò Barella, Davide Frattesi (76.Marco Verratti), Jorge Luiz Frello Filho "Jorginho" (61.Bryan Cristante), Leonardo Spinazzola (46.Federico Dimarco), Nicolò Zaniolo, Ciro Immobile (60.Federico Chiesa). Trainer: Roberto Mancini.
**Goal:** Ciro Immobile (11 penalty).

**18.06.2023    NETHERLANDS - ITALY**      **2-3(0-2)**      3rd UEFA Nations League, Third Place Play-off
Stadion De Groisch Veste, Enschede (Netherlands); Referee: Glenn Nyberg (Sweden); Attendance: 21,292
**ITA:** Gianluigi Donnarumma (Cap), Francesco Acerbi, Alessandro Buongiorno, Rafael Tolói, Federico Dimarco (74.Leonardo Spinazzola), Bryan Cristante, Marco Verratti (85.Nicolò Barella), Davide Frattesi, Giacomo Raspadori (63.Nicolò Zaniolo), Degnand Wilfried Gnonto (63.Federico Chiesa), Mateo Retegui (85.Lorenzo Pellegrini). Trainer: Roberto Mancini.
**Goals:** Federico Dimarco (6), Davide Frattesi (20), Federico Chiesa (72).

# NATIONAL TEAM PLAYERS
## (16.07.2022 – 15.07.2023)

| Name | DOB | Caps | Goals | Club | |
|------|-----|------|-------|------|---|

### Goalkeepers

| Name | DOB | Caps | Goals | Club | |
|------|-----|------|-------|------|---|
| Gianluigi DONNARUMMA | 25.02.1999 | 54 | 0 | 2022/2023: | Paris Saint-Germain FC (FRA) |
| Alex MERET | 22.03.1997 | 3 | 0 | 2022: | SSC Napoli |

### Defenders

| Name | DOB | Caps | Goals | Club | |
|------|-----|------|-------|------|---|
| Francesco ACERBI | 10.08.1988 | 31 | 1 | 2022/2023: | FC Internazionale Milano |
| Alessandro BASTONI | 13.04.1999 | 17 | 1 | 2022: | FC Internazionale Milano |
| Leonardo BONUCCI | 01.05.1987 | 121 | 8 | 2022/2023: | Juventus FC Torino |
| Alessandro BUONGIORNO | 06.06.1999 | 1 | 0 | 2023: | Torino FC |
| Matteo DARMIAN | 02.12.1989 | 38 | 1 | 2023: | FC Internazionale Milano |
| Giovanni DI LORENZO | 04.08.1993 | 28 | 3 | 2022/2023: | SSC Napoli |
| Federico DIMARCO | 10.11.1997 | 10 | 2 | 2022/2023: | FC Internazionale Milano |
| EMERSON Palmieri dos Santos | 03.08.1994 | 29 | 0 | 2022/2023: | West Ham United FC London (ENG) |
| Federico GATTI | 24.06.1998 | 2 | 0 | 2022: | Juventus FC Torino |
| Pasquale MAZZOCCHI | 27.07.1995 | 1 | 0 | 2022: | US Salernitana 1919 |
| Alessio ROMAGNOLI | 12.01.1995 | 13 | 2 | 2023: | SS Lazio Roma |
| Giorgio SCALVINI | 11.12.2003 | 4 | 0 | 2022/2023: | Atalanta Bergamasca Calcio |
| Leonardo SPINAZZOLA | 25.03.1993 | 24 | 0 | 2023: | AS Roma |
| Rafael TOLÓI | 10.10.1990 | 14 | 0 | 2022/2023: | Atalanta Bergamasca Calcio |

### Midfielders

| Name | DOB | Caps | Goals | Club | |
|------|-----|------|-------|------|---|
| Nicolò BARELLA | 07.02.1997 | 45 | 8 | 2022/2023: | FC Internazionale Milano |
| Bryan CRISTANTE | 03.03.1995 | 33 | 2 | 2022/2023: | AS Roma |
| Nicolò FAGIOLI | 12.02.2001 | 1 | 0 | 2022: | Juventus FC Torino |
| Davide FRATTESI | 22.09.1999 | 6 | 1 | 2022/2023: | US Sassuolo Calcio |
| Vincenzo GRIFO | 07.04.1993 | 9 | 4 | 2022/2023: | SC Freiburg (GER) |
| Jorge Luiz Frello Filho "JORGINHO" | 20.12.1991 | 48 | 5 | 2022: | Chelsea FC London (ENG) |
| | | | | 31.01.2023-> | Arsenal FC London (ENG) |
| Fabio MIRETTI | 03.08.2003 | 1 | 0 | 2022: | Juventus FC Torino |
| Lorenzo PELLEGRINI | 19.06.1996 | 26 | 5 | 2023: | AS Roma |
| Matteo PESSINA | 21.04.1997 | 16 | 5 | 2022/2023: | AC Monza |
| Tommaso POBEGA | 15.07.1999 | 3 | 0 | 2022/2023: | Torino FC |
| Samuele RICCI | 21.08.2001 | 2 | 0 | 2022: | Torino FC |
| Sandro TONALI | 08.05.2000 | 14 | 0 | 2022/2023: | AC Milan |
| Marco VERRATTI | 05.11.1992 | 55 | 3 | 2022/2023: | Paris Saint-Germain FC (FRA) |
| Nicolò ZANIOLO | 02.07.1999 | 13 | 2 | 2022: | AS Roma |
| | | | | 08.02.2023-> | Galatasaray SK Istanbul (TUR) |

### Forwards

| Name | DOB | Caps | Goals | Club | |
|------|-----|------|-------|------|---|
| Domenico BERARDI | 01.08.1994 | 25 | 6 | 2023: | US Sassuolo Calcio |
| Federico CHIESA | 25.10.1997 | 42 | 5 | 2022/2023: | Juventus FC Torino |
| Manolo GABBIADINI | 26.11.1991 | 13 | 2 | 2022/2023: | UC Sampdoria Genova |
| Degnand Wilfried GNONTO | 05.11.2003 | 11 | 1 | 2022/2023: | Leeds United FC (SUI) |
| Ciro IMMOBILE | 20.02.1990 | 56 | 16 | 2023: | SS Lazio Roma |
| Simone PAFUNDI | 14.03.2006 | 1 | 0 | 2022: | Udinese Calcio |
| Andrea PINAMONTI | 19.05.1999 | 1 | 0 | 2022: | US Sassuolo Calcio |
| Matteo POLITANO | 03.08.1993 | 10 | 3 | 2022/2023: | SSC Napoli |
| Giacomo RASPADORI | 18.02.2000 | 18 | 5 | 2022/2023: | SSC Napoli |
| Mateo RETEGUI | 29.04.1999 | 3 | 2 | 2023: | CA Tigre Buenos Aires (ARG) |
| Gianluca SCAMACCA | 01.01.1999 | 11 | 0 | 2022/2023: | West Ham United FC London (ENG) |

### Trainer

| Name | DOB | Record | |
|------|-----|--------|---|
| Roberto MANCINI [from 14.05.2018] | 27.11.1964 | 61 M; 37 W; 15 D; 9 L; 123-45 | |

# KAZAKHSTAN

**The Country:**
Қазақстан Республикасы (Republic of Kazakhstan)
Capital: Nur-Sultan
Surface: 2,724,900 km²
Inhabitants: 19,398,331 [2022]
Time: UTC+5/+6

**The FA:**
Қазақстанның Футбол Федерациясы (Football Federation of Kazakhstan)
5a, Momyshuly Avenue, 010000 Nur-Sultan
Tel: +7 7172 790780
Foundation date: 1914
Member of FIFA since: 1994
Member of UEFA since: 2002
Website: www.kff.kz

## NATIONAL TEAM RECORDS

| RECORDS | | |
|---|---|---|
| **First international match:** | 01.06.1992, Almaty: | Kazakhstan – Turkmenistan 1-0 |
| **Most international caps:** | Samat Smakov | - 76 caps (2000-2016) |
| **Most international goals:** | Ruslan Baltiyev | - 13 goals / 73 caps (1997-2009) |

### UEFA EUROPEAN CHAMPIONSHIP

| | |
|---|---|
| **1960** | -* |
| **1964** | - |
| **1968** | - |
| **1972** | - |
| **1976** | - |
| **1980** | - |
| **1984** | - |
| **1988** | - |
| **1992** | - |
| **1996** | - |
| **2000** | - |
| **2004** | - |
| **2008** | Qualifiers |
| **2012** | Qualifiers |
| **2016** | Qualifiers |
| **2020** | Qualifiers |

*was part of Soviet Union until 1990

### FIFA WORLD CUP

| | |
|---|---|
| **1930** | -* |
| **1934** | - |
| **1938** | - |
| **1950** | - |
| **1954** | - |
| **1958** | - |
| **1962** | - |
| **1966** | - |
| **1970** | - |
| **1974** | - |
| **1978** | - |
| **1982** | - |
| **1986** | - |
| **1990** | - |
| **1994** | Did not enter |
| **1998** | Qualifiers |
| **2002** | Qualifiers |
| **2006** | Qualifiers |
| **2010** | Qualifiers |
| **2014** | Qualifiers |
| **2018** | Qualifiers |
| **2022** | Qualifiers |

### OLYMPIC TOURNAMENTS

| | |
|---|---|
| **1908** | -* |
| **1912** | - |
| **1920** | - |
| **1924** | - |
| **1928** | - |
| **1936** | - |
| **1948** | - |
| **1952** | - |
| **1956** | - |
| **1960** | - |
| **1964** | - |
| **1968** | - |
| **1972** | - |
| **1976** | - |
| **1980** | - |
| **1984** | - |
| **1988** | - |
| **1992** | - |
| **1996** | Qualifiers |
| **2000** | Qualifiers |
| **2004** | Did not enter |
| **2008** | Qualifiers |
| **2012** | Qualifiers |
| **2016** | Qualifiers |
| **2020** | Qualifiers |

## UEFA NATIONS LEAGUE

| | |
|---|---|
| **2018/2019** | League D (Group Stage -> promoted to League C) |
| **2020/2021** | League C (Group Stage) |
| **2022/2023** | League C (Group Stage -> promoted to League B) |

## KAZAKH CLUB HONOURS IN EUROPEAN CLUB COMPETITIONS:

| European Champion Clubs' Cup (1956-1992) / UEFA Champions League (1993-2023) |
|---|
| None |

| Fairs Cup (1858-1971) / UEFA Cup (1972-2009) / UEFA Europa League (2010-2023) |
|---|
| None |

| UEFA Europa Conference League (2021-2023) |
|---|
| None |

| UEFA Super Cup (1972-2022) |
|---|
| None |

| *European Cup Winners' Cup 1961-1999** |
|---|
| None |

*defunct competition

# NATIONAL COMPETITIONS
## TABLE OF HONOURS

### KAZAKH SSR (SOVIET ERA) CHAMPIONS

| | | | | | |
|---|---|---|---|---|---|
| 1936 | Sbornaya Alma-Aty | 1960 | Yenbek Guryev | 1977 | Khimik Stepnogorsk |
| 1937 | Dinamo Alma-Ata | 1961 | Avangard Petropavlovsk | 1978 | Trud Shevchenko |
| 1938 | Dinamo Alma-Ata | 1962 | ADK Alma-Ata | 1979 | Khimik Stepnogorsk |
| 1939/1945 | *No Championship* | 1963 | Tselinnik Semipalatinsk | 1980 | Meliorator Chimkent |
| 1946 | Dinamo Alma-Ata | 1964 | ADK Alma-Ata | 1981 | Burevestnik Kustanay |
| 1947 | Lokomotiv Jambul | 1965 | ADK Alma-Ata | 1980 | Traktor Pavlodar |
| 1948 | Trudovye Rezervy Alma-Ata | 1966 | Aktyubinets Aktyubinsk | 1981 | Aktyubinets Aktyubinsk |
| 1949 | Dinamo Karaganda | 1967 | Torpedo Kokchetav | 1982 | Shakhtyor Karaganda |
| 1950 | Sbornaya Alma-Aty | 1968 | Gornyak Jezkangan | 1983 | Shakhtyor Karaganda |
| 1951 | Meliorator Chimkent | 1969 | Shakhtyor Saran' | 1984 | Tselinnik Tselinograd |
| 1952 | Meliorator Chimkent | 1970 | Stroitel Temir-Tau | 1985 | Meliorator Chimkent |
| 1953 | Meliorator Chimkent | 1971 | Yenbek Jezkangan | 1986 | Meliorator Chimkent |
| 1954 | Dinamo Alma-Ata | 1972 | Traktor Pavlodar | 1987 | Meliorator Chimkent |
| 1955 | Dinamo Alma-Ata | 1973 | Yenbek Jezkangan | 1988 | Traktor Pavlodar |
| 1956 | Sbornaya Alma-Aty | 1974 | Gornyak Nikol'sky | 1989 | Traktor Pavlodar |
| 1957 | Stroitel Alma-Ata | 1975 | Meliorator Chimkent | 1990 | Vostok Ust'-Kamenogorsk |
| 1958 | Spartak Alma-Ata | 1976 | Khimik Stepnogorsk | 1991 | Aktyubinets Aktyubinsk |
| 1959 | Spartak Alma-Ata | | | | |

| | CHAMPIONS | CUP WINNERS | BEST GOALSCORERS | |
|---|---|---|---|---|
| 1992 | FC Kairat Almaty | FC Kairat Almaty | Sergey Kogai (FC Kaysar Kyzylorda) | 21 |
| 1993 | FC Irtysh Pavlodar | FC Dostyk Almaty | Aleksandr Shmarikov (FC Taraz) | 28 |
| 1994 | FC Spartak Semey | FC Vostok Oskemen | Oleg Litvinenko (FC Taraz) | 20 |
| 1995 | FC Spartak Semey | FC Spartak Semey | Andrei Miroshnichenko (FC Spartak Semey) | 23 |
| 1996 | FC Taraz | - | Viktor Antonov (FC Irtysh Pavlodar) | 21 |
| 1997 | FC Irtysh Pavlodar | FC Kairat Almaty (1996/97) | Nurken Mazbaev (FC Taraz) | 16 |
| 1998 | FC Spartak Semey | FC Irtysh Pavlodar (1997/98) | Oleg Litvinenko (FC Spartak Semey) | 14 |
| 1999 | FC Irtysh Pavlodar | FC Kaysar Kyzylorda (1998/99) | Rejepmyrat Agabaýew (TKM, FC Kairat Almaty) | 24 |
| 2000 | FC Astana-64 | FC Kairat Almaty (1999/2000) | Nilton Pereira Mendes (BRA, FC Irtysh Pavlodar) | 21 |
| # | - | FC Astana-64 (2000/2001) | | |
| 2001 | FC Astana-64 | FC Kairat Almaty | Arsen Tlekhugov (FC Astana-64) | 30 |
| 2002 | FC Irtysh Pavlodar | FC Astana-64 | Evgeniy Lunev (FC Shakhter Karagandy) | 16 |
| 2003 | FC Irtysh Pavlodar | FC Kairat Almaty | Andrei Finonchenko (FC Shakhter Karagandy) | 18 |
| 2004 | FC Kairat Almaty | FC Taraz | Ulugbek Bakaev (UZB, FC Tobol Kostanay) Arsen Tlekhugov (FC Kairat Almaty) | 22 |
| 2005 | FC Aktobe | FC Astana-64 | Murat Tleshev (FC Irtysh Pavlodar) | 20 |
| 2006 | FC Astana-64 | FC Alma-Ata | Jafar Irismetov (UZB, FC Alma-Ata) | 17 |
| 2007 | FC Aktobe | FC Tobol Kostanay | Jafar Irismetov (UZB, FC Alma-Ata) | 17 |
| 2008 | FC Aktobe | FC Aktobe | Murat Tleshev (FC Irtysh Pavlodar) | 13 |
| 2009 | FC Aktobe | FC Atyrau | Murat Tleshev (FC Aktobe) Wladimir Baýramow (TKM, FC Tobol Kostanay) | 20 |
| 2010 | FC Tobol Kostanay | FC Lokomotiv Astana | Ulugbek Bakaev (UZB, FC Tobol Kostanay) | 16 |
| 2011 | FC Shakhter Karagandy | FC Ordabasy | Ulugbek Bakaev (UZB, FC Zhetysu Taldykorgan) | 18 |
| 2012 | FC Shakhter Karagandy | Astana FC | Ulugbek Bakaev (UZB, FC Irtysh Pavlodar) | 14 |
| 2013 | FC Aktobe | FC Shakhter Karagandy | Ihar Zenkovich (BLR, FC Shakhter Karagandy) | 15 |
| 2014 | Astana FC | FC Kairat Almaty | Foxi Kéthévoama (CTA, Astana FC) | 16 |
| 2015 | Astana FC | FC Kairat Almaty | Gerard Bi Goua Gohou (CIV, FC Kairat Almaty) | 22 |
| 2016 | Astana FC | Astana FC | Gerard Bi Goua Gohou (CIV, FC Kairat Almaty) | 22 |
| 2017 | Astana FC | FC Kairat Almaty | Gerard Bi Goua Gohou (CIV, FC Kairat Almaty) | 24 |
| 2018 | Astana FC | FC Kairat Almaty | Marcos Pinheiro Pizzelli (FC Aktobe) | 18 |
| 2019 | Astana FC Nur-Sultan | FC Kaysar Kyzylorda | Marin Tomasov (CRO, Astana FC Nur-Sultan) Aderinsola Habib Eseola (UKR, FC Kairat Almaty) | 19 |
| 2020 | FC Kairat Almaty | *Competition cancelled* | João Paulo da Silva Araújo (BRA, FC Ordabasy Shymkent) | 12 |
| 2021 | FC Tobol Kostanay | FC Kairat Almaty | Marin Tomasov (CRO, Astana FC Nur-Sultan) | 17 |
| 2022 | Astana FC | FC Ordabasy Shymkent | Pedro Miguel Pina Eugénio (POR, Astana FC Nur-Sultan) | 18 |

<u>Please note</u>: FC Lokomotiv Astana changed its name to Astana FC in 2011.

# NATIONAL CHAMPIONSHIP
## Kazakhstan Premier League 2022
### (05.03.2022 – 06.11.2022)

**Results**

**Round 1 [05-06.03.2022]**
FC Ordabasy - FC Maqtaaral 1-1(1-1)
Astana FC - Shakter Karaganda 0-3 *awarded*
FC Atyrau - FC Aqsu 0-0
FC Caspiy - FC Kyzylzhar 1-0(0-0)
FC Turan - FC Taraz 0-0
FC Kairat - FC Aktobe 2-0(0-0)
Tobol Kostanay - FC Akzhayik 1-0(0-0)

**Round 2 [10-11.03.2022]**
FC Taraz - FC Ordabasy 1-0(1-0)
FC Aqsu - Astana FC 1-0(0-0)
FC Kyzylzhar - Shakter Karaganda 0-1(0-0)
FC Caspiy - Tobol Kostanay 0-0
FC Aktobe - FC Atyrau 2-1(1-1)
FC Maqtaaral - FC Kairat 0-1(0-1)
FC Akzhayik-FC Turan 1-1(1-1) [05.10.2022]

**Round 3 [17.03.2022]**
FC Atyrau - FC Maqtaaral 2-1(2-0)
FC Kairat - FC Taraz 1-1(0-0)
FC Ordabasy - FC Akzhayik 2-0(0-0)
FC Turan - FC Caspiy 0-1(0-1)
Astana FC - FC Aktobe 1-0(1-0)
Tobol Kostanay - FC Kyzylzhar 2-0(1-0)
Shakter Kar. - FC Aqsu 4-2(3-0) [12.07.2022]

**Round 4 [03-04.04.2022]**
FC Caspiy - FC Ordabasy 2-1(2-1)
FC Aktobe - Shakter Karaganda 1-1(0-0)
FC Taraz - FC Atyrau 0-1(0-1)
FC Maqtaaral - Astana FC 0-3(0-2)
FC Kyzylzhar - FC Aqsu 2-1(1-1)
FC Akzhayik - FC Kairat 0-0
Tobol Kostanay - FC Turan 3-0(1-0)

**Round 5 [09-10.04.2022]**
FC Atyrau - FC Akzhayik 0-1(0-1)
FC Ordabasy - Tobol Kostanay 3-1(2-1)
FC Kairat - FC Caspiy 1-0(1-0)
Shakter Karaganda - FC Maqtaaral 5-1(3-0)
FC Aqsu - FC Aktobe 1-2(0-0)
FC Turan - FC Kyzylzhar 0-0
Astana FC - FC Taraz 2-1(1-1)

**Round 6 [16-17.04.2022]**
FC Akzhayik - Astana FC 1-0(1-0)
FC Caspiy - FC Atyrau 2-1(1-0)
FC Kyzylzhar - FC Aktobe 1-1(1-0)
FC Turan - FC Ordabasy 0-0
Tobol Kostanay - FC Kairat 2-2(1-1)
FC Maqtaaral - FC Aqsu 2-1(2-1)
FC Taraz - Shakter Karaganda 2-1(0-0)

**Round 7 [22-23.04.2022]**
FC Atyrau - Tobol Kostanay 2-1(0-0)
Astana FC - FC Caspiy 4-0(3-0)
Shakter Karaganda - FC Akzhayik 0-1(0-0)
FC Aktobe - FC Maqtaaral 1-0(0-0)
FC Ordabasy - FC Kyzylzhar 3-1(1-1)
FC Kairat - FC Turan 0-1(0-1)
FC Aqsu - FC Taraz 1-2(0-1)

**Round 8 [26-27.04.2022]**
FC Ordabasy - FC Kairat 2-1(1-1)
Tobol Kostanay - Astana FC 1-1(1-0)
FC Kyzylzhar - FC Maqtaaral 1-1(0-1)
FC Akzhayik - FC Aqsu 0-1(0-0)
FC Caspiy - Shakter Karaganda 4-0(1-0)
FC Turan - FC Atyrau 0-0
FC Taraz - FC Aktobe 3-0(1-0)

**Round 9 [01-02.05.2022]**
Astana FC - FC Turan 3-3(1-3)
FC Atyrau - FC Ordabasy 2-1(1-1)
Shakter Karaganda - Tobol Kostanay 4-1(1-0)
FC Aktobe - FC Akzhayik 2-1(0-1)
FC Kairat - FC Kyzylzhar 1-1(1-0)
FC Aqsu - FC Caspiy 2-0(1-0)
FC Maqtaaral - FC Taraz 0-1(0-0)

**Round 10 [07-08.05.2022]**
FC Kyzylzhar - FC Taraz 1-1(0-0)
FC Ordabasy - Astana FC 1-2(1-1)
FC Kairat - FC Atyrau 0-3(0-3)
Tobol Kostanay - FC Aqsu 2-0(1-0)
FC Akzhayik - FC Maqtaaral 0-0
FC Caspiy - FC Aktobe 2-0(0-0)
FC Turan - Shakter Karaganda 2-0(1-0)

**Round 11 [14-15.05.2022]**
Shakter Karaganda - FC Ordabasy 1-0(0-0)
FC Atyrau - FC Kyzylzhar 3-3(1-0)
Astana FC - FC Kairat 6-0(3-0)
FC Aqsu - FC Turan 2-0(1-0)
FC Aktobe - Tobol Kostanay 2-1(0-0)
FC Maqtaaral - FC Caspiy 2-1(1-0)
FC Taraz - FC Akzhayik 2-0(1-0)

**Round 12 [21-22.05.2022]**
FC Atyrau - Astana FC 1-1(0-0)
FC Kairat - Shakter Karaganda 2-0(1-0)
FC Kyzylzhar - FC Akzhayik 2-0(1-0)
Tobol Kostanay - FC Maqtaaral 4-2(0-0)
FC Caspiy - FC Taraz 2-1(2-0)
FC Ordabasy - FC Aqsu 3-0(2-0) [29.06.2022]
FC Turan - FC Aktobe 0-2(0-1) [12.07.2022]

**Round 13 [20-21.08.2022]**
Shakter Karaganda - FC Atyrau 0-0
FC Akzhayik - FC Caspiy 2-0(0-0)
FC Maqtaaral - FC Turan 2-0(0-0)
Astana FC - FC Kyzylzhar 1-0(1-0)
Tobol Kostanay - FC Taraz 2-2(2-2)
FC Aqsu - FC Kairat 1-2(0-2)
FC Aktobe - FC Ordabasy 3-1(2-1)

**Round 14 [19.06.2022]**
Shakter Karaganda - FC Kyzylzhar 1-2(1-0)
FC Ordabasy - FC Taraz 3-2(3-1)
FC Atyrau - FC Aktobe 0-2(0-0)
FC Kairat - FC Maqtaaral 1-0(0-0)
FC Turan - FC Akzhayik 1-1(1-0)
Astana FC - FC Aqsu 5-0(2-0)
Tobol Kostanay - FC Caspiy 1-0(1-0)

**Round 15 [25-26.06.2022]**
FC Akzhayik - FC Ordabasy 0-1(0-0)
FC Aqsu - Shakter Karaganda 1-1(1-0)
FC Kyzylzhar - Tobol Kostanay 1-3(1-1)
FC Caspiy - FC Turan 0-2(0-2)
FC Taraz - FC Kairat 1-1(1-1)
FC Aktobe - Astana FC 4-1(2-1)
FC Maqtaaral - FC Atyrau 1-1(0-0)

**Round 16 [01-04.07.2022]**
FC Turan - Tobol Kostanay 2-2(0-0)
Shakter Karaganda - FC Aktobe 2-3(2-0)
FC Atyrau - FC Taraz 0-0
Astana FC - FC Maqtaaral 4-0(0-0)
FC Aqsu - FC Kyzylzhar 1-0(0-0)
FC Kairat - FC Akzhayik 2-0(1-0)
FC Ordabasy - FC Caspiy 4-1(2-0)

**Round 17 [26-27.08.2022]**
FC Akzhayik - FC Atyrau 4-2(3-1)
FC Aktobe - FC Aqsu 1-0(1-0)
FC Maqtaaral - Shakter Karaganda 0-2(0-1)
FC Kyzylzhar - FC Turan 3-1(0-0)
FC Caspiy - FC Kairat 2-2(0-2)
FC Taraz - Astana FC 1-1(1-0)
Tobol Kostanay - FC Ordabasy 4-0(2-0)

**Round 18 [04-05.09.2022]**
Shakter Karaganda - FC Taraz 1-0(1-0)
FC Atyrau - FC Caspiy 3-2(0-1)
FC Aqsu - FC Maqtaaral 4-2(2-2)
FC Ordabasy - FC Turan 1-2(0-2)
FC Kairat - Tobol Kostanay 2-3(0-2)
FC Aktobe - FC Kyzylzhar 1-0(0-0)
Astana FC - FC Akzhayik 4-0(1-0)

**Round 19 [10-11.09.2022]**
FC Akzhayik - Shakter Karaganda 1-2(0-1)
FC Taraz - FC Aqsu 3-4(2-2)
FC Caspiy - Astana FC 0-3(0-1)
FC Maqtaaral - FC Aktobe 1-1(0-1)
Tobol Kostanay - FC Atyrau 0-2(0-1)
FC Kyzylzhar - FC Ordabasy 4-0(1-0)
FC Turan - FC Kairat 1-3(0-2)

**Round 20 [14-15.09.2022]**
Astana FC - Tobol Kostanay 1-2(1-1)
FC Aktobe - FC Taraz 1-0(0-0)
FC Atyrau - FC Turan 0-2(0-1)
Shakter Karaganda - FC Caspiy 0-1(0-0)
FC Aqsu - FC Akzhayik 1-0(0-0)
FC Kairat - FC Ordabasy 1-2(1-0)
FC Maqtaaral - FC Kyzylzhar 1-1(0-1)

**Round 21 [01-02.10.2022]**
FC Caspiy - FC Aqsu 1-0(1-0)
FC Ordabasy - FC Atyrau 2-0(1-0)
FC Taraz - FC Maqtaaral 0-1(0-1)
FC Kyzylzhar - FC Kairat 1-2(1-1)
Tobol Kostanay - Shakter Karaganda 3-1(1-1)
FC Akzhayik - FC Aktobe 3-1(1-0)
FC Turan - Astana FC 2-2(0-0)

**Round 22 [08-09.10.2022]**
FC Aktobe - FC Caspiy 4-0(2-0)
FC Aqsu - Tobol Kostanay 3-0(3-0)
Shakter Karaganda - FC Turan 0-0
FC Atyrau - FC Kairat 1-2(0-1)
Astana FC - FC Ordabasy 6-0(0-0)
FC Taraz - FC Kyzylzhar 0-0
FC Maqtaaral - FC Akzhayik 1-0(1-0)

**Round 23 [14-15.10.2022]**
FC Akzhayik - FC Taraz 0-0
FC Caspiy - FC Maqtaaral 2-4(2-0)
FC Ordabasy - Shakter Karaganda 1-0(0-0)
FC Turan - FC Aqsu 0-1(0-0)
FC Kyzylzhar - FC Atyrau 3-1(2-1)
Tobol Kostanay - FC Aktobe 1-0(0-0)
FC Kairat - Astana FC 0-4(0-1)

**Round 24 [23-24.10.2022]**
Shakter Karaganda - FC Kairat 0-2(0-1)
FC Akzhayik - FC Kyzylzhar 2-2(2-1)
FC Maqtaaral - Tobol Kostanay 2-1(2-0)
Astana FC - FC Atyrau 5-1(3-0)
FC Taraz - FC Caspiy 1-1(0-1)
FC Aqsu - FC Ordabasy 2-2(2-2)
FC Aktobe - FC Turan 3-2(2-1)

**Round 25** [29-30.10.2022]

FC Caspiy - FC Akzhayik 0-0
FC Taraz - Tobol Kostanay 0-2(0-2)
FC Ordabasy - FC Aktobe 2-2(0-2)
FC Kairat - FC Aqsu 2-0(0-0)
FC Kyzylzhar - Astana FC 0-2(0-1)
FC Atyrau - Shakter Karaganda 2-2(1-2)
FC Turan - FC Maqtaaral 0-3(0-2)

**Round 26** [06.11.2022]

FC Aktobe - FC Kairat 4-1(3-1)
FC Akzhayik - Tobol Kostanay 1-3(0-1)
FC Kyzylzhar - FC Caspiy 4-1(2-0)
Shakter Karaganda - Astana FC 2-3(1-2)
FC Taraz - FC Turan 2-3(0-1)
FC Aqsu - FC Atyrau 2-1(1-0)
FC Maqtaaral - FC Ordabasy 0-0

## Final Standings

| | | | | | | | | Total | | Home | | | | | Away | | | | |
|---|---|---|---|---|---|---|---|---|---|---|---|---|---|---|---|---|---|---|---|
| 1. | **Astana FC** | 26 | 16 | 5 | 5 | 65 - 24 | **53** | | 10 | 1 | 2 | 42 - 10 | | 6 | 4 | 3 | 23 - 14 |
| 2. | FC Aktobe | 26 | 16 | 4 | 6 | 43 - 28 | **52** | | 12 | 1 | 0 | 29 - 9 | | 4 | 3 | 6 | 14 - 19 |
| 3. | FC Tobol Kostanay | 26 | 14 | 5 | 7 | 46 - 33 | **47** | | 9 | 3 | 1 | 26 - 10 | | 5 | 2 | 6 | 20 - 23 |
| 4. | FC Kairat Almaty | 26 | 12 | 6 | 8 | 34 - 36 | **42** | | 6 | 2 | 5 | 15 - 15 | | 6 | 4 | 3 | 19 - 21 |
| 5. | FC Ordabasy Shymkent | 26 | 11 | 5 | 10 | 36 - 39 | **38** | | 9 | 2 | 2 | 28 - 13 | | 2 | 3 | 8 | 8 - 26 |
| 6. | FC Aqsu | 26 | 11 | 3 | 12 | 32 - 37 | **36** | | 8 | 2 | 3 | 22 - 12 | | 3 | 1 | 9 | 10 - 25 |
| 7. | FC Shakhter Karagandy | 26 | 9 | 5 | 12 | 34 - 35 | **32** | | 5 | 2 | 6 | 20 - 16 | | 4 | 3 | 6 | 14 - 19 |
| 8. | FC Maqtaaral Jetisay | 26 | 8 | 7 | 11 | 28 - 38 | **31** | | 5 | 4 | 4 | 12 - 13 | | 3 | 3 | 7 | 16 - 25 |
| 9. | FC Caspiy Aqtau | 26 | 9 | 4 | 13 | 26 - 42 | **31** | | 7 | 3 | 3 | 18 - 14 | | 2 | 1 | 10 | 8 - 28 |
| 10. | FC Kyzylzhar SK Petropavl | 26 | 7 | 9 | 10 | 33 - 32 | **30** | | 6 | 3 | 4 | 23 - 15 | | 1 | 6 | 6 | 10 - 17 |
| 11. | FC Atyrau | 26 | 7 | 8 | 11 | 30 - 39 | **29** | | 4 | 5 | 4 | 16 - 18 | | 3 | 3 | 7 | 14 - 21 |
| 12. | FC Taraz | 26 | 6 | 10 | 10 | 27 - 29 | **28** | | 4 | 4 | 5 | 16 - 15 | | 2 | 6 | 5 | 11 - 14 |
| 13. | FC Turan Turkistan (*Relegated*) | 26 | 6 | 10 | 10 | 25 - 35 | **28** | | 1 | 7 | 5 | 8 - 15 | | 5 | 3 | 5 | 17 - 20 |
| 14. | FC Akzhayik Oral (*Relegated*) | 26 | 6 | 7 | 13 | 19 - 31 | **25** | | 4 | 5 | 4 | 15 - 13 | | 2 | 2 | 9 | 4 - 18 |

| Top goalscorers: | |
|---|---|
| 18  Pedro Miguel Pina Eugénio (POR) | *Astana FC Nur-Sultan* |
| 15  Marin Tomasov (CRO) | *Astana FC Nur-Sultan* |
| 13  Andrija Filipović (CRO) | *FC Atyrau* |

# NATIONAL CUP
### Kazakhstan Kubok 2022

## Group Stage [08.07.-14.08.2022]

### Gruppe A

| | |
|---|---|
| FC Aqsu - FC Atyrau | 0-1 |
| FC Kairat Almaty - FC Ordabasy Shymkent | 2-0 |
| FC Atyrau - FC Kairat Almaty | 2-3 |
| FC Ordabasy Shymkent - FC Aqsu | 2-0 |
| FC Atyrau - FC Ordabasy Shymkent | 1-4 |
| FC Kairat Almaty - FC Aqsu | 3-2 |
| FC Ordabasy Shymkent - FC Atyrau | 1-2 |
| FC Aqsu - FC Kairat Almaty | 1-1 |
| FC Atyrau - FC Aqsu | 0-0 |
| FC Ordabasy Shymkent - FC Kairat Almaty | 1-3 |
| FC Kairat Almaty - FC Atyrau | 3-0 |
| FC Aqsu - FC Ordabasy Shymkent | 0-1 |
| *Qualified*: FC Kairat Almaty, FC Ordabasy Shymkent | |

### Gruppe B

| | |
|---|---|
| FC Kaysar Kyzylorda - FC Akzhayik Oral | 1-0 |
| FC Caspiy Aqtau - FC Kyzylzhar SK Petropavl | 1-1 |
| FC Kyzylzhar SK Petropavl - FC Kaysar Kyzylorda | 1-2 |
| FC Akzhayik Oral - FC Caspiy Aqtau | 3-1 |
| FC Caspiy Aqtau - FC Kaysar Kyzylorda | 1-2 |
| FC Akzhayik Oral - FC Kyzylzhar SK Petropavl | 1-0 |
| FC Kaysar Kyzylorda - FC Caspiy Aqtau | 1-2 |
| FC Kyzylzhar SK Petropavl - FC Akzhayik Oral | 0-2 |
| FC Akzhayik Oral - FC Kaysar Kyzylorda | 2-2 |
| FC Kyzylzhar SK Petropavl - FC Caspiy Aqtau | 1-3 |
| FC Caspiy Aqtau - FC Akzhayik Oral | 2-1 |
| FC Kaysar Kyzylorda - FC Kyzylzhar SK Petropavl | 3-1 |
| *Qualified*: FC Kaysar Kyzylorda, FC Akzhayik Oral | |

### Gruppe C

| | |
|---|---|
| FC Maqtaaral Jetisay - FC Aktobe | 3-2 |
| FC Taraz - FC Tobol Kostanay | 6-1 |
| FC Tobol Kostanay - FC Aktobe | 2-1 |
| FC Taraz - FC Maqtaaral Jetisay | 4-2 |
| FC Taraz - FC Aktobe | 0-0 |
| FC Tobol Kostanay - FC Maqtaaral Jetisay | 1-4 |
| FC Aktobe - FC Taraz | 1-1 |
| FC Maqtaaral Jetisay - FC Tobol Kostanay | 1-0 |
| FC Aktobe - FC Maqtaaral Jetisay | 1-0 |
| FC Tobol Kostanay - FC Taraz | 3-5 |
| FC Maqtaaral Jetisay - FC Taraz | 1-1 |
| FC Aktobe - FC Tobol Kostanay | 1-0 |
| *Qualified*: FC Taraz, FC Maqtaaral Jetisay | |

### Gruppe D

| | |
|---|---|
| FC Zhetysu Taldiqorghan - Astana FC Nur-Sultan | 0-0 |
| FC Shakhter Karagandy - FC Turan Turkistan | 4-0 |
| Astana FC Nur-Sultan - FC Shakhter Karagandy | 5-2 |
| FC Turan Turkistan - FC Zhetysu Taldiqorghan | 3-0 |
| FC Turan Turkistan - Astana FC Nur-Sultan | 1-1 |
| FC Zhetysu Taldiqorghan - FC Shakhter Karagandy | 0-0 |
| FC Shakhter Karagandy - FC Zhetysu Taldiqorghan | 4-2 |
| Astana FC - FC Turan Turkistan | 2-1 |
| FC Turan Turkistan - FC Shakhter Karagandy | 0-2 |
| Astana FC - FC Zhetysu Taldiqorghan | 2-2 |
| FC Zhetysu Taldiqorghan - FC Turan Turkistan | 0-0 |
| FC Shakhter Karagandy - Astana FC | 1-7 |
| *Qualified*: Astana FC, FC Shakhter Karagandy | |

### Quarter-Finals [31.08.2022]

| | | | | |
|---|---|---|---|---|
| FC Taraz - FC Shakhter Karagandy | 1-1 aet; 4-2 pen | Astana FC - FC Maqtaaral Jetisay | 1-0 |
| FC Kairat Almaty - FC Akzhayik Oral | 1-2 | FC Kaysar Kyzylorda - FC Ordabasy Shymkent | 1-1 aet; 1-4 pen |

### Semi-Finals [19.10.2022]

| | | | | |
|---|---|---|---|---|
| FC Akzhayik Oral - FC Taraz | 5-3 | Astana FC - FC Ordabasy Shymkent | 2-3 |

12.11.2022; Astana Arena, Nur-Sultan; Referee: Artem Kuchin; Attendance: 3,620
**FC Akzhayik Oral - FC Ordabasy Shymkent**                                           **4-5(2-1,4-4)**

**FC Akzhayik**: Ştefan Sicaci, Bauyrzhan Omarov, Vitaliy Pryndeta, Sergey Shustikov (Cap), Pavel Nazarenko (90+9.Ruslan Khairov), Maksym Kalenchuk (62.Batyr Mukashev), Zaven Badoyan, Rafael Sabino dos Santos (62.Amir Bilali), Ilya Kovalenko (78.Petros Avetisyan), Luka Imnadze (70.Oralkhan Omirtaev), Toma Tabatadze (78.Artur Gazdanov). Trainer: Oleg Bejenari (Moldova).

**FC Ordabasy**: Bekkhan Shayzada, Dzmitriy Borodin, Karam Sultanov, Sagadat Tursynbay, Samat Shamshi (Cap) (75.Serge Komla Nyuiadzi), Victor Cristiano Braga, Shakhboz Umarov (86.Luiz Enrique Guedes "Luizinho Guedes"), Oleksandr Batyshchev, Akmal Bakhtiyarov (82.Adilkhan Dobay), Maksim Fedin, Vsevolod Sadovskiy (75.Elkhan Astanov). Trainer: Aliaksandr Sednev (Belarus).

**Goals**: 1-0 Zaven Badoyan (7), 2-0 Toma Tabatadze (11), 2-1 Samat Shamshi (26), 2-2 Vsevolod Sadovskiy (51), 3-2 Toma Tabatadze (68), 4-2 Ilya Kovalenko (74), 4-3 Maksim Fedin (76), 4-4 Luiz Enrique Guedes "Luizinho Guedes" (90+7), 4-5 Elkhan Astanov (119 penalty).

## THE CLUBS 2022

### Football Club Aqsu

| | | |
|---|---|---|
| **Founded**: | 2018 | |
| **Stadium**: | Central Stadium, Pavlodar (11,828) | |
| **Trainer**: | Ruslan Kostyshyn (UKR) | 08.01.1977 |

| Goalkeepers: | DOB | M | (s) | G |
|---|---|---|---|---|
| Mikhail Golubnichiy | 31.01.1995 | 1 | | |
| Marsel Islamkulov | 18.04.1994 | 9 | | |
| Yevgeniy Kucherenko (UKR) | 27.08.1999 | 16 | | |
| **Defenders:** | **DOB** | **M** | **(s)** | **G** |
| Oleksiy Dytyatyev (UKR) | 07.11.1988 | 3 | | |
| Ali Gadzhibekov (RUS) | 06.08.1989 | 12 | | 1 |
| Faith Friday Obilor (NGA) | 05.03.1991 | 21 | (1) | |
| Artem Popov | 17.01.1998 | | (1) | |
| Gafurzhan Suyumbaev | 19.08.1990 | 24 | | 1 |
| Ruslan Yessimov | 28.04.1990 | 10 | | 1 |
| Ular Zhaksybaev | 20.10.1994 | 23 | (2) | 2 |
| Kayrat Zhyrgalbek uulu (KGZ) | 13.06.1993 | 23 | (2) | |
| Islam Zhilov (RUS) | 29.11.1997 | 6 | (13) | |
| **Midfielders:** | **DOB** | **M** | **(s)** | **G** |
| Aybol Abiken | 01.06.1996 | 7 | | 3 |
| Dmitriy Bachek | 13.12.2000 | 2 | (5) | |
| Mikhail Bakaev (RUS) | 05.08.1987 | 13 | (3) | |
| Gilson Sequeira da Costa (POR) | 24.09.1996 | 3 | (4) | |

| | DOB | M | (s) | G |
|---|---|---|---|---|
| Zhaslan Kairkenov | 27.03.2000 | 3 | (4) | |
| Anatoliy Krasotin | 21.02.2000 | 9 | (8) | |
| Izat Kulzhanov | 18.07.2001 | 5 | (2) | |
| May Mahlangu (RSA) | 01.05.1989 | | (3) | |
| Matvey Matvienko | 22.04.1995 | | (1) | |
| Rafail Ospanov | 05.11.1997 | | (5) | |
| Yevgen Zadoya (UKR) | 05.01.1991 | 2 | (2) | |
| Lazar Zličić (SRB) | 07.02.1997 | 11 | | 1 |
| **Forwards:** | **DOB** | **M** | **(s)** | **G** |
| Tamerlan Agimanov | 16.08.2006 | | (3) | |
| Sam Johnson (LBR) | 06.05.1993 | 3 | (2) | |
| Aslanbek Kakimov | 02.10.1993 | 14 | (4) | 3 |
| Sergey Khizhnichenko | 17.07.1991 | 3 | (3) | |
| Damir Marat | 05.11.2000 | 14 | (10) | 2 |
| Toni Brito Silva Sá (GNB) | 15.09.1993 | 11 | | 4 |
| Arman Smailov | 04.05.1997 | 2 | (17) | 2 |
| Erkebulan Tungyshbaev | 14.01.1995 | 18 | (7) | 8 |
| Miras Turlybek | 17.07.2001 | 16 | (9) | 4 |
| Georgiy Zakharenko | 12.01.1998 | 2 | (3) | |

### Football Club Aktobe

| | | |
|---|---|---|
| **Founded**: | 1967 | |
| **Stadium**: | Koblandy Batyr Stadium, Aktobe (12,729) | |
| **Trainer**: | Vladimir Mukhanov (RUS) | 20.04.1954 |
| [27.04.2022] | Petr Badlo | 24.05.1976 |
| [16.05.2022] | Andrei Karpovich | 18.01.1981 |

| Goalkeepers: | DOB | M | (s) | G |
|---|---|---|---|---|
| Stas Pokatilov | 08.12.1992 | 21 | | |
| Sasa Stamenković (SRB) | 05.01.1985 | 5 | | |
| **Defenders:** | **DOB** | **M** | **(s)** | **G** |
| Alisher Azhimov | 29.05.2001 | | (1) | |
| Temirlan Erlanov | 09.07.1993 | 19 | (1) | |
| Vladimir Ghinaitis (MDA) | 30.03.1995 | 7 | (2) | |
| Alibek Kasym | 27.05.1998 | 21 | (4) | 7 |
| Eskendir Kybyray | 14.08.1997 | 4 | (8) | |
| Dmitri Shomko | 19.03.1990 | 21 | (3) | |
| Adilkhan Tanzharikov | 25.11.1996 | 17 | (5) | |
| Ruslan Temirkhan | 10.08.1997 | | (1) | |
| **Midfielders:** | **DOB** | **M** | **(s)** | **G** |
| Joachim Adukor (LBR) | 02.05.1993 | 16 | (4) | 1 |
| Bauyrzhan Baytana | 06.05.1992 | 9 | | 1 |

| | DOB | M | (s) | G |
|---|---|---|---|---|
| Ruslan Kambolov (RUS) | 01.01.1990 | 12 | (5) | 1 |
| Arman Kenesov | 04.09.2000 | 8 | (12) | 1 |
| Yuri Logvinenko | 22.07.1988 | 8 | (7) | |
| Nikita Malyarov (RUS) | 23.10.1989 | 5 | (4) | 1 |
| Ramazan Orazov | 30.01.1998 | 17 | (5) | |
| Arturas Žulpa (LTU) | 10.06.1990 | 20 | (1) | 1 |
| **Forwards:** | **DOB** | **M** | **(s)** | **G** |
| Master Ernest Antwi Nyarko (GHA) | 09.09.1995 | 2 | (5) | |
| Vitaliy Balashov (UKR) | 15.01.1991 | 6 | (16) | 1 |
| Rogerio Alves dos Santos „China" (BRA) | 02.08.1996 | 22 | (3) | 5 |
| Gerard Bi Goua Gohou (RWA) | 29.12.1988 | 13 | (8) | 8 |
| Maksim Samorodov | 29.06.2002 | 8 | (14) | 3 |
| Serder Serderov (RUS) | 10.03.1994 | 11 | (7) | 4 |
| Hugo Vidémont (FRA) | 19.02.1993 | 14 | | 8 |

### Football Club Akzhayik Oral

| | | |
|---|---|---|
| **Founded**: | 1968 | |
| **Stadium**: | „Petr Atoyan" Stadium, Oral (8,320) | |
| **Trainer**: | Volodymyr Mazyar (UKR) | 28.09.1977 |
| [14.07.2022] | Igor Picuşceac (MDA) | 27.03.1983 |
| [21.08.2022] | Oleg Bejenari (MDA) | 17.09.1971 |

| Goalkeepers: | DOB | M | (s) | G |
|---|---|---|---|---|
| Kostyantyn Makhnovskyi (UKR) | 01.01.1989 | 3 | | |
| Ştefan Sicaci (MDA) | 08.09.1988 | 17 | | |
| Rodion Syamuk (BLR) | 11.03.1989 | 6 | | |
| **Defenders:** | **DOB** | **M** | **(s)** | **G** |
| Eldar Abdrakhmanov | 16.01.1987 | 11 | (7) | |
| Amir Bilali (ALB) | 15.05.1994 | 6 | (2) | |
| Ruslan Khairov | 18.01.1990 | | (5) | |
| Pavel Nazarenko (BLR) | 20.01.1995 | 9 | (3) | |
| Bauyrzhan Omarov | 03.08.1990 | 22 | (2) | |
| Vladimir Pokatilov | 08.12.1992 | | (3) | |
| Vitaliy Pryndeta (UKR) | 02.02.1993 | 17 | (6) | 1 |
| Miram Sapanov | 12.03.1986 | 12 | (2) | |
| Sergey Shustikov (RUS) | 05.05.1989 | 21 | (3) | 1 |
| Miloš Stamenković (SRB) | 01.06.1990 | 10 | (2) | |
| **Midfielders:** | **DOB** | **M** | **(s)** | **G** |
| Petros Avetisyan (ARM) | 07.01.1996 | 9 | (2) | 3 |
| Mate Crnčević (CRO) | 20.03.1995 | 2 | (4) | |

| | DOB | M | (s) | G |
|---|---|---|---|---|
| Maksym Kalenchuk (UKR) | 05.12.1989 | 21 | (1) | 1 |
| Batyr Mukashev | 04.02.2003 | 1 | (3) | |
| Rafael Sabino dos Santos (BRA) | 17.06.1996 | 24 | | |
| Aleksandr Vulfov (RUS) | 07.02.1998 | 3 | (3) | |
| **Forwards:** | **DOB** | **M** | **(s)** | **G** |
| Ivan Antipov | 14.01.1996 | 6 | (2) | |
| Zaven Badoyan (ARM) | 22.12.1989 | 12 | (7) | 1 |
| Artur Gazdanov (RUS) | 26.07.1992 | 13 | (9) | 1 |
| Bekzat Imangazeev | 18.02.2000 | | (9) | |
| Luka Imnadze (GEO) | 26.08.1997 | 23 | (1) | 3 |
| Rysbek Konyrov | 22.07.2002 | | (1) | |
| Igor Karpenko (UKR) | 24.09.1997 | 2 | (8) | |
| Saleta Kordić (MNE) | 19.04.1993 | | (2) | |
| Ilya Kovalenko (UKR) | 20.03.1990 | 3 | (6) | 1 |
| Oralkhan Omirtaev | 16.07.1998 | 11 | (12) | 3 |
| Ardak Saulet | 12.01.1997 | 13 | (5) | |
| Toma Tabatadze (GEO) | 17.12.1991 | 9 | (2) | 3 |

## Astana Football Club

| Founded: | 2009 (*as FC Lokomotiv Astana*) | |
|---|---|---|
| Stadium: | Astana Arena, Astana (30,200) | |
| Trainer: | Srđan Blagojević (SRB) | 06.06.1973 |
| [13.09.2022] | Grigoriy Babayan | 02.04.1980 |

| Goalkeepers: | DOB | M | (s) | G |
|---|---|---|---|---|
| Marko Milošević (SRB) | 07.02.1991 | 15 | | |
| Aleksandr Zarutskiy | 26.08.1993 | 11 | | |
| **Defenders:** | **DOB** | **M** | **(s)** | **G** |
| Abzal Beysebekov | 30.11.1992 | 11 | (7) | 1 |
| Danylo Beskorovaynyi (UKR) | 07.02.1999 | 15 | (5) | |
| Bryan Silva Garcia (BRA) | 28.03.1992 | 14 | (4) | |
| Timur Dosmagambetov | 01.05.1989 | 9 | (1) | 4 |
| Mikhail Gabyshev | 02.01.1990 | 3 | (2) | |
| Kamo Hovhannisyan (ARM) | 05.10.1992 | 23 | (1) | |
| Talgat Kusyapov | 14.02.1999 | 12 | (2) | 1 |
| Denis Polyakov (BLR) | 17.04.1991 | 18 | | 1 |
| Artem Rakhmanov (BLR) | 10.07.1990 | 7 | (6) | |
| Sagi Sovet | 15.03.2000 | 3 | (2) | |

| Midfielders: | DOB | M | (s) | G |
|---|---|---|---|---|
| Aslan Darabaev | 21.01.1989 | 23 | (1) | 2 |
| Maks Ebong (BLR) | 26.08.1999 | 22 | (1) | 2 |
| Islambek Kuat | 12.01.1993 | 6 | (5) | |
| Jérémy Manzorro (FRA) | 11.11.1991 | 16 | (3) | |
| Yuri Pertsukh | 13.05.1996 | 1 | (8) | 1 |
| Sultan Sagnaev | 14.01.2000 | | (10) | 1 |
| **Forwards:** | **DOB** | **M** | **(s)** | **G** |
| Abat Aymbetov | 07.08.1995 | 10 | (9) | 9 |
| Stanislav Basmanov | 24.06.2001 | 1 | (18) | 3 |
| Mohammed Kamara (LBR) | 31.10.1997 | 1 | (1) | |
| Keelan Lebon (FRA) | 04.07.1997 | 3 | (8) | 1 |
| Pedro Miguel Pina Eugénio (POR) | 26.06.1990 | 25 | | 18 |
| Vladislav Prokopenko | 01.07.2000 | 1 | (3) | |
| Marin Tomasov (CRO) | 31.08.1987 | 25 | | 15 |
| Rai Vloet (NED) | 08.05.1995 | 11 | (3) | 5 |

## Football Club Atyrau

| Founded: | 1980 | |
|---|---|---|
| Stadium: | Munayshy Stadium, Atyrau (8,900) | |
| Trainer: | Konstantin Gorovenko | 10.01.1977 |
| [18.08.2022] | Vyacheslav Bogatyrev | 12.10.1977 |
| [22.08.2022] | Vitaly Zhukovsky | 17.05.1984 |

| Goalkeepers: | DOB | M | (s) | G |
|---|---|---|---|---|
| Aram Hayrapetyan (ARM) | 22.11.1986 | 23 | | |
| Ilya Karavaev | 04.05.1995 | 2 | (1) | |
| Azamat Zhomartov | 19.07.1995 | 1 | | |
| **Defenders:** | **DOB** | **M** | **(s)** | **G** |
| Adi Adambaev | 04.04.2001 | 5 | (4) | |
| Pawel Baranowski (POL) | 11.10.1990 | 21 | | |
| Ravil Ibragimov | 25.12.2000 | 4 | (5) | |
| Kuanysh Kalmuratov | 27.08.1996 | 3 | (7) | |
| Matheus Bissi da Silva (BRA) | 19.03.1991 | 24 | | 2 |
| Amandyk Nabikhanov | 09.11.1997 | 18 | | 1 |
| Aleksandr Sokolenko | 23.11.1996 | 17 | (5) | |
| Soslan Takulov (RUS) | 28.04.1995 | 23 | | 1 |
| Nikolay Tarasov (RUS) | 25.02.1998 | 17 | (3) | 3 |
| Daniyar Urda | 29.05.2003 | | (1) | |
| **Midfielders:** | **DOB** | **M** | **(s)** | **G** |
| Domantas Antanavičius (LTU) | 18.11.1998 | 19 | (3) | |
| Rinat Dzhumatov | 13.10.1997 | | (1) | |
| Demir Imeri (MKD) | 27.10.1995 | 8 | (2) | 3 |

| | DOB | M | (s) | G |
|---|---|---|---|---|
| Magomed Paragulgov | 26.03.1994 | 3 | (4) | |
| Todor Petrović (SRB) | 18.08.1994 | 17 | (2) | 1 |
| Altynbek Saparov | 26.04.1995 | 4 | (11) | |
| Asylbek Seytkaliev | 29.02.1992 | 2 | (5) | |
| Oleg Soltanov | 15.04.2005 | | (1) | |
| Yuri Zavezen (RUS) | 28.01.1996 | 11 | | 1 |
| **Forwards:** | **DOB** | **M** | **(s)** | **G** |
| Pavel Dolgov (RUS) | 16.08.1996 | 4 | (3) | 1 |
| Andrija Filipović (CRO) | 18.04.1997 | 23 | (1) | 13 |
| Piotr Grzelczak (POL) | 02.03.1988 | 8 | (13) | 2 |
| Dias Kalybaev | 25.08.1999 | | (2) | |
| Anatoliy Katrich (RUS) | 09.07.1994 | 4 | (6) | |
| Denis Mitrofanov | 09.01.2002 | 4 | (4) | |
| Mukagali Pangerey | 08.02.2004 | | (4) | |
| Dmitriy Pletnev (RUS) | 16.01.1998 | 18 | (5) | 1 |
| Timur Sagyngan | 10.04.2004 | | (1) | |
| Arsen Serikkaliev | 03.01.2002 | | (1) | |
| Khusrav Toirov (TJK) | 01.08.2004 | 3 | (7) | |
| Bauyrzhan Turysbek | 15.10.1991 | | (9) | |

## Football Club Caspiy Aktau

| Founded: | 1962 | |
|---|---|---|
| Stadium: | Zhastar Stadium, Aktau (5,000) | |
| Trainer: | Nikolay Kostov (BUL) | 02.07.1963 |

| Goalkeepers: | DOB | M | (s) | G |
|---|---|---|---|---|
| Nurlybek Ayazbaev | 24.01.1991 | 20 | | |
| Risto Jankov (MKD) | 05.09.1998 | 2 | | |
| Aleksey Kozlov (RUS) | 23.01.1999 | 4 | | |
| **Defenders:** | **DOB** | **M** | **(s)** | **G** |
| Artem Baranovskiy (UKR) | 17.03.1990 | 21 | (2) | 1 |
| Madiyar Bekeshov | 10.09.2004 | | (2) | |
| Anuar Bekmyrza | 07.05.2001 | | (2) | |
| Taras Bondarenko (UKR) | 23.09.1992 | 24 | (2) | |
| Viktor Dmitrenko | 04.04.1991 | 7 | (7) | |
| Erlan Kadyrbaev | 05.10.1991 | 6 | (7) | |
| Niyaz Shugaev | 14.09.1998 | | (2) | |
| Maksat Taykenov | 14.08.1997 | 22 | | 2 |
| Ruslan Zhanysbaev | 04.11.1995 | | (1) | |
| **Midfielders:** | **DOB** | **M** | **(s)** | **G** |
| Rati Ardazishvili (GEO) | 27.01.1998 | 18 | (3) | |
| Nikola Cuckić (SRB) | 11.04.1997 | 24 | (1) | 2 |

| | DOB | M | (s) | G |
|---|---|---|---|---|
| Duman Narzildaev | 06.09.1993 | 22 | | |
| Erkebulan Nurgaliev | 12.09.1993 | 11 | (4) | 1 |
| Kuandyk Nursultanov | 24.04.1999 | | (4) | |
| Chafik Tigroudja (FRA) | 16.01.1992 | 19 | (2) | |
| **Forwards:** | **DOB** | **M** | **(s)** | **G** |
| Aslan Adil | 13.01.1998 | 17 | (7) | 2 |
| Almas Armenov | 27.01.1992 | 3 | (14) | 2 |
| Darkhan Berdibek | 31.05.2004 | 1 | (1) | |
| Pavel Kireenko (RUS) | 14.06.1994 | 26 | | 2 |
| Bekzat Kabylan | 03.03.1996 | | (4) | |
| Bakdaulet Konlimkos | 05.12.2000 | | (5) | |
| Arman Nusip | 22.01.1994 | 2 | (12) | |
| Ivan Pešić (CRO) | 06.04.1992 | 10 | | 3 |
| Ruan Ribeiro Teles (BRA) | 23.10.1997 | 12 | (7) | 6 |
| Rúben Luís Maurício Brígido (POR) | 23.06.1991 | 7 | (2) | 2 |
| Alisher Suley | 01.11.1995 | 4 | (5) | 1 |
| Maksim Vaganov | 08.08.2000 | 4 | (2) | 1 |

## Football Club Kairat Almaty

| | | | |
|---|---|---|---|
| Founded: | 1954 (*as Lokomotiv Alma-Ata*) | | |
| Stadium: | Almaty Central Stadium, Almaty (23,804) | | |
| Trainer: | Kurban Berdyev | | 25.08.1952 |
| [08.06.2022] | Kirill Keker (KGZ) | | 22.06.1979 |

| Goalkeepers: | DOB | M | (s) | G |
|---|---|---|---|---|
| Vadim Ulyanov (RUS) | 07.10.2001 | 2 | (3) | |
| Danil Ustimenko | 08.08.2000 | 24 | | |
| **Defenders:** | **DOB** | **M** | **(s)** | **G** |
| Sultanbek Astanov | 23.03.1999 | 22 | | 1 |
| Macky Frank Bagnack Mouegni (CMR) | 07.06.1995 | 7 | (1) | |
| Damir Kasabulat | 29.08.2002 | 21 | (2) | |
| Sergey Keyler | 08.11.1994 | 13 | (2) | |
| Lev Kurgin | 06.06.2002 | 5 | | |
| Egor Tkachenko | 15.04.2003 | 3 | (2) | |
| Viktor Vasin (RUS) | 06.10.1988 | 24 | | 2 |
| **Midfielders:** | **DOB** | **M** | **(s)** | **G** |
| Adam Adakhadzhiev | 23.11.1998 | | (4) | |
| Arsen Buranchiev | 12.09.2001 | 16 | (4) | |
| Rustam Emirov | 14.09.2000 | 1 | (4) | |
| Jacek Góralski (POL) | 21.09.1992 | 5 | (2) | |
| Jasurbek Jaloliddinov (UZB) | 15.05.2002 | 5 | (2) | |
| Anton Krachkovskiy (RUS) | 22.06.2002 | 16 | (5) | 1 |
| Ricardo Alves Coelho da Silva (POR) | 25.03.1993 | 13 | | |
| Andrey Ulshin | 18.04.2000 | 13 | (4) | |
| Daniyar Usenov | 18.02.2001 | 7 | (16) | |
| Adilet Sadybekov | 26.05.2002 | 10 | (1) | |
| **Forwards:** | **DOB** | **M** | **(s)** | **G** |
| Aybar Abdulla | 22.01.2002 | 1 | (1) | |
| Gulzhigit Alykulov (KGZ) | 25.11.2000 | 2 | (16) | 2 |
| João Paulo da Silva Araújo (BRA) | 02.06.1988 | 26 | | 11 |
| José Kanté Martínez (GUI) | 27.09.1990 | 8 | (2) | 6 |
| Erkebulan Seydakhmet | 04.02.2000 | 13 | (5) | |
| Artur Shushenachev | 07.04.1998 | 22 | (3) | 8 |
| Vyacheslav Shvyrev | 07.01.2001 | 7 | (14) | 2 |

## Football Club Kyzylzhar Petropavl

| | | | |
|---|---|---|---|
| Founded: | 1968 | | |
| Stadium: | Karasai Stadium, Petropavl (11,000) | | |
| Trainer: | Andrey Karpovich | | 18.01.1981 |
| [29.04.2022] | Ali Aliyev | | 27.10.1980 |

| Goalkeepers: | DOB | M | (s) | G |
|---|---|---|---|---|
| Miroslav Lobantsev (RUS) | 27.05.1995 | 25 | | |
| Vadim Petrov | 11.06.2000 | 1 | | |
| **Defenders:** | **DOB** | **M** | **(s)** | **G** |
| Aldair Adilov | 11.06.2002 | | (3) | |
| Sultan Baymagambetov | 02.09.2001 | | (1) | |
| Yuriy Bushman (UKR) | 14.05.1990 | 23 | (1) | 7 |
| Aleksandr Dovbnya (RUS) | 14.02.1996 | 2 | | |
| Ruslan Esimov | 28.04.1990 | 7 | (4) | |
| Mark Gurman | 09.02.1989 | 8 | (2) | |
| Valeri Karshakevich (BLR) | 15.02.1988 | 23 | | 2 |
| Oleg Murachev (RUS) | 22.02.1995 | 18 | (2) | |
| Mateo Mužek (CRO) | 29.04.1995 | 11 | | |
| Dmitri Schmidt | 17.11.1993 | 5 | (2) | |
| Stefan Živković (SRB) | 01.06.1990 | 6 | (2) | |
| Viktor Zyabko | 06.06.1997 | 2 | (1) | |
| **Midfielders:** | **DOB** | **M** | **(s)** | **G** |
| Gian dos Santos Martins (BRA) | 02.04.1993 | 19 | (4) | 3 |
| Artur Murza (UKR) | 13.07.2000 | 6 | (2) | |
| Moussa Koné (CIV) | 12.02.1990 | 18 | (3) | 2 |
| Rafail Ospanov | 05.11.1997 | 1 | (4) | 1 |
| Pablo Joaquin Podio (ARG) | 07.08.1989 | 22 | (2) | 1 |
| Erkin Tapalov | 03.09.1993 | 10 | (2) | |
| Sergey Tikhonovskiy (BLR) | 26.06.1990 | 9 | (9) | |
| Miras Zhenis | 30.11.2002 | | (1) | |
| **Forwards:** | **DOB** | **M** | **(s)** | **G** |
| Ubiratan Brandao de Souza (BRA) | 01.11.1995 | 2 | (3) | |
| Maksim Chikanchi (RUS) | 29.08.1998 | 3 | (7) | 1 |
| Almas Izmaylov | 30.01.2002 | | (1) | |
| Evgeniy Kozlov (RUS) | 04.02.1995 | 11 | (11) | 1 |
| Lucas Ferreira Cardoso (BRA) | 07.04.1994 | | (1) | |
| Elguja Lobjanidze (GEO) | 17.09.1992 | 9 | (1) | 7 |
| Timur Muldinov | 19.09.1993 | 11 | (13) | |
| Michaël Jordan Nkololo (COD) | 09.11.1992 | 7 | (8) | 1 |
| Andrey Panyukov (RUS) | 25.09.1994 | 5 | (3) | |
| Kirill Sidorenko (BLR) | 25.08.1995 | | (1) | |
| Pavel Yakovlev (RUS) | 07.04.1991 | 5 | (9) | 1 |
| Darko Zorić (MNE) | 12.09.1993 | 17 | (3) | 6 |

## Football Club Maqtaaral Jetisay

| | | | |
|---|---|---|---|
| Founded: | 2012 | | |
| Stadium: | „Erlan Zeykenov" Stadium, Jetisay (3,000) | | |
| Trainer: | Andrey Ferapontov | | 19.08.1975 |
| [08.09.2022] | Konstantin Gorovenko | | 10.01.1977 |

| Goalkeepers: | DOB | M | (s) | G |
|---|---|---|---|---|
| Almat Bekbaev | 14.07.1984 | 2 | (1) | |
| Serhiy Litovchenko (UKR) | 04.10.1987 | 20 | | |
| Ramil Nurmukhametov | 21.12.1987 | 2 | | |
| Zhandar Zhangaliev | 01.11.1998 | 2 | | |
| **Defenders:** | **DOB** | **M** | **(s)** | **G** |
| Ilyas Amirseitov | 22.10.1989 | 9 | (4) | |
| Dierzhon Aripov | 10.03.1997 | 10 | (5) | |
| Pavel Chikida (BLR) | 21.06.1995 | 2 | (10) | |
| Dramane Koné (CIV) | 10.11.1989 | 11 | (5) | 1 |
| Egor Potapov (RUS) | 21.09.1993 | 20 | (1) | |
| Artiom Rozgoniuc (MDA) | 01.10.1995 | 20 | (2) | 2 |
| Erbolat Rustemov | 06.10.1994 | 7 | (2) | |
| Sagi Sovet | 15.03.2000 | 3 | (1) | |
| Ruslan Yudenkov (BLR) | 28.04.1987 | 25 | | 1 |
| Artur Zapadnya (UKR) | 04.06.1990 | 9 | (4) | |
| **Midfielders:** | **DOB** | **M** | **(s)** | **G** |
| Odilzhon Abdurakhmanov (KGZ) | 18.03.1996 | 8 | | 2 |
| Rassambek Akhmatov (RUS) | 31.05.1996 | 12 | | |
| Yao Léonard Djaha (CIV) | 04.11.2001 | | (9) | |
| Sekou Doumbia (CIV) | 13.06.1994 | 11 | | |
| Rinat Dzhumatov | 13.10.1997 | 10 | (3) | |
| Aleksey Nosko (BLR) | 15.08.1996 | 10 | | 1 |
| Meyrambek Serikbay | 16.12.1999 | 5 | (6) | |
| Alibi Tuzakbaev | 08.12.1999 | 7 | (7) | |
| **Forwards:** | **DOB** | **M** | **(s)** | **G** |
| Dunaybek Ayankhan | 08.03.2000 | | (2) | |
| Aléx Bruno de Souza Silva (BRA) | 07.10.1993 | 18 | (3) | 1 |
| Sheriddin Boboev (TJK) | 21.04.1999 | 6 | (4) | |
| Ramazan Karimov | 05.07.1999 | 17 | (3) | 7 |
| Galymzhan Kenzhebek | 12.02.2003 | 3 | (19) | 3 |
| Rifat Nurmugamet | 22.05.1996 | 1 | (4) | |
| Edige Oralbay | 11.03.1997 | 1 | (6) | |
| Zhan-Ali Payruz | 12.08.1999 | 14 | (5) | 3 |
| Beknur Ryskul | 21.02.1998 | 1 | (4) | |
| Billal Sebaihi (FRA) | 31.05.1992 | 16 | (1) | 5 |
| Bekzat Zhaksybayuly | 21.12.1994 | 4 | (4) | |

## Football Club Ordabasy Shymkent

| | | |
|---|---|---|
| **Founded**: | 2000 | |
| **Stadium**: | "Kazhymukan Munaitpasov" Stadium, Shymkent (20,000) | |
| **Trainer:** | Aliaksandr Sednev (BLR) | 16.08.1973 |

| Goalkeepers: | DOB | M | (s) | G |
|---|---|---|---|---|
| Bekkhan Shayzada | 28.02.1998 | 20 | | |
| Kazhymukan Tolepbergen | 21.04.2000 | | (1) | |
| Timurbek Zakirov | 01.03.1996 | 6 | (1) | |
| **Defenders:** | **DOB** | **M** | **(s)** | **G** |
| Odil Abdumazhidov (UZB) | 01.06.2001 | 21 | (2) | 2 |
| Yevhen Chagovets (UKR) | 24.03.1998 | 5 | | |
| Dominik Dinga (SRB) | 07.04.1998 | 5 | | |
| Igor Klyushkin (RUS) | 29.01.2003 | 1 | (1) | |
| Nurali Mamirbaev | 15.02.2000 | | (1) | |
| Karam Sultanov | 15.04.1996 | 22 | | 3 |
| Sagadat Tursynbay | 26.03.1999 | 24 | | |
| **Midfielders:** | **DOB** | **M** | **(s)** | **G** |
| Oleksandr Batyshchev (UKR) | 14.09.1991 | 19 | | 1 |
| Dzmitriy Borodin (BLR) | 19.07.1999 | 9 | (2) | 3 |
| Adilkhan Dobay | 02.06.2002 | 6 | (15) | 1 |
| Sekou Doumbia (CIV) | 13.06.1994 | 8 | | |

| | DOB | M | (s) | G |
|---|---|---|---|---|
| Asludin Khadzhiev | 24.10.2000 | 3 | (3) | |
| Murodzhon Khalmatov | 20.07.2003 | | (15) | 2 |
| Samat Shamshi | 05.02.1996 | 17 | (4) | |
| Nikita Shershnev (RUS) | 19.10.2001 | 8 | (5) | |
| Victor Cristiano Braga (BRA) | 18.04.2001 | 22 | (2) | |
| **Forwards:** | **DOB** | **M** | **(s)** | **G** |
| Elkhan Astanov | 21.05.2000 | 24 | (1) | 7 |
| Akmal Bakhtiyarov | 02.06.1998 | 7 | (2) | 1 |
| Maksim Fedin | 08.06.1996 | 9 | (2) | 2 |
| Luiz Enrique "Luizinho" Guedes (BRA) | 22.05.1999 | 8 | (16) | 1 |
| Serge Komla Nyuiadzi (TOG) | 17.09.1991 | 18 | (3) | 7 |
| Vsevolod Sadovskiy (BLR) | 04.10.1996 | 13 | (7) | 4 |
| Zikrillo Sultaniyazov | 15.10.2003 | | (3) | |
| Batyrkhan Tazhibay | 07.08.2001 | | (16) | |
| Shakhboz Umarov (UZB) | 09.03.1999 | 5 | (4) | |
| Maksim Vaganov | 08.08.2000 | 6 | (5) | 1 |
| Khamza Yakudi | 12.11.2003 | | (1) | |

## Football Club Shakhter Karagandy

| | | |
|---|---|---|
| **Founded**: | 1958 | |
| **Stadium**: | Shakhter Stadium, Karaganda (19,500) | |
| **Trainer:** | Magomed Adiev (RUS) | 30.06.1977 |
| [27.04.2022] | Konstantin Emeljanov (RUS) | 28.03.1970 |
| [28.06.2022] | Vakhid Masudov | 10.10.1959 |

| Goalkeepers: | DOB | M | (s) | G |
|---|---|---|---|---|
| Igor Shatskiy | 11.05.1989 | 21 | | |
| Igor Trofimets | 20.08.1996 | 5 | | |
| Egor Tsuprikov | 27.05.1997 | | (1) | |
| **Defenders:** | **DOB** | **M** | **(s)** | **G** |
| Đorđe Ćosić (BIH) | 11.09.1995 | 22 | | 1 |
| Timur Dosmagambetov | 01.05.1989 | 13 | | 5 |
| Mikhail Gabyshev | 02.01.1990 | 10 | | |
| Filip Gligorov (MKD) | 31.07.1993 | 9 | (1) | |
| Ivan Graf (CRO) | 17.06.1987 | 12 | (2) | 1 |
| Vladimir Khozin (RUS) | 03.07.1989 | 10 | (2) | |
| Abdel Lamanje (FRA) | 27.07.1990 | 1 | (3) | |
| Kirill Malyarov (RUS) | 07.03.1997 | 11 | | |
| Temur Mustafin (RUS) | 15.04.1995 | 2 | (1) | |
| Pavel Nazarenko (BLR) | 20.01.1995 | 2 | (3) | |
| Tair Nurseitov | 11.07.2000 | | (2) | |
| Aleksandr Poznyak (BLR) | 23.07.1994 | 10 | (1) | |
| Miram Sapanov | 12.03.1986 | 11 | | |
| **Midfielders:** | **DOB** | **M** | **(s)** | **G** |
| Amir Aduev (RUS) | 11.05.1999 | 3 | (6) | |

| | DOB | M | (s) | G |
|---|---|---|---|---|
| Ansar Altynkhan | 08.11.2003 | | (2) | |
| Petros Avetisyan (ARM) | 07.01.1996 | 5 | (4) | 1 |
| Stefan Bukorac (SRB) | 15.02.1991 | 23 | | 2 |
| Róger Cañas Henao (COL) | 27.03.1990 | 25 | | 2 |
| Ibragim Dadaev | 11.06.2002 | | (3) | |
| Farkhat Musabekov (KGZ) | 03.01.1994 | 8 | (2) | 1 |
| Abylaykhan Nazymkhanov | 05.02.2002 | 14 | (9) | 1 |
| Edin Rustemović (BIH) | 06.01.1993 | 7 | (4) | |
| Almas Tyulyubay | 18.04.2001 | | (2) | |
| Ruslan Tutkyshev | 18.02.1999 | | (3) | |
| **Forwards:** | **DOB** | **M** | **(s)** | **G** |
| Temur Chogadze (GEO) | 05.05.1998 | 5 | (7) | 3 |
| Shyngys Flyuk | 28.12.2001 | | (1) | |
| Maksim Galkin | 12.07.1999 | 1 | (3) | |
| Yevgeniy Kobzar (RUS) | 09.08.1992 | 11 | (1) | 2 |
| Mykola Kovtalyuk (UKR) | 26.04.1995 | 9 | (1) | 2 |
| Roman Murtazaev | 10.09.1993 | 18 | (4) | 6 |
| Ivan Sviridov | 28.06.2002 | 6 | (8) | |
| Aydos Tattybaev | 26.04.1990 | 4 | (17) | 2 |
| Toktar Zhangylyshbay | 25.05.1993 | 8 | (13) | 1 |

## Football Club Taraz

| | | |
|---|---|---|
| **Founded**: | 1960 | |
| **Stadium**: | „Yerkebulan Babayev" Stadium, Taraz (12,527) | |
| **Trainer:** | Nurken Mazbaev | 04.06.1972 |
| [21.10.2022] | Nurmat Mirzabaev | 11.11.1972 |

| Goalkeepers: | DOB | M | (s) | G |
|---|---|---|---|---|
| Denis Kavlinov (RUS) | 10.01.1995 | 5 | | |
| Mukhamedzhan Seysen | 14.02.1999 | 21 | | |
| **Defenders:** | **DOB** | **M** | **(s)** | **G** |
| Eldos Akhmetov | 01.06.1990 | 15 | | 1 |
| Maksat Amirkhanov | 10.02.1992 | 13 | (6) | 2 |
| Berik Aytbaev | 26.06.1991 | 8 | (4) | |
| Alex Júnior Christian (HAI) | 12.05.1993 | 17 | (4) | |
| Nurlan Dairov | 26.06.1995 | 23 | | |
| Luka Gadrani (GEO) | 12.04.1997 | 20 | (1) | 1 |
| Kuanysh Kalmuratov | 27.08.1996 | 2 | (5) | |
| Adilet Kenesbek | 05.01.1996 | 19 | (2) | 1 |
| Ermek Kuantaev | 13.10.1990 | 5 | (7) | |
| Bekzat Shadmanov | 12.08.1997 | 2 | (1) | |
| Zhalgas Zhaksylykov | 16.04.2001 | 6 | (5) | |

| Midfielders: | DOB | M | (s) | G |
|---|---|---|---|---|
| Bauyrzhan Baytana | 06.05.1992 | 13 | | 2 |
| Milen Gamakov (BUL) | 12.04.1994 | 18 | (4) | 1 |
| Ersultan Kaldybekov | 12.01.2002 | 3 | (16) | |
| Bektas Nurdaulet | 22.07.1998 | 5 | (6) | |
| Marat Shakhmetov | 06.02.1989 | 15 | (10) | 1 |
| Abzal Taubay | 18.02.1995 | 14 | (7) | |
| **Forwards:** | **DOB** | **M** | **(s)** | **G** |
| Maksym Degtyarov (UKR) | 30.05.1993 | 5 | (5) | 2 |
| Jorge Elias dos Santos (BRA) | 05.06.1991 | 3 | (4) | 1 |
| Dinmukhamed Karaman | 26.06.2000 | 10 | (13) | 2 |
| Zhakyp Kozhamberdy | 26.02.1992 | 19 | (4) | 4 |
| Alisher Suley | 01.11.1995 | 1 | (7) | 1 |
| Erkebulan Toybekov | 25.06.2002 | | (3) | |
| Duman Tursynbay | 22.03.1998 | | (2) | |
| Abylaykhan Zhumabek | 19.10.2001 | 20 | (5) | 8 |
| Dauren Zhumat | 02.03.1999 | 4 | (1) | |

## Football Club Tobol Kostanay

| | Founded: | 1967 | |
|---|---|---|---|
| | Stadium: | Central Stadium, Kostanay (9,500) | |
| | Trainer: | Aleksandr Moskalenko | 18.09.1976 |
| | [20.05.2022] | Milan Milanović (SRB) | 10.01.1963 |

| Goalkeepers: | DOB | M | (s) | G |
|---|---|---|---|---|
| Timur Akmurzin (RUS) | 07.12.1997 | 9 | (1) | |
| Aleksandr Mokin | 19.06.1981 | 15 | | |
| Dmitriy Nepogodov | 17.02.1988 | 2 | | |
| **Defenders:** | **DOB** | **M** | **(s)** | **G** |
| Aleksa Amanović (MKD) | 24.10.1996 | 20 | (1) | 1 |
| Roman Asrankulov | 30.07.1999 | | (10) | |
| Bagdat Kairov | 27.04.1993 | 19 | (1) | |
| Sergey Maliy | 05.06.1990 | 22 | (1) | 4 |
| Aleksandr Marochkin | 14.07.1990 | 13 | (5) | |
| Dmitriy Miroshnichenko | 26.02.1992 | 3 | (3) | |
| Daniyar Semchenkov | 12.02.1997 | | (1) | |
| Žarko Tomašević (MNE) | 22.02.1990 | 22 | | 1 |
| **Midfielders:** | **DOB** | **M** | **(s)** | **G** |
| Dušan Jovančić (SRB) | 19.10.1990 | 24 | | 3 |

| | DOB | M | (s) | G |
|---|---|---|---|---|
| Serikzhan Muzhikov | 17.06.1989 | 11 | (3) | 4 |
| Chidi Emma Osuchukwu (NGA) | 11.10.1993 | 2 | (5) | 1 |
| Askhat Tagybergen | 09.08.1990 | 23 | (1) | 8 |
| Vladislav Vasiljev | 10.04.1997 | 13 | (9) | 1 |
| Samat Zharynbetov | 04.01.1994 | 11 | (12) | |
| **Forwards:** | **DOB** | **M** | **(s)** | **G** |
| Serges Déblé (CIV) | 01.10.1989 | 9 | (1) | 3 |
| Rudi Požeg Vancaš (SVN) | 15.03.1994 | 1 | (5) | 1 |
| Rúben Luís Maurício Brígido (POR) | 23.06.1991 | 13 | (1) | 1 |
| Igor Sergeev (UZB) | 30.04.1993 | 20 | (6) | 9 |
| Zoran Tošić (SRB) | 28.04.1987 | 21 | (2) | 5 |
| Miljan Vukadinović (SRB) | 27.12.1992 | 5 | (1) | 1 |
| Aabar Zhaksylykov | 24.07.1997 | 7 | (16) | 3 |
| Zhaslan Zhumashev | 27.09.2001 | 1 | (9) | |

## Football Club Turan Turkistan

| | Founded: | 2002 | |
|---|---|---|---|
| | Stadium: | Turkistan Arena, Turklistan (7,000) | |
| | Trainer: | Kuanysh Kabdulov | 09.07.1987 |
| | [12.06.2022] | Sergey Kogay | 14.08.1966 |
| | [01.09.2022] | Aleksandr Kuchma | 09.12.1980 |
| | [14.10.2022] | Kanat Musataev | 06.07.1970 |

| Goalkeepers: | DOB | M | (s) | G |
|---|---|---|---|---|
| Emil Balayev (AZE) | 17.04.1994 | 1 | | |
| Erzhan Tokotaev (KGZ) | 17.07.2000 | 22 | | |
| Bekzhan Toktarbay | 22.03.1997 | 3 | | |
| Dinmukhammed Zhomart | 06.12.2000 | | (1) | |
| **Defenders:** | **DOB** | **M** | **(s)** | **G** |
| Sultan Abilgazy | 22.02.1997 | 1 | (3) | |
| Zvonko Ceklić (MNE) | 11.04.1999 | 6 | (2) | |
| Olzhas Kerimzhanov | 16.05.1989 | 21 | | 2 |
| Aleksandr Kleshchenko (RUS) | 02.11.1995 | 11 | | |
| Syrbay Maulen | 26.04.1999 | | (2) | |
| Timur Rudoselskiy | 21.12.1994 | 9 | | |
| Lev Skvortsov | 02.02.2000 | 20 | (2) | |
| Kasymzhan Taipov | 19.02.1995 | 17 | (3) | 2 |
| Andrey Zaleskiy (BLR) | 20.01.1991 | 17 | (4) | |
| Ruslan Zhanysbaev | 04.11.1995 | 5 | (2) | |
| **Midfielders:** | **DOB** | **M** | **(s)** | **G** |
| Mikhail Bashilov (RUS) | 12.01.1993 | 9 | | 1 |
| Abdoulaye Diakhate (SEN) | 16.01.1988 | 22 | | 1 |
| Kuanysh Duysenbekuly | 14.08.2003 | | (2) | |
| Oleg Evdokimov (BLR) | 25.02.1994 | 8 | | 1 |

| | DOB | M | (s) | G |
|---|---|---|---|---|
| Farkhat Musabekov (KGZ) | 03.01.1994 | 7 | (3) | |
| Chidi Emma Osuchukwu (NGA) | 11.10.1993 | 10 | | 2 |
| Sanzhar Satanov | 21.09.2001 | 5 | (1) | 1 |
| Erkin Tapalov | 03.09.1993 | 5 | (4) | |
| Rakhat Usipkhanov | 19.04.2001 | 2 | (3) | |
| **Forwards:** | **DOB** | **M** | **(s)** | **G** |
| Shokhan Abzalov | 11.09.1993 | 17 | (3) | 4 |
| Temirlan Amirov | 13.04.1997 | 3 | (7) | |
| Alen Aymanov | 02.06.2002 | | (2) | |
| Kehinde Abdul Feyi Fatai (NGA) | 19.02.1990 | 1 | (4) | |
| Samir Fazli (MKD) | 22.04.1991 | 18 | (4) | 1 |
| Maksim Fedin | 08.06.1996 | 6 | | |
| Artem Gurenko (BLR) | 18.06.1994 | 3 | (6) | 1 |
| Bekzat Kabylan | 03.03.1996 | 10 | (3) | 2 |
| Aliyar Mukhammed | 20.03.2001 | 7 | (9) | 1 |
| Azat Nurgaliev | 30.06.1986 | 6 | | 1 |
| Tanat Nuserbaev | 01.01.1987 | 2 | (5) | |
| Arman Nusip | 22.01.1994 | | (2) | |
| Joálisson Santos Oliveira „Jô Santos" (BRA) | 31.03.1991 | 4 | (4) | 1 |
| Toni Brito Silva Sá (GNB) | 15.09.1993 | 7 | (2) | |
| Bakdaulet Zulfikarov | 11.03.2001 | 1 | (5) | 1 |

## SECOND LEVEL
### Kazakhstan First Division / Pervaia Liga 2022

| | | | | | | | | | |
|---|---|---|---|---|---|---|---|---|---|
| 1. | FC Okzhetpes Kokshetau (*Promoted*) | 26 | 19 | 4 | 3 | 80 | - | 22 | 61 |
| 2. | FC Kaysar Kyzylorda (*Promoted*) | 26 | 17 | 5 | 4 | 60 | - | 26 | 56 |
| 3. | FC Zhetysu Taldiqorghan | 26 | 17 | 4 | 5 | 57 | - | 23 | 52 |
| 4. | FC Kairat-Zhastar Almaty | 26 | 15 | 6 | 5 | 61 | - | 31 | 51 |
| 5. | FC Kyran Shimkent | 26 | 12 | 5 | 9 | 57 | - | 43 | 41 |
| 6. | FC Yekibastuz | 26 | 9 | 10 | 7 | 45 | - | 47 | 37 |
| 7. | FC Taraz-Karatau | 26 | 10 | 6 | 10 | 45 | - | 47 | 36 |
| 8. | FC Zhenis Nur-Sultan | 26 | 10 | 5 | 11 | 40 | - | 36 | 35 |
| 9. | FC Yassy Shymkent | 26 | 10 | 5 | 11 | 48 | - | 54 | 35 |
| 10. | FK Akademiya Ontustik Shimkent | 26 | 8 | 6 | 12 | 42 | - | 60 | 30 |
| 11. | Astana FC Jastar | 26 | 7 | 6 | 13 | 50 | - | 62 | 27 |
| 12. | Ïgilik Karatai | 26 | 6 | 3 | 17 | 27 | - | 70 | 21 |
| 13. | FC Shakhtar-Bulat Temirtau | 26 | 4 | 5 | 17 | 36 | - | 72 | 17 |
| 14. | FC Baykonur Kyzylorda (*Relegated*) | 26 | 1 | 4 | 21 | 16 | - | 71 | 7 |

## INTERNATIONAL MATCHES
(16.07.2022 – 15.07.2023)

| | | | | |
|---|---|---|---|---|
| 22.09.2022 | Astana | *Kazakhstan - Belarus* | *2-1(1-1)* | (UNL) |
| 25.09.2022 | Bakı | *Azerbaijan - Kazakhstan* | *3-0(0-0)* | (UNL) |
| 16.11.2022 | Tashkent | *Uzbekistan - Kazakhstan* | *2-0(2-0)* | (F) |
| 19.11.2022 | Abu Dhabi | *United Arab Emirates - Kazakhstan* | *2-1(1-0)* | (F) |
| 23.03.2023 | Astana | *Kazakhstan - Slovenia* | *1-2(1-0)* | (ECQ) |
| 26.03.2023 | Astana | *Kazakhstan - Denmark* | *3-2(0-2)* | (ECQ) |
| 16.06.2023 | Parma | *San Marino - Kazakhstan* | *0-3(0-1)* | (ECQ) |
| 19.06.2023 | Belfast | *Northern Ireland - Kazakhstan* | *0-1(0-0)* | (ECQ) |

**22.09.2022  KAZAKHSTAN - BELARUS**  2-1(1-1)  3rd UEFA Nations League C, Group 3
Astana Arena, Astana; Referee: Horaţiu Feşnic (Romania); Attendance: 29,637
**KAZ:** Igor Shatskiy, Mikhail Gabyshev (68.Bagdat Kairov), Nuraly Alip, Sergey Malyi, Aleksandr Marochkin, Yan Vorogovskiy, Askhat Tagybergen (Cap) [*sent off 90+4*], Aslan Darabayev, Ramazan Orazov (75.Elkhan Astanov), Baktiyar Zaynutdinov (87.Islambek Kuat), Abat Aymbetov (87.Abylayhan Zhumabek). Trainer: Magomed Adiyev (Russia).
**Goals:** Mikhail Gabyshev (18), Baktiyar Zaynutdinov (79).

**25.09.2022  AZERBAIJAN - KAZAKHSTAN**  3-0(0-0)  3rd UEFA Nations League C, Group 3
Dalğa Arena, Bakı; Referee: Harm Osmers (Germany); Attendance: 2,950
**KAZ:** Igor Shatskiy, Bagdat Kairov, Nuraly Alip [*sent off 35*], Aleksandr Marochkin, Marat Bystrov, Timur Dosmagambetov (67.Yan Vorogovskiy), Islambek Kuat (Cap), Aslan Darabayev (80.Adilet Sadybekov), Ramazan Orazov (80.Samat Zharynbetov), Elkhan Astanov (67.Abat Aymbetov), Abylayhan Zhumabek (39.Sergey Malyi). Trainer: Magomed Adiyev (Russia).

**16.11.2022  UZBEKISTAN - KAZAKHSTAN**  2-0(2-0)  Friendly International
Pakhtakor Stadium, Tashkent; Referee: Sergey Karasyov (Russia); Attendance: 5,000
**KAZ:** Igor Shatskiy, Mikhail Gabyshev (72.Bagdat Kairov), Sergey Malyi, Nuraly Alip, Aleksandr Marochkin, Timur Dosmagambetov (72.Dmitriy Shomko), Aslan Darabayev (46.Baktiyar Zaynutdinov), Askhat Tagybergen, Ramazan Orazov (67.Bauyrzhan Islamkhan), Elkhan Astanov (79.Islambek Kuat), Abat Aymbetov (72.Aybar Zhaksylykov). Trainer: Magomed Adiyev (Russia).

**19.11.2022  UNITED ARAB EMIRATES - KAZAKHSTAN**  2-1(1-0)  Friendly International
Zayed Sports City, Abu Dhabi; Referee: Zakaria Mohamed El Bana (Egypt); Attendance: n/a
**KAZ:** Igor Shatskiy, Bagdat Kairov (66.Mikhail Gabyshev), Sergey Malyi (76.Temirlan Yerlanov), Nuraly Alip, Aleksandr Marochkin [*sent off 79*], Timur Dosmagambetov (77.Dmitriy Shomko), Askhat Tagybergen (Cap) (76.Bauyrzhan Islamkhan), Islambek Kuat, Baktiyar Zaynutdinov, Elkhan Astanov (73.Maksim Samorodov), Abat Aymbetov (73.Aybar Zhaksylykov). Trainer: Magomed Adiyev (Russia).
**Goal:** Abat Aymbetov (62).

**23.03.2023  KAZAKHSTAN - SLOVENIA**  1-2(1-0)  17th EC. Qualifiers
Astana Arena, Astana; Referee: Glenn Nyberg (Sweden); Attendance: 27,122
**KAZ:** Igor Shatskiy, Mikhail Gabyshev (68.Bagdat Kairov), Sergey Malyi, Aleksandr Marochkin, Marat Bystrov (79.Temirlan Yerlanov), Yan Vorogovskiy, Aslan Darabayev (79.Abzal Beysebekov), Askhat Tagybergen (Cap), Ramazan Orazov, Maksim Samorodov (62.Bauyrzhan Islamkhan), Abat Aymbetov (62.Baktiyar Zaynutdinov). Trainer: Magomed Adiyev (Russia).
**Goal:** Maksim Samorodov (24).

**26.03.2023  KAZAKHSTAN - DENMARK**  3-2(0-2)  17th EC. Qualifiers
Astana Arena, Astana; Referee: Novak Simović (Serbia); Attendance: 28,697
**KAZ:** Igor Shatskiy, Mikhail Gabyshev (34.Lev Skvortsov), Sergey Malyi (46.Temirlan Yerlanov) , Nuraly Alip, Aleksandr Marochkin, Yan Vorogovskiy, Askhat Tagybergen (Cap), Abzal Beysebekov (83.Aslan Darabayev), Ramazan Orazov, Baktiyar Zaynutdinov (79.Bauyrzhan Islamkhan), Maksim Samorodov (78.Abat Aymbetov [sent off 90+6]). Trainer: Magomed Adiyev (Russia).
**Goals:** Baktiyar Zaynutdinov (73 penalty), Askhat Tagybergen (86), Abat Aymbetov (89).

**16.06.2023  SAN MARINO - KAZAKHSTAN**  0-3(0-1)  17th EC. Qualifiers
Stadio "Ennio Tardini", Parma (Italy); Referee: Anastasios Papapetrou (Greece); Attendance: 528
**KAZ:** Igor Shatskiy, Marat Bystrov, Nuraly Alip, Aleksandr Marochkin, Mikhail Gabyshev (78.Lev Skvortsov), Abzal Beysebekov (57.Baktiyar Zaynutdinov), Islambek Kuat, Askhat Tagybergen (Cap) (71.Arman Kenesov), Yan Vorogovskiy (78.Timur Dosmagambetov), Maksim Samorodov (71.Elkhan Astanov), Ramazan Orazov. Trainer: Magomed Adiyev (Russia).
**Goals:** Yan Vorogovskiy (37), Askhat Tagybergen (64 penalty), Baktiyar Zaynutdinov (90+5).

**19.06.2023  NORTHERN IRELAND - KAZAKHSTAN**  0-1(0-0)  17th EC. Qualifiers
Windsor Park, Belfast; Referee: Roi Reinshreiber (Israel); Attendance: 18,002
**KAZ:** Igor Shatskiy, Marat Bystrov, Nuraly Alip, Aleksandr Marochkin, Mikhail Gabyshev (68.Lev Skvortsov), Askhat Tagybergen (Cap) (81.Yerkin Tapalov), Abzal Beysebekov, Yan Vorogovskiy, Baktiyar Zaynutdinov (74.Islambek Kuat), Ramazan Orazov (81.Elkhan Astanov), Maksim Samorodov (81.Abat Aymbetov). Trainer: Magomed Adiyev (Russia).
**Goal:** Abat Aymbetov (88).

## NATIONAL TEAM PLAYERS
### (16.07.2022 – 15.07.2023)

| Name | DOB | Caps | Goals | Club |
|------|-----|------|-------|------|

### Goalkeepers

| Name | DOB | Caps | Goals | Club |
|------|-----|------|-------|------|
| Igor SHATSKIY | 11.05.1989 | 19 | 0 | 2022/2023: *FC Shakhter Karagandy* |

### Defenders

| Name | DOB | Caps | Goals | Club |
|------|-----|------|-------|------|
| Nuraly ALIP | 22.12.1999 | 25 | 0 | 2022/2023: *FK Zenit Saint Petersburg (RUS)* |
| Abzal BEYSEBEKOV | 30.11.1992 | 42 | 0 | 2023: *Astana FC* |
| Marat BYSTROV | 19.06.1992 | 19 | 0 | 2022/2023: *RFK Akhmat Grozny (RUS)* |
| Mikhail GABYSHEV | 02.01.1990 | 10 | 1 | 2022/2023: *Astana FC* |
| Bagdat KAIROV | 27.04.1993 | 11 | 0 | 2022/2023: *FC Tobol Kostanay* |
| Sergey MALYI | 05.06.1990 | 64 | 1 | 2022: *FC Tobol Kostanay* <br> 24.02.2023-> *FC Ordabasy Shymkent* |
| Aleksandr MAROCHKIN | 14.07.1990 | 34 | 0 | 2022/2023: *FC Tobol Kostanay* |
| Adilet SADYBEKOV | 26.05.2002 | 1 | 0 | 2022: *FC Kairat Almaty* |
| Dmitriy SHOMKO | 19.03.1990 | 48 | 2 | 2022: *FC Aktobe* |
| Lev SKVORTSOV | 02.02.2000 | 3 | 0 | 2023: *FK Khimki (RUS)* |
| Temirlan YERLANOV | 09.07.1993 | 17 | 1 | 2022: *FC Aktobe* <br> 24.02.2023-> *FC Ordabasy Shymkent* |

### Midfielders

| Name | DOB | Caps | Goals | Club |
|------|-----|------|-------|------|
| Elkhan ASTANOV | 21.05.2000 | 11 | 1 | 2022: *FC Ordabasy Shymkent* <br> 13.03.2023-> *Astana FC* |
| Aslan DARABAYEV | 21.01.1989 | 18 | 1 | 2022/2023: *Astana FC* |
| Timur DOSMAGAMBETOV | 01.05.1989 | 17 | 0 | 2022/2023: *Astana FC* |
| Bauyrzhan ISLAMKHAN | 23.02.1993 | 50 | 3 | 2022: *Al Ain FC (UAE); 09.11.2022-> unattached* <br> 25.02.2023-> *FC Ordabasy Shymkent* |
| Arman KENESOV | 04.09.2000 | 1 | 0 | 2023: *FC Aktobe* |
| Islambek KUAT | 12.01.1993 | 56 | 6 | 2022/2023: *Astana FC* |
| Ramazan ORAZOV | 30.01.1998 | 16 | 0 | 2022: *FC Aktobe* <br> 27.01.2023-> *FC Aqsu* <br> 12.04.2023-> *FC Tobol Kostanay* |
| Askat TAGYBERGEN | 09.08.1990 | 46 | 2 | 2022: *FC Tobol Kostanay* <br> 24.02.2023-> *FC Ordabasy Shymkent* |
| Yerkin TAPALOV | 03.09.1993 | 7 | 0 | 2023: *FC Kyzylzhar SK Petropavl* |
| Yan VOROGOVSKIY | 07.08.1996 | 33 | 3 | 2022/2023: *RWD Molenbeek (BEL)* |
| Baktiyor ZAYNUTDINOV | 02.04.1998 | 30 | 12 | 2022/2023: *FK CSKA Moskva (RUS)* |
| Samat ZHARYNBETOV | 04.01.1994 | 7 | 0 | 2022: *FC Tobol Kostanay* |

### Forwards

| Name | DOB | Caps | Goals | Club |
|------|-----|------|-------|------|
| Abat AYMBETOV | 07.08.1995 | 29 | 8 | 2022/2023: *Astana FC* |
| Maksim SAMORODOV | 29.06.2002 | 7 | 1 | 2022/2023: *FC Aktobe* |
| Aybar ZHAKSYLYKOV | 24.07.1997 | 9 | 0 | 2022: *FC Tobol Kostanay* |
| Abylayhan ZHUMABEK | 19.10.2001 | 2 | 0 | 2022: *FC Taraz* |

### Trainer

| | DOB | | | |
|------|-----|------|-------|------|
| Magomed ADIYEV (Russia) [from 27.04.2022] | 30.06.1977 | 12 M; 7 W; 1 D; 4 L; 17-14 | | |

# KOSOVO

**The Country:**
Republika e Kosovës (Republic of Kosovo)
Capital: Prishtina
Surface: 10,908 km²
Inhabitants: 1,761,985 [2022]
Time: UTC+1

**The FA:**
Federata e Futbollit e Kosovës
Rruga "28 Nëntori", nr. 171, Prishtina / Kosovë 10000
Tel: +383 38 600 220
Foundation date: 1946
Member of FIFA since: 13.05.2016
Member of UEFA since: 03.05.2016
Website: www.ffk-kosova.com

## NATIONAL TEAM RECORDS

### RECORDS

| | | |
|---|---|---|
| **First international match:** | 05.03.2014, Mitrovicë: | Kosovo – Haiti 0-0 |
| **Most international caps:** | Amir Kadri Rrahmani | - 53 caps (since 2014) |
| **Most international goals:** | Vedat Muriqi | - 24 goals / 48 caps (since 2016) |

### UEFA EUROPEAN CHAMPIONSHIP

| | |
|---|---|
| 1960 | - |
| 1964 | - |
| 1968 | - |
| 1972 | - |
| 1976 | - |
| 1980 | - |
| 1984 | - |
| 1988 | - |
| 1992 | - |
| 1996 | - |
| 2000 | - |
| 2004 | - |
| 2008 | - |
| 2012 | - |
| 2016 | - |
| 2020 | Qualifiers |

### FIFA WORLD CUP

| | |
|---|---|
| 1930 | - |
| 1934 | - |
| 1938 | - |
| 1950 | - |
| 1954 | - |
| 1958 | - |
| 1962 | - |
| 1966 | - |
| 1970 | - |
| 1974 | - |
| 1978 | - |
| 1982 | - |
| 1986 | - |
| 1990 | - |
| 1994 | - |
| 1998 | - |
| 2002 | - |
| 2006 | - |
| 2010 | - |
| 2014 | - |
| 2018 | Qualifiers |
| 2022 | Qualifiers |

### OLYMPIC TOURNAMENTS

| | |
|---|---|
| 1908 | - |
| 1912 | - |
| 1920 | - |
| 1924 | - |
| 1928 | - |
| 1936 | - |
| 1948 | - |
| 1952 | - |
| 1956 | - |
| 1960 | - |
| 1964 | - |
| 1968 | - |
| 1972 | - |
| 1976 | - |
| 1980 | - |
| 1984 | - |
| 1988 | - |
| 1992 | - |
| 1996 | - |
| 2000 | - |
| 2004 | - |
| 2008 | - |
| 2012 | - |
| 2016 | - |
| 2020 | Qualifiers |

*Please note: was part of Yugoslavia / Serbia and Montenegro / Serbia until 17.02.2008*

### UEFA NATIONS LEAGUE

| 2018/2019 | League D (Group Stage -> promoted to League C) |
|---|---|
| 2020/2021 | League C (Group Stage) |
| 2022/2023 | League C (Group Stage) |

### KOSOVO CLUB HONOURS IN EUROPEAN CLUB COMPETITIONS:

**European Champion Clubs' Cup (1956-1992) / UEFA Champions League (1993-2023)**
None

**Fairs Cup (1858-1971) / UEFA Cup (1972-2009) / UEFA Europa League (2010-2023)**
None

**UEFA Europa Conference League (2021-2023)**
None

**UEFA Super Cup (1972-2022)**
None

***European Cup Winners' Cup 1961-1999***
None

*defunct competition*

# NATIONAL COMPETITIONS
# TABLE OF HONOURS

## Kosovo Province League (within F.R. Yugoslavia)

| | CHAMPIONS | CUP WINNERS |
|---|---|---|
| 1945 | Jedinstvo Prishtina | - |
| 1946 | Jedinstvo Prishtina | - |
| 1947 | KF Trepça Mitrovicë | - |
| 1947/1948 | Proleteri Prishtina | - |
| 1948/1949 | KF Trepça Mitrovicë | - |
| 1950 | KF Trepça Mitrovicë | - |
| 1951 | Kosova Prishtina | - |
| 1952 | KF Trepça Mitrovicë | - |
| 1953/1954 | Kosova Prishtina | - |
| 1954/1955 | KF Trepça Mitrovicë | - |
| 1955/1956 | Rudari Stantërg | - |
| 1956/1957 | Rudniku Hajvali | - |
| 1957/1958 | Rudari Stantërg | - |
| 1958/1959 | FC Prishtina | - |
| 1959/1960 | Rudari Stantërg | - |
| 1960/1961 | FC Prishtina | - |
| 1961/1962 | Buduqnosti Pejë | - |
| 1962/1963 | Crvena zvezda Gjilani | - |
| 1963/1964 | Slloga Lipyan | - |
| 1964/1965 | Slloga Lipyan | - |
| 1965/1966 | Buduqnosti Pejë | - |
| 1966/1967 | Obiliqi Kastriot | - |
| 1967/1968 | FC Vëllaznimi Gjakovë | - |
| 1968/1969 | FC Vëllaznimi Gjakovë | - |
| 1969/1970 | FC Vëllaznimi Gjakovë | - |
| 1970/1971 | FC Vëllaznimi Gjakovë | - |
| 1971/1972 | FC Obiliqi | - |
| 1972/1973 | KF Fushë Kosova | - |
| 1973/1974 | FC Vëllaznimi Gjakovë | - |
| 1974/1975 | KF Liria Prizreni | - |
| 1975/1976 | RHMK Obilić | - |
| 1976/1977 | FC Prishtina | - |
| 1977/1978 | Buduqnosti Pejë | - |
| 1978/1979 | FC Prishtina | - |
| 1979/1980 | FC Vëllaznimi Gjakovë | - |
| 1980/1981 | KF Liria Prizreni | - |
| 1981/1982 | FC Vëllaznimi Gjakovë | - |
| 1982/1983 | KNI Ramiz Sadiku | - |
| 1983/1984 | KF Liria Prizreni | - |
| 1984/1985 | Crvena zvezda Gjilani | FC Vëllaznimi Gjakovë |
| 1985/1986 | FC Vëllaznimi Gjakovë | FC Vëllaznimi Gjakovë |
| 1986/1987 | KF Liria Prizreni | FC Vëllaznimi Gjakovë |
| 1987/1988 | Crvena zvezda Gjilani | *No competition* |
| 1988/1989 | Buduqnosti Pejë | *No competition* |
| 1989/1990 | FC Vëllaznimi Gjakovë | *No competition* |

## Independent League of Kosovo

| | CHAMPIONS | CUP WINNERS |
|---|---|---|
| 1990/1991 | KF Fushë-Kosova | *No competition* |
| 1991/1992 | KF Prishtina | KF Trepça Mitrovicë |
| 1992/1993 | KF Trepça Mitrovicë | KF Flamurtari Prishtina |
| 1993/1994 | KF Dukagjini Klinë | FC Prishtina |
| 1994/1995 | KF Liria Prizreni | KF Liria Prizreni |
| 1995/1996 | FC Prishtina | KF Flamurtari Prishtina |
| 1996/1997 | FC Prishtina | *Final not played* |
| 1997/1998 | *Tournament abandoned* | *No competition* |
| 1998/1999 | *No competition* | *No competition* |

## Establishment as top-league after UNMIK* take-over of Kosovo

| | CHAMPIONS | CUP WINNERS |
|---|---|---|
| 1999/2000 | FC Prishtina | SC Gjilani |
| 2000/2001 | FC Prishtina | FC Drita Gjilani |
| 2001/2002 | KF Besiana Podujevë | KF Besiana Podujevo |
| 2002/2003 | FC Drita Gjilani | KF KEK-u Obilić |
| 2003/2004 | FC Prishtina | KF Kosova Prishtina |
| 2004/2005 | KF Besa Pejë Peć | KF Besa Pejë Peć |
| 2005/2006 | KF Besa Pejë Peć | FC Prishtina |
| 2006/2007 | KF Besa Pejë Peć | KF Liria Prizreni |
| 2007/2008 | FC Prishtina | FC Vëllaznimi Gjakovë |

## After proclamation of independence

| | CHAMPIONS | CUP WINNERS |
|---|---|---|
| 2008/2009 | FC Prishtina | KF Hysi Podujevo |
| 2009/2010 | KF Trepça Mitrovicë | KF Liria Prizreni |
| 2010/2011 | KF Hysi Milloshevë | FC Prishtina |
| 2011/2012 | FC Prishtina | KF Trepça'89 Mitrovicë |
| 2012/2013 | FC Prishtina | FC Prishtina |
| 2013/2014 | KF Vushtria | KF Hajvalia |
| 2014/2015 | KF Feronikeli Glogovac | KV Feronikeli Glogovac |
| 2015/2016 | KF Feronikeli Glogovac | FC Prishtina |

*United Nations Mission in Kosovo*

Please note: Jedinstvo Prishtina changed its name to Proleteri Prishtina, Kosova Prishtina and finally to FC Prishtina.
Buduqnosti Pejë became KF Besa Pejë Peć; FC Obiliqi changed its name to RHMK Obilić and later KF KEK-u Obilić

## After membership in UEFA and FIFA

| | CHAMPIONS | CUP WINNERS | BEST GOALSCORERS | |
|---|---|---|---|---|
| 2016/2017 | KF Trepça'89 Mitrovicë | KF Llapi Podujevë | John Otto John (NGA, KF Trepça'89 Mitrovicë) | 24 |
| 2017/2018 | KF Drita Gjilan | FC Vëllaznimi Gjakovë | John Otto John (NGA, KF Trepça'89 Mitrovicë) Mirlind Daku (KF Llapi Podujevë) | 17 |
| 2018/2019 | KF Feronikeli Glogovac | KF Feronikeli Glogovac | Kastriot Rexha (KF Feronikeli Glogovac) | 21 |
| 2019/2020 | KF Drita Gjilan | KF Prishtina | Blendi Baftiu (KF Ballkani Suva Reka) Arb Manaj (KF Trepça'89 Mitrovicë) | 19 |
| 2020/2021 | KF Prishtina | KF Llapi Podujevë | Mirlind Daku (KF Ballkani Suva Reka) | 31 |
| 2021/2022 | KF Ballkani Suva Reka | KF Llapi Podujevë | Gerhard Progni (ALB, SC Gjilani) | 23 |
| 2022/2023 | KF Ballkani Suva Reka | KF Prishtina | Albion Rrahmani (KF Ballkani Suva Reka) | 22 |

# NATIONAL CHAMPIONSHIP
**Football Superleague of Kosovo 7 ALBI MALL Superliga e Kosovës 2022/2023**
(13.08.2022 – 28.05.2023)

## Results

**Round 1 [13-14.08.2022]**
SC Gjilani - KF Ferizaj 3-2
KF Trepça'89 - KF Drita Gjilan 2-2
KF Dukagjini - KF Prishtina 1-2
FK Drenica - KF Llapi 0-1
KF Malisheva - KF Ballkani 2-3 [28.09.2022]

**Round 2 [20-21.08.2022]**
KF Drita Gjilan - KF Dukagjini 1-0
KF Llapi - KF Trepça'89 2-2
KF Ferizaj - KF Prishtina 0-0
SC Gjilani - KF Malisheva 1-0
KF Ballkani - FK Drenica 1-0

**Round 3 [24-25.08.2022]**
FK Drenica - SC Gjilani 0-0
KF Malisheva - KF Ferizaj 3-1
KF Dukagjini - KF Llapi 1-1
KF Prishtina-KF Drita Gjilan 0-0 [28.09.2022]
KF Trepça'89 - KF Ballkani 1-1 [30.11.2022]

**Round 4 [27-28.08.2022]**
SC Gjilani - KF Trepça'89 3-1
KF Malisheva - FK Drenica 1-2
KF Ballkani - KF Dukagjini 1-0
KF Ferizaj - KF Drita Gjilan 1-1
KF Llapi - KF Prishtina 1-2

**Round 5 [03-04.09.2022]**
KF Drita Gjilan - KF Llapi 4-0
KF Trepça'89 - KF Malisheva 2-3
FK Drenica - KF Ferizaj 0-0
KF Dukagjini - SC Gjilani 0-1
KF Prishtina - KF Ballkani 0-1

**Round 6 [10-11.09.2022]**
FK Drenica - KF Trepça'89 2-5
KF Malisheva - KF Dukagjini 1-1
KF Ballkani - KF Drita Gjilan 0-2
KF Ferizaj - KF Llapi 2-1
SC Gjilani - KF Prishtina 1-1

**Round 7 [14-15.09.2022]**
KF Drita Gjilan - SC Gjilani 4-1
KF Prishtina - KF Malisheva 4-2
KF Dukagjini - FK Drenica 1-2
KF Trepça'89 - KF Ferizaj 1-1
KF Llapi - KF Ballkani 0-3 [04.12.2022]

**Round 8 [17-19.09.2022]**
SC Gjilani - KF Llapi 0-1
KF Malisheva - KF Drita Gjilan 2-4
FK Drenica - KF Prishtina 1-2
KF Trepça'89 - KF Dukagjini 3-0
KF Ferizaj - KF Ballkani 0-3

**Round 9 [01-02.10.2022]**
KF Drita Gjilan - FK Drenica 2-1
KF Dukagjini - KF Ferizaj 4-1
KF Llapi - KF Malisheva 1-1
KF Ballkani - SC Gjilani 2-0
KF Prishtina - KF Trepça'89 2-2 [02.11.2022]

**Round 10 [08-09.10.2022]**
KF Drita Gjilan - KF Trepça'89 3-1
KF Prishtina - KF Dukagjini 0-1
KF Ballkani - KF Malisheva 2-1
KF Ferizaj - SC Gjilani 1-1
KF Llapi - FK Drenica 3-2

**Round 11 [15-16.10.2022]**
KF Dukagjini - KF Drita Gjilan 0-1
KF Prishtina - KF Ferizaj 2-1
FK Drenica - KF Ballkani 1-1
KF Trepça'89 - KF Llapi 3-3
KF Malisheva - SC Gjilani 0-1

**Round 12 [19-20.10.2022]**
KF Drita Gjilan - KF Prishtina 1-2
KF Ferizaj - KF Malisheva 0-6
KF Ballkani - KF Trepça'89 2-0
SC Gjilani - FK Drenica 0-2
KF Llapi - KF Dukagjini 0-1 [26.10.2022]

**Round 13 [22-23.10.2022]**
KF Drita Gjilan - KF Ferizaj 1-0
KF Prishtina - KF Llapi 2-0
FK Drenica - KF Malisheva 0-0
KF Dukagjini - KF Ballkani 1-1
KF Trepça'89 - SC Gjilani 1-1

**Round 14 [29-30.10.2022]**
KF Ferizaj - FK Drenica 1-1
KF Malisheva - KF Trepça'89 4-0
KF Ballkani - KF Prishtina 1-1
SC Gjilani - KF Dukagjini 1-0
KF Llapi - KF Drita Gjilan 4-1

**Round 15 [05-06.11.2022]**
KF Dukagjini - KF Malisheva 4-0
KF Prishtina - SC Gjilani 2-2
KF Trepça'89 - FK Drenica 1-0
KF Drita Gjilan - KF Ballkani 2-2
KF Llapi - KF Ferizaj 1-2

**Round 16 [09-10.11.2022]**
FK Drenica - KF Dukagjini 0-1
KF Ferizaj - KF Trepça'89 2-3
KF Malisheva - KF Prishtina 2-1
KF Ballkani - KF Llapi 1-4
SC Gjilani - KF Drita Gjilan 1-1

**Round 17 [12-13.11.2022]**
KF Dukagjini - KF Trepça'89 1-0
KF Prishtina - FK Drenica 0-1
KF Drita Gjilan - KF Malisheva 3-1
KF Ballkani - KF Ferizaj 2-0
KF Llapi - SC Gjilani 0-1

**Round 18 [26-27.11.2022]**
FK Drenica - KF Drita Gjilan 1-3
KF Ferizaj - KF Dukagjini 0-0
SC Gjilani - KF Ballkani 0-3
KF Trepça'89 - KF Prishtina 0-3
KF Malisheva - KF Llapi 0-0

**Round 19 [11-12.02.2023]**
KF Malisheva - KF Ballkani 2-4
SC Gjilani - KF Ferizaj 0-0
FK Drenica - KF Llapi 0-1
KF Trepça'89 - KF Drita Gjilan 1-0
KF Dukagjini - KF Prishtina 1-0

**Round 20 [18-19.02.2023]**
KF Drita Gjilan - KF Dukagjini 5-1
KF Ferizaj - KF Prishtina 1-0
KF Llapi - KF Trepça'89 2-1
KF Ballkani - FK Drenica 2-1
SC Gjilani - KF Malisheva 2-2

**Round 21 [22-23.02.2023]**
KF Prishtina - KF Drita Gjilan 1-2
KF Malisheva - KF Ferizaj 1-1
FK Drenica - SC Gjilani 1-2
KF Trepça'89 - KF Ballkani 0-1
KF Dukagjini - KF Llapi 0-1

**Round 22 [25-26.02.2023]**
KF Ferizaj - KF Drita Gjilan 2-1
KF Malisheva - FK Drenica 3-1
KF Llapi - KF Prishtina 0-2
KF Ballkani - KF Dukagjini 1-1
SC Gjilani - KF Trepça'89 1-0

**Round 23 [04-05.03.2023]**
KF Drita Gjilan - KF Llapi 2-0
KF Dukagjini - SC Gjilani 0-1
FK Drenica - KF Ferizaj 1-0
KF Prishtina - KF Ballkani 2-2
KF Trepça'89 - KF Malisheva 0-0

**Round 24 [08-09.03.2023]**
FK Drenica - KF Trepça'89 1-2
KF Ferizaj - KF Llapi 2-1
KF Malisheva - KF Dukagjini 1-2
KF Ballkani - KF Drita Gjilan 1-1
SC Gjilani - KF Prishtina 0-0

**Round 25 [11-12.03.2023]**
KF Dukagjini - FK Drenica 2-0
KF Trepça'89 - KF Ferizaj 0-1
KF Drita Gjilan - SC Gjilani 1-0
KF Llapi - KF Ballkani 3-2
KF Prishtina - KF Malisheva 1-2

**Round 26 [18-19.03.2023]**
FK Drenica - KF Prishtina 0-1
KF Malisheva - KF Drita Gjilan 0-0
KF Ferizaj - KF Ballkani 0-0
SC Gjilani - KF Llapi 2-2
KF Trepça'89 - KF Dukagjini 2-1

**Round 27 [01-02.04.2023]**
KF Llapi - KF Malisheva 1-0
KF Ballkani - SC Gjilani 2-0
KF Prishtina - KF Trepça'89 4-1
KF Drita Gjilan - FK Drenica 3-0
KF Dukagjini - KF Ferizaj 3-1

**Round 28 [08-09.04.2023]**
KF Drita Gjilan - KF Trepça'89 1-1
KF Ballkani - KF Malisheva 2-2
KF Prishtina - KF Dukagjini 1-2
KF Ferizaj - SC Gjilani 2-0
KF Llapi - FK Drenica 4-0

**Round 29 [15-16.04.2023]**
KF Prishtina - KF Ferizaj 2-0
KF Trepça'89 - KF Llapi 2-1
KF Malisheva - SC Gjilani 0-2
KF Dukagjini - KF Drita Gjilan 0-0
FK Drenica - KF Ballkani 0-1

**Round 30 [22-23.04.2023]**
KF Drita Gjilan - KF Prishtina 1-0
KF Ferizaj - KF Malisheva 1-2
KF Ballkani - KF Trepça'89 7-2
SC Gjilani - FK Drenica 1-0
KF Llapi - KF Dukagjini 1-1

| Round 31 [29-30.04.2023] | Round 32 [03-04.05.2023] | Round 33 [06-07.05.2023] |
|---|---|---|
| KF Drita Gjilan - KF Ferizaj 3-0 | KF Ferizaj - FK Drenica 2-0 | KF Dukagjini - KF Malisheva 1-0 |
| FK Drenica - KF Malisheva 1-2 | KF Malisheva - KF Trepça'89 1-0 | KF Trepça'89 - FK Drenica 3-1 |
| KF Prishtina - KF Llapi 0-0 | SC Gjilani - KF Dukagjini 2-0 | KF Prishtina - SC Gjilani 0-0 |
| KF Dukagjini - KF Ballkani 1-1 | KF Llapi - KF Drita Gjilan 0-2 | KF Drita Gjilan - KF Ballkani 1-2 |
| KF Trepça'89 - SC Gjilani 0-0 | KF Ballkani - KF Prishtina 1-1 | KF Llapi - KF Ferizaj 0-0 |

| Round 34 [14.05.2023] | Round 35 [20.05.2023] | Round 36 [28.05.2023] |
|---|---|---|
| FK Drenica - KF Dukagjini 1-4 | KF Dukagjini - KF Trepça'89 3-1 | FK Drenica - KF Drita Gjilan 1-3 |
| KF Ferizaj - KF Trepça'89 1-0 | KF Prishtina - FK Drenica 4-1 | KF Ferizaj - KF Dukagjini 2-1 |
| KF Malisheva - KF Prishtina 1-1 | KF Drita Gjilan - KF Malisheva 0-1 | SC Gjilani - KF Ballkani 0-0 |
| KF Ballkani - KF Llapi 1-0 | KF Ballkani - KF Ferizaj 2-0 | KF Trepça'89 - KF Prishtina 2-1 |
| SC Gjilani - KF Drita Gjilan 1-1 | KF Llapi - SC Gjilani 2-2 | KF Malisheva - KF Llapi 3-2 |

## Final Standings

| | | Total | | | | | | | Home | | | | | | Away | | | | |
|---|---|---|---|---|---|---|---|---|---|---|---|---|---|---|---|---|---|---|---|
| 1. | **KF Ballkani Suva Reka** | 36 | 20 | 13 | 3 | 62 - 32 | **73** | 11 | 5 | 2 | 31 - 16 | 9 | 8 | 1 | 31 - 16 |
| 2. | KF Drita Gjilan | 36 | 20 | 10 | 6 | 63 - 31 | **70** | 13 | 2 | 3 | 38 - 13 | 7 | 8 | 3 | 25 - 18 |
| 3. | SC Gjilani | 36 | 13 | 15 | 8 | 34 - 34 | **54** | 7 | 8 | 3 | 19 - 16 | 6 | 7 | 5 | 15 - 18 |
| 4. | KF Dukagjini Klinë | 36 | 14 | 8 | 14 | 41 - 37 | **50** | 8 | 4 | 6 | 24 - 14 | 6 | 4 | 8 | 17 - 23 |
| 5. | KF Prishtina | 36 | 12 | 12 | 12 | 46 - 36 | **48** | 6 | 6 | 6 | 27 - 20 | 6 | 6 | 6 | 19 - 16 |
| 6. | KF Malisheva | 36 | 12 | 10 | 14 | 52 - 52 | **46** | 6 | 5 | 7 | 27 - 26 | 6 | 5 | 7 | 25 - 26 |
| 7. | KF Llapi Podujevë | 36 | 11 | 10 | 15 | 44 - 50 | **43** | 6 | 5 | 7 | 25 - 25 | 5 | 5 | 8 | 19 - 25 |
| 8. | KF Ferizaj (*Relegation Play-offs*) | 36 | 10 | 11 | 15 | 31 - 50 | **41** | 8 | 6 | 4 | 20 - 21 | 2 | 5 | 11 | 11 - 29 |
| 9. | KF Trepça'89 Mitrovicë (*Relegated*) | 36 | 10 | 10 | 16 | 46 - 62 | **40** | 7 | 7 | 4 | 24 - 20 | 3 | 3 | 12 | 22 - 42 |
| 10. | KF Drenica Skenderaj (*Relegated*) | 36 | 6 | 5 | 25 | 27 - 62 | **23** | 2 | 4 | 12 | 12 - 28 | 4 | 1 | 13 | 15 - 34 |

| Top goalscorers: | |
|---|---|
| 22  **Albion Rrahmani** | *KF Ballkani Suva Reka* |
| 14  Besnik Krasniqi | *KF Drita Gjilan* |
| 12  Marko Simonovski (MKD) | *KF Drita Gjilan* |

### Relegation Play-offs [04.06.2023]

KF Ferizaj - KF Liria Prizren      0-0 aet; 0-3 pen
KF Liria Prizren promoted for the 2023/2024 Football Superleague.

## NATIONAL CUP
### Kosovo Cup / Kupa e Kosovës 2022/2023

| Round of 32 [17.11./23-24.11.2023] | | | | |
|---|---|---|---|---|
| KF Llapi Podujevë - KF Vllaznia Požaranje | 6-2 | | KF Behar Pejë - KF Ferizaj | 3-0 *awarded* |
| KF Vëllaznimi Gjakovë - KF Prishtina | *withdrew* | | FK A&N Prizren - KF Rahoveci | 2-1 |
| KF Dukagjini Klinë - KF Rilindja 1974 | 2-0 | | KF Trepça'89 Mitrovicë - KF Kika Hogosht | 3-0 |
| KF Prizreni - KF Istogu | 2-0 aet | | KF Trepça Mitrovicë - SC Gjilani | 0-5 |
| KF Feronikeli 74 Drenas - KF 2 Korriku Prishtina | 4-1 | | KF Fushë Kosova - KF Arbëria Lipljan | 4-1 |
| KF Vushtrria - KF Drenasi | 1-0 | | KF Ramiz Sadiku Prishtina - KF Malisheva | 0-4 |
| KF Vjosa - KF Ulpiana Lipljan | 1-0 | | KF Drita Gjilan - KF Liria Prizren | 1-2 |
| KF Drenica Skenderaj - KF Flamurtari Prishtina | 2-2 aet; 7-8 pen | | KF Phönix-Banjë - KF Ballkani Suva Reka | 1-3 |

| 1/8-Finals [04-06.02.2023] | | | | |
|---|---|---|---|---|
| KF Liria Prizren - KF Llapi Podujevë | 2-3 | | SC Gjilani - KF Vjosa | 4-0 |
| KF Feronikeli 74 Drenas - KF Trepça'89 Mitrovicë | 0-3 *awarded* | | KF Behar Pejë - KF Prizreni | 3-1 |
| KF Ballkani Suva Reka - FK A&N Prizren | 2-0 | | KF Malisheva - KF Fushë Kosova | 2-0 |
| KF Flamurtari Prishtina - KF Vushtrria | 1-1 aet; 3-4 pen | | KF Prishtina - KF Dukagjini Klinë | 3-1 |

| Quarter-Finals [15.03.2023] | | | | |
|---|---|---|---|---|
| KF Trepça'89 Mitrovicë - SC Gjilani | 1-5 | | KF Vushtrria - KF Behar Pejë | 1-0 |
| KF Llapi Podujevë - KF Malisheva | 2-2 aet; 6-5 pen | | KF Prishtina - KF Ballkani Suva Reka | 2-0 |

| Semi-Finals [07.04./13.04.2022] | | | |
|---|---|---|---|
| **First Leg** | | **Second Leg** | |
| KF Llapi Podujevë - SC Gjilani | 1-2(1-2) | SC Gjilani - KF Llapi Podujevë | 1-0(1-0) |
| KF Vushtrria - KF Prishtina | 1-2(1-0) | KF Prishtina - KF Vushtrria | 6-0(3-0) |

05.06.2023; Stadiumi „Fadil Vokrri", Prishtina; Referee: Visar Kastrati; Attendance: 6,000
**SC Gjilani - KF Prishtina**                                                                                    **0-2(0-0)**

**SC Gjilani**: Enea Koliçi, Perparim Islami, Egzon Sinani, Granit Jashari, Yll Hoxha, Besar Musolli (Cap), Arbnor Ramadani (80.Oltion Bilalli), Albert Dabiqaj (89.Arbër Prekazi), Élton Pereira Gomes „Élton Calé" (80.Redon Ismaili), Baton Zabergja, Mevlan Zeka. Trainer: Zekirija Ramadani (North Macedonia).

**KF Prishtina**: Agron Kolaj, Ramiz Bytyqi, Muhamed Useini, Egzon Belica, Gledi Mici (Cap), Endrit Krasniqi (90+5.Albin Prapashtica), Kushtrim Gashi (46.Genc Hamiti), Mergim Pefqeli, Leotrim Kryeziu, Hasan Hyseni (90+1.Diar Halili), Jalen Aleix Miller Blesa (83.Bujar Pllana). Trainer: Debatik Curri (Albania).

**Goals:** 0-1 Genc Hamiti (67), 0-2 Mergim Pefqeli (74).

## THE CLUBS 2022/2023

### Klubi Futbollistik Ballkani Suva Reka

| Founded: | 1947 | |
|---|---|---|
| Stadium: | Stadiumi i Qytetit të Suharekës, Suva Reka (1,500) | |
| Trainer: | Ilir Daja (ALB) | 20.10.1966 |

| Goalkeepers: | DOB | M | (s) | G |
|---|---|---|---|---|
| Stivi Frashëri (ALB) | 29.08.1990 | 29 | | |
| Damir Ljuljanović (MNE) | 23.02.1992 | 7 | (2) | |
| **Defenders:** | **DOB** | **M** | **(s)** | **G** |
| Leonit Abazi (ALB) | 05.07.1993 | 2 | | |
| Leotrim Bekteshi | 21.04.1992 | 5 | (16) | 1 |
| Lumbardh Dellova | 01.01.1999 | 30 | | 3 |
| Rustem Hoxha (ALB) | 04.07.1991 | 1 | (7) | |
| Bajram Jashanica | 25.09.1990 | 34 | | 1 |
| Albin Kapra | 07.06.2000 | 1 | (12) | |
| Arber Potoku | 19.04.1994 | 19 | (5) | |
| Egzon Sinani | 07.06.1994 | 9 | (4) | |
| Armend Thaqi | 10.10.1992 | 36 | | 3 |
| Astrit Thaqi | 20.04.1993 | 17 | (1) | |
| Lorenc Trashi (ALB) | 19.05.1992 | 8 | (9) | |

| Midfielders: | DOB | M | (s) | G |
|---|---|---|---|---|
| Lindon Emërllahu | 07.12.2002 | 30 | | |
| Nazmi Gripshi (ALB) | 05.07.1997 | 24 | (2) | |
| Edvin Kuc (MNE) | 27.10.1993 | 29 | | 7 |
| Leonard Shala | 31.05.2003 | | (2) | |
| Qëndrim Zyba | 03.02.2001 | 23 | (7) | 2 |
| **Forwards:** | **DOB** | **M** | **(s)** | **G** |
| Albin Berisha | 14.01.2001 | 8 | (16) | 4 |
| Krenar Dulaj | 24.04.2006 | | (1) | |
| Van-Dave Harmon (LBR) | 22.09.1995 | 1 | (8) | 2 |
| Meriton Korenica | 15.12.1996 | 31 | (2) | 9 |
| Ermal Krasniqi | 07.09.1998 | 15 | (2) | 7 |
| *Lucas* Ferreira *Cardoso* (BRA) | 07.04.1994 | 3 | (2) | |
| Yoan Marc-Olivier (ENG) | 24.08.2000 | 1 | (3) | |
| Albion Rrahmani | 31.08.2000 | 31 | (4) | 22 |
| Veton Tusha | 29.12.2002 | 1 | (12) | 1 |
| Dejan Zarubica (MNE) | 11.04.1993 | 1 | (2) | |

### Klubi Futbollistik Drenica Skenderaj

| Founded: | 1958 | |
|---|---|---|
| Stadium: | Stadiumi "Bajram Aliu", Skenderaj (3,000) | |
| Trainer: | Bekim Shotani | 06.12.1974 |
| [01.03.2023] | Bledar Devolli (ALB) | 15.01.1978 |

| Goalkeepers: | DOB | M | (s) | G |
|---|---|---|---|---|
| Altin Gjokaj | 11.11.2005 | 12 | | |
| Leon Kozi (ALB) | 04.02.2003 | 3 | | |
| Arlis Shala (ALB) | 26.07.2000 | 21 | | |
| **Defenders:** | **DOB** | **M** | **(s)** | **G** |
| Arjan Abazi | | | (1) | |
| Benjamin Agyare (GHA) | 08.05.1994 | 10 | (2) | |
| Albion Avdyli | | | (1) | |
| Azem Bejta | 03.08.1990 | 29 | | |
| Arblert Beka | | 3 | (9) | |
| Ardian Hoti | 14.09.1996 | 26 | (2) | |
| Lukman Hussein (NGA) | 28.08.1996 | 12 | | |
| Veton Kabashi | 16.11.1992 | 2 | (1) | |
| Bleart Kastrati | 17.02.2003 | 6 | (2) | |
| Viktor Kuka | 25.06.1990 | 11 | | |
| Dreni Loshaj | 07.02.2002 | 1 | (1) | |
| Shkelzen Lushtaku | 22.06.1990 | 33 | | |
| Muharrem Musa | 25.06.1994 | | (2) | |
| Nii Noye Narh (NOR) | 19.12.1994 | 1 | | |
| Ermal Veliqi | 25.07.2001 | 25 | | 2 |
| Burim Veseli | 23.08.2003 | 1 | (1) | |

| Midfielders: | DOB | M | (s) | G |
|---|---|---|---|---|
| Armend Abazi | 17.08.1994 | 11 | (10) | 2 |
| Dzihan Adili (MKD) | 06.06.2002 | 1 | (2) | |
| Berat Ahmeti (ALB) | 26.01.1995 | 8 | (8) | |
| Florent Avdyli | 10.07.1993 | 5 | (4) | |
| Besfort Dervishaj | 24.09.1998 | 32 | (1) | 2 |
| Luan Dobra | 20.01.2005 | 2 | (8) | |
| Diart Geci | 21.03.2003 | 2 | (7) | |
| Erion Idrizi | | 3 | (3) | |
| Diogo Armando Lopes da Silva „Maranhão" (BRA) | 22.01.1995 | 13 | (2) | 1 |
| Faton Neziri | 10.11.2001 | 1 | (1) | |
| Endrit Shala | 22.01.2004 | 3 | (2) | |
| Arbios Thaçi | 13.10.1993 | 32 | | 1 |
| Altin Vojvoda | 15.06.1997 | 7 | | 2 |
| **Forwards:** | **DOB** | **M** | **(s)** | **G** |
| Archange Bintsouka (CGO) | 25.10.2002 | 27 | (1) | 7 |
| Zenel Gavazaj (ALB) | 02.05.2000 | 7 | (11) | 2 |
| Gentian Imeri | | 1 | | 1 |
| Osman Mëziu | 05.09.1999 | 19 | (4) | 3 |
| Yudai Miyamoto (JPN) | 10.03.1997 | 5 | | |
| Hysen Tahiri | 28.09.1992 | 2 | (4) | |
| Agim Zeka (ALB) | 06.09.1998 | 19 | (6) | 3 |

### Klubi Futbollistik Drita Gjilan

| Founded: | 1947 | |
|---|---|---|
| Stadium: | Stadiumi i Qytetit, Gjilan (15,000) | |
| Trainer: | Ardijan Nuhiji (MKD) | 07.12.1978 |
| [04.01.2023] | Arsim Thaqi | 25.05.1971 |
| [24.04.2023] | Akis Vavalis (GRE) | 21.09.1985 |

| Goalkeepers: | DOB | M | (s) | G |
|---|---|---|---|---|
| Eron Isufi | 05.08.2004 | | (1) | |
| Faton Maloku | 14.06.1991 | 27 | | |
| Florjan Smakiqi | 10.08.1998 | 9 | (1) | |
| **Defenders:** | **DOB** | **M** | **(s)** | **G** |
| Benjamin Agyare (GHA) | 08.05.1994 | 4 | (3) | |
| Prince Balde (LBR) | 23.03.1998 | 2 | (2) | 1 |
| Tun Bardhoku | 12.09.1993 | 6 | (8) | |
| Ilir Blakçori | 01.02.1993 | 31 | (1) | 1 |
| Yll Ibrahimi | 29.07.2003 | | (6) | |
| Besnik Krasniqi | 01.02.1990 | 33 | | 14 |
| Ardian Limani | 18.11.1993 | 35 | | 1 |
| Ekow Mills (GHA) | 30.07.2002 | | (1) | |
| Raddy Ovouka (CGO) | 07.12.1999 | 5 | (3) | 1 |
| Leonat Vitija | 22.08.2000 | 31 | (1) | 2 |

| Midfielders: | DOB | M | (s) | G |
|---|---|---|---|---|
| Blend Baftiu | 17.02.1998 | 36 | | 6 |
| Rron Broja | 09.04.1996 | 30 | (2) | 1 |
| *Iran* da Conceição Gonçalves *Júnior* (BRA) | 10.10.1995 | | (13) | 2 |
| Drilon Islami | 18.07.2000 | | (7) | 1 |
| Muharrem Jashari | 21.02.1998 | 24 | (7) | 4 |
| Hamdi Namani | 16.10.1994 | 20 | (11) | |
| Erion Ramushi | 16.08.2005 | | (1) | |
| **Forwards:** | **DOB** | **M** | **(s)** | **G** |
| Almir Ajzeraj | 05.10.1997 | 26 | (4) | 4 |
| Albin Krasniqi | 03.06.2001 | | (12) | |
| Almir Kryeziu | 14.12.1998 | 19 | (12) | 2 |
| Eridon Maloku | 21.01.2004 | | (1) | |
| Kastriot Selmani | 08.07.1999 | 24 | (10) | 4 |
| Marko Simonovski (MKD) | 02.01.1992 | 25 | (2) | 12 |
| Ardit Tahiri | 06.10.2002 | 9 | (25) | 6 |

## Klubi Futbollistik Dukagjini Klinë

| Founded: | 1958 | | |
|---|---|---|---|
| Stadium: | Stadiumi 18 Qershor, Klinë (1,000) | | |
| Trainer: | Armend Dallku | | 16.06.1983 |

| Goalkeepers: | DOB | M | (s) | G |
|---|---|---|---|---|
| Kenan Haxhihamza | 28.12.1996 | 28 | | |
| Altik Muhaxhiri | 09.01.1992 | 8 | (1) | |
| **Defenders:** | **DOB** | **M** | **(s)** | **G** |
| Elton Basriu (ALB) | 03.08.1987 | 34 | | |
| Ardin Dallku | 01.11.1994 | 29 | (4) | |
| Çendrim Kameraj | 13.03.1999 | 9 | (8) | |
| Rinor Kuqi | 27.04.1997 | 11 | (6) | |
| Arbër Shala | 23.12.1991 | 30 | (2) | |
| Ilir Syla | 21.05.1995 | 18 | (10) | |
| *Vitor Hugo* Leite Perusses (BRA) | 02.05.1996 | 30 | (1) | 1 |
| Melos Zenunaj | 29.08.2000 | | (2) | |
| **Midfielders:** | **DOB** | **M** | **(s)** | **G** |
| Ergyn Ahmeti | 21.12.1995 | 21 | | 1 |
| Labinot Jashanica | 16.04.1997 | 2 | (2) | |
| Vladyslav Khomutov (UKR) | 04.06.1998 | 19 | (3) | 2 |

| | DOB | M | (s) | G |
|---|---|---|---|---|
| Met Millaku | 15.11.1997 | 5 | (11) | |
| Blerind Morina | 01.01.2001 | 21 | (3) | 3 |
| Faton Neziri | 10.11.2001 | 3 | (5) | |
| Egzon Qerimi | 10.11.1993 | 3 | (4) | |
| Gentrit Salihu | 25.06.2003 | 4 | (4) | |
| Rion Selimi | 24.11.2005 | | (1) | |
| Dior Zabërgja | 18.04.1995 | 17 | (14) | 1 |
| **Forwards:** | **DOB** | **M** | **(s)** | **G** |
| Odi Henry Chibueze (NGA) | 15.11.1992 | 1 | (7) | |
| Granit Elezaj | 03.08.1996 | 2 | (7) | 1 |
| Ahmed Januzi (ALB) | 08.07.1988 | 6 | (3) | 1 |
| John Oto John (NGA) | 25.01.1998 | 22 | (10) | 9 |
| Progon Maloku (ALB) | 27.01.2000 | | (1) | |
| Altin Merlaku | 07.03.1993 | 27 | (1) | 7 |
| Marclei César Chaves *Santos* (BRA) | 18.06.1989 | 13 | (2) | 5 |
| Iljasa Zulfiu (SRB) | 27.03.1998 | 33 | (1) | 4 |

## Klubi Futbollistik Ferizaj

| Founded: | 1923 | | |
|---|---|---|---|
| Stadium: | Ferizaj Synthetic Grass Stadium, Ferizaj (1,500) | | |
| Trainer: | Arbnor Morina | | 02.06.1963 |
| [11.10.2022] | Andrej Panadić (CRO) | | 09.03.1969 |

| Goalkeepers: | DOB | M | (s) | G |
|---|---|---|---|---|
| Blend Bajraktari | 2004 | 1 | | |
| Marko Jovanovski (MKD) | 24.07.1988 | 16 | | |
| Edison Rexhepi | 28.05.2000 | 2 | | |
| Leutrim Rexhepi | 16.04.1994 | 17 | | |
| **Defenders:** | **DOB** | **M** | **(s)** | **G** |
| Qlirim Avdulli | 06.06.1999 | 17 | | |
| Behar Bardhi (MKD) | 24.03.1993 | 22 | (4) | 1 |
| Enhar Cakolli | 26.05.2000 | 11 | (6) | |
| Dardan Çerkini | 27.09.1991 | 17 | (7) | 1 |
| Gentian Emini | 03.08.1997 | 3 | (3) | |
| Filip Gligorov (MKD) | 31.07.1993 | 13 | | |
| Gentrit Halili | 14.12.2001 | 32 | | 4 |
| Donat Hasanaj | 18.09.1998 | 11 | (2) | 1 |
| Ergon Hyseni | 18.01.1994 | 19 | (8) | 1 |
| Moussa Kamara (GAM) | 03.04.1999 | 5 | (1) | |
| Jasmin Mečinović (MKD) | 22.10.1990 | 6 | (2) | |
| Elbasan Thaqi | 30.04.1991 | 3 | | |

| Midfielders: | DOB | M | (s) | G |
|---|---|---|---|---|
| Florim Berisha | 07.12.1988 | 5 | (3) | |
| Astrit Fazliu | 28.10.1987 | 13 | (8) | 3 |
| Besar Iseni (MKD) | 18.01.1997 | | (2) | |
| Drilon Islami | 18.07.2000 | 15 | | |
| Qlirim Kashtanjeva | 04.02.1999 | 4 | | |
| Helistano Manga (GNB) | 20.05.1999 | 1 | | |
| Kenan Orana | 05.04.1998 | 14 | (9) | |
| Ramush Ramadani | 15.06.2000 | 15 | (8) | 2 |
| Gentrit Ramusa | 10.09.2003 | 15 | (2) | 1 |
| Edon Sadriu | 25.05.1997 | 30 | (1) | 2 |
| Enis Sefa | 26.03.2001 | 8 | (11) | 2 |
| Bujar Shabani | 11.10.1990 | 19 | | 1 |
| Egzon Shabani | 27.08.1989 | | (4) | 1 |
| **Forwards:** | **DOB** | **M** | **(s)** | **G** |
| Betim Haxhimusa | 14.04.1992 | 17 | (5) | 4 |
| Albin Krasniqi | 03.06.2001 | 18 | | 1 |
| Mateo Panadić (CRO) | 06.10.1994 | 20 | (3) | 4 |
| Drilon Sadiku (ALB) | 27.05.2000 | 1 | (2) | |
| Erion Sadriu | | 6 | (2) | |

## Soccer Club Gjilani

| Founded: | 1945 (*as Crvena Zvezda Gjilane*) | | |
|---|---|---|---|
| Stadium: | Stadiumi i Qytetit, Gjilan (15,000) | | |
| Trainer: | Zekirija Ramadani (MKD) | | 21.01.1978 |

| Goalkeepers: | DOB | M | (s) | G |
|---|---|---|---|---|
| Enea Koliçi (ALB) | 13.02.1986 | 36 | | |
| **Defenders:** | **DOB** | **M** | **(s)** | **G** |
| Armend Halili | 22.06.1997 | 15 | (10) | |
| Yll Hoxha | 26.12.1987 | 26 | (7) | |
| Perparim Islami | 01.05.1993 | 29 | (3) | |
| Granit Jashari | 20.08.1998 | 28 | (2) | |
| Besart Krivanjeva (MKD) | 28.02.1996 | 12 | (3) | |
| Arbër Prekazi | 11.10.1989 | 23 | (4) | |
| Egzon Sinani | 07.06.1994 | 15 | (1) | |
| **Midfielders:** | **DOB** | **M** | **(s)** | **G** |
| Fabjan Beqja (ALB) | 15.02.1994 | 5 | (4) | |
| Albert Dabiqaj | 10.07.1996 | 25 | (1) | 5 |
| Redon Ismaili | 23.10.2002 | 8 | (7) | |
| Edison Kqiku | 16.01.1999 | | (5) | |

| | DOB | M | (s) | G |
|---|---|---|---|---|
| Blend Krasniqi | 08.10.2004 | | (3) | |
| Keita Lanzeni Aziz (CIV) | 28.12.1996 | | (1) | |
| Arens Mateli (ALB) | 10.07.2000 | | (5) | |
| Besar Musolli | 28.02.1989 | 28 | (1) | |
| Arbnor Ramadani | 03.06.1994 | 32 | | 2 |
| Agustín Gonzalo Torassa (ARG) | 20.10.1988 | 3 | (8) | |
| Erlis Xhemaili | 10.07.2003 | | (3) | |
| **Forwards:** | **DOB** | **M** | **(s)** | **G** |
| Oltion Bilalli | 03.01.2002 | 8 | (9) | 1 |
| Élton Pereira Gomes „Élton Calé" (BRA) | 12.07.1988 | 25 | (4) | 2 |
| Erzen Hyseni | 18.06.2004 | | (3) | |
| Shend Kelmendi | 21.09.1994 | 3 | (13) | 2 |
| Theophilus Solomon (NGA) | 18.01.1996 | 17 | (2) | 6 |
| Baton Zabergja | 18.04.2001 | 28 | (5) | 5 |
| Mevlan Zeka | 28.05.1994 | 30 | (4) | 10 |

## Klubi Futbollistik Llapi Podujevë

| Founded: | 1932 | | |
|---|---|---|---|
| Stadium: | Stadiumi „Zahir Pajaziti", Podujevë (10,000) | | |
| Trainer: | Tahir Batatina | | 12.07.1977 |

| Goalkeepers: | DOB | M | (s) | G |
|---|---|---|---|---|
| Ilir Avdyli | 20.05.1990 | 34 | | |
| Vokli Laroshi (ALB) | 06.08.2001 | 2 | | |
| **Defenders:** | **DOB** | **M** | **(s)** | **G** |
| Bianor Das Graças Lima da Silva Neto (BRA) | 28.06.1994 | 34 | | |
| Arber Bytyqi (ALB) | 16.10.2003 | 9 | (4) | |
| Martinos Christofi (CIP) | 26.07.1993 | 2 | (2) | |
| Juan Antonio Di Lorenzo (ARG) | 06.07.1998 | 4 | (1) | |
| Benjamin Emini | 20.07.1992 | 15 | | 1 |
| Fernando Augusto Rodrigues de Araujo „Fernandinho" (BRA) | 25.07.1993 | 24 | (2) | 2 |
| Bujar Idrizi | 11.12.1991 | 15 | | |
| Alex Raoul Leyi (CMR) | 29.09.2002 | 6 | (1) | |
| Bekim Maliqi | 26.07.2001 | 8 | (2) | 1 |
| Aleksandar Milić (MNE) | 24.08.1998 | 10 | | |
| Avni Selmani | 16.04.2004 | | (2) | |
| Aulon Shabani | 27.06.2003 | | (4) | |
| Diar Vokrri | 27.06.2004 | 2 | (4) | |
| **Midfielders:** | **DOB** | **M** | **(s)** | **G** |
| Arianit Hasani | 24.02.2004 | | (3) | |
| Ilir Krasniqi | 02.04.2000 | 28 | (2) | 2 |

| Gentrit Limani | 01.04.2000 | 13 | (1) | |
|---|---|---|---|---|
| Egzon Qerimi | 10.11.1993 | 1 | (4) | |
| Francisco Israel Rivera Dávalos (MEX) | 23.09.1994 | 29 | (5) | 7 |
| Robson da Silva (BRA) | 14.07.1995 | 5 | | |
| Kushtrim Shabani | 08.02.1997 | 29 | | 3 |
| Andri Stafa (ALB) | 14.02.2002 | 8 | (5) | |
| Rinor Toverlani | 05.06.2004 | | (1) | |
| **Forwards:** | **DOB** | **M** | **(s)** | **G** |
| Alef Firmino Dos Anjos (BRA) | 16.03.1998 | 17 | (4) | 5 |
| Festim Alidema | 05.10.1997 | 26 | (6) | 6 |
| Mergim Cërnavërni | 20.11.2005 | | (2) | |
| Drilon Fazliu | 17.11.2000 | 16 | (16) | 3 |
| Rinor Hoxha | 28.02.2000 | 1 | (8) | |
| Sokol Kiqina | 23.03.2002 | | (10) | |
| Albion Kurtaj | 02.11.1998 | 8 | (25) | 1 |
| Adem Maliqi | 17.07.1997 | 8 | (9) | 1 |
| Erjon Morina | 16.07.2002 | | (7) | |
| Gerhard Progni (ALB) | 06.11.1986 | 19 | (7) | 4 |
| Trimror Selimi | 06.09.2000 | 23 | (8) | 3 |

## Klubi i Futbollit Malisheva

| Founded: | 2016 | | |
|---|---|---|---|
| Stadium: | Stadiumi „Liman Gegaj", Malishevë (2,000) | | |
| Trainer: | Arsim Thaqi | | 25.05.1971 |
| [01.01.2023] | Bylbyl Sokoli | | 19.12.1958 |

| Goalkeepers: | DOB | M | (s) | G |
|---|---|---|---|---|
| Armend Blakçori | 06.08.1990 | 1 | | |
| Flamur Gashi | 06.06.2000 | 35 | | |
| **Defenders:** | **DOB** | **M** | **(s)** | **G** |
| Qlirim Avdulli | 06.06.1999 | 5 | | |
| Medin Bajrami (MKD) | 27.02.1998 | 8 | (5) | 2 |
| Faruk Bihorac (SRB) | 12.05.1996 | 16 | (1) | 1 |
| Dreni Kryeziu | 15.04.1996 | 34 | (1) | |
| Arbër Pira | 09.02.1995 | 30 | | |
| Kastriot Rapuca | 01.03.2001 | 11 | (6) | |
| Arlind Veliu | 14.06.2001 | 30 | | |
| Agon Xhaka (ALB) | 09.06.1997 | 18 | (3) | 3 |
| **Midfielders:** | **DOB** | **M** | **(s)** | **G** |
| Florent Avdyli | 10.07.1993 | 4 | (4) | |
| Kreshnik Bahtiri | 29.07.1992 | 7 | (2) | |
| Etnik Brruti | 04.03.2004 | 5 | (4) | |
| Agron Bruqi | 27.01.1993 | 7 | (9) | 1 |

| Alush Gavazaj | 24.03.1995 | 14 | (12) | 2 |
|---|---|---|---|---|
| Behar Maliqi | 22.09.1986 | 26 | | 3 |
| Ilir Mustafa | 07.08.1996 | 18 | (6) | 4 |
| Donart Vitija | 25.04.2000 | 23 | (6) | |
| Erblin Zogaj | | | (1) | |
| **Forwards:** | **DOB** | **M** | **(s)** | **G** |
| Altin Aliu | 11.11.1999 | 1 | (2) | |
| Fatjon Celani (GER) | 14.01.1992 | | (7) | |
| Fiton Hajdari | 19.09.1991 | 16 | (8) | 2 |
| Drilon Hazrollaj | 19.02.2004 | 13 | (8) | 7 |
| Adem Maliqi | 17.07.1997 | 2 | (2) | 1 |
| Yoan Marc-Olivier (ENG) | 24.08.2000 | 5 | (1) | 1 |
| Alban Shillova | 13.08.1992 | 14 | (9) | 5 |
| Ronald Sobowale (ENG) | 19.07.1997 | 23 | (4) | 11 |
| Redon Syla | 09.02.2003 | | (1) | |
| Bleart Tolaj | 07.02.2000 | 30 | (3) | 7 |

## Football Club Prishtina

| Founded: | 1922 | | |
|---|---|---|---|
| Stadium: | Stadiumi "Fadil Vokrri", Prishtina (13,500) | | |
| Trainer: | Ismet Munishi | | 03.10.1974 |
| [13.03.2023] | Debatik Curri (ALB) | | 28.12.1983 |

| Goalkeepers: | DOB | M | (s) | G |
|---|---|---|---|---|
| Ardit Nika | 12.01.1998 | 22 | | |
| Agron Kolaj | 19.03.2001 | 14 | | |
| **Defenders:** | **DOB** | **M** | **(s)** | **G** |
| Egzon Belica (MKD) | 03.09.1990 | 20 | (1) | |
| Ramiz Bytyqi | 10.01.1999 | 34 | | 1 |
| Amar Demolli | 16.07.2006 | | (1) | |
| Gentrit Dumani | 13.07.1993 | | (1) | |
| Dion Gallapeni | 22.12.2004 | | (2) | |
| Diar Halili | 02.07.2003 | | (1) | |
| Benet Ismaili | 13.03.2002 | 1 | | |
| Gledi Mici (ALB) | 06.02.1991 | 33 | | |
| Bujar Pllana | 29.10.2001 | 22 | (4) | 4 |
| Besir Ramadani (ALB) | 09.06.2000 | 9 | (7) | |
| Muhamed Useini (MKD) | 21.11.1988 | 33 | | 3 |
| **Midfielders:** | **DOB** | **M** | **(s)** | **G** |
| Endrit Baholli | 26.02.2000 | | (1) | |
| Muhamed Dubova | 14.06.2001 | | (2) | |

| Kushtrim Gashi | 15.11.1992 | 28 | | 1 |
|---|---|---|---|---|
| Genc Hamiti | 21.09.1993 | 15 | (11) | 2 |
| Hasan Hyseni | 14.04.1997 | 11 | (8) | 1 |
| Endrit Krasniqi | 26.10.1994 | 33 | | 9 |
| Korab Luma | 12.03.2005 | | (1) | |
| Mergim Pefqeli | 25.11.1993 | 27 | (1) | 2 |
| Arlind Shabani | 16.10.2001 | 3 | (9) | 1 |
| Fitim Susuri | 20.06.1998 | 2 | (9) | |
| **Forwards:** | **DOB** | **M** | **(s)** | **G** |
| Jalen Aleix Miller Blesa (ESP) | 05.02.2001 | 9 | (5) | 1 |
| Igball Jashari | 14.07.2005 | | (3) | |
| Mendurim Hoti | 23.02.1996 | 7 | (3) | 1 |
| Leotrim Kryeziu | 25.01.1999 | 34 | (1) | 8 |
| Albin Prapashtica | 08.09.2001 | 11 | (10) | 4 |
| Shefit Shefiti (ALB) | 19.02.1998 | 10 | (11) | 3 |
| Marclei César Chaves Santos (BRA) | 18.06.1989 | 2 | (9) | |
| Kreshnik Uka | 07.01.1995 | 16 | (5) | 5 |

## Klubi Futbollistik Trepça '89

| | | |
|---|---|---|
| **Founded**: | 1940 (*as KF Rudari*); re-founded 1992 (*as Minatori '89 Trepça*) | |
| **Stadium**: | Stadiumi „Riza Lushta", Mitrovica (12,000) | |
| **Trainer**: | Seid Onbashi | 06.03.1982 |

| Goalkeepers: | DOB | M | (s) | G |
|---|---|---|---|---|
| Marly Prince Heritier (CGO) | 10.04.1999 | 4 | | |
| Donat Kaçiu | 20.09.1993 | 4 | | |
| Arion Ymeri | 30.03.1995 | 28 | | |
| **Defenders:** | **DOB** | **M** | **(s)** | **G** |
| Augustine Ameworlorna (GHA) | 10.06.1999 | 33 | | |
| Valon Dedia | 31.08.2000 | 2 | (2) | |
| Gentrit Dumani | 13.07.1993 | 10 | (1) | |
| Erdin Dushi | 07.10.2002 | 29 | (2) | 3 |
| Ahmet Haliti | 01.10.1988 | 8 | | |
| Guri Hana | 27.08.2001 | 11 | (5) | |
| Happy Takalani Mashau (RSA) | 24.03.1991 | 15 | | |
| Albion Pllana | 20.08.2000 | 8 | (15) | 3 |
| Ron Raqi | 18.09.2002 | | (2) | |
| Fatmir Rexhaj | 25.05.1996 | 13 | (2) | |
| **Midfielders:** | **DOB** | **M** | **(s)** | **G** |
| Milazim Bajraktari | 13.07.2003 | | (12) | |

| | DOB | M | (s) | G |
|---|---|---|---|---|
| Rilind Nimani | 11.01.1999 | 33 | | 3 |
| Abdulah Oyekanmi (NGA) | 25.06.2003 | 16 | (8) | 4 |
| Lulzim Peci | 27.02.2002 | 15 | (12) | |
| Robert Rrahmani | 28.01.2001 | 22 | (3) | 1 |
| Samir Sahiti | 15.08.1988 | 23 | (5) | 1 |
| **Forwards:** | **DOB** | **M** | **(s)** | **G** |
| Ebenezer Adukwaw (GHA) | 03.08.2001 | 5 | (6) | 1 |
| Madi Karamo Fatty (GAM) | 11.12.1999 | 16 | (8) | 1 |
| Egzon Fazliu | 30.05.2003 | 8 | (10) | 4 |
| Armend Gashi | 29.01.2001 | 22 | (9) | 7 |
| Ardian Hasani | 03.12.2003 | 1 | (4) | |
| Christian Mba (NGA) | 12.10.1999 | 18 | | 10 |
| Ardian Muja | 09.12.1997 | 25 | | 5 |
| Ermir Rashica | 24.03.2004 | 2 | (4) | |
| Bleon Sekiraqa | 17.10.2000 | 25 | (2) | 2 |
| Daniel Tette (GHA) | 06.01.2002 | | (3) | |

## SECOND LEVEL
### First Football League of Kosovo - Liga e Parë 2022/2023

### Grupi A

| | | | | | | | | | |
|---|---|---|---|---|---|---|---|---|---|
| 1. | KF Feronikeli 74 Drenas (*Promoted*) | 27 | 17 | 6 | 4 | 49 | - | 23 | 57 |
| 2. | KF Liria Prizren (*Promotion Play-offs*) | 27 | 16 | 6 | 5 | 46 | - | 25 | 54 |
| 3. | KF Phönix-Banjë | 27 | 15 | 4 | 8 | 41 | - | 36 | 49 |
| 4. | KF Istogu | 27 | 13 | 6 | 8 | 45 | - | 36 | 45 |
| 5. | KF Trepça Mitrovicë | 27 | 10 | 6 | 11 | 47 | - | 48 | 36 |
| 6. | KF Rahoveci | 27 | 9 | 6 | 12 | 33 | - | 37 | 33 |
| 7. | KF Rilindja 1974 | 27 | 8 | 8 | 11 | 34 | - | 35 | 32 |
| 8. | KF Drenasi | 27 | 8 | 6 | 13 | 29 | - | 44 | 30 |
| 9. | FK A&N Prizren | 27 | 8 | 5 | 14 | 38 | - | 46 | 29 |
| 10. | KF Vëllaznimi Gjakovë (*Relegated*) | 27 | 2 | 5 | 20 | 15 | - | 47 | 11 |

### Grupi B

| | | | | | | | | | |
|---|---|---|---|---|---|---|---|---|---|
| 1. | KF Fushë Kosova (*Promoted*) | 27 | 17 | 8 | 2 | 47 | - | 22 | 59 |
| 2. | KF Ulpiana Lipljan (*Promotion Play-offs*) | 27 | 16 | 5 | 6 | 42 | - | 30 | 53 |
| 3. | KF Vushtrria | 27 | 13 | 7 | 7 | 39 | - | 28 | 46 |
| 4. | KF Flamurtari Prishtina | 27 | 12 | 9 | 6 | 41 | - | 26 | 45 |
| 5. | KF Vjosa | 27 | 12 | 5 | 10 | 41 | - | 40 | 41 |
| 6. | KF Vllaznia Požaranje | 27 | 7 | 7 | 13 | 35 | - | 36 | 28 |
| 7. | KF Ramiz Sadiku Prishtina | 27 | 6 | 9 | 12 | 30 | - | 39 | 27 |
| 8. | KF Kika Hogosht | 27 | 5 | 11 | 11 | 26 | - | 46 | 26 |
| 9. | KF 2 Korriku Prishtina | 27 | 5 | 9 | 13 | 27 | - | 36 | 24 |
| 10. | KF Arbëria Lipljan (*Relegated*) | 27 | 5 | 4 | 18 | 29 | - | 54 | 19 |

### Promotion Play-offs [21.05.2023]

**Semi-Final** [27.05.2023]  KF Liria Prizren - KF Ulpiana Lipljan  3-1

KF Liria Prizren were qualified for the Final against KF Ferizaj (8th placed at first level).

## INTERNATIONAL MATCHES
### (16.07.2022 – 15.07.2023)

| 24.09.2022 | Belfast | Northern Ireland - Kosovo | 2-1(0-0) | (UNL) |
|---|---|---|---|---|
| 27.09.2022 | Prishtina | Kosovo - Cyprus | 5-1(2-0) | (UNL) |
| 16.11.2022 | Prishtina | Kosovo - Armenia | 2-2(0-1) | (F) |
| 19.11.2022 | Prishtina | Kosovo - Faroe Islands | 1-1(0-0) | (F) |
| 25.03.2023 | Tel Aviv | Israel - Kosovo | 1-1(0-1) | (ECQ) |
| 28.03.2023 | Prishtina | Kosovo - Andorra | 1-1(0-0) | (ECQ) |
| 16.06.2023 | Prishtina | Kosovo - Romania | 0-0 | (ECQ) |
| 19.06.2023 | Budapest | Belarus - Kosovo | 2-1(0-0) | (ECQ) |

**24.09.2022 NORTHERN IRELAND - KOSOVO 2-1(0-0)** 3rd UEFA Nations League C, Group 2
Windsor Park, Belfast; Referee: Glenn Nyberg (Sweden); Attendance: 17,148
**KOS:** Arijanet Anan Muriqi, Florent Hadergjonaj, Betim Fazlija, Fidan Aliti, Donat Rrudhani, Ibrahim Dreshaj, Florent Muslija (78.Florian Loshaj), Bersant Celina, Milot Nexhmedin Rashica (68.Arbër Zeneli), Elbasan Rashani (87.Zymer Bytyqi), Vedat Muriqi (Cap). Trainer: Alain Giresse (France).
**Goal:** Vedat Muriqi (58).

**27.09.2022 KOSOVO - CYPRUS 5-1(2-0)** 3rd UEFA Nations League C, Group 2
Stadiumi „Fadil Vokrri", Prishtina; Referee: Kristo Tohver (Estonia); Attendance: 10,400
**KOS:** Samir Ujkani, Florent Hadergjonaj (89.Ilir Krasniqi), Amir Kadri Rrahmani (Cap) (64.Ibrahim Dreshaj), Mirlind Kryeziu, Donat Rrudhani, Betim Fazlija, Florent Muslija (89.Lindon Emërllahu), Bersant Celina, Elbasan Rashani (64.Zymer Bytyqi), Arbër Zeneli (81.Milot Nexhmedin Rashica), Vedat Muriqi. Trainer: Alain Giresse (France).
**Goals:** Florent Muslija (22), Donat Rrudhani (45+1), Elbasan Rashani (47), Vedat Muriqi (52, 84).

**16.11.2022 KOSOVO - ARMENIA 2-2(0-1)** Friendly International
Stadiumi „Fadil Vokrri", Prishtina; Referee: Eldorjan Hamiti (Albania); Attendance: 2,000
**KOS:** Visar Bekaj (Cap), Jetmir Haliti, Lumbardh Dellova, Leard Sadriu (65.Donat Rrudhani), Ilir Krasniqi (46.Lirim R. Kastrati), Eris Abedini, Muharrem Jashari, Uran Bislimi (65.Arianit Ferati), Lirim M. Kastrati, Valmir Veliu (75.Jetmir Topalli), Agon Sadiku. Trainer: Alain Giresse (France).
**Goals:** Lirim M. Kastrati (67 penalty), Donat Rrudhani (90+3).

**19.11.2022 KOSOVO - FAROE ISLANDS 1-1(0-0)** Friendly International
Stadiumi „Fadil Vokrri", Prishtina; Referee: Juxhin Xhaja (Albania); Attendance: 2,000
**KOS:** Jozef Pukaj, Lirim R. Kastrati (Cap), Kreshnik Hajrizi, Lumbardh Dellova, Donat Rrudhani, Lindon Emërllahu, Arianit Ferati, Uran Bislimi (77.Muharrem Jashari), Jetmir Topalli, Ermal Krasniqi, Agon Sadiku (63.Lirim M. Kastrati). Trainer: Alain Giresse (France).
**Goal:** Uran Bislimi (64).

**25.03.2023 ISRAEL - KOSOVO 1-1(0-1)** 17th EC. Qualifiers
Bloomfield Stadium, Tel Aviv; Referee: William Sean Collum (Scotland); Attendance: 28,935
**KOS:** Arijanet Anan Muriqi, Mërgim Vojvoda (88.Florent Hadergjonaj), Amir Kadri Rrahmani (Cap), Mirlind Kryeziu, Leart Paqarada, Ibrahim Dreshaj (88.Valon Berisha), Bersant Celina, Florent Muslija (79.Arbër Zeneli), Edon Luizim Zhegrova (67.Betim Fazlija), Milot Nexhmedin Rashica, Vedat Muriqi. Trainer: Alain Giresse (France).
**Goal:** Elazar Dasa (36 own goal).

**28.03.2023 KOSOVO - ANDORRA 1-1(0-0)** 17th EC. Qualifiers
Stadiumi "Fadil Vokrri", Prishtina; Referee: Sebastian Gishamer (Austria); Attendance: 12,600
**KOS:** Arijanet Anan Muriqi, Florent Hadergjonaj, Amir Kadri Rrahmani (Cap), Mirlind Kryeziu, Leart Paqarada (46.Donat Rrudhani), Betim Fazlija, Valon Berisha (46.Edon Zhegrova), Bersant Celina (75.Florent Muslija), Arbër Zeneli (75.Zymer Bytyqi), Milot Nexhmedin Rashica, Vedat Muriqi. Trainer: Alain Giresse (France).
**Goal:** Edon Luizim Zhegrova (59).

**16.06.2023 KOSOVO - ROMANIA 0-0** 17th EC. Qualifiers
Stadiumi „Fadil Vokrri", Prishtina; Referee: Danny Desmond Makkelie (Netherlands); Attendance: 11,000
**KOS:** Arijanet Anan Muriqi, Mërgim Vojvoda, Amir Kadri Rrahmani (Cap), Fidan Aliti, Leart Paqarada, Ibrahim Dreshaj (73.Hekuran Kryeziu), Betim Fazlija, Bersant Celina, Milot Nexhmedin Rashica (46.Edon Zhegrova), Florent Muslija (82.Jetmir Topalli), Vedat Muriqi. Trainer: Alain Giresse (France).

**19.06.2023 BELARUS - KOSOVO 2-1(0-0)** 17th EC. Qualifiers
"Szusza Ferenc" Stadion, Budapest (Hungary); Referee: Julian Weinberger (Austria); Attendance: *played behind closed doors*
**KOS:** Arijanet Anan Muriqi, Mërgim Vojvoda, Amir Kadri Rrahmani (Cap), Fidan Aliti, Leart Paqarada (25.Ermal Krasniqi), Ibrahim Dreshaj (46.Edon Zhegrova), Betim Fazlija (53.Hekuran Kryeziu), Donat Rrudhani, Florent Muslija, Bersant Celina (79.Florian Loshaj), Vedat Muriqi. Trainer: Alain Giresse (France).
**Goal:** Vedat Muriqi (87).

## NATIONAL TEAM PLAYERS
### (16.07.2022 – 15.07.2023)

| Name | DOB | Caps | Goals | Club | |
|---|---|---|---|---|---|
| **Goalkeepers** | | | | | |
| Visar BEKAJ | 24.05.1997 | 5 | 0 | 2022: | *KF Tiranë (ALB)* |
| Arijanet Anan MURIQI | 07.11.1998 | 32 | 0 | 2022/2023: | *Burnley FC (ENG)* |
| Jozef PUKAJ | 13.02.2000 | 1 | 0 | 2022: | *FC Winterthur (SUI)* |
| Samir UJKANI | 05.07.1988 | 36 | 0 | 2022: | *Empoli FC (ITA)* |
| **Defenders** | | | | | |
| Fidan ALITI | 03.10.1993 | 46 | 1 | 2022/2023: | *FC Zürich (SUI)* |
| Lumbardh DELLOVA | 01.01.1999 | 3 | 0 | 2022: | *KF Ballkani Suva Reka* |
| Ibrahim DRESHAJ | 24.01.1997 | 24 | 0 | 2022/2023: | *Fatih Karagümrük SK (TUR)* |
| Betim FAZLIJA | 25.04.1999 | 20 | 0 | 2022/2023: | *FC St. Pauli Hamburg (GER)* |
| Florent HADERGJONAJ | 31.07.1994 | 27 | 1 | 2022/2023: | *Kasımpaşa Spor Kulübü İstanbul (TUR)* |
| Kreshnik HAJRIZI | 28.05.1999 | 1 | 0 | 2022: | *FC Lugano (SUI)* |
| Jetmir HALITI | 14.09.1996 | 1 | 0 | 2022: | *Mjällby AIF Hällevik (SWE)* |
| Lirim R. KASTRATI | 02.02.1999 | 12 | 0 | 2022: | *Újpest FC (HUN)* |
| Mirlind KRYEZIU | 26.01.1997 | 10 | 0 | 2022/2023: | *FC Zürich (SUI)* |
| Leart PAQARADA | 08.10.1994 | 28 | 1 | 2023: | *FC St. Pauli Hamburg (GER)* |
| Amir Kadri RRAHMANI | 24.02.1994 | 53 | 6 | 2022/2023: | *SSC Napoli (ITA)* |
| Leard SADRIU | 22.04.2001 | 1 | 0 | 2022: | *NŠ Mura Murska Sobota (SVN)* |
| Mërgim VOJVODA | 01.02.1995 | 48 | 2 | 2023: | *Torino FC (ITA)* |
| **Midfielders** | | | | | |
| Eris ABEDINI | 29.08.1998 | 1 | 0 | 2022: | *FC Winterthur (SUI)* |
| Valon BERISHA | 07.02.1993 | 38 | 4 | 2023: | *Melbourne City FC (AUS)* |
| Uran BISLIMI | 25.09.1999 | 2 | 1 | 2022: | *FC Lugano (SUI)* |
| Zymer BYTYQI | 11.09.1996 | 18 | 1 | 2022: 31.01.2023-> | *Konyaspor Kulübü (TUR) Olympiacos SFP Peiraiás (GRE)* |
| Bersant CELINA | 09.09.1996 | 37 | 2 | 2022: 26.01.2023-> | *Kasımpaşa Spor Kulübü Istanbul (TUR) Stoke City FC (ENG)* |
| Lindon EMËRLLAHU | 07.12.2002 | 2 | 0 | 2022: | *KF Ballkani Suva Reka* |
| Arianit FERATI | 07.09.1997 | 2 | 0 | 2022: | *Fortuna Sittard (NED)* |
| Muharrem JASHARI | 21.02.1998 | 3 | 0 | 2022: | *KF Drita Gjilan* |
| Ilir KRASNIQI | 02.04.2000 | 2 | 0 | 2022: | *KF Llapi Podujevë* |
| Hekuran KRYEZIU | 12.02.1993 | 30 | 0 | 2023: | *FC Zürich (SUI)* |
| Florian LOSHAJ | 13.08.1996 | 18 | 0 | 2022: 04.02.2023-> | *KS Cracovia Kraków (POL) Istanbulspor Kulübü (TUR)* |
| Florent MUSLIJA | 06.07.1998 | 17 | 1 | 2022/2023: | *SC Paderborn 07 (GER)* |
| Milot Nexhmedin RASHICA | 28.06.1996 | 49 | 8 | 2022/2023: | *Galatasaray SK Istanbul (TUR)* |
| Donat RRUDHANI | 02.05.1999 | 10 | 2 | 2022/2023: | *BSC Young Boys Bern (SUI)* |
| Valmir VELIU | 04.06.2000 | 2 | 0 | 2022: | *Gaziantep FK (TUR)* |
| Arbër ZENELI | 25.02.1995 | 33 | 9 | 2022/2023: | *Stade de Reims (FRA)* |
| Edon Luizim ZHEGROVA | 31.03.1999 | 32 | 4 | 2023: | *Lille OSC (FRA)* |
| **Forwards** | | | | | |
| Lirim M. KASTRATI | 16.01.1999 | 19 | 2 | 2022: | *Fehérvár FC Székesfehérvár (HUN)* |
| Ermal KRASNIQI | 07.09.1998 | 2 | 0 | 2022: 10.01.2023-> | *KF Ballkani Suva Reka FC CFR 1907 Cluj-Napoca (ROU)* |
| Vedat MURIQI | 24.04.1994 | 48 | 24 | 2022/2023: | *RCD Mallorca (ESP)* |
| Elbasan RASHANI | 09.05.1993 | 24 | 5 | 2022: | *Clermont Foot 63 (FRA)* |
| Agon SADIKU | 10.03.2003 | 2 | 0 | 2022: | *FC Honka Espoo (FIN)* |
| Jetmir TOPALLI | 07.02.1998 | 6 | 0 | 2022/2023: | *Istanbulspor Kulübü (TUR)* |
| **Trainer** | | | | | |
| Alain GIRESSE (France) [23.02.2022 – 20.06.2023] | | 02.08.1952 | | 14 M; 4 W; 6 D; 4 L; 23-16 | |

# LATVIA

LATVIJA

## The Country:
Latvijas Republika (Republic of Latvia)
Capital: Rīga
Surface: 64,589 km²
Inhabitants: 1,842,226 [2022]
Time: UTC+2

## The FA:
Latvijas Futbola federācija
Olympic Sports Centre, Grostonas Street 6b, 1013 Rīga
Tel: +371 6729 2988
Foundation date: 19.06.1921
Member of FIFA since: 1922
Member of UEFA since: 1992
Website: www.lff.lv

## NATIONAL TEAM RECORDS

### RECORDS

| | | |
|---|---|---|
| **First international match:** | 24.09.1922, Rīga: | Latvia – Estonia 1-1 |
| **Most international caps:** | Vitālijs Astafjevs | - 167 caps (1992-2010) |
| **Most international goals:** | Māris Verpakovskis | - 29 goals / 104 caps (1999-2014) |

### UEFA EUROPEAN CHAMPIONSHIP

| | |
|---|---|
| 1960 | - |
| 1964 | - |
| 1968 | - |
| 1972 | - |
| 1976 | - |
| 1980 | - |
| 1984 | - |
| 1988 | - |
| 1992 | - |
| 1996 | Qualifiers |
| 2000 | Qualifiers |
| 2004 | Final Tournament (Group Stage) |
| 2008 | Qualifiers |
| 2012 | Qualifiers |
| 2016 | Qualifiers |
| 2020 | Qualifiers |

### FIFA WORLD CUP

| | |
|---|---|
| 1930 | Did not enter |
| 1934 | Did not enter |
| 1938 | *Entry not accepted by FIFA* |
| 1950 | - |
| 1954 | - |
| 1958 | - |
| 1962 | - |
| 1966 | - |
| 1970 | - |
| 1974 | - |
| 1978 | - |
| 1982 | - |
| 1986 | - |
| 1990 | - |
| 1994 | Qualifiers |
| 1998 | Qualifiers |
| 2002 | Qualifiers |
| 2006 | Qualifiers |
| 2010 | Qualifiers |
| 2014 | Qualifiers |
| 2018 | Qualifiers |
| 2022 | Qualifiers |

### OLYMPIC TOURNAMENTS

| | |
|---|---|
| 1908 | - |
| 1912 | - |
| 1920 | - |
| 1924 | - |
| 1928 | 1/8 - Finals |
| 1936 | Did not enter |
| 1948 | - |
| 1952 | - |
| 1956 | - |
| 1960 | - |
| 1964 | - |
| 1968 | - |
| 1972 | - |
| 1976 | - |
| 1980 | - |
| 1984 | - |
| 1988 | - |
| 1992 | - |
| 1996 | Qualifiers |
| 2000 | Qualifiers |
| 2004 | Qualifiers |
| 2008 | Qualifiers |
| 2012 | Qualifiers |
| 2016 | Qualifiers |
| 2020 | Qualifiers |

*was part of Soviet Union between 1940-1941 & 1944-1991

### UEFA NATIONS LEAGUE

| | |
|---|---|
| 2018/2019 | League D (Group Stage) |
| 2020/2021 | League D (Group Stage) |
| 2022/2023 | League D (Group Stage -> promoted to League C) |

### LATVIAN CLUB HONOURS IN EUROPEAN CLUB COMPETITIONS:

| European Champion Clubs' Cup (1956-1992) / UEFA Champions League (1993-2023) |
|---|
| None |

| Fairs Cup (1858-1971) / UEFA Cup (1972-2009) / UEFA Europa League (2010-2023) |
|---|
| None |

| UEFA Europa Conference League (2021-2023) |
|---|
| None |

| UEFA Super Cup (1972-2022) |
|---|
| None |

| *European Cup Winners' Cup 1961-1999** |
|---|
| None |

*defunct competition

# NATIONAL COMPETITIONS
## TABLE OF HONOURS

### LATVIAN SSR (SOVIET ERA) CHAMPIONS

| Year | Champion | Year | Champion | Year | Champion |
|------|----------|------|----------|------|----------|
| 1941 | *Championship Cancelled* | 1959 | RER Rīga | 1975 | VEF Rīga |
| 1942/1944 | *Championship Interrupted* | 1960 | ASK Rīga | 1976 | Enerģija Rīga |
| 1945 | FK Dinamo Rīga | 1961 | ASK Rīga | 1977 | Enerģija Rīga |
| 1946 | Daugava Liepāja | 1962 | ASK Rīga | 1978 | Ķīmiķis Daugavpils |
| 1947 | Daugava Liepāja | 1963 | ASK Rīga | 1979 | Elektrons Rīga |
| 1948 | Žmiļova Komanda | 1964 | ASK Rīga | 1980 | Ķīmiķis Daugavpils |
| 1949 | Sarkanais Metalurgs Liepāja | 1965 | ASK Rīga | 1981 | Elektrons Rīga |
| 1950 | AVN Rīga | 1966 | ESR Rīga | 1982 | Elektrons Rīga |
| 1951 | Sarkanais Metalurgs Liepāja | 1967 | ESR Rīga | 1983 | VEF Rīga |
| 1952 | AVN Rīga | 1968 | Starts Brocēni | 1984 | Torpedo Rīga |
| 1953 | Sarkanais Metalurgs Liepāja | 1969 | FK Venta Ventspils | 1985 | FK Alfa |
| 1954 | Sarkanais Metalurgs Liepāja | 1970 | VEF Rīga | 1986 | Torpedo Rīga |
| 1955 | Darba Rezerves Rīga | 1971 | VEF Rīga | 1987 | Torpedo Rīga |
| 1956 | Sarkanais Metalurgs Liepāja | 1972 | FK Jūrnieks | 1988 | RAF Jelgava |
| 1957 | Sarkanais Metalurgs Liepāja | 1973 | VEF Rīga | 1989 | RAF Jelgava |
| 1958 | Sarkanais Metalurgs Liepāja | 1974 | VEF Rīga | 1990 | Gauja Valmiera |

| | CHAMPIONS* | CUP WINNERS | BEST GOALSCORERS | |
|------|------------|-------------|------------------|---|
| 1910 | RV Union Rīga | - | - | |
| 1911 | Britannia FC Rīga | - | - | |
| 1912 | RV Union Rīga | - | - | |
| 1913 | SV Kaiserwald Rīga | - | - | |
| 1914 | Britannia FC Rīga | - | - | |
| 1915 | Britannia FC Rīga | - | - | |
| | ----- | ----- | ----- | |
| 1922 | Kaiserwald Rīga | - | - | |
| 1923 | Kaiserwald Rīga | - | - | |
| 1924 | RFK Rīga | - | - | |
| 1925 | RFK Rīga | - | - | |
| 1926 | RFK Rīga | - | - | |
| 1927 | Olimpia Liepaja | - | - | |
| 1928 | Olimpia Liepaja | - | - | |
| 1929 | Olimpia Liepaja | - | - | |
| 1930 | RFK Rīga | - | - | |
| 1931 | RFK Rīga | - | - | |
| 1932 | ASK Rīga | - | - | |
| 1933 | Olimpia Liepaja | - | - | |
| 1934 | RFK Rīga | - | - | |
| 1935 | RFK Rīga | - | - | |
| 1936 | Olimpia Liepaja | - | - | |
| 1937 | *No competition* | RFK Rīga | - | |
| 1938 | Olimpia Liepaja | Rīgas Vilki | - | |
| 1939 | Olimpia Liepaja | RFK Rīga | - | |
| 1940 | RFK Rīga | *No competition* | - | |
| | ----- | ----- | ----- | |
| 1991 | Skonto FC Rīga | Celtnieks Daugavpils | Vjačeslavs Ževnerovičs (Celtnieks Daugavpils) | 27 |
| 1992 | Skonto FC Rīga | Skonto FC Rīga | Vjačeslavs Ževnerovičs (VEF Riga) | 19 |
| 1993 | Skonto FC Rīga | RAF Jelgava | Aleksandrs Jeļisejevs (Skonto FC Rīga) | 20 |
| 1994 | Skonto FC Rīga | Olimpija Rīga | Vladimirs Babičevs (Skonto FC Rīga) | 14 |
| 1995 | Skonto FC Rīga | Skonto FC Rīga | Vitālijs Astafjevs (Skonto FC Rīga) | 19 |
| 1996 | Skonto FC Rīga | RAF Jelgava | Mihails Miholaps (FK Daugava Rīga) | 33 |
| 1997 | Skonto FC Rīga | Skonto FC Rīga | David Chaladze (GEO, Skonto FC Rīga) | 25 |
| 1998 | Skonto FC Rīga | Skonto FC Rīga | Viktors Dobrecovs (FK Liepājas Metalurgs) | 23 |
| 1999 | Skonto FC Rīga | FK Rīga | Viktors Dobrecovs (FK Liepājas Metalurgs) | 22 |
| 2000 | Skonto FC Rīga | Skonto FC Rīga | Vladimirs Koļesņičenko (Skonto FC Rīga) | 17 |
| 2001 | Skonto FC Rīga | Skonto FC Rīga | Mihails Miholaps (Skonto FC Rīga) | 24 |
| 2002 | Skonto FC Rīga | Skonto FC Rīga | Mihails Miholaps (Skonto FC Rīga) | 23 |
| 2003 | Skonto FC Rīga | FK Ventspils | Viktors Dobrecovs (FK Liepājas Metalurgs) | 36 |
| 2004 | Skonto FC Rīga | FK Ventspils | Aleksandr Katasonov (RUS, FK Liepājas Metalurgs) | 21 |
| 2005 | FK Liepājas Metalurgs | FK Ventspils | Viktors Dobrecovs (FK Liepājas Metalurgs) Igors Sļesarčuks (FK Venta/FK Ventspils) | 18 |
| 2006 | FK Ventspils | FK Liepājas Metalurgs | Mihails Miholaps (Skonto FC Rīga) | 15 |
| 2007 | FK Ventspils | FK Ventspils | Vits Rimkus (FK Ventspils) | 20 |
| 2008 | FK Ventspils | FK Daugava Daugavpils | Vits Rimkus (FK Ventspils) | 14 |
| 2009 | FK Liepājas Metalurgs | *No competition* | Kristaps Grebis (FK Liepājas Metalurgs) | 30 |
| 2010 | Skonto FC Rīga | FK Jelgava | Deniss Rakeļs (FK Liepājas Metalurgs) Nathan Júnior Soares de Carvalho (BRA, Skonto FC Rīga) | 18 |
| 2011 | FK Ventspils | FK Ventspils | Nathan Júnior Soares de Carvalho (BRA, Skonto FC Rīga) | 22 |

| 2012 | FC Daugava Daugavpils | Skonto FC Rīga | Mamuka Ghonghadze (GEO, FC Daugava Daugavpils) | 18 |
|---|---|---|---|---|
| 2013 | FK Ventspils | FK Ventspils | Artūrs Karašausks (Skonto FC Rīga) Andrejs Kovaļovs (FC Daugava Daugavpils) | 16 |
| 2014 | FK Ventspils | FK Jelgava | Vladislavs Gutkovskis (Skonto FC Rīga) | 28 |
| 2015 | FK Liepāja | FK Jelgava | Dāvis Ikaunieks (FK Liepaja) | 15 |
| 2016 | JPFS/FK Spartaks Jūrmala | FK Jelgava FK Ventspils (2016/2017) | Ģirts Karlsons (FK Ventspils) | 17 |
| 2017 | JPFS/FK Spartaks Jūrmala | FK Liepāja | Yevgeniy Kozlov (RUS, JPFS/FK Spartaks Jūrmala) Artūrs Karašausks (FK Liepāja) | 12 |
| 2018 | Rīga FC | Rīga FC | Darko Lemajić (SRB, Rīga FC) | 15 |
| 2019 | Rīga FC | FK Rīgas Futbola Skola | Darko Lemajić (SRB, Rīga FC / FK Rīgas Futbola Skola) | 15 |
| 2020 | Rīga FC | FK Liepāja | Luiz Paulo Hilario „Dodô" (BRA, FK Liepāja) | 18 |
| 2021 | FK Rīgas Futbola Skola | FK Rīgas Futbola Skola | Leonel Wamba Djouffo (CMR, JPFS/FK Spartaks Jūrmala) | 10 |
| 2022 | Valmiera FC | FK Auda Ķekava | Raimonds Krollis (Valmiera FC) | 24 |

*Please note: Champions of the Riga Football League (1910-1915) and Latvian Championship (1922–1940 and since 1991); RAF Jelgava was called later FK Jelgava.

## NATIONAL CHAMPIONSHIP
### Virsliga 2022
(11.03.2022 – 12.11.2022)

### Results

**Round 1 [11-13.03.2022]**
FK Liepāja - SK Super Nova 3-1(1-1)
Rīga FC - Valmiera FC 2-1(1-1)
Spartaks Jūrmala - Rīgas Futbola sk. 2-3(1-1)
BFC Daugavpils - FK Tukums 2000 2-1(1-0)
FS Metta/LU - FK Auda 0-1(0-1)

**Round 2 [18-20.03.2022]**
Valmiera FC - Spartaks Jūrmala 4-1(3-0)
FK Tukums 2000 - FS Metta/LU 2-2(2-2)
FK Liepāja - Rīga FC 1-0(1-0)
Rīgas Futbola sk. - BFC Daugavpils 4-0(1-0)
SK Super Nova - FK Auda 0-0

**Round 3 [01-02.04.2022]**
Rīga FC - SK Super Nova 2-0(2-0)
Spartaks Jūrmala - FK Liepāja 0-2(0-1)
FK Auda - FK Tukums 2000 1-0(0-0)
BFC Daugavpils - Valmiera FC 0-0
FS Metta/LU - Rīgas Futbola skola 1-1(1-1)

**Round 4 [05-07.04.2022]**
Rīga FC - Spartaks Jūrmala 3-0(1-0)
FK Liepāja - BFC Daugavpils 5-1(1-0)
Valmiera FC - FS Metta/LU 1-1(1-1)
Rīgas Futbola skola - FK Auda 0-0
SK Super Nova - FK Tukums 2000 0-1(0-1)

**Round 5 [10-11.04.2022]**
FK Auda - Valmiera FC 1-3(0-0)
BFC Daugavpils - Rīga FC 0-0
FS Metta/LU - FK Liepāja 1-5(1-2)
FK Tukums 2000 - Rīgas Futbola sk.0-10(0-7)
Spartaks Jūrmala - SK Super Nova 0-0

**Round 6 [14-15.04.2022]**
Rīga FC - FS Metta/LU 4-0(2-0)
FK Liepāja - FK Auda 1-1(0-1)
BFC Daugavpils - Spartaks Jūrmala 2-0(0-0)
Valmiera FC - FK Tukums 2000 3-0(1-0)
Rīgas Futbola skola - SK Super Nova 2-0(2-0)

**Round 7 [18-20.04.2022]**
FK Auda - Rīga FC 0-1(0-0)
FK Tukums 2000 - FK Liepāja 1-4(0-1)
SK Super Nova - BFC Daugavpils 0-0
Rīgas Futbola skola - Valmiera FC 1-3(0-2)
FS Metta/LU - Spartaks Jūrmala 2-0(1-0)

**Round 8 [23-24.04.2022]**
Rīga FC - FK Tukums 2000 1-0(0-0)
FK Liepāja - Rīgas Futbola skola 2-3(0-1)
SK Super Nova - Valmiera FC 1-5(1-2)
BFC Daugavpils - FS Metta/LU 2-0(1-0)
Spartaks Jūrmala - FK Auda 1-2(1-0)

**Round 9 [27-28.04.2022]**
Valmiera FC - FK Liepāja 3-0(0-0)
Rīgas Futbola skola - Rīga FC 2-1(1-1)
SK Super Nova - FS Metta/LU 0-1(0-0)
FK Auda-BFC Daugavpils 2-0(0-0) [06.07.22]
FK Tukums-Spartaks Jūrm.3-0(1-0) [13.07.22]

**Round 10 [30.04.-02.05.2022]**
FK Tukums 2000 - BFC Daugavpils 0-1(0-0)
Valmiera FC - Rīga FC 3-0(3-0)
Rīgas Futbola sk. - Spartaks Jūrmala 2-0(1-0)
FK Auda - FS Metta/LU 3-2(1-1)
SK Super Nova - FK Liepāja 1-3(0-1)

**Round 11 [05-06.05.2022]**
BFC Daugavpils - Rīgas Futbola sk. 1-4(1-2)
Spartaks Jūrmala - Valmiera FC 0-2(0-1)
FK Auda - SK Super Nova 4-1(3-0)
Rīga FC - FK Liepāja 0-1(0-1)
FS Metta/LU - FK Tukums 2000 3-2(2-1)

**Round 12 [09-11.05.2022]**
Valmiera FC - BFC Daugavpils 1-0(1-0)
FK Tukums 2000 - FK Auda 2-1(1-0)
FK Liepāja - Spartaks Jūrmala 0-0
SK Super Nova - Rīga FC 1-4(0-2)
Rīgas Futbola skola - FS Metta/LU 3-1(2-0)

**Round 13 [14-15.05.2022]**
BFC Daugavpils - FK Liepāja 0-4(0-0)
Spartaks Jūrmala - Rīga FC 0-4(0-3)
FK Tukums 2000 - SK Super Nova 1-1(0-1)
FK Auda - Rīgas Futbola skola 0-1(0-0)
FS Metta/LU - Valmiera FC 0-3(0-2)

**Round 14 [18-20.05.2022]**
SK Super Nova - Spartaks Jūrmala 0-3(0-2)
Rīga FC - BFC Daugavpils 2-0(1-0)
FK Liepāja - FS Metta/LU 1-0(0-0)
Rīgas Futbola sk. - FK Tukums 2000 3-0(2-0)
Valmiera FC - FK Auda 2-0(0-0)

**Round 15 [22-24.05.2022]**
Spartaks Jūrmala - BFC Daugavpils 2-0(0-0)
FS Metta/LU - Rīga FC 1-4(1-3)
SK Super Nova - Rīgas Futbola skola 0-3(0-1)
FK Auda - FK Liepāja 1-2(0-1)
FK Tukums 2000 - Valmiera FC 0-3(0-1)

**Round 16 [27-29.05.2022]**
Rīga FC - Rīgas Futbola skola 2-0(2-0)
FK Liepāja - Valmiera FC 1-3(1-1)
BFC Daugavpils - FK Auda 1-2(0-1)
FS Metta/LU - SK Super Nova 1-1(1-1)
Spartaks Jūrmala - FK Tukums 2000 1-3(0-2)

**Round 17 [17-18.06.2022]**
FK Auda - Spartaks Jūrmala 5-0(2-0)
FS Metta/LU - BFC Daugavpils 2-3(1-0)
Valmiera FC - SK Super Nova 1-0(0-0)
FK Tukums 2000 - Rīga FC 0-1(0-1)
Rīgas Futbola skola - FK Liepāja 2-2(0-1)

**Round 18 [21-22.06.2022]**
BFC Daugavpils - SK Super Nova 1-0(0-0)
Spartaks Jūrmala - FS Metta/LU 4-2(1-2)
Valmiera FC - Rīgas Futbola skola 4-0(0-0)
FK Liepāja - FK Tukums 2000 1-2(1-0)
Rīga FC - FK Auda 1-0(0-0)

**Round 19 [26-27.06.2022]**
FK Tukums 2000 - BFC Daugavpils 0-1(0-1)
Spartaks Jūrmala - Rīgas Futbola sk. 0-2(0-1)
Rīga FC - Valmiera FC 0-2(0-1)
FK Liepāja - SK Super Nova 2-0(0-0)
FS Metta/LU - FK Auda 3-0 *awarded*

**Round 20 [30.06.-03.07.2022]**
Valmiera FC - Spartaks Jūrmala 1-2(1-1)
Rīgas Futbola sk. - BFC Daugavpils 4-0(1-0)
FK Liepāja - Rīga FC 0-0
SK Super Nova - FK Auda 1-2(1-1)
FK Tukums 2000 - FS Metta/LU 2-0(1-0)

**Round 21 [16-18.07.2022]**
Valmiera FC - BFC Daugavpils 5-1(1-0)
FS Metta/LU - Rīgas Futbola skola 1-3(1-1)
Rīga FC - SK Super Nova 1-0(0-0)
FK Auda - FK Tukums 2000 3-0(1-0)
Spartaks Jūrmala - Liepāja 2-3(1-0) [14.08.22]

| Round 22 [23-24.07.2022] |
|---|
| SK Super Nova - FK Tukums 2000 2-1(1-0) |
| Valmiera FC - FS Metta/LU 6-1(1-0) |
| Rīgas Futbola skola - FK Auda 0-0 |
| Rīga FC - Spartaks Jūrmala 2-1(0-1) |
| Liepāja - BFC Daugavpils 2-1(1-1) [04.08.22] |

| Round 23 [30.07.-01.08.2022] |
|---|
| Spartaks Jūrmala - SK Super Nova 2-3(2-2) |
| FK Tukums 2000 - Rīgas Futbola sk. 0-2(0-0) |
| FS Metta/LU - FK Liepāja 2-2(0-0) |
| FK Auda - Valmiera FC 1-1(1-1) |
| Daugavpils - Rīga FC 0-4(0-1) [15.08.22] |

| Round 24 [06-08.08.2022] |
|---|
| Valmiera FC - FK Tukums 2000 6-1(4-0) |
| Rīga FC - FS Metta/LU 3-2(1-1) |
| FK Liepāja - FK Auda 1-0(1-0) |
| Rīgas Futbola skola - SK Super Nova 2-3(1-1) |
| Spartaks Jūrmala - BFC Daugavpils 2-1(1-1) |

| Round 25 [20-21.08.2022] |
|---|
| FK Tukums 2000 - FK Liepāja 2-1(2-1) |
| FS Metta/LU - Spartaks Jūrmala 0-0 |
| SK Super Nova - BFC Daugavpils 1-0(0-0) |
| FK Auda - Rīga FC 0-2(0-0) |
| Rīgas Futbola skola - Valmiera FC 2-2(1-0) |

| Round 26 [27-29.08.2022] |
|---|
| Valmiera FC - SK Super Nova 7-0(3-0) |
| BFC Daugavpils - FS Metta/LU 3-2(2-2) |
| Rīga FC - FK Tukums 2000 3-1(2-0) |
| Spartaks Jūrmala - FK Auda 0-1(0-0) |
| FK Liepāja - Rīgas Futbola skola 1-2(0-1) |

| Round 27 [03-05.09.2022] |
|---|
| Spartaks Jūrmala - FK Tukums 2000 1-3(1-1) |
| Valmiera FC - FK Liepāja 0-1(0-0) |
| SK Super Nova - FS Metta/LU 0-3(0-0) |
| Rīgas Futbola skola - Rīga FC 1-1(0-1) |
| FK Auda - BFC Daugavpils 2-0(1-0) |

| Round 28 [10-12.09.2022] |
|---|
| FK Tukums 2000 - BFC Daugavpils 0-0 |
| FK Auda - FS Metta/LU 2-1(2-0) |
| Valmiera FC - Rīga FC 3-1(1-0) |
| SK Super Nova - FK Liepāja 2-2(1-0) |
| Rīgas Futbola sk. - Spartaks Jūrmala 3-0(1-0) |

| Round 29 [16-18.09.2022] |
|---|
| Rīga FC - FK Liepāja 2-0(1-0) |
| FS Metta/LU - FK Tukums 2000 1-2(1-1) |
| Spartaks Jūrmala - Valmiera FC 1-6(1-3) |
| FK Auda - SK Super Nova 3-0(1-0) |
| Daugavpils - Rīgas Fut.sk. 1-3(1-1) [27.09.22] |

| Round 30 [30.09.-02.10.2022] |
|---|
| SK Super Nova - Rīga FC 1-4(1-2) |
| FK Tukums 2000 - FK Auda 1-0(1-0) |
| Rīgas Futbola skola - FS Metta/LU 6-0(3-0) |
| FK Liepāja - Spartaks Jūrmala 5-2(2-0) |
| Valmiera FC - BFC Daugavpils 1-1(1-1) |

| Round 31 [08-09.10.2022] |
|---|
| Spartaks Jūrmala - Rīga FC 1-3(0-3) |
| FK Tukums 2000 - SK Super Nova 2-0(1-0) |
| FK Auda - Rīgas Futbola skola 1-1(1-0) |
| FS Metta/LU - Valmiera FC 1-4(0-1) |
| BFC Daugavpils - FK Liepāja 2-3(1-2) |

| Round 32 [15-16.10.2022] |
|---|
| Valmiera FC - FK Auda 2-1(1-1) |
| FK Liepāja - FS Metta/LU 5-1(3-0) |
| SK Super Nova - Spartaks Jūrmala 1-3(1-2) |
| Rīgas Futbola sk. - FK Tukums 2000 2-2(1-0) |
| Rīga FC - BFC Daugavpils 4-0(2-0) |

| Round 33 [22-23.10.2022] |
|---|
| BFC Daugavpils - Spartaks Jūrmala 1-1(1-0) |
| FS Metta/LU - Rīga FC 0-2(0-0) |
| FK Auda - FK Liepāja 1-2(0-1) |
| SK Super Nova - Rīgas Futbola skola 0-4(0-2) |
| FK Tukums 2000 - Valmiera FC 1-1(1-0) |

| Round 34 [29-30.10.2022] |
|---|
| Spartaks Jūrmala - FS Metta/LU 2-0(1-0) |
| BFC Daugavpils - SK Super Nova 1-1(0-0) |
| Rīga FC - FK Auda 2-0(0-0) |
| FK Liepāja - FK Tukums 2000 4-1(2-0) |
| Valmiera FC - Rīgas Futbola skola 1-1(1-0) |

| Round 35 [06.11.2022] |
|---|
| FK Auda - Spartaks Jūrmala 0-1(0-1) |
| FK Tukums 2000 - Rīga FC 0-2(0-1) |
| FS Metta/LU - BFC Daugavpils 2-3(0-1) |
| Rīgas Futbola skola - FK Liepāja 0-0 |
| SK Super Nova - Valmiera FC 1-6(0-2) |

| Round 36 [12.11.2022] |
|---|
| BFC Daugavpils - FK Auda 0-1(0-0) |
| FK Liepāja - Valmiera FC 0-2(0-0) |
| FK Tukums 2000 - Spartaks Jūrmala 1-2(0-1) |
| FS Metta/LU - SK Super Nova 1-1(1-0) |
| Rīga FC - Rīgas Futbola skola 0-1(0-0) |

## Final Standings

| | | | | | | | | | Home | | | | | Away | | | |
|---|---|---|---|---|---|---|---|---|---|---|---|---|---|---|---|---|---|
| 1. | **Valmiera FC** | 36 | 26 | 7 | 3 | 101 - 25 | 85 | 14 | 2 | 2 | 53 - 11 | | 12 | 5 | 1 | 48 - 14 |
| 2. | Rīga FC | 36 | 26 | 3 | 7 | 68 - 23 | 81 | 15 | 0 | 3 | 34 - 9 | | 11 | 3 | 4 | 34 - 14 |
| 3. | FK Rīgas Futbola Skola | 36 | 22 | 10 | 4 | 83 - 32 | 76 | 9 | 7 | 2 | 39 - 15 | | 13 | 3 | 2 | 44 - 17 |
| 4. | FK Liepāja | 36 | 21 | 7 | 8 | 72 - 42 | 70 | 10 | 3 | 5 | 35 - 20 | | 11 | 4 | 3 | 37 - 22 |
| 5. | FK Auda Ķekava | 36 | 15 | 6 | 15 | 42 - 36 | 51 | 9 | 2 | 7 | 30 - 18 | | 6 | 4 | 8 | 12 - 18 |
| 6. | FK Tukums 2000 / TSS | 36 | 11 | 5 | 20 | 38 - 69 | 38 | 6 | 3 | 9 | 18 - 32 | | 5 | 2 | 11 | 20 - 37 |
| 7. | BFC Daugavpils | 36 | 9 | 7 | 20 | 30 - 67 | 38 | 5 | 6 | 7 | 18 - 27 | | 4 | 1 | 13 | 12 - 40 |
| 8. | JPFS/FK Spartaks Jūrmala | 36 | 9 | 4 | 23 | 37 - 75 | 34 | 4 | 1 | 13 | 21 - 40 | | 5 | 3 | 10 | 16 - 35 |
| 9. | FS Metta / Latvijas Universitāte Rīga (Relegation Play-offs) | 36 | 5 | 7 | 24 | 41 - 86 | 31 | 3 | 5 | 10 | 22 - 37 | | 2 | 2 | 14 | 19 - 49 |
| 10. | SK Super Nova Olaine (Relegated) | 36 | 4 | 8 | 24 | 24 - 81 | 22 | 2 | 3 | 13 | 12 - 45 | | 2 | 5 | 11 | 12 - 36 |

| Top goalscorers: | |
|---|---|
| 24 **Raimonds Krollis** | *Valmiera FC* |
| 16 Andrej Ilić (SRB) | *FK Rīgas Futbola Skola* |
| 14 Camilo Andrés Mena Márquez (COL) | *Valmiera FC* |
| 13 Luiz Paulo Hilario "Dodô" (BRA) (BRA) | *FK Liepāja* |

## Relegation Play-offs [24-27.11.2022]

FS Metta/Latvijas Universitāte Rīga - Grobiņas SC          2-0(2-0)       3-2(3-0)

FS Metta/Latvijas Universitāte Rīga remains at first level for 2023.

# NATIONAL CUP
## Latvijas Kauss 2022

### Round of 16 [09-11.07.2022]

| | | | | |
|---|---|---|---|---|
| SK Super Nova Olaine - FK Tukums 2000 / TSS | 0-2(0-0) | | Grobiņas SC - FK Liepāja | 2-1(0-1) |
| FK Rīgas Futbola Skola - JPFS/FK Spartaks Jūrmala | 4-0(0-0) | | FS Jelgava - JDFS Alberts Rīga | 2-1(1-0) |
| Skanstes SK Rīga - FC Jēkabpils / JSC | 6-1(1-0) | | Rīga FC - Valmiera FC | 0-2(0-1) |
| FK Salaspils - FS Metta/Latvijas Universitāte Rīga | 0-13(0-6) | | FK Auda Ķekava - BFC Daugavpils | 2-1(1-0) |

### Quarter-Finals [13-14.08.2022]

| | | | | |
|---|---|---|---|---|
| Grobiņas SC - Skanstes SK Rīga | 2-0(1-0) | | FK Tukums 2000 / TSS - FK Rīgas Futbola Skola | 1-4(0-1) |
| FS Jelgava - FS Metta/Latvijas Universitāte Rīga | 2-1(2-1) | | Valmiera FC - FK Auda Ķekava | 0-0 aet; 5-6 pen |

### Semi-Finals [01.09.2022]

| | | | | |
|---|---|---|---|---|
| FK Rīgas Futbola Skola - Grobiņas SC | 5-0(1-0) | | FK Auda Ķekava - FS Jelgava | 6-1(5-1) |

### Final

19.10.2022; Skonto stadions, Rīga; Referee: Edgars Maļcevs; Attendance: 2,539

**FK Auda Ķekava - FK Rīgas Futbola Skola**                    **1-0(1-0)**

**FK Auda**: Joseph Fabrice Ondoa Ebogo (Cap), Kilian Senkbeil, Vjačeslavs Isajevs, Ivo Minkevičs, Mor Talla Gaye, Manyumow Achol, Aleksejs Saveļjevs (90+2.Rafael dos Santos Resende), Daniils Ulimbaševs (72.Jegors Novikovs), Ousseynou Niang, Aboubakar Karamoko, Georgi Minchev (81.Stanislav Krapukhin). Trainer: Tomislav Stipić (Croatia).

**FK Rīgas Futbola Skola**: Pāvels Šteinbors, Jovan Vlalukin (84.Alfusainey Jatta), Vitālijs Jagodinskis, Žiga Lipušček, Petr Mareš, Stefan Panić [*sent off 78*], Tomislav Šarić, Artūrs Zjuzins (65.Elvis Stuglis), Tomáš Šimkovič (Cap) (84.Kevin Friesenbichler), Emerson Santana Deocleciano, Andrej Ilić. Trainer: Viktors Morozs.

**Goal:** 1-0 Daniils Ulimbaševs (42).

# THE CLUBS 2022

## Futbola klubs Auda Ķekava

| | |
|---|---|
| **Founded**: | 1991 |
| **Stadium**: | Audas stadions, Ķekava (520) |
| **Trainer**: | Tomislav Stipić (CRO)        01.08.1979 |

| Goalkeepers: | DOB | M | (s) | G |
|---|---|---|---|---|
| Niks Aleksandrovs | 05.05.2002 | 4 | | |
| Joseph Fabrice Ondoa Ebogo (CMR) | 24.12.1995 | 30 | | |
| Frenks Orols | 28.06.2000 | 2 | (1) | |
| Kaspars Ribaks | 02.08.1990 | | (1) | |
| **Defenders:** | DOB | M | (s) | G |
| Niko Bretschneider (GER) | 10.08.1999 | 14 | (2) | |
| Vjačeslavs Isajevs | 27.08.1993 | 11 | (1) | |
| Oleksandr Kaplienko (UKR) | 07.03.1996 | 11 | (4) | |
| João Victor Santos Menezes (BRA) | 11.11.2001 | | (1) | |
| Božo Mikulić (CRO) | 29.01.1997 | 24 | | 0 |
| Ivo Minkevičs | 28.06.1999 | 16 | (9) | |
| Mouhamed El Bachir Ngom (SEN) | 12.05.2000 | 12 | (2) | 1 |
| Jegors Novikovs | 09.02.2003 | 4 | (12) | 1 |
| Deniss Rogovs | 11.02.2003 | | (1) | |
| Kilian Senkbeil (GER) | 22.05.1999 | 5 | (4) | |
| Rendijs Šibass | 01.05.1997 | 9 | (19) | |
| Aleksandrs Solovjovs | 25.02.1988 | 5 | (4) | 1 |
| Marko Stolnik (CRO) | 08.07.1996 | 17 | | 2 |

| Midfielders: | DOB | M | (s) | G |
|---|---|---|---|---|
| Manyumow Achol (SSD) | 10.12.1999 | 23 | (6) | 1 |
| Iļja Korotkovs | 24.05.2000 | 14 | | |
| William Eseme Mukwelle (CMR) | 11.11.2002 | 7 | (8) | |
| Abiodun Omojesu Ogunniyi (NGA) | 20.12.2001 | 13 | | 2 |
| Rafael dos Santos Resende (BRA) | 05.03.2000 | 14 | (8) | |
| Bogdans Samoilovs | 13.05.2000 | | (3) | |
| Aleksejs Saveļjevs | 30.01.1999 | 19 | (9) | 1 |
| Vladimirs Stepanovs | 06.02.2000 | 9 | (4) | 3 |
| Daniils Ulimbaševs | 12.03.1992 | 29 | (3) | 2 |
| **Forwards:** | DOB | M | (s) | G |
| Mor Talla Gaye (SEN) | 26.11.1999 | 10 | (5) | 1 |
| Raivis Ķiršs | 15.01.2000 | 1 | (5) | 1 |
| Stanislav Krapukhin (RUS) | 28.03.1998 | 16 | (14) | 8 |
| Aboubakar Karamoko (CIV) | 15.10.1999 | 10 | (4) | |
| Arturs Krancmanis | 15.08.2003 | 1 | (6) | |
| Georgi Minchev (BUL) | 20.04.1995 | 9 | (4) | 3 |
| Ousseynou Niang (SEN) | 12.10.2001 | 15 | | 4 |
| Olabanjo Alexander Ogunji (NGA) | 20.01.2001 | 12 | (2) | |
| Tomislav Štrkalj (CRO) | 02.08.1996 | 17 | (3) | 8 |
| Brice Tutu (FRA) | 11.01.1998 | 13 | (3) | 5 |

## Bērnu Futbola Centrs Daugavpils

| | |
|---|---|
| **Founded**: | 11.12.2009 (*as BFC Daugava*) |
| **Stadium**: | Celtnieks stadions, Daugavpils (1,980) |
| **Trainer**: | Andrejs Kalinins        26.05.1981 |
| [01.09.2022] | Kirill Kurbatov (RUS)        06.08.1971 |

| Goalkeepers: | DOB | M | (s) | G |
|---|---|---|---|---|
| Vladislavs Kurakins | 09.07.1996 | 33 | | |
| Ņikita Šaraņins | 04.01.2003 | 3 | | |
| **Defenders:** | DOB | M | (s) | G |
| Rinalds Aizups | 31.05.2004 | 7 | (3) | |
| Dāvis Cucurs | 19.03.2000 | 16 | (4) | |
| David Idowu (NGA) | 23.06.2000 | 29 | (2) | 2 |
| Kirils Iļjins | 03.05.2001 | 33 | (1) | 1 |
| Ritus Krjauklis | 23.04.1986 | 24 | (1) | |
| Aleksejs Kudeļkins | 08.05.2002 | 20 | (4) | |
| Dmitrijs Litvinskis | 17.08.1999 | 17 | | |
| Gļebs Mihaļcovs | 15.03.2004 | 11 | (5) | |
| Shakir Seyidov (AZE) | 31.12.2000 | 5 | (3) | |
| **Midfielders:** | DOB | M | (s) | G |
| Valerijs Afanasjevs | 20.09.1982 | 18 | (8) | 2 |
| Asim Alizadə (AZE) | 05.02.2000 | 7 | (2) | |

| | DOB | M | (s) | G |
|---|---|---|---|---|
| Ralfs Baško | 10.01.2005 | | (6) | |
| Edgars Ivanovs | 07.10.2001 | 17 | (5) | |
| Johao Alberto Martínez Villegas (VEN) | 20.04.1999 | 13 | (4) | |
| Mareks Mikšto | 20.05.2003 | 9 | (4) | |
| William Eseme Mukwelle (CMR) | 11.11.2002 | 16 | (1) | 5 |
| Ervīns Piņaskins | 18.05.2006 | | (1) | |
| Milāns Tihonovičs | 30.12.2005 | | (3) | |
| Emīls Urbāns | 11.02.2005 | | (1) | |
| **Forwards:** | DOB | M | (s) | G |
| Vakhtang Bezarashvili (GEO) | 21.02.2002 | 4 | (16) | 2 |
| Rodolfo Rafael Grazziani González (COL) | 06.10.2002 | 12 | (11) | 1 |
| Dele Ola Israel (NGA) | 27.10.2001 | 32 | (1) | 3 |
| Lasha Kvaratskhelia (GEO) | 27.02.2002 | 22 | (9) | |
| Valerijs Lizunovs | 24.02.2004 | 28 | (2) | 10 |
| Joseph Agbor Yanki Bah (CMR) | 27.11.1993 | 20 | (9) | 4 |

## Futbola klubs Liepāja

**Founded**: 2014
**Stadium**: Daugava stadions, Liepāja (4,022)
**Trainer**: Kirill Alshevsky (BLR) — 27.01.1982
[04.06.2022] Tamaz Pertia (GEO) — 23.12.1974

| Goalkeepers: | DOB | M | (s) | G |
|---|---|---|---|---|
| Nikita Pinčuks | 04.01.2004 | | (1) | |
| Luka Radotić (SRB) | 17.07.2000 | | (1) | |
| Krišjānis Zviedris | 25.01.1997 | 36 | | |
| **Defenders:** | **DOB** | **M** | **(s)** | **G** |
| Kenan Hreljić (BIH) | 01.12.1997 | 9 | (3) | 1 |
| Inácio Miguel Ferreira Santos (POR) | 12.12.1995 | 15 | | 2 |
| Vjačeslavs Isajevs | 27.08.1993 | 10 | (4) | |
| Krišs Kārkliņš | 31.01.1996 | 10 | (9) | 2 |
| Seydina Keita (SEN) | 28.12.1992 | 13 | | |
| Marcos Garbellotto Silveira „Marquinhos" Pedroso (BRA) | 04.10.1993 | 10 | (6) | |
| Pablo Martín Marta Rodríguez (URU) | 28.01.1997 | 16 | | 2 |
| Yuriy Mate (UKR) | 07.01.1999 | 9 | | |
| Slaviša Radović (SRB) | 08.10.1993 | 6 | (3) | |
| Roberts Savaļnieks | 04.02.1993 | 32 | (1) | |
| Marko Simić (MNE) | 16.06.1987 | 6 | | 2 |
| Igors Tarasovs | 16.10.1988 | 4 | (1) | |
| Eduards Tīdenbergs | 18.12.1994 | 8 | (8) | 3 |
| Noah Toribio (USA) | 14.03.1999 | 4 | (2) | |

| Midfielders: | DOB | M | (s) | G |
|---|---|---|---|---|
| Ardit Deliu (ALB) | 26.10.1997 | 5 | (3) | |
| Aleksejs Grjaznovs | 01.10.1997 | 8 | (2) | |
| Nik Kapun (SVN) | 09.01.1994 | 8 | (8) | |
| Mārtiņš Ķigurs | 31.03.1997 | 6 | (2) | 4 |
| Gļebs Kļuškins | 01.10.1992 | 1 | (2) | |
| Lucas Villela Rezende (BRA) | 24.03.1994 | 27 | (7) | 9 |
| Leonel Strumia (ARG) | 29.09.1992 | 28 | (1) | |
| Yuriy Tkachuk (UKR) | 18.04.1995 | 2 | (12) | |
| Hogan Ukpa Effiong (NGA) | 28.09.2001 | 11 | (7) | 1 |
| **Forwards:** | **DOB** | **M** | **(s)** | **G** |
| Nemanja Belaković (SRB) | 08.01.1997 | 29 | (7) | 8 |
| Luiz Paulo Hilario "Dodô" (BRA) | 16.10.1987 | 31 | (2) | 13 |
| Mikhail Gordeychuk (BLR) | 23.10.1989 | 7 | (7) | 2 |
| Daniils Hvoiņickis | 08.04.1998 | | (1) | |
| Artūrs Karašausks | 29.01.1992 | 14 | (8) | 4 |
| Marks Kurtišs | 26.01.1998 | | (4) | |
| Gauthier Mankenda (COD) | 20.07.1997 | 13 | (3) | 8 |
| Ēriks Punculs | 18.01.1994 | 6 | (9) | 4 |
| Jordy Soladio Kandolo (BEL) | 12.02.1998 | 12 | | 4 |

## Futbola klubs Metta / Latvijas Universitāte Rīga

**Founded**: 02.05.2006
**Stadium**: Daugavas stadions, Rīga (10,461)
**Trainer**: Andrejs Gluščuks — 28.11.1977
[01.07.2022] Andris Riherts — 31.05.1981

| Goalkeepers: | DOB | M | (s) | G |
|---|---|---|---|---|
| Jānis Beks | 01.11.2002 | 30 | | |
| Ņikita Parfjonovs | 05.02.2004 | 1 | | |
| Alvis Sorokins | 09.02.2001 | 5 | (2) | |
| **Defenders:** | **DOB** | **M** | **(s)** | **G** |
| Daniels Fedorovičs | 07.10.2001 | 21 | (3) | |
| Ivan Harambašić (CRO) | 09.12.2000 | 6 | | |
| Gabriels Kirkils | 25.05.2001 | 18 | | |
| Jegors Novikovs | 09.02.2003 | 13 | (1) | 1 |
| Niklāvs Treimanis | 12.11.2003 | 3 | (6) | |
| Normunds Uldriķis | 29.01.2001 | 20 | (1) | 1 |
| Mikuss Vasiļevskis | 29.05.2003 | 4 | (9) | |
| Kārlis Vilnis | 03.07.2003 | 21 | (3) | 1 |
| Rūdolfs Zeņģis | 21.03.2002 | 24 | (1) | |
| **Midfielders:** | **DOB** | **M** | **(s)** | **G** |
| Daniils Čiņajevs | 03.07.2003 | 11 | (1) | |

| | DOB | M | (s) | G |
|---|---|---|---|---|
| Jānis Grīnbergs | 28.02.1999 | 30 | (2) | 1 |
| Kristupas Keršys (LTU) | 06.09.2003 | 10 | (3) | |
| Gļebs Kļuškins | 01.10.1992 | 10 | (1) | 2 |
| Jean Mbassi Zambgala (CMR) | 06.11.2003 | 12 | (3) | 2 |
| Noa Meroža | 26.07.2004 | 4 | (14) | |
| Kristofers Rēķis | 21.01.2003 | 17 | (14) | 1 |
| Lūkass Vapne | 31.08.2003 | 17 | (2) | 2 |
| Oskars Vientiess | 08.10.2002 | 33 | (1) | |
| Tomass Zants | 23.05.2003 | | (2) | |
| **Forwards:** | **DOB** | **M** | **(s)** | **G** |
| Mohamet Lamine Corréa (SEN) | 30.08.2001 | 13 | (2) | 3 |
| Bruno Melnis | 21.01.2004 | 29 | (5) | 10 |
| Yunusa Owolabi Muritala (NGA) | 02.04.2000 | 8 | (1) | 1 |
| Ingars Pūlis | 24.01.2001 | 7 | (29) | 5 |
| Artjoms Puzirevskis | 11.01.2003 | 29 | (6) | 8 |

## Rīga Football Club

**Founded**: 2014 (*as merger of FC Caramba Riga and Dinamo Rīga*)
**Stadium**: Skonto stadions, Rīga (8,087)
**Trainer**: Thorsten Fink (GER) — 29.10.1967
[16.05.2022] Kristaps Blanks — 30.06.1986
[07.06.2022] Sandro Perković (CRO) — 15.04.1984

| Goalkeepers: | DOB | M | (s) | G |
|---|---|---|---|---|
| Roberts Ozols | 10.09.1995 | 16 | | |
| Nils Puriņš | 01.08.1998 | 20 | | |
| **Defenders:** | **DOB** | **M** | **(s)** | **G** |
| Douglas Bergqvist (SWE) | 29.03.1993 | 9 | (3) | |
| Antonijs Černomordijs | 26.09.1996 | 20 | (2) | 1 |
| Gustavo Alfonso Dulanto Sanguinetti (PER) | 09.05.1995 | 4 | | |
| Raivis Andris Jurkovskis | 09.12.1996 | 26 | (1) | 1 |
| Antons Kurakins | 01.01.1990 | 8 | (6) | 1 |
| Christoph Martschinko (AUT) | 13.02.1994 | 5 | (3) | |
| Baba Musah (GHA) | 03.09.1999 | 10 | | |
| Glody Ngonda Muzinga (COD) | 31.12.1994 | 17 | (1) | 1 |
| Mouhamed El Bachir Ngom (SEN) | 12.05.2000 | 12 | (4) | |
| Armands Pētersons | 05.12.1990 | 9 | (9) | |
| Ritvars Rugins | 17.10.1989 | 3 | (5) | |
| Miloš Vranjanin (SRB) | 11.06.1996 | 8 | (1) | 1 |
| **Midfielders:** | **DOB** | **M** | **(s)** | **G** |
| Hrvoje Babec (CRO) | 28.07.1999 | 14 | (1) | 4 |
| Navarone Chesney Kai Foor (NED) | 04.02.1992 | 11 | | |
| Yuriy Kendysh (BLR) | 10.06.1990 | 29 | (2) | 6 |

| | DOB | M | (s) | G |
|---|---|---|---|---|
| Ilja Korotkovs | 24.05.2000 | 6 | (1) | |
| Mohamed Ouadah (FRA) | 31.08.1994 | | (6) | |
| Thanos Petsos (GRE) | 05.06.1991 | 15 | (5) | |
| Yuriy Vakulko (UKR) | 10.11.1997 | 14 | (12) | 1 |
| Wesley Natã Wachholz (BRA) | 18.04.1995 | 4 | (4) | 1 |
| Vladlen Yurchenko (UKR) | 22.01.1994 | 8 | (5) | 1 |
| **Forwards:** | **DOB** | **M** | **(s)** | **G** |
| Joselpho Barnes (GHA) | 12.12.2001 | 12 | (17) | 7 |
| Douglas Aurélio (BRA) | 27.03.1999 | 11 | (6) | 5 |
| Oleksandr Filippov (UKR) | 23.10.1992 | 11 | (6) | 2 |
| Gabriel Ramos da Penha (BRA) | 20.03.1996 | 26 | (5) | 10 |
| Vladimirs Kamešs | 28.10.1988 | 13 | (8) | |
| Raivis Ķiršs | 15.01.2000 | 1 | (6) | |
| Karim Loukili (MAR) | 28.04.1997 | 9 | (7) | 1 |
| Georgi Minchev (BUL) | 20.04.1995 | 1 | (15) | 1 |
| Olabanjo Alexander Ogunji (NGA) | 20.01.2001 | 4 | (3) | 1 |
| Lucas Rangel Nunes Gonçalves (BRA) | 29.12.1994 | 4 | (10) | 4 |
| Mikael Soisalo (FIN) | 24.04.1998 | 22 | (5) | 4 |
| Marcelo Luis Torres (ARG) | 06.11.1997 | 13 | (3) | 11 |
| Brice Tutu (FRA) | 11.01.1998 | 1 | (1) | |

## Futbola klubs Rīgas Futbola Skola

| Founded: | 2011 | | |
|---|---|---|---|
| Stadium: | LNK Sporta Parks, Rīga (2,300) | | |
| Trainer: | Viktors Morozs | | 30.07.1980 |

| Goalkeepers: | DOB | M | (s) | G |
|---|---|---|---|---|
| Vytautas Černiauskas (LTU) | 12.03.1989 | 22 | | |
| Jevģēnijs Nerugals | 26.02.1989 | 1 | | |
| Pāvels Šteinbors | 21.09.1985 | 13 | | |
| **Defenders:** | **DOB** | **M** | **(s)** | **G** |
| Kaspars Dubra | 20.12.1990 | 18 | (3) | |
| Vladislavs Fjodorovs | 27.09.1996 | 6 | (5) | |
| Vitālijs Jagodinskis | 28.02.1992 | 24 | | 1 |
| Jānis Krautmanis | 22.04.1997 | | (1) | |
| Žiga Lipušček (SVN) | 05.01.1997 | 25 | (2) | 3 |
| Vitālijs Maksimenko | 08.12.1990 | 11 | (6) | |
| Petr Mareš (CZE) | 17.01.1991 | 25 | (5) | 5 |
| Vladislavs Sorokins | 10.05.1997 | 20 | (8) | |
| Elvis Stuglis | 04.07.1993 | 8 | (16) | 6 |
| Jovan Vlalukin (SRB) | 21.05.1999 | 10 | (5) | |
| **Midfielders:** | **DOB** | **M** | **(s)** | **G** |
| Vladislav Galkin (RUS) | 03.04.2002 | 2 | (7) | 2 |
| Alfusainey Jatta (GAM) | 05.08.1999 | 22 | (6) | 4 |

| Stefan Panić (SRB) | 20.09.1992 | 14 | (4) | |
|---|---|---|---|---|
| Tomislav Šarić (SVN) | 24.06.1990 | 20 | (3) | 4 |
| Tomáš Šimkovič (AUT) | 16.04.1987 | 5 | (3) | |
| Karolis Uzéla (LTU) | 11.03.2000 | 3 | (2) | |
| Dmitrijs Zelenkovs | 15.05.2000 | 1 | (1) | |
| Artūrs Zjuzins | 18.06.1991 | 19 | (8) | 3 |
| Glebs Žaleiko | 27.06.2004 | 4 | (8) | |
| **Forwards:** | **DOB** | **M** | **(s)** | **G** |
| Fabricio Rodrigues da Silva Ferreira „Bill" (BRA) | 07.05.1999 | 3 | (3) | |
| Stefan Cvetković (SRB) | 12.01.1998 | 3 | (2) | |
| Ismael Diomande (CIV) | 07.12.2003 | 7 | (8) | 4 |
| Emerson Santana Deocleciano (BRA) | 27.07.1999 | 29 | (6) | 11 |
| Kevin Friesenbichler (AUT) | 06.05.1994 | 29 | (3) | 8 |
| Andrej Ilić (SRB) | 03.04.2000 | 28 | (4) | 16 |
| Cedric Kouadio (CIV) | 19.05.1999 | 7 | (5) | 2 |
| Deniss Rakels | 20.08.1992 | 8 | (12) | 10 |
| Renārs Varslavāns | 23.08.2001 | 9 | (10) | 3 |

## Jūrmalas Futbola un Peldēšanas skola/ Futbola klubs Spartaks Jūrmala

| Founded: | 2007 | | |
|---|---|---|---|
| Stadium: | Slokas stadions, Jūrmala (2,500) | | |
| Trainer: | Przemysław Łagożny (POL) | | 17.03.1992 |
| [15.05.2022] | Fabiano José Costa Flora (POR) | | 29.05.1985 |
| [23.07.2022] | Víctor Manuel Basadre Orozco (ESP) | | 16.02.1970 |
| [13.10.2022] | Oskars Kļava | | 08.08.1983 |

| Goalkeepers: | DOB | M | (s) | G |
|---|---|---|---|---|
| Iļja Isajevs | 05.12.2000 | 5 | | |
| Dāvis Ošs | 03.12.1994 | 9 | | |
| Dāvis Veisbuks | 01.03.2005 | 22 | | |
| **Defenders:** | **DOB** | **M** | **(s)** | **G** |
| Kritsters Atars | 21.04.2004 | 3 | (6) | |
| Timurs Azarovs | 23.03.2006 | | (1) | |
| Daniels Grauds | 27.07.2003 | 21 | (11) | |
| Rikardo Jagodinskis | 07.03.2005 | 1 | (1) | |
| Klāvs Kramēns | 07.07.2000 | 15 | | |
| Artūrs Ļotčikovs | 26.01.2000 | 18 | (8) | 1 |
| Mārcis Ošs | 25.07.1991 | 16 | | |
| Deniss Rogovs | 11.02.2003 | 4 | (6) | |
| Raivis Skrebels | 26.09.1999 | 34 | (1) | |
| Aleksandrs Solovjovs | 25.02.1988 | 10 | (1) | |
| **Midfielders:** | **DOB** | **M** | **(s)** | **G** |
| Markuss Alpēns | 24.01.2004 | 12 | (12) | 1 |
| Kristians Godiņš | 20.05.2004 | | (1) | |
| Oļegs Laizāns | 28.03.1987 | 36 | | 7 |

| Adam Markhiev (FIN) | 17.03.2002 | 9 | | 1 |
|---|---|---|---|---|
| Deniss Meļņiks | 07.09.2002 | 23 | (1) | |
| Abiodun Omojesu Ogunniyi (NGA) | 20.12.2001 | 17 | | 3 |
| Danila Patijčuks | 22.03.2003 | 4 | (2) | |
| Daniils Skopenko | 23.03.2000 | 3 | (4) | |
| Vladislavs Soloveičiks | 25.05.1999 | 14 | | 1 |
| Yaroslav Terekhov (UKR) | 21.04.1999 | 18 | | |
| Tin Vukmanić (CRO) | 17.04.1999 | 2 | (1) | |
| **Forwards:** | **DOB** | **M** | **(s)** | **G** |
| Kwadwo Asamoah (GHA) | 15.07.2002 | 28 | (2) | 5 |
| Algirdas Gražis | 12.06.2003 | 2 | (11) | |
| Daņiils Hvoiņickis | 08.04.1998 | 5 | (3) | |
| Heythem Kerbache (FRA) | 01.07.2000 | | (1) | |
| Arturs Krancmanis | 15.08.2003 | 4 | (10) | 1 |
| Leonardo Andriel dos Santos „Léo Gaúcho" (BRA) | 03.08.2001 | 15 | | 8 |
| Artūrs Ostapenko | 28.08.2003 | 16 | (6) | 3 |
| Kristaps Puzānovs | 06.03.2004 | | (4) | |
| Artjoms Zamullo | 23.08.2002 | 1 | (17) | 1 |
| Valentin Zekhov (RUS) | 29.04.2001 | 29 | (5) | 2 |

## Sporta Klubs Super Nova Olaine

| Founded: | 2000 | | |
|---|---|---|---|
| Stadium: | Olaines stadions, Olaine (2,500) | | |
| Trainer: | Andrejs Lapsa | | 23.04.1968 |
| [04.06.2022] | Igors Korabļovs | | 23.11.1974 |
| [29.06.2022] | Aleksandrs Koliņko | | 18.06.1975 |

| Goalkeepers: | DOB | M | (s) | G |
|---|---|---|---|---|
| Patriks Balodis | 03.12.2001 | 2 | (2) | |
| Kristaps Zommers | 07.01.1997 | 34 | | |
| **Defenders:** | **DOB** | **M** | **(s)** | **G** |
| Kritsters Atars | 21.04.2004 | 10 | (5) | 1 |
| Jegors Cīrulis | 31.07.2003 | 9 | (6) | |
| Rikardo Jagodinskis | 07.03.2005 | 7 | | |
| Roberts Jaunarājs-Janvāris | 23.03.2000 | 24 | | |
| Ņikita Koliņko | 10.06.2000 | 1 | (6) | |
| Iļja Semjonovs | 18.03.2002 | 31 | (1) | |
| Ņikita Skļarenko | 23.05.2000 | 21 | (1) | |
| Yehor Smirnov (UKR) | 03.08.1996 | 7 | | |
| Edgars Šakurovs | 16.09.2001 | 4 | (5) | |
| Roberts Zelmanis | 18.04.2001 | 34 | | 2 |
| **Midfielders:** | **DOB** | **M** | **(s)** | **G** |
| Edgars Brics | 10.04.2003 | 1 | (17) | |
| Dāvis Indrāns | 06.06.1995 | 9 | (3) | |
| Roberts Kukulis | 25.05.2007 | | (3) | |
| Jevgenijs Miņins | 17.03.2002 | 25 | (4) | 4 |

| Rihards Ozoliņš | 31.05.2001 | 28 | (2) | |
|---|---|---|---|---|
| Dmitrijs Puhovs | 04.05.2002 | | (5) | 1 |
| Alekss Regža | 16.07.1994 | 1 | (9) | |
| Ričards Rullis | 11.05.2000 | 27 | (1) | 2 |
| Vladimirs Stepanovs | 06.02.2000 | 12 | | |
| Toms Ralfs Šteinbergs | 13.02.2002 | 7 | (3) | |
| Yevgeniy Terzi (UKR) | 27.06.1997 | 14 | | 1 |
| Artjoms Troickis | 29.12.2001 | 8 | (13) | |
| **Forwards:** | **DOB** | **M** | **(s)** | **G** |
| Kirils Artjomovs | 09.05.2006 | | (2) | |
| Vüqar Əsgərov (AZE) | 14.05.1985 | 9 | (3) | |
| Kristians Černovs | 27.06.2006 | | (1) | |
| Svetoslavs Čugunovs | 10.01.2002 | 3 | (9) | |
| Algirdas Gražis | 12.06.2003 | 3 | (9) | |
| Ričards Kauliņš | 04.05.2003 | 4 | (5) | |
| Daniels Radzenieks | 22.07.2006 | | (1) | |
| Marko Regža | 20.01.1999 | 25 | (2) | 8 |
| Kristians Sprukulis | 10.10.2002 | 22 | (8) | 1 |
| Eduards Višņakovs | 10.05.1990 | 14 | | 3 |

## Futbola klubs Tukums 2000

**Founded**: 2000
**Stadium**: Tukuma pilsētas stadions, Tukums (1,000)
**Trainer**: Kristaps Dišlers     17.01.1986

| Goalkeepers: | DOB | M | (s) | G |
|---|---|---|---|---|
| Leonards Čevers | 17.05.2005 | 1 | | |
| Helmuts Saulītis | 18.05.1998 | 9 | | |
| Sergejs Vilkovs | 03.09.2002 | 26 | | |
| **Defenders:** | **DOB** | **M** | **(s)** | **G** |
| Kristaps Jansons | 26.11.2004 | 2 | (1) | |
| Robins Kokarītis | 21.10.1999 | 4 | (4) | |
| Jānis Krautmanis | 22.04.1997 | 10 | (3) | 2 |
| Markuss Kruglaužs | 28.01.2002 | 20 | (4) | 5 |
| Kristers Lībeks | 04.04.2001 | 12 | | |
| Atis Ozols | 16.03.2000 | 28 | (4) | |
| Rūdolfs Reingolcs | 01.07.2002 | 21 | (1) | |
| Niks Sliede | 08.03.2004 | 26 | (1) | |
| **Midfielders:** | **DOB** | **M** | **(s)** | **G** |
| Kaspars Anmanis | 22.01.2002 | 14 | (14) | 1 |
| Maksims Fjodorovs | 24.09.2003 | 20 | (8) | |
| Renards Krišjānis | 04.04.2002 | 3 | (8) | |
| Daniels Mīļais | 14.11.2003 | 1 | (4) | 1 |
| Ryuga Nakamura (JPN) | 24.07.2001 | 30 | (2) | 2 |
| Ričards Penka | 30.07.2004 | | (1) | |
| Pāvels Pilāts | 04.02.1997 | 5 | (4) | |
| Markus Prohorenkovs | 08.07.2005 | | (1) | |
| Bogdans Samoilovs | 13.05.2000 | 11 | (4) | 2 |
| Maksims Sidorovs | 17.09.2001 | 14 | (4) | |
| Ingars Stuglis | 12.02.1996 | 22 | (4) | 3 |
| Martins Štāls | 22.05.2005 | 9 | (1) | |
| Davis Zeltiņš | 21.08.2002 | 3 | (19) | 4 |
| **Forwards:** | **DOB** | **M** | **(s)** | **G** |
| Aleksejs Davidenkovs | 27.06.1998 | 1 | (6) | |
| Ikuto Gomi (JPN) | 09.05.2002 | 21 | (9) | 2 |
| Kristiāns Kaušelis | 14.03.2003 | 10 | (6) | 2 |
| Kristers Neilands | 09.09.2000 | 13 | | 2 |
| Kristaps Puzānovs | 06.03.2004 | 4 | (8) | 1 |
| Oskars Rubenis | 03.02.1999 | 28 | (1) | 1 |
| Ibrahima Ndiape Sow (SEN) | 15.09.2000 | 20 | (3) | 3 |
| Kristers Švāns | 30.05.1999 | 8 | (9) | 3 |

## Valmieras Football Club

**Founded**: 1996
**Stadium**: „Jānis Daliņš" stadions, Valmierā (1,250)
**Trainer**: Jurģis Kalns     05.10.1982

| Goalkeepers: | DOB | M | (s) | G |
|---|---|---|---|---|
| Vjačeslavs Kudrjavcevs | 30.03.1998 | 1 | | |
| Klāvs Lauva | 30.06.2004 | 1 | | |
| Rihards Matrevics | 18.03.1999 | 34 | | |
| **Defenders:** | **DOB** | **M** | **(s)** | **G** |
| Daniels Balodis | 10.06.1998 | 30 | | 3 |
| Artūrs Bērziņš | 01.12.2003 | | (1) | |
| Emīls Birka | 25.04.2000 | 24 | (8) | 1 |
| Pape Yaré Fall (SEN) | 09.09.2000 | 9 | (7) | 2 |
| Alvis Jaunzems | 16.06.1999 | 33 | (2) | 4 |
| Maksims Toņiševs | 12.05.2000 | 15 | (15) | |
| Roberts Veips | 22.02.2000 | 7 | (5) | |
| Roman Yakuba (UKR) | 23.04.2001 | 34 | | 1 |
| **Midfielders:** | **DOB** | **M** | **(s)** | **G** |
| Kristers Čudars | 03.09.1999 | 5 | (19) | 1 |
| Meissa Diop (SEN) | 02.02.2003 | | (8) | |
| Masaki Murata (JPN) | 29.08.1999 | 30 | (2) | 2 |
| Arthur Murza (UKR) | 13.07.2000 | | (1) | 1 |
| Kristers Penkevics | 28.01.2003 | 3 | (7) | 1 |
| Luka Silagadze (GEO) | 21.04.1999 | 13 | (19) | 5 |
| Lūkass Vapne | 31.08.2003 | 1 | (9) | 3 |
| Daisuke Yokota (JPN) | 15.06.2000 | 31 | (2) | 8 |
| Ivan Zhelizko (UKR) | 12.02.2001 | 27 | (1) | 4 |
| **Forwards:** | **DOB** | **M** | **(s)** | **G** |
| Niks Dusalijevs | 17.07.2001 | | (7) | |
| Djibril Gueyé (SEN) | 19.11.1996 | 24 | (11) | 12 |
| Jorge Duarte Rodrigues Mendes Teixeira(POR) | 08.03.1999 | | (6) | 1 |
| Raimonds Krollis | 28.10.2001 | 34 | | 24 |
| Kristers Lūsiņš | 09.05.2000 | | (8) | |
| Camilo Andrés Mena Márquez (COL) | 01.10.2002 | 32 | (3) | 14 |
| Alioune Ndoye (SEN) | 05.10.2001 | 7 | (15) | 7 |
| Kristers Neilands | 09.09.2000 | | (1) | |
| Oļģerts Raščevskis | 18.02.2003 | 1 | (1) | |

## SECOND LEVEL
### Optibet Nākotnes līga - Pirmā līga 2022

| | | | | | | | | | |
|---|---|---|---|---|---|---|---|---|---|
| 1. | FS Jelgava (*Promoted*) | 26 | 24 | 1 | 1 | 76 | - | 13 | 73 |
| 2. | Rīga FC-2 | 26 | 19 | 3 | 4 | 84 | - | 27 | 60 |
| 3. | Grobiņas SC (*Promotion Play-offs*) | 26 | 17 | 2 | 7 | 85 | - | 39 | 53 |
| 4. | Valmiera FC-2 / VSS | 26 | 17 | 1 | 8 | 90 | - | 37 | 52 |
| 5. | FK Rīgas Futbola Skola-2 | 26 | 14 | 4 | 8 | 75 | - | 43 | 46 |
| 6. | JDFS Alberts Rīga | 26 | 13 | 6 | 7 | 38 | - | 25 | 45 |
| 7. | Skanstes SK Rīga | 26 | 10 | 7 | 9 | 34 | - | 41 | 37 |
| 8. | AFA Olaine | 26 | 7 | 4 | 15 | 38 | - | 72 | 25 |
| 9. | FK Salaspils | 26 | 7 | 4 | 15 | 40 | - | 75 | 25 |
| 10. | Leevon Saldus | 26 | 6 | 5 | 15 | 34 | - | 49 | 23 |
| 11. | FK Tukums 2000 / TSS-2 | 26 | 6 | 4 | 16 | 33 | - | 66 | 22 |
| 12. | FK Dinamo Rīga (*Relegation Play-offs*) | 26 | 6 | 4 | 16 | 17 | - | 57 | 22 |
| 13. | Rēzeknes FA / BJSS (*Relegated*) | 26 | 6 | 3 | 17 | 33 | - | 70 | 21 |
| 14. | FK Smiltene / BJSS (*Relegated*) | 26 | 4 | 4 | 18 | 24 | - | 87 | 16 |

## Relegation Play-offs (2nd / 3rd Level) [20-27.11.2022]

FK Dinamo Rīga - FK Karosta Liepāja     4-2(1-2)     1-2(1-1)

FK Karosta Liepāja promoted to second level for 2023.

## INTERNATIONAL MATCHES
(16.07.2022 – 15.07.2023)

| | | | | |
|---|---|---|---|---|
| 22.09.2022 | Rīga | *Latvia - Moldova* | *1-2(0-2)* | (UNL) |
| 25.09.2022 | Andorra la Vella | *Andorra - Latvia* | *1-1(0-0)* | (UNL) |
| 16.11.2022 | Rīga | *Latvia - Estonia* | *1-1(1-1,1-1,1-1); 5-3 on penalties* | (BC) |
| 19.11.2022 | Rīga | *Latvia - Iceland* | *1-1(0-0,1-1,1-1); 7-8 on penalties* | (BC) |
| 22.03.2023 | Dublin | *Republic of Ireland - Latvia* | *3-2(2-2)* | (F) |
| 28.03.2023 | Cardiff | *Wales - Latvia* | *1-0(1-0)* | (ECQ) |
| 16.06.2023 | Rīga | *Latvia - Turkey* | *2-3(0-1)* | (ECQ) |
| 19.06.2023 | Yerevan | *Armenia - Latvia* | *2-1(1-0)* | (ECQ) |

**22.09.2022   LATVIA - MOLDOVA**          1-2(0-2)          3rd UEFA Nations League D, Group 1
Skonto stadions, Rīga; Referee: António Emanuel Carvalho Nobre (Portugal); Attendance: 6,711
**LVA:** Pāvels Šteinbors, Roberts Savaļnieks, Kaspars Dubra, Antonijs Černomordijs (Cap), Raivis Andris Jurkovskis (88.Elvis Stuglis), Kristers Tobers, Eduards Emsis, Alvis Jaunzems (57.Raimonds Krollis), Andrejs Cigaņiks (82.Dāvis Ikaunieks), Jānis Ikaunieks, Vladislavs Gutkovskis. Trainer: Dainis Kazakevičs.
**Goal:** Jānis Ikaunieks (55).

**25.09.2022   ANDORRA - LATVIA**          1-1(0-0)          3rd UEFA Nations League D, Group 1
Estadi Nacional, Andorra la Vella; Referee: Anastasios Papapetrou (Greece); Attendance: 1,102
**LVA:** Pāvels Šteinbors, Roberts Savaļnieks, Kaspars Dubra (Cap), Elvis Stuglis, Raivis Andris Jurkovskis, Kristers Tobers, Eduards Emsis (82.Igors Tarasovs), Jānis Ikaunieks, Andrejs Cigaņiks (85.Dāvis Ikaunieks), Vladislavs Gutkovskis, Raimonds Krollis. Trainer: Dainis Kazakevičs.
**Goal:** Vladislavs Gutkovskis (50).

**16.11.2022   LATVIA - ESTONIA**          1-1(1-1,1-1,1-1); 5-3 on penalties          29th Baltic Cup, Semi-Finals
Daugava stadions, Rīga; Referee: Robertas Valikonis (Lithuania); Attendance: 1,657
**LVA:** Rihards Matrevics, Raivis Andris Jurkovskis, Antonijs Černomordijs (Cap), Daniels Balodis, Roberts Savaļnieks [*sent off 90+2*], Artūrs Zjuzins, Eduards Emsis, Andrejs Cigaņiks (63.Alvis Jaunzems), Jānis Ikaunieks, Raimonds Krollis (79.Elvis Stuglis), Roberts Uldriķis (62.Dāvis Ikaunieks). Trainer: Dainis Kazakevičs.
**Goal:** Raimonds Krollis (45+2).
**Penalties:** Jānis Ikaunieks, Artūrs Zjuzins, Alvis Jaunzems, Dāvis Ikaunieks, Elvis Stuglis.

**19.11.2022   LATVIA - ICELAND**          1-1(0-0,1-1,1-1); 7-8 on penalties          29th Baltic Cup, Final
Daugava stadions, Rīga; Referee: Joonas Jaanovits (Estonia); Attendance: 997
**LVA:** Pāvels Šteinbors, Vladislavs Sorokins, Antonijs Černomordijs (Cap), Daniels Balodis, Raivis Andris Jurkovskis (80.Dāvis Ikaunieks), Eduards Emsis (88.Elvis Stuglis), Artūrs Zjuzins, Alvis Jaunzems, Andrejs Cigaņiks, Jānis Ikaunieks, Raimonds Krollis [*sent off 27*]. Trainer: Dainis Kazakevičs.
**Goal:** Andrejs Cigaņiks (67).
**Penalties:** Jānis Ikaunieks, Artūrs Zjuzins, Dāvis Ikaunieks, Alvis Jaunzems, Elvis Stuglis, Vladislavs Sorokins, Andrejs Cigaņiks, Antonijs Černomordijs (saved).

**22.03.2023   REPUBLIC OF IRELAND - LATVIA**          3-2(2-2)          Friendly International
Aviva Stadium, Dublin; Referee: Andrei Chivulete (Romania); Attendance: 41,211
**LVA:** Pāvels Šteinbors, Roberts Savaļnieks, Antonijs Černomordijs (Cap), Daniels Balodis (46.Mārcis Ošs), Vladislavs Sorokins, Kristers Tobers, Artūrs Zjuzins (71.Aleksejs Saveljevs), Andrejs Cigaņiks (71.Renārs Varslavāns), Jānis Ikaunieks (46.Alvis Jaunzems), Vladislavs Gutkovskis (56.Raimonds Krollis), Roberts Uldriķis (81.Dāvis Ikaunieks). Trainer: Dainis Kazakevičs.
**Goals:** Roberts Uldriķis (33), Artūrs Zjuzins (45+1).

**28.03.2023   WALES - LATVIA**          1-0(1-0)          17th EC. Qualifiers
Cardiff City Stadium, Cardiff; Referee: Giorgi Kruashvili (Georgia); Attendance: 32,806
**LVA:** Pāvels Šteinbors, Roberts Savaļnieks, Mārcis Ošs, Antonijs Černomordijs (Cap), Vladislavs Sorokins (46.Raivis Andris Jurkovskis), Kristers Tobers, Artūrs Zjuzins (82.Aleksejs Saveljevs), Andrejs Cigaņiks (70.Renārs Varslavāns), Jānis Ikaunieks (59.Alvis Jaunzems), Vladislavs Gutkovskis, Roberts Uldriķis (82.Raimonds Krollis). Trainer: Dainis Kazakevičs.

**16.06.2023   LATVIA - TURKEY**          2-3(0-1)          17th EC. Qualifiers
Skonto stadions, Rīga; Referee: Tamás Bognár (Hungary); Attendance: 6,287
**LVA:** Nils Tom Puriņš, Roberts Savaļnieks, Mārcis Ošs, Daniels Balodis, Raivis Andris Jurkovskis, Eduards Emsis [*sent off 82*], Kristers Tobers (Cap), Alvis Jaunzems (80.Dāvis Ikaunieks), Andrejs Cigaņiks (76.Eduards Daškevičs), Roberts Uldriķis (86.Marko Regža), Vladislavs Gutkovskis (76.Raimonds Krollis). Trainer: Dainis Kazakevičs.
**Goals:** Eduards Emsis (51), Kristers Tobers (90+4).

**19.06.2023   ARMENIA - LATVIA**          2-1(1-0)          17th EC. Qualifiers
„Vazgen Sargsyan" Hanrapetakan Stadium, Yerevan; Referee: Peter Kráľovič (Slovakia); Attendance: 13,450
**LVA:** Nils Tom Puriņš, Roberts Savaļnieks, Daniels Balodis, Mārcis Ošs (69.Elvis Stuglis), Raivis Andris Jurkovskis, Aleksejs Saveljevs, Kristers Tobers (Cap), Alvis Jaunzems (65.Maksims Toņiševs), Andrejs Cigaņiks (64.Eduards Daškevičs), Roberts Uldriķis (85.Marko Regža), Vladislavs Gutkovskis (65.Raimonds Krollis). Trainer: Dainis Kazakevičs.
**Goals:** Styopa Mkrtchyan (67 own goal).

## NATIONAL TEAM PLAYERS
### (16.07.2022 – 15.07.2023)

| Name | DOB | Caps | Goals | Club | |
|------|-----|------|-------|------|--|

### Goalkeepers

| Name | DOB | Caps | Goals | Club | |
|------|-----|------|-------|------|--|
| Rihards MATREVICS | 18.03.1999 | 2 | 0 | 2022: | *Valmiera FC* |
| Nils Tom PURIŅŠ | 01.08.1998 | 2 | 0 | 2023: | *Rīga FC* |
| Pāvels ŠTEINBORS | 21.09.1985 | 30 | 0 | 2022/2023: | *FK Rīgas Futbola Skola* |

### Defenders

| Name | DOB | Caps | Goals | Club | |
|------|-----|------|-------|------|--|
| Daniels BALODIS | 10.06.1998 | 5 | 0 | 2022/2023: | *Valmiera FC* |
| Antonijs ČERNOMORDIJS | 26.09.1996 | 30 | 1 | 2022/2023: | *Rīga FC* |
| Kaspars DUBRA | 20.12.1990 | 58 | 3 | 2022: | *FK Rīgas Futbola Skola* |
| Raivis Andris JURKOVSKIS | 09.12.1996 | 37 | 0 | 2022/2023: | *Rīga FC* |
| Mārcis OŠS | 25.07.1991 | 24 | 1 | 2023: | *FK Rīgas Futbola Skola* |
| Vladislavs SOROKINS | 10.05.1997 | 7 | 0 | 2022/2023: | *FK Rīgas Futbola Skola* |
| Elvis STUGLIS | 04.07.1993 | 10 | 0 | 2022/2023: | *FK Rīgas Futbola Skola* |
| Igors TARASOVS | 16.10.1988 | 47 | 2 | 2022: | *Ypsonas FC Limassol (CYP)* |

### Midfielders

| Name | DOB | Caps | Goals | Club | |
|------|-----|------|-------|------|--|
| Andrejs CIGAŅIKS | 12.04.1997 | 43 | 2 | 2022: / 02.01.2023-> | *FK DAC 1904 Dunajská Streda (SVK)* / *RTS Widzew Łódź* |
| Eduards DAŠKEVIČS | 12.07.2002 | 2 | 0 | 2023: | *Rīga FC* |
| Eduards EMSIS | 23.02.1996 | 26 | 2 | 2022: / 16.01.2023-> | *FC Lahti (FIN)* / *KF Egnatia Rrogozhinë (ALB)* |
| Jānis IKAUNIEKS | 16.02.1995 | 50 | 11 | 2022: / 01.01.2023-> | *Kuopion Palloseura (FIN)* / *FK Rīgas Futbola Skola* |
| Alvis JAUNZEMS | 16.06.1999 | 29 | 0 | 2022/2023: | *Valmiera FC* |
| Roberts SAVAĻNIEKS | 04.02.1993 | 51 | 2 | 2022: / 01.01.2023-> | *FK Liepāja* / *FK Rīgas Futbola Skola* |
| Aleksejs SAVELJEVS | 30.01.1999 | 11 | 1 | 2023: | *FK Auda Ķekava* |
| Kristers TOBERS | 13.12.2000 | 24 | 1 | 2022/2023: | *KS Lechia Gdańsk (POL)* |
| Maksims TOŅIŠEVS | 12.05.2000 | 1 | 0 | 2023: | *Valmiera FC* |
| Renārs VARSLAVĀNS | 23.08.2001 | 6 | 0 | 2023: | *Valmiera FC* |
| Artūrs ZJUZINS | 18.06.1991 | 60 | 9 | 2022/2023: | *FK Rīgas Futbola Skola* |

### Forwards

| Name | DOB | Caps | Goals | Club | |
|------|-----|------|-------|------|--|
| Vladislavs GUTKOVSKIS | 02.04.1995 | 43 | 11 | 2022/2023: | *RKS Raków Częstochowa (POL)* |
| Dāvis IKAUNIEKS | 07.01.1994 | 43 | 6 | 2022/2023: | *FK Jablonec (CZE)* |
| Raimonds KROLLIS | 28.10.2001 | 31 | 3 | 2022: / 20.01.2023-> | *Valmiera FC* / *Spezia Calcio La Spezia (ITA)* |
| Marko REGŽA | 20.01.1999 | 2 | 0 | 2023: | *Rīga FC* |
| Roberts ULDRIĶIS | 03.04.1998 | 41 | 7 | 2022/2023: | *SC Cambuur Leeuwarden (NED)* |

### Trainer

| Name | DOB | | | | |
|------|-----|--|--|--|--|
| Dainis KAZAKEVIČS [from 20.01.2020] | 30.03.1981 | 35 M; 10 W; 12 D; 13 L; 49-46 | | | |

# LIECHTENSTEIN

## The Country:
Fürstentum Liechtenstein (Principality of Liechtenstein)
Capital: Vaduz
Surface: 160 km²
Inhabitants: 38,387 [2022]
Time: UTC+1

## The FA:
Liechtensteiner Fussballverband
Landstrasse 149, 9494 Schaan
+423 238 24 00
Foundation date: 1934
Member of FIFA since: 1974
Member of UEFA since: 1974
Website: www.lfv.li

## NATIONAL TEAM RECORDS

### RECORDS
| | | |
|---|---|---|
| First international match: | 09.03.1982, Balzers: | Liechtenstein – Switzerland 0-1 |
| Most international caps: | Peter Karl Jehle | - 132 caps (1998-2018) |
| Most international goals: | Mario Frick | - 16 goals / 125 caps (1993-2015) |

### UEFA EUROPEAN CHAMPIONSHIP
| | |
|---|---|
| 1960 | - |
| 1964 | - |
| 1968 | - |
| 1972 | - |
| 1976 | Did not enter |
| 1980 | Did not enter |
| 1984 | Did not enter |
| 1988 | Did not enter |
| 1992 | Did not enter |
| 1996 | Qualifiers |
| 2000 | Qualifiers |
| 2004 | Qualifiers |
| 2008 | Qualifiers |
| 2012 | Qualifiers |
| 2016 | Qualifiers |
| 2020 | Qualifiers |

### FIFA WORLD CUP
| | |
|---|---|
| 1930 | - |
| 1934 | - |
| 1938 | - |
| 1950 | - |
| 1954 | - |
| 1958 | - |
| 1962 | - |
| 1966 | - |
| 1970 | - |
| 1974 | - |
| 1978 | Did not enter |
| 1982 | Did not enter |
| 1986 | Did not enter |
| 1990 | Did not enter |
| 1994 | Did not enter |
| 1998 | Qualifiers |
| 2002 | Qualifiers |
| 2006 | Qualifiers |
| 2010 | Qualifiers |
| 2014 | Qualifiers |
| 2018 | Qualifiers |
| 2022 | Qualifiers |

### OLYMPIC TOURNAMENTS
| | |
|---|---|
| 1908 | - |
| 1912 | - |
| 1920 | - |
| 1924 | - |
| 1928 | - |
| 1936 | - |
| 1948 | - |
| 1952 | - |
| 1956 | - |
| 1960 | - |
| 1964 | - |
| 1968 | - |
| 1972 | - |
| 1976 | Did not enter |
| 1980 | Did not enter |
| 1984 | Did not enter |
| 1988 | Qualifiers |
| 1992 | Did not enter |
| 1996 | Did not enter |
| 2000 | Did not enter |
| 2004 | Did not enter |
| 2008 | Qualifiers |
| 2012 | Qualifiers |
| 2016 | Qualifiers |
| 2020 | Qualifiers |

## UEFA NATIONS LEAGUE
| | |
|---|---|
| 2018/2019 | League D (Group Stage) |
| 2020/2021 | League D (Group Stage) |
| 2022/2023 | League D (Group Stage) |

## LIECHTENSTEIN CLUB HONOURS IN EUROPEAN CLUB COMPETITIONS:

### European Champion Clubs' Cup (1956-1992) / UEFA Champions League (1993-2023)
None

### Fairs Cup (1858-1971) / UEFA Cup (1972-2009) / UEFA Europa League (2010-2023)
None

### UEFA Europa Conference League (2021-2023)
None

### UEFA Super Cup (1972-2022)
None

### *European Cup Winners' Cup 1961-1999**
None

*defunct competition

|  | CHAMPIONS |
|---|---|
| 1932 | FC Vaduz (*unofficial*) |
| 1934 | FC Triesen |
| 1935 | FC Triesen |
| 1936 | FC Vaduz |
| 1937 | FC Triesen |

## CUP WINNERS

| | | | | | |
|---|---|---|---|---|---|
| 1945/1946 | FC Triesen | 1971/1972 | FC Triesen | 1997/1998 | FC Vaduz |
| 1946/1947 | FC Triesen | 1972/1973 | FC Balzers | 1998/1999 | FC Vaduz |
| 1947/1948 | FC Triesen | 1973/1974 | FC Vaduz | 1999/2000 | FC Vaduz |
| 1948/1949 | FC Vaduz | 1974/1975 | FC Triesen | 2000/2001 | FC Vaduz |
| 1949/1950 | FC Triesen | 1975/1976 | USV Eschen/Mauren | 2001/2002 | FC Vaduz |
| 1950/1951 | FC Triesen | 1976/1977 | USV Eschen/Mauren | 2002/2003 | FC Vaduz |
| 1951/1952 | FC Vaduz | 1977/1978 | USV Eschen/Mauren | 2003/2004 | FC Vaduz |
| 1952/1953 | FC Vaduz | 1978/1979 | FC Balzers | 2004/2005 | FC Vaduz |
| 1953/1954 | FC Vaduz | 1979/1980 | FC Vaduz | 2005/2006 | FC Vaduz |
| 1954/1955 | FC Schaan | 1980/1981 | FC Balzers | 2006/2007 | FC Vaduz |
| 1955/1956 | FC Vaduz | 1981/1982 | FC Balzers | 2007/2008 | FC Vaduz |
| 1956/1957 | FC Vaduz | 1982/1983 | FC Balzers | 2008/2009 | FC Vaduz |
| 1957/1958 | FC Vaduz | 1983/1984 | FC Balzers | 2009/2010 | FC Vaduz |
| 1958/1959 | FC Vaduz | 1984/1985 | FC Vaduz | 2010/2011 | FC Vaduz |
| 1959/1960 | FC Vaduz | 1985/1986 | FC Vaduz | 2011/2012 | USV Eschen/Mauren |
| 1960/1961 | FC Vaduz | 1986/1987 | USV Eschen/Mauren | 2012/2013 | FC Vaduz |
| 1961/1962 | FC Vaduz | 1987/1988 | FC Vaduz | 2013/2014 | FC Vaduz |
| 1962/1963 | FC Schaan | 1988/1989 | FC Balzers | 2014/2015 | FC Vaduz |
| 1963/1964 | FC Balzers | 1989/1990 | FC Vaduz | 2015/2016 | FC Vaduz |
| 1964/1965 | FC Triesen | 1990/1991 | FC Balzers | 2016/2017 | FC Vaduz |
| 1965/1966 | FC Vaduz | 1991/1992 | FC Vaduz | 2017/2018 | FC Vaduz |
| 1966/1967 | FC Vaduz | 1992/1993 | FC Balzers | 2018/2019 | FC Vaduz |
| 1967/1968 | FC Vaduz | 1993/1994 | FC Schaan | 2019/2020 | *Competition abandoned* |
| 1968/1969 | FC Vaduz | 1994/1995 | FC Vaduz | 2020/2021 | *Competition abandoned* |
| 1969/1970 | FC Vaduz | 1995/1996 | FC Vaduz | 2021/2022 | FC Vaduz |
| 1970/1971 | FC Vaduz | 1996/1997 | FC Balzers | 2022/2023 | FC Vaduz |

## NATIONAL CUP
### Liechtensteiner Cup 2022/2023

### 1/8-Finals [16-17/31.08.2022]

| | | | |
|---|---|---|---|
| FC Vaduz III - FC Schaan | 1-6 | FC Ruggell - USV Eschen/Mauren | 1-4 |
| FC Ruggell II - FC Vaduz II | 1-1 aet; 4-5 pen | FC Schaan II - USV Eschen/Mauren III | 3-7 |
| FC Triesenberg - FC Triesen | 5-3 | FC Triesenberg II - FC Balzers II | 1-4 |
| USV Eschen/Mauren II – FC Balzers | 0-9 | FC Triesen II - FC Vaduz | 0-18 |

### Quarter-Finals [20.09./11-12.10.2022]

| | | | |
|---|---|---|---|
| USV Eschen/Mauren III - FC Vaduz | 0-8 | FC Vaduz II - FC Balzers | 0-3 |
| FC Balzers II - FC Schaan | 3-2 | FC Triesenberg - USV Eschen/Mauren | 0-1 |

### Semi-Finals [15.03./05.04.2023]

| | | | |
|---|---|---|---|
| FC Balzers II - FC Balzers | 0-3 | USV Eschen/Mauren - FC Vaduz | 1-2 aet |

### Final

17.05.2023; Rheinpark Stadion, Vaduz; Referee: David Schärli (Switzerland); Attendance: 1,298

**FC Balzers - FC Vaduz**                                      **0-4(0-1)**

**FC Balzers**: Thomas Hobi, Aljaz Kavcic (60.Sandro Wolfinger), Tino Dietrich, Stéphane Houcine Nater, Stefan Cavigelli, Fabio Wolfinger, Emir Murati, Matti Forrer (73.Manuel Mikus), Medin Murati (25. Marc Triet), Alejandro Muñoz, Marco Wolfinger (60.Willy Pizzi). Trainer: Michele Polverino.

**FC Vaduz**: Benjamin Büchel, Fabio Fehr (60.Kristijan Dobras), Lars Mika Traber, Gabriel Isik, Dario Ulrich, Cédric Pascal Gasser, Milan Gajić (87.Ryan Fosso), Dejan Djokic (46.Elmin Rastoder), Nicolas Hasler, Tunahan Çiçek (75.Tim Väyrynen), Franklin Olanitori Sasere (46. Manuel Sutter). Trainer: Martin Stocklasa.

**Goals:** 0-1 Cédric Pascal Gasser (41), 0-2 Tunahan Çiçek (70 penalty), 0-3 Lars Mika Traber (77), 0-4 Tim Väyrynen (88).

## INTERNATIONAL MATCHES
### (16.07.2022 – 15.07.2023)

| | | | | |
|---|---|---|---|---|
| 22.09.2022 | Vaduz | *Liechtenstein - Andorra* | *0-2(0-1)* | (UNL) |
| 25.09.2022 | Chişinău | *Moldova - Liechtenstein* | *2-0(0-0)* | (UNL) |
| 16.11.2022 | Gibraltar | *Gibraltar - Liechtenstein* | *2-0(2-0)* | (F) |
| 23.03.2023 | Lisboa | *Portugal - Liechtenstein* | *4-0(1-0)* | (ECQ) |
| 26.03.2023 | Vaduz | *Liechtenstein - Iceland* | *0-7(0-2)* | (ECQ) |
| 17.06.2023 | Lëtzebuerg | *Luxembourg - Liechtenstein* | *2-0(0-0)* | (ECQ) |
| 20.06.2023 | Vaduz | *Liechtenstein - Slovakia* | *0-1(0-1)* | (ECQ) |

**22.09.2022   LIECHTENSTEIN - ANDORRA**          0-2(0-1)          3rd UEFA Nations League D, Group 1
Rheinpark Stadion, Vaduz; Referee: Juxhin Xhaja (Albania); Attendance: 914
**LIE:** Benjamin Büchel, Jens Hofer, Lars Mika Traber, Andreas Malin, Lukas Graber (46.Andrin Netzer), Simon Lüchinger (78.Marco Wolfinger), Noah Frommelt (46.Fabio Wolfinger), Maximilian Göppel, Livio Meier (46.Ridvan Kardesoglu), Nicolas Hasler (Cap), Philipp Gassner. Trainer: Martin Stocklasa.

**25.09.2022   MOLDOVA - LIECHTENSTEIN**          2-0(0-0)          3rd UEFA Nations League D, Group 1
Stadionul Zimbru, Chişinău; Referee: Stéphanie Frappart (France); Attendance: 5,774
**LIE:** Benjamin Büchel, Lars Mika Traber, Rafael Grünenfelder, Jens Hofer, Niklas Beck (86.Jakob Lorenz), Simon Lüchinger (56.Marco Wolfinger), Andrin Netzer (67.Lukas Graber), Maximilian Göppel, Aron Sele (86.Jonas Hilti), Nicolas Hasler (Cap), Philipp Gassner (56.Seyhan Yildiz). Trainer: Martin Stocklasa.

**16.11.2022   GIBRALTAR - LIECHTENSTEIN**          2-0(2-0)          Friendly International
Victoria Stadium, Gibraltar; Referee: Ahmad Faisal Al Ali (Kuwait); Attendance: 558
**LIE:** Benjamin Büchel (46.Justin Ospelt), Lars Mika Traber (61.Manuel Mikus), Jens Hofer (22.Martin Emanuel Marxer), Andreas Malin [*sent off 20*], Seyhan Yildiz, Aron Sele, Simon Lüchinger (71.Jakob Lorenz), Maximilian Göppel, Nicolas Hasler (Cap) (61.Niklas Beck), Livio Meier, Dennis Salanović (71.Noah Zinedine Frick). Trainer: Martin Stocklasa.

**23.03.2023   PORTUGAL - LIECHTENSTEIN**          4-0(1-0)          17th EC. Qualifiers
Estádio "José Alvalade", Lisboa; Referee: Espen Eskås (Norway); Attendance: 45,378
**LIE:** Benjamin Büchel, Andreas Malin (38.Simon Lüchinger), Jens Hofer, Lars Mika Traber, Sandro Wolfinger (80.Seyhan Yildiz), Nicolas Hasler (Cap), Noah Frommelt, Livio Meier (60.Fabio Wolfinger), Sandro Wieser, Aron Sele (80.Niklas Beck), Philipp Gassner (60.Jakob Lorenz). Trainer: René Pauritsch (Austria).

**26.03.2023   LIECHTENSTEIN - ICELAND**          0-7(0-2)          17th EC. Qualifiers
Rheinpark Stadion, Vaduz; Referee: Jakob Kehlet (Denmark); Attendance: 1,692
**LIE:** Benjamin Büchel, Noah Frommelt, Jens Hofer, Lars Mika Traber, Sandro Wolfinger (72.Seyhan Yildiz), Nicolas Hasler (Cap), Simon Lüchinger (46.Andrin Netzer), Sandro Wieser (77.Niklas Beck), Livio Meier (46.Fabio Wolfinger), Aron Sele, Philipp Gassner (68.Noah Zinedine Frick). Trainer: René Pauritsch (Austria).

**17.06.2023   LUXEMBOURG - LIECHTENSTEIN**          2-0(0-0)          17th EC. Qualifiers
Stade de Luxembourg, Lëtzebuerg; Referee: Oleksiy Derevinskyi (Ukraine); Attendance: 6,806
**LIE:** Benjamin Büchel, Niklas Beck, Lars Mika Traber, Andreas Malin, Livio Meier (55.Andrin Netzer), Aron Sele, Simon Lüchinger (75.Jens Hofer), Nicolas Hasler (Cap) (24.Sandro Wolfinger), Maximilian Göppel (75.Fabio Wolfinger), Ferhat Sağlam (55.Seyhan Yildiz), Dennis Salanović. Trainer: Konrad Fünfstück (Germany).

**20.06.2023   LIECHTENSTEIN - SLOVAKIA**          0-1(0-1)          17th EC. Qualifiers
Rheinpark Stadion, Vaduz; Referee: Yigal Frid (Israel); Attendance: 2,316
**LIE:** Benjamin Büchel (Cap), Jens Hofer, Lars Mika Traber, Niklas Beck, Sandro Wolfinger (62.Lukas Graber), Aron Sele (90.Julien Hasler), Simon Lüchinger (77.Colin Haas), Fabio Wolfinger (62.Livio Meier), Maximilian Göppel, Ferhat Sağlam (77.Philipp Gassner), Dennis Salanović. Trainer: Konrad Fünfstück (Germany).

## NATIONAL TEAM PLAYERS
### (16.07.2022 – 15.07.2023)

| Name | DOB | Caps | Goals | Club |
|------|-----|------|-------|------|

### Goalkeepers

| Name | DOB | Caps | Goals | Club |
|------|-----|------|-------|------|
| Benjamin BÜCHEL | 04.07.1989 | 55 | 0 | 2022/2023: *FC Vaduz* |
| Justin OSPELT | 07.09.1999 | 4 | 0 | 2022: *FC Dornbirn (AUT)* |

### Defenders

| Name | DOB | Caps | Goals | Club |
|------|-----|------|-------|------|
| Lukas GRABER | 03.05.2001 | 6 | 0 | 2022/2023: *USV Eschen/Mauren* |
| Maximilian GÖPPEL | 31.08.1997 | 53 | 2 | 2022/2023: *USV Eschen/Mauren* |
| Rafael GRÜNENFELDER | 20.03.1999 | 16 | 0 | 2022: *FC Balzers* |
| Jonas HILTI | 22.03.2000 | 1 | 0 | 2022: *FC Vaduz* |
| Jens HOFER | 01.10.1997 | 30 | 0 | 2022: *FC Biel-Bienne (SUI)* <br> 26.01.2023-> *FC Solothurn (SUI)* |
| Andreas MALIN | 31.01.1994 | 43 | 0 | 2022/2023: *FC Rot-Weiß Rankweil (AUT)* |
| Martin Emanuel MARXER | 04.10.1999 | 4 | 0 | 2022: *FC Muri-Gümlingen (SUI)* |
| Manuel MIKUS | 13.07.1999 | 1 | 0 | 2022: *FC Vaduz* |
| Lars Mika TRABER | 12.07.2000 | 8 | 0 | 2022/2023: *FC Vaduz* |
| Marco WOLFINGER | 18.04.1989 | 3 | 0 | 2022: *FC Balzers* |
| Seyhan YILDIZ | 30.04.1989 | 62 | 1 | 2022/2023: *USV Eschen/Mauren* |

### Midfielders

| Name | DOB | Caps | Goals | Club |
|------|-----|------|-------|------|
| Niklas BECK | 25.03.2001 | 12 | 0 | 2022: *FC Vaduz* <br> 01.01.2023-> *USV Eschen/Mauren* |
| Noah FROMMELT | 18.12.2000 | 21 | 0 | 2022/2023: *FC Kosova Zürich (SUI)* |
| Colin HAAS | 30.05.1996 | 1 | 0 | 2023: *FC Rugell* |
| Nicolas HASLER | 04.05.1991 | 94 | 5 | 2022/2023: *FC Vaduz* |
| Ridvan KARDESOGLU | 12.10.1996 | 10 | 0 | 2022: *FC Nensing (AUT)* |
| Jakob LORENZ | 11.09.2001 | 3 | 0 | 2022/2023: *FC Vaduz* |
| Simon LÜCHINGER | 28.11.2002 | 12 | 0 | 2022/2023: *FC Vaduz* |
| Livio MEIER | 10.01.1998 | 34 | 1 | 2022/2023: *USV Eschen/Mauren* |
| Andrin NETZER | 11.01.2002 | 10 | 0 | 2022/2023: *FC Vaduz* |
| Aron SELE | 02.09.1996 | 48 | 0 | 2022/2023: *FC Chur 97 (SUI)* |
| Sandro WIESER | 03.02.1996 | 55 | 2 | 2023: *FC Vaduz* |
| Fabio WOLFINGER | 11.05.1996 | 25 | 1 | 2022/2023: *FC Balzers* |
| Sandro WOLFINGER | 24.08.1991 | 57 | 2 | 2023: *FC Balzers* |

### Forwards

| Name | DOB | Caps | Goals | Club |
|------|-----|------|-------|------|
| Noah Zinedine FRICK | 26.10.2001 | 20 | 2 | 2022/2023: *FC Montlingen (SUI)* |
| Philipp GASSNER | 30.08.2003 | 6 | 0 | 2022/2023: *FC Dornbirn (AUT)* |
| Julien HASLER | 22.09.1989 | 1 | 0 | 2023: *FC Triesen* |
| Ferhat SAĞLAM | 10.10.2001 | 2 | 0 | 2023: *FC Vaduz* |
| Dennis SALANOVIĆ | 26.02.1996 | 52 | 4 | 2022: *FC Lahti (FIN); 01.01.2023-> unattached* <br> 08.03.2023-> *CF Talavera de la Reina (ESP)* |

### Trainer

| Name | DOB | Record |
|------|-----|--------|
| Martin STOCKLASA [01.01.2021 - 28.02.2023] | 29.05.1979 | 21 M; 0 W; 1 D; 20 L; 4-66 |
| René PAURITSCH (Austria) [01.03.2023 - 31.05.2023] | 04.02.1964 | 2 M; 0 W; 0 D; 2 L; 0-11 <br> Complete record as trainer of Liechtenstein: <br> 51 M; 4 W; 7 D; 40 L; 22-139 <br> (06.02.2013 – 19.11.2018) & (01.03.2023 – 31.05.2023) |
| Konrad FÜNFSTÜCK (Germany) [from 01.06.2023] | 07.10.1980 | 2 M; 0 W; 0 D; 2 L; 0-3 |

# LITHUANIA

## The Country:
Lietuvos Respublika (Republic of Lithuania)
Capital: Vilnius
Surface: 65,300 km²
Inhabitants: 2,840,758 [2022]
Time: UTC+2

## The FA:
Lietuvos futbolo federacija
Stadiono g. 2, 02106 Vilnius
Tel: +370 5 2638741
Foundation date: 1922
Member of FIFA since: 1923
Member of UEFA since: 1992
Website: www.lff.lt

## NATIONAL TEAM RECORDS

| | | |
|---|---|---|
| **First international match:** | 24.06.1923, Kaunas: | Lithuania – Estonia 0-5 |
| **Most international caps:** | Saulius Mikoliūnas | - 101 caps (2004-2022) |
| **Most international goals:** | Tomas Danilevičius | - 19 goals / 71 caps (1998-2014) |

### UEFA EUROPEAN CHAMPIONSHIP

| | |
|---|---|
| 1960 | - |
| 1964 | - |
| 1968 | - |
| 1972 | - |
| 1976 | - |
| 1980 | - |
| 1984 | - |
| 1988 | - |
| 1992 | - |
| 1996 | Qualifiers |
| 2000 | Qualifiers |
| 2004 | Qualifiers |
| 2008 | Qualifiers |
| 2012 | Qualifiers |
| 2016 | Qualifiers |
| 2020 | Qualifiers |

### FIFA WORLD CUP

| | |
|---|---|
| 1930 | Did not enter |
| 1934 | Qualifiers |
| 1938 | Qualifiers |
| 1950 | - |
| 1954 | - |
| 1958 | - |
| 1962 | - |
| 1966 | - |
| 1970 | - |
| 1974 | - |
| 1978 | - |
| 1982 | - |
| 1986 | - |
| 1990 | - |
| 1994 | Qualifiers |
| 1998 | Qualifiers |
| 2002 | Qualifiers |
| 2006 | Qualifiers |
| 2010 | Qualifiers |
| 2014 | Qualifiers |
| 2018 | Qualifiers |
| 2022 | Qualifiers |

### OLYMPIC TOURNAMENTS

| | |
|---|---|
| 1908 | - |
| 1912 | - |
| 1920 | - |
| 1924 | FT/Preliminary Round |
| 1928 | - |
| 1936 | - |
| 1948 | - |
| 1952 | - |
| 1956 | - |
| 1960 | - |
| 1964 | - |
| 1968 | - |
| 1972 | - |
| 1976 | - |
| 1980 | - |
| 1984 | - |
| 1988 | - |
| 1992 | - |
| 1996 | Qualifiers |
| 2000 | Qualifiers |
| 2004 | Qualifiers |
| 2008 | Qualifiers |
| 2012 | Qualifiers |
| 2016 | Qualifiers |
| 2020 | Qualifiers |

<u>Please note</u>: *was part of Soviet Union from 1944 to 1990.*

## UEFA NATIONS LEAGUE

| | |
|---|---|
| 2018/2019 | League C (Group Stage) |
| 2020/2021 | League C (Group Stage) |
| 2022/2023 | League C (Group Stage -> relegation Play-outs in March 2024) |

## LITHUANIAN CLUB HONOURS IN EUROPEAN CLUB COMPETITIONS:

### European Champion Clubs' Cup (1956-1992) / UEFA Champions League (1993-2023)
None

### Fairs Cup (1858-1971) / UEFA Cup (1972-2009) / UEFA Europa League (2010-2023)
None

### UEFA Europa Conference League (2021-2023)
None

### UEFA Super Cup (1972-2022)
None

### *European Cup Winners' Cup 1961-1999*\*
None

*\*defunct competition*

# NATIONAL COMPETITIONS
# TABLE OF HONOURS

## LITHUANIAN SSR (SOVIET ERA) CHAMPIONS

| | | | | | | |
|---|---|---|---|---|---|---|
| 1945 | Spartakas Kaunas | 1959/1960 | Elnias Šiauliai | 1975 | Dainava Alytus |
| 1946 | Dinamo Kaunas | 1960/1961 | Elnias Šiauliai | 1976 | Atmosfera Mažeikiai |
| 1947 | Lokomotyvas Kaunas | 1961/1962 | FK Atletas Kaunas | 1977 | Statybininkas Šiauliai |
| 1948 | Elnias Šiauliai | 1962/1963 | Statyba Panevėžys | 1978 | Atlantas Klaipėda |
| 1949 | Elnias Šiauliai | 1964 | Inkaras Kaunas | 1979 | Atmosfera Mažeikiai |
| 1950 | Inkaras Kaunas | 1965 | Inkaras Kaunas | 1980 | Atlantas Klaipėda |
| 1951 | Inkaras Kaunas | 1966 | Nevėžis Kėdainiai | 1981 | Atlantas Klaipėda |
| 1952 | Karininkų Namai Vilnius | 1967 | Saliutas Vilnius | 1982 | Pažanga Vilnius |
| 1953 | Elnias Šiauliai | 1968 | Statyba Panevėžys | 1983 | Pažanga Vilnius |
| 1954 | Inkaras Kaunas | 1969 | Statybininkas Šiauliai | 1984 | Atlantas Klaipėda |
| 1955 | Lima Kaunas | 1970 | FK Atletas Kaunas | 1985 | Ekranas Panevėžys |
| 1956 | Linų Audiniai Plungė | 1971 | Pažanga Vilnius | 1986 | Banga Kaunas |
| 1957 | Elnias Šiauliai | 1972 | Nevėžis Kėdainiai | 1987 | Tauras Tauragė |
| 1958 | Elnias Šiauliai | 1973 | Nevėžis Kėdainiai | 1988 | SRT Vilnius |
| 1958/1959 | Raudonoji Žvaigždė Vilnius | 1974 | Tauras Šiauliai | 1989 | Banga Kaunas |

| | CHAMPIONS | CUP WINNERS | BEST GOALSCORERS | |
|---|---|---|---|---|
| 1922 | LFLS Kaunas | - | - | |
| 1923 | LFLS Kaunas | - | - | |
| 1924 | Kovas Kaunas | - | - | |
| 1925 | Kovas Kaunas | - | - | |
| 1926 | Kovas Kaunas | - | - | |
| 1927 | LFLS Kaunas | - | - | |
| 1928 | KSS Klaipėda | - | - | |
| 1929 | KSS Klaipėda | - | - | |
| 1930 | KSS Klaipėda | - | - | |
| 1931 | KSS Klaipėda | - | - | |
| 1932 | LFLS Kaunas | - | - | |
| 1933 | Kovas Kaunas | - | - | |
| 1934 | MSK Kaunas | - | - | |
| 1935 | Kovas Kaunas | - | - | |
| 1936 | Kovas Kaunas | - | - | |
| 1937 | KSS Klaipėda | - | - | |
| 1937/1938 | KSS Klaipėda | - | - | |
| 1938/1939 | LGSF Kaunas | - | - | |
| 1939/1940 | *Competition abandoned* | - | - | |
| 1941 | *Competition not finished* | - | - | |
| 1942 | LFLS Kaunas | - | - | |
| 1942/1943 | Tauras Kaunas | - | - | |
| 1943/1944 | *Competition not finished* | - | - | |
| | ------------------------------- | ------------------------------- | ---------------------------------------------------------------- | |
| 1990 | FK Sirijus Klaipėda | FK Sirijus Klaipėda | Dalius Bajorūnas (FK Tauras Šiauliai) | 22 |
| 1991 | FK Žalgiris Vilnius | FK Žalgiris Vilnius | Egidijus Meidus (Vilija Kaunas) | 13 |
| 1991/1992 | FK Žalgiris Vilnius | FK Makabi Vilnius | Remigijus Pocius (FK Granitas Klaipėda / FK Sakalas Šiauliai) Vaidotas Šlekys (FK Ekranas Panevėžys) | 14 |
| 1992/1993 | FK Ekranas Panevėžys | FK Žalgiris Vilnius | Vaidotas Šlekys (FK Ekranas Panevėžys) | 16 |
| 1993/1994 | ROMAR Mažeikiai | FK Žalgiris Vilnius | Vaidotas Šlekys (FK Ekranas Panevėžys) Robertas Žalys (FBK Kaunas) | 16 |
| 1994/1995 | FK Inkaras-Grifas Kaunas | FK Inkaras-Grifas Kaunas | Eimantas Poderis (FK Žalgiris Vilnius / FK Inkaras-Grifas Kaunas) | 24 |
| 1995/1996 | FK Inkaras-Grifas Kaunas | FK Kareda-Sakalas Šiauliai | Edgaras Jankauskas (FK Žalgiris Vilnius) | 25 |
| 1996/1997 | FK Kareda Šiauliai | FK Žalgiris Vilnius | Remigijus Pocius (FK Kareda Šiauliai) | 14 |
| 1997/1998 | FK Kareda Šiauliai | FK Ekranas Panevėžys | Vidas Dančenka (FK Kareda Šiauliai) | 26 |
| 1998/1999 | FK Žalgiris Vilnius | FK Kareda Šiauliai | Artūras Fomenka (FK Kareda Šiauliai) | 14 |
| 1999 | FBK Kaunas | *No competition* | Nerijus Vasiliauskas (FK Žalgiris Vilnius) | 10 |
| 2000 | FBK Kaunas | FK Ekranas Panevėžys (1999/2000) | Andrius Velička (FBK Kaunas) | 26 |
| 2001 | FBK Kaunas | FK Atlantas Klaipėda (2000/01) | Remigijus Pocius (FBK Kaunas) | 22 |
| 2002 | FBK Kaunas | FBK Kaunas (2001/02) | Audrius Šlekys (FBK Kaunas) | 19 |
| 2003 | FBK Kaunas | FK Sūduva Marijampolė (2002/03) FK Žalgiris Vilnius (2003) | Ričardas Beniušis (FK Atlantas Klaipėda / FBK Kaunas) | 16 |
| 2004 | FBK Kaunas | FBK Kaunas | Povilas Lukšys (FK Ekranas Panevėžys) | 19 |
| 2005 | FK Ekranas Panevėžys | FBK Kaunas | Mantas Savėnas (FK Ekranas Panevėžys) | 27 |
| 2006 | FBK Kaunas | FK Sūduva Marijampolė | Serhiy Kuznetsov (UKR, FK Vėtra Vilnius) | 18 |
| 2007 | FBK Kaunas | *No competition* | Povilas Lukšys (FK Ekranas Panevėžys) | 26 |
| 2008 | FK Ekranas Panevėžys | FBK Kaunas (2007/08) | Rafael Pompeo Rodrigues Ledesma (BRA, FBK Kaunas) | 14 |
| 2009 | FK Ekranas Panevėžys | FK Sūduva Marijampolė (2008/09) | Valdas Trakys (FK Ekranas Panevėžys) | 20 |
| 2010 | FK Ekranas Panevėžys | FK Ekranas Panevėžys (2009/10) | Povilas Lukšys (FK Sūduva Marijampolė) | 16 |
| 2011 | FK Ekranas Panevėžys | FK Ekranas Panevėžys (2010/11) | Deivydas Matulevičius (FK Žalgiris Vilnius) | 19 |

| 2012 | FK Ekranas Panevėžys | FK Žalgiris Vilnius (2011/12) | Artūras Rimkevičius (FK Šiauliai) | 35 |
|------|----------------------|------------------------------|-----------------------------------|-----|
| 2013 | FK Žalgiris Vilnius | FK Žalgiris Vilnius (2012/13) | Nerijus Valskis (FK Sūduva Marijampolė) | 27 |
| 2014 | FK Žalgiris Vilnius | FK Žalgiris Vilnius (2013/14) | Niko Tokić (CRO, FK Šiauliai) | 19 |
| 2015 | FK Žalgiris Vilnius | FK Žalgiris Vilnius (2014/15) | Tomas Radzinevičius (FK Sūduva Marijampolė) | 28 |
| 2016 | FK Žalgiris Vilnius | FK Žalgiris Vilnius (2015/16) FK Žalgiris Vilnius (2016) | Andrija Kaluđerović (SRB, FK Žalgiris Vilnius) | 20 |
| 2017 | FK Sūduva Marijampolė | FC Stumbras Kaunas | Darvydas Šernas (FK Žalgiris Vilnius) | 18 |
| 2018 | FK Sūduva Marijampolė | FK Žalgiris Vilnius | Liviu Ion Antal (ROU, FK Žalgiris Vilnius) | 23 |
| 2019 | FK Sūduva Marijampolė | FK Sūduva Marijampolė | Tomislav Kiš (CRO, FK Žalgiris Vilnius) | 27 |
| 2020 | FK Žalgiris Vilnius | FK Panevėžys | Hugo Robin Vidémont (FRA, FK Žalgiris Vilnius) | 13 |
| 2021 | FK Žalgiris Vilnius | FK Žalgiris Vilnius | Hugo Robin Vidémont (FRA, FK Žalgiris Vilnius) | 17 |
| 2022 | FK Žalgiris Vilnius | FK Žalgiris Vilnius | Renan Henrique Oliveira Vieira (BRA, FK Žalgiris Vilnius) | 17 |

## NATIONAL CHAMPIONSHIP
### A Lyga 2022
(04.03.2022 – 23.11.2022)

### Results

**Round 1** [04-06.03.2022]
FK Žalgiris - FC Jonava 6-0(3-0)
FK Hegelmann - FK Kauno Žalgiris 2-1(0-0)
FA Šiauliai - FK Sūduva 0-0
FK Riteriai - FK Panevėžys 0-0
Banga G. - FC Džiugas 3-3(2-1) [26.03.2022]

**Round 2** [11-13.03.2022]
FK Panevėžys - FK Kauno Žalgiris 1-0(0-0)
FC Jonava - FK Hegelmann 1-4(0-3)
FC Džiugas - FK Riteriai 0-1(0-1)
FK Sūduva - Banga Gargždai 3-0(2-0)
FK Žalgiris - FA Šiauliai 0-0

**Round 3** [15-16.03.2022]
FK Hegelmann - FK Panevėžys 0-1(0-0)
FK Kauno Žalgiris - FC Džiugas 2-1(2-0)
FA Šiauliai - FC Jonava 3-0(1-0)
Banga Gargždai - FK Žalgiris 0-2(0-2)
FK Riteriai - FK Sūduva 2-0(1-0)

**Round 4** [19-20.03.2022]
FC Jonava - Banga Gargždai 1-3(0-0)
FK Sūduva - FK Kauno Žalgiris 1-1(1-0)
FC Džiugas - FK Panevėžys 0-1(0-0)
FK Hegelmann - FA Šiauliai 1-0(0-0)
FK Žalgiris - FK Riteriai 2-0(1-0)

**Round 5** [01-03.04.2022]
FK Riteriai - FC Jonava 5-0(2-0)
FK Panevėžys - FK Sūduva 2-1(0-0)
FC Džiugas - FK Hegelmann 1-1(1-0)
FK Kauno Žalgiris - FK Žalgiris 2-2(0-0)
Banga Gargždai - FA Šiauliai 0-0

**Round 6** [05-06.04.2022]
FC Jonava - FK Kauno Žalgiris 0-2(0-0)
FK Žalgiris - FK Panevėžys 0-0
FK Sūduva - FC Džiugas 1-1(0-1)
FK Hegelmann - Banga Gargždai 2-0(1-0)
FA Šiauliai - FK Riteriai 1-0(0-0)

**Round 7** [09-10.04.2022]
FK Panevėžys - FC Jonava 4-0(1-0)
FK Kauno Žalgiris - FA Šiauliai 0-0
FK Riteriai - Banga Gargždai 1-0(0-0)
FK Sūduva - FK Hegelmann 0-1(0-0)
FC Džiugas - Žalgiris 3-5(1-2) [13.04.2022]

**Round 8** [15-17.04.2022]
Banga Gargždai - FK Kauno Žalgiris 3-1(1-1)
FK Hegelmann - FK Riteriai 1-1(0-1)
FA Šiauliai - FK Panevėžys 0-3(0-2)
FC Jonava - FC Džiugas 0-1(0-0)
FK Žalgiris - FK Sūduva 0-0

**Round 9** [22-24.04.2022]
FK Kauno Žalgiris - FK Riteriai 0-1(0-0)
FK Panevėžys - Banga Gargždai 2-0(1-0)
FC Džiugas - FA Šiauliai 0-0
FK Hegelmann - FK Žalgiris 2-2(0-1)
FK Sūduva - FC Jonava 2-0(1-0)

**Round 10** [26-27.04.2022]
FC Džiugas - Banga Gargždai 0-0
FK Kauno Žalgiris - FK Hegelmann 1-3(0-2)
FK Panevėžys - FK Riteriai 3-0(2-0)
FC Jonava - FK Žalgiris 0-5(0-3)
FK Sūduva - FA Šiauliai 2-0(0-0)

**Round 11** [30.04.-01.05.2022]
FK Hegelmann - FC Jonava 4-0(2-0)
FK Kauno Žalgiris - FK Panevėžys 2-1(0-1)
FA Šiauliai - FK Žalgiris 0-1(0-1)
Banga Gargždai - FK Sūduva 0-1(0-1)
FK Riteriai - FC Džiugas 3-0(1-0)

**Round 12** [03-04.05.2022]
FK Panevėžys - FK Hegelmann 1-1(0-1)
FC Jonava - FA Šiauliai 0-3(0-1)
FC Džiugas - FK Kauno Žalgiris 1-2(0-1)
FK Sūduva - FK Riteriai 1-1(0-0)
FK Žalgiris - Banga Gargždai 2-1(1-1)

**Round 13** [14-15.05.2022]
FK Kauno Žalgiris - FK Sūduva 0-3(0-3)
FK Riteriai - FK Žalgiris 0-1(0-1)
Banga Gargždai - FC Jonava 1-1(1-1)
FK Panevėžys - FC Džiugas 1-0(0-0)
FA Šiauliai - FK Hegelmann 0-0

**Round 14** [21-22.05.2022]
FK Hegelmann - FC Džiugas 2-0(1-0)
FK Sūduva - FK Panevėžys 2-1(2-1)
FA Šiauliai - Banga Gargždai 1-1(0-1)
FK Žalgiris - FK Kauno Žalgiris 1-2(1-1)
FC Jonava - FK Riteriai 0-1(0-1) [29.05.2022]

**Round 15** [17-19.06.2022]
Banga Gargždai - FK Hegelmann 1-0(0-0)
FC Džiugas - FK Sūduva 2-2(1-1)
FK Riteriai - FA Šiauliai 1-1(0-0)
FK Kauno Žalgiris - FC Jonava 4-0(1-0)
FK Panevėžys - FK Žalgiris 0-2(0-2)

**Round 16** [21-22.06.2022]
FK Hegelmann - FK Sūduva 2-2(0-0)
Banga Gargždai - FK Riteriai 0-4(0-0)
FC Jonava - FK Panevėžys 0-5(0-3)
FA Šiauliai - FK Kauno Žalgiris 0-1(0-1)
FK Žalgiris - FC Džiugas 2-1(0-0)

**Round 17** [25-26.06.2022]
FK Panevėžys - FA Šiauliai 1-2(1-1)
FK Riteriai - FK Hegelmann 0-3(0-2)
FC Džiugas - FC Jonava 2-0(1-0)
FK Sūduva - FK Žalgiris 0-5(0-2)
FK Kauno Žalgiris - Banga Gargždai 1-1(0-1)

**Round 18** [01-03.07.2022]
FK Žalgiris - FK Hegelmann 2-1(1-0)
FC Jonava - FK Sūduva 0-4(0-0)
Banga Gargždai - FK Panevėžys 1-2(1-1)
FK Riteriai - FK Kauno Žalgiris 1-1(0-0)
FA Šiauliai - FC Džiugas 3-2(2-1)

**Round 19** [29-31.07.2022]
Banga Gargždai - FC Džiugas 1-1(0-0)
FK Riteriai - FA Šiauliai 3-1(2-0)
FC Jonava - FK Hegelmann 0-1(0-1)
Kauno Žalgiris-Sūduva 2-2(1-2) [02.08.2022]
Žalgiris - FK Panevėžys 0-1(0-1) [09.11.2022]

**Round 20** [09-10.07.2022]
FK Hegelmann - Banga Gargždai 5-0(2-0)
FC Džiugas - FK Riteriai 0-4(0-1)
Žalgiris - FK Sūduva 1-0(1-0) [27.09.2022]
FA Šiauliai - FC Jonava 2-0(2-0) [15.10.2022]
Kauno Žalgiris - Panevėžys 0-0 [05.11.2022]

**Round 21** [05-07.08.2022]
FA Šiauliai - FK Hegelmann 0-0
FC Džiugas - FC Jonava 2-2(2-0)
FK Žalgiris - Banga Gargždai 2-1(0-0)
FK Kauno Žalgiris - FK Riteriai 2-0(1-0)
FK Sūduva - FK Panevėžys 4-1(2-0)

**Round 22** [12-14.08.2022]
FK Hegelmann - FC Džiugas 5-0(2-0)
FC Jonava - FK Kauno Žalgiris 1-2(1-1)
FK Panevėžys - FA Šiauliai 1-2(0-1)
FK Riteriai - FK Žalgiris 1-5(1-2)
Banga Gargždai - FK Sūduva 0-0

**Round 23** [20-21.08.2022]
FK Hegelmann - FK Kauno Žalgiris 1-1(1-0)
FA Šiauliai - FC Džiugas 2-2(1-2)
FK Panevėžys - Banga Gargždai 2-1(2-0)
FK Žalgiris - FC Jonava 3-1(1-0)
FK Sūduva - FK Riteriai 2-1(1-1)

**Round 24** [26-28.08.2022]
Banga Gargždai - FK Riteriai 0-1(0-1)
FC Jonava - FK Sūduva 0-2(0-2)
FK Panevėžys - FC Džiugas 3-2(2-0)
FA Šiauliai - FK Kauno Žalgiris 0-3(0-1)
FK Hegelmann - FK Žalgiris 1-4(1-3)

| Round 25 [02-04.09.2022] |
|---|
| Sūduva - FA Šiauliai 2-1(1-0) [09.07.2022] |
| FK Hegelmann - FK Panevėžys 1-1(0-1) |
| FC Džiugas - FK Žalgiris 1-1(0-1) |
| FK Riteriai - FC Jonava 2-1(0-1) |
| Banga Gargždai - FK Kauno Žalgiris 0-1(0-0) |

| Round 26 [06-07.09.2022] |
|---|
| FK Sūduva - FK Hegelmann 2-1(1-0) |
| FK Kauno Žalgiris - FC Džiugas 5-1(1-0) |
| FC Jonava - Banga Gargždai 0-5(0-4) |
| FK Panevėžys - FK Riteriai 0-1(0-0) |
| Žalgiris - FA Šiauliai 5-0(3-0) [20.11.2022] |

| Round 27 [10-11.09.2022] |
|---|
| FC Džiugas - FK Sūduva 2-1(1-0) |
| FC Jonava - FK Panevėžys 1-1(1-1) |
| FK Kauno Žalgiris - FK Žalgiris 0-2(0-0) |
| FK Riteriai - FK Hegelmann 0-0 |
| FA Šiauliai - Banga Gargždai 1-1(0-0) |

| Round 28 [15-17.07.2022] |
|---|
| FA Šiauliai - FK Riteriai 3-2(2-1) |
| FK Hegelmann - FC Jonava 6-0(3-0) |
| FC Džiugas - Banga Gargždai 0-1(0-0) |
| Sūduva - Kauno Žalgiris 0-2(0-2) [19.10.22] |
| FK Panevėžys - Žalgiris 0-1(0-1) [19.10.2022] |

| Round 29 [22-24.07.2022] |
|---|
| FK Riteriai - FC Džiugas 2-1(1-1) |
| FK Panevėžys - FK Kauno Žalgiris 2-1(1-0) |
| FC Jonava - FA Šiauliai 1-3(0-1) |
| Banga Gargždai - FK Hegelmann 1-1(0-0) |
| FK Sūduva - Žalgiris 1-2(1-1) [06.11.2022] |

| Round 30 [16-18.09.2022] |
|---|
| FK Kauno Žalgiris - FC Jonava 2-1(1-1) |
| FC Džiugas - FK Hegelmann 0-1(0-1) |
| FA Šiauliai - FK Panevėžys 1-0(0-0) |
| FK Sūduva - Banga Gargždai 2-0(2-0) |
| FK Žalgiris - FK Riteriai 3-1(2-0) |

| Round 31 [01-02.10.2022] |
|---|
| FC Jonava - FC Džiugas 0-1(0-1) |
| FK Hegelmann - FA Šiauliai 2-1(1-0) |
| FK Panevėžys - FK Sūduva 2-0(0-0) |
| Riteriai - Kauno Žalgiris 2-0(0-0) [08.11.22] |
| Banga Gargždai - Žalgiris 0-2(0-2) [17.11.22] |

| Round 32 [08-09.10.2022] |
|---|
| FC Džiugas - FA Šiauliai 1-0(0-0) |
| FK Kauno Žalgiris - FK Hegelmann 1-1(1-1) |
| FC Jonava - FK Žalgiris 0-4(0-3) |
| FK Riteriai - FK Sūduva 2-3(1-3) |
| Banga Gargždai - FK Panevėžys 1-1(0-1) |

| Round 33 [21-23.10.2022] |
|---|
| FK Riteriai - Banga Gargždai 2-2(0-0) |
| FC Džiugas - FK Panevėžys 0-0 |
| FK Sūduva - FC Jonava 1-0(0-0) |
| FK Kauno Žalgiris - FA Šiauliai 1-0(1-0) |
| FK Žalgiris - FK Hegelmann 2-1(1-1) |

| Round 34 [29-30.10.2022] |
|---|
| FK Kauno Žalgiris - Banga Gargždai 3-0(1-0) |
| FA Šiauliai - FK Sūduva 2-0(2-0) |
| FC Jonava - FK Riteriai 0-3(0-0) |
| FK Žalgiris - FC Džiugas 6-0(2-0) |
| FK Panevėžys - FK Hegelmann 3-1(2-1) |

| Round 35 [11-13.11.2022] |
|---|
| Banga Gargždai - FC Jonava 2-0(1-0) |
| FC Džiugas - FK Kauno Žalgiris 0-3(0-1) |
| FK Hegelmann - FK Sūduva 2-0(2-0) |
| FA Šiauliai - FK Žalgiris 3-0(1-0) |
| FK Riteriai - FK Panevėžys 2-1(1-1) |

| Round 36 [23.11.2022] |
|---|
| FK Žalgiris - FK Kauno Žalgiris 2-3(0-2) |
| Banga Gargždai - FA Šiauliai 2-3(1-3) |
| FK Hegelmann - FK Riteriai 2-2(0-0) |
| FK Panevėžys - FC Jonava 2-1(2-1) |
| FK Sūduva - FC Džiugas 1-1(1-0) |

## Final Standings

| | | Total | | | | | | Home | | | | | | Away | | | |
|---|---|---|---|---|---|---|---|---|---|---|---|---|---|---|---|---|---|---|
| 1. | **FK Žalgiris Vilnius** | 36 | 26 | 6 | 4 | 85 - 27 | **84** | 12 | 3 | 3 | 39 - 13 | | 14 | 3 | 1 | 46 - 14 |
| 2. | FK Kauno Žalgiris Kaunas | 36 | 18 | 9 | 9 | 55 - 37 | **63** | 8 | 6 | 4 | 28 - 19 | | 10 | 3 | 5 | 27 - 18 |
| 3. | FK Panevėžys | 36 | 18 | 8 | 10 | 50 - 31 | **62** | 12 | 1 | 5 | 30 - 16 | | 6 | 7 | 5 | 20 - 15 |
| 4. | FC Hegelmann Litauen Kaunas | 36 | 16 | 13 | 7 | 62 - 32 | **61** | 10 | 6 | 2 | 41 - 16 | | 6 | 7 | 5 | 21 - 16 |
| 5. | FK Riteriai Vilnius | 36 | 17 | 8 | 11 | 53 - 41 | **59** | 9 | 5 | 4 | 29 - 20 | | 8 | 3 | 7 | 24 - 21 |
| 6. | FK Sūduva Marijampolė | 36 | 15 | 10 | 11 | 48 - 40 | **55** | 10 | 4 | 4 | 27 - 19 | | 5 | 6 | 7 | 21 - 21 |
| 7. | FA Šiauliai | 36 | 13 | 11 | 12 | 39 - 39 | **50** | 8 | 6 | 4 | 22 - 16 | | 5 | 5 | 8 | 17 - 23 |
| 8. | FK Banga Gargždai | 36 | 6 | 12 | 18 | 33 - 54 | **30** | 3 | 7 | 8 | 16 - 24 | | 3 | 5 | 10 | 17 - 30 |
| 9. | FC Džiugas Telšiai *(Relegation Play-offs)* | 36 | 5 | 12 | 19 | 34 - 67 | **27** | 3 | 7 | 8 | 16 - 25 | | 2 | 5 | 11 | 18 - 42 |
| 10. | FK Jonava *(Relegated)* | 36 | 0 | 3 | 33 | 12 - 103 | **3** | 0 | 1 | 17 | 5 - 50 | | 0 | 2 | 16 | 7 - 53 |

| Top goalscorers: | | |
|---|---|---|
| 17 | **Renan Henrique Oliveira Vieira (BRA)** | *FK Žalgiris Vilnius* |
| 13 | Vilius Armanavičius | *FC Hegelmann Litauen Kaunas* |
| 13 | Oleksij Shhebetun (UKR) | *FA Šiauliai* |
| 11 | Richard Kule Mbombo (COD) | *FK Sūduva Marijampolė* |

### Relegation Play-offs (1st / 2nd Level) [27-30.11.2022]

- FC Džiugas Telšiai      0-4(0-1)      0-1(0-0)

FC Džiugas Telšiai remains at first level for 2023.

# NATIONAL CUP
## Lietuvos futbolo taurė 2022

### Second Round [06-09.05.2022]

| | | | | |
|---|---|---|---|---|
| FK Babrungas Plungė - Baltijos FA Vilnius | 1-2(1-0,1-1) | FK Ekranas Panevėžys - FK Sūduva Marijampolė | 0-3(0-2) |
| FK Šturmas 19 Kaunas - DFK Dainava Alytus | 1-8(0-3) | FK Ataka Vilnius - FK Dembava | 3-2(2-0) |
| FK Garliava - FK Neptūnas Klaipėda | 0-2(0-1) | FM Klaipėda - FK Kauno Žalgiris Kaunas | 1-4(0-3) |
| FK Tauras Tauragė - FK Viltis Vilnius | 1-1 aet; 5-3 pen | Be1 NFA Kaunas - FC Hegelmann Litauen Kaunas | 0-3(0-1) |
| FK Granitas Vilnius - FK Venta Kuršėnai | 8-0(4-0) | FK Žalgiris Vilnius - FC Džiugas Telšiai | 3-1(0-0) |
| FKK Spartakas Ukmergė - FK TransINVEST Galinė | 0-2(0-1) | FK Medžiai Vilnius - FK Banga Gargždai | 1-2(1-1) |
| FK Utenis Utena - FK Panevėžys | 0-5(0-4) | FK Saned Joniškis - Marijampolė City FA | 3-7(0-1,3-3) |
| FK Atmosfera Mažeikiai - FK Jonava | 0-3(0-1) | FK Riteriai Vilnius - FA Šiauliai | 2-1(1-0) |

### 1/8-Finals [17-18.05./24-25.05.2022]

| | | | | |
|---|---|---|---|---|
| FK Tauras Tauragė - Marijampolė City FA | 1-4(1-1) | FK Ataka Vilnius - FK Riteriai Vilnius | 1-5(0-1) |
| DFK Dainava Alytus - FK Panevėžys | 0-2(0-0) | Baltijos FA Vilnius - FC Hegelmann Litauen Kaunas | 0-6(0-4) |
| FK Neptūnas Klaipėda - FK Žalgiris Vilnius | 0-1(0-0) | FK Sūduva Marijampolė - Banga Gargždai | 2-0(2-0) |
| FK Granitas Vilnius - FK Kauno Žalgiris Kaunas | 0-4(0-1) | FK TransINVEST Galinė - FK Jonava | 1-2(0-0) |

| Quarter-Finals [16&31.08./13.09.2022] | | | | |
|---|---|---|---|---|
| FK Jonava - FC Hegelmann Litauen Kaunas | 0-2(0-0) | FK Žalgiris Vilnius - FK Riteriai | 2-1(0-0) |
| FK Sūduva - FK Kauno Žalgiris Kaunas | 0-1(0-0) | Marijampolė City FA - FK Panevėžys | 0-2(0-2) |

| Semi-Finals [01/05.10.2022] | | | |
|---|---|---|---|
| FK Žalgiris Vilnius - FK Kauno Žalgiris Kaunas | 2-1(1-0,1-1) | FC Hegelmann Litauen Kaunas - FK Panevėžys | 0-0 aet; 4-3 pen |

## Final

16.10.2022; „Steponas Darius ir Stasys Girėnas" Stadionas, Kaunas; Referee: Manfredas Lukjančukas; Attendance: 13,589
**FK Žalgiris Vilnius - FC Hegelmann Litauen Kaunas**                                     **2-1(0-0,1-1)**

**Žalgiris Vilnius**: Edvinas Gertmonas, Saulius Mikoliūnas (Cap) (89.Mario Pavelić), Kipras Kažukolovas, Nemanja Ljubisavljević, Joël Fey d'Or Bopesu, Nicolás Martín Gorobsov, Francis Kyeremeh (74.Ovidijus Verbickas), Fabien Ourega (65.Marko Miličković), Oliver Buff (106.Petar Mamić), Renan Henrique Oliveira Vieira (89.Motiejus Burba), Mathias Kehinde Oyewusi (65.Donatas Kazlauskas). Trainer: Vladimir Cheburin (Kazakhstan).

**Hegelmann**: Rodrigo Martins Josviaki, Lukas Čerkauskas, Vilius Armalas, Samuel Odeoibo, Klaudijus Upstas (115.Salif Cissé), Yukiyoshi Karashima, Lazar Sajčić (82.Leif Estevez Fernandez), Vilius Armanavičius (Cap), Gavi Thompson (82.Matheus de Souza Marcondele), Alex Aparecido de Souza Alcântara „Negueba" (102.Ibrahim Abiodun Olaosebikan), Ignas Kružikas (74.Augustinas Klimavičius). Trainer: Andrius Skerla.

**Goals**: 1-0 Marko Miličković (76), 1-1 Samuel Odeoibo (90+3), 2-1 Mario Pavelić (110).

## THE CLUBS 2022

### Futbolo klubas Banga Gargždai

| | |
|---|---|
| **Founded**: | 1966 |
| **Stadium**: | Gargždai stadionas, Gargždai (2,323) |
| **Trainer**: | David Marques Afonso (POR)          25.06.1990 |

| Goalkeepers: | DOB | M | (s) | G |
|---|---|---|---|---|
| Mantas Bertašius | 03.05.2000 | 20 | (1) | |
| Pijus Petkevičius | 17.05.1999 | 1 | | |
| Kornelijus Smilingis | 16.04.1999 | 13 | | |
| Povilas Survila | 27.02.2001 | 2 | | |
| **Defenders:** | **DOB** | **M** | **(s)** | **G** |
| Maksim Andrejev | 09.06.2004 | | (2) | |
| Valdas Antužis | 19.06.2000 | 28 | (6) | |
| Timūras Beržonskis | 26.08.2004 | | (1) | |
| Carlos Eduardo da Silva Candido (BRA) | 17.11.1996 | 3 | (2) | 1 |
| Gonçalo Bragança de Oliveira Vieira (POR) | 31.01.1998 | 16 | | 1 |
| Mauricio Pinto (BRA) | 09.10.1996 | 23 | (1) | |
| Karolis Pliuškys | 08.06.2001 | 8 | (8) | |
| Ernestas Stočkūnas | 11.05.1998 | 30 | | 1 |
| Ricardas Šveikauskas | 09.04.1997 | 17 | | |
| Modestas Vainikaitis | 25.01.2002 | 1 | (11) | 1 |
| **Midfielders:** | **DOB** | **M** | **(s)** | **G** |
| Gabriel Pereira Brilhante (BRA) | 03.07.2002 | 3 | (7) | |
| Povilas Kasperavičius | 25.11.2007 | | (1) | |
| Justas Kerpė | 16.08.2003 | | (2) | |
| Vaidas Magdušauskas | 02.12.2003 | 13 | (3) | 1 |
| Dovydas Norvilas | 05.04.1993 | 35 | | |
| Valdas Paulauskas | 04.02.2001 | 18 | (10) | 3 |
| Mantas Petrikas | 15.01.2001 | 8 | (14) | |
| Renan Paulino de Souza (BRA) | 15.02.1995 | 32 | | 2 |
| Erikas Smulkys | 27.06.2006 | | (4) | |
| Pijus Srebalius | 24.07.2002 | 11 | (19) | 1 |
| Karolis Toleikis | 26.04.2004 | 2 | (9) | |
| Shogo Yoshikawa (JPN) | 08.04.1995 | 23 | (2) | 3 |
| Karolis Žebrauskas | 12.06.2002 | 30 | (2) | 2 |
| **Forwards:** | **DOB** | **M** | **(s)** | **G** |
| Jefferson Reis de Jesus (BRA) | 08.11.1995 | 7 | (3) | |
| Nojus Šimkus | 20.05.2005 | | (1) | |
| Ignas Venckus | 17.07.2001 | 10 | (12) | 3 |
| Robertas Vėževičius | 05.01.1986 | 23 | (4) | 9 |
| Darius Zubauskas | 11.04.2000 | 19 | (9) | 4 |

### Football Club Džiugas Telšiai

| | |
|---|---|
| **Founded**: | 1923 (*as SA Džiugas*) |
| **Stadium**: | Telšių miesto centrinis stadionas, Telšiai (2,400) |
| **Trainer**: | Marius Šluta          21.06.1984 |
| [15.06.2022] | João Manuel Lopes Prates (POR)          02.04.1973 |

| Goalkeepers: | DOB | M | (s) | G |
|---|---|---|---|---|
| Marius Paukštė | 15.12.1994 | 9 | (1) | |
| Vincentas Šarkauskas | 11.08.1999 | 27 | | |
| **Defenders:** | **DOB** | **M** | **(s)** | **G** |
| Lukas Ankudinovas | 10.08.1995 | 25 | (2) | 1 |
| Davydas Arlauskis | 18.11.1986 | 5 | | |
| Jurgis Jankauskas | 05.02.2003 | 2 | (4) | 1 |
| Adomas Mika | 25.07.1996 | 23 | | |
| Tomas Rapalavičius | 01.06.1990 | 12 | (3) | |
| Edward Sarpong (GHA) | 17.01.1997 | 26 | (7) | |
| Konstantin Shults (UKR) | 24.06.1993 | 17 | (3) | |
| Edgaras Žarskis | 04.05.1994 | 22 | | 1 |
| **Midfielders:** | **DOB** | **M** | **(s)** | **G** |
| Aldaír Caputo Ferreira (ANG) | 26.03.1998 | 15 | (2) | 2 |
| Ivo Alexandre Pereira Braz (POR) | 25.05.1995 | 12 | (10) | 4 |
| Domas Jankevičius | 14.09.2006 | | (3) | 1 |
| Leonardo Antonio „Léo Antônio" (BRA) | 09.06.1997 | 25 | (2) | 3 |
| Andrius Lipskis | 16.02.1988 | 3 | (11) | |
| Péricles Mattiello Maier (BRA) | 04.05.1999 | 17 | (4) | 2 |
| Airimas Pilipavičius | 06.08.2006 | | (3) | |
| Maksym Pyrogov (UKR) | 30.12.1996 | 24 | (5) | |
| Edvinas Sirutavičius | 01.04.2000 | | (1) | |
| Aurimas Stulga | 09.04.2006 | | (2) | |
| Domantas Šluta | 01.10.2004 | 17 | (9) | |
| Martynas Vasiliauskas | 19.11.1997 | 9 | (8) | |
| **Forwards:** | **DOB** | **M** | **(s)** | **G** |
| Nelson Djembe (CMR) | 11.03.2002 | | (1) | |
| Aivars Emsis (LVA) | 01.04.1998 | 10 | (3) | 3 |
| Jorge Eduardo Pedro Junior (BRA) | 08.09.1994 | 30 | (4) | 4 |
| Yudai Koike (JPN) | 05.11.1995 | 27 | (3) | 1 |
| Rokas Krušnauskas | 04.11.1995 | 7 | (6) | 1 |
| Noel Mbo (ENG) | 14.03.1999 | 12 | (4) | 2 |
| Dovydas Virkšas | 01.07.1997 | 9 | (21) | 3 |
| Oleksiy Zbun (UKR) | 09.06.1997 | 11 | (4) | 4 |

## Futbolo klubas Hegelmann Litauen Kaunas

**Founded:** 2009
**Stadium:** LFF Kaunas training center stadium, Kaunas (500)
**Trainer:** Andrius Skerla     29.04.1977

| Goalkeepers: | DOB | M | (s) | G |
|---|---|---|---|---|
| Ignas Plūkas | 08.12.1993 | 29 | | |
| Rodrigo Martins Josviaki (BRA) | 16.02.1995 | 7 | | |
| **Defenders:** | **DOB** | **M** | **(s)** | **G** |
| Vilius Armalas | 21.07.2000 | 8 | | |
| Lukas Čerkauskas | 12.03.1994 | 18 | (4) | |
| Matas Dedura | 17.05.2002 | | (1) | |
| Mantas Fridrikas | 13.09.1988 | 26 | (2) | 2 |
| Hugo de Figueredo Pereira (BRA) | 18.05.1992 | 26 | (1) | 2 |
| Tzlil Nehemya (ISR) | 02.03.1995 | 13 | (7) | 2 |
| Samuel Odeoibo (NGA) | 28.09.1993 | 32 | (2) | 3 |
| Rokas Rasimavičius | 21.09.2001 | 1 | (2) | |
| **Midfielders:** | **DOB** | **M** | **(s)** | **G** |
| Vilius Armanavičius | 08.05.1995 | 30 | (1) | 13 |

| | DOB | M | (s) | G |
|---|---|---|---|---|
| Leif Estevez Fernandez (GER) | 04.04.1997 | 1 | (1) | |
| Yukiyoshi Karashima (JPN) | 15.01.1997 | 30 | (1) | 6 |
| Matheus de Souza Marcondele (BRA) | 27.04.1996 | 12 | (11) | 2 |
| Ibrahim Abiodun Olaosebikan (NGA) | 19.04.2000 | 4 | (17) | |
| Lazar Sajčić (SRB) | 24.09.1996 | 24 | (6) | 7 |
| Misaki Sato (JPN) | 11.09.1998 | 3 | (24) | |
| Gavi Thompson (NGA) | 02.02.2000 | 32 | (2) | 2 |
| **Forwards:** | **DOB** | **M** | **(s)** | **G** |
| Salif Cissé (FRA) | 12.07.1992 | 14 | (13) | 2 |
| Augustinas Klimavičius | 27.04.2001 | 22 | (5) | 7 |
| Ignas Kružikas | 14.12.1998 | 13 | (18) | 2 |
| Alex Aparecido de Souza Alcântara „Negueba" (BRA) | 24.03.2001 | 26 | (7) | 8 |
| Klaudijus Upstas | 30.10.1994 | 25 | (8) | 1 |

## Football Club Jonava

**Founded:** 1946
**Stadium:** Jonavos centrinis stadionas, Jonavas (2,000)
**Trainer:** Eisvinas Utyra     14.09.1990
[23.04.2022] Yevhen Lutsenko (UKR)     10.11.1980
[14.05.2022] Martynas Matuzas     28.08.1989
[24.05.2022] Petro Kushlyk (UKR)     22.03.1951

| Goalkeepers: | DOB | M | (s) | G |
|---|---|---|---|---|
| Artem Fastov (UKR) | 23.07.2003 | 6 | (2) | |
| Orest Kostyk (UKR) | 16.04.1999 | 5 | | |
| Martynas Matuzas | 28.08.1989 | 14 | | |
| Augusto Marcelo Vantomme (ARG) | 23.06.1990 | 11 | | |
| **Defenders:** | **DOB** | **M** | **(s)** | **G** |
| David Alcides Angeloff (ARG) | 18.02.1991 | 9 | | |
| Ernest Astakhov (UKR) | 21.08.1998 | 11 | (2) | |
| Lukas Čepkauskas | 15.03.1997 | 12 | (15) | |
| Yahaya Mohammad Fawzi Ugbede-Ojo (NGA) | 28.11.2001 | 6 | (10) | |
| Airidas Kabošius | 16.04.2004 | | (4) | |
| Luiz Matheus Servo de Carvalho (BRA) | 10.01.1993 | 11 | | |
| Rokas Macijauskas | 10.02.2005 | | (3) | |
| Lucas Martorell (ARG) | 18.09.1993 | 14 | (3) | |
| Oskaras Migauskas | 15.08.2003 | | (1) | |
| Gabrielis Nikonovas | 23.04.2003 | 7 | (2) | |
| Dwight Pope (TRI) | 25.12.1992 | 1 | (4) | |
| Džiugas Raudonius | 10.01.2000 | 17 | (1) | |
| Richard Ariel Rodríguez (ARG) | 10.11.1993 | 11 | | |
| Andriy Slinkin (UKR) | 19.02.1991 | 8 | | |
| Benas Spietinis | 15.02.1996 | 9 | | |
| Andriy Spivakov (UKR) | 15.05.1995 | 7 | (3) | |
| Nojus Stankevičius | 01.02.2002 | 11 | (1) | |
| Jorge Tapia (ARG) | 10.02.2000 | 8 | (4) | |

| Midfielders: | DOB | M | (s) | G |
|---|---|---|---|---|
| Titas Buzas | 14.06.2004 | 9 | | |
| Tadas Eliošius | 01.03.1990 | 19 | (4) | 3 |
| Jehor Glušač | 21.11.2002 | 15 | (1) | |
| Vladislav Khamelyuk (UKR) | 04.05.1998 | 12 | | 1 |
| Katsuyoshi Kimishima (JPN) | 08.09.1998 | 3 | | |
| Mantas Klapatauskas | 30.12.2006 | | (1) | |
| Nahuel António Machado (ARG) | 18.04.2000 | 19 | (1) | |
| Vadym Mashchenko (UKR) | 26.07.2000 | 12 | (1) | 1 |
| Nazar Motsyk (UKR) | 23.10.1993 | 2 | (3) | |
| Arnas Neimantas | 24.10.2003 | | (2) | |
| Paulius Osauskas | 17.05.1994 | 6 | (5) | |
| Artūras Rocys | 19.08.1994 | 28 | (1) | |
| Genaras Samsonik | 16.12.2000 | 2 | (3) | 1 |
| Domas Stankevičius | 12.12.2004 | 3 | (5) | |
| Gytis Vasylius | 12.08.1999 | 4 | (8) | |
| **Forwards:** | **DOB** | **M** | **(s)** | **G** |
| Daniel Silva Araújo (BRA) | 04.05.1997 | 1 | (3) | |
| Marius Ganusauskas | 13.05.1994 | 9 | (15) | 2 |
| Juan Cruz Jorrín (ARG) | 13.02.1995 | 16 | (8) | 2 |
| Yoichi Kawachi (JPN) | 02.08.1998 | 10 | (5) | |
| Edgaras Liudžius | 14.03.2003 | | (3) | |
| Juozas Lubas | 22.05.2002 | 14 | (1) | 2 |
| Artem Radchenko (UKR) | 02.01.1995 | 13 | | |
| Denys Vasin (UKR) | 04.03.1989 | 5 | | |
| Sebastián Vásquez Gamboa (COL) | 24.05.1996 | 16 | (1) | |

## Futbolo klubas Kauno Žalgiris Kaunas

**Founded:** 2004
**Stadium:** SM Tauras stadionas, Kaunas (500)
**Trainer:** Rokas Garastas     17.08.1988

| Goalkeepers: | DOB | M | (s) | G |
|---|---|---|---|---|
| Deividas Mikelionis | 08.05.1995 | 36 | | |
| **Defenders:** | **DOB** | **M** | **(s)** | **G** |
| Martynas Dapkus | 16.02.1993 | 31 | (1) | |
| Edvinas Girdvainis | 17.01.1993 | 29 | (1) | 2 |
| Shermar Donald Emigdio Martina (CUW) | 14.04.1996 | 7 | (1) | 1 |
| Pijus Nainys | 14.02.2004 | 1 | (4) | |
| Jason Jonathan Brian Noslin (NED) | 09.02.2000 | 14 | (9) | |
| Marko Pejić (CRO) | 24.02.1995 | 24 | (3) | 1 |
| Muenfuh Seth Sincere (NGA) | 28.04.1998 | 9 | (3) | 1 |
| Egidijus Vaitkūnas | 08.08.1988 | 28 | (1) | 2 |
| **Midfielders:** | **DOB** | **M** | **(s)** | **G** |
| Michael Anaba (GHA) | 05.12.1993 | 8 | (1) | |
| Benas Anisas | 29.02.2000 | 15 | (8) | 1 |
| Mohamed Bahlouli (FRA) | 17.02.2000 | 16 | (8) | 5 |
| Olaoluwa Oyinlola Kayode (NGA) | 29.11.2002 | 5 | (6) | |

| | DOB | M | (s) | G |
|---|---|---|---|---|
| Edvinas Kloniūnas | 28.06.1998 | 7 | (16) | 1 |
| Divine Naah (GHA) | 20.04.1996 | 31 | (1) | 2 |
| Felix Kekoh Ndifor II (CMR) | 02.03.2001 | 1 | (8) | |
| Abdulgafar Opeyemi (NGA) | 01.01.2002 | | (8) | |
| Linas Pilibaitis | 05.04.1985 | 8 | (28) | 5 |
| Philipp Schellnegger (AUT) | 13.08.1997 | 7 | (1) | 2 |
| Gratas Sirgėdas | 17.12.1994 | 26 | (5) | 5 |
| Yuma Suwa (JPN) | 29.08.2000 | 4 | (4) | |
| Karolis Šilkaitis | 02.06.1996 | 30 | (2) | 2 |
| Denis Ževžikovas | 10.08.2004 | | (1) | |
| **Forwards:** | **DOB** | **M** | **(s)** | **G** |
| Anton Fase (NED) | 06.02.2000 | 15 | (2) | 9 |
| Michael Thuíque Dias Santos (BRA) | 21.03.1993 | 24 | (2) | 7 |
| Moussa Baba Sangare (CIV) | 02.02.2002 | 10 | (6) | 3 |
| Ryan Lara Trotman (BRB) | 27.06.1999 | 4 | (8) | |
| Nerijus Valskis | 04.08.1987 | 6 | (7) | 4 |

## Futbolo Klubas Panevėžys

| | | | |
|---|---|---|---|
| **Founded**: | 2015 | | |
| **Stadium**: | Aukštaitija stadionas, Panevėžys (6,600) | | |
| **Trainer**: | Valdas Urbonas | | 29.11.1967 |
| [11.09.2022] | Dainius Gleveckas | | 05.03.1977 |
| [22.09.2022] | Gino Lettieri (ITA) | | 23.12.1966 |

| Goalkeepers: | DOB | M | (s) | G |
|---|---|---|---|---|
| Ignas Driomovas | 27.04.1997 | 7 | (1) | |
| Rafael Broetto Henrique (BRA) | 18.08.1990 | 29 | | |
| **Defenders:** | **DOB** | **M** | **(s)** | **G** |
| Joshua Akpudje (NGA) | 23.07.1998 | 20 | (2) | 1 |
| Mitar Ćuković (MNE) | 06.04.1995 | 21 | (3) | 1 |
| Linas Klimavičius | 10.04.1989 | 32 | | 1 |
| Seydina Aboubakr Lamine Keita (SEN) | 28.12.1992 | 16 | | 1 |
| Matijus Remeikis | 28.03.2003 | 6 | (17) | |
| Salvador Sánchez (ARG) | 31.07.1995 | 9 | | |
| Pijus Širvys | 01.04.1998 | 30 | (2) | 1 |
| **Midfielders:** | **DOB** | **M** | **(s)** | **G** |
| Žygimantas Baguška | 09.04.2002 | | (1) | |
| Jovan Čađenović (MNE) | 13.01.1995 | 11 | (1) | 1 |
| Eimantas Dzinga | 03.02.2003 | | (1) | |
| Tautvydas Eliošius | 03.11.1991 | 22 | (13) | |
| Darius Jurgelevičius | 24.02.2003 | | (1) | |
| Ergys Kaçe (ALB) | 08.07.1993 | 3 | (3) | 1 |
| Hrysovalantis Kozoronis (GRE) | 03.08.1992 | 3 | (4) | |
| Nojus Luksys | 19.06.2004 | | (1) | |
| Jeffrey Sarpong (NED) | 03.08.1988 | 32 | (2) | 5 |
| Rokas Stanulevičius | 02.10.1994 | 22 | (3) | 3 |
| Aironas Trakšelis | 25.01.2005 | | (7) | 1 |
| Domantas Vaičekauskas | 27.09.2003 | | (2) | 1 |
| Ernestas Veliulis | 22.08.1992 | 10 | (20) | 2 |
| Wanderson Cavalcante Melo „Maranhão" (BRA) | 26.07.1994 | 27 | (3) | 5 |
| Gustas Žederštreimas | 23.01.2003 | | (3) | |
| **Forwards:** | **DOB** | **M** | **(s)** | **G** |
| Adnan Bašić (BIH) | 13.12.1996 | 1 | (11) | 1 |
| Elivelto Ribeiro Dantas (BRA) | 02.01.1992 | 33 | (1) | 6 |
| Ulysse Diallo (MLI) | 26.10.1992 | 4 | (11) | 3 |
| Nasko Milev (BUL) | 18.07.1996 | 24 | (10) | 7 |
| Ariagner Steven Smith Medina (NCA) | 13.12.1998 | 31 | (3) | 8 |
| Sebastián Vásquez (ARG) | 31.07.1995 | 3 | (5) | |

## Futbolo Klubas Riteriai Vilnius

| | | | |
|---|---|---|---|
| **Founded**: | 2005 | | |
| **Stadium**: | LFF stadionas, Vilnius (5,067) | | |
| **Trainer**: | Glenn Ståhl (SWE) | | 25.08.1971 |
| [08.05.2022] | Vaidas Sabaliauskas | | 21.02.1992 |
| [24.05.2022] | Pablo Villar Ferreiro (ESP) | | 04.09.1986 |

| Goalkeepers: | DOB | M | (s) | G |
|---|---|---|---|---|
| Armantas Vitkauskas | 23.03.1989 | 36 | | |
| **Defenders:** | **DOB** | **M** | **(s)** | **G** |
| Olaide Muhammed Badmus (NGA) | 12.04.1999 | 2 | (1) | |
| Dominykas Barauskas | 18.04.1997 | 3 | (1) | 1 |
| Valdemars Borovskis | 05.02.1984 | 30 | (4) | 1 |
| Guilherme de Souza „Choco" (BRA) | 18.01.1990 | 14 | (10) | |
| Plamen Dimov (BUL) | 29.10.1990 | 22 | | 1 |
| Akseli Kalermo (FIN) | 17.03.1997 | 27 | (2) | |
| Nemanja Lakić-Pešić (SRB) | 22.09.1991 | 10 | | 2 |
| Aleksandr Levšin | 14.08.1999 | 31 | (1) | 1 |
| Deividas Malžinskas | 01.05.1999 | 16 | (10) | |
| Marko Nikolić (SRB) | 31.03.1998 | 6 | | |
| **Midfielders:** | **DOB** | **M** | **(s)** | **G** |
| Emil Andriuškevič | 07.10.2004 | | (3) | |
| Tomas Dombrauskis | 24.09.1996 | 21 | (9) | 1 |
| Nikola Eskić (SRB) | 19.12.1997 | 15 | | |
| Felipe Bezerra Brisola (BRA) | 06.06.1990 | 10 | (1) | 1 |
| Rokas Filipavičius | 22.12.1999 | 25 | (6) | 10 |
| Luka Koberidze (GEO) | 09.09.1994 | 1 | (4) | |
| Dejan Milićević (SRB) | 10.03.1992 | 15 | | 2 |
| Matas Ramanauskas | 28.06.2000 | 14 | (10) | 2 |
| Deimantas Rimpa | 11.03.2001 | 10 | (6) | 1 |
| Armandas Šveistrys | 08.07.2002 | | (2) | |
| **Forwards:** | **DOB** | **M** | **(s)** | **G** |
| Dmytro Bilonoh (UKR) | 26.05.1995 | 6 | (22) | 8 |
| Artür Dolžnikov | 06.06.2000 | 23 | (4) | 5 |
| Mindaugas Grigaravičius | 15.07.1992 | 11 | (11) | 5 |
| Esmilis Kaušinis | 31.05.2004 | | (1) | |
| Juozas Lubas | 22.05.2002 | | (3) | |
| Lucas Dias do Nascimento Serafim (BRA) | 06.03.1997 | 13 | (8) | 2 |
| Ebuka Romanus Onah (NGA) | 24.12.2001 | 2 | (10) | |
| Gytis Paulauskas | 27.09.1999 | 27 | (4) | 8 |
| Tomáš Vestenický (SVK) | 06.04.1996 | 6 | (10) | 2 |

## Futbolo Klubas Sūduva Marijampolė

| | | | |
|---|---|---|---|
| **Founded**: | 1921 | | |
| **Stadium**: | Marijampolė Football Arena, Marijampolė (6,250) | | |
| **Trainer**: | Víctor Manuel Basadre Orozco (ESP) | | 16.02.1970 |
| [12.04.2022] | Miguel Moreira (PO) | | 06.10.1984 |
| [20.10.2022] | David Marques Pereira Silva (POR) | | 12.01.1992 |

| Goalkeepers: | DOB | M | (s) | G |
|---|---|---|---|---|
| Vilius Stebrys | 27.01.2000 | 1 | | |
| Tomas Švedkauskas | 22.06.1994 | 35 | | |
| **Defenders:** | **DOB** | **M** | **(s)** | **G** |
| Žygimantas Baltrūnas | 11.03.2002 | 1 | (3) | |
| Markas Beneta | 08.07.1993 | 31 | | 1 |
| Tautvydas Burdzilauskas | 18.05.2005 | | (1) | |
| Diogo Manuel Gonçalves Coelho (POR) | 08.07.1992 | 14 | (2) | |
| Yevgen Efremov (UKR) | 17.01.1994 | 1 | (3) | |
| Justinas Januševskis | 26.03.1994 | 27 | (2) | 1 |
| Vaidas Slavickas | 26.02.1986 | 16 | (9) | 1 |
| Nicolas Taravel (FRA) | 13.10.1994 | 23 | (4) | 1 |
| Tiago Miguel Monteiro Almeida (CPV) | 13.09.1990 | 10 | (5) | 1 |
| Modestas Vainikaitis | 25.01.2002 | | (1) | |
| Simas Venckevičius | 12.08.2005 | | (1) | |
| Aleksandar Živanović (SRB) | 08.04.1987 | 33 | | 4 |
| **Midfielders:** | **DOB** | **M** | **(s)** | **G** |
| Ernestas Burdzilauskas | 22.06.2003 | 1 | (3) | |
| Tomislav Gomelt (CRO) | 07.01.1995 | 6 | (2) | |
| João Pedro Sacramento da Silva (BRA) | 18.01.2003 | | (5) | |
| Milan Jokić (SRB) | 21.03.1995 | 16 | | |
| Povilas Leimonas | 16.11.1987 | 7 | (13) | |
| Levan Matcharashvili (GEO) | 24.03.1997 | 9 | (14) | |
| Giedrius Matulevičius | 05.03.1997 | 29 | (5) | 3 |
| Matas Miškinis | 12.10.2005 | 1 | (2) | |
| Marko Pavlovski (SRB) | 07.02.1994 | 26 | (5) | |
| Yevgen Protasov (UKR) | 23.07.1997 | 9 | (21) | 1 |
| Olivier Rommens (BEL) | 03.02.1995 | 20 | (1) | 3 |
| Ignas Skamarakas | 01.08.2006 | | (1) | |
| Xabier „Xabi" Auzmendi Arruabarrena (ESP) | 01.05.1997 | 25 | (2) | 6 |
| **Forwards:** | **DOB** | **M** | **(s)** | **G** |
| Saïd Hamulić (NED) | 12.11.2000 | 10 | (3) | 6 |
| Danylo Kondrakov (UKR) | 19.01.1998 | 12 | (3) | 4 |
| Karolis Laukžemis | 11.03.1992 | 7 | (5) | |
| Richard Kule Mbombo (COD) | 10.05.1996 | 20 | (5) | 11 |
| Simonas Urbys | 07.11.1995 | 6 | (7) | 1 |
| Linas Zingertas | 26.01.2002 | | (11) | |

## Football Academy of Šiauliai

**Founded**: 2007
**Stadium**: Šiaulių savivaldybės stadionas, Šiauliai (4,000)
**Trainer**: Mindaugas Čepas     06.08.1978

| Goalkeepers: | DOB | M | (s) | G |
|---|---|---|---|---|
| Gustas Baliutavičius | 27.08.2000 | 8 | | |
| Lukas Paukštė | 25.09.1998 | 28 | | |
| **Defenders:** | **DOB** | **M** | **(s)** | **G** |
| Nojus Vytis Audinis | 15.02.2006 | 2 | | |
| Vytas Gašpuitis | 04.03.1994 | 22 | (2) | |
| Algis Jankauskas | 27.09.1982 | 3 | (8) | |
| Rokas Lekiatas | 07.11.1998 | 35 | | 1 |
| Ernestas Pilypas | 17.05.1990 | 31 | | |
| Rimvydas Sadauskas | 21.07.1996 | 29 | (2) | |
| Gustas Zabita | 05.01.2002 | 22 | (6) | |
| **Midfielders:** | **DOB** | **M** | **(s)** | **G** |
| Sergei Amirzian | 26.12.1999 | | (10) | |
| Deividas Dovydaitis | 26.01.2003 | 16 | (15) | 1 |
| Emilis Gasiunas | 12.06.2003 | 20 | (8) | |
| Grantas Jaseliūnas | 07.01.2003 | | (1) | |

| | DOB | M | (s) | G |
|---|---|---|---|---|
| Dominykas Kubilinskas | 09.01.1999 | 19 | (7) | 1 |
| Karolis Mantinis | 23.01.2002 | 2 | (7) | |
| Kristupas Mantinis | 23.01.2002 | | (2) | |
| Gabrielius Micevičius | 25.04.2003 | 7 | (5) | 1 |
| Ronaldas Misiūnas | 16.08.1999 | | (6) | |
| Simonas Paulius | 12.05.1991 | 22 | (8) | |
| Justas Petravicius | 10.01.1996 | 12 | (1) | 2 |
| Mantas Pikčiūnas | 30.01.2003 | | (3) | |
| Juozas Radavičius | 29.12.2005 | | (1) | |
| Danielis Romanovskis | 19.06.1996 | 33 | (2) | 9 |
| Deividas Šešplaukis | 02.02.1998 | 30 | | 5 |
| **Forwards:** | **DOB** | **M** | **(s)** | **G** |
| David Arshakyan (ARM) | 16.08.1994 | 1 | (5) | |
| Eligijus Jankauskas | 22.06.1998 | 34 | (2) | 4 |
| Gabijus Micevičius | 25.04.2003 | 1 | | |
| Oleksij Shhebetun (UKR) | 02.06.1997 | 19 | | 13 |

## Futbolo klubas Žalgiris Vilnius

**Founded**: 1947
**Stadium**: LFF stadionas, Vilnius (5,067)
**Trainer**: Vladimir Cheburin (KAZ)     07.07.1965

| Goalkeepers: | DOB | M | (s) | G |
|---|---|---|---|---|
| Tomislav Duka (CRO) | 07.09.1992 | 13 | (2) | |
| Edvinas Gertmonas | 01.06.1996 | 23 | | |
| **Defenders:** | **DOB** | **M** | **(s)** | **G** |
| Joël Fey d'Or Bopesu (FRA) | 25.01.1995 | 19 | (2) | |
| Dinmukhamed Kashken (KAZ) | 04.01.2000 | 11 | (1) | |
| Kipras Kažukolovas (ENG) | 20.11.2000 | 14 | (1) | 3 |
| Nemanja Ljubisavljević (SRB) | 26.11.1996 | 23 | (1) | 1 |
| Petar Mamić (CRO) | 06.03.1996 | 28 | | 3 |
| Saulius Mikoliūnas | 02.05.1984 | 20 | (5) | 1 |
| Mario Pavelić (AUT) | 19.09.1993 | 23 | (4) | |
| Ivan Tatomirović (SRB) | 11.01.1989 | 12 | | 1 |
| **Midfielders:** | **DOB** | **M** | **(s)** | **G** |
| Oliver Buff (SUI) | 03.08.1992 | 14 | (12) | 1 |
| Nicolás Martín Gorobsov (ARG) | 25.11.1989 | 27 | (3) | 3 |
| Gustas Jarusevičius | 23.05.2003 | 10 | (12) | 1 |

| | DOB | M | (s) | G |
|---|---|---|---|---|
| Donatas Kazlauskas | 31.03.1994 | 8 | (18) | 6 |
| Mantas Kuklys | 10.06.1987 | 15 | (3) | 4 |
| Francis Kyeremeh (GHA) | 23.06.1997 | 25 | (9) | 7 |
| Marko Miličković (MNE) | 31.03.1998 | 14 | (12) | 6 |
| Fabien Ourega (FRA) | 07.12.1992 | 25 | (7) | 5 |
| Vilius Piliukaitis | 10.03.2001 | 1 | (5) | 1 |
| Matas Vareika | 27.01.2000 | | (3) | 1 |
| Ovidijus Verbickas | 04.07.1993 | 17 | (9) | 3 |
| **Forwards:** | **DOB** | **M** | **(s)** | **G** |
| Motiejus Burba | 10.08.2003 | 3 | (4) | |
| Meinardas Mikulenas | 09.07.2002 | 2 | (10) | 3 |
| Mathias Kehinde Oyewusi (NGA) | 02.02.1999 | 15 | (8) | 9 |
| Renan Henrique Oliveira Vieira (BRA) | 08.05.1997 | 18 | (11) | 17 |
| Jakub Sylvestr (SVK) | 02.02.1989 | 1 | (9) | |
| Josip Tadić (CRO) | 22.08.1987 | 15 | (3) | 6 |

## SECOND LEVEL
### LFF I Lyga 2022

| | | | | | | | | | |
|---|---|---|---|---|---|---|---|---|---|
| 1. | DFK Dainava Alytus (*Promoted*) | 30 | 21 | 4 | 5 | 69 | - | 31 | 67 |
| 2. | FK Neptūnas Klaipėda (*Promotion Play-off*) | 30 | 19 | 5 | 6 | 66 | - | 36 | 62 |
| 3. | FK Nevėžis Kėdainiai | 30 | 17 | 7 | 6 | 52 | - | 26 | 58 |
| 4. | Be1 NFA Kaunas | 30 | 15 | 12 | 3 | 39 | - | 19 | 57 |
| 5. | Marijampolė City FA | 30 | 16 | 5 | 9 | 51 | - | 41 | 53 |
| 6. | FK Babrungas Plungė | 30 | 13 | 7 | 10 | 52 | - | 34 | 46 |
| 7. | Baltijos Futbolo Akademija Vilnius | 30 | 11 | 5 | 14 | 54 | - | 47 | 38 |
| 8. | FK Ekranas Panevėžys | 30 | 12 | 5 | 13 | 48 | - | 51 | 38 |
| 9. | FK Žalgiris Vilnius "B" | 30 | 9 | 9 | 12 | 44 | - | 48 | 36 |
| 10. | FK Panevėžys „B" | 30 | 10 | 6 | 14 | 47 | - | 63 | 36 |
| 11. | FK Garliava | 30 | 9 | 6 | 15 | 27 | - | 39 | 33 |
| 12. | FA Šiauliai „B" | 30 | 10 | 3 | 17 | 33 | - | 54 | 33 |
| 13. | FK Minija Kretinga | 30 | 9 | 6 | 15 | 31 | - | 50 | 33 |
| 14. | FK Riteriai Vilnius „B" (*Relegation Play-off*) | 30 | 7 | 11 | 12 | 41 | - | 48 | 32 |
| 15. | FK Atmosfera Mažeikiai (*Relegated*) | 30 | 6 | 6 | 18 | 41 | - | 67 | 24 |
| 16. | FK Banga Gargždai „B" (*Relegated*) | 30 | 5 | 5 | 20 | 26 | - | 67 | 20 |

*3 points deducted for not meeting I Lyga license criteria.
Please note: FK Šilas Kazlų Rūda and Marijampolė football academy had merged into Marijampolė City.

### Relegation Play-offs (2nd / 3rd Level) [19-26.11.2022]

FK Šilutė - FK Riteriai Vilnius „B"            0-1(0-1)      0-4(0-1)

FK Riteriai Vilnius „B"remains at second level for 2023.

## INTERNATIONAL MATCHES
### (16.07.2022 – 15.07.2023)

| | | | | |
|---|---|---|---|---|
| 22.09.2022 | Vilnius | *Lithuania - Faroe Islands* | *1-1(1-1)* | (UNL) |
| 25.09.2022 | Lëtzebuerg | *Luxembourg - Lithuania* | *1-0(0-0)* | (UNL) |
| 16.11.2022 | Kaunas | *Lithuania - Iceland* | *0-0; 5-6 on penalties* | (BC) |
| 19.11.2022 | Tallinn | *Estonia - Lithuania* | *2-0(0-0)* | (BC) |
| 24.03.2023 | Beograd | *Serbia - Lithuania* | *2-0(1-0)* | (ECQ) |
| 27.03.2023 | Athína | *Greece - Lithuania* | *0-0* | (F) |
| 17.06.2023 | Kaunas | *Lithuania - Bulgaria* | *1-1(1-1)* | (ECQ) |
| 20.06.2023 | Budapest | *Hungary - Lithuania* | *2-0(1-0)* | (ECQ) |

**22.09.2022    LITHUANIA - FAROE ISLANDS              1-1(1-1)              3rd UEFA Nations League C, Group 1**
LFF stadionas, Vilnius; Referee: Vilhjálmur Alvar Þórarinsson (Iceland); Attendance: 2,376
**LTU:** Džiugas Bartkus, Saulius Mikoliūnas (Cap) (87.Rolandas Baravykas), Edvinas Girdvainis, Linas Klimavičius, Dominykas Barauskas, Vykintas Slivka (61.Domantas Šimkus), Linas Mėgelaitis (46.Modestas Vorobjovas), Arvydas Novikovas, Justas Lasickas (76.Artūr Dolžnikov), Paulius Golubickas (76.Titas Milašius), Fedor Černych. Trainer: Reinhold Breu (Germany).
**Goal:** Vykintas Slivka (41).

**25.09.2022    LUXEMBOURG - LITHUANIA              1-0(0-0)              3rd UEFA Nations League C, Group 1**
Stade de Luxembourg, Lëtzebuerg; Referee: Giorgi Kruashvili (Georgia); Attendance: 5,340
**LTU:** Džiugas Bartkus, Rolandas Baravykas (78.Saulius Mikoliūnas), Edvinas Girdvainis, Benas Šatkus, Dominykas Barauskas (43.Natanas Žebrauskas), Domantas Šimkus, Modestas Vorobjovas, Arvydas Novikovas, Vykintas Slivka (78.Tomas Kalinauskas), Paulius Golubickas (71.Artūr Dolžnikov), Fedor Černych (Cap). Trainer: Reinhold Breu (Germany).

**16.11.2022    LITHUANIA - ICELAND              0-0; 5-6 on penalties              29th Baltic Cup, Semi-Finals**
„Steponas Darius ir Stasys Girėnas" Stadionas, Kaunas; Referee: Andris Treimanis (Latvia); Attendance: 5,934
**LTU:** Edvinas Gertmonas, Saulius Mikoliūnas (Cap) (50.Rolandas Baravykas), Edvinas Girdvainis, Linas Klimavičius, Artemijus Tutyškinas (71.Natanas Žebrauskas), Domantas Šimkus (71.Gvidas Gineitis), Modestas Vorobjovas, Arvydas Novikovas, Justas Lasickas (88.Klaudijus Upstas), Fedor Černych, Armandas Kučys (71.Paulius Golubickas). Trainer: Reinhold Breu (Germany).
**Penalties:** Edvinas Girdvainis, Gvidas Gineitis, Arvydas Novikovas, Paulius Golubickas, Rolandas Baravykas, Natanas Žebrauskas (missed).

**19.11.2022    ESTONIA - LITHUANIA              2-0(0-0)              29th Baltic Cup, Third Place Play-off**
A. Le Coq Arena, Tallinn; Referee: Vitalijs Spasjonņikovs (Latvia); Attendance: 1,563
**LTU:** Marius Adamonis, Rolandas Baravykas, Vilius Armalas (46.Domantas Šimkus), Edvinas Girdvainis (Cap), Natanas Žebrauskas, Gvidas Gineitis, Modestas Vorobjovas, Klaudijus Upstas (66.Justas Lasickas), Paulius Golubickas (46.Fedor Černych), Tomas Kalinauskas (46.Arvydas Novikovas), Armandas Kučys (46.Linas Klimavičius). Trainer: Reinhold Breu (Germany).

**24.03.2023    SERBIA - LITHUANIA              2-0(1-0)              17th EC. Qualifiers**
Stadion "Rajko Mitić", Beograd; Referee: Lawrence Visser (Belgium); Attendance: 21,125
**LTU:** Džiugas Bartkus, Justas Lasickas, Kipras Kažukolovas, Edvinas Girdvainis, Markas Beneta (86.Rolandas Baravykas), Domantas Šimkus, Gvidas Gineitis (80.Daniel Romanovskij), Paulius Golubickas (62.Vykintas Slivka), Fedor Černych (Cap), Eligijus Jankauskas (62.Arvydas Novikovas), Gytis Paulauskas (80.Karolis Laukžemis). Trainer: Edgaras Jankauskas.

**27.03.2023    GREECE - LITHUANIA              0-0              Friendly International**
OPAP Arena, Athína; Referee: Jonathan Lardot (Belgium); Attendance: 11,950
**LTU:** Emilijus Zubas, Justas Lasickas, Kipras Kažukolovas, Edvinas Girdvainis (46.Vilius Armalas), Markas Beneta (46.Rolandas Baravykas), Gvidas Gineitis, Vykintas Slivka (78.Domantas Šimkus), Arvydas Novikovas, Daniel Romanovskij (46.Gratas Sirgedas), Fedor Černych (Cap) (60.Klaudijus Upstas), Gytis Paulauskas (46.Karolis Laukžemis). Trainer: Edgaras Jankauskas.

**17.06.2023    LITHUANIA - BULGARIA              1-1(1-1)              17th EC. Qualifiers**
„Steponas Darius ir Stasys Girėnas" Stadionas, Kaunas; Referee: Jakob Alexander Sundberg (Denmark); Attendance: 14,230
**LTU:** Edvinas Gertmonas, Justas Lasickas [*sent off 17*], Rokas Lekiatas, Edvinas Girdvainis, Markas Beneta (78.Artemijus Tutyškinas), Modestas Vorobjovas, Gvidas Gineitis, Ovidijus Verbickas (46.Klaudijus Upstas), Deividas Šešplaukis (21.Pijus Širvys), Eligijus Jankauskas (78.Gratas Sirgedas), Fedor Černych (Cap) (37.Gytis Paulauskas). Trainer: Edgaras Jankauskas.
**Goal:** Edvinas Girdvainis (15).

**20.06.2023    HUNGARY - LITHUANIA              2-0(1-0)              17th EC. Qualifiers**
Puskás Aréna, Budapest; Referee: António Emanuel Carvalho Nobre (Portugal); Attendance: 58,274
**LTU:** Edvinas Gertmonas, Rokas Lekiatas, Kipras Kažukolovas, Linas Klimavičius (Cap), Artemijus Tutyškinas (63.Markas Beneta), Gvidas Gineitis, Karolis Uzėla (46.Modestas Vorobjovas), Eligijus Jankauskas (86.Daniel Romanovskij), Gratas Sirgedas (46.Pijus Širvys), Deividas Šešplaukis (78.Armandas Kučys), Gytis Paulauskas. Trainer: Edgaras Jankauskas.

## NATIONAL TEAM PLAYERS
### (16.07.2022 – 15.07.2023)

| Name | DOB | Caps | Goals | Club | |
|------|-----|------|-------|------|---|

#### Goalkeepers

| Name | DOB | Caps | Goals | Club | |
|------|-----|------|-------|------|---|
| Marius ADAMONIS | 13.05.1997 | 1 | 0 | 2022: | *SS Lazio Roma* |
| Džiugas BARTKUS | 07.11.1989 | 12 | 0 | 2022/2023: | *Hapoel Ironi Kiryat Shmona FC (ISR)* |
| Edvinas GERTMONAS | 01.06.1996 | 6 | 0 | 2022/2023: | *FK Žalgiris Vilnius* |
| Emilijus ZUBAS | 10.07.1990 | 15 | 0 | 2023: | *Hapoel Tel Aviv FC (ISR)* |

#### Defenders

| Name | DOB | Caps | Goals | Club | |
|------|-----|------|-------|------|---|
| Vilius ARMALAS | 21.07.2000 | 2 | 0 | 2022/2023: | *FC Hegelmann Litauen Kaunas* |
| Dominykas BARAUSKAS | 18.04.1997 | 11 | 0 | 2022: | *FKS Stal Mielec (POL)* |
| Rolandas BARAVYKAS | 23.08.1995 | 35 | 2 | 2022: | *unattached* |
| | | | | 04.01.2023-> | *FCV Farul Constanţa (ROU)* |
| Markas BENETA | 08.07.1993 | 17 | 0 | 2023: | *FK Panevėžys* |
| Edvinas GIRDVAINIS | 17.01.1993 | 43 | 1 | 2022/2023: | *FK Kauno Žalgiris Kaunas* |
| Kipras KAŽUKOLOVAS | 20.11.2000 | 3 | 0 | 2023: | *FK Žalgiris Vilnius* |
| Linas KLIMAVIČIUS | 10.04.1989 | 38 | 0 | 2022/2023: | *FK Panevėžys* |
| Rokas LEKIATAS | 07.11.1998 | 2 | 0 | 2023: | *FA Šiauliai* |
| Saulius MIKOLIŪNAS | 02.05.1984 | 101 | 5 | 2022: | *FK Žalgiris Vilnius* |
| Benas ŠATKUS | 01.04.2001 | 14 | 0 | 2022: | *VfL Osnabrück (GER)* |
| Pijus ŠIRVYS | 01.04.1998 | 6 | 0 | 2023: | *FK Panevėžys* |
| Artemijus TUTYŠKINAS | 08.08.2003 | 6 | 0 | 2022/2023: | *ŁKS Łódź (POL)* |
| Natanas ŽEBRAUSKAS | 18.02.2002 | 3 | 0 | 2022: | *SpVgg Fürth (GER)* |

#### Midfielders

| Name | DOB | Caps | Goals | Club | |
|------|-----|------|-------|------|---|
| Gvidas GINEITIS | 15.04.2004 | 6 | 0 | 2022/2023: | *Torino FC (ITA)* |
| Paulius GOLUBICKAS | 19.08.1999 | 21 | 1 | 2022: | *HNK Gorica (CRO)* |
| | | | | 07.01.2023-> | *FK Žalgiris Vilnius* |
| Eligijus JANKAUSKAS | 22.06.1998 | 5 | 0 | 2023: | *FA Šiauliai* |
| Tomas KALINAUSKAS | 27.04.2000 | 2 | 0 | 2022: | *Havant & Waterlooville FC (ENG)* |
| Justas LASICKAS | 06.10.1997 | 41 | 2 | 2022/2023: | *NK Olimpija Ljubljana (SVN)* |
| Titas MILAŠIUS | 12.12.2000 | 5 | 0 | 2022: | *Bruk-Bet Termalica Nieciecza KS (POL)* |
| Linas MĖGELAITIS | 09.09.1998 | 16 | 1 | 2022: | *US Viterbese 1908 (ITA)* |
| Arvydas NOVIKOVAS | 18.12.1990 | 87 | 12 | 2022: | *Samsunspor Kulübü (TUR)* |
| | | | | 24.01.2023-> | *Hapoel Haifa FC (ISR)* |
| Daniel ROMANOVSKIJ | 19.06.1996 | 9 | 0 | 2023: | *FA Šiauliai* |
| Gratas SIRGEDAS | 17.12.1994 | 21 | 3 | 2023: | *FK Kauno Žalgiris Kaunas* |
| Vykintas SLIVKA | 29.04.1995 | 57 | 3 | 2022/2023: | *PAS Lamia (GRE)* |
| Deividas ŠEŠPLAUKIS | 03.03.1998 | 2 | 0 | 2023: | *FA Šiauliai* |
| Domantas ŠIMKUS | 10.02.1996 | 30 | 0 | 2022/2023: | *NŠ Mura Murska Sobota (SVN)* |
| Klaudijus UPSTAS | 30.10.1994 | 4 | 0 | 2022/2023: | *FC Hegelmann Litauen Kaunas* |
| Karolis UZĖLA | 11.03.2000 | 4 | 0 | 2023: | *FK Rīgas Futbola Skola (LVA)* |
| Ovidijus VERBICKAS | 04.07.1993 | 31 | 1 | 2023: | *FK Žalgiris Vilnius* |
| Modestas VOROBJOVAS | 30.12.1995 | 28 | 1 | 2022/2023: | *AFC Chindia Târgovişte (ROU)* |

#### Forwards

| Name | DOB | Caps | Goals | Club | |
|------|-----|------|-------|------|---|
| Fedor ČERNYCH | 21.05.1991 | 83 | 12 | 2022: | *Jagiellonia Białystok (POL)* |
| | | | | 08.01.2023-> | *AEL Limassol (CYP)* |
| Artūr DOLŽNIKOV | 06.01.2000 | 4 | 0 | 2022: | *FK Riteriai Vilnius* |
| Armandas KUČYS | 27.02.2003 | 5 | 0 | 2022: | *Oskarshamns AIK (SWE)* |
| | | | | 30.05.2023-> | *IFK Berga Kalmar (SWE)* |
| Karolis LAUKŽEMIS | 11.03.1992 | 31 | 2 | 2023: | *FK Banga Gargždai* |
| Gytis PAULAUSKAS | 27.09.1999 | 5 | 0 | 2023: | *KF Egnatia Rrogozhinë (ALB)* |

#### Trainer

| | DOB | | |
|--|--|--|--|
| Reinhold BREU (Germany) [28.06.2022 - 31.12.2022] | 12.09.1970 | 4 M; 0 W; 2 D; 2 L; 1-4 | |
| Edgaras JANKAUSKAS [from 01.02.2023] | 12.03.1975 | 4 M; 0 W; 2 D; 2 L; 1-5 | |
| | | Complete record as trainer of Lithuania: | |
| | | 32 M; 3 W; 7 D; 22 L; 16-62 | |
| | | (12.01.2016 – 04.12.2018) & (01.02.2023 – 20.06.2023) | |

# LUXEMBOURG

FLF

**The Country:**
Groussherzogtum Lëtzebuerg (Grand Duchy of Luxembourg)
Capital: Lëtzebuerg
Surface: 2,586.4 km²
Inhabitants: 660,809 [2023]
Time: UTC+1

**The FA:**
Fédération Luxembourgeoise de Football / Lëtzebuerger Foussballfederatioun
BP 5, Rue de Limpach, 3901 Mondercange
Tel: +352 488 665 1
Foundation date: 1908
Member of FIFA since: 1910
Member of UEFA since: 1954
Website: www.flf.lu

## NATIONAL TEAM RECORDS

### RECORDS

| | | |
|---|---|---|
| **First international match:** | 29.10.1911, Lëtzebuerg: | Luxembourg – France 1-4 |
| **Most international caps:** | Mario Mutsch | - 102 caps (2005-2019) |
| **Most international goals:** | Léon Mart | - 16 goals / 24 caps (1933-1946) |
| | Gerson Leal Rodrigues Gouveia | - 16 goals / 55 caps (since 2017) |

### UEFA EUROPEAN CHAMPIONSHIP

| | |
|---|---|
| 1960 | Did not enter |
| 1964 | Qualifiers |
| 1968 | Qualifiers |
| 1972 | Qualifiers |
| 1976 | Qualifiers |
| 1980 | Qualifiers |
| 1984 | Qualifiers |
| 1988 | Qualifiers |
| 1992 | Qualifiers |
| 1996 | Qualifiers |
| 2000 | Qualifiers |
| 2004 | Qualifiers |
| 2008 | Qualifiers |
| 2012 | Qualifiers |
| 2016 | Qualifiers |
| 2020 | Qualifiers |

### FIFA WORLD CUP

| | |
|---|---|
| 1930 | Did not enter |
| 1934 | Qualifiers |
| 1938 | Qualifiers |
| 1950 | Qualifiers |
| 1954 | Qualifiers |
| 1958 | Qualifiers |
| 1962 | Qualifiers |
| 1966 | Qualifiers |
| 1970 | Qualifiers |
| 1974 | Qualifiers |
| 1978 | Qualifiers |
| 1982 | Qualifiers |
| 1986 | Qualifiers |
| 1990 | Qualifiers |
| 1994 | Qualifiers |
| 1998 | Qualifiers |
| 2002 | Qualifiers |
| 2006 | Qualifiers |
| 2010 | Qualifiers |
| 2014 | Qualifiers |
| 2018 | Qualifiers |
| 2022 | Qualifiers |

### OLYMPIC TOURNAMENTS

| | |
|---|---|
| 1908 | - |
| 1912 | - |
| 1920 | Round 1 |
| 1924 | 1/8 - Finals |
| 1928 | 1/8 - Finals |
| 1936 | 1/8 - Finals |
| 1948 | 1/8 - Finals |
| 1952 | Round 1 |
| 1956 | - |
| 1960 | Qualifiers |
| 1964 | Did not enter |
| 1968 | Did not enter |
| 1972 | Qualifiers |
| 1976 | Qualifiers |
| 1980 | Did not enter |
| 1984 | Did not enter |
| 1988 | Did not enter |
| 1992 | Qualifiers |
| 1996 | Qualifiers |
| 2000 | Qualifiers |
| 2004 | Qualifiers |
| 2008 | Qualifiers |
| 2012 | Qualifiers |
| 2016 | Qualifiers |
| 2020 | Qualifiers |

### UEFA NATIONS LEAGUE

| | |
|---|---|
| 2018/2019 | League D (Group Stage -> promoted to League C) |
| 2020/2021 | League C (Group Stage) |
| 2022/2023 | League C (Group Stage) |

### LUXEMBOURGIAN CLUB HONOURS IN EUROPEAN CLUB COMPETITIONS:

| European Champion Clubs.Cup (1956-1992) / UEFA Champions League (1993-2023) |
|---|
| None |

| Fairs Cup (1858-1971) / UEFA Cup (1972-2009) / UEFA Europa League (2010-2023) |
|---|
| None |

| UEFA Europa Conference League (2021-2023) |
|---|
| None |

| UEFA Super Cup (1972-2022) |
|---|
| None |

| European Cup Winners' Cup 1961-1999* |
|---|
| None |

*defunct competition*

| | CHAMPIONS | CUP WINNERS | BEST GOALSCORERS | |
|---|---|---|---|---|
| 1909/1910 | Racing Club Lëtzebuerg | - | - | |
| 1910/1911 | Sporting Club Lëtzebuerg | - | - | |
| 1911/1912 | US Hollerich Bonnevoie | - | - | |
| 1912/1913 | *No competition* | - | - | |
| 1913/1914 | US Hollerich Bonnevoie | - | - | |
| 1914/1915 | US Hollerich Bonnevoie | - | - | |
| 1915/1916 | US Hollerich Bonnevoie | - | - | |
| 1916/1917 | US Hollerich Bonnevoie | - | - | |
| 1917/1918 | CS Fola Esch | - | - | |
| 1918/1919 | Sporting Club Lëtzebuerg | - | - | |
| 1919/1920 | CS Fola Esch | - | - | |
| 1920/1921 | AS la Jeunesse d'Esch/Alzette | - | - | |
| 1921/1922 | CS Fola Esch | Racing Club Lëtzebuerg | - | |
| 1922/1923 | FA Red Boys Differdange | CS Fola Esch | - | |
| 1923/1924 | CS Fola Esch | CS Fola Esch | - | |
| 1924/1925 | CA Spora Lëtzebuerg | FA Red Boys Differdange | - | |
| 1925/1926 | FA Red Boys Differdange | FA Red Boys Differdange | - | |
| 1926/1927 | Union Sportive Lëtzebuerg | FA Red Boys Differdange | - | |
| 1927/1928 | CA Spora Lëtzebuerg | CA Spora Lëtzebuerg | - | |
| 1928/1929 | CA Spora Lëtzebuerg | FA Red Boys Differdange | - | |
| 1929/1930 | CS Fola Esch | FA Red Boys Differdange | - | |
| 1930/1931 | FA Red Boys Differdange | FA Red Boys Differdange | - | |
| 1931/1932 | FA Red Boys Differdange | CA Spora Lëtzebuerg | - | |
| 1932/1933 | FA Red Boys Differdange | FC Progrès Niederkorn | - | |
| 1933/1934 | CA Spora Lëtzebuerg | FA Red Boys Differdange | - | |
| 1934/1935 | CA Spora Lëtzebuerg | AS la Jeunesse d'Esch/Alzette | - | |
| 1935/1936 | CA Spora Lëtzebuerg | FA Red Boys Differdange | - | |
| 1936/1937 | AS la Jeunesse d'Esch/Alzette | AS la Jeunesse d'Esch/Alzette | - | |
| 1937/1938 | CA Spora Lëtzebuerg | Stade Dudelange | - | |
| 1938/1939 | Stade Dudelange | Union Sportive Dudelange | - | |
| 1939/1940 | Stade Dudelange | CA Spora Lëtzebuerg | - | |
| 1940-1944 | *No competition* | *No competition* | - | |
| 1944/1945 | Stade Dudelange | FC Progrès Niederkorn | - | |
| 1945/1946 | Stade Dudelange | AS la Jeunesse d'Esch/Alzette | Camille Libar (Stade Dudelange) Paul Feller (Stade Dudelange) | 17 |
| 1946/1947 | Stade Dudelange | Union Sportive Lëtzebuerg | Camille Libar (Stade Dudelange) | 22 |
| 1947/1948 | Stade Dudelange | Stade Dudelange | Nick Kettel (Stade Dudelange) René Conrad (Union Sportive Dudelange) Charles Wagner (SC Tétange) | 18 |
| 1948/1949 | CA Spora Lëtzebuerg | Stade Dudelange | Jules Gales (CA Spora Lëtzebuerg) | 19 |
| 1949/1950 | Stade Dudelange | CA Spora Lëtzebuerg | Jules Gales (CA Spora Lëtzebuerg) | 18 |
| 1950/1951 | AS la Jeunesse d'Esch/Alzette | SC Tétange | Jules Gales (CA Spora Lëtzebuerg) | 27 |
| 1951/1952 | National Schifflange | FA Red Boys Differdange | Alphonse Schumacher (National Schifflange) | 16 |
| 1952/1953 | FC Progrès Niederkorn | FA Red Boys Differdange | Henri Fickinger (FC Progrès Niederkorn) François Müller (Red Star Mel-Belair) Roger Weydert (Union Sportive Lëtzebuerg) | 18 |
| 1953/1954 | AS la Jeunesse d'Esch/Alzette | AS la Jeunesse d'Esch/Alzette | Alphonse Schumacher (CS Fola Esch) | 29 |
| 1954/1955 | Stade Dudelange | CS Fola Esch | Alphonse Schumacher (CS Fola Esch) | 20 |
| 1955/1956 | CA Spora Lëtzebuerg | Stade Dudelange | Jean Halsdorf (Stade Dudelange) | 23 |
| 1956/1957 | Stade Dudelange | CA Spora Lëtzebuerg | François Müller (CS Grevenmacher) | 36 |
| 1957/1958 | AS la Jeunesse d'Esch/Alzette | FA Red Boys Differdange | François Jadin (Alliance Dudelange) | 17 |
| 1958/1959 | AS la Jeunesse d'Esch/Alzette | Union Sportive Lëtzebuerg | Marcel Scheer (CA Spora Lëtzebuerg) | 19 |
| 1959/1960 | AS la Jeunesse d'Esch/Alzette | National Schifflange | Louis Pilot (CS Fola Esch) | 18 |
| 1960/1961 | CA Spora Lëtzebuerg | Alliance Dudelange | Paul May (AS la Jeunesse d'Esch/Alzette) | 24 |
| 1961/1962 | Union Sportive Lëtzebuerg | Alliance Dudelange | Hans Cirelli (Alliance Dudelange) | 23 |
| 1962/1963 | AS la Jeunesse d'Esch/Alzette | Union Sportive Lëtzebuerg | Bert Heger (Stade Dudelange) | 20 |
| 1963/1964 | FC Aris Bonnevoie | Union Sportive Lëtzebuerg | Johny Leonard (Union Sportive Lëtzebuerg) | 22 |
| 1964/1965 | Stade Dudelange | CA Spora Lëtzebuerg | Johny Leonard (Union Sportive Lëtzebuerg) | 18 |
| 1965/1966 | FC Aris Bonnevoie | CA Spora Lëtzebuerg | Bert Heger (FC Aris Bonnevoie) Johny Leonard (Union Sportive Lëtzebuerg) | 23 |
| 1966/1967 | AS la Jeunesse d'Esch/Alzette | FC Aris Bonnevoie | Jemp Mertl (Union Sportive Lëtzebuerg) | 22 |
| 1967/1968 | AS la Jeunesse d'Esch/Alzette | Union Sportive Rumelange | Rainer Schönwälder (Union Sportive Lëtzebuerg) | 28 |
| 1968/1969 | FC Avenir Beggen | Union Sportive Lëtzebuerg | Bert Heger (FC Avenir Beggen) | 30 |
| 1969/1970 | AS la Jeunesse d'Esch/Alzette | Union Sportive Lëtzebuerg | Carlo Devillet (CA Spora Lëtzebuerg) | 31 |
| 1970/1971 | Union Sportive Lëtzebuerg | Jeunesse Hautcharage | Nico Braun (Union Sportive Lëtzebuerg) | 25 |
| 1971/1972 | FC Aris Bonnevoie | FA Red Boys Differdange | Furio Cardoni (Union Sportive Rumelange) Carlo Devillet (FC Aris Bonnevoie) | 21 |
| 1972/1973 | AS la Jeunesse d'Esch/Alzette | AS la Jeunesse d'Esch/Alzette | Johny Grettnich (FC Etzella Ettelbruck) Jean-Pierre Hoffmann (AS la Jeunesse d'Esch/Alz.) | 27 |
| 1973/1974 | AS la Jeunesse d'Esch/Alzette | AS la Jeunesse d'Esch/Alzette | Carlo Devillet (CA Spora Lëtzebuerg) | 23 |
| 1974/1975 | AS la Jeunesse d'Esch/Alzette | Union Sportive Rumelange | Jean-Paul Lehnen (FC Etzella Ettelbruck) | 16 |

| | | | |
|---|---|---|---|
| 1975/1976 | AS la Jeunesse d'Esch/Alzette | AS la Jeunesse d'Esch/Alzette | René Müller (FA Red Boys Differdange) | |
| | | | Albert Pissinger (FC Aris Bonnevoie) | 20 |
| 1976/1977 | AS la Jeunesse d'Esch/Alzette | FC Progrès Niederkorn | Johny Hopp (FC Progrès Niederkorn) | 19 |
| 1977/1978 | FC Progrès Niederkorn | FC Progrès Niederkorn | René Müller (FA Red Boys Differdange) | 18 |
| 1978/1979 | FA Red Boys Differdange | FA Red Boys Differdange | Aly May (FC Progrès Niederkorn) | 18 |
| 1979/1980 | AS la Jeunesse d'Esch/Alzette | CA Spora Lëtzebuerg | Robert Langers (Union Sportive Lëtzebuerg) | 26 |
| 1980/1981 | FC Progrès Niederkorn | AS la Jeunesse d'Esch/Alzette | Aly May (FC Progrès Niederkorn) | 18 |
| 1981/1982 | FC Avenir Beggen | FA Red Boys Differdange | Armin Krings (FC Avenir Beggen) | 25 |
| 1982/1983 | AS la Jeunesse d'Esch/Alzette | FC Avenir Beggen | Gérard Simon (AS la Jeunesse d'Esch/Alzette) | 23 |
| 1983/1984 | FC Avenir Beggen | FC Avenir Beggen | Armin Krings (FC Avenir Beggen) | |
| | | | Manou Scheitler (AS la Jeunesse d'Esch/Alzette) | 26 |
| 1984/1985 | AS la Jeunesse d'Esch/Alzette | FA Red Boys Differdange | Armin Krings (FC Avenir Beggen) | |
| | | | Jean-Luc Guillot (AS la Jeunesse d'Esch/Alzette) | 16 |
| 1985/1986 | FC Avenir Beggen | Union Sportive Lëtzebuerg | Armin Krings (FC Avenir Beggen) | 25 |
| 1986/1987 | AS la Jeunesse d'Esch/Alzette | FC Avenir Beggen | Armin Krings (FC Avenir Beggen) | 24 |
| 1987/1988 | AS la Jeunesse d'Esch/Alzette | AS la Jeunesse d'Esch/Alzette | Patrick Morocutti (Union Sportive Lëtzebuerg) | 26 |
| 1988/1989 | CA Spora Lëtzebuerg | Union Sportive Lëtzebuerg | Theo Scholten (AS la Jeunesse d'Esch/Alzette) | |
| | | | Markus Krahen (GER, FC Avenir Beggen) | |
| | | | Armin Krings (FC Avenir Beggen) | 21 |
| 1989/1990 | Union Sportive Lëtzebuerg | FC Swift Hesperange | Markus Krahen (GER, FC Avenir Beggen) | 30 |
| 1990/1991 | Union Sportive Lëtzebuerg | Union Sportive Lëtzebuerg | Patrick Morocutti (Union Sportive Lëtzebuerg) | 23 |
| 1991/1992 | Union Sportive Lëtzebuerg | FC Avenir Beggen | Markus Krahen (GER, FC Avenir Beggen) | 19 |
| 1992/1993 | FC Avenir Beggen | FC Avenir Beggen | Armin Krings (FC Avenir Beggen) | 23 |
| 1993/1994 | FC Avenir Beggen | FC Avenir Beggen | Stefano Fanelli (F91 Dudelange) | 19 |
| 1994/1995 | AS la Jeunesse d'Esch/Alzette | CS Grevenmacher | Yves Heinen (FC Differdange 03) | 22 |
| 1995/1996 | AS la Jeunesse d'Esch/Alzette | Union Sportive Lëtzebuerg | Mikhail Zaritski (FC Avenir Beggen) | 18 |
| 1996/1997 | AS la Jeunesse d'Esch/Alzette | AS la Jeunesse d'Esch/Alzette | Mikhail Zaritski (FC Sporting Mertzig) | |
| | | | Franco Iovino (FC Wiltz 71) | 19 |
| 1997/1998 | AS la Jeunesse d'Esch/Alzette | CS Grevenmacher | Mikhail Zaritski (FC Sporting Mertzig) | 29 |
| 1998/1999 | AS la Jeunesse d'Esch/Alzette | AS la Jeunesse d'Esch/Alzette | Frédéric Cicchirillo (FRA, (FC Sporting Mertzig) | 25 |
| 1999/2000 | F91 Dudelange | AS la Jeunesse d'Esch/Alzette | Marcel Christophe (FC Mondercange) | 26 |
| 2000/2001 | F91 Dudelange | FC Etzella Ettelbruck | Mikhail Zaritski (FC Sporting Mertzig) | 23 |
| 2001/2002 | F91 Dudelange | FC Avenir Beggen | Frédéric Cicchirillo (FRA, F91 Dudelange) | 24 |
| 2002/2003 | CS Grevenmacher | CS Grevenmacher | Daniel Huss (CS Grevenmacher) | 22 |
| 2003/2004 | AS la Jeunesse d'Esch/Alzette | F91 Dudelange | José Manuel Gomes de Andrade | |
| | | | (POR, CA Spora Lëtzebuerg) | 24 |
| 2004/2005 | F91 Dudelange | CS Pétange | Sergio Pupovac (CS Alliance 01 Lëtzebuerg) | 24 |
| 2005/2006 | F91 Dudelange | F91 Dudelange | Fatih Sözen (TUR, CS Grevenmacher) | 23 |
| 2006/2007 | F91 Dudelange | F91 Dudelange | Daniel da Mota Alves (FC Etzella Ettelbruck) | 24 |
| 2007/2008 | F91 Dudelange | CS Grevenmacher | Emmanuel Coquelet (FRA, F91 Dudelange) | 20 |
| 2008/2009 | F91 Dudelange | F91 Dudelange | Pierre Piskor (FRA, FC Differdange 03) | 30 |
| 2009/2010 | AS la Jeunesse d'Esch/Alzette | FC Differdange 03 | Daniel Huss (CS Grevenmacher) | 22 |
| 2010/2011 | F91 Dudelange | FC Differdange 03 | Sanel Ibrahimović (BIH, FC Wiltz 71) | 18 |
| 2011/2012 | F91 Dudelange | F91 Dudelange | Omar Er Rafik (MAR, FC Differdange 03) | 23 |
| 2012/2013 | CS Fola Esch | AS la Jeunesse d'Esch/Alzette | Edis Osmanović (BIH, FC Wiltz 71) | 21 |
| 2013/2014 | F91 Dudelange | FC Differdange 03 | Sanel Ibrahimović | |
| | | | (BIH, AS la Jeunesse d'Esch/Alzette) | 22 |
| 2014/2015 | CS Fola Esch | FC Differdange 03 | Sanel Ibrahimović | |
| | | | (BIH, AS la Jeunesse d'Esch/Alzette) | 21 |
| 2015/2016 | F91 Dudelange | F91 Dudelange | Julien Jahier (FRA, RFCU Lëtzebuerg) | 18 |
| 2016/2017 | F91 Dudelange | F91 Dudelange | Omar Er Rafik (MAR, FC Differdange 03) | 26 |
| 2017/2018 | F91 Dudelange | Racing FC | David Turpel (F91 Dudelange) | 33 |
| 2018/2019 | F91 Dudelange | F91 Dudelange | Samir Ali Hadji (FRA, CS Fola Esch) | 23 |
| 2019/2020 | *Championship abandoned* | *Competition abandoned* | - | |
| 2020/2021 | CS Fola Esch | *Competition abandoned* | Zachary Hadji (FRA, CS Fola Esch) | 33 |
| 2021/2022 | F91 Dudelange | Racing FC Union Lëtzebuerg | Dominik Stolz (GER, FC Swift Hesperange) | 23 |
| 2022/2023 | FC Swift Hesperange | FC Differdange 03 | Rayan Philippe (FRA, FC Swift Hesperange) | 32 |

# NATIONAL CHAMPIONSHIP
## Division Nationale BGL Ligue 2022/2023
### (06.08.2022 – 21.05.2023)

## Results

### Round 1 [06-08.08.2022]
Etzella Ettelbruck - UT Pétange 2-0
Fola Esch - UNA Strassen 2-1
FC Differdange 03 - Racing FCU 2-3
UN Käerjéng 97 - FC Wiltz 71 1-1
FC Mondercange - Victoria Rosport 5-1
US Mondorf - US Hostert 2-0
Swift Hesperange - Progrès Niedercorn 4-2
F91 Dudelange - Jeunesse d'Esch 5-0

### Round 2 [13-14.08.2022]
Racing FCU - US Mondorf 1-0
UT Pétange - Fola Esch 2-3
FC Wiltz 71 - Victoria Rosport 3-1
UNA Strassen - FC Differdange 03 3-2
Progrès Niedercorn - F91 Dudelange 2-3
US Hostert - Swift Hesperange 0-4
Jeunesse d'Esch - UN Käerjéng 97 0-0
FC Mondercange - Etzella Ettelbruck 1-2

### Round 3 [20-21.08.2022]
Victoria Rosport - Jeunesse d'Esch 1-1
Fola Esch - Etzella Ettelbruck 0-0
Swift Hesperange - Racing FCU 2-0
FC Differdange 03 - UT Pétange 1-1
UN Käerjéng 97 - Progrès Niedercorn 1-1
US Mondorf - UNA Strassen 1-2
FC Wiltz 71 - FC Mondercange 1-4
F91 Dudelange - US Hostert 3-1

### Round 4 [26-28.08.2022]
US Hostert - UN Käerjéng 97 0-1
Etzella Ettelbruck - FC Differdange 03 0-2
Progrès Niedercorn - Victoria Rosport 1-0
Jeunesse d'Esch - FC Wiltz 71 1-0
UNA Strassen - Swift Hesperange 0-4
UT Pétange - US Mondorf 4-1
FC Mondercange - Fola Esch 3-0
Racing FCU - F91 Dudelange 2-4

### Round 5 [03-04.09.2022]
Swift Hesperange - UT Pétange 3-3
F91 Dudelange - UNA Strassen 3-1
FC Differdange 03 - Fola Esch 6-0
Jeunesse d'Esch - FC Mondercange 1-1
UN Käerjéng 97 - Racing FCU 0-5
US Mondorf - Etzella Ettelbruck 3-0
Victoria Rosport - US Hostert 2-2
FC Wiltz 71 - Progrès Niedercorn 1-2

### Round 6 [10-11.09.2022]
Racing FCU - Victoria Rosport 2-2
Etzella Ettelbruck - Swift Hesperange 0-4
US Hostert - FC Wiltz 71 2-3
FC Mondercange - FC Differdange 03 0-0
UNA Strassen - UN Käerjéng 97 0-2
UT Pétange - F91 Dudelange 1-2
Fola Esch - US Mondorf 0-1
Progrès Niedercorn - Jeunesse d'Esch 2-1

### Round 7 [18.09.2022]
F91 Dudelange - Etzella Ettelbruck 4-0
Swift Hesperange - Fola Esch 8-1
Jeunesse d'Esch - US Hostert 1-2
UN Käerjéng 97 - UT Pétange 0-1
US Mondorf - FC Differdange 03 0-1
Victoria Rosport - UNA Strassen 0-0
FC Wiltz 71 - Racing FCU 1-1
Progrès Niedercorn - FC Mondercange 4-0

### Round 8 [09.10.2022]
Fola Esch - F91 Dudelange 0-2
Etzella Ettelbruck - UN Käerjéng 97 1-1
FC Differdange 03 - Swift Hesperange 1-2
US Hostert - Progrès Niedercorn 1-0
FC Mondercange - US Mondorf 1-2
Racing FCU - Jeunesse d'Esch 2-1
UNA Strassen - FC Wiltz 71 4-3
UT Pétange - Victoria Rosport 5-1

### Round 9 [16.10.2022]
F91 Dudelange - FC Differdange 03 3-1
Progrès Niedercorn - Racing FCU 0-0
US Hostert - FC Mondercange 0-0
Jeunesse d'Esch - UNA Strassen 2-0
UN Käerjéng 97 - Fola Esch 3-2
Victoria Rosport - Etzella Ettelbruck 3-1
FC Wiltz 71 - UT Pétange 0-2
Swift Hesperange - US Mondorf 4-2

### Round 10 [23.10.2022]
Fola Esch - Victoria Rosport 4-1
Etzella Ettelbruck - FC Wiltz 71 1-2
FC Differdange 03 - UN Käerjéng 97 2-2
Racing FCU - US Hostert 2-1
UNA Strassen - Progrès Niedercorn 0-1
UT Pétange - Jeunesse d'Esch 0-0
FC Mondercange - Swift Hesperange 1-2
US Mondorf - F91 Dudelange 0-7

### Round 11 [06.11.2022]
F91 Dudelange - Swift Hesperange 0-4
US Hostert - UNA Strassen 1-0
Jeunesse d'Esch - Etzella Ettelbruck 6-0
Victoria Rosport - FC Differdange 03 2-3
FC Wiltz 71 - Fola Esch 5-1
Progrès Niedercorn - UT Pétange 2-3
UN Käerjéng 97 - US Mondorf 0-2
Racing FCU - FC Mondercange 2-2

### Round 12 [13.11.2022]
Fola Esch - Jeunesse d'Esch 1-3
Etzella Ettelbruck - Progrès Niedercorn 0-1
FC Differdange 03 - FC Wiltz 71 2-1
US Mondorf - Victoria Rosport 1-6
UNA Strassen - Racing FCU 1-4
UT Pétange - US Hostert 4-1
Swift Hesperange - UN Käerjéng 97 4-2
FC Mondercange - F91 Dudelange 2-3

### Round 13 [26-27.11.2022]
Jeunesse d'Esch - FC Differdange 03 1-0
Progrès Niedercorn - Fola Esch 3-2
Racing FCU - UT Pétange 0-2
UNA Strassen - FC Mondercange 2-0
Victoria Rosport - Swift Hesperange 0-0
FC Wiltz 71 - US Mondorf 4-4
US Hostert - Etzella Ettelbruck 0-3
UN Käerjéng 97 - F91 Dudelange 2-4

### Round 14 [03-04.12.2022]
Etzella Ettelbruck - Racing FCU 0-1
FC Mondercange - UN Käerjéng 97 1-1
F91 Dudelange - Victoria Rosport 2-0
Fola Esch - US Hostert 0-1
FC Differdange 03 - Progrès Niedercorn 2-3
UT Pétange - UNA Strassen 0-1
Swift Hesperange - FC Wiltz 71 4-2
US Mondorf - Jeunesse d'Esch 3-1

### Round 15 [10-11.12.2022]
US Hostert - FC Differdange 03 0-5
UT Pétange - FC Mondercange 5-2
Swift Hesperange - Jeunesse d'Esch 2-0
Victoria Rosport - UN Käerjéng 97 3-0
Racing FCU - Fola Esch 4-2
UNA Strassen - Etzella Ettelbruck 4-1
FC Wiltz 71 - F91 Dudelange 0-3
Progrès Niedercorn - US Mondorf 4-2

### Round 16 [12.02.2023]
F91 Dudelange - Progrès Niedercorn 1-4
Fola Esch - UT Pétange 1-2
Etzella Ettelbruck - FC Mondercange 1-2
FC Differdange 03 - UNA Strassen 0-1
Swift Hesperange - US Hostert 5-1
UN Käerjéng 97 - Jeunesse d'Esch 1-4
US Mondorf - Racing FCU 0-1
Victoria Rosport - FC Wiltz 71 0-0

### Round 17 [18-19.02.2023]
FC Mondercange - FC Wiltz 71 0-3
Progrès Niedercorn - UN Käerjéng 97 1-0
Etzella Ettelbruck - Fola Esch 0-4
US Hostert - F91 Dudelange 1-4
Jeunesse d'Esch - Victoria Rosport 2-0
Racing FCU - Swift Hesperange 1-3
UNA Strassen - US Mondorf 0-1
UT Pétange - FC Differdange 03 4-2

### Round 18 [26.02.2023]
F91 Dudelange - Racing FCU 0-1
Fola Esch - FC Mondercange 2-0
FC Differdange 03 - Etzella Ettelbruck 6-0
Swift Hesperange - UNA Strassen 3-0
UN Käerjéng 97 - US Hostert 0-0
US Mondorf - UT Pétange 2-0
Victoria Rosport - Progrès Niedercorn 2-3
FC Wiltz 71 - Jeunesse d'Esch 3-2

### Round 19 [04-05.03.2023]
Fola Esch - FC Differdange 03 3-2
FC Mondercange - Jeunesse d'Esch 1-2
Etzella Ettelbruck - US Mondorf 0-3
Progrès Niedercorn - FC Wiltz 71 3-0
US Hostert - Victoria Rosport 1-3
Racing FCU - UN Käerjéng 97 1-1
UNA Strassen - F91 Dudelange 1-2
UT Pétange - Swift Hesperange 2-1

### Round 20 [11-12.03.2023]
F91 Dudelange - UT Pétange 0-1
FC Differdange 03 - FC Mondercange 2-0
Swift Hesperange - Etzella Ettelbruck 2-2
Jeunesse d'Esch - Progrès Niedercorn 0-1
UN Käerjéng 97 - UNA Strassen 1-2
US Mondorf - Fola Esch 5-0
Victoria Rosport - Racing FCU 4-2
FC Wiltz 71 - US Hostert 2-2

### Round 21 [17-19.03.2023]
UT Pétange - UN Käerjéng 97 4-1
Fola Esch - Swift Hesperange 0-3
Etzella Ettelbruck - F91 Dudelange 2-5
FC Differdange 03 - US Mondorf 2-1
US Hostert - Jeunesse d'Esch 0-1
FC Mondercange - Progrès Niedercorn 3-3
Racing FCU - FC Wiltz 71 0-1
UNA Strassen - Victoria Rosport 2-2

## Round 22 [29.03.2023]
F91 Dudelange - Fola Esch 2-1
Progrès Niedercorn - US Hostert 6-0
Swift Hesperange - FC Differdange 03 4-0
Jeunesse d'Esch - Racing FCU 1-1
US Mondorf - FC Mondercange 4-1
Victoria Rosport - UT Pétange 0-2
FC Wiltz 71 - UNA Strassen 2-1
UN Käerjéng 97 - Etzella Ett. 0-3 [05.04.23]

## Round 23 [02.04.2023]
Fola Esch - UN Käerjéng 97 3-2
Etzella Ettelbruck - Victoria Rosport 1-5
FC Differdange 03 - F91 Dudelange 0-4
FC Mondercange - US Hostert 1-0
US Mondorf - Swift Hesperange 0-4
Racing FCU - Progrès Niedercorn 1-2
UNA Strassen - Jeunesse d'Esch 2-1
UT Pétange - FC Wiltz 71 2-1

## Round 24 [08.04.2023]
F91 Dudelange - US Mondorf 4-0
Jeunesse d'Esch - UT Pétange 2-2
Progrès Niedercorn - UNA Strassen 2-1
Swift Hesperange - FC Mondercange 2-1
US Hostert - Racing FCU 1-1
UN Käerjéng 97 - FC Differdange 03 0-8
Victoria Rosport - Fola Esch 3-0
FC Wiltz 71 - Etzella Ettelbruck 3-0

## Round 25 [16.04.2023]
Fola Esch - FC Wiltz 71 1-2
Etzella Ettelbruck - Jeunesse d'Esch 3-0
FC Differdange 03 - Victoria Rosport 4-0
Swift Hesperange - F91 Dudelange 4-3
FC Mondercange - Racing FCU 0-1
US Mondorf - UN Käerjéng 97 1-1
UNA Strassen - US Hostert 2-0
UT Pétange - Progrès Niedercorn 0-2

## Round 26 [22-23.04.2023]
Victoria Rosport - US Mondorf 1-1
FC Wiltz 71 - FC Differdange 03 1-2
F91 Dudelange - FC Mondercange 5-1
Progrès Niedercorn - Etzella Ettelbruck 3-1
US Hostert - UT Pétange 0-2
Jeunesse d'Esch - Fola Esch 3-1
UN Käerjéng 97 - Swift Hesperange 0-6
Racing FCU - UNA Strassen 0-1

## Round 27 [29-30.04.2023]
FC Mondercange - UNA Strassen 0-0
Fola Esch - Progrès Niedercorn 0-4
Etzella Ettelbruck - US Hostert 1-1
F91 Dudelange - UN Käerjéng 97 4-0
FC Differdange 03 - Jeunesse d'Esch 0-2
Swift Hesperange - Victoria Rosport 5-1
US Mondorf - FC Wiltz 71 3-0
UT Pétange - Racing FCU 1-1

## Round 28 [05-07.05.2023]
Jeunesse d'Esch - US Mondorf 0-2
Progrès Niedercorn - FC Differdange 03 2-0
US Hostert - Fola Esch 0-1
UN Käerjéng 97 - FC Mondercange 2-2
Racing FCU - Etzella Ettelbruck 2-2
UNA Strassen - UT Pétange 0-3
Victoria Rosport - F91 Dudelange 2-1
FC Wiltz 71 - Swift Hesperange 0-6

## Round 29 [14.05.2023]
Fola Esch - Racing FCU 1-1
Etzella Ettelbruck - UNA Strassen 3-0
F91 Dudelange - FC Wiltz 71 1-1
FC Differdange 03 - US Hostert 1-0
Jeunesse d'Esch - Swift Hesperange 1-1
UN Käerjéng 97 - Victoria Rosport 2-1
FC Mondercange - UT Pétange 4-1
US Mondorf - Progrès Niedercorn 0-1

## Round 30 [21.05.2023]
Progrès Niedercorn - Swift Hesperange 2-2
US Hostert - US Mondorf 2-5
Jeunesse d'Esch - F91 Dudelange 4-2
Racing FCU - FC Differdange 03 0-1
UNA Strassen - Fola Esch 1-0
UT Pétange - Etzella Ettelbruck 3-2
Victoria Rosport - FC Mondercange 1-2
FC Wiltz 71 - UN Käerjéng 97 2-3

## Final Standings

| | | | | | | | | | Total | | Home | | | | | Away | | | | |
|---|---|---|---|---|---|---|---|---|---|---|---|---|---|---|---|---|---|---|---|---|
| 1. | FC Swift Hesperange | 30 | 24 | 5 | 1 | 100 | - | 28 | 77 | 13 | 2 | 0 | 56 | - | 20 | 11 | 3 | 1 | 44 | - | 8 |
| 2. | FC Progrès Niedercorn | 30 | 22 | 4 | 4 | 67 | - | 31 | 70 | 11 | 2 | 2 | 37 | - | 15 | 11 | 2 | 2 | 30 | - | 16 |
| 3. | F91 Dudelange | 30 | 22 | 1 | 7 | 86 | - | 38 | 67 | 10 | 1 | 4 | 37 | - | 16 | 12 | 0 | 3 | 49 | - | 22 |
| 4. | Union Titus Pétange | 30 | 18 | 5 | 7 | 62 | - | 38 | 59 | 9 | 2 | 4 | 37 | - | 21 | 9 | 3 | 3 | 25 | - | 17 |
| 5. | FC Differdange 03 | 30 | 14 | 3 | 13 | 60 | - | 43 | 45 | 7 | 2 | 6 | 31 | - | 20 | 7 | 1 | 7 | 29 | - | 23 |
| 6. | US Mondorf-les-Bains | 30 | 14 | 3 | 13 | 52 | - | 52 | 45 | 7 | 1 | 7 | 25 | - | 25 | 7 | 2 | 6 | 27 | - | 27 |
| 7. | AS La Jeunesse d'Esch/Alzette | 30 | 12 | 7 | 11 | 44 | - | 39 | 43 | 7 | 5 | 3 | 25 | - | 13 | 5 | 2 | 8 | 19 | - | 26 |
| 8. | Racing FC Union Lëtzebuerg | 30 | 11 | 10 | 9 | 43 | - | 39 | 43 | 4 | 4 | 7 | 20 | - | 25 | 7 | 6 | 2 | 23 | - | 14 |
| 9. | FC UNA Strassen | 30 | 12 | 3 | 15 | 33 | - | 46 | 39 | 7 | 1 | 7 | 22 | - | 26 | 5 | 2 | 8 | 11 | - | 20 |
| 10. | FC Wiltz 71 | 30 | 10 | 6 | 14 | 48 | - | 59 | 36 | 5 | 3 | 7 | 28 | - | 34 | 5 | 3 | 7 | 20 | - | 25 |
| 11. | FC Victoria Rosport | 30 | 8 | 8 | 14 | 48 | - | 58 | 32 | 5 | 6 | 4 | 24 | - | 18 | 3 | 2 | 10 | 24 | - | 40 |
| 12. | FC Mondercange | 30 | 7 | 8 | 15 | 41 | - | 55 | 29 | 4 | 4 | 7 | 23 | - | 21 | 3 | 4 | 8 | 18 | - | 34 |
| 13. | CS Fola Esch (Relegation Play-off) | 30 | 8 | 2 | 20 | 36 | - | 71 | 26 | 5 | 2 | 8 | 18 | - | 23 | 3 | 0 | 12 | 18 | - | 48 |
| 14. | UN Käerjéng 97 (Relegation Play-off) | 30 | 5 | 10 | 15 | 30 | - | 69 | 25 | 2 | 4 | 9 | 13 | - | 42 | 3 | 6 | 6 | 17 | - | 27 |
| 15. | FC Etzella Ettelbrück (Relegated) | 30 | 6 | 5 | 19 | 32 | - | 71 | 23 | 3 | 2 | 10 | 15 | - | 31 | 3 | 3 | 9 | 17 | - | 40 |
| 16. | US Hostert (Relegated) | 30 | 4 | 6 | 20 | 20 | - | 65 | 18 | 2 | 2 | 11 | 8 | - | 33 | 2 | 4 | 9 | 12 | - | 32 |

## Relegation Play-offs [25-27.05.2023]

FC Jeunesse Canach - CS Fola Esch     3-4 aet
SC Bettembourg - UN Käerjéng 97     2-3
Both CS Fola Esch and UN Käerjéng 97 remain at first level for 2023/2024.

## Top goalscorers:

| | | |
|---|---|---|
| 32 | **Rayan Philippe (FRA)** | *FC Swift Hesperange* |
| 29 | Dominik Stolz (GER) | *FC Swift Hesperange* |
| 20 | Elias Filet (FRA) | *FC Progrès Niedercorn* |
| 20 | Samir Hadji (MAR) | *F91 Dudelange* |

## NATIONAL CUP
### Coupe du Luxembourg 2022/2023

| Third Round [28-30.10.2022] | | | | |
|---|---|---|---|---|
| FC Mamer 32 - US Hostert | 2-5 | | SC Bettembourg - F91 Dudelange | 1-4 |
| Syra Mensdorf - FC Marisca Mersch | 0-2 | | US Feulen - FC Berdenia Berbourg | 1-2 |
| FC Red-Black/Egalité 07 - FC Swift Hesperange | 1-5 | | CS Grevenmacher - FC Differdange 03 | 0-2 |
| Daring Club Echternach - US Mondorf-les-Bains | 0-7 | | FC Schengen - CS Fola Esch | 1-3 aet |
| FC Mondercange - FC Victoria Rosport | 0-2 | | FC Blô-Weiss Medernach - FC Luxemburg City | 1-4 |
| AS La Jeunesse d'Esch/Alzette - FC Wiltz 71 | 0-1 | | FC Avenir Beggen - Racing FC Union Lëtzebuerg | 0-3 |
| FC CeBra 01 Cessingen - FC UNA Strassen | 1-6 | | US Rumelange - FC Jeunesse Schieren | 3-1 |
| FC Etzella Ettelbrück - Union Titus Pétange | 2-3 aet | | FC Progrès Niederkorn - UN Käerjéng 97 | 1-0 |

| 1/8-Finals [12.04.2023] | | | | |
|---|---|---|---|---|
| FC Differdange 03 - FC Swift Hesperange | 1-0 | | FC Wiltz 71 - US Hostert | 4-1 |
| US Rumelange - FC Progrès Niederkorn | 1-3 aet | | FC Luxemburg City - FC Marisca Mersch | 0-6 |
| FC Victoria Rosport - CS Fola Esch | 2-0 | | US Mondorf-les-Bains - FC UNA Strassen | 2-1 |
| Union Titus Pétange - F91 Dudelange | 2-3 | | FC Berdenia Berbourg - Racing FC Union Lëtzebuerg | 0-4 |

| Quarter-Finals [26.04.2023] | | | | |
|---|---|---|---|---|
| US Mondorf-les-Bains - Racing FC Union Lëtzebuerg | 1-0 | | FC Differdange 03 - FC Progrès Niederkorn | 3-2 |
| F91 Dudelange - FC Victoria Rosport | 2-3 aet | | FC Marisca Mersch - FC Wiltz 71 | 3-1 |

| Semi-Finals [10.05.2023] | | | | |
|---|---|---|---|---|
| FC Marisca Mersch - US Mondorf-les-Bains | 2-1 | | FC Differdange 03 - FC Victoria Rosport | 1-0 |

### Final

26.05.2023; Stade de Luxembourg, Lëtzebuerg; Referee: Ricardo Morais; Attendance: 8,385
**FC Differdange 03 - FC Marisca Mersch**                                          **4-2(0-0)**

**FC Differdange 03**: Christoffer Henri Mafoumbi, Kevin d´Anzico, Juan Bedouret, Théo Brusco, Geoffrey Franzoni (Cap), Manuel Pami Costa, Ulisses Rocha de Oliveira, Dylan Lempereur, Guillaume Trani (81.Gianluca Bei), Amine Naïfi (90.Laurent Pomponi), Érico Roberto Mendes Alves Castro (74.Gianni Monteiro Lima). Trainer: Hélder Angelino Dantas Correia Dias (Portugal).

**FC Marisca Mersch**: Stéphan Moussima, Patrick Neves Esteves, Danilo Marcelino (76.Tidiane Sacko), Valter Barros Andrade (67.Valentin Duarte), Ernest Agovic (81.Frédéric Thill), David Dadashev, Tun Held, Nicola Schreiner, Alison Martins, Joel Rodrigues da Cruz, Benjamin Bresch (Cap). Trainer: Mikhail Zaritski.

**Goals:** 1-0 Érico Roberto Mendes Alves Castro (31), 2-0 Ulisses Rocha de Oliveira (42), 2-1 Joel Rodrigues da Cruz (65), 3-1 Amine Naïfi (71), 3-2 Frédéric Thill (82), 4-2 Laurent Pomponi (90+1).

## THE CLUBS 2022/2023

### Foussballclub Déifferdeng 03

| | | |
|---|---|---|
| **Founded**: | 2003 (*as merger of FA Red Boys Differdange and AS Differdange*) | |
| **Stadium**: | Stade Municipal „Ralf Jänisch", Differdange (3,000) | |
| **Trainer**: | Pedro Miguel Resende dos Reis Morais (POR) | 19.04.1977 |
| [19.10.2022] | Stéphane Léoni (FRA) | 05.03.1976 |
| [06.03.2023] | Hélder Angelino Dantas Correia Dias (POR) | 03.04.1983 |

| Goalkeepers: | DOB | M | (s) | G |
|---|---|---|---|---|
| Andrea Amodio | 13.07.1997 | 1 | | |
| Guillaume Cappa (FRA) | 29.07.1993 | 16 | | |
| Christoffer Henri Mafoumbi (CGO) | 03.03.1994 | 12 | | |
| Rémy Pereira Fernandes | 16.09.1999 | 1 | | |
| **Defenders:** | **DOB** | **M** | **(s)** | **G** |
| Juan Bedouret (ARG) | 16.08.1998 | 24 | (2) | |
| Gianluca Bei | 17.05.1995 | 21 | (4) | 1 |
| Théo Brusco | 20.11.1999 | 22 | | 1 |
| Kevin d´Anzico | 14.08.2000 | 16 | | |
| Geoffrey Franzoni | 18.02.1991 | 25 | (1) | 1 |
| Alis Kocan | 03.06.2004 | | (1) | |
| Dylan Lempereur (FRA) | 24.10.1998 | 20 | | |
| Lucas Santos Gomes Taveira | 20.07.2005 | 1 | | |
| **Midfielders:** | **DOB** | **M** | **(s)** | **G** |
| Kilian Gulluni (FRA) | 20.04.1999 | 18 | (7) | |
| Asim Huskic | 01.03.2004 | | (2) | |

| | DOB | M | (s) | G |
|---|---|---|---|---|
| Marcelino Tambá Aires dos Reis (GNB) | 17.11.1996 | 2 | (2) | |
| Gianni Monteiro Lima | 22.12.2001 | 20 | (3) | 2 |
| Andre Manuel Silva Moreira | 11.01.2002 | 2 | (2) | |
| Amine Naïfi (FRA) | 19.12.1999 | 8 | (2) | 5 |
| Manuel Pami Costa (GNB) | 05.02.1999 | 17 | (2) | |
| *João* Paulo Ambrósio *Simões* (POR) | 28.05.2002 | 15 | (9) | 8 |
| Guillaume Trani (FRA) | 17.12.1997 | 20 | (4) | 5 |
| *Ulisses* Rocha de *Oliveira* (BRA) | 25.03.1989 | 16 | (5) | 2 |
| **Forwards:** | **DOB** | **M** | **(s)** | **G** |
| Gonçalo Jorge Almeida da Silva | 26.11.1990 | 15 | (10) | 7 |
| Érico Roberto Mendes Alves Castro (ANG) | 21.09.1992 | 17 | (5) | 12 |
| *Edgar* Jorge *Neves* da Silva (POR) | 27.04.2000 | 4 | (1) | |
| Laurent Pomponi (FRA) | 18.06.1996 | 4 | (13) | 6 |
| Alessandro Scanzano | 14.03.1996 | 1 | (3) | |
| Bertino *"Tino"* João Cabral *Barbosa* (POR) | 06.05.1992 | 8 | (6) | 8 |
| Darell Tokpa (FRA) | 02.06.2001 | 4 | (5) | |

## F91 Dudelange

| Founded: | 1991 | |
|---|---|---|
| Stadium: | Stade „Jos Nosbaum", Dudelange (2,558) | |
| Trainer: | Carlos Manuel Fangueiro Soares (POR) | 19.12.1976 |

| Goalkeepers: | DOB | M | (s) | G |
|---|---|---|---|---|
| Lucas Fox | 02.10.2000 | 22 | | |
| Jonathan Joubert | 12.09.1979 | 8 | | |
| **Defenders:** | **DOB** | **M** | **(s)** | **G** |
| Manuel da Costa (MAR) | 06.05.1986 | 1 | | |
| Vincent Decker (FRA) | 30.04.1993 | 23 | (3) | 1 |
| Jules Diouf (FRA) | 05.03.1992 | 18 | (3) | 1 |
| Mehdi Kirch | 27.01.1990 | 25 | | 1 |
| Sylvio Ouassiero (MAD) | 07.05.1994 | 22 | | 1 |
| Ismaël Sidibé (MLI) | 24.01.2002 | 5 | (1) | |
| Aldin Skenderović | 28.06.1997 | 25 | | 1 |
| Chris Stumpf | 28.08.1994 | 6 | (10) | |
| **Midfielders:** | **DOB** | **M** | **(s)** | **G** |
| Sinan Altun (FRA) | 18.06.2001 | | (1) | |
| Hugo Antunes | 06.01.2004 | | (1) | |
| Filip Bojić (CRO) | 05.10.1992 | 22 | (3) | 10 |
| *Bruno* Adelino *Freire* Fernandes (CPV) | 27.03.1999 | 12 | (4) | 2 |
| Charles Morren (BEL) | 28.02.1992 | 24 | (2) | 2 |
| Nelito Carlos da Cruz „Vova" | 29.12.1985 | 10 | (12) | 1 |
| **Forwards:** | **DOB** | **M** | **(s)** | **G** |
| Edis Agović | 12.07.1993 | 15 | (12) | 3 |
| Eliot Gashi | 15.04.1995 | 3 | (1) | |
| Samir Hadji (MAR) | 12.09.1989 | 28 | (2) | 20 |
| *João* Victo *Magno* de Souza Machado (BRA) | 15.02.1997 | 27 | (1) | 17 |
| Evann Mendes | 21.01.2004 | 4 | (8) | 1 |
| Herman Moussaki (CGO) | 10.02.1999 | 3 | (11) | 3 |
| Francisco Ninte Junior (POR) | 19.04.2003 | | (2) | |
| Dejvid Sinani | 02.04.1993 | 26 | (1) | 18 |
| Marc Thomas (FRA) | 08.05.2001 | 1 | (11) | 2 |

## Foussballclub Etzella Ettelbruck

| Founded: | 21.05.1917 | |
|---|---|---|
| Stadium: | Stade Am Deich [Stade „Wëllem Durkheim"], Ettelbruck (2,020) | |
| Trainer: | Neil Pattison | 13.03.1979 |
| [25.10.2022] | Bruno Luis Alves Freitas (POR) | 11.04.1994 |

| Goalkeepers: | DOB | M | (s) | G |
|---|---|---|---|---|
| Sergio Englaro | 03.02.2002 | 10 | | |
| Jake Galea (MLT) | 15.04.1996 | 20 | | |
| **Defenders:** | **DOB** | **M** | **(s)** | **G** |
| Florent Berisha (GER) | 01.08.2000 | 27 | (1) | 1 |
| Mirko Kramarić (CRO) | 27.01.1989 | 18 | (2) | 2 |
| Godmer Mabouba (FRA) | 23.09.1990 | 19 | (1) | |
| Pedro Moreira Bernardo | 24.11.2003 | 10 | (3) | |
| Adilson Fortes Neves | 19.12.2005 | | (1) | |
| Yanis N'Gbin | 22.10.1999 | 19 | (4) | |
| Lex Nicolay | 27.03.1997 | 29 | | |
| Anthony Nwanne (SUI) | 05.01.2001 | 5 | (1) | |
| Pol Schlesser | 12.06.1996 | 8 | (1) | |
| **Midfielders:** | **DOB** | **M** | **(s)** | **G** |
| Miguel Alves Meireles | 20.01.2006 | | (2) | |
| Raphael de Sousa | 05.03.1993 | 9 | (1) | |
| Lucas Figueiredo | 14.05.2003 | 21 | (6) | 8 |
| Noah Fernandes | 19.10.2005 | 2 | (6) | 1 |
| Till Hermandung (GER) | 10.10.1997 | 21 | (3) | 2 |
| Sven Kalisa (RWA) | 14.03.1997 | 17 | (6) | 1 |
| Gonçalo Muhongo Boa Morte Leal | 22.11.2005 | | (2) | |
| Kai Schwitz | 23.05.1997 | 2 | | |
| Jedilson Varela | 28.05.1996 | 3 | (6) | |
| **Forwards:** | **DOB** | **M** | **(s)** | **G** |
| Emro Curic (GER) | 25.07.2000 | 8 | (3) | 2 |
| Daniel Alves da Mota | 11.09.1985 | 22 | (5) | 2 |
| André Graf | 22.03.2000 | 1 | (2) | |
| Téo Herr (FRA) | 12.02.2001 | 2 | | |
| Frederick Kyereh (GER) | 18.10.1993 | 22 | (5) | 4 |
| Stefan Monteiro | 03.10.2003 | 1 | (6) | |
| Christopher Nwanne (SUI) | 05.05.1999 | | (7) | |
| Lorenzo Rapaille (BEL) | 21.11.2000 | 20 | (7) | 5 |
| Joseph Séry (FRA) | 05.08.2000 | 14 | (8) | 3 |

## Cercle sportif Fola Esch

| Founded: | 1906 | |
|---|---|---|
| Stadium: | Stade „Émile Mayrisch", Esch-sur-Alzette (3,826) | |
| Trainer: | Miguel Correia (POR) | 16.09.1971 |
| [18.10.2022] | Serge Wolf (FRA) | 11.10.1969 |
| [29.11.2022] | Stefano Bensi | 11.08.1988 |

| Goalkeepers: | DOB | M | (s) | G |
|---|---|---|---|---|
| Emmanuel Tomas Cabral (POR) | 02.08.1996 | 11 | | |
| Evan Da Costa | 07.05.2003 | 18 | | |
| Daniel Martins | 18.11.2003 | 1 | | |
| **Defenders:** | **DOB** | **M** | **(s)** | **G** |
| Denis Ahmetxhekaj | 21.02.2002 | 3 | (2) | |
| Lenny Almada Correia | 19.09.2002 | 16 | (2) | |
| Lionel Amou | 24.02.2005 | 9 | | |
| Mohamed Camara (COD) | 14.04.2000 | 10 | (4) | |
| Diego Colonato | 31.01.2005 | | (2) | |
| Gilson Delgado | 19.10.1992 | 5 | (1) | |
| André Miguel da Silva Ferreira | 16.05.1996 | 16 | (4) | |
| Julien Klein (FRA) | 07.04.1988 | 23 | | |
| Wesley Orville (BEL) | 08.08.2001 | 15 | | |
| Steve Schmidhäusler (SUI) | 18.10.2000 | 2 | | |
| Jordan Tawaba (FRA) | 22.05.1994 | 14 | | 1 |
| **Midfielders:** | **DOB** | **M** | **(s)** | **G** |
| Lucas Correia | 18.04.2002 | 18 | (4) | 5 |
| Rui Jorge Costa de Sousa | 26.12.2002 | 4 | (5) | |
| Daniel „Dani" Filipe *Freitas* Silva | 18.02.2005 | | (1) | |
| Abdulai Djabi Embaló | 30.06.2005 | | (2) | |
| Nenad Dragović | 04.06.1994 | 13 | | |
| Ilyess Jeridi (FRA) | 27.02.1997 | 22 | (2) | 3 |
| Brandon Lima Lizardo (POR) | 05.12.2003 | 3 | (9) | |
| Fabio Cerqueira Martins | 08.01.2003 | 15 | (2) | |
| Fred Paulus | 16.02.2005 | | (3) | |
| Diogo Miguel Zambujo Pimentel | 16.07.1997 | 15 | | |
| Taigo Semedo Monteiro | 03.08.2001 | 6 | (1) | |
| Bob Simon | 17.01.1996 | 7 | | |
| **Forwards:** | **DOB** | **M** | **(s)** | **G** |
| Stefano Bensi | 11.08.1988 | 6 | (1) | 2 |
| Jules Diallo (FRA) | 08.03.1993 | 17 | (7) | 5 |
| Oskar Ekeberg | 29.03.2002 | 1 | (5) | |
| Issam El Alami | 14.10.2003 | 15 | (4) | 3 |
| Yanis Lahrach (BEL) | 02.09.2002 | 7 | (10) | 1 |
| Michael Omosanya | 25.12.1999 | 2 | (1) | 1 |
| Kévin Quinol (FRA) | 07.02.1997 | 13 | (2) | 6 |
| Bruno Correia Mendes (POR) | 10.12.1994 | 17 | (9) | 4 |
| Benjamin Runser (FRA) | 04.09.1991 | 6 | (6) | 5 |

## Football Club Union Sportive Hostert

| Founded: | 1946 | | |
|---|---|---|---|
| Stadium: | Stade „Jos Becker", Hostert (1,500) | | |
| Trainer: | Lars Schäfer (GER) | | 27.08.1982 |
| [06.03.2023] | Henri Bossi | | 20.02.1958 |

| Goalkeepers: | DOB | M | (s) | G |
|---|---|---|---|---|
| Sebastian Grub (GER) | 18.10.1987 | 27 | | |
| Fabio Sebastiani | 10.12.1997 | 1 | | |
| Marius Nana Tchenga (CMR) | 27.11.1994 | 2 | | |
| **Defenders:** | **DOB** | **M** | **(s)** | **G** |
| Leo Benz (GER) | 18.04.1999 | 13 | (1) | |
| Loris Bernardy | 22.01.2001 | 22 | (1) | |
| Sékou Coulibaly (FRA) | 03.06.1994 | 21 | (1) | |
| Noah Dédenon | 08.01.2001 | 12 | (2) | |
| Amar Duračak (CRO) | 17.06.1992 | 3 | (1) | |
| Halim Meddour (FRA) | 11.02.1997 | 23 | (1) | |
| Florian Rybinski (GER) | 01.07.1999 | 3 | | |
| Cedric Steinmetz | 27.09.1999 | 20 | | 1 |
| Gédéon Tshiabuiye (FRA) | 24.07.2001 | 6 | (1) | |
| Quentin Zilli (FRA) | 16.02.1999 | 24 | | 1 |

| Midfielders: | DOB | M | (s) | G |
|---|---|---|---|---|
| Serkan Basha (ALB) | 21.01.2000 | 11 | (9) | 1 |
| Tim Ewert | 25.10.1995 | 22 | (6) | |
| Yann Ferreira | 16.01.2004 | 2 | (7) | |
| Allan Grun (FRA) | 22.01.1998 | 1 | (5) | |
| Thibault Maquart (FRA) | 31.08.1992 | 9 | (8) | |
| Anton Moroz (ROU) | 28.11.2000 | 16 | (4) | |
| **Forwards:** | **DOB** | **M** | **(s)** | **G** |
| Kevin Agović | 15.08.2000 | 8 | (12) | |
| Kilian Amehi (FRA) | 14.11.1997 | 22 | (2) | 4 |
| Julian Bidon (GER) | 22.10.1990 | 18 | (2) | 1 |
| Donovan Bonet (FRA) | 18.03.1989 | 20 | (2) | 8 |
| Ricky Borges | 28.05.1999 | | (2) | |
| Eliot Gashi | 15.04.1995 | 12 | (1) | 1 |
| Yann Hoffmann | 02.02.2002 | | (6) | 1 |
| Deniz Murić (BEL) | 06.03.1995 | 6 | (3) | |
| Moussa Touré (FRA) | 22.12.1988 | 6 | (10) | 2 |

## Association Sportive la Jeunesse d'Esch/Alzette

| Founded: | 1907 | | |
|---|---|---|---|
| Stadium: | Stade de la Frontière, Esch-sur-Alzette (4,000) | | |
| Trainer: | Henri Bossi | | 20.02.1958 |
| [17.10.2022] | Jacques Muller | | 20.03.1963 |
| [21.11.2022] | Pedro Miguel Resende dos Reis Morais (POR) | | 19.04.1977 |

| Goalkeepers: | DOB | M | (s) | G |
|---|---|---|---|---|
| Leonardo Silvestre | 11.04.2003 | 4 | (1) | |
| Kévin Sommer (FRA) | 08.11.1989 | 26 | | |
| **Defenders:** | **DOB** | **M** | **(s)** | **G** |
| Julien Bertoux (FRA) | 24.01.1993 | 9 | | |
| Maxime De Taddeo (FRA) | 11.07.1994 | 20 | (2) | |
| Adrien Kack (FRA) | 11.02.2002 | 18 | | 2 |
| Emmanuel Lapierre (FRA) | 05.08.1993 | 20 | (1) | 2 |
| Dylan Meireles | 24.12.1997 | 8 | (1) | |
| David Mendes Merces | 08.11.2000 | 2 | (4) | |
| **Midfielders:** | **DOB** | **M** | **(s)** | **G** |
| Dennis Besch | 02.04.1999 | 24 | (1) | 1 |
| Alexis Boury (FRA) | 31.10.2001 | 18 | (3) | |
| Alex de Sousa | 18.09.2003 | | (3) | |
| Aldin Derviševič | 19.08.1989 | 6 | (2) | |
| Alexis Larrière (FRA) | 20.03.1997 | 21 | (5) | 7 |

| | DOB | M | (s) | G |
|---|---|---|---|---|
| Irvin Latić | 24.05.2002 | 14 | (5) | 1 |
| Riad Ouedraogo (FRA) | 17.07.1996 | 1 | | |
| David Soares | 15.07.1995 | 22 | (4) | 1 |
| Miloš Todorović | 18.08.1995 | 28 | | 4 |
| Stancy Youbi | | | (1) | |
| **Forwards:** | **DOB** | **M** | **(s)** | **G** |
| Alexandre Arénate (GLP) | 20.07.1995 | 11 | (3) | 6 |
| Gary Bernard | 24.10.2000 | 8 | (7) | |
| Kevin dos Santos Silva Cardoso (POR) | 05.04.2002 | | (1) | |
| Andrea Deidda | 15.12.1993 | 7 | (12) | 1 |
| Maxime Deruffe (FRA) | 13.05.1988 | 12 | (9) | 1 |
| Luca Duriatti | 11.02.1998 | 9 | (9) | 2 |
| Almir Klica (MNE) | 10.11.1998 | 15 | (3) | 3 |
| Ahmed Mogni (COM) | 10.10.1991 | 12 | (2) | 4 |
| Demba Seck (FRA) | 05.01.1997 | 15 | (10) | 7 |

## Football Club Mondercange

| Founded: | 1933 | | |
|---|---|---|---|
| Stadium: | Stade Communal, Mondercange (3,300) | | |
| Trainer: | Dinis Xavier De Sousa | | 23.11.1974 |
| [20.02.2023] | Olivier Ciancanelli | | 23.10.1962 |

| Goalkeepers: | DOB | M | (s) | G |
|---|---|---|---|---|
| Teddy da Silva (FRA) | 01.06.1995 | 21 | | |
| Damien Grégorini (FRA) | 02.03.1979 | 1 | | |
| Dzemil Husovic | 18.05.2003 | 8 | | |
| **Defenders:** | **DOB** | **M** | **(s)** | **G** |
| Billy Bernard | 09.04.1991 | 10 | (2) | |
| Julian Caracciolo (FRA) | 20.05.1995 | 3 | (1) | |
| Lamine Fall (FRA) | 22.02.1994 | 20 | (3) | 1 |
| Jordan Kerstenne (BEL) | 23.04.1997 | 24 | (1) | 2 |
| Amdy Konte (SEN) | 13.07.1997 | 25 | | |
| Tom Laterza | 09.05.1992 | 21 | (1) | |
| Clayton de Sousa Moreira | 24.02.1988 | 13 | (3) | |
| Daryl Myre (FRA) | 01.09.1999 | 28 | | 2 |
| Alexandre Semedo Borges | 22.08.1989 | 1 | (1) | |
| Brandon Soares Rosa (POR) | 15.08.1998 | 19 | (3) | 1 |
| **Midfielders:** | **DOB** | **M** | **(s)** | **G** |
| Johnny Amadei (FRA) | 18.07.1992 | 13 | (10) | 3 |
| Anasse Bekhaled (FRA) | 30.10.1995 | 13 | (6) | 2 |

| | DOB | M | (s) | G |
|---|---|---|---|---|
| Paul Bossi | 22.07.1991 | 2 | (2) | |
| Kader Bourtal (FRA) | 08.10.1991 | 19 | (1) | 2 |
| Dany de Sousa | 08.11.2000 | 9 | (9) | 2 |
| Bilal El Amraoui (FRA) | 01.01.1997 | | (6) | |
| Tarek Nouidra (FRA) | 09.05.1987 | 6 | (2) | |
| *Stélvio* Rosa da Cruz (ANG) | 24.01.1989 | 19 | | |
| **Forwards:** | **DOB** | **M** | **(s)** | **G** |
| Alessandro Alunni | 19.12.1991 | 12 | (8) | 2 |
| *Flávio* António da *Silva* (POR) | 03.04.1996 | 4 | (2) | |
| Oguzhan Kaylesiz (BEL) | 06.02.1998 | 2 | (4) | |
| Sofiane Khayat (TUN) | 05.05.1999 | | (1) | |
| Alexio Alexandre dos Santos Mendes „Lélé" (POR) | 08.10.1993 | 3 | (7) | |
| El Hassane M'Barki (MAR) | 08.05.1987 | 27 | (3) | 17 |
| Eddire Mokrani (ALG) | 23.01.1991 | 2 | (4) | 2 |
| Kevin Ruppert | 16.08.1991 | 1 | (4) | |
| Faisal Sahraoui (FRA) | 14.12.1998 | | (1) | |
| Erwin Senakuku (BEL) | 01.09.1994 | 4 | (4) | 2 |

## Union sportive de Mondorf-les-Bains

| | Founded: | 1915 |
| --- | --- | --- |
| | Stadium: | Stade "John Grün", Mondorf-les-Bains (3,600) |
| | Trainer: | Manuel Correia (POR) |

Trainer date: 28.03.1976

| Goalkeepers: | DOB | M | (s) | G |
| --- | --- | --- | --- | --- |
| Erkan Agović | 24.08.2000 | 1 | | |
| Max de Cillia | 14.03.2003 | | (1) | |
| João Ricardo Silva Machado | 09.04.1999 | 29 | | |
| **Defenders:** | **DOB** | **M** | **(s)** | **G** |
| Ahmed Benhemine (FRA) | 15.01.1987 | 17 | (2) | 2 |
| Pedro Miguel Neves da Costa „Costinha" (POR) | 11.03.1994 | 21 | (2) | 1 |
| Tom de Cillia | 14.03.2003 | 1 | (1) | |
| Fatih Eren (TUR) | 17.01.1995 | 11 | (5) | |
| Sulayman Foufoué (FRA) | 09.10.2001 | 7 | | |
| Yann Matias Marques | 12.11.1996 | 19 | (2) | |
| Marcio Mendes | 04.01.2002 | 13 | (7) | 3 |
| Henid Ramdedović | 20.07.1987 | 1 | | |
| **Midfielders:** | **DOB** | **M** | **(s)** | **G** |
| Alexis Bourigeaud (FRA) | 02.07.1999 | 19 | (2) | 2 |
| *Cleidir* Paulo *Neves* Luis (POR) | 16.10.1993 | | (1) | |
| Fabio d'Alessandro | 28.06.1996 | | (1) | |
| Magnus Hansen | 26.03.2001 | 3 | (1) | |
| Dwayn Holter | 15.06.1995 | 11 | (3) | 1 |
| Dylan Nsidjine Kuete | 12.07.2000 | 20 | (1) | |
| Ricardo Couto Pinto | 14.01.1996 | 10 | (7) | 1 |
| Dzenid Ramdedović | 25.02.1992 | 8 | (2) | |
| Benjamin Schmit (BEL) | 24.01.1997 | 24 | (2) | 1 |
| Faraji Taarimte (FRA) | 17.08.1994 | 19 | (4) | 5 |
| **Forwards:** | **DOB** | **M** | **(s)** | **G** |
| Billel Abdelkadous (FRA) | 22.05.1990 | 18 | (7) | 8 |
| Sofiane Bekkouche (FRA) | 02.05.1996 | 16 | (11) | 5 |
| Sami Ben Amar (MAR) | 02.03.1998 | 4 | (3) | 1 |
| Marwane Benamra (ALG) | 09.04.1995 | 20 | (6) | 6 |
| Alhassane Keita (GUI) | 16.04.1992 | 9 | (6) | 8 |
| Diogo Fernandes Lopes (FRA) | 30.06.2002 | 18 | (8) | 7 |
| Christian Mangala (COD) | 30.06.1998 | 7 | (2) | |
| Fabrice Yao (NIG) | 29.12.1995 | 4 | (1) | |

## Football Club Progrès Niederkorn

| | Founded: | 1919 |
| --- | --- | --- |
| | Stadium: | Stade „Jos Haupert", Niederkorn (2,800) |
| | Trainer: | Jeff Strasser |

Trainer date: 05.10.1974

| Goalkeepers: | DOB | M | (s) | G |
| --- | --- | --- | --- | --- |
| Sebastien Flauss (FRA) | 19.08.1989 | 4 | | |
| Eldin Latik | 22.12.2002 | 26 | | |
| **Defenders:** | **DOB** | **M** | **(s)** | **G** |
| Oluwatobiloba Adefunyibomi Alagbe (NGA) | 24.04.2000 | 10 | | 1 |
| Florian Bohnert | 09.11.1997 | 14 | | |
| Alex Angelin Guett Guett (CMR) | 26.11.2002 | 26 | (4) | 1 |
| Hamadou Karamoko (FRA) | 31.10.1995 | 13 | | |
| Metin Karayer (FRA) | 18.05.1992 | 28 | | |
| Gérard Mersch | 08.09.1996 | 3 | (4) | |
| Vincent Peugnet (FRA) | 05.02.1998 | 25 | | 2 |
| Alexandre Sacras | 14.12.2000 | 1 | (3) | |
| Jader Soares | 19.08.1996 | 2 | | |
| **Midfielders:** | **DOB** | **M** | **(s)** | **G** |
| Brian Amofa (FRA) | 07.09.1992 | 17 | (6) | 2 |
| Yannick Bastos | 30.05.1993 | 18 | (6) | 3 |
| Emir Bijelić (BIH) | 16.01.1998 | 17 | (4) | 3 |
| Yannick Cervellera | 04.04.2001 | 1 | (2) | |
| Bilal Hend (FRA) | 18.01.2000 | 20 | (5) | 10 |
| Belmin Muratović (MNE) | 27.03.1998 | 15 | (3) | 1 |
| Ben Vogel | 22.12.1994 | 15 | (7) | 1 |
| **Forwards:** | **DOB** | **M** | **(s)** | **G** |
| Conrad Azong (GER) | 27.03.1993 | 1 | (12) | 3 |
| Mamadou Cellou Bah (GUI) | 26.02.2005 | | (1) | |
| Mayron de Almeida (BEL) | 22.11.1995 | 26 | (2) | 11 |
| Elias Filet (FRA) | 06.03.2002 | 24 | (5) | 20 |
| Ryan Klapp | 10.01.1993 | 2 | (7) | |
| Antonio Luisi | 07.10.1994 | 7 | (12) | 4 |
| Antoine Hanus Mazure | 19.09.1998 | 15 | (7) | 5 |

## Racing Football Club Union Lëtzebuerg

| | Founded: | 12.05.2005 (*as merger of Spora, Union and CS Alliance 01 Lëtzebuerg*) |
| --- | --- | --- |
| | Stadium: | Stade "Achille Hammerel", Lëtzebuerg (5,814) |
| | Trainer: | Fahrudin Kuduzović (BIH) |
| [29.04.2023] | | Julien Humbert (FRA) |

Trainer dates: 10.10.1984 / 23.06.1984

| Goalkeepers: | DOB | M | (s) | G |
| --- | --- | --- | --- | --- |
| Killian Le Roy (FRA) | 31.01.1998 | 1 | (1) | |
| Romain Ruffier (FRA) | 04.10.1989 | 29 | | |
| **Defenders:** | **DOB** | **M** | **(s)** | **G** |
| Joachim Amijekori | 14.02.2004 | 8 | (1) | |
| Judicaël Crillon (FRA) | 21.11.1988 | 4 | (1) | |
| Jonathan Hennetier (FRA) | 06.11.1991 | 28 | (1) | 1 |
| Joakim Kada (ALG) | 29.01.2001 | 22 | | 2 |
| Alexandre Laurienté (FRA) | 19.11.1989 | 27 | (2) | 1 |
| Gérard Mersch | 08.09.1996 | 2 | (1) | |
| Matis Rakotomahanina (MAD) | 19.04.2003 | 1 | | |
| Pit Simon | 17.02.1998 | 7 | (1) | 1 |
| **Midfielders:** | **DOB** | **M** | **(s)** | **G** |
| Adrian Ahmetxhekaj | 12.11.2000 | 20 | (4) | 2 |
| Dinan Amiri (ALG) | 29.05.2002 | 3 | (6) | 1 |
| Lohan Dewalque (BEL) | 28.02.2004 | 2 | (1) | |
| Mickael Garos (FRA) | 10.05.1988 | 28 | | 2 |
| Farid Ikene | 15.12.2000 | 12 | (7) | |
| Samy Kehli (FRA) | 27.01.1991 | 8 | (4) | |
| Mehdi Koussa (FRA) | 07.02.2005 | | (1) | |
| Olav Moreira | 23.09.2003 | | (1) | |
| Kevin Nakache (FRA) | 05.04.1989 | 19 | (7) | 5 |
| Abdelhakim Omrani (FRA) | 18.02.1991 | | (1) | |
| Mario Pokar (GER) | 18.01.1990 | 3 | (11) | |
| Yannick Schaus | 11.03.2000 | 10 | (6) | |
| Jérôme Simon (FRA) | 12.09.1993 | 20 | (1) | 4 |
| Delvin Skenderović | 23.01.1994 | 3 | | |
| Daniils Skopenko (LVA) | 23.03.2000 | | (1) | |
| **Forwards:** | **DOB** | **M** | **(s)** | **G** |
| Andreas Buch (GER) | 25.04.1993 | 14 | (13) | 6 |
| Emmanuel Françoise (FRA) | 08.06.1987 | 12 | (5) | 4 |
| Ronaldo Machado Pereira | 28.01.2005 | 1 | (1) | |
| Théo Mariani (FRA) | 22.05.2005 | | (1) | |
| Edvin Muratović | 15.02.1997 | 22 | (3) | 6 |
| Kablan Davy N'Goma (FRA) | 13.10.1995 | 23 | (5) | 7 |
| Yonni Rocha Fonseca | 01.04.2004 | 1 | (1) | |

## Football Club Swift Hesperange

| | Founded: | 1916 |
| --- | --- | --- |
| | Stadium: | Stade „Alphonse Theis", Hesperange (3,058) |
| | Trainer: | Pascal Carzaniga (FRA) |

Trainer date: 04.05.1971

| Goalkeepers: | DOB | M | (s) | G |
| --- | --- | --- | --- | --- |
| Youn Czekanowicz | 08.08.2000 | 1 | | |
| Geordan Dupire (FRA) | 28.09.1993 | 29 | | |
| **Defenders:** | **DOB** | **M** | **(s)** | **G** |
| Abdoul Karim Danté (MLI) | 29.10.1998 | 5 | (1) | 1 |
| Ricardo Aleixo Delgado | 22.02.1994 | 18 | (3) | 2 |
| Kevin Malget | 15.01.1991 | 15 | (1) | 3 |
| Roman Pierrard (FRA) | 11.09.1997 | 9 | (2) | |
| Jerry Prempeh (GHA) | 29.12.1988 | 26 | | 2 |
| Cédric Sacras | 28.09.1996 | 15 | (1) | 1 |
| Toufik Zeghdane (ALG) | 17.09.1992 | 15 | (4) | 1 |
| **Midfielders:** | **DOB** | **M** | **(s)** | **G** |
| El Hadi Belameiri (FRA) | 24.04.1991 | 10 | (7) | 5 |
| Clément Couturier (FRA) | 13.09.1993 | 27 | | 7 |
| Négo Ekofo (FRA) | 17.05.1997 | 17 | (2) | |
| Maxime Electeur (BEL) | 22.10.1996 | | (1) | |
| *Gustavo* Alexandre Hemkemeier (BRA) | 19.06.1997 | 2 | (3) | |
| Olivier Marques | 21.03.1992 | 4 | (13) | |
| Mohamed Morabet (GER) | 31.01.1998 | | (1) | |
| Bryan Nouvier (FRA) | 21.06.1995 | 23 | (5) | 2 |
| Jan Ostrowski | 14.04.1999 | | (1) | |
| Dominik Stolz (GER) | 04.05.1990 | 29 | | 29 |
| João Tiago Teixeira (POR) | 07.05.1996 | | (4) | 1 |
| Mehdi Terki (ALG) | 27.09.1991 | 28 | | 3 |
| **Forwards:** | **DOB** | **M** | **(s)** | **G** |
| Lado Akhalaia (MDA) | 01.07.2002 | 2 | (4) | |
| Ken Corral | 08.05.1992 | 11 | (5) | 5 |
| Maurice Deville | 31.07.1992 | 4 | (10) | |
| Achraf Drif (FRA) | 22.03.1992 | 2 | (4) | |
| Ryad Habbas (FRA) | 16.07.1997 | 1 | (5) | 2 |
| Benjamin Mokulu Tembe (COD) | 11.10.1989 | 1 | | |
| Smail Morabit (FRA) | 05.07.1988 | 2 | (5) | 2 |
| Rayan Philippe (FRA) | 23.10.2000 | 29 | (1) | 32 |
| Moussa Seydi (SEN) | 21.08.1996 | 4 | (4) | |
| Florik Shala | 19.07.1997 | 1 | (2) | |

## Uewer Nidder Käerjéng 97 Bascharage

| | Founded: | 1997 | | |
|---|---|---|---|---|
| | Stadium: | Stade um Bëchel, Hautcharage (1,000) | | |
| | Trainer: | Marc Thomé | 04.11.1963 | |
| | [20.03.2023] | Manuel Peixoto (FRA) | 18.12.1956 | |

| Goalkeepers: | DOB | M | (s) | G |
|---|---|---|---|---|
| Joé Frising | 13.01.1994 | 24 | | |
| Noah Scheidweiler | 29.08.2004 | 6 | | |
| **Defenders:** | **DOB** | **M** | **(s)** | **G** |
| Benis Belesi (BEL) | 01.06.1999 | 14 | (1) | |
| Yannick Biagui (SEN) | 21.02.1994 | 11 | (1) | 1 |
| Noé Ewert | 24.02.1997 | 19 | (3) | |
| Nicolas Fernandes (FRA) | 07.01.1988 | 18 | | 1 |
| Mathias Jänisch | 27.08.1990 | 20 | | 2 |
| Guillaume Mura (FRA) | 09.01.1986 | 21 | (1) | |
| Thomas Schroeder | 21.06.2004 | 2 | (1) | |
| Paulo Júnior Sousa Rodrigues | 05.04.2004 | 22 | (1) | |
| **Midfielders:** | **DOB** | **M** | **(s)** | **G** |
| Sam Alverdi | 23.08.1997 | 2 | (4) | |
| Luca Alverdi | 17.10.1999 | 8 | (9) | |
| Gilles Bettmer | 31.03.1989 | 2 | (7) | |
| Zidane Borges Monteiro (CPV) | 02.01.2001 | | (6) | |
| Julien Fostier | 27.08.1990 | 27 | (1) | 4 |
| Ben Klein | 04.11.2004 | 4 | (4) | |
| Mathieu Leroux (FRA) | 26.03.1996 | 13 | (4) | 2 |
| Trésor Mossi (BDI) | 28.08.2001 | 18 | (2) | |
| Seroj Titizian (ARM) | 01.02.2000 | 17 | (5) | 2 |
| **Forwards:** | **DOB** | **M** | **(s)** | **G** |
| Ivan Albanese | 14.07.1998 | 13 | (9) | 2 |
| Valerio Barbaro | 16.02.1998 | 9 | (5) | 1 |
| Jeoffrey de Oliveira (FRA) | 25.11.1999 | 12 | (4) | 2 |
| Franck M'bia Etoundi (CMR) | 30.08.1990 | 7 | (3) | 2 |
| Christivi Masombo (BEL) | 21.06.2001 | 8 | (8) | 3 |
| Deniz Muric (BEL) | 06.03.1995 | 9 | (3) | 2 |
| Resul Musolli | 12.05.2004 | 2 | (1) | |
| Stefan Lopes Rocha | 24.09.1998 | 22 | (1) | 4 |
| Hayssam Zaki (FRA) | 27.05.2003 | | (2) | |

## Football Club UNA Strassen

| | Founded: | 1922 | | |
|---|---|---|---|---|
| | Stadium: | Complexe Sportif „Jean Wirtz", Strassen (2,000) | | |
| | Trainer: | Christian Lutz (GER) | 31.10.1975 | |
| | [08.11.2022] | Carlos Teixeira | 11.01.1977 | |
| | [14.11.2022] | Arno Bonvini | 14.10.1975 | |

| Goalkeepers: | DOB | M | (s) | G |
|---|---|---|---|---|
| Emanuel Felipe Fontes Martins „Manú" | 22.03.1990 | 1 | | |
| Koray Özcan (FRA) | 01.02.1995 | 29 | | |
| **Defenders:** | **DOB** | **M** | **(s)** | **G** |
| Alen Agović | 28.11.1997 | 16 | (5) | 2 |
| Denis Agović | 13.07.1993 | 3 | (2) | |
| Kévin Bacconnier | 01.05.1993 | 19 | | 1 |
| Gauthier Bernardelli (FRA) | 21.08.1992 | 16 | (1) | 4 |
| Fabien Fonrose | 03.04.1998 | 18 | (2) | |
| Tom Schnell | 08.10.1985 | 23 | (1) | |
| Tom Siebenaler | 28.09.1990 | 15 | (2) | |
| Alan Stulin (POL) | 05.06.1990 | 16 | (1) | |
| **Midfielders:** | **DOB** | **M** | **(s)** | **G** |
| Mike Andreas (GER) | 31.01.1997 | 16 | (2) | |
| Cédric Baiverlin | 12.03.2003 | 15 | (9) | 3 |
| Kevin Kerger | 17.11.1994 | 8 | (2) | |
| Maxime Loichot (FRA) | 03.05.1998 | 10 | (4) | |
| Tony Mastrangelo | 01.09.1994 | 13 | (4) | 1 |
| Brian Moding (BEL) | 07.02.1993 | 7 | (5) | 2 |
| Diogo Pimentel | 16.07.1997 | 13 | | |
| Brian Rouffignac | 27.12.2000 | 10 | (3) | |
| Jean-Désiré Tibor (BEL) | 02.09.1993 | 8 | (4) | 1 |
| Florian Weirich (GER) | 23.09.1990 | 2 | | |
| **Forwards:** | **DOB** | **M** | **(s)** | **G** |
| Brian Babit (FRA) | 21.03.1993 | 20 | (3) | 5 |
| Blaise Baillet (BEL) | 30.12.1999 | 4 | (17) | 2 |
| Dany Camilo Almeida | 12.01.2001 | 15 | (11) | 4 |
| Cédric Cossou (FRA) | 20.04.1997 | 6 | (2) | |
| Nicolas Perez (FRA) | 26.10.1990 | 27 | (2) | 6 |
| Marcus Ragnell (SWE) | 15.05.2005 | | (1) | |
| Pedro Santos | 29.09.2005 | | (3) | 1 |

## Union Titus Pétange

| | Founded: | 2015 | | |
|---|---|---|---|---|
| | Stadium: | Stade Municipal "Jérémy Schulz", Pétange (2,400) | | |
| | Trainer: | Yannick Sambea Kakoko (GER) | 26.01.1990 | |

| Goalkeepers: | DOB | M | (s) | G |
|---|---|---|---|---|
| André Barrela | 22.01.2001 | 25 | | |
| Hugo Wolf (FRA) | 01.04.2000 | 5 | | |
| **Defenders:** | **DOB** | **M** | **(s)** | **G** |
| *Lucas* Lima *Carnevalli* (BRA) | 29.03.1995 | 8 | (7) | |
| Sascha Heil (GER) | 04.05.1999 | 18 | (1) | 1 |
| Jérémy Mawatu (FRA) | 12.08.1997 | 24 | (1) | |
| Jonathan Nsanzimana (GER) | 06.01.2004 | 3 | | |
| José Francisco Monteiro Peti „Zé Peti" (POR) | 27.05.2002 | 3 | (2) | |
| Marian Sarr (GAM) | 30.01.1995 | 25 | (1) | 1 |
| Sambou Sarr (SEN) | 11.11.2000 | 20 | (4) | |
| Mike Schneider | 01.02.1995 | 13 | (3) | 3 |
| Fabio Ezequiel Teixeira | 13.05.2004 | 1 | (2) | |
| **Midfielders:** | **DOB** | **M** | **(s)** | **G** |
| Alexander Laukart (GER) | 25.10.1998 | 9 | | |
| Ayman Ouhatti (MAR) | 15.01.2001 | 17 | (4) | |
| Gianluigi Pitisci (BEL) | 22.10.2002 | 4 | (4) | |
| Valentin Steinmetz (FRA) | 12.12.1997 | 23 | (2) | 3 |
| Denis Stumpf | 09.09.1997 | 19 | (4) | 1 |
| Patrik Teixeira Pinto | 10.05.1996 | 14 | (6) | |
| Axel Vitris (FRA) | 18.01.2002 | 2 | (3) | 2 |
| **Forwards:** | **DOB** | **M** | **(s)** | **G** |
| Artur Abreu Pereira | 11.08.1994 | 24 | (3) | 15 |
| António Pedro Pina Gomes (POR) | 29.08.2000 | 16 | (7) | 3 |
| Rubén Gonçalves Matheus | 03.02.2003 | 10 | (14) | 3 |
| Kai Merk (KGZ) | 28.08.1998 | 18 | (2) | 11 |
| Balsa Perković (SRB) | 14.01.2005 | 3 | (11) | 1 |
| Eric Preljević | 31.07.2004 | | (4) | |
| Kempes Tekiela (GER) | 15.10.1997 | 26 | (1) | 16 |

## Football Club Victoria Rosport

| | Founded: | 01.10.1928 | |
|---|---|---|---|
| | Stadium: | VictoriArena, Rosport (1,000) | |
| | Trainer: | Martin Forkel (GER) | 22.07.1979 |

| Goalkeepers: | DOB | M | (s) | G |
|---|---|---|---|---|
| Niklas Bürger (GER) | 07.10.1992 | 29 | | |
| Bobby Jiang | 08.05.1999 | 1 | | |
| **Defenders:** | **DOB** | **M** | **(s)** | **G** |
| Juri Amidon | 30.07.2001 | 9 | (3) | |
| Eric Brandenburger | 08.09.1998 | 28 | | 1 |
| Gilles Feltes | 06.12.1995 | 29 | | 3 |
| Albert Ferreira | 14.02.2005 | 10 | (2) | 1 |
| Gonçalo Rodrigues Fernandes | 05.10.2002 | 25 | (2) | 3 |
| Dāvis Sprūds (LVA) | 28.12.1998 | 25 | (1) | 2 |
| Johannes Steinbach (GER) | 02.07.1992 | 27 | (1) | 8 |
| Philimon Tawiah (GHA) | 11.12.1998 | 8 | (6) | |
| Oege-Sietse van Lingen (NED) | 21.10.1999 | 10 | (4) | 6 |
| **Midfielders:** | **DOB** | **M** | **(s)** | **G** |
| Michel Bechtold | 01.07.1995 | 20 | (6) | |
| Gabriel Gaspar Pereira | 20.07.1990 | 12 | (9) | 2 |
| Kevin Marques | 16.01.1998 | 28 | | 1 |
| Yannick Paulos | 25.05.2004 | | (1) | |
| Mike Tchantchou | 21.08.1998 | | (5) | |
| Ben Kader Zoundi (BEL) | 08.09.1997 | 3 | (3) | |
| **Forwards:** | **DOB** | **M** | **(s)** | **G** |
| Yan Bouché | 19.03.1999 | 24 | (2) | 5 |
| Ernesto Carratala-Jiménez (GER) | 10.11.1999 | 15 | (12) | 9 |
| Sam Crowther (NED) | 03.04.2000 | 11 | (5) | 5 |
| Raul Ferreira | 18.11.2002 | | (2) | |
| Glen Habimana (RWA) | 13.11.2001 | 6 | (9) | 2 |
| Joé Neves Araujo | 06.12.2004 | 10 | (10) | |

## Football Club Wiltz 71

| | |
|---|---|
| **Founded**: | 12.03.1971 |
| **Stadium**: | Stade „Christophe Turpel", Wiltz (3,000) |
| **Trainer**: | David Vandenbroeck (BEL)    12.07.1985 |

| Goalkeepers: | DOB | M | (s) | G |
|---|---|---|---|---|
| Olivier Mabille | 01.03.1988 | 1 | | |
| Ralph Schon | 20.01.1990 | 29 | | |
| **Defenders:** | **DOB** | **M** | **(s)** | **G** |
| Ben Biver | 31.10.1997 | 25 | (2) | |
| Gilson Delgado Freitas | 19.10.1992 | 9 | | |
| Dany Fernandes | 09.05.1994 | | (1) | |
| Randy Giargiana (BEL) | 22.11.1995 | 17 | (6) | 2 |
| Peter Guinari | 02.06.2001 | 16 | (1) | |
| Damien Humblet | 21.09.1996 | 21 | | 1 |
| Célestin Lilango Nzanga | 01.05.1997 | 7 | (1) | |
| Moise Ngwisani (COD) | 28.01.1998 | 16 | (4) | 2 |
| Rick Brito Oliveira | 25.11.2000 | 7 | (2) | |
| Andy Rodrigues | 11.05.2003 | 9 | (1) | |

| Midfielders: | DOB | M | (s) | G |
|---|---|---|---|---|
| Emir Burkić (SVN) | 27.07.1993 | 1 | (1) | |
| Bakary Jaiteh (GAM) | 30.11.1999 | 18 | | 3 |
| Junior Malick Belporo (CMR) | 21.10.1994 | | (2) | |
| Luca Napoleone | 30.09.1993 | 18 | (8) | 5 |
| Chris Philipps | 08.03.1994 | 20 | (1) | 5 |
| Lenn Scheuer | 18.09.2003 | | (2) | |
| Christophe Schroeder | 24.05.2000 | 12 | (7) | |
| Luigi Vaccaro (BEL) | 26.03.1991 | 14 | (9) | 2 |
| **Forwards:** | **DOB** | **M** | **(s)** | **G** |
| Redouane Boulbrachène (FRA) | 25.11.1996 | 6 | (5) | 1 |
| Kevin Alexandre Delgado Martins | 13.03.2002 | 2 | (11) | 1 |
| Mirza Jašarević (BIH) | 12.12.1999 | 9 | (10) | 3 |
| Benjamin Romeyns (BEL) | 27.05.2001 | 26 | (3) | 11 |
| David Timmermans (BEL) | 10.04.1993 | 23 | (4) | 7 |
| Bigen Yala Lusala (BEL) | 20.10.1992 | 24 | (2) | 4 |

## SECOND LEVEL
### Éierepromotioun / Promotion d'Honneur 2022/2023

| | | | | | | | | |
|---|---|---|---|---|---|---|---|---|
| 1. | FC Schifflange 95 (*Promoted*) | 30 | 20 | 4 | 6 | 62 - 37 | 64 |
| 2. | FC Marisca Mersch (*Promoted*) | 30 | 17 | 7 | 6 | 65 - 43 | 58 |
| 3. | SC Bettembourg (*Promotion Play-off*) | 30 | 15 | 7 | 8 | 69 - 52 | 52 |
| 4. | FC Jeunesse Canach (*Promotion Play-off*) | 30 | 16 | 3 | 11 | 67 - 48 | 51 |
| 5. | FC Rodange 91 | 30 | 15 | 6 | 9 | 63 - 50 | 51 |
| 6. | US Rumelange | 30 | 14 | 5 | 11 | 54 - 49 | 47 |
| 7. | FC Mamer 32 | 30 | 12 | 8 | 10 | 63 - 46 | 44 |
| 8. | FC Alisontia Steinsel | 30 | 11 | 10 | 9 | 44 - 44 | 43 |
| 9. | FC Berdenia Berbourg | 30 | 12 | 6 | 12 | 47 - 47 | 42 |
| 10. | FC Blô-Weiss Medernach | 30 | 12 | 3 | 15 | 39 - 48 | 39 |
| 11. | FC Yellow Boys Weiler-la-Tour | 30 | 11 | 5 | 14 | 59 - 55 | 38 |
| 12. | CS Grevenmacher | 30 | 10 | 7 | 13 | 53 - 54 | 37 |
| 13. | FC Jeunesse Junglinster (*Relegation Play-off*) | 30 | 10 | 7 | 13 | 41 - 52 | 37 |
| 14. | FC Luxembourg City (*Relegation Play-off*) | 30 | 8 | 8 | 14 | 42 - 56 | 32 |
| 15. | FC Atert Bissen (*Relegated*) | 30 | 6 | 6 | 18 | 40 - 76 | 24 |
| 16. | FC Jeunesse Schieren (*Relegated*) | 30 | 3 | 4 | 23 | 36 - 87 | 13 |

## Relegation Play-offs [2nd / 3rd Level]

| | |
|---|---|
| FC Jeunesse Junglinster - FC Avenir Beggen | 1-5 |
| FC Luxembourg City - FC Koeppchen Wormeldange | 2-2 aet; 3-4 pen |

Both FC Avenir Beggen and FC Koeppchen Wormeldange will play at second level in 2023/2024.

## INTERNATIONAL MATCHES
### (16.07.2022 – 15.07.2023)

| | | | | |
|---|---|---|---|---|
| 22.09.2022 | Istanbul | *Turkey - Luxembourg* | *3-3(1-2)* | (UNL) |
| 25.09.2022 | Lëtzebuerg | *Luxembourg - Lithuania* | *1-0(0-0)* | (UNL) |
| 17.11.2022 | Lëtzebuerg | *Luxembourg - Hungary* | *2-2(1-1)* | (F) |
| 20.11.2022 | Lëtzebuerg | *Luxembourg - Bulgaria* | *0-0* | (F) |
| 23.03.2023 | Trnava | *Slovakia - Luxembourg* | *0-0* | (ECQ) |
| 26.03.2023 | Lëtzebuerg | *Luxembourg - Portugal* | *0-6(0-4)* | (ECQ) |
| 09.06.2023 | Lëtzebuerg | *Luxembourg - Malta* | *0-1(0-0)* | (F) |
| 17.06.2023 | Lëtzebuerg | *Luxembourg - Liechtenstein* | *2-0(0-0)* | (ECQ) |
| 20.06.2023 | Zenica | *Bosnia and Herzegovina - Luxembourg* | *0-2(0-1)* | (ECQ) |

**22.09.2022    TURKEY - LUXEMBOURG        3-3(1-2)**        3rd UEFA Nations League C, Group 1
Başakşehir "Fatih Terim" Stadyumu, Istanbul; Referee: Tobias Stieler (Germany); Attendance: 12,708
**LUX:** Anthony Moris, Marvin Martins Santos da Graça (53.Florian Bohnert), Laurent Jans (Cap), Maxime Chanot (46.Lars Christian Krogh Gerson), Michael Gonçalves Pinto, Sébastien Thill, Leandro Barreiro Martins, Vincent Thill (75.Timothé Rupil), Yvandro Borges Sanches, Danel Sinani, Gerson Leal Rodrigues Correia (85.Aldin Skenderovic). Trainer: Luc Aloyse Yvon Holtz.
**Goals:** Marvin Martins Santos da Graça (8), Danel Sinani (37), Gerson Leal Rodrigues Correia (69).

**25.09.2022    LUXEMBOURG - LITHUANIA        1-0(0-0)**        3rd UEFA Nations League C, Group 1
Stade de Luxembourg, Lëtzebuerg; Referee: Giorgi Kruashvili (Georgia); Attendance: 5,340
**LUX:** Anthony Moris, Marvin Martins Santos da Graça (90.Florian Bohnert), Laurent Jans (Cap), Maxime Chanot, Michael Gonçalves Pinto, Sébastien Thill (90+6.Diogo Miguel Zambujo Pimentel), Leandro Barreiro Martins, Vincent Thill (79.Lars Christian Krogh Gerson), Yvandro Borges Sanches (90.Timothé Rupil), Danel Sinani, Gerson Leal Rodrigues Correia. Trainer: Luc Aloyse Yvon Holtz.
**Goal:** Gerson Leal Rodrigues Correia (89).

**17.11.2022    LUXEMBOURG - HUNGARY        2-2(1-1)**        Friendly International
Stade de Luxembourg, Lëtzebuerg; Referee: Jonathan Lardot (Belgium); Attendance: 3,571
**LUX:** Anthony Moris (46.Ralph Schon), Laurent Jans (Cap), Enes Mahmutović, Michael Gonçalves Pinto, Florian Bohnert, Mathias Flag Olesen (46.Sébastien Thill), Leandro Barreiro Martins, Yvandro Borges Sanches (71.Alessio Curci), Dejvid Sinani (59.Fabio Lohei), Danel Sinani, Gerson Leal Rodrigues Correia (90+2.Timothé Rupil). Trainer: Luc Aloyse Yvon Holtz.
**Goals:** Gerson Leal Rodrigues Correia (7 penalty), Alessio Curci (78).

**20.11.2022    LUXEMBOURG - BULGARIA        0-0**        Friendly International
Stade de Luxembourg, Lëtzebuerg; Referee: Manfredas Lukjančukas (Lithuania); Attendance: 4,700
**LUX:** Ralph Schon, Laurent Jans (Cap), Enes Mahmutović, Maxime Chanot (46.Dirk Delfin Carlson), Michael Gonçalves Pinto, Mathias Flag Olesen (46.Gerson Leal Rodrigues Correia), Leandro Barreiro Martins, Vincent Thill (59.Timothé Rupil), Florian Bohnert (90+2.Sébastien Thill), Alessio Curci (59.Yvandro Borges Sanches), Danel Sinani [*sent off 87*]. Trainer: Luc Aloyse Yvon Holtz.

**23.03.2023    SLOVAKIA - LUXEMBOURG        0-0**        17th EC. Qualifiers
Štadión "Antona Malatinského", Trnava; Referee: Rade Obrenovič (Slovenia); Attendance: 3,523
**LUX:** Anthony Moris, Maxime Chanot, Lars Christian Krogh Gerson, Mathias Flag Olesen (64.Vincent Thill), Michael Gonçalves Pinto, Florian Bohnert (84.Timothé Rupil), Christopher Martins Pereira (Cap), Leandro Barreiro Martins, Yvandro Borges Sanches (64.Laurent Jans), Gerson Leal Rodrigues Correia, Danel Sinani (84.Sébastien Thill). Trainer: Luc Aloyse Yvon Holtz.

**26.03.2023    LUXEMBOURG - PORTUGAL        0-6(0-4)**        17th EC. Qualifiers
Stade de Luxembourg, Lëtzebuerg; Referee: Radu Marian Petrescu (Romania); Attendance: 9,231
**LUX:** Anthony Moris, Laurent Jans (Cap), Maxime Chanot, Lars Christian Krogh Gerson (46.Dirk Delfin Carlson), Marvin Martins Santos da Graça (46.Florian Bohnert), Michael Gonçalves Pinto, Leandro Barreiro Martins, Christopher Martins Pereira (82.Sébastien Thill), Vincent Thill (70.Yvandro Borges Sanches), Gerson Leal Rodrigues Correia, Danel Sinani (46.Mathias Flag Olesen). Trainer: Luc Aloyse Yvon Holtz.

**09.06.2023    LUXEMBOURG - MALTA        0-1(0-0)**        Friendly International
Stade de Luxembourg, Lëtzebuerg; Referee: Eldorjan Hamiti (Albania); Attendance: 4,028
**LUX:** Ralph Schon (46.Tiago Pereira Cardoso), Maxime Chanot (65.Fabio Lohei), Dirk Delfin Carlson, Laurent Jans (Cap), Florian Bohnert (87.David Jonathans), Mathias Flag Olesen, Christopher Martins Pereira (74.Dejvid Sinani), Leandro Barreiro Martins, Timothé Rupil (65.Alessio Curci), Yvandro Borges Sanches (74.Eldin Dzogović), Gerson Leal Rodrigues Correia. Trainer: Luc Aloyse Yvon Holtz.

**17.06.2023    LUXEMBOURG - LIECHTENSTEIN        2-0(0-0)**        17th EC. Qualifiers
Stade de Luxembourg, Lëtzebuerg; Referee: Oleksiy Derevinskyi (Ukraine); Attendance: 6,806
**LUX:** Anthony Moris, Marvin Martins Santos da Graça (90.Eldin Dzogovic), Maxime Chanot, Enes Mahmutović, Laurent Jans (Cap) (46.Florian Bohnert), Christopher Martins Pereira, Leandro Barreiro Martins, Vincent Thill (46.Gerson Leal Rodrigues Correia, Alessio Curci (46.Mathias Flag Olesen), Yvandro Borges Sanches (90.Timothé Rupil), Danel Sinani. Trainer: Luc Aloyse Yvon Holtz.
**Goals:** Danel Sinani (59), Gerson Leal Rodrigues Correia (89).

**20.06.2023    BOSNIA AND HERZEGOVINA - LUXEMBOURG        0-2(0-1)**        17th EC. Qualifiers
Stadion Bilino Polje, Zenica; Referee: Gal Leibovitz (Israel); Attendance: 8,600
**LUX:** Anthony Moris, Enes Mahmutović, Maxime Chanot, Laurent Jans (Cap), Christopher Martins Pereira, Florian Bohnert, Mathias Flag Olesen, Leandro Barreiro Martins, Alessio Curci (58.Marvin Martins Santos da Graça), Yvandro Borges Sanches (83.Dirk Delfin Carlson), Danel Sinani (90+1.Dejvid Sinani). Trainer: Luc Aloyse Yvon Holtz.
**Goals:** Yvandro Borges Sanches (4), Danel Sinani (74).

## NATIONAL TEAM PLAYERS
### (16.07.2022 – 15.07.2023)

| Name | DOB | Caps | Goals | Club |
|---|---|---|---|---|
| **Goalkeepers** | | | | |
| Anthony MORIS | 29.04.1990 | 57 | 0 | 2022/2023: *Royale Union Saint-Gilloise (BEL)* |
| Tiago PEREIRA Cardoso | 07.04.2006 | 1 | 0 | 2023: *Borussia VfL Mönchengladbach (GER)* |
| Ralph SCHON | 20.01.1990 | 18 | 0 | 2022/2023: *FC Wiltz 71* |
| **Defenders** | | | | |
| Dirk Delfin CARLSON | 01.04.1998 | 48 | 0 | 2022: *ADO Den Haag (NED)* <br> 06.02.2023-> *SKN St. Pölten (AUT)* |
| Maxime CHANOT | 21.11.1989 | 62 | 3 | 2022/2023: *New York City FC (USA)* |
| Eldin DZOGOVIĆ | 08.06.2003 | 3 | 0 | 2023: *1. FC Magdeburg (GER)* |
| Laurent JANS | 05.08.1992 | 95 | 1 | 2022/2023: *SV Waldhof Mannheim (GER)* |
| Lars Christian Krogh GERSON | 05.02.1990 | 92 | 4 | 2022/2023: *Kongsvinger IL (NOR)* |
| Fabio LOHEI | 12.04.2005 | 2 | 0 | 2022/2023: *FC Metz (FRA)* |
| Enes MAHMUTOVIĆ | 22.05.1997 | 25 | 0 | 2022/2023: *PFC CSKA Sofia (BUL)* |
| Marvin MARTINS Santos da Graça | 17.02.1995 | 28 | 3 | 2022/2023: *FK Austria Wien (AUT)* |
| Michael "Mica" Gonçalves PINTO | 04.06.1993 | 28 | 1 | 2022/2023: *Sparta Rotterdam (NED)* |
| **Midfielders** | | | | |
| Leandro BARREIRO Martins | 03.01.2000 | 48 | 2 | 2022/2023: *1. FSV Mainz 05 (GER)* |
| Christopher MARTINS Pereira | 19.02.1997 | 60 | 1 | 2023: *FK Spartak Moskva (RUS)* |
| Mathias Flaga OLESEN | 21.03.2001 | 13 | 0 | 2022/2023: *1.FC Köln (GER)* |
| Diogo Miguel Zambujo PIMENTEL | 16.07.1997 | 1 | 0 | 2022: *CS Fola Esch* |
| Gerson Leal Rodrigues Correia | 20.06.1995 | 55 | 16 | 2022/2023: *Al Wahda FC Abu Dhabi (UAE)* |
| Timothé RUPIL | 12.06.2003 | 9 | 0 | 2022/2023: *1. FSV Mainz 05 (GER)* |
| Aldin SKENDEROVIĆ | 28.06.1997 | 27 | 0 | 2022: *F91 Dudelange* |
| Sébastien THILL | 01.02.1994 | 32 | 2 | 2022/2023: *FC Hansa Rostock (GER)* |
| Vincent THILL | 04.02.2000 | 48 | 3 | 2022/2023: *AIK Stockholm (SWE)* |
| **Forwards** | | | | |
| Florian BOHNERT | 09.11.1997 | 39 | 1 | 2022: *FC Progrès Niederkorn* <br> 01.01.2023-> *SC Bastia (FRA)* |
| Yvandro BORGES Sanches | 24.05.2004 | 21 | 2 | 2022/2023: *Borussia VfL Mönchengladbach (GER)* |
| Alessio CURCI | 16.02.2022 | 5 | 1 | 2022/2023: *1. FSV Mainz 05 (GER)* |
| David JONATHANS | 26.01.2004 | 1 | 0 | 2023: *FC Bayern München (GER)* |
| Danel SINANI | 05.04.1997 | 55 | 11 | 2022: *Norwich City FC (ENG)* <br> 31.01.2023-> *Wigan Athletic FC (ENG)* <br> 31.05.2023-> *Norwich City FC (ENG)* |
| Dejvid SINANI | 02.04.1993 | 3 | 0 | 2022/2023: *F91 Dudelange* |
| **Trainer** | | | | |
| Luc Aloyse Yvon HOLTZ [from 03.08.2010] | 14.06.1969 | | | 124 M; 28 W; 24 D; 72 L; 104-236 |

# MALTA

## The Country:
Republic of Malta (Repubblika ta' Malta)
Capital: Valletta
Surface: 316 km²
Inhabitants: 519,562 [2021]
Time: UTC+1

## The FA:
Assoċjazzjoni tal-Futbol ta' Malta
Millennium Stand, Floor 2 National Stadium, Ta'Qali, ATD4000 Malta
Tel: +356 23 386 000
Foundation date: 1900
Member of FIFA since: 1959
Member of UEFA since: 1960
Website: www.mfa.com.mt

## NATIONAL TEAM RECORDS

| RECORDS | | |
|---|---|---|
| **First international match:** | 24.02.1957, Gzira: | Malta – Austria 2-3 |
| **Most international caps:** | Michael Mifsud | - 143 caps (2000-2020) |
| **Most international goals:** | Michael Mifsud | - 42 goals / 143 caps (2000-2020) |

| UEFA EUROPEAN CHAMPIONSHIP | |
|---|---|
| 1960 | Did not enter |
| 1964 | Qualifiers |
| 1968 | Did not enter |
| 1972 | Qualifiers |
| 1976 | Qualifiers |
| 1980 | Qualifiers |
| 1984 | Qualifiers |
| 1988 | Qualifiers |
| 1992 | Qualifiers |
| 1996 | Qualifiers |
| 2000 | Qualifiers |
| 2004 | Qualifiers |
| 2008 | Qualifiers |
| 2012 | Qualifiers |
| 2016 | Qualifiers |
| 2020 | Qualifiers |

| FIFA WORLD CUP | |
|---|---|
| 1930 | Did not enter |
| 1934 | Did not enter |
| 1938 | Did not enter |
| 1950 | Did not enter |
| 1954 | Did not enter |
| 1958 | Did not enter |
| 1962 | Did not enter |
| 1966 | Did not enter |
| 1970 | Did not enter |
| 1974 | Qualifiers |
| 1978 | Qualifiers |
| 1982 | Qualifiers |
| 1986 | Qualifiers |
| 1990 | Qualifiers |
| 1994 | Qualifiers |
| 1998 | Qualifiers |
| 2002 | Qualifiers |
| 2006 | Qualifiers |
| 2010 | Qualifiers |
| 2014 | Qualifiers |
| 2018 | Qualifiers |
| 2022 | Qualifiers |

| OLYMPIC TOURNAMENTS | |
|---|---|
| 1908 | - |
| 1912 | - |
| 1920 | - |
| 1924 | - |
| 1928 | - |
| 1936 | - |
| 1948 | - |
| 1952 | - |
| 1956 | - |
| 1960 | Did not enter |
| 1964 | Did not enter |
| 1968 | Did not enter |
| 1972 | *Withdrew* |
| 1976 | Did not enter |
| 1980 | Did not enter |
| 1984 | Did not enter |
| 1988 | Did not enter |
| 1992 | Qualifiers |
| 1996 | Qualifiers |
| 2000 | Qualifiers |
| 2004 | Qualifiers |
| 2008 | Qualifiers |
| 2012 | Qualifiers |
| 2016 | Qualifiers |
| 2020 | Qualifiers |

## UEFA NATIONS LEAGUE

| 2018/2019 | League D (Group Stage) |
|---|---|
| 2020/2021 | League D (Group Stage) |
| 2022/2023 | League D (Group Stage) |

## MALTESE CLUB HONOURS IN EUROPEAN CLUB COMPETITIONS:

| European Champion Clubs' Cup (1956-1992) / UEFA Champions League (1993-2023) |
|---|
| None |
| **Fairs Cup (1858-1971) / UEFA Cup (1972-2009) / UEFA Europa League (2010-2023)** |
| None |
| **UEFA Europa Conference League (2021-2023)** |
| None |
| **UEFA Super Cup (1972-2022)** |
| None |
| *European Cup Winners' Cup 1961-1999\** |
| None |

*\*defunct competition*

# NATIONAL COMPETITIONS
## TABLE OF HONOURS

| | CHAMPIONS | CUP WINNERS | BEST GOALSCORERS | |
|---|---|---|---|---|
| 1909/1910 | Floriana FC | - | Salvu Samuele (Floriana FC) | 4 |
| 1910/1911 | *No championship* | - | - | |
| 1911/1912 | Floriana FC | - | *not known* | |
| 1912/1913 | Floriana FC | - | *not known* | |
| 1913/1914 | Hamrun Spartans FC | - | *not known* | |
| 1914/1915 | Valletta United FC | - | *not known* | |
| 1915/1916 | *No championship* | - | - | |
| 1916/1917 | St. George's FC | - | *not known* | |
| 1917/1918 | Hamrun Spartans FC | - | *not known* | |
| 1918/1919 | The King's Own Malta Regiment | - | *not known* | |
| 1919/1920 | Sliema Wanderers FC | - | *not known* | |
| 1920/1921 | Floriana FC | - | *not known* | |
| 1921/1922 | Floriana FC | - | *not known* | |
| 1922/1923 | Sliema Wanderers FC | - | *not known* | |
| 1923/1924 | Sliema Wanderers FC | - | *not known* | |
| 1924/1925 | Floriana FC | - | *not known* | |
| 1925/1926 | Sliema Wanderers FC | - | *not known* | |
| 1926/1927 | Floriana FC | - | *not known* | |
| 1927/1928 | Floriana FC | - | *not known* | |
| 1928/1929 | Floriana FC | - | P. Friggieri (Floriana FC) | 4 |
| 1929/1930 | Sliema Wanderers FC | - | *not known* | |
| 1930/1931 | Floriana FC | - | C. Cauchi (Floriana FC) | 4 |
| 1931/1932 | Valletta United FC | - | *not known* | |
| 1932/1933 | Sliema Wanderers FC | - | *not known* | |
| 1933/1934 | Sliema Wanderers FC | - | A. Brincat (Sliema Wanderers FC) | 2 |
| 1934/1935 | Floriana FC | Sliema Wanderers FC | Tony Nicholl (Sliema Wanderers FC) | 11 |
| 1935/1936 | Sliema Wanderers FC | Sliema Wanderers FC | Anton Mayerhoffer (AUT, Floriana FC) | 3 |
| 1936/1937 | Floriana FC | Sliema Wanderers FC | George Albert Bond (ENG, Floriana FC) | 4 |
| 1937/1938 | Sliema Wanderers FC | Floriana FC | Tony Nicholl (Sliema Wanderers FC) C. Cauchi (Floriana FC) | 5 |
| 1938/1939 | Sliema Wanderers FC | Melita FC St. Julian's | Tony Nicholl (Sliema Wanderers FC) | 8 |
| 1939/1940 | Sliema Wanderers FC | Sliema Wanderers FC | Tony Nicholl (Sliema Wanderers FC) | 18 |
| 1940-1944 | *No championship* | - | - | |
| 1944/1945 | Valletta FC | Floriana FC | Tony Nicholl (Sliema Athletics FC) | 6 |
| 1945/1946 | Valletta FC | Sliema Wanderers FC | *not known* | |
| 1946/1947 | Hamrun Spartans FC | Floriana FC | Maurice Decesare (Melita FC St. Julian's) C. Galea (Floriana FC) | 11 |
| 1947/1948 | Valletta FC | Sliema Wanderers FC | Freddie Landolina (Hamrun Spartans FC) | 16 |
| 1948/1949 | Sliema Wanderers FC | Floriana FC | Salvinu Schembri (Valletta FC) Tony Nicholl (Sliema Wanderers FC) | 11 |
| 1949/1950 | Floriana FC | Floriana FC | Pace (Valletta FC) | 16 |
| 1950/1951 | Floriana FC | Sliema Wanderers FC | Pullu Demanuele (Valletta FC) | 14 |
| 1951/1952 | Floriana FC | Sliema Wanderers FC | Lolly Borg (Floriana FC) | 17 |
| 1952/1953 | Floriana FC | Floriana FC | Pace (Valletta FC) | 9 |
| 1953/1954 | Sliema Wanderers FC | Floriana FC | Tony Nicholl (Sliema Wanderers FC) | 12 |
| 1954/1955 | Floriana FC | Floriana FC | Lolly Borg (Floriana FC) Tony Cauchi (Floriana FC) | 13 |
| 1955/1956 | Sliema Wanderers FC | Sliema Wanderers FC | Sammy Nicholl (Sliema Wanderers FC) | 15 |
| 1956/1957 | Sliema Wanderers FC | Floriana FC | Sammy Nicholl (Sliema Wanderers FC) | 14 |
| 1957/1958 | Floriana FC | Floriana FC | Pullu Demanuele (Floriana FC) | 14 |
| 1958/1959 | Valletta FC | Sliema Wanderers FC | A. Cassar (Hamrun Spartans FC) | 11 |
| 1959/1960 | Valletta FC | Valletta FC | F. Zammit (Valletta FC) M. Azzopardi (Valletta FC) | 12 |
| 1960/1961 | Hibernians FC Paola | Floriana FC | Tony Cauchi (Floriana FC) | 12 |
| 1961/1962 | Floriana FC | Hibernians FC Paola | Tony Cauchi (Floriana FC) | 17 |
| 1962/1963 | Valletta FC | Sliema Wanderers FC | M. Azzopardi (Valletta FC) | 20 |
| 1963/1964 | Sliema Wanderers FC | Valletta FC | A. Borg (Valletta FC) | 11 |
| 1964/1965 | Sliema Wanderers FC | Sliema Wanderers FC | Joseph Cini (Sliema Wanderers FC) | 12 |
| 1965/1966 | Sliema Wanderers FC | Floriana FC | John Bonnett (Sliema Wanderers FC) Ronald Cocks (Sliema Wanderers FC) | 6 |
| 1966/1967 | Hibernians FC Paola | Floriana FC | A. Delia (Hibernians FC Paola) | 8 |
| 1967/1968 | Floriana FC | Sliema Wanderers FC | Joseph Cini (Sliema Wanderers FC) | 10 |
| 1968/1969 | Hibernians FC Paola | Sliema Wanderers FC | C. Cassar (Hibernians FC Paola) | 9 |
| 1969/1970 | Floriana FC | Hibernians FC Paola | Joseph Cini (Sliema Wanderers FC) Ronald Cocks (Sliema Wanderers FC) | 7 |
| 1970/1971 | Sliema Wanderers FC | Hibernians FC Paola | Raymond Xuereb (Floriana FC) | 5 |
| 1971/1972 | Sliema Wanderers FC | Floriana FC | Tony Giglio (Valletta FC) | 9 |
| 1972/1973 | Floriana FC | Gżira United FC | C. Borg (Hamrun Spartans FC) | 10 |
| 1973/1974 | Valletta FC | Sliema Wanderers FC | T. Camilleri (Sliema Wanderers FC) | 9 |
| 1974/1975 | Floriana FC | Valletta FC | Raymond Xuereb (Floriana FC) | 17 |

| | | | | |
|---|---|---|---|---|
| 1975/1976 | Sliema Wanderers FC | Floriana FC | Richard Aquilina (Sliema Wanderers FC) | 9 |
| 1976/1977 | Floriana FC | Valletta FC | Raymond Xuereb (Floriana FC) | 16 |
| 1977/1978 | Valletta FC | Valletta FC | Leonard Farrugia (Valletta FC) | 16 |
| 1978/1979 | Hibernians FC Paola | Sliema Wanderers FC | C. Brincat (Marsa FC) | 11 |
| 1979/1980 | Valletta FC | Hibernians FC Paola | Emanuel Fabri (Sliema Wanderers FC) Leonard Farrugia (Valletta FC) F. Cristiano (Valletta FC) | 15 |
| 1980/1981 | Hibernians FC Paola | Floriana FC | Ernest Spiteri-Gonzi (Hibernians FC Paola) | 13 |
| 1981/1982 | Hibernians FC Paola | Hibernians FC Paola | Ernest Spiteri-Gonzi (Hibernians FC Paola) | 12 |
| 1982/1983 | Hamrun Spartans FC | Hamrun Spartans FC | Leo Refalo (Hamrun Spartans FC) | 7 |
| 1983/1984 | Valletta FC | Hamrun Spartans FC | Georgi Ivanov (BUL, Hamrun Spartans FC) Charles Muscat (Żurrieq FC) | 7 |
| 1984/1985 | Rabat Ajax FC | Żurrieq FC | Leonard Farrugia (Valletta FC) | 9 |
| 1985/1986 | Rabat Ajax FC | Rabat Ajax FC | Gianluca De Ponti (ITA, Żurrieq FC) | 8 |
| 1986/1987 | Hamrun Spartans FC | Hamrun Spartans FC | Carmel Busuttil (Rabat Ajax FC) | 10 |
| 1987/1988 | Hamrun Spartans FC | Hamrun Spartans FC | Barry Gallagher (ENG, Hamrun Spartans FC) | 7 |
| 1988/1989 | Sliema Wanderers FC | Hamrun Spartans FC | Joseph Zarb (Valletta FC) | 11 |
| 1989/1990 | Valletta FC | Sliema Wanderers FC | Joseph Zarb (Valletta FC) | 17 |
| 1990/1991 | Hamrun Spartans FC | Valletta FC | Joseph Zarb (Valletta FC) | 12 |
| 1991/1992 | Valletta FC | Hamrun Spartans FC | Stefan Sultana (Hamrun Spartans FC) | 22 |
| 1992/1993 | Floriana FC | Floriana FC | Carl Zachhau (DEN, Hibernians FC Paola) | 22 |
| 1993/1994 | Hibernians FC Paola | Floriana FC | Carl Zachhau (DEN, Hibernians FC Paola) Joseph Zarb (Valletta FC) | 17 |
| 1994/1995 | Hibernians FC Paola | Valletta FC | Carl Saunders (ENG, Sliema Wanderers FC) | 18 |
| 1995/1996 | Sliema Wanderers FC | Valletta FC | Aldrin Muscat (Sliema Wanderers FC) | 18 |
| 1996/1997 | Valletta FC | Valletta FC | Danilo Dončić (SRB, Valletta FC) | 32 |
| 1997/1998 | Valletta FC | Hibernians FC Paola | Joseph Brincat (Birkirkara FC/Floriana FC) | 19 |
| 1998/1999 | Valletta FC | Valletta FC | Gilbert Agius (Valletta FC) | 20 |
| 1999/2000 | Birkirkara FC | Sliema Wanderers FC | Michael Mifsud (Sliema Wanderers FC) | 21 |
| 2000/2001 | Valletta FC | Valletta FC | Michael Mifsud (Sliema Wanderers FC) | 30 |
| 2001/2002 | Hibernians FC Paola | Birkirkara FC | Danilo Dončić (SRB, Sliema Wanderers FC) | 32 |
| 2002/2003 | Sliema Wanderers FC | Birkirkara FC | Adrian Mifsud (Hibernians FC Paola) Danilo Dončić (SRB, Sliema Wanderers FC) Michael Galea (Birkirkara FC) | 18 |
| 2003/2004 | Sliema Wanderers FC | Sliema Wanderers FC | Danilo Dončić (SRB, Sliema Wanderers FC) | 19 |
| 2004/2005 | Sliema Wanderers FC | Birkirkara FC | Andrew Cohen (Hibernians FC Paola) | 21 |
| 2005/2006 | Birkirkara FC | Hibernians FC Paola | Michael Galea (Birkirkara FC) | 19 |
| 2006/2007 | Marsaxlokk FC | Hibernians FC Paola | Daniel Bogdanović (Marsaxlokk FC) | 31 |
| 2007/2008 | Valletta FC | Birkirkara FC | Omar Sebastián Monesterolo (ARG, Valletta FC) | 19 |
| 2008/2009 | Hibernians FC Paola | Sliema Wanderers FC | Terence Scerri (Hibernians FC Paola) | 26 |
| 2009/2010 | Birkirkara FC | Valletta FC | Camilo Sanvezzo (BRA, Qormi FC) | 24 |
| 2010/2011 | Valletta FC | Floriana FC | Alfred Effiong (NGA, Marsaxlokk FC) | 17 |
| 2011/2012 | Valletta FC | Hibernians FC Paola | Obinna Obiefule (NGA, Marsaxlokk FC/Mosta FC) | 34 |
| 2012/2013 | Birkirkara FC | Hibernians FC Paola | José Luis Negrín (ESP, Melita FC St. Julian's/Rabat Ajax FC) | 22 |
| 2013/2014 | Valletta FC | Valletta FC | Jhonnattann Benites da Conceiçao (BRA, Birkirkara FC) Edison Luiz dos Santos "Tarabai" (BRA, Hibernians FC Paola) | 21 |
| 2014/2015 | Hibernians FC Paola | Birkirkara FC | Jorginho (BRA, Hibernians FC Paola) Edison Luiz dos Santos "Tarabai" (BRA, Hibernians FC Paola) | 25 |
| 2015/2016 | Valletta FC | Sliema Wanderers FC | Mario Fontanella (ITA, Floriana FC) | 20 |
| 2016/2017 | Hibernians FC Paola | Floriana FC | Bojan Kaljević (MNE, Balzan FC) | 23 |
| 2017/2018 | Valletta FC | Valletta FC | Amadou Samb (SEN, Gżira United FC) | 21 |
| 2018/2019 | Valletta FC | Balzan FC | Taylon Nicolas Correa Marcolino (BRA, Hibernians FC Paola) | 19 |
| 2019/2020 | Floriana FC | *Competition abandoned* | Kristian Keqi (ALB, Floriana FC) | 14 |
| 2020/2021 | Hamrun Spartans FC | *Competition abandoned* | Kevin Duvan Ante Rosero (COL, Santa Luċija FC) | 17 |
| 2021/2022 | Hibernians FC Paola | Floriana FC | Máxuell Maia da Silva (BRA, Gżira United FC) | 17 |
| 2022/2023 | Hamrun Spartans FC | | Jefferson Mateus de Assis Estácio (BRA, Gżira United FC) | 20 |

## NATIONAL CHAMPIONSHIP
### Maltese Premier League 2022/2023
(19.08.2022 – 22.04.2023)

### Results

**Round 1** [19-21.08.2022]
Birkirkara FC - Sirens FC 2-0(0-0)
Balzan FC - Żebbuġ Rangers 3-1(2-1)
Gżira United - St. Luċija FC 3-1(3-1)
Mosta FC - Gudja United 1-2(0-1)
Floriana FC - Pietà Hotspurs 2-0(2-0)
Valletta FC - Hibernians FC 1-1(0-0)
Hamrun Sp. - Marsaxlokk 1-0(1-0) [07.09.22]

**Round 2** [26-29.08.2022]
Gudja United - Gżira United 3-3(2-1)
Pietà Hotspurs - Valletta FC 0-6(0-3)
Sirens FC - Floriana FC 2-2(2-0)
Marsaxlokk FC - Mosta FC 1-4(1-3)
Żebbuġ Rangers - Birkirkara FC 1-2(1-1)
St. Luċija FC - Balzan FC 0-2(0-2)
Hibernians FC - Hamrun Spartans 1-4(0-2)

**Round 3** [03-04.09.2022]
Birkirkara FC - Floriana FC 1-0(0-0)
Balzan FC - Gudja United 0-1(0-1)
Żebbuġ Rangers - St. Luċija FC 2-0(0-0)
Valletta FC - Sirens FC 0-0
Gżira United - Marsaxlokk FC 0-0
Mosta FC - Hibernians FC 0-5(0-2)
Hamrun Spartans - Pietà Hotspurs 2-0(2-0)

**Round 4** [09-11.09.2022]
Gudja United - Żebbuġ Rangers 2-1(2-0)
Floriana FC - Valletta FC 1-0(0-0)
Pietà Hotspurs - Mosta FC 1-4(0-1)
Sirens FC - Ħamrun Spartans 0-2(0-1)
Marsaxlokk FC - Balzan FC 1-2(1-0)
Hibernians FC - Gżira United 1-2(1-0)
St. Luċija FC - Birkirkara FC 0-4(0-0)

**Round 5** [01-02.10.2022]
Ħamrun Spartans - Floriana FC 2-0(1-0)
Mosta FC - Sirens FC 1-1(1-1)
St. Luċija FC - Gudja United 1-3(0-1)
Żebbuġ Rangers - Marsaxlokk FC 0-3(0-2)
Birkirkara FC - Valletta FC 3-0(1-0)
Gżira United - Pietà Hotspurs 4-0(1-0)
Balzan FC - Hibernians FC 0-2(0-2)

**Round 6** [07-09.10.2022]
Hibernians FC - Żebbuġ Rangers 1-0(0-0)
Valletta FC - Ħamrun Spartans 0-1(0-1)
Marsaxlokk FC - St. Luċija FC 2-2(2-1)
Gudja United - Birkirkara FC 1-1(1-0)
Floriana FC - Mosta FC 1-1(1-0)
Sirens FC - Gżira United 0-3(0-2)
Pietà Hotspurs - Balzan FC 2-3(0-1)

**Round 7** [15-17.10.2022]
Birkirkara FC - Ħamrun Spartans 0-0
Mosta FC - Valletta FC 3-1(0-0)
Żebbuġ Rangers - Pietà Hotspurs 0-1(0-0)
Gżira United - Floriana FC 1-0(1-0)
St. Luċija FC - Hibernians FC 2-3(1-1)
Balzan FC - Sirens FC 0-0
Gudja United - Marsaxlokk FC 1-2(0-0)

**Round 8** [21-23.10.2022]
Sirens FC - Żebbuġ Rangers 3-3(1-3)
Ħamrun Spartans - Mosta FC 2-1(1-0)
Hibernians FC - Gudja United 2-1(1-1)
Valletta FC - Gżira United 0-0
Pietà Hotspurs - St. Luċija FC 1-2(1-1)
Floriana FC - Balzan FC 0-0
Marsaxlokk FC - Birkirkara FC 1-0(0-0)

**Round 9** [29-30.10.2022]
Birkirkara FC - Mosta FC 1-2(1-2)
Balzan FC - Valletta FC 1-3(1-0)
St. Luċija FC - Sirens FC 0-0
Żebbuġ Rangers - Floriana FC 0-1(0-0)
Gudja United - Pietà Hotspurs 1-0(1-0)
Gżira United - Ħamrun Spartans 1-2(1-1)
Marsaxlokk FC - Hibernians FC 1-1(0-0)

**Round 10** [04-06.11.2022]
Mosta FC - Gżira United 0-2(0-1)
Hibernians FC - Birkirkara FC 1-1(0-1)
Pietà Hotspurs - Marsaxlokk FC 1-1(0-0)
Sirens FC - Gudja United 2-0(1-0)
Floriana FC - St. Luċija FC 1-0(0-0)
Valletta FC - Żebbuġ Rangers 3-0(0-0)
Ħamrun Spartans - Balzan FC 1-0(0-0)

**Round 11** [12-13.11.2022]
Birkirkara FC - Gżira United 1-1(1-1)
Hibernians FC - Pietà Hotspurs 2-1(2-0)
St. Luċija FC - Valletta FC 0-2(0-1)
Gudja United - Floriana FC 0-3(0-2)
Balzan FC - Mosta FC 1-2(0-1)
Marsaxlokk FC - Sirens FC 1-2(0-0)
Żebbuġ R.-Ħamrun Sp. 4-2(2-1) [27.11.2022]

**Round 12** [03-04.12.2022]
Sirens FC - Hibernians FC 0-1(0-1)
Gżira United - Balzan FC 0-1(0-1)
Floriana FC - Marsaxlokk FC 1-1(0-1)
Ħamrun Spartans - St. Luċija FC 2-0
Pietà Hotspurs - Birkirkara FC 1-5(0-2)
Mosta FC - Żebbuġ Rangers 2-0(0-0)
Valletta FC - Gudja United 0-1(0-1)

**Round 13** [10-12.12.2022]
Birkirkara FC - Balzan FC 2-1(1-1)
Pietà Hotspurs - Sirens FC 0-1(0-0)
Żebbuġ Rangers - Gżira United 0-2(0-1)
Gudja United - Ħamrun Spartans 0-1(0-0)
Marsaxlokk FC - Valletta FC 1-2(1-0)
St. Luċija FC - Mosta FC 1-2(0-1)
Hibernians FC - Floriana FC 1-0(1-0)

**Round 14** [15-17.12.2022]
St. Luċija FC - Gżira United 0-1(0-1)
Sirens FC - Birkirkara FC 1-0(1-0)
Żebbuġ Rangers - Balzan FC 2-3(1-1)
Gudja United - Mosta FC 2-1(1-1)
Marsaxlokk FC - Ħamrun Spartans 0-1(0-0)
Pietà Hotspurs - Floriana FC 1-3(0-1)
Hibernians FC - Valletta FC 0-4(0-0)

**Round 15** [07-08.01.2023]
Gżira United - Gudja United 1-1(0-0)
Floriana FC - Sirens FC 1-0(0-0)
Birkirkara FC - Żebbuġ Rangers 5-0(4-0)
Balzan FC - St. Luċija FC 3-1(2-1)
Mosta FC - Marsaxlokk FC 2-1(1-1)
Valletta FC - Pietà Hotspurs 1-1(1-1)
Ħamrun Spartans - Hibernians FC 1-0(0-0)

**Round 16** [20-22.01.2023]
St. Luċija FC - Żebbuġ Rangers 2-1(1-0)
Hibernians FC - Mosta FC 2-0(1-0)
Floriana FC - Birkirkara FC 1-2(0-0)
Gudja United - Balzan FC 0-1(0-1)
Marsaxlokk FC - Gżira United 0-3(0-0)
Pietà Hotspurs - Ħamrun Spartans 1-2(0-1)
Sirens FC - Valletta FC 3-3(0-2) [01.02.2023]

**Round 17** [28-29.01.2023]
Gżira United - Hibernians FC 2-0(1-0)
Birkirkara FC - St. Luċija FC 2-0(1-0)
Żebbuġ Rangers - Gudja United 2-0(1-0)
Mosta FC - Pietà Hotspurs 4-0(0-0)
Balzan FC - Marsaxlokk FC 0-0
Valletta FC - Floriana FC 0-0
Ħamrun Spartans - Sirens FC 3-0(2-0)

**Round 18** [04-05.02.2023]
Floriana FC - Ħamrun Spartans 0-1(0-0)
Gudja United - St. Luċija FC 3-0(0-0)
Sirens FC - Mosta FC 1-2(1-1)
Pietà Hotspurs - Gżira United 0-6(0-2)
Hibernians FC - Balzan FC 1-2(0-0)
Valletta FC - Birkirkara FC 1-1(1-1)
Marsaxlokk FC - Żebbuġ Rangers 1-1(1-0)

**Round 19** [11-12.02.2023]
Birkirkara FC - Gudja United 3-1(2-0)
Ħamrun Spartans - Valletta FC 1-0(1-0)
Żebbuġ Rangers - Hibernians FC 0-2(0-1)
Balzan FC - Pietà Hotspurs 3-2(1-2)
Gżira United - Sirens FC 1-0(1-0)
St. Luċija FC - Marsaxlokk FC 0-1(0-0)
Mosta FC - Floriana FC 2-0(1-0)

**Round 20** [18-19.02.2023]
Floriana FC - Gżira United 1-1(1-1)
Marsaxlokk FC - Gudja United 1-1(1-1)
Pietà Hotspurs - Żebbuġ Rangers 0-2(0-0)
Hibernians FC - St. Luċija FC 3-2(1-1)
Valletta FC - Mosta FC 0-0
Ħamrun Spartans - Birkirkara FC 0-0
Sirens FC - Balzan FC 1-3(0-0)

**Round 21** [04-05.03.2023]
St. Luċija FC - Pietà Hotspurs 2-1(1-0)
Żebbuġ Rangers - Sirens FC 0-1(0-0)
Gudja United - Hibernians FC 1-4(0-2)
Gżira United - Valletta FC 1-2(0-1)
Birkirkara FC - Marsaxlokk FC 1-1(0-0)
Mosta FC - Ħamrun Spartans 1-2(0-2)
Balzan FC - Floriana FC 3-1(3-0)

**Round 22** [10-12.03.2023]
Valletta FC - Balzan FC 0-0
Ħamrun Spartans - Gżira United 1-0(0-0)
Hibernians FC - Marsaxlokk FC 1-3(0-2)
Floriana FC - Żebbuġ Rangers 1-0(0-0)
Mosta FC - Birkirkara FC 1-1(1-1)
Sirens FC - St. Luċija FC 2-1(1-1)
Pietà Hotspurs - Gudja United 3-1(2-1)

**Round 23** [01-02.04.2023]
Gżira United - Mosta FC 1-2(1-1)
Gudja United - Sirens FC 0-1(0-0)
Żebbuġ Rangers - Valletta FC 1-5(0-2)
Balzan FC - Ħamrun Spartans 0-4(0-3)
Marsaxlokk FC - Pietà Hotspurs 1-2(1-1)
Birkirkara FC - Hibernians FC 5-0(4-0)
St. Luċija FC - Floriana FC 0-2(0-0)

**Round 24** [08-10.04.2023]
Gżira United - Birkirkara FC 1-3(0-1)
Floriana FC - Gudja United 1-1(1-0)
Pietà Hotspurs - Hibernians FC 1-4(1-2)
Sirens FC - Marsaxlokk FC 3-2(2-2)
Mosta FC - Balzan FC 2-3(1-1)
Valletta FC - St. Luċija FC 0-1(0-1)
Ħamrun Spartans - Żebbuġ Rangers 4-0(1-0)

**Round 25** [14-15.04.2023]
Marsaxlokk FC - Floriana FC 1-5(0-4)
Birkirkara FC - Pietà Hotspurs 3-2(2-0)
Gudja United - Valletta FC 1-2(0-2)
Hibernians FC - Sirens FC 1-1(1-0)
St. Luċija FC - Ħamrun Spartans 1-1(0-1)
Balzan FC - Gżira United 0-2(0-1)
Żebbuġ Rangers - Mosta FC 0-5(0-2)

**Round 26** [20-22.04.2023]
Sirens FC - Pietà Hotspurs 0-0
Valletta FC - Marsaxlokk FC 1-1(1-0)
Balzan FC - Birkirkara FC 2-1(1-0)
Gżira United - Żebbuġ Rangers 4-0(0-0)
Mosta FC - St. Luċija FC 2-1(0-1)
Floriana FC - Hibernians FC 2-5(1-2)
Ħamrun Spartans - Gudja United 2-0(2-0)

| | | Total | | | | | | | Home | | | | | Away | | | | |
|---|---|---|---|---|---|---|---|---|---|---|---|---|---|---|---|---|---|---|
| 1. | **Hamrun Spartans FC** | 26 | 22 | 3 | 1 | 45 | - | 10 | 69 | 12 | 1 | 0 | 22 - 1 | 10 | 2 | 1 | 23 - 9 |
| 2. | Birkirkara FC | 26 | 14 | 8 | 4 | 50 | - | 20 | 50 | 9 | 3 | 1 | 29 - 8 | 5 | 5 | 3 | 21 - 12 |
| 3. | Gżira United FC | 26 | 14 | 6 | 6 | 46 | - | 19 | 48 | 6 | 2 | 5 | 20 - 12 | 8 | 4 | 1 | 26 - 7 |
| 4. | Balzan FC | 26 | 14 | 4 | 8 | 37 | - | 32 | 46 | 5 | 2 | 6 | 16 - 20 | 9 | 2 | 2 | 21 - 12 |
| 5. | Hibernians FC Paola | 26 | 14 | 4 | 8 | 45 | - | 37 | 46 | 6 | 2 | 5 | 17 - 21 | 8 | 2 | 3 | 28 - 16 |
| 6. | Mosta FC | 26 | 14 | 4 | 8 | 47 | - | 33 | 46 | 6 | 2 | 5 | 21 - 19 | 8 | 2 | 3 | 26 - 14 |
| 7. | Floriana FC | 26 | 10 | 7 | 9 | 30 | - | 26 | 37 | 5 | 5 | 3 | 13 - 12 | 5 | 2 | 6 | 17 - 14 |
| 8. | Valletta FC | 26 | 9 | 10 | 7 | 37 | - | 23 | 37 | 1 | 9 | 3 | 7 - 7 | 8 | 1 | 4 | 30 - 16 |
| 9. | Sirens FC San Pawl il-Baħar | 26 | 8 | 9 | 9 | 25 | - | 32 | 33 | 4 | 4 | 5 | 18 - 22 | 4 | 5 | 4 | 7 - 10 |
| 10. | Gudja United FC | 26 | 8 | 5 | 13 | 28 | - | 39 | 29 | 4 | 2 | 7 | 15 - 20 | 4 | 3 | 6 | 13 - 19 |
| 11. | Marsaxlokk FC | 26 | 5 | 10 | 11 | 28 | - | 38 | 25 | 1 | 4 | 8 | 12 - 26 | 4 | 6 | 3 | 16 - 12 |
| 12. | Santa Luċija FC (*Relegation Play-offs*) | 26 | 4 | 3 | 19 | 20 | - | 49 | 15 | 2 | 2 | 9 | 9 - 23 | 2 | 1 | 10 | 11 - 26 |
| 13. | Żebbuġ Rangers FC (*Relegated*) | 26 | 4 | 2 | 20 | 21 | - | 58 | 14 | 3 | 0 | 10 | 12 - 27 | 1 | 2 | 10 | 9 - 31 |
| 14. | Pietà Hotspurs FC (*Relegated*) | 26 | 3 | 3 | 20 | 22 | - | 65 | 12 | 1 | 1 | 11 | 12 - 40 | 2 | 2 | 9 | 10 - 25 |

<u>Please note</u>: Hibernians FC Paola and Balzan FC finished equal on points, A play-off decider determines the fourth place and Qualification for the UEFA Europa Conference League

**Fourth Place Play-offs** [01.05.2023]

Hibernians FC Paola - Balzan FC      2-3(0-1,2-2)

**Relegation Play-offs** [28.04.2023]

Santa Luċija FC - Żejtun Corinthians FC      2-0(1-0)
Santa Luċija FC remains at first level for 2023/2024.

| Top goalscorers: | | |
|---|---|---|
| **20** | **Jefferson Mateus de Assis Estácio (BRA)** | *Gżira United FC* |
| 18 | Elvis Mashike Sukisa (COD) | *Hamrun Spartans FC* |
| 14 | Ángel Yesid Torres Quiñones (COL) | *Balzan FC* |
| 14 | Jurgen Degabriele | *Hibernians FC Paola* |

# NATIONAL CUP
## Maltese FA Trophy 2022/2023

### Round of 32 [13-15.01.2023]

| | | | | |
|---|---|---|---|---|
| Hibernians FC Paola - Żurrieq FC | 3-1(2-1) | Gudja United FC - Naxxar Lions FC | 2-1(1-1) |
| Sirens FC San Pawl il-Baħar - Mqabba FC | 1-0(0-0) | Gżira United FC - Sliema Wanderers FC | 2-0(1-0) |
| Birkirkara FC - Nadur Youngsters FC Nadur | 4-0(2-0) | Pietà Hotspurs FC - Xewkija Tigers FC | 2-0(1-0) |
| Attard FC - Kerċem Ajax FC | 2-8(1-4) | Hamrun Spartans FC - Għajnsielem FC | 3-1(0-0,1-1) |
| Balzan FC - Tarxien Rainbows FC | 4-0(2-0) | Melita FC St. Julian's - Mosta FC | 0-3(0-2) |
| Mtarfa FC - Qala Saints FC | 1-2(0-0) | Floriana FC - Santa Luċija FC | 0-1(0-1) |
| Żejtun Corinthians FC - Marsaxlokk FC | 0-5(0-2) | San Ġwann FC - Mġarr United FC | 3-1(2-1) |
| Valletta FC - Żabbar St. Patrick FC | 5-1(1-1) | Swieqi United FC - Żebbuġ Rangers FC | 1-0(0-0) |

### 1/8-Finals [07-08./15.02.2023]

| | | | | |
|---|---|---|---|---|
| Mosta FC - Swieqi United FC | 1-1 aet; 3-2 pen | Gżira United FC - Qala Saints FC | 3-0(2-0) |
| Pietà Hotspurs FC - San Ġwann FC | 0-2(0-0) | Valletta FC - Hamrun Spartans FC | 1-2(1-0) |
| Balzan FC - Birkirkara FC | 2-2 aet; 4-5 pen | Santa Luċija FC - Marsaxlokk FC | 0-2(0-0) |
| Hibernians FC Paola - Kerċem Ajax FC | 8-0(4-0) | Gudja United FC - Sirens FC San Pawl il-Baħar | 1-0(0-0) |

### Quarter-Finals [25-26.02.2023]

| | | | | |
|---|---|---|---|---|
| Gżira United FC - Gudja United FC | 1-1 aet; 4-3 pen | Mosta FC - San Ġwann FC | 5-0(2-0) |
| Birkirkara FC - Hamrun Spartans FC | 1-0(1-0) | Hibernians FC Paola - Marsaxlokk FC | 0-1(0-0) |

### Semi-Finals [25-26.04.2023]

| | | | | |
|---|---|---|---|---|
| Marsaxlokk FC - Gżira United FC | 1-1 aet; 5-4 pen | Birkirkara FC - Mosta FC | 4-3(1-0) |

### Final

30.04.2023; Ta' Qali National Stadium, Attard; Referee: Tristan Farrugia Cann; Attendance: 4,128
**Birkirkara FC - Marsaxlokk FC**      **2-0(0-0)**

**Birkirkara FC**: Amary Sylla, Kurt Zammit, Cain Attard, Osvaldo Iorio Forestero, Diego Pires Dall'Oca, Simon Zibo, Yannick Yankam (90+1.Neil Micallef), Denis Custodio Ribeiro, Alex da Paixão Alves „Lecão" (88.Kevin Tulimieri),  Paul Mbong (70.Andrei Cosmin Ciolacu), Enzo Daniel Cabrera (90+1.Jean Paul Farrugia). Trainer: Giovanni Tedesco (Italy).

**Marsaxlokk FC**: Marko Drobnjak, Óscar Matías Carniello (81.Claudio Bonanni), Leandro Damián Aguirre, Dejan Vuković, Juan Cruz Aguilar, Ryan Scicluna (81.Terence Vella), Santiago Ferraris, Peter Xuereb (59.Edafe Uzeh), Ayrton Attard, Santiago Fabián Moracci (59.Kristian Keqi), Tiago Adan Fonseca. Trainer: Dragan Đurđević (Serbia).

**Goals:** 1-0 Osvaldo Iorio Forestero (77), 2-0 Claudio Bonanni (85 own goal).

# THE CLUBS 2022/2023

## Balzan Football Club

| Founded: | 1937 | | |
|---|---|---|---|
| Stadium: | St. Aloysius Sports and Recreational Complex, Birkirkara (100) | | |
| Trainer: | Oliver Spiteri | | 04.07.1970 |

| Goalkeepers: | DOB | M | (s) | G |
|---|---|---|---|---|
| Rudi Briffa | 21.08.1996 | 8 | | |
| Jonathan Debono | 17.07.1985 | 18 | | |
| **Defenders:** | **DOB** | **M** | **(s)** | **G** |
| Samir Arab | 25.03.1994 | 17 | (5) | |
| Ivan Božović (SRB) | 26.05.1990 | 22 | | |
| Zak Grech | 21.07.1999 | | (4) | |
| Momčilo Rašo (MNE) | 06.02.1997 | 23 | (1) | 2 |
| Diver Duván Torres Quiñónes (COL) | 15.02.1999 | 7 | (3) | |
| Nikola Žerjal (SRB) | 10.07.1997 | 6 | (1) | |
| Miloš Zlatković (SRB) | 01.01.1997 | 12 | (1) | 1 |
| **Midfielders:** | **DOB** | **M** | **(s)** | **G** |
| Leonardo Agius | 17.09.2002 | | (1) | |
| Adam Bradshaw | 31.10.2001 | 1 | (12) | |
| Nikola Braunović | 21.07.1997 | 14 | (4) | |
| Milan Đurić (SRB) | 03.10.1987 | 3 | | |
| Paul Fenech | 20.12.1986 | 24 | (1) | |

| Neil Frendo | 04.01.1999 | | (1) | |
|---|---|---|---|---|
| Jake Grech | 06.02.2004 | | (1) | |
| Marcus Grima | 22.07.2000 | 22 | (3) | |
| Benjamin Hili | 16.02.2004 | 5 | (7) | |
| Luca Mallia | 04.04.1998 | | (5) | |
| Bogdan Mladenović (SRB) | 04.04.1996 | 4 | (10) | |
| Delvin N'Dinga (CGO) | 14.03.1988 | 2 | (6) | 1 |
| **Forwards:** | **DOB** | **M** | **(s)** | **G** |
| Aleksa Andrejić (SRB) | 24.01.1993 | 16 | | 2 |
| Gabriel Diego Farrugia | 14.05.2004 | | (1) | |
| Aidan Friggieri | 28.04.1998 | 1 | (1) | |
| Suleiman Jalu (NED) | 20.03.2000 | 4 | (4) | |
| Bojan Kaljević (MNE) | 25.01.1986 | 11 | (15) | 6 |
| Uroš Ljubomirac (SRB) | 12.04.1990 | 10 | | 2 |
| *Matheus* Nogueira Albuquerque de Souza (BRA) | 15.09.1993 | 18 | (6) | 7 |
| Ángel Yesid Torres Quiñones (COL) | 06.04.2000 | 21 | (1) | 14 |
| Alexander Satariano | 25.10.2001 | 17 | (7) | 2 |

## Birkirkara Football Club

| Founded: | 1950 | | |
|---|---|---|---|
| Stadium: | Mġarr Ground, Imgarr (300) | | |
| Trainer: | Giovanni Tedesco (ITA) | | 26.01.2022 |

| Goalkeepers: | DOB | M | (s) | G |
|---|---|---|---|---|
| Giacomo Nava (ITA) | 27.01.1997 | 20 | | |
| Amary Sylla | 16.09.2001 | 6 | (2) | |
| **Defenders:** | **DOB** | **M** | **(s)** | **G** |
| Cain Attard | 10.09.1994 | 25 | | 1 |
| Adam Camilleri | 29.01.2002 | | (1) | |
| Alessandro Coppola (ITA) | 13.03.2000 | 20 | | 2 |
| Osvaldo Iorio Forestero (URU) | 02.08.2000 | 18 | (6) | 5 |
| Enrico Pepe | 12.11.1989 | 19 | (1) | |
| Nemanja Radojević (SRB) | 05.02.1992 | 2 | | 1 |
| Kurt Zammit | 26.02.1996 | 23 | (2) | |
| **Midfielders:** | **DOB** | **M** | **(s)** | **G** |
| Nathan Cross | 01.09.2004 | | (1) | |
| Diego Pires *Dall'Oca* (BRA) | 13.09.1995 | 9 | (5) | |
| Matteo Fedele (SUI) | 20.07.1992 | 7 | (3) | 1 |
| Kaiden Fenech | 17.11.2005 | | (1) | |

| Matteo Gambin | 04.05.2004 | | (6) | |
|---|---|---|---|---|
| Neil Micallef | 12.01.1999 | 2 | (13) | |
| Ryan Scicluna | 30.07.1993 | 1 | (2) | |
| Yannick Yankam | 12.12.1997 | 25 | | 5 |
| Simon Zibo (GHA) | 30.11.1997 | 18 | | 2 |
| **Forwards:** | **DOB** | **M** | **(s)** | **G** |
| Enzo Daniel Cabrera (ARG) | 20.11.1999 | 22 | (3) | 13 |
| Andrei Cosmin Ciolacu (ROU) | 09.08.1992 | 4 | (5) | 2 |
| Mathias Conti | 05.03.2004 | | (2) | 1 |
| Federico Matías Falcone (ARG) | 21.02.1990 | 2 | (6) | 1 |
| Jean Paul Farrugia | 21.03.1992 | | (12) | |
| Alex da Paixão Alves „Lecão" (BRA) | 17.01.1993 | 18 | (5) | 6 |
| Paul Mbong | 02.09.2001 | 20 | (5) | 4 |
| *Denis* Custodio Ribeiro (BRA) | 09.09.1998 | 10 | (11) | 1 |
| Kevin Tulimieri (ITA) | 15.03.1992 | 15 | (8) | 3 |
| Jed Valletta | 20.08.2003 | | (4) | |

## Floriana Football Club

| Founded: | 1894 | | |
|---|---|---|---|
| Stadium: | Independence Arena, Floriana (3,000) | | |
| Trainer: | Gianluca Atzori (ITA) | | 06.03.1971 |

| Goalkeepers: | DOB | M | (s) | G |
|---|---|---|---|---|
| Reece Cutajar | 15.06.2005 | 2 | (2) | |
| Duncan Formosa | 30.06.2000 | 5 | (1) | |
| Georgi Kitanov (BUL) | 06.03.1995 | 19 | | |
| **Defenders:** | **DOB** | **M** | **(s)** | **G** |
| Emiliano Callegari Torre (ARG) | 26.02.1996 | 19 | | 1 |
| Zachary Cassar | 02.11.1998 | 8 | (7) | 1 |
| Oualid El Hasni (TUN) | 09.08.1993 | 25 | | 3 |
| Raul Formosa | 16.02.2005 | | (1) | |
| Alejandro Garzia | 21.03.2002 | 10 | (7) | 1 |
| Christian Rutjens Oliva (ESP) | 05.01.1998 | 8 | | |
| Owen Spiteri | 02.11.2002 | 13 | (3) | 1 |
| Lorenzo Trillò (ITA) | 20.05.1997 | 19 | (7) | 3 |
| **Midfielders:** | **DOB** | **M** | **(s)** | **G** |
| Luca Accarino | 19.05.2004 | 3 | (1) | |
| Ulises Jesús Arias (ARG) | 05.08.1996 | 21 | | 1 |
| Jan Busuttil | 06.03.1999 | 21 | (4) | 4 |

| Christopher Junior Buttigieg | 11.05.2005 | | (1) | |
|---|---|---|---|---|
| Neil Cassar | 12.03.2004 | | (3) | |
| Lorenzo De Grazia (ITA) | 01.04.1995 | 12 | (4) | |
| Matías Nicolás García (ARG) | 22.07.1996 | 12 | (2) | |
| Eden Hershkovitz (ISR) | 23.08.1997 | 2 | (6) | |
| Fernando Ezequiel Juárez (ARG) | 23.08.1998 | 7 | | |
| Eman Micallef | 03.10.2003 | | (2) | |
| Sindre Osestad (NOR) | 02.10.1999 | 5 | | |
| Adam Magri Overend | 03.05.2000 | 21 | (4) | 1 |
| Kemar David Reid (JAM) | 15.08.1994 | 20 | (5) | 5 |
| **Forwards:** | **DOB** | **M** | **(s)** | **G** |
| Andrei Cosmin Ciolacu (ROU) | 09.08.1992 | 5 | (10) | 3 |
| Alen Melunović (SRB) | 26.01.1990 | 4 | (5) | |
| Kyrian Nwoko | 04.07.1997 | 2 | (7) | |
| James Scicluna | 04.03.1998 | | (12) | |
| Mattia Veselji | 14.03.2002 | 15 | (6) | 5 |
| Carlo Zammit Lonardelli | 29.04.2001 | 8 | (9) | 1 |

## Gudja United Football Club

| Founded: | 1945 | | |
|---|---|---|---|
| Stadium: | „Louis Azzopardi" Stadium, Gudja (1,000) | | |
| Trainer: | Andrea Agostinelli (ITA) | | 20.04.1957 |
| [12.04.2023] | Ludvic Bartolo | | |

| Goalkeepers: | DOB | M | (s) | G |
|---|---|---|---|---|
| James Pisani | 14.02.1995 | 2 | | |
| Glenn Zammit | 05.08.1987 | 24 | | |
| **Defenders:** | **DOB** | **M** | **(s)** | **G** |
| Joseph Attard | 14.10.2002 | 3 | (6) | |
| Juan Andrés Bolaños Ramírez (COL) | 22.07.1991 | 20 | | |
| Neil Anthony Micallef | 23.11.1998 | 21 | (1) | |
| Karl Micallef | 08.09.1996 | 22 | (1) | 1 |
| *André Fausto* Prates Rodrigues Júnior (BRA) | 02.05.1994 | 18 | | 2 |
| Farid Romero Zúñiga (COL) | 08.09.1998 | 13 | (7) | 1 |
| **Midfielders:** | **DOB** | **M** | **(s)** | **G** |
| Jean Claude Bugeja Aboumehdi | 10.02.2004 | 1 | (3) | |
| James Arthur (GHA) | 17.02.1989 | 24 | | |
| Ayrton Azzopardi | 12.09.1993 | 3 | (2) | 1 |
| Johan Bezzina | 30.05.1994 | 9 | (5) | 3 |

| *Samuel Gomes* da Mata (BRA) | 20.08.1999 | 17 | (1) | 3 |
|---|---|---|---|---|
| John Mintoff | 23.08.1988 | 6 | (9) | |
| Matias Roberto Muchardi (ARG) | 09.02.1988 | 15 | (1) | 1 |
| Tatsuro Nagamatsu (JPN) | 23.04.1995 | 9 | (8) | 6 |
| Nicolas Navarrete (ARG) | 29.08.1995 | 19 | (5) | 2 |
| Neil Tabone | 01.10.1997 | 13 | (3) | |
| Hubert Vella | 07.02.1994 | 13 | (6) | |
| **Forwards:** | **DOB** | **M** | **(s)** | **G** |
| Shaisen Attard | 29.10.2004 | 6 | (5) | |
| Llywelyn Cremona | 07.05.1995 | | (1) | |
| Tensior Gusman | 24.01.1997 | | (2) | |
| Divaio Kolf (NED) | 19.07.2003 | | (3) | |
| Vito Plut (SVN) | 08.07.1988 | 24 | (1) | 6 |
| Ahinga Selemani (USA) | 15.03.1996 | 4 | (7) | 1 |

## Gżira United Football Club

| Founded: | 1947 | | |
| Stadium: | Gżira Football Ground, Gżira (n/a) | | |
| Trainer: | Darren Abdilla | | 10.07.1979 |

| Goalkeepers: | DOB | M | (s) | G |
|---|---|---|---|---|
| David Cassar | 24.11.1987 | 3 | (2) | |
| Krassimir Zammit | 06.05.2002 | | (1) | |
| Darijan Radelić Žarkov (CRO) | 21.07.1992 | 23 | | |
| **Defenders:** | **DOB** | **M** | **(s)** | **G** |
| Marko Ćosić (CRO) | 02.03.1994 | 26 | | |
| Marcelo Dias | 29.09.1985 | 24 | | 1 |
| *Gabriel* Bohrer *Mentz* (BRA) | 11.08.1998 | 22 | | 2 |
| Luis Carlos Riascos Torres (COL) | 17.09.2001 | 17 | (3) | 2 |
| Luke Tabone | 12.08.1997 | 20 | (2) | 1 |
| Thiago Espíndola de Paula „Thiaguinho" (BRA) | 14.05.1993 | 1 | (7) | 1 |
| **Midfielders:** | **DOB** | **M** | **(s)** | **G** |
| Mohamed Alouzi | 15.07.2003 | | (1) | |
| Jean Paul Attard | 28.05.2001 | | (1) | |
| Andy Borg | 27.06.2004 | | (15) | |

| | DOB | M | (s) | G |
|---|---|---|---|---|
| Ricardo Calixto Correa Duarte (URU) | 20.07.1994 | 6 | (6) | |
| Izaak Ellul | 11.08.2004 | | (1) | |
| *Ewertton* José Costa Silva (BRA) | 10.08.1997 | 4 | (1) | |
| Clive Gauci | 24.04.1996 | 4 | (6) | |
| Hytem Kabar | 23.07.2003 | | (1) | |
| Jackson David Mendoza Usuga (COL) | 20.04.1998 | 7 | (11) | |
| Nicky Muscat | 13.07.1996 | 20 | (4) | 1 |
| Stephen Pisani | 07.08.1992 | 18 | (5) | 1 |
| Zachary Scerri | 08.03.1996 | 22 | (3) | 1 |
| **Forwards:** | **DOB** | **M** | **(s)** | **G** |
| Brooklyn Borg | 08.01.2004 | | (20) | |
| *Jefferson Mateus* de Assis Estácio (BRA) | 21.10.1994 | 25 | | 20 |
| Toni Kolega (CRO) | 10.10.1998 | 24 | (2) | 2 |
| Lucas Ribeiro de Oliveira „Macula" (BRA) | 10.06.2000 | 1 | (7) | 2 |
| Máxuell Maia da Silva „Máxuell Samurai" (BRA) | 30.09.1991 | 19 | (3) | 11 |

## Hamrun Spartans Football Club

| Founded: | 1907 | | |
| Stadium: | "Victor Tedesco" Stadium, Hamrun (6,000) | | |
| Trainer: | Branko Nišević (SRB) | | 31.08.1971 |

| Goalkeepers: | DOB | M | (s) | G |
|---|---|---|---|---|
| Henry Bonello | 13.10.1988 | 20 | | |
| Anthony Curmi | 20.11.1982 | | (1) | |
| Pablo Guillermo *Sánchez* Niño (ENG) | 20.10.1995 | 4 | | |
| Steve Sultana | 07.09.1990 | | (1) | |
| Winiston Cristian Santos „Tom" (BRA) | 30.10.1991 | 2 | | |
| **Defenders:** | **DOB** | **M** | **(s)** | **G** |
| Zeron Azzopardi | 09.08.2004 | | (1) | |
| Steve Borg | 15.05.1988 | 19 | (1) | 1 |
| Rodrigo Callegari Torre (ARG) | 22.06.1997 | 8 | (7) | |
| *Vinícius* de Freitas Ribeiro (BRA) | 07.03.1993 | 1 | (13) | |
| Sven Xerri | 10.02.2005 | | (6) | |
| **Midfielders:** | **DOB** | **M** | **(s)** | **G** |
| Leon Borg | 27.10.2003 | | (2) | 1 |
| Bjorn Buhagiar | 10.02.2004 | | (1) | |
| Ryan Camenzuli | 08.09.1994 | 25 | (1) | 1 |
| Juan Carlos Corbalan | 03.03.1997 | 21 | (1) | 1 |

| | DOB | M | (s) | G |
|---|---|---|---|---|
| *Emerson* Marcelina (BRA) | 24.02.1991 | 25 | | 1 |
| Matteo Fedele (SUI) | 20.07.1992 | 3 | (2) | |
| Matthew Guillaumier | 09.04.1998 | 25 | | 4 |
| Matthew Mifsud | 14.02.2002 | | (2) | |
| **Forwards:** | **DOB** | **M** | **(s)** | **G** |
| Shaisen Attard | 29.10.2004 | | (7) | |
| Ognjen Bjeličić (SRB) | 29.07.1997 | 21 | | |
| *Cláudio* Henrique da Silva Barboza „Murici" (BRA) | 13.05.1998 | 2 | (1) | |
| Ailton Jorge dos Santos Soares "Dodô" (CPV) | 06.12.1990 | 10 | (13) | 3 |
| *Ederson* Bruno Domingos (BRA) | 21.08.1989 | 18 | (7) | 2 |
| Kalle Holmberg (SWE) | 03.03.1993 | 4 | (5) | |
| *Jonny* Robert do Nascimento Torres (BRA) | 18.05.1998 | 18 | (7) | 5 |
| Elvis Mashike Sukisa (COD) | 06.06.1994 | 23 | (3) | 18 |
| Joseph Essien Mbong | 15.07.1997 | 5 | (5) | |
| Luke Montebello | 13.08.1995 | 11 | (11) | 6 |
| Roko Prša (CRO) | 16.02.1996 | 21 | | 2 |
| Mousa Balla Sowe (GAM) | 02.02.1997 | | (1) | |

## Hibernians Football Club Paola

| Founded: | 1922 | | |
| Stadium: | "Tony Bezzina" Stadium, Paola (2,968) | | |
| Trainer: | Andrea Pisanu (ITA) | | 07.01.1982 |
| [07.02.2023] | Silvio Vella | | 08.02.1967 |

| Goalkeepers: | DOB | M | (s) | G |
|---|---|---|---|---|
| Justin Haber | 09.06.1981 | 11 | | |
| Marko Jovičić (SRB) | 02.02.1995 | 2 | | |
| Ibrahim Koné (GUI) | 05.12.1989 | 13 | | |
| **Defenders:** | **DOB** | **M** | **(s)** | **G** |
| Andrei Agius | 12.08.1986 | 9 | (6) | |
| Ferdinando Apap | 29.07.1992 | 23 | | 5 |
| Matthew Ellul | 23.05.2002 | | (2) | 1 |
| Zachary Grech | 25.08.2000 | 9 | (10) | |
| Gabriel Izquier Artiles „Gabri Izquier" (ESP) | 29.04.1993 | 18 | (2) | |
| *Gonzalo* Llerena Bravo (ESP) | 25.05.1990 | 19 | (3) | 1 |
| *Rodolfo* dos Santos *Soares* (BRA) | 20.05.1985 | 10 | (2) | |
| Kurt Shaw | 01.04.1999 | 13 | (3) | 1 |
| Mathias Vallejo (USA) | 04.01.2004 | 1 | (1) | |
| Joseph Zerafa | 31.05.1988 | 6 | (6) | |

| Midfielders: | DOB | M | (s) | G |
|---|---|---|---|---|
| Arziel Borg | 27.04.2003 | | (1) | |
| Ali Diakité (CIV) | 03.03.1993 | 23 | (2) | 1 |
| Jake Grech | 18.11.1997 | 23 | (3) | 13 |
| Bjorn Kristensen | 05.04.1993 | 22 | (3) | |
| Dunstan Vella | 27.04.1996 | 12 | (7) | |
| **Forwards:** | **DOB** | **M** | **(s)** | **G** |
| Isaiah Chukunyere | 28.04.2005 | | (2) | |
| Jurgen Degabriele | 10.10.1996 | 21 | (3) | 14 |
| Eduardo Andrés Mangles Herrera (NED) | 01.11.2004 | | (3) | |
| *Jairo* Morillas Rivero (ESP) | 02.07.1993 | 2 | (12) | |
| Gabriel Mensah (GHA) | 05.10.1995 | 6 | (11) | |
| Yunusa Owolabi Muritala (NGA) | 02.04.2000 | 20 | (4) | 7 |
| João Vítor de Oliveira Florêncio „Robinho" (BRA) | 25.12.1997 | 6 | (3) | 2 |
| Brian Thaylor Lubanzadio Aldama (ANG) | 27.02.1994 | 17 | (7) | |

## Marsaxlokk Football Club

| Founded: | 1949 (*as Marsaxlokk White Stars*) | | |
| Stadium: | Marsaxlokk Ground, Marsaxlokk (150) | | |
| Trainer: | Pablo César Doffo (ARG) | | 06.04.1983 |
| [23.03.2023] | Dragan Đurđević (SRB) | | 18.04.1981 |

| Goalkeepers: | DOB | M | (s) | G |
|---|---|---|---|---|
| Marko Drobnjak (SRB) | 17.05.1995 | 20 | | |
| José Luis Gamonal Ruiz (CHI) | 09.10.1989 | 2 | | |
| José María Gobbi (ARG) | 08.10.1992 | 3 | | |
| Fredrick Tabone | 08.11.1988 | 1 | | |
| **Defenders:** | **DOB** | **M** | **(s)** | **G** |
| Leandro Damián Aguirre (ARG) | 08.02.1989 | 21 | | 1 |
| Claudio Bonanni (ITA) | 05.03.1997 | 5 | (1) | 1 |
| Óscar Matías Carniello (ARG) | 18.09.1988 | 14 | | 1 |
| Timothy Tabone Desira | 15.07.1995 | 1 | | |
| Emerson Vella | 09.09.1991 | 5 | (8) | |
| Dejan Vuković | 04.01.1993 | 22 | (1) | |
| **Midfielders:** | **DOB** | **M** | **(s)** | **G** |
| Juan Cruz Aguilar (ARG) | 08.02.1996 | 18 | (1) | |
| Conor Borg | 13.05.1997 | 3 | (2) | |
| Kaylon Dimech | 08.10.2004 | | (2) | |
| Santiago Ferraris (ARG) | 26.02.1999 | 21 | (2) | 2 |
| *Jeferson Mendes* da Silva (BRA) | 25.12.2001 | 2 | | |

| | DOB | M | (s) | G |
|---|---|---|---|---|
| Kristian Keqi (ALB) | 28.07.1996 | 17 | (1) | 3 |
| Dale Mifsud | 26.09.2003 | 3 | (5) | |
| Peter Paul Sammut | 28.12.1991 | 1 | (4) | |
| Ryan Scicluna | 30.07.1993 | 10 | | |
| Walter Omar Serrano (ARG) | 02.07.1986 | 11 | | 2 |
| Ryan Tonna | 27.04.2001 | | (4) | |
| Edafe Uzeh (NGA) | 22.03.1988 | 8 | (10) | |
| Peter Xuereb | 07.05.1992 | 19 | (1) | 2 |
| **Forwards:** | **DOB** | **M** | **(s)** | **G** |
| Daniel Agius | 15.11.1996 | 16 | (5) | 1 |
| Ayrton Attard | 05.11.2000 | 20 | (4) | 5 |
| Alfred Effiong | 29.11.1984 | | (8) | |
| Santiago Fabián Moracci (ARG) | 20.03.2001 | 12 | (10) | 2 |
| Vamara Sanogo (FRA) | 22.04.1995 | 2 | (4) | |
| *Tiago Adan* Fonseca (BRA) | 14.03.1988 | 21 | (2) | 4 |
| Terence Vella | 20.04.1990 | 3 | (6) | 1 |
| *Wellington* Valentim de Sousa (BRA) | 11.12.1994 | 5 | (9) | |

## Mosta Football Club

| Goalkeepers: | DOB | M | (s) | G |
|---|---|---|---|---|
| Ini Etim Akpan (NGA) | 03.08.1984 | 26 | | |
| **Defenders:** | **DOB** | **M** | **(s)** | **G** |
| Jacob Akrong (GHA) | 31.12.1992 | 16 | (3) | 5 |
| Duane Bonnici | 10.10.1995 | 15 | (7) | 1 |
| Jonas Rodriguez Ekani (CMR) | 13.10.1992 | 19 | (2) | |
| Tyron Farrugia | 22.02.1989 | 12 | (6) | 1 |
| Ibe Joseph Feargod (NGA) | 01.03.2004 | 1 | (5) | |
| Steve Kingue (CMR) | 23.01.2000 | 11 | (5) | |
| Jake Vassallo | 21.06.2004 | 20 | (3) | |
| **Midfielders:** | **DOB** | **M** | **(s)** | **G** |
| Geoffrey Acheampong (GHA) | 28.01.1997 | 14 | | 1 |
| Nathan Agius | 16.11.2003 | 1 | (14) | |
| Roderick Briffa | 24.08.1981 | 22 | (2) | 1 |
| Boubakary Diarra (FRA) | 30.08.1993 | 23 | (1) | 1 |

**Founded**: 1935
**Stadium**: "Charles Abela" Memorial Stadium, Mosta (600)
**Trainer**: Joe Grech

| | DOB | M | (s) | G |
|---|---|---|---|---|
| Chibueze Glamour Eziefula (NGA) | 15.02.2003 | 2 | (5) | 1 |
| Clayton Failla | 08.01.1986 | 24 | | 7 |
| Patrick Mensah (GHA) | 04.10.2001 | 4 | (2) | |
| Gianluca Sciberras | 02.08.2002 | 4 | (8) | |
| Precious Linus Tenebe (NGA) | 13.06.2004 | 7 | (15) | |
| Kaishu Yamazaki (JPN) | 12.07.1997 | 4 | (2) | |
| **Forwards:** | **DOB** | **M** | **(s)** | **G** |
| Tobi Akiti (NGA) | 20.04.2001 | 4 | (3) | |
| Zachary Brincat | 24.06.1998 | 20 | (2) | 10 |
| Férébory Doré (CGO) | 21.01.1989 | 3 | (5) | |
| Evo Christ Ememe (NGA) | 30.04.2001 | 25 | | 10 |
| Nsumoh Johnson Kalu (NGA) | 14.06.2001 | 2 | (8) | |
| William Legault | 21.06.2003 | | (6) | 1 |
| Victor Ifeanyi Mbata (NGA) | 25.07.2002 | | (6) | |
| Chidera Micheal Okoh (NGA) | 05.04.2003 | 7 | (8) | 8 |

## Pietà Hotspurs Football Club

| Goalkeepers: | DOB | M | (s) | G |
|---|---|---|---|---|
| Dele Alampasu (NGA) | 24.12.1996 | 11 | | |
| Reeves Cini | 14.01.2002 | 11 | (1) | |
| Jake Farrugia | 07.03.2004 | | (1) | |
| Simone Moschin | 20.01.1996 | 4 | | |
| **Defenders:** | **DOB** | **M** | **(s)** | **G** |
| Clinton Bangura (AUT) | 22.03.1998 | 23 | | 1 |
| Kaydon Catania | 01.12.2005 | 1 | (3) | |
| Ivin Farrugia | 02.06.2005 | 4 | (3) | 1 |
| Ivin Gatt | 25.05.2005 | | (1) | |
| Thomas Howland | 01.09.2005 | | (2) | |
| Zean Leonardi | 05.03.2003 | 25 | | |
| Ganiu Atanda Ogungbe (NGA) | 01.12.1992 | 19 | | |
| Daniel Zerafa | 08.04.1994 | 14 | (2) | 1 |
| **Midfielders:** | **DOB** | **M** | **(s)** | **G** |
| Terence Agius | 15.01.1994 | 16 | (5) | 1 |
| Ange Belibi (BEL) | 11.12.2001 | 4 | (2) | |
| Kurt Briffa | 22.06.2003 | 5 | (11) | |
| Luca Gatt | 21.12.1999 | | (5) | |

**Founded**: 1968
**Stadium**: "Tony Bezzina" Stadium, Paola (2,968)
**Trainer**: Rodney Bugeja    14.10.1978

| | DOB | M | (s) | G |
|---|---|---|---|---|
| Jake Ghio | 08.09.2001 | 23 | (2) | 1 |
| Sheldon Mizzi | 08.01.2002 | 4 | (5) | |
| Samuel Okoh | 18.09.2001 | 21 | (5) | 1 |
| Temitope Abraham Ojo (NGA) | 08.12.1998 | 21 | | 2 |
| Nigel Scerri | 12.02.2004 | | (1) | |
| Alan Schembri Wismayer | 03.04.1996 | 14 | (10) | |
| Gabriel Xuereb | 28.01.2003 | | (9) | |
| Ito Yasukaze (JPN) | 10.11.1998 | 4 | | |
| **Forwards:** | **DOB** | **M** | **(s)** | **G** |
| Anis Ajroud (TUN) | 30.03.2002 | | (1) | |
| Latif Amadu (GHA) | 20.08.1993 | 6 | (3) | |
| Sékou Camara (GUI) | 23.09.1997 | 7 | (5) | 1 |
| Armen Hovhannisyan (ARM) | 07.03.2000 | 10 | | 4 |
| Paul Lapira | 05.02.1998 | 2 | (5) | |
| Kian Leonardi | 20.02.2005 | 11 | (11) | 3 |
| Davi Rodrigues Miranda „Marinho" (BRA) | 19.05.1999 | 4 | (3) | |
| Yuto Morita (JPN) | 26.05.2001 | 3 | (8) | 1 |
| Takuma Yamaguchi (JPN) | 20.10.1998 | 19 | (5) | 3 |

## Santa Luċija Football Club

| Goalkeepers: | DOB | M | (s) | G |
|---|---|---|---|---|
| Dylan Ciappara | 12.07.2002 | 5 | | |
| Matthew Calleja Cremona | 14.09.1994 | 20 | | |
| Makoto Kikushima (JPN) | 22.06.1999 | 1 | | |
| **Defenders:** | **DOB** | **M** | **(s)** | **G** |
| Brady Agius | 05.09.2002 | | (3) | |
| Binu Bairam (ROU) | 19.11.2000 | 24 | (1) | 1 |
| *Diego* Fracarolli Pacheco (BRA)Diego | | 12 | (5) | |
| Lorenzo Soares Fonseca (CPV) | 17.01.1998 | 19 | | |
| Zvi Jie (NED) | 17.03.2002 | 3 | (4) | |
| Michael Johnson | 11.05.1994 | 7 | (3) | |
| Sheldon Mizzi | 08.01.2002 | | (1) | |
| Jurgen Pisani | 03.09.1992 | 26 | | 1 |
| Nicolas Pulis | 29.01.1998 | 19 | (1) | 1 |
| Thomas Rier (NED) | 13.01.2000 | 7 | (1) | |
| *Rodolfo* dos Santos *Soares* (BRA) | 20.05.1985 | 9 | | 1 |
| Dexter Xuereb | 21.09.1997 | 21 | (3) | |

**Founded**: 1974
**Stadium**: Grawnd Santa Luċija, Santa Luċija (1,000)
**Trainer**: Pablo Cortés Sánchez (ESP)    1991
[03.11.2022]    Vincenzo Potenza (ITA)    03.05.1970

| Midfielders: | DOB | M | (s) | G |
|---|---|---|---|---|
| Liam Ayad (CIV) | 27.06.1998 | 20 | (3) | 1 |
| Emerson Camilleri | 01.05.2002 | 2 | (4) | |
| Liam McKay | 22.05.2001 | 2 | (6) | |
| Reon Saito (JPN) | 16.04.1999 | 1 | (6) | |
| Jan Tanti | 14.04.1998 | 3 | (11) | 1 |
| Yevgeniy Terzi (UKR) | 27.06.1997 | 11 | | 2 |
| Matthias Vella | 29.10.2002 | 3 | (3) | |
| Jamie Zerafa | 02.03.1998 | 4 | (8) | |
| **Forwards:** | **DOB** | **M** | **(s)** | **G** |
| Miguel Ángel Alba (ARG) | 14.08.1988 | 12 | (9) | |
| Jamie Carbone | 16.08.2002 | 2 | (15) | 1 |
| Robert Gegedosh (UKR) | 02.05.1993 | 10 | (1) | |
| Francisco Eliomar Rodrigues Farias "Léo Bahia" (BRA) | 19.05.1991 | 23 | (2) | 6 |
| Érick Andrés Moreno Serna (COL) | 24.11.1991 | 2 | (7) | |
| Kyrian Nwoko | 04.07.1997 | 5 | (3) | 2 |
| Meghon Valpoort (CUW) | 31.07.2000 | 13 | (1) | 2 |

## Sirens Football Club San Pawl il-Baħar

| Goalkeepers: | DOB | M | (s) | G |
|---|---|---|---|---|
| Andrea Cassar | 19.12.1992 | 11 | | |
| Matthew Grech | 19.02.1996 | 15 | | |
| Andriy Etienne Vella | 15.05.2005 | | (1) | |
| **Defenders:** | **DOB** | **M** | **(s)** | **G** |
| Adrian Borg | 20.05.1989 | 15 | (5) | 1 |
| Krist Borg | 28.12.2005 | | (1) | |
| Gary Camilleri | 05.08.1999 | 18 | | |
| Alex Cini | 28.10.1991 | 21 | (1) | 1 |
| *Gabriel* Ventura (BRA) | 05.04.1997 | 13 | | |
| Kevin Muscat | 26.05.2004 | | (1) | |
| Armah Vaikainah (LBR) | 17.06.1995 | 14 | | |
| Andreas Vella | 27.01.2001 | 2 | (6) | |
| Jacob Walker | 31.07.1997 | 18 | (1) | 2 |
| *Weder* Soares da *Silva* (BRA) | 07.07.1992 | 7 | (2) | |
| Daniel Zarb | 23.02.2005 | 1 | (1) | |

**Founded**: 1968
**Stadium**: Sirens Stadium, San Pawl il-Baħar (600)
**Trainer**: Winston Muscat    29.08.1969

| Midfielders: | DOB | M | (s) | G |
|---|---|---|---|---|
| Sean Cipriott | 10.09.1997 | 15 | | 1 |
| Ricardo Calixto Correa Duarte (URU) | 20.07.1994 | 8 | (1) | 1 |
| Kemmu Degran Jackson (JAM) | 11.07.1995 | 18 | (6) | |
| Miguel Maggi | 19.06.2005 | | (6) | |
| *Marcelo* Muniz (BRA) | 14.01.1991 | 19 | (2) | 1 |
| Kei Sano (JPN) | 03.04.1992 | 19 | (4) | 6 |
| Stéphane Sessègnon (BEN) | 01.06.1984 | 8 | (11) | |
| Rei Tachikawa (JPN) | 18.01.1998 | 23 | | 2 |
| **Forwards:** | **DOB** | **M** | **(s)** | **G** |
| Siraj Arab | 25.03.1994 | 4 | (11) | |
| Promise Oluwatobi Emmanuel David (CAN) | 03.07.2001 | 1 | (6) | |
| Ivan Kolev (BUL) | 15.10.1995 | 16 | (3) | 3 |
| Paulo Vyctor Bento do Vale (BRA) | 21.03.1996 | 17 | (1) | 5 |
| *Wellington* Oliveira Vieira „Petinha" (BRA) | 20.01.1993 | 3 | (5) | |

## Valletta Football Club

| | Founded: | 1943 | | |
|---|---|---|---|---|
| | Stadium: | Sirens Stadium, San Pawl il-Baħar (600) | | |
| | Trainer: | Thane Micallef | | 18.04.1985 |

| Goalkeepers: | DOB | M | (s) | G |
|---|---|---|---|---|
| Cain Formosa | 26.11.2000 | 8 | | |
| Alessandro Guarnone (ITA) | 27.03.1999 | 18 | | |
| **Defenders:** | **DOB** | **M** | **(s)** | **G** |
| Jean Borg | 08.01.1998 | 14 | (1) | |
| Ryan Camilleri | 22.05.1988 | 5 | (1) | |
| Kayden Farrugia | 02.04.2006 | | (1) | |
| Christian Gauci | 26.12.2001 | 11 | (7) | 1 |
| Bradley Kamdem (FRA) | 18.08.1994 | 20 | | |
| Peter Ohaka | 04.09.2006 | | (2) | |
| Enzo Adrián Ruiz (ARG) | 20.06.1989 | 20 | (1) | |
| Eslit Sala | 09.05.2000 | 19 | (2) | 1 |
| **Midfielders:** | **DOB** | **M** | **(s)** | **G** |
| Tristan Caruana | 15.09.1991 | 9 | (10) | |
| Shaun Dimech | 08.08.2001 | 21 | (3) | 5 |
| Sheldon MacKay | 20.09.2003 | 1 | (3) | |
| Josiah Mallia | 13.08.2005 | | (1) | |

| | DOB | M | (s) | G |
|---|---|---|---|---|
| Rowen Muscat | 05.06.1991 | 7 | (2) | |
| Brandon Paiber | 05.06.1995 | 23 | (1) | 5 |
| Enmy Manuel Peña Beltré (DOM) | 17.09.1992 | 21 | (2) | 1 |
| **Forwards:** | **DOB** | **M** | **(s)** | **G** |
| Oke Akpoveta (NGA) | 12.12.1991 | 10 | (2) | 4 |
| Jake Azzopardi | 13.02.2006 | | (2) | |
| Zak Barbara | 07.02.2005 | | (3) | |
| Kilian Bevis | 13.02.1998 | 22 | | 6 |
| Llywelyn Cremona | 07.05.1995 | 2 | (9) | |
| Federico Matías Falcone (ARG) | 21.02.1990 | 11 | | 4 |
| *Flávio* dos Santos da Silva Cheveresan *"Carioca"* (BRA) | 11.12.1988 | 2 | (8) | 1 |
| William Jebor (LBR) | 10.11.1991 | | (9) | |
| Isaiah Micallef | 28.04.2004 | | (2) | |
| Nilton Soares Rodrigues „Niltinho" (BRA) | 11.09.1993 | 4 | (2) | |
| Jean-Marie Ulrich N'Nomo N'Gong (FRA) | 28.02.1996 | 14 | (6) | 3 |
| Joseph Willy (NGA) | 08.05.1997 | 9 | (7) | |
| Andrea Zammit | 05.04.2003 | 15 | (9) | 6 |

## Żebbuġ Rangers Football Club

| | Founded: | 1943 | | |
|---|---|---|---|---|
| | Stadium: | Żebbuġ Ground, Żebbuġ (1,000) | | |
| | Trainer: | Brian Spiteri | | |

| Goalkeepers: | DOB | M | (s) | G |
|---|---|---|---|---|
| Jamie Azzopardi | 01.09.1997 | 23 | | |
| Miguel Chetcuti | 26.01.2000 | 3 | (1) | |
| **Defenders:** | **DOB** | **M** | **(s)** | **G** |
| Travis Bartolo | 05.04.1995 | 9 | (11) | |
| Kurt Bondin | 03.06.2002 | 12 | (10) | 1 |
| Shaun Bugeja | 03.08.1995 | 24 | | 2 |
| Paul Galea | 16.11.2002 | | (1) | |
| Joseph Gaetano Gesualdi | 15.02.1992 | 12 | (9) | |
| *Henrique* Marcelino *Motta* (BRA) | 10.01.1991 | 11 | | 1 |
| *Leandro Almeida* da Silva (BRA) | 14.03.1987 | 24 | | |
| Roberto Enrique Sánchez (ARG) | 05.01.1995 | 23 | | 1 |
| Gianluca Tanti | 09.06.2003 | | (3) | |
| Randall Vella | 16.04.1992 | 12 | (8) | |

| | DOB | M | (s) | G |
|---|---|---|---|---|
| *Wilker* Rocha *Santos* (BRA) | 26.07.1994 | 14 | (3) | |
| **Midfielders:** | **DOB** | **M** | **(s)** | **G** |
| Stefan Janković (SRB) | 25.06.1997 | 17 | (2) | |
| Glen Mifsud | 10.01.2002 | 2 | (6) | |
| Ayrton Mizzi | 21.02.1996 | 16 | (9) | |
| Jordan Sciberras | 22.03.1999 | 5 | (14) | |
| Almir de Jesús Soto Maldonado (COL) | 17.07.1994 | 16 | (6) | |
| Yanis Tonna | 07.02.1992 | 13 | (2) | |
| **Forwards:** | **DOB** | **M** | **(s)** | **G** |
| Shamison Buttigieg | 16.06.2003 | | (2) | |
| Charles Lokolingoy (AUS) | 02.03.1997 | 26 | | 11 |
| Stanimir Milošković (SRB) | 21.12.1983 | 14 | (11) | 1 |
| Jeferson Fernandes Macedo „Perdigão" (BRA) | 17.07.1991 | 10 | (5) | 1 |
| Miguel Antonio Pérez Jiménez (COL) | 22.09.1992 | | (4) | 1 |

## SECOND LEVEL
### Maltese Challenge League 2022/2023

| First Phase | | | | | | | | |
|---|---|---|---|---|---|---|---|---|
| 1. Sliema Wanderers FC | 17 | 15 | 2 | 0 | 40 | - | 10 | 47 |
| 2. Naxxar Lions FC | 17 | 13 | 2 | 2 | 40 | - | 15 | 41 |
| 3. Żejtun Corinthians FC | 17 | 11 | 0 | 6 | 35 | - | 22 | 33 |
| 4. Tarxien Rainbows FC | 17 | 9 | 5 | 3 | 34 | - | 19 | 32 |
| 5. Żurrieq FC | 17 | 9 | 2 | 6 | 33 | - | 28 | 29 |
| 6. Melita FC St. Julian's | 17 | 7 | 5 | 5 | 29 | - | 22 | 26 |
| 7. Fgura United FC | 17 | 7 | 4 | 6 | 41 | - | 25 | 25 |
| 8. Marsa FC | 17 | 6 | 6 | 5 | 27 | - | 23 | 24 |
| 9. Swieqi United FC | 17 | 6 | 6 | 5 | 33 | - | 31 | 24 |
| 10. St. Andrews FC | 17 | 6 | 4 | 7 | 23 | - | 27 | 22 |
| 11. Lija Athletic FC | 17 | 5 | 5 | 7 | 28 | - | 32 | 20 |
| 12. Attard FC | 17 | 5 | 4 | 8 | 19 | - | 30 | 19 |
| 13. San Ġwann FC | 17 | 5 | 3 | 9 | 20 | - | 34 | 18 |
| 14. Marsaskala FC | 17 | 4 | 3 | 10 | 28 | - | 39 | 15 |
| 15. Mqabba FC | 17 | 4 | 3 | 10 | 21 | - | 36 | 15 |
| 16. Qrendi FC | 17 | 3 | 5 | 9 | 19 | - | 36 | 14 |
| 17. Mtarfa FC | 17 | 4 | 2 | 11 | 11 | - | 28 | 14 |
| 18. Vittoriosa Stars FC Birgu | 17 | 3 | 1 | 13 | 14 | - | 38 | 10 |

Please note: teams ranked 1-6 were qualified for the Promotion Play-offs (Top Six), while teams ranked 7-18 were qualified for the Relegation Play-offs (Play-Out).

| Top Six | | | | | | | | |
|---|---|---|---|---|---|---|---|---|
| 1. Sliema Wanderers FC (*Promoted*) | 27 | 24 | 3 | 0 | 66 | - | 15 | 75 |
| 2. Naxxar Lions FC (*Promoted*) | 27 | 19 | 3 | 5 | 58 | - | 28 | 60 |
| 3. Żejtun Corinthians FC (*Promotion Play-offs*) | 27 | 15 | 2 | 10 | 51 | - | 45 | 47 |
| 4. Tarxien Rainbows FC | 27 | 13 | 7 | 7 | 55 | - | 32 | 46 |
| 5. Żurrieq FC | 27 | 10 | 2 | 15 | 38 | - | 59 | 32 |
| 6. Melita FC St. Julian's | 27 | 9 | 7 | 11 | 42 | - | 36 | 34 |

| | | | | | | | | | |
|---|---|---|---|---|---|---|---|---|---|

<table>
<tr><td colspan="10" align="center">Play-Out</td></tr>
<tr><td>7.</td><td>Swieqi United FC</td><td>28</td><td>14</td><td>8</td><td>6</td><td>53</td><td>-</td><td>38</td><td>50</td></tr>
<tr><td>8.</td><td>Fgura United FC</td><td>28</td><td>11</td><td>8</td><td>9</td><td>57</td><td>-</td><td>39</td><td>41</td></tr>
<tr><td>9.</td><td>St. Andrews FC</td><td>28</td><td>11</td><td>7</td><td>10</td><td>37</td><td>-</td><td>40</td><td>40</td></tr>
<tr><td>10.</td><td>Lija Athletic FC</td><td>28</td><td>11</td><td>6</td><td>11</td><td>51</td><td>-</td><td>54</td><td>39</td></tr>
<tr><td>11.</td><td>Attard FC</td><td>28</td><td>10</td><td>7</td><td>11</td><td>39</td><td>-</td><td>45</td><td>37</td></tr>
<tr><td>12.</td><td>Marsa FC</td><td>28</td><td>9</td><td>8</td><td>11</td><td>40</td><td>-</td><td>42</td><td>35</td></tr>
<tr><td>13.</td><td>San Ġwann FC (Relegated)</td><td>28</td><td>9</td><td>7</td><td>12</td><td>33</td><td>-</td><td>45</td><td>34</td></tr>
<tr><td>14.</td><td>Qrendi FC (Relegated)</td><td>28</td><td>8</td><td>7</td><td>13</td><td>38</td><td>-</td><td>52</td><td>31</td></tr>
<tr><td>15.</td><td>Marsaskala FC (Relegated)</td><td>28</td><td>7</td><td>8</td><td>13</td><td>50</td><td>-</td><td>57</td><td>29</td></tr>
<tr><td>16.</td><td>Mqabba FC (Relegated)</td><td>28</td><td>6</td><td>4</td><td>18</td><td>29</td><td>-</td><td>56</td><td>22</td></tr>
<tr><td>17.</td><td>Vittoriosa Stars FC Birgu (Relegated)</td><td>28</td><td>6</td><td>4</td><td>18</td><td>27</td><td>-</td><td>57</td><td>22</td></tr>
<tr><td>18.</td><td>Mtarfa FC (Relegated)</td><td>28</td><td>5</td><td>6</td><td>17</td><td>21</td><td>45</td><td></td><td>21</td></tr>
</table>

## NATIONAL TEAM

### INTERNATIONAL MATCHES
#### (16.07.2022 – 15.07.2023)

| | | | | |
|---|---|---|---|---|
| 23.09.2022 | Tallinn | *Estonia - Malta* | *2-1(1-0)* | (UNL) |
| 27.09.2022 | Attard | *Malta - Israel* | *2-1(0-1)* | (F) |
| 17.11.2022 | Attard | *Malta - Greece* | *2-2(0-1)* | (F) |
| 20.11.2022 | Attard | *Malta - Republic of Ireland* | *0-1(0-0)* | (F) |
| 23.03.2023 | Skopje | *North Macedonia - Malta* | *2-1(0-0)* | (ECQ) |
| 26.03.2023 | Attard | *Malta - Italy* | *0-2(0-2)* | (ECQ) |
| 09.06.2023 | Lëtzebuerg | *Luxembourg - Malta* | *0-1(0-0)* | (F) |
| 16.06.2023 | Attard | *Malta - England* | *0-4(0-3)* | (ECQ) |
| 19.06.2023 | Trnava | *Ukraine - Malta* | *1-0(0-0)* | (ECQ) |

**23.09.2022     ESTONIA - MALTA                    2-1(1-0)                    3<sup>rd</sup> UEFA Nations League D, Group 2**

A. Le Coq Arena, Tallinn; Referee: Daniel Siebert (Germany); Attendance: 5,539
**MLT:** Henry Bonello, Cain Attard (72.Shaun Dimech), Enrico Pepe, Jean Borg [*sent off 45+4*], Joseph Essien Mbong, Matthew Guillaumier (Cap), Brandon Diego Paiber (72.Jurgen Degabriele), Ryan Camenzuli, Alexander Satariano (89.Luke Montebello), Jodi Jay Felice Jones (46.Steve Borg), Teddy Teuma.rainer: Devis Mangia (Italy).
**Goal:** Teddy Teuma (51 penalty).

**27.09.2022     MALTA - ISRAEL                    2-1(0-1)                    Friendly International**

Ta'Qali National Stadium, Attard; Referee: Eldorjan Hamiti (Albania); Attendance: n/a
**MLT:** Henry Bonello, Enrico Pepe, Steve Borg (Cap) (60.Ferdinando Apap), Jean Borg (78.Luke Montebello), Joseph Essien Mbong, Matthew Guillaumier, Bjorn Kristensen (60.Teddy Teuma), Ryan Camenzuli, Jan Busuttil (46.Jodi Jay Felice Jones), Shaun Dimech (71.Alexander Satariano), Jurgen Degabriele (46.James Dominic Brown). Trainer: Devis Mangia (Italy).
**Goals:** Alexander Satariano (84), Ferdinando Apap (86).

**17.11.2022     MALTA - GREECE                    2-2(0-1)                    Friendly International**

Ta'Qali National Stadium, Attard; Referee: Alain Durieux (Luxembourg); Attendance: n/a
**MLT:** Henry Bonello, Enrico Pepe, Steve Borg (Cap) (46.Ferdinando Apap), Jean Borg (80.Karl Micallef), Paul Mbong (80.Bjorn Kristensen), Teddy Teuma, Matthew Guillaumier, Ryan Camenzuli, Joseph Essien Mbong (52.Juan Carlos Corbalan), Jurgen Degabriele (80.Alexander Satariano), Shaun Dimech (80.Jodi Jay Felice Jones). Trainer: Gilbert Agius.
**Goals:** Jurgen Degabriele (55), Teddy Teuma (67 penalty).

**20.11.2022     MALTA - REPUBLIC OF IRELAND        0-1(0-0)                    Friendly International**

Ta'Qali National Stadium, Attard; Referee: Chrysovalantis Theouli (Cyprus); Attendance: n/a
**MLT:** Henry Bonello, Enrico Pepe, Ferdinando Apap (73.Kurt Shaw), Jean Borg, Joseph Essien Mbong, Matthew Guillaumier (Cap), Bjorn Kristensen (20.Dunstan Vella; 52.Stephen Pisani), Ryan Camenzuli, Teddy Teuma (88.Kyrian Nwoko), Jodi Jay Felice Jones (66.Luke David Gambin), Alexander Satariano (72.Luke Montebello). Trainer: Gilbert Agius.

**23.03.2023     NORTH MACEDONIA - MALTA           2-1(0-0)                    17<sup>th</sup> EC. Qualifiers**

Nacionalna Arena "Toše Proeski", Skopje; Referee: Kristo Tohver (Estonia); Attendance: 9,991
**MLT:** Henry Bonello, Joseph Essien Mbong, Steve Borg (Cap), Cain Attard, Ferdinando Apap, Ryan Camenzuli (77.Juan Carlos Corbalan), Bjorn Kristensen (77.Yannick Yankam), Matthew Guillaumier, Teddy Teuma (84.Brandon Diego Paiber), Paul Mbong (67.Shaun Dimech), Alexander Satariano (84.Jodi Jay Felice Jones). Trainer: Michele Marcolini (Italy).
**Goal:** Yannick Yankam (86).

**26.03.2023     MALTA - ITALY                    0-2(0-2)                    17<sup>th</sup> EC. Qualifiers**

Ta'Qali National Stadium, Attard; Referee: Georgi Kabakov (Bulgaria); Attendance: 16,015
**MLT:** Henry Bonello, Joseph Essien Mbong, Steve Borg (Cap), Ferdinando Apap (83.James Dominic Brown), Cain Attard (63.Zach Muscat), Juan Carlos Corbalan, Matthew Guillaumier, Nikolai Muscat (76.Teddy Teuma), Yannick Yankam, Jodi Jay Felice Jones (76.Shaun Dimech), Alexander Satariano (64.Kyrian Nwoko). Trainer: Michele Marcolini (Italy).

**09.06.2023     LUXEMBOURG - MALTA               0-1(0-0)                    Friendly International**

Stade de Luxembourg, Lëtzebuerg; Referee: Eldorjan Hamiti (Albania); Attendance: 4,028
**MLT:** Henry Bonello, Zach Muscat, Ferdinando Apap (82.Jean Borg), Steve Borg (Cap), Joseph Essien Mbong (76.Juan Carlos Corbalan), Jake Grech (46.Bjorn Kristensen), Matthew Guillaumier, Yannick Yankam, Ryan Camenzuli, Jodi Jay Felice Jones, Luke Montebello (46.Kyrian Nwoko). Trainer: Michele Marcolini (Italy).
**Goal:** Kyrian Nwoko (64).

**16.06.2023**  **MALTA - ENGLAND**  **0-4(0-3)**  17<sup>th</sup> EC. Qualifiers

Ta'Qali National Stadium, Attard; Referee: Igor Pajac (Croatia); Attendance: 16,277
**MLT:** Henry Bonello, Zach Muscat, Ferdinando Apap, Steve Borg (Cap), Joseph Essien Mbong, Matthew Guillaumier (46.Yannick Yankam), Bjorn Kristensen (60.Nikolai Muscat), Teddy Teuma, Cain Attard (87.Juan Carlos Corbalan), Jodi Jay Felice Jones (76.Jurgen Degabriele), Kyrian Nwoko (60.Alexander Satariano). Trainer: Michele Marcolini (Italy).

**19.06.2023**  **UKRAINE - MALTA**  **1-0(0-0)**  17<sup>th</sup> EC. Qualifiers

Štadión "Antona Malatinského", Trnava (Slovakia); Referee: Ruddy Buquet (France); Attendance: 7,543
**MLT:** Henry Bonello (45+3.Matthew Grech), Zach Muscat, Steve Borg (Cap), Jean Borg, Joseph Essien Mbong (87.Jurgen Degabriele), Teddy Teuma (87.Jake Grech), Yannick Yankam, Matthew Guillaumier, Ryan Camenzuli, Jodi Jay Felice Jones (62.Shaun Dimech), Kyrian Nwoko (46.Alexander Satariano). Trainer: Michele Marcolini (Italy).

| NATIONAL TEAM PLAYERS | | | | |
|---|---|---|---|---|
| (16.07.2022 – 15.07.2023) | | | | |

| Name | DOB | Caps | Goals | *Club* |
|---|---|---|---|---|
| **Goalkeepers** | | | | |
| Henry BONELLO | 13.10.1988 | 49 | 0 | 2022/2023: *Hamrun Spartans FC* |
| Matthew GRECH | 19.02.1996 | 1 | 0 | 2023: *Sirens FC San Pawl il-Bahar* |
| **Defenders** | | | | |
| Ferdinando APAP | 29.07.1992 | 17 | 1 | 2022/2023: *Hibernians FC Paola* |
| Jean BORG | 08.01.1998 | 17 | 0 | 2022: *Valletta FC* 19.01.2023-> *Fidelis Andria 2018 (ITA)* |
| Steve BORG | 15.05.1988 | 75 | 3 | 2022/2023: *Hamrun Spartans FC* |
| James Dominic BROWN | 12.01.1998 | 3 | 0 | 2022/2023: *St. Johnstone FC Perth (SCO)* |
| Karl MICALLEF | 08.09.1996 | 8 | 0 | 2022: *Gudja United FC* |
| Zach MUSCAT | 22.08.1993 | 60 | 3 | 2023: *SC Farense (POR)* |
| Enrico PEPE | 12.11.1989 | 17 | 0 | 2022: *Birkirkara FC* |
| Kurt SHAW | 01.04.1999 | 19 | 0 | 2022: *Hibernians FC Paola* |
| **Midfielders** | | | | |
| Cain ATTARD | 10.09.1994 | 18 | 2 | 2022/2023: *Birkirkara FC* |
| Ryan CAMENZULI | 08.09.1994 | 34 | 0 | 2022/2023: *Hamrun Spartans FC* |
| Juan Carlos CORBALAN | 13.03.1997 | 22 | 1 | 2022/2023: *Hamrun Spartans FC* |
| Jake GRECH | 18.11.1997 | 23 | 0 | 2023: *Hibernians FC Paola* |
| Matthew GUILLAUMIER | 09.04.1998 | 28 | 2 | 2022/2023: *Hamrun Spartans FC* |
| Bjorn KRISTENSEN | 05.04.1993 | 38 | 0 | 2022/2023: *Hibernians FC Paola* |
| Joseph Essien MBONG | 15.07.1997 | 49 | 3 | 2022: *Hapoel Ironi Kiryat Shmona FC (ISR)* 14.01.2023-> *Hamrun Spartans FC* |
| Nikolai MUSCAT | 13.07.1996 | 6 | 0 | 2023: *Gżira United FC* |
| Brandon Diego PAIBER | 05.06.1995 | 8 | 0 | 2022/2023: *Valletta FC* |
| Stephen PISANI | 07.08.1992 | 37 | 0 | 2022: *Gżira United FC* |
| Teddy TEUMA | 30.09.1993 | 31 | 1 | 2022/2023: *Royale Union Saint-Gilloise (BEL)* |
| Dunstan VELLA | 27.04.1996 | 15 | 0 | 2022: *Hibernians FC Paola* |
| Yannick YANKAM | 12.11.1997 | 5 | 1 | 2023: *Birkirkara FC* |
| **Forwards** | | | | |
| Jan BUSUTTIL | 06.03.1999 | 4 | 1 | 2022: *Floriana FC* |
| Jurgen DEGABRIELE | 10.10.1996 | 24 | 5 | 2022/2023: *Hibernians FC Paola* |
| Shaun DIMECH | 08.08.2001 | 19 | 2 | 2022/2023: *Valletta FC* |
| Luke David GAMBIN | 16.03.1993 | 36 | 1 | 2022: *Sutton United FC (ENG)* |
| Jodi Jay Felice JONES | 22.10.1997 | 9 | 0 | 2022: *Oxford United FC (ENG)* 26.01.2023-> *Notts County FC (ENG)* |
| Paul MBONG | 02.09.2001 | 15 | 0 | 2022/2023: *Birkirkara FC* |
| Luke MONTEBELLO | 13.08.1995 | 27 | 0 | 2022/2023: *Hamrun Spartans FC* |
| Kyrian NWOKO | 04.07.1997 | 25 | 4 | 2022: *Floriana FC* 27.01.2023-> *Santa Luċija FC* |
| Alexander SATARIANO | 25.10.2001 | 27 | 3 | 2022/2023: *Balzan FC* |
| **Trainer** | | | | |
| Devis MANGIA (Italy) [30.12.2019 – 30.09.2022] | 06.06.1974 | 28 M; 10 W; 5 D; 13 L; 33-47 | | |
| Gilbert AGIUS [08.11. – 14.12.2022] | 21.02.1974 | 2 M; 0 W; 1 D; 1 L; 2-3 | | |
| Michele MARCOLINI (Italy) [from 01.01.2023] | 02.10.1975 | 5 M; 1 W; 0 D; 4 L; 2-9 | | |

# MOLDOVA

## The Country:
Republica Moldova (Republic of Moldova)
Capital: Chişinău
Surface: 33,846 km²
Inhabitants: 2,512,758 [2023]
Time: UTC+2

## The FA:
Federaţia Moldovenească de Fotbal
Strada Tricolorului 39, 2012 Chişinău
Tel: +373 22 210 413
Foundation date: 1990
Member of FIFA since: 1994
Member of UEFA since: 1993
Website: www.fmf.md

## NATIONAL TEAM RECORDS

| RECORDS | | |
|---|---|---|
| **First international match:** | 02.07.1991, Chişinău: | Moldova – Georgia 2-4 |
| **Most international caps:** | Alexandru Ion Epureanu | - 100 caps (2006-2021) |
| **Most international goals:** | Ion Nicolăescu | - 12 goals / 35 caps (since 2018) |

### UEFA EUROPEAN CHAMPIONSHIP

| | |
|---|---|
| 1960 | - |
| 1964 | - |
| 1968 | - |
| 1972 | - |
| 1976 | - |
| 1980 | - |
| 1984 | - |
| 1988 | - |
| 1992 | - |
| 1996 | Qualifiers |
| 2000 | Qualifiers |
| 2004 | Qualifiers |
| 2008 | Qualifiers |
| 2012 | Qualifiers |
| 2016 | Qualifiers |
| 2020 | Qualifiers |

### FIFA WORLD CUP

| | |
|---|---|
| 1930 | - |
| 1934 | - |
| 1938 | - |
| 1950 | - |
| 1954 | - |
| 1958 | - |
| 1962 | - |
| 1966 | - |
| 1970 | - |
| 1974 | - |
| 1978 | - |
| 1982 | - |
| 1986 | - |
| 1990 | - |
| 1994 | Did Not Enter |
| 1998 | Qualifiers |
| 2002 | Qualifiers |
| 2006 | Qualifiers |
| 2010 | Qualifiers |
| 2014 | Qualifiers |
| 2018 | Qualifiers |
| 2022 | Qualifiers |

### OLYMPIC TOURNAMENTS

| | |
|---|---|
| 1908 | - |
| 1912 | - |
| 1920 | - |
| 1924 | - |
| 1928 | - |
| 1936 | - |
| 1948 | - |
| 1952 | - |
| 1956 | - |
| 1960 | - |
| 1964 | - |
| 1968 | - |
| 1972 | - |
| 1976 | - |
| 1980 | - |
| 1984 | - |
| 1988 | - |
| 1992 | Did not enter |
| 1996 | Qualifiers |
| 2000 | Qualifiers |
| 2004 | Qualifiers |
| 2008 | Qualifiers |
| 2012 | Qualifiers |
| 2016 | Qualifiers |
| 2020 | Qualifiers |

*was part of Soviet Union between 1940-1991*

## UEFA NATIONS LEAGUE

| 2018/2019 | League D (Group Stage -> promoted to League C) |
|---|---|
| 2020/2021 | League C (Group Stage -> Relegation play-outs -> relegated to League D) |
| 2022/2023 | League D (Group Stage) |

## MOLDOVAN CLUB HONOURS IN EUROPEAN CLUB COMPETITIONS:

| European Champion Clubs' Cup (1956-1992) / UEFA Champions League (1993-2023) |
|---|
| None |

| Fairs Cup (1858-1971) / UEFA Cup (1972-2009) / UEFA Europa League (2010-2023) |
|---|
| None |

| UEFA Europa Conference League (2021-2023) |
|---|
| None |

| UEFA Super Cup (1972-2022) |
|---|
| None |

| *European Cup Winners' Cup 1961-1999** |
|---|
| None |

*defunct competition*

# NATIONAL COMPETITIONS
## TABLE OF HONOURS

| | | | | | | | |
|---|---|---|---|---|---|---|---|
| 1945 | Dinamo Chişinău | 1961 | KSKhI Chişinău | 1977 | Stroitel Tiraspol |
| 1946 | Dinamo Chişinău | 1962 | Universitet Chişinău | 1978 | Nistru Tiraspol |
| 1947 | Dinamo Chişinău | 1963 | Temp Tiraspol | 1979 | Nistru Ciobruciu |
| 1948 | Dinamo Chişinău | 1964 | Temp Tiraspol' | 1980 | Nistru Ciobruciu |
| 1949 | Burevestnik Bender | 1965 | Energhia Tiraspol | 1981 | Grănicerul Glodeni |
| 1950 | Krasnoe Znamia Chişinău | 1966 | Stroindustria Bălţi | 1982 | Grănicerul Glodeni |
| 1951 | Krasnoe Znamia Chişinău | 1967 | Nistrul Bender | 1983 | Grănicerul Glodeni |
| 1952 | Dinamo Chişinău | 1968 | Temp Tiraspol | 1984 | Grănicerul Glodeni |
| 1953 | Dinamo Chişinău | 1969 | Politehnik Chişinău | 1985 | Iskra-Stal |
| 1954 | KSKhI Chişinău | 1970 | Politehnik Chişinău | 1986 | Avangard Lazovsk |
| 1955 | Burevestnik Bender | 1971 | Pişcevik Bender | 1987 | Tekstilshchik Tiraspol |
| 1956 | Spartak Tiraspol | 1972 | Kolhoz im. Lenina Edineţ | 1988 | Tighina Bender |
| 1957 | KSKhI Chişinău | 1973 | Pişcevik Bender | 1989 | Tekstilshchik Tiraspol |
| 1958 | Moldavkabel' Bender | 1974 | Dinamo Chişinău | 1990 | Moldovgidromaş Chişinău |
| 1959 | NIISVIV Chişinău | 1975 | Dinamo Chişinău | 1991 | Speranţa Nisporeni |
| 1960 | Tiraspol | 1976 | Stroitel Tiraspol | | |

| | CHAMPIONS | CUP WINNERS | BEST GOALSCORERS | |
|---|---|---|---|---|
| 1992 | FC Zimbru Chişinău | FC Bugeac Comrat | Serghei Alexandrov (FC Bugeac Comrat) Oleg Flentea (FC Constructorul Chişinău) | 13 |
| 1992/1993 | FC Zimbru Chişinău | FC Tiligul-Tiras Tiraspol | Vladimir Kosse (FC Tiligul-Tiras Tiraspol) | 30 |
| 1993/1994 | FC Zimbru Chişinău | FC Tiligul-Tiras Tiraspol | Vladimir Kosse (FC Tiligul-Tiras Tiraspol) | 24 |
| 1994/1995 | FC Zimbru Chişinău | FC Tiligul-Tiras Tiraspol | Vladislav Gavriliuc (FC Nistru Otaci / FC Zimbru Chişinău) | 20 |
| 1995/1996 | FC Zimbru Chişinău | FC Constructorul Chişinău | Vladislav Gavriliuc (FC Zimbru Chişinău) | 34 |
| 1996/1997 | FC Constructorul Chişinău | FC Zimbru Chişinău | Serghei Rogaciov (FC Constructorul Chişinău / FC Olimpia Bălţi) | 35 |
| 1997/1998 | FC Zimbru Chişinău | FC Zimbru Chişinău | Serghei Clescenco (FC Zimbru Chişinău) | 25 |
| 1998/1999 | FC Zimbru Chişinău | FC Sheriff Tiraspol | Serghei Rogaciov (FC Sheriff Tiraspol) | 21 |
| 1999/2000 | FC Zimbru Chişinău | FC Constructorul Chişinău | Serghei Rogaciov (FC Sheriff Tiraspol) | 20 |
| 2000/2001 | FC Sheriff Tiraspol | FC Sheriff Tiraspol | Ruslan Barburoş (Haiducul Sporting Hânceşti / FC Agro Chişinău / FC Sheriff Tiraspol) David Mujiri (GEO, FC Sheriff Tiraspol) | 17 |
| 2001/2002 | FC Sheriff Tiraspol | FC Sheriff Tiraspol | Ruslan Barburoş (FC Sheriff Tiraspol) | 17 |
| 2002/2003 | FC Sheriff Tiraspol | FC Zimbru Chişinău | Serghei Dadu (FC Tiraspol / FC Sheriff Tiraspol) | 19 |
| 2003/2004 | FC Sheriff Tiraspol | FC Zimbru Chişinău | Vladimir Shishelov (UZB, FC Zimbru Chişinău) | 15 |
| 2004/2005 | FC Sheriff Tiraspol | FC Nistru Otaci | Cătălin Sergiu Lichioiu (ROU, FC Nistru Otaci) | 16 |
| 2005/2006 | FC Sheriff Tiraspol | FC Sheriff Tiraspol | Aliaksei Kuchuk (BLR, FC Sheriff Tiraspol) | 13 |
| 2006/2007 | FC Sheriff Tiraspol | FC Zimbru Chişinău | Aliaksei Kuchuk (BLR, FC Sheriff Tiraspol) | 17 |
| 2007/2008 | FC Sheriff Tiraspol | FC Sheriff Tiraspol | Igor Picuşceac (FC Tiraspol / FC Sheriff Tiraspol) | 14 |
| 2008/2009 | FC Sheriff Tiraspol | FC Sheriff Tiraspol | Oleg Andronic (FC Zimbru Chişinău) | 16 |
| 2009/2010 | FC Sheriff Tiraspol | FC Sheriff Tiraspol | Alexandru Maximov (FC Viitorul Orhei) Jymmy Dougllas França (BRA, FC Sheriff Tiraspol) | 13 |
| 2010/2011 | FC Dacia Chişinău | FC Iskra-Stal Rîbniţa | Gheorghe Boghiu (FC Milsami Orhei) | 26 |
| 2011/2012 | FC Sheriff Tiraspol | FC Milsami Orhei | Wilfried Bendjamin Balima (BFA, FC Sheriff Tiraspol) | 18 |
| 2012/2013 | FC Sheriff Tiraspol | FC Tiraspol | Gheorghe Boghiu (FC Milsami Orhei) | 16 |
| 2013/2014 | FC Sheriff Tiraspol | FC Zimbru Chişinău | Luvannor Henrique de Sousa Silva (BRA, FC Sheriff Tiraspol) | 26 |
| 2014/2015 | FC Milsami Orhei | FC Sheriff Tiraspol | Ricardo Cavalcante Mendes "Ricardinho" (BRA, FC Sheriff Tiraspol) | 19 |
| 2015/2016 | FC Sheriff Tiraspol | FC Zaria Bălţi | Danijel Subotić (SUI, FC Sheriff Tiraspol) | 12 |
| 2016/2017 | FC Sheriff Tiraspol | FC Sheriff Tiraspol | Ricardo Cavalcante Mendes "Ricardinho" (BRA, FC Sheriff Tiraspol) | 15 |
| 2017 | FC Sheriff Tiraspol | FC Milsami Orhei (2017/18) | Vitalie Damaşcan (FC Sheriff Tiraspol) | 13 |
| 2018 | FC Sheriff Tiraspol | FC Sheriff Tiraspol (2018/19) | Vladimir Ambros (CS Petrocub Hînceşti) | 12 |
| 2019 | FC Sheriff Tiraspol | CS Petrocub Hînceşti (2019/20) | Yuri Kendysh (BLR, FC Sheriff Tiraspol) | 13 |
| 2020/2021 | FC Sheriff Tiraspol | FC Sfântul Gheorghe Suruceni | Frank Andersson Castañeda Vélez (COL, FC Sheriff Tiraspol) | 28 |
| 2021/2022 | FC Sheriff Tiraspol | FC Sheriff Tiraspol | Vladimir Ambros (CS Petrocub Hînceşti) | 17 |
| 2022/2023 | FC Sheriff Tiraspol | FC Sheriff Tiraspol | Ibrahim Akanbi Rasheed (NGA, FC Sheriff Tiraspol) Alexandru Dedov (FC Zimbru Chişinău) | 8 |

# NATIONAL CHAMPIONSHIP
## Divizia Naţională – Super Liga 2022/2023
### (30.07.2022 – 20.05.2023)

## Phase I - Results

**Round 1** [30-31.07.2022]
Dacia Buiucani - CSF Bălţi 0-0
FC Zimbru - FC Sheriff 1-1(0-0)
Petrocub Hînceşti - FC Sf. Gheorghe 0-2(0-1)
Milsami Orhei - Dinamo-Auto 0-0

**Round 2** [06-07.08.2022]
Dinamo-Auto - FC Zimbru 0-0
FC Sfântul Gheorghe - FC Sheriff 1-3(1-2)
Petrocub Hînceşti - Dacia Buiucani 1-0(1-0)
CSF Bălţi - Milsami Orhei 1-1(0-0)

**Round 3** [13-14.08.2022]
Dacia Buiucani-FC Sfântul Gheorghe 2-0(1-0)
FC Zimbru - CSF Bălţi 0-3(0-1)
FC Sheriff - Dinamo-Auto 2-0(1-0)
Milsami Orhei - Petrocub Hînceşti 1-0(1-0)

**Round 4** [20-21.08.2022]
FC Sfântul Gheorghe - Dinamo-Auto 3-0(2-0)
Petrocub Hînceşti - FC Zimbru 2-2(0-1)
Dacia Buiucani - Milsami Orhei 0-2(0-2)
CSF Bălţi - FC Sheriff 0-3(0-1)

**Round 5** [27-29.08.2022]
Dinamo-Auto - CSF Bălţi 0-1(0-0)
FC Zimbru - Dacia Buiucani 3-4(0-0)
Milsami Orhei - FC Sfântul Gheorghe 2-3(2-1)
FC Sheriff - Petrocub Hînceşti 1-1(1-1)

**Round 6** [03-04.09.2022]
Dacia Buiucani - FC Sheriff 0-2(0-1)
Petrocub Hînceşti - Dinamo-Auto 4-0(1-0)
FC Sfântul Gheorghe - CSF Bălţi 1-2(0-0)
Milsami Orhei - FC Zimbru 1-0(1-0)

**Round 7** [10-12.09.2022]
Dinamo-Auto - Dacia Buiucani 2-0(1-0)
FC Zimbru - FC Sfântul Gheorghe 3-3(0-3)
FC Sheriff - Milsami Orhei 2-0(1-0)
CSF Bălţi - Petrocub Hînceşti 0-1(0-0)

**Round 8** [16-18.09.2022]
Dinamo-Auto - Milsami Orhei 1-1(1-0)
CSF Bălţi - Dacia Buiucani 0-1(0-0)
FC Sf. Gheorghe - Petrocub Hînceşti 1-2(0-1)
FC Sheriff - FC Zimbru 0-0

**Round 9** [01-02.10.2022]
FC Zimbru - Dinamo-Auto 2-1(2-1)
Milsami Orhei - CSF Bălţi 1-0(0-0)
Dacia Buiucani - Petrocub Hînceşti 0-0
FC Sheriff - FC Sfântul Gheorghe 3-0(0-0)

**Round 10** [08-09.10.2022]
FC Sfântul Gheorghe-Dacia Buiucani 1-0(1-0)
Petrocub Hînceşti - Milsami Orhei 2-1(0-1)
Dinamo-Auto - FC Sheriff 0-1(0-1)
CSF Bălţi - FC Zimbru 0-2(0-0)

**Round 11** [15-16.10.2022]
Dinamo-Auto - FC Sfântul Gheorghe 0-2(0-1)
Milsami Orhei - Dacia Buiucani 1-1(0-0)
FC Zimbru - Petrocub Hînceşti 2-1(1-1)
FC Sheriff - CSF Bălţi 2-1(1-0)

**Round 12** [22-23.10.2022]
Dacia Buiucani - FC Zimbru 0-0
CSF Bălţi - Dinamo-Auto 1-0(0-0)
FC Sfântul Gheorghe - Milsami Orhei 1-0(0-0)
Petrocub Hînceşti - FC Sheriff 1-0(1-0)

**Round 13** [27-30.10.2022]
Dinamo-Auto - Petrocub Hînceşti 1-4(1-2)
FC Zimbru - Milsami Orhei 1-1(0-0)
CSF Bălţi - FC Sfântul Gheorghe 4-0(1-0)
FC Sheriff - Dacia Buiucani 2-1(0-0)

**Round 14** [09.11.2022]
FC Sfântul Gheorghe - FC Zimbru 0-1(0-1)
Milsami Orhei - FC Sheriff 0-2(0-1)
Dacia Buiucani - Dinamo-Auto 5-0(3-0)
Petrocub Hînceşti - CSF Bălţi 1-0(0-0)

## Final Standings

| | | Total | | | | | | | Home | | | | | Away | | |
|---|---|---|---|---|---|---|---|---|---|---|---|---|---|---|---|---|
| 1. | FC Sheriff Tiraspol | 14 | 10 | 3 | 1 | 24 - 6 | **33** | 5 | 2 | 0 | 12 - 3 | 5 | 1 | 1 | 12 - 3 |
| 2. | CS Petrocub Hînceşti | 14 | 8 | 3 | 3 | 20 - 11 | **27** | 5 | 1 | 1 | 11 - 5 | 3 | 2 | 2 | 9 - 6 |
| 3. | FC Zimbru Chişinău | 14 | 4 | 7 | 3 | 17 - 17 | **19** | 2 | 3 | 2 | 12 - 14 | 2 | 4 | 1 | 5 - 3 |
| 4. | FC Sfântul Gheorghe Suruceni | 14 | 6 | 1 | 7 | 18 - 22 | **19** | 3 | 0 | 4 | 8 - 8 | 3 | 1 | 3 | 10 - 14 |
| 5. | FC Milsami Orhei | 14 | 4 | 5 | 5 | 12 - 14 | **17** | 3 | 2 | 2 | 6 - 6 | 1 | 3 | 3 | 6 - 8 |
| 6. | CSF Bălţi | 14 | 5 | 2 | 7 | 13 - 13 | **17** | 2 | 1 | 4 | 6 - 8 | 3 | 1 | 3 | 7 - 5 |
| 7. | FC Dacia Buiucani Chişinău *(Relegation Play-offs)* | 14 | 4 | 4 | 6 | 14 - 14 | **16** | 2 | 3 | 2 | 7 - 4 | 2 | 1 | 4 | 7 - 10 |
| 8. | FC Dinamo-Auto Tiraspol *(Relegation Play-offs)* | 14 | 1 | 3 | 10 | 5 - 26 | **0** | 1 | 2 | 4 | 4 - 9 | 0 | 1 | 6 | 1 - 17 |

*Please note*: FC Dinamo-Auto Tiraspol - 6 points deducted for match-fixing!

Top-6 teams were qualified for the Phase II (Championship Play-offs). Teams ranked 7-8 were qualified for the Promotion/Relegation Play-offs with Liga 1 teams.

## Phase II - Results

**Round 1** [11-13.03.2023]
FC Zimbru - FC Sfântul Gheorghe 0-0
Petrocub Hînceşti - Milsami Orhei 2-1(0-1)
FC Sheriff - CSF Bălţi 1-0(0-0)

**Round 2** [17-19.03.2023]
FC Sfântul Gheorghe - CSF Bălţi 1-1(1-0)
Milsami Orhei - FC Zimbru 0-3(0-1)
FC Sheriff - Petrocub Hînceşti 1-0(1-0)

**Round 3** [01-02.04.2023]
FC Zimbru - FC Sheriff 0-2(0-1)
FC Sfântul Gheorghe - Milsami Orhei 1-1(0-1)
Petrocub Hînceşti - CSF Bălţi 0-0

**Round 4** [09.04.2023]
CSF Bălţi - Milsami Orhei 2-2(1-0)
FC Sheriff - FC Sfântul Gheorghe 1-0(1-0)
Petrocub Hînceşti - FC Zimbru 3-2(3-1)

**Round 5** [15.04.2023]
FC Sfântul Gheorghe - Petrocub Hînceşti 0-0
FC Zimbru - CSF Bălţi 1-0(1-0)
FC Sheriff - Milsami Orhei 2-1(1-1)

**Round 6** [22.04.2023]
FC Sfântul Gheorghe - FC Zimbru 0-2(0-1)
CSF Bălţi - FC Sheriff 1-1(0-1)
Milsami Orhei - Petrocub Hînceşti 0-2(0-1)

**Round 7** [29-30.04.2023]
CSF Bălţi - FC Sfântul Gheorghe 0-2(0-1)
FC Zimbru - Milsami Orhei 0-1(0-0)
Petrocub Hînceşti - FC Sheriff 1-1(1-0)

**Round 8** [06-07.05.2023]
FC Sheriff - FC Zimbru 0-0
Milsami Orhei - FC Sfântul Gheorghe 3-0(2-0)
CSF Bălţi - Petrocub Hînceşti 0-3(0-2)

**Round 9** [13-14.05.2023]
Milsami Orhei - CSF Bălţi 1-0(0-0)
FC Sfântul Gheorghe - FC Sheriff 0-2(0-2)
FC Zimbru - Petrocub Hînceşti 1-2(1-2)

**Round 10** [20.05.2023]
CSF Bălţi - FC Zimbru 1-1(0-0)
Petrocub Hînceşti - FC Sf. Gheorghe 3-0(2-0)
Milsami Orhei - FC Sheriff 0-4(0-3)

| Final Standings | | | | | | | | | | | | | | | |
|---|---|---|---|---|---|---|---|---|---|---|---|---|---|---|---|
| | | **Total** | | | | | | | **Home** | | | | **Away** | | |
| 1. **FC Sheriff Tiraspol** | 10 | 7 | 3 | 0 | 15 - 3 | **24** | 5 | 2 | 0 | 10 - 2 | 2 | 1 | 0 | 5 - 1 |
| 2. **CS Petrocub Hînceşti** | 10 | 6 | 3 | 1 | 16 - 6 | **21** | 4 | 2 | 0 | 12 - 4 | 2 | 1 | 1 | 4 - 2 |
| 3. **FC Zimbru Chişinău** | 10 | 3 | 3 | 4 | 10 - 9 | **12** | 1 | 1 | 3 | 2 - 5 | 2 | 2 | 1 | 8 - 4 |
| 4. **FC Milsami Orhei** | 10 | 3 | 2 | 5 | 10 - 16 | **11** | 2 | 0 | 2 | 4 - 5 | 1 | 2 | 3 | 6 - 11 |
| 5. **FC Sfântul Gheorghe Suruceni**\*\* | 10 | 1 | 4 | 5 | 4 - 13 | **7** | 0 | 3 | 2 | 2 - 6 | 1 | 1 | 3 | 2 - 7 |
| 6. **CSF Bălţi** | 10 | 0 | 5 | 5 | 5 - 13 | **5** | 0 | 2 | 1 | 3 - 5 | 0 | 3 | 4 | 2 - 8 |

\*\**Please note*: FC Sfântul Gheorghe Suruceni were dissolved at end of season.

| Top goalscorers: | | |
|---|---|---|
| 8 | **Ibrahim Akanbi Rasheed (NGA)** | *FC Sheriff Tiraspol* |
| 8 | **Alexandru Dedov** | *FC Zimbru Chişinău* |
| 7 | Marius Iosipoi | *CS Petrocub Hînceşti* |
| 6 | Radu Gînsari | *FC Milsami Orhei* |

## NATIONAL CUP
### Cupa Moldovei 2022/2023

| 1/8-Finals [18-19.10.2022] | | | |
|---|---|---|---|
| FC Iskra Rîbniţa - FC Dacia Buiucani Chişinău | 0-7(0-0) | FC Floreşti - CS Petrocub Hînceşti | 2-2 aet; 2-4 pen |
| Locomotiva Ocniţa - FC Milsami Orhei | 0-2(0-0) | FC Speranţa Drochia - FC Sheriff Tiraspol | 0-6(0-4) |
| FC La Familia Bender - FC Sfântul Gheorghe Suruceni | 0-5(0-0,0-0) | FC Zimbru Chişinău - FC Victoria Chişinău | 3-0(1-0) |
| FC Dinamo-Auto Tiraspol - Univer Oguzsport Comrat | 0-2/(0-0,0-0) | CSF Bălţi - FC Stăuceni | 4-0(0-0) |

| Quarter-Finals [04-05.03./05.04.2023] | | | |
|---|---|---|---|
| **First Leg** | | **Second Leg** | |
| FC Dacia Buiucani Chişinău - FC Sheriff Tiraspol | 0-3(0-2) | FC Sheriff Tiraspol - FC Dacia Buiucani Chişinău | 3-1(1-0) |
| FC Milsami Orhei - CS Petrocub Hînceşti | 0-3(0-1) | CS Petrocub Hînceşti - FC Milsami Orhei | 3-1(2-1) |
| FC Sfântul Gheorghe Suruceni - FC Zimbru Chişinău | 0-0 | FC Zimbru Chişinău - FC Sfântul Gheorghe Suruceni | 3-3 aet; 6-7 pen |
| CSF Bălţi - Univer Oguzsport Comrat | 5-0(3-0) | Univer Oguzsport Comrat - CSF Bălţi | 1-4(1-0) |

| Semi-Finals [26.04./03.05.2023] | | | |
|---|---|---|---|
| **First Leg** | | **Second Leg** | |
| FC Sfântul Gheorghe Suruceni - CSF Bălţi | 1-0(0-0) | CSF Bălţi - FC Sfântul Gheorghe Suruceni | 3-1(1-0,1-1) |
| FC Sheriff Tiraspol - Petrocub Hînceşti | 2-0(1-0) | Petrocub Hînceşti - FC Sheriff Tiraspol | 0-1(0-0) |

### Final

28.05.2023; Stadionul Municipal, Hînceşti; Referee: Petru Stoianov; Attendance: 1,185
**FC Sheriff Tiraspol - CSF Bălţi**                                 **0-0 aet; 7-6 on penalties**

**FC Sheriff**: Maksim Koval, Renan Guedes Borges, Munashe Garananga, Stjepan Radeljić, Armel Zohouri (117.Gaby Kiki), Cédric Badolo, Moussa Kyabou (117.Abdoul Moumouni), Mouhamed Diop, Amine Talal (Cap) (88.Bubacarr Tambedou), Ricardo Cavalcante Mendes „Ricardinho" (99.Michael Steven López), Abdoul Tapsoba (117.Iyayi Believe Atiemwen). Trainer: Roberto Bordin (Italy).

**CSF Bălţi**: Stanislav Namaşco, Andrei Rusnac (Cap), Denis Furtună, Welington Matsukichi da Silva Taira, Nathanael Bongo Mbourou, Nichita Moţpan, Federico Nsue Nguema, Vadim Yakovlev, Daniel Danu (72.Petru Neagu), Zotsara Randriambololona, Serafim Cojocari. Trainer: Veaceslav Rusnac.

**Penalties:** Petru Neagu 0-1; Cédric Badolo (saved); Nichita Moţpan 0-2; Iyayi Believe Atiemwen 1-2; Andrei Rusnac 1-3; Renan Guedes Borges 2-3; Denis Furtună 2-4; Gaby Kiki 3-4; Zotsara Randriambololona (saved); Bubacarr Tambedou 4-4; Serafim Cojocari 4-5; Michael Steven López 5-5; Vadim Yakovlev 5-6; Stjepan Radeljić 6-6; Welington Matsukichi da Silva Taira (saved); Mouhamed Diop 7-6.

## THE CLUBS 2022/2023

### Clubul Sportiv de Fotbal Bălţi

| Founded: | 1984 (*as Zaria Bălţi*) | | |
|---|---|---|---|
| Stadium: | Stadionul Orăşenesc, Bălţi (5,953) | | |
| Trainer: | Serghei Cebotari | | 21.02.1981 |
| [11.10.2022] | Veaceslav Rusnac | | 27.08.1975 |

| Goalkeepers: | DOB | M | (s) | G |
|---|---|---|---|---|
| Stanislav Namaşco | 10.11.1986 | 15 | | |
| Victor Străistari | 21.06.1999 | 9 | | |
| **Defenders:** | **DOB** | **M** | **(s)** | **G** |
| Álvaro Bely Medina (ARG) | 21.03.1994 | 18 | (1) | 1 |
| Vladislav Boico | 27.09.2006 | | (3) | |
| Denis Furtună | 13.10.1999 | 20 | (3) | |
| Valeriu Gaiu | 06.02.2001 | 9 | (3) | |
| Anatolie Prepeliţă | 06.08.1997 | 6 | | 1 |
| Welington Matsukichi da Silva *Taira* (BRA) | 10.04.1996 | 24 | | 2 |
| Ivan Voropai | 21.04.1998 | 9 | | |
| **Midfielders:** | **DOB** | **M** | **(s)** | **G** |
| Nathanael Bongo Mbourou (GAB) | 24.08.1996 | 10 | | |
| Ruslan Chelari | 27.02.1999 | 7 | (3) | |

| | | | | |
|---|---|---|---|---|
| Serafim Cojocari | 07.01.2001 | 13 | (2) | 3 |
| Daniel Danu | 26.08.2002 | 20 | (3) | 2 |
| Nichita Moţpan | 17.07.2001 | 10 | | |
| Federico Nsue Nguema (EQG) | 20.04.1997 | 10 | | |
| Zotsara Randriambololona (MAD) | 22.04.1994 | 23 | (1) | 1 |
| Andrei Rusnac | 22.09.1996 | 21 | (1) | 1 |
| Vadim Yakovlev (KAZ) | 29.07.2003 | 9 | (11) | |
| **Forwards:** | **DOB** | **M** | **(s)** | **G** |
| Vadim Gulceac | 06.08.1998 | 7 | (2) | 2 |
| Serghei Mişcov | 25.04.2003 | 2 | (15) | 1 |
| Petru Neagu | 13.08.1999 | 7 | (13) | |
| Miracle Chinaza Nwautobo (NGA) | 25.10.2011 | 12 | (6) | 2 |
| Nichita Picus | 13.09.2002 | 3 | (7) | 1 |
| Nichita Cambura | 28.01.2005 | | (1) | |

## Fotbal Club Dacia Buiucani

**Founded**: 25.09.2097
**Stadium**: Stadionul Suruceni, Suruceni (1,500)
**Trainer**: Andrei Martin 27.06.1974

| Goalkeepers: | DOB | M | (s) | G |
|---|---|---|---|---|
| Sebastian Iulian Agachi | 25.09.2000 | 13 | | |
| Victor Dodon | 01.03.2004 | 1 | | |
| **Defenders:** | **DOB** | **M** | **(s)** | **G** |
| Roman Bejan | 01.08.2003 | 2 | (1) | |
| Maxim Cojocaru | 29.10.1999 | | (1) | |
| Vadim Cravcescu | 07.03.1985 | 3 | | |
| Vitalie Dumbrava | 23.04.2004 | 1 | (2) | 1 |
| Ştefan Efros | 08.05.1990 | 9 | | 1 |
| Maxim Focşa | 21.04.1992 | 13 | | 2 |
| Ion Ghimp | 11.09.1996 | 13 | (1) | |
| Alexandru Gutium | 15.07.2003 | 10 | (4) | |
| Mihai Ţipac | 20.11.2000 | 10 | (2) | |

| Midfielders: | DOB | M | (s) | G |
|---|---|---|---|---|
| Vasile Bîtlan | 31.01.2004 | 14 | | 3 |
| Ilie Botnari | 25.07.2003 | 3 | (8) | |
| Gheorghe Brînzaniuc | 06.05.2001 | 7 | (4) | |
| Dumitru Demian | 08.02.1999 | 9 | (2) | 1 |
| Cristian Păscăluţă | 08.09.2005 | | (3) | |
| Artur Pătraş | 01.10.1988 | 10 | (3) | 1 |
| Dumitru Reniţă | 02.12.1999 | | (8) | |
| Eugen Zasaviţchi | 24.11.1992 | 13 | | |
| **Forwards:** | **DOB** | **M** | **(s)** | **G** |
| Dumitru Bivol | 03.10.2001 | 7 | (5) | |
| Vadim Crîcimari | 22.08.1988 | 1 | (1) | |
| Daniel Dosca | 20.02.2003 | 3 | (7) | 3 |
| Oleg Martin | 21.10.1999 | | (7) | |
| Nicu Namolovan | 28.01.2002 | 12 | (2) | 2 |

## Football Club Dinamo-Auto Tiraspol

**Founded**: 24.07.2009
**Stadium**: Stadionul Dinamo-Auto, Tiraspol (1,300)
**Trainer**: Oleg Bejenari 17.09.1971
[06.08.2022] Anatol Teslev 15.09.1947
[09.09.2022] Novruz Azimov (AZE) 19.03.1960
[01.01.2023] Cüneyt Karakuş (TUR) 20.11.1965

| Goalkeepers: | DOB | M | (s) | G |
|---|---|---|---|---|
| Ivan Marcov | 09.10.2004 | 2 | (1) | |
| Dallian Gislain Toung Allogho (GAB) | 08.06.1996 | 12 | | |
| **Defenders:** | **DOB** | **M** | **(s)** | **G** |
| Andrew Vivien Anomerawani Ombenidjouwa (GAB) | 08.07.2001 | 3 | (8) | |
| Alexandr Calîn | 26.06.2005 | 2 | (3) | |
| Stane Essono (GAB) | 28.05.1998 | 10 | (4) | |
| Habib Omar Fofana (CIV) | 16.11.1998 | 10 | | |
| Mekhrubon Karimov (TJK) | 19.01.2004 | 12 | | 1 |
| Maxim Manastîrlî | 01.03.2004 | | (1) | |
| Urie-Michel Mboula (GAB) | 30.04.2003 | 9 | (2) | |
| Javier Mum Boho (EQG) | 24.01.2001 | 13 | | |
| Constantin Stamov | 01.03.2004 | | (4) | |

| Midfielders: | DOB | M | (s) | G |
|---|---|---|---|---|
| Furkan Akin (TUR) | 18.09.2000 | 13 | | 1 |
| Nathanael Bongo Mbourou (GAB) | 24.08.1996 | 10 | (1) | |
| Peter Ngozi Kings (NGA) | 04.04.2001 | 8 | (1) | |
| Federico Nsue Nguema (EQG) | 20.04.1997 | 13 | (1) | |
| Warren Lloyd Mac Starsky Ondo (GAB) | 31.01.2003 | 3 | (5) | |
| Kabir Salimshoev (TJK) | 01.08.2004 | 3 | (6) | |
| José Fidel Sipi Bita (EQG) | 07.01.2001 | 10 | (3) | |
| Vadim Şleahtiţchi | 02.02.2005 | 2 | (4) | |
| **Forwards:** | **DOB** | **M** | **(s)** | **G** |
| Eric Bekale Biyoghe (GAB) | 04.03.2000 | 8 | (4) | |
| Rody Junior Effaghe (GAB) | 11.04.2004 | 11 | (3) | 3 |

## Football Club Milsami Orhei

**Founded**: 2005
**Stadium**: Complexul Sportiv Raional, Orhei (2,539)
**Trainer**: Serghei Dubrovin 04.01.1952

| Goalkeepers: | DOB | M | (s) | G |
|---|---|---|---|---|
| Victor Buga | 29.06.1994 | 9 | (1) | |
| Mihail Cioban | 03.02.2001 | 1 | | |
| Emil Tîmbur | 21.07.1997 | 14 | | |
| **Defenders:** | **DOB** | **M** | **(s)** | **G** |
| Vadim Bolohan | 15.08.1986 | 12 | | |
| Igor Bondarenco | 28.06.1995 | 19 | (4) | |
| Vadim Dijinari | 01.04.1999 | 12 | | |
| Dinu Graur | 27.12.1994 | 9 | (1) | |
| Gabriel Holban | 24.10.2003 | | (2) | |
| Aleksandar Isaevski (MKD) | 19.05.1995 | 10 | | |
| Valerii Macriţchii | 13.02.1996 | 10 | (2) | |
| Prohor Nihaev | 29.08.2006 | 5 | (8) | 1 |
| Petru Racu | 17.07.1987 | 14 | (1) | |
| Yaroslav Terekhov (UKR) | 21.04.1999 | 9 | | |
| Vladislav Zavalişca | 30.01.2003 | | (3) | |

| Midfielders: | DOB | M | (s) | G |
|---|---|---|---|---|
| Vitus Amougui (CMR) | 15.01.1991 | 9 | (4) | |
| Gheorghe Andronic | 25.09.1991 | 6 | (5) | |
| Alexandru Antoniuc | 23.05.1989 | 23 | | 2 |
| Alexandr Belousov | 14.05.1998 | 12 | (1) | 1 |
| Igor Lambarskiy (RUS) | 26.11.1992 | 9 | (3) | |
| Evgheni Oancea | 05.01.1996 | 2 | (4) | |
| Daniel Pîslă | 14.06.1986 | 9 | (10) | 3 |
| Danu Spătaru | 24.05.1994 | 10 | | 1 |
| **Forwards:** | **DOB** | **M** | **(s)** | **G** |
| Mamadou Camara (MLI) | 18.02.2001 | 12 | (5) | 3 |
| Radu Gînsari | 10.12.1991 | 22 | | 6 |
| Sergiu Istrati | 07.08.1988 | 11 | (9) | 1 |
| Sergiu Nazar | 02.07.1997 | 1 | (10) | |
| Artiom Puntus | 31.05.1995 | 8 | (2) | 2 |
| Dumitru Rogac | 07.11.1998 | 6 | (4) | 1 |

## Club Sportiv Petrocub Hînceşti

**Founded**: 1994
**Stadium**: Stadionul Municipal, Hînceşti (1,500)
**Trainer**: Ivan Tabanov 07.08.1966

| Goalkeepers: | DOB | M | (s) | G |
|---|---|---|---|---|
| Cristian Avram | 27.07.1994 | 15 | | |
| Nicolae Cebotari | 24.05.1997 | 1 | | |
| Igor Mostovei | 25.09.1999 | 8 | | |
| **Defenders:** | **DOB** | **M** | **(s)** | **G** |
| Cristian Axenti | 04.01.2004 | | (1) | |
| Ianus Jaman | 16.05.2004 | | (3) | |
| Ion Jardan | 10.01.1990 | 23 | | |
| Victor Mudrac | 03.03.1994 | 22 | | 2 |
| Maxim Potîrniche | 13.06.1989 | 21 | (1) | 2 |
| Ioan-Calin Revenco | 26.06.2000 | 22 | (1) | 1 |
| Artiom Rozgoniuc | 01.10.1995 | 10 | | |
| **Midfielders:** | **DOB** | **M** | **(s)** | **G** |
| Alexandru Bejan | 07.05.1996 | 7 | (14) | |
| Victor Bogaciuc | 17.10.1999 | 20 | | 5 |
| Tudor Butucel | 14.08.2003 | | (9) | |

| | DOB | M | (s) | G |
|---|---|---|---|---|
| Nicky Cleşcenco | 23.07.2001 | 2 | (2) | 1 |
| Maxim Cojocaru | 13.01.1998 | 20 | (1) | 2 |
| Corneliu Cotogoi | 23.06.2001 | 4 | (12) | |
| Alexandru Graur | 11.02.2001 | 1 | (2) | |
| Teodor Lungu | 12.06.1995 | 5 | (2) | 1 |
| Mihai Lupan | 08.09.2004 | 3 | (17) | 1 |
| Mihai Plătică | 15.03.1990 | 6 | | 2 |
| Sergiu Plătică | 05.06.1991 | 22 | | 2 |
| Iaser Ţurcan | 07.01.1998 | 4 | (3) | 1 |
| **Forwards:** | **DOB** | **M** | **(s)** | **G** |
| Vladimir Ambros | 30.12.1993 | 17 | (1) | 5 |
| Ruslan Bînzaru | 18.05.2002 | 1 | (4) | |
| Artem Fedorov (UKR) | 18.09.1998 | 3 | (10) | 1 |
| Marius Iosipoi | 28.04.2000 | 21 | (1) | 7 |
| Constantin Sandu | 15.09.1993 | 6 | (7) | 1 |

## Fotbal Club Sfântul Gheorghe Suruceni

| Founded: | 2003 |
| Stadium: | Stadionul Suruceni, Suruceni (1,500) |
| Trainer: | Nicolae Mandricenco | 12.03.1958 |

| Goalkeepers: | DOB | M | (s) | G |
|---|---|---|---|---|
| Valeriu Butucel | 09.08.2005 | 1 | | |
| Nicolae Calancea | 29.08.1986 | 14 | | |
| Victor Străistari | 21.06.1999 | 9 | | |
| Defenders: | DOB | M | (s) | G |
| Ion Borș | 25.07.2002 | 20 | | |
| Eduardo de Sousa Santos „Eduardo Kau" (BRA) | 17.01.1999 | 4 | | |
| Artiom Litviakov | 23.10.1996 | 3 | (7) | |
| Cedric Ngah (CMR) | 17.10.1998 | 18 | (2) | 1 |
| Petru Ojog | 17.07.1990 | 13 | (7) | |
| Yevhen Smirnov (UKR) | 16.04.1993 | 8 | (1) | |
| Serghei Svinarenco | 18.09.1996 | 14 | (2) | |
| Mihail Ștefan | 07.08.2001 | 16 | (4) | 1 |
| Midfielders: | DOB | M | (s) | G |
| Calin Calaidjoglu | 18.01.2001 | 17 | (6) | 2 |
| Ruslan Chelari | 27.02.1999 | 3 | (4) | |
| Andrei Cojocari | 21.01.1987 | 11 | (2) | |
| Vitalie Guțu | 28.08.2005 | | (4) | |
| Maximilian Ihekuna (NGA) | 15.09.2001 | 18 | (4) | |
| Daniel Lisu | 02.04.2002 | 16 | (6) | 1 |
| Teodor Lungu | 12.06.1995 | 2 | | |
| Vadim Paireli | 08.11.1995 | 13 | (9) | 2 |
| Dan Pușcaș | 01.06.2001 | 18 | (4) | 1 |
| Alexandru Suvorov | 02.02.1987 | 7 | (11) | 3 |
| Forwards: | DOB | M | (s) | G |
| Keinus Bunga (BEL) | 01.08.1997 | 12 | (6) | 1 |
| Marin Căruntu | 28.11.1997 | 14 | (7) | 2 |
| Yaniv Edery (FRA) | 23.06.2003 | | (3) | |
| Jibril Ibrahimi (NGA) | 01.02.2002 | 5 | | 5 |
| Theocharis Pozatzidis (GRE) | 18.02.1999 | 8 | (9) | 3 |

## Fotbal Club Sheriff Tiraspol

| Founded: | 04.04.1997 |
| Stadium: | Stadionul Sheriff, Tiraspol (12,798) |
| Trainer: | Stjepan Tomas (CRO) | 03.06.1976 |
| [25.10.2022] | Victor Mihailov | 18.12.1981 |
| [09.01.2023] | Roberto Bordin (ITA) | 10.01.1965 |

| Goalkeepers: | DOB | M | (s) | G |
|---|---|---|---|---|
| Razak Abalora (GHA) | 04.09.1996 | 10 | | |
| Dumitru Celeadnic | 23.04.1992 | 9 | | |
| Maksim Koval (UKR) | 09.12.1992 | 5 | | |
| Defenders: | DOB | M | (s) | G |
| Christ Eneme Bekale (GAB) | 20.03.1999 | | (7) | |
| Serafim Cojocari | 07.01.2001 | | (1) | |
| Stefanos Evangelou (GRE) | 12.05.1998 | 4 | | |
| Munashe Garananga (ZIM) | 18.01.2001 | 3 | (2) | |
| Heron Crespo da Silva (BRA) | 17.08.2000 | 9 | (4) | |
| Keston Anthony Julien (TRI) | 26.10.1998 | 8 | (4) | 1 |
| Gaby Kiki (CMR) | 15.02.1995 | 18 | (1) | 3 |
| Patrick Kpozo (GHA) | 15.07.1997 | 13 | (2) | |
| Stjepan Radeljić (BIH) | 05.09.1997 | 16 | (2) | 1 |
| Renan Guedes Borges (BRA) | 19.01.1998 | 9 | (7) | |
| Armel Zohouri (CIV) | 05.04.2001 | 15 | (2) | 1 |
| Midfielders: | DOB | M | (s) | G |
| Steve Brahim Joshep Omar Ambri (GNB) | 12.08.1997 | 7 | (1) | 4 |
| Giannis-Fivos Botos (GRE) | 20.12.2000 | 4 | (3) | 1 |
| Cédric Badolo (BFA) | 04.11.1998 | 14 | (4) | 1 |
| Mouhamed Diop (SEN) | 30.09.2000 | 17 | (3) | 4 |
| Moussa Kyabou (MLI) | 18.04.1998 | 8 | (2) | |
| Regi Lushkja (ALB) | 17.05.1996 | 2 | (7) | |
| Abdoul Moumouni (NIG) | 07.08.2002 | 6 | (3) | |
| Charles Petro (MWI) | 08.02.2001 | 5 | (1) | |
| Mudasiru Salifu (GHA) | 01.04.1997 | 11 | (1) | |
| Amine Talal (MAR) | 05.06.1996 | 8 | (2) | 1 |
| Forwards: | DOB | M | (s) | G |
| Danil Ankudinov (KAZ) | 31.07.2003 | | (4) | |
| Iyayi Believe Atiemwen (NGA) | 24.01.1996 | 9 | (5) | 3 |
| Nichita Covali | 07.09.2002 | | (1) | |
| Felipe dos Reis Pereira Vizeu do Carmo Linhares (BRA) | 12.03.1997 | 2 | (4) | 2 |
| Origbaajo Ismaila (NGA) | 04.08.1998 | 3 | (5) | 2 |
| Michael Steven López (ARG) | 19.08.1997 | 3 | (2) | |
| Abou Ouattara (BFA) | 26.12.1999 | 5 | (4) | 2 |
| José Vitor Rodrigues Da Silva Santos „Pernambuco" (BRA) | 28.04.1998 | 6 | (4) | 1 |
| Ibrahim Akanbi Rasheed (NGA) | 09.05.1999 | 16 | (3) | 8 |
| Ricardo Cavalcante Mendes „Ricardinho" (BRA) | 04.09.1989 | 4 | (3) | |
| Bubacarr Tambedou (GAM) | 05.04.2002 | 2 | (5) | 1 |
| Abdoul Tapsoba (BFA) | 23.08.2001 | 9 | | 2 |
| Kay Tejan (NED) | 03.02.1997 | 3 | (5) | 1 |
| Momo Yansane (GUI) | 29.07.1997 | 1 | | |

## Fotbal Club Zimbru Chișinău

| Founded: | 1947 |
| Stadium: | Stadionul Zimbru, Chișinău (10,400) |
| Trainer: | Vlad Goian | 14.11.1970 |
| [31.08.2022] | Lilian Popescu | 15.11.1973 |

| Goalkeepers: | DOB | M | (s) | G |
|---|---|---|---|---|
| Sebastian Agachi | 25.09.2000 | 2 | | |
| Nikos Giannakopoulos (GRE) | 19.02.1993 | 22 | | |
| Defenders: | DOB | M | (s) | G |
| Ștefan Burghiu | 28.03.1991 | 19 | | 2 |
| Kenroy Campbell (JAM) | 30.05.2002 | 11 | (5) | 2 |
| Alexei Ciopa | 27.10.1998 | 6 | (4) | |
| Maxim Cojocaru | 29.10.1999 | 6 | (2) | |
| Cătălin Cucoș | 29.09.2003 | 6 | | |
| Valeriu Gaiu | 06.02.2001 | 2 | (4) | |
| Alexandru Gău | 27.01.2004 | | (1) | |
| Ivanilson Joaquim Monteiro Magalhães (POR) | 04.04.1999 | 5 | (3) | |
| Nikolaos Karanikas (GRE) | 04.03.1992 | 3 | (3) | |
| Andrei Macrițchii | 13.02.1996 | 9 | (1) | |
| Alexandru Misarăș (ROU) | 06.05.1997 | 16 | | |
| Evgheni Pleșco | 25.02.2001 | 4 | (1) | |
| Veaceslav Posmac | 07.11.1990 | 1 | | |
| Cristian Ursu | 12.02.1998 | 3 | (2) | |
| Donny van Iperen (NED) | 29.03.1995 | 2 | | |
| Midfielders: | DOB | M | (s) | G |
| Gheorghe Andronic | 25.09.1991 | 4 | (1) | |
| Gheorghe Anton | 27.01.1993 | 6 | (6) | |
| Rachid Baldé (GNB) | 24.02.2000 | 3 | (2) | |
| Iulian Bejan | 04.03.2004 | 6 | (5) | |
| Octavian Bulat | 23.08.2000 | | (8) | |
| Marius Curoș | 30.10.2003 | 2 | (4) | |
| Denis Dedechko (UKR) | 02.07.1987 | 10 | | |
| Alexandru Dedov | 26.07.1989 | 22 | | 8 |
| Maximiliano Do Sacramento Castro (NED) | 23.02.2002 | | (2) | |
| Mihail Ghecev | 05.11.1997 | 8 | | 1 |
| Maxim Mihaliov | 22.08.1986 | 8 | (5) | 2 |
| Vlad Răileanu | 09.01.2003 | 11 | (9) | 1 |
| Eugeniu Sidorenco | 19.03.1989 | 14 | (6) | 4 |
| Forwards: | DOB | M | (s) | G |
| Emmanuel Alaribe (NGA) | 24.08.2000 | 9 | | 4 |
| Amâncio José Pinto Fortes (ANG) | 18.04.1990 | 5 | (3) | 1 |
| Mihai Cozari | 07.02.2004 | | (1) | |
| Ilie Damașcan | 12.10.1995 | 16 | (3) | |
| Rostislav Garganciuc | 16.04.2003 | | (1) | |
| Petru Leucă | 19.07.1990 | | (6) | |
| Fabian Pegza | 24.10.2005 | | (1) | |
| Steve Rubanguka (RWA) | 14.10.1996 | 19 | (2) | |
| Shakhrom Samiev (TJK) | 08.02.2001 | 4 | (4) | 1 |

# SECOND LEVEL
## Divizia A 2022/2023

### Phase I

#### Group A

| | | | | | | | | |
|---|---|---|---|---|---|---|---|---|
| 1. FC Floreşti | 10 | 7 | 0 | 3 | 15 | - | 8 | 21 |
| 2. FC Făleşti | 10 | 6 | 1 | 3 | 22 | - | 16 | 19 |
| 3. FC Sheriff-2 Tiraspol | 10 | 5 | 3 | 2 | 28 | - | 6 | 18 |
| 4. FCM Ungheni | 10 | 5 | 1 | 4 | 20 | - | 15 | 16 |
| 5. FC Speranis Nisporeni | 10 | 3 | 1 | 6 | 17 | - | 27 | 10 |
| 6. FC Sucleia | 10 | 1 | 0 | 9 | 10 | - | 40 | 3 |

#### Group B

| | | | | | | | | |
|---|---|---|---|---|---|---|---|---|
| 1. FC Victoria Chişinău | 10 | 8 | 0 | 2 | 41 | - | 9 | 24 |
| 2. CF Spartanii Sportul Selemet | 10 | 8 | 0 | 2 | 25 | - | 11 | 24 |
| 3. FC Speranţa Drochia | 10 | 4 | 1 | 5 | 14 | - | 14 | 13 |
| 4. FC Văsieni | 10 | 4 | 0 | 6 | 13 | - | 24 | 12 |
| 5. FC Olimp Comrat | 10 | 2 | 2 | 6 | 12 | - | 28 | 8 |
| 6. FC Real Succes Chişinău | 10 | 2 | 1 | 7 | 13 | - | 32 | 7 |

Winners and Runners-up of each group were qualified for the Phase II Group 1 (Promotion Round with 2 teams of Super Liga Phase I), while all other teams were qualified for the Phase II Group 2.

### Phase II

#### Group 1 (Promotion Round)

| | | | | | | | | |
|---|---|---|---|---|---|---|---|---|
| 1. FC Dacia Buiucani Chişinău (*Promoted*) | 10 | 8 | 2 | 0 | 26 | - | 3 | 26 |
| 2. FC Floreşti | 10 | 7 | 1 | 2 | 23 | - | 8 | 22 |
| 3. FC Dinamo-Auto Tiraspol | 10 | 5 | 2 | 3 | 22 | - | 9 | 17 |
| 4. CF Spartanii Sportul Selemet | 10 | 4 | 1 | 5 | 17 | - | 20 | 13 |
| 5. FC Victoria Chişinău | 10 | 3 | 0 | 7 | 16 | - | 25 | 9 |
| 6. FC Făleşti | 10 | 0 | 0 | 10 | 9 | - | 48 | 0 |

#### Group 2

| | | | | | | | | |
|---|---|---|---|---|---|---|---|---|
| 1. FC Sheriff-2 Tiraspol | 7 | 5 | 1 | 1 | 24 | - | 5 | 16 |
| 2. FC Speranis Nisporeni | 7 | 5 | 1 | 1 | 22 | - | 6 | 16 |
| 3. FC Văsieni | 7 | 4 | 1 | 2 | 18 | - | 14 | 13 |
| 4. FC Sucleia | 7 | 3 | 1 | 3 | 9 | - | 18 | 10 |
| 5. FC Speranţa Drochia | 7 | 3 | 1 | 3 | 10 | - | 14 | 10 |
| 6. FC Real Succes Chişinău | 7 | 2 | 1 | 4 | 9 | - | 18 | 7 |
| 7. FC Olimp Comrat | 7 | 1 | 2 | 4 | 9 | - | 13 | 5 |
| 8. FCM Ungheni | 7 | 1 | 0 | 6 | 5 | - | 18 | 3 |

Teams ranked 2-6 from Group 1 and teams ranked 2-6 from Group 2 advanced to the Promotion Play-offs.
FC Olimp Comrat and FCM Ungheni renonced to enter Play-offs, while FC Sheriff-2 Tiraspol (as reserve team) were not eligible to participate.

### Promotion Play-offs

| First Round [06.05.2023] | | |
|---|---|---|
| FC Speranis Nisporeni - FC Speranţa Drochia | 4-0(0-0) |
| FC Văsieni - FC Sucleia | 6-1(2-0) |

| Second Round [14.05.2023] | | |
|---|---|---|
| CF Spartanii Sportul Selemet - FC Real Succes Chişinău | 7-1(2-0) |
| FC Dinamo-Auto Tiraspol - FC Speranis Nisporeni | 2-2(1-0,1-1,2-2); 5-4 pen |
| FC Floreşti - FC Văsieni | 2-0(0-0) |
| FC Victoria Chişinău - FC Făleşti | 6-2(0-1) |

| Semi-Finals [19.05.2023] | | |
|---|---|---|
| FC Dinamo-Auto Tiraspol - CF Spartanii Sportul Selemet | 2-0(1-0) |
| FC Floreşti - FC Victoria Chişinău | 3-3(1-1,2-2,3-3); 6-7 pen |

| Final [24.05.2023] | | |
|---|---|---|
| FC Dinamo-Auto Tiraspol - FC Victoria Chişinău | 5-1(3-0) |

Both FC Dinamo-Auto Tiraspol and FC Victoria Chişinău failed to obtain license to compete at first Level in 2023/2024.
As a consequence, **FC Floreşti** and **CF Spartanii Sportul Selemet** were promoted instead!

## INTERNATIONAL MATCHES
### (16.07.2022 – 15.07.2023)

| | | | | |
|---|---|---|---|---|
| 22.09.2022 | Rīga | *Latvia - Moldova* | *1-2(0-2)* | (UNL) |
| 25.09.2022 | Chişinău | *Moldova - Liechtenstein* | *2-0(0-0)* | (UNL) |
| 16.11.2022 | Chişinău | *Moldova - Azerbaijan* | *1-2(0-2)* | (F) |
| 20.11.2022 | Chişinău | *Moldova - Romania* | *0-5(0-2)* | (F) |
| 24.03.2023 | Chişinău | *Moldova - Faroe Islands* | *1-1(0-1)* | (ECQ) |
| 27.03.2023 | Chişinău | *Moldova - Czech Republic* | *0-0* | (ECQ) |
| 17.06.2023 | Tiranë | *Albania - Moldova* | *2-0(0-0)* | (ECQ) |
| 20.06.2023 | Chişinău | *Moldova - Poland* | *3-2(0-2)* | (ECQ) |

**22.09.2022　LATVIA - MOLDOVA　　　　　1-2(0-2)　　　　3rd UEFA Nations League D, Group 1**
Skonto stadions, Rīga; Referee: António Emanuel Carvalho Nobre (Portugal); Attendance: 6,711
**MDA:** Dumitru Celeadnic, Veaceslav Posmac, Igor Armaş, Artur Crăciun, Mihail Caimacov, Artur Ioniţă (Cap), Ioan-Călin Revenco, Nichita Moţpan (84.Eugeniu Cociuc), Sergiu Plătică (84.Ion Jardan), Ion Nicolăescu (73.Virgiliu Postolachi), Vitalie Damaşcan (90+5.Maxim Cojocaru). Trainer: Serghei Cleşcenco.
**Goals:** Ioan-Călin Revenco (26), Ion Nicolăescu (45).

**25.09.2022　MOLDOVA - LIECHTENSTEIN　　　2-0(0-0)　　　3rd UEFA Nations League D, Group 1**
Stadionul Zimbru, Chişinău; Referee: Stéphanie Frappart (France); Attendance: 5,774
**MDA:** Dumitru Celeadnic, Alexandr Belousov (81.Maxim Cojocaru), Igor Armaş, Vadim Bolohan (81.Veaceslav Posmac), Artur Crăciun, Sergiu Plătică, Artur Ioniţă (Cap), Vadim Raţă, Nichita Moţpan (57.Virgiliu Postolachi), Ion Nicolăescu (76.Victor Stînă), Vitalie Damaşcan. Trainer: Serghei Cleşcenco.
**Goals:** Victor Stînă (90+2, 90+4).

**16.11.2022　MOLDOVA - AZERBAIJAN　　　　1-2(0-2)　　　　Friendly International**
Stadionul Zimbru, Chişinău; Referee: Denys Shurman (Ukraine); Attendance: 3,742
**MDA:** Dumitru Celeadnic, Daniel Dumbravanu, Iurie Iovu, Igor Armaş, Artur Ioniţă (Cap) (84.Mihail Plătică), Eugeniu Cociuc (46.Virgiliu Postolachi), Ioan-Călin Revenco, Oleg Reabciuk, Mihail Caimacov (66.Nichita Moţpan), Vadim Raţă (84.Nicky Serghei Clescenco), Vitalie Damaşcan (66.Victor Stînă). Trainer: Serghei Cleşcenco.
**Goal:** Nichita Moţpan (90+2).

**20.11.2022　MOLDOVA - ROMANIA　　　　　0-5(0-2)　　　　Friendly International**
Stadionul Zimbru, Chişinău; Referee: Yaşar Kemal Uğurlu (Turkey); Attendance: 6,145
**MDA:** Dumitru Celeadnic, Sergiu Plătică (46.Ioan-Călin Revenco), Igor Armaş, Vadim Bolohan, Daniel Dumbravanu (46.Iurie Iovu), Oleg Reabciuk, Artur Ioniţă (Cap) (75.Mihail Plătică), Vadim Raţă, Nichita Moţpan (75.Victor Stînă), Vitalie Damaşcan, Virgiliu Postolachi (61.Mihail Caimacov). Trainer: Serghei Cleşcenco.

**24.03.2023　MOLDOVA - FAROE ISLANDS　　　1-1(0-1)　　　　17th EC. Qualifiers**
Stadionul Zimbru, Chişinău; Referee: Nicolas Walsh (Scotland); Attendance: 4,732
**MDA:** Dorian Răilean, Veaceslav Posmac, Artur Crăciun, Victor Mudrac (73.Serafim Cojocari), Mihail Caimacov, Vadim Raţă (Cap), Ioan-Călin Revenco, Sergiu Plătică (73.Victor Stînă), Vitalie Damaşcan, Virgiliu Postolachi (46.Nichita Moţpan), Ion Nicolăescu. Trainer: Serghei Cleşcenco.
**Goal:** Ion Nicolăescu (87 penalty).

**27.03.2023　MOLDOVA - CZECH REPUBLIC　　　0-0　　　　　17th EC. Qualifiers**
Stadionul Zimbru, Chişinău; Referee: Daniel Schlager (Germany); Attendance: 5,120
**MDA:** Dorian Răilean, Veaceslav Posmac, Artur Crăciun, Victor Mudrac, Ioan-Călin Revenco (83.Sergiu Plătică), Mihail Caimacov, Vadim Raţă (Cap), Nichita Moţpan (59.Virgiliu Postolachi), Serafim Cojocari, Ion Nicolăescu (83.Victor Stînă), Vitalie Damaşcan (14.Maxim Cojocaru). Trainer: Serghei Cleşcenco.

**17.06.2023　ALBANIA - MOLDOVA　　　　　2-0(0-0)　　　　17th EC. Qualifiers**
Arena Kombëtare, Tiranë; Referee: Dennis Higler (Netherlands); Attendance: 20,944
**MDA:** Dorian Răilean, Veaceslav Posmac, Artur Crăciun, Victor Mudrac, Vladyslav Baboglo (73.Sergiu Plătică), Ioan-Călin Revenco (73.Serafim Cojocari), Vadim Raţă (Cap), Nichita Moţpan (55.Victor Stînă), Oleg Reabciuk, Ion Nicolăescu (65.Virgiliu Postolachi), Vitalie Damaşcan (56.Maxim Cojocaru). Trainer: Serghei Cleşcenco.

**20.06.2023　MOLDOVA - POLAND　　　　　3-2(0-2)　　　　17th EC. Qualifiers**
Stadionul Zimbru, Chişinău; Referee: Filip Glova (Slovakia); Attendance: 9,442
**MDA:** Dorian Răilean, Veaceslav Posmac (Cap), Artur Crăciun, Victor Mudrac, Ioan-Călin Revenco, Vladyslav Baboglo, Cristian Dros (46.Nichita Moţpan), Oleg Reabciuk, Maxim Cojocaru, Vitalie Damaşcan (46.Virgiliu Postolachi), Ion Nicolăescu (85.Serafim Cojocari). Trainer: Serghei Cleşcenco.
**Goals:** Ion Nicolăescu (48, 79), Vladyslav Baboglo (85).

## NATIONAL TEAM PLAYERS
(16.07.2022 – 15.07.2023)

| Name | DOB | Caps | Goals | Club |
|---|---|---|---|---|
| **Goalkeepers** | | | | |
| Dumitru CELEADNIC | 23.04.1992 | 6 | 0 | 2022: *FC Sheriff Tiraspol* |
| Dorian RĂILEAN | 13.10.1993 | 10 | 0 | 2023: *FC Unirea Dej (ROU)* |
| **Defenders** | | | | |
| Igor ARMAŞ | 14.07.1987 | 83 | 6 | 2022: *FC Voluntari (ROU)* |
| Vladyslav BABOGLO | 14.11.1998 | 2 | 1 | 2023: *FK Oleksandriya (UKR)* |
| Alexandr BELOUSOV | 14.05.1998 | 5 | 0 | 2022: *FC Milsami Orhei* |
| Vadim BOLOHAN | 15.08.1986 | 40 | 1 | 2022: *FC Milsami Orhei* |
| Artur CRĂCIUN | 29.06.1998 | 16 | 0 | 2022/2023: *Hapoel Kfar Saba FC (ISR)* |
| Daniel DUMBRAVANU | 22.07.2001 | 5 | 0 | 2022: *APOEL Nicosia (CYP)* |
| Iurie IOVU | 06.07.2002 | 3 | 0 | 2022/2023: *NK Istra 1961 Pula (SVN)* |
| Ion JARDAN | 10.01.1990 | 49 | 0 | 2022: *CS Petrocub Hînceşti* |
| Victor MUDRAC | 03.03.1994 | 12 | 0 | 2023: *CS Petrocub Hînceşti* |
| Veaceslav POSMAC | 07.11.1990 | 63 | 2 | 2022/2023: *Boluspor Kulübü (TUR)* |
| Oleg REABCIUK | 16.01.1998 | 41 | 0 | 2022/2023: *Olympiacos SFP Peiraiás (GRE)* |
| Ioan-Călin REVENCO | 26.06.2000 | 17 | 1 | 2022/2023: *CS Petrocub Hînceşti* |
| **Midfielders** | | | | |
| Mihail CAIMACOV | 22.07.1998 | 20 | 1 | 2022/2023: *FK Torpedo Moskva (RUS)* |
| Eugeniu COCIUC | 11.05.1993 | 29 | 0 | 2022: *FC Pyunik Yerevan (ARM)* |
| Serafim COJOCARI | 07.01.2001 | 4 | 0 | 2023: *CSF Bălţi* |
| Cristian DROS | 15.04.1998 | 15 | 0 | 2023: *FC Slavia Mozyr (BLR)* |
| Artur IONIŢĂ | 17.08.1990 | 67 | 3 | 2022: *Pisa SC (ITA)* |
| Nichita MOŢPAN | 17.07.2001 | 10 | 2 | 2022: *Hapoel Haifa FC (ISR)* <br> 31.12.2022-> *CSF Bălţi* |
| Mihail PLĂTICĂ | 15.03.1990 | 9 | 1 | 2022: *CS Petrocub Hînceşti* |
| Sergiu PLĂTICĂ | 09.06.1991 | 40 | 0 | 2022/2023: *CS Petrocub Hînceşti* |
| Vadim RAŢĂ | 05.03.1993 | 37 | 1 | 2022/2023: *FC Voluntari (ROU)* |
| Victor STÎNĂ | 20.03.1998 | 8 | 2 | 2022/2023: *Panserraikós GS Serres (GRE)* |
| **Forwards** | | | | |
| Nicky Serghei CLEŞCENCO | 23.07.2001 | 4 | 0 | 2022: *FC Sion (SUI)* |
| Maxim COJOCARU | 13.01.1998 | 13 | 0 | 2022/2023: *CS Petrocub Hînceşti* |
| Vitalie DAMAŞCAN | 24.01.1999 | 28 | 2 | 2022/2023: *FC Voluntari (ROU)* |
| Ion NICOLĂESCU | 07.09.1998 | 35 | 12 | 2022: *FK DAC Dunajská Streda (SVK)* <br> 23.09.2022-> *Beitar Jersusalem FC (ISR)* |
| Virgiliu POSTOLACHI | 17.03.2000 | 11 | 0 | 2022/2023: *FC UT Arad (ROU)* |
| **Trainer** | | | | |
| Serghei CLEŞCENCO [from 03.12.2021] | 20.05.1972 | | | 16 M; 6 W; 3 D; 7 L; 19-27 |

# MONTENEGRO

**The Country:**
Crna Gora (Montenegro)
Capital: Podgorica
Surface: 13,812 km²
Inhabitants: 602,445 [2023]
Time: UTC+1

**The FA:**
Fudbalski savez Crne Gore
Bulevar Veljka Vlahovića bb ME, 81000 Podgorica
Tel: +382 20 445 600
Foundation date: 1931
Member of FIFA since: 2007
Member of UEFA since: 2007
Website: www.fscg.me

## NATIONAL TEAM RECORDS

| RECORDS | | |
|---|---|---|
| **First international match:** | 24.03.2007, Podgorica: | Montenegro – Hungary 2-1 |
| **Most international caps:** | Fatos Bećiraj | - 86 caps (2009-2022) |
| **Most international goals:** | Stevan Jovetić | - 31 goals / 68 caps (since 2007) |

| UEFA EUROPEAN CHAMPIONSHIP | |
|---|---|
| 1960 | - |
| 1964 | - |
| 1968 | - |
| 1972 | - |
| 1976 | - |
| 1980 | - |
| 1984 | - |
| 1988 | - |
| 1992 | - |
| 1996 | - |
| 2000 | - |
| 2004 | - |
| 2008 | - |
| 2012 | Qualifiers |
| 2016 | Qualifiers |
| 2020 | Qualifiers |

| FIFA WORLD CUP | |
|---|---|
| 1930 | - |
| 1934 | - |
| 1938 | - |
| 1950 | - |
| 1954 | - |
| 1958 | - |
| 1962 | - |
| 1966 | - |
| 1970 | - |
| 1974 | - |
| 1978 | - |
| 1982 | - |
| 1986 | - |
| 1990 | - |
| 1994 | - |
| 1998 | - |
| 2002 | - |
| 2006 | - |
| 2010 | Qualifiers |
| 2014 | Qualifiers |
| 2018 | Qualifiers |
| 2022 | Qualifiers |

| OLYMPIC TOURNAMENTS | |
|---|---|
| 1908 | - |
| 1912 | - |
| 1920 | - |
| 1924 | - |
| 1928 | - |
| 1936 | - |
| 1948 | - |
| 1952 | - |
| 1956 | - |
| 1960 | - |
| 1964 | - |
| 1968 | - |
| 1972 | - |
| 1976 | - |
| 1980 | - |
| 1984 | - |
| 1988 | - |
| 1992 | - |
| 1996 | - |
| 2000 | - |
| 2004 | - |
| 2008 | - |
| 2012 | Qualifiers |
| 2016 | Qualifiers |
| 2020 | Qualifiers |

*was part of Yugoslavia/Serbia until 2006*

| UEFA NATIONS LEAGUE | |
|---|---|
| 2018/2019 | League C (Group Stage) |
| 2020/2021 | League C (Group Stage -> promoted to League B) |
| 2022/2023 | League B (Group Stage) |

## MONTENEGRIN CLUB HONOURS IN EUROPEAN CLUB COMPETITIONS:

| European Champion Clubs.Cup (1956-1992) / UEFA Champions League (1993-2023) |
|---|
| None |
| **Fairs Cup (1858-1971) / UEFA Cup (1972-2009) / UEFA Europa League (2010-2023)** |
| None |
| **UEFA Europa Conference League (2021-2023)** |
| None |
| **UEFA Super Cup (1972-2022)** |
| None |
| *European Cup Winners' Cup 1961-1999\** |
| None |

*defunct competition*

# NATIONAL COMPETITIONS
## TABLE OF HONOURS

|  | CHAMPIONS | CUP WINNERS | BEST GOALSCORERS | |
|---|---|---|---|---|
| 2006/2007 | FK Zeta Golubovci | FK Rudar Pljevlja | Damir Čakar (FK Rudar Pljevlja) | |
|  |  |  | Žarko Korać (FK Zeta Golubovci) | 16 |
| 2007/2008 | FK Budućnost Podgorica | FK Mogren Budva | Ivan Jablan (FK Lovćen Cetinje) | 13 |
| 2008/2009 | FK Mogren Budva | OFK Petrovac | Fatos Bećiraj (FK Budućnost Podgorica) | 18 |
| 2009/2010 | FK Rudar Pljevlja | FK Rudar Pljevlja | Ivan Bošković (OFK Grbalj) | 28 |
| 2010/2011 | FK Mogren Budva | FK Rudar Pljevlja | Ivan Vuković (FK Budućnost Podgorica) | 20 |
| 2011/2012 | FK Budućnost Podgorica | FK Čelik Nikšić | Admir Adrović (FK Budućnost Podgorica) | 22 |
| 2012/2013 | FK Sutjeska Nikšić | FK Budućnost Podgorica | Admir Adrović (FK Budućnost Podgorica) | |
|  |  |  | Žarko Korać (FK Zeta Golubovci) | 15 |
| 2013/2014 | FK Sutjeska Nikšić | FK Lovćen Cetinje | Stefan Mugoša (OFK Titograd Podgorica) | 15 |
| 2014/2015 | FK Rudar Pljevlja | FK Mladost Podgorica | Goran Vujović (FK Sutjeska Nikšić) | 21 |
| 2015/2016 | FK Mladost Podgorica | FK Rudar Pljevlja | Marko Šćepanović (FK Mladost Podgorica) | 19 |
| 2016/2017 | FK Budućnost Podgorica | FK Sutjeska Nikšić | Zoran Petrović (OFK Titograd Podgorica) | 14 |
| 2017/2018 | FK Sutjeska Nikšić | FK Mladost Podgorica | Igor Ivanović (FK Sutjeska Nikšić) | 14 |
| 2018/2019 | FK Sutjeska Nikšić | FK Budućnost Podgorica | Nikola Krstović (FK Zeta Golubovci) | 17 |
| 2019/2020 | FK Budućnost Podgorica | *Competition cancelled* | Marko Ćetković (FK Sutjeska Nikšić) | 10 |
| 2020/2021 | FK Budućnost Podgorica | FK Budućnost Podgorica | Božo Marković (FK Sutjeska Nikšić) | 16 |
| 2021/2022 | FK Sutjeska Nikšić | FK Budućnost Podgorica | Adnan Bašić (BIH, OFK Petrovac) | 14 |
| 2022/2023 | FK Budućnost Podgorica | FK Sutjeska Nikšić | Tyrone Conraad (NED, FK Sutjeska Nikšić) | 26 |

# NATIONAL CHAMPIONSHIP
## Prva Crnogorska Fudbal Liga 2022/2023
### (23.07.2022 – 25.05.2023)

## Results

**Round 1 [23-24.07.2022]**
FK Jedinstvo - Sutjeska Nikšić 1-1(1-1)
FK Jezero - Rudar Pljevlja 3-1(2-1)
Arsenal Tivat - OFK Petrovac 0-2(0-1)
FK Mornar - Dečić Tuzi 0-1(0-1)
Iskra Danilov. - Budućnost 1-1(0-1) [24.08.22]

**Round 2 [30-31.07.2022]**
Dečić Tuzi - Iskra Danilovgrad 3-0(1-0)
Rudar Pljevlja - FK Mornar 1-0(0-0)
Sutjeska Nikšić - FK Jezero 3-0(2-0)
Arsenal Tivat - FK Jedinstvo 1-0(0-0)
OFK Petrovac - FK Budućnost 4-2(1-1)

**Round 3 [06-07.08.2022]**
FK Jedinstvo - OFK Petrovac 0-1(0-1)
FK Jezero - Arsenal Tivat 2-1(0-1)
Iskra Danilovgrad - Rudar Pljevlja 0-0
FK Mornar - Sutjeska Nikšić 2-1(2-0)
FK Budućnost - Dečić Tuzi 0-2(0-0)

**Round 4 [16.08.2022]**
Rudar Pljevlja - FK Budućnost 0-1(0-0)
Sutjeska Nikšić - Iskra Danilovgrad 3-0(1-0)
FK Jedinstvo - FK Jezero 0-1(0-0)
Arsenal Tivat - FK Mornar 2-1(0-0)
OFK Petrovac - Dečić Tuzi 2-2(1-2)

**Round 5 [20-21.08.2022]**
FK Jezero - OFK Petrovac 2-2(0-0)
FK Budućnost - Sutjeska Nikšić 2-0(0-0)
Iskra Danilovgrad - Arsenal Tivat 2-3(0-1)
FK Mornar - FK Jedinstvo 2-2(0-0)
Dečić Tuzi - Rudar Pljevlja 5-1(3-1)

**Round 6 [27-28.08.2022]**
Sutjeska Nikšić - Dečić Tuzi 3-0(1-0)
FK Jezero - FK Mornar 3-1(1-0)
OFK Petrovac - Rudar Pljevlja 0-0
FK Jedinstvo - Iskra Danilovgrad 2-1(1-0)
Arsenal Tivat - FK Budućnost 0-4(0-1)

**Round 7 [03-04.09.2022]**
Dečić Tuzi - Arsenal Tivat 2-4(0-3)
Iskra Danilovgrad - FK Jezero 2-1(1-1)
Rudar Pljevlja - Sutjeska Nikšić 0-0
FK Mornar - OFK Petrovac 1-0(1-0)
FK Budućnost - FK Jedinstvo 3-0(2-0)

**Round 8 [10-11.09.2022]**
OFK Petrovac - Sutjeska Nikšić 0-4(0-3)
Arsenal Tivat - Rudar Pljevlja 0-2(0-0)
FK Jedinstvo - Dečić Tuzi 1-2(0-1)
FK Jezero - FK Budućnost 0-0
FK Mornar - Iskra Danilovgrad 0-0

**Round 9 [17.09.2022]**
Sutjeska Nikšić - Arsenal Tivat 2-1(1-0)
Rudar Pljevlja - FK Jedinstvo 0-3(0-0)
Iskra Danilovgrad - OFK Petrovac 1-2(1-1)
Dečić Tuzi - FK Jezero 1-1(1-0)
FK Budućnost - FK Mornar 2-0(1-0)

**Round 10 [01-02.10.2022]**
Sutjeska Nikšić - FK Jedinstvo 5-0(2-0)
Rudar Pljevlja - FK Jezero 2-1(1-0)
Dečić Tuzi - FK Mornar 3-1(1-1)
OFK Petrovac - Arsenal Tivat 1-2(0-1)
FK Budućnost - Iskra Danilovgrad 0-1(0-0)

**Round 11 [09.10.2022]**
FK Mornar - Rudar Pljevlja 2-2(1-1)
FK Jedinstvo - Arsenal Tivat 2-2(2-2)
FK Budućnost - OFK Petrovac 3-3(0-2)
Iskra Danilovgrad - Dečić Tuzi 0-0
FK Jezero - Sutjeska Nikšić 1-0(0-0)

**Round 12 [15-16.10.2022]**
Rudar Pljevlja - Iskra Danilovgrad 3-1(1-0)
Arsenal Tivat - FK Jezero 1-1(1-0)
OFK Petrovac - FK Jedinstvo 1-1(1-0)
Dečić Tuzi - FK Budućnost 0-0
Sutjeska Nikšić - FK Mornar 1-1(0-0)

**Round 13 [21-22.10.2022]**
FK Jezero - FK Jedinstvo 0-2(0-1)
Dečić Tuzi - OFK Petrovac 1-1(0-1)
Iskra Danilovgrad - Sutjeska Nikšić 1-2(0-2)
FK Mornar - Arsenal Tivat 0-1(0-0)
FK Budućnost - Rudar Pljevlja 2-1(0-1)

**Round 14 [29-30.10.2022]**
OFK Petrovac - FK Jezero 2-1(2-1)
Arsenal Tivat - Iskra Danilovgrad 3-0(0-0)
FK Jedinstvo - FK Mornar 1-0(0-0)
Rudar Pljevlja - Dečić Tuzi 1-1(1-0)
Sutjeska Nikšić - FK Budućnost 0-1(0-1)

**Round 15 [06.11.2022]**
Rudar Pljevlja - OFK Petrovac 0-1(0-0)
Iskra Danilovgrad - FK Jedinstvo 1-3(0-2)
FK Budućnost - Arsenal Tivat 2-0(1-0)
FK Mornar - FK Jezero 1-0(1-0)
Dečić Tuzi - Sutjeska Nikšić 1-2(1-1)

**Round 16 [12.11.2022]**
FK Jezero - Iskra Danilovgrad 0-0
FK Jedinstvo - FK Budućnost 0-1(0-0)
Sutjeska Nikšić - Rudar Pljevlja 4-0(2-0)
OFK Petrovac - FK Mornar 1-2(1-0)
Arsenal Tivat - Dečić Tuzi 1-2(0-1)

**Round 17 [26-27.11.2022]**
Dečić Tuzi - FK Jedinstvo 0-1(0-0)
Iskra Danilovgrad - FK Mornar 2-1(1-1)
Rudar Pljevlja - Arsenal Tivat 0-0
FK Budućnost - FK Jezero 2-1(0-1)
Sutjeska Nikšić - OFK Petrovac 2-0(0-0)

**Round 18 [03.12.2022]**
FK Jedinstvo - Rudar Pljevlja 0-0
FK Jezero - Dečić Tuzi 0-0
FK Mornar - FK Budućnost 1-2(0-1)
OFK Petrovac - Iskra Danilovgrad 1-0(0-0)
Arsenal Tivat - Sutjeska Nikšić 2-2(0-1)

| Round 19 [07.12.2022] |
|---|
| Arsenal Tivat - OFK Petrovac 1-1(0-1) |
| FK Jedinstvo - Sutjeska Nikšić 0-4(0-1) |
| FK Jezero - Rudar Pljevlja 0-0 |
| Iskra Danilovgrad - FK Budućnost 3-0(1-0) |
| FK Mornar - Dečić Tuzi 1-0(0-0) [10.12.2022] |

| Round 20 [18.02.2023] |
|---|
| Rudar Pljevlja - FK Mornar 0-1(0-0) |
| Arsenal Tivat - FK Jedinstvo 1-0(1-0) |
| Dečić Tuzi - Iskra Danilovgrad 0-2(0-0) |
| Sutjeska Nikšić - FK Jezero 4-2(2-1) |
| OFK Petrovac - FK Budućnost 1-1(0-1) |

| Round 21 [23.02.2023] |
|---|
| FK Jezero - Arsenal Tivat 1-0(0-0) |
| FK Jedinstvo - OFK Petrovac 2-1(0-0) |
| Iskra Danilovgrad - Rudar Pljevlja 2-1(1-0) |
| FK Mornar - Sutjeska Nikšić 3-2(0-1) |
| FK Budućnost - Dečić Tuzi 1-0(0-0) |

| Round 22 [28.02.2023] |
|---|
| Sutjeska Nikšić - Iskra Danilovgrad 2-1(1-0) |
| Arsenal Tivat - FK Mornar 0-0 |
| OFK Petrovac - Dečić Tuzi 2-1(2-0) |
| FK Jedinstvo - FK Jezero 2-1(1-0) [19.04.23] |
| Rudar Pljevlja- Budućnost 1-1(0-0) [19.04.23] |

| Round 23 [04.03.2023] |
|---|
| FK Jezero - OFK Petrovac 1-1(1-0) |
| Dečić Tuzi - Rudar Pljevlja 1-0(0-0) |
| Iskra Danilovgrad - Arsenal Tivat 0-1(0-0) |
| FK Mornar - FK Jedinstvo 1-0(0-0) |
| FK Budućnost - Sutjeska Nikšić 1-1(0-1) |

| Round 24 [08.03.2023] |
|---|
| FK Jedinstvo - Iskra Danilovgrad 2-1(2-0) |
| Arsenal Tivat - FK Budućnost 1-1(1-1) |
| FK Jezero - FK Mornar 0-0 |
| OFK Petrovac - Rudar Pljevlja 2-3(2-1) |
| Sutjeska Nikšić - Dečić Tuzi 1-1(0-0) |

| Round 25 [12-13.03.2023] |
|---|
| FK Mornar - OFK Petrovac 0-1(0-0) |
| Rudar Pljevlja - Sutjeska Nikšić 1-4(0-2) |
| FK Budućnost - FK Jedinstvo 4-0(2-0) |
| Dečić Tuzi - Arsenal Tivat 0-0 |
| Iskra Danilovgrad - FK Jezero 1-1(0-0) |

| Round 26 [18.03.2023] |
|---|
| FK Jedinstvo - Dečić Tuzi 0-0 |
| Arsenal Tivat - Rudar Pljevlja 0-1(0-1) |
| FK Jezero - FK Budućnost 1-2(0-1) |
| FK Mornar - Iskra Danilovgrad 0-0 |
| OFK Petrovac - Sutjeska Nikšić 1-1(0-1) |

| Round 27 [01.04.2023] |
|---|
| Rudar Pljevlja - FK Jedinstvo 1-2(0-1) |
| FK Budućnost - FK Mornar 2-0(0-0) |
| Iskra Danilovgrad - OFK Petrovac 2-2(1-1) |
| Dečić Tuzi - FK Jezero 1-1(0-0) |
| Sutjeska Nikšić - Arsenal Tivat 2-2(1-1) |

| Round 28 [05.04.2023] |
|---|
| Rudar Pljevlja - FK Jezero 0-0 |
| OFK Petrovac - Arsenal Tivat 0-3(0-0) |
| Dečić Tuzi - FK Mornar 1-1(1-0) |
| FK Budućnost - Iskra Danilovgrad 3-0(0-0) |
| Sutjeska Nikšić - FK Jedinstvo 3-4(1-2) |

| Round 29 [09.04.2023] |
|---|
| Iskra Danilovgrad - Dečić Tuzi 1-3(0-2) |
| FK Jezero - Sutjeska Nikšić 0-0 |
| FK Jedinstvo - Arsenal Tivat 0-0 |
| FK Mornar - Rudar Pljevlja 2-0(1-0) |
| FK Budućnost - OFK Petrovac 4-4(2-1) |

| Round 30 [15.04.2023] |
|---|
| Sutjeska Nikšić - FK Mornar 4-1(1-1) |
| Rudar Pljevlja - Iskra Danilovgrad 3-1(2-0) |
| Arsenal Tivat - FK Jezero 1-0(1-0) |
| OFK Petrovac - FK Jedinstvo 2-3(1-1) |
| Dečić Tuzi - FK Budućnost 4-3(1-1) |

| Round 31 [23.04.2023] |
|---|
| FK Mornar - Arsenal Tivat 0-1(0-0) |
| FK Jezero - FK Jedinstvo 2-1(1-0) |
| Iskra Danilovgrad - Sutjeska Nikšić 0-2(0-0) |
| Dečić Tuzi - OFK Petrovac 3-0(2-0) |
| FK Budućnost - Rudar Pljevlja 2-1(2-1) |

| Round 32 [29.04.2023] |
|---|
| FK Jedinstvo - FK Mornar 3-1(0-1) |
| Arsenal Tivat - Iskra Danilovgrad 2-3(2-2) |
| Rudar Pljevlja - Dečić Tuzi 0-0 |
| OFK Petrovac - FK Jezero 1-0(0-0) |
| Sutjeska Nikšić - FK Budućnost 2-2(2-0) |

| Round 33 [07.05.2023] |
|---|
| Rudar Pljevlja - OFK Petrovac 4-2(2-1) |
| Iskra Danilovgrad - FK Jedinstvo 1-1(0-0) |
| FK Budućnost - Arsenal Tivat 1-0(1-0) |
| Dečić Tuzi - Sutjeska Nikšić 0-3(0-2) |
| FK Mornar - FK Jezero 1-0(0-0) |

| Round 34 [14.05.2023] |
|---|
| FK Jezero - Iskra Danilovgrad 2-0(1-0) |
| FK Jedinstvo - FK Budućnost 1-3(1-2) |
| Sutjeska Nikšić - Rudar Pljevlja 2-1(1-0) |
| OFK Petrovac - FK Mornar 0-1(0-1) |
| Arsenal Tivat - Dečić Tuzi 0-0 |

| Round 35 [21.05.2023] |
|---|
| Dečić Tuzi - FK Jedinstvo 2-0(2-0) |
| Iskra Danilovgrad - FK Mornar 1-1(0-1) |
| Rudar Pljevlja - Arsenal Tivat 1-2(0-1) |
| FK Budućnost - FK Jezero 1-3(0-0) |
| Sutjeska Nikšić - OFK Petrovac 2-1(0-0) |

| Round 36 [25.05.2023] |
|---|
| FK Jedinstvo - Rudar Pljevlja 3-4(2-1) |
| FK Jezero - Dečić Tuzi 2-1(1-0) |
| FK Mornar - FK Budućnost 0-1(0-1) |
| OFK Petrovac - Iskra Danilovgrad 4-1(3-0) |
| Arsenal Tivat - Sutjeska Nikšić 0-1(0-0) |

### Final Standings

| | | Total | | | | | | Home | | | | | Away | | | |
|---|---|---|---|---|---|---|---|---|---|---|---|---|---|---|---|---|---|
| 1. | FK Budućnost Podgorica | 36 | 20 | 10 | 6 | 61 - 37 | 70 | 12 | 3 | 3 | 35 - 17 | 8 | 7 | 3 | 26 - 20 |
| 2. | FK Sutjeska Nikšić | 36 | 20 | 10 | 6 | 75 - 34 | 70 | 12 | 4 | 2 | 45 - 18 | 8 | 6 | 4 | 30 - 16 |
| 3. | FK Arsenal Tivat | 36 | 13 | 11 | 12 | 39 - 39 | 50 | 5 | 6 | 7 | 16 - 21 | 8 | 5 | 5 | 23 - 18 |
| 4. | FK Dečić Tuzi | 36 | 12 | 14 | 10 | 44 - 37 | 50 | 7 | 6 | 5 | 28 - 21 | 5 | 8 | 5 | 16 - 16 |
| 5. | FK Jedinstvo Bijelo Polje | 36 | 13 | 8 | 15 | 43 - 54 | 47 | 6 | 5 | 7 | 20 - 24 | 7 | 3 | 8 | 23 - 30 |
| 6. | OFK Petrovac | 36 | 11 | 12 | 13 | 50 - 57 | 45 | 6 | 5 | 7 | 25 - 28 | 5 | 7 | 6 | 25 - 29 |
| 7. | FK Jezero Plav | 36 | 10 | 13 | 13 | 35 - 38 | 43 | 8 | 8 | 2 | 20 - 12 | 2 | 5 | 11 | 15 - 26 |
| 8. | FK Mornar Bar (Relegation Play-offs) | 36 | 11 | 9 | 16 | 30 - 41 | 42 | 8 | 4 | 6 | 17 - 14 | 3 | 5 | 10 | 13 - 27 |
| 9. | FK Rudar Pljevlja (Relegation Play-offs) | 36 | 9 | 11 | 16 | 36 - 51 | 38 | 5 | 6 | 7 | 18 - 21 | 4 | 5 | 9 | 18 - 30 |
| 10. | FK Iskra Danilovgrad (Relegated) | 36 | 7 | 10 | 19 | 33 - 58 | 31 | 4 | 7 | 7 | 21 - 25 | 3 | 3 | 12 | 12 - 33 |

| Top goalscorers: | |
|---|---|
| 26  Tyrone Conraad (NED) | *FK Sutjeska Nikšić* |
| 13  Žarko Korać | *FK Jedinstvo Bijelo Polje* |
| 10  Mendy Mamadou (SEN) | *OFK Petrovac* |

### Promotion / Relegation Play-offs [30.05.-03.06.2023]

| | | |
|---|---|---|
| FK Mornar Bar - FK Berane | 2-0(1-0) | 2-0(1-0) |
| FK Kom Zlatica - FK Rudar Pljevlja | 1-1(1-0) | 1-2(0-2) |

Both FK Mornar Bar and FK Rudar Pljevlja will play at first level in 2023/2024.

### 1/8-Finals [07.09.2022]

| | | | | |
|---|---|---|---|---|
| FK Jedinstvo Bijelo Polje - OFK Mladost DG Podgorica | 3-1(2-1) | FK Podgorica - FK Iskra Danilovgrad | 0-3(0-2) |
| FK Sutjeska Nikšić - FK Jezero | 1-0(1-0) | FK Zeta Golubovci - FK Rudar Pljevlja | 1-3(0-3) |
| FK Bokelj Kotor - FK Arsenal Tivat | 2-3(1-0) | FK Mornar Bar - OFK Petrovac | 2-0(0-0) |
| FK Podgorica - FK Igalo | 3-0(0-0) | FK Dečić Tuzi - FK Budućnost Podgorica | 1-1 aet; 5-4 pen |

### Quarter-Finals [26.10.2022]

| | | | |
|---|---|---|---|
| FK Arsenal Tivat - FK Jedinstvo Bijelo Polje | 0-0 aet; 5-3 pen | FK Dečić Tuzi - FK Podgorica | 2-0(1-0) |
| FK Rudar Pljevlja - FK Sutjeska Nikšić | 0-2(0-1) | FK Iskra Danilovgrad - FK Mornar Bar | 1-1 aet; 5-3 pen |

### Semi-Finals [19.04./03.05.2023]

| First Leg | | Second Leg | |
|---|---|---|---|
| FK Sutjeska Nikšić - FK Dečić Tuzi | 3-1(1-0) | FK Dečić Tuzi - FK Sutjeska Nikšić | 1-1(0-1) |
| FK Iskra Danilovgrad - FK Arsenal Tivat | 1-3(0-2) | FK Arsenal Tivat - FK Iskra Danilovgrad | 1-3 aet; 4-1 pen |

### Final

29.05.2023; Stadion pod Goricom, Podgorica; Referee: Miloš Savović; Attendance: 3,500

**FK Sutjeska Nikšić - FK Arsenal Tivat**    **1-1(1-0,1-1,1-1); 4-3 on penalties**

**FK Sutjeska Nikšić**: Suad Ličina, Anto Babić (26.Amir Bilali), Marko Vučić, Nikola Stijepović, Srdjan Krstović (91.Aleksandar Vlahović), Marko Matanović, Igor Pajović (91.Božo Marković), Novica Eraković (68.Dušan Vuković), Wajdi Sahli, Tyrone Conraad (104.Ognjen Đinović), Vuk Striković (68.Jovan Nikolić). Trainer: Nenad Brnović.

**FK Arsenal Tivat**: Igor Nikić, Marko Dragičević (120.Nikola Braletić), Ćetko Manojlović, Mirko Todorović (72.Nikola Čelebić), Radule Živković, Jovan Mirković, Danilo Bakić, Julián Montenegro (72.Andjelo Rudović), Boris Došljak (80.Boban Đorđević), Jasmin Muhović, Ivan Bulatović (104.Petar Mališić). Trainer: Radislav Dragićević.

**Goals**: 0-1 Ćetko Manojlović (27), 1-1 Wajdi Sahli (85).

**Penalties**: Andjelo Rudović (missed); Marko Vučić (missed); Danilo Bakić 0-1; Marko Matanović 1-1; Jasmin Muhović (missed); Božo Marković 2-1; Nikola Čelebić 2-2; Dušan Vuković 3-2; Ćetko Manojlović 3-3; Wajdi Sahli 4-3.

# THE CLUBS 2022/2023

## Fudbalski klub Arsenal Tivat

| | |
|---|---|
| **Founded**: | 1914 |
| **Stadium**: | Stadion u Parku, Tivat (2,000) |
| **Trainer**: | Radislav Dragićević        13.09.1971 |

| Goalkeepers: | DOB | M | (s) | G |
|---|---|---|---|---|
| Igor Nikić | 25.08.2000 | 36 | | |
| **Defenders:** | **DOB** | **M** | **(s)** | **G** |
| Marko Čavor | 05.07.1999 | 19 | (5) | |
| Nikola Čelebić | 04.07.1989 | 17 | (3) | |
| Marko Dragičević | 01.06.2003 | 12 | (9) | |
| Filip Jezdović (SRB) | 09.11.1998 | 2 | (9) | |
| Ćetko Manojlović | 03.01.1991 | 33 | | 3 |
| Stefan Mršulja | 15.12.1999 | 12 | (5) | |
| Bogdan Rašo | 06.10.2000 | 4 | (1) | |
| Mirko Todorović (SRB) | 22.08.1985 | 23 | (5) | |
| Radule Živković (SRB) | 20.10.1990 | 15 | (1) | |
| **Midfielders:** | **DOB** | **M** | **(s)** | **G** |
| Danilo Bakić | 28.10.1995 | 32 | | 2 |
| Nemanja Bojanić | 04.02.2006 | | (3) | |
| Luka Bojić | 04.09.1992 | 1 | (2) | |
| Nikola Braletić | 25.02.2004 | | (1) | |
| Aleksa Ćetković | 13.02.2004 | 13 | (2) | |

| | DOB | M | (s) | G |
|---|---|---|---|---|
| Jovan Dašić | 29.03.2003 | 15 | (2) | 4 |
| Petar Mališić | 04.09.2001 | 4 | (8) | |
| Jovan Mirković | 30.08.2001 | 16 | (12) | |
| Julián Montenegro (ARG) | 23.03.1989 | 31 | (2) | 8 |
| Velibor Mršulja | 18.06.1991 | 2 | (11) | |
| Aleksandar Mujkić (SWE) | 20.01.2001 | | (4) | |
| Andjelo Rudović | 03.05.1996 | 8 | (6) | 2 |
| Đorđe Štešević | 02.06.2002 | | (7) | |
| Stefan Vulanović | 06.07.2004 | | (1) | |
| **Forwards:** | **DOB** | **M** | **(s)** | **G** |
| Marko Brnović | 27.06.2003 | 1 | (3) | |
| Ivan Bulatović | 16.02.1996 | 30 | (3) | 6 |
| Boris Došljak | 04.06.1989 | 31 | (3) | 7 |
| Boban Đorđević | 20.02.1997 | 4 | (10) | 1 |
| Božo Marković | 26.10.1989 | 11 | (5) | 2 |
| Jasmin Muhović | 02.04.1989 | 19 | (16) | 2 |
| Dejan Pepić | 27.07.1993 | 5 | (4) | |
| *Sávio Oliveira dos Santos (BRA)* | 17.11.1994 | | (3) | 1 |

## Fudbalski Klub Budućnost Podgorica

| | |
|---|---|
| **Founded**: | 1925 |
| **Stadium**: | Stadion pod Goricom, Podgorica (15,230) |
| **Trainer**: | Aleksandar Nedović — 05.09.1978 |
| [09.08.2022] | Miodrag Džudović — 06.09.1979 |

| Goalkeepers: | DOB | M | (s) | G |
|---|---|---|---|---|
| Miloš Dragojević | 03.02.1989 | 25 | | |
| Đorđije Pavličić | 03.12.1996 | 11 | | |
| **Defenders:** | **DOB** | **M** | **(s)** | **G** |
| Vladan Adžić | 05.07.1987 | 26 | | 1 |
| Damjan Dakić | 28.04.2004 | 15 | (4) | 1 |
| Uroš Ignjatović (SRB) | 18.02.2001 | 35 | | 1 |
| Ivan Novović | 26.04.1989 | 2 | (5) | 1 |
| Andrija Ražnatović | 24.12.2000 | 34 | | 4 |
| Marko Simić | 16.06.1987 | 26 | (1) | 4 |
| Bodin Tomašević | 12.05.2006 | 1 | | |
| Nikola Vuković | 05.12.2004 | 1 | | |
| Petar Vuković | 27.02.2002 | 1 | | |
| **Midfielders:** | **DOB** | **M** | **(s)** | **G** |
| Vasilije Adžić | 12.05.2006 | 8 | (15) | 3 |
| Marko Bakić | 01.11.1993 | 10 | (2) | 5 |
| Aleksa Ćetković | 13.02.2004 | | (1) | |
| Jovan Dašić | 29.03.2003 | 3 | (3) | |
| Miomir Đuričković | 26.07.1997 | 25 | (9) | 2 |
| Petar Grbić | 07.08.1988 | 16 | | 2 |
| Branislav Janković | 08.02.1992 | 4 | (6) | |
| Pablo Ángel Ariel Lucero (ARG) | 16.04.1999 | 18 | (6) | 3 |
| Luka Mirković | 01.11.1990 | 10 | (13) | |
| Marko Pavlovski (SRB) | 07.02.1994 | 9 | (5) | 1 |
| Vladimir Perišić | 26.08.2004 | 4 | (15) | |
| Anđelo Rudović | 03.05.1996 | 2 | (12) | |
| Balša Sekulić | 10.06.1998 | 15 | (1) | 6 |
| Petar Sekulović | 14.08.1998 | 3 | (7) | |
| Vasilije Terzić | 12.05.1999 | 24 | (6) | 2 |
| **Forwards:** | **DOB** | **M** | **(s)** | **G** |
| Viktor Đukanović | 29.01.2004 | 14 | (3) | 1 |
| Filip Knežević (SRB) | 08.11.1991 | 8 | (6) | 2 |
| Lazar Mijović | 12.03.2003 | 5 | (1) | 3 |
| Stefan Milošević | 23.06.1996 | 9 | (7) | 5 |
| Marko Mrvaljević | 05.06.2001 | 8 | (23) | 6 |
| Marko Perović | 05.03.2006 | | (1) | |
| Zoran Petrović | 14.07.1997 | 24 | (5) | 8 |

## Fudbalski klub Dečić Tuzi

| | |
|---|---|
| **Founded**: | 1926 |
| **Stadium**: | Stadion „Tuško Polje", Tuzi (2,000) |
| **Trainer**: | Vladimir Janković (SRB) — 01.08.1970 |
| [23.09.2022] | Derviš Hadžiosmanović (BIH) — 09.08.1959 |
| [04.01.2023] | Vladimir Gaćinović (SRB) — 03.01.1966 |
| [19.03.2023] | Juraj Jarábek (SVK) — 03.10.1962 |

| Goalkeepers: | DOB | M | (s) | G |
|---|---|---|---|---|
| Dušan Marković (SRB) | 03.04.1998 | 35 | | |
| Pavle Velimirović | 11.04.1990 | 1 | | |
| **Defenders:** | **DOB** | **M** | **(s)** | **G** |
| Igor Ćuković | 06.06.1993 | 19 | | 1 |
| Jonathan Drešaj | 15.03.2000 | 31 | | |
| Robert Đelaj | 23.09.2002 | 18 | (5) | |
| Pjeter Ljuljđuraj | 29.06.1992 | 20 | (7) | 1 |
| Aleksandar Šofranac | 21.10.1990 | 6 | (1) | |
| Marko Tući | 04.12.1998 | 26 | (1) | 2 |
| Radule Živković (SRB) | 20.10.1990 | 1 | | |
| **Midfielders:** | **DOB** | **M** | **(s)** | **G** |
| Adil Adžović | 21.04.2002 | | (3) | |
| Anel Asović | | | (1) | |
| Andrej Bajović | 06.06.2003 | 18 | (8) | 2 |
| Matija Božanović | 13.04.1994 | 6 | (6) | |
| Draško Božović | 30.06.1988 | 33 | | 5 |
| Velizar Janketić | 15.11.1996 | 2 | (4) | |
| Anđelko Jovanović | 18.11.1999 | | (9) | |
| Danilo Marković | 15.07.1998 | 3 | (7) | |
| Aleksa Marušić | 08.06.1999 | 2 | (14) | 1 |
| Jovan Nikolić | 21.07.1991 | 15 | (2) | |
| *Pedro* Sass Petrazzi (BRA) | 15.09.1990 | 9 | (4) | |
| Lazar Stanišić | 08.09.2004 | 8 | (10) | 2 |
| Leon Ujkaj | 03.03.1997 | 13 | (1) | |
| Erjon Vuçaj (ALB) | 25.12.1990 | 14 | (11) | 2 |
| Milan Vušurović | 18.04.1995 | 9 | (3) | 3 |
| Darko Zorić | 12.09.1993 | 1 | | |
| **Forwards:** | **DOB** | **M** | **(s)** | **G** |
| Fatos Bećiraj | 05.05.1988 | 15 | (3) | 5 |
| Ilir Camaj | 24.06.1996 | 4 | (5) | 1 |
| Boris Cmiljanić | 17.03.1996 | 19 | (6) | 7 |
| Stefan Denković (SRB) | 16.06.1991 | 15 | | 6 |
| Igor Ivanović | 09.09.1990 | 15 | (1) | 2 |
| Predrag Kašćelan | 30.06.1990 | 4 | (1) | |
| Bojan Pavićević | 02.07.2004 | | (2) | |
| Danilo Pešukić | 20.09.2000 | 18 | (16) | 2 |
| Oliver Šarkić | 23.07.1997 | 16 | (1) | 2 |

## Fudbalski klub Iskra Danilovgrad

| | |
|---|---|
| **Founded**: | 1919 |
| **Stadium**: | Stadion „Braće Velašević", Danilovgrad (2,000) |
| **Trainer**: | Milivoje Novović — 29.02.1984 |
| [05.09.2022] | Aleksandar Nedović — 05.09.1978 |
| [10.04.2023] | Mladen Lambulić (SRB) — 09.07.1972 |

| Goalkeepers: | DOB | M | (s) | G |
|---|---|---|---|---|
| Marko Kordić | 22.02.1995 | 35 | | |
| Vojislav Radusinović | 13.02.1998 | 1 | | |
| **Defenders:** | **DOB** | **M** | **(s)** | **G** |
| Stefan Knežević | 07.05.1997 | 2 | (3) | |
| Nikola Kumburović | 13.11.1999 | 15 | (1) | |
| Filip Mitrović | 17.11.1993 | 20 | (5) | |
| Ognjen Obradović | 15.03.2000 | 28 | (3) | 4 |
| Andrej Pupović | 09.06.2001 | 13 | (5) | |
| Danilo Rađen (USA) | 21.06.1994 | 12 | (1) | 2 |
| Nemanja Raspopović | | | (1) | |
| Đorđe Šaletić | 06.01.2002 | 32 | | 1 |
| Aleksa Tomašević | 30.11.2002 | | (1) | |
| Petar Vukčević | 02.03.2001 | 12 | (2) | |
| Nikola Vukotić | 09.01.2003 | 19 | (4) | |
| **Midfielders:** | **DOB** | **M** | **(s)** | **G** |
| Vladimir Boljević | 17.01.1988 | 27 | (7) | 3 |
| Savo Gazivoda | 18.07.1994 | 1 | (13) | 1 |
| Branislav Janković | 08.02.1992 | 12 | (2) | |
| Miloš Kalezić | 09.08.1993 | 16 | | 2 |
| Damir Kojašević | 03.06.1987 | 12 | (4) | 2 |
| Danilo Marković | 15.07.1998 | 11 | (2) | |
| Ivan Marković (SRB) | 20.06.1994 | 6 | (9) | 1 |
| Halil Muharemović | 06.11.1997 | 21 | (7) | 4 |
| Bogdan Obradović | 02.05.2002 | 2 | (21) | |
| Pavle Pavićević | 04.10.2002 | | (5) | |
| Petar Pavlićević | 10.05.2000 | 9 | (13) | 1 |
| Filip Perović | 18.07.2006 | | | |
| Žarko Popović | 11.10.1999 | 30 | (3) | 5 |
| Andrija Rajović (DEN) | 07.06.2001 | 2 | (5) | |
| Vladislav Rogošić | 21.09.1994 | | (5) | |
| Arihiro Sentoku (JPN) | 09.12.1998 | 9 | (6) | |
| Matija Uskoković | 18.04.2004 | | (1) | |
| **Forwards:** | **DOB** | **M** | **(s)** | **G** |
| Mario Gjolaj | 06.04.2002 | 10 | (8) | 1 |
| Andrija Kolundzić | 23.09.2002 | 6 | (8) | 1 |
| Darko Nikač | 15.09.1990 | 28 | (5) | 1 |
| Mihailo Perović | 23.01.1997 | 5 | (1) | 2 |

## Fudbalski klub Jedinstvo Bijelo Polje

| | Founded: | 1922 | | |
| --- | --- | --- | --- | --- |
| | Stadium: | Gradski stadion, Bijelo Polje (5,000) | | |
| | Trainer: | Vuko Bogavac | | 23.02.1971 |

| Goalkeepers: | DOB | M | (s) | G |
| --- | --- | --- | --- | --- |
| Sergej Joksimović | 16.08.2002 | 35 | | |
| Filip Rosandić | 27.03.1997 | 1 | | |
| **Defenders:** | **DOB** | **M** | **(s)** | **G** |
| Ermin Alić | 23.02.1992 | 11 | (2) | |
| Uroš Blagojević (SRB) | 21.03.2002 | 1 | (1) | |
| Sead Dacić | 10.11.1997 | 29 | (1) | 3 |
| Momčilo Dulović | 25.05.1992 | 28 | (2) | 1 |
| Mladen Kovačević (SRB) | 23.09.2002 | 4 | (12) | |
| Radule Krulanović | 30.06.1999 | 17 | (9) | |
| Amir Muzurović | 17.10.2001 | 7 | (2) | 2 |
| Srđan Šćepanović | 20.10.1994 | 17 | (2) | 1 |
| Lazar Šekularac | 11.10.2006 | 2 | (3) | |
| **Midfielders:** | **DOB** | **M** | **(s)** | **G** |
| Haris Banda | 14.05.1993 | 29 | | 1 |

| | DOB | M | (s) | G |
| --- | --- | --- | --- | --- |
| Marko Bugarin | 16.08.1999 | 9 | (5) | |
| Djordjije Cvijović | 01.01.2000 | 27 | (5) | |
| Nikola Cvijović | 13.12.1998 | 2 | (6) | |
| Luka Đorđević (SRB) | 05.05.2001 | 27 | (3) | 3 |
| Orhan Hajrović | 16.05.1996 | 25 | (6) | 4 |
| Mirza Idrizović | 10.12.1997 | 27 | (2) | 4 |
| Danis Kolić | | 1 | (17) | 1 |
| Bojan Vlaović | 06.02.2000 | 23 | (3) | 1 |
| **Forwards:** | **DOB** | **M** | **(s)** | **G** |
| Bojan Bojić (SRB) | 03.03.2000 | 11 | (15) | 1 |
| Žarko Korać | 11.06.1987 | 26 | (3) | 13 |
| Eniks Kriještorac | 17.01.1999 | 2 | (4) | |
| Alija Krnić | 02.01.1998 | 24 | (4) | 4 |
| Aleksa Mrđa (BIH) | 15.08.1999 | 10 | (20) | 3 |
| Aldin Mušović | 10.11.2002 | 1 | (18) | 1 |

## Fudbalski klub Jezero Plav

| | Founded: | 1934 | | |
| --- | --- | --- | --- | --- |
| | Stadium: | Stadion pod Racinom, Plav (2,500) | | |
| | Trainer: | Rade Petrović-Njegoš | | 21.09.1982 |

| Goalkeepers: | DOB | M | (s) | G |
| --- | --- | --- | --- | --- |
| Igor Asanović | 20.04.1992 | 21 | | |
| Stefan Kastratović | 04.01.1994 | 15 | | |
| **Defenders:** | **DOB** | **M** | **(s)** | **G** |
| Radoš Dedić | 17.05.1993 | 23 | (4) | 1 |
| Milun Joković | 24.02.2003 | | (3) | |
| Nikola Jovićević | 04.01.1996 | 20 | (3) | |
| Jovan Pajović | 28.08.1996 | 32 | (1) | 5 |
| Ilija Radunović | 01.08.1993 | 25 | (2) | |
| Matija Stijepović | 30.12.1999 | 25 | (4) | |
| Petar Vuković | 27.02.2002 | 13 | (1) | |
| **Midfielders:** | **DOB** | **M** | **(s)** | **G** |
| Aldin Adžović | 18.04.1994 | 19 | | 2 |
| Srđan Bošković | 24.12.1996 | 16 | (8) | 1 |
| Mohamed Cherif (GER) | 08.05.2000 | | (4) | |
| Amel Đešević | | | (3) | |
| Kōhei Katō (JPN) | 14.06.1989 | 15 | | |
| Damir Kojašević | 03.06.1987 | 11 | (1) | 1 |

| | DOB | M | (s) | G |
| --- | --- | --- | --- | --- |
| Davor Kontić | 30.10.1999 | 27 | (2) | 1 |
| Ivan Marković (SRB) | 20.06.1994 | 3 | (5) | |
| Andrew Marveggio (AUS) | 22.04.1992 | 7 | (7) | |
| Vojin Pavlović | 09.11.1993 | 34 | | 7 |
| Milisav Perošević | 05.04.2002 | | (6) | |
| Saša Radenović | 26.04.1991 | | (10) | |
| Edis Redžepagić | 27.07.1997 | 8 | (7) | 3 |
| Naoaki Senaga (JPN) | 19.07.1998 | 10 | (9) | |
| Marko Šimun | 16.06.2001 | 2 | (5) | |
| Idriz Toskić | 12.10.1995 | | (2) | |
| **Forwards:** | **DOB** | **M** | **(s)** | **G** |
| Armin Bošnjak | 20.04.1994 | 30 | (5) | 6 |
| Balša Ćetković | 20.12.2003 | 5 | (10) | |
| Anil Julević | 01.11.2002 | | (2) | |
| Takeru Komiya (JPN) | 14.08.2001 | 1 | (5) | |
| Alden Škrijelj | 18.10.2000 | 7 | (11) | |
| Balša Tošković | 01.01.2003 | 25 | (10) | 7 |
| Marko Vuković | 20.03.1996 | 2 | (7) | |

## Fudbalski klub Mornar Bar

| | Founded: | 1923 | | |
| --- | --- | --- | --- | --- |
| | Stadium: | Stadion Topolica, Bar (2,500) | | |
| | Trainer: | Andrija Delibašić | | 24.04.1981 |
| [02.05.2023] | | Zoran Đurašković (SRB) | | 07.07.1975 |

| Goalkeepers: | DOB | M | (s) | G |
| --- | --- | --- | --- | --- |
| Stefan Popović | 11.01.1993 | 29 | | |
| Stojan Vukčević | 03.09.2000 | 7 | (1) | |
| **Defenders:** | **DOB** | **M** | **(s)** | **G** |
| Jovan Baošić | 07.07.1995 | 22 | (2) | 1 |
| Matija Božanović | 13.04.1994 | 13 | (1) | |
| Velimir Ljutica | 01.11.2005 | 20 | (3) | 1 |
| Lukas Rošić (CRO) | 26.09.1997 | 4 | (2) | |
| Siniša Stevanović (SRB) | 12.01.1989 | 30 | | |
| Balša Vukotić | 27.07.2004 | 20 | (2) | 3 |
| **Midfielders:** | **DOB** | **M** | **(s)** | **G** |
| Andrej Cvijović | 11.12.2001 | 7 | (14) | |
| Marko Ćetković | 10.07.1986 | 26 | (6) | 6 |
| Savo Gazivoda | 18.07.1994 | 1 | (6) | |
| Enes Habibović | 28.06.2003 | 1 | (1) | |
| Anđelko Jovanović | 18.11.1999 | 5 | (8) | 1 |
| Demir Kajević | 20.04.1989 | 24 | (4) | 1 |
| Andrija Kaluđerović | 29.10.1993 | 30 | (2) | |
| Lazar Lambulić | 12.03.2000 | 18 | (14) | |

| | DOB | M | (s) | G |
| --- | --- | --- | --- | --- |
| Blagota Marković | 09.01.2002 | 4 | (1) | |
| Danijel Nikolić | 24.02.2004 | 1 | (1) | |
| Iori Okamoto (JPN) | 27.12.1998 | | (1) | |
| Petar Sekulović | 14.08.1998 | 13 | (6) | 1 |
| Ermin Seratlić | 21.09.1990 | 5 | (13) | |
| Demir Škrijelj | 10.07.1997 | 8 | (13) | |
| Milan Smiljanić (SRB) | 19.11.1986 | 17 | (1) | |
| **Forwards:** | **DOB** | **M** | **(s)** | **G** |
| Fatos Bećiraj | 05.05.1988 | 12 | (4) | 2 |
| Petar Grbić | 07.08.1988 | 13 | (4) | 1 |
| Boško Guzina | 30.04.1996 | 4 | (5) | 1 |
| Benjamin Kacić | 28.06.1991 | | (5) | |
| Edin Karamanaga | 06.02.2004 | | (5) | |
| Aleksa Maraš | 09.10.2001 | 4 | (5) | 1 |
| Rodney Michael (SLE) | 10.08.1999 | 10 | (2) | |
| Igor Poček | 23.12.1994 | 7 | (8) | |
| Milivoje Raičević | 21.07.1993 | 16 | (7) | 4 |
| Aleksandar Vujačić | 19.03.1990 | 25 | (4) | 5 |

## Omladinski fudbalski klub Petrovac

**Founded**: 1969
**Stadium**: Stadion "Mitar Mićo Goliš", Petrovac (1,630)
**Trainer**: Mladen Lambulić (SRB)   09.07.1972
[09.03.2023]   Dušan Ivanović

| Goalkeepers: | DOB | M | (s) | G |
|---|---|---|---|---|
| Milan Jelovac | 06.08.1993 | 28 | | |
| Danilo Radošević | 10.12.2002 | 8 | | |
| **Defenders:** | **DOB** | **M** | **(s)** | **G** |
| Danilo Dragićević | 31.08.2004 | 2 | (1) | |
| Filip Femić | 25.02.2003 | | (3) | 1 |
| Marko Franeta | | 2 | | |
| Luka Malešević | 01.08.1998 | 16 | | |
| Vuk Matejić | | | (1) | |
| Zoran Mikijelj | 13.12.1991 | 20 | (2) | 1 |
| Aleksandar Milić | 24.08.1998 | 15 | | |
| Vasilije Radenović | 10.05.1994 | 28 | (2) | 2 |
| Stefan Radinović | 09.12.1999 | 16 | (9) | |
| Mihailo Vojvodić | 20.09.2003 | 5 | (11) | |
| Aleksa Vujović | 23.05.2005 | 2 | (1) | |
| Igor Zonjić | 16.10.1991 | 7 | (2) | 1 |
| **Midfielders:** | **DOB** | **M** | **(s)** | **G** |
| Aldin Adžović | 18.04.1994 | 11 | (5) | 2 |
| Dejan Boljević | 30.05.1990 | 30 | (4) | 3 |
| Balša Boričić | 07.01.1997 | 10 | (13) | 1 |
| Miloš Brnović | 26.04.2000 | 14 | (1) | 1 |
| *Caíque* Augusto Correia Chagas (BRA) | 26.04.1994 | 29 | | 2 |
| Nemanja Carević | 08.04.2004 | 8 | (18) | 1 |
| Vukas Dragović | 12.12.2005 | | (2) | |
| Marko Marković | 05.09.1987 | 10 | (6) | |
| Vuko Vicković | 09.02.2004 | 1 | (3) | |
| Jovan Vujović (BIH) | 20.01.1996 | 13 | (7) | |
| Boris Žujović | | | (1) | |
| **Forwards:** | **DOB** | **M** | **(s)** | **G** |
| Slobodan Babić (SRB) | 04.03.2000 | 15 | (19) | 5 |
| Balša Dubljević | 02.12.2001 | 18 | (14) | 1 |
| Rodrigo Faust (ARG) | 14.09.1995 | 21 | (5) | 8 |
| Mendy Mamadou (SEN) | 04.10.1998 | 30 | (2) | 10 |
| Dejan Perović | 19.08.2002 | 22 | (11) | 4 |
| Nikola Zvrko | 07.03.1995 | 15 | (19) | 3 |

## Fudbalski klub Rudar Pljevlja

**Founded**: 1920
**Stadium**: Stadion pod Golubinjom, Pljevlja (5,140)
**Trainer**: Srđan Nikić   28.05.1978
[21.09.2022]   Dragan Aničić (SRB)   04.11.1970

| Goalkeepers: | DOB | M | (s) | G |
|---|---|---|---|---|
| Lazar Baltić | 27.03.2002 | 1 | (1) | |
| Dušan Mrdak | 27.07.2004 | 1 | (1) | |
| Azir Muminović (BIH) | 18.04.1997 | 34 | | |
| **Defenders:** | **DOB** | **M** | **(s)** | **G** |
| Miloš Bakrač | 25.02.1992 | 31 | | |
| Luka Boričić | 18.05.2002 | 28 | (3) | 2 |
| Stefan Janjić (BIH) | 11.02.1996 | 11 | (1) | 1 |
| Nemanja Kartal | 17.07.1994 | 11 | (1) | |
| Ljubomir Pejović | 26.05.2003 | 30 | (1) | 1 |
| Stefan Radojičić (SRB) | 30.05.2001 | 12 | (3) | |
| Jovan Vujisić | 09.10.2003 | 3 | (1) | |
| **Midfielders:** | **DOB** | **M** | **(s)** | **G** |
| Uroš Bulatović | 07.12.2004 | 1 | (3) | |
| Marko Burzanović | 13.01.1998 | 1 | (2) | |
| Arsenije Čepić | | 1 | (5) | |
| Aleksa Golubović | 19.11.2002 | 23 | (8) | 1 |
| Hiroki Harada (JPN) | 23.05.1998 | 3 | (14) | |
| Velizar Janketić | 15.11.1996 | 14 | (2) | 7 |
| Duje Javorčić (CRO) | 25.11.1999 | 7 | (9) | |
| Ognjen Kasalica | 16.10.2002 | 1 | (11) | |
| Veljko Krstonijević | 30.12.2001 | | (1) | |
| Ognjen Peličić | 05.02.1999 | 24 | (3) | |
| Matija Rovčanin | | | (1) | |
| Irfan Šahman | 05.10.1993 | 34 | | 1 |
| Miloš Zečević | 28.01.1999 | 7 | (6) | 1 |
| Dušan Zivković (SRB) | 31.07.1996 | 18 | | 2 |
| **Forwards:** | **DOB** | **M** | **(s)** | **G** |
| Ivan Bojović | 20.02.2001 | 23 | (3) | 4 |
| Kristijan Ernec | 19.01.2003 | | (1) | |
| Ognjen Gašević | 02.04.2002 | 33 | | 2 |
| Stefan Golubović | 02.09.2005 | 3 | (12) | 1 |
| Ljubomir Kovačević | 23.02.2000 | 2 | (8) | 1 |
| Stefan Nikolić | 16.04.1990 | 10 | (5) | 3 |
| Danin Talović | 08.03.1995 | 20 | (3) | 5 |
| Dejan Tumbas (SRB) | 05.08.1999 | 9 | (5) | 4 |

## Fudbalski klub Sutjeska Nikšić

**Founded**: 1927
**Stadium**: Stadion kraj Bistrice, Nikšić (5,214)
**Trainer**: Milija Savović   08.02.1979
[12.08.2022]   Nenad Brnović   18.01.1980

| Goalkeepers: | DOB | M | (s) | G |
|---|---|---|---|---|
| Vladan Giljen | 12.07.1989 | 31 | | |
| Suad Ličina | 08.02.1995 | 5 | (3) | |
| **Defenders:** | **DOB** | **M** | **(s)** | **G** |
| Anto Babić | 25.01.2000 | 35 | | 2 |
| Amir Bilali (ALB) | 15.05.1994 | 12 | (1) | 1 |
| Miloš Drinčić | 14.02.1999 | 19 | | |
| Ognjen Đinović | 12.09.2003 | 2 | (11) | |
| Dragan Grivić | 12.02.1996 | 29 | (1) | 8 |
| Adrijan Rudović | 10.06.1995 | 2 | (2) | |
| Aleksandar Vlahović | 10.03.2000 | 5 | (3) | |
| Marko Vučić | 30.12.1996 | 16 | (6) | 3 |
| **Midfielders:** | **DOB** | **M** | **(s)** | **G** |
| Nikola Đurković | 15.04.2003 | | (4) | |
| Novica Eraković | 12.11.1999 | 32 | (1) | 5 |
| Miloš Kalezić | 09.08.1993 | 1 | (11) | |
| Srdjan Krstović | 05.08.2000 | 33 | | 3 |
| Marko Matanović | 17.07.2000 | 27 | (8) | 3 |
| Jovan Nikolić | 21.07.1991 | 4 | (9) | |
| Igor Pajović | 01.06.2002 | 5 | (17) | |
| Wajdi Sahli (TUN) | 17.04.1997 | 13 | (19) | 6 |
| Nikola Stijepović | 02.11.1993 | 29 | (4) | |
| Ilija Tučević | 18.10.1995 | 11 | (12) | |
| Dušan Zivković (SRB) | 31.07.1996 | 8 | (3) | 1 |
| Lazar Žižić | 21.08.2003 | 1 | (7) | 1 |
| **Forwards:** | **DOB** | **M** | **(s)** | **G** |
| Zakaria El Mabruk Al Harish (LBY) | 23.10.1998 | 1 | | |
| Petar Aničić | 12.07.2004 | | (1) | |
| Tyrone Conraad (NED) | 07.04.1997 | 28 | (5) | 26 |
| Filip Knežević (SRB) | 08.11.1991 | 7 | (2) | 2 |
| Božo Marković | 26.10.1989 | 1 | (12) | |
| Fahd Saad Mohamed (LBY) | 10.06.2004 | | (8) | 1 |
| Yulian Nenov (BUL) | 17.11.1994 | | (1) | |
| Vuk Striković | 10.06.2002 | 17 | (8) | 9 |
| Dušan Vuković | 06.08.2002 | 22 | (11) | 4 |

| | | | | | | | | | |
|---|---|---|---|---|---|---|---|---|---|
| 1. | OFK Mladost DG Podgorica[1] (*Promoted*) | 32 | 16 | 6 | 10 | 38 | - | 38 | 53 |
| 2. | FK Kom Zlatica (*Promotion Play-offs*) | 32 | 14 | 7 | 11 | 39 | - | 34 | 49 |
| 3. | FK Berane[1] (*Promotion Play-offs*) | 32 | 14 | 7 | 11 | 30 | - | 24 | 48 |
| 4. | FK Bokelj Kotor | 32 | 12 | 11 | 9 | 34 | - | 27 | 47 |
| 5. | FK Podgorica | 32 | 11 | 11 | 10 | 36 | - | 33 | 44 |
| 6. | OFK Grbalj Radanovići | 32 | 10 | 9 | 13 | 26 | - | 29 | 39 |
| 7. | FK Otrant-Olympic Ulcinj | 32 | 9 | 11 | 12 | 32 | - | 38 | 38 |
| 8. | FK Igalo | 32 | 9 | 11 | 12 | 33 | - | 34 | 38 |
| 9. | FK Zeta Golubovci (*Relegated*) | 32 | 9 | 7 | 16 | 30 | - | 41 | 34 |
| 10. | OFK Nikšić (*Relegated*) | (*withdrew*) | | | | | | | |

Please note: OFK Nikšić withdrew from the league due to the financial reasons.
[1] *1 point deducted.*

## NATIONAL TEAM

### INTERNATIONAL MATCHES
### (16.07.2022 – 15.07.2023)

| | | | | |
|---|---|---|---|---|
| 23.09.2022 | Zenica | *Bosnia and Herzegovina - Montenegro* | *1-0(1-0)* | (UNL) |
| 26.09.2022 | Podgorica | *Montenegro - Finland* | *0-2(0-0)* | (UNL) |
| 17.11.2022 | Podgorica | *Montenegro - Slovakia* | *2-2(0-1)* | (F) |
| 20.11.2022 | Ljubljana | *Slovenia - Montenegro* | *1-0(1-0)* | (F) |
| 24.03.2023 | Razgrad | *Bulgaria - Montenegro* | *0-1(0-0)* | (ECQ) |
| 27.03.2023 | Podgorica | *Montenegro - Serbia* | *0-2(0-0)* | (ECQ) |
| 17.06.2023 | Podgorica | *Montenegro - Hungary* | *0-0* | (ECQ) |
| 20.06.2023 | Podgorica | *Montenegro - Czech Republic* | *1-4(0-1)* | (F) |

**23.09.2022    BOSNIA AND HERZEGOVINA - MONTENEGRO    1-0(1-0)    3rd UEFA Nations League B, Group 3**
Stadion Bilino Polje, Zenica; Referee: Szymon Marciniak (Poland); Attendance: 12,050
MNE: Milan Mijatović, Marko Vešović, Igor Vujačić, Žarko Tomašević, Risto Radunović, Aleksandar Šćekić (70.Sead Hakšabanović), Marko Janković (81.Driton Camaj), Vukan Savićević (46.46.Nikola Vukčević), Adam Marušić, Milutin Osmajić (46.Stefan Mugoša), Stevan Jovetić (Cap) (70.Uroš Đurđević). Trainer: Miodrag Radulović.

**26.09.2022    MONTENEGRO - FINLAND    0-2(0-0)    3rd UEFA Nations League B, Group 3**
Stadion Goricom, Podgorica; Referee: François Letexier (France); Attendance: 2,522
MNE: Milan Mijatović, Marko Vešović, Igor Vujačić, Žarko Tomašević [*sent off 17*], Risto Radunović (25.Saša Balić), Vladimir Jovović (63.Marko Vukčević), Nikola Vukčević, Marko Janković, Sead Hakšabanović (32.Driton Camaj), Stevan Jovetić (Cap) (33.Aleksandar Šćekić), Stefan Mugoša (62.Uroš Đurđević). Trainer: Miodrag Radulović.

**17.11.2022    MONTENEGRO - SLOVAKIA    2-2(0-1)    Friendly International**
Stadion pod Goricom, Podgorica; Referee: Irfan Peljto (Bosnia and Herzegovina); Attendance: 1,109
MNE: Lazar Carević, Marko Vešović (58.Dušan Bakić), Nikola Šipčić, Stefan Savić (Cap), Risto Radunović, Marko Janković (70.Vukan Savićević), Stefan Lončar (70.Nikola Vukčević), Adam Marušić, Vladimir Jovović (46.Driton Camaj), Nikola Krstović (90+4.Žarko Tomašević), Stefan Mugoša (46.Novica Eraković). Trainer: Miodrag Radulović.
**Goals:** Stefan Savić (76, 90+7 penalty).

**20.11.2022    SLOVENIA - MONTENEGRO    1-0(1-0)    Friendly International**
Stadion Stožice, Ljubljana; Referee: Christopher Jäger (Austria); Attendance: 11,165
MNE: Matija Šarkić, Adam Marušić (46.Dušan Bakić), Stefan Savić (Cap), Žarko Tomašević, Andrija Vukčević, Novica Eraković (59.Aleksandar Šćekić), Stefan Lončar (59.Nikola Vukčević), Vukan Savićević (77.Marko Tuci), Vladimir Jovović (90+3.Miloš Milović), Nikola Krstović, Stefan Mugoša (67.Risto Radunović). Trainer: Miodrag Radulović.

**24.03.2023    BULGARIA - MONTENEGRO    0-1(0-0)    17th EC. Qualifiers**
Huvepharma Arena, Razgrad; Referee: Əliyar Ağayev (Azerbaijan); Attendance: 21,125
MNE: Milan Mijatović, Marko Vešović, Igor Vujačić, Stefan Savić (Cap), Risto Radunović, Aleksandar Šćekić, Adam Marušić (83.Stefan Mugoša), Marko Bakić (46.Stevan Jovetić), Vukan Savićević, Sead Hakšabanović (46.Vladimir Jovović; 79.Stefan Lončar), Nikola Krstović (71.Milutin Osmajić). Trainer: Miodrag Radulović.
**Goal:** Nikola Krstović (70).

**27.03.2023    MONTENEGRO - SERBIA    0-2(0-0)    17th EC. Qualifiers**
Stadion pod Goricom, Podgorica; Referee: Clément Turpin (France); Attendance: 9,831
MNE: Milan Mijatović, Igor Vujačić, Stefan Savić (Cap), Žarko Tomašević (41.Nikola Šipčić), Marko Vešović, Vukan Savićević (70.Vladimir Jovović), Sead Hakšabanović (77.Driton Camaj), Aleksandar Šćekić (76.Stefan Lončar), Adam Marušić, Stevan Jovetić (Cap) (71.Milutin Osmajić), Nikola Krstović. Trainer: Miodrag Radulović.

**17.06.2023    MONTENEGRO - HUNGARY    0-0    17th EC. Qualifiers**
Stadion pod Goricom, Podgorica; Referee: Jesús Gil Manzano (Spain); Attendance: 6,761
MNE: Milan Mijatović, Igor Vujačić, Stefan Savić, Žarko Tomašević, Marko Vešović (72.Marko Vukčević), Marko Janković, Vukan Savićević (82.Stefan Lončar), Aleksandar Šćekić (61.Miloš Raičković), Andrija Vukčević, Nikola Krstović (72.Milutin Osmajić), Stevan Jovetić (Cap) (82.Sead Hakšabanović). Trainer: Miodrag Radulović.

**20.06.2023** **MONTENEGRO - CZECH REPUBLIC** **1-4(0-1)** Friendly International

Stadion pod Goricom, Podgorica; Referee: Matthew De Gabriele (Malta); Attendance: 1,792

**MNE:** Matija Šarkić, Žarko Tomašević, Miloš Milović (46.Vladan Bubanja), Stefan Savić (Cap), Risto Radunović, Marko Vukčević, Marko Janković (46.Stefan Lončar), Marko Bakić (59.Driton Camaj), Vukan Savićević (46.Andrija Radulović), Milutin Osmajić (77.Dušan Bakić), Stefan Mugoša (58.Nikola Krstović). Trainer: Miodrag Radulović.

**Goal:** Driton Camaj (66).

## NATIONAL TEAM PLAYERS
### (16.07.2022 – 15.07.2023)

| Name | DOB | Caps | Goals | Club | |
|---|---|---|---|---|---|
| **Goalkeepers** | | | | | |
| Lazar CAREVIĆ | 16.03.1999 | 2 | 0 | 2022: | FK Vojvodina Novi Sad (SRB) |
| Milan MIJATOVIĆ | 26.07.1987 | 31 | 0 | 2022/2023: | Al Adalah FC Al Hulaylah (KSA) |
| Matija ŠARKIĆ | 23.07.1997 | 7 | 0 | 2022: | Wolverhampton Wanderers FC (ENG) |
| | | | | 25.01.2023-> | Stoke City FC (ENG) |
| **Defenders** | | | | | |
| Saša BALIĆ | 29.01.1990 | 14 | 0 | 2022: | Korona Kielce (POL) |
| Adam MARUŠIĆ | 17.10.1992 | 54 | 3 | 2022/2023: | SS Lazio Roma (ITA) |
| Miloš MILOVIĆ | 22.12.1995 | 3 | 0 | 2022: | FK Voždovac Beograd (SRB) |
| | | | | 28.01.2023-> | FK Navbahor Namangan (UZB) |
| Risto RADUNOVIĆ | 04.05.1992 | 29 | 1 | 2022/2023: | SC FCSB Bucureşti (ROU) |
| Stefan SAVIĆ | 08.01.1991 | 68 | 7 | 2022/2023: | Club Atlético de Madrid (ESP) |
| Nikola ŠIPČIĆ | 17.05.1995 | 6 | 0 | 2022/2023: | CD Tenerife (ESP) |
| Žarko TOMAŠEVIĆ | 22.02.1990 | 61 | 5 | 2022: | FC Tobol Kostanay (KAZ) |
| | | | | 15.01.2023-> | Astana FC (KAZ) |
| Igor VUJAČIĆ | 08.08.1994 | 28 | 0 | 2022/2023: | FK Partizan Beograd (SRB) |
| Andrija VUKČEVIĆ | 11.10.1996 | 4 | 0 | 2022/2023: | HNK Rijeka (CRO) |
| **Midfielders** | | | | | |
| Marko BAKIĆ | 01.11.1993 | 23 | 0 | 2023: | OFI Heraklion (GRE) |
| Vladan BUBANJA | 21.02.1999 | 1 | 0 | 2023: | NK Lokomotiva Zagreb (CRO) |
| Driton CAMAJ | 07.03.1997 | 6 | 1 | 2022/2023: | Kisvárda FC (HUN) |
| Novica ERAKOVIĆ | 12.11.1999 | 4 | 0 | 2022: | FK Sutjeska Nikšić |
| Sead HAKŠABANOVIĆ | 04.05.1999 | 33 | 1 | 2022/2023: | Celtic FC Glasgow (SCO) |
| Marko JANKOVIĆ | 09.07.1995 | 41 | 1 | 2022/2023: | Qarabağ FK Bakı (AZE) |
| Vladimir JOVOVIĆ | 26.10.1994 | 51 | 0 | 2022/2023: | FK Jablonec (CZE) |
| Stefan LONČAR | 19.02.1996 | 8 | 0 | 2022: | FK Novi Pazar (SRB) |
| | | | | 26.01.2023-> | Debreceni VSC (HUN) |
| Milutin OSMAJIĆ | 25.07.1999 | 17 | 1 | 2022/2023: | FC de Vizela (POR) |
| Andrija RADULOVIĆ | 03.07.2002 | 1 | 0 | 2023: | FK Radnik Surdulica (SRB) |
| Miloš RAIČKOVIĆ | 02.12.1993 | 15 | 0 | 2023: | FC Aktobe (KAZ) |
| Vukan SAVIĆEVIĆ | 29.01.1994 | 18 | 0 | 2022/2023: | Giresunspor Kulübü (TUR) |
| Aleksandar ŠĆEKIĆ | 12.12.1991 | 39 | 0 | 2022: | Dibba Al Fujairah FC (UAE) |
| | | | | 05.01.2023-> | Hapoel Haifa FC (ISR) |
| Marko TUCI | 04.12.1998 | 1 | 0 | 2022: | FK Dečić Tuzi |
| Marko VEŠOVIĆ | 28.08.1991 | 48 | 2 | 2022/2023: | Qarabağ FK Bakı (AZE) |
| Marko VUKČEVIĆ | 07.06.1993 | 16 | 1 | 2022/2023: | FC UT Arad (ROU) |
| Nikola VUKČEVIĆ | 13.12.1991 | 51 | 1 | 2022: | Al Ahli SC Doha (QAT) |
| **Forwards** | | | | | |
| Dušan BAKIĆ | 23.02.1999 | 3 | 0 | 2022/2023: | FC Dinamo Minsk (BLR) |
| Uroš ĐURĐEVIĆ | 02.03.1994 | 10 | 0 | 2022: | Real Sporting de Gijón (ESP) |
| Stevan JOVETIĆ | 02.11.1989 | 68 | 31 | 2022/2023: | Hertha BSC Berlin (GER) |
| Nikola KRSTOVIĆ | 05.04.2000 | 9 | 1 | 2022/2023: | FK DAC Dunajská Streda (SVK) |
| Stefan MUGOŠA | 23.02.1992 | 49 | 15 | 2022/2023: | Vissel Kobe (JPN) |
| **Trainer** | | | | | |
| Miodrag RADULOVIĆ [from 29.12.2020] | 23.10.1967 | 26 M; 7 W; 7 D; 12 L; 26-34 | | | |

# NETHERLANDS

## The Country:
Nederland (Netherlands)
Capital: Amsterdam
Surface: 41,543 km²
Inhabitants: 17,923,200 [2023]
Time: UTC+1

## The FA:
Koninklijke Nederlandse Voetbalbond
Woudenbergseweg 56-58 Postbus 515 3700, Am Zeist
Tel: +31 343 499 201
Foundation date: 1889
Member of FIFA since: 1904
Member of UEFA since: 1954
Website: www.knvb.nl

## NATIONAL TEAM RECORDS

### RECORDS

| | |
|---|---|
| **First international match:** | 30.04.1905, Antwerpen: Belgium – Netherlands 1-4 |
| **Most international caps:** | Wesley Benjamin Sneijder - 134 caps (2003-2018) |
| **Most international goals:** | Robin van Persie - 50 goals / 102 caps (2005-2017) |

### UEFA EUROPEAN CHAMPIONSHIP

| | |
|---|---|
| 1960 | Did not enter |
| 1964 | Qualifiers |
| 1968 | Qualifiers |
| 1972 | Qualifiers |
| 1976 | Final Tournament (3rd Place) |
| 1980 | Final Tournament (Group Stage) |
| 1984 | Qualifiers |
| **1988** | **Final Tournament (Winners)** |
| 1992 | Final Tournament (Semi-Finals) |
| 1996 | Final Tournament (Quarter-Finals) |
| 2000 | Final Tournament (Semi-Finals) |
| 2004 | Final Tournament (Semi-Finals) |
| 2008 | Final Tournament (Quarter-Finals) |
| 2012 | Final Tournament (Group Stage) |
| 2016 | Qualifiers |
| 2020 | Final Tournament (2nd Round of 16) |

### FIFA WORLD CUP

| | |
|---|---|
| 1930 | Did not enter |
| 1934 | Final Tournament (1st Round) |
| 1938 | Final Tournament (1st Round) |
| 1950 | Did not enter |
| 1954 | Did not enter |
| 1958 | Qualifiers |
| 1962 | Qualifiers |
| 1966 | Qualifiers |
| 1970 | Qualifiers |
| 1974 | Final Tournament (Runners-up) |
| 1978 | Final Tournament (Runners-up) |
| 1982 | Qualifiers |
| 1986 | Qualifiers |
| 1990 | Final Tournament (2nd Round of 16) |
| 1994 | Final Tournament (Quarter-Finals) |
| 1998 | Final Tournament (4th Place) |
| 2002 | Qualifiers |
| 2006 | Final Tournament (2nd Round of 16) |
| 2010 | Final Tournament (Runners-up) |
| 2014 | Final Tournament (3rd Place) |
| 2018 | Qualifiers |
| 2022 | Final Tournament (Quarter-Finals) |

### OLYMPIC TOURNAMENTS

| | |
|---|---|
| 1908 | 3rd Place |
| 1912 | 3rd Place |
| 1920 | 3rd Place |
| 1924 | 4th Place |
| 1928 | 1/8 - Finals |
| 1936 | Did not enter |
| 1948 | 1/8 - Finals |
| 1952 | Qualifiers |
| 1956 | Did not enter |
| 1960 | Qualifiers |
| 1964 | Qualifiers |
| 1968 | Qualifiers |
| 1972 | Qualifiers |
| 1976 | Qualifiers |
| 1980 | Qualifiers |
| 1984 | Qualifiers |
| 1988 | Qualifiers |
| 1992 | Qualifiers |
| 1996 | Qualifiers |
| 2000 | Qualifiers |
| 2004 | Qualifiers |
| 2008 | Quarter-Finals |
| 2012 | Qualifiers |
| 2016 | Qualifiers |
| 2020 | Qualifiers |

### UEFA NATIONS LEAGUE

| | |
|---|---|
| 2018/2019 | League A (Group Stage -> Final Tournament – Runners-up) |
| 2020/2021 | League A (Group Stage) |
| 2022/2023 | League A (Group Stage -> Final Tournament – 4th Place) |

## NETHERLANDIAN CLUB HONOURS IN EUROPEAN CLUB COMPETITIONS:

| European Champion Clubs' Cup (1956-1992) / UEFA Champions League (1993-2023) | | |
|---|---|---|
| AFC Ajax Amsterdam | 4 | 1970/1971, 1971/1972, 1972/1973, 1994/1995 |
| Feyenoord Rotterdam | 1 | 1969/1970 |
| PSV Eindhoven | 1 | 1987/1988 |
| **Fairs Cup (1858-1971) / UEFA Cup (1972-2009) / UEFA Europa League (2010-2023)** | | |
| Feyenoord Rotterdam | 2 | 1973/1974, 2001/2002 |
| PSV Eindhoven | 1 | 1977/1978 |
| AFC Ajax Amsterdam | 1 | 1991/1992 |
| **UEFA Europa Conference League (2021-2023)** | | |
| None | | |
| **UEFA Super Cup (1972-2022)** | | |
| AFC Ajax Amsterdam | 2 | 1973, 1995 |
| ***European Cup Winners' Cup 1961-1999**** | | |
| AFC Ajax Amsterdam | 1 | 1986/1987 |

*defunct competition

# NATIONAL COMPETITIONS
## TABLE OF HONOURS

| | CHAMPIONS* | CUP WINNERS | BEST GOALSCORERS | |
|---|---|---|---|---|
| 1888/1889 | VV Concordia Rotterdam | - | - | |
| 1889/1890 | HFC Haarlem | - | - | |
| 1890/1891 | HVV Den Haag | - | - | |
| 1891/1892 | RAP Amsterdam | - | - | |
| 1892/1893 | HFC Haarlem | - | - | |
| 1893/1894 | RAP Amsterdam | - | - | |
| 1894/1895 | HFC Haarlem | - | - | |
| 1895/1896 | HVV Den Haag | - | - | |
| 1896/1897 | RAP Amsterdam | - | - | |
| 1897/1898 | RAP Amsterdam | - | - | |
| 1898/1899 | RAP Amsterdam | RAP Amsterdam | - | |
| 1899/1900 | HVV Den Haag | Velocitas Breda | - | |
| 1900/1901 | HVV Den Haag | HBS Craeyenhout | - | |
| 1901/1902 | HVV Den Haag | Haarlem | - | |
| 1902/1903 | HVV Den Haag | HVV Den Haag | - | |
| 1903/1904 | HBS Craeyenhout | HFC Haarlem | - | |
| 1904/1905 | HVV Den Haag | VOC Rotterdam | - | |
| 1905/1906 | HBS Craeyenhout | VV Concordia Rotterdam | - | |
| 1906/1907 | HVV Den Haag | VOC Rotterdam | - | |
| 1907/1908 | Quick Den Haag | HBS Craeyenhout 2 | - | |
| 1908/1909 | Sparta Rotterdam | Quick Den Haag 2 | - | |
| 1909/1910 | HVV Den Haag | Quick Den Haag 2 | - | |
| 1910/1911 | Sparta Rotterdam | Quick Den Haag | - | |
| 1911/1912 | Sparta Rotterdam | HFC Haarlem | - | |
| 1912/1913 | Sparta Rotterdam | Koninklijke HFC Haarlem | - | |
| 1913/1914 | HVV Den Haag | Dordrechtsche FC | - | |
| 1914/1915 | Sparta Rotterdam | Koninklijke HFC Haarlem | - | |
| 1915/1916 | Willem II Tilburg | Quick Den Haag | - | |
| 1916/1917 | Go Ahead Eagles Deventer | AFC Ajax Amsterdam | - | |
| 1917/1918 | AFC Ajax Amsterdam | Racing Club Heemstede | - | |
| 1918/1919 | AFC Ajax Amsterdam | *No competition* | - | |
| 1919/1920 | Be Quick 1887 Groningen | CVV Rotterdam | - | |
| 1920/1921 | NAC Breda | Schoten Harlem | - | |
| 1921/1922 | Go Ahead Eagles Deventer | *No competition* | - | |
| 1922/1923 | Racing Club Heemstede | *No competition* | - | |
| 1923/1924 | SC Feijenoord Rotterdam | *No competition* | - | |
| 1924/1925 | HBS Craeyenhout | Zaanlandsche FC | - | |
| 1925/1926 | SC Enschede | LONGA Lichtenvoorde | - | |
| 1926/1927 | Heracles Almelo | VUC Den Haag | - | |
| 1927/1928 | SC Feijenoord Rotterdam | Racing Club Heemstede | - | |
| 1928/1929 | PSV Eindhoven | *No competition* | - | |
| 1929/1930 | Go Ahead Eagles Deventer | SC Feijenoord Rotterdam | - | |
| 1930/1931 | AFC Ajax Amsterdam | *No competition* | - | |
| 1931/1932 | AFC Ajax Amsterdam | DFC | - | |
| 1932/1933 | Go Ahead Eagles Deventer | *No competition* | - | |
| 1933/1934 | AFC Ajax Amsterdam | Velocitas Groningen | - | |
| 1934/1935 | PSV Eindhoven | SC Feijenoord Rotterdam | - | |
| 1935/1936 | SC Feijenoord Rotterdam | Roermond FC | - | |
| 1936/1937 | AFC Ajax Amsterdam | FC Eindhoven | - | |
| 1937/1938 | SC Feijenoord Rotterdam | VSV Velsen | - | |
| 1938/1939 | AFC Ajax Amsterdam | FC Wageningen | - | |
| 1939/1940 | SC Feijenoord Rotterdam | *No competition* | - | |
| 1940/1941 | Heracles Almelo | *No competition* | - | |
| 1941/1942 | ADO Den Haag | *No competition* | - | |
| 1942/1943 | ADO Den Haag | AFC Ajax Amsterdam | - | |
| 1943/1944 | AVV De Volewijckers Amsterdam | Willem II Tilburg | - | |
| 1944/1945 | *No competition* | *No competition* | - | |
| 1945/1946 | HFC Haarlem | *No competition* | - | |
| 1946/1947 | AFC Ajax Amsterdam | *No competition* | - | |
| 1947/1948 | BVV Den Bosch | FC Wageningen | - | |
| 1948/1949 | Schiedamse VV | Quick 1888 Nijmegen | - | |
| 1949/1950 | SV Limburgia Brunssum | PSV Eindhoven | - | |
| 1950/1951 | PSV Eindhoven | *No competition* | - | |
| 1951/1952 | Willem II Tilburg | *No competition* | - | |
| 1952/1953 | Racing Club Heemstede | *No competition* | - | |
| 1953/1954 | FC Eindhoven | *No competition* | - | |
| 1954/1955 | Willem II Tilburg | *No competition* | - | |
| 1955/1956 | Rapid JC Kerkrade | *No competition* | - | |
| 1956/1957 | AFC Ajax Amsterdam | Fortuna '54 Geleen | Coenraad Henrik Dillen (PSV Eindhoven) | 43 |
| 1957/1958 | VV DOS Utrecht | Sparta Rotterdam | Leonard Canjels (NAC Breda) | 32 |
| 1958/1959 | Sparta Rotterdam | VVV | Leonard Canjels (NAC Breda) | 34 |
| 1959/1960 | AFC Ajax Amsterdam | *No competition* | Hendrik Groot (AFC Ajax Amsterdam) | 38 |

| Season | Champion | Cup Winner | Top Scorer | Goals |
|---|---|---|---|---|
| 1960/1961 | SC Feijenoord Rotterdam | AFC Ajax Amsterdam | Hendrik Groot (AFC Ajax Amsterdam) | 41 |
| 1961/1962 | SC Feijenoord Rotterdam | Sparta Rotterdam | Dick Tol (FC Volendam) | 27 |
| 1962/1963 | PSV Eindhoven | Willem II Tilburg | Pierre Kerkhofs (PSV Eindhoven) | 22 |
| 1963/1964 | DWS Amsterdam | Fortuna '54 Geleen | Frans Geurtsen (DWS Amsterdam) | 28 |
| 1964/1965 | SC Feijenoord Rotterdam | SC Feijenoord Rotterdam | Frans Geurtsen (DWS Amsterdam) | 23 |
| 1965/1966 | AFC Ajax Amsterdam | Sparta Rotterdam | Wilhelmus Martinus Leonardus Johannes van der Kuijlen (PSV Eindhoven) Piet Kruiver (SC Feijenoord Rotterdam) | 23 |
| 1966/1967 | AFC Ajax Amsterdam | AFC Ajax Amsterdam | Hendrik Johannes Cruijff (AFC Ajax Amsterdam) | 33 |
| 1967/1968 | AFC Ajax Amsterdam | ADO Den Haag | Ove Kindvall (SWE, SC Feijenoord Rotterdam) | 28 |
| 1968/1969 | SC Feijenoord Rotterdam | SC Feijenoord Rotterdam | Dirk Wouter Johannes van Dijk (FC Twente Enschede) Bengt Ove Kindvall (SWE, SC Feijenoord Rotterdam) | 30 |
| 1969/1970 | AFC Ajax Amsterdam | AFC Ajax Amsterdam | Wilhelmus Martinus Leonardus Johannes van der Kuijlen (PSV Eindhoven) | 26 |
| 1970/1971 | SC Feijenoord Rotterdam | AFC Ajax Amsterdam | Bengt Ove Kindvall (SWE, SC Feijenoord Rotterdam) | 24 |
| 1971/1972 | AFC Ajax Amsterdam | AFC Ajax Amsterdam | Hendrik Johannes Cruijff (AFC Ajax Amsterdam) | 25 |
| 1972/1973 | AFC Ajax Amsterdam | NAC Breda | Franciscus Janssens (NEC Nijmegen) Willy Brokamp (MVV Maastricht) | 18 |
| 1973/1974 | SC Feyenoord Rotterdam | PSV Eindhoven | Wilhelmus Martinus Leonardus Johannes van der Kuijlen (PSV Eindhoven) | 27 |
| 1974/1975 | PSV Eindhoven | FC Den Haag | Geertruida Maria Geels (AFC Ajax Amsterdam) | 30 |
| 1975/1976 | PSV Eindhoven | PSV Eindhoven | Geertruida Maria Geels (AFC Ajax Amsterdam) | 29 |
| 1976/1977 | AFC Ajax Amsterdam | FC Twente Enschede | Geertruida Maria Geels (AFC Ajax Amsterdam) | 34 |
| 1977/1978 | PSV Eindhoven | AZ'67 Alkmaar | Geertruida Maria Geels (AFC Ajax Amsterdam) | 30 |
| 1978/1979 | AFC Ajax Amsterdam | AFC Ajax Amsterdam | Cornelis Kist (AZ'67 Alkmaar) | 34 |
| 1979/1980 | AFC Ajax Amsterdam | SC Feyenoord Rotterdam | Cornelis Kist (AZ'67 Alkmaar) | 27 |
| 1980/1981 | AZ'67 Alkmaar '67 | AZ'67 Alkmaar | Geertruida Maria Geels (Sparta Rotterdam) | 22 |
| 1981/1982 | AFC Ajax Amsterdam | AZ'67 Alkmaar | Willem Cornelis Nicolaas Kieft (AFC Ajax) | 32 |
| 1982/1983 | AFC Ajax Amsterdam | AFC Ajax Amsterdam | Peter Houtman (SC Feyenoord Rotterdam) | 30 |
| 1983/1984 | SC Feyenoord Rotterdam | SC Feyenoord Rotterdam | Marcel van Basten (AFC Ajax Amsterdam) | 28 |
| 1984/1985 | AFC Ajax Amsterdam | FC Utrecht | Marcel van Basten (AFC Ajax Amsterdam) | 22 |
| 1985/1986 | PSV Eindhoven | AFC Ajax Amsterdam | Marcel van Basten (AFC Ajax Amsterdam) | 37 |
| 1986/1987 | PSV Eindhoven | AFC Ajax Amsterdam | Marcel van Basten (AFC Ajax Amsterdam) | 31 |
| 1987/1988 | PSV Eindhoven | PSV Eindhoven | Willem Cornelis Nicolaas Kieft (PSV Eindhoven) | 29 |
| 1988/1989 | PSV Eindhoven | PSV Eindhoven | Romário de Souza Faria (BRA, PSV Eindhoven) | 19 |
| 1989/1990 | AFC Ajax Amsterdam | PSV Eindhoven | Romário de Souza Faria (BRA, PSV Eindhoven) | 23 |
| 1990/1991 | PSV Eindhoven | SC Feyenoord Rotterdam | Romário de Souza Faria (BRA, PSV Eindhoven) Dennis Nicolaas Maria Bergkamp (AFC Ajax) | 25 |
| 1991/1992 | PSV Eindhoven | SC Feyenoord Rotterdam | Dennis Nicolaas Maria Bergkamp (AFC Ajax Amsterdam) | 24 |
| 1992/1993 | SC Feyenoord Rotterdam | AFC Ajax Amsterdam | Dennis Nicolaas Maria Bergkamp (AFC Ajax Amsterdam) | 26 |
| 1993/1994 | AFC Ajax Amsterdam | SC Feyenoord Rotterdam | Jari Olavi Litmanen (FIN, AFC Ajax Amsterdam) | 26 |
| 1994/1995 | AFC Ajax Amsterdam | SC Feyenoord Rotterdam | Ronaldo Luís Nazário de Lima (BRA, PSV Eindhoven) | 30 |
| 1995/1996 | AFC Ajax Amsterdam | PSV Eindhoven | Luc Gilbert Cyrille Nilis (BEL, PSV Eindhoven) | 21 |
| 1996/1997 | PSV Eindhoven | Roda JC Kerkrade | Luc Gilbert Cyrille Nilis (BEL, PSV Eindhoven) | 21 |
| 1997/1998 | AFC Ajax Amsterdam | AFC Ajax Amsterdam | Nikolaos Machlas (GRE, SBV Vitesse Arnhem) | 34 |
| 1998/1999 | SC Feyenoord Rotterdam | AFC Ajax Amsterdam | Rutgerus Johannes Martinus van Nistelrooy (PSV Eindhoven) | 31 |
| 1999/2000 | PSV Eindhoven | Roda JC Kerkrade | Rutgerus Johannes Martinus van Nistelrooy (PSV Eindhoven) | 29 |
| 2000/2001 | PSV Eindhoven | FC Twente Enschede | Mateja Kežman (SRB, PSV Eindhoven) | 24 |
| 2001/2002 | AFC Ajax Amsterdam | AFC Ajax Amsterdam | Petrus Ferdinandus Johannes van Hooijdonk (SC Feyenoord Rotterdam) | 24 |
| 2002/2003 | PSV Eindhoven | FC Utrecht | Mateja Kežman (SRB, PSV Eindhoven) | 35 |
| 2003/2004 | AFC Ajax Amsterdam | FC Utrecht | Mateja Kežman (SRB, PSV Eindhoven) | 31 |
| 2004/2005 | PSV Eindhoven | PSV Eindhoven | Dirk Kuyt (SC Feyenoord Rotterdam) | 29 |
| 2005/2006 | PSV Eindhoven | AFC Ajax Amsterdam | Dirk Jan Klaas Huntelaar (SC Heerenveen/AFC Ajax Amsterdam) | 33 |
| 2006/2007 | PSV Eindhoven | AFC Ajax Amsterdam | Afonso Alves Martins Júnior (BRA, SC Heerenveen) | 34 |
| 2007/2008 | PSV Eindhoven | SC Feyenoord Rotterdam | Dirk Jan Klaas Huntelaar (AFC Ajax Amsterdam) | 33 |
| 2008/2009 | AZ Alkmaar | SC Heerenveen | Mounir El Hamdaoui (MAR, AZ Alkmaar) | 23 |
| 2009/2010 | FC Twente Enschede | AFC Ajax Amsterdam | Luis Alberto Suárez Díaz (URU, AFC Ajax Amsterdam) | 35 |
| 2010/2011 | AFC Ajax Amsterdam | FC Twente Enschede | Björn Vleminckx (BEL, NEC Nijmegen) | 23 |
| 2011/2012 | AFC Ajax Amsterdam | PSV Eindhoven | Bas Dost (SC Heerenveen) | 32 |
| 2012/2013 | AFC Ajax Amsterdam | AZ Alkmaar | Wilfried Guemiand Bony (CIV, SBV Vitesse Arnhem) | 31 |
| 2013/2014 | AFC Ajax Amsterdam | PEC Zwolle | Alfreð Finnbogason (ISL, SC Heerenveen) | 29 |
| 2014/2015 | PSV Eindhoven | FC Groningen | Memphis Depay (PSV Eindhoven) | 22 |
| 2015/2016 | PSV Eindhoven | Feyenoord Rotterdam | Vincent Petrus Anna Sebastiaan Janssen (AZ Alkmaar) | 27 |
| 2016/2017 | Feyenoord Rotterdam | SBV Vitesse Arnhem | Nicolai Mick Jørgensen (DEN, Feyenoord Rotterdam) | 21 |
| 2017/2018 | PSV Eindhoven | Feyenoord Rotterdam | Alireza Jahanbakhsh (IRN, AZ Alkmaar) | 21 |
| 2018/2019 | AFC Ajax Amsterdam | AFC Ajax Amsterdam | Luuk de Jong (PSV Eindhoven) Dušan Tadić (SRB, AFC Ajax Amsterdam) | 28 |
| 2019/2020 | *Championship cancelled* | *Competition cancelled* | - | |
| 2020/2021 | AFC Ajax Amsterdam | AFC Ajax Amsterdam | Georgios Giakoumakis (GRE, VVV-Venlo) | 26 |

| 2021/2022 | AFC Ajax Amsterdam | PSV Eindhoven | Sébastien Romain Teddy Haller (CIV, AFC Ajax Amsterdam) | 21 |
| 2022/2023 | Feyenoord Rotterdam | PSV Eindhoven | Anastasios Douvikas (GRE, FC Utrecht) Xavier Quentin Shay Simons (PSV Eindhoven) | 19 |

*National Champions (1888–1956), Eredivisie (since 1956)

## NATIONAL CHAMPIONSHIP
### Eredivisie 2022/2023
(05.08.2022 – 28.05.2023)

### Results

**Round 1** [05-07.08.2022]
SC Heerenveen - Sparta Rotterdam 0-0
Fortuna Sittard - AFC Ajax 2-3(1-0)
SC Cambuur - Excelsior 0-2(0-2)
PSV Eindhoven - FC Emmen 4-1(3-0)
RKC Waalwijk - FC Utrecht 2-2(2-0)
FC Groningen - FC Volendam 2-2(2-1)
Vitesse - Feyenoord 2-5(1-2)
NEC Nijmegen - FC Twente 0-1(0-0)
AZ Alkmaar - Go Ahead Eagles 2-0(0-0)

**Round 2** [12-14.08.2022]
Excelsior - Vitesse 3-1(2-1)
Go Ahead Eagles - PSV Eindhoven 2-5(1-3)
FC Emmen - RKC Waalwijk 1-1(0-0)
FC Utrecht - SC Cambuur 0-0
Feyenoord - SC Heerenveen 0-0
FC Volendam - NEC Nijmegen 1-4(1-2)
AFC Ajax - FC Groningen 6-1(3-1)
FC Twente - Fortuna Sittard 3-0(2-0)
Sparta Rotterdam - AZ Alkmaar 2-3(1-1)

**Round 3** [20-21.08.2022]
Vitesse - SC Heerenveen 0-4(0-2)
Fortuna Sittard - SC Cambuur 1-4(1-0)
FC Emmen - FC Utrecht 3-2(1-2)
FC Groningen - Go Ahead Eagles 1-0(1-0)
Sparta Rotterdam - AFC Ajax 0-1(0-1)
RKC Waalwijk - Feyenoord 0-1(0-0)
Eindhoven - Volendam 7-1(3-1) [31.08.22]
FC Twente - Excelsior 4-0(2-0) [31.08.22]
AZ Alkmaar - Nijmegen 1-1(0-0) [01.09.22]

**Round 4** [26-28.08.2022]
NEC Nijmegen - FC Groningen 1-1(0-0)
Go Ahead Eagles - Sparta Rotterdam 0-1(0-1)
Vitesse - RKC Waalwijk 2-2(0-1)
Feyenoord - FC Emmen 4-0(0-0)
SC Heerenveen - Fortuna Sittard 2-1(2-0)
FC Utrecht - AFC Ajax 0-2(0-2)
Excelsior - PSV Eindhoven 1-6(0-3)
FC Volendam - FC Twente 1-0(0-0)
SC Cambuur - AZ Alkmaar 0-1(0-0)

**Round 5** [02-04.09.2022]
Fortuna Sittard - FC Utrecht 3-4(0-0)
AFC Ajax - SC Cambuur 4-0(2-0)
FC Twente - PSV Eindhoven 2-1(2-0)
Sparta Rotterdam - FC Volendam 4-0(1-0)
Go Ahead Eagles - Feyenoord 3-4(2-2)
RKC Waalwijk - Excelsior 5-2(1-2)
FC Emmen - AZ Alkmaar 0-3(0-3)
SC Heerenveen - NEC Nijmegen 0-0
FC Groningen - Vitesse 0-1(0-0)

**Round 6** [09-11.09.2022]
FC Volendam - Go Ahead Eagles 2-3(1-1)
NEC Nijmegen - Fortuna Sittard 1-1(0-0)
AFC Ajax - SC Heerenveen 5-0(2-0)
Excelsior - FC Emmen 2-1(0-1)
FC Utrecht - Vitesse 1-0(0-0)
PSV Eindhoven - RKC Waalwijk 1-0(0-0)
SC Cambuur - FC Groningen 0-1(0-0)
AZ Alkmaar - FC Twente 1-1(0-0)
Feyenoord - Sparta Rotterdam 3-0(2-0)

**Round 7** [16-18.09.2022]
FC Utrecht - NEC Nijmegen 0-0
Sparta Rotterdam - FC Groningen 2-1(0-0)
Vitesse - FC Volendam 1-1(0-1)
RKC Waalwijk - SC Cambuur 5-1(1-1)
Fortuna Sittard - Excelsior 1-0(0-0)
Go Ahead Eagles - FC Emmen 2-0(1-0)
PSV Eindhoven - Feyenoord 4-3(2-2)
SC Heerenveen - FC Twente 2-1(2-1)
AZ Alkmaar - AFC Ajax 2-1(2-1)

**Round 8** [01-02.10.2022]
SC Cambuur - PSV Eindhoven 3-0(0-0)
FC Groningen - AZ Alkmaar 1-4(1-2)
AFC Ajax - Go Ahead Eagles 1-1(1-0)
FC Twente - Vitesse 3-0(1-0)
Fortuna Sittard - FC Volendam 2-0(2-0)
Excelsior - FC Utrecht 0-1(0-1)
NEC Nijmegen - Feyenoord 1-1(1-1)
RKC Waalwijk - Sparta Rotterdam 2-2(1-1)
FC Emmen - SC Heerenveen 0-0

**Round 9** [07-09.10.2022]
FC Groningen - RKC Waalwijk 2-3(1-1)
FC Volendam - AFC Ajax 2-4(0-2)
Sparta Rotterdam - FC Emmen 3-1(1-0)
NEC Nijmegen - Excelsior 1-1(0-0)
Go Ahead Eagles - SC Cambuur 0-0
Feyenoord - FC Twente 2-0(1-0)
FC Utrecht - AZ Alkmaar 1-2(0-1)
SC Heerenveen - PSV Eindhoven 0-1(0-0)
Vitesse - Fortuna Sittard 1-2(1-1)

**Round 10** [14-16.10.2022]
FC Emmen - FC Volendam 1-1(0-0)
Fortuna Sittard - RKC Waalwijk 0-0
Go Ahead Eagles - SC Heerenveen 1-1(0-0)
SC Cambuur - Vitesse 0-3(0-1)
Sparta Rotterdam - NEC Nijmegen 2-0(2-0)
FC Twente - FC Groningen 3-0(0-0)
PSV Eindhoven - FC Utrecht 6-1(3-1)
AZ Alkmaar - Feyenoord 1-3(1-1)
AFC Ajax - Excelsior 7-1(3-0)

**Round 11** [22-23.10.2022]
Feyenoord - Fortuna Sittard 1-1(0-1)
RKC Waalwijk - AFC Ajax 1-4(1-1)
Vitesse - FC Emmen 2-1(2-0)
Excelsior - AZ Alkmaar 2-1(2-0)
SC Cambuur - FC Twente 1-0(0-0)
FC Groningen - PSV Eindhoven 4-2(3-1)
NEC Nijmegen - Go Ahead Eagles 3-3(1-2)
FC Utrecht - Sparta Rotterdam 3-1(1-0)
FC Volendam - SC Heerenveen 1-3(1-1)

**Round 12** [29-30.10.2022]
SC Heerenveen - FC Utrecht 1-2(1-1)
Sparta Rotterdam - Fortuna Sittard 3-1(1-1)
Go Ahead Eagles - Excelsior 3-1(2-0)
FC Emmen - FC Groningen 0-0
FC Twente - RKC Waalwijk 3-0(2-0)
PSV Eindhoven - NEC Nijmegen 3-0(1-0)
AZ Alkmaar - FC Volendam 2-1(2-0)
AFC Ajax - Vitesse 2-2(1-1) [09.11.2022]
Feyenoord - SC Cambuur 1-0(1-0) [10.11.22]

**Round 13** [04-06.11.2022]
SC Cambuur - NEC Nijmegen 0-1(0-1)
Vitesse - Sparta Rotterdam 0-4(0-0)
Fortuna Sittard - FC Emmen 1-0(1-0)
Excelsior - SC Heerenveen 0-1(0-0)
FC Utrecht - FC Groningen 2-1(0-1)
FC Twente - Go Ahead Eagles 1-1(1-0)
FC Volendam - Feyenoord 0-2(0-2)
AFC Ajax - PSV Eindhoven 1-2(0-1)
RKC Waalwijk - AZ Alkmaar 3-1(1-1)

**Round 14** [11-13.11.2022]
Sparta Rotterdam - FC Twente 1-1(0-0)
FC Volendam - FC Utrecht 0-4(0-1)
FC Emmen - AFC Ajax 3-3(1-3)
PSV Eindhoven - AZ Alkmaar 0-1(0-1)
NEC Nijmegen - RKC Waalwijk 6-1(1-1)
FC Groningen - Fortuna Sittard 2-3(1-0)
SC Heerenveen - SC Cambuur 2-1(1-1)
Feyenoord - Excelsior 5-1(2-1)
Go Ahead Eagles - Vitesse 2-2(2-0)

**Round 15** [06-08.01.2023]
FC Twente - FC Emmen 2-0(1-0)
RKC Waalwijk - SC Heerenveen 0-0
AZ Alkmaar - Vitesse 1-0(0-0)
Fortuna Sittard - Go Ahead Eagles 0-2(0-2)
PSV Eindhoven - Sparta Rotterdam 0-0
FC Utrecht - Feyenoord 1-1(1-0)
NEC Nijmegen - AFC Ajax 1-1(0-1)
SC Cambuur - FC Volendam 0-3(0-2)
Excelsior - FC Groningen 1-0(0-0)

**Round 16** [14-15.01.2023]
SC Heerenveen - AZ Alkmaar 0-2(0-1)
FC Volendam - RKC Waalwijk 2-1(0-0)
Sparta Rotterdam - Excelsior 1-0(0-0)
AFC Ajax - FC Twente 0-0
Vitesse - NEC Nijmegen 0-0
Fortuna Sittard - PSV Eindhoven 2-2(1-0)
Go Ahead Eagles - FC Utrecht 2-2(1-2)
FC Groningen - Feyenoord 0-3(0-2)
FC Emmen - SC Cambuur 0-0

**Round 17** [20-22.01.2023]
Excelsior - FC Volendam 2-0(1-0)
NEC Nijmegen - FC Emmen 3-1(2-1)
PSV Eindhoven - Vitesse 1-0(0-0)
SC Cambuur - Sparta Rotterdam 0-3(0-2)
SC Heerenveen - FC Groningen 3-1(1-1)
FC Twente - FC Utrecht 2-0(1-0)
Feyenoord - AFC Ajax 1-1(1-0)
AZ Alkmaar - Fortuna Sittard 3-1(2-1)
Waalwijk - Go Ahead 3-1(1-1) [01.02.2023]

**Round 18** [24-26.01.2023]
FC Emmen - PSV Eindhoven 1-0(1-0)
Sparta Rotterdam - RKC Waalwijk 0-0
Go Ahead Eagles - AZ Alkmaar 1-4(0-1)
Vitesse - FC Twente 2-2(1-1)
Fortuna Sittard - SC Heerenveen 2-0(0-0)
FC Utrecht - Excelsior 1-0(1-0)
Feyenoord - NEC Nijmegen 2-0(2-0)
FC Groningen - SC Cambuur 0-1(0-0)
AFC Ajax - FC Volendam 1-1(0-0)

## Round 19 [28-29.01.2023]

PSV Eindhoven - Go Ahead Eagles 2-0(1-0)
RKC Waalwijk - FC Emmen 2-0(2-0)
SC Heerenveen - Vitesse 1-3(1-2)
NEC Nijmegen - Sparta Rotterdam 1-1(0-0)
AZ Alkmaar - FC Utrecht 5-5(3-3)
FC Twente - Feyenoord 1-1(0-1)
Excelsior - AFC Ajax 1-4(1-2)
FC Volendam - FC Groningen 3-2(1-0)
SC Cambuur - Fortuna Sittard 1-2(1-0)

## Round 20 [03-05.02.2023]

Fortuna Sittard - Sparta Rotterdam 0-0
FC Volendam - AZ Alkmaar 1-1(0-0)
FC Emmen - Vitesse 2-2(1-2)
FC Utrecht - SC Heerenveen 1-0(0-0)
Excelsior - RKC Waalwijk 0-0
SC Cambuur - AFC Ajax 0-5(0-2)
Feyenoord - PSV Eindhoven 2-2(0-1)
Go Ahead Eagles - NEC Nijmegen 1-0(1-0)
FC Groningen - FC Twente 1-1(0-1)

## Round 21 [10-12.02.2023]

AZ Alkmaar - Excelsior 5-0(5-0)
NEC Nijmegen - SC Cambuur 0-0
PSV Eindhoven - FC Groningen 6-0(1-0)
FC Emmen - Fortuna Sittard 0-1(0-0)
Sparta Rotterdam - Go Ahead Eagles 2-1(1-0)
SC Heerenveen - Feyenoord 1-2(0-2)
Vitesse - FC Utrecht 2-0(0-0)
AFC Ajax - RKC Waalwijk 3-1(0-1)
FC Twente - FC Volendam 3-0(3-0)

## Round 22 [17-19.02.2023]

RKC Waalwijk - Fortuna Sittard 3-1(0-0)
FC Volendam - Vitesse 2-0(1-0)
FC Groningen - FC Emmen 1-1(1-1)
Feyenoord - AZ Alkmaar 2-1(1-1)
SC Cambuur - SC Heerenveen 1-2(1-1)
FC Utrecht - PSV Eindhoven 2-2(1-1)
Go Ahead Eagles - FC Twente 2-0(2-0)
AFC Ajax - Sparta Rotterdam 4-0(2-0)
Excelsior - NEC Nijmegen 0-3(0-1)

## Round 23 [24-26.02.2023]

Sparta Rotterdam - FC Utrecht 0-3(0-0)
FC Groningen - Excelsior 3-0(1-0)
SC Heerenveen - RKC Waalwijk 1-4(1-0)
AZ Alkmaar - SC Cambuur 2-1(1-0)
NEC Nijmegen - FC Volendam 3-0(0-0)
Fortuna Sittard - Feyenoord 2-4(0-3)
FC Emmen - Go Ahead Eagles 2-2(1-1)
Vitesse - AFC Ajax 1-2(1-1)
PSV Eindhoven - FC Twente 3-1(1-0)

## Round 24 [03-05.03.2023]

FC Utrecht - Fortuna Sittard 1-2(0-0)
Vitesse - AZ Alkmaar 0-1(0-1)
FC Volendam - FC Emmen 3-1(0-0)
Feyenoord - FC Groningen 1-0(0-0)
FC Twente - SC Heerenveen 3-3(1-1)
Excelsior - Sparta Rotterdam 1-4(1-1)
RKC Waalwijk - PSV Eindhoven 0-1(0-1)
AFC Ajax - NEC Nijmegen 1-0(0-0)
SC Cambuur - Go Ahead Eagles 4-1(2-1)

## Round 25 [11-12.03.2023]

FC Emmen - Excelsior 2-0(0-0)
Fortuna Sittard - FC Twente 0-3(0-0)
AZ Alkmaar - FC Groningen 1-0(1-0)
Sparta Rotterdam - Vitesse 3-1(2-1)
NEC Nijmegen - FC Utrecht 2-2(1-0)
SC Heerenveen - AFC Ajax 2-4(1-3)
PSV Eindhoven - SC Cambuur 5-2(1-1)
Feyenoord - FC Volendam 2-1(0-1)
Go Ahead - Waalwijk 3-2(2-1) [19.04.2023]

## Round 26 [17-19.03.2023]

FC Volendam - Fortuna Sittard 2-1(1-0)
FC Utrecht - Go Ahead Eagles 1-2(1-1)
FC Emmen - Sparta Rotterdam 0-2(0-1)
RKC Waalwijk - NEC Nijmegen 1-3(0-3)
FC Groningen - SC Heerenveen 0-2(0-2)
AFC Ajax - Feyenoord 2-3(2-1)
Excelsior - SC Cambuur 4-1(4-0)
Vitesse - PSV Eindhoven 1-1(0-1)
FC Twente - AZ Alkmaar 2-1(2-0)

## Round 27 [01-02.04.2023]

AZ Alkmaar - SC Heerenveen 1-1(0-1)
Excelsior - FC Twente 0-0
NEC Nijmegen - PSV Eindhoven 2-4(0-3)
SC Cambuur - FC Emmen 1-2(0-0)
RKC Waalwijk - Vitesse 1-0(1-0)
Go Ahead Eagles - AFC Ajax 0-0
FC Utrecht - FC Volendam 0-0
Sparta Rotterdam - Feyenoord 1-3(1-1)
Fortuna Sittard - FC Groningen 3-1(2-0)

## Round 28 [07-09.04.2023]

FC Groningen - FC Utrecht 1-2(1-1)
Vitesse - Go Ahead Eagles 2-0(1-0)
AZ Alkmaar - Sparta Rotterdam 0-1(0-1)
PSV Eindhoven - Excelsior 4-0(1-0)
SC Heerenveen - FC Volendam 2-1(2-1)
FC Twente - SC Cambuur 4-0(3-0)
FC Emmen - NEC Nijmegen 0-0
AFC Ajax - Fortuna Sittard 4-0(2-0)
Feyenoord - RKC Waalwijk 5-1(3-0)

## Round 29 [14-16.04.2023]

Excelsior - Go Ahead Eagles 2-1(0-0)
RKC Waalwijk - FC Groningen 2-1(0-0)
Sparta Rotterdam - SC Heerenveen 4-0(1-0)
NEC Nijmegen - Vitesse 1-4(0-2)
FC Utrecht - FC Twente 1-0(0-0)
FC Volendam - PSV Eindhoven 2-3(0-2)
SC Cambuur - Feyenoord 0-3(0-1)
AFC Ajax - FC Emmen 3-1(2-0)
Fortuna Sittard - AZ Alkmaar 0-3(0-2)

## Round 30 [21-25.04.2023]

FC Volendam - SC Cambuur 2-0(1-0)
SC Heerenveen - FC Emmen 2-3(1-0)
Vitesse - Excelsior 0-0
FC Twente - Sparta Rotterdam 3-3(1-2)
Go Ahead Eagles - Fortuna Sittard 2-0(1-0)
PSV Eindhoven - AFC Ajax 3-0(1-0)
Feyenoord - FC Utrecht 3-1(1-0)
AZ Alkmaar - RKC Waalwijk 3-0(1-0)
FC Groningen - NEC Nijmegen 0-1(0-0)

## Round 31 [05-07.05.2023]

RKC Waalwijk - FC Volendam 4-1(2-0)
Sparta Rotterdam - PSV Eindhoven 0-1(0-0)
NEC Nijmegen - SC Heerenveen 2-3(1-1)
SC Cambuur - FC Utrecht 0-3(0-2)
AFC Ajax - AZ Alkmaar 0-0
FC Emmen - FC Twente 0-3(0-0)
Excelsior - Feyenoord 0-2(0-1)
Go Ahead Eagles - FC Groningen 1-1(1-1)
Fortuna Sittard - Vitesse 2-0(0-0)

## Round 32 [12-16.05.2023]

FC Twente - NEC Nijmegen 4-0(1-0)
FC Volendam - Sparta Rotterdam 2-1(1-1)
SC Heerenveen - Excelsior 0-0
FC Utrecht - RKC Waalwijk 2-0(0-0)
Vitesse - SC Cambuur 2-0(0-0)
Feyenoord - Go Ahead Eagles 3-0(2-0)
AZ Alkmaar - FC Emmen 5-1(5-0)
PSV Eindhoven - Fortuna Sittard 2-1(1-1)
FC Groningen - AFC Ajax 2-3(1-1)

## Round 33 [21.05.2023]

AFC Ajax - FC Utrecht 3-1(1-0)
FC Emmen - Feyenoord 1-3(1-1)
Excelsior - Fortuna Sittard 3-0(0-0)
Go Ahead Eagles - FC Volendam 3-0(1-0)
NEC Nijmegen - AZ Alkmaar 0-3(0-2)
PSV Eindhoven - SC Heerenveen 3-3(1-2)
RKC Waalwijk - FC Twente 0-5(0-2)
Sparta Rotterdam - SC Cambuur 4-1(3-1)
Vitesse - FC Groningen 6-0(2-0)

## Round 34 [28.05.2023]

AZ Alkmaar - PSV Eindhoven 1-2(0-0)
SC Cambuur - RKC Waalwijk 4-0(2-0)
Feyenoord - Vitesse 0-1(0-1)
Fortuna Sittard - NEC Nijmegen 1-1(0-0)
FC Groningen - Sparta Rotterdam 0-5(0-1)
SC Heerenveen - Go Ahead Eagles 2-0(1-0)
FC Twente - AFC Ajax 3-1(0-1)
FC Utrecht - FC Emmen 3-2(1-1)
FC Volendam - Excelsior 3-2(3-0)

## Final Standings

| # | Team | Total P | W | D | L | GF | - | GA | Pts | Home W | D | L | GF | - | GA | Away W | D | L | GF | - | GA |
|---|------|--------|---|---|---|----|---|----|-----|--------|---|---|----|---|----|--------|---|---|----|---|----|
| 1. | **Feyenoord Rotterdam** | 34 | 25 | 7 | 2 | 81 | - | 30 | **82** | 12 | 4 | 1 | 37 | - | 10 | 13 | 3 | 1 | 44 | - | 20 |
| 2. | PSV Eindhoven | 34 | 23 | 6 | 5 | 89 | - | 40 | **75** | 14 | 2 | 1 | 54 | - | 14 | 9 | 4 | 4 | 35 | - | 26 |
| 3. | AFC Ajax Amsterdam | 34 | 20 | 9 | 5 | 86 | - | 38 | **69** | 10 | 5 | 2 | 47 | - | 14 | 10 | 4 | 3 | 39 | - | 24 |
| 4. | AZ Alkmaar | 34 | 20 | 7 | 7 | 68 | - | 35 | **67** | 9 | 5 | 3 | 36 | - | 20 | 11 | 2 | 4 | 32 | - | 15 |
| 5. | FC Twente Enschede | 34 | 18 | 10 | 6 | 66 | - | 27 | **64** | 13 | 4 | 0 | 46 | - | 11 | 5 | 6 | 6 | 20 | - | 16 |
| 6. | Sparta Rotterdam | 34 | 17 | 8 | 9 | 60 | - | 37 | **59** | 10 | 2 | 5 | 32 | - | 18 | 7 | 6 | 4 | 28 | - | 19 |
| 7. | FC Utrecht | 34 | 15 | 9 | 10 | 55 | - | 50 | **54** | 8 | 5 | 4 | 20 | - | 15 | 7 | 4 | 6 | 35 | - | 35 |
| 8. | SC Heerenveen | 34 | 12 | 10 | 12 | 44 | - | 50 | **46** | 6 | 3 | 8 | 21 | - | 26 | 6 | 7 | 4 | 23 | - | 24 |
| 9. | RKC Waalwijk | 34 | 11 | 8 | 15 | 50 | - | 64 | **41** | 9 | 3 | 5 | 34 | - | 26 | 2 | 5 | 10 | 16 | - | 38 |
| 10. | SBV Vitesse Arnhem | 34 | 10 | 10 | 14 | 45 | - | 50 | **40** | 5 | 6 | 6 | 24 | - | 25 | 5 | 4 | 8 | 21 | - | 25 |
| 11. | Go Ahead Eagles Deventer | 34 | 10 | 10 | 14 | 46 | - | 56 | **40** | 7 | 6 | 4 | 28 | - | 23 | 3 | 4 | 10 | 18 | - | 33 |
| 12. | NEC Nijmegen | 34 | 8 | 15 | 11 | 42 | - | 45 | **39** | 3 | 9 | 5 | 28 | - | 28 | 5 | 6 | 6 | 14 | - | 17 |
| 13. | Fortuna Sittard | 34 | 10 | 6 | 18 | 39 | - | 62 | **36** | 5 | 4 | 8 | 21 | - | 28 | 5 | 2 | 10 | 18 | - | 34 |
| 14. | FC Volendam | 34 | 10 | 6 | 18 | 42 | - | 71 | **36** | 9 | 1 | 7 | 29 | - | 32 | 1 | 5 | 11 | 13 | - | 39 |
| 15. | SBV Excelsior Rotterdam | 34 | 9 | 5 | 20 | 32 | - | 71 | **32** | 8 | 2 | 7 | 22 | - | 26 | 1 | 3 | 13 | 10 | - | 45 |
| 16. | FC Emmen (*Relegation Play-offs*) | 34 | 6 | 10 | 18 | 33 | - | 65 | **28** | 3 | 9 | 5 | 16 | - | 23 | 3 | 1 | 13 | 17 | - | 42 |
| 17. | SC Cambuur Leeuwarden (*Relegated*) | 34 | 5 | 4 | 25 | 26 | - | 69 | **19** | 3 | 0 | 14 | 14 | - | 33 | 2 | 4 | 11 | 12 | - | 36 |
| 18. | FC Groningen (*Relegated*) | 34 | 4 | 6 | 24 | 31 | - | 75 | **18** | 3 | 3 | 11 | 20 | - | 34 | 1 | 3 | 13 | 11 | - | 41 |

<u>Please note</u>: teams ranked 5-8 were qualified for the European competition Play-offs.

## Top goalscorers:

| | | |
|---|---|---|
| 19 | **Anastasios Douvikas (GRE)** | *FC Utrecht* |
| 19 | **Xavier Quentin Shay Simons** | *PSV Eindhoven* |
| 16 | Sydney van Hooijdonk | *SC Heerenveen* |
| 15 | Santiago Tomás Giménez (MEX) | *Feyenoord Rotterdam* |

## European competition Play-offs

| Semi-Finals [01-04.06.2023] | | | |
|---|---|---|---|
| | SC Heerenveen - FC Twente Enschede | 1-2(1-1) | 0-4(0-3) |
| | FC Utrecht - Sparta Rotterdam | 1-2(0-2) | 1-0 aet; 4-5 pen |

| Final [08-11.06.2023] | | | |
|---|---|---|---|
| | Sparta Rotterdam - **FC Twente Enschede** | 1-1(0-0) | 0-1(0-0) |

## Promotion / Relegation Play-offs (1st / 2nd Level)

| First Round [22-23/26-27.05.2023] | | | |
|---|---|---|---|
| | FC Eindhoven - Almere City FC | 1-0(0-0) | 1-3(0-0,1-1) |
| | VVV-Venlo - Willem II Tilburg | 3-2(2-2) | 2-2(0-2,1-2) |
| | NAC Breda - MVV Maastricht | 1-0(1-0) | 4-1(3-0) |

| Semi-Finals [30-31.05./03.06.2023] | | | |
|---|---|---|---|
| | VVV-Venlo - Almere City FC | 1-1(1-1) | 1-1 aet; 0-2 pen |
| | NAC Breda - FC Emmen | 1-2(0-2) | 0-2(0-0) |

| Final [06-11.06.2023] | | | |
|---|---|---|---|
| | Almere City FC - FC Emmen | 2-0(0-0) | 2-1(0-0) |

**Almere City FC** promoted to 2023/2024 Eredivisie.

# NATIONAL CUP
## KNVB 2022/2023

### Second Round [10-12.01.2023]

| | | | | |
|---|---|---|---|---|
| FC Twente Enschede - SC Telstar Velsen | 3-1(2-0) | De Treffers Groesbeek - SC Cambuur | 1-0(1-0) |
| Kozakken Boys Werkendam - ADO Den Haag | 1-3(0-1) | SC Heerenveen - FC Volendam | 2-0(0-0) |
| HV & CV Quick Den Haag - VBV De Graafschap D. | 1-4(1-3) | FC Den Bosch - AFC Ajax Amsterdam | 0-2(0-1) |
| NAC Breda - FC Eindhoven | 2-1(0-1,1-1) | Heracles Almelo - Go Ahead Eagles Deventer | 0-1(0-0) |
| Sparta Rotterdam - PSV Eindhoven | 1-2(0-2) | SV Urk - VV Katwijk | 0-3(0-1) |
| SBV Excelsior Rotterdam - AZ Alkmaar | 1-4(1-3) | Blauw Geel '38 Veghel - FC Utrecht | 1-3(0-3) |
| VVV-Venlo - FC Emmen | 2-3(0-2) | FC Groningen - SV Spakenburg | 2-3(0-2) |
| Almere City FC - NEC Nijmegen | 0-4(0-2) | Feyenoord Rotterdam - PEC Zwolle | 3-1(2-1) |

### 1/8-Finals [07-09.02.2023]

| | | | | |
|---|---|---|---|---|
| AZ Alkmaar - FC Utrecht | 1-2(0-0,1-1) | SV Spakenburg - VV Katwijk | 1-1 aet; 4-1 pen |
| VBV De Graafschap Doet. - De Treffers Groesbeek | 3-0(0-0) | Feyenoord Rotterdam - NEC Nijmegen | 4-4 aet; 5-3 pen |
| NAC Breda - SC Heerenveen | 1-2(1-1) | FC Twente Enschede - AFC Ajax Amsterdam | 0-1(0-0) |
| PSV Eindhoven - FC Emmen | 3-1(2-0) | ADO Den Haag - Go Ahead Eagles Deventer | 1-0(0-0) |

### Quarter-Finals [28.02.-02.03.2023]

| | | | | |
|---|---|---|---|---|
| FC Utrecht - SV Spakenburg | 1-4(0-1) | PSV Eindhoven - ADO Den Haag | 3-1(2-0) |
| SC Heerenveen - Feyenoord Rotterdam | 0-1(0-0) | VBV De Graafschap Doet. - AFC Ajax Amsterdam | 0-3(0-2) |

| Semi-Finals [04-05.04.2023] | | | |
|---|---|---|---|
| SV Spakenburg - PSV Eindhoven | 1-2(0-1) | Feyenoord Rotterdam - AFC Ajax Amsterdam | 1-2(1-1) |

## Final

30.04.2023; Stadion Feijenoord, Rotterdam; Referee: Dennis Higler; Attendance: 40,650

**AFC Ajax Amsterdam - PSV Eindhoven**                    **1-1(1-0,1-1,1-1); 2-3 on penalties**

**AFC Ajax:** Gerónimo Rulli, Jorge Eduardo Sánchez Ramos (46.Devyne Rensch), Edson Omar Álvarez Velázquez, Jurriën David Norman Timber, Jorrel Hato (75.Owen Wijndal), Davy Klaassen (116.Silvano Vos), Florian Grillitsch (68.Calvin Bassey Ughelumba), Dušan Tadić (Cap), Steven Berghuis (75.Francisco Fernandes da Conceição), Steven Charles Bergwijn (116.Mika Godts), Brian Brobbey. Trainer: John Gilbert Alan Heitinga.

**PSV Eindhoven:** Joël Drommel, Jordan Teze (76.Phillipp Mwene), André Ramalho Silva, Jarrad Branthwaite, Patrick van Aanholt, Joey Veerman, Ibrahim Sangaré, Guus Til (59.Anwar El Ghazi), Johan Bakayoko (59.Thorgan Ganael Francis Hazard), Xavier Quentin Shay Simons (98.Érick Gabriel Gutiérrez Galaviz), Luuk de Jong (Cap) (105.Fábio Daniel Soares Silva). Trainer: Rutgerus Johannes Martinus van Nistelrooij.

**Goals:** 1-0 Jarrad Branthwaite (42 own goal), 1-1 Thorgan Ganael Francis Hazard (67).

**Penalties:** Dušan Tadić 1-0; Thorgan Ganael Francis Hazard 1-1; Brian Brobbey (missed); André Ramalho Silva (saved); Jurriën David Norman Timber (missed); Ibrahim Sangaré (missed); Mika Godts 2-1; Anwar El Ghazi 2-2; Edson Omar Álvarez Velázquez (saved); Fábio Daniel Soares Silva 2-3.

## THE CLUBS 2022/2023

### Amsterdamsche Football Club Ajax

| Founded: | 18.03.1900 | | |
|---|---|---|---|
| Stadium: | "Johann Cruijff" ArenA, Amsterdam (55,500) | | |
| Trainer: | Alfred Schreuder | | 02.11.1972 |
| [27.01.2023] | John Gilbert Alan Heitinga | | 15.11.1983 |

| Goalkeepers: | DOB | M | (s) | G |
|---|---|---|---|---|
| Remko Pasveer | 08.11.1983 | 15 | | |
| Gerónimo Rulli (ARG) | 20.05.1992 | 19 | | |
| **Defenders:** | **DOB** | **M** | **(s)** | **G** |
| Youri Baas | 17.03.2003 | 2 | (4) | |
| Calvin Bassey Ughelumba (NGA) | 31.12.1999 | 20 | (5) | 1 |
| Daley Blind | 09.03.1990 | 11 | (2) | |
| Jorrel Hato | 07.03.2006 | 6 | (5) | |
| Lisandro Magallán Orueta (ARG) | 27.09.1993 | | (2) | |
| Youri Regeer | 18.08.2003 | | (3) | |
| Devyne Rensch | 18.01.2003 | 26 | | 3 |
| Jorge Eduardo Sánchez Ramos (MEX) | 10.12.1997 | 11 | (6) | 2 |
| Perr Schuurs | 26.11.1999 | 1 | (1) | |
| Jurriën David Norman Timber | 17.06.2001 | 34 | | 2 |
| Owen Wijndal | 28.11.1999 | 15 | (5) | |
| **Midfielders:** | **DOB** | **M** | **(s)** | **G** |
| Edson Omar Álvarez Velázquez (MEX) | 24.10.1997 | 30 | (1) | 3 |
| Steven Berghuis | 19.12.1991 | 25 | (4) | 9 |
| Kian Fitz-Jim | 05.07.2003 | | (2) | |
| Florian Grillitsch (AUT) | 07.08.1995 | 4 | (6) | |
| Davy Klaassen | 21.02.1993 | 21 | (12) | 8 |
| Kenneth Ina Dorothea Taylor | 16.05.2002 | 29 | (3) | 8 |
| Silvano Vos | 16.03.2005 | | (2) | |
| **Forwards:** | **DOB** | **M** | **(s)** | **G** |
| *Antony* Matheus dos Santos (BRA) | 24.02.2000 | 2 | | 1 |
| Steven Charles Bergwijn | 08.10.1997 | 28 | (4) | 12 |
| Brian Brobbey | 01.02.2002 | 17 | (15) | 13 |
| *Francisco* Fernandes da *Conceição* (POR) | 14.12.2002 | 4 | (15) | |
| Mika Godts | 07.06.2005 | | (3) | |
| Mohammed Kudus (GHA) | 02.08.2000 | 19 | (11) | 11 |
| Lorenzo Lucca (ITA) | 10.09.2000 | | (14) | 2 |
| Lucas Ariel Ocampos (ARG) | 11.07.1994 | 1 | (3) | |
| Christian Rasmussen (DEN) | 19.01.2003 | | (2) | |
| Dušan Tadić (SRB) | 20.11.1988 | 34 | | 11 |

### Alkmaar Zaanstreek Alkmaar

| Founded: | 10.05.1967 | |
|---|---|---|
| Stadium: | AFAS Stadion, Alkmaar (19,478) | |
| Trainer: | Pascal Jansen | 02.05.1973 |

| Goalkeepers: | DOB | M | (s) | G |
|---|---|---|---|---|
| Mathew Ryan (AUS) | 08.04.1992 | 18 | | |
| Hobie Verhulst | 02.04.1993 | 16 | | |
| **Defenders:** | **DOB** | **M** | **(s)** | **G** |
| Sam Beukema | 17.11.1998 | 24 | (2) | 2 |
| Mees de Wit | 17.04.1998 | 2 | (20) | 2 |
| Maxim Dekker | 21.04.2004 | 10 | (3) | 1 |
| Wouter Goes | 10.06.2004 | 8 | | 1 |
| Pantelis Hatzidiakos (GRE) | 18.01.1997 | 33 | | |
| Milos Kerkez (HUN) | 07.11.2003 | 33 | | 3 |
| Rolando Maximiliano "Bruno" Martins Indi | 08.02.1992 | 4 | | |
| Yukinari Sugawara (JPN) | 28.06.2000 | 26 | (5) | 3 |
| Zinho Vanheusden (BEL) | 29.07.1999 | 2 | (5) | |
| Aslak Witry (NOR) | 10.03.1996 | | (2) | |
| **Midfielders:** | **DOB** | **M** | **(s)** | **G** |
| Riechedly Bazoer | 12.10.1996 | 1 | (15) | |
| Zico Buurmeester | 07.06.2002 | | (7) | 1 |
| Jordy Clasie | 27.06.1991 | 33 | | 3 |
| Fedde de Jong | 13.06.2003 | 1 | (1) | |
| Dani de Wit | 28.01.1998 | 15 | (3) | 5 |
| Peer Koopmeiners | 04.05.2000 | | (6) | |
| Djordje Mihailovic (USA) | 10.11.1998 | 5 | (10) | 1 |
| Sven Mijnans | 09.03.2000 | 14 | (1) | 4 |
| Tijjani Reijnders | 29.07.1998 | 34 | | 3 |
| **Forwards:** | **DOB** | **M** | **(s)** | **G** |
| Håkon Evjen (NOR) | 14.02.2000 | 6 | (2) | |
| Jesper Karlsson (SWE) | 25.07.1998 | 21 | (2) | 9 |
| Mayckel Lahdo (SWE) | 30.12.2002 | 1 | (24) | 2 |
| Mexx Meerdink | 24.07.2003 | 1 | (5) | |
| Jens Odgaard (DEN) | 31.03.1999 | 28 | (1) | 9 |
| Vangelis Pavlidis (GRE) | 21.11.1998 | 22 | (3) | 12 |
| Myron van Brederode | 06.07.2003 | 16 | (9) | 4 |
| Yusuf Barası (TUR) | 31.03.2003 | | (11) | |

## Sportclub Cambuur Leeuwarden

| Founded: | 19.06.1964 | | |
|---|---|---|---|
| Stadium: | Cambuurstadion, Leeuwarden (10,500) | | |
| Trainer: | Henk de Jong | | 27.08.1964 |
| [20.10.2022] | Pascal Bosschaart & | | 28.02.1980 |
| | Martijn Barto | | 23.08.1984 |
| [14.11.2022] | Sjors Ultee | | 23.05.1987 |

| Goalkeepers: | DOB | M | (s) | G |
|---|---|---|---|---|
| *João* Manuel Neves *Virgínia* (POR) | 10.10.1999 | 17 | | |
| Brett Minnema | 06.01.2002 | 1 | | |
| Robbin Ruiter | 25.03.1987 | 16 | | |
| Defenders: | DOB | M | (s) | G |
| Alex Bangura (SLE) | 13.07.1999 | 28 | (1) | 1 |
| Léon Bergsma | 25.01.1997 | 21 | (3) | |
| Calvin Leonardus Mac-Intosch (SUR) | 09.08.1989 | 6 | (5) | |
| Doke Schmidt | 07.04.1992 | 20 | (5) | |
| Floris Smand | 20.01.2003 | 22 | (1) | |
| Sekou Sylla (GUI) | 09.01.1999 | 2 | (3) | |
| Marco Tol | 25.04.1998 | 22 | (2) | 1 |
| Sai van Wermeskerken (JPN) | 28.06.1994 | 18 | (6) | 1 |
| Midfielders: | DOB | M | (s) | G |
| Michael Breij | 15.01.1997 | 16 | (16) | 2 |
| Navarone Foor | 04.02.1992 | 15 | | 2 |
| Mees Hoedemakers | 18.02.1998 | 25 | (4) | 3 |
| Jamie Jacobs | 03.12.1997 | 18 | (9) | 2 |

| | DOB | M | (s) | G |
|---|---|---|---|---|
| Robin Maulun (FRA) | 23.11.1996 | 3 | (4) | |
| Mitchel Paulissen | 21.04.1993 | 23 | (6) | 2 |
| Vincent Pichel | 12.11.2001 | | (4) | |
| Ben Rienstra | 05.06.1990 | 1 | (3) | |
| Jasper ter Heide | 29.03.1999 | 1 | (3) | 1 |
| Daniël van Kaam | 23.06.2000 | 26 | (1) | 1 |
| Forwards: | DOB | M | (s) | G |
| Remco Balk | 02.03.2001 | 12 | (18) | 1 |
| Tom Boere | 24.11.1992 | 7 | (6) | |
| Sam Hendriks | 25.01.1995 | | (1) | |
| Bjørn Maars Johnsen (NOR) | 06.11.1991 | 10 | (3) | 3 |
| Mimoun Mahi (MAR) | 13.03.1994 | 7 | (5) | 1 |
| Felix Mambimbi (SUI) | 18.01.2001 | 3 | (5) | |
| David Sambissa (GAB) | 11.01.1996 | 2 | (16) | 1 |
| Milan Smit | 13.02.2003 | 3 | (10) | 1 |
| Roberts Uldriķis (LVA) | 03.04.1998 | 14 | (14) | 1 |
| Silvester van der Water | 30.09.1996 | 15 | (8) | 1 |

## Football Club Emmen

| Founded: | 21.08.1925 | | |
|---|---|---|---|
| Stadium: | De Oude Meerdijk, Merdijk (8,600) | | |
| Trainer: | Dick Lukkien | | 28.03.1972 |

| Goalkeepers: | DOB | M | (s) | G |
|---|---|---|---|---|
| Eric Oelschlägel (GER) | 20.09.1995 | 9 | | |
| Mickey van der Hart | 13.06.1994 | 25 | | |
| Defenders: | DOB | M | (s) | G |
| Miguel Gianpierre Araujo Blanco (PER) | 24.10.1994 | 30 | (1) | 1 |
| Mohamed Bouchouari (BEL) | 15.11.2000 | 18 | (8) | 1 |
| Lorenzo Burnet | 11.01.1991 | 17 | (2) | |
| Maurilio de Lannoy | 07.11.2003 | | (1) | |
| Julius Dirksen | 02.03.2003 | 15 | (12) | |
| Jeff Hardeveld | 27.02.1995 | 4 | (2) | |
| Michaël Heylen (BEL) | 03.01.1994 | 2 | (9) | |
| Arnaud Luzayadio (FRA) | 19.07.1999 | | (1) | |
| Mike te Wierik | 08.06.1992 | 14 | | |
| Keziah Veendorp | 17.02.1997 | 33 | | |
| Jeroen Veldmate | 08.11.1988 | 25 | | 3 |
| Dennis Vos | 28.11.2001 | 3 | (3) | |

| Midfielders: | DOB | M | (s) | G |
|---|---|---|---|---|
| Lucas Bernadou (FRA) | 24.09.2000 | 22 | (8) | 2 |
| Mark Diemers | 11.10.1993 | 31 | (1) | 2 |
| Ahmed El Messaoudi (MAR) | 03.08.1995 | 16 | (9) | 2 |
| Maikel Kieftenbeld | 26.06.1990 | 1 | | |
| Azzeddine Toufiqui (FRA) | 25.04.1999 | | (5) | |
| Jari Vlak | 15.08.1998 | 18 | (13) | 1 |
| Forwards: | DOB | M | (s) | G |
| Jeremy Antonisse (CUW) | 29.03.2002 | 11 | (2) | 1 |
| Jasin Assehnoun (FIN) | 26.12.1998 | 4 | (25) | 1 |
| Oussama Darfalou (ALG) | 29.09.1993 | | (8) | |
| Metehan Güçlü (FRA) | 02.04.1999 | | (1) | |
| Danny Hoesen | 15.01.1991 | 1 | (3) | |
| Fernando José Pacheco Rivas (PER) | 26.06.1999 | | (9) | |
| Ole Romeny | 20.06.2000 | 29 | (4) | 11 |
| *Rui* Jorge Monteiro *Mendes* (POR) | 10.11.1999 | 16 | (2) | 1 |
| Ben Scholte | 10.08.2001 | 1 | (6) | |
| Richairo Živković (CUW) | 05.09.1996 | 29 | (3) | 5 |

## Stichting Betaald Voetbal Excelsior Rotterdam

| Founded: | 23.07.1902 | | |
|---|---|---|---|
| Stadium: | Stadion Woudestein [Van Donge & De Roo], Rotterdam (4,500) | | |
| Trainer: | Marinus Dijkhuizen | | 04.01.1972 |

| Goalkeepers: | DOB | M | (s) | G |
|---|---|---|---|---|
| Norbert Alblas | 12.12.1994 | | (1) | |
| Stijn van Gassel | 18.10.1996 | 34 | | |
| Defenders: | DOB | M | (s) | G |
| Maxime Awoudja (GER) | 02.02.1998 | 2 | (8) | |
| Redouan el Yaakoubi | 25.01.1996 | 33 | | 3 |
| Siebe Horemans (BEL) | 02.06.1998 | 33 | (1) | 3 |
| Nathangelo Alexandro Markelo (CUW) | 07.01.1999 | 3 | (11) | |
| Sven Nieuwpoort | 13.04.1993 | 22 | (1) | |
| Kik Pierie | 20.07.2000 | 7 | | 1 |
| Serano Seymor | 04.01.2002 | 10 | (11) | 1 |
| Nathan Tjoe-a-On | 22.12.2001 | 24 | (5) | 1 |
| Arthur Zagré (FRA) | 04.10.2001 | 8 | (1) | |
| Midfielders: | DOB | M | (s) | G |
| Yassin Ayoub (MAR) | 06.03.1994 | 9 | (6) | |
| Marouan Azarkan | 08.12.2001 | 26 | (1) | 3 |

| | DOB | M | (s) | G |
|---|---|---|---|---|
| Julian Baas | 16.04.2002 | 27 | (6) | 3 |
| Joshua Eijgenraam | 18.02.2002 | 5 | (8) | |
| Adrian Fein (GER) | 18.03.1999 | 8 | (6) | |
| Kenzo Goudmijn | 18.12.2001 | 33 | (1) | 4 |
| Peer Koopmeiners | 04.05.2000 | 16 | (3) | |
| Noah Naujoks | 02.05.2002 | 4 | (6) | |
| Forwards: | DOB | M | (s) | G |
| Luuk Admiraal | 15.03.2002 | | (1) | |
| Nikolas Agrafiotis (SRB) | 25.04.2000 | 5 | (12) | 2 |
| Vicente Besuijen | 10.04.2001 | | (2) | |
| Jacky Donkor (BEL) | 12.11.1998 | | (6) | |
| Couhaib Driouech (MAR) | 17.04.2002 | 27 | (6) | 3 |
| Raphaël Eyongo | 21.05.2003 | | (5) | |
| Reda Kharchouch | 27.08.1995 | 13 | (16) | 2 |
| Lazaros Lamprou (GRE) | 19.12.1997 | 16 | (12) | 4 |
| Mike van Duinen | 06.11.1991 | 9 | (19) | |

## Feyenoord Rotterdam

**Founded**: 19.07.1908
**Stadium**: Stadion Feijenoord, Rotterdam (47,500)
**Trainer**: Arne Slot    17.09.1978

| Goalkeepers: | DOB | M | (s) | G |
|---|---|---|---|---|
| Justin Bijlow | 22.01.1998 | 25 | | |
| Timon Wellenreuther (GER) | 03.12.1995 | 9 | | |
| **Defenders:** | **DOB** | **M** | **(s)** | **G** |
| Mimeirhel Benita | 17.11.2003 | | (2) | |
| Fredrik André Bjørkan (NOR) | 21.08.1998 | 1 | | |
| Lutsharel Geertruida | 18.07.2000 | 29 | (1) | 3 |
| Dávid Hancko (SVK) | 13.12.1997 | 31 | | 2 |
| Quilindschy Hartman | 14.11.2001 | 21 | (2) | 2 |
| Neraysho Kasanwirjo | 18.02.2002 | 1 | (4) | |
| Marcos Johan López Lanfranco (PER) | 20.11.1999 | 6 | (13) | |
| Marcus Pedersen (NOR) | 16.07.2000 | 25 | (4) | 1 |
| Jacob Rasmussen (DEN) | 28.05.1997 | 8 | (2) | 1 |
| Gernot Trauner (AUT) | 25.03.1992 | 18 | (1) | |
| **Midfielders:** | **DOB** | **M** | **(s)** | **G** |
| Fredrik Aursnes (NOR) | 10.12.1995 | 2 | | |
| Cole John Bassett (USA) | 28.07.2001 | | (1) | |
| Ezequiel Eduardo Bullaude (ARG) | 26.10.2000 | | (9) | |
| Antoni Milambo | 03.04.2005 | | (3) | |
| Noah Naujoks | 02.05.2002 | | (2) | |
| Orkun Kökçü (TUR) | 29.12.2000 | 31 | (1) | 8 |
| Sebastian Szymański (POL) | 10.05.1999 | 24 | (5) | 9 |
| Mo Taabouni | 29.03.2002 | | (5) | |
| Quinten Timber | 17.06.2001 | 19 | (5) | 2 |
| Jens Toornstra | 04.04.1989 | | (3) | |
| Mats Wieffer | 16.11.1999 | 18 | (7) | 1 |
| **Forwards:** | **DOB** | **M** | **(s)** | **G** |
| *Danilo* Pereira Da Silva (BRA) | 07.04.1999 | 14 | (20) | 10 |
| Javairô Dilrosun | 22.06.1998 | 23 | (8) | 5 |
| Santiago Tomás Giménez (MEX) | 18.04.2001 | 21 | (11) | 15 |
| Oussama Idrissi (MAR) | 26.02.1996 | 17 | (10) | 4 |
| *Igor* Guilherme Barbosa da *Paixão* (BRA) | 28.06.2000 | 15 | (13) | 7 |
| Alireza Jahanbakhsh (IRN) | 11.08.1993 | 12 | (16) | 5 |
| Patrik Wålemark (SWE) | 14.10.2001 | 4 | (11) | 2 |

## Fortuna Sittard

**Founded**: 01.07.1968
**Stadium**: Fortuna Sittard Stadion, Sittard (10,300)
**Trainer**: Sjors Ultee    23.05.1987
[22.08.2022] Dominik Vergoossen    20.03.1972
[09.09.2022] Julio Velázquez Santiago (ESP)    05.10.1981

| Goalkeepers: | DOB | M | (s) | G |
|---|---|---|---|---|
| Ivor Pandur (CRO) | 25.03.2000 | 31 | | |
| Yanick van Osch | 24.03.1997 | 3 | | |
| **Defenders:** | **DOB** | **M** | **(s)** | **G** |
| George Cox (ENG) | 14.01.1998 | 25 | (2) | |
| *Ivo* Daniel Ferreira Mendonça *Pinto* (POR) | 07.01.1990 | 26 | (3) | |
| Roel Janssen | 16.06.1990 | | (5) | |
| Stipe Radić (CRO) | 10.06.2000 | 3 | (4) | |
| *Rodrigo* Guth (BRA) | 10.11.2000 | 33 | (1) | 1 |
| Dimitrios Siovas (GRE) | 16.09.1988 | 22 | (2) | 1 |
| Mike van Beijnen | 07.03.1999 | | (1) | |
| Rémy Vita (MAD) | 01.04.2001 | 10 | (17) | 2 |
| Joaquín „*Ximo*" *Navarro* Jiménez (ESP) | 23.01.1990 | 14 | (1) | |
| **Midfielders:** | **DOB** | **M** | **(s)** | **G** |
| Cole John Bassett (USA) | 28.07.2001 | 2 | (8) | |
| Kristijan Bistrović (CRO) | 09.04.1998 | 13 | | 1 |
| Deroy d'Encarnação Duarte (CPV) | 04.07.1999 | 17 | (9) | 1 |
| Doğan Erdoğan (TUR) | 22.08.1996 | 19 | (8) | |
| Arianit Ferati (GER) | 07.09.1997 | 18 | (9) | 1 |
| Oğuzhan Özyakup (TUR) | 23.09.1992 | 18 | (4) | 3 |
| Vasilios Sourlis (GRE) | 16.11.2002 | | (2) | |
| Mickaël Tirpan (BEL) | 23.10.1993 | 5 | | |
| **Forwards:** | **DOB** | **M** | **(s)** | **G** |
| Thomas Buitink | 14.06.2000 | 3 | (10) | |
| Gianmarco Cangiano (ITA) | 16.11.2001 | | (5) | |
| Iñigo *Córdoba* Querejeta (ESP) | 13.03.1997 | 29 | (2) | 5 |
| Paul Gladon | 18.03.1992 | 13 | (14) | 7 |
| Tijjani Noslin | 07.07.1999 | 18 | (13) | 5 |
| Mats Seuntjens | 17.04.1992 | 10 | (2) | |
| Tunahan Taşçı (TUR) | 29.04.2002 | | (10) | |
| *Úmaro* Embaló (POR) | 06.05.2001 | 18 | (9) | 3 |
| Burak Yılmaz (TUR) | 15.07.1985 | 24 | (2) | 9 |

## Go Ahead Eagles Deventer

**Founded**: 02.12.1902
**Stadium**: Stadion De Adelaarshorst, Deventer (10,000)
**Trainer**: René Hake    18.12.1971

| Goalkeepers: | DOB | M | (s) | G |
|---|---|---|---|---|
| Jeffrey de Lange | 01.04.1998 | 34 | | |
| **Defenders:** | **DOB** | **M** | **(s)** | **G** |
| Jamal Amofa | 25.11.1998 | 27 | (4) | |
| Aventis Aventisian (GRE) | 17.08.2002 | | (2) | |
| Justin Bakker | 03.03.1998 | 3 | | |
| Mats Deijl | 15.07.1997 | 32 | | 2 |
| Jay Idzes | 02.06.2000 | 32 | | 1 |
| *José* Manuel *Fontán* Mondragón (ESP) | 11.02.2000 | 12 | (9) | 1 |
| Bas Kuipers | 17.08.1994 | 21 | (2) | 3 |
| Federico Mattiello (ITA) | 14.07.1995 | | (6) | |
| Gerrit Nauber (GER) | 13.04.1992 | 12 | (7) | |
| Fredrik Oppegård (NOR) | 07.08.2002 | 4 | (4) | |
| Pim Saathof | 28.12.2003 | | (3) | |
| **Midfielders:** | **DOB** | **M** | **(s)** | **G** |
| Xander Blomme (BEL) | 21.06.2002 | 5 | (3) | 1 |
| Evert Linthorst | 03.03.2000 | 16 | (7) | 1 |
| Enric Llansana | 12.04.2001 | 14 | (7) | |
| Philippe Rommens (BEL) | 20.08.1997 | 28 | | 3 |
| Tesfaldet Simon Tekie (SWE) | 04.06.1997 | 4 | (4) | |
| **Forwards:** | **DOB** | **M** | **(s)** | **G** |
| Bobby Adekanye | 14.02.1999 | 28 | (3) | 6 |
| Martijn Berden | 29.07.1997 | | (5) | |
| *Dario* Serra Álvarez (ESP) | 20.01.2003 | | (4) | 1 |
| Oliver Edvardsen (NOR) | 19.03.1999 | 26 | (2) | 7 |
| Rashaan Fernandes | 29.07.1998 | 7 | (12) | |
| Isac Lidberg (SWE) | 08.09.1998 | 33 | | 7 |
| Jahnoah Markelo | 04.01.2003 | | (5) | |
| Sylla Sow | 08.08.1996 | | (24) | 1 |
| Finn Stokkers | 18.04.1996 | 11 | (13) | 3 |
| Willum Willumsson (ISL) | 23.10.1998 | 25 | (2) | 8 |

## Football Club Groningen

| Founded: | 16.06.1971 | | |
|---|---|---|---|
| Stadium: | Stadion Euroborg, Groningen (22,550) | | |
| Trainer: | Frank Wormuth (GER) | | 13.09.1960 |
| [02.12.2022] | Dennis van der Ree | | 19.04.1979 |

| Goalkeepers: | DOB | M | (s) | G |
|---|---|---|---|---|
| Jan de Boer | 20.05.2000 | 2 | (1) | |
| Peter Leeuwenburgh | 23.03.1994 | 8 | | |
| Michael Verrips | 03.12.1996 | 24 | | |
| **Defenders:** | **DOB** | **M** | **(s)** | **G** |
| Radinio Balker | 03.09.1998 | 31 | | 1 |
| Mads Bech (DEN) | 07.01.1999 | 10 | (1) | |
| Thijmen Blokzijl | 25.02.2005 | 13 | (2) | |
| Matěj Chaluš (CZE) | 02.02.1998 | 4 | (4) | |
| Damil Dankerlui Wadilie (SUR) | 24.08.1996 | 6 | (12) | |
| Yahya Kalley (SWE) | 20.03.2001 | | (5) | |
| Neraysho Kasanwirjo | 18.02.2002 | 14 | (1) | |
| Isak Määttä (NOR) | 19.09.2001 | 32 | (1) | |
| Nordin Musampa | 13.10.2001 | 5 | (3) | |
| Marin Šverko (CRO) | 04.02.1998 | 2 | (3) | |
| Mike te Wierik | 08.06.1992 | 13 | (2) | |
| Liam van Gelderen | 23.03.2001 | 13 | (4) | 1 |
| Jetro Willems | 30.03.1994 | 6 | (1) | |
| **Midfielders:** | **DOB** | **M** | **(s)** | **G** |
| Laros Duarte | 28.02.1997 | 19 | (6) | 2 |

| | DOB | M | (s) | G |
|---|---|---|---|---|
| Johan Hove (NOR) | 07.09.2000 | 18 | | 2 |
| Daleho Irandust (SWE) | 04.06.1998 | 9 | (8) | |
| Ramon Pascal Lundqvist (SWE) | 10.05.1997 | 4 | (9) | |
| Ragnar Oratmangoen | 21.01.1998 | 13 | (6) | |
| Joey Pelupessy | 15.05.1993 | 14 | (5) | 1 |
| Jorg Schreuders | 09.09.2004 | 4 | (1) | |
| Aimar Sher (SWE) | 20.12.2002 | | (6) | |
| Tomáš Suslov (SVK) | 07.06.2002 | 26 | (4) | 1 |
| Luciano Valente (ITA) | 04.10.2003 | 9 | (11) | |
| **Forwards:** | **DOB** | **M** | **(s)** | **G** |
| Paulos Abraham (SWE) | 16.07.2002 | 5 | (3) | |
| Oliver Antman (FIN) | 15.08.2001 | 8 | (3) | 2 |
| Patrick Joosten | 14.04.1996 | | (1) | |
| Florian Krüger (GER) | 13.02.1999 | 12 | (10) | 4 |
| Elvis Manu | 13.08.1993 | 8 | (2) | |
| Cyril Ngonge (BEL) | 26.05.2000 | 8 | (4) | 3 |
| Ricardo Pepi (USA) | 09.01.2003 | 28 | (1) | 12 |
| Romano Postema | 07.02.2002 | | (2) | |
| Jørgen Strand Larsen (NOR) | 06.02.2000 | 4 | | 1 |
| Thom van Bergen | 06.01.2004 | 2 | (10) | |

## Sportclub Heerenveen

| Founded: | 20.07.1920 | | |
|---|---|---|---|
| Stadium: | "Abe Lenstra" Stadion, Heerenveen (27,224) | | |
| Trainer: | Kees van Wonderen | | 04.01.1969 |

| Goalkeepers: | DOB | M | (s) | G |
|---|---|---|---|---|
| Jan Bekkema | 09.04.1996 | | (1) | |
| Xavier Mous | 04.08.1995 | 16 | | |
| Andries Noppert | 07.04.1994 | 18 | | |
| **Defenders:** | **DOB** | **M** | **(s)** | **G** |
| Hussein Ali (SWE) | 01.03.2002 | | (5) | |
| Paweł Bochniewicz (POL) | 30.01.1996 | 33 | | 2 |
| Jeffrey Bruma | 13.11.1991 | 8 | (2) | |
| Rami Kaib (TUN) | 08.05.1997 | 5 | (16) | 1 |
| Mats Köhlert (GER) | 02.05.1998 | 31 | | 1 |
| Joost van Aken | 13.05.1994 | 11 | (4) | |
| Sven van Beek | 28.07.1994 | 15 | | |
| Milan van Ewijk | 08.09.2000 | 34 | | 6 |
| Syb van Ottele | 02.02.2002 | 12 | (8) | 1 |

| Midfielders: | DOB | M | (s) | G |
|---|---|---|---|---|
| Rami Al Hajj (SWE) | 17.09.2001 | 7 | (10) | |
| Tibor Halilović (CRO) | 18.03.1995 | 7 | (12) | |
| Thom Haye | 09.02.1995 | 30 | (1) | 2 |
| Simon Olsson (SWE) | 14.09.1997 | 27 | (6) | |
| Anas Tahiri (BEL) | 15.05.1995 | 30 | (2) | 1 |
| Pelle van Amersfoort | 01.04.1996 | 13 | (6) | 3 |
| Timo Zaal | 09.02.2004 | | (1) | |
| **Forwards:** | **DOB** | **M** | **(s)** | **G** |
| Alex Timossi Andersson (SWE) | 19.01.2001 | 1 | (11) | |
| Antoine Colassin (BEL) | 26.02.2001 | 8 | (14) | 3 |
| Daniel Karlsbakk (NOR) | 07.04.2003 | 1 | (9) | |
| Ché Nunnely | 04.02.1999 | 7 | (6) | 1 |
| Osame Sahraoui (NOR) | 11.06.2001 | 12 | (3) | 1 |
| Amin Sarr (SWE) | 11.03.2001 | 18 | (1) | 5 |
| Sydney van Hooijdonk | 06.02.2000 | 30 | (3) | 16 |

## Nijmegen Eendracht Combinatie

| Founded: | 15.11.1900 | | |
|---|---|---|---|
| Stadium: | Goffertstadion, Nijmegen (12,500) | | |
| Trainer: | Rogier Meijer | | 05.09.1981 |

| Goalkeepers: | DOB | M | (s) | G |
|---|---|---|---|---|
| Mattijs Branderhorst | 31.12.1993 | 2 | | |
| Jacobus Antonius Peter Cillessen | 22.04.1989 | 32 | | |
| **Defenders:** | **DOB** | **M** | **(s)** | **G** |
| Ilias Bronkhorst | 10.05.1997 | | (4) | |
| Souffian el Karouani (MAR) | 19.10.2000 | 33 | | 2 |
| Iván Márquez Álvarez (ESP) | 09.06.1994 | 31 | | 3 |
| Joris Kramer | 02.08.1996 | 11 | (11) | |
| Terry Lartey Sanniez | 10.08.1996 | 1 | (8) | |
| Philippe Sandler | 10.02.1997 | 20 | (1) | 1 |
| Bart van Rooij | 26.05.2001 | 33 | | |
| Calvin Verdonk | 26.04.1997 | 10 | (7) | |

| Midfielders: | DOB | M | (s) | G |
|---|---|---|---|---|
| Andri Baldursson (ISL) | 10.01.2002 | 1 | (10) | |
| Jordy Bruijn | 23.07.1996 | 4 | (15) | 2 |
| Dirk Proper | 24.02.2002 | 32 | | 1 |
| Lasse Schöne (DEN) | 27.05.1986 | 32 | | 1 |
| Oussama Tannane (MAR) | 23.03.1994 | 25 | | 6 |
| **Forwards:** | **DOB** | **M** | **(s)** | **G** |
| Ibrahim Cissoko | 26.03.2003 | 9 | (17) | 2 |
| Landry Dimata (BEL) | 01.09.1997 | 25 | (5) | 10 |
| Mikkel Duelund (DEN) | 29.06.1997 | 11 | (4) | 1 |
| Magnus Mattsson (DEN) | 25.02.1999 | 23 | (2) | 4 |
| Anthony Musaba | 06.12.2000 | 2 | (14) | 1 |
| Pedro David Rosendo Marques (POR) | 25.04.1998 | 7 | (23) | 5 |
| Elayis Tavşan | 30.04.2001 | 30 | (2) | 3 |

## Philips Sport Vereniging Eindhoven

| | |
|---|---|
| Founded: | 31.08.1913 |
| Stadium: | Philips Stadion, Eindhoven (36,500) |
| Trainer: | Rutgerus Johannes Martinus van Nistelrooij 01.07.1976 |
| [24.05.2023] | Fredericus Jacobus Rutten 05.12.1962 |

| Goalkeepers: | DOB | M | (s) | G |
|---|---|---|---|---|
| Walter Daniel Benítez (ARG) | 19.01.1993 | 30 | | |
| Joël Drommel | 16.11.1996 | 4 | | |
| **Defenders:** | **DOB** | **M** | **(s)** | **G** |
| André Ramalho Silva (BRA) | 16.02.1992 | 20 | (8) | |
| Olivier Boscagli (FRA) | 18.11.1997 | 2 | (5) | 1 |
| Jarrad Branthwaite (ENG) | 27.06.2002 | 21 | (6) | 2 |
| Ki-Jana Delano Hoever | 18.01.2002 | 2 | (3) | |
| Mauro Jaqueson Júnior Ferreira dos Santos (BRA) | 06.05.1999 | 3 | (3) | |
| Philipp Max (GER) | 30.09.1993 | 12 | (2) | |
| Phillipp Mwene (AUT) | 29.01.1994 | 19 | (6) | |
| Armando Obispo | 05.03.1999 | 21 | (1) | 2 |
| Fredrik Oppegård (NOR) | 07.08.2002 | 1 | (2) | |
| Jordan Teze | 30.09.1999 | 23 | (4) | |
| Patrick van Aanholt | 29.08.1990 | 13 | (2) | 1 |
| **Midfielders:** | **DOB** | **M** | **(s)** | **G** |
| Érick Gabriel Gutiérrez Galaviz (MEX) | 15.06.1995 | 13 | (17) | 2 |
| Richard Ledezma (USA) | 06.09.2000 | 1 | (6) | |
| Ibrahim Sangaré (CIV) | 02.12.1997 | 26 | (3) | 5 |
| Xavier Quentin Shay Simons | 21.04.2003 | 34 | | 19 |
| Guus Til | 22.12.1997 | 19 | (11) | 9 |
| Marco van Ginkel | 01.12.1992 | | (1) | |
| Joey Veerman | 19.11.1998 | 30 | (3) | 4 |
| **Forwards:** | **DOB** | **M** | **(s)** | **G** |
| Johan Bakayoko (BEL) | 20.04.2003 | 17 | (6) | 5 |
| Carlos Vinícius Alves Morais (BRA) | 25.03.1995 | | (1) | |
| Luuk de Jong | 27.08.1990 | 23 | (1) | 14 |
| Anwar El Ghazi | 03.05.1995 | 12 | (11) | 8 |
| Fábio Daniel Soares Silva (POR) | 19.07.2002 | 5 | (9) | 4 |
| Fodé Fofana | 26.10.2002 | | (1) | |
| Cody Mathès Gakpo | 07.05.1999 | 14 | | 9 |
| Thorgan Ganael Francis Hazard (BEL) | 29.03.1993 | 1 | (8) | 1 |
| Chukwunonso Tristan Madueke (ENG) | 10.03.2002 | 2 | (3) | 1 |
| Ismael Saibari (MAR) | 18.07.2001 | 5 | (12) | |
| Sávio Moreira de Oliveira (BRA) | 10.04.2004 | | (6) | |
| Yorbe Vertessen (BEL) | 08.01.2001 | 1 | (7) | |

## Rooms Katholieke Combinatie Waalwijk

| | |
|---|---|
| Founded: | 26.08.1940 |
| Stadium: | Mandemakers Stadion, Waalwijk (7,500) |
| Trainer: | Joseph Oosting 29.01.1972 |

| Goalkeepers: | DOB | M | (s) | G |
|---|---|---|---|---|
| Joel Dinis Castro Pereira (POR) | 28.06.1996 | 2 | | |
| Etienne Vaessen | 26.07.1995 | 32 | | |
| **Defenders:** | **DOB** | **M** | **(s)** | **G** |
| Shawn Adewoye (BEL) | 29.06.2000 | 33 | | 1 |
| Juriën Gaari (CUW) | 23.12.1993 | 33 | | |
| Julian Lelieveld | 24.11.1997 | 34 | | 2 |
| Thierry Lutonda (BEL) | 27.10.2000 | 32 | (1) | 1 |
| Lars Nieuwpoort | 29.10.1994 | 6 | (4) | |
| Dario Van Den Buijs (BEL) | 12.09.1995 | 24 | (2) | 3 |
| Luuk Wouters | 08.06.1999 | 1 | (5) | |
| **Midfielders:** | **DOB** | **M** | **(s)** | **G** |
| Vurnon Anita (CUW) | 04.04.1989 | 30 | (4) | 2 |
| Sebbe Augustijns (BEL) | 03.09.1999 | | (6) | |
| Iliass Bel Hassani | 16.09.1992 | 20 | (1) | 5 |
| Pelle Clement | 19.05.1996 | 30 | (3) | 2 |
| Kevin Felida (CUW) | 11.11.1999 | | (6) | |
| Chris Lokesa (BEL) | 07.11.2004 | | (1) | |
| Hans Mulder | 27.04.1987 | | (2) | |
| Yassin Oukili (MAR) | 03.01.2001 | 20 | (11) | 3 |
| Mats Seuntjens | 17.04.1992 | 18 | (1) | 4 |
| Patrick Vroegh | 29.11.1999 | 5 | (11) | |
| **Forwards:** | **DOB** | **M** | **(s)** | **G** |
| Saïd Riad Bakari (COM) | 22.09.1994 | 2 | (24) | |
| Zakaria Bakkali (BEL) | 26.01.1996 | 1 | (17) | 3 |
| Mika Biereth (DEN) | 08.02.2003 | 2 | (10) | 2 |
| Lennerd Daneels (BEL) | 10.04.1998 | 3 | | |
| Florian Jozefzoon (SUR) | 09.02.1991 | 9 | (17) | 5 |
| Julen Lobete Cienfuegos (ESP) | 18.09.2000 | 12 | (17) | 4 |
| Michiel Kramer | 03.12.1988 | 24 | (3) | 12 |
| Roy Kuijpers | 17.01.2000 | 1 | (15) | |

## Sparta Rotterdam

| | |
|---|---|
| Founded: | 01.04.1888 |
| Stadium: | Stadion Sparta, Rotterdam (11,000) |
| Trainer: | Maurice Steijn 20.11.1973 |

| Goalkeepers: | DOB | M | (s) | G |
|---|---|---|---|---|
| Nick Olij | 01.08.1995 | 32 | | |
| Youri Schoonderwaldt | 13.03.2000 | 2 | | |
| **Defenders:** | **DOB** | **M** | **(s)** | **G** |
| Dirk Abels | 13.06.1997 | 12 | (14) | 1 |
| Adil Auassar | 06.10.1986 | 22 | (7) | |
| Mike Eerdhuijzen | 13.07.2000 | 12 | (13) | |
| Aaron Meijers | 28.10.1987 | 1 | (12) | |
| Rick Meissen | 24.02.2002 | | (4) | |
| Michael „Mica" Gonçalves Pinto (LUX) | 04.06.1993 | 33 | | 3 |
| Omar Rekik (TUN) | 20.12.2001 | | (6) | |
| Shurandy Sambo | 19.08.2001 | 28 | (2) | 2 |
| Dylan van Wageningen | 18.01.2003 | | (1) | |
| Bart Vriends | 09.05.1991 | 29 | (1) | 2 |
| **Midfielders:** | **DOB** | **M** | **(s)** | **G** |
| Jonathan de Guzmán | 13.09.1987 | 17 | (4) | 2 |
| Joshua Kitolano (NOR) | 03.08.2001 | 29 | (5) | 4 |
| Sven Mijnans | 09.03.2000 | 16 | (3) | 3 |
| Younes Gaston Namli (DEN) | 20.06.1994 | 17 | (9) | 1 |
| Pedro Alemañ Serna (ESP) | 21.03.2002 | | (5) | |
| Rayvien Rosario (CUW) | 11.04.2004 | | (1) | |
| Jeremy van Mullem | 18.03.1999 | 7 | (20) | |
| Arno Verschueren (BEL) | 08.04.1997 | 28 | (3) | 9 |
| **Forwards:** | **DOB** | **M** | **(s)** | **G** |
| Patrick Brouwer | 19.03.2001 | | (2) | |
| Charles-Andreas Brym (CAN) | 08.08.1998 | | (2) | |
| Mario Engels (GER) | 22.10.1993 | | (9) | 1 |
| Jason Eyenga-Lokilo (COD) | 17.09.1998 | 3 | (4) | |
| Tobias Lauritsen (NOR) | 30.08.1997 | 34 | | 12 |
| Dano Lourens | 04.03.2004 | | (1) | |
| Elias Hoff Melkersen (NOR) | 31.12.2002 | | (2) | |
| Koki Saito (JPN) | 10.08.2001 | 19 | (7) | 7 |
| Mohammed Tahiri (MAR) | 22.01.2001 | | (6) | |
| Vito van Crooij | 29.01.1996 | 33 | (1) | 12 |

## Football Club Twente Enschede

| | |
|---|---|
| Founded: | 01.07.1965 |
| Stadium: | Stadion De Groisch Veste, Enschede (30,205) |
| Trainer: | Ron Jans 29.09.1958 |

| Goalkeepers: | DOB | M | (s) | G |
|---|---|---|---|---|
| Przemysław Tytoń (POL) | 04.01.1987 | 1 | | |
| Lars Unnerstall (GER) | 20.07.1990 | 33 | | |
| **Defenders:** | **DOB** | **M** | **(s)** | **G** |
| Joshua Brenet | 20.03.1994 | 28 | (4) | 7 |
| Max Bruns | 06.11.2002 | 4 | (5) | |
| Luca Everink | 09.02.2001 | | (3) | |
| Mees Hilgers | 13.05.2001 | 25 | (3) | 1 |
| Julio José Pleguezuelo Selva (ESP) | 26.01.1997 | 11 | (12) | 2 |
| Robin Pröpper | 23.09.1993 | 29 | | 1 |
| Alfons Sampsted (ISL) | 06.04.1998 | 5 | (7) | |
| Gijs Smal | 31.08.1997 | 34 | | 2 |
| **Midfielders:** | **DOB** | **M** | **(s)** | **G** |
| Wout Brama | 21.08.1986 | | (11) | |
| Mathias Kjølø (NOR) | 27.06.2001 | 11 | (11) | |
| Michal Sadílek (CZE) | 31.05.1999 | 12 | (2) | 2 |
| Anass Salah-Eddine | 18.01.2002 | 7 | (7) | |
| Casper Staring | 01.02.2001 | | (1) | |
| Sem Steijn | 17.11.2001 | 12 | (15) | 6 |
| Michel Vlap | 02.06.1997 | 27 | (5) | 3 |
| Ramiz Zerrouki (ALG) | 26.05.1998 | 32 | | 1 |
| **Forwards:** | **DOB** | **M** | **(s)** | **G** |
| Vaclav Černý (CZE) | 17.10.1997 | 29 | (3) | 13 |
| Denilho Cleonise | 08.12.2001 | 2 | (11) | 1 |
| Virgil Misidjan | 24.07.1993 | 26 | (5) | 8 |
| Daan Rots | 25.07.2001 | 5 | (17) | |
| Sander Sybrandy | 31.03.2004 | | (1) | |
| Christos Tzolis (GRE) | 30.01.2002 | 5 | (5) | 1 |
| Manfred Alonso Ugalde Arce (CRC) | 25.05.2002 | 8 | (16) | 8 |
| Ricky van Wolfswinkel | 27.01.1989 | 28 | (6) | 9 |

## Football Club Utrecht

| Founded: | 01.07.1970 | |
|---|---|---|
| Stadium: | Stadion Galgenwaard, Utrecht (23,750) | |
| Trainer: | Hendrikus Fraser | 07.07.1966 |
| [14.12.2022] | Aleksandar Ranković (SRB) | 31.08.1978 |
| [28.12.2022] | Michael Silberbauer (DEN) | 07.07.1981 |

| Goalkeepers: | DOB | M | (s) | G |
|---|---|---|---|---|
| Vasilis Barkas (GRE) | 30.05.1994 | 32 | | |
| Fabian de Keijzer | 10.05.2000 | 2 | | |
| **Defenders:** | **DOB** | **M** | **(s)** | **G** |
| Ramon Hendriks | 18.07.2001 | 4 | | |
| Sean Klaiber (SUR) | 31.07.1994 | 25 | (3) | 1 |
| Ruben Kluivert | 21.05.2001 | 3 | (10) | |
| Modibo Sagnan (FRA) | 14.04.1999 | 22 | (1) | 1 |
| Hidde ter Avest | 20.05.1997 | 9 | (11) | |
| Mike van der Hoorn | 15.10.1992 | 24 | (1) | 1 |
| Djevencio van der Kust | 30.04.2001 | 7 | (1) | |
| Mark van der Maarel | 12.08.1989 | 24 | (5) | |
| Nick Viergever | 03.08.1989 | 18 | (1) | 2 |
| Django Warmerdam | 02.09.1995 | 2 | (4) | |
| Arthur Zagré (FRA) | 04.10.2001 | | (2) | |
| **Midfielders:** | **DOB** | **M** | **(s)** | **G** |
| Can Bozdoğan (GER) | 05.04.2001 | 15 | (9) | 1 |
| Luuk Brouwers | 03.05.1998 | 18 | (6) | |
| Victor Jensen (DEN) | 08.02.2000 | 4 | (8) | 1 |

| | DOB | M | (s) | G |
|---|---|---|---|---|
| Zakaria Labyad (MAR) | 09.03.1993 | 3 | (4) | 1 |
| Albert-Nicolas Lottin (FRA) | 29.08.2001 | | (1) | |
| Bart Ramselaar | 29.06.1996 | 3 | (6) | |
| Rocco Robert Shein (EST) | 14.07.2003 | | (5) | |
| Jens Toornstra | 04.04.1989 | 28 | | 1 |
| Sander van de Streek | 24.03.1993 | 26 | (2) | 9 |
| **Forwards:** | **DOB** | **M** | **(s)** | **G** |
| Taylor Anthony Booth (USA) | 31.05.2001 | 20 | (4) | 2 |
| Othmane Boussaid (BEL) | 07.03.2000 | 25 | (7) | 3 |
| Anthony Descotte (BEL) | 03.08.2003 | 1 | (5) | 1 |
| Bas Leon Dost | 31.05.1989 | 14 | (8) | 9 |
| Anastasios Douvikas (GRE) | 02.08.1999 | 24 | (8) | 19 |
| Naoki Maeda (JPN) | 17.11.1994 | 3 | (8) | |
| Mimoun Mahi | 13.03.1994 | | (2) | |
| Daishawn Orpheo Marvin Redan (SUR) | 02.02.2001 | 10 | (4) | 1 |
| Derensili Sanches Fernandes | 28.05.2001 | | (3) | |
| Moussa Sylla (FRA) | 25.11.1999 | 5 | (5) | 1 |
| Amin Younes (GER) | 06.08.1993 | 3 | (7) | |

## Stichting Betaald Voetbal Vitesse Arnhem

| Founded: | 14.05.1892 | |
|---|---|---|
| Stadium: | GelreDome, Arnhem (21,248) | |
| Trainer: | Thomas Letsch (GER) | 26.08.1968 |
| [26.09.2022] | Phillip John-William Cocu | 29.10.1970 |

| Goalkeepers: | DOB | M | (s) | G |
|---|---|---|---|---|
| Jeroen Houwen | 18.02.1996 | 2 | (1) | |
| Daan Reiziger | 18.06.2001 | 6 | (2) | |
| Kjell Scherpen | 23.01.2000 | 26 | | |
| **Defenders:** | **DOB** | **M** | **(s)** | **G** |
| Carlens Arcus (HAI) | 28.06.1996 | 28 | (2) | 1 |
| Enzo Cornelisse | 01.01.2003 | 15 | (5) | |
| Mitchell Dijks | 09.02.1993 | 3 | (4) | |
| Francisco Reis Ferreira „Ferro" (POR) | 26.03.1997 | 6 | (3) | |
| Ryan Flamingo | 31.12.2002 | 30 | (3) | 3 |
| Tomáš Hájek (CZE) | 01.12.1991 | 2 | (5) | |
| Nicolas Isimat-Mirin (FRA) | 15.11.1991 | 13 | (3) | |
| Melle Meulensteen | 04.07.1999 | 31 | (1) | 1 |
| Dominik Oroz (CRO) | 29.10.2000 | 11 | (5) | 1 |
| Maximilian Wittek (GER) | 21.08.1995 | 31 | | 3 |
| Romaric Yapi (FRA) | 13.07.2000 | 3 | (13) | |

| **Midfielders:** | **DOB** | **M** | **(s)** | **G** |
|---|---|---|---|---|
| Matúš Bero (SVK) | 06.09.1995 | 31 | | 5 |
| Toni Domgjoni (KOS) | 04.09.1998 | 3 | (4) | |
| Daan Huisman | 26.07.2002 | | (2) | |
| Kacper Kozłowski (POL) | 16.10.2003 | 26 | (3) | 2 |
| Million Manhoef | 03.01.2002 | 27 | (6) | 9 |
| Davy Pröpper | 02.09.1991 | 1 | (1) | |
| Sondre Tronstad (NOR) | 26.08.1995 | 21 | (7) | 2 |
| Marco van Ginkel | 01.12.1992 | 13 | | 2 |
| Gabriel Vidović (GER) | 01.12.2003 | 14 | (11) | 4 |
| **Forwards:** | **DOB** | **M** | **(s)** | **G** |
| Nikolai Baden Frederiksen (DEN) | 18.05.2000 | 5 | (8) | 2 |
| Bartosz Białek (POL) | 11.11.2001 | 18 | (7) | 5 |
| Thomas Buitink | 14.01.2000 | 1 | (7) | |
| Gyan de Regt | 18.08.2003 | | (2) | |
| Miliano Jonathans | 05.04.2004 | | (12) | |
| Mohamed Sankoh | 16.10.2003 | 6 | (15) | 2 |
| Simon van Duivenbooden | 11.05.2002 | 1 | (8) | 1 |

## Football Club Volendam

| Founded: | 01.06.1977 | |
|---|---|---|
| Stadium: | Kras Stadion, Volendam (7,384) | |
| Trainer: | Wilhelmus Maria Jonk | 12.10.1966 |

| Goalkeepers: | DOB | M | (s) | G |
|---|---|---|---|---|
| Barry Lauwers | 29.11.1999 | 1 | | |
| Filip Stanković (SRB) | 25.02.2002 | 33 | | |
| **Defenders:** | **DOB** | **M** | **(s)** | **G** |
| Oskar Buur Rasmussen (DEN) | 31.03.1998 | 11 | (5) | 1 |
| Achraf Douiri | 27.11.1999 | 5 | (4) | |
| Joshua Hughson Flint (ENG) | 13.10.2000 | 8 | (4) | |
| Dean James | 30.04.2000 | 4 | (3) | |
| Xavier Mbuyamba | 31.12.2001 | 28 | | 5 |
| Damon Mirani | 13.05.1996 | 29 | (2) | 3 |
| Derry John Murkin (ENG) | 27.07.1999 | 32 | | |
| Deron Payne | 25.09.2002 | 1 | (2) | |
| Brian Plat | 05.04.2000 | 26 | (3) | |
| Givairo Read | 02.06.2006 | | (1) | |
| Billy van Duijl | 04.10.2005 | 2 | (1) | |
| **Midfielders:** | **DOB** | **M** | **(s)** | **G** |
| Joey Antonioli | 15.12.2003 | | (1) | |
| Franco Antonucci (BEL) | 20.06.1999 | 10 | (7) | 2 |

| | DOB | M | (s) | G |
|---|---|---|---|---|
| Benaissa Benamar (MAR) | 08.04.1997 | 24 | (5) | 2 |
| Carel Eiting | 11.02.1998 | 34 | | 3 |
| Flip Klomp | 18.10.2001 | | (1) | |
| Imran Nazih | 25.01.2006 | | (3) | |
| Gaetano Oristanio (ITA) | 28.09.2002 | 24 | (3) | 1 |
| Walid Ould-Chikh | 06.11.1999 | 4 | (23) | 1 |
| Florent Sanchez Da Silva (FRA) | 02.04.2003 | 8 | (5) | 1 |
| Calvin Twigt | 30.01.2003 | 16 | | 1 |
| **Forwards:** | **DOB** | **M** | **(s)** | **G** |
| Jordi Blom | 05.06.2002 | | (2) | |
| Ibrahim el Kadiri | 23.01.2002 | 8 | (9) | |
| Darius Johnson (GRN) | 15.03.2000 | | (2) | |
| Robert Mühren | 18.05.1989 | 21 | (7) | 5 |
| Bilal Ould-Chikh (MAR) | 28.07.1997 | 10 | (7) | 2 |
| Daryl van Mieghem | 05.12.1989 | 22 | (8) | 8 |
| Henk Veerman | 26.02.1991 | 11 | (18) | 4 |
| Lequincio Zeefuik | 26.11.2004 | 2 | (12) | 2 |

## SECOND LEVEL
### Eerste Divisie 2022/2023

| | | | | | | | | | |
|---|---|---|---|---|---|---|---|---|---|
| 1. | Heracles Almelo (*Promoted*) | 38 | 27 | 4 | 7 | 103 | - | 42 | 85 |
| 2. | PEC Zwolle (*Promoted*) | 38 | 27 | 4 | 7 | 99 | - | 43 | 85 |
| 3. | Almere City FC | 38 | 21 | 7 | 10 | 58 | - | 41 | 70 |
| 4. | Willem II Tilburg | 38 | 19 | 11 | 8 | 68 | - | 40 | 68 |
| 5. | MVV Maastricht | 38 | 18 | 5 | 15 | 65 | - | 65 | 59 |
| 6. | NAC Breda | 38 | 18 | 5 | 15 | 64 | - | 64 | 59 |
| 7. | VVV-Venlo | 38 | 16 | 10 | 12 | 56 | - | 51 | 58 |
| 8. | FC Eindhoven | 38 | 16 | 10 | 12 | 58 | - | 54 | 58 |
| 9. | SC Telstar Velsen | 38 | 14 | 11 | 13 | 39 | - | 52 | 53 |
| 10. | VBV De Graafschap Doetinchem | 38 | 15 | 7 | 16 | 64 | - | 54 | 52 |
| 11. | Jong AZ Alkmaar* | 38 | 14 | 9 | 15 | 60 | - | 58 | 51 |
| 12. | ADO Den Haag | 38 | 13 | 12 | 13 | 51 | - | 57 | 51 |
| 13. | Jong Ajax Amsterdam* | 38 | 12 | 10 | 16 | 69 | - | 72 | 46 |
| 14. | Jong PSV Eindhoven* | 38 | 12 | 9 | 17 | 59 | - | 63 | 45 |
| 15. | SV Roda JC Kerkrade | 38 | 12 | 7 | 19 | 49 | - | 59 | 43 |
| 16. | Helmond Sport | 38 | 11 | 10 | 17 | 39 | - | 57 | 43 |
| 17. | Tot Ons Plezier Oss | 38 | 10 | 7 | 21 | 45 | - | 76 | 37 |
| 18. | FC Dordrecht | 38 | 9 | 8 | 21 | 41 | - | 68 | 35 |
| 19. | FC Den Bosch | 38 | 10 | 5 | 23 | 46 | - | 85 | 35 |
| 20. | Jong FC Utrecht* | 38 | 7 | 7 | 24 | 33 | - | 65 | 28 |

Teams ranked 3-8 were qualified for the Promotion Play-offs.
*Reserve teams are not eligible to be promoted.

## NATIONAL TEAM

### INTERNATIONAL MATCHES
#### (16.07.2022 – 15.07.2023)

| | | | | |
|---|---|---|---|---|
| 22.09.2022 | Warszawa | *Poland - Netherlands* | *0-2(0-1)* | (UNL) |
| 25.09.2022 | Amsterdam | *Netherlands - Belgium* | *1-0(0-0)* | (UNL) |
| 21.11.2022 | Doha | *Senegal - Netherlands* | *0-2(0-0)* | (WC) |
| 25.11.2022 | Al Rayyan | *Netherlands - Ecuador* | *1-1(1-0)* | (WC) |
| 29.11.2022 | Al Khor | *Netherlands - Qatar* | *2-0(1-0)* | (WC) |
| 03.12.2022 | Al Rayyan | *Netherlands - United States* | *3-1(2-0)* | (WC) |
| 09.12.2022 | Lusail | *Netherlands - Argentina* | *2-2(0-1,2-2,2-2); 3-4 pen* | (WC) |
| 24.03.2023 | Paris | *France - Netherlands* | *4-0(3-0)* | (ECQ) |
| 27.03.2023 | Rotterdam | *Netherlands - Gibraltar* | *3-0(1-0)* | (ECQ) |
| 14.06.2023 | Rotterdam | *Netherlands - Croatia* | *2-4(1-0,2-2)* | (UNL) |
| 18.06.2023 | Enschede | *Netherlands - Italy* | *2-3(0-2)* | (UNL) |

**22.09.2022 POLAND - NETHERLANDS**     **0-2(0-1)**     3rd UEFA Nations League A, Group 4
Stadion Narodowy, Warszawa; Referee: Alejandro José Hernández Hernández (Spain); Attendance: 56,673
**NED:** Remko Jurian Pasveer, Denzel Justus Morris Dumfries, Virgil van Dijk (Cap), Nathan Benjamin Aké, Daley Blind, Frenkie de Jong (46.Marten Elco de Roon), Jurriën David Norman Timber, Cody Mathès Gakpo, Teun Koopmeiners (6.Steven Berghuis; 75.Kenneth Ina Dorothea Taylor), Memphis Depay (52.Vincent Petrus Anna Sebastiaan Janssen), Steven Charles Bergwijn (75.Wout Weghorst). Trainer: Louis van Gaal.
**Goals:** Cody Mathès Gakpo (13), Steven Charles Bergwijn (60).

**25.09.2022 NETHERLANDS - BELGIUM**     **1-0(0-0)**     3rd UEFA Nations League A, Group 4
"Johan Cruyff" Arena, Amsterdam; Referee: Anthony Taylor (England); Attendance: 52,314
**NED:** Remko Jurian Pasveer, Denzel Justus Morris Dumfries, Virgil van Dijk (Cap), Daley Blind, Nathan Benjamin Aké (46.Tyrell Malacia), Marten Elco de Roon, Jurriën David Norman Timber (65.Stefan de Vrij), Davy Klaassen (90+2.Ryan Jiro Gravenberch), Vincent Petrus Anna Sebastiaan Janssen (46.Kenneth Ina Dorothea Taylor), Steven Berghuis (31.Cody Mathès Gakpo), Steven Charles Bergwijn. Trainer: Louis van Gaal.
**Goal:** Virgil van Dijk (73).

**21.11.2022 SENEGAL - NETHERLANDS**     **0-2(0-0)**     22nd FIFA WC. Group Stage.
Al Thumama Stadium, Doha (Qatar); Referee: Wilton Pereira Sampaio (Brazil); Attendance: 41,721
**NED:** Andries Noppert, Denzel Justus Morris Dumfries, Matthijs de Ligt, Virgil van Dijk (Cap), Nathan Benjamin Aké, Daley Blind, Steven Berghuis (79.Teun Koopmeiners), Frenkie de Jong, Cody Mathès Gakpo (90+4.Marten Elco de Roon), Vincent Petrus Anna Sebastiaan Janssen (62.Memphis Depay), Steven Charles Bergwijn (79.Davy Klaassen). Trainer: Louis van Gaal.
**Goals:** Cody Mathès Gakpo (84), Davy Klaassen (90+9).

**25.11.2022 NETHERLANDS - ECUADOR**     **1-1(1-0)**     22nd FIFA WC. Group Stage.
Khalifa International Stadium, Al Rayyan (Qatar); Referee: Mustapha Ghorbal (Algeria); Attendance: 44,833
**NED:** Andries Noppert, Jurriën David Norman Timber, Virgil van Dijk (Cap), Nathan Benjamin Aké, Denzel Justus Morris Dumfries, Teun Koopmeiners (79.Marten Elco de Roon), Frenkie de Jong, Daley Blind, Davy Klaassen (69.Steven Berghuis), Cody Mathès Gakpo (79.Wout François Maria Weghorst), Steven Charles Bergwijn (46.Memphis Depay). Trainer: Louis van Gaal.
**Goal:** Cody Mathès Gakpo (6).

**29.11.2022**   **NETHERLANDS - QATAR**                          **2-0(1-0)**                          22<sup>nd</sup> FIFA WC. Group Stage.

Al Bayt Stadium, Al Khor; Referee: Bakary Papa Gassama (Gambia); Attendance: 66,784
**NED:** Andries Noppert, Jurriën David Norman Timber, Virgil van Dijk (Cap), Nathan Benjamin Aké, Denzel Justus Morris Dumfries, Marten Elco de Roon (83.Teun Koopmeiners), Frenkie de Jong (86.Kenneth Ina Dorothea Taylor), Daley Blind, Davy Klaassen (66.Steven Berghuis), Cody Mathès Gakpo (82.Wout François Maria Weghorst), Memphis Depay (66.Vincent Petrus Anna Sebastiaan Janssen). Trainer: Louis van Gaal.
**Goals:** Cody Mathès Gakpo (26), Frenkie de Jong (49).

**03.12.2022**   **NETHERLANDS - UNITED STATES**                 **3-1(2-0)**                          22<sup>nd</sup> FIFA WC. 2<sup>nd</sup> Round of 16.

Khalifa International Stadium, Al Rayyan (Qatar); Referee: Wilton Pereira Sampaio (Brazil); Attendance: 44,846
**NED:** Andries Noppert, Jurriën David Norman Timber, Virgil van Dijk (Cap), Nathan Benjamin Aké (90+3.Matthijs de Ligt), Denzel Justus Morris Dumfries, Marten Elco de Roon (46.Steven Charles Bergwijn), Frenkie de Jong, Daley Blind, Davy Klaassen (46.Teun Koopmeiners), Cody Mathès Gakpo (90+3.Wout François Maria Weghorst), Memphis Depay (82.Xavi Quentin Shay Simons). Trainer: Louis van Gaal.
**Goals:** Memphis Depay (10), Daley Blind (45+1), Denzel Justus Morris Dumfries (81).

**09.12.2022**   **NETHERLANDS - ARGENTINA**              **2-2(0-1,2-2,2-2); 3-4 on penalties**      22<sup>nd</sup> FIFA WC. Quarter-Finals.

Lusail Stadium, Lusail (Qatar); Referee: Antonio Miguel Mateu Lahoz (Spain); Attendance: 88,235
**NED:** Andries Noppert, Jurriën David Norman Timber, Virgil van Dijk (Cap), Nathan Benjamin Aké, Denzel Justus Morris Dumfries [*sent off 120+9*], Marten Elco de Roon (46.Teun Koopmeiners), Frenkie de Jong, Daley Blind (64.Luuk de Jong), Cody Mathès Gakpo (113.Noa Noëll Lang), Memphis Depay (78.Wout François Maria Weghorst), Steven Charles Bergwijn (46.Steven Berghuis). Trainer: Louis van Gaal.
**Goals:** Wout François Maria Weghorst (83, 90+11).
**Penalties:** Virgil van Dijk (saved), Steven Berghuis (saved), Teun Koopmeiners, Wout François Maria Weghorst, Luuk de Jong.

**24.03.2023**   **FRANCE - NETHERLANDS**                       **4-0(3-0)**                          17<sup>th</sup> EC. Qualifiers

Stade de France, Saint-Denis, Paris; Referee: Maurizio Mariani (Italy); Attendance: 77,328
**NED:** Jacobus Antonius Peter Cillessen, Lutsharel Geertruida (87.Tyrell Malacia), Virgil van Dijk (Cap), Nathan Benjamin Aké, Marten Elco de Roon (67.Daley Blind), Jurriën David Norman Timber, Kenneth Ina Dorothea Taylor (35.Wout Weghorst), Georginio Gregion Emile Wijnaldum, Xavier Quentin Shay Simons (68.Davy Klaassen), Steven Berghuis (68.Donyell Malen), Memphis Depay. Trainer: Ronald Koeman.

**27.03.2023**   **NETHERLANDS - GIBRALTAR**                    **3-0(1-0)**                          17<sup>th</sup> EC. Qualifiers

Stadion Feijenoord, Rotterdam; Referee: Morten Krogh (Denmark); Attendance: 36,327
**NED:** Jacobus Antonius Peter Cillessen, Denzel Justus Morris Dumfries, Virgil van Dijk (Cap), Matthijs de Ligt (76.Tyrell Malacia), Nathan Benjamin Aké, Mats Wieffer (63.Daley Blind), Georginio Gregion Emile Wijnaldum (46.Cody Mathès Gakpo), Steven Berghuis (46.Donyell Malen), Xavier Quentin Shay Simons, Wout Weghorst, Memphis Depay (63.Davy Klaassen). Trainer: Ronald Koeman.
**Goals:** Memphis Depay (23), Nathan Benjamin Aké (50, 82).

**14.06.2023**   **NETHERLANDS - CROATIA**                    **2-4(1-0,2-2)**                        3<sup>rd</sup> UEFA Nations League, Semi-Finals

Stadion Feijenoord, Rotterdam; Referee: István Kovács (Romania); Attendance: 39,359
**NED:** Justin Bijlow, Denzel Justus Morris Dumfries (85.Noa Noëll Lang), Lutsharel Geertruida, Virgil van Dijk (Cap), Nathan Benjamin Aké (106.Tyrell Malacia), Frenkie de Jong, Mats Wieffer (75.Georginio Gregion Emile Wijnaldum), Teun Koopmeiners, Cody Mathès Gakpo (106.Marten Elco de Roon), Xavier Quentin Shay Simons (64.Wout Weghorst), Donyell Malen (75.Steven Charles Bergwijn). Trainer: Ronald Koeman.
**Goals:** Donyell Malen (34), Noa Noëll Lang (90+6).

**18.06.2023**   **NETHERLANDS - ITALY**                        **2-3(0-2)**                          3<sup>rd</sup> UEFA Nations League, Third Place Play-off

Stadion De Groisch Veste, Enschede (Netherlands); Referee: Glenn Nyberg (Sweden); Attendance: 21,292
**NED:** Justin Bijlow, Denzel Justus Morris Dumfries, Lutsharel Geertruida (46.Georginio Gregion Emile Wijnaldum), Virgil van Dijk (Cap), Nathan Benjamin Aké, Frenkie de Jong, Mats Wieffer (76.Johannes Cornelis Maria Veerman), Cody Mathès Gakpo, Xavier Quentin Shay Simons (63.Teun Koopmeiners), Noa Noëll Lang (46.Wout Weghorst), Donyell Malen (46.Steven Charles Bergwijn). Trainer: Ronald Koeman.
**Goals:** Steven Charles Bergwijn (68), Georginio Gregion Emile Wijnaldum (90).

## NATIONAL TEAM PLAYERS
### (16.07.2022 – 15.07.2023)

| Name | DOB | Caps | Goals | Club |
|---|---|---|---|---|
| **Goalkeepers** | | | | |
| Justin BIJLOW | 22.01.1998 | 8 | 0 | 2022/2023: *Feyenoord Rotterdam* |
| Jacobus Antonius Peter "Jasper" CILLESSEN | 22.04.1989 | 65 | 0 | 2023: *NEC Nijmegen* |
| Andries NOPPERT | 07.04.1994 | 5 | 0 | 2022: *SC Heerenveen* |
| Remko Jurian PASVEER | 08.11.1983 | 2 | 0 | 2022: *AFC Ajax Amsterdam* |
| **Defenders** | | | | |
| Nathan Benjamin AKÉ | 18.02.1995 | 38 | 5 | 2022/2023: *Manchester City FC (ENG)* |
| Daley BLIND | 09.03.1990 | 101 | 3 | 2022: *AFC Ajax Amsterdam* <br> 05.01.2023-> *FC Bayern München (GER)* |
| Matthijs DE LIGT | 12.08.1999 | 41 | 2 | 2022/2023: *FC Bayern München (GER)* |
| Stefan DE VRIJ | 05.02.1992 | 59 | 3 | 2022: *FC Internazionale Milano (ITA)* |
| Denzel Justus Morris DUMFRIES | 18.04.1996 | 45 | 6 | 2022/2023: *FC Internazionale Milano (ITA)* |
| Lutsharel GEERTRUIDA | 18.07.2000 | 3 | 0 | 2023: *Feyenoord Rotterdam* |
| Tyrell MALACIA | 17.08.1999 | 9 | 0 | 2022/2023: *Manchester United FC (ENG)* |
| Jurriën David Norman TIMBER | 17.06.2001 | 15 | 0 | 2022/2023: *AFC Ajax Amsterdam* |
| Virgil VAN DIJK | 08.07.1991 | 58 | 6 | 2022/2023: *Liverpool FC (ENG)* |
| **Midfielders** | | | | |
| Frenkie DE JONG | 12.05.1997 | 52 | 2 | 2022/2023: *FC Barcelona (ESP)* |
| Marten Elco DE ROON | 29.03.1991 | 37 | 0 | 2022/2023: *Atalanta Bergamasca Calcio (ITA)* |
| Ryan Jiro GRAVENBERCH | 16.05.2002 | 11 | 1 | 2022: *FC Bayern München (GER)* |
| Davy KLAASSEN | 21.02.1993 | 41 | 10 | 2022/2023: *AFC Ajax Amsterdam* |
| Teun KOOPMEINERS | 28.02.1998 | 17 | 1 | 2022/2023: *Atalanta Bergamasca Calcio (ITA)* |
| Xavier Quentin Shay SIMONS | 21.04.2003 | 5 | 0 | 2022/2023: *PSV Eindhoven* |
| Kenneth Ina Dorothea TAYLOR | 16.05.2002 | 4 | 0 | 2022/2023: *AFC Ajax Amsterdam* |
| Johannes Cornelis Maria VEERMAN | 19.11.1998 | 1 | 0 | 2023: *PSV Eindhoven* |
| Mats WIEFFER | 16.11.1999 | 3 | 0 | 2023: *Feyenoord Rotterdam* |
| Georginio Gregion Emile WIJNALDUM | 11.11.1990 | 90 | 27 | 2022/2023: *AS Roma (ITA)* |
| **Forwards** | | | | |
| Steven BERGHUIS | 19.12.1991 | 45 | 2 | 2022/2023: *AFC Ajax Amsterdam* |
| Steven Charles BERGWIJN | 08.10.1997 | 30 | 8 | 2022/2023: *AFC Ajax Amsterdam* |
| Luuk DE JONG | 27.08.1990 | 39 | 8 | 2022: *PSV Eindhoven* |
| Memphis DEPAY | 13.02.1994 | 88 | 44 | 2022: *FC Barcelona (ESP)* <br> 20.01.2023-> *Club Atlético de Madrid (ESP)* |
| Cody Mathès GAKPO | 07.05.1999 | 17 | 6 | 2022: *PSV Eindhoven* <br> 01.01.2023-> *Liverpool FC (ENG)* |
| Vincent Petrus Anna Sebastiaan JANSSEN | 15.06.1994 | 22 | 7 | 2022: *Royal Antwerp FC (BEL)* |
| Noa Noëll LANG | 17.06.1999 | 8 | 2 | 2022/2023: *Club Brugge KV (BEL)* |
| Donyell MALEN | 19.01.1999 | 23 | 5 | 2023: *BV Borussia Dortmund (GER)* |
| Wout François Maria WEGHORST | 07.08.1992 | 23 | 5 | 2022: *Beşiktaş JK Istanbul (TUR)* <br> 13.01.2023-> *Manchester United FC (ENG)* |
| **Trainer** | | | | |
| Aloysius Paulus Maria "Louis" VAN GAAL [04.08.2021 – 31.12.2022] | 08.08.1951 | | | 20 M; 14 W; 6 D; 0 L; 51-17 <br> Complete record as trainer of Netherlands: <br> 63 M; 40 W; 19 D; 4 L; 150-48 <br> (02.09.2000 – 10.11.2001) & (15.08.2012 – 12.07.2014) & <br> (04.08.2021 – 31.12.2022) |
| Ronald KOEMAN [from 01.01.2023] | 21.03.1963 | | | 4 M; 1 W; 0 D; 3 L; 7-11 <br> Complete record as trainer of Netherlands: <br> 24 M; 12 W; 5 D; 7 L; 50-29 <br> (06.02.2018 – 18.08.2020) & (from 01.01.2023) |

# NORTH MACEDONIA

### The Country:
Република Северна Македонија (Republic of North Macedonia)
Capital: Skopje
Surface: 25,713 km²
Inhabitants: 1,836,713 [2021]
Time: UTC+1

### The FA:
Fudbalska Federacija na Severna Makedonija
bul. Asnom br.21, 1000 Skopje
Tel: +389 2 312 92 91
Foundation date: 1926
Member of FIFA since: 1926/1994
Member of UEFA since: 1954/1994
Website: www.ffm.mk

## NATIONAL TEAM RECORDS

### RECORDS

| | | |
|---|---|---|
| **First international match:** | 13.10.1993, Kranj: | Slovenia – Macedonia 1-4 |
| **Most international caps:** | Goran Pandev | - 122 caps (2001-2021) |
| **Most international goals:** | Goran Pandev | - 38 goals / 122 caps (2001-2021) |

### UEFA EUROPEAN CHAMPIONSHIP

| | |
|---|---|
| 1960 | - |
| 1964 | - |
| 1968 | - |
| 1972 | - |
| 1976 | - |
| 1980 | - |
| 1984 | - |
| 1988 | - |
| 1992 | - |
| 1996 | Qualifiers |
| 2000 | Qualifiers |
| 2004 | Qualifiers |
| 2008 | Qualifiers |
| 2012 | Qualifiers |
| 2016 | Qualifiers |
| 2020 | Final Tournament (Group Stage) |

### FIFA WORLD CUP

| | |
|---|---|
| 1930 | - |
| 1934 | - |
| 1938 | - |
| 1950 | - |
| 1954 | - |
| 1958 | - |
| 1962 | - |
| 1966 | - |
| 1970 | - |
| 1974 | - |
| 1978 | - |
| 1982 | - |
| 1986 | - |
| 1990 | - |
| 1994 | Did not enter |
| 1998 | Qualifiers |
| 2002 | Qualifiers |
| 2006 | Qualifiers |
| 2010 | Qualifiers |
| 2014 | Qualifiers |
| 2018 | Qualifiers |
| 2022 | Qualifiers |

### OLYMPIC TOURNAMENTS

| | |
|---|---|
| 1908 | - |
| 1912 | - |
| 1920 | - |
| 1924 | - |
| 1928 | - |
| 1936 | - |
| 1948 | - |
| 1952 | - |
| 1956 | - |
| 1960 | - |
| 1964 | - |
| 1968 | - |
| 1972 | - |
| 1976 | - |
| 1980 | - |
| 1984 | - |
| 1988 | - |
| 1992 | Did not enter |
| 1996 | Qualifiers |
| 2000 | Qualifiers |
| 2004 | Qualifiers |
| 2008 | Qualifiers |
| 2012 | Qualifiers |
| 2016 | Qualifiers |
| 2020 | Qualifiers |

*was part of Yugoslavia until 08.09.1991*

### UEFA NATIONS LEAGUE

| | |
|---|---|
| 2018/2019 | League D (Group Stage -> promoted to League C) |
| 2020/2021 | League C (Group Stage) |
| 2022/2023 | League C (Group Stage) |

### MACEDONIAN CLUB HONOURS IN EUROPEAN CLUB COMPETITIONS:

| European Champion Clubs' Cup (1956-1992) / UEFA Champions League (1993-2023) |
|---|
| None |

| Fairs Cup (1858-1971) / UEFA Cup (1972-2009) / UEFA Europa League (2010-2023) |
|---|
| None |

| UEFA Europa Conference League (2021-2023) |
|---|
| None |

| UEFA Super Cup (1972-2022) |
|---|
| None |

| *European Cup Winners' Cup 1961-1999** |
|---|
| None |

*defunct competition*

# NATIONAL COMPETITIONS
## TABLE OF HONOURS

### Royal League
### (territory of Vardarska Banovina belonging to the Kingdom of Yugoslavia)

| | CHAMPIONS |
|---|---|
| 1929 | Pobeda Skopje |
| 1930 | Jug Skopje, SSK Skopje, Sparta Skopje* |
| 1931 | Championship not finished |
| 1932 | SSK Skopje |
| 1933 | SSK Skopje |
| 1934 | SSK Skopje |
| 1935 | Championship not finished |
| 1936 | Gragjanski Skopje |
| 1937 | Championship not finished |
| 1938 | Gragjanski Skopje |
| 1939 | Gragjanski Skopje |
| 1940 | SSK Skopje |
| 1941 | SSK Skopje |

*All 3 teams finished with equal number of points*

### As part of Bulgaria

| | CHAMPIONS |
|---|---|
| 1942 | Makedonija Skopje |
| 1943 | ZhSK Skopje |
| 1944 | ZhSK Skopje |

### Republic League (within F.R. Yugoslavia)

| | | | | | | |
|---|---|---|---|---|---|---|
| 1944/1945 | Makedonija Skopje | 1960/1961 | Pelister Bitola | 1976/1977 | Rabotnichki Skopje |
| 1945/1946 | Pobeda Skopje | 1961/1962 | Pobeda Prilep | 1977/1978 | Tikvesh Kavadarci |
| 1946/1947 | Makedonija Skopje | 1962/1963 | Pobeda Prilep | 1978/1979 | Pobeda Prilep |
| 1947/1948 | Dinamo Skopje | 1963/1964 | Bregalnica Shtip | 1979/1980 | Rabotnichki Skopje |
| 1948/1949 | 11 Oktomvri Kumanovo | 1964/1965 | Teteks Tetovo | 1980/1981 | Pobeda Prilep |
| 1949/1950 | Rabotnik Bitola | 1965/1966 | Rabotnichki Skopje | 1981/1982 | Pelister Bitola |
| 1950/1951 | Rabotnik Bitola | 1966/1967 | Bregalnica Shtip | 1982/1983 | Belasica Strumica |
| 1951/1952 | Rabotnichki Skopje | 1967/1968 | Rabotnichki Skopje | 1983/1984 | Bregalnica Shtip |
| 1952/1953 | Pobeda Prilep | 1968/1969 | Teteks Tetovo | 1984/1985 | Teteks Tetovo |
| 1953/1954 | Rabotnichki Skopje | 1969/1970 | MIK Skopje | 1985/1986 | Pobeda Prilep |
| 1954/1955 | Rabotnichki Skopje | 1970/1971 | Kumanovo | 1986/1987 | Metalurg Skopje |
| 1955/1956 | Vardar Skopje | 1971/1972 | Tikvesh Kavadarci | 1987/1988 | Belasica Strumica |
| 1956/1957 | Rabotnichki Skopje | 1972/1973 | Rabotnichki Skopje | 1988/1989 | Borec-Titov Veles |
| 1957/1958 | Rabotnichki Skopje | 1973/1974 | Teteks Tetovo | 1989/1990 | Balkan Skopje |
| 1958/1959 | Pobeda Prilep | 1974/1975 | Pelister Bitola | 1990/1991 | Makedonija Skopje |
| 1959/1960 | Pelister Bitola | 1975/1976 | Bregalnica Shtip | 1991/1992 | Sasa Makedonska Kamenica |

### After proclamation of independence - Macedonian First League

| | CHAMPIONS | CUP WINNERS | BEST GOALSCORERS | |
|---|---|---|---|---|
| 1992/1993 | FK Vardar Skopje | FK Vardar Skopje | Saša Ćirić (FK Vardar Skopje) | 36 |
| 1993/1994 | FK Vardar Skopje | FK Sileks Kratovo | Zoran Boshkovski (FK Sileks Kratovo) | 21 |
| 1994/1995 | FK Vardar Skopje | FK Vardar Skopje | Saša Ćirić (FK Vardar Skopje) | 35 |
| 1995/1996 | FK Sileks Kratovo | FK Sloga Jugomagnat Skopje | Zoran Boshkovski (FK Sileks Kratovo) | 20 |
| 1996/1997 | FK Sileks Kratovo | FK Sileks Kratovo | Vancho Micevski (FK Sileks Kratovo) Miroslav Gjokić (FK Sileks Kratovo) | 16 |
| 1997/1998 | FK Sileks Kratovo | FK Vardar Skopje | Vancho Atanasov (FK Belasica Stremica) | 12 |
| 1998/1999 | FK Sloga Jugomagnat Skopje | FK Vardar Skopje | Rogério Oliveira da Costa (FK Pobeda Prilep) | 22 |
| 1999/2000 | FK Sloga Jugomagnat Skopje | FK Sloga Jugomagnat Skopje | Argjend Beqiri (FK Sloga Jugomagnat Skopje) | 19 |
| 2000/2001 | FK Sloga Jugomagnat Skopje | FK Pelister Bitola | Argjend Beqiri (FK Sloga Jugomagnat Skopje) | 27 |
| 2001/2002 | FK Vardar Skopje | FK Pobeda Prilep | Miroslav Gjokić (FK Pobeda Prilep) | 22 |
| 2002/2003 | FK Vardar Skopje | FK Cementarnica 55 Skopje | Ljubiša Savić (FK Bregalnica Štip / FK Sloga Jugomagnat Skopje) | 25 |
| 2003/2004 | FK Pobeda Prilep | FK Sloga Jugomagnat Skopje | Dragan Dimitrovski (FK Pobeda Prilep) | 25 |
| 2004/2005 | FK Rabotnički Skopje | KF Bashkimi Kumanovo | Aleksandar Stojanovski (FK Belasica Stremica) Stevica Ristić (FK Sileks Kratovo) | 26 |
| 2005/2006 | FK Rabotnički Skopje | FK Makedonija Gjorče Petrov | Stevica Ristić (FK Sileks Kratovo) | 27 |
| 2006/2007 | FK Pobeda Prilep | FK Vardar Skopje | Boban Janchevski (KF Bashkimi Kumanovo / KF Renova Džepčište) | 26 |
| 2007/2008 | FK Rabotnički Skopje | FK Rabotnički Skopje | Ivica Gligorovski (FK Milano Kumanovo) | 15 |
| 2008/2009 | FK Makedonija Gjorče Petrov | FK Rabotnički Skopje | Ivica Gligorovski (FK Milano Kumanovo) | 14 |
| 2009/2010 | KF Renova Džepčište | FK Teteks Tetovo | Bobi Bozhinovski (FK Rabotnički Skopje) | 15 |
| 2010/2011 | KF Shkëndija Tetovo | FK Metalurg Skopje | Hristijan Kirovski (FK Skopje) | 20 |
| 2011/2012 | FK Vardar Skopje | KF Renova Džepčište | Filip Ivanovski (FK Vardar Skopje) | 24 |
| 2012/2013 | FK Vardar Skopje | FK Teteks Tetovo | Jovan Kostovski (FK Vardar Skopje) | 22 |
| 2013/2014 | FK Rabotnički Skopje | FK Rabotnički Skopje | Dejan Blazhevski (FK Horizont Turnovo) | 19 |
| 2014/2015 | FK Vardar Skopje | FK Rabotnički Skopje | Izair Emini (KF Renova Džepčište) | 20 |
| 2015/2016 | FK Vardar Skopje | KF Shkëndija Tetovo | Besart Ibraimi (KF Shkëndija Tetovo) | 26 |
| 2016/2017 | FK Vardar Skopje | FK Pelister Bitola | Besart Ibraimi (KF Shkëndija Tetovo) | 20 |

| 2017/2018 | KF Shkëndija Tetovo | KF Shkëndija Tetovo | Ferhan Hasani (KF Shkëndija Tetovo) | |
| | | | Besart Ibraimi (KF Shkëndija Tetovo) | 22 |
| 2018/2019 | KF Shkëndija Tetovo | Fudb. Akademija Pandev Strumica | Vlatko Stojanovski (KF Renova Džepčište) | 18 |
| 2019/2020 | FK Vardar Skopje | *Competition cancelled* | Daniel Avramovski (FK Vardar Skopje) | 11 |
| 2020/2021 | KF Shkëndija Tetovo | FK Sileks Kratovo | Besart Ibraimi (KF Shkëndija Tetovo) | 24 |
| 2021/2022 | KF Shkupi Čair | FK Makedonija Gjorče Petrov | Sunday Damilare Adetunji (NGA, KF Shkupi Čair) | 20 |
| 2022/2023 | FC Struga Trim-Lum | FK Makedonija Gjorče Petrov | Besart Ibraimi (FC Struga Trim-Lum) | 18 |

Please note: FK Sloga Jugomagnat Skopje became KF Shkupi Čair in 2009.

# NATIONAL CHAMPIONSHIP
## Macedonian First Football League – Prva Liga 2022/2023
### (06.08.2022 – 14.05.2023)

## Results

Please note: KF Renova Džepčište withdrew prior to the start of the season due to financial problems.

**Round 1 [06-07.08.2022]**
FC Struga - FK Pobeda 3-0(1-0)
Akademija Pandev - FK Bregalnica 1-2(1-0)
Sileks Kratovo - FK Rabotnički 2-0(0-0)
KF Shkëndija - FK Skopje 2-0(1-0) [17.08.22]
GFK Tikvesh - KF Shkupi 3-1(2-0) [07.09.22]

**Round 2 [13-14.08.2022]**
KF Shkupi - Makedonija GP 2-1(0-0)
FK Bregalnica - FC Struga 0-1(0-0)
FK Rabotnički - Akademija Pandev 0-5(0-3)
KF Shkëndija - Sileks Kratovo 1-1(1-0)
FK Pobeda - GFK Tikvesh 0-1(0-1)

**Round 3 [20-21.08.2022]**
Makedonija GP - FK Pobeda 4-1(3-1)
Akademija Pandev - KF Shkëndija 0-1(0-0)
Sileks Kratovo - FK Skopje 3-1(1-0)
FC Struga - FK Rabotnički 2-1(1-1)
GFK Tikvesh - FK Bregalnica 1-1(0-1)

**Round 4 [27-28.08.2022]**
Sileks Kratovo - Akademija Pandev 1-1(1-1)
FK Bregalnica - Makedonija GP 1-0(0-0)
FK Rabotnički - GFK Tikvesh 2-0(2-0)
FK Skopje - KF Shkupi 0-2(0-1)
KF Shkëndija - FC Struga 0-2(0-0)

**Round 5 [31.08.2022]**
Akademija Pandev - FK Skopje 3-0(1-0)
KF Shkupi - FK Pobeda 1-1(1-0)
Makedonija GP - FK Rabotnički 1-1(0-0)
FC Struga - Sileks Kratovo 2-1(1-0)
GFK Tikvesh - KF Shkëndija 1-3(1-2)

**Round 6 [04.09.2022]**
Akademija Pandev - FC Struga 0-3(0-1)
FK Bregalnica - KF Shkupi 2-0(0-0)
FK Skopje - FK Pobeda 1-0(1-0)
KF Shkëndija - Makedonija GP 1-1(0-0)
Sileks Kratovo - GFK Tikvesh 3-2(1-0)

**Round 7 [10-11.09.2022]**
Makedonija GP - Sileks Kratovo 0-1(0-0)
KF Shkupi - FK Rabotnički 5-0(4-0)
FK Pobeda - FK Bregalnica 1-0(0-0)
FC Struga - FK Skopje 3-0(1-0)
GFK Tikvesh - Akademija Pandev 2-1(2-1)

**Round 8 [17-18.09.2022]**
Akademija Pandev - Makedonija GP 0-1(0-1)
FK Rabotnički - FK Pobeda 1-0(1-0)
KF Shkëndija - KF Shkupi 0-0
FC Struga - GFK Tikvesh 2-0(1-0)
FK Skopje - FK Bregalnica 0-0

**Round 9 [01-02.10.2022]**
Makedonija GP - FC Struga 1-1(0-0)
FK Bregalnica - FK Rabotnički 1-3(0-1)
KF Shkupi - Sileks Kratovo 0-0
FK Pobeda - KF Shkëndija 1-3(1-1)
GFK Tikvesh - FK Skopje 2-0(1-0)

**Round 10 [08-09.10.2022]**
GFK Tikvesh - Makedonija GP 4-0(2-0)
Akademija Pandev - KF Shkupi 0-1(0-0)
FK Skopje - FK Rabotnički 0-0
KF Shkëndija - FK Bregalnica 0-0
Sileks Kratovo - FK Pobeda 0-3(0-1)

**Round 11 [15-16.10.2022]**
FK Bregalnica - Sileks Kratovo 2-3(2-1)
FK Rabotnički - KF Shkëndija 2-4(1-1)
Makedonija GP - FK Skopje 2-0(1-0)
FK Pobeda - Akademija Pandev 1-1(0-0)
KF Shkupi - FC Struga 1-0(0-0)

**Round 12 [25-26.10.2022]**
FK Bregalnica - Akademija Pandev 1-0(0-0)
FK Rabotnički - Sileks Kratovo 0-1(0-1)
KF Shkupi - GFK Tikvesh 4-2(3-0)
FK Skopje - KF Shkëndija 0-1(0-1)
FK Pobeda - FC Struga 2-0(1-0)

**Round 13 [30.10.2022]**
Akademija Pandev - FK Rabotnički 0-2(0-1)
Makedonija GP - KF Shkupi 1-1(0-1)
Sileks Kratovo - KF Shkëndija 1-1(0-0)
FC Struga - FK Bregalnica 2-2(1-1)
GFK Tikvesh - FK Pobeda 1-0(1-0)

**Round 14 05-06.11.2022 [ ]**
FK Skopje - Sileks Kratovo 0-0
FK Bregalnica - GFK Tikvesh 2-1(1-0)
FK Rabotnički - FC Struga 1-1(0-0)
KF Shkëndija - Akademija Pandev 1-1(1-0)
FK Pobeda - Makedonija GP 1-3(1-1)

**Round 15 [12-13.11.2022]**
Akademija Pandev - Sileks Kratovo 3-0(1-0)
KF Shkupi - FK Skopje 3-1(2-1)
FC Struga - KF Shkëndija 1-0(1-0)
GFK Tikvesh - FK Rabotnički 3-0(1-0)
Makedonija GP - FK Bregalnica 0-0

**Round 16 [26-27.11.2022]**
Sileks Kratovo - FC Struga 1-2(0-2)
FK Rabotnički - Makedonija GP 2-0(2-0)
FK Skopje - Akademija Pandev 2-1(0-0)
KF Shkëndija - GFK Tikvesh 0-0
FK Pobeda - KF Shkupi 0-6(0-3)

**Round 17 [04.12.2022]**
KF Shkupi - FK Bregalnica 3-1(1-1)
Makedonija GP - KF Shkëndija 1-3(0-1)
FK Pobeda - FK Skopje 0-0
FC Struga - Akademija Pandev 1-0(0-0)
GFK Tikvesh - Sileks Kratovo 0-2(0-0)

**Round 18 [11.12.2022]**
Akademija Pandev - GFK Tikvesh 0-2(0-1)
FK Bregalnica - FK Pobeda 2-2(2-0)
FK Rabotnički - KF Shkupi 2-4(0-3)
FK Skopje - FC Struga 1-1(0-0)
Sileks Kratovo - Makedonija GP 1-3(0-2)

**Round 19 [19.02.2023]**
FK Bregalnica - FK Skopje 0-0
KF Shkupi - KF Shkëndija 2-0(1-0)
Makedonija GP - Akademija Pandev 0-1(0-0)
FK Pobeda - FK Rabotnički 0-2(0-1)
GFK Tikvesh - FC Struga 1-1(1-0)

**Round 20 [25-26.02.2023]**
FC Struga - Makedonija GP 0-0
FK Rabotnički - FK Bregalnica 0-1(0-1)
FK Skopje - GFK Tikvesh 0-0
KF Shkëndija - FK Pobeda 1-0(0-0)
Sileks Kratovo - KF Shkupi 2-1(2-0)

**Round 21 [04-05.03.2023]**
FK Rabotnički - FK Skopje 4-0(1-0)
KF Shkupi - Akademija Pandev 3-3(3-2)
FK Bregalnica - KF Shkëndija 0-0
Makedonija GP - GFK Tikvesh 3-0(1-0)
FK Pobeda - Sileks Kratovo 1-4(0-1)

**Round 22 [08.03.2023]**
Akademija Pandev - FK Pobeda 3-0(1-0)
FK Skopje - Makedonija GP 1-1(0-1)
KF Shkëndija - FK Rabotnički 3-1(2-0)
Sileks Kratovo - FK Bregalnica 1-2(0-1)
FC Struga - KF Shkupi 2-1(1-0)

**Round 23 [11-12.03.2023]**
Sileks Kratovo - FK Skopje 3-1(1-0)
FK Bregalnica - FK Pobeda 4-0(2-0)
FC Struga - Makedonija GP 0-0
KF Shkupi - FK Rabotnički 3-1(3-1)
KF Shkëndija - Akademija Pandev 2-1(2-0)

**Round 24 [18-19.03.2023]**
Akademija Pandev - KF Shkupi 1-1(0-1)
FK Pobeda - Sileks Kratovo 1-5(0-2)
FK Rabotnički - FC Struga 0-1(0-1)
GFK Tikvesh - Makedonija GP 0-1(0-0)
FK Skopje - KF Shkëndija 0-2(0-1)

**Round 25 [02.04.2023]**
FK Bregalnica - GFK Tikvesh 0-0
FC Struga - Akademija Pandev 3-1(3-0)
KF Shkupi - FK Skopje 0-1(0-1)
Makedonija GP - FK Rabotnički 2-1(1-1)
KF Shkëndija - FK Pobeda 2-0(1-0)

**Round 26 [09.04.2023]**
Akademija Pandev - FK Rabotnički 0-0
FK Bregalnica - Makedonija GP 2-1(0-0)
FK Skopje - FC Struga 1-1(0-1)
FK Pobeda - KF Shkupi 0-6(0-1)
GFK Tikvesh - Sileks Kratovo 0-0

**Round 27 [15.04.2023]**
FC Struga - FK Pobeda 6-2(2-1)
Makedonija GP - Akademija Pandev 0-0
FK Rabotnički - FK Skopje 1-0(0-0)
KF Shkëndija - GFK Tikvesh 4-1(1-0)
Sileks Kratovo - FK Bregalnica 0-0

| Round 28 [22-23.04.2023] |
|---|
| FK Bregalnica - KF Shkëndija 0-1(0-0) |
| FK Skopje - Akademija Pandev 1-1(0-1) |
| FK Pobeda - FK Rabotnički 0-1(0-1) |
| Sileks Kratovo - Makedonija GP 1-0(1-0) |
| GFK Tikvesh - KF Shkupi 0-0 |

| Round 29 [26.04.2023] |
|---|
| Akademija Pandev - FK Pobeda 2-0(0-0) |
| FC Struga - GFK Tikvesh 2-0(1-0) |
| KF Shkupi - FK Bregalnica 3-0(1-0) |
| Makedonija GP - FK Skopje 2-1(1-0) |
| KF Shkëndija - Sileks Kratovo 0-0 |

| Round 30 [29-30.04.2023] |
|---|
| KF Shkëndija - Makedonija GP 3-1(2-1) |
| FK Bregalnica - FC Struga 0-3(0-2) |
| FK Pobeda - FK Skopje 0-4(0-2) |
| Sileks Kratovo - KF Shkupi 0-2(0-0) |
| GFK Tikvesh - FK Rabotnički 1-3(0-2) |

| Round 31 [07.05.2023] |
|---|
| Akademija Pandev - GFK Tikvesh 1-4(0-1) |
| FC Struga - Sileks Kratovo 3-0(1-0) |
| KF Shkupi - KF Shkëndija 2-1(1-1) |
| Makedonija GP - FK Pobeda 7-0(4-0) |
| FK Rabotnički - FK Bregalnica 5-4(3-2) |

| Round 32 [10.05.2023] |
|---|
| FK Bregalnica - Akademija Pandev 1-1(0-0) |
| KF Shkupi - Makedonija GP 3-0(2-0) |
| KF Shkëndija - FC Struga 1-2(0-0) |
| Sileks Kratovo - FK Rabotnički 2-0(2-0) |
| GFK Tikvesh - FK Skopje 4-0(0-0) |

| Round 33 [14.05.2023] |
|---|
| Akademija Pandev - Sileks Kratovo 2-2(2-2) |
| FC Struga - KF Shkupi 2-1(0-1) |
| FK Skopje - FK Bregalnica 1-2(1-1) |
| FK Pobeda - GFK Tikvesh 1-4(1-0) |
| FK Rabotnički - KF Shkëndija 1-2(0-0) |

## Final Standings

| | | | | | | | | | Home | | | | | Away | | | |
|---|---|---|---|---|---|---|---|---|---|---|---|---|---|---|---|---|---|
| 1. | **FC Struga Trim-Lum** | 30 | 20 | 8 | 2 | 53 - 19 | **68** | 13 | 3 | 0 | 34 - 9 | | 7 | 5 | 2 | 19 - 10 |
| 2. | KF Shkupi Čair | 30 | 17 | 7 | 6 | 62 - 27 | **58** | 11 | 3 | 1 | 35 - 12 | | 6 | 4 | 5 | 27 - 15 |
| 3. | KF Shkëndija Tetovo | 30 | 16 | 9 | 5 | 43 - 23 | **57** | 7 | 7 | 2 | 21 - 11 | | 9 | 2 | 3 | 22 - 12 |
| 4. | FK Sileks Kratovo | 30 | 13 | 9 | 8 | 41 - 34 | **48** | 7 | 3 | 5 | 21 - 19 | | 6 | 6 | 3 | 20 - 15 |
| 5. | FK Bregalnica 2008 Štip | 30 | 10 | 11 | 9 | 33 - 34 | **41** | 6 | 5 | 5 | 18 - 16 | | 4 | 6 | 4 | 15 - 18 |
| 6. | GFK Tikvesh 1930 Kavadarci | 30 | 11 | 7 | 12 | 40 - 37 | **40** | 7 | 4 | 4 | 23 - 13 | | 4 | 3 | 8 | 17 - 24 |
| 7. | FK Makedonija Gjorče Petrov Skopje | 30 | 10 | 9 | 11 | 37 - 33 | **39** | 6 | 5 | 3 | 24 - 11 | | 4 | 4 | 8 | 13 - 22 |
| 8. | FK Rabotnički Skopje | 30 | 11 | 4 | 15 | 37 - 48 | **37** | 6 | 1 | 7 | 21 - 23 | | 5 | 3 | 8 | 16 - 25 |
| 9. | Fudbalska Akademija Pandev Strumica | 30 | 6 | 10 | 14 | 34 - 38 | **28** | 4 | 3 | 8 | 16 - 19 | | 2 | 7 | 6 | 18 - 19 |
| 10. | FK Skopje (*Relegation Play-offs*) | 30 | 4 | 10 | 16 | 17 - 44 | **22** | 2 | 8 | 4 | 8 - 12 | | 2 | 2 | 12 | 9 - 32 |
| 11. | FK Pobeda AD Prilep (*Relegated*) | 30 | 3 | 4 | 23 | 18 - 78 | **13** | 2 | 2 | 11 | 9 - 40 | | 1 | 2 | 12 | 9 - 38 |
| 12. | KF Renova Džepčište (*Relegated*) | 0 | 0 | 0 | 0 | 0 - 0 | **0** | | | | | | | | | |

| Top goalscorers: | |
|---|---|
| 18 **Besart Ibraimi** | *FC Struga Trim-Lum* |
| 12 Bunjamin Shabani | *FC Struga Trim-Lum* |
| 11 Sunday Damilare Adetunji (NGA) | *KF Shkupi Čair* |
| 11 Renaldo Showayne Cephas (JAM) | *KF Shkupi Čair* |

## Relegation Play-offs [21.05.2023]

FK Skopje - FK Vardar Skopje      0-3(0-1)
FK Vardar Skopje promoted for the 2023/2ß024 Prva Liga..

# NATIONAL CUP
## Kup na Makedonija 2022/2023

### First Round [14.09.2022]

| | | | | |
|---|---|---|---|---|
| FK Belasica Strumica - KF Shkupi Čair | 1-3 | FK Teteks Tetovo - Fud. Akademija Pandev Strumica | 0-6 | |
| FK Karaorman Struga - KF Shkëndija Tetovo | 0-3 | FK Vardar Negotino - FC Struga Trim-Lum | 1-2 | |
| KF Gostivari - FK Pelister Bitola | 0-1 | FK Karbinci - FK Pobeda AD Prilep | 0-6 | |
| FK Sasa Makedonska Kamenica - FK Vardar Skopje | 0-3 | FK Sloga 1934 Vinica - FK Bregalnica 2008 Štip | 0-3 | |
| FK Kožuf Gevgelija - GFK Tikvesh 1930 Kavadarci | 0-2 | KF Zajazi Zajas - FK Voska Sport Ohrid | 0-3 *awarded* | |
| BVK Konjare - FK Rabotnički Skopje | 0-5 | FK Ljuboten Tetovo - KF Renova Džepčište | 3-0 *awarded* | |
| FK Crno Buki ZL - FK Skopje | 0-3 *awarded* | KF Fortuna 1975 Çento - FK Borec Veles | 5-3 | |

### 1/8-Finals [05.19.10.2022]

| | | | |
|---|---|---|---|
| FC Struga Trim-Lum - FK Rabotnički Skopje | 2-1 | KF Shkupi Čair - FK Voska Sport Ohrid | 6-0 |
| FK Bregalnica 2008 Štip - FK Pelister Bitola | 1-0 | KF Shkëndija Tetovo - FK Skopje | 5-0 |
| FK Vardar Skopje - KF Fortuna 1975 Çento | 4-0 | GFK Tikvesh 1930 Kavadarci - FK Sileks Kratovo | 0-1 |
| Fudbalska Akademija Pandev Str.-FK Ljuboten Tet. | 9-0 | FK Pobeda AD Prilep-FK Makedonija Gjorče Petrov | 0-2 |

### Quarter-Finals [09.11.2022]

| | | | |
|---|---|---|---|
| FK Sileks Kratovo - FK Vardar Skopje | 0-0 aet; 3-2 pen | KF Shkupi Čair - KF Shkëndija Tetovo | 0-3 *awarded* |
| FK Makedonija Gjorče Petrov - F. Akademija Pandev | 1-0 | FC Struga Trim-Lum - FK Bregalnica 2008 Štip | 2-0 |

### Semi-Finals [05.04.2023]

| | | | |
|---|---|---|---|
| FC Struga Trim-Lum - Sileks Kratovo | 1-0 | KF Shkëndija Tetovo-FK Makedonija Gjorče Petrov | 1-1 aet; 3-4 pen |

20.05.2023; "Petar Miloševski" Training Center, Skopje; Referee: Igor Stojchevski; Attendance: 0,000
**FC Struga Trim-Lum - FK Makedonija Gjorče Petrov**                    **1-1(0-1,1-1,1-1); 0-2 on penalties**

**FC Struga**: Vedran Kjosevski, Medzit Neziri, Edis Malikji (46.Fatjon Jusufi), Besart Krivanjeva, Sava Radić, Zija Merxhani, Bunjamin Shabani (Cap), Besmir Bojku, Valentin Kochoski (65.Flamur Tairi), Besart Ibraimi (74.Hogan Ukpa Effiong), Suhejlj Muharem (46.Marjan Radeski). Trainer: Shpëtim Duro (Albania).

**FK Makedonija**: Hristijan Stevkovski, Filip Mishevski (Cap), Bojan Ilievski, Andrey Yago da Silva Mesquita Almeida, Dragan Stojkov (33.Adama Samake), Georgi Stoilov (106.Emir Skenderi), Stefan Lazarevikj (116.Hristijan Pecov), Samir Fazli, Kristijan Stojkovski (74.Esmin Lichina), Jovan Popzlatanov (85.Filip Aleksovski), Arbin Vosha (74.Matheus Lemos da Silva). Trainer: Goran Simov (Serbia).

**Goals:** 0-1 Filip Mishevski (28 penalty), 1-1 Fatjon Jusufi (77).

**Penalties:** Flamur Tairi (missed); Filip Mishevski (saved); Marjan Radeski (missed); Esmin Lichina 0-1; Medzit Neziri (missed); Filip Aleksovski (saved); Bunjamin Shabani (saved); Emir Skenderi 0-2.

## THE CLUBS 2022/2023

### Fudbalska Akademija Pandev Strumica

| | | | | |
|---|---|---|---|---|
| Founded: | 2010 | | | |
| Stadium: | Stadion „Blagoj Istatov", Strumica (9,200) | | | |
| Trainer: | Gjorgje Stojchev | | 18.04.1986 | |
| [07.09.2022] | Aleksandar Vasoski | | 21.11.1979 | |
| [07.05.2023] | Toni Atanasov | | 04.01.1975 | |

| Goalkeepers: | DOB | M | (s) | G |
|---|---|---|---|---|
| Marko Alchevski | 16.04.2002 | 19 | | |
| Marko Jovanovski | 24.07.1988 | 11 | | |
| **Defenders:** | **DOB** | **M** | **(s)** | **G** |
| Federico Acosta (ARG) | 30.03.1996 | 20 | | |
| David Bosheski | 19.02.2003 | | (1) | |
| Mite Cikarski | 06.01.1993 | 8 | (6) | 1 |
| Dime Dimov | 25.07.1994 | 29 | | |
| Nahuel Ismael Franco (ARG) | 12.09.2001 | 4 | (4) | |
| Tomislav Iliev | 02.12.1993 | 10 | (4) | |
| Zoran Ivanovski | 07.05.2000 | 8 | (10) | |
| Georgije Jankulov | 25.11.2001 | 13 | | |
| Dušan Joković (SRB) | 04.07.1999 | 7 | | 1 |
| Kosta Manev (FIN) | 07.04.1993 | 5 | | |
| Agron Rufati | 06.04.1999 | 10 | | 1 |
| Nikolce Sarkoski | 08.03.1994 | 5 | | |
| Andrej Velkov | 07.02.2006 | | (1) | |
| **Midfielders:** | **DOB** | **M** | **(s)** | **G** |
| Hakan Akgül (TUR) | 19.03.2003 | | (11) | |
| Bojan Dimoski | 23.11.2001 | 24 | (2) | |
| Gjorge Djekov | 18.10.2005 | | (2) | |

| Ilija Donov | 31.08.2001 | 16 | (8) | 1 |
|---|---|---|---|---|
| Martin Gjorgievski | 28.02.2005 | 11 | (8) | 2 |
| Vane Krstevski | 28.04.2003 | 19 | (9) | 5 |
| Mladen Ljumovic | 03.12.1991 | | (1) | |
| Bojan Najdenov | 27.08.1991 | 11 | | |
| Goran Tomovski | 21.07.1998 | 11 | (12) | 1 |
| Mario Vrdoljak (CRO) | 21.07.1993 | 12 | (1) | 1 |
| **Forwards:** | **DOB** | **M** | **(s)** | **G** |
| Neat Abdulai | 17.07.2001 | | (3) | |
| Viktor Angelov | 27.03.1994 | 6 | (5) | 1 |
| Matej Cvetanoski | 18.08.1997 | 4 | (2) | |
| Mikheili Ergemlidze (GEO) | 28.09.1999 | 7 | (5) | 3 |
| Ivan Galevski | 15.11.1996 | 7 | (4) | |
| Marko Gjorgjievski | 18.04.2000 | 7 | (6) | |
| Kostadin Kapsarov | 21.05.2005 | | (1) | |
| Dimitar Mitrovski | 28.01.1999 | 13 | (1) | 3 |
| Saško Pandev | 01.05.1987 | | (5) | |
| Kire Stojanov | 28.08.2005 | | (2) | |
| Dimitar Trajkov | 08.08.2004 | 9 | (18) | 6 |
| Kristijan Velinovski | 31.05.1999 | 24 | (3) | 6 |

### Fudbalski klub Bregalnica Štip

| | | | | |
|---|---|---|---|---|
| Founded: | 1921 | | | |
| Stadium: | Stadion Gradski, Štip (4,000) | | | |
| Trainer: | Ilčo Gjorgioski | | 11.12.1971 | |
| [11.11.2022] | Lazar Ilijev | | 25.03.1987 | |
| [21.12.2022] | Goran Zdravkov | | 11.11.1980 | |

| Goalkeepers: | DOB | M | (s) | G |
|---|---|---|---|---|
| David Denkovski | 17.08.2000 | 2 | (1) | |
| Nemanja Šćekić (MNE) | 17.12.1991 | 28 | | |
| **Defenders:** | **DOB** | **M** | **(s)** | **G** |
| Alexander Borja Córdoba (COL) | 25.10.1998 | 5 | (17) | |
| Mihail Dimitrievski | 11.07.2002 | 16 | (12) | |
| Sebastián Herrera Cardona (COL) | 23.01.1995 | 10 | (1) | 1 |
| Stefan Kocev | 23.02.1994 | 12 | (3) | |
| Halid Lwaliwa (UGA) | 22.08.1996 | 20 | | |
| Daniel Mojsov | 25.12.1987 | 20 | (2) | 1 |
| Angjelo Nikolovski | 10.11.2001 | | (2) | |
| Aleksandar Ristevski | 11.05.1992 | 26 | (1) | 3 |
| Goran Siljanovski | 01.07.1990 | 27 | (1) | 1 |
| **Midfielders:** | **DOB** | **M** | **(s)** | **G** |
| Mario Adjijev | 14.09.2005 | | (1) | |
| Dimitrij Dimitrievski | 11.07.2002 | 8 | (16) | |
| Patrik Džalto (CRO) | 19.02.1997 | | (2) | |

| Blagoj Hadji-Kimov | 19.06.2005 | | (1) | |
|---|---|---|---|---|
| Adis Hadžanović (BIH) | 02.01.1993 | 13 | (9) | |
| David Kalpachki | 01.06.2000 | 13 | (1) | 1 |
| Faysel Kasmi (BEL) | 31.10.1995 | 12 | (1) | |
| Petar Kolev | 28.06.2005 | | (1) | |
| Dino Miholov | 29.01.2005 | | (1) | |
| Ivan Nikolov | 17.02.2002 | 27 | (1) | 5 |
| Marko Sofijanoski | 24.06.2004 | | (1) | |
| Mateo Sofijanoski | 24.06.2004 | | (6) | |
| **Forwards:** | **DOB** | **M** | **(s)** | **G** |
| Marijan Altiparmakovski | 18.07.1991 | 14 | (10) | 1 |
| Zoran Andonov | 09.06.2000 | 13 | (1) | 1 |
| Darko Dodev | 16.01.1998 | 26 | (3) | 7 |
| Milan Đokić (SRB) | 12.09.1997 | 10 | (14) | 3 |
| Gjorgi Gjorgiev | 18.06.1996 | 24 | (4) | 8 |
| Ljupche Kudev | 07.12.2003 | 4 | (7) | 1 |

## Fudbalski klub Makedonija Gjorče Petrov Skopje

| | Founded: | 1932 | | |
|---|---|---|---|---|
| | Stadium: | Stadion „Gjorče Petrov", Skopje (3,000) | | |
| | Trainer: | Muharem Bajrami | | 29.11.1985 |
| | [14.03.2023] | Goran Simov (SRB) | | 31.03.1975 |

| Goalkeepers: | DOB | M | (s) | G |
|---|---|---|---|---|
| Hristijan Stevkovski | 27.02.1999 | 28 | | |
| Stefan Tasev | 08.07.2004 | 2 | | |
| **Defenders:** | **DOB** | **M** | **(s)** | **G** |
| *Andrey Yago* da Silva Mesquita Almeida(BRA) | 29.12.1997 | 10 | | |
| Bojan Ilievski | 01.09.1999 | 18 | (4) | |
| Aleksandar Isaevski | 19.05.1995 | | (2) | |
| Esmin Lichina | 20.03.1998 | 20 | (2) | 1 |
| Jhon Edy Mena Pérez (COL) | 06.06.1997 | | (8) | 1 |
| Filip Mishevski | 01.11.1991 | 29 | | 6 |
| Hristijan Pecov | 30.04.1994 | 10 | (2) | |
| Maksim Slavkov | 26.08.2005 | 3 | (1) | |
| Fisnik Zuka | 03.09.1995 | 11 | (4) | |
| **Midfielders:** | **DOB** | **M** | **(s)** | **G** |
| Agan Abazi | 09.10.2002 | 3 | (8) | 1 |
| Ermadin Adem | 07.07.1990 | 10 | (2) | |
| Sefer Emini | 15.07.2000 | 2 | | 2 |
| Martin Jovanovikj | 04.03.2006 | | (1) | |
| Stefan Lazarevikj | 18.02.1997 | 19 | (4) | |
| *Matheus* Lemos da Silva (BRA) | 24.04.1997 | 21 | (8) | 1 |
| Adama Samake (CIV) | 29.12.2002 | 23 | (3) | 2 |
| Darko Sekovski | 20.02.2006 | | (3) | |
| Georgi Stoilov | 25.08.1995 | 19 | (4) | |
| Dragan Stojkov | 23.02.1988 | 10 | (2) | |
| **Forwards:** | **DOB** | **M** | **(s)** | **G** |
| Filip Aleksovski | 25.03.2000 | 4 | (20) | 4 |
| Altin Aliji | 25.08.2006 | | (2) | |
| Khalid Abdul Basit (GHA) | 10.08.1996 | | (6) | 1 |
| Samir Fazli | 22.04.1991 | 9 | (4) | 2 |
| Fahrudin Gjurgjevikj | 17.02.1992 | 6 | (5) | 1 |
| Vukašin Jovković (SRB) | 12.01.2001 | 1 | (2) | 1 |
| Jovan Popzlatanov | 06.07.1996 | 11 | (3) | |
| Emir Skenderi | 01.04.2000 | 12 | (11) | 5 |
| Aleksej Slavkov | 26.08.2005 | 1 | (1) | |
| Kristijan Stojkovski | 17.09.1991 | 23 | (3) | 2 |
| Arbin Vosha | 04.08.2001 | 25 | (4) | 5 |
| Vanja Vučićević (SRB) | 22.03.1998 | | (6) | 1 |

## Fudbalski klub Pobeda Prilep

| | Founded: | 2010 (*as Viktorija Prilep*) | | |
|---|---|---|---|---|
| | Stadium: | Stadion "Goce Delčev", Prilep (15,000) | | |
| | Trainer: | Boban Babunski | | 05.05.1968 |
| | [05.01.2023] | Blagojche Damevski | | 17.10.1981 |

| Goalkeepers: | DOB | M | (s) | G |
|---|---|---|---|---|
| Daniel Kotevski | 16.08.1999 | 6 | (3) | |
| Vasilij Marinovski | 09.07.2005 | | (2) | |
| Antonio Shemkoski | 14.08.2004 | 2 | | |
| Darko Tofiloski | 13.01.1986 | 22 | (1) | |
| **Defenders:** | **DOB** | **M** | **(s)** | **G** |
| Antonio Bosheski | 03.09.1995 | 9 | (3) | |
| Sufjan Chajani | 24.12.2004 | 2 | (4) | |
| Metodija Delov | 02.06.1993 | 9 | (4) | |
| Ognjen Đurković (SRB) | 11.12.2001 | 18 | | 3 |
| Boban Gjorcheski | 09.10.2004 | 2 | | |
| Agon Hani | 06.04.1998 | 19 | (3) | |
| Teofan Ilijoski Kiseski | 19.03.1998 | 1 | (2) | |
| Vane Jovanov | 28.12.1998 | 5 | (3) | 1 |
| Hristijan Kocev | 30.03.2000 | 1 | (6) | |
| Leonid Kofilovski | 24.10.2004 | 6 | | |
| Igor Panoski | 18.03.1999 | 14 | (4) | 1 |
| Anatolij Petejchuk | 22.10.2002 | 7 | (6) | 1 |
| Miodrag Petković (SRB) | 10.09.2003 | 1 | (4) | |
| Marko Simunovic | 10.04.2000 | 4 | (1) | |
| Stefan Spirkoski | 30.04.1999 | 1 | (1) | |
| Oliver Stoimenovski | 26.03.1999 | 7 | | |
| Filip Stomnaroski | 03.10.1995 | 18 | | 1 |
| **Midfielders:** | **DOB** | **M** | **(s)** | **G** |
| Armend Aliu | 26.04.1996 | 8 | (4) | |
| Andrej Arizankoski | 08.05.2005 | 10 | (7) | |
| Amos Gubam Dadet (NGA) | 30.11.1999 | 22 | | 1 |
| David Debreslioski | 24.08.2004 | 2 | (1) | |
| Vladimir Dujovski | 30.06.1996 | 5 | (4) | |
| Saleem Fawakhry | 04.04.1999 | 3 | (5) | |
| Besnik Ferati | 19.04.2000 | 7 | (3) | 1 |
| Dimitri Kochoski | 20.10.2004 | 1 | (3) | |
| Jordancho Naumovski | 15.02.1995 | 11 | (1) | |
| Hristijan Pop-Antoski | 06.01.2004 | | (1) | |
| Hamza Ramani | 17.09.2002 | 12 | (1) | 1 |
| Bojan Spirkoski | 22.04.1995 | 13 | (1) | 1 |
| Mile Todorov | 20.08.1999 | 9 | (2) | |
| Viktor Tosheski | 01.11.2004 | | (1) | |
| Luka Trajkoski | 08.02.2000 | 6 | (1) | |
| **Forwards:** | **DOB** | **M** | **(s)** | **G** |
| Murat Adili | 22.09.1992 | 1 | (4) | |
| Amasihohu James Akugbe (BEL) | 04.07.2000 | 9 | (1) | |
| Eric Amo (GHA) | 15.06.2003 | 2 | (1) | |
| Vasilije Delibašić (MNE) | 14.03.2003 | 7 | (5) | 1 |
| Ivan Galevski | 15.11.1996 | 5 | (6) | 1 |
| Andrej Kudijan | 04.09.1997 | 10 | (3) | 1 |
| Atdhe Mazari | 02.06.2001 | 16 | | 4 |
| Martin Milanoski | 05.02.2005 | 1 | (3) | |
| Mario Naumoski | 31.08.2000 | 9 | (3) | |
| Filip Spirkoski | 08.06.2000 | 1 | (4) | |
| Filip Todoroski | 09.06.2003 | 6 | (8) | |
| Dino Varoshanoski | 01.04.2004 | | (1) | |

## Fudbalski klub Rabotnički Skopje

| | Founded: | 04.10.1937 | | |
|---|---|---|---|---|
| | Stadium: | Nacionalna Arena "Toše Proeski", Skopje (36,460) | | |
| | Trainer: | Ljupcho Markovski | | 24.02.1967 |
| | [12.09.2022] | Stojan Ignatov | | 22.12.1979 |
| | [01.10.2022] | Milan Ilievski | | 21.07.1982 |

| Goalkeepers: | DOB | M | (s) | G |
|---|---|---|---|---|
| Igor Aleksovski | 24.02.1995 | 28 | | |
| Filip Ilikj | 26.01.1997 | 2 | | |
| Petar Jakimov | 08.08.2005 | | (1) | |
| **Defenders:** | **DOB** | **M** | **(s)** | **G** |
| Sabahudin Alomerović | 29.06.1997 | 26 | (2) | |
| Stefan Despotovski (SRB) | 23.01.2003 | 12 | | |
| Dejan Đuric (SRB) | 27.10.1998 | 22 | | 1 |
| Fatih Ismaili | 29.08.1997 | 17 | | |
| Bojan Ivanov | 07.10.1994 | | (1) | |
| Andrej Kirovski | 11.02.1999 | 6 | (3) | |
| David Ljushev | 28.05.2004 | | (2) | |
| Martin Miserdovski | 11.11.2002 | 6 | (4) | 1 |
| Dimitrij Poposki | 10.11.2002 | 1 | (3) | |
| **Midfielders:** | **DOB** | **M** | **(s)** | **G** |
| Armend Alimi | 11.12.1987 | 21 | (7) | |
| Matej Angelov | 11.07.2004 | 19 | (8) | |
| Filip Boshkovski | 28.10.2000 | 15 | (9) | |
| Muhamed Elmas | 31.01.2006 | | (2) | |
| Feta Fetai | 11.05.2005 | 5 | (8) | |
| Ivo Janakievski | 09.06.1993 | 7 | (8) | 1 |
| Todor Nikolovski | 23.10.1996 | | (2) | |
| *Rafael Goes* da Silva Cavalcanti (BRA) | 08.05.2001 | 3 | (4) | |
| Dimitar Todorovski | 07.03.2002 | 21 | (9) | 1 |
| **Forwards:** | **DOB** | **M** | **(s)** | **G** |
| Aimé Marcelin Gando Biala (CMR) | 27.02.1997 | 19 | (5) | 6 |
| Metodi Maksimov | 20.08.2002 | 13 | (1) | 3 |
| Nikola Manojlov | 01.02.2006 | 1 | (7) | |
| Kire Markoski | 20.02.1995 | 10 | | 2 |
| Atdhe Mazari | 02.06.2001 | 12 | | 3 |
| Anes Rušević (SRB) | 02.12.1996 | 22 | (7) | 9 |
| Nikolce Sharkoski | 08.03.1994 | 13 | (7) | 1 |
| Mario Stankovski | 06.09.1999 | 1 | (9) | |
| Filip Todoroski | 09.06.2003 | 1 | (6) | |
| Nikola Velichkovski | 13.09.2005 | | (7) | |
| Krste Velkoski | 20.02.1988 | 27 | (1) | 8 |

## Klubi Futbollit Renova Džepčište

| Founded: | 2003 |
| Stadium: | Stadion Tetovo, Tetovo (15,000) |
| Trainer: | - |

## Klubi Futbollistik Shkëndija Tetovo

| Founded: | 27.08.1979 | | |
| Stadium: | Stadion Tetovo, Tetovo (15,000) | | |
| Trainer: | Artim Sakiri | 23.09.1973 |
| [15.09.2022] | Qatip Osmani | 29.06.1969 |

| Goalkeepers: | DOB | M | (s) | G |
|---|---|---|---|---|
| Ferat Ramani | 28.10.1994 | 1 | | |
| Davor Taleski | 19.05.1995 | 13 | | |
| Kostadin Zahov | 08.11.1987 | 16 | | |
| **Defenders:** | **DOB** | **M** | **(s)** | **G** |
| Egzon Bejtulai | 07.01.1994 | 23 | (1) | |
| Klisman Cake (ALB) | 02.05.1999 | 24 | (1) | 3 |
| Ardijan Cuculi | 19.07.1987 | 8 | (5) | |
| Metodi Maksimov | 20.08.2002 | 12 | | |
| Mihail Manevski | 25.02.1999 | | (1) | |
| Mevlan Murati | 05.03.1994 | 14 | (4) | |
| Medzit Neziri | 02.09.1990 | 8 | (4) | |
| Almir Rexhepi (ALB) | 04.04.2001 | 3 | (3) | 1 |
| Leard Sadriu (KOS) | 22.04.2001 | 1 | | |
| Bashkim Velija | 01.08.1993 | 20 | (4) | 1 |
| Jan Vondra (CZE) | 13.09.1995 | 3 | | |
| **Midfielders:** | **DOB** | **M** | **(s)** | **G** |
| Sabit Bilali | 15.08.1997 | 6 | (5) | 1 |
| Bruno Dita (ALB) | 18.02.1993 | 19 | (5) | 1 |
| Memetriza Hamza | 09.02.2004 | | (1) | |
| Ferhan Hasani | 18.06.1990 | 21 | (4) | 2 |
| Mustafa Mujezinović (BIH) | 06.05.1993 | 2 | (9) | 1 |
| Amir Nuhija | 25.01.2005 | 1 | (1) | |
| Kamer Qaka (ALB) | 11.04.1995 | 8 | (4) | |
| Florent Ramadani | 27.08.2000 | 10 | (13) | 1 |
| Reshat Ramadani | 30.06.2003 | 12 | (4) | |
| Ennur Totre | 29.10.1996 | 13 | (1) | |
| **Forwards:** | **DOB** | **M** | **(s)** | **G** |
| Eraldo Çinari (ALB) | 11.10.1996 | 14 | | 8 |
| Ljupco Doriev | 13.09.1995 | 20 | (5) | 10 |
| Dashmir Elezi | 21.11.2004 | 13 | (3) | 1 |
| Lorik Jakupi | 03.09.2005 | 1 | (4) | |
| Nasko Milev (BUL) | 18.07.1996 | 12 | (1) | 3 |
| Valmir Nafiu | 23.04.1994 | | (10) | |
| Zani Nazifi | 01.02.2005 | | (2) | |
| Adenis Shala (KOS) | 23.10.1998 | 21 | (9) | 7 |
| Vlatko Stojanovski | 23.04.1997 | 6 | (8) | 2 |
| *Vagner* Gonçalves Nogueira de Souza (BRA) | 27.04.1996 | 5 | (5) | 1 |

## Klubi Futbollistik Shkupi Čair

| Founded: | 1927 | | |
| Stadium: | Stadion Čair, Skopje (6,000) | | |
| Trainer: | Goce Sedloski | 10.04.1974 |
| [22.03.2023] | Cihat Arslan (TUR) | 09.02.1970 |

| Goalkeepers: | DOB | M | (s) | G |
|---|---|---|---|---|
| Artan Iljazi | 24.02.1999 | 4 | | |
| Kristijan Naumovski | 17.09.1988 | 26 | | |
| **Defenders:** | **DOB** | **M** | **(s)** | **G** |
| Xhelil Abdulla | 25.09.1991 | 7 | (3) | |
| Melos Bajrami (KOS) | 29.09.2001 | 13 | (1) | 1 |
| Vladica Brdarovski | 07.02.1990 | 22 | (3) | |
| Sufjan Chajani | 24.12.2004 | | (1) | |
| Besir Demiri (ALB) | 01.08.1994 | 4 | (7) | 1 |
| Darko Ilieski | 14.10.1991 | 7 | (2) | 1 |
| Gagi Margvelashvili (GEO) | 30.10.1996 | 21 | (4) | 4 |
| Mario Mladenovski | 16.09.2000 | 17 | (4) | 1 |
| Idriz Osmanivikj | 25.01.2004 | | (1) | |
| Mario Richkov | 04.05.2004 | 10 | | |
| Faustin Senghor (SEN) | 02.01.1994 | 2 | | |
| Blerton Sheji | 21.10.2000 | 6 | (17) | |
| Angelce Timovski | 13.11.1994 | 4 | (10) | |
| **Midfielders:** | **DOB** | **M** | **(s)** | **G** |
| Kristijan Ackovski | 15.02.1998 | 8 | (10) | |
| Ali Adem | 01.06.2000 | 11 | (11) | 1 |
| Freddy Antonio Álvarez Rodríguez (CRC) | 26.04.1995 | 26 | (3) | 10 |
| Albert Diène (SEN) | 12.02.1998 | 15 | (9) | 1 |
| *Queven* da Silva Inacio (BRA) | 21.11.1998 | 21 | (3) | 3 |
| Omer Sulejman | 06.04.2005 | | (2) | |
| Kristijan Trapanovski | 14.08.1999 | 14 | (13) | 5 |
| Aleks Zlatkov | 19.03.2002 | 7 | (2) | |
| **Forwards:** | **DOB** | **M** | **(s)** | **G** |
| Sunday Damilare Adetunji (NGA) | 10.12.1997 | 26 | | 11 |
| Renaldo Showayne Cephas (JAM) | 08.12.1999 | 22 | (7) | 11 |
| Mamadou Danfa (SEN) | 06.03.2001 | 11 | (12) | 4 |
| Pepi Gjorgiev | 04.10.1994 | 2 | (11) | 2 |
| Walid Hamidi (ALG) | 16.10.1996 | 24 | (3) | 5 |
| Ardit Nesimi (DEN) | 19.09.2003 | | (2) | |

## Fudbalski klub Sileks Kratovo

| Founded: | 1965 |
| Stadium: | Stadion Gradski, Kratovo (6,000) |
| Trainer: | Gorazd Mihajlov | 21.08.1974 |

| Goalkeepers: | DOB | M | (s) | G |
|---|---|---|---|---|
| Matej Andov | 16.11.2001 | 2 | | |
| Daniel Božinovski | 08.07.1989 | 24 | | |
| Metodija Velkovski | 24.05.2000 | 4 | | |
| **Defenders:** | **DOB** | **M** | **(s)** | **G** |
| Faruk Bihorać (SRB) | 12.05.1996 | 3 | (1) | |
| Kristijan Eftimov | 01.09.1999 | 9 | (4) | |
| Igor Janevski | 09.02.2004 | 3 | (7) | |
| Georgije Jankulov | 25.11.2001 | 1 | (4) | |
| Arsim Ljamalari | 22.07.1994 | 26 | | 3 |
| Mihail Manevski | 25.02.1999 | 18 | (4) | |
| Marko Marinković (SRB) | 06.01.1994 | 1 | (1) | |
| Miloš Nikolić (SRB) | 22.02.1989 | 15 | (5) | |
| Andrej Petkoski | 01.07.1998 | 14 | (4) | |
| Bojan Rajkov | 14.07.1998 | 19 | (5) | |
| Andrej Richkov | 23.09.1998 | 9 | (3) | |
| Nikola Risteski | 20.12.1996 | 5 | (3) | |
| **Midfielders:** | **DOB** | **M** | **(s)** | **G** |
| Burhan Aliji | 29.09.1989 | 8 | (13) | 1 |
| Darko Angjeleski | 19.07.1999 | 14 | (7) | |
| Hristijan Georgievski | 12.04.2003 | | (5) | |
| Robert Kocev | 14.06.1994 | | (1) | |
| David Manasievski | 25.09.2001 | 19 | (9) | 4 |
| Stefan Milosavljević (SRB) | 09.05.1992 | 10 | (3) | 2 |
| Vladimir Petrović (SRB) | 15.02.1997 | 15 | (2) | 1 |
| Hamza Ramani | 17.09.2002 | 9 | (4) | 1 |
| Viktor Serafimovski | 24.10.1995 | 26 | | 1 |
| Filip Stojchevski | 04.02.1999 | 13 | (10) | 2 |
| **Forwards:** | **DOB** | **M** | **(s)** | **G** |
| Dejan Cvetanoski | 15.05.1990 | | (12) | |
| Amar Emurli | 04.01.2003 | 1 | (1) | |
| Marko Gjorgjievski | 18.04.2000 | 10 | (2) | 6 |
| Aleksandar Katanić (SRB) | 15.08.1995 | 4 | (7) | 4 |
| Damjan Masevski | 06.03.2001 | 4 | (15) | 3 |
| Filip Obadović (SRB) | 19.08.1997 | 9 | (5) | 6 |
| Marjan Ristovski | 25.07.1996 | 29 | | 5 |
| Tomislav Turčin (CRO) | 31.05.1997 | 6 | (2) | |

## Fudbalski klub Skopje

| Founded: | 1960 | |
|---|---|---|
| Stadium: | Stadion Železarnica, Skopje (3,000) | |
| Trainer: | Slavcho Georgievski | 30.03.1980 |
| [06.03.2023] | Mirsad Jonuz | 09.04.1962 |

| Goalkeepers: | DOB | M | (s) | G |
|---|---|---|---|---|
| Andreja Efremov | 02.09.1992 | 22 | | |
| Petar Mitev | 30.01.1998 | 8 | (1) | |
| **Defenders:** | DOB | M | (s) | G |
| Kristijan Churlinov | 23.02.2001 | 25 | | |
| Hristijan Dimov | 23.03.2000 | 14 | (3) | 1 |
| Gordijan Hristovski | 21.04.2003 | 5 | (1) | |
| Jasmin Mecinović | 22.10.1990 | 13 | | |
| Dino Najdoski | 08.05.1992 | 26 | | |
| Sodiq Anthony Rasheed (NGA) | 30.04.2000 | 13 | | |
| Filip Stojanovski | 01.12.1996 | | (3) | |
| Gorast Stojmenov | 26.06.2002 | 1 | | |
| Blagoja Todorovski | 11.06.1985 | 8 | | |
| **Midfielders:** | DOB | M | (s) | G |
| Marko Andonovski | 30.01.2001 | 1 | (1) | |
| Martin Blaževski | 13.05.1992 | 8 | | |
| Mrgim Dani | 16.04.1994 | | (11) | |
| Filip Duranski | 17.07.1991 | 11 | | |
| Hristijan Georgievski | 12.04.2003 | 5 | (5) | |
| Leonid Ignatov | 04.01.2002 | 22 | (2) | 1 |

| | DOB | M | (s) | G |
|---|---|---|---|---|
| Alpaj Jusuf | 26.03.1998 | | (2) | |
| David Kalpachki | 01.06.2000 | 16 | | |
| Bozidar Mitrevski | 07.01.2001 | 9 | (9) | |
| Mihailo Mitrov | 05.03.1995 | 1 | (4) | |
| Paul-Henry Moussinga Mouasso (CMR) | 25.10.1997 | 17 | (4) | 1 |
| Mario Nastevski | 10.04.1995 | 6 | (10) | 1 |
| Lazar Peev | 19.06.1997 | 2 | (10) | |
| Mile Todorov | 20.08.1999 | 12 | (1) | 1 |
| **Forwards:** | DOB | M | (s) | G |
| Anid Abazi | 09.10.2002 | 4 | (6) | 1 |
| Izet Ajrullahu | 08.05.1998 | 8 | (6) | |
| Amasihohu James Akugbe (BEL) | 04.07.2000 | 9 | (3) | |
| Antonio Bozhinoski | 16.01.2000 | 20 | (4) | |
| Besmir Daci | 29.09.2004 | 3 | (3) | 1 |
| Bujar Hajdari | 23.08.2002 | 12 | (15) | 6 |
| Mustafa Jusuf | 01.04.2000 | 3 | (2) | |
| Hristijan Kirovski | 12.10.1985 | 4 | (3) | 1 |
| Seydou Koné (MLI) | 04.11.2002 | 3 | (6) | 1 |
| Fikret Livoreka | 04.09.2005 | | (2) | |
| Azer Omeragikj | 14.07.2002 | 19 | (4) | 2 |

## Football Club Struga Trim-Lum

| Founded: | 2015 | |
|---|---|---|
| Stadium: | Stadion Gradska Plaža, Struga (2,500) | |
| Trainer: | Srgjan Zaharievski | 12.09.1973 |
| [01.03.2023] | Shpëtim Duro (ALB) | 24.12.1959 |

| Goalkeepers: | DOB | M | (s) | G |
|---|---|---|---|---|
| Kristijan Kitanovski | 03.10.2002 | 1 | (1) | |
| Vedran Kjosevski (BIH) | 22.05.1995 | 24 | | |
| Raif Mirseloski | 29.11.1984 | 5 | | |
| **Defenders:** | DOB | M | (s) | G |
| Darko Ilieski | 14.10.1995 | 15 | | 2 |
| Ard Kasami | 03.01.1998 | 21 | (3) | |
| Besart Krivanjeva | 28.02.1996 | 13 | | |
| Edis Malikji | 04.05.1995 | 11 | (8) | |
| Zija Merxhani | 22.10.1995 | 25 | (2) | 2 |
| Medzit Neziri | 02.09.1990 | 13 | | |
| Miklovan Pere (ALB) | 19.05.1991 | 8 | (15) | |
| Sava Radić (SRB) | 04.03.1998 | 26 | | 1 |
| **Midfielders:** | DOB | M | (s) | G |
| Besmir Bojku | 03.01.1995 | 26 | (1) | 1 |

| | DOB | M | (s) | G |
|---|---|---|---|---|
| Jusuf Kaba | 04.02.2004 | | (2) | |
| Valentin Kochoski | 01.03.1997 | 14 | (14) | 1 |
| Arbri Pengu (POR) | 16.05.2003 | 1 | (1) | |
| Bunjamin Shabani | 30.01.1991 | 29 | | 12 |
| Flamur Tairi | 24.11.1990 | 3 | (15) | |
| Hogan Ukpa Effiong (NGA) | 28.09.2001 | 18 | (9) | 2 |
| Arion Ziba | 22.11.2001 | | (1) | |
| **Forwards:** | DOB | M | (s) | G |
| Besart Ibraimi | 17.12.1986 | 25 | (4) | 18 |
| Abdulhadi Jahja | 03.06.1999 | 12 | (10) | |
| Fatjon Jusufi | 17.12.1995 | 6 | (18) | 1 |
| Hristijan Maleski | 04.05.2002 | 18 | (5) | 7 |
| Suhejlj Muharem | 25.08.2001 | 11 | (4) | 2 |
| Marjan Radeski | 10.02.1995 | 5 | (7) | 2 |

## Gradski Fudbalski Klub Tikvesh 1930

| Founded: | 21.12.1930 | |
|---|---|---|
| Stadium: | Stadion Gradski, Kavadarci (7,500) | |
| Trainer: | Vlatko Kostov | 01.09.1965 |
| [08.09.2022] | Gjorgji Mojsov | 10.06.1985 |

| Goalkeepers: | DOB | M | (s) | G |
|---|---|---|---|---|
| Martin Davkov | 18.12.1998 | 16 | | |
| Stojan Dimovski | 19.09.1982 | 14 | | |
| **Defenders:** | DOB | M | (s) | G |
| Almir Ćubara (BIH) | 21.11.1997 | 13 | | |
| Gligor Donchev | 04.05.1998 | 11 | (6) | 1 |
| Aleksandar Gjurkovski | 11.02.2002 | 15 | (1) | |
| Daniel Karcheski | 07.03.1992 | 23 | (6) | 1 |
| Stefan Kostov | 31.10.1996 | 6 | (1) | |
| Stefan Naumcheski | 07.08.2000 | 27 | (1) | |
| Aleksandar Varelovski | 08.05.1988 | 28 | (1) | 3 |
| **Midfielders:** | DOB | M | (s) | G |
| Nikolay Hristov (BUL) | 01.08.1989 | 25 | (1) | 1 |
| Neven Kostadinov | 16.04.2006 | | (6) | |
| Andrej Lazarov | 08.09.1999 | 26 | (3) | 1 |
| Bojan Memov | 04.05.2005 | | (1) | |

| | DOB | M | (s) | G |
|---|---|---|---|---|
| Uroš Mirković (SRB) | 08.08.1990 | 7 | (21) | 1 |
| Stojan Petkovski | 24.01.1996 | 3 | (14) | |
| Gjoko Spasov | 28.11.2006 | | (4) | |
| Dragan Stojkov | 23.02.1988 | 6 | (6) | |
| Riste Temelkov | 02.10.1997 | 12 | (8) | 1 |
| **Forwards:** | DOB | M | (s) | G |
| Ivan Ivanovski | 27.06.1995 | 19 | (3) | 9 |
| Daniel Milovanovikj | 10.08.1998 | 15 | (9) | 4 |
| Aleksandar Mishov | 21.07.1998 | 13 | (14) | 7 |
| Kjire Mitkov | 20.01.2002 | | (1) | |
| Viktor Naumovski | 07.09.2001 | | (1) | |
| Anael Barga Ngoba (CMR) | 08.10.1998 | 18 | (5) | 6 |
| Ediz Spahiu | 18.03.2001 | 16 | (11) | 5 |
| Danail Tasev | 26.04.2002 | 17 | (9) | |
| Martin Todorov | 11.08.2003 | | (4) | |

## SECOND LEVEL
### Vtora Liga 2022/2023

| | | | | | | | | | | | |
|---|---|---|---|---|---|---|---|---|---|---|---|
| 1. | FK Voska Sport Ohrid (*Promoted*) | 30 | 23 | 6 | 1 | 84 | - | 25 | 75 |
| 2. | KF Gostivari* (*Promoted*) | 30 | 23 | 7 | 0 | 71 | - | 11 | 73 |
| 3. | FK Vardar Skopje (*Promotion Play-offs*) | 30 | 19 | 6 | 5 | 55 | - | 20 | 63 |
| 4. | FK Pelister Bitola | 30 | 17 | 7 | 6 | 64 | - | 26 | 58 |
| 5. | FK Detonit Plačkovica Radoviš | 30 | 14 | 8 | 8 | 43 | - | 35 | 50 |
| 6. | KF Besa Dobërdoll | 30 | 15 | 3 | 12 | 43 | - | 29 | 48 |
| 7. | GFK Ohrid | 30 | 12 | 5 | 13 | 31 | - | 35 | 41 |
| 8. | KF Arsimi 1973 Çegran | 30 | 12 | 4 | 14 | 41 | - | 35 | 40 |
| 9. | FK Kožuf Gevgelija | 30 | 10 | 6 | 14 | 40 | - | 54 | 36 |
| 10. | FK Belasica Strumica | 30 | 10 | 5 | 15 | 36 | - | 47 | 35 |
| 11. | FK Karaorman Struga | 30 | 9 | 7 | 14 | 30 | - | 40 | 34 |
| 12. | FK Sasa Makedonska Kamenica | 30 | 8 | 7 | 15 | 31 | - | 49 | 31 |
| 13. | FK Teteks Tetovo (*Relegation Play-offs*) | 30 | 9 | 4 | 17 | 31 | - | 78 | 31 |
| 14. | FK Lokomotiva Skopje (*Relegated*) | 30 | 8 | 6 | 16 | 35 | - | 41 | 30 |
| 15. | FK Sloga 1934 Vinica (*Relegated*) | 30 | 6 | 7 | 17 | 26 | - | 47 | 25 |
| 16. | FK Borec Veles (*Relegated*) | 30 | 0 | 2 | 28 | 13 | - | 102 | 2 |

*3 points deducted*

### Relegation Play-offs [28.05.2023]

| | |
|---|---|
| GFK Osogovo Kočani - FK Teteks Tetovo | 1-6(0-2) |
| KF Bashkimi Kumanovo – Vëllazërimi J 1977 | 3-0(2-0) |
| FK Novaci - FK Vardar Negotino | 1-1(1-0,1-1,1-1); 2-3 pen |

FK Teteks Tetovo, KF Bashkimi Kumanovo and FK Vardar Negotino will play at second level in 2023/2024.

## NATIONAL TEAM

### INTERNATIONAL MATCHES
#### (16.07.2022 – 15.07.2023)

| | | | | |
|---|---|---|---|---|
| 23.09.2022 | Tbilisi | *Georgia - North Macedonia* | 2-0(1-0) | (UNL) |
| 26.09.2022 | Skopje | *North Macedonia - Bulgaria* | 0-1(0-0) | (UNL) |
| 22.10.2022 | Abu Dhabi | *Saudi Arabia - North Macedonia* | 1-0(0-0) | (F) |
| 17.11.2022 | Skopje | *North Macedonia - Finland* | 1-1(0-1) | (F) |
| 20.11.2022 | Skopje | *North Macedonia - Azerbaijan* | 1-3(1-1) | (F) |
| 23.03.2023 | Skopje | *North Macedonia - Malta* | 2-1(0-0) | (ECQ) |
| 27.03.2023 | Skopje | *North Macedonia - Faroe Islands* | 1-0(0-0) | (F) |
| 16.06.2023 | Skopje | *North Macedonia - Ukraine* | 2-3(2-0) | (ECQ) |
| 19.06.2023 | Manchester | *England - North Macedonia* | 7-0(3-0) | (ECQ) |

**23.09.2022    GEORGIA - NORTH MACEDONIA        2-0(1-0)**        3rd UEFA Nations League C, Group 4
"Boris Paichadze" Dinamo Arena, Tbilisi; Referee: Ivan Kružliak (Slovakia); Attendance: 54,200
**MKD:** Stole Dimitrievski, Gjoko Zajkov, Darko Velkovski (72.Nikola Serafimov), Visar Musliu, Ezgjan Alioski, Eljif Elmas, Stefan Spirovski (68.Aleksandar Trajkovski), Enis Bardi (Cap) (84.Agon Elezi), Stefan Aškovski (68.Todor Todoroski), Bojan Miovski, Milan Ristovski (73.Jani Atanasov). Trainer: Blagoja Milevski.

**26.09.2022    NORTH MACEDONIA - BULGARIA        0-1(0-0)**        3rd UEFA Nations League C, Group 4
Nacionalna Arena "Toše Proeski", Skopje; Referee: Julian Weinberger (Austria); Attendance: 20,173
**MKD:** Stole Dimitrievski, Egzon Bejtulai, Gjoko Zajkov, Visar Musliu, Todor Todoroski [*sent off 14*], Eljif Elmas, Enis Bardi (Cap), Aleksandar Trajkovski (22.Stefan Aškovski; 85.Dorian Babunski), Ezgjan Alioski, Bojan Miovski (61.Stefan Spirovski), Milan Ristovski (61.Ljupcho Doriev). Trainer: Blagoja Milevski.

**22.10.2022    SAUDI ARABIA - NORTH MACEDONIA        1-0(0-0)**        Friendly International
Zayed Sports City Stadium, Abu Dhabi (United Arab Emirates); Referee: Sultan Mohamed Saleh Yousif Alha Al Hammadi (United Arab Emirates); Attendance: n/a
**MKD:** Kristijan Naumovski (58.Igor Aleksovski), Darko Velkovski (Cap) (64.Zija Merdjani), Vladica Brdarovski, Kristijan Toševski (79.Bojan Ilievski), Ali Adem (58.Ivan Nikolov), Bojan Dimoski, Egzon Bejtulai (88.Mario Mladenovski), Ferhan Hasani (58.Kristijan Trapanovski), Metodi Maksimov (58.Bunjamin Shabani), Besart Ibraimi (46.Vlatko Stojanovski), Ljupcho Doriev. Trainer: Blagoja Milevski.

**17.11.2022    NORTH MACEDONIA - FINLAND        1-1(0-1)**        Friendly International
Nacionalna Arena "Toše Proeski", Skopje; Referee: Novak Simović (Serbia); Attendance: 2,000
**MKD:** Stole Dimitrievski, Egzon Bejtulai (46.Ljupcho Doriev), Nikola Serafimov, Visar Musliu (59.Darko Velkovski), Ezgjan Alioski, Stefan Spirovski (46.Bojan Miovski), Boban Nikolov (59.Valon Ethemi), Stefan Ristovski (Cap), Enis Bardi, Eljif Elmas (87.Agon Elezi), Ilija Nestorovski (59.Jani Atanasov). Trainer: Blagoja Milevski.
**Goal:** Enis Bardi (75 penalty).

**20.11.2022**    **NORTH MACEDONIA - AZERBAIJAN**      **1-3(1-1)**        Friendly International
Nacionalna Arena "Toše Proeski", Skopje; Referee: Enea Jorgji (Albania); Attendance: 1,000
**MKD:** Damjan Šiškovski, Stefan Ristovski (Cap) (77.Egzon Bejtulai), Nikola Serafimov, Visar Musliu, Stefan Aškovski (76.Dorian Babunski), David Babunski (56.Valon Ethemi), Boban Nikolov [*sent off 52*], Ljupcho Doriev (83.Martin Mircevski), Enis Bardi, Eljif Elmas (76.Bojan Dimoski), Ilija Nestorovski (56.Jani Atanasov). Trainer: Blagoja Milevski.
**Goal:** Enis Bardi (29 penalty).

**23.03.2023**    **NORTH MACEDONIA - MALTA**      **2-1(0-0)**        17th EC. Qualifiers
Nacionalna Arena "Toše Proeski", Skopje; Referee: Kristo Tohver (Estonia); Attendance: 9,991
**MKD:** Stole Dimitrievski, Darko Velkovski (58.Darko Churlinov), Gjoko Zajkov (90+2.Kire Ristevski), Visar Musliu, Stefan Ristovski (Cap), Enis Bardi, Jani Atanasov, Ezgjan Alioski (78.Stefan Aškovski), Eljif Elmas, Bojan Miovski (78.Milan Ristovski), Aleksandar Trajkovski (58.Ilija Nestorovski). Trainer: Blagoja Milevski.
**Goals:** Eljif Elmas (66), Darko Churlinov (72).

**27.03.2023**    **NORTH MACEDONIA - FAROE ISLANDS**      **1-0(0-0)**        Friendly International
Nacionalna Arena "Toše Proeski", Skopje; Referee: Miloš Savović (Montenegro); Attendance: 500
**MKD:** Damjan Šiškovski, Stefan Ristovski, Darko Velkovski (79.Jovan Manev), Kire Ristevski (Cap), Ezgjan Alioski, Jani Atanasov (70.Agon Elezi), Enis Bardi, Darko Churlinov (79.Stefan Aškovski), Valon Ethemi (69.David Babunski), Ilija Nestorovski (54.Bojan Miovski), Milan Ristovski (54.Eljif Elmas). Trainer: Blagoja Milevski.
**Goal:** Bojan Miovski (82).

**16.06.2023**    **NORTH MACEDONIA - UKRAINE**      **2-3(2-0)**        17th EC. Qualifiers
Nacionalna Arena "Toše Proeski", Skopje; Referee: Lukas Fähndrich (Switzerland); Attendance: 14,370
**MKD:** Stole Dimitrievski, Stefan Ristovski (Cap), Gjoko Zajkov, Visar Musliu [*sent off 73*], Ezgjan Alioski, Arijan Ademi (65.Jani Atanasov), Eljif Elmas, Enis Bardi, Stefan Aškovski (65.Vladica Brdarovski; 90+1.Dorian Babunski), Ilija Nestorovski (65.Milan Ristovski), Aleksandar Trajkovski (75.Ljupcho Doriev). Trainer: Blagoja Milevski.
**Goals:** Enis Bardi (31 penalty), Eljif Elmas (39).

**19.06.2023**    **ENGLAND - NORTH MACEDONIA**      **7-0(3-0)**        17th EC. Qualifiers
Old Trafford, Manchester; Referee: István Kovács (Romania); Attendance: 70,708
**MKD:** Stole Dimitrievski, Stefan Aškovski, Darko Velkovski, Gjoko Zajkov (57.Nikola Serafimov), Stefan Ristovski (Cap) (46.Egzon Bejtulai), Ezgjan Alioski, Arijan Ademi (57.Jani Atanasov), Enis Bardi (67.David Babunski), Eljif Elmas, Ilija Nestorovski, Aleksandar Trajkovski (57.Dorian Babunski). Trainer: Blagoja Milevski.

| NATIONAL TEAM PLAYERS | | | | |
|---|---|---|---|---|
| (16.07.2022 – 15.07.2023) | | | | |

| Name | DOB | Caps | Goals | *Club* |
|---|---|---|---|---|
| **Goalkeepers** | | | | |
| Igor ALEKSOVSKI | 24.02.1995 | **1** | **0** | 2022: *FK Rabotnički Skopje* |
| Stole DIMITRIEVSKI | 25.12.1993 | **62** | **0** | 2022/2023: *Rayo Vallecano de Madrid (ESP)* |
| Kristijan NAUMOVSKI | 17.09.1988 | **7** | **0** | 2022: *KF Shkupi Čair* |
| Damjan ŠIŠKOVSKI | 18.03.1995 | **9** | **0** | 2022/2023: *Doxa Katokopias FC (CYP)* |
| **Defenders** | | | | |
| Stefan AŠKOVSKI | 24.02.1992 | **22** | **0** | 2022/2023: *PAS Lamia (GRE)* |
| Egzon BEJTULAI | 07.01.1994 | **27** | **0** | 2022/2023: *KF Shkëndija Tetovo* |
| Vladica BRDAROVSKI | 07.02.1990 | **9** | **0** | 2022/2023: *KF Shkupi Čair* |
| Bojan DIMOSKI | 23.11.2001 | **3** | **0** | 2022: *Fudbalska Akademija Pandev Strumica* |
| Bojan ILIEVSKI | 01.09.1999 | **1** | **0** | 2022: *FK Makedonija Gjorče Petrov Skopje* |
| Metodi MAKSIMOV | 20.08.2002 | **1** | **0** | 2022: *FK Rabotnički Skopje* |
| Jovan MANEV | 25.01.2001 | **1** | **0** | 2023: *Adana Demirspor Kulübü (TUR)* |
| Zija MERDJANI | 22.10.1995 | **1** | **0** | 2022: *FC Struga Trim-Lum* |
| Mario MLADENOVSKI | 16.09.2000 | **2** | **0** | 2022: *KF Shkupi Čair* |
| Visar MUSLIU | 13.11.1994 | **51** | **1** | 2022/2023: *FC Ingolstadt 04 (GER)* |
| Kire RISTEVSKI | 22.10.1990 | **59** | **0** | 2023: *FC Pyunik Yerevan (ARM)* |
| Stefan RISTOVSKI | 12.02.1992 | **82** | **2** | 2022/2023: *GNK Dinamo Zagreb (CRO)* |
| Nikola SERAFIMOV | 11.08.1999 | **6** | **0** | 2022/2023: *Fehérvár FC Székesfehérvár (HUN)* |
| Todor TODOROSKI | 26.02.1999 | **6** | **0** | 2022: *Sumqayıt FK (AZE)* |
| Kristijan TOŠEVSKI | 06.05.1994 | **9** | **0** | 2022: *KF Tiranë (ALB)* |
| Darko VELKOVSKI | 21.06.1995 | **48** | **3** | 2022/2023: *Al Ettifaq FC Dammam (KSA)* |
| Gjoko ZAJKOV | 10.02.1995 | **25** | **1** | 2022: *FK Vorskla Poltava (UKR)* <br> 12.01.2023-> *CS Universitatea Craiova* |

## Midfielders

| | | | | | |
|---|---|---|---|---|---|
| Ali ADEM | 01.06.2000 | 1 | 0 | 2022: | KF Shkupi Čair |
| Arijan ADEMI | 29.05.1991 | 30 | 4 | 2023: | Beijing Guoan FC (CHN) |
| Ezgjan ALIOSKI | 12.02.1992 | 67 | 12 | 2022/2023: | Fenerbahçe SK Istanbul (TUR) |
| Jani ATANASOV | 31.10.1999 | 8 | 0 | 2022: | HNK Hajduk Split (CRO) |
| | | | | 23.01.2023-> | KS Cracovia Kraków (POL) |
| David BABUNSKI | 01.03.1994 | 15 | 0 | 2022/2023: | Mezőkövesdi SE (HUN) |
| Enis BARDI | 02.07.1995 | 56 | 14 | 2022/2023: | Trabzonspor Kulübü (TUR) |
| Darko CHURLINOV | 11.07.2000 | 19 | 4 | 2023: | Burnley FC (ENG) |
| Agon ELEZI | 01.03.2001 | 3 | 0 | 2022/2023: | NK Varaždin (CRO) |
| Eljif ELMAS | 27.09.1999 | 50 | 11 | 2022/2023: | SSC Napoli (ITA) |
| Valon ETHEMI | 03.10.1997 | 4 | 0 | 2022/2023: | İstanbulspor (TUR) |
| Ferhan HASANI | 18.06.1990 | 43 | 2 | 2022: | KF Shkëndija Tetovo |
| Boban NIKOLOV | 28.07.1994 | 48 | 4 | 2022: | SC FCSB Bucureşti (ROU) |
| Ivan NIKOLOV | 17.02.2002 | 1 | 0 | 2022: | FK Bregalnica 2008 Štip |
| Bunjamin SHABANI | 30.01.1991 | 1 | 0 | 2022: | FC Struga Trim-Lum |
| Stefan SPIROVSKI | 23.08.1990 | 55 | 1 | 2022: | FC Pyunik Yerevan (ARM) |

## Forwards

| | | | | | |
|---|---|---|---|---|---|
| Dorian BABUNSKI | 29.08.1996 | 7 | 0 | 2022/2023: | Debreceni VSC (HUN) |
| Ljupcho DORIEV | 13.09.1995 | 8 | 0 | 2022/2023: | KF Shkëndija Tetovo |
| Besart IBRAIMI | 17.12.1986 | 16 | 0 | 2022: | FC Struga Trim-Lum |
| Bojan MIOVSKI | 24.06.1999 | 15 | 2 | 2022/2023: | Aberdeen FC (SCO) |
| Martin MIRCEVSKI | 11.02.1997 | 1 | 0 | 2022: | FK TSC Bačka Topola (SRB) |
| Ilija NESTOROVSKI | 12.03.1990 | 52 | 10 | 2022/2023: | Udinese Calcio (ITA) |
| Milan RISTOVSKI | 08.04.1998 | 18 | 3 | 2022/2023: | FC Spartak Trnava (SVK) |
| Vlatko STOJANOVSKI | 23.04.1997 | 10 | 2 | 2022: | KF Shkëndija Tetovo |
| Aleksandar TRAJKOVSKI | 05.09.1992 | 84 | 20 | 2022/2023: | Al-Fayha FC Al Majma'ah (KSA) |
| Kristijan TRAPANOVSKI | 14.08.1999 | 1 | 0 | 2022: | KF Shkupi Čair |

## Trainer

| | | |
|---|---|---|
| Blagoja MILEVSKI [from 01.08.2021] | 25.03.1971 | 22 M; 8 W; 5 D; 9 L; 29-32 |

# NORTHERN IRELAND

## The Country:
Tuaisceart Éireann (Northern Ireland)
Capital: Belfast
Surface: 14,130 km²
Inhabitants: 1,903,175 [2021]
Time: UTC

## The FA:
Irish Football Association
National Football Stadium Donegal Avenue BT12 6LW, Belfast
Tel: +44 28 9066 9458
Foundation date: 1880
Member of FIFA since: 1911
Member of UEFA since: 1954
Website: www.irishfa.com

## NATIONAL TEAM RECORDS

### RECORDS
| | | |
|---|---|---|
| First international match: | 18.02.1882, Belfast: | Ireland – England 0-13 |
| Most international caps: | Steven Davis | - 140 caps (since 2005) |
| Most international goals: | David Jonathan Healy | - 36 goals / 95 caps (2000-2013) |

### UEFA EUROPEAN CHAMPIONSHIP
| | |
|---|---|
| 1960 | Did not enter |
| 1964 | Qualifiers |
| 1968 | Qualifiers |
| 1972 | Qualifiers |
| 1976 | Qualifiers |
| 1980 | Qualifiers |
| 1984 | Qualifiers |
| 1988 | Qualifiers |
| 1992 | Qualifiers |
| 1996 | Qualifiers |
| 2000 | Qualifiers |
| 2004 | Qualifiers |
| 2008 | Qualifiers |
| 2012 | Qualifiers |
| 2016 | Final Tournament (2nd Round of 16) |
| 2020 | Qualifiers |

### FIFA WORLD CUP
| | |
|---|---|
| 1930 | Did not enter |
| 1934 | Did not enter |
| 1938 | Did not enter |
| 1950 | Qualifiers |
| 1954 | Qualifiers |
| 1958 | Final Tournament (Quarter-Finals) |
| 1962 | Qualifiers |
| 1966 | Qualifiers |
| 1970 | Qualifiers |
| 1974 | Qualifiers |
| 1978 | Qualifiers |
| 1982 | Final Tournament (2nd Round) |
| 1986 | Final Tournament (Group Stage) |
| 1990 | Qualifiers |
| 1994 | Qualifiers |
| 1998 | Qualifiers |
| 2002 | Qualifiers |
| 2006 | Qualifiers |
| 2010 | Qualifiers |
| 2014 | Qualifiers |
| 2018 | Qualifiers |
| 2022 | Qualifiers |

### OLYMPIC TOURNAMENTS
| | |
|---|---|
| 1908 | - |
| 1912 | - |
| 1920 | - |
| 1924 | - |
| 1928 | - |
| 1936 | - |
| 1948 | - |
| 1952 | - |
| 1956 | - |
| 1960 | - |
| 1964 | - |
| 1968 | - |
| 1972 | - |
| 1976 | - |
| 1980 | - |
| 1984 | - |
| 1988 | - |
| 1992 | - |
| 1996 | - |
| 2000 | - |
| 2004 | - |
| 2008 | - |
| 2012 | - |
| 2016 | - |
| 2020 | - |

### UEFA NATIONS LEAGUE
| | |
|---|---|
| 2018/2019 | League B (Group Stage) |
| 2020/2021 | League B (Group Stage -> relegated to League C) |
| 2022/2023 | League C (Group Stage) |

### NORTHERN IRISH CLUB HONOURS IN EUROPEAN CLUB COMPETITIONS:

| European Champion Clubs.Cup (1956-1992) / UEFA Champions League (1993-2023) |
|---|
| None |

| Fairs Cup (1858-1971) / UEFA Cup (1972-2009) / UEFA Europa League (2010-2023) |
|---|
| None |

| UEFA Europa Conference League (2021-2023) |
|---|
| None |

| UEFA Super Cup (1972-2022) |
|---|
| None |

| *European Cup Winners' Cup 1961-1999** |
|---|
| None |

*defunct competition

# NATIONAL COMPETITIONS
## TABLE OF HONOURS

| | CHAMPIONS | CUP WINNERS | BEST GOALSCORERS | |
|---|---|---|---|---|
| 1880/1881 | - | Moyola Park AFC | - | |
| 1881/1882 | - | Queen's Island FC Belfast | - | |
| 1882/1883 | - | Cliftonville FAC | - | |
| 1883/1884 | - | Distillery FC Ballyskeagh | - | |
| 1884/1885 | - | Distillery FC Ballyskeagh | - | |
| 1885/1886 | - | Distillery FC Ballyskeagh | - | |
| 1886/1887 | - | Ulster FC Ballynafeigh | - | |
| 1887/1888 | - | Cliftonville FAC | - | |
| 1888/1889 | - | Distillery FC Ballyskeagh | - | |
| 1889/1890 | - | Gordon Highlanders | - | |
| 1890/1891 | Linfield FC Belfast | Linfield FC Belfast | Robert Hill (Linfield FC Belfast) | 20 |
| 1891/1892 | Linfield FC Belfast | Linfield FC Belfast | Tim Morrison (Linfield FC Belfast) | 21 |
| 1892/1893 | Linfield FC Belfast | Linfield FC Belfast | Robert Hill (Linfield FC Belfast) James Percy (Cliftonville FAC) | 9 |
| 1893/1894 | Glentoran FC Belfast | Distillery FC Ballyskeagh | Michael McErlean (Linfield FC Belfast) | 9 |
| 1894/1895 | Linfield FC Belfast | Linfield FC Belfast | George Gaukrodger (Linfield FC Belfast) Joe McAllen (Linfield FC Belfast) | 4 |
| 1895/1896 | Distillery FC Ballyskeagh | Distillery FC Ballyskeagh | - | |
| 1896/1897 | Glentoran FC Belfast | Cliftonville FAC | Johnny Darling (Linfield FC Belfast) Richard Peden (Linfield FC Belfast) | 6 |
| 1897/1898 | Linfield FC Belfast | Linfield FC Belfast | - | |
| 1898/1899 | Distillery FC Ballyskeagh | Linfield FC Belfast | - | |
| 1899/1900 | Belfast Celtic FC | Cliftonville FAC | - | |
| 1900/1901 | Distillery FC Ballyskeagh | Cliftonville FAC | - | |
| 1901/1902 | Linfield FC Belfast | Linfield FC Belfast | - | |
| 1902/1903 | Distillery FC Ballyskeagh | Distillery FC Ballyskeagh | - | |
| 1903/1904 | Linfield FC Belfast | Linfield FC Belfast | - | |
| 1904/1905 | Glentoran FC Belfast | Distillery FC Ballyskeagh | - | |
| 1905/1906 | Cliftonville FAC Distillery FC Ballyskeagh (shared) | Shelbourne FC Dublin | - | |
| 1906/1907 | Linfield FC Belfast | Cliftonville FAC | - | |
| 1907/1908 | Linfield FC Belfast | Bohemians FC Dublin | - | |
| 1908/1909 | Linfield FC Belfast | Cliftonville FAC | - | |
| 1909/1910 | Cliftonville FAC | Distillery FC Ballyskeagh | - | |
| 1910/1911 | Linfield FC Belfast | Shelbourne FC Dublin | - | |
| 1911/1912 | Glentoran FC Belfast | Linfield FC Belfast | - | |
| 1912/1913 | Glentoran FC Belfast | Linfield FC Belfast | - | |
| 1913/1914 | Linfield FC Belfast | Glentoran FC Belfast | - | |
| 1914/1915 | Belfast Celtic FC | Linfield FC Belfast | - | |
| 1915/1916 | *No competition* | Linfield FC Belfast | - | |
| 1916/1917 | *No competition* | Glentoran FC Belfast | - | |
| 1917/1918 | *No competition* | Belfast Celtic FC | - | |
| 1918/1919 | *No competition* | Linfield FC Belfast | - | |
| 1919/1920 | Belfast Celtic FC | Shelbourne FC Dublin | - | |
| 1920/1921 | Glentoran FC Belfast | Glentoran FC Belfast | - | |
| 1921/1922 | Linfield FC Belfast | Linfield FC Belfast | - | |
| 1922/1923 | Linfield FC Belfast | Linfield FC Belfast | - | |
| 1923/1924 | Queen's Island FC Belfast | Queen's Island FC Belfast | - | |
| 1924/1925 | Glentoran FC Belfast | Distillery FC Ballyskeagh | - | |
| 1925/1926 | Belfast Celtic FC | Belfast Celtic FC | - | |
| 1926/1927 | Belfast Celtic FC | Ards FC Newtownards | Joseph Gardiner Absolom Bambrick (Glentoran FC Belfast) | 28 |
| 1927/1928 | Belfast Celtic FC | Willowfield FC | - | |
| 1928/1929 | Belfast Celtic FC | Ballymena FC | Joseph Gardiner Absolom Bambrick (Linfield FC Belfast) | 43 |
| 1929/1930 | Linfield FC Belfast | Linfield FC Belfast | Joseph Gardiner Absolom Bambrick (Linfield FC Belfast) | 50 |
| 1930/1931 | Glentoran FC Belfast | Linfield FC Belfast | Fred Roberts (Glentoran FC Belfast) | 55 |
| 1931/1932 | Linfield FC Belfast | Glentoran FC Belfast | - | |
| 1932/1933 | Belfast Celtic FC | Glentoran FC Belfast | Joseph Gardiner Absolom Bambrick (Linfield FC Belfast) | 40 |
| 1933/1934 | Linfield FC Belfast | Linfield FC Belfast | - | |
| 1934/1935 | Linfield FC Belfast | Glentoran FC Belfast | - | |
| 1935/1936 | Belfast Celtic FC | Linfield FC Belfast | - | |
| 1936/1937 | Belfast Celtic FC | Belfast Celtic FC | - | |
| 1937/1938 | Belfast Celtic FC | Belfast Celtic FC | - | |
| 1938/1939 | Belfast Celtic FC | Linfield FC Belfast | - | |
| 1939/1940 | Belfast Celtic FC | Ballymena United FC | - | |
| 1940/1941 | *No competition* | Belfast Celtic FC | - | |
| 1941/1942 | *No competition* | Linfield FC Belfast | - | |
| 1942/1943 | *No competition* | Belfast Celtic FC | - | |
| 1943/1944 | *No competition* | Belfast Celtic FC | - | |
| 1944/1945 | *No competition* | Linfield FC Belfast | - | |

| | | | | |
|---|---|---|---|---|
| 1945/1946 | *No competition* | Linfield FC Belfast | - | |
| 1946/1947 | *No competition* | Belfast Celtic FC | - | |
| 1947/1948 | Belfast Celtic FC | Linfield FC Belfast | James Jones (Belfast Celtic FC) | 28 |
| 1948/1949 | Linfield FC Belfast | Derry City FC | William Simpson (Linfield FC Belfast) | 19 |
| 1949/1950 | Linfield FC Belfast | Linfield FC Belfast | Sammy Hughes (Glentoran FC Belfast) | 23 |
| 1950/1951 | Glentoran FC Belfast | Glentoran FC Belfast | Sammy Hughes (Glentoran FC Belfast) Walter Allen (Portadown FC) | 23 |
| 1951/1952 | Glenavon FC Lurgan | Ards FC Newtownards | James Jones (Glenavon FC Lurgan) | 27 |
| 1952/1953 | Glentoran FC Belfast | Linfield FC Belfast | Sammy Hughes (Glentoran FC Belfast) | 28 |
| 1953/1954 | Linfield FC Belfast | Derry City FC | James Jones (Glenavon FC Lurgan) | 32 |
| 1954/1955 | Linfield FC Belfast | Dundela FC Belfast | Francis Coyle (Coleraine FC) | 20 |
| 1955/1956 | Linfield FC Belfast | Distillery FC Ballyskeagh | James Jones (Glenavon FC Lurgan) | 26 |
| 1956/1957 | Glenavon FC Lurgan | Glenavon FC Lurgan | James Jones (Glenavon FC Lurgan) | 33 |
| 1957/1958 | Ards FC Newtownards | Ballymena United FC | John Edward Thompson Milburn (Linfield FC Belfast) | 29 |
| 1958/1959 | Linfield FC Belfast | Glenavon FC Lurgan | John Edward Thompson Milburn (Linfield FC Belfast) | 26 |
| 1959/1960 | Glenavon FC Lurgan | Linfield FC Belfast | James Jones (Glenavon FC Lurgan) | 29 |
| 1960/1961 | Linfield FC Belfast | Glenavon FC Lurgan | Trevor Thompson (Glentoran FC Belfast) | 22 |
| 1961/1962 | Linfield FC Belfast | Linfield FC Belfast | Mick Lynch (Ards FC Newtownards) | 20 |
| 1962/1963 | Distillery FC Ballyskeagh | Linfield FC Belfast | Joe Meldrum (Distillery FC Ballyskeagh) | 27 |
| 1963/1964 | Glentoran FC Belfast | Derry City FC | Trevor Thompson (Linfield FC Belfast) | 21 |
| 1964/1965 | Derry City FC | Coleraine FC | Kenny Halliday (Coleraine FC) Dennis Guy (Glenavon FC Lurgan) | 19 |
| 1965/1966 | Linfield FC Belfast | Glentoran FC Belfast | Sammy Pavis (Linfield FC Belfast) | 28 |
| 1966/1967 | Glentoran FC Belfast | Crusaders FC Belfast | Sammy Pavis (Linfield FC Belfast) | 25 |
| 1967/1968 | Glentoran FC Belfast | Crusaders FC Belfast | Sammy Pavis (Linfield FC Belfast) | 30 |
| 1968/1969 | Linfield FC Belfast | Ards FC Newtownards | Danny Hale (Derry City FC) | 21 |
| 1969/1970 | Glentoran FC Belfast | Linfield FC Belfast | Des Dickson (Coleraine FC) | 21 |
| 1970/1971 | Linfield FC Belfast | Distillery FC Ballyskeagh | Bryan Hamilton (Linfield FC Belfast) | 18 |
| 1971/1972 | Glentoran FC Belfast | Coleraine FC | Peter Watson (Distillery FC Ballyskeagh) Des Dickson (Coleraine FC) | 15 |
| 1972/1973 | Crusaders FC Belfast | Glentoran FC Belfast | Des Dickson (Coleraine FC) | 23 |
| 1973/1974 | Coleraine FC | Ards FC Newtownards | Des Dickson (Coleraine FC) | 24 |
| 1974/1975 | Linfield FC Belfast | Coleraine FC | Martin Malone (Portadown FC) | 15 |
| 1975/1976 | Crusaders FC Belfast | Carrick Rangers FC | Des Dickson (Coleraine FC) | 23 |
| 1976/1977 | Glentoran FC Belfast | Coleraine FC | Ronnie McAteer (Crusaders FC Belfast) | 20 |
| 1977/1978 | Linfield FC Belfast | Linfield FC Belfast | Warren Feeney (Glentoran FC Belfast) | 17 |
| 1978/1979 | Linfield FC Belfast | Cliftonville FAC | Tommy Armstrong (Ards FC Newtownards) | 21 |
| 1979/1980 | Linfield FC Belfast | Linfield FC Belfast | James Martin (Glentoran FC Belfast) | 17 |
| 1980/1981 | Glentoran FC Belfast | Ballymena United FC | Des Dickson (Coleraine FC) Paul Malone (Ballymena United FC) | 18 |
| 1981/1982 | Linfield FC Belfast | Linfield FC Belfast | Gary Blackledge (Glentoran FC Belfast) | 18 |
| 1982/1983 | Linfield FC Belfast | Glentoran FC Belfast | James Campbell (Ards FC Newtownards) | 15 |
| 1983/1984 | Linfield FC Belfast | Ballymena United FC | Martin McGaughey (Linfield FC Belfast) Trevor Anderson (Linfield FC Belfast) | 15 |
| 1984/1985 | Linfield FC Belfast | Glentoran FC Belfast | Martin McGaughey (Linfield FC Belfast) | 34 |
| 1985/1986 | Linfield FC Belfast | Glentoran FC Belfast | Trevor Anderson (Linfield FC Belfast) | 14 |
| 1986/1987 | Linfield FC Belfast | Glentoran FC Belfast | Ray McCoy (Coleraine FC) Gary Macartney (Glentoran FC Belfast) | 14 |
| 1987/1988 | Glentoran FC Belfast | Glentoran FC Belfast | Martin McGaughey (Linfield FC Belfast) | 18 |
| 1988/1989 | Linfield FC Belfast | Ballymena United FC | Stephen Baxter (Linfield FC Belfast) | 17 |
| 1989/1990 | Portadown FC | Glentoran FC Belfast | Martin McGaughey (Linfield FC Belfast) | 19 |
| 1990/1991 | Portadown FC | Portadown FC | Stephen Derek McBride (Glenavon FC Lurgan) | 22 |
| 1991/1992 | Glentoran FC Belfast | Glenavon FC Lurgan | Harry McCourt (Omagh Town FAC) Stephen Derek McBride (Glenavon FC Lurgan) | 18 |
| 1992/1993 | Linfield FC Belfast | Bangor FC | Steve Cowan (Portadown FC) | 23 |
| 1993/1994 | Linfield FC Belfast | Linfield FC Belfast | Darren Erskine (Ards FC Newtownards) Stephen Derek McBride (Glenavon FC Lurgan) | 22 |
| 1994/1995 | Crusaders FC Belfast | Linfield FC Belfast | Glenn Ferguson (Glenavon FC Lurgan) | 27 |
| 1995/1996 | Portadown FC | Glentoran FC Belfast | Garry Andrew Haylock (Portadown FC) | 19 |
| 1996/1997 | Crusaders FC Belfast | Glenavon FC Lurgan | Garry Andrew Haylock (Portadown FC) | 16 |
| 1997/1998 | Cliftonville FAC | Glentoran FC Belfast | Vincent Thomas Arkins (Portadown FC) | 22 |
| 1998/1999 | Glentoran FC Belfast | Portadown FC | Vincent Thomas Arkins (Portadown FC) | 19 |
| 1999/2000 | Linfield FC Belfast | Glentoran FC Belfast | Vincent Thomas Arkins (Portadown FC) | 29 |
| 2000/2001 | Linfield FC Belfast | Glentoran FC Belfast | David James Larmour (Linfield FC Belfast) | 17 |
| 2001/2002 | Portadown FC | Linfield FC Belfast | Vincent Thomas Arkins (Portadown FC) | 30 |
| 2002/2003 | Glentoran FC Belfast | Coleraine FC | Vincent Thomas Arkins (Portadown FC) | 29 |
| 2003/2004 | Linfield FC Belfast | Glentoran FC Belfast | Glenn Ferguson (Linfield FC Belfast) | 25 |
| 2004/2005 | Glentoran FC Belfast | Portadown FC | Christopher Morgan (Glentoran FC Belfast) | 19 |
| 2005/2006 | Linfield FC Belfast | Linfield FC Belfast | Peter Thompson (Linfield FC Belfast) | 25 |
| 2006/2007 | Linfield FC Belfast | Linfield FC Belfast | Gary Hamilton (Glentoran FC Belfast) | 27 |
| 2007/2008 | Linfield FC Belfast | Linfield FC Belfast | Peter Thompson (Linfield FC Belfast) | 29 |
| 2008/2009 | Glentoran FC Belfast | Crusaders FC Belfast | Curtis Allen (Lisburn Distillery FC Ballyskeagh) | 19 |
| 2009/2010 | Linfield FC Belfast | Linfield FC Belfast | Rory Christopher Patterson (Coleraine FC) | 30 |
| 2010/2011 | Linfield FC Belfast | Linfield FC Belfast | Peter Thompson (Linfield FC Belfast) | 23 |
| 2011/2012 | Linfield FC Belfast | Linfield FC Belfast | Gary Kyle McCutcheon (Ballymena United FC) | 27 |

| 2012/2013 | Cliftonville FAC | Glentoran FC Belfast | Liam Boyce (Cliftonville FAC) | 29 |
|---|---|---|---|---|
| 2013/2014 | Cliftonville FAC | Glenavon FC Lurgan | Joseph Anthony Gormley (Cliftonville FAC) | 27 |
| 2014/2015 | Crusaders FC Belfast | Glentoran FC Belfast | Joseph Anthony Gormley (Cliftonville FAC) | 31 |
| 2015/2016 | Crusaders FC Belfast | Glenavon FC Lurgan | Paul Heatley (Crusaders FC Belfast) Andrew Waterworth (Linfield FC Belfast) | 22 |
| 2016/2017 | Linfield FC Belfast | Linfield FC Belfast | Andrew Mitchell (Dungannon Swifts) | 25 |
| 2017/2018 | Crusaders FC Belfast | Coleraine FC | Joseph Anthony Gormley (Cliftonville FAC) | 22 |
| 2018/2019 | Linfield FC Belfast | Crusaders FC Belfast | Joseph Anthony Gormley (Cliftonville FAC) | 20 |
| 2019/2020 | Linfield FC Belfast | Glentoran FC Belfast | Joseph Anthony Gormley (Cliftonville FAC) | 18 |
| 2020/2021 | Linfield FC Belfast | Linfield FC Belfast | Shayne Francis Lavery (Linfield FC Belfast) | 23 |
| 2021/2022 | Linfield FC Belfast | Crusaders FC Belfast | Jay Donnelly (Glentoran FC Belfast) | 25 |
| 2022/2023 | Larne FC | Crusaders FC Belfast | Matthew Shevlin (Coleraine FC) | 23 |

## NATIONAL CHAMPIONSHIP
### NIFL / Danske Bank PremiershipPremiership 2022/2023
#### (21.08.2022 – 29.04.2023)

### Regular Season - Results

**Round 1** [12-14.08.2022]
Larne FC - Glentoran FC 0-0
Ballymena United - Glenavon FC 2-2(2-1)
Carrick Rangers - Newry City 2-1(1-1)
Coleraine FC - Cliftonville FAC 3-1(2-0)
Crusaders FC - Dungannon Swifts 5-1(2-1)
Linfield FC - Portadown FC 4-0(1-0)

**Round 2** [19-21.08.2022]
Glentoran FC - Crusaders FC 3-1(1-1)
Cliftonville FAC - Carrick Rangers 3-2(1-2)
Dungannon Swifts-Ballymena United 0-2(0-0)
Glenavon FC - Larne FC 1-2(1-1)
Portadown FC - Coleraine FC 0-2(0-1)
Newry City - Linfield FC 1-3(1-2)

**Round 3** [23.08.2022]
Ballymena United - Cliftonville FAC 1-2(1-1)
Carrick Rangers - Coleraine FC 2-4(1-2)
Crusaders FC - Portadown FC 2-1(0-1)
Dungannon Swifts - Glentoran FC 0-1(0-0)
Glenavon FC-Newry City 1-5(0-3) [30.08.22]
Linfield FC - Larne FC 1-0(0-0) [22.11.22]

**Round 4** [26-28.08.2022]
Coleraine FC - Glenavon FC 1-3(1-1)
Larne FC - Ballymena United 3-0(1-0)
Portadown FC - Glentoran FC 0-3(0-2)
Cliftonville FAC - Dungannon Swifts 4-2(2-1)
Newry City - Crusaders FC 1-2(1-0)
Carrick Rangers - Linfield FC 2-1(1-0)

**Round 5** [02-03.09.2022]
Crusaders FC - Larne FC 1-1(0-0)
Dungannon Swifts - Coleraine FC 0-5(0-4)
Ballymena United - Linfield FC 0-4(0-2)
Glenavon FC - Carrick Rangers 2-2(2-1)
Glentoran FC - Newry City 3-0(0-0)
Portadown FC - Cliftonville FAC 1-2(1-2)

**Round 6**
Linfield FC - Glenavon 3-2(1-1) [18.10.22]
Carrick R. - Portadown FC 2-0(1-0) [08.11.22]
Coleraine - Crusaders FC 1-2(1-2) [08.11.22]
Larne FC - Dungannon 4-0(2-0) [08.11.22]
Newry City-Ballymena U. 3-2(2-1) [08.11.22]
Cliftonville - Glentoran 1-0(0-0) [20.12.22]

**Round 7** [16-17.09.2022]
Crusaders FC - Linfield FC 2-1(0-0)
Newry City - Dungannon Swifts 1-0(0-0)
Ballymena United - Carrick Rangers 0-1(0-0)
Glenavon FC - Cliftonville FAC 0-1(0-0)
Glentoran FC - Coleraine FC 1-0(0-0)
Portadown FC - Larne FC 0-1(0-1)

**Round 8** [23.09.2022]
Carrick Rangers - Larne FC 0-1(0-0)
Coleraine FC - Newry City 2-0(0-0)
Crusaders FC - Ballymena United 3-0(2-0)
Dungannon Swifts - Portadown FC 2-0(1-0)
Glenavon - Glentoran FC 2-1(0-1) [08.11.22]
Linfield FC - Cliftonville FAC 0-0 [08.11.22]

**Round 9** [30.09.-01.10.2022]
Portadown FC - Glenavon FC 1-1(1-0)
Carrick Rangers - Crusaders FC 4-3(2-2)
Cliftonville FAC - Newry City 4-0(4-0)
Dungannon Swifts - Linfield FC 0-1(0-1)
Larne FC - Coleraine FC 2-0(1-0)
Glentoran - Ballymena U. 1-0(0-0) [14.03.23]

**Round 10** [07-08.10.2022]
Cliftonville FAC - Crusaders FC 0-0
Glentoran FC - Carrick Rangers 5-0(4-0)
Newry City - Larne FC 0-2(0-0)
Ballymena United - Portadown FC 2-0(1-0)
Coleraine FC - Linfield FC 0-0
Glenavon FC - Dungannon Swifts 5-0(0-0)

**Round 11** [14-15.10.2022]
Larne FC - Cliftonville FAC 4-0(1-0)
Linfield FC - Glentoran FC 0-3(0-0)
Ballymena United - Coleraine FC 2-1(1-0)
Carrick Rangers - Dungannon Swifts 3-0(1-0)
Crusaders FC - Glenavon FC 3-2(1-1)
Portadown FC - Newry City 1-3(0-0)

**Round 12** [21-22.10.2022]
Dungannon Swifts - Ballymena U. 1-1(1-1)
Coleraine FC - Cliftonville FAC 2-4(1-2)
Crusaders FC - Portadown FC 4-0(2-0)
Glenavon FC - Carrick Rangers 4-2(2-1)
Linfield FC - Larne FC 2-4(1-2)
Newry City - Glentoran FC 0-1(0-1)

**Round 13** [28-29.10.2022]
Glenavon FC - Ballymena United 3-2(0-1)
Glentoran FC - Larne FC 4-0(1-0)
Cliftonville FAC - Carrick Rangers 1-0(0-0)
Coleraine FC - Portadown FC 4-0(2-0)
Dungannon Swifts - Crusaders FC 0-2(0-1)
Newry City - Linfield FC 0-2(0-1)

**Round 14** [04-05.11.2022]
Ballymena United - Newry City 3-0(1-0)
Larne FC - Crusaders FC 4-1(4-0)
Carrick Rangers - Coleraine FC 0-1(0-0)
Cliftonville FAC - Glenavon FC 2-2(1-0)
Glentoran FC - Dungannon Swifts 3-1(1-1)
Portadown FC - Linfield FC 0-3(0-0)

**Round 15** [11-14.11.2022]
Coleraine FC - Glentoran FC 0-0
Dungannon Swifts - Cliftonville FAC 0-2(0-1)
Linfield FC - Glenavon FC 1-0(0-0)
Portadown FC - Larne FC 0-5(0-2)
Newry City - Carrick Rangers 4-1(1-1)
Crusaders FC - Ballymena United 0-1(0-0)

**Round 16** [18-20.11.2022]
Ballymena United - Linfield FC 0-2(0-1)
Larne FC - Dungannon Swifts 2-1(0-1)
Carrick Rangers - Portadown FC 2-0(0-0)
Crusaders FC - Newry City 4-0(2-0)
Glenavon FC - Coleraine FC 0-0
Glentoran FC - Cliftonville FAC 0-1(0-1)

**Round 17** [25-26.11.2022]
Larne FC - Coleraine FC 0-2(0-2)
Carrick Rangers - Ballymena United 0-2(0-0)
Cliftonville FAC - Newry City 2-0(1-0)
Dungannon Swifts - Glenavon FC 1-0(0-0)
Portadown FC - Glentoran FC 0-2(0-1)
Linfield FC - Crusaders FC 0-0

**Round 18** [02-04.12.2022]
Glenavon FC - Larne FC 0-1(0-0)
Ballymena United - Cliftonville FAC 4-1(1-0)
Coleraine FC - Dungannon Swifts 2-0(2-0)
Crusaders FC - Glentoran FC 3-2(2-1)
Linfield FC - Carrick Rangers 1-2(1-0)
Newry City - Portadown FC 3-0* *awarded*
*originally 1-3, Portadown FC fielded an ineligible player*

**Round 19** [09-10.12.2022]
Coleraine FC - Crusaders FC 2-0(1-0)
Dungannon Swifts - Carrick Rangers 4-1(2-0)
Larne FC - Newry City 2-0(1-0)
Portadown FC - Ballymena United 1-0(1-0)
Cliftonville - Linfield FC 1-0(1-0) [10.01.23]
Glentoran FC - Glenavon FC 0-0 [28.02.23]

**Round 20** [17.12.2022]
Cliftonville FAC - Portadown FC 4-1(2-1)
Linfield FC - Dungannon Swifts 4-0(2-0)
Glenavon FC - Crusaders 4-2(2-0) [10.01.23]
Newry City - Coleraine 1-2(0-1) [10.01.23]
Ballymena U. - Larne 0-3(0-1) [21.02.23]
Carrick R. - Glentoran FC 1-5(0-2) [07.03.23]

**Round 21** [26.12.2022]
Glentoran FC - Linfield FC 1-2(0-1)
Coleraine FC - Ballymena United 2-0(2-0)
Crusaders FC - Cliftonville FAC 3-0(2-0)
Dungannon Swifts - Newry City 2-0(1-0)
Glenavon FC - Portadown FC 2-1(0-0)
Larne FC - Carrick Rangers 0-0

**Round 22** [02.01.2023]
Ballymena United - Glentoran FC 2-0(1-0)
Carrick Rangers - Crusaders FC 0-3(0-2)
Cliftonville FAC - Larne FC 2-1(0-0)
Linfield FC - Coleraine FC 0-0
Portadown FC - Dungannon Swifts 0-0
Newry City - Glenavon 0-1(0-1) [04.03.23]

**Round 23** [13-14.01.2023]
Carrick Rangers - Cliftonville FAC 3-3(1-3)
Ballymena United-Dungannon Swifts 2-0(0-0)
Coleraine FC - Portadown FC 4-1(3-1)
Crusaders FC - Newry City 3-1(1-0)
Glenavon FC - Linfield FC 1-6(1-1)
Glentoran FC - Larne FC 0-1(0-0)

**Round 24** [21.01.2023]
Cliftonville FAC - Coleraine FC 2-2(1-0)
Dungannon Swifts - Glenavon 2-1(1-1)
Larne FC - Crusaders FC 0-0
Linfield FC - Ballymena United 3-0(2-0)
Newry City - Glentoran 1-3(0-2)
Portadown - Carrick R. 1-3(1-1) [04.03.23]

**Round 25** [24.01.2023]
Ballymena United - Newry City 0-0
Coleraine FC - Carrick Rangers 1-0(0-0)
Crusaders FC - Linfield FC 2-1(1-0)
Glenavon FC - Cliftonville FAC 1-3(0-1)
Glentoran FC - Dungannon Swifts 6-0(5-0)
Larne FC - Portadown FC 2-0(1-0)

**Round 26** [28-30.01.2023]
Carrick Rangers - Glenavon FC 1-1(0-0)
Cliftonville FAC - Ballymena United 4-0(2-0)
Dungannon Swifts - Coleraine FC 0-3(0-1)
Portadown FC - Linfield FC 1-6(1-2)
Newry City - Larne FC 0-0
Glentoran FC - Crusaders FC 2-0(0-0)

**Round 27** [10-11.02.2023]
Larne FC - Glenavon FC 3-0(2-0)
Newry City - Carrick Rangers 0-2(0-1)
Ballymena United - Portadown FC 0-0
Coleraine FC - Glentoran FC 2-2(1-1)
Crusaders FC - Dungannon Swifts 3-0(1-0)
Linfield FC - Cliftonville FAC 1-0(0-0)

**Round 28** [14.02.2023]
Carrick Rangers - Ballymena United 1-0(1-0)
Cliftonville FAC - Portadown FC 3-0(1-0)
Coleraine FC - Newry City 1-0(1-0)
Dungannon Swifts - Larne FC 3-0(0-0)
Glenavon FC - Crusaders FC 2-2(0-0)
Glentoran FC - Linfield FC 3-0(1-0)

**Round 29** [17-18.02.2023]
Ballymena United - Glentoran FC 1-3(1-1)
Newry City - Dungannon Swifts 0-2(0-1)
Crusaders FC - Coleraine FC 2-0(1-0)
Larne FC - Cliftonville FAC 2-1(1-0)
Linfield FC - Carrick Rangers 2-0(0-0)
Portadown FC - Glenavon FC 3-1(1-0)

**Round 30** [24-25.02.2023]
Portadown FC - Dungannon Swifts 3-1(1-0)
Ballymena United - Crusaders FC 0-0
Carrick Rangers - Larne FC 2-3(0-0)
Cliftonville FAC - Glentoran FC 2-1(2-0)
Glenavon FC - Newry City 0-2(0-2)
Linfield FC - Coleraine FC 2-0(1-0)

**Round 31** [07-11.03.2023]
Coleraine FC - Ballymena United 3-1(2-1)
Larne FC - Linfield FC 0-0
Dungannon Swifts - Carrick Rangers 0-1(0-1)
Glentoran FC - Glenavon FC 0-2(0-1)
Newry City - Portadown FC 3-4(2-2)
Crusaders - Cliftonville 2-2(1-1) [13.03.23]

**Round 32** [17-18.03.2023]
Larne FC - Ballymena United 1-0(1-0)
Carrick Rangers - Glentoran FC 0-4(0-0)
Cliftonville FAC - Dungannon Swifts 1-2(0-0)
Glenavon FC - Coleraine FC 2-1(0-1)
Linfield FC - Newry City 7-0(4-0)
Portadown FC - Crusaders FC 2-2(1-0)

**Round 33** [24-25.03.2023]
Dungannon Swifts - Linfield FC 0-5(0-2)
Coleraine FC - Larne FC 0-0
Crusaders FC - Carrick Rangers 3-0(0-0)
Newry City - Cliftonville FAC 1-2(0-0)
Glentoran - Portadown FC 5-1(3-0) [01.04.23]
Ballymena U. - Glenavon 0-1(0-1) [03.04.23]

## Final Standings

| | | | | | | | | | |
|---|---|---|---|---|---|---|---|---|---|
| 1. | Larne FC | 33 | 22 | 7 | 4 | 57 | - | 18 | 73 |
| 2. | Linfield FC Belfast | 33 | 21 | 5 | 7 | 70 | - | 25 | 68 |
| 3. | Cliftonville FAC | 33 | 20 | 6 | 7 | 61 | - | 41 | 66 |
| 4. | Glentoran FC Belfast | 33 | 20 | 4 | 9 | 68 | - | 24 | 64 |
| 5. | Crusaders FC Belfast | 33 | 18 | 8 | 7 | 65 | - | 37 | 62 |
| 6. | Coleraine FC | 33 | 17 | 7 | 9 | 53 | - | 30 | 58 |
| 7. | Glenavon FC Lurgan | 33 | 11 | 8 | 14 | 50 | - | 57 | 41 |
| 8. | Carrick Rangers FC | 33 | 11 | 4 | 18 | 41 | - | 65 | 37 |
| 9. | Ballymena United FC | 33 | 9 | 5 | 19 | 30 | - | 49 | 32 |
| 10. | Newry City AFC | 33 | 7 | 2 | 24 | 31 | - | 66 | 23 |
| 11. | Dungannon Swifts FC | 33 | 7 | 2 | 24 | 22 | - | 76 | 23 |
| 12. | Portadown FC | 33 | 4 | 4 | 25 | 23 | - | 83 | 16 |

Teams ranked 1-6 were qualified for the Championship Round, while teams ranked 7-12 were qualified for the Relegation Round.

## Relegation Round

### Results

**Round 34** [07.04.2023]
Carrick Rangers - Newry City 0-2(0-2)
Glenavon FC - Dungannon Swifts 1-1(1-0)
Portadown FC - Ballymena United 1-0(1-0)

**Round 35** [11.04.2023]
Carrick Rangers - Dungannon Swifts 2-0(1-0)
Glenavon FC - Ballymena United 3-2(1-0)
Portadown FC - Newry City 0-1(0-1)

**Round 36** [15.04.2023]
Ballymena United-Dungannon Swifts 2-0(0-0)
Newry City - Glenavon FC 0-1(0-0)
Portadown FC - Carrick Rangers 3-1(2-0)

**Round 37** [22.04.2023]
Carrick Rangers - Glenavon FC 1-3(0-1)
Dungannon Swifts - Portadown FC 3-2(1-0)
Newry City - Ballymena United 2-2(1-1)

**Round 38** [29.04.2023]
Ballymena United - Carrick Rangers 1-0(0-0)
Dungannon Swifts - Newry City 2-1(1-1)
Glenavon FC - Portadown FC 0-0

## Championship Round

### Results

**Round 34** [07.04.2023]
Cliftonville FAC - Coleraine FC 2-2(1-1)
Larne FC - Glentoran FC 2-0(2-0)
Linfield FC - Crusaders FC 0-0

**Round 35** [11-12.04.2023]
Cliftonville FAC - Larne FC 0-2(0-1)
Crusaders FC - Coleraine FC 3-1(0-1)
Linfield FC - Glentoran FC 1-1(1-0)

**Round 36** [14-15.04.2023]
Crusaders FC - Larne FC 0-2(0-1)
Coleraine FC - Linfield FC 0-1(0-0)
Glentoran FC - Cliftonville FAC 3-0(3-0)

**Round 37** [21-22.04.2023]
Larne FC - Linfield FC 1-1(1-0)
Cliftonville FAC - Crusaders FC 3-3(0-1)
Glentoran FC - Coleraine FC 3-0(3-0)

**Round 38** [29.04.2023]
Cliftonville FAC - Linfield FC 0-2(0-1)
Coleraine FC - Larne FC 3-0(0-0)
Crusaders FC - Glentoran FC 1-2(0-1)

## Final Standings

| | | Total | | | | | | Home | | | | | | Away | | | | |
|---|---|---|---|---|---|---|---|---|---|---|---|---|---|---|---|---|---|---|
| 1. | **Larne FC** | 38 | 25 | 8 | 5 | 64 - 22 | **83** | 12 | 5 | 1 | 32 - 6 | | 13 | 3 | 4 | 32 - 16 |
| 2. | Linfield FC Belfast | 38 | 23 | 8 | 7 | 75 - 27 | **77** | 11 | 5 | 2 | 35 - 12 | | 12 | 3 | 5 | 40 - 15 |
| 3. | Glentoran FC Belfast | 38 | 23 | 5 | 10 | 77 - 28 | **74** | 13 | 1 | 4 | 43 - 9 | | 10 | 4 | 6 | 34 - 19 |
| 4. | Cliftonville FAC | 38 | 20 | 8 | 10 | 66 - 53 | **68** | 12 | 5 | 3 | 41 - 22 | | 8 | 3 | 7 | 25 - 31 |
| 5. | Crusaders FC Belfast | 38 | 19 | 10 | 9 | 72 - 45 | **67** | 15 | 2 | 3 | 49 - 17 | | 4 | 8 | 6 | 23 - 28 |
| 6. | Coleraine FC | 38 | 18 | 8 | 12 | 59 - 39 | **62** | 11 | 4 | 4 | 33 - 15 | | 7 | 4 | 8 | 26 - 24 |
| 7. | Glenavon FC Lurgan | 38 | 14 | 10 | 14 | 58 - 61 | **52** | 8 | 5 | 7 | 34 - 36 | | 6 | 5 | 7 | 24 - 25 |
| 8. | Carrick Rangers FC | 38 | 12 | 4 | 22 | 45 - 74 | **40** | 8 | 2 | 10 | 28 - 37 | | 4 | 2 | 12 | 17 - 37 |
| 9. | Ballymena United FC | 38 | 11 | 6 | 21 | 37 - 55 | **39** | 8 | 4 | 7 | 22 - 20 | | 3 | 2 | 14 | 15 - 35 |
| 10. | Newry City AFC | 38 | 9 | 3 | 26 | 37 - 71 | **30** | 4 | 2 | 13 | 21 - 32 | | 5 | 1 | 13 | 16 - 39 |
| 11. | Dungannon Swifts FC (*Relegation Play-offs*) | 38 | 9 | 3 | 26 | 28 - 84 | **30** | 7 | 1 | 10 | 17 - 31 | | 2 | 2 | 16 | 11 - 53 |
| 12. | Portadown FC (*Relegated*) | 38 | 6 | 5 | 27 | 29 - 88 | **23** | 5 | 3 | 11 | 18 - 37 | | 1 | 2 | 16 | 11 - 51 |

Teams ranked 3-4 and 6-7 were qualified for the UEFA Europa Conference League Play-offs.

### Top goalscorers:

| | | |
|---|---|---|
| 23 | **Matthew Shevlin** | *Coleraine FC* |
| 19 | Matthew Fitzpatrick | *Glenavon FC Lurgan* |
| 18 | Ronan Hale (IRL) | *Cliftonville FAC* |

### Relegation Play-offs [30.05.-01.06.2023]

| | | |
|---|---|---|
| Annagh United FC Portadown - Dungannon Swifts FC | 2-1(1-1) | 0-2(0-1) |

Dungannon Swifts FC remains at first level for 2023/2024.

### UEFA Europa Conference League Play-offs

**Semi-Finals [10.05.2023]**

| | |
|---|---|
| Cliftonville FAC - Coleraine FC | 2-1(2-0) |
| Glentoran FC Belfast - Glenavon FC Lurgan | 5-0(2-0) |

**Final [13.05.2023]**

| | |
|---|---|
| **Glentoran FC Belfast** - Cliftonville FAC | 2-0(2-0) |

## NATIONAL CUP
### Irish Cup 2022/2023

**Fifth Round [06-07.01.2023]**

| | | | | |
|---|---|---|---|---|
| Dundela FC Belfast - Cliftonville FAC | 0-5(0-2) | | Institute FC Derry - Annagh United | 4-0(3-0) |
| Knockbreda FC Belfast - St Mary's Youth FC | 2-0(1-0) | | Larne FC - Crumlin United FC | 3-0(1-0) |
| Ballinamallard United FC - Glenavon FC Lurgan | 1-2(0-0) | | Linfield FC Belfast - Warrenpoint Town FC | 3-0(1-0) |
| Ballyclare Comrades FC - Dollingstown FC | 1-0(1-0) | | Moyola Park AFC - Glentoran FC Belfast | 0-2(0-2) |
| Bangor FC - Tandragee Rovers FC | 4-0(1-0) | | Newington FC - Ballymoney United FC | 2-1(0-0) |
| Carrick Rangers FC - Ballymena United FC | 1-1 aet; 0-3 pen | | Newry City AFC - Harland & Wolff Welders FC | 1-2(1-1) |
| Coleraine FC - Loughgall FC | 3-1(0-1) | | Portadown FC - Banbridge Town FC | 2-0(1-0) |
| Crusaders FC Belfast - Dergview FC Castlederg | 6-0(1-0) | | Dungannon Swifts FC - Ards FC Newtownards | 3-1(1-0) |

**1/8-Finals [03-04.02.2023]**

| | | | | |
|---|---|---|---|---|
| Bangor FC - Crusaders FC Belfast | 1-2(0-1) | | Glenavon FC Lurgan - Harland & Wolff Welders FC | 0-1(0-0) |
| Knockbreda FC Belfast - Dungannon Swifts FC | 1-2(1-0) | | Larne FC - Linfield FC Belfast | 1-1 aet; 4-3 pen |
| Ballymena United FC - Newington FC | 4-1(2-0) | | Portadown FC - Glentoran FC Belfast | 0-3(0-1) |
| Cliftonville FAC - Coleraine FC | 2-2 aet; 3-1 pen | | Institute FC Derry - Ballyclare Comrades FC | 0-1(0-0) |

**Quarter-Finals [03-04.03.2023]**

| | | | | |
|---|---|---|---|---|
| Harland & Wolff Welders FC Belfast - Larne FC | 0-1(0-0) | | Cliftonville FAC - Dungannon Swifts FC | 1-2(0-0) |
| Ballyclare Comrades FC - Ballymena United FC | 1-3(1-0,1-1) | | Crusaders FC Belfast - Glentoran FC Belfast | 1-0(1-0) |

**Semi-Finals [31.03.-01.04.2023]**

| | | | | |
|---|---|---|---|---|
| Larne FC - Ballymena United FC | 0-2(0-0) | | Dungannon Swifts FC - Crusaders FC Belfast | 0-1(0-0) |

**Final**

07.05.2023; Windsor Park, Belfast; Referee: Tim Marshall; Attendance: 9,688

**Ballymena United FC - Crusaders FC Belfast**　　　　　　　　　　　　**0-4(0-1)**

**Ballymena**: Jordan Williamson, Robert McVarnock (56.Mikey Place), Craig Farquhar, Scott Whiteside, Ross Redman (56.Jordan Gibson), Sean Graham (85.Andy McGrory), Steven McCullough, Douglas Wilson (78.Kenneth Kane), Joshua Kelly (Cap), Ryan Waide, David McDaid. Trainer: David Jeffrey.

**Crusaders**: Jonny Tuffey, Daniel Larmour (85.Chris Hegarty), Rory McKeown, Jarlath O'Rourke, Jordan Forsythe, Philip Lowry (Cap), Robbie Weir (85.Ben Kennedy), Jude Winchester (72.Declan Caddell), Ross Clarke (85.Gary Thompson), Paul Heatley, Adam Lecky (83.Jordan Owens). Trainer: Stephen Baxter.

**Goals:** 0-1 Ross Clarke (12), 0-2 Adam Lecky (53), 0-3 Philip Lowry (65), 0-4 Paul Heatley (69).

# THE CLUBS 2022/2023

Please note: appearances and goals are including statistics of both regular season and play-offs (Championship Round & Relegation Round).

## Ballymena United Football Club

| Founded: | 07.04.1928 | | | |
|---|---|---|---|---|
| Stadium: | The Showgrounds, Ballymena (3,824) | | | |
| Trainer: | David Jeffrey | | 28.10.1962 | |

| Goalkeepers: | DOB | M | (s) | G |
|---|---|---|---|---|
| Sean O'Neill | 11.04.1988 | 25 | (2) | |
| Marcus Thompson | 25.04.2006 | 1 | | |
| Jordan Williamson | 23.05.1995 | 12 | | |
| **Defenders:** | **DOB** | **M** | **(s)** | **G** |
| Craig Farquhar | 09.05.2003 | 9 | (2) | 1 |
| Sean Graham | 20.11.2000 | 24 | (2) | 3 |
| Conor Keeley | 12.12.1997 | 17 | | 2 |
| Caolan Loughran | 09.01.1995 | | (1) | |
| Steven McCullough | 30.08.1994 | 27 | (6) | |
| Robert McVarnock | 20.10.1999 | 9 | (6) | |
| Ross Redman | 23.11.1989 | 26 | (2) | 1 |
| Scott Whiteside | 16.06.1997 | 34 | (2) | |
| **Midfielders:** | **DOB** | **M** | **(s)** | **G** |
| Jordan Gibson | 23.06.1995 | 25 | (10) | 4 |

| Jack Henderson | 17.06.2000 | 14 | (11) | 1 |
|---|---|---|---|---|
| Joshua Kelly | 08.03.1999 | 31 | (3) | 4 |
| Andy McGrory | 15.12.1991 | 6 | (10) | 1 |
| Kym Nelson | 18.07.1995 | 28 | (4) | 4 |
| Mikey Place (IRL) | 09.04.1998 | 29 | (5) | 3 |
| Lewis Tennant | 22.08.2004 | | (1) | |
| George Tipton | 03.11.2002 | 1 | (7) | |
| Evan Tweed (IRL) | 01.03.1999 | 6 | (2) | |
| Douglas Wilson | 03.03.1994 | 20 | | 1 |
| **Forwards:** | **DOB** | **M** | **(s)** | **G** |
| Kenneth Kane | 13.08.1999 | 15 | (15) | |
| David McDaid | 03.12.1990 | 32 | | 7 |
| Paul McElroy | 07.07.1994 | 6 | (3) | 1 |
| David Parkhouse | 24.10.1999 | 3 | (6) | |
| Ryan Waide | 12.02.2000 | 18 | (11) | 4 |

## Carrick Rangers Football Club

| Founded: | 1939 | | | |
|---|---|---|---|---|
| Stadium: | Loughshore Hotel Arena, Carrickfergus (2,100) | | | |
| Trainer: | Stuart King (ENG) | | 20.03.1981 | |

| Goalkeepers: | DOB | M | (s) | G |
|---|---|---|---|---|
| Ross Glendinning | 18.05.1993 | 37 | | |
| Aaron Hogg | 14.01.1988 | 1 | | |
| **Defenders:** | **DOB** | **M** | **(s)** | **G** |
| Benjamin Buchanan-Rolleston | 03.02.2002 | 1 | (4) | |
| Jim Ervin | 05.06.1985 | 34 | | |
| Kurtis Forsythe | 28.09.2002 | 33 | (2) | |
| Reece Glendinning | 09.06.1995 | 35 | (2) | |
| Matthew Mulholland | 04.03.2001 | | (1) | |
| Cameron Stewart | 11.03.1997 | 15 | (2) | 2 |
| Mark Surgenor | 19.12.1985 | 12 | (11) | |
| Ben Tilney (ENG) | 28.02.1997 | 38 | | 2 |
| **Midfielders:** | **DOB** | **M** | **(s)** | **G** |
| Lloyd Anderson | 09.03.1998 | 33 | (4) | 6 |
| Joshua Andrews | 12.06.2004 | | (2) | |
| Kyle Cherry | 13.05.1993 | 17 | (10) | 3 |
| Jamal Dupree | 11.08.1997 | 1 | (7) | |

| Steven Gordon | 27.07.1993 | 17 | | 1 |
|---|---|---|---|---|
| Scott Graham | 27.08.2004 | | (2) | |
| Ronan Kalla | 08.03.2003 | 3 | (26) | |
| Daniel Kelly | 06.01.1993 | 2 | | |
| Andy Mitchell | 06.04.1992 | 28 | (3) | 4 |
| Paul Waite | 26.10.2001 | | (1) | |
| **Forwards:** | **DOB** | **M** | **(s)** | **G** |
| Curtis Allen | 22.02.1988 | 12 | (1) | 7 |
| David Cushley | 22.07.1989 | 34 | (1) | 7 |
| Alex Gawne | 22.05.2001 | 16 | (15) | |
| Aodhán Gillen | 03.03.2001 | 2 | (7) | |
| Nedas Maculaitis | 06.08.1999 | 14 | (2) | 4 |
| Emmett McGuckin | 07.03.1991 | 31 | (3) | 6 |
| Peter McKiernan | 06.06.2002 | | (17) | |
| James McLaughlin | 06.03.1990 | 1 | (7) | |
| Stewart Nixon | 08.05.1997 | 1 | (4) | |

## Cliftonville Football & Athletic Club

| Founded: | 1879 | | | |
|---|---|---|---|---|
| Stadium: | Solitude Stadium, Belfast (3,054) | | | |
| Trainer: | Paddy McLaughlin | | 10.10.1979 | |
| [19.04.2023] | Declan O'Hara | | 04.02.1983 | |

| Goalkeepers: | DOB | M | (s) | G |
|---|---|---|---|---|
| Gerard Doherty (IRL) | 24.08.1981 | 1 | (1) | |
| Nathan Gartside | 08.03.1998 | 36 | | |
| Fynn Michael Cordell Talley (ENG) | 14.09.2002 | 1 | | |
| **Defenders:** | **DOB** | **M** | **(s)** | **G** |
| Jonathan Addis | 27.09.1992 | 31 | (4) | 2 |
| Odhran Casey | 09.04.2002 | 10 | (17) | |
| Colin Coates | 26.10.1985 | 17 | (7) | 1 |
| Levi Ives | 28.07.1997 | 9 | (3) | 1 |
| Jamie McDonagh | 08.05.1996 | 18 | (14) | |
| Jamie Robinson (IRL) | 18.03.2002 | 9 | (2) | |
| Luke Turner (IRL) | 20.05.2002 | 34 | (1) | 1 |
| **Midfielders:** | **DOB** | **M** | **(s)** | **G** |
| Chris Curran | 05.01.1991 | 7 | (20) | 1 |

| Ronan Doherty | 10.01.1996 | 33 | (2) | 2 |
|---|---|---|---|---|
| Chris Gallagher | 30.03.1999 | 37 | | 1 |
| Rory Hale (IRL) | 27.11.1996 | 34 | (2) | 7 |
| Kris Lowe | 06.01.1996 | 33 | | 1 |
| Stephen Mallon (IRL) | 07.02.1999 | 2 | (1) | |
| Donal Rocks | 13.07.2000 | | (2) | |
| Gerard Storey | 05.02.2002 | | (1) | |
| Aaron Traynor | 24.07.1990 | 3 | (6) | |
| **Forwards:** | **DOB** | **M** | **(s)** | **G** |
| Ryan Curran | 13.10.1993 | 23 | (3) | 14 |
| Joe Gormley | 26.11.1989 | 18 | (20) | 10 |
| Ronan Hale (IRL) | 08.09.1998 | 37 | | 18 |
| Sean Moore | 13.08.2005 | 20 | (11) | 5 |
| David Parkhouse | 24.10.1999 | 5 | (9) | 1 |

## Coleraine Football Club

| Founded: | 1927 | | | |
|---|---|---|---|---|
| Stadium: | The Showgrounds, Coleraine (4,843) | | | |
| Trainer: | Oran Kearney | | 29.07.1978 | |

| Goalkeepers: | DOB | M | (s) | G |
|---|---|---|---|---|
| Gareth Deane | 14.06.1994 | 23 | | |
| Martin Gallagher | 26.10.1990 | 15 | | |
| **Defenders:** | **DOB** | **M** | **(s)** | **G** |
| Rodney Brown | 13.08.1995 | 8 | (1) | 1 |
| Kieran Farren (IRL) | 21.11.2000 | 23 | (1) | 1 |
| Dean Jarvis | 01.06.1992 | 32 | (1) | 2 |
| Lyndon Kane | 15.02.1997 | 34 | | 1 |
| Conor McDermott | 18.09.1997 | 34 | (1) | |
| Adam Mullan | 24.10.1995 | 11 | (2) | |
| Stephen O'Donnell | 01.09.1992 | 29 | (1) | |
| **Midfielders:** | **DOB** | **M** | **(s)** | **G** |
| Sean Carlin | 06.11.2004 | | (1) | |
| Josh Carson | 03.06.1993 | 31 | (1) | 3 |
| Eamon Fyfe | 01.04.1998 | 2 | (12) | 1 |
| Alfie Gaston | 11.10.2007 | | (1) | |

| Jamie Glackin | 16.02.1995 | 30 | | 5 |
|---|---|---|---|---|
| Aaron Jarvis | 10.05.1997 | 14 | (9) | 1 |
| Stephen Lowry | 14.10.1986 | 5 | (4) | |
| Lee Lynch (IRL) | 27.11.1991 | 26 | (8) | 2 |
| Evan McLaughlin | 30.03.2002 | 8 | (12) | 3 |
| Jack O'Mahony | 26.01.2000 | 13 | (14) | |
| Andy Scott | 19.06.2000 | 11 | (4) | 2 |
| Matthew Shevlin | 07.12.1998 | 36 | (1) | 23 |
| **Forwards:** | **DOB** | **M** | **(s)** | **G** |
| Senan Devine | 12.01.2007 | 2 | | |
| Michael McCrudden | 31.07.1991 | 8 | (20) | 4 |
| Conor McKendry | 21.10.1998 | 21 | (6) | 5 |
| Corey McLaughlin | 12.02.2004 | | (1) | |
| James McLaughlin | 06.03.1990 | 2 | (11) | 1 |
| Jack Patton | 29.06.2005 | | (1) | |

## Crusaders Football Club Belfast

**Founded**: 1898
**Stadium**: Seaview Stadium, Belfast (3,208)
**Trainer**: Stephen Baxter 01.10.1965

| Goalkeepers: | DOB | M | (s) | G |
|---|---|---|---|---|
| Tom Murphy (IRL) | 26.08.2000 | 2 | | |
| Jonny Tuffey | 20.01.1987 | 36 | | |
| **Defenders:** | **DOB** | **M** | **(s)** | **G** |
| Lewis Barr | 20.04.2003 | 4 | (2) | |
| Billy Joe Burns | 28.04.1989 | 33 | | 2 |
| Declan Caddell | 13.04.1988 | 6 | (10) | 1 |
| Chris Hegarty | 13.08.1992 | 22 | (6) | 2 |
| Daniel Larmour | 03.09.1998 | 29 | (2) | 2 |
| Rory McKeown | 08.04.1993 | 12 | (5) | |
| Joshua Robinson | 30.06.1993 | 15 | (4) | |
| Cameron Stewart | 20.02.2003 | 1 | (3) | |
| **Midfielders:** | **DOB** | **M** | **(s)** | **G** |
| Corrie Burns | 08.08.2003 | | (1) | |
| Ross Clarke | 17.05.1993 | 29 | (3) | 5 |
| Jordan Forsythe | 11.02.1991 | 32 | | 10 |
| Ben Kennedy | 12.01.1997 | 2 | | 2 |
| Philip Lowry | 15.07.1989 | 35 | | 17 |
| Jarlath O'Rourke | 13.02.1995 | 28 | | 2 |
| Gary Thompson | 26.05.1990 | 7 | (12) | |
| Robbie Weir | 09.12.1988 | 16 | (12) | |
| Jude Winchester | 13.04.1993 | 30 | (2) | 1 |
| **Forwards:** | **DOB** | **M** | **(s)** | **G** |
| Jay Boyd | 09.01.2003 | 1 | (5) | 1 |
| Dean Ebbe (IRL) | 16.07.1994 | 11 | (14) | 1 |
| Paul Heatley | 30.06.1987 | 27 | | 11 |
| Adam Lecky | 03.05.1991 | 24 | (9) | 7 |
| Jonathan McMurray | 19.09.1994 | 6 | (11) | 1 |
| Jordan Owens | 09.07.1989 | 4 | (22) | 3 |
| McCauley Snelgrove (ENG) | 09.09.2002 | 6 | (3) | 2 |

## Dungannon Swifts Football Club

**Founded**: 1949
**Stadium**: Stangmore Park, Dungannon (2,000)
**Trainer**: Dean Shiels 01.02.1985

| Goalkeepers: | DOB | M | (s) | G |
|---|---|---|---|---|
| Declan Dunne | 31.03.2000 | 34 | | |
| Adam Groogan | 21.05.2003 | 1 | | |
| Dwayne Nelson | 05.09.1984 | 3 | | |
| **Defenders:** | **DOB** | **M** | **(s)** | **G** |
| Mayowa Animasahun (IRL) | 08.08.2003 | 22 | (7) | 2 |
| Brendan Barr (IRL) | 05.05.2001 | 12 | (4) | |
| Garry Breen (IRL) | 17.03.1989 | 9 | (1) | |
| Darren Cole (SCO) | 03.01.1992 | 2 | | |
| Caolin Coyle | 23.04.2000 | 4 | (7) | |
| Dean Curry | 11.12.1994 | 14 | (3) | |
| Caolan Marron | 04.07.1998 | 23 | | |
| Cahal McGinty | 29.09.2000 | 18 | (11) | |
| Oran O'Kane | 10.11.2003 | 4 | (3) | |
| Michael Ruddy | 05.08.1993 | 24 | (1) | |
| John Scott | 05.06.2001 | 13 | (2) | |
| **Midfielders:** | **DOB** | **M** | **(s)** | **G** |
| Gerardo Alfredo Bruna Blanco (ARG) | 29.01.1991 | 15 | (7) | 1 |
| Ryan Donnelly | 04.09.2006 | 1 | | |
| Lewis Francis | 15.04.2004 | 1 | | |
| Ben Gallagher | 30.03.2002 | 3 | (16) | |
| Tomas Galvin | 22.09.2004 | | (1) | |
| James Knowles | 06.04.1993 | 34 | (2) | 5 |
| Padraig Lynch | 01.05.2004 | 3 | (9) | 1 |
| Ryan Mayse | 07.12.1993 | 18 | (8) | 2 |
| Ruairi McDonald | 11.03.1997 | | (3) | |
| Ethan McGee | 23.08.2002 | 34 | | 3 |
| Steven Scott | 05.10.2004 | 5 | (12) | |
| Odhran Skelton | 11.03.2004 | 1 | | |
| Corey Smith | 24.01.2005 | 1 | (11) | 1 |
| Adam Towe | 08.03.2005 | | (1) | |
| **Forwards:** | **DOB** | **M** | **(s)** | **G** |
| Sam Anderson | 14.07.2006 | | (1) | |
| Rhyss Campbell | 30.11.1998 | 30 | (1) | 4 |
| James Convie | 01.07.2002 | 2 | (7) | |
| Ben Cushnie | 07.08.2001 | 9 | (10) | |
| Terry Devlin | 06.11.2003 | 4 | | |
| Jordan Jenkins | 28.02.2000 | 9 | (2) | 1 |
| Joe McCready | 24.07.1990 | 23 | (9) | 1 |
| Joseph Moore (SCO) | 17.06.2001 | 3 | (8) | 2 |
| Michael O'Connor (IRL) | 31.07.1998 | 22 | (10) | 3 |
| Darragh Stewart | 20.03.2004 | | (1) | |
| Marc Walsh (IRL) | 15.03.2001 | 17 | (14) | 2 |
| Kenny Ximenes (TLS) | 04.04.2005 | | (1) | |

## Glenavon Football Club Lurgan

**Founded**: 1889
**Stadium**: Mourneview Park, Lurgan (3,302)
**Trainer**: Gary Hamilton 06.10.1980

| Goalkeepers: | DOB | M | (s) | G |
|---|---|---|---|---|
| Rory Brown (IRL) | 25.05.2000 | 36 | | |
| Mark Matthews | 17.04.2002 | 2 | | |
| **Defenders:** | **DOB** | **M** | **(s)** | **G** |
| Calum Birney | 19.04.1993 | 24 | (4) | |
| Andrew Doyle | 28.10.1990 | 10 | (6) | 1 |
| Micheal Glynn | 12.03.2002 | 13 | (1) | 3 |
| Mark Haughey | 23.01.1991 | 7 | (1) | 1 |
| Sean Jones-Carey | 16.01.2004 | | (2) | |
| Conor Kerr | 07.06.1999 | 19 | (4) | |
| Harry Lynch | 16.05.2006 | 1 | | |
| Aaron Rogers | 04.09.1996 | 13 | (1) | |
| Danny Wallace | 21.10.1994 | 33 | | 3 |
| Sean Ward | 12.01.1984 | 33 | (1) | |
| **Midfielders:** | **DOB** | **M** | **(s)** | **G** |
| Chris Atherton | 19.10.2008 | | (2) | |
| Isaac Baird | 16.03.2004 | 29 | (6) | 1 |
| Jamie Doran | 11.02.2004 | 12 | (7) | 2 |
| Robert Garrett | 05.05.1988 | 19 | (4) | 1 |
| Jack Malone (IRL) | 05.04.2000 | 22 | (5) | 4 |
| Conor McCloskey | 29.01.1992 | 12 | (15) | 3 |
| Robbie Norton | 16.04.1998 | 1 | | |
| Michael O'Connor | 06.10.1987 | 9 | (7) | 1 |
| Conor Scannell | 28.01.2004 | 6 | (5) | 1 |
| Matthew Snoddy | 02.06.1993 | 22 | (13) | 1 |
| Jordan Stewart | 31.03.1995 | 5 | | |
| **Forwards:** | **DOB** | **M** | **(s)** | **G** |
| Eoin Bradley | 31.12.1983 | 13 | (9) | 4 |
| Peter Campbell | 16.09.1997 | 30 | (1) | 4 |
| Josh Doyle (IRL) | 19.06.2002 | 3 | (9) | 2 |
| Matthew Fitzpatrick | 02.09.1994 | 34 | | 19 |
| Gary Hamilton | 06.10.1980 | | (2) | |
| Cohen Henderson | 29.07.2006 | 2 | (2) | 1 |
| Aaron Prendergast | 30.01.2004 | 8 | (19) | 4 |

## Glentoran Football Club Belfast

**Founded:** 1882
**Stadium:** The Oval, Belfast (6,054)
**Trainer:** Michael McDermott — 07.02.1974
[17.01.2023] Rodney Joseph McAree — 19.08.1974

| Goalkeepers: | DOB | M | (s) | G |
|---|---|---|---|---|
| Aaron McCarey (IRL) | 14.01.1992 | 36 | | |
| Oliver Webber | 26.06.2000 | 2 | | |
| **Defenders:** | **DOB** | **M** | **(s)** | **G** |
| Bobby Burns | 07.10.1999 | 32 | (3) | 9 |
| Joe Crowe | 20.04.1998 | 4 | (12) | |
| Marcus Kane | 08.12.1991 | 27 | (4) | |
| Rhys Marshall | 16.01.1995 | 38 | | 2 |
| Patrick McClean | 22.11.1996 | 19 | (1) | 2 |
| Luke McCullough | 15.02.1994 | 24 | (1) | 1 |
| Harry Murphy | 22.10.2003 | 4 | (2) | |
| James Singleton | 22.08.1995 | 20 | (10) | 2 |
| Malachy Smith | 08.04.2001 | | (4) | |
| Aaron Wightman | 23.02.2004 | 9 | (11) | |
| Aidan Wilson (SCO) | 02.01.1999 | 26 | (1) | 4 |

| Midfielders: | DOB | M | (s) | G |
|---|---|---|---|---|
| Seanan Clucas | 08.11.1992 | 3 | (2) | |
| Terry Devlin | 06.11.2003 | 27 | (6) | 4 |
| Conor McMenamin | 24.08.1995 | 27 | (1) | 10 |
| Sean Murray (IRL) | 11.10.1993 | 8 | (7) | 1 |
| Ciarán O'Connor (IRL) | 04.07.1996 | | (1) | |
| Hrvoje Plum (CRO) | 28.05.1994 | 12 | (13) | 1 |
| **Forwards:** | **DOB** | **M** | **(s)** | **G** |
| Jay Donnelly | 10.04.1995 | 28 | (6) | 12 |
| Rory Donnelly | 18.02.1992 | 20 | (13) | 3 |
| Shay McCartan | 18.05.1994 | 23 | (4) | 5 |
| Niall McGinn | 20.07.1987 | 15 | (2) | 8 |
| Junior Ogedi-Uzokwe (ENG) | 03.03.1994 | 5 | (8) | 2 |
| Daniel Purkis | 10.06.1995 | 9 | (25) | 8 |
| Ally Roy | 26.07.1997 | | (15) | 1 |
| Rhys Walsh | 08.07.2006 | | (1) | |

## Larne Football Club

**Founded:** 1889
**Stadium:** Inver Park, Larne (2,732)
**Trainer:** Tiernan Lynch — 27.03.1980

| Goalkeepers: | DOB | M | (s) | G |
|---|---|---|---|---|
| Rohan Ferguson (SCO) | 06.12.1997 | 34 | | |
| Jack Cameron McIntyre (ENG) | 18.10.2002 | 3 | | |
| James Pardington (ENG) | 20.07.2000 | 1 | | |
| **Defenders:** | **DOB** | **M** | **(s)** | **G** |
| Cian Bolger (IRL) | 12.03.1992 | 31 | (1) | 2 |
| Sean Brown | 01.02.2005 | 1 | | |
| Tomas Cosgrove | 11.12.1992 | 36 | | 2 |
| Aaron Donnelly | 22.03.2000 | 33 | | |
| Micheal Glynn | 12.03.2002 | 16 | (1) | 1 |
| Graham Kelly (IRL) | 16.10.1997 | 4 | (17) | |
| Ben Walker | 28.04.2005 | | (1) | |
| Shaun Want (SCO) | 09.02.1997 | 32 | | |
| Albert Watson | 08.09.1985 | 8 | (8) | 1 |
| **Midfielders:** | **DOB** | **M** | **(s)** | **G** |
| Ben Doherty | 24.03.1997 | 21 | | 4 |
| Shea Gordon | 16.05.1998 | 16 | (16) | 1 |

| | DOB | M | (s) | G |
|---|---|---|---|---|
| Jeff Hughes | 29.05.1985 | 6 | (7) | |
| Max Hutchison (SCO) | 16.01.2001 | | (3) | |
| Daniel Kearns (IRL) | 26.08.1991 | 2 | (16) | |
| Thomas Maguire | 09.09.1999 | 1 | (10) | |
| Leroy Millar | 01.09.1995 | 36 | | 10 |
| Mark Randall (ENG) | 28.09.1989 | 16 | (10) | 2 |
| Andy Scott | 19.06.2000 | | (7) | |
| Dylan Sloan | 15.04.2004 | | (5) | |
| Fuad Sule (IRL) | 20.01.1997 | 31 | (4) | 1 |
| Joseph Thomson (SCO) | 14.01.1997 | 15 | (2) | 3 |
| **Forwards:** | **DOB** | **M** | **(s)** | **G** |
| Billy Junior Banda (IRL) | 01.06.1998 | | (4) | |
| Lee Bonis | 03.08.1999 | 34 | | 15 |
| Matthew Lusty | 14.07.2003 | 1 | (5) | |
| Paul O'Neill | 07.01.2000 | 27 | (7) | 13 |
| Andrew Ryan (SCO) | 29.09.1994 | 13 | (1) | 7 |
| Randy Wolters (NED) | 06.04.1990 | | (2) | |

## Linfield Football Club Belfast

**Founded:** 1886
**Stadium:** Windsor Park, Belfast (18,434)
**Trainer:** David Jonathan Healy — 05.08.1979

| Goalkeepers: | DOB | M | (s) | G |
|---|---|---|---|---|
| Christopher Johns | 13.05.1995 | 38 | | |
| David Walsh | 05.07.2002 | | (1) | |
| **Defenders:** | **DOB** | **M** | **(s)** | **G** |
| Jimmy Callacher | 11.06.1991 | 25 | | 2 |
| Matthew Clarke | 03.03.1994 | 35 | | 1 |
| Danny Finlayson | 19.01.2001 | 32 | (2) | 1 |
| Ben Hall | 16.01.1997 | 2 | | |
| Ryan McKay | 10.12.2004 | 1 | (1) | |
| Michael Newberry | 30.12.1997 | 14 | (1) | 1 |
| Conor Pepper (IRL) | 04.05.1994 | 3 | (7) | |
| Niall Quinn | 02.08.1993 | | (9) | 1 |
| Sam Roscoe (ENG) | 16.06.1998 | 36 | | 3 |
| **Midfielders:** | **DOB** | **M** | **(s)** | **G** |
| Joel Cooper | 29.02.1996 | 32 | (1) | 12 |
| Stephen Fallon | 03.03.1997 | 11 | (2) | 1 |
| Max Haygarth (ENG) | 21.01.2002 | 2 | (7) | 1 |

| | DOB | M | (s) | G |
|---|---|---|---|---|
| Kyle McClean | 03.10.1998 | 12 | (16) | 1 |
| Liam McStravick | 27.11.2004 | | (3) | 1 |
| Kirk Millar | 07.08.1992 | 25 | (3) | 4 |
| Jamie Mulgrew | 05.06.1986 | 31 | (5) | |
| Cammy Palmer | 15.05.2000 | 15 | (7) | 2 |
| Chris Shields (IRL) | 27.12.1990 | 31 | (4) | 6 |
| Jordan Stewart | 31.03.1995 | | (3) | |
| Eetu Vertainen (FIN) | 11.05.1999 | 19 | (11) | 17 |
| **Forwards:** | **DOB** | **M** | **(s)** | **G** |
| Rhys Annett | 06.11.2004 | | (1) | |
| Andrew Clarke | 12.12.2002 | 9 | (13) | 3 |
| Ethan Devine | 08.02.2001 | 6 | (24) | 5 |
| Braiden Graham | 07.11.2007 | | (1) | |
| Kyle Joseph George Lafferty | 16.09.1987 | 5 | (3) | |
| Robbie McDaid | 23.10.1996 | 20 | (4) | 6 |
| Chris McKee | 07.05.2002 | 14 | (15) | 6 |

## Newry City Athletic Football Club

**Founded:** 1918 (*as Newry Town FC*); re-founded 2013
**Stadium:** The Showgrounds, Newry (2,275)
**Trainer:** Darren Mullen — 23.06.1972

| Goalkeepers: | DOB | M | (s) | G |
|---|---|---|---|---|
| Niall Brady (IRL) | 02.02.2002 | 5 | | |
| Shane Halpenny (IRL) | 07.01.2004 | | (1) | |
| Steven Maguire | 14.12.1984 | 33 | | |
| **Defenders:** | **DOB** | **M** | **(s)** | **G** |
| Mohamed Boudiaf (IRL) | 15.06.2002 | | (3) | |
| Noel Healy | 27.07.1997 | 38 | | 1 |
| Darren King | 16.10.1985 | 31 | (1) | |
| Andy Martin | 22.03.1997 | 21 | (2) | |
| Ryan McGivern | 08.01.1990 | 30 | (3) | |
| Stephen Moan | 04.09.1990 | 22 | (2) | |
| Dale Montgomery | 19.04.1991 | 28 | (3) | |
| Manny Omrore (ENG) | 18.11.1998 | 6 | (4) | |
| Donal Scullion | 08.06.2004 | 24 | (7) | 2 |
| **Midfielders:** | **DOB** | **M** | **(s)** | **G** |
| Declan Carville | 13.12.1989 | 1 | (30) | 2 |
| Philip Donnelly (IRL) | 29.04.1992 | 23 | (6) | 1 |

| | DOB | M | (s) | G |
|---|---|---|---|---|
| Brian Healy | 24.08.2004 | 8 | (27) | 2 |
| Sean McCaul | 09.03.2004 | | (2) | |
| Liam McNamee (IRL) | 15.01.2003 | | (1) | |
| Ciarán O'Connor (IRL) | 04.07.1996 | 1 | (4) | 1 |
| Donal Rocks | 13.07.2000 | 10 | (8) | 1 |
| Dylan Sloan | 15.04.2004 | 5 | (4) | |
| **Forwards:** | **DOB** | **M** | **(s)** | **G** |
| Olajuwon Bamidele Adeyemo (NGA) | 13.02.1995 | 10 | (3) | 1 |
| Jamie Clarke | 18.06.1989 | 2 | (7) | |
| Lorcan Forde | 07.11.1999 | 13 | (3) | 2 |
| Daniel Hughes | 03.05.1992 | 26 | (2) | 5 |
| Ebuka Kwelele (IRL) | 11.06.2002 | | (5) | |
| Tommy Lockhart | 20.12.1993 | 34 | | 1 |
| Matthew Lusty | 14.07.2003 | 4 | (5) | |
| John McGovern | 17.10.2002 | 17 | (2) | 5 |
| Paul McGovern | 09.01.2008 | | (1) | |
| James Teelan | 17.10.2002 | 26 | (10) | 10 |

## Portadown Football Club

| Founded: | 1887 | |
|---|---|---|
| Stadium: | Shamrock Park, Portadown (3,940) | |
| Trainer: | Paul Doolin (IRL) | 26.03.1963 |
| [26.10.2022] | Niall Currie | 12.09.1972 |

| Goalkeepers: | DOB | M | (s) | G |
|---|---|---|---|---|
| Jethren Keith Barr (RSA) | 13.09.1995 | 27 | | |
| Ondřej Mastný (CZE) | 08.03.2002 | 9 | | |
| Ruadhán McKenna | 01.03.2002 | 2 | | |
| **Defenders:** | **DOB** | **M** | **(s)** | **G** |
| Jason Akiotu (ENG) | 11.03.1998 | 8 | | |
| Howard Beverland | 30.03.1990 | 4 | (2) | |
| Gledis Cakaj (IRL) | 26.09.2003 | 5 | (1) | |
| Lee Chapman | 09.11.1994 | 11 | (4) | |
| Reece Jordan | 06.03.2005 | 12 | (3) | |
| Barney McKeown | 29.06.2001 | 25 | (3) | 1 |
| Patrick McNally | 20.08.1994 | 29 | (1) | 1 |
| Chris Rodgers | 03.01.1991 | 15 | | |
| Tumelo Tlou (IRL) | 12.03.2002 | 3 | (2) | |
| Lee Upton | 24.08.2001 | 27 | (1) | 1 |
| **Midfielders:** | **DOB** | **M** | **(s)** | **G** |
| Joshua Archer | 21.07.2003 | 25 | (4) | 3 |
| Oisin Conaty | 17.02.2003 | 11 | | 1 |
| Zach Cowan | 20.09.2005 | | (1) | |
| Leo Donnellan (IRL) | 07.07.1998 | 12 | (3) | |

| | DOB | M | (s) | G |
|---|---|---|---|---|
| Katlego Keabetswe Mashigo (RSA) | 26.01.2001 | 1 | (7) | |
| Eoghan McCawl | 31.01.1996 | 16 | | |
| Mark Russell (SCO) | 22.03.1996 | 32 | (4) | 1 |
| Billy-Jay Stedman (ENG) | 03.11.1999 | 7 | (12) | |
| Stephen Teggart | 19.01.1998 | 24 | (9) | 2 |
| Luke Wilson | 15.02.2000 | 22 | (4) | 1 |
| **Forwards:** | **DOB** | **M** | **(s)** | **G** |
| Alberto Baldé Almánzar (DOM) | 21.03.2002 | 19 | (10) | 1 |
| Jack Evans | 08.08.2000 | | (3) | |
| Cathair Friel | 25.05.1993 | 13 | (3) | 3 |
| Bennie Igiehon (ENG) | 03.11.1993 | | (11) | 1 |
| Jordan Jenkins | 28.02.2000 | 20 | | 3 |
| Paul McElroy | 07.07.1994 | 13 | | 6 |
| Jonah Mitchell | 23.06.1999 | 1 | (9) | |
| Joseph Moore (SCO) | 17.06.2001 | 7 | (5) | |
| Gregory Moorhouse (IRL) | 10.07.1994 | 10 | | 3 |
| Alan O'Sullivan (IRL) | 24.03.1995 | 3 | (10) | 3 |
| Igor Rutkowski (POL) | 05.05.2004 | 2 | (8) | |
| Don De Dieu Tantale (FRA) | 23.02.2001 | 2 | (5) | |
| Mathew Walker | 19.02.2003 | 1 | (5) | |

## SECOND LEVEL
### NIFL Championship 2022/2023

### Regular Season

| | | | | | | | | |
|---|---|---|---|---|---|---|---|---|
| 1. | Loughgall FC | 33 | 21 | 6 | 6 | 65 - 20 | 69 |
| 2. | Warrenpoint Town FC | 33 | 19 | 6 | 8 | 61 - 40 | 63 |
| 3. | Annagh United FC Portadown | 33 | 16 | 7 | 10 | 51 - 37 | 55 |
| 4. | Dundela FC Belfast | 33 | 17 | 3 | 13 | 49 - 46 | 54 |
| 5. | Ards FC Newtownards | 33 | 14 | 5 | 14 | 64 - 62 | 47 |
| 6. | Ballyclare Comrades FC | 33 | 12 | 11 | 10 | 56 - 54 | 47 |
| 7. | Harland & Wolff Welders FC Belfast | 33 | 14 | 4 | 15 | 56 - 53 | 46 |
| 8. | Ballinamallard United FC | 33 | 12 | 10 | 11 | 42 - 50 | 46 |
| 9. | Institute FC Derry | 33 | 9 | 7 | 17 | 45 - 54 | 34 |
| 10. | Newington FC | 33 | 9 | 6 | 18 | 50 - 65 | 33 |
| 11. | Dergview FC Castlederg | 33 | 9 | 6 | 18 | 45 - 63 | 33 |
| 12. | Knockbreda FC Belfast | 33 | 7 | 7 | 19 | 39 - 79 | 28 |

Team ranked 1-6 were qualified for the Promotion Group, while teams ranked 7-12 were qualified for the Relegation Group.

### Promotion Group

| | | | | | | | | |
|---|---|---|---|---|---|---|---|---|
| 1. | Loughgall FC (*Promoted*) | 38 | 23 | 8 | 7 | 76 - 25 | 77 |
| 2. | Warrenpoint Town FC* | 38 | 21 | 8 | 9 | 67 - 45 | 71 |
| 3. | Annagh United FC Portadown (*Promotion Play-offs*) | 38 | 17 | 8 | 13 | 58 - 43 | 59 |
| 4. | Dundela FC Belfast | 38 | 18 | 4 | 16 | 57 - 58 | 58 |
| 5. | Ards FC Newtownards | 38 | 17 | 5 | 16 | 72 - 75 | 56 |
| 6. | Ballyclare Comrades FC | 38 | 14 | 13 | 11 | 66 - 63 | 55 |

### Relegation Group

| | | | | | | | | |
|---|---|---|---|---|---|---|---|---|
| 7. | Harland & Wolff Welders FC Belfast | 38 | 17 | 4 | 17 | 69 - 65 | 55 |
| 8. | Ballinamallard United FC | 38 | 14 | 10 | 14 | 50 - 59 | 52 |
| 9. | Newington FC | 38 | 12 | 7 | 19 | 64 - 73 | 43 |
| 10. | Dergview FC Castlederg | 38 | 11 | 8 | 19 | 51 - 68 | 41 |
| 11. | Institute FC Derry | 38 | 10 | 8 | 20 | 50 - 63 | 38 |
| 12. | Knockbreda FC Belfast (*Relegation Play-offs*) | 38 | 8 | 9 | 21 | 47 - 90 | 33 |

*Please note: as Warrenpoint Town FC were denied a license for the 2023/2024 season, Institute FC Derry remained at the second level and Knockbreda FC Belfast took their place in the Relegation Play-offs.

### Relegation Play-offs [2nd / 3rd level] [30.05.-03.06.2023]

| | | |
|---|---|---|
| Ballymacash Rangers FC - Knockbreda FC Belfast | 2-4(1-1) | 0-0 |

Knockbreda FC Belfast remains at second level for 2023/2024.

## INTERNATIONAL MATCHES
(16.07.2022 – 15.07.2023)

| 22.09.2022 | Belfast | *Northern Ireland - Kosovo* | *2-1(0-0)* | (UNL) |
|---|---|---|---|---|
| 25.09.2022 | Athína | *Greece - Northern Ireland* | *3-1(1-1)* | (UNL) |
| | | | | |
| 23.03.2023 | Serravalle | *San Marino - Northern Ireland* | *0-2(0-1)* | (ECQ) |
| 26.03.2023 | Belfast | *Northern Ireland - Finland* | *0-1(0-1)* | (ECQ) |
| 16.06.2023 | København | *Denmark - Northern Ireland* | *1-0(0-0)* | (ECQ) |
| 19.06.2023 | Belfast | *Northern Ireland - Kazakhstan* | *0-1(0-0)* | (ECQ) |

**22.09.2022    NORTHERN IRELAND - KOSOVO            2-1(0-0)**                3rd UEFA Nations League C, Group 2
Windsor Park, Belfast; Referee: Glenn Nyberg (Sweden); Attendance: 17,148
**NIR:** Bailey Peacock-Farrell, Jonathan Grant Evans, Thomas Michael Flanagan, Patrick James Coleman McNair, Jamal Piaras Lewis (76.Shane Kevin Ferguson), Conor Bradley, Steven Davis (Cap) (90+1.Alistair Edward McCann), Corry John Evans (76.Gavin Whyte), George Alan Saville (67.Jordan Andrew Thompson), Dion Elie Charles (76.Shayne Francis Lavery), Joshua Brendan David Magennis. Trainer: Ian Robert Baraclough (England).
**Goals:** Gavin Whyte (82), Joshua Brendan David Magennis (90+3).

**25.09.2022    GREECE - NORTHERN IRELAND            3-1(1-1)**                3rd UEFA Nations League C, Group 2
Stádio "Georgios Kamaras", Athína; Referee: Filip Glova (Slovakia); Attendance: 5,871
**NIR:** Bailey Peacock-Farrell, Conor Bradley (68.Dion Elie Charles), Jonathan Grant Evans (Cap), Thomas Michael Flanagan, Patrick James Coleman McNair, Jamal Piaras Lewis (76.Shane Kevin Ferguson), Steven Davis, Alistair Edward McCann, Jordan Andrew Thompson (9.George Alan Saville), Shayne Francis Lavery (67.Gavin Whyte), Joshua Brendan David Magennis (76.Conor McMenamin). Trainer: Ian Robert Baraclough (England).
**Goal:** Shayne Francis Lavery (18).

**23.03.2023    SAN MARINO - NORTHERN IRELAND        0-2(0-1)**                17th EC. Qualifiers
San Marino Stadium, Serravalle; Referee: Gergő Bognár (Hungary); Attendance: 2,099
**NIR:** Bailey Peacock-Farrell, Ciaron Maurice Brown (82.Isaac Jude Price), Craig George Cathcart (Cap), Daniel George Ballard (67.Cameron Alexander McGeehan), Conor Bradley, George Alan Saville (73.Jordan Andrew Thompson), Dion Elie Charles, Patrick James Coleman McNair, Jamal Piaras Lewis (73.Shane Kevin Ferguson), Shea Charles, Conor James Washington (57.Joshua Brendan David Magennis). Trainer: Michael Andrew Martin O'Neill.
**Goals:** Dion Elie Charles (24, 55).

**26.03.2023    NORTHERN IRELAND - FINLAND           0-1(0-1)**                17th EC. Qualifiers
Windsor Park, Belfast; Referee: Ivan Kružliak (Slovakia); Attendance: 17,936
**NIR:** Bailey Peacock-Farrell, Ciaron Maurice Brown, Daniel George Ballard (50.Joshua Brendan David Magennis), Craig George Cathcart (Cap), Conor Bradley, Jordan Andrew Thompson (79.George Alan Saville), Dion Elie Charles, Patrick James Coleman McNair, Jamal Piaras Lewis, Shea Charles (79.Isaac Jude Price), Conor James Washington (69.Gavin Whyte). Trainer: Michael Andrew Martin O'Neill.

**16.06.2023    DENMARK - NORTHERN IRELAND           1-0(0-0)**                17th EC. Qualifiers
Parken Stadium, København; Referee: Daniel Stefański (Poland); Attendance: 35,701
**NIR:** Bailey Peacock-Farrell, Ciaron Maurice Brown, Jonathan Grant Evans (Cap), Patrick James Coleman McNair, Conor Bradley (77.Conor McMenamin), Shea Charles (69.Jordan Andrew Thompson), Alistair Edward McCann (85.Callum Marshall), George Alan Saville, Trai Hume, Isaac Jude Price (77.Dale Taylor), Shayne Francis Lavery (69.Dion Elie Charles). Trainer: Michael Andrew Martin O'Neill.

**19.06.2023    NORTHERN IRELAND - KAZAKHSTAN        0-1(0-0)**                17th EC. Qualifiers
Windsor Park, Belfast; Referee: Roi Reinshreiber (Israel); Attendance: 18,002
**NIR:** Bailey Peacock-Farrell, Patrick James Coleman McNair, Craig George Cathcart, Jonathan Grant Evans (Cap) (63.Conor McMenamin), Trai Hume, George Alan Saville, Shea Charles, Jordan Andrew Thompson (84.Ciaron Maurice Brown), Dion Elie Charles (72.Shayne Francis Lavery), Alistair Edward McCann (71.Dale Taylor), Isaac Jude Price. Trainer: Michael Andrew Martin O'Neill.

## NATIONAL TEAM PLAYERS
### (16.07.2022 – 15.07.2023)

| Name | DOB | Caps | Goals | Club |
|------|-----|------|-------|------|
| **Goalkeepers** | | | | |
| Bailey PEACOCK-FARRELL | 29.10.1996 | 39 | 0 | 2022/2023: *Burnley FC (ENG)* |
| **Defenders** | | | | |
| Daniel George BALLARD | 22.09.1999 | 18 | 2 | 2023: *Sunderland AFC (ENG)* |
| Conor BRADLEY | 09.07.2003 | 13 | 0 | 2022/2023: *Bolton Wanderers FC (ENG)* |
| Ciaron Maurice BROWN | 14.01.1998 | 16 | 0 | 2023: *Oxford United FC (ENG)* |
| Craig George CATHCART | 06.02.1989 | 72 | 2 | 2023: *Watford FC (ENG)* |
| Jonathan Grant EVANS | 03.01.1988 | 102 | 5 | 2022/2023: *Leicester City FC (ENG)* |
| Thomas Michael FLANAGAN | 21.10.1991 | 15 | 0 | 2022/2023: *Shrewsbury Town FC (ENG)* |
| Trai HUME | 18.03.2002 | 4 | 0 | 2023: *Sunderland AFC (ENG)* |
| Jamal Piaras LEWIS | 25.01.1998 | 30 | 0 | 2022/2023: *Newcastle United FC (ENG)* |
| Patrick James Coleman McNAIR | 27.04.1995 | 62 | 6 | 2022/2023: *Middlesbrough FC (ENG)* |
| **Midfielders** | | | | |
| Shea CHARLES | 05.11.2003 | 8 | 0 | 2023: *Manchester City FC (ENG)* |
| Steven DAVIS | 01.01.1985 | 140 | 13 | 2022: *Rangers FC Glasgow (SCO)* |
| Corry John EVANS | 17.07.1990 | 70 | 2 | 2022: *Sunderland AFC (ENG)* |
| Shane Kevin FERGUSON | 12.07.1991 | 57 | 2 | 2022/2023: *Rotherham United FC (ENG)* |
| Alistair Edward McCANN | 04.12.1999 | 18 | 1 | 2022/2023: *Preston North End FC (ENG)* |
| Cameron Alexander McGEEHAN | 06.04.1995 | 1 | 0 | 2023: *KV Oostende (BEL)* |
| Conor McMENAMIN | 24.08.1995 | 6 | 0 | 2022/2023: *Glentoran FC Belfast* |
| Isaac Jude PRICE | 26.09.2003 | 4 | 0 | 2023: *Everton FC Liverpool (ENG)* |
| George Alan SAVILLE | 01.06.1993 | 46 | 0 | 2022/2023: *Millwall FC London (ENG)* |
| Jordan Andrew THOMPSON | 03.01.1997 | 30 | 0 | 2022/2023: *Stoke City FC (ENG)* |
| Gavin WHYTE | 31.01.1996 | 30 | 5 | 2022/2023: *Cardiff City FC (WAL)* |
| **Forwards** | | | | |
| Dion Elie CHARLES | 07.10.1995 | 17 | 2 | 2022/2023: *Bolton Wanderers FC (ENG)* |
| Shayne Francis LAVERY | 08.12.1998 | 19 | 3 | 2022/2023: *Blackpool FC (ENG)* |
| Joshua Brendan David MAGENNIS | 15.05.1990 | 71 | 10 | 2022/2023: *Wigan Athletic FC (ENG)* |
| Callum MARSHALL | 28.11.2004 | 1 | 0 | 2023: *West Ham United FC London (ENG)* |
| Dale TAYLOR | 12.12.2003 | 3 | 0 | 2023: *Nottingham Forest FC (ENG)* |
| Conor James WASHINGTON | 18.05.1992 | 37 | 6 | 2023: *Rotherham United FC (ENG)* |

| Trainer | | |
|---------|---|---|
| Ian Robert BARACLOUGH (England) [27.06.2020 – 21.10.2022] | 04.12.1970 | 28 M; 6 W; 8 D; 14 L; 27-36 |
| Michael Andrew Martin O'NEILL [from 07.12.2022] | 05.07.1969 | 4 M; 1 W; 0 D; 3 L; 2-3 Complete record as trainer of Northern Ireland: 76 M; 27 W; 18 D; 31 L; 77-86 (29.02.2012 – 19.11.2019) & (from 07.12.2022) |

# NORWAY

**The Country:**
Kongeriket Norge (Kingdom of Norway)
Capital: Oslo
Surface: 385,203 km²
Inhabitants: 5,425,270 [2022]
Time: UTC+1

**The FA:**
Norges Fotballforbund
Postboks 5000, Ullevaal Stadion, 0840 Oslo
Tel: +47 21 02 93 00
Founded: 1902
Member of FIFA since: 1908
Member of UEFA since: 1954
Website: www.fotball.no

## NATIONAL TEAM RECORDS

### RECORDS

| | | |
|---|---|---|
| **First international match:** | 12.07.1908, Göteborg: | Sweden – Norway 11-3 |
| **Most international caps:** | John Arne Semundseth Riise | - 110 caps (2000-2013) |
| **Most international goals:** | Jørgen Juve | - 33 goals / 45 caps (1928-1937) |

### UEFA EUROPEAN CHAMPIONSHIP

| | |
|---|---|
| 1960 | Qualifiers |
| 1964 | Qualifiers |
| 1968 | Qualifiers |
| 1972 | Qualifiers |
| 1976 | Qualifiers |
| 1980 | Qualifiers |
| 1984 | Qualifiers |
| 1988 | Qualifiers |
| 1992 | Qualifiers |
| 1996 | Qualifiers |
| 2000 | Final Tournament (Group Stage) |
| 2004 | Qualifiers |
| 2008 | Qualifiers |
| 2012 | Qualifiers |
| 2016 | Qualifiers |
| 2020 | Qualifiers |

### FIFA WORLD CUP

| | |
|---|---|
| 1930 | Did not enter |
| 1934 | Did not enter |
| 1938 | Final Tournament (1st Round) |
| 1950 | Did not enter |
| 1954 | Qualifiers |
| 1958 | Qualifiers |
| 1962 | Qualifiers |
| 1966 | Qualifiers |
| 1970 | Qualifiers |
| 1974 | Qualifiers |
| 1978 | Qualifiers |
| 1982 | Qualifiers |
| 1986 | Qualifiers |
| 1990 | Qualifiers |
| 1994 | Final Tournament (Group Stage) |
| 1998 | Final Tournament (2nd Round of 16) |
| 2002 | Qualifiers |
| 2006 | Qualifiers |
| 2010 | Qualifiers |
| 2014 | Qualifiers |
| 2018 | Qualifiers |
| 2022 | Qualifiers |

### OLYMPIC TOURNAMENTS

| | |
|---|---|
| 1908 | - |
| 1912 | Final Tournament (Quarter-Finals) |
| 1920 | Final Tournament (Quarter-Finals) |
| 1924 | Did not enter |
| 1928 | Did not enter |
| 1936 | Final Tournament (3rd Place) |
| 1948 | Did not enter |
| 1952 | Final Tournament (Round 1) |
| 1956 | Did not enter |
| 1960 | Qualifiers |
| 1964 | Did not enter |
| 1968 | Did not enter |
| 1972 | Did not enter |
| 1976 | Qualifiers |
| 1980 | Qualifiers |
| 1984 | Final Tournament (Group Stage) |
| 1988 | Qualifiers |
| 1992 | Qualifiers |
| 1996 | Qualifiers |
| 2000 | Qualifiers |
| 2004 | Qualifiers |
| 2008 | Qualifiers |
| 2012 | Qualifiers |
| 2016 | Qualifiers |
| 2020 | Qualifiers |

### UEFA NATIONS LEAGUE

| | |
|---|---|
| 2018/2019 | League C (Group Stage -> promoted to League B) |
| 2020/2021 | League B (Group Stage) |
| 2022/2023 | League B (Group Stage) |

### NORWEGIAN CLUB HONOURS IN EUROPEAN CLUB COMPETITIONS:

| European Champion Clubs.Cup (1956-1992) / UEFA Champions League (1993-2023) |
|---|
| None |

| Fairs Cup (1858-1971) / UEFA Cup (1972-2009) / UEFA Europa League (2010-2023) |
|---|
| None |

| UEFA Europa Conference League (2021-2023) |
|---|
| None |

| UEFA Super Cup (1972-2022) |
|---|
| None |

| European Cup Winners' Cup 1961-1999* |
|---|
| None |

*defunct competition

# NATIONAL COMPETITIONS
## TABLE OF HONOURS

| | CHAMPIONS | CUP WINNERS | BEST GOALSCORERS | |
|---|---|---|---|---|
| 1902 | - | Sportsklubben Grane | - | |
| 1903 | - | Odds BK Skien | - | |
| 1904 | - | Odds BK Skien | - | |
| 1905 | - | Odds BK Skien | - | |
| 1906 | - | Odds BK Skien | - | |
| 1907 | - | Mercantile FK | - | |
| 1908 | - | Lyn 1896 FK Oslo | - | |
| 1909 | - | Lyn 1896 FK Oslo | - | |
| 1910 | - | Lyn 1896 FK Oslo | - | |
| 1911 | - | Lyn 1896 FK Oslo | - | |
| 1912 | - | Mercantile FK | - | |
| 1913 | - | Odds BK Skien | - | |
| 1914 | - | Frigg Oslo FK | - | |
| 1915 | - | Odds BK Skien | - | |
| 1916 | - | Frigg Oslo FK | - | |
| 1917 | - | Sarpsborg FK | - | |
| 1918 | - | Kvik FK Fredrikshald | - | |
| 1919 | - | Odds BK Skien | - | |
| 1920 | - | FK Ørn-Horten | - | |
| 1921 | - | Frigg Oslo FK Oslo | - | |
| 1922 | - | Odds BK Skien | - | |
| 1923 | - | SK Brann Bergen | - | |
| 1924 | - | Odds BK Skien | - | |
| 1925 | - | SK Brann Bergen | - | |
| 1926 | - | Odds BK Skien | - | |
| 1927 | - | FK Ørn-Horten | - | |
| 1928 | - | FK Ørn-Horten | - | |
| 1929 | - | Sarpsborg FK | - | |
| 1930 | - | FK Ørn-Horten | - | |
| 1931 | - | Odds BK Skien | - | |
| 1932 | - | Fredrikstad FK | - | |
| 1933 | - | Mjøndalen IF | - | |
| 1934 | - | Mjøndalen IF | - | |
| 1935 | - | Fredrikstad FK | - | |
| 1936 | - | Fredrikstad FK | - | |
| 1937 | - | Mjøndalen IF | - | |
| 1937/1938 | Fredrikstad FK | Fredrikstad FK | - | |
| 1938/1939 | Fredrikstad FK | Sarpsborg FK | - | |
| 1939/1940 | *Championship abandoned* | Fredrikstad FK | - | |
| 1940/1941 | *No competition* | *No competition* | - | |
| 1941/1942 | *No competition* | *No competition* | - | |
| 1942/1943 | *No competition* | *No competition* | - | |
| 1943/1944 | *No competition* | *No competition* | - | |
| 1944/1945 | *No competition* | Lyn 1896 FK Oslo | - | |
| 1945/1946 | *No competition* | Lyn 1896 FK Oslo | - | |
| 1946/1947 | *No competition* | Skeid Fotball Oslo | - | |
| 1947/1948 | SK Freidig Trondheim | Sarpsborg FK | - | |
| 1948/1949 | Fredrikstad FK | Sarpsborg FK | Arvid Havnås (Sandefjord BK) | 12 |
| 1949/1950 | IF Fram Larvik | Fredrikstad FK | Reidar Dørum (FK Ørn-Horten) | 13 |
| 1950/1951 | Fredrikstad FK | Sarpsborg FK | John Sveinsson (Lyn 1896 FK Oslo) | 19 |
| 1951/1952 | Fredrikstad FK | IL Sparta Sparsborg | Jan Tangen (Strømmen IF) | 15 |
| 1952/1953 | Larvik Turn & Idrettsforening | Viking FK Stavanger | Gunnar Thoresen (Larvik Turn & Idrettsforening) Per Jacobsen (Odds BK Skien) | 15 |
| 1953/1954 | Fredrikstad FK | Skeid Fotball Oslo | Gunnar Thoresen (Larvik Turn & Idrettsforening) | 15 |
| 1954/1955 | Larvik Turn & Idrettsforening | Skeid Fotball Oslo | Harald Hennum (Skeid Fotball Oslo) | 13 |
| 1955/1956 | Larvik Turn & Idrettsforening | Skeid Fotball Oslo | Willy Fossli (Asker Fotball) | 17 |
| 1956/1957 | Fredrikstad FK | Fredrikstad FK | Per Kristoffersen (Fredrikstad FK) | 15 |
| 1957/1958 | Viking FK Stavanger | Skeid Fotball Oslo | Harald Hennum (Skeid Fotball Oslo) | 17 |
| 1958/1959 | Lillestrøm SK | Viking FK Stavanger | Reidar Sundby (Larvik Turn & Idrettsforening) | 13 |
| 1959/1960 | Fredrikstad FK | Rosenborg BK Trondheim | Per Kristoffersen (Fredrikstad FK) | 13 |
| 1960/1961 | Fredrikstad FK | Fredrikstad FK | Per Kristoffersen (Fredrikstad FK) | 15 |
| 1961/1962 | SK Brann Bergen | SK Gjøvik-Lyn | Rolf Birger Pedersen (SK Brann Bergen) | 26 |
| 1963 | SK Brann Bergen | Skeid Fotball Oslo | Leif Eriksen (Vålerenga Fotball Oslo) | 16 |
| 1964 | Lyn 1896 FK Oslo | Rosenborg BK Trondheim | Ole Stavrum (Lyn 1896 FK Oslo) | 18 |
| 1965 | Vålerenga Fotball Oslo | Skeid Fotball Oslo | Harald Berg (Lyn 1896 FK Oslo) | 19 |
| 1966 | Skeid Fotball Oslo | Fredrikstad FK | Per Kristoffersen (Fredrikstad FK) | 20 |
| 1967 | Rosenborg BK Trondheim | Lyn 1896 FK Oslo | Odd Iversen (Rosenborg BK Trondheim) | 17 |
| 1968 | Lyn 1896 FK Oslo | Lyn 1896 FK Oslo | Odd Iversen (Rosenborg BK Trondheim) | 30 |
| 1969 | Rosenborg BK Trondheim | Strømsgodset IF Drammen | Odd Iversen (Rosenborg BK Trondheim) | 26 |
| 1970 | Strømsgodset IF Drammen | Strømsgodset IF Drammen | Steinar Pettersen (Strømsgodset IF Drammen) | 16 |
| 1971 | Rosenborg BK Trondheim | Rosenborg BK Trondheim | Jan Fuglset (Fredrikstad IF) | 17 |
| 1972 | Viking FK Stavanger | SK Brann Bergen | Egil Solberg (Mjøndalen IF) | |

| | | | | |
|---|---|---|---|---|
| | | | Johannes Vold (Viking FK Stavanger) | 16 |
| 1973 | Viking FK Stavanger | Strømsgodset IF Drammen | Stein Karlsen (Hamarkameratene) | 17 |
| 1974 | Viking FK Stavanger | Skeid Fotball Oslo | Odd Berg (Molde FK) | 13 |
| 1975 | Viking FK Stavanger | FK Bodø/Glimt | Arne Dokken (Lillestrøm SK) | 18 |
| 1976 | Lillestrøm SK | SK Brann Bergen | Jan Fuglset (Molde FK) | 17 |
| 1977 | Lillestrøm SK | Lillestrøm SK | Trygve Johannessen (Viking FK Stavanger) | 17 |
| 1978 | IK Start Kristiansand | Lillestrøm SK | Tom Lund (Lillestrøm SK) | 17 |
| 1979 | Viking FK Stavanger | Viking FK Stavanger | Odd Iversen (Vålerenga Fotball Oslo) | 16 |
| 1980 | IK Start Kristiansand | Vålerenga Fotball Oslo | Arne Dokken (Lillestrøm SK) | 14 |
| 1981 | Vålerenga Fotball Oslo | Lillestrøm SK | Pål Jacobsen (Vålerenga Fotball Oslo) | 16 |
| 1982 | Viking FK Stavanger | SK Brann Bergen | Tor Arne Granerud (Hamarkameratene) Trygve Johannessen (Viking FK Stavanger) | 11 |
| 1983 | Vålerenga Fotball Oslo | Moss FK | Olav Nysæter (Kongsvinger IL) | 14 |
| 1984 | Vålerenga Fotball Oslo | Fredrikstad FK | Sverre Brandhaug (Rosenborg BK Trondheim) | 13 |
| 1985 | Rosenborg BK Trondheim | Lillestrøm SK | Jørn Andersen (Vålerenga Fotball Oslo) | 23 |
| 1986 | Lillestrøm SK | Tromsø IL | Arve Seland (IK Start Kristiansand) | 12 |
| 1987 | Moss FK | Bryne FK | Jan Kristian Fjærestad (Moss FK) | 18 |
| 1988 | Rosenborg BK Trondheim | Rosenborg BK Trondheim | Jan Åge Fjørtoft (Lillestrøm SK) | 14 |
| 1989 | Lillestrøm SK | Viking FK Stavanger | Jahn Ivar Jakobsen (Rosenborg BK Trondheim) | 18 |
| 1990 | Rosenborg BK Trondheim | Rosenborg BK Trondheim | Tore André Dahlum (IK Start Kristiansand) | 20 |
| 1991 | Viking FK Stavanger | Strømsgodset IF Drammen | Karl Petter Løken (Rosenborg BK Trondheim) | 12 |
| 1992 | Rosenborg BK Trondheim | Rosenborg BK Trondheim | Kjell Roar Kaasa (Kongsvinger IL) | 17 |
| 1993 | Rosenborg BK Trondheim | FK Bodø/Glimt | Mons Ivar Mjelde (Lillestrøm SK) | 19 |
| 1994 | Rosenborg BK Trondheim | Molde FK | Harald Martin Brattbakk (Rosenborg BK Trondheim) | 17 |
| 1995 | Rosenborg BK Trondheim | Rosenborg BK Trondheim | Harald Martin Brattbakk (Rosenborg BK Trondheim) | 26 |
| 1996 | Rosenborg BK Trondheim | Tromsø IL | Harald Martin Brattbakk (Rosenborg BK Trondheim) | 28 |
| 1997 | Rosenborg BK Trondheim | Vålerenga Fotball Oslo | Sigurd Rushfeldt (Rosenborg BK Trondheim) | 27 |
| 1998 | Rosenborg BK Trondheim | Stabæk Fotball Bærum | Sigurd Rushfeldt (Rosenborg BK Trondheim) | 25 |
| 1999 | Rosenborg BK Trondheim | Rosenborg BK Trondheim | Rune Lange (Tromsø IL) | 23 |
| 2000 | Rosenborg BK Trondheim | Odd Grenland Skien | Thorstein Helstad (SK Brann Bergen) | 18 |
| 2001 | Rosenborg BK Trondheim | Viking FK Stavanger | Frode Johnsen (Rosenborg BK Trondheim) Thorstein Helstad (SK Brann Bergen) Clayton Zane (AUS, Lillestrøm SK) | 17 |
| 2002 | Rosenborg BK Trondheim | Vålerenga Fotball Oslo | Harald Martin Brattbakk (Rosenborg BK Trondheim) | 17 |
| 2003 | Rosenborg BK Trondheim | Rosenborg BK Trondheim | Harald Martin Brattbakk (Rosenborg BK Trondheim) | 17 |
| 2004 | Rosenborg BK Trondheim | SK Brann Bergen | Frode Johnsen (Rosenborg BK Trondheim) | 19 |
| 2005 | Vålerenga Fotball Oslo | Molde FK | Ole Martin Årst (Tromsø IL) | 16 |
| 2006 | Rosenborg BK Trondheim | Fredrikstad FK | Daniel Nannskog (SWE, Stabæk Fotball Bærum) | 19 |
| 2007 | SK Brann Bergen | Lillestrøm SK | Thorstein Helstad (SK Brann Bergen) | 22 |
| 2008 | Stabæk Fotball Bærum | Vålerenga Fotball Oslo | Daniel Nannskog (SWE, Stabæk Fotball Bærum) | 16 |
| 2009 | Rosenborg BK Trondheim | Aalesunds FK | Rade Prica (SWE, Rosenborg BK Trondheim) | 17 |
| 2010 | Rosenborg BK Trondheim | Strømsgodset IF Drammen | Baye Djiby Fall (SEN, Molde FK) | 16 |
| 2011 | Molde FK | Aalesunds FK | Mustafa Abdellaoue (Tromsø IL) | 17 |
| 2012 | Molde FK | IL Hødd Ulsteinvik | Péter Kovács (HUN, Strømsgodset IF Drammen) Zdeněk Ondrášek (CZE, Tromsø IL) | 14 |
| 2013 | Strømsgodset IF Drammen | Molde FK | Frode Johnsen (Odds BK Skien) | 16 |
| 2014 | Molde FK | Molde FK | Viðar Örn Kjartansson (ISL, Vålerenga Fotball Oslo) | 25 |
| 2015 | Rosenborg BK Trondheim | Rosenborg BK Trondheim | Alexander Toft Søderlund (Rosenborg BK Trondheim) | 22 |
| 2016 | Rosenborg BK Trondheim | Rosenborg BK Trondheim | Christian Gytkjær (DEN, Rosenborg BK Trondheim) | 19 |
| 2017 | Rosenborg BK Trondheim | Lillestrøm SK | Nicklas Bendtner (DEN, Rosenborg BK Trondheim) | 19 |
| 2018 | Rosenborg BK Trondheim | Rosenborg BK Trondheim | Bi Sylvestre Franck Fortune Boli (CIV, Stabæk Fotball Bærum) | 17 |
| 2019 | Molde FK | Viking FK Stavanger | Torgeir Børven (Odds BK Skien) | 21 |
| 2020 | FK Bodø/Glimt | Competition cancelled | Kasper Junker (DEN, FK Bodø/Glimt) | 27 |
| 2021 | FK Bodø/Glimt | Molde FK (21/22) | Anthony Ohikhuaeme Omoijuanfo (Molde FK) | 27 |
| 2022 | Molde FK | SK Brann Bergen (22/23) | Amahl William D'vaz Pellegrino (FK Bodø/Glimt) | 25 |

Please note: the Norwegian Championship was called Norgesserien (1937–1948), Hovedserien (1948–1962), 1. divisjon (1963–1989), Tippeligaen (1990–2016) and Eliteserien (since 2017).

# NATIONAL CHAMPIONSHIP
## Eliteserien 2022
### (02.04.2022 – 13.11.2022)

## Results

### Round 1 [02-03.04.2022]
Hamarkameratene - Lillestrøm 2-2(2-0)
Molde FK - Vålerenga 1-0(0-0)
Aalesunds FK - Kristiansund 1-0(0-0)
FK Haugesund - Sandefjord 1-3(0-3)
FK Jerv - Strømsgodset 1-0(0-0)
Odds BK - Tromsø IL 2-0(1-0)
Sarpsborg 08 - Viking 0-1(0-0)
FK Bodø/Glimt - Rosenborg 2-2(0-1)

### Round 2 [09-10.04.2022]
Lillestrøm - FK Jerv 4-0(2-0)
Sandefjord - FK Bodø/Glimt 1-2(0-1)
Kristiansund - Sarpsborg 08 2-3(0-3)
Rosenborg - Odds BK 1-0(1-0)
Strømsgodset - Molde FK 1-3(1-0)
Tromsø IL - Hamarkameratene 2-1(1-1)
Vålerenga - FK Haugesund 2-1(2-1)
Viking - Aalesunds FK 1-0(0-0)

### Round 3 [18.04.2022]
Aalesunds FK - Tromsø IL 2-2(1-0)
FK Haugesund - Strømsgodset 0-1(0-0)
FK Jerv - Kristiansund 1-0(1-0)
Hamarkameratene - Sandefjord 3-0(1-0)
Molde FK - Lillestrøm 1-2(0-1)
Odds BK - Viking 2-1(0-0)
Sarpsborg 08 - Rosenborg 1-1(1-0)
FK Bodø/Glimt - Vålerenga 5-1(2-0)

### Round 4 [23-24.04.2022]
Odds BK - Aalesunds FK 2-3(0-2)
Strømsgodset - Sandefjord 0-5(0-2)
Kristiansund - Hamarkameratene 2-2(1-1)
Lillestrøm - FK Haugesund 1-0(0-0)
Tromsø IL - Sarpsborg 08 2-5(1-2)
Vålerenga - FK Jerv 1-0(0-0)
Viking - FK Bodø/Glimt 2-0(1-0)
Rosenborg - Molde FK 0-0

### Round 5 [07-08.05.2022]
Sarpsborg 08 - Odds BK 1-0(0-0)
Molde FK - Viking 3-4(3-1)
FK Bodø/Glimt - Lillestrøm 1-1(0-1)
FK Haugesund - Kristiansund 2-0(1-0)
FK Jerv - Tromsø IL 1-1(1-1)
Sandefjord - Vålerenga 1-3(0-2)
Strømsgodset - Rosenborg 3-0(3-0)
Hamarkameratene - Aalesunds FK 0-0

### Round 6 [16.05.2022]
Aalesunds FK - Molde FK 0-2(0-2)
FK Bodø/Glimt - Tromsø IL 1-1(0-0)
Kristiansund - Strømsgodset 0-3(0-2)
Lillestrøm - Sarpsborg 08 1-0(0-0)
Odds BK - FK Haugesund 0-4(0-2)
Rosenborg - Sandefjord 3-0(1-0)
Viking - FK Jerv 3-0(0-0)
Vålerenga - Hamarkameratene 1-1(0-0)

### Round 7 [21-22.05.2022]
Sandefjord - Lillestrøm 1-4(1-3)
Molde FK - Kristiansund 2-1(2-0)
FK Haugesund - FK Bodø/Glimt 1-4(0-3)
FK Jerv - Odds BK 0-1(0-0)
Sarpsborg 08 - Aalesunds FK 1-2(1-1)
Strømsgodset - Vålerenga 3-2(3-0)
Tromsø IL - Viking 1-1(0-0)
Hamarkameratene - Rosenborg 1-1(0-1)

### Round 8 [25-26.05.2022]
Aalesunds FK - FK Jerv 2-1(0-0)
FK Bodø/Glimt - Strømsgodset 2-2(2-1)
Odds BK - Sandefjord 0-1(0-1)
Viking - Hamarkameratene 1-1(1-0)
Lillestrøm - Vålerenga 2-0(0-0)
Rosenborg - FK Haugesund 3-3(1-3)
Sarpsborg 08 - Molde FK 1-2(0-0)
Kristiansund-Tromsø IL 1-1(0-1) [03.08.2022]

### Round 9 [28-29.05.2022]
Hamarkameratene - Odds BK 1-2(0-2)
Strømsgodset - Viking 3-2(1-1)
FK Haugesund - Aalesunds FK 2-2(1-1)
FK Jerv - Sarpsborg 08 0-5(0-2)
Molde FK - FK Bodø/Glimt 3-1(1-0)
Tromsø IL - Lillestrøm 2-2(1-0)
Vålerenga - Rosenborg 0-4(0-0)
Sandefjord-Kristiansund 2-0(1-0) [27.07.2022]

### Round 10 [18-19.06.2022]
Sarpsborg 08 - Strømsgodset 5-1(4-1)
Kristiansund - FK Bodø/Glimt 0-2(0-0)
FK Jerv - Hamarkameratene 1-2(0-2)
Lillestrøm - Rosenborg 3-1(2-1)
Odds BK - Molde FK 1-2(0-0)
Tromsø IL - FK Haugesund 1-1(0-0)
Viking - Sandefjord 1-2(1-0)
Aalesunds FK - Vålerenga 2-2(1-0)

### Round 11 [25-26.06.2022]
FK Haugesund - Viking 4-2(1-2)
Rosenborg - Kristiansund 3-1(2-1)
FK Bodø/Glimt - Aalesunds FK 2-0(0-0)
Hamarkameratene - Sarpsborg 08 3-2(2-2)
Sandefjord - Tromsø IL 2-2(1-0)
Strømsgodset - Lillestrøm 3-0(0-0)
Vålerenga - Odds BK 0-1(0-0)
Molde FK - FK Jerv 1-1(0-0) [06.07.2022]

### Round 12 [02-03.07.2022]
Tromsø IL - Vålerenga 1-0(0-0) [12.05.2022]
FK Jerv - FK Haugesund 1-0(0-0)
Odds BK - FK Bodø/Glimt 3-2(1-1)
Aalesunds FK - Strømsgodset 1-0(0-0)
Hamarkameratene - Molde FK 0-0
Kristiansund - Lillestrøm 1-3(1-0)
Sarpsborg 08 - Sandefjord 4-3(2-2)
Viking - Rosenborg 1-1(0-1)

### Round 13 [09-12.07.2022]
FK Bodø/Glimt - Sarpsborg 08 4-1(2-1)
Strømsgodset - Odds BK 0-0
Lillestrøm - Viking 0-1(0-0)
Molde FK - Tromsø IL 5-1(3-1)
Rosenborg - FK Jerv 3-2(2-1)
Vålerenga - Kristiansund 3-0(0-0)
FK Haugesund - Hamarkameratene 1-1(1-1)
Sandefjord - Aalesunds FK 2-2(1-1)

### Round 14 [16-17.07.2022]
FK Jerv - Sandefjord 1-2(0-0)
Hamarkameratene - FK Bodø/Glimt 0-2(0-0)
Molde FK - FK Haugesund 1-0(0-0)
Odds BK - Lillestrøm 1-1(0-0)
Sarpsborg 08 - Vålerenga 0-1(0-1)
Viking - Kristiansund 2-1(0-0)
Aalesunds FK - Rosenborg 0-0
Tromsø IL - Strømsgodset 1-0(1-0) [31.08.22]

### Round 15 [23-24.07.2022]
Lillestrøm - Aalesunds FK 2-0(2-0) [28.04.22]
FK Bodø/Glimt - FK Jerv 5-0(4-0)
Rosenborg - Tromsø IL 3-0(2-0)
FK Haugesund - Sarpsborg 08 3-1(2-1)
Kristiansund - Odds BK 2-2(2-0)
Sandefjord - Molde FK 2-3(1-1)
Vålerenga - Viking 4-2(3-1)
Strømsgodset - Hamarkameratene 1-1(0-0)

### Round 16 [30-31.07.2022]
Viking - FK Haugesund 5-1(2-1) [30.04.2022]
Aalesunds FK - FK Bodø/Glimt 1-2(1-2)
Hamarkameratene - Kristiansund 0-1(0-1)
Odds BK - Rosenborg 2-3(1-0)
Tromsø IL - Sandefjord 3-0(2-0)
FK Jerv - Vålerenga 2-5(1-3)
Molde FK - Strømsgodset 3-0(1-0)
Sarpsborg 08 - Lillestrøm 0-2(0-0)

### Round 17 [06-07.08.2022]
FK Bodø/Glimt - Odds BK 7-0(4-0)
Rosenborg - Hamarkameratene 2-1(1-1)
FK Haugesund - FK Jerv 3-1(1-0)
Kristiansund - Molde FK 2-3(2-2)
Lillestrøm - Tromsø IL 1-1(0-1)
Sandefjord - Viking 2-2(2-0)
Strømsgodset - Sarpsborg 08 3-1(2-0)
Vålerenga - Aalesunds FK 4-0(0-0)

### Round 18 [12-14.08.2022]
Molde FK - Odds BK 3-0(2-0) [11.05.2022]
Viking - Strømsgodset 0-0 [12.05.2022]
Sandefjord - Rosenborg 2-5(2-2)
Sarpsborg 08 - FK Bodø/Glimt 1-4(0-2)
Aalesunds FK - FK Haugesund 1-2(0-0)
FK Jerv - Lillestrøm 1-0(0-0)
Tromsø IL - Kristiansund 2-1(1-0)
Hamarkameratene - Vålerenga 1-1(0-1)

### Round 19 [20-21.08.2022]
FK Bodø/Glimt - Hamarkameratene 2-2(1-0)
Odds BK - Sarpsborg 08 1-0(1-0)
FK Haugesund - Molde FK 0-1(0-1)
Lillestrøm - Sandefjord 3-0(1-0)
Strømsgodset - FK Jerv 6-0(1-0)
Vålerenga - Tromsø IL 1-0(0-0)
Rosenborg - Aalesunds FK 2-1(1-1)
Kristiansund - Viking 2-1(2-1) [31.08.2022]

### Round 20 [27-28.08.2022]
FK Jerv - FK Bodø/Glimt 0-2(0-1)
Sandefjord - Strømsgodset 2-2(0-0)
Aalesunds FK - Odds BK 1-1(1-1)
Hamarkameratene - FK Haugesund 1-0(1-0)
Lillestrøm - Kristiansund 1-1(1-0)
Molde FK - Sarpsborg 08 4-1(3-1)
Viking - Vålerenga 1-2(0-1)
Tromsø IL - Rosenborg 4-3(2-3)

### Round 21 [03-04.09.2022]
FK Bodø/Glimt - Molde FK 1-4(1-2)
FK Haugesund - Tromsø IL 2-1(1-1)
Kristiansund - Sandefjord 3-1(2-0)
Odds BK - FK Jerv 2-1(2-1)
Rosenborg - Viking 4-1(2-0)
Sarpsborg 08 - Hamarkameratene 2-1(0-1)
Strømsgodset - Aalesunds FK 1-2(0-2)
Vålerenga - Lillestrøm 3-1(2-0)

| Round 22 [10-11.09.2022] |
|---|
| Sandefjord - Odds BK 1-3(1-1) |
| Lillestrøm - Strømsgodset 2-1(2-0) |
| Aalesunds FK - Sarpsborg 08 1-3(0-2) |
| FK Jerv - Molde FK 2-4(0-1) |
| Hamarkameratene - Viking 1-2(1-1) |
| Kristiansund - Vålerenga 3-2(1-1) |
| Tromsø IL - FK Bodø/Glimt 3-2(2-0) |
| FK Haugesund - Rosenborg 2-1(1-1) |

| Round 23 [17-18.09.2022] |
|---|
| Odds BK - Hamarkameratene 2-0(0-0) |
| FK Bodø/Glimt - FK Haugesund 1-1(0-0) |
| Rosenborg - Lillestrøm 3-1(2-0) |
| Sarpsborg 08 - FK Jerv 4-3(2-3) |
| Strømsgodset - Kristiansund 4-1(2-0) |
| Vålerenga - Sandefjord 4-0(2-0) |
| Viking - Tromsø IL 2-2(1-0) |
| Molde FK - Aalesunds FK 3-0(1-0) |

| Round 24 [01-02.10.2022] |
|---|
| Tromsø IL - Molde FK 0-1(0-1) |
| Lillestrøm - FK Bodø/Glimt 1-4(1-1) |
| Vålerenga - Strømsgodset 4-0(4-0) |
| Aalesunds FK - Viking 2-1(0-0) |
| FK Haugesund - Odds BK 2-2(1-1) |
| Hamarkameratene - FK Jerv 2-1(1-0) |
| Sandefjord - Sarpsborg 08 1-1(1-0) |
| Kristiansund - Rosenborg 4-4(3-1) |

| Round 25 [08-09.10.2022] |
|---|
| Sarpsborg 08 - FK Haugesund 4-0(3-0) |
| FK Bodø/Glimt - Sandefjord 4-1(0-1) |
| Molde FK - Hamarkameratene 5-0(4-0) |
| Odds BK - Kristiansund 1-1(1-1) |
| Strømsgodset - Tromsø IL 1-2(1-1) |
| Viking - Lillestrøm 0-3(0-1) |
| Rosenborg - Vålerenga 3-0(2-0) |
| FK Jerv - Aalesunds FK 0-1(0-1) [19.10.2022] |

| Round 26 [15-16.10.2022] |
|---|
| Tromsø IL - Odds BK 3-2(1-1) |
| Rosenborg - Strømsgodset 3-0(2-0) |
| Aalesunds FK - Hamarkameratene 0-0 |
| Kristiansund - FK Haugesund 0-1(0-1) |
| Sandefjord - FK Jerv 1-2(1-2) |
| Vålerenga - FK Bodø/Glimt 0-6(0-3) |
| Viking - Sarpsborg 08 0-1(0-1) |
| Lillestrøm - Molde FK 0-1(0-0) |

| Round 27 [22-23.10.2022] |
|---|
| Hamarkameratene - Strømsgodset 1-1(1-1) |
| Odds BK - Vålerenga 2-1(1-0) |
| Aalesunds FK - Sandefjord 1-0(0-0) |
| FK Bodø/Glimt - Kristiansund 5-0(2-0) |
| FK Haugesund - Lillestrøm 0-1(0-1) |
| FK Jerv - Viking 2-2(0-0) |
| Sarpsborg 08 - Tromsø IL 1-1(0-0) |
| Molde FK - Rosenborg 2-1(1-0) |

| Round 28 [29-30.10.2022] |
|---|
| Strømsgodset - FK Haugesund 1-2(1-1) |
| Vålerenga - Sarpsborg 08 3-3(2-2) |
| Kristiansund - Aalesunds FK 4-0(2-0) |
| Lillestrøm - Odds BK 0-2(0-0) |
| Rosenborg - FK Bodø/Glimt 3-2(0-1) |
| Sandefjord - Hamarkameratene 1-2(0-1) |
| Tromsø IL - FK Jerv 2-2(0-0) |
| Viking - Molde FK 1-4(0-2) |

| Round 29 [06.11.2022] |
|---|
| Aalesunds FK - Lillestrøm 2-1(1-1) |
| FK Bodø/Glimt - Viking 5-4(2-2) |
| FK Haugesund - Vålerenga 1-1(0-0) |
| FK Jerv - Rosenborg 2-4(0-2) |
| Hamarkameratene - Tromsø IL 1-2(0-0) |
| Molde FK - Sandefjord 2-1(1-0) |
| Odds BK - Strømsgodset 5-1(2-1) |
| Sarpsborg 08 - Kristiansund 2-2(1-2) |

| Round 30 [13.11.2022] |
|---|
| Kristiansund - FK Jerv 1-1(1-1) |
| Lillestrøm - Hamarkameratene 3-1(1-1) |
| Rosenborg - Sarpsborg 08 2-3(1-2) |
| Sandefjord - FK Haugesund 2-2(0-2) |
| Strømsgodset - FK Bodø/Glimt 2-4(1-1) |
| Tromsø IL - Aalesunds FK 2-2(1-2) |
| Vålerenga - Molde FK 1-2(1-0) |
| Viking - Odds BK 1-1(1-0) |

## Final Standings

| | | Total | | | | | | | Home | | | | | Away | | | | |
|---|---|---|---|---|---|---|---|---|---|---|---|---|---|---|---|---|---|---|
| 1. | **Molde FK** | 30 | 25 | 3 | 2 | 71 - 25 | 78 | 12 | 1 | 2 | 39 - 13 | 13 | 2 | 0 | 32 - 12 |
| 2. | FK Bodø/Glimt | 30 | 18 | 6 | 6 | 86 - 41 | 60 | 8 | 6 | 1 | 47 - 20 | 10 | 0 | 5 | 39 - 21 |
| 3. | Rosenborg BK Trondheim | 30 | 16 | 8 | 6 | 69 - 44 | 56 | 12 | 2 | 1 | 38 - 15 | 4 | 6 | 5 | 31 - 29 |
| 4. | Lillestrøm SK | 30 | 16 | 5 | 9 | 49 - 34 | 53 | 9 | 2 | 4 | 24 - 13 | 7 | 3 | 5 | 25 - 21 |
| 5. | Odds BK Skien | 30 | 13 | 6 | 11 | 43 - 45 | 45 | 8 | 1 | 6 | 26 - 22 | 5 | 5 | 5 | 17 - 23 |
| 6. | Vålerenga Fotball Oslo | 30 | 13 | 5 | 12 | 52 - 49 | 44 | 9 | 2 | 4 | 31 - 21 | 4 | 3 | 8 | 21 - 28 |
| 7. | Tromsø IL | 30 | 10 | 13 | 7 | 46 - 49 | 43 | 8 | 5 | 2 | 29 - 23 | 2 | 8 | 5 | 17 - 26 |
| 8. | Sarpsborg 08 FF | 30 | 12 | 5 | 13 | 57 - 54 | 41 | 6 | 3 | 6 | 27 - 24 | 6 | 2 | 7 | 30 - 30 |
| 9. | Aalesunds FK | 30 | 10 | 9 | 11 | 32 - 45 | 39 | 6 | 5 | 4 | 17 - 17 | 4 | 4 | 7 | 15 - 28 |
| 10. | FK Haugesund | 30 | 10 | 8 | 12 | 42 - 46 | 38 | 6 | 4 | 5 | 24 - 22 | 4 | 4 | 7 | 18 - 24 |
| 11. | Viking FK Stavanger | 30 | 9 | 8 | 13 | 48 - 54 | 35 | 5 | 5 | 5 | 21 - 19 | 4 | 3 | 8 | 27 - 35 |
| 12. | Strømsgodset IF Drammen | 30 | 9 | 6 | 15 | 44 - 55 | 33 | 7 | 2 | 6 | 32 - 25 | 2 | 4 | 9 | 12 - 30 |
| 13. | Hamarkameratene | 30 | 6 | 13 | 11 | 33 - 43 | 31 | 4 | 6 | 5 | 17 - 17 | 2 | 7 | 6 | 16 - 26 |
| 14. | Sandefjord Fotball (Relegation Play-offs) | 30 | 6 | 6 | 18 | 42 - 68 | 24 | 1 | 6 | 8 | 23 - 35 | 5 | 0 | 10 | 19 - 33 |
| 15. | Kristiansund BK (Relegated) | 30 | 5 | 8 | 17 | 37 - 60 | 23 | 4 | 5 | 6 | 27 - 29 | 1 | 3 | 11 | 10 - 31 |
| 16. | FK Jerv Grimstad (Relegated) | 30 | 5 | 5 | 20 | 30 - 69 | 20 | 4 | 2 | 9 | 15 - 29 | 1 | 3 | 11 | 15 - 40 |

| Top goalscorers: | |
|---|---|
| **25 Amahl William D'vaz Pellegrino** | **FK Bodø/Glimt** |
| 16 Hugo Vegard Vetlesen | FK Bodø/Glimt |
| 15 David Datro Fofana (CIV) | Molde FK |
| 15 Tobias Heintz | Sarpsborg 08 FF |
| 15 Casper Tengstedt (DEN) | Rosenborg BK Trondheim |

## Relegation Play-offs [16-19.11.2022]

Sandefjord Fotball - Kongsvinger IL Toppfotball        4-0(2-0)        1-2(1-0)

Sandefjord Fotball remains at first level for 2023.

## NATIONAL CUP
### Norgesmesterskapet 2022/2023

### Third Round [29-30.06./10.08./17.08./28.09./12.10.2022]

| | | | | |
|---|---|---|---|---|
| Byåsen Toppfotball - Sandefjord Fotball | 1-2(0-1) | KFUM-Kameratene Oslo - Sogndal Fotball | 1-1 aet; 4-5 pen |
| Kjelsås Fotball - Skeid Oslo | 3-3 aet; 3-4 pen | Sandnes Ulf - Rosenborg BK Trondheim | 0-2(0-1) |
| Moss FK - IK Start Kristiansand | 0-3(0-1) | Ullensaker/Kisa IL - Ranheim IL Trondheim | 0-2(0-1) |
| Sotra SK - FK Haugesund | 0-1(0-0) | SK Brann Bergen - Fredrikstad FK | 6-0(2-0) |
| FK Gjøvik-Lyn - Stabæk Fotball Bærum | 0-7(0-3) | FK Jerv Grimstad - Odds BK Skien | 2-3(1-2,2-2) |
| Eidsvold Turnforening - Molde FK | 1-4(1-1) | Hamarkameratene - Tromsø IL | 0-0 aet; 5-6 pen |
| Lillestrøm SK - Aalesunds FK | 1-0(1-0) | Tromsdalen UIL - Bryne FK | 0-1(0-0) |
| Vålerenga Fotball Oslo - FK Bodø/Glimt | 0-1(0-0) | Viking FK Stavanger - Kristiansund BK | 1-0(0-0,0-0) |

### 1/8-Finals [05/12.03.2023]

| | | | | |
|---|---|---|---|---|
| Ranheim IL Trondheim - FK Bodø/Glimt | 0-4(0-1) | Sogndal Fotball - Lillestrøm SK | 1-2(1-1) |
| SK Brann Bergen - FK Haugesund | 3-1(2-0) | IK Start Kristiansand - Tromsø IL | 1-1 aet; 4-5 pen |
| Stabæk Fotball Bærum - Bryne FK | 5-0(1-0) | Sandefjord Fotball - Odds BK Skien | 4-1(4-0) |
| Skeid Oslo - Molde FK | 1-3(1-1) | Viking FK Stavanger - Rosenborg BK Trondheim | 2-0(0-0) |

### Quarter-Finals [18-19.03.2023]

| | | | | |
|---|---|---|---|---|
| Stabæk Fotball Bærum - Molde FK | 1-1 aet; 9-8 pen | Tromsø IL - Lillestrøm SK | 2-3(1-0,2-2) |
| FK Bodø/Glimt - Viking FK Stavanger | 5-3(0-2) | SK Brann Bergen - Sandefjord Fotball | 3-0(3-0) |

### Semi-Finals [26.04.2023]

| | | | | |
|---|---|---|---|---|
| Stabæk Fotball Bærum - SK Brann Bergen | 0-2(0-1) | Lillestrøm SK - FK Bodø/Glimt | 1-0(1-0) |

### Final

20.05.2023; Ullevaal Stadion, Oslo; Referee: Tore Hansen; Attendance: 25,532
**SK Brann Bergen - Lillestrøm SK**                                                        **2-0(1-0)**

**SK Brann Bergen**: Mathias Dyngeland, Svenn Crone, Japhet Sery Larsen, Ruben Kristiansen (77.Fredrik Pallesen Knudsen), David Møller Wolfe, Mathias Rasmussen, Sivert Heltne Nilsen (Cap), Felix Horn Myhre, Ole Didrik Blomberg (90+3.Thore Baardsen Pedersen), Bård Finne (90+2.Niklas Fernando Nygård Castro), Frederik Lindbøg Børsting (77.Niklas Jensen Wassberg). Trainer: Eirik Horneland.

**Lillestrøm SK**: Mads Christiansen, Espen Garnås (70.Magnus Knudsen), Lunan Ruben Gabrielsen, Vetle Skjærvik, Lars Mogstad Ranger (28.Eskil Edh), Vetle Dragsnes (79.Andreas Aalen Vindheim), Ylldren Ibrahimaj (70.Kristoffer Tønnessen), Vebjørn Alvestad Hoff, Gjermund Åsen (Cap) (70.Tobias Hammer Svendsen), Thomas Lehne Olsen, Akor Jerome Adams. Trainer: Geir Bakke.

**Goals:** 1-0 Ole Didrik Blomberg (16), 2-0 Bård Finne (62).

## THE CLUBS 2022

### Aalesunds Fotballklubb

| | |
|---|---|
| **Founded**: | 25.06.1914 |
| **Stadium**: | Color Line Stadion, Ålesund (10,778) |
| **Trainer**: | Lars Arne Nilsen          06.04.1964 |

| Goalkeepers: | DOB | M | (s) | G |
|---|---|---|---|---|
| Sten Grytebust | 25.10.1989 | 30 | | |
| **Defenders:** | **DOB** | **M** | **(s)** | **G** |
| Alexander Juel Andersen (DEN) | 29.01.1991 | 19 | (1) | |
| David Fällman (SWE) | 04.02.1990 | 26 | (2) | |
| Petar Golubović (SRB) | 13.07.1994 | 23 | (2) | 1 |
| Nikolai Hopland | 24.07.2004 | 9 | (8) | 1 |
| John Shoguto Kitolano | 18.10.1999 | 5 | (3) | |
| Isak Dybvik Määttä | 19.09.2001 | 15 | | 3 |
| Jeppe Moe | 03.08.1995 | | (8) | |
| Simen Rafn | 16.02.1992 | 20 | (8) | 1 |
| Besim Šerbečić (BIH) | 01.05.1998 | 26 | | |
| **Midfielders:** | **DOB** | **M** | **(s)** | **G** |
| Kristoffer Barmen | 19.08.1993 | 20 | (6) | 2 |
| Dario Čanađija (CRO) | 17.04.1994 | 20 | (1) | 1 |

| | DOB | M | (s) | G |
|---|---|---|---|---|
| Fredrik Haugen | 13.06.1992 | 7 | (11) | |
| Torbjørn Kallevåg | 21.08.1993 | 11 | (15) | 2 |
| Gilbert Koomson (GHA) | 09.09.1994 | 5 | (5) | 1 |
| Henrik Melland | 29.03.2005 | | (1) | |
| Erikson Spinola Lima „Nenass" (CPV) | 05.07.1995 | 24 | (5) | 2 |
| Erlend Segberg | 12.04.1997 | 10 | (5) | |
| Oscar Solnørdal | 23.10.2002 | | (6) | 1 |
| **Forwards:** | **DOB** | **M** | **(s)** | **G** |
| Alexander Ammitzbøll (DEN) | 17.02.1999 | 2 | (7) | |
| Mamadou Diaw (SEN) | 02.01.2001 | | (7) | |
| Moses Ebiye (NGA) | 28.04.1997 | 10 | (2) | 5 |
| Sigurd Haugen | 17.07.1997 | 13 | | 7 |
| Björn Martin Kristiansen | 04.05.2002 | 1 | (4) | |
| Simen Nordli | 25.12.1999 | 23 | (6) | 3 |
| Kristoffer Ødemarksbakken | 05.12.1995 | 11 | (17) | 2 |

## Fotballklubben Bodø/Glimt

Founded: 19.09.2016
Stadium: Aspmyra Stadion, Bodø (5,635)
Trainer: Kjetil Knutsen     02.10.1968

| Goalkeepers: | DOB | M | (s) | G |
|---|---|---|---|---|
| Nikita Haikin (RUS) | 11.07.1995 | 27 | | |
| Julian Rekdahl Faye Lund | 20.05.1999 | 3 | (1) | |
| **Defenders:** | **DOB** | **M** | **(s)** | **G** |
| Isak Amundsen | 14.10.1999 | 9 | (5) | 2 |
| Marius Høibråten | 23.01.1995 | 27 | (1) | 1 |
| Sigurd Kvile | 26.02.2000 | | (1) | |
| Marius Lode | 11.03.1993 | 6 | (4) | |
| Brede Moe | 15.12.1991 | 16 | | 1 |
| Alfons Sampsted (ISL) | 06.04.1998 | 30 | | 1 |
| Japhet Sery Larsen (DEN) | 10.04.2000 | 5 | (5) | |
| Brice Wembangomo | 18.12.1996 | 27 | (1) | 2 |
| **Midfielders:** | **DOB** | **M** | **(s)** | **G** |
| Patrick Berg | 24.11.1997 | 10 | | 1 |
| Albert Grønbæk Erlykke | 23.05.2001 | 9 | (3) | 2 |
| Sondre Fet | 17.01.1997 | 1 | | |
| Elias Hagen | 20.01.2000 | 17 | (5) | |
| Anders Konradsen | 18.07.1990 | | (7) | |

| | DOB | M | (s) | G |
|---|---|---|---|---|
| Morten Konradsen | 03.05.1996 | | (4) | |
| Ulrik Saltnes | 10.11.1992 | 23 | (4) | 6 |
| Fredrik Sjøvold | 17.08.2003 | | (4) | |
| Ask Tjærandsen-Skau | 14.01.2001 | | (4) | |
| Hugo Vegard Vetlesen | 29.02.2000 | 28 | (1) | 16 |
| Gaute Høberg Vetti | 02.09.1998 | 2 | (6) | |
| **Forwards:** | **DOB** | **M** | **(s)** | **G** |
| Victor Okoh Boniface (NGA) | 23.12.2000 | 5 | (10) | 6 |
| Runar Espejord | 26.02.1996 | 19 | (8) | 12 |
| Gilbert Koomson (GHA) | 09.09.1994 | 4 | (10) | |
| Joel Mugisha Mvuka | 12.11.2002 | 15 | (11) | 2 |
| Lasse Nordås | 10.02.2002 | 1 | | |
| Amahl William D'vaz Pellegrino | 18.06.1990 | 23 | (4) | 25 |
| Lars-Jørgen Salvesen | 19.02.1996 | 5 | (8) | 2 |
| Ola Selvaag Solbakken | 07.09.1998 | 12 | (3) | 4 |
| Sondre Sørli | 30.10.1995 | 6 | (11) | 1 |
| Nino Žugelj (SVN) | 25.04.2000 | | (7) | 1 |

## Hamarkameratene

Founded: 10.06.1918
Stadium: Briskeby Stadion, Hamar (7,800)
Trainer: Jakob Saldern Stein Michelsen     30.09.1980

| Goalkeepers: | DOB | M | (s) | G |
|---|---|---|---|---|
| Nicholas George Hagen Godoy (GUA) | 02.08.1996 | 23 | | |
| Lars Jendal | 24.04.1999 | 7 | | |
| **Defenders:** | **DOB** | **M** | **(s)** | **G** |
| Clément Bayiha (CAN) | 08.03.1999 | 2 | (6) | |
| Julian Fletcher Dunn-Johnson (CAN) | 11.07.2000 | 3 | (1) | |
| Fernán José Faerrón Tristán (CRC) | 22.08.2000 | 6 | (5) | |
| Vegard Kongsro | 07.08.1998 | 22 | (4) | 2 |
| Markus Lund Nakkim | 21.07.1996 | 4 | (1) | |
| Hasan Kuruçay (TUR) | 31.08.1997 | 28 | | 4 |
| Amin Nouri | 10.01.1990 | 11 | (9) | 1 |
| Halvor Rødølen Opsahl | 08.10.2002 | 23 | (1) | |
| Vetle Skjærvik | 15.09.2000 | 25 | (1) | |
| **Midfielders:** | **DOB** | **M** | **(s)** | **G** |
| Mørten Bjørlo | 04.10.1995 | 11 | (5) | 1 |
| Eduards Daškevičs (LVA) | 12.07.2002 | | (8) | |

| | DOB | M | (s) | G |
|---|---|---|---|---|
| Kristian Eriksen | 18.07.1995 | 16 | | 4 |
| Kobe Hernández-Foster (USA) | 26.06.2002 | 10 | (9) | 1 |
| Aleksander Melgalvis | 10.08.1989 | 25 | (1) | 4 |
| Kristian Lønstad Onsrud | 22.07.1994 | 19 | (4) | 3 |
| Emil Sildnes | 29.01.1993 | 6 | (14) | |
| Fredrik Sjølstad | 29.03.1994 | 25 | (2) | 2 |
| Oliver Sørensen Jensen (DEN) | 10.03.2002 | 3 | (3) | |
| Benjamin Thoresen Faraas | 08.09.2005 | | (10) | 1 |
| **Forwards:** | **DOB** | **M** | **(s)** | **G** |
| Jonas Enkerud | 25.04.1990 | 25 | (4) | 4 |
| Rilwan Olanrewaju Hassan (NGA) | 09.02.1991 | 1 | (5) | |
| Pål Alexander Kirkevold | 10.11.1990 | 24 | (3) | 4 |
| Victor Stange Lind | 12.07.2003 | 6 | (1) | |
| Marcus Pedersen | 08.06.1990 | 3 | (7) | |
| Yuriy Yakovenko (UKR) | 03.09.1993 | 2 | (10) | 1 |

## Fotballklubben Haugesund

Founded: 28.10.1993
Stadium: Haugesund Sparebank Arena, Haugesund (8,754)
Trainer: Jostein Grindhaug     20.02.1973

| Goalkeepers: | DOB | M | (s) | G |
|---|---|---|---|---|
| Egil Selvik | 30.07.1997 | 30 | | |
| **Defenders:** | **DOB** | **M** | **(s)** | **G** |
| Anders Bærtelsen (DEN) | 09.05.2000 | 28 | | |
| Ulrik Fredriksen | 17.06.1999 | 9 | (5) | |
| Thore Pedersen | 11.08.1996 | 14 | (7) | |
| Søren Reese (DEN) | 29.07.1993 | 29 | | 3 |
| Nikolas Walstad | 14.02.1997 | 19 | (8) | 1 |
| **Midfielders:** | **DOB** | **M** | **(s)** | **G** |
| Bruno Miguel Santos Leite (POR) | 26.03.1995 | | (8) | 1 |
| Magnus Christensen (DEN) | 20.08.1997 | 10 | (4) | 1 |
| Sander Håvik Innvær | 11.10.2004 | | (1) | |
| Kevin Martin Krygård | 17.05.2000 | 30 | | |
| Torje Naustdal | 26.04.2000 | 2 | (5) | |

| | DOB | M | (s) | G |
|---|---|---|---|---|
| Vegard Solheim | 10.08.2004 | | (4) | |
| Peter Therkildsen (DEN) | 13.06.1998 | 29 | | 2 |
| Christos Zafeiris | 23.02.2003 | 29 | | 4 |
| **Forwards:** | **DOB** | **M** | **(s)** | **G** |
| Julius Eskesen (DEN) | 16.03.1999 | 17 | (9) | 3 |
| Hilary Chukwah Gong (NGA) | 10.10.1998 | | (12) | 1 |
| Joacim Holtan | 08.08.1998 | 1 | (13) | |
| Alioune Ndour (SEN) | 21.10.1997 | 18 | | 9 |
| Bilal Njie | 13.06.1998 | 13 | (10) | 6 |
| Martin Samuelsen | 17.04.1997 | 6 | (12) | 1 |
| Mads Sande | 22.03.1998 | 25 | (4) | 6 |
| Alexander Søderlund | 03.08.1987 | 21 | (5) | 4 |
| Sebastian Tounekti (TUN) | 13.07.2002 | | (5) | |

## Fotballklubben Jerv Grimstad

Founded: 05.08.1921
Stadium: J.J. Ugland Stadion – Levermyr, Grimstad (3,300)
Trainer: Arne Sandstø     21.10.1966

| Goalkeepers: | DOB | M | (s) | G |
|---|---|---|---|---|
| Øystein Øvretveit | 25.06.1994 | 25 | | |
| Amund Wichne | 12.05.1997 | 5 | | |
| **Defenders:** | **DOB** | **M** | **(s)** | **G** |
| Daniel Michael Rodriguez Arrocha (DEN) | 09.01.1995 | 12 | (3) | |
| Henrik Bredeli | 01.04.1998 | 9 | (3) | |
| Mathias Haarup (DEN) | 10.02.1996 | 23 | (5) | 1 |
| Ole Martin Kolskogen | 20.01.2001 | 22 | (2) | |
| Iman Mafi | 09.07.1994 | 8 | (10) | |
| Dylan Teddy Ngallot Mboumbouni (CTA) | 20.02.1996 | 6 | (2) | |
| John Olav Norheim | 05.04.1995 | 29 | | 2 |
| Kristian Novak | 19.10.1998 | | (8) | |
| Erik Tore Sandberg | 27.02.2000 | 14 | (12) | |
| Torje Wichne | 12.05.1997 | 28 | (1) | |
| **Midfielders:** | **DOB** | **M** | **(s)** | **G** |
| Erik Brenden | 07.01.1994 | 20 | (1) | 3 |

| | DOB | M | (s) | G |
|---|---|---|---|---|
| Leandro Fernandes (NED) | 25.12.1999 | 12 | (3) | |
| Bendik Kristiansen | 20.11.2002 | | (1) | |
| Thomas Ness | 05.10.1998 | | (4) | |
| Ask Tjærandsen-Skau | 14.01.2001 | 7 | (3) | 1 |
| Mikael Ugland | 24.01.2000 | 6 | (15) | 5 |
| Mathias Wichmann (DEN) | 06.08.1991 | 27 | (2) | 1 |
| **Forwards:** | **DOB** | **M** | **(s)** | **G** |
| Rodney Antwi (NED) | 03.11.1995 | 2 | (6) | |
| Jeremy Cijntje (CUW) | 08.01.1998 | 3 | (5) | |
| Amadou Diallo (GUI) | 21.06.1994 | 14 | (14) | 3 |
| Luis Willis Alves Furtado (CPV) | 04.09.1997 | 13 | (5) | 2 |
| Daniel Håkans (FIN) | 26.10.2000 | 7 | | 1 |
| Erlend Hustad | 03.01.1997 | 13 | (8) | |
| Felix Schröter (GER) | 23.01.1996 | 3 | (9) | 5 |
| Doğuhan Aral Şimşir (DEN) | 19.06.2002 | 13 | (7) | 3 |
| Peter Wilson (SWE) | 09.10.1996 | 9 | (1) | 2 |

## Kristiansund Ballklubb

**Founded**: 02.09.2003
**Stadium**: Kristiansund Stadion, Kristiansund (4,444)
**Trainer**: Christian Michelsen  14.03.1976

| Goalkeepers: | DOB | M | (s) | G |
|---|---|---|---|---|
| Mor Mbaye (SEN) | 03.01.1996 | 7 | | |
| Sean McDermott (IRL) | 30.05.1993 | 23 | | |
| **Defenders:** | **DOB** | **M** | **(s)** | **G** |
| Christoffer Aasbak | 22.07.1993 | 14 | | 1 |
| Marius Alm | 03.12.1997 | 2 | (1) | |
| Isaac Annan (GHA) | 09.09.2001 | 1 | (5) | |
| Amin Soleiman Askar | 01.10.1985 | 5 | (14) | |
| Aliou Coly (SEN) | 10.12.1992 | 8 | (6) | |
| Henrik Gjesdal | 19.07.1993 | | (8) | |
| Nikolai Søyset Hopland | 24.07.2004 | 1 | (1) | |
| Andreas Hopmark | 06.07.1991 | 21 | (2) | 2 |
| Sebastian Jarl | 11.01.2000 | 20 | (4) | |
| Sigurd Kvile | 26.02.2000 | 3 | (1) | |
| Snorre Strand Nilsen | 14.01.1997 | 30 | | 2 |
| Martin Sjølstad | 09.07.2000 | | (2) | |
| Dan Peter Ulvestad | 04.04.1989 | 18 | | 1 |
| Max Normann Williamsen | 24.07.2003 | 16 | (9) | 2 |

| Midfielders: | DOB | M | (s) | G |
|---|---|---|---|---|
| David Agbo (GHA) | 01.04.2000 | | (12) | |
| Heine Gikling Bruseth | 06.04.2004 | | (1) | |
| Paweł Chrupałła | 16.03.2003 | | (9) | |
| Amidou Diop (SEN) | 25.02.1992 | 28 | | 4 |
| Jesper Isaksen | 13.10.1999 | 15 | (5) | |
| Liridon Kalludra (SWE) | 05.11.1991 | 15 | (13) | 1 |
| Sander Erik Kartum | 03.10.1995 | 24 | (4) | 2 |
| **Forwards:** | **DOB** | **M** | **(s)** | **G** |
| Bendik Bye | 09.03.1990 | 20 | (9) | 9 |
| Torgil Gjertsen | 12.03.1992 | 21 | (9) | 1 |
| Moses Mawa | 04.08.1996 | 5 | (2) | |
| Faris Pemi Moumbagna (CMR) | 01.07.2000 | 11 | (3) | 5 |
| Agon Mucolli (ALB) | 26.09.1998 | 5 | (4) | 1 |
| Mikkel Rakneberg | 28.02.2002 | | (3) | |
| Oskar Sivertsen | 15.02.2004 | | (2) | |
| Marius Weidel | 13.06.2005 | | (1) | |
| Brynjólfur Darri Willumsson (ISL) | 12.08.2000 | 17 | (8) | 4 |

## Lillestrøm Sportsklubb

**Founded**: 02.04.1917
**Stadium**: Åråsen Stadion, Lillestrøm (11,500)
**Trainer**: Geir Bakke  23.10.1969

| Goalkeepers: | DOB | M | (s) | G |
|---|---|---|---|---|
| Mads Christiansen | 21.10.2000 | 30 | | 1 |
| **Defenders:** | **DOB** | **M** | **(s)** | **G** |
| Vetle Dragsnes | 06.02.1994 | 30 | | 5 |
| Espen Garnås | 31.12.1994 | 27 | (1) | 2 |
| Igoh Ogbu (NGA) | 08.02.2000 | 28 | | 3 |
| Tom Peder Pettersson (SWE) | 25.03.1990 | 14 | (2) | 3 |
| Lars Mogstad Ranger | 12.03.1999 | 18 | (4) | |
| Colin Rösler | 22.04.2000 | 9 | (5) | |
| Philip Slørdahl | 14.11.2000 | | (1) | |
| **Midfielders:** | **DOB** | **M** | **(s)** | **G** |
| Gjermund Åsen | 22.05.1991 | 22 | (4) | 2 |
| Eskil Edh | 04.08.2002 | 17 | (2) | 1 |
| Frederik Holst (DEN) | 24.09.1994 | 3 | (10) | |

| | DOB | M | (s) | G |
|---|---|---|---|---|
| Kaan Kairinen (FIN) | 22.12.1998 | 14 | (8) | 1 |
| Magnus Knudsen | 15.06.2001 | 26 | (1) | 3 |
| Marius Lundemo | 11.04.1994 | | (3) | |
| Ifeanyi Matthew (NGA) | 20.01.1997 | 29 | | 2 |
| Henrik Langaas Skogvold | 14.07.2004 | | (4) | |
| **Forwards:** | **DOB** | **M** | **(s)** | **G** |
| Akor Jerome Adams (NGA) | 29.01.2000 | 15 | (8) | 8 |
| Hólmbert Aron Friðjónsson (ISL) | 19.04.1993 | 8 | (19) | 5 |
| Pål André Helland | 04.01.1990 | 2 | (12) | 2 |
| Ylldren Ibrahimaj (KOS) | 24.12.1995 | 27 | (3) | 4 |
| Thomas Lehne Olsen | 29.06.1991 | 10 | (1) | 5 |
| Elias Sebastian Solberg | 03.03.2004 | | (1) | |
| Tobias Hammer Svendsen | 31.08.1999 | 1 | (13) | |
| Doğuhan Aral Şimşir (DEN) | 19.06.2002 | | (6) | |

## Molde Fotballklubb

**Founded**: 19.06.1911
**Stadium**: Aker Stadion, Molde (11,249)
**Trainer**: Erling Moe  22.07.1970

| Goalkeepers: | DOB | M | (s) | G |
|---|---|---|---|---|
| Jacob Karlstrøm | 09.01.1997 | 26 | | |
| Oliver Petersen | 26.09.2001 | 4 | | |
| **Defenders:** | **DOB** | **M** | **(s)** | **G** |
| Martin Bjørnbak | 22.03.1992 | 15 | (2) | |
| Anders Rønne Børset | 22.02.2006 | | (1) | |
| Eirik Haugan | 27.08.1997 | 22 | (4) | 1 |
| Kristoffer Haugen | 21.02.1994 | 17 | (2) | 3 |
| Erling Knudtzon | 15.12.1988 | 13 | (13) | 2 |
| Martin Linnes | 20.09.1991 | 23 | | 4 |
| Mathias Fjørtoft Løvik | 06.12.2003 | 9 | (4) | |
| Birk Risa | 13.02.1998 | 26 | | |
| Benjamin Tiedemann Hansen (DEN) | 07.02.1994 | 23 | (2) | |
| **Midfielders:** | **DOB** | **M** | **(s)** | **G** |
| Johan Bakke | 01.04.2004 | 1 | (7) | |

| | DOB | M | (s) | G |
|---|---|---|---|---|
| Emil Breivik | 11.06.2000 | 22 | (5) | 1 |
| Magnus Wolff Eikrem | 08.08.1990 | 16 | (5) | 6 |
| Kristian Eriksen | 18.07.1995 | 10 | (3) | 2 |
| Magnus Grødem | 14.08.1998 | 15 | (12) | 7 |
| Etzaz Hussain | 27.01.1993 | 9 | (9) | 2 |
| Markus André Kaasa | 15.07.1997 | 17 | (8) | 9 |
| Sivert Mannsverk | 08.05.2002 | 22 | (3) | 1 |
| Niklas Ødegård | 29.03.2004 | 1 | (10) | 1 |
| **Forwards:** | **DOB** | **M** | **(s)** | **G** |
| Eirik Andersen | 21.09.1992 | 3 | (1) | 1 |
| Mathis Bolly (CIV) | 14.11.1990 | | (9) | |
| Ola Brynhildsen | 27.04.1999 | 12 | (7) | 11 |
| David Datro Fofana (CIV) | 22.12.2002 | 19 | (5) | 15 |
| Rafik Zekhnini | 12.01.1998 | 5 | (10) | 2 |

## Odds Ballklubb Skien

**Founded**: 31.03.1894
**Stadium**: Skagerak Arena, Skien (11,767)
**Trainer**: Pål Arne Johansen  16.02.1977

| Goalkeepers: | DOB | M | (s) | G |
|---|---|---|---|---|
| Leopold Wahlstedt (SWE) | 04.07.1999 | 30 | | |
| **Defenders:** | **DOB** | **M** | **(s)** | **G** |
| Josef Brian Baccay | 29.04.2001 | 18 | (5) | |
| Odin Luras Bjørtuft | 19.12.1998 | 27 | | 1 |
| Kevin Egell-Johnsen | 13.05.2000 | 1 | (2) | |
| Steffen Hagen | 08.03.1986 | 28 | | |
| John Kitolano | 18.10.1999 | 1 | (4) | |
| Magnus Lekven | 13.01.1988 | 1 | (5) | |
| Ivan Mesík (SVK) | 01.06.2001 | 5 | (5) | |
| Espen Ruud | 26.02.1984 | 23 | (3) | 3 |
| Jesper Svenungsen Skau | 19.05.2003 | | (3) | |
| Gilli Rólantsson Sørensen (FRO) | 11.08.1992 | 16 | (6) | |
| **Midfielders:** | **DOB** | **M** | **(s)** | **G** |
| Vebjørn Hoff | 13.02.1996 | 11 | | 3 |
| Filip Rønningen Jørgensen | 27.05.2002 | 25 | (3) | 3 |

| | DOB | M | (s) | G |
|---|---|---|---|---|
| Joshua Kitolano | 03.08.2001 | 16 | | |
| Salomon Owusu (GHA) | 28.10.1995 | 29 | (1) | 1 |
| Thomas Grevsnes Rekdal | 16.03.2001 | 1 | (2) | |
| **Forwards:** | **DOB** | **M** | **(s)** | **G** |
| Syver Aas | 15.01.2004 | 2 | (22) | |
| Valentin Adama Diomandé | 14.02.1990 | 1 | (1) | 1 |
| Dennis Gjengaar | 24.02.2004 | 7 | (3) | 5 |
| Mikael Ingebrigtsen | 21.07.1996 | 18 | (6) | 4 |
| Milan Jevtović (SRB) | 13.06.1993 | 23 | (6) | 10 |
| Flamur Kastrati (KOS) | 14.11.1991 | 1 | (5) | |
| Tobias Lauritsen | 30.08.1997 | 13 | (2) | 6 |
| Abel William Stensrud | 23.05.2002 | 5 | (11) | 2 |
| Faniel Temesgen Tewelde | 09.09.2006 | | (2) | |
| Conrad Wallem | 09.06.2000 | 28 | (1) | 4 |
| Philipp Zulechner (AUT) | 12.04.1990 | | (2) | |

## Rosenborg Ballklub Trondheim

| | | |
|---|---|---|
| **Founded**: | 19.05.1917 | |
| **Stadium**: | Lerkendal Stadion, Trondheim (21,421) | |
| **Trainer**: | Kjetil André Rekdal | 06.11.1968 |

| Goalkeepers: | DOB | M | (s) | G |
|---|---|---|---|---|
| André Hansen | 17.12.1989 | 30 | | |
| Sander Tangvik | 29.11.2002 | | (1) | |
| **Defenders:** | **DOB** | **M** | **(s)** | **G** |
| Adam Andersson (SWE) | 11.11.1996 | 1 | (4) | |
| Jonathan Augustinsson (SWE) | 30.03.1996 | | (3) | |
| Renzo Giampaoli (ARG) | 07.01.2000 | 10 | (14) | |
| Markus Henriksen | 25.07.1992 | 29 | | |
| Adrian Nilsen Pereira | 31.08.1999 | 11 | (10) | 2 |
| Samuel Jarard Rogers (USA) | 17.05.1999 | 21 | (2) | 6 |
| Håkon Røsten | 21.02.2005 | | (3) | |
| **Midfielders:** | **DOB** | **M** | **(s)** | **G** |
| Tobias Børkeeiet | 18.04.1999 | 27 | | 2 |
| Marius Sivertsen Broholm | 26.12.2004 | | (9) | |
| Paweł Chrupałła | 16.03.2003 | | (4) | 1 |
| Leo Erik Jean Cornic | 02.01.2001 | 10 | (2) | 3 |
| Vebjørn Hoff | 13.02.1996 | | (10) | |
| Carl Holse (DEN) | 02.06.1999 | 25 | (3) | 3 |
| Victor Jensen (DEN) | 08.02.2000 | 25 | (3) | 5 |
| Sverre Halseth Nypan | 19.12.2006 | 2 | | |
| Erlend Dahl Reitan | 11.09.1997 | 29 | (1) | 3 |
| Olaus Skarsem | 02.07.1998 | 20 | (5) | |
| Per Ciljan Skjelbred | 16.06.1987 | 4 | (15) | |
| Edvard Tagseth | 23.01.2001 | 20 | (7) | 1 |
| Pavle Vagić (SWE) | 24.01.2000 | 10 | (1) | |
| **Forwards:** | **DOB** | **M** | **(s)** | **G** |
| Bryan Fiabema | 16.02.2003 | 5 | (6) | 1 |
| Noah Jean Holm | 23.05.2001 | 8 | (3) | 1 |
| Magnus Holte | 27.03.2006 | | (1) | |
| Kristall Máni Ingason (ISL) | 18.01.2002 | 2 | (6) | 2 |
| Ole Christian Sæter | 30.03.1996 | 18 | (2) | 14 |
| Casper Tengstedt (DEN) | 01.06.2000 | 14 | | 15 |
| Stefano Holmquist Vecchia (SWE) | 23.01.1995 | 9 | (7) | 9 |

## Sandefjord Fotball

| | | |
|---|---|---|
| **Founded**: | 10.09.1998 | |
| **Stadium**: | Release (Sandefjord) Arena, Sandefjord (6,582) | |
| **Trainer**: | Hans Erik Ødegaard & | 20.01.1974 |
| | Andreas Ulrik Tegström (SWE) | 18.01.1979 |

| Goalkeepers: | DOB | M | (s) | G |
|---|---|---|---|---|
| Hugo Keto (FIN) | 09.02.1998 | 10 | | |
| Jacob Storevik | 29.07.1996 | 20 | | |
| **Defenders:** | **DOB** | **M** | **(s)** | **G** |
| Fredrik Flo | 10.10.1996 | 6 | (2) | 1 |
| Sander Moen Foss | 31.12.1998 | 2 | | |
| Mats Haakenstad | 14.11.1993 | 19 | (3) | 2 |
| Quint Jansen (NED) | 10.09.1990 | 20 | (4) | 2 |
| Lars Markmanrud | 01.03.2001 | 12 | (4) | 1 |
| Fredrik Mani Pålerud | 24.02.1994 | 8 | (4) | |
| Philip Alexander Kolberg Slørdahl | 14.11.2000 | 3 | (2) | |
| Ian Smeulers (NED) | 12.01.2000 | 28 | | |
| Jesper Taaje | 25.10.1997 | 26 | (1) | 2 |
| **Midfielders:** | **DOB** | **M** | **(s)** | **G** |
| Benjamin Hellum Andersen | 21.06.2005 | | (1) | |
| Keanin Ayer Boya (RSA) | 21.04.2000 | 7 | (11) | 3 |
| Fréderic Bikoro Akieme Nchama (EQG) | 17.03.1996 | 1 | (8) | |
| William Kurtović (SWE) | 22.06.1996 | 25 | (1) | 2 |
| Filip Loftesnes-Bjune | 08.04.2005 | | (3) | |
| Sander Risan Mørk | 06.12.2000 | 5 | | |
| Aleksander Nilsson (SWE) | 05.09.2002 | 15 | | |
| Amer Ordagić (BIH) | 05.05.1993 | 10 | (6) | |
| Harmeet Singh | 12.11.1990 | 6 | (8) | 1 |
| André Sødlund | 22.12.1996 | | (1) | |
| Vetle Walle Egeli | 02.02.2004 | 5 | (3) | |
| Albin Winbo (SWE) | 27.10.1997 | 5 | (8) | 1 |
| **Forwards:** | **DOB** | **M** | **(s)** | **G** |
| Youssef Chaib | 12.08.1996 | 1 | (10) | 1 |
| Sivert Gussiås | 18.08.1999 | 1 | (24) | |
| Sebastian Holm Mathisen | 30.06.2005 | | (2) | |
| Wally Njie | 20.12.2002 | | (1) | |
| Franklin Nyenetue | 16.11.2000 | 15 | (12) | 2 |
| Mohamed Ofkir | 04.08.1996 | 29 | | 12 |
| Rubén Herráiz Alcaraz „Rufo" | 13.01.1993 | 10 | (1) | 1 |
| Alexander Ruud Tveter | 07.03.1991 | 29 | | 8 |
| Deyver Antonio Vega Álvarez (CRC) | 19.09.1992 | 12 | (7) | 2 |

## Sarpsborg 08 Fotballforening

| | | |
|---|---|---|
| **Founded**: | 15.01.2008 | |
| **Stadium**: | Sarpsborg Stadion, Sarpsborg (8,022) | |
| **Trainer**: | Stefan Bo Anders Billborn | 15.11.1972 |

| Goalkeepers: | DOB | M | (s) | G |
|---|---|---|---|---|
| Anders Kristiansen | 17.03.1990 | 19 | | |
| Simen Vidtun Nilsen | 03.03.2000 | 10 | | |
| Leander Øy | 24.10.2003 | 1 | (1) | |
| **Defenders:** | **DOB** | **M** | **(s)** | **G** |
| Anders Hagelskjær (DEN) | 16.02.1997 | 10 | | |
| Jørgen Horn | 07.06.1987 | 11 | (4) | |
| Magnar Ødegaard | 11.05.1993 | 14 | (8) | 1 |
| Anton Skipper (DEN) | 31.03.2000 | 7 | (2) | |
| Joachim Soltvedt | 09.09.1995 | 24 | (4) | 4 |
| Joachim Thomassen | 04.05.1988 | 6 | (4) | |
| Bjørn Inge Utvik | 28.02.1996 | 19 | (1) | |
| Eirik Wichne | 12.05.1997 | 15 | (9) | |
| **Midfielders:** | **DOB** | **M** | **(s)** | **G** |
| Martin Høyland | 17.09.1995 | 1 | (15) | |
| Jonathan Lindseth | 25.02.1996 | 15 | | 2 |
| Mikkel Maigaard Jakobsen (DEN) | 20.09.1995 | 23 | (4) | 9 |
| Serge-Junior Martinsson Ngouali (GAB) | 23.01.1992 | 29 | | 1 |
| Laurent Mendy (SEN) | 27.11.2001 | | (1) | |
| Anton Salétros (SWE) | 12.04.1996 | 28 | | 5 |
| Simon Hjalmar Friedel Tibbling (SWE) | 07.09.1994 | 10 | (4) | 2 |
| Victor Torp Odergaard (DEN) | 30.07.1999 | 9 | (4) | 2 |
| **Forwards:** | **DOB** | **M** | **(s)** | **G** |
| Gustav Per Fredrik Engvall (SWE) | 29.04.1996 | 13 | | 1 |
| Ole Jørgen Halvorsen | 02.10.1987 | 13 | (15) | |
| Tobias Heintz | 13.07.1998 | 28 | (1) | 15 |
| Aboubacar Dit Boubou Konté (MLI) | 02.03.2001 | | (4) | |
| Guillermo Molins (SWE) | 26.09.1988 | 15 | (12) | 6 |
| Rashad Muhammed (FRA) | 25.09.1993 | 1 | (3) | |
| Kristian Opseth | 06.01.1990 | 3 | (9) | 2 |
| Aridon Racaj (KOS) | 12.03.2005 | | (1) | |
| Steffen Skålevik | 31.01.1993 | 6 | (20) | 5 |

## Strømsgodset Toppfotball Drammen

| | | |
|---|---|---|
| **Founded**: | 10.02.1907 | |
| **Stadium**: | Marienlyst Stadion, Drammen (8,935) | |
| **Trainer**: | Håkon Wibe-Lund & | 05.09.1980 |
| | Bjørn Petter Ingebretsen | 26.05.1967 |

| Goalkeepers: | DOB | M | (s) | G |
|---|---|---|---|---|
| Viljar Myhra | 21.07.1996 | 30 | | |
| **Defenders:** | **DOB** | **M** | **(s)** | **G** |
| Eirik Espelid Blikstad | 16.05.2004 | | (2) | |
| Ernest Boahene (GHA) | 06.03.2000 | | (11) | 1 |
| Thomas Grøgaard | 08.02.1994 | 30 | | 1 |
| Niklas Gunnarsson | 27.04.1991 | 19 | (3) | 1 |
| Sondre Fosnæss Hanssen | 25.05.2001 | 3 | (5) | |
| Fabian Holst-Larsen | 30.12.2004 | 3 | (5) | |
| Ari Leifsson (ISL) | 19.04.1998 | 10 | | |
| Gustav Valsvik | 26.05.1993 | 30 | | 3 |
| Lars Christopher Vilsvik | 18.10.1988 | 23 | (1) | 2 |
| **Midfielders:** | **DOB** | **M** | **(s)** | **G** |
| Emmanuel Danso (GHA) | 10.11.2000 | | (4) | |
| Johan Hove | 07.09.2000 | 30 | | 11 |
| Jack Ipalibo (NGA) | 06.04.1998 | 18 | (4) | 4 |
| Kreshnik Krasniqi | 22.12.2000 | 5 | (5) | |
| Andreas Waterfield Skjold | 02.02.2003 | | (1) | |
| Herman Stengel | 26.08.1995 | 29 | | 3 |
| Jonas Torissen Therkelsen | 05.05.2003 | 1 | (3) | |
| **Forwards:** | **DOB** | **M** | **(s)** | **G** |
| Jonatan Braut Brunes | 07.08.2000 | 8 | (5) | 3 |
| Ole Enersen | 06.09.2002 | 11 | (8) | 1 |
| Fred Friday (NGA) | 22.05.1995 | 16 | (10) | 5 |
| Tobias Fjeld Gulliksen | 09.07.2003 | 16 | (6) | 2 |
| Lars-Jørgen Salvesen | 19.02.1996 | 12 | (3) | 5 |
| Halldor Stenevik | 02.02.2000 | 25 | (2) | |
| Kristoffer Tokstad | 05.07.1991 | 11 | (10) | 1 |
| Albert Palmberg Thorsen | 23.04.2003 | | (8) | |

## Tromsø Idrettslag

| Founded: | 15.09.1920 | | |
| Stadium: | Alfheim Stadion, Tromsø (6,687) | | |
| Trainer: | Gaute Ugelstad Helstrup | | 15.05.1976 |

| Goalkeepers: | DOB | M | (s) | G |
|---|---|---|---|---|
| Jakob Haugaard (DEN) | 01.05.1992 | 29 | | |
| Simon Edmund Thomas (CAN) | 12.04.1990 | 1 | | |
| **Defenders:** | **DOB** | **M** | **(s)** | **G** |
| Mikkel Konradsen Ceide | 03.09.2001 | | (2) | |
| Jostein Gundersen | 02.04.1996 | 22 | (1) | 2 |
| Anders Jenssen | 10.10.1993 | 17 | (8) | |
| Warren Kamanzi | 11.11.2000 | 14 | (14) | 4 |
| Oskar Aron Opsahl | 25.08.2001 | | (2) | |
| Casper Øyvann | 07.12.1999 | 13 | (4) | |
| Christophe Psyché (FRA) | 28.07.1988 | 27 | | 2 |
| Niklas Vesterlund (DEN) | 06.06.1999 | 23 | | 2 |
| Isak Kjelsrud Vik | 22.01.2003 | | (6) | |

| Midfielders: | DOB | M | (s) | G |
|---|---|---|---|---|
| Kent-Are Antonsen | 12.02.1995 | 18 | (6) | 2 |
| Tobias Hafstad | 01.06.2002 | | (6) | |
| Ruben Jenssen | 04.05.1988 | 27 | | 2 |
| Eric Bugale Kitolano | 02.09.1997 | 23 | (6) | 13 |
| Lasse Nilsen | 21.02.1995 | 23 | (4) | 1 |
| Runar Norheim | 14.02.2005 | 2 | (10) | 1 |
| Sakarias Opsahl | 17.07.1999 | 30 | | 3 |
| Felix Winther (DEN) | 18.05.2000 | 6 | (20) | 1 |
| **Forwards:** | **DOB** | **M** | **(s)** | **G** |
| Elias Aarflot | 25.11.2003 | | (1) | |
| Moses Ebiye (NGA) | 28.04.1997 | 11 | (5) | 2 |
| August Mikkelsen | 24.10.2000 | 26 | | 7 |
| Lasse Selvåg Nordås | 10.02.2002 | 10 | (4) | 2 |
| Jasse Tuominen (FIN) | 12.11.1995 | 8 | (18) | 1 |

## Viking Fotballklubb Stavanger

| Founded: | 10.08.1899 | | |
| Stadium: | SR-Bank Arena (Viking Stadion), Stavanger (15,900) | | |
| Trainer: | Morten Jensen & | | 09.03.1981 |
| | Bjarte Andre Lunde Aarsheim | | 14.01.1975 |

| Goalkeepers: | DOB | M | (s) | G |
|---|---|---|---|---|
| Patrik Sigurður Gunnarsson (ISL) | 15.11.2000 | 28 | | |
| Arild Østbø | 19.04.1991 | 2 | | |
| **Defenders:** | **DOB** | **M** | **(s)** | **G** |
| Sondre Bjørshol | 30.04.1994 | 27 | (2) | |
| David Brekalo (SVN) | 03.12.1998 | 26 | | 2 |
| Djibril Thialaw Diop (SEN) | 06.01.1999 | 7 | | 1 |
| Shayne Pattynama (NED) | 11.08.1998 | 14 | (4) | |
| Sebastian Sebulonsen | 27.01.2000 | 12 | (3) | 4 |
| Gianni Ryan Stensness (AUS) | 07.02.1999 | 16 | (2) | |
| Viljar Vevatne | 07.12.1994 | 17 | (5) | 1 |
| Rolf Daniel Vikstøl | 22.02.1989 | 5 | (7) | 1 |
| **Midfielders:** | **DOB** | **M** | **(s)** | **G** |
| Sondre Auklend | 10.06.2003 | | (1) | |
| Yann-Erik de Lanlay | 14.05.1992 | 11 | (10) | 1 |
| Samúel Friðjónsson (ISL) | 22.02.1996 | 11 | (5) | 1 |

| Herman Johan Haugen | 25.04.2000 | 5 | (7) | 1 |
|---|---|---|---|---|
| Kristoffer Løkberg | 22.01.1992 | 19 | (3) | 4 |
| Naatan Skyttä (FIN) | 07.05.2002 | 7 | (3) | |
| Markus Solbakken | 25.07.2000 | 27 | | 1 |
| Harald Tangen | 03.01.2001 | 15 | (10) | 1 |
| Fredrik Torsteinbø | 13.03.1991 | 3 | (11) | |
| **Forwards:** | **DOB** | **M** | **(s)** | **G** |
| Edvin Austbø | 01.05.2005 | | (7) | 1 |
| Veton Berisha | 13.04.1994 | 12 | | 8 |
| Kevin Kabran (SWE) | 22.11.1993 | 20 | (10) | 5 |
| Daniel Karlsbakk | 07.04.2003 | 11 | (10) | 2 |
| Simen Kvia-Egeskog | 26.05.2003 | | (2) | |
| Niklas Sandberg | 18.05.1995 | 12 | (12) | 2 |
| Sander Svendsen | 06.08.1997 | 6 | (5) | 1 |
| Mai Traoré (GUI) | 24.11.1999 | 3 | (20) | 4 |
| Zlatko Tripić | 02.12.1992 | 14 | (6) | 5 |

## Vålerenga Fotball Oslo

| Founded: | 29.07.1913 | | |
| Stadium: | Intility Arena, Oslo (16,555) | | |
| Trainer: | Dag-Eilev Fagermo | | 28.01.1967 |

| Goalkeepers: | DOB | M | (s) | G |
|---|---|---|---|---|
| Kjetil Haug | 12.06.1998 | 12 | | |
| Sondre Løvseth Rossbach | 07.02.1996 | 1 | (1) | |
| Magnus Smelhus Sjøeng | 23.03.2002 | 17 | | |
| **Defenders:** | **DOB** | **M** | **(s)** | **G** |
| Brynjar Ingi Bjarnason (ISL) | 06.12.1999 | 12 | (2) | |
| Vegar Hedenstad | 26.06.1991 | 27 | | 2 |
| Simen Kristiansen Juklerød | 18.05.1994 | 8 | (1) | |
| Ivan Näsberg | 22.04.1996 | 13 | | 1 |
| Brage Skaret | 28.04.2002 | | (1) | |
| Ken Remi Stefan Strandberg | 25.07.1990 | 6 | | 1 |
| Jonatan Tollås | 01.07.1990 | 20 | (4) | 1 |
| Leonard Žuta (MKD) | 09.08.1992 | 21 | (2) | 2 |
| **Midfielders:** | **DOB** | **M** | **(s)** | **G** |
| Henrik Bjørdal | 04.02.1997 | 21 | (3) | 4 |
| Tobias Christensen | 11.05.2000 | 15 | (13) | 2 |

| Mathias Johnrud Emilsen | 08.06.2003 | | (1) | |
|---|---|---|---|---|
| Odin Thiago Holm | 18.01.2003 | 15 | (7) | 2 |
| Fredrik Jensen | 18.05.1993 | 20 | (6) | |
| Magnus Riisnæs | 04.11.2004 | | (14) | |
| Petter Strand | 24.08.1994 | 26 | (3) | |
| **Forwards:** | **DOB** | **M** | **(s)** | **G** |
| Torgeir Børven | 03.12.1991 | 12 | (1) | 5 |
| Aron Dønnum | 20.04.1998 | 9 | (2) | 2 |
| Jones El-Abdellaoui | 12.01.2006 | | (2) | |
| Jacob Emil Dicko Eng | 14.09.2004 | 8 | (13) | 4 |
| Taofeek Ismaheel (NGA) | 16.07.2000 | 4 | (5) | |
| Seedy Jatta | 18.03.2003 | 3 | (17) | 1 |
| Viðar Örn Kjartansson (ISL) | 11.03.1990 | 9 | (1) | 4 |
| Amor Layouni (TUN) | 03.10.1992 | 18 | (2) | 8 |
| Osame Sahraoui | 11.06.2001 | 27 | (2) | 6 |
| Henrik Udahl | 12.01.1997 | 6 | (17) | 4 |

## SECOND LEVEL
### First Division / OBOS-ligaen 2022

| | | | | | | | | | |
|---|---|---|---|---|---|---|---|---|---|
| 1. | SK Brann Bergen (*Promoted*) | 30 | 26 | 3 | 1 | 95 | - | 16 | 81 |
| 2. | Stabæk Fotball Bærum (*Promoted*) | 30 | 16 | 10 | 4 | 62 | - | 28 | 58 |
| 3. | IK Start Kristiansand (*Promotion Play-offs*) | 30 | 16 | 6 | 8 | 63 | - | 38 | 54 |
| 4. | KFUM-Kameratene Oslo (*Promotion Play-offs*) | 30 | 15 | 7 | 8 | 61 | - | 48 | 52 |
| 5. | Sandnes Ulf (*Promotion Play-offs*) | 30 | 14 | 5 | 11 | 54 | - | 52 | 47 |
| 6. | Kongsvinger IL Toppfotball (*Promotion Play-offs*) | 30 | 13 | 7 | 10 | 43 | - | 37 | 46 |
| 7. | Sogndal Fotball | 30 | 12 | 7 | 11 | 55 | - | 53 | 43 |
| 8. | Ranheim IL Trondheim | 30 | 12 | 7 | 11 | 49 | - | 52 | 43 |
| 9. | Mjøndalen IF | 30 | 13 | 3 | 14 | 39 | - | 47 | 42 |
| 10. | Fredrikstad FK | 30 | 9 | 8 | 13 | 46 | - | 51 | 35 |
| 11. | Byrne FK | 30 | 9 | 8 | 13 | 42 | - | 52 | 35 |
| 12. | Raufoss IL | 30 | 9 | 8 | 13 | 35 | - | 54 | 35 |
| 13. | Åsane Fotball | 30 | 8 | 8 | 14 | 42 | - | 67 | 32 |
| 14. | Skeid Oslo (*Relegation Play-offs*) | 30 | 8 | 4 | 18 | 39 | - | 54 | 28 |
| 15. | Grorud IL Oslo (*Relegated*) | 30 | 4 | 8 | 18 | 34 | - | 69 | 20 |
| 16. | IL Stjørdals-Blink (*Relegated*) | 30 | 4 | 5 | 21 | 30 | - | 71 | 17 |

| | | |
|---|---|---|
| **Promotion Play-offs** | | |

| | | |
|---|---|---|
| **First Round** [03.11.2022] | Sandnes Ulf - Kongsvinger IL Toppfotball | 0-1(0-0) |
| **Second Round** [08.11.2022] | KFUM-Kameratene Oslo - Kongsvinger IL Toppfotball | 1-2(1-0) |
| **Third Round** [13.11.2022] | IK Start Kristiansand - Kongsvinger IL Toppfotball | 0-1(0-0) |

Kongsvinger IL Toppfotball qualified for the First Level Relegation/Promotion Play-offs .

| | | |
|---|---|---|
| **Relegation Play-offs (2nd / 3rd Level)** [02-05.11.2022] | | |

| | | |
|---|---|---|
| Skeid Oslo – Arendal Fotball | 6-0(2-0) | 2-1(0-0) |

Skeid Oslo remains at second level for 2023.

| | |
|---|---|
| **NATIONAL TEAM** | |

| | |
|---|---|
| **INTERNATIONAL MATCHES** (16.07.2022 – 15.07.2023) | |

| | | | | |
|---|---|---|---|---|
| 24.09.2022 | Ljubljana | *Slovenia - Norway* | *2-1(0-0)* | (UNL) |
| 27.09.2022 | Oslo | *Norway - Serbia* | *0-2(0-1)* | (UNL) |
| 17.11.2022 | Dublin | *Republic of Ireland - Norway* | *1-2(0-1)* | (F) |
| 20.11.2022 | Oslo | *Norway - Finland* | *1-1(0-1)* | (F) |
| | | | | |
| 25.03.2023 | Málaga | *Spain - Norway* | *3-0(1-0)* | (ECQ) |
| 28.03.2023 | Batumi | *Georgia - Norway* | *1-1(0-1)* | (ECQ) |
| 17.06.2023 | Oslo | *Norway - Scotland* | *1-2(0-0)* | (ECQ) |
| 20.06.2023 | Oslo | *Norway - Cyprus* | *3-1(1-0)* | (ECQ) |

**24.09.2022    SLOVENIA - NORWAY              2-1(0-0)**              3rd UEFA Nations League B, Group 4
Stadion Stožice, Ljubljana; Referee: Lawrence Visser (Belgium); Attendance: 14,824
**NOR:** Ørjan Håskold Nyland, Julian Ryerson, Leo Skiri Østigård, Andreas Schjølberg Hanche-Olsen, Birger Solberg Meling, Sander Gard Bolin Berge, Kristian Thorstvedt (61.Morten Thorsby), Martin Ødegaard (Cap) (71.Fredrik Aursnes), Mohamed Amine Elyounoussi (70.Mats Møller Dæhli), Alexander Sørloth (62.Jørgen Strand Larsen), Erling Braut Haaland. Trainer: Ståle Solbakken.
**Goal:** Erling Braut Håland (47).

**27.09.2022    NORWAY - SERBIA              0-2(0-1)**              3rd UEFA Nations League B, Group 4
Ullevaal Stadion, Oslo; Referee: Antonio Miguel Mateu Lahoz (Spain); Attendance: 24,364
**NOR:** Ørjan Håskold Nyland, Julian Ryerson (57.Marcus Holmgren Pedersen), Leo Skiri Østigård, Andreas Schjølberg Hanche-Olsen (78.Patrick Berg), Birger Solberg Meling (74.Fredrik André Bjørkan), Fredrik Aursnes (57.Kristoffer Vassbakk Ajer), Martin Ødegaard (Cap), Sander Gard Bolin Berge, Mohamed Amine Elyounoussi (57.Jørgen Strand Larsen), Alexander Sørloth, Erling Braut Haaland. Trainer: Ståle Solbakken.

**17.11.2022    REPUBLIC OF IRELAND - NORWAY              1-2(0-1)**              Friendly International
Aviva Stadium, Dublin; Referee: Allard Lindhout (Netherlands); Attendance: 41,120
**NOR:** Ørjan Håskold Nyland, Marcus Holmgren Pedersen (65.Julian Ryerson), Leo Skiri Østigård, Ken Remi Stefan Strandberg, Fredrik André Bjørkan (66.Birger Solberg Meling), Patrick Berg (90+2.Stian Rode Gregersen), Martin Ødegaard (Cap), Morten Thorsby (74.Ola Brynhildsen), Mohamed Amine Elyounoussi, Ola Selvaag Solbakken (63.Kristoffer Zachariassen), Jørgen Strand Larsen (74.Ohi Anthony Kwoeme Omoijuanfo). Trainer: Ståle Solbakken.
**Goals:** Leo Skiri Østigård (40), Ohi Anthony Kwoeme Omoijuanfo (85).

**20.11.2022    NORWAY - FINLAND              1-1(0-1)**              Friendly International
Ullevaal Stadion, Oslo; Referee: Morten Krogh (Denmark); Attendance: 13,347
**NOR:** Ørjan Håskold Nyland, Marcus Holmgren Pedersen (56.Julian Ryerson), Leo Skiri Østigård, Ken Remi Stefan Strandberg (46.Stian Rode Gregersen), Birger Solberg Meling, Patrick Berg, Martin Ødegaard (Cap), Kristoffer Zachariassen (46.Ola Brynhildsen), Mohamed Amine Elyounoussi (66.Hugo Vegard Vetlesen), Mats Møller Dæhli (46.Ola Selvaag Solbakken), Alexander Sørloth. Trainer: Ståle Solbakken.
**Goal:** Alexander Sørloth (46).

**25.03.2023    SPAIN - NORWAY              3-0(1-0)**              17th EC. Qualifiers
Estadio La Rosaleda, Málaga; Referee: Benoît Bastien (France); Attendance: 29,214
**NOR:** Ørjan Håskold Nyland, Marcus Holmgren Pedersen (74.Julian Ryerson), Leo Skiri Østigård, Ken Remi Stefan Strandberg, Birger Solberg Meling (74.Fredrik André Bjørkan), Patrick Berg, Martin Ødegaard (Cap), Fredrik Aursnes, Sander Gard Bolin Berge (74.Ola Selvaag Solbakken), Mohamed Amine Elyounoussi (74.Jørgen Strand Larsen), Alexander Sørloth (86.Ola Brynhildsen). Trainer: Ståle Solbakken.

**28.03.2023    GEORGIA - NORWAY              1-1(0-1)**              17th EC. Qualifiers
Batumi Stadium, Batumi; Referee: Andris Treimanis (Latvia); Attendance: 20,300
**NOR:** Ørjan Håskold Nyland, Marcus Holmgren Pedersen (90+5.Julian Ryerson), Leo Skiri Østigård, Ken Remi Stefan Strandberg, Birger Solberg Meling, Patrick Berg (90+5.Kristian Thorstvedt), Martin Ødegaard (Cap), Fredrik Aursnes, Ola Selvaag Solbakken (82.Ola Brynhildsen), Mohamed Amine Elyounoussi (78.Sander Gard Bolin Berge), Alexander Sørloth. Trainer: Ståle Solbakken.
**Goal:** Alexander Sørloth (15).

**17.06.2023**   **NORWAY - SCOTLAND**                         **1-2(0-0)**                              17th EC. Qualifiers
Ullevaal Stadion, Oslo; Referee: Matej Jug (Slovenia); Attendance: 25,791
**NOR:** Ørjan Håskold Nyland, Julian Ryerson, Leo Skiri Østigård, Ken Remi Stefan Strandberg, Birger Solberg Meling, Patrick Berg (84.Jørgen Strand Larsen), Martin Ødegaard (Cap), Fredrik Aursnes (84.Kristian Thorstvedt), Ola Selvaag Solbakken (63.Sander Gard Bolin Berge), Alexander Sørloth (79.Mohamed Amine Elyounoussi), Erling Braut Haaland (84.Mats Møller Dæhli). Trainer: Ståle Solbakken.
**Goal:** Erling Braut Haaland (61 penalty).

**20.06.2023**   **NORWAY - CYPRUS**                           **3-1(1-0)**                              17th EC. Qualifiers
Ullevaal Stadion, Oslo; Referee: Aleksandar Stavrev (North Macedonia); Attendance: 23,643
**NOR:** Ørjan Håskold Nyland, Julian Ryerson (59.Brice Wembangomo), Leo Skiri Østigård, Ken Remi Stefan Strandberg, Birger Solberg Meling, Patrick Berg (74.Kristian Thorstvedt), Martin Ødegaard (Cap), Fredrik Aursnes (87.Kristoffer Velde), Ola Selvaag Solbakken (58.Sander Gard Bolin Berge), Alexander Sørloth, Erling Braut Haaland (87.Bård Finne). Trainer: Ståle Solbakken.
**Goals:** Ola Selvaag Solbakken (12), Erling Braut Haaland (56 penalty, 60).

## NATIONAL TEAM PLAYERS
### (16.07.2022 – 15.07.2023)

| Name | DOB | Caps | Goals | Club | |
|------|-----|------|-------|------|---|

### Goalkeepers

| Name | DOB | Caps | Goals | Club | |
|------|-----|------|-------|------|---|
| Ørjan Håskold NYLAND | 10.09.1990 | 46 | 0 | 2022/2023: | *Reading FC (ENG)* |

### Defenders

| Name | DOB | Caps | Goals | Club | |
|------|-----|------|-------|------|---|
| Kristoffer Vassbakk AJER | 17.04.1998 | 27 | 0 | 2022: | *Brentford FC London (ENG)* |
| Fredrik André BJØRKAN | 21.08.1998 | 9 | 0 | 2022: / 08.01.2023-> | *Feyenoord Rotterdam (NED)* / *FK Bodø/Glimt* |
| Stian Rode GREGERSEN | 17.05.1995 | 7 | 0 | 2022: | *FC Girondins de Bordeaux (FRA)* |
| Andreas Schjølberg HANCHE-OLSEN | 17.01.1997 | 14 | 0 | 2022: | *KAA Gent (BEL)* |
| Birger Solberg MELING | 17.12.1994 | 37 | 0 | 2022/2023: | *Stade Rennais FC (FRA)* |
| Marcus Holmgren PEDERSEN | 16.07.2000 | 18 | 0 | 2022/2023: | *Feyenoord Rotterdam (NED)* |
| Julian RYERSON | 17.11.1997 | 11 | 0 | 2022: / 17.01.2023-> | *1.FC Union Berlin (GER)* / *BV 09 Borussia Dortmund (GER)* |
| Ken Remi Stefan STRANDBERG | 25.07.1990 | 33 | 1 | 2022/2023: | *Vålerenga Fotball Oslo* |
| Brice WEMBANGOMO | 18.12.1996 | 1 | 0 | 2023: | *FK Bodø/Glimt* |
| Leo Skiri ØSTIGÅRD | 28.11.1999 | 13 | 1 | 2022/2023: | *SSC Napoli (ITA)* |

### Midfielders

| Name | DOB | Caps | Goals | Club | |
|------|-----|------|-------|------|---|
| Fredrik AURSNES | 10.12.1995 | 14 | 0 | 2022/2023: | *Sport Lisboa e Benfica (POR)* |
| Patrick BERG | 24.11.1997 | 18 | 0 | 2022/2023: | *FK Bodø/Glimt* |
| Sander Gard Bolin BERGE | 14.02.1998 | 36 | 1 | 2022/2023: | *Sheffield United FC (ENG)* |
| Ola BRYNHILDSEN | 27.04.1999 | 4 | 0 | 2022/2023: | *Molde FK* |
| Mohamed Amine ELYOUNOUSSI | 04.08.1994 | 52 | 9 | 2022/2023: | *Southampton FC (ENG)* |
| Mats MØLLER Dæhli | 02.03.1995 | 36 | 2 | 2022/2023: | *1. FC Nürnberg (GER)* |
| Ola Selvaag SOLBAKKEN | 07.09.1998 | 8 | 1 | 2022: / 02.01.2023-> | *FK Bodø/Glimt* / *AS Roma (ITA)* |
| Morten THORSBY | 05.05.1996 | 17 | 0 | 2022: | *1.FC Union Berlin (GER)* |
| Kristoffer VELDE | 09.09.1999 | 1 | 0 | 2023: | *KKS Lech Poznań (POL)* |
| Hugo Vegard VETLESEN | 29.02.2000 | 1 | 0 | 2022: | *FK Bodø/Glimt* |
| Kristoffer ZACHARIASSEN | 27.01.1994 | 3 | 0 | 2022: | *Ferencvárosi TC (HUN)* |
| Martin ØDEGAARD | 17.12.1998 | 51 | 2 | 2022/2023: | *Arsenal FC London (ENG)* |

### Forwards

| Name | DOB | Caps | Goals | Club | |
|------|-----|------|-------|------|---|
| Bård FINNE | 13.02.1995 | 1 | 0 | 2023: | *SK Brann Bergen* |
| Erling Braut HAALAND | 21.07.2000 | 25 | 24 | 2022/2023: | *Manchester City FC (ENG)* |
| Ohi Anthony Kwoeme OMOIJUANFO | 10.01.1994 | 2 | 1 | 2022: | *Brøndby IF (DEN)* |
| Jørgen STRAND Larsen | 06.02.2000 | 6 | 0 | 2022/2023: | *RC Celta de Vigo (ESP)* |
| Alexander SØRLOTH | 05.12.1995 | 49 | 16 | 2022/2023: | *Real Sociedad de Fútbol San Sebastián (ESP)* |
| Kristian THORSTVEDT | 13.03.1999 | 21 | 4 | 2022/2023: | *US Sassuolo Calcio (ITA)* |

### Trainer

| Name | DOB | Record | | | | |
|------|-----|--------|---|---|---|---|
| Ståle SOLBAKKEN [from 07.12.2020] | 27.02.1968 | 26 M; 13 W; 6 D; 7 L; 43-26 | | | | |

# POLAND

**The Country:**
Rzeczpospolita Polska (Republic of Poland)
Capital: Warszawa
Surface: 312,679 km²
Inhabitants: 38,036,118 [2022]
Time: UTC+1

**The FA:**
Polski Związek Piłki Nożnej
Bitwy Warszawskiej 1920 r.7, 02-366, Warszawa
Tel: +48 732 122 222
Founded: 1919
Member of FIFA since: 1923
Member of UEFA since: 1954
Website: www.pzpn.pl

## NATIONAL TEAM RECORDS

### RECORDS

| | | |
|---|---|---|
| **First international match:** | 18.12.1921, Budapest: | Hungary – Poland 1-0 |
| **Most international caps:** | Robert Lewandowski | - 142 caps (since 2008) |
| **Most international goals:** | Robert Lewandowski | - 79 goals / 142 caps (since 2008) |

### UEFA EUROPEAN CHAMPIONSHIP

|  |  |
|---|---|
| 1960 | Qualifiers |
| 1964 | Qualifiers |
| 1968 | Qualifiers |
| 1972 | Qualifiers |
| 1976 | Qualifiers |
| 1980 | Qualifiers |
| 1984 | Qualifiers |
| 1988 | Qualifiers |
| 1992 | Qualifiers |
| 1996 | Qualifiers |
| 2000 | Qualifiers |
| 2004 | Qualifiers |
| 2008 | Final Tournament (Group Stage) |
| 2012 | Final Tournament (Group Stage) |
| 2016 | Final Tournament (Quarter-Finals) |
| 2020 | Final Tournament (Group Stage) |

### FIFA WORLD CUP

|  |  |
|---|---|
| 1930 | Did not enter |
| 1934 | Qualifiers |
| 1938 | Final Tournament (1st Round) |
| 1950 | Did not enter |
| 1954 | *Withdrew* |
| 1958 | Qualifiers |
| 1962 | Qualifiers |
| 1966 | Qualifiers |
| 1970 | Qualifiers |
| 1974 | Final Tournament (3rd Place) |
| 1978 | Final Tournament (Round 2) |
| 1982 | Final Tournament (3rd Place) |
| 1986 | Final Tournament (2nd Round of 16) |
| 1990 | Qualifiers |
| 1994 | Qualifiers |
| 1998 | Qualifiers |
| 2002 | Final Tournament (Group Stage) |
| 2006 | Final Tournament (Group Stage) |
| 2010 | Qualifiers |
| 2014 | Qualifiers |
| 2018 | Final Tournament (Group Stage) |
| 2022 | Final Tournament (2nd Round of 16) |

### OLYMPIC TOURNAMENTS

|  |  |
|---|---|
| 1908 | - |
| 1912 | - |
| 1920 | - |
| 1924 | Preliminary Round |
| 1928 | Did not enter |
| 1936 | 4th Place |
| 1948 | Did not enter |
| 1952 | Round 1 |
| 1956 | Did not enter |
| 1960 | Group Stage |
| 1964 | Qualifiers |
| 1968 | Qualifiers |
| 1972 | **Winners** |
| 1976 | Runners-up |
| 1980 | Qualifiers |
| 1984 | Qualifiers |
| 1988 | Qualifiers |
| 1992 | Runners-up |
| 1996 | Qualifiers |
| 2000 | Qualifiers |
| 2004 | Qualifiers |
| 2008 | Qualifiers |
| 2012 | Qualifiers |
| 2016 | Qualifiers |
| 2020 | Qualifiers |

### UEFA NATIONS LEAGUE

|  |  |
|---|---|
| 2018/2019 | League A (Group Stage) |
| 2020/2021 | League A (Group Stage) |
| 2022/2023 | League A (Group Stage) |

### POLISH CLUB HONOURS IN EUROPEAN CLUB COMPETITIONS:

| European Champion Clubs' Cup (1956-1992) / UEFA Champions League (1993-2023) |
|---|
| None |

| Fairs Cup (1858-1971) / UEFA Cup (1972-2009) / UEFA Europa League (2010-2023) |
|---|
| None |

| UEFA Europa Conference League (2021-2023) |
|---|
| None |

| UEFA Super Cup (1972-2022) |
|---|
| None |

| *European Cup Winners' Cup 1961-1999\** |
|---|
| None |

*\*defunct competition*

# NATIONAL COMPETITIONS
## TABLE OF HONOURS

| | CHAMPIONS | CUP WINNERS | BEST GOALSCORERS | |
|---|---|---|---|---|
| 1920 | *Championship abandoned* | - | - | |
| 1921 | KS Cracovia Kraków | - | - | |
| 1922 | LKS Pogoń Lwów | - | - | |
| 1923 | LKS Pogoń Lwów | - | - | |
| 1924 | *No competition* | - | - | |
| 1925 | LKS Pogoń Lwów | - | - | |
| 1926 | LKS Pogoń Lwów | Wisła Kraków | - | |
| 1927 | Wisła Kraków | - | Henryk Reyman (Wisła Kraków) | 37 |
| 1928 | Wisła Kraków | - | Ludwik Gintel (KS Cracovia Kraków) | 28 |
| 1929 | KS Warta Poznań | - | Rochus Nastula (Czarni Lwów) | 25 |
| 1930 | KS Cracovia Kraków | - | Karol Kossok (KS Cracovia Kraków) | 24 |
| 1931 | RKS Garbarnia Kraków | - | Walerian Kisieliński (Wisła Kraków) | 24 |
| 1932 | KS Cracovia Kraków | - | Kajetan Kryszkiewicz (KS Warta Poznań) | 16 |
| 1933 | KS Ruch Wielkie Hajduki Chorzów | - | Artur Woźniak (Wisła Kraków) | 19 |
| 1934 | KS Ruch Wielkie Hajduki Chorzów | - | Ernst Wilimowski (KS Ruch Wielkie Hajduki Chorzów) | 33 |
| 1935 | KS Ruch Wielkie Hajduki Chorzów | - | Michał Matyas (LKS Pogoń Lwów) | 22 |
| 1936 | KS Ruch Wielkie Hajduki Chorzów | - | Teodor Peterek (KS Ruch Wielkie Hajduki Chorzów) Ernst Wilimowski (KS Ruch Wielkie Hajduki Chorzów) | 18 |
| 1937 | KS Cracovia Kraków | - | Artur Woźniak (Wisła Kraków) | 12 |
| 1938 | KS Ruch Wielkie Hajduki Chorzów | - | Teodor Peterek (KS Ruch Wielkie Hajduki Chorzów) | 21 |
| 1939 | *Championship abandoned* | - | Ernst Wilimowski (KS Ruch Wielkie Hajduki Chorzów) | 12 |
| 1940 | *No competition* | - | - | |
| 1941 | *No competition* | - | - | |
| 1942 | *No competition* | - | - | |
| 1943 | *No competition* | - | - | |
| 1944 | *No competition* | - | - | |
| 1945 | *No competition* | - | - | |
| 1946 | Polonia Warszawa | - | - | |
| 1947 | KS Warta Poznań | - | - | |
| 1948 | KS Cracovia Kraków | - | Józef Kohut (Wisła Kraków) | 31 |
| 1949 | Wisła Kraków | - | Teodor Anioła (KKS Lech Poznań) | 20 |
| 1950 | Wisła Kraków | - | Teodor Anioła (KKS Lech Poznań) | 21 |
| 1951 | Unia Chorzów | Unia Chorzów | Teodor Anioła (KKS Lech Poznań) | 20 |
| 1952 | Unia Chorzów | Kolejarz Warszawa | Gerard Cieślik (Unia Chorzów) | 11 |
| 1953 | Unia Chorzów | WKS Gwardia Warszawa (1953/54) | Gerard Cieślik (Unia Chorzów) | 24 |
| 1954 | KS Polonia Bytom | WKS Gwardia Warszawa | Henryk Kempny (KS Polonia Bytom) Ernst Pohl (Legia Warszawa) | 13 |
| 1955 | CWKS Warszawa | CWKS Warszawa | Stanisław Hachorek (WKS Gwardia Warszawa) | 16 |
| 1956 | CWKS Warszawa | CWKS Warszawa | Henryk Kempny (Legia Warszawa) | 21 |
| 1957 | KS Górnik Zabrze | ŁKS Łódź | Lucjan Brychczy (Legia Warszawa) | 19 |
| 1958 | ŁKS Łódź | *No competition* | Władysław Soporek (ŁKS Łódź) | 19 |
| 1959 | KS Górnik Zabrze | *No competition* | Jan Liberda (KS Polonia Bytom) Ernst Pohl (KS Górnik Zabrze) | 21 |
| 1960 | Ruch Chorzów | *No competition* | Marian Norkowski (Polonia Bydgoszcz) | 17 |
| 1961 | KS Górnik Zabrze | *No competition* | Ernst Pohl (KS Górnik Zabrze) | 24 |
| 1962 | KS Polonia Bytom | Zagłębie Sosnowiec | Jan Liberda (KS Polonia Bytom) | 16 |
| 1962/1963 | KS Górnik Zabrze | Zagłębie Sosnowiec | Marian Kielec (MKS Pogoń Szczecin) | 18 |
| 1963/1964 | KS Górnik Zabrze | CWKS Warszawa | Lucjan Brychczy (Legia Warszawa) Józef Gałeczka (Zagłębie Sosnowiec) Jerzy Wilim (TS Szombierki Bytom) | 18 |
| 1964/1965 | KS Górnik Zabrze | KS Górnik Zabrze | Lucjan Brychczy (Legia Warszawa) | 18 |
| 1965/1966 | KS Górnik Zabrze | CWKS Warszawa | Włodzimierz Lubański (KS Górnik Zabrze) | 23 |
| 1966/1967 | KS Górnik Zabrze | Wisła Kraków | Włodzimierz Lubański (KS Górnik Zabrze) | 18 |
| 1967/1968 | Ruch Chorzów | KS Górnik Zabrze | Włodzimierz Lubański (KS Górnik Zabrze) | 24 |
| 1968/1969 | CWKS Legia Warszawa | KS Górnik Zabrze | Włodzimierz Lubański (KS Górnik Zabrze) | 22 |
| 1969/1970 | CWKS Legia Warszawa | KS Górnik Zabrze | Andrzej Jarosik (Zagłębie Sosnowiec) | 18 |
| 1970/1971 | KS Górnik Zabrze | KS Górnik Zabrze | Andrzej Jarosik (Zagłębie Sosnowiec) | 13 |
| 1971/1972 | KS Górnik Zabrze | KS Górnik Zabrze | Ryszard Szymczak (WKS Gwardia Warszawa) | 16 |
| 1972/1973 | FKS Stal Mielec | CWKS Legia Warszawa | Grzegorz Lato (FKS Stal Mielec) | 13 |
| 1973/1974 | Ruch Chorzów | Ruch Chorzów | Zdzisław Kapka (Wisła Kraków) | 15 |
| 1974/1975 | Ruch Chorzów | Stal Rzeszów | Grzegorz Lato (FKS Stal Mielec) | 19 |
| 1975/1976 | FKS Stal Mielec | KS Śląsk Wrocław | Kazimierz Kmiecik (Wisła Kraków) | 20 |
| 1976/1977 | KS Śląsk Wrocław | Zagłębie Sosnowiec | Włodzimierz Mazur (Zagłębie Sosnowiec) | 17 |
| 1977/1978 | Wisła Kraków | Zagłębie Sosnowiec | Kazimierz Kmiecik (Wisła Kraków) | 15 |
| 1978/1979 | Ruch Chorzów | MZKS Arka Gdynia | Kazimierz Kmiecik (Wisła Kraków) | 17 |
| 1979/1980 | TS Szombierki Bytom | CWKS Legia Warszawa | Kazimierz Kmiecik (Wisła Kraków) | 24 |
| 1980/1981 | RTS Widzew Łódź | CWKS Legia Warszawa | Krzysztof Adamczyk (Legia Warszawa) | 18 |
| 1981/1982 | RTS Widzew Łódź | KKS Lech Poznań | Grzegorz Kapica (TS Szombierki Bytom) | 15 |
| 1982/1983 | KKS Lech Poznań | KS Lechia Gdańsk | Mirosław Okoński (KKS Lech Poznań) | |

| | | | Mirosław Tłokiński (RTS Widzew Łódź) | 15 |
|---|---|---|---|---|
| 1983/1984 | KKS Lech Poznań | KKS Lech Poznań | Włodzimierz Ciołek (Górnik Wałbrzych) | 14 |
| 1984/1985 | KS Górnik Zabrze | RTS Widzew Łódź | Leszek Iwanicki (LKP Motor Lublin) | 14 |
| 1985/1986 | KS Górnik Zabrze | GKS Katowice | Andrzej Zgutczyński (KS Górnik Zabrze) | 20 |
| 1986/1987 | KS Górnik Zabrze | KS Śląsk Wrocław | Marek Leśniak (MKS Pogoń Szczecin) | 24 |
| 1987/1988 | KS Górnik Zabrze | KKS Lech Poznań | Dariusz Dziekanowski (Legia Warszawa) | 20 |
| 1988/1989 | Ruch Chorzów | CWKS Legia Warszawa | Krzysztof Warzycha (Ruch Chorzów) | 24 |
| 1989/1990 | KKS Lech Poznań | CWKS Legia Warszawa | Andrzej Juskowiak (KKS Lech Poznań) | 18 |
| 1990/1991 | Zagłębie Lubin | GKS Katowice | Tomasz Dziubiński (Wisła Kraków) | 21 |
| 1991/1992 | KKS Lech Poznań | MKS Miedź Legnica | Jerzy Podbrożny (KKS Lech Poznań) Mirosław Waligóra (KS Hutnik Kraków) | 20 |
| 1992/1993 | KKS Lech Poznań | GKS Katowice | Jerzy Podbrożny (KKS Lech Poznań) | 25 |
| 1993/1994 | Legia Warszawa | Legia Warszawa | Zenon Burzawa (Sokół Pniewy) | 21 |
| 1994/1995 | Legia Warszawa | Legia Warszawa | Bogusław Cygan (FKS Stal Mielec) | 16 |
| 1995/1996 | RTS Widzew Łódź | Ruch Chorzów | Marek Koniarek (RTS Widzew Łódź) | 29 |
| 1996/1997 | RTS Widzew Łódź | Legia Warszawa | Mirosław Trzeciak (ŁKS Łódź) | 18 |
| 1997/1998 | ŁKS Łódź | KS Amica Wronki | Arkadiusz Bąk (Polonia Warszawa) Sylwester Czereszewski (Legia Warszawa) Mariusz Śrutwa (Ruch Chorzów) | 14 |
| 1998/1999 | Wisła Kraków | KS Amica Wronki | Tomasz Frankowski (Wisła Kraków) | 21 |
| 1999/2000 | Polonia Warszawa | KS Amica Wronki | Adam Kompała (KS Górnik Zabrze) | 19 |
| 2000/2001 | Wisła Kraków | Polonia Warszawa | Tomasz Frankowski (Wisła Kraków) | 18 |
| 2001/2002 | Legia Warszawa | Wisła Kraków | Maciej Żurawski (Wisła Kraków) | 21 |
| 2002/2003 | Wisła Kraków | Wisła Kraków | Stanko Svitlica (SRB, Legia Warszawa) | 24 |
| 2003/2004 | Wisła Kraków | KKS Lech Poznań | Maciej Żurawski (Wisła Kraków) | 20 |
| 2004/2005 | Wisła Kraków | KS Dyskobolia Grodzisk Wielkopolski | Tomasz Frankowski (Wisła Kraków) | 25 |
| 2005/2006 | Legia Warszawa | Wisła Płock | Grzegorz Piechna (Korona Kielce) | 21 |
| 2006/2007 | Zagłębie Lubin | KS Dyskobolia Grodzisk Wielkopolski | Piotr Reiss (KKS Lech Poznań) | 15 |
| 2007/2008 | Wisła Kraków | Legia Warszawa | Paweł Brożek (Wisła Kraków) | 23 |
| 2008/2009 | Wisła Kraków | KKS Lech Poznań | Paweł Brożek (Wisła Kraków) Takesure Chinyama (ZIM, Legia Warszawa) | 19 |
| 2009/2010 | KKS Lech Poznań | Jagiellonia Białystok | Robert Lewandowski (KKS Lech Poznań) | 18 |
| 2010/2011 | Wisła Kraków | Legia Warszawa | Tomasz Frankowski (Jagiellonia Białystok) | 14 |
| 2011/2012 | KS Śląsk Wrocław | Legia Warszawa | Artjoms Rudņevs (LVA, KKS Lech Poznań) | 22 |
| 2012/2013 | Legia Warszawa | Legia Warszawa | Róbert Demjan (SVK, TS Podbeskidzie Bielsko-Biała) | 14 |
| 2013/2014 | Legia Warszawa | SP Zawisza Bydgoszcz | Marcin Robak (GKS Piast Gliwice / MKS Pogoń Szczecin) | 22 |
| 2014/2015 | KKS Lech Poznań | Legia Warszawa | Kamil Wilczek (GKS Piast Gliwice) | 20 |
| 2015/2016 | Legia Warszawa | Legia Warszawa | Nemanja Nikolić (HUN, Legia Warszawa) | 28 |
| 2016/2017 | Legia Warszawa | MZKS Arka Gdynia | Marco Filipe Lopes Paixão (POR, KS Lechia Gdańsk) Marcin Robak (KKS Lech Poznań) | 18 |
| 2017/2018 | Legia Warszawa | Legia Warszawa | Carlos Daniel López Huesca "Carlitos" (ESP, Wisła Kraków) | 24 |
| 2018/2019 | GKS Piast Gliwice | KS Lechia Gdańsk | Igor Angulo Alboniga (ESP, KS Górnik Zabrze) | 24 |
| 2019/2020 | Legia Warszawa | KS Cracovia Kraków | Christian Lund Gytkjær (DEN, KKS Lech Poznań) | 24 |
| 2020/2021 | Legia Warszawa | RKS Raków Częstochowa | Tomáš Pekhart (CZE, Legia Warszawa) | 22 |
| 2021/2022 | KKS Lech Poznań | RKS Raków Częstochowa | Iván López Álvarez „Ivi" (ESP, RKS Raków Częstochowa) | 20 |
| 2022/2023 | RKS Raków Częstochowa | Legia Warszawa | Marc Gual Huguet (ESP, Jagiellonia Białystok) | 16 |

Ruch Chorzów = KS Ruch Wielkie Hajduki Chorzów (1927-1939), Unia Chorzów (1949-1954), Unia-Ruch Chorzów (1955).
Legia Warszawa = CWKS Warszawa (1950-1967), CWKS Legia Warszawa (1967-1990).

## NATIONAL CHAMPIONSHIP
### Ekstraklasa 2022/2023
(15.07.2022 – 27.05.2023)

### Results

**Round 1 [15-18.07.2022]**
Raków Częstochowa - Warta Poznań 1-0(0-0)
Zagłębie Lubin - Śląsk Wrocław 0-0
Lech Poznań - Stal Mielec 0-2(0-1)
Jagiellonia Białystok - Piast Gliwice 2-0(1-0)
Korona Kielce - Legia Warszawa 1-1(0-0)
Radomiak Radom - Miedź Legnica 1-1(0-0)
Wisła Płock - Lechia Gdańsk 3-0(1-0)
Pogoń Szczecin - Widzew Łódź 2-1(1-1)
Górnik Zabrze - Cracovia Kraków 0-2(0-2)

**Round 2 [22-25.07.2022]**
Warta Poznań - Wisła Płock 0-4(0-3)
Jagiellonia Białystok - Widzew Łódź 0-2(0-0)
Cracovia Kraków - Korona Kielce 2-0(1-0)
Legia Warszawa - Zagłębie Lubin 2-0(1-0)
Śląsk Wrocław - Pogoń Szczecin 2-1(1-1)
Stal Mielec - Radomiak Radom 1-0(0-0)
Piast Gliw. - Raków Częst. 0-1(0-0) [06.10.22]
Lechia Gd. - Górnik Z. 2-1(0-1) [18.11.22]
Miedź Leg. - Lech Poznań 2-2(1-1) [01.02.23]

**Round 3 [29.07.-01.08.2022]**
Piast Gliwice - Zagłębie Lubin 0-1(0-0)
Cracovia Kraków - Legia Warszawa 3-0(1-0)
Radomiak Radom - Górnik Zabrze 0-3(0-2)
Miedź Legnica - Warta Poznań 1-2(1-1)
Pogoń Szczecin-Jagiellonia Białystok 1-0(1-0)
Lech Poznań - Wisła Płock 1-3(0-1)
Raków Częstochowa - Stal Mielec 3-2(1-1)
Widzew Łódź - Lechia Gdańsk 2-3(1-2)
Korona Kielce - Śląsk Wrocław 3-1(2-0)

## Round 4 [05-08.08.2022]
Stal Mielec - Cracovia Kraków 2-0(1-0)
Legia Warszawa - Piast Gliwice 2-0(0-0)
Lechia Gdańsk - Korona Kielce 0-1(0-1)
Jagiellonia B. - Radomiak Radom 1-2(1-0)
Śląsk Wrocław - Widzew Łódź 0-0
Warta Poznań - Pogoń Szczecin 1-2(0-2)
Zagłębie Lubin - Lech Poznań 1-1(0-0)
Górnik Zabrze - Raków Częstochowa 1-0(1-0)
Wisła Płock - Miedź Legnica 4-1(2-1)

## Round 5 [12-15.08.2022]
Miedź Legnica - Zagłębie Lubin 0-1(0-0)
Widzew Łódź - Legia Warszawa 1-2(0-2)
Cracovia Kraków - Piast Gliwice 0-1(0-0)
Górnik Zabrze - Stal Mielec 1-3(1-2)
Pogoń Szczecin - Wisła Płock 2-2(1-0)
Radomiak Radom - Lechia Gdańsk 4-1(2-1)
Raków Częstochowa - Jagiellonia B. 2-2(2-0)
Lech Poznań - Śląsk Wrocław 0-1(0-1)
Korona Kielce - Warta Poznań 0-1(0-1)

## Round 6 [19-21.08.2022]
Jagiellonia Białystok-Miedź Legnica 2-1(0-1)
Legia Warszawa - Górnik Zabrze 2-2(0-1)
Wisła Płock - Korona Kielce 2-1(1-0)
Śląsk Wrocław - Cracovia Kraków 1-1(1-1)
Warta Poznań - Widzew Łódź 0-1(0-0)
Zagłębie Lubin - Radomiak Radom 0-1(0-0)
Piast Gliwice - Stal Mielec 4-0(1-0)
Raków Częst. - Pogoń Sz. 1-0(0-0) [31.08.22]
Lechia Gdańsk - Lech Po. 0-3(0-2) [31.08.22]

## Round 7 [26-28.08.2022]
Górnik Zabrze - Jagiellonia Białystok 1-1(0-1)
Stal Mielec - Legia Warszawa 0-1(0-0)
Radomiak Radom - Korona Kielce 0-2(0-1)
Miedź Legnica - Lechia Gdańsk 2-1(1-0)
Pogoń Szczecin - Zagłębie Lubin 3-0(1-0)
Widzew Łódź - Wisła Płock 2-1(1-0)
Cracovia Kraków - Warta Poznań 0-2(0-0)
Śląsk Wrocław-Raków Częstochowa 1-4(0-1)
Lech Poznań - Piast Gliwice 1-0(1-0)

## Round 8 [02-05.09.2022]
Legia Warszawa - Radomiak Radom 1-0(0-0)
Stal Mielec - Śląsk Wrocław 2-0(1-0)
Lechia Gdańsk - Warta Poznań 0-0
Cracovia Kr. - Raków Częstochowa 3-0(2-0)
Zagłębie Lubin - Jagiellonia B. 1-1(0-0)
Korona Kielce - Pogoń Szczecin 1-2(0-2)
Lech Poznań - Widzew Łódź 2-0(0-0)
Piast Gliwice - Miedź Legnica 2-1(1-1)
Wisła Płock - Górnik Zabrze 1-1(1-0)

## Round 9 [09-12.09.2022]
Warta Poznań - Zagłębie Lubin 2-2(1-1)
Widzew Łódź - Cracovia Kraków 2-0(1-0)
Śląsk Wrocław - Lechia Gdańsk 2-1(0-1)
Radomiak Radom - Wisła Płock 2-0(1-0)
Górnik Zabrze - Piast Gliwice 3-3(2-2)
Miedź Legnica - Korona Kielce 2-2(1-0)
Pogoń Szczecin - Lech Poznań 2-2(1-1)
Raków Częstochowa - Legia Warsz. 4-0(1-0)
Jagiellonia Białystok - Stal Mielec 4-0(3-0)

## Round 10 [16-18.09.2022]
Piast Gliwice - Śląsk Wrocław 1-1(1-1)
Legia Warszawa - Miedź Legnica 3-2(2-2)
Stal Mielec - Widzew Łódź 0-3(0-0)
Lechia Gdańsk - Jagiellonia B. 2-2(0-1)
Raków Częstochowa - Radomiak R. 3-0(1-0)
Cracovia Kraków - Pogoń Szczecin 1-0(1-0)
Korona Kielce - Górnik Zabrze 1-2(1-1)
Zagłębie Lubin - Wisła Płock 2-1(1-1)
Warta Poznań - Lech Poznań 0-1(0-0)

## Round 11 [30.09.-03.10.2022]
Radomiak Radom - Cracovia Kraków 0-2(0-1)
Wisła Płock - Piast Gliwice 1-0(0-0)
Górnik Zabrze - Zagłębie Lubin 2-3(1-2)
Lech Poznań - Legia Warszawa 0-0
Pogoń Szczecin - Lechia Gdańsk 2-1(2-1)
Miedź Legnica - Stal Mielec 0-2(0-2)
Jagiellonia Białystok - Korona Kielce 4-1(1-1)
Widzew Łódź - Raków Częstochowa 0-0
Śląsk Wrocław - Warta Poznań 0-2(0-1)

## Round 12 [07-10.10.2022]
Stal Mielec - Pogoń Szczecin 4-2(2-1)
Jagiellonia Białystok - Wisła Płock 1-1(0-1)
Śląsk Wrocław - Górnik Zabrze 4-1(2-0)
Legia Warszawa - Warta Poznań 1-0(1-0)
Cracovia Kraków - Lechia Gdańsk 0-1(0-0)
Zagłębie Lubin - Korona Kielce 1-0(1-0)
Lech Poznań - Radomiak Radom 1-0(1-0)
Raków Częstochowa-Miedź Legnica 1-0(1-0)
Piast Gliwice - Widzew Łódź 1-2(0-1)

## Round 13 [14-16.10.2022]
Korona Kielce - Stal Mielec 0-2(0-2)
Wisła Płock - Legia Warszawa 2-1(0-0)
Radomiak Radom - Śląsk Wrocław 2-0(0-0)
Lechia Gdańsk-Raków Częstochowa 0-3(0-2)
Warta Poznań - Jagiellonia Białystok 2-0(0-0)
Pogoń Szczecin - Piast Gliwice 1-1(0-1)
Miedź Legnica - Cracovia Kraków 1-1(0-1)
Widzew Łódź - Zagłębie Lubin 3-0(1-0)
Górnik Zabrze - Lech Poznań 1-2(1-1)

## Round 14 [21-24.10.2022]
Widzew Łódź - Miedź Legnica 1-0(1-0)
Stal Mielec - Wisła Płock 1-1(1-0)
Legia Warszawa - Pogoń Szczecin 1-1(1-0)
Raków Częstochowa - Korona Kielce 1-0(0-0)
Warta Poznań - Górnik Zabrze 0-0
Śląsk Wrocław-Jagiellonia Białystok 2-2(1-1)
Cracovia Kraków - Lech Poznań 0-0
Piast Gliwice - Radomiak Radom 1-2(1-1)
Zagłębie Lubin - Lechia Gdańsk 0-3(0-1)

## Round 15 [28-31.10.2022]
Miedź Legnica - Pogoń Szczecin 2-4(2-2)
Górnik Zabrze - Widzew Łódź 3-0(3-0)
Korona Kielce - Piast Gliwice 1-1(1-0)
Jagiellonia B. - Legia Warszawa 2-5(1-3)
Wisła Płock - Śląsk Wrocław 1-2(0-0)
Zagłębie Lubin - Cracovia Kraków 0-2(0-0)
Lechia Gdańsk - Stal Mielec 1-0(0-0)
Lech Poznań - Raków Częstochowa 1-2(0-0)
Radomiak Radom - Warta Poznań 2-3(0-2)

## Round 16 [04-06.11.2022]
Stal Mielec - Zagłębie Lubin 3-0(0-0)
Legia Warszawa - Lechia Gdańsk 2-1(0-0)
Piast Gliwice - Warta Poznań 0-2(0-1)
Cracovia Kraków - Jagiellonia B. 1-0(0-0)
Pogoń Szczecin - Górnik Zabrze 1-4(1-1)
Raków Częstochowa - Wisła Płock 7-1(4-1)
Miedź Legnica - Śląsk Wrocław 1-0(1-0)
Widzew Łódź - Radomiak Radom 1-3(0-2)
Lech Poznań - Korona Kielce 3-2(1-0)

## Round 17 [11-13.11.2022]
Warta Poznań - Stal Mielec 1-1(0-0)
Wisła Płock - Cracovia Kraków 1-0(0-0)
Korona Kielce - Widzew Łódź 0-1(0-0)
Górnik Zabrze - Miedź Legnica 0-3(0-2)
Jagiellonia Białystok - Lech Poznań 1-2(1-1)
Zagłębie Lubin-Raków Częstochowa 1-2(0-2)
Radomiak Radom - Pogoń Szczecin 1-2(0-0)
Lechia Gdańsk - Piast Gliwice 1-3(0-1)
Śląsk Wrocław - Legia Warszawa 0-0

## Round 18 [27-30.01.2023]
Miedź Legnica - Radomiak Radom 0-0
Stal Mielec - Lech Poznań 0-0
Warta Poznań - Raków Częstochowa 1-1(1-0)
Widzew Łódź - Pogoń Szczecin 3-3(0-1)
Śląsk Wrocław - Zagłębie Lubin 0-3(0-1)
Piast Gliwice - Jagiellonia Białystok 1-1(0-0)
Legia Warszawa - Korona Kielce 3-2(2-0)
Lechia Gdańsk - Wisła Płock 1-0(0-0)
Cracovia Kraków - Górnik Zabrze 2-0(1-0)

## Round 19 [03-06.02.2023]
Widzew Łódź - Jagiellonia Białystok 1-1(0-0)
Raków Częstochowa - Piast Gliwice 1-0(1-0)
Górnik Zabrze - Lechia Gdańsk 1-1(1-0)
Zagłębie Lubin - Legia Warszawa 1-2(0-1)
Radomiak Radom - Stal Mielec 1-0(1-0)
Lech Poznań - Miedź Legnica 1-0(1-0)
Pogoń Szczecin - Śląsk Wrocław 0-2(0-0)
Korona Kielce - Cracovia Kraków 2-1(1-0)
Wisła Płock - Warta Poz. 1-0(0-0) [08.03.23]

## Round 20 [10-13.02.2023]
Stal Mielec - Raków Częstochowa 0-0
Lechia Gdańsk - Widzew Łódź 0-0
Śląsk Wrocław - Korona Kielce 1-1(0-0)
Wisła Płock - Lech Poznań 0-1(0-1)
Jagiellonia Białystok-Pogoń Szczecin 2-0(0-0)
Zagłębie Lubin - Piast Gliwice 0-2(0-2)
Górnik Zabrze - Radomiak Radom 0-0
Legia Warszawa - Cracovia Kraków 2-2(0-1)
Warta Poznań - Miedź Legnica 1-1(0-0)

## Round 21 [17-20.02.2023]
Cracovia Kraków - Stal Mielec 2-1(0-1)
Widzew Łódź - Śląsk Wrocław 1-0(0-0)
Korona Kielce - Lechia Gdańsk 1-0(1-0)
Raków Częstochowa - Górnik Zabrze 2-0(1-0)
Pogoń Szczecin - Warta Poznań 3-1(1-1)
Miedź Legnica - Wisła Płock 2-1(1-1)
Lech Poznań - Zagłębie Lubin 1-2(1-2)
Piast Gliwice - Legia Warszawa 0-1(0-0)
Radomiak Radom - Jagiellonia Białystok 0-0

## Round 22 [24-27.02.2023]
Jagiellonia B. - Raków Częstochowa 1-2(1-1)
Legia Warszawa - Widzew Łódź 2-2(1-0)
Piast Gliwice - Cracovia Kraków 2-1(0-0)
Warta Poznań - Korona Kielce 5-1(3-0)
Lechia Gdańsk - Radomiak Radom 1-3(0-2)
Stal Mielec - Górnik Zabrze 0-1(0-0)
Wisła Płock - Pogoń Szczecin 0-1(0-0)
Śląsk Wrocław - Lech Poznań 2-1(1-0)
Zagłębie Lubin - Miedź Legnica 2-1(0-0)

## Round 23 [03-06.03.2023]
Stal Mielec - Piast Gliwice 0-2(0-0)
Lech Poznań - Lechia Gdańsk 5-0(2-0)
Widzew Łódź - Warta Poznań 0-2(0-1)
Korona Kielce - Wisła Płock 1-0(0-0)
Górnik Zabrze - Legia Warszawa 0-1(0-1)
Miedź Legnica - Jagiellonia B. 1-1(1-1)
Pogoń Sz. - Raków Częstochowa 0-2(0-1)
Cracovia Kraków - Śląsk Wrocław 1-1(0-1)
Radomiak Radom - Zagłębie Lubin 0-1(0-1)

## Round 24 [10-13.03.2023]
Lechia Gdańsk - Miedź Legnica 4-0(0-0)
Raków Częstochowa-Śląsk Wrocław 4-1(1-0)
Korona Kielce - Radomiak Radom 2-1(1-1)
Zagłębie Lubin - Pogoń Szczecin 0-1(0-0)
Jagiellonia Białystok - Górnik Zabrze 2-1(2-1)
Warta Poznań - Cracovia Kraków 0-0
Piast Gliwice - Lech Poznań 0-1(0-0)
Legia Warszawa - Stal Mielec 2-0(0-0)
Wisła Płock - Widzew Łódź 1-1(1-0)

**Round 25** [17-19.03.2023]
Górnik Zabrze - Wisła Płock 3-2(0-2)
Radomiak Radom - Legia Warszawa 0-2(0-1)
Śląsk Wrocław - Stal Mielec 1-1(1-1)
Jagiellonia Białystok-Zagłębie Lubin 2-2(0-1)
Pogoń Szczecin - Korona Kielce 0-0
Raków Częstochowa - Cracovia Kr. 4-1(1-1)
Warta Poznań - Lechia Gdańsk 2-0(1-0)
Miedź Legnica - Piast Gliwice 0-1(0-1)
Widzew Łódź - Lech Poznań 1-2(0-0)

**Round 26** [31.03.-03.04.2023]
Zagłębie Lubin - Warta Poznań 0-0
Piast Gliwice - Górnik Zabrze 1-0(1-0)
Korona Kielce - Miedź Legnica 1-0(1-0)
Legia Warszawa - Raków Częstoch. 3-1(2-1)
Lechia Gdańsk - Śląsk Wrocław 0-0
Wisła Płock - Radomiak Radom 1-1(0-0)
Cracovia Kraków - Widzew Łódź 1-1(0-0)
Lech Poznań - Pogoń Szczecin 2-2(1-1)
Stal Mielec - Jagiellonia Białystok 1-1(0-1)

**Round 27** [06-10.04.2023]
Śląsk Wrocław - Piast Gliwice 0-1(0-0)
Górnik Zabrze - Korona Kielce 1-1(0-1)
Wisła Płock - Zagłębie Lubin 2-0(0-0)
Widzew Łódź - Stal Mielec 0-2(0-1)
Pogoń Szczecin - Cracovia Kraków 3-2(2-1)
Lech Poznań - Warta Poznań 2-0(1-0)
Jagiellonia B. - Lechia Gdańsk 1-0(0-0)
Radomiak Radom - Raków Częstochowa 0-0
Miedź Legnica - Legia Warszawa 2-2(1-1)

**Round 28** [14-17.04.2023]
Warta Poznań - Śląsk Wrocław 3-1(2-1)
Zagłębie Lubin - Górnik Zabrze 0-2(0-0)
Cracovia Kraków - Radomiak Radom 3-0(1-0)
Korona Kielce - Jagiellonia Białystok 2-1(0-1)
Lechia Gdańsk - Pogoń Szczecin 0-1(0-0)
Piast Gliwice - Wisła Płock 1-0(1-0)
Raków Częstochowa - Widzew Łódź 2-0(1-0)
Legia Warszawa - Lech Poznań 2-2(1-0)
Stal Mielec - Miedź Legnica 1-1(0-0)

**Round 29** [21-24.04.2023]
Wisła Płock - Jagiellonia Białystok 2-4(2-1)
Warta Poznań - Legia Warszawa 1-0(0-0)
Lechia Gdańsk - Cracovia Kraków 1-2(0-1)
Miedź Legnica-Raków Częstochowa 0-2(0-1)
Pogoń Szczecin - Stal Mielec 4-2(2-0)
Korona Kielce - Zagłębie Lubin 2-2(2-2)
Widzew Łódź - Piast Gliwice 3-0(0-2)
Górnik Zabrze - Śląsk Wrocław 2-0(2-0)
Radomiak Radom - Lech Poznań 1-1(1-0)

**Round 30** [28.04.-01.05.2023]
Legia Warszawa - Wisła Płock 2-0(1-0)
Raków Częstochowa-Lechia Gdańsk 4-0(1-0)
Jagiellonia Białystok - Warta Poznań 3-1(3-0)
Zagłębie Lubin - Widzew Łódź 2-0(1-0)
Piast Gliwice - Pogoń Szczecin 0-0
Śląsk Wrocław - Radomiak Radom 0-1(0-1)
Stal Mielec - Korona Kielce 0-0
Lech Poznań - Górnik Zabrze 0-1(0-1)
Cracovia Kraków - Miedź Legnica 1-1(0-1)

**Round 31** [05-08.05.2023]
Jagiellonia Białystok-Śląsk Wrocław 1-1(0-1)
Górnik Zabrze - Warta Poznań 2-0(1-0)
Radomiak Radom - Piast Gliwice 0-1(0-1)
Lech Poznań - Cracovia Kraków 3-0(3-0)
Lechia Gdańsk - Zagłębie Lubin 1-3(1-1)
Wisła Płock - Stal Mielec 0-0
Korona Kielce - Raków Częstochowa 1-0(1-0)
Pogoń Szczecin - Legia Warszawa 2-1(1-0)
Miedź Legnica - Widzew Łódź 0-1(0-0)

**Round 32** [12-15.05.2023]
Piast Gliwice - Korona Kielce 2-1(0-0)
Legia Warszawa - Jagiellonia B. 5-1(1-1)
Śląsk Wrocław - Wisła Płock 3-1(1-1)
Cracovia Kraków - Zagłębie Lubin 0-1(0-0)
Widzew Łódź - Górnik Zabrze 2-3(1-2)
Stal Mielec - Lechia Gdańsk 0-0
Pogoń Szczecin - Miedź Legnica 3-2(1-1)
Raków Częstochowa - Lech Poznań 0-2(0-1)
Warta Poznań - Radomiak Radom 1-2(0-2)

**Round 33** [19-22.05.2023]
Zagłębie Lubin - Stal Mielec 2-0(2-0)
Korona Kielce - Lech Poznań 0-3(0-1)
Jagiellonia Białystok - Cracovia Kr. 1-1(1-0)
Górnik Zabrze - Pogoń Szczecin 2-1(0-0)
Lechia Gdańsk - Legia Warszawa 1-0(0-0)
Śląsk Wrocław - Miedź Legnica 4-2(2-0)
Radomiak Radom - Widzew Łódź 3-1(2-1)
Wisła Płock - Raków Częstochowa 1-2(1-0)
Warta Poznań - Piast Gliwice 1-1(1-1)

**Round 34** [27.05.2023]
Stal Mielec - Warta Poznań 1-0(1-0)
Cracovia Kraków - Wisła Płock 3-0(1-0)
Lech Poznań - Jagiellonia Białystok 2-0(1-0)
Legia Warszawa - Śląsk Wrocław 3-1(2-1)
Miedź Legnica - Górnik Zabrze 0-0
Piast Gliwice - Lechia Gdańsk 3-0 *awarded*
Pogoń Szczecin - Radomiak Radom 4-0(1-0)
Raków Częstochowa-Zagłębie Lubin 1-1(0-0)
Widzew Łódź - Korona Kielce 0-3(0-2)

## Final Standings

| | | Total | | | | | | Home | | | | | Away | | | |
|---|---|---|---|---|---|---|---|---|---|---|---|---|---|---|---|---|---|
| 1. | **RKS Raków Częstochowa** | 34 | 23 | 6 | 5 | 63 - 24 | **75** | 14 | 2 | 1 | 41 - 10 | 9 | 4 | 4 | 22 - 14 |
| 2. | Legia Warszawa | 34 | 19 | 9 | 6 | 57 - 37 | **66** | 12 | 5 | 0 | 38 - 17 | 7 | 4 | 6 | 19 - 20 |
| 3. | KKS Lech Poznań | 34 | 17 | 10 | 7 | 51 - 29 | **61** | 9 | 2 | 6 | 25 - 15 | 8 | 8 | 1 | 26 - 14 |
| 4. | MKS Pogoń Szczecin | 34 | 17 | 9 | 8 | 57 - 46 | **60** | 10 | 4 | 3 | 33 - 23 | 7 | 5 | 5 | 24 - 23 |
| 5. | GKS Piast Gliwice | 34 | 15 | 8 | 11 | 40 - 31 | **53** | 7 | 4 | 6 | 20 - 15 | 8 | 4 | 5 | 20 - 16 |
| 6. | KS Górnik Zabrze | 34 | 13 | 9 | 12 | 45 - 43 | **48** | 6 | 5 | 6 | 23 - 23 | 7 | 4 | 6 | 22 - 20 |
| 7. | KS Cracovia Kraków | 34 | 12 | 10 | 12 | 41 - 35 | **46** | 8 | 5 | 4 | 23 - 10 | 4 | 5 | 8 | 18 - 25 |
| 8. | KS Warta Poznań | 34 | 12 | 9 | 13 | 37 - 35 | **45** | 5 | 7 | 5 | 21 - 18 | 7 | 2 | 8 | 16 - 17 |
| 9. | Zagłębie Lubin | 34 | 12 | 9 | 13 | 35 - 44 | **45** | 4 | 5 | 8 | 13 - 20 | 8 | 4 | 5 | 22 - 24 |
| 10. | RKS Radomiak Radom | 34 | 12 | 8 | 14 | 34 - 41 | **44** | 5 | 4 | 8 | 17 - 20 | 7 | 4 | 6 | 17 - 21 |
| 11. | FKS Stal Mielec | 34 | 11 | 10 | 13 | 36 - 40 | **43** | 6 | 7 | 4 | 18 - 14 | 5 | 3 | 9 | 18 - 26 |
| 12. | RTS Widzew Łódź | 34 | 11 | 8 | 15 | 38 - 47 | **41** | 5 | 3 | 9 | 22 - 28 | 6 | 5 | 6 | 16 - 19 |
| 13. | Korona Kielce | 34 | 11 | 8 | 15 | 39 - 48 | **41** | 8 | 3 | 6 | 19 - 19 | 3 | 5 | 9 | 20 - 29 |
| 14. | Jagiellonia Białystok | 34 | 9 | 14 | 11 | 48 - 49 | **41** | 8 | 4 | 5 | 30 - 22 | 1 | 10 | 6 | 18 - 27 |
| 15. | WKS Śląsk Wrocław | 34 | 9 | 11 | 14 | 35 - 48 | **38** | 6 | 6 | 5 | 23 - 23 | 3 | 5 | 9 | 12 - 25 |
| 16. | Wisła Płock *(Relegated)* | 34 | 10 | 7 | 17 | 41 - 50 | **37** | 8 | 4 | 5 | 23 - 16 | 2 | 3 | 12 | 18 - 34 |
| 17. | KS Lechia Gdańsk *(Relegated)* | 34 | 8 | 6 | 20 | 28 - 56 | **30** | 5 | 4 | 8 | 15 - 22 | 3 | 2 | 12 | 13 - 34 |
| 18. | MKS Miedź Legnica *(Relegated)* | 34 | 4 | 11 | 19 | 33 - 55 | **23** | 3 | 7 | 7 | 16 - 23 | 1 | 4 | 12 | 17 - 32 |

## Top goalscorers:

| | | |
|---|---|---|
| 16 | **Marc Gual Huguet (ESP)** | *Jagiellonia Białystok* |
| 14 | Jesús Imaz Ballesté (ESP) | *Jagiellonia Białystok* |
| 13 | Kamil Grosicki | *MKS Pogoń Szczecin* |
| 12 | Josué Filipe Soares Pesqueira (POR) | *Legia Warszawa* |
| 12 | Jakub Łukowski | *Korona Kielce* |

## NATIONAL CUP
### Puchar Polski 2022/2023

**Second Round [12.10./18-20.10.2022]**

| | | | | | |
|---|---|---|---|---|---|
| KS Lechia Zielona Góra - Jagiellonia Białystok | 3-1(2-1) | | Resovia Rzeszów - KS Cracovia Kraków | 4-3(2-3) |
| Rekord Bielsko-Biała - MKS Pogoń Szczecin | 3-3 aet; 11-12 pen | | MKS Sandecja Nowy Sącz - KS Warta Poznań | 2-1(1-0) |
| Zagłębie Sosnowiec - RKS Raków Częstochowa | 0-1(0-0) | | LKP Motor Lublin - Zagłębie Lubin | 1-0(0-0,0-0) |
| FKS Stal Mielec - GKS Piast Gliwice | 0-3(0-0,0-0) | | TS Wisła Kraków - MKS Puszcza Niepołomice | 2-2 aet; 6-5 pen |
| KKS 1925 Kalisz - KS Olimpia Elblag | 2-0(1-0) | | KKS Lech Poznań - WKS Śląsk Wrocław | 1-3(1-1) |
| GKS Górnik Łęczna - Korona Kielce | 1-0(0-0) | | MKP Pogoń Siedlce - MKS Chrobry Głogów | 3-1(2-0) |
| Wisła Płock - Legia Warszawa | 0-3(0-1) | | SP Zawisza Bydgoszcz - RKS Radomiak Radom | 1-3(1-1) |
| KS Radunia Stężyca - KS Lechia Gdańsk | 1-4(1-2) | | GKS Katowice - KS Górnik Zabrze | 1-2(1-0) |

**1/8-Finals [08-10.11.2022]**

| | | | | | |
|---|---|---|---|---|---|
| KKS 1925 Kalisz - KS Górnik Zabrze | 3-3 aet; 5-3 pen | | MKS Pogoń Szczecin - RKS Raków Częstochowa | 0-1(0-0) |
| GKS Górnik Łęczna - GKS Piast Gliwice | 1-0(0-0,0-0) | | MKS Sandecja Nowy Sącz - WKS Śląsk Wrocław | 0-3 awarded |
| KS Lechia Gdańsk - Legia Warszawa | 2-2 aet; 2-4 pen | | KS Lechia Zielona Góra - RKS Radomiak Radom | 0-0 aet; 3-1 pen |
| LKP Motor Lublin - TS Wisła Kraków | 1-0(0-0) | | MKP Pogoń Siedlce - Resovia Rzeszów | 1-0(0-0) |

**Quarter-Finals [28.02.-01.03.2023]**

| | | | | | |
|---|---|---|---|---|---|
| KS Lechia Zielona Góra - Legia Warszawa | 0-3(0-2) | | KKS 1925 Kalisz - WKS Śląsk Wrocław | 3-0(3-0) |
| MKP Pogoń Siedlce - GKS Górnik Łęczna | 0-1(0-0) | | LKP Motor Lublin - RKS Raków Częstochowa | 0-3(0-1) |

**Semi-Finals [04-05.04.2023]**

| | | | | | |
|---|---|---|---|---|---|
| KKS 1925 Kalisz - Legia Warszawa | 0-1(0-1) | | GKS Górnik Łęczna - RKS Raków Częstochowa | 0-1(0-0) |

**Final**

02.05.2023; Stadion Narodowy, Warszawa; Referee: Piotr Lasyk; Attendance: 44,701
**Legia Warszawa - RKS Raków Częstochowa**     **0-0 aet; 6-5 on penalties**

**Legia Warszawa**: Kacper Tobiasz, Yuri Oliveira Ribeiro [*sent off 6*], Rafał Augustyniak, Artur Jędrzejczyk, Paweł Wszołek, Bartosz Slisz, Josué Filipe Soares Pesqueira (Cap) (106.Patryk Sokołowski), Bartosz Kapustka (86.Jurgen Çelhaka), Filip Mladenović [*sent off 120+6 on the bench*] (106.Makana Baku), Ernest Muçi (43.Maik Nawrocki), Tomáš Pekhart (62.Maciej Rosołek). Trainer: Kosta Runjaić (Germany).

**Raków Częstochowa**: Kacper Trelowski, Stratos Svarnas, Tomáš Petrášek (Cap) (46.Patryk Kun; 91.Wiktor Długosz), Zoran Arsenić, Fran Tudor, Ben Lederman (68.Bartosz Nowak), Giannis Papanikolaou, Jean Carlos Silva Rocha [*sent off 120+6*], Vladyslav Kochergin, Iván „Ivi" López Álvarez (98.Mateusz Wdowiak), Vladislavs Gutkovskis (68.Fabian Piasecki). Trainer: Marek Papszun.

**Penalties:** Bartosz Slisz 1-0; Fran Tudor 1-1; Maciej Rosołek 2-1; Stratos Svarnas 2-2; Rafał Augustyniak 3-1; Fabian Piasecki 3-3; Patryk Sokołowski 4-3; Bartosz Nowak 4-4; Paweł Wszołek 5-4; Jean Carlos Silva Rocha 5-5; Maik Nawrocki 6-5; Mateusz Wdowiak (saved).

## THE CLUBS 2022/2023

### Miejski Klub Sportowy Cracovia Kraków

| | | |
|---|---|---|
| **Founded**: | 13.06.1906 | |
| **Stadium**: | Stadion "Marszałek Józef Piłsudski", Kraków (15,016) | |
| **Trainer**: | Jacek Zieliński | 22.03.1961 |

| Goalkeepers: | DOB | M | (s) | G |
|---|---|---|---|---|
| Lukáš Hrošło (SVK) | 19.04.1987 | 3 | | |
| Karol Niemczycki | 05.07.1999 | 31 | | |
| **Defenders:** | **DOB** | **M** | **(s)** | **G** |
| Virgil Eugen Ghiţă (ROU) | 04.06.1998 | 34 | | 3 |
| Arttu Hoskonen (FIN) | 16.04.1997 | 9 | (2) | 1 |
| David Jablonský (CZE) | 08.10.1991 | 14 | (1) | 1 |
| Paweł Jaroszyński | 02.10.1994 | 12 | (9) | |
| Jakub Jugas (CZE) | 05.05.1992 | 24 | (2) | 1 |
| Kamil Pestka | 22.08.1998 | 6 | | |
| Cornel Emilian Râpă (ROU) | 16.01.1990 | 19 | (7) | |
| Matej Rodin (CRO) | 13.02.1996 | 14 | | 1 |
| Michal Sipľak (SVK) | 02.02.1996 | 13 | (8) | |
| **Midfielders:** | **DOB** | **M** | **(s)** | **G** |
| Jani Atanasov (MKD) | 31.10.1999 | 10 | (5) | 1 |
| Mateusz Bochnak | 11.02.1998 | 9 | (7) | 2 |
| Mathias Hebo (DEN) | 02.08.1995 | 11 | (1) | 1 |
| Kacper Jodłowski | 30.05.1999 | | (4) | |

| | DOB | M | (s) | G |
|---|---|---|---|---|
| Otar Kakabadze (GEO) | 27.06.1995 | 20 | (7) | 1 |
| Karol Knap | 12.09.2001 | 17 | (13) | 2 |
| Bartłomiej Kolec | 02.03.2004 | | (1) | |
| Florian Loshaj (KOS) | 13.08.1996 | 7 | (8) | 1 |
| Takuto Oshima (JPN) | 01.06.1998 | 26 | (6) | 1 |
| Filip Rózga | 07.08.2006 | | (1) | |
| Michał Stachera | 18.01.2001 | 1 | | |
| **Forwards:** | **DOB** | **M** | **(s)** | **G** |
| Filip Balaj (SVK) | 02.08.1997 | | (6) | |
| Benjamin Källman (FIN) | 17.06.1998 | 24 | (10) | 6 |
| Yevgen Konoplyanka (UKR) | 29.09.1989 | 12 | (14) | 2 |
| Patryk Makuch | 11.04.1999 | 24 | (8) | 6 |
| Jakub Myszor | 07.06.2002 | 9 | (11) | 2 |
| Michał Rakoczy | 30.03.2002 | 25 | (5) | 7 |
| Kacper Śmiglewski | 07.01.2005 | | (3) | |
| Sebastian Strózik | 15.05.1999 | | (1) | |
| Patryk Zaucha | 19.04.2000 | | (1) | |

## Klub Sportowy Górnik Zabrze

**Founded**: 14.12.1948
**Stadium**: Stadion „Ernest Pohl", Zabrze (24,563)
**Trainer**: Bartosch Gaul (GER)    05.10.1987
[18.03.2023]   Jan Urban    14.05.1962

| Goalkeepers: | DOB | M | (s) | G |
|---|---|---|---|---|
| Daniel Bielica | 30.04.1999 | 24 | | |
| Kevin Broll (GER) | 23.08.1995 | 10 | | |
| **Defenders:** | **DOB** | **M** | **(s)** | **G** |
| Emil Bergström (SWE) | 19.05.1993 | 23 | (2) | 2 |
| Rafał Janicki | 05.07.1992 | 14 | (2) | |
| Erik Janža (SVN) | 21.06.1993 | 32 | | 2 |
| Richard Jensen (FIN) | 17.03.1996 | 28 | (1) | 1 |
| Aleksander Paluszek | 09.04.2001 | 10 | (7) | 3 |
| Boris Sekulić (SVK) | 21.10.1991 | 9 | (2) | 1 |
| Kryspin Szcześniak | 08.01.2001 | 11 | (3) | |
| Jakub Szymański | 05.07.2002 | 1 | (2) | |
| Norbert Wojtuszek | 05.10.2001 | 8 | (10) | |
| **Midfielders:** | **DOB** | **M** | **(s)** | **G** |
| Robin Roger Kamber (SUI) | 15.02.1996 | 1 | (3) | |
| Jonatan Kotzke (GER) | 18.03.1990 | 11 | (5) | |
| Krzysztof Kubica | 25.05.2000 | | (4) | |
| Alasana Manneh (GAM) | 08.04.1998 | 4 | | |
| Jean Jules Sepp Mvondo (CMR) | 23.04.1998 | 20 | (7) | |
| Bartosz Nowak | 25.08.1993 | 2 | | 1 |
| Damian Rasak | 08.02.1996 | 12 | | 2 |
| Dariusz Stalmach | 08.12.2005 | | (3) | |
| Blaž Vrhovec (SVN) | 20.02.1992 | 6 | (7) | |
| Nikodem Zielonka | 17.08.2004 | | (1) | |
| **Forwards:** | **DOB** | **M** | **(s)** | **G** |
| Mateusz Cholewiak | 05.02.1990 | 7 | (15) | |
| Robert Dadok | 24.12.1996 | 15 | (13) | 4 |
| Daniel „Dani" Pacheco Lobato (ESP) | 05.01.1991 | 19 | (9) | 2 |
| Krzysztof Kolanko | 03.08.2006 | | (4) | |
| Piotr Krawczyk | 29.12.1994 | 12 | (12) | 4 |
| Amadej Maroša (SVN) | 07.02.1994 | | (5) | |
| Kanji Okunuki (JPN) | 11.08.1999 | 18 | (8) | 4 |
| Paweł Olkowski | 13.02.1990 | 20 | (6) | 1 |
| Lukas Podolski (GER) | 04.06.1985 | 25 | (4) | 6 |
| Anthony van den Hurk (CUW) | 09.01.1993 | 2 | (4) | 1 |
| Szymon Włodarczyk | 05.01.2003 | 18 | (12) | 9 |
| Daisuke Yokota (JPN) | 15.06.2000 | 12 | (1) | 2 |

## Jagiellonia Białystok Sportowa Spółka Akcyjna

**Founded**: 30.05.1920
**Stadium**: Stadion Miejski, Białystok (22,432)
**Trainer**: Maciej Stolarczyk    15.01.1972
[04.04.2023]   Adrian Siemieniec    13.01.1992

| Goalkeepers: | DOB | M | (s) | G |
|---|---|---|---|---|
| Sławomir Abramowicz | 09.06.2004 | 2 | (1) | |
| Zlatan Alomerović (GER) | 15.06.1991 | 32 | | |
| **Defenders:** | **DOB** | **M** | **(s)** | **G** |
| Israel Puerto Pineda (ESP) | 15.06.1993 | 23 | (3) | |
| Jakub Lewicki | 17.09.2005 | 14 | (5) | 1 |
| Miłosz Matysik | 26.04.2004 | 10 | (5) | |
| Bojan Nastić (BIH) | 06.07.1994 | 19 | (2) | |
| Pawel Olszewski | 07.06.1999 | 3 | (8) | |
| Michał Pazdan | 21.09.1987 | 12 | (2) | 1 |
| Mateusz Skrzypczak | 22.08.2000 | 23 | (3) | 1 |
| Dušan Stojinović (SVN) | 26.08.2000 | 9 | (3) | |
| Bogdan Ionuţ Ţîru (ROU) | 15.03.1994 | 15 | | |
| Bartłomiej Wdowik | 25.09.2000 | 16 | (10) | |
| **Midfielders:** | **DOB** | **M** | **(s)** | **G** |
| Jesús Imaz Ballesté (ESP) | 26.09.1990 | 32 | (1) | 14 |
| Juan del Carmen Cámara Mesa (ESP) | 13.02.1994 | 3 | (5) | |
| Wojciech Łaski | 21.05.2000 | 2 | (10) | 1 |
| Rui Filipe da Cunha Correia „Nené" (POR) | 10.06.1995 | 25 | (5) | 5 |
| Aurélien Nguiamba (FRA) | 18.01.1999 | 5 | (6) | |
| Martin Pospíšil (CZE) | 26.06.1991 | 9 | (7) | |
| Taras Romanczuk | 14.11.1991 | 22 | (2) | 1 |
| Michal Sáček (CZE) | 19.09.1996 | 12 | (2) | |
| Oliwier Wojciechowski | 05.04.2005 | 3 | (4) | |
| **Forwards:** | **DOB** | **M** | **(s)** | **G** |
| Bartosz Bida | 21.02.2001 | 10 | (5) | |
| Maciej Bortniczuk | 06.09.2001 | 2 | (8) | 1 |
| Fedor Černych (LTU) | 21.05.1991 | 9 | (7) | 1 |
| Mateusz Kowalski | 21.07.2005 | 1 | (10) | 2 |
| Tomasz Kupisz | 02.01.1990 | 4 | (12) | 1 |
| Marc Gual Huguet (ESP) | 13.03.1996 | 27 | (4) | 16 |
| Camilo Andrés Mena Márquez (COL) | 01.10.2002 | 1 | (6) | |
| Tomáš Přikrýl (CZE) | 04.07.1992 | 26 | (4) | 1 |
| Andrzej Trubeha | 22.11.1997 | 3 | (4) | |
| Maciej Twarowski | 13.03.2001 | | (1) | |

## Korona Kielce

**Founded**: 10.07.1973
**Stadium**: Suzuki Arena [Stadion Miejski w Kielcach], Kielce (15,550)
**Trainer**: Leszek Ojrzyński    31.05.1972
[29.10.2022]   Kamil Kuzera    11.03.1983

| Goalkeepers: | DOB | M | (s) | G |
|---|---|---|---|---|
| Konrad Forenc | 17.07.1992 | 20 | | |
| Marcel Zapytowski | 08.01.2001 | 14 | | |
| **Defenders:** | **DOB** | **M** | **(s)** | **G** |
| Saša Balić (MNE) | 29.01.1990 | 11 | | |
| Marius Ionuţ Briceag (ROU) | 06.04.1992 | 17 | | |
| Adrian Danek | 01.08.1994 | 13 | (5) | |
| Marcus Valdez Pereira Godinho (CAN) | 28.06.1997 | 6 | (9) | 1 |
| Bartosz Kwiecień | 07.05.1994 | | (5) | |
| Piotr Malarczyk | 01.08.1991 | 17 | | 3 |
| Kyrylo Petrov (UKR) | 22.06.1990 | 25 | (1) | 2 |
| Roberto Corral García (ESP) | 14.09.1997 | 3 | (2) | |
| Łukasz Sierpina | 27.03.1988 | 3 | (3) | |
| Grzegorz Szymusik | 04.06.1998 | 3 | (4) | |
| Miłosz Trojak | 05.05.1994 | 33 | | 1 |
| Dawid Więckowski | 07.11.2001 | 2 | | |
| Dominick Lukasz Zator (CAN) | 18.09.1994 | 17 | | 1 |
| Mario Zebić (CRO) | 17.12.1995 | 5 | (3) | |
| **Midfielders:** | **DOB** | **M** | **(s)** | **G** |
| Ronaldo Octavian Andrei Deaconu (ROU) | 13.05.1997 | 23 | (4) | 2 |
| Adam Deja | 24.06.1993 | 15 | (4) | |
| Oskar Sewerzyński | 12.08.2001 | 8 | (7) | |
| Marcin Szpakowski | 26.09.2001 | 8 | (13) | |
| Dalibor Takáč (SVK) | 11.10.1997 | 15 | (12) | |
| **Forwards:** | **DOB** | **M** | **(s)** | **G** |
| Dawid Błanik | 15.04.1997 | 11 | (16) | 3 |
| Adam Frączczak | 07.08.1987 | 2 | (7) | |
| Jacek Kiełb | 10.01.1988 | 2 | (19) | |
| Jakub Konstantyn | 26.06.2002 | | (1) | |
| Kacper Kostorz | 21.08.1999 | | (12) | 2 |
| Jakub Łukowski | 25.05.1996 | 34 | | 12 |
| Janusz Nojszewski | 18.04.2003 | | (5) | |
| David González Plata „Nono"(ESP) | 28.05.1991 | 16 | | |
| Jacek Podgórski | 23.06.1996 | 16 | (12) | 1 |
| Yevgeniy Shikavka (BLR) | 15.10.1992 | 22 | (9) | 6 |
| Hubert Szulc | 27.08.2004 | | (1) | |
| Bartosz Śpiączka | 19.08.1991 | 13 | (4) | 4 |
| Luka Zarandia (GEO) | 17.02.1996 | | (7) | |

## Kolejowy Klub Sportowy Lech Poznań

**Founded**: 19.03.1922
**Stadium**: Stadion Miejski, Poznań (43,269)
**Trainer**: Joseph Antonius van den Brom (NED)  04.10.1966

| Goalkeepers: | DOB | M | (s) | G |
|---|---|---|---|---|
| Filip Bednarek | 26.09.1992 | 32 | | |
| Dominik Holec (SVK) | 28.07.1994 | 1 | | |
| Artur Rudko (UKR) | 07.05.1992 | 1 | | |
| **Defenders:** | **DOB** | **M** | **(s)** | **G** |
| Alan Czerwiński | 02.02.1993 | 17 | (5) | |
| Filip Dagerstål (SWE) | 01.02.1997 | 18 | (2) | |
| Barry James Douglas (SCO) | 04.09.1989 | 12 | (4) | |
| Michał Gurgul | 30.01.2006 | 1 | (2) | |
| *Joel* Vieira *Pereira* (POR) | 28.09.1996 | 24 | (7) | |
| Antonio Milić (CRO) | 10.03.1994 | 22 | (1) | 1 |
| Maksymilian Pingot | 01.04.2003 | 4 | (1) | |
| *Pedro* Miguel Braga *Rebocho* (POR) | 23.01.1995 | 17 | (2) | |
| Bartosz Salamon | 01.05.1991 | 7 | (3) | |
| Ľubomír Šatka (SVK) | 02.12.1995 | 13 | | 1 |
| Mateusz Żukowski | 23.11.2001 | | (3) | |

| Midfielders: | DOB | M | (s) | G |
|---|---|---|---|---|
| *Afonso* Gamelas de Pinho *Sousa* (POR) | 03.05.2000 | 16 | (8) | 4 |
| Adriel Ba Loua (CIV) | 25.07.1996 | 8 | (12) | |
| *João* Pedro Reis *Amaral* (POR) | 07.09.1991 | 6 | (15) | 2 |
| Jesper Karlström (SWE) | 21.06.1995 | 27 | (4) | 1 |
| Nika Kvekveskiri (GEO) | 29.05.1992 | 19 | (9) | 2 |
| Filip Marchwiński | 10.01.2002 | 17 | (10) | 5 |
| Radosław Murawski | 22.04.1994 | 22 | (9) | 1 |
| Kristoffer Velde (NOR) | 09.09.1999 | 20 | (10) | 8 |
| **Forwards:** | **DOB** | **M** | **(s)** | **G** |
| Jakub Antczak | 29.04.2004 | | (1) | |
| Mikael Ishak (SWE) | 31.03.1993 | 20 | (3) | 11 |
| Michał Krzysztof Skóraś | 15.02.2000 | 26 | (6) | 9 |
| Artur Sobiech | 12.06.1990 | 5 | (10) | 3 |
| Filip Szymczak | 06.05.2002 | 12 | (9) | 2 |
| Georgi Tsitaishvili (GEO) | 18.11.2000 | 7 | (5) | 1 |
| Filip Wilak | 06.08.2003 | | (3) | |

## Klub Sportowy Lechia Gdańsk Spółka Akcyjna

**Founded**: 07.08.1945
**Stadium**: Polsat Plus Arena, Gdańsk (43,615)
**Trainer**: Tomasz Kaczmarek  20.09.1984
[31.08.2022]  Maciej Kalkowski  18.07.1974
[19.09.2022]  Marcin Kaczmarek  02.01.1974
[21.03.2023]  David Badía Cequier (ESP)  04.09.1974

| Goalkeepers: | DOB | M | (s) | G |
|---|---|---|---|---|
| Michał Buchalik | 03.02.1989 | 4 | (1) | |
| Dušan Kuciak (SVK) | 21.05.1985 | 30 | | |
| **Defenders:** | **DOB** | **M** | **(s)** | **G** |
| Joel Abu Hanna (ISR) | 22.01.1998 | 13 | (1) | |
| Jakub Bartkowski | 07.11.1991 | 13 | (3) | 1 |
| Henrik Castegren (SWE) | 28.03.1996 | 7 | | |
| *Conrado* Buchanelli Holz (BRA) | 03.04.1997 | 16 | (5) | |
| Filip Koperski | 24.02.2004 | 2 | (5) | |
| Mario Maloča (CRO) | 04.05.1989 | 26 | (1) | 1 |
| Michał Nalepa | 22.01.1993 | 22 | (1) | 2 |
| Rafał Pietrzak | 30.01.1992 | 30 | (4) | |
| David Stec (AUT) | 10.05.1994 | 13 | (4) | |
| **Midfielders:** | **DOB** | **M** | **(s)** | **G** |
| Jan Biegański | 04.12.2002 | | (4) | |
| Joeri de Kamps (NED) | 10.02.1992 | 6 | (4) | |

| | DOB | M | (s) | G |
|---|---|---|---|---|
| Maciej Gajos | 19.03.1991 | 22 | (7) | 4 |
| Jakub Kałuziński | 31.10.2002 | 11 | (13) | |
| Jarosław Kubicki | 07.08.1995 | 27 | (4) | 2 |
| Tomasz Neugebauer | 08.05.2003 | 1 | (1) | |
| Kristers Tobers (LVA) | 13.12.2000 | 22 | (5) | |
| **Forwards:** | **DOB** | **M** | **(s)** | **G** |
| Christian Clemens (GER) | 04.08.1991 | 5 | (5) | |
| Bassekou Diabaté (MLI) | 15.04.2000 | 10 | (13) | |
| İlkay Durmuş (TUR) | 01.05.1994 | 22 | (3) | 1 |
| *Flávio* Emanuel Lopes *Paixão* (POR) | 19.09.1984 | 19 | (7) | 7 |
| Kevin Friesenbichler (AUT) | 06.05.1994 | 5 | (7) | |
| Dominik Piła | 06.05.2001 | 7 | (8) | |
| Kacper Sezonienko | 23.03.2003 | 8 | (16) | |
| Marco Terrazzino (GER) | 15.04.1991 | 12 | (15) | 1 |
| Łukasz Zjawiński | 11.07.2001 | | (2) | |
| Łukasz Zwoliński | 24.02.1993 | 21 | (6) | 9 |

## Legia Warszawa

**Founded**: 1916
**Stadium**: Stadion "Marszałek Józef Piłsudski", Warszawa (31,800)
**Trainer**: Kosta Runjaić (GER)  04.06.1971

| Goalkeepers: | DOB | M | (s) | G |
|---|---|---|---|---|
| Dominik Hładun | 17.09.1995 | 7 | | |
| Kacper Tobiasz | 04.11.2002 | 27 | | |
| **Defenders:** | **DOB** | **M** | **(s)** | **G** |
| Joel Abu Hanna (ISR) | 22.01.1998 | 1 | | |
| Rafał Augustyniak | 14.10.1993 | 18 | (7) | 4 |
| Artur Jędrzejczyk | 04.11.1987 | 24 | (2) | |
| Mattias Johansson (SWE) | 16.02.1992 | 10 | (1) | 1 |
| Filip Mladenović (SRB) | 15.08.1991 | 25 | (1) | 6 |
| Maik Nawrocki | 07.02.2001 | 23 | (2) | 4 |
| Lindsay Rose (MRI) | 08.02.1992 | 10 | (7) | 1 |
| Mateusz Wieteska | 11.02.1997 | 2 | | |
| *Yuri* Oliveira *Ribeiro* (POR) | 24.01.1997 | 20 | (4) | 1 |
| **Midfielders:** | **DOB** | **M** | **(s)** | **G** |
| Jurgen Çelhaka (ALB) | 06.12.2000 | 2 | (6) | |
| Jakub Jędrasik | 07.04.2005 | | (1) | |

| | DOB | M | (s) | G |
|---|---|---|---|---|
| *Josué* Filipe Soares Pesqueira (POR) | 17.09.1990 | 32 | | 12 |
| Bartosz Kapustka | 23.12.1996 | 23 | (6) | 2 |
| Igor Kharatin (UKR) | 02.02.1995 | 3 | (6) | |
| Róbert Pich (SVK) | 12.11.1988 | 4 | (13) | |
| Bartosz Slisz | 29.03.1999 | 30 | (2) | |
| Patryk Sokołowski | 25.09.1994 | 4 | (14) | |
| Igor Strzałek | 19.01.2004 | 2 | (11) | |
| Paweł Wszołek | 30.04.1992 | 32 | (2) | 7 |
| **Forwards:** | **DOB** | **M** | **(s)** | **G** |
| Makana Baku (GER) | 08.04.1998 | 12 | (10) | |
| Carlos Daniel López Huesca „Carlitos" (ESP) | 12.06.1990 | 11 | (10) | 1 |
| Lirim M. Kastrati (KOS) | 16.01.1999 | | (1) | |
| Blaž Kramer (SVN) | 01.06.1996 | | (12) | 1 |
| Ernest Muçi (ALB) | 19.03.2001 | 24 | (8) | 5 |
| Tomáš Pekhart (CZE) | 26.05.1989 | 9 | (4) | 5 |
| Maciej Rosołek | 02.09.2001 | 19 | (15) | 5 |

## Miejski Klub Sportowy Miedź Legnica

| | | |
|---|---|---|
| **Founded**: | 14.09.1971 | |
| **Stadium**: | Stadion im. Orła Białego, Kielce (6,864) | |
| **Trainer**: | Wojciech Łobodziński | 20.10.1982 |
| [11.10.2022] | Radosław Bella | 09.08.1987 |
| [17.10.2022] | Grzegorz Mokry | 19.01.1985 |

| Goalkeepers: | DOB | M | (s) | G |
|---|---|---|---|---|
| Mateusz Abramowicz | 08.11.1992 | 20 | | |
| Stefanos Kapino (GRE) | 18.03.1994 | 4 | | |
| Paweł Lenarcik | 21.03.1995 | 10 | | |
| **Defenders:** | **DOB** | **M** | **(s)** | **G** |
| Jon *Aurtenetxe* Borde (ESP) | 03.01.1992 | 6 | (2) | |
| Jurich Christopher Alexander Carolina (CUW) | 15.07.1998 | 21 | (2) | |
| Jens Martin Gammelby (DEN) | 05.02.1995 | 4 | (2) | |
| Levent Gülen (SUI) | 24.02.1994 | 26 | (1) | |
| Michael Kostka (GER) | 13.12.2003 | 9 | (18) | |
| Carlos Julio Martínez Rivas (DOM) | 04.02.1994 | 11 | (1) | |
| Giannis Masouras (GRE) | 24.08.1996 | 10 | (4) | 1 |
| Hubert Matynia | 04.11.1995 | 18 | (4) | |
| Nemanja Mijušković (MNE) | 04.03.1992 | 28 | | 2 |
| Andrzej Niewulis | 21.04.1989 | 15 | | 1 |
| Maciej Śliwa | 22.05.2001 | 2 | (6) | 1 |
| Dimitar Velkovski (BUL) | 22.01.1995 | 11 | (3) | |

| Midfielders: | DOB | M | (s) | G |
|---|---|---|---|---|
| Jerónimo Cacciabué (ARG) | 24.01.1998 | 7 | (4) | |
| Víctor Moya Martínez „Chuca" (ESP) | 10.06.1997 | 25 | (5) | 6 |
| Maxime Dominguez (SUI) | 01.02.1996 | 27 | (2) | 1 |
| Dawid Drachal | 31.01.2005 | 7 | (9) | 1 |
| Kamil Drygas | 07.09.1991 | 14 | (3) | 2 |
| Marcin Garuch | 14.09.1988 | | (1) | |
| Mehdi Lehaire (BEL) | 22.01.2000 | | (7) | |
| Szymon Matuszek | 07.01.1989 | 6 | (8) | 1 |
| Santiago Naveda Lara (MEX) | 16.04.2001 | 11 | (6) | 1 |
| Damian Tront | 27.10.1994 | 8 | (2) | |
| **Forwards:** | **DOB** | **M** | **(s)** | **G** |
| Emmanuel Agbor (CMR) | 21.06.2003 | | (1) | |
| Ángelo José Henríquez Iturra (CHI) | 13.04.1994 | 26 | (3) | 7 |
| Olaf Kobacki | 10.07.2001 | 15 | (9) | 1 |
| *Koldo Obieta* Alberdi (ESP) | 08.10.1993 | 12 | (17) | 3 |
| Luciano Narsingh (NED) | 13.09.1990 | 18 | (11) | 5 |
| Kamil Zapolnik | 09.09.1992 | 3 | (9) | |

## Gliwicki Klub Sportowy Piast Gliwice

| | | |
|---|---|---|
| **Founded**: | 18.06.1945 | |
| **Stadium**: | Stadion Miejski im. Piotra Wieczorka, Gliwice (10,037) | |
| **Trainer**: | Waldemar Fornalik | 11.04.1963 |
| [27.10.2022] | Aleksandar Vuković (SRB) | 25.08.1979 |

| Goalkeepers: | DOB | M | (s) | G |
|---|---|---|---|---|
| František Plach (SVK) | 08.03.1992 | 33 | (1) | |
| Jakub Szmatuła | 22.03.1981 | 1 | | |
| **Defenders:** | **DOB** | **M** | **(s)** | **G** |
| Jakub Czerwiński | 06.08.1991 | 33 | | 1 |
| Jakub Holúbek (SVK) | 12.01.1991 | 7 | (14) | |
| Tomáš Huk (SVK) | 22.12.1994 | 1 | | |
| Alexandros Katranis (GRE) | 04.05.1998 | 28 | (2) | |
| *Miguel Muñoz* Fernández (ESP) | 22.11.1996 | 4 | (2) | |
| Tomasz Mokwa | 10.02.1993 | 8 | (3) | |
| Ariel Mosór | 19.02.2003 | 28 | | |
| Arkadiusz Pyrka | 20.09.2002 | 29 | (4) | 2 |
| Constantin Reiner (AUT) | 11.07.1997 | 11 | (1) | 2 |
| **Midfielders:** | **DOB** | **M** | **(s)** | **G** |
| Michał Chrapek | 03.04.1992 | 30 | (1) | 4 |
| Patryk Dziczek | 25.03.1998 | 20 | (4) | 3 |
| Tom Hateley (ENG) | 12.09.1989 | 17 | (14) | |
| Michał Kaput | 18.02.1998 | 3 | (13) | |
| Szczepan Mucha | 29.02.2004 | 1 | (5) | |
| Grzegorz Tomasiewicz | 05.05.1996 | 32 | (1) | 3 |
| **Forwards:** | **DOB** | **M** | **(s)** | **G** |
| Michael Ameyaw | 16.09.2000 | 16 | (11) | 4 |
| *Jorge Félix* Muñoz García (ESP) | 22.08.1991 | 18 | (11) | 3 |
| Damian Kądzior | 16.06.1992 | 17 | (4) | 3 |
| Gabriel Kirejczyk | 12.02.2003 | 4 | (6) | |
| Rauno Sappinen (EST) | 23.01.1996 | 5 | (6) | 1 |
| Alex Sobczyk (AUT) | 20.05.1997 | | (10) | |
| Alberto *Toril* Domingo (ESP) | 01.06.1997 | 3 | (8) | |
| Kamil Wilczek | 14.01.1988 | 25 | (3) | 9 |

## Morski Klub Sportowy Pogoń Szczecin

| | | |
|---|---|---|
| **Founded**: | 21.04.1948 | |
| **Stadium**: | Stadion „Florian Krygier", Szczecin (18,027) | |
| **Trainer**: | Jens Otto Andreas Gustafsson (SWE) | 15.10.1978 |

| Goalkeepers: | DOB | M | (s) | G |
|---|---|---|---|---|
| Bartosz Klebaniuk | 03.04.2002 | 4 | (1) | |
| Dante Stipica (CRO) | 30.05.1991 | 30 | | |
| **Defenders:** | **DOB** | **M** | **(s)** | **G** |
| Jakub Bartkowski | 07.11.1991 | 13 | (1) | 1 |
| Leonardo Koutris (GRE) | 23.07.1995 | 16 | | 2 |
| Léonardo „*Léo*" Borges Da Silva (BRA) | 03.01.2001 | 9 | (6) | |
| Danijel Lončar (CRO) | 26.06.1997 | 6 | (2) | |
| *Luís* Carlos Machado *Mata* (POR) | 06.07.1997 | 8 | (5) | |
| Mariusz Malec | 04.04.1995 | 15 | (9) | |
| Paweł Stolarski | 28.01.1996 | 8 | (8) | |
| Konstantinos Triantafyllopoulos (GRE) | 03.04.1993 | 17 | (6) | |
| Linus Wahlqvist (SWE) | 11.11.1996 | 12 | | |
| Benedikt Zech (AUT) | 03.11.1990 | 30 | | |
| **Midfielders:** | **DOB** | **M** | **(s)** | **G** |
| Vahan Bichakhchyan (ARM) | 09.07.1999 | 13 | (18) | 6 |
| Damian Dąbrowski | 27.08.1992 | 32 | | 4 |
| Kamil Drygas | 07.09.1991 | 1 | (11) | 1 |
| Mariusz Fornalczyk | 15.01.2003 | 1 | (10) | |
| Alexander Gorgon (AUT) | 28.10.1988 | 6 | (11) | 3 |
| Kamil Grosicki | 08.06.1988 | 34 | | 13 |
| Sebastian Kowalczyk | 22.08.1998 | 25 | (9) | 6 |
| Rafał Kurzawa | 29.01.1993 | 11 | (6) | |
| Mateusz Łęgowski | 29.01.2003 | 24 | (2) | 3 |
| Adrian Przyborek | 01.01.2007 | | (3) | |
| Yadegar Rostami (IRN) | 02.01.2004 | | (1) | |
| Kacper Smoliński | 07.02.2001 | 2 | (1) | 1 |
| Marcel Wędrychowski | 13.01.2002 | 8 | (13) | 1 |
| **Forwards:** | **DOB** | **M** | **(s)** | **G** |
| Pontus Almqvist (SWE) | 10.07.1999 | 16 | (11) | 5 |
| *Jean Carlos* Silva Rocha (BRA) | 10.05.1996 | 6 | (9) | 1 |
| Kacper Kostorz | 21.08.1999 | | (1) | |
| Michał Kucharczyk | 20.03.1991 | 5 | (5) | |
| Luka Zahovič (SVN) | 15.11.1995 | 22 | (10) | 6 |

## Radomiak Radom

**Founded**: 1910
**Stadium**: Stadion Lekkoatletyczno-Piłkarski w Radomiu, Radom (4,501)
**Trainer**: Mariusz Lewandowski   18.05.1979
[16.04.2023] Constantin Gâlcă (ROU)   08.03.1972

| Goalkeepers: | DOB | M | (s) | G |
|---|---|---|---|---|
| Gabriel Kobylak | 20.02.2002 | 29 | | |
| Filip Majchrowicz | 09.02.2000 | 3 | | |
| Jakub Ojrzyński | 19.02.2003 | 1 | | |
| Albert Posiadała | 25.02.2003 | 1 | | |
| **Defenders:** | **DOB** | **M** | **(s)** | **G** |
| Dawid Abramowicz | 16.05.1991 | 31 | | 4 |
| Mike Cestor Botuli (COD) | 30.04.1992 | 13 | (3) | |
| Mateusz Cichocki | 31.01.1992 | 21 | (1) | |
| Mateusz Grzybek | 30.03.1996 | 16 | | 2 |
| Damian Jakubik | 25.03.1990 | 17 | (2) | |
| *Pedro Justiniano* Almeida Gomes (POR) | 18.04.2000 | 10 | (2) | |
| *Raphael Rossi* Branco (BRA) | 25.07.1990 | 28 | (2) | 2 |
| **Midfielders:** | **DOB** | **M** | **(s)** | **G** |
| Roberto Emanuel Oliveira Alves (SUI) | 08.06.1997 | 31 | (1) | 3 |
| Thabo Cele (RSA) | 15.01.1997 | 12 | (8) | |
| Francisco „Chico" Augusto Neto *Ramos* (POR) | 10.04.1995 | 9 | | |
| Christos Donis (GRE) | 09.10.1994 | 13 | (2) | |
| *Filipe* Guterres *Nascimento* (POR) | 07.01.1995 | 13 | | 3 |

| | DOB | M | (s) | G |
|---|---|---|---|---|
| Luiz Gustavo Novaes Palhares „Luizão"(BRA) | 20.02.1998 | 4 | (7) | |
| Daniel Łukasik | 28.04.1991 | 3 | (6) | |
| Jakub Nowakowski | 11.10.2001 | 3 | (12) | |
| Dariusz Pawłowski | 25.02.1999 | 4 | (9) | |
| *Tiago* Manuel Maio *Matos* (POR) | 22.01.2001 | | (3) | |
| **Forwards:** | **DOB** | **M** | **(s)** | **G** |
| Alberto „Berto" Cayarga Fernández (ESP) | 17.09.1996 | 11 | (5) | |
| Frank Andersson Castañeda Vélez (COL) | 17.07.1994 | 7 | (5) | 1 |
| Michał Feliks | 19.03.1999 | 2 | (8) | 1 |
| *Leândro* Rossi Pereira (BRA) | 26.11.1988 | 7 | (8) | |
| Leonardo Miramar *Rocha* (POR) | 23.05.1997 | 13 | | 6 |
| *Lisandro* Pedro Varela *Semedo* (CPV) | 12.03.1996 | 23 | (9) | 3 |
| *Luís* Miguel Vieira Babo *Machado* (POR) | 04.11.1992 | 26 | (2) | 4 |
| *Maurides* Roque Junior (BRA) | 10.03.1994 | 13 | (3) | 4 |
| Krystian Okoniewski | 24.01.2005 | | (6) | |
| Daniel Pik | 20.07.2000 | 6 | (19) | |
| Jean Franco Sarmiento Campo (COL) | 07.02.1997 | 4 | (6) | |
| Dominik Sokół | 16.05.1999 | | (7) | |

## Robotniczy Klub Sportowy Raków Częstochowa

**Founded**: 1921
**Stadium**: Miejski Stadion Piłkarski Raków, Płock (5,500)
**Trainer**: Marek Papszun   08.08.1974

| Goalkeepers: | DOB | M | (s) | G |
|---|---|---|---|---|
| Vladan Kovačević (BIH) | 11.04.1998 | 28 | | |
| Kacper Trelowski | 19.08.2003 | 6 | | |
| **Defenders:** | **DOB** | **M** | **(s)** | **G** |
| Zoran Arsenić (CRO) | 02.06.1994 | 30 | (1) | |
| Andrzej Niewulis | 21.04.1989 | | (1) | |
| Tomáš Petrášek (CZE) | 02.03.1992 | 7 | (6) | 1 |
| Bogdan Racoviţan (FRA) | 06.06.2000 | 12 | (1) | 1 |
| Milan Rundić (SRB) | 29.03.1992 | 16 | (2) | |
| Stratos Svarnas (GRE) | 11.11.1997 | 29 | | 3 |
| **Midfielders:** | **DOB** | **M** | **(s)** | **G** |
| Gustav Berggren (SWE) | 07.09.1997 | 5 | (20) | 1 |
| Marcin Cebula | 06.12.1995 | 3 | (10) | 1 |
| Szymon Czyż | 08.07.2001 | 5 | (3) | |
| *Fábio* Miguel dos Santos *Sturgeon* (POR) | 04.02.1994 | | (1) | |
| Valeriane Gvilia (GEO) | 24.05.1994 | 1 | | |
| Vladyslav Kochergin (UKR) | 30.04.1996 | 26 | (7) | 8 |

| | DOB | M | (s) | G |
|---|---|---|---|---|
| Tobiasz Kubik | 29.01.2003 | | (1) | |
| Patryk Kun | 20.04.1995 | 21 | (3) | 2 |
| Ben Lederman | 08.05.2000 | 11 | (13) | |
| Bartosz Nowak | 25.08.1993 | 21 | (8) | 9 |
| Giannis Papanikolaou (GRE) | 18.11.1998 | 29 | (2) | 1 |
| Igor Sapała | 11.10.1995 | 1 | | |
| Deian Cristian Sorescu (ROU) | 29.08.1997 | 8 | (3) | 2 |
| Daniel Szeląpgowski | 02.09.2002 | | (4) | |
| Fran Tudor (CRO) | 27.09.1995 | 28 | (3) | 2 |
| Mateusz Wdowiak | 28.08.1996 | 10 | (20) | 3 |
| **Forwards:** | **DOB** | **M** | **(s)** | **G** |
| Wiktor Długosz | 01.07.2000 | 3 | (15) | |
| Vladislavs Gutkovskis (LVA) | 02.04.1995 | 19 | (13) | 8 |
| Iván „Iví" López Álvarez (ESP) | 29.06.1994 | 24 | (3) | 9 |
| *Jean Carlos* Silva Rocha (BRA) | 10.05.1996 | 14 | (2) | 3 |
| Sebastian Musiolik | 19.05.1996 | 2 | (15) | |
| Fabian Piasecki | 04.05.1995 | 15 | (8) | 6 |

## Fabryczny Klub Sportowy Stal Mielec

**Founded**: 10.04.1939
**Stadium**: Stadion Miejski, Mielec (6,864)
**Trainer**: Adam Majewski   24.12.1973
[20.03.2023] Kamil Kiereś   16.07.1974

| Goalkeepers: | DOB | M | (s) | G |
|---|---|---|---|---|
| Bartosz Mrozek | 23.02.2000 | 34 | | |
| **Defenders:** | **DOB** | **M** | **(s)** | **G** |
| Dominykas Barauskas (LTU) | 18.04.1997 | 7 | (1) | |
| Marcin Flis | 10.02.1994 | 26 | | |
| Arkadiusz Kasperkiewicz | 29.09.1994 | 24 | (3) | 1 |
| Kamil Kruk | 13.03.2000 | 17 | (3) | 2 |
| *Leândro* Messias dos Santos (BRA) | 29.12.1983 | | (10) | |
| Mateusz Matras | 23.01.1991 | 31 | | 2 |
| **Midfielders:** | **DOB** | **M** | **(s)** | **G** |
| Alexander „Álex" Vallejo Mínguez (ESP) | 16.01.1992 | 10 | (4) | |
| Bartłomiej Ciepiela | 24.05.2001 | 8 | (9) | 1 |
| Fryderyk Gerbowski | 17.01.2003 | 11 | (11) | 2 |
| Krystian Getinger | 29.08.1988 | 34 | | |
| Koki Hinokio (JPN) | 26.02.2001 | 8 | (6) | 1 |

| | DOB | M | (s) | G |
|---|---|---|---|---|
| Fabian Hiszpański | 26.10.1993 | 22 | (9) | 1 |
| Krystian Kardyś | 03.08.2002 | | (3) | |
| Przemysław Maj | 06.04.2003 | 2 | (3) | |
| Mateusz Mak | 14.11.1991 | 8 | (17) | 2 |
| David Poręba (USA) | 01.12.2002 | | (1) | |
| Adam Ratajczyk | 12.06.2002 | 12 | (4) | 1 |
| Bogdan Vaštšuk (ESZ) | 04.10.1995 | 2 | (3) | |
| Piotr Wlazło | 03.06.1989 | 33 | | 4 |
| Maciej Wolski | 29.03.1997 | 13 | (12) | |
| Paweł Żyra | 07.04.1998 | 10 | (9) | 1 |
| **Forwards:** | **DOB** | **M** | **(s)** | **G** |
| Maciej Domański | 05.09.1990 | 27 | (7) | 4 |
| Saïd Hamulić (BIH) | 12.11.2000 | 14 | (3) | 9 |
| Mikołaj Lebedyński | 14.10.1990 | 10 | (17) | |
| Rauno Sappinen (EST) | 23.01.1996 | 11 | (3) | 3 |

## Wrocławski Klub Sportowy Śląsk Wrocław Spółka Akcyjna

| | | | |
|---|---|---|---|
| **Founded:** | 18.03.1946 | | |
| **Stadium:** | Stadion Wrocław (Tarczyński Arena), Wrocław (45,105) | | |
| **Trainer:** | Ivan Đurđević (SRB) | | 05.02.1977 |
| [21.04.2023] | Jacek Magiera | | 01.01.1977 |

| Goalkeepers: | DOB | M | (s) | G |
|---|---|---|---|---|
| Rafał Leszczyński | 26.04.1992 | 20 | | |
| Michał Szromnik | 04.03.1993 | 14 | | |
| **Defenders:** | **DOB** | **M** | **(s)** | **G** |
| Łukasz Bejger | 11.01.2002 | 21 | | 2 |
| Diogo Sousa Verdasca (POR) | 26.10.1996 | 20 | (1) | |
| Daniel Grétarsson (ISL) | 02.10.1995 | 25 | (3) | 1 |
| Patryk Janasik | 25.08.1997 | 15 | (4) | |
| Martin Konczkowski | 14.09.1993 | 20 | (3) | |
| Mariusz Pawelec | 14.04.1986 | | (1) | |
| Konrad Poprawa | 04.06.1998 | 28 | (1) | |
| Mateusz Stawny | 23.10.2003 | 1 | (1) | |
| Víctor García Marín (ESP) | 31.05.1994 | 25 | (4) | |
| **Midfielders:** | **DOB** | **M** | **(s)** | **G** |
| Dawid Bałdyga | 08.01.2003 | | (1) | |
| Karol Borys | 28.09.2006 | 2 | (4) | |
| Adrian Bukowski | 18.03.2003 | 8 | (1) | |
| Łukasz Gerstenstein | 06.10.2004 | | (1) | |
| Javier Hyjek | 12.01.2001 | 3 | (6) | |
| Adrian Łyszczarz | 22.08.1999 | 5 | (13) | 1 |
| Matías Nahuel Leiva Esquivel (ESP) | 22.11.1996 | 20 | (9) | 3 |
| Patrick Olsen (DEN) | 23.04.1994 | 26 | (1) | 3 |
| Michał Rzuchowski | 27.12.1993 | 10 | (9) | |
| Petr Schwarz (CZE) | 12.11.1991 | 22 | (3) | 3 |
| Marcel Żyłła | 14.01.2000 | | (2) | |
| **Forwards:** | **DOB** | **M** | **(s)** | **G** |
| Sebastian Bergier | 20.12.1999 | | (7) | |
| Cayetano „Caye" Quintana Hernández (ESP) | 20.12.1993 | 11 | (7) | |
| Erik Alexander Expósito Hernández (ESP) | 23.06.1996 | 26 | (3) | 7 |
| Dennis Jastrzembski (GER) | 20.02.2000 | 12 | (16) | 2 |
| Piotr Samiec-Talar | 02.11.2001 | 11 | (8) | 1 |
| Patryk Szwedzik | 02.12.2001 | 2 | (7) | |
| John Yeboah (GER) | 23.06.2000 | 27 | (5) | 10 |

## Klub Sportowy Warta Poznań

| | | | |
|---|---|---|---|
| **Founded:** | 15.06.1912 | | |
| **Stadium:** | Stadion Dyskobolii, Grodzisk Wielkopolski (5,383) | | |
| **Trainer:** | Dawid Szulczek | | 26.01.1990 |

| Goalkeepers: | DOB | M | (s) | G |
|---|---|---|---|---|
| Jędrzej Grobelny | 28.06.2001 | 5 | (1) | |
| Adrian Lis | 28.05.1992 | 29 | | |
| **Defenders:** | **DOB** | **M** | **(s)** | **G** |
| Jan Grzesik | 21.10.1994 | 27 | (3) | 4 |
| Robert Ivanov (FIN) | 19.09.1994 | 31 | | 1 |
| Bartosz Kieliba | 01.08.1990 | | (2) | |
| Kamil Kościelny | 04.08.1991 | 8 | (11) | |
| Konrad Matuszewski | 04.10.2001 | 27 | (4) | |
| Wiktor Pleśnierowicz | 29.03.2001 | 5 | (10) | |
| Dimitrios Stavropoulos (GRE) | 01.05.1997 | 28 | (3) | 2 |
| Dawid Szymonowicz | 07.07.1995 | 33 | | 1 |
| **Midfielders:** | **DOB** | **M** | **(s)** | **G** |
| Jędrzej Hanuszczak | 23.03.2008 | | (1) | |
| Jakub Kiełb | 15.07.1993 | 10 | (9) | |
| Michał Kopczyński | 15.06.1992 | 18 | (10) | 1 |
| Mateusz Kupczak | 20.02.1992 | 15 | (4) | |
| Niilo Mäenpää (FIN) | 14.01.1998 | 19 | (12) | |
| Miguel Mariz Luís (POR) | 27.02.1999 | 21 | (7) | 2 |
| Jakub Paszkowski | 16.09.2006 | | (2) | |
| Mikołaj Rakowski | 16.03.2002 | | (1) | |
| Szymon Sarbinowski | 24.03.2004 | | (3) | |
| Miłosz Szczepański | 22.03.1998 | 18 | (9) | 4 |
| Maciej Żurawski | 22.12.2000 | 17 | (14) | 4 |
| **Forwards:** | **DOB** | **M** | **(s)** | **G** |
| Milan Corryn (BEL) | 04.04.1999 | 2 | (6) | 1 |
| Enis Destan (TUR) | 15.06.2002 | 3 | (18) | 1 |
| Michał Jakóbowski | 08.09.1992 | 1 | (2) | |
| Wiktor Kamiński | 23.02.2004 | | (2) | |
| Jayson Papeau (FRA) | 30.06.1996 | | (1) | |
| Stefan Savić (AUT) | 09.01.1994 | 7 | (8) | 3 |
| Kajetan Szmyt | 29.05.2002 | 19 | (12) | 3 |
| Adam Zreľák (SVK) | 05.05.1994 | 31 | | 8 |

## Robotnicze Towarzystwo Sportowe Widzew Łódź

| | | | |
|---|---|---|---|
| **Founded:** | 14.09.1971 | | |
| **Stadium:** | Stadion Widzewa, Łódź (18,018) | | |
| **Trainer:** | Janusz Niedźwiedź | | 23.01.1982 |

| Goalkeepers: | DOB | M | (s) | G |
|---|---|---|---|---|
| Henrich Ravas (SVK) | 16.08.1997 | 33 | | |
| Jakub Wrąbel | 08.06.1996 | 1 | | |
| **Defenders:** | **DOB** | **M** | **(s)** | **G** |
| Bozhidar Chorbadzhiyski (BUL) | 08.08.1995 | 5 | (6) | |
| Adam Dębiński | 07.07.2004 | | (1) | |
| Martin Kreuzriegler (AUT) | 10.01.1994 | 18 | (12) | 3 |
| Patryk Stępiński | 16.01.1995 | 32 | (1) | |
| Serafin Szota | 04.03.1999 | 25 | (2) | |
| Mateusz Żyro | 28.10.1998 | 25 | (5) | |
| **Midfielders:** | **DOB** | **M** | **(s)** | **G** |
| Andrejs Cigaņiks (LVA) | 12.04.1997 | 10 | (5) | 1 |
| Karol Danielak | 29.09.1991 | 9 | (5) | 1 |
| Ignacy Dawid | 15.01.2003 | | (1) | |
| Fábio Alexandre da Silva Nunes (POR) | 24.07.1992 | 13 | (1) | |
| Marek Hanousek (CZE) | 06.08.1991 | 29 | (1) | 2 |
| Dominik Kun | 22.06.1993 | 22 | (11) | 4 |
| Juliusz Letniowski | 08.04.1998 | 16 | (15) | 1 |
| Patryk Lipski | 12.06.1994 | 2 | (8) | 2 |
| Mato Miloš (CRO) | 30.06.1993 | 19 | (5) | 1 |
| Juljan Shehu (ALB) | 06.09.1998 | 9 | (15) | |
| Jakub Sypek | 07.04.2001 | 2 | (13) | 1 |
| Ernest Terpiłowski | 14.09.2001 | 25 | | 3 |
| Filip Zawadzki | 01.07.2004 | 1 | (2) | |
| Paweł Zieliński | 17.07.1990 | 13 | (10) | |
| **Forwards:** | **DOB** | **M** | **(s)** | **G** |
| Kristoffer Hansen (NOR) | 12.08.1994 | 2 | (21) | 3 |
| Jordi Sánchez Ribas (ESP) | 11.11.1994 | 23 | (6) | 6 |
| Mateusz Kempski | 21.03.2003 | | (1) | |
| Bartłomiej Pawłowski | 13.11.1992 | 31 | (1) | 10 |
| Łukasz Zjawiński | 11.07.2001 | 9 | (10) | |

## Wisła Płock Spółka Akcyjna

| | | | |
|---|---|---|---|
| **Founded**: | 1947 | | |
| **Stadium**: | Stadion „Kazimierza Górski" [Orlen], Płock (12,800) | | |
| **Trainer**: | Pavol Staňo (SVK) | | 29.09.1977 |
| [16.05.2023] | Marek Saganowski | | 31.10.1978 |

| Goalkeepers: | DOB | M | (s) | G |
|---|---|---|---|---|
| Bartłomiej Gradecki | 26.12.1999 | 14 | | |
| Krzysztof Kamiński | 26.11.1990 | 20 | | |
| **Defenders:** | **DOB** | **M** | **(s)** | **G** |
| Paweł Chrupałła (NOR) | 16.03.2003 | | (2) | |
| Adam Chrzanowski | 31.03.1999 | 14 | (3) | |
| Igor Drapiński | 31.05.2004 | 2 | (5) | |
| Steve Kapuadi (FRA) | 30.04.1998 | 26 | | |
| Anton Krivotsyuk (AZE) | 20.08.1998 | 8 | (1) | 1 |
| Damian Michalski | 17.05.1998 | 6 | | |
| Jakub Rzeźniczak | 26.10.1986 | 24 | (1) | |
| Jakub Szymański | 05.07.2002 | 6 | | |
| Martin Šulek (SVK) | 15.01.1998 | 14 | (6) | |
| Piotr Tomasik | 31.10.1987 | 24 | (3) | |
| Kristián Vallo (SVK) | 02.06.1998 | 17 | (5) | 2 |
| **Midfielders:** | **DOB** | **M** | **(s)** | **G** |
| Radosław Cielemęcki | 19.02.2003 | 1 | (4) | |
| Dominik Furman | 06.07.1992 | 31 | (2) | |
| Miroslav Gono (SVK) | 01.11.2000 | 1 | (3) | |

| | DOB | M | (s) | G |
|---|---|---|---|---|
| Martin Hašek (CZE) | 03.10.1995 | | (3) | |
| Krzysztof Janus | 25.03.1986 | | (1) | |
| Filip Lesniak (SVK) | 14.05.1996 | 15 | (14) | |
| Michał Mokrzycki | 29.12.1997 | 1 | (2) | |
| Aleksander Pawlak | 14.11.2001 | 18 | (5) | 1 |
| Damian Rasak | 08.02.1996 | 9 | (8) | |
| Mateusz Szwoch | 19.03.1993 | 27 | (1) | 2 |
| Damian Warchoł | 19.07.1995 | 2 | (18) | 3 |
| **Forwards:** | **DOB** | **M** | **(s)** | **G** |
| Antonio David Álvarez Rey „Davo" (ESP) | 18.12.1994 | 16 | (2) | 9 |
| Dawid Kocyła | 23.07.2002 | 6 | (14) | 2 |
| Marko Kolar (CRO) | 31.05.1995 | 8 | (18) | 4 |
| Milan Kvocera (SVK) | 01.01.1998 | | (10) | |
| Mateusz Lewandowski | 04.03.1999 | 4 | (12) | 2 |
| Łukasz Sekulski | 03.11.1990 | 19 | (8) | 6 |
| Bartosz Śpiączka | 19.08.1991 | 11 | (2) | 2 |
| Tomasz Walczak | 17.08.2005 | | (3) | |
| Rafał Wolski | 10.11.1992 | 30 | | 7 |

## Zagłębie Lubin Spółka Akcyjna

| | | | |
|---|---|---|---|
| **Founded**: | 10.09.1945 | | |
| **Stadium**: | Stadion Miejski w Lubinie, Lubin (16,068) | | |
| **Trainer**: | Piotr Stokowiec | | 25.05.1972 |
| [08.11.2022] | Paweł Karmelita | | 28.08.1977 |
| [29.11.2022] | Waldemar Fornalik | | 11.04.1963 |

| Goalkeepers: | DOB | M | (s) | G |
|---|---|---|---|---|
| Kacper Bieszczad | 11.09.2002 | 15 | | |
| Jasmin Burić (BIH) | 18.02.1987 | 5 | | |
| Sokratis Dioudis (GRE) | 03.02.1993 | 14 | | |
| **Defenders:** | **DOB** | **M** | **(s)** | **G** |
| Mateusz Bartolewski | 12.01.1998 | 7 | (4) | |
| Kacper Chodyna | 24.05.1999 | 28 | (5) | 7 |
| Guram Giorbelidze (GEO) | 25.02.1996 | 13 | (2) | |
| Mateusz Grzybek | 30.03.1996 | 13 | (3) | |
| Jarosław Jach | 17.02.1994 | 25 | | 1 |
| Bartłomiej Kłudka | 14.05.2002 | 19 | (2) | |
| Bartosz Kopacz | 21.05.1992 | 28 | | 1 |
| Luís Carlos Machado *Mata* (POR) | 06.07.1997 | 3 | | |
| Aleks Ławniczak | 05.05.1999 | 25 | (2) | |
| Arkadiusz Woźniak | 01.06.1990 | 3 | (8) | |
| **Midfielders:** | **DOB** | **M** | **(s)** | **G** |
| Koki Hinokio (JPN) | 26.02.2001 | 2 | (6) | |
| Filip Kocaba | 13.11.2004 | 1 | (2) | |

| | DOB | M | (s) | G |
|---|---|---|---|---|
| Łukasz Łakomy | 18.01.2001 | 32 | (2) | 4 |
| Tomasz Makowski | 19.07.1999 | 16 | (12) | 1 |
| Tomasz Pieńko | 05.01.2004 | 10 | (21) | 3 |
| Marko Poletanović (SRB) | 20.07.1993 | 18 | (6) | 1 |
| Adam Ratajczyk | 12.06.2002 | | (3) | |
| Filip Starzyński | 27.05.1991 | 25 | (7) | 1 |
| Jakub Żubrowski | 21.03.1992 | 1 | (1) | |
| **Forwards:** | **DOB** | **M** | **(s)** | **G** |
| Rafael Adamski | 21.11.2001 | 9 | (10) | 2 |
| Damjan Bohar (SVN) | 18.10.1991 | 22 | (2) | 3 |
| Cheikhou Dieng (SEN) | 23.11.1993 | 3 | (3) | |
| Martin Doležal (CZE) | 03.05.1990 | 11 | (9) | 2 |
| Tornike Gaprindashvili (GEO) | 20.07.1997 | 11 | (12) | 2 |
| Szymon Kobusiński | 04.05.1998 | | (5) | |
| Dawid Kurminowski | 24.02.1999 | 11 | (3) | 4 |
| Jakub Świerczok | 28.12.1992 | 2 | (3) | |
| Saša Živec (SVN) | 02.04.1991 | 2 | (12) | 2 |

## SECOND LEVEL
### I liga 2022/2023

| | | | | | | | | | |
|---|---|---|---|---|---|---|---|---|---|
| 1. | ŁKS Łódź (*Promoted*) | 34 | 19 | 9 | 6 | 58 | - | 36 | 66 |
| 2. | KS Ruch Chorzów (*Promoted*) | 34 | 17 | 11 | 6 | 48 | - | 33 | 62 |
| 3. | Bruk-Bet Termalica Nieciecza KS (*Promotion Play-offs*) | 34 | 16 | 13 | 5 | 55 | - | 37 | 61 |
| 4. | TS Wisła Kraków (*Promotion Play-offs*) | 34 | 18 | 6 | 10 | 61 | - | 38 | 60 |
| 5. | MKS Puszcza Niepołomice (*Promotion Play-offs*) | 34 | 16 | 10 | 8 | 49 | - | 36 | 58 |
| 6. | ZKS Stal Rzeszów (*Promotion Play-offs*) | 34 | 14 | 9 | 11 | 56 | - | 43 | 51 |
| 7. | TS Podbeskidzie Bielsko-Biała | 34 | 12 | 13 | 9 | 56 | - | 47 | 49 |
| 8. | MZKS Arka Gdynia | 34 | 13 | 9 | 12 | 56 | - | 45 | 48 |
| 9. | MKS Chrobry Głogów | 34 | 12 | 10 | 12 | 44 | - | 53 | 46 |
| 10. | GKS Katowice | 34 | 10 | 14 | 10 | 41 | - | 39 | 44 |
| 11. | Zagłębie Sosnowiec | 34 | 10 | 12 | 12 | 33 | - | 43 | 42 |
| 12. | GKS Górnik Łęczna | 34 | 9 | 13 | 12 | 40 | - | 45 | 40 |
| 13. | GKS Tychy | 34 | 10 | 9 | 15 | 46 | - | 52 | 39 |
| 14. | CWKS Resovia Rzeszów | 34 | 9 | 11 | 14 | 43 | - | 51 | 38 |
| 15. | OKS Odra Opole | 34 | 10 | 7 | 17 | 39 | - | 48 | 37 |
| 16. | KS Skra Częstochowa (*Relegated*) | 34 | 9 | 4 | 21 | 18 | - | 49 | 31 |
| 17. | MKS Chojniczanka Chojnice (*Relegated*) | 34 | 5 | 12 | 17 | 35 | - | 57 | 27 |
| 18. | MKS Sandecja Nowy Sącz (*Relegated*) | 34 | 5 | 12 | 17 | 28 | - | 54 | 27 |

### Promotion Play-offs (1st / 2nd Level)

| **Play-offs Semi-Finals (06.06.2023)** | Bruk-Bet Termalica Nieciecza KS - ZKS Stal Rzeszów | 2-0(1-0) |
|---|---|---|
| | TS Wisła Kraków - MKS Puszcza Niepołomice | 1-4(0-2) |
| **Play-offs Final (11.06.2023)** | Bruk-Bet Termalica Nieciecza KS - MKS Puszcza Niepołomice | 2-3(0-0,2-2) |

**MKS Puszcza Niepołomice** were promoted to the Ekstraklasa 2023/2024.

## INTERNATIONAL MATCHES
(16.07.2022 – 15.07.2023)

| 22.09.2022 | Warszawa | *Poland - Netherlands* | *0-2(0-1)* | (UNL) |
|---|---|---|---|---|
| 25.09.2022 | Cardiff | *Wales - Poland* | *0-1(0-0)* | (UNL) |
| 16.11.2022 | Warszawa | *Poland - Chile* | *1-0(0-0)* | (F) |
| 22.11.2022 | Doha | *Mexico - Poland* | *0-0* | (WC) |
| 26.11.2022 | Al Rayyan | *Poland - Saudi Arabia* | *2-0(1-0)* | (WC) |
| 30.11.2022 | Doha | *Poland - Argentina* | *0-2(0-0)* | (WC) |
| 04.12.2022 | Doha | *France - Poland* | *3-1(1-0)* | (WC) |
| | | | | |
| 24.03.2023 | Praha | *Czech Republic - Poland* | *3-1(2-0)* | (ECQ) |
| 27.03.2023 | Warszawa | *Poland - Albania* | *1-0(1-0)* | (ECQ) |
| 16.06.2023 | Warszawa | *Poland - Germany* | *1-0(1-0)* | (F) |
| 20.06.2023 | Chişinău | *Moldova - Poland* | *3-2(0-2)* | (ECQ) |

**22.09.2022    POLAND - NETHERLANDS                0-2(0-1)**                 3rd UEFA Nations League A, Group 4
Stadion Narodowy, Warszawa; Referee: Alejandro José Hernández Hernández (Spain); Attendance: 56,673
**POL:** Wojciech Tomasz Szczęsny, Jan Kacper Bednarek, Jakub Piotr Kiwior, Kamil Jacek Glik, Przemysław Frankowski (79.Bartosz Bereszyński), Grzegorz Krychowiak, Karol Linetty (46.Arkadiusz Krystian Milik), Nicola Zalewski (79.Michał Krzysztof Skóraś), Sebastian Szymański (70.Mateusz Andrzej Klich), Piotr Zieliński (86.Mateusz Łęgowski), Robert Lewandowski (Cap). Trainer: Czesław Michniewicz.

**25.09.2022    WALES - POLAND                0-1(0-0)**                 3rd UEFA Nations League A, Group 4
Cardiff City Stadium, Cardiff; Referee: Andris Treimanis (Latvia); Attendance: 31,520
**POL:** Wojciech Tomasz Szczęsny, Jan Kacper Bednarek, Jakub Piotr Kiwior, Kamil Jacek Glik, Bartosz Bereszyński (90.Robert Gumny), Szymon Piotr Żurkowski (83.Sebastian Szymański), Piotr Zieliński, Grzegorz Krychowiak, Nicola Zalewski, Karol Grzegorz Świderski (65.Krzysztof Piątek), Robert Lewandowski (Cap). Trainer: Czesław Michniewicz.
**Goal:** Karol Grzegorz Świderski (58).

**16.11.2022    POLAND - CHILE                1-0(0-0)**                 Friendly International
Stadion Wojska Polskiego, Warszawa; Referee: Harm Osmers (Germany); Attendance: 27,900
**POL:** Łukasz Skorupski, Jakub Piotr Kiwior, Jan Kacper Bednarek (79.Mateusz Wieteska), Kamil Jacek Glik (Cap) (46.Bartosz Bereszyński), Robert Gumny, Szymon Piotr Żurkowski, Sebastian Szymański, Grzegorz Krychowiak (67.Damian Dawid Szymański), Przemysław Frankowski (67.Kamil Paweł Grosicki), Arkadiusz Krystian Milik (59.Krzysztof Piątek), Karol Grzegorz Świderski (59.Jakub Kamiński). Trainer: Czesław Michniewicz.
**Goal:** Krzysztof Piątek (85).

**22.11.2022    MEXICO - POLAND                0-0**                 22nd FIFA WC. Group Stage.
Stadium 974, Doha (Qatar); Referee: Christopher James Beath (Australia); Attendance: 39,369
**POL:** Wojciech Tomasz Szczęsny, Bartosz Bereszyński, Kamil Jacek Glik, Jakub Piotr Kiwior, Matthew Stuart Cash, Jakub Kamiński, Grzegorz Krychowiak, Sebastian Szymański (71.Przemysław Frankowski), Piotr Sebastian Zieliński (87.Arkadiusz Krystian Milik), Nicola Zalewski (46.Krystian Bielik), Robert Lewandowski (Cap). Trainer: Czesław Michniewicz.

**26.11.2022    POLAND - SAUDI ARABIA                2-0(1-0)**                 22nd FIFA WC. Group Stage.
Education City Stadium, Al Rayyan (Qatar); Referee: Wilton Pereira Sampaio (Brazil); Attendance: 44,259
**POL:** Wojciech Tomasz Szczęsny, Bartosz Bereszyński, Kamil Jacek Glik, Jakub Piotr Kiwior, Matthew Stuart Cash, Krystian Bielik, Grzegorz Krychowiak, Przemysław Frankowski, Piotr Sebastian Zieliński (63.Jakub Kamiński), Arkadiusz Krystian Milik (71.Krzysztof Piątek), Robert Lewandowski (Cap). Trainer: Czesław Michniewicz.
**Goals:** Piotr Sebastian Zieliński (39), Robert Lewandowski (82).

**30.11.2022    POLAND - ARGENTINA                0-2(0-0)**                 22nd FIFA WC. Group Stage.
Stadium 974, Doha (Qatar); Referee: Danny Desmond Makkelie (Netherlands); Attendance: 44,089
**POL:** Wojciech Tomasz Szczęsny, Matthew Stuart Cash, Kamil Jacek Glik, Jakub Piotr Kiwior, Bartosz Bereszyński (72.Artur Marcin Jędrzejczyk), Piotr Sebastian Zieliński, Krystian Bielik (62.Damian Dawid Szymański), Grzegorz Krychowiak (83. Krzysztof Piątek), Przemysław Frankowski (46.Jakub Kamiński), Robert Lewandowski (Cap), Karol Grzegorz Świderski (46.Michał Krzysztof Skóraś). Trainer: Czesław Michniewicz.

**04.12.2022    FRANCE - POLAND                3-1(1-0)**                 22nd FIFA WC. 2nd Round of 16.
Al Thumama Stadium, Doha (Qatar); Referee: Jesús Noel Valenzuela Sáez (Venezuela); Attendance: 40,989
**POL:** Wojciech Tomasz Szczęsny, Matthew Stuart Cash, Kamil Jacek Glik, Jakub Piotr Kiwior (87.Jan Kacper Bednarek), Bartosz Bereszyński, Jakub Kamiński (71.Nicola Zalewski), Piotr Sebastian Zieliński, Grzegorz Krychowiak (71.Krystian Bielik), Sebastian Szymański (64.Arkadiusz Krystian Milik), Przemysław Frankowski (87.Kamil Paweł Grosicki), Robert Lewandowski (Cap). Trainer: Czesław Michniewicz.
**Goal:** Robert Lewandowski (90+9 penalty).

**24.03.2023    CZECH REPUBLIC - POLAND                3-1(2-0)**                 17th EC. Qualifiers
Eden Arena, Praha; Referee: Anastasios Sidiropoulos (Greece); Attendance: 19,045
**POL:** Wojciech Tomasz Szczęsny, Matthew Stuart Cash (9.Robert Gumny), Jan Kacper Bednarek, Jakub Piotr Kiwior, Michał Karbownik (46.Michał Krzysztof Skóraś), Karol Linetty (76.Damian Dawid Szymański), Krystian Bielik (46.Karol Grzegorz Świderski), Sebastian Szymański (64.Nicola Zalewski), Piotr Zieliński, Przemysław Frankowski, Robert Lewandowski (Cap). Trainer: Fernando Manuel Fernandes da Costa Santos (Portugal).
**Goal:** Damian Dawid Szymański (87).

**27.03.2023    POLAND - ALBANIA                1-0(1-0)**                 17th EC. Qualifiers
Stadion Narodowy, Warszawa; Referee: Slavko Vinčić (Slovenia); Attendance: 56,227
**POL:** Wojciech Tomasz Szczęsny, Przemysław Frankowski, Bartosz Salamon, Jan Kacper Bednarek, Jakub Piotr Kiwior, Karol Linetty (78.Damian Dawid Szymański), Karol Grzegorz Świderski (88.Sebastian Szymański), Piotr Zieliński, Jakub Kamiński, Nicola Zalewski (68.Michał Krzysztof Skóraś), Robert Lewandowski (Cap). Trainer: Fernando Manuel Fernandes da Costa Santos (Portugal).
**Goal:** Karol Grzegorz Świderski (41).

**16.06.2023**  **POLAND - GERMANY**  1-0(1-0)  Friendly International
Stadion Narodowy, Warszawa; Referee: Orel Grinfeld (Israel); Attendance: 57,098
**POL:** Wojciech Tomasz Szczęsny, Bartosz Bereszyński (72.Przemysław Frankowski), Tomasz Karol Kędziora, Jakub Piotr Kiwior, Jan Kacper Bednarek, Jakub Kamiński, Sebastian Szymański (46.Karol Linetty), Jakub Błaszczykowski (Cap) (17.Michał Krzysztof Skóraś), Piotr Zieliński (65.Bartosz Piotr Slisz), Damian Dawid Szymański (77.Krystian Bielik), Robert Lewandowski (46.Arkadiusz Krystian Milik). Trainer: Fernando Manuel Fernandes da Costa Santos (Portugal).
**Goal:** Jakub Piotr Kiwior (31).

**20.06.2023**  **MOLDOVA - POLAND**  3-2(0-2)  17th EC. Qualifiers
Stadionul Zimbru, Chişinău; Referee: Filip Glova (Slovakia); Attendance: 9,442
**POL:** Wojciech Tomasz Szczęsny, Tomasz Karol Kędziora, Jan Kacper Bednarek, Jakub Piotr Kiwior, Przemysław Frankowski (64.Bartosz Bereszyński), Damian Dawid Szymański (83.Karol Linetty), Piotr Zieliński, Sebastian Szymański, Nicola Zalewski (64.Jakub Kamiński), Arkadiusz Krystian Milik (73.Karol Grzegorz Świderski), Robert Lewandowski (Cap). Trainer: Fernando Manuel Fernandes da Costa Santos (Portugal).
**Goals:** Arkadiusz Krystian Milik (12), Robert Lewandowski (34).

| NATIONAL TEAM PLAYERS (16.07.2022 – 15.07.2023) | | | | |
|---|---|---|---|---|
| **Name** | **DOB** | **Caps** | **Goals** | *Club* |
| **Goalkeepers** | | | | |
| Łukasz SKORUPSKI | 05.05.1991 | 8 | 0 | 2022: *Bologna FC 1909 (ITA)* |
| Wojciech Tomasz SZCZĘSNY | 18.04.1990 | 74 | 0 | 2022/2023: *Juventus FC Torino (ITA)* |
| **Defenders** | | | | |
| Jan Kacper BEDNAREK | 12.04.1996 | 50 | 1 | 2022/2023: *Southampton FC (ENG)* |
| Bartosz BERESZYŃSKI | 12.07.1992 | 52 | 0 | 2022: *UC Sampdoria Genova (ITA)* / 07.01.2023-> *SSC Napoli (ITA)* |
| Matthew Stuart CASH | 07.08.1997 | 12 | 1 | 2022/2023: *Aston Villa FC Birmingham (ENG)* |
| Kamil Jacek GLIK | 03.02.1988 | 103 | 6 | 2022/2023: *Benevento Calcio (ITA)* |
| Robert GUMNY | 04.06.1998 | 6 | 0 | 2022/2023: *FC Augsburg (GER)* |
| Artur Marcin JĘDRZEJCZYK | 04.11.1987 | 41 | 3 | 2022: *Legia Warszawa* |
| Michał KARBOWNIK | 13.03.2001 | 4 | 0 | 2023: *TSV Fortuna Düsseldorf (GER)* |
| Tomasz Karol KĘDZIORA | 11.06.1994 | 28 | 1 | 2023: *PAOK Thessaloníki (GRE)* |
| Jakub Piotr KIWIOR | 15.02.2000 | 13 | 1 | 2022: *Spezia Calcio La Spezia (ITA)* / 23.01.2023-> *Arsenal FC London (GER)* |
| Bartosz SALAMON | 01.05.1991 | 11 | 0 | 2023: *KKS Lech Poznań* |
| Mateusz WIETESKA | 11.02.1997 | 2 | 0 | 2022: *Clermont Foot 63 (FRA)* |
| **Midfielders** | | | | |
| Krystian BIELIK | 04.01.1998 | 11 | 0 | 2022/2023: *Birmingham City FC (ENG)* |
| Przemysław FRANKOWSKI | 12.04.1995 | 34 | 1 | 2022/2023: *Racing Club de Lens (FRA)* |
| Kamil Paweł GROSICKI | 08.06.1988 | 88 | 17 | 2022: *MKS Pogoń Szczecin* |
| Jakub KAMIŃSKI | 05.06.2002 | 11 | 1 | 2022/2023: *VfL Wolfsburg (GER)* |
| Mateusz Andrzej KLICH | 13.06.1990 | 41 | 2 | 2022: *Leeds United FC (ENG)* |
| Grzegorz KRYCHOWIAK | 29.01.1990 | 98 | 5 | 2022: *Al-Shabab FC Riyadh (KSA)* |
| Karol LINETTY | 02.02.1995 | 46 | 5 | 2022/2023: *Torino FC (ITA)* |
| Mateusz ŁĘGOWSKI | 29.01.2003 | 1 | 0 | 2022: *MKS Pogoń Szczecin* |
| Michał Krzysztof SKÓRAŚ | 15.02.2000 | 5 | 0 | 2022/2023: *KKS Lech Poznań* |
| Bartosz Piotr SLISZ | 29.03.1999 | 2 | 0 | 2023: *Legia Warszawa* |
| Damian Dawid SZYMAŃSKI | 16.06.1995 | 14 | 2 | 2022/2023: *AEK Athína (GRE)* |
| Sebastian SZYMAŃSKI | 10.05.1999 | 24 | 1 | 2022/2023: *Feyenoord Rotterdam (NED)* |
| Nicola ZALEWSKI | 23.01.2002 | 12 | 0 | 2022/2023: *AS Roma (ITA)* |
| Piotr Sebastian ZIELIŃSKI | 20.05.1994 | 82 | 10 | 2022/2023: *SSC Napoli (ITA)* |
| Szymon Piotr ŻURKOWSKI | 25.09.1997 | 7 | 0 | 2022: *ACF Fiorentina (POL)* |
| **Forwards** | | | | |
| Jakub BŁASZCZYKOWSKI | 14.12.1985 | 109 | 21 | 2022/2023: *TS Wisła Kraków* |
| Robert LEWANDOWSKI | 21.08.1988 | 142 | 79 | 2022/2023: *FC Barcelona (ESP)* |
| Arkadiusz Krystian MILIK | 28.02.1994 | 69 | 17 | 2022/2023: *Juventus FC Torino (ITA)* |
| Krzysztof PIĄTEK | 01.07.1995 | 27 | 11 | 2022/2023: *US Salernitana 1919 (ITA)* |
| Karol Grzegorz ŚWIDERSKI | 23.01.1997 | 22 | 89 | 2022/2023: *Charlotte FC (USA)* |
| **Trainer** | | | | |
| Czesław MICHNIEWICZ [31.01.2022 – 31.12.2022] | 12.02.1970 | 13 M; 5 W; 3 D; 5 L; 13-18 | | |
| FERNANDO Manuel Fernandes da Costa SANTOS (Portugal) [from 24.01.2023] | 10.10.1954 | 4 M; 2 W; 0 D; 2 L; 5-6 | | |

# PORTUGAL

**The Country:**
República Portuguesa (Portuguese Republic)
Capital: Lisboa
Surface: 92,212 km²
Inhabitants: 10,467,366 [2022]
Time: UTC

**The FA:**
Federação Portuguesa de Futebol
Avenida das Seleções 1495-433, Cruz Quebrada - Dafundo
Tel: +351 213 252 700
Founded: 31.03.1914
Member of FIFA since: 1923
Member of UEFA since: 1954
Website: www.fpf.pt

## NATIONAL TEAM RECORDS

### RECORDS

| | |
|---|---|
| **First international match:** | 18.12.1921, Madrid: Spain – Portugal 3-1(2-0) |
| **Most international caps:** | Cristiano Ronaldo dos Santos Aveiro - 200 caps (since 2003) |
| **Most international goals:** | Cristiano Ronaldo dos Santos Aveiro - 123 goals / 200 caps (since 2003) |

### UEFA EUROPEAN CHAMPIONSHIP

|  |  |
|---|---|
| 1960 | Qualifiers |
| 1964 | Qualifiers |
| 1968 | Qualifiers |
| 1972 | Qualifiers |
| 1976 | Qualifiers |
| 1980 | Qualifiers |
| 1984 | Final Tournament (Semi-Finals) |
| 1988 | Qualifiers |
| 1992 | Qualifiers |
| 1996 | Final Tournament (Quarter-Finals) |
| 2000 | Final Tournament (Semi-Finals) |
| 2004 | Final Tournament (Runners-up) |
| 2008 | Final Tournament (Quarter-Finals) |
| 2012 | Final Tournament (Semi-Finals) |
| 2016 | **Final Tournament (Winners)** |
| 2020 | Final Tournament (2nd Round of 16) |

### FIFA WORLD CUP

|  |  |
|---|---|
| 1930 | Did not enter |
| 1934 | Qualifiers |
| 1938 | Qualifiers |
| 1950 | Qualifiers |
| 1954 | Qualifiers |
| 1958 | Qualifiers |
| 1962 | Qualifiers |
| 1966 | Final Tournament (3rd Place) |
| 1970 | Qualifiers |
| 1974 | Qualifiers |
| 1978 | Qualifiers |
| 1982 | Qualifiers |
| 1986 | Final Tournament (Group Stage) |
| 1990 | Qualifiers |
| 1994 | Qualifiers |
| 1998 | Qualifiers |
| 2002 | Final Tournament (Group Stage) |
| 2006 | Final Tournament (4th Place) |
| 2010 | Final Tournament (2nd Round of 16) |
| 2014 | Final Tournament (Group Stage) |
| 2018 | Final Tournament (2nd Round of 16) |
| 2022 | Final Tournament (Quarter-Finals) |

### OLYMPIC TOURNAMENTS

|  |  |
|---|---|
| 1908 | - |
| 1912 | - |
| 1920 | - |
| 1924 | - |
| 1928 | Quarter-Finals |
| 1936 | Did not enter |
| 1948 | Did not enter |
| 1952 | Did not enter |
| 1956 | Did not enter |
| 1960 | Did not enter |
| 1964 | Did not enter |
| 1968 | Did not enter |
| 1972 | Did not enter |
| 1976 | Did not enter |
| 1980 | Did not enter |
| 1984 | Qualifiers |
| 1988 | Qualifiers |
| 1992 | Qualifiers |
| 1996 | 4th Place |
| 2000 | Qualifiers |
| 2004 | Group Stage |
| 2008 | Qualifiers |
| 2012 | Qualifiers |
| 2016 | Quarter-Finals |
| 2020 | Qualifiers |

### UEFA NATIONS LEAGUE

|  |  |
|---|---|
| 2018/2019 | League A (Group Stage -> Final Tournament: **Winners)** |
| 2020/2021 | League A (Group Stage) |
| 2022/2023 | League A (Group Stage) |

### FIFA CONFEDERATIONS CUP 1992-2017

2017 (3rd Place)

### PORTUGUESE CLUB HONOURS IN EUROPEAN CLUB COMPETITIONS:

| European Champion Clubs.Cup (1956-1992) / UEFA Champions League (1993-2023) | | |
|---|---|---|
| Sport Lisboa e Benfica | 2 | 1960/1961, 1961/1962 |
| FC do Porto | 2 | 1986/1987, 2003/2004 |
| **Fairs Cup (1858-1971) / UEFA Cup (1972-2009) / UEFA Europa League (2010-2023)** | | |
| FC do Porto | 2 | 2002/2003, 2010/2011 |
| **UEFA Europa Conference League (2021-2023)** | | |
| None | | |
| **UEFA Super Cup (1972-2022)** | | |
| FC do Porto | 1 | 1987 |
| *European Cup Winners' Cup 1961-1999\** | | |
| Sporting Clube de Portugal Lisboa | 1 | 1963/1964 |

*defunct competition*

# NATIONAL COMPETITIONS
# TABLE OF HONOURS

## Campeonato de Portugal (1922–1938)*

*created in 1922 and played in cup system, with all the clubs participating in elimination rounds, the winners were named Champions of Portugal. The league sytem started in 1934.

| CHAMPIONS | |
|---|---|
| 1922 | FC do Porto |
| 1922/1923 | Sporting Clube de Portugal Lisboa |
| 1923/1924 | SC Olhanense |
| 1924/1925 | FC do Porto |
| 1925/1926 | CS Marítimo Funchal |
| 1926/1927 | CF Os Belenenses Lisboa |
| 1927/1928 | Carcavelinhos FC |
| 1928/1929 | CF Os Belenenses Lisboa |
| 1929/1930 | Sport Lisboa e Benfica |

| CHAMPIONS | |
|---|---|
| 1930/1931 | Sport Lisboa e Benfica |
| 1931/1932 | FC do Porto |
| 1932/1933 | CF Os Belenenses Lisboa |
| 1933/1934 | Sporting Clube de Portugal Lisboa |
| 1934/1935 | Sport Lisboa e Benfica |
| 1935/1936 | Sporting Clube de Portugal Lisboa |
| 1936/1937 | FC do Porto |
| 1937/1938 | Sporting Clube de Portugal Lisboa |

| | CHAMPIONS* | CUP WINNERS | BEST GOALSCORERS | |
|---|---|---|---|---|
| 1934/1935 | FC do Porto | - | Manuel Esteves Soeiro Vasques (Sporting Clube de Portugal Lisboa) | 14 |
| 1935/1936 | Sport Lisboa e Benfica | - | Artur de Sousa "Pinga" (FC do Porto) | 21 |
| 1936/1937 | Sport Lisboa e Benfica | - | Manuel Esteves Soeiro Vasques (Sporting Clube de Portugal Lisboa) | 24 |
| 1937/1938 | Sport Lisboa e Benfica | - | Fernando Baptista de Seixas Peyroteo de Vasconcelos (Sporting Clube de Portugal Lisboa) | 34 |
| 1938/1939 | FC do Porto | Associação Académica de Coimbra | José Monteiro "Costuras" (FC do Porto) | 18 |
| 1939/1940 | FC do Porto | Sport Lisboa e Benfica | Fernando Baptista de Seixas Peyroteo de Vasconcelos (Sporting Clube de Portugal Lisboa) Slavko Kodrnja (CRO, FC do Porto) | 29 |
| 1940/1941 | Sporting Clube de Portugal Lisboa | Sporting Clube de Portugal Lisboa | Fernando Baptista de Seixas Peyroteo de Vasconcelos (Sporting Clube de Portugal Lisboa) | 29 |
| 1941/1942 | Sport Lisboa e Benfica | CF Os Belenenses Lisboa | Manuel BeloCorreia Dias (FC do Porto) | 36 |
| 1942/1943 | Sport Lisboa e Benfica | Sport Lisboa e Benfica | Júlio Correia da Silva "Julinho" (Sport Lisboa e Benfica) | 24 |
| 1943/1944 | Sporting Clube de Portugal Lisboa | Sport Lisboa e Benfica | Francisco Rodrigues (Vitória FC Setúbal) | 28 |
| 1944/1945 | Sport Lisboa e Benfica | Sporting Clube de Portugal Lisboa | Francisco Rodrigues (Vitória FC Setúbal) | 21 |
| 1945/1946 | CF Os Belenenses Lisboa | Sporting Clube de Portugal Lisboa | Fernando Baptista de Seixas Peyroteo de Vasconcelos (Sporting Clube de Portugal Lisboa) | 37 |
| 1946/1947 | Sporting Clube de Portugal Lisboa | *No competition* | Fernando Baptista de Seixas Peyroteo de Vasconcelos (Sporting Clube de Portugal Lisboa) | 43 |
| 1947/1948 | Sporting Clube de Portugal Lisboa | Sporting Clube de Portugal Lisboa | António Araújo (FC do Porto) | 36 |
| 1948/1949 | Sporting Clube de Portugal Lisboa | Sport Lisboa e Benfica | Fernando Baptista de Seixas Peyroteo de Vasconcelos (Sporting Clube de Portugal Lisboa) | 40 |
| 1949/1950 | Sport Lisboa e Benfica | *No competition* | Júlio Correia da Silva "Julinho" (Sport Lisboa e Benfica) | 29 |
| 1950/1951 | Sporting Clube de Portugal Lisboa | Sport Lisboa e Benfica | Manuel Soeiro Vasques (Sporting Clube de Portugal Lisboa) | 29 |
| 1951/1952 | Sporting Clube de Portugal Lisboa | Sport Lisboa e Benfica | José Pinto de Carvalho Santos Águas (Sport Lisboa e Benfica) | 28 |
| 1952/1953 | Sporting Clube de Portugal Lisboa | Sport Lisboa e Benfica | Sebastião Lucas da Fonseca „Matateu" (CF Os Belenenses Lisboa) | 29 |
| 1953/1954 | Sporting Clube de Portugal Lisboa | Sporting Clube de Portugal Lisboa | João Baptista Martins (Sporting Clube de Portugal Lisboa) | 31 |
| 1954/1955 | Sport Lisboa e Benfica | Sport Lisboa e Benfica | Sebastião Lucas da Fonseca „Matateu" (CF Os Belenenses Lisboa) | 32 |
| 1955/1956 | FC do Porto | FC do Porto | José Pinto de Carvalho Santos Águas (Sport Lisboa e Benfica) | 28 |
| 1956/1957 | Sport Lisboa e Benfica | Sport Lisboa e Benfica | José Pinto de Carvalho Santos Águas (Sport Lisboa e Benfica) | 30 |
| 1957/1958 | Sporting Clube de Portugal Lisboa | FC do Porto | Arsénio Trindade Duarte (GD CUF do Barreiro) | 23 |
| 1958/1959 | FC do Porto | Sport Lisboa e Benfica | José Pinto de Carvalho Santos Águas (Sport Lisboa e Benfica) | 26 |
| 1959/1960 | Sport Lisboa e Benfica | CF Os Belenenses Lisboa | Edmur Pinto Ribeiro (Vitória SC Guimarães) | 25 |
| 1960/1961 | Sport Lisboa e Benfica | Leixões SC Porto | José Pinto de Carvalho Santos Águas (Sport Lisboa e Benfica) | 27 |
| 1961/1962 | Sporting Clube de Portugal Lisboa | Sport Lisboa e Benfica | Azumir Luis Casimiro Veríssimo (BRA, FC do Porto) | 23 |
| 1962/1963 | Sport Lisboa e Benfica | Sporting Clube de Portugal Lisboa | José Augusto Costa Sénica Torres (Sport Lisboa e Benfica) | 26 |
| 1963/1964 | Sport Lisboa e Benfica | Sport Lisboa e Benfica | Eusébio da Silva Ferreira (Sport Lisboa e Benfica) | 28 |
| 1964/1965 | Sport Lisboa e Benfica | Vitória FC Setúbal | Eusébio da Silva Ferreira (Sport Lisboa e Benfica) | 28 |
| 1965/1966 | Sporting Clube de Portugal Lisboa | Sporting Clube de Braga | Eusébio da Silva Ferreira (Sport Lisboa e Benfica) Ernesto de Figueiredo (Sporting Clube de Portugal) | 25 |
| 1966/1967 | Sport Lisboa e Benfica | Vitória FC Setúbal | Eusébio da Silva Ferreira (Sport Lisboa e Benfica) | 31 |

| | | | |
|---|---|---|---|
| 1967/1968 | Sport Lisboa e Benfica | FC do Porto | Eusébio da Silva Ferreira (Sport Lisboa e Benfica) | 43 |
| 1968/1969 | Sport Lisboa e Benfica | Sport Lisboa e Benfica | Manuel António Leitão da Silva (Associação Académica de Coimbra) | 19 |
| 1969/1970 | Sporting Clube de Portugal Lisboa | Sport Lisboa e Benfica | Eusébio da Silva Ferreira (Sport Lisboa e Benfica) | 20 |
| 1970/1971 | Sport Lisboa e Benfica | Sporting Clube de Portugal Lisboa | Artur Jorge Braga Melo Teixeira (Sport Lisboa e Benfica) | 23 |
| 1971/1972 | Sport Lisboa e Benfica | Sport Lisboa e Benfica | Artur Jorge Braga Melo Teixeira (Sport Lisboa e Benfica) | 27 |
| 1972/1973 | Sport Lisboa e Benfica | Sporting Clube de Portugal Lisboa | Eusébio da Silva Ferreira (Sport Lisboa e Benfica) | 40 |
| 1973/1974 | Sporting Clube de Portugal Lisboa | Sporting Clube de Portugal Lisboa | Héctor Casimiro Yazalde (ARG, Sporting Clube de Portugal Lisboa) | 46 |
| 1974/1975 | Sport Lisboa e Benfica | Boavista FC do Porto | Héctor Casimiro Yazalde (ARG, Sporting Clube de Portugal Lisboa) | 30 |
| 1975/1976 | Sport Lisboa e Benfica | Boavista FC do Porto | Rui Manuel Trindade Jordão (Sport Lisboa e Benfica) | 30 |
| 1976/1977 | Sport Lisboa e Benfica | FC do Porto | Fernando Mendes Soares Gomes (FC do Porto) | 26 |
| 1977/1978 | FC do Porto | Sporting Clube de Portugal Lisboa | Fernando Mendes Soares Gomes (FC do Porto) | 25 |
| 1978/1979 | FC do Porto | Boavista FC do Porto | Fernando Mendes Soares Gomes (FC do Porto) | 27 |
| 1979/1980 | Sporting Clube de Portugal Lisboa | Sport Lisboa e Benfica | Rui Manuel Trindade Jordão (Sporting Clube de Portugal Lisboa) | 31 |
| 1980/1981 | Sport Lisboa e Benfica | Sport Lisboa e Benfica | Tamagnini Manuel Gomes Batista "Nené" (Sport Lisboa e Benfica) | 20 |
| 1981/1982 | Sporting Clube de Portugal Lisboa | Sporting Clube de Portugal Lisboa | Jacques Pereira (FC do Porto) | 27 |
| 1982/1983 | Sport Lisboa e Benfica | Sport Lisboa e Benfica | Fernando Mendes Soares Gomes (FC do Porto) | 36 |
| 1983/1984 | Sport Lisboa e Benfica | FC do Porto | Fernando Mendes Soares Gomes (FC do Porto) Tamagnini Manuel Gomes Batista "Nené" (Sport Lisboa e Benfica) | 21 |
| 1984/1985 | FC do Porto | Sport Lisboa e Benfica | Fernando Mendes Soares Gomes (FC do Porto) | 39 |
| 1985/1986 | FC do Porto | Sport Lisboa e Benfica | Manuel José Tavares Fernandes (Sporting Clube de Portugal Lisboa) | 30 |
| 1986/1987 | Sport Lisboa e Benfica | Sport Lisboa e Benfica | Paulo Roberto Bacinello "Paulinho Cascavel" (BRA, Vitória SC Guimarães) | 22 |
| 1987/1988 | FC do Porto | FC do Porto | Paulo Roberto Bacinello "Paulinho Cascavel" (BRA, Sporting Clube de Portugal Lisboa) | 23 |
| 1988/1989 | Sport Lisboa e Benfica | CF Os Belenenses Lisboa | Vata Matanu Garcia (ANG, Sport Lisboa e Benfica) | 16 |
| 1989/1990 | FC do Porto | CF Estrela da Amadora | Mats Magnusson (SWE, Sport Lisboa e Benfica) | 33 |
| 1990/1991 | Sport Lisboa e Benfica | FC do Porto | José Rui Lopes Águas (Sport Lisboa e Benfica) | 25 |
| 1991/1992 | FC do Porto | Boavista FC do Porto | Richard Daddy Owubokiri (NGA, Boavista FC do Porto) | 30 |
| 1992/1993 | FC do Porto | Sport Lisboa e Benfica | Jorge Paulo Cadete Santos Reis (Sporting Clube de Portugal Lisboa) | 18 |
| 1993/1994 | Sport Lisboa e Benfica | FC do Porto | Rashidi Yekini (NGA, Vitória FC Setúbal) | 21 |
| 1994/1995 | FC do Porto | Sporting Clube de Portugal Lisboa | Hassan Nader (MAR, SC Farense) | 21 |
| 1995/1996 | FC do Porto | Sport Lisboa e Benfica | Domingos José Paciência Oliveira (FC do Porto) | 25 |
| 1996/1997 | FC do Porto | Boavista FC do Porto | Mário Jardel de Almeida Ribeiro (BRA, FC do Porto) | 30 |
| 1997/1998 | FC do Porto | FC do Porto | Mário Jardel de Almeida Ribeiro (BRA, FC do Porto) | 26 |
| 1998/1999 | FC do Porto | SC Beira-Mar Aveiro | Mário Jardel de Almeida Ribeiro (BRA, FC do Porto) | 36 |
| 1999/2000 | Sporting Clube de Portugal Lisboa | FC do Porto | Mário Jardel de Almeida Ribeiro (BRA, FC do Porto) | 37 |
| 2000/2001 | Boavista FC do Porto | FC do Porto | Renivaldo Pereira de Jesus "Pena" (BRA, FC do Porto) | 22 |
| 2001/2002 | Sporting Clube de Portugal Lisboa | Sporting Clube de Portugal Lisboa | Mário Jardel de Almeida Ribeiro (BRA, Sporting Clube de Portugal Lisboa) | 42 |
| 2002/2003 | FC do Porto | FC do Porto | Fary Faye (SEN, SC Beira-Mar Aveiro) | 18 |
| 2003/2004 | FC do Porto | Sport Lisboa e Benfica | Benedict Saul McCarthy (RSA, FC do Porto) | 20 |
| 2004/2005 | Sport Lisboa e Benfica | Vitória FC Setúbal | Liédson da Silva Muniz (BRA, Sporting Clube de Portugal Lisboa) | 25 |
| 2005/2006 | FC do Porto | FC do Porto | Albert Meyong Zé (CMR, CF Os Belenenses Lisboa) | 17 |
| 2006/2007 | FC do Porto | Sporting Clube de Portugal Lisboa | Liédson da Silva Muniz (BRA, Sporting Clube de Portugal Lisboa) | 15 |
| 2007/2008 | FC do Porto | Sporting Clube de Portugal Lisboa | Lisandro López (ARG, FC do Porto) | 24 |
| 2008/2009 | FC do Porto | FC do Porto | Ânderson Miguel da Silva "Nenê" (BRA, CD Nacional Funchal) | 20 |
| 2009/2010 | Sport Lisboa e Benfica | FC do Porto | Óscar René Cardozo Marín (PAR, Sport Lisboa e Benfica) | 26 |
| 2010/2011 | FC do Porto | FC do Porto | Givanildo Vieira de Sousa "Hulk" (BRA, FC do Porto) | 23 |
| 2011/2012 | FC do Porto | Associação Académica de Coimbra | Óscar René Cardozo Marín (PAR, Sport Lisboa e Benfica) | 20 |
| 2012/2013 | FC do Porto | Vitória SC Guimarães | Jackson Arley Martínez Valencia (COL, FC do Porto) | 26 |
| 2013/2014 | Sport Lisboa e Benfica | Sport Lisboa e Benfica | Jackson Arley Martínez Valencia (COL, FC do Porto) | 20 |
| 2014/2015 | Sport Lisboa e Benfica | Sporting Clube de Portugal Lisboa | Jackson Arley Martínez Valencia (COL, FC do Porto) | 21 |

| 2015/2016 | Sport Lisboa e Benfica | Sporting Clube de Braga | Jonas Gonçalves Oliveira (BRA, Sport Lisboa e Benfica) | 32 |
| 2016/2017 | Sport Lisboa e Benfica | Sport Lisboa e Benfica | Bas Dost (NED, Sporting Clube de Portugal Lisboa) | 34 |
| 2017/2018 | FC do Porto | Desportivo das Aves | Jonas Gonçalves Oliveira (BRA, Sport Lisboa e Benfica) | 34 |
| 2018/2019 | Sport Lisboa e Benfica | Sporting Clube de Portugal Lisboa | Haris Seferović (SUI, Sport Lisboa e Benfica) | 23 |
| 2019/2020 | FC do Porto | FC do Porto | Carlos Vinícius Alves Morais (BRA, Sport Lisboa e Benfica) Luis Miguel Afonso Fernandes "Pizzi" (Sport Lisboa e Benfica) Mehdi Taremi (IRN, Rio Ave FC Vila do Conde) | 18 |
| 2020/2021 | Sporting Clube de Portugal Lisboa | Sporting Clube de Braga | Pedro António Pereira Gonçalves (Sporting Clube de Portugal Lisboa) | 23 |
| 2021/2022 | FC do Porto | FC do Porto | Darwin Gabriel Núñez Ribeiro (URU, Sport Lisboa e Benfica) | 26 |
| 2022/2023 | Sport Lisboa e Benfica | FC do Porto | Mehdi Taremi (IRN, FC do Porto) | 22 |

*Please note: Campeonato da Liga da Primeira Divisão (1934-1938), Campeonato Nacional da Primeira Divisão (1938-1999), Primeira Liga (since 1999).

## NATIONAL CHAMPIONSHIP
### Primeira Liga 2022/2023
(05.08.2022 – 27.05.2023)

### Results

**Round 1 [05-08.08.2022]**
Benfica - Arouca 4-0(3-0)
Rio Ave - Vizela 0-1(0-0)
GD Estoril - Famalicão 2-0(2-0)
FC Porto - Marítimo 5-1(3-0)
Santa Clara - Casa Pia 0-0
SC Braga - Sporting 3-3(2-2)
Portimonense - Boavista 0-1(0-1)
GD Chaves - Vitória Guimarães 0-1(0-1)
Gil Vicente - Paços de Ferreira 1-0(0-0)

**Round 2 [12-15.08.2022]**
Famalicão - SC Braga 0-3(0-2)
Casa Pia - Benfica 0-1(0-0)
Sporting - Rio Ave 3-0(1-0)
Boavista - Santa Clara 2-1(0-1)
Vizela - FC Porto 0-1(0-0)
Vitória Guimarães - GD Estoril 1-0(1-0)
Marítimo - GD Chaves 1-2(1-0)
Arouca - Gil Vicente 1-0(1-0)
Paços de Ferreira - Portimonense 0-3(0-1)

**Round 3 [19-22.08.2022]**
GD Estoril - Rio Ave 2-2(1-0)
Santa Clara - Arouca 1-2(0-0)
GD Chaves - Vizela 1-1(1-1)
FC Porto - Sporting 3-0(1-0)
Casa Pia - Boavista 2-0(0-0)
SC Braga - Marítimo 5-0(2-0)
Portimonense - Vitória Guimarães 2-1(0-0)
Gil Vicente - Famalicão 0-0
Benfica - Paços de Ferr. 3-2(2-1) [30.08.2022]

**Round 4 [26-29.08.2022]**
Paços de Ferreira - GD Estoril 0-3(0-2)
Marítimo - Portimonense 0-1(0-1)
Boavista - Benfica 0-3(0-1)
Sporting - GD Chaves 0-2(0-0)
Famalicão - Santa Clara 1-0(1-0)
Arouca - SC Braga 0-6(0-4)
Rio Ave - FC Porto 3-1(3-0)
Vitória Guimarães - Casa Pia 0-1(0-1)
Vizela - Gil Vicente 2-2(2-2)

**Round 5 [02-05.09.2022]**
Benfica - Vizela 2-1(0-1)
GD Estoril - Sporting 0-2(0-2)
SC Braga - Vitória Guimarães 1-0(0-0)
Gil Vicente - FC Porto 0-2(0-2)
Casa Pia - Arouca 0-0
Santa Clara - Marítimo 2-1(0-0)
Portimonense - Famalicão 1-0(0-0)
Boavista - Paços de Ferreira 1-0(0-0)
GD Chaves - Rio Ave 1-1(1-0)

**Round 6 [09-12.09.2022]**
Vitória Guimarães - Santa Clara 1-0(0-0)
Famalicão - Benfica 0-1(0-0)
Sporting - Portimonense 4-0(2-0)
FC Porto - GD Chaves 3-0(1-0)
Paços de Ferreira - Casa Pia 2-3(1-0)
Arouca - Boavista 1-2(1-1)
Marítimo - Gil Vicente 1-2(1-0)
Rio Ave - SC Braga 2-3(0-2)
Vizela - GD Estoril 0-1(0-1)

**Round 7 [16-18.09.2022]**
Portimonense - GD Chaves 1-0(1-0)
Santa Clara - Paços de Ferreira 1-1(1-0)
Gil Vicente - Rio Ave 2-2(0-1)
GD Estoril - FC Porto 1-1(1-0)
Boavista - Sporting 2-1(1-0)
Arouca - Vitória Guimarães 2-2(1-0)
Benfica - Marítimo 5-0(1-0)
Casa Pia - Famalicão 1-0(0-0)
SC Braga - Vizela 2-0(0-0)

**Round 8 [30.09.-03.10.2022]**
Sporting - Gil Vicente 3-1(2-0)
FC Porto - SC Braga 4-1(2-0)
Vizela - Portimonense 1-0(1-0)
GD Chaves - GD Estoril 1-1(1-0)
Vitória Guimarães - Benfica 0-0
Rio Ave - Santa Clara 1-0(1-0)
Paços de Ferreira - Arouca 1-1(0-0)
Famalicão - Boavista 4-0(2-0)
Marítimo - Casa Pia 1-2(1-1)

**Round 9 [07-10.10.2022]**
Gil Vicente - GD Estoril 0-1(0-0)
Santa Clara - Sporting 1-2(0-1)
Benfica - Rio Ave 4-2(3-1)
Portimonense - FC Porto 0-2(0-1)
Paços de Ferreira - Vitória Guimarães 0-1(0-1)
Boavista - Marítimo 1-1(1-0)
Casa Pia - Vizela 0-1(0-0)
SC Braga - GD Chaves 0-1(0-1)
Arouca - Famalicão 4-1(1-1)

**Round 10 [21-24.10.2022]**
FC Porto - Benfica 0-1(0-0)
Famalicão - Paços de Ferreira 2-1(1-1)
GD Estoril - SC Braga 0-2(0-2)
Sporting - Casa Pia 3-1(0-1)
Vizela - Santa Clara 0-1(0-0)
Marítimo - Arouca 1-1(1-1)
GD Chaves - Gil Vicente 3-1(0-1)
Vitória Guimarães - Boavista 3-2(1-1)
Rio Ave - Portimonense 1-0(1-0)

**Round 11 [28-31.10.2022]**
Paços de Ferreira - Marítimo 0-1(0-1)
Santa Clara - FC Porto 1-1(0-1)
Benfica - GD Chaves 5-0(3-0)
Arouca - Sporting 1-0(0-0)
Boavista - Vizela 2-2(1-2)
Portimonense - GD Estoril 1-1(0-1)
Casa Pia - Rio Ave 1-0(0-0)
Gil Vicente - SC Braga 0-1(0-0)
Vitória Guimarães - Famalicão 3-2(1-0)

**Round 12 [04-07.11.2022]**
Gil Vicente - Portimonense 1-2(1-1)
Vizela - Arouca 0-1(0-1)
FC Porto - Paços de Ferreira 4-0(3-0)
Sporting - Vitória Guimarães 3-0(2-0)
Rio Ave - Boavista 1-0(0-0)
Marítimo - Famalicão 0-0
SC Braga - Casa Pia 0-1(0-1)
GD Estoril - Benfica 1-5(0-3)
GD Chaves - Santa Clara 0-0

**Round 13 [12-14.11.2022]**
Arouca - Rio Ave 0-1(0-0)
Boavista - FC Porto 1-4(0-1)
Paços de Ferreira - Vizela 0-2(0-0)
Vitória Guimarães - Marítimo 1-0(0-0)
Benfica - Gil Vicente 3-1(2-1)
Casa Pia - GD Chaves 1-2(1-0)
Portimonense - SC Braga 1-2(1-0)
Famalicão - Sporting 1-2(0-2)
Santa Clara - GD Estoril 3-1(2-1)

**Round 14 [28-30.12.2022]**
Rio Ave - Marítimo 1-1(1-1) [23.12.2022]
Portimonense - Casa Pia 1-2(1-1)
FC Porto - Arouca 5-1(3-0)
Gil Vicente - Santa Clara 1-0(1-0)
Sporting - Paços de Ferreira 3-0(3-0)
GD Chaves - Famalicão 0-2(0-1)
Vizela - Vitória Guimarães 3-0(1-0)
SC Braga - Benfica 3-0(2-0)
GD Estoril - Boavista 2-1(0-1) [09.02.2023]

**Round 15 [05-08.01.2023]**
Santa Clara - SC Braga 0-4(0-2)
Benfica - Portimonense 1-0(1-0)
Famalicão - Vizela 2-1(1-0)
Arouca - GD Estoril 2-0(1-0)
Vitória Guimarães - Rio Ave 0-0
Casa Pia - FC Porto 0-0
Paços de Ferreira - GD Chaves 1-0(0-0)
Marítimo - Sporting 1-0(0-0)
Boavista - Gil Vicente 1-0(1-0)

## Round 16 [13-16.01.2023]
Portimonense - Santa Clara 0-0
Vizela - Marítimo 3-0(2-0)
Rio Ave - Paços de Ferreira 0-1(0-1)
SC Braga - Boavista 1-0(0-0)
GD Chaves - Arouca 1-1(1-0)
Benfica - Sporting 2-2(1-1)
FC Porto - Famalicão 4-1(3-0)
GD Estoril - Casa Pia 2-0(1-0)
Gil Vicente - Vitória Guimarães 2-1(1-1)

## Round 17 [20-23.01.2023]
Arouca - Portimonense 4-0(2-0)
Sporting - Vizela 2-1(0-0)
Paços de Ferreira - SC Braga 1-2(0-0)
Santa Clara - Benfica 0-3(0-2)
Vitória Guimarães - FC Porto 0-1(0-1)
Marítimo - GD Estoril 1-0(1-0)
Casa Pia - Gil Vicente 1-3(0-0)
Famalicão - Rio Ave 0-0
Boavista - GD Chaves 1-1(1-0)

## Round 18 [29.01.-01.02.2023]
Casa Pia - Santa Clara 2-1(0-0)
Vizela - Rio Ave 3-1(0-1)
Boavista - Portimonense 4-2(0-0)
Famalicão - GD Estoril 1-0(0-0)
Vitória Guimarães - GD Chaves 2-1(1-0)
Paços de Ferreira - Gil Vicente 2-1(1-0)
Arouca - Benfica 0-3(0-1)
Marítimo - FC Porto 0-2(0-0)
Sporting - SC Braga 5-0(1-0)

## Round 19 [04-06.02.2023]
Santa Clara - Boavista 2-2(0-1)
Benfica - Casa Pia 3-0(2-0)
GD Estoril - Vitória Guimarães 0-1(0-1)
GD Chaves - Marítimo 2-1(2-1)
SC Braga - Famalicão 4-1(1-0)
FC Porto - Vizela 2-0(1-0)
Gil Vicente - Arouca 1-1(1-1)
Portimonense - Paços de Ferreira 1-0(0-0)
Rio Ave - Sporting 0-1(0-0)

## Round 20 [10-13.02.2023]
Paços de Ferreira-Benfica 0-2(0-2) [26.01.23]
Vizela - GD Chaves 0-0
Arouca - Santa Clara 1-0(0-0)
Vitória Guimarães - Portimonense 1-0(1-0)
Famalicão - Gil Vicente 0-1(0-0)
Sporting - FC Porto 1-2(0-0)
Marítimo - SC Braga 1-2(1-2)
Rio Ave - GD Estoril 2-0(0-0)
Boavista - Casa Pia 0-0

## Round 21 [17-20.02.2023]
Gil Vicente - Vizela 1-1(0-0)
GD Estoril - Paços de Ferreira 1-3(0-2)
Portimonense - Marítimo 2-1(0-1)
FC Porto - Rio Ave 1-0(1-0)
Santa Clara - Famalicão 1-3(0-0)
SC Braga - Arouca 2-0(1-0)
Casa Pia - Vitória Guimarães 0-0
GD Chaves - Sporting 2-3(1-1)
Benfica - Boavista 3-1(0-0)

## Round 22 [24-27.02.2023]
Famalicão - Portimonense 1-0(0-0)
Arouca - Casa Pia 2-0(0-0)
Marítimo - Santa Clara 3-1(0-1)
Vizela - Benfica 0-2(0-1)
Rio Ave - GD Chaves 1-0(0-0)
Paços de Ferreira - Boavista 1-3(0-1)
FC Porto - Gil Vicente 1-2(1-2)
Sporting - GD Estoril 2-0(1-0)
Vitória Guimarães - SC Braga 2-1(2-0)

## Round 23 [03-06.03.2023]
Boavista - Arouca 0-0
Benfica - Famalicão 2-0(1-0)
GD Estoril - Vizela 0-3(0-2)
Portimonense - Sporting 0-1(0-0)
GD Chaves - FC Porto 1-3(0-2)
Gil Vicente - Marítimo 2-0(1-0)
Santa Clara - Vitória Guimarães 1-3(0-3)
SC Braga - Rio Ave 2-0(1-0)
Casa Pia - Paços de Ferreira 2-1(0-1)

## Round 24 [10-13.03.2023]
FC Porto - GD Estoril 3-2(2-1)
GD Chaves - Portimonense 2-0(1-0)
Paços de Ferreira - Santa Clara 1-0(0-0)
Vitória Guimarães - Arouca 0-2(0-0)
Vizela - SC Braga 0-4(0-1)
Rio Ave - Gil Vicente 2-1(2-0)
Marítimo - Benfica 0-3(0-1)
Sporting - Boavista 3-0(2-0)
Famalicão - Casa Pia 1-0(1-0)

## Round 25 [17-19.03.2023]
Santa Clara - Rio Ave 0-2(0-0)
Portimonense - Vizela 0-1(0-0)
Benfica - Vitória Guimarães 5-1(3-0)
Arouca - Paços de Ferreira 1-1(0-0)
GD Estoril - GD Chaves 0-2(0-1)
Casa Pia - Marítimo 2-0(1-0)
SC Braga - FC Porto 0-0
Boavista - Famalicão 1-2(0-0)
Gil Vicente - Sporting 0-0 [05.04.2023]

## Round 26 [31.03.-03.04.2023]
GD Estoril - Gil Vicente 1-0(1-0)
Vizela - Casa Pia 3-1(1-1)
Vitória Guimarães - Paços de Ferreira 0-0
Sporting - Santa Clara 3-0(2-0)
GD Chaves - SC Braga 1-2(1-1)
Marítimo - Boavista 4-2(2-0)
Rio Ave - Benfica 0-1(0-0)
FC Porto - Portimonense 1-0(1-0)
Famalicão - Arouca 0-1(0-0)

## Round 27 [07-10.04.2023]
Santa Clara - Vizela 0-1(0-1)
Benfica - FC Porto 1-2(1-1)
Boavista - Vitória Guimarães 2-1(1-0)
Arouca - Marítimo 1-0(1-0)
Paços de Ferreira - Famalicão 1-3(1-1)
Portimonense - Rio Ave 2-2(0-1)
SC Braga - GD Estoril 4-1(1-0)
Casa Pia - Sporting 3-4(2-2)
Gil Vicente - GD Chaves 0-0

## Round 28 [14-17.04.2023]
Famalicão - Vitória Guimarães 2-1(1-0)
GD Estoril - Portimonense 0-1(0-0)
Marítimo - Paços de Ferreira 3-1(2-0)
GD Chaves - Benfica 1-0(0-0)
FC Porto - Santa Clara 2-1(1-0)
Rio Ave - Casa Pia 1-1(0-1)
SC Braga - Gil Vicente 1-0(1-0)
Sporting - Arouca 1-1(0-1)
Vizela - Boavista 1-1(0-0)

## Round 29 [21-24.04.2023]
Casa Pia - SC Braga 0-1(0-0)
Famalicão - Marítimo 3-2(0-2)
Boavista - Rio Ave 3-2(3-1)
Paços de Ferreira - FC Porto 0-2(0-0)
Portimonense - Gil Vicente 1-0(0-0)
Benfica - GD Estoril 1-0(1-0)
Santa Clara - GD Chaves 1-1(0-0)
Arouca - Vizela 1-0(1-0)
Vitória Guimarães - Sporting 0-2(0-0)

## Round 30 [28-30.04.2023]
Rio Ave - Arouca 1-0(0-0)
Marítimo - Vitória Guimarães 1-2(0-1)
SC Braga - Portimonense 4-1(3-1)
Vizela - Paços de Ferreira 1-2(0-2)
GD Chaves - Casa Pia 1-0(1-0)
Gil Vicente - Benfica 0-2(0-0)
GD Estoril - Santa Clara 3-0(2-0)
FC Porto - Boavista 1-0(0-0)
Sporting - Famalicão 2-1(1-0)

## Round 31 [05-08.05.2023]
Casa Pia - Portimonense 1-1(0-0)
Santa Clara - Gil Vicente 3-2(2-0)
Boavista - GD Estoril 1-0(0-0)
Benfica - SC Braga 1-0(0-0)
Marítimo - Rio Ave 2-2(1-2)
Vitória Guimarães - Vizela 3-0(2-0)
Paços de Ferreira - Sporting 0-4(0-2)
Famalicão - GD Chaves 1-2(0-0)
Arouca - FC Porto 0-1(0-1)

## Round 32 [12-15.05.2023]
Gil Vicente - Boavista 3-1(1-0)
Vizela - Famalicão 0-0
GD Chaves - Paços de Ferreira 2-0(0-0)
Portimonense - Benfica 1-5(1-3)
Sporting - Marítimo 2-1(0-1)
Rio Ave - Vitória Guimarães 0-1(0-0)
SC Braga - Santa Clara 5-3(3-1)
FC Porto - Casa Pia 2-1(0-1)
GD Estoril - Arouca 2-0(0-0)

## Round 33 [19-21.05.2023]
Marítimo - Vizela 1-0(0-0)
Santa Clara - Portimonense 1-0(1-0)
Arouca - GD Chaves 1-0(0-0)
Boavista - SC Braga 1-1(0-0)
Famalicão - FC Porto 2-4(2-2)
Vitória Guimarães - Gil Vicente 1-0(0-0)
Casa Pia - GD Estoril 2-2(0-0)
Paços de Ferreira - Rio Ave 3-1(1-1)
Sporting - Benfica 2-2(2-0)

## Round 34 [26-27.05.2023]
Rio Ave - Famalicão 2-2(0-2)
Vizela - Sporting 1-2(1-1)
Gil Vicente - Casa Pia 1-0(0-0)
GD Chaves - Boavista 1-4(0-2)
GD Estoril - Marítimo 3-1(1-0)
Benfica - Santa Clara 3-0(2-0)
FC Porto - Vitória Guimarães 3-0(3-0)
Portimonense - Arouca 0-2(0-0)
SC Braga - Paços de Ferreira 3-0(2-0)

## Final Standings

| | | | Total | | | | | | Home | | | | | Away | | | |
|---|---|---|---|---|---|---|---|---|---|---|---|---|---|---|---|---|---|
| 1. | **Sport Lisboa e Benfica** | 34 | 28 | 3 | 3 | 82 - 20 | 87 | 15 | 1 | 1 | 48 - 12 | 13 | 2 | 2 | 34 - 8 |
| 2. | FC do Porto | 34 | 27 | 4 | 3 | 73 - 22 | 85 | 15 | 0 | 2 | 44 - 11 | 12 | 4 | 1 | 29 - 11 |
| 3. | Sporting Clube de Braga | 34 | 25 | 3 | 6 | 75 - 30 | 78 | 13 | 2 | 2 | 40 - 11 | 12 | 1 | 4 | 35 - 19 |
| 4. | Sporting Clube de Portugal Lisboa | 34 | 23 | 5 | 6 | 71 - 32 | 74 | 13 | 2 | 2 | 42 - 12 | 10 | 3 | 4 | 29 - 20 |
| 5. | FC de Arouca | 34 | 15 | 9 | 10 | 36 - 37 | 54 | 10 | 2 | 5 | 22 - 17 | 5 | 7 | 5 | 14 - 20 |
| 6. | Vitória SC Guimarães | 34 | 16 | 5 | 13 | 34 - 39 | 53 | 10 | 3 | 4 | 18 - 12 | 6 | 2 | 9 | 16 - 27 |
| 7. | GD Chaves | 34 | 12 | 10 | 12 | 35 - 40 | 46 | 6 | 5 | 6 | 20 - 21 | 6 | 5 | 6 | 15 - 19 |
| 8. | FC Famalicão | 34 | 13 | 5 | 16 | 39 - 47 | 44 | 9 | 1 | 7 | 21 - 19 | 4 | 4 | 9 | 18 - 28 |
| 9. | Boavista FC Porto | 34 | 12 | 8 | 14 | 43 - 54 | 44 | 8 | 6 | 3 | 23 - 21 | 4 | 2 | 11 | 20 - 33 |
| 10. | Casa Pia Atlético Clube Lisboa | 34 | 11 | 8 | 15 | 31 - 40 | 41 | 6 | 5 | 6 | 18 - 17 | 5 | 3 | 9 | 13 - 23 |
| 11. | FC de Vizela | 34 | 11 | 7 | 16 | 34 - 38 | 40 | 5 | 4 | 8 | 18 - 19 | 6 | 3 | 8 | 16 - 19 |
| 12. | Rio Ave FC Vila do Conde | 34 | 10 | 10 | 14 | 36 - 43 | 40 | 8 | 3 | 6 | 18 - 14 | 2 | 7 | 8 | 18 - 29 |
| 13. | Gil Vicente FC Barcelos | 34 | 10 | 7 | 17 | 32 - 41 | 37 | 6 | 6 | 5 | 15 - 14 | 4 | 1 | 12 | 17 - 27 |
| 14. | GD Estoril Praia | 34 | 10 | 5 | 19 | 33 - 49 | 35 | 7 | 2 | 8 | 20 - 24 | 3 | 3 | 11 | 13 - 25 |
| 15. | Portimonense SC Portimão | 34 | 10 | 4 | 20 | 25 - 48 | 34 | 6 | 3 | 8 | 14 - 21 | 4 | 1 | 12 | 11 - 27 |
| 16. | CS Marítimo Funchal *(Relegation Play-offs)* | 34 | 7 | 5 | 22 | 32 - 63 | 26 | 6 | 3 | 8 | 21 - 23 | 1 | 2 | 14 | 11 - 40 |
| 17. | FC Paços de Ferreira *(Relegated)* | 34 | 6 | 5 | 23 | 26 - 62 | 23 | 3 | 2 | 12 | 13 - 33 | 3 | 3 | 11 | 13 - 29 |
| 18. | CD Santa Clara Açores *(Relegated)* | 34 | 5 | 7 | 22 | 26 - 58 | 22 | 4 | 5 | 8 | 18 - 29 | 1 | 2 | 14 | 8 - 29 |

## Top goalscorers:

| | | |
|---|---|---|
| 22 | **Mehdi Taremi (IRN)** | *FC do Porto* |
| 19 | Gonçalo Matias Ramos | *Sport Lisboa e Benfica* |
| 17 | João Mário Naval da Costa Eduardo | *Sport Lisboa e Benfica* |
| 17 | Francisco José "Fran" Navarro Aliaga (ESP) | *Gil Vicente FC Barcelos* |

## Relegation Play-offs [03-11.06.2023]

CF Estrela da Amadora - CS Marítimo Funchal     2-1(1-0)     1-2 aet; 3-2 pen
CF Estrela da Amadora were promoted to Primeira Liga 2023/2024.

# NATIONAL CUP
## Taça de Portugal 2022/2023

### Fourth Round [08-10.11.2022]

| | | | | |
|---|---|---|---|---|
| Länk FC Vilaverdense - FC de Oliveira do Hospital | 7-0(5-0) | | FC Famalicão - Dumiense FC | 4-1(3-0) |
| Gil Vicente FC Barcelos - FC de Arouca | 1-4(1-2) | | CD Rabo de Peixe - AD Sanjoanense | 2-0(1-0) |
| Varzim SC - SC São João de Vêr | 1-0(1-0) | | SC Beira-Mar Aveiro - Pevidém SC | 3-2(0-1) |
| CD Mafra - FC do Porto | 0-3(0-2) | | Casa Pia Atlético Clube Lisboa - Valadares Gaia FC | 2-0(2-0) |
| Académico de Viseu FC - AD Camacha Santa Cruz | 3-0(2-0) | | Vitória SC Guimarães - FC de Vizela | 2-1(1-0,1-1) |
| CA Pêro Pinheiro - Vitória FC Setúbal | 1-4(0-2) | | GD Estoril Praia - Sport Lisboa e Benfica | 0-1(0-0) |
| CD Nacional Funchal - CD Tondela | 1-0(0-0) | | B-SAD Lisboa - AD Machico | 4-0(3-0) |
| Leixões SC Porto - SC Farense Faro | 3-1(2-0) | | SC de Braga - Moreirense FC Moreira de Cónegos | 2-1(1-1) |

### 1/8-Finals [10-12.01.2023]

| | | | | |
|---|---|---|---|---|
| Leixões SC Porto - FC Famalicão | 1-2(0-0,1-1) | | Sporting Clube de Braga - Vitória SC Guimarães | 3-2(0-2) |
| Varzim SC - Sport Lisboa e Benfica | 0-2(0-1) | | Académico de Viseu FC - SC Beira-Mar | 2-0(1-0) |
| Länk FC Vilaverdense - B-SAD Lisboa | 1-4(0-2) | | FC do Porto - FC de Arouca | 4-0(1-0) |
| CD Nacional Funchal - CD Rabo de Peixe | 1-0(1-0) | | Vitória FC Setúbal - Casa Pia Atlético Clube Lisboa | 0-1(0-1) |

### Quarter-Finals [08-09.02.2023]

| | | | | |
|---|---|---|---|---|
| FC Famalicão - B-SAD Lisboa | 4-1(1-0) | | Casa Pia Atlético Clube - CD Nacional Funchal | 2-5(0-1,2-2) |
| Académico de Viseu FC - FC do Porto | 0-1(0-0) | | Sporting Clube de Braga - Sport Lisboa e Benfica | 1-1 aet; 5-4 pen |

### Semi-Finals [12-25.04./26.04.-04.05.2023]

| First Leg | | | Second Leg | |
|---|---|---|---|---|
| CD Nacional Funchal - Sporting Clube de Braga | 0-5(0-2) | | Sporting Clube de Braga - CD Nacional Funchal | 2-2(1-0) |
| FC Famalicão - FC do Porto | 1-2(1-1) | | FC do Porto - FC Famalicão | 3-2(1-1,1-2) |

### Final

04.06.2023; Estádio Nacional, Oeiras, Lisboa; Referee: João Pedro Silva Pinheiro; Attendance: 35,000
**Sporting Clube de Braga - FC do Porto**     **0-2(0-0)**

**SC Braga**: Matheus Magalhães, Victor Gómez (70.Simon Bokoté Banza), Tormena (74.Pizzi), Sikou Niakaté [*sent off 79*], Cristián Alexis Borja González (58.Josafat Wooding Mendes), André Horta (Cap) (58.Uroš Račić), Almoatasembellah Ali Mohamed Al Musrati, Iuri Medeiros (58.Álvaro Djaló), Bruma, Ricardo Horta, Abel Ruiz. Trainer: Artur Jorge Torres Gomes Araújo Amorim.

**FC do Porto**: Cláudio Ramos, Pepe (Cap), Marcano, Wendell [*sent off 62*], Pepê, Stephen Antunes Eustáquio (90+3.Marko Grujić), Andrés Mateus Uribe Villa, Otávio (90+3.Gabriel Veron), Galeno (90+3.André Franco), Evanilson (44.Toni Martínez; 67.Zaidu Sanusi), Mehdi Taremi. Trainer: Sérgio Paulo Merceiro Da Conceição.

**Goals:** 0-1 André Horta (53 own goal), 0-2 Otávio (81).

## Futebol Clube de Arouca

**Founded**: 25.12.1951
**Stadium**: Estádio Municipal de Arouca, Arouca (5,000)
**Trainer**: Armando Evangelista Macedo Freitas     03.11.1973

| Goalkeepers: | DOB | M | (s) | G |
|---|---|---|---|---|
| Ignacio De Arruabarrena Fernández (URU) | 16.01.1997 | 30 | | |
| *João* Nuno Figueiredo *Valido* | 03.03.2000 | | (1) | |
| *Thiago* Rodrigues da Silva (BRA) | 12.06.1996 | 1 | | |
| Emilijus Zubas (LTU) | 10.07.1990 | 3 | | |
| **Defenders:** | **DOB** | **M** | **(s)** | **G** |
| Nino Galović (CRO) | 06.07.1992 | 14 | (5) | |
| *João* Othávio *Basso* (BRA) | 13.01.1997 | 32 | | 3 |
| Bogdan Milovanov (UKR) | 19.04.1998 | 11 | (4) | |
| Jerome Osei Opoku (ENG) | 14.10.1998 | 21 | (3) | |
| Mateus *Quaresma* Correia (BRA) | 22.08.1996 | 31 | (1) | 1 |
| *Rafael* Tavares Gomes *Fernandes* | 28.06.2002 | 1 | (1) | |
| *Tiago* Alexandre Sousa *Esgaio* | 01.08.1995 | 25 | (1) | |
| José Manuel Velázquez Rodríguez (VEN) | 08.09.1990 | | (2) | |
| *Weverson* Moreira da Costa (BRA) | 05.07.2000 | 1 | (3) | |
| **Midfielders:** | **DOB** | **M** | **(s)** | **G** |
| *David* Martins *Simão* | 15.05.1990 | 30 | (1) | |

| | DOB | M | (s) | G |
|---|---|---|---|---|
| Yaw Moses (GHA) | 07.01.1999 | 2 | (10) | |
| *Oriol Busquets* Mas (ESP) | 20.01.1999 | 13 | (11) | |
| *Pedro* Manuel da Silva *Moreira* | 15.03.1989 | | (6) | |
| Alan Nahuel Ruíz (ARG) | 19.08.1993 | 31 | | 3 |
| Ismaila Wafougossani Soro (CIV) | 07.05.1998 | 22 | (4) | |
| Morlaye Sylla (GUI) | 27.07.1998 | 23 | (10) | 4 |
| Victor Gabriel Moura de Oliveira „Vitinho"(BRA) | 04.01.2000 | 2 | (7) | |
| **Forwards:** | **DOB** | **M** | **(s)** | **G** |
| *Antony* Alves Santos (BRA) | 08.09.2001 | 26 | (7) | 6 |
| *Arsénio* Martins Lafuente Nunes | 30.08.1989 | 8 | (23) | |
| Bruno Henrique Marques Torres „*Bruninho*" (BRA) | 22.02.1999 | | (17) | 1 |
| André Watshini Bukia (COD) | 03.03.1995 | 13 | (1) | 2 |
| Oday Ibrahim Mohammad Dabbagh (PLE) | 03.12.1998 | 11 | (3) | 7 |
| Yusuf Lawal (NGA) | 23.03.1998 | | (9) | |
| Benjamin Stanley Michel (USA) | 23.10.1997 | 1 | (11) | 1 |
| Rafael „*Rafa*" Sebastián *Mújica* García (ESP) | 29.10.1998 | 22 | (5) | 8 |

## Sport Lisboa e Benfica

**Founded**: 28.02.1904
**Stadium**: Estádio do Sport Lisboa e Benfica [da Luz], Lisboa (64,642)
**Trainer**: Roger Schmidt (GER)     13.03.1967

| Goalkeepers: | DOB | M | (s) | G |
|---|---|---|---|---|
| *Samuel* Jumpe *Soares* | 15.06.2002 | | (1) | |
| Odisseas Vlachodimos (GRE) | 26.04.1994 | 34 | | |
| **Defenders:** | **DOB** | **M** | **(s)** | **G** |
| Alejandro „*Álex*" Grimaldo García (ESP) | 20.09.1995 | 33 | | 5 |
| *António* João Pereira Albuquerque Tavares *Silva* | 30.10.2003 | 30 | | 3 |
| Alexander Hartmann Bah (DEN) | 09.12.1997 | 21 | (7) | 1 |
| John Anthony Brooks (USA) | 28.01.1993 | | (2) | |
| *Gilberto* Moraes Junior (BRA) | 07.03.1993 | 8 | (12) | 2 |
| *Lucas Verissimo* da Silva (BRA) | 02.07.1995 | | (2) | |
| Felipe Rodrigues da Silva „*Morato*" (BRA) | 30.06.2001 | 7 | (2) | 1 |
| Nicolás Hernán Otamendi (ARG) | 12.02.1988 | 31 | | 1 |
| Mihailo Ristić (SRB) | 31.10.1995 | 1 | (6) | 1 |
| Jan Bert Lieve Vertonghen (BEL) | 24.04.1987 | | (1) | |
| **Midfielders:** | **DOB** | **M** | **(s)** | **G** |
| Fredrik Aursnes (NOR) | 10.12.1995 | 24 | (4) | 2 |
| Francisco Leonel Lima Silva Machado „Chiquinho" | 19.07.1995 | 14 | (11) | 1 |
| *Diogo* António Cupido *Gonçalves* | 06.02.1997 | 2 | (8) | |

| | DOB | M | (s) | G |
|---|---|---|---|---|
| Enzo Jeremías Fernández (ARG) | 17.01.2001 | 17 | | 1 |
| *Florentino* Ibrain Morris Luís | 19.08.1999 | 25 | (8) | |
| *João Mário* Naval da Costa Eduardo | 19.01.1993 | 33 | | 17 |
| *João* Pedro Goncalves *Neves* | 27.09.2004 | 6 | (11) | 1 |
| *Cher Ndour* (ITA) | 27.07.2004 | | (1) | |
| Julian Weigl (GER) | 08.09.1995 | | (2) | |
| **Forwards:** | **DOB** | **M** | **(s)** | **G** |
| *David Neres* Campos (BRA) | 03.03.1997 | 22 | (9) | 6 |
| Julian Draxler (GER) | 20.09.1993 | 4 | (6) | 1 |
| *Gonçalo* Manuel Ganchinho *Guedes* | 29.11.1996 | 4 | (8) | 1 |
| *Gonçalo* Matias *Ramos* | 20.06.2001 | 30 | | 19 |
| *Henrique* Pereira *Araújo* | 19.01.2002 | | (5) | |
| Petar Musa (CRO) | 04.03.1998 | 2 | (28) | 7 |
| *Rafa*el Alexandre Fernandes Ferreira da *Silva* | 17.05.1993 | 26 | (2) | 8 |
| *Rodrigo* Cunha Pereira de *Pinho* (BRA) | 30.05.1991 | | (2) | |
| Andreas Rædergård Schjelderup (NOR) | 01.06.2004 | | (1) | |
| Casper Tengstedt (DEN) | 01.06.2000 | | (4) | |
| Roman Yaremchuk (UKR) | 27.11.1995 | | (2) | |

## Boavista Futebol Clube Porto

**Founded**: 01.08.1903
**Stadium**: Estádio do Bessa, Porto (28,263)
**Trainer**: Armando Gonçalves Teixeira Petit     25.09.1976

| Goalkeepers: | DOB | M | (s) | G |
|---|---|---|---|---|
| *César* Bernardo Dutra (BRA) | 27.01.1992 | 5 | | |
| *João* Pedro Oliveira *Gonçalves* | 05.11.2000 | 1 | | |
| *Rafael* Wihby *Bracali* (BRA) | 05.05.1981 | 28 | | |
| **Defenders:** | **DOB** | **M** | **(s)** | **G** |
| Rodrigo Abascal Barros (URU) | 14.01.1994 | 27 | | |
| Reginald Jacob Cannon (USA) | 11.06.1998 | 26 | (4) | |
| *Filipe* Miguel Neves *Ferreira* | 27.09.1990 | 4 | (3) | |
| Yanis Hamache (ALG) | 13.07.1999 | 2 | | |
| *Júlio* Augusto *Dabó* (GNB) | 13.03.2004 | | (3) | |
| Sopuruchukwu Bruno Onyemaechi (NGA) | 03.04.1999 | 29 | | 1 |
| *Pedro* Jorge Gonçalves *Malheiro* | 21.01.2001 | 31 | (1) | |
| *Ricardo* Luís Chaby *Mangas* | 19.03.1998 | 22 | (5) | 4 |
| *Robson* Alves Reis (BRA) | 21.05.2000 | 1 | (5) | |
| Vincent Julien Sasso (FRA) | 16.02.1991 | 23 | (1) | 4 |
| **Midfielders:** | **DOB** | **M** | **(s)** | **G** |
| Bernardo Silva Conceição „Berna" | 15.09.2003 | | (1) | |

| | DOB | M | (s) | G |
|---|---|---|---|---|
| Ibrahima Camará (GUI) | 25.01.1999 | 12 | (12) | |
| *Joel* Filipe Organista da *Silva* | 11.02.2003 | | (7) | |
| Gaïus Makouta (CGO) | 25.07.1997 | 31 | (1) | 2 |
| Sebastián Pérez Cardona (COL) | 29.03.1993 | 29 | | 3 |
| Miguel Silva *Reisinho* | 09.04.1999 | | (3) | |
| Ilija Vukotić (MNE) | 07.01.1999 | 5 | (8) | |
| Masaki Watai (JPN) | 18.07.1999 | 5 | (10) | 1 |
| **Forwards:** | **DOB** | **M** | **(s)** | **G** |
| Róbert Boženík (SVK) | 18.11.1999 | 9 | (14) | 4 |
| *Bruno* Miguel Ponces *Lourenço* | 02.02.1998 | 21 | (8) | 4 |
| Kenji Joel Gorré (CUW) | 29.09.1994 | 16 | (14) | 2 |
| *Luís* Miguel Castelo *Santos* | 20.01.2000 | 2 | (7) | |
| Martim Miguel Carneiro Tavares | 10.11.2003 | 2 | (20) | 2 |
| Yusupha Njie (GAM) | 03.01.1994 | 23 | (4) | 13 |
| *Salvador* José Milhazes *Agra* | 11.11.1991 | 20 | (10) | 3 |
| *Tiago* André Rajão *Machado* | 02.04.2004 | | (2) | |
| *Tiago* Fontoura Fonseca *Morais* | 03.09.2003 | | (2) | |

## Sporting Clube de Braga

**Founded**: 19.01.1921
**Stadium**: Estádio Municipal de Braga, Braga (30,286)
**Trainer**: Artur Jorge Torres Gomes Araújo Amorim · 01.01.1972

| Goalkeepers: | DOB | M | (s) | G |
|---|---|---|---|---|
| Lukáš Horníček (CZE) | 13.07.2002 | | (1) | |
| *Matheus* Lima *Magalhães* (BRA) | 29.03.1992 | 32 | | |
| *Tiago* Magalhães de *Sá* | 11.01.1995 | 2 | (1) | |
| **Defenders:** | **DOB** | **M** | **(s)** | **G** |
| Cristián Alexis Borja González (COL) | 18.02.1993 | 8 | (6) | |
| *Bruno* Miguel Ferreira *Rodrigues* | 08.06.2001 | 1 | | |
| José *Dinis Pinto* Magalhães Rodrigues | 24.08.2000 | | (1) | |
| *Fabiano* Josué de Souza *Silva* (BRA) | 14.03.2000 | 11 | (1) | |
| Josafat Wooding Mendes (SWE) | 31.12.2002 | 2 | (2) | 1 |
| Sikou Niakaté (MLI) | 10.07.1999 | 25 | (1) | 3 |
| *Nuno* Miguel Ribeiro da Cruz Jerónimo *Sequeira* | 19.08.1990 | 24 | (3) | 1 |
| *Paulo* André Rodrigues de *Oliveira* | 08.01.1992 | 15 | (5) | |
| Serdar Saatçı (TUR) | 14.02.2003 | 2 | (1) | |
| Vítor *Tormena* de Farias (BRA) | 04.01.1996 | 26 | (1) | 1 |
| *Victor Gómez* Perea (ESP) | 01.04.2000 | 23 | (3) | |
| **Midfielders:** | **DOB** | **M** | **(s)** | **G** |
| Almoatasembellah Ali Mohamed Al Musrati (LBY) | 06.04.1996 | 28 | | 3 |
| *André* de *Castro* Pereira | 02.04.1988 | 3 | (21) | 1 |
| *André* Filip Luz *Horta* | 07.11.1996 | 27 | (5) | 1 |
| Jean-Baptiste Gorby (FRA) | 25.07.2002 | | (7) | |
| *Pedro* Eliezer Carvalho *Santos* | 12.10.2000 | | (3) | |
| Luis Miguel Afonso Fernandes „Pizzi" | 06.10.1989 | 3 | (13) | 2 |
| Uroš Račić (SRB) | 17.03.1998 | 12 | (13) | 1 |
| **Forwards:** | **DOB** | **M** | **(s)** | **G** |
| *Abel Ruiz* Ortega (ESP) | 28.01.2000 | 26 | (8) | 8 |
| *Álvaro Djaló* Dias Fernandes (GNB) | 16.08.1999 | 2 | (22) | 2 |
| Simon Bokoté Banza (FRA) | 13.08.1996 | 15 | (15) | 11 |
| Armindo Tué Na Bangna „Bruma" | 24.10.1994 | 13 | (3) | 4 |
| *Hernâni Infande* Tchuda da Silva (GNB) | 03.04.2001 | 1 | (2) | |
| *Iuri* José Picanço *Medeiros* | 10.07.1994 | 29 | (1) | 10 |
| Diego Lainez Leyva (MEX) | 09.06.2000 | 1 | (5) | 1 |
| *Ricardo* Jorge Luz *Horta* | 15.09.1994 | 30 | | 14 |
| *Rodrigo* Martins *Gomes* | 07.07.2003 | 1 | (14) | 1 |
| Vítor Manuel Carvalho Oliveira „*Vitinha*" | 15.03.2000 | 12 | (5) | 7 |

## Casa Pia Atlético Clube Lisboa

**Founded**: 03.07.1920
**Stadium**: Estádio Nacional, Lisboa (37,593)
**Trainer**: Filipe Gonçalo Pinto Martins · 29.05.1978

| Goalkeepers: | DOB | M | (s) | G |
|---|---|---|---|---|
| *João* Victor Donna *Bravim* (BRA) | 03.05.1998 | 1 | | |
| *Lucas Paes* Souza (BRA) | 07.12.1997 | 2 | | |
| *Ricardo* Jorge Cecília Batista | 19.11.1986 | 31 | | |
| **Defenders:** | **DOB** | **M** | **(s)** | **G** |
| *Derick* Theodoro Santos *Poloni* (BRA) | 01.09.1993 | 17 | (6) | |
| Eduardo Enrique Fereira Peñaranda (VEN) | 29.09.2000 | 1 | (2) | |
| *Fernando* Lopes dos Santos *Varela* (CPV) | 26.11.1987 | 25 | (2) | 1 |
| *João* Aniceto Grandela *Nunes* | 19.11.1995 | 17 | (9) | 1 |
| Leonardo „*Léo*" da Costa *Bolgado* (BRA) | 20.08.1998 | 4 | (7) | 1 |
| *Leonardo* Filipe Cruz *Lelo* | 30.03.2000 | 25 | (2) | 1 |
| *Lucas* Soares de Almeida (BRA) | 04.05.1998 | 25 | (2) | 1 |
| Duplexe Tchamba Bangou (CMR) | 10.07.1998 | 4 | (1) | |
| *Vasco* Herculano Salgado Cunha Mango *Fernandes* | 12.11.1986 | 27 | (3) | |
| Nermin Zolotić (BIH) | 07.07.1993 | 25 | (4) | |
| **Midfielders:** | **DOB** | **M** | **(s)** | **G** |
| *Afonso* Miguel Castro Vilhena *Taira* | 17.06.1992 | 26 | (6) | |
| *Ângelo* Pelegrinelli *Neto* (BRA) | 02.09.1991 | 20 | (7) | 2 |
| Benedito Mambuene Mukendi „Beni" (ANG) | 21.05.2002 | 10 | (4) | |
| Carlos Miguel Pereira Fernandes „Cuca" | 09.01.1991 | 2 | (18) | |
| *Diogo* Costa *Pinto* | 29.06.1999 | 5 | (12) | |
| Yan Brice Eteki (CMR) | 26.08.1997 | 4 | (13) | |
| Takahiro Kunimoto (JPN) | 08.10.1997 | 17 | (7) | 1 |
| *Romário* Miguel Silva Baró | 25.01.2000 | 11 | (7) | |
| Victor Emanuel Araújo Ferreira „Vitó" | 18.09.1997 | | (4) | |
| **Forwards:** | **DOB** | **M** | **(s)** | **G** |
| *Anderson* Cordeiro Costa (BRA) | 10.10.1998 | | (2) | |
| Carnejy Antoine (FRA) | 27.07.1991 | | (6) | 1 |
| *Clayton* Fernandes Silva (BRA) | 11.01.1999 | 11 | (18) | 4 |
| Wanderson *Felippe Cardoso* dos Santos (BRA) | 04.10.1994 | 5 | (6) | 4 |
| Saviour Amunde Godwin (NGA) | 22.08.1996 | 28 | (2) | 4 |
| Francisco Pedro Tiago Silva „Kiki Silva" | 14.02.1998 | | (1) | |
| Leonardo „*Léo*" Natel Vieira (BRA) | 14.03.1997 | | (4) | |
| Clecildo *Rafael* Martins de Souza Ladislau (BRA) | 17.03.1989 | 18 | (8) | 6 |
| Yuki Soma (JPN) | 25.02.1997 | 13 | (5) | 2 |

## Grupo Desportivo de Chaves

**Founded**: 27.09.1949
**Stadium**: Estádio Municipal "Eng.Manuel Branco Teixeira", Chaves (8,400)
**Trainer**: Vítor Fernando de Carvalho Campelos · 11.05.1975

| Goalkeepers: | DOB | M | (s) | G |
|---|---|---|---|---|
| *Gonçalo Filipe* Jesus Pinto | 30.04.2000 | | (1) | |
| *Paulo Vítor* Fagundes dos Anjos (BRA) | 21.11.1988 | 30 | | |
| *Rodrigo Moura* do Nascimento (BRA) | 25.01.1996 | 4 | | |
| **Defenders:** | **DOB** | **M** | **(s)** | **G** |
| *Bruno* Alberto *Langa* (MOZ) | 31.10.1997 | 29 | | |
| *Eduardo* Salvador Rosa Oliveira *Borges* | 27.05.2002 | | (4) | |
| Elosman *Euller* Silva Cavalcante (BRA) | 04.01.1995 | 13 | (8) | 1 |
| *Guilherme* Willian da Silva (BRA) | 21.10.2000 | | (2) | |
| *Hélder* Gomes *Morim* | 14.05.2001 | | (7) | |
| *João* Pedro Araújo *Correia* | 05.09.1996 | 19 | (5) | |
| *João* Ricardo Pereira *Queirós* | 22.04.1998 | 3 | (2) | |
| *Nélson* Macedo *Monte* | 20.07.1995 | 29 | (2) | |
| Carlos dos Santos Rodrigues „Ponck" (CPV) | 13.01.1995 | 20 | (1) | |
| *Sandro* Plínio Rosa da *Cruz* | 12.05.2001 | 4 | (9) | |
| Habib Sylla (CIV) | 12.02.1999 | 7 | (2) | |
| Steven da Sousa Vitória (CAN) | 11.01.1987 | 30 | (1) | 7 |
| **Midfielders:** | **DOB** | **M** | **(s)** | **G** |
| Ricardo Martins Guimarães „Guima" | 14.11.1995 | 22 | (7) | |
| *João* Pedro Fortes Bachiessa „*Batxi*" | 01.05.1998 | 4 | | 1 |
| *João* Sabino *Mendes* Neto Saraiva | 21.10.1994 | 30 | (1) | 2 |
| *João Pedro* Almeida Machado | 03.04.1993 | 6 | (8) | |
| *João* Rafael Brito *Teixeira* | 06.02.1994 | 32 | | 5 |
| *Kevin* Lenini Gonçalves Pereira de Pina (CPV) | 27.01.1997 | 5 | | |
| Nwankwo Emeka Obiora (NGA) | 12.07.1991 | 5 | (7) | 1 |
| Sidy Sarr (SEN) | 05.06.1996 | 1 | (4) | |
| **Forwards:** | **DOB** | **M** | **(s)** | **G** |
| Issah Abass (GHA) | 26.09.1998 | 14 | (12) | 4 |
| Bernardo Martins Sousa „Benny" | 27.03.2000 | 15 | (14) | |
| Héctor *Hernández* Marrero (ESP) | 14.09.1995 | 16 | (6) | 7 |
| Joarlem Batista Santos „Jô" (BRA) | 01.05.1995 | 2 | (18) | 1 |
| Jonathan „*Jonny*" *Arriba* Monroy (ESP) | 01.11.2001 | 8 | (5) | 1 |
| Olávio Vieira dos Santos Júnior „Juninho" (BRA) | 21.11.1996 | 21 | (9) | 4 |
| Fábio *Patrick* dos Reis dos Santos Fernandes (CPV) | 13.12.1993 | | (6) | |
| Luther Wesley Singh (RSA) | 05.08.1997 | 5 | (17) | |

## Grupo Desportivo Estoril Praia

| | Founded: | 17.05.1939 | | | |
|---|---|---|---|---|---|
| | Stadium: | Estádio "António Coimbra da Mota", Estoril (8,015) | | | |
| | Trainer: | Nélson Alexandre da Silva Veríssimo | 17.04.1977 | | |
| [28.02.2023] | | José Ricardo Ribeiro Soares | 11.11.1974 | | |

| Goalkeepers: | DOB | M | (s) | G |
|---|---|---|---|---|
| *Daniel* Alexis Leite *Figueira* | 20.07.1998 | 32 | | |
| *Pedro* José Moreira *Silva* | 13.02.1997 | 2 | (1) | |
| **Defenders:** | **DOB** | **M** | **(s)** | **G** |
| *Bernardo* Maria Morais Cardoso *Vital* | 29.12.2000 | 25 | (1) | |
| Shaquil Delos (FRA) | 16.06.1999 | 4 | (6) | |
| Gonçalo Lago Pontes Esteves | 27.02.2004 | 2 | (1) | |
| João Carlos Reis Graça „Joãozinho" | 02.07.1989 | 30 | | 1 |
| Lucas Henrique da Silva „Lucas Áfrico" (BRA) | 05.02.1995 | 4 | (2) | |
| Edson André Sitoe „Mexer" (MOZ) | 08.09.1988 | 11 | (3) | |
| *Pedro* Miguel Costa *Álvaro* | 02.03.2000 | 29 | (1) | 1 |
| *Tiago* Carvalho *Santos* | 23.07.2002 | 28 | (2) | |
| *Volnei* Feltes (BRA) | 15.04.2000 | | (1) | |
| **Midfielders:** | **DOB** | **M** | **(s)** | **G** |
| Francisco Oliveira "Chico" *Geraldes* | 18.04.1995 | 21 | (5) | 4 |
| Rafik Guitane (FRA) | 26.05.1999 | 9 | (4) | |
| *João* António Antunes *Carvalho* | 09.03.1997 | 27 | (2) | 1 |
| *João* Pedro da Costa *Gamboa* | 31.08.1996 | 14 | (3) | |
| *João* Miguel Vieira Freitas Silva *Marques* | 13.02.2002 | 4 | (7) | |
| James Léa Siliki (FRA) | 12.06.1996 | 7 | (15) | 3 |
| Mor Ndiaye (SEN) | 22.11.2000 | 14 | (12) | |
| Loreintz Rosier (FRA) | 14.08.1998 | 12 | | |
| Mabrouk Rouaï (FRA) | 01.11.2000 | | (2) | |
| **Forwards:** | **DOB** | **M** | **(s)** | **G** |
| Mohamed Elias Achouri (TUN) | 10.02.1999 | | (2) | |
| *Arthur* Gomes *Lourenço* (BRA) | 03.07.1998 | 4 | | 1 |
| Yusuf Isa Bamidele (NGA) | 22.02.2001 | | (5) | 1 |
| *Carlos Eduardo* Ferreira de Souza (BRA) | 10.10.1996 | 9 | (4) | 2 |
| *Cassiano* Dias Moreira (BRA) | 16.06.1989 | 10 | (5) | 2 |
| *Erison* Danilo de Souza (BRA) | 13.04.1999 | 10 | (1) | 2 |
| *Gilson* Benchimol *Tavares* | 29.12.2001 | 1 | (10) | |
| *João* Carlos Cardoso *Santo* (BRA) | 01.03.1995 | 5 | (18) | 2 |
| Alejandro José Marqués Méndez (VEN) | 04.08.2000 | 7 | (8) | 3 |
| *Rodrigo* Miguel Forte Paes *Martins* | 15.09.1998 | 15 | (15) | 3 |
| *Sérgio* Pereira *Andrade* | 29.01.2001 | 1 | (6) | 1 |
| *Tiago* Filipe Alves *Araújo* | 27.03.2001 | 8 | (17) | 1 |
| *Tiago* Maria Antunes *Gouveia* | 18.06.2001 | 29 | | 5 |

## Futebol Clube de Famalicão

| | Founded: | 21.08.1931 | | | |
|---|---|---|---|---|---|
| | Stadium: | Estádio Municipal 22 de Junho, Vila Nova de Famalicão (5,307) | | | |
| | Trainer: | Rui Pedro Teixeira de Jesus da Silva | 14.03.1977 | | |
| [22.09.2022] | | João Pedro Ramos Borges Sousa | 04.08.1971 | | |

| Goalkeepers: | DOB | M | (s) | G |
|---|---|---|---|---|
| *Luiz* Lúcio Reis *Júnior* (BRA) | 14.01.2001 | 33 | | |
| Ivan Zlobin (RUS) | 07.03.1997 | 1 | | |
| **Defenders:** | **DOB** | **M** | **(s)** | **G** |
| *Alexandre* Manuel *Penetra* Correia | 09.09.2001 | 29 | | 2 |
| Dylan Batubinsika (FRA) | 15.02.1996 | 2 | | |
| Hernán De La Fuente (ARG) | 07.01.1997 | 6 | (1) | |
| *Diogo* Lucas *Queirós* | 05.01.1999 | | (1) | |
| *Francisco* Sampaio *Moura* | 16.08.1999 | 23 | (5) | 2 |
| *Martín* Aguirregabiria Padilla (ESP) | 10.05.1996 | 2 | (15) | |
| Enea Mihaj (ALB) | 05.07.1998 | 25 | | |
| *Otávio* Ataíde da Silva (BRA) | 21.04.2002 | 8 | (1) | |
| *Riccieli* Eduardo da Silva Júnior (BRA) | 17.09.1998 | 30 | | |
| *Rúben* Alexandre Rocha *Lima* | 03.10.1989 | 14 | (4) | 1 |
| **Midfielders:** | **DOB** | **M** | **(s)** | **G** |
| *André* Luis Gomes *Simões* | 16.12.1989 | 2 | (7) | |
| Santiago Colombatto (ARG) | 17.01.1997 | 31 | (2) | 3 |
| *David* José Gomes Oliveira *Tavares* | 18.03.1999 | | (5) | |
| Gustavo Enrique Giordano Amaro *Assunção* Da Silva (BRA) | 30.03.2000 | 9 | (13) | 1 |
| *Gustavo* Filipe Alves Freitas Azevedo *Sá* | 11.11.2004 | 4 | (11) | |
| *Iván* Jaime Pajuelo (ESP) | 26.09.2000 | 21 | (3) | 9 |
| *Pedro* David *Brazão* Teixeira | 30.12.2002 | 4 | (2) | |
| Judilson Mamadú Tuncará Gomes „Pelé" (GNB) | 29.09.1991 | 7 | (5) | |
| *Zaydou* Youssouf (FRA) | 11.07.1999 | 25 | (7) | 2 |
| **Forwards:** | **DOB** | **M** | **(s)** | **G** |
| Alejandro „*Álex*" *Millán* Iranzo (ESP) | 07.11.1999 | 10 | (3) | 2 |
| Jhonder Leonel Cádiz Fernández (VEN) | 29.07.1995 | 14 | (10) | 4 |
| *Denílson* Pereira Junior (BRA) | 18.07.1995 | 4 | (7) | |
| Mihai-Alexandru Dobre (ROU) | 30.08.1998 | 11 | (6) | 2 |
| *Heriberto* Moreno Borges *Tavares* | 19.02.1997 | 2 | (2) | |
| *Ivo* Tiago dos Santos *Rodrigues* | 30.03.1995 | 26 | (4) | 2 |
| Junior Kadile (FRA) | 16.12.2002 | 8 | (6) | 1 |
| *Leandro* Mário Baldé *Sanca* | 04.01.2000 | 4 | (10) | 2 |
| *Pablo Felipe* Pereira de Jesus (BRA) | 02.01.2004 | 9 | (6) | 2 |
| José Luis Rodríguez Francis (PAN) | 19.06.1998 | 6 | (1) | |
| *Rui* Pedro da Rocha *Fonte* | 23.04.1990 | 3 | (15) | 1 |
| *Théo* Luis *Fonseca* | 11.06.2000 | 1 | (4) | |

## Gil Vicente Futebol Clube Barcelos

| | Founded: | 1924 | | | |
|---|---|---|---|---|---|
| | Stadium: | Estádio Cidade de Barcelos, Barcelos (12,504) | | | |
| | Trainer: | Ivo Ricardo Abreu Vieira | 10.01.1976 | | |
| [03.11.2022] | | Carlos Manuel Gomes da Cunha | 17.10.1971 | | |
| [14.11.2022] | | Pedro Daniel da Cunha Pereira de Sousa | 03.10.1984 | | |

| Goalkeepers: | DOB | M | (s) | G |
|---|---|---|---|---|
| *Andrew* da Silva Ventura (BRA) | 01.07.2001 | 23 | (1) | |
| Stanislav Kritsyuk (RUS) | 01.12.1990 | 11 | | |
| **Defenders:** | **DOB** | **M** | **(s)** | **G** |
| *Adrián Marín* Gómez (ESP) | 09.01.1997 | 29 | (2) | |
| Rui Filipe Caetano Moura „Carraça" | 01.03.1993 | 20 | (6) | |
| *Danilo* Filipe Melo *Veiga* | 25.09.2002 | 8 | (1) | |
| *Gabriel* Pereira *Magalhães* dos Santos (BRA) | 07.05.2000 | 4 | (3) | |
| Emmanuel Hackman (GHA) | 14.05.1995 | 2 | | |
| *Henrique* Martins *Gomes* | 30.11.1995 | 5 | (4) | |
| *Lucas* de Souza *Cunha* (BRA) | 23.01.1997 | 15 | | |
| *Manuel* Alberto Cunha *Lopes* | 29.05.2000 | 5 | | |
| *Rúben* Miguel Marques dos Santos *Fernandes* | 06.05.1986 | 24 | (2) | |
| *Tomás* Lemos *Araújo* | 16.05.2002 | 21 | (1) | 1 |
| José Carlos Teixeira Lopes Reis Gonçalves „Zé Carlos" | 31.07.1998 | 4 | (4) | |
| **Midfielders:** | **DOB** | **M** | **(s)** | **G** |
| Giorgi Aburjania (GEO) | 02.01.1995 | 18 | (9) | |
| *André* Filipe Encarnação *Simões* | 17.08.2003 | | (2) | |
| Kanya Fujimoto (JPN) | 01.07.1999 | 32 | (2) | |
| *Matheus* Bueno Batista (BRA) | 30.07.1998 | 4 | (10) | |
| *Pedro* Miguel Amorim Pereira Silva „Tiba" | 31.08.1988 | 15 | (11) | 1 |
| *Vitor* Carvalho Vieira (BRA) | 27.05.1997 | 31 | | 3 |
| Roan Roberto Wilson Gordon (CRC) | 01.05.2002 | 1 | (4) | |
| **Forwards:** | **DOB** | **M** | **(s)** | **G** |
| Ali Alipour (IRN) | 11.11.1995 | 5 | (10) | 2 |
| Mizuki Arai (JPN) | 14.04.1997 | 2 | (6) | |
| Bilel Aouacheria (FRA) | 02.04.1994 | 8 | (16) | 1 |
| Juan Manuel Boselli Graf (URU) | 09.11.1999 | 15 | (12) | 1 |
| *Boubacar* Rafael Neto *Hanne* | 26.02.1999 | | (2) | |
| Laurindo Dilson Maria Aurélio „Depú" (ANG) | 08.01.2000 | | (5) | |
| *Élder* Santana Conceição (BRA) | 07.04.1993 | | (5) | |
| Francisco „*Fran*" José *Navarro* Aliaga (ESP) | 03.02.1998 | 34 | | 17 |
| *Kevin* Villodres Medina (ESP) | 26.02.2001 | 7 | (14) | |
| *Marlon* Douglas de Sales Silva (BRA) | 15.09.1997 | 4 | (6) | |
| Jorge *Miguel* Castro *Monteiro* | 24.07.2003 | | (1) | |
| *Murilo* de Souza Costa (BRA) | 31.10.1994 | 27 | (1) | 5 |

## Club Sport Marítimo Funchal

| Founded: | 20.09.1910 | | |
|---|---|---|---|
| Stadium: | Estádio do Marítimo, Funchal (10,932) | | |
| Trainer: | Vasco César Freire de Seabra | 15.09.1983 |
| [08.09.2022] | João Alexandre Oliveira Nunes Henriques | 31.10.1972 |
| [14.12.2022] | José Manuel Martins Teixeira Gomes | 28.08.1970 |

| Goalkeepers: | DOB | M | (s) | G |
|---|---|---|---|---|
| Giorgi Makaridze (GEO) | 31.03.1990 | 6 | | |
| Marcelo Henrique Passos Carné (BRA) | 06.02.1990 | 14 | | |
| João Miguel Macedo Silva | 07.04.1995 | 8 | | |
| Matouš Trmal (CZE) | 02.10.1998 | 6 | | |
| Defenders: | DOB | M | (s) | G |
| Cláudio Winck Neto (BRA) | 15.04.1994 | 27 | (7) | 6 |
| Dylan João Raymond Collard (MRI) | 16.04.2000 | | (1) | |
| Fábio Diogo Agrela Ferreira „Fábio China" | 07.07.1992 | 4 | (6) | |
| Fernando de Lacerda Gomes (GNB) | 03.02.2002 | | (2) | |
| Leonardo „Leo" de Andrade Silva (BRA) | 18.04.1998 | 12 | | 1 |
| Matheus de Mello Costa (BRA) | 26.01.1995 | 13 | (7) | |
| Moisés Castillo Mosquera (COL) | 24.05.2001 | 16 | (4) | |
| Paulo Sérgio Mota „Paulinho" | 13.07.1991 | 8 | (2) | |
| Renê Ferreira Dos Santos (BRA) | 21.04.1992 | 13 | (1) | 1 |
| Vitor Costa de Brito (BRA) | 01.07.1994 | 28 | | 2 |
| Zainadine Abdula Mulungo Chavango Júnior (MOZ) | 24.06.1988 | 23 | (1) | |
| Midfielders: | DOB | M | (s) | G |
| André António Rosário Teles | 06.04.1997 | | (2) | |
| Stefano Beltrame (ITA) | 08.02.1993 | 13 | (7) | |
| Diogo Alexandre Almeida Mendes | 24.01.1998 | 15 | (5) | |
| João Afonso Crispim (BRA) | 09.02.1995 | 18 | (6) | |

| | DOB | M | (s) | G |
|---|---|---|---|---|
| Miguel Ferreira de Sousa | 19.09.1998 | 3 | | |
| Rafael Alexandre Sousa Gancho Brito | 19.01.2002 | 7 | (6) | |
| Joel Soñora (USA) | 15.09.1996 | 2 | (2) | |
| Valdemir de Oliveira Soares (BRA) | 12.03.1997 | 15 | (3) | 1 |
| Luciano Gastón Vega Albornoz (ARG) | 04.09.1999 | | (7) | |
| Bruno Alexandre Vieira Almeida „Xadas" | 02.12.1997 | 30 | (2) | 3 |
| Forwards: | DOB | M | (s) | G |
| André Filipe Cunha Vidigal | 17.08.1998 | 28 | (4) | 8 |
| Antonio Zarzana Pérez (ESP) | 21.03.2002 | 3 | (3) | |
| Geny Cipriano Catamo (MOZ) | 26.01.2001 | 3 | (6) | 1 |
| Clésio Palmirim David Baúque (GNB) | 11.10.1994 | | (2) | |
| José Edgar Andrade da Costa | 14.04.1987 | 3 | (18) | |
| Félix Alexandre Andrade Sanches Correia | 22.01.2001 | 8 | (5) | 2 |
| Stanley Guzorochi Kanu (NGA) | 17.01.1999 | | (5) | |
| Leonardo Augusto dos Santos Pereira „Léo"(BRA) | 29.06.2000 | 7 | (3) | |
| Carlos Percy Liza Espinoza (PER) | 10.04.2000 | 3 | (8) | 1 |
| Pablo Moreno Taboada (ESP) | 03.05.2002 | 12 | (7) | |
| Jesús Andrés Ramírez Díaz (VEN) | 04.05.1998 | 5 | (17) | 1 |
| José Brayan Riascos Valencia (COL) | 10.10.1994 | 10 | (6) | 3 |
| Rubén André Fernandes Marques | 20.09.2002 | 1 | | |
| Diederrick Joel Tagueu Tadjo (CMR) | 06.12.1993 | 10 | (4) | 1 |

## Futebol Clube Paços de Ferreira

| Founded: | 05.04.1950 | | |
|---|---|---|---|
| Stadium: | Estádio Capital do Móvel, Paços de Ferreira (9,076) | | |
| Trainer: | Paulo César Silva Peixoto | 12.05.1980 |
| [18.10.2022] | José Albano Ferreira da Mota | 25.02.1964 |
| [15.12.2022] | Marco Daniel Faria de Freitas Paiva | 14.07.1987 |
| [01.01.2023] | Paulo César Silva Peixoto | 12.05.1980 |

| Goalkeepers: | DOB | M | (s) | G |
|---|---|---|---|---|
| Jordi Martins Almeida (BRA) | 03.09.1993 | 6 | | |
| José Pedro Ferreira Oliveira | 06.04.2002 | 3 | | |
| José Carlos Coentrão Marafona | 08.05.1987 | 16 | | |
| Igor Vekič (SVN) | 06.05.1998 | 9 | (1) | |
| Defenders: | DOB | M | (s) | G |
| Vitorino Gabriel Pacheco Antunes | 01.04.1987 | 31 | | 1 |
| Erick Steven Ferigra Burnham (ECU) | 07.02.1999 | 12 | (4) | |
| Fernando Manuel Ferreira Fonseca | 14.03.1997 | 2 | (4) | |
| Flávio da Silva Ramos (BRA) | 12.05.1994 | 9 | | |
| João Miguel Ribeiro Vigário | 20.11.1995 | | (1) | |
| Jorge Fernando dos Santos Silva | 22.03.1996 | 3 | (14) | |
| Luís Pedro Alves Bastos | 10.09.2001 | 4 | (4) | |
| Jóbson de Brito Gonzaga „Maracás" (BRA) | 27.04.1994 | 17 | | |
| Nuno Miguel Reis Lima | 16.03.2001 | 27 | (1) | 1 |
| Pedro Luís Machado Ganchas | 31.05.2000 | 2 | (3) | |
| Tiago Abiola Delfim Almeida Ilori | 26.02.1993 | 3 | | |
| Midfielders: | DOB | M | (s) | G |
| Osvaldo Nicolás Fabián Gaitán (ARG) | 23.02.1988 | 24 | (3) | 3 |
| Jordan William Holsgrove (SCO) | 10.09.1999 | 21 | (3) | 2 |

| | DOB | M | (s) | G |
|---|---|---|---|---|
| Abbas Ibrahim (NGA) | 02.01.1998 | 3 | (4) | |
| Luíz Carlos Martins Moreira (BRA) | 05.07.1985 | 13 | (7) | |
| Matchoi Bobó Djaló | 10.04.2003 | 14 | (8) | 1 |
| Paulo Guilherme Gonçalves Bernardo | 24.01.2002 | 9 | (4) | 2 |
| Rui Miguel Guerra Pires | 22.03.1998 | 30 | (1) | |
| Tiago Miguel Hora Ribeiro | 14.03.2002 | 1 | (4) | |
| Bastien Toma (SUI) | 24.06.1999 | 4 | (8) | |
| Forwards: | DOB | M | (s) | G |
| Adrián Butzke Benavides (ESP) | 30.03.1999 | 13 | (13) | 6 |
| Alexandre Xavier Pereira Guedes | 11.02.1994 | 10 | (6) | 1 |
| Arthur de Oliveira Sales (BRA) | 03.07.2002 | 3 | (9) | |
| Juan Antonio Delgado Baeza (CHI) | 05.03.1993 | 31 | | |
| Fábio Roberto Gomes Netto (BRA) | 25.05.1997 | 1 | (8) | |
| Hernâni Infande Tchuda da Silva (GNB) | 03.04.2001 | 4 | (6) | 1 |
| Kayky da Silva Chagas (BRA) | 11.06.2003 | 3 | (5) | |
| N'dri Philippe Koffi (FRA) | 09.03.2002 | 7 | (5) | 2 |
| Lucas da Silva de Jesus (BRA) | 30.01.1998 | | (1) | |
| Mauro Meireles Couto | 15.11.2005 | 1 | (4) | |
| Ichnygel Gerzjomir Minguel Thomas (CUW) | 01.02.2001 | 23 | (11) | 4 |
| José Uilton Silva de Jesus (BRA) | 25.07.1992 | 15 | (14) | 1 |

## Portimonense Sporting Clube Portimão

| Founded: | 14.08.1914 | |
|---|---|---|
| Stadium: | Estádio Municipal, Portimão (6,204) | |
| Trainer: | Paulo Sérgio Bento Brito | 19.02.1968 |

| Goalkeepers: | DOB | M | (s) | G |
|---|---|---|---|---|
| Kosuke Nakamura (JPN) | 27.02.1995 | 30 | | |
| Samuel Portugal Lima (BRA) | 29.03.1994 | 4 | | |
| Defenders: | DOB | M | (s) | G |
| João Victor Tornich „Alemão" (BRA) | 06.11.2002 | 4 | (1) | |
| Filipe do Bem Relvas Vitó Oliveira | 20.09.1999 | 33 | | |
| Gonçalo Faria Costa | 18.02.2000 | 2 | (7) | |
| Lucas Alves de Araujo (BRA) | 22.07.1992 | 6 | (1) | |
| Fahd Moufi (MAR) | 05.05.1996 | 31 | | 1 |
| Zié Mohamed Ouattara (CIV) | 09.01.2000 | 12 | (10) | 1 |
| Park Ji-soo (KOR) | 13.06.1994 | 14 | | |
| David Samuel Custódio Lima „Pastor" (BRA) | 20.02.2000 | | (1) | |
| Pedro Henrique de Oliveira Correia „Pedrão" (BRA) | 03.05.1997 | 29 | | 2 |
| Moustapha Seck (SEN) | 23.02.1996 | 27 | (2) | |
| Sérgio Manuel Fernandes da Conceição | 12.11.1996 | 1 | (3) | |
| Wagner Leonardo Calvelo De Souza (BRA) | 23.07.1999 | 1 | | |
| Willyan da Silva Rocha (BRA) | 27.01.1995 | 4 | | |
| Midfielders: | DOB | M | (s) | G |
| Bruno Miguel Carapeto Reis | 20.07.1999 | | (4) | |
| Carlos Vinicios Santos de Jesus „Carlinhos"(BRA) | 22.06.1994 | 8 | (1) | |

| | DOB | M | (s) | G |
|---|---|---|---|---|
| Mohamed Diaby (FRA) | 03.09.1996 | 15 | (10) | 1 |
| Ewerton da Silva Pereira (BRA) | 01.12.1992 | 6 | (6) | 1 |
| Henrique Jocú | 09.09.2001 | 6 | (8) | |
| Gustavo Klismahn Dimarães Miranda (BRA) | 23.11.1999 | 9 | (6) | |
| Lucas Queiroz Canteiro „Luquinha" (BRA) | 03.10.2000 | 11 | (6) | 2 |
| Maurício José Da Silveira Junior (BRA) | 21.10.1988 | 11 | (3) | 3 |
| Lucas de Souza Ventura „Nonoca" (BRA) | 19.05.1998 | 8 | (5) | |
| Paulo Estrela Moreira Alves | 20.02.1999 | 19 | (7) | 2 |
| Pedro Miguel Cunha Sá | 01.12.1993 | 11 | (2) | |
| Forwards: | DOB | M | (s) | G |
| Anderson de Oliveira da Silva (BRA) | 16.07.1998 | 5 | (1) | |
| Wilinton Aponzá Carabali (COL) | 29.03.2000 | | (1) | |
| Yony Alexander González Copete (COL) | 11.07.1994 | 10 | (6) | |
| Ricardo Manuel Pinho Matos | 25.03.2000 | 1 | (14) | 1 |
| Bryan Giovanni Róchez Mejía (HON) | 01.01.1995 | 7 | (14) | 1 |
| Rui Pedro Ribeiro Fernandes Duarte Gomes | 04.09.1997 | 8 | (22) | 1 |
| Adewale Oluwafemi Sapara (NGA) | 27.01.1995 | 1 | (4) | |
| Welinton Júnior Ferreira dos Santos (BRA) | 08.06.1993 | 24 | | 6 |
| Yago Cariello Ribeiro „Yago Caju" (BRA) | 27.07.1999 | 16 | (9) | 3 |

## Futebol Clube do Porto

| Founded: | 28.09.1893 | | |
|---|---|---|---|
| Stadium: | Estádio do Dragão, Porto (50,033) | | |
| Trainer: | Sérgio Paulo Merceiro Da Conceição | | 15.11.1974 |

| Goalkeepers: | DOB | M | (s) | G |
|---|---|---|---|---|
| Cláudio Pires Morais Ramos | 16.11.1991 | 1 | | |
| Diogo Meireles Costa | 19.09.1999 | 33 | | |
| **Defenders:** | **DOB** | **M** | **(s)** | **G** |
| David Mota Veiga Teixeira Carmo | 19.07.1999 | 7 | (2) | |
| Fábio Rafael Rodrigues Cardoso | 19.04.1994 | 14 | (3) | 2 |
| João Mário Neto Lopes | 03.01.2000 | 15 | (3) | 1 |
| Iván Marcano Sierra (ESP) | 23.06.1987 | 25 | | 4 |
| Képler Laveran Lima Ferreira „Pepe" | 26.02.1983 | 22 | (2) | |
| Rodrigo Fernandes da Conceição | 02.01.2000 | 6 | (10) | |
| Zaidu Sanusi (NGA) | 13.06.1997 | 10 | (8) | |
| Wendell Nascimento Borges (BRA) | 20.07.1993 | 24 | (2) | 1 |
| Wilson Migueis Manafá Jancó | 23.07.1994 | 5 | (2) | |
| **Midfielders:** | **DOB** | **M** | **(s)** | **G** |
| André Filipe Russo Franco | 12.04.1998 | 6 | (11) | 2 |
| Bernardo Pereira Folha | 23.03.2002 | 1 | (4) | |

| | DOB | M | (s) | G |
|---|---|---|---|---|
| Bruno Xavier Almeida Costa | 19.04.1997 | 4 | (2) | |
| Stephen Antunes Eustáquio (CAN) | 21.12.1996 | 19 | (10) | 2 |
| Marko Grujić (SRB) | 13.04.1996 | 14 | (10) | 1 |
| Otávio Edmilson da Silva Monteiro | 09.02.1995 | 25 | (2) | 5 |
| Eduardo Gabriel Aquino Cossa „Pepê" (BRA) | 24.02.1997 | 28 | (6) | 4 |
| Andrés Mateus Uribe Villa (COL) | 21.03.1991 | 29 | (2) | 4 |
| Vasco José Cardoso Sousa | 03.04.2003 | | (1) | |
| **Forwards:** | **DOB** | **M** | **(s)** | **G** |
| Francisco Evanilson de Lima Barbosa (BRA) | 06.10.1999 | 18 | (5) | 7 |
| Gabriel Veron Fonseca de Souza (BRA) | 03.09.2002 | 2 | (15) | |
| Wenderson Rodrigues do Nascimento Galeno (BRA) | 21.10.1997 | 20 | (11) | 8 |
| Gonçalo Oscar Albuquerque Borges | 29.03.2001 | | (10) | |
| Daniel Namaso Edi-Mesumbe Loader (ENG) | 28.08.2000 | 5 | (17) | 3 |
| Abraham Ayomide Marcus (NGA) | 02.01.2000 | | (1) | |
| Mehdi Taremi (IRN) | 18.07.1992 | 31 | (2) | 22 |
| Antonio „Toni" Martínez López (ESP) | 30.06.1997 | 10 | (21) | 5 |

## Rio Ave Futebol Clube Vila do Conde

| Founded: | 18.01.1939 | | |
|---|---|---|---|
| Stadium: | Estádio dos Arcos, Vila do Conde (5,300) | | |
| Trainer: | Luís Carlos Batalha Freire | | 03.11.1985 |

| Goalkeepers: | DOB | M | (s) | G |
|---|---|---|---|---|
| Jhonatan Luiz da Siqueira (BRA) | 08.05.1991 | 32 | | |
| Audenirton Soares da Silva „Magrão" (BRA) | 15.05.2000 | 2 | | |
| **Defenders:** | **DOB** | **M** | **(s)** | **G** |
| Aderlan Leandro De Jesus Santos (BRA) | 09.04.1989 | 32 | | 1 |
| João Pedro Loureiro da Costa „Costinha" | 26.03.2000 | 33 | | 3 |
| João Diogo Fonseca Ferreira | 22.03.2001 | | (8) | |
| Jorge Karseladze | 18.03.2005 | | (2) | |
| Josué Humberto Gonçalves Leal Sá | 17.06.1992 | 17 | (1) | |
| Miguel Raimundo Nóbrega | 17.04.2000 | 6 | (5) | |
| Renato Pantalon (CRO) | 27.10.1997 | 21 | (1) | 1 |
| Patrick William Sá De Oliveira (BRA) | 03.06.1997 | 23 | (3) | 2 |
| Pedro Miguel Gaspar Amaral | 25.08.1997 | 11 | (1) | 1 |
| Sávio Antônio Alves (BRA) | 26.05.1995 | | (14) | |
| **Midfielders:** | **DOB** | **M** | **(s)** | **G** |
| Miguel Baeza Pérez (ESP) | 27.03.2000 | 14 | (8) | |
| Bruno Santos Ventura | 27.02.2001 | 1 | (2) | |

| | DOB | M | (s) | G |
|---|---|---|---|---|
| Gonçalo Rosa Gonçalves Pereira Rodrigues „Guga" | 18.07.1997 | 33 | | 2 |
| João Salazar da Graça | 18.06.1995 | 12 | (7) | 1 |
| Julien Lomboto Lompombi (FRA) | 13.05.2002 | | (1) | |
| Amine Oudrhiri (MAR) | 04.11.1992 | 8 | (11) | |
| Andreas Samaris (GRE) | 13.06.1989 | 19 | (5) | |
| Vítor Hugo Gomes da Silva | 25.12.1987 | 7 | (13) | |
| **Forwards:** | **DOB** | **M** | **(s)** | **G** |
| André Filipe Ferreira Coelho Pereira | 05.05.1995 | 12 | (9) | 1 |
| Emmanuel Okyere Boateng (GHA) | 23.05.1996 | 21 | (7) | 6 |
| Fábio Ronaldo Costa Conceição | 28.04.2001 | 22 | (9) | 3 |
| Hernâni Jorge Santos Fortes | 20.08.1991 | 5 | (16) | 2 |
| Jorge Samuel Figueiredo Fernandes „Joca" | 30.01.1996 | 6 | | |
| Paulo Vitor Fernandes Pereira (BRA) | 24.06.1994 | 11 | (14) | 1 |
| Leonardo Acevedo Ruiz (COL) | 18.04.1996 | 8 | (17) | 4 |
| André Filipe Alves Monteiro „Ukra" | 16.03.1988 | 2 | (13) | |
| Abdul-Aziz Yakubu (GHA) | 10.11.1998 | 16 | (1) | 7 |
| José Manuel Silva Oliveira "Zé Manuel" | 23.10.1990 | | (1) | |

## Clube Desportivo Santa Clara Ponta Delgada

| Founded: | 31.01.1921 | | |
|---|---|---|---|
| Stadium: | Estádio de São Miguel, Ponta Delgada (13,277) | | |
| Trainer: | Mário Fernando Magalhães da Silva | | 24.04.1977 |
| [06.01.2023] | António Jorge Rocha Simão | | 12.08.1976 |
| [26.02.2023] | Danildo José São Pedro Accioly Filho (BRA) | | 30.03.1981 |

| Goalkeepers: | DOB | M | (s) | G |
|---|---|---|---|---|
| Gabriel Batista de Souza (BRA) | 03.06.1998 | 26 | | |
| Marco André Rocha Pereira | 01.12.1987 | 8 | | |
| **Defenders:** | **DOB** | **M** | **(s)** | **G** |
| Kennedy Boateng (GHA) | 29.11.1996 | 26 | | 3 |
| Diogo dos Santos Cabral „Calila" | 10.10.1998 | 6 | (9) | |
| Ítalo Fernando Assis Goncalves (BRA) | 18.02.2002 | 12 | | |
| Matheus Nunes Fagundes de Araújo (BRA) | 01.03.2001 | 13 | (7) | |
| Eulânio Ângelo Chipela Gomes „Nanu" (GNB) | 17.05.1994 | 5 | (6) | |
| Paulo Eduardo Ferreira Godinho (BRA) | 14.02.2002 | 5 | (3) | |
| Paulo Henrique Rodrigues Cabral | 23.10.1996 | 17 | (2) | |
| Pierre Emmanuel Sagna (SEN) | 21.08.1990 | 23 | (1) | |
| Cristian Marcelo González Tassano (URU) | 23.07.1996 | 11 | (2) | 1 |
| Xavier „Xavi" Quintillà Guasch (ESP) | 23.08.1996 | 8 | (5) | 1 |
| Ygor Nogueira de Paula (BRA) | 27.03.1995 | 12 | | 1 |
| **Midfielders:** | **DOB** | **M** | **(s)** | **G** |
| Adriano Firmino dos Santos da Silva (BRA) | 04.11.1999 | 27 | (4) | 1 |
| Anderson Carvalho Santos (BRA) | 20.05.1990 | 5 | (6) | |
| Bruno André Cavaco Jordão | 12.10.1998 | 9 | (2) | 1 |

| | DOB | M | (s) | G |
|---|---|---|---|---|
| João José Pereira da Costa „Costinha" | 25.08.1992 | 8 | (5) | |
| Kento Misao (JPN) | 16.04.1996 | 11 | (6) | |
| Pedro Henrique Rodrigues Bicalho (BRA) | 23.04.2001 | 2 | (3) | |
| Rildo Gonçalves de Amorim Filho (BRA) | 21.01.2000 | 7 | (16) | 3 |
| Rodrigo Ribeiro Valente | 15.02.2001 | | (5) | |
| Rúben Alexandre Gomes Oliveira | 14.12.1994 | | (1) | |
| Victor Bobsin Pereira (BRA) | 12.01.2000 | 18 | (6) | |
| **Forwards:** | **DOB** | **M** | **(s)** | **G** |
| Allano Brendon de Souza Lima (BRA) | 24.04.1995 | 15 | (5) | 1 |
| André Miguel Pinto Lopes „Andrézinho" | 01.12.1996 | 4 | (14) | 1 |
| Bruno Filipe Pereira Soares Almeida | 09.09.1996 | 17 | (5) | 1 |
| Gabriel Silva Vieira (BRA) | 22.03.2002 | 24 | (9) | 5 |
| Walter Rodrigo González Sosa (PAR) | 21.05.1995 | 4 | (2) | |
| João Marcos Lima Cândido (BRA) | 11.05.2000 | 2 | (2) | |
| Matheus Barcelos da Silva „Babi" (BRA) | 18.07.1997 | 15 | (11) | 5 |
| Ricardo Jorge Oliveira António „Ricardinho" | 06.08.1998 | 21 | (4) | |
| Rui Pedro Silva Costa | 20.02.1996 | | (1) | |
| Filip Stevanović (SRB) | 25.09.2002 | | (7) | |
| Kyosuke Tagawa (JPN) | 11.02.1999 | 13 | (14) | 2 |

## Sporting Clube de Portugal Lisboa

**Founded**: 01.07.1906
**Stadium**: Estádio "José Alvalade", Lisboa (50,095)
**Trainer**: Rúben Filipe Marques Amorim — 27.01.1985

| Goalkeepers: | DOB | M | (s) | G |
|---|---|---|---|---|
| *Antonio Adán* Garrido (ESP) | 13.05.1987 | 31 | | |
| Franco Israel Wibmer (URU) | 22.04.2000 | 3 | | |
| **Defenders:** | **DOB** | **M** | **(s)** | **G** |
| Héctor *Bellerín* Moruno (ESP) | 19.03.1995 | 6 | (4) | 1 |
| *Chico* Faria Camará *Lamba* | 10.03.2003 | | (1) | |
| Sebastián Coates Nion (URU) | 07.10.1990 | 30 | | 1 |
| Ousmane Diomande (CIV) | 04.12.2003 | 11 | (2) | 1 |
| *Flávio* Basilua Jacinto *Nazinho* | 20.07.2003 | 2 | (1) | |
| *Gonçalo* Bernardo *Inácio* | 25.08.2001 | 26 | (7) | 1 |
| *José* Martínez *Marsà* (ESP) | 04.03.2002 | 2 | | |
| *Matheus Reis* de Lima (BRA) | 18.02.1995 | 26 | (7) | 1 |
| Luís Carlos Novo *Neto* | 26.05.1988 | 4 | (2) | |
| *Pedro* Antonio *Porro* Sauceda (ESP) | 13.09.1999 | 12 | (2) | 2 |
| *Ricardo* Sousa *Esgaio* | 16.05.1993 | 15 | (10) | 1 |
| Jeremiah St. Juste (NED) | 19.10.1996 | 7 | (14) | 1 |
| **Midfielders:** | **DOB** | **M** | **(s)** | **G** |
| Sotirios Alexandropoulos (GRE) | 26.11.2001 | | (6) | |
| *Dário* Cassia Luis *Essugo* | 14.03.2005 | 3 | (1) | |
| *Mateus* Gonçalo Espanha *Fernandes* | 10.07.2004 | 1 | (2) | |
| *Matheus* Luiz *Nunes* (BRA) | 27.08.1998 | 2 | | 1 |
| Hidemasa Morita (JPN) | 10.05.1995 | 21 | (8) | 6 |
| Mateo Tanlongo (ARG) | 12.08.2003 | | (9) | |
| Manuel Ugarte Ribeiro (URU) | 11.04.2001 | 28 | (3) | |
| **Forwards:** | **DOB** | **M** | **(s)** | **G** |
| *Arthur Gomes* Lourenço (BRA) | 03.07.1998 | 6 | (18) | 1 |
| Marcus Edwards (ENG) | 03.12.1998 | 27 | (6) | 7 |
| Abdul Fatawu Issahaku (GHA) | 08.03.2004 | 1 | (5) | |
| Jovane Eduardo Borges Cabral (CPV) | 14.06.1998 | | (4) | |
| *Nuno* Miguel Gomes dos *Santos* | 13.02.1995 | 25 | (6) | 8 |
| João Paulo Dias Fernandes „*Paulinho*" | 09.11.1992 | 14 | (8) | 5 |
| *Pedro* António Pereira *Gonçalves* | 28.06.1998 | 33 | | 15 |
| Diogo Filipe Costa Rocha „*Rochinha*" | 03.05.1995 | 3 | (13) | 1 |
| *Rodrigo* Duarte *Ribeiro* (BRA) | 28.04.2005 | | (2) | |
| Francisco António Machado Mota Castro *Trincão* | 29.12.1999 | 26 | (8) | 10 |
| Youssef Chermiti | 24.05.2004 | 9 | (7) | 3 |

## Vitória Sport Clube de Guimarães

**Founded**: 22.09.1922
**Stadium**: Estádio "D. Afonso Henriques", Guimarães (30,007)
**Trainer**: João Miguel da Cunha Teixeira "Moreno" — 19.08.1981

| Goalkeepers: | DOB | M | (s) | G |
|---|---|---|---|---|
| *Bruno* Miguel Semedo *Varela* | 04.11.1994 | 27 | | |
| *Celton* Anssumane *Biai* | 13.08.2000 | 5 | | |
| Pedro *Rafael* Silva *Oliveira* | 28.09.2003 | 2 | | |
| **Defenders:** | **DOB** | **M** | **(s)** | **G** |
| *Afonso* Manuel Abreu de *Freitas* | 07.04.2000 | 25 | (1) | 1 |
| *André* Fonseca *Amaro* | 13.08.2002 | 27 | | 1 |
| Ibrahima Bamba (CIV) | 22.04.2002 | 27 | (1) | |
| *Bruno* Miguel Boialvo *Gaspar* (ANG) | 21.04.1993 | 1 | (6) | |
| *Hélder* José Oliveira *Sá* | 10.11.2002 | 9 | (1) | |
| *Jorge* Filipe Oliveira *Fernandes* | 02.04.1997 | 3 | (2) | |
| Miguel Ângelo Gomes Ferreira *Magalhães* | 16.11.2002 | 23 | (1) | |
| Ryoya Ogawa (JPN) | 24.11.1996 | 2 | (4) | |
| Mamadou Tounkara (FRA) | 14.12.2001 | 11 | (3) | |
| Mikel Villanueva Álvarez (VEN) | 14.04.1993 | 29 | | 1 |
| **Midfielders:** | **DOB** | **M** | **(s)** | **G** |
| *Alfa Semedo* Esteves (GNB) | 30.08.1997 | | (1) | |
| Domingos *André* Ribeiro *Almeida* | 30.05.2000 | 3 | | |
| *André* Filipe Brás *André* | 26.08.1989 | 16 | (4) | 1 |
| Daniel „*Dani*" Filipe Bandeira e *Silva* | 11.04.2000 | 17 | (13) | 1 |
| *Gonçalo* Teixeira Nogueira | 28.12.2003 | | (2) | |
| Nicolas Janvier (FRA) | 11.08.1998 | 4 | (15) | 1 |
| *Manuel* Jorge *Silva* | 12.06.2001 | 1 | | |
| Matheus Salgueiro Pains „Matheus Índio" (BRA) | 27.08.1999 | | (8) | |
| *Tiago* Rafael Maia *Silva* | 02.06.1993 | 26 | (2) | 5 |
| *Tomás* Romano Pereira dos Santos *Händel* | 27.11.2000 | 6 | (3) | 1 |
| José Carlos Natário Ferreira „*Zé Carlos*" | 30.10.2001 | 8 | (7) | |
| **Forwards:** | **DOB** | **M** | **(s)** | **G** |
| *Alisson* Pelegrini *Safira* (BRA) | 17.03.1995 | 8 | (14) | 5 |
| *Anderson* Oliveira *Silva* (BRA) | 21.11.1997 | 14 | (16) | 4 |
| *André* Oliveira *Silva* (BRA) | 03.06.1997 | 21 | (2) | 6 |
| Antonio Cortés Heredia „*Antoñín*" (ESP) | 16.04.2000 | | (3) | |
| Jason Bahamboula (FRA) | 15.06.2001 | | (1) | |
| *Diogo* Miguel Faria *Ferreira* | 09.09.2001 | | (1) | |
| Michael Andrew Johnston (SCO) | 19.04.1999 | 15 | (10) | 1 |
| João Pedro Ferreira Silva „*Jota Silva*" | 01.08.1999 | 22 | (8) | 2 |
| *Nélson* Conceição da Luz (ANG) | 04.02.1998 | 10 | (19) | 3 |
| *Rúben* Barcelos De Sousa *Lameiras* | 22.12.1994 | 12 | (7) | 1 |

## Futebol Clube de Vizela

**Founded**: 01.01.1939
**Stadium**: Estádio do FC Vizela, Vizela (6,100)
**Trainer**: Álvaro Adriano Teixeira Pacheco — 25.06.1971
[30.11.2022] Manuel Jorge da Silva Cruz "Tulipa" — 16.10.1972

| Goalkeepers: | DOB | M | (s) | G |
|---|---|---|---|---|
| Fabijan Buntić (CRO) | 24.02.1997 | 33 | | |
| *Luiz Felipe* da Silva Nunes (BRA) | 24.04.1997 | 1 | | |
| **Defenders:** | **DOB** | **M** | **(s)** | **G** |
| Mohamed Aidara (CIV) | 06.11.1996 | 1 | (5) | |
| *Anderson* de Jesús Santos (BRA) | 02.03.1995 | 30 | | 3 |
| *Bruno* Ricardo Valdez *Wilson* | 27.12.1996 | 23 | (1) | |
| *Carlos Isaac* Muñoz Obejero (ESP) | 30.04.1998 | 3 | (6) | |
| Ivanildo Jorge Mendes *Fernandes* | 26.03.1996 | 17 | (3) | |
| *Hugo* Silva *Oliveira* | 10.02.2002 | | (1) | |
| *Igor* de Carvalho *Julião* (BRA) | 23.08.1994 | 19 | (1) | 1 |
| Christian Neiva Afonso „*Kiki*" | 10.12.1994 | 26 | (2) | 1 |
| *Matheus Pereira* de Souza (BRA) | 21.12.2000 | 8 | (10) | 1 |
| **Midfielders:** | **DOB** | **M** | **(s)** | **G** |
| Alejandro Alvarado Jr. (USA) | 29.07.2003 | | (5) | |
| *Claudemir* Domingues de Souza (BRA) | 27.03.1988 | 17 | (5) | |
| *Diego* Gabriel Silva *Rosa* (BRA) | 12.10.2002 | 3 | (6) | |
| Alexis Méndez (USA) | 06.09.2000 | 12 | (18) | 1 |
| Monsuru Abdulsalam Opeyemi (NGA) | 11.08.2003 | 1 | | |
| *Pedro Ortíz* Bernat (ESP) | 19.08.2000 | 5 | (4) | |
| *Raphael* Gregorio *Guzzo* | 06.01.1995 | 29 | (1) | 2 |
| Osama Jabar Shafia Rashid (IRQ) | 13.01.1992 | 4 | (14) | 1 |
| Fábio Samuel Amorim Silva „*Samu*" | 21.04.1996 | 32 | (1) | 3 |
| *Tómas* Costa *Silva* | 15.10.1999 | 12 | (10) | 1 |
| **Forwards:** | **DOB** | **M** | **(s)** | **G** |
| Francis Cann (GHA) | 06.02.1998 | | (3) | |
| Friday Ubi Etim (NGA) | 21.05.2002 | 1 | (18) | 2 |
| Francisco Miguel Ribeiro Tomé Tavares „*Kiko*" *Bondoso* | 17.11.1995 | 34 | | 2 |
| Matías Rafael Lacava González (VEN) | 24.10.2002 | 2 | (13) | 1 |
| *Nuno* Gonçalo Rocha *Moreira* | 16.06.1999 | 22 | (7) | 1 |
| Milutin Osmajić (MNE) | 25.07.1999 | 26 | (5) | 8 |
| Andrés de Jesús Sarmiento Salas (COL) | 15.01.1998 | | (4) | |
| Alexander Schmidt (AUT) | 19.01.1998 | 3 | (7) | |
| Kévin Lucien Zohi (MLI) | 19.12.1996 | 10 | (15) | 2 |

## SECOND LEVEL
### LigaPro 2022/2023

| | | | | | | | | | | |
|---|---|---|---|---|---|---|---|---|---|---|
| 1. | Moreirense FC Moreira de Cónegos (*Promoted*) | 34 | 24 | 7 | 3 | 77 | - | 38 | 79 |
| 2. | SC Farense Faro (*Promoted*) | 34 | 21 | 6 | 7 | 57 | - | 34 | 69 |
| 3. | CF Estrela da Amadora (*Promotion Play-offs*) | 34 | 16 | 15 | 3 | 55 | - | 35 | 63 |
| 4. | Académico de Viseu FC | 34 | 14 | 11 | 9 | 51 | - | 45 | 53 |
| 5. | FC do Porto "B"* | 34 | 14 | 9 | 11 | 48 | - | 40 | 51 |
| 6. | CD Mafra | 34 | 12 | 11 | 11 | 46 | - | 49 | 47 |
| 7. | UD Vilafranquense | 34 | 12 | 10 | 12 | 42 | - | 36 | 46 |
| 8. | CD Feirense Santa Maria da Feira | 34 | 11 | 13 | 10 | 43 | - | 37 | 46 |
| 9. | SC União Torreense | 34 | 13 | 5 | 16 | 38 | - | 41 | 44 |
| 10. | UD Oliveirense | 34 | 11 | 10 | 13 | 51 | - | 50 | 43 |
| 11. | CD Tondela | 34 | 8 | 16 | 10 | 35 | - | 35 | 40 |
| 12. | FC de Penafiel | 34 | 9 | 12 | 13 | 36 | - | 47 | 39 |
| 13. | CD Nacional Funchal | 34 | 10 | 9 | 15 | 35 | - | 46 | 39 |
| 14. | Sport Lisboa e Benfica "B"* | 34 | 10 | 8 | 16 | 52 | - | 58 | 38 |
| 15. | Leixões SC Porto | 34 | 10 | 9 | 15 | 38 | - | 49 | 38 |
| 16. | B-SAD Lisboa (*Relegation Play-offs*) | 34 | 9 | 8 | 17 | 41 | - | 59 | 35 |
| 17. | CD Trofense (*Relegated*) | 34 | 8 | 8 | 18 | 31 | - | 51 | 32 |
| 18. | Sporting da Covilhã (*Relegated*) | 34 | 7 | 7 | 20 | 31 | - | 57 | 28 |

*Please note: reserve teams are ineligible to promotion.

### Relegation Play-offs (2nd / 3rd Level) [21-29.05.2022]

Länk FC Vilaverdense - B-SAD Lisboa                1-1(1-1)        1-0(1-0)

Länk FC Vilaverdense promoted to the second level for 2023/2024.

## NATIONAL TEAM

### INTERNATIONAL MATCHES
#### (16.07.2022 – 15.07.2023)

| | | | | |
|---|---|---|---|---|
| 24.09.2022 | Praha | *Czech Republic - Portugal* | *0-4(0-2)* | (UNL) |
| 27.09.2022 | Braga | *Portugal - Spain* | *0-1(0-0)* | (UNL) |
| 17.11.2022 | Lisboa | *Portugal - Nigeria* | *4-0(2-0)* | (F) |
| 24.11.2022 | Doha | *Portugal - Ghana* | *3-2(0-0)* | (WC) |
| 28.11.2022 | Lusail | *Portugal - Uruguay* | *2-0(0-0)* | (WC) |
| 02.12.2022 | Al Rayyan | *Korea Republic - Portugal* | *2-1(1-1)* | (WC) |
| 06.12.2022 | Lusail | *Portugal - Switzerland* | *6-1(2-0)* | (WC) |
| 10.12.2022 | Doha | *Morocco - Portugal* | *1-0(1-0)* | (WC) |
| | | | | |
| 23.03.2023 | Lisboa | *Portugal - Liechtenstein* | *4-0(1-0)* | (ECQ) |
| 26.03.2023 | Lëtzebuerg | *Luxembourg - Portugal* | *0-6(0-4)* | (ECQ) |
| 17.06.2023 | Lisboa | *Portugal - Bosnia and Herzegovina* | *3-0(1-0)* | (ECQ) |
| 20.06.2023 | Reykjavík | *Iceland - Portugal* | *0-1(0-0)* | (ECQ) |

**24.09.2022    CZECH REPUBLIC - PORTUGAL        0-4(0-2)        3rd UEFA Nations League A, Group 2**
Fortuna Arena, Praha; Referee: Srđan Jovanović (Serbia); Attendance: 19,322
**POR:** Diogo Costa, Diogo Dalot, Danilo Pereira (83.João Mário), Rúben Dias, Mário Rui, Rúben Neves, William Carvalho (7.João Palhinha), Bruno Fernandes (77.Matheus Nunes), Bernardo Silva (67.Ricardo Horta), Cristiano Ronaldo (Cap), Rafael Leão (67.Diogo Jota). Trainer: Fernando Manuel Fernandes da Costa Santos.
**Goals:** Diogo Dalot (33), Bruno Fernandes (45+2), Diogo Dalot (52), Diogo Jota (82).

**27.09.2022    PORTUGAL - SPAIN        0-1(0-0)        3rd UEFA Nations League A, Group 2**
Estadio Municipal de Braga, Braga; Referee: Daniele Orsato (Italy); Attendance: 28,196
**POR:** Diogo Costa, João Cancelo, Danilo Pereira, Rúben Dias, Nuno Mendes, William Carvalho (78.Rafael Leão), Rúben Neves (89.João Félix), Bruno Fernandes, Bernardo Silva (73.João Mário), Diogo Jota (78.Vitinha), Cristiano Ronaldo (Cap). Trainer: Fernando Manuel Fernandes da Costa Santos.

**17.11.2022    PORTUGAL - NIGERIA        4-0(2-0)        Friendly International**
Estádio "José Alvalade", Lisboa; Referee: Chrysovalantis Theouli (Cyprus); Attendance: 43,621
**POR:** Rui Patrício (Cap), Diogo Dalot, António Silva, Rúben Dias (46.Raphaël Guerreiro), Nuno Mendes (46.Vitinha), Otávio (76.Ricardo Horta), William Carvalho, André Silva (66.Gonçalo Ramos), Bruno Fernandes (46.Pepe), Bernardo Silva (46.João Mário), João Félix. Trainer: Fernando Manuel Fernandes da Costa Santos.
**Goals:** Bruno Fernandes (9, 35 penalty), Gonçalo Ramos (82), João Mário (84).

**24.11.2022    PORTUGAL - GHANA        3-2(0-0)        22nd FIFA WC. Group Stage.**
Stadium 974, Doha (Qatar); Referee: Ismail Elfath (United States); Attendance: 42,662
**POR:** Diogo Costa, João Cancelo, Rúben Dias, Danilo Pereira, Raphaël Guerreiro, Bernardo Silva (88. João Palhinha), Rúben Neves (77.Rafael Leão), Otávio (56.William Carvalho), Bruno Fernandes, Cristiano Ronaldo (Cap) (88.Gonçalo Ramos), João Félix (88. João Mário). Trainer: Fernando Manuel Fernandes da Costa Santos.
**Goals:** Cristiano Ronaldo (65 penalty), João Félix (78), Rafael Leão (80).

**28.11.2022**   **PORTUGAL - URUGUAY**                                        **2-0(0-0)**                          22<sup>nd</sup> FIFA WC. Group Stage.
Lusail Stadium, Lusail (Qatar); Referee: Alireza Faghani (Iran); Attendance: 88,668
**POR:** Diogo Costa, João Cancelo, Rúben Dias, Pepe, Nuno Mendes (42.Raphaël Guerreiro), Rúben Neves (69.Rafael Leão), Bernardo Silva, William Carvalho (82.João Palhinha), Bruno Fernandes, Cristiano Ronaldo (Cap) (82.Gonçalo Ramos), João Félix (82. Matheus Nunes). Trainer: Fernando Manuel Fernandes da Costa Santos.
**Goals:** Bruno Fernandes (54, 90+3 penalty).

**02.12.2022**   **KOREA REPUBLIC - PORTUGAL**                    **2-1(1-1)**                          22<sup>nd</sup> FIFA WC. Group Stage.
Education City Stadium, Al Rayyan (Qatar); Referee: Facundo Raúl Tello Figueroa (Argentina); Attendance: 44,097
**POR:** Diogo Costa, Diogo Dalot, Pepe, António Silva, João Cancelo, Matheus Nunes (65.Rafael Leão), Rúben Neves (65.João Palhinha), Vitinha (81.William Carvalho), Ricardo Horta, Cristiano Ronaldo (Cap) (65.André Silva), João Mário (81.Bernardo Silva). Trainer: Fernando Manuel Fernandes da Costa Santos.
**Goal:** Ricardo Horta (5).

**06.12.2022**   **PORTUGAL - SWITZERLAND**                         **6-1(2-0)**                          22<sup>nd</sup> FIFA WC. 2<sup>nd</sup> Round of 16.
Lusail Stadium, Lusail (Qatar); Referee: César Arturo Ramos Palazuelos (Mexico); Attendance: 83,720
**POR:** Diogo Costa, Diogo Dalot, Pepe (Cap), Rúben Dias, Raphaël Guerreiro, Otávio (74.Vitinha), William Carvalho, Bernardo Silva (81.Rúben Neves), Bruno Fernandes (87.Rafael Leão), Gonçalo Ramos (74.Ricardo Horta), João Félix (74. Cristiano Ronaldo). Trainer: Fernando Manuel Fernandes da Costa Santos.
**Goals:** Gonçalo Ramos (17), Pepe (33), Gonçalo Ramos (51), Raphaël Guerreiro (55), Gonçalo Ramos (67), Rafael Leão (90+2).

**10.12.2022**   **MOROCCO - PORTUGAL**                               **1-0(1-0)**                          22<sup>nd</sup> FIFA WC. Quarter-Finals.
Al Thumama Stadium, Doha (Qatar); Referee: Facundo Raúl Tello Figueroa (Argentina); Attendance: 44,198
**POR:** Diogo Costa, Diogo Dalot (79.Ricardo Horta), Pepe (Cap), Rúben Dias, Raphaël Guerreiro (51.João Cancelo), Rúben Neves (51.Cristiano Ronaldo), Otávio (69.Vitinha), Bernardo Silva, Bruno Fernandes, Gonçalo Ramos (69.Rafael Leão), João Félix. Trainer: Fernando Manuel Fernandes da Costa Santos.

**23.03.2023**   **PORTUGAL - LIECHTENSTEIN**                      **4-0(1-0)**                                              17<sup>th</sup> EC. Qualifiers
Estádio "José Alvalade", Lisboa; Referee: Espen Eskås (Norway); Attendance: 45,378
**POR:** Rui Patrício, Danilo Pereira (67.Rúben Neves), Rúben Dias, Gonçalo Inácio, João Cancelo, Bruno Fernandes (89.João Mário), João Palhinha, Raphaël Guerreiro, Bernardo Silva (78.Vitinha), João Félix (67.Rafael Leão), Cristiano Ronaldo (Cap) (78.Gonçalo Ramos). Trainer: Roberto Martínez Montoliú (Spain).
**Goals:** João Cancelo (8), Bernardo Silva (47), Cristiano Ronaldo (51 penalty, 63).

**26.03.2023**   **LUXEMBOURG - PORTUGAL**                        **0-6(0-4)**                                              17<sup>th</sup> EC. Qualifiers
Stade de Luxembourg, Lëtzebuerg; Referee: Radu Marian Petrescu (Romania); Attendance: 9,231
**POR:** Rui Patrício, Danilo Pereira, Rúben Dias, António Silva, Diogo Dalot, João Palhinha (86.Diogo Jota), Bruno Fernandes (75.Rafael Leão), Nuno Mendes, Bernardo Silva (64.Rúben Neves), João Félix (75.Otávio), Cristiano Ronaldo (Cap) (64.Gonçalo Ramos). Trainer: Roberto Martínez Montoliú (Spain).
**Goals:** Cristiano Ronaldo (9), João Félix (15), Bernardo Silva (18), Cristiano Ronaldo (31), Otávio (77), Rafael Leão (88).

**17.06.2023**   **PORTUGAL - BOSNIA AND HERZEGOVINA**    **3-0(1-0)**                                   17<sup>th</sup> EC. Qualifiers
Estádio do Sport Lisboa e Benfica, Lisboa; Referee: Davide Massa (Italy); Attendance: 55,058
**POR:** Diogo Costa, Danilo Pereira, Rúben Dias, António Silva, João Cancelo, Bruno Fernandes, João Palhinha (87.Diogo Jota), Raphaël Guerreiro (78.Nélson Semedo), Bernardo Silva (87.Otávio), João Félix (62.Rúben Neves), Cristiano Ronaldo (Cap). Trainer: Roberto Martínez Montoliú (Spain).
**Goals:** Bernardo Silva (44), Bruno Fernandes (77, 90+3).

**20.06.2023**   **ICELAND - PORTUGAL**                                 **0-1(0-0)**                                              17<sup>th</sup> EC. Qualifiers
Laugardalsvöllur, Reykjavík; Referee: Daniel Siebert (Germany); Attendance: 9,517
**POR:** Diogo Costa, Danilo Pereira (84.Otávio), Pepe, Rúben Dias, Diogo Dalot, Bruno Fernandes (84.Vitinha), Rúben Neves (67.Gonçalo Inácio), João Cancelo (67.Raphaël Guerreiro), Bernardo Silva (90+3.Diogo Jota), Rafael Leão, Cristiano Ronaldo (Cap). Trainer: Roberto Martínez Montoliú (Spain).
**Goals:** Cristiano Ronaldo (89).

## NATIONAL TEAM PLAYERS
### (16.07.2022 – 15.07.2023)

| Name | DOB | Caps | Goals | Club |
|---|---|---|---|---|
| **Goalkeepers** | | | | |
| DIOGO Meireles da COSTA | 19.09.1999 | 14 | 0 | 2022/2023: *FC do Porto* |
| RUI Pedro dos Santos PATRÍCIO | 15.02.1988 | 107 | 0 | 2022/2023: *AS Roma (ITA)* |
| **Defenders** | | | | |
| ANTÓNIO João Pereira Albuquerque Tavares da SILVA | 30.10.2003 | 5 | 0 | 2022/2023: *Sport Lisboa e Benfica* |
| DANILO Luís Hélio PEREIRA | 09.09.1991 | 68 | 2 | 2022/2023: *Paris Saint-Germain FC (FRA)* |
| José DIOGO DALOT Teixeira | 18.03.1999 | 12 | 0 | 2022/2023: *Manchester United FC (ENG)* |
| GONÇALO Bernardo INÁCIO | 25.08.2001 | 2 | 0 | 2023: *Sporting Clube de Portugal Lisboa* |
| JOÃO Pedro Cavaco CANCELO | 27.05.1994 | 44 | 8 | 2022: *Manchester City FC (ENG)* <br> 31.01.2023-> *FC Bayern München (GER)* |
| MÁRIO RUI Silva Duarte | 27.05.1991 | 12 | 0 | 2022: *SSC Napoli (ITA)* |
| NÉLSON Cabral SEMEDO "Nelsinho" | 16.11.1993 | 25 | 0 | 2023: *Wolverhampton Wanderers FC (ENG)* |
| NUNO Alexandre Tavares MENDES | 19.06.2002 | 19 | 0 | 2022/2023: *Paris Saint-Germain FC (FRA)* |
| Képler Laveran Lima Ferreira "PEPE" | 26.02.1983 | 134 | 8 | 2022/2023: *FC do Porto* |
| RAPHAËL Adelino José GUERREIRO | 22.12.1993 | 64 | 4 | 2022/2023: *BV Borussia Dortmund (GER)* |
| RÚBEN Santos Gato Alves DIAS | 14.05.1997 | 48 | 2 | 2022/2023: *Manchester City FC (ENG)* |
| **Midfielders** | | | | |
| BRUNO Miguel Borges FERNANDES | 08.09.1994 | 57 | 15 | 2022/2023: *Manchester United FC (ENG)* |
| JOÃO MÁRIO Naval da Costa Eduardo | 19.01.1993 | 56 | 3 | 2022/2023: *Sport Lisboa e Benfica* |
| JOÃO Maria Lobo Alves PALHINHA Gonçalves | 09.07.1995 | 21 | 2 | 2022/2023: *Fulham FC London (ENG)* |
| MATHEUS Luiz NUNES | 27.08.1998 | 11 | 1 | 2022: *Wolverhampton Wanderers FC (ENG)* |
| OTÁVIO Edmilson da Silva Monteiro | 09.02.1995 | 14 | 3 | 2022/2023: *FC do Porto* |
| RAFAEL Alexandre da Conceição LEÃO | 10.06.1999 | 19 | 3 | 2022/2023: *AC Milan (ITA)* |
| RÚBEN Diogo da Silva NEVES | 13.03.1997 | 41 | 0 | 2022/2023: *Wolverhampton Wanderers FC (ENG)* |
| Vítor Machado Ferreira "VITINHA" | 13.02.2000 | 10 | 0 | 2022/2023: *Paris Saint-Germain FC (FRA)* |
| WILLIAM Silva de CARVALHO | 07.04.1992 | 80 | 5 | 2022: *Real Betis Balompié Sevilla (ESP)* |
| **Forwards** | | | | |
| ANDRÉ Miguel Valente SILVA | 06.11.1995 | 53 | 19 | 2022: *RasenBallsport Leipzig (GER)* |
| BERNARDO Mota Veiga de Carvalho e SILVA | 10.08.1994 | 82 | 11 | 2022/2023: *Manchester City FC (ENG)* |
| CRISTIANO RONALDO dos Santos Aveiro | 05.02.1985 | 200 | 123 | 2022: *Manchester United FC (ENG)* <br> 22.11.2022-> *unattached* <br> 01.01.2023-> *Al-Nassr FC Riyadh (KSA)* |
| Diogo José Teixeira da Silva "DIOGO JOTA" | 04.12.1996 | 32 | 10 | 2022/2023: *Liverpool FC (ENG)* |
| GONÇALO Matias RAMOS | 20.06.2001 | 7 | 4 | 2022/2023: *Sport Lisboa e Benfica* |
| JOÃO FÉLIX Sequeira | 10.11.1999 | 31 | 5 | 2022: *Club Atlético de Madrid (ESP)* <br> 11.01.2023-> *Chelsea FC London (ENG)* |
| RICARDO Jorge Luz HORTA | 15.09.1994 | 9 | 2 | 2022: *Sporting Clube de Braga* |
| **Trainer** | | | | |
| FERNANDO Manuel Fernandes da Costa SANTOS [23.09.2014 - 15.12.2022] | 10.10.1954 | 109 M; 67 W; 23 D; 19 L; 226-81 | | |
| Roberto MARTÍNEZ Montoliú (Spain) [from 09.01.2023] | 13.07.1973 | 4 M; 4 W; 0 D; 0 L; 14-0 | | |

# REPUBLIC OF IRELAND

## The Country:
Éire (Republic of Ireland)
Capital: Dublin
Surface: 70,273 km²
Inhabitants: 5,123,536 [2022]
Time: UTC

## The FA:
Football Association of Ireland
National Sports Campus, Abbotstown, Dublin 15, D15 X8PD
Tel: +353 1 8999 500
Founded: 1921
Member of FIFA since: 1923
Member of UEFA since: 1954
Website: www.fai.ie

## NATIONAL TEAM RECORDS

### RECORDS
| | | |
|---|---|---|
| **First international match:** | 21.03.1926, Torino: | Italy – Republic of Ireland 3-0 |
| **Most international caps:** | Robert David Keane | - 146 caps (1998-2016) |
| **Most international goals:** | Robert David Keane | - 68 goals / 146 caps (1998-2016) |

### UEFA EUROPEAN CHAMPIONSHIP
| | |
|---|---|
| 1960 | Qualifiers |
| 1964 | Qualifiers |
| 1968 | Qualifiers |
| 1972 | Qualifiers |
| 1976 | Qualifiers |
| 1980 | Qualifiers |
| 1984 | Qualifiers |
| 1988 | Final Tournament (Group Stage) |
| 1992 | Qualifiers |
| 1996 | Qualifiers |
| 2000 | Qualifiers |
| 2004 | Qualifiers |
| 2008 | Qualifiers |
| 2012 | Final Tournament (Group Stage) |
| 2016 | Final Tournament (2nd Round of 16) |
| 2020 | Qualifiers |

### FIFA WORLD CUP
| | |
|---|---|
| 1930 | Did not enter |
| 1934 | Qualifiers |
| 1938 | Qualifiers |
| 1950 | Qualifiers |
| 1954 | Qualifiers |
| 1958 | Qualifiers |
| 1962 | Qualifiers |
| 1966 | Qualifiers |
| 1970 | Qualifiers |
| 1974 | Qualifiers |
| 1978 | Qualifiers |
| 1982 | Qualifiers |
| 1986 | Qualifiers |
| 1990 | Final Tournament (Quarter-Finals) |
| 1994 | Final Tournament (2nd Round of 16) |
| 1998 | Qualifiers |
| 2002 | Final Tournament (2nd Round of 16) |
| 2006 | Qualifiers |
| 2010 | Qualifiers |
| 2014 | Qualifiers |
| 2018 | Qualifiers |
| 2022 | Qualifiers |

### OLYMPIC TOURNAMENTS
| | |
|---|---|
| 1908 | - |
| 1912 | - |
| 1920 | - |
| 1924 | Quarter-Finals |
| 1928 | - |
| 1936 | - |
| 1948 | Preliminary Round |
| 1952 | Did not enter |
| 1956 | Did not enter |
| 1960 | Qualifiers |
| 1964 | Did not enter |
| 1968 | Did not enter |
| 1972 | Qualifiers |
| 1976 | Qualifiers |
| 1980 | Qualifiers |
| 1984 | Did not enter |
| 1988 | Qualifiers |
| 1992 | Qualifiers |
| 1996 | Qualifiers |
| 2000 | Qualifiers |
| 2004 | Qualifiers |
| 2008 | Qualifiers |
| 2012 | Qualifiers |
| 2016 | Qualifiers |
| 2020 | Qualifiers |

### UEFA NATIONS LEAGUE
| | |
|---|---|
| 2018/2019 | League B (Group Stage) |
| 2020/2021 | League B (Group Stage) |
| 2022/2023 | League B (Group Stage) |

### IRISH CLUB HONOURS IN EUROPEAN CLUB COMPETITIONS:

| European Champion Clubs.Cup (1956-1992) / UEFA Champions League (1993-2023) |
|---|
| None |

| Fairs Cup (1858-1971) / UEFA Cup (1972-2009) / UEFA Europa League (2010-2023) |
|---|
| None |

| UEFA Europa Conference League (2021-2023) |
|---|
| None |

| UEFA Super Cup (1972-2022) |
|---|
| None |

| *European Cup Winners' Cup 1961-1999** |
|---|
| None |

*defunct competition

## NATIONAL COMPETITIONS
## TABLE OF HONOURS

| | CHAMPIONS | CUP WINNERS | BEST GOALSCORERS | |
|---|---|---|---|---|
| 1921/1922 | St. James' Gate | St. James' Gate FC Dublin | Jack Kelly (St. James' Gate FC Dublin) | 11 |
| 1922/1923 | Shamrock Rovers FC Dublin | Alton United | Bob Fullam (Shamrock Rovers FC Dublin) | 27 |
| 1923/1924 | Bohemian FC Dublin | Athlone Town FC | Dave Roberts (Bohemian FC Dublin) | 20 |
| 1924/1925 | Shamrock Rovers FC Dublin | Shamrock Rovers FC Dublin | Billy Farrell (Shamrock Rovers FC Dublin) | 25 |
| 1925/1926 | Shelbourne FC Dublin | Fordsons FC Cork | Billy Farrell (Shamrock Rovers FC Dublin) | 24 |
| 1926/1927 | Shamrock Rovers FC Dublin | Drumcondra | David Byrne (Shamrock Rovers FC Dublin) John McMillan (Shelbourne FC Dublin) | 17 |
| 1927/1928 | Bohemian FC Dublin | Bohemian FC Dublin | Charlie Heinemann (Fordsons FC Cork) | 24 |
| 1928/1929 | Shelbourne FC Dublin | Shamrock Rovers FC Dublin | Eddie Carroll (Dundalk FC) | 17 |
| 1929/1930 | Bohemian FC Dublin | Shamrock Rovers FC Dublin | Johnny Ledwidge (Shelbourne FC Dublin) | 16 |
| 1930/1931 | Shelbourne FC Dublin | Shamrock Rovers FC Dublin | Alec Hair (Shelbourne FC Dublin) | 29 |
| 1931/1932 | Shamrock Rovers FC Dublin | Shamrock Rovers FC Dublin | Pearson Ferguson (Cork FC) Jack Forster (Waterford FC) | 21 |
| 1932/1933 | Dundalk FC | Shamrock Rovers FC Dublin | George Ebbs (St. James' Gate FC Dublin) | 20 |
| 1933/1934 | Bohemian FC Dublin | Cork FC | Alf Rigby (St. James' Gate FC Dublin) | 13 |
| 1934/1935 | Dolphin | Bohemian FC Dublin | Alf Rigby (St. James' Gate FC Dublin) | 17 |
| 1935/1936 | Bohemian FC Dublin | Shamrock Rovers FC Dublin | Jimmy Turnbull (Cork FC) | 37 |
| 1936/1937 | Sligo Rovers FC | Waterford FC | Bob Slater (Shelbourne FC Dublin, Waterford FC) | 20 |
| 1937/1938 | Shamrock Rovers FC Dublin | St. James' Gate FC Dublin | Willie Byrne (St. James' Gate FC Dublin) | 25 |
| 1938/1939 | Shamrock Rovers FC Dublin | Shelbourne FC Dublin | Paddy Bradshaw (St. James' Gate FC Dublin) | 22 |
| 1939/1940 | St. James' Gate | Shamrock Rovers FC Dublin | Paddy Bradshaw (St. James' Gate FC Dublin) | 29 |
| 1940/1941 | Cork United FC | Cork United FC | Mick O'Flanagan (Bohemian FC Dublin) | 19 |
| 1941/1942 | Cork United FC | Dundalk FC | Tommy Byrne (Limerick FC) | 20 |
| 1942/1943 | Cork United FC | Drumcondra | Sean McCarthy (Cork United FC) | 16 |
| 1943/1944 | Shelbourne FC Dublin | Shamrock Rovers FC Dublin | Sean McCarthy (Cork United FC) | 16 |
| 1944/1945 | Cork United FC | Shamrock Rovers FC Dublin | Sean McCarthy (Cork United FC) | 26 |
| 1945/1946 | Cork United FC | Drumcondra FC Dublin | Paddy O'Leary (Cork United FC) | 15 |
| 1946/1947 | Shelbourne FC Dublin | Cork United FC | Paddy Coad (Shamrock Rovers FC Dublin) Alf Hanson (Shelbourne FC Dublin) | 11 |
| 1947/1948 | Drumcondra FC Dublin | Shamrock Rovers FC Dublin | Sean McCarthy (Cork United FC) | 13 |
| 1948/1949 | Drumcondra FC Dublin | Dundalk FC | Bernard Lester (Transport FC Dublin) Eugene Noonan (Waterford FC) Paddy O'Leary (Cork Athletic FC) | 12 |
| 1949/1950 | Cork Athletic FC | Transport FC Dublin | Dave McCulloch   (Waterford FC) | 19 |
| 1950/1951 | Cork Athletic FC | Cork Athletic FC | Dessie Glynn (Drumcondra FC Dublin) | 20 |
| 1951/1952 | St. Patrick's Athletic FC Dublin | Dundalk FC | Shay Gibbons (St. Patrick's Athletic FC Dublin) | 26 |
| 1952/1953 | Shelbourne FC Dublin | Cork Athletic FC | Shay Gibbons (St. Patrick's Athletic FC Dublin) | 22 |
| 1953/1954 | Shamrock Rovers FC Dublin | Drumcondra FC Dublin | Danny Jordan (Bohemian FC Dublin) | 14 |
| 1954/1955 | St. Patrick's Athletic FC Dublin | Shamrock Rovers FC Dublin | Jimmy Gauld (Waterford FC) | 30 |
| 1955/1956 | St. Patrick's Athletic FC Dublin | Shamrock Rovers FC Dublin | Shay Gibbons (St. Patrick's Athletic FC Dublin) | 21 |
| 1956/1957 | Shamrock Rovers FC Dublin | Drumcondra FC Dublin | Tommy Hamilton (Shamrock Rovers FC Dublin) Donal Leahy (Evergreen United FC Cork) | 15 |
| 1957/1958 | Drumcondra FC Dublin | Dundalk FC | Donal Leahy (Evergreen United FC Cork) | 16 |
| 1958/1959 | Shamrock Rovers FC Dublin | St. Patrick's Athletic FC Dublin | Donal Leahy (Evergreen United FC Cork) | 22 |
| 1959/1960 | Limerick FC | Shelbourne FC Dublin | Austin Noonan (Cork Celtic FC) | 27 |
| 1960/1961 | Drumcondra FC Dublin | St. Patrick's Athletic FC Dublin | Dan McCaffrey (Drumcondra FC Dublin) | 29 |
| 1961/1962 | Shelbourne FC Dublin | Shamrock Rovers FC Dublin | Eddie Bailham (Shamrock Rovers FC Dublin) | 21 |
| 1962/1963 | Dundalk FC | Shelbourne FC Dublin | Mick Lynch (Waterford FC) | 12 |
| 1963/1964 | Shamrock Rovers FC Dublin | Shamrock Rovers FC Dublin | Eddie Bailham (Shamrock Rovers FC Dublin) Jimmy Hasty (Dundalk FC) Johnny Kingston (Cork Hibernians FC) | 18 |
| 1964/1965 | Drumcondra FC Dublin | Shamrock Rovers FC Dublin | Jackie Mooney (Shamrock Rovers FC Dublin) | 16 |
| 1965/1966 | Waterford FC | Shamrock Rovers FC Dublin | Mick Lynch (Waterford FC) | 17 |
| 1966/1967 | Dundalk FC | Shamrock Rovers FC Dublin | Johnny Brooks (Sligo Rovers FC) Danny Hale (Dundalk FC) | 15 |
| 1967/1968 | Waterford FC | Shamrock Rovers FC Dublin | Carl Davenport (Cork Celtic FC) Ben Hannigan (Dundalk FC) | 15 |
| 1968/1969 | Waterford FC | Shamrock Rovers FC Dublin | Mick Leech (Shamrock Rovers FC Dublin) | 19 |
| 1969/1970 | Waterford FC | Bohemian FC Dublin | Brendan Bradley (Finn Harps FC Ballybofey) | 18 |
| 1970/1971 | Cork Hibernians FC | Limerick FC | Brendan Bradley (Finn Harps FC Ballybofey) | 20 |
| 1971/1972 | Waterford FC | Cork Hibernians FC | Alfie Hale (Waterford FC) Tony Marsden (Cork Hibernians FC) | 22 |
| 1972/1973 | Waterford FC | Cork Hibernians FC | Alfie Hale (Waterford FC) Terry Harkin (Finn Harps FC Ballybofey) | 20 |
| 1973/1974 | Cork Celtic FC | Finn Harps FC Ballybofey | Terry Flanagan (Bohemian FC Dublin) Turlough O'Connor (Bohemian FC Dublin) | 18 |
| 1974/1975 | Bohemian FC Dublin | Home Farm FC Dublin | Brendan Bradley (Finn Harps FC Ballybofey) | 21 |
| 1975/1976 | Dundalk FC | Bohemian FC Dublin | Brendan Bradley (Finn Harps FC Ballybofey) | 29 |
| 1976/1977 | Sligo Rovers FC | Dundalk FC | Syd Wallace (Waterford FC) | 16 |
| 1977/1978 | Bohemian FC Dublin | Shamrock Rovers FC Dublin | Turlough O'Connor (Bohemian FC Dublin) | 24 |
| 1978/1979 | Dundalk FC | Dundalk FC | John Delamere (Sligo Rovers FC, Shelbourne FC Dublin) | 17 |
| 1979/1980 | Limerick United FC | Waterford FC | Alan Campbell (Shamrock Rovers FC Dublin) | 22 |

| Season | Champion | Runner-up | Top scorer | Goals |
|---|---|---|---|---|
| 1980/1981 | Athlone Town FC | Dundalk FC | Eugene Davis (Athlone Town FC) | 23 |
| 1981/1982 | Dundalk FC | Limerick United FC | Michael O'Connor (Athlone Town FC) | 22 |
| 1982/1983 | Athlone Town FC | Sligo Rovers FC | Noel Larkin (Athlone Town FC) | 18 |
| 1983/1984 | Shamrock Rovers FC Dublin | UCD | Alan Campbell (Shamrock Rovers FC Dublin) | 24 |
| 1984/1985 | Shamrock Rovers FC Dublin | Shamrock Rovers FC Dublin | Thomas Gaynor (Limerick City FC) Michael O'Connor (Athlone Town FC) | 17 |
| 1985/1986 | Shamrock Rovers FC Dublin | Shamrock Rovers FC Dublin | Tommy Gaynor (Limerick City FC) | 15 |
| 1986/1987 | Shamrock Rovers FC Dublin | Shamrock Rovers FC Dublin | Michael Byrne (Shamrock Rovers FC Dublin) | 12 |
| 1987/1988 | Dundalk FC | Dundalk FC | Jonathan Speak (Derry City FC) | 24 |
| 1988/1989 | Derry City FC | Derry City FC | William Robert Hamilton (NIR, Limerick City FC) | 21 |
| 1989/1990 | St. Patrick's Athletic FC Dublin | Bray Wanderers FC | Mark Ennis (St. Patrick's Athletic FC Dublin) | 19 |
| 1990/1991 | Dundalk FC | Galway United FC | Peter Hanrahan (Dundalk FC) | 18 |
| 1991/1992 | Shelbourne FC Dublin | Bohemian FC Dublin | John Caulfield (Cork City FC) | 16 |
| 1992/1993 | Cork City FC | Shelbourne FC Dublin | Pat Morley (Cork City FC) | 20 |
| 1993/1994 | Shamrock Rovers FC Dublin | Sligo Rovers FC | Stephen Geoghegan (Shamrock Rovers FC Dublin) | 23 |
| 1994/1995 | Dundalk FC | Derry City FC | John Caulfield (Cork City FC) | 16 |
| 1995/1996 | St. Patrick's Athletic FC Dublin | Shelbourne FC Dublin | Stephen Geoghegan (Shelbourne FC Dublin) | 19 |
| 1996/1997 | Derry City FC | Shelbourne FC Dublin | Anthony Cousins (Shamrock Rovers FC Dublin) Stephen Geoghegan (Shelbourne FC Dublin) | 16 |
| 1997/1998 | St. Patrick's Athletic FC Dublin | Cork City FC | Stephen Geoghegan (Shelbourne FC Dublin) | 17 |
| 1998/1999 | St. Patrick's Athletic FC Dublin | Bray Wanderers FC | Trevor Molloy (St. Patrick's Athletic FC Dublin) | 15 |
| 1999/2000 | Shelbourne FC Dublin | Shelbourne FC Dublin | Patrick Morley (Cork City FC) | 20 |
| 2000/2001 | Bohemian FC Dublin | Bohemian FC Dublin | Glen Crowe (Bohemian FC Dublin) | 25 |
| 2001/2002 | Shelbourne FC Dublin | Dundalk FC | Glen Crowe (Bohemian FC Dublin) | 21 |
| 2002/2003 | Bohemian FC Dublin | Derry City FC (2000) | Glen Crowe (Bohemian FC Dublin) | 18 |
| 2003 | Shelbourne FC Dublin | Longford Town FC | Jason Byrne (Shelbourne FC Dublin) | 21 |
| 2004 | Shelbourne FC Dublin | Longford Town FC | Jason Byrne (Shelbourne FC Dublin) | 25 |
| 2005 | Cork City FC | Drogheda United FC | Jason Byrne (Shelbourne FC Dublin) | 22 |
| 2006 | Shelbourne FC Dublin | Derry City FC | Jason Byrne (Shelbourne FC Dublin) | 15 |
| 2007 | Drogheda United FC | Cork City FC | Dave Mooney (Longford Town FC) | 19 |
| 2008 | Bohemian FC Dublin | Bohemian FC Dublin | Dave Mooney (Cork City FC) Mark Quigley (St. Patrick's Athletic FC Dublin) Mark Farren (Derry City FC) | 15 |
| 2009 | Bohemian FC Dublin | Sporting Fingal | Gary Michael Nolan Twigg (SCO, Shamrock Rovers FC Dublin) | 24 |
| 2010 | Shamrock Rovers FC Dublin | Sligo Rovers FC | Gary Michael Nolan Twigg (SCO, Shamrock Rovers FC Dublin) | 20 |
| 2011 | Shamrock Rovers FC Dublin | Sligo Rovers FC | Eamon Zayed (LBY, Derry City FC) | 22 |
| 2012 | Sligo Rovers FC | Derry City FC | Gary Michael Nolan Twigg (SCO, Shamrock Rovers FC Dublin) | 22 |
| 2013 | St. Patrick's Athletic FC Dublin | Sligo Rovers FC | Rory Christopher Patterson (NIR, Derry City FC) | 18 |
| 2014 | Dundalk FC | St. Patrick's Athletic FC Dublin | Patrick James Hoban (Dundalk FC) Christopher Joseph Fagan (St. Patrick's Athletic FC Dublin) | 20 |
| 2015 | Dundalk FC | Dundalk FC | Richard Patrick Towell (Dundalk FC) | 25 |
| 2016 | Dundalk FC | Cork City FC | Seán Patrick Maguire (Cork City FC) | 18 |
| 2017 | Cork City FC | Cork City FC | Seán Patrick Maguire (Cork City FC) | 20 |
| 2018 | Dundalk FC | Dundalk FC | Patrick James Hoban (Dundalk FC) | 29 |
| 2019 | Dundalk FC | Shamrock Rovers FC | Joseph Ogedi Junior Chukwuemka Ogedi-Uzokwe (ENG, Derry City FC) | 14 |
| 2020 | Shamrock Rovers FC Dublin | Dundalk FC | Patrick James Hoban (Dundalk FC) | 10 |
| 2021 | Shamrock Rovers FC Dublin | St. Patrick's Athletic FC Dublin | Georgie Kelly (Bohemian FC Dublin) | 21 |
| 2022 | Shamrock Rovers FC Dublin | Derry City FC | Aidan Keena (Sligo Rovers FC) | 18 |

## NATIONAL CHAMPIONSHIP
### League of Ireland Premier Division 2022
(18.02.2022 – 06.11.2022)

### Results

**Round 1 [18.02.2022]**
Dundalk FC - Derry City 2-2(1-1)
Shelbourne FC - St. Patrick's Athletic 0-3(0-1)
Shamrock Rovers - UC Dublin 3-0(2-0)
Finn Harps-Drogheda Unit. 2-2(2-1)[04.04.22]
Sligo Rov. - Bohemian FC 0-1(0-1) [05.04.22]

**Round 2 [25.02.2022]**
Bohemian FC - Dundalk FC 2-2(2-1)
Derry City - Shamrock Rovers 2-1(0-0)
Drogheda United - Shelbourne FC 0-2(0-0)
St. Patrick's Athletic - Sligo Rovers 1-2(0-1)
UC Dublin - Finn Harps 0-0

**Round 3 [28.02.2022]**
Bohemian FC - St. Patrick's Athletic 1-0(0-0)
Derry City - Sligo Rovers 0-0
Dundalk FC - Finn Harps 3-0(1-0)
UC Dublin - Shelbourne FC 0-0
Shamrock Rovers - Drogheda United 3-1(2-0)

**Round 4 [04-05.03.2022]**
Drogheda United - UC Dublin 4-2(3-0)
Shelbourne FC - Derry City 0-1(0-0)
St. Patrick's Athl. - Shamrock Rovers 1-0(0-0)
Finn Harps - Bohemian FC 1-1(0-0)
Sligo Rovers - Dundalk FC 0-0

**Round 5 [11.03.2022]**
Drogheda United - Sligo Rovers 0-3(0-3)
Shelbourne FC - Dundalk FC 1-1(0-0)
Finn Harps - St. Patrick's Athletic 0-2(0-0)
Shamrock Rovers - Bohemian FC 1-0(1-0)
UC Dublin - Derry City 0-2(0-0) [04.04.2022]

**Round 6 [14.03.2022]**
Bohemian FC - Shelbourne FC 1-1(0-0)
Derry City - Drogheda United 2-0(1-0)
Dundalk FC - Shamrock Rovers 0-0
Sligo Rovers - Finn Harps 3-1(2-0)
St. Patrick's Athletic - UC Dublin 2-0(1-0)

**Round 7 [18.03.2022]**
UC Dublin - Bohemian FC 1-1(0-1)
Derry City - St. Patrick's Athletic 2-1(1-0)
Drogheda United - Dundalk FC 1-0(0-0)
Shelbourne FC - Finn Harps 0-3(0-1)
Shamrock Rovers - Sligo Rovers 2-2(0-2)

**Round 8 [01.04.2022]**
Bohemian FC - Derry City 1-2(1-0)
Dundalk FC - UC Dublin 2-0(1-0)
St. Patrick's Athl. - Drogheda United 1-1(0-1)
Sligo Rovers - Shelbourne FC 0-1(0-1)
Finn Harps - Shamrock Rovers 0-3(0-1)

**Round 9 [08-09.04.2022]**
Drogheda United - Bohemian FC 1-1(0-1)
Shelbourne FC - Shamrock Rovers 1-2(0-1)
St. Patrick's Athletic - Dundalk FC 0-0
Finn Harps - Derry City 1-2(0-1)
Sligo Rovers - UC Dublin 2-2(1-0)

**Round 10 [15.04.2022]**
Bohemian FC - Finn Harps 2-2(0-1)
Derry City - Shelbourne FC 1-2(1-0)
Dundalk FC - Sligo Rovers 2-1(2-0)
UC Dublin - Drogheda United 0-2(0-0)
Shamrock Rovers - St. Patrick's Athl. 1-0(0-0)

**Round 11 [18.04.2022]**
Shelbourne FC - Bohemian FC 1-4(1-2)
UC Dublin - St. Patrick's Athletic 1-2(0-0)
Finn Harps - Sligo Rovers 0-1(0-1)
Shamrock Rovers - Dundalk FC 1-0(0-0)
Drogheda United - Derry City 1-1(1-1)

**Round 12 [22-23.04.2022]**
Bohemian FC - Shamrock Rovers 1-3(0-2)
Derry City - UC Dublin 7-1(5-0)
Dundalk FC - Shelbourne FC 2-1(0-0)
St. Patrick's Athletic - Finn Harps 2-0(1-0)
Sligo Rovers - Drogheda United 3-2(2-1)

**Round 13 [29.04.2022]**
Bohemian FC - UC Dublin 3-0(1-0)
Dundalk FC - Drogheda United 4-1(1-0)
St. Patrick's Athletic - Derry City 0-4(0-3)
Sligo Rovers - Shamrock Rovers 1-1(0-1)
Finn Harps - Shelbourne FC 1-0(0-0)

**Round 14 [06.05.2022]**
Derry City - Bohemian FC 1-1(1-1)
Drogheda United - St. Patrick's Athl. 0-4(0-2)
Shelbourne FC - Sligo Rovers 2-1(2-0)
UC Dublin - Dundalk FC 2-2(0-1)
Shamrock Rovers - Finn Harps 3-1(3-1)

**Round 15 [13-14.05.2022]**
Dundalk FC - Bohemian FC 3-1(0-1)
Shelbourne FC - Drogheda United 1-0(0-0)
Shamrock Rovers - Derry City 1-0(0-0)
Finn Harps - UC Dublin 0-1(0-0)
Sligo Rovers - St. Patrick's Athletic 1-1(1-0)

**Round 16 [19-20.05.2022]**
UC Dublin - Shamrock Rovers 0-3(0-3)
Bohemian FC - Sligo Rovers 2-1(0-0)
Derry City - Dundalk FC 1-2(0-1)
Drogheda United - Finn Harps 3-1(0-0)
St. Patrick's Athletic - Shelbourne FC 1-2(1-1)

**Round 17 [23.05.2022]**
Drogheda United - Shamrock Rovers 1-0(1-0)
Shelbourne FC - UC Dublin 2-0(1-0)
Sligo Rovers - Derry City 2-1(1-1)
St. Patrick's Athletic - Bohemian FC 3-0(2-0)
Finn Harps - Dundalk FC 0-1(0-0)

**Round 18 [27.05.2022]**
Bohemian FC - Drogheda United 1-1(1-0)
Derry City - Finn Harps 2-2(1-1)
Dundalk FC - St. Patrick's Athletic 1-0(1-0)
UC Dublin - Sligo Rovers 1-1(0-0)
Shamrock Rovers - Shelbourne FC 2-0(2-0)

**Round 19**
St. Patrick's-Shamrock R. 1-2(0-0) [27.06.22]
Drogheda - UC Dublin 1-1(1-1) [01.08.22]
Shelbourne - Derry City 0-1(0-0) [29.08.22]
Sligo Rov. - Dundalk 0-3* *awarded* [29.08.22]
Finn Harps-Bohemian FC 0-2(0-0) [24.09.22]

*originally 2-0, Sligo Rovers FC fielded a suspended player.*

**Round 20 [17-18.06.2022]**
Bohemian FC - Shelbourne FC 1-0(1-0)
Derry City - Drogheda United 1-1(1-0)
Dundalk FC - Shamrock Rovers 1-0(0-0)
St. Patrick's Athletic - UC Dublin 2-1(0-0)
Sligo Rovers - Finn Harps 3-0(2-0)

**Round 21 [24.06.2022]**
Drogheda United - Sligo Rovers 0-0
Shelbourne FC - Dundalk FC 0-0
UC Dublin - Derry City 0-1(0-0)
Shamrock Rovers - Bohemian FC 1-0(0-0)
Finn Harps - St. Patrick's Athletic 2-2(0-1)

**Round 22 [01-02.07.2022]**
Bohemian FC - Derry City 2-3(0-1)
Dundalk FC - UC Dublin 0-0(0-0)
St. Patrick's Athletic - Drogheda 3-0(1-0)
Finn Harps - Shamrock Rovers 0-1(0-1)
Sligo Rovers - Shelbourne FC 3-1(2-1)

**Round 23 [07-08.07.2022]**
Derry City - St. Patrick's Athl. 0-0 [09.05.22]
Shamrock Rov.-Sligo Rov. 3-1(0-0) [09.05.22]
UC Dublin - Bohemian FC 1-3(1-2)
Drogheda United - Dundalk FC 1-0(1-0)
Shelbourne FC - Finn Harps 3-1(2-1)

**Round 24 [15-17.07.2022]**
Drogheda United - Bohemian FC 0-1(0-0)
St. Patrick's Athletic - Dundalk FC 1-1(1-0)
Finn Harps - Derry City 1-2(1-0)
Sligo Rovers - UC Dublin 0-2(0-1)
Shelbourne FC - Shamrock Rov 0-0 [22.09.22]

**Round 25 [22-23.07.2022]**
Dundalk FC - Finn Harps 3-0(3-0)
UC Dublin - Shelbourne FC 0-2(0-0)
Shamrock Rovers - Drogheda United 1-1(0-0)
Bohemian - St. Patrick's 1-3(0-2) [29.08.22]
Derry City - Sligo Rovers 1-0(1-0) [13.09.22]

**Round 26 [05-07.08.2022]**
Dundalk FC - Derry City 1-1(0-1)
Finn Harps - Drogheda United 3-0(2-0)
Sligo Rovers - Bohemian FC 2-1(0-0)
Shamrock R. - UC Dublin 1-0(1-0) [26.09.22]
Shelbourne - St. Patrick's 4-4(2-2) [03.10.22]

**Round 27 [12-14.08.2022]**
Bohemian FC - Dundalk FC 0-1(0-1)
Derry City - Shamrock Rovers 0-0
Drogheda United - Shelbourne FC 3-1(1-1)
UC Dublin - Finn Harps 2-1(1-1)
St. Patrick's Athletic - Sligo Rovers 1-0(1-0)

**Round 28 [19-21.08.2022]**
Drogheda United - Derry City 1-1(0-1)
Shelbourne FC - Bohemian FC 1-1(0-1)
UC Dublin - St. Patrick's Athletic 1-2(0-1)
Finn Harps - Sligo Rovers 3-2(2-0)
Shamrock Rovers - Dundalk FC 3-0(2-0)

**Round 29 [02-03.09.2022]**
Bohemian FC - Shamrock Rovers 1-0(0-0)
Derry City - UC Dublin 3-0(1-0)
Dundalk FC - Shelbourne FC 0-0
St. Patrick's Athletic - Finn Harps 2-1(2-1)
Sligo Rovers - Drogheda United 2-0(1-0)

**Round 30 [09-11.09.2022]**
Derry City - Bohemian FC 1-0(1-0)
Drogheda - St. Patrick's Athletic 0-2(0-0)
Shelbourne FC - Sligo Rovers 0-2(0-1)
UC Dublin - Dundalk FC 3-2(0-1)
Shamrock Rovers - Finn Harps 5-1(4-0)

**Round 31 [30.09.-01.10.2022]**
Bohemian FC - UC Dublin 1-0(1-0)
Dundalk FC - Drogheda United 2-0(2-0)
St. Patrick's Athletic - Derry City 0-1(0-0)
Finn Harps - Shelbourne FC 1-1(0-0)
Sligo Rovers - Shamrock Rovers 1-3(0-2)

**Round 32 [07-09.10.2022]**
Bohemian FC - Drogheda United 0-1(0-0)
Derry City - Finn Harps 3-0(1-0)
Dundalk FC - St. Patrick's Athletic 1-2(1-1)
UC Dublin - Sligo Rovers 0-2(0-1)
Shamrock Rovers - Shelbourne FC 3-2(1-2)

**Round 33 [14-16.10.2022]**
St. Patrick's Athletic - Bohemian FC 3-1(1-0)
Finn Harps - Dundalk FC 1-2(0-2)
Drogheda United - Shamrock Rovers 1-1(1-1)
Shelbourne - UC Dublin 1-1(1-0) [24.10.2022]
Sligo Rovers - Derry City 0-0 [24.10.2022]

**Round 34 [21.10.2022]**
Bohemian FC - Finn Harps 2-2(0-0)
Derry City - Shelbourne FC 1-1(0-0)
Dundalk FC - Sligo Rovers 3-3(1-1)
UC Dublin - Drogheda United 2-1(1-1)
Shamrock Rov - St. Patrick's Athletic 4-1(2-1)

**Round 35 [28-30.10.2022]**
Dundalk FC - Bohemian FC 2-1(2-0)
Shelbourne FC - Drogheda United 6-0(4-0)
Sligo Rovers - St. Patrick's Athletic 1-0(0-0)
Finn Harps - UC Dublin 1-3(1-1)
Shamrock Rovers - Derry City 1-0(1-0)

**Round 36 [06.11.2022]**
Bohemian FC - Sligo Rovers 3-1(1-0)
Derry City - Dundalk FC 0-1(0-1)
Drogheda United - Finn Harps 2-0(1-0)
St. Patrick's Athletic - Shelbourne FC 4-0(3-0)
UC Dublin - Shamrock Rovers 0-2(0-1)

## Final Standings

| | | Total | | | | | Home | | | | | Away | | | | |
|---|---|---|---|---|---|---|---|---|---|---|---|---|---|---|---|---|
| 1. | **Shamrock Rovers FC Dublin** | 36 | 24 | 7 | 5 | 61 - 22 | **79** | 16 | 2 | 0 | 39 - 10 | 8 | 5 | 5 | 22 - 12 |
| 2. | Derry City FC | 36 | 18 | 12 | 6 | 53 - 27 | **66** | 8 | 7 | 3 | 28 - 13 | 10 | 5 | 3 | 25 - 14 |
| 3. | Dundalk FC | 36 | 18 | 12 | 6 | 53 - 30 | **66** | 12 | 5 | 1 | 35 - 13 | 6 | 7 | 5 | 18 - 17 |
| 4. | St. Patrick's Athletic FC Dublin | 36 | 18 | 7 | 11 | 57 - 37 | **61** | 10 | 3 | 5 | 28 - 16 | 8 | 4 | 6 | 29 - 21 |
| 5. | Sligo Rovers FC | 36 | 13 | 10 | 13 | 47 - 44 | **49** | 8 | 5 | 5 | 24 - 20 | 5 | 5 | 8 | 23 - 24 |
| 6. | Bohemian FC Dublin | 36 | 12 | 10 | 14 | 45 - 46 | **46** | 7 | 5 | 6 | 25 - 23 | 5 | 5 | 8 | 20 - 23 |
| 7. | Shelbourne FC Dublin | 36 | 10 | 11 | 15 | 40 - 49 | **41** | 5 | 6 | 7 | 23 - 25 | 5 | 5 | 8 | 17 - 24 |
| 8. | Drogheda United FC | 36 | 9 | 11 | 16 | 34 - 58 | **38** | 7 | 6 | 5 | 20 - 21 | 2 | 5 | 11 | 14 - 37 |
| 9. | University College Dublin AFC (*Relegation Play-offs*) | 36 | 6 | 8 | 22 | 28 - 67 | **26** | 3 | 5 | 10 | 14 - 29 | 3 | 3 | 12 | 14 - 38 |
| 10. | Finn Harps FC Ballybofey (*Relegated*) | 36 | 4 | 8 | 24 | 33 - 71 | **20** | 3 | 4 | 11 | 17 - 28 | 1 | 4 | 13 | 16 - 43 |

### Top goalscorers:

| | | |
|---|---|---|
| 18 | **Aidan Keena** | *Sligo Rovers FC* |
| 14 | Eoin Doyle | *St. Patrick's Athletic FC Dublin* |
| 11 | Graham Dylan Burke | *Shamrock Rovers FC* |
| 11 | Jamie McGonigle (NIR) | *Derry City FC* |
| 11 | Sean Boyd | *Shelbourne FC Dublin* |

## Relegation Play-offs [11.11.2022]

University College Dublin AFC - Waterford FC                    1-0(1-0)
University College Dublin AFC remains at first level for 2023.

# NATIONAL CUP
## FAI Cup 2022

### First Round [29-31.07.2022]

| | | | | |
|---|---|---|---|---|
| Maynooth University Town FC - Villa FC | 2-1(0-0) | Derry City FC - Oliver Bond Celtic FC | 7-0(4-0) |
| Treaty United FC Limerick - Usher Celtic FC | 5-0(1-0) | Lucan United FC - Killester Donnycarney FC | 3-0(2-0) |
| Dundalk FC - Longford Town FC | 4-0(0-0) | Salthill Devon FC - Malahide United FC | 2-2 aet; 5-6 pen |
| University College Dublin AFC - Cockhill Celtic | 3-0(2-0) | Bonagee United FC Letterkenny - Pike Rovers FC | 6-0(3-0) |
| Drogheda United FC - Athlone Town AFC | 5-1(3-0) | St. Patrick's Athletic FC Dublin - Waterford FC | 2-3(2-3) |
| Bray Wanderers FC - Shelbourne FC Dublin | 0-3(0-2) | Bluebell United FC - Galway United FC | 0-7(0-3) |
| Finn Harps FC Ballybofey - Bohemian FC Dublin | 1-3(1-2) | Cobh Ramblers FC - Cork City FC | 0-1(0-1) |
| Bangor Celtic FC Dublin - Shamrock Rovers FC | 0-4(0-1) | Sligo Rovers FC - Wexford FC Crossabeg | 1-2(0-0,1-1) |

### 1/8-Finals [26-28.08.2022]

| | | | |
|---|---|---|---|
| Lucan United FC - Bohemian FC Dublin | 0-2(0-2) | Bonagee United FC - Shelbourne FC Dublin | 0-4(0-1) |
| Derry City FC - Cork City FC | 2-0(1-0) | Maynooth University Town - Treaty United FC | 0-3(0-1) |
| Galway United FC - University College Dublin AFC | 2-3(1-1) | Malahide United FC - Waterford FC | 0-6(0-4) |
| Wexford FC Crossabeg - Dundalk FC | 2-3(0-1,2-2) | Drogheda United FC - Shamrock Rovers FC Dublin | 1-2(0-1,1-1) |

### Quarter-Finals [16-18.09.2022]

| | | | |
|---|---|---|---|
| Treaty United FC Limerick - U. College Dublin AFC | 4-1(2-0) | Shelbourne FC Dublin - Bohemian FC Dublin | 3-0(2-0) |
| Waterford FC - Dundalk FC | 3-2(2-1) | Derry City FC - Shamrock Rovers FC Dublin | 3-1(1-0,1-1) |

### Semi-Finals [16.10.2022]

| | | | |
|---|---|---|---|
| Derry City FC - Treaty United FC Limerick | 2-1(2-1) | Waterford FC - Shelbourne FC Dublin | 0-1(0-1) |

### Final

13.11.2022; Aviva Stadium, Dublin; Referee: Damien MacGraith; Attendance: 32,412
**Derry City FC - Shelbourne FC Dublin**                    **4-0(2-0)**

**Derry City**: Brian Maher, Ronan Boyce, Shane McEleney (82.Ciarán Coll), Mark Gerard Connolly, Cameron McJannett, Cameron Dummigan, William Luke Patching (89.Jordan John McEneff), Patrick McEleney (Cap), Ryan Graydon (82.Joseph Thomson), Michael Duffy (89.Brandon Kavanagh), Jamie McGonigle (76.Oluwaseun Ewerogba Akintunde). Trainer: Ruaidhri Higgins (Northern Ireland).

**Shelbourne FC**: Brendan Clarke, John Ross Wilson, Stephan Negru, Luke Byrne (Cap), Shane Anthony Griffin, Shane Farrell (46.Brian McManus), Jonathan Lunney, Gavin Molloy (70.Mark Coyle), Aodh Dervin (64.Kameron Malcom Ledwidge), Jack Moylan, Sean Boyd. Trainer: Damien Anthony Duff.

**Goals:** 1-0 Jamie McGonigle (18), 2-0 Cameron McJannett (35), 3-0 Cameron McJannett (61), 4-0 Jordan John McEneff (90+2 penalty).

## Bohemian Football Club Dublin

| | | | |
|---|---|---|---|
| **Founded**: | 06.09.1890 | | |
| **Stadium**: | Dalymount Park, Dublin (3,640) | | |
| **Trainer**: | Keith Long | | 14.11.1973 |
| [30.08.2022] | Derek Pender | | 02.10.1983 |
| [14.10.2022] | Declan Devine | | 15.09.1973 |

| Goalkeepers: | DOB | M | (s) | G |
|---|---|---|---|---|
| Reece Byrne | 20.11.2004 | 1 | | |
| Jon McCracken (SCO) | 24.05.2000 | 5 | | |
| Tadhg Ryan | 01.03.1997 | 12 | | |
| James Anthony Talbot | 24.04.1997 | 18 | | |
| **Defenders:** | **DOB** | **M** | **(s)** | **G** |
| Ryan Burke | 23.11.2000 | 4 | (1) | |
| Cian Byrne | 31.01.2003 | | (1) | |
| Jordan Doherty | 29.08.2000 | 23 | (9) | 1 |
| Rory Feely | 03.01.1997 | 21 | (6) | 2 |
| James Finnerty | 01.02.1999 | 3 | (4) | |
| Grant Dean Horton (ENG) | 13.09.2001 | 11 | | 1 |
| Ciaran Kelly | 04.07.1998 | 31 | (3) | 1 |
| Joshua Kerr (SCO) | 24.02.1998 | 6 | | |
| Jake McCormack | 04.08.2004 | | (1) | |
| Max Murphy | 02.06.2001 | 17 | (7) | |
| Samuel James Packham (ENG) | 08.11.2001 | 5 | (1) | |
| Tyreke Wilson | 02.12.1999 | 22 | (3) | 1 |
| **Midfielders:** | **DOB** | **M** | **(s)** | **G** |
| Derinsola Adewale | 28.06.2005 | | (1) | |
| Liam Burt (SCO) | 01.02.1999 | 20 | (8) | 6 |
| James Clarke | 28.01.2001 | 12 | (1) | 3 |
| Laurenz Dehl (GER) | 12.12.2001 | 1 | | |
| Dawson Devoy | 20.11.2001 | 20 | (2) | 8 |
| Aaron Doran | 23.05.2003 | 1 | (1) | |
| Jordan Michael Flores (ENG) | 04.10.1995 | 22 | (6) | 3 |
| Conor Thomas Levingston | 21.01.1998 | 21 | (4) | |
| Stephen Anthony Mallon | 07.02.1999 | 4 | (6) | 1 |
| Declan McDaid (SCO) | 22.11.1995 | 9 | (6) | 2 |
| John Joshua McKiernan (ENG) | 18.01.2002 | | (1) | |
| James McManus | 01.03.2005 | 4 | (9) | |
| Jamie Mullins | 29.09.2004 | 3 | (14) | |
| John Anthony James O'Sullivan | 18.09.1993 | 5 | (3) | 1 |
| Kristopher David Twardek (CAN) | 08.03.1997 | 24 | (5) | 1 |
| **Forwards:** | **DOB** | **M** | **(s)** | **G** |
| Jonathan Afolabi | 14.01.2000 | | (3) | |
| Ryan Michael McClean Cassidy | 02.03.2001 | 1 | (7) | |
| Alistair Coote (SCO) | 11.06.1998 | 26 | (4) | 2 |
| Lido Lotefa (COD) | 08.04.2000 | | (2) | |
| Joseph Ogedi Junior Chukwuemka Ogedi-Uzokwe (ENG) | 03.03.1994 | 14 | (5) | 4 |
| Promise Omochere (NGA) | 18.10.2000 | 19 | (3) | 5 |
| Ethon Sean O'Driscoll Varian | 11.08.2002 | 11 | (2) | 2 |

## Derry City Football Club

| | | | |
|---|---|---|---|
| **Founded**: | 1928 | | |
| **Stadium**: | "Ryan McBride" Brandywell Stadium, Derry (3,700) | | |
| **Trainer**: | Ruaidhri Higgins (NIR) | | 23.10.1984 |

| Goalkeepers: | DOB | M | (s) | G |
|---|---|---|---|---|
| Nathan James Gartside (NIR) | 08.03.1998 | 2 | | |
| Brian Maher | 01.11.2000 | 34 | | |
| **Defenders:** | **DOB** | **M** | **(s)** | **G** |
| Ronan Boyce | 12.05.2001 | 24 | (4) | 3 |
| Ciarán Coll | 19.08.1991 | 12 | (6) | |
| Mark Gerard Connolly | 16.12.1991 | 11 | | |
| Cameron Dummigan (NIR) | 02.06.1996 | 33 | | 2 |
| Daniel Patrick Lafferty (NIR) | 18.05.1989 | 14 | (11) | |
| Daithí McCallion (NIR) | 08.04.2005 | | (1) | |
| Shane McEleney (NIR) | 31.01.1991 | 27 | (3) | |
| Cameron McJannett (ENG) | 06.09.1998 | 34 | | 2 |
| Eoin Toal (NIR) | 15.02.1999 | 19 | (1) | 1 |
| **Midfielders:** | **DOB** | **M** | **(s)** | **G** |
| Sadou Diallo (ENG) | 10.06.1999 | 11 | (2) | 1 |
| Declan Glass (SCO) | 07.06.2000 | 2 | (2) | |
| Ciaron Harkin (NIR) | 15.01.1996 | 2 | | |
| Brandon Kavanagh | 21.09.2000 | 23 | (8) | 1 |
| Jack Malone | 05.04.2000 | 1 | (2) | |
| Patrick McEleney (NIR) | 26.09.1992 | 21 | (6) | 1 |
| Jordan John McEneff | 08.01.2001 | | (3) | |
| Evan McLaughlin (NIR) | 30.03.2002 | | (12) | |
| William Luke Patching (ENG) | 18.10.1998 | 31 | (2) | 10 |
| Gerard Ciaran Storey (NIR) | 05.02.2002 | | (1) | |
| Joseph Thomson (SCO) | 14.01.1997 | 20 | (12) | 4 |
| **Forwards:** | **DOB** | **M** | **(s)** | **G** |
| Oluwaseun Ewerogba Akintunde (ENG) | 29.03.1996 | 14 | (19) | 6 |
| Michael Duffy (NIR) | 28.07.1994 | 8 | (5) | 3 |
| Cian Kavanagh | 03.01.2003 | 1 | (5) | 1 |
| Ryan Graydon | 11.04.1999 | 9 | (4) | 3 |
| Jamie McGonigle (NIR) | 05.03.1996 | 26 | (9) | 11 |
| Caoimhin Porter (NIR) | 01.04.2003 | 3 | | |
| Matthew Smith (SCO) | 13.03.1997 | 14 | (5) | 3 |

## Drogheda United Football Club

| | | | |
|---|---|---|---|
| **Founded**: | 1919 | | |
| **Stadium**: | Head in The Game Park, Drigheda (3,500) | | |
| **Trainer**: | Kevin Doherty | | 18.04.1990 |

| Goalkeepers: | DOB | M | (s) | G |
|---|---|---|---|---|
| Fiachra Pagel | | | (1) | |
| Samuel James Long (ENG) | 12.11.2002 | 15 | | |
| Colin McCabe | 06.01.1997 | 20 | | |
| Lee Steacy | 18.01.1993 | 1 | | |
| **Defenders:** | **DOB** | **M** | **(s)** | **G** |
| Keith Cowan | 23.08.1985 | 22 | (4) | |
| Dane Massey | 17.04.1988 | 28 | (3) | |
| Dylan Molloy | 07.11.2003 | | (2) | |
| Georgie Poynton | 28.08.1997 | 22 | (5) | 1 |
| Andrew Quinn | 24.01.2002 | 28 | (2) | |
| Callum Ralph | 03.02.2004 | | (2) | |
| Sean Patrick Roughan | 31.08.2003 | 15 | | |
| Evan Weir | 16.04.2002 | 24 | (3) | 4 |
| **Midfielders:** | **DOB** | **M** | **(s)** | **G** |
| Ryan Brennan | 11.11.1991 | 11 | (14) | 6 |
| James Clarke | 28.01.2001 | 18 | (5) | 1 |
| Gary Richard Deegan | 28.09.1987 | 33 | | 1 |
| Dylan Grimes | 10.03.1998 | 17 | (9) | |
| Luke Heeney | 06.02.1999 | 11 | (5) | |
| Mark Hughes | 28.04.1993 | 3 | (3) | |
| Darragh Markey | 23.05.1997 | 21 | (3) | 1 |
| Darragh Noone | 28.04.1997 | 5 | (4) | |
| Darragh Nugent | 01.03.2001 | 25 | (7) | 2 |
| Dayle Rooney | 24.02.1994 | 28 | (7) | 5 |
| Emre Topcu | 21.08.2005 | 1 | (3) | |
| **Forwards:** | **DOB** | **M** | **(s)** | **G** |
| Victor Arong (NGA) | 09.09.2004 | | (4) | |
| Mohamed Boudiaf | 15.06.2002 | | (2) | |
| Killian Cailloce | 09.12.2005 | | (1) | |
| Adam Foley (NIR) | 11.12.1989 | 12 | (10) | 2 |
| Chris Lyons | 08.05.1993 | 16 | (12) | 4 |
| Stevan Stanic-Floody (AUS) | 01.08.2003 | | (1) | |
| Dean Williams | 09.02.2000 | 20 | (10) | 6 |

## Dundalk Football Club

| | | |
|---|---|---|
| **Founded**: | 1903 | |
| **Stadium**: | Oriel Park, Dundalk (4,500) | |
| **Trainer**: | Stephen O'Donnell | 15.01.1986 |
| [20.04.2021] | James Magilton (NIR) | 06.05.1969 |
| [16.06.2021] | Vinny Perth | 02.08.1976 |

| Goalkeepers: | DOB | M | (s) | G |
|---|---|---|---|---|
| Peter Cherrie (SCO) | 01.10.1983 | 3 | | |
| Nathan Shepperd (WAL) | 10.09.2000 | 33 | | |
| **Defenders:** | **DOB** | **M** | **(s)** | **G** |
| Samuel Bone (ENG) | 06.02.1998 | 23 | (9) | 1 |
| Andrew Boyle | 07.03.1991 | 31 | (1) | |
| Mark Gerard Connolly | 16.12.1991 | 20 | | 1 |
| Brian Gartland | 04.11.1986 | 4 | (1) | |
| Darragh John Leahy | 15.04.1998 | 28 | | 3 |
| Lewis Jon Macari (SCO) | 08.02.2002 | 33 | (1) | 1 |
| Robert McCourt | 06.04.1998 | 2 | (1) | |
| **Midfielders:** | **DOB** | **M** | **(s)** | **G** |
| Joseph Anthony Adams (WAL) | 13.02.2001 | 20 | (13) | |
| Robert Benson | 07.05.1992 | 19 | (10) | 3 |
| Paul Doyle | 10.04.1998 | 16 | (9) | 2 |

| | DOB | M | (s) | G |
|---|---|---|---|---|
| Mark Hanratty | 19.07.2002 | 1 | (2) | |
| Alfie Lewis (ENG) | 28.09.1999 | 11 | (1) | 1 |
| John Martin | 05.01.1999 | 10 | (21) | 2 |
| John Mountney | 22.02.1993 | 7 | (3) | |
| Gregory Sloggett | 03.07.1996 | 30 | (2) | 1 |
| Keith Ward | 12.10.1990 | 10 | (22) | 5 |
| Daniel Patrick Williams (WAL) | 19.04.2001 | 7 | (3) | |
| **Forwards:** | **DOB** | **M** | **(s)** | **G** |
| Steven Bradley (SCO) | 17.03.2002 | 23 | (9) | 6 |
| Runar Hauge (NOR) | 01.09.2001 | 5 | (4) | 2 |
| Patrick Jefferson Hoban | 28.07.1991 | 21 | (4) | 9 |
| Daniel Kelly | 21.05.1996 | 20 | (3) | 6 |
| David McMillan | 14.12.1988 | 9 | (19) | 2 |
| Ryan O'Kane (NIR) | 16.08.2003 | 10 | (8) | 2 |

## Finn Harps Football Club Ballybofey

| | | |
|---|---|---|
| **Founded**: | 1954 | |
| **Stadium**: | Finn Park, Ballybofey (6,000) | |
| **Trainer**: | Oliver Horgan | 17.02.1968 |

| Goalkeepers: | DOB | M | (s) | G |
|---|---|---|---|---|
| Mark Anthony McGinley | 26.03.1990 | 20 | | |
| James Karl McKeown (ENG) | 24.07.1989 | 12 | | |
| Gavin Mulreany | 18.03.1998 | 4 | | |
| **Defenders:** | **DOB** | **M** | **(s)** | **G** |
| Erol Alkan (TUR) | 16.02.1994 | 3 | (4) | |
| Gary Boylan | 24.04.1996 | 12 | | |
| Ethan Boyle | 04.01.1997 | 32 | | 4 |
| Regan Donelon | 17.04.1996 | 25 | | |
| Damien Duffy | 12.11.2002 | | (1) | |
| José Carrillo Mancilla (ESP) | 04.03.1995 | 17 | (6) | 1 |
| Shaun McDermott | 19.02.2002 | | (1) | |
| Liam McGing (AUS) | 11.12.1998 | 3 | (2) | |
| Harry Nicolson (SCO) | 16.01.2001 | 2 | (5) | |
| Rob Slevin | 14.07.1998 | 28 | (2) | |
| Conor Tourish | 02.03.1995 | 24 | (3) | 5 |
| David Webster | 07.04.1990 | 9 | | |

| Midfielders: | DOB | M | (s) | G |
|---|---|---|---|---|
| Ryan Michael Connolly | 13.01.1992 | 25 | (1) | 2 |
| Dylan Duncan (ENG) | 25.01.1999 | 7 | (8) | |
| Bastien Charles Patrick Héry (MAD) | 23.03.1992 | 9 | (9) | |
| Nathan Logue-Cunningham | 04.02.2001 | | (1) | |
| Adam McCaffrey | 13.12.2002 | | (2) | |
| Barry McNamee (NIR) | 17.02.1992 | 34 | | 3 |
| Elie Gael N'Zeyi (FRA) | 17.10.1997 | 23 | | |
| Ryan Gavin Rainey | 11.10.1996 | 27 | (5) | 1 |
| Mark Anthony Timlin | 07.11.1994 | 5 | (20) | 1 |
| **Forwards:** | **DOB** | **M** | **(s)** | **G** |
| Jesse Devers | 11.01.1997 | 4 | (6) | |
| Robert Jones (SCO) | 22.09.1995 | 5 | (7) | 2 |
| Yousef Mahdy | 20.01.1998 | 12 | (8) | 1 |
| Eric Lemond McWoods (USA) | 21.10.1995 | 18 | (7) | 5 |
| Filip Mihaljević (CRO) | 09.03.1992 | 31 | (5) | 6 |
| Sean O'Donnell | 02.05.2004 | | (3) | |
| Luke Rudden | 23.04.2002 | 1 | (20) | 1 |
| Jaime Siaj Romero (JOR) | 16.12.1995 | 4 | (5) | 1 |

## St. Patrick's Athletic Football Club Dublin

| | | |
|---|---|---|
| **Founded**: | 1929 | |
| **Stadium**: | Richmond Park, Dublin (5,340) | |
| **Trainer**: | Timothy Clancy | 08.06.1984 |

| Goalkeepers: | DOB | M | (s) | G |
|---|---|---|---|---|
| Joseph Tetteh Anang (ENG) | 08.06.2000 | 24 | | |
| David Odumosu | 23.03.2001 | 2 | | |
| Daniel Rogers | 23.03.1994 | 10 | | |
| **Defenders:** | **DOB** | **M** | **(s)** | **G** |
| James Abankwah | 16.01.2004 | 5 | (6) | |
| Patrick Barrett | 22.07.1993 | 2 | | |
| Ian Bermingham | 08.01.1989 | 6 | (6) | |
| Anthony Patrick Breslin | 13.02.1997 | 31 | (1) | 2 |
| Harry Wolliam Brockbank (ENG) | 26.09.1998 | 9 | (2) | |
| Barry Noel Cotter | 04.12.1998 | 10 | (1) | 2 |
| Sam Curtis | 01.12.2005 | 18 | | |
| Tom Grivosti (ENG) | 15.06.1999 | 29 | (1) | 1 |
| Joseph Redmond | 23.01.2000 | 36 | | 1 |
| Jack David Scott (NIR) | 22.09.2002 | 12 | (4) | 1 |
| **Midfielders:** | **DOB** | **M** | **(s)** | **G** |
| Darragh Burns (NIR) | 06.08.2002 | 18 | (4) | 4 |

| | DOB | M | (s) | G |
|---|---|---|---|---|
| Christopher Forrester | 17.12.1992 | 34 | | 5 |
| Jamie Lennon | 09.05.1998 | 9 | (3) | |
| Darius Lipsiuc | 16.09.2005 | | (1) | |
| Jason McClelland | 03.05.1997 | 8 | (12) | 1 |
| Ben McCormack | 04.04.2003 | 7 | (10) | 2 |
| Adam Murphy | 08.04.2005 | 1 | (3) | |
| Adam Kieran O'Reilly | 11.05.2001 | 30 | (4) | 2 |
| Thijs Timmermans (NED) | 25.07.1998 | 6 | (1) | 1 |
| **Forwards:** | **DOB** | **M** | **(s)** | **G** |
| Serge Atakayi (FIN) | 30.01.1999 | 10 | (3) | 4 |
| Ronan Liam Coughlan | 02.10.1995 | 3 | (7) | |
| Eoin Doyle | 12.03.1988 | 34 | (2) | 14 |
| Mark Doyle | 19.11.1996 | 18 | (14) | 5 |
| Billy King (SCO) | 12.05.1994 | 20 | (9) | 4 |
| Tunde Owolabi (BEL) | 26.07.1996 | 4 | (24) | 5 |
| Kyle Robinson | 08.11.2002 | | (7) | 1 |

## Shamrock Rovers Football Club Dublin

| | | |
|---|---|---|
| **Founded**: | 1899 | |
| **Stadium**: | Tallaght Stadium, Dublin (8,000) | |
| **Trainer**: | Stephen Bradley | 19.11.1984 |

| Goalkeepers: | DOB | M | (s) | G |
|---|---|---|---|---|
| Alan Mannus (NIR) | 19.05.1982 | 34 | | |
| Léon-Maurice Pöhls (GER) | 01.05.1997 | 2 | (1) | |
| **Defenders:** | **DOB** | **M** | **(s)** | **G** |
| Daniel Cleary | 09.03.1996 | 10 | (1) | 4 |
| Barry Noel Cotter | 04.12.1998 | 6 | (9) | 1 |
| Kieran Cruise | 03.01.2004 | | (1) | |
| Sean Gannon | 11.07.1991 | 17 | (9) | 1 |
| Lee Grace | 01.12.1992 | 28 | (2) | |
| Sean Hoare | 15.03.1994 | 28 | (5) | 2 |
| Sean Kavanagh | 20.01.1994 | 15 | (4) | |
| Carl Lennox | 24.10.2004 | | (1) | |
| Roberto Carlos Lopes (CPV) | 17.06.1992 | 26 | (1) | 1 |
| Andrew Lyons | 02.08.2000 | 26 | (5) | 7 |
| **Midfielders:** | **DOB** | **M** | **(s)** | **G** |
| Jack Byrne | 24.04.1996 | 25 | (4) | 2 |

| | DOB | M | (s) | G |
|---|---|---|---|---|
| Justin Ferizaj | 13.01.2005 | 2 | (3) | |
| Ronan Michael Finn | 21.12.1987 | 18 | (4) | |
| Daniel Mândroiu | 20.10.1998 | 15 | (3) | 7 |
| Christopher John McCann | 21.07.1987 | 5 | (8) | |
| Gary O'Neill | 27.01.1995 | 29 | (3) | |
| Simon Power | 13.05.1998 | | (3) | 1 |
| Viktor Serdenyuk (UKR) | 27.01.1996 | 1 | (2) | |
| Richard Towell | 17.07.1991 | 16 | (12) | 2 |
| Dylan Billy Watts | 11.04.1997 | 24 | (7) | 2 |
| **Forwards:** | **DOB** | **M** | **(s)** | **G** |
| Graham Dylan Burke | 21.09.1993 | 15 | (11) | 11 |
| Aidomo Emakhu | 26.10.2003 | 1 | (21) | 1 |
| Neil Farrugia | 19.05.1999 | 11 | (12) | 3 |
| Rory Nicholas Gaffney | 23.10.1989 | 31 | (4) | 10 |
| Aaron Greene | 02.01.1990 | 11 | (22) | 4 |
| Gideon Tetteh | 30.05.2005 | | (2) | |

## Shelbourne Football Club Dublin

| Goalkeepers: | DOB | M | (s) | G |
|---|---|---|---|---|
| Brendan Clarke | 17.09.1985 | 29 | | |
| Lewis Webb (WAL) | 12.09.2001 | 7 | | |
| **Defenders:** | **DOB** | **M** | **(s)** | **G** |
| Luke Browne | 06.10.2005 | | (1) | |
| Luke Byrne | 08.07.1993 | 34 | | |
| Shane Anthony Griffin | 08.09.1994 | 26 | (2) | |
| Joshua Giurgi | 18.06.2002 | 2 | (5) | |
| Conor Kane | 05.11.1998 | 27 | | |
| Kameron Malcom Ledwidge | 07.04.2001 | 21 | (13) | 1 |
| Stephan Negru | 24.07.2002 | 6 | | 1 |
| Aaron O'Driscoll | 04.04.1999 | 21 | (4) | |
| Adam Thomas (NZL) | 01.04.1992 | 4 | | |
| John Ross Wilson | 13.12.1998 | 25 | (5) | 1 |
| **Midfielders:** | **DOB** | **M** | **(s)** | **G** |
| Mark Coyle | 13.02.1997 | 15 | (6) | 1 |

| Founded: | 1895 | | | |
|---|---|---|---|---|
| Stadium: | Tolka Park, Drumcondra (4,400) | | | |
| Trainer: | Damien Anthony Duff | | | 02.03.1979 |

| Aodh Dervin | 21.07.1999 | 19 | (11) | 1 |
|---|---|---|---|---|
| Gavin Hodgins | 06.06.2005 | 1 | (4) | |
| Jonathan Lunney | 02.02.1998 | 19 | (6) | 2 |
| Jordan John McEneff | 08.01.2001 | 6 | (7) | |
| Brian McManus | 29.11.2001 | 15 | (9) | 2 |
| Gavin Molloy | 19.10.2001 | 15 | (4) | 2 |
| Jack Moylan | 01.09.2001 | 26 | (1) | 7 |
| Kyle O'Connor | 14.03.2003 | | (1) | |
| **Forwards:** | **DOB** | **M** | **(s)** | **G** |
| Stanley Anaebonam | 14.04.1999 | | (9) | |
| Sean Boyd | 20.06.1998 | 21 | (8) | 11 |
| Daniel Clive Carr (TRI) | 29.05.1994 | 8 | (19) | 2 |
| Shane Farrell | 26.06.2000 | 30 | (4) | 6 |
| Jad Hakiki | 23.06.2004 | 7 | (3) | |
| Daniel Thomas Hawkins (ENG) | 22.04.2001 | 2 | (3) | 1 |
| Matthew Smith (SCO) | 13.03.1997 | 10 | (1) | 2 |

## Sligo Rovers Football Club

| Goalkeepers: | DOB | M | (s) | G |
|---|---|---|---|---|
| Richard Brush (ENG) | 26.11.1984 | 8 | | |
| Edward McGinty | 05.08.1999 | 19 | | |
| Luke McNicholas | 01.01.2000 | 8 | | |
| Conor Walsh | 17.03.2005 | 1 | | |
| **Defenders:** | **DOB** | **M** | **(s)** | **G** |
| Lewis Banks (ENG) | 14.04.1997 | 23 | (4) | 1 |
| Shane Blaney | 20.01.1999 | 22 | (3) | |
| Garry Buckley | 19.08.1993 | 17 | | 2 |
| Éanna Clancy | 26.02.2004 | 1 | (4) | |
| Cameron James Evans (WAL) | 23.02.2001 | 1 | (1) | |
| Colm Horgan | 02.07.1994 | 17 | (4) | 1 |
| Seamas Keogh | 28.02.2002 | 1 | (15) | 1 |
| Patrick Kirk | 02.06.1998 | 27 | (6) | 1 |
| Robert McCourt | 06.04.1998 | 9 | (1) | |
| Nando Zen Pijnaker (NZL) | 25.02.1999 | 28 | (3) | 1 |

| Founded: | 1928 | | | |
|---|---|---|---|---|
| Stadium: | The Showgrounds, Sligo (3,873) | | | |
| Trainer: | Liam Buckley | | | 14.04.1960 |
| [22.05.2022] | John Russell | | | 18.05.1985 |

| Midfielders: | DOB | M | (s) | G |
|---|---|---|---|---|
| Kailin Barlow | 28.06.2003 | 3 | (9) | |
| Gregory Bolger | 09.09.1988 | 21 | (5) | |
| Robert Lee Burton (WAL) | 26.12.1999 | 9 | (3) | |
| Mark Byrne | 12.08.2000 | 3 | (7) | |
| David Cawley | 17.09.1991 | 13 | (9) | 2 |
| Adam McDonnell | 14.05.1997 | 29 | (3) | 3 |
| Niall Morahan | 30.05.2000 | 19 | (8) | |
| Karl O'Sullivan | 31.10.1999 | 20 | (9) | 3 |
| **Forwards:** | **DOB** | **M** | **(s)** | **G** |
| William Fitzgerald | 19.05.1999 | 31 | (4) | 2 |
| Jordan Patrick Dear Hamilton (CAN) | 17.03.1996 | 7 | (6) | 2 |
| Cillian Heaney | 18.04.2001 | | (12) | |
| Aidan Keena | 25.04.1999 | 30 | (2) | 18 |
| Frank Liivak (EST) | 07.07.1996 | 13 | (2) | 4 |
| Max Andrew Mata (NZL) | 10.07.2000 | 16 | (11) | 7 |

## University College Dublin Association Football Club

| Goalkeepers: | DOB | M | (s) | G |
|---|---|---|---|---|
| Lorcan Healy | 23.05.2000 | 17 | (1) | |
| Kian Moore | 31.03.2003 | 19 | (1) | |
| **Defenders:** | **DOB** | **M** | **(s)** | **G** |
| Luke Boore | 28.03.1999 | 2 | | |
| Ryan Bowden | 19.08.2003 | | (1) | |
| Mark Dignam | 17.04.1999 | 16 | (7) | 2 |
| Jamie Duggan | | 2 | | |
| Alex Dunne | 05.08.2002 | 12 | (4) | |
| Michael Gallagher | 09.07.2000 | 25 | (3) | |
| Harry McEvoy | 16.08.2001 | | (1) | |
| Harvey O'Brien | 31.10.2000 | 2 | (1) | |
| Evan Osam | 17.08.1977 | 31 | (1) | |
| John Ryan | 21.01.2004 | 9 | (11) | |
| Sam Todd (NIR) | 28.04.1998 | 34 | | 2 |
| Eric Yoro | 19.02.2004 | 14 | | |
| **Midfielders:** | **DOB** | **M** | **(s)** | **G** |
| Sean Brennan | 05.07.2001 | 23 | (5) | |
| Evan Caffrey | 27.02.2003 | 31 | (5) | 2 |
| Aaron Corish | | 1 | (2) | |

| Founded: | 1895 | | | |
|---|---|---|---|---|
| Stadium: | UCD Bowl, Dublin (3,000) | | | |
| Trainer: | Andrew Myler | | | 02.12.1975 |

| Dylan Duffy | 28.11.2002 | 25 | (6) | 3 |
|---|---|---|---|---|
| Eoin Farrell | 27.03.2002 | 2 | (2) | |
| Donal Higgins | 10.09.2001 | 17 | (14) | 2 |
| Tobi Jinad | 09.05.2003 | 1 | | |
| Dara Keane | 24.12.1998 | 20 | (1) | 2 |
| Jack Keaney | 18.01.1999 | 26 | (3) | 1 |
| Adam Lennon | 04.08.2002 | | (6) | |
| Daniel Norris | 17.02.2003 | 4 | (6) | |
| Harry O'Connor | 27.09.2005 | | (4) | |
| Matthew Scott | 08.02.2003 | | (1) | |
| Adam Verdon | 25.01.2002 | 7 | (6) | |
| **Forwards:** | **DOB** | **M** | **(s)** | **G** |
| Lennon Gill | 24.08.2004 | 2 | (4) | |
| John Haist | 05.12.1995 | 2 | (7) | |
| Liam Kerrigan | 09.05.2000 | 17 | (2) | 2 |
| Thomas Lonergan | 02.01.2004 | 11 | (8) | 6 |
| Alex Nolan I | 20.03.2003 | 9 | (17) | 2 |
| Alex Nolan II | 13.02.2005 | | (1) | |
| Colm Whelan | 29.06.2000 | 15 | | 4 |

Please note: Bray Wanderers FC and Cabinteely FC merged in the pre-season to create a revamped Bray Wanderers.

| | | | | | | | | | |
|---|---|---|---|---|---|---|---|---|---|
| 1. | Cork City FC (*Promoted*) | 32 | 20 | 8 | 4 | 63 | - | 22 | 68 |
| 2. | Waterford FC (*Promotion Play-offs*) | 32 | 20 | 4 | 8 | 70 | - | 34 | 64 |
| 3. | Galway United FC (*Promotion Play-offs*) | 32 | 17 | 9 | 6 | 56 | - | 30 | 60 |
| 4. | Longford Town FC (*Promotion Play-offs*) | 32 | 14 | 10 | 8 | 49 | - | 41 | 52 |
| 5. | Treaty United FC Limerick (*Promotion Play-offs*) | 32 | 11 | 11 | 10 | 37 | - | 43 | 44 |
| 6. | Wexford FC Crossabeg | 32 | 10 | 11 | 11 | 45 | - | 47 | 41 |
| 7. | Bray Wanderers FC | 32 | 6 | 9 | 17 | 30 | - | 62 | 27 |
| 8. | Athlone Town FC | 32 | 7 | 3 | 22 | 44 | - | 75 | 24 |
| 9. | Cobh Ramblers FC | 32 | 4 | 5 | 23 | 37 | - | 78 | 17 |

### Promotion Play-offs (1st / 2nd Level)

| | | | |
|---|---|---|---|
| **Semi-Finals [26/29-30.10.2022]** | Treaty United FC Limerick - Waterford FC | 1-4(0-2) | 3-3(3-1) |
| | Longford Town FC - Galway United FC | 2-2(1-0) | 0-3(0-1) |
| **Final [04.11.2022]** | Galway United FC - Waterford FC | 0-3(0-2) | |

Waterford FC were qualified for the Promotion/Relegation Play-off.

## NATIONAL TEAM

### INTERNATIONAL MATCHES
#### (16.07.2022 – 15.07.2023)

| | | | | |
|---|---|---|---|---|
| 24.09.2022 | Glasgow | *Scotland - Republic of Ireland* | *2-1(1-1)* | (UNL) |
| 27.09.2022 | Dublin | *Republic of Ireland - Armenia* | *3-2(1-0)* | (UNL) |
| 17.11.2022 | Dublin | *Republic of Ireland - Norway* | *1-2(0-1)* | (F) |
| 20.11.2022 | Attard | *Malta - Republic of Ireland* | *0-1(0-0)* | (F) |
| 22.03.2023 | Dublin | *Republic of Ireland - Latvia* | *3-2(2-2)* | (F) |
| 27.03.2023 | Dublin | *Republic of Ireland - France* | *0-1(0-0)* | (ECQ) |
| 16.06.2023 | Athína | *Greece - Republic of Ireland* | *2-1(1-1)* | (ECQ) |
| 19.06.2023 | Dublin | *Republic of Ireland - Gibraltar* | *3-0(0-0)* | (ECQ) |

**24.09.2022 SCOTLAND - REPUBLIC OF IRELAND 2-1(1-1)** 3rd UEFA Nations League B, Group 1
Hampden Park, Glasgow; Referee: Sandro Schärer (Switzerland); Attendance: 48,853
**IRL:** Gavin Okeroghene Bazunu, Dara Joseph O'Shea, Nathan Michael Collins, John Egan (Cap), Jason Paul Knight, Jayson Patrick Molumby (76.Alan James Browne), Matthew James Doherty (76.Séamus Coleman), Joshua Jon Cullen, James Joseph McClean (83.Robert Brady), Michael Oluwadurotimi Obafemi (60.Chiedozie Ogbene), Troy Daniel Parrott (76.Callum Jack Robinson). Trainer: Stephen Kenny.
**Goal:** John Egan (18).

**27.09.2022 REPUBLIC OF IRELAND - ARMENIA 3-2(1-0)** 3rd UEFA Nations League B, Group 1
Aviva Stadium, Dublin; Referee: Rade Obrenovič (Slovenia); Attendance: 41,719
**IRL:** Gavin Okeroghene Bazunu, Dara Joseph O'Shea, Nathan Michael Collins, John Egan (Cap), Jason Paul Knight (76.Alan James Browne), Jayson Patrick Molumby (51.Conor Hourihane), Matthew James Doherty, Jeffrey Patrick Hendrick, Robert Brady, Michael Oluwadurotimi Obafemi (86.Scott Andrew Hogan), Troy Daniel Parrott (76.Callum Jack Robinson). Trainer: Stephen Kenny.
**Goals:** John Egan (18), Michael Oluwadurotimi Obafemi (52), Robert Brady (90+1 penalty).

**17.11.2022 REPUBLIC OF IRELAND - NORWAY 1-2(0-1)** Friendly International
Aviva Stadium, Dublin; Referee: Allard Lindhout (Netherlands); Attendance: 41,120
**IRL:** Gavin Okeroghene Bazunu, Matthew James Doherty, Nathan Michael Collins, John Egan (Cap), Dara Joseph O'Shea, Callum Joshua Ryan O'Dowda (75.Robert Brady), Joshua Jon Cullen, Jayson Patrick Molumby (82.Jeffrey Patrick Hendrick), Alan James Browne (89.Evan Joe Ferguson), Callum Jack Robinson, Michael Oluwadurotimi Obafemi (75.Chiedozie Ogbene). Trainer: Stephen Kenny.
**Goal:** Alan James Browne (69).

**20.11.2022 MALTA - REPUBLIC OF IRELAND 0-1(0-0)** Friendly International
Ta'Qali National Stadium, Attard; Referee: Chrysovalantis Theouli (Cyprus); Attendance: n/a
**IRL:** Caoimhin Odhrán Kelleher, Séamus Coleman (Cap), Nathan Michael Collins, John Egan, Matthew James Doherty, Alan James Browne (66.Jeffrey Patrick Hendrick), Joshua Jon Cullen, Jamie Terence McGrath, James Joseph McClean (66.Callum Joshua Ryan O'Dowda), Callum Jack Robinson (85.Mark Sykes), Chiedozie Ogbene (76.Evan Joe Ferguson). Trainer: Stephen Kenny.
**Goal:** Callum Jack Robinson (55).

**22.03.2023 REPUBLIC OF IRELAND - LATVIA 3-2(2-2)** Friendly International
Aviva Stadium, Dublin; Referee: Andrei Chivulete (Romania); Attendance: 41,211
**IRL:** Caoimhin Odhrán Kelleher, Andrew Abiola Omobamidele (63.John Egan), Nathan Michael Collins, Dara Joseph O'Shea, Matthew James Doherty (Cap) (63.Chiedozie Ogbene), Alan James Browne, Jayson Patrick Molumby, William Anthony Patrick Smallbone (82.Jeffrey Patrick Hendrick), Callum Joshua Ryan O'Dowda (77.James Joseph McClean), Evan Joe Ferguson (73.Troy Daniel Parrott), Michael Oluwadurotimi Obafemi (63.Michael Andrew Johnston). Trainer: Stephen Kenny.
**Goals:** Callum Joshua Ryan O'Dowda (6), Evan Joe Ferguson (17), Chiedozie Ogbene (65).

**27.03.2023**    **REPUBLIC OF IRELAND - FRANCE**      **0-1(0-0)**      17<sup>th</sup> EC. Qualifiers

Aviva Stadium, Dublin; Referee: Artur Manuel Ribeiro Soares Dias (Portugal); Attendance: 50,219
**IRL:** Gavin Okeroghene Bazunu, Dara Joseph O'Shea (78.Alan James Browne), Nathan Michael Collins, John Egan, Séamus Coleman (Cap), Joshua Jon Cullen, Jayson Patrick Molumby (86.Michael Oluwadurotimi Obafemi), Matthew James Doherty (77.James Joseph McClean), Jason Paul Knight (77.Michael Andrew Johnston), Chiedozie Ogbene, Evan Joe Ferguson (65.Adam Uche Idah). Trainer: Stephen Kenny.

**16.06.2023**    **GREECE - REPUBLIC OF IRELAND**      **2-1(1-1)**      17<sup>th</sup> EC. Qualifiers

OPAP Arena, Athína; Referee: Harald Lechner (Austria); Attendance: 17,452
**IRL:** Gavin Okeroghene Bazunu, Darragh Patrick Lenihan (89.Troy Daniel Parrott), Nathan Michael Collins, John Egan (Cap), Joshua Jon Cullen, Jayson Patrick Molumby (81.Michael Oluwadurotimi Obafemi), Matthew James Doherty [*sent off90+5*], Callum Joshua Ryan O'Dowda (53.James Joseph McClean), William Anthony Patrick Smallbone (53.Jason Paul Knight), Evan Joe Ferguson, Adam Uche Idah (46.Michael Andrew Johnston). Trainer: Stephen Kenny.
**Goal:** Nathan Michael Collins (29).

**19.06.2023**    **REPUBLIC OF IRELAND - GIBRALTAR**      **3-0(0-0)**      17<sup>th</sup> EC. Qualifiers

Aviva Stadium, Dublin; Referee: Marian Alexandru Barbu (Romania); Attendance: 42,156
**IRL:** Gavin Okeroghene Bazunu, Dara Joseph O'Shea, Nathan Michael Collins (46.Michael Andrew Johnston), John Egan, Joshua Jon Cullen, Jason Paul Knight (84.Jeffrey Patrick Hendrick), William Anthony Patrick Smallbone (72.Alan James Browne), Jamie Terence McGrath, James Joseph McClean (Cap), Evan Joe Ferguson (84.Adam Uche Idah), Michael Oluwadurotimi Obafemi (57.Troy Daniel Parrott). Trainer: Stephen Kenny.
**Goals:** Michael Andrew Johnston (52), Evan Joe Ferguson (59), Adam Uche Idah (90+2).

| NATIONAL TEAM PLAYERS | | | |
|---|---|---|---|
| (16.07.2022 – 15.07.2023) | | | |

| Name | DOB | Caps | Goals | Club |
|---|---|---|---|---|
| **Goalkeepers** | | | | |
| Gavin Okeroghene BAZUNU | 20.02.2002 | 16 | 0 | 2022/2023: *Southampton FC (ENG)* |
| Caoimhín Odhrán KELLEHER | 23.11.1998 | 10 | 0 | 2022/2023: *Liverpool FC (ENG)* |
| **Defenders** | | | | |
| Séamus COLEMAN | 11.10.1988 | 68 | 1 | 2022/2023: *Everton FC Liverpool (ENG)* |
| Nathan Michael COLLINS | 30.04.2001 | 14 | 2 | 2022/2023: *Wolverhampton Wanderers FC (ENG)* |
| Matthew James DOHERTY | 16.01.1992 | 36 | 1 | 2022: *Tottenham Hotspur FC London (ENG)* <br> 31.01.2023-> *Club Atlético de Madrid (ESP)* |
| John EGAN | 20.10.1992 | 34 | 3 | 2022/2023: *Sheffield United FC (ENG)* |
| Darragh Patrick LENIHAN | 16.03.1994 | 4 | 0 | 2023: *Blackburn Rovers FC (ENG)* |
| Callum Joshua Ryan O'DOWDA | 23.04.1995 | 27 | 1 | 2022/2023: *Cardiff City FC (WAL)* |
| Dara Joseph O'SHEA | 04.03.1999 | 19 | 0 | 2022/2023: *West Bromwich Albion FC (ENG)* |
| Andrew Abiola OMOBAMIDELE | 23.06.2002 | 6 | 0 | 2023: *Norwich City FC (ENG)* |
| Mark SYKES | 04.08.1977 | 1 | 0 | 2022: *Bristol City FC (ENG)* |
| **Midfielders** | | | | |
| Robert BRADY | 14.0.1992 | 60 | 9 | 2022: *Preston North End FC (ENG)* |
| Alan James BROWNE | 15.04.1995 | 30 | 5 | 2022/2023: *Preston North End FC (ENG)* |
| Jeffrey Patrick HENDRICK | 31.01.1992 | 79 | 2 | 2022/2023: *Reading FC (ENG)* |
| Conor HOURIHANE | 02.02.1991 | 36 | 1 | 2022: *Derby County FC (ENG)* |
| Jason Paul KNIGHT | 13.02.2001 | 20 | 1 | 2022/2023: *Derby County FC (ENG)* |
| James Joseph McCLEAN | 22.04.1989 | 100 | 11 | 2022/2023: *Wigan Athletic FC (ENG)* |
| Jamie Terence McGRATH | 30.09.1996 | 8 | 0 | 2022/2023: *Dundee United FC (SCO)* |
| Jayson Patrick MOLUMBY | 06.08.1999 | 20 | 0 | 2022/2023: *West Bromwich Albion FC (ENG)* |
| Chiedozie OGBENE | 01.05.1997 | 15 | 4 | 2022/2023: *Rotherham United FC (ENG)* |
| William Anthony Patrick SMALLBONE | 21.02.2000 | 3 | 0 | 2023: *Stoke City FC (ENG)* |
| **Forwards** | | | | |
| Joshua Jon CULLEN | 07.04.1996 | 26 | 0 | 2022/2023: *Burnley FC (ENG)* |
| Evan Joe FERGUSON | 19.10.2004 | 6 | 2 | 2022/2023: *Brighton & Hove Albion FC* |
| Scott Andrew HOGAN | 13.04.1992 | 12 | 0 | 2022: *Birmingham City FC (ENG)* |
| Adam Uche IDAH | 11.02.2001 | 16 | 1 | 2023: *Norwich City FC (ENG)* |
| Michael Andrew JOHNSTON | 19.04.1999 | 4 | 1 | 2023: *Vitória SC Guimarães (POR)* |
| Michael Oluwadurotimi OBAFEMI | 06.07.2000 | 11 | 2 | 2022: *Swansea City AFC (WAL)* <br> 29.01.2023-> *Burnley FC (ENG)* |
| Troy Daniel PARROTT | 04.02.2002 | 20 | 4 | 2022/2023: *Preston North End FC (ENG)* |
| Callum Jack ROBINSON | 02.02.1995 | 34 | 8 | 2022: *Cardiff City FC (WAL)* |
| **Trainer** | | | | |
| Stephen KENNY [from 04.04.2020] | 30.10.1971 | | | 34 M; 10 W; 11 D; 13 L; 41-33 |

# ROMANIA

## The Country:
Română (Romania)
Capital: Bucureşti
Surface: 238,397 km²
Inhabitants: 19,892,812 [2023]
Time: UTC+2

## The FA:
Federaţia Română de Fotbal
Casa Fotbalului, Str. Serg. Vasile Şerbanică 12, 22186 Bucureşti
Tel: +40 314 337 037
Founded: 1909
Member of FIFA since: 1923
Member of UEFA since: 1954
Website: www.frf.ro

## NATIONAL TEAM RECORDS

### RECORDS
| | | |
|---|---|---|
| **First international match:** | 08.06.1922, Beograd: | Yugoslavia – Romania 1-2 |
| **Most international caps:** | Dorinel Ionel Munteanu | - 134 caps (1991-2007) |
| **Most international goals:** | Gheorghe Hagi | - 35 goals / 125 caps (1983-2000) |
| | Adrian Mutu | - 35 goals / 77 caps (2000-2013) |

### UEFA EUROPEAN CHAMPIONSHIP
| | |
|---|---|
| 1960 | Qualifiers |
| 1964 | Qualifiers |
| 1968 | Qualifiers |
| 1972 | Qualifiers |
| 1976 | Qualifiers |
| 1980 | Qualifiers |
| 1984 | Final Tournament (Group Stage) |
| 1988 | Qualifiers |
| 1992 | Qualifiers |
| 1996 | Final Tournament (Group Stage) |
| 2000 | Final Tournament (Quarter-Finals) |
| 2004 | Qualifiers |
| 2008 | Final Tournament (Group Stage) |
| 2012 | Qualifiers |
| 2016 | Final Tournament (Group Stage) |
| 2020 | Qualifiers |

### FIFA WORLD CUP
| | |
|---|---|
| 1930 | Final Tournament (Group Stage) |
| 1934 | Final Tournament (1st Round) |
| 1938 | Final Tournament (1st Round) |
| 1950 | Did not enter |
| 1954 | Qualifiers |
| 1958 | Qualifiers |
| 1962 | *Withdrew* |
| 1966 | Qualifiers |
| 1970 | Final Tournament (Group Stage) |
| 1974 | Qualifiers |
| 1978 | Qualifiers |
| 1982 | Qualifiers |
| 1986 | Qualifiers |
| 1990 | Final Tournament (2nd Round of 16) |
| 1994 | Final Tournament (Quarter-Finals) |
| 1998 | Final Tournament (2nd Round of 16) |
| 2002 | Qualifiers |
| 2006 | Qualifiers |
| 2010 | Qualifiers |
| 2014 | Qualifiers |
| 2018 | Qualifiers |
| 2022 | Qualifiers |

### OLYMPIC TOURNAMENTS
| | |
|---|---|
| 1908 | - |
| 1912 | - |
| 1920 | - |
| 1924 | - |
| 1928 | 1/8 - Finals |
| 1936 | Did not enter |
| 1948 | Did not enter |
| 1952 | Preliminary Round |
| 1956 | Did not enter |
| 1960 | Qualifiers |
| 1964 | Quarter-Finals |
| 1968 | Qualifiers |
| 1972 | Qualifiers |
| 1976 | Qualifiers |
| 1980 | Qualifiers |
| 1984 | Qualifiers |
| 1988 | Qualifiers |
| 1992 | Qualifiers |
| 1996 | Qualifiers |
| 2000 | Qualifiers |
| 2004 | Qualifiers |
| 2008 | Qualifiers |
| 2012 | Qualifiers |
| 2016 | Qualifiers |
| 2020 | Final Tournament (Group Stage) |

## UEFA NATIONS LEAGUE
| | |
|---|---|
| 2018/2019 | League C (Group Stage -> promoted to League B) |
| 2020/2021 | League B (Group Stage) |
| 2022/2023 | League B (Group Stage -> relegated to League C) |

## ROMANIAN CLUB HONOURS IN EUROPEAN CLUB COMPETITIONS:

| European Champion Clubs.Cup (1956-1992) / UEFA Champions League (1993-2023) | | |
|---|---|---|
| FC Steaua Bucureşti | 1 | 1985/1986 |
| **Fairs Cup (1858-1971) / UEFA Cup (1972-2009) / UEFA Europa League (2010-2023)** | | |
| None | | |
| **UEFA Europa Conference League (2021-2023)** | | |
| None | | |
| **UEFA Super Cup (1972-2022)** | | |
| FC Steaua Bucureşti | 1 | 1986 |
| ***European Cup Winners' Cup 1961-1999**** | | |
| None | | |

*defunct competition

# NATIONAL COMPETITIONS
## TABLE OF HONOURS

| | CHAMPIONS* | CUP WINNERS | BEST GOALSCORERS | |
|---|---|---|---|---|
| 1909/1910 | Olympia Bucureşti | - | - | |
| 1910/1911 | Olympia Bucureşti | - | - | |
| 1911/1912 | United Ploieşti | - | - | |
| 1912/1913 | Colentina AC Bucureşti | - | - | |
| 1913/1914 | Colentina AC Bucureşti | - | - | |
| 1914/1915 | Româno-Americană Bucureşti | - | - | |
| 1915/1916 | Prahova Ploieşti | - | - | |
| 1916/1917 | *No competition* | - | - | |
| 1917/1918 | *No competition* | - | - | |
| 1918/1919 | *No competition* | - | - | |
| 1919/1920 | AS Venus Bucureşti | - | - | |
| 1920/1921 | AS Venus Bucureşti | - | - | |
| 1921/1922 | Chinezul Timişoara | - | - | |
| 1922/1923 | Chinezul Timişoara | - | - | |
| 1923/1924 | Chinezul Timişoara | - | - | |
| 1924/1925 | Chinezul Timişoara | - | - | |
| 1925/1926 | Chinezul Timişoara | - | - | |
| 1926/1927 | Chinezul Timişoara | - | - | |
| 1927/1928 | CS Colţea Braşov | - | - | |
| 1928/1929 | AS Venus Bucureşti | - | - | |
| 1929/1930 | FC Juventus Bucureşti | - | - | |
| 1930/1931 | UD Reşiţa | - | - | |
| 1931/1932 | AS Venus Bucureşti | - | - | |
| 1932/1933 | FC Ripensia Timişoara | - | - | |
| 1933/1934 | AS Venus Bucureşti | FC Ripensia Timişoara | Ştefan Dobay (FC Ripensia Timişoara) | 25 |
| 1934/1935 | FC Ripensia Timişoara | ACS CFR Bucureşti | Ştefan Dobay (FC Ripensia Timişoara) | 24 |
| 1935/1936 | FC Ripensia Timişoara | FC Ripensia Timişoara | Ştefan Barbu (ACS CFR Bucureşti) | 23 |
| 1936/1937 | AS Venus Bucureşti | FC Rapid Bucureşti | Ştefan Dobay (FC Ripensia Timişoara) Traian Iordache (Unirea Tricolor Bucureşti) | 21 |
| 1937/1938 | FC Ripensia Timişoara | FC Rapid Bucureşti | Árpád Thierjung (Chinezul Timişoara) | 22 |
| 1938/1939 | AS Venus Bucureşti | FC Rapid Bucureşti | Adalbert Marksteiner [Béla Marosvári] (FC Ripensia Timişoara) | 21 |
| 1939/1940 | AS Venus Bucureşti | FC Rapid Bucureşti | Ştefan Auer II [István Avar] (FC Rapid Bucureşti) | 21 |
| 1940/1941 | Unirea Tricolor Bucureşti | FC Rapid Bucureşti | Ion Bogdan (FC Rapid Bucureşti) Valeriu Niculescu (Unirea Tricolor Bucureşti) | 21 |
| 1941/1942 | *No competition* | FC Rapid Bucureşti | - | |
| 1942/1943 | *No competition* | CFR Turnu Severin | - | |
| 1943/1944 | *No competition* | *No competition* | - | |
| 1944/1945 | *No competition* | *No competition* | - | |
| 1945/1946 | *No competition* | *No competition* | - | |
| 1946/1947 | IT Arad | *No competition* | Ladislau Bonyhádi (IT Arad) | 26 |
| 1947/1948 | IT Arad | IT Arad | Ladislau Bonyhádi (IT Arad) | 49 |
| 1948/1949 | IC Oradea | CSCA Bucureşti | Gheorghe Váczi (IC Oradea) | 24 |
| 1950 | Flamura Roşie Arad | CCA Bucureşti | Andrei Rădulescu (Locomotiva Bucureşti) | 18 |
| 1951 | CCA Bucureşti | CCA Bucureşti | Gheorghe Váczi (Progresul Oradea) | 23 |
| 1952 | CCA Bucureşti | CCA Bucureşti | Titus Ozon (CS Dinamo Bucureşti) | 17 |
| 1953 | CCA Bucureşti | Flamura Roşie Arad | Titus Ozon (CS Dinamo Bucureşti) | 12 |
| 1954 | Flamura Roşie Arad | Metalul Reşiţa | Alexandru Ene I (CS Dinamo Bucureşti) | 20 |
| 1955 | CS Dinamo Bucureşti | CCA Bucureşti | Ion Ciosescu (Ştiinţa Timişoara) | 18 |
| 1956 | CCA Bucureşti | Progresul Oradea | Ion Alecsandrescu (CCA Bucureşti) | 18 |
| 1957/1958 | FC Petrolul Ploieşti | CS Ştiinţa Timişoara | Ion Ciosescu (CS Ştiinţa Timişoara) | 21 |
| 1958/1959 | FC Petrolul Ploieşti | CS Dinamo Bucureşti | Gheorghe Ene (CS Rapid Bucureşti) | 17 |
| 1959/1960 | CCA Bucureşti | Progresul Bucureşti | Gheorghe Constantin (CCA Bucureşti) | 20 |
| 1960/1961 | CCA Bucureşti | Arieşul Turda | Gheorghe Constantin (CCA Bucureşti) | 22 |
| 1961/1962 | CS Dinamo Bucureşti | CSA Steaua Bucureşti | Gheorghe Constantin (CSA Steaua Bucureşti) | 24 |
| 1962/1963 | CS Dinamo Bucureşti | FC Petrolul Ploieşti | Ion Gheorghe Ionescu (CS Rapid Bucureşti) | 20 |
| 1963/1964 | CS Dinamo Bucureşti | CS Dinamo Bucureşti | Constantin Frăţilă (CS Dinamo Bucureşti) Cornel Pavlovici (CSA Steaua Bucureşti) | 19 |
| 1964/1965 | CS Dinamo Bucureşti | Ştiinţa Cluj | Mihai Adam (Ştiinţa Cluj) | 18 |
| 1965/1966 | FC Petrolul Ploieşti | CSA Steaua Bucureşti | Ion Gheorghe Ionescu (CS Rapid Bucureşti) | 24 |
| 1966/1967 | CS Rapid Bucureşti | CSA Steaua Bucureşti | Ion Oblemenco (Universitatea Craiova) | 17 |
| 1967/1968 | CSA Steaua Bucureşti | CS Dinamo Bucureşti | Mihai Adam (CS Universitatea Cluj) | 15 |
| 1968/1969 | UT Arad | CSA Steaua Bucureşti | Florea Dumitrache (CS Dinamo Bucureşti) | 22 |
| 1969/1970 | UT Arad | CSA Steaua Bucureşti | Ion Oblemenco (CS Universitatea Craiova) | 19 |
| 1970/1971 | CS Dinamo Bucureşti | CSA Steaua Bucureşti | Constantin Moldoveanu (Politehnica Iaşi) Florea Dumitrache (CS Dinamo Bucureşti) Gheorghe Tătaru (CSA Steaua Bucureşti) | 15 |
| 1971/1972 | FC Argeş Piteşti | CS Rapid Bucureşti | Ion Oblemenco (CS Universitatea Craiova) | 20 |
| 1972/1973 | CS Dinamo Bucureşti | CS Chimia Râmnicu Vâlcea | Ion Oblemenco (CS Universitatea Craiova) | 21 |
| 1973/1974 | CS Universitatea Craiova | CSM Jiul Petroşani | Mihai Adam (CFR Cluj-Napoca) | 23 |
| 1974/1975 | CS Dinamo Bucureşti | CS Rapid Bucureşti | Dudu Georgescu (CS Dinamo Bucureşti) | 33 |

| | | | | |
|---|---|---|---|---|
| 1975/1976 | CSA Steaua Bucureşti | CSA Steaua Bucureşti | Dudu Georgescu (CS Dinamo Bucureşti) | 31 |
| 1976/1977 | CS Dinamo Bucureşti | CS Universitatea Craiova | Dudu Georgescu (CS Dinamo Bucureşti) | 47 |
| 1977/1978 | CSA Steaua Bucureşti | CS Universitatea Craiova | Dudu Georgescu (CS Dinamo Bucureşti) | 24 |
| 1978/1979 | FC Argeş Piteşti | CSA Steaua Bucureşti | Marin Radu II (FC Argeş Piteşti) | 22 |
| 1979/1980 | CS Universitatea Craiova | CS Politehnica Timişoara | Septimiu Câmpeanu II (CS Universitatea Cluj) | 24 |
| 1980/1981 | CS Universitatea Craiova | CS Universitatea Craiova | Marin Radu II (FC Argeş Piteşti) | 28 |
| 1981/1982 | CS Dinamo Bucureşti | CS Dinamo Bucureşti | Anghel Iordănescu (CSA Steaua Bucureşti) | 20 |
| 1982/1983 | CS Dinamo Bucureşti | CS Universitatea Craiova | Petre Grosu (FC Bihor Oradea) | 20 |
| 1983/1984 | CS Dinamo Bucureşti | CS Dinamo Bucureşti | Marcel Coraş (CF Sportul Studenţesc Bucureşti) | 20 |
| 1984/1985 | CSA Steaua Bucureşti | CSA Steaua Bucureşti | Gheorghe Hagi (CF Sportul Studenţesc Bucureşti) | 20 |
| 1985/1986 | CSA Steaua Bucureşti | CS Dinamo Bucureşti | Gheorghe Hagi (CF Sportul Studenţesc Bucureşti) | 31 |
| 1986/1987 | CSA Steaua Bucureşti | CSA Steaua Bucureşti | Rodion Gorun Cămătaru (CS Dinamo Bucureşti) | 44 |
| 1987/1988 | CSA Steaua Bucureşti | CSA Steaua Bucureşti | Victor Piţurcă (CSA Steaua Bucureşti) | 34 |
| 1988/1989 | CSA Steaua Bucureşti | CSA Steaua Bucureşti | Dorin Mateuţ (CS Dinamo Bucureşti) | 43 |
| 1989/1990 | CS Dinamo Bucureşti | CS Dinamo Bucureşti | Gavril Balint (CSA Steaua Bucureşti) | 19 |
| 1990/1991 | CS Universitatea Craiova | CS Universitatea Craiova | Ovidiu Cornel Hanganu (FC Corvinul Hunedoara) | 24 |
| 1991/1992 | CS Dinamo Bucureşti | CSA Steaua Bucureşti | Gábor Gerstenmájer (CS Dinamo Bucureşti) | 21 |
| 1992/1993 | CSA Steaua Bucureşti | FC Universitatea Craiova | Ilie Dumitrescu (CSA Steaua Bucureşti) | 24 |
| 1993/1994 | CSA Steaua Bucureşti | ACF Gloria Bistriţa | Gheorghe Craioveanu (FC Universitatea Craiova) | 21 |
| 1994/1995 | CSA Steaua Bucureşti | FC Petrolul Ploieşti | Gheorghe Craioveanu (FC Universitatea Craiova) | 27 |
| 1995/1996 | CSA Steaua Bucureşti | CSA Steaua Bucureşti | Ion Vlădoiu (CSA Steaua Bucureşti) | 25 |
| 1996/1997 | CSA Steaua Bucureşti | CSA Steaua Bucureşti | Sabin Ilie (CSA Steaua Bucureşti) | 31 |
| 1997/1998 | CSA Steaua Bucureşti | UFC Rapid Bucureşti | Constantin Barbu (FC Argeş Piteşti)<br>Ion Vasile Oană (ACF Gloria Bistriţa) | 22 |
| 1998/1999 | UFC Rapid Bucureşti | FC Steaua Bucureşti | Ioan Viorel Ganea (ACF Gloria Bistriţa) | 28 |
| 1999/2000 | FC Dinamo Bucureşti | FC Dinamo Bucureşti | Marian Savu (FC Naţional Bucureşti) | 20 |
| 2000/2001 | FC Steaua Bucureşti | FC Dinamo Bucureşti | Marius Constantin Niculae (FC Dinamo Bucureşti) | 20 |
| 2001/2002 | FC Dinamo Bucureşti | UFC Rapid Bucureşti | Cătălin Cursaru (FCM Bacău) | 17 |
| 2002/2003 | UFC Rapid Bucureşti | FC Dinamo Bucureşti | Claudiu Nicu Răducanu (FC Steaua Bucureşti) | 21 |
| 2003/2004 | FC Dinamo Bucureşti | FC Dinamo Bucureşti | Ionel Daniel Dănciulescu (FC Dinamo Bucureşti) | 21 |
| 2004/2005 | FC Steaua Bucureşti | FC Dinamo Bucureşti | Gheorghe Bucur (CF Sportul Studenţesc Bucureşti)<br>Claudiu Iulian Niculescu (FC Dinamo Bucureşti) | 21 |
| 2005/2006 | FC Steaua Bucureşti | UFC Rapid Bucureşti | Ionuţ Costinel Mazilu (CF Sportul Studenţesc Bucureşti) | 22 |
| 2006/2007 | FC Dinamo Bucureşti | UFC Rapid Bucureşti | Claudiu Iulian Niculescu (FC Dinamo Bucureşti) | 18 |
| 2007/2008 | FC CFR 1907 Cluj-Napoca | FC CFR 1907 Cluj-Napoca | Ionel Daniel Dănciulescu (FC Dinamo Bucureşti) | 21 |
| 2008/2009 | FC Unirea Urziceni | FC CFR 1907 Cluj-Napoca | Gheorghe Bucur (FC Timişoara)<br>Florin Constantin Costea (FC Universitatea Craiova) | 17 |
| 2009/2010 | FC CFR 1907 Cluj-Napoca | FC CFR 1907 Cluj-Napoca | Andrei Cristea (FC Dinamo Bucureşti) | 16 |
| 2010/2011 | ASC Oţelul Galaţi | FC Steaua Bucureşti | Ianis Alin Zicu (FC Timişoara) | 18 |
| 2011/2012 | FC CFR 1907 Cluj-Napoca | FC Dinamo Bucureşti | Wesley Lopes da Silva (BRA, FC Vaslui) | 27 |
| 2012/2013 | FC Steaua Bucureşti | FC Petrolul Ploieşti | Raul Andrei Rusescu (FC Steaua Bucureşti) | 21 |
| 2013/2014 | FC Steaua Bucureşti | AFC Astra Giurgiu | Liviu Ion Antal (FC Vaslui) | 14 |
| 2014/2015 | FC Steaua Bucureşti | FC Steaua Bucureşti | Grégory Tadé (FRA, FC CFR 1907 Cluj-Napoca) | 18 |
| 2015/2016 | AFC Astra Giurgiu | FC CFR 1907 Cluj-Napoca | Adrian Ioan Hora (CS Pandurii Târgu Jiu) | 19 |
| 2016/2017 | FC Viitorul Constanţa | FC Voluntari | Azdren Llullaku (ALB, CS Gaz Metan Mediaş) | 16 |
| 2017/2018 | FC CFR 1907 Cluj-Napoca | CS Universitatea Craiova | Marius George Ţucudean (FC Viitorul Constanţa, FC CFR 1907 Cluj-Napoca)<br>Harlem-Eddy Gnohéré (FRA, FCSB Bucureşti) | 15 |
| 2018/2019 | FC CFR 1907 Cluj-Napoca | FC Viitorul Constanţa | Marius George Ţucudean (FC CFR 1907 Cluj-Napoca) | 18 |
| 2019/2020 | FC CFR 1907 Cluj-Napoca | SC FCSB Bucureşti | Gabriel Cristian Iancu (FC Viitorul Constanţa) | 18 |
| 2020/2021 | FC CFR 1907 Cluj-Napoca | CS Universitatea Craiova | Florin Lucian Tănase (SC FCSB Bucureşti) | 24 |
| 2021/2022 | FC CFR 1907 Cluj-Napoca | ACS Sepsi OSK Sfântu Gheorghe | Florin Lucian Tănase (SC FCSB Bucureşti) | 20 |
| 2022/2023 | FCV Farul Constanţa | ACS Sepsi OSK Sfântu Gheorghe | Marko Dugandžić (CRO, FC Rapid 1923 Bucureşti) | 22 |

* Romanian Football Championship (1909–1921), Divizia A (1921–2006), Liga I (since 2006).

Club name changements:

**FC Rapid Bucureşti** = ACS CFR Bucureşti (1923-1936), FC Rapid Bucureşti (1936-1945), CFR Bucureşti (1945-1949), Locomotiva Bucureşti (1949-1958), CS Rapid Bucureşti (1958-1992), UFC Rapid Bucureşti (1992-2016), Academia Rapid Bucureşti (2017), FC Rapid Bucureşti (since 2018).
**UT Arad** = IT Arad (1945–1949), Flamura Roşie Arad (1950–1957), UT Arad (1958–2014), UTA Bătrâna Doamnă Arad (2014–2017), UT Arad (since 2017).
**ACS CAO Oradea** = CA Oradea (1919-1940), Nagyváradi AC (1940-1944), Libertatea Oradea (1945-1948), IC Oradea (1948-1951), Progresul Oradea (1951-1958), CS Oradea (1958-1961), Crişana Oradea (1961-1963).
**FCSB Bucureşti** = ASA Bucureşti (1947-1948), CSCA Bucureşti (1948-1950), CCA Bucureşti (1950-1961), CSA Steaua Bucureşti (1961-1998), FC Steaua Bucureşti (1998-2017), FCSB Bucureşti (since 2017).
**FC Dinamo Bucureşti** = CS Dinamo Bucureşti (1945-1992), FC Dinamo Bucureşti (since 1992).
**ACS Poli Timişoara** = SS Politehnica Timişoara (1921-1948), CSU Timişoara (1948-1950), CS Ştiinţa Timişoara (1950-1966), CS Politehnica Timişoara (1966-1969), FC Ripensia Timişoata (1969), CS Politehnica Timişoara (1969-1992), FC Politehnica Timişoara (1992-2012), ACS Poli Timişoara (since 2012).
**FC Universitatea Cluj-Napoca** = Universitatea Cluj (1919-1948), CSU Cluj (1948-1949), Ştiinţa Cluj (1949-1966), CS Universitatea Cluj (1966-1974), CS Universitatea Cluj-Napoca (1974-1992), FC Universitatea Cluj-Napoca (since 1992).
**CS Universitatea Craiova** = CSU Craiova (1948-1950), Ştiinţa Craiova (1950-1966), CS Universitatea Craiova (1966-1992), FC Universitatea Craiova (1992-2011), CS Universitatea Craiova (since 2013).

# NATIONAL CHAMPIONSHIP
## Liga I 2022/2023
### (15.07.2022 – 28.05.2023)

**Regular Season - Results**

**Round 1** [15-18.07.2022]
AFC Hermannstadt - CS Mioveni 3-0(1-0)
CS Univ. Craiova - Sepsi OSK 2-2(1-0)
FC Argeş - UT Arad 2-0(1-0)
CFR Cluj - Rapid Bucureşti 1-0(1-0)
FCV Farul - FC U Craiova 2-1(2-0)
FCSB Bucureşti - Universitatea Cluj 1-1(0-1)
FC Botoşani - Chindia Târgovişte 3-2(3-1)
Petrolul Ploieşti - FC Voluntari 0-1(0-0)

**Round 2** [22-25.07.2022]
CS Mioveni - FCV Farul 0-2(0-0)
FC Voluntari - FC Botoşani 0-1(0-0)
Sepsi OSK - FC Argeş 4-0(0-0)
FC U Craiova - CFR Cluj 3-1(1-1)
Universitatea Cluj-CS Univ. Craiova 1-1(1-0)
Rapid Bucureşti - FCSB Bucureşti 2-0(2-0)
Chindia Târgovişte - Hermannstadt 1-1(1-1)
UT Arad - Petrolul Ploieşti 2-0(1-0)

**Round 3** [29.07.-01.08.2022]
FC Argeş - Universitatea Cluj 3-1(1-1)
FCV Farul - Chindia Târgovişte 0-0
FC Voluntari - UT Arad 3-0(2-0)
CFR Cluj - CS Mioveni 4-2(3-1)
Petrolul Ploieşti - Sepsi OSK 1-1(0-0)
CS Univ. Craiova - Rapid Bucureşti 0-1(0-0)
FCSB Bucureşti - FC U Craiova 1-1(0-0)
AFC Hermannstadt - FC Botoşani 1-1(0-0)

**Round 4** [05-08.08.2022]
Universitatea Cluj - Petrolul Ploieşti 0-1(0-1)
CS Mioveni - FCSB Bucureşti 1-1(1-0)
Rapid Bucureşti - FC Argeş 2-1(1-0)
Sepsi OSK - UT Arad 0-0
Chindia Târgovişte - CFR Cluj 0-2(0-2)
FC U Craiova - CS Univ. Craiova 1-2(0-2)
AFC Hermannstadt - FC Voluntari 2-1(2-1)
FC Botoşani - FCV Farul 1-1(1-1)

**Round 5** [12-15.08.2022]
FC Argeş - FC U Craiova 0-2(0-1)
UT Arad - Universitatea Cluj 2-1(1-1)
Petrolul Ploieşti - Rapid Bucureşti 1-0(1-0)
CS Univ. Craiova - CS Mioveni 1-0(1-0)
CFR Cluj - FC Botoşani 0-1(0-1)
FCSB Bucureşti - Chindia Târgovişte 3-2(0-2)
FC Voluntari - Sepsi OSK 0-0
FCV Farul - AFC Hermannstadt 0-0

**Round 6** [19-22.08.2022]
CS Mioveni - FC Argeş 0-1(0-0)
FC U Craiova - Petrolul Ploieşti 0-1(0-1)
Rapid Bucureşti - UT Arad 1-0(1-0)
Universitatea Cluj - Sepsi OSK 0-1(0-0)
FCV Farul - FC Voluntari 2-1(0-1)
Chindia-CS Univ. Craiova 1-1(0-1) [29.11.22]
Hermannstadt - CFR Cluj 2-3(1-2) [30.11.22]
Botoşani-FCSB Bucureşti 2-3(1-2) [01.12.22]

**Round 7** [26-29.08.2022]
FC Voluntari - Universitatea Cluj 0-0
UT Arad - FC U Craiova 2-1(2-0)
Petrolul Ploieşti - CS Mioveni 0-0
Sepsi OSK - Rapid Bucureşti 1-2(1-2)
FC Argeş - Chindia Târgovişte 2-1(0-1)
CFR Cluj - FCV Farul 1-3(1-1)
FCSB Bucureşti - AFC Hermannstadt 2-2(1-1)
CS Univ. Craiova - FC Botoşani 1-0(0-0)

**Round 8** [30.08.-01.09.2022]
CS Mioveni - UT Arad 1-1(1-1)
FC U Craiova - Sepsi OSK 1-0(1-0)
Rapid Bucureşti - Universitatea Cluj 1-0(0-0)
Chindia Târgovişte - Petrolul Ploieşti 2-3(0-2)
CFR Cluj - FC Voluntari 4-0(1-0)
FCV Farul - FCSB Bucureşti 3-1(2-0)
FC Botoşani - FC Argeş 0-0
Hermannstadt - CS Univ. Craiova 1-0(0-0)

**Round 9** [02-05.09.2022]
Sepsi OSK - CS Mioveni 0-1(0-0)
Universitatea Cluj - FC U Craiova 1-1(1-1)
UT Arad - Chindia Târgovişte 1-1(0-1)
FC Voluntari - Rapid Bucureşti 0-1(0-0)
Petrolul Ploieşti - FC Botoşani 2-1(1-0)
FC Argeş - AFC Hermannstadt 0-1(0-0)
CS Univ. Craiova - FCV Farul 4-3(2-3)
FCSB Bucureşti-CFR Cluj 0-1(0-0) [15.12.22]

**Round 10** [09-12.09.2022]
FC Botoşani - UT Arad 1-2(0-2)
Chindia Târgovişte - Sepsi OSK 1-2(1-1)
AFC Hermannstadt - Petrolul Ploieşti 2-1(1-1)
FC U Craiova - Rapid Bucureşti 1-0(0-0)
FCV Farul - FC Argeş 3-0(1-0)
CFR Cluj - CS Univ. Craiova 2-0(2-0)
CS Mioveni - Universitatea Cluj 0-1(0-1)
FCSB Bucureşti - FC Voluntari 1-1(0-0)

**Round 11** [16-19.09.2022]
FC Voluntari - FC U Craiova 1-0(1-0)
Petrolul Ploieşti - FCV Farul 1-3(0-2)
UT Arad - AFC Hermannstadt 1-2(1-1)
Sepsi OSK - FC Botoşani 7-0(2-0)
Rapid Bucureşti - CS Mioveni 2-1(1-1)
Universit. Cluj - Chindia Târgovişte 1-0(0-0)
CS Univ. Craiova - FCSB Bucureşti 2-1(1-1)
FC Argeş - CFR Cluj 0-1(0-0)

**Round 12** [30.09.-03.10.2022]
CS Univ. Craiova - FC Voluntari 1-1(0-0)
CS Mioveni - FC U Craiova 2-2(2-2)
CFR Cluj - Petrolul Ploieşti 1-0(0-0)
AFC Hermannstadt - Sepsi OSK 1-2(1-0)
FCV Farul - UT Arad 2-0(1-0)
FCSB Bucureşti - FC Argeş 3-2(1-1)
FC Botoşani - Universitatea Cluj 1-1(0-0)
Chindia Târgovişte - Rapid Bucureşti 2-1(1-0)

**Round 13** [07-10.10.2022]
FC Voluntari - CS Mioveni 3-1(2-1)
FC Argeş - CS Univ. Craiova 1-0(0-0)
Universitatea Cluj - Hermannstadt 1-0(0-0)
Rapid Bucureşti - FC Botoşani 1-0(1-0)
Sepsi OSK - FCV Farul 0-1(0-1)
Petrolul Ploieşti - FCSB Bucureşti 0-2(0-1)
FC U Craiova - Chindia Târgovişte 0-1(0-0)
UT Arad - CFR Cluj 1-1(0-1)

**Round 14** [14-17.10.2022]
FC Argeş - FC Voluntari 0-0
AFC Hermannstadt - Rapid Bucureşti 0-2(0-0)
FC Botoşani - FC U Craiova 1-0(0-0)
FCV Farul - Universitatea Cluj 2-1(1-0)
CS Univ. Craiova - Petrolul Ploieşti 2-1(0-0)
Chindia Târgovişte - CS Mioveni 1-0(0-0)
FCSB Bucureşti - UT Arad 2-1(1-0)
CFR Cluj - Sepsi OSK 2-1(1-1)

**Round 15** [21-24.10.2022]
Rapid Bucureşti - FCV Farul 1-1(0-1)
FC Voluntari - Chindia Târgovişte 0-3(0-1)
FC U Craiova - AFC Hermannstadt 1-1(0-0)
CS Mioveni - FC Botoşani 0-0
UT Arad - CS Univ. Craiova 1-2(1-1)
Universitatea Cluj - CFR Cluj 1-2(0-1)
Petrolul Ploieşti - FC Argeş 2-0(1-0)
Sepsi OSK - FCSB Bucureşti 0-1(0-0)

**Round 16** [28-31.10.2022]
Chindia Târgovişte - FC Botoşani 2-2(1-1)
FC U Craiova - FCV Farul 1-2(1-1)
FC Voluntari - Petrolul Ploieşti 0-1(0-1)
Sepsi OSK - CS Univ. Craiova 1-0(0-0)
UT Arad - FC Argeş 0-1(0-1)
Rapid Bucureşti - CFR Cluj 2-1(1-0)
CS Mioveni - AFC Hermannstadt 0-2(0-0)
Universitatea Cluj - FCSB Bucureşti 2-1(2-0)

**Round 17** [04-07.11.2022]
FC Botoşani - FC Voluntari 0-1(0-0)
FCV Farul - CS Mioveni 2-1(1-1)
FC Argeş - Sepsi OSK 0-5(0-2)
Petrolul Ploieşti - UT Arad 2-1(0-0)
CS Univ. Craiova-Universitatea Cluj 1-0(0-0)
Hermannstadt - Chindia Târgovişte 0-1(0-0)
FCSB Bucureşti - Rapid Bucureşti 3-1(2-0)
CFR Cluj - FC U Craiova 3-1(2-0)

**Round 18** [11-14.11.2022]
Sepsi OSK - Petrolul Ploieşti 2-0(1-0)
Chindia Târgovişte - FCV Farul 1-1(0-0)
Rapid Bucureşti - CS Univ. Craiova 2-2(1-2)
UT Arad - FC Voluntari 1-1(1-1)
CS Mioveni - CFR Cluj 0-1(0-0)
FC U Craiova - FCSB Bucureşti 0-2(0-2)
Universitatea Cluj - FC Argeş 1-1(0-1)
FC Botoşani - AFC Hermannstadt 0-0

**Round 19** [02-05.12.2022]
UT Arad - Sepsi OSK 1-4(1-1)
Petrolul Ploieşti - Universitatea Cluj 2-0(1-0)
FC Voluntari - AFC Hermannstadt 3-0(1-0)
CS Univ. Craiova - FC U Craiova 0-2(0-0)
FCV Farul - FC Botoşani 8-0(2-0)
CFR Cluj - Chindia Târgovişte 2-0(1-0)
FC Argeş - Rapid Bucureşti 1-1(0-1)
FCSB Bucureşti - CS Mioveni 5-1(2-0)

**Round 20** [09-14.12.2022]
Sepsi OSK - FC Voluntari 1-1(1-0)
AFC Hermannstadt - FCV Farul 4-0(1-0)
Universitatea Cluj - UT Arad 0-0
FC Botoşani - CFR Cluj 1-1(0-1)
Chindia Târgovişte - FCSB Bucureşti 0-2(0-1)
FC U Craiova - FC Argeş 1-0(0-0)
CS Mioveni - CS Univ. Craiova 0-1(0-1)
Rapid Bucureşti - Petrolul Ploieşti 3-1(1-0)

**Round 21** [16-20.12.2022]
FC Voluntari - FCV Farul 1-1(0-1)
Sepsi OSK - Universitatea Cluj 2-1(1-0)
CS Univ. Craiova-Chindia Târgovişte 3-0(2-0)
FC Argeş - CS Mioveni 2-2(2-0)
Petrolul Ploieşti - FC U Craiova 1-1(1-0)
UT Arad - Rapid Bucureşti 1-1(1-0)
FCSB Bucureşti - FC Botoşani 1-0(0-0)
CFR Cluj - AFC Hermannstadt 0-1(0-0)

| Round 22 [20-23.01.2023] |
|---|
| Universitatea Cluj - FC Voluntari 2-1(1-0) |
| Rapid Bucureşti - Sepsi OSK 3-0(3-0) |
| CS Mioveni - Petrolul Ploieşti 1-0(1-0) |
| FC Botoşani - CS Univ. Craiova 1-0(1-0) |
| FC U Craiova - UT Arad 1-1(1-0) |
| AFC Hermannstadt - FCSB Bucureşti 0-1(0-0) |
| Chindia Târgovişte - FC Argeş 1-1(1-0) |
| FCV Farul - CFR Cluj 0-3(0-0) |

| Round 23 [27-30.01.2023] |
|---|
| Universitatea Cluj - Rapid Bucureşti 0-0 |
| UT Arad - CS Mioveni 1-2(0-2) |
| Petrolul Ploieşti - Chindia Târgovişte 1-2(1-0) |
| CS Univ. Craiova - Hermannstadt 2-0(0-0) |
| FC Argeş - FC Botoşani 0-2(0-1) |
| FCSB Bucureşti - FCV Farul 2-3(0-0) |
| FC Voluntari - CFR Cluj 0-1(0-0) |
| Sepsi OSK - FC U Craiova 4-0(3-0)[16.03.23] |

| Round 24 [03-06.02.2023] |
|---|
| Chindia Târgovişte - UT Arad 2-1(1-1) |
| FC U Craiova - Universitatea Cluj 5-0(3-0) |
| AFC Hermannstadt - FC Argeş 1-1(1-1) |
| Rapid Bucureşti - FC Voluntari 4-1(2-0) |
| CS Mioveni - Sepsi OSK 1-1(0-1) |
| CFR Cluj - FCSB Bucureşti 0-1(0-0) |
| FC Botoşani - Petrolul Ploieşti 5-0(3-0) |
| FCV Farul - CS Univ. Craiova 2-1(2-0) |

| Round 25 [10-13.02.2023] |
|---|
| Universitatea Cluj - CS Mioveni 2-2(1-2) |
| Rapid Bucureşti - FC U Craiova 1-2(0-1) |
| UT Arad - FC Botoşani 3-1(3-1) |
| CS Univ. Craiova - CFR Cluj 2-0(0-0) |
| FC Argeş - FCV Farul 0-0 |
| FC Voluntari - FCSB Bucureşti 1-2(0-1) |
| Sepsi OSK - Chindia Târgovişte 2-2(1-2) |
| Petrolul Ploieşti - AFC Hermannstadt 2-0(2-0) |

| Round 26 [17-20.02.2023] |
|---|
| Chindia Târgov. - Universitatea Cluj 2-2(0-1) |
| CS Mioveni - Rapid Bucureşti 0-0 |
| AFC Hermannstadt - UT Arad 0-0 |
| FCV Farul - Petrolul Ploieşti 2-0(1-0) |
| CFR Cluj - FC Argeş 3-1(2-0) |
| FCSB Bucureşti - CS Univ. Craiova 1-1(1-0) |
| FC Botoşani - Sepsi OSK 1-1(1-1) |
| FC U Craiova - FC Voluntari 2-1(0-1) |

| Round 27 [24-27.02.2023] |
|---|
| FC U Craiova - CS Mioveni 2-1(1-0) |
| UT Arad - FCV Farul 0-1(0-0) |
| Sepsi OSK - AFC Hermannstadt 2-1(1-0) |
| Universitatea Cluj - FC Botoşani 2-0(1-0) |
| Rapid Bucureşti - Chindia Târgovişte 2-0(0-0) |
| FC Voluntari - CS Univ. Craiova 1-0(0-0) |
| FC Argeş - FCSB Bucureşti 1-2(0-0) |
| Petrolul Ploieşti - CFR Cluj 2-5(0-1) |

| Round 28 [28.02.-02.03.2023] |
|---|
| Hermannstadt - Universitatea Cluj 0-1(0-1) |
| Chindia Târgovişte - FC U Craiova 0-0 |
| FCV Farul - Sepsi OSK 2-0(2-0) |
| CS Mioveni - FC Voluntari 0-3(0-1) |
| CS Univ. Craiova - FC Argeş 1-0(0-0) |
| FC Botoşani - Rapid Bucureşti 1-2(0-1) |
| CFR Cluj - UT Arad 2-1(1-0) |
| FCSB Bucureşti - Petrolul Ploieşti 4-1(2-1) |

| Round 29 [03-06.03.2023] |
|---|
| Universitatea Cluj - FCV Farul 2-0(1-0) |
| FC U Craiova - FC Botoşani 1-0(1-0) |
| Rapid Bucureşti - AFC Hermannstadt 0-1(0-1) |
| CS Mioveni - Chindia Târgovişte 2-0(1-0) |
| Petrolul Ploieşti - CS Univ. Craiova 0-1(0-1) |
| UT Arad - FCSB Bucureşti 3-1(1-1) |
| FC Voluntari - FC Argeş 0-0 |
| Sepsi OSK - CFR Cluj 2-2(1-2) |

| Round 30 [10-13.03.2023] |
|---|
| FC Botoşani - CS Mioveni 1-1(1-0) |
| CS Univ. Craiova - UT Arad 2-1(0-1) |
| FC Argeş - Petrolul Ploieşti 0-1(0-1) |
| FCV Farul - Rapid Bucureşti 2-1(1-1) |
| FCSB Bucureşti - Sepsi OSK 1-0(1-0) |
| AFC Hermannstadt - FC U Craiova 1-0(0-0) |
| Chindia Târgovişte - FC Voluntari 1-1(0-1) |
| CFR Cluj - Universitatea Cluj 4-0(3-0) |

## Final Standings

| | | | | | | | | | Home | | | | Away | | |
|---|---|---|---|---|---|---|---|---|---|---|---|---|---|---|---|
| 1. | FCV Farul Constanţa | 30 | 19 | 7 | 4 | 54 - 28 | 64 | 12 | 2 | 1 | 32 - 9 | 7 | 5 | 3 | 22 - 19 |
| 2. | FC CFR 1907 Cluj-Napoca | 30 | 20 | 3 | 7 | 54 - 28 | 63 | 11 | 0 | 4 | 29 - 12 | 9 | 3 | 3 | 25 - 16 |
| 3. | SC FCSB Bucureşti | 30 | 17 | 6 | 7 | 51 - 35 | 57 | 8 | 5 | 2 | 30 - 18 | 9 | 1 | 5 | 21 - 17 |
| 4. | CS Universitatea Craiova | 30 | 16 | 6 | 8 | 37 - 27 | 54 | 11 | 2 | 2 | 24 - 12 | 5 | 4 | 6 | 13 - 15 |
| 5. | FC Rapid 1923 Bucureşti | 30 | 15 | 7 | 8 | 40 - 26 | 52 | 10 | 3 | 2 | 27 - 12 | 5 | 4 | 6 | 13 - 14 |
| 6. | ACS Sepsi OSK Sfântu Gheorghe | 30 | 11 | 9 | 10 | 47 - 30 | 42 | 6 | 4 | 5 | 27 - 13 | 5 | 5 | 5 | 20 - 17 |
| 7. | FC Universitatea Craiova 1948 | 30 | 11 | 7 | 12 | 34 - 33 | 40 | 8 | 2 | 5 | 20 - 13 | 3 | 5 | 7 | 14 - 20 |
| 8. | ACS Petrolul Ploieşti | 30 | 11 | 3 | 16 | 28 - 44 | 36 | 6 | 3 | 6 | 17 - 18 | 5 | 0 | 10 | 11 - 26 |
| 9. | AS FC Universitatea Cluj | 30 | 8 | 10 | 12 | 25 - 37 | 34 | 6 | 6 | 3 | 16 - 11 | 2 | 4 | 9 | 9 - 26 |
| 10. | FC Voluntari | 30 | 8 | 10 | 12 | 28 - 32 | 34 | 5 | 4 | 6 | 13 - 11 | 3 | 6 | 6 | 15 - 21 |
| 11. | FC Botoşani | 30 | 7 | 11 | 12 | 29 - 44 | 32 | 4 | 7 | 4 | 19 - 15 | 3 | 4 | 8 | 10 - 29 |
| 12. | AFC Chindia Târgovişte | 30 | 7 | 11 | 12 | 32 - 42 | 32 | 3 | 8 | 4 | 17 - 20 | 4 | 3 | 8 | 15 - 22 |
| 13. | AFC Hermannstadt Sibiu* | 30 | 11 | 8 | 11 | 30 - 29 | 32 | 6 | 3 | 6 | 18 - 14 | 5 | 5 | 5 | 12 - 15 |
| 14. | FC Argeş Piteşti | 30 | 6 | 9 | 15 | 21 - 41 | 27 | 4 | 4 | 7 | 12 - 19 | 2 | 5 | 8 | 9 - 22 |
| 15. | FC UT Arad | 30 | 6 | 9 | 15 | 29 - 41 | 27 | 5 | 4 | 6 | 20 - 20 | 1 | 5 | 9 | 9 - 21 |
| 16. | CS Mioveni | 30 | 4 | 10 | 16 | 23 - 45 | 22 | 2 | 6 | 7 | 8 - 16 | 2 | 4 | 9 | 15 - 29 |

*9 points deducted due to financial debts.

Teams ranked 1-6 were qualified for the Championship Play-offs, while teams ranked 7-16 were qualified for the Relegation Play-out.
In both rounds, points from Regular Season were halved and rounded upwards and no other records carried over from the Regular season.

## Relegation Play-out

### Results

| Round 1 [17-20.03.2023] |
|---|
| FC Voluntari - AFC Hermannstadt 1-1(1-0) |
| Petrolul Ploieşti - UT Arad 1-0(0-0) |
| FC Botoşani - Chindia Târgovişte 1-0(0-0) |
| FC U Craiova - CS Mioveni 3-0(0-0) |
| Universitatea Cluj - FC Argeş 2-0(1-0) |

| Round 2 [31.03.-03.04.2023] |
|---|
| FC U Craiova - Petrolul Ploieşti 0-1(0-0) |
| UT Arad - Universitatea Cluj 2-0(2-0) |
| AFC Hermannstadt - FC Botoşani 1-1(0-0) |
| FC Argeş - FC Voluntari 0-2(0-2) |
| CS Mioveni - Chindia Târgovişte 0-1(0-0) |

| Round 3 [08-10.04.2023] |
|---|
| FC Voluntari - UT Arad 1-1(1-1) |
| Universitatea Cluj - FC U Craiova 1-3(0-3) |
| Chindia Târgovişte - Hermannstadt 1-2(1-0) |
| FC Botoşani - FC Argeş 1-0(0-0) |
| Petrolul Ploieşti - CS Mioveni 2-0(2-0) |

| Round 4 [14-17.04.2023] |
|---|
| FC U Craiova - FC Voluntari 3-3(1-0) |
| UT Arad - FC Botoşani 0-2(0-2) |
| CS Mioveni - AFC Hermannstadt 0-2(0-1) |
| Petrolul Ploieşti - Universitatea Cluj 0-2(0-2) |
| FC Argeş - Chindia Târgovişte 1-0(1-0) |

| Round 5 [22-24.04.2023] |
|---|
| AFC Hermannstadt - FC Argeş 2-1(2-0) |
| FC Botoşani - FC U Craiova 0-0 |
| Chindia Târgovişte - UT Arad 2-1(1-0) |
| Universitatea Cluj - CS Mioveni 1-0(0-0) |
| FC Voluntari - Petrolul Ploieşti 2-2(1-1) |

| Round 6 [28.04.-02.05.2023] |
|---|
| FC U Craiova - Chindia Târgovişte 1-0(1-0) |
| CS Mioveni - FC Argeş 0-2(0-1) |
| Petrolul Ploieşti - FC Botoşani 1-0(0-0) |
| Universitatea Cluj - FC Voluntari 2-3(2-1) |
| UT Arad - AFC Hermannstadt 1-0(0-0) |

FC Voluntari - CS Mioveni 1-0(1-0)
Chindia Târgovişte - Petrolul Ploieşti 1-2(1-0)
FC Botoşani - Universitatea Cluj 0-0
AFC Hermannstadt - FC U Craiova 0-0
FC Argeş - UT Arad 2-2(0-2)

**Round 8** [12-14.05.2023]
FC Voluntari - FC Botoşani 2-0(1-0)
Petrolul Ploieşti - AFC Hermannstadt 0-1(0-0)
Universitatea Cluj - Chindia Târgov. 2-0(1-0)
CS Mioveni - UT Arad 0-2(0-0)
FC U Craiova - FC Argeş 2-1(2-0)

**Round 9** [19-20.05.2023]
Hermannstadt - Universitatea Cluj 1-2(1-0)
UT Arad - FC U Craiova 1-1(0-0)
FC Argeş - Petrolul Ploieşti 3-0(1-0)
Chindia Târgovişte - FC Voluntari 2-2(0-2)
FC Botoşani - CS Mioveni 5-1(2-1)

### Final Standings

| | | | | | Total | | | Home | | | | Away | | | |
|---|---|---|---|---|---|---|---|---|---|---|---|---|---|---|---|
| 7. | FC Universitatea Craiova 1948 | 9 | 4 | 4 | 1 | 13 - 7 | 36 | 3 | 1 | 1 | 9 - 5 | 1 | 3 | 0 | 4 - 2 |
| 8. | ACS Petrolul Ploieşti | 9 | 5 | 1 | 3 | 9 - 9 | 34 | 3 | 0 | 2 | 4 - 3 | 2 | 1 | 1 | 5 - 6 |
| 9. | FC Voluntari | 9 | 4 | 5 | 0 | 17 - 11 | 34 | 2 | 3 | 0 | 7 - 4 | 2 | 2 | 0 | 10 - 7 |
| 10. | AS FC Universitatea Cluj | 9 | 5 | 1 | 3 | 12 - 9 | 33 | 3 | 0 | 2 | 8 - 6 | 2 | 1 | 1 | 4 - 3 |
| 11. | FC Botoşani | 9 | 4 | 3 | 2 | 10 - 5 | 31 | 3 | 2 | 0 | 7 - 1 | 1 | 1 | 2 | 3 - 4 |
| 12. | AFC Hermannstadt Sibiu | 9 | 4 | 3 | 2 | 10 - 7 | 31 | 1 | 2 | 1 | 4 - 4 | 3 | 1 | 1 | 6 - 3 |
| 13. | FC UT Arad (*Relegation Play-offs*) | 9 | 3 | 3 | 3 | 10 - 9 | 26 | 2 | 1 | 1 | 4 - 3 | 1 | 2 | 2 | 6 - 6 |
| 14. | FC Argeş Piteşti (*Relegation Play-offs*) | 9 | 3 | 1 | 5 | 10 - 11 | 24 | 2 | 1 | 1 | 6 - 4 | 1 | 0 | 4 | 4 - 7 |
| 15. | AFC Chindia Târgovişte (*Relegated*) | 9 | 2 | 1 | 6 | 7 - 12 | 23 | 1 | 1 | 2 | 6 - 7 | 1 | 0 | 4 | 1 - 5 |
| 16. | CS Mioveni (*Relegated*) | 9 | 0 | 0 | 9 | 1 - 19 | 11 | 0 | 0 | 4 | 0 - 7 | 0 | 0 | 5 | 1 - 12 |

FC Universitatea Craiova 1948 and FC Voluntari were qualified for the European competiton play-offs Semi-Final.
ACS Petrolul Ploieşti failed to onbtain a UEFA lience.

### Championship Play-offs

#### Results

**Round 1** [18-19.03.2023]
FCSB Bucureşti - CS Univ. Craiova 1-1(0-1)
FCV Farul - Sepsi OSK 2-1(1-0)
CFR Cluj - Rapid Bucureşti 2-2(2-1)

**Round 2** [01-03.04.2023]
Rapid Bucureşti - FCV Farul 1-1(0-0)
CS Univ. Craiova - CFR Cluj 1-1(0-0)
Sepsi OSK - FCSB Bucureşti 1-2(1-2)

**Round 3** [08-10.04.2023]
FCV Farul - CS Univ. Craiova 3-2(1-1)
CFR Cluj - FCSB Bucureşti 1-1(1-0)
Sepsi OSK - Rapid Bucureşti 2-0(1-0)

**Round 4** [15-17.04.2023]
CFR Cluj - Sepsi OSK 2-1(1-1)
CS Univ. Craiova - Rapid Bucureşti 3-1(1-1)
FCSB Bucureşti - FCV Farul 2-1(1-0)

**Round 5** [21-23.04.2023]
Sepsi OSK - CS Univ. Craiova 1-2(0-0)
FCV Farul - CFR Cluj 1-0(0-0)
Rapid Bucureşti - FCSB Bucureşti 1-0(1-0)

**Round 6** [29.04.-01.05.2023]
Sepsi OSK - FCV Farul 1-1(0-0)
CS Univ. Craiova - FCSB Bucureşti 1-2(0-1)
Rapid Bucureşti - CFR Cluj 3-1(3-1)

**Round 7** [06-08.05.2023]
FCV Farul - Rapid Bucureşti 7-2(4-0)
CFR Cluj - CS Univ. Craiova 1-1(0-0)
FCSB Bucureşti - Sepsi OSK 3-1(1-0)

**Round 8** [12-14.05.2023]
Rapid Bucureşti - Sepsi OSK 0-0
CS Univ. Craiova - FCV Farul 1-1(0-1)
FCSB Bucureşti - CFR Cluj 1-0(0-0)

**Round 9** [20-22.05.2023]
Sepsi OSK - CFR Cluj 1-2(1-1)
FCV Farul - FCSB Bucureşti 3-2(1-2)
Rapid Bucureşti - CS Univ. Craiova 2-3(1-1)

**Round 10** [27-28.05.2023]
FCSB Bucureşti - Rapid Bucureşti 1-5(0-3)
CFR Cluj - FCV Farul 1-2(1-1)
CS Univ. Craiova - Sepsi OSK 0-1(0-0)

### Final Standings

| | | | | | Total | | | Home | | | | Away | | | |
|---|---|---|---|---|---|---|---|---|---|---|---|---|---|---|---|
| 1. | **FCV Farul Constanţa** | 10 | 6 | 3 | 1 | 22 - 13 | 53 | 5 | 0 | 0 | 16 - 7 | 1 | 3 | 1 | 6 - 6 |
| 2. | SC FCSB Bucureşti | 10 | 5 | 2 | 3 | 15 - 15 | 46 | 3 | 1 | 1 | 8 - 8 | 2 | 1 | 2 | 7 - 7 |
| 3. | FC CFR 1907 Cluj-Napoca | 10 | 2 | 4 | 4 | 11 - 14 | 42 | 1 | 3 | 1 | 7 - 7 | 1 | 1 | 3 | 4 - 7 |
| 4. | CS Universitatea Craiova | 10 | 3 | 4 | 3 | 15 - 14 | 40 | 1 | 2 | 2 | 6 - 6 | 2 | 2 | 1 | 9 - 8 |
| 5. | FC Rapid 1923 Bucureşti | 10 | 3 | 3 | 4 | 17 - 20 | 38 | 2 | 2 | 1 | 7 - 5 | 1 | 1 | 3 | 10 - 15 |
| 6. | ACS Sepsi OSK Sfântu Gheorghe | 10 | 2 | 2 | 6 | 10 - 14 | 29 | 1 | 1 | 3 | 6 - 7 | 1 | 1 | 3 | 4 - 7 |

FC CFR 1907 Cluj-Napoca were qualified for the European competiton play-offs Final.

### Top goalscorers:

| | | |
|---|---|---|
| 22 | **Marko Dugandžić (CRO)** | *FC Rapid 1923 Bucureşti* |
| 20 | Andrea Compagno (ITA) | *FC Universitatea Craiova 1948 & FCSB Bucureşti* |
| 16 | Sebastian Árpád Mailat | *FC Botoşani* |

| **Semi-Final** [26.05.2023] | FC Universitatea Craiova 1948 - FC Voluntari | 3-3(1-0,3-3,3-3); 5-4 pen |
|---|---|---|
| **Final** [01.06.2023] | FC CFR 1907 Cluj-Napoca - FC Universitatea Craiova 1948 | 1-0(0-0,0-0) |

**Relegation Play-offs** [28-29.05.-03-04.06.2023]

| | | |
|---|---|---|
| FC Gloria Buzău - FC UT Arad | 0-0 | 1-5(0-1) |
| FC Dinamo Bucureşti - FC Argeş Piteşti | 6-1(4-0) | 2-4(1-2) |

Both FC UT Arad and FC Dinamo Bucureşti will play at first level in 2023/2024.

# NATIONAL CUP
## Cupa României 2022/2023

**Group Stage** [18.10.-08.12.2022]

| **Group A** | |
|---|---|
| FC Dinamo Bucureşti - FC Universitatea Craiova 1948 | 0-0 |
| AFC Unirea 04 Slobozia - FC Voluntari | 0-1(0-0) |
| ACS Petrolul Ploieşti - ACS Sepsi OSK Sfântu Gheorghe | 1-3(0-0) |
| AFC Unirea 04 Slobozia - ACS Petrolul Ploieşti | 0-0 |
| FC Dinamo Bucureşti - ACS Sepsi OSK Sfântu Gheorghe | 2-3(0-1) |
| FC Universitatea Craiova 1948- FC Voluntari | 1-0(1-0) |
| ACS Sepsi OSK Sfântu Gheorghe - FC Voluntari | 4-0(2-0) |
| ACS Petrolul Ploieşti - FC Universitatea Craiova 1948 | 0-1(0-0) |
| AFC Unirea 04 Slobozia - FC Dinamo Bucureşti | 3-3(1-3) |
| *Qualified*: ACS Sepsi OSK Sfântu Gheorghe, FC Universit.Craiova 1948 | |

| **Group B** | |
|---|---|
| FC Gloria Buzău - FC Botoşani | 0-1(0-0) |
| FC UT Arad - SC FCSB Bucureşti | 2-2(1-1) |
| ACS SC Oţelul Galaţi - CS Mioveni | 0-1(0-1) |
| CS Mioveni - FC Botoşani | 1-0(0-0) |
| FC Gloria Buzău - FC UT Arad | 1-3(1-2) |
| ACS SC Oţelul Galaţi - SC FCSB Bucureşti | 0-0 |
| FC Botoşani - SC FCSB Bucureşti | 0-2(0-0) |
| CS Mioveni - FC UT Arad | 0-3(0-1) |
| ACS SC Oţelul Galaţi - FC Gloria Buzău | 0-2(0-1) |
| *Qualified*: FC UT Arad, CS Mioveni | |

| **Group C** | |
|---|---|
| CSM Alexandria - FCV Farul Constanţa | 2-2(1-1) |
| CSC Dumbrăviţa - FC Rapid 1923 Bucureşti | 1-4(1-1) |
| AS FC Universitatea Cluj - FC CFR 1907 Cluj-Napoca | 1-1(0-1) |
| FC Rapid 1923 Bucureşti - FCV Farul Constanţa | 0-2(0-1) |
| CSM Alexandria - AS FC Universitatea Cluj | 0-4(0-1) |
| CSC Dumbrăviţa - FC CFR 1907 Cluj-Napoca | 0-5(0-0) |
| CSM Alexandria - CSC Dumbrăviţa | 0-4(0-2) |
| FCV Farul Constanţa - FC CFR 1907 Cluj-Napoca | 0-0 |
| AS FC Universitatea Cluj - FC Rapid 1923 Bucureşti | 0-0 |
| *Qualified*: FC CFR 1907 Cluj-Napoca, AS FC Universitatea Cluj | |

| **Group D** | |
|---|---|
| CS Ocna Mureş - AFC Chindia Târgovişte | 1-0(1-0) |
| AFC Hermannstadt Sibiu - CS Universitatea Craiova | 0-2(0-1) |
| CS Minaur Baia Mare - FC Argeş Piteşti | 0-0 |
| CS Minaur Baia Mare - AFC Hermannstadt Sibiu | 2-3(0-1) |
| AFC Chindia Târgovişte - FC Argeş Piteşti | 1-1(1-1) |
| CS Ocna Mureş - CS Universitatea Craiova | 1-1(0-1) |
| FC Argeş Piteşti - CS Universitatea Craiova | 2-1(0-0) |
| AFC Hermannstadt Sibiu - AFC Chindia Târgovişte | 4-1(3-1) |
| CS Ocna Mureş - CS Minaur Baia Mare | 0-6(0-1) |
| *Qualified*: AFC Hermannstadt Sibiu, FC Argeş Piteşti | |

**Quarter-Finals** [04-06.04.2023]

| | | | | |
|---|---|---|---|---|
| FC UT Arad - FC Universitatea Craiova 1948 | 1-0(1-0) | | ACS Sepsi OSK Sfântu Gheorghe - CS Mioveni | 4-1(0-0) |
| AFC Hermannstadt Sibiu - AS FC Universitatea Cluj | 1-2(1-0) | | FC CFR 1907 Cluj-Napoca - FC Argeş Piteşti | 1-0(0-0) |

**Semi-Finals** [26-27.04.2023]

| | | | | |
|---|---|---|---|---|
| ACS Sepsi OSK Sf. G. - FC CFR 1907 Cluj-Napoca | 3-0(2-0) | | AS FC Universitatea Cluj - FC UT Arad | 1-0(1-0) |

**Final**

24.05.2023; Stadionul Municipal, Sibiu; Referee: Cătălin Popa; Attendance: 11,813
**ACS Sepsi OSK Sfântu Gheorghe - AS FC Universitatea Cluj**　　　　　　　　　　**0-0 aet; 5-4 on penalties**

**Sepsi OSK**: Roland-Csaba Niczuly (Cap), Denis Ciobotariu (86.Radoslav Dimitrov), Branislav Niňaj, Mihai Bălaşa (86.Márk Tamás), Andres Dumitrescu, Jonathan Yoni Emanuel Rodríguez, Nicolae Păun (90+22.Roland Varga), Mario Júnior Rondón Fernández (46.Adnan Aganović), Cosmin Matei (75.Ion Gheorghe), Marius Ştefănescu, Pavol Šafranko (75.Alexandru Tudorie). Trainer: Cristiano Bergodi (Italy).

**Universitatea Cluj**: Andrei Gorcea, Ivan Martić, Andrei Piţian, Andrei Miron, Alexandru Chipciu (Cap), Ioan Filip (80.José Gomes „Zé Gomes"), Gabriel Simion, Martin Remacle (90+9.Ely Ernesto Lopes Fernandes), Dan Nistor, Ovidiu Bic, Mamadou Thiam (90+9.Dragoş Tescan). Trainer: Ioan Ovidiu Sabău.

**Penalties:** Roland Varga 1-0; Alexandru Chipciu 1-1; Jonathan Yoni Emanuel Rodríguez (saved); Ovidiu Bic 1-2; Alexandru Tudorie 2-2; Dragoş Tescan 2-3; Ion Gheorghe 3-3; Ely Ernesto Lopes Fernandes (saved); Marius Ştefănescu 4-3; Dan Nistor 4-4; Adnan Aganović (missed); José Gomes „Zé Gomes" (saved); Márk Tamás 5-4; Ivan Martić (saved).

Please note: appearances and goals are including statistics of both regular season and play-offs (Championship or Relegation).

## Asociaţia Sport Club Campionii Fotbal Club Argeş Piteşti

| | | |
|---|---|---|
| **Founded**: | 06.08.1953 (*as Dinamo Piteşti*) | |
| **Stadium**: | Stadionul „Nicolae Dobrin", Piteşti (15,000) | |
| **Trainer**: | Constantin Schumacher | 08.05.1976 |
| [26.10.2022] | Marius Croitoru | 02.10.1980 |
| [08.03.2023] | Dragoş Radu | 02.06.1981 |
| [15.03.2023] | Bogdan Vintilă | 27.02.1972 |

| Goalkeepers: | DOB | M | (s) | G |
|---|---|---|---|---|
| Alexandru Greab | 26.05.1992 | 7 | (2) | |
| George Micle | 08.11.2001 | 7 | (1) | |
| Sebastian Micu | 19.05.2001 | 1 | | |
| Cătălin Straton | 09.10.1989 | 24 | | |
| **Defenders:** | **DOB** | **M** | **(s)** | **G** |
| Zorhan Ludovic Bassong (CAN) | 07.05.1999 | 6 | (2) | |
| *Brendon* Lucas da Silva Estevam (BRA) | 20.05.1995 | 6 | (2) | |
| Mike Cestor Botuli (COD) | 30.04.1992 | 16 | | |
| Marius Constantin | 25.10.1984 | 21 | (2) | |
| Alin Dobrosavlevici | 24.10.1994 | 15 | (5) | |
| *Fábio* André Freitas *Vianna* (POR) | 08.10.1998 | 12 | (3) | |
| Iasmin Latovlevici | 11.05.1986 | 9 | (2) | |
| Claudiu Moisie | 13.05.2000 | | (2) | |
| Facundo Emanuel Rizzi (ARG) | 28.08.1997 | 15 | (1) | |
| Andrei Tofan | 02.08.1996 | 30 | (4) | 1 |
| Grigore Turda | 30.07.1997 | 17 | (3) | 1 |
| Mario Zebić (CRO) | 17.12.1995 | 10 | (1) | 1 |
| **Midfielders:** | **DOB** | **M** | **(s)** | **G** |
| Bryan Alcéus (HAI) | 01.02.1996 | 8 | (8) | |
| Horaţiu Răzvan Covaci | 10.10.2003 | | (2) | |
| Geani Creţu | 12.01.2000 | 10 | (7) | |
| David Croitoru | 09.08.2003 | | (1) | |
| Antonio Jakoliš (CRO) | 28.02.1992 | 20 | (12) | 1 |
| Derlis David Meza Colli (PAR) | 15.08.1988 | 24 | (10) | |
| Atair *Mimito* Rocha Biai (GNB) | 12.12.1997 | 9 | (2) | |
| Tony Njiké (FRA) | 29.01.1998 | 34 | | |
| Martin Raynov (BUL) | 25.04.1992 | 6 | (2) | |
| Ionuţ Şerban | 09.03.1992 | 8 | (10) | 1 |
| Andrei Tîrcoveanu | 22.05.1997 | 3 | (5) | |
| **Forwards:** | **DOB** | **M** | **(s)** | **G** |
| Dorian Bertrand (MAD) | 21.05.1993 | 13 | (11) | 2 |
| Boubacar Hanne (POR) | 26.02.1999 | 2 | (5) | |
| Andreiaş Cristian Calcan | 09.04.1994 | 23 | (12) | 3 |
| Enzo Célestine (FRA) | 24.07.1997 | | (7) | |
| Julio Donisa (MAD) | 15.01.1994 | 4 | (5) | |
| Paul Arnold Garita (CMR) | 18.06.1993 | 32 | (4) | 12 |
| Alexandru Işfan | 31.01.2000 | 21 | | 4 |
| Wesley Jobello (FRA) | 23.01.1994 | 6 | (8) | 1 |
| Kevin Koubemba (CGO) | 23.03.1993 | 10 | (4) | 2 |
| Gino Oprescu | 18.08.2005 | | (1) | |
| Yanis Pîrvu | 02.04.2007 | | (6) | |

## Fotbal Club Botoşani

| | | |
|---|---|---|
| **Founded**: | 2001 | |
| **Stadium**: | Stadionul Municipal, Botoşani (7,782) | |
| **Trainer**: | Mihai Răzvan Teja | 22.09.1978 |
| [10.12.2022] | Alin Bejan | 14.09.1975 |
| [17.11.2022] | Mihai Ciobanu | 27.05.1960 |
| [10.12.2022] | Flavius Stoican | 24.11.1976 |

| Goalkeepers: | DOB | M | (s) | G |
|---|---|---|---|---|
| Răzvan Ducan | 09.02.2001 | 9 | | |
| Eduard Pap | 01.07.1994 | 30 | | |
| **Defenders:** | **DOB** | **M** | **(s)** | **G** |
| Kévin Gnonher Boli (CIV) | 21.06.1991 | 11 | (1) | |
| Victor Dican | 11.10.2000 | 37 | (1) | 1 |
| Andrei Dragu | 07.10.1999 | 27 | (8) | 2 |
| Narcis Cosmin Ilaş | 27.03.2007 | 1 | | |
| Kassim M'Dahoma (COM) | 26.01.1997 | | (1) | |
| Ayrton Mboko (BEL) | 23.10.1997 | 6 | (2) | |
| Gabriel Mutombo (FRA) | 19.01.1996 | 14 | | 1 |
| Andrei Patache | 29.10.1987 | 12 | (7) | 1 |
| Júnior Udeme Pius (NGA) | 20.12.1995 | 9 | | |
| Rijad Sadiku (BIH) | 18.01.2000 | 12 | (7) | |
| Shaquill Sno (NED) | 05.01.1996 | 12 | (4) | 2 |
| Alin Şeroni | 26.03.1987 | 18 | (7) | 1 |
| Alexandru Ţigănaşu | 12.06.1990 | 32 | | 1 |
| **Midfielders:** | **DOB** | **M** | **(s)** | **G** |
| Marius Cioiu | 01.11.1999 | 4 | (11) | |
| Gabriel David | 11.02.2003 | | (2) | |
| George Dragomir | 06.08.2003 | | (2) | |
| Eduard Marian Florescu | 27.06.1997 | 11 | (9) | 3 |
| Antoni Ivanov (BUL) | 11.09.1995 | 30 | (3) | |
| Franco Gabriel Mussis (ARG) | 19.04.1992 | 8 | (4) | |
| Ovidiu Ioan Perianu | 16.04.2002 | 9 | (3) | |
| Charles Petro (MWI) | 08.02.2001 | 9 | | |
| Virgile Pinson (FRA) | 22.02.1996 | 3 | (15) | |
| Elad Shahaf (ISR) | 13.01.1998 | 5 | (7) | |
| Yacouba Sylla (MLI) | 29.11.1990 | 9 | (6) | |
| Andrei Tîrcoveanu | 22.05.1997 | 3 | (8) | |
| Cyril Zabou (FRA) | 18.06.1996 | 16 | (6) | |
| **Forwards:** | **DOB** | **M** | **(s)** | **G** |
| Andrei Burlacu | 12.01.1997 | | (5) | |
| Sekou Camara (GUI) | 20.07.1997 | 14 | (19) | 5 |
| Iulian Cărăuşu | 03.07.2005 | | (2) | |
| Cătălin Golofca | 21.04.1990 | | (7) | |
| Sergej Grubač (MNE) | 29.05.2000 | | (4) | |
| Sebastian Mailat | 12.12.1997 | 35 | (1) | 16 |
| Mateus Barbosa Santos „Mateus Criciúma" (BRA) | 19.01.1999 | 13 | (1) | |
| Petar Petkovski (MKD) | 03.01.1997 | 2 | (8) | |
| Mihai Roman I | 16.10.1984 | 2 | (16) | |
| Mihai Alexandru Roman II | 31.05.1992 | 22 | (10) | 5 |
| Junior Tallo (CIV) | 21.12.1992 | 3 | (1) | |
| Terrence Tisdell (LBR) | 16.03.1998 | 1 | (3) | 1 |

## Fotbal Club Căile Ferate Române 1907 Cluj-Napoca

| | | |
|---|---|---|
| **Founded**: | 1907 (*as Kolozsvári Vasutas Sport Club*) | |
| **Stadium**: | Stadionul "Dr. Constantin Rădulescu", Cluj-Napoca (23,500) | |
| **Trainer**: | Dan Vasile Petrescu | 22.12.1967 |

| Goalkeepers: | DOB | M | (s) | G |
|---|---|---|---|---|
| Cristian Emanuel Bălgrădean | 21.03.1988 | 3 | | |
| Răzvan Sava | 21.06.2002 | 3 | | |
| Simone Scuffet (ITA) | 31.05.1996 | 34 | | |
| **Defenders:** | **DOB** | **M** | **(s)** | **G** |
| Rareş Bălan | 19.01.2000 | 1 | (1) | |
| Christopher Braun (GER) | 15.07.1991 | 23 | (7) | 1 |
| Karlo Bručić (CRO) | 17.04.1992 | 3 | | |
| Andrei Andonie Burcă | 15.04.1993 | 28 | | |
| Mário Jorge Melico Paulino "Camora" | 10.11.1986 | 26 | (3) | 1 |
| Daniel Graovac (BIH) | 08.08.1993 | 2 | | |
| Denis Kolinger (CRO) | 14.01.1994 | 18 | (3) | 1 |
| Cephas Malele (ANG) | 08.01.1994 | 12 | (6) | 4 |
| Cristian Marian Manea | 09.08.1997 | 28 | (2) | 5 |
| Andrei Peteleu | 20.08.1992 | 1 | (6) | |
| Bogdan Ţîru | 15.03.1994 | 1 | (4) | |
| Jefferson *Yuri* De Sousa *Matias* (BRA) | 10.02.1995 | 30 | (4) | 4 |
| **Midfielders:** | **DOB** | **M** | **(s)** | **G** |
| Nana Boateng (GHA) | 10.05.1994 | 31 | (1) | 3 |
| Mihai Cătălin Bordeianu | 18.11.1991 | 9 | (4) | |
| Lovro Cvek (CRO) | 06.07.1995 | 19 | (11) | 2 |
| Ciprian Ioan Deac | 16.02.1986 | 28 | (3) | 6 |
| Alin Fică | 14.06.2001 | 5 | (2) | |
| Adrian Gîdea | 13.03.2000 | | (4) | |
| Ovidiu Hoban | 27.12.1982 | 3 | (19) | 1 |
| Vito Hammershøy-Mistrati (DEN) | 15.06.1992 | | (5) | 1 |
| Karlo Muhar (CRO) | 17.01.1996 | 27 | (5) | 5 |
| Claudiu Adrian Mihai Petrila | 07.11.2000 | 22 | (16) | 3 |
| *Roger* Junio Rodrigues Figueira (BRA) | 01.03.1996 | 5 | (12) | |
| **Forwards:** | **DOB** | **M** | **(s)** | **G** |
| Daniel Birligea | 19.04.2000 | 16 | (15) | 5 |
| Sergiu Buş | 02.11.1992 | | (4) | |
| Gabriel Debeljuh (CRO) | 28.09.1996 | 2 | (2) | 2 |
| Marko Dugandžić (CRO) | 07.04.1994 | 1 | | |
| Rangelo Maria Janga (CUW) | 16.04.1992 | 21 | (9) | 10 |
| *Jefté* Betancor Sánchez (ESP) | 06.07.1993 | 4 | (3) | 1 |
| Ermal Krasniqi (KOS) | 07.09.1998 | 15 | (3) | 4 |
| Anton Maglica (CRO) | 11.11.1991 | 2 | (8) | 1 |
| Adrian Păun | 01.04.1995 | 2 | (3) | |
| Emmanuel Kwaku Yeboah (GHA) | 25.02.2003 | 15 | (16) | 3 |

## Asociaţia Fotbal Club Chindia Târgovişte

| | | | | |
|---|---|---|---|---|
| **Founded**: | 11.08.2010 | | | |
| **Stadium**: | Stadionul „Eugen Popescu", Târgovişte (8,400) | | | |
| **Trainer**: | Adrian Mihalcea | | 24.05.1976 | |
| [21.09.2022] | Anton Petrea | | 09.03.1975 | |

| Goalkeepers: | DOB | M | (s) | G |
|---|---|---|---|---|
| Cătălin Căbuz | 18.06.1996 | 34 | | |
| Dinu Moldovan | 03.05.1990 | 5 | (1) | |
| **Defenders:** | **DOB** | **M** | **(s)** | **G** |
| Costel Avram | 11.06.2002 | | (1) | |
| Deian Boldor | 03.02.1995 | 20 | (5) | 1 |
| Tiberiu Căpuşă | 06.04.1998 | 33 | (1) | 1 |
| Daniel Celea | 06.07.1995 | 34 | | 2 |
| Constantin Cristian Dima | 21.07.1999 | | (1) | |
| Cornel Dinu | 09.06.1989 | 7 | (9) | |
| *Esteban* Obiang Obono (EQG) | 07.05.1998 | 19 | (8) | 1 |
| Adrian Ioniţă | 11.03.2000 | 20 | (7) | |
| **Midfielders:** | **DOB** | **M** | **(s)** | **G** |
| Rassambeck Akhmatov (FRA) | 31.05.1996 | 27 | (2) | 1 |
| Cosmin Atanase | 03.01.2001 | 2 | (9) | 1 |
| Cristian Cherchez | 01.02.1991 | | (5) | |
| Jérémy Jimmy Théophile Corinus (FRA) | 16.03.1997 | 12 | (2) | |

| Marco Alexandru Dulca | 11.05.1999 | 19 | | |
|---|---|---|---|---|
| Denis Dumitraşcu | 27.04.1995 | 24 | (11) | |
| Alexandru Jipa | 14.09.2001 | | (2) | |
| Aly Ndom (FRA) | 30.05.1996 | | (1) | |
| Juan Pablo Passaglia (ARG) | 24.05.1989 | 8 | (8) | |
| Ovidiu Perianu | 16.04.2002 | 4 | (5) | |
| Doru Popadiuc | 18.02.1995 | 31 | (3) | 8 |
| Andrei Şerban | 31.10.2000 | 14 | (16) | 2 |
| Modestas Vorobjovas (LTU) | 30.12.1995 | 22 | (11) | |
| **Forwards:** | **DOB** | **M** | **(s)** | **G** |
| Sergiu Buş | 02.11.1992 | 2 | (14) | |
| Nasser Chamed (COM) | 04.10.1993 | 8 | (11) | |
| Godberg Cooper (ITA) | 20.08.1997 | 11 | (16) | 5 |
| Sergej Grubač (MNE) | 29.05.2000 | | (10) | |
| Andreas Mihaiu | 19.08.1998 | 2 | (9) | 1 |
| Cristian Neguţ | 09.12.1995 | 34 | (1) | 6 |
| Daniel Popa | 14.07.1995 | 37 | | 9 |

## Fotbal Club Viitorul Farul Constanţa

| | | | | |
|---|---|---|---|---|
| **Founded**: | 2009 (*as Viitorul Constanţa*) | | | |
| **Stadium**: | Stadionul Viitorul, Constanţa (4,554) | | | |
| **Trainer**: | Gheorghe Hagi | | 05.02.1965 | |

| Goalkeepers: | DOB | M | (s) | G |
|---|---|---|---|---|
| Mihai Aioani | 07.11.1999 | 39 | | |
| Alexandru Buzbuchi | 31.10.1993 | 1 | | |
| **Defenders:** | **DOB** | **M** | **(s)** | **G** |
| Rolandas Baravykas (LTU) | 23.08.1995 | 2 | (1) | |
| Romario Sandu Benzar | 26.03.1992 | 4 | (2) | |
| Daniel Bîrzu | 28.05.2002 | | (2) | |
| Radu Boboc | 24.04.1999 | | (1) | |
| Kévin Boli (CIV) | 21.06.1991 | 7 | (6) | |
| Andrei Borza | 12.11.2005 | 16 | (17) | 3 |
| *Gustavo* Henrique *Maríns* Silva (BRA) | 11.02.2002 | 1 | (4) | |
| David Kiki (BEN) | 25.11.1993 | 35 | (3) | 1 |
| Ionuţ Larie | 16.01.1987 | 39 | | 3 |
| Sebastian Mladen | 11.12.1991 | 4 | | |
| Mihai Popescu | 07.05.1993 | 29 | (1) | 1 |
| Dan Sîrbu | 22.04.2003 | 15 | (15) | |
| **Midfielders:** | **DOB** | **M** | **(s)** | **G** |
| Andrei Artean | 14.08.1993 | 39 | (1) | 3 |
| Tudor Cristian Băluţă | 27.03.1999 | 27 | (5) | 6 |
| Luca Banu | 31.01.2005 | | (2) | |
| Carlos Casap | 29.12.1998 | 4 | (25) | 1 |

| Jérémy Jimmy Théophile Corinus (FRA) | 16.03.1997 | 1 | (3) | |
|---|---|---|---|---|
| Kevin Doukouré (CIV) | 30.03.1999 | 4 | (23) | 1 |
| Constantin Grameni | 23.10.2002 | 33 | (6) | 6 |
| Robert Andrei Ion | 05.09.2000 | 1 | (2) | |
| Dragoş Ionuţ Nedelcu | 16.02.1997 | 23 | (6) | 1 |
| Nicolas Popescu | 02.01.2003 | | (1) | |
| Eduard Rădăslăvescu | 30.07.2004 | | (1) | |
| **Forwards:** | **DOB** | **M** | **(s)** | **G** |
| Denis Alibec | 05.01.1991 | 29 | (2) | 14 |
| Luca Andronache | 26.07.2003 | | (3) | |
| Ionuţ Cojocaru | 28.07.2003 | | (3) | |
| Mateus Barbosa Santos „Mateus Criciúma" (BRA) | 19.01.1999 | 2 | (11) | 2 |
| Adrian Mazilu | 13.09.2005 | 14 | (5) | 6 |
| Robert Moldoveanu | 08.03.1999 | 1 | (6) | 1 |
| Vlad Morar | 01.08.1993 | 9 | (12) | 4 |
| Louis Munteanu | 16.06.2002 | 26 | (3) | 10 |
| Adrian Petre | 11.02.1998 | 1 | (2) | 2 |
| Alexi Pitu | 05.06.2002 | 19 | (1) | 5 |
| Enes Sali | 23.02.2006 | 3 | (16) | 2 |
| Alexandru Stoian | 15.12.2007 | | (1) | |
| Gabriel Andrei Torje | 22.11.1989 | 12 | (4) | 3 |

## Sport Club Fotbal Club FCSB Bucureşti

| | | | | |
|---|---|---|---|---|
| **Founded**: | 07.06.1947 (*as AS Armata Bucureşti*) | | | |
| **Stadium**: | Arena Naţională, Bucureşti (55,634) | | | |
| **Trainer**: | Anton Petrea | | 09.03.1975 | |
| [26.07.2022] | Nicolae Dică | | 09.05.1980 | |
| [01.11.2022] | Mihai Pintilii | | 09.11.1984 | |
| [30.11.2022] | Leonard Strizu | | 26.08.1967 | |
| [03.03.2023] | Mihai Pintilii | | 09.11.1984 | |
| [30.03.2023] | Ilias Charalampous (CYP) | | 25.09.1980 | |

| Goalkeepers: | DOB | M | (s) | G |
|---|---|---|---|---|
| Ştefan Târnovanu | 09.05.2000 | 37 | | |
| Andrei Vlad | 15.04.1999 | 3 | | |
| **Defenders:** | **DOB** | **M** | **(s)** | **G** |
| Radu Ştefăniţă Boboc | 24.04.1999 | 5 | | |
| Rachid Ahmed Bouhenna (ALG) | 29.06.1991 | 4 | | |
| Valentin Iulian Creţu | 02.01.1989 | 12 | (5) | |
| Iulian Lucian Cristea | 17.07.1994 | 7 | (7) | |
| Joyskim Dawa Tchakonte (CMR) | 09.04.1996 | 33 | (2) | 3 |
| Denis Hăruţ | 25.02.1999 | 5 | (4) | |
| Alexandru Pantea | 11.09.2003 | 10 | (7) | |
| Risto Radunović (MNE) | 04.05.1992 | 31 | | 1 |
| Sorin Şerban | 17.03.2000 | 2 | | |
| Joonas Tamm (EST) | 02.02.1992 | 32 | (3) | 3 |
| **Midfielders:** | **DOB** | **M** | **(s)** | **G** |
| Andrei Cordea | 24.06.1999 | 27 | (10) | 7 |
| Marco Alexandru Dulca | 11.05.1999 | 3 | (2) | |
| Malcom Edjouma (FRA) | 08.10.1996 | 23 | (6) | 9 |
| Alexandru Musi | 17.04.2004 | 1 | (2) | |

| Boban Nikolov (MKD) | 28.07.1994 | | (11) | |
|---|---|---|---|---|
| Răzvan Oaidă | 02.03.1998 | 11 | (11) | |
| Darius Olaru | 03.03.1998 | 34 | (3) | 1 |
| Ovidiu Marian Popescu | 27.02.1994 | 8 | (9) | 1 |
| Vadim Raţă (MDA) | 05.05.1993 | 2 | | |
| Eduard Rădăslăvescu | 30.07.2004 | 1 | (13) | 1 |
| Deian Sorescu | 29.08.1997 | 17 | (1) | 2 |
| Adrian Şut | 30.04.1999 | 30 | (2) | 5 |
| Florin Lucian Tănase | 30.12.1994 | 2 | | 1 |
| **Forwards:** | **DOB** | **M** | **(s)** | **G** |
| Florinel Coman | 10.04.1998 | 28 | (7) | 8 |
| Andrea Compagno (ITA) | 22.04.1996 | 26 | (1) | 15 |
| Ioan Andrei Vasile Dumiter | 10.04.1999 | | (1) | |
| Ivan Mamut (CRO) | 30.04.1997 | | (2) | |
| David Raul Miculescu | 02.05.2001 | 11 | (25) | 3 |
| Billel Omrani (FRA) | 02.06.1993 | 6 | (16) | 2 |
| Octavian George Popescu | 27.12.2002 | 24 | (12) | 4 |
| Gheorghe Bogdan Rusu | 09.04.1990 | 2 | (1) | |
| Ianis Ilie Stoica | 08.12.2002 | 3 | (3) | |

## Asociaţia Fotbal Club Hermannstadt Sibiu

**Founded**: 29.07.2015
**Stadium**: Stadionul Municipal, Sibiu (13,013)
**Trainer**: Constantin Marius Măldărăşanu — 19.04.1975

| Goalkeepers: | DOB | M | (s) | G |
|---|---|---|---|---|
| Plamen Iliev (BUL) | 30.11.1991 | 5 | | |
| Karlo Letica (CRO) | 11.02.1997 | 25 | | |
| Vlad Muţiu | 02.02.1995 | 9 | | |
| **Defenders:** | DOB | M | (s) | G |
| Florin Bejan | 28.03.1991 | 25 | (2) | 1 |
| Mihai Butean | 14.09.1996 | 35 | | 1 |
| Cornel Ene | 21.07.1993 | 7 | (1) | |
| Saeed Issah (GHA) | 11.01.2000 | 3 | (4) | |
| Paolo Medina Etienne (MEX) | 28.05.1999 | 8 | (3) | |
| Raul Opruţ | 04.01.1998 | 34 | | 2 |
| Ionuţ Stoica | 06.01.1988 | 31 | | 2 |
| **Midfielders:** | DOB | M | (s) | G |
| Baba Alhassan (GHA) | 03.01.2000 | 21 | (9) | 6 |
| Paul Antoche | 21.06.1992 | 17 | (2) | |
| Ionuţ Biceanu | 26.02.1994 | 31 | (7) | |
| Dragoş Iancu | 29.09.2002 | | (11) | |
| Sota Mino (JPN) | 20.10.1994 | 32 | (4) | |
| Alexandru Ilie Răuţă | 17.06.1992 | 7 | (9) | |
| **Forwards:** | DOB | M | (s) | G |
| Matko Babić (CRO) | 28.07.1998 | | (23) | 1 |
| Silviu Balaure | 06.02.1996 | 28 | (11) | 4 |
| Cristian Bărbuţ | 22.04.1995 | 1 | (10) | |
| Valentin Buhăcianu | 28.10.1993 | 1 | (15) | |
| Adrian Ioan Hora | 21.08.1988 | 1 | (1) | |
| Gabriel Iancu | 15.04.1994 | 7 | (2) | 1 |
| Vesel Limaj (GER) | 01.12.1996 | 8 | (7) | 1 |
| Ionuţ Eugen Năstăsie | 07.01.1992 | 2 | (12) | |
| Alexandru Oroian | 27.01.2001 | 20 | (13) | 2 |
| Daniel Paraschiv | 24.04.1999 | 38 | (1) | 14 |
| Petrişor Petrescu | 29.06.1993 | 14 | (20) | 1 |
| Călin Popescu | 15.11.2001 | 19 | (11) | |

## Clubul Sportiv Mioveni

**Founded**: 15.08.2000 (as AS Mioveni 2000)
**Stadium**: Stadionul Orăşenesc, Mioveni (10,000)
**Trainer**: Alexandru Pelici — 10.01.1974
[24.08.2022] Flavius Stoican — 24.11.1976
[01.11.2022] Marius Stoica — 23.08.1969
[05.12.2022] Adrian Matei — 29.02.1968
[14.01.2023] Nicolae Dică — 09.05.1980
[26.04.2023] George Cotiga — 12.10.1989

| Goalkeepers: | DOB | M | (s) | G |
|---|---|---|---|---|
| Laurenţiu Bucur | 08.09.2005 | | (1) | |
| Flavius Croitoru | 13.07.1992 | 5 | | |
| Alexandru Greab | 26.05.1992 | 13 | | |
| Iustin Popescu | 01.09.1993 | 17 | | |
| Valentin Sima | 20.10.1997 | 4 | | |
| **Defenders:** | DOB | M | (s) | G |
| Ionuţ Balaur | 06.06.1989 | 22 | (3) | 1 |
| Ionuţ Burnea | 12.08.1992 | 13 | (6) | |
| Cornel Alexandru Ene | 21.07.1993 | 3 | (2) | |
| *Guilherme* Gomes Garutti (BRA) | 08.03.1994 | 33 | | 1 |
| Alexandru Iacob | 14.04.1989 | 7 | (1) | |
| Marcos "Marquinhos" Garbellotto Silveira Pedroso (BRA) | 04.10.1993 | 11 | (1) | |
| Dylan Teddy Ngallot Mboumbouni (CTA) | 20.02.1996 | 2 | (3) | |
| Dorinel Oancea | 02.04.1997 | 18 | (1) | |
| Teodor Peştişor | 08.11.2004 | | (1) | |
| Adrian Scarlatache | 05.12.1986 | 28 | | 3 |
| Daniel Şerbănică | 25.06.1996 | 11 | (3) | |
| Shaquill Sno (NED) | 05.01.1996 | 12 | (2) | |
| Răzvan Trif | 09.10.1997 | 10 | (4) | |
| **Midfielders:** | DOB | M | (s) | G |
| Amine Benchaib (BEL) | 18.06.1998 | 9 | (6) | 3 |
| Adrian Cierpka (POL) | 06.01.1995 | | (1) | |
| Valentin Coşereanu | 17.07.1991 | 6 | (17) | |
| Emanuel Dat | 18.01.2001 | 1 | (1) | |
| Remus Guţea | 18.04.2005 | 3 | (4) | 1 |
| Brent Lepistu (EST) | 26.03.1993 | 4 | (4) | |
| Mihai Lixandru | 05.06.2001 | 27 | (3) | 1 |
| Andrei Militaru | 03.04.2005 | | (1) | |
| Vlad Mitrea | 23.01.2001 | | (1) | |
| Andrei Panait | 16.05.1989 | 23 | (3) | |
| Vlad Pop | 31.08.2000 | 24 | (5) | |
| Daniel Toma | 22.04.2000 | 6 | (16) | |
| Szilard Vereş | 27.01.1996 | 3 | | |
| **Forwards:** | DOB | M | (s) | G |
| Liviu Antal | 02.06.1989 | 16 | (14) | 2 |
| Ştefan Blănaru | 20.02.1989 | 11 | (3) | |
| Andrei Burlacu | 12.01.1997 | 1 | (6) | |
| Alexandru Buziuc | 15.03.1994 | 14 | (12) | 2 |
| Amateo Andrei Căprescu | 23.10.2004 | 1 | (2) | |
| Nicolae Cârnaţ | 08.04.1998 | 13 | (13) | 1 |
| Amadou Diallo (GUI) | 21.06.1994 | 6 | (6) | |
| Cristian Cosmin Dumitru | 13.12.2001 | 1 | (3) | |
| Junior Kabananga Kalonji (COD) | 04.04.1989 | 1 | (9) | |
| Blerim Krasniqi (ALB) | 05.07.1996 | 12 | (11) | 2 |
| Ionuţ Rădescu | 20.03.1995 | 19 | (14) | |
| Bogdan Rusu | 09.04.1990 | 18 | (2) | 7 |
| Albert Voinea | 06.12.1992 | 1 | (1) | |

## Asociaţia Clubul Sportiv Petrolul Ploieşti

**Founded**: 31.12.1924 (as FC Juventus Bucureşti)
**Stadium**: Stadionul "Ilie Oană", Ploieşti (15,073)
**Trainer**: Nicolae Constantin — 03.12.1973
[07.02.2023] Florin Cristian Pârvu — 02.04.1975

| Goalkeepers: | DOB | M | (s) | G |
|---|---|---|---|---|
| Raul Avram | 26.06.1993 | 2 | | |
| Andreas Leitner (AUT) | 25.03.1994 | 11 | | |
| Octavian Vâlceanu | 13.10.1996 | 26 | | |
| **Defenders:** | DOB | M | (s) | G |
| Cosmin Florin Achim | 19.09.1995 | 3 | (2) | |
| Florin Borţa | 21.06.1999 | 19 | (7) | |
| Seniko Doua (CIV) | 01.11.2001 | 12 | (4) | 2 |
| Ricardo Grigore | 07.04.1999 | 3 | | |
| Marian Fernando *Huja* (POR) | 05.08.1999 | 20 | | |
| Félix *Mathaus* Lima Santos (CPV) | 28.11.1990 | 25 | | 2 |
| Bart Meijers (NED) | 10.01.1997 | 38 | | 1 |
| Alberto Nicolaie Olaru | 23.03.1998 | | (2) | |
| Paul Papp | 11.11.1989 | 12 | | |
| Georgi Pashov (BUL) | 04.03.1990 | 12 | (4) | |
| Gabriel Sebastian Tamaş | 09.11.1983 | 13 | | 2 |
| Valentin Ţicu | 19.09.2000 | 37 | (1) | 1 |
| Mihai Velisar | 30.08.1998 | 2 | (3) | |
| **Midfielders:** | DOB | M | (s) | G |
| Mario Bratu | 07.06.2002 | 5 | (16) | 1 |
| Constantin Budescu | 19.02.1989 | 8 | (9) | 3 |
| Eugen Cebotaru (MDA) | 16.10.1984 | 3 | (13) | |
| Marius Iulian Cioiu | 01.11.1999 | 8 | (4) | 1 |
| Ismaël Diomandé (CIV) | 28.08.1992 | 1 | (3) | 1 |
| Lucian Dumitriu | 21.09.1992 | 17 | (18) | 2 |
| Mario Ioniţă | 17.03.2007 | | (1) | |
| *Jair* Tavares da Silva (BRA) | 03.08.1994 | 33 | (1) | 3 |
| *Jefferson* Nogueira Junior (BRA) | 22.01.1994 | 4 | (2) | |
| Stefan Purtić (SRB) | 06.08.1998 | 6 | (7) | 1 |
| Takayuki Seto (JPN) | 05.02.1986 | 30 | (5) | |
| Cosmin Tucaliuc | 13.05.2000 | | (12) | |
| **Forwards:** | DOB | M | (s) | G |
| Raul Bucur | 24.12.2002 | | (1) | |
| Gheorghe-Teodor Grozav | 29.09.1990 | 36 | (2) | 10 |
| Okechukwu Christian Irobiso (NGA) | 28.05.1993 | 27 | (5) | 7 |
| Mirko Ivanovski (MKD) | 31.10.1989 | 9 | (5) | |
| Harrison Manzala Tusumgama (COD) | 06.03.1994 | | (3) | |
| Simon Moise Măzărache | 10.01.1993 | 4 | (10) | |
| Robert Moldoveanu | 08.03.1999 | 3 | (8) | |
| Mihnea Rădulescu | 17.09.2005 | | (1) | |

## Fotbal Club Rapid 1923 București

| Founded: | 25.06.1923 (*as CFR București*) | | |
| Stadium: | Stadionul Rapid-Giulești, București (14,047) | | |
| Trainer: | Adrian Mutu | 08.01.1979 | |

| Goalkeepers: | DOB | M | (s) | G |
|---|---|---|---|---|
| Virgil Drăghia | 31.07.1990 | 1 | | |
| Horațiu Moldovan | 20.01.1998 | 39 | | |
| George Ungureanu | 01.04.2007 | | (1) | |
| **Defenders:** | **DOB** | **M** | **(s)** | **G** |
| Claudiu Belu-Iordache | 07.11.1993 | 5 | | |
| Damien Dussaut (FRA) | 08.11.1994 | 1 | | |
| Dragoș Grigore | 07.09.1986 | 27 | (1) | 2 |
| Paul Iacob | 21.06.1996 | 13 | (4) | 3 |
| Cristian Ignat | 29.01.2003 | 1 | (2) | |
| Iraneuton Sousa *Morais* Junior (BRA) | 22.07.1986 | 36 | | 2 |
| Răzvan Onea | 19.05.1998 | 31 | (2) | 1 |
| Cristian Ionuț Săpunaru | 05.04.1984 | 39 | | 4 |
| Florin Ștefan | 09.05.1996 | 7 | (6) | |
| **Midfielders:** | **DOB** | **M** | **(s)** | **G** |
| Cristian Alexandru Albu | 17.08.1993 | 28 | (4) | 3 |
| Andrei Ciobanu | 18.01.1998 | 6 | (7) | |
| Ljuban Crepulja (CRO) | 02.09.1993 | 17 | (3) | |

| Alexandru Crivac | 06.05.2002 | | (1) | |
|---|---|---|---|---|
| Xian Emmers (BEL) | 20.07.1999 | 18 | (6) | 1 |
| Alexandru Ioniță | 14.12.1994 | 29 | (5) | 2 |
| Mattias Käit (EST) | 29.06.1998 | 28 | (3) | 2 |
| Alexandru Irinel Măţan | 29.08.1999 | 2 | (4) | |
| Romario Moise | 21.09.1996 | | (1) | |
| Ștefan Pănoiu | 23.09.2002 | 16 | (21) | 3 |
| Alexandru Stan | 07.02.1989 | | (2) | |
| **Forwards:** | **DOB** | **M** | **(s)** | **G** |
| Funsho Ibrahim Bamgboye (NGA) | 09.01.1999 | 6 | (6) | 3 |
| Valentin Costache | 02.08.1998 | 15 | (9) | |
| Marko Dugandžić (CRO) | 07.04.1994 | 33 | (4) | 22 |
| Kevin Luckassen (NED) | 27.07.1993 | 7 | (15) | 2 |
| Hervin Ongenda (FRA) | 24.06.1995 | 1 | (3) | |
| Jayson Papeau (FRA) | 30.06.1996 | 5 | (15) | |
| Antonio Sefer | 22.04.2000 | 27 | (10) | 6 |
| Jakub Vojtuš (SVK) | 22.10.1993 | 2 | (3) | |

## Asociația Club Sportiv Sepsi Oltul Sport Klub Sfântu Gheorghe

| Founded: | 2011 | | |
| Stadium: | Sepsi Arena, Sfântu Gheorghe (8,400) | | |
| Trainer: | Leontin Florian Grozavu | 19.08.1967 | |
| [28.09.2021] | Róbert Ilyés | 04.02.1974 | |
| [10.10.2021] | Cristiano Bergodi (ITA) | 14.10.1964 | |

| Goalkeepers: | DOB | M | (s) | G |
|---|---|---|---|---|
| Răzvan Began | 12.08.1996 | 4 | | |
| Roland-Csaba Niczuly | 21.09.1995 | 36 | | |
| **Defenders:** | **DOB** | **M** | **(s)** | **G** |
| Mihai Bălașa | 14.01.1995 | 20 | (2) | 1 |
| Denis Ciobotariu | 10.06.1998 | 25 | (3) | 2 |
| Radoslav Dimitrov (BUL) | 12.08.1988 | 21 | (6) | |
| Andres Dumitrescu | 11.03.2001 | 25 | (5) | 1 |
| Rareș Ispas | 26.08.2000 | 15 | (5) | |
| Bogdan Alexandru Mitrea | 29.09.1987 | 5 | | 1 |
| Branislav Niňaj (SVK) | 17.05.1994 | 30 | (4) | |
| Márk Tamás (HUN) | 28.10.1993 | 16 | (2) | 1 |
| **Midfielders:** | **DOB** | **M** | **(s)** | **G** |
| Anass Achahbar (NED) | 13.01.1994 | 1 | (13) | 1 |
| Adnan Aganović (CRO) | 03.10.1987 | 27 | (6) | 2 |
| *Francisco Santos* Silva Júnior (POR) | 18.01.1992 | 8 | (13) | |

| Ion Gheorghe | 08.10.1999 | 15 | (15) | 2 |
|---|---|---|---|---|
| Cosmin Matei | 30.09.1991 | 29 | (6) | 6 |
| Ákos Nistor | 20.11.2004 | | (1) | |
| Enriko Papa (ALB) | 12.03.1993 | 6 | (10) | |
| Nicolae Păun | 19.01.1999 | 31 | (5) | 4 |
| Jonathan Yoni Emanuel Rodríguez (ARG) | 07.06.1990 | 24 | (7) | |
| Marius Ștefănescu | 14.08.1998 | 26 | (4) | 6 |
| Roland Varga (HUN) | 23.01.1990 | 5 | (7) | |
| **Forwards:** | **DOB** | **M** | **(s)** | **G** |
| Stefan Aškovski (MKD) | 24.02.1992 | | (1) | |
| Cristi Bărbuț | 22.04.1995 | 7 | (7) | |
| Vitalie Damașcan (MDA) | 24.01.1999 | 2 | (3) | 1 |
| Cătălin Golofca | 21.04.1990 | 3 | (8) | 2 |
| Mario Júnior Rondón Fernández (VEN) | 26.03.1986 | 23 | (17) | 9 |
| Pavol Šafranko (SVK) | 16.11.1994 | 18 | (12) | 5 |
| Alexandru Tudorie | 19.03.1996 | 18 | (18) | 11 |

## Asociația Sportivă Fotbal Club Universitatea Cluj

| Founded: | 23.11.1919 (*as SS Studenţilor Universitari Cluj*); re-founded 2016 | | |
| Stadium: | Cluj Arena, Cluj-Napoca (30,201) | | |
| Trainer: | Erik Augustin Lincar | 16.10.1978 | |
| [25.08.2022] | Eugen Neagoe | 22.08.1967 | |
| [02.01.2023] | Ioan Ovidiu Sabău | 12.02.1968 | |

| Goalkeepers: | DOB | M | (s) | G |
|---|---|---|---|---|
| Laurenţiu Constantin Brănescu | 30.03.1994 | 3 | | |
| Andrei Gorcea | 02.08.2001 | 25 | | |
| Plamen Iliev (BUL) | 30.11.1991 | 11 | | |
| **Defenders:** | **DOB** | **M** | **(s)** | **G** |
| Rolandas Baravykas (LTU) | 23.08.1995 | 2 | (2) | |
| Alexandru Bota | 31.03.2008 | | (1) | |
| Marius Ionuţ Briceag | 06.04.1992 | 16 | (3) | 1 |
| Ivan Goranov (BUL) | 10.06.1992 | 4 | (4) | |
| Florin Ilie | 18.06.1992 | 22 | (2) | |
| Denis Ispas | 05.09.1993 | 26 | (2) | 1 |
| Ivan Martić (CRO) | 02.10.1990 | 13 | | |
| Andrei Miron | 28.05.1994 | 13 | (1) | |
| Dorinel Oancea | 02.04.1997 | 13 | (4) | |
| Andrei Piţian | 16.11.1995 | 17 | (5) | |
| Paul Ovidiu Pîrvulescu | 11.08.1988 | 4 | (1) | |
| Roberto Romeo (ITA) | 27.04.1990 | 6 | (2) | |
| Ștefan Marinel Vlădoiu | 28.12.1998 | 12 | (2) | |
| **Midfielders:** | **DOB** | **M** | **(s)** | **G** |
| Ovidiu Bic | 23.02.1994 | 29 | (4) | 2 |

| Ioan Filip | 20.05.1989 | 22 | (15) | 3 |
|---|---|---|---|---|
| Lóránd Fülöp | 24.07.1997 | 10 | (10) | 2 |
| Cătălin Florin Hlistei | 24.08.1994 | 1 | (3) | |
| Dan Nistor | 06.05.1988 | 11 | (1) | 3 |
| Florin Flavius Purece | 06.11.1991 | 6 | (8) | |
| Martin Remacle (BEL) | 16.05.1997 | 18 | (11) | 5 |
| *Romário* Santos Pires (BRA) | 16.01.1989 | 18 | (6) | 1 |
| Gabriel Simion | 22.05.1998 | 18 | (7) | |
| **Forwards:** | **DOB** | **M** | **(s)** | **G** |
| Adrian Bălan | 14.03.1990 | 13 | (15) | 4 |
| Alexandru Boiciuc (MDA) | 21.08.1997 | | (8) | |
| Alexandru Chipciu | 18.05.1989 | 33 | (1) | 1 |
| *Ely* Ernesto Lopes Fernandes (CPV) | 04.11.1990 | 9 | (6) | 1 |
| Florian Haită | 29.10.2000 | 9 | (7) | |
| Albert Hofman | 10.04.2003 | 2 | (2) | |
| Ovidiu Horșia | 30.10.2000 | 2 | (5) | |
| Ianis Stoica | 08.12.2002 | 4 | (6) | |
| Dragoș Tescan | 15.09.1999 | 6 | (6) | 1 |
| Mamadou Thiam (SEN) | 20.03.1995 | 23 | (4) | 9 |
| José Gomes „Zé Gomes" (POR) | 08.04.1999 | 8 | (8) | 1 |

## Universitatea Craiova 1948 Club Sportiv

| Founded: | 1948; re-founded 2013 | |
|---|---|---|
| Stadium: | Stadionul "Ion Oblemenco", Craiova (30,929) | |
| Trainer: | László Balint | 29.03.1979 |
| [09.08.2022] | Mirel Matei Rădoi | 22.03.1981 |
| [08.12.2022] | Dragoş Bon | 13.06.1980 |
| [01.01.2023] | Eugen Neagoe | 22.08.1967 |

| Goalkeepers: | DOB | M | (s) | G |
|---|---|---|---|---|
| Giedrius Arlauskis (LTU) | 01.12.1987 | 7 | | |
| David Lazăr | 08.08.1991 | 15 | | |
| Mirko Pigliacelli (ITA) | 30.06.1993 | 1 | | |
| Laurenţiu Popescu | 18.01.1997 | 17 | | |
| **Defenders:** | **DOB** | **M** | **(s)** | **G** |
| Juraj Badelj (CRO) | 24.08.2003 | 6 | (1) | |
| Nicuşor Silviu Bancu | 18.09.1992 | 13 | | |
| *Basilio* Ndong Owono Nchama (EQG) | 17.01.1999 | 14 | (1) | |
| Denis Benga | 24.07.2005 | 1 | (1) | |
| Marius Valerică Găman | 25.02.1989 | 8 | (7) | |
| Ivan Martić (CRO) | 02.10.1990 | 7 | (3) | |
| Bogdan Mitrea | 29.09.1987 | 19 | | 2 |
| Paul Papp | 11.11.1989 | 16 | (1) | 1 |
| *Raúl* Michel Melo da *Silva* (BRA) | 04.11.1989 | 18 | (5) | |
| Vladimir Ionuţ Screciu | 13.01.2000 | 34 | (2) | |
| Bogdan Ilie Vătăjelu | 24.04.1993 | 24 | (1) | 1 |
| Ştefan Marinel Vlădoiu | 28.12.1998 | 11 | (5) | |
| Gjoko Zajkov (MKD) | 10.02.1995 | 16 | | |

| Midfielders: | DOB | M | (s) | G |
|---|---|---|---|---|
| Ştefan Baiaram | 31.12.2002 | 21 | (6) | 3 |
| Mihai Căpăţînă | 16.12.1995 | 16 | (14) | |
| Alexandru Creţu | 24.04.1992 | 27 | (7) | 7 |
| Eduard Marian Florescu | 27.06.1997 | 1 | | |
| Alexandru Mateiu | 10.12.1989 | 18 | (15) | |
| Dan Nicolae Nistor | 06.05.1988 | 15 | (5) | 2 |
| Ante Roguljić (CRO) | 11.03.1996 | 5 | (22) | 1 |
| David Sala | 24.08.2004 | 2 | (4) | |
| Ionuţ Vînă | 20.02.1995 | 3 | (2) | |
| **Forwards:** | **DOB** | **M** | **(s)** | **G** |
| George Cîmpanu | 08.10.2000 | 16 | (15) | 4 |
| Marian Danciu | 24.04.2002 | | (2) | |
| *Gustavo* Di Mauro Vagenin (BRA) | 14.11.1991 | | (2) | 2 |
| Sergiu Hanca | 04.04.1992 | 5 | (5) | 1 |
| Alexandru Işfan | 31.01.2000 | 13 | (3) | |
| Andrei Virgil Ivan | 04.01.1997 | 30 | (5) | 14 |
| Elvir Koljič (BIH) | 08.07.1995 | 9 | (16) | 5 |
| Jovan Marković | 23.03.2001 | 23 | (14) | 7 |
| Rivaldo Vitor Borba Ferreira Júnior „Rivaldinho" (BRA) | 29.04.1995 | 9 | (14) | 1 |

## Fotbal Club Universitatea Craiova 1948

| Founded: | 1991 (*as FC Universitatea Craiova*) | |
|---|---|---|
| Stadium: | Stadionul "Ion Oblemenco", Craiova (30,929) | |
| Trainer: | Marius Croitoru | 02.10.1980 |
| [11.10.2022] | Paul Răducan | 14.12.1967 |
| [09.11.2022] | Nicolò Napoli (ITA) | 07.02.1962 |

| Goalkeepers: | DOB | M | (s) | G |
|---|---|---|---|---|
| Ionuţ Gurău | 27.03.1999 | 20 | | |
| Robert Popa | 05.03.2003 | 19 | (2) | |
| **Defenders:** | **DOB** | **M** | **(s)** | **G** |
| *André* Lourenço *Duarte* (POR) | 12.09.1997 | 39 | | |
| Danny Agostinho Henriques (NED) | 29.07.1997 | 16 | | |
| Gabriel Enache | 18.08.1990 | 5 | (3) | |
| Ricardo Florin Grigore | 07.04.1999 | 4 | (6) | |
| Jérémy Huyghebaert (BEL) | 07.01.1989 | 27 | (3) | |
| Matheus *Mascarenhas* dos Santos Raimundo (BRA) | 27.07.1998 | 10 | (5) | |
| Radu Alexandru Negru | 17.04.1999 | 35 | | |
| Kyriakos Papadopoulos (GRE) | 23.02.1992 | 7 | (2) | |
| Lorenzo Paramatti (ITA) | 02.01.1995 | 14 | (6) | |
| **Midfielders:** | **DOB** | **M** | **(s)** | **G** |
| Vlad Achim | 07.04.1989 | 28 | (1) | 1 |
| Dragoş Albu | 15.03.2001 | 22 | | 3 |
| Samuel Asamoah (GHA) | 23.03.1994 | 25 | (3) | |

| | DOB | M | (s) | G |
|---|---|---|---|---|
| Juan Francisco Bauza (ARG) | 03.05.1996 | 25 | (4) | 4 |
| *Giovanni* Piccolomo (BRA) | 04.04.1994 | 4 | (6) | |
| Mario Ilie | 17.01.2007 | | (1) | |
| François Marquet (BEL) | 17.04.1995 | 2 | (12) | |
| Ionuţ Zanfir | 21.08.2000 | | (2) | |
| **Forwards:** | **DOB** | **M** | **(s)** | **G** |
| William Baeten (BEL) | 07.02.1997 | 28 | (3) | 4 |
| Yassine Bahassa (FRA) | 21.05.1992 | 22 | (14) | 5 |
| Claudiu Bălan | 22.06.1994 | 1 | (5) | |
| Vladislav Blănuţă (MDA) | 12.01.2002 | 3 | (7) | 1 |
| Aurelian Chiţu | 25.03.1991 | 23 | (10) | 10 |
| Andrea Compagno (ITA) | 22.04.1996 | 7 | | 5 |
| George Ganea | 26.05.1999 | 16 | (12) | 4 |
| Gabriel Cristian Iancu | 15.04.1994 | 7 | (8) | 2 |
| Jibril Ibrahimi (NGA) | 01.12.2002 | | (4) | |
| Sékou Sidibé (BEL) | 05.05.2001 | 5 | (14) | 3 |
| Benjamin Van Durmen (BEL) | 20.03.1997 | 15 | (10) | 3 |

## Fotbal Club Uzina Textilă Arad

| Founded: | 18.04.1945 | |
|---|---|---|
| Stadium: | Stadionul „Francisc von Neuman", Arad (12,700) | |
| Trainer: | Ilie Poenaru | 11.11.1976 |
| [01.11.2022] | László Bálint | 29.03.1979 |
| [25.04.2023] | Mircea Rednic | 09.04.1962 |

| Goalkeepers: | DOB | M | (s) | G |
|---|---|---|---|---|
| Dragoş Balauru | 11.11.1989 | 9 | | |
| Florin Iacob | 16.08.1993 | 22 | | |
| Danylo Kucher (UKR) | 25.01.1997 | 8 | | |
| **Defenders:** | **DOB** | **M** | **(s)** | **G** |
| Yacoub Aly Abeid (MTN) | 11.12.1997 | 19 | (2) | 1 |
| Alexandru Benga | 15.06.1989 | 38 | | 2 |
| Romario Benzar | 26.03.1992 | 7 | (2) | |
| Andrei Chindriş | 12.01.1999 | 18 | (4) | |
| Mihai Dobrescu | 12.09.1992 | 10 | (5) | |
| *Erico* Constantino da Silva (BRA) | 20.07.1989 | 10 | (3) | |
| Erion Hoxhallari (ALB) | 15.10.1995 | 23 | (3) | 1 |
| Cristian Maxim | 26.04.2003 | | (2) | |
| Marko Vukčević (MNE) | 07.06.1993 | 25 | (4) | |
| **Midfielders:** | **DOB** | **M** | **(s)** | **G** |
| Paul Anton | 10.05.1991 | 18 | (9) | |
| Idriz Batha (ALB) | 28.03.1992 | 31 | (3) | 1 |
| Juan Bautista Cascini (ARG) | 04.06.1997 | 22 | (10) | 2 |
| Fabiano Cibi | 22.03.2005 | | (1) | |
| Damian Isac | 31.01.2001 | 6 | (5) | |

| | DOB | M | (s) | G |
|---|---|---|---|---|
| Salvatore Gioacchin Marrone | 05.05.2001 | | (2) | |
| Florentin Matei | 15.04.1993 | 4 | (8) | |
| Rareş Pop | 14.06.2005 | 24 | (1) | 3 |
| *Roger* Junio Rodrigues Ferreira (BRA) | 01.03.1996 | 12 | (2) | 1 |
| Raul Şteau | 22.04.2001 | 7 | (14) | |
| Desley Ubbink (NED) | 15.06.1993 | 22 | (11) | 3 |
| **Forwards:** | **DOB** | **M** | **(s)** | **G** |
| Orhan Ademi (SUI) | 28.10.1991 | | (8) | |
| Joseph Enziwanne Godwin (NGA) | 15.07.2003 | | (1) | |
| Wesley Georges Jobello (FRA) | 23.01.1994 | 7 | (10) | |
| Claudiu Keşerü | 02.12.1986 | 11 | (15) | 3 |
| David Miculescu | 02.05.2001 | 3 | | 2 |
| Stefan Milošević (MNE) | 23.06.1996 | 11 | (5) | 4 |
| Claudiu Negoescu | 23.03.2003 | | (6) | |
| Philip Porwei Otele (NGA) | 15.04.1999 | 23 | (11) | 5 |
| Patrick Paşcalău | 10.12.2005 | | (4) | |
| Virgiliu Postolachi (MDA) | 17.03.2000 | 28 | (9) | 10 |
| Albert Stahl | 11.01.1999 | 9 | (14) | |
| *Willie* Hortencio *Barbosa* (BRA) | 15.05.1993 | 2 | (9) | |

## Fotbal Club Voluntari

| | Founded: | 2010 (*as Inter Voluntari*) | | |
|---|---|---|---|---|
| | Stadium: | Stadionul „Anghel Iordănescu", Voluntari (4,600) | | |
| | Trainer: | Liviu Ciobotariu | | 26.03.1971 |

| Goalkeepers: | DOB | M | (s) | G |
|---|---|---|---|---|
| Jesús *Fernández* Collado (ESP) | 11.06.1988 | 2 | | |
| Mihai Popa | 12.10.2000 | 37 | | |
| **Defenders:** | **DOB** | **M** | **(s)** | **G** |
| Cosmin Achim | 19.09.1995 | 3 | (4) | 1 |
| Naser Aliji (ALB) | 27.12.1993 | 32 | (4) | |
| Vlăduț Andreș | 23.05.2000 | 1 | (4) | |
| Igor Armaş (MDA) | 14.07.1987 | 38 | | |
| Cristian Costin | 17.06.1998 | 26 | (9) | 1 |
| Patricio Martín Matricardi (ARG) | 07.01.1994 | 35 | | 1 |
| Cristian Ignacio Paz (ARG) | 24.04.1995 | 4 | (6) | |
| Ricardo José Veiga Varzim „Ricardinho" (POR) | 24.03.1994 | 28 | (1) | 1 |
| Alexandru Vlad | 06.12.1989 | 5 | (8) | |
| **Midfielders:** | **DOB** | **M** | **(s)** | **G** |
| Doru Andrei | 03.02.2003 | | (2) | |
| Lukáš Droppa (CZE) | 22.04.1989 | 11 | (3) | 1 |
| Lóránd Fülöp | 24.07.1997 | | (5) | |
| Omar Nicolás Govea García (MEX) | 18.01.1996 | 9 | (1) | 1 |

| | DOB | M | (s) | G |
|---|---|---|---|---|
| *Hélder* Luís Lopes Vieira *Tavares* (CPV) | 26.12.1989 | 14 | (20) | |
| Salvatore Gioacchin Marrone | 05.05.2001 | 2 | (2) | |
| Ulrich Meleke (CIV) | 24.05.1999 | 30 | (2) | |
| Nicolas Popescu | 02.01.2003 | | (3) | |
| Vadim Raţă (MDA) | 05.05.1993 | 33 | | 1 |
| Rúnar Sigurjónsson (ISL) | 18.06.1990 | 11 | (1) | 4 |
| Roberto-Niculae Voican | 06.02.2003 | 1 | (4) | |
| **Forwards:** | **DOB** | **M** | **(s)** | **G** |
| Vitalie Damaşcan (MDA) | 24.01.1999 | 27 | | 9 |
| Ioan Andrei Vasile Dumiter | 10.04.1999 | 1 | (14) | 1 |
| Daniel Florea | 17.04.1988 | 11 | (21) | 5 |
| *Marcelo* André Veiga *Lopes* (POR) | 21.04.1994 | 25 | (11) | 5 |
| Aymar Meleke (CIV) | 24.05.1999 | | (2) | 1 |
| George Merloi | 15.10.1999 | 1 | (22) | |
| Alexandru Munteanu | 07.01.2002 | | (1) | |
| Adam Nemec (SVK) | 02.09.1985 | 34 | (3) | 10 |
| Robert Popescu | 09.03.2003 | | (2) | |
| Mihai Răduţ | 18.03.1990 | 8 | (14) | 1 |

## SECOND LEVEL
### Liga II 2022/2023

### Regular Season

| | | | | | | | | | |
|---|---|---|---|---|---|---|---|---|---|
| 1. | CSA Steaua Bucureşti | 19 | 12 | 4 | 3 | 37 | - | 18 | 40 |
| 2. | ACSM Politehnica Iaşi | 19 | 12 | 4 | 3 | 30 | - | 14 | 40 |
| 3. | ACS SC Oţelul Galaţi | 19 | 10 | 6 | 3 | 21 | - | 12 | 36 |
| 4. | FC Unirea Dej | 19 | 8 | 8 | 3 | 30 | - | 25 | 32 |
| 5. | FC Gloria Buzău | 19 | 8 | 7 | 4 | 27 | - | 21 | 31 |
| 6. | FC Dinamo Bucureşti | 19 | 9 | 4 | 6 | 27 | - | 18 | 31 |
| 7. | AFC Unirea 04 Slobozia | 19 | 8 | 7 | 4 | 30 | - | 17 | 31 |
| 8. | CS Concordia Chiajna | 19 | 9 | 2 | 8 | 22 | - | 17 | 29 |
| 9. | FC Braşov | 19 | 7 | 7 | 5 | 26 | - | 20 | 28 |
| 10. | CSM Slatina | 19 | 6 | 9 | 4 | 18 | - | 11 | 27 |
| 11. | FK Csíkszereda Miercurea Ciuc | 19 | 7 | 5 | 7 | 25 | - | 18 | 26 |
| 12. | ACS Viitorul Pandurii Târgu Jiu | 19 | 8 | 1 | 10 | 22 | - | 28 | 25 |
| 13. | CSC 1599 Şelimbăr | 19 | 6 | 6 | 7 | 19 | - | 22 | 24 |
| 14. | CSC Dumbrăviţa | 19 | 7 | 3 | 9 | 24 | - | 34 | 24 |
| 15. | FC Metaloglobus Bucureşti | 19 | 6 | 3 | 10 | 18 | - | 22 | 21 |
| 16. | AFC Progresul Spartac Bucureşti | 19 | 3 | 8 | 8 | 17 | - | 28 | 17 |
| 17. | FC Ripensia Timişoara | 19 | 4 | 4 | 11 | 16 | - | 23 | 16 |
| 18. | CS Minaur Baia Mare | 19 | 3 | 7 | 9 | 18 | - | 29 | 16 |
| 19. | SSU Politehnica Timişoara | 19 | 2 | 7 | 10 | 13 | - | 29 | 13 |
| 20. | AFC Unirea Constanţa | 19 | 4 | 0 | 15 | 15 | - | 49 | 12 |

Team ranked 1-6 were qualified for the Promotion Play-off Round, while teams ranked 7-20 were qualified for the Play-out Round.

### Promotion Play-off Round

| | | | | | | | | | |
|---|---|---|---|---|---|---|---|---|---|
| 1. | ACSM Politehnica Iaşi (*Promoted*) | 10 | 5 | 5 | 0 | 20 | - | 8 | 60 |
| 2. | CSA Steaua Bucureşti | 10 | 3 | 3 | 4 | 16 | - | 18 | 52 |
| 3. | ACS SC Oţelul Galaţi (*Promoted*) | 10 | 4 | 1 | 5 | 8 | - | 13 | 49 |
| 4. | FC Dinamo Bucureşti (*Promotion Play-offs*) | 10 | 4 | 3 | 3 | 16 | - | 12 | 46 |
| 5. | FC Gloria Buzău (*Promotion Play-offs*) | 10 | 2 | 5 | 3 | 9 | - | 11 | 42 |
| 6. | FC Unirea Dej | 10 | 1 | 5 | 4 | 2 | - | 9 | 40 |

<u>Please note</u>: CSA Steaua Bucureşti were not eligible for promotion.

### Play-out Round – Group A

| | | | | | | | | | |
|---|---|---|---|---|---|---|---|---|---|
| 1. | FK Csíkszereda Miercurea Ciuc | 6 | 4 | 1 | 1 | 12 | - | 6 | 39 |
| 2. | CSC 1599 Şelimbăr | 6 | 4 | 0 | 2 | 9 | - | 7 | 36 |
| 3. | AFC Unirea 04 Slobozia | 6 | 0 | 3 | 3 | 7 | - | 11 | 34 |
| 4. | CSM Slatina | 6 | 2 | 1 | 3 | 2 | - | 5 | 34 |
| 5. | FC Metaloglobus Bucureşti (*Relegation Play-offs*) | 6 | 3 | 2 | 1 | 12 | - | 6 | 32 |
| 6. | CS Minaur Baia Mare (*Relegated*) | 6 | 1 | 3 | 2 | 3 | - | 4 | 22 |
| 7. | SSU Politehnica Timişoara (*Relegated*) | 6 | 2 | 0 | 4 | 5 | | 11 | 19 |

### Play-out Round – Group B

| | | | | | | | | | |
|---|---|---|---|---|---|---|---|---|---|
| 1. | FC Braşov | 6 | 5 | 1 | 0 | 23 | - | 5 | 44 |
| 2. | CS Concordia Chiajna | 6 | 3 | 1 | 2 | 8 | - | 6 | 39 |
| 3. | CSC Dumbrăviţa | 6 | 3 | 0 | 3 | 12 | - | 8 | 33 |
| 4. | ACS Viitorul Pandurii Târgu Jiu | 6 | 2 | 1 | 3 | 10 | - | 11 | 32 |
| 5. | AFC Progresul Spartac Bucureşti (*Relegation Play-offs*) | 6 | 4 | 0 | 2 | 15 | - | 7 | 29 |
| 6. | AFC Unirea Constanţa (*Relegated*) | 6 | 2 | 0 | 4 | 5 | - | 27 | 18 |
| 7. | FC Ripensia Timişoara (*Relegated*) | 6 | 0 | 1 | 5 | 2 | | 11 | 17 |

FC Metaloglobus Bucureşti - AFC Progresul Spartac Bucureşti    1-1(1-1)    0-0 aet; 5-3 pen
FC Metaloglobus Bucureşti remains at second level.

## NATIONAL TEAM

| Date | City | Match | Score | Comp |
|---|---|---|---|---|
| 23.09.2022 | Helsinki | *Finland - Romania* | *1-1(1-0)* | (UNL) |
| 26.09.2022 | Bucureşti | *Romania - Bosnia and Herzegovina* | *4-1(1-0)* | (UNL) |
| 17.11.2022 | Cluj-Napoca | *Romania - Slovenia* | *1-2(0-2)* | (F) |
| 20.11.2022 | Chişinău | *Moldova - Romania* | *0-5(0-2)* | (F) |
| 25.03.2023 | Andorra la Vella | *Andorra - Romania* | *0-2(0-1)* | (ECQ) |
| 28.03.2023 | Bucureşti | *Romania - Belarus* | *2-1(2-0)* | (ECQ) |
| 16.06.2023 | Prishtina | *Kosovo - Romania* | *0-0* | (ECQ) |
| 19.06.2023 | Luzern | *Switzerland - Romania* | *2-2(2-0)* | (ECQ) |

**23.09.2022    FINLAND - ROMANIA    1-1(1-0)    3<sup>rd</sup> UEFA Nations League B, Group 3**
Olympiastadion, Helsinki; Referee: Carlos del Cerro Grande (Spain); Attendance: 20,130
**ROU:** Ionuţ Andrei Radu, Andrei Florin Raţiu, Adrián Rus, Ionuţ Nedelcearu, Nicuşor Silviu Bancu, Marius Mihai Marin (Cap), Răzvan Gabriel Marin (90+1.Alexandru Cicâldău), Florin Lucian Tănase (66.Nicolae Claudiu Stanciu), Dennis Man (66.Andrei Ioan Cordea), Deian Cristian Sorescu (79.Denis Mihai Drăguş), Denis Alibec (67.George Alexandru Puşcaş). Trainer: Edward Marius Iordănescu.
**Goal:** Florin Lucian Tănase (52).

**26.09.2022    ROMANIA - BOSNIA AND HERZEGOVINA    4-1(1-0)    3<sup>rd</sup> UEFA Nations League B, Group 3**
Stadionul Rapid-Giuleşti, Bucureşti; Referee: Halil Umut Meler (Turkey); Attendance: 12,693
**ROU:** Ionuţ Andrei Radu, Andrei Florin Raţiu, Adrián Rus (83.Ionuţ Nedelcearu), Andrei Andonie Burcă, Nicuşor Silviu Bancu, Darius Dumitru Olaru, Răzvan Gabriel Marin (64.Tudor Cristian Băluţă), Dennis Man (64.Andrei Ioan Cordea), Nicolae Claudiu Stanciu (Cap), Deian Cristian Sorescu (56.Mário Jorge Malico Paulino "Camora"), Denis Alibec (64.George Alexandru Puşcaş). Trainer: Edward Marius Iordănescu.
**Goals:** Dennis Man (38), George Alexandru Puşcaş (73), Andrei Florin Raţiu (79), George Alexandru Puşcaş (86).

**17.11.2022    ROMANIA - SLOVENIA    1-2(0-2)    Friendly International**
Cluj Arena, Cluj-Napoca; Referee: Nicolas Laforge (Belgium); Attendance: 6,845
**ROU:** Horaţiu Alexandru Moldovan, Cristian Marian Manea, Ionuţ Nedelcearu (73.Radu Matei Drăguşin), Andrei Andonie Burcă, Bogdan Ilie Vătăjelu (60.Raul Marian Opruţ), Marius Mihai Marin, Alexandru Cicâldău (60.Darius Dumitru Olaru), Răzvan Gabriel Marin (Cap) (84.Daniel Boloca), Andrei Ioan Cordea (46.Olimpiu Vasile Moruţan), Denis Mihai Drăguş (73.Claudiu Adrian Mihai Petrila), George Alexandru Puşcaş. Trainer: Edward Marius Iordănescu.
**Goal:** Denis Mihai Drăguş (64).

**20.11.2022    MOLDOVA - ROMANIA    0-5(0-2)    Friendly International**
Stadionul Zimbru, Chişinău; Referee: Yaşar Kemal Uğurlu (Turkey); Attendance: 6,145
**ROU:** Ştefan Târnovanu, Cristian Marian Manea (70.Alexandru Grigoraş Pantea), Adrián Rus, Andrei Andonie Burcă (Cap) (69.Radu Matei Drăguşin), Raul Marian Opruţ, Darius Dumitru Olaru, Tudor Cristian Băluţă, Olimpiu Vasile Moruţan (62.Antonio Valentin Sefer), Alexandru Cicâldău (77.Nicolae Ionuţ Păun), Denis Mihai Drăguş (62.Marius Ştefănescu), George Alexandru Puşcaş (59.Daniel George Paraschiv). Trainer: Edward Marius Iordănescu.
**Goals:** Olimpiu Vasile Moruţan (9), Denis Mihai Drăguş (40), Alexandru Cicâldău (61), Daniel George Paraschiv (71 penalty), Adrián Rus (88).

**25.03.2023    ANDORRA - ROMANIA    0-2(0-1)    17<sup>th</sup> EC. Qualifiers**
Estadi Nacional, Andorra la Vella; Referee: Dario Bel (Croatia); Attendance: 2,927
**ROU:** Ionuţ Andrei Radu, Andrei Florin Raţiu, Radu Matei Drăguşin, Andrei Andonie Burcă, Deian Cristian Sorescu, Darius Dumitru Olaru (65.Marius Mihai Marin), Răzvan Gabriel Marin (65.Tudor Cristian Băluţă), Olimpiu Vasile Moruţan (72.Mihai Alexandru Dobre), Nicolae Claudiu Stanciu (Cap) (78.Florin Lucian Tănase), Dennis Man (72.Octavian George Popescu), Denis Alibec. Trainer: Edward Marius Iordănescu.
**Goals:** Dennis Man (35), Denis Alibec (50).

**28.03.2023    ROMANIA - BELARUS    2-1(2-0)    17<sup>th</sup> EC. Qualifiers**
Arena Naţională, Bucureşti; Referee: Allard Lindhout (Netherlands); Attendance: 27,837
**ROU:** Ionuţ Andrei Radu, Cristian Marian Manea, Radu Matei Drăguşin, Andrei Andonie Burcă, Raul Marian Opruţ, Tudor Cristian Băluţă (44.Alexandru Cicâldău), Răzvan Gabriel Marin, Nicolae Claudiu Stanciu (Cap) (77.Marius Mihai Marin), Olimpiu Vasile Moruţan (65.Mihai Alexandru Dobre), Dennis Man (65.Octavian George Popescu), Denis Alibec (77.Florin Lucian Tănase). Trainer: Edward Marius Iordănescu.
**Goals:** Nicolae Claudiu Stanciu (17), Andrei Andonie Burcă (19).

**16.06.2023    KOSOVO - ROMANIA    0-0    17<sup>th</sup> EC. Qualifiers**
Stadiumi „Fadil Vokrri", Prishtina; Referee: Danny Desmond Makkelie (Netherlands); Attendance: 11,000
**ROU:** Horaţiu Alexandru Moldovan, Cristian Marian Manea, Andrei Andonie Burcă, Radu Matei Drăguşin, Mário Jorge Malico Paulino "Camora" (23.Deian Cristian Sorescu), Tudor Cristian Băluţă, Marius Mihai Marin, Nicolae Claudiu Stanciu (Cap) (86.Ianis Hagi), Dennis Man (61.Olimpiu Vasile Moruţan), Florinel Teodor Coman (61.Valentin Mihai Mihăilă), George Alexandru Puşcaş (86.Denis Alibec). Trainer: Edward Marius Iordănescu.

**19.06.2023    SWITZERLAND - ROMANIA    2-2(2-0)    17<sup>th</sup> EC. Qualifiers**
Swissporarena, Lucerne; Referee: Daniele Orsato (Italy); Attendance: 14,400
**ROU:** Horaţiu Alexandru Moldovan, Cristian Marian Manea, Radu Matei Drăguşin, Ionuţ Nedelcearu, Andrei Andonie Burcă, Deian Cristian Sorescu (73.Darius Dumitru Olaru), Nicolae Claudiu Stanciu (Cap), Vladimir Ionuţ Screciu (84.Alexandru Cicâldău), Ianis Hagi (57.Valentin Mihai Mihăilă), Florinel Teodor Coman (58.Olimpiu Vasile Moruţan), Denis Alibec (73.George Alexandru Puşcaş). Trainer: Edward Marius Iordănescu.
**Goals:** Valentin Mihai Mihăilă (89, 90+2).

## NATIONAL TEAM PLAYERS
### (16.07.2022 – 15.07.2023)

| Name | DOB | Caps | Goals | Club |
|------|-----|------|-------|------|
| **Goalkeepers** | | | | |
| Horaţiu Alexandru MOLDOVAN | 20.01.1998 | 3 | 0 | 2022/2023: *FC Rapid 1923 Bucureşti* |
| Ionuţ Andrei RADU | 28.05.1997 | 4 | 0 | 2022: *US Cremonese (ITA)* / 25.01.2023-> *AJ Auxerre (FRA)* |
| Ştefan TÂRNOVANU | 09.05.2000 | 1 | 0 | 2022: *SC FCSB Bucureşti* |
| **Defenders** | | | | |
| Nicuşor Silviu BANCU | 18.09.1992 | 28 | 2 | 2022: *CS Universitatea Craiova* |
| Andrei Andonie BURCĂ | 15.04.1993 | 19 | 1 | 2022/2023: *FC CFR 1907 Cluj-Napoca* |
| Mário Jorge Malico Paulino "CAMORA" | 10.11.1986 | 10 | 0 | 2022/2023: *FC CFR 1907 Cluj-Napoca* |
| Radu Matei DRĂGUŞIN | 03.02.2002 | 7 | 0 | 2022/2023: *Genoa C&FC (ITA)* |
| Cristian Marian MANEA | 09.08.1997 | 23 | 2 | 2022/2023: *FC CFR 1907 Cluj-Napoca* |
| Ionuţ NEDELCEARU | 25.04.1996 | 25 | 2 | 2022/2023: *US Città di Palermo (ITA)* |
| Raul Marian OPRUŢ | 04.01.1998 | 3 | 0 | 2022/2023: *AFC Hermannstadt Sibiu* |
| Alexandru Grigoraş PANTEA | 11.09.2003 | 1 | 0 | 2022: *SC FCSB Bucureşti* |
| Andrei Florin RAŢIU | 20.06.1998 | 11 | 1 | 2022/2023: *SD Huesca (ESP)* |
| Adrián RUS | 18.03.1996 | 17 | 1 | 2022: *Pisa SC (ITA)* |
| Bogdan Ilie VĂTĂJELU | 24.04.1993 | 1 | 0 | 2022: *CS Universitatea Craiova* |
| **Midfielders** | | | | |
| Daniel BOLOCA | 22.12.1998 | 1 | 0 | 2022: *Frosinone Calcio (ITA)* |
| Tudor Cristian BĂLUŢĂ | 27.03.1999 | 12 | 0 | 2022/2023: *FCV Farul Constanţa* |
| Alexandru CICÂLDĂU | 08.07.1997 | 30 | 4 | 2022/2023: *Al Ittihad Kalba Sports & Cultural Club (UAE)* |
| Florinel Teodor COMAN | 10.04.1998 | 7 | 0 | 2023: *SC FCSB Bucureşti* |
| Andrei Ioan CORDEA | 24.06.1999 | 5 | 0 | 2022: *SC FCSB Bucureşti* |
| Mihai Alexandru DOBRE | 30.08.1998 | 2 | 0 | 2023: *FC Famalicão (POR)* |
| Ianis HAGI | 22.10.1998 | 26 | 2 | 2023: *Rangers FC Glasgow (SCO)* |
| Dennis MAN | 26.08.1998 | 19 | 6 | 2022/2023: *Parma Calcio 1913 (ITA)* |
| Marius Mihai MARIN | 30.08.1998 | 11 | 0 | 2022/2023: *Pisa SC (ITA)* |
| Răzvan Gabriel MARIN | 23.05.1996 | 46 | 2 | 2022/2023: *Empoli FC (ITA)* |
| Valentin Mihai MIHĂILĂ | 02.02.2000 | 12 | 3 | 2023: *Parma Calcio 1913 (ITA)* |
| Olimpiu Vasile MORUŢAN | 25.04.1999 | 9 | 1 | 2022/2023: *Pisa SC (ITA)* |
| Darius Dumitru OLARU | 03.03.1998 | 11 | 0 | 2022/2023: *SC FCSB Bucureşti* |
| Claudiu Adrian Mihai PETRILA | 07.11.2000 | 1 | 0 | 2022: *FC CFR 1907 Cluj-Napoca* |
| Octavian George POPESCU | 27.12.2002 | 7 | 0 | 2023: *SC FCSB Bucureşti* |
| Nicolae Ionuţ PĂUN | 19.01.1999 | 2 | 0 | 2022: *ACS Sepsi OSK Sfântu Gheorghe* |
| Vladimir Ionuţ SCRECIU | 13.01.2000 | 1 | 0 | 2023: *CS Universitatea Craiova* |
| Antonio Valentin SEFER | 22.04.2000 | 1 | 0 | 2022: *FC Rapid 1923 Bucureşti* |
| Deian Cristian SORESCU | 29.08.1997 | 12 | 0 | 2022: *RKS Raków Częstochowa (POL)* / 14.01.2023-> *SC FCSB Bucureşti* |
| Nicolae Claudiu STANCIU | 07.05.1993 | 60 | 12 | 2022/2023: *Wuhan Three Towns FC (CHN)* |
| Marius ŞTEFĂNESCU | 14.08.1999 | 2 | 0 | 2022: *ACS Sepsi OSK Sfântu Gheorghe* |
| Florin Lucian TĂNASE | 30.12.1994 | 17 | 2 | 2022/2023: *Al Jazira SCC Abu Dhabi (UAE)* |
| **Forwards** | | | | |
| Denis ALIBEC | 05.01.1991 | 31 | 3 | 2022/2023: *FCV Farul Constanţa* |
| Denis Mihai DRĂGUŞ | 06.07.1999 | 5 | 2 | 2022: *R Standard Liège (BEL)* |
| Daniel George PARASCHIV | 24.04.1999 | 1 | 1 | 2022: *AFC Hermannstadt Sibiu* |
| George Alexandru PUŞCAŞ | 08.04.1996 | 36 | 10 | 2022/2023: *Genoa C&FC (ITA)* |
| **Trainer** | | | | |
| Edward Marius IORDĂNESCU [from 26.01.2022] | 16.06.1978 | | | 14 M; 5 W; 4 D; 5 L; 20-16 |

# RUSSIA

## The Country:
Российская Федерация (Russian Federation)
Capital: Moskva
Surface: 17,098,246 km²
Inhabitants: 147,182,123 [2022]
Time: UTC+2 to +12

## The FA:
Российский Футбольный Союз (Russian Football Union)
Ulitsa Narodnaya 7, 115 172 Moskva
Tel: +7 495 926 1300
Founded: 19.01.1912
Member of FIFA since: 1912-1917 and since 1992
Member of UEFA since: 1954
Website: www.rfs.ru

## NATIONAL TEAM RECORDS

### RECORDS

| | | |
|---|---|---|
| **First international match:** | 30.06.1912, Stockholm: | Finland – Russia 2-1 |
| **Most international caps:** | Sergey Ignashevich | - 127 caps (2002-2018) |
| **Most international goals:** | Aleksandr Kerzhakov | - 30 goals / 91 caps (2002-2016) |
| | Artyom Dzyuba | - 30 goals / 55 caps (since 2011) |

### UEFA EUROPEAN CHAMPIONSHIP

|  |  |
|---|---|
| 1960 | -* |
| 1964 | - |
| 1968 | - |
| 1972 | - |
| 1976 | - |
| 1980 | - |
| 1984 | - |
| 1988 | - |
| 1992 | - |
| 1996 | Final Tournament (Group Stage) |
| 2000 | Qualifiers |
| 2004 | Final Tournament (Group Stage) |
| 2008 | Final Tournament (Semi-Finals) |
| 2012 | Final Tournament (Group Stage) |
| 2016 | Final Tournament (Group Stage) |
| 2020 | Final Tournament (Group Stage) |

*from 1960 to 1992 as Soviet Union/C.I.S.

### FIFA WORLD CUP

|  |  |
|---|---|
| 1930 | -** |
| 1934 | - |
| 1938 | - |
| 1950 | - |
| 1954 | - |
| 1958 | - |
| 1962 | - |
| 1966 | - |
| 1970 | - |
| 1974 | - |
| 1978 | - |
| 1982 | - |
| 1986 | - |
| 1990 | - |
| 1994 | Final Tournament (Group Stage) |
| 1998 | Qualifiers |
| 2002 | Final Tournament (Group Stage) |
| 2006 | Qualifiers |
| 2010 | Qualifiers |
| 2014 | Final Tournament (Group Stage) |
| 2018 | Final Tournament (Quarter-Finals) |
| 2022 | *Disqualified* |

**from 1930 to 1990 as Soviet Union

### OLYMPIC TOURNAMENTS

|  |  |
|---|---|
| 1908 | - |
| 1912 | Quarter-Finals |
| 1920 | - |
| 1924 | - |
| 1928 | - |
| 1936 | - |
| 1948 | - |
| 1952 | - |
| 1956 | - |
| 1960 | - |
| 1964 | - |
| 1968 | - |
| 1972 | - |
| 1976 | - |
| 1980 | - |
| 1984 | - |
| 1988 | - |
| 1992 | - |
| 1996 | Qualifiers |
| 2000 | Qualifiers |
| 2004 | Qualifiers |
| 2008 | Qualifiers |
| 2012 | Qualifiers |
| 2016 | Qualifiers |
| 2020 | Qualifiers |

## UEFA NATIONS LEAGUE

|  |  |
|---|---|
| 2018/2019 | League B (Group Stage) |
| 2020/2021 | League B (Group Stage) |
| 2022/2023 | *Disqualified* (Relegated to League C) |

## FIFA CONFEDERATIONS CUP 1992-2017

2017 (Group Stage)

## RUSSIAN CLUB HONOURS IN EUROPEAN CLUB COMPETITIONS:

| European Champion Clubs.Cup (1956-1992) / UEFA Champions League (1993-2023) | | |
|---|---|---|
| None | | |

| Fairs Cup (1858-1971) / UEFA Cup (1972-2009) / UEFA Europa League (2010-2023) | | |
|---|---|---|
| PFK CSKA Moskva | 1 | 2004/2005 |
| FK Zenit Saint Petersburg | 1 | 2007/2008 |

| UEFA Europa Conference League (2021-2023) | | |
|---|---|---|
| None | | |

| UEFA Super Cup (1972-2022) | | |
|---|---|---|
| FK Zenit Saint Petersburg | 1 | 2008 |

| European Cup Winners' Cup 1961-1999* |
|---|
| None |

*defunct competition*

# NATIONAL COMPETITIONS
# TABLE OF HONOURS

| Football championship of Russian Empire | |
|---|---|
| 1912 | Saint Petersburg |
| 1913 | Odessa |
| 1914 | *Championship cancelled* |

| Football championship of Russian SFSR among city teams | |
|---|---|
| 1920 | Moskva |
| 1921 | *No competition* |
| 1922 | Moskva |
| 1923 | *No competition* |
| 1924 | Leningrad |
| 1925 | *No competition* |
| 1926 | *No competition* |
| 1927 | Moskva |
| 1928 | Moskva |
| 1929 | *No competition* |
| 1930 | *No competition* |
| 1931 | Moskva |
| 1932 | Leningrad |
| 1933 | *No competition* |
| 1934 | Voronezh |
| 1935 | *No competition* |

## Soviet League (1936–1991)

| | CHAMPIONS | CUP WINNERS | BEST GOALSCORERS | |
|---|---|---|---|---|
| 1936 (spring) | Dinamo Moskva | - | Mikhail Semichastny (Dinamo Moskva) | 6 |
| 1936 (autumn) | Spartak Moskva | Lokomotiv Moskva | Georgy Glazkov (Spartak Moskva) | 7 |
| 1937 | Dinamo Moskva | Dinamo Moskva | Boris Paichadze (Dinamo Tbilisi) Leonid Rumyantsev (Spartak Moskva) Vasily Smirnov (Dinamo Moskva) | 8 |
| 1938 | Spartak Moskva | Spartak Moskva | Makar Goncharenko (Dinamo Kiev) | 19 |
| 1939 | Spartak Moskva | Spartak Moskva | Grigory Fedotov (CDKA Moskva) | 21 |
| 1940 | Dinamo Moskva | *No competition* | Grigory Fedotov (CDKA Moskva) Sergey Solovyov (Dinamo Moskva) | 21 |
| 1941 | *No competition* | *No competition* | - | |
| 1942 | *No competition* | *No competition* | - | |
| 1943 | *No competition* | *No competition* | - | |
| 1944 | *No competition* | Zenit Leningrad | - | |
| 1945 | Dinamo Moskva | CDKA Moskva | Vsevolod Bobrov (CDKA Moskva) | 24 |
| 1946 | CDKA Moskva | Spartak Moskva | Aleksandr Ponomaryov (Torpedo Moskva) | 18 |
| 1947 | CDKA Moskva | Spartak Moskva | Vsevolod Bobrov (CDKA Moskva) Valentin Nikolayev (CDKA Moskva) Sergey Solovyov (Dinamo Moskva) | 14 |
| 1948 | CDKA Moskva | CDKA Moskva | Sergey Solovyov (Dinamo Moskva) | 25 |
| 1949 | Dinamo Moskva | Torpedo Moskva | Nikita Simonyan (Spartak Moskva) | 26 |
| 1950 | CDKA Moskva | Spartak Moskva | Nikita Simonyan (Spartak Moskva) | 34 |
| 1951 | CDSA Moskva | CDSA Moskva | Avtandil Gogoberidze (Dinamo Tbilisi) | 16 |
| 1952 | Spartak Moskva | Torpedo Moskva | Andrey Zazroyev (Dinamo Kiev) | 11 |
| 1953 | Spartak Moskva | Dinamo Moskva | Nikita Simonyan (Spartak Moskva) | 14 |
| 1954 | Dinamo Moskva | Dynamo Kiev | Anatoli Ilyin (Spartak Moskva) Vladimir Ilyin (Dinamo Moskva) Antonin Sochnev (Trudovye Reservy Leningrad) | 11 |
| 1955 | Dinamo Moskva | CDSA Moskva | Eduard Streltsov (Torpedo Moskva) | 15 |
| 1956 | Spartak Moskva | *No competition* | Vasily Buzunov (ODO Sverdlovsk) | 17 |
| 1957 | Dinamo Moskva | Lokomotiv Moskva | Vasily Buzunov (CSK MO Moskva) | 16 |
| 1958 | Spartak Moskva | Spartak Moskva | Anatoli Ilyin (Spartak Moskva) | 19 |
| 1959 | Dinamo Moskva | - | Zaur Kaloyev (Dinamo Tbilisi) | 16 |
| 1960 | Torpedo Moskva | Torpedo Moskva (1959/60) | Zaur Kaloyev (Dinamo Tbilisi) Gennady Gusarov (Torpedo Moskva) | 20 |
| 1961 | Dinamo Kiev | Shakhtyor Stalino | Gennady Gusarov (Torpedo Moskva) | 22 |
| 1962 | Spartak Moskva | Shakhtyor Stalino | Mikhail Mustygin (Belarus Minsk) | 17 |
| 1963 | Dinamo Moskva | Spartak Moskva | Oleg Kopaev (SKA Rostov-na-Donu) | 27 |
| 1964 | Dinamo Tbilisi | Dynamo Kiev | Vladimir Fedotov (CSKA Moskva) | 16 |
| 1965 | Torpedo Moskva | Spartak Moskva | Oleg Kopaev (SKA Rostov-na-Donu) | 18 |
| 1966 | Dinamo Kiev | Dynamo Kiev (1965/66) | Ilya Datunashvili (Dinamo Tbilisi) | 20 |
| 1967 | Dinamo Kiev | Dinamo Moskva (1966/67) | Mikhail Mustygin (Dinamo Minsk) | 19 |
| 1968 | Dinamo Kiev | Torpedo Moskva (1967/68) | Georgi Gavasheli (Dinamo Tbilisi) Berador Abduraimov (Pakhtakor Tashkent) | 22 |
| 1969 | Spartak Moskva | Karpaty Lviv | Nikolai Osyanin (Spartak Moskva) Vladimir Proskurin (SKA Rostov-na-Donu) Dzhemal Kherhadze (Torpedo Kutaisi) | 16 |

| 1970 | CSKA Moskva | Dinamo Moskva | Givi Nodia (Dinamo Tbilisi) | 17 |
|---|---|---|---|---|
| 1971 | Dinamo Kiev | Spartak Moskva | Eduard Malofeev (Dinamo Minsk) | 16 |
| 1972 | Zarya Voroshilovgrad | Torpedo Moskva | Oleg Blokhin (Dinamo Kiev) | 14 |
| 1973 | Ararat Yerevan | Ararat Yerevan | Oleg Blokhin (Dinamo Kiev) | 18 |
| 1974 | Dinamo Kiev | Dynamo Kiev | Oleg Blokhin (Dinamo Kiev) | 20 |
| 1975 | Dinamo Kiev | Ararat Yerevan | Oleg Blokhin (Dinamo Kiev) | 18 |
| 1976 (spring) | Dinamo Moskva | - | Arkady Andreasian (Ararat Yerevan) | 8 |
| 1976 (autumn) | Torpedo Moskva | Dinamo Tbilisi | Aleksandr Markin (Zenit Leningrad) | 13 |
| 1977 | Dinamo Kiev | Dinamo Moskva | Oleg Blokhin (Dinamo Kiev) | 17 |
| 1978 | Dinamo Tbilisi | Dynamo Kiev | Georgi Yartsev (Spartak Moskva) | 19 |
| 1979 | Spartak Moskva | Dinamo Tbilisi | Vitali Starukhin (Shakhtar Donetsk) | 26 |
| 1980 | Dinamo Kiev | Shakhtar Donetsk | Sergey Andreev (SKA Rostov-na-Donu) | 20 |
| 1981 | Dinamo Kiev | SKA Rostov-on-Don | Ramaz Shengelia (Dinamo Tbilisi) | 23 |
| 1982 | Dinamo Minsk | Dynamo Kiev | Andrei Yakubik (Pakhtakor Tashkent) | 23 |
| 1983 | Dnipro Dnipropetrovsk | Shakhtar Donetsk | Yuriy Gavrilov (Spartak Moskva) | 18 |
| 1984 | Zenit Leningrad | Dinamo Moskva | Sergey Andreev (SKA Rostov-na-Donu) | 20 |
| 1985 | Dinamo Kiev | Dynamo Kiev | Oleg Protasov (Dnipro Dnipropetrovsk) | 35 |
| 1986 | Dinamo Kiev | Torpedo Moskva | Aleksandr Borodyuk (Dinamo Moskva) | 21 |
| 1987 | Spartak Moskva | Dynamo Kiev | Oleg Protasov (Dnipro Dnipropetrovsk) | 18 |
| 1988 | Dnipro Dnipropetrovsk | Metalist Kharkiv | Yevhen Shakhov (Dnipro Dnipropetrovsk) Aleksandr Borodyuk (Dinamo Moskva) | 16 |
| 1989 | Spartak Moskva | Dnipro Dnipropetrovsk | Sergey Rodionov (Spartak Moskva) | 16 |
| 1990 | Dinamo Kiev | Dynamo Kiev | Oleg Protasov (Dinamo Kiev) Valery Shmarov (Spartak Moskva) | 12 |
| 1991 | CSKA Moskva | CSKA Moskva | Igor Kolyvanov (Dinamo Moskva) | 18 |

**Russian League (1992–present)**

| | CHAMPIONS | CUP WINNERS | BEST GOALSCORERS | |
|---|---|---|---|---|
| 1992 | FK Spartak Moskva | FK Spartak Moskva | Vali Gasimov (AZE, FK Dinamo Moskva) | 16 |
| 1993 | FK Spartak Moskva | FK Torpedo Moskva | Viktor Panchenko (FK KamAZ Naberezhnye Chelny) | 21 |
| 1994 | FK Spartak Moskva | FK Spartak Moskva | Igor Simutenkov (FK Dinamo Moskva) | 21 |
| 1995 | FK Alania Vladikavkaz | FK Dinamo Moskva | Oleg Veretennikov (Rotor Volgograd) | 25 |
| 1996 | FK Spartak Moskva | FK Lokomotiv Moskva | Aleksandr Maslov (FK Rostselmash Rostov-na-Donu) | 23 |
| 1997 | FK Spartak Moskva | FK Lokomotiv Moskva | Oleg Veretennikov (FK Rotor Volgograd) | 22 |
| 1998 | FK Spartak Moskva | FK Spartak Moskva | Oleg Veretennikov (FK Rotor Volgograd) | 22 |
| 1999 | FK Spartak Moskva | FK Zenit Saint Petersburg | Georgi Demetradze (GEO, FK Alania Vladikavkaz) | 21 |
| 2000 | FK Spartak Moskva | FK Lokomotiv Moskva | Dmitriy Loskov (FK Lokomotiv Moskva) | 18 |
| 2001 | FK Spartak Moskva | FK Lokomotiv Moskva | Dmitriy Vyazmikin (FK Torpedo Moskva) | 18 |
| 2002 | FK Lokomotiv Moskva | PFK CSKA Moskva | Rolan Gusev (PFK CSKA Moskva) Dmitriy Kirichenko (PFK CSKA Moskva) | 15 |
| 2003 | PFK CSKA Moskva | FK Spartak Moskva | Dmitriy Loskov (FK Lokomotiv Moskva) | 14 |
| 2004 | FK Lokomotiv Moskva | FK Terek Grozny | Aleksandr Kerzhakov (FK Zenit Saint Petersburg) | 18 |
| 2005 | PFK CSKA Moskva | PFK CSKA Moskva | Dmitriy Kirichenko (FK Moskva) | 14 |
| 2006 | PFK CSKA Moskva | PFK CSKA Moskva | Roman Pavlyuchenko (FK Spartak Moskva) | 18 |
| 2007 | FK Zenit Saint Petersburg | FK Lokomotiv Moskva | Roman Pavlyuchenko (FK Spartak Moskva) Roman Adamov (FK Moskva) | 14 |
| 2008 | FK Rubin Kazan | PFK CSKA Moskva | Vágner Silva de Souza "Vágner Love" (BRA, PFK CSKA Moskva) | 20 |
| 2009 | FK Rubin Kazan | PFK CSKA Moskva | Welliton Soares de Morais (BRA, FK Spartak Moskva) | 21 |
| 2010 | FK Zenit Saint Petersburg | FK Zenit Saint Petersburg | Welliton Soares de Morais (BRA, FK Spartak Moskva) | 19 |
| 2010/2011 | - | PFK CSKA Moskva | - | |
| 2011/2012 | FK Zenit Saint Petersburg | FK Rubin Kazan | Seydou Doumbia (CIV, PFK CSKA Moskva) | 28 |
| 2012/2013 | PFK CSKA Moskva | PFK CSKA Moskva | Yura Movsisyan (ARM, FK Spartak Moskva) Francisco Wánderson do Carmo Carneiro (BRA, FK Krasnodar) | 13 |
| 2013/2014 | PFK CSKA Moskva | FK Rostov | Seydou Doumbia (CIV, PFK CSKA Moskva) | 18 |
| 2014/2015 | FK Zenit Saint Petersburg | FK Lokomotiv Moskva | Givanildo Vieira de Sousa "Hulk" (BRA, FK Zenit Saint Petersburg) | 15 |
| 2015/2016 | PFK CSKA Moskva | FK Zenit Saint Petersburg | Fyodor Smolov (FK Krasnodar) | 20 |
| 2016/2017 | FK Spartak Moskva | FK Lokomotiv Moskva | Fyodor Smolov (FK Krasnodar) | 18 |
| 2017/2018 | FK Lokomotiv Moskva | FK Tosno | Quincy Anton Promes (NED, FK Spartak Moskva) | 15 |
| 2018/2019 | FK Zenit Saint Petersburg | FK Lokomotiv Moskva | Fedor Chalov (PFK CSKA Moskva) | 15 |
| 2019/2020 | FK Zenit Saint Petersburg | FK Zenit Saint Petersburg | Sardar Azmoun (IRN, FK Zenit Saint Petersburg) Artyom Dzyuba (FK Zenit Saint Petersburg) | 17 |
| 2020/2021 | FK Zenit Saint Petersburg | FK Lokomotiv Moskva | Artyom Dzyuba (FK Zenit Saint Petersburg) | 20 |
| 2021/2022 | FK Zenit Saint Petersburg | FK Spartak Moskva | Gamid Agalarov (FK Ufa) | 19 |
| 2022/2023 | FK Zenit Saint Petersburg | PFK CSKA Moskva | Malcom Filipe Silva de Oliveira (BRA, FK Zenit Saint Petersburg) | 23 |

## Results

### Round 1 [15-17.07.2022]
FK Khimki - FK Zenit 1-1(0-1)
CSKA Moskva - FK Ural 2-0(1-0)
FK Orenburg - Krylia Sovetov 2-4(1-0)
Akhmat Grozny - Spartak Moskva 1-1(1-0)
Torpedo Moskva - PFK Sochi 1-3(0-2)
Lokomotiv M. - Nizhny Novgorod 1-1(0-0)
Dinamo Moskva - FK Rostov 1-1(1-0)
FK Krasnodar - Fakel Voronezh 2-2(2-1)

### Round 2 [22-24.07.2022]
FK Zenit - Krylia Sovetov 3-0(3-0)
CSKA Moskva - PFK Sochi 3-0(1-0)
FK Orenburg - FK Ural 3-0(0-0)
FK Krasnodar - Spartak Moskva 1-4(0-1)
FK Khimki - Nizhny Novgorod 3-0(0-0)
Dinamo Moskva - Torpedo Moskva 4-0(3-0)
Akhmat Grozny - Fakel Voronezh 2-1(1-1)
Lokomotiv Moskva - FK Rostov 2-2(1-1)

### Round 3 [29-31.07.2022]
FK Ural - FK Krasnodar 1-3(0-1)
Fakel Voronezh - Dinamo Moskva 3-3(0-2)
FK Zenit - Lokomotiv Moskva 5-0(0-0)
PFK Sochi - Akhmat Grozny 2-1(1-0)
Nizhny Novgorod - CSKA Moskva 2-2(0-2)
Krylia Sovetov - Torpedo Moskva 1-1(0-1)
Spartak Moskva - FK Orenburg 4-1(3-0)
FK Rostov - FK Khimki 1-0(1-0)

### Round 4 [06-07.08.2022]
FK Ural - Spartak Moskva 0-2(0-2)
CSKA Moskva - Fakel Voronezh 4-1(0-1)
Akhmat Grozny - FK Zenit 0-0
FK Krasnodar - Lokomotiv Moskva 3-0(0-0)
Torpedo Moskva - FK Khimki 1-3(1-1)
Krylia Sovetov - Dinamo Moskva 0-2(0-1)
FK Rostov - FK Orenburg 2-1(1-0)
PFK Sochi - Nizhny Novgorod 2-1(2-0)

### Round 5 [12-14.08.2022]
Fakel Voronezh - FK Ural 0-0
Lokomotiv Moskva - Krylia Sovetov 1-1(0-0)
FK Zenit - CSKA Moskva 2-1(1-0)
Dinamo Moskva - FK Krasnodar 0-0
FK Khimki - Akhmat Grozny 1-3(0-2)
FK Orenburg - Torpedo Moskva 1-0(1-0)
Nizhny Novgorod - FK Rostov 3-4(1-2)
Spartak Moskva - PFK Sochi 3-0(0-0)

### Round 6 [19-21.08.2022]
Krylia Sovetov - Fakel Voronezh 1-1(0-0)
FK Ural - Nizhny Novgorod 0-1(0-0)
FK Khimki - Lokomotiv Moskva 0-3(0-2)
Dinamo Moskva - Spartak Moskva 1-0(1-0)
FK Rostov - PFK Sochi 2-2(0-1)
CSKA Moskva - Akhmat Grozny 4-2(3-1)
FK Zenit - Torpedo Moskva 2-0(0-0)
FK Krasnodar - FK Orenburg 2-0(1-0)

### Round 7 [26-28.08.2022]
PFK Sochi - FK Khimki 4-1(3-0)
Nizhny Novgorod - Dinamo Moskva 2-2(0-2)
Fakel Voronezh - Spartak Moskva 1-4(1-0)
Akhmat Grozny - Krylia Sovetov 1-2(1-1)
FK Ural - FK Zenit 0-4(0-0)
Lokomotiv Moskva - FK Orenburg 5-1(3-1)
Torpedo Moskva - FK Krasnodar 1-4(0-2)
FK Rostov - CSKA Moskva 0-0

### Round 8 [03-05.09.2022]
FK Orenburg - FK Khimki 3-1(2-1)
Nizhny Novgorod - Fakel Voronezh 3-1(0-1)
FK Krasnodar - PFK Sochi 2-1(0-0)
Dinamo Moskva - FK Ural 2-1(1-1)
Krylia Sovetov - CSKA Moskva 0-1(0-0)
Lokomotiv Moskva - Akhmat Grozny 1-2(1-1)
Spartak Moskva - FK Zenit 1-2(1-0)
Torpedo Moskva - FK Rostov 0-1(0-0)

### Round 9 [09-11.09.2022]
PFK Sochi - Dinamo Moskva 2-1(2-1)
FK Khimki - Krylia Sovetov 0-0
CSKA Moskva - FK Krasnodar 4-1(2-0)
Akhmat Grozny - Nizhny Novgorod 1-3(0-1)
FK Ural - Torpedo Moskva 2-0(0-0)
Fakel Voronezh - Lokomotiv Moskva 2-0(1-0)
FK Zenit - FK Orenburg 8-0(5-0)
FK Rostov - Spartak Moskva 4-2(2-1)

### Round 10 [17-18.09.2022]
FK Ural - Akhmat Grozny 1-2(0-1)
Torpedo Moskva - CSKA Moskva 1-0(1-0)
FK Rostov - Krylia Sovetov 2-1(1-1)
Dinamo Moskva - FK Zenit 0-2(0-1)
Nizhny Novgorod - FK Orenburg 0-2(0-1)
FK Krasnodar - FK Khimki 3-1(2-0)
PFK Sochi - Fakel Voronezh 1-1(1-1)
Spartak Moskva-Lokomotiv Moskva 1-0(1-0)

### Round 11 [01-03.10.2022]
FK Orenburg - PFK Sochi 4-1(3-0)
FK Khimki - CSKA Moskva 1-2(0-2)
Lokomotiv Moskva - FK Ural 2-4(0-2)
Fakel Voronezh - Torpedo Moskva 2-2(2-1)
FK Zenit - FK Rostov 3-1(1-0)
Akhmat Grozny - Dinamo Moskva 2-1(2-0)
Nizhny Novgorod - Spartak Moskva 1-2(1-0)
Krylia Sovetov - FK Krasnodar 0-0

### Round 12 [07-09.10.2022]
FK Ural - FK Khimki 2-1(1-0)
Fakel Voronezh - FK Zenit 1-1(1-1)
CSKA Moskva - Dinamo Moskva 1-1(1-1)
PFK Sochi - Lokomotiv Moskva 4-0(1-0)
Spartak Moskva - Krylia Sovetov 5-2(1-1)
FK Orenburg - Akhmat Grozny 2-1(1-0)
Torpedo Moskva - Nizhny Novgorod 0-0
FK Rostov - FK Krasnodar 3-2(0-2)

### Round 13 [14-16.10.2022]
FK Rostov - FK Ural 1-2(1-1)
FK Khimki - Fakel Voronezh 0-0
Torpedo Moskva-Lokomotiv Moskva 0-1(0-0)
FK Krasnodar - Akhmat Grozny 2-3(1-2)
Dinamo Moskva - FK Orenburg 3-2(1-1)
Krylia Sovetov - PFK Sochi 2-0(2-0)
Nizhny Novgorod - FK Zenit 0-3(0-2)
CSKA Moskva - Spartak Moskva 2-2(1-0)

### Round 14 [22-24.10.2022]
Nizhny Novgorod - FK Krasnodar 0-2(0-1)
Fakel Voronezh - FK Rostov 1-1(0-0)
Lokomotiv Moskva-Dinamo Moskva 1-3(1-1)
FK Orenburg - CSKA Moskva 2-2(1-2)
Spartak Moskva - FK Khimki 5-0(2-0)
Akhmat Grozny - Torpedo Moskva 1-0(1-0)
FK Ural - Krylia Sovetov 2-1(1-0)
FK Zenit - PFK Sochi 7-0(4-0)

### Round 15 [28-30.10.2022]
FK Orenburg - Fakel Voronezh 4-1(2-0)
Dinamo Moskva - FK Khimki 6-1(3-0)
Akhmat Grozny - FK Rostov 1-2(1-0)
Lokomotiv Moskva - CSKA Moskva 0-1(0-1)
Krylia Sovetov - Nizhny Novgorod 2-1(0-1)
PFK Sochi - FK Ural 2-2(1-1)
Spartak Moskva - Torpedo Moskva 1-0(0-0)
FK Krasnodar - FK Zenit 0-1(0-0)

### Round 16 [04-06.11.2022]
FK Khimki - FK Orenburg 2-0(0-0)
PFK Sochi - Spartak Moskva 1-1(1-1)
Fakel Voronezh - FK Krasnodar 3-3(1-2)
FK Zenit - Akhmat Grozny 1-2(0-2)
CSKA Moskva - Nizhny Novgorod 0-1(0-0)
FK Ural - Lokomotiv Moskva 2-2(0-1)
Torpedo Moskva - Krylia Sovetov 0-2(0-1)
FK Rostov - Dinamo Moskva 2-1(0-0)

### Round 17 [11-13.11.2022]
Nizhny Novgorod - Akhmat Grozny 3-2(1-0)
FK Ural - Fakel Voronezh 2-0(1-0)
Krylia Sovetov - FK Rostov 1-3(0-2)
Torpedo Moskva - FK Zenit 0-0(0-0)
Lokomotiv Moskva-Spartak Moskva 1-2(0-2)
FK Orenburg - FK Krasnodar 5-1(3-1)
FK Khimki - PFK Sochi 0-2(0-1)
Dinamo Moskva - CSKA Moskva 2-1(1-0)

### Round 18 [03-05.03.2023]
Fakel Voronezh - FK Khimki 1-1(1-1)
Spartak Moskva - FK Ural 2-2(1-1)
Akhmat Grozny - FK Orenburg 3-1(2-1)
FK Zenit - Nizhny Novgorod 3-0(1-0)
FK Rostov - Lokomotiv Moskva 1-3(0-1)
Dinamo Moskva - Krylia Sovetov 1-0(0-0)
FK Krasnodar - Torpedo Moskva 2-2(0-1)
PFK Sochi - CSKA Moskva 2-0(0-0)

### Round 19 [10-12.03.2023]
PFK Sochi - FK Orenburg 0-4(0-1)
Torpedo Moskva - FK Ural 0-1(0-0)
Akhmat Grozny - Lokomotiv Moskva 0-1(0-1)
Spartak Moskva - Fakel Voronezh 3-2(2-2)
FK Krasnodar - Dinamo Moskva 3-1(1-1)
FK Zenit - FK Khimki 3-2(1-0)
CSKA Moskva - Krylia Sovetov 4-0(3-0)
FK Rostov - Nizhny Novgorod 2-1(0-0)

### Round 20 [18-19.03.2023]
FK Orenburg - Spartak Moskva 2-0(2-0)
FK Ural - Dinamo Moskva 0-1(0-0)
Fakel Voronezh - PFK Sochi 3-0(1-0)
Lokomotiv Moskva - FK Krasnodar 3-2(0-2)
FK Khimki - FK Rostov 0-1(0-1)
Krylia Sovetov - Akhmat Grozny 0-1(0-0)
Nizhny Novgorod - Torpedo M. 0-3* awarded
CSKA Moskva - FK Zenit 1-0(0-0)

*originally 1-1; FK Nizhny Novgorod fielded
an ineligible player.

### Round 21 [01-02.04.2023]
Dinamo Moskva - PFK Sochi 0-2(0-0)
Nizhny Novgorod - Lokomotiv M. 0-4(0-3)
Spartak Moskva - Akhmat Grozny 0-0
FK Zenit - FK Ural 2-0(0-0)
FK Khimki - FK Krasnodar 0-6(0-1)
Krylia Sovetov - FK Orenburg 1-1(1-1)
Fakel Voronezh - CSKA Moskva 0-2(0-1)
FK Rostov - Torpedo Moskva 2-1(1-0)

**Round 22** [08-10.04.2023]
Torpedo Moskva - Fakel Voronezh 2-0(1-0)
Akhmat Grozny - FK Ural 2-0(1-0)
Spartak Moskva - Dinamo Moskva 3-3(2-2)
PFK Sochi - Krylia Sovetov 1-2(0-0)
CSKA Moskva - FK Khimki 3-0(2-0)
FK Krasnodar - Nizhny Novgorod 3-1(2-0)
Lokomotiv Moskva - FK Zenit 1-2(1-1)
FK Orenburg - FK Rostov 2-2(2-0)

**Round 23** [15-16.04.2023]
Dinamo Moskva - Nizhny Novgorod 3-1(0-0)
Krylia Sovetov - FK Khimki 0-0
PFK Sochi - FK Krasnodar 0-2(0-1)
FK Ural - CSKA Moskva 1-2(0-1)
Torpedo Moskva - Spartak Moskva 1-2(0-2)
FK Orenburg - Lokomotiv Moskva 1-4(1-3)
Fakel Voronezh - Akhmat Grozny 1-1(0-1)
FK Rostov - FK Zenit 0-0

**Round 24** [22-24.04.2023]
FK Khimki - Torpedo Moskva 4-2(1-1)
Fakel Voronezh - FK Orenburg 1-3(1-2)
FK Zenit - Dinamo Moskva 3-1(0-1)
FK Ural - FK Rostov 1-3(0-1)
Nizhny Novgorod - Krylia Sovetov 2-1(1-1)
Akhmat Grozny - PFK Sochi 1-0(0-0)
CSKA Moskva - Lokomotiv Moskva 1-1(1-0)
Spartak Moskva - FK Krasnodar 4-3(0-1)

**Round 25** [28-30.04.2023]
Dinamo Moskva - Fakel Voronezh 0-2(0-0)
Krylia Sovetov - FK Zenit 1-5(1-2)
Akhmat Grozny - CSKA Moskva 1-3(0-2)
FK Krasnodar - FK Ural 1-1(1-1)
Spartak Moskva - FK Rostov 1-1(0-0)
FK Orenburg - Nizhny Novgorod 1-0(0-0)
PFK Sochi - Torpedo Moskva 3-1(2-0)
Lokomotiv Moskva - FK Khimki 5-1(1-0)

**Round 26** [06-08.05.2023]
FK Khimki - Dinamo Moskva 0-1(0-0)
Torpedo Moskva - Akhmat Grozny 1-5(0-3)
FK Rostov - Fakel Voronezh 0-2(0-0)
Nizhny Novgorod - FK Ural 0-0
CSKA Moskva - FK Orenburg 2-1(1-0)
FK Zenit - Spartak Moskva 3-2(2-1)
FK Krasnodar - Krylia Sovetov 2-1(1-1)
Lokomotiv Moskva - PFK Sochi 3-0(2-0)

**Round 27** [13-14.05.2023]
FK Ural - FK Orenburg 2-1(0-0)
FK Khimki - Spartak Moskva 1-1(1-0)
FK Zenit - FK Krasnodar 2-2(1-0)
CSKA Moskva - Torpedo Moskva 3-0(2-0)
Krylia Sovetov - Lokomotiv Moskva 1-1(1-0)
Dinamo Moskva - Akhmat Grozny 0-3(0-1)
Fakel Voronezh - Nizhny Novgorod 1-0(0-0)
PFK Sochi - FK Rostov 1-0(0-0)

**Round 28** [20-22.05.2023]
Lokomotiv Moskva - Fakel Voronezh 1-0(0-0)
FK Orenburg - FK Zenit 2-2(1-1)
Torpedo Moskva - Dinamo Moskva 0-3(0-2)
Akhmat Grozny - FK Khimki 3-0(1-0)
Krylia Sovetov - FK Ural 3-0(1-0)
Spartak Moskva - CSKA Moskva 2-1(1-1)
FK Krasnodar - FK Rostov 3-0(3-0)
Nizhny Novgorod - PFK Sochi 4-0(0-0)

**Round 29** [27-28.05.2023]
FK Khimki - FK Ural 0-3(0-2)
Torpedo Moskva - FK Orenburg 1-3(1-1)
FK Krasnodar - CSKA Moskva 0-0
PFK Sochi - FK Zenit 1-1(1-0)
Spartak Moskva - Nizhny Novgorod 0-0
Dinamo Moskva-Lokomotiv Moskva 2-4(1-1)
Fakel Voronezh - Krylia Sovetov 2-1(1-0)
FK Rostov - Akhmat Grozny 3-2(2-2)

**Round 30** [03.06.2023]
Akhmat Grozny - FK Krasnodar 2-2(0-0)
FK Orenburg - Dinamo Moskva 3-0(2-0)
Krylia Sovetov - Spartak Moskva 1-0(0-0)
Lokomotiv Moskva-Torpedo Moskva 3-1(0-0)
Nizhny Novgorod - FK Khimki 2-0(1-0)
FK Ural - PFK Sochi 1-0(0-0)
FK Zenit - Fakel Voronezh 1-0(0-0)
CSKA Moskva - FK Rostov 4-1(4-0)

## Final Standings

| | | | | | | | | Home | | | | | Away | | | | |
|---|---|---|---|---|---|---|---|---|---|---|---|---|---|---|---|---|---|
| 1. | **FK Zenit Saint Petersburg** | 30 | 21 | 7 | 2 | 74 - 20 | **70** | 13 | 1 | 1 | 48 - 11 | 8 | 6 | 1 | 26 - 9 |
| 2. | PFK CSKA Moskva | 30 | 17 | 7 | 6 | 56 - 27 | **58** | 11 | 3 | 1 | 38 - 11 | 6 | 4 | 5 | 18 - 16 |
| 3. | FK Spartak Moskva | 30 | 15 | 9 | 6 | 60 - 38 | **54** | 9 | 5 | 1 | 35 - 17 | 6 | 4 | 5 | 25 - 21 |
| 4. | FK Rostov | 30 | 15 | 8 | 7 | 48 - 44 | **53** | 9 | 3 | 3 | 25 - 20 | 6 | 5 | 4 | 23 - 24 |
| 5. | RFK Akhmat Grozny | 30 | 15 | 5 | 10 | 51 - 39 | **50** | 7 | 3 | 5 | 21 - 17 | 8 | 2 | 5 | 30 - 22 |
| 6. | FK Krasnodar | 30 | 13 | 9 | 8 | 62 - 46 | **48** | 8 | 4 | 3 | 29 - 18 | 5 | 5 | 5 | 33 - 28 |
| 7. | FK Orenburg | 30 | 14 | 4 | 12 | 58 - 55 | **46** | 10 | 3 | 2 | 37 - 19 | 4 | 1 | 10 | 21 - 36 |
| 8. | FK Lokomotiv Moskva | 30 | 13 | 6 | 11 | 54 - 46 | **45** | 6 | 3 | 6 | 30 - 23 | 7 | 3 | 5 | 24 - 23 |
| 9. | FK Dinamo Moskva | 30 | 13 | 6 | 11 | 49 - 45 | **45** | 8 | 2 | 5 | 25 - 20 | 5 | 4 | 6 | 24 - 25 |
| 10. | PFK Sochi | 30 | 11 | 5 | 14 | 37 - 54 | **38** | 8 | 4 | 3 | 26 - 18 | 3 | 1 | 11 | 11 - 36 |
| 11. | FK Ural Yekaterinburg | 30 | 10 | 6 | 14 | 33 - 45 | **36** | 6 | 1 | 8 | 17 - 23 | 4 | 5 | 6 | 16 - 22 |
| 12. | PFK Krylia Sovetov Samara | 30 | 8 | 8 | 14 | 32 - 45 | **32** | 4 | 6 | 5 | 14 - 17 | 4 | 2 | 9 | 18 - 28 |
| 13. | FK Pari Nizhny Novgorod (*Relegation Play-offs*) | 30 | 8 | 6 | 16 | 33 - 50 | **30** | 5 | 3 | 7 | 22 - 28 | 3 | 3 | 9 | 11 - 22 |
| 14. | FK Fakel Voronezh (*Relegation Play-offs*) | 30 | 6 | 12 | 12 | 36 - 48 | **30** | 4 | 8 | 3 | 22 - 22 | 2 | 4 | 9 | 14 - 26 |
| 15. | FK Khimki (*Relegated*) | 30 | 4 | 6 | 20 | 25 - 67 | **18** | 3 | 4 | 8 | 13 - 25 | 1 | 2 | 12 | 12 - 42 |
| 16. | FK Torpedo Moskva (*Relegated*) | 30 | 3 | 4 | 23 | 22 - 61 | **13** | 2 | 1 | 12 | 9 - 30 | 1 | 3 | 11 | 13 - 31 |

## Top goalscorers:

| | | |
|---|---|---|
| 23 | **Malcom Filipe Silva de Oliveira (BRA)** | *FK Zenit Saint Petersburg* |
| 20 | Quincy Anton Promes (NED) | *FK Spartak Moskva* |
| 19 | Fyodor Chalov | *PFK CSKA Moskva* |

## Relegation Play-offs [07-10.06.2023]

| | | |
|---|---|---|
| FK Yenisey Krasnoyarsk - FK Fakel Voronezh | 0-1(0-0) | 0-2(0-1) |
| FK Rodina Moskva - FK Pari Nizhny Novgorod | 0-3(0-1) | 2-0(2-0) |

FK Fakel Voronezh and FK Pari Nizhny Novgorod will play in the 2023/2024 Premier League.

# NATIONAL CUP
## Kubok Rossii (Кубок России) 2022/2023

### Russian Premier League Path

#### Quarter-Finals [22-23.02./28.02.-01.03.2023]

| First Leg | | Second Leg | |
|---|---|---|---|
| FK Rostov - FK Ural Yekaterinburg | 1-1(0-1) | FK Ural Yekaterinburg - FK Rostov | 2-1(1-0) |
| FK Lokomotiv Moskva - FK Spartak Moskva | 0-1(0-1) | FK Spartak Moskva - FK Lokomotiv Moskva | 4-2(1-1) |
| PFK Krylia Sovetov Samara - FK Dinamo Moskva | 2-1(0-0) | FK Dinamo Moskva - PFK Krylia Sovetov Samara | 1-1(0-1) |
| PFK CSKA Moskva - FK Krasnodar | 3-0(2-0) | FK Krasnodar - PFK CSKA Moskva | 1-0(0-0) |

#### Semi-Finals [14-15.03./04-05.04.2023]

| First Leg | | Second Leg | |
|---|---|---|---|
| FK Spartak Moskva - FK Ural Yekaterinburg | 1-1(1-0) | FK Ural Yekaterinburg - FK Spartak Moskva | 2-1(1-0) |
| PFK Krylia Sovetov Samara - PFK CSKA Moskva | 2-2(0-0) | PFK CSKA Moskva - PFK Krylia Sovetov Samara | 1-0(0-0) |

#### Final [19.04./03.05.2023]

| | |
|---|---|
| PFK CSKA Moskva - FK Ural Yekaterinburg | 1-1(0-0) |
| FK Ural Yekaterinburg - PFK CSKA Moskva | 1-2(0-1) |

PFK CSKA Moskva were qualified for the Kubok Rossii Final.

---

### Region Path

#### Quarter-Finals – Stage 1 [25-27.02.2023]

| | | | |
|---|---|---|---|
| FK Volga Ulyanovsk - FK Zenit Saint Petersburg | 0-3(0-1) | FK Ufa - RFK Akhmat Grozny | 1-2(0-2) |
| FK Akron Tolyatti - FK Torpedo Moskva | 2-0(2-0) | FK Zvezda Saint Petersburg - FK Pari Nizhny Novgorod | 0-2(0-1) |

#### Quarter-Finals – Stage 2 [14-16.03.2023]

| | | | |
|---|---|---|---|
| FK Akron Tolyatti - FK Lokomotiv Moskva | 1-1 aet; 7-6 pen | FK Zenit Saint Petersburg - FK Dinamo Moskva | 1-1 aet; 4-5 pen |
| RFK Akhmat Grozny - FK Krasnodar | 0-3(0-1) | FK Pari Nizhny Novgorod - FK Rostov | 0-1(0-0) |

#### Semi-Finals – Stage 1 [04-06.04.2023]

| | | | |
|---|---|---|---|
| FK Dinamo Moskva - FK Akron Tolyatti | 0-0 aet; 1-4 pen | FK Krasnodar - FK Rostov | 1-1 aet; 5-3 pen |

#### Semi-Finals – Stage 2 [19.04.2023]

| | | | |
|---|---|---|---|
| FK Akron Tolyatti - FK Spartak Moskva | 2-1(2-0) | FK Krasnodar - PFK Krylia Sovetov Samara | 2-2 aet; 3-0 pen |

#### Final – Stage 1 [03.05.2023]

| | |
|---|---|
| FK Krasnodar - FK Akron Tolyatti | 0-0 aet; 4-2 pen |

#### Final – Stage 2 [17.05.2023]

| | |
|---|---|
| FK Krasnodar - FK Ural Yekaterinburg | 2-1(1-1) |

FK Krasnodar were qualified for the Kubok Rossii Final.

### Final

11.06.2023; Luzhniki Stadion, Moskva; Referee: Vladislav Bezborodov; Attendance: 53,425
**FK Krasnodar - PFK CSKA Moskva**    **1-1(0-1,1-1,1-1); 5-6 on penalties**

**FK Krasnodar**: Stanislav Agkatsev, Sergey Petrov (83.Sergey Volkov), Georgiy Harutyunyan, Junior Osmar Ignacio Alonso Mujica, Cristian Leonel Ramírez Zambrano, Kevin Lenini Gonçalves Pereira de Pina (83.Aleksandr Chernikov), Eduard Spertsyan (Cap), João Pedro Fortes Bachiessa „João Batxi", Aleksey Ionov (46.Ilzat Akhmetov), Olakunle Junior Olusegun, Jhon Andrés Córdoba Copete. Trainer: Vladimir Ivić (Serbia).

**CSKA Moskva**: Igor Akinfeev (Cap), Moisés Roberto Barbosa, Willyan da Silva Rocha, Igor Diveev, Kirill Nababkin (69.Milan Gajić), Konstantin Kuchaev (46.Víctor Felipe Méndez Obando), Saša Zdjelar, Baktiyor Zaynutdinov (73.Jorge Andrés Carrascal Guardo), Ivan Oblyakov (63.Anton Zabolotniy), Jesús Manuel Medina Maldonado, Fedor Chalov. Trainer: Vladimir Fedotov.

**Goals:** 0-1 Fedor Chalov (32), 1-1 Jhon Andrés Córdoba Copete (50).

**Penalties:** Fedor Chalov 0-1; Eduard Spertsyan 1-1; Igor Diveev 1-2; Ilzat Akhmetov 2-2; Moisés Roberto Barbosa (missed); Jhon Andrés Córdoba Copete 3-2; Milan Gajić 3-3; João Pedro Fortes Bachiessa „João Batxi" (saved); Jesús Manuel Medina Maldonado 3-4; Junior Osmar Ignacio Alonso Mujica 4-4; Jorge Andrés Carrascal Guardo 4-5; Cristian Leonel Ramírez Zambrano 5-5; Anton Zabolotniy 5-6; Olakunle Junior Olusegun (saved).

## Respublikanskiy Fudbolnij Klub Akhmat Grozny

**Founded**: 1958
**Stadium**: Akhmat-Arena, Grozny (30,597)
**Trainer**: Andrey Talalayev — 05.10.1972
[11.09.2022] Yuriy Nagaytsev (LVA) — 19.04.1973
[22.09.2022] Sergei Tashuyev — 01.01.1959

| Goalkeepers: | DOB | M | (s) | G |
|---|---|---|---|---|
| Mikhail Oparin | 22.05.1993 | 1 | (1) | |
| Georgi Sheliya (GEO) | 11.12.1988 | 29 | | |
| Rizvan Tashaev | 05.10.2003 | | (1) | |
| **Defenders:** | **DOB** | **M** | **(s)** | **G** |
| Miroslav Bogosavac (SRB) | 14.10.1996 | 24 | (1) | |
| Marat Bystrov (KAZ) | 19.06.1992 | 19 | (1) | |
| Zoran Nižić (CRO) | 11.10.1989 | 7 | (4) | |
| Miloš Šatara (BIH) | 28.10.1995 | 6 | | |
| Andrei Semyonov | 24.03.1989 | 18 | (1) | |
| Darko Todorović (BIH) | 05.05.1997 | 12 | (2) | 1 |
| Rizvan Utsiev | 07.02.1988 | 13 | (3) | |
| Yuriy Zhuravlev | 29.06.1996 | 10 | (2) | 1 |
| **Midfielders:** | **DOB** | **M** | **(s)** | **G** |
| Zaim Divanović (MNE) | 09.12.2000 | 2 | (3) | |
| Kirill Folmer | 25.02.2000 | | (3) | |
| Vladislav Kamilov | 29.08.1995 | 13 | (7) | 2 |
| Evgeny Kharin | 11.06.1995 | 19 | (7) | 5 |
| Minkail Matsuev | 03.02.2000 | | (1) | |
| Lechi Sadulayev | 08.01.2000 | 21 | (1) | 2 |
| Anton Shvets | 26.04.1993 | 24 | (3) | 2 |
| Artiom Timofeev | 12.01.1994 | 25 | (1) | 8 |
| Aleksandr Troshechkin | 23.04.1996 | 11 | (8) | 2 |
| Magomed Yakuev | 07.06.2004 | | (2) | |
| **Forwards:** | **DOB** | **M** | **(s)** | **G** |
| Gamid Agalarov | 16.07.2000 | 8 | (14) | 3 |
| Islam Alsultanov | 18.08.2001 | | (1) | |
| Bernard Berisha (KOS) | 24.10.1991 | 16 | (4) | 5 |
| Ilya Chernyak (BLR) | 19.05.2002 | | (2) | |
| Bi Néné Junior Gbamblé (CIV) | 09.05.2002 | 3 | (2) | 1 |
| Vladimir Ilyin | 20.05.1992 | 8 | (19) | 4 |
| Vladsilav Karapuzov | 06.01.2000 | 8 | (10) | 2 |
| Mohamed Konaté (CIV) | 12.12.1997 | 17 | (7) | 11 |
| Ivan Oleynikov | 24.08.1998 | 16 | (8) | 2 |

## Profesionalniy Fudbolnij Klub CSKA [Central Sport Club of the Army] Moskva

**Founded**: 27.08.1911
**Stadium**: VEB Arena, Moskva (30,457)
**Trainer**: Vladimir Fedotov — 12.08.1966

| Goalkeepers: | DOB | M | (s) | G |
|---|---|---|---|---|
| Igor Akinfeev | 08.04.1986 | 29 | | |
| Vladislav Torop | 07.11.2003 | 1 | | |
| **Defenders:** | **DOB** | **M** | **(s)** | **G** |
| Ilya Agapov | 21.01.2001 | 1 | (1) | |
| *Bruno* da Lara *Fuchs* (BRA) | 01.04.1999 | 2 | (2) | |
| Igor Diveev | 27.09.1999 | 20 | | 2 |
| Milan Gajić (SRB) | 28.01.1996 | 27 | (2) | |
| Matvey Lukin | 27.04.2004 | 1 | (1) | |
| *Moisés* Roberto Barbosa (BRA) | 11.03.1995 | 22 | (2) | |
| Kirill Nababkin | 08.09.1986 | 17 | (5) | 1 |
| Egor Noskov | 24.03.2003 | 1 | (3) | |
| Georgiy Shchennikov | 27.04.1991 | 2 | (1) | |
| Willyan da Silva Rocha (BRA) | 27.01.1995 | 22 | | 3 |
| **Midfielders:** | **DOB** | **M** | **(s)** | **G** |
| Jorge Andrés Carrascal Guardo (COL) | 25.05.1998 | 16 | (10) | 6 |
| Nikita Ermakov | 19.01.2003 | | (22) | |
| Konstantin Kuchaev | 18.03.1998 | 10 | (4) | 2 |
| Víctor Felipe Méndez Obando (CHI) | 23.09.1999 | 22 | (4) | |
| Maksim Mukhin | 04.11.2001 | 9 | (8) | 1 |
| Ivan Oblyakov | 05.07.1998 | 22 | (6) | 8 |
| Baktiyor Zaynutdinov (KAZ) | 02.04.1998 | 19 | (2) | 1 |
| Saša Zdjelar (SRB) | 20.03.1995 | 21 | (6) | |
| **Forwards:** | **DOB** | **M** | **(s)** | **G** |
| Fedor Chalov | 10.04.1998 | 29 | (1) | 19 |
| Adolfo Julián Gaich (ARG) | 26.02.1999 | | (8) | 1 |
| Kirill Glebov | 10.11.2005 | 1 | (5) | |
| Jesús Manuel Medina Maldonado (PAR) | 30.04.1997 | 24 | (1) | 8 |
| Egor Ushakov | 02.12.2002 | 1 | (3) | |
| Vladislav Yakovlev | 14.02.2002 | | (9) | |
| Anton Zabolotniy | 13.06.1991 | 11 | (13) | 3 |

## Fudbolnij Klub Dinamo Moskva

**Founded**: 18.04.1923
**Stadium**: VTB Arena, Moskva (26,319)
**Trainer**: Slaviša Jokanović (SRB) — 16.08.1968
[15.05.2023] Pavel Alpatov — 29.05.1990

| Goalkeepers: | DOB | M | (s) | G |
|---|---|---|---|---|
| Igor Leshchuk | 20.02.1996 | 6 | | |
| Anton Shunin | 27.01.1987 | 24 | | |
| **Defenders:** | **DOB** | **M** | **(s)** | **G** |
| Elazar Dasa (ISR) | 03.12.1992 | 18 | (4) | |
| Roberto Fernández Urbieta (PAR) | 07.06.2000 | 19 | | 2 |
| Diego Sebastián Laxalt Suárez (URU) | 07.02.1993 | 6 | (3) | |
| Milan Majstorović (SRB) | 21.02.2005 | 4 | (5) | |
| Nicolás Marichal Pérez (URU) | 17.03.2001 | 11 | (3) | |
| Sergey Parshivlyuk | 18.03.1989 | 13 | (6) | 1 |
| Saba Sazonov | 01.02.2002 | 22 | (2) | 1 |
| Dmitriy Skopintsev | 02.03.1997 | 23 | (6) | 1 |
| Guillermo Varela Olivera (URU) | 24.03.1993 | 1 | | |
| **Midfielders:** | **DOB** | **M** | **(s)** | **G** |
| Daniil Fomin | 02.03.1997 | 28 | | 5 |
| Luka Gagnidze (GEO) | 28.02.2003 | 12 | (8) | |
| Aleksandr Kutitskiy | 01.01.2002 | 14 | (8) | |
| Denis Makarov | 18.02.1998 | 19 | (6) | 4 |
| Nikola Moro (CRO) | 12.03.1998 | 6 | | |
| Mathias Antonsen Normann (NOR) | 28.05.1996 | 9 | (5) | |
| Arsen Zakharyan | 26.05.2003 | 27 | | 4 |
| **Forwards:** | **DOB** | **M** | **(s)** | **G** |
| Ulvi Babaev | 30.03.2004 | | (1) | |
| Yaroslav Gladyshev | 05.05.2003 | 7 | (19) | 5 |
| Vyacheslav Grulev | 23.03.1999 | 11 | (15) | 3 |
| Vladislav Karapuzov | 06.01.2000 | | (4) | |
| Daniil Lesovoy | 12.01.1998 | 1 | (12) | |
| Nicolas Brice Moumi Ngamaleu (CMR) | 09.07.1994 | 15 | (4) | 2 |
| Fedor Smolov | 09.02.1990 | 20 | (4) | 10 |
| Konstantin Tyukavin | 22.06.2002 | 14 | (14) | 9 |

## Fudbolnij Klub Fakel Voronezh

| | | | | |
|---|---|---|---|---|
| **Founded**: | 1947 | | | |
| **Stadium**: | Tsentralnyi Profsoyuz Stadion, Voronezh (31,793) | | | |
| **Trainer:** | Oleg Vasilenko | | 06.10.1973 | |
| [06.09.2022] | Dmitri Pyatibratov | | 24.05.1976 | |
| [01.05.2023] | Vadim Evseev | | 08.01.1976 | |

| Goalkeepers: | DOB | M | (s) | G |
|---|---|---|---|---|
| Aleksey Gorodovoy | 10.08.1993 | 6 | | |
| Ilya Svinov | 25.09.2000 | 24 | | |
| **Defenders:** | DOB | M | (s) | G |
| Sergey Bozhin | 12.09.1994 | 21 | | 2 |
| Sergei Bryzgalov | 15.11.1992 | 3 | | |
| Vasily Cherov | 13.01.1996 | 14 | (11) | |
| Aslan Dashaev | 19.02.1989 | 5 | (1) | 2 |
| Igor Kalinin | 11.11.1995 | 14 | (1) | |
| Ruslan Magal | 24.09.1991 | 7 | (18) | 1 |
| Vladislav Masternoy | 17.11.1995 | 2 | (9) | |
| Evgeniy Morozov | 14.02.2001 | 25 | | 2 |
| Evgeniy Shlyakov | 30.08.1991 | 9 | (1) | |
| Mikhail Smirnov | 03.06.1990 | 1 | | |
| Kirill Suslov | 26.10.1991 | 18 | (5) | |
| **Midfielders:** | DOB | M | (s) | G |
| Roman Akbashev | 01.11.1991 | 24 | (4) | 6 |

| | DOB | M | (s) | G |
|---|---|---|---|---|
| Daniil Chernyakov | 07.01.2001 | 2 | (2) | |
| Oleg Dmitriev | 18.11.1995 | 12 | (4) | |
| Irakli Kvekveskiri (GEO) | 12.03.1990 | 21 | (6) | 3 |
| Andrey Mendel | 17.04.1995 | 16 | (10) | 1 |
| Réda Rabeï (ALG) | 12.07.1994 | 4 | (6) | 1 |
| Alikhan Shavaev | 05.01.1993 | | (9) | |
| Vyacheslav Yakimov | 05.01.1998 | 11 | (1) | |
| **Forwards:** | DOB | M | (s) | G |
| Ilnur Alshin | 31.08.1993 | 21 | (2) | 1 |
| Khyzyr Appaev | 27.01.1990 | 27 | (1) | 3 |
| Mohamed Amine Brahimi (FRA) | 17.09.1998 | 11 | (2) | |
| Nikita Ershov | 17.09.2002 | | (1) | |
| Georgiy Gongadze | 20.03.1996 | 18 | (10) | 9 |
| Matvey Ivakhnov | 21.07.2003 | | (10) | 1 |
| Maksim Maksimov | 04.11.1995 | 9 | (15) | 4 |
| Evgeniy Markov | 07.07.1994 | 5 | (4) | |

## Fudbolnij Klub Khimki

| | | | | |
|---|---|---|---|---|
| **Founded**: | 1997 | | | |
| **Stadium**: | Arena Khimki, Khimki (18,636) | | | |
| **Trainer:** | Sergei Yuran | | 11.06.1969 | |
| [10.08.2022] | Nikolai Pisarev | | 23.11.1968 | |
| [02.09.2022] | Spartak Gogniyev | | 19.01.1981 | |
| [03.04.2023] | Rinat Bilyaletdinov | | 17.08.1957 | |
| [11.04.2023] | Andrey Talalayev | | 05.10.1972 | |

| Goalkeepers: | DOB | M | (s) | G |
|---|---|---|---|---|
| Vitaliy Gudiev | 22.04.1995 | 7 | (1) | |
| Ilya Lantratov | 11.11.1995 | 14 | | |
| Anton Mitryushkin | 08.02.1996 | 9 | | |
| **Defenders:** | DOB | M | (s) | G |
| Nikola Antić (SRB) | 04.01.1994 | 11 | | |
| Kirill Bozhenov | 07.12.2000 | 9 | (2) | |
| Artur Cherniy | 11.12.2000 | 5 | (6) | |
| Irakli Chezhiya | 22.05.1992 | 7 | (1) | |
| Egor Danilkin | 01.08.1995 | 4 | (1) | |
| Oleksandr Filin (UKR) | 25.06.1996 | 11 | | |
| Petar Golubović (SRB) | 13.07.1994 | 12 | | |
| Sergey Gorshkov | 29.11.1999 | | (2) | |
| Brian Oladapo Idowu (NGA) | 18.05.1992 | 13 | (3) | |
| Danila Kalin | 29.06.2002 | | (1) | |
| Leonardo „Leo" de Andrade Silva (BRA) | 18.04.1998 | 12 | | |
| Vitaliy Lystsov | 11.07.1995 | 8 | | |
| Stefan Melentijević (SRB) | 20.03.2004 | 5 | (3) | |
| Aleksey Nikitin | 27.01.1992 | 7 | (2) | |
| Lev Skvortsov (KAZ) | 02.02.2000 | 7 | (1) | |
| Cristian Marcelo González Tassano (URU) | 23.07.1996 | 5 | (1) | |
| Dmitry Tikhiy | 29.10.1992 | 9 | | |
| Zahar Volkaw (BLR) | 12.08.1997 | 8 | (2) | |
| Artyom Yuran | 24.06.1997 | | (2) | |

| Midfielders: | DOB | M | (s) | G |
|---|---|---|---|---|
| Mory Gbane (CIV) | 25.12.2000 | 12 | (10) | |
| Nemanja Glavčić (SRB) | 19.02.1997 | 7 | (10) | 1 |
| Denis Glushakov | 27.01.1987 | 13 | (1) | |
| Ayaz Guliev | 27.11.1996 | 16 | (3) | |
| Janio Bikel Figueiredo da Silva (POR) | 28.06.1995 | 11 | | |
| Ilya Kamyshev | 13.07.1997 | 2 | (6) | |
| Georgiy Karginov | 29.01.2001 | | (1) | |
| Danil Kazantsev | 05.01.2001 | 2 | (5) | |
| David Kobesov | 06.01.2000 | 1 | (3) | |
| Lachezar Kotev (BUL) | 05.01.1998 | | (2) | |
| Butta Magomedov | 25.12.1997 | 19 | (3) | 5 |
| **Forwards:** | DOB | M | (s) | G |
| Kemal Ademi (SUI) | 23.01.1996 | | (1) | |
| Aleksandr Dolgov | 24.09.1998 | 11 | (14) | 4 |
| Dzhambulat Dulaev | 18.10.1999 | | (3) | |
| Vladimir Khubulov | 02.03.2001 | 4 | (4) | 1 |
| Ilya Kukharchuk | 02.08.1990 | 4 | (4) | 2 |
| Aleksandr Lomovitskiy | 27.01.1998 | 13 | (2) | 1 |
| Marcos Guilherme de Almeida Santos Matos (BRA) | 05.08.1995 | 5 | (5) | 1 |
| Danil Massurenko | 22.05.1999 | | (1) | |
| Reziuan Mirzov | 22.06.1993 | 12 | (12) | 4 |
| Aleksandr Rudenko | 15.03.1999 | 20 | (5) | 4 |
| Ilya Sadygov | 29.09.2000 | 5 | (15) | 1 |
| Aleksandr Zuev | 26.06.1996 | 10 | (4) | |

## Fudbolnij Klub Krasnodar

| | | | | |
|---|---|---|---|---|
| **Founded**: | 22.02.2008 | | | |
| **Stadium**: | Krasnodar Stadion, Krasnodar (34,291) | | | |
| **Trainer:** | Aleksandr Storozhuk | | 10.08.1981 | |
| [04.01.2023] | Vladimir Ivić (SRB) | | 07.05.1977 | |

| Goalkeepers: | DOB | M | (s) | G |
|---|---|---|---|---|
| Stanislav Agkatsev | 09.01.2002 | 3 | | |
| Matvey Safonov | 25.02.1999 | 27 | | |
| **Defenders:** | DOB | M | (s) | G |
| Junior Osmar Ignacio Alonso Mujica (PAR) | 09.02.1993 | 12 | | 1 |
| Sergey Borodin | 30.01.1999 | 10 | | 1 |
| Georgiy Harutyunyan (ARM) | 09.08.2004 | 2 | | |
| Oleg Isaenko | 31.01.2000 | 1 | (2) | |
| Kaio Fernando da Silva Pantaleão (BRA) | 18.09.1995 | 20 | | |
| Vyacheslav Litvinov | 01.04.2001 | 10 | (8) | |
| Sergey Petrov | 02.01.1991 | 9 | (10) | 1 |
| Dmitriy Pivovarov | 21.03.2000 | | (1) | |
| Cristian Leonel Ramírez Zambrano (ECU) | 12.08.1994 | 26 | (1) | 2 |
| Egor Sorokin | 04.11.1995 | 6 | (1) | |
| Mikhail Sukhoruchenko | 13.04.2003 | | (1) | |
| Sergey Volkov | 09.09.2002 | 24 | (3) | 1 |
| **Midfielders:** | DOB | M | (s) | G |
| Ilzat Akhmetov | 31.12.1997 | 10 | (17) | 2 |
| Mihajlo Banjac (SRB) | 10.11.1999 | 16 | (11) | 3 |
| Aleksandr Chernikov | 01.02.2000 | 11 | (2) | |
| Kady Iuri Borges Malinowski (BRA) | 02.05.1996 | 6 | (1) | 3 |
| Kevin Lenini Gonçalves Pereira de Pina (CPV) | 27.01.1997 | 14 | (1) | 1 |

| | DOB | M | (s) | G |
|---|---|---|---|---|
| David Kokoev | 29.08.2002 | | (1) | |
| Dmitriy Kratkov | 15.01.2002 | | (2) | |
| Nikita Krivtsov | 18.08.2002 | 15 | (5) | 6 |
| Aleks Matsukatov | 11.01.1999 | | (1) | |
| Ifeany David Ndouka (NGA) | 02.12.2003 | | (1) | |
| Eduard Spertsyan (ARM) | 07.06.2000 | 26 | (2) | 10 |
| Vyacheslav Yakimov | 05.01.1998 | 1 | (4) | |
| **Forwards:** | DOB | M | (s) | G |
| Ruslan Apekov | 08.06.2000 | | (2) | |
| Moses David Cobnan (NGA) | 10.09.2002 | 6 | (4) | |
| Jhon Andrés Córdoba Copete (COL) | 11.05.1993 | 22 | (1) | 14 |
| Aleksey Ionov | 18.02.1989 | 20 | (7) | 7 |
| João Pedro Fortes Bachiessa „João Batxi" (POR) | 01.05.1998 | 9 | (5) | 3 |
| Rustam Khalnazarov | 20.07.2000 | | | |
| Aleksandr Koksharov | 20.12.2004 | 1 | (6) | 1 |
| Maksim Kutovoy | 01.07.2001 | | (1) | 1 |
| Irakliy Manelov | 19.09.2002 | 3 | (1) | |
| Jonathan Theophilus Okoronkwo (NGA) | 13.09.2003 | | (1) | |
| Olakunle Junior Olusegun (NGA) | 23.04.2002 | 19 | (5) | 5 |
| Vladislav Samko | 03.01.2002 | | (3) | |
| Magomed-Shapi Suleymanov | 16.12.1999 | 1 | (3) | |

## Professionalnij Fudbolnij Klub Krylia Sovetov Samara

| | |
|---|---|
| **Founded:** | 12.04.1942 |
| **Stadium:** | Solidarnost Samara Arena, Samara (44,918) |
| **Trainer:** | Igor Osinjkin     04.06.1965 |

| Goalkeepers: | DOB | M | (s) | G |
|---|---|---|---|---|
| Evgeni Frolov | 05.02.1988 | 2 | (1) | |
| Ivan Lomaev | 21.01.1999 | 22 | | |
| Bogdan Ovsyannikov | 05.01.1999 | 6 | | |
| **Defenders:** | **DOB** | **M** | **(s)** | **G** |
| Mateo Barać (CRO) | 20.07.1994 | 4 | (4) | |
| Glenn Bijl (NED) | 13.07.1995 | 28 | | 2 |
| Roman Evgenyev | 23.02.1999 | 26 | (3) | |
| *Fernando* Peixoto *Costanza* (BRA) | 29.11.1998 | 11 | (2) | 3 |
| Ilya Gaponov | 25.10.1997 | 9 | (7) | 1 |
| Yuriy Gorshkov | 13.03.1999 | 24 | | |
| Nikolai Rasskazov | 04.01.1998 | 7 | (5) | 1 |
| Aleksandr Soldatenkov | 28.12.1996 | 25 | | |
| Georgiy Zotov | 12.01.1990 | 3 | (9) | |
| **Midfielders:** | **DOB** | **M** | **(s)** | **G** |
| Sergey Babkin | 25.09.2002 | 6 | (10) | 1 |
| Dmitriy Ivanisenya (UKR) | 11.01.1994 | 2 | | |
| Aleksandr Kovalenko | 08.08.2003 | 22 | (1) | 1 |
| Danil Lipovoy | 22.09.1999 | 1 | (4) | |
| Amar Rahmanović (BIH) | 13.05.1994 | 12 | (5) | 1 |
| Artyom Sokolov | 01.04.2003 | 7 | (5) | |
| Maksim Vityugov | 01.02.1998 | 16 | (12) | |
| Denis Yakuba | 26.05.1996 | 6 | (4) | 1 |
| **Forwards:** | **DOB** | **M** | **(s)** | **G** |
| Aleksandar Ćirković (SRB) | 21.09.2001 | 3 | (9) | 1 |
| Benjamín Antonio Garré (ARG) | 11.07.2000 | 11 | (2) | 3 |
| Maksim Glushenkov | 28.07.1999 | 16 | | 5 |
| Vladimir Khubulov | 02.03.2001 | | (13) | |
| Sergei Pinyaev | 02.11.2004 | 9 | (2) | 3 |
| Vladislav Shitov | 07.05.2003 | 5 | (18) | 2 |
| Vladimir Sychevoy Pisarskiy | 27.02.1996 | 9 | (2) | |
| Dmitri Tsypchenko | 29.06.1999 | 13 | (11) | 3 |
| Roman Yezhov | 02.09.1997 | 21 | (1) | 3 |
| Aleksandr Zuev | 26.06.1996 | 4 | (6) | |

## Fudbolnij Klub Lokomotiv Moskva

| | | |
|---|---|---|
| **Founded:** | 23.07.1922 | |
| **Stadium:** | RZD Arena, Moskva (27,320) | |
| **Trainer:** | Josef Zinnbauer (GER) | 01.05.1970 |
| [13.10.2022] | Andrei Fyodorov (UZB) | 10.04.1971 |
| [13.11.2022] | Mikhail Galaktionov | 21.05.1984 |

| Goalkeepers: | DOB | M | (s) | G |
|---|---|---|---|---|
| Guilherme Alvim Marinato | 12.12.1985 | 3 | | |
| Daniil Khudyakov | 09.01.2004 | 14 | | |
| Ilya Lantratov | 11.11.1995 | 13 | | |
| **Defenders:** | **DOB** | **M** | **(s)** | **G** |
| Germán Andrés Conti (ARG) | 03.06.1994 | 3 | | |
| Tin Jedvaj (CRO) | 28.11.1995 | 12 | (2) | |
| Ivan Kuzmichev | 20.10.2000 | 12 | (1) | |
| *Lucas Fasson* dos Santos (BRA) | 30.05.2001 | 2 | (1) | |
| Stanislav Magkeev | 27.03.1999 | 18 | (1) | |
| Mark Mampassi (UKR) | 12.03.2003 | 4 | (3) | |
| Mario Mitaj (ALB) | 06.08.2003 | 4 | (10) | |
| Maksim Nenakhov | 13.12.1998 | 19 | (1) | 1 |
| Egor Pogostnov | 01.03.2004 | 9 | | |
| Igor Smolnikov | 08.08.1988 | 1 | (5) | |
| Nair Tiknizyan (ARM) | 12.05.1999 | 27 | (2) | 4 |
| Dmitri Zhivoglyadov | 29.05.1994 | 12 | (4) | |
| **Midfielders:** | **DOB** | **M** | **(s)** | **G** |
| Sergey Babkin | 25.09.2002 | | (1) | |
| Dmitry Barinov | 11.09.1996 | 26 | (1) | 2 |
| Alexis Beka Beka (FRA) | 29.03.2001 | 1 | (1) | |
| Artyom Karpukas | 13.06.2002 | 27 | | 2 |
| Daniil Kulikov | 24.06.1998 | 3 | (10) | |
| Konstantin Maradishvili | 07.02.2000 | 5 | (16) | 2 |
| Anton Miranchuk | 17.10.1995 | 19 | (9) | 8 |
| Maksim Petrov | 18.01.2001 | | (1) | |
| Mikhail Shchetinin | 08.07.2005 | 1 | (2) | |
| Rifat Zhemaletdinov | 20.09.1996 | 4 | (7) | |
| **Forwards:** | **DOB** | **M** | **(s)** | **G** |
| Abdula Bagamaev | 18.10.2004 | | (1) | |
| Artyom Dzyuba | 22.08.1988 | 11 | | 8 |
| Maksim Glushenkov | 28.07.1999 | 10 | (3) | 5 |
| Ivan Ignatyev | 06.01.1999 | 9 | (11) | 5 |
| Wilson Isidor (FRA) | 27.08.2000 | 12 | (8) | 8 |
| François Kamano (GUI) | 02.05.1996 | 26 | (2) | 3 |
| Gyrano Kerk (NED) | 02.12.1995 | 11 | (6) | 2 |
| Pedro Gabriel Pereira Lopes „Pedrinho" (BRA) | 10.11.1999 | 3 | (3) | |
| Sergei Pinyaev | 02.11.2004 | 7 | (2) | 2 |
| Marko Rakonjac (MNE) | 25.04.2000 | 2 | (10) | |
| Vadim Rakov | 09.01.2005 | | (9) | |

## Fudbolnij Klub Orenburg

| | |
|---|---|
| **Founded:** | 1976 |
| **Stadium:** | Gazovik Stadion, Orenburg (10,046) |
| **Trainer:** | Marcel Lička (CZE)     17.07.1977 |

| Goalkeepers: | DOB | M | (s) | G |
|---|---|---|---|---|
| Evgeniy Goshev | 17.06.1997 | 8 | (1) | |
| Aleksey Kenyaikin | 23.08.1998 | 11 | | |
| Nikolay Sysuev | 19.05.1999 | 11 | | |
| **Defenders:** | **DOB** | **M** | **(s)** | **G** |
| Aleksandr Ektov | 30.01.1996 | 20 | (5) | 3 |
| Renato Gojković (BIH) | 10.09.1995 | 21 | (3) | 1 |
| Danila Khotulev | 01.10.2002 | 13 | (1) | |
| Andrey Malykh | 24.08.1988 | 7 | (1) | |
| Aljaksandr Paulawez (BLR) | 13.08.1996 | 5 | (2) | |
| Matías Damián Pérez (ARG) | 03.03.1999 | 10 | | |
| Vladimir Poluyakhtov | 11.07.1989 | 8 | (12) | |
| Kiryl Pyachenin (BLR) | 18.03.1997 | 15 | (4) | |
| Mikhail Sivakov (BLR) | 16.01.1988 | 21 | (3) | |
| Mateo Stamatov (BUL) | 22.03.1999 | 12 | (3) | |
| **Midfielders:** | **DOB** | **M** | **(s)** | **G** |
| Timur Ayupov | 26.07.1993 | 17 | (6) | 4 |
| Ivan Bašić (BIH) | 30.04.2002 | 7 | (8) | 2 |
| César Gabriel Florentín (ARG) | 13.03.1999 | 19 | (1) | 2 |
| Batraz Gurtsiev | 12.12.1998 | 2 | (6) | |
| Kiryl Kaplenka (BLR) | 15.06.1999 | 14 | (6) | 2 |
| Danil Kapustyanskiy | 30.10.2004 | | (6) | 1 |
| Yury Kavalyow (BLR) | 27.01.1993 | 9 | (11) | 2 |
| Nikolai Titkov | 18.08.2000 | 3 | (13) | |
| Lucas Gabriel Vera (ARG) | 18.04.1997 | 25 | (2) | 2 |
| **Forwards:** | **DOB** | **M** | **(s)** | **G** |
| Diego Emmanuel Acosta Curtido (PAR) | 12.11.2002 | | (2) | |
| Brian Ezequiel Mansilla (ARG) | 16.04.1997 | 17 | (5) | 4 |
| Jimmy Marín Vílchez (CRC) | 08.10.1997 | 16 | (9) | 7 |
| Vladimir Obukhov | 08.02.1992 | 4 | (7) | 2 |
| Stepan Oganesyan | 28.09.2001 | 6 | (14) | 2 |
| Vladimir Sychevoy Pisarskiy | 27.02.1996 | 12 | (3) | 14 |
| Dmitri Vorobyev | 28.11.1997 | 17 | (5) | 8 |

## Fudbolnij Klub Pari Nizhny Novgorod

| Founded: | 2015 | | |
|---|---|---|---|
| Stadium: | Nizhny Novgorod Stadion, Nizhny Novgorod (44,899) | | |
| Trainer: | Mikhail Galaktionov | | 21.05.1984 |
| [11.11.2022] | Anton Khazov | | 28.04.1979 |
| [31.12.2022] | Artyom Gorlov | | 23.06.1987 |
| [04.04.2023] | Sergei Yuran | | 11.06.1969 |

| Goalkeepers: | DOB | M | (s) | G |
|---|---|---|---|---|
| Nikita Goylo | 10.08.1998 | 11 | | |
| Artur Nigmatullin | 17.05.1991 | 19 | | |
| **Defenders:** | **DOB** | **M** | **(s)** | **G** |
| Ilya Agapov | 21.01.2001 | 13 | | |
| Viktor Aleksandrov | 14.02.2002 | 14 | (3) | 2 |
| Kirill Gotsuk | 10.09.1992 | 27 | | 3 |
| Ákos Kecskés (HUN) | 04.01.1996 | 1 | | |
| Daniil Kornyushin | 08.10.2001 | 11 | (3) | |
| Lucas Gabriel Masoero Masi (ARG) | 01.02.1995 | 20 | (2) | |
| Elmir Nabiullin | 08.03.1995 | 5 | (4) | |
| Daniil Penchikov | 21.03.1998 | 4 | | |
| Dmitriy Stotskiy | 01.12.1989 | 22 | (3) | 2 |
| Ibrokhimkhalil Yuldashev (UZB) | 14.02.2001 | 14 | (14) | 2 |
| **Midfielders:** | **DOB** | **M** | **(s)** | **G** |
| Ilya Berkovskiy | 15.03.2000 | 3 | (3) | |
| Denis Glushakov | 27.01.1987 | 4 | (3) | 1 |

| | DOB | M | (s) | G |
|---|---|---|---|---|
| Nikita Kakkoev | 22.08.1999 | 17 | (4) | 1 |
| Nikolai Kalinskiy | 22.09.1993 | 18 | (4) | 4 |
| David Kobesov | 06.01.2000 | | (2) | |
| Mamadou Maiga (MLI) | 10.02.1995 | 21 | (1) | 1 |
| Yaroslav Mikhailov | 28.04.2003 | 16 | (5) | 1 |
| Dmitry Rybchinsky | 19.08.1998 | 17 | (9) | 2 |
| Albert Sharipov | 11.04.1993 | 10 | (7) | |
| Konstantin Shiltsov | 07.05.2002 | 1 | (9) | |
| Artyom Sokolov | 01.04.2003 | 3 | (3) | |
| Ilya Zhigulev | 01.02.1996 | 4 | (8) | |
| **Forwards:** | **DOB** | **M** | **(s)** | **G** |
| Vyacheslav Krotov | 14.02.1993 | 13 | (10) | 2 |
| Timur Suleymanov | 17.03.2000 | 21 | (7) | 10 |
| Vladislav Yakovlev | 14.02.2002 | 4 | (7) | 1 |
| Momo Yansane (GUI) | 29.07.1997 | 5 | (11) | |
| Felicio Mendes João *Milson* (ANG) | 12.10.1999 | 7 | (9) | 2 |
| Edgar Sevikyan | 08.08.2001 | 5 | (5) | |

## Fudbolnij Klub Rostov

| Founded: | 1930 | | |
|---|---|---|---|
| Stadium: | Rostov Arena, Rostov-na-Donu (45,000) | | |
| Trainer: | Valeriy Karpin | | 02.02.1969 |

| Goalkeepers: | DOB | M | (s) | G |
|---|---|---|---|---|
| Sergey Pesyakov | 16.12.1988 | 30 | | |
| **Defenders:** | **DOB** | **M** | **(s)** | **G** |
| Evgeniy Chernov | 23.10.1992 | 19 | (4) | 2 |
| Andrey Langovich | 28.05.2003 | 11 | (11) | 2 |
| Viktor Melekhin | 16.12.2003 | 20 | (4) | |
| Maksim Osipenko | 16.05.1994 | 26 | | 6 |
| Danila Prokhin | 24.05.2001 | 11 | (8) | 1 |
| Aleksandr Silyanov | 17.02.2001 | 29 | (1) | 2 |
| Denis Terentyev | 13.08.1992 | 5 | (11) | |
| **Midfielders:** | **DOB** | **M** | **(s)** | **G** |
| Khoren Bayramyan (ARM) | 07.01.1992 | 20 | (3) | 1 |
| Danil Glebov | 03.11.1999 | 28 | | 4 |

| | DOB | M | (s) | G |
|---|---|---|---|---|
| Ivan Komarov | 15.04.2003 | 2 | (9) | |
| Aleksey Mironov | 01.01.2000 | 14 | (12) | 1 |
| Alyaksandr Syalyava (BLR) | 17.05.1992 | 4 | (8) | 1 |
| Daniil Utkin | 12.10.1999 | 22 | (5) | 3 |
| **Forwards:** | **DOB** | **M** | **(s)** | **G** |
| Egor Golenkov | 07.07.1999 | 5 | (24) | |
| Nikolay Komlichenko | 29.06.1995 | 26 | | 10 |
| Stepan Melnikov | 25.04.2002 | 1 | (9) | 1 |
| Artyom Ntumba | 19.04.2003 | | (7) | |
| Dmitriy Poloz | 12.07.1991 | 20 | (5) | 8 |
| Kirill Shchetinin | 17.01.2002 | 20 | (10) | 1 |
| David Tosevski (MKD) | 16.07.2001 | | (2) | |
| Roman Tugarev | 22.07.1998 | 17 | (7) | 1 |

## Professionalnij Fudbolnij Klub Sochi

| Founded: | 06.06.2018 | | |
|---|---|---|---|
| Stadium: | Fisht Olympic Stadion, Sochi (47,659) | | |
| Trainer: | Vadim Garanin | | 29.11.1970 |
| [25.12.2022] | Kurban Berdyev (TKM) | | 25.08.1952 |
| [10.04.2023] | Dmitri Khokhlov | | 22.12.1975 |

| Goalkeepers: | DOB | M | (s) | G |
|---|---|---|---|---|
| Denis Adamov | 20.02.1998 | 16 | (1) | |
| Soslan Dzhanaev | 13.03.1987 | 9 | | |
| Nikolay Zabolotniy | 16.04.1990 | 5 | | |
| **Defenders:** | **DOB** | **M** | **(s)** | **G** |
| Vanja Drkušič (SVN) | 30.10.1999 | 26 | | 1 |
| Artyom Makarchuk | 09.11.1995 | 25 | (4) | 1 |
| Timofey Margasov | 12.06.1992 | 21 | (5) | |
| Artyom Meshchaninov | 19.02.1996 | 13 | (4) | |
| Ivan Miladinović (SRB) | 14.08.1994 | 7 | (2) | |
| Moussa Sissako (MLI) | 10.11.2000 | 2 | (8) | 1 |
| Sergey Terekhov | 27.06.1990 | 27 | | |
| Igor Yurganov | 10.12.1993 | 19 | (1) | |
| Kirill Zaika | 07.10.1992 | 10 | (5) | 2 |
| **Midfielders:** | **DOB** | **M** | **(s)** | **G** |
| Victorien Angban (CIV) | 29.09.1996 | 6 | (1) | |

| | DOB | M | (s) | G |
|---|---|---|---|---|
| Amir Batyrev (CAN) | 11.03.2002 | 2 | (7) | |
| Kirill Kravtsov | 14.06.2002 | 12 | (12) | 1 |
| *Miguel* Silveira dos Santos (BRA) | 26.03.2003 | | (2) | |
| Christian Fernando Noboa Tello (ECU) | 09.04.1985 | 24 | (2) | 11 |
| Timofey Shipunov | 20.07.2003 | 3 | (12) | 2 |
| Ibrahim Tsallagov | 12.12.1990 | 13 | (5) | 1 |
| Kirill Ushatov | 24.01.2000 | | (7) | |
| Artur Yusupov | 01.09.1989 | 25 | (1) | 3 |
| **Forwards:** | **DOB** | **M** | **(s)** | **G** |
| Nikita Burmistrov | 06.07.1989 | 13 | (8) | |
| Luka Đorđević (MNE) | 09.07.1994 | 7 | (6) | 2 |
| João Natailton Ramos dos Santos „Joãozinho" (BRA) | 25.12.1988 | 12 | (11) | 3 |
| Daniil Martovoy | 24.05.2003 | | (1) | |
| Georgi Melkadze | 04.04.1997 | 18 | (6) | 5 |
| Vladislav Sarveli | 01.10.1997 | 15 | (11) | 4 |

## Fudbolnij Klub Spartak Moskva

| Founded: | 18.04.1922 | | |
|---|---|---|---|
| Stadium: | Otkritie Arena, Moskva (44,307) | | |
| Trainer: | Guillermo Abascal Pérez (ESP) | | 13.04.1989 |

| Goalkeepers: | DOB | M | (s) | G |
|---|---|---|---|---|
| Aleksandr Maksimenko | 19.03.1998 | 3 | | |
| Aleksandr Selikhov | 07.04.1994 | 27 | | |
| **Defenders:** | **DOB** | **M** | **(s)** | **G** |
| Maximiliano Caufriez (BEL) | 16.02.1997 | | (1) | |
| Nikita Chernov | 14.01.1996 | 17 | (7) | |
| Daniil Denisov | 21.10.2002 | 26 | (3) | 1 |
| Alexis David Duarte Pereira (PAR) | 12.03.2000 | 5 | (2) | |
| Georgi Dzhikiya | 21.11.1993 | 21 | (1) | |
| Leon Klassen | 29.05.2000 | 2 | (9) | |
| Daniil Khlusevich | 26.02.2001 | 22 | (4) | |
| Pavel Maslov | 14.04.2000 | 6 | (13) | 1 |
| Miha Mevlja (SVN) | 12.06.1990 | 2 | (2) | |
| Nikolai Rasskazov | 04.01.1998 | | (4) | |
| Maciej Rybus (POL) | 19.08.1989 | 3 | (5) | 1 |
| *Tomás* Franco *Tavares* (POR) | 07.03.2001 | 10 | (3) | |

| Midfielders: | DOB | M | (s) | G |
|---|---|---|---|---|
| Mikhail Ignatov | 04.05.2000 | 18 | (3) | 2 |
| Ruslan Litvinov | 18.08.2001 | 22 | (3) | 3 |
| Christopher Pereira Martins (LUX) | 19.02.1997 | 13 | (5) | 2 |
| Victor Moses (NGA) | 12.12.1990 | 3 | (7) | 2 |
| Danil Prutsev | 25.03.2000 | 17 | (10) | 1 |
| Nail Umyarov | 27.06.2000 | 10 | (2) | |
| Roman Zobnin | 11.02.1994 | 28 | (1) | 4 |
| Daniil Zorin | 22.02.2004 | | (2) | |
| **Forwards:** | **DOB** | **M** | **(s)** | **G** |
| Keita Baldé (SEN) | 08.03.1995 | 6 | (6) | 3 |
| Pavel Meleshin | 25.03.2004 | | (8) | 1 |
| Shamar Amaro Nicholson (JAM) | 16.03.1997 | 10 | (12) | 3 |
| Quincy Anton Promes (NED) | 04.01.1992 | 25 | (2) | 20 |
| Vitaliy Shitov | 07.05.2003 | | (1) | |
| Aleksandr Sobolev | 07.03.1997 | 23 | (3) | 13 |
| Anton Zinkovskiy | 14.04.1996 | 11 | (17) | 3 |

## Fudbolnij Klub Torpedo Moskva

| Founded: | 17.08.1924 | |
|---|---|---|
| Stadium: | Luzhniki Stadion, Moskva (81,000) | |
| Trainer: | Aleksandr Borodyuk | 30.11.1962 |
| [18.08.2022] | Nikolai Kovardayev | 24.09.1970 |
| [13.10.2022] | Andrey Talalayev | 05.10.1972 |
| [22.03.2023] | Josep Clotet Ruiz (ESP) | 28.04.1977 |

| Goalkeepers: | DOB | M | (s) | G |
|---|---|---|---|---|
| Egor Baburin | 09.08.1993 | 21 | | |
| Vitaliy Botnar | 19.05.2001 | 4 | | |
| Aleksandr Dovbnya | 10.04.1987 | 5 | (1) | |
| **Defenders:** | **DOB** | **M** | **(s)** | **G** |
| Oleg Kozhemyakin | 30.05.1995 | 22 | (4) | |
| Ilya Kutepov | 29.07.1993 | 9 | | |
| Egor Proshkin | 15.01.1999 | 6 | (6) | |
| Bojan Roganović (MNE) | 28.09.2000 | 11 | (2) | |
| Artyom Samsonov | 06.02.1989 | 20 | (2) | |
| Evgeniy Shlyakov | 30.08.1991 | 8 | | |
| Aleksey Shumskikh | 01.07.1990 | 2 | (1) | |
| Igor Smolnikov | 08.08.1988 | 15 | (1) | 1 |
| Stefan Šapić (SRB) | 26.02.1997 | 3 | (2) | 1 |
| Ivan Temnikov | 28.01.1989 | 1 | (3) | |
| Raman Yuzapchuk (BLR) | 24.07.1997 | 11 | (1) | |
| Yuriy Zhuravlev | 29.06.1996 | 3 | | |
| **Midfielders:** | **DOB** | **M** | **(s)** | **G** |
| Mihail Caimacov (MDA) | 22.07.1998 | 5 | (5) | 1 |
| Mario Ćurić (CRO) | 28.09.1998 | 12 | (5) | 1 |
| Ivan Enin | 06.02.1994 | 18 | (4) | |
| Damien Vincent Denis Le Tallec (FRA) | 19.04.1990 | 6 | (3) | |
| Ravil Netfullin | 03.03.1993 | 18 | (3) | 1 |

| | DOB | M | (s) | G |
|---|---|---|---|---|
| Aleksandr Orekhov | 24.05.2002 | 4 | (1) | |
| Aleksey Pomerko | 03.05.1990 | 7 | (1) | 1 |
| Bogdan Reichman | 26.05.2002 | 2 | (6) | |
| Aleksandr Ryazantsev | 05.09.1986 | 9 | (7) | |
| Igor Savić (BIH) | 08.10.2000 | 12 | (3) | |
| Artyom Simonyan (ARM) | 20.02.1995 | 1 | (1) | |
| Aleksey Usanov | 14.01.2001 | 2 | | |
| **Forwards:** | **DOB** | **M** | **(s)** | **G** |
| *André* Felipe Ribeiro de Souza (BRA) | 27.09.1990 | 3 | (2) | 1 |
| Maksim Danilin | 26.05.2001 | | (2) | |
| Khojimat Erkinov (UZB) | 29.05.2001 | 13 | (7) | |
| Jair Diego Alves de Brito „Jajá" (BRA) | 15.04.2001 | | (7) | |
| Amur Kalmykov | 29.05.1994 | 2 | (3) | |
| David Karaev | 10.03.1995 | 25 | (4) | 2 |
| Márk Koszta (HUN) | 26.09.1996 | 1 | (3) | |
| Ilya Kukharchuk | 02.08.1990 | 5 | (4) | 1 |
| Dzyanis Laptev (BLR) | 01.08.1991 | 2 | (2) | |
| Igor Lebedenko | 27.05.1983 | 11 | (12) | 2 |
| José Yordy Reyna Serna Sánchez (PER) | 17.09.1993 | 11 | (1) | 1 |
| Ilya Stefanovich | 23.06.1996 | 8 | (5) | 5 |
| Mukhammad Sultonov | 22.12.1992 | 4 | (5) | |
| Dzambolat Tsallagov | 01.01.2000 | | (2) | |
| Maksim Turishchev | 05.03.2002 | 8 | (17) | |

## Fudbolnij Klub Ural Yekaterinburg

| Founded: | 1930 | |
|---|---|---|
| Stadium: | Central Stadion, Yekaterinburg (35,696) | |
| Trainer: | Igor Shalimov | 02.02.1969 |
| [08.08.2022] | Yevgeni Averyanov | 31.03.1979 |
| [15.08.2022] | Viktar Hancharenka (BLR) | 10.06.1977 |

| Goalkeepers: | DOB | M | (s) | G |
|---|---|---|---|---|
| Nikita Alekseev | 09.01.2002 | 1 | | |
| Ilya Pomazun | 16.08.1996 | 29 | | |
| **Defenders:** | **DOB** | **M** | **(s)** | **G** |
| Silvije Begić (CRO) | 03.06.1993 | 13 | (2) | |
| Mingiyan Beveev | 30.11.1995 | 20 | (5) | |
| Vladis Emmerson Illoy Ayyet (CGO) | 07.10.1995 | 18 | (4) | 1 |
| Egor Filipenko (BLR) | 10.04.1988 | 13 | | 1 |
| Aleksey Gerasimov | 15.04.1993 | 6 | (3) | |
| Leo Goglichidze | 29.04.1997 | 19 | (7) | |
| Denys Kulakov (UKR) | 01.05.1986 | 15 | (4) | |
| Ivan Kuzmichev | 20.10.2000 | 6 | (1) | |
| Artyom Mamin | 25.07.1997 | 7 | (2) | |
| **Midfielders:** | **DOB** | **M** | **(s)** | **G** |
| Eric Cosmin Bicfalvi (ROU) | 05.02.1988 | 21 | (5) | 4 |
| Ilya Bykovskiy | 16.02.2001 | 4 | (3) | 1 |
| Ibrahima Cissé (GUI) | 28.02.1994 | 14 | (3) | |
| Andrey Egorychev | 14.02.1993 | 20 | (1) | 2 |
| Roman Emelyanov | 08.05.1992 | | (2) | |

| | DOB | M | (s) | G |
|---|---|---|---|---|
| Aleksey Evseev | 30.03.1994 | | (1) | |
| Yuri Gazinskiy | 20.07.1989 | 12 | (2) | 3 |
| Ilya Ishkov | 25.05.2005 | | (1) | |
| Igor Konovalov | 08.07.1996 | 4 | (2) | |
| Danijel Miškić (CRO) | 11.10.1993 | 26 | (1) | 3 |
| Vyacheslav Podberezkin | 21.06.1992 | 9 | (4) | |
| Oleg Shatov | 29.07.1990 | 1 | (3) | |
| Fanil Sungatulin | 24.12.2001 | 10 | (14) | |
| Luka Tsulukidze (GEO) | 08.02.2004 | | (1) | |
| Oston Urunov (UZB) | 19.12.2000 | | (2) | |
| Yuriy Zheleznov | 15.11.2002 | 1 | (13) | |
| **Forwards:** | **DOB** | **M** | **(s)** | **G** |
| Ramazan Gadzhimuradov | 09.01.1998 | 6 | (4) | |
| Aleksey Kashtanov | 13.03.1996 | 17 | (11) | 5 |
| Lazar Ranđelović (SRB) | 05.08.1997 | 15 | (3) | 3 |
| Evgeniy Tatarinov | 06.02.1999 | 1 | (9) | |
| Rai Hendrikus Martinus Vloet (NED) | 08.05.1995 | 8 | (7) | 4 |
| Aleksandr Yushin | 04.04.1995 | 14 | (12) | 5 |

## Fudbolnij Klub Zenit Saint Petersburg

| Founded: | 25.05.1925 | |
|---|---|---|
| Stadium: | Gazprom Arena (Krestovsky Stadium), Saint Petersburg (67,800) | |
| Trainer: | Sergei Semak | 27.02.1976 |

| Goalkeepers: | DOB | M | (s) | G |
|---|---|---|---|---|
| Mikhail Kerzhakov | 28.01.1987 | 23 | (1) | |
| Daniil Odoevskiy | 22.01.2003 | 4 | | |
| Aleksandr Vasyutin | 04.03.1995 | 3 | | |
| **Defenders:** | **DOB** | **M** | **(s)** | **G** |
| Arsen Adamov | 20.10.1999 | 1 | (8) | |
| Nuraly Alip (KAZ) | 22.12.1999 | 6 | (2) | |
| Dmitriy Chistyakov | 13.01.1994 | 9 | (6) | |
| *Douglas* dos *Santos* Justino de Melo (BRA) | 22.03.1994 | 27 | (1) | |
| Vyacheslav Karavayev | 20.05.1995 | 23 | (1) | |
| Danil Krugovoy | 28.05.1998 | 5 | (14) | |
| Dejan Lovren (CRO) | 05.07.1989 | 15 | | 1 |
| *Robert Renan* Alves Barbosa (BRA) | 11.10.2003 | 9 | | |
| Rodrigo de Souza Prado „Rodrigão" (BRA) | 11.09.1995 | 21 | (1) | 1 |
| **Midfielders:** | **DOB** | **M** | **(s)** | **G** |
| Wilmar Enrique Barrios Teherán (COL) | 16.10.1993 | 27 | (1) | 1 |

| | DOB | M | (s) | G |
|---|---|---|---|---|
| Cláudio Luiz Rodrigues Parise Leonel „Claudinho" (BRA) | 28.01.1997 | 19 | (5) | 5 |
| Aleksandr Erokhin | 13.10.1989 | 1 | (19) | 2 |
| Danila Kozlov | 19.01.2005 | | (2) | |
| Daler Kuzyaev | 15.01.1993 | 22 | (4) | 5 |
| Yaroslav Mikhailov | 28.04.2003 | | (1) | |
| Vladislav Saus | 06.08.2003 | | (1) | |
| Marcus *Wendel* Valle da Silva (BRA) | 28.08.1997 | 24 | (1) | 8 |
| **Forwards:** | **DOB** | **M** | **(s)** | **G** |
| Zelimkhan Bakaev | 01.07.1996 | 1 | (16) | 1 |
| Aleksey Baranovsky | 25.01.2005 | | (3) | |
| Zander Mateo Cassierra Cabezas (COL) | 13.04.1997 | 17 | (9) | 2 |
| *Gustavo* Mantuan (BRA) | 20.06.2001 | 4 | (18) | 6 |
| *Malcom* Filipe Silva de Oliveira (BRA) | 26.02.1997 | 27 | | 23 |
| Andrey Mostovoy | 05.11.1997 | 23 | (6) | 8 |
| Ivan Sergeev | 11.05.1995 | 14 | (12) | 10 |
| Aleksey Sutormin | 10.01.1994 | 5 | (9) | |

| | | | | | | | | | |
|---|---|---|---|---|---|---|---|---|---|
| 1. | FK Rubin Kazan (*Promoted*) | 34 | 19 | 12 | 3 | 53 | - | 27 | 69 |
| 2. | FK Baltika Kaliningrad (*Promoted*) | 34 | 18 | 13 | 3 | 56 | - | 30 | 67 |
| 3. | FK Alania Vladikavkaz* | 34 | 17 | 11 | 6 | 56 | - | 35 | 62 |
| 4. | FK Yenisey Krasnoyarsk (*Promotion Play-offs*) | 34 | 13 | 15 | 6 | 43 | - | 35 | 54 |
| 5. | FK Rodina Moskva (*Promotion Play-offs*) | 34 | 13 | 11 | 10 | 42 | - | 38 | 50 |
| 6. | FK Neftekhimik Nizhnekamsk | 34 | 12 | 11 | 11 | 34 | - | 33 | 47 |
| 7. | FK Shinnik Yaroslavl | 34 | 13 | 7 | 14 | 36 | - | 41 | 46 |
| 8. | FK Dinamo Makhachkala | 34 | 12 | 10 | 12 | 25 | - | 29 | 46 |
| 9. | FK Akron Tolyatti | 34 | 10 | 16 | 8 | 38 | - | 36 | 46 |
| 10. | FK SKA-Khabarovsk | 34 | 11 | 11 | 12 | 50 | - | 39 | 44 |
| 11. | FK KAMAZ Naberezhnye Chelny | 34 | 11 | 11 | 12 | 35 | - | 36 | 44 |
| 12. | FK Volgar Astrakhan | 34 | 11 | 11 | 12 | 37 | - | 41 | 44 |
| 13. | FK Arsenal Tula | 34 | 11 | 8 | 15 | 37 | - | 46 | 41 |
| 14. | FK Kuban Krasnodar | 34 | 9 | 10 | 15 | 36 | - | 41 | 37 |
| 15. | FK Veles Moskva (*Relegated*) | 34 | 9 | 6 | 19 | 35 | - | 55 | 33 |
| 16. | FK Ufa (*Relegated*) | 34 | 8 | 8 | 18 | 35 | - | 46 | 32 |
| 17. | FK Krasnodar-2 (*Relegated*) | 34 | 8 | 7 | 19 | 32 | - | 54 | 31 |
| 18. | FK Volga Ulyanovsk (*Relegated*) | 34 | 6 | 12 | 16 | 23 | - | 41 | 30 |

*Please note: FK Alania Vladikavkaz failed to receive a license for the 2023/2024 Premier League.

## NATIONAL TEAM

### INTERNATIONAL MATCHES
#### (16.07.2022 – 15.07.2023)

| | | | | |
|---|---|---|---|---|
| 24.09.2022 | Bishkek | *Kyrgyz Republic - Russia* | *1-2(1-1)* | (F) |
| 17.11.2022 | Dushanbe | *Tajikistan - Russia* | *0-0* | (F) |
| 20.11.2022 | Tashkent | *Uzbekistan - Russia* | *0-0* | (F) |
| 23.03.2023 | Tehran | *Iran - Russia* | *1-1(0-1)* | (F) |
| 26.03.2023 | Saint Petersburg | *Russia - Iraq* | *2-0(0-0)* | (F) |

**24.09.2022    KYRGYZ REPUBLIC - RUSSIA        1-2(1-1)                    Friendly International**
„Dolen Omurzakov" Stadium, Bishkek; Referee: Daniyar Sakhi (Kazakhstan); Attendance: n/a
**RUS:** Matvei Safonov, Vyacheslav Karavayev (46.Daniil Khlusevich), Maksim Osipenko (46.Aleksandr Silyanov), Danil Krugovoy (46.Andrey Mostovoy), Sergey Borodin (46.Daler Kuzyayev), Roman Yezhov (46.Maksim Glushenkov), Zelimkhan Bakayev (46.Artyom Makarchuk), Daniil Fomin (46.Daniil Utkin), Danil Glebov (Cap) (46.Georgiy Dzhikiya), Aleksandr Kovalenko (46.Dmitriy Barinov), Aleksandr Sobolev (46.Nikolay Komlichenko). Trainer: Valeriy Karpin.
**Goals:** Aleksandr Sobolev (30 penalty), Daniil Utkin (89).

**17.11.2022    TAJIKISTAN - RUSSIA        0-0                    Friendly International**
Pamir Stadium, Dushanbe; Referee: Ilgiz Tantashev (Uzbekistan); Attendance: 20,000
**RUS:** Aleksandr Selikhov (46.Sergey Pesyakov; 54.Anton Shunin), Maksim Osipenko, Aleksandr Soldatenkov, Daniil Khlusevich, Artyom Makarchuk, Anton Miranchuk (46.Arsen Zakharyan), Daniil Utkin, Danil Glebov (Cap), Lechi Sadulayev (79.Andrey Mostovoy), Sergey Pinyayev (84.Daniil Fomin), Fyodor Chalov (46.Vladimir Pisarskiy). Trainer: Valeriy Karpin.

**20.11.2022    UZBEKISTAN - RUSSIA        0-0                    Friendly International**
Pakhtakor Stadium, Tashkent; Referee: Daniyar Sakhi (Kazakhstan); Attendance: n/a
**RUS:** Anton Shunin, Georgiy Dzhikiya (Cap) (64.Maksim Osipenko), Vyacheslav Karavayev (63.Artyom Makarchuk), Aleksandr Silyanov (69.Anton Miranchuk), Daler Kuzyayev, Dmitriy Barinov, Daniil Fomin, Andrey Mostovoy, Ruslan Litvinov, Arsen Zakharyan (76.Sergey Pinyayev), Aleksandr Sobolev (77.Nikolay Komlichenko). Trainer: Valeriy Karpin.

**23.03.2023    IRAN - RUSSIA        1-1(0-1)                    Friendly International**
Azadi Stadium, Tehran; Referee: Ilgiz Tantashev (Uzbekistan); Attendance: 15,000
**RUS:** Matvei Safonov, Vyacheslav Karavayev, Maksim Osipenko, Daler Kuzyayev (Cap) (87.Danil Prutsev), Anton Miranchuk (78.Daniil Fomin), Anton Zinkovskiy (87.Ilzat Akhmetov), Daniil Khlusevich (88.Aleksandr Silyanov), Ruslan Litvinov, Danil Glebov, Arsen Zakharyan (69.Ivan Oblyakov), Nikolay Komlichenko (78.Konstantin Tyukavin). Trainer: Valeriy Karpin.
**Goal:** Anton Miranchuk (28 penalty).

**26.03.2023    RUSSIA - IRAQ        2-0(0-0)                    Friendly International**
Krestovsky Stadium, Saint Petersburg; Referee: Akhrol Riskullaev (Uzbekistan); Attendance: 23,818
**RUS:** Sergey Pesyakov, Maksim Osipenko (66.Daniil Khlusevich), Aleksandr Silyanov, Daniil Denisov, Daniil Fomin (Cap) (67.Daler Kuzyayev [*sent off 90+3*]), Ivan Oblyakov (80.Vyacheslav Karavayev), Danil Prutsev (46.Anton Miranchuk), Ruslan Litvinov, Sergey Pinyayev (71.Anton Zinkovskiy), Danil Glebov, Aleksandr Sobolev (74.Konstantin Tyukavin). Trainer: Valeriy Karpin.
**Goals:** Anton Miranchuk (50), Sergey Pinyayev (58).

## NATIONAL TEAM PLAYERS
### (16.07.2022 – 15.07.2023)

| Name | DOB | Caps | Goals | Club | |
|---|---|---|---|---|---|

### Goalkeepers

| Name | DOB | Caps | Goals | Club | |
|---|---|---|---|---|---|
| Sergey PESYAKOV | 16.12.1988 | 2 | 0 | 2022/2023: | *FK Rostov* |
| Matvei SAFONOV | 25.02.1999 | 9 | 0 | 2022/2023: | *FK Krasnodar* |
| Aleksandr SELIKHOV | 07.04.1994 | 1 | 0 | 2022: | *FK Spartak Moskva* |
| Anton SHUNIN | 27.01.1987 | 15 | 0 | 2022: | *FK Dinamo Moskva* |

### Defenders

| Name | DOB | Caps | Goals | Club | |
|---|---|---|---|---|---|
| Sergey BORODIN | 30.01.1999 | 1 | 0 | 2022: | *Beitar Jerusalem FC (ISR)* |
| Daniil DENISOV | 21.10.2002 | 1 | 0 | 2023: | *FK Spartak Moskva* |
| Georgiy DZHIKIYA | 21.11.1993 | 43 | 2 | 2022: | *FK Spartak Moskva* |
| Vyacheslav KARAVAYEV | 20.05.1995 | 24 | 2 | 2022/2023: | *FK Zenit Saint Petersburg* |
| Daniil KHLUSEVICH | 26.02.2001 | 4 | 0 | 2022/2023: | *FK Spartak Moskva* |
| Danil KRUGOVOY | 28.05.1998 | 1 | 0 | 2022: | *FK Zenit Saint Petersburg* |
| Ruslan LITVINOV | 18.08.2001 | 3 | 0 | 2022/2023: | *FK Spartak Moskva* |
| Artyom MAKARCHUK | 09.11.1995 | 3 | 0 | 2022: | *PFK Sochi* |
| Maksim OSIPENKO | 16.05.1994 | 8 | 0 | 2022/2023: | *FK Rostov* |
| Aleksandr SILYANOV | 17.02.2001 | 4 | 0 | 2022/2023: | *FK Lokomotiv Moskva* |
| Aleksandr SOLDATENKOV | 28.12.1996 | 1 | 0 | 2022: | *PFK Krylia Sovetov Samara* |

### Midfielders

| Name | DOB | Caps | Goals | Club | |
|---|---|---|---|---|---|
| Ilzat AKHMETOV | 31.12.1997 | 9 | 0 | 2023: | *FK Krasnodar* |
| Zelimkhan BAKAYEV | 01.07.1996 | 13 | 1 | 2022: | *FK Zenit Saint Petersburg* |
| Dmitriy BARINOV | 11.09.1996 | 15 | 0 | 2022: | *FK Lokomotiv Moskva* |
| Daniil FOMIN | 02.03.1997 | 13 | 0 | 2022/2023: | *FK Dinamo Moskva* |
| Danil GLEBOV | 03.11.1999 | 6 | 0 | 2022/2023: | *FK Rostov* |
| Aleksandr KOVALENKO | 08.08.2003 | 1 | 0 | 2022: | *PFK Krylia Sovetov Samara* |
| Daler KUZYAYEV | 15.01.1993 | 46 | 2 | 2022/2023: | *FK Zenit Saint Petersburg* |
| Anton MIRANCHUK | 17.10.1995 | 23 | 5 | 2022/2023: | *FK Lokomotiv Moskva* |
| Andrey MOSTOVOY | 05.11.1997 | 13 | 1 | 2022: | *FK Zenit Saint Petersburg* |
| Ivan OBLYAKOV | 05.07.1998 | 4 | 0 | 2023: | *PFK CSKA Moskva* |
| Sergey PINYAYEV | 02.11.2004 | 3 | 1 | 2022/2023: | *FK Lokomotiv Moskva* |
| Danil PRUTSEV | 25.03.2000 | 2 | 0 | 2023: | *FK Spartak Moskva* |
| Lechi SADULAYEV | 08.01.2000 | 1 | 0 | 2022: | *RFK Akhmat Grozny* |
| Daniil UTKIN | 12.10.1999 | 2 | 1 | 2022: | *FK Rostov* |
| Roman YEZHOV | 02.09.1997 | 1 | 0 | 2022: | *PFK Krylia Sovetov Samara* |
| Arsen ZAKHARYAN | 26.05.2003 | 7 | 0 | 2022/2023: | *FK Dinamo Moskva* |
| Anton ZINKOVSKIY | 04.04.1996 | 2 | 0 | 2023: | *FK Spartak Moskva* |

### Forwards

| Name | DOB | Caps | Goals | Club | |
|---|---|---|---|---|---|
| Fyodor CHALOV | 10.04.1998 | 4 | 0 | 2022: | *PFK CSKA Moskva* |
| Maksim GLUSHENKOV | 28.07.1999 | 1 | 0 | 2022: | *FK Lokomotiv Moskva* |
| Nikolay KOMLICHENKO | 29.06.1995 | 6 | 1 | 2022/2023: | *FK Rostov* |
| Vladimir PISARSKIY | 27.02.1996 | 1 | 0 | 2022: | *FK Orenburg* |
| Aleksandr SOBOLEV | 07.03.1997 | 11 | 4 | 2022/2023: | *FK Spartak Moskva* |
| Konstantin TYUKAVIN | 22.06.2002 | 3 | 0 | 2023: | *FK Dinamo Moskva* |

### Trainer

| Name | DOB | Record | |
|---|---|---|---|
| Valeriy KARPIN [from 26.07.2021] | 02.09.1963 | 12 M; 7 W; 4 D; 1 L; 18-4 | |

# SAN MARINO

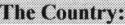

SAN MARINO

### The Country:
Repubblica di San Marino (Republic of San Marino)
Capital: San Marino
Surface: 61,2 km²
Inhabitants: 33,600 [2021]
Time: UTC+1

### The FA:
Federazione Sammarinese Giuoco Calcio
Strada di Montecchio 17, 47890 San Marino
Tel: +378 0549 990 515
Founded: 1931
Member of FIFA since: 1988
Member of UEFA since: 1988
Website: www.fsgc.sm

## NATIONAL TEAM RECORDS

| RECORDS | |
|---|---|
| **First international match:** | 23.08.1986, Serravalle:   San Marino – Canada Olympic Team 0-1 |
| **Most international caps:** | Matteo Giampaolo Vitaioli        - 85 caps (since 2007) |
| **Most international goals:** | Andy Selva        - 8 goals / 73 caps (1998-2016) |

| UEFA EUROPEAN CHAMPIONSHIP | |
|---|---|
| 1960 | Did not enter |
| 1964 | Did not enter |
| 1968 | Did not enter |
| 1972 | Did not enter |
| 1976 | Did not enter |
| 1980 | Did not enter |
| 1984 | Did not enter |
| 1988 | Did not enter |
| 1992 | Qualifiers |
| 1996 | Qualifiers |
| 2000 | Qualifiers |
| 2004 | Qualifiers |
| 2008 | Qualifiers |
| 2012 | Qualifiers |
| 2016 | Qualifiers |
| 2020 | Qualifiers |

| FIFA WORLD CUP | |
|---|---|
| 1930 | Did not enter |
| 1934 | Did not enter |
| 1938 | Did not enter |
| 1950 | Did not enter |
| 1954 | Did not enter |
| 1958 | Did not enter |
| 1962 | Did not enter |
| 1966 | Did not enter |
| 1970 | Did not enter |
| 1974 | Did not enter |
| 1978 | Did not enter |
| 1982 | Did not enter |
| 1986 | Did not enter |
| 1990 | Did not enter |
| 1994 | Qualifiers |
| 1998 | Qualifiers |
| 2002 | Qualifiers |
| 2006 | Qualifiers |
| 2010 | Qualifiers |
| 2014 | Qualifiers |
| 2018 | Qualifiers |
| 2022 | Qualifiers |

| OLYMPIC TOURNAMENTS | |
|---|---|
| 1908 | - |
| 1912 | - |
| 1920 | - |
| 1924 | - |
| 1928 | - |
| 1936 | Did not enter |
| 1948 | Did not enter |
| 1952 | Did not enter |
| 1956 | Did not enter |
| 1960 | Did not enter |
| 1964 | Did not enter |
| 1968 | Did not enter |
| 1972 | Did not enter |
| 1976 | Did not enter |
| 1980 | Did not enter |
| 1984 | Did not enter |
| 1988 | Did not enter |
| 1992 | Did not enter |
| 1996 | Qualifiers |
| 2000 | Did not enter |
| 2004 | Qualifiers |
| 2008 | Qualifiers |
| 2012 | Qualifiers |
| 2016 | Qualifiers |
| 2020 | Qualifiers |

## UEFA NATIONS LEAGUE

| 2018/2019 | League D (Group Stage) |
|---|---|
| 2020/2021 | League D (Group Stage) |
| 2022/2023 | League D (Group Stage) |

## SAN MARINESE CLUB HONOURS IN EUROPEAN CLUB COMPETITIONS:

| European Champion Clubs' Cup (1956-1992) / UEFA Champions League (1993-2023) |
|---|
| None |
| **Fairs Cup (1858-1971) / UEFA Cup (1972-2009) / UEFA Europa League (2010-2023)** |
| None |
| **UEFA Europa Conference League (2021-2023)** |
| None |
| **UEFA Super Cup (1972-2022)** |
| None |
| *European Cup Winners' Cup 1961-1999\** |
| None |

*defunct competition*

<u>Please note</u>: until the introduction of a regular championship in 1985/86, the Coppa Titano was the only annual tournament for San Marinese clubs.

### CUP WINNERS 1937-1985

| Year | Winner | | Year | Winner |
|------|--------|--|------|--------|
| 1937 | AC Libertas Borgo Maggiore | | 1970 | SP Tre Penne Città di San Marino |
| 1938-1949 | *No competition* | | 1971 | SP Tre Fiori Fiorentino |
| 1950 | AC Libertas Borgo Maggiore | | 1972 | FC Domagnano |
| 1951-1953 | *No competition* | | 1973 | *Competition abandoned* |
| 1954 | AC Libertas Borgo Maggiore | | 1974 | SP Tre Fiori Fiorentino |
| 1955-1957 | *No competition* | | 1975 | SP Tre Fiori Fiorentino |
| 1958 | AC Libertas Borgo Maggiore | | 1976 | SS Juvenes Serravalle |
| 1959 | AC Libertas Borgo Maggiore | | 1977 | SS Juvenes Serravalle |
| 1960 | *No competition* | | 1978 | SS Juvenes Serravalle |
| 1961 | AC Libertas Borgo Maggiore | | 1979 | SS Juvenes Serravalle |
| 1962-1964 | *No competition* | | 1980 | SS Cosmos Serravalle |
| 1965 | SS Juvenes Serravalle | | 1981 | SS Cosmos Serravalle |
| 1966 | SP Tre Fiori Fiorentino | | 1982 | SP Tre Penne Città di San Marino |
| 1967 | SP Tre Penne Città di San Marino | | 1983 | SP Tre Penne Città di San Marino |
| 1968 | SS Juvenes Serravalle | | 1984 | SS Juvenes Serravalle |
| 1969 | *Competition abandoned* | | 1985 | SP Tre Fiori Fiorentino |

| | CHAMPIONS | CUP WINNERS | BEST GOALSCORERS | |
|--|-----------|-------------|------------------|--|
| 1985/1986 | SC Faetano | SP La Fiorita Montegiardino | - | |
| 1986/1987 | SP La Fiorita Montegiardino | AC Libertas Borgo Maggiore | - | |
| 1987/1988 | SP Tre Fiori Fiorentino | FC Domagnano | - | |
| 1988/1989 | FC Domagnano | AC Libertas Borgo Maggiore | - | |
| 1989/1990 | SP La Fiorita Montegiardino | FC Domagnano | - | |
| 1990/1991 | SC Faetano | AC Libertas Borgo Maggiore | - | |
| 1991/1992 | SS Montevito Fiorentino | FC Domagnano | - | |
| 1992/1993 | SP Tre Fiori Fiorentino | SC Faetano | - | |
| 1993/1994 | SP Tre Fiori Fiorentino | SC Faetano | - | |
| 1994/1995 | SP Tre Fiori Fiorentino | SS Cosmos Serravalle | - | |
| 1995/1996 | AC Libertas Borgo Maggiore | FC Domagnano | - | |
| 1996/1997 | SS Folgore/Falciano Serravalle | SS Murata | - | |
| 1997/1998 | SS Folgore/Falciano Serravalle | SC Faetano | Damiano Vannucci (SS Virtus Acquaviva) | 21 |
| 1998/1999 | SC Faetano | SS Cosmos Serravalle | - | |
| 1999/2000 | SS Folgore/Falciano Serravalle | SP Tre Penne Città di San Marino | - | |
| 2000/2001 | SS Cosmos Serravalle | FC Domagnano | - | |
| 2001/2002 | FC Domagnano | FC Domagnano | - | |
| 2002/2003 | FC Domagnano | FC Domagnano | - | |
| 2003/2004 | SS Pennarossa Chiesanuova | SS Pennarossa Chiesanuova | Damiano Vannucci (SS Virtus Acquaviva) | 15 |
| 2004/2005 | FC Domagnano | SS Pennarossa Chiesanuova | Matteo Pazzaglia (SS Montevito Fiorentino) | 19 |
| 2005/2006 | SS Murata | AC Libertas Borgo Maggiore | - | |
| 2006/2007 | SS Murata | SS Murata | - | |
| 2007/2008 | SS Murata | SS Murata | - | |
| 2008/2009 | SP Tre Fiori Fiorentino | AC Juvenes/Dogana | - | |
| 2009/2010 | SP Tre Fiori Fiorentino | SP Tre Fiori Fiorentino | Simon Parma (SS Virtus Acquaviva) | 13 |
| 2010/2011 | SP Tre Fiori Fiorentino | AC Juvenes/Dogana | Jose Hirsch (SS Virtus Acquaviva) Marco Fantini (AC Juvenes/Dogana) Roberto Gatti (ITA, SS Murata) Alessandro Giunta (ITA, SP Tre Fiori Fiorentino) Francesco Viroli (ITA, SC Faetano) | 13 |
| 2011/2012 | SP Tre Penne Città di San Marino | SP La Fiorita Montegiardino | Cristian Rubén Menin (SS SS Cosmos Serravalle) Simon Parma (SP La Fiorita Montegiardino) | 11 |
| 2012/2013 | SP Tre Penne Città di San Marino | SP La Fiorita Montegiardino | Alberto Cannini (SP Tre Fiori Fiorentino) Denis Iencinella (FC Fiorentino) | 17 |
| 2013/2014 | SP La Fiorita Montegiardino | AC Libertas Borgo Maggiore | Valentin Grigore (ROU, SS Cosmos Serravalle) Giacomo Gualtieri (SP La Fiorita Montegiardino) | 18 |
| 2014/2015 | SS Folgore/Falciano Serravalle | SS Folgore/Falciano Serravalle | Daniele Friguglietti (ITA, San Giovanni) | 16 |
| 2015/2016 | SP Tre Penne Città di San Marino | SP La Fiorita Montegiardino | Marco Martini (ITA, SP La Fiorita Montegiardino) | 20 |
| 2016/2017 | SP La Fiorita Montegiardino | SP Tre Penne Città di San Marino | Marco Martini (ITA, SP La Fiorita Montegiardino) | 27 |
| 2017/2018 | SP La Fiorita Montegiardino | SP La Fiorita Montegiardino | Imre Badalassi (ITA, SP Tre Fiori Fiorentino) | 18 |
| 2018/2019 | SP Tre Penne Città di San Marino | SP Tre Fiori Fiorentino | Andrea Compagno (ITA, SP Tre Fiori Fiorentino) | 22 |
| 2019/2020 | SP Tre Fiori Fiorentino | *Competition cancelled* | Eric Fedeli (ITA, SS Murata Città di San Marino) | 16 |
| 2020/2021 | SS Folgore Falciano Calcio | SP La Fiorita Montegiardino | Imre Badalassi (ITA, SS Folgore Falciano Calcio) | 13 |
| 2021/2022 | SP La Fiorita Montegiardino | SP Tre Fiori Fiorentino | Imre Badalassi (ITA, SP Tre Penne Città di S.M.) | 24 |
| 2022/2023 | SP Tre Penne Città di San Marino | SS Virtus Acquaviva | Matteo Prandelli (ITA, SS Cosmos Serravalle) | 23 |

# NATIONAL CHAMPIONSHIP
## Campionato Sammarinese di Calcio 2022/2023
### (02.09.2022 – 20.05.2023)

## Results

### Round 1 [02-04.09.2022]
FC Domagnano - SS Virtus 1-2
SS Pennarossa - SS San Giovanni 4-0
FC Fiorentino - AC Juvenes/Dogana 0-4
SS Cosmos - SS Murata 4-1
SP La Fiorita - SP Cailungo 2-0
SP Tre Fiori - SC Faetano 4-0
AC Libertas - SS Folgore/Falciano 0-0

### Round 2 [09-11.09.2022]
SS Folgore/Falciano - SP La Fiorita 0-1
SP Cailungo - SP Tre Penne 0-2
SC Faetano - AC Libertas 1-3
AC Juvenes/Dogana - FC Domagnano 1-1
SS Murata - SS Pennarossa 2-4
SS San Giovanni - SS Cosmos 0-3
SS Virtus - SP Tre Fiori 1-2

### Round 3 [16-18.09.2022]
SP Tre Fiori - SP Cailungo 2-2
SS Cosmos - SC Faetano 4-0
FC Fiorentino - SS Virtus 1-2
SS Pennarossa - SS Folgore/Falciano 4-0
SP La Fiorita - AC Juvenes/Dogana 1-0
SS San Giovanni - SS Murata 0-2
SP Tre Penne - FC Domagnano 2-0(1-0)

### Round 4 [30.09.-02.10.2022]
AC Juvenes/Dogana - SS Murata 0-2
FC Domagnano - FC Fiorentino 1-1
SP La Fiorita - SS Cosmos 2-0
SS Virtus - AC Libertas 1-1
SP Cailungo - SS San Giovanni 0-3
SC Faetano - SS Folgore/Falciano 0-3
SP Tre Penne - SP Tre Fiori 2-1

### Round 5 [08-09.10.2022]
FC Domagnano - SP La Fiorita 0-1
SS Murata - SP Tre Penne 1-4
SP Tre Fiori - AC Libertas 1-2
SS Folgore/Falciano - SS San Giovanni 1-2
SS Cosmos - SS Pennarossa 1-0
FC Fiorentino - SC Faetano 2-5
AC Juvenes/Dogana - SS Virtus 1-3

### Round 6 [14-16.10.2022]
SS San Giovanni - FC Fiorentino 4-3
SS Virtus - SP La Fiorita 2-0
SS Pennarossa - SP Tre Fiori 0-1
SS Folgore/Falciano - SS Murata 4-1
SP Cailungo - FC Domagnano 0-0
AC Libertas - SS Cosmos 1-1
SP Tre Penne - AC Juvenes/Dogana 2-2

### Round 7 [21-22.10.2022]
SS Murata - SC Faetano 0-2
SP Cailungo - SS Pennarossa 2-1
FC Domagnano - SS Folgore/Falciano 2-1
AC Juvenes/Dogana - SS Cosmos 0-2
SP Tre Fiori - SS San Giovanni 1-0
FC Fiorentino - AC Libertas 3-2
SP La Fiorita - SP Tre Penne 0-1

### Round 8 [04-06.11.2022]
SS San Giovanni - SC Faetano 0-2
FC Fiorentino - SP La Fiorita 0-1
AC Libertas - SP Cailungo 1-1
SS Murata - SP Tre Fiori 0-1
SS Virtus - SP Tre Penne 0-0
SS Pennarossa - FC Domagnano 2-2
SS Folgore/Falciano - AC Juvenes/Dogana 1-2

### Round 9 [11-13.11.2022]
FC Domagnano - SS Cosmos 1-2
AC Juvenes/Dogana - SS San Giovanni 1-2
SP Tre Fiori - SS Folgore/Falciano 2-0
SP Tre Penne - FC Fiorentino 1-1
SP Cailungo - SS Virtus 1-3
SC Faetano - SS Pennarossa 2-1
SP La Fiorita - AC Libertas 1-0

### Round 10 [25-27.11.2022]
AC Libertas - SP Tre Penne 0-1
SS Cosmos - FC Fiorentino 4-0
SS Pennarossa - SP La Fiorita 1-2
SP Tre Fiori - FC Domagnano 2-1
SS Folgore/Falciano - SP Cailungo 4-1
SC Faetano - AC Juvenes/Dogana 3-3
SS Murata - SS Virtus 1-2

### Round 11 [03-04.12.2022]
SP Cailungo - SS Murata 4-1
FC Domagnano - AC Libertas 1-1
SP La Fiorita - SC Faetano 4-0
SS Virtus - SS Cosmos 0-0
FC Fiorentino - SP Tre Fiori 0-3
AC Juvenes/Dogana - SS Pennarossa 3-1
SP Tre Penne - SS San Giovanni 3-1

### Round 12 [09-11.12.2022]
SS Pennarossa - FC Fiorentino 1-1
SS Cosmos - SP Tre Penne 1-0
SC Faetano - SP Cailungo 3-0
AC Libertas - AC Juvenes/Dogana 2-1
SS San Giovanni - FC Domagnano 1-1
SS Murata - SP La Fiorita 1-2
SS Folgore/Falciano - SS Virtus 1-1

### Round 13 [17-18.12.2022]
AC Libertas - SS Pennarossa 3-3
SP Tre Penne - SS Folgore/Falciano 1-2
SS Virtus - SC Faetano 3-1
SP Cailungo - SS Cosmos 0-0
FC Fiorentino - SS Murata 1-0
AC Juvenes/Dogana - SP Tre Fiori 0-1
SP La Fiorita - SS San Giovanni 2-2

### Round 14 [07-08.01.2023]
SP Cailungo - FC Fiorentino 2-2
SS San Giovanni - SS Virtus 0-2
SP Tre Fiori - SP La Fiorita 1-1
SS Folgore/Falciano - SS Cosmos 0-4
SC Faetano - FC Domagnano 1-4
SS Murata - AC Libertas 2-3
SS Pennarossa - SP Tre Penne 1-4

### Round 15 [14-15.01.2023]
FC Fiorentino - SS Folgore/Falciano 1-1
AC Juvenes/Dogana - SP-Cailungo 0-2
AC Libertas - SS San Giovanni 1-0
SS Virtus - SS Pennarossa 0-1
SS Cosmos - SP Tre Fiori 1-1
FC Domagnano - SS Murata 2-2
SP Tre Penne - SC Faetano 2-0

### Round 16 [20-22.01.2023]
SS Murata - SS Cosmos 2-3
SC Faetano - SP Tre Fiori 1-2
SS Folgore/Falciano - AC Libertas 2-3
SS Virtus - FC Domagnano 5-2
AC Juvenes/Dogana - FC Fiorentino 1-2
SS San Giovanni - SS Pennarossa 1-1
SP Cailungo - SP La Fiorita 0-1 [08.02.2023]

### Round 17 [28-29.01.2023]
SS Cosmos - SS San Giovanni 4-0
FC Domagnano - AC Juvenes/Dogana 1-3
SS Pennarossa - SS Murata 2-3
SP Tre Penne - SP Cailungo 3-0
SP La Fiorita - SS Folgore/Falciano 2-0
AC Libertas - SC Faetano 2-1
SP Tre Fiori - SS Virtus 1-1

### Round 18 [03-05.02.2023]
SP Cailungo - SP Tre Fiori 0-3
SS Virtus - FC Fiorentino 1-1
FC Domagnano - SP Tre Penne 1-2
SS Folgore/Falciano - SS Pennarossa 2-1
SC Faetano - SS Cosmos 0-2
AC Juvenes/Dogana - SP La Fiorita 0-1
SS Murata - SS San Giovanni 3-1

### Round 19 [11-12.02.2023]
SS Cosmos - SP La Fiorita 1-1
SS San Giovanni - SP Cailungo 1-1
SS Murata - AC Juvenes/Dogana 2-2
SP Tre Fiori - SP Tre Penne 1-2
SS Folgore/Falciano - SC Faetano 0-0
AC Libertas - SS Virtus 2-2
FC Fiorentino - FC Domagnano 0-0

### Round 20 [18-19.02.2023]
SC Faetano - FC Fiorentino 0-2
SS Pennarossa - SS Cosmos 0-4
SS San Giovanni - SS Folgore/Falciano 2-3
SP La Fiorita - FC Domagnano 2-3
AC Libertas - SP Tre Fiori 0-0
SP Tre Penne - SS Murata 2-0
SS Virtus - AC Juvenes/Dogana 1-0

### Round 21 [25-26.02.2023]
AC Juvenes/Dogana - SP Tre Penne 0-1
SS Murata - SS Folgore/Falciano 0-2
SP La Fiorita - SS Virtus 0-1
FC Fiorentino - SS San Giovanni 1-3
SP Tre Fiori - SS Pennarossa 2-0
FC Domagnano - SP Cailungo 3-0
SS Cosmos - AC Libertas 1-0 [14.03.2023]

### Round 22 [03-05.03.2023]
AC Libertas - FC Fiorentino 3-3
SS San Giovanni - SP Tre Fiori 0-2
SS Cosmos - AC Juvenes/Dogana 4-0
SC Faetano - SS Murata 2-5
SS Pennarossa - SP Cailungo 3-0
SS Folgore/Falciano - FC Domagnano 0-2
SP Tre Penne - SP La Fiorita 1-1

### Round 23 [07-08.03.2023]
SC Faetano - SS San Giovanni 0-1
SP Tre Fiori - SS Murata 0-1
SP Cailungo - AC Libertas 1-2
SP La Fiorita - FC Fiorentino 3-1
FC Domagnano - SS Pennarossa 0-1
SP Tre Penne - SS Virtus 2-1
AC Juvenes/Dogana - SS Folgore/Falciano 2-0

### Round 24 [11-12.03.2023]
SS Virtus - SP Cailungo 4-2
FC Fiorentino - SP Tre Penne 1-5
SS Cosmos - FC Domagnano 2-0
AC Libertas - SP La Fiorita 1-1
SS San Giovanni - AC Juvenes/Dogana 0-1
SS Pennarossa - SC Faetano 0-2
SS Folgore/Falciano - SP Tre Fiori 0-2

| Round 25 [17-19.03.2023] | | Round 26 [01-02.04.2023] | | Round 27 [05-06.04.2023] | |
|---|---|---|---|---|---|
| SP Tre Penne - AC Libertas | 4-0 | SS San Giovanni - SP Tre Penne | 2-3 | AC Juvenes/Dogana - AC Libertas | 0-3 |
| SP Cailungo - SS Folgore/Falciano | 2-4 | AC Libertas - FC Domagnano | 3-0 | SP Tre Penne - SS Cosmos | 2-2 |
| SP La Fiorita - SS Pennarossa | 2-0 | SS Pennarossa - AC Juvenes/Dogana | 1-4 | FC Domagnano - SS San Giovanni | 3-0 |
| FC Fiorentino - SS Cosmos | 0-1 | SS Cosmos - SS Virtus | 1-1 | SP Cailungo - SC Faetano | 5-2 |
| AC Juvenes/Dogana - SC Faetano | 2-2 | SP Tre Fiori - FC Fiorentino | 2-1 | SS Virtus - SS Folgore/Falciano | 2-0 |
| FC Domagnano - SP Tre Fiori | 1-3 | SS Murata - SP Cailungo | 2-1 | FC Fiorentino - SS Pennarossa | 2-5 |
| SS Virtus - SS Murata | 5-0 | SC Faetano - SP La Fiorita | 0-3 | SP La Fiorita - SS Murata | 2-0 |

| Round 28 [11-12.04.2023] | | Round 29 [15-16.04.2023] | | Round 30 [22-23.04.2023] | |
|---|---|---|---|---|---|
| SS Murata - FC Fiorentino | 2-1 | SS Cosmos - SS Folgore/Falciano | 5-0 | SS Folgore/Falciano - FC Fiorentino | 1-0 |
| SS Pennarossa - AC Libertas | 0-7 | AC Libertas - SS Murata | 0-0 | SS San Giovanni - AC Libertas | 1-3 |
| SS San Giovanni - SP La Fiorita | 1-1 | SS Virtus - SS San Giovanni | 2-0 | SP Cailungo - AC Juvenes/Dogana | 1-6 |
| SP Tre Fiori - AC Juvenes/Dogana | 4-1 | SP Tre Penne - SS Pennarossa | 2-0 | SS Pennarossa - SS Virtus | 1-3 |
| SS Cosmos - SP Cailungo | 5-1 | FC Domagnano - SC Faetano | 2-3 | SP Tre Fiori - SS Cosmos | 0-2 |
| SS Folgore/Falciano - SP Tre Penne | 0-4 | FC Fiorentino - SP Cailungo | 6-0 | SS Murata - FC Domagnano | 5-1 |
| SC Faetano - SS Virtus | 2-2 | SP La Fiorita - SP Tre Fiori | 1-0 | SC Faetano - SP Tre Penne | 0-2 |

## Final Standings

| | | Total | | | | | | | Home | | | | | | Away | | | | |
|---|---|---|---|---|---|---|---|---|---|---|---|---|---|---|---|---|---|---|---|---|
| 1. | SP Tre Penne Città di San Marino | 28 | 21 | 5 | 2 | 60 | - | 19 | 68 | 9 | 4 | 1 | 29 | - | 11 | 12 | 1 | 1 | 31 | - | 8 |
| 2. | SS Cosmos Serravalle | 28 | 20 | 7 | 1 | 64 | - | 13 | 67 | 11 | 3 | 0 | 38 | - | 5 | 9 | 4 | 1 | 26 | - | 8 |
| 3. | SP La Fiorita Montegiardino | 28 | 18 | 6 | 4 | 41 | - | 17 | 60 | 10 | 1 | 3 | 24 | - | 8 | 8 | 5 | 1 | 17 | - | 9 |
| 4. | SS Virtus Acquaviva | 28 | 16 | 9 | 3 | 53 | - | 25 | 57 | 8 | 4 | 2 | 27 | - | 10 | 8 | 5 | 1 | 26 | - | 15 |
| 5. | SP Tre Fiori Fiorentino | 28 | 17 | 5 | 6 | 45 | - | 21 | 56 | 7 | 3 | 4 | 23 | - | 14 | 10 | 2 | 2 | 22 | - | 7 |
| 6. | AC Libertas Borgo Maggiore | 28 | 12 | 11 | 5 | 49 | - | 33 | 47 | 4 | 9 | 1 | 19 | - | 14 | 8 | 2 | 4 | 30 | - | 19 |
| 7. | SS Folgore Falciano Calcio Serravalle | 28 | 9 | 4 | 15 | 32 | - | 49 | 31 | 4 | 2 | 8 | 16 | - | 24 | 5 | 2 | 7 | 16 | - | 25 |
| 8. | SS Murata Città di San Marino | 28 | 9 | 3 | 16 | 41 | - | 57 | 30 | 4 | 1 | 9 | 23 | - | 29 | 5 | 2 | 7 | 18 | - | 28 |
| 9. | AC Juvenes/Dogana Serravalle | 28 | 8 | 5 | 15 | 40 | - | 46 | 29 | 2 | 2 | 10 | 11 | - | 23 | 6 | 3 | 5 | 29 | - | 23 |
| 10. | FC Domagnano | 28 | 6 | 8 | 14 | 36 | - | 48 | 26 | 3 | 3 | 8 | 19 | - | 22 | 3 | 5 | 6 | 17 | - | 26 |
| 11. | SC Faetano | 28 | 7 | 4 | 17 | 35 | - | 63 | 25 | 2 | 2 | 10 | 15 | - | 33 | 5 | 2 | 7 | 20 | - | 30 |
| 12. | SS Pennarossa Chiesanuova | 28 | 7 | 4 | 17 | 39 | - | 57 | 25 | 3 | 2 | 9 | 20 | - | 33 | 4 | 2 | 8 | 19 | - | 24 |
| 13. | SS San Giovanni Borgo Maggiore | 28 | 6 | 5 | 17 | 28 | - | 54 | 23 | 1 | 4 | 9 | 13 | - | 28 | 5 | 1 | 8 | 15 | - | 26 |
| 14. | FC Fiorentino | 28 | 5 | 8 | 15 | 37 | - | 58 | 23 | 3 | 2 | 9 | 18 | - | 32 | 2 | 6 | 6 | 19 | - | 26 |
| 15. | SP Cailungo Borgo Maggiore | 28 | 4 | 6 | 18 | 29 | - | 69 | 18 | 3 | 3 | 8 | 18 | - | 30 | 1 | 3 | 10 | 11 | - | 39 |

**Top goalscorer**: Matteo Prandelli (ITA, SS Cosmos Serravalle) – 23 goals

Teams ranked 2-7 were qualified for the Play-offs Quarter-Finals, while teams ranked 8-11 were qualified for the Play-offs First Round, which will determine the club which will play in the 2023-2024 UEFA Europa Conference League.

## Europa Conference League Play-offs

| First Round [26.04.2023] | SS Murata Città di San Marino - SC Faetano | 0-1 | |
|---|---|---|---|
| | AC Juvenes/Dogana Serravalle - FC Domagnano | 3-2 | |

| Quarter-Finals [29-30.04./03.05.2023] | AC Libertas Borgo Maggiore - SP Tre Fiori Fiorentino | 2-1 | 1-1 |
|---|---|---|---|
| | SS Virtus Acquaviva* - SS Folgore Falciano Calcio Serravalle | 1-1 | 1-1 |
| | SS Cosmos Serravalle - SC Faetano | 4-1 | 3-0 |
| | SP La Fiorita Montegiardino - AC Juvenes/Dogana Serravalle | 2-0 | 3-0 |

*qualified by having better record in the championship.*

| Semi-Finals [06-07./13.05.2023] | SS Cosmos Serravalle - AC Libertas Borgo Maggiore | 2-0 | 1-0 |
|---|---|---|---|
| | SS Virtus Acquaviva - SP La Fiorita Montegiardino | 0-0 | 1-2 |

| 4th – 5th Place Play-off [19.05.2023] | AC Libertas Borgo Maggiore - SS Virtus Acquaviva | 1-2 | |
|---|---|---|---|

| Final / 2nd - 3rd Place [20.05.2023] | **SS Cosmos Serravalle** - SP La Fiorita Montegiardino | 2-1 | |
|---|---|---|---|

## NATIONAL CUP
### Coppa Titano Final 2022/2023

### 1/8-Finals [04-05./18-19.10.2022]

| First Leg | | Second Leg | |
|---|---|---|---|
| SS Cosmos Serravalle - SS Virtus Acquaviva | 0-1(0-1) | SS Virtus Acquaviva - SS Cosmos Serravalle | 1-1(0-1,0-1) |
| FC Domagnano - AC Libertas Borgo Maggiore | 0-2(0-0) | AC Libertas Borgo Maggiore - FC Domagnano | 6-2(3-1) |
| FC Fiorentino - SP La Fiorita Montegiardino | 0-5(0-2) | SP La Fiorita Montegiardino - FC Fiorentino | 3-1(2-0) |
| SC Faetano - SS Murata Città di San Marino | 3-1(1-1) | SS Murata Città di San Marino - SC Faetano | 4-0(2-0) |
| SS San Giovanni Borgo Maggiore - SS Folgore/Falciano | 0-0 | SS Folgore/Falciano - SS San Giovanni Borgo Maggiore | 3-2(1-0,2-2) |
| SP Tre Penne Città di San Marino - SS Pennarossa | 0-0 | SS Pennarossa - SP Tre Penne Città di San Marino | 1-4(0-2) |
| AC Juvenes/Dogana Serravalle - SP Cailungo | 2-1(0-1) | SP Cailungo - AC Juvenes/Dogana Serravalle | 1-1(0-0) |

### Quarter-Finals [30.11./14.12.2022]

| First Leg | | Second Leg | |
|---|---|---|---|
| SP Tre Fiori - SS Virtus Acquaviva | 1-0(1-0) | SS Virtus Acquaviva - SP Tre Fiori | 3-1(1-0) |
| SP Tre Penne C. di San Marino - AC Juvenes/Dogana | 1-3(0-0) | AC Juvenes/Dogana - SP Tre Penne C. di San Marino | 0-3(0-2) |
| SS Murata Città di San Marino - SS Folgore/Falciano | 1-1(1-1) | SS Folgore/Falciano - SS Murata Città di San Marino | 3-2(1-0,2-2) |
| AC Libertas B. Maggiore - SP La Fiorita Montegiardino | 1-1(0-1) | SP La Fiorita Montegiardino-AC Libertas B. Maggiore | 0-1(0-1) |

### Semi-Finals [25.01./08.02.2023]

| First Leg | | Second Leg | |
|---|---|---|---|
| SS Virtus Acquaviva - SS Folgore/Falciano | 3-0(2-0) | SS Folgore/Falciano - SS Virtus Acquaviva | 1-0(1-0) |
| SP Tre Penne Città di San Marino - AC Libertas | 2-0(1-0) | AC Libertas - SP Tre Penne Città di San Marino | 0-2(0-0) |

### Final

27.05.2023; Campo Sportivo di Montecchio; Referee: Antonio Ucini; Attendance: n/a
**SS Virtus Acquaviva - SP Tre Penne Città di San Marino**          **3-1(3-1)**

**SS Virtus**: Andrea Battistini, Manuel Battistini (Cap), Nicola Gori [*sent off 90*], Alex Nodari, Roberto Sabato, Alessandro Golinucci, Matteo Pedrini (86.Mattia Pirini), Elia Ciacci, Ivan Buonocunto, Loris Tortori (79.Aron Giacomoni), Nicola Angeli (89.Luca Sorrentino). Trainer: Luigi Bizzotto (Italy).

**SP Tre Penne**: Mattia Migani, Giacomo Nigretti (68.Fabio Giovagnoli), Nicolas Lombardi, Antonio Barretta, Piero Cauterucci (62.Davide Cesarini), Luca Righini, Michael Battistini (62.Andrea Montanari), Nicola Gai (Cap), Lorenzo Dormi, Luca Ceccaroli, Imre Badalassi. Trainer: Stefano Ceci.

**Goals:** 1-0 Elia Ciacci (6), 2-0 Ivan Buonocunto (32), 3-0 Matteo Pedrini (35), 3-1 Imre Badalassi (39).

## THE CLUBS 2022/2023

Please note: appearances and goals are including statistics of regular season and play-offs (Championship & Europa Conference League).

### Società Polisportiva Cailungo Borgo Maggiore

| | |
|---|---|
| **Founded**: | 1974 |
| **Stadium**: | Stadio Fonte Dell'Ovo, Città di San Marino (500) |
| **Trainer**: | Cristian Protti                     17.04.1973 |

| Goalkeepers: | DOB | M | (s) | G |
|---|---|---|---|---|
| Elia Benedettini | 22.06.1995 | 27 | (1) | |
| Marco Morelli (ITA) | 24.09.1986 | 2 | (1) | |
| **Defenders:** | **DOB** | **M** | **(s)** | **G** |
| Juri Biordi | 1995 | 20 | (3) | |
| Mattia Censoni | 31.03.1996 | 1 | (12) | |
| Matteo Ferrari (ITA) | 23.02.1994 | 16 | (4) | 1 |
| Manuel Iuzzolino (ITA) | 05.05.1990 | 21 | (2) | 1 |
| Daniele Lusini (ITA) | 10.03.1982 | 17 | (1) | |
| Jair Alexander Mutis Terazza (COL) | 02.06.1999 | 11 | (8) | |
| Filippo Quaranta | 11.09.1998 | 26 | | 2 |
| Luca Ricci (ITA) | 25.03.1993 | 3 | | |
| Nicola Zafferani | 06.11.1991 | 11 | (6) | 2 |
| **Midfielders:** | **DOB** | **M** | **(s)** | **G** |
| Michele Cervellini | 14.04.1988 | 14 | (5) | |

| | DOB | M | (s) | G |
|---|---|---|---|---|
| Tommaso Conti (ITA) | 18.06.1992 | | (8) | |
| Alessandro Giangrandi (ITA) | 09.12.1996 | 25 | (1) | 2 |
| Alessandro Liverani | 12.10.2000 | 3 | (4) | |
| Manuel Muccioli (ITA) | 12.12.1996 | 21 | (4) | |
| Armando Senja (ALB) | 26.07.1997 | 19 | (5) | 4 |
| **Forwards:** | **DOB** | **M** | **(s)** | **G** |
| Joel Apezteguía Hijuelos (CUB) | 17.12.1983 | 14 | (3) | 2 |
| Armando Aruci | 10.07.1989 | 8 | (1) | |
| Karim Abdoul Bara (CUB) | 22.09.1997 | 22 | (2) | 3 |
| Francesco Canini (ITA) | 08.05.2002 | 13 | (1) | 8 |
| Cristian Intilla (ITA) | 04.09.2001 | 1 | (4) | |
| Espedito Marinaro (ITA) | 10.09.1992 | 11 | (11) | 2 |
| Alessandro Morri | 12.06.2003 | 2 | (8) | 1 |
| Andrea Muccioli (ITA) | 26.04.1997 | | (2) | |

Please note: Elia Benedettini was used also as a field player in Round 29 (as substitute), while Marco Morelli was used also as a field player in Round 28 (as substitute) & 30.

## Società Sportiva Cosmos Serravalle

**Founded**: 1979
**Stadium**: San Marino Stadium, Serravalle (7,000)
**Trainer**: Nicola Berardi     05.08.1969

| Goalkeepers: | DOB | M | (s) | G |
|---|---|---|---|---|
| Lorenzo Batori (ITA) | 07.11.1993 | | (1) | |
| Aldo Simoncini | 30.08.1986 | 33 | | |
| **Defenders:** | **DOB** | **M** | **(s)** | **G** |
| Alberto Celli | 24.06.1985 | | (1) | |
| Alessandro Cucchi (ITA) | 18.03.2000 | 7 | (9) | |
| Alessandro D'Addario | 09.09.1997 | 29 | (2) | 1 |
| Roberto Di Maio | 21.09.1982 | 30 | | 2 |
| Alberto Guerra | 13.01.2004 | 7 | (7) | |
| Manuel Maggioli (ITA) | 06.04.2000 | 23 | (3) | 1 |
| Mirko Palazzi | 21.03.1987 | 30 | (1) | |
| Thomas Raschi | 11.07.1996 | | (6) | |
| **Midfielders:** | **DOB** | **M** | **(s)** | **G** |
| Lorenzo Capicchioni | 19.01.2002 | 12 | (3) | 2 |
| Simone Errico (ITA) | 30.04.1992 | 29 | (1) | 4 |
| Simone Loiodice (ITA) | 16.03.1989 | 28 | (1) | 3 |

| | DOB | M | (s) | G |
|---|---|---|---|---|
| Mattia Lualdi (ITA) | 26.07.1992 | | (1) | |
| Lorenzo Pastorelli (ITA) | 10.06.2001 | 29 | (2) | 5 |
| Francesco Perrotta (ITA) | 27.08.1981 | | (1) | 1 |
| Gianmarco Savelli (ITA) | 20.04.2001 | 9 | (23) | 3 |
| Giacomo Valentini | 26.06.2001 | 1 | (10) | |
| **Forwards:** | **DOB** | **M** | **(s)** | **G** |
| Paolo Basile (ITA) | 08.06.1992 | | (2) | |
| Tommaso Bastianelli (ITA) | 09.03.2003 | | (1) | |
| Emilio Docente (ITA) | 11.12.1983 | 3 | (8) | 2 |
| Tommaso Guidi (ITA) | 21.10.1998 | 20 | (6) | 10 |
| Lorenzo Nisi (ITA) | 25.04.1999 | 15 | (4) | 5 |
| Matteo Prandelli (ITA) | 18.11.1988 | 23 | (8) | 23 |
| Filippo Righini (ITA) | 14.09.1992 | 2 | (8) | 1 |
| Matteo Sapucci (ITA) | 02.02.1998 | 3 | (12) | 2 |
| Riccardo Zulli (ITA) | 08.09.2000 | 30 | (1) | 10 |

## Football Club Domagnano

**Founded**: 1966
**Stadium**: Campo sportivo, Domagnano (500)
**Trainer**: Simone Amadori
[17.02.2023]   Nicola Ranocchini     04.04.1985

| Goalkeepers: | DOB | M | (s) | G |
|---|---|---|---|---|
| Davide Colonna | 10.11.2000 | 28 | | |
| Simone Guidi | 14.06.2000 | 1 | (1) | |
| Alessandro Marcaccini | 05.07.1973 | 1 | | |
| **Defenders:** | **DOB** | **M** | **(s)** | **G** |
| Samuel Averhoff | 19.11.1999 | 5 | (12) | |
| Filippo Baffoni (ITA) | 25.09.1991 | 11 | (2) | |
| Giovanni Bonini | 05.09.1986 | 17 | (6) | |
| Claudio Cola (ITA) | 24.04.1986 | 5 | (1) | |
| Angelo Faetanini | 17.01.1993 | 7 | (3) | |
| Luciano Ferraro (ARG) | 04.04.1994 | 24 | | |
| Simone Nanni | 03.08.2000 | 20 | (6) | 1 |
| Luca Olivieri (ITA) | 23.12.1995 | 16 | | |
| Michael Parma (ITA) | 28.03.1998 | 16 | (2) | |
| Filippo Ricchi | 29.01.2004 | | (7) | |

| Midfielders: | DOB | M | (s) | G |
|---|---|---|---|---|
| Nicolò Bacchiocchi (ITA) | 26.02.1991 | 27 | (1) | 2 |
| Nicolò Brolli (ITA) | 03.04.2002 | | (1) | |
| Alessio Cangini (ITA) | 05.01.1991 | 7 | | 1 |
| Mattia Ceccaroli (ITA) | 03.02.1999 | 22 | (1) | 6 |
| Lorenzo Crescentini | 20.10.2004 | | (13) | |
| Manuel Mazzoli (ITA) | 21.08.1984 | 10 | (8) | 1 |
| Giuliano Morena (ITA) | 14.08.1992 | 10 | (1) | |
| Mattia Ramundo (ITA) | 19.11.1993 | | (3) | |
| Kevin Zonzini | 11.08.1997 | 20 | | 4 |
| **Forwards:** | **DOB** | **M** | **(s)** | **G** |
| Nicolò Angelini | 15.03.1992 | 13 | (16) | 6 |
| Daniele Babboni | 09.01.2000 | 15 | (10) | 2 |
| Eric Fedeli (ITA) | 13.01.1992 | 26 | (2) | 10 |
| Mathias Grassi | 23.03.2004 | | (1) | |
| Ramiro Martín Lago (ARG) | 14.10.1987 | 8 | (3) | |
| Tommaso Lombardi (ITA) | 01.02.2001 | 10 | (1) | 2 |

Please note: Alessandro Marcaccini was used as a field player in Round 27.

## Società Calcio Faetano

**Founded**: 1962
**Stadium**: San Marino Stadium, Serravalle (7,000)
**Trainer**: Danilo Girolomoni (ITA)     22.11.1982

| Goalkeepers: | DOB | M | (s) | G |
|---|---|---|---|---|
| Michele Magnani | 12.09.2003 | 1 | (1) | |
| Riccardo Porcellini (ITA) | 03.05.2005 | 30 | | |
| **Defenders:** | **DOB** | **M** | **(s)** | **G** |
| Domenico Barretta (ITA) | 26.06.2000 | | (3) | |
| Christian Bocchetti (ITA) | 24.06.2002 | 7 | (2) | |
| Ignacio Carabajal (ITA) | 04.11.1997 | 5 | (2) | |
| Giacomo Casali | 14.02.2004 | 1 | (3) | |
| Alex Della Valle | 13.06.1990 | 18 | (4) | |
| Ciro Eboli (ITA) | 04.09.2000 | 14 | (13) | 1 |
| Abdoul Aziz Soumah (ITA) | 22.01.1993 | 19 | (9) | |
| Luca Terenzi | 10.05.2004 | 26 | (1) | 3 |
| Luca Tomassoni (ITA) | 21.11.1994 | 28 | | |
| **Midfielders:** | **DOB** | **M** | **(s)** | **G** |
| Alessio Bertuccini (ITA) | 04.07.2005 | 1 | (10) | |

| | DOB | M | (s) | G |
|---|---|---|---|---|
| Nicolò Borioni (ITA) | 31.07.2002 | 5 | (17) | |
| Luciano Composto (ARG) | 28.01.2003 | 13 | (17) | 2 |
| Assane Fall (SEN) | 26.02.1994 | 27 | | 1 |
| Mattia Giardi | 15.12.1991 | 19 | (1) | |
| Arneld Kalemi (ALB) | 03.03.2001 | 19 | (5) | 3 |
| Mattia Pellegrino (ITA) | 10.03.1999 | | (2) | |
| Alberto Persici (ITA) | 04.04.2000 | 27 | | 1 |
| Alessandro Pini (ITA) | 03.03.1996 | 24 | (4) | 1 |
| Alessandro Renzi | 16.02.2003 | | (8) | |
| Vincenzo Ruocco (ITA) | 05.04.2004 | 5 | (8) | |
| **Forwards:** | **DOB** | **M** | **(s)** | **G** |
| Gianluca Ferrario (ITA) | 16.08.1996 | 19 | (2) | 8 |
| Tommaso Gatti | 14.07.2003 | 8 | (12) | 2 |
| Marseljan Mema (ALB) | 13.02.1997 | 25 | (1) | 15 |

## Football Club Fiorentino

**Founded**: 1974
**Stadium**: Campo Sportivo, Fiorentino (700)
**Trainer**: Enrico Malandri (ITA)     30.05.1983

| Goalkeepers: | DOB | M | (s) | G |
|---|---|---|---|---|
| Michele Berardi | 30.11.1991 | 1 | (1) | |
| Luca Bianchi (ITA) | 07.01.1990 | 27 | | |
| **Defenders:** | **DOB** | **M** | **(s)** | **G** |
| Nicolò Accosta (ITA) | 31.08.2004 | 2 | (1) | |
| Maximiliano Baizan | 23.03.1993 | 4 | (14) | |
| Luca Bottoni (ITA) | 12.08.1996 | 22 | (1) | |
| Giovanni De Rosa (ITA) | 12.06.2002 | 10 | (2) | |
| Luca Filippi (ITA) | 27.09.1988 | 25 | | 2 |
| Mirko Paglialonga (ITA) | 19.09.1983 | 12 | (4) | |
| Moussa Tall (SEN) | 30.09.2003 | 20 | (1) | 2 |
| Alessandro Terenzi | 23.05.2000 | | (3) | |
| **Midfielders:** | **DOB** | **M** | **(s)** | **G** |
| Nicola D'Addario | 21.12.2003 | 17 | (10) | 1 |

| | DOB | M | (s) | G |
|---|---|---|---|---|
| Andrea Borgagni | 21.10.1996 | | (9) | |
| Pietro Calzolari | 28.10.1991 | 18 | (5) | |
| Matias Colagiovanni (ARG) | 16.01.1991 | 18 | (3) | 1 |
| Cristiano De Lorenzis (ITA) | 01.08.2004 | | (1) | |
| Andrea Dolcini | 14.04.2003 | 24 | (1) | 1 |
| Christian Maccagno (ITA) | 05.06.1983 | | (1) | |
| Armando Marino (ITA) | 21.08.2004 | | (15) | 2 |
| Francesco Mastrota (ITA) | 25.06.2002 | 20 | (3) | 1 |
| Alessandro Molinari | 14.05.1989 | 16 | (8) | 1 |
| Lorenzo Sottile (ITA) | 13.04.1996 | 13 | (10) | 5 |
| **Forwards:** | **DOB** | **M** | **(s)** | **G** |
| Fabrizio Castellazzi (ITA) | 29.07.1984 | 16 | (6) | 3 |
| Adolfo Hirsch | 31.01.1986 | 21 | (2) | 4 |
| Alessandro Torsani (ITA) | 02.11.2000 | 22 | (1) | 14 |

## Società Sportiva Folgore Falciano Calcio Serravalle

| Founded: | 1972 | | |
| Stadium: | San Marino Stadium, Serravalle (7,000) | | |
| Trainer: | Omar Lepri (ITA) | | 10.05.1977 |

| Goalkeepers: | DOB | M | (s) | G |
|---|---|---|---|---|
| Andrea Mignani (ITA) | 02.06.1998 | 5 | | |
| Francesco Pollini (ITA) | 01.11.1994 | 25 | | |
| **Defenders:** | **DOB** | **M** | **(s)** | **G** |
| Oleg Ankotovych (UKR) | 11.08.2004 | | (4) | |
| Cristian Brolli | 28.02.1992 | 9 | (2) | 1 |
| Alex Cavalli | 26.02.1992 | | (4) | |
| Dario De Luigi (ITA) | 19.03.1990 | 10 | (1) | |
| Giacomo Francioni | 25.10.2000 | 1 | (2) | |
| Alex Gattei Colonna (ITA) | 16.07.1988 | 8 | | 2 |
| Daniel Piscaglia (ITA) | 06.12.1992 | 25 | | |
| Roberto Rosini (ITA) | 27.09.1991 | 7 | (2) | |
| Andrea Sabbadini (ITA) | 21.05.1985 | | (3) | |
| Francesco Sartori (ITA) | 07.03.1993 | 22 | (2) | 5 |
| Fabio Sottile (ITA) | 05.02.1993 | 24 | | |

| Midfielders: | DOB | M | (s) | G |
|---|---|---|---|---|
| Muhamed Ahmetovic (ITA) | 19.07.1999 | 4 | (9) | |
| Alessio Cangini (ITA) | 05.01.1991 | 11 | (1) | |
| Alan Cerquetti | 01.08.1989 | | (3) | |
| Enrico Golinucci | 16.07.1991 | 23 | (4) | 1 |
| Riccardo Montanari (ITA) | 06.08.1991 | 28 | | 1 |
| Andrea Nucci (ITA) | 06.09.1986 | 2 | (1) | |
| Andrea Pasini (ITA) | 04.01.1997 | 3 | | |
| Matteo Serafini (ITA) | 13.02.1994 | 27 | | 4 |
| **Forwards:** | **DOB** | **M** | **(s)** | **G** |
| Marco Bernardi | 02.01.1994 | 28 | (1) | 3 |
| Marco Di Marzio (ITA) | 16.07.2000 | 19 | (7) | 4 |
| William Edoardo Garcia (ITA) | 13.05.2002 | 2 | (6) | |
| Matteo Giardi | 14.04.1997 | 1 | (13) | 1 |
| Alessandro Mami (ITA) | 24.07.1992 | 11 | (17) | 3 |
| Daniele Santoni (ITA) | 13.10.1992 | 15 | (1) | 2 |
| Mattia Urbinati (ITA) | 17.12.1995 | 20 | (5) | 6 |

## Associazione Calcio Juvenes/Dogana Serravalle

| Founded: | 2000 (as merger of SS Juvenes Serravalle and GS Dogana) | | |
| Stadium: | San Marino Stadium, Serravalle (7,000) | | |
| Trainer: | Manuel Amati (ITA) | | 01.01.1980 |

| Goalkeepers: | DOB | M | (s) | G |
|---|---|---|---|---|
| Denis Broccoli | 10.08.1988 | 1 | (1) | |
| Fabio Gentilini (ITA) | 09.09.1984 | 30 | | |
| **Defenders:** | **DOB** | **M** | **(s)** | **G** |
| Maicol Acquarelli (ITA) | 21.09.1993 | 12 | (9) | |
| Gianmaria Borghini (ITA) | 04.03.1997 | 28 | (1) | 2 |
| Giacomo Borghini (ITA) | 27.07.2001 | 27 | (2) | 2 |
| Alex Cavalli | 26.02.1992 | | (1) | |
| Michele Cevoli | 22.07.1998 | 21 | (2) | 1 |
| Adrian Alexandre Eacock (ENG) | 22.03.1992 | | (1) | |
| Federico Muccioli | 20.06.1996 | 4 | (7) | |
| Filippo Santi | 23.01.2001 | 22 | (4) | |
| Alexander Adrian Radu (ROU) | 21.03.1996 | | (3) | |
| **Midfielders:** | **DOB** | **M** | **(s)** | **G** |
| Alberto Baldazzi | 08.11.2001 | 7 | (8) | |

| | DOB | M | (s) | G |
|---|---|---|---|---|
| Gabriele Ciccarelli (ITA) | 23.02.1994 | 11 | (8) | |
| Riccardo Colonna | 10.04.1999 | 28 | (2) | 2 |
| Nicholas Lisi | 18.05.2004 | 2 | (7) | |
| Davide Lisi (ITA) | 16.07.2001 | 6 | (3) | |
| Lorenzo Meluzzi (ITA) | 18.10.1994 | 17 | (9) | 1 |
| Filippo Pasolini | 22.02.2003 | 13 | (2) | 2 |
| Giacomo Valentini | 26.06.2001 | 9 | (2) | |
| **Forwards:** | **DOB** | **M** | **(s)** | **G** |
| Gianluca Benedetti (ITA) | 04.11.1995 | 22 | (8) | 6 |
| Eric D'Angeli (ITA) | 04.05.2000 | 18 | (13) | 3 |
| Davide Merli (ITA) | 08.02.2000 | 22 | (8) | 11 |
| Lorenzo Pasquinelli | 18.11.2002 | 4 | (7) | 3 |
| Mario Antonio Salvemini (ITA) | 08.02.1992 | 17 | (7) | 4 |
| Francesco Stella (ITA) | 25.05.1995 | 16 | (8) | 5 |
| Federico Tumidei | 30.09.2001 | 4 | (14) | 1 |

## Società Polisportiva La Fiorita Montegiardino

| Founded: | 1967 | | |
| Stadium: | Stadio "Igor Crescentini", Montegiardino (700) | | |
| Trainer: | Oscar Lasagni (ITA) | | 04.10.1971 |
| [31.12.2022] | Thomas Manfredini (ITA) | | 27.05.1980 |

| Goalkeepers: | DOB | M | (s) | G |
|---|---|---|---|---|
| Gianluca Vivan (ITA) | 27.12.1983 | 31 | | |
| Simone Venturini (ITA) | 27.05.1998 | 2 | | |
| **Defenders:** | **DOB** | **M** | **(s)** | **G** |
| Nicholas Arrigoni (ITA) | 09.01.1995 | 15 | (3) | |
| Andrea Brighi (ITA) | 29.07.1992 | 22 | (1) | |
| Lorenzo Fatica (ITA) | 31.08.1988 | 27 | (3) | 4 |
| Marco Gasperoni (ITA) | 18.02.1992 | 20 | (2) | 2 |
| Andrea Grandoni | 23.03.1997 | 9 | (1) | |
| Nicola Greco (ITA) | 30.06.2000 | 26 | (5) | 1 |
| Alessandro Romagna (ITA) | 19.05.1994 | 3 | | |
| Daniel Santo Sorbara (ITA) | 30.01.2004 | 1 | | |
| **Midfielders:** | **DOB** | **M** | **(s)** | **G** |
| Armando Amati (ITA) | 15.01.1995 | 21 | (5) | 4 |
| Galip Arapi (ALB) | 20.01.2001 | 8 | (8) | 1 |
| Jacopo Berardi | 23.02.2004 | | (1) | |

| | DOB | M | (s) | G |
|---|---|---|---|---|
| Luca Bonifazi | 12.11.1982 | | (5) | |
| Andrea Grassi (ITA) | 30.09.1993 | 23 | (6) | 1 |
| Atiljo Hoxha (ALB) | 21.12.2004 | | (1) | |
| Lorenzo Lunadei | 12.07.1997 | 15 | (12) | |
| Nicola Palazzi (ITA) | 26.09.1996 | 18 | (6) | |
| Matteo Semprini | 30.03.1995 | 11 | (14) | |
| Pio Staiano (ITA) | 01.01.2004 | 1 | (9) | |
| Tommaso Zafferani | 19.02.1996 | 18 | (12) | 1 |
| **Forwards:** | **DOB** | **M** | **(s)** | **G** |
| Sami Abouzziane (MAR) | 16.09.2001 | 6 | (10) | 1 |
| Enrico Bartolini (ITA) | 24.11.1981 | 9 | (2) | 4 |
| Samuel Pancotti | 31.10.2000 | 23 | (9) | 6 |
| Danilo Rinaldi | 18.04.1986 | 20 | (6) | 9 |
| Raffaele Russo (ITA) | 04.09.2002 | 13 | (4) | 7 |
| Laye Signate (SEN) | 12.01.2001 | | (7) | |
| Matteo Vitaioli | 27.10.1989 | 21 | (3) | 7 |

## Associazione Calcio Libertas Borgo Maggiore

| Founded: | 1928 | | |
| Stadium: | Campo sportivo, Borgo Maggiore (1,000) | | |
| Trainer: | Gabriele Cardini (ITA) | | 21.05.1973 |
| [15.11.2022] | Floriano Sperindio | | 17.08.1973 |

| Goalkeepers: | DOB | M | (s) | G |
|---|---|---|---|---|
| Nicolò Battistini (ITA) | 03.07.1999 | 3 | (1) | |
| Pasquale Savastano (ITA) | 12.12.2003 | 1 | | |
| Matteo Zavoli | 06.07.1996 | 29 | | |
| **Defenders:** | **DOB** | **M** | **(s)** | **G** |
| Lorenzo Costa (ITA) | 01.03.1992 | 23 | (1) | |
| Angelo Gregorio (ITA) | 11.04.1991 | 18 | | |
| Filippo Guglielmi (ITA) | 16.03.2001 | 29 | (3) | 1 |
| Dario Merendino (ITA) | 14.11.1983 | 10 | (12) | |
| Andrea Mingucci (ITA) | 27.11.1998 | 21 | (4) | |
| Diego Moretti | 07.02.2000 | 14 | (6) | |
| Marcello Morini | 25.11.1996 | 2 | (6) | |
| Bruno Perretta (ARG) | 26.12.1998 | 15 | (1) | 2 |
| Federico Pesaresi (ITA) | 09.08.1996 | 12 | (4) | 1 |
| **Midfielders:** | **DOB** | **M** | **(s)** | **G** |
| Mario Barone (ITA) | 13.06.1984 | 23 | (2) | 4 |

| | DOB | M | (s) | G |
|---|---|---|---|---|
| Martin Bastos Moncalvo (URU) | 19.10.1994 | 15 | (7) | 1 |
| Alex Gasperoni | 30.06.1984 | 8 | (10) | |
| Lorenzo Gasperoni | 03.01.1990 | 14 | (8) | 1 |
| Fabio Giovagnoli (ITA) | 10.06.1992 | 2 | (3) | |
| Gian Luca Morelli (ITA) | 13.02.1985 | 14 | (5) | |
| Thomas Sapori (ITA) | 18.08.2001 | 27 | (5) | 6 |
| Francesco Stacchini | 18.01.1997 | 3 | (4) | |
| **Forwards:** | **DOB** | **M** | **(s)** | **G** |
| Armando Aruci | 10.07.1989 | 10 | (1) | 3 |
| Federico Barlafante (ITA) | 06.06.2000 | 13 | (6) | 3 |
| Mohamed Ben Kacem (MAR) | 27.02.1994 | 11 | (8) | 5 |
| Marco Bucci (ITA) | 19.07.1999 | 23 | (9) | 7 |
| Antonio Iovino (ITA) | 25.07.2002 | | (1) | |
| Hamdi Kuqi (ITA) | 15.06.2002 | 1 | (6) | 2 |
| Emiliano Olcese (ARG) | 14.05.1983 | 22 | (7) | 15 |

## Società Sportiva Murata Città di San Marino

| | | | | |
|---|---|---|---|---|
| **Founded**: | 1966 | | | |
| **Stadium**: | Campo sportivo, Montegiardino (1,000) | | | |
| **Trainer**: | Roberto Sarti | | 13.10.1967 | |
| [21.12.2022] | Giuseppe Angelini (ITA) | | 14.03.1965 | |

| Goalkeepers: | DOB | M | (s) | G |
|---|---|---|---|---|
| Moussa Gueye (SEN) | 31.12.1995 | 14 | | |
| Mattia Manzaroli | 03.10.1991 | 12 | | |
| Achille Terenzi | 21.07.2002 | 3 | | |
| **Defenders:** | **DOB** | **M** | **(s)** | **G** |
| Nicola Carlini | 07.11.2002 | 7 | (4) | |
| Mattia Costantini (ITA) | 24.07.1989 | 21 | (2) | |
| Xhulio Gega (ALB) | 17.02.1995 | 24 | (3) | 3 |
| Cristian Grieco (ITA) | 27.10.1998 | 20 | (5) | 1 |
| Giacomo Matteoni | 11.04.2002 | 13 | (1) | |
| Nicolò Ricci (ITA) | 06.06.1999 | 5 | (9) | |
| Thomas Rosti | 03.05.2001 | 6 | (5) | |
| Carlo Valentini | 15.03.1982 | 15 | (6) | 1 |
| Fabio Vitaioli | 05.04.1984 | 20 | (3) | |

| Midfielders: | DOB | M | (s) | G |
|---|---|---|---|---|
| Matteo Gaiani (ITA) | 02.01.1995 | 27 | | 4 |
| Samel Gjorretaj (ALB) | 04.01.2002 | 11 | (14) | |
| Luca Patregnani (ITA) | 08.04.1985 | 9 | | |
| Mattia Sarti | 14.01.2003 | 3 | (11) | |
| Jacopo Semprini (ITA) | 06.05.2002 | 13 | | 5 |
| Alex Toccaceli | 16.01.2002 | 19 | (7) | 1 |
| Davide Venerucci | 08.06.1997 | 6 | (9) | |
| **Forwards:** | **DOB** | **M** | **(s)** | **G** |
| Matteo Baldini (ITA) | 02.10.1998 | 8 | (4) | 2 |
| Andrea Comuniello (ITA) | 27.04.1995 | 20 | (8) | 4 |
| Mario Dulcetti (ITA) | 18.03.2004 | | (6) | |
| Nicolas Ferraro (ITA) | 17.08.1995 | 16 | (10) | 4 |
| Raul Ura (ITA) | 10.09.1998 | 27 | (1) | 15 |

## Società Sportiva Pennarossa Chiesanuova

| | | | | |
|---|---|---|---|---|
| **Founded**: | 1968 | | | |
| **Stadium**: | Campo sportivo, Chiesanuova (300) | | | |
| **Trainer**: | Andrea Farabegoli (ITA) | | 01.08.1976 | |
| [23.11.2022] | Massimo Gori (ITA) | | 29.05.1961 | |

| Goalkeepers: | DOB | M | (s) | G |
|---|---|---|---|---|
| Simone Benedettini | 21.01.1997 | 23 | | |
| Youssef Boujir (MAR) | 11.11.2005 | 2 | (2) | |
| Moussa Gueye (SEN) | 31.12.1995 | 2 | | |
| Eugenio Marconi | 22.10.1998 | 1 | | |
| **Defenders:** | **DOB** | **M** | **(s)** | **G** |
| Nicholas Arrigoni (ITA) | 09.01.1995 | 10 | | |
| Gianvito Battiata (ITA) | 22.10.2003 | 3 | (5) | |
| Daniele Conti (ITA) | 06.06.1990 | 22 | | 1 |
| Manuel De Biagi | 07.03.2002 | 4 | (4) | |
| Mirko Mantovani | 14.11.1986 | 14 | (2) | |
| Riccardo Mezzadri (ITA) | 14.04.1986 | 20 | (3) | 1 |
| Luca Righi | 01.04.1995 | 10 | (4) | |
| Antonio Stelitano (ITA) | 22.10.1987 | 26 | (1) | |
| Alberto Tomassini | 19.02.2002 | 11 | | |
| Simone Vittori | 19.04.2004 | 6 | (3) | |

| Midfielders: | DOB | M | (s) | G |
|---|---|---|---|---|
| Muhamed Ahmetovic (ITA) | 19.07.1999 | 4 | (6) | |
| Ismail Bahi (MAR) | 03.11.2001 | 13 | (1) | 2 |
| Maicol Berretti | 01.05.1989 | 12 | (3) | |
| Alessio Boschi (ITA) | 22.11.2005 | | (1) | |
| Luca Cecchetti | 03.07.2000 | 15 | (7) | 3 |
| Alessandro Conti (ITA) | 07.01.1998 | 14 | (3) | 2 |
| Carmine Pietro Giordano (ITA) | 12.07.2003 | 1 | (6) | |
| Anxhelo Isaraj (ALB) | 25.12.1991 | 9 | (4) | |
| Riccardo Michelotti | 13.09.1999 | 19 | (4) | 1 |
| Enzo Zago (ITA) | 27.06.2000 | 24 | (1) | 4 |
| **Forwards:** | **DOB** | **M** | **(s)** | **G** |
| Gianmarco Baschetti | 29.04.1991 | 4 | (8) | |
| Mohamed Ben Kacem (MAR) | 27.02.1994 | 10 | | 7 |
| Luciano Baltazar Franchelli (ARG) | 28.07.2003 | 6 | (2) | |
| Valerio Scalise (ITA) | 04.09.2002 | | (2) | |
| Francesco Ottaviani (ITA) | 17.09.2000 | 3 | (8) | |
| Mattia Stefanelli | 12.03.1993 | 20 | (1) | 17 |

## Società Sportiva San Giovanni Borgo Maggiore

| | | | | |
|---|---|---|---|---|
| **Founded**: | 1948 | | | |
| **Stadium**: | Stadio Borgo Maggiore, Borgo Maggiore (1,000) | | | |
| **Trainer**: | Marco Tognacci | | 15.10.1970 | |

| Goalkeepers: | DOB | M | (s) | G |
|---|---|---|---|---|
| Mirco De Angelis | 03.03.2000 | 25 | | |
| Manuel Nigro (ITA) | 21.10.2004 | 4 | | |
| **Defenders:** | **DOB** | **M** | **(s)** | **G** |
| Luca Angelini (ITA) | 17.09.1989 | 20 | (1) | 2 |
| Giacomo Conti | 21.07.1999 | 22 | (1) | |
| Alex de Biagi | 02.01.2000 | 8 | (11) | |
| Alessandro Giambalvo | 23.04.2003 | 3 | (6) | |
| Alex Giuliano (ITA) | 05.01.1995 | 14 | (4) | |
| Stefano Sartini | 02.05.2000 | 20 | (5) | |
| Enea Senja (ALB) | 10.01.1999 | 18 | (3) | |
| Manuel Serafini (ITA) | 30.11.1999 | 6 | (8) | |
| **Midfielders:** | **DOB** | **M** | **(s)** | **G** |
| Francesco Angelini (ITA) | 23.01.2003 | 2 | (6) | |

| | DOB | M | (s) | G |
|---|---|---|---|---|
| Federico Berardi (ITA) | 17.09.1997 | 23 | (4) | |
| Francesco Boldrini (ITA) | 09.01.1995 | 18 | (3) | 1 |
| Andrea Celli (ITA) | 27.11.1996 | 11 | (10) | 1 |
| Andrea Corinti (ITA) | 23.11.1998 | 22 | (5) | 3 |
| Gabriele Della Croce (ITA) | 20.06.2000 | | (1) | |
| Kevin Lisi (ITA) | 16.11.2001 | 20 | (1) | 3 |
| Massimiliano Morini | 05.04.2004 | 1 | (7) | |
| Giulio Strologo (ITA) | 01.08.1991 | 14 | (10) | |
| **Forwards:** | **DOB** | **M** | **(s)** | **G** |
| Mihail Bruma (ROU) | 22.12.1995 | 24 | (2) | 6 |
| Simone Greppi (ITA) | 03.09.2001 | 10 | (6) | 4 |
| Lorenzo Montebelli (ITA) | 12.10.1999 | 8 | (16) | |
| Nicola Sartini (ITA) | 04.07.1999 | 15 | (12) | 6 |

Please note: Manuel Nigro was used also as field player in Round 27.

## Società Polisportiva Tre Fiori Fiorentino

| Founded: | 1949 | | |
|---|---|---|---|
| Stadium: | Stadio di Fiorentino, Fiorentino (1,000) | | |
| Trainer: | Andy Selva | | 23.05.1976 |
| [24.04.2023] | Giorgio Leoni | | 04.09.1950 |

| Goalkeepers: | DOB | M | (s) | G |
|---|---|---|---|---|
| Alex Castagnoli | 13.04.1989 | 2 | (1) | |
| Alessandro Semprini | 29.01.1994 | 28 | | |
| **Defenders:** | **DOB** | **M** | **(s)** | **G** |
| Christian Boldini (ITA) | 21.07.2004 | | (2) | |
| Umberto De Lucia (ITA) | 07.01.1992 | 28 | | 4 |
| Nicola Della Valle (ITA) | 19.05.1997 | 6 | (7) | |
| Eros Grani (ITA) | 17.02.1999 | 17 | (1) | |
| Angelo Gregorio (ITA) | 11.04.1991 | 8 | (1) | |
| Lautaro Rubén Jara (ARG) | 14.01.1994 | 9 | (2) | |
| Kevin Martin (ITA) | 24.03.1995 | 23 | (5) | |
| Giacomo Matteoni | 11.04.2002 | 5 | (2) | |
| Davide Simoncini | 30.08.1986 | 1 | (1) | |
| **Midfielders:** | **DOB** | **M** | **(s)** | **G** |
| Luca Censoni | 18.07.1996 | 10 | (8) | 1 |
| Andrea De Falco (ITA) | 19.06.1986 | 21 | (1) | 3 |
| Federico Dolcini | 22.03.2000 | 20 | (8) | 2 |

| | DOB | M | (s) | G |
|---|---|---|---|---|
| Lorenzo Falzetta (ITA) | 28.03.2000 | 26 | (3) | 3 |
| Adam Adami Martins (BRA) | 24.06.1992 | 19 | (3) | 1 |
| Francesco Muci (ITA) | 29.05.2003 | | (3) | |
| Giacomo Pracucci (ITA) | 21.01.1997 | 4 | (7) | |
| Thomas Rastelli | 07.03.2002 | 18 | (10) | 2 |
| Luigi Rizzo (ITA) | 24.02.1997 | 8 | (7) | |
| Davide Savino (ITA) | 23.08.2001 | 4 | (3) | 1 |
| Andrea Tamagnini | 27.09.1997 | 6 | (13) | 1 |
| **Forwards:** | **DOB** | **M** | **(s)** | **G** |
| Tommaso Bernardi (ITA) | 08.04.2001 | 18 | (10) | 4 |
| Federico Ciccione (ITA) | 03.01.2001 | | (10) | 1 |
| Bojan Gjurchinoski (MKD) | 13.04.1994 | 23 | (5) | 9 |
| Massimo Goh (ITA) | 01.02.1999 | 7 | (1) | 2 |
| Lamine Tall (SEN) | 05.12.2001 | 10 | (4) | 8 |
| Emanuele Smecca (ITA) | 2003 | | (2) | |
| Michael Traini (ITA) | 21.07.1988 | 9 | (2) | 4 |

## Società Polisportiva Tre Penne Città di San Marino

| Founded: | 1956 | | |
|---|---|---|---|
| Stadium: | Stadio Fonte Dell'Ovo, Città di San Marino (500) | | |
| Trainer: | Stefano Ceci | | 16.10.1969 |

| Goalkeepers: | DOB | M | (s) | G |
|---|---|---|---|---|
| Mattia Migani (ITA) | 10.03.1992 | 27 | | |
| Emanuele Semprini (ITA) | 25.12.1988 | 1 | | |
| **Defenders:** | **DOB** | **M** | **(s)** | **G** |
| Antonio Barretta (ITA) | 19.09.1995 | 19 | (4) | 1 |
| Piero Cauterucci (ITA) | 06.04.1999 | 2 | (7) | 2 |
| Davide Cesarini | 16.02.1995 | 5 | (10) | |
| Nicolas Lombardi (ITA) | 21.05.1995 | 27 | | 1 |
| Giuseppe Maio (ITA) | 16.10.2004 | | (2) | |
| Giacomo Nigretti (ITA) | 28.04.1999 | 25 | | 4 |
| Riccardo Tisselli (ITA) | 29.07.1997 | 11 | (3) | 1 |
| Paolo Vandi (ITA) | 23.09.1994 | 26 | (1) | 2 |
| **Midfielders:** | **DOB** | **M** | **(s)** | **G** |
| Michael Battistini | 08.10.1996 | 11 | (12) | |

| | DOB | M | (s) | G |
|---|---|---|---|---|
| Enrico Cibelli | 14.07.1987 | 2 | (11) | |
| Raffaele Alessandro Coppola (ITA) | 16.09.2003 | | (3) | |
| Nicola Gai (ITA) | 06.12.1987 | 25 | | 9 |
| Fabio Giovagnoli (ITA) | 10.06.1992 | 1 | (4) | |
| Andrea Montanari (ITA) | 10.11.1986 | 22 | | |
| Luca Righini (ITA) | 25.12.1990 | 24 | | 10 |
| Giacomo Zafferani | 16.07.1996 | | (1) | |
| **Forwards:** | **DOB** | **M** | **(s)** | **G** |
| Imre Badalassi (ITA) | 08.02.1995 | 27 | (1) | 14 |
| Luca Ceccaroli | 05.07.1995 | 21 | (4) | 7 |
| Lorenzo Dormi (ITA) | 11.02.1995 | 15 | (5) | 4 |
| Mirko Malagoli (ITA) | 16.11.2002 | | (5) | |
| Riccardo Pieri (ITA) | 27.10.1994 | 17 | (9) | 4 |
| Michele Stellato (ITA) | 27.09.2001 | | (4) | |

## Società Sportiva Virtus Acquaviva

| Founded: | 1964 | | |
|---|---|---|---|
| Stadium: | Stadio di Acquaviva, Acquaviva (2,000) | | |
| Trainer: | Luigi Bizzotto (ITA) | | 08.03.1960 |

| Goalkeepers: | DOB | M | (s) | G |
|---|---|---|---|---|
| Andrea Battistini (ITA) | 10.08.2000 | 3 | | |
| Alex Passaniti (ITA) | 13.11.1998 | 26 | | |
| Alex Stimac | 22.06.1996 | 1 | | |
| **Defenders:** | **DOB** | **M** | **(s)** | **G** |
| Manuel Battistini | 22.07.1994 | 29 | (1) | |
| Nicolò Castiglioni (ITA) | 16.07.1996 | 13 | (13) | |
| Aron Giacomoni | 22.08.1987 | 17 | (2) | |
| Nicola Gori (ITA) | 08.05.1997 | 17 | (6) | |
| Alex Nodari (ITA) | 15.02.1982 | 31 | (1) | |
| Roberto Sabato (ITA) | 28.07.1987 | 26 | (2) | 5 |
| **Midfielders:** | **DOB** | **M** | **(s)** | **G** |
| Mariano Alvarez | 05.02.1996 | 1 | | |
| Ivan Buonocunto (ITA) | 24.02.1986 | 30 | (2) | 8 |

| | DOB | M | (s) | G |
|---|---|---|---|---|
| Elia Ciacci | 13.11.2001 | 20 | (13) | |
| Lorenzo Contadini (ITA) | 05.10.1994 | 8 | (18) | |
| Alessandro Golinucci (ITA) | 10.10.1994 | 20 | (5) | 1 |
| Jacopo Muggeo (ITA) | 19.08.1990 | 3 | (14) | |
| Matteo Pedrini (ITA) | 16.01.2000 | 11 | (3) | 3 |
| Mattia Pirini (ITA) | 18.11.1992 | 18 | (7) | |
| Pietro Sopranzi | 29.01.1998 | 10 | (12) | 8 |
| **Forwards:** | **DOB** | **M** | **(s)** | **G** |
| Filippo Albini (ITA) | 16.09.2000 | 6 | (2) | 1 |
| Nicola Angeli (ITA) | 28.05.1989 | 22 | (4) | 11 |
| Simone Benincasa (ITA) | 25.01.2001 | 18 | (4) | 4 |
| Luca Sorrentino (ITA) | 08.05.1994 | 17 | (13) | 9 |
| Oleksander Tadzhybayev (UKR) | 10.04.1994 | | (1) | |
| Loris Tortori (ITA) | 13.10.1988 | 16 | (3) | 7 |

Please note: Manuel Battistini was used also as goalkeeper in 2 matches (Round 29 & 30); Nicola Angeli played as goalkeeper in 1 match (4th Place play-off).

## INTERNATIONAL MATCHES
### (16.07.2022 – 15.07.2023)

| | | | | |
|---|---|---|---|---|
| 21.09.2022 | Serravalle | *San Marino - Seychelles* | *0-0* | (F) |
| 26.09.2022 | Serravalle | *San Marino - Estonia* | *0-4(0-1)* | (UNL) |
| 17.11.2022 | Gros Islet | *Saint Lucia - San Marino* | *1-1(1-0)* | (F) |
| 20.11.2022 | Gros Islet | *Saint Lucia - San Marino* | *1-0(0-0)* | (F) |
| | | | | |
| 23.03.2023 | Serravalle | *San Marino - Northern Ireland* | *0-2(0-1)* | (ECQ) |
| 26.03.2023 | Ljubljana | *Slovenia - San Marino* | *2-0(0-0)* | (ECQ) |
| 16.06.2023 | Parma | *San Marino - Kazakhstan* | *0-3(0-1)* | (ECQ) |
| 19.06.2023 | Helsinki | *Finland - San Marino* | *6-0(2-0)* | (ECQ) |

**21.09.2022　SAN MARINO - SEYCHELLES　　　0-0　　　　　Friendly International**
San Marino Stadium, Serravalle; Referee: David Šmajc (Slovenia); Attendance: 367
**SMR:** Elia Benedettini, Alessandro D'Addario (82.Adolfo José Hirsch), Filippo Fabbri, Dante Carlos Rossi, Mirko Palazzi, Andrea Grandoni (46.Mattia Stefanelli), Marcello Mularoni (82.David Tomassini), Alessandro Golinucci (87.Lorenzo Lunadei), Michael Battistini, Luca Ceccaroli (59.Fabio Ramón Tomassini), Matteo Giampaolo Vitaioli (Cap) (60.Alessandro Tosi). Trainer: Fabrizio Constantini (Italy).

**26.09.2022　SAN MARINO - ESTONIA　　　0-4(0-1)　　　3rd UEFA Nations League D, Group 2**
San Marino Stadium, Serravalle; Referee: Kateryna Monzul (Ukraine); Attendance: 608
**SMR:** Elia Benedettini, Simone Franciosi, Mirko Palazzi (Cap), Alessandro Tosi, Tommaso Zafferani (46.Manuel Battistini), Michael Battistini (65.Enrico Golinucci), Alessandro Golinucci (66.Marcello Mularoni), Lorenzo Lunadei, Andrea Grandoni (46.Alessandro D'Addario), Danilo Ezequiel Rinaldi, Fabio Ramón Tomassini (84.Matteo Giampaolo Vitaioli). Trainer: Fabrizio Constantini (Italy).

**17.11.2022　SAINT LUCIA - SAN MARINO　　　1-1(1-0)　　　　　Friendly International**
"Daren Sammy" Cricket Ground, Gros Islet; Referee: Moet Gaymes (Saint Vincent and the Grenadines); Attendance: 750
**SMR:** Elia Benedettini, Michele Cevoli, Andrea Grandoni (57.Adolfo José Hirsch), Mirko Palazzi, Alessandro Tosi, Alessandro D'Addario (69.David Tomassini), Marcello Mularoni (57.Lorenzo Lazzari), Lorenzo Capicchioni, Alessandro Golinucci (81.Pietro Sopranzi), Matteo Giampaolo Vitaioli (Cap) (69.Samuel Pancotti), Danilo Ezequiel Rinaldi (81.Mattia Stefanelli). Trainer: Fabrizio Constantini (Italy).
**Goal:** Lorenzo Lazzari (90+4).

**20.11.2022　SAINT LUCIA - SAN MARINO　　　1-0(0-0)　　　　　Friendly International**
"Daren Sammy" Cricket Ground, Gros Islet; Referee: Reon Radix (Grenada); Attendance: 3,723
**SMR:** Aldo Junior Simoncini, Michele Cevoli, Mirko Palazzi (Cap), Alessandro Tosi, Simone Franciosi (84.Mattia Ceccaroli), Enrico Golinucci (46.Alessandro Golinucci), Lorenzo Capicchioni, Tommaso Zafferani (72.Adolfo José Hirsch), Fabio Ramón Tomassini (60.Samuel Pancotti), Lorenzo Lazzari (84.David Tomassini), Danilo Ezequiel Rinaldi (60.Matteo Giampaolo Vitaioli). Trainer: Fabrizio Constantini (Italy).

**23.03.2023　SAN MARINO - NORTHERN IRELAND　　　0-2(0-1)　　　17th EC. Qualifiers**
San Marino Stadium, Serravalle; Referee: Gergő Bognár (Hungary); Attendance: 2,099
**SMR:** Elia Benedettini, Manuel Battistini, Dante Carlos Rossi (46.Michele Cevoli), Roberto Di Maio, Mirko Palazzi (Cap) (46.Alessandro Tosi), Filippo Fabbri, Lorenzo Capicchioni (72.Michael Battistini), Alessandro Golinucci, Lorenzo Lazzari, Filippo Berardi (60.Danilo Ezequiel Rinaldi), Nicola Nanni (85.Matteo Giampaolo Vitaioli). Trainer: Fabrizio Constantini (Italy).

**26.03.2023　SLOVENIA - SAN MARINO　　　2-0(0-0)　　　17th EC. Qualifiers**
Stadion Stožice, Ljubljana; Referee: Nathan Verboomen (Belgium); Attendance: 10,282
**SMR:** Elia Benedettini, Alessandro D'Addario, Michele Cevoli, Filippo Fabbri (73.Simone Franciosi), Dante Carlos Rossi (46.Roberto Di Maio), Alessandro Tosi, Michael Battistini, Alessandro Golinucci, Lorenzo Lunadei (73.Matteo Giampaolo Vitaioli), Filippo Berardi (59.Lorenzo Lazzari), Nicola Nanni (Cap) (86.Danilo Ezequiel Rinaldi). Trainer: Fabrizio Constantini (Italy).

**16.06.2023　SAN MARINO - KAZAKHSTAN　　　0-3(0-1)　　　17th EC. Qualifiers**
Stadio "Ennio Tardini", Parma (Italy); Referee: Anastasios Papapetrou (Greece); Attendance: 528
**SMR:** Elia Benedettini, Manuel Battistini (Cap), Roberto Di Maio, Filippo Fabbri (82.Michele Cevoli), Dante Carlos Rossi, Alessandro Tosi (65.Adolfo José Hirsch), Lorenzo Capicchioni (80.Matteo Giampaolo Vitaioli), Alessandro Golinucci, Lorenzo Lazzari, Filippo Berardi (65.Luca Ceccaroli), Nicola Nanni (80.Michael Battistini). Trainer: Fabrizio Constantini (Italy).

**19.06.2023　FINLAND - SAN MARINO　　　6-0(2-0)　　　17th EC. Qualifiers**
Olympiastadion, Helsinki; Referee: Genc Nuza (Kosovo); Attendance: 32,812
**SMR:** Elia Benedettini, Alessandro D'Addario, Roberto Di Maio (89.Simone Franciosi), Filippo Fabbri, Dante Carlos Rossi, Alessandro Tosi (78.Manuel Battistini), Alessandro Golinucci (Cap), Lorenzo Lunadei (66.Marcello Mularoni), Michael Battistini (78.Enrico Golinucci), Filippo Berardi (66.Matteo Giampaolo Vitaioli), Nicola Nanni. Trainer: Fabrizio Constantini (Italy).

| Name | DOB | Caps | Goals | Club | |
|---|---|---|---|---|---|

### Goalkeepers

| Name | DOB | Caps | Goals | Club | |
|---|---|---|---|---|---|
| Elia BENEDETTINI | 22.06.1995 | 43 | 0 | 2022/2023: | SP Cailungo Borgo Maggiore |
| Aldo Junior SIMONCINI | 30.08.1986 | 64 | 0 | 2022: | SS Cosmos Serravalle |

### Defenders

| Name | DOB | Caps | Goals | Club | |
|---|---|---|---|---|---|
| Manuel BATTISTINI | 11.07.1994 | 51 | 0 | 2022/2023: | SS Virtus Acquaviva |
| Mattia CECCAROLI | 03.02.1999 | 1 | 0 | 2022: | FC Domagnano |
| Michele CEVOLI | 22.07.1998 | 18 | 0 | 2022/2023: | AC Juvenes/Dogana Serravalle |
| Alessandro D'ADDARIO | 09.09.1997 | 24 | 0 | 2022/2023: | SS Cosmos Serravalle |
| Roberto DI MAIO | 21.09.1982 | 4 | 0 | 2023: | SS Cosmos Serravalle |
| Filippo FABBRI | 07.01.2002 | 20 | 1 | 2022/2023: | Olbia Calcio 1905 (ITA) |
| Simone FRANCIOSI | 03.09.2001 | 4 | 0 | 2022/2023: | A.S.D. Valfoglia (ITA) |
| Andrea GRANDONI | 23.03.1997 | 36 | 0 | 2022: | SP La Fiorita Montegiardino |
| Mirko PALAZZI | 21.03.1987 | 73 | 1 | 2022/2023: | SS Cosmos Serravalle |
| Dante Carlos ROSSI | 12.07.1987 | 24 | 0 | 2022/2023: | ASD Tropical Coriano (ITA) |
| Alessandro TOSI | 28.04.2001 | 8 | 0 | 2022/2023: | ASD Victor San Marino Acquaviva |

### Midfielders

| Name | DOB | Caps | Goals | Club | |
|---|---|---|---|---|---|
| Michael BATTISTINI | 08.10.1996 | 20 | 0 | 2022/2023: | SP Tre Penne Città di San Marino |
| Lorenzo CAPICCHIONI | 19.01.2002 | 4 | 0 | 2022: | ASD Riccione 1929 (ITA) |
| | | | | 26.01.2023-> | SS Cosmos Serravalle |
| Luca CECCAROLI | 05.07.1995 | 17 | 0 | 2022/2023: | SP Tre Penne Città di San Marino |
| Alessandro GOLINUCCI | 10.10.1994 | 42 | 0 | 2022/2023: | SS Virtus Acquaviva |
| Enrico GOLINUCCI | 16.07.1991 | 40 | 0 | 2022/2023: | SS Folgore Falciano Calcio Serravalle |
| Lorenzo LAZZARI | 04.08.2001 | 5 | 1 | 2022/2023: | ASD Victor San Marino Acquaviva |
| Lorenzo LUNADEI | 12.07.1997 | 32 | 0 | 2022/2023: | SP La Fiorita Montegiardino |
| Marcello MULARONI | 08.09.1998 | 35 | 0 | 2022/2023: | ASD Tropical Coriano (ITA) |
| Danilo Ezequiel RINALDI | 18.04.1986 | 51 | 1 | 2022/2023: | SP La Fiorita Montegiardino |
| Tommaso ZAFFERANI | 19.02.1996 | 19 | 0 | 2022: | SP La Fiorita Montegiardino |

### Forwards

| Name | DOB | Caps | Goals | Club | |
|---|---|---|---|---|---|
| Filippo BERARDI | 18.05.1997 | 25 | 1 | 2023: | AC Sammaurese (ITA) |
| Adolfo José HIRSCH | 31.01.1986 | 59 | 0 | 2022/2023: | FC Fiorentino |
| Nicola NANNI | 02.05.2000 | 31 | 1 | 2023: | Olbia Calcio 1905 (ITA) |
| Samuel PANCOTTI | 31.10.2000 | 2 | 0 | 2022: | SP La Fiorita Montegiardino |
| Pietro SOPRANZI | 29.01.1998 | 1 | 0 | 2022: | SS Virtus Acquaviva |
| Mattia STEFANELLI | 12.03.1993 | 17 | 1 | 2022: | SS Pennarossa Chiesanuova |
| David TOMASSINI | 14.03.2000 | 14 | 1 | 2022: | ASD Tropical Coriano (ITA) |
| Fabio Ramón TOMASSINI | 05.02.1996 | 32 | 0 | 2022: | US Pietracuta San Leo (ITA) |
| Matteo Giampaolo VITAIOLI | 27.10.1989 | 85 | 1 | 2022/2023: | SP La Fiorita Montegiardino |

### Trainer

| Name | DOB | Record | |
|---|---|---|---|
| Fabrizio CONSTANTINI (Italy) [from 27.11.2021] | 03.06.1968 | 14 M; 0 W; 2 D; 12 L; 2-29 | |

# SCOTLAND

## The Country:
Scotland
Capital: Edinburgh
Surface: 77,933 km²
Inhabitants: 5,480,000 [2021]
Time: UTC

## The FA:
Scottish Football Association
Hampden Park G42, 9AY Glasgow
Tel: +44 141 616 6000
Founded: 1873
Member of FIFA since: 1910
Member of UEFA since: 1954
Website: www.scottishfa.co.uk

## NATIONAL TEAM RECORDS

| RECORDS | | |
|---|---|---|
| **First international match:** | 30.11.1872, Glasgow: | Scotland – England 0-0 |
| **Most international caps:** | Kenneth Mathieson Dalglish | - 102 caps (1971-1986) |
| **Most international goals:** | Denis Law | - 30 goals / 55 caps (1958-1974) |
| | Kenneth Mathieson Dalglish | - 30 goals / 102 caps (1971-1986) |

| UEFA EUROPEAN CHAMPIONSHIP | |
|---|---|
| 1960 | Did not enter |
| 1964 | Did not enter |
| 1968 | Qualifiers |
| 1972 | Qualifiers |
| 1976 | Qualifiers |
| 1980 | Qualifiers |
| 1984 | Qualifiers |
| 1988 | Qualifiers |
| 1992 | Final Tournament (Group Stage) |
| 1996 | Final Tournament (Group Stage) |
| 2000 | Qualifiers |
| 2004 | Qualifiers |
| 2008 | Qualifiers |
| 2012 | Qualifiers |
| 2016 | Qualifiers |
| 2020 | Final Tournament (Group Stage) |

| FIFA WORLD CUP | |
|---|---|
| 1930 | Did not enter |
| 1934 | Did not enter |
| 1938 | Did not enter |
| 1950 | *Withdrew after being qualified* |
| 1954 | Final Tournament (Group Stage) |
| 1958 | Final Tournament (Group Stage) |
| 1962 | Qualifiers |
| 1966 | Qualifiers |
| 1970 | Qualifiers |
| 1974 | Final Tournament (Group Stage) |
| 1978 | Final Tournament (Group Stage) |
| 1982 | Final Tournament (Group Stage) |
| 1986 | Final Tournament (Group Stage) |
| 1990 | Final Tournament (Group Stage) |
| 1994 | Qualifiers |
| 1998 | Final Tournament (Group Stage) |
| 2002 | Qualifiers |
| 2006 | Qualifiers |
| 2010 | Qualifiers |
| 2014 | Qualifiers |
| 2018 | Qualifiers |
| 2022 | Qualifiers |

| OLYMPIC TOURNAMENTS | |
|---|---|
| 1908 | - |
| 1912 | - |
| 1920 | - |
| 1924 | - |
| 1928 | - |
| 1936 | - |
| 1948 | - |
| 1952 | - |
| 1956 | - |
| 1960 | - |
| 1964 | - |
| 1968 | - |
| 1972 | - |
| 1976 | - |
| 1980 | - |
| 1984 | - |
| 1988 | - |
| 1992 | - |
| 1996 | - |
| 2000 | - |
| 2004 | - |
| 2008 | - |
| 2012 | - |
| 2016 | - |
| 2020 | - |

## UEFA NATIONS LEAGUE

| 2018/2019 | League C (Group Stage -> promoted to League B) |
|---|---|
| 2020/2021 | League B (Group Stage) |
| 2022/2023 | League B (Group Stage -> promoted to League A) |

## SCOTTISH CLUB HONOURS IN EUROPEAN CLUB COMPETITIONS:

| European Champion Clubs.Cup (1956-1992) / UEFA Champions League (1993-2023) | | |
|---|---|---|
| Celtic FC Glasgow | 1 | 1966/1967 |
| **Fairs Cup (1858-1971) / UEFA Cup (1972-2009) / UEFA Europa League (2010-2023)** | | |
| None | | |
| **UEFA Europa Conference League (2021-2023)** | | |
| None | | |
| **UEFA Super Cup (1972-2022)** | | |
| Aberdeen FC | 1 | 1983 |
| ***European Cup Winners' Cup 1961-1999**** | | |
| Rangers FC Glasgow | 1 | 1971/1972 |
| Aberdeen FC | 1 | 1982/1983 |

*defunct competition

# NATIONAL COMPETITIONS
## TABLE OF HONOURS

| | CHAMPIONS | CUP WINNERS | BEST GOALSCORERS | |
|---|---|---|---|---|
| 1873/1874 | - | Queen's Park FC Glasgow | - | |
| 1874/1875 | - | Queen's Park FC Glasgow | - | |
| 1875/1876 | - | Queen's Park FC Glasgow | - | |
| 1876/1877 | - | Vale of Leven FC Alexandria | - | |
| 1877/1878 | - | Vale of Leven FC Alexandria | - | |
| 1878/1879 | - | Vale of Leven FC Alexandria | - | |
| 1879/1880 | - | Queen's Park FC Glasgow | - | |
| 1880/1881 | - | Queen's Park FC Glasgow | - | |
| 1881/1882 | - | Queen's Park FC Glasgow | - | |
| 1882/1883 | - | Dumbarton FC | - | |
| 1883/1884 | - | Queen's Park FC Glasgow | - | |
| 1884/1885 | - | Renton FC | - | |
| 1885/1886 | - | Queen's Park FC Glasgow | - | |
| 1886/1887 | - | Hibernian FC Edinburgh | - | |
| 1887/1888 | - | Renton FC | - | |
| 1888/1889 | - | Third Lanark AC Glasgow | - | |
| 1889/1890 | - | Queen's Park FC Glasgow | - | |
| 1890/1891 | Dumbarton FC Rangers FC Glasgow [joint winners] | Heart of Midlothian FC Edinburgh | Jack Bell (Dumbarton FC) | 20 |
| 1891/1892 | Dumbarton FC | Celtic FC Glasgow | Jack Bell (Dumbarton FC) | 23 |
| 1892/1893 | Celtic FC Glasgow | Queen's Park FC Glasgow | Sandy McMahon (Celtic FC Glasgow) John Campbell (Celtic FC Glasgow) | 11 |
| 1893/1894 | Celtic FC Glasgow | Rangers FC Glasgow | Sandy McMahon (Celtic FC Glasgow) | 16 |
| 1894/1895 | Heart of Midlothian FC Edinburgh | St. Bernard's FC Edinburgh | James Miller (Clyde FC Cumbernauld) | 12 |
| 1895/1896 | Celtic FC Glasgow | Heart of Midlothian FC Edinburgh | Allan Martin (Celtic FC Glasgow) | 19 |
| 1896/1897 | Heart of Midlothian FC Edinburgh | Rangers FC Glasgow | Willie Taylor (Heart of Midlothian FC Edinburgh) | 12 |
| 1897/1898 | Celtic FC Glasgow | Rangers FC Glasgow | Robert Hamilton (Rangers FC Glasgow) | 18 |
| 1898/1899 | Rangers FC Glasgow | Celtic FC Glasgow | Robert Hamilton (Rangers FC Glasgow) | 25 |
| 1899/1900 | Rangers FC Glasgow | Celtic FC Glasgow | Robert Hamilton (Rangers FC Glasgow) William Michael (Heart of Midlothian FC Edinburgh) | 15 |
| 1900/1901 | Rangers FC Glasgow | Heart of Midlothian FC Edinburgh | Robert Hamilton (Rangers FC Glasgow) | 20 |
| 1901/1902 | Rangers FC Glasgow | Hibernian FC Edinburgh | William Maxwell (Third Lanark AC Glasgow) | 10 |
| 1902/1903 | Hibernian FC Edinburgh | Rangers FC Glasgow | David Reid (Hibernian FC Edinburgh) | 14 |
| 1903/1904 | Third Lanark AC Glasgow | Celtic FC Glasgow | Robert Hamilton (Rangers FC Glasgow) | 28 |
| 1904/1905 | Celtic FC Glasgow | Third Lanark AC Glasgow | Robert Hamilton (Rangers FC Glasgow) James Quinn (Celtic FC Glasgow) | 19 |
| 1905/1906 | Celtic FC Glasgow | Heart of Midlothian FC Edinburgh | James Quinn (Celtic FC Glasgow) | 20 |
| 1906/1907 | Celtic FC Glasgow | Celtic FC Glasgow | James Quinn (Celtic FC Glasgow) | 29 |
| 1907/1908 | Celtic FC Glasgow | Celtic FC Glasgow | Jock Simpson (Falkirk FC) | 32 |
| 1908/1909 | Celtic FC Glasgow | *No competition* | John Hunter (Dundee FC) | 29 |
| 1909/1910 | Celtic FC Glasgow | Dundee FC | James Quinn (Celtic FC Glasgow) Jock Simpson (Falkirk FC) | 24 |
| 1910/1911 | Rangers FC Glasgow | Celtic FC Glasgow | William Reid (Rangers FC Glasgow) | 38 |
| 1911/1912 | Rangers FC Glasgow | Celtic FC Glasgow | William Reid (Rangers FC Glasgow) | 33 |
| 1912/1913 | Rangers FC Glasgow | Falkirk FC | James Reid (Airdrieonians FC) | 30 |
| 1913/1914 | Celtic FC Glasgow | Celtic FC Glasgow | James Reid (Airdrieonians FC) | 27 |
| 1914/1915 | Celtic FC Glasgow | *No competition* | Tom Gracie (Heart of Midlothian FC Edinburgh) James Richardson (Ayr United FC) | 29 |
| 1915/1916 | Celtic FC Glasgow | *No competition* | James McColl (Celtic FC Glasgow) | 34 |
| 1916/1917 | Celtic FC Glasgow | *No competition* | Herbert George Yarnall (ENG, Airdrieonians FC) | 39 |
| 1917/1918 | Rangers FC Glasgow | *No competition* | Hugh Ferguson (Motherwell FC) | 35 |
| 1918/1919 | Celtic FC Glasgow | *No competition* | David McLean (Rangers FC Glasgow) | 29 |
| 1919/1920 | Rangers FC Glasgow | Kilmarnock FC | Hugh Ferguson (Motherwell FC) | 33 |
| 1920/1921 | Rangers FC Glasgow | Partick Thistle FC Glasgow | Hugh Ferguson (Motherwell FC) | 43 |
| 1921/1922 | Celtic FC Glasgow | Greenock Morton FC | Duncan Walker (St. Mirren FC Paisley) | 45 |
| 1922/1923 | Rangers FC Glasgow | Celtic FC Glasgow | John White (Heart of Midlothian FC Edinburgh) | 30 |
| 1923/1924 | Rangers FC Glasgow | Airdrieonians FC | David Halliday (Dundee FC) | 38 |
| 1924/1925 | Rangers FC Glasgow | Celtic FC Glasgow | William Alexander Devlin (Cowdenbeath FC) | 33 |
| 1925/1926 | Celtic FC Glasgow | St. Mirren FC Paisley | William Alexander Devlin (Cowdenbeath FC) | 40 |
| 1926/1927 | Rangers FC Glasgow | Celtic FC Glasgow | James Edward McGrory (Celtic FC Glasgow) | 49 |
| 1927/1928 | Rangers FC Glasgow | Rangers FC Glasgow | James Edward McGrory (Celtic FC Glasgow) | 47 |
| 1928/1929 | Rangers FC Glasgow | Kilmarnock FC | Evelyn Morrison (Falkirk FC) | 43 |
| 1929/1930 | Rangers FC Glasgow | Rangers FC Glasgow | Benjamin Collard Yorston (Aberdeen FC) | 38 |
| 1930/1931 | Rangers FC Glasgow | Celtic FC Glasgow | Bernard Joseph Battles Jr. (Heart of Midlothian FC Edinburgh) | 44 |
| 1931/1932 | Motherwell FC | Rangers FC Glasgow | William MacFadyen (Motherwell FC) | 52 |
| 1932/1933 | Rangers FC Glasgow | Celtic FC Glasgow | William MacFadyen (Motherwell FC) | 45 |
| 1933/1934 | Rangers FC Glasgow | Rangers FC Glasgow | James Smith (Rangers FC Glasgow) | 41 |
| 1934/1935 | Rangers FC Glasgow | Rangers FC Glasgow | James Smith (Rangers FC Glasgow) | 36 |
| 1935/1936 | Celtic FC Glasgow | Rangers FC Glasgow | James Edward McGrory (Celtic FC Glasgow) | 50 |

| Season | Champion | Runner-up | Top scorer | Goals |
|---|---|---|---|---|
| 1936/1937 | Rangers FC Glasgow | Celtic FC Glasgow | David Wilson (Hamilton Academical) | 34 |
| 1937/1938 | Celtic FC Glasgow | East Fife FC Methil | Andrew Black (Heart of Midlothian FC Edinburgh) | 40 |
| 1938/1939 | Rangers FC Glasgow | Clyde FC Cumbernauld | Alexander Venters (Rangers FC Glasgow) | 35 |
| 1939/1940 | *No competition* | *No competition* | - | |
| 1940/1941 | *No competition* | *No competition* | - | |
| 1941/1942 | *No competition* | *No competition* | - | |
| 1942/1943 | *No competition* | *No competition* | - | |
| 1943/1944 | *No competition* | *No competition* | - | |
| 1944/1945 | *No competition* | *No competition* | - | |
| 1945/1946 | *No competition* | *No competition* | - | |
| 1946/1947 | Rangers FC Glasgow | Aberdeen FC | Robert Carmichael Mitchell (Third Lanark AC Glasgow) | 22 |
| 1947/1948 | Hibernian FC Edinburgh | Rangers FC Glasgow | Archie Aikman (Falkirk FC) | 20 |
| 1948/1949 | Rangers FC Glasgow | Rangers FC Glasgow | Alexander Gair Stott (Dundee FC) | 30 |
| 1949/1950 | Rangers FC Glasgow | Rangers FC Glasgow | Willie Bauld (Heart of Midlothian FC Edinburgh) | 30 |
| 1950/1951 | Hibernian FC Edinburgh | Celtic FC Glasgow | Lawrance Reilly (Hibernian FC Edinburgh) | 22 |
| 1951/1952 | Hibernian FC Edinburgh | Motherwell FC | Lawrance Reilly (Hibernian FC Edinburgh) | 27 |
| 1952/1953 | Rangers FC Glasgow | Rangers FC Glasgow | Lawrance Reilly (Hibernian FC Edinburgh) Charlie Fleming (East Fife FC Methil) | 30 |
| 1953/1954 | Celtic FC Glasgow | Celtic FC Glasgow | James Wardhaugh (Heart of Midlothian FC Edinburgh) | 27 |
| 1954/1955 | Aberdeen FC | Clyde FC Cumbernauld | Willie Bauld (Heart of Midlothian FC Edinburgh) | 21 |
| 1955/1956 | Rangers FC Glasgow | Heart of Midlothian FC Edinburgh | James Wardhaugh (Heart of Midlothian FC Edinburgh) | 28 |
| 1956/1957 | Rangers FC Glasgow | Falkirk FC | Hugh Baird (Airdrieonians FC) | 33 |
| 1957/1958 | Heart of Midlothian FC Edinburgh | Clyde FC Cumbernauld | James Wardhaugh (Heart of Midlothian FC Edinburgh) James Murray (Heart of Midlothian FC Edinburgh) | 28 |
| 1958/1959 | Rangers FC Glasgow | St. Mirren FC Paisley | Joseph Henry Baker (Hibernian FC Edinburgh) | 25 |
| 1959/1960 | Heart of Midlothian FC Edinburgh | Rangers FC Glasgow | Joseph Henry Baker (Hibernian FC Edinburgh) | 42 |
| 1960/1961 | Rangers FC Glasgow | Dunfermline Athletic FC | Alexander Harley (Third Lanark AC Glasgow) | 42 |
| 1961/1962 | Dundee FC | Rangers FC Glasgow | Alan John Gilzean (Dundee FC) | 24 |
| 1962/1963 | Rangers FC Glasgow | Rangers FC Glasgow | James Millar (Rangers FC Glasgow) | 27 |
| 1963/1964 | Rangers FC Glasgow | Rangers FC Glasgow | Alan John Gilzean (Dundee FC) | 32 |
| 1964/1965 | Kilmarnock FC | Celtic FC Glasgow | Jim Forrest (Rangers FC Glasgow) | 30 |
| 1965/1966 | Celtic FC Glasgow | Rangers FC Glasgow | James McBride (Celtic FC Glasgow) Alexander Chapman Ferguson (Dunfermline Athletic FC) | 31 |
| 1966/1967 | Celtic FC Glasgow | Celtic FC Glasgow | Thomas Stephen Chalmers (Celtic FC Glasgow) | 21 |
| 1967/1968 | Celtic FC Glasgow | Dunfermline Athletic FC | Robert Lennox (Celtic FC Glasgow) | 32 |
| 1968/1969 | Celtic FC Glasgow | Celtic FC Glasgow | Kenneth Cameron (Dundee United FC) | 26 |
| 1969/1970 | Celtic FC Glasgow | Aberdeen FC | Colin Anderson Stein (Rangers FC Glasgow) | 24 |
| 1970/1971 | Celtic FC Glasgow | Celtic FC Glasgow | Henry Anthony Hood (Celtic FC Glasgow) | 22 |
| 1971/1972 | Celtic FC Glasgow | Celtic FC Glasgow | Joseph Montgomery Harper (Aberdeen FC) | 33 |
| 1972/1973 | Celtic FC Glasgow | Rangers FC Glasgow | Alan Fordyce Gordon (Hibernian FC Edinburgh) | 27 |
| 1973/1974 | Celtic FC Glasgow | Celtic FC Glasgow | John Kelly Deans (Celtic FC Glasgow) | 26 |
| 1974/1975 | Rangers FC Glasgow | Celtic FC Glasgow | Andrew Mullen Gray (Dundee United FC) William Pettigrew (Motherwell FC) | 20 |
| 1975/1976 | Rangers FC Glasgow | Rangers FC Glasgow | Kenneth Mathieson Dalglish (Celtic FC Glasgow) | 24 |
| 1976/1977 | Celtic FC Glasgow | Celtic FC Glasgow | William Pettigrew (Motherwell FC) | 21 |
| 1977/1978 | Rangers FC Glasgow | Rangers FC Glasgow | Derek Joseph Johnstone (Rangers FC Glasgow) | 25 |
| 1978/1979 | Celtic FC Glasgow | Rangers FC Glasgow | Andrew Ritchie (Greenock Morton FC) | 22 |
| 1979/1980 | Aberdeen FC | Celtic FC Glasgow | Douglas McKenzie Somner (St. Mirren FC Paisley) | 25 |
| 1980/1981 | Celtic FC Glasgow | Rangers FC Glasgow | Francis Peter McGarvey (Celtic FC Glasgow) | 23 |
| 1981/1982 | Celtic FC Glasgow | Aberdeen FC | George McKinley Cassidy McCluskey (Celtic FC Glasgow) | 21 |
| 1982/1983 | Dundee United FC | Aberdeen FC | Charles Nicholas (Celtic FC Glasgow) | 29 |
| 1983/1984 | Aberdeen FC | Aberdeen FC | Brian John McClair (Celtic FC Glasgow) | 23 |
| 1984/1985 | Aberdeen FC | Celtic FC Glasgow | Douglas Francis McDougall (Aberdeen FC) | 22 |
| 1985/1986 | Celtic FC Glasgow | Aberdeen FC | Alistair Murdoch McCoist (Rangers FC Glasgow) | 24 |
| 1986/1987 | Rangers FC Glasgow | St. Mirren FC Paisley | Brian John McClair (Celtic FC Glasgow) | 35 |
| 1987/1988 | Celtic FC Glasgow | Celtic FC Glasgow | Tommy Coyne (Dundee FC) | 33 |
| 1988/1989 | Rangers FC Glasgow | Celtic FC Glasgow | Mark Edward McGhee (Celtic FC Glasgow) Charles Nicholas (Aberdeen FC) | 16 |
| 1989/1990 | Rangers FC Glasgow | Aberdeen FC | John Grant Robertson (Heart of Midlothian FC Edinburgh) | 17 |
| 1990/1991 | Rangers FC Glasgow | Motherwell FC | Tommy Coyne (Celtic FC Glasgow) | 18 |
| 1991/1992 | Rangers FC Glasgow | Rangers FC Glasgow | Alistair Murdoch McCoist (Rangers FC Glasgow) | 34 |
| 1992/1993 | Rangers FC Glasgow | Rangers FC Glasgow | Alistair Murdoch McCoist (Rangers FC Glasgow) | 34 |
| 1993/1994 | Rangers FC Glasgow | Dundee United FC | Mark Wayne Hateley (ENG, Rangers FC Glasgow) | 22 |
| 1994/1995 | Rangers FC Glasgow | Celtic FC Glasgow | Tommy Coyne (Motherwell FC) | 16 |
| 1995/1996 | Rangers FC Glasgow | Rangers FC Glasgow | Petrus Ferdinandus Johannes van Hooijdonk (NED, Celtic FC Glasgow) | 26 |
| 1996/1997 | Rangers FC Glasgow | Kilmarnock FC | Jorge Paulo Cadete Santos Reis (POR, Celtic FC Glasgow) | 25 |
| 1997/1998 | Celtic FC Glasgow | Heart of Midlothian FC Edinburgh | Marco Negri (ITA, Rangers FC Glasgow) | 32 |
| 1998/1999 | Rangers FC Glasgow | Rangers FC Glasgow | Henrik Edward Larsson (SWE, Celtic FC Glasgow) | 29 |

| | | | |
|---|---|---|---|
| 1999/2000 | Rangers FC Glasgow | Rangers FC Glasgow | Mark Anthony Viduka (AUS, Celtic FC Glasgow) | 25 |
| 2000/2001 | Celtic FC Glasgow | Celtic FC Glasgow | Henrik Edward Larsson (SWE, Celtic FC Glasgow) | 35 |
| 2001/2002 | Celtic FC Glasgow | Rangers FC Glasgow | Henrik Edward Larsson (SWE, Celtic FC Glasgow) | 29 |
| 2002/2003 | Rangers FC Glasgow | Rangers FC Glasgow | Henrik Edward Larsson (SWE, Celtic FC Glasgow) | 28 |
| 2003/2004 | Celtic FC Glasgow | Celtic FC Glasgow | Henrik Edward Larsson (SWE, Celtic FC Glasgow) | 30 |
| 2004/2005 | Rangers FC Glasgow | Celtic FC Glasgow | John Hartson (WAL, Celtic FC Glasgow) | 25 |
| 2005/2006 | Celtic FC Glasgow | Heart of Midlothian FC Edinburgh | Kris Boyd (Kilmarnock FC / Rangers FC Glasgow) | 32 |
| 2006/2007 | Celtic FC Glasgow | Celtic FC Glasgow | Kris Boyd (Rangers FC Glasgow) | 20 |
| 2007/2008 | Celtic FC Glasgow | Rangers FC Glasgow | Scott Douglas McDonald (AUS, Celtic FC Glasgow) | 25 |
| 2008/2009 | Rangers FC Glasgow | Rangers FC Glasgow | Kris Boyd (Rangers FC Glasgow) | 27 |
| 2009/2010 | Rangers FC Glasgow | Dundee United FC | Kris Boyd (Rangers FC Glasgow) | 23 |
| 2010/2011 | Rangers FC Glasgow | Celtic FC Glasgow | Kenneth Miller (Rangers FC Glasgow) | 21 |
| 2011/2012 | Celtic FC Glasgow | Heart of Midlothian FC Edinburgh | Gary Hooper (ENG, Celtic FC Glasgow) | 24 |
| 2012/2013 | Celtic FC Glasgow | Celtic FC Glasgow | Michael Higdon (ENG, Motherwell FC) | 26 |
| 2013/2014 | Celtic FC Glasgow | St. Johnstone FC Perth | Kristian Arran Commons (Celtic FC Glasgow) | 27 |
| 2014/2015 | Celtic FC Glasgow | Inverness Caledonian Thistle FC | Adam Christopher Rooney (IRL, Aberdeen FC) | 18 |
| 2015/2016 | Celtic FC Glasgow | Hibernian FC Edinburgh | Leigh Griffiths (Celtic FC Glasgow) | 31 |
| 2016/2017 | Celtic FC Glasgow | Celtic FC Glasgow | Liam Boyce (NIR, Ross County FC Dingwall) | 23 |
| 2017/2018 | Celtic FC Glasgow | Celtic FC Glasgow | Kris Boyd (Kilmarnock FC) | 18 |
| 2018/2019 | Celtic FC Glasgow | Celtic FC Glasgow | Alfredo José Morelos Aviléz (COL, Rangers FC Glasgow) | 18 |
| 2019/2020 | Celtic FC Glasgow | Celtic FC Glasgow | Odsonne Édouard (FRA, Celtic FC Glasgow) | 22 |
| 2020/2021 | Rangers FC Glasgow | St. Johnstone FC Perth | Odsonne Édouard (FRA, Celtic FC Glasgow) | 18 |
| 2021/2022 | Celtic FC Glasgow | Rangers FC Glasgow | Georgios Giakoumakis (GRE, Celtic FC Glasgow) Regan Evans Charles-Cook (GRN, Ross County FC) | 13 |
| 2022/2023 | Celtic FC Glasgow | Celtic FC Glasgow | Kyogo Furuhashi (JPN, Celtic FC Glasgow) | 27 |

# NATIONAL CHAMPIONSHIP
## Scottish Premiership 2022/2023
(30.07.2022 – 28.05.2023)

## Results

**Round 1 [30-31.07.2022]**
Livingston FC - Rangers FC 1-2(1-0)
Kilmarnock FC - Dundee United 1-1(0-1)
Heart of Midlothian-Ross County FC 2-1(0-0)
St. Johnstone FC - Hibernian FC 0-1(0-0)
St. Mirren FC - Motherwell FC 0-1(0-1)
Celtic FC - Aberdeen FC 2-0(1-0)

**Round 2 [06-07.08.2022]**
Aberdeen FC - St. Mirren FC 4-1(3-0)
Rangers FC - Kilmarnock FC 2-0(0-0)
Motherwell FC - St. Johnstone FC 1-2(0-1)
Ross County FC - Celtic FC 1-3(0-0)
Hibernian FC - Heart of Midlothian 1-1(0-1)
Dundee United - Livingston FC 0-1(0-0)

**Round 3 [13-14.08.2022]**
Aberdeen FC - Motherwell FC 2-3(1-1)
Rangers FC - St. Johnstone FC 4-0(1-0)
Livingston FC - Hibernian FC 2-1(1-0)
St. Mirren FC - Ross County FC 1-0(0-0)
Kilmarnock FC - Celtic FC 0-5(0-3)
Heart of Midlothian - Dundee United 4-1(1-0)

**Round 4 [20-21.08.2022]**
Hibernian FC - Rangers FC 2-2(0-1)
Dundee United - St. Mirren FC 0-3(0-1)
Motherwell FC - Livingston FC 1-0(0-0)
Ross County FC - Kilmarnock FC 1-0(0-0)
St. Johnstone FC - Aberdeen FC 0-1(0-0)
Celtic FC - Heart of Midlothian 2-0(1-0)

**Round 5 [27-28.08.2022]**
Aberdeen FC - Livingston FC 5-0(1-0)
Kilmarnock FC - Motherwell FC 2-1(0-1)
Rangers FC - Ross County FC 4-0(2-0)
St. Mirren FC - Hibernian FC 1-0(1-0)
Dundee United - Celtic FC 0-9(0-4)
Heart of Midlothian - St. Johnstone 3-2(2-1)

**Round 6 [03.09.2022]**
Celtic FC - Rangers FC 4-0(3-0)
Hibernian FC - Kilmarnock FC 1-0(1-0)
Livingston FC - Heart of Midlothian 1-0(1-0)
Motherwell FC - Dundee United 0-0
Ross County FC - Aberdeen FC 1-1(0-0)
St. Johnstone FC - St. Mirren FC 3-0(1-0)

**Round 7 [04-05.10.2022]**
Ross County FC - Motherwell FC 0-5(0-1)
Kilmarnock FC - St. Johnstone FC 2-1(1-0)
Dundee U. - Hibernian FC 1-0(1-0) [11.10.22]
Aberdeen - Rangers FC 2-3(1-1) [20.12.22]
Celtic FC - Livingston FC 2-1(2-1) [21.12.22]
Heart of M. - St. Mirren 1-0(1-0) [13.01.23]

**Round 8 [17-18.09.2022]**
Rangers FC - Dundee United 2-1(1-0)
Hibernian FC - Aberdeen FC 3-1(1-1)
Livingston FC - Kilmarnock FC 1-0(1-0)
St. Johnstone FC - Ross County FC 0-0
St. Mirren FC - Celtic FC 2-0(1-0)
Motherwell FC - Heart of Midlothian 0-3(0-1)

**Round 9 [01.10.2022]**
Heart of Midlothian - Rangers FC 0-4(0-2)
Celtic FC - Motherwell FC 2-1(1-1)
Dundee United - St. Johnstone FC 1-2(0-2)
Aberdeen FC - Kilmarnock FC 4-1(3-1)
Ross County FC - Hibernian FC 0-2(0-0)
St. Mirren FC - Livingston FC 2-1(0-0)

**Round 10 [08-09.10.2022]**
St. Johnstone FC - Celtic FC 1-2(0-1)
Rangers FC - St. Mirren FC 4-0(2-0)
Hibernian FC - Motherwell FC 1-0(0-0)
Livingston FC - Ross County FC 0-1(0-0)
Dundee United - Aberdeen FC 4-0(2-0)
Kilmarnock FC - Heart of Midlothian 2-2(0-0)

**Round 11 [15-16.10.2022]**
Celtic FC - Hibernian FC 6-1(3-0)
Livingston FC - St. Johnstone FC 1-0(1-0)
Ross County FC - Dundee United 1-1(1-0)
St. Mirren FC - Kilmarnock FC 0-0
Motherwell FC - Rangers FC 1-2(0-0)
Aberdeen FC - Heart of Midlothian 2-0(0-0)

**Round 12 [21-22.10.2022]**
Hibernian FC - St. Johnstone FC 1-2(1-0)
Heart of Midlothian - Celtic FC 3-4(1-1)
Kilmarnock FC - Ross County FC 1-0(1-0)
Rangers FC - Livingston FC 1-1(0-1)
Motherwell FC - Aberdeen FC 1-2(0-1)
St. Mirren FC - Dundee United 2-1(1-0)

**Round 13 [29-30.10.2022]**
Dundee United - Motherwell FC 0-1(0-1)
Rangers FC - Aberdeen FC 4-1(2-1)
Hibernian FC - St. Mirren FC 3-0(1-0)
St. Johnstone FC - Kilmarnock FC 1-0(1-0)
Livingston FC - Celtic FC 0-3(0-1)
Ross County FC-Heart of Midlothian 1-2(1-2)

**Round 14 [04-06.11.2022]**
Aberdeen FC - Hibernian FC 4-1(1-0)
Kilmarnock FC - Livingston FC 2-3(2-1)
Celtic FC - Dundee United 4-2(2-1)
Ross County FC - St. Mirren FC 3-2(1-2)
St. Johnstone FC - Rangers FC 2-1(1-0)
Heart of Midlothian - Motherwell FC 3-2(1-0)

**Round 15 [08-09.11.2022]**
Hibernian FC - Ross County FC 0-2(0-1)
Livingston FC - Aberdeen FC 2-1(2-0)
Dundee United - Kilmarnock FC 4-0(3-0)
Rangers FC - Heart of Midlothian 1-0(0-0)
Motherwell FC - Celtic FC 1-2(0-1)
St. Mirren FC - St. Johnstone FC 2-2(1-1)

## Round 16 [12.11.2022]
St. Mirren FC - Rangers FC 1-1(0-0)
Celtic FC - Ross County FC 2-1(0-0)
Kilmarnock FC - Hibernian FC 1-0(0-0)
Heart of Midlothian - Livingston FC 1-1(0-0)
St. Johnstone FC - Motherwell FC 1-1(1-1)
Aberdeen FC - Dundee United 1-0(1-0)

## Round 17 [15-17.12.2022]
Rangers FC - Hibernian FC 3-2(1-2)
Aberdeen FC - Celtic FC 0-1(0-0)
Heart of Midlothian - Kilmarnock FC 3-1(2-0)
Ross County FC - St. Johnstone FC 1-2(1-0)
Motherwell - St. Mirren 2-1(2-1) [15.02.23]
Livingston - Dundee Unit. 1-1(1-0) [08.03.23]

## Round 18 [23-24.12.2022]
Ross County FC - Rangers FC 0-1(0-1)
Motherwell FC - Kilmarnock FC 2-2(1-0)
Celtic FC - St. Johnstone FC 4-1(3-0)
St. Mirren FC - Aberdeen FC 3-1(1-1)
Dundee United - Heart of Midlothian 2-2(1-1)
Hibernian FC - Livingston FC 4-0(3-0)

## Round 19 [28.12.2022]
Dundee United - Ross County FC 3-0(1-0)
Kilmarnock FC - Aberdeen FC 2-1(2-0)
Rangers FC - Motherwell FC 3-0(2-0)
Livingston FC - St. Mirren FC 1-1(0-0)
St. Johnstone FC-Heart of Midlothian 2-3(0-2)
Hibernian FC - Celtic FC 0-4(0-2)

## Round 20 [02.01.2023]
Rangers FC - Celtic FC 2-2(0-1)
Aberdeen FC - Ross County FC 0-0
Kilmarnock FC - St. Mirren FC 0-0
Heart of Midlothian - Hibernian FC 3-0(2-0)
Livingston FC - Motherwell FC 1-1(1-1)
St. Johnstone FC - Dundee United 0-1(0-0)

## Round 21 [07-08.01.2023]
Celtic FC - Kilmarnock FC 2-0(1-0)
Aberdeen FC - St. Johnstone FC 2-0(0-0)
Ross County FC - Livingston FC 0-2(0-0)
St. Mirren FC - Heart of Midlothian 1-1(1-0)
Motherwell FC - Hibernian FC 2-3(0-1)
Dundee United - Rangers FC 0-2(0-0)

## Round 22 [14-18.01.2023]
Hibernian FC - Dundee United 2-2(1-2)
Motherwell FC - Ross County FC 1-1(0-0)
St. Johnstone FC - Livingston FC 2-4(0-3)
Celtic FC - St. Mirren FC 4-0(2-0)
Heart of Midlothian - Aberdeen FC 5-0(4-0)
Kilmarnock FC - Rangers FC 2-3(1-1)

## Round 23 [28-29.01.2023]
Rangers FC - St. Johnstone FC 2-0(1-0)
Hibernian FC - Aberdeen FC 6-0(3-0)
Ross County FC - Kilmarnock FC 3-0(1-0)
St. Mirren FC - Motherwell FC 1-0(1-0)
Livingston FC - Heart of Midlothian 0-0
Dundee United - Celtic FC 0-2(0-0)

## Round 24 [31.01.-01.02.2023]
Ross County FC - Hibernian FC 1-1(0-1)
Celtic FC - Livingston FC 3-0(3-0)
Aberdeen FC - St. Mirren FC 1-3(0-0)
Kilmarnock FC - Dundee United 1-0(1-0)
Heart of Midlothian - Rangers FC 0-3(0-2)
Motherwell FC - St. Johnstone FC 0-2(0-1)

## Round 25 [04-05.02.2023]
Aberdeen FC - Motherwell FC 3-1(1-0)
Rangers FC - Ross County FC 2-1(1-0)
Heart of Midlothian - Dundee United 3-1(0-1)
Livingston FC - Kilmarnock FC 3-1(3-0)
St. Mirren FC - Hibernian FC 0-1(0-0)
St. Johnstone FC - Celtic FC 1-4(1-3)

## Round 26 [18-19.02.2023]
Celtic FC - Aberdeen FC 4-0(2-0)
Dundee United - St. Johnstone FC 1-2(0-1)
Hibernian FC - Kilmarnock FC 2-0(1-0)
Livingston FC - Rangers FC 0-3(0-1)
St. Mirren FC - Ross County FC 1-0(1-0)
Motherwell FC - Heart of Midlothian 2-0(1-0)

## Round 27 [25.02.2023]
Aberdeen FC - Livingston FC 1-0(1-0)
Kilmarnock FC - Motherwell FC 1-1(1-0)
Ross County FC - Dundee United 4-0(2-0)
St. Johnstone FC - St. Mirren FC 1-0(0-0)
Celtic-Heart of Midlothian 3-1(1-1) [08.03.23]
Hibernian - Rangers FC 1-4(1-2) [08.03.23]

## Round 28 [04-05.03.2023]
Rangers FC - Kilmarnock FC 3-1(3-0)
Heart of Midlothian - St. Johnstone 3-0(1-0)
Livingston FC - Hibernian FC 1-4(1-2)
Ross County FC - Motherwell FC 0-2(0-0)
Dundee United - Aberdeen FC 1-3(0-0)
St. Mirren FC - Celtic FC 1-5(1-0)

## Round 29 [18.03.2023]
Motherwell FC - Rangers FC 2-4(1-1)
Celtic FC - Hibernian FC 3-1(0-1)
Dundee United - St. Mirren FC 1-1(1-0)
Aberdeen FC - Heart of Midlothian 3-0(3-0)
Kilmarnock FC - St. Johnstone FC 1-1(1-0)
Livingston FC - Ross County FC 2-1(2-0)

## Round 30 [01-02.04.2023]
Kilmarnock FC - Heart of Midlothian 2-1(2-1)
Rangers FC - Dundee United 2-0(1-0)
Hibernian FC - Motherwell FC 1-3(0-1)
St. Johnstone FC - Aberdeen FC 0-1(0-1)
St. Mirren FC - Livingston FC 3-0(3-0)
Ross County FC - Celtic FC 0-2(0-1)

## Round 31 [08-09.04.2023]
Celtic FC - Rangers FC 3-2(1-1)
Aberdeen FC - Kilmarnock FC 2-0(1-0)
Heart of Midlothian - St. Mirren FC 0-2(0-0)
Motherwell FC - Livingston FC 3-0(3-0)
St. Johnstone FC - Ross County FC 0-2(0-1)
Dundee United - Hibernian FC 2-1(1-0)

## Round 32 [14-16.04.2023]
Ross County FC - Aberdeen FC 0-1(0-1)
Hibernian FC - Heart of Midlothian 1-0(0-0)
Rangers FC - St. Mirren FC 5-2(1-1)
Livingston FC - St. Johnstone FC 2-0(2-0)
Motherwell FC - Dundee United 1-2(1-0)
Kilmarnock FC - Celtic FC 1-4(1-4)

## Round 33 [22-23.04.2023]
Heart of Midlothian - Ross County 6-1(4-0)
Celtic FC - Motherwell FC 1-1(1-0)
Dundee United - Livingston FC 2-0(1-0)
St. Johnstone FC - Hibernian FC 1-1(1-1)
St. Mirren FC - Kilmarnock FC 0-2(0-2)
Aberdeen FC - Rangers FC 2-0(0-0)

## Final Standings

| | | | | | | | | |
|---|---|---|---|---|---|---|---|---|
| 1. | Celtic FC Glasgow | 33 | 30 | 2 | 1 | 103 - 25 | 92 |
| 2. | Rangers FC Glasgow | 33 | 25 | 4 | 4 | 81 - 34 | 79 |
| 3. | Aberdeen FC | 33 | 17 | 2 | 14 | 52 - 52 | 53 |
| 4. | Heart of Midlothian FC Edinburgh | 33 | 14 | 6 | 13 | 56 - 49 | 48 |
| 5. | Hibernian FC Edinburgh | 33 | 13 | 5 | 15 | 49 - 52 | 44 |
| 6. | St. Mirren FC Paisley | 33 | 12 | 8 | 13 | 38 - 49 | 44 |
| 7. | Livingston FC | 33 | 12 | 6 | 15 | 33 - 52 | 42 |
| 8. | Motherwell FC | 33 | 10 | 7 | 16 | 44 - 48 | 37 |
| 9. | St. Johnstone FC Perth | 33 | 9 | 6 | 18 | 34 - 54 | 33 |
| 10. | Dundee United FC | 33 | 8 | 7 | 18 | 36 - 58 | 31 |
| 11. | Kilmarnock FC | 33 | 8 | 7 | 18 | 29 - 58 | 31 |
| 12. | Ross County FC Dingwall | 33 | 7 | 6 | 20 | 28 - 52 | 27 |

Teams ranked 1-6 were qualified for the Championship Round, while teams ranked 7-12 were qualified for the Relegation Round.

**Round 34** [06.05.2023]
Motherwell FC - Kilmarnock FC 2-0(1-0)
Ross County FC - Livingston FC 2-0(1-0)
St. Johnstone FC - Dundee United 1-0(1-0)

**Round 35** [13.05.2023]
Dundee United - Ross County FC 1-3(1-1)
Kilmarnock FC - Livingston FC 2-0(0-0)
St. Johnstone FC - Motherwell FC 0-2(0-0)

**Round 36** [20.05.2023]
Kilmarnock FC - St. Johnstone FC 0-1(0-1)
Livingston FC - Dundee United 2-1(1-1)
Motherwell FC - Ross County FC 1-0(0-0)

**Round 37** [24.05.2023]
Dundee United - Kilmarnock FC 0-3(0-2)
Livingston FC - Motherwell FC 1-1(0-1)
Ross County FC - St. Johnstone FC 3-3(0-1)

**Round 38** [28.05.2023]
Kilmarnock FC - Ross County FC 3-1(1-0)
Motherwell FC - Dundee United 3-2(1-1)
St. Johnstone FC - Livingston FC 2-0(1-0)

### Final Standings

| | | Total | | | | | | Home | | | | Away | | |
|---|---|---|---|---|---|---|---|---|---|---|---|---|---|---|
| 7. Motherwell FC | 38 | 14 | 8 | 16 | 53 - 51 | 50 | 7 | 3 | 9 | 26 - 28 | 7 | 5 | 7 | 27 - 23 |
| 8. Livingston FC | 38 | 13 | 7 | 18 | 36 - 60 | 46 | 9 | 5 | 5 | 22 - 22 | 4 | 2 | 13 | 14 - 38 |
| 9. St. Johnstone FC Perth | 38 | 12 | 7 | 19 | 41 - 59 | 43 | 5 | 4 | 10 | 18 - 25 | 7 | 3 | 9 | 23 - 34 |
| 10. Kilmarnock FC | 38 | 11 | 7 | 20 | 37 - 62 | 40 | 9 | 5 | 5 | 26 - 26 | 2 | 2 | 15 | 11 - 36 |
| 11. Ross County FC Dingwall *(Relegation Play-offs)* | 38 | 9 | 7 | 22 | 37 - 60 | 34 | 5 | 4 | 10 | 22 - 30 | 4 | 3 | 12 | 15 - 30 |
| 12. Dundee United FC *(Relegated)* | 38 | 8 | 7 | 23 | 40 - 70 | 31 | 6 | 2 | 11 | 23 - 35 | 2 | 5 | 12 | 17 - 35 |

### Results

**Round 34** [06-07.05.2023]
Hibernian FC - St. Mirren FC 2-1(2-0)
Heart of Midlothian - Celtic FC 0-2(0-0)
Rangers FC - Aberdeen FC 1-0(0-0)

**Round 35** [13.05.2023]
Rangers FC - Celtic FC 3-0(2-0)
Aberdeen FC - Hibernian FC 0-0
St. Mirren FC - Heart of Midlothian 2-2(2-0)

**Round 36** [20-21.05.2023]
Heart of Midlothian - Aberdeen FC 2-1(1-1)
Celtic FC - St. Mirren FC 2-2(1-2)
Hibernian FC - Rangers FC 1-3(0-1)

**Round 37** [24.05.2023]
Aberdeen FC - St. Mirren FC 3-0(2-0)
Hibernian FC - Celtic FC 4-2(0-1)
Rangers FC - Heart of Midlothian 2-2(1-1)

**Round 38** [27.05.2023]
Celtic FC - Aberdeen FC 5-0(2-0)
Heart of Midlothian - Hibernian FC 1-1(1-1)
St. Mirren FC - Rangers FC 0-3(0-1)

### Final Standings

| | | Total | | | | | | Home | | | | Away | | |
|---|---|---|---|---|---|---|---|---|---|---|---|---|---|---|
| 1. **Celtic FC Glasgow** | 38 | 32 | 3 | 3 | 114 - 34 | 99 | 17 | 2 | 0 | 58 - 14 | 15 | 1 | 3 | 56 - 20 |
| 2. Rangers FC Glasgow | 38 | 29 | 5 | 4 | 93 - 37 | 92 | 16 | 3 | 0 | 50 - 13 | 13 | 2 | 4 | 43 - 24 |
| 3. Aberdeen FC | 38 | 18 | 3 | 17 | 56 - 60 | 57 | 13 | 2 | 4 | 41 - 14 | 5 | 1 | 13 | 15 - 46 |
| 4. Heart of Midlothian FC Edinburgh | 38 | 15 | 9 | 14 | 63 - 57 | 54 | 12 | 2 | 5 | 43 - 27 | 3 | 7 | 9 | 20 - 30 |
| 5. Hibernian FC Edinburgh | 38 | 15 | 7 | 16 | 57 - 59 | 52 | 10 | 3 | 6 | 36 - 27 | 5 | 4 | 10 | 21 - 32 |
| 6. St. Mirren FC Paisley | 38 | 12 | 10 | 16 | 43 - 61 | 46 | 9 | 5 | 5 | 23 - 21 | 3 | 5 | 11 | 20 - 40 |

| Top goalscorers: | |
|---|---|
| 27 **Kyogo Furuhashi (JPN)** | *Celtic FC Glasgow* |
| 25 Kevin van Veen (NED) | *Motherwell FC* |
| 24 Lawrence Shakland | *Heart of Midlothian FC Edinburgh* |

### Relegation Play-offs [01-04.06.2023]

Partick Thistle FC Glasgow - Ross County FC Dingwall         2-0(2-0)      1-3(1-3,1-3); 4-5 pen

Ross County FC Dingwall remains at first level for the 2023/2024 season.

### Fourth Round [21-24.01./31.01.2023]

| | | | | |
|---|---|---|---|---|
| Celtic FC Glasgow - Greenock Morton FC | 5-0(4-0) | Hamilton Academical FC-Ross County FC Dingwall | 0-0 aet; 5-3 pen |
| Kilmarnock FC - Dumbarton FC | 1-0(0-0) | St. Johnstone FC - Rangers FC Glasgow | 0-1(0-1) |
| Dundee United FC - University of Stirling FC | 3-0(1-0) | Hibernian FC Edinburgh - Heart of Midlothian FC | 0-3(0-1) |
| St. Mirren FC Paisley - Dundee FC | 0-0 aet; 3-0 pen | Darvel FC - Aberdeen FC | 1-0(1-0) |
| Partick Thistle FC Glasgow-Dunfermline Athletic FC | 1-1 aet; 4-2 pen | Elgin City FC - Drumchapel United FC | 2-1(1-1) |
| Arbroath FC - Motherwell FC | 0-2(0-1) | Linlithgow Rose FC - Raith Rovers FC Kirkcaldy | 0-2(0-0) |
| Alloa Athletic FC - Falkirk FC | 1-2(1-1) | Inverness Caledonian Thistle FC - Queen's Park FC | 3-0 awarded |
| Stenhousemuir FC - Livingston FC | 1-3(1-0) | Cove Rangers FC - Ayr United FC | 0-3(0-1) |

### 1/8-Finals [10-13.02.2023]

| | | | | |
|---|---|---|---|---|
| Hamilton Academical FC - Heart of Midlothian FC | 0-2(0-1) | Ayr United FC - Elgin City FC | 4-1(0-1,1-1) |
| Raith Rovers FC Kirkcaldy - Motherwell FC | 3-1(2-0) | Celtic FC Glasgow - St. Mirren FC Paisley | 5-1(1-0) |
| Livingston FC - Inverness Caledonian Thistle FC | 0-3(0-0) | Rangers FC Glasgow - Partick Thistle FC Glasgow | 3-2(0-1) |
| Dundee United FC - Kilmarnock FC | 0-1(0-0) | Darvel FC - Falkirk FC | 1-5(0-2) |

### Quarter-Finals [10-13.03.2023]

| | | | | |
|---|---|---|---|---|
| Inverness Caledonian Thistle FC - Kilmarnock FC | 2-1(1-1) | Rangers FC Glasgow - Raith Rovers FC Kirkcaldy | 3-0(1-0) |
| Heart of Midlothian FC Edinburgh - Celtic FC Glasgow | 0-3(0-2) | Falkirk FC - Ayr United FC | 2-1(0-1) |

### Semi-Finals [29-30.04.2023]

| | | | |
|---|---|---|---|
| Falkirk FC - Inverness Caledonian Thistle FC | 0-3(0-2) | Rangers FC Glasgow - Celtic FC Glasgow | 0-1(0-1) |

### Final

03.06.2023; Hampden Park, Glasgow; Referee: John Beaton; Attendance: 47,247
**Celtic FC Glasgow - Inverness Caledonian Thistle FC**     **3-1(1-0)**

**Celtic**: Charles Joseph John Hart, Alistair William Johnston, Tomoki Iwata, Carl Anders Theodor Starfelt, Greg John Taylor, Matthew Sean O'Riley (76.Sead Hakšabanović), Callum William McGregor (Cap), Reo Hatate (76.David Turnbull), João Pedro Neves Filipe „Jota" (90+2.James Forrest), Kyogo Furuhashi (59.Oh Hyun-gyu), Daizen Maeda (46.Liel Abada). Trainer: Angelos Postecoglou (Australia).

**Inverness**: Mark Ridgers, Wallace Duffy, Daniel Gerard Devine (75.Zak Delaney), Robbie Deas, Cameron Harper, Scott Allardice (81.Aaron Brian Doran Cogan), David Carson, Sean Welsh (Cap), Jay Henderson (68.Daniel MacKay), William Robert Mckay (75.Austin Samuels), Nathan Edward Shaw (81.Roddy MacGregor). Trainer: William Dodds.

**Goals:** 1-0 Kyogo Furuhashi (38), 2-0 Liel Abada (65), 2-1 William Robert Mckay (84), 3-1 João Pedro Neves Filipe „Jota" (90+1).

## THE CLUBS 2022/2023

Please note: appearances and goals are including statistics of both regular season and play-offs (Championship Round & Relegation Round).

### Aberdeen Football Club

| | | |
|---|---|---|
| **Founded**: | 14.04.1903 | |
| **Stadium**: | Pittodrie Stadium, Aberdeen (20,866) | |
| **Trainer**: | James Michael Goodwin (IRL) | 20.11.1981 |
| [29.01.2023] | Barry Gordon George Robson | 07.11.1978 |

| Goalkeepers: | DOB | M | (s) | G |
|---|---|---|---|---|
| Jay Gorter (NED) | 30.05.2000 | 4 | | |
| Joseph Peter Lewis (ENG) | 06.10.1987 | 3 | | |
| Kelle Willem Roos (NED) | 31.05.1992 | 31 | | |
| **Defenders:** | **DOB** | **M** | **(s)** | **G** |
| Hayden Coulson (ENG) | 17.06.1998 | 19 | (9) | |
| Angus MacDonald (ENG) | 15.10.1992 | 15 | | |
| Jack MacKenzie | 04.07.2000 | 10 | (8) | |
| Jack Milne | 10.02.2003 | | (1) | |
| Matthew William Pollock (ENG) | 28.09.2001 | 15 | | 2 |
| Jayden De'Chante Richardson (ENG) | 04.09.2000 | 16 | (3) | |
| Liam Scales (IRL) | 08.08.1998 | 30 | (1) | 1 |
| Anthony Kelvin Stewart (ENG) | 18.09.1992 | 21 | | 1 |
| **Midfielders:** | **DOB** | **M** | **(s)** | **G** |
| Connor Barron | 29.08.2002 | 11 | (6) | 1 |
| Leighton Owen Clarkson (ENG) | 19.10.2001 | 32 | (2) | 5 |
| Johnathan Hayes (IRL) | 09.07.1987 | 24 | (6) | 1 |

| | | | | |
|---|---|---|---|---|
| Ross McCrorie | 18.03.1998 | 33 | | 2 |
| Patrik Myslovič (SVK) | 28.05.2001 | | (4) | |
| Dante Polvara (USA) | 21.06.2000 | 1 | (2) | |
| Ylber Ramadani (ALB) | 12.04.1996 | 37 | | 1 |
| Graeme Garry Shinnie | 04.08.1991 | 13 | | 2 |
| **Forwards:** | **DOB** | **M** | **(s)** | **G** |
| Alfie Bavidge | 11.04.2006 | | (5) | |
| Vicente Besuijen (NED) | 10.04.2001 | 9 | (9) | 3 |
| Luis Henrique Barros Lopes „Duk" (POR) | 16.02.2000 | 29 | (8) | 16 |
| Ryan Duncan | 18.01.2004 | 8 | (15) | 1 |
| Matthew Kennedy (NIR) | 01.11.1994 | 15 | (6) | 2 |
| Dilan Kumar Markanday (ENG) | 20.08.2001 | | (3) | |
| Bojan Miovski (MKD) | 24.06.1999 | 37 | | 16 |
| Shayden Jermaine Morris (ENG) | 30.03.2002 | | (13) | |
| Christian Ramírez (USA) | 04.04.1991 | 1 | (8) | |
| Callum Roberts (ENG) | 14.04.1997 | | (3) | |
| Marley Joseph Watkins (WAL) | 17.10.1990 | 4 | (22) | 1 |

## Celtic Football Club Glasgow

**Founded**: 06.11.1887
**Stadium**: Celtic Park, Glasgow (60,411)
**Trainer**: Angelos Postecoglou (AUS)  27.08.1965

| Goalkeepers: | DOB | M | (s) | G |
|---|---|---|---|---|
| Scott Bain | 22.11.1991 | 1 | | |
| Charles Joseph John Hart (ENG) | 19.04.1987 | 37 | | |
| **Defenders:** | **DOB** | **M** | **(s)** | **G** |
| Oliver Abildgaard Nielsen (DEN) | 10.06.1996 | | (6) | |
| Alexandro Ezequiel Bernabéi (ARG) | 24.09.2000 | 9 | (6) | 1 |
| Cameron Carter-Vickers (USA) | 31.12.1997 | 29 | | |
| Moritz Jenz (GER) | 30.04.1999 | 10 | (1) | 2 |
| Alistair William Johnston (CAN) | 08.10.1998 | 14 | | 1 |
| Josip Juranović (CRO) | 16.08.1995 | 9 | (1) | 1 |
| Yuki Kobayashi (JPN) | 18.07.2000 | 5 | | |
| Anthony Ralston | 16.11.1998 | 14 | (2) | |
| Carl Anders Theodor Starfelt (SWE) | 01.06.1995 | 26 | (2) | 3 |
| Greg John Taylor | 05.11.1997 | 28 | (3) | 3 |
| Stephen Welsh | 19.01.2000 | 4 | | 1 |
| **Midfielders:** | **DOB** | **M** | **(s)** | **G** |
| Reo Hatate (JPN) | 21.11.1997 | 29 | (3) | 6 |
| Tomoki Iwata (JPN) | 07.04.1997 | 6 | (7) | |
| James McCarthy (IRL) | 12.11.1990 | | (2) | |
| Callum William McGregor | 14.06.1993 | 31 | | 4 |
| Aaron Frank Mooy (AUS) | 15.09.1990 | 13 | (16) | 4 |
| Matthew Sean O'Riley (ENG) | 21.11.2000 | 32 | (6) | 3 |
| Ben Summers | 16.06.2004 | | (2) | |
| David Turnbull | 10.07.1999 | 6 | (22) | 4 |
| Rocco Vata (IRL) | 18.04.2005 | | (4) | |
| **Forwards:** | **DOB** | **M** | **(s)** | **G** |
| Liel Abada (ISR) | 03.10.2001 | 13 | (21) | 10 |
| James Forrest | 07.07.1991 | 5 | (11) | 4 |
| Kyogo Furuhashi (JPN) | 20.01.1995 | 31 | (5) | 27 |
| Georgios Giakoumakis (GRE) | 09.12.1994 | 4 | (15) | 6 |
| Sead Hakšabanović (MNE) | 04.05.1999 | 8 | (18) | 5 |
| João Pedro Neves Filipe „Jota" (POR) | 30.03.1999 | 26 | (7) | 11 |
| Daizen Maeda (JPN) | 20.10.1997 | 25 | (10) | 8 |
| Oh Hyun-gyu (KOR) | 12.04.2001 | 3 | (13) | 6 |

## Dundee United Football Club

**Founded**: 24.05.1909
**Stadium**: Tannadice Park, Dundee (14,223)
**Trainer**: John James Ross  05.06.1976
[30.08.2022]  Liam Fox  02.02.1984
[01.03.2023]  James Michael Goodwin (IRL)  20.11.1981

| Goalkeepers: | DOB | M | (s) | G |
|---|---|---|---|---|
| Mark Romano Birighitti (AUS) | 17.04.1991 | 26 | | |
| Carljohan Daniel Viktor Eriksson (FIN) | 25.04.1995 | 9 | | |
| Jack Newman | 12.02.2002 | 3 | (1) | |
| **Defenders:** | **DOB** | **M** | **(s)** | **G** |
| Loick Denis Henry Ayina (FRA) | 20.04.2003 | 12 | | |
| Aziz Eraltay Behich (AUS) | 16.12.1990 | 31 | | 3 |
| Ryan Christopher Edwards (ENG) | 07.10.1993 | 29 | (3) | |
| Kieran Freeman | 20.03.2000 | 22 | (2) | 1 |
| Ross Graham | 20.02.2001 | 12 | (3) | |
| Scott McMann | 09.07.1996 | 28 | (2) | |
| Charlie Mulgrew | 06.03.1986 | 18 | (1) | 1 |
| Liam Smith | 10.04.1996 | 27 | (1) | 1 |
| **Midfielders:** | **DOB** | **M** | **(s)** | **G** |
| Mathew Anim Cudjoe (GHA) | 11.11.2003 | 2 | (10) | |
| Arnaud Djoum (BEL) | 02.05.1989 | 8 | (8) | |
| Ian Andrew Harkes (USA) | 30.03.1995 | 25 | (5) | 2 |
| Dylan James Christopher Levitt (WAL) | 17.11.2000 | 24 | (3) | 5 |
| Jamie McGrath (IRL) | 30.09.1996 | 29 | (3) | 8 |
| Archie Alexander Meekison | 04.05.2002 | 1 | (6) | |
| Peter Ian Pawlett | 03.02.1991 | 5 | (7) | |
| **Forwards:** | **DOB** | **M** | **(s)** | **G** |
| Sadat Anaku (UGA) | 09.12.2000 | 2 | (12) | |
| Nicholas Alexander McCormack Clark | 03.06.1991 | | (3) | |
| Steven Kenneth Fletcher | 26.03.1987 | 30 | (3) | 9 |
| Kai Fotheringham | 18.04.2003 | 3 | (8) | |
| Rory Iain MacLeod | 03.02.2006 | 2 | (13) | |
| Glenn Middleton | 01.01.2000 | 21 | (8) | 2 |
| Ilmari Niskanen (FIN) | 27.10.1997 | 8 | (12) | 1 |
| Craig Sibbald | 18.05.1995 | 29 | (6) | 1 |
| Miller Thomson | 20.07.2004 | | (3) | |
| Anthony Paul Watt | 29.12.1993 | 12 | (5) | 4 |

## Heart of Midlothian Football Club Edinburgh

**Founded**: 1874
**Stadium**: Tynecastle Park, Edinburgh (19,852)
**Trainer**: Robert Neilson  19.06.1980
[10.04.2023]  Steven John Naismith  14.09.1986

| Goalkeepers: | DOB | M | (s) | G |
|---|---|---|---|---|
| Alexander Clark | 26.06.1992 | 20 | (1) | |
| Craig Anthony Gordon | 31.12.1982 | 16 | | |
| Ross Stewart | 10.04.1995 | 2 | (1) | |
| **Defenders:** | **DOB** | **M** | **(s)** | **G** |
| Nathaniel Caleb Atkinson (AUS) | 13.06.1999 | 11 | (7) | 1 |
| Alexander William Cochrane (ENG) | 21.04.2000 | 30 | (4) | 2 |
| Craig Halkett | 29.05.1995 | 5 | (1) | |
| James Clayton Hill (ENG) | 10.01.2002 | 13 | (1) | |
| Stephen Kingsley | 23.07.1994 | 16 | (5) | |
| Lewis Neilson | 15.05.2003 | 4 | (6) | |
| Kye Francis Rowles (AUS) | 24.06.1998 | 27 | (2) | 1 |
| Toby Peter Sibbick (ENG) | 23.05.1999 | 27 | (5) | |
| Michael Smith (NIR) | 04.09.1988 | 23 | (5) | 2 |
| **Midfielders:** | **DOB** | **M** | **(s)** | **G** |
| Cameron Peter Devlin (AUS) | 07.06.1998 | 26 | (4) | 1 |
| Alan Forrest | 09.09.1996 | 16 | (19) | 4 |
| Jorge Edward Grant (ENG) | 19.12.1994 | 10 | (18) | 2 |
| Andy Halliday | 11.10.1991 | 19 | (9) | 3 |
| Peter Haring (AUT) | 02.06.1993 | 10 | (6) | |
| Orestis Kiomourtzoglou (GER) | 07.05.1998 | 11 | (12) | |
| Gary Mackay-Steven | 31.08.1990 | 3 | (1) | |
| Connor Smith | 01.02.2002 | 1 | (6) | |
| **Forwards:** | **DOB** | **M** | **(s)** | **G** |
| Liam Boyce (NIR) | 08.04.1991 | 4 | (1) | 1 |
| Joshua Lloyd Ginnelly (ENG) | 24.03.1997 | 26 | (4) | 12 |
| Euan Henderson | 29.06.2000 | | (3) | |
| Stephen Peter Humphrys (ENG) | 15.09.1997 | 7 | (12) | 3 |
| Garang Mawien Kuol (AUS) | 15.09.2004 | 1 | (7) | 1 |
| Barrie McKay | 30.12.1994 | 29 | (8) | 4 |
| Yutaro Oda (JPN) | 12.08.2001 | 7 | (5) | 1 |
| Lawrence Shankland | 10.08.1995 | 33 | (4) | 24 |
| Robert Snodgrass | 07.09.1987 | 21 | (2) | 1 |

## Hibernian Football Club Edinburgh

**Founded:** 06.08.1875
**Stadium:** Easter Road Stadium, Edinburgh (20,421)
**Trainer:** Lee David Johnson (ENG)　　07.06.1981

| Goalkeepers: | DOB | M | (s) | G |
|---|---|---|---|---|
| David James Marshall | 05.03.1985 | 38 | | |
| **Defenders:** | **DOB** | **M** | **(s)** | **G** |
| Rocky Bushiri (BEL) | 30.11.1999 | 13 | (2) | |
| Marijan Čabraja (CRO) | 25.02.1997 | 18 | (7) | |
| Chris Cadden | 19.09.1996 | 34 | (3) | 1 |
| Allan Delferriere (BEL) | 03.03.2002 | | (1) | |
| Michael Devlin | 03.10.1993 | | (1) | |
| Conrad Jonathan Egan-Riley (ENG) | 02.01.2003 | 13 | (1) | |
| William Thomas Fish (ENG) | 17.02.2003 | 18 | (3) | 3 |
| Paul Thomas Hanlon | 20.01.1990 | 33 | (1) | 1 |
| Oscar MacIntyre | 23.07.2004 | | (2) | |
| David Kyle McClelland (NIR) | 10.02.2002 | | (1) | |
| Lewis Miller (AUS) | 24.08.2000 | 3 | (9) | |
| Ryan Thomas Porteous | 25.03.1999 | 21 | | 3 |
| Lewis Stevenson | 05.01.1988 | 20 | (8) | 1 |
| **Midfielders:** | **DOB** | **M** | **(s)** | **G** |
| Josh Campbell | 06.05.2000 | 28 | (8) | 8 |
| Jake Billy Doyle-Hayes (IRL) | 30.12.1998 | 9 | (8) | |
| Ewan Henderson | 27.03.2000 | 11 | (19) | 1 |
| James Alexander Jeggo (AUS) | 12.02.1992 | 16 | | |
| Nohan Kenneh (ENG) | 10.01.2003 | 13 | (2) | 1 |
| Kyle Magennis | 26.08.1998 | 7 | (6) | 2 |
| Demetri Kareem Mitchell (ENG) | 11.01.1997 | 1 | (2) | |
| Joseph Peter Newell (ENG) | 15.03.1993 | 33 | (1) | 1 |
| **Forwards:** | **DOB** | **M** | **(s)** | **G** |
| Momodou Bojang (GAM) | 19.06.2001 | | (5) | |
| Martin Callie Boyle (AUS) | 25.04.1993 | 10 | (2) | 5 |
| Christian Rhys Doidge (WAL) | 25.08.1992 | 1 | (4) | |
| Matthew Timothy Hoppe (USA) | 13.03.2001 | 3 | (6) | 1 |
| *Jair* Veiga Vieira *Tavares* (POR) | 13.02.2001 | 2 | (6) | |
| Mykola Kukharevych (UKR) | 01.07.2001 | 10 | (5) | 5 |
| Aiden John McGeady (IRL) | 04.04.1986 | 6 | (3) | |
| Harry McKirdy (ENG) | 29.03.1997 | 5 | (17) | |
| Elias Melkersen (NOR) | 31.12.2002 | 5 | (8) | |
| Kevin Michael Nisbet | 08.03.1997 | 16 | (3) | 12 |
| Josh O'Connor | 16.06.2004 | | (2) | |
| Élie Youan (FRA) | 07.04.1999 | 31 | (5) | 9 |

## Kilmarnock Football Club

**Founded:** 05.01.1869
**Stadium:** The BBSP Stadium Rugby Park, Kilmarnock (15,003)
**Trainer:** Derek John McInnes　　05.07.1971

| Goalkeepers: | DOB | M | (s) | G |
|---|---|---|---|---|
| Zachary Hemming (ENG) | 07.03.2000 | 10 | | |
| Samuel Colin Walker (ENG) | 02.10.1991 | 28 | | |
| **Defenders:** | **DOB** | **M** | **(s)** | **G** |
| Luke Chambers (ENG) | 24.06.2004 | 13 | (1) | |
| Benjamin Joshua Chrisene (ENG) | 12.01.2004 | 11 | (2) | |
| Abraham Jeriel Richard Dorsett (ENG) | 04.05.2002 | 10 | (1) | 1 |
| Lewis Mayo | 19.03.2000 | 32 | (2) | |
| Jack Sanders (ENG) | 18.03.1999 | | (4) | |
| Christopher Martin Thomas Stokes (ENG) | 08.03.1991 | 10 | (5) | 2 |
| Ashton John Taylor (WAL) | 02.09.1990 | 29 | (3) | 4 |
| Joseph Harris Wright (WAL) | 26.02.1995 | 31 | (3) | 5 |
| **Midfielders:** | **DOB** | **M** | **(s)** | **G** |
| Ryan Alebiosu (ENG) | 17.12.2001 | 14 | (9) | |
| Blair Alston | 23.03.1992 | 6 | (10) | |
| Liam Francis Peadar Donnelly (NIR) | 07.03.1996 | 17 | (5) | 2 |
| Bradley Joseph Lyons (NIR) | 26.05.1997 | 5 | (14) | 1 |
| Kerr McInroy | 31.08.2000 | 7 | (5) | |
| Fraser Murray | 07.05.1999 | 4 | (15) | |
| Liam Polworth | 12.10.1994 | 19 | (7) | 1 |
| Alan Thomas Daniel Power (IRL) | 23.01.1988 | 25 | (7) | |
| David Watson | 12.02.2005 | 8 | (2) | |
| **Forwards:** | **DOB** | **M** | **(s)** | **G** |
| Daniel Armstrong | 11.10.1997 | 31 | (6) | 9 |
| Innes Cameron | 22.08.2000 | 5 | (11) | 1 |
| Christian Rhys Doidge (WAL) | 25.08.1992 | 21 | (6) | 3 |
| Jordan Lewis Jones (NIR) | 24.10.1994 | '14 | (8) | |
| Kyle Joseph George Lafferty (NIR) | 16.09.1987 | 8 | (4) | 1 |
| Rory McKenzie | 07.10.1993 | 30 | (6) | |
| Scott Robinson | 12.03.1992 | 6 | (10) | 2 |
| Oliver Shaw | 12.03.1998 | 7 | (5) | |
| Ayodeji Sotona (IRL) | 07.12.2002 | | (2) | |
| Kyle Thomas Vassell (NIR) | 07.02.1993 | 14 | | 4 |
| Bobby Wales | 23.06.2005 | 2 | (8) | |
| Steven Warnock | 12.06.2003 | | (1) | |
| Calum Waters | 10.03.1996 | 1 | (1) | |

## Livingston Football Club

**Founded:** 1943
**Stadium:** Almondvale Stadium, Livingston (9,713)
**Trainer:** David Paul Martindale　　13.07.1974

| Goalkeepers: | DOB | M | (s) | G |
|---|---|---|---|---|
| Shamal Tyrell George (ENG) | 06.01.1998 | 32 | | |
| Jack Hamilton | 22.03.1994 | 2 | (1) | |
| Ivan Konovalov (RUS) | 18.08.1994 | 4 | | |
| **Defenders:** | **DOB** | **M** | **(s)** | **G** |
| Morgan Marc Boyes (WAL) | 22.04.2001 | 15 | (7) | 1 |
| Jamie Brandon | 05.02.1998 | 1 | (7) | |
| Phillip Čančar (AUS) | 11.05.2001 | 1 | (2) | |
| Luiyi Ramón de Lucas Pérez (DOM) | 31.08.1994 | 8 | (2) | |
| Nicholas Devlin | 17.10.1993 | 38 | | 2 |
| Jack Joseph Fitzwater (ENG) | 23.09.1997 | 26 | (2) | 1 |
| Sean Kelly | 01.11.1993 | 29 | (1) | 2 |
| Jackson Longridge | 12.04.1995 | 3 | (6) | |
| Stephen Ayomide Oluwagbenga Obileye (ENG) | 02.09.1994 | 22 | (3) | 1 |
| Thomas Peter Wilson Parkes (ENG) | 15.01.1992 | 2 | (2) | |
| James Penrice | 22.12.1998 | 16 | (13) | 3 |
| **Midfielders:** | **DOB** | **M** | **(s)** | **G** |
| Dylan Bahamboula (FRA) | 22.05.1995 | 9 | (11) | 1 |
| Romeni Scott Bitsindou (BEL) | 11.05.1996 | | (1) | |
| Jason Derek Holt | 19.02.1993 | 26 | (9) | |
| Stephen Kelly | 13.04.2000 | 24 | (7) | 5 |
| Cristian Alexis Montaño Castillo (COL) | 11.12.1991 | 25 | (6) | 4 |
| Joshua Kearney Mullin | 23.09.1992 | | (1) | |
| Stéphane Richi Oméonga (BEL) | 27.03.1996 | 18 | (12) | |
| Scott Pittman | 09.07.1992 | 27 | (6) | |
| Andrew Shinnie | 17.07.1989 | 21 | (12) | 1 |
| **Forwards:** | **DOB** | **M** | **(s)** | **G** |
| Bruce Anderson | 23.09.1998 | 21 | (9) | 6 |
| Steven Bradley | 17.03.2002 | 12 | (4) | 1 |
| Kurtis Owen Guthrie (ENG) | 21.04.1993 | 6 | (10) | |
| Esmaël Ruti Tavares Cruz da Silva Gonçalves (GNB) | 25.06.1991 | 1 | (7) | |
| Joel Jonathan Nouble (ENG) | 19.01.1996 | 29 | (1) | 7 |

## Motherwell Football Club

| | Founded: | 17.05.1886 | | |
|---|---|---|---|---|
| | Stadium: | Fir Park, Motherwell (13,677) | | |
| | Trainer: | Steven Hammell | | 18.02.1982 |
| | [11.02.2023] | Stuart Kettlewell | | 04.06.1984 |

| Goalkeepers: | DOB | M | (s) | G | | | DOB | M | (s) | G |
|---|---|---|---|---|---|---|---|---|---|---|
| Liam Patrick Kelly | 23.01.1996 | 38 | | | Lennon Miller | 25.08.2006 | 1 | (3) | |
| **Defenders:** | **DOB** | **M** | **(s)** | **G** | Joshua Francis Morris (ENG) | 30.09.1991 | 3 | (6) | |
| Shane Blaney (IRL) | 20.01.1999 | 4 | (4) | | Harrison Theodore Paton (CAN) | 23.05.1998 | 2 | (5) | |
| Jake Carroll (IRL) | 11.08.1991 | 1 | | | Callum Slattery (ENG) | 08.02.1999 | 23 | (6) | 4 |
| Dan Patrick Casey (IRL) | 29.10.1997 | 12 | | | Kian Speirs | 22.05.2004 | | (1) | |
| Walter James Byrne Furlong (IRL) | 07.06.2002 | 15 | (1) | | Ross Tierney (IRL) | 06.03.2001 | 4 | (14) | 2 |
| Sondre Solholm Johansen (NOR) | 07.07.1995 | 18 | (1) | 1 | **Forwards:** | **DOB** | **M** | **(s)** | **G** |
| Max Johnston | 26.12.2003 | 13 | (4) | 3 | Rolando James Aarons (JAM) | 16.11.1995 | | (2) | |
| Ricki Lamie | 20.06.1993 | 22 | (2) | | Jack Aitchison | 05.03.2000 | 2 | (8) | |
| Paul McGinn | 22.10.1990 | 36 | | | Oliver Crankshaw (ENG) | 12.08.1998 | 2 | (2) | |
| Bevis Mugabi (UGA) | 01.05.1995 | 4 | (9) | 1 | Joseph Isiah Efford (USA) | 29.08.1996 | 4 | (5) | 1 |
| Stephen Gerard O'Donnell | 11.05.1992 | 14 | (13) | | Robert Mahon (IRL) | 06.06.2003 | | (1) | |
| Matthew Luke Penney (ENG) | 11.02.1998 | 16 | | | Mikael Mandron (FRA) | 11.10.1994 | 8 | (2) | 1 |
| **Midfielders:** | **DOB** | **M** | **(s)** | **G** | Stuart McKinstry | 18.09.2002 | 10 | (11) | 4 |
| Calum James Butcher (ENG) | 26.02.1991 | 13 | | | Louis Elliott Moult (ENG) | 14.05.1992 | 1 | (6) | 1 |
| Dean Cornelius | 11.04.2001 | 17 | (15) | | Jonathan Chiedozie Obika (ENG) | 12.09.1990 | 5 | (4) | 1 |
| Riku Danzaki (JPN) | 31.05.2000 | 1 | (2) | | Luca Ross | 11.08.2006 | | (1) | |
| Sean Richard Goss (ENG) | 01.10.1995 | 38 | | 1 | Connor Shields | 29.07.1997 | 15 | (4) | |
| Barry Maguire | 27.04.1998 | 4 | (6) | | Blair Spittal | 19.12.1995 | 36 | | 6 |
| | | | | | Kevin van Veen (NED) | 01.06.1991 | 36 | (2) | 25 |

## Rangers Football Club Glasgow

| | Founded: | 1872 | | |
|---|---|---|---|---|
| | Stadium: | Ibrox Park Stadium, Glasgow (50,987) | | |
| | Trainer: | Giovanni Christiaan van Bronckhorst (NED) | | 05.02.1975 |
| | [28.11.2022] | Michael Beale (ENG) | | 04.09.1980 |

| Goalkeepers: | DOB | M | (s) | G | | | DOB | M | (s) | G |
|---|---|---|---|---|---|---|---|---|---|---|
| Robbie McCrorie | 18.03.1998 | 4 | | | Alexander Lowry | 23.06.2003 | 1 | (4) | |
| Allan James McGregor | 31.01.1982 | 24 | | | John David Lundstram (ENG) | 18.02.1994 | 32 | (5) | 5 |
| Jonathan Peter McLaughlin | 09.09.1987 | 10 | | | Charlie Liam McCann (IRL) | 24.04.2002 | 1 | | |
| **Defenders:** | **DOB** | **M** | **(s)** | **G** | Nicolas Thierry Raskin (BEL) | 23.02.2001 | 11 | (1) | |
| Borna Barišić (CRO) | 10.11.1992 | 27 | (3) | 1 | Bailey Rice | 04.10.2006 | | (1) | |
| Benjamin Keith Davies (ENG) | 11.08.1995 | 25 | (2) | | James Hoban Sands (USA) | 06.07.2000 | 10 | (7) | |
| Adam Devine | 25.03.2003 | 3 | (3) | | **Forwards:** | **DOB** | **M** | **(s)** | **G** |
| Connor Lambert Goldson (ENG) | 18.12.1992 | 25 | | 2 | Antonio Čolak (CRO) | 17.09.1993 | 18 | (7) | 14 |
| Leon Thomson King | 14.01.2004 | 9 | (6) | | Ryan Kent (ENG) | 11.11.1996 | 28 | (1) | 3 |
| John Souttar | 25.09.1996 | 8 | (4) | 1 | Thomas Morris Lawrence (WAL) | 13.01.1994 | 4 | (1) | 2 |
| James Henry Tavernier (ENG) | 31.10.1991 | 38 | | 16 | Zakariya Lovelace (ENG) | 23.01.2006 | | (1) | |
| Rıdvan Yılmaz (TUR) | 21.05.2001 | 8 | (1) | | Arron Lyall | 27.09.2003 | | (1) | |
| **Midfielders:** | **DOB** | **M** | **(s)** | **G** | Rabbi Matondo (WAL) | 09.09.2000 | 9 | (10) | |
| Scott Nathaniel Arfield (CAN) | 01.11.1988 | 7 | (24) | 5 | Ross McCausland (NIR) | 12.05.2003 | | (1) | |
| Todd Owen Cantwell (ENG) | 27.02.1998 | 15 | (1) | 6 | Alfredo José Morelos Aviléz (COL) | 21.06.1996 | 15 | (17) | 11 |
| Steven Davis (NIR) | 01.01.1985 | 3 | (5) | 1 | Kemar Roofe (ENG) | 06.01.1993 | | (3) | 1 |
| Ianis Hagi (ROU) | 22.10.1998 | 3 | (5) | 1 | Fashion Sakala (ZAM) | 14.03.1997 | 22 | (7) | 12 |
| Ryan Jack | 27.02.1992 | 19 | (7) | 1 | Malik Leon Tillman (USA) | 28.05.2002 | 22 | (6) | 10 |
| Glen Adjei Kamara (FIN) | 28.10.1995 | 12 | (10) | 1 | Robbie Ure | 26.02.2004 | | (2) | |
| | | | | | Scott Wright | 08.08.1997 | 5 | (18) | |

## Ross County Football Club Dingwall

| | Founded: | 1929 | | |
|---|---|---|---|---|
| | Stadium: | Victoria Park, Dingwall (6,541) | | |
| | Trainer: | Malcolm George Mackay | | 19.02.1972 |

| Goalkeepers: | DOB | M | (s) | G | | | DOB | M | (s) | G |
|---|---|---|---|---|---|---|---|---|---|---|
| Ross Laidlaw | 12.07.1992 | 38 | | | Nohan Kenneh (ENG) | 10.01.2003 | 13 | (3) | |
| **Defenders:** | **DOB** | **M** | **(s)** | **G** | Victor Loturi (CAN) | 21.05.2001 | 20 | (7) | |
| Jack Baldwin (ENG) | 30.06.1993 | 27 | (2) | 1 | Benjamin Alan Paton (CAN) | 05.05.2000 | 3 | (4) | |
| George Harmon (ENG) | 08.12.2000 | 28 | (2) | 2 | Jordan Roy Tillson (ENG) | 05.03.1993 | 19 | (9) | 1 |
| Alex Iacovitti | 02.09.1997 | 36 | | 3 | **Forwards:** | **DOB** | **M** | **(s)** | **G** |
| Callum Charles Johnson (ENG) | 23.10.1996 | 14 | (4) | | William Akio (SSD) | 23.07.1998 | 2 | (10) | 1 |
| Ben Purrington (ENG) | 20.05.1996 | 11 | | | Eamonn Brophy | 10.03.1996 | 8 | | 3 |
| Connor Steven Randall (ENG) | 21.10.1995 | 23 | (1) | | Owura Nsiah Edwards (ENG) | 10.04.2001 | 15 | (14) | 3 |
| Dylan Smith | 21.06.2006 | 5 | (8) | | Jordi Hiwula-Mayifuila (ENG) | 21.09.1994 | 10 | (11) | 1 |
| Keith Watson | 14.11.1989 | 19 | (9) | | Simon Murray | 15.03.1992 | 5 | (9) | 2 |
| **Midfielders:** | **DOB** | **M** | **(s)** | **G** | Kazeem Aderemi Olaigbe (BEL) | 02.01.2003 | 7 | (12) | |
| Ross Callachan | 04.09.1993 | 17 | (7) | 1 | Alexander Kinloch Samuel (WAL) | 20.09.1995 | 3 | (7) | 1 |
| David Cancola (AUT) | 23.10.1996 | 22 | (8) | 2 | Dominic James Samuel (ENG) | 01.04.1994 | 3 | (8) | |
| Yan Dhanda (ENG) | 14.12.1998 | 23 | (7) | 5 | Joshua Samuel Sims (ENG) | 28.03.1997 | 10 | (10) | |
| Gwion Dafydd Rhys Edwards (WAL) | 01.03.1993 | 4 | (1) | | Josh Stones (ENG) | 12.11.2003 | | (6) | |
| | | | | | Jordan White | 04.02.1992 | 33 | (5) | 11 |

## St. Johnstone Football Club Perth

| | | |
|---|---|---|
| Founded: | 1884 | |
| Stadium: | McDiarmid Park, Perth (10,696) | |
| Trainer: | Callum Iain Davidson | 25.06.1976 |
| [16.04.2023] | Steven George MacLean | 23.08.1982 |

| Goalkeepers: | DOB | M | (s) | G |
|---|---|---|---|---|
| Remi Luke Matthews (ENG) | 10.02.1994 | 34 | | |
| Elliot Charles Parish (ENG) | 20.05.1990 | 2 | | |
| Ross Sinclair | 07.05.2001 | 2 | | |
| **Defenders:** | **DOB** | **M** | **(s)** | **G** |
| James Dominic Brown (ENG) | 12.01.1998 | 23 | (3) | 1 |
| Andrew MacLaren Considine | 01.04.1987 | 32 | | 1 |
| Tony Gallacher | 23.07.1999 | 2 | (3) | |
| Liam Gordon | 26.01.1996 | 29 | (3) | 2 |
| Ryan James McGowan (AUS) | 15.08.1989 | 28 | | 1 |
| Alexander Paul Mitchell (ENG) | 07.10.2001 | 25 | (4) | 1 |
| Adam Montgomery | 18.07.2002 | 26 | (2) | |
| **Midfielders:** | **DOB** | **M** | **(s)** | **G** |
| Cameron Ballantyne II | 22.04.2000 | 3 | | |
| Graham Carey (IRL) | 20.05.1989 | 24 | (6) | 3 |
| Alistair Crawford | 30.07.1991 | 2 | (14) | 2 |
| Murray Davidson | 07.03.1988 | 1 | (3) | |
| Melker Hallberg (SWE) | 20.10.1995 | 28 | (2) | 2 |
| Maksym Kucheriaviy (UKR) | 09.05.2002 | 1 | (3) | |
| Cameron MacPherson | 29.12.1998 | 17 | (6) | |
| Daniel Shaquille Jabari Phillips (TRI) | 18.01.2001 | 16 | (7) | |
| David Wotherspoon (CAN) | 16.01.1990 | 7 | (15) | |
| Drey Jermaine Wright (ENG) | 30.04.1995 | 37 | (1) | 7 |
| **Forwards:** | **DOB** | **M** | **(s)** | **G** |
| Thelonius Bair (CAN) | 27.08.1999 | 6 | (21) | 1 |
| Nicholas Clark | 03.06.1991 | 19 | (1) | 4 |
| Christopher Kane | 05.09.1994 | | (2) | 1 |
| Stevie May | 03.11.1992 | 30 | (7) | 9 |
| Connor McLennan | 05.10.1999 | 7 | (19) | 1 |
| James Murphy | 28.08.1989 | 15 | (9) | 3 |
| Michael Francis O'Halloran | 06.01.1991 | | (4) | |
| Zak Rudden | 06.02.2000 | 2 | (10) | 1 |

## St. Mirren Football Club Paisley

| | | |
|---|---|---|
| Founded: | 1877 | |
| Stadium: | St. Mirren Park, St. Mirren (7,937) | |
| Trainer: | Stephen Robinson (NIR) | 10.12.1974 |

| Goalkeepers: | DOB | M | (s) | G |
|---|---|---|---|---|
| Trevor Carson (NIR) | 05.03.1988 | 37 | | |
| Peter Urminský (SVK) | 24.05.1999 | 1 | | |
| **Defenders:** | **DOB** | **M** | **(s)** | **G** |
| Charles Dunne (IRL) | 13.02.1993 | 31 | (2) | |
| Marcus Fraser | 23.06.1994 | 33 | (1) | |
| Declan Gallagher | 13.02.1991 | 21 | (6) | 2 |
| Joseph James Gordan Shaughnessy (IRL) | 06.07.1992 | 14 | (8) | 1 |
| Thierry Small (ENG) | 01.08.2004 | 7 | (7) | |
| Ryan Strain (AUS) | 02.04.1997 | 35 | (1) | 4 |
| Richard Neil Peter Tait | 02.12.1989 | 7 | (5) | 1 |
| Scott Tanser (ENG) | 23.10.1994 | 23 | (7) | |
| Richard Taylor (ENG) | 02.10.2000 | 7 | (4) | |
| **Midfielders:** | **DOB** | **M** | **(s)** | **G** |
| Keanu Kole Baccus (AUS) | 07.06.1998 | 30 | (3) | 2 |
| Caolan Boyd-Munce (NIR) | 26.01.2000 | 1 | (2) | |
| Ethan Erhahon | 09.05.2001 | 20 | | |
| Ryan Flynn | 04.09.1988 | 3 | (17) | |
| Alexandros Gogić (CYP) | 13.04.1994 | 23 | (7) | 2 |
| Jay Henderson | 07.03.2002 | | (3) | |
| Mark O'Hara | 12.12.1995 | 34 | (1) | 10 |
| Dylan Reid | 01.03.2005 | | (2) | |
| **Forwards:** | **DOB** | **M** | **(s)** | **G** |
| Jonah Ananias Paul Ayunga (KEN) | 24.05.1997 | 16 | (3) | 3 |
| Eamonn Brophy | 10.03.1996 | 1 | (11) | |
| Alex Greive (NZL) | 13.05.1999 | 12 | (16) | 4 |
| Lewis Jamieson | 17.04.2002 | 1 | (6) | |
| Greg Kiltie | 18.01.1997 | 18 | (17) | 2 |
| Curtis Main (ENG) | 20.06.1992 | 36 | (1) | 9 |
| Kieran Offord | 28.03.2004 | | (9) | |
| Olutoyosi Tajudeen Olusanya (ENG) | 14.10.1997 | | (1) | |
| Fraser Taylor | 20.02.2003 | | (3) | |
| Anthony Paul Watt | 29.12.1993 | 7 | (3) | 1 |

## SECOND LEVEL
### Scottish Championship 2022/2023

| | | | | | | | | |
|---|---|---|---|---|---|---|---|---|
| 1. | Dundee FC (*Promoted*) | 36 | 17 | 12 | 7 | 66 - 40 | 63 |
| 2. | Ayr United FC | 36 | 16 | 10 | 10 | 61 - 43 | 58 |
| 3. | Queen's Park FC Glasgow | 36 | 17 | 7 | 12 | 63 - 52 | 58 |
| 4. | Partick Thistle FC Glasgow | 36 | 16 | 9 | 11 | 65 - 45 | 57 |
| 5. | Greenock Morton FC | 36 | 15 | 12 | 9 | 53 - 43 | 57 |
| 6. | Inverness Caledonian Thistle FC | 36 | 15 | 10 | 11 | 52 - 47 | 55 |
| 7. | Raith Rovers FC Kirkcaldy | 36 | 11 | 10 | 15 | 46 - 49 | 43 |
| 8. | Arbroath FC | 36 | 6 | 16 | 14 | 29 - 47 | 34 |
| 9. | Hamilton Academical FC (*Relegation Play-offs*) | 36 | 7 | 10 | 19 | 31 - 63 | 31 |
| 10. | Cove Rangers FC (*Relegated*) | 36 | 7 | 10 | 19 | 38 - 75 | 31 |

Please note: runners-up were qualified for the Premiership Play-offs Semi-Finals, while teams ranked 3-4 were qualified for the Premiership Play-offs Quarter-Finals.

### Premiership Play-offs

| Quarter-Finals [09-12.05.2023] | Partick Thistle FC Glasgow - Queen's Park FC Glasgow | 4-3(2-1) | 4-0(3-0) |
|---|---|---|---|
| Semi-Finals [19-26.05.2023] | Partick Thistle FC Glasgow - Ayr United FC | 3-0(1-0) | 5-0(2-0) |

Partick Thistle FC Glasgow were qualified for the Promotion Play-offs.

### Relegation Play-offs (2nd / 3rd Level)

| Semi-Finals [09-13.05.2023] | Airdrieonians FC - Falkirk FC | 6-2(5-0) | 1-0(1-0) |
|---|---|---|---|
| | Alloa Athletic FC - Hamilton Academical FC | 1-0(1-0) | 2-5(2-4) |
| Final [17-20.05.2023] | Airdrieonians FC - Hamilton Academical FC | 1-0(0-0) | 1-2 aet; 6-5 pen |

Airdrieonians FC promoted for the Scottish Championship 2023/2024.

## INTERNATIONAL MATCHES
### (16.07.2022 – 15.07.2023)

| | | | | |
|---|---|---|---|---|
| 21.09.2022 | Glasgow | *Scotland - Ukraine* | 3-0(0-0) | (UNL) |
| 24.09.2022 | Glasgow | *Scotland - Republic of Ireland* | 2-1(1-1) | (UNL) |
| 27.09.2022 | Kraków | *Ukraine - Scotland* | 0-0 | (UNL) |
| 16.11.2022 | Diyarbakır | *Turkey - Scotland* | 2-1(1-0) | (F) |
| 25.03.2023 | Glasgow | *Scotland - Cyprus* | 3-0(1-0) | (ECQ) |
| 28.03.2023 | Glasgow | *Scotland - Spain* | 2-0(1-0) | (ECQ) |
| 17.06.2023 | Oslo | *Norway - Scotland* | 1-2(0-0) | (ECQ) |
| 20.06.2023 | Glasgow | *Scotland - Georgia* | 2-0(1-0) | (ECQ) |

**21.09.2022    SCOTLAND - UKRAINE    3-0(0-0)    3rd UEFA Nations League B, Group 1**
Hampden Park, Glasgow; Referee: Maurizio Mariani (Italy); Attendance: 42,846
**SCO:** Craig Sinclair Gordon, Nathan Kenneth Patterson (26.Aaron Buchanan Hickey), Jack William Hendry, Scott Fraser McKenna, Kieran Tierney (85.Greg John Taylor), Callum William McGregor, Scott Francis McTominay, John McGinn (Cap), Stuart Armstrong (76.Ryan Fraser), Ryan Christie (85.Kenneth McLean), Ché Zach Everton Fred Adams (76.Lyndon John Dykes). Trainer: Stephen Clarke.
**Goals:** John McGinn (70), Lyndon John Dykes (80, 87).

**24.09.2022    SCOTLAND - REPUBLIC OF IRELAND    2-1(1-1)    3rd UEFA Nations League B, Group 1**
Hampden Park, Glasgow; Referee: Sandro Schärer (Switzerland); Attendance: 48,853
**SCO:** Craig Sinclair Gordon, Aaron Buchanan Hickey (58.Anthony Ralston), Jack William Hendry, Scott Fraser McKenna, Kieran Tierney (42.Greg John Taylor), Callum William McGregor, Scott Francis McTominay, Stuart Armstrong (58.Ryan Fraser), John McGinn (Cap), Ryan Christie (85.Kenneth McLean), Lyndon John Dykes (85.Ché Zach Everton Fred Adams). Trainer: Stephen Clarke.
**Goals:** Jack William Hendry (50), Ryan Christie (82 penalty).

**27.09.2022    UKRAINE - SCOTLAND    0-0    3rd UEFA Nations League B, Group 1**
Stadion Cracovii im. Józefa Piłsudskiego, Kraków (Poland); Referee: Anastasios Sidiropoulos (Greece); Attendance: 13,534
**SCO:** Craig Sinclair Gordon, Aaron Buchanan Hickey (90+1.Anthony Ralston), Ryan Thomas Porteous, Jack William Hendry, Greg John Taylor (71.Stephen Kingsley), Callum William McGregor, Ryan Jack (72.Stuart Armstrong), Kenneth McLean, John McGinn (Cap), Ryan Fraser (72.Ryan Christie), Ché Zach Everton Fred Adams (79.Lyndon John Dykes). Trainer: Stephen Clarke.

**16.11.2022    TURKEY - SCOTLAND    2-1(1-0)    Friendly International**
Diyarbakır Stadyumu, Diyarbakır; Referee: Visar Kastrati (Kosovo); Attendance: 28 348
**SCO:** Craig Sinclair Gordon, Kieran Tierney, Grant Campbell Hanley (46.Scott Fraser McKenna), Jack William Hendry, Ryan Fraser (46.Calvin William Ramsay), Scott Francis McTominay (79.Lewis Ferguson), Billy Clifford Gilmour (67.Ryan Jack), Andrew Henry Robertson (Cap), John McGinn, Stuart Armstrong (67.Ryan Christie), Lyndon John Dykes (79.Jacob Samuel Brown). Trainer: Stephen Clarke.
**Goal:** John McGinn (62).

**25.03.2023    SCOTLAND - CYPRUS    3-0(1-0)    17th EC. Qualifiers**
Hampden Park, Glasgow; Referee: Duje Strukan (Croatia); Attendance: 48,195
**SCO:** Angus Fraser James Gunn, Kieran Tierney, Grant Campbell Hanley, Ryan Thomas Porteous, Aaron Buchanan Hickey (79.Nathan Kenneth Patterson), Callum William McGregor, Ryan Jack (67.Ryan Christie), Andrew Henry Robertson (Cap), John McGinn, Stuart Armstrong (67.Scott Francis McTominay), Ché Zach Everton Fred Adams (57.Lyndon John Dykes). Trainer: Stephen Clarke.
**Goals:** John McGinn (21), Scott Francis McTominay (87, 90+3).

**28.03.2023    SCOTLAND - SPAIN    2-0(1-0)    17th EC. Qualifiers**
Hampden Park, Glasgow;Referee: Sandro Schärer (Switzerland) [46.replaced by the fourth official Lukas Fähndrich (Switzerland)]; Attendance: 47,976
**SCO:** Angus Fraser James Gunn, Kieran Tierney (75.Liam David Ian Cooper), Grant Campbell Hanley, Ryan Thomas Porteous, Aaron Buchanan Hickey (82.Nathan Kenneth Patterson), Callum William McGregor, Scott Francis McTominay, Andrew Henry Robertson (Cap), John McGinn (83.Lewis Ferguson), Ryan Christie (74.Kenneth McLean), Lyndon John Dykes (89.Lawrence Shankland). Trainer: Stephen Clarke.
**Goals:** Scott Francis McTominay (7, 51).

**17.06.2023    NORWAY - SCOTLAND    1-2(0-0)    17th EC. Qualifiers**
Ullevaal Stadion, Oslo; Referee: Matej Jug (Slovenia); Attendance: 25,791
**SCO:** Angus Fraser James Gunn, Kieran Tierney (65.Liam David Ian Cooper), Jack William Hendry, Ryan Thomas Porteous (79.Kenneth McLean), Aaron Buchanan Hickey, Callum William McGregor (78.Billy Clifford Gilmour), Scott Francis McTominay, Andrew Henry Robertson (Cap), John McGinn (90+1.Dominic John Hyam), Ryan Christie (78.Stuart Armstrong), Lyndon John Dykes. Trainer: Stephen Clarke.
**Goals:** Lyndon John Dykes (87), Kenneth McLean (89).

**20.06.2023    SCOTLAND - GEORGIA    2-0(1-0)    17th EC. Qualifiers**
Hampden Park, Glasgow; Referee: István Vad (Hungary); Attendance: 50,062
**SCO:** Angus Fraser James Gunn, Kieran Tierney (78.John Francis Souttar), Jack William Hendry, Ryan Thomas Porteous, Aaron Buchanan Hickey, Callum William McGregor (78.Ryan Jack), Scott Francis McTominay, Andrew Henry Robertson (Cap), John McGinn (90+2.Ryan Christie), Billy Clifford Gilmour (86.Kenneth McLean), Lyndon John Dykes (78.Kevin Michael Nisbet). Trainer: Stephen Clarke.
**Goals:** Callum William McGregor (6), Scott Francis McTominay (47).

## NATIONAL TEAM PLAYERS
### (16.07.2022 – 15.07.2023)

| Name | DOB | Caps | Goals | Club | |
|------|-----|------|-------|------|---|

### Goalkeepers

| Name | DOB | Caps | Goals | | Club |
|------|-----|------|-------|---|------|
| Craig Sinclair GORDON | 31.12.1982 | 74 | 0 | 2022: | *Heart of Midlothian FC Edinburgh* |
| Angus Fraser James GUNN | 02.01.1966 | 4 | 0 | 2023: | *Norwich City FC (ENG)* |

### Defenders

| Name | DOB | Caps | Goals | | Club |
|------|-----|------|-------|---|------|
| Liam David Ian COOPER | 30.08.1991 | 16 | 0 | 2023: | *Leeds United FC (ENG)* |
| Grant Campbell HANLEY | 20.11.1991 | 48 | 2 | 2022/2023: | *Norwich City FC (ENG)* |
| Jack William HENDRY | 07.05.1995 | 23 | 3 | 2022: | *US Cremonese (ITA)* |
| | | | | 26.01.2023-> | *Club Brugge KV (BEL)* |
| Aaron Buchanan HICKEY | 10.06.2002 | 11 | 0 | 2022/2023: | *Brentford FC London (ENG)* |
| Dominic John HYAM | 20.12.1995 | 1 | 0 | 2023: | *Blackburn Rovers FC (ENG)* |
| Stephen KINGSLEY | 23.07.1994 | 1 | 0 | 2022: | *Heart of Midlothian FC Edinburgh* |
| Scott Fraser McKENNA | 12.11.1996 | 29 | 1 | 2022: | *Nottingham Forest FC (ENG)* |
| Nathan Kenneth PATTERSON | 16.10.2001 | 13 | 1 | 2022/2023: | *Everton FC Liverpool (ENG)* |
| Ryan Thomas PORTEOUS | 25.03.1999 | 5 | 0 | 2022: | *Hibernian FC Edinburgh* |
| | | | | 27.01.2023-> | *Watford FC (ENG)* |
| Anthony RALSTON | 16.11.1998 | 6 | 1 | 2022: | *Celtic FC Glasgow* |
| Calvin William RAMSAY | 31.07.2003 | 1 | 0 | 2022: | *Liverpool FC (ENG)* |
| Andrew Henry ROBERTSON | 11.03.1994 | 64 | 3 | 2022/2023: | *Liverpool FC (ENG)* |
| John Francis SOUTTAR | 25.09.1996 | 7 | 1 | 2023: | *Rangers FC Glasgow* |
| Greg John TAYLOR | 05.11.1997 | 10 | 0 | 2022: | *Celtic FC Glasgow* |
| Kieran TIERNEY | 05.06.1997 | 39 | 1 | 2022/2023: | *Arsenal FC London (ENG)* |

### Midfielders

| Name | DOB | Caps | Goals | | Club |
|------|-----|------|-------|---|------|
| Stuart ARMSTRONG | 30.03.1992 | 42 | 4 | 2022/2023: | *Southampton FC (ENG)* |
| Lewis FERGUSON | 24.08.1999 | 6 | 0 | 2022/2023: | *Bologna FC 1909 (ITA)* |
| Billy Clifford GILMOUR | 11.06.2001 | 18 | 0 | 2022/2023: | *Brighton & Hove Albion FC (ENG)* |
| Ryan JACK | 27.02.1992 | 16 | 0 | 2022/2023: | *Rangers FC Glasgow* |
| John McGINN | 18.10.1994 | 56 | 16 | 2022/2023: | *Aston Villa FC Birmingham (ENG)* |
| Callum William McGREGOR | 14.06.1993 | 53 | 3 | 2022/2023: | *Celtic FC Glasgow* |
| Kenneth McLEAN | 08.01.1992 | 31 | 2 | 2022/2023: | *Norwich City FC (ENG)* |
| Scott Francis McTOMINAY | 08.12.1996 | 41 | 6 | 2022/2023: | *Manchester United FC (ENG)* |

### Forwards

| Name | DOB | Caps | Goals | | Club |
|------|-----|------|-------|---|------|
| Ché Zach Everton Fred ADAMS | 13.07.1996 | 23 | 5 | 2022/2023: | *Southampton FC (ENG)* |
| Jacob Samuel BROWN | 10.04.1998 | 6 | 0 | 2022: | *Stoke City FC (ENG)* |
| Ryan CHRISTIE | 22.02.1995 | 39 | 5 | 2022/2023: | *AFC Bournemouth (ENG)* |
| Lyndon John DYKES | 07.10.1995 | 30 | 9 | 2022/2023: | *Queens Park Rangers FC London (ENG)* |
| Ryan FRASER | 24.02.1994 | 26 | 4 | 2022: | *Newcastle United FC (ENG)* |
| Kevin Michael NISBET | 08.03.1997 | 11 | 1 | 2023: | *Millwall FC London (ENG)* |
| Lawrence SHANKLAND | 10.08.1995 | 5 | 0 | 2023: | *Heart of Midlothian FC Edinburgh* |

### Trainer

| Name | DOB | |
|------|-----|---|
| Stephen "Steve" CLARKE [from 20.05.2019] | 29.08.1963 | 45 M; 23 W; 10 D; 12 L; 66-49 |

# SERBIA

## The Country:
Република Србија (Republic of Serbia)
Capital: Beograd
Surface: 77,474 km²
Inhabitants: 6,647,003 [2022]
Time: UTC+1

## The FA:
Fudbalski savez Srbije
Terazije 35, CP 263, 11000 Beograd
Tel: +381 11 3233 447
Founded: 1919
Member of FIFA since: 1921
Member of UEFA since: 1954
Website: www.fss.rs

## NATIONAL TEAM RECORDS

### RECORDS
| | | |
|---|---|---|
| **First international match:** | 28.08.1920, Antwerpen: | Czechoslovakia – Yugoslavia 7-0 |
| **Most international caps:** | Branislav Ivanović | - 105 caps (2005-2018) |
| **Most international goals:** | Aleksandar Mitrović | - 52 goals / 81 caps (since 2013) |

### UEFA EUROPEAN CHAMPIONSHIP*
| | |
|---|---|
| 1960 | Final Tournament (Runners-up) |
| 1964 | Qualifiers |
| 1968 | Final Tournament (Runners-up) |
| 1972 | Qualifiers |
| 1976 | Final Tournament (4th Place) |
| 1980 | Qualifiers |
| 1984 | Final Tournament (Group Stage) |
| 1988 | Qualifiers |
| 1992 | *Qualified / Suspended* |
| 1996 | *Suspended* |
| 2000 | Final Tournament (Quarter-Finals) |
| 2004 | Qualifiers |
| 2008 | Qualifiers |
| 2012 | Qualifiers |
| 2016 | Qualifiers |
| 2020 | Qualifiers |

### FIFA WORLD CUP*
| | |
|---|---|
| 1930 | Final Tournament (4th Place) |
| 1934 | Qualifiers |
| 1938 | Qualifiers |
| 1950 | Final Tournament (Group Stage) |
| 1954 | Final Tournament (Quarter-Finals) |
| 1958 | Final Tournament (Quarter-Finals) |
| 1962 | Final Tournament (4th Place) |
| 1966 | Qualifiers |
| 1970 | Qualifiers |
| 1974 | Final Tournament (2nd Round) |
| 1978 | Qualifiers |
| 1982 | Final Tournament (Group Stage) |
| 1986 | Qualifiers |
| 1990 | Final Tournament (Quarter-Finals) |
| 1994 | *Suspended* |
| 1998 | Final Tournament (2nd Round of 16) |
| 2002 | Qualifiers |
| 2006 | Final Tournament (Group Stage) |
| 2010 | Final Tournament (Group Stage) |
| 2014 | Qualifiers |
| 2018 | Final Tournament (Group Stage) |
| 2022 | Final Tournament (Group Stage) |

### OLYMPIC TOURNAMENTS*
| | |
|---|---|
| 1908 | - |
| 1912 | - |
| 1920 | Round 1 |
| 1924 | Qualifiers |
| 1928 | 1/8 - Finals |
| 1936 | Did not enter |
| 1948 | Runners-up |
| 1952 | Runners-up |
| 1956 | Runners-up |
| 1960 | **Winners** |
| 1964 | Quarter-Finals |
| 1968 | Did not enter |
| 1972 | Qualifiers |
| 1976 | Qualifiers |
| 1980 | 4th Place |
| 1984 | 3rd Place |
| 1988 | Group Stage |
| 1992 | Qualifiers |
| 1996 | *Suspended* |
| 2000 | Qualifiers |
| 2004 | Group Stage |
| 2008 | Group Stage |
| 2012 | Qualifiers |
| 2016 | Qualifiers |
| 2020 | Qualifiers |

*as Yugoslavia (1930-2002), Serbia and Montenegro (2002-2006).*

### UEFA NATIONS LEAGUE
| | |
|---|---|
| 2018/2019 | League C (Group Stage -> promoted to League B) |
| 2020/2021 | League B (Group Stage) |
| 2022/2023 | League B (Group Stage -> promoted to League A) |

## SERBIAN CLUB HONOURS IN EUROPEAN CLUB COMPETITIONS:

| European Champion Clubs.Cup (1956-1992) / UEFA Champions League (1993-2023) | | |
|---|---|---|
| FK Crvena Zvezda Beograd | 1 | 1990/1991 |

| Fairs Cup (1858-1971) / UEFA Cup (1972-2009) / UEFA Europa League (2010-2023) |
|---|
| None |

| UEFA Europa Conference League (2021-2023) |
|---|
| None |

| UEFA Super Cup (1972-2022) |
|---|
| None |

| *European Cup Winners' Cup 1961-1999** |
|---|
| None |

*defunct competition*

# NATIONAL COMPETITIONS
## TABLE OF HONOURS

### Kingdom of Yugoslavia (1923–1940)

| | CHAMPIONS | CUP WINNERS | BEST GOALSCORERS | |
|---|---|---|---|---|
| 1923 | HŠK Građanski Zagreb | HAŠK Zagreb | Dragan Jovanović (SK Jugoslavija Beograd) | 4 |
| 1924 | SK Jugoslavija Beograd | Zagreb XI | Dragan Jovanović (SK Jugoslavija Beograd) | 6 |
| 1925 | SK Jugoslavija Beograd | Zagreb XI | Dragan Jovanović (SK Jugoslavija Beograd) | 4 |
| 1926 | HŠK Građanski Zagreb | Zagreb XI | Dušan Petković (SK Jugoslavija Beograd) | 4 |
| 1927 | NK Hajduk Split | Beograd XI | Kuzman Sotirović (BSK Beograd) | 6 |
| 1928 | HŠK Građanski Zagreb | *No competition* | Ljubo Benčić (NK Hajduk Split) | 8 |
| 1929 | NK Hajduk Split | *No competition* | Đorđe Vujadinović (BSK Beograd) | 10 |
| 1930 | HŠK Concordia Zagreb | *No competition* | Blagoje Marjanović (BSK Beograd) | 10 |
| 1930/1931 | BSK Beograd | *No competition* | Đorđe Vujadinović (BSK Beograd) | 12 |
| 1931/1932 | HŠK Concordia Zagreb | *No competition* | Svetislav Valjarević (HŠK Concordia Zagreb) | 10 |
| 1932/1933 | BSK Beograd | *No competition* | Vladimir Kragić (NK Hajduk Split) | 21 |
| 1933/1934 | *No competition* | BSK Beograd | - | |
| 1934/1935 | BSK Beograd | *No competition* | Leo Lemešić (NK Hajduk Split) | 18 |
| 1935/1936 | BSK Beograd | SK Jugoslavija | Blagoje Marjanović (BSK Beograd) | 5 |
| 1936/1937 | HŠK Građanski Zagreb | *No competition* | Blagoje Marjanović (BSK Beograd) | 21 |
| 1937/1938 | HAŠK Zagreb | *No competition* | August Lešnik (HŠK Građanski Zagreb) | 17 |
| 1938/1939 | BSK Beograd | *No competition* | August Lešnik (HŠK Građanski Zagreb) | 22 |
| 1939/1940 | HŠK Građanski Zagreb | HŠK Građanski Zagreb | Svetislav Glišović (BSK Beograd) | 10 |

### SFR Yugoslavia (1945–1992)

| | CHAMPIONS | CUP WINNERS | BEST GOALSCORERS | |
|---|---|---|---|---|
| 1945 | S.R. Serbia | *No competition* | Stjepan Bobek (JNA) | 8 |
| 1946/1947 | FK Partizan Beograd | FK Partizan Beograd | Franjo Wölfl (NK Dinamo Zagreb) | 28 |
| 1947/1948 | NK Dinamo Zagreb | FK Crvena Zvezda Beograd | Franjo Wölfl (NK Dinamo Zagreb) | 22 |
| 1948/1949 | FK Partizan Beograd | FK Crvena Zvezda Beograd | Frane Matošić (NK Hajduk Split) | 17 |
| 1950 | NK Hajduk Split | FK Crvena Zvezda Beograd | Marko Valok (FK Partizan Beograd) | 17 |
| 1951 | FK Crvena Zvezda Beograd | NK Dinamo Zagreb | Kosta Tomašević (FK Crvena Zvezda Beograd) | 16 |
| 1952 | NK Hajduk Split | FK Partizan Beograd | Stanoje Jocić (BSK Beograd) | 13 |
| 1952/1953 | FK Crvena Zvezda Beograd | BSK Beograd | Todor Živanović (FK Crvena Zvezda Beograd) | 17 |
| 1953/1954 | NK Dinamo Zagreb | FK Partizan Beograd | Stjepan Bobek (FK Partizan Beograd) | 21 |
| 1954/1955 | NK Hajduk Split | BSK Beograd | Predrag Marković (BSK Beograd) Kosta Tomašević (FK Spartak Subotica) Bernard Vukas (NK Hajduk Split) | 20 |
| 1955/1956 | FK Crvena Zvezda Beograd | *No competition* | Muhamed Mujić (FK Velež Mostar) Tihomir Ognjanov (FK Spartak Subotica) Todor Veselinović (FK Vojvodina Novi Sad) | 21 |
| 1956/1957 | FK Crvena Zvezda Beograd | FK Partizan Beograd | Todor Veselinović (FK Vojvodina Novi Sad) | 28 |
| 1957/1958 | NK Dinamo Zagreb | FK Crvena Zvezda Beograd | Todor Veselinović (FK Vojvodina Novi Sad) | 19 |
| 1958/1959 | FK Crvena Zvezda Beograd | FK Crvena Zvezda Beograd | Bora Kostić (FK Crvena Zvezda Beograd) | 25 |
| 1959/1960 | FK Crvena Zvezda Beograd | NK Dinamo Zagreb | Bora Kostić (FK Crvena Zvezda Beograd) | 19 |
| 1960/1961 | FK Partizan Beograd | FK Vardar Skoplje | Zoran Prljinčević (FK Radnički Beograd) Todor Veselinović (FK Vojvodina Novi Sad) | 16 |
| 1961/1962 | FK Partizan Beograd | OFK Beograd | Dražan Jerković (NK Dinamo Zagreb) | 16 |
| 1962/1963 | FK Partizan Beograd | NK Dinamo Zagreb | Mišo Smajlović (FK Željezničar Sarajevo) | 18 |
| 1963/1964 | FK Crvena Zvezda Beograd | FK Crvena Zvezda Beograd | Asim Ferhatović (FK Sarajevo) | 19 |
| 1964/1965 | FK Partizan Beograd | NK Dinamo Zagreb | Zlatko Dračić (NK Zagreb) | 23 |
| 1965/1966 | FK Vojvodina Novi Sad | OFK Beograd | Petar Nadoveza (NK Hajduk Split) | 21 |
| 1966/1967 | FK Sarajevo | NK Hajduk Split | Mustafa Hasanagić (FK Partizan Beograd) | 18 |
| 1967/1968 | FK Crvena Zvezda Beograd | FK Crvena Zvezda Beograd | Slobodan Santrač (OFK Beograd) | 22 |
| 1968/1969 | FK Crvena Zvezda Beograd | NK Dinamo Zagreb | Vojin Lazarević (FK Crvena Zvezda Beograd) | 22 |
| 1969/1970 | FK Crvena Zvezda Beograd | FK Crvena Zvezda Beograd | Slobodan Santrač (OFK Beograd) Dušan Bajević (FK Velež Mostar) | 20 |
| 1970/1971 | NK Hajduk Split | FK Crvena Zvezda Beograd | Petar Nadoveza (NK Hajduk Split) Božo Janković (FK Željezničar Sarajevo) | 20 |
| 1971/1972 | FK Željezničar Sarajevo | NK Hajduk Split | Slobodan Santrač (OFK Beograd) | 33 |
| 1972/1973 | FK Crvena Zvezda Beograd | NK Hajduk Split | Slobodan Santrač (OFK Beograd) Vojin Lazarević (FK Crvena Zvezda Beograd) | 25 |
| 1973/1974 | NK Hajduk Split | NK Hajduk Split | Danilo Popivoda (Olimpija Ljubljana) | 17 |
| 1974/1975 | NK Hajduk Split | NK Hajduk Split | Dušan Savić (FK Crvena Zvezda Beograd) Boško Đorđević (FK Partizan Beograd) | 20 |
| 1975/1976 | FK Partizan Beograd | NK Hajduk Split | Nenad Bjeković (FK Partizan Beograd) | 24 |
| 1976/1977 | FK Crvena Zvezda Beograd | NK Rijeka | Zoran Filipović (FK Crvena Zvezda Beograd) | 21 |
| 1977/1978 | FK Partizan Beograd | NK Rijeka | Radomir Savić (FK Sarajevo) | 21 |
| 1978/1979 | NK Hajduk Split | NK Dinamo Zagreb | Dušan Savić (FK Crvena Zvezda Beograd) | 24 |
| 1979/1980 | FK Crvena Zvezda Beograd | FK Crvena Zvezda Beograd | Safet Sušić (FK Sarajevo) Dragoljub Kostić (FK Napredak Kruševac) | 17 |
| 1980/1981 | FK Crvena Zvezda Beograd | FK Velež Mostar | Milan Radović (NK Rijeka) | 26 |
| 1981/1982 | NK Dinamo Zagreb | FK Crvena Zvezda Beograd | Snješko Cerin (NK Dinamo Zagreb) | 19 |

| 1982/1983 | FK Partizan Beograd | NK Dinamo Zagreb | Sulejman Halilović (NK Dinamo Vinkovci) | 18 |
|---|---|---|---|---|
| 1983/1984 | FK Crvena Zvezda Beograd | NK Hajduk Split | Darko Pančev (FK Vardar Skoplje) | 19 |
| 1984/1985 | FK Sarajevo | FK Crvena Zvezda Beograd | Zlatko Vujović (NK Hajduk Split) | 25 |
| 1985/1986 | FK Partizan Beograd | FK Velež Mostar | Davor Čop (NK Dinamo Vinkovci) | 20 |
| 1986/1987 | FK Vardar Skoplje | NK Hajduk Split | Radmilo Mihajlović (FK Željezničar Sarajevo) | 23 |
| 1987/1988 | FK Crvena Zvezda Beograd | FK Borac Banja Luka | Duško Milinković (FK Rad Beograd) | 16 |
| 1988/1989 | FK Vojvodina Novi Sad | FK Partizan Beograd | Davor Šuker (NK Osijek) | 18 |
| 1989/1990 | FK Crvena Zvezda Beograd | FK Crvena Zvezda Beograd | Darko Pančev (FK Crvena Zvezda Beograd) | 25 |
| 1990/1991 | FK Crvena Zvezda Beograd | NK Hajduk Split | Darko Pančev (FK Crvena Zvezda Beograd) | 34 |
| 1991/1992 | FK Crvena Zvezda Beograd | *No competition* | Darko Pančev (FK Crvena Zvezda Beograd) | 25 |

## First League of Serbia and Montenegro (1992–2006)

| | CHAMPIONS | CUP WINNERS | BEST GOALSCORERS | |
|---|---|---|---|---|
| 1992/1993 | FK Partizan Beograd | FK Crvena Zvezda Beograd | Anto Drobnjak (FK Crvena Zvezda Beograd) Vesko Mihajlović (FK Vojvodina Novi Sad) | 22 |
| 1993/1994 | FK Partizan Beograd | FK Partizan Beograd | Savo Milošević (FK Partizan Beograd) | 21 |
| 1994/1995 | FK Crvena Zvezda Beograd | FK Crvena Zvezda Beograd | Savo Milošević (FK Partizan Beograd) | 30 |
| 1995/1996 | FK Partizan Beograd | FK Crvena Zvezda Beograd | Vojislav Budimirović (FK Čukarički) | 23 |
| 1996/1997 | FK Partizan Beograd | FK Crvena Zvezda Beograd | Zoran Jovičić (FK Crvena Zvezda Beograd) | 21 |
| 1997/1998 | FK Obilić Beograd | FK Partizan Beograd | Saša Marković (FK Železnik Beograd/ FK Crvena Zvezda Beograd) | 27 |
| 1998/1999 | FK Partizan Beograd | FK Crvena Zvezda Beograd | Dejan Osmanović (FK Hajduk Kula) | 16 |
| 1999/2000 | FK Crvena Zvezda Beograd | FK Crvena Zvezda Beograd | Mateja Kežman (FK Partizan Beograd) | 27 |
| 2000/2001 | FK Crvena Zvezda Beograd | FK Partizan Beograd | Petar Divić (OFK Beograd) | 27 |
| 2001/2002 | FK Partizan Beograd | FK Crvena Zvezda Beograd | Zoran Đurašković (FK Mladost Lučani) | 27 |
| 2002/2003 | FK Partizan Beograd | FK Sartid Smederevo | Zvonimir Vukić (FK Partizan Beograd) | 22 |
| 2003/2004 | FK Crvena Zvezda Beograd | FK Crvena Zvezda Beograd | Nikola Žigić (FK Crvena Zvezda Beograd) | 19 |
| 2004/2005 | FK Partizan Beograd | FK Železnik Beograd | Marko Pantelić (FK Crvena Zvezda Beograd) | 21 |
| 2005/2006 | FK Crvena Zvezda Beograd | FK Crvena Zvezda Beograd | Srđan Radonjić (FK Partizan Beograd) | 20 |

## Serbian Superliga (since 2006)

| | CHAMPIONS | CUP WINNERS | BEST GOALSCORERS | |
|---|---|---|---|---|
| 2006/2007 | FK Crvena Zvezda Beograd | FK Crvena Zvezda Beograd | Srđan Baljak (FK Banat Zrenjanin) | 18 |
| 2007/2008 | FK Partizan Beograd | FK Partizan Beograd | Nenad Jestrović (FK Crvena Zvezda Beograd) | 13 |
| 2008/2009 | FK Partizan Beograd | FK Partizan Beograd | Lamine Diarra (SEN, FK Partizan Beograd) | 19 |
| 2009/2010 | FK Partizan Beograd | FK Crvena Zvezda Beograd | Dragan Mrđa (FK Vojvodina Novi Sad) | 22 |
| 2010/2011 | FK Partizan Beograd | FK Partizan Beograd | Ivica Iliev (FK Partizan Beograd) Andrija Kaluđerović (FK Crvena Zvezda Beograd) | 13 |
| 2011/2012 | FK Partizan Beograd | FK Crvena Zvezda Beograd | Darko Spalević (FK Radnički Kragujevac) | 19 |
| 2012/2013 | FK Partizan Beograd | FK Jagodina | Miloš Stojanović (FK Jagodina) | 19 |
| 2013/2014 | FK Crvena Zvezda Beograd | FK Vojvodina Novi Sad | Dragan Mrđa (FK Crvena Zvezda Beograd) | 19 |
| 2014/2015 | FK Partizan Beograd | FK Čukarički | Patrick Friday Eze (NGA, FK Mladost Lučani) | 15 |
| 2015/2016 | FK Crvena Zvezda Beograd | FK Partizan Beograd | Aleksandar Katai (FK Crvena Zvezda Beograd) | 21 |
| 2016/2017 | FK Partizan Beograd | FK Partizan Beograd | Uroš Đurđević (FK Partizan Beograd) Leonardo da Silva Souza (BRA, FK Partizan Beograd) | 24 |
| 2017/2018 | FK Crvena Zvezda Beograd | FK Partizan Beograd | Aleksandar Pešić (FK Crvena Zvezda Beograd) | 25 |
| 2018/2019 | FK Crvena Zvezda Beograd | FK Partizan Beograd | Nermin Haskić (BIH, FK Radnički Niš) | 24 |
| 2019/2020 | FK Crvena Zvezda Beograd | FK Vojvodina Novi Sad | Nenad Lukić (TSC Bačka Topola) Vladimir Silađi (TSC Bačka Topola) Nikola Petković (FK Javor Ivanjica) | 16 |
| 2020/2021 | FK Crvena Zvezda Beograd | FK Crvena Zvezda Beograd | Milan Makarić (FK Radnik Surdulica) | 25 |
| 2021/2022 | FK Crvena Zvezda Beograd | FK Crvena Zvezda Beograd | Ricardo Jorge Pires Gomes (CPV, FK Partizan Beograd) | 29 |
| 2022/2023 | FK Crvena Zvezda Beograd | FK Crvena Zvezda Beograd | Ricardo Jorge Pires Gomes (CPV, FK Partizan Beograd) | 20 |

## Regular Season - Results

### Round 1 [08-11.07.2022]
FK Voždovac - FK Novi Pazar 1-0(1-0)
FK Čukarički - Bačka Topola 1-4(0-1)
FK Javor - Partizan 0-4(0-1)
Mladost Lučani - Spartak Subotica 1-1(0-1)
Vojvodina - FK Napredak 1-0(0-0)
Radnik Surdulica - Mladost GAT 1-2(0-1)
Crvena Zvezda - Radnički Niš 4-0(3-0)
FK Kolubara - Radnički 1923 1-1(1-1)

### Round 2 [15-17.07.2022]
FK Novi Pazar - FK Čukarički 1-2(1-1)
Radnički Niš - Partizan 3-3(1-1)
Spartak Subotica - Radnik Surdulica 2-0(1-0)
Mladost GAT - Vojvodina 0-4(0-1)
Crvena Zvezda - FK Kolubara 5-0(5-0)
Bačka Topola - FK Javor 0-0
Radnički 1923 - Mladost Lučani 1-0(0-0)
FK Napredak - FK Voždovac 0-0

### Round 3 [22-24.07.2022]
FK Javor - FK Novi Pazar 2-1(2-1)
Partizan - Bačka Topola 0-0
Radnik Surdulica - Radnički 1923 0-0
FK Čukarički - FK Napredak 1-0(1-0)
Mladost Lučani - Crvena Zvezda 1-2(0-1)
Vojvodina - Spartak Subotica 0-0
FK Voždovac - Mladost GAT 0-0
FK Kolubara-Radnički Niš 1-0(1-0) [17.08.22]

### Round 4 [29-31.07.2022]
FK Novi Pazar - Partizan 1-0(1-0)
Crvena Zvezda - Radnik Surdulica 6-0(1-0)
Radnički 1923 - Vojvodina 0-2(0-0)
FK Napredak - FK Javor 2-4(0-1)
Spartak Subotica - FK Voždovac 3-0(1-0)
Radnički Niš - Bačka Topola 0-3(0-0)
FK Kolubara - Mladost Lučani 3-2(2-1)
Mladost GAT - FK Čukarički 0-2(0-1)

### Round 5 [05-08.08.2022]
FK Voždovac - Radnički 1923 1-0(0-0)
Bačka Topola - FK Novi Pazar 0-1(0-0)
Mladost Lučani - Radnički Niš 2-2(1-1)
Radnik Surdulica - FK Kolubara 0-0
FK Čukarički - Spartak Subotica 2-0(0-0)
FK Javor - Mladost GAT 2-1(1-1)
Partizan - FK Napredak 1-0(1-0) [20.10.22]
Vojvodina-Crvena Zvezda 0-2(0-0) [20.10.22]

### Round 6 [12-15.08.2022]
Radnički Niš - FK Novi Pazar 1-3(0-1)
FK Napredak - Bačka Topola 0-0
FK Kolubara - Vojvodina 2-2(1-0)
Crvena Zvezda - FK Voždovac 4-0(2-0)
Mladost Lučani - Radnik Surdulica 3-2(1-1)
Spartak Subotica - FK Javor 2-2(2-1)
Mladost GAT - Partizan 0-1(0-0)
Radnički 1923 - FK Čukarički 1-1(1-0)

### Round 7 [19-22.08.2022]
FK Novi Pazar - FK Napredak 2-1(1-0)
Vojvodina - Mladost Lučani 1-1(0-0)
FK Javor - Radnički 1923 0-1(0-0)
Radnik Surdulica - Radnički Niš 1-3(0-1)
Bačka Topola - Mladost GAT 3-0(2-0)
FK Voždovac - FK Kolubara 1-0(0-0)
Partizan - Spartak Subot. 0-1(0-0) [10.11.22]
Čukarički-Crvena Zvezda 0-2(0-1) [10.11.22]

### Round 8 [25-28.08.2022]
Radnik Surdulica - Vojvodina 1-1(1-0)
Mladost GAT - FK Novi Pazar 1-2(0-2)
Radnički Niš - FK Napredak 3-2(1-2)
Spartak Subotica - Bačka Topola 0-0
Mladost Lučani - FK Voždovac 1-2(0-0)
FK Kolubara - FK Čukarički 3-2(3-1)
Crvena Zvezda - FK Javor 4-1(1-1)
Radnički 1923 - Partizan 0-1(0-0)

### Round 9 [30.08.-01.09.2022]
FK Novi Pazar - Spartak Subotica 2-0(1-0)
FK Napredak - Mladost GAT 1-0(1-0)
Vojvodina - Radnički Niš 3-0(1-0)
FK Javor - FK Kolubara 0-1(0-1)
FK Voždovac - Radnik Surdulica 4-1(1-1)
Bačka Topola - Radnički 1923 2-0(1-0)
Partizan - Crvena Zvezda 1-1(0-1)
FK Čukarički - Mladost Lučani 3-1(2-1)

### Round 10 [03-05.09.2022]
Radnički Niš - Mladost GAT 1-1(1-1)
Spartak Subotica - FK Napredak 1-2(0-1)
Vojvodina - FK Voždovac 2-1(0-0)
FK Kolubara - Partizan 1-5(1-4)
Crvena Zvezda - Bačka Topola 1-1(1-1)
Radnički 1923 - FK Novi Pazar 1-3(1-1)
Mladost Lučani - FK Javor 4-1(3-1)
Radnik Surdulica - FK Čukarički 0-4(0-3)

### Round 11 [10-12.09.2022]
FK Napredak - Radnički 1923 1-0(1-0)
Bačka Topola - FK Kolubara 3-1(1-0)
Mladost GAT - Spartak Subotica 1-0(1-0)
FK Novi Pazar - Crvena Zvezda 1-2(1-1)
FK Čukarički - Vojvodina 2-0(2-0)
Partizan - Mladost Lučani 6-0(2-0)
FK Javor - Radnik Surdulica 2-2(0-0)
FK Voždovac - Radnički Niš 1-0(0-0)

### Round 12 [16-19.09.2022]
Radnički 1923 - Mladost GAT 3-0(2-0)
Mladost Lučani - Bačka Topola 2-5(1-2)
FK Voždovac - FK Čukarički 0-3(0-2)
Vojvodina - FK Javor 2-0(1-0)
Crvena Zvezda - FK Napredak 1-0(0-0)
Radnik Surdulica - Partizan 0-2(0-1)
FK Kolubara - FK Novi Pazar 1-0(1-0)
Radnički Niš - Spartak Subotica 3-0(1-0)

### Round 13 [30.09.-03.10.2022]
FK Novi Pazar - Mladost Lučani 3-1(1-1)
Bačka Topola - Radnik Surdulica 2-1(1-1)
FK Javor - FK Voždovac 0-2(0-1)
FK Napredak - FK Kolubara 4-0(3-0)
Spartak Subotica - Radnički 1923 1-2(1-2)
Mladost GAT - Crvena Zvezda 0-4(0-1)
Partizan - Vojvodina 4-1(2-0)
FK Čukarički - Radnički Niš 2-2(1-1)

### Round 14 [07-10.10.2022]
Radnik Surdulica - FK Novi Pazar 1-1(1-1)
Mladost Lučani - FK Napredak 3-1(1-0)
FK Kolubara - Mladost GAT 0-0
Vojvodina - Bačka Topola 1-2(1-2)
FK Čukarički - FK Javor 3-0(1-0)
Crvena Zvezda - Spartak Subotica 3-0(3-0)
FK Voždovac - Partizan 0-4(0-3)
Radnički Niš - Radnički 1923 1-3(0-2)

### Round 15 [14-16.10.2022]
Mladost GAT - Mladost Lučani 1-1(1-0)
FK Novi Pazar - Vojvodina 1-1(1-0)
Bačka Topola - FK Voždovac 3-0(1-0)
Spartak Subotica - FK Kolubara 2-1(0-1)
FK Javor - Radnički Niš 0-2(0-1)
FK Napredak - Radnik Surdulica 1-0(0-0)
Radnički 1923 - Crvena Zvezda 0-1(0-0)
Partizan - FK Čukarički 3-2(1-1)

### Round 16 [22-24.10.2022]
Bačka Topola - FK Čukarički 1-1(1-0)
Radnički 1923 - FK Kolubara 3-0(1-0)
Radnički Niš - Crvena Zvezda 1-2(0-0)
FK Novi Pazar - FK Voždovac 0-0
Partizan - FK Javor 3-3(2-1)
Mladost GAT - Radnik Surdulica 2-1(0-1)
Spartak Subotica - Mladost Lučani 1-1(0-0)
FK Napredak - Vojvodina 0-2(0-1)

### Round 17 [29-30.10.2022]
FK Javor - Bačka Topola 0-1(0-0)
FK Čukarički - FK Novi Pazar 2-2(1-1)
FK Voždovac - FK Napredak 0-0
Vojvodina - Mladost GAT 2-0(1-0)
Radnik Surdulica - Spartak Subotica 2-0(0-0)
FK Kolubara - Crvena Zvezda 0-2(0-1)
Mladost Lučani - Radnički 1923 0-0
Partizan - Radnički Niš 4-0(2-0)

### Round 18 [04-06.11.2022]
Mladost GAT - FK Voždovac 1-2(0-1)
FK Novi Pazar - FK Javor 3-1(0-1)
FK Napredak - FK Čukarički 0-0
Radnički 1923 - Radnik Surdulica 1-0(0-0)
Radnički Niš - FK Kolubara 1-1(0-1)
Spartak Subotica - Vojvodina 1-1(0-0)
Crvena Zvezda - Mladost Lučani 2-0(1-0)
Bačka Topola - Partizan 2-3(1-1)

### Round 19 [11-13.11.2022]
FK Javor - FK Napredak 2-1(0-1)
Mladost Lučani - FK Kolubara 2-0(1-0)
Bačka Topola - Radnički Niš 1-0(1-0)
Vojvodina - Radnički 1923 2-1(0-0)
Radnik Surdulica - Crvena Zvezda 1-2(0-1)
Partizan - FK Novi Pazar 1-0(0-0)
FK Čukarički - Mladost GAT 2-0(2-0)
FK Voždovac - Spartak Subotica 2-0(1-0)

### Round 20 [03-05.02.2023]
FK Kolubara - Radnik Surdulica 1-0(1-0)
Radnički 1923 - FK Voždovac 0-1(0-1)
Radnički Niš - Mladost Lučani 2-1(0-1)
Crvena Zvezda - Vojvodina 1-1(1-1)
Spartak Subotica - FK Čukarički 1-3(0-1)
FK Napredak - Partizan 0-1(0-0)
FK Novi Pazar - Bačka Topola 2-1(0-0)
Mladost GAT - FK Javor 2-3(1-2)

### Round 21 [10-12.02.2023]
Radnik Surdulica - Mladost Lučani 1-0(0-0)
FK Čukarički - Radnički 1923 3-2(0-0)
FK Voždovac - Crvena Zvezda 0-6(0-3)
Bačka Topola - FK Napredak 2-0(2-0)
Vojvodina - FK Kolubara 3-0(1-0)
Partizan - Mladost GAT 0-4(0-2)
FK Javor - Spartak Subotica 1-0(1-0)
FK Novi Pazar - Radnički Niš 0-0

**Round 22** [17-19.02.2023]
Mladost Lučani - Vojvodina 1-1(0-1)
FK Kolubara - FK Voždovac 1-0(0-0)
Radnički Niš - Radnik Surdulica 0-0
Crvena Zvezda - FK Čukarički 3-0(2-0)
FK Napredak - FK Novi Pazar 0-1(0-0)
Radnički 1923 - FK Javor 0-0
Mladost GAT - Bačka Topola 1-2(1-2)
Spartak Subotica - Partizan 1-2(0-1)

**Round 23** [23-27.02.2023]
FK Napredak - Radnički Niš 2-0(0-0)
FK Voždovac - Mladost Lučani 1-1(0-1)
Vojvodina - Radnik Surdulica 1-1(1-1)
FK Čukarički - FK Kolubara 3-0(0-0)
FK Javor - Crvena Zvezda 0-2(0-1)
Bačka Topola - Spartak Subotica 2-2(2-0)
FK Novi Pazar - Mladost GAT 1-0(0-0)
Partizan - Radnički 1923 1-1(1-0)

**Round 24** [28.02.-03.03.2023]
Radnički Niš - Vojvodina 1-4(0-2)
Radnik Surdulica - FK Voždovac 2-0(0-0)
Mladost GAT - FK Napredak 0-1(0-1)
Spartak Subotica - FK Novi Pazar 2-0(1-0)
Mladost Lučani - FK Čukarički 0-1(0-0)
Radnički 1923 - Bačka Topola 0-2(0-2)
FK Kolubara - FK Javor 1-0(0-0)
Crvena Zvezda - Partizan 1-0(1-0)

**Round 25** [05-08.03.2023]
FK Čukarički - Radnik Surdulica 1-0(0-0)
FK Napredak - Spartak Subotica 1-1(1-0)
FK Voždovac - Vojvodina 0-0
FK Novi Pazar - Radnički 1923 1-0(1-0)
FK Javor - Mladost Lučani 1-1(0-1)
Mladost GAT - Radnički Niš 0-0
Bačka Topola - Crvena Zvezda 1-2(0-1)
Partizan - FK Kolubara 1-1(1-0)

**Round 26** [11-13.03.2023]
Radnički 1923 - FK Napredak 3-0(2-0)
Vojvodina - FK Čukarički 3-2(2-0)
Spartak Subotica - Mladost GAT 0-0
Radnički Niš - FK Voždovac 2-3(0-1)
Radnik Surdulica - FK Javor 0-0
Crvena Zvezda - FK Novi Pazar 5-1(2-1)
Mladost Lučani - Partizan 0-3(0-0)
FK Kolubara - Bačka Topola 0-1(0-0)

**Round 27** [17-19.03.2023]
Partizan - Radnik Surdulica 1-2(0-2)
Mladost GAT - Radnički 1923 1-2(0-1)
FK Novi Pazar - FK Kolubara 0-1(0-0)
FK Javor - Vojvodina 1-1(0-1)
Bačka Topola - Mladost Lučani 2-1(2-0)
Spartak Subotica - Radnički Niš 0-1(0-1)
FK Napredak - Crvena Zvezda 1-1(0-1)
FK Čukarički - FK Voždovac 3-1(1-1)

**Round 28** [31.03.-02.04.2023]
FK Kolubara - FK Napredak 0-1(0-0)
Mladost Lučani - FK Novi Pazar 1-3(1-1)
Radnički 1923 - Spartak Subotica 2-2(1-1)
FK Voždovac - FK Javor 0-1(0-0)
Crvena Zvezda - Mladost GAT 4-2(2-2)
Vojvodina - Partizan 2-1(0-0)
Radnik Surdulica - Bačka Topola 0-1(0-0)
Radnički Niš - FK Čukarički 0-2(0-2)

**Round 29** [04-07.04.2023]
FK Napredak - Mladost Lučani 0-0
Partizan - FK Voždovac 1-0(1-0)
Mladost GAT - FK Kolubara 0-0
Spartak Subotica - Crvena Zvezda 1-4(1-2)
FK Novi Pazar - Radnik Surdulica 1-0(0-0)
Radnički 1923 - Radnički Niš 1-0(0-0)
FK Javor - FK Čukarički 1-2(0-0)
Bačka Topola - Vojvodina 1-1(1-0)

**Round 30** [10-12.04.2023]
Mladost Lučani - Mladost GAT 0-0
FK Kolubara - Spartak Subotica 2-1(0-0)
Crvena Zvezda - Radnički 1923 2-0(1-0)
Vojvodina - FK Novi Pazar 2-0(0-0)
FK Voždovac - Bačka Topola 1-3(1-2)
Radnički Niš - FK Javor 1-0(1-0)
Radnik Surdulica - FK Napredak 1-0(1-0)
FK Čukarički - Partizan 1-0(0-0) [20.04.2023]

## Final Standings

| | | | | | | | | | | |
|---|---|---|---|---|---|---|---|---|---|---|
| 1. | FK Crvena Zvezda Beograd | 30 | 26 | 4 | 0 | 81 | - | 14 | 82 |
| 2. | FK TSC Bačka Topola | 30 | 18 | 8 | 4 | 52 | - | 22 | 62 |
| 3. | FK Čukarički Beograd | 30 | 19 | 5 | 6 | 56 | - | 31 | 62 |
| 4. | FK Partizan Beograd | 30 | 17 | 6 | 7 | 57 | - | 28 | 57 |
| 5. | FK Vojvodina Novi Sad | 30 | 14 | 12 | 4 | 47 | - | 27 | 54 |
| 6. | FK Novi Pazar | 30 | 15 | 5 | 10 | 37 | - | 31 | 50 |
| 7. | FK Voždovac Beograd | 30 | 11 | 6 | 13 | 24 | - | 42 | 39 |
| 8. | FK Radnički 1923 Kragujevac | 30 | 10 | 7 | 13 | 29 | - | 30 | 37 |
| 9. | FK Kolubara Lazarevac | 30 | 10 | 7 | 13 | 23 | - | 45 | 37 |
| 10. | FK Napredak Kruševac | 30 | 8 | 7 | 15 | 22 | - | 31 | 31 |
| 11. | FK Radnički Niš | 30 | 7 | 8 | 15 | 30 | - | 51 | 29 |
| 12. | FK Javor Ivanjica | 30 | 7 | 8 | 15 | 28 | - | 49 | 29 |
| 13. | FK Spartak Subotica | 30 | 5 | 10 | 15 | 26 | - | 43 | 25 |
| 14. | FK Mladost Lučani | 30 | 4 | 11 | 15 | 32 | - | 52 | 23 |
| 15. | FK Radnik Surdulica | 30 | 5 | 8 | 17 | 21 | 44 | | 23 |
| 16. | FK Mladost GAT Novi Sad | 30 | 4 | 8 | 18 | 20 | 45 | | 20 |

Teams ranked 1-8 were qualified for the Championship Round, while teams ranked 9-16 were qualified for the Relegation Round.

## Relegation Round

### Results

**Round 31** [21-23.04.2023]
Radnički Niš - Mladost GAT 0-1(0-0)
FK Kolubara - Mladost Lučani 0-1(0-1)
FK Napredak - Spartak Subotica 1-0(1-0)
FK Javor - Radnik Surdulica 0-0

**Round 32** [25-27.04.2023]
Mladost GAT - FK Kolubara 1-0(1-0)
Mladost Lučani - FK Napredak 0-1(0-0)
Spartak Subotica - FK Javor 3-2(1-1)
Radnik Surdulica - Radnički Niš 1-0(0-0)

**Round 33** [30.04.-02.05.2023]
Radnički Niš - Mladost Lučani 1-2(0-0)
FK Napredak - Radnik Surdulica 0-1(0-0)
FK Kolubara - Spartak Subotica 0-3(0-1)
FK Javor - Mladost GAT 0-0

**Round 34** [07-09.05.2023]
Mladost GAT - Spartak Subotica 1-1(0-0)
FK Javor - FK Kolubara 2-0(1-0)
Mladost Lučani - Radnik Surdulica 2-0(2-0)
FK Napredak - Radnički Niš 1-2(1-2)

**Round 35** [14-15.05.2023]
FK Kolubara - FK Napredak 2-2(1-1)
Radnički Niš - FK Javor 3-3(2-1)
Radnik Surdulica - Mladost GAT 1-1(0-0)
Spartak Subotica - Mladost Lučani 2-0(0-0)

**Round 36** [22.05.2023]
Radnik Surdulica - FK Kolubara 2-1(1-1)
FK Javor - Mladost Lučani 0-1(0-0)
Mladost GAT - FK Napredak 0-0
Radnički Niš - Spartak Subotica 0-1(0-1)

**Round 37** [27.05.2023]
FK Kolubara - Radnički Niš 2-1(0-0)
Mladost Lučani - Mladost GAT 2-1(0-0)
FK Napredak - FK Javor 0-1(0-0)
Spartak Subotica - Radnik Surdulica 2-2(2-0)

| | | | | | | | | | | | | | | | | | |
|---|---|---|---|---|---|---|---|---|---|---|---|---|---|---|---|---|---|
| 9. | FK Napredak Kruševac | 37 | 10 | 9 | 18 | 27 | - | 37 | 39 | 6 | 6 | 7 | 15 - 14 | 4 | 3 | 11 | 12 - 23 |
| 10. | FK Spartak Subotica | 37 | 9 | 12 | 16 | 38 | - | 49 | 39 | 6 | 6 | 6 | 25 - 23 | 3 | 6 | 10 | 13 - 26 |
| 11. | FK Mladost Lučani | 37 | 9 | 11 | 17 | 40 | - | 57 | 38 | 6 | 5 | 7 | 25 - 26 | 3 | 6 | 10 | 15 - 31 |
| 12. | FK Javor Ivanjica | 37 | 9 | 10 | 18 | 35 | - | 56 | 37 | 5 | 5 | 9 | 14 - 23 | 4 | 5 | 9 | 21 - 33 |
| 14. | FK Radnički Niš (Relegation Play-offs) | 37 | 9 | 8 | 20 | 37 | - | 61 | 35 | 5 | 4 | 10 | 24 - 34 | 4 | 4 | 10 | 13 - 27 |
| 15. | FK Radnik Surdulica (Relegation Play-offs) | 37 | 8 | 11 | 18 | 28 | - | 50 | 35 | 6 | 6 | 6 | 15 - 18 | 2 | 5 | 12 | 13 - 32 |
| 13. | FK Kolubara Lazarevac (Relegated)* | 37 | 11 | 8 | 18 | 28 | - | 57 | 35 | 9 | 4 | 6 | 21 - 24 | 2 | 4 | 12 | 7 - 33 |
| 16. | FK Mladost GAT Novi Sad (Relegated) | 37 | 6 | 12 | 19 | 25 | - | 49 | 30 | 3 | 5 | 10 | 12 - 26 | 3 | 7 | 9 | 13 - 23 |

*Please note: FK Kolubara Lazarevac get 6 points deducted due to match fixing.

## Championship Round

### Results

**Round 31** [21-23.04.2023]
FK Voždovac - Radnički 1923 2-1(1-0)
Vojvodina - FK Novi Pazar 4-0(2-0)
Crvena Zvezda - Bačka Topola 4-1(1-1)
FK Čukarički - Partizan 1-0(1-0)

**Round 32** [26-27.04.2023]
FK Novi Pazar - FK Voždovac 0-1(0-0)
Radnički 1923 - Vojvodina 2-2(1-1)
Partizan - Crvena Zvezda 0-0
Bačka Topola - FK Čukarički 1-0(0-0)

**Round 33** [29.04.-01.05.2023]
FK Novi Pazar - Radnički 1923 0-1(0-0)
Vojvodina - FK Voždovac 2-0(1-0)
Crvena Zvezda - FK Čukarički 4-0(2-0)
Bačka Topola - Partizan 1-3(1-1)

**Round 34** [08.05.2023]
Radnički 1923 - Bačka Topola 1-4(1-2)
FK Čukarički - Vojvodina 1-0(1-0)
FK Voždovac - Crvena Zvezda 0-2(0-1)
Partizan - FK Novi Pazar 2-0(1-0)

**Round 35** [13-15.05.2023]
FK Čukarički - FK Novi Pazar 4-0(1-0)
Crvena Zvezda - Vojvodina 2-1(1-0)
Bačka Topola - FK Voždovac 2-0(0-0)
Partizan - Radnički 1923 2-1(1-1)

**Round 36** [20-21.05.2023]
Radnički 1923 - Crvena Zvezda 1-1(0-0)
Vojvodina - Partizan 2-2(1-1)
FK Voždovac - FK Čukarički 1-1(0-1)
FK Novi Pazar - Bačka Topola 1-4(0-0)

**Round 37** [27-28.05.2023]
Partizan - FK Voždovac 2-1(2-0)
Bačka Topola - Vojvodina 1-1(0-0)
FK Čukarički - Radnički 1923 2-1(2-1)
Crvena Zvezda - FK Novi Pazar 2-2(0-0)

### Final Standings

| | | | | Total | | | | | | Home | | | | | Away | | | |
|---|---|---|---|---|---|---|---|---|---|---|---|---|---|---|---|---|---|---|
| 1. | **FK Crvena Zvezda Beograd** | 37 | 30 | 7 | 0 | 96 | - | 19 | 97 | 16 | 3 | 0 | 58 - 10 | 14 | 4 | 0 | 38 - 9 |
| 2. | FK TSC Bačka Topola | 37 | 22 | 9 | 6 | 66 | - | 32 | 75 | 10 | 5 | 4 | 31 - 17 | 12 | 4 | 2 | 35 - 15 |
| 3. | FK Čukarički Beograd | 37 | 23 | 6 | 8 | 65 | - | 38 | 75 | 15 | 2 | 2 | 37 - 15 | 8 | 4 | 6 | 28 - 23 |
| 4. | FK Partizan Beograd | 37 | 21 | 8 | 8 | 68 | - | 34 | 71 | 10 | 6 | 3 | 33 - 18 | 11 | 2 | 5 | 35 - 16 |
| 5. | FK Vojvodina Novi Sad | 37 | 16 | 15 | 6 | 59 | - | 35 | 63 | 12 | 4 | 2 | 33 - 13 | 4 | 11 | 4 | 26 - 22 |
| 6. | FK Novi Pazar | 37 | 15 | 6 | 16 | 40 | - | 49 | 51 | 9 | 3 | 6 | 20 - 16 | 6 | 3 | 10 | 20 - 33 |
| 7. | FK Voždovac Beograd | 37 | 13 | 7 | 17 | 29 | - | 52 | 46 | 7 | 5 | 6 | 15 - 23 | 6 | 2 | 11 | 14 - 29 |
| 8. | FK Radnički 1923 Kragujevac | 37 | 11 | 9 | 17 | 37 | - | 43 | 42 | 6 | 5 | 7 | 20 - 20 | 5 | 4 | 10 | 17 - 23 |

### Top goalscorers:

| | | |
|---|---|---|
| 20 | **Ricardo Jorge Pires Gomes (CPV)** | *FK Partizan Beograd* |
| 17 | Aleksandar Katai | *FK Crvena Zvezda Beograd* |
| 13 | Petar Ratkov | *FK TSC Bačka Topola* |
| 13 | Nikola Čumić | *FK Vojvodina Novi Sad* |

## Relegation Play-offs [31.05.-04.06.2023]

| | | |
|---|---|---|
| FK Inđija - FK Radnički Niš | 3-1(2-0) | 0-3(0-1) |
| FK Grafičar Beograd - FK Radnik Surdulica | 1-1(0-0) | 0-2(0-1) |

Both FK Radnički Niš and FK Radnik Surdulica are remaining at first level.

## NATIONAL CUP
### Kup Srbije 2022/2023

#### First Round [28-29.09./12.10./19.10./01.11.2022]

| | | | | |
|---|---|---|---|---|
| FK Radnički Srem. Mitrovica - FK Partizan Beograd | 1-1 aet; 2-0 pen | FK Jagodina - FK Novi Pazar | 1-2(1-1) |
| FK Mačva Šabac - FK Crvena Zvezda Beograd | 0-2(0-0) | FK Loznica - FK TSC Bačka Topola | 1-2(0-0) |
| FK Indija - FK Napredak Kruševac | 0-2(0-1) | FK Polet Ljubić - FK Radnik Surdulica | 0-1(0-1) |
| FK Javor Ivanjica - FK Radnički Niš | 0-0 aet; 5-6 pen | FK Zlatibor Čajetina - FK Čukarički Beograd | 0-2(0-1) |
| FK Železničar Pančevo - RFK Novi Sad 1921 | 3-0(1-0) | FK Kabel Novi Sad - FK Metalac Gornji Milanovac | 0-0 aet; 4-5 pen |
| FK IMT Beograd - FK Radnički 1923 Kragujevac | 2-1(0-0) | FK Mladost GAT Novi Sad - FK Voždovac Beograd | 2-0(1-0) |
| OFK Žarkovo - FK Kolubara Lazarevac | 1-1 aet; 4-5 pen | FK Rad Beograd - FK Spartak Subotica | 0-2(0-0) |
| FK Radnički Beograd - FK Mladost Lučani | 2-1(0-1) | FK Grafičar Beograd - FK Vojvodina Novi Sad | 1-1 aet; 0-3 pen |

#### 1/8-Finals [09.11.2022 & 15.03.2023]

| | | | | |
|---|---|---|---|---|
| FK Radnički Beograd - FK Radnik Surdulica | 1-2(0-1) | FK Vojvodina Novi Sad-FK Mladost GAT Novi Sad | 2-1(0-1) |
| FK TSC Bačka Topola - FK Železničar Pančevo | 2-0(2-0) | FK Radnički Sremska Mitrovica - FK Crvena Zvezda | 1-3(1-1) |
| FK Radnički Niš - FK IMT Beograd | 3-0(1-0) | FK Metalac Go. Milanovac - FK Čukarički Beograd | 0-2(0-1) |
| FK Novi Pazar - FK Kolubara Lazarevac | 2-1(2-1) | FK Spartak Subotica - FK Napredak Kruševac | 0-1(0-1) |

#### Quarter-Finals [03-04.05.2023]

| | | | | |
|---|---|---|---|---|
| FK Napredak Kruševac - FK Crvena Zvezda Beograd | 0-0 aet; 2-4 pen | FK Radnik Surdulica - FK Čukarički Beograd | 0-1(0-1) |
| FK TSC Bačka Topola - FK Novi Pazar | 4-0(2-0) | FK Radnički Niš - FK Vojvodina Novi Sad | 0-1(0-1) |

#### Semi-Finals [17-18.05.2023]

| | | | | |
|---|---|---|---|---|
| FK TSC Bačka Topola - FK Crvena Zvezda Beograd | 0-3(0-1) | FK Vojvodina Novi Sad - FK Čukarički Beograd | 0-1(0-0) |

#### Final

25.05.2023; Stadion „Rajko Mitić", Beograd; Referee: Milan Mitić; Attendance: 6,000
**FK Crvena Zvezda Beograd - FK Čukarički Beograd**          **2-1(0-1)**

**Crvena Zvezda**: Milan Borjan (Cap), Alex Vigo Gamaliel (58.Lazar Nikolić), Strahinja Eraković, Aleksandar Dragović, Irakli Azarovi (79.Milan Rodić), Guélor Kanga (58.Kings Kangwa), Srđan Mijailović, Mirko Ivanić, Osman Bukari, Aleksandar Katai (72.Marko Rakonjac), Aleksandar Pešić. Trainer: Miloš Milojević.

**FK Čukarički**: Nemanja Belić, Viktor Rogan, Uroš Drezgić, Bojan Kovačević (81.Luka Stojanović), Nemanja Tošić, Marko Dočić (Cap), Miladin Stevanović, Igor Miladinović (81.Stefan Tomović), Đorđe Ivanović (86.Almir Aganspahić), Luka Adžić (64.Samuel Owusu), Muhammed Badamosi. Trainer: Dušan Kerkez (Bosnia and Herzegovina).

**Goals:** 0-1 Marko Dočić (21), 1-1 Aleksandar Pešić (61), 2-1 Aleksandar Pešić (76).

## THE CLUBS 2022/2023

<u>Please note</u>: appearances and goals are including statistics of both regular season and play-offs (Championship Round & Relegation Round).

### Fudbalski Klub Crvena Zvezda Beograd

| | |
|---|---|
| **Founded:** | 04.03.1945 |
| **Stadium:** | Stadion „Rajko Mitić", Beograd (51,755) |
| **Trainer:** | Dejan Stanković          11.09.1978 |
| [27.08.2022] | Miloš Milojević          29.09.1982 |

| Goalkeepers: | DOB | M | (s) | G |
|---|---|---|---|---|
| Milan Borjan (CAN) | 23.10.1987 | 33 | | |
| Nikola Vasiljević | 24.06.1996 | 4 | | |
| **Defenders:** | **DOB** | **M** | **(s)** | **G** |
| Irakli Azarovi (GEO) | 21.02.2002 | 10 | (10) | |
| Vuk Bogdanović | 03.04.2002 | | (1) | |
| Aleksandar Dragović (AUT) | 06.03.1991 | 29 | (3) | |
| Strahinja Eraković | 22.01.2001 | 31 | (2) | |
| Marko Gobeljić | 13.09.1992 | 11 | (4) | 2 |
| Stefan Leković | 09.01.2004 | 5 | (7) | 1 |
| Nemanja Milunović | 31.05.1989 | 16 | (4) | |
| Lazar Nikolić | 01.08.1999 | 4 | (4) | |
| Radovan Pankov | 05.08.1995 | 1 | (3) | |
| Milan Rodić | 02.04.1991 | 24 | (2) | 1 |
| Uroš Spajić | 13.02.1993 | 2 | (1) | 1 |
| Alex Vigo Gamaliel (ARG) | 28.04.1999 | 12 | (1) | 2 |
| **Midfielders:** | **DOB** | **M** | **(s)** | **G** |
| Mirko Ivanić (MNE) | 13.09.1993 | 24 | (5) | 8 |
| Guélor Kanga (GAB) | 01.09.1990 | 29 | (1) | 10 |
| Kings Kangwa (ZAM) | 06.04.1999 | 20 | (12) | 8 |
| Nenad Krstičić | 03.07.1990 | | (4) | |

| | DOB | M | (s) | G |
|---|---|---|---|---|
| Srđan Mijailović | 10.11.1993 | 22 | (3) | |
| Stefan Mitrović | 15.08.2002 | 17 | (15) | 5 |
| Veljko Nikolić | 29.08.1999 | 3 | (6) | 1 |
| Egor Prutsev (RUS) | 23.12.2002 | 4 | (6) | |
| Sékou Junior Sanogo (CIV) | 05.05.1989 | 3 | (9) | |
| Slavoljub Srnić | 12.01.1992 | 4 | (11) | |
| Nikola Stanković | 24.04.2003 | 2 | (4) | |
| **Forwards:** | **DOB** | **M** | **(s)** | **G** |
| El Fardou Mohamed Ben Nabouhane (COM) | 10.06.1989 | 5 | (6) | 2 |
| Osman Bukari (GHA) | 13.12.1998 | 25 | (4) | 12 |
| Kalifa Coulibaly (MLI) | 21.08.1991 | | (4) | 1 |
| Aleksandar Katai | 06.02.1991 | 27 | (8) | 17 |
| Vladimir Lučić | 28.06.2002 | | (2) | |
| Jovan Mijatović | 11.07.2005 | 4 | (8) | 1 |
| Nikola Mituljikić | 20.01.2003 | | (7) | |
| Ibrahim Mustapha (GHA) | 18.06.2000 | 1 | (11) | |
| Ohikhuaeme Anthony Kwoeme Omoijuanfo(NOR) | 10.01.1994 | 1 | (1) | 1 |
| Milan Pavkov | 09.02.1994 | 3 | (1) | 5 |
| Aleksandar Pešić | 21.05.1992 | 25 | (3) | 11 |
| Marko Rakonjac (MNE) | 25.04.2000 | 6 | (7) | 4 |

## Fudbalski Klub Čukarički Beograd

**Founded:** 04.07.1926 (*as Čukarički SK*)
**Stadium:** Stadion Čukarički, Beograd (4,070)
**Trainer:** Dušan Kerkez (BIH)     01.05.1976

| Goalkeepers: | DOB | M | (s) | G |
|---|---|---|---|---|
| Nemanja Belić | 24.04.1987 | 19 | | |
| Novak Mićović | 25.10.2001 | 13 | (1) | |
| Zoran Popović | 28.05.1988 | 5 | | |
| **Defenders:** | **DOB** | **M** | **(s)** | **G** |
| Uroš Drezgić | 04.10.2002 | 26 | (1) | 2 |
| Marko Gajić | 10.03.1992 | 3 | (5) | |
| Aleksa Koloni | 01.07.2005 | | (1) | |
| Bojan Kovačević | 22.05.2004 | 15 | (2) | 1 |
| Radovan Pankov | 05.08.1995 | 14 | | 1 |
| Darko Puškarić | 13.07.1985 | 7 | | |
| Viktor Rogan | 12.12.2002 | 15 | (7) | 1 |
| Bojan Roganović (MNE) | 28.09.2000 | 4 | (2) | |
| Vojin Serafimović | 14.10.2005 | 2 | (3) | |
| Miladin Stevanović | 11.02.1996 | 24 | (2) | |
| Nemanja Tošić | 23.01.1997 | 30 | (1) | 3 |
| Nikola Vujadinović (MNE) | 31.07.1986 | 8 | (1) | 1 |
| **Midfielders:** | **DOB** | **M** | **(s)** | **G** |
| Marko Dočić | 21.04.1993 | 28 | (3) | 11 |
| Stefan Kovač (BIH) | 14.01.1999 | 20 | (5) | 1 |
| Jovan Lukić | 20.01.2002 | 1 | (9) | |
| Srđan Mijailović | 10.11.1993 | 8 | | |
| Igor Miladinović | 08.06.2003 | 2 | (9) | |
| Samuel Owusu (GHA) | 28.03.1996 | 21 | (8) | 1 |
| Nikola Petković | 23.02.2003 | 6 | (10) | |
| Sambou Sissoko (MLI) | 29.06.2000 | 15 | (9) | |
| Luka Stojanović | 04.01.1994 | 1 | (8) | 5 |
| Matija Stojanović | 24.11.2005 | | (1) | |
| Stefan Tomović | 14.10.2001 | 14 | (11) | 5 |
| **Forwards:** | **DOB** | **M** | **(s)** | **G** |
| Luka Adžić | 17.09.1998 | 10 | (12) | 2 |
| Almir Aganspahić (BIH) | 12.09.1996 | 2 | (9) | 1 |
| Muhammed Badamosi (GAM) | 27.12.1998 | 33 | (3) | 11 |
| Stefan Čolović | 16.04.1994 | 1 | (1) | |
| Đorđe Ivanović | 20.11.1995 | 29 | (6) | 9 |
| Aleksa Janković | 12.04.2000 | 2 | (5) | 1 |
| Vladimir Lučić | 28.06.2002 | 23 | (5) | 3 |
| Uroš Miladinović | 16.06.2004 | | (1) | |
| Ibrahima N'Diaye (SEN) | 06.12.1994 | 5 | (12) | 3 |
| Mihajlo Spasojević | 15.02.2004 | 1 | (12) | 2 |

## Fudbalski Klub Javor Ivanjica

**Founded:** 1912
**Stadium:** Stadion FK Javor, Ivanjica (3,000)
**Trainer:** Igor Bondžulić     05.10.1980
[04.10.2022] Mladen Dodić     20.08.1969
[25.05.2023] Milovan Milović     24.10.1980

| Goalkeepers: | DOB | M | (s) | G |
|---|---|---|---|---|
| Strahinja Manojlović (BIH) | 11.08.2002 | 18 | | |
| Boris Velimirović | 08.09.2001 | 2 | | |
| Aleksandar Vulić | 08.06.2001 | 17 | | |
| **Defenders:** | **DOB** | **M** | **(s)** | **G** |
| Bratislav Đukić | 29.09.1999 | 11 | (12) | |
| Srđan Grabež | 02.04.1991 | 13 | | |
| Milan Ilić | 07.02.2000 | 13 | (1) | |
| Kosta Janjić | 22.05.2000 | 3 | | |
| Boris Kopitović (MNE) | 17.09.1994 | 18 | (1) | 1 |
| Nemanja Miletić | 26.07.1991 | 15 | | |
| Stefan Milošević | 07.04.1995 | 5 | (2) | |
| Lazar Nikolić | 01.08.1999 | 18 | | 2 |
| Milan Obradović | 27.12.1999 | 33 | | |
| Igor Petrović | 03.11.2000 | 1 | (2) | |
| Đorđe Skoko | 03.06.2003 | 1 | | |
| Kristijan Tojčić (BIH) | 06.12.1999 | 26 | (6) | |
| Stefan Vico (MNE) | 28.02.1995 | 1 | (2) | |
| **Midfielders:** | **DOB** | **M** | **(s)** | **G** |
| Miloš Adamović | 19.06.1988 | 16 | (1) | |
| Boubacari Doucouré (FRA) | 19.03.1999 | 29 | | 2 |
| Milan Đurić | 03.10.1987 | 5 | (7) | |
| Luka Gojković | 28.11.1999 | 31 | (3) | 6 |
| Milan Marčić | 14.03.1996 | 16 | | 1 |
| Stefan Vukašinović | 24.07.2003 | | (1) | |
| Damir Salihović | 28.08.2001 | | (3) | |
| **Forwards:** | **DOB** | **M** | **(s)** | **G** |
| Radivoj Bosić | 01.12.2000 | 7 | (8) | 1 |
| Norman Odale Campbell (JAM) | 24.11.1999 | 29 | (6) | 7 |
| Dino Dolmagić | 26.02.1994 | 9 | (11) | |
| *Eliomar* Correia Silva (BRA) | 16.03.1988 | 7 | (20) | 1 |
| Petar Gigić | 07.03.1997 | 33 | (2) | 8 |
| Pavle Ivelja | 20.01.1998 | 2 | (7) | |
| Luka Luković | 11.10.1996 | 15 | (3) | 2 |
| Marko Maletić (BIH) | 25.10.1993 | | (14) | |
| Ugochukwu Ogbonnaya Oduenyi (NGA) | 03.02.1996 | | (3) | |
| Luka Ratković | 09.04.1997 | 5 | (13) | 1 |
| Ibrahim Tanko (GHA) | 30.04.1999 | 8 | (25) | 2 |

## Fudbalski Klub Kolubara Lazarevac

**Founded:** 1919
**Stadium:** Stadion Kolubara, Kolubara (2,500)
**Trainer:** Dejan Đurđević     04.07.1967
[18.10.2022] Veroljub Dukanac     13.09.1973

| Goalkeepers: | DOB | M | (s) | G |
|---|---|---|---|---|
| Balša Popović (MNE) | 10.06.2000 | 7 | (1) | |
| Dejan Stanivuković | 19.06.1994 | 30 | | |
| **Defenders:** | **DOB** | **M** | **(s)** | **G** |
| Emir Azemović (MNE) | 06.01.1997 | 6 | | |
| Vasilije Bakić | 24.05.2000 | 28 | (1) | |
| Igor Cvetojević | 01.07.2001 | 2 | | 1 |
| Ivan Ćorković | 10.05.2001 | 4 | (9) | |
| Nikola Janković | 07.06.1993 | 16 | | |
| Nenad Kočović | 20.02.1995 | 30 | (3) | |
| Stefan Marjanović | 25.07.1994 | 10 | (2) | 1 |
| Ilija Miličević | 20.06.2001 | 13 | (3) | 1 |
| Andrija Radovanović | 15.09.2000 | 14 | (10) | |
| Andreja Stojanović | 12.11.1998 | 2 | | |
| Ivan Tatomirović | 11.01.1989 | 3 | (2) | |
| Nikola Vasiljević | 30.06.1991 | 10 | (5) | 1 |
| **Midfielders:** | **DOB** | **M** | **(s)** | **G** |
| Mehmed Ćosić (BIH) | 25.06.1997 | 9 | (6) | 1 |
| Uroš Đuranović (MNE) | 01.02.1994 | 13 | (2) | 4 |
| Petar Đuričković | 20.06.1991 | 4 | (3) | 1 |
| Miloš Filipović | 09.05.1990 | 15 | (1) | 2 |
| Goran Lončar | 27.08.2001 | 15 | (5) | |
| Nemanja Milojević (GRE) | 23.02.1998 | 30 | (4) | 4 |
| Bogdan Mladenović | 04.04.1996 | | (1) | |
| Donald Molls Ntchamda (CMR) | 14.07.1998 | 1 | (9) | |
| Nemanja Nikolić (MNE) | 01.01.1988 | 24 | (5) | |
| Dimitrije Petronijević | 21.06.2001 | 11 | (3) | |
| Vukasin Radosavljević | 19.01.2006 | | (1) | |
| Damir Sadiković (BIH) | 07.04.1995 | 16 | (13) | 2 |
| Slobodan Simović | 22.05.1989 | 7 | (2) | |
| Abdul Musa Zubairu (NGA) | 03.10.1998 | 4 | (5) | |
| **Forwards:** | **DOB** | **M** | **(s)** | **G** |
| Nemanja Andrić | 13.06.1987 | | (9) | |
| Dražen Bagarić (CRO) | 12.11.1992 | 6 | (10) | |
| Miloš Đokić | 06.09.1991 | 22 | (9) | 1 |
| Vanja Ilić | 03.01.1999 | 16 | (12) | 2 |
| Veljko Ilić | 20.10.2005 | 1 | (3) | |
| Haris Kadrić (SVN) | 16.03.2000 | 8 | (10) | 1 |
| Srđan Kočić | 16.02.1999 | 10 | (2) | |
| Marko Mrkić | 20.08.1996 | 1 | (3) | 1 |
| Dejan Tumbas | 05.08.1999 | 2 | (6) | |
| Ante Vukušic (CRO) | 04.06.1991 | 17 | (10) | 4 |
| Luka Vulin | 07.07.2003 | | (2) | |

## Fudbalski Klub Mladost Lučani

| Founded: | 1952 | | |
|---|---|---|---|
| Stadium: | Stadion Mladost, Lučani (5,944) | | |
| Trainer: | Dragiša Žunić | | 29.06.1978 |
| [19.03.2023] | Milorad Kosanović | | 04.01.1951 |
| [13.04.2023] | Tomislav Sivić | | 29.08.1966 |

| Goalkeepers: | DOB | M | (s) | G |
|---|---|---|---|---|
| Miloš Ostojić | 21.04.1996 | 4 | | |
| Željko Samčović | 12.09.2002 | 20 | | |
| Luka Savić | 17.06.2001 | 4 | (1) | |
| Saša Stamenković | 05.01.1985 | 9 | | |
| **Defenders:** | **DOB** | **M** | **(s)** | **G** |
| Filip Babić | 27.05.1995 | 12 | (2) | |
| Nikola Ćirković | 04.12.1991 | 32 | | |
| David Dunđerski | 28.10.1999 | 10 | (4) | 1 |
| Nikola Leković | 19.12.1989 | 31 | | 1 |
| Stefan Maksimović | 13.04.2002 | 5 | | |
| Nemanja Mićević | 28.01.1999 | 5 | (2) | |
| Ivan Milošević | 03.11.1984 | 23 | | 1 |
| Nenad Perović | 20.06.2002 | | (1) | |
| Sava Pribaković | 04.02.2003 | | (1) | |
| Igor Radovanović | 13.04.2003 | 2 | (3) | |
| Darko Stanojević | 12.04.1987 | 3 | (2) | |
| Aleksandar Varjačić | 23.05.1991 | 7 | (4) | 1 |
| Mihailo Vesnić | 05.01.2001 | 14 | (4) | 1 |
| Nemanja Žunić | 09.09.2003 | 13 | (2) | 1 |
| **Midfielders:** | **DOB** | **M** | **(s)** | **G** |
| Nenad Adamović | 12.01.1989 | 4 | (7) | 1 |

| | DOB | M | (s) | G |
|---|---|---|---|---|
| Regis Samuel Baha (CMR) | 21.10.1996 | 24 | (6) | |
| Đorđe Gordić | 05.11.2004 | 14 | (2) | 3 |
| Aleksandar Ješić | 13.09.1994 | 17 | (8) | |
| Milan Marčić | 14.03.1996 | 7 | (3) | |
| Miroslav Maričić | 21.01.1998 | 5 | (4) | |
| Vukasin Marković | 13.06.2001 | | (1) | |
| Vladimir Radivojević | 04.02.1986 | 17 | (12) | 4 |
| Žarko Udovičić | 31.08.1987 | 22 | (11) | 1 |
| Marko Veličković | 12.10.2004 | | (2) | |
| Filip Žunić | 16.05.2002 | 7 | (1) | |
| **Forwards:** | **DOB** | **M** | **(s)** | **G** |
| Đorđe Babić | 04.08.2000 | | (3) | |
| Milan Bojović | 13.04.1987 | 19 | | 11 |
| Nikola Jojić | 15.09.2003 | 35 | (2) | 7 |
| Ognjen Milanović | 04.10.2001 | | (4) | |
| Marko Mirić | 26.03.1987 | 27 | | 4 |
| Jovan Mitrović | 18.05.2003 | | (2) | |
| Marko Pelivanović | 17.08.2004 | | (1) | |
| Vladimir Siladi | 23.04.1993 | 5 | (8) | 1 |
| Uros Sremčević | 24.04.2006 | | (10) | |
| Stefan Stanisavljević | 16.01.2002 | 4 | (7) | 1 |
| Nemanja Tomić | 21.01.1988 | 6 | (3) | 1 |

## Fudbalski Klub Mladost GAT Novi Sad

| Founded: | 1972 | | |
|---|---|---|---|
| Stadium: | Stadion Karađorđe, Novi Sad (14,458) | | |
| Trainer: | Branko Žigić | | 30.12.1981 |
| [02.08.2022] | Aleksandar Linta | | 22.10.1975 |
| [22.09.2022] | Ljubomir Ristovski | | 29.11.1969 |
| [09.03.2023] | Nenad Lalatović | | 22.12.1977 |

| Goalkeepers: | DOB | M | (s) | G |
|---|---|---|---|---|
| Marko Knežević | 29.03.1989 | 12 | | |
| Aleksa Milojević | 08.01.2000 | 25 | | |
| **Defenders:** | **DOB** | **M** | **(s)** | **G** |
| Đorđe Ćosić (BIH) | 11.09.1995 | 17 | | |
| Emmanuel Hackman (TOG) | 14.05.1995 | 14 | (1) | |
| Miljan Ilić | 23.05.1993 | 25 | (6) | |
| Nikola Janković | 07.06.1993 | 13 | (3) | 1 |
| Vladimir Kovačević | 11.11.1992 | 18 | | |
| Marko Mandić | 11.03.1999 | 13 | (5) | |
| Miloš Milovanović | 09.12.1987 | 6 | (4) | |
| Bojan Mlađović | 16.10.1995 | 6 | (2) | |
| Nikola Stanković | 18.12.1993 | 6 | (2) | |
| Strahinja Tanasijević | 12.06.1997 | 15 | | |
| Nikola Vujadinović (MNE) | 31.07.1986 | 12 | | |
| **Midfielders:** | **DOB** | **M** | **(s)** | **G** |
| Lazar Arsić | 24.09.1991 | 8 | (12) | |
| Miroslav Bjeloš | 29.10.1990 | 5 | (6) | |
| Đorđe Denić | 01.04.1996 | 23 | (2) | 1 |
| Srđan Dimitrov | 28.07.1992 | 15 | (2) | 1 |
| Romain Thierry Marie Gall (USA) | 31.01.1995 | 4 | (3) | 1 |
| Branimir Jočić | 10.07.1994 | 9 | (5) | |

| | DOB | M | (s) | G |
|---|---|---|---|---|
| Novica Maksimović | 04.04.1988 | 30 | (1) | 6 |
| Miroslav Maričić | 21.01.1998 | 7 | (4) | |
| Saša Marković | 13.03.1991 | 9 | (7) | 1 |
| Aleksa Marušić (MNE) | 08.06.1999 | 3 | (7) | 1 |
| Dušan Mijić | 17.06.1993 | 5 | (4) | |
| Danilo Miladinović | 28.02.2002 | | (4) | |
| Jovan Mituljikić | 20.01.2003 | 5 | (9) | 1 |
| Danilo Sekulić | 18.04.1990 | 6 | (8) | |
| **Forwards:** | **DOB** | **M** | **(s)** | **G** |
| Ilija Babić | 03.08.2002 | 15 | (13) | |
| *Cristian* Daniel Dal Bello Fagundes (BRA) | 13.12.1999 | 10 | (4) | 1 |
| Zoran Karać | 30.06.1995 | | (2) | |
| Aleksandar Katanić | 15.08.1995 | 6 | (10) | |
| Nemanja Milić | 25.05.1990 | 14 | (3) | 3 |
| Milan Mirosavljev | 24.04.1995 | 9 | (1) | 2 |
| Nikola Popović | 31.05.1994 | 16 | (2) | |
| Dragoljub Radoman (MNE) | 09.01.2004 | 1 | (4) | |
| Andrija Radulović (MNE) | 03.07.2002 | 16 | (1) | 4 |
| Milan Savić (BIH) | 19.05.2000 | | (4) | |
| Mile Savković | 03.11.1992 | 1 | (2) | |
| Milan Vidakov | 19.08.2000 | 8 | (13) | 2 |

## Fudbalski Klub Napredak Kruševac

| Founded: | 08.12.1946 | | |
|---|---|---|---|
| Stadium: | Stadion Mladost, Kruševac (10,331) | | |
| Trainer: | Dušan Đorđević | | 23.04.1970 |
| [22.02.2023] | Dragan Perišić | | 27.10.1979 |

| Goalkeepers: | DOB | M | (s) | G |
|---|---|---|---|---|
| Nikola Petrić | 11.05.1991 | 31 | | |
| Vladimir Savić | 12.03.1996 | 6 | | |
| **Defenders:** | **DOB** | **M** | **(s)** | **G** |
| Nemanja Đeković | 09.05.2003 | 24 | (4) | 2 |
| Stefan Jovanović | 07.04.1994 | 31 | | 1 |
| Dejan Kerkez | 20.01.1996 | 31 | | 1 |
| Nemanja Kojičić | 22.08.1997 | 4 | (1) | |
| Ognjen Mršić | 13.02.1999 | 9 | (1) | |
| Vladimir Prijović | 26.06.2002 | 12 | (3) | 1 |
| Josip Projić | 23.08.1987 | 3 | (3) | |
| Nikola Vukajlović | 13.05.1996 | 25 | (5) | |
| **Midfielders:** | **DOB** | **M** | **(s)** | **G** |
| Klemen Bolha (SVN) | 19.03.1993 | 17 | (7) | |
| Nikola Knežević | 10.03.2003 | 8 | (7) | |
| Nemanja Krstić | 05.08.1994 | 28 | (6) | 3 |
| Luka Laban | 07.04.2004 | 1 | (5) | |

| | DOB | M | (s) | G |
|---|---|---|---|---|
| Petar Mićin | 29.09.1998 | 12 | (4) | |
| Marko Pantić | 18.06.1998 | 8 | (14) | |
| Marko Putinčanin | 16.12.1987 | 26 | (1) | 3 |
| Uroš Rasković | 02.09.2000 | | (2) | |
| Nikola Stanković | 24.04.2003 | 11 | (4) | |
| **Forwards:** | **DOB** | **M** | **(s)** | **G** |
| Nebojša Bastajić | 20.08.1990 | 28 | (3) | 5 |
| Bojan Čečarić | 10.10.1993 | 17 | (15) | 2 |
| Miloš Džugurdić | 02.12.1992 | | (1) | |
| Đorđe Jovanović | 17.08.2001 | 12 | (16) | 1 |
| Srđan Kočić | 16.02.1999 | 1 | (9) | |
| Uroš Ljubomirac | 12.04.1990 | 10 | (5) | |
| Bojan Matić | 22.12.1991 | 21 | (8) | 3 |
| Mark Roosnupp (EST) | 12.05.1997 | 2 | (10) | |
| Mlađan Stevanović | 01.01.1995 | 2 | (9) | |
| Marko Šarić | 28.11.1998 | 27 | (8) | 5 |
| Jovan Zogović | 11.02.2001 | | (8) | |

## Fudbalski Klub Novi Pazar

| | | | | |
|---|---|---|---|---|
| **Founded**: | 1928 | | | |
| **Stadium**: | Gradski stadion, Novi Pazar (12,000) | | | |
| **Trainer**: | Vladimir Gaćinović | | | 03.01.1966 |
| [15.10.2022] | Damir Čakar (MNE) | | | 28.06.1973 |
| [25.10.2022] | Izet Ljajić | | | 12.08.1970 |
| [14.12.2022] | Aleksandar Stanković | | | 07.03.1981 |
| [24.03.2023] | Davor Berber | | | 22.05.1977 |

| Goalkeepers: | DOB | M | (s) | G |
|---|---|---|---|---|
| Almin Kahrimanović | 03.10.2003 | 2 | | |
| Filip Kljajić | 16.08.1990 | 26 | | |
| Lazar Slavković | 03.03.2002 | 9 | | |
| **Defenders:** | **DOB** | **M** | **(s)** | **G** |
| Ensar Brunčević | 13.02.1999 | | (4) | |
| Slavko Damjanović | 02.11.1992 | 3 | (1) | |
| Milan Joksimović | 09.02.1990 | 33 | (1) | 2 |
| Filip Jović | 27.02.2000 | 25 | (6) | |
| Numan Kurdić (BIH) | 01.07.1999 | 14 | (3) | |
| Periša Pešukić (MNE) | 07.12.1997 | 31 | | |
| Slobodan Rubežić | 21.03.2000 | 35 | | 2 |
| Vahid Zimonjić | 14.07.2000 | 3 | (11) | |
| **Midfielders:** | **DOB** | **M** | **(s)** | **G** |
| Adetunji Rasaq Adeshina (NGA) | 02.12.2004 | 2 | (2) | |
| Semir Alić | 27.03.2004 | 3 | (9) | |
| Petar Đuričković | 20.06.1991 | 11 | (4) | |
| Mitar Ergelaš | 05.08.2002 | 12 | (11) | 1 |
| Miloš Filipović | 09.05.1990 | 6 | (4) | |
| Sead Islamović | 24.09.1999 | 13 | (4) | 1 |

| Danko Kiković | 21.09.1994 | 10 | (10) | |
|---|---|---|---|---|
| Kemal Koninčanin | 07.06.2005 | | (2) | |
| Stefan Lončar (MNE) | 19.02.1996 | 18 | | 1 |
| Igor Maksimović | 31.07.1999 | 3 | (2) | |
| Miloš Mijić | 22.11.1989 | 24 | (8) | 5 |
| Miljan Momčilović | 17.03.2001 | 24 | (3) | 1 |
| Mustafa Mujezinović (BIH) | 06.05.1993 | 1 | (10) | |
| Samir Radovac (BIH) | 25.01.1996 | 5 | (10) | |
| **Forwards:** | **DOB** | **M** | **(s)** | **G** |
| Nikola Bogdanovski (MKD) | 25.01.1999 | 14 | (14) | 2 |
| Hamza Bronja | 27.08.2004 | | (2) | |
| Zoran Danoski (MKD) | 20.10.1990 | 4 | (3) | 2 |
| Ibrahim Fijuljanin | 08.02.2004 | | (4) | |
| Nenad Gavrić | 12.12.1991 | 9 | (10) | 1 |
| Andrija Majdevac | 07.08.1997 | 29 | (1) | 12 |
| Bojica Nikčević (MNE) | 04.02.2000 | 25 | (2) | 7 |
| Luka Ratković | 09.04.1997 | 4 | (2) | |
| Slobodan Stanojlović | 28.12.2001 | 9 | (14) | 3 |
| Marko Vučić (MNE) | 30.12.1996 | | (3) | |

## Fudbalski Klub Partizan Beograd

| | | | | |
|---|---|---|---|---|
| **Founded**: | 04.10.1945 | | | |
| **Stadium**: | Stadion Partizan, Beograd (29,775) | | | |
| **Trainer**: | Ilija Stolica | | | 07.07.1978 |
| [13.08.2022] | Gordan Petrić | | | 30.07.1969 |
| [27.02.2023] | Igor Duljaj | | | 29.10.1979 |

| Goalkeepers: | DOB | M | (s) | G |
|---|---|---|---|---|
| Aleksandar Popović | 27.09.1999 | 28 | | |
| Nemanja Stevanović | 08.05.1992 | 9 | | |
| **Defenders:** | **DOB** | **M** | **(s)** | **G** |
| Aleksander Filipović | 20.12.1994 | 20 | | 2 |
| Mihajlo Ilić | 04.06.2003 | 6 | (2) | |
| Svetozar Marković | 23.03.2000 | 21 | (1) | 2 |
| Siniša Saničanin (BIH) | 24.04.1995 | 16 | (1) | 1 |
| Zlatan Šehović | 08.08.2000 | 2 | (7) | 1 |
| Slobodan Urošević | 15.04.1994 | 35 | | 4 |
| Igor Vujačić (MNE) | 08.08.1994 | 32 | (1) | 2 |
| Marko Živković | 17.05.1994 | 14 | (5) | 1 |
| **Midfielders:** | **DOB** | **M** | **(s)** | **G** |
| Erickson Patrick Correia Andrade I (CPV) | 09.02.1993 | 11 | (5) | |
| Kristijan Belić | 25.03.2001 | 19 | (3) | 1 |
| Andrés Felipe Colorado Sánchez (COL) | 01.12.1998 | 12 | (2) | 1 |
| Ljubomir Fejsa | 14.08.1988 | 12 | (11) | |

| Janko Jevremović | 14.07.2004 | | (8) | |
|---|---|---|---|---|
| Bibras Natcho (ISR) | 18.02.1988 | 30 | (6) | 12 |
| Danilo Pantić | 26.10.1996 | 12 | (6) | 1 |
| Mihajlo Petković | 27.05.2004 | 5 | (2) | 1 |
| Mateja Stjepanović | 20.02.2004 | | (1) | |
| Hamidou Traoré (MLI) | 07.10.1996 | 10 | (4) | |
| Saša Zdjelar | 20.03.1995 | 3 | | |
| **Forwards:** | **DOB** | **M** | **(s)** | **G** |
| Samed Baždar | 31.01.2004 | 5 | (22) | 4 |
| Fousséni Diabaté (MLI) | 18.10.1995 | 26 | (6) | 2 |
| Filip Holender (HUN) | 27.07.1994 | | (1) | |
| Nemanja Jović | 08.08.2002 | 7 | (15) | 2 |
| Aleksandar Lutovac | 28.06.1997 | 3 | (7) | 1 |
| Queensy Miquel Saymon Wensley (NED) | 19.08.1995 | 27 | (6) | 7 |
| Andrija Pavlović | 16.11.1993 | 6 | (12) | 2 |
| Ricardo Jorge Pires Gomes (CPV) | 18.12.1991 | 34 | (1) | 20 |
| Nikola Terzić | 28.09.2000 | 2 | (6) | 1 |

## Fudbalski Klub Radnički 1923 Kragujevac

| | | | | |
|---|---|---|---|---|
| **Founded**: | 31.05.1923 | | | |
| **Stadium**: | Stadion Čika Dača, Kragujevac (15,100) | | | |
| **Trainer**: | Dejan Joksimović | | | 24.10.1974 |

| Goalkeepers: | DOB | M | (s) | G |
|---|---|---|---|---|
| Stojan Leković | 07.08.2001 | 22 | | |
| Ognjen Lukić | 04.07.2003 | 1 | | |
| Milos Mladenović | 20.11.2001 | 7 | | |
| Lazar Raičević | 22.02.1998 | 7 | | |
| **Defenders:** | **DOB** | **M** | **(s)** | **G** |
| Dušan Cvetinović | 24.12.1988 | 15 | | |
| Filip Ivanović | 13.02.1992 | 30 | (1) | |
| Marko Janković | 29.08.2000 | | (1) | |
| Luka Malić (BIH) | 07.05.2000 | 2 | (1) | |
| Nikola Miličić | 04.07.2004 | 20 | (7) | |
| Milan Mitrović | 02.07.1988 | 14 | | |
| Ljubiša Pecelj | 29.09.1993 | 24 | (1) | 1 |
| Dajan Ponjević | 10.02.1989 | 13 | (4) | |
| Luka Slavković | 02.01.2007 | | (1) | |
| Vladimír Tomović | 31.05.2003 | 5 | (2) | |
| Aleksandar Varjačić | 23.05.1991 | 2 | (2) | |
| Nikola Vlajković | 13.09.1995 | 23 | (1) | |
| **Midfielders:** | **DOB** | **M** | **(s)** | **G** |
| Miloš Brnović (MNE) | 26.04.2000 | 1 | (11) | |
| Vasilije Đurić | 18.07.1998 | 9 | (5) | 2 |
| Nikola Kovačević | 14.04.1994 | 2 | (2) | |

| Damjan Krajišnik | 24.04.1997 | 26 | (7) | 4 |
|---|---|---|---|---|
| Miloš Milisavljević | 26.10.1992 | 2 | (1) | |
| Luka Milojević | 09.06.2003 | | (4) | |
| Luka Milunović | 21.12.1992 | 10 | (6) | 3 |
| Dragoljub Srnić | 12.01.1992 | 12 | (9) | |
| Miloš Vidović | 03.10.1989 | 28 | (1) | 4 |
| Uroš Vidović | 09.06.1994 | 1 | (8) | |
| Luka Zorić | 02.08.1998 | 17 | (13) | 4 |
| **Forwards:** | **DOB** | **M** | **(s)** | **G** |
| Charles Geoffrey Chinedu (NGA) | 01.10.1997 | 6 | (4) | 2 |
| Stefan Čolović | 16.04.1994 | 22 | (2) | 2 |
| *Evandro* da Silva (BRA) | 14.01.1997 | 13 | (8) | 1 |
| Đorđe Jovanović | 09.03.2003 | 6 | (12) | |
| Đorđe Maksimović | 09.10.1999 | 5 | (20) | |
| Marko Mirić | 26.03.1987 | 6 | | |
| Aleksandar Petrović | 16.08.2004 | | (1) | |
| Nikola Ristović | 16.01.2001 | | (1) | |
| Dušan Stoiljković | 05.09.1994 | 11 | (8) | 2 |
| Marko Šimić (CRO) | 23.01.1988 | 5 | (1) | 1 |
| Nemanja Tomić | 21.01.1988 | 12 | (4) | 3 |
| Vojo Ubiparip | 10.05.1988 | 3 | (6) | 1 |
| Milutin Vidosavljević | 21.02.2001 | 25 | (4) | 7 |

## Fudbalski Klub Radnički Niš

| | | |
|---|---|---|
| **Founded**: | 24.04.1923 | |
| **Stadium**: | Stadion Čair, Niš (18,151) | |
| **Trainer**: | Tomislav Sivić | 29.08.1966 |
| [12.08.2022] | Saša Mrkić | 16.12.1967 |
| [05.09.2022] | Nenad Lalatović | 06.09.2022 |
| [08.03.2023] | Dragan Šarac | 27.09.1975 |

| Goalkeepers: | DOB | M | (s) | G |
|---|---|---|---|---|
| Marko Drobnjak | 17.05.1995 | 4 | | |
| Filip Dujmović (BIH) | 12.03.1999 | 1 | | |
| Dragan Rosić | 15.11.1996 | 19 | | |
| Dimitrije Stevanović | 27.08.2004 | 13 | | |
| **Defenders:** | **DOB** | **M** | **(s)** | **G** |
| Nikola Aksentijević | 09.03.1993 | 12 | (1) | |
| Nikola Andrić | 23.05.1992 | 6 | (1) | |
| Lazar Đorđević | 14.07.1992 | 1 | | |
| Amougou Ignace Thierry Etongou (CMR) | 22.09.1999 | 14 | (2) | |
| Filip Frei (SUI) | 07.01.2001 | 2 | (3) | |
| Maka Gakou (FRA) | 13.03.2000 | 6 | (4) | |
| Nemanja Jovičić | 13.04.2000 | 1 | (4) | |
| Stefan Marjanović | 25.07.1994 | 16 | (1) | |
| Bojan Mlađović | 16.10.1995 | 2 | | 1 |
| Milan Savić | 04.04.1994 | 21 | (3) | |
| Nikola Stajić | 08.09.2001 | 5 | (4) | |
| Andreja Stojanović | 12.11.1998 | 25 | (3) | |
| Anton Tolordava (GEO) | 02.08.1996 | 6 | | |
| Boris Varga | 14.08.1993 | 11 | | |
| Mbouri Basile Yamkam (CMR) | 02.01.1998 | 32 | (1) | |
| **Midfielders:** | **DOB** | **M** | **(s)** | **G** |
| Lazar Arsić | 24.09.1991 | | (1) | |

| | DOB | M | (s) | G |
|---|---|---|---|---|
| Marko Đurišić | 17.07.1997 | 8 | (4) | |
| Saša Marjanović | 13.11.1987 | 16 | (13) | 4 |
| Aleksandar Mesarović | 27.09.1998 | 18 | (13) | |
| Petar Mićin | 29.09.1998 | 13 | (3) | 1 |
| Ryohei Michibuchi (JPN) | 16.06.1994 | 2 | (2) | |
| Stefan Mitrović | 15.08.2002 | 2 | | |
| Giorgi Papunashvili (GEO) | 02.09.1995 | 1 | (2) | |
| Lazar Pavlović | 02.11.2001 | 9 | (3) | |
| Aleksandr Pejović | 28.12.1990 | 32 | (1) | 4 |
| **Forwards:** | **DOB** | **M** | **(s)** | **G** |
| Ognjen Ajdar | 05.04.2003 | | (19) | |
| Nemanja Belaković | 08.01.1997 | 13 | (3) | 2 |
| Stefan Cvetković | 12.01.1998 | 12 | (13) | 2 |
| Stefan Dimić | 01.05.1993 | 13 | (2) | 2 |
| Aleksa Dušanić | 05.02.2003 | | (2) | |
| Lazar Jovanović | 13.07.1993 | 5 | | 1 |
| Saša Jovanović | 30.08.1993 | 10 | (14) | 1 |
| Stefan Mihajlović | 24.06.1994 | | (1) | |
| Sava Petrov | 18.06.1998 | 27 | (8) | 2 |
| Matija Petrović | 13.06.2004 | 1 | (5) | |
| Miljan Škrbić | 18.09.1995 | 8 | (10) | 7 |
| Nikola Štulić | 08.09.2001 | 17 | (2) | 10 |
| Branislav Tomić | 12.02.1995 | 3 | (8) | |

## Fudbalski Klub Radnik Surdulica

| | | |
|---|---|---|
| **Founded**: | 1926 | |
| **Stadium**: | Stadion Surdulica, Surdulica (3,312) | |
| **Trainer**: | Aleksandar Linta | 22.10.1975 |
| [02.08.2022] | Dragan Radojičić (MNE) | 02.08.2022 |
| [09.09.2022] | Dragan Perišić (MNE) | 27.10.1979 |
| [20.10.2022] | Simo Krunić (BIH) | 03.01.1967 |
| [01.01.2023] | Slavoljub Đorđević | 15.02.1981 |

| Goalkeepers: | DOB | M | (s) | G |
|---|---|---|---|---|
| Stefan Ranđelović | 27.01.1999 | 31 | | |
| Nikola Vujanac | 22.06.1991 | 6 | | |
| **Defenders:** | **DOB** | **M** | **(s)** | **G** |
| Sadick Abubakar (GHA) | 02.02.1998 | 18 | (1) | 1 |
| Taras Bondarenko (UKR) | 23.09.1992 | 17 | | 2 |
| Dušan Hodžić (BIH) | 31.10.1993 | 12 | (3) | |
| Nikola Ignjatović | 02.02.1998 | 4 | (3) | |
| Milan Jezdimirović | 05.09.1996 | 2 | (1) | |
| Ranko Jokić | 22.04.1999 | 24 | (8) | 1 |
| Uroš Lazić | 15.03.2003 | 13 | (4) | |
| Leandro Climaco Pinto (BRA) | 24.01.1994 | 5 | (1) | |
| Dušan Stevanović | 22.06.1996 | 24 | | |
| Uroš Stojanović | 23.08.1995 | 26 | (7) | 1 |
| **Midfielders:** | **DOB** | **M** | **(s)** | **G** |
| Siniša Babić | 13.02.1991 | 11 | (3) | |
| Viktor Lukić | 06.10.2000 | 1 | (9) | |
| Ousman Marong (GAM) | 21.06.1999 | 2 | (8) | |
| Predrag Medić | 21.05.1998 | 8 | (1) | |
| Andrija Milić | 15.07.2001 | 2 | (6) | |

| | DOB | M | (s) | G |
|---|---|---|---|---|
| Vuk Mitošević | 12.02.1991 | 1 | (2) | |
| Davor Nedeljković | 04.02.1996 | 5 | (5) | 1 |
| Mihailo Oreščanin | 07.09.1997 | 30 | (2) | 2 |
| Filip Petrović | 12.05.2002 | 3 | (8) | |
| Edin Rustemović (BIH) | 06.01.1993 | 22 | | 1 |
| Nemanja Subotić | 23.01.1992 | 16 | (16) | 1 |
| **Forwards:** | **DOB** | **M** | **(s)** | **G** |
| Vukasin Bogdanović | 04.10.2002 | 12 | (8) | |
| Nikola Bogdanovski (MKD) | 25.01.1999 | 2 | (2) | |
| Zoran Danoski (MKD) | 20.10.1990 | 18 | (2) | 2 |
| Dejan Drazić | 26.09.1995 | 8 | (6) | |
| Borko Duronjić | 24.09.1997 | 17 | (12) | 2 |
| Vasilije Janjić | 25.01.1995 | 1 | (5) | |
| Veljko Jovanović | 02.07.2001 | 1 | (3) | |
| Petar Kunić (BIH) | 15.07.1993 | 7 | (19) | 3 |
| Milan Makarić | 04.10.1995 | 15 | (3) | |
| Uroš Milovanović | 18.10.2000 | 3 | (3) | |
| Andrija Radulović (MNE) | 03.07.2002 | 18 | | 5 |
| Miloš Spasić | 29.07.1997 | 19 | | 5 |
| Luka Velikić | 01.01.2001 | 3 | (3) | |

## Fudbalski Klub Spartak Subotica

| | | |
|---|---|---|
| **Founded**: | 21.04.1945 | |
| **Stadium**: | Gradski stadion, Subotica (13,000) | |
| **Trainer**: | Slavko Petrović | 10.08.1958 |
| [22.09.2022] | Ljubiša Dunđerski | 26.05.1972 |
| [27.03.2023] | Milan Milanović | 10.01.1963 |

| Goalkeepers: | DOB | M | (s) | G |
|---|---|---|---|---|
| Mišo Dubljanić (MNE) | 20.12.1999 | 10 | | |
| Filip Manojlović | 25.04.1996 | 27 | | |
| **Defenders:** | **DOB** | **M** | **(s)** | **G** |
| Nikolaos Baxevanos (GRE) | 16.07.1999 | 4 | (2) | |
| Mihailo Bogićević (SUI) | 30.05.1998 | 16 | (4) | |
| Marko Bugarin (MNE) | 16.08.1999 | 9 | (3) | |
| Dženan Bureković (BIH) | 29.05.1995 | 1 | (2) | |
| David Dunđerski | 28.10.1999 | 5 | (3) | |
| Aleksa Đurasović II (MNE) | 21.04.2004 | | (5) | |
| Stefan Filipović | 21.06.1994 | 12 | (2) | |
| Jovan Marinković | 12.09.1996 | 9 | (4) | |
| Ognjen Mitrović | 30.06.1999 | 8 | (1) | |
| Miloš Ostojić | 03.08.1991 | 24 | (1) | |
| Aleksandar Tanasin | 15.11.1991 | 23 | (7) | 1 |
| Aleksandar Vidović | 12.05.2001 | | (1) | |
| Vladimir Vitorović | 03.10.2000 | 22 | (6) | 1 |
| **Midfielders:** | **DOB** | **M** | **(s)** | **G** |
| Morice Abraham (TAN) | 13.08.2003 | | (15) | |

| | DOB | M | (s) | G |
|---|---|---|---|---|
| Edmund Addo (GHA) | 17.05.2000 | 14 | (2) | |
| Aleksa Đurasović I | 23.12.2002 | 17 | (13) | 1 |
| Noboru Shimura (JPN) | 11.03.1993 | 29 | (2) | 2 |
| Petar Stanić | 14.08.2001 | 21 | (9) | 3 |
| Srđan Šćepanović | 23.10.1998 | 4 | (5) | |
| Andrej Todoroski (MKD) | 19.04.1999 | 18 | (11) | 5 |
| Miloš Tošeski (MKD) | 24.02.1998 | 9 | (7) | 1 |
| Janko Tumbasević | 14.01.1985 | 22 | (10) | 2 |
| Vladan Vidaković | 14.03.1999 | 2 | | |
| **Forwards:** | **DOB** | **M** | **(s)** | **G** |
| Luka Bijelović | 11.04.2001 | 29 | (2) | 8 |
| Radivoj Bosić | 01.12.2000 | 2 | (5) | |
| Srđan Hrstić | 18.07.2003 | 22 | (5) | 6 |
| Marko Obradović | 30.06.1991 | 12 | (5) | 2 |
| Kwaku Osei (GHA) | 17.08.2000 | 1 | (4) | |
| Milos Rošević | 13.05.2001 | 4 | (12) | |
| Nikola Srećković | 26.04.1996 | 31 | (3) | 6 |
| Lazar Stajković | 18.12.2003 | | (4) | |
| Vojo Ubiparip | 10.05.1988 | | (8) | |

## Fudbalski Klub Topolyai Sport Club Bačka Topola

| | Founded: | 1913 (*as Topolyai Sport Club*) | | |
|---|---|---|---|---|
| | Stadium: | TSC Arena, Bačka Topola (4,500) | | |
| | Trainer: | Žarko Lazetić | | 22.02.1982 |

| Goalkeepers: | DOB | M | (s) | G |
|---|---|---|---|---|
| Nenad Filipović | 24.04.1987 | 2 | | |
| Veljko Ilić | 21.07.2003 | 35 | | |
| **Defenders:** | **DOB** | **M** | **(s)** | **G** |
| Goran Antonić | 03.11.1990 | 23 | (4) | 2 |
| Dušan Cvetinović | 24.12.1988 | 7 | (2) | |
| Miloš Cvetković | 06.01.1990 | 31 | (1) | 2 |
| Josip Čalušić (CRO) | 11.10.1993 | 29 | (2) | 2 |
| Nemanja Krsmanović | 09.05.2003 | | (1) | |
| Vukašin Krstić | 13.04.2003 | 2 | (4) | |
| Nemanja Petrović | 17.04.1992 | 30 | (2) | 4 |
| Nemanja Stojić | 15.01.1998 | 36 | | 1 |
| Aranđel Stojković | 02.03.1995 | 25 | (4) | 1 |
| **Midfielders:** | **DOB** | **M** | **(s)** | **G** |
| Mihajlo Banjac | 10.11.1999 | 1 | | 1 |
| Boubacari Doucouré (FRA) | 19.03.1999 | | (1) | |
| Ifet Đakovac | 05.12.1997 | 34 | | 10 |
| Luka Ilić | 02.07.1999 | 22 | (3) | 6 |
| Miljan Krpić | 03.07.2003 | | (12) | |
| Nikola Kuveljić | 06.04.1997 | 20 | (8) | |
| Mihajlo Milosavić | 14.07.2004 | | (1) | |
| Ivan Milosavljević | 19.03.2000 | 14 | (16) | 1 |
| Martin Mircevski (MKD) | 11.02.1997 | 8 | (10) | 7 |
| Milán Rádin | 25.06.1991 | 7 | (3) | |
| Saša Tomanović | 20.09.1989 | 5 | (10) | |
| **Forwards:** | **DOB** | **M** | **(s)** | **G** |
| Nikola Čolić | 17.08.2002 | | (2) | |
| Saša Jovanović | 15.12.1991 | 33 | (1) | 10 |
| Petar Ratkov | 18.08.2003 | 31 | (5) | 13 |
| Jug Stanojev | 29.07.1999 | 3 | (13) | 1 |
| Slobodan Stanojlović | 28.12.2001 | | (6) | 1 |
| Adrian Szőke (HUN) | 01.07.1998 | | (3) | |
| Nikolas Špalek (SVK) | 12.02.1997 | | (4) | |
| Stefan Vukić | 29.06.1995 | 9 | (18) | 3 |

## Fudbalski Klub Vojvodina Novi Sad

| | Founded: | 06.03.1914 | | |
|---|---|---|---|---|
| | Stadium: | Stadion Karađorđe, Novi Sad (14,458) | | |
| | Trainer: | Milan Rastavac | | 01.11.1973 |
| [25.02.2023] | | Radoslav Batak (MNE) | | 15.08.1977 |

| Goalkeepers: | DOB | M | (s) | G |
|---|---|---|---|---|
| Lazar Carević (MNE) | 16.03.1999 | 35 | | |
| Nikola Simić | 21.12.1996 | 2 | (1) | |
| **Defenders:** | **DOB** | **M** | **(s)** | **G** |
| Filip Antonijević | 24.07.2000 | 7 | (2) | |
| Marko Bjeković | 21.09.2000 | 14 | (5) | |
| Vuk Bogdanović | 03.04.2002 | | (2) | |
| Stefan Đorđević | 13.03.1991 | 23 | (1) | |
| Igor Jeličić | 28.02.2000 | 26 | (2) | |
| Boris Kopitović (MNE) | 17.09.1994 | 1 | | |
| Milan Lazarević | 10.01.1997 | 25 | (4) | 1 |
| Nemanja Ljubisavljević | 26.11.1996 | 8 | (4) | |
| Mamadou Traoré (MLI) | 03.10.1994 | 28 | (3) | 1 |
| Uroš Vitas | 06.07.1992 | 17 | (1) | |
| **Midfielders:** | **DOB** | **M** | **(s)** | **G** |
| Aleksandar Busnić | 04.12.1997 | 10 | (12) | 2 |
| Vladimir Miletić | 05.03.2003 | 5 | (7) | |
| Radomir Milosavljević | 28.07.1992 | 18 | (8) | 2 |
| Uroš Nikolić | 14.12.1993 | 12 | (12) | 8 |
| Mirko Topić | 05.02.2001 | 27 | (8) | |
| Dejan Zukić | 07.05.2001 | 16 | (16) | 3 |
| **Forwards:** | **DOB** | **M** | **(s)** | **G** |
| Yves Baraye (SEN) | 22.06.1992 | 17 | (17) | 5 |
| Nebojša Bastajić | 20.08.1990 | 1 | (2) | |
| Nikola Čumić | 20.11.1998 | 25 | (4) | 13 |
| Uroš Kabić | 01.01.2004 | 7 | (12) | 2 |
| Filip Malbašić | 18.11.1992 | 20 | (9) | 6 |
| Jovan Milošević | 31.07.2005 | 6 | (12) | 3 |
| Mihajlo Nešković | 09.02.2000 | 4 | (3) | |
| Nemanja Nikolić | 19.10.1992 | 25 | (6) | 4 |
| Veljko Simić | 17.02.1995 | 26 | (8) | 7 |
| Milan Vidakov | 19.08.2000 | 1 | (3) | |
| Ivan Vukčević (MNE) | 04.12.2001 | 1 | (7) | |

## Fudbalski Klub Voždovac Beograd

| | Founded: | 1912 | | |
|---|---|---|---|---|
| | Stadium: | Stadion Shopping Center, Beograd (5,175) | | |
| | Trainer: | Nebojša Jandrić | | 02.10.1975 |
| [19.08.2022] | | Nikola Puača | | 03.01.1982 |

| Goalkeepers: | DOB | M | (s) | G |
|---|---|---|---|---|
| Andrija Katić | 17.02.2002 | 14 | | |
| Miloš Krunić | 22.11.1996 | 23 | (1) | |
| **Defenders:** | **DOB** | **M** | **(s)** | **G** |
| Filip Damjanović | 02.07.1998 | 35 | | |
| Damjan Daničić | 24.01.2000 | 4 | (6) | |
| Mateja Đorđević | 17.01.2003 | 21 | (4) | |
| Vukašin Đurđević | 24.01.2004 | | (1) | 1 |
| Nikola Đuričić | 12.12.1999 | 13 | (3) | |
| Stefan Hajdin | 15.04.1994 | 19 | | 2 |
| Dušan Joković | 04.07.1999 | 1 | (1) | |
| Marko Mijailović | 14.08.1997 | 29 | (4) | 1 |
| Miloš Milović (MNE) | 22.12.1995 | 16 | | 1 |
| Nenad Nikić (BIH) | 08.07.2001 | 1 | (3) | |
| Nikola Zečević | 16.06.2004 | 7 | (4) | |
| **Midfielders:** | **DOB** | **M** | **(s)** | **G** |
| Edin Ajdinović | 07.06.2001 | 18 | (10) | 1 |
| Marko Đurišić | 17.07.1997 | 7 | (2) | |
| Marko Ivezić | 02.12.2001 | 27 | (2) | |
| Bogdan Jočić | 11.01.2001 | 12 | (10) | 1 |
| Aleksa Matić | 20.09.2002 | 12 | (3) | |
| Predrag Medić | 21.05.1998 | 2 | (7) | |
| Ivan Milosavljević | 19.03.2000 | | (2) | |
| Matija Mitrović | 12.12.2004 | | (4) | |
| Martin Novaković | 05.01.2001 | 1 | (8) | |
| Vladan Novevski | 13.05.2002 | 4 | (4) | |
| Stefan Purtić | 06.08.1998 | 12 | (5) | |
| Arihiro Sentoku (JPN) | 09.12.1998 | 4 | (7) | 1 |
| **Forwards:** | **DOB** | **M** | **(s)** | **G** |
| Borisav Burmaz | 21.04.2001 | 24 | (7) | 6 |
| Aleksandar Ćirković | 21.09.2001 | 5 | | |
| Dušan Dodić | 09.03.2004 | | (1) | |
| Haris Kadrić (SVN) | 16.03.2000 | 1 | (9) | 1 |
| Obren Kljajić (BIH) | 18.09.2003 | | (2) | |
| Andrija Lazarevič | 03.04.2004 | 11 | (3) | |
| Branislav Marković | 12.10.1998 | 1 | (6) | |
| Mihajlo Nešković | 09.02.2000 | 21 | (2) | 2 |
| Miloš Pantović | 24.08.2002 | 29 | (2) | 7 |
| Dragan Stoisavljević | 25.11.2003 | 2 | (9) | |
| Danilo Teodorović (BIH) | 21.05.2002 | 10 | (14) | 3 |
| Veljko Trifunović | 04.08.1998 | 2 | (11) | 1 |
| Nikša Vujanović (MNE) | 03.03.2001 | 19 | (8) | 1 |

### Regular Season

| | | | | | | | | | | |
|---|---|---|---|---|---|---|---|---|---|---|
| 1. | FK IMT Beograd | 30 | 18 | 7 | 5 | 45 | - | 27 | 61 |
| 2. | FK Železničar Pančevo | 30 | 17 | 6 | 7 | 47 | - | 25 | 57 |
| 3. | FK Grafičar Beograd | 30 | 15 | 5 | 10 | 57 | - | 38 | 50 |
| 4. | FK Radnički Sremska Mitrovica | 30 | 11 | 12 | 7 | 30 | - | 26 | 45 |
| 5. | FK Jedintsvo Ub | 30 | 12 | 8 | 10 | 32 | - | 26 | 44 |
| 6. | RFK Novi Sad 1921 | 30 | 12 | 7 | 11 | 34 | - | 31 | 43 |
| 7. | FK Inđija | 30 | 10 | 13 | 7 | 38 | - | 30 | 43 |
| 8. | FK Radnički Beograd | 30 | 12 | 4 | 14 | 27 | - | 35 | 40 |
| 9. | FK Sloboda Užice | 30 | 7 | 16 | 7 | 33 | - | 34 | 37 |
| 10. | OFK Vršac | 30 | 10 | 7 | 13 | 28 | - | 33 | 37 |
| 11. | FK Mačva Šabac | 30 | 8 | 13 | 9 | 28 | - | 31 | 37 |
| 12. | FK Metalac Gornji Milanovac | 30 | 9 | 8 | 13 | 29 | - | 36 | 35 |
| 13. | FK Trayal Kruševac | 30 | 9 | 8 | 13 | 29 | - | 37 | 35 |
| 14. | FK Loznica | 30 | 7 | 10 | 13 | 28 | - | 45 | 31 |
| 15. | FK Rad Beograd | 30 | 5 | 13 | 12 | 32 | - | 46 | 28 |
| 16. | FK Zlatibor Čajetina | 30 | 4 | 11 | 15 | 26 | - | 43 | 23 |

Team ranked 1-8 were qualified for the Promotion Round, while teams ranked 9-16 were qualified for the Relegation Round.

### Promotion Round

| | | | | | | | | | | |
|---|---|---|---|---|---|---|---|---|---|---|
| 1. | FK IMT Beograd (*Promoted*) | 37 | 22 | 9 | 6 | 63 | - | 36 | 75 |
| 2. | FK Železničar Pančevo (*Promoted*) | 37 | 20 | 8 | 9 | 63 | - | 35 | 68 |
| 3. | FK Grafičar Beograd (*Promotion Play-offs*) | 37 | 17 | 9 | 11 | 65 | - | 46 | 60 |
| 4. | FK Inđija (*Promotion Play-offs*) | 37 | 13 | 15 | 9 | 46 | - | 35 | 54 |
| 5. | FK Radnički Sremska Mitrovica | 37 | 13 | 14 | 10 | 43 | - | 38 | 53 |
| 6. | FK Jedintsvo Ub | 37 | 14 | 11 | 12 | 45 | - | 38 | 53 |
| 7. | RFK Novi Sad 1921 | 37 | 14 | 8 | 15 | 44 | - | 51 | 50 |
| 8. | FK Radnički Beograd | 37 | 13 | 6 | 18 | 32 | - | 50 | 45 |

### Relegation Round

| | | | | | | | | | | |
|---|---|---|---|---|---|---|---|---|---|---|
| 9. | FK Sloboda Užice | 37 | 11 | 18 | 8 | 42 | - | 41 | 51 |
| 10. | OFK Vršac | 37 | 13 | 9 | 15 | 39 | - | 42 | 48 |
| 11. | FK Mačva Šabac | 37 | 11 | 15 | 11 | 37 | - | 40 | 48 |
| 12. | FK Metalac Gornji Milanovac | 37 | 12 | 12 | 13 | 42 | - | 42 | 48 |
| 13. | FK Loznica (*Relegation*) | 37 | 10 | 11 | 16 | 40 | - | 54 | 41 |
| 14. | FK Trayal Kruševac (*Relegation*) | 37 | 10 | 10 | 17 | 37 | - | 46 | 40 |
| 15. | FK Zlatibor Čajetina (*Relegation*) | 37 | 7 | 12 | 18 | 36 | - | 54 | 33 |
| 16. | FK Rad Beograd (*Relegation*) | 37 | 5 | 15 | 17 | 37 | - | 63 | 30 |

# NATIONAL TEAM

## INTERNATIONAL MATCHES
### (16.07.2022 – 15.07.2023)

| | | | | |
|---|---|---|---|---|
| 24.09.2022 | Beograd | *Serbia - Sweden* | *4-1(2-1)* | (UNL) |
| 27.09.2022 | Oslo | *Norway - Serbia* | *0-2(0-1)* | (UNL) |
| 18.11.2022 | Arad | *Bahrain - Serbia* | *1-5(1-1)* | (F) |
| 24.11.2022 | Lusail | *Brazil - Serbia* | *2-0(0-0)* | (WC) |
| 28.11.2022 | Al Wakrah | *Cameroon - Serbia* | *3-3(1-2)* | (WC) |
| 02.12.2022 | Doha | *Serbia - Switzerland* | *2-3(2-2)* | (WC) |
| 26.01.2023 | Los Angeles | *United States - Serbia* | *1-2(1-1)* | (F) |
| 24.03.2023 | Beograd | *Serbia - Lithuania* | *2-0(1-0)* | (ECQ) |
| 27.03.2023 | Podgorica | *Montenegro - Serbia* | *0-2(0-0)* | (ECQ) |
| 16.06.2023 | Wien | *Serbia - Jordan* | *3-2(1-0)* | (F) |
| 20.06.2023 | Razgrad | *Bulgaria - Serbia* | *1-1(0-0)* | (ECQ) |

**24.09.2022    SERBIA - SWEDEN                4-1(2-1)              3rd UEFA Nations League B, Group 4**
Stadion „Rajko Mitić", Beograd; Referee: Georgi Kabakov (Bulgaria); Attendance: 14,122
**SRB:** Vanja Milinković-Savić, Stefan Mitrović, Srđan Babić, Erhan Mašović, Andrija Živković (46.Darko Lazović), Saša Lukić, Sergej Milinković-Savić, Dušan Tadić (Cap) (84.Stefan Mitrović), Filip Kostić (84.Ivan Ilić), Dušan Vlahović (90.Luka Jović), Aleksandar Mitrović (72.Uroš Račić). Trainer: Trainer: Dragan Stojković.
**Goals:** Aleksandar Mitrović (18, 45+1, 50), Saša Lukić (70).

**27.09.2022    NORWAY - SERBIA                0-2(0-1)              3rd UEFA Nations League B, Group 4**
Ullevaal Stadion, Oslo; Referee: Antonio Miguel Mateu Lahoz (Spain); Attendance: 24,364
**SRB:** Vanja Milinković-Savić, Miloš Veljković, Stefan Mitrović, Strahinja Pavlović (89.Srđan Babić), Ivan Ilić, Saša Lukić, Andrija Živković (72.Darko Lazović), Filip Kostić (72.Nemanja Radonjić), Dušan Tadić (Cap) (90+3.Filip Đuričić), Dušan Vlahović, Aleksandar Mitrović (90+3.Luka Jović). Trainer: Trainer: Dragan Stojković.
**Goals:** Dušan Vlahović (42), Aleksandar Mitrović (54).

**18.11.2022    BAHRAIN - SERBIA                    1-5(1-1)                    Friendly International**
Al Muharraq Stadium, Arad; Referee: Khalid Saleh Al Turais (Saudi Arabia); Attendance: 4,000
**SRB:** Vanja Milinković-Savić, Strahinja Pavlović, Nikola Milenković (79.Strahinja Eraković), Stefan Mitrović (46.Darko Lazović), Ivan Ilić (70.Nemanja Maksimović), Nemanja Gudelj, Andrija Živković (46.Dušan Vlahović), Filip Mladenović, Sergej Milinković-Savić (60.Marko Grujić), Dušan Tadić (Cap) (60.Filip Đuričić), Luka Jović. Trainer: Trainer: Dragan Stojković.
**Goals:** Dušan Tadić (8, 50), Dušan Vlahović (51), Filip Đuričić (87), Luka Jović (89).

**24.11.2022    BRAZIL - SERBIA                    2-0(0-0)                    22ⁿᵈ FIFA WC. Group Stage.**
Lusail Stadium, Lusail (Qatar); Referee: Alireza Faghani (Iran); Attendance: 88,103
**SRB:** Vanja Milinković-Savić, Nikola Milenković, Miloš Veljković, Strahinja Pavlović, Andrija Živković (57.Nemanja Radonjić), Saša Lukić (66.Darko Lazović), Nemanja Gudelj (57.Ivan Ilić), Sergej Milinković-Savić, Filip Mladenović (66.Dušan Vlahović), Dušan Tadić (Cap), Aleksandar Mitrović (83.Nemanja Maksimović). Trainer: Trainer: Dragan Stojković.

**28.11.2022    CAMEROON - SERBIA                    3-3(1-2)                    22ⁿᵈ FIFA WC. Group Stage.**
Al Janoub Stadium, Al Wakrah (Qatar); Referee: Mohammed Abdulla Hassan Mohamed (United Arab Emirates); Attendance: 39,789
**SRB:** Vanja Milinković-Savić, Nikola Milenković, Miloš Veljković (78.Srđan Babić), Strahinja Pavlović (55.Stefan Mitrović), Andrija Živković (78.Nemanja Radonjić), Saša Lukić, Nemanja Maksimović, Sergej Milinković-Savić (78.Marko Grujić), Filip Kostić (90+2.Filip Đuričić), Dušan Tadić (Cap), Aleksandar Mitrović. Trainer: Trainer: Dragan Stojković.
**Goals:** Strahinja Pavlović (45+1), Sergej Milinković-Savić (45+3), Aleksandar Mitrović (53).

**02.12.2022    SERBIA - SWITZERLAND                    2-3(2-2)                    22ⁿᵈ FIFA WC. Group Stage.**
Stadium 974, Doha (Qatar); Referee: Fernando Andrés Rapallini (Argentina); Attendance: 41,378
**SRB:** Vanja Milinković-Savić, Nikola Milenković, Miloš Veljković (55.Nemanja Gudelj), Strahinja Pavlović, Andrija Živković (78.Nemanja Radonjić), Sergej Milinković-Savić (68.Nemanja Maksimović), Saša Lukić, Filip Kostić, Dušan Tadić (Cap) (78.Filip Đuričić), Aleksandar Mitrović, Dušan Vlahović (55.Luka Jović). Trainer: Trainer: Dragan Stojković.
**Goals:** Aleksandar Mitrović (25), Dušan Vlahović (35).

**26.01.2023    UNITED STATES - SERBIA                    1-2(1-1)                    Friendly International**
BMO [Bank of Montreal] Stadium, Los Angeles; Referee: Daneon Parchment (Jamaica); Attendance: 11,745
**SRB:** Đorđe Petrović (46.Dragan Rosić), Marko Mijailović, Ranko Veselinović, Nemanja Stojić, Nemanja Petrović, Nikola Petković (81.Luka Bijelović), Mirko Topić (46.Nikola Štulić), Veljko Simić (Cap) (76.Filip Damjanović), Luka Ilić (62.Marko Ivezić), Vladimir Lučić (62.Miloš Pantović), Dejan Joveljić. Trainer: Trainer: Dragan Stojković.
**Goals:** Luka Ilić (43), Veljko Simić (46).

**24.03.2023    SERBIA - LITHUANIA                    2-0(1-0)                    17ᵗʰ EC. Qualifiers**
Stadion "Rajko Mitić", Beograd; Referee: Lawrence Visser (Belgium); Attendance: 21,125
**SRB:** Vanja Milinković-Savić, Strahinja Pavlović, Strahinja Eraković, Nemanja Gudelj, Andrija Živković (80.Nikola Milenković), Saša Lukić (72.Ivan Ilić), Marko Grujić, Filip Kostić, Dušan Tadić (Cap) (72.Lazar Vujadin Samardžić), Dušan Vlahović (63.Sergej Milinković-Savić), Aleksandar Mitrović (80.Dejan Joveljić). Trainer: Trainer: Dragan Stojković.
**Goals:** Dušan Tadić (16), Dušan Vlahović (53).

**27.03.2023    MONTENEGRO - SERBIA                    0-2(0-0)                    17ᵗʰ EC. Qualifiers**
Stadion pod Goricom, Podgorica; Referee: Clément Turpin (France); Attendance: 9,831
**SRB:** Vanja Milinković-Savić, Strahinja Pavlović, Nikola Milenković, Nemanja Gudelj, Ivan Ilić (46.Andrija Živković), Marko Grujić (81.Saša Lukić), Filip Đuričić (46.Dušan Vlahović), Sergej Milinković-Savić, Dušan Tadić (Cap) (89.Strahinja Eraković), Aleksandar Mitrović (85.Uroš Račić). Trainer: Trainer: Dragan Stojković.
**Goals:** Dušan Vlahović (78, 90+6).

**16.06.2023    SERBIA - JORDAN                    3-2(1-0)                    Friendly International**
"Fritz Horr" Stadion, Wien (Austria); Referee: Stefan Ebner (Austria); Attendance: 8,854
**SRB:** Predrag Rajković, Strahinja Eraković, Srđan Babić, Erhan Mašović, Darko Lazović (74.Andrija Živković), Uroš Račić (63.Sergej Milinković-Savić), Marko Grujić, Filip Đuričić (63.Ivan Ilić), Filip Kostić (Cap) (46.Filip Mladenović), Đorđe Jovanović (46.Dejan Joveljić), Lazar Vujadin Samardžić (46.Dušan Tadić). Trainer: Trainer: Dragan Stojković.
**Goals:** Strahinja Eraković (7), Dejan Joveljić (83, 88).

**20.06.2023    BULGARIA - SERBIA                    1-1(0-0)                    17ᵗʰ EC. Qualifiers**
Ludogorets Arena, Razgrad; Referee: Craig Pawson (England); Attendance: 6,700
**SRB:** Vanja Milinković-Savić, Nemanja Gudelj, Nikola Milenković, Strahinja Pavlović, Saša Lukić (58.Đorđe Jovanović), Nemanja Maksimović (81.Marko Grujić), Andrija Živković (71.Darko Lazović), Filip Kostić (71.Filip Mladenović), Sergej Milinković-Savić, Dušan Tadić (Cap), Dejan Joveljić. Trainer: Trainer: Dragan Stojković.
**Goal:** Darko Lazović (90+6).

## NATIONAL TEAM PLAYERS
### (16.07.2022 – 15.07.2023)

| Name | DOB | Caps | Goals | Club | |
|---|---|---|---|---|---|
| **Goalkeepers** | | | | | |
| Vanja MILINKOVIĆ-SAVIĆ | 20.02.1997 | 13 | 0 | 2022/2023: | Torino FC (ITA) |
| Đorđe PETROVIĆ | 08.10.1999 | 2 | 0 | 2023: | New England Revolution Boston (USA) |
| Predrag RAJKOVIĆ | 31.10.1995 | 29 | 0 | 2023: | RCD Mallorca (ESP) |
| Dragan ROSIĆ | 15.11.1996 | 1 | 0 | 2023: | FK Radnički Niš |
| **Defenders** | | | | | |
| Srđan BABIĆ | 22.04.1996 | 4 | 0 | 2022/2023: | UD Almería (ESP) |
| Filip DAMJANOVIĆ | 02.07.1998 | 1 | 0 | 2023: | FK Voždovac Beograd |
| Strahinja ERAKOVIĆ | 22.01.2001 | 5 | 0 | 2022/2023: | FK Crvena Zvezda Beograd |
| Erhan MAŠOVIĆ | 22.11.1998 | 3 | 0 | 2022/2023: | VfL Bochum (GER) |
| Marko MIJAILOVIĆ | 14.08.1997 | 1 | 0 | 2023: | FK Voždovac Beograd |
| Nikola MILENKOVIĆ | 12.10.1997 | 45 | 3 | 2022/2023: | ACF Fiorentina (ITA) |
| Stefan MITROVIĆ | 22.05.1990 | 36 | 0 | 2022: | Getafe CF (ESP) |
| Filip MLADENOVIĆ | 15.08.1991 | 24 | 1 | 2022/2023: | Legia Warszawa (POL) |
| Strahinja PAVLOVIĆ | 24.05.2001 | 28 | 2 | 2022/2023: | FC Red Bull Salzburg (AUT) |
| Nemanja PETROVIĆ | 17.04.1992 | 1 | 0 | 2023: | FK TSC Bačka Topola |
| Nemanja STOJIĆ | 15.01.1998 | 1 | 0 | 2023: | FK TSC Bačka Topola |
| Miloš VELJKOVIĆ | 26.09.1995 | 24 | 0 | 2022: | SV Werder Bremen (GER) |
| Ranko VESELINOVIĆ | 24.03.1999 | 2 | 0 | 2023: | Vancouver Whitecaps FC (CAN) |
| **Midfielders** | | | | | |
| Luka BIJELOVIĆ | 11.04.2001 | 1 | 0 | 2023: | FK Spartak Subotica |
| Filip ĐURIČIĆ | 30.01.1992 | 41 | 5 | 2022/2023: | UC Sampdoria Genova (ITA) |
| Marko GRUJIĆ | 13.04.1996 | 23 | 0 | 2022/2023: | FC do Porto (POR) |
| Nemanja GUDELJ | 16.11.1991 | 54 | 1 | 2022/2023: | Sevilla FC (ESP) |
| Ivan ILIĆ | 17.03.2001 | 10 | 0 | 2022: | Hellas Verona FC (ITA) |
| | | | | 30.01.2023-> | Torino FC (ITA) |
| Luka ILIĆ | 02.07.1999 | 1 | 1 | 2023: | FK TSC Bačka Topola |
| Marko IVEZIĆ | 02.12.2001 | 1 | 0 | 2023: | FK Voždovac Beograd |
| Filip KOSTIĆ | 01.11.1992 | 55 | 3 | 2022/2023: | Juventus FC Torino (ITA) |
| Darko LAZOVIĆ | 15.09.1990 | 29 | 1 | 2022/2023: | Hellas Verona FC (ITA) |
| Saša LUKIĆ | 13.08.1996 | 38 | 2 | 2022: | Torino FC (ITA) |
| | | | | 31.01.2023-> | Fulham FC London (ENG) |
| Vladimir LUČIĆ | 28.06.2002 | 1 | 0 | 2023: | FK Čukarički Beograd |
| Nemanja MAKSIMOVIĆ | 26.01.1995 | 44 | 0 | 2022/2023: | Getafe CF (ESP) |
| Sergej MILINKOVIĆ-SAVIĆ | 27.02.1995 | 43 | 7 | 2022/2023: | SS Lazio Roma (ITA) |
| Stefan MITROVIĆ | 15.08.2002 | 1 | 0 | 2022: | FK Crvena Zvezda Beograd |
| Miloš PANTOVIĆ | 24.08.2002 | 1 | 0 | 2023: | FK Voždovac Beograd |
| Nikola PETKOVIĆ | 23.02.2003 | 1 | 0 | 2023: | FK Čukarički Beograd |
| Nemanja RADONJIĆ | 15.02.1996 | 39 | 5 | 2022: | Torino FC (ITA) |
| Uroš RAČIĆ | 17.03.1998 | 11 | 0 | 2022/2023: | Sporting Clube de Braga (POR) |
| Lazar Vujadin SAMARDŽIĆ | 24.02.2002 | 2 | 0 | 2023: | Udinese Calcio (ITA) |
| Veljko SIMIĆ | 17.02.1995 | 1 | 1 | 2023: | FK Vojvodina Novi Sad |
| Dušan TADIĆ | 20.11.1988 | 98 | 21 | 2022/2023: | AFC Ajax Amsterdam (NED) |
| Mirko TOPIĆ | 05.02.2001 | 1 | 0 | 2023: | FK Vojvodina Novi Sad |
| Andrija ŽIVKOVIĆ | 11.07.1996 | 36 | 1 | 2022/2023: | PAOK Thessaloníki )GRE) |
| **Forwards** | | | | | |
| Đorđe JOVANOVIĆ | 15.02.1999 | 3 | 0 | 2023: | Maccabi Tel Aviv FC (ISR) |
| Dejan JOVELJIĆ | 07.08.1999 | 6 | 2 | 2023: | Los Angeles Galaxy (USA) |
| Luka JOVIĆ | 23.12.1997 | 30 | 10 | 2022: | ACF Fiorentina (ITA) |
| Aleksandar MITROVIĆ | 16.09.1994 | 81 | 52 | 2022/2023: | Fulham FC London (ENG) |
| Nikola ŠTULIĆ | 08.09.2001 | 1 | 0 | 2023: | FK Radnički Niš |
| Dušan VLAHOVIĆ | 28.01.2000 | 21 | 13 | 2022/2023: | Juventus FC Torino (ITA) |
| **Trainer** | | | | | |
| Dragan STOJKOVIĆ [from 03.03.2021] | 03.03.1965 | | | 29 M; 18 W; 6 D; 5 L; 61-32 | |

# SLOVAKIA

**The Country:**
Slovenská republika (Slovak Republic)
Capital: Bratislava
Surface: 49,035 km²
Inhabitants: 5,460,185 [2022]
Time: UTC+1

**The FA:**
Slovenský futbalový zväz
Tomášikova 30C, 821 01 Bratislava
Tel: +421 2 3910 3100
Founded: 04.11.1938
Member of FIFA since: 1994
Member of UEFA since: 1993
Website: www.futbalsfz.sk

## NATIONAL TEAM RECORDS

| RECORDS | | |
|---|---|---|
| **First international match:** | 27.08.1939, Bratislava: | Slovakia – Germany 2-0 |
| **Most international caps:** | Marek Hamšik | - 138 caps (2007-2023) |
| **Most international goals:** | Marek Hamšik | - 26 goals / 138 caps (2007-2023) |

### UEFA EUROPEAN CHAMPIONSHIP

| | |
|---|---|
| 1960 | - |
| 1964 | - |
| 1968 | - |
| 1972 | - |
| 1976 | - |
| 1980 | - |
| 1984 | - |
| 1988 | - |
| 1992 | - |
| 1996 | Qualifiers |
| 2000 | Qualifiers |
| 2004 | Qualifiers |
| 2008 | Qualifiers |
| 2012 | Qualifiers |
| 2016 | Final Tournament (2nd Round of 16) |
| 2020 | Final Tournament (Group Stage) |

### FIFA WORLD CUP

| | |
|---|---|
| 1930 | - |
| 1934 | - |
| 1938 | - |
| 1950 | - |
| 1954 | - |
| 1958 | - |
| 1962 | - |
| 1966 | - |
| 1970 | - |
| 1974 | - |
| 1978 | - |
| 1982 | - |
| 1986 | - |
| 1990 | - |
| 1994 | - |
| 1998 | Qualifiers |
| 2002 | Qualifiers |
| 2006 | Qualifiers |
| 2010 | Final Tournament (2nd Round of 16) |
| 2014 | Qualifiers |
| 2018 | Qualifiers |
| 2022 | Qualifiers |

### OLYMPIC TOURNAMENTS

| | |
|---|---|
| 1908 | - |
| 1912 | - |
| 1920 | - |
| 1924 | - |
| 1928 | - |
| 1936 | - |
| 1948 | - |
| 1952 | - |
| 1956 | - |
| 1960 | - |
| 1964 | - |
| 1968 | - |
| 1972 | - |
| 1976 | - |
| 1980 | - |
| 1984 | - |
| 1988 | - |
| 1992 | - |
| 1996 | Qualifiers |
| 2000 | Group Stage |
| 2004 | Qualifiers |
| 2008 | Qualifiers |
| 2012 | Qualifiers |
| 2016 | Qualifiers |
| 2020 | Qualifiers |

*Please note: was part of Czechoslovakia 1918-1939 and 1945-1992.*

## UEFA NATIONS LEAGUE

| 2018/2019 | League B (Group Stage) |
|---|---|
| 2020/2021 | League B (Group Stage -> relegated to League C) |
| 2022/2023 | League C (Group Stage) |

## SLOVAK CLUB HONOURS IN EUROPEAN CLUB COMPETITIONS:

| European Champion Clubs.Cup (1956-1992) / UEFA Champions League (1993-2023) | | |
|---|---|---|
| None | | |
| **Fairs Cup (1858-1971) / UEFA Cup (1972-2009) / UEFA Europa League (2010-2023)** | | |
| None | | |
| **UEFA Europa Conference League (2021-2023)** | | |
| None | | |
| **UEFA Super Cup (1972-2022)** | | |
| None | | |
| ***European Cup Winners' Cup 1961-1999*** | | |
| ŠK Slovan Bratislava* | 1 | 1968/1969 |
| *represented Czechoslovakia | | |

*defunct competition

# NATIONAL COMPETITIONS
## TABLE OF HONOURS

<u>Please note</u>: Slovakia was part of Czechoslovakia (1918–1993). First Slovak championship [Zväzové Majstrovstvá Slovenska] was played between Slovak teams (1925–1933).

### Zväzové Majstrovstvá Slovenska (1925-1933)

|  | CHAMPIONS |
|---|---|
| 1925 | 1. ČsŠK Bratislava |
| 1925/1926 | 1. ČsŠK Bratislava |
| 1926/1927 | 1. ČsŠK Bratislava |
| 1927/1928 | SK Žilina |
| 1928/1929 | SK Žilina |
| 1929/1930 | 1. ČsŠK Bratislava |
| 1930/1931 | Ligeti SC Bratislava |
| 1931/1932 | 1. ČsŠK Bratislava |
| 1932/1933 | SC Rusj Uzhorod |

### Slovenská liga (1939–1945)

|  | CHAMPIONS |
|---|---|
| 1938/1939 | Sparta Považská Bystrica |
| 1939/1940 | ŠK Bratislava |
| 1940/1941 | ŠK Bratislava |
| 1941/1942 | ŠK Bratislava |
| 1942/1943 | OAP Bratislava |
| 1943/1944 | ŠK Bratislava |

|  | CHAMPIONS | CUP WINNERS | BEST GOALSCORERS | |
|---|---|---|---|---|
| 1993/1994 | ŠK Slovan Bratislava | ŠK Slovan Bratislava | Pavol Diňa (DAC Dunajska Streda) | 19 |
| 1994/1995 | ŠK Slovan Bratislava | FK Inter Bratislava | Robert Semenik (MFK Dukla Banská Bystrica) | 18 |
| 1995/1996 | ŠK Slovan Bratislava | FC Chemlon Humenné | Robert Semenik (1. FC Košice) | 29 |
| 1996/1997 | 1. FC Košice | ŠK Slovan Bratislava | Jozef Kožlej (1. FC Košice) | 22 |
| 1997/1998 | 1. FC Košice | FC Spartak Trnava | Ľubomír Luhový (FC Spartak Trnava) | 17 |
| 1998/1999 | ŠK Slovan Bratislava | ŠK Slovan Bratislava | Martin Fabuš (TJ Ozeta Dukla Trenčín) | 19 |
| 1999/2000 | FK Inter Bratislava | FK Inter Bratislava | Szilárd Németh (FK Inter Bratislava) | 16 |
| 2000/2001 | FK Inter Bratislava | FK Inter Bratislava | Szilárd Németh (FK Inter Bratislava) | 23 |
| 2001/2002 | MŠK Žilina | FK VTJ Koba Senec | Marek Mintál (MŠK Žilina) | 21 |
| 2002/2003 | MŠK Žilina | FK Matador Púchov | Marek Mintál (MŠK Žilina) Martin Fabuš (Laugaricio Trenčín / MŠK Žilina) | 20 |
| 2003/2004 | MŠK Žilina | FC Artmedia Petržalka | Roland Števko (MFK Ružomberok) | 17 |
| 2004/2005 | Artmedia Bratislava | MFK Dukla Banská Bystrica | Filip Šebo (FC Artmedia Petržalka) | 22 |
| 2005/2006 | MFK Ružomberok | MFK Ružomberok | Róbert Rák (FC Nitra) Erik Jendrišek (MFK Ružomberok) | 21 |
| 2006/2007 | MŠK Žilina | FC ViOn Zlaté Moravce | Tomáš Oravec (FC Artmedia Petržalka) | 16 |
| 2007/2008 | FC Artmedia Petržalka | FC Artmedia Petržalka | Ján Novák (MFK Košice) | 17 |
| 2008/2009 | ŠK Slovan Bratislava | MFK Košice | Pavol Masaryk (ŠK Slovan Bratislava) | 15 |
| 2009/2010 | MŠK Žilina | ŠK Slovan Bratislava | Róbert Rák (FC Nitra) | 18 |
| 2010/2011 | ŠK Slovan Bratislava | ŠK Slovan Bratislava | Filip Šebo (ŠK Slovan Bratislava) | 22 |
| 2011/2012 | MŠK Žilina | MŠK Žilina | Pavol Masaryk (MFK Ružomberok) | 18 |
| 2012/2013 | ŠK Slovan Bratislava | ŠK Slovan Bratislava | David Depetris (AS Trenčín) | 16 |
| 2013/2014 | ŠK Slovan Bratislava | MFK Košice | Tomáš Malec (AS Trenčín) | 14 |
| 2014/2015 | AS Trenčín | AS Trenčín | Matej Jelić (CRO, MŠK Žilina) Jan Kalabiška (CZE, FK Senica) | 19 |
| 2015/2016 | AS Trenčín | AS Trenčín | Gino Ronald van Kessel (CUW, AS Trenčín) | 17 |
| 2016/2017 | MŠK Žilina | ŠK Slovan Bratislava | Filip Hlohovský (MŠK Žilina) Seydouba Soumah (GUI, ŠK Slovan Bratislava) | 20 |
| 2017/2018 | FC Spartak Trnava | ŠK Slovan Bratislava | Samuel Mráz (MŠK Žilina) | 21 |
| 2018/2019 | ŠK Slovan Bratislava | FC Spartak Trnava | Andraž Šporar (SVN, ŠK Slovan Bratislava) | 29 |
| 2019/2020 | ŠK Slovan Bratislava | ŠK Slovan Bratislava | Andraž Šporar (SVN, ŠK Slovan Bratislava) | 12 |
| 2020/2021 | ŠK Slovan Bratislava | ŠK Slovan Bratislava | Dawid Kuminowski (POL, MŠK Žilina) | 19 |
| 2021/2022 | ŠK Slovan Bratislava | FC Spartak Trnava | Jakub Kadák (AS Trenčín) | 13 |
| 2022/2023 | ŠK Slovan Bratislava | FC Spartak Trnava | Nikola Krstović (MNE, FK DAC 1904 Dunajská Streda) | 18 |

## NATIONAL CHAMPIONSHIP
### Slovak Fortuna Liga 2022/2023
(15.07.2022 – 20.05.2023)

### Regular Season - Results

**Round 1** [15-17.07.2022]
MFK Zemplín - Banská Bystrica 2-0(0-0)
AS Trenčín - MŠK Žilina 0-0
Spartak Trnava - Zlaté Moravce 2-0(1-0)
FK Železiarne - Slovan Bratislava 2-1(1-0)
Dunajská Streda - Tatran L. Mikuláš 2-1(0-0)
MFK Skalica - MFK Ružomberok 0-2(0-2)

**Round 2** [22-24.07.2022]
Zlaté Moravce - MFK Skalica 2-2(1-1)
Tatran L. Mikuláš - MFK Zemplín 1-1(1-1)
Slovan Bratislava - AS Trenčín 4-0(1-0)
MŠK Žilina - Dunajská Streda 1-1(1-0)
MFK Ružomberok - FK Železiarne 2-2(1-1)
Spartak Trnava - Banská Bystrica 1-2(0-1)

**Round 3** [29-31.07.2022]
MŠK Žilina - Banská Bystrica 4-1(2-0)
MFK Skalica - AS Trenčín 2-0(1-0)
Slovan Bratislava - MFK Zemplín 4-2(0-2)
Dunajská Streda - Zlaté Moravce 3-0(1-0)
Spartak Trnava - FK Železiarne 1-1(1-0)
Tatran L. Mikuláš - MFK Ružomberok 0-0

**Round 4** [05-07.08.2022]
AS Trenčín - MFK Zemplín 3-1(1-1)
Banská Bystrica - MFK Ružomberok 2-3(2-0)
Zlaté Moravce - Tatran L. Mikuláš 1-1(1-1)
FK Železiarne - Dunajská Streda 0-0
Slovan Bratislava - MFK Skalica 3-0(1-0)
Spartak Trnava - MŠK Žilina 2-2(0-1)

**Round 5** [12-14.08.2022]
MFK Skalica - FK Železiarne 1-1(0-1)
MŠK Žilina - Zlaté Moravce 1-0(0-0)
MFK Ružomberok - AS Trenčín 0-0
Tatran L. Mikuláš - Slovan Bratislava 1-5(1-1)
MFK Zemplín - Spartak Trnava 0-4(0-1)
Dunajská Streda - Banská Bystrica 3-0(1-0)

**Round 6** [19-21.08.2022]
FK Železiarne - Banská Bystrica 3-1(2-0)
AS Trenčín - Tatran L. Mikuláš 2-1(1-0)
MFK Zemplín - MFK Skalica 3-1(1-0)
Spartak Trnava - Dunajská Streda 3-1(1-0)
Zlaté Moravce - MFK Ružomberok 2-2(0-1)
Slovan Bratislava - MŠK Žilina 3-1(2-0)

**Round 7 [26-28.08.2022]**
MŠK Žilina - MFK Zemplín 2-0(1-0)
Banská Bystrica - Zlaté Moravce 4-2(1-1)
Dunajská Streda - AS Trenčín 1-2(1-0)
Tatran L. Mikuláš - FK Železiarne 2-5(0-2)
MFK Skalica - Spartak Trnava 1-1(0-0)
MFK Ružomberok-Slovan Bratislava 0-1(0-0)

**Round 8 [30-31.08.2022]**
FK Železiarne - Zlaté Moravce 0-0
MFK Skalica - MŠK Žilina 1-0(1-0)
AS Trenčín - Banská Bystrica 0-2(0-1)
MFK Zemplín - MFK Ružomberok 1-1(0-0)
Spartak Trnava - Tatran L. Mikuláš 1-0(0-0)
Slovan Bratislava - Dunajská Streda 1-1(0-1)

**Round 9 [02-04.09.2022]**
MŠK Žilina - FK Železiarne 0-1(0-0)
Banská Bystrica - Slovan Bratislava 0-1(0-0)
Dunajská Streda - MFK Zemplín 1-0(0-0)
Tatran L. Mikuláš - MFK Skalica 0-0
Zlaté Moravce - AS Trenčín 1-0(1-0)
MFK Ružomberok - Spartak Trnava 3-2(3-1)

**Round 10 [09-11.09.2022]**
MFK Ružomberok - MŠK Žilina 0-2(0-2)
Tatran L. Mikuláš - Banská Bystrica 1-2(1-0)
MFK Skalica - Dunajská Streda 1-1(0-0)
AS Trenčín - Spartak Trnava 0-2(0-1)
MFK Zemplín - Železiarne 1-0(1-0)[12.10.22]
Slovan Br. - Zlaté Moravce 4-1(2-1)[24.11.22]

**Round 11 [16-18.09.2022]**
Banská Bystrica - MFK Skalica 0-0
MŠK Žilina - Tatran L. Mikuláš 4-2(3-1)
FK Železiarne - AS Trenčín 2-0(2-0)
Zlaté Moravce - MFK Zemplín 0-1(0-1)
Spartak Trnava - Slovan Bratislava 0-0
Dunajská St.-Ružomberok 1-0(1-0) [24.11.22]

**Round 12 [30.09.-02.10.2022]**
MFK Ružomberok - MFK Skalica 2-0(1-0)
Banská Bystrica - MFK Zemplín 3-1(1-0)
Tatran L. Mikuláš - Dunajská Streda 0-1(0-1)
MŠK Žilina - AS Trenčín 1-1(0-0)
Slovan Bratislava - FK Železiarne 3-1(0-0)
Zlaté Moravce - Spartak Trnava 0-3(0-1)

**Round 13 [07-09.10.2022]**
FK Železiarne - MFK Ružomberok 0-2(0-1)
Banská Bystrica - Spartak Trnava 0-2(0-1)
MFK Skalica - Zlaté Moravce 0-2(0-1)
MFK Zemplín - Tatran L. Mikuláš 1-2(1-0)
Dunajská Streda - MŠK Žilina 5-2(2-1)
AS Trenčín - Slovan Bratislava 4-0(2-0)

**Round 14 [14-16.10.2022]**
Zlaté Moravce - Dunajská Streda 2-2(0-0)
AS Trenčín - MFK Skalica 3-1(0-0)
Banská Bystrica - MŠK Žilina 2-1(1-1)
MFK Ružomberok-Tatran L. Mikuláš 1-1(0-1)
FK Železiarne - Spartak Trnava 3-1(2-0)
MFK Zemplín - Slovan Bratislava 0-1(0-0)

**Round 15 [21-23.10.2022]**
MFK Skalica - Slovan Bratislava 1-4(0-3)
Tatran L. Mikuláš - Zlaté Moravce 1-2(0-0)
MFK Ružomberok - Banská Bystrica 1-1(0-0)
MFK Zemplín - AS Trenčín 2-0(0-0)
MŠK Žilina - Spartak Trnava 1-2(0-1)
Dunajská Streda - FK Železiarne 2-1(0-0)

**Round 16 [28-30.10.2022]**
Zlaté Moravce - MŠK Žilina 4-0(2-0)
AS Trenčín - MFK Ružomberok 0-0
FK Železiarne - MFK Skalica 0-2(0-1)
Slovan Bratislava - Tatran L. Mikuláš 1-0(0-0)
Banská Bystrica - Dunajská Streda 1-3(1-1)
Spartak Trnava - Zemplín 4-1(3-0) [24.11.22]

**Round 17 [04-06.11.2022]**
Banská Bystrica - FK Železiarne 0-2(0-1)
Dunajská Streda - Spartak Trnava 1-0(0-0)
Tatran L. Mikuláš - AS Trenčín 1-1(0-0)
MFK Skalica - MFK Zemplín 0-0
MŠK Žilina - Slovan Bratislava 4-1(3-0)
Ružomberok - Zlaté Morav.2-2(1-0)[27.11.22]

**Round 18 [11-13.11.2022]**
Spartak Trnava - MFK Skalica 2-1(0-1)
AS Trenčín - Dunajská Streda 0-4(0-0)
FK Železiarne - Tatran L. Mikuláš 1-0(1-0)
MFK Zemplín - MŠK Žilina 3-2(1-1)
Zlaté Moravce - Banská Bystrica 4-4(0-1)
Slovan Bratislava-MFK Ružomberok 2-0(0-0)

**Round 19 [10-12.02.2023]**
Banská Bystrica - AS Trenčín 3-0(2-0)
Tatran L. Mikuláš - Spartak Trnava 1-2(1-1)
MFK Ružomberok - MFK Zemplín 1-0(1-0)
MŠK Žilina - MFK Skalica 1-0(0-0)
Zlaté Moravce - FK Železiarne 1-1(0-1)
Dunajská Streda - Slovan Bratislava 1-1(1-0)

**Round 20 [17-19.02.2023]**
Spartak Trnava - MFK Ružomberok 0-2(0-0)
AS Trenčín - Zlaté Moravce 1-1(1-0)
MFK Zemplín - Dunajská Streda 0-2(0-1)
Slovan Bratislava - Banská Bystrica 2-2(0-2)
MFK Skalica - Tatran L. Mikuláš 3-0(1-0)
FK Železiarne - MŠK Žilina 3-1(1-0)

**Round 21 [24-26.02.2023]**
FK Železiarne - MFK Zemplín 2-2(1-2)
Banská Bystrica - Tatran L. Mikuláš 2-0(1-0)
Dunajská Streda - MFK Skalica 2-1(0-1)
Spartak Trnava - AS Trenčín 3-2(3-0)
Zlaté Moravce - Slovan Bratislava 1-1(0-1)
MŠK Žilina - MFK Ružomberok 2-0(1-0)

**Round 22 [04.03.2023]**
AS Trenčín - FK Železiarne 1-1(1-0)
Tatran L. Mikuláš - MŠK Žilina 1-2(1-1)
MFK Ružomberok - Dunajská Streda 0-1(0-0)
MFK Skalica - Banská Bystrica 1-2(0-0)
MFK Zemplín - Zlaté Moravce 0-0
Slovan Bratislava - Spartak Trnava 4-1(3-0)

**Final Standings**

| | | | | | | | | | |
|---|---|---|---|---|---|---|---|---|---|
| 1. | FK DAC 1904 Dunajská Streda | 22 | 14 | 6 | 2 | 39 | - | 17 | 48 |
| 2. | ŠK Slovan Bratislava | 22 | 14 | 5 | 3 | 47 | - | 23 | 47 |
| 3. | FC Spartak Trnava | 22 | 12 | 4 | 6 | 39 | - | 26 | 40 |
| 4. | FK Železiarne Podbrezová | 22 | 9 | 8 | 5 | 32 | - | 24 | 35 |
| 5. | MŠK Žilina | 22 | 9 | 4 | 9 | 34 | - | 33 | 31 |
| 6. | MFK Dukla Banská Bystrica | 22 | 9 | 4 | 9 | 34 | - | 37 | 31 |
| 7. | MFK Ružomberok | 22 | 7 | 9 | 6 | 24 | - | 22 | 30 |
| 8. | MFK Zemplín Michalovce | 22 | 6 | 5 | 11 | 22 | - | 34 | 23 |
| 9. | FC ViOn Zlaté Moravce | 22 | 4 | 11 | 7 | 28 | - | 35 | 23 |
| 10. | AS Trenčín | 22 | 5 | 7 | 10 | 20 | - | 33 | 22 |
| 11. | MFK Skalica | 22 | 4 | 7 | 11 | 19 | - | 31 | 19 |
| 12. | MFK Tatran Liptovský Mikuláš | 22 | 1 | 6 | 15 | 17 | - | 40 | 9 |

Teams ranked 1-6 were qualified for the Championship Round, while teams ranked 7-12 were qualified for the Relegation Round.

**Round 23** [10-11.03.2023]
AS Trenčín - MFK Ružomberok 0-3(0-1)
Tatran L. Mikuláš - MFK Skalica 0-3(0-2)
Zlaté Moravce - MFK Zemplín 2-5(0-3)

**Round 24** [18.03.2023]
MFK Skalica - AS Trenčín 2-0(2-0)
MFK Ružomberok - Zlaté Moravce 2-0(0-0)
MFK Zemplín - Tatran L. Mikuláš 0-0

**Round 25** [31.03.-01.04.2023]
Zlaté Moravce - MFK Skalica 0-0
MFK Zemplín - MFK Ružomberok 2-2(0-0)
Tatran L. Mikuláš - AS Trenčín 0-2(0-0)

**Round 26** [08.04.2023]
Zlaté Moravce - Tatran L. Mikuláš 0-1(0-1)
AS Trenčín - MFK Zemplín 3-3(1-1)
MFK Skalica - MFK Ružomberok 1-1(0-1)

**Round 27** [15.04.2023]
MFK Zemplín - MFK Skalica 1-1(1-0)
AS Trenčín - Zlaté Moravce 2-1(0-0)
MFK Ružomberok-Tatran L. Mikuláš 3-0(1-0)

**Round 28** [21-22.04.2023]
MFK Ružomberok - AS Trenčín 4-1(2-0)
MFK Skalica - Zlaté Moravce 0-1(0-0)
Tatran L. Mikuláš - MFK Zemplín 1-3(1-3)

**Round 29** [28-29.04.2023]
AS Trenčín - Tatran L. Mikuláš 2-2(0-2)
Zlaté Moravce - MFK Ružomberok 1-0(0-0)
MFK Skalica - MFK Zemplín 3-2(2-1)

**Round 30** [06.05.2023]
MFK Ružomberok - MFK Skalica 1-2(0-1)
MFK Zemplín - AS Trenčín 0-2(0-2)
Tatran L. Mikuláš - Zlaté Moravce 1-1(1-1)

**Round 31** [12-13.05.2023]
Zlaté Moravce - AS Trenčín 1-2(1-1)
MFK Ružomberok - MFK Zemplín 2-0(0-0)
MFK Skalica - Tatran L. Mikuláš 4-0(1-0)

**Round 32** [20.05.2023]
Tatran L. Mikuláš-MFK Ružomberok 2-1(1-1)
MFK Zemplín - Zlaté Moravce 1-0(1-0)
AS Trenčín - MFK Skalica 1-3(1-1)

## Final Standings

| | | Total | | | | | | Home | | | | Away | | |
|---|---|---|---|---|---|---|---|---|---|---|---|---|---|---|
| 7. MFK Ružomberok | 32 | 12 | 11 | 9 | 43 - 31 | **47** | 7 | 5 | 4 | 24 - 15 | 5 | 6 | 5 | 19 - 16 |
| 8. MFK Skalica | 32 | 10 | 10 | 12 | 38 - 38 | **40** | 6 | 5 | 5 | 21 - 17 | 4 | 5 | 7 | 17 - 21 |
| 9. AS Trenčín | 32 | 9 | 9 | 14 | 35 - 52 | **36** | 5 | 6 | 5 | 22 - 25 | 4 | 3 | 9 | 13 - 27 |
| 10. MFK Zemplín Michalovce | 32 | 9 | 9 | 14 | 39 - 50 | **36** | 6 | 5 | 5 | 17 - 18 | 3 | 4 | 9 | 22 - 32 |
| 11. FC ViOn Zlaté Moravce (*Relegation Play-offs*) | 32 | 6 | 13 | 13 | 35 - 49 | **31** | 3 | 8 | 5 | 22 - 25 | 3 | 5 | 8 | 13 - 24 |
| 12. MFK Tatran Liptovský Mikuláš (*Relegated*) | 32 | 3 | 9 | 20 | 24 - 59 | **18** | 1 | 5 | 10 | 13 - 31 | 2 | 2 | 10 | 11 - 28 |

MFK Ružomberok were qualified for the Europa Conference League play-offs.

## Championship Round

**Round 23** [11-12.03.2023]
Spartak Trnava - FK Železiarne 6-1(3-0)
Slovan Bratislava - MŠK Žilina 0-1(0-1)
Banská Bystrica - Dunajská Streda 2-3(0-3)

**Round 24** [17-19.03.2023]
MŠK Žilina - Banská Bystrica 6-4(1-2)
FK Železiarne - Slovan Bratislava 1-2(1-1)
Dunajská Streda - Spartak Trnava 3-1(1-0)

**Round 25** [01-02.04.2023]
Banská Bystrica - FK Železiarne 3-1(2-1)
Spartak Trnava - Slovan Bratislava 0-0
Dunajská Streda - MŠK Žilina 1-0(1-0)

**Round 26** [07-09.04.2023]
FK Železiarne - MŠK Žilina 3-2(1-2)
Banská Bystrica - Spartak Trnava 2-0(0-0)
Slovan Bratislava - Dunajská Streda 2-1(0-0)

**Round 27** [14-16.04.2023]
Dunajská Streda - FK Železiarne 2-1(0-1)
MŠK Žilina - Spartak Trnava 1-1(0-0)
Slovan Bratislava - Banská Bystrica 4-0(1-0)

**Round 28** [22-23.04.2023]
FK Železiarne - Banská Bystrica 1-2(1-0)
MŠK Žilina - Slovan Bratislava 2-4(1-2)
Spartak Trnava - Dunajská Streda 1-1(1-0)

**Round 29** [28-30.04.2023]
Slovan Bratislava - Spartak Trnava 1-0(1-0)
Banská Bystrica - MŠK Žilina 1-1(1-1)
FK Železiarne - Dunajská Streda 2-0(1-0)

**Round 30** [05-07.05.2023]
MŠK Žilina - FK Železiarne 0-1(0-1)
Spartak Trnava - Banská Bystrica 0-1(0-0)
Dunajská Streda - Slovan Bratislava 2-3(1-1)

**Round 31** [13.05.2023]
MŠK Žilina - Dunajská Streda 0-1(0-0)
Banská Bystrica - Slovan Bratislava 1-2(0-1)
FK Železiarne - Spartak Trnava 0-3(0-1)

**Round 32** [20.05.2023]
Spartak Trnava - MŠK Žilina 4-2(2-1)
Dunajská Streda - Banská Bystrica 1-0(1-0)
Slovan Bratislava - FK Železiarne 0-1(0-0)

## Final Standings

| | | Total | | | | | | Home | | | | Away | | |
|---|---|---|---|---|---|---|---|---|---|---|---|---|---|---|
| 1. **ŠK Slovan Bratislava** | 32 | 21 | 6 | 5 | 65 - 32 | **69** | 12 | 2 | 2 | 38 - 12 | 9 | 4 | 3 | 27 - 20 |
| 2. FK DAC 1904 Dunajská Streda | 32 | 20 | 7 | 5 | 54 - 29 | **67** | 13 | 1 | 2 | 31 - 13 | 7 | 6 | 3 | 23 - 16 |
| 3. FC Spartak Trnava | 32 | 15 | 7 | 10 | 55 - 38 | **52** | 8 | 5 | 3 | 30 - 17 | 7 | 2 | 7 | 25 - 21 |
| 4. FK Železiarne Podbrezová | 32 | 13 | 8 | 11 | 44 - 44 | **47** | 8 | 3 | 5 | 23 - 19 | 5 | 5 | 6 | 21 - 25 |
| 5. MFK Dukla Banská Bystrica | 32 | 13 | 5 | 14 | 50 - 56 | **44** | 7 | 2 | 7 | 26 - 22 | 6 | 3 | 7 | 24 - 34 |
| 6. MŠK Žilina | 32 | 11 | 6 | 15 | 49 - 53 | **39** | 8 | 3 | 5 | 30 - 20 | 3 | 3 | 10 | 19 - 33 |

Teams ranked 4-6 were qualified for the Europa Conference League play-offs.

| Top goalscorers: | |
|---|---|
| 18  Nikola Krstović (MNE) | *FK DAC 1904 Dunajská Streda* |
| 15  Aleksandar Čavrić (SRB) | *ŠK Slovan Bratislava* |
| 15  Róbert Polievka | *MFK Dukla Banská Bystrica* |

## Europa Conference League Play-offs [23-26.05.2023]

| | | |
|---|---|---|
| **Semi-Finals** | FK Železiarne Podbrezová - MFK Ružomberok | 0-3(0-3) |
| | MFK Dukla Banská Bystrica - MŠK Žilina | 1-3(0-1) |
| **Final** | **MŠK Žilina** - MFK Ružomberok | 3-1(1-0) |

## Relegation Play-offs [23-26.05.2023]

FC Tatran Prešov - FC ViOn Zlaté Moravce                    1-0(1-0)          0-3(0-1)
FC ViOn Zlaté Moravce remains at first level for 2023/2024.

# NATIONAL CUP
## Slovenský Pohár 2022/2023

### Fourth Round [11/18-19/25-26.10.& 09.11.2022]

| | | | | |
|---|---|---|---|---|
| FC Košice - KFC Komárno | 2-3(1-1) | FK Brezno - MŠK Púchov | 1-3(0-2) |
| FK Pohronie Žiar nad Hronom - MFK Tatran L. Mikuláš | 0-1(0-1) | ŠTK 1914 Šamorín - MŠK Žilina | 2-1(0-0) |
| FK Humenné - FK DAC 1904 Dunajská Streda | 2-1(0-1) | FK Lokomotíva D. Nova Ves - MFK Ružomberok | 0-3(0-1) |
| 1. MFK Kežmarok - MFK Dukla Banská Bystrica | 0-1(0-1) | Spartak Myjava - MFK Dolný Kubín | 4-1(2-1) |
| FK MŠK Považská Bystrica - FC ViOn Zlaté Moravce | 2-2 aet;7-8 pen | FK Dubnica - MFK Zemplín Michalovce | 0-3(0-2) |
| FC Tatran Prešov - FK Železiarne Podbrezová | 1-0(1-0) | SK Odeva Lipany - MFK Skalica | 0-1(0-1) |
| OK Častkovce - TJ Jednota Bánová | 1-2(0-2) | ŠKF Sereď - FC Spartak Trnava | 0-3(0-1) |
| FK Slavoj Trebišov - AS Trenčín | 0-4(0-1) | MŠK Tesla Stropkov - ŠK Slovan Bratislava | 2-3(0-3) |

### 1/8-Finals [08-09.11.2022 & 07.02.2023]

| | | | |
|---|---|---|---|
| KFC Komárno - FC ViOn Zlaté Moravce | 2-0(0-0) | ŠTK 1914 Šamorín - MŠK Púchov | 1-1 aet; 4-3 pen |
| FK Humenné - FC Tatran Prešov | 0-1(0-1) | TJ Jednota Bánová - MFK Tatran Liptovský Mikuláš | 0-3(0-0) |
| MFK Skalica - MFK Ružomberok | 1-1 aet; 4-3 pen | AS Trenčín - Spartak Myjava | 5-0(2-0) |
| FC Spartak Trnava - MFK Zemplín Michalovce | 2-2 aet; 4-3 pen | MFK Dukla Banská Bystrica - ŠK Slovan Bratislava | 1-2(1-1) |

### Quarter-Finals [28.02./01.03./07-08.03.2023]

| | | | |
|---|---|---|---|
| KFC Komárno - FC Spartak Trnava | 0-2(0-0) | FC Tatran Prešov - AS Trenčín | 0-1(0-1) |
| ŠTK 1914 Šamorín ŠK Slovan Bratislava | 1-1 aet; 3-4 pen | MFK Tatran Liptovský Mikuláš - MFK Skalica | 2-2 aet; 3-4 pen |

### Semi-Finals [15.03./12.04. & 05.04./19.04.2023]

| First Leg | | Second Leg | |
|---|---|---|---|
| AS Trenčín - FC Spartak Trnava | 1-2(0-0) | FC Spartak Trnava - AS Trenčín | 3-0(1-0) |
| ŠK Slovan Bratislava - MFK Skalica | 2-1(1-1) | MFK Skalica - ŠK Slovan Bratislava | 3-3(1-0,3-2) |

### Final

01.05.2023; Štadión "Antona Malatinského", Trnava; Referee: Michal Očenáš; Attendance: 15,427
**FC Spartak Trnava - ŠK Slovan Bratislava**                    **3-1(0-0,1-1)**

**Spartak Trnava:** Martin Vantruba, Kristián Koštrna, Lukáš Štetina, Sebastián Kóša (72.Milan Ristovski), Filip Twardzik, Martin Bukata (80.Jakub Paur), Kyriakos Savvidis, Roman Procházka (Cap) (80.Dyjan Carlos De Azevedo), Kelvin Ofori (116.Alex Iván), Abdulrahman Taiwo (120+2.Samuel Štefánik), Erik Daniel (106.Kazeem Bolaji Soliu). Trainer: Michal Gašparík.

**Slovan Bratislava:** Martin Trnovský, Jurij Medveděv (115.Filip Lichý), Guram Kashia, Vernon De Marco Morlacchi (Cap), Lukáš Pauschek (115.Lucas Lovat), Jaba Kankava, Juraj Kucka, Andre Jay Green (84.Uche Henry Agbo), Giorgi Chakvetadze (84.Malik Abubakari), Sharani Zuberu (66.Jaromír Zmrhal), Aleksandar Čavrić (99.Tigran Barseghyan). Trainer: Vladimír Weiss.

**Goals:** 0-1 Andre Jay Green (57), 1-1 Abdulrahman Taiwo (85), 2-1 Jakub Paur (110), 3-1 Filip Twardzik (120+5 penalty).

# THE CLUBS 2022/2023

Please note: appearances and goals includes statistics of both regular season and play-offs (Championship or Relegation Round).

## Mestský futbalový klub Dukla Banská Bystrica

**Founded**: 01.07.1965 (*as VTJ Dukla Banská Bystrica*)
**Stadium**: Národný Atletický Štadión, Banská Bystrica (7,900)
**Trainer**: Michal Šťasný (CZE)  19.08.1978

| Goalkeepers: | DOB | M | (s) | G |
|---|---|---|---|---|
| Matúš Hruška | 17.09.1994 | 32 | | |
| **Defenders:** | **DOB** | **M** | **(s)** | **G** |
| Adam Červeň | 20.08.2003 | 1 | | |
| Nicolás Ezequiel Gorosito (ARG) | 17.08.1988 | 11 | (1) | 1 |
| Ľuboš Kupčík | 03.03.1989 | 8 | (6) | |
| Cyriaque Mayounga Ngolou (FRA) | 04.10.2000 | | (2) | |
| Lukáš Migaľa | 04.07.1990 | 19 | (4) | |
| Marián Pišoja | 16.06.2000 | 15 | (7) | |
| Patrik Prikryl | 19.09.1992 | 4 | | |
| Martin Slaninka | 26.03.1996 | | (1) | |
| Adrián Slávik | 12.04.1999 | 23 | (8) | 1 |
| Jakub Uhrinčať | 07.02.2001 | 25 | | 1 |
| Ľubomír Willwéber | 11.09.1992 | 30 | | 2 |
| Timotej Zahumenský | 17.07.1995 | 26 | (3) | |
| **Midfielders:** | **DOB** | **M** | **(s)** | **G** |
| Andrija Balić (CRO) | 11.08.1997 | 11 | | 5 |

| | DOB | M | (s) | G |
|---|---|---|---|---|
| Gabriel Demian | 04.12.2004 | | (2) | |
| Michal Faško | 24.08.1994 | 25 | (1) | 7 |
| Lukáš Gašparovič | 17.02.1993 | 2 | (10) | |
| Adam Hanes | 17.06.2002 | 4 | (16) | 1 |
| Matúš Köröš | 17.11.2003 | 1 | (3) | |
| Branislav Ľupták | 05.06.1991 | 28 | (3) | |
| Peter Mazán | 13.05.1990 | | (3) | |
| Dávid Richtárech | 22.04.1996 | 22 | (1) | |
| **Forwards:** | **DOB** | **M** | **(s)** | **G** |
| David Alberto Depetris (ARG) | 11.11.1988 | 4 | (15) | 9 |
| Matej Franko | 14.02.2001 | 10 | (17) | 2 |
| David Jackuliak | 02.08.2003 | | (5) | |
| Adrián Kačerík | 02.08.1997 | 3 | (10) | |
| Róbert Polievka | 09.06.1996 | 27 | | 15 |
| Martin Rymarenko | 09.04.1999 | 21 | (2) | 6 |
| Samuel Svetlík | 03.08.2004 | | (4) | |

## Futbalový klub DAC 1904 Dunajská Streda

**Founded**: 1904 (*as Dunaszerdahelyi Atlétikai Club*)
**Stadium**: MOL Aréna, Dunajská Streda (12,700)
**Trainer**: Adrián Guľa  29.06.1975

| Goalkeepers: | DOB | M | (s) | G |
|---|---|---|---|---|
| Samuel Petráš | 10.04.1999 | 25 | | |
| Dániel Veszelinov (HUN) | 05.07.2001 | 7 | | |
| **Defenders:** | **DOB** | **M** | **(s)** | **G** |
| Alejandro „Álex" Méndez García (ESP) | 28.07.2001 | 3 | (4) | |
| Carlos Alexandre "Alex" Reis Pinto (POR) | 08.07.1998 | 26 | | |
| César Rodolfo Blackman Camarena (PAN) | 02.04.1998 | 21 | (6) | 2 |
| Andrejs Ciganiks (LVA) | 12.04.1997 | 4 | (3) | |
| Éric Javier Davis Grajales (PAN) | 31.03.1991 | 2 | (2) | |
| Damian Kachút | 09.06.2004 | | (1) | |
| Dominik Kružliak | 10.07.1996 | 15 | (10) | 2 |
| Mateus Brunetti Valor (BRA) | 18.11.1999 | 23 | (2) | 1 |
| Ahmet Muhamedbegović (AUT) | 30.10.1998 | 14 | (5) | |
| Spyros Risvanis (GRE) | 03.01.1994 | 17 | (1) | |
| **Midfielders:** | **DOB** | **M** | **(s)** | **G** |
| Milan Dimun | 19.09.1996 | 24 | (6) | 2 |
| Enis Fazlagić (MKD) | 27.03.2000 | 4 | (2) | |
| Željko Gavrić (SRB) | 05.12.2000 | 14 | (1) | 2 |

| | DOB | M | (s) | G |
|---|---|---|---|---|
| Miroslav Káčer | 02.02.1996 | 27 | | 1 |
| Zsolt Kalmár (HUN) | 09.06.1995 | 13 | (13) | 8 |
| Sebastián Nebyla | 25.01.2002 | 9 | (15) | 3 |
| Sainey Njie (GAM) | 30.08.2001 | 2 | | |
| Ammar Ramadan (SYR) | 05.01.2001 | 10 | (17) | 4 |
| Riquelme Rodrigues Mendes (BRA) | 02.10.2002 | | (2) | |
| Dominik Veselovský | 19.07.2002 | 18 | (5) | 2 |
| **Forwards:** | **DOB** | **M** | **(s)** | **G** |
| Yhoan Many Andzouana (CGO) | 13.12.1996 | 25 | (2) | 2 |
| Norbert Balogh (HUN) | 21.02.1996 | 3 | (4) | |
| Csaba János Hahn (HUN) | 15.03.1995 | 1 | (2) | |
| Nikola Krstović (MNE) | 05.04.2000 | 25 | (2) | 18 |
| Lukas Leginus | 24.04.2000 | 3 | (1) | |
| Brahim Moumou (GER) | 06.05.2001 | 1 | (1) | |
| Ioannis Niarchos (GRE) | 26.06.2002 | 7 | (6) | |
| Ion Nicolăescu (MDA) | 07.09.1998 | 1 | (8) | 1 |
| Martin Rymarenko | 09.04.1999 | | (2) | |
| Regő Szánthó (HUN) | 22.11.2000 | 8 | (14) | 4 |

## Mestský futbalový klub Ružomberok

**Founded**: 1906 (*as Rózsahegyi Sport Club*)
**Stadium**: Štadión pod Čebraťom, Ružomberok (4,817)
**Trainer**: Peter Struhár  17.01.1984

| Goalkeepers: | DOB | M | (s) | G |
|---|---|---|---|---|
| Tomáš Frühwald | 23.09.2002 | 13 | | |
| Ivan Krajčírik | 15.06.2000 | 14 | | |
| Dominik Ťapaj | 10.05.2004 | 5 | | |
| **Defenders:** | **DOB** | **M** | **(s)** | **G** |
| Lukáš Fabiš | 05.05.1998 | 24 | (4) | |
| Matej Madleňák | 07.02.1999 | 26 | (3) | 3 |
| Matúš Malý | 11.07.2001 | 14 | (7) | |
| Ján Maslo | 05.02.1986 | 26 | | 2 |
| Alexander Mojžiš | 02.01.1999 | 26 | | |
| Adam Morong | 16.06.1993 | 8 | (4) | |
| Mário Mrva | 16.02.1999 | 5 | (5) | 1 |
| Alexander Selecký | 08.10.2002 | 14 | (1) | |
| Viktor Úradník | 11.08.2004 | 2 | (2) | |
| **Midfielders:** | **DOB** | **M** | **(s)** | **G** |
| Martin Chrien | 08.09.1995 | 19 | (6) | 1 |
| Krištof Domonkos | 17.08.1998 | 11 | (4) | 1 |

| | DOB | M | (s) | G |
|---|---|---|---|---|
| Michal Dopater | 26.02.2001 | | (3) | |
| Gabriel Halabrín | 21.04.2003 | 3 | (8) | |
| Matej Kochan | 21.11.1992 | 2 | | |
| Filip Lichý | 25.01.2001 | 9 | (1) | 1 |
| Oliver Luterán | 06.09.2001 | 17 | (9) | |
| Adrián Macejko | 26.04.2003 | 3 | (13) | 1 |
| Jakub Rakyta | 05.02.2003 | 1 | (5) | |
| Kevin Švehla | 22.07.2003 | 1 | (4) | |
| Marek Zsigmund | 20.04.1997 | 20 | | |
| **Forwards:** | **DOB** | **M** | **(s)** | **G** |
| Tomáš Bobček | 08.09.2001 | 21 | (2) | 5 |
| Martin Boda | 02.02.1997 | 3 | (5) | 2 |
| Štefan Gerec | 10.11.1992 | 23 | (9) | 8 |
| Marko Kelemen | 29.04.2000 | 7 | (18) | 3 |
| Martin Regáli | 12.10.1993 | 17 | | 7 |
| Samuel Šefčík | 04.11.1996 | 7 | (5) | 6 |
| Adam Tučný | 21.05.2002 | 11 | (11) | 1 |

## Mestský futbalový klub Skalica

**Founded:** 1920 (*as ŠK Skalica*)
**Stadium:** Štadión MFK Skalica, Skalica (1,500)
**Trainer:** Juraj Jarábek 03.10.1962
[22.12.2022] Pavol Majerník 31.12.1978

| Goalkeepers: | DOB | M | (s) | G |
|---|---|---|---|---|
| Martin Junas | 09.03.1996 | 24 | | |
| Igor Šemrinec | 22.11.1987 | 8 | (1) | |
| **Defenders:** | **DOB** | **M** | **(s)** | **G** |
| Filip Blažek | 11.03.1998 | 31 | | |
| Martin Černek | 30.12.1994 | 13 | (12) | |
| Peter Čögley | 11.08.1988 | 16 | | |
| Haiderson Hurtado Palomino (COL) | 25.11.1995 | 15 | (1) | 2 |
| Adam Krčik | 16.03.1996 | 14 | | |
| Adam Morong | 16.06.1993 | 14 | | 2 |
| Oliver Podhorín | 06.07.1992 | 13 | (8) | |
| Ondřej Rudzan (CZE) | 25.08.1998 | 17 | | 1 |
| Marek Václav | 26.07.1996 | 6 | (9) | |
| **Midfielders:** | **DOB** | **M** | **(s)** | **G** |
| Denis Baumgartner | 02.02.1998 | 5 | (14) | 1 |
| Tomáš Brigant | 11.10.1994 | | (1) | |

| | DOB | M | (s) | G |
|---|---|---|---|---|
| Andrej Fábry | 01.03.1997 | 19 | (11) | 11 |
| Mário Hollý | 25.04.2000 | 27 | (3) | 2 |
| Jakub Kousal (CZE) | 06.09.2002 | 4 | (8) | 1 |
| Martin Mášik | 08.01.1999 | 8 | (12) | 1 |
| Martin Nagy | 05.09.1990 | 28 | | 1 |
| Martin Petr (CZE) | 14.03.1999 | 1 | | |
| Denis Potoma | 15.02.2000 | 3 | (12) | |
| Ján Vlasko | 11.01.1990 | 19 | (10) | 6 |
| **Forwards:** | **DOB** | **M** | **(s)** | **G** |
| Roman Haša (CZE) | 15.02.1993 | 21 | (9) | 3 |
| Žan Medved (SVN) | 14.06.1999 | 5 | (3) | 1 |
| Jaroslav Mihalík | 27.07.1994 | 9 | (3) | 1 |
| Daniel Šebesta | 24.10.1991 | 3 | (13) | |
| Ondřej Štursa (CZE) | 17.06.2000 | | (1) | |
| Jakub Švec | 23.07.2000 | | (10) | 1 |
| Yann Michael Yao (CIV) | 20.06.1997 | 29 | (3) | 4 |

## Športový klub Slovan Bratislava

**Founded:** 03.05.1919 (*as 1. ČsŠK Bratislava*)
**Stadium:** Štadión Tehelné pole, Bratislava (22,500)
**Trainer:** Vladimír Weiss 22.09.1964

| Goalkeepers: | DOB | M | (s) | G |
|---|---|---|---|---|
| Adrián Chovan | 08.10.1995 | 17 | (2) | |
| Adam Hrdina | 12.02.2004 | 1 | | |
| Martin Trnovský | 07.06.2000 | 14 | | |
| **Defenders:** | **DOB** | **M** | **(s)** | **G** |
| Myenty Abena (SUR) | 12.12.1994 | 9 | (1) | |
| Vernon De Marco Morlacchi | 18.11.1992 | 21 | (4) | 2 |
| Guram Kashia (GEO) | 04.07.1987 | 20 | (2) | 2 |
| Richard Križan | 23.09.1997 | 9 | (4) | |
| Maudo Lamine Jarjué (GAM) | 30.09.1997 | 2 | | |
| Lucas Lovat (BRA) | 15.01.1997 | 21 | (3) | 1 |
| Jurij Medveděv (CZE) | 18.06.1996 | 16 | (4) | |
| Lukáš Pauschek | 09.12.1992 | 11 | (2) | |
| Siemen Voet (BEL) | 03.02.2000 | 10 | | |
| **Midfielders:** | **DOB** | **M** | **(s)** | **G** |
| Uche Henry Agbo (NGA) | 04.12.1995 | 8 | (8) | 1 |
| Tigran Barseghyan (ARM) | 22.09.1993 | 10 | (16) | 5 |
| Giorgi Chakvetadze (GEO) | 29.08.1999 | 18 | (7) | 1 |

| | DOB | M | (s) | G |
|---|---|---|---|---|
| Dávid Holman (HUN) | 17.03.1993 | 2 | (2) | 1 |
| Jaba Kankava (GEO) | 18.03.1986 | 20 | (6) | 1 |
| Juraj Kucka | 26.02.1987 | 21 | (7) | 6 |
| Filip Lichý | 25.01.2001 | 2 | (4) | |
| Alen Mustafić (BIH) | 05.07.1999 | 12 | (5) | |
| Ibrahim Danda Rabiu (NGA) | 15.03.1991 | 2 | (2) | |
| Vladimír Weiss | 30.11.1989 | 16 | (4) | 9 |
| Jaromír Zmrhal (CZE) | 02.08.1993 | 13 | (12) | 3 |
| **Forwards:** | **DOB** | **M** | **(s)** | **G** |
| Malik Abubakari (GHA) | 10.05.2000 | 9 | (5) | 2 |
| Adler da Silva Parreira (SUI) | 28.12.1998 | | (3) | |
| Aleksandar Čavrić (SRB) | 18.05.1994 | 21 | (9) | 15 |
| Andre Jay Green (ENG) | 26.07.1998 | 15 | (10) | 6 |
| Dávid Hrnčár | 10.12.1997 | 12 | (4) | 5 |
| Žan Medved (SVN) | 14.06.1999 | 3 | (5) | |
| Eric Kleybel Ramírez Matheus (VEN) | 20.11.1998 | 12 | (4) | 3 |
| Iván Šaponjić (SRB) | 02.08.1997 | 4 | (10) | 2 |
| Sharani Zuberu (GHA) | 07.01.2000 | 1 | (8) | |

## Football Club Spartak Trnava

**Founded:** 30.05.1923 (*as TŠS Trnava*)
**Stadium:** Štadión "Antona Malatinského", Trnava (19,200)
**Trainer:** Michal Gašparík 19.12.1981

| Goalkeepers: | DOB | M | (s) | G |
|---|---|---|---|---|
| Dobrivoj Rusov | 13.01.1993 | 1 | | |
| Dominik Takáč | 12.01.1999 | 23 | | |
| Martin Vantruba | 07.02.1998 | 8 | | |
| **Defenders:** | **DOB** | **M** | **(s)** | **G** |
| Kazeem Bolaji Soliu (NGA) | 13.12.2002 | 5 | (6) | |
| Matej Čurma | 27.03.1996 | 9 | (9) | |
| Sebastián Kóša | 13.09.2003 | 22 | (5) | 2 |
| Kristián Koštrna | 15.12.1993 | 30 | (1) | 1 |
| Lukáš Štetina | 28.07.1991 | 30 | | |
| Gergely Tumma | 10.02.2000 | | (3) | |
| Filip Twardzik (CZE) | 10.02.1993 | 12 | | 3 |
| Marek Ujlaky | 03.12.2003 | 1 | (5) | |
| Tomáš Vaško | 05.02.2004 | | (1) | |
| **Midfielders:** | **DOB** | **M** | **(s)** | **G** |
| Martin Bukata | 02.10.1993 | 19 | (6) | 4 |
| Erik Daniel (CZE) | 04.02.1992 | 23 | (3) | 4 |

| | DOB | M | (s) | G |
|---|---|---|---|---|
| Patrik Karhan | 19.06.2003 | | (4) | |
| Martin Mikovič | 12.09.1990 | 19 | (1) | 2 |
| Kelvin Ofori (GHA) | 27.07.2001 | 10 | (1) | 2 |
| Azeez Oseni (NGA) | 16.10.2002 | 7 | (7) | 2 |
| Jakub Paur | 04.07.1992 | 9 | (13) | 2 |
| Roman Procházka | 14.03.1989 | 22 | (2) | 2 |
| Kyriakos Savvidis (GRE) | 20.06.1995 | 27 | (1) | 4 |
| Samuel Štefánik | 16.11.1991 | 19 | (8) | 5 |
| **Forwards:** | **DOB** | **M** | **(s)** | **G** |
| Sudais Ali Baba (NGA) | 25.08.2000 | | (2) | |
| Dyjan Carlos De *Azevedo* (BRA) | 23.06.1991 | 6 | (18) | |
| Yusuf Isa Bamidele (NGA) | 22.02.2001 | 8 | | 2 |
| Kelvin Boateng (GHA) | 24.03.2000 | 4 | (12) | 1 |
| Alex Iván | 26.03.1997 | 5 | (10) | |
| Miłosz Kozak (POL) | 23.05.1997 | | (1) | |
| Milan Ristovski (MKD) | 08.04.1998 | 15 | (13) | 3 |
| Abdulrahman Taiwo (NGA) | 05.08.1998 | 18 | (3) | 14 |

## Mestský Futbalový klub Tatran Liptovský Mikuláš

| | | |
|---|---|---|
| **Founded**: | 1934 | |
| **Stadium**: | Národné tréningové centrum, Poprad (5,700) | |
| **Trainer:** | Jozef Kostelník | 14.09.1970 |
| [22.11.2022] | Marek Fabuľa | 05.08.1975 |
| [27.02.2023] | Ivan Lisivka | 10.05.1986 |
| [10.03.2023] | Ondrej Desiatnik | 25.09.1975 |

| Goalkeepers: | DOB | M | (s) | G |
|---|---|---|---|---|
| Denis Gröger (CZE) | 17.02.1999 | 4 | (1) | |
| Dávid Húska | 30.09.2003 | 1 | | |
| Martin Polaček | 02.04.1990 | 7 | | |
| Dominik Sváček (CZE) | 24.02.1997 | 20 | | |
| **Defenders:** | **DOB** | **M** | **(s)** | **G** |
| Imrich Bedecs | 12.12.1991 | 24 | (2) | 2 |
| Tomás Krajčí | 2006 | | (1) | |
| Dávid Krčík | 28.06.1999 | 1 | | |
| Samuel Kuchárik | 24.06.2004 | | (2) | |
| Mário Mihál | 27.02.2001 | 6 | | |
| Mihajlo Popović (SRB) | 01.01.1993 | 20 | (3) | 3 |
| Jaroslav Soukup | 13.12.2006 | | (2) | |
| Ivan Spychka (UKR) | 18.01.1991 | 12 | | 1 |
| Gergely Tumma | 10.02.2000 | 9 | | |
| Richard Župa | 27.04.1998 | 13 | (7) | |
| **Midfielders:** | **DOB** | **M** | **(s)** | **G** |
| Lukáš Bielák | 14.12.1986 | 10 | (1) | |
| Dávid Filinský | 18.01.1999 | 12 | | |
| Tomáš Gerát | 15.06.1993 | 25 | (1) | 1 |

| | DOB | M | (s) | G |
|---|---|---|---|---|
| Adrián Kačerík | 02.08.1997 | 13 | (4) | 2 |
| Ivan Kotora | 27.06.1991 | | (4) | |
| Martin Nečas (CZE) | 04.09.1998 | 19 | (9) | |
| Strahinja Pavišić (SRB) | 29.05.1996 | 5 | (3) | |
| Tomáš Staš | 13.07.1996 | 14 | (8) | 1 |
| Christián Steinhübel | 02.10.1994 | 5 | (5) | 2 |
| Marko Totka | 12.09.2000 | 14 | (3) | |
| Rastislav Václavík | 28.02.1997 | 25 | (2) | 4 |
| **Forwards:** | **DOB** | **M** | **(s)** | **G** |
| Richard Bartoš | 28.06.1992 | 12 | (1) | |
| René Dedič | 07.08.1993 | 6 | (2) | 1 |
| Tobiáš Diviš | 02.12.2003 | 8 | (7) | |
| Peter Ďungel | 06.09.1993 | 4 | (5) | |
| David Adeniyi Fadairo (NGA) | 07.11.2000 | 1 | (3) | |
| Adam Gaži | 01.03.2003 | 15 | (7) | 1 |
| Erik Jendrišek | 26.10.1986 | 21 | (9) | 5 |
| Ľuboslav Laura | 05.07.1994 | 18 | (8) | 1 |
| Adam Matoš | 17.02.2002 | 2 | (5) | |
| Peter Voško | 17.08.2000 | 6 | (18) | |

## Asociácia športov Trenčín

| | | |
|---|---|---|
| **Founded**: | 1992 (*as TJ Ozeta Dukla Trenčín*) | |
| **Stadium**: | Štadión Sihoť, Trenčín (10,000) | |
| **Trainer:** | Peter Hyballa (GER) | 05.12.1975 |
| [27.07.2022] | Marián Zimen | 03.08.1980 |
| [27.03.2023] | František Straka (CZE) | 28.05.1958 |

| Goalkeepers: | DOB | M | (s) | G |
|---|---|---|---|---|
| Michal Kukučka | 12.04.2002 | 24 | | |
| Josimar José Évora Dias „Vózinha" (CPV) | 03.06.1986 | 8 | (1) | |
| **Defenders:** | **DOB** | **M** | **(s)** | **G** |
| Samuel Bagín | 08.02.2004 | 12 | (1) | 2 |
| Lukáš Ďuriška | 16.08.1992 | 6 | (6) | |
| Strahinja Kerkez (CYP) | 13.12.2002 | | (1) | |
| Samuel Kozlovský | 19.11.1999 | 20 | (1) | |
| Kingsley Madu (NGA) | 12.12.1995 | 10 | | 1 |
| Šimon Mičuda | 28.01.2004 | 10 | (8) | |
| Kelvin Spencer Pires (CPV) | 05.06.2000 | 24 | (3) | 4 |
| Lazar Stojsavljević (SRB) | 05.05.1998 | 25 | | 3 |
| Roman Šebeň | 09.03.2003 | 2 | (5) | |
| Reuben Yem (NGA) | 29.10.1997 | 17 | (3) | |
| **Midfielders:** | **DOB** | **M** | **(s)** | **G** |
| Filip Bainović (SRB) | 23.06.1996 | 24 | (6) | 6 |
| Artur Gajdoš | 20.01.2004 | 25 | (4) | 6 |
| Dominik Hollý | 11.11.2003 | 15 | (4) | 1 |

| | DOB | M | (s) | G |
|---|---|---|---|---|
| Rahim Ibrahim (GHA) | 10.06.2001 | 11 | (7) | 1 |
| Matúš Kmeť | 27.06.2000 | 21 | (10) | 2 |
| Samuel Lavrinčík | 10.07.2001 | 17 | (6) | |
| Adewale Oladoye (NGA) | 25.08.2001 | 6 | (5) | |
| Cristian Ezequiel Ramírez (ARG) | 29.03.1995 | | (4) | |
| **Forwards:** | **DOB** | **M** | **(s)** | **G** |
| Lucas Demitra | 09.04.2003 | 7 | (7) | |
| Philip Azango Elayo (NGA) | 21.05.1997 | 7 | (2) | 1 |
| Dabney dos Santos Souza (NED) | 31.07.1996 | 2 | (8) | |
| Chinonso Emeka (NGA) | 30.08.2001 | 7 | (4) | 4 |
| *Eynel* Domingo Rocha *Soares* (CPV) | 25.10.1998 | 30 | | 2 |
| Adam Gaži | 01.03.2003 | | (2) | |
| Njegoš Kupusović (SRB) | 22.02.2001 | 18 | (11) | 1 |
| Lukáš Letenay | 19.04.2001 | 1 | (12) | |
| Lekan Okunola (NGA) | 04.08.2003 | 1 | (8) | |
| Ľuboš Praženka | 20.06.2005 | 1 | (5) | |
| Witan Sulaeman (IDN) | 08.10.2001 | 1 | (9) | 1 |

## Mestský Futbalový klub Zemplín Michalovce

| | | |
|---|---|---|
| **Founded**: | 1912 (*as NAC Michalovce*) | |
| **Stadium**: | Mestský futbalový štadión, Michalovce (4,440) | |
| **Trainer:** | Norbert Hrnčár | 09.06.1970 |
| [16.05.2023] | Vladimír Rusnák | 19.08.1965 |

| Goalkeepers: | DOB | M | (s) | G |
|---|---|---|---|---|
| Andriy Kozhukhar (UKR) | 20.07.1999 | 5 | | |
| Benjamín Szaráz | 09.03.1998 | 27 | | |
| **Defenders:** | **DOB** | **M** | **(s)** | **G** |
| Alejandro „*Alex*" *Méndez* García (ESP) | 28.07.2001 | 18 | | |
| Zvonko Ceklić (MNE) | 11.04.1999 | 4 | (2) | |
| Michal Jeřábek (CZE) | 10.09.1993 | 17 | | 1 |
| Juraj Kotula | 30.09.1995 | 29 | | |
| Daniel Magda | 25.11.1997 | 15 | (7) | 1 |
| Saša Marjanović (BIH) | 05.02.2002 | 13 | | |
| Michal Ranko | 19.02.1994 | 16 | (4) | 1 |
| Filip Vaško | 11.08.1999 | 16 | (9) | |
| Polydefkis Volanakis (GRE) | 25.04.2003 | 13 | (1) | |
| **Midfielders:** | **DOB** | **M** | **(s)** | **G** |
| Matúš Begala | 07.04.2001 | 11 | (14) | |

| | DOB | M | (s) | G |
|---|---|---|---|---|
| Wisdom Kanu (NGA) | 27.03.1994 | 25 | (6) | 6 |
| Sainey Njie (GAM) | 30.08.2001 | 22 | (1) | |
| Brian *Peña* Perez-Vico (ESP) | 20.06.2002 | 28 | (2) | 6 |
| David Petrik | 14.06.2005 | | (12) | 1 |
| Kristi Qose (ALB) | 10.06.1995 | 7 | (4) | |
| Yushi Shimamura (JPN) | 20.12.1999 | | (7) | |
| Tibor Slebodník | 21.09.2000 | 7 | (18) | |
| Igor Žofčák | 10.04.1983 | 6 | (18) | 3 |
| **Forwards:** | **DOB** | **M** | **(s)** | **G** |
| Usman Issa Adekunle (NGA) | 20.12.1997 | 4 | (11) | 3 |
| Adler da Silva Parreira (SUI) | 28.12.1998 | 11 | (6) | 4 |
| Lukáš Jánošík | 05.03.1994 | 28 | (3) | 5 |
| Matija Krivokapić (MNE) | 19.03.2003 | | (3) | |
| Matúš Marcin | 06.04.1994 | 29 | (1) | 7 |
| Zoran Záhradník | 19.08.2005 | 1 | (7) | |

## Football Club Viliam Ondrejka Zlaté Moravce

| Founded: | 1995 | |
|---|---|---|
| Stadium: | Štadión FC ViOn, Zlaté Moravce (4,006) | |
| Trainer: | Ján Kocian | 13.03.1958 |
| [06.10.2022] | Ivan Galád | 10.04.1963 |

| Goalkeepers: | DOB | M | (s) | G |
|---|---|---|---|---|
| Patrik Lukáč | 05.12.1994 | 32 | | |
| **Defenders:** | **DOB** | **M** | **(s)** | **G** |
| Stephano Alves de *Almeida* (BRA) | 17.09.1993 | 24 | (3) | 5 |
| Denys Balan (UKR) | 18.08.1993 | 5 | (1) | |
| Martin Bednár | 22.04.1999 | 19 | (3) | |
| Matúš Čonka | 15.10.1990 | 21 | (1) | |
| Nazariy Gavrylyuk (UKR) | 07.02.2003 | 1 | (2) | |
| Michal Pintér | 04.02.1994 | 22 | | 2 |
| Samuel Šuľa | 12.04.2000 | 26 | (2) | 1 |
| Alden Šuvalija (BIH) | 03.03.2002 | 21 | (2) | 1 |
| Martin Toml (CZE) | 25.03.1996 | 15 | (3) | |
| **Midfielders:** | **DOB** | **M** | **(s)** | **G** |
| Adam Brenkus | 08.01.1999 | 4 | (22) | 7 |
| Denis Duga | 05.09.1994 | 24 | (6) | 2 |
| Tomáš Ďubek | 22.01.1987 | 20 | (8) | 2 |
| Tomce Grozdanovski (MKD) | 14.03.2000 | 1 | (3) | |
| Timotej Múdry | 04.04.2000 | 23 | (3) | |
| Anton Sloboda | 10.07.1987 | 12 | (4) | |
| **Forwards:** | **DOB** | **M** | **(s)** | **G** |
| Roman Čerepkai | 06.04.2002 | 6 | (5) | 3 |
| Lucas Demitra | 09.04.2003 | 3 | (4) | |
| Tomáš Horák | 03.08.1998 | 1 | (8) | 1 |
| Kenneth Tig-Ishor Ikugar (NGA) | 27.10.2000 | 6 | (8) | 1 |
| Alexandros Kyziridis (GRE) | 16.09.2000 | 2 | (1) | |
| Egy Maulana Vikri (IDN) | 07.07.2000 | 1 | (5) | |
| Karol Mondek | 02.06.1991 | 29 | (2) | 2 |
| Ioannis Niarchos (GRE) | 26.06.2002 | 12 | (4) | 5 |
| Patrik Pinte | 06.01.1997 | 17 | (12) | 1 |
| Sebastián Rák | 31.07.2003 | | (1) | |
| Tomáš Vestenický | 06.04.1996 | 5 | (8) | 1 |

## Futbalový klub Železiarne Podbrezová

| Founded: | 1920 (*as RTJ Podbrezová*) | |
|---|---|---|
| Stadium: | ZELPO Aréna, Podbrezová (4,061) | |
| Trainer: | Roman Skuhravý (CZE) | 06.01.1975 |

| Goalkeepers: | DOB | M | (s) | G |
|---|---|---|---|---|
| Richard Ludha | 08.11.2000 | 30 | | |
| Matěj Luksch (CZE) | 19.06.1998 | 1 | | |
| Ivan Rehák | 27.04.2001 | 1 | | |
| **Defenders:** | **DOB** | **M** | **(s)** | **G** |
| Marek Bartoš | 13.10.1996 | 31 | | 4 |
| Boris Godál | 27.05.1987 | 14 | | 4 |
| Matej Grešák | 31.05.1999 | 27 | (2) | |
| Peter Kováčik | 01.12.2001 | 13 | (2) | 2 |
| Matej Oravec | 30.03.1998 | 11 | (2) | |
| Nicolas Šikula | 15.05.2003 | 4 | (16) | |
| **Midfielders:** | **DOB** | **M** | **(s)** | **G** |
| Mikuláš Bakaľa | 04.01.2001 | 31 | (1) | 1 |
| Damián Bariš | 09.12.1994 | 10 | (13) | 1 |
| Patrik Blahút | 07.10.1997 | 8 | (2) | 1 |
| Michal Breznaník | 16.12.1985 | 3 | (12) | |
| Samuel Ďatko | 24.06.2001 | 31 | (1) | 3 |
| Šimon Faško | 09.04.2006 | 10 | (2) | |
| Erik Grendel | 13.10.1988 | 8 | (7) | |
| Christophe Kabongo (CZE) | 27.08.2003 | 6 | (4) | 5 |
| Vladimír Kukoľ | 08.05.1986 | 6 | (19) | |
| Martin Lupták | 28.02.2004 | | (1) | |
| Filip Mielke | 09.04.2005 | | (1) | |
| René Paraj | 04.08.1992 | 23 | | 2 |
| Jozef Špyrka | 30.05.1999 | 9 | (4) | 1 |
| Martin Talakov (MKD) | 09.03.2003 | 3 | (9) | |
| Marcel Vasil | 09.02.2001 | 2 | (6) | |
| **Forwards:** | **DOB** | **M** | **(s)** | **G** |
| Usman Issa Adekunle (NGA) | 20.12.1997 | 2 | (3) | |
| Moses David Cobnan (NGA) | 10.09.2002 | 17 | (1) | 9 |
| Adam Horvát | 18.02.2004 | 1 | (5) | |
| Marek Kuzma | 22.06.1988 | 18 | (5) | 3 |
| Andy Masaryk | 07.04.2005 | 1 | (5) | 1 |
| Daniel Pavúk | 03.02.1998 | 26 | (5) | 5 |
| Moussa Sangare (CIV) | 02.02.2002 | 5 | (6) | 1 |

## Mestský Športový klub Žilina

| Founded: | 20.06.1908 (*as Zsolnai Testgyakorlók Köre*) | |
|---|---|---|
| Stadium: | Štadión pod Dubňom, Žilina (11,253) | |
| Trainer: | Jaroslav Hynek | 05.09.1975 |

| Goalkeepers: | DOB | M | (s) | G |
|---|---|---|---|---|
| Samuel Belaník | 26.08.2003 | 1 | | |
| Ľubomír Belko | 04.02.2002 | 25 | | |
| Matej Slávik | 05.08.1994 | 4 | (1) | |
| Marek Teplan | 07.07.2002 | 2 | | |
| **Defenders:** | **DOB** | **M** | **(s)** | **G** |
| Benson Anang (GHA) | 01.05.2000 | 3 | (2) | 1 |
| Krisztián Bari | 06.02.2001 | 27 | (3) | 3 |
| Dominik Javorček | 02.11.2002 | 4 | (6) | 2 |
| Adam Kopas | 16.08.1999 | 20 | (3) | 2 |
| Samuel Kopásek | 22.05.2003 | 3 | (5) | |
| Patrik Leitner | 07.02.2002 | 22 | (1) | |
| Ján Minárik | 25.07.1997 | 11 | (2) | |
| James Willy Ndjeungoue (CMR) | 04.04.2003 | 2 | (2) | |
| Tomáš Nemčík | 19.04.2001 | 25 | | |
| Richmond Owusu (GHA) | 02.02.2003 | 2 | (7) | |
| Matúš Rusnák | 19.12.1999 | 24 | (3) | |
| Branislav Sluka | 23.01.1999 | 1 | (3) | |
| Andrej Stojchevski (MKD) | 26.05.2003 | 19 | (5) | 3 |
| **Midfielders:** | **DOB** | **M** | **(s)** | **G** |
| Xavier Rodrigue Adang Mveng (CMR) | 07.06.2004 | 1 | | |
| Samuel Gidi (GHA) | 15.04.2004 | 24 | (7) | 3 |
| Patrik Iľko | 16.02.2001 | 11 | (17) | 1 |
| Patrik Myslovič | 28.05.2001 | 18 | | 4 |
| Mário Sauer | 15.05.2004 | 8 | (7) | |
| **Forwards:** | **DOB** | **M** | **(s)** | **G** |
| Henry Addo (GHA) | 01.05.2003 | | (5) | 1 |
| Dávid Ďuriš | 22.03.1999 | 25 | (5) | 8 |
| Anton Loic Essomba Bikoula (CMR) | 01.12.2003 | 3 | (5) | |
| Roland Galčík | 30.07.2001 | 16 | (14) | 3 |
| Timotej Jambor | 04.04.2003 | 21 | (5) | 8 |
| Taofiq Jibril (NGA) | 23.04.1998 | 6 | (9) | 1 |
| Adrián Kaprálik | 10.06.2002 | 24 | (7) | 9 |
| Boris Krstič (SRB) | 25.06.2003 | | (2) | |
| Vladimir Trabalik | 02.11.2002 | | (2) | |

# SECOND LEVEL
## 2. Liga 2022/2023

| | | | | | | | | | | |
|---|---|---|---|---|---|---|---|---|---|---|
| 1. | FC Košice (*Promoted*) | 30 | 20 | 6 | 4 | 61 | - | 21 | 66 |
| 2. | FC Tatran Prešov (*Promotion Play-offs*) | 30 | 20 | 2 | 8 | 49 | - | 24 | 62 |
| 3. | KFC Komárno | 30 | 14 | 11 | 5 | 41 | - | 26 | 53 |
| 4. | MŠK Žilina „B" | 30 | 14 | 5 | 11 | 63 | - | 53 | 47 |
| 5. | FK Pohronie Žiar nad Hronom | 30 | 11 | 11 | 8 | 45 | - | 41 | 44 |
| 6. | ŠK Slovan Bratislava U-21 | 30 | 12 | 7 | 11 | 43 | - | 45 | 43 |
| 7. | Spartak Myjava | 30 | 12 | 7 | 11 | 46 | - | 41 | 43 |
| 8. | FC ŠTK 1914 Šamorín | 30 | 12 | 4 | 14 | 44 | - | 50 | 40 |
| 9. | MŠK Považská Bystrica | 30 | 10 | 10 | 10 | 52 | - | 48 | 40 |
| 10. | MŠK Púchov | 30 | 11 | 5 | 14 | 47 | - | 44 | 38 |
| 11. | FK Slavoj Trebišov | 30 | 10 | 6 | 14 | 32 | - | 44 | 36 |
| 12. | FC Petržalka Bratislava | 30 | 8 | 10 | 12 | 40 | - | 43 | 34 |
| 13. | MFK Dolný Kubín | 30 | 10 | 4 | 16 | 36 | - | 60 | 34 |
| 14. | FK Humenné | 30 | 7 | 11 | 12 | 24 | - | 35 | 32 |
| 15. | FK Rača (*Relegated*) | 30 | 6 | 8 | 16 | 25 | - | 52 | 26 |
| 16. | FK Dubnica nad Váhom (*Relegated*) | 30 | 6 | 7 | 17 | 38 | - | 59 | 25 |

# NATIONAL TEAM

## INTERNATIONAL MATCHES
### (16.07.2022 – 15.07.2023)

| | | | | |
|---|---|---|---|---|
| 22.09.2022 | Trnava | *Slovakia - Azerbaijan* | *1-2(0-1)* | (UNL) |
| 25.09.2022 | Bačka Topola | *Slovakia - Belarus* | *1-1(0-1)* | (UNL) |
| 17.11.2022 | Podgorica | *Montenegro - Slovakia* | *2-2(0-1)* | (F) |
| 20.11.2022 | Bratislava | *Slovakia - Chile* | *0-0* | (F) |
| 23.03.2023 | Trnava | *Slovakia - Luxembourg* | *0-0* | (ECQ) |
| 26.03.2023 | Bratislava | *Slovakia - Bosnia and Herzegovina* | *2-0(2-0)* | (ECQ) |
| 17.06.2023 | Reykjavík | *Iceland - Slovakia* | *1-2(1-1)* | (ECQ) |
| 20.06.2023 | Vaduz | *Liechtenstein - Slovakia* | *0-1(0-1)* | (ECQ) |

**22.09.2022    SLOVAKIA - AZERBAIJAN      1-2(0-1)      3rd UEFA Nations League C, Group 3**
Štadión "Antona Malatinského", Trnava; Referee: William Sean Collum (Scotland); Attendance: 2,875
**SVK:** Marek Rodák, Kristián Vallo, Ľubomír Šatka, Milan Škriniar (Cap), Dávid Hancko, Stanislav Lobotka, László Bénes (83.Samuel Mráz), Matúš Bero (83.Dávid Ďuriš), Martin Regáli (63.Christián Herc), Erik Jirka, Róbert Boženík (74.Adam Zreľák). Trainer: Francesco Calzona (Italy).
**Goal:** Erik Jirka (90+3).

**25.09.2022    SLOVAKIA - BELARUS      1-1(0-1)      3rd UEFA Nations League C, Group 3**
TSC Arena, Bačka Topola (Serbia); Referee: Nikola Dabanović (Montenegro); Attendance: 524
**SVK:** Marek Rodák, Peter Pekarík, Ľubomír Šatka, Milan Škriniar (Cap), Dávid Hancko, Stanislav Lobotka, László Bénes (74.Patrik Hrošovský), Juraj Kucka (87.Samuel Mráz), Erik Jirka, Dávid Ďuriš (74.Matúš Bero), Róbert Boženík (60.Adam Zreľák). Trainer: Francesco Calzona (Italy).
**Goal:** Adam Zreľák (65).

**17.11.2022    MONTENEGRO - SLOVAKIA      2-2(0-1)      Friendly International**
Stadion pod Goricom, Podgorica; Referee: Irfan Peljto (Bosnia and Herzegovina); Attendance: 1,109
**SVK:** Martin Dúbravka, Kristián Vallo (40.Peter Pekarík), Milan Škriniar (Cap), Ľubomír Šatka, Dávid Hancko, Stanislav Lobotka, Juraj Kucka, Ondrej Duda (83.László Bénes), Matúš Bero (84.Martin Regáli), Dávid Ďuriš (45+1.Tomáš Suslov), Róbert Boženík (83.Adam Zreľák [*sent off 90+5*]). Trainer: Francesco Calzona (Italy).
**Goals:** Dávid Hancko (15), Juraj Kucka (47).

**20.11.2022    SLOVAKIA - CHILE      0-0      Friendly International**
Štadion Tehelné pole, Bratislava; Referee: Ondřej Berka (Czech Republic); Attendance: 19,757
**SVK:** Martin Dúbravka, Peter Pekarík, Milan Škriniar, Ľubomír Šatka, Vernon De Marco Morlacchi (80.Adam Obert), Stanislav Lobotka, László Bénes (70.Patrik Hrošovský), Marek Hamšík (Cap) (89.Martin Regáli), Tomáš Suslov (89.Adrián Kaprálik), Ondrej Duda (70.Matúš Bero), Róbert Boženík (80.Dávid Strelec). Trainer: Francesco Calzona (Italy).

**23.03.2023    SLOVAKIA - LUXEMBOURG      0-0      17th EC. Qualifiers**
Štadión "Antona Malatinského", Trnava; Referee: Rade Obrenovič (Slovenia); Attendance: 3,523
**SVK:** Martin Dúbravka, Peter Pekarík (82.Michal Tomič), Ľubomír Šatka, Norbert Gyömbér, Dávid Hancko, Stanislav Lobotka, Juraj Kucka (Cap), Ondrej Duda (80.László Bénes), Tomáš Suslov (73.Róbert Mak), Lukáš Haraslín, Róbert Polievka (73.Róbert Boženík). Trainer: Francesco Calzona (Italy).

**26.03.2023    SLOVAKIA - BOSNIA AND HERZEGOVINA      2-0(2-0)      17th EC. Qualifiers**
Štadion Tehelné pole, Bratislava; Referee: Marco Di Bello (Italy); Attendance: 6,052
**SVK:** Martin Dúbravka, Peter Pekarík, Denis Vavro, Norbert Gyömbér, Dávid Hancko, Stanislav Lobotka (90+2.Patrik Hrošovský), Juraj Kucka (Cap), Ondrej Duda (69.László Bénes), Lukáš Haraslín (90+2.Matúš Bero), Róbert Mak (58.Tomáš Suslov), Róbert Polievka (69.Adam Zreľák). Trainer: Francesco Calzona (Italy).
**Goals:** Róbert Mak (13), Lukáš Haraslín (40).

**17.06.2023**   **ICELAND - SLOVAKIA**                     **1-2(1-1)**                          17th EC. Qualifiers
Laugardalsvöllur, Reykjavík; Referee: Donald Robertson (Scotland); Attendance: 7,555
**SVK:** Martin Dúbravka, Peter Pekarík, Denis Vavro, Milan Škriniar, Dávid Hancko, Stanislav Lobotka, Marek Hamšík (Cap) (81.Matúš Bero), Juraj Kucka, Ivan Schranz (81.Dávid Ďuriš), Róbert Mak (57.Tomáš Suslov), Róbert Polievka (57.Róbert Boženík). Trainer: Francesco Calzona (Italy).
**Goals:** Juraj Kucka (27), Tomáš Suslov (69).

**20.06.2023**   **LIECHTENSTEIN - SLOVAKIA**              **0-1(0-1)**                          17th EC. Qualifiers
Rheinpark Stadion, Vaduz; Referee: Yigal Frid (Israel); Attendance: 2,316
**SVK:** Martin Dúbravka, Peter Pekarík, Milan Škriniar, Denis Vavro (90.Norbert Gyömbér), Dávid Hancko, Stanislav Lobotka (89.Patrik Hrošovský), Marek Hamšík (Cap) (77.Matúš Bero), Juraj Kucka, Tomáš Suslov, Róbert Mak (62.Dávid Ďuriš), Róbert Polievka (77.Dávid Strelec). Trainer: Francesco Calzona (Italy).
**Goal:** Denis Vavro (45+1).

## NATIONAL TEAM PLAYERS
### (16.07.2022 – 15.07.2023)

| Name | DOB | Caps | Goals | Club |
|---|---|---|---|---|
| **Goalkeepers** | | | | |
| Martin DÚBRAVKA | 15.01.1989 | 35 | 0 | 2022: *Manchester United FC (ENG)* |
| | | | | 01.01.2023-> *Newcastle United FC (ENG)* |
| Marek RODÁK | 13.12.1996 | 19 | 0 | 2022: *Fulham FC London (ENG)* |
| **Defenders** | | | | |
| Vernon DE MARCO Morlacchi | 18.11.1992 | 6 | 1 | 2022: *ŠK Slovan Bratislava* |
| Norbert GYÖMBÉR | 03.07.1992 | 33 | 0 | 2023: *US Salernitana 1919 (ITA)* |
| Dávid HANCKO | 13.12.1997 | 29 | 2 | 2022/2023: *Feyenoord Rotterdam (NED)* |
| Adam OBERT | 23.08.2002 | 1 | 0 | 2022: *Cagliari Calcio (ITA)* |
| Peter PEKARÍK | 30.10.1986 | 119 | 2 | 2022/2023: *Hertha BSC Berlin (GER)* |
| Ľubomír ŠATKA | 02.12.1995 | 32 | 0 | 2022/2023: *KKS Lech Poznań (POL)* |
| Milan ŠKRINIAR | 11.02.1995 | 60 | 3 | 2022/2023: *FC Internazionale Milano (ITA)* |
| Michal TOMIČ | 30.03.1999 | 1 | 0 | 2023: *FK Mladá Boleslav (CZE)* |
| Kristián VALLO | 02.06.1998 | 2 | 0 | 2022: *Wisła Płock (POL)* |
| Denis VAVRO | 10.04.1996 | 13 | 1 | 2023: *FC København (DEN)* |
| **Midfielders** | | | | |
| Matúš BERO | 06.09.1995 | 28 | 1 | 2022/2023: *SBV Vitesse Arnhem (NED)* |
| László BÉNES | 09.09.1997 | 13 | 1 | 2022/2023: *Hamburger SV (GER)* |
| Ondrej DUDA | 05.12.1994 | 63 | 10 | 2022: *1. FC Köln (GER)* |
| | | | | 29.01.2023-> *Hellas Verona FC (ITA)* |
| Marek HAMŠÍK | 27.07.1987 | 138 | 26 | 2022/2023: *Trabzonspor Kulübü (TUR)* |
| Lukáš HARASLÍN | 26.05.1996 | 29 | 3 | 2023: *AC Sparta Praha (CZE)* |
| Christián HERC | 30.09.1998 | 4 | 0 | 2022: *Grasshopper Club Zürich (SUI)* |
| Patrik HROŠOVSKÝ | 22.04.1992 | 49 | 0 | 2022/2023: *KRC Genk (BEL)* |
| Erik JIRKA | 19.09.1997 | 9 | 2 | 2022: *FC Viktoria Plzeň (CZE)* |
| Juraj KUCKA | 26.02.1987 | 99 | 12 | 2022/2023: *ŠK Slovan Bratislava* |
| Stanislav LOBOTKA | 25.11.1994 | 47 | 3 | 2022/2023: *SSC Napoli (ITA)* |
| Dávid STRELEC | 04.04.2001 | 17 | 2 | 2022: *Spezia Calcio La Spezia (ITA)* |
| | | | | 31.01.2023-> *Reggina 1914 (ITA)* |
| Tomáš SUSLOV | 07.06.2002 | 20 | 2 | 2022/2023: *FC Groningen (NED)* |
| **Forwards** | | | | |
| Róbert BOŽENÍK | 18.11.1999 | 31 | 5 | 2022/2023: *Boavista FC Porto (POR)* |
| Dávid ĎURIŠ | 22.03.1999 | 5 | 0 | 2022/2023: *MŠK Žilina* |
| Adrián KAPRÁLIK | 10.06.2002 | 1 | 0 | 2022: *MŠK Žilina* |
| Róbert MAK | 08.03.1991 | 77 | 15 | 2023: *Sydney FC (AUS)* |
| Samuel MRÁZ | 13.05.1997 | 6 | 1 | 2022: *CD Mirandés (ESP)* |
| Róbert POLIEVKA | 09.06.1996 | 4 | 0 | 2023: *MFK Dukla Banská Bystrica* |
| Martin REGÁLI | 12.10.1993 | 4 | 0 | 2022: *MFK Ružomberok* |
| Ivan SCHRANZ | 13.09.1993 | 17 | 3 | 2023: *SK Slavia Praha (CZE)* |
| Adam ZREĽÁK | 05.05.1994 | 9 | 3 | 2022/2023: *KS Warta Poznań (POL)* |

| National team coach | | |
|---|---|---|
| Francesco CALZONA (Italy) [from 09.07.2022] | 24.10.1968 | 8 M; 3 W; 4 D; 1 L; 9-6 |

# SLOVENIA

## The Country:
Republika Slovenija (Republic of Slovenia)
Capital: Ljubljana
Surface: 20,273 km²
Inhabitants: 2,116,972 [2022]
Time: UTC+1

## The FA:
Nogometna zveza Slovenije
Predoslje 40 a, p.p. 130, 4000 Kranj
Tel: +386 4 27 59 400
Founded: 23.04.1920
Member of FIFA since: 1992
Member of UEFA since: 1992
Website: www.nzs.si

## NATIONAL TEAM RECORDS

| RECORDS | | |
|---|---|---|
| **First international match:** | 03.06.1992, Tallinn: | Estonia – Slovenia 1-1 |
| **Most international caps:** | Boštjan Cesar | - 101 caps (2003-2018) |
| **Most international goals:** | Zlatko Zahovič | - 35 goals / 80 caps (1992-2004) |

### UEFA EUROPEAN CHAMPIONSHIP

| | |
|---|---|
| 1960 | - |
| 1964 | - |
| 1968 | - |
| 1972 | - |
| 1976 | - |
| 1980 | - |
| 1984 | - |
| 1988 | - |
| 1992 | - |
| 1996 | Qualifiers |
| 2000 | Final Tournament (Group Stage) |
| 2004 | Qualifiers |
| 2008 | Qualifiers |
| 2012 | Qualifiers |
| 2016 | Qualifiers |
| 2020 | Qualifiers |

### FIFA WORLD CUP

| | |
|---|---|
| 1930 | - |
| 1934 | - |
| 1938 | - |
| 1950 | - |
| 1954 | - |
| 1958 | - |
| 1962 | - |
| 1966 | - |
| 1970 | - |
| 1974 | - |
| 1978 | - |
| 1982 | - |
| 1986 | - |
| 1990 | - |
| 1994 | Did not enter |
| 1998 | Qualifiers |
| 2002 | Final Tournament (Group Stage) |
| 2006 | Qualifiers |
| 2010 | Final Tournament (Group Stage) |
| 2014 | Qualifiers |
| 2018 | Qualifiers |
| 2022 | Qualifiers |

### OLYMPIC TOURNAMENTS

| | |
|---|---|
| 1908 | - |
| 1912 | - |
| 1920 | - |
| 1924 | - |
| 1928 | - |
| 1936 | - |
| 1948 | - |
| 1952 | - |
| 1956 | - |
| 1960 | - |
| 1964 | - |
| 1968 | - |
| 1972 | - |
| 1976 | - |
| 1980 | - |
| 1984 | - |
| 1988 | - |
| 1992 | - |
| 1996 | Qualifiers |
| 2000 | Qualifiers |
| 2004 | Qualifiers |
| 2008 | Qualifiers |
| 2012 | Qualifiers |
| 2016 | Qualifiers |
| 2020 | Qualifiers |

*Please note: was part of Yugoslavia between 1930-1990*

## UEFA NATIONS LEAGUE

| | |
|---|---|
| 2018/2019 | League C (Group Stage) |
| 2020/2021 | League C (Group Stage -> promoted to League B) |
| 2022/2023 | League B (Group Stage) |

## SLOVENIAN CLUB HONOURS IN EUROPEAN CLUB COMPETITIONS:

| European Champion Clubs.Cup (1956-1992) / UEFA Champions League (1993-2023) |
|---|
| None |

| Fairs Cup (1858-1971) / UEFA Cup (1972-2009) / UEFA Europa League (2010-2023) |
|---|
| None |

| UEFA Europa Conference League (2021-2023) |
|---|
| None |

| UEFA Super Cup (1972-2022) |
|---|
| None |

| *European Cup Winners' Cup 1961-1999** |
|---|
| None |

*\*defunct competition*

| | CHAMPIONS | CUP WINNERS | BEST GOALSCORERS | |
|---|---|---|---|---|
| 1991/1992 | NK Olimpija Ljubljana | NK Maribor | Zoran Ubavič (NK Olimpija Ljubljana) | 29 |
| 1992/1993 | NK Olimpija Ljubljana | NK Olimpija Ljubljana | Sašo Udovič (ND Slovan Ljubljana) | 25 |
| 1993/1994 | NK Olimpija Ljubljana | NK Maribor | Štefan Škaper (NK Beltinci) | 23 |
| 1994/1995 | NK Olimpija Ljubljana | NK Mura Murska Sobota | Štefan Škaper (NK Beltinci) | 25 |
| 1995/1996 | ND Gorica | NK Olimpija Ljubljana | Ermin Šiljak (NK Olimpija Ljubljana) | 28 |
| 1996/1997 | NK Maribor | NK Maribor | Faik Kamberović (BIH, NK Celje) | 21 |
| 1997/1998 | NK Maribor | NK Rudar Velenje | Ismet Ekmečić (NK Olimpija Ljubljana) | 21 |
| 1998/1999 | NK Maribor | NK Maribor | Novica Nikčević (SRB, ND Gorica) | 17 |
| 1999/2000 | NK Maribor | NK Olimpija Ljubljana | Kliton Bozgo (ALB, NK Maribor) | 24 |
| 2000/2001 | NK Maribor | ND Gorica | Damir Pekič (NK Celje) | 23 |
| 2001/2002 | NK Maribor | ND Gorica | Romano Obilinović (CRO, NK Primorje Ajdovščina) | 16 |
| 2002/2003 | NK Maribor | NK Olimpija Ljubljana | Marko Kmetec (NK Ljubljana / NK Olimpija Ljubljana) | 21 |
| 2003/2004 | ND Gorica | NK Maribor | Dražen Žeželj (NK Ljubljana / NK Primorje Ajdovščina) | 19 |
| 2004/2005 | ND Gorica | NK Celje | Kliton Bozgo (ALB, NK Maribor) | 18 |
| 2005/2006 | ND Gorica | FC Koper | Miran Burgič (ND Gorica) | 24 |
| 2006/2007 | NK Domžale | FC Koper | Nikola Nikezić (MNE, NK Domžale / ND Gorica) | 22 |
| 2007/2008 | NK Domžale | NK Interblock Ljubljana | Dario Zahora (CRO, NK Domžale) | 22 |
| 2008/2009 | NK Maribor | NK Interblock Ljubljana | Etien Velikonja (ND Gorica) | 17 |
| 2009/2010 | FC Koper | NK Maribor | Milan Osterc (FC Koper) | 23 |
| 2010/2011 | NK Maribor | NK Domžale | Marcos Magno Morales Tavares (BRA, NK Maribor) | 16 |
| 2011/2012 | NK Maribor | NK Maribor | Dare Vršič (NK Olimpija Ljubljana) | 22 |
| 2012/2013 | NK Maribor | NK Maribor | Marcos Magno Morales Tavares (BRA, NK Maribor) | 17 |
| 2013/2014 | NK Maribor | ND Gorica | Mate Eterović (CRO, NK Rudar Velenje) | 19 |
| 2014/2015 | NK Maribor | FC Koper | Marcos Magno Morales Tavares (BRA, NK Maribor) | 17 |
| 2015/2016 | NK Olimpija Ljubljana | NK Maribor | Rok Kronaveter (NK Olimpija Ljubljana) Jean-Philippe Mendy (FRA, NK Maribor) Andraž Šporar (NK Olimpija Ljubljana) | 17 |
| 2016/2017 | NK Maribor | NK Domžale | John Mary Honi Uzuegbunam (CMR, NK Rudar Velenje) | 17 |
| 2017/2018 | NK Olimpija Ljubljana | NK Olimpija Ljubljana | Luka Zahović (NK Maribor) | 18 |
| 2018/2019 | NK Maribor | NK Olimpija Ljubljana | Luka Zahović (NK Maribor) | 18 |
| 2019/2020 | NK Celje | NŠ Mura Murska Sobota | Ante Vukušic (CRO, NK Olimpija Ljubljana) | 26 |
| 2020/2021 | NŠ Mura Murska Sobota | NK Olimpija Ljubljana | Jan Mlakar (NK Maribor) Nardin Mulahusejnović (BIH, FC Koper) | 14 |
| 2021/2022 | NK Maribor | FC Koper | Ognjen Mudrinski (SRB, NK Maribor) | 17 |
| 2022/2023 | NK Olimpija Ljubljana | NK Olimpija Ljubljana | Žan Vipotnik (NK Maribor) | 20 |

## NATIONAL CHAMPIONSHIP
### Prva liga Slovenije 2022/2023
(15.07.2022 – 20.05.2023)

### Results

**Round 1** [15-18.07.2022]
FC Koper - NK Tabor 2-1(0-0)
NK Domžale - NK Celje 0-0
NK Maribor - NK Radomlje 0-3(0-2)
Olimpija Ljubljana - NŠ Mura 2-0(0-0)
ND Gorica - NK Bravo 2-0(1-0)

**Round 2** [22-24.07.2022]
NK Radomlje - NK Celje 1-1(0-0)
NK Maribor - ND Gorica 3-2(2-1)
NK Bravo - FC Koper 1-0(1-0)
NK Tabor - Olimpija Ljubljana 0-1(0-1)
NŠ Mura - NK Domžale 4-3(1-3)

**Round 3** [29-31.07.2022]
ND Gorica - NK Radomlje 0-1(0-1)
NK Domžale - NK Tabor 1-1(1-0)
Olimpija Ljubljana - NK Bravo 1-0(0-0)
FC Koper - NK Maribor 2-1(1-1)
NK Celje - NŠ Mura 3-3(0-2)

**Round 4** [05-08.08.2022]
NK Tabor - NK Celje 1-0(0-0)
NK Bravo - NK Domžale 0-1(0-1)
NK Radomlje - NŠ Mura 1-1(1-0)
NK Maribor - Olimpija Ljubljana 0-2(0-1)
ND Gorica - FC Koper 1-2(0-1)

**Round 5** [12-15.08.2022]
NK Celje - NK Bravo 1-0(1-0)
NŠ Mura - NK Tabor 2-2(0-1)
FC Koper - NK Radomlje 5-0(2-0)
NK Domžale - NK Maribor 3-2(1-1)
Olimpija Ljubljana - ND Gorica 2-0(0-0)

**Round 6** [19-22.08.2022]
NK Radomlje - NK Tabor 0-0
NK Bravo - NŠ Mura 0-1(0-0)
FC Koper - Olimpija Ljubljana 0-2(0-1)
NK Maribor - NK Celje 2-2(2-2)
ND Gorica - NK Domžale 0-0

**Round 7** [26-28.08.2022]
NK Tabor - NK Bravo 0-4(0-1)
NK Celje - ND Gorica 1-0(0-0)
Olimpija Ljubljana - NK Radomlje 2-1(1-0)
NK Domžale - FC Koper 0-2(0-0)
NŠ Mura - NK Maribor 0-1(0-0)

**Round 8** [02-05.09.2022]
ND Gorica - NŠ Mura 0-0
FC Koper - NK Celje 0-2(0-2)
NK Maribor - NK Tabor 2-2(0-1)
Olimpija Ljubljana - NK Domžale 3-2(0-2)
NK Radomlje - NK Bravo 1-1(0-0)

**Round 9** [09-11.09.2022]
NK Domžale - NK Radomlje 3-1(0-1)
NK Tabor - ND Gorica 1-3(1-2)
NK Celje - Olimpija Ljubljana 4-3(0-2)
NK Bravo - NK Maribor 0-1(0-0)
NŠ Mura - FC Koper 2-1(1-0)

| Round 10 [17-18.09.2022] |
|---|
| NK Tabor - FC Koper 0-2(0-1) |
| NŠ Mura - Olimpija Ljubljana 2-3(2-1) |
| NK Bravo - ND Gorica 2-0(2-0) |
| NK Radomlje - NK Maribor 0-5(0-2) |
| NK Celje - NK Domžale 2-1(0-1) |

| Round 11 [01-02.10.2022] |
|---|
| NK Domžale - NŠ Mura 2-2(1-1) |
| Olimpija Ljubljana - NK Tabor 2-0(1-0) |
| FC Koper - NK Bravo 2-0(1-0) |
| ND Gorica - NK Maribor 1-4(0-3) |
| NK Celje - NK Radomlje 2-1(1-1) |

| Round 12 [08-10.10.2022] |
|---|
| NK Tabor - NK Domžale 1-1(0-1) |
| NK Maribor - FC Koper 1-0(0-0) |
| NK Bravo - Olimpija Ljubljana 6-1(2-0) |
| NŠ Mura - NK Celje 3-1(0-1) |
| NK Radomlje - ND Gorica 1-1(1-1) |

| Round 13 [14-16.10.2022] |
|---|
| NK Celje - NK Tabor 1-0(1-0) |
| NK Domžale - NK Bravo 0-0 |
| FC Koper - ND Gorica 1-1(0-1) |
| Olimpija Ljubljana - NK Maribor 1-0(0-0) |
| NŠ Mura - NK Radomlje 3-0(2-0) |

| Round 14 [22-24.10.2022] |
|---|
| NK Maribor - NK Domžale 0-3(0-1) |
| NK Tabor - NŠ Mura 0-4(0-4) |
| ND Gorica - Olimpija Ljubljana 0-0 |
| NK Bravo - NK Celje 2-0(1-0) |
| NK Radomlje - FC Koper 2-2(1-1) |

| Round 15 [28.10.-02.11.2022] |
|---|
| NK Domžale - ND Gorica 5-1(2-0) |
| NK Tabor - NK Radomlje 2-1(0-1) |
| NK Celje - NK Maribor 3-3(1-1) |
| Olimpija Ljubljana - FC Koper 2-1(2-1) |
| NŠ Mura - NK Bravo 1-0(1-0) |

| Round 16 [04-06.11.2022] |
|---|
| FC Koper - NK Domžale 1-1(1-1) |
| ND Gorica - NK Celje 0-2(0-1) |
| NK Radomlje - Olimpija Ljubljana 0-1(0-1) |
| NK Bravo - NK Tabor 2-1(0-1) |
| NK Maribor - NŠ Mura 5-1(3-1) |

| Round 17 [12-13.11.2022] |
|---|
| NK Bravo - NK Radomlje 1-1(1-0) |
| NK Domžale - Olimpija Ljubljana 0-3(0-0) |
| NK Tabor - NK Maribor 0-4(0-3) |
| NK Celje - FC Koper 1-1(0-1) |
| NŠ Mura - ND Gorica 2-0(1-0) |

| Round 18 [29.11.-01.12.2022] |
|---|
| ND Gorica - NK Tabor 1-1(0-1) |
| NK Maribor - NK Bravo 3-0(3-0) |
| NK Radomlje - NK Domžale 0-2(0-0) |
| FC Koper - NŠ Mura 0-0 |
| Olimpija Ljubljana - NK Celje 0-0 |

| Round 19 [06-08.12.2022] |
|---|
| ND Gorica - NK Bravo 0-0 |
| NK Maribor - NK Radomlje 7-0(4-0) |
| FC Koper - NK Tabor 5-1(2-0) |
| NK Domžale - NK Celje 2-1(0-0) |
| Olimpija Ljubljana - NŠ Mura 0-0 |

| Round 20 [10-12.12.2022] |
|---|
| NK Bravo - FC Koper 0-1(0-1) |
| NK Tabor - Olimpija Ljubljana 0-8(0-2) |
| NK Maribor - ND Gorica 2-1(1-1) |
| NK Radomlje - NK Celje 0-3(0-1) |
| NŠ Mura - NK Domžale 0-1(0-1) |

| Round 21 [11-12.02.2023] |
|---|
| Olimpija Ljubljana - NK Bravo 2-1(0-0) |
| NK Celje - NŠ Mura 2-1(1-0) |
| ND Gorica - NK Radomlje 1-1(0-0) |
| FC Koper - NK Maribor 0-1(0-1) |
| NK Domžale - NK Tabor 0-4(0-1) |

| Round 22 [18-19.02.2023] |
|---|
| NK Tabor - NK Celje 2-2(1-1) |
| NK Radomlje - NŠ Mura 0-0 |
| ND Gorica - FC Koper 2-2(1-2) |
| NK Bravo - NK Domžale 0-2(0-1) |
| NK Maribor - Olimpija Ljubljana 2-0(2-0) |

| Round 23 [21-23.02.2023] |
|---|
| FC Koper - NK Radomlje 1-2(0-1) |
| NŠ Mura - NK Tabor 2-2(0-2) |
| NK Celje - NK Bravo 1-1(1-1) |
| Olimpija Ljubljana - ND Gorica 4-3(2-1) |
| NK Domžale - NK Maribor 1-1(1-0) |

| Round 24 [25-26.02.2023] |
|---|
| NK Bravo - NŠ Mura 0-0 |
| NK Radomlje - NK Tabor 0-0 |
| FC Koper - Olimpija Ljubljana 0-1(0-0) |
| NK Maribor - NK Celje 2-0(2-0) |
| ND Gorica - NK Domžale 0-2(0-1) |

| Round 25 [04-05.03.2023] |
|---|
| NK Celje - ND Gorica 0-1(0-0) |
| NK Domžale - FC Koper 0-0 |
| Olimpija Ljubljana - NK Radomlje 1-0(0-0) |
| NK Tabor - NK Bravo 1-1(1-0) |
| NŠ Mura - NK Maribor 2-1(2-1) |

| Round 26 [10-12.03.2023] |
|---|
| ND Gorica - NŠ Mura 1-1(0-0) |
| NK Maribor - NK Tabor 1-1(0-0) |
| FC Koper - NK Celje 0-1(0-0) |
| Olimpija Ljubljana - NK Domžale 1-4(0-3) |
| NK Radomlje - NK Bravo 3-1(1-1) |

| Round 27 [15-16.03.2023] |
|---|
| NK Bravo - NK Maribor 2-3(0-3) |
| NK Domžale - NK Radomlje 1-2(0-1) |
| NK Celje - Olimpija Ljubljana 0-1(0-0) |
| NK Tabor - ND Gorica 0-1(0-0) |
| NŠ Mura - FC Koper 1-2(0-0) |

| Round 28 [18-19.03.2023] |
|---|
| NK Radomlje - NK Maribor 1-1(1-1) |
| NK Celje - NK Domžale 1-0(0-0) |
| NK Bravo - ND Gorica 2-1(0-0) |
| NK Tabor - FC Koper 0-1(0-1) |
| NŠ Mura - Olimpija Ljubljana 2-1(2-1) |

| Round 29 [01-02.04.2023] |
|---|
| NK Celje - NK Radomlje 1-1(1-0) |
| ND Gorica - NK Maribor 0-3(0-1) |
| FC Koper - NK Bravo 1-0(1-0) |
| Olimpija Ljubljana - NK Tabor 1-0(1-0) |
| NK Domžale - NŠ Mura 0-0 |

| Round 30 [08-10.04.2023] |
|---|
| NK Tabor - NK Domžale 1-1(1-1) |
| NK Radomlje - ND Gorica 2-0(1-0) |
| NK Maribor - FC Koper 3-1(1-0) |
| NK Bravo - Olimpija Ljubljana 1-0(0-0) |
| NŠ Mura - NK Celje 0-2(0-1) |

| Round 31 [14-16.04.2023] |
|---|
| FC Koper - ND Gorica 1-0(0-0) |
| NŠ Mura - NK Radomlje 1-1(1-1) |
| NK Domžale - NK Bravo 2-2(0-1) |
| NK Celje - NK Tabor 0-0 |
| Olimpija Ljubljana - NK Maribor 2-0(1-0) |

| Round 32 [22-23.04.2023] |
|---|
| NK Radomlje - FC Koper 1-1(1-1) |
| NK Tabor - NŠ Mura 1-2(0-0) |
| NK Maribor - NK Domžale 1-0(0-0) |
| ND Gorica - Olimpija Ljubljana 2-2(1-1) |
| NK Bravo - NK Celje 0-3(0-1) |

| Round 33 [28-30.04.2023] |
|---|
| NK Domžale - ND Gorica 1-1(1-0) |
| NŠ Mura - NK Bravo 0-1(0-0) |
| NK Celje - NK Maribor 3-1(1-0) |
| NK Tabor - NK Radomlje 1-2(1-0) |
| Olimpija Ljubljana - FC Koper 3-2(2-1) |

| Round 34 [02-04.05.2023] |
|---|
| NK Maribor - NŠ Mura 3-1(2-1) |
| NK Radomlje - Olimpija Ljubljana 2-1(0-1) |
| ND Gorica - NK Celje 1-2(1-0) |
| NK Bravo - NK Tabor 1-1(1-0) |
| FC Koper - NK Domžale 2-3(1-2) |

| Round 35 [13-14.05.2023] |
|---|
| NŠ Mura - ND Gorica 4-2(1-2) |
| NK Domžale - Olimpija Ljubljana 2-1(1-0) |
| NK Celje - FC Koper 2-0(1-0) |
| NK Tabor - NK Maribor 1-1(0-0) |
| NK Bravo - NK Radomlje 0-1(0-0) |

| Round 36 [19-20.05.2023] |
|---|
| ND Gorica - NK Tabor 1-0(1-0) |
| NK Maribor - NK Bravo 1-1(0-0) |
| Olimpija Ljubljana - NK Celje 0-2(0-1) |
| FC Koper - NŠ Mura 1-2(1-0) |
| NK Radomlje - NK Domžale 1-0(0-0) |

## Final Standings

| | | | | | | | | Home | | | | | Away | | | | |
|---|---|---|---|---|---|---|---|---|---|---|---|---|---|---|---|---|---|
| 1. **NK Olimpija Ljubljana** | 36 | 23 | 4 | 9 | 60 - 39 | 73 | 14 | 2 | 2 | 29 - 16 | 9 | 2 | 7 | 31 - 23 |
| 2. NK Celje | 36 | 19 | 10 | 7 | 53 - 34 | 67 | 11 | 5 | 2 | 29 - 18 | 8 | 5 | 5 | 24 - 16 |
| 3. NK Maribor | 36 | 18 | 8 | 10 | 70 - 43 | 62 | 10 | 4 | 4 | 37 - 21 | 8 | 4 | 6 | 33 - 22 |
| 4. NK Domžale | 36 | 13 | 13 | 10 | 50 - 42 | 52 | 5 | 9 | 4 | 23 - 24 | 8 | 4 | 6 | 27 - 18 |
| 5. NŠ Mura Murska Sobota | 36 | 13 | 13 | 10 | 50 - 45 | 52 | 9 | 3 | 6 | 31 - 24 | 4 | 10 | 4 | 19 - 21 |
| 6. FC Koper | 36 | 14 | 8 | 14 | 46 - 40 | 50 | 7 | 3 | 8 | 24 - 19 | 7 | 5 | 6 | 22 - 21 |
| 7. NK Radomlje | 36 | 10 | 14 | 12 | 35 - 53 | 44 | 4 | 10 | 4 | 16 - 21 | 6 | 4 | 8 | 19 - 32 |
| 8. NK Bravo Ljubljana | 36 | 9 | 9 | 18 | 33 - 41 | 36 | 7 | 3 | 8 | 20 - 18 | 2 | 6 | 10 | 13 - 23 |
| 9. ND Gorica (*Relegation Play-offs*) | 36 | 5 | 12 | 19 | 31 - 57 | 27 | 2 | 9 | 7 | 13 - 23 | 3 | 3 | 12 | 18 - 34 |
| 10. NK Tabor Sežana (*Relegated*) | 36 | 3 | 15 | 18 | 29 - 63 | 24 | 2 | 5 | 11 | 12 - 39 | 1 | 10 | 7 | 17 - 24 |

| Top goalscorers: | |
|---|---|
| 20  **Žan Vipotnik** | *NK Maribor* |
| 19  Mirlind Daku (KOS) | *NŠ Mura Murska Sobota* |
| 14  Aljoša Matko | *NK Celje* |

## Relegation Play-offs [25-28.05.2023]

NK Aluminij Kidričevo - ND Gorica                                   3-1(1-1)          1-1(1-1)

NK Aluminij Kidričevo promoted to the first level for 2023/2024.

# NATIONAL CUP
## Pokal Nogometne zveze Slovenije 2022/2023

### Third Round [08-10.11.2022]

| | | | | |
|---|---|---|---|---|
| NK Hotiza - NK Domžale | 0-7(0-4) | NK Idrija - NK Aluminij Kidričevo | 1-5(0-2) |
| KNK Fužinar - ŠD Cven | 4-1(3-0) | NK Rogaška - NK Odranci | 7-0(2-0) |
| NK Nafta Lendava 1903- NK Triglav Kranj | 1-1 aet; 5-4 pen | NK Celje - NŠ Mura Murska Sobota | 2-1(1-0) |
| NK Radenska Slatina - NK Bistrica Slov. Bistrica | 0-3 *awarded* | NK Olimpija Ljubljana - NK Ljutomer | 4-1(2-0) |
| NK Bravo Ljubljana - NK Britof | 9-0(7-0) | NK Maribor - NK Krka Novo Mesto | 3-1(0-1) |
| ŠD Videm - NK Dob | 2-2 aet; 8-7 pen | NK Tabor Sežana - NK Šenčur | 2-1(1-1,1-1) |
| DNŠ Zavrč - NK Serdica | 2-0(1-0) | NK Rudar Velenje - NK Dobrovce | 4-1(2-0) |
| ND Primorje Ajdovščina - NK Zagorje | 8-0(2-0) | FC Koper - SD Cirkulane | 6-0(2-0) |

### 1/8-Finals [07-09.03.2023]

| | | | | |
|---|---|---|---|---|
| ND Primorje Ajdovščina - DNŠ Zavrč | 6-1(4-0) | NK Rudar Velenje - NK Maribor | 0-4(0-1) |
| NK Celje - ŠD Videm | 3-0(2-0) | NK Aluminij Kidričevo - KNK Fužinar | 4-2(1-1) |
| FC Koper - NK Domžale | 2-0(0-0,0-0) | NK Nafta Lendava 1903- NK Olimpija Ljubljana | 1-3(0-3) |
| NK Tabor Sežana - NK Rogaška | 0-1(0-0) | NK Bistrica Slov. Bistrica - NK Bravo Ljubljana | 1-0(0-0) |

### Quarter-Finals [05-06.04.2023]

| | | | | |
|---|---|---|---|---|
| NK Aluminij Kidričevo - FC Koper | 1-0(0-0) | NK Rogaška - NK Bistrica Slovenska Bistrica | 0-2(0-2) |
| NK Maribor - ND Primorje Ajdovščina | 3-1(2-0) | NK Olimpija Ljubljana - NK Celje | 0-0 aet; 6-5 pen |

### Semi-Finals [25-26.04.2023]

| | | | |
|---|---|---|---|
| NK Bistrica Slovenska Bistrica - NK Maribor | 1-3(0-0) | NK Olimpija Ljubljana - NK Aluminij Kidričevo | 2-1(2-1) |

### Final

06.05.2023; Stadion Z'dežele, Celje; Referee: Bojan Mertik; Attendance: 9,217
**NK Olimpija Ljubljana - NK Maribor**                                  **2-1(0-0,0-0)**

**NK Olimpija**: Matevž Vidovšek, Marcel Ratnik, Đorđe Crnomarković, David de Senna Fernandes Sualehe, Aljaž Krefl (83.Justas Lasickas), Agustin Doffo (119.Anes Krdžalić), Timi Max Elšnik, Mario Kvesić, Svit Sešlar, Aldair Adulai Djaló Baldé (83.Rui Pedro da Silva e Sousa), Admir Bristrić. Trainer: Albert Riera Ortega (Spain).

**NK Maribor**: Ažbe Jug, Max Watson, Luka Uskoković, Ignacio Guerrico, Martin Milec (88.Andraž Žinič), Jan Repas (113.Ishaq Kayode Rafiu), Marin Laušić (90+3.Luka Božičković), Marko Božič (80.Rok Kronaveter; 113.Nemanja Mitrovič), Marko Tolić (106.Arnel Jakupović), Ivan Brnić, Žan Vipotnik. Trainer: Damir Krznar (Croatia).

**Goals:** 1-0 Justas Lasickas (103), 1-1 Nemanja Mitrovič (113), 2-1 Timi Max Elšnik (120+10 penalty).

# THE CLUBS 2022/2023

## Nogometni klub Bravo Ljubljana

| | | |
|---|---|---|
| **Founded**: | 2006 | |
| **Stadium**: | Šiška Sports Park, Ljubljana (2,308) | |
| **Trainer**: | Dejan Grabić | 21.09.1980 |
| [01.03.2023] | Aleš Arnol | 28.09.1984 |

| Goalkeepers: | DOB | M | (s) | G |
|---|---|---|---|---|
| Gal Fink | 18.04.2002 | 16 | | |
| Matija Orbanić (CRO) | 29.05.2000 | 20 | | |
| **Defenders:** | **DOB** | **M** | **(s)** | **G** |
| Matija Burin | 25.03.2001 | 3 | | |
| Nemanja Jakšić (SRB) | 11.07.1995 | 35 | | 1 |
| Maro Katinić (CRO) | 13.04.2004 | 16 | | 1 |
| Matija Kavčič | 11.07.1997 | 35 | (1) | |
| Mitja Križan | 05.06.1997 | 21 | (1) | 2 |
| Almin Kurtović | 16.03.2000 | 29 | (6) | 3 |
| Stefan Milić (MNE) | 06.07.2000 | 14 | | |
| Mark Španring | 13.06.2001 | 20 | (4) | |
| Žan Trontelj | 21.01.2000 | 5 | (13) | |
| Gašper Vodeb | 30.06.2003 | 1 | (2) | |

| Midfielders: | DOB | M | (s) | G |
|---|---|---|---|---|
| Lan Hribar | 24.07.2005 | | (2) | |
| Martin Kramarič | 14.11.1997 | 30 | (1) | 11 |
| Gal Puconja | 21.04.2004 | 1 | (5) | |
| Nsana Claudelion Etienne Simon (FRA) | 11.03.2000 | 25 | (3) | 2 |
| Tamar Svetlin | 30.07.2001 | 20 | (3) | 2 |
| Ivan Šaranić (CRO) | 12.05.2003 | 6 | (8) | |
| Gasper Trdin | 28.03.1998 | 30 | (3) | |
| **Forwards:** | **DOB** | **M** | **(s)** | **G** |
| Denis Bušnja (CRO) | 14.04.2000 | 7 | (8) | 1 |
| David Flakus Bosilj | 01.02.2002 | 19 | (8) | 2 |
| Gal Kurež | 27.04.2001 | | (7) | |
| Luka Marjanac (BIH) | 24.01.2003 | 2 | (10) | |
| Loren Maružin (CRO) | 04.12.1997 | 5 | (11) | 1 |
| Beno Selan | 02.01.2005 | 12 | (4) | |
| Luka Štor | 05.07.1998 | 24 | (6) | 6 |

## Nogometni klub Celje

**Founded**: 28.12.1919 (*as SK Celje*)
**Stadium**: Stadion Z'dežele, Celje (13,059)
**Trainer**: Roman Pilipchuk (RUS)  27.07.1967

| Goalkeepers: | DOB | M | (s) | G |
|---|---|---|---|---|
| Matko Obradović (CRO) | 11.05.1991 | 15 | | |
| Florijan Raduha | 01.04.1997 | 2 | | |
| Matjaž Rozman | 03.01.1987 | 19 | | |
| **Defenders:** | **DOB** | **M** | **(s)** | **G** |
| Nejc Ajhmajer | 22.04.2003 | 14 | (1) | |
| Amadej Brecl | 06.04.1997 | 2 | (2) | |
| Žan Flis | 30.07.1997 | 5 | | |
| Žan Karničnik | 18.09.1994 | 15 | (1) | |
| Lukas Mačak | 26.01.2005 | | (7) | 1 |
| Nino Milić | 01.05.2004 | 5 | (4) | |
| Grigori Morozov (RUS) | 06.06.1994 | 13 | (1) | |
| Klemen Nemanič | 07.11.1996 | 5 | | |
| Dušan Stojinović | 26.08.2000 | 11 | (1) | |
| Daniel Štefulj (CRO) | 08.11.1999 | 6 | (1) | |
| Damjan Vukliševič | 28.06.1995 | 24 | (1) | 4 |
| David Zec | 05.01.2000 | 34 | | 2 |
| **Midfielders:** | **DOB** | **M** | **(s)** | **G** |
| Luka Bobičanec (CRO) | 23.05.1993 | 11 | (1) | |
| Vasilije Janjičić (SUI) | 02.11.1998 | 4 | (11) | 3 |
| Nino Kouter | 19.12.1993 | 31 | (3) | 2 |
| Ivan Maevski (BLR) | 05.05.1988 | | (2) | 1 |
| Denis Popovič | 15.10.1989 | 27 | | 4 |
| Tamar Svetlin | 30.07.2001 | 1 | (3) | |
| Jon Šporn | 22.05.1997 | 10 | (3) | |
| Tomislav Tomić (BIH) | 16.11.1990 | | (2) | |
| Matic Vrbanec | 28.10.1996 | 19 | (9) | |
| Mark Zabukovnik | 27.12.2000 | 23 | (5) | 2 |
| **Forwards:** | **DOB** | **M** | **(s)** | **G** |
| Gregor Bajde | 29.04.1994 | 9 | (16) | 3 |
| Lovro Bizjak | 12.11.1993 | 15 | (7) | 2 |
| Ivan Božić (CRO) | 08.06.1997 | 7 | (1) | 1 |
| Bi Nene Junior Gbamblé (CIV) | 09.05.2002 | 11 | (4) | 2 |
| Chukwubuikem Ikwuemesi (NGA) | 05.08.2001 | 24 | (6) | 9 |
| Miroslav Iličić (CRO) | 17.04.1998 | 1 | (1) | |
| Domen Justinek | 18.03.2004 | | (1) | |
| Ibrahim Kargbo (BEL) | 03.01.2000 | 4 | (3) | |
| Tin Matić (CRO) | 23.10.1997 | 4 | (17) | 1 |
| Aljoša Matko | 29.03.2000 | 25 | (4) | 14 |

## Nogometni klub Domžale

**Founded**: 07.11.1920 (*as SK Disk Domžale*)
**Stadium**: Domžale Sports Park, Domžale (3,100)
**Trainer**: Simon Rožman  06.04.1983

| Goalkeepers: | DOB | M | (s) | G |
|---|---|---|---|---|
| Ajdin Mulalič | 13.09.1994 | 28 | | |
| Gašper Tratnik | 04.01.2000 | 8 | | |
| **Defenders:** | **DOB** | **M** | **(s)** | **G** |
| Enes Alić (BIH) | 03.09.1999 | 11 | (3) | |
| Amadej Brecl | 06.04.1997 | 8 | (3) | 2 |
| Andrej Đurić (SRB) | 21.09.2003 | 30 | (1) | 2 |
| Elmedin Fazlić (SUI) | 18.07.2002 | 4 | (4) | |
| Mitja Ilenič | 26.12.2004 | 15 | (1) | |
| Tilen Klemenčič | 21.08.1995 | 5 | | |
| Mirko Mutavčić | 29.01.2001 | 14 | (5) | 2 |
| Abraham Nnamdi Nwankwo (NGA) | 22.07.2001 | 12 | (1) | |
| Christian Schoissengeyr (DOM) | 18.10.1994 | 14 | (2) | |
| Andraž Žinič | 12.02.1999 | | (2) | |
| **Midfielders:** | **DOB** | **M** | **(s)** | **G** |
| Nermin Hodžić (BIH) | 13.07.1994 | 21 | (3) | |
| Zeni Husmani (MKD) | 28.11.1990 | 18 | (2) | |
| Benjamin Markuš | 30.01.2001 | 25 | (8) | |
| Daniel Offenbacher (AUT) | 18.02.1992 | 5 | (10) | |
| Nick Perc | 27.05.2003 | 7 | (7) | 1 |
| Janez Pišek | 04.05.1998 | 10 | (2) | 1 |
| Jošt Pišek | 10.03.2002 | 23 | (7) | 2 |
| Žiga Repas | 29.05.2001 | 21 | (5) | 4 |
| Mark Strajnar | 19.12.2003 | 16 | (5) | 2 |
| Luka Topalović | 23.02.2006 | 5 | (5) | 1 |
| **Forwards:** | **DOB** | **M** | **(s)** | **G** |
| Bartol Barišić (CRO) | 01.01.2003 | 10 | (15) | 7 |
| Ivan Durdov (CRO) | 17.07.2000 | 16 | (1) | 7 |
| Mirza Hasanbegović (BIH) | 19.07.2001 | 4 | (5) | 1 |
| Arnel Jakupović (AUT) | 29.05.1998 | 13 | (7) | 2 |
| Nikola Jovićević (MNE) | 30.09.2003 | 1 | (1) | |
| Franko Kovačević (CRO) | 08.08.1999 | 30 | | 12 |
| Awosanya Oluwatobilola Dimeji (NGA) | 15.01.2003 | | (3) | |
| Matej Podlogar | 23.02.1991 | 6 | (20) | 2 |
| Emir Saitoski (MKD) | 08.05.2003 | 8 | (10) | |
| Slobodan Vuk | 15.09.1989 | 8 | (8) | 2 |

## Nogometno društvo Gorica

**Founded**: 1947 (*as FD Gorica*)
**Stadium**: Nova Gorica Sports Park, Gorica (3,100)
**Trainer**: Miran Srebrnič  08.01.1970
[02.03.2023] Edoardo Reja (ITA)  10.10.1945
[17.04.2023] Agron Šalja  20.08.1972

| Goalkeepers: | DOB | M | (s) | G |
|---|---|---|---|---|
| Matevž Dajčar | 05.02.2002 | 12 | | |
| Uroš Likar | 01.10.1999 | 24 | | |
| **Defenders:** | **DOB** | **M** | **(s)** | **G** |
| Jan Andrejašič | 16.09.1995 | 5 | (7) | |
| Ahmed Awua Ankrah (ITA) | 03.01.2002 | 24 | (6) | |
| Filip Brekalo (CRO) | 20.01.2003 | 14 | | |
| Denis Cerovec (CRO) | 04.04.1991 | 20 | (2) | 1 |
| Denis Klinar | 21.02.1992 | 2 | (2) | |
| Alen Krajnc | 01.07.1995 | 24 | (7) | 3 |
| Nejc Mevlja | 12.06.1990 | 31 | | 2 |
| Vahid Selimović (LUX) | 03.04.1997 | 7 | (1) | |
| Matija Širok | 31.05.1991 | 22 | (2) | |
| Jošt Urbančič | 12.04.2001 | 19 | | |
| **Midfielders:** | **DOB** | **M** | **(s)** | **G** |
| Alessandro Ahmetaj (ITA) | 02.01.2000 | 20 | (8) | 2 |
| Luka Baruca | 09.01.2003 | 7 | (7) | |
| Darko Hrka | 20.11.1999 | 29 | (4) | |
| Matej Jukić (CRO) | 07.04.1997 | 10 | (16) | 1 |
| Steven Juncaj (USA) | 08.03.1998 | 7 | (3) | |
| Žan Leban | 10.08.1999 | 5 | (10) | |
| Leon Marinič | 21.11.1997 | 8 | (7) | 1 |
| Tilen Mlakar | 26.04.1995 | 1 | (8) | |
| Zvonimir Petrović (BIH) | 11.12.2000 | 23 | (4) | |
| Luka Stankovski (MKD) | 02.09.2002 | 9 | (1) | 2 |
| **Forwards:** | **DOB** | **M** | **(s)** | **G** |
| Tino Agić (CRO) | 30.04.2002 | 15 | (11) | |
| Žan Bešir | 17.10.2000 | 1 | (13) | |
| Ranaldo Biggs (JAM) | 11.07.2002 | | (1) | |
| Miroslav Iličić (CRO) | 17.04.1998 | 6 | (13) | 2 |
| Bernard Karrica (ALB) | 07.01.2001 | 10 | (5) | 1 |
| Dario Kolobarić | 06.02.2000 | 13 | (1) | 5 |
| Samuel Obi (NGA) | 29.05.2003 | | (1) | |
| Luka Vekič | 10.04.1995 | 8 | (16) | 3 |
| Etien Velikonja | 26.12.1988 | 20 | (5) | 6 |

## Football Club Koper

**Founded:** 1920
**Stadium:** Stadion Bonifika, Koper (4,047)
**Trainer:** Zoran Zeljković 09.05.1980

| Goalkeepers: | DOB | M | (s) | G |
|---|---|---|---|---|
| David Adam | 15.11.1993 | | (1) | |
| Adnan Golubovič | 22.07.1995 | 36 | | |
| **Defenders:** | **DOB** | **M** | **(s)** | **G** |
| Karlo Bilić (CRO) | 06.09.1993 | 6 | (5) | |
| Vid Koderman | 18.04.2003 | 9 | (2) | |
| Žiga Laci | 20.07.2002 | 1 | | |
| Maj Mittendorfer | 11.05.2000 | 23 | (5) | |
| Ivan Novoselec (CRO) | 19.06.1995 | 24 | | 2 |
| Matej Palčič | 21.06.1993 | 22 | (4) | |
| Michael Pavlović | 12.06.2001 | 9 | (2) | |
| Franjo Prce (CRO) | 07.01.1996 | 8 | (1) | |
| Aleksander Rajčevič | 17.11.1986 | 5 | (3) | |
| Milan Šimčák (SVK) | 23.08.1995 | 18 | (3) | |
| Žan Žužek | 26.01.1997 | 4 | | |
| **Midfielders:** | **DOB** | **M** | **(s)** | **G** |
| Maks Barišič | 06.03.1995 | 2 | (5) | 1 |
| Žan Benedičič | 03.10.1995 | 13 | (16) | 4 |
| Omar Correia (FRA) | 10.04.2000 | 28 | (2) | 2 |
| Cristojaye Damarrio Daley (JAM) | 23.08.2002 | 1 | (1) | |
| Rene Hrvatin | 08.12.2006 | | (1) | |
| Luka Kambič | 20.12.1998 | 19 | (7) | 2 |
| Andrej Kotnik | 04.08.1995 | 26 | (6) | 12 |
| Nikola Krajinović (CRO) | 09.11.1999 | 18 | (15) | |
| William Milovanović (SWE) | 06.05.2002 | 1 | (2) | |
| Rudi Požeg Vancaš | 15.03.1994 | 17 | (4) | 2 |
| Riad Silajdžić | 13.02.2005 | | (1) | |
| David Stanojević | 07.05.2004 | | (1) | |
| Danilo Šipovac (BIH) | 17.04.2000 | 2 | (5) | |
| Luka Tičić | 25.10.2000 | 26 | (3) | 1 |
| **Forwards:** | **DOB** | **M** | **(s)** | **G** |
| Bright Edomwonyi (NGA) | 24.07.1994 | 22 | (4) | 9 |
| Matthias Fanimo (ENG) | 28.01.1994 | 4 | (4) | |
| Anis Jašaragič | 09.08.1999 | 8 | (14) | 5 |
| Dario Kolobarić | 06.02.2000 | 5 | (10) | |
| Timothé Nkada (FRA) | 20.07.1999 | 4 | (7) | |
| Wilkims Ochieng (KEN) | 15.02.2003 | 5 | (2) | |
| Bede Amarachi Osuji (NGA) | 21.01.1996 | 21 | (4) | 5 |
| Kaheem Anthony Parris (JAM) | 06.01.2000 | 7 | | 1 |
| Luka Šušnjara | 04.04.1997 | 2 | (6) | |

## Nogometni klub Maribor

**Founded:** 12.12.1960
**Stadium:** Stadion Ljudski vrt, Maribor (11,709)
**Trainer:** Radovan Karanović 03.10.1968
[16.08.2022] Damir Krznar (CRO) 10.07.1972

| Goalkeepers: | DOB | M | (s) | G |
|---|---|---|---|---|
| Menno Bergsen (NED) | 26.08.1999 | 13 | | |
| Ažbe Jug | 03.03.1992 | 19 | (1) | |
| Samo Pridgar | 10.03.2003 | 4 | | |
| **Defenders:** | **DOB** | **M** | **(s)** | **G** |
| Ignacio Guerrico (ARG) | 09.07.1998 | 16 | (12) | |
| Sven Karič | 07.03.1998 | 26 | (2) | 1 |
| Vid Koderman | 18.04.2003 | 1 | | |
| Martin Milec | 20.09.1991 | 18 | (1) | 1 |
| Nemanja Mitrovič | 15.10.1992 | 11 | (1) | 1 |
| Mirko Mutavčić | 29.01.2001 | 1 | | |
| Gregor Sikošek | 13.02.1994 | 17 | (4) | 1 |
| Luka Uskoković (MNE) | 10.04.1996 | 21 | (4) | |
| Max Watson (SWE) | 03.02.1996 | 23 | (1) | 3 |
| Andraž Žinič | 12.02.1999 | 14 | (4) | |
| **Midfielders:** | **DOB** | **M** | **(s)** | **G** |
| Aljaž Antolin | 02.08.2002 | 26 | (6) | |
| Marko Božič (AUT) | 14.05.1998 | 20 | (11) | 5 |
| Luka Božičković (BIH) | 02.09.2003 | 1 | (10) | 1 |
| Tine Čuk | 15.02.2005 | 1 | (6) | |
| Rok Kronaveter | 07.12.1986 | 16 | (17) | 3 |
| Altin Kryeziu | 03.01.2002 | | (4) | |
| Marin Laušić (CRO) | 26.06.2001 | 9 | (14) | 2 |
| Marcel Lorber | 26.04.2004 | | (2) | |
| Rok Maher | 20.07.2001 | 1 | | |
| Aleks Pihler | 15.01.1994 | 1 | (1) | |
| Jan Repas | 19.03.1997 | 33 | | 5 |
| Marko Tolić (CRO) | 05.07.1996 | 24 | (4) | 7 |
| Vladan Vidaković (SRB) | 14.03.1999 | 4 | (4) | |
| **Forwards:** | **DOB** | **M** | **(s)** | **G** |
| Denis Alijagić (BIH) | 10.04.2003 | | (3) | |
| Roko Baturina (CRO) | 20.06.2000 | 11 | (8) | 5 |
| Ivan Brnić (CRO) | 23.08.2001 | 27 | (7) | 7 |
| Josip Iličić | 29.01.1988 | 7 | (4) | 2 |
| Arnel Jakupović (AUT) | 29.05.1998 | 5 | (7) | 2 |
| Ishaq Kayode Rafiu (NGA) | 16.12.2000 | | (5) | |
| Rok Sirk | 10.09.1993 | 1 | (12) | 1 |
| Danijel Šturm | 04.01.1999 | 1 | (2) | |
| Marcos Tavares | 01.06.2004 | | (1) | |
| Žan Vipotnik | 18.03.2002 | 23 | (7) | 20 |
| Nino Žugelj | 25.04.2000 | 1 | | 1 |

## Nogometna šola Mura Murska Sobota

**Founded:** 14.05.2012
**Stadium:** Mestni stadion Fazanerija, Murska Sobota (4,506)
**Trainer:** Damir Čontala 27.07.1984
[28.02.2023] Dejan Grabić 21.09.1980

| Goalkeepers: | DOB | M | (s) | G |
|---|---|---|---|---|
| Klemen Mihelak | 31.12.2001 | 26 | | |
| Matko Obradović (CRO) | 11.05.1991 | 10 | | |
| **Defenders:** | **DOB** | **M** | **(s)** | **G** |
| Gregor Balažic | 12.02.1988 | 19 | (6) | 2 |
| Amar Beganović (BIH) | 25.11.1999 | 32 | (1) | 2 |
| Miha Kompan Breznik | 05.10.2003 | | (2) | |
| Žiga Kous | 27.10.1992 | 23 | (6) | |
| Srđan Kuzmić | 16.01.2004 | 17 | (8) | |
| Matic Maruško | 30.11.1990 | 25 | (3) | 1 |
| Darrick-Kobie Morris (CRO) | 15.07.1995 | 22 | (2) | 3 |
| Klemen Pučko | 27.01.1996 | 11 | (8) | |
| Leard Sadriu (KOS) | 22.04.2001 | 10 | (2) | |
| **Midfielders:** | **DOB** | **M** | **(s)** | **G** |
| Luka Bobičanec (CRO) | 23.05.1993 | 12 | (3) | 2 |
| Timotej Brkić | 18.07.2005 | 3 | | |
| Tio Cipot | 20.04.2003 | 16 | (2) | 2 |
| Jaka Domjan | 05.05.2004 | 1 | (1) | |
| Niko Kasalo | 31.12.2005 | 5 | (4) | 1 |
| Alen Kozar | 07.04.1995 | | (11) | |
| Nik Lorbek | 17.04.1996 | 4 | (4) | |
| Dardan Shabanhaxhaj (AUT) | 23.04.2001 | 14 | (11) | 1 |
| Domantas Šimkus (LTU) | 10.02.1996 | 7 | (8) | |
| Filippo Tripi (ITA) | 06.01.2002 | 12 | (1) | |
| Lazar Zličić (SRB) | 07.02.1997 | 10 | (5) | 2 |
| **Forwards:** | **DOB** | **M** | **(s)** | **G** |
| Mihajlo Baić (SRB) | 21.11.2002 | | (2) | |
| Kai Cipot | 28.04.2001 | 34 | | 2 |
| Mirlind Daku (KOS) | 01.01.1998 | 31 | (2) | 19 |
| Nikola Jovićević (MNE) | 30.09.2003 | | (10) | 1 |
| Mihael Klepač (CRO) | 19.09.1997 | 24 | (8) | 7 |
| Josip Majić (CRO) | 05.07.1994 | | (6) | |
| Nikola Petković (SRB) | 23.09.1996 | 7 | (9) | 3 |
| Ivan Šarić (CRO) | 16.01.2001 | 7 | (8) | |
| Martin Šroler | 02.11.1998 | 14 | (15) | 2 |

## Nogometni klub Olimpija Ljubljana

| Founded: | 02.03.2005 (*as NK Bežigrad Ljubljana*) | | |
| Stadium: | Stadion Stožice, Ljubljana (16,038) | | |
| Trainer: | Albert Riera Ortega (ESP) | 15.04.1982 | |

| Goalkeepers: | DOB | M | (s) | G |
|---|---|---|---|---|
| Žan Mauricio | 16.11.2004 | | (1) | |
| Denis Pintol | 07.02.2000 | 9 | | |
| Matevž Vidovšek | 30.10.1999 | 27 | | |
| **Defenders:** | **DOB** | **M** | **(s)** | **G** |
| Đorđe Crnomarković (SRB) | 10.09.1993 | 22 | (4) | 1 |
| *David* de Senna Fernandes *Sualehe* (POR) | 23.03.1997 | 18 | (12) | 1 |
| Pasco Estrada (AUT) | 12.03.2002 | 19 | (14) | 1 |
| Mateo Karamatić (AUT) | 28.09.2001 | 14 | (7) | |
| Aljaž Krefl | 20.02.1994 | 18 | (7) | |
| Ivan Lagundžić (CRO) | 14.06.1999 | 1 | | |
| Justas Lasickas (LTU) | 06.10.1997 | 19 | (9) | |
| Goran Milović (CRO) | 29.01.1989 | 9 | (12) | |
| Marcel Ratnik | 23.12.2003 | 27 | (4) | 1 |
| **Midfielders:** | **DOB** | **M** | **(s)** | **G** |
| Agustin Doffo (ARG) | 25.05.1995 | 31 | (1) | |
| Nemanja Gavrić | 20.10.2003 | 1 | (6) | 1 |

| | DOB | M | (s) | G |
|---|---|---|---|---|
| Vall Janković | 29.03.2004 | | (1) | |
| Anes Krdžalić (BIH) | 28.08.2004 | 9 | (6) | 3 |
| Mario Kvesić (BIH) | 12.01.1992 | 32 | (3) | 12 |
| Marin Pilj (CRO) | 03.12.1996 | 3 | (2) | |
| Ivan Posavec (CRO) | 05.07.1998 | 6 | (4) | |
| Svit Sešlar | 09.01.2002 | 34 | | 9 |
| **Forwards:** | **DOB** | **M** | **(s)** | **G** |
| Aldair Adulai Djaló Baldé (GNB) | 31.01.1992 | 12 | (17) | 2 |
| Admir Bristrić (BIH) | 28.04.2003 | 6 | (8) | 4 |
| Timi Max Elšnik | 29.04.1998 | 29 | (4) | 7 |
| Mustafa Nukić | 03.12.1990 | 21 | (4) | 7 |
| Ivan Prtajin (CRO) | 14.05.1996 | | (1) | |
| *Rui Pedro* da Silva e Sousa (POR) | 20.03.1998 | 20 | (7) | 6 |
| *Samuel* Lopes Robalo *Pedro* (POR) | 24.04.2001 | 3 | (10) | 1 |
| Dino Špehar (CRO) | 08.02.1994 | 1 | (5) | |
| Almedin Ziljkić (BIH) | 25.02.1996 | 5 | (11) | 1 |

## Nogometni klub Radomlje

| Founded: | 1972 | | |
| Stadium: | Domžale Sports Park, Domžale (3,100) | | |
| Trainer: | Nermin Bašić (BIH) | 24.11.1983 | |
| [22.12.2022] | Oliver Bogatinov | 26.09.1978 | |

| Goalkeepers: | DOB | M | (s) | G |
|---|---|---|---|---|
| Luka Baš | 30.04.2002 | 4 | (1) | |
| Emil Velić | 06.02.1995 | 32 | | |
| **Defenders:** | **DOB** | **M** | **(s)** | **G** |
| Gaber Dobrovoljc | 27.01.1993 | 8 | (1) | |
| Luka Guček | 29.01.1999 | 8 | (1) | |
| Tin Hrvoj (CRO) | 06.06.2001 | 22 | (10) | |
| Rok Jazbec | 23.09.1995 | 3 | (9) | 1 |
| Uroš Korun | 25.05.1987 | 25 | (3) | 2 |
| Stipo Marković (BIH) | 03.12.1993 | 29 | (3) | |
| Vicko Ševelj (CRO) | 19.09.2000 | 29 | (2) | |
| Rok Štorman | 04.09.2004 | 1 | | |
| Vedran Vrhovac (BIH) | 20.11.1998 | 15 | (5) | |
| **Midfielders:** | **DOB** | **M** | **(s)** | **G** |
| Luka Cerar | 26.05.1993 | 19 | (10) | 1 |
| Ivan Čalušić (CRO) | 12.09.1999 | 4 | | |
| Mario Čuić (CRO) | 22.04.2001 | 30 | (4) | 1 |
| Ognjen Gnjatić (BIH) | 16.10.1991 | 3 | (3) | |

| | DOB | M | (s) | G |
|---|---|---|---|---|
| Klemen Justin | 12.06.2002 | | (5) | |
| Matej Malenšek | 27.05.2005 | | (1) | |
| Darly N'Landu (FRA) | 14.07.2000 | 13 | (9) | 1 |
| Sandi Nuhanović | 05.12.1998 | 30 | (5) | 4 |
| Samsondin Ouro (GER) | 02.03.2000 | 19 | (2) | 3 |
| Andrej Pogačar | 20.08.2002 | 4 | (12) | |
| Leon Sever | 09.04.1998 | 9 | (15) | |
| Madžid Šošić (BIH) | 12.08.2002 | 18 | (12) | 3 |
| Anel Žulić | 07.11.2004 | 16 | (2) | |
| **Forwards:** | **DOB** | **M** | **(s)** | **G** |
| Filip Čuić (BIH) | 22.02.2003 | 10 | (13) | 5 |
| Nedim Hadžić (BIH) | 19.03.1999 | 8 | (5) | 2 |
| Janko Ivetić | 23.02.2001 | | (3) | |
| Ismir Nadarević (BIH) | 29.08.2003 | | (7) | |
| Ester Sokler | 04.06.1999 | 24 | (6) | 10 |
| Francesco Tahiraj (ALB) | 21.09.1996 | 13 | (6) | |
| Pape Thiam (SEN) | 08.05.2002 | | (1) | |

## Nogometni klub Tabor Sežana

| Founded: | 1923 | | |
| Stadium: | Stadion „Rajko Štolfa“, Sežana (1,310) | | |
| Trainer: | Dušan Kosič | 23.04.1971 | |

| Goalkeepers: | DOB | M | (s) | G |
|---|---|---|---|---|
| Alen Jurca | 15.01.2001 | 1 | | |
| Jan Koprivec | 15.07.1988 | 35 | | |
| **Defenders:** | **DOB** | **M** | **(s)** | **G** |
| Mihael Briški (CRO) | 02.01.1999 | 28 | | 3 |
| Zacharie Iscaye (FRA) | 02.10.2000 | 5 | (16) | |
| Thadèe Kaleba (FRA) | 20.04.1999 | 21 | (2) | |
| Milan Kocič | 16.02.1990 | 12 | (1) | 1 |
| Denis Christ Damsen Kouao (CIV) | 23.11.1996 | 27 | (3) | 2 |
| Elvis Letaj (CRO) | 26.09.2003 | 16 | (1) | |
| Mark Pabai (LBR) | 30.09.2000 | 4 | (4) | |
| Andraž Struna | 23.04.1989 | 1 | (3) | |
| Aleksandar Zeljković | 04.07.1999 | 3 | (9) | |
| **Midfielders:** | **DOB** | **M** | **(s)** | **G** |
| Tim Bajnoci | 26.06.1905 | | (1) | |
| Miha Breznik | 05.10.2003 | 7 | | |
| Dragoslav Burkic (AUT) | 01.07.2000 | | (1) | |
| Dino Halilović (CRO) | 08.02.1998 | 8 | (4) | 2 |
| Nabil Khali (FRA) | 05.04.1998 | 16 | (9) | 1 |
| Alen Korošec | 17.11.2001 | 35 | (1) | 1 |
| Sacha Marasović (FRA) | 06.01.1998 | 16 | | 3 |
| Til Mavretič | 19.11.1997 | 1 | | |

| | DOB | M | (s) | G |
|---|---|---|---|---|
| Žiga Ovsenek | 21.01.1998 | 29 | (2) | 1 |
| Mark Seliškar | 16.01.2002 | 1 | (6) | |
| Lan Štravs | 04.03.2000 | 5 | (4) | 2 |
| Abdullah Talal Hameed (IRQ) | 20.11.1995 | 5 | (2) | |
| Tom Tolić (CRO) | 09.04.1999 | 5 | (3) | 1 |
| Tim Vatovec | 10.12.2003 | | (15) | |
| Milan Vukotić (MNE) | 05.10.2002 | | (5) | |
| Adrian Zeljković | 19.08.2002 | 29 | (1) | 1 |
| Diego Živulić (CRO) | 23.03.1992 | 12 | (1) | |
| **Forwards:** | **DOB** | **M** | **(s)** | **G** |
| Žan Bešir | 17.10.2000 | | (7) | |
| *Coba* Gomes da Costa (ESP) | 26.07.2002 | 5 | (8) | |
| Henry Crinacoba (FRA) | 17.05.2004 | | (2) | |
| Robert Čakš | 31.01.2001 | | (4) | |
| Boucif El Afghani (FRA) | 20.08.1997 | 1 | (9) | 1 |
| Manji Moses Gimsay (NGA) | 29.09.1999 | 1 | (1) | |
| Tom Kljun | 29.01.2004 | 10 | (3) | |
| Fahd Ndzengue (GAB) | 07.07.2000 | 14 | (10) | 2 |
| Stevan Nikolić (SRB) | 28.09.2002 | 5 | (3) | |
| Miloš Savić (AUT) | 02.05.2002 | 2 | (3) | |
| Jakoslav Stanković | 10.04.2001 | 22 | (10) | 4 |
| Luka Šušnjara | 04.04.1997 | 14 | (1) | 2 |

## SECOND LEVEL
### Slovenian Second League 2022/2023

| | | | | | | | | | |
|---|---|---|---|---|---|---|---|---|---|
| 1. | NK Rogaška Slatina (*Promoted*) | 30 | 21 | 5 | 4 | 52 | - | 23 | 68 |
| 2. | NK Aluminij Kidričevo (*Promotion Play-offs*) | 30 | 19 | 7 | 4 | 58 | - | 23 | 64 |
| 3. | ND Ilirija 1911 Ljubljana | 30 | 16 | 6 | 8 | 55 | - | 30 | 54 |
| 4. | NK Krka Novo Mesto | 30 | 14 | 11 | 5 | 46 | - | 28 | 53 |
| 5. | ND Beltinci | 30 | 12 | 8 | 10 | 47 | - | 45 | 44 |
| 6. | NK Nafta Lendava 1903 | 30 | 11 | 8 | 11 | 50 | - | 43 | 41 |
| 7. | ND Primorje Ajdovščina | 30 | 10 | 11 | 9 | 42 | - | 40 | 41 |
| 8. | NK Brinje Grosuplje | 30 | 11 | 5 | 14 | 30 | - | 37 | 38 |
| 9. | NK Bistrica Slovenska Bistrica | 30 | 9 | 10 | 11 | 39 | - | 40 | 37 |
| 10. | ND Bilje | 30 | 10 | 7 | 13 | 40 | - | 53 | 37 |
| 11. | NK Jadran Dekani | 30 | 7 | 14 | 9 | 27 | - | 29 | 35 |
| 12. | NK Triglav Kranj | 30 | 10 | 5 | 15 | 33 | - | 52 | 35 |
| 13. | NK Rudar Velenje | 30 | 7 | 11 | 12 | 41 | - | 51 | 32 |
| 14. | NK Fužinar Ravne na Koroškem | 30 | 8 | 7 | 15 | 39 | - | 56 | 31 |
| 15. | NK Krško (*Relegated*) | 30 | 6 | 6 | 18 | 36 | - | 59 | 24 |
| 16. | NK Dob (*Relegated*) | 30 | 4 | 9 | 17 | 37 | - | 63 | 21 |

## NATIONAL TEAM

### INTERNATIONAL MATCHES
#### (16.07.2022 – 15.07.2023)

| | | | | |
|---|---|---|---|---|
| 24.09.2022 | Ljubljana | *Slovenia - Norway* | *2-1(0-0)* | (UNL) |
| 27.09.2022 | Stockholm | *Sweden - Slovenia* | *1-1(1-1)* | (UNL) |
| 17.11.2022 | Cluj-Napoca | *Romania - Slovenia* | *1-2(0-2)* | (F) |
| 20.11.2022 | Ljubljana | *Slovenia - Montenegro* | *1-0(1-0)* | (F) |
| 23.03.2023 | Astana | *Kazakhstan - Slovenia* | *1-2(1-0)* | (ECQ) |
| 26.03.2023 | Ljubljana | *Slovenia - San Marino* | *2-0(0-0)* | (ECQ) |
| 16.06.2023 | Helsinki | *Finland - Slovenia* | *2-0(1-0)* | (ECQ) |
| 19.06.2023 | Ljubljana | *Slovenia - Denmark* | *1-1(1-1)* | (ECQ) |

**24.09.2022  SLOVENIA - NORWAY**  **2-1(0-0)**  3rd UEFA Nations League B, Group 4
Stadion Stožice, Ljubljana; Referee: Lawrence Visser (Belgium); Attendance: 14,824
**SVN:** Jan Oblak (Cap), Žan Karničnik (90+3.David Brekalo), Miha Blažič, Jaka Bijol, Gregor Sikošek, Benjamin Verbič (71.Sandi Lovrić), Adam Gnezda Čerin (90+3.Jon Gorenc Stankovič), Jasmin Kurtič, Petar Stojanović, Benjamin Šeško, Andraž Šporar (88.Domen Črnigoj). Trainer: Matjaž Kek.
**Goals:** Andraž Šporar (69), Benjamin Šeško (81).

**27.09.2022  SWEDEN - SLOVENIA**  **1-1(1-1)**  3rd UEFA Nations League B, Group 4
Friends Arena, Stockholm; Referee: Felix Zwayer (Germany); Attendance: 22,895
**SVN:** Jan Oblak (Cap), Žan Karničnik, Miha Blažič, Jaka Bijol, Gregor Sikošek (64.Jure Balkovec), Adam Gnezda Čerin, Jon Gorenc Stankovič (71.Timi Max Elšnik), Petar Stojanović, Benjamin Verbič (85.Sandi Lovrić), Jan Mlakar (64.Domen Črnigoj), Benjamin Šeško. Trainer: Matjaž Kek.
**Goal:** Benjamin Šeško (28).

**17.11.2022  ROMANIA - SLOVENIA**  **1-2(0-2)**  Friendly International
Cluj Arena, Cluj-Napoca; Referee: Nicolas Laforge (Belgium); Attendance: 6,845
**SVN:** Jan Oblak (Cap), Petar Stojanović, Miha Blažič (46.Miha Mevlja), Jaka Bijol, Jure Balkovec (70.Gregor Sikošek), Adam Gnezda Čerin, Jasmin Kurtič (85.Jon Gorenc Stankovič), Sandi Lovrić (46.Žan Karničnik), Benjamin Verbič (78.Tomi Horvat), Benjamin Šeško, Andraž Šporar (46.Andres Vombergar). Trainer: Matjaž Kek.
**Goals:** Benjamin Šeško (26), Andraž Šporar (32).

**20.11.2022  SLOVENIA - MONTENEGRO**  **1-0(1-0)**  Friendly International
Stadion Stožice, Ljubljana; Referee: Christopher Jäger (Austria); Attendance: 11,165
**SVN:** Jan Oblak (Cap), Petar Stojanović (72.Žan Karničnik), Miha Blažič, Jaka Bijol, Gregor Sikošek, Adam Gnezda Čerin (90+3.David Brekalo), Jasmin Kurtič, Benjamin Verbič (81.Jon Gorenc Stankovič), Miha Zajc (68.Tomi Horvat), Benjamin Šeško (81.Luka Zahovič), Andraž Šporar. Trainer: Matjaž Kek.
**Goal:** Miha Zajc (42).

**23.03.2023  KAZAKHSTAN - SLOVENIA**  **1-2(1-0)**  17th EC. Qualifiers
Astana Arena, Astana; Referee: Glenn Nyberg (Sweden); Attendance: 27,122
**SVN:** Jan Oblak (Cap), Žan Karničnik, Jaka Bijol, Miha Blažič (5.David Brekalo), Jure Balkovec (46.Miha Zajc), Adam Gnezda Čerin, Jon Gorenc Stankovič, Petar Stojanović, Benjamin Verbič (70.Sandi Lovrić), Žan Celar (70.Žan Vipotnik), Benjamin Šeško. Trainer: Matjaž Kek.
**Goals:** David Brekalo (47), Žan Vipotnik (78).

**26.03.2023  SLOVENIA - SAN MARINO**  **2-0(0-0)**  17th EC. Qualifiers
Stadion Stožice, Ljubljana; Referee: Nathan Verboomen (Belgium); Attendance: 10,282
**SVN:** Jan Oblak (Cap), Petar Stojanović, David Brekalo, Jaka Bijol (36.Vanja Drkušić), Žan Karničnik (58.Jure Balkovec), Adam Gnezda Čerin, Sandi Lovrić, Benjamin Verbič (82.Tomi Horvat), Miha Zajc (82.Jon Gorenc Stankovič), Benjamin Šeško, Andres Vombergar (58.Žan Vipotnik). Trainer: Matjaž Kek.
**Goals:** Benjamin Šeško (56), Roberto Di Maio (60 own goal).

**16.06.2023**    **FINLAND - SLOVENIA**        **2-0(1-0)**          17th EC. Qualifiers

Olympiastadion, Helsinki; Referee: Guillermo Cuadra Fernández (Spain); Attendance: 32,560
**SVN:** Vid Belec, Žan Karničnik, David Brekalo, Jaka Bijol (Cap), Jure Balkovec, Adam Gnezda Čerin, Miha Zajc (79.Timi Max Elšnik), Petar Stojanović (78.Benjamin Verbič), Sandi Lovrić (65.Jan Mlakar), Benjamin Šeško (86.Žan Celar), Andraž Šporar (65.Žan Vipotnik). Trainer: Matjaž Kek.

**19.06.2023**    **SLOVENIA - DENMARK**        **1-1(1-1)**          17th EC. Qualifiers

Stadion Stožice, Ljubljana; Referee: François Letexier (France); Attendance: 14,382
**SVN:** Matevž Vidovšek, Žan Karničnik, David Brekalo, Jaka Bijol (Cap), Erik Janža, Timi Max Elšnik, Adam Gnezda Čerin, Petar Stojanović, Jan Mlakar (90+2.Benjamin Verbič), Benjamin Šeško, Andraž Šporar (81.Žan Vipotnik). Trainer: Matjaž Kek.
**Goal:** Andraž Šporar (25).

## NATIONAL TEAM PLAYERS
### (16.07.2022 – 15.07.2023)

| Name | DOB | Caps | Goals | Club | |
|---|---|---|---|---|---|
| **Goalkeepers** | | | | | |
| Vid BELEC | 06.06.1990 | 19 | 0 | 2023: | APOEL Nicosia (CYP) |
| Jan OBLAK | 07.01.1993 | 56 | 0 | 2022/2023: | Club Atlético de Madrid (ESP) |
| Matevž VIDOVŠEK | 30.10.1999 | 1 | 0 | 2023: | NK Olimpija Ljubljana |
| **Defenders** | | | | | |
| Jure BALKOVEC | 09.09.1994 | 29 | 0 | 2022/2023: | Alanyaspor Kulübü (TUR) |
| Miha BLAŽIČ | 08.05.1993 | 25 | 0 | 2022/2023: | Angers SCO (FRA) |
| David BREKALO | 03.12.1998 | 10 | 1 | 2022/2023: | Viking FK Stavanger (NOR) |
| Vanja DRKUŠIĆ | 30.10.1999 | 1 | 0 | 2023: | PFK Sochi (RUS) |
| Erik JANŽA | 21.06.1993 | 2 | 0 | 2023: | KS Górnik Zabrze (POL) |
| Žan KARNIČNIK | 18.09.1984 | 18 | 0 | 2022: | PFC Ludogorets Razgrad (BUL) |
| | | | | 01.01.2023-> | NK Celje |
| Miha MEVLJA | 12.06.1990 | 50 | 2 | 2022: | FK Spartak Moskva (RUS) |
| Gregor SIKOŠEK | 13.02.1994 | 11 | 0 | 2022: | NK Maribor |
| Petar STOJANOVIĆ | 07.10.1995 | 45 | 2 | 2022/2023: | Empoli FC (ITA) |
| **Midfielders** | | | | | |
| Jaka BIJOL | 05.02.1999 | 39 | 1 | 2022/2023: | Udinese Calcio (ITA) |
| Domen ČRNIGOJ | 18.11.1995 | 26 | 3 | 2022: | Venezia FC (ITA) |
| Timi Max ELŠNIK | 29.04.1998 | 4 | 0 | 2022/2023: | NK Olimpija Ljubljana |
| Adam GNEZDA Čerin | 16.07.1999 | 21 | 2 | 2022/2023: | PAE Panathinaïkos Athína (GRE) |
| Tomi HORVAT | 24.03.1999 | 4 | 0 | 2022/2023: | SK Sturm Graz (AUT) |
| Jasmin KURTIĆ | 10.01.1989 | 83 | 2 | 2022: | PAOK Thessaloníki (GRE) |
| Sandi LOVRIĆ | 28.03.1998 | 28 | 3 | 2022/2023: | Udinese Calcio (ITA) |
| Jon Gorenc STANKOVIČ | 14.01.1996 | 17 | 1 | 2022/2023: | SK Sturm Graz (AUT) |
| Benjamin VERBIČ | 27.11.1993 | 51 | 5 | 2022/2023: | PAE Panathinaïkos Athína (GRE) |
| Miha ZAJC | 01.07.1994 | 38 | 8 | 2022/2023: | Fenerbahçe SK İstanbul (TUR) |
| **Forwards** | | | | | |
| Žan CELAR | 14.03.1999 | 8 | 0 | 2023: | FC Lugano (SUI) |
| Jan MLAKAR | 23.10.1998 | 8 | 1 | 2022/2023: | HNK Hajduk Split (CRO) |
| Benjamin ŠEŠKO | 31.05.2003 | 21 | 6 | 2022/2023: | FC Red Bull Salzburg (AUT) |
| Andraž ŠPORAR | 27.02.1994 | 44 | 8 | 2022/2023: | PAE Panathinaïkos Athína (GRE) |
| Žan VIPOTNIK | 18.03.2002 | 4 | 0 | 2023: | NK Maribor |
| Andres VOMBERGAR | 20.11.1994 | 2 | 0 | 2022/2023: | CA San Lorenzo de Almagro Buenos Aires(ARG) |
| Luka ZAHOVIČ | 15.11.1995 | 14 | 0 | 2022: | MKS Pogoń Szczecin (POL) |
| **National team coach** | | | | | |
| Matjaž KEK [from 27.11.2019] | 09.09.1961 | | | 44 M; 18 W; 15 D; 11 L; 63-41 Complete record as trainer of Slovenia: 93 M; 39 W; 23 D; 31 L; 124-86 (07.02.2007 – 11.10.2011) & (from 27.11.2019) | |

# SPAIN

## The Country:
Reino de España (Kingdom of Spain)
Capital: Madrid
Surface: 505,990 km²
Inhabitants: 48,196,693 [2023]
Time: UTC

## The FA:
Real Federación Española de Fútbol
Ramón y Cajal, s/n Apartado postal 385, 28230 Las Rozas (Madrid)
Tel: +34 914 959 800
Founded: 14.10.1909
Member of FIFA since: 1913
Member of UEFA since: 1954
Website: www.rfef.es

## NATIONAL TEAM RECORDS

### RECORDS
| | | |
|---|---|---|
| **First international match:** | 28.08.1920, Bruxelles: | Spain - Denmark 1-0 |
| **Most international caps:** | Sergio Ramos García | - 180 caps (since 2005) |
| **Most international goals:** | David Villa Sánchez | - 59 goals / 98 caps (2005-2017) |

| UEFA EUROPEAN CHAMPIONSHIP | | FIFA WORLD CUP | | OLYMPIC TOURNAMENTS | |
|---|---|---|---|---|---|
| 1960 | Qualifiers | 1930 | Did not enter | 1908 | - |
| 1964 | **Final Tournament (Winners)** | 1934 | Final Tournament (Quarter-Finals) | 1912 | - |
| 1968 | Qualifiers | 1938 | *Withdrew* | 1920 | Final Tournament (Quarter-Finals) |
| 1972 | Qualifiers | 1950 | Final Tournament (4th Place) | 1924 | Preliminary Round |
| 1976 | Qualifiers | 1954 | Qualifiers | 1928 | Quarter-Finals |
| 1980 | Final Tournament (Group Stage) | 1958 | Qualifiers | 1936 | Did not enter |
| 1984 | Final Tournament (Runners-up) | 1962 | Final Tournament (Group Stage) | 1948 | Did not enter |
| 1988 | Final Tournament (Group Stage) | 1966 | Final Tournament (Group Stage) | 1952 | Did not enter |
| 1992 | Qualifiers | 1970 | Qualifiers | 1956 | Did not enter |
| 1996 | Final Tournament (Quarter-Finals) | 1974 | Qualifiers | 1960 | Did not enter |
| 2000 | Final Tournament (Quarter-Finals) | 1978 | Final Tournament (Group Stage) | 1964 | Qualifiers |
| 2004 | Final Tournament (Group Stage) | 1982 | Final Tournament (2nd Round) | 1968 | Final Tournament (Quarter-Finals) |
| 2008 | **Final Tournament (Winners)** | 1986 | Final Tournament (Quarter-Finals) | 1972 | Qualifiers |
| 2012 | **Final Tournament (Winners)** | 1990 | Final Tournament (2nd Round of 16) | 1976 | Final Tournament (Group Stage) |
| 2016 | Final Tournament (2nd Round of 16) | 1994 | Final Tournament (Quarter-Finals) | 1980 | Final Tournament (Group Stage) |
| 2020 | Final Tournament (Semi-Finals) | 1998 | Final Tournament (Group Stage) | 1984 | Qualifiers |
| | | 2002 | Final Tournament (Quarter-Finals) | 1988 | Qualifiers |
| | | 2006 | Final Tournament (2nd Round of 16) | 1992 | **Winners** |
| | | 2010 | **Final Tournament (Winners)** | 1996 | Final Tournament (Quarter-Finals) |
| | | 2014 | Final Tournament (Group Stage) | 2000 | Final Tournament (Runners-up) |
| | | 2018 | Final Tournament (2nd Round of 16) | 2004 | Qualifiers |
| | | 2022 | Final Tournament (2nd Round of 16) | 2008 | Qualifiers |
| | | | | 2012 | Final Tournament (Group Stage) |
| | | | | 2016 | Qualifiers |
| | | | | 2020 | Final Tournament (Runners-up) |

### UEFA NATIONS LEAGUE
| | |
|---|---|
| 2018/2019 | League A (Group Stage) |
| 2020/2021 | League A (Group Stage -> Final Tournament – Runners-up) |
| 2022/2023 | League A (Group Stage -> Final Tournament – **Winners**) |

### FIFA CONFEDERATIONS CUP 1992-2017
2009 (3rd Place), 2013 (Runners-up)

## SPANISH CLUB HONOURS IN EUROPEAN CLUB COMPETITIONS:

| European Champion Clubs.Cup (1956-1992) / UEFA Champions League (1993-2023) | | |
|---|---|---|
| Real Madrid CF | 14 | 1955/1956, 1956/1957, 1957/1958, 1958/1959, 1959/1960, 1965/1966, 1997/1998, 1999/2000, 2001/2002, 2013/2014, 2015/2016, 2016/2017, 2017/2018, 2021/2022 |
| FC Barcelona | 5 | 1991/1992, 2005/2006, 2008/2009, 2010/2011, 2014/2015 |
| **Fairs Cup (1858-1971) / UEFA Cup (1972-2009) / UEFA Europa League (2010-2023)** | | |
| Sevilla FC | 7 | 2005/2006, 2006/2007, 2013/2014, 2014/2015, 2015/2016, 2019/2020, 2022/2023 |

| | | | |
|---|---|---|---|
| FC Barcelona | **3** | 1955-1958, 1958-1960, 1965/1966 | |
| Club Atlético de Madrid | **3** | 2009/2010, 2011/2012, 2017/2018 | |
| Valencia CF | **3** | 1961/1962, 1962/1963, 2003/2004 | |
| Real Madrid CF | **2** | 1984/1985, 1985/1986 | |
| Real Zaragoza | **1** | 1963/1964 | |
| Villarreal CF | **1** | 2020/2021 | |

| UEFA Europa Conference League (2021-2023) | | |
|---|---|---|
| None | | |

| UEFA Super Cup (1972-2022) | | |
|---|---|---|
| FC Barcelona | **5** | 1992, 1997, 2009, 2011, 2015 |
| Real Madrid CF | **5** | 2002, 2014, 2016, 2017, 2022 |
| Club Atlético de Madrid | **3** | 2010, 2012, 2018 |
| Valencia CF | **2** | 1980, 2004 |
| Sevilla FC | **1** | 2006 |

| *European Cup Winners' Cup 1961-1999** | | |
|---|---|---|
| FC Barcelona | **4** | 1978/1979, 1981/1982, 1988/1989, 1996/1997 |
| Club Atlético de Madrid | **1** | 1961/1962 |
| Valencia CF | **1** | 1979/1980 |
| Real Zaragoza | **1** | 1994/1995 |

*defunct competition*

# NATIONAL COMPETITIONS
## TABLE OF HONOURS

| | CHAMPIONS | CUP WINNERS | BEST GOALSCORERS | |
|---|---|---|---|---|
| 1903 | - | Athletic Club Bilbao | - | |
| 1904 | - | Athletic Club Bilbao | - | |
| 1905 | - | Madrid FC | - | |
| 1906 | - | Madrid FC | - | |
| 1907 | - | Madrid FC | - | |
| 1908 | - | Madrid FC | - | |
| 1909 | - | Real Sociedad de Fútbol San Sebastián | - | |
| 1910 | - | FC Barcelona (FEF)* Athletic Club Bilbao (UECF)** | - | |
| 1911 | - | Athletic Club Bilbao | - | |
| 1912 | - | FC Barcelona | - | |
| 1913 | - | Racing Club de Irún (FEF) FC Barcelona (UECF) | - | |
| 1914 | - | Athletic Club Bilbao | - | |
| 1915 | - | Athletic Club Bilbao | - | |
| 1916 | - | Athletic Club Bilbao | - | |
| 1917 | - | Madrid FC | - | |
| 1918 | - | Real Unión Club de Irún | - | |
| 1919 | - | Arenas Club de Getxo | - | |
| 1920 | - | FC Barcelona | - | |
| 1921 | - | Athletic Club Bilbao | - | |
| 1922 | - | FC Barcelona | - | |
| 1923 | - | Athletic Club Bilbao | - | |
| 1924 | - | Real Unión Club de Irún | - | |
| 1925 | - | FC Barcelona | - | |
| 1926 | - | FC Barcelona | - | |
| 1927 | - | Real Unión Club de Irún | - | |
| 1928 | - | FC Barcelona | - | |
| 1929 | FC Barcelona | RCD Español Barcelona | Francisco "Paco" Bienzobas Ocáriz (Real Sociedad de Fútbol San Sebastián) | 14 |
| 1929/1930 | Athletic Club Bilbao | Athletic Club Bilbao | Guillermo Gorostiza Paredes (Athletic Club Bilbao) | 19 |
| 1930/1931 | Athletic Club Bilbao | Athletic Club Bilbao | Agustín Sauto Arana "Bata" (Athletic Club Bilbao) | 27 |
| 1931/1932 | Real Madrid FC | Athletic Club Bilbao | Guillermo Gorostiza Paredes (Athletic Club Bilbao) | 12 |
| 1932/1933 | Real Madrid FC | Athletic Club Bilbao | Manuel Olivares Lapeña (Real Madrid FC) | 16 |
| 1933/1934 | Athletic Club Bilbao | Real Madrid FC | Isidro Lángara Galarraga (Real Oviedo CF) | 27 |
| 1934/1935 | Real Betis Balompié Sevilla | Sevilla FC | Isidro Lángara Galarraga (Real Oviedo CF) | 26 |
| 1935/1936 | Athletic Club Bilbao | Real Madrid FC | Isidro Lángara Galarraga (Real Oviedo CF) | 27 |
| 1936/1937 | *League Cancelled* | *No competition* | - | |
| 1937/1938 | *League Cancelled* | *No competition* | - | |
| 1938/1939 | *League Cancelled* | Sevilla FC | - | |
| 1939/1940 | Atlético Aviación Madrid | RCD Español Barcelona | Víctor Unamuno Ibarzabal (Athletic Club Bilbao) | 22 |
| 1940/1941 | Atlético Aviación Madrid | Valencia CF | Prudencio Sánchez Fernández "Pruden" (Atlético Aviación Madrid) | 30 |
| 1941/1942 | Valencia CF | CF Barcelona | Edmundo Suárez Trabanco "Mundo" (Valencia CF) | 27 |
| 1942/1943 | Atlético Club de Bilbao | Atlético Club de Bilbao | Mariano Martín Alonso (CF Barcelona) | 32 |
| 1943/1944 | Valencia CF | Atlético Club de Bilbao | Edmundo Suárez Trabanco "Mundo" (Valencia CF) | 27 |
| 1944/1945 | CF Barcelona | Atlético Club de Bilbao | Pedro Telmo Zarraonandía Montoya (Atlético Club de Bilbao) | 19 |
| 1945/1946 | Sevilla FC | Real Madrid CF | Pedro Telmo Zarraonandía Montoya (Atlético Club de Bilbao) | 24 |
| 1946/1947 | Valencia CF | Real Madrid CF | Pedro Telmo Zarraonandía Montoya (Atlético Club de Bilbao) | 34 |

| | | | |
|---|---|---|---|
| 1947/1948 | CF Barcelona | Sevilla FC | Manuel Fernández Fernández "Pahiño" (RC Celta de Vigo) | 23 |
| 1948/1949 | CF Barcelona | Valencia CF | César Rodríguez Álvarez (CF Barcelona) | 28 |
| 1949/1950 | Club Atlético de Madrid | Atlético Club de Bilbao | Pedro Telmo Zarraonandía Montoya (Atlético Club de Bilbao) | 25 |
| 1950/1951 | Club Atlético de Madrid | CF Barcelona | Pedro Telmo Zarraonandía Montoya (Atlético Club de Bilbao) | 38 |
| 1951/1952 | CF Barcelona | CF Barcelona | Manuel Fernández Fernández "Pahiño" (Real Madrid CF) | 28 |
| 1952/1953 | CF Barcelona | CF Barcelona | Pedro Telmo Zarraonandía Montoya (Atlético Club de Bilbao) | 24 |
| 1953/1954 | Real Madrid CF | Valencia CF | Alfredo Stéfano Di Stéfano Laulhé (Real Madrid CF) | 27 |
| 1954/1955 | Real Madrid CF | Atlético Club de Bilbao | Juan Arza Iñigo (Sevilla FC) | 28 |
| 1955/1956 | Atlético Club de Bilbao | Atlético Club de Bilbao | Alfredo Stéfano Di Stéfano Laulhé (Real Madrid CF) | 24 |
| 1956/1957 | Real Madrid CF | CF Barcelona | Alfredo Stéfano Di Stéfano Laulhé (Real Madrid CF) | 31 |
| 1957/1958 | Real Madrid CF | Atlético Club de Bilbao | Manuel Badenes Calduch (Real Valladolid CF) Alfredo Stéfano Di Stéfano Laulhé (Real Madrid CF) Ricardo de la Virgen (Valencia CF) | 19 |
| 1958/1959 | CF Barcelona | CF Barcelona | Alfredo Stéfano Di Stéfano Laulhé (Real Madrid CF | 23 |
| 1959/1960 | CF Barcelona | Club Atlético de Madrid | Ferenc Puskás (HUN, Real Madrid CF) | 26 |
| 1960/1961 | Real Madrid CF | Club Atlético de Madrid | Ferenc Puskás (HUN, Real Madrid CF) | 27 |
| 1961/1962 | Real Madrid CF | Real Madrid CF | Juan Roberto Seminario Rodríguez (PER, Real Zaragoza) | 25 |
| 1962/1963 | Real Madrid CF | CF Barcelona | Ferenc Puskás (HUN, Real Madrid CF) | 26 |
| 1963/1964 | Real Madrid CF | Real Zaragoza | Ferenc Puskás (HUN, Real Madrid CF) | 20 |
| 1964/1965 | Real Madrid CF | Club Atlético de Madrid | Cayetano Ré Ramírez (PAR, CF Barcelona) | 25 |
| 1965/1966 | Club Atlético de Madrid | Real Zaragoza | Luciano Sánchez Rodríguez "Vavá" (Elche CF) | 19 |
| 1966/1967 | Real Madrid CF | Valencia CF | Waldo Machado da Silva (BRA, Valencia CF) | 24 |
| 1967/1968 | Real Madrid CF | CF Barcelona | Fidel Uriarte Macho (Atlético Club de Bilbao) | 22 |
| 1968/1969 | Real Madrid CF | Atlético Club de Bilbao | Amancio Amaro Varela (Club Atlético de Madrid) José Eulogio Gárate Ormaechea (Real Madrid CF) | 14 |
| 1969/1970 | Club Atlético de Madrid | Real Madrid CF | Amancio Amaro Varela (Real Madrid CF) José Luis Aragonés Suárez (Club Atlético de Madrid) José Eulogio Gárate Ormaechea (Club Atlético de Madrid) | 16 |
| 1970/1971 | Valencia CF | CF Barcelona | José Eulogio Gárate Ormaechea (Club Atlético de Madrid) Carles Rexach i Cerdà (CF Barcelona) | 17 |
| 1971/1972 | Real Madrid CF | Club Atlético de Madrid | Enrique Porta Guíu (Granada CF) | 20 |
| 1972/1973 | Club Atlético de Madrid | Athletic Club Bilbao | Mariano Arias Chamorro "Marianín" (Real Oviedo CF) | 19 |
| 1973/1974 | CF Barcelona | Real Madrid CF | Enrique Castro González "Quini" (Real Sporting de Gijón) | 20 |
| 1974/1975 | Real Madrid CF | Real Madrid CF | Carlos Ruiz Herrero (Athletic Club Bilbao) | 19 |
| 1975/1976 | Real Madrid CF | Club Atlético de Madrid | Enrique Castro González "Quini" (Real Sporting de Gijón) | 21 |
| 1976/1977 | Club Atlético de Madrid | Real Betis Balompié Sevilla | Mario Alberto Kempes Chiodi (ARG, Valencia CF) | 24 |
| 1977/1978 | Real Madrid CF | FC Barcelona | Mario Alberto Kempes Chiodi (ARG, Valencia CF) | 28 |
| 1978/1979 | Real Madrid CF | Valencia CF | Johann Krankl (AUT, FC Barcelona) | 29 |
| 1979/1980 | Real Madrid CF | Real Madrid CF | Enrique Castro González "Quini" (Real Sporting de Gijón) | 24 |
| 1980/1981 | Real Sociedad de Fútbol San Sebastián | FC Barcelona | Enrique Castro González "Quini" (FC Barcelona) | 20 |
| 1981/1982 | Real Sociedad de Fútbol San Sebastián | Real Madrid CF | Enrique Castro González "Quini" (FC Barcelona) | 26 |
| 1982/1983 | Athletic Club Bilbao | FC Barcelona | Hipólito Rincón Povedano (Real Betis Balompié Sevilla) | 20 |
| 1983/1984 | Athletic Club Bilbao | Athletic Club Bilbao | Jorge Orosmán da Silva Echeverrito (URU, Real Valladolid CF) Juan Gómez González "Juanito" (Real Madrid CF) | 17 |
| 1984/1985 | FC Barcelona | Club Atlético de Madrid | Hugo Sánchez Márquez (MEX, Club Atlético de Madrid) | 19 |
| 1985/1986 | Real Madrid CF | Real Zaragoza | Hugo Sánchez Márquez (MEX, Real Madrid CF) | 22 |
| 1986/1987 | Real Madrid CF | Real Sociedad de Fútbol San Sebastián | Hugo Sánchez Márquez (MEX, Real Madrid CF) | 34 |
| 1987/1988 | Real Madrid CF | FC Barcelona | Hugo Sánchez Márquez (MEX, Real Madrid CF) | 29 |
| 1988/1989 | Real Madrid CF | Real Madrid CF | Baltazar Maria de Morais Júnior (BRA, Club Atlético de Madrid) | 35 |
| 1989/1990 | Real Madrid CF | FC Barcelona | Hugo Sánchez Márquez (MEX, Real Madrid CF) | 38 |
| 1990/1991 | FC Barcelona | Club Atlético de Madrid | Emilio Butragueño Santos (Real Madrid CF) | 19 |
| 1991/1992 | FC Barcelona | Club Atlético de Madrid | Manuel Sánchez Delgado "Manolo" (Club Atlético de Madrid) | 27 |
| 1992/1993 | FC Barcelona | Real Madrid CF | José Roberto Gama de Oliveira "Bebeto" (RC Deportivo La Coruña) | 29 |
| 1993/1994 | FC Barcelona | Real Zaragoza | Romário de Souza Faria (BRA, FC Barcelona) | 30 |
| 1994/1995 | Real Madrid CF | RC Deportivo La Coruña | Iván Luis Zamorano Zamora (CHI, Real Madrid CF) | 28 |
| 1995/1996 | Club Atlético de Madrid | Club Atlético de Madrid | Juan Antonio Pizzi Torroja (CD Tenerife) | 31 |
| 1996/1997 | Real Madrid CF | FC Barcelona | Ronaldo Luís Nazário de Lima (BRA, FC Barcelona) | 34 |
| 1997/1998 | FC Barcelona | FC Barcelona | Christian Vieri (Club Atlético de Madrid) | 24 |
| 1998/1999 | FC Barcelona | Valencia CF | Raúl González Blanco (Real Madrid CF) | 25 |
| 1999/2000 | RC Deportivo La Coruña | RCD Espanyol Barcelona | Salvador Ballesta Vialcho "Salva" (Real Racing Club de Santander) | 27 |
| 2000/2001 | Real Madrid CF | Real Zaragoza | Raúl González Blanco (Real Madrid CF) | 24 |
| 2001/2002 | Valencia CF | RC Deportivo La Coruña | Diego Tristán Herrera (RC Deportivo La Coruña) | 21 |
| 2002/2003 | Real Madrid CF | RCD Mallorca | Rudolphus Antonius "Roy" Makaay (NED, RC Deportivo La Coruña) | 29 |
| 2003/2004 | Valencia CF | Real Zaragoza | Ronaldo Luís Nazário de Lima (BRA, Real Madrid CF) | 25 |
| 2004/2005 | FC Barcelona | Real Betis Balompié Sevilla | Diego Forlán Corazzo (URU, Villarreal CF) | 25 |
| 2005/2006 | FC Barcelona | RCD Espanyol Barcelona | Samuel Eto'o Fils (CMR, FC Barcelona) | 26 |
| 2006/2007 | Real Madrid CF | Sevilla FC | Rutgerus Johannes Martinus "Ruud" van Nistelrooy (NED, Real Madrid CF) | 25 |

| | | | | |
|---|---|---|---|---|
| 2007/2008 | Real Madrid CF | Valencia CF | Daniel González Güiza (RCD Mallorca) | 27 |
| 2008/2009 | FC Barcelona | FC Barcelona | Diego Forlán Corazzo (URU, Club Atlético de Madrid) | 32 |
| 2009/2010 | FC Barcelona | Sevilla FC | Lionel Andrés Messi Cuccittini (ARG, FC Barcelona) | 34 |
| 2010/2011 | FC Barcelona | Real Madrid CF | Cristiano Ronaldo dos Santos Aveiro (POR, Real Madrid CF) | 40 |
| 2011/2012 | Real Madrid CF | FC Barcelona | Lionel Andrés Messi Cuccittini (ARG, FC Barcelona) | 50 |
| 2012/2013 | FC Barcelona | Club Atlético de Madrid | Lionel Andrés Messi Cuccittini (ARG, FC Barcelona) | 46 |
| 2013/2014 | Club Atlético de Madrid | Real Madrid CF | Cristiano Ronaldo dos Santos Aveiro (POR, Real Madrid CF) | 31 |
| 2014/2015 | FC Barcelona | FC Barcelona | Cristiano Ronaldo dos Santos Aveiro (POR, Real Madrid CF) | 48 |
| 2015/2016 | FC Barcelona | FC Barcelona | Luis Alberto Suárez Díaz (URU, FC Barcelona) | 40 |
| 2016/2017 | Real Madrid CF | FC Barcelona | Lionel Andrés Messi Cuccittini (ARG, FC Barcelona) | 37 |
| 2017/2018 | FC Barcelona | FC Barcelona | Lionel Andrés Messi Cuccittini (ARG, FC Barcelona) | 34 |
| 2018/2019 | FC Barcelona | Valencia CF | Lionel Andrés Messi Cuccittini (ARG, FC Barcelona) | 36 |
| 2019/2020 | Real Madrid CF | Real Sociedad de Fútbol San Sebastián | Lionel Andrés Messi Cuccittini (ARG, FC Barcelona) | 25 |
| 2020/2021 | Club Atlético de Madrid | FC Barcelona | Lionel Andrés Messi Cuccittini (ARG, FC Barcelona) | 30 |
| 2021/2022 | Real Madrid CF | Real Betis Balompié Sevilla | Karim Mostafa Benzema (FRA, Real Madrid CF) | 28 |
| 2022/2023 | FC Barcelona | Real Madrid CF | Robert Lewandowski (POL, FC Barcelona) | 23 |

*FEF = Federación Española de Fútbol; **UECF = Unión Española de Clubes de Fútbol

## NATIONAL CHAMPIONSHIP
### La Liga 2022/2023
(12.08.2022 – 04.06.2023)

### Results

**Round 1 [12-15.08.2022]**
Osasuna - Sevilla FC 2-1(1-1)
Celta Vigo - Espanyol Barcelona 2-2(1-0)
Valladolid - Villarreal 0-3(0-0)
FC Barcelona - Rayo Vallecano 0-0
Cádiz - Real Sociedad 0-1(0-1)
Valencia - Girona 1-0(1-0)
UD Almería - Real Madrid 1-2(1-0)
Athletic Bilbao - RCD Mallorca 0-0
Getafe - Atlético Madrid 0-3(0-1)
Real Betis - Elche 3-0(2-0)

**Round 2 [19-22.08.2022]**
Espanyol Barcelona-Rayo Vallecano 0-2(0-1)
Sevilla FC - Valladolid 1-1(0-0)
Osasuna - Cádiz 2-0(1-0)
RCD Mallorca - Real Betis 1-2(0-1)
Celta Vigo - Real Madrid 1-4(1-2)
Athletic Bilbao - Valencia 1-0(1-0)
Atlético Madrid - Villarreal 0-2(0-0)
Real Sociedad - FC Barcelona 1-4(1-1)
Elche - UD Almería 1-1(1-1)
Girona - Getafe 3-1(1-0)

**Round 3 [26-29.08.2022]**
Girona - Celta Vigo 0-1(0-0)
Real Betis - Osasuna 1-0(1-0)
Elche - Real Sociedad 0-1(0-1)
Rayo Vallecano - RCD Mallorca 0-2(0-1)
UD Almería - Sevilla FC 2-1(1-1)
Getafe - Villarreal 0-0
FC Barcelona - Valladolid 4-0(2-0)
Espanyol Barcelona - Real Madrid 1-3(1-1)
Cádiz - Athletic Bilbao 0-4(0-1)
Valencia - Atlético Madrid 0-1(0-0)

**Round 4 [02-05.09.2022]**
Celta Vigo - Cádiz 3-0(0-0)
RCD Mallorca - Girona 1-1(0-0)
Real Madrid - Real Betis 2-1(1-1)
Real Sociedad - Atlético Madrid 1-1(0-1)
Sevilla FC - FC Barcelona 0-3(0-2)
Osasuna - Rayo Vallecano 1-0(1-0)
Athletic Bilbao - Espanyol Barcelona 0-1(0-0)
Villarreal - Elche 4-0(2-0)
Valencia - Getafe 5-1(3-0)
Valladolid - UD Almería 1-0(0-0)

**Round 5 [09-12.09.2022]**
Girona - Valladolid 2-1(1-1)
Rayo Vallecano - Valencia 2-1(1-0)
Espanyol Barcelona - Sevilla FC 2-3(1-3)
Cádiz - FC Barcelona 0-4(0-0)
Atlético Madrid - Celta Vigo 4-1(1-0)
Real Madrid - RCD Mallorca 4-1(1-1)
Elche - Athletic Bilbao 1-4(0-4)
Getafe - Real Sociedad 2-1(1-0)
Real Betis - Villarreal 1-0(0-0)
UD Almería - Osasuna 0-1(0-1)

**Round 6 [16-18.09.2022]**
Valladolid - Cádiz 0-1(0-0)
RCD Mallorca - UD Almería 1-0(1-0)
FC Barcelona - Elche 3-0(2-0)
Valencia - Celta Vigo 3-0(1-0)
Athletic Bilbao - Rayo Vallecano 3-2(3-1)
Osasuna - Getafe 0-2(0-1)
Villarreal - Sevilla FC 1-1(0-1)
Real Betis - Girona 2-1(1-1)
Real Sociedad - Espanyol Barcelona 2-1(2-1)
Atlético Madrid - Real Madrid 1-2(0-2)

**Round 7 [30.09.-03.10.2022]**
Athletic Bilbao - UD Almería 4-0(2-0)
Cádiz - Villarreal 0-0
Getafe - Valladolid 2-3(2-2)
Sevilla FC - Atlético Madrid 0-2(0-1)
RCD Mallorca - FC Barcelona 0-1(0-1)
Espanyol Barcelona - Valencia 2-2(0-0)
Celta Vigo - Real Betis 1-0(1-0)
Girona - Real Sociedad 3-5(2-2)
Real Madrid - Osasuna 1-1(1-0)
Rayo Vallecano - Elche 2-1(1-1)

**Round 8 [07-10.10.2022]**
Osasuna - Valencia 1-2(0-1)
UD Almería - Rayo Vallecano 3-1(3-0)
Atlético Madrid - Girona 2-1(1-0)
Sevilla FC - Athletic Bilbao 1-1(1-0)
Getafe - Real Madrid 0-1(0-1)
Valladolid - Real Betis 0-0
Cádiz - Espanyol Barcelona 2-2(1-0)
Real Sociedad - Villarreal 1-0(1-0)
FC Barcelona - Celta Vigo 1-0(1-0)
Elche - RCD Mallorca 1-1(1-0)

**Round 9 [14-17.10.2022]**
Rayo Vallecano - Getafe 0-0
Girona - Cádiz 1-1(0-0)
Valencia - Elche 2-2(2-1)
RCD Mallorca - Sevilla FC 0-1(0-0)
Athletic Bilbao - Atlético Madrid 0-1(0-0)
Celta Vigo - Real Sociedad 1-2(1-1)
Real Madrid - FC Barcelona 3-1(2-0)
Espanyol Barcelona - Valladolid 1-0(0-0)
Real Betis - UD Almería 3-1(1-0)
Villarreal - Osasuna 2-0(1-0)

**Round 10 [18-20.10.2022]**
Sevilla FC - Valencia 1-1(0-1)
Getafe - Athletic Bilbao 2-2(1-1)
Atlético Madrid - Rayo Vallecano 1-1(1-0)
Cádiz - Real Betis 0-0
Valladolid - Celta Vigo 4-1(1-1)
Real Sociedad - RCD Mallorca 1-0(1-0)
Elche - Real Madrid 0-3(0-1)
UD Almería - Girona 3-2(3-0)
Osasuna - Espanyol Barcelona 1-0(0-0)
FC Barcelona - Villarreal 3-0(3-0)

**Round 11 [22-24.10.2022]**
Rayo Vallecano - Cádiz 5-1(2-0)
Valladolid - Real Sociedad 1-0(1-0)
Valencia - RCD Mallorca 1-2(0-0)
Real Madrid - Sevilla FC 3-1(1-0)
Espanyol Barcelona - Elche 2-2(1-1)
Real Betis - Atlético Madrid 1-2(0-0)
Girona - Osasuna 1-1(1-1)
Villarreal - UD Almería 2-1(0-1)
FC Barcelona - Athletic Bilbao 4-0(3-0)
Celta Vigo - Getafe 1-1(0-1)

**Round 12 [28-31.10.2022]**
RCD Mallorca - Espanyol Barcelona 1-1(0-0)
UD Almería - Celta Vigo 3-1(0-1)
Cádiz - Atlético Madrid 3-2(1-0)
Sevilla FC - Rayo Vallecano 0-1(0-0)
Valencia - FC Barcelona 0-1(0-0)
Osasuna - Valladolid 2-0(2-0)
Real Madrid - Girona 1-1(0-0)
Athletic Bilbao - Villarreal 1-0(0-0)
Real Sociedad - Real Betis 0-2(0-0)
Elche - Getafe 0-1(0-0)

**Round 13 [04-07.11.2022]**
Girona - Athletic Bilbao 2-1(0-0)
Getafe - Cádiz 0-0
Valladolid - Elche 2-1(1-0)
Celta Vigo - Osasuna 1-2(1-2)
FC Barcelona - UD Almería 2-0(0-0)
Atlético Madrid-Espanyol Barcelona 1-1(0-0)
Real Sociedad - Valencia 1-1(1-1)
Villarreal - RCD Mallorca 0-2(0-1)
Real Betis - Sevilla FC 1-1(1-0)
Rayo Vallecano - Real Madrid 3-2(2-2)

**Round 14 [08-10.11.2022]**
Elche - Girona 1-2(1-1)
Athletic Bilbao - Valladolid 3-0(1-0)
Osasuna - FC Barcelona 1-2(1-0)
Sevilla FC - Real Sociedad 1-2(1-2)
UD Almería - Getafe 1-0(1-0)
Espanyol Barcelona - Villarreal 0-1(0-0)
RCD Mallorca - Atlético Madrid 1-0(1-0)
Rayo Vallecano - Celta Vigo 0-0
Valencia - Real Betis 3-0(0-0)
Real Madrid - Cádiz 2-1(1-0)

**Round 15 [29-31.12.2022]**
Girona - Rayo Vallecano 2-2(1-1)
Real Betis - Athletic Bilbao 0-0
Atlético Madrid - Elche 2-0(0-0)
Getafe - RCD Mallorca 2-0(0-0)
Celta Vigo - Sevilla FC 1-1(1-0)
Cádiz - UD Almería 1-1(0-1)
Valladolid - Real Madrid 0-2(0-0)
FC Barcelona - Espanyol Barcelona 1-1(1-0)
Villarreal - Valencia 2-1(1-1)
Real Sociedad - Osasuna 2-0(1-0)

**Round 16 [06-09.01.2023]**
Elche - Celta Vigo 0-1(0-1)
Valencia - Cádiz 0-1(0-1)
Villarreal - Real Madrid 2-1(0-0)
RCD Mallorca - Valladolid 1-0(0-0)
Espanyol Barcelona - Girona 2-2(0-1)
UD Almería - Real Sociedad 0-2(0-0)
Rayo Vallecano - Real Betis 1-2(1-2)
Sevilla FC - Getafe 2-1(1-0)
Atlético Madrid - FC Barcelona 0-1(0-1)
Athletic Bilbao - Osasuna 0-0

**Round 17 [13-16.01.2023]**
Celta Vigo - Villarreal 1-1(0-1)
Valladolid - Rayo Vallecano 0-1(0-0)
Girona - Sevilla FC 2-1(0-1)
Osasuna - RCD Mallorca 1-0(0-0)
Real Sociedad - Athletic Bilbao 3-1(2-1)
Getafe - Espanyol Barcelona 1-2(1-1)
UD Almería - Atlético Madrid 1-1(1-1)
Cádiz - Elche 1-1(1-0)
Real Betis - FC Barcelona 1-2(0-0) [01.02.23]
Real Madrid - Valencia 2-0(0-0) [02.02.2023]

**Round 18 [20-23.01.2023]**
RCD Mallorca - Celta Vigo 1-0(0-0)
Rayo Vallecano - Real Sociedad 0-2(0-2)
Espanyol Barcelona - Real Betis 1-0(1-0)
Atlético Madrid - Valladolid 3-0(3-0)
Sevilla FC - Cádiz 1-0(0-0)
Villarreal - Girona 1-0(0-0)
Elche - Osasuna 1-1(0-1)
FC Barcelona - Getafe 1-0(1-0)
Athletic Bilbao - Real Madrid 0-2(0-1)
Valencia - UD Almería 2-2(0-0)

**Round 19 [27-30.01.2023]**
UD Almería - Espanyol Barcelona 3-1(1-0)
Cádiz - RCD Mallorca 2-0(2-0)
Girona - FC Barcelona 0-1(0-0)
Sevilla FC - Elche 3-0(3-0)
Getafe - Real Betis 0-1(0-0)
Valladolid - Valencia 1-0(0-0)
Osasuna - Atlético Madrid 0-1(0-0)
Celta Vigo - Athletic Bilbao 1-0(0-0)
Real Madrid - Real Sociedad 0-0
Villarreal - Rayo Vallecano 0-1(0-0)

**Round 20 [03-06.02.2023]**
Athletic Bilbao - Cádiz 4-1(3-1)
Espanyol Barcelona - Osasuna 1-1(0-1)
Elche - Villarreal 3-1(2-1)
Atlético Madrid - Getafe 1-1(0-0)
Real Betis - Celta Vigo 3-4(2-2)
RCD Mallorca - Real Madrid 1-0(1-0)
Girona - Valencia 1-0(0-0)
Real Sociedad - Valladolid 0-1(0-0)
FC Barcelona - Sevilla FC 3-0(0-0)
Rayo Vallecano - UD Almería 2-0(0-0)

**Round 21 [10-15.02.2023]**
Cádiz - Girona 2-0(2-0)
UD Almería - Real Betis 2-3(1-2)
Sevilla FC - RCD Mallorca 2-0(2-0)
Valencia - Athletic Bilbao 1-2(1-1)
Getafe - Rayo Vallecano 1-1(0-1)
Celta Vigo - Atlético Madrid 0-1(0-0)
Valladolid - Osasuna 0-0
Villarreal - FC Barcelona 0-1(0-1)
Espanyol Barcelona - Real Sociedad 2-3(0-1)
Real Madrid - Elche 4-0(3-0)

**Round 22 [17-20.02.2023]**
Girona - UD Almería 6-2(4-0)
Real Sociedad - Celta Vigo 1-1(1-0)
Real Betis - Valladolid 2-1(2-1)
RCD Mallorca - Villarreal 4-2(2-1)
Osasuna - Real Madrid 0-2(0-0)
Elche - Espanyol Barcelona 0-1(0-0)
Rayo Vallecano - Sevilla FC 1-1(0-1)
Atlético Madrid - Athletic Bilbao 1-0(0-0)
FC Barcelona - Cádiz 2-0(2-0)
Getafe - Valencia 1-0(0-0)

**Round 23 [24-27.02.2023]**
Elche - Real Betis 2-3(2-0)
Espanyol Barcelona - RCD Mallorca 2-1(1-1)
Cádiz - Rayo Vallecano 1-0(0-0)
Real Madrid - Atlético Madrid 1-1(0-0)
Valencia - Real Sociedad 1-0(1-0)
Athletic Bilbao - Girona 2-3(1-3)
Celta Vigo - Valladolid 3-0(2-0)
UD Almería - FC Barcelona 1-0(1-0)
Sevilla FC - Osasuna 2-3(0-1)
Villarreal - Getafe 2-1(1-1)

**Round 24 [03-06.03.2023]**
Real Sociedad - Cádiz 0-0
Getafe - Girona 3-2(3-0)
UD Almería - Villarreal 0-2(0-0)
RCD Mallorca - Elche 0-1(0-0)
Atlético Madrid - Sevilla FC 6-1(2-1)
Valladolid - Espanyol Barcelona 2-1(1-0)
FC Barcelona - Valencia 1-0(1-0)
Rayo Vallecano - Athletic Bilbao 0-0
Real Betis - Real Madrid 0-0
Osasuna - Celta Vigo 0-0

**Round 25 [10-13.03.2023]**
Cádiz - Getafe 2-2(1-0)
Real Madrid - Espanyol Barcelona 3-1(2-1)
Elche - Valladolid 1-1(0-1)
Celta Vigo - Rayo Vallecano 3-0(0-0)
Valencia - Osasuna 1-0(0-0)
RCD Mallorca - Real Sociedad 1-1(0-1)
Sevilla FC - UD Almería 2-1(1-1)
Villarreal - Real Betis 1-1(0-1)
Athletic Bilbao - FC Barcelona 0-1(0-1)
Girona - Atlético Madrid 0-1(0-0)

**Round 26 [17-19.03.2023]**
Valladolid - Athletic Bilbao 1-3(0-1)
UD Almería - Cádiz 1-1(0-0)
Rayo Vallecano - Girona 2-2(2-1)
Espanyol Barcelona - Celta Vigo 1-3(0-2)
Atlético Madrid - Valencia 3-0(1-0)
Real Betis - RCD Mallorca 1-0(0-0)
Osasuna - Villarreal 0-3(0-1)
Real Sociedad - Elche 2-0(0-0)
Getafe - Sevilla FC 2-0(0-0)
FC Barcelona - Real Madrid 2-1(1-1)

**Round 27 [31.03.-03.04.2023]**
RCD Mallorca - Osasuna 0-0
Girona - Espanyol Barcelona 2-1(0-0)
Athletic Bilbao - Getafe 0-0
Cádiz - Sevilla FC 0-2(0-0)
Elche - FC Barcelona 0-4(0-1)
Celta Vigo - UD Almería 2-2(2-2)
Real Madrid - Valladolid 6-0(4-0)
Villarreal - Real Sociedad 2-0(0-0)
Atlético Madrid - Real Betis 1-0(0-0)
Valencia - Rayo Vallecano 1-1(0-1)

**Round 28 [07-10.04.2023]**
Sevilla FC - Celta Vigo 2-2(1-0)
Osasuna - Elche 2-1(0-1)
Espanyol Barcelona - Athletic Bilbao 1-2(0-1)
Real Sociedad - Getafe 2-0(1-0)
Real Madrid - Villarreal 2-3(1-1)
Valladolid - RCD Mallorca 3-3(1-0)
Real Betis - Cádiz 0-2(0-0)
UD Almería - Valencia 2-1(0-0)
Rayo Vallecano - Atlético Madrid 1-2(0-2)
FC Barcelona - Girona 0-0

**Round 29 [14-17.04.2023]**
Rayo Vallecano - Osasuna 2-1(2-0)
Villarreal - Valladolid 1-2(0-2)
Athletic Bilbao - Real Sociedad 2-0(1-0)
Real Betis - Espanyol Barcelona 3-1(2-0)
Cádiz - Real Madrid 0-2(0-0)
Girona - Elche 2-0(1-0)
Getafe - FC Barcelona 0-0
Atlético Madrid - UD Almería 2-1(2-1)
Valencia - Sevilla FC 0-2(0-0)
Celta Vigo - RCD Mallorca 0-1(0-1)

**Round 30 [21-23.04.2023]**
Espanyol Barcelona - Cádiz 0-0
Osasuna - Real Betis 3-2(3-1)
UD Almería - Athletic Bilbao 1-2(0-1)
Real Sociedad - Rayo Vallecano 2-1(0-0)
Valladolid - Girona 1-0(1-0)
Real Madrid - Celta Vigo 2-0(1-0)
Elche - Valencia 0-2(0-2)
FC Barcelona - Atlético Madrid 1-0(1-0)
RCD Mallorca - Getafe 3-1(0-1)
Sevilla FC - Villarreal 2-1(1-0)

| Round 31 [25-27.04.2023] |
|---|
| Cádiz - Osasuna 0-1(0-0) |
| Girona - Real Madrid 4-2(2-1) |
| Real Betis - Real Sociedad 0-0 |
| Atlético Madrid - RCD Mallorca 3-1(1-1) |
| Getafe - UD Almería 1-2(0-1) |
| Celta Vigo - Elche 1-0(0-0) |
| Rayo Vallecano - FC Barcelona 2-1(1-0) |
| Valencia - Valladolid 2-1(0-1) |
| Villarreal - Espanyol Barcelona 4-2(0-1) |
| Athletic Bilbao - Sevilla FC 0-1(0-0) |

| Round 32 [28.04.-01.05.2023] |
|---|
| Osasuna - Real Sociedad 0-2(0-1) |
| Elche - Rayo Vallecano 4-0(1-0) |
| Real Madrid - UD Almería 4-2(3-1) |
| FC Barcelona - Real Betis 4-0(3-0) |
| Cádiz - Valencia 2-1(1-0) |
| Villarreal - Celta Vigo 3-1(2-1) |
| Espanyol Barcelona - Getafe 1-0(1-0) |
| Valladolid - Atlético Madrid 2-5(1-3) |
| RCD Mallorca - Athletic Bilbao 1-1(0-0) |
| Sevilla FC - Girona 0-2(0-1) |

| Round 33 [02-04.05.2023] |
|---|
| FC Barcelona - Osasuna 1-0(0-0) |
| UD Almería - Elche 2-1(1-0) |
| Real Sociedad - Real Madrid 2-0(0-0) |
| Valencia - Villarreal 1-1(0-0) |
| Atlético Madrid - Cádiz 5-1(2-0) |
| Getafe - Celta Vigo 1-0(1-0) |
| Girona - RCD Mallorca 2-1(1-0) |
| Sevilla FC - Espanyol Barcelona 3-2(1-2) |
| Athletic Bilbao - Real Betis 0-1(0-1) |
| Rayo Vallecano - Valladolid 2-1(0-0) |

| Round 34 [12-15.05.2023] |
|---|
| RCD Mallorca - Cádiz 1-0(1-0) |
| Real Sociedad - Girona 2-2(2-2) |
| Osasuna - UD Almería 3-1(0-0) |
| Villarreal - Athletic Bilbao 5-1(2-1) |
| Real Madrid - Getafe 1-0(0-0) |
| Celta Vigo - Valencia 1-2(0-1) |
| Elche - Atlético Madrid 0-1(0-1) |
| Valladolid - Sevilla FC 3-0(0-0) |
| Espanyol Barcelona - FC Barcelona 2-4(0-3) |
| Real Betis - Rayo Vallecano 3-1(2-0) |

| Round 35 [19-21.05.2023] |
|---|
| Cádiz - Valladolid 2-0(0-0) |
| Girona - Villarreal 1-2(1-1) |
| Athletic Bilbao - Celta Vigo 2-1(1-0) |
| Getafe - Elche 1-1(1-1) |
| UD Almería - RCD Mallorca 3-0(2-0) |
| FC Barcelona - Real Sociedad 1-2(0-1) |
| Rayo Vallecano-Espanyol Barcelona 1-2(1-1) |
| Atlético Madrid - Osasuna 3-0(1-0) |
| Valencia - Real Madrid 1-0(1-0) |
| Sevilla FC - Real Betis 0-0 |

| Round 36 [23-25.05.2023] |
|---|
| Celta Vigo - Girona 1-1(1-0) |
| Real Sociedad - UD Almería 1-0(1-0) |
| Valladolid - FC Barcelona 3-1(2-0) |
| Elche - Sevilla FC 1-1(1-1) |
| Villarreal - Cádiz 2-0(2-0) |
| Real Madrid - Rayo Vallecano 2-1(1-0) |
| Real Betis - Getafe 0-1(0-0) |
| Espanyol Barcelona-Atlético Madrid 3-3(0-2) |
| RCD Mallorca - Valencia 1-0(0-0) |
| Osasuna - Athletic Bilbao 2-0(0-0) |

| Round 37 [27-28.05.2023] |
|---|
| Sevilla FC - Real Madrid 1-2(1-1) |
| Athletic Bilbao - Elche 0-1(0-0) |
| Atlético Madrid - Real Sociedad 2-1(1-0) |
| FC Barcelona - RCD Mallorca 3-0(2-0) |
| Cádiz - Celta Vigo 1-0(0-0) |
| Getafe - Osasuna 2-1(1-1) |
| Girona - Real Betis 1-2(1-0) |
| Valencia - Espanyol Barcelona 2-2(1-1) |
| Rayo Vallecano - Villarreal 2-1(0-0) |
| UD Almería - Valladolid 0-0 |

| Round 38 [04.06.2023] |
|---|
| Osasuna - Girona 2-1(0-0) |
| Villarreal - Atlético Madrid 2-2(1-1) |
| RCD Mallorca - Rayo Vallecano 3-0(0-0) |
| Real Madrid - Athletic Bilbao 1-1(0-0) |
| Real Sociedad - Sevilla FC 2-1(1-0) |
| Real Betis - Valencia 1-1(1-1) |
| Celta Vigo - FC Barcelona 2-1(1-0) |
| Espanyol Barcelona - UD Almería 3-3(1-1) |
| Elche - Cádiz 1-1(0-1) |
| Valladolid - Getafe 0-0 |

## Final Standings

| | | | | | | | Total | | Home | | | | | Away | | | | |
|---|---|---|---|---|---|---|---|---|---|---|---|---|---|---|---|---|---|---|
| 1. | FC Barcelona | 38 | 28 | 4 | 6 | 70 - 20 | 88 | 15 | 3 | 1 | 37 - 4 | 13 | 1 | 5 | 33 - 16 |
| 2. | Real Madrid CF | 38 | 24 | 6 | 8 | 75 - 36 | 78 | 13 | 5 | 1 | 44 - 16 | 11 | 1 | 7 | 31 - 20 |
| 3. | Club Atlético de Madrid | 38 | 23 | 8 | 7 | 70 - 33 | 77 | 13 | 3 | 3 | 41 - 15 | 10 | 5 | 4 | 29 - 18 |
| 4. | Real Sociedad de Fútbol San Sebastián | 38 | 21 | 8 | 9 | 51 - 35 | 71 | 11 | 5 | 3 | 26 - 16 | 10 | 3 | 6 | 25 - 19 |
| 5. | Villarreal CF | 38 | 19 | 7 | 12 | 59 - 40 | 64 | 12 | 3 | 4 | 36 - 18 | 7 | 4 | 8 | 23 - 22 |
| 6. | Real Betis Balompié Sevilla | 38 | 17 | 9 | 12 | 46 - 41 | 60 | 9 | 5 | 5 | 26 - 18 | 8 | 4 | 7 | 20 - 23 |
| 7. | CA Osasuna Pamplona | 38 | 15 | 8 | 15 | 37 - 42 | 53 | 11 | 1 | 7 | 24 - 21 | 4 | 7 | 8 | 13 - 21 |
| 8. | Athletic Club Bilbao | 38 | 14 | 9 | 15 | 47 - 43 | 51 | 8 | 3 | 8 | 22 - 15 | 6 | 6 | 7 | 25 - 28 |
| 9. | RCD Mallorca | 38 | 14 | 8 | 16 | 37 - 43 | 50 | 10 | 5 | 4 | 22 - 12 | 4 | 3 | 12 | 15 - 31 |
| 10. | Girona FC | 38 | 13 | 10 | 15 | 58 - 55 | 49 | 10 | 3 | 6 | 35 - 26 | 3 | 7 | 9 | 23 - 29 |
| 11. | Rayo Vallecano de Madrid | 38 | 13 | 10 | 15 | 45 - 53 | 49 | 9 | 5 | 5 | 28 - 22 | 4 | 5 | 10 | 17 - 31 |
| 12. | Sevilla FC | 38 | 13 | 10 | 15 | 47 - 54 | 49 | 7 | 5 | 7 | 24 - 25 | 6 | 5 | 8 | 23 - 29 |
| 13. | RC Celta de Vigo | 38 | 11 | 10 | 17 | 43 - 53 | 43 | 7 | 6 | 6 | 26 - 21 | 4 | 4 | 11 | 17 - 32 |
| 14. | Cádiz CF | 38 | 10 | 12 | 16 | 30 - 53 | 42 | 7 | 6 | 6 | 19 - 23 | 3 | 6 | 10 | 11 - 30 |
| 15. | Getafe CF | 38 | 10 | 12 | 16 | 34 - 45 | 42 | 7 | 6 | 6 | 21 - 20 | 3 | 6 | 10 | 13 - 25 |
| 16. | Valencia CF | 38 | 11 | 9 | 18 | 42 - 45 | 42 | 8 | 5 | 6 | 27 - 19 | 3 | 4 | 12 | 15 - 26 |
| 17. | Unión Deportiva Almería | 38 | 11 | 8 | 19 | 49 - 65 | 41 | 10 | 3 | 6 | 29 - 22 | 1 | 5 | 13 | 20 - 43 |
| 18. | Real Valladolid CF (Relegated) | 38 | 11 | 7 | 20 | 33 - 63 | 40 | 8 | 4 | 7 | 21 - 25 | 3 | 3 | 13 | 12 - 38 |
| 19. | RCD Espanyol Barcelona (Relegated) | 38 | 8 | 13 | 17 | 52 - 69 | 37 | 4 | 7 | 8 | 27 - 35 | 4 | 6 | 9 | 25 - 34 |
| 20. | Elche CF (Relegated) | 38 | 5 | 10 | 23 | 30 - 67 | 25 | 3 | 6 | 10 | 18 - 29 | 2 | 4 | 13 | 12 - 38 |

| Top goalscorers: | |
|---|---|
| 23 **Robert Lewandowski (POL)** | *FC Barcelona* |
| 19 Karim Mostafa Benzema (FRA) | *Real Madrid CF* |
| 16 José Luis Mato Sanmartín "Joselu" | *RCD Espanyol Barcelona* |
| 15 Antoine Griezmann (FRA) | *Club Atlético de Madrid* |
| 15 Borja Iglesias Quintas | *Real Betis Balompié Sevilla* |
| 15 Vedat Muriqi (KOS) | *RCD Mallorca* |

# NATIONAL CUP
## Copa del Rey 2022/2023

### Second Round [20-22.12.2022]

| | | | | |
|---|---|---|---|---|
| CD Guadalajara - Elche CF | 0-3(0-1) | | Juventud Torremolinos CF - Sevilla FC | 0-3(0-1) |
| CD Diocesano Cáceres - Getafe CF | 0-2(0-1) | | CD Arnedo - CA Osasuna Pamplona | 1-3(0-3) |
| CF Intercity Alicante - CD Mirandés | 2-0(1-0) | | CD Coria - Real Sociedad de Fútbol San Sebastián | 0-5(0-3) |
| Real Unión Club Irun - RCD Mallorca | 0-1(0-1) | | UD Logroñés - Albacete Balompié | 0-0 aet; 4-3 pen |
| Sestao River Club - Athletic Club Bilbao | 0-1(0-1) | | AD Ceuta FC - UD Ibiza | 3-2(2-2) |
| CD Guijuelo - Villarreal CF | 1-2(1-1,1-1) | | Pontevedra CF - CD Tenerife | 2-1(2-0) |
| AD Alcorcón - FC Cartagena | 1-1 aet; 2-4 pen | | Gernika Club - RC Celta de Vigo | 0-3(0-1) |
| CD Atlético Paso - RCD Espanyol Barcelona | 0-1(0-0) | | CP Cacereño - Girona FC | 2-1(1-1) |
| Atlético Saguntino - Rayo Vallecano de Madrid | 0-0 aet; 1-3 pen | | Linares Deportivo - Real Racing Club Santander | 1-0(0-0) |
| CD Ibiza - SD Eibar | 1-0(0-0) | | CD Eldense - Burgos CF | 1-0(1-0) |
| AD Mérida - Deportivo Alavés Vitoria-Gasteiz | 0-1(0-1) | | CD Arenteiro - Club Atlético de Madrid | 1-3(1-1) |
| CD Numancia - Real Sporting de Gijón | 0-3(0-2) | | Club Gimnàstic de Tarragona - Málaga CF | 2-1(1-1) |
| Levante UD Valencia - FC Andorra | 2-1(2-0) | | CF La Nucía - UD Las Palmas | 0-0 aet; 6-5 pen |
| Arenas Club de Getxo - Real Valladolid CF | 1-5(1-2) | | Real Oviedo - Granada CF | 1-0(1-0) |

### Third Round [03-05.01.2023]

| | | | | |
|---|---|---|---|---|
| CF La Nucía - Valencia CF | 0-3(0-2) | | Pontevedra CF - RCD Mallorca | 0-2(0-0,0-0) |
| FC Cartagena - Villarreal CF | 1-5(1-0) | | Linares Deportivo - Sevilla FC | 0-5(0-2) |
| RCD Espanyol Barcelona - RC Celta de Vigo | 3-1(0-1,1-1) | | Real Oviedo - Club Atlético de Madrid | 0-2(0-1) |
| CP Cacereño - Real Madrid CF | 0-1(0-0) | | CF Intercity Alicante - FC Barcelona | 3-4(0-1,3-3) |
| AD Ceuta FC - Elche CF | 1-0(1-0) | | Deportivo Alavés Vitoria-Gasteiz-Real Valladolid CF | 1-0(1-0) |
| Levante UD Valencia - Getafe CF | 3-2(0-1) | | CD Ibiza - Real Betis Balompié Sevilla | 1-4(1-0) |
| Real Sporting de Gijón - Rayo Vallecano de Madrid | 2-0(0-0) | | Club Gimnàstic Tarragona - CA Osasuna Pamplona | 1-2(0-1,1-1) |
| UD Logroñés - Real Sociedad San Sebastián | 0-1(0-1) | | CD Eldense - Athletic Club Bilbao | 1-6(0-2) |

### 1/8-Finals [17-19.01.2023]

| | | | | |
|---|---|---|---|---|
| Real Sociedad San Sebastián - RCD Mallorca | 1-0(1-0) | | Levante UD Valencia - Club Atlético de Madrid | 0-2(0-0) |
| Deportivo Alavés Vitoria-Gasteiz - Sevilla FC | 0-1(0-0) | | Real Betis Balompié Sevilla - CA Osasuna Pamplona | 2-2 aet; 2-4 pen |
| Real Sporting de Gijón - Valencia CF | 0-4(0-3) | | AD Ceuta FC - FC Barcelona | 0-5(0-1) |
| Athletic Club Bilbao - RCD Espanyol Barcelona | 1-0(1-0) | | Villarreal CF - Real Madrid CF | 2-3(2-0) |

### Quarter-Finals [25-26.01.2023]

| | | | | |
|---|---|---|---|---|
| FC Barcelona - Real Sociedad San Sebastián | 1-0(0-0) | | Valencia CF - Athletic Club Bilbao | 1-3(1-2) |
| CA Osasuna Pamplona - Sevilla FC | 2-1(0-0,1-1) | | Real Madrid CF - Club Atlético de Madrid | 3-1(0-1,1-1) |

### Semi-Finals [01-02.03./04-05.04.2023]

| First Leg | | | Second Leg | |
|---|---|---|---|---|
| CA Osasuna Pamplona - Athletic Club Bilbao | 1-0(0-0) | | Athletic Club Bilbao - CA Osasuna Pamplona | 1-1(1-0,1-0) |
| Real Madrid CF - FC Barcelona | 0-1(0-1) | | FC Barcelona - Real Madrid CF | 0-4(0-1) |

### Final

06.05.2023; Estadio La Cartuja, Sevilla; Referee: José María Sánchez Martínez; Attendance: 55,579

**Real Madrid CF - CA Osasuna Pamplona**                                        **2-1(1-0)**

**Real Madrid**: Thibaut Nicolas Marc Courtois, Dani Carvajal, Eder Militão, David Olatukunbo Alaba, Eduardo Celmi Camavinga, Aurélien Djani Tchouaméni (69.Antonio Rüdiger), Federico Santiago Valverde Dipetta, Toni Kroos (82.Luka Modrić), Rodrygo (82.Marco Asensio), Karim Mostafa Benzema (Cap), Vinícius Júnior. Trainer: Carlo Ancelotti (Italy).

**Osasuna Pamplona**: Sergio Herrera, Rubén Peña (75.Kike Barja), Aridane, David García (Cap), Juan Cruz, Lucas Torró (86.Pablo Ibáñez), Moncayola, Aimar Oroz, Moi Gómez (86.Kike García), Ante Budimir (70.Luis Ezequiel Ávila), Abde Ezzalzouli (75.Rubén García). Trainer: Jagoba Arrasate Elustondo.

**Goals:** 1-0 Rodrygo (2), 1-1 Lucas Torró (58), 2-1 Rodrygo (70).

## Unión Deportiva Almería

**Founded**: 26.07.1989 (*as Almería CF*)
**Stadium**: Power Horse Stadium, Almería (15,274)
**Trainer**: Joan Francesc Ferrer Sicilia "Rubi"      01.01.1970

| Goalkeepers: | DOB | M | (s) | G |
|---|---|---|---|---|
| *Fernando* Martínez Rubio | 10.06.1990 | 37 | | |
| Diego *Mariño* Villar | 09.05.1990 | | (1) | |
| Fernando *Pacheco* Flores | 18.05.1992 | 1 | | |
| **Defenders:** | **DOB** | **M** | **(s)** | **G** |
| Sergio *Akieme* Rodríguez (EQG) | 16.12.1997 | 27 | (2) | 1 |
| Alejandro *Pozo* Pozo | 22.02.1999 | 20 | (10) | |
| Alejandro „*Álex*" *Centelles* Plaza | 30.08.1999 | 11 | (4) | 1 |
| Srđan Babić (SRB) | 22.04.1996 | 33 | (1) | 3 |
| Juan Brandáriz Movilla „*Chumi*" | 02.03.1999 | 15 | (6) | 1 |
| *Kaiky* Fernandes Melo (BRA) | 12.01.2004 | 7 | (6) | |
| Houboulang Mendes (FRA) | 04.05.1998 | 11 | (3) | |
| *Rodrigo* Ely (ITA) | 03.11.1993 | 36 | | |
| **Midfielders:** | **DOB** | **M** | **(s)** | **G** |
| *Arnau Puigmal* Martínez | 10.01.2001 | 7 | (15) | 1 |
| *César* de la Hoz López | 30.03.1992 | 18 | (7) | 1 |
| Iñigo *Eguaras* Álvarez | 07.03.1992 | 10 | (15) | 1 |

| | | | | |
|---|---|---|---|---|
| José Carlos *Lazo* Romero | 16.02.1996 | | (1) | |
| Gonzalo Julián *Melero* Manzanares | 02.01.1994 | 24 | (3) | 4 |
| Francisco *Portillo* Soler | 13.06.1990 | 4 | (23) | 2 |
| Lucas Gastón Robertone (ARG) | 18.03.1997 | 34 | (3) | 2 |
| Samuel de Almeida Costa „*Samú*" (POR) | 27.11.2000 | 22 | (10) | 1 |
| **Forwards:** | **DOB** | **M** | **(s)** | **G** |
| Francisco José „*Curro*" *Sánchez* Rodríguez | 03.01.1996 | | (2) | |
| Adrián *Embarba* Blázquez | 07.05.1992 | 18 | (11) | 4 |
| *Dyego* Wilverson Ferreira *Sousa* (POR) | 14.09.1989 | 3 | (17) | |
| *Lázaro* Vinicius Marques (BRA) | 12.03.2002 | 7 | (12) | 6 |
| Leonardo Micali Carrilho Baptistão „*Leo Baptistão*" (BRA) | 26.08.1992 | 24 | (4) | 5 |
| Marko Marezi Milovanović (SRB) | 04.08.2003 | | (2) | |
| Largie Ramazani (BEL) | 27.02.2001 | 13 | (20) | 3 |
| Umar Sadiq Mesbah (NGA) | 02.02.1997 | 3 | | 2 |
| Luis Javier Suárez Charris (COL) | 02.12.1997 | 18 | (3) | 4 |
| El Bilal Touré (MLI) | 03.10.2001 | 15 | (6) | 7 |

## Athletic Club Bilbao

**Founded**: 1898
**Stadium**: Estadio San Mamés, Bilbao (53,289)
**Trainer**: Ernesto Valverde Tejedor      09.02.1964

| Goalkeepers: | DOB | M | (s) | G |
|---|---|---|---|---|
| *Julen Agirrezabala* Astúlez | 26.12.2000 | 7 | (1) | |
| *Unai Simón* Mendibil | 11.06.1997 | 31 | | |
| **Defenders:** | **DOB** | **M** | **(s)** | **G** |
| *Aitor Paredes* Casamichana | 29.04.2000 | 9 | (7) | |
| Mikel *Balenziaga* Oruesagasti | 29.02.1988 | 1 | (2) | |
| Ander *Capa* Rodríguez | 08.02.1992 | 1 | (6) | |
| Óscar *de Marcos* Arana | 14.04.1989 | 32 | (5) | 1 |
| Iñigo *Lekue* Martínez | 04.05.1993 | 14 | (6) | |
| Iñigo *Martínez* Berridi | 17.05.1991 | 15 | | 1 |
| Daniel *Vivian* Moreno | 05.07.1999 | 26 | (3) | 1 |
| *Yeray* Álvarez López | 24.01.1995 | 27 | (1) | 1 |
| *Yuri* Berchiche Izeta | 10.02.1990 | 27 | (2) | 1 |
| **Midfielders:** | **DOB** | **M** | **(s)** | **G** |
| *Ander Herrera* Agüera | 14.08.1989 | 9 | (8) | |

| | | | | |
|---|---|---|---|---|
| Daniel „*Dani*" *García* Carrillo | 24.05.1990 | 18 | (7) | |
| Iker *Muniain* Goñi | 19.12.1992 | 19 | (11) | |
| Oihan *Sancet* Tirapu | 25.04.2000 | 32 | (4) | 10 |
| Unai *Vencedor* París | 15.11.2000 | | (10) | |
| Mikel *Vesga* Arruti | 08.04.1993 | 28 | (8) | 3 |
| Oier *Zarraga* Egaña | 04.01.1999 | 6 | (20) | |
| **Forwards:** | **DOB** | **M** | **(s)** | **G** |
| Alejandro „*Álex*" *Berenguer* Remiro | 04.07.1995 | 26 | (11) | 4 |
| Gorka *Guruzeta* Rodríguez | 12.09.1996 | 17 | (13) | 6 |
| Iñaki *Williams* Arthuer | 15.06.1994 | 34 | (2) | 10 |
| Malcom Abdulai *Ares* Djalo | 12.10.2001 | | (8) | |
| Jon *Morcillo* Conesa | 15.09.1998 | | (10) | |
| Nicholas „*Nico*" *Williams* Arthuer | 12.07.2002 | 32 | (4) | 6 |
| Raúl *García* Escudero | 11.07.1986 | 6 | (29) | 2 |
| Asier *Villalibre* Molina | 30.09.1997 | 1 | (4) | |

## Club Atlético de Madrid

**Founded**: 26.04.1903 (*as Athletic Club de Madrid*)
**Stadium**: Estadio Metropolitano, Madrid (68,456)
**Trainer**: Diego Pablo Simeone (ARG)      28.04.1970

| Goalkeepers: | DOB | M | (s) | G |
|---|---|---|---|---|
| *Antonio Gomis* Alemañ | 20.05.2003 | | (1) | |
| Ivo Grbić (CRO) | 18.01.1996 | 10 | (2) | |
| Jan Oblak (SVN) | 07.01.1993 | 28 | | |
| **Defenders:** | **DOB** | **M** | **(s)** | **G** |
| Matthew James Doherty (IRL) | 16.01.1992 | | (2) | |
| *Felipe* Augusto de Almeida *Monteiro* (BRA) | 16.05.1989 | 2 | (1) | |
| José María *Giménez* de Vargas (URU) | 20.01.1995 | 26 | (2) | 2 |
| *Mario Hermoso* Canseco | 18.06.1995 | 24 | (2) | 3 |
| Nahuel Molina Lucero (ARG) | 06.04.1998 | 33 | | 4 |
| Sergio *Reguilón* Rodríguez | 16.12.1996 | 2 | (9) | |
| *Reinildo* Isnard Mandava (MOZ) | 21.01.1994 | 22 | | |
| Stefan Savić (MNE) | 08.01.1991 | 22 | | |
| **Midfielders:** | **DOB** | **M** | **(s)** | **G** |
| Rodrigo Javier De Paul (ARG) | 24.05.1994 | 24 | (6) | 2 |
| Jorge Resurrección Merodio „*Koke*" | 08.01.1992 | 30 | (3) | |

| | | | | |
|---|---|---|---|---|
| Geoffrey Edwin Kondogbia (CTA) | 15.02.1993 | 10 | (10) | |
| Thomas Benoît Lemar (FRA) | 12.11.1995 | 17 | (10) | 1 |
| *Marcos Llorente* Moreno | 30.01.1995 | 21 | (1) | 1 |
| *Pablo Barrios* Rivas | 15.06.2003 | 6 | (15) | |
| *Saúl* Ñíguez Esclapez | 21.11.1994 | 11 | (20) | 3 |
| Axel Laurent Angel Lambert Witsel (BEL) | 12.01.1989 | 25 | (8) | |
| **Forwards:** | **DOB** | **M** | **(s)** | **G** |
| *Álvaro* Borja *Morata* Martín | 23.10.1992 | 23 | (13) | 13 |
| *Carlos Martín* Domínguez | 22.04.2002 | | (4) | |
| Yannick Ferreira-Carrasco (BEL) | 04.09.1993 | 26 | (9) | 7 |
| Ángel Martín Correa Martínez (ARG) | 09.03.1995 | 13 | (22) | 9 |
| Memphis Depay (NED) | 13.02.1994 | 3 | (5) | 4 |
| Antoine Griezmann (FRA) | 21.03.1991 | 31 | (7) | 15 |
| João Félix Sequeira (POR) | 10.11.1999 | 7 | (7) | 4 |
| *Matheus* Santos Carneiro da *Cunha* (BRA) | 27.05.1999 | 2 | (9) | |

## Futbol Club Barcelona

**Founded**: 29.11.1899 (*as Foot-Ball Club Barcelona*)
**Stadium**: Estadio Camp Nou, Barcelona (99,354)
**Trainer**: Xavier Hernández Creus "Xavi"      25.01.1980

| Goalkeepers: | DOB | M | (s) | G |
|---|---|---|---|---|
| Iñaki Peña Sotorres | 02.03.1999 | | (2) | |
| Marc-André ter Stegen (GER) | 30.04.1992 | 38 | | |
| **Defenders:** | **DOB** | **M** | **(s)** | **G** |
| Alejandro „*Álex*" *Baldé* Martínez | 18.10.2003 | 30 | (3) | 1 |
| Ronald Federico Araújo da Silva (URU) | 07.03.1999 | 21 | (1) | |
| *Chadi Riad* Dnanou | 17.06.2003 | | (1) | |
| Andreas Bødtker Christensen (DEN) | 10.04.1996 | 22 | (1) | 1 |
| *Eric García* Martret | 09.01.2001 | 15 | (9) | 1 |
| *Héctor Bellerín* Moruno | 19.03.1995 | 1 | (2) | |
| *Jordi Alba* Ramos | 21.03.1989 | 14 | (10) | 2 |
| Jules Olivier Koundé (FRA) | 12.11.1998 | 28 | (1) | 1 |
| *Marcos Alonso* Mendoza | 28.12.1990 | 11 | (13) | 1 |
| Gerard *Piqué* i Bernabéu | 02.02.1987 | 4 | (2) | |
| *Sergi Roberto* Carnicer | 07.02.1992 | 15 | (8) | 4 |
| **Midfielders:** | **DOB** | **M** | **(s)** | **G** |
| *Aleix Garrido* Cañizares | 22.02.2004 | | (1) | |

| | | | | |
|---|---|---|---|---|
| Sergio *Busquets* Burgos | 16.07.1988 | 28 | (2) | |
| Frenkie de Jong (NED) | 12.05.1997 | 29 | (4) | 2 |
| Pablo Martín Páez Gavira „*Gavi*" | 05.08.2004 | 30 | (6) | 2 |
| Franck Yannick Kessié (CIV) | 19.12.1996 | 7 | (21) | 1 |
| *Pablo Torre* Carral | 03.04.2003 | 1 | (7) | |
| Pedro González López „*Pedri*" | 25.11.2002 | 22 | (4) | 6 |
| **Forwards:** | **DOB** | **M** | **(s)** | **G** |
| *Ángel Alarcón* Galiot | 15.05.2004 | | (4) | |
| Anssumane „*Ansu*" *Fati* Vieira | 31.10.2002 | 12 | (24) | 7 |
| Pierre-Emerick Emiliano François Aubameyang (GAB) | 18.06.1989 | | (1) | |
| Masour Ousmane Dembélé (FRA) | 15.05.1997 | 16 | (9) | 5 |
| Memphis Depay (NED) | 13.02.1994 | 2 | | 1 |
| *Ferrán Torres* García | 29.02.2000 | 14 | (19) | 4 |
| Lamine Yamal Nasraoui Ebana | 13.07.2007 | | (1) | |
| Robert Lewandowski (POL) | 21.08.1988 | 33 | (1) | 23 |
| Raphael Dias Belloli „*Raphinha*" (BRA) | 14.12.1996 | 25 | (11) | 7 |

## Cádiz Club de Fútbol

| | Founded: | 10.09.1910 | | |
|---|---|---|---|---|
| | Stadium: | Estadio Nuevo Mirandilla, Cádiz (20,724) | | |
| | Trainer: | Sergio González Soriano | 10.11.1976 | |

| Goalkeepers: | DOB | M | (s) | G |
|---|---|---|---|---|
| Jeremías Conán Ledesma (ARG) | 13.02.1993 | 34 | | |
| *David Gil* Mohedano | 11.01.1994 | 4 | | |
| **Defenders:** | **DOB** | **M** | **(s)** | **G** |
| Santiago Arzamendia Duarte (PAR) | 05.05.1998 | 5 | (7) | |
| Juan Torres Ruiz „*Cala*" | 26.11.1989 | 1 | (2) | |
| *Carlos García*-Die Sánchez | 07.07.2000 | | (1) | |
| Víctor *Chust* García | 05.03.2000 | 10 | (4) | 1 |
| Luis Alfonso Espino García (URU) | 05.01.1992 | 35 | (1) | |
| Rafael Jiménez Jarque „*Fali*" | 12.08.1993 | 22 | (3) | |
| Isaac Carcelén Valencia „*Iza*" | 23.04.1993 | 25 | (2) | |
| *Jorge Meré* Pérez | 17.04.1997 | 6 | (4) | |
| *Joseba Zaldua* Bengoetxea | 24.06.1992 | 7 | (3) | |
| *Luis Hernández* Rodríguez | 14.04.1989 | 35 | | |
| Mamadou „*Momo*" Mbaye (SEN) | 28.06.1998 | 7 | (7) | |
| *Raúl Parra* Artal | 26.11.1999 | 4 | (2) | |
| **Midfielders:** | **DOB** | **M** | **(s)** | **G** |
| Tomás Jesús Alarcón Vergara (CHI) | 19.01.1999 | 2 | (2) | |
| Rubén *Alcaraz* Jiménez | 01.05.1991 | 22 | (9) | 3 |
| Alejandro Fernández Iglesias „*Álex*" | 15.10.1992 | 17 | (11) | 3 |
| Antonio *Blanco* Conde | 23.07.2000 | 2 | (1) | |
| Youba Diarra (MLI) | 24.03.1998 | 1 | (4) | |
| Gonzalo Escalante (ARG) | 27.03.1993 | 13 | (1) | 4 |
| Federico San Emeterio Díaz „*Fede*" | 16.03.1997 | 24 | (9) | |
| José María Martín Bejarano-Serrano „*José Mari*" | 06.12.1987 | 2 | (16) | |
| **Forwards:** | **DOB** | **M** | **(s)** | **G** |
| Alberto Álvaro *Perea* Correoso | 19.12.1990 | 1 | | |
| *Álvaro Giménez* Candela | 19.05.1995 | | (1) | |
| *Álvaro Negredo* Sánchez | 20.08.1985 | 9 | (12) | 1 |
| Theo Bongonda Mbul'Ofeko Batombo (BEL) | 20.11.1995 | 24 | (7) | 4 |
| Christopher "*Chris*" *Ramos* De la Flor | 16.01.1997 | 7 | (8) | 1 |
| José Antonio *De la Rosa* Garrido | 28.07.2004 | | (2) | |
| Mamady Diarra (MLI) | 26.06.2000 | 1 | (1) | |
| *Iván Alejo* Peralta | 10.02.1995 | 13 | (18) | |
| Anthony Rubén Lozano Colón (HON) | 25.04.1993 | 14 | (14) | 1 |
| *Lucas Pérez* Martínez | 10.09.1988 | 5 | (9) | 3 |
| Awer Bul Mabil (AUS) | 15.09.1995 | 1 | (4) | |
| Francisco Mwepu (ZAM) | 29.02.2000 | | (1) | |
| Brian Alexis Ocampo Ferreira (URU) | 25.06.1999 | 15 | (3) | 1 |
| *Roger Martí* Salvador | 03.01.1991 | 8 | (6) | 1 |
| *Rubén Sobrino* Pozuelo | 01.06.1992 | 28 | (5) | 3 |
| *Sergi Guardiola* Navarro | 29.05.1991 | 14 | (3) | 3 |

## Real Club Celta de Vigo

| | Founded: | 23.08.1923 | | |
|---|---|---|---|---|
| | Stadium: | Estadio Abanca-Balaídos, Vigo (29,000) | | |
| | Trainer: | Eduardo Germán Coudet (ARG) | 12.09.1974 | |
| [02.11.2022] | | Carlos Augusto Soares da Costa Faria Carvalhal (POR) | 04.12.1965 | |

| Goalkeepers: | DOB | M | (s) | G |
|---|---|---|---|---|
| *Iván Villar* Martínez | 09.07.1997 | 19 | | |
| Agustín Federico Marchesín (ARG) | 16.03.1988 | 19 | | |
| **Defenders:** | **DOB** | **M** | **(s)** | **G** |
| Joseph Aidoo (GHA) | 29.09.1995 | 35 | | 3 |
| *Carlos Domínguez* Cáceres | 11.02.2001 | 1 | (2) | |
| *Fernando Medrano* Gastañaga | 26.03.2000 | | (1) | |
| *Hugo Mallo* Novegil | 22.06.1991 | 26 | | |
| Javier „*Javi*" *Galán* Gil | 19.11.1994 | 36 | (1) | |
| *Kevin Vázquez* Comesaña | 23.03.1993 | 6 | (4) | |
| *Óscar Mingueza* García | 13.05.1999 | 13 | (8) | |
| *Unai Núñez* Gestoso | 30.01.1997 | 35 | (1) | |
| **Midfielders:** | **DOB** | **M** | **(s)** | **G** |
| Francisco José "*Fran*" *Beltrán* Peinado | 03.02.1999 | 33 | (3) | |
| Gabriel „*Gabri*" *Veiga* Novas | 27.05.2002 | 28 | (8) | 11 |
| *Hugo Sotelo* Gómez | 19.12.2003 | | (1) | |
| Luca Daniel de la Torre (USA) | 23.05.1998 | 16 | (12) | |
| *Óscar Rodríguez* Arnaiz | 28.06.1998 | 19 | (14) | 2 |
| Williot Theo Swedberg (SWE) | 01.02.2004 | | (4) | |
| Renato Fabrizio Tapia Cortijo (PER) | 28.07.1995 | 16 | (12) | |
| **Forwards:** | **DOB** | **M** | **(s)** | **G** |
| *Carles Pérez* Sayol | 16.02.1998 | 23 | (12) | 3 |
| Franco Emanuel Cervi (ARG) | 26.05.1994 | 21 | (15) | |
| *Gonçalo* Mendes *Paciência* (POR) | 01.08.1994 | 5 | (20) | 2 |
| *Iago Aspas* Juncal | 01.08.1987 | 31 | (6) | 12 |
| *Miguel Rodríguez* Vidal | 29.04.2003 | 3 | (4) | 1 |
| *Pablo Durán* Fernández | 25.05.2001 | | (4) | |
| Haris Seferović (SUI) | 22.02.1992 | 10 | (8) | 3 |
| Augusto Jorge Mateo Solari (ARG) | 03.01.1992 | 3 | (9) | |
| Jørgen Strand Larsen (NOR) | 06.02.2000 | 20 | (12) | 4 |

## Elche Club de Fútbol

| | Founded: | 1923 | | |
|---|---|---|---|---|
| | Stadium: | Estadio „Martínez Valero", Elche, (31,388) | | |
| | Trainer: | Francisco Javier Rodríguez Vílchez | 17.06.1978 | |
| [05.10.2022] | | Alberto Gallego Laencuentra | 16.03.1974 | |
| [12.10.2022] | | Jorge Francisco Almirón Quintana (ARG) | 19.06.1971 | |
| [07.11.2022] | | Sergio Martínez Mantecón | 08.06.1980 | |
| [17.11.2022] | | Pablo Machín Díez | 07.04.1975 | |
| [21.03.2023] | | Sebastián Andrés Beccacece (ARG) | 17.12.1980 | |

| Goalkeepers: | DOB | M | (s) | G |
|---|---|---|---|---|
| *Édgar Badía* Guardiola | 12.02.1992 | 36 | | |
| Axel Wilfredo Werner (ARG) | 28.02.1996 | 2 | | |
| **Defenders:** | **DOB** | **M** | **(s)** | **G** |
| Pedro *Bigas* Rigo | 15.05.1990 | 25 | (3) | |
| Lautaro Emanuel Blanco (ARG) | 19.02.1999 | 9 | (8) | |
| *Carlos Clerc* Martínez | 21.02.1992 | 31 | (1) | |
| John *Chetauya* Nwankwo Donald Okeh | 25.09.2000 | 13 | (1) | |
| *Diego González* Polanco | 28.01.1995 | 8 | (8) | |
| Federico Fernández (ARG) | 21.02.1989 | 1 | | |
| Nicolás Ezequiel Fernández Marcau (ARG) | 11.01.2000 | 3 | (15) | |
| *Gonzalo Cacicedo Verdú* | 21.10.1988 | 9 | (7) | 1 |
| *José Ángel Carmona* Navarro | 29.01.2002 | 8 | (1) | 1 |
| *Pol* Mikel *Lirola* Kosok | 13.08.1997 | 7 | (5) | 1 |
| Lisandro Magallán Orueta (ARG) | 27.09.1993 | 11 | (3) | |
| Johan Andrés Mojica Palacio (COL) | 21.08.1992 | 3 | | |
| Helibelton Palacios Zapata (COL) | 11.06.1993 | 23 | (1) | |
| Enzo Pablo Roco Roco (CHI) | 16.08.1992 | 19 | (3) | |
| **Midfielders:** | **DOB** | **M** | **(s)** | **G** |
| Alejandro *Alfaro* Cascales | 15.06.2002 | | (1) | |
| Pape Cheikh Diop (SEN) | 08.08.1997 | | (2) | |
| Domingos Quina (POR) | 18.11.1999 | 2 | (8) | |
| Gerard *Gumbau* Garriga | 18.12.1994 | 31 | (4) | 1 |
| Randy Nteka (FRA) | 06.12.1997 | 10 | (4) | |
| *Omar Mascarell* González | 02.02.1993 | 28 | | |
| Javier Matías Pastore (ARG) | 20.06.1989 | | (1) | |
| José Raúl Gutiérrez Parejo „*Raúl Guti*" | 30.12.1996 | 12 | (16) | |
| **Forwards:** | **DOB** | **M** | **(s)** | **G** |
| *Álex Collado* Gutiérrez | 22.04.1999 | 8 | (7) | 1 |
| Lucas Ariel Boyé (ARG) | 28.02.1996 | 29 | (6) | 7 |
| *Fidel* Chaves De La Torre | 27.10.1989 | 21 | (6) | 3 |
| José Antonio Ferrández Pomares „*Josan*" | 03.12.1989 | 9 | (17) | 1 |
| *Pere Milla* Peña | 23.09.1992 | 21 | (10) | 6 |
| Ezequiel Ponce Martínez (ARG) | 29.03.1997 | 8 | (26) | 4 |
| *Roger Martí* Salvador | 03.01.1991 | 8 | (4) | |
| José Antonio „*Tete*" *Morente* Oliva | 04.12.1996 | 23 | (9) | 4 |

## Reial Club Deportiu Espanyol de Barcelona

| | | | |
|---|---|---|---|
| **Founded**: | 28.10.1900 | | |
| **Stadium**: | RCDE Stadium [Estadi Cornellà-El Prat], Barcelona (40,000) | | |
| **Trainer**: | Diego Martínez Penas | | 16.12.1980 |
| [03.04.2023] | Luis García Fernández | | 06.02.1981 |

| Goalkeepers: | DOB | M | (s) | G |
|---|---|---|---|---|
| *Álvaro Fernández* Llorente | 13.04.1998 | 11 | | |
| *Joan García* Pons | 04.05.2001 | 1 | | |
| Benjamin Pascal Lecomte (FRA) | 26.04.1991 | 10 | | |
| Fernando *Pacheco* Flores | 18.05.1992 | 16 | | |
| **Defenders:** | **DOB** | **M** | **(s)** | **G** |
| Adrià Giner *Pedrosa* | 13.05.1998 | 2 | (5) | |
| *Brian Oliván* Herrero | 01.04.1994 | 29 | (1) | 1 |
| Leandro Daniel Cabrera Sasía (URU) | 17.06.1991 | 31 | (1) | |
| Omar El Hilali (MAR) | 12.09.2003 | 1 | (4) | |
| *Fernando Calero* Villa | 14.09.1995 | 20 | (7) | |
| César Jasib Montes Castro (MEX) | 24.02.1997 | 18 | (2) | 3 |
| *Óscar Gil* Regaño | 26.04.1998 | 31 | (2) | |
| Ronaël Pierre-Gabriel (FRA) | 13.06.1998 | 2 | (6) | 1 |
| *Rubén Sánchez* Sáez | 04.02.2001 | 9 | (9) | |
| *Sergi Gómez* Solà | 28.03.1992 | 26 | (3) | |
| *Simo* Wassim Keddari Boulif | 03.02.2005 | | (7) | |
| **Midfielders:** | **DOB** | **M** | **(s)** | **G** |
| Keidi Bare (ALB) | 28.08.1997 | 4 | (14) | |
| *Denis Suárez* Fernández | 06.01.1994 | 11 | (7) | |
| Eduardo „*Edu*" *Expósito* Jaén | 01.08.1996 | 13 | (15) | 2 |
| *José Gragera* Amado | 14.05.2000 | 5 | (4) | 1 |
| *Pol Lozano* Vizuete | 06.10.1999 | | (4) | |
| *Roger Martínez* Santamaria | 05.04.2004 | | (1) | |
| *Sergi Darder* Moll | 22.12.1993 | 38 | | 6 |
| *Vinicius* de Souza Costa (BRA) | 17.06.1999 | 27 | (7) | 1 |
| **Forwards:** | **DOB** | **M** | **(s)** | **G** |
| *Adrián Embarba* Blázquez | 07.05.1992 | | (1) | |
| *Aleix Vidal* Parreu | 21.08.1989 | 10 | (15) | |
| Martin Christensen Braithwaite (DEN) | 05.06.1991 | 29 | (2) | 10 |
| Daniel „*Dani*" *Gómez* Alcón | 30.07.1998 | | (8) | |
| *Javier Puado* Díaz | 25.05.1998 | 25 | (12) | 7 |
| José Luis Mato Sanmartín „*Joselu*" | 27.03.1990 | 33 | (1) | 16 |
| Luca Warrick Daeovie Koleosho (USA) | 15.09.2004 | | (4) | 1 |
| José Carlos *Lazo* Romero | 16.02.1996 | | (10) | 1 |
| Nicolás „*Nico*" *Melamed* Ribaudo | 11.04.2001 | 16 | (16) | 1 |
| Nabil Zoubdi Touaizi (MAR) | 01.02.2001 | | (1) | |

## Getafe Club de Fútbol

| | | | |
|---|---|---|---|
| **Founded**: | 08.07.1983 | | |
| **Stadium**: | Estadio Coliseum „Alfonso Pérez", Getafe (16,500) | | |
| **Trainer**: | Enrique "Quique" Sánchez Flores | | 05.02.1965 |
| [29.04.2023] | José Bordalás Jiménez | | 05.03.1964 |

| Goalkeepers: | DOB | M | (s) | G |
|---|---|---|---|---|
| *David Soria* Solís | 04.04.1993 | 38 | | |
| **Defenders:** | **DOB** | **M** | **(s)** | **G** |
| Omar Federico Alderete Fernández (PAR) | 26.12.1996 | 23 | (2) | 1 |
| Alejandro „*Álex*" *Revuelta* Montero | 16.04.2000 | | (1) | |
| Pedro Gastón Álvarez Sosa (URU) | 24.03.2000 | 16 | (6) | 2 |
| Jordan Kévin Amavi (FRA) | 09.03.1994 | 1 | (4) | |
| Fabrizio Germán Angileri (ARG) | 15.03.1994 | 7 | (8) | |
| Dakonam Djené (TOG) | 31.12.1991 | 33 | | |
| *Domingos* de Sousa Coutinho Meneses *Duarte* (POR) | 10.03.1995 | 30 | (1) | |
| Juan Antonio *Iglesias* Sánchez | 03.07.1998 | 21 | (11) | 1 |
| Stefan Mitrovič (SRB) | 22.05.1990 | 18 | (4) | |
| Damián Nicolás Suárez Suárez (URU) | 27.04.1988 | 26 | (2) | 1 |
| **Midfielders:** | **DOB** | **M** | **(s)** | **G** |
| *Ángel Algobia* Esteves | 23.06.1999 | 11 | (15) | |
| Mauro Wilney Arambarri Rosa (URU) | 30.09.1995 | 13 | | |
| *Carles Aleñá* Castillo | 05.01.1998 | 26 | (9) | 2 |
| *Gonzalo Villar* del Fraile | 23.03.1998 | 3 | (13) | |
| *Luis Milla* Manzanares | 07.10.1994 | 22 | (5) | |
| Nemanja Maksimović (SRB) | 26.01.1995 | 26 | (3) | |
| Jaime *Seoane* Valenciano | 22.01.1997 | 2 | (14) | |
| **Forwards:** | **DOB** | **M** | **(s)** | **G** |
| Munir El Haddadi Mohamed (MAR) | 01.09.1995 | 10 | (18) | 3 |
| *Borja Mayoral* Moya | 05.04.1997 | 33 | (2) | 8 |
| Jaime *Mata* Arnaiz | 24.10.1988 | 5 | (13) | 1 |
| Juan Miguel *Latasa* Fernández Layos | 23.03.2001 | 2 | (16) | 1 |
| Moisés Parra Gutiérrez „*Moi Parra*" | 24.06.2002 | | (1) | |
| Cristian Portugués Manzanera „*Portu*" | 21.05.1992 | 17 | (17) | |
| Enes Ünal (TUR) | 10.05.1997 | 35 | | 14 |

## Girona Futbol Club

| | | | |
|---|---|---|---|
| **Founded**: | 23.07.1930 | | |
| **Stadium**: | Estadi Montilivi, Girona (13,400) | | |
| **Trainer**: | Miguel Ángel Sánchez Muñoz "Míchel" | | 30.10.1975 |

| Goalkeepers: | DOB | M | (s) | G |
|---|---|---|---|---|
| Paulo Dino Gazzaniga Farias (ARG) | 02.01.1992 | 28 | | |
| *Juan Carlos* Martín Corral | 20.01.1988 | 10 | | |
| **Defenders:** | **DOB** | **M** | **(s)** | **G** |
| *Arnau Martínez* López | 25.04.2003 | 32 | (1) | 3 |
| Santiago Ignacio Bueno Sciutto (URU) | 09.11.1998 | 34 | | |
| Alexander Martín Marquinho Callens Asín (PER) | 04.05.1992 | | (6) | |
| *David López* Silva | 09.10.1989 | 19 | (1) | 3 |
| Bernardo José Espinosa Zúñiga (COL) | 11.07.1989 | 14 | (6) | 1 |
| Javier „*Javi*" *Hernández* Carrera | 02.05.1998 | 13 | (12) | 1 |
| Juan Pedro Ramírez López „*Juanpe*" | 30.04.1991 | 17 | (2) | 1 |
| *Miguel Gutiérrez* Ortega | 27.07.2001 | 27 | (7) | 2 |
| *Yan* Bueno *Couto* (BRA) | 03.06.2002 | 12 | (13) | 1 |
| **Midfielders:** | **DOB** | **M** | **(s)** | **G** |
| *Aleix García* Serrano | 28.06.1997 | 26 | (4) | 1 |
| Ricard *Artero* Ruiz | 05.02.2003 | | (7) | |
| *Borja García* Freire | 02.11.1990 | 10 | (1) | 1 |
| Yangel Clemente Herrera Ravelo (VEN) | 07.01.1998 | 12 | (8) | 2 |
| *Iván Martín* Núñez | 14.02.1999 | 18 | (6) | 3 |
| *Oriol Romeu* Vidal | 24.09.1991 | 33 | | 2 |
| *Ramón Terrats* Espacio | 18.10.2000 | 2 | (6) | |
| *Reinier* Jesus Carvalho (BRA) | 19.01.2002 | 5 | (13) | 2 |
| Samuel „*Samu*" *Sáiz* Alonso | 22.01.1991 | 1 | (7) | 2 |
| **Forwards:** | **DOB** | **M** | **(s)** | **G** |
| Valentín Mariano José Castellanos Giménez(ARG) | 03.10.1998 | 33 | (2) | 13 |
| *Joel Roca* Casals | 07.06.2005 | | (5) | |
| Manuel „*Manu*" Javier *Vallejo* Galván | 14.02.1997 | 2 | (5) | |
| *Óscar Ureña* García | 31.05.2003 | 1 | (2) | |
| *Rodrigo Riquelme* Reche | 02.04.2000 | 25 | (9) | 4 |
| Cristhian Ricardo Stuani Curbelo (URU) | 12.10.1986 | 8 | (24) | 9 |
| Viktor Tsygankov (UKR) | 15.11.1997 | 17 | (2) | 3 |
| Laureano Antonio „*Toni*" *Villa* Suárez | 07.01.1995 | 12 | (12) | 1 |
| *Valery* Fernández Estrada | 23.11.1999 | 7 | (18) | |

## Real Club Deportivo Mallorca

**Founded:** 05.03.1916
**Stadium:** Estadio Mallorca Son Moix, Palma de Mallorca (23,142)
**Trainer:** Javier Aguirre Onaindía (MEX)  01.12.1958

| Goalkeepers: | DOB | M | (s) | G |
|---|---|---|---|---|
| Dominik Greif (SVK) | 06.04.1997 | 1 | | |
| Leonardo „Leo" Román Riquelme | 06.07.2000 | 1 | | |
| Predrag Rajković (SRB) | 31.10.1995 | 36 | | |
| **Defenders:** | **DOB** | **M** | **(s)** | **G** |
| Hans Carl Ludwig Augustinsson (SWE) | 21.04.1994 | 1 | (3) | |
| José Manuel Arias Copete | 10.10.1999 | 27 | (1) | 1 |
| Braian Ezequiel Cufré (ARG) | 15.12.1996 | 2 | (3) | |
| Giovanni Alessandro González Apud (URU) | 20.09.1994 | 9 | (6) | |
| Dennis Hadžikadunić (BIH) | 09.07.1998 | 7 | (1) | |
| Jaume Vincent Costa Jordá | 18.03.1988 | 30 | (2) | |
| Josep Antoni Gayá Martínez | 07.07.2000 | 1 | (1) | |
| Matija Nastasić (SRB) | 28.03.1993 | 10 | (4) | 1 |
| Pablo Carmine Maffeo Becerra | 12.07.1997 | 34 | (1) | 2 |
| Antonio José Raíllo Arenas | 08.10.1991 | 31 | | 2 |
| Franco Matías Russo Panos (ARG) | 25.10.1994 | 2 | (1) | |
| Martin Valjent (SVK) | 11.12.1995 | 30 | | |

| Midfielders: | DOB | M | (s) | G |
|---|---|---|---|---|
| Antonio Sánchez Navarro | 22.04.1997 | 11 | (21) | |
| Iddrisu Baba (GHA) | 22.01.1996 | 20 | (9) | |
| Rodrigo Andrés Battaglia (ARG) | 12.07.1991 | 8 | (7) | |
| Daniel „Dani" Rodríguez Vázquez | 06.06.1988 | 26 | (9) | 3 |
| Clément Grenier (FRA) | 07.01.1991 | 6 | (15) | |
| Lee Kang-in (KOR) | 19.02.2001 | 33 | (3) | 6 |
| Manuel „Manu" Morlanes Ariño | 12.01.1999 | 9 | (3) | 1 |
| Rubén Quintanilla Rodríguez | 03.04.2002 | | (1) | |
| Iñigo Ruiz de Galarreta | 06.08.1993 | 28 | (2) | |
| **Forwards:** | **DOB** | **M** | **(s)** | **G** |
| Abdón Prats Bastidas | 07.12.1992 | 2 | (24) | 1 |
| Ángel Luís Rodríguez Díaz | 26.04.1987 | 2 | (15) | 1 |
| Javier Llabrés Expósito | 11.09.2002 | | (1) | |
| Philana Tinotenda Kadewere (ZIM) | 05.01.1996 | 5 | (10) | 1 |
| Júnior Waka Lible Lago „Lago Júnior" (CIV) | 31.12.1990 | | (5) | |
| Vedat Muriqi (KOS) | 24.04.1994 | 34 | (1) | 15 |
| Amath Ndiaye Diedhiou (SEN) | 16.07.1996 | 12 | (16) | 2 |

## Club Atlético Osasuna Pamplona

**Founded:** 24.10.1920
**Stadium:** Estadio El Sadar, Pamplona (23,576)
**Trainer:** Jagoba Arrasate Elustondo  22.04.1978

| Goalkeepers: | DOB | M | (s) | G |
|---|---|---|---|---|
| Aitor Fernández Abarisketa | 03.05.1991 | 21 | | |
| Sergio Herrera Pirón | 05.06.1993 | 17 | | |
| **Defenders:** | **DOB** | **M** | **(s)** | **G** |
| Aridane Hernández Umpiérrez | 23.03.1989 | 20 | (3) | |
| David García Zubiria | 14.02.1994 | 31 | (1) | 2 |
| Diego Moreno Garbayo | 21.06.2001 | 7 | (4) | |
| Jorge Herrando Oroz | 28.02.2001 | 1 | | |
| Juan Cruz Álvaro Armada | 28.07.1992 | 21 | (6) | |
| Manuel "Manu" Sánchez de la Peña | 24.08.2000 | 22 | (9) | |
| Ignacio „Nacho" Vidal Miralles | 24.01.1995 | 15 | (5) | |
| Rubén Peña Jiménez | 18.07.1991 | 14 | (6) | |
| Unai García Lugea | 03.02.1992 | 20 | (1) | |
| **Midfielders:** | **DOB** | **M** | **(s)** | **G** |
| Aimar Oroz Huarte | 27.11.2001 | 23 | (8) | 3 |

| | DOB | M | (s) | G |
|---|---|---|---|---|
| Darko Brašanac (SRB) | 12.02.1992 | 9 | (16) | 1 |
| Iker Muñoz Cameros | 05.11.2002 | 2 | (6) | |
| Lucas Torró Marset | 19.07.1994 | 31 | (2) | 1 |
| Jon Moncayola Tollar | 13.05.1998 | 25 | (12) | 1 |
| Pablo Ibáñez Lumbreras | 20.09.1998 | 12 | (13) | |
| Roberto Torres Morales | 07.03.1989 | | (2) | |
| **Forwards:** | **DOB** | **M** | **(s)** | **G** |
| Luis Ezequiel Ávila (ARG) | 06.02.1994 | 23 | (6) | 8 |
| Ante Budimir (CRO) | 22.07.1991 | 22 | (9) | 8 |
| Abde Ezzalzouli (MAR) | 17.12.2001 | 19 | (9) | 4 |
| Iker Benito Sánchez | 10.08.2002 | 2 | (2) | |
| Enrique Barja Afonso „Kike Barja" | 01.04.1997 | 15 | (12) | 1 |
| Enrique García Martínez „Kike García" | 25.11.1989 | 7 | (28) | 2 |
| Moisés „Moi" Gómez Bordonado | 23.06.1994 | 28 | (5) | 3 |
| Rubén García Santos | 14.07.1993 | 11 | (18) | 2 |

## Rayo Vallecano de Madrid

**Founded:** 29.05.1924
**Stadium:** Campo de Fútbol de Vallecas, Madrid (14,708)
**Trainer:** Andoni Iraola Sagarna  22.06.1982

| Goalkeepers: | DOB | M | (s) | G |
|---|---|---|---|---|
| Diego López Rodríguez | 03.11.1981 | 1 | (1) | |
| Stole Dimitrievski (MKD) | 25.12.1993 | 37 | | |
| **Defenders:** | **DOB** | **M** | **(s)** | **G** |
| Iván Balliu Campeny (ALB) | 01.01.1992 | 37 | | |
| Alejandro Catena Marugán | 28.10.1994 | 35 | | 1 |
| Francisco „Fran" José García Torres | 14.08.1999 | 38 | | 2 |
| Florian Grégoire Claude Lejeune (FRA) | 20.05.1991 | 31 | | 4 |
| Mario Hernández Fernández | 25.01.1999 | 1 | (2) | |
| Mario Suárez Mata | 24.02.1987 | | (2) | |
| Khalid Abdul Mumin Suleman (GHA) | 06.06.1998 | 9 | (7) | |
| Josep „Pep" María Chavarría Pérez | 10.04.1998 | 2 | (14) | |
| Esteban Ariel Saveljić (ARG) | 20.05.1991 | | (1) | |
| **Midfielders:** | **DOB** | **M** | **(s)** | **G** |
| Ismaila Pathé Ciss (SEN) | 16.03.1994 | 12 | (20) | 1 |
| Diego Méndez Molero | 29.08.2003 | | (1) | |

| | DOB | M | (s) | G |
|---|---|---|---|---|
| José Ángel Pozo la Rosa | 15.03.1996 | 1 | (7) | |
| Randy Nteka (FRA) | 06.12.1997 | | (10) | |
| Óscar Valentín Martín Luengo | 20.08.1994 | 29 | (5) | |
| Santiago „Santi" Comesaña Veiga | 05.10.1996 | 29 | (6) | 3 |
| Óscar Guido Trejo (ARG) | 26.04.1988 | 28 | (6) | 3 |
| Unai López Cabrera | 30.10.1995 | 12 | (22) | 1 |
| **Forwards:** | **DOB** | **M** | **(s)** | **G** |
| Álvaro García Rivera | 27.10.1992 | 34 | (1) | 5 |
| Andrés Martín García | 11.07.1999 | 3 | (6) | |
| Tiago Manuel Dias Correia „Bebé" (POR) | 12.07.1990 | | (4) | |
| Radamel Falcao García Zárate (COL) | 10.02.1986 | 3 | (24) | 2 |
| Isaac „Isi" Palazón Camacho | 27.12.1994 | 36 | (1) | 9 |
| Pablo Muñoz Crespo | 04.09.2003 | | (2) | |
| Raúl de Tomás Gómez | 17.10.1994 | 9 | (10) | 4 |
| Salvador Sánchez Ponce „Salvi" | 30.03.1991 | 4 | (20) | |
| Sergio Camello Pérez | 10.02.2001 | 27 | (11) | 6 |

## Real Betis Balompié Sevilla

**Founded:** 12.09.1907
**Stadium:** Estadio "Benito Villamarín", Sevilla (60,721)
**Trainer:** Manuel Luis Pellegrini Ripamonti (CHI)  16.09.1953

| Goalkeepers: | DOB | M | (s) | G |
|---|---|---|---|---|
| Claudio Andrés Bravo Muñoz (CHI) | 13.04.1983 | 12 | | |
| Rui Tiago Dantas da Silva (POR) | 07.02.1994 | 26 | | |
| **Defenders:** | **DOB** | **M** | **(s)** | **G** |
| Abner Vinicius Da Silva Santos (BRA) | 27.05.2000 | 7 | (6) | |
| Alexandre „Álex" Moreno Lopera | 08.06.1993 | 15 | | |
| Aitor Ruibal García | 22.03.1996 | 15 | (11) | |
| Édgar González Estrada | 01.04.1997 | 18 | (7) | |
| Félix Martí Garreta | 21.04.2004 | 1 | | |
| Francisco „Fran" Javier Delgado Rojano | 11.07.2001 | | (1) | |
| Juan Miranda González | 19.01.2000 | 16 | (5) | 3 |
| Luiz Felipe Ramos Marchi (ITA) | 22.03.1997 | 22 | (1) | |
| Martín Montoya Torralbo | 14.04.1991 | 6 | | |
| Germán Alejo Pezzella (ARG) | 27.06.1991 | 29 | (2) | |
| Youssouf Sabaly (SEN) | 05.03.1993 | 19 | (4) | 1 |
| Víctor Ruiz Torre | 25.01.1989 | 5 | (5) | |

| Midfielders: | DOB | M | (s) | G |
|---|---|---|---|---|
| Edgar Paul Akouokou (CIV) | 20.12.1997 | 3 | (9) | |
| Sergio Canales Madrazo | 16.02.1991 | 28 | (3) | 4 |
| Nabil Fekir (FRA) | 18.07.1993 | 12 | (3) | 2 |
| José Andrés Guardado Hernández (MEX) | 28.09.1986 | 16 | (10) | 1 |
| Rodrigo Sánchez Rodríguez „Rodri" | 16.05.2000 | 19 | (11) | 2 |
| Guido Rodríguez (ARG) | 12.04.1994 | 33 | (1) | 1 |
| William Silva de Carvalho (POR) | 07.04.1992 | 31 | (2) | 3 |
| **Forwards:** | **DOB** | **M** | **(s)** | **G** |
| Ayoze Pérez Gutiérrez | 29.07.1993 | 17 | (2) | 3 |
| Borja Iglesias Quintas | 17.01.1993 | 29 | (6) | 15 |
| Joaquín Sánchez Rodríguez | 21.07.1981 | 2 | (20) | |
| Juan Cruz Díaz Espósito | 25.04.2000 | 1 | (5) | 1 |
| Juan Miguel Jiménez López „Juanmi" | 20.05.1993 | 9 | (13) | 4 |
| Lorenzo Morón García „Loren" | 30.12.1993 | | (2) | |
| Luiz Henrique André Rosa da Silva (BRA) | 02.01.2001 | 21 | (12) | 1 |
| Roberto „Rober" González Bayón | 06.01.2001 | | (2) | |
| Willian José da Silva (BRA) | 23.11.1991 | 6 | (22) | 2 |

## Real Madrid Club de Fútbol

**Founded**: 06.03.1902 (*as Madrid Football Club*)
**Stadium**: Estadio "Santiago Bernabéu", Madrid (65,000)
**Trainer**: Carlo Ancelotti (ITA)                    10.06.1959

| Goalkeepers: | DOB | M | (s) | G |
|---|---|---|---|---|
| Thibaut Nicolas Marc Courtois (BEL) | 11.05.1992 | 31 | | |
| Andriy Lunin (UKR) | 11.02.1999 | 7 | | |
| **Defenders:** | **DOB** | **M** | **(s)** | **G** |
| David Olatukunbo Alaba (AUT) | 24.06.1992 | 21 | (2) | 1 |
| *Álvaro Odriozola* Arzallus | 14.12.1995 | | (3) | |
| Daniel *„Dani"* Carvajal Ramos | 11.01.1992 | 20 | (7) | |
| *Eder* Gabriel *Militão* (BRA) | 18.01.1998 | 30 | (3) | 5 |
| *Jesús Vallejo* Lázaro | 05.01.1997 | | (1) | |
| *Lucas Vázquez* Iglesias | 01.07.1991 | 12 | (11) | 4 |
| Ferland Mendy (FRA) | 08.06.1995 | 17 | (1) | |
| José Ignacio Fernández Iglesias *„Nacho"* | 18.01.1990 | 18 | (9) | 1 |
| Antonio Rüdiger (GER) | 03.03.1993 | 26 | (7) | 1 |
| **Midfielders:** | **DOB** | **M** | **(s)** | **G** |
| Sergio *Arribas* Calvo | 30.09.2001 | | (2) | |

| | DOB | M | (s) | G |
|---|---|---|---|---|
| Eduardo Celmi Camavinga (FRA) | 10.11.2002 | 21 | (16) | |
| Carlos Henrique Casimiro *„Casemiro"* (BRA) | 23.02.1992 | | (1) | |
| Daniel *„Dani"* Ceballos Fernández | 07.08.1996 | 19 | (11) | |
| Toni Kroos (GER) | 04.01.1990 | 25 | (5) | 2 |
| Luka Modrić (CRO) | 09.09.1985 | 19 | (14) | 4 |
| Aurélien Djani Tchouaméni (FRA) | 27.01.2000 | 24 | (9) | |
| Federico Santiago Valverde Dipetta (URU) | 22.07.1998 | 29 | (5) | 7 |
| **Forwards:** | **DOB** | **M** | **(s)** | **G** |
| Karim Mostafa Benzema (FRA) | 19.12.1987 | 24 | | 19 |
| Eden Michael Hazard (BEL) | 07.01.1991 | 2 | (4) | |
| *Marco Asensio* Willemsen | 21.01.1996 | 15 | (16) | 9 |
| *Mariano Díaz* Mejía (DOM) | 01.08.1993 | 1 | (8) | |
| Álvaro Daniel *Rodríguez* Muñoz | 14.07.2004 | | (6) | 1 |
| *Rodrygo* Silva de Goes (BRA) | 09.01.2001 | 25 | (9) | 9 |
| *Vinícius* José Paixão de Oliveira *Júnior* (BRA) | 12.07.2000 | 32 | (1) | 10 |

## Real Sociedad de Fútbol San Sebastián

**Founded**: 07.09.1909
**Stadium**: Estadio Anoeta [Reale Arena], San Sebastián (39,500)
**Trainer**: Imanol Alguacil Barrenetxea                    04.07.1971

| Goalkeepers: | DOB | M | (s) | G |
|---|---|---|---|---|
| Alejandro *Remiro* Gargallo | 24.03.1995 | 38 | | |
| **Defenders:** | **DOB** | **M** | **(s)** | **G** |
| *Aihen Muñoz* Capellán | 16.08.1997 | 20 | (3) | |
| *Álex Sola* López Ocaña | 09.06.1999 | 3 | (7) | |
| *Andoni Gorosabel* Espinosa | 04.08.1996 | 19 | (8) | |
| *Aritz Elustondo* Irribaría | 28.03.1994 | 16 | (9) | |
| *Diego Rico* Salguero | 23.02.1993 | 18 | (2) | |
| *Jon Pacheco* Dozagarat | 08.01.2001 | 12 | (5) | |
| Robin Aimé Robert Le Normand | 11.11.1996 | 31 | (2) | |
| Igor *Zubeldía* Elorza | 30.03.1997 | 29 | (2) | 1 |
| **Midfielders:** | **DOB** | **M** | **(s)** | **G** |
| *Brais Méndez* Portela | 07.01.1997 | 28 | (6) | 8 |
| *David* Josué Jiménez *Silva* | 08.01.1986 | 25 | (3) | 2 |
| Ander *Guevara* Lajo | 07.07.1997 | 2 | (6) | |
| Asier Illarramendi Andonegu *„Illarra"* | 08.03.1990 | 13 | (11) | 1 |
| *Jon Magunazelaia* Argoitia | 13.07.2001 | | (2) | |

| | DOB | M | (s) | G |
|---|---|---|---|---|
| *Martín Zubimendi* Ibáñez | 02.02.1999 | 35 | (1) | 1 |
| *Mikel Merino* Zazón | 22.06.1996 | 28 | (5) | 2 |
| Jon Ander *Olasagasti* Imizcoz | 16.08.2000 | | (3) | |
| *Pablo Marín* Tejada | 03.07.2003 | 3 | (7) | |
| *Robert Navarro* Muñoz | 12.04.2002 | 1 | (16) | |
| Beñat *Turrientes* Imaz | 31.01.2002 | 1 | (5) | |
| **Forwards:** | **DOB** | **M** | **(s)** | **G** |
| *Ander Barrenetxea* Muguruza | 27.12.2001 | 9 | (14) | 3 |
| *Ander Martín* Odriozola | 16.11.2000 | | (3) | |
| *Carlos Fernández* Luna | 22.05.1996 | 8 | (16) | 1 |
| Mohamed-Ali Cho (FRA) | 19.01.2004 | 5 | (14) | 1 |
| Alexander Isak (SWE) | 21.09.1999 | 2 | | 1 |
| *Jon Karrikaburu* Jaimerena | 19.09.2002 | | (6) | |
| Takefusa Kubo (JPN) | 04.06.2001 | 29 | (6) | 9 |
| *Mikel Oyarzabal* Ugarte | 21.04.1997 | 14 | (9) | 4 |
| Umar Sadiq Mesbah (NGA) | 02.02.1997 | 1 | (1) | 1 |
| Alexander Sørloth (NOR) | 05.12.1995 | 28 | (6) | 12 |

## Sevilla Fútbol Club

**Founded**: 25.01.1890
**Stadium**: Estadio "Ramón Sánchez Pizjuán", Sevilla (43,883)
**Trainer**: Julen Lopetegui Agote                    28.09.1966
[06.10.2022] Jorge Luis Sampaoli Moya (ARG)                    13.03.1960
[21.02.2023] José Luis Mendilibar Etxebarria                    14.03.1961

| Goalkeepers: | DOB | M | (s) | G |
|---|---|---|---|---|
| Yassine Bounou *„Bono"* (MAR) | 05.04.1991 | 25 | | |
| Marko Dmitrović (SRB) | 24.01.1992 | 13 | (2) | |
| **Defenders:** | **DOB** | **M** | **(s)** | **G** |
| Marcos Javier Acuña (ARG) | 28.10.1991 | 21 | (9) | 3 |
| *Alex* Nicolao *Telles* (BRA) | 15.12.1992 | 15 | (12) | |
| Loïc Badé (FRA) | 11.04.2000 | 16 | (3) | 1 |
| *Diego Hormigo* Iturralde | 16.04.2003 | 1 | | |
| *Jesús Navas* González | 21.11.1985 | 21 | (11) | |
| *José Ángel Carmona* Navarro | 29.01.2002 | 5 | (5) | 2 |
| Enrique Jesús *„Kike" Salas* Valiente | 23.04.2002 | 4 | (2) | 1 |
| Marcos do Nascimento Teixeira *„Marcão"* (BRA) | 05.06.1996 | 4 | (1) | |
| Gonzalo Ariel Montiel (ARG) | 01.01.1997 | 17 | (11) | |
| Tanguy-Austin Nianzou Kouassi (FRA) | 07.06.2002 | 16 | (3) | 1 |
| Karim Rekik (NED) | 02.12.1994 | 15 | (1) | 1 |
| **Midfielders:** | **DOB** | **M** | **(s)** | **G** |
| *Carlos Álvarez* Rivera | 06.08.2003 | | (1) | |
| Thomas Joseph Delaney (DEN) | 03.09.1991 | 2 | (6) | |
| *Fernando* Francisco Reges (BRA) | 25.07.1987 | 19 | (3) | |
| Nemanja Gudelj (SRB) | 16.11.1991 | 31 | (3) | 3 |

| | DOB | M | (s) | G |
|---|---|---|---|---|
| Pape Alassane Gueye (SEN) | 24.01.1999 | 15 | (1) | 1 |
| Francisco Román Alarcón Suárez *„Isco"* | 21.04.1992 | 10 | (2) | |
| Adnan Januzaj (BEL) | 05.02.1995 | 1 | (1) | |
| *Joan Jordán* Moreno | 06.07.1994 | 19 | (4) | |
| *Manuel Bueno* Sebastián | 27.07.2004 | 2 | | |
| *Óliver Torres* Muñoz | 10.11.1994 | 27 | (5) | 3 |
| *Pedro Ortíz* Bernat | 19.08.2000 | | (1) | |
| Ivan Rakitić (CRO) | 10.03.1988 | 21 | (10) | 1 |
| **Forwards:** | **DOB** | **M** | **(s)** | **G** |
| *Bryan Gil* Salvatierra | 11.02.2001 | 10 | (7) | 2 |
| Jesús Manuel Corona Ruiz (MEX) | 06.01.1993 | 1 | (3) | 1 |
| Kasper Dolberg Rasmussen (DEN) | 06.10.1997 | 2 | (2) | |
| Youssef En-Nesyri (MAR) | 01.06.1997 | 17 | (14) | 8 |
| Alejandro Darío Gómez (ARG) | 15.02.1988 | 11 | (8) | 1 |
| *Iván Romero* de Ávila Araque | 10.04.2001 | | (1) | |
| Érik Manuel Lamela Cordero (ARG) | 04.03.1992 | 20 | (12) | 6 |
| Lucas Ariel Ocampos (ARG) | 11.07.1994 | 11 | (8) | 4 |
| Rafael Mir Vicente *„Rafa Mir"* | 18.06.1997 | 16 | (10) | 6 |
| Jesús Joaquín Fernández Sáez de la Torre *„Suso"* | 19.11.1993 | 10 | (15) | 2 |

## Valencia Club de Fútbol

| | | |
|---|---|---|
| **Founded:** | 18.03.1909 | |
| **Stadium:** | Estadio Mestalla, Valencia (49,430) | |
| **Trainer:** | Gennaro Ivan Gattuso (ITA) | 09.01.1978 |
| [31.01.2023] | Salvador González Marco "Voro" | 09.101.963 |
| [14.02.2023] | Rubén Baraja Vegas | 11.07.1975 |

| Goalkeepers: | DOB | M | (s) | G |
|---|---|---|---|---|
| Giorgi Mamardashvili (GEO) | 29.09.2000 | 38 | | |
| **Defenders:** | **DOB** | **M** | **(s)** | **G** |
| Eray Cömert (SUI) | 04.02.1998 | 19 | (4) | 1 |
| *Cristhian* Andrey *Mosquera* Ibargüen | 27.06.2004 | 1 | (2) | |
| Mouctar Diakhaby (FRA) | 19.12.1996 | 28 | (1) | 3 |
| Dimitri Foulquier (GLP) | 23.03.1993 | 17 | (13) | |
| Gabriel Armando de Abreu „*Gabriel Paulista*" (BRA) | 26.11.1990 | 18 | (3) | 1 |
| José Luis *Gayà* Peña | 25.05.1995 | 31 | | 1 |
| *Jesús Vázquez* Alcalde | 02.01.2003 | 3 | (7) | |
| Cenk Özkaçar (TUR) | 06.10.2000 | 14 | (3) | |
| *Thierry* Rendall *Correia* (POR) | 09.03.1999 | 24 | (3) | |
| Antonio Latorre Grueso „*Toni Lato*" | 21.11.1997 | 9 | (15) | 1 |
| **Midfielders:** | **DOB** | **M** | **(s)** | **G** |
| Domingos *André* Ribeiro *Almeida* (POR) | 30.05.2000 | 29 | (5) | 2 |
| *Carlos Soler* Barragán | 02.01.1997 | 3 | | 1 |
| *Hugo Guillamón* Sammartín | 31.01.2000 | 19 | (6) | 1 |
| Javier „*Javi*" *Guerra* Moreno | 13.05.2003 | 6 | (4) | 1 |
| Moriba Kourouma Kourouma (GUI) | 19.01.2003 | 10 | (14) | |
| Yunus Dimoara Musah (USA) | 29.11.2002 | 26 | (7) | |
| Nicolás „*Nico*" *González* Iglesias | 03.01.2002 | 18 | (8) | 1 |
| **Forwards:** | **DOB** | **M** | **(s)** | **G** |
| *Alberto Mari* Sánchez | 11.07.2001 | | (5) | 1 |
| Édinson Roberto Cavani Gómez (URU) | 14.02.1987 | 20 | (5) | 5 |
| *Diego López* Noguerol | 13.05.2002 | 5 | (5) | 3 |
| Francisco „*Fran*" *Pérez* Martínez | 09.09.2002 | | (7) | |
| Maximiliano Gómez González (URU) | 14.08.1996 | | (3) | |
| *Hugo Duro* Perales | 10.11.1999 | 12 | (18) | 1 |
| Justin Dean Kluivert (NED) | 05.05.1999 | 15 | (11) | 6 |
| Marcos Andre De Sousa Mendonça „*Maranhão*" (BRA) | 20.10.1996 | 3 | (14) | 1 |
| Samuel „*Samu*" *Castillejo* Azuaga | 18.01.1995 | 17 | (8) | 4 |
| *Samuel* Dias *Lino* (BRA) | 23.12.1999 | 33 | (5) | 6 |

## Real Valladolid Club de Fútbol

| | | |
|---|---|---|
| **Founded**: | 20.06.1928 | |
| **Stadium**: | Estadi „José Zorilla", Valladolid (28,012) | |
| **Trainer**: | José Rojo Martín "Pacheta" | 23.03.1968 |
| [04.04.2023] | Paulo César Pezzolano Suárez (URU) | 25.04.1983 |

| Goalkeepers: | DOB | M | (s) | G |
|---|---|---|---|---|
| *Álvaro Aceves* Catalina | 26.07.2003 | | (1) | |
| Sergio *Asenjo* Andrés | 28.06.1989 | 10 | | |
| *Jordi Masip* López | 03.01.1989 | 28 | | |
| **Defenders:** | **DOB** | **M** | **(s)** | **G** |
| Zouhair Feddal Agharbi (MAR) | 23.12.1989 | 4 | (4) | |
| *David Torres* Ortiz | 05.03.2003 | 2 | (5) | |
| Jawad El Yamiq (MAR) | 29.02.1992 | 19 | (6) | 1 |
| Sergio *Escudero* Palomo | 02.09.1989 | 17 | (6) | 1 |
| *Iván Fresneda* Corraliza | 28.09.2004 | 18 | (4) | |
| Javier „*Javi*" *Sánchez* de Felipe | 14.03.1997 | 28 | (4) | 1 |
| *Joaquín* Fernández Moreno | 31.05.1996 | 24 | (3) | 1 |
| *Lucas* Oliveira *Rosa* (BRA) | 03.04.2000 | 11 | (6) | |
| *Luis* Jesús *Pérez* Maqueda | 04.02.1995 | 15 | (3) | |
| Lucas René Olaza Catrofe (URU) | 21.07.1994 | 16 | (7) | |
| **Midfielders:** | **DOB** | **M** | **(s)** | **G** |
| Álvaro *Aguado* Méndez | 01.05.1996 | 18 | (16) | 1 |
| Selim Amallah (MAR) | 15.11.1996 | 3 | (4) | 2 |
| Martin Hongla Yma (CMR) | 16.03.1998 | 15 | (1) | |
| Enrique „*Kike*" *Pérez* Muñoz | 14.02.1997 | 28 | (8) | 1 |
| Mickaël Ramon Vincent Malsa (MTQ) | 12.10.1995 | | (5) | |
| Ramón Rodríguez Jiménez „*Monchu*" | 13.09.1999 | 23 | (10) | 3 |
| *Roque Mesa* Quevedo | 07.06.1989 | 20 | (9) | 2 |
| Anuar Mohamed Tuhami (MAR) | 15.01.1995 | 3 | | 1 |
| **Forwards:** | **DOB** | **M** | **(s)** | **G** |
| Babatunde Akinsola Jimoh (NGA) | 10.03.2003 | | (1) | |
| Sekou Gassama Cissokho (SEN) | 06.05.1995 | | (1) | |
| *Iván Sánchez* Aguayo | 23.09.1992 | 13 | (12) | 1 |
| Robert *Kenedy* Nunes do Nascimento (BRA) | 08.02.1996 | 2 | (10) | |
| Cyle Christopher Larin (CAN) | 17.04.1995 | 16 | (3) | 8 |
| Darwin Daniel Machís Marcano (VEN) | 07.02.1993 | 7 | (4) | |
| *Manuel Pozo* Guerrero | 12.12.2001 | | (1) | |
| Juan José Narváez Solarte (COL) | 12.02.1995 | 1 | (4) | |
| Óscar *Plano* Pedreño | 11.02.1991 | 22 | (11) | 1 |
| Gonzalo Jordy Plata Jiménez (ECU) | 01.11.2000 | 26 | (8) | 1 |
| *Roberto Arroyo* Gregorio | 25.08.2003 | | (1) | |
| *Sergi Guardiola* Navarro | 29.05.1991 | 8 | (6) | |
| *Sergio León* Limones | 06.01.1989 | 14 | (15) | 6 |
| Laureano Antonio „*Toni*" *Villa* Suárez | 07.01.1995 | 1 | (1) | |
| Shon Zalman Weissman (ISR) | 14.02.1996 | 6 | (9) | 1 |

## Villarreal Club de Fútbol

| | | |
|---|---|---|
| **Founded**: | 10.03.1923 | |
| **Stadium**: | Estadio de la Cerámica, Villarreal (23,008) | |
| **Trainer**: | Unai Emery Etxegoien | 03.11.1971 |
| [26.10.2022] | Enrique "*Quique*" *Setién* Solar | 27.09.1958 |

| Goalkeepers: | DOB | M | (s) | G |
|---|---|---|---|---|
| Filip Jørgensen (DEN) | 16.04.2002 | 2 | | |
| José Manuel *Reina* Páez | 31.08.1982 | 22 | | |
| Gerónimo Rulli (ARG) | 20.05.1992 | 14 | | |
| **Defenders:** | **DOB** | **M** | **(s)** | **G** |
| *Alberto Moreno* Pérez | 05.07.1992 | 14 | (10) | |
| Mamadou Ibra Mbacke Fall (SEN) | 21.11.2002 | | (1) | |
| Juan Marcos Foyth (ARG) | 12.01.1998 | 22 | (4) | 1 |
| *Jorge Cuenca* Barreno | 17.11.1999 | 5 | (5) | |
| Francisco „*Kiko*" *Femenía* Far | 02.02.1991 | 13 | (7) | |
| Aïssa Mandi (ALG) | 22.10.1991 | 16 | (5) | |
| Johan Andrés Mojica Palacio (COL) | 21.08.1992 | 5 | (12) | |
| *Pau* Francisco *Torres* | 16.01.1997 | 34 | | 1 |
| Alfonso *Pedraza* Sag | 09.04.1996 | 20 | (6) | |
| *Raúl Albiol* Tortajada | 04.09.1985 | 24 | (1) | |
| **Midfielders:** | **DOB** | **M** | **(s)** | **G** |
| *Alberto Del Moral* Saelices | 20.07.2000 | | (1) | |
| Alejandro „*Álex*" *Baena* Rodríguez | 20.07.2001 | 19 | (16) | 6 |
| Étienne Capoue (FRA) | 11.07.1988 | 22 | (6) | 3 |
| Francis Coquelin (FRA) | 13.05.1991 | 9 | (7) | 1 |
| Daniel „*Dani*" *Parejo* Muñoz | 16.04.1989 | 37 | | 3 |
| Giovani Lo Celso (ARG) | 09.04.1996 | 14 | (8) | 2 |
| Manuel „*Manu*" *Morlanes* Ariño | 12.01.1999 | 2 | (2) | |
| *Ramón Terrats* Espacio | 18.10.2000 | 11 | (5) | 1 |
| Manuel *Trigueros* Muñoz | 17.10.1991 | 8 | (15) | |
| **Forwards:** | **DOB** | **M** | **(s)** | **G** |
| Samuel Chukwueze (NGA) | 22.05.1999 | 27 | (10) | 6 |
| *Diego Collado* Raya | 09.01.2001 | | (2) | |
| Arnaut Danjuma Adam Groeneveld (NED) | 31.01.1997 | 6 | (4) | 2 |
| Fernando „*Fer*" *Niño* Rodríguez | 24.10.2000 | | (3) | |
| *Gerard Moreno* Balagueró | 07.04.1992 | 14 | (7) | 7 |
| Haissem Hassan (FRA) | 08.02.2002 | | (2) | |
| Nicolas Jackson (SEN) | 20.06.2001 | 16 | (10) | 12 |
| *Jorge Pascual* Medina | 09.04.2003 | | (2) | 1 |
| *José* Luis *Morales* Nogales | 23.07.1987 | 11 | (18) | 7 |
| *Yeremi* Jesús *Pino* Santos | 20.10.2002 | 31 | (5) | 4 |

## SECOND LEVEL
### Segunda División 2022/2023

| | | | | | | | | | | | |
|---|---|---|---|---|---|---|---|---|---|---|---|
| 1. | Granada CF (*Promoted*) | 42 | 22 | 9 | 11 | 55 | - | 30 | 75 |
| 2. | UD Las Palmas (*Promoted*) | 42 | 18 | 18 | 6 | 49 | - | 29 | 72 |
| 3. | Levante UD Valencia | 42 | 18 | 18 | 6 | 46 | - | 30 | 72 |
| 4. | Deportivo Alavés Vitoria-Gasteiz | 42 | 19 | 14 | 9 | 47 | - | 33 | 71 |
| 5. | SD Eibar | 42 | 19 | 14 | 9 | 45 | - | 36 | 71 |
| 6. | Albacete Balompié | 42 | 17 | 16 | 9 | 58 | - | 47 | 67 |
| 7. | FC Andorra | 42 | 16 | 11 | 15 | 47 | - | 37 | 59 |
| 8. | Real Oviedo CF | 42 | 16 | 11 | 15 | 34 | - | 35 | 59 |
| 9. | FC Cartagena | 42 | 16 | 10 | 16 | 47 | - | 49 | 58 |
| 10. | CD Tenerife | 42 | 14 | 15 | 13 | 42 | - | 37 | 57 |
| 11. | Burgos CF | 42 | 13 | 15 | 14 | 33 | - | 35 | 54 |
| 12. | Real Racing Club Santander | 42 | 14 | 12 | 16 | 39 | - | 40 | 54 |
| 13. | Real Zaragoza | 42 | 12 | 17 | 13 | 40 | - | 39 | 53 |
| 14. | CD Leganés | 42 | 14 | 11 | 17 | 37 | - | 42 | 53 |
| 15. | SD Huesca | 42 | 11 | 19 | 12 | 36 | - | 36 | 52 |
| 16. | CD Mirandés | 42 | 13 | 13 | 16 | 48 | - | 54 | 52 |
| 17. | Real Sporting de Gijón | 42 | 11 | 17 | 14 | 43 | - | 48 | 50 |
| 18. | Villarreal CF "B" | 42 | 13 | 11 | 18 | 49 | - | 55 | 50 |
| 19. | SD Ponferradina (*Relegated*) | 42 | 9 | 17 | 16 | 40 | - | 53 | 44 |
| 20. | Málaga CF (*Relegated*) | 42 | 10 | 14 | 18 | 37 | - | 44 | 44 |
| 21. | UD Ibiza (*Relegated*) | 42 | 7 | 13 | 22 | 33 | - | 66 | 34 |
| 22. | CD Lugo (*Relegated*) | 42 | 6 | 13 | 23 | 27 | - | 57 | 31 |

Teams ranked 3-6 were qualified for the Promotion Play-offs.

### Promotion Play-offs

| **Semi-Finals [03-07/08.06.2023]** | SD Eibar - Deportivo Alavés Vitoria-Gasteiz | 1-1(0-1) | 0-2(0-1) |
|---|---|---|---|
| | Albacete Balompié - Levante UD Valencia | 1-3(1-2) | 0-3(0-2) |
| **Play-off Finals [11-17.06.2023]** | Deportivo Alavés Vitoria-Gasteiz - Levante UD Valencia | 0-0 | 1-0(0-0) |

Deportivo Alavés Vitoria-Gasteiz promoted to La Liga 2023/2024.

## NATIONAL TEAM

### INTERNATIONAL MATCHES
### (16.07.2022 – 15.07.2023)

| | | | | |
|---|---|---|---|---|
| 24.09.2022 | Zaragoza | *Spain - Switzerland* | *1-2(0-1)* | (UNL) |
| 27.09.2022 | Braga | *Portugal - Spain* | *0-1(0-0)* | (UNL) |
| 17.11.2022 | Amman | *Jordan - Spain* | *1-3(0-1)* | (F) |
| 23.11.2022 | Doha | *Spain - Costa Rica* | *7-0(3-0)* | (WC) |
| 27.11.2022 | Al Khor | *Spain - Germany* | *1-1(0-0)* | (WC) |
| 01.12.2022 | Al Rayyan | *Japan - Spain* | *2-1(0-1)* | (WC) |
| 06.12.2022 | Al Rayyan | *Morocco - Spain* | *0-0; 3-0 pen* | (WC) |
| 25.03.2023 | Málaga | *Spain - Norway* | *3-0(1-0)* | (ECQ) |
| 28.03.2023 | Glasgow | *Scotland - Spain* | *2-0(1-0)* | (ECQ) |
| 15.06.2023 | Enschede | *Spain - Italy* | *2-1(1-1)* | (UNL) |
| 18.06.2023 | Rotterdam | *Croatia - Spain* | *0-0; 4-5 pen* | (UNL) |

**24.09.2022    SPAIN - SWITZERLAND**          **1-2(0-1)**          3rd UEFA Nations League A, Group 2
Estadio La Romareda, Zaragoza; Referee: Clément Turpin (France); Attendance: 31,804
**ESP:** Unai Simón, César Azpilicueta (87.Carlos Soler), Eric García, Pau Torres, Jordi Alba, Sergio Busquets (Cap), Gavi, Pedri (70.Marcos Llorente), Ferran Torres (63.Yeremi Pino), Pablo Sarabia (63.Nico Williams), Marco Asensio (63.Borja Iglesias). Trainer: Luis Enrique Martínez García.
**Goal:** Jordi Alba (51).

**27.09.2022    PORTUGAL - SPAIN**          **0-1(0-0)**          3rd UEFA Nations League A, Group 2
Estadio Municipal de Braga, Braga; Referee: Daniele Orsato (Italy); Attendance: 28,196
**ESP:** Unai Simón, Dani Carvajal, Hugo Guillamón (46.Sergio Busquets), Pau Torres, José Gayá, Rodri, Koke (Cap) (60.Gavi), Carlos Soler (60.Pedri), Ferran Torres (73.Nico Williams), Pablo Sarabia (60.Yeremi Pino), Álvaro Morata. Trainer: Luis Enrique Martínez García.
**Goal:** Álvaro Morata (88).

**17.11.2022    JORDAN - SPAIN**          **1-3(0-1)**          Friendly International
Amman International Stadium, Amman; Referee: Ahmed Abu Bakar Said Al Kaf (Oman); Attendance: 20,000
**ESP:** Robert Sánchez (46.David Raya), Dani Carvajal (46.César Azpilicueta), Eric García (72.Rodri), Pau Torres, Aymeric Laporte (58.Jordi Alba), Koke (Cap) (58.Daniel Olmo), Gavi (58.Ferran Torres), Carlos Soler, Pablo Sarabia (58.Yeremi Pino), Ansu Fati (72.Nico Williams), Marco Asensio. Trainer: Luis Enrique Martínez García.
**Goals:** Ansu Fati (13), Gavi (56), Nico Williams (84).

**23.11.2022**    SPAIN - COSTA RICA                     7-0(3-0)                          22nd FIFA WC. Group Stage.
Al Thumama Stadium, Doha (Qatar); Referee: Mohammed Abdulla Hassan Mohamed (United Arab Emirates); Attendance: 40,013
**ESP:** Unai Simón, César Azpilicueta, Aymeric Laporte, Jordi Alba (64.Alejandro Balde), Rodri, Gavi, Sergio Busquets (Cap) (64.Koke), Pedri (57.Carlos Soler), Ferran Torres (57.Álvaro Morata), Marco Asensio (69.Nico Williams), Dani Olmo. Trainer: Luis Enrique Martínez García.
**Goals:** Dani Olmo (11), Marco Asensio (21), Ferran Torres (31 penalty, 54), Gavi (74), Carlos Soler (90), Álvaro Morata (90+2).

**27.11.2022**    SPAIN - GERMANY                        1-1(0-0)                          22nd FIFA WC. Group Stage.
Al Bayt Stadium, Al Khor (Qatar); Referee: Danny Desmond Makkelie (Netherlands); Attendance: 68,895
**ESP:** Unai Simón, Dani Carvajal, Aymeric Laporte, Jordi Alba (82.Alejandro Balde), Rodri, Gavi (66.Koke), Sergio Busquets (Cap), Pedri, Ferran Torres (54.Álvaro Morata), Marco Asensio (66.Nico Williams), Dani Olmo. Trainer: Luis Enrique Martínez García.
**Goal:** Álvaro Morata (62).

**01.12.2022**    JAPAN - SPAIN                          2-1(0-1)                          22nd FIFA WC. Group Stage.
Khalifa International Stadium, Al Rayyan (Qatar); Referee: Victor Miguel de Freitas Gomes (South Africa); Attendance: 44,851
**ESP:** Unai Simón, César Azpilicueta (46.Dani Carvajal), Pau Torres, Alejandro Balde (68.Jordi Alba), Rodri, Sergio Busquets (Cap), Gavi (68.Ansu Fati), Pedri, Nico Williams (57.Ferran Torres), Álvaro Morata (57.Marco Asensio), Dani Olmo. Trainer: Luis Enrique Martínez García.
**Goal:** Álvaro Morata (11).

**06.12.2022**    MOROCCO - SPAIN                   0-0; 3-0 on penalties                22nd FIFA WC. 2nd Round of 16.
Education City Stadium, Al Rayyan (Qatar); Referee: Fernando Andrés Rapallini (Argentina); Attendance: 44,667
**ESP:** Unai Simón, Aymeric Laporte, Jordi Alba (82.Alejandro Balde), Rodri, Gavi (63.Carlos Soler), Sergio Busquets (Cap), Pedri, Ferran Torres (57.Álvaro Morata; 118.Pablo Sarabia), Marco Asensio (63.Álvaro Morata), Dani Olmo (98.Ansu Fati). Trainer: Luis Enrique Martínez García.
**Penalties:** Pablo Sarabia (missed), Carlos Soler (saved), Sergio Busquets (saved).

**25.03.2023**    SPAIN - NORWAY                         3-0(1-0)                          17th EC. Qualifiers
Estadio La Rosaleda, Málaga; Referee: Benoît Bastien (France); Attendance: 29,214
**ESP:** Kepa Arrizabalaga, Dani Carvajal, Nacho, Aymeric Laporte, Alejandro Balde, Mikel Merino (81.Fabián Ruiz), Rodri, Iago Aspas (58.Dani Ceballos), Daniel Olmo (67.Yeremi Pino), Gavi (58.Mikel Oyarzabal), Álvaro Morata (Cap) (81.Joselu). Trainer: Luis de la Fuente Castillo.
**Goals:** Dani Olmo (13), Joselu (84, 85).

**28.03.2023**    SCOTLAND - SPAIN                       2-0(1-0)                          17th EC. Qualifiers
Hampden Park, Glasgow;Referee: Sandro Schärer (Switzerland) [46.replaced by the fourth official Lukas Fähndrich (Switzerland)]; Attendance: 47,976
**ESP:** Kepa Arrizabalaga, Pedro Porro (46.Dani Carvajal), David García, Iñigo Martínez, José Gayá, Rodri (Cap), Mikel Merino (57.Iago Aspas), Dani Ceballos (79.Gavi), Yeremi Pino, Mikel Oyarzabal (46.Nico Williams), Joselu (66.Borja Iglesias). Trainer: Luis de la Fuente Castillo.

**15.06.2023**    SPAIN - ITALY                          2-1(1-1)                          3rd UEFA Nations League, Semi-Finals
De Grolsch Veste, Enschede (Netherlands); Referee: Slavko Vinčić (Slovenia); Attendance: 24,558
**ESP:** Unai Simón, Jesús Navas, Robin Le Normand, Aymeric Laporte, Jordi Alba (Cap), Mikel Merino (74.Fabián Ruiz), Rodri, Rodrigo (46.Marco Asensio), Gavi (68.Sergio Canales), Yeremi Pino (74.Ansu Fati), Álvaro Morata (84.Joselu). Trainer: Luis de la Fuente Castillo.
**Goals:** Yeremi Pino (3), Joselu (88).

**18.06.2023**    CROATIA - SPAIN                   0-0 aet; 4-5 on penalties            3rd UEFA Nations League, Final
Stadion Feijenoord, Rotterdam (Netherlands); Referee: Felix Zwayer (Germany); Attendance: 41,110
**ESP:** Unai Simón, Jesús Navas (97.Dani Carvajal), Robin Le Normand (78.Nacho), Aymeric Laporte, Jordi Alba (Cap), Fabián Ruiz (78.Mikel Merino), Rodri, Marco Asensio, Gavi (87.Daniel Olmo), Yeremi Pino (66.Ansu Fati), Álvaro Morata (66.Joselu). Trainer: Luis de la Fuente Castillo.
**Penalties:** Joselu, Rodri, Mikel Merino, Marco Asensio, Aymeric Laporte (missed), Dani Carvajal.

## NATIONAL TEAM PLAYERS
(16.07.2022 – 15.07.2023)

| Name | DOB | Caps | Goals | Club | |
|---|---|---|---|---|---|

### Goalkeepers

| Name | DOB | Caps | Goals | Club | |
|---|---|---|---|---|---|
| DAVID RAYA Martín | 15.09.1995 | 2 | 0 | 2022: | *Brentford FC London (ENG)* |
| KEPA ARRIZABALAGA Revuelta | 03.10.1994 | 13 | 0 | 2023: | *Chelsea FC London (ENG)* |
| ROBERT Lynch SÁNCHEZ | 18.11.1997 | 2 | 0 | 2022: | *Brighton & Hove Albion FC (ENG)* |
| UNAI SIMÓN Mendibil | 11.06.1997 | 33 | 0 | 2022/2023: | *Athletic Club Bilbao* |

### Defenders

| Name | DOB | Caps | Goals | Club | |
|---|---|---|---|---|---|
| ALEJANDRO BALDE Martínez | 18.10.2003 | 5 | 0 | 2022/2023: | *FC Barcelona* |
| AYMERIC Jean Louis Gérard Alphonse LAPORTE | 27.05.1994 | 22 | 1 | 2022/2023: | *Manchester City FC (ENG)* |
| CÉSAR AZPILICUETA Tanco | 28.08.1989 | 44 | 1 | 2022: | *Chelsea FC London (ENG)* |
| Daniel "DANI" CARVAJAL Ramos | 11.01.1992 | 36 | 0 | 2022/2023: | *Real Madrid CF* |
| DAVID GARCÍA Zubiria | 14.02.1994 | 1 | 0 | 2023: | *CA Osasuna Pamplona* |
| ERIC GARCÍA Martret | 09.01.2001 | 19 | 0 | 2022: | *FC Barcelona* |
| HUGO GUILLAMÓN Sanmartín | 31.01.2000 | 3 | 1 | 2022: | *Valencia CF* |
| IÑIGO MARTÍNEZ Berridi | 17.05.1991 | 20 | 1 | 2023: | *Athletic Club Bilbao* |
| JESÚS NAVAS González | 21.11.1985 | 48 | 5 | 2023: | *Sevilla FC* |
| JORDI ALBA Ramos | 21.03.1989 | 93 | 9 | 2022/2023: | *FC Barcelona* |
| JOSÉ Luis GAYÀ Peña | 25.03.1995 | 19 | 3 | 2022/2023: | *Valencia CF* |
| José Ignacio Fernández Iglesias "NACHO" | 18.01.1990 | 24 | 1 | 2023: | *Real Madrid CF* |
| PAU Francisco TORRES | 16.01.1997 | 23 | 1 | 2022: | *Villarreal CF* |
| PEDRO Antonio PORRO Sauceda | 13.09.1999 | 2 | 0 | 2023: | *Tottenham Hotspur FC London (ENG)* |
| ROBIN Aimé Robert LE NORMAND | 11.11.1996 | 2 | 0 | 2023: | *Real Sociedad de Fútbol San Sebastián* |

### Midfielders

| Name | DOB | Caps | Goals | Club | |
|---|---|---|---|---|---|
| CARLOS SOLER Barragán | 02.01.1997 | 14 | 4 | 2022: | *Paris Saint-Germain FC (FRA)* |
| Daniel „DANI" CEBALLOS Fernández | 07.08.1996 | 13 | 1 | 2023: | *Real Madrid CF* |
| DANIEL OLMO Carvajal | 07.05.1998 | 31 | 6 | 2022/2023: | *RasenBallsport Leipzig (GER)* |
| FABIÁN RUIZ Peña | 03.04.1996 | 18 | 1 | 2023: | *Paris Saint-Germain FC (FRA)* |
| Pablo Martín Páez Gavira "GAVI" | 05.08.2004 | 21 | 3 | 2022/2023: | *FC Barcelona* |
| Joge Resurrección Merodio "KOKE" | 08.01.1992 | 70 | 0 | 2022: | *Club Atlético de Madrid* |
| MARCO ASENSIO Willemsen | 21.01.1996 | 37 | 2 | 2022/2023: | *Real Madrid CF* |
| MARCOS LLORENTE Moreno | 30.01.1995 | 18 | 0 | 2022: | *Club Atlético de Madrid* |
| MIKEL MERINO Zazón | 22.06.1996 | 15 | 0 | 2023: | *Real Sociedad de Fútbol San Sebastián* |
| PABLO SARABIA García | 11.05.1992 | 26 | 9 | 2022: | *Paris Saint-Germain FC (FRA)* |
| Pedro González López "PEDRI" | 25.11.2002 | 18 | 0 | 2022: | *FC Barcelona* |
| Rodrigo Hernández Cascante "RODRI" | 22.06.1996 | 43 | 1 | 2022/2023: | *Manchester City FC (ENG)* |
| SERGIO BUSQUETS i Burgos | 16.07.1988 | 143 | 2 | 2022: | *FC Barcelona* |
| SERGIO CANALES Madrazo | 16.02.1991 | 11 | 1 | 2023: | *Real Betis Balompié Sevilla* |

### Forwards

| Name | DOB | Caps | Goals | Club | |
|---|---|---|---|---|---|
| ÁLVARO Borja MORATA Martín | 23.10.1992 | 64 | 30 | 2022/2023: | *Club Atlético de Madrid* |
| Anssumane "ANSU" FATI Vieira | 31.10.2002 | 9 | 2 | 2022/2023: | *FC Barcelona* |
| BORJA IGLESIAS Quintás | 17.01.1993 | 2 | 0 | 2022/2023: | *Real Betis Balompié Sevilla* |
| FERRAN TORRES García | 29.02.2000 | 35 | 15 | 2022: | *FC Barcelona* |
| IAGO ASPAS Juncal | 01.08.1987 | 20 | 6 | 2023: | *RC Celta de Vigo* |
| José Luis Sanmartín Mato "JOSELU" | 27.03.1990 | 4 | 3 | 2023: | *RCD Espanyol Barcelona* |
| MIKEL OYARZABAL Ugarte | 21.04.1997 | 23 | 6 | 2023: | *Real Sociedad de Fútbol San Sebastián* |
| Nicholas "NICO" WILLIAMS Arthuer | 12.07.2002 | 8 | 1 | 2022/2023: | *Athletic Club Bilbao* |
| RODRIGO Moreno Machado | 06.03.1991 | 28 | 8 | 2023: | *Leeds United FC (ENG)* |
| YEREMI Jesús PINO Santos | 20.10.2002 | 11 | 2 | 2022/2023: | *Villarreal CF* |

### Trainer

| Name | DOB | | | | |
|---|---|---|---|---|---|
| LUIS ENRIQUE Martínez García [09.07.2018 – 10.03.2019] & [19.11.2019 – 08.12.2022] | 08.05.1970 | 49 M; 28 W; 14 D; 7 L; 104-38 | | | |
| Luis DE LA FUENTE Castillo [from 01.01.2023] | 21.06.1961 | 4 M; 2 W; 1 D; 1 L; 5-3 | | | |

# SWEDEN

## The Country:
Konungariket Sverige (Kingdom of Sweden)
Capital: Stockholm
Surface: 450,295 km²
Inhabitants: 10,481,937 [2022]
Time: UTC+1

## The FA:
Svenska Fotbollsförbundet
Evenemangsgatan 31A, PO Box 1216, 171 23 Solna
Tel: +46 8 735 0900
Founded: 1904
Member of FIFA since: 1904
Member of UEFA since: 1954
Website: www.svenskfotboll.se

## NATIONAL TEAM RECORDS

### RECORDS
| | | |
|---|---|---|
| **First international match:** | 12.07.1908, Göteborg: | Sweden – Norway 11-3 |
| **Most international caps:** | Anders Gunnar Svensson | - 148 caps (1999-2013) |
| **Most international goals:** | Zlatan Ibrahimović | - 62 goals / 118 caps (since 2001) |

### UEFA EUROPEAN CHAMPIONSHIP
| | |
|---|---|
| 1960 | Did not enter |
| 1964 | Qualifiers |
| 1968 | Qualifiers |
| 1972 | Qualifiers |
| 1976 | Qualifiers |
| 1980 | Qualifiers |
| 1984 | Qualifiers |
| 1988 | Qualifiers |
| 1992 | Final Tournament (Semi-Finals) |
| 1996 | Qualifiers |
| 2000 | Final Tournament (Group Stage) |
| 2004 | Final Tournament (Quarter-Finals) |
| 2008 | Final Tournament (Group Stage) |
| 2012 | Final Tournament (Group Stage) |
| 2016 | Final Tournament (Group Stage) |
| 2020 | Final Tournament (2nd Round of 16) |

### FIFA WORLD CUP
| | |
|---|---|
| 1930 | Did not enter |
| 1934 | Final Tournament (Quarter-Finals) |
| 1938 | Final Tournament (4th Place) |
| 1950 | Final Tournament (3rd Place) |
| 1954 | Qualifiers |
| 1958 | Final Tournament (Runners-up) |
| 1962 | Qualifiers |
| 1966 | Qualifiers |
| 1970 | Final Tournament (Group Stage) |
| 1974 | Final Tournament (2nd Round) |
| 1978 | Final Tournament (Group Stage) |
| 1982 | Qualifiers |
| 1986 | Qualifiers |
| 1990 | Final Tournament (Group Stage) |
| 1994 | Final Tournament (3rd Place) |
| 1998 | Qualifiers |
| 2002 | Final Tournament (2nd Round of 16) |
| 2006 | Final Tournament (2nd Round of 16) |
| 2010 | Qualifiers |
| 2014 | Qualifiers |
| 2018 | Final Tournament (Quarter-Finals) |
| 2022 | Qualifiers |

### OLYMPIC TOURNAMENTS
| | |
|---|---|
| 1908 | 4th Place |
| 1912 | Round 1 |
| 1920 | Quarter-Finals |
| 1924 | 3rd Place |
| 1928 | Did not enter |
| 1936 | 1/8 - Finals |
| 1948 | **Winners** |
| 1952 | 3rd Place |
| 1956 | Did not enter |
| 1960 | Did not enter |
| 1964 | Qualifiers |
| 1968 | Did not enter |
| 1972 | Did not enter |
| 1976 | Did not enter |
| 1980 | Did not enter |
| 1984 | Did not enter |
| 1988 | Quarter-Finals |
| 1992 | Quarter-Finals |
| 1996 | Qualifiers |
| 2000 | Qualifiers |
| 2004 | Qualifiers |
| 2008 | Qualifiers |
| 2012 | Qualifiers |
| 2016 | Group Stage |
| 2020 | Qualifiers |

## UEFA NATIONS LEAGUE
| | |
|---|---|
| 2018/2019 | League B (Group Stage -> promoted to League A) |
| 2020/2021 | League A (Group Stage -> relegated to League B) |
| 2022/2023 | League B (Group Stage -> relegated to League C) |

## SWEDISH CLUB HONOURS IN EUROPEAN CLUB COMPETITIONS:

| European Champion Clubs.Cup (1956-1992) / UEFA Champions League (1993-2023) | | |
|---|---|---|
| None | | |
| **Fairs Cup (1858-1971) / UEFA Cup (1972-2009) / UEFA Europa League (2010-2023)** | | |
| IFK Göteborg | 2 | 10981/1982, 1986/1987 |
| **UEFA Europa Conference League (2021-2023)** | | |
| None | | |
| **UEFA Super Cup (1972-2022)** | | |
| None | | |
| ***European Cup Winners' Cup 1961-1999\**** | | |
| None | | |

*defunct competition

# NATIONAL COMPETITIONS
## TABLE OF HONOURS

| | CHAMPIONS* | CUP WINNERS | BEST GOALSCORERS | |
|---|---|---|---|---|
| 1896 | Örgryte IS Göteborg | - | - | |
| 1897 | Örgryte IS Göteborg | - | - | |
| 1898 | Örgryte IS Göteborg | - | - | |
| 1899 | Örgryte IS Göteborg | - | - | |
| 1900 | AIK Stockholm | - | - | |
| 1901 | AIK Stockholm | - | - | |
| 1902 | Örgryte IS Göteborg | - | - | |
| 1903 | Göteborgs IF | - | - | |
| 1904 | Örgryte IS Göteborg | - | - | |
| 1905 | Örgryte IS Göteborg | - | - | |
| 1906 | Örgryte IS Göteborg | - | - | |
| 1907 | Örgryte IS Göteborg | - | - | |
| 1908 | IFK Göteborg | - | - | |
| 1909 | Örgryte IS Göteborg | - | - | |
| 1910 | IFK Göteborg | - | - | |
| 1911 | AIK Stockholm | - | - | |
| 1912 | Djurgårdens IF Stockholm | - | - | |
| 1913 | Örgryte IS Göteborg | - | - | |
| 1914 | AIK Stockholm | - | - | |
| 1915 | Djurgårdens IF Stockholm | - | - | |
| 1916 | AIK Stockholm | - | - | |
| 1917 | Djurgårdens IF Stockholm | - | - | |
| 1918 | IFK Göteborg | - | - | |
| 1919 | GAIS Göteborg | - | - | |
| 1920 | Djurgårdens IF Stockholm | - | - | |
| 1921 | IFK Eskilstuna | - | - | |
| 1922 | GAIS Göteborg | - | - | |
| 1923 | AIK Stockholm | - | - | |
| 1924 | Fässbergs IF Mölndal | - | - | |
| 1925 | Brynäs IF Gävle | - | - | |
| ---------- | ---------- | ---------- | ---------- | |
| 1930/1931 | GAIS Göteborg | - | John Nilsson (GAIS Göteborg) | 26 |
| 1931/1932 | AIK Stockholm | - | Carl-Erik Holmberg (Örgryte IS Göteborg) | 29 |
| 1932/1933 | Helsingborgs IF | - | Torsten Bunke (Helsingborgs IF) | 21 |
| 1933/1934 | Helsingborgs IF | - | Sven Jonasson (IF Elfsborg Borås) | 20 |
| 1934/1935 | IFK Göteborg | - | Harry Andersson (IK Sleipner Norrköping) | 23 |
| 1935/1936 | IF Elfsborg Borås | - | Sven Jonasson (IF Elfsborg Borås) | 24 |
| 1936/1937 | AIK Stockholm | - | Olle Zethlerlund (AIK Stockholm) | 23 |
| 1937/1938 | IK Sleipner Norrköping | - | Curt Hjelm (IK Sleipner Norrköping) | 13 |
| 1938/1939 | IF Elfsborg Borås | - | Erik Persson (AIK Stockholm) Ove Andersson (Malmö FF) Yngve Lindgren (Örgryte IS Göteborg) | 16 |
| 1939/1940 | IF Elfsborg Borås | - | Anders Pålsson (Helsingborgs IF) | 17 |
| 1940/1941 | Helsingborgs IF | Helsingborgs IF | Stig Nyström (IK Brage Borlänge) | 17 |
| 1941/1942 | IFK Göteborg | GAIS Göteborg | Sven Jacobsson (GAIS Göteborg) | 20 |
| 1942/1943 | IFK Norrköping | IFK Norrköping | Gunnar Nordahl (Degerfors IF) | 16 |
| 1943/1944 | Malmö FF | Malmö FF | Leif Larsson (IFK Göteborg) | 19 |
| 1944/1945 | IFK Norrköping | IFK Norrköping | Gunnar Nordahl (IFK Norrköping) | 27 |
| 1945/1946 | IFK Norrköping | Malmö FF | Gunnar Nordahl (IFK Norrköping) | 25 |
| 1946/1947 | IFK Norrköping | Malmö FF | Gunnar Gren (IFK Göteborg) | 18 |
| 1947/1948 | IFK Norrköping | Råå IF | Gunnar Nordahl (IFK Norrköping) | 18 |
| 1948/1949 | Malmö FF | AIK Stockholm | Carl-Johan Franck (Helsingborgs IF) | 19 |
| 1949/1950 | Malmö FF | AIK Stockholm | Ingvar Rydell (Malmö FF) | 22 |
| 1950/1951 | Malmö FF | Malmö FF | Hasse Jeppson (Djurgårdens IF Stockholm) | 17 |
| 1951/1952 | IFK Norrköping | *No competition* | Karl-Alfred Jacobsson (GAIS Göteborg) | 17 |
| 1952/1953 | Malmö FF | Malmö FF | Karl-Alfred Jacobsson (GAIS Göteborg) | 24 |
| 1953/1954 | GAIS Göteborg | *No competition* | Karl-Alfred Jacobsson (GAIS Göteborg) | 21 |
| 1954/1955 | Djurgårdens IF Stockholm | *No competition* | Kurt Hamrin (AIK Stockholm) | 22 |
| 1955/1956 | IFK Norrköping | *No competition* | Sylve Bengtsson (Halmstads BK) | 22 |
| 1956/1957 | IFK Norrköping | *No competition* | Harry Bild (IFK Norrköping) | 19 |
| 1957/1958 | IFK Göteborg | *No competition* | Bertil Johansson (IFK Göteborg) Henry Källgren (IFK Norrköping) | 27 |
| 1959 | Djurgårdens IF Stockholm | *No competition* | Rune Börjesson (Örgryte IS Göteborg) | 21 |
| 1960 | IFK Norrköping | *No competition* | Rune Börjesson (Örgryte IS Göteborg) | 24 |
| 1961 | IF Elfsborg Borås | *No competition* | Bertil Johansson (IFK Göteborg) | 20 |
| 1962 | IFK Norrköping | *No competition* | Leif Skiöld (Djurgårdens IF Stockholm) | 21 |
| 1963 | IFK Norrköping | *No competition* | Lars Heinermann (Degerfors IF) Bo Larsson (Malmö FF) | 17 |
| 1964 | Djurgårdens IF Stockholm | *No competition* | Krister Granbom (Helsingborgs IF) | 22 |
| 1965 | Malmö FF | *No competition* | Bo Larsson (Malmö FF) | 28 |
| 1966 | Djurgårdens IF Stockholm | *No competition* | Ove Kindvall (IFK Norrköping) | 20 |
| 1967 | Malmö FF | Malmö FF | Dag Szepanski (Malmö FF) | 22 |
| 1968 | Östers IF Växjö | *No competition* | Ove Eklund (Åtvidabergs FF) | 16 |

| | | | | |
|------|------|------|------|------|
| 1969 | IFK Göteborg | IFK Norrköping (1968/69) | Reine Almqvist (IFK Göteborg) | 16 |
| 1970 | Malmö FF | Åtvidabergs FF (1969/70) | Bo Larsson (Malmö FF) | 16 |
| 1971 | Malmö FF | Åtvidabergs FF (1970/71) | Roland Sandberg (Åtvidabergs FF) | 17 |
| 1972 | Åtvidabergs FF | Landskrona BoIS (1971/72) | Ralf Edström (Åtvidabergs FF) Roland Sandberg (Åtvidabergs FF) | 16 |
| 1973 | Åtvidabergs FF | Malmö FF (1972/73) | Jan Mattsson (Östers IF Växjö) | 20 |
| 1974 | Malmö FF | Malmö FF (1973/74) | Jan Mattsson (Östers IF Växjö) | 22 |
| 1975 | Malmö FF | Malmö FF (1974/75) | Jan Mattsson (Östers IF Växjö) | 31 |
| 1976 | Halmstads BK | AIK Stockholm (1975/76) | Rutger Backe (Halmstads BK) | 21 |
| 1977 | Malmö FF | Östers IF Växjö (1976/77) | Reine Almqvist (IFK Göteborg) Mats Aronsson (Landskrona BoIS) | 15 |
| 1978 | Östers IF Växjö | Malmö FF (1977/78) | Tommy Berggren (Djurgårdens IF Stockholm) | 19 |
| 1979 | Halmstads BK | IFK Göteborg (1978/79) | Mats Werner (Hammarby IF) | 14 |
| 1980 | Östers IF Växjö | Malmö FF (1979/80) | Billy Ohlsson (Hammarby IF) | 19 |
| 1981 | Östers IF Växjö | Kalmar FF (1980/81) | Torbjörn Nilsson (IFK Göteborg) | 20 |
| 1982 | IFK Göteborg | IFK Göteborg (1981/82) | Dan Corneliusson (IFK Göteborg) | 12 |
| 1983 | IFK Göteborg | IFK Göteborg (1982/83) | Thomas Ahlström (IF Elfsborg Borås) | 16 |
| 1984 | IFK Göteborg | Malmö FF (1983/84) | Billy Ohlsson (Hammarby IF) | 14 |
| 1985 | Örgryte IS Göteborg | AIK Stockholm (1984/85) | Sören Börjesson (Örgryte IS Göteborg) Peter Karlsson (Kalmar FF) William Lansdowne (ENG, Kalmar FF) | 10 |
| 1986 | Malmö FF | Malmö FF (1985/86) | Johnny Ekström (IFK Göteborg) | 13 |
| 1987 | IFK Göteborg | Kalmar FF (1986/87) | Lasse Larsson (Malmö FF) | 19 |
| 1988 | Malmö FF | IFK Norrköping (1987/88) | Dan Martin Nataniel Dahlin (Malmö FF) | 17 |
| 1989 | IFK Norrköping | Malmö FF (1988/89) | Jan Hellström (IFK Norrköping) | 16 |
| 1990 | IFK Göteborg | Djurgårdens IF Stockholm (1989/90) | Kaj Eskelinen (IFK Göteborg) | 10 |
| 1991 | IFK Göteborg | IFK Norrköping (1990/91) IFK Göteborg (1991) | Bernt Kennet Andersson (IFK Göteborg) | 13 |
| 1992 | AIK Stockholm | No competition | Hans Eklund (Östers IF Växjö) | 16 |
| 1993 | IFK Göteborg | Degerfors IF (1992/93) | Henrik Bertilsson (Halmstads BK) Mats Lilienberg (Trelleborgs FF) | 18 |
| 1994 | IFK Göteborg | IFK Norrköping (1993/94) | Niclas Kindvall (IFK Norrköping) | 23 |
| 1995 | IFK Göteborg | Halmstads BK (1994/95) | Niklas Skoog (Västra Frölunda IF) | 17 |
| 1996 | IFK Göteborg | AIK Stockholm (1995/96) | Andreas Andersson (IFK Göteborg) | 19 |
| 1997 | Halmstads BK | AIK Stockholm (1996/97) | Mats Lilienberg (Halmstads BK) Christer Mattiasson (IF Elfsborg Borås) Dan Sahlin (Örebro SK) | 14 |
| 1998 | AIK Stockholm | Helsingborgs IF (1997/98) | Arild Stavrum (Helsingborgs IF) | 18 |
| 1999 | Helsingborgs IF | AIK Stockholm (1998/99) | Marcus Allbäck (Örgryte IS Göteborg) | 15 |
| 2000 | Halmstads BK | Örgryte IS Göteborg (1999/2000) | Fredrik Berglund (IF Elfsborg Borås) | 18 |
| 2001 | Hammarby IF | IF Elfsborg Borås (2000/01) | Stefan Selaković (Halmstads BK) | 15 |
| 2002 | Djurgårdens IF Stockholm | Djurgårdens IF Stockholm | Peter Emeka Ijeh (NGA, Malmö FF) | 24 |
| 2003 | Djurgårdens IF Stockholm | IF Elfsborg Borås | Niklas Skoog (Malmö FF) | 22 |
| 2004 | Malmö FF | Djurgårdens IF Stockholm | Markus Rosenberg (Halmstads BK) | 14 |
| 2005 | Djurgårdens IF Stockholm | Djurgårdens IF Stockholm | Gunnar Heiðar Þorvaldsson (ISL, Halmstads BK) | 16 |
| 2006 | IF Elfsborg Borås | Helsingborgs IF | Ariclenes da Silva Ferreira "Ari" (BRA, Kalmar FF) | 15 |
| 2007 | IFK Göteborg | Kalmar FF | Bengt Eric Marcus Berg (IFK Göteborg) Razak Omotoyossi (BEN, Helsingborgs IF) | 14 |
| 2008 | Kalmar FF | IFK Göteborg | Patrik Ingelsten (Kalmar FF) | 19 |
| 2009 | AIK Stockholm | AIK Stockholm | Tobias Hysén (IFK Göteborg) Francisco Wánderson do Carmo Carneiro (BRA, GAIS Göteborg) | 18 |
| 2010 | Malmö FF | Helsingborgs IF | Alexander Gerndt (Gefle IF / Helsingborgs IF) | 20 |
| 2011 | Helsingborgs IF | Helsingborgs IF | Mathias Ranégie (BK Häcken Göteborg / Malmö FF) | 21 |
| 2012 | IF Elfsborg Borås | No competition | Abdul Majeed Waris (GHA, BK Häcken Göteborg) | 23 |
| 2013 | Malmö FF | IFK Göteborg (2012/13) | Imad Khalili (IFK Norrköping / Helsingborgs IF) | 15 |
| 2014 | Malmö FF | IF Elfsborg Borås (2013/14) | Lasse Vibe (IFK Göteborg) | 23 |
| 2015 | IFK Norrköping | IFK Göteborg (2014/15) | Emir Kujović (IFK Norrköping) | 21 |
| 2016 | Malmö FF | BK Häcken Göteborg (2015/16) | John Owoeri (NGA, BK Häcken Göteborg) | 17 |
| 2017 | Malmö FF | Östersunds FK (2016/17) | Karl Albin Elis Holmberg (IFK Norrköping) Magnus Lennart Eriksson (Djurgårdens IF Stockholm) | 14 |
| 2018 | AIK Stockholm | Djurgårdens IF Stockholm (2017/18) | Paulo José de Oliveira „Paulinho" (BRA, BK Häcken Göteborg) | 20 |
| 2019 | Djurgårdens IF Stockholm | BK Häcken Göteborg (2018/2019) | Mohamed Buya Turay (SLE, Djurgårdens IF Stockholm) | 15 |
| 2020 | Malmö FF | IFK Göteborg (2019/2020) | Christoffer Åke Sven Nyman (IFK Norrköping) | 18 |
| 2021 | Malmö FF | Hammarby IF Stockholm (2020/2021) | Samuel Adeniyi Adegbenro (NGA, IFK Norrköping) | 17 |
| 2022 | BK Häcken Göteborg | Malmö FF (2021/2022) | Alexander Thomas Jeremejeff (BK Häcken Göteborg) | 22 |

*Svenska Mästerskapet (1896–1925), Allsvenskan (1931–1981), Allsvenskan Play-offs (1982–1990), Mästerskapsserien (1991–1992), Allsvenskan (since 1993).

# NATIONAL CHAMPIONSHIP
## Allsvenskan 2022
### (02.04.2022 – 06.11.2022)

## Results

### Round 1 [02-04.04.2022]
Hammarby IF - Helsingborgs IF 2-1(1-0)
BK Häcken - AIK Stockholm 4-2(2-1)
IFK Göteborg - IFK Värnamo 2-1(1-0)
IK Sirius - GIF Sundsvall 2-1(0-1)
IFK Norrköping - Varbergs BoIS 0-1(0-0)
Kalmar FF - Malmö FF 0-1(0-0)
IF Elfsborg - Mjällby AIF 0-2(0-0)
Djurgårdens IF - Degerfors IF 3-1(1-0)

### Round 2 [09-11.04.2022]
GIF Sundsvall - Hammarby IF 1-5(1-4)
Degerfors IF - BK Häcken 1-2(0-1)
Helsingborgs IF - IFK Göteborg 0-1(0-1)
Varbergs BoIS - Kalmar FF 0-3(0-2)
AIK Stockholm - IFK Norrköping 1-0(1-0)
Mjällby AIF - Djurgårdens IF 1-0(0-0)
IFK Värnamo - IK Sirius 0-0
Malmö FF - IF Elfsborg 1-1(1-0)

### Round 3 [15-17.04.2022]
Hammarby IF - Mjällby AIF 2-0(0-0)
Djurgårdens IF - IFK Norrköping 2-1(0-1)
Varbergs BoIS - GIF Sundsvall 2-0(2-0)
Kalmar FF - Degerfors IF 2-0(1-0)
Malmö FF - AIK Stockholm 3-0(2-0)
BK Häcken - IFK Göteborg 0-2(0-1)
IF Elfsborg - IFK Värnamo 4-1(1-0)
IK Sirius - Helsingborgs IF 1-0(1-0)

### Round 4 [20-21.04.2022]
AIK Stockholm - Varbergs BoIS 1-0(1-0)
IFK Göteborg - Djurgårdens IF 1-1(1-0)
IFK Norrköping - BK Häcken 1-1(1-1)
Mjällby AIF - IK Sirius 3-0(1-0)
GIF Sundsvall - Kalmar FF 1-0(0-0)
Degerfors IF - Hammarby IF 0-1(0-1)
Helsingborgs IF - IF Elfsborg 1-0(1-0)
IFK Värnamo - Malmö FF 0-0

### Round 5 [24-26.04.2022]
AIK Stockholm - Djurgårdens IF 1-0(1-0)
Varbergs BoIS - Mjällby AIF 0-0
Helsingborgs IF - BK Häcken 1-1(0-0)
IF Elfsborg - GIF Sundsvall 3-1(1-1)
IK Sirius - Hammarby IF 0-3(0-1)
IFK Värnamo - Degerfors IF 2-0(1-0)
Malmö FF - IFK Göteborg 1-0(0-0)
Kalmar FF - IFK Norrköping 1-2(0-2)

### Round 6 [30.04.-02.05.2022]
Djurgårdens IF - IK Sirius 4-0(2-0)
Degerfors IF - IF Elfsborg 0-6(0-4)
Mjällby AIF - Helsingborgs IF 2-1(1-1)
BK Häcken - Varbergs BoIS 3-1(2-0)
GIF Sundsvall - AIK Stockholm 0-2(0-0)
IFK Göteborg - Kalmar FF 1-2(1-0)
IFK Norrköping - IFK Värnamo 2-0(0-0)
Hammarby IF - Malmö FF 0-0

### Round 7 [07-09.05.2022]
AIK Stockholm - IFK Göteborg 1-0(0-0)
Malmö FF - Mjällby AIF 2-0(2-0)
Kalmar FF - Hammarby IF 2-0(2-0)
Varbergs BoIS - IK Sirius 0-2(0-0)
Helsingborgs IF - IFK Norrköping 0-1(0-0)
GIF Sundsvall - Degerfors IF 2-3(0-0)
IFK Värnamo - BK Häcken 1-2(1-1)
IF Elfsborg - Djurgårdens IF 0-0

### Round 8 [14-16.05.2022]
Mjällby AIF - IFK Värnamo 1-1(0-1)
IK Sirius - IF Elfsborg 2-0(0-0)
BK Häcken - Kalmar FF 3-1(1-1)
Hammarby IF - AIK Stockholm 3-3(2-1)
Degerfors IF - Helsingborgs IF 2-1(1-0)
IFK Göteborg - Varbergs BoIS 1-1(1-0)
IFK Norrköping - GIF Sundsvall 5-1(4-0)
Djurgårdens IF - Malmö FF 4-0(2-0)

### Round 9 [21-23.05.2022]
AIK Stockholm - IK Sirius 2-2(2-2)
Helsingborgs IF - IFK Värnamo 1-4(1-0)
Hammarby IF - IFK Norrköping 3-0(1-0)
IF Elfsborg - IFK Göteborg 3-1(2-1)
Varbergs BoIS - Degerfors IF 2-1(1-0)
Kalmar FF - Djurgårdens IF 1-0(0-0)
Malmö FF - BK Häcken 1-2(0-0)
GIF Sundsvall - Mjällby AIF 2-0(0-0)

### Round 10 [28-29.05.2022]
IFK Göteborg - GIF Sundsvall 2-0(0-0)
Mjällby AIF - Kalmar FF 1-1(1-0)
BK Häcken - IK Sirius 4-3(2-1)
Degerfors IF - Malmö FF 0-2(0-2)
Djurgårdens IF - Varbergs BoIS 4-0(2-0)
IFK Norrköping - IF Elfsborg 2-2(1-2)
Helsingborgs IF - AIK Stockholm 1-2(1-0)
IFK Värnamo - Hammarby IF 1-0(0-0)

### Round 11 [26-27.06.2022]
Degerfors IF - AIK Stockholm 1-1(1-1)
Hammarby IF - BK Häcken 2-2(0-0)
Mjällby AIF - IFK Norrköping 1-1(0-0)
GIF Sundsvall - Djurgårdens IF 2-5(1-4)
IF Elfsborg - Varbergs BoIS 4-1(1-1)
IK Sirius - IFK Göteborg 1-2(1-1)
Kalmar FF - IFK Värnamo 1-0(1-0)
Malmö FF - Helsingborgs IF 2-1(1-1)

### Round 12 [01-04.07.2022]
GIF Sundsvall - Malmö FF 2-1(2-1)
AIK Stockholm - Mjällby AIF 0-1(0-1)
Helsingborgs IF - Kalmar FF 1-1(0-1)
Djurgårdens IF - Hammarby IF 1-0(0-0)
Varbergs BoIS - IFK Värnamo 3-0(1-0)
BK Häcken - IF Elfsborg 1-1(1-1)
IFK Norrköping - IK Sirius 0-1(0-0)
IFK Göteborg - Degerfors IF 2-0(2-0)

### Round 13 [09-11.07.2022]
Malmö FF - Varbergs BoIS 3-0(1-0)
Degerfors IF - IFK Norrköping 1-1(0-1)
IF Elfsborg - AIK Stockholm 2-2(1-1)
Mjällby AIF - BK Häcken 1-2(1-0)
Kalmar FF - IK Sirius 1-1(1-1)
Hammarby IF - IFK Göteborg 3-0(1-0)
Helsingborgs IF - Djurgårdens IF 0-2(0-1)
IFK Värnamo - GIF Sundsvall 1-1(1-0)

### Round 14 [16-18.07.2022]
IFK Norrköping - Malmö FF 0-2(0-1)
Djurgårdens IF - IFK Värnamo 5-0(2-0)
AIK Stockholm - Kalmar FF 1-0(1-0)
Hammarby IF - IF Elfsborg 3-0(2-0)
IFK Göteborg - Mjällby AIF 1-1(1-0)
IK Sirius - Degerfors IF 2-0(1-0)
GIF Sundsvall - BK Häcken 1-5(1-1)
Varbergs BoIS - Helsingborgs IF 0-0

### Round 15 [23-25.07.2022]
Malmö FF - IK Sirius 3-1(1-0)
Mjällby AIF - Degerfors IF 2-1(0-0)
Helsingborgs IF - GIF Sundsvall 1-0(1-0)
IFK Värnamo - AIK Stockholm 2-3(0-1)
BK Häcken - Djurgårdens IF 1-2(1-0)
Kalmar FF - IF Elfsborg 1-0(0-0)
IFK Norrköping - IFK Göteborg 0-2(0-1)
Varbergs BoIS - Hammarby IF 0-3(0-2)

### Round 16 [30.07.-01.08.2022]
Djurgårdens-Helsingborgs 2-2(1-2) [05.05.22]
AIK Stockholm-Malmö FF 2-0(1-0)[11.05.22]
Degerfors IF - Kalmar FF 2-1(1-1)
GIF Sundsvall - Varbergs BoIS 1-3(0-3)
Hammarby IF - IFK Värnamo 1-2(0-0)
IF Elfsborg - BK Häcken 4-4(2-1)
IK Sirius - Mjällby AIF 0-1(0-0)
IFK Göteborg - IFK Norrköping 2-0(1-0)

### Round 17 [06-08.08.2022]
IFK Norrköping - Degerfors IF 2-0(1-0)
Hammarby IF - GIF Sundsvall 3-0(1-0)
IK Sirius - Malmö FF 0-3(0-2)
Kalmar FF - AIK Stockholm 1-0(0-0)
Mjällby AIF - IF Elfsborg 1-1(1-0)
IFK Värnamo - Djurgårdens IF 0-0
BK Häcken - Helsingborgs IF 5-0(1-0)
Varbergs BoIS - IFK Göteborg 0-4(0-1)

### Round 18 [13-15.08.2022]
Helsingborgs IF - IK Sirius 0-0
AIK Stockholm - IFK Värnamo 2-2(1-1)
Djurgårdens IF - Kalmar FF 3-2(2-0)
Malmö FF - GIF Sundsvall 3-1(3-0)
Degerfors IF - Varbergs BoIS 1-1(0-0)
IF Elfsborg - IFK Norrköping 1-1(1-0)
BK Häcken - Mjällby AIF 1-0(0-0)
IFK Göteborg - Hammarby IF 0-1(0-0)

### Round 19 [20-22.08.2022]
Varbergs BoIS - Djurgårdens IF 2-2(2-0)
Mjällby AIF - Malmö FF 1-0(1-0)
IFK Värnamo - IF Elfsborg 1-1(1-0)
IFK Norrköping - AIK Stockholm 2-4(0-3)
GIF Sundsvall - Helsingborgs IF 1-2(0-1)
IK Sirius - BK Häcken 0-1(0-0)
Kalmar FF - IFK Göteborg 1-0(0-0)
Hammarby IF - Degerfors IF 5-1(2-1)

### Round 20 [27-29.08.2022]
BK Häcken - IFK Värnamo 4-1(1-0)
Degerfors IF - GIF Sundsvall 3-1(1-1)
AIK Stockholm - Hammarby IF 2-2(1-1)
IFK Göteborg - IK Sirius 2-0(1-0)
Varbergs BoIS - IFK Norrköping 1-1(0-1)
Helsingborgs IF - Mjällby AIF 0-1(0-0)
Malmö FF - Kalmar FF 0-1(0-0)
Djurgårdens IF - IF Elfsborg 2-1(2-0)

### Round 21 [04-05.09.2022]
BK Häcken - Degerfors IF 2-2(1-0)
IK Sirius - Djurgårdens IF 0-1(0-1)
AIK Stockholm - GIF Sundsvall 4-0(1-0)
IF Elfsborg - Malmö FF 3-2(1-1)
Kalmar FF - Varbergs BoIS 1-0(1-0)
Mjällby AIF - IFK Göteborg 1-4(0-3)
IFK Värnamo - Helsingborgs IF 3-2(2-1)
IFK Norrköping - Hammarby IF 4-1(0-1)

| Round 22 [10-12.09.2022] | |
|---|---|
| IK Sirius - IFK Värnamo | 2-3(0-2) |
| Degerfors IF - Mjällby AIF | 0-0 |
| Hammarby IF - Djurgårdens IF | 0-0 |
| GIF Sundsvall - IF Elfsborg | 0-2(0-2) |
| Malmö FF - IFK Norrköping | 2-1(0-1) |
| Varbergs BoIS - AIK Stockholm | 2-0(0-0) |
| Kalmar FF - BK Häcken | 1-1(1-0) |
| IFK Göteborg - Helsingborgs IF | 1-3(1-2) |

| Round 23 [17-18.09.2022] | |
|---|---|
| BK Häcken - Hammarby IF | 1-1(0-1) |
| IFK Norrköping - Kalmar FF | 2-2(1-0) |
| IFK Värnamo - Varbergs BoIS | 1-0(0-0) |
| Helsingborgs IF - Malmö FF | 1-2(1-1) |
| IF Elfsborg - IK Sirius | 3-0(2-0) |
| Mjällby AIF - GIF Sundsvall | 1-1(0-0) |
| AIK Stockholm - Degerfors IF | 1-1(1-0) |
| Djurgårdens IF - IFK Göteborg | 3-0(2-0) |

| Round 24 [01-03.10.2022] | |
|---|---|
| Malmö FF - Hammarby IF | 0-0 |
| Degerfors IF - Djurgårdens IF | 3-0(1-0) |
| GIF Sundsvall - IFK Norrköping | 1-3(0-2) |
| Varbergs BoIS - BK Häcken | 1-1(1-0) |
| IK Sirius - AIK Stockholm | 1-1(0-0) |
| Kalmar FF - Helsingborgs IF | 2-0(1-0) |
| IFK Värnamo - Mjällby AIF | 2-1(1-1) |
| IFK Göteborg - IF Elfsborg | 1-3(1-2) |

| Round 25 [08-10.10.2022] | |
|---|---|
| Degerfors IF - IK Sirius | 0-0 |
| IF Elfsborg - Kalmar FF | 0-2(0-2) |
| Malmö FF - IFK Värnamo | 0-0 |
| GIF Sundsvall - IFK Göteborg | 3-2(3-0) |
| AIK Stockholm - Helsingborgs IF | 2-0(0-0) |
| Djurgårdens IF - BK Häcken | 0-1(0-1) |
| IFK Norrköping - Mjällby AIF | 2-2(1-0) |
| Hammarby IF - Varbergs BoIS | 5-1(3-0) |

| Round 26 [14-17.10.2022] | |
|---|---|
| IF Elfsborg - Degerfors IF | 1-1(0-0) |
| BK Häcken - GIF Sundsvall | 4-1(1-1) |
| Helsingborgs IF - Varbergs BoIS | 1-3(0-2) |
| IK Sirius - IFK Norrköping | 2-0(2-0) |
| IFK Värnamo - Kalmar FF | 1-3(1-1) |
| Djurgårdens IF - AIK Stockholm | 1-2(0-1) |
| Mjällby AIF - Hammarby IF | 0-3(0-3) |
| IFK Göteborg - Malmö FF | 2-1(0-0) |

| Round 27 [19-20.10.2022] | |
|---|---|
| AIK Stockholm - BK Häcken | 1-2(0-1) |
| IFK Norrköping - Helsingborgs IF | 2-0(1-0) |
| GIF Sundsvall - IFK Värnamo | 1-2(1-1) |
| Varbergs BoIS - IF Elfsborg | 0-3(0-0) |
| Degerfors IF - IFK Göteborg | 3-1(0-1) |
| Kalmar FF - Mjällby AIF | 1-2(0-1) |
| Malmö FF - Djurgårdens IF | 2-3(2-0) |
| Hammarby IF - IK Sirius | 1-1(0-0) |

| Round 28 [23-24.10.2022] | |
|---|---|
| Helsingborgs IF - Degerfors IF | 1-2(0-1) |
| IF Elfsborg - Hammarby IF | 2-1(1-0) |
| BK Häcken - Malmö FF | 2-1(1-0) |
| Djurgårdens IF - GIF Sundsvall | 4-0(2-0) |
| IK Sirius - Kalmar FF | 0-0 |
| Mjällby AIF - Varbergs BoIS | 4-1(1-0) |
| IFK Värnamo - IFK Norrköping | 1-1(0-1) |
| IFK Göteborg - AIK Stockholm | 1-0(0-0) |

| Round 29 [29-31.10.2022] | |
|---|---|
| Degerfors IF - IFK Värnamo | 0-0 |
| IFK Göteborg - BK Häcken | 0-4(0-3) |
| Mjällby AIF - AIK Stockholm | 1-2(0-1) |
| GIF Sundsvall - IK Sirius | 2-3(1-1) |
| Hammarby IF - Kalmar FF | 4-2(1-0) |
| Varbergs BoIS - Malmö FF | 2-5(0-1) |
| IF Elfsborg - Helsingborgs IF | 3-0(1-0) |
| IFK Norrköping - Djurgårdens IF | 0-1(0-0) |

| Round 30 [06.11.2022] | |
|---|---|
| AIK Stockholm - IF Elfsborg | 0-1(0-0) |
| BK Häcken - IFK Norrköping | 3-3(2-2) |
| Djurgårdens IF - Mjällby AIF | 0-1(0-1) |
| Helsingborgs IF - Hammarby IF | 0-2(0-0) |
| IK Sirius - Varbergs BoIS | 2-3(0-3) |
| Kalmar FF - GIF Sundsvall | 4-0(1-0) |
| Malmö FF - Degerfors IF | 2-2(1-1) |
| IFK Värnamo - IFK Göteborg | 1-4(0-1) |

## Final Standings

| | | Total | | | | | | Home | | | | | | Away | | | | |
|---|---|---|---|---|---|---|---|---|---|---|---|---|---|---|---|---|---|---|
| 1. | **BK Häcken Göteborg** | 30 | 18 | 10 | 2 | 69 | - | 37 | **64** | 9 | 4 | 2 | 38 | - | 21 | 9 | 6 | 0 | 31 | - | 16 |
| 2. | Djurgårdens IF Stockholm | 30 | 17 | 6 | 7 | 55 | - | 25 | **57** | 11 | 1 | 3 | 38 | - | 11 | 6 | 5 | 4 | 17 | - | 14 |
| 3. | Hammarby IF Stockholm | 30 | 16 | 8 | 6 | 60 | - | 27 | **56** | 9 | 5 | 1 | 37 | - | 13 | 7 | 3 | 5 | 23 | - | 14 |
| 4. | Kalmar FF | 30 | 15 | 6 | 9 | 41 | - | 27 | **51** | 10 | 2 | 3 | 20 | - | 7 | 5 | 4 | 6 | 21 | - | 20 |
| 5. | AIK Stockholm | 30 | 14 | 8 | 8 | 45 | - | 36 | **50** | 8 | 4 | 3 | 21 | - | 11 | 6 | 4 | 5 | 24 | - | 25 |
| 6. | IF Elfsborg Borås | 30 | 13 | 10 | 7 | 55 | - | 35 | **49** | 8 | 5 | 2 | 33 | - | 19 | 5 | 5 | 5 | 22 | - | 16 |
| 7. | Malmö FF | 30 | 13 | 7 | 10 | 44 | - | 34 | **46** | 8 | 4 | 3 | 25 | - | 13 | 5 | 3 | 7 | 19 | - | 21 |
| 8. | IFK Göteborg | 30 | 14 | 3 | 13 | 42 | - | 39 | **45** | 7 | 3 | 5 | 19 | - | 18 | 7 | 0 | 8 | 23 | - | 21 |
| 9. | Mjällby AIF Hällevik | 30 | 11 | 10 | 9 | 33 | - | 33 | **43** | 5 | 6 | 4 | 21 | - | 20 | 6 | 4 | 5 | 12 | - | 13 |
| 10. | IFK Värnamo | 30 | 9 | 10 | 11 | 34 | - | 47 | **37** | 5 | 6 | 4 | 17 | - | 18 | 4 | 4 | 7 | 17 | - | 29 |
| 11. | IK Sirius Uppsala | 30 | 9 | 8 | 13 | 31 | - | 42 | **35** | 6 | 2 | 7 | 17 | - | 17 | 3 | 6 | 6 | 14 | - | 25 |
| 12. | IFK Norrköping | 30 | 8 | 10 | 12 | 40 | - | 42 | **34** | 5 | 4 | 6 | 24 | - | 20 | 3 | 6 | 6 | 16 | - | 22 |
| 13. | Degerfors IF | 30 | 7 | 10 | 13 | 32 | - | 49 | **31** | 5 | 6 | 4 | 17 | - | 18 | 2 | 4 | 9 | 15 | - | 31 |
| 14. | Varbergs BoIS (*Relegation Play-offs*) | 30 | 8 | 7 | 15 | 31 | - | 57 | **31** | 4 | 5 | 6 | 15 | - | 25 | 4 | 2 | 9 | 16 | - | 32 |
| 15. | Helsingborgs IF (*Relegated*) | 30 | 4 | 5 | 21 | 22 | - | 52 | **17** | 2 | 3 | 10 | 9 | - | 22 | 2 | 2 | 11 | 13 | - | 30 |
| 16. | GIF Sundsvall (*Relegated*) | 30 | 4 | 2 | 24 | 28 | - | 80 | **14** | 4 | 0 | 11 | 20 | - | 38 | 0 | 2 | 13 | 8 | - | 42 |

| Top goalscorers: | | |
|---|---|---|
| 22 | **Alexander Thomas Jeremejeff** | **BK Häcken Göteborg** |
| 20 | Carl Marcus Christer Antonsson | *IFK Värnamo* |
| 13 | Bengt Erik Marcus Berg | *IFK Göteborg* |

## Relegation Play-offs [10-13.11.2022]

Östers IF Växjö - Varbergs BoIS  1-2(1-1)  1-2(0-1)

Varbergs BoIS remains at first level for 2023.

## Group Stage [18.02.-05.03.2023]

### Group 1

| | |
|---|---|
| BK Häcken Göteborg - Jönköpings Södra IF | 5-0(1-0) |
| FC Trollhättan - Halmstads BK | 0-1(0-1) |
| FC Trollhättan - BK Häcken Göteborg | 1-6(1-3) |
| Halmstads BK - Jönköpings Södra IF | 3-1(1-1) |
| Jönköpings Södra IF - FC Trollhättan | 0-1(0-1) |
| BK Häcken Göteborg - Halmstads BK | 2-1(2-1) |

*Qualified*: BK Häcken Göteborg

### Group 2

| | |
|---|---|
| Djurgårdens IF Stockholm - Landskrona BoIS | 6-1(3-0) |
| IF Brommapojkarna - Örebro SK | 1-2(0-1) |
| Örebro SK - Djurgårdens IF Stockholm | 1-2(0-1) |
| IF Brommapojkarna - Landskrona BoIS | 2-3(1-1) |
| Landskrona BoIS - Örebro SK | 0-2(0-0) |
| Djurgårdens IF Stockholm - IF Brommapojkarna | 2-1(2-1) |

*Qualified*: Djurgårdens IF Stockholm

### Group 3

| | |
|---|---|
| Hammarby IF Stockholm - IK Brage Borlänge | 4-1(1-0) |
| GIF Sundsvall - Norrby IF Borås | 1-1(1-0) |
| Norrby IF Borås - Hammarby IF Stockholm | 0-3(0-1) |
| GIF Sundsvall - IK Brage Borlänge | 0-2(0-1) |
| IK Brage Borlänge - Norrby IF Borås | 5-0(3-0) |
| Hammarby IF Stockholm - GIF Sundsvall | 8-0(5-0) |

*Qualified*: Hammarby IF Stockholm

### Group 4

| | |
|---|---|
| Onsala BK - Helsingborgs IF | 0-5(0-3) |
| Kalmar FF - Trelleborgs FF | 3-2(2-1) |
| Onsala BK - Kalmar FF | 0-3(0-1) |
| Helsingborgs IF - Trelleborgs FF | 1-3(0-2) |
| Trelleborgs FF - Onsala BK | 1-0(1-0) |
| Kalmar FF - Helsingborgs IF | 4-1(2-0) |

*Qualified*: Kalmar FF

### Group 5

| | |
|---|---|
| Varbergs BoIS - Östersunds FK | 1-0(0-0) |
| AIK Stockholm - Västerås SK Fotboll | 1-1(1-1) |
| Varbergs BoIS - Västerås SK Fotboll | 0-2(0-2) |
| Östersunds FK - AIK Stockholm | 0-3(0-1) |
| Västerås SK Fotboll - Östersunds FK | 2-2(1-1) |
| AIK Stockholm - Varbergs BoIS | 3-0(1-0) |

*Qualified*: AIK Stockholm

### Group 6

| | |
|---|---|
| Malmö FF - Skövde AIK | 2-0(2-0) |
| IFK Luleå - Degerfors IF | 0-2(0-0) |
| IFK Luleå - Malmö FF | 0-1(0-0) |
| Degerfors IF - Skövde AIK | 1-0(1-0) |
| Skövde AIK - IFK Luleå | 3-1(2-0) |
| Malmö FF - Degerfors IF | 2-1(0-0) |

*Qualified*: Malmö FF

### Group 7

| | |
|---|---|
| GAIS Göteborg - IFK Norrköping | 0-1(0-1) |
| IFK Göteborg - Utsiktens BK | 3-2(3-1) |
| GAIS Göteborg - IFK Göteborg | 2-1(0-1) |
| IFK Norrköping - Utsiktens BK | 3-3(0-1) |
| Utsiktens BK - GAIS Göteborg | 0-2(0-0) |
| IFK Göteborg - IFK Norrköping | 0-4(0-2) |

*Qualified*: IFK Norrköping

### Group 8

| | |
|---|---|
| Mjällby AIF Hällevik - Dalkurd FF Uppsala | 1-0(0-0) |
| Oskarshamns AIK - IK Sirius Uppsala | 1-4(1-1) |
| Oskarshamns AIK - Mjällby AIF Hällevik | 1-2(1-1) |
| IK Sirius Uppsala - Dalkurd FF Uppsala | 4-0(1-0) |
| Dalkurd FF Uppsala - Oskarshamns AIK | 5-2(1-1) |
| Mjällby AIF Hällevik - IK Sirius Uppsala | 3-2(0-1) |

*Qualified*: Mjällby AIF Hällevik

## Quarter-Finals [11-13.03.2023]

| | | | |
|---|---|---|---|
| BK Häcken Göteborg - IFK Norrköping | 3-0(1-0) | Djurgårdens IF Stockholm - Malmö FF | 2-2 aet; 5-3 pen |
| Kalmar FF - Mjällby AIF Hällevik | 0-0 aet; 4-5 pen | Hammarby IF Stockholm - AIK Stockholm | 2-1(1-1) |

## Semi-Finals [18-19.03.2023]

| | | | |
|---|---|---|---|
| Mjällby AIF Hällevik - Hammarby IF Stockholm | 1-0(1-0) | BK Häcken Göteborg - Djurgårdens IF Stockholm | 3-0(2-0) |

## Final

18.05.2023; Strandvallen, Hällevik; Referee: Mohammed Al Hakim; Attendance: 5,832

**Mjällby AIF Hällevik - BK Häcken Göteborg**                    **1-4(0-2)**

**Mjällby AIF**: Noel Törnqvist, Colin Rösler, Ivan Kričak, Tom Peder Pettersson (65.Noah Eile), Herman Johansson, Otto Rosengren, Arvid Brorsson (65.Max Johannes Whitta Fenger), Adam Ståhl (82.Mamudu Moro), Viktor Gustafson (Cap) (65.David Löfqvist), Noah Persson (82.Elliot Stroud), Eric Alexander Johansson. Trainer: Anders Torstensson.

**BK Häcken**: Peter Abrahamsson, Valgeir Lunddal Friðriksson, Simon Sandberg (68.Johan Hammar), Even Hovland, Kristoffer Lund (79.Kadir Hodžić), Samuel Gustafson (Cap), Akoua Amane Romeo, Mikkel Rygaard, Ibrahim Sadiq (46.Momodou Sonko), Lars Olden Larsen (76.Tomas Totland), Bénie Adama Traoré (68.Ola Williams Kamara). Trainer: Per-Mathias Högmo.

**Goals:** 0-1 Ibrahim Sadiq (45+1), 0-2 Ibrahim Sadiq (45+4), 0-3 Mikkel Rygaard (48), 0-4 Samuel Gustafson (66), 1-4 Max Johannes Whitta Fenger (85).

## Allmänna Idrottsklubben Stockholm

| | | | | |
|---|---|---|---|---|
| **Founded**: | 15.02.1891 | | | |
| **Stadium**: | Friends Arena, Stockholm (50,000) | | | |
| **Trainer**: | Bartosz Grzelak (POL) | | 02.11.1978 | |
| [19.08.2022] | Henok Goitom (ERI) | | 22.09.1984 | |
| [18.10.2022] | Peter Wennberg | | 04.12.1975 | |

| Goalkeepers: | DOB | M | (s) | G |
|---|---|---|---|---|
| Budimir Janošević (SRB) | 21.10.1989 | 2 | | |
| Kristoffer Nordfeldt | 23.06.1989 | 28 | | |
| **Defenders:** | **DOB** | **M** | **(s)** | **G** |
| Axel Björnström | 10.09.1995 | 11 | (15) | |
| Per Karlsson | 02.01.1986 | 1 | (6) | |
| Mikael Lustig | 13.12.1986 | 23 | (4) | 2 |
| Joe Mendes | 31.12.2002 | 18 | (6) | |
| Alexander Milošević | 30.01.1992 | 16 | | 2 |
| Erick Ouma Otieno (KEN) | 27.09.1996 | 25 | (1) | 2 |
| Sotirios Papagiannopoulos | 05.09.1990 | 26 | (2) | 1 |
| Collins Sichenje Lusaka (KEN) | 19.09.2003 | 4 | (4) | |
| **Midfielders:** | **DOB** | **M** | **(s)** | **G** |
| Gabriel Victor David Andersson | 22.10.2004 | | (1) | |
| Yasin Ayari | 06.10.2003 | 15 | (9) | 4 |
| Jesper Ismaila Ceesay | 20.10.2001 | 2 | (6) | |

| | DOB | M | (s) | G |
|---|---|---|---|---|
| Bilal Hussein | 22.04.2000 | 23 | (1) | |
| Sebastian Bengt Ulf Larsson | 06.06.1985 | 26 | (1) | 5 |
| Tom Strannegård | 29.04.2002 | | (3) | |
| Vincent Thill (LUX) | 04.02.2000 | 10 | (1) | 1 |
| **Forwards:** | **DOB** | **M** | **(s)** | **G** |
| Amar Abdirahman Ahmed | 19.02.2004 | 5 | (4) | 1 |
| Taha Ayari | 10.05.2005 | 1 | (4) | |
| Nabil Bahoui | 05.02.1991 | 18 | (5) | 6 |
| Zachary Elbouzedi (IRL) | 05.04.1998 | 12 | (13) | 1 |
| John Alberto Fernando Andres Luigi Olof Guidetti | 15.04.1992 | 11 | (3) | 5 |
| Jordan Larsson | 20.06.1997 | 11 | | 3 |
| Benjamin Mbunga Kimpioka | 21.02.2000 | 5 | (11) | 1 |
| Henry Atola Meja (KEN) | 21.12.2001 | | (3) | |
| Erik Ring | 24.04.2002 | 8 | (9) | |
| Nicolás Marcelo Stefanelli (ARG) | 22.11.1994 | 29 | | 9 |

## Degerfors Idrottsförening

| | | |
|---|---|---|
| **Founded**: | 13.01.1907 | |
| **Stadium**: | Stora Valla, Degerfors (7,500) | |
| **Trainer**: | Andreas Holmberg | 17.08.1984 |

| Goalkeepers: | DOB | M | (s) | G |
|---|---|---|---|---|
| Jeffrey Joseph Gal (USA) | 06.04.1993 | 9 | (1) | |
| Alfie Malik Whiteman (ENG) | 02.10.1998 | 21 | | |
| **Defenders:** | **DOB** | **M** | **(s)** | **G** |
| Elyas Bouzaiene | 08.09.1997 | 13 | (3) | 1 |
| Gustav Granath | 15.02.1997 | 27 | | |
| Anton Kralj | 12.03.1998 | 10 | (3) | |
| Gustaf Johan Lagerbielke | 10.04.2000 | 14 | | 3 |
| Ronald Mukiibi (UGA) | 16.09.1991 | 1 | (2) | |
| Sebastian Ohlsson | 31.12.1992 | 26 | | 1 |
| Sean Sabetkar | 28.04.1995 | 10 | (5) | |
| **Midfielders:** | **DOB** | **M** | **(s)** | **G** |
| Diego de Jesús Campos Ballestero (CRC) | 01.10.1995 | 22 | (7) | 5 |
| Adam Carlén | 27.06.2000 | 23 | (6) | |

| | DOB | M | (s) | G |
|---|---|---|---|---|
| Christos Gravius | 14.10.1997 | 25 | | |
| Daniel Krezić (MKD) | 03.05.1996 | | (10) | |
| Erik Lindell | 14.02.1996 | 9 | (11) | |
| Rasmus Örqvist | 18.10.1998 | 25 | (3) | 3 |
| Justin Salmon (LBR) | 25.01.1999 | 13 | (5) | 1 |
| **Forwards:** | **DOB** | **M** | **(s)** | **G** |
| Johan Bertilsson | 15.02.1988 | 10 | (18) | 1 |
| Nikola Đurđić (SRB) | 01.04.1986 | 11 | (8) | 2 |
| Omar Faraj | 09.03.2002 | 15 | (1) | 4 |
| Joseph-Claude Agyeman Gyau (USA) | 16.09.1992 | 22 | | |
| Chriss-Albin Alexander Mörfelt | 10.01.2000 | 2 | (3) | 1 |
| Adhavan Rajamohan | 21.02.1993 | 4 | (13) | |
| Abdelrahman Saidi | 13.08.1999 | 9 | (2) | 5 |
| Dijan Vukojević | 12.09.1995 | 9 | (14) | 3 |

## Djurgårdens Idrottsförening Stockholm

| | | |
|---|---|---|
| **Founded**: | 12.03.1891 | |
| **Stadium**: | Tele2 Arena, Stockholm (30,000) | |
| **Trainer**: | Thomas Lagerlöf & | 15.11.1971 |
| | Kim Bergstrand | 18.04.1968 |

| Goalkeepers: | DOB | M | (s) | G |
|---|---|---|---|---|
| Aleksandr Vasyutin (RUS) | 04.03.1995 | 2 | | |
| Jacob Widell Zetterström | 11.07.1998 | 28 | | |
| **Defenders:** | **DOB** | **M** | **(s)** | **G** |
| Pierre Bengtsson | 12.04.1988 | 13 | (4) | |
| Marcus Andreas Danielson | 08.04.1989 | 12 | (1) | 1 |
| Hjalmar Ekdal | 21.10.1998 | 23 | (1) | 3 |
| Isak Malcolm Kwaku Hien | 13.01.1999 | 14 | (3) | 2 |
| Piotr Johansson | 28.02.1995 | 27 | (1) | |
| Melker Olle Jonsson | 10.07.2002 | | (1) | |
| Elliot Käck | 18.09.1989 | | (2) | |
| Jesper Löfgren | 03.05.1997 | 10 | (11) | |
| **Midfielders:** | **DOB** | **M** | **(s)** | **G** |
| Elias Andersson | 31.01.1996 | 16 | (9) | 2 |
| Emmanuel Justine Rabby Banda (ZAM) | 29.09.1997 | 8 | (19) | 4 |
| Leo Cornic (NOR) | 02.01.2001 | 2 | (3) | |

| | DOB | M | (s) | G |
|---|---|---|---|---|
| Magnus Eriksson | 08.04.1990 | 28 | (1) | 3 |
| Hampus Finndell | 06.06.2000 | 26 | (1) | 5 |
| Isak Alemayehu Mulugeta | 11.10.2006 | | (1) | |
| Rasmus Vilhelm Schüller (FIN) | 18.06.1991 | 23 | | 1 |
| Besard Šabović | 05.01.1998 | 3 | (9) | 1 |
| **Forwards:** | **DOB** | **M** | **(s)** | **G** |
| Albion Ademi (ALB) | 19.02.1999 | | (3) | |
| Joel Asoro | 27.04.1999 | 15 | (14) | 6 |
| Amadou Doumbouya (GUI) | 12.10.2002 | 3 | (5) | |
| Victor Edvardsen | 14.01.1996 | 25 | (3) | 9 |
| Alexandros Garcia Tsotidis | 19.07.2004 | | (1) | |
| Sead Hakšabanović (MNE) | 04.05.1999 | 11 | | 2 |
| Kalle Holmberg | 03.03.1993 | 3 | (11) | 2 |
| Haris Radetinac (BIH) | 28.10.1985 | 23 | (6) | 5 |
| Gustav Wikheim (NOR) | 18.03.1993 | 15 | (11) | 6 |

## Idrottsföreningen Elfsborg Borås

| | | |
|---|---|---|
| **Founded**: | 26.06.1904 (*as Borås Fotbollslag*) | |
| **Stadium**: | Borås Arena, Borås (16,899) | |
| **Trainer**: | Bo Jimmy Thelin | 14.03.1978 |

| Goalkeepers: | DOB | M | (s) | G |
|---|---|---|---|---|
| Tim Rönning | 15.02.1999 | 16 | | |
| Hákon Rafn Valdimarsson (ISL) | 13.10.2001 | 14 | | |
| **Defenders:** | **DOB** | **M** | **(s)** | **G** |
| Gustav Henriksson | 03.02.1998 | 4 | (1) | 1 |
| Rasmus Sebastian Holmén | 29.04.1992 | 15 | | |
| Bo Niklas Hult | 13.02.1990 | 11 | (2) | |
| Gustaf Johan Lagerbielke | 10.04.2000 | 5 | (1) | |
| Johan Larsson | 05.05.1990 | 24 | (1) | 2 |
| Maudo Lamine Jarjué (GAM) | 30.09.1997 | 9 | (1) | 1 |
| Simon Strand | 25.05.1993 | 17 | (6) | |
| Leo Väisänen (FIN) | 23.07.1997 | 27 | | |
| Oliver Zandén | 14.08.2001 | 8 | (5) | 2 |
| **Midfielders:** | **DOB** | **M** | **(s)** | **G** |
| Michael Baidoo (GHA) | 14.05.1999 | 14 | (7) | 8 |
| Emmanuel Boateng (GHA) | 17.06.1997 | 18 | (5) | |

| | DOB | M | (s) | G |
|---|---|---|---|---|
| Kevin Holmén | 13.12.2001 | | (4) | |
| Simon Olsson | 14.09.1997 | 15 | | 4 |
| Timothy Noor Ouma (KEN) | 10.06.2004 | | (1) | |
| André Rømer (DEN) | 18.07.1993 | 25 | | 1 |
| Noah Söderberg | 21.08.2001 | 17 | (7) | 3 |
| Besfort Zeneli | 21.11.2002 | | (2) | |
| **Forwards:** | **DOB** | **M** | **(s)** | **G** |
| Oscar Aga (NOR) | 06.01.2001 | 1 | (12) | 2 |
| Rasmus Alm | 17.08.1995 | 20 | (6) | 6 |
| Alexander Bernhardsson | 08.09.1998 | 10 | (16) | 7 |
| Jack Cooper-Love | 25.12.2001 | | (2) | |
| Per Frick | 14.04.1992 | 20 | (3) | 2 |
| Sveinn Aron Guðjohnsen (ISL) | 12.05.1998 | 10 | (19) | 5 |
| Jeppe Okkels (DEN) | 27.07.1999 | 16 | (13) | 2 |
| Jacob Ondrejka | 02.09.2002 | 14 | (16) | 4 |
| Ahmed Qasem | 12.07.2003 | | (6) | 1 |

# Idrottsföreningen Kamraterna Göteborg

**Founded**: 04.10.1904
**Stadium**: Gamla Ullevi Stadion, Göteborg (18,600)
**Trainer**: Mikael Stahre — 05.07.1975

| Goalkeepers: | DOB | M | (s) | G |
|---|---|---|---|---|
| Pontus Jacob Ragne Dahlberg | 21.01.1999 | 4 | | |
| Warner Hahn (SUR) | 15.06.1992 | 26 | | |
| **Defenders:** | **DOB** | **M** | **(s)** | **G** |
| Johan Bångsbo | 10.02.2003 | 18 | (1) | 1 |
| Mattias Bjärsmyr | 03.01.1986 | 15 | (1) | |
| Felix Eriksson | 21.05.2004 | | (2) | |
| Alai Ghasem | 16.02.2003 | 1 | (3) | |
| Alexander Jallow | 03.03.1998 | 19 | | 1 |
| Carl Johansson | 23.05.1994 | 27 | | 1 |
| Emil Salomonsson | 28.04.1989 | 12 | (11) | 1 |
| Tim van Assema (NED) | 31.01.2002 | | (2) | |
| Oscar Wendt | 24.10.1985 | 28 | | |
| **Midfielders:** | **DOB** | **M** | **(s)** | **G** |
| Amir Fouad Aboud Al Ammari (IRQ) | 27.07.1997 | 3 | (8) | |
| Filip Ambrož (CRO) | 01.12.2003 | | (1) | |
| Hussein Carneil | 09.05.2003 | 15 | (9) | 1 |
| Sebastian Eriksson | 31.01.1989 | 7 | (10) | 1 |
| Abundance Salaou (CIV) | 05.07.2004 | 4 | (3) | |
| Karl Gustav Johan Svensson | 07.02.1987 | 28 | | 1 |
| Simon Thern | 18.09.1992 | 20 | (2) | 2 |
| Kevin Yakob | 10.10.2000 | 11 | (4) | 4 |
| **Forwards:** | **DOB** | **M** | **(s)** | **G** |
| Suleiman Abdullahi (NGA) | 10.12.1996 | | (5) | |
| Hosam Aiesh (SYR) | 14.04.1995 | 20 | (6) | 2 |
| Bengt Erik Marcus Berg | 17.08.1986 | 26 | | 13 |
| Linus Carlstrand | 31.08.2004 | | (5) | |
| Eman Marković (NOR) | 08.05.1999 | 11 | (2) | 1 |
| Gustaf Norlin | 09.01.1997 | 20 | (10) | 10 |
| Alfons Nygaard | 20.04.2002 | | (1) | |
| Saidu Salisu (NGA) | 14.02.2002 | | (1) | |
| Tobias Sana | 11.07.1989 | 6 | | |
| Erik Sorga (EST) | 08.07.1999 | | (8) | 1 |
| Oscar Ingemar Kristoffer Vilhelmsson | 02.10.2003 | 9 | (2) | 2 |

# Hammarby Idrottsförening Fotbollförening Stockholm

**Founded**: 07.03.1897
**Stadium**: Tele2 Arena, Stockholm (30,000)
**Trainer**: Martí Cifuentes Corvillo (ESP) — 07.07.1982

| Goalkeepers: | DOB | M | (s) | G |
|---|---|---|---|---|
| Davor Blažević | 07.02.1993 | 13 | (1) | |
| Oliver Dovin | 11.07.2002 | 17 | | |
| **Defenders:** | **DOB** | **M** | **(s)** | **G** |
| Nathaniel Adjei (GHA) | 21.08.2002 | 1 | (2) | |
| Mads Fenger (DEN) | 10.09.1990 | 25 | (1) | 1 |
| Mohanad Abdulkadhim Qasim Al Jebur (IRQ) | 10.04.1997 | 25 | (1) | 3 |
| Edvin Kurtulus (KOS) | 05.03.2000 | 25 | (2) | 2 |
| Richárd Magyar | 03.05.1991 | 7 | (1) | |
| Bjørn Paulsen (DEN) | 02.07.1991 | 2 | (11) | 1 |
| Shaquille Pinas (SUR) | 19.03.1998 | 9 | (5) | |
| Simon Sandberg | 25.03.1994 | 24 | (3) | |
| Dennis Widgren | 28.03.1994 | 1 | (7) | |
| **Midfielders:** | **DOB** | **M** | **(s)** | **G** |
| Jeppe Andersen (DEN) | 06.12.1992 | 15 | (12) | 1 |
| Nahir Besara | 25.02.1991 | 27 | (3) | 11 |
| Darijan Bojanić | 28.12.1994 | 26 | (3) | 4 |
| Dennis Collander | 09.05.2002 | 3 | (2) | |
| Alper Demirol | 01.10.2002 | 2 | (11) | |
| Abbe Khalili | 07.06.1992 | | (3) | |
| Fredrik Hammar | 26.02.2001 | | (1) | |
| Loret Sadiku (ALB) | 28.07.1991 | 19 | (2) | |
| Williot Swedberg | 01.02.2004 | 9 | (1) | 5 |
| Pavle Vagić | 24.01.2000 | 1 | (11) | |
| **Forwards:** | **DOB** | **M** | **(s)** | **G** |
| Veton Berisha (NOR) | 13.04.1994 | 12 | (2) | 4 |
| David Concha Salas (ESP) | 20.11.1996 | 1 | (12) | |
| Jusef Erabi | 08.06.2003 | | (7) | |
| Mayckel Lahdo | 30.12.2002 | 4 | (6) | 1 |
| Gustav Ludwigson | 20.10.1993 | 29 | | 11 |
| Joel Nilsson | 11.07.1994 | 11 | (11) | 5 |
| Abdelrahman Saidi | 13.08.1999 | 10 | (7) | 3 |
| Astrit Selmani (KOS) | 13.05.1997 | 8 | (5) | 2 |
| Bubacarr Trawally (GAM) | 10.11.1994 | 4 | (5) | 2 |

# Bollklubben Häcken Göteborg

**Founded**: 02.08.1940
**Stadium**: Bravida Arena (Nya Rambergsvallen), Göteborg (6,500)
**Trainer**: Per-Mathias Högmo — 01.12.1959

| Goalkeepers: | DOB | M | (s) | G |
|---|---|---|---|---|
| Peter Abrahamsson | 18.07.1988 | 27 | | |
| Johan Brattberg | 28.12.1996 | 2 | | |
| Jonathan Rasheed | 21.11.1991 | 1 | (1) | |
| **Defenders:** | **DOB** | **M** | **(s)** | **G** |
| Valgeir Lunddal Friðriksson (ISL) | 24.09.2001 | 22 | (4) | |
| Johan Hammar | 22.02.1994 | 29 | | 2 |
| Kadir Hodžić | 05.08.1994 | 1 | (7) | |
| Even Hovland (NOR) | 14.02.1989 | 30 | | 4 |
| Sebastian Lagerlund | 14.09.2002 | | (1) | |
| Kristoffer Lund (DEN) | 14.05.2002 | 23 | (2) | |
| Franklin Tebo Uchenna (NGA) | 15.01.2000 | 1 | (8) | |
| Tomas Totland (NOR) | 28.09.1999 | 14 | (9) | |
| **Midfielders:** | **DOB** | **M** | **(s)** | **G** |
| Romeo Amane (CIV) | 20.02.2003 | 6 | (12) | 1 |
| Gustav Berggren | 07.09.1997 | 14 | | 2 |
| Alexander Faltsetas | 04.07.1987 | | (3) | |
| Erik Friberg | 10.02.1986 | 1 | (17) | |
| Samuel Gustafson | 11.01.1995 | 28 | | 1 |
| Simon Gustafson | 11.01.1995 | 13 | (1) | |
| Mikkel Rygaard (DEN) | 25.12.1990 | 26 | (2) | 11 |
| **Forwards:** | **DOB** | **M** | **(s)** | **G** |
| Leo Bengtsson | 26.05.1998 | 12 | (1) | 1 |
| Alexander Thomas Jeremejeff | 12.10.1993 | 25 | (2) | 22 |
| Lars Olden Larsen (NOR) | 17.09.1998 | 10 | (9) | 4 |
| William Nilsson | 24.10.2004 | | (1) | |
| Ibrahim Sadiq (GHA) | 07.05.2000 | 11 | (8) | 7 |
| Tobias Tigjani Sana | 11.07.1989 | 5 | (1) | 1 |
| Momodou Sonko | 31.01.2005 | | (2) | |
| Filip Trpcevski (MKD) | 04.05.2003 | | (6) | |
| Blair Sebastian Turgott (JAM) | 22.05.1994 | 8 | (15) | 2 |
| Oscar Uddenäs | 17.08.2002 | 20 | (8) | 7 |
| Ali Youssef (TUN) | 05.08.2000 | 1 | (3) | 1 |

## Helsingborgs Idrottsförening

| Founded: | 04.06.1907 | | |
|---|---|---|---|
| Stadium: | Olympiastadion, Helsingborg (16,500) | | |
| Trainer: | Jörgen Lennartsson | | 10.04.1965 |
| [22.05.2022] | Mattias Lindström & | | 18.04.1980 |
| | Álvaro Marcio Santos (BRA) | | 30.01.1980 |

| Goalkeepers: | DOB | M | (s) | G |
|---|---|---|---|---|
| Kalle Joelsson | 21.03.1998 | 25 | | |
| Anders Lindegaard (DEN) | 13.04.1984 | 5 | | |
| **Defenders:** | **DOB** | **M** | **(s)** | **G** |
| Simon Bengtsson | 23.04.2004 | 2 | (1) | |
| Viljormur Davidsen (FRO) | 19.07.1991 | 27 | (1) | |
| Emil Hellman | 20.04.2001 | 6 | (5) | |
| Andreas Landgren | 17.03.1989 | | (4) | |
| Philip Rejnhold Olsen (DEN) | 21.03.1996 | 13 | | |
| Thomas Pauck Rogne (NOR) | 29.06.1990 | 13 | | |
| Ali Suljić | 18.09.1997 | 11 | | |
| Ravy Tsouka Dozi (CGO) | 23.12.1994 | 15 | | |
| Charlie Weberg | 22.05.1998 | 9 | (1) | 1 |
| Casper Widell | 05.05.2003 | 23 | | |
| **Midfielders:** | **DOB** | **M** | **(s)** | **G** |
| Benjamin Acquah (GHA) | 29.12.2000 | 9 | (1) | 1 |
| Sumar Almadjed | 13.03.1996 | | (1) | |
| Diego César de Oliveira „Diego Fumaça" (BRA) | 18.12.1994 | 3 | (7) | |
| Albert Ejupi | 28.08.1992 | 10 | | |
| Alexander Daniel Faltsetas | 04.07.1987 | 13 | | |
| Armin Gigović | 06.04.2002 | 14 | (2) | 2 |
| Ervin Gigović | 16.09.2003 | 2 | (2) | |
| Abdul Rahman Khalili | 07.06.1992 | 11 | (1) | |
| Lucas Lingman (FIN) | 25.01.1998 | 14 | (1) | |
| Dennis Olsson | 10.06.1999 | 5 | (7) | 2 |
| **Forwards:** | **DOB** | **M** | **(s)** | **G** |
| Amin Al Hamawi | 17.12.2003 | 5 | (4) | 2 |
| Assad Al Islam Al Hamlawi | 27.10.2000 | 3 | (7) | 1 |
| Taha Ali | 01.07.1998 | 27 | (2) | 3 |
| Joseph Amoako (GHA) | 13.09.2002 | 3 | (6) | |
| Rasmus Jönsson | 27.01.1990 | 10 | (17) | |
| Arian Kabashi | 14.03.1997 | 8 | (6) | 1 |
| Adam Kaied | 02.03.2002 | 3 | (9) | |
| Rasmus Karjalainen (FIN) | 04.04.1996 | | (7) | |
| Wilhelm Loeper | 30.03.1998 | 10 | (6) | 1 |
| Viktor Lundberg | 04.03.1991 | | (3) | |
| Amar Muhsin | 27.12.1997 | 8 | (5) | 4 |
| Anton Nilsson | 26.02.2004 | | (2) | |
| Anthony van den Hurk (CUW) | 09.01.1993 | 14 | | 3 |
| Rasmus Wiedesheim-Paul | 08.02.1999 | 9 | (4) | 1 |

## Kalmar Fotbollsförening

| Founded: | 15.06.1910 (as IF Göta) | | |
|---|---|---|---|
| Stadium: | Guldfågeln Arena, Kalmar (12,000) | | |
| Trainer: | Henrik Rydström | | 16.02.1976 |

| Goalkeepers: | DOB | M | (s) | G |
|---|---|---|---|---|
| Jakob Kindberg | 07.02.1994 | 1 | (1) | |
| Ricardo Henrique Schuck Friedrich (BRA) | 18.02.1993 | 29 | | |
| **Defenders:** | **DOB** | **M** | **(s)** | **G** |
| Douglas Bergqvist | 29.03.1993 | 8 | (2) | |
| Johan Karlsson | 20.06.2001 | 12 | (1) | 1 |
| Axel Lindahl | 04.04.1995 | 18 | (8) | 1 |
| Sebastian Nilsson | 01.02.2003 | | (1) | |
| Davíð Kristján Ólafsson (ISL) | 15.05.1995 | 28 | (1) | 2 |
| Lars Sætra (NOR) | 24.07.1991 | 27 | (3) | 3 |
| Rasmus Sjöstedt | 28.02.1992 | 25 | (2) | |
| Johan Stenmark | 26.02.1999 | | (9) | |
| **Midfielders:** | **DOB** | **M** | **(s)** | **G** |
| Victor Backman | 16.03.2001 | 2 | (8) | |
| Oliver Berg (NOR) | 28.08.1993 | 29 | | 9 |
| Isak Bjerkebo | 19.01.2003 | | (10) | 1 |
| Nahom Girmai Netabay | 28.08.1994 | 23 | (3) | 2 |
| Carl Gustafsson | 18.03.2000 | 30 | | 1 |
| Leon Isa | 01.02.2005 | | (1) | |
| Erik Israelsson | 25.02.1989 | | (7) | |
| Isak Jansson | 31.01.2002 | 11 | (3) | 1 |
| Kevin Jensen | 15.06.2001 | 1 | (7) | |
| Sebastian Nanasi | 16.05.2002 | 16 | | 5 |
| Romário Pereira Sipião (BRA) | 10.08.1985 | 28 | (2) | 1 |
| **Forwards:** | **DOB** | **M** | **(s)** | **G** |
| Papa Alioune Diouf (SEN) | 22.06.1989 | 2 | (6) | 1 |
| Filip Sachpekidis | 03.07.1997 | 6 | (12) | 3 |
| Noah Shamoun | 08.12.2002 | 11 | (16) | 3 |
| Simon Skrabb (FIN) | 19.01.1995 | 23 | (4) | 3 |

## Malmö Fotbollförening

| Founded: | 24.02.1910 | | |
|---|---|---|---|
| Stadium: | Eleda Stadion, Malmö (22,500) | | |
| Trainer: | Miloš Milojević (SRB) | | 29.09.1982 |
| [29.07.2022] | Andreas Georgson | | 02.09.1985 |
| [06.09.2022] | Åge Hareide (NOR) | | 23.09.1953 |

| Goalkeepers: | DOB | M | (s) | G |
|---|---|---|---|---|
| Johan Dahlin | 08.09.1986 | 19 | | |
| Ismael Diarra Diawara (MLI) | 11.11.1994 | 11 | (3) | |
| **Defenders:** | **DOB** | **M** | **(s)** | **G** |
| Felix Beijmo | 31.01.1998 | 24 | (3) | 1 |
| Joseph Ceesay | 03.06.1998 | 6 | (4) | |
| Matěj Chaluš (CZE) | 02.02.1998 | 4 | (6) | |
| Dennis Hadžikadunić (BIH) | 09.07.1998 | 23 | (2) | 1 |
| Jonas Knudsen (DEN) | 16.09.1992 | 7 | (3) | |
| Eric Larsson | 15.07.1991 | 9 | (4) | |
| Niklas Moisander (FIN) | 29.09.1985 | 8 | | |
| Lasse Nielsen (DEN) | 08.01.1988 | 23 | | |
| Martin Tony Waikwa Olsson | 17.05.1988 | 13 | (3) | |
| **Midfielders:** | **DOB** | **M** | **(s)** | **G** |
| Samuel Adrian | 02.03.1998 | | (1) | |
| Anders Christiansen (DEN) | 08.06.1990 | 16 | (4) | 2 |
| Hugo Emanuel Larsson | 27.06.2004 | 10 | (17) | 1 |
| Carl Oscar Johan Lewicki | 14.07.1992 | 9 | (2) | |
| Emmanuel Addoquaye Lomotey (GHA) | 19.12.1997 | 2 | (1) | |
| Adi Nalić (BIH) | 01.12.1997 | 2 | (2) | |
| Sebastian Nanasi | 16.05.2002 | 2 | (7) | |
| Sergio Fernando Peña Flores (PER) | 28.09.1995 | 17 | (2) | 1 |
| Erdal Rakip (MKD) | 13.02.1996 | 19 | (6) | 1 |
| Mahamé Siby (FRA) | 07.07.1996 | 2 | | |
| Nils Ola Toivonen | 03.07.1986 | 12 | (13) | 6 |
| Moustafa Zeidan Khalili | 07.06.1998 | 11 | (4) | 3 |
| **Forwards:** | **DOB** | **M** | **(s)** | **G** |
| Abdul Malik Abubakari (GHA) | 10.05.2000 | 3 | (5) | 2 |
| Jo Inge Berget (NOR) | 11.09.1990 | 16 | (6) | 2 |
| Veljko Birmančević (SRB) | 05.03.1998 | 13 | (5) | 5 |
| Mohamed Buya Turay (SLE) | 10.01.1995 | 8 | (2) | 1 |
| Romain Thierry Marie Gall (USA) | 31.01.1995 | 2 | (1) | |
| Søren Rieks (DEN) | 07.04.1987 | 10 | (5) | 2 |
| Patriot Sejdiu (KOS) | 05.05.2000 | 10 | (9) | 4 |
| Isaac Kiese Thelin | 24.06.1992 | 19 | (4) | 12 |

## Mjällby Allmänna Idrottsförening Hällevik

| Founded: | 01.04.1939 | | | |
| Stadium: | Strandvallen, Hällevik (6,750) | | | |
| Trainer: | Andreas Brännström | | 10.05.1976 | |

| Goalkeepers: | DOB | M | (s) | G |
|---|---|---|---|---|
| Samuel Brolin | 29.09.2000 | 29 | | |
| Noel Törnqvist | 01.02.2002 | 1 | | |
| **Defenders:** | **DOB** | **M** | **(s)** | **G** |
| Jesper Thomas Valter Merbom Adolfsson | 15.01.1999 | | (2) | |
| Carlos Moros Gracia (ESP) | 15.04.1993 | 28 | | 4 |
| Noah Eile | 19.07.2002 | 22 | | |
| Josip Filipović (CRO) | 08.05.1996 | | (1) | |
| Jetmir Haliti (KOS) | 14.09.1996 | 20 | (3) | |
| Ivan Kričak (SRB) | 19.07.1996 | 18 | (6) | 1 |
| Adam Ståhl | 08.10.1994 | 24 | (1) | 1 |
| Magnus Finne Wørts (DEN) | 08.02.1999 | 7 | (4) | |
| **Midfielders:** | **DOB** | **M** | **(s)** | **G** |
| Amir Fouad Aboud Al Ammari (IRQ) | 27.07.1997 | 10 | (2) | 1 |
| Andreas Blomqvist | 05.05.1992 | | (12) | |

| Viktor Gustafson | 22.03.1995 | 20 | | 4 |
|---|---|---|---|---|
| Jesper Gustavsson | 29.10.1994 | 28 | | 1 |
| David Löfqvist | 06.08.1986 | 11 | (16) | 2 |
| Noah Persson | 16.07.2003 | 26 | (3) | 1 |
| Otto Rosengren | 16.05.2003 | 21 | (5) | |
| **Forwards:** | **DOB** | **M** | **(s)** | **G** |
| Jacob Bergström | 26.04.1995 | 8 | (7) | 2 |
| Herman Johansson | 16.10.1997 | 12 | (16) | 3 |
| Mamudu Moro (GHA) | 07.03.1995 | 18 | (9) | 2 |
| Albin Mörfelt | 10.01.2000 | 4 | (6) | |
| Silas Nwankwo (NGA) | 12.12.2003 | 17 | (11) | 8 |
| Heradi Rashidi | 24.07.1994 | 2 | (9) | |
| Taylor Silverholt | 04.04.2001 | | (2) | |
| Azeez Temitope Yusuf (NGA) | 09.03.2002 | | (2) | |
| Rasmus Wiedesheim-Paul | 08.02.1999 | 4 | (9) | |

## Idrottsföreningen Kamraterna Norrköping

| Founded: | 29.05.1897 | | | |
| Stadium: | Nya Parken, Norrköping (15,734) | | | |
| Trainer: | Rikard Norling | | 04.06.1971 | |
| [12.07.2022] | Vedran Vučičević (SRB) | | 11.05.1981 | |
| [08.08.2022] | Glen Riddersholm (DEN) | | 24.04.1972 | |

| Goalkeepers: | DOB | M | (s) | G |
|---|---|---|---|---|
| Oscar Jansson | 23.12.1990 | 30 | | |
| **Defenders:** | **DOB** | **M** | **(s)** | **G** |
| Viktor Agardius | 23.10.1989 | 11 | (2) | 1 |
| Egzon Binaku (ALB) | 27.08.1995 | 2 | (9) | |
| Filip Dagerstål | 01.02.1997 | 11 | | |
| Godswill Ekpolo (NGA) | 14.05.1995 | 23 | (5) | |
| Anton Mikael Eriksson | 05.03.2000 | 17 | | |
| Marco Lund (DEN) | 30.06.1996 | 12 | (4) | |
| Theodore Rask | 01.05.2000 | | (1) | |
| Ralf Linus Wahlqvist | 11.11.1996 | 26 | | |
| **Midfielders:** | **DOB** | **M** | **(s)** | **G** |
| Ishaq Abdulrazak (NGA) | 05.05.2002 | 10 | | |
| Daniel Eid (NOR) | 14.10.1998 | 22 | (6) | 1 |
| Fritiof Hellichius | 03.08.2003 | 1 | (5) | |
| Jean Carlos de Brito (BRA) | 09.06.1995 | 8 | | |

| Jacob Ortmark | 29.08.1997 | 28 | | 6 |
|---|---|---|---|---|
| Dino Salihović | 02.12.2002 | 2 | (8) | |
| Maic Sema | 02.12.1988 | 2 | (20) | 1 |
| Arnór Sigurðsson (ISL) | 15.05.1999 | 11 | | 6 |
| Ari Freyr Skúlason (ISL) | 14.05.1987 | 21 | (6) | |
| Christopher Nilsson Telo | 04.11.1989 | 1 | (5) | |
| **Forwards:** | **DOB** | **M** | **(s)** | **G** |
| Jonathan Levi | 23.01.1996 | 29 | | 6 |
| Lucas Urbano Dias de Lima | 02.04.2002 | 1 | (11) | |
| Andri Lucas Guðjohnsen (ISL) | 29.01.2002 | 2 | (11) | |
| Eman Marković (NOR) | 08.05.1999 | 10 | (5) | 1 |
| Christoffer Nyman | 05.10.1992 | 26 | (3) | 11 |
| Laorent Shabani | 19.08.1999 | 12 | (5) | 3 |
| Darrell Kamdem Tibell | 20.02.2002 | | (3) | |
| Arnór Ingvi Traustason (ISL) | 30.04.1993 | 12 | | 3 |

## Idrottsklubben Sirius Uppsala

| Founded: | 1907 | | | |
| Stadium: | Studenternas IP, Uppsala (10,038) | | | |
| Trainer: | Daniel Bäckström | | 22.12.1987 | |

| Goalkeepers: | DOB | M | (s) | G |
|---|---|---|---|---|
| David Mitov Nilsson (MKD) | 12.01.1991 | 13 | | |
| Hannes Sveijer | 28.04.2002 | 3 | | |
| Tommi Vaiho | 13.09.1988 | 14 | | |
| **Defenders:** | **DOB** | **M** | **(s)** | **G** |
| Tim Björkström | 08.01.1991 | 22 | (4) | 1 |
| Kristopher Da Graca | 16.01.1998 | 14 | (8) | |
| Johan Karlsson | 20.06.2001 | 3 | (10) | |
| Karl Larson | 28.10.1991 | 2 | (10) | 2 |
| Marcus Mathisen (DEN) | 27.02.1996 | 25 | | 3 |
| Patrick Nwadike | 29.08.1998 | 3 | (2) | 1 |
| Isak Ssewankambo | 27.02.1996 | 9 | | |
| Jakob Axel Krister Voelkerling-Persson | 27.09.2000 | 6 | (7) | 1 |
| Trond Dennis Widgren | 28.03.1994 | 13 | (1) | |
| Kevin Wright (SLE) | 28.12.1995 | 2 | (6) | |
| **Midfielders:** | **DOB** | **M** | **(s)** | **G** |
| Adam Hellborg | 30.07.1998 | 9 | (14) | 1 |

| Patrik Karlsson Lagemyr | 18.12.1996 | 14 | (3) | 1 |
|---|---|---|---|---|
| Filip Olsson | 24.04.1999 | 3 | (13) | |
| Óli Valur Ómarsson (ISL) | 09.01.2003 | 5 | (8) | |
| Jamie Roche | 05.04.2001 | 26 | (1) | |
| Filip Rogić | 14.06.1993 | 27 | | 1 |
| Daniel Tom John Stensson | 24.03.1997 | 15 | | 1 |
| Adam Wikman | 15.12.2003 | 2 | | |
| Moustafa Zeidan | 07.06.1998 | 7 | (1) | 1 |
| **Forwards:** | **DOB** | **M** | **(s)** | **G** |
| Aron Bjarnason (ISL) | 14.10.1995 | 28 | (2) | 4 |
| Christian Kouakou | 20.04.1995 | 24 | (2) | 7 |
| Tashreeq Matthews (RSA) | 12.09.2000 | 9 | (3) | 2 |
| Laorent Shabani (ALB) | 19.08.1999 | 11 | | 1 |
| Yukiya Sugita (JPN) | 22.04.1993 | 10 | (14) | 1 |
| Edi Sylisufaj (KOS) | 08.03.2000 | 11 | (16) | 1 |
| Antonio Yakoub | 12.06.2002 | | (3) | |

## Gymnastik- och Idrottsföreningen Sundsvall

| Founded: | 25.08.1903 | | | |
| Stadium: | NP3 Arena (Idrottsparken), Sundswall (8,000) | | | |
| Trainer: | Henrik Åhnstrand | | 29.07.1979 | |
| [29.07.2022] | Brian Clarhaut (USA) | | 11.04.1986 | |

| Goalkeepers: | DOB | M | (s) | G |
|---|---|---|---|---|
| Andreas Andersson | 27.02.1991 | 14 | | |
| Oscar Jonsson | 24.01.1997 | 12 | (1) | |
| Gustav Molin | 21.10.2002 | 4 | (1) | |
| **Defenders:** | **DOB** | **M** | **(s)** | **G** |
| Alexander Blomqvist | 03.08.1994 | 24 | (1) | 1 |
| Niklas Dahlström | 28.05.1997 | 1 | (4) | |
| Edwin Dellkrans | 17.04.2003 | | (2) | |
| Anton Eriksson | 05.03.2000 | 11 | | |
| Gabriel Venceslau Fernandes Castro (POR) | 15.11.2000 | 4 | (2) | |
| Forrest Baldwin Lasso (USA) | 11.05.1993 | 22 | | |
| Rasmus Lindkvist | 16.05.1990 | 22 | (1) | |
| Robert Lundström | 01.11.1989 | 25 | (1) | 1 |
| Dennis Olsson | 03.10.1994 | 20 | (9) | |
| Teodor Stenshagen | 11.02.2001 | 7 | (6) | |

| Midfielders: | DOB | M | (s) | G |
|---|---|---|---|---|
| Erik Andersson | 03.05.1997 | 22 | (2) | 2 |
| Johan Bengtsson | 01.01.2004 | | (4) | |
| Marcus Burman | 09.08.1996 | 4 | (16) | |
| Jesper Carström | 18.05.2002 | | (3) | |
| Joe Benny Corona Crespín (USA) | 09.07.1990 | 22 | (3) | |
| Peter Makrillos (AUS) | 04.09.1995 | 7 | (4) | 1 |
| Ludvig Nåvik | 02.11.2003 | 12 | (15) | |
| Paya Pichkah | 21.03.2000 | 11 | (10) | |
| Pontus Silfwer | 14.08.1991 | 15 | (9) | |
| Daniel Stensson | 24.03.1997 | 9 | | 1 |
| **Forwards:** | **DOB** | **M** | **(s)** | **G** |
| Ronaldo Damus (HAI) | 12.09.1999 | 15 | (10) | 5 |
| Pontus Engblom | 03.11.1991 | 25 | (2) | 11 |
| Alexander Larsson | 14.01.2004 | | (13) | |
| Saku Ylätupa (FIN) | 04.08.1999 | 22 | (5) | 5 |

## Varbergs Boll- och Idrottssällskap

**Founded**: 25.03.1925
**Stadium**: Varberg Energi Arena (Påskbergsvallen), Varberg (4,500)
**Trainer**: Joakim Persson    03.04.1975

| Goalkeepers: | DOB | M | (s) | G |
|---|---|---|---|---|
| Fredrik Andersson | 25.10.1988 | 27 | | |
| Stojan Lukić (BIH) | 28.12.1979 | 3 | (1) | |
| **Defenders:** | **DOB** | **M** | **(s)** | **G** |
| Jon Birkfeldt | 03.06.1996 | 19 | (3) | 1 |
| Johan Tobias Carlsson | 28.07.1995 | 13 | (1) | 1 |
| Joakim Lindner | 22.03.1991 | 25 | (1) | 1 |
| Gideon Mensah (GHA) | 09.10.2000 | 10 | (6) | 1 |
| Oliver Stanišić | 10.02.1994 | 20 | | 1 |
| Óskar Sverrisson (ISL) | 26.11.1992 | 7 | (5) | |
| Hampus Zackrisson | 24.08.1994 | 5 | (4) | |
| **Midfielders:** | **DOB** | **M** | **(s)** | **G** |
| André Boman | 15.11.2001 | 22 | (5) | |
| Eliton Pardinho Toreta Júnior (BRA) | 26.01.1998 | 7 | (11) | 1 |
| Filipe Sissé (POR) | 22.06.2001 | 5 | (5) | 2 |
| Alexander Johansson | 30.10.1995 | 24 | (5) | 6 |
| Victor Karlsson | 18.05.2001 | 2 | (4) | |
| Luke Gareth Le Roux (RSA) | 10.03.2000 | 26 | | 1 |

| | DOB | M | (s) | G |
|---|---|---|---|---|
| Anton Liljenbäck | 21.02.1995 | 19 | (3) | 2 |
| Ismet Lushaku (KOS) | 22.09.2000 | 16 | (6) | |
| Jacob Redenfors | 30.04.2004 | | (1) | |
| Joel Sundström | 15.08.2001 | | (8) | |
| Robin Tranberg | 06.02.1993 | 16 | (7) | 1 |
| Albin Winbo | 27.10.1997 | 4 | (7) | 1 |
| **Forwards:** | **DOB** | **M** | **(s)** | **G** |
| Oliver Alfonsi | 03.06.2003 | 14 | (10) | 2 |
| Filip Bohman | 24.11.1996 | 6 | (6) | 1 |
| Jaheem Burke | 19.08.2001 | | (7) | 1 |
| Flamur Dzelili | 09.09.1999 | | (3) | |
| Simon Karlsson Adjei | 10.11.1993 | 3 | (3) | 1 |
| Dion Krasniqi | 24.08.2003 | 1 | (7) | |
| Des Kunst (NED) | 12.10.1999 | 6 | (7) | |
| Montader Madjed | 07.04.2005 | 2 | (4) | |
| Tashreeq Matthews (RSA) | 12.09.2000 | 5 | (5) | |
| Robin Simović | 29.05.1991 | 23 | (1) | 7 |

## Idrottsföreningen Kamraterna Värnamo

**Founded**: 1912
**Stadium**: Finnvedsvallen, Värnamo (5,000)
**Trainer**: Kim Hellberg    01.02.1988

| Goalkeepers: | DOB | M | (s) | G |
|---|---|---|---|---|
| Hampus Gustafsson | 20.06.2001 | 1 | | |
| Jonathan Ayola Ursin Rasheed | 21.11.1991 | 2 | | |
| Pilip Vaitsiakhovich (BLR) | 26.03.1990 | 27 | | |
| **Defenders:** | **DOB** | **M** | **(s)** | **G** |
| Bernardo Vilar Estevão Jeronimo (BRA) | 12.02.1998 | 6 | (5) | |
| Francis de Vries (NZL) | 28.11.1994 | 10 | (1) | |
| Victor Eriksson | 17.09.2000 | 30 | | |
| Victor Larsson | 19.04.2000 | 24 | (4) | |
| Albin Zackarias Lohikangas | 20.08.1998 | 5 | (4) | |
| Hampus Näsström | 18.12.1994 | 7 | (18) | |
| Evaldo Nascimento Lamaur Neto „Netinho"(BRA) | 05.04.1994 | 14 | (6) | 1 |
| Robin Tihi (FIN) | 16.03.2002 | 27 | (1) | |
| Felix Wennergrund | 26.03.2001 | 1 | (3) | |
| Freddy Winsth | 15.07.1990 | 17 | (2) | |

| Midfielders: | DOB | M | (s) | G |
|---|---|---|---|---|
| David Mikael Edvardsson | 05.03.2002 | 1 | (6) | |
| Erick Brendon Pinheiro da Silva (BRA) | 23.05.1995 | 1 | (6) | |
| Oscar Johansson | 06.05.1995 | 28 | | 3 |
| William Kenndal | 04.04.1996 | 22 | (7) | |
| Abdussalam Magashy (NGA) | 06.04.1998 | 26 | (4) | 4 |
| Charlie Vindehall | 08.05.1996 | 7 | (18) | 1 |
| **Forwards:** | **DOB** | **M** | **(s)** | **G** |
| Carl Marcus Christer Antonsson | 08.05.1991 | 30 | | 20 |
| Haris Avdiu | 21.10.1997 | | (3) | |
| Edvin Bećirović | 29.03.2000 | 2 | (9) | |
| Jesper Dickman | 10.04.2001 | | (1) | |
| Christian Moses (SLE) | 10.08.1993 | | (4) | |
| Moonga Simba | 08.05.2000 | | (11) | |
| Wenderson Oliveira do Nascimento (BRA) | 27.04.1999 | 26 | (1) | 1 |
| Ajdin Zeljković | 26.12.1997 | 16 | | 2 |

## SECOND LEVEL
### Superettan 2022

| | | | | | | | | | |
|---|---|---|---|---|---|---|---|---|---|
| 1. | IF Brommapojkarna (*Promoted*) | 30 | 19 | 5 | 6 | 64 | - | 40 | 62 |
| 2. | Halmstads BK (*Promoted*) | 30 | 17 | 5 | 8 | 57 | - | 32 | 56 |
| 3. | Östers IF Växjö (*Promotion Play-offs*) | 30 | 13 | 9 | 8 | 47 | - | 35 | 48 |
| 4. | Trelleborgs FF | 30 | 13 | 6 | 11 | 46 | - | 49 | 45 |
| 5. | Skövde AIK | 30 | 11 | 11 | 8 | 40 | - | 39 | 44 |
| 6. | Landskrona BoIS | 30 | 11 | 11 | 8 | 40 | - | 42 | 44 |
| 7. | IK Brage Borlänge | 30 | 11 | 9 | 10 | 44 | - | 40 | 42 |
| 8. | AFC Eskilstuna | 30 | 12 | 4 | 14 | 48 | - | 46 | 40 |
| 9. | Västerås SK Fotboll | 30 | 10 | 10 | 10 | 50 | - | 49 | 40 |
| 10. | Örebro SK | 30 | 10 | 7 | 13 | 33 | - | 38 | 37 |
| 11. | Utsiktens BK Västra | 30 | 10 | 7 | 13 | 40 | - | 46 | 37 |
| 12. | Jönköpings Södra IF | 30 | 9 | 9 | 12 | 41 | - | 51 | 36 |
| 13. | Örgryte IS Göteborg (*Relegation Play-offs*) | 30 | 8 | 11 | 11 | 45 | - | 44 | 35 |
| 14. | Östersunds FK (*Relegation Play-offs*) | 30 | 7 | 10 | 13 | 32 | - | 44 | 31 |
| 15. | Norrby IF Borås (*Relegated*) | 30 | 8 | 7 | 15 | 33 | - | 47 | 31 |
| 16. | Dalkurd FF Uppsala (*Relegated*) | 30 | 8 | 5 | 17 | 37 | - | 55 | 29 |

## Relegation Play-offs (2nd / 3rd Level) [10-13.11.2022]

| | | |
|---|---|---|
| Sandvikens IF - Örgryte IS Göteborg | 0-2(0-1) | 3-2(0-1) |
| Falkenbergs FF - Östersunds FK | 1-1(1-1) | 0-2(0-0) |

Both Örgryte IS Göteborg and Östersunds FK remain at second level for 2022.

## INTERNATIONAL MATCHES
(16.07.2022 – 15.07.2023)

| 24.09.2022 | Beograd | Serbia - Sweden | 4-1(2-1) | (UNL) |
| 27.09.2022 | Stockholm | Sweden - Slovenia | 1-1(1-1) | (UNL) |
| 16.11.2022 | Girona | Mexico - Sweden | 1-2(0-0) | (F) |
| 19.11.2022 | Malmö | Sweden - Algeria | 2-0(1-0) | (F) |
| | | | | |
| 09.01.2023 | Faro/Loulé | Sweden - Finland | 2-0(1-0) | (F) |
| 12.01.2023 | Faro/Loulé | Sweden - Iceland | 2-1(0-1) | (F) |
| 24.03.2023 | Stockholm | Sweden - Belgium | 0-3(0-1) | (ECQ) |
| 27.03.2023 | Stockholm | Sweden - Azerbaijan | 5-0(1-0) | (ECQ) |
| 16.06.2023 | Stockholm | Sweden - New Zealand | 4-1(3-1) | (F) |
| 20.06.2023 | Wien | Austria - Sweden | 2-0(0-0) | (ECQ) |

**24.09.2022**    **SERBIA - SWEDEN**      **4-1(2-1)**      3rd UEFA Nations League B, Group 4
Stadion „Rajko Mitić", Beograd; Referee: Georgi Kabakov (Bulgaria); Attendance: 14,122
**SWE:** Robin Patrick Olsen, Daniel Andreas Sundgren, Isak Malcolm Kwaku Hien, Victor Jörgen Nilsson Lindelöf (Cap), Hans Carl Ludwig Augustinsson, Jens-Lys Michel Cajuste (46.Mats Kristoffer Olsson), Mattias Olof Svanberg, Viktor Johan Anton Claesson (64.Anthony David Junior Elanga), Dejan Kuluševski (64.Mikael Ishak), Emil Peter Forsberg (74.Jesper Kewe Karlström), Viktor Gyökeres (64.Robin Kwamina Quaison). Trainer: Jan Olof Andersson.
**Goal:** Viktor Johan Anton Claesson (15).

**27.09.2022**    **SWEDEN - SLOVENIA**      **1-1(1-1)**      3rd UEFA Nations League B, Group 4
Friends Arena, Stockholm; Referee: Felix Zwayer (Germany); Attendance: 22,895
**SWE:** Robin Patrick Olsen, Eric Joel Andersson, Victor Jörgen Nilsson Lindelöf (Cap), Isak Malcolm Kwaku Hien (88.Mikael Ishak), Hans Carl Ludwig Augustinsson, Mats Kristoffer Olsson (79.Mattias Olof Svanberg), Jesper Kewe Karlström, Viktor Johan Anton Claesson (70.Anthony David Junior Elanga), Emil Peter Forsberg, Dejan Kuluševski, Robin Kwamina Quaison (70.Viktor Gyökeres). Trainer: Jan Olof Andersson.
**Goal:** Emil Peter Forsberg (42).

**16.11.2022**    **MEXICO - SWEDEN**      **1-2(0-0)**      Friendly International
Estadi Montilivi, Girona (Spain); Referee: César Soto Grado (Spain); Attendance: 5,395
**SWE:** Bo Kristoffer Nordfeldt, Emil Alfons Holm, Victor Jörgen Nilsson Lindelöf (Cap), Isak Malcolm Kwaku Hien, Hans Carl Ludwig Augustinsson (82.Ken Nlata Sema), Samuel Gustafson, Jesper Kewe Karlström (69.Emil Peter Forsberg), Marcus Christer Rohdén (83.Magnus Eriksson), Mattias Olof Svanberg, Anthony David Junior Elanga (69.Robin Kwamina Quaison), Viktor Gyökeres (69.Mikael Ishak). Trainer: Jan Olof Andersson.
**Goals:** Marcus Christer Rohdén (54), Mattias Olof Svanberg (84).

**19.11.2022**    **SWEDEN - ALGERIA**      **2-0(1-0)**      Friendly International
Malmö Stadion, Malmö; Referee: Espen Eskås (Norway); Attendance: 13,486
**SWE:** Robin Patrick Olsen, Emil Alfons Holm, Victor Jörgen Nilsson Lindelöf (Cap) (46.Aiham Hanz Ousou), Isak Malcolm Kwaku Hien, Hans Carl Ludwig Augustinsson, Samuel Gustafson, Mats Kristoffer Olsson (66.Jesper Kewe Karlström), Mattias Olof Svanberg (75.Marcus Christer Rohdén), Viktor Johan Anton Claesson (66.Anthony David Junior Elanga), Emil Peter Forsberg (67.Karl Jesper Karlsson), Viktor Gyökeres (84.Robin Kwamina Quaison). Trainer: Jan Olof Andersson.
**Goals:** Emil Peter Forsberg (45+3), Viktor Johan Anton Claesson (47).

**09.01.2023**    **SWEDEN - FINLAND**      **2-0(1-0)**      Friendly International
Estádio Algarve, Faro/Loulé (Portugal); Referee: Vitor Jorge Fernandes Ferreira (Portugal); Attendance: n/a
**SWE:** Leopold Wahlstedt, André Peder Boman, Victor Kim Ludwig Eriksson, Hjalmar Ekdal, Noah Karl Anders Persson, Alexander Olof Bernhardsson, Samuel Gustafson (Cap) (82.Carl Ivar Gustafsson), Hugo Emanuel Larsson (68.Bilal Hussein), Yasin Abbas Ayari (82.Algot Sebastian Nanasi), Moustafa Zeidan Khalili (68.Omar Faraj), Christoffer Åke Sven Nyman (82.Joel Joshogene Asoro). Trainer: Jan Olof Andersson.
**Goals:** Christoffer Åke Sven Nyman (38), Joel Joshogene Asoro (90+3).

**12.01.2023**    **SWEDEN - ICELAND**      **2-1(0-1)**      Friendly International
Estádio Algarve, Faro/Loulé (Portugal); Referee: Luís Miguel Branco Godinho (Portugal); Attendance: 212
**SWE:** Jacob Mikael Widell Zetterström (46.Oliver Lukas Dozae Nnonyelu Dovin), Josafat Woodling Mendes, Gustaf Johan Lagerbielke, Edvin Kurtulus (Cap), Nils Erik Elias Andersson, Armin Gigović (77.Samuel Gustafson), Carl Ivar Gustafsson (63.Omar Faraj), Jacob Axel Per Ondrejka, Algot Sebastian Nanasi (79.Yasin Abbas Ayari), Joel Joshogene Asoro (84.Moustafa Zeidan Khalili), Victor Kaj Edvardsen (63.Bilal Hussein). Trainer: Jan Olof Andersson.
**Goals:** Nils Erik Elias Andersson (85), Jacob Ondrejka (90+4).

**24.03.2023**    **SWEDEN - BELGIUM**      **0-3(0-1)**      17th EC. Qualifiers
Friends Arena, Stockholm; Referee: Orel Grinfeld (Israel); Attendance: 49,296
**SWE:** Robin Patrick Olsen, Ralf Linus Wahlqvist, Victor Jörgen Nilsson Lindelöf (Cap), Hjalmar Ekdal, Hans Carl Ludwig Augustinsson (85.Gabriel Gudmundsson), Samuel Gustafson, Mats Kristoffer Olsson (64.Viktor Gyökeres), Mattias Olof Svanberg, Emil Peter Forsberg (73.Viktor Johan Anton Claesson), Dejan Kuluševski, Alexander Isak (73.Zlatan Ibrahimović). Trainer: Jan Olof Andersson.

**27.03.2023**    **SWEDEN - AZERBAIJAN**      **5-0(1-0)**      17th EC. Qualifiers
Friends Arena, Stockholm; Referee: Stéphanie Frappart (France); Attendance: 23,674
**SWE:** Robin Patrick Olsen, Ralf Linus Wahlqvist, Victor Jörgen Nilsson Lindelöf (Cap), Hjalmar Ekdal (46.Isak Malcolm Kwaku Hien), Gabriel Gudmundsson, Mattias Olof Svanberg, Samuel Gustafson, Dejan Kuluševski (82.Karl Jesper Karlsson), Emil Peter Forsberg (70.Jesper Kewe Karlström), Viktor Gyökeres (87.Anthony David Junior Elanga), Alexander Isak (70.Viktor Johan Anton Claesson). Trainer: Jan Olof Andersson.
**Goals:** Emil Peter Forsberg (38), Bəhlul Mustafazadə (65 own goal), Viktor Gyökeres (79), Karl Jesper Karlsson (88), Anthony David Junior Elanga (89).

**16.06.2023**     **SWEDEN - NEW ZEALAND**            **4-1(3-1)**            Friendly International

Friends Arena, Stockholm; Referee: Craig Pawson (England); Attendance: 20,528
**SWE:** Bo Kristoffer Nordfeldt, Daniel Andreas Sundgren, Carl Anders Theodor Starfelt, Hjalmar Ekdal (76.Edvin Kurtulus), Gabriel Gudmundsson (46.Ken Nlata Sema), Jens-Lys Michel Cajuste (61.Hugo Emanuel Larsson), Mats Kristoffer Olsson (46.Jesper Kewe Karlström), Marcus Christer Rohdén, Karl Jesper Karlsson, Viktor Johan Anton Claesson (Cap) (61.Anthony David Junior Elanga), Robin Kwamina Quaison. Trainer: Jan Olof Andersson.
**Goals:** Karl Jesper Karlsson (39), Robin Kwamina Quaison (44), Karl Jesper Karlsson (45), Anthony David Junior Elanga (90+2).

**20.06.2023**     **AUSTRIA - SWEDEN**              **2-0(0-0)**            17th EC. Qualifiers

"Ernst Happel" Stadion, Wien; Referee: Marco Guida (Italy); Attendance: 46,300
**SWE:** Robin Patrick Olsen, Ralf Linus Wahlqvist, Isak Malcolm Kwaku Hien, Victor Jörgen Nilsson Lindelöf (Cap), Martin Tony Waikwa Olsson, Albin Ekdal (46.Jesper Kewe Karlström), Samuel Gustafson, Mattias Olof Svanberg (87.Viktor Johan Anton Claesson), Emil Peter Forsberg (76.Karl Jesper Karlsson), Dejan Kuluševski (87.Anthony David Junior Elanga), Alexander Isak (76.Viktor Gyökeres). Trainer: Jan Olof Andersson.

## NATIONAL TEAM PLAYERS
### (16.07.2022 – 15.07.2023)

| Name | DOB | Caps | Goals | Club |
|---|---|---|---|---|
| **Goalkeepers** | | | | |
| Oliver Lukas Dozae Nnonyelu DOVIN | 11.07.2002 | 1 | 0 | 2023: *Hammarby IF Stockholm* |
| Bo Kristoffer NORDFELDT | 23.06.1989 | 17 | 0 | 2022/2023: *AIK Stockholm* |
| Robin Patrick OLSEN | 08.01.1990 | 66 | 0 | 2022/2023: *Aston Villa FC Birmingham (ENG)* |
| Leopold WAHLSTEDT | 04.07.1999 | 1 | 0 | 2023: *Odds BK Skien (NOR)* |
| Jacob Mikael Widell ZETTERSTRÖM | 11.07.1998 | 1 | 0 | 2023: *Djurgårdens IF Stockholm* |
| **Defenders** | | | | |
| Nils Erik Elias ANDERSSON | 31.01.1996 | 1 | 1 | 2023: *Djurgårdens IF Stockholm* |
| Eric Joel ANDERSSON | 11.11.1996 | 9 | 0 | 2022: *FC Midtjylland Herning (DEN)* |
| Hans Carl Ludwig AUGUSTINSSON | 21.04.1994 | 51 | 2 | 2022: *Aston Villa FC Birmingham (ENG)* <br> 30.01.2023-> *RCD Mallorca (ESP)* |
| André Peder BOMAN | 15.11.2001 | 1 | 0 | 2023: *Varbergs BoIS* |
| Hjalmar EKDAL | 21.10.1998 | 6 | 0 | 2022: *Djurgårdens IF Stockholm* <br> 21.01.2023-> *Burnley FC (ENG)* |
| Victor Kim Ludwig ERIKSSON | 17.09.2000 | 1 | 0 | 2023: *IFK Värnamo* |
| Gabriel GUDMUNDSSON | 29.04.1999 | 5 | 0 | 2023: *Lille OSC (FRA)* |
| Isak Malcolm Kwaku HIEN | 13.01.1999 | 6 | 0 | 2022/2023: *Hellas Verona FC (ITA)* |
| Emil Alfons HOLM | 13.05.2000 | 2 | 0 | 2022: *Spezia Calcio La Spezia (ITA)* |
| Edvin KURTULUS | 05.03.2000 | 4 | 0 | 2023: *Hammarby IF Stockholm* |
| Gustaf Johan LAGERBIELKE | 10.04.2000 | 1 | 0 | 2023: *IF Elfsborg Borås* |
| Victor Jörgen Nilsson LINDELÖF | 17.07.1994 | 59 | 3 | 2022/2023: *Manchester United FC (ENG)* |
| Josafat Woodling MENDES | 31.12.2002 | 1 | 0 | 2023: *AIK Stockholm* |
| Martin Tony Waikwa OLSSON | 17.05.1988 | 56 | 5 | 2023: *Malmö FF* |
| Aiham Hanz OUSOU | 09.01.2000 | 1 | 0 | 2022: *SK Slavia Praha (CZE)* |
| Noah Karl Anders PERSSON | 16.07.2003 | 1 | 0 | 2023: *Mjällby AIF Hällevik* |
| Ken Nlata SEMA | 30.09.1993 | 15 | 0 | 2022/2023: *Watford FC (ENG)* |
| Carl Anders Theodor STARFELT | 01.06.1995 | 6 | 0 | 2023: *Celtic FC Glasgow (SCO)* |
| Daniel Andreas SUNDGREN | 22.11.1990 | 3 | 0 | 2022/2023: *Maccabi Haifa FC (ISR)* |
| Ralf Linus WAHLQVIST | 11.11.1996 | 9 | 0 | 2023: *MKS Pogoń Szczecin* |

## Midfielders

| Name | Date of Birth | M | G | Year | Club |
|---|---|---|---|---|---|
| Yasin Abbas AYARI | 06.10.2003 | 2 | 0 | 2023: | *AIK Stockholm* |
| Alexander Olof BERNHARDSSON | 08.09.1998 | 1 | 0 | 2023: | *IF Elfsborg Borås* |
| Jens-Lys Michel CAJUSTE | 10.08.1999 | 15 | 0 | 2022/2023: | *Stade de Reims (FRA)* |
| Viktor Johan Anton CLAESSON | 02.01.1992 | 69 | 13 | 2022/2023: | *FC København (DEN)* |
| Albin EKDAL | 28.07.1989 | 67 | 0 | 2023: | *Spezia Calcio La Spezia (ITA)* |
| Anthony David Junior ELANGA | 27.04.2002 | 12 | 3 | 2022/2023: | *Manchester United FC (ENG)* |
| Magnus Lennart ERIKSSON | 08.04.1990 | 4 | 0 | 2022: | *Djurgårdens IF Stockholm* |
| Emil Peter FORSBERG | 23.10.1991 | 81 | 20 | 2022/2023: | *RasenBallsport Leipzig (GER)* |
| Armin GIGOVIĆ | 06.04.2002 | 1 | 0 | 2023: | *FK Rostov (RUS)* |
| Samuel GUSTAFSON | 11.01.1995 | 7 | 0 | 2022/2023: | *BK Häcken Göteborg* |
| Carl Ivar GUSTAFSSON | 18.03.2000 | 2 | 0 | 2023: | *Kalmar FF* |
| Bilal HUSSEIN | 22.04.2000 | 2 | 0 | 2023: | *AIK Stockholm* |
| Karl Jesper KARLSSON | 25.07.1998 | 11 | 3 | 2022/2023: | *AZ Alkmaar (NED)* |
| Jesper Kewe KARLSTRÖM | 21.06.1995 | 13 | 0 | 2022/2023: | *KKS Lech Poznań* |
| Hugo Emanuel LARSSON | 27.06.2004 | 2 | 0 | 2023: | *Malmö FF* |
| Algot Sebastian NANASI | 16.05.2002 | 2 | 0 | 2023: | *Malmö FF* |
| Mats Kristoffer OLSSON | 30.06.1995 | 45 | 0 | 2022/2023: | *FC Midtjylland Herning (DEN)* |
| Jacob Axel Per ONDREJKA | 02.09.2002 | 1 | 0 | 2023: | *IF Elfsborg Borås* |
| Marcus Christer ROHDÉN | 11.05.1991 | 18 | 2 | 2022/2023: | *Frosinone Calcio (ITA)* |
| Mattias Olof SVANBERG | 05.01.1999 | 28 | 2 | 2022/2023: | *VfL Wolfsburg (GER)* |

## Forwards

| Name | Date of Birth | M | G | Year | Club |
|---|---|---|---|---|---|
| Joel Joshogene ASORO | 27.04.1999 | 2 | 1 | 2023: | *Djurgårdens IF Stockholm* |
| Victor Kaj EDVARDSEN | 14.01.1996 | 1 | 0 | 2023: | *Djurgårdens IF Stockholm* |
| Omar FARAJ | 09.03.2002 | 2 | 0 | 2023: | *AIK Stockholm* |
| Viktor GYÖKERES | 04.06.1998 | 14 | 3 | 2022/2023: | *Coventry City FC (ENG)* |
| Zlatan IBRAHIMOVIĆ | 03.10.1981 | 122 | 62 | 2023: | *AC Milan (ITA)* |
| Alexander ISAK | 21.09.1999 | 40 | 9 | 2023: | *Newcastle United FC (ENG)* |
| Mikael ISHAK | 31.03.1993 | 7 | 1 | 2022: | *KKS Lech Poznań (POL)* |
| Dejan KULUŠEVSKI | 25.04.2000 | 30 | 2 | 2022/2023: | *Tottenham Hotspur FC London (ENG)* |
| Christoffer Åke Sven NYMAN | 05.10.1992 | 11 | 2 | 2023: | *IFK Norrköping* |
| Robin Kwamina QUAISON | 09.10.1993 | 47 | 13 | 2022/2023: | *Al-Ettifaq FC Dammam (KSA)* |
| Moustafa ZEIDAN Khalili | 07.06.1998 | 2 | 0 | 2023: | *Malmö FF* |

## Trainer

| Name | Date of Birth | Record |
|---|---|---|
| Jan Olof "Janne" ANDERSSON [from 23.06.2016] | 29.09.1962 | 88 M; 45 W; 14 D; 29 L; 139-89 |

# SWITZERLAND

## The Country:
Schweizerische Eidgenossenschaft (Swiss Confederation)
Capital: Bern
Surface: 41,285 km²
Inhabitants: 8,636,896 [2020]
Time: UTC+1

## The FA:
Schweizerischer Fussballverband
Worbstrasse 48, Postfach 3000, Bern 15
Tel: +41 31 950 8111
Founded: 07.04.1895
Member of FIFA since: 1904
Member of UEFA since: 1954
Website: www.football.ch

## NATIONAL TEAM RECORDS

### RECORDS
| | | |
|---|---|---|
| First international match: | 12.02.1905, Paris: | France – Switzerland 1-0 |
| Most international caps: | Heinz Hermann | - 118 caps (1978-1991) |
| Most international goals: | Alexander Frei | - 42 goals / 84 caps (2001-2011) |

### UEFA EUROPEAN CHAMPIONSHIP
| | |
|---|---|
| 1960 | Did not enter |
| 1964 | Qualifiers |
| 1968 | Qualifiers |
| 1972 | Qualifiers |
| 1976 | Qualifiers |
| 1980 | Qualifiers |
| 1984 | Qualifiers |
| 1988 | Qualifiers |
| 1992 | Qualifiers |
| 1996 | Final Tournament (Group Stage) |
| 2000 | Qualifiers |
| 2004 | Final Tournament (Group Stage) |
| 2008 | Final Tournament (Group Stage) |
| 2012 | Qualifiers |
| 2016 | Final Tournament (2nd Round of 16) |
| 2020 | Final Tournament (Quarter-Finals) |

### FIFA WORLD CUP
| | |
|---|---|
| 1930 | Did not enter |
| 1934 | Final Tournament (Quarter-Finals) |
| 1938 | Final Tournament (Quarter-Finals) |
| 1950 | Final Tournament (Group Stage) |
| 1954 | Final Tournament (Quarter-Finals) |
| 1958 | Qualifiers |
| 1962 | Final Tournament (Group Stage) |
| 1966 | Final Tournament (Group Stage) |
| 1970 | Qualifiers |
| 1974 | Qualifiers |
| 1978 | Qualifiers |
| 1982 | Qualifiers |
| 1986 | Qualifiers |
| 1990 | Qualifiers |
| 1994 | Final Tournament (2nd Round of 16) |
| 1998 | Qualifiers |
| 2002 | Qualifiers |
| 2006 | Final Tournament (2nd Round of 16) |
| 2010 | Final Tournament (Group Stage) |
| 2014 | Final Tournament (2nd Round of 16) |
| 2018 | Final Tournament (2nd Round of 16) |
| 2022 | Final Tournament (2nd Round of 16) |

### OLYMPIC TOURNAMENTS
| | |
|---|---|
| 1908 | - |
| 1912 | - |
| 1920 | - |
| 1924 | Runners-up |
| 1928 | 1/8 - Finals |
| 1936 | Did not enter |
| 1948 | Did not enter |
| 1952 | Did not enter |
| 1956 | Did not enter |
| 1960 | Qualifiers |
| 1964 | Qualifiers |
| 1968 | Qualifiers |
| 1972 | Qualifiers |
| 1976 | Did not enter |
| 1980 | Did not enter |
| 1984 | Did not enter |
| 1988 | Qualifiers |
| 1992 | Qualifiers |
| 1996 | Qualifiers |
| 2000 | Qualifiers |
| 2004 | Qualifiers |
| 2008 | Qualifiers |
| 2012 | Group Stage |
| 2016 | Qualifiers |
| 2020 | Qualifiers |

### UEFA NATIONS LEAGUE
| | |
|---|---|
| 2018/2019 | League A (Group Stage -> Final Tournament: 4th Place) |
| 2020/2021 | League A (Group Stage) |
| 2022/2023 | League A (Group Stage) |

### SWISS CLUB HONOURS IN EUROPEAN CLUB COMPETITIONS:

#### European Champion Clubs' Cup (1956-1992) / UEFA Champions League (1993-2023)
None

#### Fairs Cup (1858-1971) / UEFA Cup (1972-2009) / UEFA Europa League (2010-2023)
None

#### UEFA Europa Conference League (2021-2023)
None

#### UEFA Super Cup (1972-2022)
None

#### European Cup Winners' Cup 1961-1999*
None

*defunct competition

# NATIONAL COMPETITIONS
## TABLE OF HONOURS

| | CHAMPIONS | CUP WINNERS | BEST GOALSCORERS | |
|---|---|---|---|---|
| 1898/1899 | Anglo-American Club FC Zürich | - | - | |
| 1899/1900 | Grasshopper Club Zürich | - | - | |
| 1900/1901 | Grasshopper Club Zürich | - | - | |
| 1901/1902 | FC Zürich | - | - | |
| 1902/1903 | BSC Young Boys Bern | - | - | |
| 1903/1904 | FC St. Gallen | - | - | |
| 1904/1905 | Grasshopper Club Zürich | - | - | |
| 1905/1906 | FC Winterthur | - | - | |
| 1906/1907 | Servette FC Genève | - | - | |
| 1907/1908 | FC Winterthur | - | - | |
| 1908/1909 | BSC Young Boys Bern | - | - | |
| 1909/1910 | BSC Young Boys Bern | - | - | |
| 1910/1911 | BSC Young Boys Bern | - | - | |
| 1911/1912 | FC Aarau | - | - | |
| 1912/1913 | Montriond Lausanne | - | - | |
| 1913/1914 | FC Aarau | - | - | |
| 1914/1915 | SC Brühl St. Gallen | - | - | |
| 1915/1916 | Cantonal Neuchâtel | - | - | |
| 1916/1917 | FC Winterthur | - | - | |
| 1917/1918 | Servette FC Genève | - | - | |
| 1918/1919 | Étoile La Chaux-de-Fonds | - | - | |
| 1919/1920 | BSC Young Boys Bern | - | - | |
| 1920/1921 | Grasshopper Club Zürich | - | - | |
| 1921/1922 | Servette FC Genève | - | - | |
| 1922/1923 | *Title not awarded* | - | - | |
| 1923/1924 | FC Zürich | - | - | |
| 1924/1925 | Servette FC Genève | - | - | |
| 1925/1926 | Servette FC Genève | Grasshopper Club Zürich | - | |
| 1926/1927 | Grasshopper Club Zürich | Grasshopper Club Zürich | - | |
| 1927/1928 | Grasshopper Club Zürich | Servette FC Genève FC | - | |
| 1928/1929 | BSC Young Boys Bern | Urania Genève Sport | - | |
| 1929/1930 | Servette FC Genève | BSC Young Boys Bern | - | |
| 1930/1931 | Grasshopper Club Zürich | FC Lugano | - | |
| 1931/1932 | FC Lausanne-Sport | Grasshopper Club Zürich | - | |
| 1932/1933 | Servette FC Genève | FC Basel | - | |
| 1933/1934 | Servette FC Genève | Grasshopper Club Zürich | Leopold Kielholz (Servette FC Genève) | 40 |
| 1934/1935 | FC Lausanne-Sport | FC Lausanne-Sport | Engelbert Bösch (AUT, FC Bern) | 27 |
| 1935/1936 | FC Lausanne-Sport | Young Fellows FC Zürich | Willy Jäggi (FC Lausanne-Sport) | 27 |
| 1936/1937 | Grasshopper Club Zürich | Grasshopper Club Zürich | Alessandro Frigerio Payán (Young Fellows FC Zürich) | 23 |
| 1937/1938 | FC Lugano | Grasshopper Club Zürich | Numa Monnard (FC Basel) | 20 |
| 1938/1939 | Grasshopper Club Zürich | FC Lausanne-Sport | Josef Artimovics (AUT, FC Grenchen) | 15 |
| 1939/1940 | Servette FC Genève | Grasshopper Club Zürich | Georges Aeby (Servette FC Genève) | 22 |
| 1940/1941 | FC Lugano | Grasshopper Club Zürich | Alessandro Frigerio Payán (FC Lugano) | 26 |
| 1941/1942 | Grasshopper Club Zürich | Grasshopper Club Zürich | Alessandro Frigerio Payán (FC Lugano) | 23 |
| 1942/1943 | Grasshopper Club Zürich | Grasshopper Club Zürich | Lauro Amadò (Grasshopper Club Zürich) | 31 |
| 1943/1944 | FC Lausanne-Sport | FC Lausanne-Sport | Erich Andres (Young Fellows FC Zürich) | 23 |
| 1944/1945 | Grasshopper Club Zürich | BSC Young Boys Bern | Hans-Peter Friedländer (Grasshopper Club Zürich) | 26 |
| 1945/1946 | Servette FC Genève | Grasshopper Club Zürich | Hans-Peter Friedländer (Grasshopper Club Zürich) | 25 |
| 1946/1947 | FC Biel-Bienne | FC Basel | Lauro Amadò (Grasshopper Club Zürich) Hans Blaser (BSC Young Boys Bern) | 19 |
| 1947/1948 | AC Bellinzona | FC La Chaux-de-Fonds | Josef Righetti (FC Grenchen) | 26 |
| 1948/1949 | FC Lugano | Servette FC Genève FC | Jacques Fatton (Servette FC Genève) | 21 |
| 1949/1950 | Servette FC Genève | FC Lausanne-Sport | Jacques Fatton (Servette FC Genève) | 32 |
| 1950/1951 | FC Lausanne-Sport | FC La Chaux-de-Fonds | Hans-Peter Friedländer (FC Lausanne-Sport) | 23 |
| 1951/1952 | Grasshopper Club Zürich | Grasshopper Club Zürich | Josef Hügi (FC Basel) | 24 |
| 1952/1953 | FC Basel | BSC Young Boys Bern | Josef Hügi (FC Basel) Eugen Meier (BSC Young Boys Bern) | 32 |
| 1953/1954 | FC La Chaux-de-Fonds | FC La Chaux-de-Fonds | Josef Hügi (FC Basel) | 29 |
| 1954/1955 | FC La Chaux-de-Fonds | FC La Chaux-de-Fonds | Marcel Mauron (FC La Chaux-de-Fonds) | 30 |
| 1955/1956 | Grasshopper Club Zürich | Grasshopper Club Zürich | Branislav Vukosavljević (YUG, Grasshopper Club Zürich) | 33 |
| 1956/1957 | BSC Young Boys Bern | FC La Chaux-de-Fonds | Adrien Kauer (FC La Chaux-de-Fonds) | 29 |
| 1957/1958 | BSC Young Boys Bern | BSC Young Boys Bern | Ernst Wechselberger (GER, BSC Young Boys Bern) | 22 |
| 1958/1959 | BSC Young Boys Bern | FC Grenchen | Eugen Meier (BSC Young Boys Bern) | 24 |
| 1959/1960 | BSC Young Boys Bern | FC Luzern | Willy Schneider (BSC Young Boys Bern) | 25 |
| 1960/1961 | Servette FC Genève | FC La Chaux-de-Fonds | Giuliano Robbiani (Grasshopper Club Zürich) | 27 |
| 1961/1962 | Servette FC Genève | FC Lausanne-Sport | Jacques Fatton (Servette FC Genève) | 25 |
| 1962/1963 | FC Zürich | FC Basel | Peter von Burg (FC Zürich) | 24 |

| | | | |
|---|---|---|---|
| 1963/1964 | FC La Chaux-de-Fonds | FC Lausanne-Sport | Michel Desbiolles (Servette FC Genève) | 23 |
| 1964/1965 | FC Lausanne-Sport | FC Sion | Rolf Blättler (Grasshopper Club Zürich) Pierre Kerkhoffs (NED, FC Lausanne-Sport) | 19 |
| 1965/1966 | FC Zürich | FC Zürich | Rolf Blättler (Grasshopper Club Zürich) | 28 |
| 1966/1967 | FC Basel | FC Basel | Rolf Blättler (Grasshopper Club Zürich) | 24 |
| 1967/1968 | FC Zürich | FC Lugano | Friedrich Künzli (FC Zürich) | 28 |
| 1968/1969 | FC Basel | FC St. Gallen | Hans-Otto Peters (GER, FC Biel-Bienne) | 24 |
| 1969/1970 | FC Basel | FC Zürich | Friedrich Künzli (FC Zürich) | 19 |
| 1970/1971 | Grasshopper Club Zürich | Servette FC Genève FC | Walter Müller (BSC Young Boys Bern) | 19 |
| 1971/1972 | FC Basel | FC Zürich | Herbert Dimmeler (FC Winterthur) Bernd Dörfel (GER, Servette FC Genève) | 17 |
| 1972/1973 | FC Basel | FC Zürich | Ottmar Hitzfeld (FC Basel) Jan-Olof Grahn (FC Lausanne-Sport) | 18 |
| 1973/1974 | FC Zürich | FC Sion | Daniel Jeandupeux (FC Zürich) | 22 |
| 1974/1975 | FC Zürich | FC Basel | Ilija Katić (FC Zürich) | 23 |
| 1975/1976 | FC Zürich | FC Zürich | Peter Risi (FC Zürich) | 33 |
| 1976/1977 | FC Basel | BSC Young Boys Bern | Franco Cucinotta (ITA, FC Zürich) | 28 |
| 1977/1978 | Grasshopper Club Zürich | Servette FC Genève FC | Friedrich Künzli (FC Lausanne-Sport) | 21 |
| 1978/1979 | Servette FC Genève | Servette FC Genève FC | Peter Risi (FC Zürich) | 16 |
| 1979/1980 | FC Basel | FC Sion | Claudio Sulser (Grasshopper Club Zürich) | 25 |
| 1980/1981 | FC Zürich | FC Lausanne-Sport | Peter Risi (FC Luzern) | 18 |
| 1981/1982 | Grasshopper Club Zürich | FC Sion | Claudio Sulser (Grasshopper Club Zürich) | 23 |
| 1982/1983 | Grasshopper Club Zürich | Grasshopper Club Zürich | Jean-Paul Brigger (Servette FC Genève) | 23 |
| 1983/1984 | Grasshopper Club Zürich | Servette FC Genève FC | Georges Bregy (FC Sion) | 21 |
| 1984/1985 | Servette FC Genève | FC Aarau | Dominique Cina (FC Sion) | 24 |
| 1985/1986 | BSC Young Boys Bern | FC Sion | Steen Thychosen (DEN, FC Lausanne-Sport) | 21 |
| 1986/1987 | Neuchâtel Xamax FCS | BSC Young Boys Bern | John Hartmann Eriksen (DEN, Servette FC Genève) | 28 |
| 1987/1988 | Neuchâtel Xamax FCS | Grasshopper Club Zürich | John Hartmann Eriksen (DEN, Servette FC Genève) | 36 |
| 1988/1989 | FC Luzern | Grasshopper Club Zürich | Karl-Heinz Rummenigge (GER, Servette FC Genève) | 24 |
| 1989/1990 | Grasshopper Club Zürich | Grasshopper Club Zürich | Iván Luis Zamorano Zamora (CHI, FC St. Gallen) | 23 |
| 1990/1991 | Grasshopper Club Zürich | FC Sion | Dario Zuffi (BSC Young Boys Bern) | 17 |
| 1991/1992 | FC Sion | FC Luzern | Miklos Jon Molnar (DEN, Servette FC Genève) | 18 |
| 1992/1993 | FC Aarau | FC Lugano | „Sonny" Anderson da Silva (BRA, Servette FC Genève) | 20 |
| 1993/1994 | Servette FC Genève | Grasshopper Club Zürich | Élber de Souza (BRA, Grasshopper Club Zürich) | 21 |
| 1994/1995 | Grasshopper Club Zürich | FC Sion | Petar Aleksandrov (BUL, Neuchâtel Xamax FCS) | 24 |
| 1995/1996 | Grasshopper Club Zürich | FC Sion | Petar Aleksandrov (BUL, FC Luzern) Viorel Dinu Moldovan (ROU, Neuchâtel Xamax FCS) | 19 |
| 1996/1997 | FC Sion | FC Sion | Viorel Dinu Moldovan (ROU, Grasshopper Club Zürich) | 27 |
| 1997/1998 | Grasshopper Club Zürich | FC Lausanne-Sport | Shabani Christophe Nonda (COD, FC Zürich) | 24 |
| 1998/1999 | Servette FC Genève | FC Lausanne-Sport | Alexandre Rey (Servette FC Genève) | 19 |
| 1999/2000 | FC St. Gallen | FC Zürich | Charles Amoah (GHA, FC St. Gallen) | 25 |
| 2000/2001 | Grasshopper Club Zürich | Servette FC Genève FC | Stéphane Chapuisat (Grasshopper Club Zürich) Christian Eduardo Giménez (ARG, FC Lugano) | 21 |
| 2001/2002 | FC Basel | FC Basel | Christian Eduardo Giménez (ARG, FC Lugano) Richard Darío Núñez Pereyra (URU, Grasshopper Club Zürich) | 28 |
| 2002/2003 | Grasshopper Club Zürich | FC Basel | Richard Darío Núñez Pereyra (URU, Grasshopper Club Zürich) | 27 |
| 2003/2004 | FC Basel | FC Will 1900 | Stéphane Chapuisat (BSC Young Boys Bern) | 23 |
| 2004/2005 | FC Basel | FC Zürich | Christian Eduardo Giménez (ARG, FC Basel) | 27 |
| 2005/2006 | FC Zürich | FC Sion | Alhassane Keita Otchico (GUI, FC Zürich) | 20 |
| 2006/2007 | FC Zürich | FC Basel | Mladen Petrić (CRO, FC Basel) | 19 |
| 2007/2008 | FC Basel | FC Basel | Hakan Yakin (BSC Young Boys Bern) | 24 |
| 2008/2009 | FC Zürich | FC Sion | Seydou Doumbia (CIV, BSC Young Boys Bern) | 20 |
| 2009/2010 | FC Basel | FC Basel | Seydou Doumbia (CIV, BSC Young Boys Bern) | 30 |
| 2010/2011 | FC Basel | FC Sion | Alexander Frei (FC Basel) | 27 |
| 2011/2012 | FC Basel | FC Basel | Alexander Frei (FC Basel) | 24 |
| 2012/2013 | FC Basel | Grasshopper Club Zürich | Ezequiel Óscar Scarione (ARG, FC St. Gallen) | 21 |
| 2013/2014 | FC Basel | FC Zürich | Shkëlzen Taib Gashi (ALB, Grasshopper Club Zürich) | 19 |
| 2014/2015 | FC Basel | FC Sion | Shkëlzen Taib Gashi (ALB, FC Basel) | 21 |
| 2015/2016 | FC Basel | FC Zürich | Moanes Daobur (ISR, Grasshopper Club Zürich) | 19 |
| 2016/2017 | FC Basel | FC Basel | Seydou Doumbia (CIV, FC Basel) | 20 |
| 2017/2018 | BSC Young Boys Bern | FC Zürich | Albian Afrim Ajeti (FC Basel) | 17 |
| 2018/2019 | BSC Young Boys Bern | FC Basel | Guillaume Hoarau (FRA, BSC Young Boys Bern) | 24 |
| 2019/2020 | BSC Young Boys Bern | BSC Young Boys Bern | Jean-Pierre Nsamé (CMR, BSC Young Boys Bern) | 32 |
| 2020/2021 | BSC Young Boys Bern | FC Luzern | Jean-Pierre Nsamé (CMR, BSC Young Boys Bern) | 19 |
| 2021/2022 | FC Zürich | FC Lugano | Theoson-Jordan Siebatcheu Pefok (USA, BSC Young Boys Bern) | 22 |
| 2022/2023 | BSC Young Boys Bern | BSC Young Boys Bern | Jean-Pierre Junior Nsame (CMR, BSC Young Boys Bern) | 21 |

Name changements of first level: Serie A (1898–1931), National League (1931–1944), National League A (1944–2003), Super League (since 2003).

# NATIONAL CHAMPIONSHIP
## Swiss Super League 2022/2023
### (16.07.2022 – 29.05.2023)

**Results**

**Round 1 [16-17.07.2022]**
Young Boys - FC Zürich 4-0(0-0)
FC Winterthur - FC Basel 1-1(1-0)
FC Lugano - FC Sion 2-3(0-1)
Servette Genève - FC St. Gallen 1-0(1-0)
Luzern - Grasshopper Club 1-1(1-1) [10.08.22]

**Round 2 [23-24.07.2022]**
FC Zürich - FC Luzern 0-0
FC St. Gallen - FC Winterthur 2-0(2-0)
FC Basel - Servette Genève 1-1(1-0)
FC Sion - Young Boys 0-3(0-2)
Grasshopper Club - FC Lugano 2-1(1-0)

**Round 3 [30-31.07.2022]**
FC St. Gallen - FC Zürich 2-0(2-0)
FC Sion - Servette Genève 0-0
FC Winterthur - FC Lugano 1-4(1-3)
Young Boys - Grasshopper Club 1-1(1-0)
FC Luzern - FC Basel 0-2(0-1) [09.11.2022]

**Round 4 [06-07.08.2022]**
Servette Genève - FC Winterthur 1-0(0-0)
Grasshopper Club - FC St. Gallen 3-2(2-2)
FC Zürich - FC Sion 0-3(0-0)
FC Basel - Young Boys 0-0
FC Lugano - FC Luzern 1-2(0-1)

**Round 5 [13-14.08.2022]**
FC Sion - Grasshopper Club 2-2(1-0)
FC St. Gallen - FC Luzern 4-1(1-0)
FC Winterthur - FC Zürich 1-1(0-0)
FC Basel - FC Lugano 0-2(0-0)
Young Boys - Servette Genève 3-0(1-0)

**Round 6 [27-28.08.2022]**
FC Luzern - FC Sion 2-0(2-0)
Servette Genève - Grasshopper Club 3-1(1-1)
FC Lugano - FC St. Gallen 2-3(1-2)
FC Winterthur - Young Boys 1-5(1-1)
FC Zürich - FC Basel 2-4(1-1)

**Round 7 [03-04.09.2022]**
FC Sion - FC Basel 2-1(1-0)
FC Zürich - FC Lugano 1-2(1-1)
FC Luzern - Servette Genève 0-2(0-1)
FC St. Gallen - Young Boys 2-1(0-0)
Grasshopper Club - FC Winterthur 3-0(1-0)

**Round 8 [10-11.09.2022]**
FC St. Gallen - FC Sion 1-2(0-2)
FC Winterthur - FC Luzern 0-6(0-4)
Servette Genève - FC Zürich 3-2(2-1)
FC Basel - Grasshopper Club 5-1(2-1)
Young Boys - FC Lugano 3-0(2-0)

**Round 9 [01-02.10.2022]**
FC Basel - FC St. Gallen 3-2(2-1)
Grasshopper Club - FC Zürich 1-1(0-1)
FC Sion - FC Winterthur 1-3(1-1)
FC Lugano - Servette Genève 1-0(1-0)
FC Luzern - Young Boys 1-2(1-1)

**Round 10 [08-09.10.2022]**
Grasshopper Club - FC Sion 4-4(3-1)
Young Boys - FC St. Gallen 2-1(1-1)
Servette Genève - FC Luzern 1-1(1-0)
FC Lugano - FC Basel 1-0(1-0)
FC Zürich - FC Winterthur 0-0

**Round 11 [15-16.10.2022]**
FC Sion - FC Luzern 2-0(1-0)
FC Winterthur - Grasshopper Club 1-0(0-0)
FC St. Gallen - FC Lugano 1-1(1-0)
FC Zürich - Young Boys 0-0
Servette Genève - FC Basel 0-0

**Round 12 [18-20.10.2022]**
FC Winterthur - FC Sion 1-0(1-0)
FC Lugano - Young Boys 1-4(1-1)
FC Luzern - FC St. Gallen 3-3(2-2)
FC Basel - FC Zürich 0-0
Grasshopper Club - Servette Genève 2-3(0-0)

**Round 13 [22-23.10.2022]**
Young Boys - FC Sion 1-1(0-0)
FC Luzern - FC Lugano 3-1(0-0)
FC Basel - FC Winterthur 3-1(2-0)
FC St. Gallen - Servette Genève 1-1(0-1)
FC Zürich - Grasshopper Club 1-4(0-2)

**Round 14 [29-30.10.2022]**
Grasshopper Club - FC Luzern 1-3(1-2)
Servette Genève - FC Lugano 2-2(2-1)
FC Sion - FC Zürich 0-1(0-1)
FC Winterthur - FC St. Gallen 1-0(1-0)
Young Boys - FC Basel 3-1(2-0)

**Round 15 [05-06.11.2022]**
FC St. Gallen - Grasshopper Club 2-1(1-0)
FC Luzern - FC Winterthur 1-1(0-1)
Servette Genève - Young Boys 0-0
FC Basel - FC Sion 0-0
FC Lugano - FC Zürich 2-0(1-0)

**Round 16 [12-13.11.2022]**
FC Sion - FC St. Gallen 2-7(1-5)
Grasshopper Club - FC Basel 1-0(1-0)
FC Zürich - Servette Genève 4-1(1-0)
FC Lugano - FC Winterthur 3-1(2-1)
Young Boys - FC Luzern 3-0(2-0)

**Round 17 [21-22.01.2023]**
FC Luzern - FC Zürich 2-2(0-0)
Grasshopper Club - Young Boys 1-2(0-1)
FC Sion - FC Lugano 2-3(1-2)
FC St. Gallen - FC Basel 1-1(1-1)
FC Winterthur - Servette 1-2(0-0) [15.02.23]

**Round 18 [28-29.01.2023]**
FC Lugano - Grasshopper Club 1-1(0-1)
FC Basel - FC Luzern 2-3(1-0)
Young Boys - FC Winterthur 5-1(3-1)
FC Zürich - FC St. Gallen 1-0(0-0)
Servette Genève - FC Sion 2-2(2-0)

**Round 19 [04-05.02.2023]**
Grasshopper Club - FC Basel 1-0(0-0)
FC St. Gallen - Servette Genève 3-0(2-0)
FC Sion - FC Zürich 0-1(0-0)
FC Luzern - Young Boys 1-1(1-0)
FC Winterthur - FC Lugano 1-0(1-0)

**Round 20 [11-12.02.2023]**
Servette Genève - Grasshopper Club 2-1(1-0)
FC Basel - FC Sion 3-1(1-1)
FC Lugano - FC Luzern 1-1(1-1)
FC Zürich - FC Winterthur 1-1(1-1)
Young Boys - FC St. Gallen 5-1(2-1)

**Round 21 [18-19.02.2023]**
FC Winterthur - FC Sion 1-1(1-0)
Young Boys - FC Lugano 1-1(0-1)
FC St. Gallen - FC Luzern 2-2(1-1)
FC Basel - Servette Genève 2-2(0-1)
Grasshopper Club - FC Zürich 1-2(1-0)

**Round 22 [25-26.02.2023]**
FC Sion - FC St. Gallen 0-4(0-1)
FC Zürich - Young Boys 2-2(1-0)
FC Luzern - Grasshopper Club 1-0(0-0)
FC Lugano - FC Basel 2-2(2-0)
Servette Genève - FC Winterthur 1-1(1-0)

**Round 23 [04-05.03.2023]**
FC Winterthur - Young Boys 1-1(0-1)
FC Luzern - FC Basel 0-1(0-1)
FC St. Gallen - Grasshopper Club 1-1(1-1)
FC Sion - FC Lugano 1-1(0-1)
FC Zürich - Servette Genève 1-1(0-0)

**Round 24 [11-12.03.2023]**
Young Boys - FC Sion 4-0(2-0)
FC Lugano - FC Zürich 2-0(2-0)
Servette Genève - FC Luzern 0-3 Wert.
FC Basel - FC St. Gallen 1-1(0-0)
Grasshopper Club - FC Winterthur 2-1(1-0)

**Round 25 [18-19.03.2023]**
FC Zürich - FC Luzern 2-1(1-1)
FC Sion - Grasshopper Club 1-2(1-1)
FC Winterthur - FC St. Gallen 1-0(0-0)
FC Lugano - Servette Genève 1-1(0-0)
Young Boys - FC Basel 3-0(0-0)

**Round 26 [01-02.04.2023]**
Servette Genève - Young Boys 2-1(0-1)
FC Basel - FC Winterthur 2-0(1-0)
Grasshopper Club - FC Lugano 2-1(1-0)
FC Luzern - FC Sion 1-2(0-0)
FC St. Gallen - FC Zürich 2-2(1-1)

**Round 27 [08-10.04.2023]**
FC Zürich - FC Basel 1-1(1-1)
FC Sion - Servette Genève 2-2(1-1)
FC Lugano - FC St. Gallen 1-1(1-0)
FC Winterthur - FC Luzern 1-2(0-1)
Young Boys - Grasshopper Club 2-0(0-0)

**Round 28 [15-16.04.2023]**
Servette Genève - FC Lugano 0-0
FC Luzern - FC Zürich 4-1(2-1)
FC St. Gallen - FC Winterthur 2-3(2-3)
FC Basel - Young Boys 1-1(0-1)
Grasshopper Club - FC Sion 1-3(0-1)

**Round 29 [22-23.04.2023]**
FC Winterthur - Grasshopper Club 1-2(0-2)
Young Boys - Servette Genève 6-1(4-0)
FC Basel - FC Luzern 0-2(0-0)
FC Lugano - FC Sion 2-0(0-0)
FC Zürich - FC St. Gallen 1-0(0-0)

**Round 30 [25-27.04.2023]**
Grasshopper Club - Young Boys 4-1(2-1)
FC St. Gallen - FC Lugano 1-2(1-2)
Servette Genève - FC Zürich 4-0(2-0)
FC Luzern - FC Winterthur 3-1(1-1)
FC Sion - FC Basel 1-2(1-2)

| Round 31 [29-30.04.2023] | |
|---|---|
| FC Lugano - Grasshopper Club | 5-1(1-1) |
| Servette Genève - FC St. Gallen | 1-1(1-1) |
| FC Zürich - FC Sion | 2-2(1-2) |
| FC Winterthur - FC Basel | 1-4(1-2) |
| Young Boys - FC Luzern | 5-1(3-1) |

| Round 32 [06-07.05.2023] | |
|---|---|
| FC Sion - FC Winterthur | 0-1(0-1) |
| FC St. Gallen - Young Boys | 0-2(0-0) |
| FC Luzern - FC Lugano | 2-2(2-0) |
| FC Basel - FC Zürich | 0-2(0-0) |
| Grasshopper Club - Servette Genève | 2-3(1-1) |

| Round 33 [13-14.05.2023] | |
|---|---|
| Grasshopper Club - FC Luzern | 2-0(0-0) |
| Servette Genève - FC Sion | 5-0(3-0) |
| Young Boys - FC Zürich | 1-1(1-1) |
| FC Lugano - FC Winterthur | 2-1(2-1) |
| FC St. Gallen - FC Basel | 6-1(3-0) |

| Round 34 [20-21.05.2023] | |
|---|---|
| FC Winterthur - Servette Genève | 0-1(0-0) |
| FC Luzern - FC St. Gallen | 1-1(1-1) |
| FC Sion - Young Boys | 0-2(0-1) |
| FC Basel - FC Lugano | 1-1(1-0) |
| FC Zürich - Grasshopper Club | 2-1(1-1) |

| Round 35 [25.05.2023] | |
|---|---|
| FC Lugano - Young Boys | 2-0(0-0) |
| FC Sion - FC Luzern | 1-2(1-0) |
| FC Winterthur - FC Zürich | 0-2(0-2) |
| Grasshopper Club - FC St. Gallen | 2-2(1-1) |
| Servette Genève - FC Basel | 3-3(1-1) |

| Round 36 [29.05.2023] | |
|---|---|
| FC Basel - Grasshopper Club | 3-1(0-0) |
| FC Luzern - Servette Genève | 0-1(0-1) |
| FC St. Gallen - FC Sion | 4-0(3-0) |
| FC Zürich - FC Lugano | 2-3(0-2) |
| Young Boys - FC Winterthur | 2-1(1-0) |

## Final Standings

| | | | | | | | | Total | | Home | | | | Away | | | |
|---|---|---|---|---|---|---|---|---|---|---|---|---|---|---|---|---|---|
| 1. | **BSC Young Boys Bern** | 36 | 21 | 11 | 4 | 82 - 30 | **74** | 14 | 4 | 0 | 54 - 11 | 7 | 7 | 4 | 28 - 19 |
| 2. | Servette FC Genève | 36 | 14 | 16 | 6 | 53 - 48 | **58** | 8 | 9 | 1 | 31 - 18 | 6 | 7 | 5 | 22 - 30 |
| 3. | FC Lugano | 36 | 15 | 12 | 9 | 59 - 47 | **57** | 9 | 5 | 4 | 32 - 21 | 6 | 7 | 5 | 27 - 26 |
| 4. | FC Luzern | 36 | 13 | 11 | 12 | 56 - 52 | **50** | 5 | 7 | 6 | 26 - 24 | 8 | 4 | 6 | 30 - 28 |
| 5. | FC Basel | 36 | 11 | 14 | 11 | 51 - 50 | **47** | 6 | 8 | 4 | 27 - 21 | 5 | 6 | 7 | 24 - 29 |
| 6. | FC St. Gallen | 36 | 11 | 12 | 13 | 66 - 52 | **45** | 8 | 6 | 4 | 37 - 21 | 3 | 6 | 9 | 29 - 31 |
| 7. | Grasshopper Club Zürich | 36 | 12 | 8 | 16 | 56 - 64 | **44** | 9 | 3 | 6 | 35 - 29 | 3 | 5 | 10 | 21 - 35 |
| 8. | FC Zürich | 36 | 10 | 14 | 12 | 41 - 55 | **44** | 5 | 8 | 5 | 23 - 26 | 5 | 6 | 7 | 18 - 29 |
| 9. | FC Winterthur | 36 | 8 | 8 | 20 | 32 - 66 | **32** | 5 | 4 | 9 | 15 - 32 | 3 | 4 | 11 | 17 - 34 |
| 10. | FC Sion (*Relegation Play-offs*) | 36 | 7 | 10 | 19 | 41 - 73 | **31** | 2 | 4 | 12 | 17 - 37 | 5 | 6 | 7 | 24 - 36 |

Please note: no club were directly relegated. Next year's Swiss Super League will be played with 12 teams.

| Top goalscorers: | |
|---|---|
| 21 **Jean-Pierre Junior Nsame (CMR)** | *BSC Young Boys Bern* |
| 19 Cedric Jan Itten | *BSC Young Boys Bern* |
| 16 Žan Celar (SVN) | *FC Lugano* |
| 14 Emmanuel Delan Junior Latte Lath (CIV) | *FC St. Gallen* |

## Relegation Play-offs [03-06.06.2023]

| FC Sion - FC Stade Lausanne Ouchy | 0-2(0-1) | 2-4(2-2) |
|---|---|---|

FC Stade Lausanne Ouchy were promoted for the Swiss Super League 2023/2024.

## NATIONAL CUP
### Schweizer Cup 2022/2023

### Second Round [16-18.09.2022]

| | | | |
|---|---|---|---|
| Neuchâtel Xamax FCS - FC Thun 1898 | 1-2(1-1) | FC La Chaux-de-Fonds - Servette FC Genève | 0-2(0-0) |
| FC Meyrin - FC Winterthur | 0-4(0-1) | AC Arbedo-Castione - FC Sarmenstorf | 6-0(3-0) |
| FC Köniz - FC Wohlen | 1-2(0-1) | FC Stade Lausanne Ouchy - BSC Young Boys Bern | 0-1(0-0) |
| FC Rotkreuz - SC Kriens | 2-1(0-1,1-1) | FC Schaffhausen – Yverdon-Sport FC | 4-1(3-1) |
| AC Bellinzona - FC Luzern | 0-1(0-0,0-0) | FC Breitenrain Bern - FC Lugano | 0-4(0-0) |
| FC Rapperswil-Jona - FC Sion | 0-2(0-1) | FC Aarau - FC Basel | 1-3(1-1,1-1) |
| Etoile Carouge FC - FC St. Gallen | 2-4(2-1) | FC Portalban/Gletterens - FC Wil 1900 | 0-2(0-0) |
| FC Goldstern - Grasshopper Club Zürich | 0-3(0-0) | FC Lausanne-Sport - FC Zürich | 3-2(1-2,2-2) |

### 1/8-Finals [08-09.11.2022/31.01.-01.02.2023]

| | | | |
|---|---|---|---|
| FC Rotkreuz - FC Schaffhausen | 2-1(0-1) | FC Wohlen - Servette FC Genève | 2-5(1-0,1-1) |
| AC Arbedo-Castione - FC St. Gallen | 0-5(0-2) | FC Lugano - FC Winterthur | 1-0(0-0) |
| FC Wil 1900 - FC Sion | 1-2(0-0,0-0) | FC Thun 1898 - FC Luzern | 2-2 aet; 4-2 pen |
| FC Lausanne-Sport - BSC Young Boys Bern | 1-5(1-2) | Grasshopper Club Zürich - FC Basel | 3-5(1-2) |

### Quarter-Finals [28.02.-02.03.2023]

| | | | |
|---|---|---|---|
| FC Thun 1898 - BSC Young Boys Bern | 0-5(0-1) | FC Sion - FC Lugano | 0-3(0-0) |
| FC St. Gallen - FC Basel | 1-2(1-0,1-1) | FC Rotkreuz - Servette FC Genève | 0-3(0-2) |

### Semi-Finals [04-05.04.2023]

| | | | |
|---|---|---|---|
| FC Basel - BSC Young Boys Bern | 2-4(0-2) | Servette FC Genève - FC Lugano | 2-2 aet; 3-5 pen |

04.06.2023; Stadion Wankdorf, Bern; Referee: Lukas Fähndrich; Attendance: 31,500
**BSC Young Boys Bern - FC Lugano**                                      **3-2(2-0)**

**Young Boys Bern**: Marvin Keller, Lewin Blum, Aurèle Amenda, Cédric Zesiger, Ulisses Garcia, Sandro Lauper (5.Cheikh Niasse; 90+3.Fabian Lustenberger), Christian Fassnacht (Cap), Filip Ugrinić (81.Kastriot Imeri), Fabian Rieder, Meschack Elia Lina (90+3.Joël Almada Monteiro), Jean-Pierre Junior Nsame (90+3.Mohamed Camara). Trainer: Raphaël Wicky.

**FC Lugano**: Amir Saipi, Allan Arigoni (87.Boris Babić), Ousmane Doumbia, Albian Hajdari (77.Jhon Jairo Espínoza Izquierdo), Milton Nahuel Valenzuela, Jonathan Maximiliano Sabbatini Perfecto (Cap), Hadj Mahmoud (46.Kreshnik Hajrizi), Uran Bislimi (46.Mattia Bottani), Renato Steffen, Ignacio Aliseda, Žan Celar (66.Mohammed Amoura). Trainer: Mattia Croci-Torti.

**Goals:** 1-0 Jean-Pierre Junior Nsame (20), 2-0 Jean-Pierre Junior Nsame (45+3), 2-1 Mattia Bottani (53), 3-1 Meschack Elia Lina (85), 3-2 Renato Steffen (87).

# THE CLUBS 2022/2023

## Fussball Club Basel 1893

| | | | |
|---|---|---|---|
| **Founded**: | 15.11.1893 | | |
| **Stadium**: | St. Jakob-Park, Basel (37,994) | | |
| **Trainer**: | Alexander Frei | | 15.07.1979 |
| [07.02.2023] | Heiko Vogel (GER) | | 21.11.1975 |

| Goalkeepers: | DOB | M | (s) | G |
|---|---|---|---|---|
| Marvin Hitz | 18.09.1987 | 32 | | |
| Mirko Salvi | 14.02.1994 | 4 | (2) | |
| **Defenders:** | **DOB** | **M** | **(s)** | **G** |
| Kasim Adams (GHA) | 22.06.1995 | 25 | (3) | 1 |
| Marvin Akahomen | 15.07.2007 | 1 | (1) | |
| *Arnau Comas* Freixas (ESP) | 11.04.2000 | 13 | | 2 |
| Riccardo Calafiori (ITA) | 19.05.2002 | 21 | (2) | |
| Nasser Djiga (BFA) | 15.11.2002 | 1 | | |
| Noah Katterbach (GER) | 13.04.2001 | 3 | (3) | |
| Michael Lang | 08.02.1991 | 22 | (5) | 1 |
| Andrea Padula (ITA) | 04.04.1996 | | (2) | |
| Andy Pelmard (FRA) | 12.03.2000 | 29 | (5) | |
| *Sergio López* Galache (ESP) | 08.04.1999 | 16 | (5) | 1 |
| Hugo Vogel (FRA) | 04.01.2004 | 2 | | |
| **Midfielders:** | **DOB** | **M** | **(s)** | **G** |
| Wouter Burger (NED) | 16.02.2001 | 23 | (7) | 4 |
| Andy Diouf (FRA) | 17.05.2003 | 26 | (8) | |

| Emmanuel Essiam (GHA) | 19.12.2003 | 2 | (2) | |
|---|---|---|---|---|
| Fabian Frei | 08.01.1989 | 15 | (8) | 1 |
| Darian Males | 03.05.2001 | 21 | (7) | 4 |
| Brian Adriano Ogechukwu Onyegbule (GER) | 23.06.2006 | | (1) | |
| Taulant Xhaka (ALB) | 28.03.1991 | 18 | (2) | |
| **Forwards:** | **DOB** | **M** | **(s)** | **G** |
| Kanga Liam Aaron Akalé (FRA) | 20.04.2005 | | (1) | |
| Mohamed Zeki Amdouni | 04.12.2000 | 23 | (9) | 12 |
| Jean-Kévin Augustin (FRA) | 16.06.1997 | 8 | (12) | 3 |
| Bradley Fink | 17.04.2003 | 12 | (13) | 5 |
| *Hugo Novoa* Ramos (ESP) | 24.01.2003 | 5 | (7) | 1 |
| Anton Kade (GER) | 17.01.2004 | 10 | (8) | |
| Sayfallah Ltaief (TUN) | 22.04.2000 | 1 | (5) | |
| Liam Alan Millar (CAN) | 27.09.1999 | 15 | (11) | |
| Dan Assane Ndoye (SEN) | 25.10.2000 | 25 | (7) | 4 |
| Kaly Sène (SEN) | 28.05.2001 | 1 | (4) | |
| Ádám Csaba Szalai (HUN) | 09.12.1987 | 1 | (4) | |
| Andi Zeqiri | 22.06.1999 | 21 | (9) | 11 |

## Grasshopper Club Zürich

| | | | |
|---|---|---|---|
| **Founded**: | 01.09.1886 | | |
| **Stadium**: | Letzigrund Stadion, Zürich (26,104) | | |
| **Trainer**: | Giorgio Contini | | 04.01.1974 |

| Goalkeepers: | DOB | M | (s) | G |
|---|---|---|---|---|
| André Campos Moreira (POR) | 02.12.1995 | 28 | | |
| Justin Hammel | 02.12.2000 | 8 | (1) | |
| **Defenders:** | **DOB** | **M** | **(s)** | **G** |
| Bendegúz Bolla (HUN) | 22.11.1999 | 32 | (1) | 2 |
| Teruki Hara (JPN) | 30.07.1998 | 5 | (7) | |
| Florian Hoxha (KOS) | 22.02.2001 | | (2) | |
| Li Lei (CHN) | 30.05.1992 | 4 | (2) | |
| Noah Loosli | 23.01.1997 | 24 | (6) | 1 |
| Georg Margreitter (AUT) | 07.11.1988 | 10 | (7) | |
| Eliseu Mendja Nadjack Soares Cassamá(GNB) | 06.02.1994 | 3 | (4) | |
| Ayumu Seko (JPN) | 07.06.2000 | 30 | (1) | |
| *Tomás* Aresta Branco Machado *Ribeiro* (POR) | 30.04.1999 | 24 | (3) | 3 |
| **Midfielders:** | **DOB** | **M** | **(s)** | **G** |
| Amir Abrashi (ALB) | 27.03.1990 | 22 | (5) | |
| Noah Blasucci | 19.06.1999 | | (2) | |

| Christián Herc (SVK) | 30.09.1998 | 18 | (14) | 5 |
|---|---|---|---|---|
| Dion Kacuri | 11.02.2004 | 2 | (11) | 1 |
| Hayao Kawabe (JPN) | 08.09.1995 | 33 | | 9 |
| Tsiy William Ndenge (GER) | 13.06.1997 | 21 | (6) | 4 |
| Petar Pušić | 25.01.1999 | 13 | (21) | 5 |
| Dominik Schmid | 10.03.1998 | 34 | | |
| Meritan Shabani (GER) | 15.03.1999 | 14 | (12) | 3 |
| **Forwards:** | **DOB** | **M** | **(s)** | **G** |
| Renat Dadashov (AZE) | 17.05.1999 | 22 | (12) | 8 |
| Filipe de Carvalho Ferreira | 01.12.2003 | 3 | (15) | 1 |
| Shkelqim Demhasaj (KOS) | 19.04.1996 | 7 | (6) | 3 |
| *Guilherme Schettine* Guimarães (BRA) | 10.10.1995 | 13 | (6) | 6 |
| Jeong Sang-bin (KOR) | 01.04.2002 | 2 | (5) | |
| Francis Momoh (NGA) | 25.03.2001 | 5 | (6) | 1 |
| Giotto Morandi | 04.03.1999 | 19 | (13) | 2 |

## Football Club Lugano

| | | |
|---|---|---|
| **Founded**: | 1908; re-founded 2004 (*as AC Lugano*) | |
| **Stadium**: | Stadio Cornaredo, Lugano (6,390) | |
| **Trainer**: | Mattia Croci-Torti | 10.04.1982 |

| Goalkeepers: | DOB | M | (s) | G |
|---|---|---|---|---|
| Serif Berbić | 25.11.2001 | 1 | | |
| Sebastian Osigwe Ogenna (NGA) | 26.03.1994 | 7 | | |
| Amir Saipi | 08.07.2000 | 28 | | |
| **Defenders:** | **DOB** | **M** | **(s)** | **G** |
| Allan Arigoni | 04.11.1998 | 21 | (5) | 1 |
| Fabio Daprelà | 19.02.1991 | 25 | | |
| Noah De Queiroz | 10.12.2002 | | (1) | 1 |
| Jhon Jairo Espínoza Izquierdo (ECU) | 24.02.1999 | 8 | (8) | |
| Mickaël Facchinetti | 15.02.1991 | | (9) | |
| Albian Hajdari | 18.05.2003 | 14 | (4) | |
| Kreshnik Hajrizi (KOS) | 28.05.1999 | 16 | (3) | 1 |
| Lukas Mai (GER) | 31.03.2000 | 16 | (3) | |
| Milton Nahuel Valenzuela (ARG) | 13.08.1998 | 28 | (2) | 2 |
| Reto Ziegler | 16.01.1986 | 10 | | 2 |
| **Midfielders:** | **DOB** | **M** | **(s)** | **G** |
| Uran Bislimi (KOS) | 25.09.1999 | 15 | (15) | 2 |

| Mattia Bottani | 24.05.1991 | 16 | (10) | 1 |
|---|---|---|---|---|
| Ousmane Doumbia (CIV) | 21.05.1992 | 34 | (1) | 2 |
| Adrian Durrer | 13.07.2001 | 3 | (1) | |
| Maren Haile-Selassie | 13.03.1999 | 8 | (7) | 1 |
| Roman Macek (CZE) | 18.04.1997 | 13 | (16) | |
| Hadj Mahmoud (TUN) | 24.04.2000 | 5 | (14) | 1 |
| Chinwendu Johan Nkame (NGA) | 07.01.1998 | 1 | (2) | |
| Jonathan Maximiliano Sabbatini Perfecto (URU) | 31.03.1988 | 35 | | 3 |
| **Forwards:** | **DOB** | **M** | **(s)** | **G** |
| Ignacio Aliseda (ARG) | 14.03.2000 | 15 | (8) | 8 |
| Mohammed Amoura (ALG) | 09.05.2000 | 10 | (21) | 8 |
| Johann Angstmann (USA) | 16.01.2003 | | (1) | |
| Boris Babić | 10.11.1997 | 5 | (21) | 2 |
| Alessandro Casciato (ITA) | 30.05.2000 | | (1) | |
| Žan Celar (SVN) | 14.03.1999 | 26 | (4) | 16 |
| Hicham Mahou (FRA) | 02.07.1999 | 11 | (7) | 1 |
| Renato Steffen | 03.11.1991 | 25 | (3) | 7 |

## Fussball-Club Luzern

**Founded**: 12.08.1901
**Stadium**: Swissporarena, Luzern (16,490)
**Trainer**: Mario Frick (LIE)    07.09.1974

| Goalkeepers: | DOB | M | (s) | G |
|---|---|---|---|---|
| Pascal Loretz | 01.06.2003 | 8 | | |
| Marius Müller (GER) | 12.07.1993 | 25 | | |
| Vaso Vasić (SRB) | 26.04.1990 | 3 | | |
| **Defenders:** | **DOB** | **M** | **(s)** | **G** |
| Ismajl Beka (KOS) | 31.10.1999 | 19 | (3) | 1 |
| Marco Burch | 19.10.2000 | 24 | (1) | 3 |
| Rúben Dantas Fernandes | 19.05.2003 | 1 | | |
| Mohamed Dräger (TUN) | 25.06.1996 | 24 | (7) | 3 |
| Martin Frýdek (CZE) | 24.03.1992 | 29 | | 3 |
| Luca Jaquez | 02.06.2003 | 8 | (2) | |
| Leny Meyer | 01.07.2004 | 2 | (2) | |
| Severin Ottiger | 20.04.2003 | 10 | (2) | |
| Denis Simani (ALB) | 13.10.1991 | 22 | | |
| Mauricio Willimann Rangel (MEX) | 16.01.2003 | | (1) | |
| **Midfielders:** | **DOB** | **M** | **(s)** | **G** |
| Nicky Beloko | 16.02.2000 | 30 | | 2 |
| Samuele Campo | 06.07.1995 | | (9) | |
| Mamady Diambou (MLI) | 11.11.2002 | 3 | (10) | |
| Pius Dorn (GER) | 24.09.1996 | 34 | | 4 |
| Lorik Emini (KOS) | 29.08.1999 | 2 | (4) | |
| Christian Gentner (GER) | 14.08.1985 | 3 | (7) | 1 |
| Ardon Jashari | 30.07.2002 | 34 | | 1 |
| Jakub Kadák (SVK) | 14.12.2000 | 7 | (3) | 1 |
| Max Meyer (GER) | 18.09.1995 | 28 | (1) | 11 |
| Noah Rupp | 13.08.2003 | | (1) | |
| Pascal Schürpf | 15.07.1989 | 21 | (9) | 5 |
| Mihailo Stevanović | 04.01.2002 | | (1) | |
| **Forwards:** | **DOB** | **M** | **(s)** | **G** |
| Asumah Abubakar (POR) | 10.05.1997 | 14 | (14) | 3 |
| Joaquín Matías Ardaiz de los Santos (URU) | 11.01.1999 | 5 | (10) | |
| Luuk Breedijk | 20.02.2004 | | (6) | 1 |
| Sofyan Chader (FRA) | 12.05.2000 | 12 | (9) | 4 |
| Benjamin Mbunga Kimpioka (SWE) | 21.02.2000 | 1 | (5) | 1 |
| Thibault Klidjé (TOG) | 10.07.2001 | 4 | (10) | |
| Ibrahima N'Diaye (SEN) | 06.07.1998 | 1 | (2) | |
| Dejan Sorgić (SRB) | 15.09.1989 | 15 | (8) | 8 |
| Varol Tasar (TUR) | 04.10.1996 | | (3) | |
| Nando Toggenburger | 17.03.2004 | | (4) | |
| Lars Villiger | 29.04.2003 | 7 | (4) | 1 |

## Servette Football Club Genève 1890

**Founded**: 20.03.1890
**Stadium**: Stade de Genève, Genève (28,833)
**Trainer**: Alain Geiger    05.11.1960

| Goalkeepers: | DOB | M | (s) | G |
|---|---|---|---|---|
| Jérémy Frick | 08.03.1993 | 35 | | |
| Edin Omeragić | 20.03.2002 | 1 | | |
| **Defenders:** | **DOB** | **M** | **(s)** | **G** |
| Valton Behrami | 16.03.2004 | | (1) | |
| Anthony Baron (GLP) | 29.12.1992 | 12 | (5) | |
| Moritz Bauer (AUT) | 25.01.1992 | 7 | (3) | 1 |
| Gaël Clichy (FRA) | 26.07.1985 | 27 | | 1 |
| Moussa Diallo (FRA) | 27.01.1997 | 12 | (3) | |
| *Diogo* Pinheiro *Monteiro* (POR) | 28.01.2005 | 1 | (2) | |
| Issa Kaloga | 27.02.2004 | | (1) | |
| Théo Magnin | 09.08.2003 | 1 | (7) | |
| Melingo Kevin Mbabu | 19.04.1995 | 16 | | |
| Steve Rouiller | 10.07.1990 | 17 | (5) | 1 |
| Yoan Severin (FRA) | 24.01.1997 | 28 | | 2 |
| Baba Souare | 07.03.1999 | | (2) | |
| Nicolas Vouilloz | 11.05.2001 | 28 | (3) | |
| **Midfielders:** | **DOB** | **M** | **(s)** | **G** |
| Alexis Antunes | 31.07.2000 | 15 | (13) | 2 |
| Sidiki Camara | 23.08.2002 | | (2) | |
| Boris Cespedes (BOL) | 19.06.1995 | 8 | (9) | |
| Timothé Cognat (FRA) | 25.01.1998 | 33 | (1) | 2 |
| Samba Diba (SEN) | 24.12.2003 | 3 | (12) | |
| David Douline (FRA) | 28.05.1993 | 18 | | 1 |
| Théo Valls (FRA) | 18.12.1995 | 6 | (20) | 3 |
| **Forwards:** | **DOB** | **M** | **(s)** | **G** |
| Chris Vianney Bedia (CIV) | 05.03.1996 | 21 | (2) | 12 |
| Mohamed Chaïbi (FRA) | 12.10.1996 | | (2) | |
| Enzo Crivelli (FRA) | 06.02.1995 | 3 | (16) | 4 |
| Boubacar Fofana (FRA) | 07.09.1998 | 5 | (17) | 3 |
| Dereck Kutesa | 06.12.1997 | 23 | (6) | 3 |
| Dimitri Oberlin | 27.09.1997 | | (4) | |
| Alexandre Dias Patricio | 17.02.2004 | | (3) | |
| Patrick Pflücke (GER) | 30.11.1996 | 31 | (5) | 6 |
| Ronny Rodelin (FRA) | 18.11.1989 | 12 | (12) | 1 |
| Miroslav Stevanović (BIH) | 29.07.1990 | 33 | (2) | 9 |
| Hussayn Touati (FRA) | 03.10.2001 | | (11) | 2 |

## Football Club de Sion

**Founded**: 1909
**Stadium**: Stade Tourbillon, Sion (14,283)
**Trainer**: Paolo Tramezzani (ITA)    30.07.1970
[21.11.2022] Fabio Celestini    31.10.1975
[07.03.2023] David Bettoni (FRA)    23.11.1971
[16.05.2023] Paolo Tramezzani (ITA)    30.07.1970

| Goalkeepers: | DOB | M | (s) | G |
|---|---|---|---|---|
| Kevin Fickentscher | 06.07.1988 | 3 | | |
| Heinz Lindner (AUT) | 17.07.1990 | 28 | | |
| Alexandros Safarikas (GRE) | 26.08.1999 | 5 | (1) | |
| **Defenders:** | **DOB** | **M** | **(s)** | **G** |
| *Baltazar* Costa Rodrigues de Oliveira (BRA) | 06.05.2000 | 25 | (1) | |
| Dimitri Cavaré (GLP) | 05.02.1995 | 20 | (4) | 1 |
| Gora Diouf (SEN) | 20.09.2003 | 5 | (1) | |
| Dennis Iapichino | 27.07.1990 | 8 | (7) | |
| Numa Lavanchy | 25.08.1993 | 32 | (1) | |
| François Moubandje | 21.06.1990 | 3 | (1) | |
| Gilles Richard | 23.02.2003 | | (1) | |
| Nathanaël Saintini (GLP) | 30.05.2000 | 27 | | |
| Joël Schmied | 23.09.1998 | 17 | (7) | 1 |
| Reto Ziegler | 16.01.1986 | 14 | (1) | |
| **Midfielders:** | **DOB** | **M** | **(s)** | **G** |
| Musa Araz | 17.01.1994 | 27 | (4) | 2 |
| Wylan Cyprien (FRA) | 28.01.1995 | 17 | (1) | 3 |
| Anto Grgić | 28.11.1996 | 28 | (3) | 2 |
| *José Aguilar* Martínez (ESP) | 05.02.2001 | | (2) | |
| Denis-Will Poha (FRA) | 28.05.1997 | 21 | (9) | 1 |
| Luca Zuffi | 27.03.1990 | 7 | (13) | 1 |
| **Forwards:** | **DOB** | **M** | **(s)** | **G** |
| Mario Balotelli Barwuah (ITA) | 12.08.1990 | 14 | (4) | 6 |
| Kevin Bua | 11.08.1993 | 13 | (15) | 1 |
| Ilyas Chouaref (FRA) | 12.12.2000 | 21 | (11) | 1 |
| Yassin Fortuné (FRA) | 30.01.1999 | 4 | (3) | 1 |
| Kevin Halabaku (KOS) | 29.11.2001 | 2 | (18) | |
| Cleilton Monteiro da Costa „Itaitinga" (BRA) | 04.10.1998 | 24 | (4) | 4 |
| Gaëtan Karlen | 07.06.1993 | 2 | (17) | |
| Giovanni-Guy Yann Sio (CIV) | 31.03.1989 | 12 | (15) | 9 |
| Filip Stojilković | 04.01.2000 | 14 | (4) | 5 |
| Abdel Zagré (BFA) | 09.03.2004 | 3 | (3) | |

## Fussballclub St. Gallen 1879

**Founded**: 19.04.1879
**Stadium**: Kybunpark, St. Gallen (19,456)
**Trainer**: Peter Zeidler (GER)  08.08.1962

| Goalkeepers: | DOB | M | (s) | G |
|---|---|---|---|---|
| Lawrence Ati-Zigi (GHA) | 29.11.1996 | 33 | | |
| Lukas Watkowiak (GER) | 06.03.1996 | 3 | (1) | |
| **Defenders:** | **DOB** | **M** | **(s)** | **G** |
| Daouda Guindo (MLI) | 14.10.2002 | 14 | (1) | 1 |
| Michael Kempter (PHI) | 12.01.1995 | 9 | (1) | |
| Alessandro Kräuchi | 03.06.1998 | | (5) | |
| Matej Maglica (CRO) | 25.09.1998 | 27 | (4) | 1 |
| Isaac Schmidt | 07.12.1999 | 20 | (9) | 2 |
| Leonidas Stergiou | 03.03.2002 | 30 | (5) | |
| Basil Stillhart | 24.03.1994 | 23 | (3) | 3 |
| Patrick Sutter | 18.01.1999 | 20 | (4) | |
| Albert Vallçi (AUT) | 02.07.1995 | 14 | (8) | |
| **Midfielders:** | **DOB** | **M** | **(s)** | **G** |
| Ricardo Azevedo Alves | 02.12.2001 | 4 | (9) | |
| Lukas Görtler (GER) | 15.06.1994 | 30 | | 9 |
| Stefano Guidotti (ITA) | 16.06.1999 | 1 | (8) | |
| *Jordi* Quintillà Guasch (ESP) | 25.10.1993 | 34 | (1) | 1 |
| Gregory Karlen | 30.01.1995 | 9 | (11) | 3 |
| Randy Schneider | 27.08.2001 | 2 | (12) | |
| *Víctor Ruiz* Abril (ESP) | 02.11.1993 | 2 | | |
| Christian Witzig | 09.01.2001 | 25 | (7) | 3 |
| **Forwards:** | **DOB** | **M** | **(s)** | **G** |
| Chadrac Akolo Ababa (COD) | 01.04.1995 | 17 | (15) | 7 |
| Alessio Besio | 18.03.2004 | | (4) | |
| Fabrizio Cavegn | 28.08.2002 | | (4) | |
| Leon Dajaku (GER) | 12.04.2001 | 5 | (7) | |
| Willem Geubbels (FRA) | 16.08.2001 | 2 | (15) | 2 |
| Jérémy Guillemenot | 06.01.1998 | 29 | (3) | 11 |
| Emmanuel Latte Lath (CIV) | 01.01.1999 | 21 | (10) | 14 |
| Noha Ndombasi Nlandu (FRA) | 28.04.2001 | | (11) | |
| Fabian Schubert (AUT) | 29.08.1994 | 6 | (2) | 3 |
| Julian Tobias Emilio von Moos | 01.04.2001 | 16 | (5) | 4 |

## Fussballclub Winterthur

**Founded**: 1896
**Stadium**: Stadion Schützenwiese, Winterthur (8,400)
**Trainer**: Bruno George Berner  21.11.1977

| Goalkeepers: | DOB | M | (s) | G |
|---|---|---|---|---|
| Timothy Bruce Fayulu (COD) | 24.07.1999 | 11 | | |
| Markus Kuster (AUT) | 22.02.1994 | 20 | | |
| Jozef Pukaj (KOS) | 13.02.2000 | 5 | (1) | |
| **Defenders:** | **DOB** | **M** | **(s)** | **G** |
| Souleymane Diaby (CIV) | 08.10.1999 | 22 | (8) | |
| Adrian Gantenbein | 18.04.2001 | 17 | (6) | |
| Roy Gelmi | 01.03.1995 | 21 | (2) | |
| Michael José Barroso Gonçalves | 10.03.1995 | 18 | (8) | |
| Granit Lekaj | 23.02.1990 | 27 | | |
| Tobias Schättin | 05.06.1997 | 18 | (8) | |
| Yannick Schmid | 11.05.1995 | 24 | | |
| **Midfielders:** | **DOB** | **M** | **(s)** | **G** |
| Eris Abedini (KOS) | 29.08.1998 | 12 | (15) | |
| Remo Arnold | 17.01.1997 | 24 | (4) | |
| Carmine Chiappetta | 09.03.2003 | 1 | (5) | |
| Thibault Corbaz | 07.01.1994 | 17 | (10) | |
| Matteo di Giusto | 18.08.2000 | 35 | | 6 |
| Noe Holenstein | 25.03.2004 | 1 | (7) | 1 |
| Hekuran Kryeziu (KOS) | 12.02.1993 | 9 | (14) | |
| Gëzim Rexhep Pepsi (KOS) | 12.07.1998 | | (1) | |
| Samir Ramizi (SRB) | 24.07.1991 | 23 | (2) | 5 |
| Francisco José Rodríguez Araya | 14.09.1995 | 11 | (12) | 2 |
| Stephan Vinicius Seiler | 16.09.2000 | | (7) | 1 |
| Laurin Vögele | 21.08.2004 | | (2) | |
| **Forwards:** | **DOB** | **M** | **(s)** | **G** |
| Joaquín Matías Ardaiz de los Santos (URU) | 11.01.1999 | 16 | | 5 |
| Samuel Ballet | 12.03.2001 | 6 | (14) | 1 |
| Roman Buess | 21.09.1992 | 23 | (11) | 6 |
| Nishan Burkart | 31.01.2000 | 20 | (4) | 3 |
| Florian Kamberi (ALB) | 08.03.1995 | 4 | (9) | 1 |
| Sayfallah Ltaief (TUN) | 22.04.2000 | 6 | (9) | 1 |
| Neftali Manzambi | 23.04.1997 | 5 | (14) | |

## Berner Sport Club Young Boys

**Founded**: 14.03.1898
**Stadium**: Wankdorf Stadion, Bern (31,789)
**Trainer**: Raphaël Wicky  26.04.1977

| Goalkeepers: | DOB | M | (s) | G |
|---|---|---|---|---|
| Marvin Keller | 03.07.2002 | 3 | | |
| Anthony Racioppi | 31.12.1998 | 18 | (1) | |
| David von Ballmoos | 30.12.1994 | 15 | | |
| **Defenders:** | **DOB** | **M** | **(s)** | **G** |
| Aurèle Amenda | 31.07.2003 | 11 | (5) | |
| Loris Benito | 07.01.1992 | 11 | (8) | |
| Lewin Blum | 27.07.2001 | 24 | (7) | 1 |
| Mohamed Camara (GUI) | 28.08.1997 | 11 | (1) | |
| Ulisses Garcia | 11.01.1996 | 23 | (4) | 1 |
| Jordan Lefort (FRA) | 09.08.1993 | 1 | (1) | |
| Fabian Lustenberger | 02.05.1988 | 20 | (6) | |
| Quentin Maceiras | 10.10.1995 | 4 | (3) | |
| Kevin Rüegg | 05.08.1998 | 7 | (3) | |
| Cédric Zesiger | 24.06.1998 | 30 | (1) | 2 |
| **Midfielders:** | **DOB** | **M** | **(s)** | **G** |
| Miguel Chaiwa (ZAM) | 07.06.2004 | 2 | (4) | |
| Christian Fassnacht | 11.11.1993 | 26 | (3) | 8 |
| Kastriot Imeri | 27.06.2000 | 15 | (12) | 5 |
| Alexandre Tounde Dimitri Jankewitz | 25.12.2001 | | (3) | |
| Sandro Lauper | 25.10.1996 | 14 | (6) | 2 |
| Cheikh Niasse (SEN) | 19.01.2000 | 20 | (6) | |
| Fabian Rieder | 16.02.2002 | 31 | (2) | 7 |
| Donat Rrudhani (KOS) | 02.05.1999 | 6 | (19) | |
| Vincent Sierro | 08.10.1995 | 8 | (7) | 1 |
| Filip Ugrinić | 05.01.1999 | 20 | (9) | 1 |
| **Forwards:** | **DOB** | **M** | **(s)** | **G** |
| Meschack Elia Lina (COD) | 06.08.1997 | 20 | (11) | 7 |
| Cedric Jan Itten | 27.12.1996 | 20 | (11) | 19 |
| *Joël* Almada *Monteiro* (POR) | 05.08.1999 | 7 | (21) | 1 |
| Wilfried Kanga (FRA) | 21.02.1998 | 2 | | 3 |
| Nicolas Moumi Ngamaleu (CMR) | 09.07.1994 | 4 | (3) | 1 |
| Jean-Pierre Junior Nsame (CMR) | 01.05.1993 | 23 | (10) | 21 |

## Fussballclub Zürich

| | |
|---|---|
| **Founded**: | 01.08.1896 |
| **Stadium**: | Letzigrund Stadion, Zürich (26,104) |
| **Trainer**: | Franco Foda (GER) | 23.04.1966 |
| [23.09.2022] | Genesio Colatrella | 31.12.1971 |
| [10.10.2022] | Bo Henriksen (DEN) | 07.02.1975 |

| Goalkeepers: | DOB | M | (s) | G |
|---|---|---|---|---|
| Yanick Brecher | 25.05.1993 | 34 | | |
| Živko Kostadinović | 10.04.1992 | 2 | | |
| **Defenders:** | **DOB** | **M** | **(s)** | **G** |
| Fidan Aliti (KOS) | 03.10.1993 | 27 | (2) | |
| Marc Hornschuh (GER) | 02.03.1991 | 7 | (12) | 1 |
| Lindrit Kamberi | 07.10.1999 | 25 | (7) | 1 |
| Nikola Katić (CRO) | 10.10.1996 | 22 | | 1 |
| Mirlind Kryeziu (KOS) | 26.01.1997 | 12 | (2) | 1 |
| Karol Mets (EST) | 16.05.1993 | 9 | (4) | |
| Bećir Omeragić | 20.01.2002 | 18 | (5) | |
| **Midfielders:** | **DOB** | **M** | **(s)** | **G** |
| *Adriàn Guerrero* Aguilar (ESP) | 28.01.1998 | 28 | | 1 |
| Donis Avdijaj (KOS) | 25.08.1996 | 4 | (3) | |
| Nikola Boranijašević (SRB) | 19.05.1992 | 33 | | |
| Cheick Condé (GUI) | 26.07.2000 | 26 | (4) | 1 |
| Blerim Džemaili | 12.04.1986 | 13 | (8) | 5 |
| Ramon Guzzo | 05.07.2004 | | (1) | |

| | DOB | M | (s) | G |
|---|---|---|---|---|
| Selmin Hodža | 24.05.2003 | 2 | (4) | |
| Mathew Ifeanyi (NGA) | 20.01.1997 | 12 | (1) | 2 |
| Bledian Krasniqi | 17.06.2001 | 20 | (12) | 1 |
| Antonio Marchesano | 18.01.1991 | 28 | (5) | 2 |
| Jonathan Yula Okita (COD) | 05.10.1996 | 19 | (10) | 7 |
| Fabian Rohner | 17.08.1998 | 6 | (21) | 1 |
| Stephan Seiler | 16.09.2000 | 3 | (3) | |
| Ole Kristian Selnæs (NOR) | 07.07.1994 | 10 | (6) | |
| **Forwards:** | **DOB** | **M** | **(s)** | **G** |
| Daniel Afriyie (GHA) | 26.06.2001 | | (2) | |
| Degnand Wilfried Gnonto (ITA) | 05.11.2003 | 4 | (2) | |
| Akaki Gogia (GER) | 18.01.1992 | 1 | (1) | |
| Calixte Ligue | 21.03.2005 | 1 | (8) | 1 |
| Ivan Santini (CRO) | 21.05.1989 | 3 | (8) | |
| Roko Šimić (CRO) | 10.09.2003 | 4 | (12) | 4 |
| Aiyegun Tosin (BEN) | 26.06.1998 | 23 | (4) | 12 |
| Bogdan Vyunnyk (UKR) | 21.05.2002 | | (7) | |

## SECOND LEVEL
### Swiss Challenge League 2022/2023

| | | | | | | | | | |
|---|---|---|---|---|---|---|---|---|---|
| 1. | Yverdon-Sport FC (*Promoted*) | 36 | 20 | 6 | 10 | 64 | - 53 | 66 |
| 2. | FC Lausanne-Sport (*Promoted*) | 36 | 17 | 10 | 9 | 58 | - 43 | 61 |
| 3. | FC Stade Lausanne Ouchy (*Promotion Play-offs*) | 36 | 17 | 9 | 10 | 70 | - 53 | 60 |
| 4. | FC Aarau | 36 | 15 | 12 | 9 | 63 | - 57 | 57 |
| 5. | FC Wil 1900 | 36 | 16 | 8 | 12 | 62 | - 52 | 56 |
| 6. | FC Thun | 36 | 12 | 13 | 11 | 62 | - 55 | 49 |
| 7. | FC Schaffhausen | 36 | 12 | 8 | 16 | 51 | - 59 | 44 |
| 8. | FC Vaduz | 36 | 7 | 16 | 13 | 54 | - 56 | 37 |
| 9. | AC Bellinzona | 36 | 11 | 4 | 21 | 38 | - 71 | 37 |
| 10. | Neuchâtel Xamax FCS (*Relegation Play-offs*) | 36 | 4 | 12 | 20 | 42 | - 65 | 24 |

## Relegation Play-offs [31.05.-03.06.2023]

FC Rapperswil-Jona - Neuchâtel Xamax FCS                    1-3(0-3)          0-3(0-0)
Neuchâtel Xamax FCS remains at second level for 2023/2024.

### INTERNATIONAL MATCHES
(16.07.2022 – 15.07.2023)

| | | | | |
|---|---|---|---|---|
| 24.09.2022 | Zaragoza | Spain - Switzerland | 1-2(0-1) | (UNL) |
| 27.09.2022 | St. Gallen | Switzerland - Czech Republic | 2-1(2-1) | (UNL) |
| 17.11.2022 | Abu Dhabi | Ghana - Switzerland | 2-0(0-0) | (F) |
| 24.11.2022 | Al Wakrah | Switzerland - Cameroon | 1-0(0-0) | (WC) |
| 28.11.2022 | Doha | Brazil - Switzerland | 1-0(0-0) | (WC) |
| 02.12.2022 | Doha | Serbia - Switzerland | 2-3(2-2) | (WC) |
| 06.12.2022 | Lusail | Portugal - Switzerland | 6-1(2-0) | (WC) |
| | | | | |
| 25.03.2023 | Novi Sad | Belarus - Switzerland | 0-5(0-3) | (ECQ) |
| 28.03.2023 | Genève | Switzerland - Israel | 3-0(1-0) | (ECQ) |
| 16.06.2023 | Andorra la Vella | Andorra - Switzerland | 1-2(0-2) | (ECQ) |
| 19.06.2023 | Luzern | Switzerland - Romania | 2-2(2-0) | (ECQ) |

**24.09.2022    SPAIN - SWITZERLAND         1-2(0-1)**         3rd UEFA Nations League A, Group 2
Estadio La Romareda, Zaragoza; Referee: Clément Turpin (France); Attendance: 31,804
**SUI:** Yann Sommer, Silvan Dominic Widmer, Nico Elvedi, Manuel Obafemi Akanji, Ricardo Iván Rodríguez Araya (46.Renato Steffen), Granit Xhaka (Cap), Remo Marco Freuler, Mohameth Djibril Ibrahima Sow (68.Denis Lemi Zakaria Lako Lado), Xherdan Shaqiri (68.Dan Assane Ndoye), Rubén Estephan Vargas Martínez (78.Michel Aebischer), Breel Donald Embolo (86.Haris Seferović). Trainer: Murat Yakin.
**Goals:** Manuel Obafemi Akanji (21), Breel Donald Embolo (59).

**27.09.2022    SWITZERLAND - CZECH REPUBLIC    2-1(2-1)**         3rd UEFA Nations League A, Group 2
Kybunpark, St. Gallen; Referee: Irfan Peljto (Bosnia and Herzegovina); Attendance: 13,353
**SUI:** Yann Sommer, Silvan Dominic Widmer, Fabian Lukas Schär, Nico Elvedi, Ricardo Iván Rodríguez Araya, Granit Xhaka (Cap), Remo Marco Freuler (90+3.Ardon Jashari), Mohameth Djibril Ibrahima Sow (79.Denis Lemi Zakaria Lako Lado), Xherdan Shaqiri (65.Renato Steffen), Rubén Estephan Vargas Martínez (79.Mohamed Zeki Amdouni), Breel Donald Embolo (65.Haris Seferović). Trainer: Murat Yakin.
**Goals:** Remo Marco Freuler (29), Breel Donald Embolo (30).

**17.11.2022    GHANA - SWITZERLAND         2-0(0-0)**         Friendly International
Zayed Sports City Stadium, Abu Dhabi (United Arab Emirates); Referee: Ahmed Eisa Mohamed Darwish (United Arab Emirates); Attendance: 650
**SUI:** Yann Sommer, Silvan Dominic Widmer (62.Christian Fassnacht), Fabian Lukas Schär (65.Haris Seferović), Eray Ervin Cömert, Manuel Obafemi Akanji (46.Nico Elvedi), Granit Xhaka (Cap), Denis Lemi Zakaria Lako Lado, Remo Marco Freuler (46.Noah Okafor), Xherdan Shaqiri, Rubén Estephan Vargas Martínez (62.Renato Steffen), Breel Donald Embolo (46.Michel Aebischer). Trainer: Murat Yakin.

**24.11.2022    SWITZERLAND - CAMEROON       1-0(0-0)**         22nd FIFA WC. Group Stage.
Al Janoub Stadium, Al Wakrah (Qatar); Referee: Facundo Raúl Tello Figueroa (Argentina); Attendance: 39,089
**SUI:** Yann Sommer, Silvan Dominic Widmer, Manuel Obafemi Akanji, Nico Elvedi, Ricardo Iván Rodríguez Araya (90.Eray Ervin Cömert), Remo Marco Freuler, Granit Xhaka (Cap), Mohameth Djibril Ibrahima Sow (72.Fabian Frei), Xherdan Shaqiri (72.Noah Okafor), Rubén Estephan Vargas Martínez (81. Fabian Rieder), Breel Donald Embolo (72.Haris Seferović). Trainer: Murat Yakin.
**Goal:** Breel Donald Embolo (48).

**28.11.2022    BRAZIL - SWITZERLAND        1-0(0-0)**         22nd FIFA WC. Group Stage.
Stadium 974, Doha (Qatar); Referee: Iván Arcides Barton Cisneros (El Salvador); Attendance: 43,649
**SUI:** Yann Sommer, Silvan Dominic Widmer (86.Fabian Frei), Manuel Obafemi Akanji, Nico Elvedi, Ricardo Iván Rodríguez Araya, Remo Marco Freuler, Granit Xhaka (Cap), Fabian Rieder (58.Renato Steffen), Mohameth Djibril Ibrahima Sow (76.Michel Aebischer), Rubén Estephan Vargas Martínez (58.Edimilson Fernandes Ribeiro), Breel Donald Embolo (76.Haris Seferović). Trainer: Murat Yakin.

**02.12.2022    SERBIA - SWITZERLAND        2-3(2-2)**         22nd FIFA WC. Group Stage.
Stadium 974, Doha (Qatar); Referee: Fernando Andrés Rapallini (Argentina); Attendance: 41,378
**SUI:** Gregor Kobel, Silvan Dominic Widmer, Manuel Obafemi Akanji, Fabian Lukas Schär, Ricardo Iván Rodríguez Araya, Remo Marco Freuler, Granit Xhaka (Cap), Mohameth Djibril Ibrahima Sow (72.Edimilson Fernandes Ribeiro), Xherdan Shaqiri (72.Denis Lemi Zakaria Lako Lado), Rubén Estephan Vargas Martínez (81.Christian Fassnacht), Breel Donald Embolo (90+6.Noah Okafor). Trainer: Murat Yakin.
**Goals:** Xherdan Shaqiri (20), Breel Donald Embolo (44), Remo Marco Freuler (48).

**06.12.2022    PORTUGAL - SWITZERLAND       6-1(2-0)**         22nd FIFA WC. 2nd Round of 16.
Lusail Stadium, Lusail (Qatar); Referee: César Arturo Ramos Palazuelos (Mexico); Attendance: 83,720
**SUI:** Yann Sommer, Fabian Lukas Schär (46.Eray Ervin Cömert), Manuel Obafemi Akanji, Ricardo Iván Rodríguez Araya, Remo Marco Freuler (54.Denis Lemi Zakaria Lako Lado), Edimilson Fernandes Ribeiro, Granit Xhaka (Cap), Mohameth Djibril Ibrahima Sow (54.Haris Seferović), Xherdan Shaqiri, Rubén Estephan Vargas Martínez (66.Noah Okafor), Breel Donald Embolo (89.Ardon Jashari). Trainer: Murat Yakin.
**Goal:** Manuel Obafemi Akanji (58).

**25.03.2023    BELARUS - SWITZERLAND        0-5(0-3)**         17th EC. Qualifiers
Karađorđe Stadium, Novi Sad (Serbia); Referee: Alejandro José Hernández Hernández (Spain); Attendance: *played behind closed doors*
**SUI:** Yann Sommer, Silvan Dominic Widmer, Nico Elvedi, Manuel Obafemi Akanji (82.Cédric Zesiger), Ricardo Iván Rodríguez Araya, Granit Xhaka (Cap) (66.Fabian Rieder), Remo Marco Freuler, Denis Lemi Zakaria Lako Lado, Renato Steffen (58.Mohamed Zeki Amdouni), Rubén Estephan Vargas Martínez (66.Christian Fassnacht), Cedric Jan Itten (59.Noah Okafor). Trainer: Murat Yakin.
**Goals:** Renato Steffen (4, 17, 29), Granit Xhaka (62), Mohamed Zeki Amdouni (65).

**28.03.2023    SWITZERLAND - ISRAEL        3-0(1-0)**         17th EC. Qualifiers
Stade de Genève, Genève; Referee: Nikola Dabanović (Montenegro); Attendance: 14,819
**SUI:** Yann Sommer, Silvan Dominic Widmer, Nico Elvedi, Manuel Obafemi Akanji, Ricardo Iván Rodríguez Araya (85.Edimilson Fernandes Ribeiro), Granit Xhaka (Cap), Remo Marco Freuler, Denis Lemi Zakaria Lako Lado (74.Fabian Rieder), Rubén Estephan Vargas Martínez (74.Christian Fassnacht), Cedric Jan Itten (68.Noah Okafor), Mohamed Zeki Amdouni (68.Renato Steffen). Trainer: Murat Yakin.
**Goals:** Rubén Estephan Vargas Martínez (39), Mohamed Zeki Amdouni (48), Silvan Dominic Widmer (52).

**16.06.2023**   **ANDORRA - SWITZERLAND**                    **1-2(0-2)**                    17<sup>th</sup> EC. Qualifiers

Estadi Nacional, Andorra la Vella; Referee: Balázs Berke (Hungary); Attendance: 2,490
**SUI:** Gregor Kobel, Nico Elvedi, Manuel Obafemi Akanji, Ricardo Iván Rodríguez Araya, Granit Xhaka (Cap), Remo Marco Freuler, Edimilson Fernandes Ribeiro, Xherdan Shaqiri (61.Renato Steffen), Denis Lemi Zakaria Lako Lado (74.Mohameth Djibril Ibrahima Sow), Rubén Estephan Vargas Martínez (61.Steven Zuber), Mohamed Zeki Amdouni (61.Andi Avdi Zeqiri). Trainer: Murat Yakin.
**Goals:** Remo Marco Freuler (7), Mohamed Zeki Amdouni (33).

**19.06.2023**   **SWITZERLAND - ROMANIA**                    **2-2(2-0)**                    17<sup>th</sup> EC. Qualifiers

Swissporarena, Lucerne; Referee: Daniele Orsato (Italy); Attendance: 14,400
**SUI:** Yann Sommer, Nico Elvedi, Manuel Obafemi Akanji, Ricardo Iván Rodríguez Araya, Granit Xhaka (Cap), Remo Marco Freuler, Edimilson Fernandes Ribeiro (90.Fabian Lukas Schär), Xherdan Shaqiri (90+1.Uran Bislimi), Denis Lemi Zakaria Lako Lado (75.Mohameth Djibril Ibrahima Sow), Rubén Estephan Vargas Martínez (75.Renato Steffen), Mohamed Zeki Amdouni (59.Haris Seferović). Trainer: Murat Yakin.
**Goals:** Mohamed Zeki Amdouni (28, 41).

| NATIONAL TEAM PLAYERS<br>(16.07.2022 – 15.07.2023) | | | | |
|---|---|---|---|---|
| **Name** | **DOB** | **Caps** | **Goals** | *Club* |

| **Goalkeepers** | | | | |
|---|---|---|---|---|
| Gregor KOBEL | 06.12.1997 | 5 | 0 | 2022/2023: *BV Borussia 09 Dortmund (GER)* |
| Yann SOMMER | 17.12.1988 | 83 | 0 | 2022: *Borussia VfL Mönchengladbach (GER)*<br>19.01.2023-> *FC Bayern München (GER)* |

| **Defenders** | | | | |
|---|---|---|---|---|
| Manuel Obafemi AKANJI | 19.07.1995 | 51 | 2 | 2022/2023: *Manchester City FC (ENG)* |
| Eray Ervin CÖMERT | 04.02.1998 | 12 | 0 | 2022: *Valencia CF (ESP)* |
| Nico ELVEDI | 30.09.1996 | 47 | 1 | 2022/2023: *Borussia VfL Mönchengladbach (GER)* |
| Fabian FREI | 08.01.1989 | 24 | 3 | 2022: *FC Basel* |
| Ricardo Iván RODRÍGUEZ Araya | 25.08.1992 | 108 | 9 | 2022/2023: *Torino FC (ITA)* |
| Fabian Lukas SCHÄR | 20.12.1991 | 76 | 8 | 2022/2023: *Newcastle United FC (ENG)* |
| Silvan Dominic WIDMER | 05.03.1993 | 39 | 3 | 2022/2023: *1. FSV Mainz 05 (GER)* |
| Cédric ZESIGER | 24.06.1998 | 2 | 0 | 2023: *BSC Young Boys Bern* |

| **Midfielders** | | | | |
|---|---|---|---|---|
| Michel AEBISCHER | 06.01.1997 | 13 | 0 | 2022: *Bologna FC 1909 (ITA)* |
| Uran BISLIMI | 25.09.1999 | 1 | 0 | 2023: *FC Lugano* |
| Christian FASSNACHT | 11.11.1993 | 19 | 4 | 2022/2023: *BSC Young Boys Bern* |
| Edimilson FERNANDES Ribeiro | 15.04.1996 | 28 | 2 | 2022/2023: *1. FSV Mainz 05 (GER)* |
| Remo Marco FREULER | 15.04.1992 | 57 | 7 | 2022/2023: *Nottingham Forest FC (ENG)* |
| Ardon JASHARI | 30.07.2002 | 2 | 0 | 2022: *FC Luzern* |
| Fabian RIEDER | 16.02.2002 | 4 | 0 | 2022/2023: *BSC Young Boys Bern* |
| Xherdan SHAQIRI | 10.10.1991 | 114 | 26 | 2022/2023: *Chicago Fire SC (USA)* |
| Mohameth Djibril Ibrahima SOW | 06.02.1997 | 38 | 0 | 2022/2023: *Eintracht Frankfurt (GER)* |
| Renato STEFFEN | 03.11.1991 | 33 | 4 | 2022/2023: *FC Lugano* |
| Granit XHAKA | 27.09.1992 | 115 | 13 | 2022/2023: *Arsenal FC London (ENG)* |
| Denis Lemi ZAKARIA Lako Lado | 20.11.1996 | 49 | 3 | 2022/2023: *Chelsea FC London (ENG)* |
| Steven ZUBER | 17.08.1991 | 52 | 10 | 2023: *AEK Athína (GRE)* |

| **Forwards** | | | | |
|---|---|---|---|---|
| Mohamed Zeki AMDOUNI | 04.12.2000 | 5 | 5 | 2022/2023: *FC Basel* |
| Breel Donald EMBOLO | 14.02.1997 | 63 | 13 | 2022: *AS Monaco FC (FRA)* |
| Cedric Jan ITTEN | 27.12.1996 | 9 | 4 | 2023: *BSC Young Boys Bern* |
| Dan Assane NDOYE | 25.10.2000 | 1 | 0 | 2022: *FC Basel* |
| Noah OKAFOR | 24.05.2000 | 14 | 2 | 2022/2023: *FC Red Bull Salzburg (AUT)* |
| Haris SEFEROVIĆ | 22.02.1992 | 93 | 25 | 2022: *Galatasaray SK Istanbul (TUR)*<br>31.01.2023-> *RC Celta de Vigo (ESP)* |
| Rubén Estephan VARGAS Martínez | 05.08.1998 | 35 | 5 | 2022/2023: *FC Augsburg (GER)* |
| Andi Avdi ZEQIRI | 22.06.1999 | 8 | 0 | 2023: *FC Augsburg (GER)* |

| **Trainer** | | | |
|---|---|---|---|
| Murat YAKIN [from 09.08.2021] | 15.09.1974 | 24 M; 12 W; 5 D; 7 L; 38-28 | |

# TURKEY

### The Country:
Türkiye Cumhuriyeti (Republic of Turkey)
Capital: Ankara
Surface: 783,356 km²
Inhabitants: 85,279,553 [2022]
Time: UTC+3

### The FA:
Türkiye Futbol Federasyonu
Hasan Dogan Milli Takimlar Kamp ve Egitim Tesisleri Riva Beykoz, Istanbul
Tel: +90 0 216 554 51 00
Founded: 1923
Member of FIFA since: 1923
Member of UEFA since: 1962
Website: www.tff.org

## NATIONAL TEAM RECORDS

| RECORDS | | | |
|---|---|---|---|
| **First international match:** | 26.10.1923, Istanbul: | Turkey – Romania 2-2 | |
| **Most international caps:** | Rüştü Reçber | - 120 caps (1994-2012) | |
| **Most international goals:** | Hakan Şükür | - 51 goals / 112 caps (1992-2007) | |

### UEFA EUROPEAN CHAMPIONSHIP

|  |  |
|---|---|
| 1960 | Qualifiers |
| 1964 | Qualifiers |
| 1968 | Qualifiers |
| 1972 | Qualifiers |
| 1976 | Qualifiers |
| 1980 | Qualifiers |
| 1984 | Qualifiers |
| 1988 | Qualifiers |
| 1992 | Qualifiers |
| 1996 | Final Tournament (Group Stage) |
| 2000 | Final Tournament (Quarter-Finals) |
| 2004 | Qualifiers |
| 2008 | Final Tournament (Semi-Finals) |
| 2012 | Qualifiers |
| 2016 | Final Tournament (Group Stage) |
| 2020 | Final Tournament (Group Stage) |

### FIFA WORLD CUP

|  |  |
|---|---|
| 1930 | Did not enter |
| 1934 | *Withdrew* |
| 1938 | Did not enter |
| 1950 | *Qualified but withdrew* |
| 1954 | Final Tournament (Group Stage) |
| 1958 | *Withdrew* |
| 1962 | Qualifiers |
| 1966 | Qualifiers |
| 1970 | Qualifiers |
| 1974 | Qualifiers |
| 1978 | Qualifiers |
| 1982 | Qualifiers |
| 1986 | Qualifiers |
| 1990 | Qualifiers |
| 1994 | Qualifiers |
| 1998 | Qualifiers |
| 2002 | Final Tournament (3rd Place) |
| 2006 | Qualifiers |
| 2010 | Qualifiers |
| 2014 | Qualifiers |
| 2018 | Qualifiers |
| 2022 | Qualifiers |

### OLYMPIC TOURNAMENTS

|  |  |
|---|---|
| 1908 | - |
| 1912 | - |
| 1920 | - |
| 1924 | Preliminary Round |
| 1928 | 1/8 - Finals |
| 1936 | 1/8 - Finals |
| 1948 | Quarter-Finals |
| 1952 | Quarter-Finals |
| 1956 | *Withdrew* |
| 1960 | Group Stage |
| 1964 | Qualifiers |
| 1968 | Qualifiers |
| 1972 | Qualifiers |
| 1976 | Qualifiers |
| 1980 | Group Stage |
| 1984 | *Withdrew* |
| 1988 | Qualifiers |
| 1992 | Qualifiers |
| 1996 | Qualifiers |
| 2000 | Qualifiers |
| 2004 | Qualifiers |
| 2008 | Qualifiers |
| 2012 | Qualifiers |
| 2016 | Qualifiers |
| 2020 | Qualifiers |

### UEFA NATIONS LEAGUE

|  |  |
|---|---|
| 2018/2019 | League B (Group Stage) |
| 2020/2021 | League B (Group Stage -> relegated to League C) |
| 2022/2023 | League C (Group Stage -> promoted to League B) |

### FIFA CONFEDERATIONS CUP 1992-2017
2003 (3rd Place)

### TURKISH CLUB HONOURS IN EUROPEAN CLUB COMPETITIONS:

| European Champion Clubs.Cup (1956-1992) / UEFA Champions League (1993-2023) | | |
|---|---|---|
| None | | |
| **Fairs Cup (1858-1971) / UEFA Cup (1972-2009) / UEFA Europa League (2010-2023)** | | |
| Galatasaray SK Istanbul | 1 | 1999/2000 |
| **UEFA Europa Conference League (2021-2023)** | | |
| None | | |
| **UEFA Super Cup (1972-2022)** | | |
| Galatasaray SK Istanbul | 1 | 2000 |
| ***European Cup Winners' Cup 1961-1999**** | | |
| None | | |

*defunct competition

# NATIONAL COMPETITIONS
## TABLE OF HONOURS

### Turkish Football Championship (1924–1951)*

| | CHAMPIONS |
|---|---|
| 1924 | Harbiye Ankara |
| 1925-1926 | *No competition* |
| 1927 | Muhafizgücü SK Ankara |
| 1928 - 1931 | *No competition* |
| 1932 | Istanbulspor |
| 1933 | Fenerbahçe SK Istanbul |
| 1934 | Beşiktaş JK Istanbul |
| 1935 | Fenerbahçe SK Istanbul |
| 1936 - 1939 | *No competition* |
| 1940 | Eskişehir Demirspor |
| 1941 | Gençlerbirliği Ankara SK Ankara |
| 1942 | Harp Okulu SK Ankara |
| 1943 | *No competition* |
| 1944 | Fenerbahçe SK Istanbul |
| 1945 | Harp Okulu SK Ankara |
| 1946 | Gençlerbirliği Ankara SK Ankara |
| 1947 | Ankara Demirspor |
| 1948 | *No competition* |
| 1949 | MKE Ankaragücü SK |
| 1950 | Göztepe SK İzmir |
| 1951 | Beşiktaş JK Istanbul |

*Not recognized by Turkish FA.

### National Division (1937–1950)*

| | CHAMPIONS |
|---|---|
| 1937 | Fenerbahçe SK Istanbul |
| 1938 | Güneş SK Istanbul |
| 1939 | Galatasaray SK Istanbul |
| 1940 | Fenerbahçe SK Istanbul |
| 1941 | Beşiktaş JK Istanbul |
| 1942 | *No competition* |
| 1943 | Fenerbahçe SK Istanbul |
| 1944 | Beşiktaş JK Istanbul |
| 1945 | Fenerbahçe SK Istanbul |
| 1946 | Fenerbahçe SK Istanbul |
| 1947 | Beşiktaş JK Istanbul |
| 1948 | *No competition* |
| 1949 | *No competition* |
| 1950 | Fenerbahçe SK Istanbul |

| | CHAMPIONS | CUP WINNERS | BEST GOALSCORERS | |
|---|---|---|---|---|
| 1956/1957** | Beşiktaş JK Istanbul | - | Nazmi Bilge (Beşiktaş JK Istanbul) | 8 |
| 1957/1958** | Beşiktaş JK Istanbul | - | Lefter Küçükandonyadis (Fenerbahçe SK Istanbul) | |
| | | | Metin Oktay (Galatasaray SK Istanbul) | 10 |
| 1958/1959 | Fenerbahçe SK Istanbul | - | Metin Oktay (Galatasaray SK Istanbul) | 11 |
| 1959/1960 | Beşiktaş JK Istanbul | - | Metin Oktay (Galatasaray SK Istanbul) | 33 |
| 1960/1961 | Fenerbahçe SK Istanbul | - | Metin Oktay (Galatasaray SK Istanbul) | 36 |
| 1961/1962 | Galatasaray SK Istanbul | - | Fikri Elma (Ankara Demirspor) | 21 |
| 1962/1963 | Galatasaray SK Istanbul | Galatasaray SK Istanbul | Metin Oktay (Galatasaray SK Istanbul) | 38 |
| 1963/1964 | Fenerbahçe SK Istanbul | Galatasaray SK Istanbul | Güven Önüt (Beşiktaş JK Istanbul) | 19 |
| 1964/1965 | Fenerbahçe SK Istanbul | Galatasaray SK Istanbul | Metin Oktay (Galatasaray SK Istanbul) | 17 |
| 1965/1966 | Beşiktaş JK Istanbul | Galatasaray SK Istanbul | Ertan Adatepe (MKE Ankaragücü SK) | 20 |
| 1966/1967 | Beşiktaş JK Istanbul | Altay SK İzmir | Ertan Adatepe (MKE Ankaragücü SK) | 18 |
| 1967/1968 | Fenerbahçe SK Istanbul | Fenerbahçe SK Istanbul | Fevzi Zemzem (Göztepe SK İzmir) | 19 |
| 1968/1969 | Galatasaray SK Istanbul | Göztepe SK İzmir | Metin Oktay (Galatasaray SK Istanbul) | 17 |
| 1969/1970 | Fenerbahçe SK Istanbul | Göztepe SK İzmir | Fethi Heper (Eskişehirspor Kulübü) | 13 |
| 1970/1971 | Galatasaray SK Istanbul | Eskişehirspor Kulübü | Ogün Altıparmak (Fenerbahçe SK Istanbul) | 16 |
| 1971/1972 | Galatasaray SK Istanbul | MKE Ankaragücü SK | Fethi Heper (Eskişehirspor Kulübü) | 20 |
| 1972/1973 | Galatasaray SK Istanbul | Galatasaray SK Istanbul | Osman Arpacıoğlu (Fenerbahçe SK Istanbul) | 16 |
| 1973/1974 | Fenerbahçe SK Istanbul | Fenerbahçe SK Istanbul | Cemil Turan (Fenerbahçe SK Istanbul) | 14 |
| 1974/1975 | Fenerbahçe SK Istanbul | Beşiktaş JK Istanbul | Ömer Kaner (Eskişehirspor Kulübü) | 14 |
| 1975/1976 | Trabzonspor Kulübü | Galatasaray SK Istanbul | Cemil Turan (Fenerbahçe SK Istanbul) | |
| | | | Ali Osman Renklibay (MKE Ankaragücü SK) | 17 |
| 1976/1977 | Trabzonspor Kulübü | Trabzonspor Kulübü | Necmi Perekli (Trabzonspor Kulübü) | 18 |
| 1977/1978 | Fenerbahçe SK Istanbul | Trabzonspor Kulübü | Cemil Turan (Fenerbahçe SK Istanbul) | 17 |
| 1978/1979 | Trabzonspor Kulübü | Fenerbahçe SK Istanbul | Özer Umdu (Adanaspor AŞ) | 15 |
| 1979/1980 | Trabzonspor Kulübü | Altay SK İzmir | Mustafa Denizli (Altay SK İzmir) | |
| | | | Bahtiyar Yorulmaz (Bursaspor Kulübü) | 12 |
| 1980/1981 | Trabzonspor Kulübü | MKE Ankaragücü SK | Bora Öztürk (Adanaspor AŞ) | 15 |
| 1981/1982 | Beşiktaş JK Istanbul | Galatasaray SK Istanbul | Selçuk Yula (Fenerbahçe SK Istanbul) | 16 |
| 1982/1983 | Fenerbahçe SK Istanbul | Fenerbahçe SK Istanbul | Selçuk Yula (Fenerbahçe SK Istanbul) | 19 |
| 1983/1984 | Trabzonspor Kulübü | Trabzonspor Kulübü | Tarik Hodžić (YUG, Galatasaray SK Istanbul) | 16 |
| 1984/1985 | Fenerbahçe SK Istanbul | Galatasaray SK Istanbul | Aykut Yiğit (Sakaryaspor Kulübü) | 20 |
| 1985/1986 | Beşiktaş JK Istanbul | Bursaspor Kulübü | Tanju Çolak (Samsunspor Kulübü) | 33 |
| 1986/1987 | Galatasaray SK Istanbul | Gençlerbirliği Ankara | Tanju Çolak (Samsunspor Kulübü) | 25 |
| 1987/1988 | Galatasaray SK Istanbul | Sakaryaspor Kulübü | Tanju Çolak (Galatasaray SK Istanbul) | 39 |
| 1988/1989 | Fenerbahçe SK Istanbul | Beşiktaş JK Istanbul | Aykut Kocaman (Fenerbahçe SK Istanbul) | 29 |
| 1989/1990 | Beşiktaş JK Istanbul | Beşiktaş JK Istanbul | Feyyaz Uçar (Beşiktaş JK Istanbul) | 28 |
| 1990/1991 | Beşiktaş JK Istanbul | Galatasaray SK Istanbul | Tanju Çolak (Galatasaray SK Istanbul) | 31 |
| 1991/1992 | Beşiktaş JK Istanbul | Trabzonspor Kulübü | Aykut Kocaman (Fenerbahçe SK Istanbul) | 25 |
| 1992/1993 | Galatasaray SK Istanbul | Galatasaray SK Istanbul | Tanju Çolak (Fenerbahçe SK Istanbul) | 27 |
| 1993/1994 | Galatasaray SK Istanbul | Beşiktaş JK Istanbul | Bülent Uygun (Fenerbahçe SK Istanbul) | 22 |
| 1994/1995 | Beşiktaş JK Istanbul | Trabzonspor Kulübü | Aykut Kocaman (Fenerbahçe SK Istanbul) | 27 |
| 1995/1996 | Fenerbahçe SK Istanbul | Galatasaray SK Istanbul | Shota Arveladze (GEO, Trabzonspor Kulübü) | 25 |
| 1996/1997 | Galatasaray SK Istanbul | Kocaelispor Kulübü | Hakan Şükür (Galatasaray SK Istanbul) | 38 |

| 1997/1998 | Galatasaray SK Istanbul | Beşiktaş JK Istanbul | Hakan Şükür (Galatasaray SK Istanbul) | 33 |
|---|---|---|---|---|
| 1998/1999 | Galatasaray SK Istanbul | Galatasaray SK Istanbul | Hakan Şükür (Galatasaray SK Istanbul) | 19 |
| 1999/2000 | Galatasaray SK Istanbul | Galatasaray SK Istanbul | Serkan Aykut (Samsunspor Kulübü) | 30 |
| 2000/2001 | Fenerbahçe SK Istanbul | Gençlerbirliği Ankara | Okan Yılmaz (Bursaspor Kulübü) | 23 |
| 2001/2002 | Galatasaray SK Istanbul | Kocaelispor Kulübü | Arif Erdem (Galatasaray SK Istanbul) İlhan Mansız (Beşiktaş JK Istanbul) | 21 |
| 2002/2003 | Beşiktaş JK Istanbul | Trabzonspor Kulübü | Okan Yılmaz (Bursaspor Kulübü) | 24 |
| 2003/2004 | Fenerbahçe SK Istanbul | Trabzonspor Kulübü | Zafer Biryol (Atiker Konyaspor Kulübü) | 25 |
| 2004/2005 | Fenerbahçe SK Istanbul | Galatasaray SK Istanbul | Fatih Tekke (Trabzonspor Kulübü) | 31 |
| 2005/2006 | Galatasaray SK Istanbul | Beşiktaş JK Istanbul | Gökhan Ünal (Kayseri Erciyesspor Kulübü) | 25 |
| 2006/2007 | Fenerbahçe SK Istanbul | Beşiktaş JK Istanbul | Alexsandro de Souza "Alex" (BRA, Fenerbahçe SK Istanbul) | 19 |
| 2007/2008 | Galatasaray SK Istanbul | Kayseri Erciyesspor Kulübü | Semih Şentürk (Fenerbahçe SK Istanbul) | 17 |
| 2008/2009 | Beşiktaş JK Istanbul | Beşiktaş JK Istanbul | Milan Baroš (CZE, Galatasaray SK Istanbul) | 20 |
| 2009/2010 | Bursaspor Kulübü | Trabzonspor Kulübü | Ariza Makukula (POR, Kayseri Erciyesspor Kulübü) | 21 |
| 2010/2011 | Fenerbahçe SK Istanbul | Beşiktaş JK Istanbul | Alexsandro de Souza "Alex" (BRA, Fenerbahçe SK Istanbul) | 28 |
| 2011/2012 | Galatasaray SK Istanbul | Fenerbahçe SK Istanbul | Burak Yılmaz (Trabzonspor Kulübü) | 33 |
| 2012/2013 | Galatasaray SK Istanbul | Fenerbahçe SK Istanbul | Burak Yılmaz (Galatasaray SK Istanbul) | 24 |
| 2013/2014 | Fenerbahçe SK Istanbul | Galatasaray SK Istanbul | Aatif Chahechouhe (MAR, Sivasspor Kulübü) | 17 |
| 2014/2015 | Galatasaray SK Istanbul | Galatasaray SK Istanbul | José Fernando Viana de Santana "Fernandão" (BRA, Bursaspor Kulübü) | 22 |
| 2015/2016 | Beşiktaş JK Istanbul | Galatasaray SK Istanbul | Mario Gómez García (Beşiktaş JK Istanbul) | 26 |
| 2016/2017 | Beşiktaş JK Istanbul | Atiker Konyaspor Kulübü | Vágner Silva de Souza (BRA, Alanyaspor) | 23 |
| 2017/2018 | Galatasaray SK Istanbul | Akhisar Belediyespor Gençlik SK | Bafétimbi Gomis (FRA, Galatasaray SK Istanbul) | 29 |
| 2018/2019 | Galatasaray SK Istanbul | Galatasaray SK Istanbul | Mbaye Diagne (SEN, Kasımpaşa Spor Kulübü / Galatasaray SK Istanbul) | 30 |
| 2019/2020 | Istanbul Başakşehir FK | Trabzonspor Kulübü | Alexander Sørloth (NOR, Trabzonspor Kulübü) | 24 |
| 2020/2021 | Beşiktaş JK Istanbul | Beşiktaş JK Istanbul | Aaron Salem Boupendza Pozzi (GAB, Hatayspor Antakya) | 22 |
| 2021/2022 | Trabzonspor Kulübü | Sivasspor Kulübü | Umut Bozok (Kasımpaşa SK Istanbul) | 20 |
| 2022/2023 | Galatasaray SK Istanbul | Fenerbahçe SK Istanbul | Enner Remberto Valencia Lastra (ECU, Fenerbahçe SK) | 29 |

**recognized by Turkish FA only since 2002.*

## NATIONAL CHAMPIONSHIP
### Süper Lig 2022/2023
(05.08.2022 – 07.06.2023)

### Results

**Round 1** [05-08.08.2022]
İstanbulspor - Trabzonspor 0-2(0-1)
Sivasspor - Gaziantep 1-1(0-1)
Beşiktaş - Kayserispor 1-0(0-0)
Giresunspor - Adana Demirspor 2-3(0-2)
Fatih Karagümrük - Alanyaspor 2-4(0-2)
Antalyaspor - Galatasaray 0-1(0-0)
Istanbul Başakşehir - Kasımpaşa 4-0(2-0)
Ankaragücü - Konyaspor 0-0
Fenerbahçe - Ümraniyespor 3-3(2-1)

**Round 2** [12-15.08.2022]
Trabzonspor - Hatayspor 1-0(0-0)
Kayserispor - İstanbulspor 1-0(1-0)
Adana Demirspor - Sivasspor 3-0(1-0)
Galatasaray - Giresunspor 0-1(0-0)
Gaziantep - Ankaragücü 1-0(0-0)
Ümraniyespor - Antalyaspor 0-1(0-0)
Alanyaspor - Beşiktaş 3-3(1-3)
Konyaspor - Istanbul Başakşehir 0-0
Kasımpaşa - Fenerbahçe 0-6(0-3)

**Round 3** [19-22.08.2022]
Ümraniyespor - Galatasaray 0-1(0-0)
Giresunspor - Kasımpaşa 1-0(0-0)
Hatayspor - Gaziantep 1-2(1-1)
Antalyaspor - Trabzonspor 5-2(2-1)
Istanbul Başakşehir - Kayserispor 2-0(1-0)
Beşiktaş - Fatih Karagümrük 4-1(2-0)
İstanbulspor - Konyaspor 0-4(0-2)
Sivasspor - Alanyaspor 1-1(1-0)
Fenerbahçe - Adana Demirspor 4-2(2-0)

**Round 4** [26-29.08.2022]
Gaziantep - Antalyaspor 5-2(1-2)
Fatih Karagümrük - Ankaragücü 4-1(2-0)
Adana Demirspor - Ümraniyespor 1-0(1-0)
Alanyaspor - İstanbulspor 0-1(0-0)
Kasımpaşa - Hatayspor 1-0(1-0)
Kayserispor - Giresunspor 3-0(1-0)
Trabzonspor - Galatasaray 0-0
Konyaspor - Fenerbahçe 1-0(0-0)
Beşiktaş - Sivasspor 3-1(3-0)

**Round 5** [02-04.09.2022]
Ümraniyespor - Trabzonspor 0-1(0-0)
Istanbul Başakşehir - Alanyaspor 2-0(1-0)
Sivasspor - Fatih Karagümrük 0-0
Fenerbahçe - Kayserispor 2-0(1-0)
Giresunspor - Konyaspor 0-1(0-0)
Hatayspor - Adana Demirspor 1-1(1-0)
Ankaragücü - Beşiktaş 2-3(1-2)
Antalyaspor - Kasımpaşa 0-2(0-1)
Galatasaray - Gaziantep 2-1(1-1)

**Round 6** [09-12.09.2022]
Alanyaspor - Ankaragücü 2-1(0-0)
Konyaspor - Hatayspor 1-0(0-0)
Fatih Karagümrük - Giresunspor 1-1(0-0)
Sivasspor - İstanbulspor 1-1(0-0)
Gaziantep - Ümraniyespor 1-1(0-0)
Kasımpaşa - Galatasaray 2-3(1-1)
Kayserispor - Antalyaspor 1-0(0-0)
Beşiktaş - Istanbul Başakşehir 0-1(0-0)
Adana Demirspor - Trabzonspor 3-2(1-1)

**Round 7** [16-18.09.2022]
Galatasaray - Konyaspor 2-1(1-1)
Hatayspor - Kayserispor 0-4(0-2)
Ümraniyespor - Kasımpaşa 1-2(0-1)
Antalyaspor - Adana Demirspor 0-3(0-1)
İstanbulspor - Beşiktaş 2-2(1-2)
Istanbul Başakşehir - Fatih Karagümrük 0-0
Trabzonspor - Gaziantep 3-2(2-2)
Ankaragücü - Sivasspor 2-1(2-0)
Fenerbahçe - Alanyaspor 5-0(3-0)

**Round 8** [01-03.10.2022]
Kasımpaşa - Gaziantep 1-0(0-0)
Ankaragücü - Istanbul Başakşehir 1-2(0-1)
Kayserispor - Trabzonspor 1-2(1-0)
Adana Demirspor - Galatasaray 0-0
Alanyaspor - Giresunspor 1-1(0-0)
Sivasspor - Hatayspor 1-2(1-2)
Konyaspor - Ümraniyespor 1-0(1-0)
Beşiktaş - Fenerbahçe 0-0
Fatih Karagümrük - İstanbulspor 1-2(1-0)

**Round 9** [07-10.10.2022]
Gaziantep - Adana Demirspor 1-1(0-0)
İstanbulspor - Ankaragücü 1-2(0-1)
Antalyaspor - Konyaspor 1-1(0-0)
Giresunspor - Beşiktaş 0-1(0-1)
Ümraniyespor - Kayserispor 2-2(0-1)
Hatayspor - Alanyaspor 1-0(0-0)
Fenerbahçe - Fatih Karagümrük 5-4(2-2)
Istanbul Başakşehir - Sivasspor 0-2(0-1)
Trabzonspor - Kasımpaşa 0-0

## Round 10 [14-17.10.2022]
Alanyaspor - Antalyaspor 3-2(1-0)
Fatih Karagümrük - Hatayspor 3-0(2-0)
Kasımpaşa - Adana Demirspor 1-4(0-2)
Kayserispor - Galatasaray 2-1(2-0)
Konyaspor - Gaziantep 0-1(0-0)
Istanbul Başakşehir - İstanbulspor 2-0(1-0)
Beşiktaş - Trabzonspor 2-2(1-2)
Ankaragücü - Fenerbahçe 0-3(0-2)
Sivasspor - Giresunspor 3-0(2-0)

## Round 11 [21-24.10.2022]
Antalyaspor - İstanbulspor 2-1(1-1)
Ümraniyespor - Fatih Karagümrük 1-3(1-1)
Trabzonspor - Sivasspor 1-0(1-0)
Fenerbahçe - Istanbul Başakşehir 1-0(0-0)
Kasımpaşa - Kayserispor 0-1(0-1)
Adana Demirspor - Konyaspor 1-1(1-1)
Galatasaray - Alanyaspor 2-2(2-0)
Giresunspor - Ankaragücü 1-1(0-0)
Hatayspor - Beşiktaş 2-1(0-1)

## Round 12 [28-31.10.2022]
Fatih Karagümrük - Galatasaray 0-2(0-0)
Konyaspor - Kasımpaşa 1-1(0-0)
Alanyaspor - Gaziantep 2-0(1-0)
Ankaragücü - Hatayspor 4-1(1-0)
Beşiktaş - Ümraniyespor 5-2(2-1)
Kayserispor - Adana Demirspor 2-2(0-1)
İstanbulspor - Fenerbahçe 2-5(0-2)
Istanbul Başakşehir - Giresunspor 3-1(1-0)
Sivasspor - Antalyaspor 0-2(0-2)

## Round 13 [04-07.11.2022]
Kasımpaşa - Ankaragücü 1-1(0-0)
Ümraniyespor - Alanyaspor 3-1(2-0)
Giresunspor - İstanbulspor 3-2(1-1)
Galatasaray - Beşiktaş 2-1(1-1)
Gaziantep - Kayserispor 1-2(0-1)
Antalyaspor - Fatih Karagümrük 4-2(3-2)
Trabzonspor - Konyaspor 2-2(2-1)
Fenerbahçe - Sivasspor 1-0(0-0)
Hatayspor - Istanbul Başakşehir 3-3(1-0)

## Round 14 [11-13.11.2022]
Alanyaspor - Adana Demirspor 0-0
Ankaragücü - Trabzonspor 1-1(0-0)
Sivasspor - Ümraniyespor 2-2(1-1)
Fenerbahçe - Giresunspor 1-2(1-0)
Istanbul Başakşehir - Galatasaray 0-7(0-3)
Fatih Karagümrük - Gaziantep 3-3(1-2)
İstanbulspor - Hatayspor 0-1(0-1)
Kayserispor - Konyaspor 1-2(1-2)
Beşiktaş - Antalyaspor 0-0 [26.02.2023]

## Round 15 [23-25.12.2022]
Antalyaspor - Ankaragücü 0-2(0-0)
Ümraniyespor - Istanbul Başakşehir 1-3(1-1)
Hatayspor - Giresunspor 1-1(0-0)
Kasımpaşa - Sivasspor 1-2(1-1)
Trabzonspor - Fenerbahçe 2-0(0-0)
Adana Demirspor-Fatih Karagümrük 2-1(2-1)
Gaziantep - Beşiktaş 1-1(0-0)
Konyaspor - Alanyaspor 2-2(1-0)
Galatasaray - İstanbulspor 2-1(2-0)

## Round 16 [27-29.12.2022]
Ankaragücü - Ümraniyespor 1-2(1-1)
Istanbul Başakşehir - Antalyaspor 2-0(0-0)
Fenerbahçe - Hatayspor 4-0(2-0)
Alanyaspor - Kayserispor 3-1(2-0)
İstanbulspor - Kasımpaşa 2-1(1-1)
Fatih Karagümrük - Trabzonspor 4-1(2-1)
Giresunspor - Gaziantep 2-1(1-0)
Sivasspor - Galatasaray 1-2(0-1)
Beşiktaş - Adana Demirspor 1-0(1-0)

## Round 17 [03-05.01.2023]
Ümraniyespor - Hatayspor 2-2(1-1)
Antalyaspor - Fenerbahçe 1-2(1-0)
Kasımpaşa - Alanyaspor 4-1(2-0)
Kayserispor - Fatih Karagümrük 2-4(0-2)
Galatasaray - Ankaragücü 2-1(2-1)
Konyaspor - Sivasspor 2-2(2-1)
Gaziantep - Istanbul Başakşehir 1-1(0-1)
Adana Demirspor - İstanbulspor 6-0(1-0)
Trabzonspor - Giresunspor 3-0(1-0)

## Round 18 [07-09.01.2023]
Hatayspor - Antalyaspor 0-0
Beşiktaş - Kasımpaşa 2-1(2-0)
Fatih Karagümrük - Konyaspor 3-3(2-0)
Ankaragücü - Kayserispor 2-1(1-1)
Giresunspor - Ümraniyespor 0-1(0-0)
Fenerbahçe - Galatasaray 0-3(0-1)
Istanbul Başakş. - Adana Demirspor 2-1(0-0)
Alanyaspor - Trabzonspor 5-0(3-0)
İstanbulspor - Gaziantep 1-1(0-1)

## Round 19 [13-15.01.2023]
Kayserispor - Sivasspor 4-1(3-0)
Galatasaray - Hatayspor 4-0(3-0)
Antalyaspor - Giresunspor 2-2(1-1)
Adana Demirspor - Ankaragücü 3-1(0-0)
Konyaspor - Beşiktaş 1-2(1-0)
Trabzonspor - Istanbul Başakşehir 1-0(1-0)
Ümraniyespor - İstanbulspor 0-2(0-2)
Kasımpaşa - Fatih Karagümrük 2-2(1-0)
Gaziantep - Fenerbahçe 1-2(0-1)

## Round 20 [20-23.01.2023]
Adana Demirspor - Giresunspor 1-1(0-1)
Kasımpaşa - Istanbul Başakşehir 1-3(1-0)
Galatasaray - Antalyaspor 2-1(0-0)
Gaziantep - Sivasspor 1-2(0-1)
Alanyaspor - Fatih Karagümrük 2-2(1-1)
Kayserispor - Beşiktaş 0-2(0-2)
Trabzonspor - İstanbulspor 4-0(1-0)
Konyaspor - Ankaragücü 0-1(0-0)
Ümraniyespor - Fenerbahçe 1-2(0-0)

## Round 21 [27-29.01.2023]
Beşiktaş - Alanyaspor 3-0(1-0)
Sivasspor - Adana Demirspor 1-2(0-1)
Ankaragücü - Gaziantep 0-2(0-0)
Hatayspor - Trabzonspor 2-1(0-1)
Antalyaspor - Ümraniyespor 3-2(1-1)
Giresunspor - Galatasaray 0-4(0-1)
İstanbulspor - Kayserispor 2-4(2-1)
Fenerbahçe - Kasımpaşa 5-1(2-1)
Istanbul Başakşehir - Konyaspor 2-0(1-0)

## Round 22 [31.01.-02.02.2023]
Alanyaspor - Sivasspor 0-3(0-2)
Fatih Karagümrük - Beşiktaş 1-1(0-1)
Gaziantep - Hatayspor 4-1(1-1)
Kasımpaşa - Giresunspor 5-1(3-1)
Galatasaray - Ümraniyespor 3-2(1-2)
Trabzonspor - Antalyaspor 2-0(1-0)
Kayserispor - Istanbul Başakşehir 1-0(0-0)
Konyaspor - İstanbulspor 0-1(0-0)
Adana Demirspor - Fenerbahçe 1-1(0-0)

## Round 23 [04-05.02.2023]
Ankaragücü - Fatih Karagümrük 0-2(0-1)
Sivasspor - Beşiktaş 1-0(1-0)
Antalyaspor - Gaziantep 1-0(1-0)
İstanbulspor - Alanyaspor 2-1(0-0)
Hatayspor - Kasımpaşa 1-0(0-0)
Galatasaray - Trabzonspor 2-1(1-1)
Fenerbahçe - Konyaspor 4-0(2-0) [25.02.23]
Giresunspor - Kayserispor 1-2(0-2) [25.02.23]
Ümraniyespor - Adana D. 1-1(0-0) [26.02.23]

## Round 24 [03-06.03.2023]
Alanyaspor - Istanbul Başakşehir 1-0(0-0)
Fatih Karagümrük - Sivasspor 4-3(1-1)
Trabzonspor - Ümraniyespor 1-2(0-0)
Kayserispor - Fenerbahçe 1-2(0-1)
Konyaspor - Giresunspor 0-0
Adana Demirspor - Hatayspor 3-0 *awarded*
Beşiktaş - Ankaragücü 2-1(1-0)
Gaziantep - Galatasaray 0-3 *awarded*
Kasımpaşa - Antalyaspor 3-1(2-1)

## Round 25 [10-13.03.2023]
Giresunspor - Fatih Karagümrük 2-2(2-1)
Antalyaspor - Kayserispor 4-0(1-0)
Galatasaray - Kasımpaşa 1-0(0-0)
Ankaragücü - Alanyaspor 2-0(1-0)
Trabzonspor - Adana Demirspor 4-1(1-1)
Hatayspor - Konyaspor 0-3 *awarded*
Istanbul Başakşehir - Beşiktaş 0-2(0-1)
Ümraniyespor - Gaziantep 3-0 *awarded*
İstanbulspor - Sivasspor 3-0(1-0)

## Round 26 [17-19.03.2023]
Konyaspor - Galatasaray 2-1(0-1)
Kasımpaşa - Ümraniyespor 1-1(1-1)
Adana Demirspor - Antalyaspor 2-0(2-0)
Beşiktaş - İstanbulspor 3-1(1-0)
Fatih Karagümrük - Istanbul Başakş. 2-2(1-1)
Sivasspor - Ankaragücü 2-0(1-0)
Alanyaspor - Fenerbahçe 1-3(1-0)
Gaziantep - Trabzonspor 0-3 *awarded*
Kayserispor - Hatayspor 3-0 *awarded*

## Round 27 [01-03.04.2023]
Istanbul Başakşehir - Ankaragücü 1-0(1-0)
Trabzonspor - Kayserispor 3-4(1-2)
Galatasaray - Adana Demirspor 2-0(0-0)
Gaziantep - Kasımpaşa 0-3 *awarded*
Hatayspor - Sivasspor 0-3 *awarded*
Ümraniyespor - Konyaspor 2-2(0-0)
Giresunspor - Alanyaspor 2-2(0-1)
Fenerbahçe - Beşiktaş 2-4(1-0)
İstanbulspor - Fatih Karagümrük 0-1(0-1)

## Round 28 [07-10.04.2023]
Konyaspor - Antalyaspor 1-1(1-1)
Adana Demirspor - Gaziantep 3-0 *awarded*
Alanyaspor - Hatayspor 3-0 *awarded*
Ankaragücü - İstanbulspor 3-2(2-0)
Kasımpaşa - Trabzonspor 2-0(1-0)
Sivasspor - Istanbul Başakşehir 1-1(1-0)
Beşiktaş - Giresunspor 3-1(2-1)
Kayserispor - Ümraniyespor 3-1(1-1)
Fatih Karagümrük - Fenerbahçe 1-2(1-0)

## Round 29 [14-16.04.2023]
Antalyaspor - Alanyaspor 3-1(2-1)
Galatasaray - Kayserispor 6-0(4-0)
Gaziantep - Konyaspor 0-3 *awarded*
Hatayspor - Fatih Karagümrük 0-3 *awarded*
Adana Demirspor - Kasımpaşa 5-0(3-0)
İstanbulspor - Istanbul Başakşehir 1-0(1-0)
Fenerbahçe - Ankaragücü 2-1(0-0)
Giresunspor - Sivasspor 1-0(1-0)
Trabzonspor - Beşiktaş 0-0

## Round 30 [18-20.04.2023]
Alanyaspor - Galatasaray 1-4(1-2)
Fatih Karagümrük - Ümraniyespor 4-2(2-1)
Beşiktaş - Hatayspor 3-0 *awarded*
İstanbulspor - Antalyaspor 3-3(2-1)
Kayserispor - Kasımpaşa 0-0
Istanbul Başakşehir - Fenerbahçe 1-2(1-0)
Konyaspor - Adana Demirspor 1-2(1-1)
Ankaragücü - Giresunspor 3-1(0-1)
Sivasspor - Trabzonspor 4-1(2-1)

| Round 31 [22-24.04.2023] |
|---|
| Ümraniyespor - Beşiktaş 0-2(0-1) |
| Gaziantep - Alanyaspor 0-3 *awarded* |
| Hatayspor - Ankaragücü 0-3 *awarded* |
| Kasımpaşa - Konyaspor 1-2(1-2) |
| Adana Demirspor - Kayserispor 5-3(4-3) |
| Galatasaray - Fatih Karagümrük 3-3(2-3) |
| Giresunspor - Istanbul Başakşehir 2-4(0-4) |
| Antalyaspor - Sivasspor 1-2(0-2) |
| Fenerbahçe - İstanbulspor 3-3(1-0) |

| Round 32 [28.04.-01.05.2023] |
|---|
| Alanyaspor - Ümraniyespor 1-0(1-0) |
| Istanbul Başakşehir - Hatayspor 3-0 *awarded* |
| Kayserispor - Gaziantep 3-0 *awarded* |
| Fatih Karagümrük - Antalyaspor 0-1(0-1) |
| Konyaspor - Trabzonspor 2-1(1-1) |
| Ankaragücü - Kasımpaşa 0-0 |
| Sivasspor - Fenerbahçe 1-3(0-3) |
| Beşiktaş - Galatasaray 3-1(1-1) |
| İstanbulspor - Giresunspor 1-0(1-0) |

| Round 33 [06-08.05.2023] |
|---|
| Antalyaspor - Beşiktaş 1-3(1-0) |
| Adana Demirspor - Alanyaspor 4-2(2-2) |
| Gaziantep - Fatih Karagümrük 0-3 *awarded* |
| Hatayspor - İstanbulspor 0-3 *awarded* |
| Ümraniyespor - Sivasspor 4-1(2-1) |
| Konyaspor - Kayserispor 2-2(0-0) |
| Giresunspor - Fenerbahçe 1-1(0-1) |
| Galatasaray - Istanbul Başakşehir 1-0(1-0) |
| Trabzonspor - Ankaragücü 2-0(1-0) |

| Round 34 [16-18.05.2023] |
|---|
| Sivasspor - Kasımpaşa 1-2(0-0) |
| Alanyaspor - Konyaspor 0-3(0-1) |
| İstanbulspor - Galatasaray 0-2(0-1) |
| Beşiktaş - Gaziantep 3-0 *awarded* |
| Giresunspor - Hatayspor 3-0 *awarded* |
| Istanbul Başakşehir - Ümraniyespor 1-1(1-0) |
| Ankaragücü - Antalyaspor 1-1(0-0) |
| Fatih Karagümrük-Adana Demirspor 2-3(1-0) |
| Fenerbahçe - Trabzonspor 3-1(1-0) |

| Round 35 [20-22.05.2023] |
|---|
| Kasımpaşa - İstanbulspor 1-0(0-0) |
| Galatasaray - Sivasspor 2-0(1-0) |
| Kayserispor - Alanyaspor 0-4(0-2) |
| Gaziantep - Giresunspor 0-3 *awarded* |
| Hatayspor - Fenerbahçe 0-3 *awarded* |
| Ümraniyespor - Ankaragücü 1-2(1-1) |
| Adana Demirspor - Beşiktaş 1-4(1-1) |
| Antalyaspor - Istanbul Başakşehir 0-0 |
| Trabzonspor - Fatih Karagümrük 4-1(3-1) |

| Round 36 [30.05.2023] |
|---|
| Alanyaspor - Kasımpaşa 1-3(0-0) |
| Ankaragücü - Galatasaray 1-4(1-2) |
| Fenerbahçe - Antalyaspor 2-0(1-0) |
| Giresunspor - Trabzonspor 2-4(0-2) |
| Hatayspor - Ümraniyespor 0-3 *awarded* |
| Istanbul Başakşehir - Gaziantep 3-0 *awarded* |
| İstanbulspor - Adana Demirspor 0-2(0-1) |
| Fatih Karagümrük - Kayserispor 2-0(2-0) |
| Sivasspor - Konyaspor 1-0(1-0) |

| Round 37 [03-04.06.2023] |
|---|
| Antalyaspor - Hatayspor 3-0 *awarded* |
| Gaziantep - İstanbulspor 0-3 *awarded* |
| Konyaspor - Fatih Karagümrük 1-1(1-1) |
| Adana Demirspor - Istanbul Başakş. 2-3(1-2) |
| Kasımpaşa - Beşiktaş 2-5(0-2) |
| Kayserispor - Ankaragücü 0-1(0-1) |
| Trabzonspor - Alanyaspor 5-1(4-1) |
| Ümraniyespor - Giresunspor 0-1(0-1) |
| Galatasaray - Fenerbahçe 3-0(1-0) |

| Round 38 [06-07.06.2023] |
|---|
| Fenerbahçe - Gaziantep 3-0 *awarded* |
| Hatayspor - Galatasaray 0-3 *awarded* |
| Fatih Karagümrük - Kasımpaşa 3-0(1-0) |
| Sivasspor - Kayserispor 1-1(1-1) |
| Istanbul Başakşehir - Trabzonspor 3-1(1-0) |
| Ankaragücü - Adana Demirspor 1-2(0-1) |
| Beşiktaş - Konyaspor 3-3(2-1) |
| Giresunspor - Antalyaspor 2-0(1-0) |
| İstanbulspor - Ümraniyespor 4-0(1-0) |

## Final Standings

| | | | | | | | | Home | | | | | Away | | | | |
|---|---|---|---|---|---|---|---|---|---|---|---|---|---|---|---|---|---|
| 1. | **Galatasaray SK Istanbul** | 36 | 28 | 4 | 4 | 83 - 27 | **88** | 15 | 2 | 1 | 41 - 15 | 13 | 2 | 3 | 42 - 12 |
| 2. | Fenerbahçe SK Istanbul | 36 | 25 | 5 | 6 | 87 - 42 | **80** | 13 | 2 | 3 | 50 - 24 | 12 | 3 | 3 | 37 - 18 |
| 3. | Beşiktaş JK Istanbul | 36 | 23 | 9 | 4 | 78 - 36 | **78** | 13 | 4 | 1 | 41 - 15 | 10 | 5 | 3 | 37 - 21 |
| 4. | Adana Demirspor Kulübü | 36 | 20 | 9 | 7 | 76 - 45 | **69** | 12 | 4 | 2 | 46 - 19 | 8 | 5 | 5 | 30 - 26 |
| 5. | Istanbul Başakşehir FK | 36 | 18 | 8 | 10 | 54 - 37 | **62** | 12 | 2 | 4 | 31 - 17 | 6 | 6 | 6 | 23 - 20 |
| 6. | Trabzonspor Kulübü | 36 | 17 | 6 | 13 | 64 - 54 | **57** | 12 | 4 | 2 | 38 - 13 | 5 | 2 | 11 | 26 - 41 |
| 7. | Fatih Karagümrük SK | 36 | 13 | 12 | 11 | 75 - 63 | **51** | 7 | 5 | 6 | 40 - 31 | 6 | 7 | 5 | 35 - 32 |
| 8. | Konyaspor Kulübü | 36 | 12 | 15 | 9 | 49 - 41 | **51** | 5 | 8 | 5 | 18 - 18 | 7 | 7 | 4 | 31 - 23 |
| 9. | Kayserispor Kulübü | 36 | 15 | 5 | 16 | 55 - 61 | **47** | 9 | 2 | 7 | 28 - 22 | 6 | 3 | 9 | 27 - 39 |
| 10. | Kasımpaşa Spor Kulübü Istanbul | 36 | 12 | 7 | 17 | 45 - 61 | **43** | 7 | 3 | 8 | 29 - 33 | 5 | 4 | 9 | 16 - 28 |
| 11. | MKE Ankaragücü SK | 36 | 12 | 6 | 18 | 43 - 53 | **42** | 6 | 4 | 8 | 24 - 28 | 6 | 2 | 10 | 19 - 25 |
| 12. | Istanbulspor Kulübü | 36 | 12 | 5 | 19 | 47 - 63 | **41** | 6 | 3 | 9 | 24 - 31 | 6 | 2 | 10 | 23 - 32 |
| 13. | Antalyaspor Kulübü | 36 | 11 | 8 | 17 | 46 - 55 | **41** | 8 | 3 | 7 | 31 - 26 | 3 | 5 | 10 | 15 - 29 |
| 14. | Sivasspor Kulübü | 36 | 11 | 8 | 17 | 46 - 54 | **41** | 5 | 7 | 6 | 23 - 21 | 6 | 1 | 11 | 23 - 33 |
| 15. | Alanyaspor Kulübü | 36 | 11 | 8 | 17 | 54 - 70 | **41** | 8 | 4 | 6 | 29 - 27 | 3 | 4 | 11 | 25 - 43 |
| 16. | Giresunspor Kulübü (*Relegated*) | 36 | 10 | 10 | 16 | 42 - 60 | **40** | 6 | 4 | 8 | 25 - 29 | 4 | 6 | 8 | 17 - 31 |
| 17. | Ümraniyespor Kulübü (*Relegated*) | 36 | 7 | 9 | 20 | 47 - 64 | **30** | 3 | 4 | 11 | 22 - 29 | 4 | 5 | 9 | 25 - 35 |
| 18. | Gaziantep FK (*withdrawn*) | 36 | 6 | 7 | 23 | 31 - 72 | **25** | 3 | 4 | 11 | 17 - 37 | 3 | 3 | 12 | 14 - 35 |
| 19. | Hatayspor Kulübü Antakya (*withdrawn*) | 36 | 6 | 5 | 25 | 19 - 83 | **23** | 4 | 4 | 10 | 12 - 37 | 2 | 1 | 15 | 7 - 46 |

Please note: on 12.02.2023, Gaziantep FK and Hatayspor Kulübü Antakya withdrew from the league following the 2023 Turkey-Syria earthquake and were not relegated at the end of the season. All their results for upcoming matches were awarded as 3-0 wins for the opponents.

| Top goalscorers: | |
|---|---|
| 29 **Enner Remberto Valencia Lastra (ECU)** | *Fenerbahçe SK Istanbul* |
| 23 Mbaye Diagne (SEN) | *Fatih Karagümrük SK* |
| 22 Mauro Emanuel Icardi Riveiro (ARG) | *Galatasaray SK Istanbul* |
| 20 Fabio Borini (ITA) | *Fatih Karagümrük SK* |

### Fifth Round [20-22.12.2022]

| | | | | |
|---|---|---|---|---|
| Kasımpaşa SK Istanbul - Ümraniyespor Kulübü | 1-2(0-0) | | Alanyaspor Kulübü - Eyüpspor Kulübü | 3-2(0-1,2-2) |
| MKE Ankaragücü SK - Tuzlaspor Kulübü | 2-0(1-0) | | Trabzonspor Kulübü - Samsunspor | 3-0(2-0) |
| Sivasspor Kulübü - Esenler Erokspor Kulübü | 5-2(3-1) | | Beşiktaş JK Istanbul - Şanlıurfaspor SK | 4-2(0-2) |
| Antalyaspor Kulübü - Manisa FK | 1-0(0-0) | | Kayserispor Kulübü - Gençlerbirliği SK Ankara | 2-0(0-0) |
| Istanbul Başakşehir FK - Göztepe SK İzmir | 3-1(3-0) | | Konyaspor Kulübü - Bodrumspor | 3-2(0-0,1-1) |
| Fenerbahçe SK Istanbul - Istanbulspor Kulübü | 3-1(2-0) | | Gaziantep FK - Boluspor Kulübü | 3-1(1-0) |
| Giresunspor Kulübü - Karacabey Belediyespor | 0-5(0-2) | | Adana Demirspor Kulübü - Çaykur Rizespor Kulübü | 3-4(0-2,2-2) |
| Fatih Karagümrük SK - Uşakspor | 3-0(1-0) | | Galatasaray SK Istanbul - Ankara Keçiörengücü SK | 1-0(0-0) |

### 1/8-Finals [17-19.01.2023]

| | | | | |
|---|---|---|---|---|
| Sivasspor Kulübü - Karacabey Belediyespor | 3-0(1-0) | | MKE Ankaragücü SK - Beşiktaş JK Istanbul | 1-1 aet; 4-3 pen |
| Antalyaspor Kulübü - Kayserispor Kulübü | 0-2(0-0,0-0) | | Ümraniyespor Kulübü - Trabzonspor Kulübü | 1-4(1-0,1-1) |
| Alanyaspor Kulübü - Galatasaray SK Istanbul | 1-2(0-2) | | Gaziantep FK - Konyaspor Kulübü | 1-1 aet; 7-6 pen |
| Fatih Karagümrük SK - Istanbul Başakşehir FK | 2-2 aet; 3-5 pen | | Fenerbahçe SK Istanbul - Çaykur Rizespor Kulübü | 2-1(1-1) |

### Quarter-Finals [04-06.04.2023]

| | | | | |
|---|---|---|---|---|
| MKE Ankaragücü SK - Trabzonspor Kulübü | 3-1(0-1) | | Galatasaray SK Istanbul - Istanbul Başakşehir FK | 2-3(1-2) |
| Sivasspor Kulübü - Gaziantep FK | 3-0 awarded | | Fenerbahçe SK Istanbul - Kayserispor Kulübü | 4-1(2-1) |

### Semi-Finals [03-04.05./24-25.05.2023]

| First Leg | | | Second Leg | |
|---|---|---|---|---|
| Sivasspor Kulübü - Fenerbahçe SK Istanbul | 0-0 | | Fenerbahçe SK Istanbul - Sivasspor Kulübü | 3-0(0-0) |
| Istanbul Başakşehir FK - MKE Ankaragücü SK | 1-0(0-0) | | MKE Ankaragücü SK - Istanbul Başakşehir FK | 2-2(1-0,2-1) |

### Final

11.06.2023; "Gürsel Aksel" Spor ve Sağlıklı Yaşam Merkezi, İzmir; Referee: Atilla Karaoğlan; Attendance: 12,182

**Fenerbahçe SK Istanbul - Istanbul Başakşehir FK**                    **2-0(2-0)**

**Fenerbahçe**: Irfan Can Eğribayat, Ferdi Kadıoğlu, Serdar Aziz, Attila Árpád Szalai, Luan Peres Petroni, Arda Güler (90.Mert Hakan Yandaş), Willian Souza Arão da Silva, Miha Zajc (74.Bright Osayi-Samuel), İrfan Kahveci (85.Diego Martín Rossi Marachlian), Michy Batshuayi Atunga (90.Serdar Dursun), Enner Remberto Valencia Lastra (Cap) (74.İsmail Yüksek). Trainer: Jorge Fernando Pinheiro de Jesus (Portugal).

**Istanbul Başakşehir**: Muhammed Şengezer, Ömer Ali Şahiner, Leonardo Campos Duarte Da Silva „Léo", Ahmed Touba (77.Danijel Aleksić), Caner Erkin (34.Lucas Pedro Alves de Lima), Serdar Gürler (34.Adnan Januzaj), Berkay Özcan, Lucas Rodrigo Biglia (Cap) (34.Eden Kartsev), Deniz Türüç (85.Şener Özbayraklı), Philippe Paulin Kény, João Vitor Brandão Figueiredo. Trainer: Emre Belözoğlu.

**Goals:** 1-0 Michy Batshuayi Atunga (1), 2-0 Michy Batshuayi Atunga (29).

## THE CLUBS 2022/2023

### Adana Demirspor Kulübü

| Founded: | 28.12.1940 | |
|---|---|---|
| Stadium: | Yeni Adana Stadyumu, Adana (33,543) | |
| Trainer: | Vincenzo Montella (ITA) | 18.06.1974 |

| Goalkeepers: | DOB | M | (s) | G | | | DOB | M | (s) | G |
|---|---|---|---|---|---|---|---|---|---|---|
| Ertaç Özbir | 25.10.1989 | 32 | | | Furkan Soyalp | 12.06.1995 | 1 | (5) | |
| Goran Karačić (BIH) | 18.08.1996 | 1 | | | Gökhan Inler (SUI) | 27.06.1984 | 10 | (18) | 2 |
| Vedat Karakuş | 28.02.1998 | 1 | | | Jorge Emanuel Morel Barrios (PAR) | 22.01.1998 | 9 | (3) | 1 |
| **Defenders:** | DOB | M | (s) | G | Badou N'Diaye (SEN) | 27.10.1990 | 32 | | 8 |
| Abdurrahim Dursun | 01.12.1998 | 1 | (7) | | Benjamin Stambouli (FRA) | 13.08.1990 | 25 | (5) | 1 |
| İsmail Çokçalış | 21.06.2000 | 5 | (1) | | Yusuf Erdoğan | 07.08.1992 | 2 | (3) | |
| Kévin Manuel Rodrigues (POR) | 05.03.1994 | 33 | | 2 | Yusuf Sarı | 20.11.1998 | 17 | (14) | 5 |
| Jovan Manev (MKD) | 25.01.2001 | 4 | (4) | | **Forwards:** | DOB | M | (s) | G |
| Mert Çetin | 01.01.1997 | 7 | (3) | | David Babajide Akintola (NGA) | 13.01.1996 | 21 | (8) | 6 |
| Yaroslav Rakitskiy (UKR) | 03.08.1989 | 8 | | | Britt Curtis Assombalonga (COD) | 06.12.1992 | 4 | (8) | 2 |
| Samet Akaydın | 13.03.1994 | 16 | | 2 | Mario Balotelli Barwuah (ITA) | 12.08.1990 | | (2) | |
| Semih Güler | 30.11.1994 | 22 | (8) | | Berk Yıldız | 09.01.1996 | | (6) | |
| Jonas Svensson (NOR) | 06.03.1993 | 29 | | | Artyom Dzyuba (RUS) | 22.08.1988 | 2 | (2) | 1 |
| Tayyip Sanuç | 17.12.1999 | 2 | (1) | 1 | Gökhan Töre | 20.01.1992 | | (3) | 1 |
| **Midfielders:** | DOB | M | (s) | G | Fredrik Gulbrandsen (NOR) | 10.09.1992 | 6 | (17) | 2 |
| Younès Belhanda (MAR) | 25.02.1990 | 27 | (3) | 12 | Cherif Ndiaye (SEN) | 23.01.1996 | 8 | (4) | 8 |
| Birkir Bjarnason (ISL) | 27.05.1988 | 2 | (7) | | Samuel Bakia Nongoh (CMR) | 04.03.2004 | 1 | (1) | |
| Emre Akbaba | 04.10.1992 | 22 | (5) | 7 | Henry Chukwuemeka Onyekuru (NGA) | 05.06.1997 | 24 | (4) | 8 |
| Erhun Öztumer | 29.05.1991 | | (4) | | Salih Kavrazlı | 16.03.2002 | | (1) | |

## Alanyaspor Kulübü

**Founded**: 1948
**Stadium**: Kırbıyık Holding Stadyumu, Alanya (10,130)
**Trainer**: Francesco Farioli (ITA)    10.04.1989
[27.02.2023] Ersun Yanal    17.12.1961
[22.04.2023] Ömer Erdoğan    03.05.1977

| Goalkeepers: | DOB | M | (s) | G |
|---|---|---|---|---|
| Yusuf Karagöz | 05.10.1999 | 4 | (1) | |
| Alex Rúnarsson (ISL) | 18.02.1995 | 30 | | |
| **Defenders:** | **DOB** | **M** | **(s)** | **G** |
| Ahmet Gülay | 13.01.2003 | | (1) | |
| Jure Balkovec (SVN) | 09.09.1994 | 21 | (8) | 4 |
| Cagan Erciyas | 04.02.2003 | 1 | | |
| Zouhair Feddal (MAR) | 23.12.1989 | 5 | | |
| Furkan Bayır | 09.02.2000 | 31 | (1) | 1 |
| Joher Rassoul (SEN) | 31.12.1995 | 10 | (3) | |
| Tayfur Bingöl | 11.01.1993 | 1 | (3) | |
| **Midfielders:** | **DOB** | **M** | **(s)** | **G** |
| Idrissa Doumbia (CIV) | 14.04.1998 | 15 | (10) | 2 |
| Efkan Bekiroğlu | 14.09.1995 | 17 | (8) | 4 |
| Fatih Aksoy | 06.11.1997 | 25 | (2) | |
| Leroy Fer (NED) | 05.01.1990 | 26 | (4) | 1 |
| Zinedine Ferhat (ALG) | 01.03.1993 | 12 | (11) | 1 |
| Arnaud Lusamba (FRA) | 04.01.1997 | 16 | (12) | 1 |
| *Pedro* Miguel Almeida Lopes *Pereira* (POR) | 22.01.1998 | 18 | (8) | |
| Oussama Targhalline (MAR) | 20.05.2002 | 2 | (4) | |
| Ümit Akdağ | 06.10.2003 | | (1) | |
| Umut Güneş | 16.03.2000 | 22 | (5) | 2 |
| Yusuf Özdemir | 10.01.2001 | 17 | (8) | 2 |
| **Forwards:** | **DOB** | **M** | **(s)** | **G** |
| Daniel João Santos *Candeias* (POR) | 25.02.1988 | 17 | (10) | 1 |
| Famara Diédhiou (SEN) | 15.12.1992 | | (2) | |
| Efecan Karaca | 16.11.1989 | 28 | | 5 |
| Erencan Yardımcı | 04.02.2002 | 3 | (11) | 3 |
| Moustafa Hassan Mohamed Abdelmonem Mahgoub (EGY) | 05.03.1993 | 21 | (3) | 10 |
| *Ivan* Ricardo Neves Abreu *Cavaleiro* (POR) | 18.10.1993 | 12 | (10) | 2 |
| Efthimios Koulouris (GRE) | 06.03.1996 | 4 | (6) | 3 |
| Oğuz Aydın | 27.10.2000 | 9 | (19) | 1 |
| *Wilson* Bruno Naval da Costa *Eduardo* (ANG) | 08.07.1990 | 7 | (9) | 4 |

## Makina ve Kimya Endüstrisi Ankaragücü Spor Kulübü

**Founded**: 31.08.1910
**Stadium**: Eryaman Stadyumu, Ankara (20,560)
**Trainer**: Mustafa Dalcı    01.07.1973
[29.08.2022] Ömer Erdoğan    03.05.1977
[20.02.2023] Sedat Ağçay    22.09.1981
[23.03.2023] Tolunay Kafkas    31.03.1968

| Goalkeepers: | DOB | M | (s) | G |
|---|---|---|---|---|
| Bahadır Güngördü | 16.01.1996 | 11 | (3) | |
| Doğukan Kaya | 16.01.2000 | 1 | | |
| Gökhan Akkan | 01.01.1995 | 23 | | |
| **Defenders:** | **DOB** | **M** | **(s)** | **G** |
| Arda Kızıldağ | 15.10.1998 | 5 | (2) | |
| Arda Ünyay | 18.01.2007 | | (1) | |
| Hasan Ali Kaldırım | 09.12.1989 | 6 | (2) | |
| Matěj Hanousek (CZE) | 02.06.1993 | 8 | (3) | |
| Stelios Kitsiou (GRE) | 28.09.1993 | 10 | (2) | 1 |
| Kévin Malcuit (FRA) | 31.07.1991 | 19 | (1) | 1 |
| *Marlon* Rodrigues Xavier (BRA) | 20.05.1997 | 11 | (2) | |
| Mert Can | 07.02.2005 | | (1) | |
| Nihad Mujakić (BIH) | 15.04.1998 | 32 | | |
| Oğuz Ceylan | 15.12.1990 | 8 | (4) | |
| Sinan Osmanoğlu | 09.01.1990 | 1 | (1) | |
| Uroš Radaković (SRB) | 31.03.1994 | 22 | | 1 |
| Yasin Güreler | 02.07.1991 | 10 | (4) | 1 |
| **Midfielders:** | **DOB** | **M** | **(s)** | **G** |
| Abdullah Durak | 01.04.1987 | 2 | (1) | |
| Ali Kaan Güneren | 08.04.2000 | | (3) | |
| Atakan Çankaya | 25.06.1998 | 15 | (5) | |
| İbrahim Yılmaz Çiçek | 17.09.2006 | | (1) | |
| Şahverdi Çetin (GER) | 28.09.2000 | | (1) | |
| Lamine Diack (SEN) | 15.11.2000 | 14 | (12) | 2 |
| Andrej Đokanović (BIH) | 01.03.2001 | 6 | (8) | |
| Pedro Filipe Barbosa Moreira „Pedrinho" (POR) | 20.12.1992 | 17 | (11) | |
| Pedro Filipe Figueiredo Rodrigues „Pêpê" (POR) | 20.05.1997 | 1 | (5) | |
| Taylan Antalyalı | 08.01.1995 | 27 | (3) | 3 |
| Tolga Ciğerci | 23.03.1992 | 16 | | 2 |
| Ghayas Zahid (NOR) | 08.09.1994 | 18 | (10) | 2 |
| **Forwards:** | **DOB** | **M** | **(s)** | **G** |
| Gboly Ariyibi (USA) | 18.01.1995 | 2 | (8) | |
| Giorgi Beridze (GEO) | 12.05.1997 | 20 | (9) | 4 |
| Tasos Chatzigiovannis (GRE) | 31.05.1997 | 7 | (18) | 1 |
| Eren Derdiyok (SUI) | 12.06.1988 | | (1) | |
| Emre Kılınç | 23.08.1994 | 24 | (4) | 2 |
| Fıratcan Üzüm | 04.06.1999 | 3 | (7) | |
| Gökhan Töre | 20.01.1992 | 1 | (2) | |
| *Jesé* Rodríguez Ruíz (ESP) | 26.02.1993 | 6 | (8) | 2 |
| Federico Macheda (ITA) | 22.08.1991 | 4 | (7) | |
| Felicio Mendes João *Milson* (ANG) | 12.10.1999 | 5 | (5) | 5 |
| Bevic Moussiti-Oko (CGO) | 28.01.1995 | | (8) | |
| Ali Sowe (GAM) | 14.06.1994 | 30 | (2) | 12 |

## Antalyaspor Kulübü

**Founded**: 02.07.1966
**Stadium**: Antalya Stadyumu [Corendon Airlines Park], Antalya (32,537)
**Trainer**: Nuri Şahin    05.09.1988

| Goalkeepers: | DOB | M | (s) | G |
|---|---|---|---|---|
| Alperen Uysal | 01.01.1994 | 10 | | |
| Ataberk Dadakdeniz | 05.08.1999 | 1 | | |
| Ruud Boffin (BEL) | 05.11.1987 | 7 | | |
| *Hèlton* Brant Aleixo Leite (BRA) | 02.11.1990 | 17 | | |
| **Defenders:** | **DOB** | **M** | **(s)** | **G** |
| Bünyamin Balcı | 31.05.2000 | 32 | (2) | |
| Cemali Sertel | 06.01.2000 | 7 | (11) | |
| Emrecan Uzunhan | 26.02.2001 | 8 | (4) | |
| Sherel Floranus (CUW) | 23.08.1998 | 5 | (7) | |
| Amar Gerxhaliu (KOS) | 26.04.2002 | 2 | (2) | |
| Güray Vural | 11.06.1988 | 30 | | 4 |
| Fedor Kudryashov (RUS) | 05.04.1987 | 10 | (3) | |
| Christian Luyindama Nekadio (COD) | 08.01.1994 | 5 | | |
| Ömer Toprak | 21.07.1989 | 20 | (3) | 1 |
| Veysel Sarı | 25.07.1988 | 27 | (4) | 2 |
| **Midfielders:** | **DOB** | **M** | **(s)** | **G** |
| Erkan Eyibil | 15.06.2001 | | (1) | |
| *Fernando* Lucas Martins (BRA) | 03.03.1992 | 30 | | 5 |
| Alfredo Gomes Ribeiro „Fredy" (ANG) | 27.03.1990 | 18 | (8) | 3 |
| Mustafa Erdilman | 01.01.2004 | | (5) | |
| Hakan Özmert | 03.06.1985 | 1 | (8) | |
| Shoya Nakajima (JPN) | 23.08.1994 | 6 | (9) | |
| Erdal Rakip (MKD) | 13.02.1996 | 9 | (6) | |
| Soner Aydoğdu | 05.01.1991 | 7 | (6) | |
| Bálint Szabó (HUN) | 18.01.2001 | | (1) | |
| Ufuk Akyol | 27.08.1997 | 17 | (9) | |
| **Forwards:** | **DOB** | **M** | **(s)** | **G** |
| Bertuğ Yıldırım | 12.07.2002 | 2 | (11) | 2 |
| Doğukan Sinik | 21.01.1999 | 11 | (1) | 3 |
| Houssameddine Ghacha (ALG) | 25.10.1995 | 10 | (15) | |
| Gökdeniz Bayrakdar | 23.11.2001 | 3 | (10) | 2 |
| Sinan Gümüş (GER) | 15.01.1994 | 4 | (10) | |
| Sam Larsson (SWE) | 10.04.1993 | 25 | (5) | 2 |
| *Luiz Adriano* Souza da Silva (BRA) | 12.04.1987 | 15 | (4) | 2 |
| Admir Mehmedi (SUI) | 16.03.1991 | 3 | (7) | |
| Alassane Ndao (SEN) | 20.12.1996 | 16 | (1) | 1 |
| Haji Amir Wright (USA) | 27.03.1998 | 27 | (1) | 15 |

## Beşiktaş Jimnastik Kulübü Istanbul

**Founded:** 04.03.1903
**Stadium:** Vodafone Park, Istanbul (42,590)
**Trainer:** Valérien Ismaël (FRA)　28.09.1975
[28.10.2022] Şenol Güneş　01.06.1952

| Goalkeepers: | DOB | M | (s) | G |
|---|---|---|---|---|
| Emre Bilgin | 26.02.2004 | 2 | | |
| Ersin Destanoğlu | 01.01.2001 | 9 | | |
| Mert Günok | 01.03.1989 | 23 | | |
| **Defenders:** | **DOB** | **M** | **(s)** | **G** |
| Onur Bulut (GER) | 16.04.1994 | 6 | (2) | |
| Omar Colley (GAM) | 24.10.1992 | 10 | | |
| Emrecan Uzunhan | 26.02.2001 | 1 | (2) | |
| Francisco Javier "Javi" Montero Rubio (ESP) | 14.01.1999 | 2 | (1) | |
| Arthur Masuaku (COD) | 07.11.1993 | 30 | (1) | 2 |
| Valentin Rosier (FRA) | 19.08.1996 | 26 | (1) | 1 |
| Romain Ghanem Paul Saïss (MAR) | 26.03.1990 | 21 | (4) | 1 |
| Tayfur Bingöl | 11.01.1993 | 6 | (20) | 2 |
| Tayyip Sanuç | 17.12.1999 | 19 | (1) | 2 |
| Umut Meraş | 20.12.1995 | 4 | (11) | |
| Welinton Souza Silva (BRA) | 10.04.1989 | 10 | (4) | |
| **Midfielders:** | **DOB** | **M** | **(s)** | **G** |
| Bamidele Jermaine Alli (ENG) | 11.04.1996 | 10 | (3) | 2 |
| Gedson Carvalho Fernandes (POR) | 09.01.1999 | 29 | (4) | 3 |
| Rachid Ghezzal (ALG) | 09.05.1992 | 7 | (4) | 2 |

| | DOB | M | (s) | G |
|---|---|---|---|---|
| Amir Hadžiahmetović (BIH) | 08.03.1997 | 12 | | 1 |
| Atiba Hutchinson (CAN) | 08.02.1983 | 1 | (4) | 1 |
| Josef de Souza Dias (BRA) | 11.02.1989 | 9 | (1) | 1 |
| Kartal Kyara Yılmaz | 04.11.2000 | 1 | (2) | |
| Kerem Kesgin | 05.11.2000 | | (6) | |
| Alexandru Iulian Maxim (ROU) | 08.07.1990 | 2 | (9) | |
| Necip Uysal | 24.01.1991 | 8 | (13) | |
| Salih Uçan | 06.01.1994 | 28 | (1) | 3 |
| Berkay Vardar (AZE) | 14.01.2003 | 3 | (2) | |
| **Forwards:** | **DOB** | **M** | **(s)** | **G** |
| Vincent Pate Aboubakar (CMR) | 22.01.1992 | 15 | (1) | 13 |
| Tyler Dominic Boyd (USA) | 30.12.1994 | | (1) | |
| Cenk Tosun | 07.06.1991 | 22 | (10) | 15 |
| Kenan Karaman | 05.03.1994 | | (2) | |
| Jackson Muleka Kyanvubu (COD) | 04.10.1999 | 14 | (15) | 5 |
| Georges-Kévin N'Koudou (CMR) | 13.02.1995 | 13 | (7) | 4 |
| Nathan Redmond (ENG) | 06.03.1994 | 15 | (10) | 5 |
| Semih Kılıçsoy | 15.08.2005 | | (4) | |
| Wout François Maria Weghorst (NED) | 07.08.1992 | 16 | | 8 |

## Fatih Karagümrük Spor Kulübü Istanbul

**Founded:** 1926
**Stadium:** Atatürk Olimpiyat Stadı, Istanbul (76,761)
**Trainer:** Andrea Pirlo (ITA)　19.05.1979
[24.05.2023] Alparslan Erdem　11.12.1988

| Goalkeepers: | DOB | M | (s) | G |
|---|---|---|---|---|
| Batuhan Şen | 03.02.1999 | 18 | | |
| Cem Kablan | 01.01.2000 | | (1) | |
| Emiliano Viviano (ITA) | 01.12.1985 | 16 | (1) | |
| **Defenders:** | **DOB** | **M** | **(s)** | **G** |
| Davide Biraschi (ITA) | 02.07.1994 | 28 | (1) | 2 |
| Bruno Miguel Ferreira Rodrigues (POR) | 08.06.2001 | 3 | (2) | |
| Burak Bekaroğlu | 16.04.1997 | 2 | | |
| Caner Erkin | 04.10.1988 | 12 | | |
| Steven Roy Caulker (SLE) | 29.12.1991 | 4 | (2) | 1 |
| Ibrahim Drešević (KOS) | 24.01.1997 | 32 | | 1 |
| Efecan Mızrakcı | 09.01.2004 | | (1) | |
| Emir Tintiş | 12.01.2004 | 1 | | |
| Rayyan Baniya | 18.02.1999 | 25 | | 2 |
| Salih Dursun | 12.07.1991 | 9 | (13) | 1 |
| **Midfielders:** | **DOB** | **M** | **(s)** | **G** |
| Andrea Bertolacci (ITA) | 11.01.1991 | 11 | (3) | |
| Jakup Jimmy Durmaz (SWE) | 22.03.1989 | 11 | (1) | |
| Adem Ljajić (SRB) | 29.09.1991 | | (9) | |

| | DOB | M | (s) | G |
|---|---|---|---|---|
| Levent Mercan (GER) | 10.12.2000 | 23 | (6) | 2 |
| Lawrence Anwan Nicholas (NGA) | 17.05.2001 | 5 | (14) | |
| Magomed Ozdoev (RUS) | 05.11.1992 | 32 | | 5 |
| Matteo Ricci (ITA) | 27.05.1994 | 14 | (2) | 1 |
| Otabek Shukurov (UZB) | 22.06.1996 | 23 | (5) | 1 |
| Adnan Uğur (BEL) | 28.06.2001 | 1 | (10) | |
| **Forwards:** | **DOB** | **M** | **(s)** | **G** |
| Fabio Borini (ITA) | 29.03.1991 | 29 | (1) | 19 |
| Burak Kapacak | 08.12.1999 | 1 | (12) | 1 |
| Colin Kâzım-Richards | 26.08.1986 | 2 | (15) | |
| Ebrima Colley (GAM) | 01.02.2000 | 18 | (9) | 1 |
| Brahim Darri (NED) | 14.09.1994 | | (1) | |
| Mbaye Diagne (SEN) | 28.10.1991 | 28 | (5) | 23 |
| Sofiane Féghouli (ALG) | 26.12.1989 | 3 | (6) | |
| Kerim Frei | 19.11.1993 | 5 | (13) | 3 |
| Jean Evrard Kouassi (CIV) | 25.09.1994 | 9 | (3) | 3 |
| Saba Lobzhanidze (GEO) | 18.12.1994 | 8 | (2) | 2 |
| Ahmed Musa (NGA) | 14.10.1992 | 1 | (2) | |
| Samed Onur | 15.07.2002 | | (6) | |

## Fenerbahçe Spor Kulübü Istanbul

**Founded:** 03.05.1907 (as Fenerbahçe Futbol Kulübü)
**Stadium:** „Şükrü Saracoğlu" Stadyumu, Istanbul (47,834)
**Trainer:** Jorge Fernando Pinheiro de Jesus (POR)　24.07.1954

| Goalkeepers: | DOB | M | (s) | G |
|---|---|---|---|---|
| Altay Bayındır | 14.04.1998 | 26 | | |
| Irfan Can Eğribayat | 30.06.1998 | 8 | | |
| **Defenders:** | **DOB** | **M** | **(s)** | **G** |
| Ezgjan Alioski (MKD) | 12.02.1992 | 9 | (8) | 1 |
| Gustavo Henrique Vernes (BRA) | 24.03.1993 | 12 | (1) | 2 |
| Ferdi Kadıoğlu | 07.10.1999 | 32 | | 3 |
| Paolo Mauricio Lemos Merladett (URU) | 28.12.1995 | 2 | | |
| Luan Peres Petroni (BRA) | 19.07.1994 | 9 | (2) | 1 |
| Jayden Oosterwolde (NED) | 26.04.2001 | 2 | (1) | |
| Samet Akaydın | 13.03.1994 | 17 | | |
| Serdar Aziz | 23.10.1990 | 11 | (3) | |
| Attila Árpád Szalai (HUN) | 20.01.1998 | 32 | | 2 |
| **Midfielders:** | **DOB** | **M** | **(s)** | **G** |
| Arda Güler | 25.02.2005 | 11 | (9) | 4 |
| İrfan Kahveci | 15.07.1995 | 19 | (8) | 4 |
| İsmail Yüksek | 26.01.1999 | 7 | (12) | |

| | DOB | M | (s) | G |
|---|---|---|---|---|
| Lincoln Henrique Oliveira dos Santos (BRA) | 07.11.1998 | 14 | (7) | |
| Mert Hakan Yandaş | 19.08.1994 | 5 | (10) | |
| Miguel Crespo da Silva (POR) | 11.09.1996 | 14 | (9) | 3 |
| Bright Osayi-Samuel (NGA) | 31.12.1997 | 10 | (13) | |
| Willian Souza Arão da Silva (BRA) | 12.03.1992 | 28 | (3) | |
| Miha Zajc (SVN) | 01.07.1994 | 12 | (11) | 3 |
| **Forwards:** | **DOB** | **M** | **(s)** | **G** |
| Michy Batshuayi Atunga (BEL) | 02.10.1993 | 16 | (3) | 12 |
| Mërgim Berisha (GER) | 11.05.1998 | | (1) | 1 |
| Armindo Tué Na Bangna „Bruma" (POR) | 24.10.1994 | | (1) | |
| Emre Mor | 24.07.1997 | 11 | (17) | 2 |
| João Pedro Geraldino dos Santos Galvão (BRA) | 09.03.1992 | 10 | (10) | 4 |
| Joshua Christian Kojo King (NOR) | 15.01.1992 | 9 | (7) | 4 |
| Diego Martín Rossi Marachlian (URU) | 05.03.1998 | 17 | (16) | 4 |
| Serdar Dursun | 19.10.1991 | 3 | (15) | 1 |
| Enner Remberto Valencia Lastra (ECU) | 04.11.1989 | 28 | (3) | 29 |

## Galatasaray Spor Kulübü Istanbul

| Founded: | 30.10.1905 (*as Galata-Serai Football Club*) | |
|---|---|---|
| Stadium: | Nef Stadyumu, Istanbul (52,580) | |
| Trainer: | Okan Buruk | 19.10.1973 |

| Goalkeepers: | DOB | M | (s) | G |
|---|---|---|---|---|
| Okan Koçuk | 27.07.1995 | 1 | (1) | |
| Néstor Fernando Muslera Micol (URU) | 16.06.1986 | 33 | | |
| **Defenders:** | DOB | M | (s) | G |
| Abdülkerim Bardakçı | 07.09.1994 | 30 | | 3 |
| Sam Adekugbe (CAN) | 16.01.1995 | 6 | | |
| Sacha Boey (CMR) | 13.09.2000 | 31 | | 1 |
| Léo Dubois (FRA) | 14.09.1994 | 9 | (12) | 1 |
| Emin Bayram | 02.04.2003 | 4 | (3) | |
| Emre Taşdemir | 08.08.1995 | 5 | | 1 |
| Kaan Ayhan | 10.11.1994 | 1 | (4) | |
| Kazımcan Karataş | 16.01.2003 | 8 | (3) | |
| Victor Nelsson (DEN) | 14.10.1998 | 33 | | |
| Patrick van Aanholt (NED) | 29.08.1990 | 9 | (1) | |
| **Midfielders:** | DOB | M | (s) | G |
| Baran Aksaka | 29.01.2003 | | (1) | |
| Berkan Kutlu | 25.01.1998 | 6 | (18) | |
| Alexandru Cicâldău (ROU) | 08.07.1997 | | (1) | |
| Emre Akbaba | 04.10.1992 | 3 | (2) | |
| Hamza Akman | 27.09.2004 | | (1) | |
| Juan Manuel *Mata* García (ESP) | 28.04.1988 | 3 | (13) | 3 |
| Fredrik Midtsjø (NOR) | 11.08.1993 | 5 | (16) | 1 |
| *Sérgio* Miguel Relvas de *Oliveira* (POR) | 02.06.1992 | 29 | (3) | 4 |
| Taylan Antalyalı | 08.01.1995 | | (1) | |
| Lucas Sebastián Torreira Di Pascua (URU) | 11.02.1996 | 28 | (3) | |
| **Forwards:** | DOB | M | (s) | G |
| Barış Yılmaz | 23.05.2000 | 8 | (17) | 4 |
| Yusuf Demir (AUT) | 02.06.2003 | | (5) | |
| Emre Kılınç | 23.08.1994 | | (2) | |
| Bafétimbi Gomis (FRA) | 06.08.1985 | 7 | (16) | 8 |
| Mauro Emanuel Icardi Riveiro (ARG) | 19.02.1993 | 21 | (3) | 22 |
| Kerem Aktürkoğlu | 21.10.1998 | 31 | (3) | 9 |
| Dries Mertens (BEL) | 06.05.1987 | 27 | (3) | 6 |
| Milot Rashica (KOS) | 28.06.1996 | 20 | (6) | 4 |
| Haris Seferović (SUI) | 22.02.1992 | 4 | (6) | |
| Nicolò Zaniolo (ITA) | 02.07.1999 | 2 | (8) | 5 |
| Yunus Akgün | 07.07.2000 | 10 | (15) | 1 |

## Gaziantep Futbol Kulübü

| Founded: | 1988 (*as Sankospor*) | |
|---|---|---|
| Stadium: | Kalyon Stadyumu, Gaziantep (33,502) | |
| Trainer: | Erol Bulut | 30.01.1975 |
| [27.01.2023] | Erdal Güneş | 29.03.1982 |

| Goalkeepers: | DOB | M | (s) | G |
|---|---|---|---|---|
| Günay Güvenc | 25.06.1991 | 22 | | |
| **Defenders:** | DOB | M | (s) | G |
| Arda Kızıldağ | 15.10.1998 | 5 | (3) | 1 |
| Ertuğrul Ersoy | 13.02.1997 | 18 | | 2 |
| Papy Djilobodji (SEN) | 01.12.1988 | 18 | (1) | 1 |
| Matěj Hanousek (CZE) | 02.06.1993 | 13 | (7) | |
| İbrahim Pehlivan | 21.08.1993 | 6 | (4) | |
| Stelios Kitsiou (GRE) | 28.09.1993 | 20 | | 1 |
| Ömürcan Artan | 27.07.1999 | 3 | (2) | |
| Alin Dorinel Toşca (ROU) | 14.03.1992 | 6 | (2) | |
| **Midfielders:** | DOB | M | (s) | G |
| Abdulkadir Parmak | 28.12.1994 | 3 | (6) | |
| Onurhan Babuşcu (AUT) | 05.09.2003 | | (2) | |
| Furkan Soyalp | 12.06.1995 | 16 | (4) | 1 |
| Marko Jevtović (SRB) | 24.07.1993 | 21 | | 3 |
| Alexandru Iulian Maxim (ROU) | 08.07.1990 | 21 | | 4 |
| Alexander Merkel (KAZ) | 22.02.1992 | 8 | (6) | 2 |
| Lazar Marković (SRB) | 02.03.1994 | 12 | (7) | 4 |
| Mirza Cihan | 26.10.2000 | 1 | (9) | |
| Luka Stankovski (MKD) | 02.09.2002 | | (5) | |
| **Forwards:** | DOB | M | (s) | G |
| Torgeir Børven (NOR) | 03.12.1991 | | (1) | |
| *João* Vitor Brandão *Figueiredo* (BRA) | 27.05.1996 | 21 | (1) | 7 |
| Mustafa Eskihellaç | 05.05.1997 | 11 | (3) | 1 |
| Tomas Pekhart (CZE) | 26.05.1989 | 3 | (9) | 1 |
| Ángelo Nicolás Sagal Tapia (CHI) | 18.04.1993 | 11 | (4) | 2 |
| Valmir Veliu (KOS) | 04.06.2000 | 3 | (12) | 1 |

## Giresunspor Kulübü

| Founded: | 1967 | |
|---|---|---|
| Stadium: | Çotanak Spor Kompleksi, Giresun (22,028) | |
| Trainer: | Hakan Keleş | 08.01.1972 |
| [04.05.2023] | İrfan Buz | 15.04.1967 |

| Goalkeepers: | DOB | M | (s) | G |
|---|---|---|---|---|
| Ferhat Kaplan | 07.01.1989 | 11 | (2) | |
| Onurcan Piri | 28.09.1994 | 23 | | |
| **Defenders:** | DOB | M | (s) | G |
| Alper Uludağ | 11.12.1990 | 28 | (3) | 1 |
| Ramón Gínes Arias Quinteros (URU) | 27.07.1992 | 30 | (1) | |
| Faruk Genç | 16.02.2000 | 5 | (8) | 1 |
| Hayrullah Bilazer | 20.05.1995 | 31 | | |
| Kadir Seven | 05.05.2003 | 7 | (8) | |
| Alexis Rafael Pérez Fontanilla (COL) | 25.03.1994 | 25 | | |
| Faustin Senghor (SEN) | 02.01.1994 | | (5) | |
| Sergen Piçinciol | 11.10.1995 | 3 | (2) | |
| Talha Ülvan (BEL) | 20.04.2001 | 1 | (6) | |
| **Midfielders:** | DOB | M | (s) | G |
| Jorman David Campuzano Puentes (COL) | 30.04.1996 | 25 | (2) | 2 |
| Doğan Davas | 22.08.1997 | 4 | (20) | 1 |
| Erol Çan Akdağ | 18.08.1996 | | (4) | |
| Brandley Kuwas (CUW) | 19.09.1992 | 12 | (15) | 1 |
| Robert Andrés Mejía Navarrete (COL) | 06.10.2000 | 26 | (3) | 1 |
| Murat Akpınar | 24.01.1999 | 7 | (23) | |
| Rahmetullah Berişbek | 22.03.1999 | | (18) | 1 |
| Görkem Sağlam (GER) | 11.04.1998 | 25 | (4) | 1 |
| Vukan Savičević (MNE) | 29.01.1994 | 13 | (13) | 1 |
| Hamidou Traoré (MLI) | 07.10.1996 | 3 | | |
| **Forwards:** | DOB | M | (s) | G |
| Rijad Bajić (BIH) | 06.05.1994 | 34 | | 14 |
| *Borja Sainz* Eguskiza (ESP) | 21.02.2001 | 32 | | 9 |
| Mert Kurt | 25.10.2002 | | (7) | |
| Oğulcan Cağlayan | 22.03.1996 | | (8) | |
| Sergio Antonio Da Luz Junior „Serginho" (BRA) | 06.04.1995 | 29 | | 2 |

## Hatayspor Kulübü Antakya

| Founded: | 1967 | |
|---|---|---|
| Stadium: | „Yeni Hatay" Stadyumu, Antakya (25,000) | |
| Trainer: | Serkan Özbalta | 05.02.1979 |
| [21.09.2022] | Volkan Demirel | 27.10.1981 |

| Goalkeepers: | DOB | M | (s) | G |
|---|---|---|---|---|
| Erce Kardeşler | 14.03.1994 | 21 | | |
| **Defenders:** | DOB | M | (s) | G |
| Samuel Ayomide Adekugbe (CAN) | 16.01.1995 | 16 | (2) | |
| Burak Bekaroğlu | 16.04.1997 | 3 | | |
| Burak Öksüz | 25.01.1996 | 10 | (1) | 1 |
| Engin Can Aksoy | 14.11.2003 | 1 | (1) | |
| Simon Falette (GUI) | 19.02.1992 | 6 | (2) | |
| Kaan Kanak | 06.10.1990 | 8 | (8) | 1 |
| Kâmil Çörekçi | 01.02.1992 | 16 | (1) | |
| Kerim Alıcı | 24.06.1997 | 4 | | |
| Recep Burak Yilmaz | 27.11.1995 | 9 | (1) | |
| Ognjen Vranješ (BIH) | 24.10.1989 | 14 | (1) | |
| **Midfielders:** | DOB | M | (s) | G |
| Rayane Aabid (FRA) | 19.01.1992 | 14 | (7) | |
| Mehdi Boudjemaa (FRA) | 07.04.1998 | 14 | (5) | |
| Jeremy Dudziak (TUN) | 28.08.1995 | 1 | (2) | |
| Muhammed Mert (BEL) | 09.02.1995 | | (3) | |
| Musa Çağıran | 17.11.1992 | 5 | (7) | |
| Onur Ergün | 15.11.1992 | 14 | (6) | 1 |
| *Rúben* Tiago Rodrigues *Ribeiro* (POR) | 01.08.1987 | 15 | (4) | |
| **Forwards:** | DOB | M | (s) | G |
| Christian Twasam Atsu (GHA) † **06.02.2023** | 10.01.1992 | | (3) | 1 |
| Bertuğ Yıldırım | 12.07.2002 | 9 | (7) | 4 |
| Ayoub El Kaabi (MAR) | 25.06.1993 | 20 | (1) | 8 |
| Mohammed Kamara (LBR) | 31.10.1997 | | (1) | |
| Saba Lobzhanidze (GEO) | 18.12.1994 | 18 | (3) | 1 |
| Sadık Baş | 11.05.1994 | 2 | (5) | |
| Dylan Saint-Louis (CGO) | 26.04.1995 | 3 | (5) | |
| Kévin Olivier Soni (CMR) | 17.04.1998 | | (3) | |
| Kevin Varga (HUN) | 30.03.1996 | 2 | (9) | |
| José Luís Mendes Andrade „Zé Luís" (CPV) | 24.01.1991 | 6 | (8) | 2 |

## Istanbul Başakşehir Futbol Kulübü

**Founded:** 1990 (*as Istanbul Büyükşehir Belediyespor*); re-founded 2004
**Stadium:** Başakşehir „Fatih Terim" Stadyumu, Istanbul (17,156)
**Trainer:** Emre Belözoğlu    07.09.1980

| Goalkeepers: | DOB | M | (s) | G |
|---|---|---|---|---|
| Deniz Dilmen | 05.06.2005 | 1 | | |
| Muhammed Şengezer | 05.01.1997 | 12 | | |
| Volkan Babacan | 11.08.1988 | 21 | | |
| **Defenders:** | **DOB** | **M** | **(s)** | **G** |
| Ayberk Kaygısız | 11.08.2004 | | (2) | |
| Caner Erkin | 04.10.1988 | 3 | (4) | |
| Alexandru Epureanu (MDA) | 27.09.1986 | 4 | | |
| Hasan Ali Kaldırım | 09.12.1989 | 5 | (1) | |
| Edgar Miguel Ié (GNB) | 01.05.1994 | 2 | (1) | |
| Uilson de Souza Paula Junior "Junior Caiçara" (BRA) | 27.04.1989 | 6 | (6) | |
| Leonardo Campos Duarte Da Silva „Léo" (BRA) | 17.07.1996 | 28 | (2) | |
| *Lucas* Pedro Alves de *Lima* (BRA) | 10.10.1991 | 26 | (3) | 1 |
| Youssouf Nyange Ndayishimiye (BDI) | 27.10.1998 | 17 | | 4 |
| Ömer Ali Şahiner | 02.01.1992 | 23 | (4) | 1 |
| Şener Özbayraklı | 23.01.1990 | 8 | (2) | |
| Ahmed Touba (ALG) | 13.03.1998 | 21 | (3) | |
| Wu Shaocong (CHN) | 20.03.2000 | 1 | (2) | |
| **Midfielders:** | **DOB** | **M** | **(s)** | **G** |
| Danijel Aleksić (SRB) | 30.04.1991 | 18 | (12) | 8 |
| Okechukwu Godson Azubuike (NGA) | 19.04.1997 | | (1) | |
| Berkay Aydoğmuş | 07.01.2004 | 1 | (2) | |
| Berkay Özcan | 15.02.1998 | 26 | (7) | 3 |
| Lucas Rodrigo Biglia (ARG) | 30.01.1986 | 18 | (7) | |
| Enzo Vito Gabriel Crivelli (FRA) | 06.02.1995 | | (1) | |
| Deniz Türüç | 29.01.1993 | 22 | (8) | 7 |
| Adnan Januzaj (BEL) | 05.02.1995 | 6 | (5) | 2 |
| Eden Kartsev (ISR) | 11.04.2000 | 1 | (2) | |
| Mahmut Tekdemir | 20.01.1988 | 21 | (3) | |
| Francis Beny Nzaba (CGO) | 17.07.2002 | | (2) | |
| Mesut Özil (GER) | 15.10.1988 | 1 | (3) | |
| **Forwards:** | **DOB** | **M** | **(s)** | **G** |
| Batuhan Çelik | 12.01.2005 | | (3) | |
| Nacer Chadli (BEL) | 02.08.1989 | 1 | | 1 |
| Mounir Chouiar (FRA) | 23.01.1999 | 12 | (4) | 1 |
| *João* Vitor Brandão *Figueiredo* (BRA) | 27.05.1996 | 10 | (2) | 3 |
| Philippe Paulin Kény (SEN) | 18.05.1999 | 11 | (15) | 4 |
| Muhammet Arslantaş | 27.01.2001 | | (2) | |
| Stefano Okaka (ITA) | 09.08.1989 | 12 | (9) | 1 |
| Serdar Gürler | 14.09.1991 | 20 | (11) | 6 |
| Patryk Szysz (POL) | 01.04.1998 | 9 | (16) | 3 |
| Bertrand Isidore Traoré (BFA) | 06.09.1995 | 7 | (5) | 2 |

## İstanbulspor Kulübü

**Founded:** 04.01.1926
**Stadium:** Necmi Kadıoğlu Stadyumu, Istanbul (7,500)
**Trainer:** Osman Zeki Korkmaz    02.05.1982
[25.10.2022] Fatih Tekke    09.09.1977

| Goalkeepers: | DOB | M | (s) | G |
|---|---|---|---|---|
| Alp Arda | 07.06.1995 | 2 | | |
| David Jensen (DEN) | 25.03.1992 | 32 | | |
| **Defenders:** | **DOB** | **M** | **(s)** | **G** |
| Simon Deli (CIV) | 27.10.1991 | 8 | (2) | |
| Demeaco Duhaney (ENG) | 13.10.1998 | 18 | | 1 |
| Okan Erdoğan (GER) | 29.09.1998 | 30 | | |
| Ertuğrul Ersoy | 13.02.1997 | | (5) | |
| Mehmet Yeşil | 31.05.1998 | 26 | (7) | 1 |
| Adi Mehremić (BIH) | 26.04.1992 | 7 | (8) | 1 |
| Inainfe Michael Ologo (NGA) | 05.04.2003 | 4 | (3) | |
| Oğuzhan Berber | 10.04.1992 | 14 | (4) | |
| Tuncer Duhan Aksu | 11.09.1997 | 25 | (3) | |
| Ali Yaşar (BEL) | 08.03.1995 | 17 | (8) | 1 |
| **Midfielders:** | **DOB** | **M** | **(s)** | **G** |
| Abdullah Dijlan Aydın | 16.06.2000 | | (1) | |
| Mahamadou Ba (MLI) | 21.09.1999 | 14 | (1) | 1 |
| Aldin Čajić (BIH) | 11.09.1992 | | (8) | |
| Patrick Ebert (GER) | 17.03.1987 | | (7) | |
| Eslem Öztürk | 01.12.1997 | | (1) | |
| Kerem Şen | 14.06.2002 | 2 | (5) | 1 |
| Florian Loshaj (KOS) | 13.08.1996 | 4 | (4) | |
| Melih Kabasakal | 18.02.1996 | 15 | (2) | 1 |
| Muammer Sarıkaya | 09.02.1998 | 25 | (6) | 1 |
| Eduart Rroca (ALB) | 28.07.1993 | 20 | (3) | 3 |
| Onur Ergün | 15.11.1992 | 6 | (4) | 1 |
| Vefa Temel | 03.11.2002 | | (2) | |
| Ferhat Yazgan (GER) | 20.10.1992 | 2 | | |
| **Forwards:** | **DOB** | **M** | **(s)** | **G** |
| Kristal Abazaj (ALB) | 06.07.1996 | 2 | (3) | |
| Emir Gültekin | 02.10.2000 | 11 | (16) | 2 |
| Valon Ethemi (ALB) | 03.10.1997 | 27 | (3) | 12 |
| Jason Eyenga-Lokilo (COD) | 17.09.1998 | 13 | (3) | 4 |
| Emeka Friday Eze (NGA) | 26.09.1996 | 13 | (2) | 4 |
| Sindrit Guri (ALB) | 23.10.1993 | 2 | (10) | |
| Ibrahim Yilmaz | 06.02.1994 | 15 | (2) | |
| Kağan Miray Bağış | 10.04.1998 | | (9) | |
| Raymond Owusu (GHA) | 20.04.2002 | | (1) | |
| Jetmir Topalli (KOS) | 07.02.1998 | 20 | (8) | 5 |
| Valmir Veliu (KOS) | 04.06.2000 | | (1) | |

## Kasımpaşa Spor Kulübü Istanbul

**Founded:** 15.01.1921
**Stadium:** „Recep Tayyip Erdoğan" Stadyumu, Istanbul (14,234)
**Trainer:** Sami Uğurlu    27.04.1978
[17.08.2022] Şenol Can    03.04.1983
[22.11.2022] Selçuk İnan    10.02.1985
[04.04.2023] Kemal Özdeş    10.05.1970

| Goalkeepers: | DOB | M | (s) | G |
|---|---|---|---|---|
| Erdem Canpolat (GER) | 13.04.2001 | 9 | (1) | |
| Günay Güvenc | 25.06.1991 | 8 | | |
| Ertuğrul Taşkıran | 05.11.1989 | 18 | | |
| **Defenders:** | **DOB** | **M** | **(s)** | **G** |
| Mortadha Ben Ouanes (TUN) | 02.07.1994 | 27 | (2) | 4 |
| Jeffrey Kevin van Homoet Bruma (NED) | 13.11.1991 | 8 | (2) | |
| Papy Djilobodji (SEN) | 01.12.1988 | 10 | | 1 |
| Ryan Henk Donk (SUR) | 30.03.1986 | 19 | (1) | 1 |
| *Fabiano* Josué de Souza Silva (BRA) | 14.03.2000 | 9 | | |
| Feyzi Yıldırım | 23.01.1996 | | (2) | |
| Daniel Graovac (BIH) | 08.08.1993 | 11 | (3) | |
| Florent Hadergjonaj (KOS) | 31.07.1994 | 23 | (2) | 3 |
| Raoul Petretta (ITA) | 24.03.1997 | 6 | (3) | 1 |
| Recep Yemişci | 01.01.1999 | 1 | | |
| Sadık Çiftpinar | 01.01.1993 | 11 | (1) | 1 |
| Tarkan Serbest | 02.05.1994 | 8 | (3) | |
| Taylan Aydin | 10.02.2006 | | (1) | |
| Mickaël Tirpan (BEL) | 23.10.1993 | 21 | (2) | |
| Yasin Özcan | 20.04.2006 | 15 | (4) | 2 |
| **Midfielders:** | **DOB** | **M** | **(s)** | **G** |
| Ali Demirel | 02.01.2003 | 2 | (6) | |
| Aytaç Kara | 23.03.1993 | 15 | (17) | 3 |
| Bersant Celina (KOS) | 09.09.1996 | 12 | (6) | 1 |
| Valentin Eysseric (FRA) | 25.03.1992 | 30 | (2) | 3 |
| Turgay Gemicibaşı (GER) | 23.04.1996 | 3 | (3) | |
| Haris Hajradinović (BIH) | 18.02.1994 | 27 | (6) | 2 |
| Hasan Emre Yeşilyurt | 18.08.2000 | 1 | | |
| Mickaël Malsa (MTQ) | 12.10.1995 | 10 | | 1 |
| Oğuzhan Efe Yilmaz | 17.06.2003 | | (1) | |
| Selim Dilli | 26.05.1998 | | (1) | |
| Yunus Mallı | 24.02.1992 | | (9) | |
| **Forwards:** | **DOB** | **M** | **(s)** | **G** |
| Stéphane Bahoken (FRA) | 28.05.1992 | 18 | (8) | 4 |
| Mounir Chouiar (FRA) | 23.01.1999 | 12 | (4) | 2 |
| Ahmet Engin (GER) | 09.08.1996 | 6 | (21) | 1 |
| Erdem Çetinkaya | 29.03.2001 | | (2) | |
| Mamadou Fall (SEN) | 31.12.1991 | 34 | | 8 |
| Ali Gholizadeh (IRN) | 10.03.1996 | 1 | (3) | |
| Berat Kalkan (MKD) | 02.03.2003 | | (10) | |
| Bengali-Fodé Koita (GUI) | 21.10.1990 | 7 | (7) | 3 |
| Mustafa Eskihellaç | 05.05.1997 | 3 | (2) | |
| Tunay Torun | 21.04.1990 | | (9) | |

## Kayseri Spor Kulübü

**Founded**: 1966
**Stadium**: „Kadir Has" Stadyumu, Kayseri (32,864)
**Trainer**: Çağdaş Atan     28.02.1980

| Goalkeepers: | DOB | M | (s) | G |
|---|---|---|---|---|
| Bilal Bayazıt (NED) | 08.04.1999 | 30 | | |
| Cenk Gönen | 21.02.1988 | 4 | (1) | |
| **Defenders:** | **DOB** | **M** | **(s)** | **G** |
| Arif Kocaman | 14.09.2003 | 12 | (2) | 1 |
| Onur Bulut (GER) | 16.04.1994 | 21 | | 3 |
| Lionel Carole (FRA) | 12.04.1991 | 23 | | |
| Majid Hosseini (IRN) | 20.06.1996 | 24 | (1) | 2 |
| Dimitrios Kolovetsios (GRE) | 16.10.1991 | 29 | (1) | |
| Ramazan Civelek | 22.01.1996 | 12 | (17) | 2 |
| **Midfielders:** | **DOB** | **M** | **(s)** | **G** |
| Yaw Ackah (GHA) | 01.06.1999 | 4 | (11) | |
| Ahmet Malatyalı | 10.07.2003 | | (1) | |
| Joseph Attamah (GHA) | 22.05.1994 | 7 | (2) | |
| Baran Gezek | 26.08.2005 | 1 | (4) | |
| Berat Eskin | 13.10.2004 | | (2) | |

| | DOB | M | (s) | G |
|---|---|---|---|---|
| Andrea Bertolacci (ITA) | 11.01.1991 | 3 | (4) | 1 |
| *Gustavo* Campanharo (BRA) | 04.04.1992 | 21 | (3) | |
| Ali Karimi (IRN) | 11.02.1994 | 10 | (10) | 2 |
| Olivier Kemen (FRA) | 20.07.1996 | 23 | (4) | 3 |
| Bernard Mensah (GHA) | 17.10.1994 | 20 | (7) | 5 |
| Anthony Uzodimma (NGA) | 17.04.1999 | 8 | (8) | 1 |
| **Forwards:** | **DOB** | **M** | **(s)** | **G** |
| *Carlos* Manuel Cardoso *Mané* (POR) | 11.03.1994 | 18 | (7) | 4 |
| Emrah Başsan | 17.04.1992 | 13 | (13) | 2 |
| Mario Gavranović (SUI) | 24.11.1989 | 14 | (8) | 4 |
| Gökhan Sazdağı | 20.09.1994 | 20 | (11) | 1 |
| İlhan Parlak | 18.01.1987 | 4 | (18) | 2 |
| *Miguel* Felipe Nunes *Cardoso* (POR) | 19.06.1994 | 28 | (3) | 7 |
| Mustafa Pektemek | 11.08.1988 | 2 | (10) | |
| Mame Thiam (SEN) | 09.10.1992 | 22 | (5) | 9 |
| Talha Sarıarslan | 18.01.2004 | 1 | (5) | |

## Konyaspor Kulübü

**Founded**: 22.06.1922
**Stadium**: Konya Büyükşehir Stadyumu, Konya (42,000)
**Trainer**: İlhan Palut     12.11.1976
[17.01.2023]   Aleksandar Stanojević (SRB)     28.10.1973

| Goalkeepers: | DOB | M | (s) | G |
|---|---|---|---|---|
| Erhan Erentürk | 30.05.1995 | 5 | | |
| Ibrahim Šehić (BIH) | 02.09.1988 | 29 | | |
| **Defenders:** | **DOB** | **M** | **(s)** | **G** |
| Adil Demirbağ | 10.12.1997 | 27 | | |
| Ahmet Oğuz | 16.01.1993 | 31 | | |
| Francisco Javier Calvo Quesada (CRC) | 08.07.1992 | 31 | | 3 |
| Cebrail Karayel | 15.08.1994 | 3 | (13) | |
| *Guilherme* Haubert Sityá (BRA) | 01.04.1990 | 34 | | 2 |
| Kahraman Demirtaş | 01.05.1994 | 2 | (5) | |
| Uğurcan Yazğılı | 09.04.1999 | 8 | (6) | 1 |
| Karahan Yasir Subaşı | 01.01.1996 | | (1) | |
| **Midfielders:** | **DOB** | **M** | **(s)** | **G** |
| Andreas Bouchalakis (GRE) | 05.04.1993 | 11 | (1) | |
| *Bruno* Lourenço Pinto de Almeida *Paz* (POR) | 23.04.1998 | 10 | (18) | 1 |
| Amir Hadžiahmetović (BIH) | 08.03.1997 | 18 | | 3 |
| Robert Murić (CRO) | 12.03.1996 | 7 | (21) | |
| Oğulcan Ülgün | 11.05.1998 | 5 | (13) | 2 |

| | DOB | M | (s) | G |
|---|---|---|---|---|
| Domagoj Pavičić (CRO) | 09.03.1994 | 2 | (5) | |
| Alejandro *Pozuelo* Melero (ESP) | 20.09.1991 | 11 | (1) | 4 |
| Amar Rahmanović (BIH) | 13.05.1994 | 3 | (2) | |
| Niko Rak (CRO) | 26.07.2003 | | | |
| Soner Dikmen | 01.09.1993 | 29 | (3) | 5 |
| **Forwards:** | **DOB** | **M** | **(s)** | **G** |
| *Amilton* Minervino da Silva (BRA) | 12.08.1989 | 2 | (5) | |
| Zymer Bytyqi (KOS) | 11.09.1996 | 18 | (1) | |
| Endri Çekiçi (ALB) | 23.11.1996 | 13 | (7) | 2 |
| Sokol Çikalleshi (ALB) | 27.07.1990 | 1 | (1) | |
| Mame Diouf (SEN) | 16.12.1987 | 17 | (11) | 9 |
| Mahir Emreli (AZE) | 01.07.1997 | 7 | (5) | 2 |
| Uche Ikpeazu (UGA) | 28.02.1995 | | (15) | |
| Mehmet Büyüksayar | 08.05.2004 | | (7) | |
| Konrad Michalak (POL) | 19.09.1997 | 21 | (5) | |
| Marlos Moreno Durán (COL) | 20.09.1996 | 12 | | 1 |
| Muhammed Demir | 10.01.1992 | 17 | (4) | 6 |

## Sivasspor Kulübü

**Founded**: 09.05.1967
**Stadium**: 4 Eylül Stadyumu, Sivas (27,532)
**Trainer**: Rıza Çalımbay     02.02.1963

| Goalkeepers: | DOB | M | (s) | G |
|---|---|---|---|---|
| Ali Vural | 10.07.1990 | 30 | | |
| Muammer Yıldırım | 14.09.1990 | 5 | (1) | |
| **Defenders:** | **DOB** | **M** | **(s)** | **G** |
| Alaaddin Okumuş | 23.08.1995 | 6 | (8) | |
| Aaron Appindangoyé (GAB) | 20.02.1992 | 14 | (4) | |
| Samba Camara (MLI) | 14.11.1992 | 6 | (5) | |
| Caner Osmanpaşa | 15.01.1988 | 23 | | 2 |
| Dimitrios Goutas (GRE) | 04.04.1994 | 30 | (1) | |
| Murat Paluli | 09.08.1994 | 19 | (1) | |
| Uğur Çiftçi | 04.05.1992 | 20 | (3) | |
| Ziya Erdal | 05.01.1988 | 12 | (5) | |
| **Midfielders:** | **DOB** | **M** | **(s)** | **G** |
| Charilaos Charisis (GRE) | 12.01.1995 | 21 | (5) | 1 |
| Isaac Cofie (GHA) | 20.09.1991 | 9 | (6) | 2 |
| Erdoğan Yeşilyurt | 06.11.1993 | 26 | (4) | 3 |
| Emre Gökay | 18.02.2006 | 1 | (2) | 1 |

| | DOB | M | (s) | G |
|---|---|---|---|---|
| Hakan Arslan | 18.07.1988 | 14 | (15) | 1 |
| Kader Keita (FRA) | 06.11.2000 | 11 | (4) | |
| Kerem Atakan Kesgin | 05.11.2000 | 2 | | |
| Mehmet Albayrak | 05.01.2004 | | (1) | |
| Dia Saba (ISR) | 18.11.1992 | 11 | (2) | 5 |
| Samuel „*Samu*" *Sáiz* Alonso (ESP) | 22.01.1991 | 11 | (2) | 4 |
| Fredrik Ulvestad (NOR) | 17.06.1992 | 22 | (6) | 1 |
| Robin Yalçın (GER) | 25.01.1994 | 13 | (9) | 1 |
| **Forwards:** | **DOB** | **M** | **(s)** | **G** |
| Karol Angielski (POL) | 20.03.1996 | 2 | (13) | |
| Jordy Josué Caicedo Medina (ECU) | 18.11.1997 | 5 | (9) | 3 |
| Max Gradel (CIV) | 30.11.1987 | 25 | (5) | 7 |
| Leke Samson James (NGA) | 01.11.1992 | 7 | (7) | 3 |
| Ahmed Musa (NGA) | 14.10.1992 | 3 | (14) | |
| Clinton Mua N'Jie (CMR) | 15.08.1993 | 16 | (13) | 2 |
| Mustapha Yatabaré (MLI) | 26.01.1986 | 21 | (6) | 6 |

## Trabzonspor Kulübü

| | | |
|---|---|---|
| **Founded**: | 02.08.1967 | |
| **Stadium**: | „Şenol Güneş" Stadyumu, Trabzon (40,782) | |
| **Trainer**: | Abdullah Avcı | 31.07.1963 |
| [08.03.2023] | Orhan Ak | 29.09.1979 |
| [05.04.2023] | İhsan Gündüz Derelioğlu | 15.11.1961 |
| [18.04.2023] | Nenad Bjelica (CRO) | 20.08.1971 |

| Goalkeepers: | DOB | M | (s) | G |
|---|---|---|---|---|
| Muhammet Tepe | 01.01.2001 | 4 | (1) | |
| Uğurcan Çakır | 05.04.1996 | 31 | | |
| **Defenders:** | **DOB** | **M** | **(s)** | **G** |
| Arif Boşluk | 06.06.2003 | 3 | (3) | |
| Marc *Bartra* Aregall (ESP) | 15.01.1991 | 25 | (4) | 4 |
| *Bruno* da Silva *Peres* (BRA) | 01.03.1990 | 7 | | |
| Stefano Wilfred Denswil (NED) | 07.05.1993 | 12 | (7) | 1 |
| Eren Elmalı | 07.07.2000 | 31 | (2) | |
| Hüseyin Türkmen | 01.01.1998 | 12 | (2) | |
| Jens Stryger Larsen (DEN) | 21.02.1991 | 26 | (6) | 1 |
| Oğuzhan Yılmaz | 02.07.2006 | | (1) | |
| Serkan Asan | 28.04.1999 | 1 | (3) | |
| Taha Altıkardeş | 22.08.2003 | 2 | (1) | |
| *Vitor Hugo* Franchescoli de Souza (BRA) | 20.05.1991 | 19 | (1) | 1 |
| Yusuf Erdoğan | 07.08.1992 | | (4) | |
| **Midfielders:** | **DOB** | **M** | **(s)** | **G** |
| Abdülkadir Ömür | 25.06.1999 | 21 | (8) | 2 |
| Anastasios Bakasetas (GRE) | 28.06.1993 | 26 | (1) | 8 |
| Enis Bardhi (MKD) | 02.07.1995 | 12 | (18) | 6 |
| Berat Özdemir | 23.05.1998 | | (1) | |
| Doğucan Haspolat | 11.02.2000 | 10 | (9) | 1 |
| Dorukhan Toköz | 21.05.1996 | 4 | (2) | |
| Emirhan Zaman | 19.05.2003 | 1 | | |
| Jean-Philippe Gbamin (CIV) | 25.09.1995 | 8 | (11) | |
| Marek Hamšík (SVK) | 27.07.1987 | 11 | (12) | 3 |
| Salih Malkoçoğlu | 23.02.2005 | | (1) | |
| Manolis Siopis (GRE) | 14.05.1994 | 26 | (4) | |
| Yusuf Yazıcı | 29.01.1997 | 7 | (6) | 3 |
| **Forwards:** | **DOB** | **M** | **(s)** | **G** |
| Andreas Evald Cornelius (DEN) | 16.03.1993 | 4 | | 1 |
| Jorge *Djaniny* Tavares Semedo (CPV) | 21.03.1991 | 8 | (9) | |
| Maximiliano Gómez González (URU) | 14.08.1996 | 23 | (3) | 5 |
| Mahmoud Ahmed Ibrahim Hassan „Trézéguet" (EGY) | 01.10.1994 | 24 | (4) | 11 |
| Jean Evrard Kouassi (CIV) | 25.09.1994 | | (5) | |
| Montassir Lahtimi (MAR) | 01.04.2001 | 1 | (7) | |
| Lazar Marković (SRB) | 02.03.1994 | 4 | (4) | 1 |
| Naci Ünüvar | 13.06.2003 | 1 | (7) | 1 |
| Edin Višća (BIH) | 17.02.1990 | 10 | (3) | 2 |
| Poyraz Efe Yildirim | 15.01.2005 | | (1) | |
| Umut Bozok | 19.09.1996 | 11 | (16) | 8 |

## Ümraniyespor Kulübü

| | | |
|---|---|---|
| **Founded**: | 1938 | |
| **Stadium**: | Ümraniye Belediyesi Şehir Stadyumu, Ümraniye (3,513) | |
| **Trainer**: | Recep Uçar | 22.09.1975 |
| [20.04.2023] | Mustafa Er | 11.01.1980 |

| Goalkeepers: | DOB | M | (s) | G |
|---|---|---|---|---|
| Anıl Demir | 04.11.1996 | 1 | | |
| Berke Özer | 25.05.2000 | 5 | | |
| Orkun Özdemir | 23.04.1995 | 18 | (2) | |
| Serkan Kırıntılı | 15.02.1985 | 10 | | |
| **Defenders:** | **DOB** | **M** | **(s)** | **G** |
| *Allyson* Aires dos Santos (BRA) | 23.10.1990 | 15 | | |
| Deniz Tabak | 05.01.2004 | | (1) | |
| Alexandru Epureanu (MDA) | 27.09.1986 | 13 | | |
| Emre Nefiz | 24.11.1994 | | (1) | |
| Tomislav Glumac (CRO) | 14.05.1991 | 27 | | 2 |
| Ermir Lenjani (ALB) | 05.08.1989 | 14 | (4) | |
| Mert Yılmaz | 08.03.1999 | 1 | (2) | |
| Mustafa Eser | 29.08.2001 | 8 | (3) | |
| Onur Atasayar | 01.01.1995 | 18 | | |
| Strahil Popov (BUL) | 31.08.1990 | 20 | (2) | |
| Yusuf Saitoğlu | 01.01.2003 | 1 | | |
| **Midfielders:** | **DOB** | **M** | **(s)** | **G** |
| Batuhan Arıcı | 20.01.2003 | 1 | | |
| Beren Küçükbaşarık | 27.05.2005 | | (1) | |
| Doğukan Saral | 31.01.2003 | | (1) | |
| Fatih Şanlıtürk | 01.01.2003 | 1 | (5) | |
| Nika Gagnidze (GEO) | 20.03.2001 | | (2) | |
| Kartal Yılmaz | 04.11.2000 | 15 | (8) | |
| Antonio Mršić (CRO) | 05.06.1987 | 12 | (18) | 6 |
| Oğuz Gürbulak | 10.08.1992 | 20 | (8) | 1 |
| Isaac Sackey (GHA) | 04.04.1994 | 23 | (7) | |
| Jesse Sekidika (NGA) | 14.07.1996 | 9 | (4) | 1 |
| Serkan Göksu | 19.05.1993 | 23 | (6) | |
| Yunus Mertoğlu | 20.04.2001 | 1 | (1) | |
| **Forwards:** | **DOB** | **M** | **(s)** | **G** |
| Bel Durel Avounou (CGO) | 25.09.1997 | 20 | (7) | 5 |
| Adel Bettaieb (FRA) | 28.01.1997 | 7 | (14) | |
| Yonathan Alexander Del Valle Rodríguez (VEN) | 28.05.1990 | 8 | (10) | 1 |
| Paulo Bartolome Hermenegildo Da Costa „Geraldo" (ANG) | 23.11.1991 | 22 | (7) | 1 |
| Valentin Gheorghe (ROU) | 14.02.1997 | 11 | (13) | 1 |
| Güneş Güventürk | 18.07.2005 | | (1) | |
| Tobi Olarenwaju Ayobami Kayode (NGA) | 08.05.1993 | 5 | (6) | 3 |
| Metehan Mimaroğlu | 07.07.1994 | 2 | (8) | |
| Onur Ayik | 28.01.1990 | 14 | (16) | 2 |
| Osman Erdoğan | 16.07.2004 | | (1) | |
| Umut Nayir | 28.06.1993 | 29 | (2) | 17 |

## SECOND LEVEL
### TFF First League 2022/2023

| | | | | | | | | |
|---|---|---|---|---|---|---|---|---|
| 1. | Samsunspor Kulübü Derneği (*Promoted*) | 36 | 23 | 9 | 4 | 70 - 26 | 78 |
| 2. | Çaykur Rizespor Kulübü (*Promoted*) | 36 | 18 | 14 | 4 | 64 - 35 | 68 |
| 3. | Pendikspor Kulübü (*Promotion Play-offs Finals*) | 36 | 19 | 10 | 7 | 65 - 36 | 67 |
| 4. | Bodrumspor (*Promotion Play-offs*) | 36 | 18 | 8 | 10 | 55 - 34 | 62 |
| 5. | Sakaryaspor Kulübü Derneği (*Promotion Play-offs*) | 36 | 20 | 2 | 14 | 59 - 47 | 62 |
| 6. | Eyüp Spor Kulübü (*Promotion Play-offs*) | 36 | 18 | 8 | 10 | 40 - 30 | 62 |
| 7. | Göztepe SK İzmir (*Promotion Play-offs*) | 36 | 17 | 9 | 10 | 45 - 31 | 60 |
| 8. | Manisa Futbol Kulübü | 36 | 15 | 11 | 10 | 53 - 47 | 56 |
| 9. | Ankara Keçiörengücü SK | 36 | 16 | 8 | 12 | 59 - 47 | 56 |
| 10. | Bandırmaspor Kulübü | 36 | 15 | 10 | 11 | 55 - 58 | 55 |
| 11. | Boluspor Kulübü | 36 | 14 | 10 | 12 | 44 - 46 | 52 |
| 12. | Altay SK İzmir[1] | 36 | 11 | 10 | 15 | 45 - 48 | 40 |
| 13. | Erzurumspor Futbol Kulübü[1] | 36 | 11 | 9 | 16 | 43 - 48 | 39 |
| 14. | Tuzlaspor Kulübü | 36 | 11 | 5 | 20 | 42 - 52 | 38 |
| 15. | Gençlerbirliği SK Ankara | 36 | 10 | 8 | 18 | 46 - 55 | 38 |
| 16. | Altınordu FK İzmir (*Relegated*) | 36 | 9 | 8 | 19 | 41 - 57 | 35 |
| 17. | Adanaspor AŞ (*withdrew*) | 36 | 6 | 7 | 23 | 32 - 76 | 25 |
| 18. | Denizlispor Kulübü[1] (*Relegated*) | 36 | 7 | 5 | 24 | 35 - 67 | 23 |
| 19. | Yeni Malatya Spor Kulübü[1] (*withdrew*) | 36 | 4 | 7 | 25 | 22 - 81 | 16 |

[1]*3 points deducted for licensing problems.*

Please note: Adanaspor AŞ and Y withdrew from the league following the 2023 Turkey-Syria earthquake and were not relegated at the end of the season.
The match Göztepe SK İzmir - Altay SK İzmir was suspended after an attack on a goalkeeper, both sides would be considered defeated 3-0.

## Promotion Play-offs

| | | | |
|---|---|---|---|
| **Quarter-Finals [26.05.2023]** | Bodrumspor - Göztepe SK İzmir | 3-1(2-0) | |
| | Sakaryaspor Kulübü Derneği - Eyüp Spor Kulübü | 0-1(0-0,0-0) | |
| **Semi-Finals [31.05.-04.06.2023]** | Eyüp Spor Kulübü - Bodrumspor | 1-0(1-0) | 0-2(0-0) |
| **Final [08.06.2023]** | Pendikspor Kulübü - Bodrumspor | 2-1(2-1) | |

**Pendikspor Kulübü** promoted to the 2023/2024 Süper Lig.


# NATIONAL TEAM

## INTERNATIONAL MATCHES
### (16.07.2022 – 15.07.2023)

| | | | | |
|---|---|---|---|---|
| 22.09.2022 | Istanbul | *Turkey - Luxembourg* | *3-3(2-0)* | (UNL) |
| 25.09.2022 | Tórshavn | *Faroe Islands - Turkey* | *2-1(0-0)* | (UNL) |
| 16.11.2022 | Diyarbakır | *Turkey - Scotland* | *2-1(1-0)* | (F) |
| 19.11.2022 | Gaziantep | *Turkey - Czech Republic* | *2-1(1-0)* | (F) |
| 25.03.2023 | Yerevan | *Armenia - Turkey* | *1-2(1-1)* | (ECQ) |
| 28.03.2023 | Bursa | *Turkey - Croatia* | *0-2(0-2)* | (ECQ) |
| 16.06.2023 | Rīga | *Latvia - Turkey* | *2-3(0-1)* | (ECQ) |
| 19.06.2023 | Samsun | *Turkey - Wales* | *2-0(0-0)* | (ECQ) |

**22.09.2022 TURKEY - LUXEMBOURG 3-3(2-0)** 3rd UEFA Nations League C, Group 1
Başakşehir "Fatih Terim" Stadyumu, Istanbul; Referee: Tobias Stieler (Germany); Attendance: 12,708
**TUR:** Uğurcan Çakır, Mehmet Zeki Çelik, Kaan Ayhan, Çağlar Söyüncü (Cap) (46.Tolga Ciğerci), Eren Elmalı, Orkun Kökçü (81.İsmail Yüksek), Ferdi Kadıoğlu, Cengiz Ünder (78.Yunus Akgün), Muhammed Kerem Aktürkoğlu (73.Serdar Dursun), Halil İbrahim Dervişoğlu (46.İrfan Can Kahveci), Enes Ünal. Trainer: Stefan Kuntz (Germany).
**Goals:** Cengiz Ünder (16 penalty), Maxime Chanot (33 own goal), İsmail Yüksek (87).

**25.09.2022 FAROE ISLANDS - TURKEY 2-1(0-0)** 3rd UEFA Nations League C, Group 1
Tórsvøllur, Tórshavn; Referee: Serhiy Boiko (Ukraine); Attendance: 2,056
**TUR:** Altay Bayındır, Mehmet Zeki Çelik, Ozan Muhammed Kabak, Kaan Ayhan (Cap), Eren Elmalı (82.Umut Bozok), Berkan İsmail Kutlu (59.Halil İbrahim Dervişoğlu), Yunus Akgün (60.İsmail Yüksek), İrfan Can Kahveci, Ferdi Kadıoğlu, Muhammed Kerem Aktürkoğlu (60.Serdar Gürler), Serdar Dursun. Trainer: Stefan Kuntz (Germany).
**Goal:** Serdar Gürler (89).

**16.11.2022 TURKEY - SCOTLAND 2-1(1-0)** Friendly International
Diyarbakır Stadyumu, Diyarbakır; Referee: Visar Kastrati (Kosovo); Attendance: 28 348
**TUR:** Uğurcan Çakır, Cenk Özkaçar, Ozan Muhammed Kabak, Çağlar Söyüncü, Mehmet Zeki Çelik, Orkun Kökçü (46.Salih Özcan), Hakan Çalhanoğlu (Cap) (69.Deniz Türüç), Ferdi Kadıoğlu (34.Eren Elmalı), Cengiz Ünder (81.İsmail Yüksek), İrfan Can Kahveci (81.Muhammed Kerem Aktürkoğlu), Cenk Tosun (69.Enes Ünal). Trainer: Stefan Kuntz (Germany).
**Goals:** Ozan Muhammed Kabak (40), Cengiz Ünder (49).

**19.11.2022 TURKEY - CZECH REPUBLIC 2-1(1-0)** Friendly International
Kalyon Stadyumu, Gaziantep; Referee: William Sean Collum (Scotland); Attendance: 29,017
**TUR:** Doğan Alemdar, Çağlar Söyüncü (60.Cenk Özkaçar), Samet Akaydin, Ozan Muhammed Kabak (60.Tayyib Talha Sanuç), Onur Bulut, Hakan Çalhanoğlu (Cap) (80.Berkay Özcan), Salih Özcan, Eren Elmalı, Cengiz Ünder (80.İsmail Yüksek), Doğukan Sinik (68.Arda Güler), Enes Ünal (68.Cenk Tosun). Trainer: Stefan Kuntz (Germany).
**Goals:** Enes Ünal (31), Hakan Çalhanoğlu (70).

**25.03.2023 ARMENIA - TURKEY 1-2(1-1)** 17th EC. Qualifiers
„Vazgen Sargsyan" Hanrapetakan Stadium, Yerevan; Referee: José María Sánchez Martínez (Spain); Attendance: 14,125
**TUR:** Fehmi Mert Günok, Çağlar Söyüncü, Merih Demiral (46.Salih Özcan), Ozan Muhammed Kabak, Onur Bulut, Orkun Kökçü (74.İsmail Yüksek), Hakan Çalhanoğlu (Cap), Ferdi Kadıoğlu (74.Eren Elmalı), Cengiz Ünder, Cenk Tosun (46.Muhammed Kerem Aktürkoğlu), Enes Ünal (85.Umut Nayir). Trainer: Stefan Kuntz (Germany).
**Goals:** Orkun Kökçü (35), Muhammed Kerem Aktürkoğlu (64).

**28.03.2023 TURKEY - CROATIA 0-2(0-2)** 17th EC. Qualifiers
Bursa Büyükşehir Belediye Stadyumu, Bursa; Referee: Andreas Ekberg (Sweden); Attendance: 37,750
**TUR:** Fehmi Mert Günok, Mehmet Zeki Çelik, Merih Demiral, Çağlar Söyüncü, Ferdi Kadıoğlu, Salih Özcan, Orkun Kökçü (67.Arda Güler), Hakan Çalhanoğlu (Cap) (38.İsmail Yüksek), Cengiz Ünder (81.Cenk Tosun), Muhammed Kerem Aktürkoğlu (67.Barış Alper Yılmaz), Enes Ünal (81.Umut Nayir). Trainer: Stefan Kuntz (Germany).

**16.06.2023 LATVIA - TURKEY 2-3(0-1)** 17th EC. Qualifiers
Skonto stadions, Rīga; Referee: Tamás Bognár (Hungary); Attendance: 6,287
**TUR:** Fehmi Mert Günok, Mehmet Zeki Çelik (71.Eren Elmalı), Merih Demiral, Abdülkerim Bardakcı, Ferdi Kadıoğlu (89.Ozan Muhammed Kabak), Orkun Kökçü (78.Salih Özcan), Hakan Çalhanoğlu (Cap), Cengiz Ünder, Arda Güler (71.Barış Alper Yılmaz), Muhammed Kerem Aktürkoğlu (89.İrfan Can Kahveci), Umut Nayir. Trainer: Stefan Kuntz (Germany).
**Goals:** Abdülkerim Bardakcı (23), Cengiz Ünder (61), İrfan Can Kahveci (90+5).

**19.06.2023**  **TURKEY - WALES**  2-0(0-0)  17th EC. Qualifiers

Samsun 19 Mayıs Stadium, Samsun; Referee: Fabio Maresca (Italy); Attendance: 28,766
**TUR:** Fehmi Mert Günok, Mehmet Zeki Çelik (60.Eren Elmalı), Merih Demiral, Abdülkerim Bardakcı, Ferdi Kadıoğlu (73.İrfan Can Kahveci), Salih Özcan (60.Arda Güler), Orkun Kökçü (89.Salih Uçan), Hakan Çalhanoğlu (Cap), Cengiz Ünder, Muhammed Kerem Aktürkoğlu (46.Umut Nayir), Barış Alper Yılmaz. Trainer: Stefan Kuntz (Germany).
**Goals:** Umut Nayir (72), Arda Güler (80).

## NATIONAL TEAM PLAYERS
### (16.07.2022 – 15.07.2023)

| Name | DOB | Caps | Goals | Club |
|------|-----|------|-------|------|
| **Goalkeepers** | | | | |
| ALTAY Bayındır | 14.04.1998 | 5 | 0 | 2022: *Fenerbahçe SK Istanbul* |
| DOĞAN Alemdar | 29.10.2002 | 2 | 0 | 2022: *Stade Rennais FC (FRA)* |
| FEHMI Mert Günok | 01.03.1989 | 26 | 0 | 2023: *Beşiktaş JK Istanbul* |
| UĞURCAN Çakır | 05.04.1996 | 22 | 0 | 2022: *Trabzonspor Kulübü* |
| **Defenders** | | | | |
| ABDÜLKERIM Bardakcı | 07.09.1994 | 2 | 1 | 2023: *Galatasaray SK Istanbul* |
| CENK Özkaçar | 06.10.2000 | 3 | 0 | 2022: *Valencia CF (ESP)* |
| ÇAĞLAR Söyüncü | 23.05.1996 | 53 | 2 | 2022/2023: *Leicester City FC (ENG)* |
| EREN Elmalı | 07.07.2000 | 9 | 0 | 2022/2023: *Trabzonspor Kulübü* |
| FERDI Kadıoğlu | 07.10.1999 | 11 | 0 | 2022/2023: *Fenerbahçe SK Istanbul* |
| KAAN Ayhan | 10.11.1994 | 51 | 5 | 2022: *US Sassuolo Calcio (ITA)* |
| MERIH Demiral | 05.03.1998 | 39 | 2 | 2023: *Atalanta Bergamasca Calcio (ITA)* |
| ONUR Bulut | 16.04.1994 | 2 | 0 | 2022: *Kayserispor Kulübü* <br> 08.02.2023-> *Beşiktaş JK Istanbul* |
| OZAN Muhammed Kabak | 25.03.2000 | 22 | 1 | 2022/2023: *TSG 1899 Hoffenheim (GER)* |
| SAMET Akaydin | 13.03.1994 | 1 | 0 | 2022: *Adana Demirspor Kulübü* |
| TAYYIB Talha Sanuç | 17.12.1999 | 1 | 0 | 2022: *Beşiktaş JK Istanbul* |
| Mehmet ZEKI Çelik | 17.02.1997 | 38 | 2 | 2022/2023: *AS Roma (ITA)* |
| **Midfielders** | | | | |
| ARDA Güler | 25.02.2005 | 4 | 1 | 2022/2023: *Fenerbahçe SK Istanbul* |
| BERKAN İsmail Kutlu | 25.01.1998 | 7 | 0 | 2022: *Galatasaray SK Istanbul* |
| BERKAY Özcan | 15.02.1998 | 7 | 0 | 2022: *Istanbul Başakşehir FK* |
| DENIZ Türüç | 29.01.1993 | 12 | 2 | 2022: *Istanbul Başakşehir FK* |
| HAKAN Çalhanoğlu | 08.02.1994 | 78 | 17 | 2022/2023: *FC Internazionale Milano (ITA)* |
| İRFAN Can Kahveci | 15.07.1995 | 26 | 2 | 2022/2023: *Fenerbahçe SK Istanbul* |
| İSMAIL Yüksek | 26.01.1999 | 6 | 1 | 2022/2023: *Fenerbahçe SK Istanbul* |
| Muhammed KEREM Aktürkoğlu | 21.10.1998 | 21 | 4 | 2022/2023: *Galatasaray SK Istanbul* |
| ORKUN Kökçü | 29.12.2000 | 22 | 2 | 2022/2023: *Feyenoord Rotterdam (NED)* |
| SALIH Özcan | 11.01.1998 | 11 | 0 | 2022/2023: *BV 09 Borussia Dortmund (GER)* |
| SALIH Uçan | 06.01.1994 | 2 | 0 | 2023: *Beşiktaş JK Istanbul* |
| TOLGA Ciğerci | 23.03.1992 | 4 | 0 | 2022: *MKE Ankaragücü SK* |
| **Forwards** | | | | |
| BARIŞ Alper Yılmaz | 23.05.2000 | 5 | 0 | 2023: *Galatasaray SK Istanbul* |
| CENGIZ Ünder | 14.07.1997 | 49 | 16 | 2022/2023: *Olympique de Marseille (FRA)* |
| CENK Tosun | 07.06.1991 | 49 | 18 | 2022/2023: *Beşiktaş JK Istanbul* |
| DOĞUKAN Sinik | 21.01.1999 | 6 | 2 | 2022: *Hull City AFC (ENG)* |
| ENES Ünal | 10.05.1997 | 32 | 2 | 2022/2023: *Getafe CF (ESP)* |
| HALIL İbrahim Dervişoğlu | 08.12.1999 | 15 | 6 | 2022: *Burnley FC (ENG)* |
| SERDAR Dursun | 19.10.1991 | 10 | 7 | 2022: *Fenerbahçe SK Istanbul* |
| SERDAR Gürler | 14.09.1991 | 8 | 1 | 2022: *Istanbul Başakşehir FK* |
| UMUT Bozok | 19.09.1996 | 1 | 0 | 2022: *Trabzonspor Kulübü* |
| UMUT Nayir | 28.06.1993 | 4 | 1 | 2023: *Ümraniyespor Kulübü* |
| YUNUS Akgün | 07.07.2000 | 5 | 1 | 2022: *Galatasaray SK Istanbul* |
| **Trainer** | | | | |
| Stefan KUNTZ (Germany) [from 19.09.2021] | 30.10.1962 | | | 18 M; 12 W; 2 D; 4 L; 43-21 |

# UKRAINE

UKRAINE

## The Country:
Україна (Ukraine)
Capital: Kyiv
Surface: 603,628 km²
Inhabitants: 36,744,636 [2023]
Time: UTC+2

## The FA:
Федерація Футболу України [Football Federation of Ukraine]
Provulok Laboratornyi, 7-A P.O. Box 55, 01133 Kyiv
Tel: +380 44 521 0521
Founded: 1991
Member of FIFA since: 1992
Member of UEFA since: 1992
Website: uaf.ua

## NATIONAL TEAM RECORDS

| RECORDS | | |
|---|---|---|
| First international match: | 29.04.1992, Uzhgorod: | Ukraine – Hungary 1-3 |
| Most international caps: | Anatoliy Tymoshchuk | - 144 caps (2000-2016) |
| Most international goals: | Andriy Shevchenko | - 48 goals / 111 caps (1995-2012) |

### UEFA EUROPEAN CHAMPIONSHIP

| | |
|---|---|
| 1960 | - |
| 1964 | - |
| 1968 | - |
| 1972 | - |
| 1976 | - |
| 1980 | - |
| 1984 | - |
| 1988 | - |
| 1992 | - |
| 1996 | Qualifiers |
| 2000 | Qualifiers |
| 2004 | Qualifiers |
| 2008 | Qualifiers |
| 2012 | Final Tournament (Group Stage) |
| 2016 | Final Tournament (Group Stage) |
| 2020 | Final Tournament (Quarter-Finals) |

### FIFA WORLD CUP

| | |
|---|---|
| 1930 | - |
| 1934 | - |
| 1938 | - |
| 1950 | - |
| 1954 | - |
| 1958 | - |
| 1962 | - |
| 1966 | - |
| 1970 | - |
| 1974 | - |
| 1978 | - |
| 1982 | - |
| 1986 | - |
| 1990 | - |
| 1994 | Did not enter |
| 1998 | Qualifiers |
| 2002 | Qualifiers |
| 2006 | Final Tournament (Quarter-Finals) |
| 2010 | Qualifiers |
| 2014 | Qualifiers |
| 2018 | Qualifiers |
| 2022 | Qualifiers |

### OLYMPIC TOURNAMENTS

| | |
|---|---|
| 1908 | - |
| 1912 | - |
| 1920 | - |
| 1924 | - |
| 1928 | - |
| 1936 | - |
| 1948 | - |
| 1952 | - |
| 1956 | - |
| 1960 | - |
| 1964 | - |
| 1968 | - |
| 1972 | - |
| 1976 | - |
| 1980 | - |
| 1984 | - |
| 1988 | - |
| 1992 | - |
| 1996 | Qualifiers |
| 2000 | Qualifiers |
| 2004 | Qualifiers |
| 2008 | Qualifiers |
| 2012 | Qualifiers |
| 2016 | Qualifiers |
| 2020 | Qualifiers |

*was part of Soviet Union between 1930-1990

### UEFA NATIONS LEAGUE

| | |
|---|---|
| 2018/2019 | League B (Group Stage -> promoted to League A) |
| 2020/2021 | League A (Group Stage -> relegated to League B) |
| 2022/2023 | League B (Group Stage) |

## UKRAINIAN CLUB HONOURS IN EUROPEAN CLUB COMPETITIONS:

| European Champion Clubs' Cup (1956-1992) / UEFA Champions League (1993-2023) | | |
|---|---|---|
| None | | |
| **Fairs Cup (1858-1971) / UEFA Cup (1972-2009) / UEFA Europa League (2010-2023)** | | |
| FK Shakhtar Donetsk | 1 | 2008/2009 |
| **UEFA Europa Conference League (2021-2023)** | | |
| None | | |
| **UEFA Super Cup (1972-2022)** | | |
| FK Dinamo Kyiv** | 1 | 1975 |
| ***European Cup Winners' Cup 1961-1999*** | | |
| FK Dinamo Kyiv** | 2 | 1974/1975, 1985/1986 |
| **represented the Soviet Union | | |

*defunct competition

# NATIONAL COMPETITIONS
# TABLE OF HONOURS

## Championship of cities

|  | CHAMPIONS |
|------|-----------|
| 1921 | Kharkiv |
| 1922 | Kharkiv |
| 1923 | Kharkiv |
| 1924 | Kharkiv |
| 1925 | *No competition* |
| 1926 | *No competition* |
| 1927 | Kharkiv |
| 1928 | Kharkiv |
| 1929 | *No competition* |
| 1930 | *No competition* |
| 1931 | Kyiv |
| 1932 | Kharkiv |
| 1933 | *No competition* |
| 1934 | Kharkiv |
| 1935 | Dnipropetrovsk |

## Championship of the Proletarian Sports Society Dinamo

|  | CHAMPIONS |
|------|-----------|
| 1929 | Dinamo Kharkiv |
| 1931 | Dinamo Kyiv |
| 1932 | Dinamo Kharkiv |
| 1933 | Dinamo Kyiv |
| 1934 | Dinamo Kharkiv |
| 1935 | Dinamo Kyiv |

## UKRAINIAN SSR (SOVIET ERA) CHAMPIONS

| Year | Champion | Year | Champion | Year | Champion |
|------|----------|------|----------|------|----------|
| 1936 | Zavod Ordzhonikidze Kramators'k | 1958 | Arsenal Kyiv | 1975 | Krivbas Kryvyi Rih |
| 1937 | Spartak Dnipropetrovs'k | 1959 | Avangard Zhovti Vody | 1976 | Krivbas Kryvyi Rih |
| 1938 | Dzerzhynec Voroshylovgrad | 1960 | Metalurg Zaporizhzhya | 1977 | SKA Odesa |
| 1939 | Lokomotyv Zaporizhzhya | 1961 | Chornomorets Odesa | 1978 | Metalist Kharkiv |
| 1940 | Lokomotyv Zaporizhzhya | 1962 | Trudovi Rezervy Voroshylovgrad | 1979 | Kolos Nikopil |
| 1941-1945 | *No competition* | 1963 | SKA Odesa | 1980 | SKA Kyiv |
| 1946 | Spartak Uzhgorod | 1964 | Lokomotyv Vinnytsa | 1981 | Krivbas Kryvyi Rih |
| 1947 | Bil'shovyk Mukacheve | 1965 | SKA L'viv | 1982 | Bukovyna Chernivtsi |
| 1948 | Torpedo Odesa | 1966 | Avangard Zhovti Vody | 1983 | SKA Kyiv |
| 1949 | Pishevik Odesa | 1967 | Avtomobilist Zhytomyr | 1984 | Nyva Vinnytsa |
| 1950 | Spartak Uzhgorod | 1968 | Avangard Ternopil | 1985 | Tavrya Simferopil |
| 1951 | Budinok ofitseriv Kyiv | 1969 | Spartak Ivano-Frankivs'k | 1986 | Zarya Voroshylovgrad |
| 1952 | Metalurg Zaporizhzhya | 1970 | Metalurg Zaporizhzhya | 1987 | Tavrya Simferopil |
| 1953 | Spartak Uzhgorod | 1971 | Krivbas Kryvyi Rih | 1988 | Bukovyna Chernivtsi |
| 1954 | Mashinobudivnik Kyiv | 1972 | Spartak Ivano-Frankivs'k | 1989 | Volyn Lutsk |
| 1955 | Spartak Stanislav | 1973 | Tavria Simferopil | 1990 | Bukovyna Chernivtsi |
| 1956 | Shakhtar Stakhanov | 1974 | Sudostroitel Nikolaev | 1991 | Karpaty Lviv |
| 1957 | SKVO Odesa |  |  |  |  |

|  | CHAMPIONS | CUP WINNERS | BEST GOALSCORERS |  |
|------|-----------|-------------|------------------|----|
| 1992 | SC Tavriya Simferopol | FK Chornomorets Odesa | Yuriy Hudymenko (SC Tavriya Simferopol) | 12 |
| 1992/1993 | FK Dinamo Kyiv | FK Dinamo Kyiv | Serhiy Husyev (FK Chornomorets Odesa) | 17 |
| 1993/1994 | FK Dinamo Kyiv | FK Chornomorets Odesa | Tymerlan Huseinov (FK Chornomorets Odesa) | 18 |
| 1994/1995 | FK Dinamo Kyiv | FK Shakhtar Donetsk | Arsen Avakov (TJK, FK Metalurh Zaporizhya) | 21 |
| 1995/1996 | FK Dinamo Kyiv | FK Dinamo Kyiv | Tymerlan Huseinov (FK Chornomorets Odesa) | 20 |
| 1996/1997 | FK Dinamo Kyiv | FK Shakhtar Donetsk | Oleh Matveyev (FK Shakhtar Donetsk) | 21 |
| 1997/1998 | FK Dinamo Kyiv | FK Dinamo Kyiv | Serhiy Rebrov (FK Dinamo Kyiv) | 22 |
| 1998/1999 | FK Dinamo Kyiv | FK Dinamo Kyiv | Andriy Shevchenko (FK Dinamo Kyiv) | 18 |
| 1999/2000 | FK Dinamo Kyiv | FK Dinamo Kyiv | Maksim Shatskikh (UZB, FK Dinamo Kyiv) | 20 |
| 2000/2001 | FK Dinamo Kyiv | FK Shakhtar Donetsk | Andrij Vorobej (FK Shakhtar Donetsk) | 21 |
| 2001/2002 | FK Shakhtar Donetsk | FK Shakhtar Donetsk | Serhiy Shyshchenko (FK Metalurh Donetsk) | 12 |
| 2002/2003 | FK Dinamo Kyiv | FK Dinamo Kyiv | Maksim Shatskikh (UZB, FK Dinamo Kyiv) | 22 |
| 2003/2004 | FK Dinamo Kyiv | FK Shakhtar Donetsk | Giorgi Demetradze (GEO, FK Metalurh Donetsk) | 18 |
| 2004/2005 | FK Shakhtar Donetsk | FK Dinamo Kyiv | Olexandr Kosyrin (FK Chornomorets Odesa) | 14 |
| 2005/2006 | FK Shakhtar Donetsk | FK Dinamo Kyiv | Evaeverson Lemos da Silva "Brandão" (FK Shakhtar Donetsk) Emmanuel Osei Okoduwa (NGA, FK Arsenal Kyiv) | 15 |
| 2006/2007 | FK Dinamo Kyiv | FK Dinamo Kyiv | Oleksandr Hladkyi (FK Kharkhiv) | 13 |
| 2007/2008 | FK Shakhtar Donetsk | FK Shakhtar Donetsk | Marko Dević (FK Metalist Kharkhiv) | 19 |
| 2008/2009 | FK Dinamo Kyiv | FK Vorskla Poltava | Olexander Kowpak (SC Tavriya Simferopol) | 17 |
| 2009/2010 | FK Shakhtar Donetsk | SC Tavriya Simferopol | Artem Milevsky (FK Dinamo Kyiv) | 17 |
| 2010/2011 | FK Shakhtar Donetsk | FK Shakhtar Donetsk | Yevhen Seleznyov (FC Dnipro Dnipropetrovsk) | 17 |
| 2011/2012 | FK Shakhtar Donetsk | FK Shakhtar Donetsk | Yevhen Seleznyov (FK Shakhtar Donetsk) Maicon Pereira de Oliveira (VRA, FK Volyn Lutsk) | 14 |
| 2012/2013 | FK Shakhtar Donetsk | FK Shakhtar Donetsk | Henrikh Mkhitaryan (ARM, FK Shakhtar Donetsk) | 25 |
| 2013/2014 | FK Shakhtar Donetsk | FK Dinamo Kyiv | Luiz Adriano de Souza da Silva (FK Shakhtar Donetsk) | 20 |
| 2014/2015 | FK Dinamo Kyiv | FK Dinamo Kyiv | Alex Teixeira Santos (BRA, FK Shakhtar Donetsk) Eric Cosmin Bicfalvi (ROU, FK Volyn Lutsk) | 17 |
| 2015/2016 | FK Dinamo Kyiv | FK Shakhtar Donetsk | Alex Teixeira Santos (BRA, FK Shakhtar Donetsk) | 22 |

| | | | | |
|---|---|---|---|---|
| 2016/2017 | FK Shakhtar Donetsk | FK Shakhtar Donetsk | Andriy Yarmolenko (FK Dinamo Kyiv) | 15 |
| 2017/2018 | FK Shakhtar Donetsk | FK Shakhtar Donetsk | Facundo Ferreyra (ARG, FK Shakhtar Donetsk) | 21 |
| 2018/2019 | FK Shakhtar Donetsk | FK Shakhtar Donetsk | Aluísio Chaves Ribeiro Moraes Júnior (FK Shakhtar Donetsk) | 19 |
| 2019/2020 | FK Shakhtar Donetsk | FK Dinamo Kyiv | Aluísio Chaves Ribeiro Moraes Júnior (FK Shakhtar Donetsk) | 20 |
| 2020/2021 | FK Dinamo Kyiv | FK Dinamo Kyiv | Vladyslav Kulach (FK Vorskla Poltava) | 15 |
| 2021/2022 | *Championship cancelled* | *Competition cancelled* | - | |
| 2022/2023 | FK Shakhtar Donetsk | *Competition not held* | Artem Dovbyk (SC Dnipro-1) | 24 |

## NATIONAL CHAMPIONSHIP
### Ukrainian Premier League 2022/2023
(23.08.2022 – 04.06.2023)

Please note: all matches were played without audience. Due to the Russian invasion, matches were played only in venues belonging to Western Ukraine.

**Round 1** [23-24.08.2022]
Shakhtar Donetsk - Metalist 1925 0-0
Zorya Luhansk - Vorskla Poltava 3-1(2-0)
Chornomorets - NK Veres 0-1(0-1)
Kolos Kovalivka - Kryvbas K. Rih 1-0(1-0)
Rukh Lviv - Metalist Kharkiv 1-2(1-1)
FK Mynai - FK Lviv 0-1(0-0) [25.09.22]
Inhulets P. - Dinamo Kyiv 1-2(0-2) [17.11.22]
SC Dnipro-1 - Oleksandriya 1-1(1-1) [11.05.23]

**Round 2** [27-29.08.2022]
FK Lviv - Zorya Luhansk 2-3(1-1)
Vorskla Poltava - NK Veres 1-2(1-0)
Metalist 1925 - Chornomorets 0-0
Kolos Kovalivka - Rukh Lviv 2-0(1-0)
Shakhtar Donetsk - Kryvbas K. Rih 1-0(0-0)
Dinamo Kyiv - SC Dnipro-1 0-3(0-1)
Metalist Kharkiv - Inhulets Petrove 1-1(1-0)
FK Oleksandriya - FK Mynai 2-1(1-0)

**Round 3** [02-05.09.2022]
Rukh Lviv - Shakhtar Donetsk 0-1(0-0)
SC Dnipro-1 - NK Veres 2-0(1-0)
Zorya Luhansk - Dinamo Kyiv 3-2(2-0)
Metalist 1925 - Vorskla Poltava 3-2(0-1)
Chornomorets - Inhulets Petrove 1-1(0-1)
Kryvbas Kryvyi Rih - FK Lviv 0-0
FK Mynai - Kolos Kovalivka 1-1(1-1)
FK Oleksandriya - Metalist Kharkiv 1-3(1-1)

**Round 4** [09-12.09.2022]
Rukh Lviv - Zorya Luhansk 3-1(1-0)
Kryvbas Kryvyi Rih - NK Veres 0-1(0-1)
Shakhtar Donetsk - Chornomorets 2-1(0-1)
SC Dnipro-1 - Metalist 1925 3-0(0-0)
Kolos Kovalivka - Metalist Kharkiv 1-0(0-0)
Dinamo Kyiv - FK Lviv 1-0(1-0)
Vorskla Poltava - FK Oleksandriya 0-0
Inhulets Petrove - FK Mynai 1-2(0-1)

**Round 5** [30.09.-02.10.2022]
NK Veres - Rukh Lviv 2-2(2-1)
Metalist 1925 - Kolos Kovalivka 2-0(2-0)
Inhulets Petrove - Vorskla Poltava 0-1(0-1)
FK Lviv - SC Dnipro-1 0-3(0-2)
Metalist Kharkiv - Shakhtar Donetsk 1-6(0-4)
FK Mynai - Dinamo Kyiv 0-1(0-0)
Chornomorets - FK Oleksandriya 1-2(0-0)
Zorya Luhansk - Kryvbas Kryvyi Rih 2-2(2-1)

**Round 6** [07-09.10.2022]
NK Veres - Metalist Kharkiv 1-2(0-1)
Kolos Kovalivka - Inhulets Petrove 0-0
Vorskla Poltava - Chornomorets 2-1(0-0)
SC Dnipro-1 - Zorya Luhansk 3-0(1-0)
Kryvbas Kryvyi Rih - FK Mynai 0-0
Dinamo Kyiv - Rukh Lviv 3-0(1-0)
Oleksandriya-Metalist 1925 3-3(1-2) [27.02.23]
FK Lviv - Shakhtar Donetsk 1-2(0-0)[12.04.23]

**Round 7** [14-16.10.2022]
Inhulets Pet. - Oleksandriya 1-2(0-1) [25.08.22]
FK Mynai - NK Veres 1-1(0-1)
Metalist 1925 - FK Lviv 2-2(2-1)
Metalist Kharkiv - Vorskla Poltava 3-2(1-0)
Rukh Lviv - SC Dnipro-1 2-3(1-1)
Shakhtar Donetsk - Dinamo Kyiv 3-1(1-0)
Zorya Luhansk-Kolos Kov. 2-2(1-1) [01.12.22]
Chornomorets-Kryvbas K.R. 0-1(0-1)[02.12.22]

**Round 8** [18-19.10.2022]
FK Lviv - NK Veres 1-3(1-1)
FK Oleksandriya - Kryvbas K. Rih 2-0(1-0)
Chornomorets - Zorya Luhansk 0-4(0-3)
SC Dnipro-1 - Inhulets Petrove 2-2(1-0)
Vorskla Poltava - Rukh Lviv 0-1(0-1)
Shakhtar Donetsk - Kolos Kovalivka 3-0(1-0)
Metalist 1925 - FK Mynai 0-1(0-0)
Dinamo Kyiv - Metalist Kh. 3-0(2-0) [30.11.22]

**Round 9** [22-24.10.2022]
FK Oleksandriya - FK Lviv 2-0(1-0)
Dinamo Kyiv - Vorskla Poltava 1-1(1-1)
Metalist Kharkiv - SC Dnipro-1 0-1(0-0)
NK Veres - Zorya Luhansk 0-1(0-0)
Rukh Lviv - Metalist 1925 1-1(1-0)
Kryvbas Kryvyi Rih-Inhulets Petrove 2-1(0-0)
Kolos Kovalivka - Chornomorets 1-1(0-1)
FK Mynai - Shakhtar Don. 1-4(1-3) [28.02.23]

**Round 10** [28-31.10.2022]
Metalist 1925 - Zorya Luhansk 0-3(0-2)
Vorskla Poltava - FK Mynai 2-0(1-0)
Shakhtar Donetsk - FK Oleksandriya 2-2(1-1)
SC Dnipro-1 - Chornomorets 1-0(1-0)
FK Lviv - Metalist Kharkiv 1-1(0-1)
Dinamo Kyiv - Kryvbas Kryvyi Rih 3-1(2-1)
Kolos Kovalivka - NK Veres 2-0(0-0)
Inhulets Pet. - Rukh Lviv 1-0(1-0) [19.04.23]

**Round 11** [04-06.11.2022]
Vorskla Poltava - FK Lviv 1-0(0-0)
FK Oleksandriya - Kolos Kovalivka 4-1(1-0)
Zorya Luhansk - Metalist Kharkiv 3-2(0-0)
Metalist 1925 - NK Veres 1-4(0-1)
Shakhtar Donetsk - Inhulets Petrove 3-0(1-0)
SC Dnipro-1 - FK Mynai 3-1(0-0)
Rukh Lviv - Kryvbas Kryvyi Rih 2-1(0-0)
Chornomorets - Dinamo Kyiv 0-3(0-1)

**Round 12** [08-10.11.2022]
Inhulets Petrove - Zorya Luhansk 1-0(1-0)
Metalist Kharkiv - Metalist 1925 0-0
Kryvbas Kryvyi Rih-Vorskla Poltava 1-0(0-0)
Kolos Kovalivka - SC Dnipro-1 1-3(1-2)
NK Veres - Shakhtar Donetsk 0-2(0-1)
FK Lviv - Rukh Lviv 2-1(2-0)
FK Mynai - Chornomorets 0-1(0-1)
Dinamo Kyiv - FK Oleksandriya 3-1(1-0)

**Round 13** [13-14.11.2022]
Vorskla Poltava - SC Dnipro-1 1-1(0-1)
FK Oleksandriya - NK Veres 3-2(1-1)
Dinamo Kyiv - Kolos Kovalivka 0-0
Metalist 1925 - Inhulets Petrove 2-1(1-1)
Shakhtar Donetsk - Zorya Luhansk 2-2(1-1)
Metalist Kharkiv - Kryvbas K. Rih 0-1(0-0)
Chornomorets - FK Lviv 2-0(0-0)
Rukh Lviv - FK Mynai 1-1(1-0)

**Round 14** [18-21.11.2022]
Zorya Luhansk - FK Oleksandriya 4-1(0-0)
SC Dnipro-1 - Shakhtar Donetsk 2-1(1-1)
Kolos Kovalivka - Vorskla Poltava 1-2(0-1)
FK Mynai - Metalist Kharkiv 1-0(0-0)
Kryvbas Kryvyi Rih - Metalist 1925 0-2(0-2)
Inhulets Petrove - FK Lviv 0-1(0-0)
NK Veres - Dinamo Kyiv 0-1(0-1)
Rukh Lviv-Chornomorets 2-2(0-2) [07.12.22]

**Round 15** [23-28.11.2022]
Shakhtar Donetsk - Vorskla Poltava 3-2(1-0)
Chornomorets - Metalist Kharkiv 0-0
Inhulets Petrove - NK Veres 1-0(1-0)
Dinamo Kyiv - Metalist 1925 0-0
FK Lviv - Kolos Kovalivka 0-1(0-0)
Zorya Luhansk - FK Mynai 1-0(0-0)
FK Oleksandriya - Rukh Lviv 1-1(0-0)
Kryvbas Kryvyi Rih - SC Dnipro-1 2-1(1-1)

**Round 16** [03-06.03.2023]
Kryvbas K. Rih - Kolos Kovalivka 1-0(0-0)
FK Oleksandriya - SC Dnipro-1 2-2(1-1)
Dinamo Kyiv - Inhulets Petrove 0-2(0-2)
NK Veres - Chornomorets 1-3(0-1)
Metalist Kharkiv - Rukh Lviv 1-2(0-1)
Vorskla Poltava - Zorya Luhansk 2-3(2-0)
Metalist 1925 - Shakhtar Donetsk 0-7(0-4)
FK Lviv - FK Mynai 1-0(0-0)

**Round 17** [11-12.03.2023]
FK Mynai - FK Oleksandriya 1-1(1-0)
Inhulets Petrove - Metalist Kharkiv 2-1(1-0)
Zorya Luhansk - FK Lviv 3-1(1-0)
Chornomorets - Metalist 1925 1-1(1-1)
SC Dnipro-1 - Dinamo Kyiv 0-1(0-1)
NK Veres - Vorskla Poltava 2-2(0-1)
Kryvbas K. Rih - Shakhtar Donetsk 0-3(0-0)
Rukh Lviv - Kolos Kovalivka 0-1(0-0)

**Round 18** [17-19.03.2023]
Metalist Kharkiv - FK Oleksandriya 0-0
Vorskla Poltava - Metalist 1925 0-0
Dinamo Kyiv - Zorya Luhansk 0-1(0-0)
FK Lviv - Kryvbas Kryvyi Rih 2-2(0-1)
NK Veres - SC Dnipro-1 0-1(0-1)
Inhulets Petrove - Chornomorets 1-2(0-2)
Kolos Kovalivka - FK Mynai 0-1(0-1)
Shakhtar Donetsk - Rukh Lviv 2-0(2-0)

| Round 19 [01-02.04.2023] |
|---|
| FK Mynai - Inhulets Petrove 1-2(1-0) |
| Metalist Kharkiv - Kolos Kovalivka 0-0 |
| NK Veres - Kryvbas Kryvyi Rih 1-2(0-0) |
| FK Oleksandriya - Vorskla Poltava 3-0(2-0) |
| FK Lviv - Dinamo Kyiv 0-2(0-0) |
| Metalist 1925 - SC Dnipro-1 0-3(0-0) |
| Zorya Luhansk - Rukh Lviv 3-0(1-0) |
| Chornomorets - Shakhtar Donetsk 2-2(2-2) |

| Round 20 [07-09.04.2023] |
|---|
| Vorskla Poltava - Inhulets Petrove 1-0(0-0) |
| Dinamo Kyiv - FK Mynai 2-0(1-0) |
| Kryvbas Kryvyi Rih - Zorya Luhansk 1-0(0-0) |
| Shakhtar Donetsk - Metalist Kharkiv 1-0(0-0) |
| Rukh Lviv - NK Veres 0-0 |
| SC Dnipro-1 - FK Lviv 5-2(3-0) |
| FK Oleksandriya - Chornomorets 1-1(0-1) |
| Kolos Kovalivka - Metalist 1925 3-0(2-0) |

| Round 21 [14-16.04.2023] |
|---|
| FK Mynai - Kryvbas Kryvyi Rih 1-0(1-0) |
| Inhulets Petrove - Kolos Kovalivka 0-1(0-1) |
| Rukh Lviv - Dinamo Kyiv 1-1(1-1) |
| Metalist Kharkiv - NK Veres 5-5(4-3) |
| Metalist 1925 - FK Oleksandriya 0-0 |
| Zorya Luhansk - SC Dnipro-1 2-1(0-0) |
| Shakhtar Donetsk - FK Lviv 2-0(1-0) |
| Chornomorets - Vorskla Poltava 0-1(0-0) |

| Round 22 [21-24.04.2023] |
|---|
| Kolos Kovalivka - Zorya Luhansk 0-1(0-1) |
| Vorskla Poltava - Metalist Kharkiv 3-2(3-1) |
| NK Veres - FK Mynai 1-1(0-0) |
| Dinamo Kyiv - Shakhtar Donetsk 1-1(0-1) |
| FK Lviv - Metalist 1925 0-2(0-1) |
| Kryvbas Kryvyi Rih - Chornomorets 2-3(0-1) |
| SC Dnipro-1 - Rukh Lviv 3-2(2-2) |
| FK Oleksandriya - Inhulets Petrove 0-0 |

| Round 23 [28-29.04.2023] |
|---|
| Metalist Kharkiv - Dinamo Kyiv 1-3(0-0) |
| NK Veres - FK Lviv 3-2(2-2) |
| Kolos Kovalivka - Shakhtar Donetsk 1-3(1-0) |
| FK Mynai - Metalist 1925 1-1(0-0) |
| Zorya Luhansk - Chornomorets 3-1(2-1) |
| Inhulets Petrove - SC Dnipro-1 0-2(0-0) |
| Kryvbas K. Rih - FK Oleksandriya 2-1(0-0) |
| Rukh Lviv - Vorskla Poltava 1-1(0-0) |

| Round 24 [03-04.05.2023] |
|---|
| SC Dnipro-1 - Metalist Kharkiv 5-0(3-0) |
| Shakhtar Donetsk - FK Mynai 1-0(1-0) |
| FK Lviv - FK Oleksandriya 0-1(0-1) |
| Zorya Luhansk - NK Veres 1-0(0-0) |
| Chornomorets - Kolos Kovalivka 3-0(1-0) |
| Inhulets Petrove - Kryvbas Kryvyi Rih 0-0 |
| Metalist 1925 - Rukh Lviv 0-0 |
| Vorskla Poltava - Dinamo Kyiv 1-2(1-1) |

| Round 25 [07-08.05.2023] |
|---|
| Metalist Kharkiv - FK Lviv 1-0(0-0) |
| Chornomorets - SC Dnipro-1 1-2(0-0) |
| FK Oleksandriya - Shakhtar Donetsk 1-1(1-0) |
| Kryvbas Kryvyi Rih - Dinamo Kyiv 0-1(0-0) |
| FK Mynai - Vorskla Poltava 2-0(1-0) |
| Rukh Lviv - Inhulets Petrove 3-0(1-0) |
| NK Veres - Kolos Kovalivka 0-1(0-1) |
| Zorya Luhansk - Metalist 1925 3-0(1-0) |

| Round 26 [13-15.05.2023] |
|---|
| Dinamo Kyiv - Chornomorets 2-3(0-2) |
| Inhulets Petrove - Shakhtar Donetsk 0-2(0-0) |
| FK Lviv - Vorskla Poltava 0-2(0-0) |
| Metalist Kharkiv - Zorya Luhansk 0-5(0-4) |
| NK Veres - Metalist 1925 1-0(0-0) |
| Kryvbas Kryvyi Rih - Rukh Lviv 1-0(0-0) |
| FK Mynai - SC Dnipro-1 0-1(0-0) |
| Kolos Kovalivka - FK Oleksandriya 0-2(0-2) |

| Round 27 [19-21.05.2023] |
|---|
| SC Dnipro-1 - Kolos Kovalivka 2-1(0-1) |
| Vorskla Poltava - Kryvbas K. Rih 1-0(0-0) |
| Shakhtar Donetsk - NK Veres 2-1(1-0) |
| Chornomorets - FK Mynai 0-1(0-0) |
| Zorya Luhansk - Inhulets Petrove 2-0(1-0) |
| FK Oleksandriya - Dinamo Kyiv 1-5(1-2) |
| Metalist 1925 - Metalist Kharkiv 2-0(0-0) |
| Rukh Lviv - FK Lviv 2-0(0-0) |

| Round 28 [24-25.05.2023] |
|---|
| SC Dnipro-1 - Vorskla Poltava 1-2(1-2) |
| Kolos Kovalivka - Dinamo Kyiv 0-3(0-1) |
| NK Veres - FK Oleksandriya 2-2(1-2) |
| Zorya Luhansk - Shakhtar Donetsk 0-3(0-1) |
| FK Mynai - Rukh Lviv 0-0 |
| Inhulets Petrove - Metalist 1925 0-0 |
| FK Lviv - Chornomorets 0-1(0-1) |
| Kryvbas K. Rih - Metalist Kharkiv 2-0(1-0) |

| Round 29 [28-29.05.2023] |
|---|
| FK Oleksandriya - Zorya Luhansk 0-2(0-2) |
| Shakhtar Donetsk - SC Dnipro-1 3-0(1-0) |
| Dinamo Kyiv - NK Veres 3-0(0-0) |
| FK Lviv - Inhulets Petrove 0-2(0-0) |
| Metalist 1925 - Kryvbas Kryvyi Rih 0-2(0-0) |
| Metalist Kharkiv - FK Mynai 1-2(1-0) |
| Chornomorets - Rukh Lviv 1-3(1-2) |
| Vorskla Poltava - Kolos Kovalivka 2-0(0-0) |

| Round 30 [04.06.2023] |
|---|
| SC Dnipro-1 - Kryvbas Kryvyi Rih 1-0(0-0) |
| Kolos Kovalivka - FK Lviv 1-0(1-0) |
| Metalist 1925 - Dinamo Kyiv 1-1(1-1) |
| Metalist Kharkiv - Chornomorets 0-3(0-0) |
| FK Mynai - Zorya Luhansk 0-3(0-2) |
| Rukh Lviv - FK Oleksandriya 0-0 |
| NK Veres - Inhulets Petrove 1-0(0-0) |
| Vorskla Poltava - Shakhtar Donetsk 2-1(1-0) |

## Final Standings

| | | Total | | | | | | Home | | | | | Away | | | |
|---|---|---|---|---|---|---|---|---|---|---|---|---|---|---|---|---|---|
| 1. | **FK Shakhtar Donetsk** | 30 | 22 | 6 | 2 | 69 - 21 | **72** | 12 | 3 | 0 | 30 - 9 | 10 | 3 | 2 | 39 - 12 |
| 2. | SC Dnipro-1 | 30 | 21 | 4 | 5 | 61 - 27 | **67** | 11 | 2 | 2 | 34 - 13 | 10 | 2 | 3 | 27 - 14 |
| 3. | FK Zorya Luhansk | 30 | 21 | 4 | 5 | 64 - 31 | **67** | 11 | 3 | 1 | 35 - 17 | 10 | 1 | 4 | 29 - 14 |
| 4. | FK Dinamo Kyiv | 30 | 18 | 6 | 6 | 51 - 25 | **60** | 7 | 4 | 4 | 22 - 13 | 11 | 2 | 2 | 29 - 12 |
| 5. | FK Vorskla Poltava | 30 | 13 | 6 | 11 | 38 - 37 | **45** | 8 | 3 | 4 | 19 - 13 | 5 | 3 | 7 | 19 - 24 |
| 6. | FK Oleksandriya | 30 | 10 | 14 | 6 | 42 - 39 | **44** | 6 | 6 | 3 | 26 - 22 | 4 | 8 | 3 | 16 - 17 |
| 7. | FK Kryvbas Kryvyi Rih | 30 | 12 | 5 | 13 | 26 - 30 | **41** | 8 | 2 | 5 | 14 - 13 | 4 | 3 | 8 | 12 - 17 |
| 8. | FK Kolos Kovalivka | 30 | 10 | 6 | 14 | 23 - 36 | **36** | 6 | 2 | 7 | 14 - 16 | 4 | 4 | 7 | 9 - 20 |
| 9. | FK Chornomorets Odesa | 30 | 9 | 8 | 13 | 35 - 40 | **36** | 2 | 4 | 9 | 12 - 22 | 7 | 4 | 4 | 23 - 18 |
| 10. | FK Mynai Uzhhorod | 30 | 8 | 9 | 13 | 22 - 33 | **35** | 3 | 5 | 7 | 10 - 17 | 5 | 4 | 6 | 12 - 16 |
| 11. | FK Rukh Lviv | 30 | 7 | 11 | 12 | 31 - 37 | **32** | 4 | 7 | 4 | 19 - 15 | 3 | 4 | 8 | 12 - 22 |
| 12. | FC Metalist 1925 Kharkiv | 30 | 6 | 14 | 10 | 23 - 42 | **32** | 4 | 5 | 6 | 13 - 26 | 2 | 9 | 4 | 10 - 16 |
| 13. | NK Veres Rivne (*Relegation Play-offs*) | 30 | 8 | 7 | 15 | 35 - 45 | **31** | 3 | 4 | 8 | 15 - 22 | 5 | 3 | 7 | 20 - 23 |
| 14. | FK Inhulets Petrove (*Relegation Play-offs*) | 30 | 8 | 7 | 15 | 22 - 34 | **31** | 5 | 2 | 8 | 10 - 15 | 3 | 5 | 7 | 12 - 19 |
| 15. | FC Metalist Kharkiv (*Relegated*) | 30 | 5 | 7 | 18 | 27 - 58 | **22** | 2 | 5 | 8 | 14 - 31 | 3 | 2 | 10 | 13 - 27 |
| 16. | FK Lviv* (*Relegated*) | 30 | 3 | 4 | 23 | 18 - 52 | **13** | 2 | 2 | 11 | 10 - 26 | 1 | 2 | 12 | 8 - 26 |

*Please note: FK Lviv suspended its activity for the next season.

| Top goalscorers: | |
|---|---|
| **24  Artem Dovbyk** | *SC Dnipro-1* |
| 13  Nazariy Rusyn | *FK Zorya Luhansk* |
| 13  Taulant Seferi (ALB) | *FK Vorskla Poltava* |

## Relegation Play-offs [10-14.06.2023]

| | | |
|---|---|---|
| FK Inhulets Petrove - FC LNZ Cherkasy | 1-1(0-0) | 1-2(0-2) |
| MFK Metalurh Zaporizhzhia - NK Veres Rivne | 1-0(1-0) | 1-6(0-3) |

Both FC LNZ Cherkasy and NK Veres Rivne will play in the Ukrainian Premier League 2023/2024.

## Futbolnij Klub Chornomorets Odesa

| | Founded: | 26.03.1936 | | | |
|---|---|---|---|---|---|
| | Stadium: | Chornomorets Stadium, Odesa (34,164) | | | |
| | Trainer: | Roman Hryhorchuk | | 22.03.1965 | |

| Goalkeepers: | DOB | M | (s) | G |
|---|---|---|---|---|
| Dmytro Nepogodov | 17.02.1988 | 21 | | |
| Yevgen Past | 16.03.1988 | 8 | (1) | |
| Danylo Varakuta | 04.11.2001 | 1 | (1) | |
| **Defenders:** | **DOB** | **M** | **(s)** | **G** |
| Maksym Biliy | 21.06.1990 | 4 | (2) | |
| Luka Guček (SVN) | 29.01.1999 | 10 | | |
| Manjrekar James (CAN) | 05.08.1993 | 13 | | 1 |
| Ilya Putrya | 15.05.1998 | 26 | | 2 |
| Volodymyr Salyuk | 25.06.2002 | 23 | (4) | 2 |
| Yevgen Selin | 09.05.1988 | 8 | (1) | 1 |
| Serhiy Sukhanov | 06.04.1995 | | (1) | |
| Maxim Voytikhovskiy | 07.01.1999 | 2 | (12) | 1 |
| Vitaliy Yermakov | 07.06.1992 | 23 | (2) | 3 |
| **Midfielders:** | **DOB** | **M** | **(s)** | **G** |
| Ivan Bobko | 10.12.1990 | 10 | (2) | 1 |
| Inal Chertkoev | 08.10.1999 | | (1) | |
| Oleksandr Demchenko | 13.02.1996 | 12 | (1) | 3 |
| Guy Hadida (ISR) | 23.07.1995 | 7 | (2) | 2 |

| | DOB | M | (s) | G |
|---|---|---|---|---|
| Serhiy Kravchenko | 24.04.1983 | 8 | (1) | |
| Ivan Lytvynenko | 10.04.2001 | | (1) | |
| Vladyslav Naumets | 07.03.1999 | 9 | (4) | |
| Serhiy Petko | 23.01.1994 | 1 | (1) | |
| Rodion Plaksa | 22.01.2002 | 5 | (3) | |
| Serhiy Politylo | 09.01.1989 | 17 | (7) | |
| Oleksandr Vasyliev | 27.04.1994 | 14 | | |
| Yevgen Zadoya | 05.01.1991 | | (2) | |
| **Forwards:** | **DOB** | **M** | **(s)** | **G** |
| Danyil Alefirenko | 19.04.2000 | 13 | (1) | 8 |
| Artur Avagimyan | 16.01.1997 | 6 | (6) | |
| Ziguy Badibanga (BEL) | 26.11.1991 | 15 | (6) | 2 |
| Maksym Bragaru | 21.07.2002 | 29 | | 2 |
| Realdo Fili (ALB) | 14.05.1996 | 2 | (4) | |
| Oleksandr Gladkiy | 24.08.1987 | 4 | (17) | 1 |
| Kevin Koubemba (CGO) | 23.03.1993 | 9 | (4) | |
| Orest Kuzyk | 17.05.1995 | 20 | (6) | 1 |
| Andriy Shtogrin | 14.12.1998 | 4 | (13) | |
| Dmytro Yusov | 11.05.1993 | 12 | (7) | 4 |

## Sport Club Dnipro-1

| | Founded: | 10.03.2017 | | | |
|---|---|---|---|---|---|
| | Stadium: | Avanhard Arena, Uzhhorod (12,000) | | | |
| | Trainer: | Oleksandr Kucher | | 22.10.1982 | |

| Goalkeepers: | DOB | M | (s) | G |
|---|---|---|---|---|
| *Max Walef* Araújo da Silva (BRA) | 23.10.1993 | 16 | | |
| Vladyslav Rybak | 05.07.2001 | 13 | | |
| Valeriy Yurchuk | 12.04.1990 | 1 | | |
| **Defenders:** | **DOB** | **M** | **(s)** | **G** |
| Volodymyr Adamyuk | 17.07.1991 | 23 | (1) | 3 |
| Gabriel Dal Toé *Busanello* (BRA) | 29.10.1998 | 6 | (1) | |
| *Gabriel Gomes* Ferreira (BRA) | 23.08.1999 | 3 | (2) | |
| Serhiy Gorbunov | 14.03.1994 | 2 | (3) | |
| Yanis Hamache (ALG) | 13.07.1999 | 10 | (1) | 2 |
| *Hayner* Willian Monjardim Cordeiro (BRA) | 02.10.1995 | 4 | (11) | |
| Oleksandr Kaplienko | 07.03.1996 | 7 | | |
| Mykyta Kononov | 22.01.2003 | | (4) | |
| Serhiy Loginov | 24.08.1990 | 1 | (7) | 1 |
| Ronald Alberto Matarrita Ulate (CRC) | 09.07.1994 | 3 | (6) | |
| Yevgeniy Pasich | 13.07.1993 | 7 | (5) | |
| Eduard Sarapiy | 12.05.1999 | 29 | | 5 |
| Oleksandr Svatok | 27.09.1994 | 25 | | |

| Midfielders: | DOB | M | (s) | G |
|---|---|---|---|---|
| Ruslan Babenko | 08.07.1992 | 23 | (1) | |
| Farès Bahlouli (FRA) | 08.04.1995 | | (5) | |
| Domingo Felipe Blanco (ARG) | 22.04.1995 | 19 | | 3 |
| Oleksiy Gutsulyak | 25.12.1997 | 22 | (2) | 7 |
| Igor Kogut | 07.03.1996 | 3 | (25) | 3 |
| Valeriy Luchkevych | 11.01.1996 | | (2) | |
| Oleksandr Pikhalyonok | 07.05.1997 | 30 | | 6 |
| Valentyn Rubchynskiy | 15.02.2002 | 22 | (6) | 1 |
| Volodymyr Tanchyk | 17.10.1991 | 9 | (14) | |
| Vyacheslav Tankovskiy | 16.08.1995 | 3 | (4) | |
| **Forwards:** | **DOB** | **M** | **(s)** | **G** |
| Artem Dovbyk | 21.06.1997 | 29 | (1) | 24 |
| Artem Gromov | 14.01.1990 | 4 | (5) | 1 |
| Oleksandr Nazarenko | 01.02.2000 | 8 | (15) | 1 |
| João Gabriel Martins *Peglow* (BRA) | 07.01.2002 | 8 | (5) | 3 |
| Evgen Pidlepenets | 10.11.1998 | | (8) | 1 |

## Futbolnij Klub Dinamo Kyiv

| | Founded: | 13.05.1927 | | | |
|---|---|---|---|---|---|
| | Stadium: | NSC Olimpiyskiy Stadium, Kyiv (70,050) | | | |
| | Trainer: | Mircea Lucescu (ROU) | | 29.07.1945 | |
| | [26.04.2023] | Oleksandr Shovkovskiy | | 02.01.1975 | |

| Goalkeepers: | DOB | M | (s) | G |
|---|---|---|---|---|
| Denis Boyko | 29.01.1988 | 3 | (1) | |
| Georgiy Bushchan | 31.05.1994 | 8 | | |
| Ruslan Neshcheret | 22.01.2002 | 19 | (1) | |
| **Defenders:** | **DOB** | **M** | **(s)** | **G** |
| Anton Bol | 08.01.2003 | | (3) | |
| Mykyta Burda | 24.03.1995 | 1 | | |
| Vladyslav Dubinchak | 01.07.1998 | 13 | (5) | |
| Maksym Dyachuk | 21.07.2003 | 14 | | |
| Oleksandr Karavayev | 02.06.1992 | 13 | (7) | |
| Tomasz Kędziora (POL) | 11.06.1994 | 6 | (3) | |
| Mykyta Kravchenko | 14.06.1997 | 1 | (2) | |
| Denys Popov | 17.02.1999 | 16 | (2) | 1 |
| Oleksandr Syrota | 11.06.2000 | 15 | (4) | 1 |
| Oleksandr Tymchyk | 20.01.1997 | 16 | (3) | 1 |
| Kostiantyn Vivcharenko | 10.06.2002 | 14 | (8) | 2 |
| Ilya Zabarniy | 01.09.2002 | 14 | | |
| **Midfielders:** | **DOB** | **M** | **(s)** | **G** |
| Oleksandr Andriyevskiy | 25.06.1994 | 11 | (5) | 3 |
| Vitaliy Buyalskiy | 06.01.1993 | 27 | | 12 |

| | DOB | M | (s) | G |
|---|---|---|---|---|
| Denys Garmash | 19.04.1990 | 4 | (20) | 1 |
| Vladyslav Kabaev | 01.09.1995 | 19 | (2) | |
| Justin Lonwijk (NED) | 21.12.1999 | 11 | (7) | 1 |
| Reshat Ramadani (MKD) | 30.06.2003 | | (1) | |
| Mykola Shaparenko | 04.10.1998 | 1 | (4) | |
| Volodymyr Shepelyev | 01.06.1997 | 18 | (3) | 1 |
| Serhiy Sydorchuk | 02.05.1991 | 25 | (2) | |
| Anton Tsarenko | 17.06.2004 | 3 | (8) | 1 |
| Viktor Tsyhankov | 15.11.1997 | 13 | | 6 |
| Oleksandr Yatsyk | 03.01.2003 | | (2) | |
| **Forwards:** | **DOB** | **M** | **(s)** | **G** |
| Artem Besedin | 31.03.1996 | 4 | (5) | |
| Samba Diallo (SEN) | 05.01.2003 | | (1) | |
| Vladyslav Kulach | 07.05.1993 | | (2) | |
| Olabiran Blessing Muyiwa (NGA) | 07.09.1998 | 10 | (1) | 1 |
| Kaheem Anthony Parris (JAM) | 06.01.2000 | 3 | (10) | |
| Eric Kleybel Ramírez Matheus (VEN) | 20.11.1998 | 3 | (10) | 3 |
| Vladyslav Vanat | 04.01.2002 | 21 | (4) | 12 |
| Nazar Voloshyn | 17.06.2003 | 4 | (9) | 3 |

## Futbolnij Klub Inhulets Petrove

| | | | |
|---|---|---|---|
| Founded: | 2013 | | |
| Stadium: | Inhulets Stadium, Petrove (1,869) | | |
| Trainer: | Serhiy Lavrynenko | 17.02.1975 | |
| [13.11.2022] | Mladen Bartulović (CRO) | 05.10.1986 | |
| [29.12.2022] | Serhiy Kovalets | 05.09.1968 | |

| Goalkeepers: | DOB | M | (s) | G |
|---|---|---|---|---|
| Oleg Bilyk | 11.01.1998 | 7 | (1) | |
| Danylo Kucher | 25.01.1997 | 5 | (1) | |
| Oleksiy Palamarchuk | 22.07.1991 | 17 | | |
| Roman Pidkivka | 09.05.1995 | 1 | | |
| **Defenders:** | **DOB** | **M** | **(s)** | **G** |
| Serhiy Chenbay | 06.11.1992 | 12 | | |
| Maksym Kovalyov | 20.03.1989 | 22 | | 3 |
| Maksym Melnychuk | 18.09.1999 | 3 | (5) | |
| Dmitri Nagiyev (AZE) | 27.11.1995 | 26 | (1) | |
| Vitaliy Pavlov | 25.06.1988 | 12 | | |
| Dmytro Pospelov | 19.10.1991 | 12 | (6) | |
| Taras Sakiv | 19.11.1997 | 11 | (1) | |
| Artem Smoliakov | 29.05.2003 | 24 | (4) | 2 |
| Vladyslav Sydorenko | 24.10.1997 | 8 | (8) | |
| **Midfielders:** | **DOB** | **M** | **(s)** | **G** |
| Vladislav Klymenko | 19.06.1994 | 24 | (3) | 1 |

| | DOB | M | (s) | G |
|---|---|---|---|---|
| Andriy Korobenko | 28.05.1997 | 8 | (9) | |
| Yuriy Kozyrenko | 27.11.1999 | 6 | (8) | |
| Oleksandr Kucherenko | 01.10.1991 | 24 | (2) | 1 |
| Andriy Kukharuk | 13.12.1995 | 22 | (2) | |
| Oleg Osypenko | 10.10.2001 | 1 | | |
| Denys Rezepov | 11.02.2002 | 5 | (7) | |
| Yevgen Zaporozhets | 20.09.1994 | 22 | (2) | 1 |
| **Forwards:** | **DOB** | **M** | **(s)** | **G** |
| Andriy Blyznychenko | 24.07.1994 | | (4) | |
| Viktor Blyznychenko | 29.09.2002 | 5 | (4) | |
| Ivan Golovkin | 24.05.2000 | 7 | (6) | 1 |
| Oleksandr Kozak | 25.07.1994 | 16 | (4) | 3 |
| Danylo Kravchuk | 02.07.2001 | 2 | (10) | 1 |
| Maksym Marusych | 17.07.1993 | 7 | (18) | 2 |
| Volodymyr Odaryuk | 13.02.1994 | 10 | (14) | 3 |
| Artem Sitalo | 01.08.1989 | 11 | (6) | 3 |

## Futbolnij Klub Kolos Kovalivka

| | | |
|---|---|---|
| Founded: | 2012 | |
| Stadium: | Kolos Stadium, Kovalivka (5,050) | |
| Trainer: | Yaroslav Vyshnyak | 22.07.1982 |

| Goalkeepers: | DOB | M | (s) | G |
|---|---|---|---|---|
| Kiril Fesiun | 07.08.2002 | 1 | | |
| Yevgen Volynets | 26.08.1993 | 29 | | |
| **Defenders:** | **DOB** | **M** | **(s)** | **G** |
| Serhiy Chobotenko | 16.01.1997 | 26 | | 2 |
| Oleksandr Chornomorets | 05.04.1993 | 22 | | |
| Roman Goncharenko | 16.11.1993 | 15 | (1) | 1 |
| Mykyta Kravchenko | 14.06.1997 | 13 | | |
| Denys Kuzyk | 18.09.2002 | 2 | (2) | |
| Yevgen Novak | 01.02.1989 | 14 | (2) | |
| Mikalaj Solatau (BLR) | 11.11.1994 | 16 | (1) | |
| Vladyslav Yemets | 09.09.1997 | 11 | (1) | |
| Oleksy Zozulya | 15.04.1992 | 5 | (2) | |
| **Midfielders:** | **DOB** | **M** | **(s)** | **G** |
| Andriy Bogdanov | 21.01.1990 | 15 | (5) | |
| Oleg Ilyin | 08.06.1997 | 19 | (9) | 1 |

| | DOB | M | (s) | G |
|---|---|---|---|---|
| Oleh Kryvoruchko | 10.11.2004 | | (4) | |
| Vadym Milko | 22.08.1986 | 25 | (2) | 4 |
| Pavlo Orikhovskiy | 13.05.1996 | 26 | (2) | 8 |
| Yevgeniy Smyrnyi | 18.08.1998 | 13 | (5) | |
| Andrii Solovyov | 23.08.2002 | | (1) | |
| Yevgen Zadoya | 05.01.1991 | 1 | (5) | |
| **Forwards:** | **DOB** | **M** | **(s)** | **G** |
| Denys Bezborodko | 31.05.1994 | 16 | (8) | 2 |
| Serhiy Bolbat | 13.06.1993 | 21 | (7) | 1 |
| Artem Husol | 05.01.2006 | | (4) | |
| Yevgeniy Isaenko | 07.08.2000 | 4 | (15) | |
| Volodymyr Lysenko | 20.04.1988 | 11 | (9) | |
| Serhiy Myakushko | 15.04.1993 | 17 | (7) | 2 |
| Kiril Popov | 01.05.2003 | 4 | (20) | |
| Vladyslav Veleten | 01.10.2002 | 4 | (9) | 1 |

## Futbolnij Klub Kryvbas Kriyvyi Rih

| | | |
|---|---|---|
| Founded: | 1959 | |
| Stadium: | NSC Olimpiyskiy Stadium, Kyiv (70,050) | |
| Trainer: | Yuriy Vernydub | 22.01.1966 |

| Goalkeepers: | DOB | M | (s) | G |
|---|---|---|---|---|
| Andriy Klishchuk | 03.07.1992 | 13 | | |
| Bohdan Sarnavskiy | 29.01.1995 | 17 | | |
| **Defenders:** | **DOB** | **M** | **(s)** | **G** |
| Danilo Beskorovayniy | 07.02.1999 | 14 | | |
| Junior Yvan Nyabeye Dibango (CMR) | 10.03.2002 | 22 | (1) | |
| Dragan Lovrić (CRO) | 03.01.1996 | 8 | | |
| Yevgen Opanasenko | 25.08.1990 | 3 | (4) | |
| Andriy Ponedelnik | 28.02.1997 | 14 | (8) | 1 |
| Dmytro Semenov | 04.11.1999 | 7 | (1) | |
| Tymur Stetskov | 27.01.1998 | 20 | (6) | 2 |
| Vitaliy Vernydub | 17.10.1987 | 11 | | 1 |
| Ivan Zotko | 09.07.1996 | 2 | (3) | |
| Volodymyr Yakimets | 03.03.1998 | 18 | (1) | |
| **Midfielders:** | **DOB** | **M** | **(s)** | **G** |
| Yevhen Banada | 29.02.1992 | 14 | (4) | |
| Rifet Kapić (BIH) | 03.07.1995 | 23 | | 6 |

| | DOB | M | (s) | G |
|---|---|---|---|---|
| Zakhar Karpus | 07.04.2005 | | (3) | |
| Dmytro Khomchenovskiy | 16.04.1990 | 26 | (1) | |
| Tymur Korablin | 02.01.2002 | | (11) | 1 |
| Klim Prykhodko | 09.02.2000 | 6 | (5) | 1 |
| Vyacheslav Ryabov | 21.06.1989 | 6 | (3) | |
| Vladyslav Semotyuk | 14.11.2000 | 3 | (3) | |
| Denys Shevchenko | 03.04.2003 | 1 | (5) | |
| Mykyta Tatarkov | 04.01.1995 | 20 | (6) | |
| **Forwards:** | **DOB** | **M** | **(s)** | **G** |
| Roman Debelko | 08.08.1993 | 13 | (7) | 4 |
| Oleksiy Khoblenko | 04.04.1994 | 6 | (2) | 1 |
| Maksym Lunyov | 22.05.1998 | 8 | (3) | 1 |
| Artur Mykytyshyn | 14.07.2003 | 12 | (8) | 1 |
| Daniel Sosah (NIG) | 21.09.1998 | 4 | (2) | |
| Denys Ustymenko | 12.04.1999 | 8 | (11) | |
| Nazar Voloshyn | 17.06.2003 | 13 | | 4 |
| Maksym Zaderaka | 07.09.1994 | 18 | (8) | 2 |

## Futbolnij Klub Lviv

| | | |
|---|---|---|
| **Founded**: | 2006 | |
| **Stadium**: | Skif Stadium, Lviv (4,033) | |
| **Trainer:** | Oleg Dulub (BLR) | 20.09.1965 |
| [21.03.2023] | Anatoliy Bezsmertniy | 21.01.1969 |
| [01.06.2023] | Roman Handzyn | 16.10.1991 |

| Goalkeepers: | DOB | M | (s) | G |
|---|---|---|---|---|
| Oleksandr Ilyushchenkov | 23.03.1990 | 10 | | |
| Ilia Olkhovyi | 30.05.2003 | 3 | | |
| Ivan Ponomarenko | 10.05.1998 | 4 | | |
| Oleksandr Rybka | 10.04.1987 | 11 | | |
| Valeriy Yurchuk | 12.04.1990 | 2 | | |
| **Defenders:** | **DOB** | **M** | **(s)** | **G** |
| Andriy Busko | 20.05.1997 | 7 | | |
| Oleksiy Dytyatev | 07.11.1988 | 8 | (1) | |
| *Guilherme Silva* Souza (BRA) | 12.06.2001 | 2 | (1) | |
| *Higor* Gabriel Fernandes Alves (BRA) | 28.04.1999 | 11 | | |
| Borys Krushynskiy | 10.05.2002 | 8 | (6) | 1 |
| Denys Kuzyk | 18.09.2002 | 12 | (1) | |
| Mykola Kyrychok | 16.05.2006 | | (2) | |
| Nazariy Muravskiy | 03.02.2000 | 13 | (1) | |
| Taras Mykhavko | 30.05.2005 | 2 | (2) | |
| Roman Nykytyuk | 09.09.1993 | 14 | (9) | |
| Pavlo Polegenko | 06.01.1995 | 9 | | |
| Maxim Sasovskiy | 23.08.2001 | 8 | (4) | |
| Yaroslav Shandra | 15.06.2006 | | (1) | |
| Serhiy Siminin | 09.10.1987 | 7 | (3) | |
| Oula Abass Traoré (BFA) | 29.09.1995 | 3 | | |
| Artem Vovkun | 07.09.2001 | 11 | (9) | |
| **Midfielders:** | **DOB** | **M** | **(s)** | **G** |
| Akhmed Alibekov | 29.05.1998 | 11 | (2) | |

| | DOB | M | (s) | G |
|---|---|---|---|---|
| Oleksandr Belyaev | 04.10.1999 | 11 | (3) | 1 |
| Ivan Bokalo | 25.04.2006 | | (1) | |
| Vitaliy Boyko | 03.12.1997 | 12 | (1) | 1 |
| Denys Dovbetskiy | 27.01.2004 | | (1) | |
| Maksym Gryso | 14.05.1996 | 24 | | |
| Leonardo Antonio „Léo Antônio" (BRA) | 09.06.1997 | 5 | | |
| Vladyslav Mendruk | 16.01.2006 | | (1) | |
| Maksym Mudriy | 05.05.2003 | 1 | | |
| *Murilo* de Souza Felisberto (BRA) | 17.05.1996 | | (1) | |
| Roman Mykhailiv | 31.01.2003 | 2 | (4) | |
| Vitaliy Mykhailiv | 11.10.2005 | 2 | (10) | |
| Artem Mylchenko | 22.07.2000 | 25 | (3) | 1 |
| Bohdan Myshenko | 29.12.1994 | 9 | (10) | |
| Mykhaylo Shyshka | 05.07.1994 | 8 | (3) | |
| Ivijan Svržnjak (CRO) | 02.08.2001 | 11 | (1) | 2 |
| Oleksandr Vasyliev | 27.04.1994 | 13 | | 1 |
| Andriy Yakymiv | 15.06.1997 | 2 | (4) | |
| **Forwards:** | **DOB** | **M** | **(s)** | **G** |
| Yaroslav Bogunov | 04.09.1993 | 9 | (5) | 2 |
| Vladyslav Bugay | 27.10.1997 | 24 | (5) | 4 |
| Aderinsola Habib Eseola | 28.06.1991 | 2 | (6) | |
| Vladyslav Herych | 07.11.2005 | | (3) | |
| Nazariy Nych | 19.02.1994 | 11 | (3) | 1 |
| Artur Remenyak | 09.08.2000 | 3 | (13) | 2 |
| Bohdan-Yulian Vyshynskiy | 27.02.2005 | | (1) | |

## Futbolnij Klub Metalist Kharkiv

| | | |
|---|---|---|
| **Founded**: | 11.12.1925 | |
| **Stadium**: | Avanhard Arena, Uzhhorod (12,000) | |
| **Trainer:** | Oleh Ratiy | 05.07.1970 |
| [27.01.2023] | Perica Ognjenović (SRB) | 24.02.1977 |

| Goalkeepers: | DOB | M | (s) | G |
|---|---|---|---|---|
| Danyil Ermolov | 03.12.2000 | 13 | | |
| Orest Kostyk | 16.04.1999 | 11 | (1) | |
| Oleksandr Rybka | 10.04.1987 | 6 | | |
| **Defenders:** | **DOB** | **M** | **(s)** | **G** |
| *Anderson* da Silveira Ribeiro „Pico" (BRA) | 04.11.1988 | | (1) | |
| Kyrylo Digtyar | 25.11.2007 | 1 | (1) | |
| Vitaliy Fedoriv | 21.10.1987 | 5 | | |
| Oleksandr Kapliyenko | 07.03.1996 | 13 | (1) | 2 |
| Yegor Klymenchuk | 11.11.1997 | 5 | (4) | |
| Pathy Malumandsoko (FRA) | 11.05.2000 | 4 | (1) | 1 |
| Oleksandr Mizyuk | 31.05.1995 | 27 | (2) | 1 |
| Oleksandr Nikolyshyn | 20.07.2004 | 4 | (2) | |
| Bohdan Porokh | 05.08.2000 | 14 | (3) | 1 |
| Daniil Prykhodko | 16.03.2006 | | (1) | |
| *Roberto Corral* García (ESP) | 14.09.1997 | 9 | (1) | |
| Yuriy Romaniuk | 06.05.1997 | 21 | (1) | 1 |
| *Samuel* Michels Valencio (BRA) | 06.06.1999 | 2 | (6) | |
| Volodymyr Shopin | 09.05.1991 | 3 | (2) | |
| Kyrylo Vlaha | 22.10.2006 | 3 | (1) | |

| Midfielders: | DOB | M | (s) | G |
|---|---|---|---|---|
| Maksym Bagachanskiy | 05.06.2002 | 4 | (15) | |
| Igor Chaykovskiy | 07.10.1991 | 14 | (2) | |
| Alex Chidomere | 12.08.2002 | 11 | (5) | 2 |
| Yehor Demchenko | 25.07.1997 | 14 | (8) | 1 |
| Yegor Kartushov | 05.01.1991 | 23 | (1) | 1 |
| Vladyslav Naumets | 07.03.1999 | 8 | (7) | 1 |
| Serhiy Panasenko | 09.03.1992 | 15 | (10) | 3 |
| Andriy Ralyuchenko | 08.06.1995 | 23 | (4) | |
| Hennadiy Synchuk | 10.07.2006 | 2 | (2) | |
| Vyacheslav Tankovskiy | 16.08.1995 | 14 | | |
| Oleksandr Tsvirenko | 26.02.2006 | | (1) | |
| **Forwards:** | **DOB** | **M** | **(s)** | **G** |
| Bohdan Boychuk | 30.05.1996 | 7 | (2) | 2 |
| Danylo Kaidalov | 02.02.2006 | | (2) | |
| Danylo Knysh | 03.03.1996 | 3 | (8) | |
| Dmytro Korkishko | 04.05.1990 | 8 | (5) | 1 |
| Evgen Pidlepenets | 10.11.1998 | 13 | (1) | 2 |
| Maksym Pryadun | 17.02.1997 | 26 | (2) | 9 |
| Yevheniy Ryazantsev | 28.01.2002 | 3 | (12) | |
| Dmitro Shamych | 15.05.2001 | 1 | (1) | |

## Futbolnij Klub Metalist 1925 Kharkiv

| | | |
|---|---|---|
| **Founded**: | 17.08.2016 | |
| **Stadium**: | NSC Olimpiyskiy Stadium, Kyiv (70,050) | |
| **Trainer:** | Valeriy Kryventsov | 31.07.1973 |
| [23.10.2022] | Edmar Galovskiy | 16.06.1980 |

| Goalkeepers: | DOB | M | (s) | G |
|---|---|---|---|---|
| Oleh Mozil | 07.04.1996 | 23 | | |
| Ihor Potimkov | 17.10.2003 | | (2) | |
| Denys Sydorenko | 18.04.1989 | 7 | (1) | |
| **Defenders:** | **DOB** | **M** | **(s)** | **G** |
| Mykyta Bezugliy | 01.08.1995 | 28 | (1) | 3 |
| Dmytro Kapinus | 28.04.2003 | 13 | (5) | 1 |
| Ivan Kovalenko | 10.03.1999 | 4 | (1) | |
| Igor Kurilo | 03.05.1993 | 27 | (1) | |
| Yuriy Potimkov | 01.08.2002 | 1 | (3) | |
| Mykhailo Rudavskiy | 26.05.2001 | 5 | (6) | |
| Mykhaylo Shershen | 27.04.1995 | 10 | (3) | 1 |
| Yevgeniy Tkachuk | 27.06.1991 | 8 | (2) | 1 |
| Maksym Zhychykov | 07.11.1992 | 24 | (1) | |
| **Midfielders:** | **DOB** | **M** | **(s)** | **G** |
| Vladyslav Dmytrenko | 24.05.2000 | 8 | (13) | 1 |
| Artem Gabelok | 02.01.1995 | 28 | | 2 |
| Dmytro Kravchenko | 25.02.1995 | 20 | (6) | |

| | DOB | M | (s) | G |
|---|---|---|---|---|
| Yaroslav Martynyuk | 20.02.1989 | 21 | (4) | 2 |
| Rostyslav Rusyn | 26.10.1995 | 22 | (3) | 4 |
| Andriy Tkachuk | 18.11.1987 | 2 | (7) | |
| Beka Vachiberadze (GEO) | 05.03.1996 | 16 | (5) | 1 |
| *Wendel* da Silva Ramos (BRA) | 01.04.2001 | | (3) | |
| **Forwards:** | **DOB** | **M** | **(s)** | **G** |
| Abdulla Abdulaiev | 12.02.2002 | 1 | (7) | |
| Andriy Boryachuk | 23.04.1996 | 8 | | 3 |
| Kostyantyn Bychek | 21.04.2000 | 14 | (7) | 2 |
| Andriy Chyruk | 08.01.2001 | 8 | (12) | 1 |
| Artem Dudik | 02.01.1997 | | (3) | |
| *Igor Henrique* da Silva Nogueira (BRA) | 27.02.2004 | | (4) | |
| Vladyslav Ostrovskiy | 13.09.2004 | 3 | (6) | |
| Vitaliy Ponomar | 31.05.1990 | 1 | | |
| Andriy Remenyuk | 03.02.1999 | 25 | (4) | |
| Vadym Solohub | 11.03.2004 | | (1) | |
| Illia Zubkov | 21.04.1998 | 3 | (2) | |

## Futbolnij Klub Mynai Uzhhorod

| Founded: | 2015 | | |
|---|---|---|---|
| Stadium: | Mynai Arena, Uzhhorod (1,312) | | |
| Trainer: | Volodymyr Sharan | | 18.09.1971 |

| Goalkeepers: | DOB | M | (s) | G |
|---|---|---|---|---|
| Aleksandr Bandura | 30.05.1986 | 28 | | |
| Oleksandr Kemkin | 05.08.2002 | 1 | (1) | |
| German Penkov | 26.05.1994 | 1 | | |
| **Defenders:** | **DOB** | **M** | **(s)** | **G** |
| Andriy Buleza | 25.01.2004 | 12 | (2) | |
| Bohdan Chuev | 23.02.2000 | 5 | (9) | |
| Taras Dmytruk | 09.03.2000 | 5 | (8) | |
| Igor Gonchar | 10.01.1993 | 25 | (3) | |
| Oleg Gorin | 02.02.2000 | 19 | (2) | |
| Yuriy Kravchuk | 06.04.1994 | 13 | (3) | 2 |
| Oleksandr Melnyk | 10.02.2000 | 11 | (2) | |
| Dmytro Nemchaninov | 27.01.1990 | 28 | | |
| Ivan Trubochkin | 17.03.1993 | 16 | (3) | 1 |
| **Midfielders:** | **DOB** | **M** | **(s)** | **G** |
| Mihail Ghecev (MDA) | 05.11.1997 | 9 | (7) | 1 |
| Dmytro Kasimov | 14.08.1999 | 1 | (5) | |
| Oleksiy Khakhlyov | 06.02.1999 | 14 | | 1 |
| Eldar Kuliyev | 24.03.2002 | 14 | | 1 |
| Ruslan Palamar | 09.08.1993 | 1 | (8) | 1 |
| Serhiy Petko | 23.01.1994 | 7 | (5) | 1 |
| Valeriy Rogozynskiy | 03.09.1995 | 11 | (17) | |
| Mykhaylo Shyshka | 05.07.1994 | 5 | (7) | |
| Yegor Tverdokhlib | 17.12.2000 | 29 | (1) | 5 |
| Vadym Vitenchuk | 13.01.1997 | 28 | | 2 |
| Nazariy Vorobchak | 22.03.2000 | 17 | (2) | 2 |
| **Forwards:** | **DOB** | **M** | **(s)** | **G** |
| Anton Baydal | 08.02.2000 | 2 | (10) | |
| Danylo Golub | 03.07.2003 | | (7) | 1 |
| Danylo Kolesnyk | 22.09.2001 | 1 | (14) | |
| Yuriy Kolomoyets | 22.03.1990 | 5 | (10) | |
| Yevhen Seleznyov | 20.07.1985 | | (1) | |
| Oleg Vyshnevskiy | 04.10.1995 | 22 | (5) | 4 |

## Futbolnij Klub Oleksandriya

| Founded: | 1948 | | |
|---|---|---|---|
| Stadium: | NSC Olimpiyskiy Stadium, Kyiv (70,050) | | |
| Trainer: | Yuriy Hura | | 08.08.1976 |
| [21.12.2022] | Ruslan Rotan | | 29.10.1981 |

| Goalkeepers: | DOB | M | (s) | G |
|---|---|---|---|---|
| Oleg Bilyk | 11.01.1998 | 11 | | |
| Valentin Gorokh | 14.02.2001 | 4 | | |
| Mykyta Shevchenko | 26.01.1993 | 15 | (1) | |
| **Defenders:** | **DOB** | **M** | **(s)** | **G** |
| Vladyslav Baboglo | 14.11.1998 | 26 | (1) | |
| Valeriy Bondarenko | 03.02.1994 | 12 | (3) | |
| Demyan Chubatiy | 16.03.2004 | | (2) | |
| Maksym Dyachuk | 21.07.2003 | 4 | (1) | |
| Serhiy Loginov | 24.08.1990 | 12 | (1) | 2 |
| Oleksandr Melnyk | 10.02.2000 | 3 | (1) | |
| Denys Miroshnichenko | 11.10.1994 | 27 | (2) | 4 |
| Roman Savchenko | 17.02.2004 | 1 | (1) | |
| Danil Skorko | 06.04.2002 | 5 | (6) | |
| Andriy Tsurikov | 05.10.1992 | 21 | (2) | 5 |
| **Midfielders:** | **DOB** | **M** | **(s)** | **G** |
| Bohdan Biloshevskiy | 12.01.2000 | 2 | (1) | |
| Oleksandr Demchenko | 13.02.1996 | 12 | (1) | 1 |
| Kyrylo Dryshlyuk | 16.09.1999 | 7 | (5) | |
| Vladyslav Kalitvintsev | 04.01.1993 | 16 | (4) | 2 |
| Yuriy Kopyna | 04.07.1996 | 11 | (5) | |
| Denys Kostyshyn | 31.08.1997 | 1 | (2) | 1 |
| Kyrylo Kovalets | 02.07.1993 | 17 | (8) | 5 |
| Ivan Matyushenko | 29.04.2003 | | (7) | |
| Emil Mustafaiev | 24.09.2001 | 12 | (7) | 2 |
| Mykola Mykhaylenko | 22.05.2001 | 13 | (1) | 2 |
| Serhiy Rybalka | 01.04.1990 | 24 | (3) | 4 |
| Kyrylo Sigeyev | 16.05.2004 | 10 | (5) | 2 |
| Daniil Vashchenko | 02.10.2005 | | (1) | |
| Vikentii Voloshyn | 17.04.2001 | 4 | (14) | |
| **Forwards:** | **DOB** | **M** | **(s)** | **G** |
| Artur Avagimyan | 16.01.1997 | 1 | (7) | |
| Serhiy Gryn | 06.06.1994 | | (1) | |
| Bohdan Kobzar | 22.04.2002 | 7 | (13) | 1 |
| Oleg Kozhushko | 17.02.1998 | 14 | (14) | |
| Andriy Kulakov | 28.04.1999 | 12 | (2) | 1 |
| Artem Shulianskiy | 11.04.2001 | 5 | (14) | 1 |
| Maksym Tretyakov | 06.03.1996 | 21 | (1) | 7 |

## Futbolnij Klub Rukh Lviv

| Founded: | 2003 | | |
|---|---|---|---|
| Stadium: | Ukraina Stadium, Lviv (27,925) | | |
| Trainer: | Leonid Kuchuk (BLR) | | 27.08.1959 |
| [22.03.2023] | Vitaliy Ponomaryov | | 07.12.1974 |

| Goalkeepers: | DOB | M | (s) | G |
|---|---|---|---|---|
| Dmytro Ledviy | 26.08.2003 | 3 | | |
| Yuriy Pankiv | 03.11.1984 | 27 | | |
| **Defenders:** | **DOB** | **M** | **(s)** | **G** |
| Maksym Biliy | 21.06.1990 | 1 | | |
| Roman Didyk | 02.12.2002 | 23 | (1) | 1 |
| Vitaliy Kholod | 15.01.2004 | 4 | (5) | |
| Andrii Kitela | 13.12.2004 | 3 | (2) | |
| Rostyslav Lyakh | 12.10.2000 | 27 | (2) | |
| Vitaliy Roman | 15.04.2003 | 22 | (1) | |
| Bohdan Slyubyk | 11.02.2004 | 15 | (3) | |
| Denis Slyusar | 27.05.2002 | 18 | | 1 |
| Oleksiy Sych | 01.04.2001 | 3 | | |
| Oleg Veremiyenko | 13.02.1999 | 1 | | |
| **Midfielders:** | **DOB** | **M** | **(s)** | **G** |
| Oleksiy Dovgiy | 02.11.1989 | 18 | (4) | 4 |
| *Edson* Fernando da Silva Gomes (BRA) | 24.04.1998 | 4 | (1) | |
| Valeriy Fedorchuk | 05.10.1988 | 6 | (2) | |
| Maryan Mysyk | 02.10.1996 | 10 | (8) | |
| Denis Pidgurskiy | 27.05.2003 | 10 | (3) | |
| Ostap Prytula | 24.06.2000 | 7 | (16) | |
| Marko Sapuha | 29.05.2003 | 18 | | 1 |
| *Talles* Brener de Paula (BRA) | 12.05.1998 | 25 | (3) | 7 |
| **Forwards:** | **DOB** | **M** | **(s)** | **G** |
| Fabricio Oscar Alvarenga (ARG) | 17.02.1996 | 13 | (5) | |
| Bohdan Boychuk | 30.05.1996 | 5 | (6) | |
| Bright Enobakhare (NGA) | 08.02.1998 | 1 | | |
| Yaroslav Karabin | 19.11.2002 | 7 | (17) | 3 |
| Yuriy Klymchuk | 05.05.1997 | 27 | | 9 |
| Ilya Kvasnytsya | 20.03.2003 | | (8) | |
| Ruslan Nepeypiev | 03.06.2003 | | (1) | |
| Vasyl Runich | 31.01.2000 | 4 | (15) | 2 |
| Viv Efosa Solomon-Otabor (NGA) | 02.01.1996 | 28 | | 3 |
| Andriy Stolyarchuk | 04.07.2004 | | (2) | |
| Denys Teslyuk | 11.04.2003 | | (2) | |

## Futbolnij Klub Shakhtar Donetsk

**Founded**: 24.05.1936
**Stadium**: NSC Olimpiyskiy Stadium, Kyiv (70,050)
**Trainer**: Igor Jovićević (CRO)  30.11.1973

| Goalkeepers: | DOB | M | (s) | G |
|---|---|---|---|---|
| Andriy Pyatov | 28.06.1984 | 2 | | |
| Oleksiy Shevchenko | 24.02.1992 | | (1) | |
| Anatoliy Trubin | 01.08.2001 | 28 | | |
| **Defenders:** | **DOB** | **M** | **(s)** | **G** |
| Valeriy Bondar | 27.02.1999 | 25 | (1) | 1 |
| Marian Farina | 28.08.2003 | 1 | | |
| Giorgi Gocholeishvili (GEO) | 14.02.2001 | 9 | (4) | 1 |
| Yukhym Konoplya | 26.08.1999 | 15 | (3) | 2 |
| Viktor Kornienko | 14.02.1999 | | (1) | |
| Serhiy Kryvtsov | 15.03.1991 | 9 | | |
| Eduard Kozik | 19.04.2003 | | (3) | |
| *Lucas Taylor* Maia Reis (BRA) | 10.04.1995 | 4 | (6) | 1 |
| Mykola Matvienko | 02.05.1996 | 27 | (1) | 2 |
| Bohdan Mykhaylychenko | 21.03.1997 | 18 | (7) | 2 |
| Yaroslav Rakitskiy | 03.08.1989 | 13 | | 1 |
| **Midfielders:** | **DOB** | **M** | **(s)** | **G** |
| Artem Bondarenko | 21.08.2000 | 25 | (3) | 9 |
| Neven Đurasek (CRO) | 15.08.1998 | 12 | (6) | 1 |

| | DOB | M | (s) | G |
|---|---|---|---|---|
| Anton Glushchenko | 20.04.2004 | | (1) | |
| Dmytro Kryskiv | 06.10.2000 | 12 | (6) | 5 |
| Yegor Nazaryna | 10.07.1997 | 7 | (13) | |
| Oleh Ocheretko | 25.03.2003 | 3 | (10) | |
| Taras Stepanenko | 08.08.1989 | 26 | | 3 |
| Georgiy Sudakov | 01.09.2002 | 27 | (2) | 5 |
| Andriy Totovytskyy | 20.01.1993 | 2 | (7) | |
| Oleksandr Zubkov | 03.08.1996 | 13 | (4) | 5 |
| **Forwards:** | **DOB** | **M** | **(s)** | **G** |
| Andriy Boryachuk | 23.04.1996 | | (2) | |
| Kevin Jesús Kelsy Genez (VEN) | 27.07.2004 | 4 | (10) | 5 |
| Mykhaylo Mudryk | 05.01.2001 | 11 | (1) | 7 |
| Ivan Petryak | 13.03.1994 | 4 | (9) | 1 |
| Marian Shved | 16.07.1997 | 4 | (6) | 2 |
| Danylo Sikan | 16.04.2001 | 14 | (12) | 9 |
| Khusrav Toirov (TJK) | 01.08.2004 | | (2) | |
| Dmytro Topalov | 12.03.1998 | 3 | (8) | |
| Lassina Traoré (BFA) | 12.01.2001 | 12 | (9) | 5 |


## Narodnyy Klub Veres Rivne

**Founded**: 1957
**Stadium**: Avanhard Stadium, Rivne (4,650)
**Trainer**: Yuriy Virt  04.05.1974

| Goalkeepers: | DOB | M | (s) | G |
|---|---|---|---|---|
| Bohdan Kogut | 10.10.1987 | 27 | (1) | |
| Vadym Yushchyshyn | 23.11.1999 | 3 | | |
| **Defenders:** | **DOB** | **M** | **(s)** | **G** |
| Denys Balan | 18.08.1993 | 10 | | |
| Roman Gagun | 16.07.1993 | 26 | (1) | |
| Danyil Khondak | 19.04.2001 | 3 | | 1 |
| Vasil Kurko | 25.04.1995 | 19 | (8) | |
| Mykola Kvasniy | 04.01.1995 | 2 | (3) | |
| Oleksandr Matkobozhyk | 03.01.1998 | 2 | (1) | 1 |
| Roman Miroshnyk | 03.01.1994 | 11 | | |
| Yevgeniy Pasich | 13.07.1993 | 13 | | |
| Semen Vovchenko | 13.06.1999 | 29 | | 3 |
| **Midfielders:** | **DOB** | **M** | **(s)** | **G** |
| Vitaliy Dakhnovskiy | 10.02.1999 | 19 | (10) | 3 |
| Mihail Ghecev (MDA) | 05.11.1997 | | (1) | |

| | DOB | M | (s) | G |
|---|---|---|---|---|
| Dmytro Hodia | 10.03.2005 | | (2) | |
| Dmytro Klyots | 15.04.1996 | 27 | | 5 |
| Valeriy Kucherov | 11.08.1993 | 27 | | 3 |
| Oleksansdr Lebedenko | 13.08.1989 | 17 | (12) | 1 |
| Gennadiy Pasich | 13.07.1993 | 24 | | 1 |
| Stanislav Sharay | 25.05.1997 | 16 | (8) | 1 |
| Serhiy Shestakov | 12.04.1990 | 1 | (5) | |
| Dmytro Shukh | 08.11.2004 | | (2) | |
| Vladyslav Tyshyninov | 20.03.2000 | | (1) | |
| Maksym Vadovsky | 12.08.2003 | | (1) | |
| **Forwards:** | **DOB** | **M** | **(s)** | **G** |
| Andriy Blyznychenko | 24.07.1994 | 11 | (4) | 5 |
| Mykola Gayduchyk | 30.12.1999 | 22 | (7) | 3 |
| Mykhaylo Sergiychuk | 29.07.1991 | 2 | (12) | 1 |
| Vladyslav Sharay | 25.05.1997 | 12 | (16) | 3 |
| Mykhaylo Shestakov | 12.04.1990 | 7 | (18) | 3 |


## Futbolnij Klub Vorskla Poltava

**Founded**: 1955
**Stadium**: Avanhard Arena, Uzhhorod (12,000)
**Trainer**: Viktor Skrypnyk  19.11.1969

| Goalkeepers: | DOB | M | (s) | G |
|---|---|---|---|---|
| Pavlo Isenko | 21.07.2003 | 15 | | |
| Dmytro Riznyk | 30.01.1999 | 15 | | |
| **Defenders:** | **DOB** | **M** | **(s)** | **G** |
| Andriy Batsula | 06.02.1992 | 19 | (4) | |
| Volodymyr Chesnakov | 12.02.1988 | 15 | (2) | 1 |
| *Felipe* Rodrigues dos Santos „Diadema" (BRA) | 31.10.1995 | 11 | (7) | 2 |
| Daniil Khrypchuk | 09.12.2003 | 2 | (2) | |
| Vasyl Kravets | 20.08.1997 | 25 | | 3 |
| Ilya Krupskiy | 02.10.2004 | 2 | (5) | |
| *Lucas* Pereira *Ramires* Constante (BRA) | 27.04.2002 | 4 | (5) | |
| Maksym Melnychuk | 18.09.1999 | 2 | (1) | |
| Igor Perduta | 15.11.1990 | 27 | | |
| Serhiy Yavorskiy | 05.07.1989 | 9 | (4) | |
| Gjoko Zajkov (MKD) | 10.02.1995 | 12 | (2) | |
| **Midfielders:** | **DOB** | **M** | **(s)** | **G** |
| Artem Chelyadin | 29.12.1999 | 18 | (8) | 1 |
| Dmytro Chernysh | 10.08.2004 | | (5) | |

| | DOB | M | (s) | G |
|---|---|---|---|---|
| Ibrahim Kane (MLI) | 23.06.2000 | 9 | (2) | 1 |
| Yuriy Kozyrenko | 27.11.1999 | | (4) | |
| Andriy Kravchuk | 26.02.1999 | 3 | (2) | 1 |
| Artem Kulakovskiy | 11.02.2002 | | (6) | |
| Ivan Nesterenko | 23.07.2003 | 2 | (5) | |
| Yevgen Pavlyuk | 18.08.2002 | 16 | (1) | 1 |
| Aleksandr Sklyar | 26.02.1991 | 22 | (3) | 4 |
| Ardit Toli (ALB) | 12.07.1997 | 4 | (6) | |
| Ennur Totre (MKD) | 29.10.1996 | 2 | (1) | |
| Vladlen Yurchenko | 22.01.1994 | 15 | (2) | 1 |
| **Forwards:** | **DOB** | **M** | **(s)** | **G** |
| Danylo Kravchuk | 02.07.2001 | | (1) | |
| *Marlyson* Conceição Oliveira (BRA) | 17.12.1997 | 8 | (3) | 3 |
| Denys Oliynyk | 16.06.1987 | 18 | (5) | 2 |
| *Ricardo Lopes* Pereira (BRA) | 28.10.1990 | 2 | (5) | |
| Rodel Kurai Richards (ENG) | 05.09.2000 | | (1) | |
| Taulant Seferi (ALB) | 15.11.1996 | 26 | (2) | 13 |
| Ruslan Stepanyuk | 16.01.1992 | 27 | (3) | 5 |

## Futbolnij Klub Zorya Luhansk

| Founded: | 1923 |
|---|---|
| Stadium: | Dinamo Stadium, Kyiv (16,873) |
| Trainer: | Patrick van Leeuwen (NED) |

| Goalkeepers: | DOB | M | (s) | G |
|---|---|---|---|---|
| Dmytro Matsapura | 10.03.2000 | 15 | | |
| Oleksandr Saputin | 13.11.2003 | 15 | | |
| **Defenders:** | **DOB** | **M** | **(s)** | **G** |
| Arseniy Batagov | 05.03.2002 | 30 | | 1 |
| Bohdan Butko | 13.01.1991 | 25 | | 2 |
| Oleg Danchenko | 01.08.1994 | 15 | | |
| Maksym Imerekov | 23.01.1991 | 28 | | 4 |
| Igor Kiryukhantsev | 29.01.1996 | 11 | | 5 |
| Yaroslav Kysyl | 31.05.2003 | | (1) | |
| Pavlo Polegenko | 06.01.1995 | | (12) | |
| Maksym Smiyan | 11.04.2002 | 4 | (5) | |
| Igor Snurnitsyn | 07.03.2000 | 8 | (6) | |
| Roman Vantukh | 04.07.1998 | 12 | (9) | 1 |
| **Midfielders:** | **DOB** | **M** | **(s)** | **G** |
| Akhmed Alibekov | 29.05.1998 | | (1) | |
| Volodymyr Brazhko | 23.01.2002 | 23 | (6) | 7 |
| Serhiy Buletsa | 16.02.1999 | 28 | | 7 |
| Kyrylo Dryshlyuk | 16.09.1999 | 4 | (9) | |

08.08.1969

| | DOB | M | (s) | G |
|---|---|---|---|---|
| Ilya Gulko | 17.11.2002 | | (1) | |
| Vladyslav Kabaev | 01.09.1995 | 1 | | |
| Oleksiy Khakhlyov | 06.02.1999 | 1 | (11) | |
| Maksym Khlan | 27.01.2003 | 1 | (7) | |
| Mykola Mykhaylenko | 22.05.2001 | | (5) | |
| Dmytro Myshnyov | 26.01.1994 | 13 | (13) | 3 |
| Yegor Nazaryna | 10.07.1997 | 4 | | 1 |
| Yevhen Shakhov | 30.11.1990 | 13 | (4) | 4 |
| **Forwards:** | **DOB** | **M** | **(s)** | **G** |
| Danyil Alefirenko | 19.04.2000 | | (5) | 1 |
| Denys Antyukh | 30.07.1997 | 15 | (10) | 3 |
| Denys Bezborodko | 31.05.1994 | 1 | | 2 |
| Vyacheslav Churko | 10.05.1993 | 13 | (3) | 2 |
| *Cristian* Daniel Dal Bello Fagundes (BRA) | 13.12.1999 | 6 | | |
| Eduardo Antonio Guerrero Locano (PAN) | 21.02.2000 | 9 | (1) | 5 |
| Maksym Lunyov | 22.05.1998 | 1 | (9) | |
| Denys Nahnoyniy | 03.02.2002 | 7 | (6) | 1 |
| Vladyslav Pogorilyi | 03.09.2003 | | (11) | 1 |
| Nazariy Rusyn | 25.10.1998 | 27 | (3) | 13 |

# SECOND LEVEL
## Ukrainian First League 2022/2023

### Regular Season

#### Group A

| | | | | | | | | | |
|---|---|---|---|---|---|---|---|---|---|
| 1. | FK Polissia Zhytomyr | 14 | 13 | 1 | 0 | 34 | - | 6 | 40 |
| 2. | FK Karpaty Lviv | 14 | 9 | 1 | 4 | 22 | - | 13 | 28 |
| 3. | FK Epicenter Kamianets-Podilskiy | 14 | 8 | 3 | 3 | 17 | - | 11 | 27 |
| 4. | FK Nyva Ternopil | 14 | 5 | 5 | 4 | 15 | - | 8 | 20 |
| 5. | FK Prykarpattia Ivano-Frankivsk | 14 | 4 | 3 | 7 | 11 | - | 22 | 15 |
| 6. | FK Dinaz Vyshhorod | 14 | 2 | 4 | 8 | 14 | - | 28 | 10 |
| 7. | FSK Bukovyna Chernivtsi | 14 | 2 | 3 | 9 | 9 | - | 21 | 9 |
| 8. | FSK Mariupol | 14 | 1 | 4 | 9 | 12 | - | 25 | 7 |

#### Group B

| | | | | | | | | | |
|---|---|---|---|---|---|---|---|---|---|
| 1. | FC LNZ Cherkasy | 14 | 9 | 3 | 2 | 22 | - | 6 | 30 |
| 2. | FK Obolon Kyiv | 14 | 9 | 2 | 3 | 20 | - | 9 | 29 |
| 3. | FK Kremin Kremenchuk | 14 | 6 | 3 | 5 | 28 | - | 24 | 21 |
| 4. | MFK Metalurh Zaporizhzhia | 14 | 5 | 5 | 4 | 17 | - | 16 | 20 |
| 5. | FC Chernihiv | 14 | 4 | 4 | 6 | 13 | - | 17 | 16 |
| 6. | SK Poltava | 14 | 4 | 3 | 7 | 15 | - | 19 | 15 |
| 7. | FK Skoruk Tomakivka | 14 | 3 | 5 | 6 | 15 | - | 22 | 14 |
| 8. | FK Hirnyk-Sport Horishni Plavni | 14 | 1 | 5 | 8 | 8 | - | 25 | 8 |

Team ranked 1-4 of each group were qualified for the Promotion Round, while teams ranked 5-8 of each group were qualified for the Relegation Round.

#### Promotion Round

| | | | | | | | | | |
|---|---|---|---|---|---|---|---|---|---|
| 1. | FK Polissia Zhytomyr (*Promoted*) | 14 | 10 | 2 | 2 | 25 | - | 9 | 32 |
| 2. | FK Obolon Kyiv (*Promoted*) | 14 | 8 | 5 | 1 | 19 | - | 8 | 29 |
| 3. | FC LNZ Cherkasy (*Promotion Play-offs*) | 14 | 6 | 4 | 4 | 19 | - | 12 | 22 |
| 4. | MFK Metalurh Zaporizhzhia (*Promotion Play-offs*) | 14 | 6 | 3 | 5 | 18 | - | 16 | 21 |
| 5. | FK Karpaty Lviv | 14 | 5 | 3 | 6 | 12 | - | 16 | 18 |
| 6. | FK Epicenter Kamianets-Podilskiy | 14 | 4 | 3 | 7 | 12 | - | 17 | 15 |
| 7. | FK Nyva Ternopil | 14 | 0 | 8 | 6 | 10 | - | 17 | 8 |
| 8. | FK Kremin Kremenchuk | 14 | 1 | 4 | 9 | 11 | - | 31 | 7 |

#### Group B

| | | | | | | | | | |
|---|---|---|---|---|---|---|---|---|---|
| 1. | FK Prykarpattia Ivano-Frankivsk | 14 | 6 | 6 | 2 | 21 | - | 11 | 24 |
| 2. | FK Skoruk Tomakivka* | 14 | 5 | 8 | 1 | 18 | - | 9 | 23 |
| 3. | FSK Bukovyna Chernivtsi | 14 | 5 | 6 | 3 | 18 | - | 14 | 21 |
| 4. | FK Dinaz Vyshhorod | 14 | 5 | 6 | 3 | 16 | - | 17 | 21 |
| 5. | FC Chernihiv | 14 | 5 | 4 | 5 | 15 | - | 16 | 19 |
| 6. | SK Poltava | 14 | 4 | 4 | 6 | 16 | - | 22 | 16 |
| 7. | FSK Mariupol (*Relegation Play-offs*) | 14 | 3 | 3 | 8 | 18 | - | 23 | 12 |
| 8. | FK Hirnyk-Sport Horishni Plavni | 14 | 2 | 5 | 7 | 12 | - | 22 | 11 |

* FK Skoruk Tomakivka withdrew for the next season due to destructions caused by the Russian invasion.

FK Khust - FSK Mariupol                                                          1-1(0-0)                    1-0(0-0)

FK Khust promoted for the 2023/2024 Ukrainian First League.
FSK Mariupol was not relegated as a result of FK Skoruk Tomakivka's withdrawal for the next season.

## NATIONAL TEAM

### INTERNATIONAL MATCHES
(16.07.2022 – 15.07.2023)

| | | | | |
|---|---|---|---|---|
| 21.09.2022 | Glasgow | *Scotland - Ukraine* | *3-0(0-0)* | (UNL) |
| 24.09.2022 | Yerevan | *Armenia - Ukraine* | *0-5(0-1)* | (UNL) |
| 27.09.2022 | Kraków | *Ukraine - Scotland* | *0-0* | (UNL) |
| | | | | |
| 26.03.2023 | London | *England - Ukraine* | *2-0(2-0)* | (ECQ) |
| 12.06.2023 | Bremen | *Germany - Ukraine* | *3-3(1-2)* | (F) |
| 16.06.2023 | Skopje | *North Macedonia - Ukraine* | *2-3(2-0)* | (ECQ) |
| 19.06.2023 | Trnava | *Ukraine - Malta* | *1-0(0-0)* | (ECQ) |

**21.09.2022    SCOTLAND - UKRAINE**                    **3-0(0-0)**                    3ʳᵈ UEFA Nations League B, Group 1
Hampden Park, Glasgow; Referee: Maurizio Mariani (Italy); Attendance: 42,846
**UKR:** Anatoliy Trubin, Oleksandr Karavayev, Valeriy Bondar , Mykola Matviyenko, Bohdan Mykhaylichenko, Taras Stepanenko (46.Serhiy Sydorchuk), Oleksandr Pikhalyonok (83.Oleksandr Zubkov), Ruslan Malinovskiy, Andriy Yarmolenko (Cap) (67.Viktor Tsyhankov), Mykhaylo Mudryk (83.Danylo Ihnatenko), Artem Dovbyk (67.Roman Yaremchuk). Trainer: Oleksandr Petrakov.

**24.09.2022    ARMENIA - UKRAINE**                    **0-5(0-1)**                    3ʳᵈ UEFA Nations League B, Group 1
„Vazgen Sargsyan" Hanrapetakan Stadium, Yerevan; Referee: João Pedro da Silva Pinheiro (Portugalia); Attendance: 7,200
**UKR:** Andriy Lunin, Illya Zabarniy, Taras Kacharaba, Serhiy Kryvtsov (78.Mykola Matviyenko), Oleksandr Tymchyk, Danylo Ihnatenko, Serhiy Sydorchuk (Cap) (46.Oleksandr Pikhalyonok), Vitaliy Mykolenko, Oleksandr Zubkov (71.Mykhaylo Mudryk), Viktor Tsyhankov (67.Andriy Yarmolenko), Roman Yaremchuk (67.Artem Dovbyk). Trainer: Oleksandr Petrakov.
**Goals:** Oleksandr Tymchyk (22), Oleksandr Zubkov (57), Artem Dovbyk (69), Danylo Ihnatenko (81), Artem Dovbyk (84).

**27.09.2022    UKRAINE - SCOTLAND**                    **0-0**                    3ʳᵈ UEFA Nations League B, Group 1
Stadion Cracovii im. Józefa Piłsudskiego, Kraków (Poland); Referee: Anastasios Sidiropoulos (Greece); Attendance: 13,534
**UKR:** Andriy Lunin, Oleksandr Tymchyk, Illya Zabarniy, Mykola Matviyenko, Vitaliy Mykolenko, Taras Stepanenko, Ruslan Malinovskiy (87.Oleksandr Pikhalyonok), Danylo Ihnatenko, Andriy Yarmolenko (Cap) (87.Oleksandr Zubkov), Mykhaylo Mudryk (75.Viktor Tsyhankov), Artem Dovbyk (75.Roman Yaremchuk). Trainer: Oleksandr Petrakov.

**26.03.2023    ENGLAND - UKRAINE**                    **2-0(2-0)**                    17ᵗʰ EC. Qualifiers
Wembley Stadium, London; Referee: Serdar Gözübüyük (Netherlands); Attendance: 83,947
**UKR:** Anatoliy Trubin, Oleksandr Karavayev (61.Vitaliy Buyalskiy), Oleksandr Svatok, Mykola Matviyenko, Vitaliy Mykolenko (62.Eduard Sobol), Taras Stepanenko (90.Yevhen Konoplyanka), Oleksandr Zinchenko (Cap), Heorhiy Sudakov, Ruslan Malinovskiy, Mykhaylo Mudryk (61.Viktor Tsyhankov), Roman Yaremchuk (74.Artem Dovbyk). Trainer: Ruslan Rotan.

**12.06.2023    GERMANY - UKRAINE**                    **3-3(1-2)**                    Friendly International
Weserstadion, Bremen; Referee: Anastasios Sidiropoulos (Greece); Attendance: 35,795
**UKR:** Anatoliy Trubin, Oleksandr Tymchyk, Illya Zabarniy, Mykola Matviyenko, Vitaliy Mykolenko (78.Eduard Sobol), Taras Stepanenko (65.Danylo Ihnatenko), Heorhiy Sudakov, Viktor Tsyhankov (71.Oleksandr Zubkov), Mykhaylo Mudryk (78.Oleksandr Pikhalyonok), Andriy Yarmolenko (Cap) (65.Ruslan Malinovskiy), Artem Dovbyk (64.Vladyslav Vanat). Trainer: Serhiy Rebrov.
**Goals:** Viktor Tsyhankov (19), Amntonio Rüdiger (23 own goal), Viktor Tsyhankov (56).

**16.06.2023    NORTH MACEDONIA - UKRAINE**                    **2-3(2-0)**                    17ᵗʰ EC. Qualifiers
Nacionalna Arena "Toše Proeski", Skopje; Referee: Lukas Fähndrich (Switzerland); Attendance: 14,370
**UKR:** Anatoliy Trubin, Oleksandr Tymchyk (46.Yukhym Konoplya), Illya Zabarniy, Mykola Matviyenko, Vitaliy Mykolenko, Taras Stepanenko, Andriy Yarmolenko (Cap) (66.Ruslan Malinovskiy), Heorhiy Sudakov, Viktor Tsyhankov (90+3.Oleksandr Zubkov), Mykhaylo Mudryk (90.Serhiy Sydorchuk), Artem Dovbyk (46.Vladyslav Vanat). Trainer: Serhiy Rebrov.
**Goals:** Illya Zabarniy (62), Yukhym Konoplya (67), Viktor Tsyhankov (83).

**19.06.2023    UKRAINE - MALTA**                    **1-0(0-0)**                    17ᵗʰ EC. Qualifiers
Štadión "Antona Malatinského", Trnava (Slovakia); Referee: Ruddy Buquet (France); Attendance: 7,543
**UKR:** Anatoliy Trubin, Yukhym Konoplya, Illya Zabarniy, Serhiy Kryvtsov, Mykola Matviyenko (46.Vitaliy Mykolenko), Taras Stepanenko, Ruslan Malinovskiy (63.Vitaliy Buyalskiy), Heorhiy Sudakov, Andriy Yarmolenko (Cap) (81.Serhiy Sydorchuk), Viktor Tsyhankov (90+5.Oleksandr Svatok), Vladyslav Vanat (63.Artem Dovbyk). Trainer: Serhiy Rebrov.
**Goal:** Viktor Tsyhankov (72 penalty).

## NATIONAL TEAM PLAYERS
### (16.07.2022 – 15.07.2023)

| Name | DOB | Caps | Goals | Club |
|------|-----|------|-------|------|

### Goalkeepers

| Name | DOB | Caps | Goals | Club |
|------|-----|------|-------|------|
| Andriy LUNIN | 11.02.1999 | 9 | 0 | 2022: *Real Madrid CF (ESP)* |
| Anatoliy TRUBIN | 01.08.2001 | 7 | 0 | 2022/2023: *FK Shakhtar Donetsk* |

### Defenders

| Name | DOB | Caps | Goals | Club |
|------|-----|------|-------|------|
| Valeriy BONDAR | 27.02.1999 | 3 | 0 | 2022: *FK Shakhtar Donetsk* |
| Taras KACHARABA | 07.01.1995 | 3 | 0 | 2022: *SK Slavia Praha (CZE)* |
| Oleksandr KARAVAYEV | 02.06.1992 | 47 | 2 | 2022/2023: *FK Dinamo Kyiv* |
| Yukhym KONOPLYA | 26.08.1999 | 5 | 1 | 2023: *FK Shakhtar Donetsk* |
| Serhiy KRYVTSOV | 15.03.1991 | 32 | 0 | 2022: *FK Shakhtar Donetsk* <br> 31.01.2023-> *CIF Miami (USA)* |
| Mykola MATVIYENKO | 02.05.1996 | 58 | 0 | 2022/2023: *FK Shakhtar Donetsk* |
| Bohdan MYKHAYLICHENKO | 21.03.1997 | 7 | 0 | 2022: *FK Shakhtar Donetsk* |
| Vitaliy MYKOLENKO | 29.05.1999 | 32 | 1 | 2022/2023: *Everton FC Liverpool (ENG)* |
| Eduard SOBOL | 20.04.1995 | 29 | 0 | 2023: *Racing Club de Strasbourg (FRA)* |
| Oleksandr SVATOK | 27.09.1994 | 2 | 0 | 2023: *SC Dnipro-1* |
| Oleksandr TYMCHYK | 20.01.1997 | 14 | 1 | 2022/2023: *FK Dinamo Kyiv* |
| Illya ZABARNIY | 01.09.2002 | 27 | 1 | 2022: *FK Dinamo Kyiv* <br> 31.01.2023-> *AFC Bournemouth (ENG)* |

### Midfielders

| Name | DOB | Caps | Goals | Club |
|------|-----|------|-------|------|
| Vitaliy BUYALSKIY | 06.01.1993 | 11 | 0 | 2023: *FK Dinamo Kyiv* |
| Danylo IHNATENKO | 13.03.1997 | 6 | 1 | 2022/2023: *FC Girondins de Bordeaux (FRA)* |
| Yevhen KONOPLYANKA | 29.09.1989 | 87 | 21 | 2023: *KS Cracovia Kraków (POL)* |
| Ruslan MALINOVSKIY | 04.05.1993 | 55 | 7 | 2022: *Atalanta Bergamasca Calcio (ITA)* <br> 09.01.2023-> *Olympique de Marseille (FRA)* |
| Mykhaylo MUDRYK | 05.01.2001 | 11 | 0 | 2022: *FK Shakhtar Donetsk* <br> 15.01.2023-> *Chelsea FC London (ENG)* |
| Oleksandr PIKHALYONOK | 07.05.1997 | 6 | 0 | 2022/2023: *SC Dnipro-1* |
| Taras STEPANENKO | 08.08.1989 | 77 | 4 | 2022/2023: *FK Shakhtar Donetsk* |
| Heorhiy SUDAKOV | 01.09.2002 | 7 | 0 | 2023: *FK Shakhtar Donetsk* |
| Serhiy SYDORCHUK | 02.05.1991 | 56 | 3 | 2022/2023: *FK Dinamo Kyiv* |
| Viktor TSYHANKOV | 15.11.1997 | 47 | 11 | 2022: *FK Dinamo Kyiv* <br> 17.01.2023-> *Girona FC (ESP)* |
| Oleksandr ZINCHENKO | 15.12.1996 | 53 | 8 | 2023: *Arsenal FC London (ENG)* |
| Oleksandr ZUBKOV | 03.08.1996 | 26 | 2 | 2022/2023: *FK Shakhtar Donetsk* |

### Forwards

| Name | DOB | Caps | Goals | Club |
|------|-----|------|-------|------|
| Artem DOVBYK | 21.06.1997 | 18 | 6 | 2022/2023: *SC Dnipro-1* |
| Vladyslav VANAT | 04.01.2002 | 3 | 0 | 2023: *FK Dinamo Kyiv* |
| Roman YAREMCHUK | 27.11.1995 | 43 | 13 | 2022/2023: *Club Brugge KV (BEL)* |
| Andriy YARMOLENKO | 23.10.1989 | 115 | 45 | 2022/2023: *Al Ain FC (UAE)* |

### Trainer

| Name | DOB | Record | |
|------|-----|--------|---|
| Oleksandr PETRAKOV [18.08.2021 - 31.12.2022] | 06.08.1957 | 15 M; 6 W; 7 D; 2 L; 23-13 | |
| Ruslan ROTAN [28.02. – 06.06.2023] | 29.10.1981 | 1 M; 0 W; 0 D; 1 L; 0-2 | |
| Serhiy REBROV [from 07.06.2023] | 03.06.1974 | 3 M; 2 W; 1 D; 0 L; 7-5 | |

# WALES

**The Country:**
Cymru (Wales)
Capital: Cardiff
Surface: 20,779 km²
Inhabitants: 3,267,501 [2022]
Time: UTC

**The FA:**
Football Association of Wales
Hensol, Vanguard Way 72, 8JY Glamorgan
Tel: +44 29 2043 5830
Founded: 1876
Member of FIFA: 1910-1920; 1924-1928; since 1946
Member of UEFA since: 1954
Website: www.faw.cymru

## NATIONAL TEAM RECORDS

### RECORDS

| | | |
|---|---|---|
| **First international match:** | 25.03.1876, Glasgow: | Scotland – Wales 4-0 |
| **Most international caps:** | Gareth Frank Bale | - 111 caps (2006-2022) |
| **Most international goals:** | Gareth Frank Bale | - 41 goals / 111 caps (2006-2022) |

### UEFA EUROPEAN CHAMPIONSHIP

| | |
|---|---|
| 1960 | Did not enter |
| 1964 | Qualifiers |
| 1968 | Qualifiers |
| 1972 | Qualifiers |
| 1976 | Qualifiers |
| 1980 | Qualifiers |
| 1984 | Qualifiers |
| 1988 | Qualifiers |
| 1992 | Qualifiers |
| 1996 | Qualifiers |
| 2000 | Qualifiers |
| 2004 | Qualifiers |
| 2008 | Qualifiers |
| 2012 | Qualifiers |
| 2016 | Final Tournament (Semi-Finals) |
| 2020 | Final Tournament (2nd Round of 16) |

### FIFA WORLD CUP

| | |
|---|---|
| 1930 | *Not a FIFA member* |
| 1934 | *Not a FIFA member* |
| 1938 | *Not a FIFA member* |
| 1950 | Qualifiers |
| 1954 | Qualifiers |
| 1958 | Final Tournament (Quarter-Finals) |
| 1962 | Qualifiers |
| 1966 | Qualifiers |
| 1970 | Qualifiers |
| 1974 | Qualifiers |
| 1978 | Qualifiers |
| 1982 | Qualifiers |
| 1986 | Qualifiers |
| 1990 | Qualifiers |
| 1994 | Qualifiers |
| 1998 | Qualifiers |
| 2002 | Qualifiers |
| 2006 | Qualifiers |
| 2010 | Qualifiers |
| 2014 | Qualifiers |
| 2018 | Qualifiers |
| 2022 | Final Tournament (Group Stage) |

### OLYMPIC TOURNAMENTS

| | |
|---|---|
| 1908 | - |
| 1912 | - |
| 1920 | - |
| 1924 | - |
| 1928 | - |
| 1936 | - |
| 1948 | - |
| 1952 | - |
| 1956 | - |
| 1960 | - |
| 1964 | - |
| 1968 | - |
| 1972 | - |
| 1976 | - |
| 1980 | - |
| 1984 | - |
| 1988 | - |
| 1992 | - |
| 1996 | - |
| 2000 | - |
| 2004 | - |
| 2008 | - |
| 2012 | - |
| 2016 | - |
| 2020 | - |

### UEFA NATIONS LEAGUE

| | |
|---|---|
| 2018/2019 | League B (Group Stage) |
| 2020/2021 | League B (Group Stage -> promoted to League A) |
| 2022/2023 | League A (Group Stage -> relegated to League B) |

### WELSH CLUB HONOURS IN EUROPEAN CLUB COMPETITIONS:

**European Champion Clubs.Cup (1956-1992) / UEFA Champions League (1993-2023)**

None

**Fairs Cup (1858-1971) / UEFA Cup (1972-2009) / UEFA Europa League (2010-2023)**

None

**UEFA Europa Conference League (2021-2023)**

None

**UEFA Super Cup (1972-2022)**

None

***European Cup Winners' Cup 1961-1999\****

None

*\*defunct competition*

# NATIONAL COMPETITIONS
## TABLE OF HONOURS

### CUP WINNERS 1878-1992

| Year | Winner | Year | Winner | Year | Winner |
|------|--------|------|--------|------|--------|
| 1877/1878 | Wrexham AFC | 1916/1917 | *No competition* | 1954/1955 | Barry Town United FC |
| 1878/1879 | Newtown White Stars FC | 1917/1918 | *No competition* | 1955/1956 | Cardiff City FC |
| 1879/1880 | Ruabon Druids FC | 1918/1919 | *No competition* | 1956/1957 | Wrexham AFC |
| 1880/1881 | Ruabon Druids FC | 1919/1920 | Cardiff City FC | 1957/1958 | Wrexham AFC |
| 1881/1882 | Ruabon Druids FC | 1920/1921 | Wrexham AFC | 1958/1959 | Cardiff City FC |
| 1882/1883 | Wrexham AFC | 1921/1922 | Cardiff City FC | 1959/1960 | Wrexham AFC |
| 1883/1884 | Oswestry Town FC Shropshire(ENG) | 1922/1923 | Cardiff City FC | 1960/1961 | Swansea Town AFC |
| 1884/1885 | Ruabon Druids FC | 1923/1924 | Wrexham AFC | 1961/1962 | Bangor City FC |
| 1885/1886 | Ruabon Druids FC | 1924/1925 | Wrexham AFC | 1962/1963 | Borough United FC |
| 1886/1887 | Chirk AAA FC | 1925/1926 | Ebbw Vale FC | 1963/1964 | Cardiff City FC |
| 1887/1888 | Chirk AAA FC | 1926/1927 | Cardiff City FC | 1964/1965 | Cardiff City FC |
| 1888/1889 | Bangor City FC | 1927/1928 | Cardiff City FC | 1965/1966 | Swansea Town AFC |
| 1889/1890 | Chirk AAA FC | 1928/1929 | Connah's Quay & Shotton FC | 1966/1967 | Cardiff City FC |
| 1890/1891 | Shrewsbury Town FC (ENG) | 1929/1930 | Cardiff City FC | 1967/1968 | Cardiff City FC |
| 1891/1892 | Chirk AAA FC | 1930/1931 | Wrexham AFC | 1968/1969 | Cardiff City FC |
| 1892/1893 | Wrexham AFC | 1931/1932 | Swansea Town AFC | 1969/1970 | Cardiff City FC |
| 1893/1894 | Chirk AAA FC | 1932/1933 | Chester City FC (ENG) | 1970/1971 | Cardiff City FC |
| 1894/1895 | Newtown AFC | 1933/1934 | Bristol City FC (ENG) | 1971/1972 | Wrexham AFC |
| 1895/1896 | Bangor City FC | 1934/1935 | Tranmere Rovers FC (ENG) | 1972/1973 | Cardiff City FC |
| 1896/1897 | Wrexham AFC | 1935/1936 | Crewe Alexandra FC (ENG) | 1973/1974 | Cardiff City FC |
| 1897/1898 | Ruabon Druids FC | 1936/1937 | Crewe Alexandra FC (ENG) | 1974/1975 | Wrexham AFC |
| 1898/1899 | Ruabon Druids FC | 1937/1938 | Shrewsbury Town FC (ENG) | 1975/1976 | Cardiff City FC |
| 1899/1900 | Aberystwyth Town FC | 1938/1939 | South Liverpool FC (ENG) | 1976/1977 | Shrewsbury Town FC (ENG) |
| 1900/1901 | Oswestry Town FC (ENG) | 1939/1940 | Wellington Town FC (ENG) | 1977/1978 | Wrexham AFC |
| 1901/1902 | Wellington Town FC (ENG) | 1940/1941 | *No competition* | 1978/1979 | Shrewsbury Town FC (ENG) |
| 1902/1903 | Wrexham AFC | 1941/1942 | *No competition* | 1979/1980 | Newport County AFC |
| 1903/1904 | Ruabon Druids FC | 1942/1943 | *No competition* | 1980/1981 | Swansea City FC |
| 1904/1905 | Wrexham AFC | 1943/1944 | *No competition* | 1981/1982 | Swansea City FC |
| 1905/1906 | Wellington Town FC (ENG) | 1944/1945 | *No competition* | 1982/1983 | Swansea City FC |
| 1906/1907 | Oswestry Town FC (ENG) | 1945/1946 | *No competition* | 1983/1984 | Shrewsbury Town FC (ENG) |
| 1907/1908 | Chester City FC (ENG) | 1946/1947 | Chester City FC (ENG) | 1984/1985 | Shrewsbury Town FC (ENG) |
| 1908/1909 | Wrexham AFC | 1947/1948 | Lovell's Athletic FC | 1985/1986 | Wrexham AFC |
| 1909/1910 | Wrexham AFC | 1948/1949 | Merthyr Tydfil FC | 1986/1987 | Merthyr Tydfil FC |
| 1910/1911 | Wrexham AFC | 1949/1950 | Swansea Town AFC | 1987/1988 | Cardiff City FC |
| 1911/1912 | Cardiff City | 1950/1951 | Merthyr Tydfil FC | 1988/1989 | Swansea City FC |
| 1912/1913 | Swansea Town AFC | 1951/1952 | Rhyl FC | 1989/1990 | Hereford United FC (ENG) |
| 1913/1914 | Wrexham AFC | 1952/1953 | Rhyl FC | 1990/1991 | Swansea City FC |
| 1914/1915 | Wrexham AFC | 1953/1954 | Flint Town United FC | 1991/1992 | Cardiff City FC |
| 1915/1916 | *No competition* | | | | |

| | CHAMPIONS* | CUP WINNERS | BEST GOALSCORERS | |
|------|-----------|-------------|------------------|---|
| 1992/1993 | Cwmbrân Town AFC | Cardiff City FC | Steve Woods (Ebbw Vale FC) | 29 |
| 1993/1994 | Bangor City FC | Barry Town United FC | Dave Taylor (Porthmadog FC) | 43 |
| 1994/1995 | Bangor City FC | Wrexham AFC | Frank Mottram (Bangor City FC) | 31 |
| 1995/1996 | Barry Town United FC | Llansantffraid FC | Ken McKenna (Conwy United FC) | 38 |
| 1996/1997 | Barry Town United FC | Barry Town United FC | Anthony Bird (Barry Town United FC) | 42 |
| 1997/1998 | Barry Town United FC | Bangor City FC | Eifion Wyn Williams (Barry Town United FC) | 40 |
| 1998/1999 | Barry Town United FC | Inter CableTel Cardiff | Eifion Wyn Williams (Barry Town United FC) | 28 |
| 1999/2000 | Total Network Solutions | Bangor City FC | Chris Summers (Cwmbrân Town AFC) | 28 |
| 2000/2001 | Barry Town United FC | Barry Town United FC | Graham Evans (Caersws FC) | 25 |
| 2001/2002 | Barry Town United FC | Barry Town United FC | Marc Lloyd-Williams (Bangor City FC) | 47 |
| 2002/2003 | Barry Town United FC | Barry Town United FC | Graham Evans (Caersws FC) | 24 |
| 2003/2004 | Rhyl FC | Rhyl FC | Graham Evans (Caersws FC) | 24 |
| 2004/2005 | Total Network Solutions | Total Network Solutions | Marc Lloyd-Williams (Total Network Solutions) | 31 |
| 2005/2006 | Total Network Solutions | Rhyl FC | Rhys Griffiths (Port Talbot Town FC) | 28 |
| 2006/2007 | The New Saints FC | Carmarthen Town FC | Rhys Griffiths (Llanelli Town AFC) | 30 |
| 2007/2008 | Llanelli Town AFC | Bangor City FC | Rhys Griffiths (Llanelli Town AFC) | 40 |
| 2008/2009 | Rhyl FC | Bangor City FC | Rhys Griffiths (Llanelli Town AFC) | 31 |
| 2009/2010 | The New Saints FC | Bangor City FC | Rhys Griffiths (Llanelli Town AFC) | 30 |
| 2010/2011 | Bangor City FC | Llanelli Town AFC | Rhys Griffiths (Llanelli Town AFC) | 25 |
| 2011/2012 | The New Saints FC | The New Saints FC | Rhys Griffiths (Llanelli Town AFC) | 24 |
| 2012/2013 | The New Saints FC | Prestatyn Town FC | Michael Wilde (The New Saints FC) | 25 |
| 2013/2014 | The New Saints FC | The New Saints FC | Chris Venables (Aberystwyth Town FC) | 20 |
| 2014/2015 | The New Saints FC | The New Saints FC | Chris Venables (Aberystwyth Town FC) | 28 |
| 2015/2016 | The New Saints FC | The New Saints FC | Chris Venables (Bala Town FC) | 20 |
| 2016/2017 | The New Saints FC | Bala Town FC | Jason Oswell (ENG, Newtown AFC) | 22 |
| 2017/2018 | The New Saints FC | Connah's Quay Nomads FC | Gregory Alexander Draper (NZL, The New Saints FC) | 11 |
| 2018/2019 | The New Saints FC | The New Saints FC | Steven Anthony Tames (ENG, Bala Town FC) | 17 |

| 2019/2020 | Connah's Quay Nomads FC | *Competition postponed* | Chris Venables (Bala Town FC) | 22 |
|---|---|---|---|---|
| 2020/2021 | Connah's Quay Nomads FC | *No competition* | Chris Venables (Bala Town FC) | 24 |
| 2021/2022 | The New Saints FC | The New Saints FC | Declan Joseph McManus (SCO, The New Saints FC) | 24 |
| 2022/2023 | The New Saints FC | The New Saints FC | Declan Joseph McManus (SCO, The New Saints FC) | 29 |

Please note: Championship called League of Wales (1992–2002) and Welsh Premier League (since 2002).

## NATIONAL CHAMPIONSHIP
### Cymru Premier League 2022/2023
#### (12.08.2022 – 22.04.2023)

### Regular Season - Results

**Round 1 [12-14.08.2022]**
Airbus UK - Aberystwyth Town 1-2(0-1)
Metropolitan - Connah's Quay 2-0(1-0)
Haverfordwest - Caernarfon Town 1-0(0-0)
Newtown AFC - The New Saints 0-0
Pontypridd - Flint Town 0-1(0-1)
Penybont FC - Bala Town 2-0(0-0)

**Round 2 [19-20.08.2022]**
Connah's Quay - Airbus UK 1-0(0-0)
Newtown AFC - Flint Town 0-2(0-2)
Bala Town - Haverfordwest 1-1(0-1)
Caernarfon Town - Pontypridd 2-0(0-0)
The New Saints - Penybont FC 1-0(0-0)
Aberystwyth Town - Metropolitan 0-4(0-3)

**Round 3 [26-27.08.2022]**
Bala Town - Newtown AFC 3-0(2-0)
The New Saints - Connah's Quay 2-1(1-1)
Caernarfon Town - Metropolitan 5-1(3-1)
Haverfordwest - Airbus UK 3-0(1-0)
Penybont FC - Flint Town 2-1(0-1)
Pontypridd - Aberystwyth Town 2-1(1-0)

**Round 4 [30.08.2022]**
Airbus UK - Flint Town 1-3(1-0)
Metropolitan - Pontypridd 3-0(1-0)
Connah's Quay - Bala Town 1-0(1-0)
Newtown AFC - Caernarfon Town 2-1(2-0)
Penybont FC - Haverfordwest 3-2(1-1)
Aberystwyth Town - The New Saints 0-2(0-0)

**Round 5 [02-03.09.2022]**
Caernarfon Town - Airbus UK 3-1(0-1)
Aberystwyth Town - Bala Town 1-4(0-1)
Metropolitan - Flint Town 1-0(0-0)
Connah's Quay - Penybont FC 2-0(1-0)
Haverfordwest - Newtown AFC 2-3(2-1)
Pontypridd - The New Saints 0-2(0-1)

**Round 6 [06-07.01.2023]**
Flint Town - Aberystwyth Town 1-1(0-1)
Penybont FC - Caernarfon Town 5-1(3-0)
Airbus UK - Metropolitan 0-2(0-0)
Bala Town - Pontypridd 3-0(1-0)
Newtown AFC - Connah's Quay 0-0
The New Saints - Haverfordwest 3-1(2-0)

**Round 7 [16-17.09.2022]**
Aberystwyth Town - Connah's Quay 2-1(0-0)
Caernarfon Town - Haverfordwest 2-1(1-0)
Metropolitan - The New Saints 0-7(0-3)
Flint Town - Bala Town 1-1(0-0)
Pontypridd - Airbus UK 1-0(0-0)
Newtown AFC - Penybont FC 2-3(0-2)

**Round 8 [23-24.09.2022]**
Airbus UK - Newtown AFC 4-4(2-2)
Penybont FC - Aberystwyth Town 3-1(2-1)
Bala Town - Metropolitan 2-0(0-0)
Connah's Quay - Pontypridd 1-0(1-0)
Haverfordwest - Flint Town 1-1(1-1)
New Saints - Caernarfon 3-0(2-0) [25.10.22]

**Round 9 [27.09.2022]**
Caernarfon Town - Connah's Quay 0-2(0-0)
The New Saints - Flint Town 6-2(2-1)
Haverfordwest - Metropolitan 1-0(0-0)
Newtown AFC - Bala Town 0-2(0-1)
Penybont FC - Pontypridd 1-1(1-1)
Aberystwyth Town - Airbus UK 2-1(1-0)

**Round 10 [30.09.-01.10.2022]**
Airbus UK - Bala Town 0-6(0-4)
The New Saints - Newtown AFC 4-1(3-1)
Metropolitan - Aberystwyth Town 2-1(2-0)
Connah's Quay - Haverfordwest 1-0(0-0)
Flint Town - Penybont FC 1-1(1-1)
Pontypridd - Caernarfon Town 3-1(1-0)

**Round 11 [14-15.10.2022]**
Caernarfon Town - Flint Town 2-0(0-0)
Pontypridd - Newtown AFC 1-4(0-3)
Aberystwyth Town - Haverfordwest 2-1(1-0)
Airbus UK - Penybont FC 0-3(0-1)
Bala Town - The New Saints 0-5(0-2)
Connah's Quay - Metropolitan 2-0(1-0)

**Round 12 [21-22.10.2022]**
Caernarfon Town-Aberystwyth Town 2-1(1-0)
Haverfordwest - Bala Town 1-4(1-0)
Newtown AFC - Metropolitan 0-1(0-1)
Penybont FC - Connah's Quay 0-1(0-0)
The New Saints - Pontypridd 2-0(2-0)
Flint Town - Airbus UK 1-0(0-0)

**Round 13 [28-29.10.2022]**
Connah's Quay - Newtown AFC 3-1(2-0)
Aberystwyth Town - Flint Town 2-1(0-0)
Airbus UK - Pontypridd 0-4(0-3)
Bala Town - Penybont FC 1-1(0-1)
Metropolitan - Caernarfon Town 0-3(0-0)
Haverfordwest - The New Saints 1-3(0-2)

**Round 14 [04-06.11.2022]**
Bala Town - Aberystwyth Town 3-0(2-0)
Newtown AFC - Airbus UK 2-1(2-0)
Caernarfon Town - Penybont FC 0-2(0-1)
Flint Town - Haverfordwest 0-1(0-0)
The New Saints - Metropolitan 4-0(2-0)
Pontypridd - Connah's Quay 0-5(0-4)

**Round 15 [18-19.11.2022]**
Connah's Quay - Caernarfon Town 3-3(0-1)
Aberystwyth Town - Pontypridd 2-1(2-1)
Airbus UK - Haverfordwest 1-2(1-0)
Metropolitan - Bala Town 1-0(0-0)
Flint Town - Newtown AFC 1-4(1-0)
Penybont FC - The New Saints 0-0

**Round 16 [02.12.2022]**
Airbus UK - Connah's Quay 1-2(0-1)
Bala Town - Flint Town 1-0(0-0)
Caernarfon Town - Newtown AFC 2-3(1-2)
Haverfordwest - Penybont FC 2-1(2-0)
Pontypridd - Metropolitan 0-1(0-0)
The New Saints-Aberystwyth Town 11-0(4-0)

**Round 17 [10-11.12.2022]**
Flint Town - Metropolitan 1-1(0-1)
Newtown AFC - Haverfordwest 2-0(1-0)
Connah's-Aberystwyth T. 3-0(1-0) [20.12.22]
Caernarfon - New Saints 0-1(0-0) [03.01.23]
Penybont FC - Airbus UK 2-0(0-0) [03.01.23]
Pontypridd - Bala Town 2-1(2-1) [03.01.2023]

**Round 18 [16.12.2022]**
Metropolitan - Haverfordwest 2-0(1-0)
Newtown AFC - Pontypridd 4-2(3-1)
Airbus UK - Caernarfon 0-3(0-2) [10.01.23]
Bala Town - Connah's Quay 0-0 [10.01.23]
Flint T. - The New Saints 1-8(1-4) [10.01.23]
Aberystwyth - Penybont 0-3(0-2) [10.01.23]

**Round 19 [22-23.12.2022]**
Metropolitan - Newtown AFC 2-1(1-1)
Bala Town - Airbus UK 2-1(0-0)
Connah's Quay - The New Saints 1-1(0-0)
Flint Town - Caernarfon Town 2-1(1-0)
Haverfordwest - Aberystwyth Town 3-1(2-1)
Pontypridd - Penybont FC 0-1(0-0)

**Round 20 [26.12.2022]**
Aberystwyth Town - Newtown AFC 1-2(1-2)
Caernarfon Town - Bala Town 1-5(1-2)
Connah's Quay - Flint Town 2-0(0-0)
Penybont FC - Metropolitan 1-3(0-1)
Pontypridd - Haverfordwest 3-2(2-1)
The New Saints - Airbus UK 7-0(3-0)

**Round 21 [30-31.12.2022]**
Newtown AFC - Aberystwyth Town 6-1(1-0)
Bala Town - Caernarfon Town 3-0(2-0)
Metropolitan - Penybont FC 0-0
Airbus UK - The New Saints 0-8(0-6)
Flint Town - Connah's Quay 0-0
Haverfordwest - Pontypridd 1-1(0-0)

**Round 22 [21.01.2023]**
Aberystwyth Town-Caernarfon Town 2-1(1-0)
Metropolitan - Airbus UK 3-1(1-0)
Flint Town - Pontypridd 4-1(2-0)
Penybont - Newtown 3-0(3-0) [28.01.23]
New Saints - Bala Town 3-0(1-0) [31.01.23]
Haverfordwest - Connah's 2-1(2-1) [31.01.23]

## Final Standings

| | | | | | | | | |
|---|---|---|---|---|---|---|---|---|
| 1. | The New Saints FC | 22 | 19 | 3 | 0 | 83 - 8 | 60 |
| 2. | Connah's Quay Nomads FC | 22 | 13 | 5 | 4 | 33 - 14 | 44 |
| 3. | Penybont FC Bridgend | 22 | 12 | 5 | 5 | 37 - 19 | 41 |
| 4. | Cardiff Metropolitan University FC | 22 | 13 | 2 | 7 | 29 - 29 | 41 |
| 5. | Bala Town FC | 22 | 12 | 4 | 6 | 42 - 21 | 40 |
| 6. | Newtown AFC | 22 | 10 | 3 | 9 | 41 - 39 | 33 |
| 7. | Haverfordwest County AFC | 22 | 8 | 3 | 11 | 29 - 35 | 27 |
| 8. | Caernarfon Town FC | 22 | 8 | 1 | 13 | 33 - 41 | 25 |
| 9. | Flint Town United FC | 22 | 6 | 6 | 10 | 24 - 37 | 24 |
| 10. | Aberystwyth Town FC | 22 | 7 | 1 | 14 | 23 - 58 | 22 |
| 11. | Pontypridd United AFC | 22 | 6 | 2 | 14 | 22 - 42 | 20 |
| 12. | Airbus UK Broughton FC | 22 | 0 | 1 | 21 | 13 - 66 | -2 |

Teams ranked 1-6 were qualified for the Championship Round, while teams ranked 7-12 were qualified for the Relegation Round.

## Relegation Round

**Round 23 [11.02.2023]**
Caernarfon Town - Haverfordwest 2-0(0-0)
Flint Town - Aberystwyth Town 5-0(2-0)
Pontypridd - Airbus UK 4-0(2-0)

**Round 24 [17-18.02.2023]**
Airbus UK - Caernarfon Town 0-2(0-0)
Aberystwyth Town - Pontypridd 3-3(1-0)
Haverfordwest - Flint Town 3-1(2-1)

**Round 25 [24-25.02.2023]**
Airbus UK - Aberystwyth Town 1-7(0-2)
Caernarfon Town - Flint Town 2-2(1-1)
Pontypridd - Haverfordwest 2-1(1-1)

**Round 26 [11.03.2023]**
Aberystwyth Town - Haverfordwest 0-1(0-0)
Flint Town - Airbus UK 2-1(1-1)
Pontypridd - Caernarfon Town 1-0(1-0)

**Round 27 [17-18.03.2023]**
Caernarfon Town-Aberystwyth Town 0-1(0-1)
Flint Town - Pontypridd 0-0
Haverfordwest - Airbus UK 4-0(1-0)

**Round 28 [25.03.2023]**
Haverfordwest - Caernarfon Town 2-2(1-1)
Aberystwyth Town - Flint Town 1-0(0-0)
Airbus UK - Pontypridd 0-3(0-2)

**Round 29 [31.03.-01.04.2023]**
Caernarfon Town - Airbus UK 4-0(2-0)
Flint Town - Haverfordwest 0-2(0-2)
Pontypridd - Aberystwyth Town 1-1(1-0)

**Round 30 [07-08.04.2023]**
Haverfordwest - Pontypridd 2-0(1-0)
Aberystwyth Town - Airbus UK 1-1(0-0)
Flint Town - Caernarfon 2-3(2-1) [19.04.23]

**Round 31 [14-15.04.2023]**
Airbus UK - Flint Town 1-3(0-1)
Caernarfon Town - Pontypridd 1-2(0-0)
Haverfordwest - Aberystwyth Town 1-1(0-1)

**Round 32 [22.04.2023]**
Aberystwyth Town-Caernarfon Town 3-2(1-2)
Pontypridd - Flint Town 3-2(1-1)
Airbus UK - Haverfordwest 1-4(1-1)

## Championship Round

**Round 23 [11.02.2023]**
Metropolitan - The New Saints 3-2(1-2)
Bala Town - Penybont FC 0-0
Newtown AFC - Connah's Quay 1-1(1-0)

**Round 24 [17-18.02.2023]**
Penybont FC - Metropolitan 2-1(1-0)
Connah's Quay - Bala Town 1-1(1-0)
The New Saints - Newtown AFC 1-0(1-0)

**Round 25 [25.02.2023]**
The New Saints - Penybont FC 1-1(1-0)
Connah's Quay - Metropolitan 2-1(1-0)
Newtown AFC - Bala Town 3-2(0-1)

**Round 26 [10-13.03.2023]**
Metropolitan - Newtown AFC 0-0
Penybont FC - Connah's Quay 1-1(0-0)
The New Saints - Bala Town 2-1(1-1)

**Round 27 [17-18.03.2023]**
Connah's Quay - The New Saints 0-0
Bala Town - Metropolitan 0-0
Newtown AFC - Penybont FC 0-1(0-0)

**Round 28 [24-25.03.2023]**
Connah's Quay - Newtown AFC 2-0(0-0)
The New Saints - Metropolitan 7-1(4-1)
Penybont FC - Bala Town 2-2(1-0)

**Round 29 [31.03.-01.04.2023]**
Metropolitan - Penybont FC 2-3(1-0)
Bala Town - Connah's Quay 1-2(1-2)
Newtown AFC - The New Saints 0-5(0-2)

**Round 30 [07-08.04.2023]**
Bala Town - Newtown AFC 1-2(0-0)
Penybont FC - The New Saints 2-5(0-2)
Metropolitan - Connah's Quay 0-2(0-2)

**Round 31 [14-15.04.2023]**
Bala Town - The New Saints 0-2(0-0)
Newtown AFC - Metropolitan 1-2(0-0)
Connah's Quay - Penybont FC 0-0

**Round 32 [22.04.2023]**
The New Saints - Connah's Quay 4-1(1-0)
Metropolitan - Bala Town 2-1(2-0)
Penybont FC - Newtown AFC 2-1(0-1)

## Final Standings

| | | | | Total | | | | | Home | | | | | Away | | | |
|---|---|---|---|---|---|---|---|---|---|---|---|---|---|---|---|---|---|
| 1. | **The New Saints FC** | 32 | 26 | 5 | 1 | 112 - 17 | **83** | 15 | 1 | 0 | 61 - 9 | | 11 | 4 | 1 | 51 - 8 |
| 2. | Connah's Quay Nomads FC | 32 | 17 | 10 | 5 | 45 - 23 | **61** | 11 | 5 | 0 | 25 - 7 | | 6 | 5 | 5 | 20 - 16 |
| 3. | Penybont FC Bridgend[1] | 32 | 16 | 10 | 6 | 51 - 32 | **52** | 9 | 4 | 3 | 31 - 20 | | 7 | 6 | 3 | 18 - 12 |
| 4. | Cardiff Metropolitan University FC | 32 | 16 | 4 | 12 | 41 - 49 | **52** | 10 | 2 | 4 | 23 - 21 | | 6 | 2 | 8 | 18 - 28 |
| 5. | Bala Town FC | 32 | 12 | 8 | 12 | 51 - 37 | **44** | 7 | 5 | 4 | 21 - 14 | | 5 | 3 | 8 | 30 - 23 |
| 6. | Newtown AFC | 32 | 12 | 5 | 15 | 49 - 56 | **41** | 6 | 3 | 7 | 23 - 24 | | 6 | 2 | 8 | 26 - 32 |
| 7. | Haverfordwest County AFC | 32 | 14 | 5 | 13 | 49 - 44 | **47** | 9 | 4 | 3 | 30 - 19 | | 5 | 1 | 10 | 19 - 25 |
| 8. | Pontypridd United AFC | 32 | 12 | 5 | 15 | 41 - 52 | **41** | 9 | 1 | 6 | 23 - 23 | | 3 | 4 | 9 | 18 - 29 |
| 9. | Caernarfon Town FC | 32 | 12 | 3 | 17 | 51 - 54 | **39** | 8 | 1 | 7 | 28 - 22 | | 4 | 2 | 10 | 23 - 32 |
| 10. | Aberystwyth Town FC | 32 | 11 | 5 | 16 | 41 - 73 | **38** | 8 | 2 | 6 | 22 - 28 | | 3 | 3 | 10 | 19 - 45 |
| 11. | Flint Town United FC (*Relegated*) | 32 | 9 | 8 | 15 | 41 - 53 | **35** | 5 | 6 | 5 | 22 - 25 | | 4 | 2 | 10 | 19 - 28 |
| 12. | Airbus UK Broughton FC[1] (*Relegated*) | 32 | 0 | 2 | 30 | 18 - 100 | **-4** | 0 | 1 | 15 | 11 - 58 | | 0 | 1 | 15 | 7 - 42 |

Teams ranked 4-7 were qualified for the European Conference League.
[1] *6 points deducted for fielding ineligible players.*

## Top goalscorers:

| | | |
|---|---|---|
| 29 | **Declan Joseph McManus (SCO)** | *The New Saints FC* |
| 15 | Ryan Brobbel (NIR) | *The New Saints FC* |
| 14 | Jordan Davies | *Haverfordwest County AFC* |
| 14 | Aaron John Williams (ENG) | *Newtown AFC* |

## European Conference League Play-offs

| **Semi-Finals [05-06.05.2023]** | Bala Town FC - Newtown AFC | 2-4(1-2) |
|---|---|---|
| | Cardiff Metropolitan University FC - Haverfordwest County AFC | 0-0 aet; 3-4 pen |

| **Final [13.05.2023]** | Newtown AFC - **Haverfordwest County AFC** | 1-1(1-1,1-1,1-1); 3-4 pen |
|---|---|---|

# NATIONAL CUP
## Welsh Cup 2022/2023

### Third Round [11-12.11.2022]

| | | | | |
|---|---|---|---|---|
| Penydarren Boys & Girls - Trethomas Bluebirds AFC | 1-0 | Cwmbran Celtic FC - Carmarthen Town AFC | 4-3 |
| The New Saints FC - Caernarfon Town FC | 2-1 | Buckley Town FC - Prestatyn Town FC | 2-0 |
| Connah's Quay Nomads FC - Colwyn Bay FC | 4-0 | Aberystwyth Town - Newtown AFC | 1-3 |
| Cefn Druids AFC - Llanelli Town AFC | 3-4 | Airbus UK Broughton FC - Trefelin Boys & Girls Club | 2-1 |
| Ruthin Town FC - Pontypridd United AFC | 3-4 | Bala Town FC - Flint Town United FC | 2-0 |
| Pontardawe Town FC - Pill FC Pillgwenlly | 3-1 | Hakin United Milford Haven - Holywell Town FC | 1-5 |
| Guilsfield FC - Goytre United FC | 6-3 | Mold Alexandra FC - Briton Ferry Llansawel AFC | 0-4 |
| Conwy Borough FC - Penybont FC Bridgend | 0-3 | Barry Town United FC - Gresford Athletic FC | 0-2 |

### 1/8-Finals [14/25.01.2023]

| | | | | |
|---|---|---|---|---|
| Guilsfield FC - Holywell Town FC | 1-2(0-2) | Pontardawe Town FC - Airbus UK Broughton FC | 1-1 aet; 4-5 pen |
| Gresford Athletic FC - Penybont FC Bridgend | 0-2(0-1) | Bala Town FC - Pontypridd United AFC | 2-1(1-0) |
| Briton Ferry Llansawel AFC - Buckley Town FC | 2-2 aet; 8-7 pen | Llanelli Town AFC - Connah's Quay Nomads FC | 0-2(0-1) |
| The New Saints FC - Newtown AFC | 7-0(4-0) | Penydarren Boys & Girls - Cwmbran Celtic FC | 2-3(0-3) |

### Quarter-Finals [04-05.02.2023]

| | | | | |
|---|---|---|---|---|
| Cwmbran Celtic FC - The New Saints FC | 1-3(1-1) | Connah's Quay Nomads FC - Airbus UK Broughton | 5-0(1-0) |
| Bala Town FC - Briton Ferry Llansawel AFC | 2-0(0-0) | Penybont FC Bridgend - Holywell Town FC | 2-1(0-1) |

### Semi-Finals [03-04.03.2023]

| | | | | |
|---|---|---|---|---|
| Bala Town FC - Connah's Quay Nomads FC | 3-2(0-1) | Penybont FC Bridgend - The New Saints FC | 0-2(0-2) |

### Final

30.04.2023; Nantporth Stadium, Bangor; Referee: Nicholas Pratt; Attendance: n/a
**The New Saints FC - Bala Town FC**                    **6-0(1-0)**

**The New Saints FC**: Connor Roberts, Chris Marriott, Blaine Hudson, Daniel Davies, Ryan Astles, Jon Routledge (80.Daniel Williams), Daniel Redmond, Ryan Brobbel, Leo Smith (66.Ben Clark), Declan Joseph McManus (74.Jordan Lee Raymond Williams), Joshua Daniels (80.Adrian Cieślewicz). Trainer: Craig Harrison (England).

**Bala Town FC**: Alex Ramsay, Antony Kay, Nathan Peate, Naim Arsan, David Edwards, Kieran Smith (62.George Newell), Nathan Burke, Oliver Shannon, Lassana Nalatche Mendes (64.Luke Wall), Paul Rutherford (87.James Davies), Chris Venables (62.Ross White). Trainer: Colin Caton.

**Goals:** 1-0 Declan Joseph McManus (19), 2-0 Daniel Redmond (51), 3-0 Ryan Brobbel (56), 4-0 Jordan Lee Raymond Williams (87), 5-0 Adrian Cieślewicz (88), 6-0 Ryan Brobbel (90+1).

Please note: appearances and goals includes statistics of both regular season and play-offs (Championship and Relegation).

## Aberystwyth Town Football Club

| Founded: | 1884 | |
|---|---|---|
| Stadium: | Park Avenue, Aberystwyth (5,000) | |
| Trainer: | Anthony Simon Williams | 20.09.1977 |

| Goalkeepers: | DOB | M | (s) | G |
|---|---|---|---|---|
| Leigh Jenkins | 16.10.1991 | 4 | | |
| Matthew Turner | 27.03.2002 | 13 | | 1 |
| Lewis Webb | 12.09.2001 | 15 | | |
| Defenders: | DOB | M | (s) | G |
| Louis Bradford (ENG) | 21.02.2002 | 26 | | 3 |
| Benjamin Erickson | 04.12.2000 | 4 | (2) | |
| Harri Horwood | 24.04.2000 | 16 | (1) | |
| Jamie Jones | 16.01.2004 | | (4) | |
| Billy Kirkman (ENG) | 26.02.2004 | 12 | | |
| Sam Litchfield | 17.03.1993 | 27 | (1) | 2 |
| Philip Perry | 23.09.2002 | 4 | (4) | |
| Jack Rimmer | 29.03.1999 | 13 | (2) | |
| Liam Walsh | 26.07.1996 | 12 | | |

| Midfielders: | DOB | M | (s) | G |
|---|---|---|---|---|
| Harry Arnison (ENG) | 12.03.2002 | 26 | | 5 |
| Jake Canavan (ENG) | 17.12.2003 | 6 | (3) | 1 |
| Charley Edge | 14.05.1997 | 11 | (4) | |
| Jonathan Evans | 10.03.1993 | 19 | (8) | 8 |
| Iwan Lewis | 19.06.1993 | 32 | | 2 |
| Jack Thorn (ENG) | 22.03.2001 | 31 | | 2 |
| Forwards: | DOB | M | (s) | G |
| Cameron Allen | 04.05.2005 | 1 | (4) | |
| Mark Cadwallader (ENG) | 08.07.1988 | 8 | (2) | 5 |
| Alex Darlington | 26.12.1988 | 8 | (13) | 4 |
| Steffan Davies | 14.07.1989 | 11 | (8) | |
| Niall Flint (ENG) | 15.08.1997 | 29 | (1) | 6 |
| John Owen | 18.08.1992 | 16 | (6) | 1 |
| Sam Phillips | 24.02.1999 | 8 | (8) | |

## Airbus UK Broughton Football Club

| Founded: | 1946 [as Vickers-Armstrong] | |
|---|---|---|
| Stadium: | The Airfield, Broughton (1,600) | |
| Trainer: | Steve O'Shaughnessy | 13.10.1967 |
| [19.10.2022] | Jamie Lee Reed | 02.09.1976 |
| [21.04.2023] | Mark Allen | 02.09.1976 |

| Goalkeepers: | DOB | M | (s) | G |
|---|---|---|---|---|
| Lewis Dutton | 03.06.2001 | 28 | | |
| Mike Jones (ENG) | 16.06.1993 | 3 | | |
| Bradley Kelly (ENG) | 24.10.2003 | 1 | | |
| Defenders: | DOB | M | (s) | G |
| Lewis Bevan | | | (2) | |
| Gareth Edwards | 20.07.1983 | 15 | (2) | |
| Reward Mwakona (ENG) | 16.06.1998 | 10 | (5) | |
| Billy Nicholas | 10.01.2003 | 3 | | |
| Elliott Orton | 13.03.2004 | 8 | (2) | |
| Owen Payne | 02.04.2001 | 20 | (3) | 1 |
| Philip Perry (ENG) | 23.09.2002 | 5 | | |
| Jake Phillips | 31.01.1997 | 28 | (1) | 1 |
| Daniel Roberts | 26.05.2000 | 6 | | 1 |
| Steve Tomassen (ENG) | 03.09.1993 | 20 | (3) | 2 |
| Sean Wilson (ENG) | 02.03.2003 | 3 | | |
| Midfielders: | DOB | M | (s) | G |
| Johnny Black (NIR) | 26.02.1988 | | (1) | |
| Beau Cornish | 05.11.2001 | 22 | (6) | 1 |
| Jamie Crowther | 10.02.1992 | 18 | (5) | |

| | DOB | M | (s) | G |
|---|---|---|---|---|
| Aaron Edwards (ENG) | 17.02.2004 | 1 | | |
| Ryan Edwards | 22.06.1988 | 21 | (1) | |
| Tyler Ryan McManus (ENG) | | 12 | (5) | |
| Joe Palmer | 13.08.1999 | 26 | (2) | 1 |
| George Peers | 23.09.2000 | 21 | (1) | 1 |
| Sam Rickett (ENG) | 12.12.2002 | 10 | (2) | |
| Thomas Williams (ENG) | 31.10.2003 | 1 | (1) | |
| Forwards: | DOB | M | (s) | G |
| Sam Frederick Baker (ENG) | 02.12.2004 | | (6) | |
| Michael Burke (ENG) | 19.10.2002 | 9 | (8) | |
| Kaiden Anthony Cooke | | 2 | (12) | 1 |
| Craig Curran (ENG) | 23.08.1989 | 6 | (2) | |
| Mamudo Dabo (POR) | 10.11.1997 | 5 | (4) | 1 |
| Adam Davies (ENG) | 13.10.1996 | 16 | (3) | 4 |
| Lloyd Dean (ENG) | 17.07.1988 | 5 | (3) | |
| Jake Eyre | 02.11.1995 | 12 | (3) | 3 |
| Brad Knight (ENG) | 30.08.2004 | 4 | (7) | |
| Jeanny Leblanc-Akpo (ENG) | 03.02.2002 | 7 | (4) | |
| Finn Savage | 23.04.2002 | 4 | (8) | 1 |

## Bala Town Football Club

| Founded: | 1880 | |
|---|---|---|
| Stadium: | Maes Tegid Stadium, Bala (3,000) | |
| Trainer: | Colin Caton | 22.08.1970 |

| Goalkeepers: | DOB | M | (s) | G |
|---|---|---|---|---|
| Harry Lloyd | 30.04.1997 | 8 | (1) | |
| Alex Ramsay | 15.07.1993 | 24 | | |
| Defenders: | DOB | M | (s) | G |
| Naim Arsan | 14.12.1993 | 27 | (2) | |
| Nathan Peate | 02.05.1991 | 28 | | 4 |
| Oliver Southern (ENG) | 14.01.2002 | 18 | (2) | |
| Ross White | 23.06.1996 | 26 | (2) | |
| Calum Woods (ENG) | 05.02.1987 | 1 | | |
| Midfielders: | DOB | M | (s) | G |
| Michael Ashworth (ENG) | 11.10.2003 | | (2) | |
| Nathan Burke (ENG) | 15.09.1995 | 8 | (1) | 1 |
| David Edwards | 03.02.1986 | 22 | (1) | 2 |
| Soulayman El Amri (ITA) | 11.05.1998 | | (7) | |
| Ethan Jones (ENG) | 16.10.2004 | | (5) | |

| | DOB | M | (s) | G |
|---|---|---|---|---|
| Antony Kay (ENG) | 21.10.1982 | 24 | | 2 |
| Lassana Nalatche Mendes (GNB) | 26.12.1996 | 27 | (2) | 4 |
| Elis Puw | 05.03.2006 | | (1) | |
| Oliver Shannon (ENG) | 12.09.1995 | 22 | (8) | 3 |
| Kieran Smith (ENG) | 03.06.1992 | 24 | | 3 |
| Forwards: | DOB | M | (s) | G |
| Christoph Aziamale (GER) | 18.12.1997 | | (1) | |
| James Davies | 02.10.1993 | 1 | (19) | 1 |
| Alex Fletcher (ENG) | 30.08.2004 | | (1) | |
| George Newell (ENG) | 27.01.1997 | 27 | (3) | 9 |
| Adam Roscrow | 17.02.1995 | 8 | (4) | 7 |
| Paul Rutherford (ENG) | 10.07.1987 | 11 | (12) | |
| Chris Venables | 23.07.1985 | 27 | (1) | 7 |
| Luke Wall (ENG) | 11.11.1996 | 19 | (7) | 7 |

## Caernarfon Town Football Club

**Founded**: 1937
**Stadium**: The Oval, Caernarfon (3,000)
**Trainer**: Huw Griffiths — 09.02.1977
[18.03.2023] Richard Owain Davies — 03.07.1985

| Goalkeepers: | DOB | M | (s) | G |
|---|---|---|---|---|
| Tyler French | 14.10.1996 | 1 | (1) | |
| Joshua Tibbetts (ENG) | 05.07.1998 | 27 | | |
| Ryan Woods | 21.10.1990 | 4 | | |
| **Defenders:** | **DOB** | **M** | **(s)** | **G** |
| Dion Donohue | 26.08.1993 | 13 | (1) | 2 |
| Harold Essien (ENG) | 22.12.2001 | | (4) | |
| Cai Griffith | 17.07.2005 | 3 | (3) | |
| Guto Wyn Griffith | | | (1) | |
| Gruffydd John | 22.06.1994 | 30 | | 1 |
| Alec Takunda Mudimu (ZIM) | 08.04.1995 | 2 | (3) | |
| Cai Powell-Roberts | 03.08.1999 | 10 | (2) | |
| Aaron Simpson | 19.10.1995 | 15 | (1) | |
| Ryan Williams | 07.10.1998 | 12 | (2) | |
| **Midfielders:** | **DOB** | **M** | **(s)** | **G** |
| Rhys Alun | 13.11.1997 | 2 | (8) | 1 |
| Laurence Bell (ENG) | 01.09.1992 | 20 | (2) | 2 |
| Sion Bradley | 20.02.1998 | 25 | (5) | 4 |
| Iwan Cartwright | 09.08.1996 | 29 | | 1 |
| Noah Edwards | 30.05.1996 | 29 | | 2 |
| Caio Evans | 18.12.2004 | | (2) | |
| Joe Faux (AUS) | 06.08.1996 | 26 | (4) | 7 |
| Danny Gosset | 30.09.1994 | 22 | (4) | 1 |
| Rob Hughes | 22.04.1992 | 13 | (11) | 4 |
| Darren Thomas | 20.01.1987 | 23 | (4) | 6 |
| Ben Wynne (ENG) | 20.04.2002 | 20 | (8) | 5 |
| **Forwards:** | **DOB** | **M** | **(s)** | **G** |
| Osian Evans | 13.07.2006 | | (13) | |
| Michael Peter Hayes (ENG) | 21.11.1987 | 1 | (1) | |
| Gruffydd Michael Wyn Jones | 31.01.2005 | | (1) | |
| Lloyd Marsh-Hughes | 27.04.2001 | 17 | (6) | 6 |
| Fabrizio Murtas | 03.07.2005 | | (8) | |
| Fidel O'Rourke | 05.02.2002 | 8 | (2) | 7 |

## Cardiff Metropolitan University Football Club

**Founded**: 2000 (*as UWIC Inter Cardiff*)
**Stadium**: Cyncoed Campus, Cardiff (1,620)
**Trainer**: Ryan Jenkins — 14.01.1984
[30.01.2023] Christian Edwards — 25.11.1975

| Goalkeepers: | DOB | M | (s) | G |
|---|---|---|---|---|
| Alex Lang | 10.10.1999 | 32 | | |
| **Defenders:** | **DOB** | **M** | **(s)** | **G** |
| Matthew Chubb (ENG) | 31.08.1998 | 27 | | 2 |
| Christopher Jack Craven | 03.10.2000 | 30 | | 1 |
| Jac Tomos Davies | 28.02.2001 | 4 | (3) | |
| Alaric Jones | 09.02.2001 | 12 | (6) | |
| Emlyn Lewis | 14.06.1996 | 31 | | 1 |
| Kyle McCarthy | 12.04.1993 | 25 | | |
| Cian Williams | 11.04.2003 | 5 | (6) | |
| **Midfielders:** | **DOB** | **M** | **(s)** | **G** |
| Chris Baker | 29.11.1993 | 30 | | 2 |
| Charlie Bullock | 01.08.2004 | | (2) | |
| Charlie Corsby (ENG) | 14.10.1991 | 4 | (5) | |
| Craig Davies | 18.10.2000 | 1 | (13) | 1 |
| Harris Feltham (ENG) | 19.09.2003 | | (2) | |
| Dixon Kabongo | 21.11.2003 | 11 | (11) | |
| Tom Price | 26.11.1999 | 19 | (1) | |
| Jack Veale (ENG) | 01.10.2002 | 4 | (6) | 1 |
| **Forwards:** | **DOB** | **M** | **(s)** | **G** |
| Dan Bowen | 11.09.2004 | | (1) | |
| Eliot Evans | 26.11.1991 | 29 | (1) | 9 |
| Elliot Humphries | 28.06.2005 | | (1) | |
| Samuel Jones | 08.12.1998 | 30 | | 9 |
| Harry Owen (ENG) | 15.02.1996 | 32 | | 4 |
| Lewis Rees | 01.07.2002 | 26 | (4) | 9 |
| Brandon Roberts | 26.08.2003 | | (2) | |

## Connah's Quay Nomads Football Club

**Founded**: 1946
**Stadium**: Deeside Stadium, Connah's Quay (1,500)
**Trainer**: Neil David Gibson — 10.10.1979

| Goalkeepers: | DOB | M | (s) | G |
|---|---|---|---|---|
| Andrew Firth (ENG) | 26.09.1996 | 32 | | |
| **Defenders:** | **DOB** | **M** | **(s)** | **G** |
| John Disney (IRL) | 15.05.1992 | 31 | | 1 |
| Ryan Harrington | 03.10.1998 | 27 | (3) | 2 |
| Danny Holmes (ENG) | 06.01.1989 | 16 | (3) | |
| George Horan (ENG) | 18.02.1982 | 27 | (1) | 4 |
| Benjamin Nash | 23.07.1998 | 30 | (1) | 4 |
| Kris Owens (ENG) | 07.12.1998 | 2 | (2) | |
| Dan Roberts | 26.05.2000 | 2 | (1) | |
| **Midfielders:** | **DOB** | **M** | **(s)** | **G** |
| Callum Bratley (ENG) | 12.03.1995 | 20 | (4) | |
| Aeron Edwards | 16.02.1988 | 11 | (7) | 1 |
| Harry Franklin (NIR) | 02.12.1999 | 11 | (7) | 4 |
| Callum Morris (ENG) | 01.09.1992 | 26 | (2) | 4 |
| Arnaldo Paulo Fernandes Mendes (POR) | 08.07.1993 | 17 | (10) | 2 |
| Anderson Rene Pinto Nogueira (POR) | 11.02.1994 | | (5) | |
| Ryan Stratulis (ENG) | 18.04.2003 | 11 | (4) | 2 |
| Josh Williams | 13.07.2004 | 18 | (2) | 1 |
| **Forwards:** | **DOB** | **M** | **(s)** | **G** |
| Mike Hayes (ENG) | 21.11.1987 | 9 | (9) | 5 |
| Luca Daniel Hogan | | | (7) | |
| Jack Kenny (ENG) | 14.10.1991 | 11 | | 2 |
| Joe Malkin (ENG) | 18.07.1998 | 9 | (6) | 3 |
| Michael Wilde | 27.08.1983 | 23 | (1) | 10 |
| Aron Williams | 08.11.1995 | 19 | (2) | |

## Flint Town United Football Club

**Founded**: 1886
**Stadium**: Cae-y-Castell Stadium, Flint (1,000)
**Trainer**: Lee Anthony Fowler — 10.06.1983

| Goalkeepers: | DOB | M | (s) | G |
|---|---|---|---|---|
| Harry Allen (ENG) | 01.11.2001 | 26 | | |
| Dawid Szczepaniak (POL) | 13.04.2000 | 6 | | |
| **Defenders:** | **DOB** | **M** | **(s)** | **G** |
| Bobby Beaumont | 25.03.2002 | 30 | | 2 |
| Brandon Diau (CGO) | 02.06.1993 | 30 | | 4 |
| Tyler Garratt (ENG) | 26.10.1996 | 16 | (2) | |
| Alec Takunda Mudimu (ZIM) | 08.04.1995 | 4 | (1) | |
| Harry Owen | 14.07.2003 | 29 | | 3 |
| Morgan Elliot Roberts (ENG) | 20.12.2000 | 1 | (3) | |
| Anthony Stephens | 21.01.1994 | 23 | | 2 |
| **Midfielders:** | **DOB** | **M** | **(s)** | **G** |
| Jordan Carroll (IRL) | 24.10.2000 | 20 | (8) | 1 |
| Larnell Cole (ENG) | 09.03.1993 | 8 | (9) | 2 |
| Harvey Drazdauskas | 11.04.2006 | | (1) | |
| Soulayman El Amri (ITA) | 11.05.1998 | | (1) | |
| Liam Ellis (ENG) | 16.04.2003 | | (2) | |
| Danny Harrison (ENG) | 04.11.1982 | 31 | | 3 |
| Ben Daniel Hughes | 12.10.2004 | 8 | (17) | 1 |
| Omar Ibrahim | 04.07.2000 | 13 | (7) | |
| Ashton Mather (ENG) | 03.04.2005 | | (1) | |
| Jay Owen | 14.01.1991 | 24 | | 1 |
| **Forwards:** | **DOB** | **M** | **(s)** | **G** |
| Jean-Louis Akpa-Akpro (CIV) | 04.01.1985 | 29 | (1) | 7 |
| Harley Brindley-Peagram | 12.11.2005 | | (6) | |
| Mark Cadwallader (ENG) | 08.07.1988 | 7 | (1) | 1 |
| Zack Clarke | 25.01.2003 | 9 | | 6 |
| Jack Hindle (ENG) | 29.10.1993 | 5 | (5) | |
| Callum Huxley | 07.10.2001 | | (1) | |
| Rhys Kavanagh (ENG) | 29.09.1998 | 7 | (5) | 1 |
| Jayden Major (ENG) | 29.08.2002 | 3 | (4) | |
| Okera Simmonds (ENG) | 25.12.1999 | 23 | (3) | 7 |

## Haverfordwest County Association Football Club

| | | |
|---|---|---|
| **Founded**: | 1899 | |
| **Stadium**: | Bridge Meadow Stadium, Haverfordwest (2,100) | |
| **Trainer**: | Anthony Pennock | 10.04.1971 |

| Goalkeepers: | DOB | M | (s) | G |
|---|---|---|---|---|
| Lewis Brass (ENG) | 26.08.1996 | 2 | | |
| John Chesters | 14.07.2006 | | (1) | |
| Lee Idzi | 08.02.1988 | 8 | (1) | |
| Zac Maxwell Jones (NZL) | 27.11.2000 | 22 | (1) | |
| **Defenders:** | **DOB** | **M** | **(s)** | **G** |
| Rhys Abbruzzese | 28.03.1998 | 30 | | 2 |
| Oscar Borg (ENG) | 05.09.1997 | 7 | (1) | |
| Lucas Davies | 12.02.2005 | | (1) | |
| Ryan George | 27.11.2001 | 7 | (10) | |
| Iori Humphreys | 24.03.2004 | 6 | (7) | 1 |
| Lee Jenkins | 30.08.2001 | 31 | | 1 |
| Kyle Patten | 21.07.1994 | 14 | (3) | 1 |
| Dylan Rees | 17.09.1996 | 25 | | 2 |
| Jazz Richards | 12.04.1991 | 15 | (1) | 1 |
| **Midfielders:** | **DOB** | **M** | **(s)** | **G** |
| Ioan Evans | 22.09.2001 | 10 | (8) | 3 |
| Harri John | 04.04.2006 | 9 | (10) | |
| Henry Jones | 18.09.1993 | 15 | (4) | 2 |
| Elliot Scotcher | 03.03.1994 | 11 | (2) | 1 |
| Corey Shephard | 28.12.1997 | 8 | (4) | 1 |
| Jamie Veale | 28.11.1996 | 22 | (5) | 3 |
| Ricky Watts | 07.11.1991 | 12 | (7) | |
| Seth Woodhouse | | | (1) | |
| **Forwards:** | **DOB** | **M** | **(s)** | **G** |
| Jordan Davies | 16.11.1995 | 30 | (2) | 14 |
| Elliott Dugan (ENG) | 18.09.2000 | 8 | (10) | 2 |
| Ben Fawcett | 07.09.2000 | 24 | (1) | 6 |
| Daniel Hawkins | 22.04.2001 | 4 | (2) | 2 |
| Daniel James | 30.11.2004 | | (3) | |
| Jack Leahy (ENG) | 17.09.2002 | 4 | (5) | 1 |
| Ivan Watkins | 28.12.2001 | 1 | (4) | |
| Jack Wilson | 12.04.2001 | 27 | (2) | 6 |

## Newtown Association Football Club

| | | |
|---|---|---|
| **Founded**: | 1875 | |
| **Stadium**: | Latham Park, Newtown (5,000) | |
| **Trainer**: | Chris Hughes (SCO) | 12.09.1979 |

| Goalkeepers: | DOB | M | (s) | G |
|---|---|---|---|---|
| Josh Hyde | 07.12.2004 | | (1) | |
| David Jones | 03.02.1990 | 32 | | |
| **Defenders:** | **DOB** | **M** | **(s)** | **G** |
| Matthew Jones | 14.07.1999 | 13 | (12) | 2 |
| Kieran Mills-Evans | 11.10.1992 | 17 | (2) | 2 |
| Callum Roberts | 16.10.1998 | 22 | | 1 |
| Ryan Sears | 30.12.1998 | 29 | | |
| Shane Sutton | 31.01.1989 | 24 | | |
| Brett Taylor (ENG) | 22.12.2000 | 6 | (3) | |
| Craig Williams | 21.12.1987 | 19 | (3) | |
| **Midfielders:** | **DOB** | **M** | **(s)** | **G** |
| Henry Cowans (ENG) | 02.10.1996 | 20 | (8) | 2 |
| Dylan Downs (ENG) | 14.09.2003 | | (8) | |
| Zevai Gabriel (ENG) | | | (2) | |
| George Hughes (ENG) | 23.03.1999 | 27 | (3) | |
| Nick Rushton | 03.02.1992 | 26 | (4) | 6 |
| Jake Walker (ENG) | 03.11.2000 | 24 | (6) | 2 |
| Theo Jay Wharton (SKN) | 15.11.1994 | 3 | (10) | |
| **Forwards:** | **DOB** | **M** | **(s)** | **G** |
| Nigel Aris (ENG) | 29.01.2003 | 11 | (12) | 3 |
| Hannoch Boakye (ITA) | | | (3) | |
| Rhys Hesden (ENG) | 20.10.2002 | 1 | (8) | 1 |
| Zeli Ismail (ENG) | 12.12.1993 | 13 | (5) | 4 |
| Lifumpa Mwandwe (ENG) | 29.12.2000 | 4 | (1) | |
| Louis Robles (ENG) | 11.09.1996 | 30 | | 10 |
| Macauley Taylor | 27.10.1999 | | (3) | |
| Devon Torry | | | (4) | |
| Aaron John Williams (ENG) | 21.10.1993 | 31 | (1) | 14 |

## Penybont Football Club Bridgend

| | | |
|---|---|---|
| **Founded**: | 2013 (as merger of Bridgend Town AFC and Bryntirion Athletic FC) | |
| **Stadium**: | Bryntirion Park, Bridgend (3,000) | |
| **Trainer**: | Rhys Griffiths | 01.03.1980 |

| Goalkeepers: | DOB | M | (s) | G |
|---|---|---|---|---|
| Kelland Absalom | 05.01.1998 | 23 | | |
| Alexander Pennock | 07.02.2001 | 9 | | |
| **Defenders:** | **DOB** | **M** | **(s)** | **G** |
| Billy Borge | 22.05.1998 | 22 | (4) | 1 |
| Jak Carson | | | (1) | |
| Mael Davies | 10.10.1998 | 24 | (3) | |
| Daniel Jefferies | 30.01.1999 | 23 | | |
| Mark Little (ENG) | 20.08.1988 | 26 | (1) | |
| Kane Owen | 22.10.1994 | 29 | | 6 |
| Luke Sylvester | 12.09.1998 | | (1) | |
| Josh Yorwerth | 28.02.1995 | 18 | (1) | 2 |
| **Midfielders:** | **DOB** | **M** | **(s)** | **G** |
| Łewis Clutton | 31.08.2001 | 4 | (14) | 1 |
| Ashley Evans | 18.07.1989 | 18 | (2) | |
| Lewis Harling | 11.06.1992 | 13 | (1) | 1 |
| Shaun MacDonald | 17.06.1988 | 16 | (2) | |
| Ryan Reynolds | 15.09.2000 | 18 | (9) | 7 |
| Kai Whitmore (ENG) | 17.02.2001 | 20 | (12) | 2 |
| **Forwards:** | **DOB** | **M** | **(s)** | **G** |
| Kostya Georgievsky (NIR) | 28.06.1996 | 18 | (4) | 4 |
| Rhys Griffiths | 01.03.1980 | 1 | (1) | 1 |
| Rhys Kavanagh (ENG) | 29.09.1998 | 10 | (2) | 5 |
| Keyon Reffell | 06.10.1990 | 24 | (5) | 5 |
| Sam Snaith | 05.05.2000 | 4 | (17) | 1 |
| Tom Tweedy | 15.09.2004 | 1 | (13) | 1 |
| Nathan Wood | 23.04.1997 | 31 | (1) | 11 |

## Pontypridd United Association Football Club

| | | |
|---|---|---|
| **Founded**: | 1992 [as Pontypridd Town AFC] | |
| **Stadium**: | USW Sports Park, Treforest (1,000) | |
| **Trainer**: | Andrew Stokes | 20.12.1985 |

| Goalkeepers: | DOB | M | (s) | G |
|---|---|---|---|---|
| Ashley Morris | 31.07.1984 | 24 | | |
| George Ratcliffe | 12.09.2004 | 8 | | |
| **Defenders:** | **DOB** | **M** | **(s)** | **G** |
| Lee Baldock | 19.01.1992 | 3 | (5) | |
| Harrison Bright | 23.02.2004 | 3 | (4) | |
| Luke Cummings | 25.10.1991 | 18 | | 1 |
| Oliver Dalton | 12.05.1990 | 3 | (1) | |
| Thomas Davies | 11.11.2003 | 9 | | 4 |
| Joe Evans | 26.11.1997 | 23 | (2) | 3 |
| Jordan Knott | 13.09.1993 | 20 | (4) | |
| Harrison Lewis | 18.02.2004 | | (1) | |
| Ben Margetson | 01.09.2000 | 10 | | 2 |
| Dave Vincent | 17.06.1990 | 14 | (3) | 1 |
| Joe Woodiwiss | 10.11.2002 | 7 | (1) | |
| Jarrad Wright | 13.09.1992 | 22 | (1) | 3 |
| **Midfielders:** | **DOB** | **M** | **(s)** | **G** |
| James Bloom | 11.08.1991 | 4 | (4) | 1 |
| Clayton Green | 27.02.1994 | 27 | | 3 |
| Joe Hunt | 18.11.1999 | 20 | | |
| Jack Karadogan | 04.02.2004 | 4 | (3) | |
| Kieran Lewis | 26.06.1993 | 25 | | 2 |
| Kurtis Rees | 14.02.1994 | 16 | (6) | 1 |
| Elliot Richards | 10.09.1991 | 8 | (6) | 1 |
| James Saddler | 11.01.1992 | 7 | (6) | |
| Lewys Morgan Twamley | 26.05.2003 | 12 | (7) | |
| **Forwards:** | **DOB** | **M** | **(s)** | **G** |
| Ben Ahmun | 02.02.1992 | 28 | (2) | 13 |
| Oliver Jay Amos | 16.08.2004 | | (6) | |
| Aaron Hillier | 23.10.2003 | | (1) | |
| Corey Jenkins | 14.02.1991 | 6 | (9) | |
| Owain Jones | 01.10.1996 | 8 | (8) | 3 |
| Jamal Salawu (ENG) | 06.12.2003 | | (2) | |
| Danny Williams | 18.02.2000 | 23 | (4) | 2 |

## The New Saints of Oswestry Town & Llansantffraid Football Club

| | |
|---|---|
| **Founded**: | 1959 |
| **Stadium**: | Park Hall Stadium, Oswestry (England) (2,034) |
| **Trainer**: | Craig Harrison (ENG)   10.11.1977 |

| Goalkeepers: | DOB | M | (s) | G |
|---|---|---|---|---|
| Connor Roberts | 08.12.1992 | 32 | | |
| **Defenders:** | **DOB** | **M** | **(s)** | **G** |
| Ryan Astles | 01.07.1994 | 31 | (1) | 3 |
| Ashley Baker | 30.10.1996 | 7 | (5) | 2 |
| Daniel Davies | 28.06.1995 | 21 | (5) | 5 |
| Keston Davies | 02.10.1996 | 11 | (1) | |
| Blaine Hudson (ENG) | 28.10.1991 | 7 | (3) | |
| Billy Kirkman (ENG) | 26.02.2004 | 1 | (4) | |
| Chris Marriott (ENG) | 24.09.1989 | 24 | (1) | 2 |
| Josh Pask (ENG) | 01.11.1997 | 4 | (2) | |
| **Midfielders:** | **DOB** | **M** | **(s)** | **G** |
| Ryan Brobbel (NIR) | 05.03.1993 | 25 | (5) | 15 |
| Jake Canavan (ENG) | 17.12.2003 | | (7) | 2 |

| | DOB | M | (s) | G |
|---|---|---|---|---|
| Ben Clark | 14.10.2000 | 16 | (8) | 13 |
| Daniel Redmond (ENG) | 02.03.1991 | 30 | (1) | 5 |
| Jon Routledge (ENG) | 23.11.1989 | 25 | (5) | 1 |
| Leo Smith | 15.05.1998 | 18 | (9) | 4 |
| Daniel Williams | 19.04.2001 | 15 | (7) | 2 |
| **Forwards:** | **DOB** | **M** | **(s)** | **G** |
| Adrian Cieślewicz (POL) | 16.11.1990 | 15 | (14) | 8 |
| Gwion Dafydd | 11.03.2005 | 3 | (11) | 8 |
| Joshua Daniels (IRL) | 22.02.1996 | 28 | (2) | 5 |
| Joshua Lock | 13.08.2004 | | (1) | |
| Declan Joseph McManus (SCO) | 03.08.1994 | 21 | (4) | 29 |
| Reece Warder (ENG) | 30.09.2003 | | (2) | |
| Jordan Lee Raymond Williams (ENG) | 13.12.1992 | 3 | (5) | 1 |
| Adam Wilson (ENG) | 10.04.2000 | 15 | (3) | 7 |

## SECOND LEVEL
### 2022/2023

#### Cymru North

| | | | | | | | | | | |
|---|---|---|---|---|---|---|---|---|---|---|
| 1. | Colwyn Bay FC (*Promoted*) | 30 | 27 | 2 | 1 | 101 | - | 24 | 83 |
| 2. | Holywell Town FC | 30 | 26 | 1 | 3 | 75 | - | 22 | 79 |
| 3. | Llandudno FC | 30 | 20 | 6 | 4 | 70 | - | 23 | 66 |
| 4. | Guilsfield FC | 30 | 17 | 6 | 7 | 58 | - | 37 | 57 |
| 5. | Ruthin Town FC | 30 | 16 | 3 | 11 | 48 | - | 44 | 51 |
| 6. | Prestatyn Town FC | 30 | 14 | 4 | 12 | 66 | - | 50 | 46 |
| 7. | Cefn Druids AFC | 30 | 13 | 4 | 13 | 48 | - | 64 | 43 |
| 8. | Buckley Town FC | 30 | 12 | 6 | 12 | 53 | - | 61 | 42 |
| 9. | Mold Alexandra FC | 30 | 10 | 5 | 15 | 41 | - | 52 | 35 |
| 10. | Gresford Athletic FC | 30 | 10 | 5 | 15 | 32 | - | 43 | 35 |
| 11. | Porthmadog FC | 30 | 10 | 3 | 17 | 36 | - | 53 | 33 |
| 12. | Llanidloes Town FC | 30 | 7 | 6 | 17 | 42 | - | 63 | 27 |
| 13. | Chirk AAA FC | 30 | 5 | 11 | 14 | 32 | - | 49 | 26 |
| 14. | Conwy Borough FC (*Relegated*) | 30 | 5 | 8 | 17 | 33 | - | 64 | 23 |
| 15. | Penrhyncoch FC (*Relegated*) | 30 | 3 | 7 | 20 | 31 | - | 72 | 16 |
| 16. | Holyhead Hotspur FC (*Relegated*) | 30 | 2 | 9 | 19 | 24 | - | 69 | 15 |

#### Cymru South

| | | | | | | | | | | |
|---|---|---|---|---|---|---|---|---|---|---|
| 1. | Barry Town United FC (*Promoted*) | 30 | 25 | 3 | 2 | 78 | - | 25 | 78 |
| 2. | Llanelli Town AFC | 30 | 19 | 5 | 6 | 63 | - | 34 | 62 |
| 3. | Briton Ferry Llansawel AFC | 30 | 17 | 9 | 4 | 72 | - | 33 | 60 |
| 4. | Carmarthen Town AFC | 30 | 16 | 4 | 10 | 66 | - | 41 | 52 |
| 5. | Cambrian & Clydach Vale Boys & Girls Club | 30 | 14 | 5 | 11 | 64 | - | 53 | 47 |
| 6. | Afan Lido FC Port Talbot | 30 | 13 | 8 | 9 | 61 | - | 52 | 47 |
| 7. | Llantwit Major FC | 30 | 13 | 6 | 11 | 46 | - | 40 | 45 |
| 8. | Cwmbran Celtic FC | 30 | 10 | 8 | 12 | 62 | - | 53 | 38 |
| 9. | Pontardawe Town FC | 30 | 12 | 1 | 17 | 51 | - | 73 | 37 |
| 10. | Ammanford AFC | 30 | 8 | 9 | 13 | 40 | - | 57 | 33 |
| 11. | Taff's Well AFC | 30 | 8 | 8 | 14 | 50 | - | 54 | 32 |
| 12. | Goytre United FC | 30 | 8 | 8 | 14 | 45 | - | 67 | 32 |
| 13. | Abergavenny Town FC | 30 | 9 | 5 | 16 | 35 | - | 60 | 32 |
| 14. | Trefelin Boys & Girls Club (*Relegated*) | 30 | 7 | 6 | 17 | 47 | - | 70 | 27 |
| 15. | Swansea University FC (*Relegated*) | 30 | 6 | 8 | 16 | 30 | - | 64 | 26 |
| 16. | Ynyshir Albions FC (*Relegated*) | 30 | 7 | 3 | 20 | 33 | - | 67 | 24 |

## INTERNATIONAL MATCHES
### (16.07.2022 – 15.07.2023)

| 22.09.2022 | Bruxelles | *Belgium - Wales* | *2-1(2-0)* | (UNL) |
|---|---|---|---|---|
| 25.09.2022 | Cardiff | *Wales - Poland* | *0-1(0-0)* | (UNL) |
| 21.11.2022 | Al Rayyan | *United States - Wales* | *1-1(1-0)* | (WC) |
| 25.11.2022 | Al Rayyan | *Wales - Iran* | *0-2(0-0)* | (WC) |
| 29.11.2022 | Al Rayyan | *Wales - England* | *0-3(0-0)* | (WC) |
| | | | | |
| 25.03.2023 | Split | *Croatia - Wales* | *1-1(1-0)* | (ECQ) |
| 28.03.2023 | Cardiff | *Wales - Latvia* | *1-0(1-0)* | (ECQ) |
| 16.06.2023 | Cardiff | *Wales - Armenia* | *2-4(1-2)* | (ECQ) |
| 19.06.2023 | Samsun | *Turkey - Wales* | *2-0(0-0)* | (ECQ) |

**22.09.2022   BELGIUM - WALES**          **2-1(2-0)**          3rd UEFA Nations League A, Group 4
Stade "Roi Baudouin", Bruxelles,; Referee: Ali Palabıyık (Turkey); Attendance: 28,463
**WAL:** Wayne Robert Hennessey (Cap), Rhys Llewelyn Norrington-Davies (84.Tyler D'Whyte Roberts), Joseph Peter Rodon, Christopher James Mepham, Connor Richard John Roberts, Ethan Kwame Colm Raymond Ampadu, Matthew Robert Smith (64.Joseff John Morrell), Neco Shay Williams, Brennan Price Johnson, Daniel Owen James, Kieffer Roberto Francisco Moore (64.Gareth Frank Bale). Trainer: Robert John Page.
**Goal:** Kieffer Roberto Francisco Moore (50).

**25.09.2022   WALES - POLAND**          **0-1(0-0)**          3rd UEFA Nations League A, Group 4
Cardiff City Stadium, Cardiff; Referee: Andris Treimanis (Latvia); Attendance: 31,520
**WAL:** Wayne Robert Hennessey, Rhys Llewelyn Norrington-Davies (58.Kieffer Roberto Francisco Moore), Joseph Peter Rodon, Benjamin Cabango, Connor Richard John Roberts (85.Benjamin Sorba William Thomas), Dylan James Christopher Levitt (72.Rubin James Colwill), Joseff John Morrell, Neco Shay Williams, Brennan Price Johnson, Daniel Owen James, Gareth Frank Bale (Cap). Trainer: Robert John Page.

**21.11.2022   UNITED STATES - WALES**          **1-1(1-0)**          22nd FIFA WC. Group Stage.
„Ahmad bin Ali" Stadium, Al Rayyan (Qatar); Referee: Abdulrahman Ibrahim Al Jassim (Qatar); Attendance: 43,418
**WAL:** Wayne Robert Hennessey, Christopher James Mepham, Joseph Peter Rodon, Benjamin Thomas Davies, Connor Richard John Roberts, Ethan Kwame Colm Raymond Ampadu (90+5.Joseff John Morrell), Aaron James Ramsey, Harry Wilson (90+3.Benjamin Sorba William Thomas), Neco Shay Williams (79.Brennan Price Johnson), Gareth Frank Bale (Cap), Daniel Owen James (46.Kieffer Roberto Francisco Moore). Trainer: Robert John Page.
**Goal:** Gareth Frank Bale (82 penalty).

**25.11.2022   WALES - IRAN**          **0-2(0-0)**          22nd FIFA WC. Group Stage.
„Ahmad bin Ali" Stadium, Al Rayyan (Qatar); Referee: Mario Alberto Escobar Toca (Guatemala); Attendance: 40,875
**WAL:** Wayne Robert Hennessey [*sent off 86*], Christopher James Mepham, Joseph Peter Rodon, Benjamin Thomas Davies, Connor Richard John Roberts (57.Brennan Price Johnson), Aaron James Ramsey (87.Daniel Ward), Ethan Kwame Colm Raymond Ampadu (77.Joseph Michael Allen), Harry Wilson (57.Daniel Owen James), Neco Shay Williams, Gareth Frank Bale (Cap), Kieffer Roberto Francisco Moore. Trainer: Robert John Page.

**29.11.2022   WALES - ENGLAND**          **0-3(0-0)**          22nd FIFA WC. Group Stage.
„Ahmad bin Ali" Stadium, Al Rayyan (Qatar); Referee: Slavko Vinčić (Slovenia); Attendance: 44,297
**WAL:** Daniel Ward, Neco Shay Williams (36.Connor Richard John Roberts), Christopher James Mepham, Joseph Peter Rodon, Benjamin Thomas Davies (59.Joseff John Morrell), Aaron James Ramsey, Ethan Kwame Colm Raymond Ampadu, Joseph Michael Allen (81.Rubin James Colwill), Gareth Frank Bale (Cap) (46.Brennan Price Johnson), Kieffer Roberto Francisco Moore, Daniel Owen James (77.Harry Wilson). Trainer: Robert John Page.

**25.03.2023   CROATIA - WALES**          **1-1(1-0)**          17th EC. Qualifiers
Stadion Poljud, Split; Referee: João Pedro da Silva Pinheiro (Portugal); Attendance: 33,474
**WAL:** Daniel Ward, Connor Richard John Roberts, Joseph Peter Rodon, Christopher James Mepham, Neco Shay Williams, Ethan Kwame Colm Raymond Ampadu, Joseff John Morrell (90+2.Jordan Anthony James), Aaron James Ramsey (Cap) (64.Wesley James Burns), Daniel Owen James (64.Nathan Paul Broadhead), Kieffer Roberto Francisco Moore (70.Thomas William Bradshaw), Harry Wilson (64.Benjamin Sorba William Thomas). Trainer: Robert John Page.
**Goal:** Nathan Paul Bradhead (90+3).

**28.03.2023   WALES - LATVIA**          **1-0(1-0)**          17th EC. Qualifiers
Cardiff City Stadium, Cardiff; Referee: Giorgi Kruashvili (Georgia); Attendance: 32,806
**WAL:** Daniel Ward, Neco Shay Williams, Christopher James Mepham, Joseph Peter Rodon, Connor Richard John Roberts, Ethan Kwame Colm Raymond Ampadu, Joseff John Morrell, Daniel Owen James (73.Nathan Paul Broadhead), Aaron James Ramsey (Cap) (90+2.Oliver Joseph Cooper) , Harry Wilson (90+4.Benjamin Cabango), Kieffer Roberto Francisco Moore. Trainer: Robert John Page.
**Goal:** Kieffer Roberto Francisco Moore (41).

**16.06.2023   WALES - ARMENIA**          **2-4(1-2)**          17th EC. Qualifiers
Cardiff City Stadium, Cardiff; Referee: Georgi Kabakov (Bulgaria); Attendance: 32,774
**WAL:** Daniel Ward, Connor Richard John Roberts, Joseph Peter Rodon (67.Neco Shay Williams), Christopher James Mepham, Benjamin Thomas Davies, Ethan Kwame Colm Raymond Ampadu, Aaron James Ramsey (Cap) (67.Joseff John Morrell), Harry Wilson (82.Thomas William Bradshaw), Brennan Price Johnson (70.David Robert Brooks), Daniel Owen James (82.Nathan Paul Broadhead), Kieffer Roberto Francisco Moore [*sent off 78*]. Trainer: Robert John Page.
**Goals:** Daniel Owen James (10), Harry Wilson (72).

**19.06.2023   TURKEY - WALES**          **2-0(0-0)**          17th EC. Qualifiers
Samsun 19 Mayıs Stadium, Samsun; Referee: Fabio Maresca (Italy); Attendance: 28,766
**WAL:** Daniel Ward, Connor Richard John Roberts, Christopher James Mepham, Joseph Peter Rodon, Neco Shay Williams, Ethan Kwame Colm Raymond Ampadu, Joseff John Morrell [*sent off 41*], Harry Wilson (84.Nathan Paul Broadhead), Aaron James Ramsey (Cap) (84. Jordan Anthony James), Daniel Owen James (62.Thomas William Bradshaw), Brennan Price Johnson (46.Benjamin Cabango). Trainer: Robert John Page.

## NATIONAL TEAM PLAYERS
### (16.07.2022 – 15.07.2023)

| Name | DOB | Caps | Goals | Club | |
|------|-----|------|-------|------|-|

### Goalkeepers

| Name | DOB | Caps | Goals | Club | |
|------|-----|------|-------|------|-|
| Wayne Robert HENNESSEY | 24.01.1987 | 108 | 0 | 2022: | *Nottingham Forest FC (ENG)* |
| Daniel WARD | 22.06.1993 | 32 | 0 | 2022/2023: | *Leicester City FC (ENG)* |

### Defenders

| Name | DOB | Caps | Goals | Club | |
|------|-----|------|-------|------|-|
| Benjamin CABANGO | 30.05.2000 | 7 | 0 | 2022/2023: | *Swansea City AFC* |
| Benjamin Thomas DAVIES | 24.04.1993 | 78 | 1 | 2022/2023: | *Tottenham Hotspur FC London (ENG)* |
| Christopher James MEPHAM | 05.10.1997 | 40 | 0 | 2022/2023: | *AFC Bournemouth (ENG)* |
| Rhys Llewelyn NORRINGTON-DAVIES | 22.04.1999 | 13 | 1 | 2022: | *Sheffield United FC (ENG)* |
| Connor Richard John ROBERTS | 23.09.1995 | 48 | 3 | 2022/2023: | *Burnley FC (ENG)* |
| Joseph Peter RODON | 22.10.1997 | 37 | 0 | 2022/2023: | *Stade Rennais FC (FRA)* |
| Neco Shay WILLIAMS | 13.04.2001 | 30 | 2 | 2022/2023: | *Nottingham Forest FC (ENG)* |

### Midfielders

| Name | DOB | Caps | Goals | Club | |
|------|-----|------|-------|------|-|
| Joseph Michael ALLEN | 14.03.1990 | 74 | 2 | 2022: | *Swansea City AFC* |
| Ethan Kwame Colm Raymond AMPADU | 14.09.2000 | 44 | 0 | 2022/2023: | *Spezia Calcio La Spezia (ITA)* |
| David Robert BROOKS | 08.07.1997 | 22 | 2 | 2023: | *AFC Bournemouth (ENG)* |
| Wesley James BURNS | 23.11.1994 | 4 | 0 | 2023: | *Ipswich Town FC (ENG)* |
| Rubin James COLWILL | 27.04.2002 | 8 | 1 | 2022: | *Cardiff City FC* |
| Oliver Joseph COOPER | 14.12.1999 | 1 | 0 | 2023: | *Swansea City AFC* |
| Jordan Anthony JAMES | 02.07.2004 | 2 | 0 | 2023: | *Birmingham City FC (ENG)* |
| Dylan James Christopher LEVITT | 17.11.2000 | 13 | 0 | 2022: | *Dundee United FC (SCO)* |
| Joseff John MORRELL | 03.01.1997 | 36 | 0 | 2022/2023: | *Portsmouth FC (ENG)* |
| Aaron James RAMSEY | 26.12.1990 | 82 | 20 | 2022/2023: | *OGC Nice (FRA)* |
| Matthew Robert SMITH | 22.11.1999 | 19 | 0 | 2022: | *Milton Keynes Dons FC (ENG)* |
| Benjamin Sorba William THOMAS | 25.01.1999 | 8 | 0 | 2022:<br>25.01.2023-> | *Huddersfield Town FC (ENG)*<br>*Blackburn Rovers FC (ENG)* |
| Harry WILSON | 22.03.1997 | 46 | 6 | 2022/2023: | *Fulham FC London (ENG)* |

### Forwards

| Name | DOB | Caps | Goals | Club | |
|------|-----|------|-------|------|-|
| Gareth Frank BALE | 16.07.1989 | 111 | 41 | 2022: | *Los Angeles FC (USA)* |
| Thomas William BRADSHAW | 27.07.1992 | 6 | 0 | 2023: | *Millwall FC London (ENG)* |
| Nathan Paul BROADHEAD | 05.04.1998 | 4 | 1 | 2023: | *Ipswich Town FC (ENG)* |
| Daniel Owen JAMES | 10.11.1997 | 45 | 6 | 2022/2023: | *Fulham FC London (ENG)* |
| Brennan Price JOHNSON | 23.05.2001 | 20 | 2 | 2022/2023: | *Nottingham Forest FC (ENG)* |
| Kieffer Roberto Francisco MOORE | 08.08.1992 | 34 | 10 | 2022/2023: | *AFC Bournemouth (ENG)* |
| Tyler D'Whyte ROBERTS | 12.01.1999 | 20 | 0 | 2022: | *Leeds United FC (ENG)* |

### Trainer

| Name | DOB | | | | |
|------|-----|---|---|---|-|
| Robert John PAGE [03.11.2020] | 03.09.1974 | 32 M; 9 W; 10 D; 13 L; 33-44 | | | |